GUIDE TO THE PRESIDENCY

THE PRESIDENCY

Fourth Edition ★ Volume I

Michael Nelson, Editor

CQ PRESS

A Division of Congressional Quarterly Inc.
Washington, D.C.

CQ Press
1255 22nd Street, NW, Suite 400
Washington, DC 20037

Phone: 202-729-1900; toll-free, 1-866-4CQ-PRESS (1-866-427-7737)

Web: www.cqpress.com

Cover design: Malcolm McGaughy/McGaughy Design

Cover photo: John Aikins/Corbis

Interior design and composition by Judy Myers, graphic designer.

Illustration credits and acknowledgments begin on page 1889, volume II, which is to be
considered an extension of the copyright page.

∞ The paper used in this publication exceeds the requirements of the American National
Standard for Information Sciences—Permanence of Paper for Printed Library Materials,
ANSI Z39.48-1992.

Printed and bound in the United States of America

11 10 09 08 07   1 2 3 4 5

Library of Congress Cataloging-in-Publication Data

Guide to the presidency / Michael Nelson, editor. — 4th ed.
    p. cm.
 Includes bibliographical references and index.
 ISBN 978-0-87289-362-7 (hardcover, volume 1 : alk. paper) — ISBN 978-0-87289-363-4
(hardcover, volume 2 : alk. paper) — ISBN 978-0-87289-364-1 (hardcover, set : alk. paper)
 1. Presidents—United States. I. Nelson, Michael, 1949- II. Title.

JK516.C57 2007
352.230973—dc22

2007025322

★ SUMMARY TABLE OF CONTENTS

Volume I

Volume II

★ TABLE OF CONTENTS

Volume I

Volume I . . .

Volume I . . .

Volume I . . .

Volume I . . .

Volume II

Volume II . . .

Volume II . . .

★ FOREWORD

CQ Press's *Guide to the Presidency* is one of the few reference books that I always take with me on my working summer "vacation" on Cape Cod. I find it an indispensable book—and so, I think, will every American historian and biographer, every political scientist, and every student of international relations. Certainly it ought to be on the desk of every member of Congress, and every aspirant for the presidency should make it his or her bible.

These imposing volumes are, first of all, a compendium of all the basic facts concerning the American presidency. Here are short, accurate, and insightful biographical sketches of every American president. These are fair-minded but not bland. For instance, the pre-presidential years of Warren G. Harding are said to have been devoted to "drinking, playing poker, and developing political allies." Richard M. Nixon is considered "tainted" by the Watergate scandal, because "he had participated in the cover-up of illegal administration activities." Even more refreshing are the biographies of every first lady. Where else could one learn that Ida McKinley had frequent bouts of epilepsy, that Edith Roosevelt carried bouquets of flowers to avoid having to shake hundreds of hands during public receptions, and that Mamie Eisenhower suffered not from alcoholism but from a chronic inner ear condition that caused her to lose her balance and bump into things? Careful, brief biographies of every vice president bring to mind such forgotten figures as Richard M. Johnson, vice president during the Van Buren administration who had an African-American mistress, Julia Chinn, and attempted to introduce his mixed-blood daughters as equals in virulently racist Washington society.

Here, too, are readily accessible tables of the popular and electoral votes for each presidential and vice presidential candidate in every national election since 1789, together with a list of Also-Rans—candidates who received some electoral votes but did not become president or vice president. One appendix presents the cabinet members of every administration.

But this *Guide* is far more than a mere encyclopedia of facts. The body of the book consists of long, careful monographs, each written by an expert, on the structure and basic functions of the presidential office. Beginning with the brief, general provisions of the Constitution providing for a chief executive, the authors trace the slow, and often unsteady, evolution of the office, from George Washington's small staff of three departments (plus an attorney general), operating on a budget of about $4 million a year, to the present vast proliferation, with a federal executive bureaucracy that in 2004 consisted of almost 1.7 million employees.

These admirable chapters authoritatively examine the president's numerous, and often overlapping, roles, as legislative leader, chief diplomat, commander in chief, head of state, party leader, and chief economist. Others offer insightful accounts of how presidents and vice presidents are nominated and how these practices have changed over time. A revealing section traces the evolution of the role of the president as chief executive officer. As late as 1884, Woodrow Wilson, in *Congressional Government*, described the president's day-to-day business of running the government as "mere administration"—"usually not much above routine." But in subsequent decades the duties have so enormously expanded as to make nearly impossible demands on the time, energy, and health of the occupant of the White House. It was appropriate for Clinton Rossiter to introduce his authoritative 1956 study of the presidency with a quotation from *Macbeth*: "Methought I heard a voice cry, 'Sleep no more!' "

Valuable as history, several of these chapters are illuminating guides to present-day issues. Chapters new to this edition of the work are "Unilateral Powers of the Presidency" and "The Presidency and Popular Culture."

An especially valuable section of the *Guide* deals with the president and the federal bureaucracy. Featuring the brief, amusing boxed insert "Bureaucratic Lingo," it traces the remorseless growth of the civil service and shows how the bureaucracy not merely implements but also makes policy—independently of the president and of Congress. It makes it easier to understand the frustration so many presidents have felt toward the bureaucracy. Franklin D. Roosevelt, explaining why his numerous attempts to bring about changes in the State Department, the Treasury Department, and even the military were so often unsuccessful said it was "like punching a feather bed. You punch it with your right and you punch it with your left until you are finally exhausted, and then you find the damn bed just as it was before you started punching."

Largely a record of the success of the American presidency, the *Guide* also contains warnings of the fragility of the institution. Its sad chronicle of ten attempts to assassinate American presidents, from Andrew Jackson to Ronald Reagan, warns of the dangers hidden behind the panoply of power. The *Guide* also analyzes the three instances in U.S. history of serious attempts to remove a president from office. Whatever the merits in each case, the impeachment proceedings against Andrew Johnson, Richard M. Nixon, and Bill Clinton suggest how easy it is to arouse partisanship and prejudice against a vulnerable incumbent.

A notable feature of the *Guide* is the attention it gives to the vice presidency. For most of U.S. history it has been an office without meaningful functions and so inconsequential that in 1828 Daniel Webster declined nomination saying, "I do not propose to be buried until I am dead." Indeed, the office has generally been so unimportant that because of deaths and resignations, the country has been without a vice president for one-fifth of its history—and has suffered no ill consequences. Only in recent years, beginning with Walter Mondale, has the vice president begun to serve as a close adviser to the president. That shift is important because, as the *Guide* notes, nine vice presidents—more than one-fifth of those who have served in the office—have become chief executive on the death (or, in Nixon's case, resignation) of the president.

My only complaint about the *Guide* is that it contains so much fascinating miscellaneous information that I become easily sidetracked when I am doing research. Where else could I discover that at George Washington's first inauguration, no Bible could be found in Federal Hall in New York City, and aides had to rush out and borrow one from St. John's Masonic Lodge No. 1, a few blocks away on Wall Street? Or that John Adams, whom some recent historians have praised as a paragon of democratic leadership, campaigned to have Congress authorize the ostentatious presidential title of "His Highness the President of the United States and Protector of the Rights of the Same"? Or that Massachusetts did not ratify the Twelfth Amendment—the 1804 amendment providing for separate balloting for president and vice president—until 1961? Or that British scholar Harold J. Laski once called Franklin D. Roosevelt's New Deal a "pill to cure an earthquake"? Or that Americans lived—for the most part quite unaware—in a state of national emergency from 1933 to 1975? Or, on a lighter note, that Andrew Johnson's daughter, Martha Johnson Patterson, who presided over the White House during her father's administration because of the illness of her mother, put cows on the White House lawn to provide the first family with milk and butter?

But these are minor diversions in this magisterial work, which Michael Nelson has so ably planned and so intelligently edited. He has given us the fullest and best account of the origins and history of that distinctive American contribution to the science of politics, the presidency.

DAVID HERBERT DONALD
Charles Warren Professor of
American History Emeritus
Harvard University

★ PREFACE

The presidency is both a person and an office. At any given moment, the powers and duties of the presidency are entrusted fully to the person who is the president. To a great degree, the presidency has been shaped and defined by the forty-three individuals who, as of this writing, have held the office. Historical periods often are described in terms of the presidents who dominated them: the "Age of Jackson," the "Lincoln years," the "New Deal period" of Franklin D. Roosevelt, the "Reagan era."

But the presidency is more than the persons who have served as president. It is also an office, an enduring and evolving institution that is deeply embedded in an interactive network of other institutions: Congress, the Supreme Court, the departments and agencies of the bureaucracy, the news media, interest groups, political parties, the public, and the nations of the world.

Plan of the Book

By design and execution, *Guide to the Presidency* reflects the individualism of the presidency. The two volumes of the book are laced with descriptions of every president's accomplishments and failures, virtues and foibles. Even a quick glance at the table of contents and the index will attest to the detailed information the *Guide* provides on each president. Part VIII consists of illustrated biographies of every president, from George Washington to George W. Bush (Chapter 35), the vice presidents, from John Adams to Richard B. Cheney (Chapter 36), and the first ladies, from Martha Washington to Laura Bush (Chapter 37). Part VII delves into the daily life of the president (Chapter 32), the role of the first lady, the first family, and the president's friends (chapter 33), and the developing role of former presidents (Chapter 34).

The institutional character of the presidency is manifested in several ways, all of which are described in this book.

- *The presidency is a constitutional office.* It has been shaped by its design at the Constitutional Convention in 1787 and by later constitutional amendments, Supreme Court decisions, and customs and precedents. Chapter 1 offers an extensive description of the constitutional beginnings of the presidency, and the six chapters that constitute Part

III thoroughly examine the various powers of the office, most of them constitutional in origin. Constitutional aspects of the presidency also are noted throughout the book. Part II, for example, examines the processes of presidential selection, succession, and removal. New chapters, added for the fourth edition of the book, treat the unilateral powers of the presidency and depictions of the presidency in popular culture.

- *The presidency is a historical office.* During its more than two centuries of existence, the presidency has evolved in response to changing social, economic, and political conditions—domestically and internationally. Chapter 2, which plots chronologically the development of the presidency, is one of only several places in the *Guide* where the history of the office is described. Chapter 6, for example, consists of an election-by-election history of presidential contests.

- *The presidency is the nation's supreme elective office.* Part II offers full treatment of presidential selection and removal—not just the history, rules, strategies, and processes of presidential nominations and elections, but also the methods provided by the Constitution for presidential selection under special circumstances, such as the death, resignation, or disability of the president.

- *The presidency is a highly public and political office.* Indeed, it is as public and political after an election as it is during a campaign as evidenced by the ongoing importance of presidential appearances (Chapter 16). Presidential leadership depends heavily on the support or acquiescence of those groups outside government whose relations with the presidency are also described in Part IV—the political parties (Chapter 17), the mass media (Chapter 18), the public (Chapter 20), and interest groups (Chapter 21). In addition, a new chapter in this edition treats the place of the presidency in popular culture (Chapter 19).

- *The presidency is the chief office of the executive branch.* This branch comprises the White House staff, the cabinet, and the numerous departments and agencies of the federal bureaucracy. Its major players and major components are described extensively in Part V.

• *The presidency is part of a multibranch system of government.* Throughout the *Guide,* attention is paid to the separation of powers and the checks and balances that characterize the American constitutional system, but the interactions of the presidency with Congress (Chapter 29), the Supreme Court (Chapter 30), and the bureaucracy (Chapter 31) are specifically the subject of Part VI.

The *Guide* also covers the vice presidency—its origins and history (Chapter 3), the processes of vice presidential selection (Chapter 5) and removal (Chapter 8), and the office of the vice president (Chapter 23).

Thus the *Guide to the Presidency* explains in two volumes the origins, evolution, and contemporary workings of the most important office of the U.S. political system. The book has been written and edited to make this material readily accessible. The thirty-seven chapters of the *Guide,* in eight parts, are each devoted to a particular subject, but these topics are not discrete because few aspects of the presidency are unrelated to others. The subject of one chapter, therefore, may be mentioned in several different contexts throughout the book. The president's relationship with the public, for example, is the focus of Part IV, but this relationship is also discussed in Part I (in Chapter 2, on the history of the office) and in Part II (in Chapter 5, on the electoral process). Easily visible cross-references in each chapter guide the reader to other relevant discussions as well as to documents, tables, and figures in the appendixes. This overlap provides complete treatment of a topic in one place but also allows readers to discover and pursue related subjects.

Continuing the tradition of CQ Press's other major reference works—*Guide to Congress, Guide to the U.S. Supreme Court,* and *Guide to U.S. Elections*—the material in *Guide to the Presidency* is descriptive, factual, unbiased, and easy to understand. Writing in a highly readable style, the authors have distilled for the average reader the widely accepted expertise of scholars who study the presidency. For readers who want to delve further into the scholarly literature, the notes and selected bibliographies at the end of each chapter show the way.

The reference materials section in the *Guide* supplements the text with documents, tables, and charts. Included are excerpts from more than forty documents highly significant to the presidency, with explanatory headnotes. The tables list, among other things, electoral votes for all presidential elections and cabinet members from the administration of George Washington through that of George W. Bush.

The photographs and other images deserve special mention. The *Guide* is lavishly illustrated with hundreds of pictures chosen to instruct as well as to add visual interest. Some were selected to familiarize students with the classic pictures from the presidency—such as the shot of an exuberant Truman displaying a "Dewey Defeats Truman" headline.

Others capture unique moments—such as a young Bill Clinton meeting John F. Kennedy. Other illustrations highlight little-known facts of presidential history—such as the cartoon from the 1840 election showing the origin of the expression "OK." Boxed material throughout the chapters emphasizes important, interesting, and current events.

Changes in the Fourth Edition

Readers familiar with the award-winning earlier editions of the *Guide to the Presidency* will find that this edition is, if anything, even better. It has been thoroughly updated to incorporate the events and personalities of the George W. Bush presidency and to address budgetary and economic issues, emerging political trends, recent Supreme Court appointments, and the new challenges posed by the "war on terrorism" and the war in Iraq.

This edition also has been updated to incorporate new academic research on the presidency published during the 1990s and 2000s. The new scholarship infuses every chapter, but is especially apparent in two entirely new chapters: one on the unilateral powers of the presidency and one on depictions of the president in popular culture.

Several highly respected scholars specializing in the presidency have joined the roster of contributors to this edition, including Meena Bose, David A. Crockett, Matthew Dickinson, Matthew Kerbel, Andrew C. Rudalevige, Greg Smith, Mary Stuckey, Daniel J. Tichenor, and Shirley Anne Warshaw.

Perhaps the most striking improvement in the fourth edition is its design and layout, which features numerous changes to enhance readability and visual presentation.

Acknowledgments

The current edition of the *Guide* is the work of numerous dedicated scholars and authors, many of whom have participated in all four editions. Major contributors are noted in the opening pages of Volume I and in each chapter.

At CQ Press, preparation of the Fourth edition was overseen by acquisitions editor Mary Carpenter and development editor David Arthur under the direction of Andrea Pedolsky, chief of library reference editorial acquisitions. Sally Ryman once again handled production along with managing editor Joan Gossett and editorial coordinator Belinda Josey. Freelance editors Jon Preimesberger and Colleen McGuiness were the principle copy editors. Indexing of this edition was carried out by Indexing Partners LLC.

The efforts of many people have brought this project through successive editions, but the work of a few deserve individual mention. David R. Tarr, former executive editor of CQ Press, kept alive the idea of the *Guide* during its conceptual stages, then provided thoughtful direction and support in the second edition and returned as sponsoring editor for the third edition. Freelance copy editor Sabra Bissette

Ledent was instrumental in the original and second editions and served as the lead editor for the third edition, with responsibility for much of the content. Nola Healy Lynch, former developmental editor at CQ Press, wrote the working outline of the first edition in the 1980s, and presidential scholar Thomas E. Cronin reviewed the initial plan of the book. Margaret Seawell, formerly a senior editor at CQ Press, was the principal editor of the first edition. Much of her seminal work on original manuscripts remains intact. The work of these editors was ably carried forward by CQ Press acquisitions editor Shana Wagger, who served as both developmental and supervisory editor of the second edition.

John L. Moore, former assistant director of CQ Press, edited several chapters in the first and second editions and compiled the original reference materials. In the third edi-tion, he revised the chapters on elections and the president and the media.

The authors of the *Guide* displayed unusual dedication in meeting the demands of a rigorous review and editing process. I commend them for their stamina as well as for their scholarship. In addition to the contributors to the new volume, freelance writers Harrison Donnelly, Richard A. Karno, Margaret C. Thompson, and James Brian Watts deserve warm acknowledgment.

Finally, I and the other writers and staff owe a great deal to our friends and especially our families, who stood by while we worked on the *Guide*. Their support and good cheer count for much.

MICHAEL NELSON
Rhodes College

MICHAEL NELSON, *Professor of Political Science, Rhodes College:* Chapter 1, Constitutional Beginnings; Chapter 3, History of the Vice Presidency; Chapter 4, Rating the Presidents; Chapter 5, The Electoral Process and Taking Office; Chapter 7, Selection by Succession; Chapter 8, Removal of the President and the Vice President; Chapter 23, Office of the Vice President; Chapter 34, Former Presidents; Chapter 35, Biographies of the Presidents; Chapter 36, Biographies of the Vice Presidents; Chapter 37, Biographies of the First Ladies; headnotes to Documents and Texts.

HAROLD F. BASS JR., *Professor of Political Science and Dean of the School of Social Sciences, Ouachita Baptist University:* Chapter 16, Presidential Appearances; Chapter 17, The President and Political Parties.

W. CRAIG BLEDSOE, *Professor of Political Science and Provost, Lipscomb University:* Chapter 26, Presidential Commissions.

MEENA BOSE, *Peter S. Kalikow Chair in Presidential Studies, Hofstra University:* Chapter 13, Chief Diplomat; Chapter 14, Commander in Chief.

MARK E. BYRNES, *Professor of Political Science, Middle Tennessee State University:* Chapter 31, The President and the Bureaucracy.

DAVID A. CROCKETT, *Associate Professor of Political Science, Trinity University:* Chapter 20, Public Support and Opinion.

MATTHEW DICKINSON, *Professor of Political Science, Middlebury College:* Chapter 12, Legislative Leader.

DAVID HERBERT DONALD, *Charles Warren Professor of American History Emeritus, Harvard University:* Foreword.

JIM GRANATO, *Director, University of Houston Center for Public Policy, and Associate Professor, Department of Political Science:* Chapter 15, Chief Economist.

DEBORAH KALB, *Washington, D.C., Author:* Chapter 6, Chronology of Presidential Elections; Chapter 27, Housing of the Executive Branch; Chapter 28, Executive Branch Pay and Perquisites; Chapter 32, Daily Life of the President; Chapter 33, The First Lady, The First Family, and the President's Friends.

MATTHEW KERBEL, *Professor of Political Science, Villanova University:* Chapter 18, The President and the News Media.

SIDNEY M. MILKIS, *White Burkett Miller Professor and Chair of the Department of Politics, University of Virginia:* Chapter 2, History of the Presidency.

STEPHEN L. ROBERTSON, *Adjunct Professor of Political Science, Middle Tennessee State University:* Chapter 22, Executive Office of the President: White House Office.

ANDREW C. RUDALEVIGE, *Associate Professor of Political Science, Dickinson College:* Chapter 9, Unilateral Powers of the Presidency.

GREG SMITH, *Associate Professor of Communication, Georgia State University:* Chapter 19, The Presidency and Popular Culture.

ROBERT J. SPITZER, *Distinguished Service Professor of Political Science, State University of New York—Cortland:* Chapter 29, The President and Congress.

MARY STUCKEY, *Professor of Communication and Political Science, Georgia State University:* Chapter 10, Chief of State; Chapter 19, The Presidency and Popular Culture.

DANIEL J. TICHENOR, *Associate Professor of Political Science, Rutgers University:* Chapter 21, The President and Interest Groups.

JOHN R. VILE, *Professor and Chair of Political Science, Middle Tennessee State University:* Chapter 30, The President and the Supreme Court.

SHIRLEY ANNE WARSHAW, *Professor of Political Science, Gettysburg College:* Chapter 11, Chief Administrator; Chapter 24, Executive Office of the President: Supporting Organizations; Chapter 25, The Cabinet and Executive Departments.

★ CONTRIBUTORS TO PREVIOUS EDITIONS

HAROLD F. BASS JR., *Professor of Political Science and Dean of the School of Social Sciences, Ouachita Baptist University:* Public Support and Opinion; The President and Interest Groups.

ADRIEL BETTELHEIM, *Senior Writer for* CQ Weekly: Executive Office of the President: Supporting Organizations; The Cabinet and Executive Departments; Government Agencies and Corporations.

W. CRAIG BLEDSOE, *Professor of Political Science and Provost, Lipscomb University:* Chief Executive; Executive Branch Pay and Perquisites; Executive Office of the President: Supporting Organizations; Cabinet and Executive Departments; Government Agencies and Corporations; Presidential Commissions.

CHRISTOPHER J. BOSSO, *Professor of Political Science and Associate Dean School of Social Science, Public Affairs, and Public Policy, Northeastern University:* Chief Executive; Legislative Leader.

MARK E. BYRNES, *Professor of Political Science, Middle Tennessee State University:* The President and the Bureaucracy.

DANIEL C. DILLER, *Washington, D.C., Author on Politics and International Relations:* Chief Diplomat; Commander in Chief; Chief of State; Chief Economist; Biographies of the Presidents; Biographies of the Vice Presidents.

CHARLES C. EUCHNER, *Former Executive Director, Rappaport Institute for Greater Boston in affiliation with the Taubman Center at the Kennedy School of Government, Harvard University:* The Electoral Process; Taking Office; Chronology of Presidential Elections; Presidential Appearances; Public Support and Opinion; The President and Interest Groups.

JIM GRANATO, *Director, University of Houston Center for Public Policy, and Associate Professor, Department of Political Science:* Chief Economist.

DEBORAH KALB, *Washington, D.C., Author:* Executive Office of the President: Supporting Organizations.

MARTHA JOYNT KUMAR, *Professor of Political Science, Towson University:* The President and the News Media.

JOHN ANTHONY MALTESE, *Associate Professor of Political Science, University of Georgia:* The Electoral Process; Taking Office.

SIDNEY M. MILKIS, *White Burkett Miller Professor and Chair of the Department of Politics, University of Virginia:* History of the Presidency.

JOHN MOORE, *Washington, D.C., Author on Elections and Politics:* Chronology of Presidential Elections; The President and the News Media.

DEAN J. PETERSON, *Assistant Professor of Economics, Seattle University:* Chief Economist.

STEPHEN L. ROBERTSON, *Adjunct Professor of Political Science, Middle Tennessee State University:* Daily Life of the President; The First Lady, the First Family, and the President's Friends; Executive Office of the President: White House Office.

MARK J. ROZELL, *Professor of Public Policy, George Mason University:* Chief Executive.

LESLIE RIGBY, *Washington, D.C., Author on Governmental Affairs and Public Policy:* Executive Office of the President: Supporting Organizations; Cabinet and Executive Departments; Government Agencies and Corporations.

MARGARET H. SEAWELL, *Executive Editor, Sage Publications:* Housing of the Executive Branch.

ROBERT J. SPITZER, *Distinguished Service Professor of Political Science, State University of New York—Cortland:* The President and Congress.

JOHN R. VILE, *Professor and Chair of Political Science, Middle Tennessee State University:* The President and the Supreme Court.

STEPHEN H. WIRLS, *Associate Professor of Political Science, Rhodes College:* Chief Diplomat; Commander in Chief.

MARGARET JANE WYSZOMIRSKI, *Professor, School of Public Policy and Management, Ohio State University:* Removal of the President.

chapter 1

Constitutional Beginnings

by Michael Nelson

The constitutional convention of 1787 was, as Connecticut governor Samuel Huntington told the delegates to his state's constitutional ratifying convention, "a new event in the history of mankind. Heretofore, most governments have been formed by tyrants and imposed on mankind by force. Never before did a people, in a time of peace and tranquility, meet together by their representatives and, with calm deliberation, frame for themselves a system of government." [1] In the midst of this "new event," nothing was newer than the American presidency, an invention unlike any other national executive in history. Its inventors—the fifty-five convention delegates—drew on their personal and professional experience, study of history and philosophy, understanding of political reality, and individual and collective wits in designing the office.

The convention's most important clusters of decisions involved *number and selection* (the series of choices that made the presidency a single-person office whose incumbent is selected by an independent national constituency), *term and removal* (the former fixed in length, the latter difficult to achieve), and *powers and institutional separation* (which made the presidency one of three separated institutions sharing the powers of the national government).

Although the presidency has been modified several times by constitutional amendments, the basic design of the Framers remains as it was more than two centuries ago.

ANTECEDENTS

As with any invention, the presidency had antecedents, all of which influenced the form the office took in the Constitution. The delegates to the convention had long experience with British executives—the king in London and his appointed governors in the American colonies. Delegates also were influenced by their careful study of political philosophy. After independence was declared in 1776, delegates had the benefit of a decade's worth of experience with governments of their own design, under both the various state constitutions and the Articles of Confederation, which defined and created a national government. These experiences, more than anything else, set the stage for the calling of the Constitutional Convention and the creation of the presidency.

British and Colonial Executives

During their long years as colonists, Americans became well acquainted with the British form of government, which is best described as a constitutional monarchy. Great Britain was headed by a king (or, less frequently, a queen) who assumed the throne through inheritance and reigned for life. The monarch's power was limited by the power of Parliament, the British legislature. The king could order the nation into war, for example, but his order would prevail only if Parliament was willing to appropriate the funds to finance the effort. Conversely, Parliament could pass laws, but the king could veto them. Parliament was a bicameral, or two-house, legislature—it consisted of the House of Commons, which was elected, and the House of Lords, which was made up of hereditary peers with lifetime tenure.

The British form of government was more than just the most familiar one to the American colonists—many of them also regarded it as the best that human beings ever had devised. Basic liberties seemed better safeguarded by Britain's constitutional monarchy than by any other government in history. British wealth and power exceeded that of any other Western nation. Indeed, Great Britain seemed to have solved what traditionally had been regarded as an insolvable problem of classical political philosophy—that is, the inherent limitations of each of the three basic forms of government that were identified by Aristotle: monarchy (rule by one person), aristocracy (rule by an elite), and democracy (rule by the people). [2] Because, as the problem usually was formulated, those who were entrusted to reign on behalf of the whole society ended up using power for selfish ends, monarchy inevitably degenerated into despotism, aristocracy into oligarchy, and democracy into anarchy, then tyranny. The British remedy, developed over several centuries, was to meliorate these tendencies by blending elements of all three forms of government into one—monarchy in the king, aristocracy in the House of Lords, and democracy in the House of Commons—and by allowing each element to check and balance the others.

The governments of most of Britain's American colonies were similar in structure to the British national government: a governor appointed by the king; an upper house of the legislature, which in most colonies was appointed by the governor; and a lower house of the legislature, which was elected by the people. Royal governors were armed with substantial powers, including the right to cast an absolute, or final, veto over colonial legislation, the right to create courts and appoint judges, and even the right to prorogue, or dissolve, the legislature. But politically astute governors exercised these powers cautiously because only the legislature was empowered to appropriate the funds to finance a colony's government and pay its governor's salary.

For all their virtues, the British and colonial governments were prone to abuse by executives who were hungry for power. King George III, who reigned during the American Revolution, used government contracts, jobs, and other forms of patronage as virtual bribes to ensure the support of members of Parliament. Some colonial governors employed similar practices with their legislatures.[3] In 1776 the colonists' anger about these abuses of power was expressed fervently in the Declaration of Independence. The Declaration is best known for its ringing preamble ("all men are created equal"; "Life, Liberty and the pursuit of Happiness"), but it mainly consisted of a long and detailed indictment of executive "injuries and usurpations, all having in direct object the establishment of an absolute Tyranny over these States."

The lesson many Americans drew from their experience with the British and colonial governments was that liberty is threatened by executive power and safeguarded by legislative power. As James Wilson, the Scottish-born Pennsylvanian who signed the Declaration, fought in the Revolutionary War, and later served as a Pennsylvania delegate to the Constitutional Convention, observed:

> Before [the Revolution], the executive and judicial powers of the government were placed neither in the people, nor in those who professed to receive them under the authority of the people. They were derived from a different and a foreign source: they were regulated by foreign maxims; they were directed to a foreign purpose. Need we be surprised, then, that they were objects of aversion and distrust? . . . On the other hand, our assemblies were chosen by ourselves: they were guardians of our rights, the objects of our confidence, and the anchor of our political hopes. Every power which could be placed in them, was thought to be safely placed: every extension of that power was considered as an extension of our own security.[4]

Political Philosophy

Various scholars have argued that the Framers were guided in their thinking about government in general and the executive in particular by one or another work or school of political philosophy. The *Second Treatise of Government* (1690) by John Locke, the British philosopher; *L'Esprit des Lois* (The Spirit of the Laws, 1748) by the French philosopher Baron de Montesquieu; and numerous writings of David Hume and other philosophers of the Scottish Enlightenment—all have their champions as the main philosophical inspiration of the Constitution.

In truth, the Framers were guided by all of these works, as well as by their studies of modern and ancient government. James Madison, for example, compiled a document called "Vices of the Political System of the United States," which cataloged his objections to the state constitutions of the 1770s and 1780s on the basis of general precepts of governance that he had derived from his research. John Adams, although not present at the Constitutional Convention (he was in London serving as the U.S. ambassador to the Court of Saint James), wrote and circulated a book in 1787 called *Defense of the Constitutions of Government of the United States of America.* Although rather aristocratic in tone, it argued for separation of powers and a bicameral legislature.

Drawn from these varied sources, the basic political philosophy of the Framers was grounded in several widely shared ideas: a belief in the fundamental rights of life, liberty, and property; an understanding of the threat that human nature's darker side posed to the preservation of these rights; and a commitment to the importance of having a republican form of government, characterized by separation of powers, as a means of averting this threat. *(See box, The Framers' Philosophy, p. 5.)*

State Constitutions

During the course of the Revolutionary War, seventeen constitutions were written by the thirteen newly independent states. (Some states began with one constitution, then quickly replaced it with another.) Revulsion against their experience with the British executive—the king in London and the royal governors in the colonial capitals—led almost all of the authors of state constitutions to provide for weak governors and strong legislatures. As Wilson wryly observed, under independence "the executive and the judicial as well as the legislative authority was now the child of the people; but to the two former, the people behaved like stepmothers. The legislature was still discriminated by excessive partiality; and into its lap, every good and precious gift was profusely thrown."[5]

In the decade after independence was declared, state governors typically were elected by the legislature for a brief term (one year, in most cases) and were ineligible for reelec-

THE FRAMERS' PHILOSOPHY

In his book *1787: The Grand Convention*, Clinton Rossiter, a preeminent scholar of the founding period, summarized the basic political philosophy of the Framers by enumerating the clusters of interconnected ideas about human nature and public institutions that underlay their approach to the writing of the Constitution.[1]

The first of these clusters, according to Rossiter, involved natural law and the basic human nature that derives from it:

"The political and social world is governed by laws as certain and universal as those which govern the physical world. Whether direct commands of God, necessities of nature, or simply hard lessons of history, these laws have established a moral order that men ignore at their peril. . . .

"The nature of man, which is an expression of the law of nature, is a durable mix of ennobling excellencies and degrading imperfections. Man's 'good' qualities, which need all the support they can get from education, religion, and government, are sociability, reasonableness, generosity, and the love of liberty; his 'bad' qualities, which flourish quite unaided, are selfishness, passion, greed, and corruptibility.

"Many things can corrupt a man, but none more drastically than the taste and touch of political power. . . ."

In the Framers' philosophy, Rossiter continues, the law of nature guarantees people certain fundamental rights—notably, life, liberty, property, conscience, and the pursuit of happiness—to which every individual is equally entitled.

From these rights flow an understanding of the proper role of government:

"The purpose of government is to protect men in the enjoyment of their natural rights, secure their persons and property against violence, remove obstructions to their pursuit of happiness, help them to live virtuous and useful lives, adjust the complexity of their social relations, and in general fill those limited but essential collective needs that they cannot fill as individuals or in families."

The proper design of government is a different matter, more difficult to determine than government's proper role:

"The nature of government, like the nature of man, is a mixture of good and bad—'good' because it has been ordained by the law of nature to serve some of the most basic needs of men, 'bad' because it can always get out of hand and turn arbitrary, corrupt, wicked, and oppressive. . . .

"The best form that has ever been devised or even imagined is republican government, which is to say, popular, representative, responsible, and non-hereditary. . . .

"The one agency essential to republican government is a representative legislature. Its basic function is to act as an instrument of consent through which the people tax and restrict themselves.

"The fact of legislative primacy does not mean, however, that all authority should be lodged in the representative assembly. In those governments that are stable as well as republican the total sum of permissible power is divided among three branches: a legislature, preferably bicameral; an executive, preferably single; and a judiciary, necessarily independent." A government in which several institutions share powers "is most likely to strike the right balance between the urges of liberty and the needs of authority."

1. All of the quotations that follow are from Clinton Rossiter, *1787: The Grand Convention* (London: MacGibbon and Kee, 1968), 60–64.

---

tion. They were forced to share their powers with a council of some sort, which made them, in the assessment of the historian Gordon Wood, "little more than chairmen of their executive boards."[6] (Indeed, at the Constitutional Convention, Gov. Edmund Randolph of Virginia opposed the proposal to make the presidency a unitary office by saying that, as governor, he was merely "a member of the executive.") Such powers as the governors had were meager. Most state constitutions made vague grants of authority to their chief executives and, by specifically denying them the right to veto legislation and to make appointments, rendered them incapable of defending even those modest powers from legislative encroachment. In his *Notes on the State of Virginia*, Thomas Jefferson described the result in his home state:

All the powers of government, legislative, executive and judiciary, result to the legislative body. . . . The [state constitutional] convention, which passed the ordinance of government, laid its foundation on this basis, that the legislative, executive and judiciary departments should be separate and distinct, so that no person should exercise the powers of more than one of them at the same time. But no barrier was provided between these several powers. The judiciary and executive members were left dependent on

the legislative for their subsistence in office and some of them for their continuance in it. If therefore the legislature assumes executive and judiciary powers, no opposition is likely to be made; nor, if made, can it be effectual; because in that case they may put their proceedings in the form of an act of assembly, which will render them obligatory on the other branches.[7]

The constitution of the state of New York offered a striking exception to the general practice of weak governors and strong legislatures. New York's governor was elected by the people, not the legislature, for a term of three years, not one, and, rather than being confined to one term, could be reelected as often as the voters wanted. (George Clinton, the first governor to be chosen under the New York constitution, was elected seven times, for a total of twenty-one years.) The executive power of New York was unitary, exercised by the governor alone and not shared with a council. The governor was empowered to veto legislation, subject to a vote to override by the legislature, and to make appointments, subject to legislative confirmation. Finally, the powers of New York's governor were defined by the state constitution in detail, much as the powers of the president would be in the U.S. Constitution:

ARTICLE XVIII. . . . The governor . . . shall by virtue of his office, be general and commander in chief of all the militia, and admiral of the navy of this state; . . . he shall have power to convene the assembly and senate on extraordinary occasions; to prorogue them from time to time, provided such prorogations shall not exceed sixty days in the space of any one year; and, at his discretion, to grant reprieves and pardons to persons convicted of crimes, other than treason and murder, in which he may suspend the execution of the sentence, until it shall be reported to the legislature at their subsequent meeting; and they shall either pardon or direct the execution of the criminal, or grant a further reprieve.

ARTICLE XIX. . . . It shall be the duty of the governor to inform the legislature of the condition of the state so far as may concern his department; to recommend such matters to their consideration as shall appear to him to concern its good government, welfare and prosperity; to correspond with the Continental Congress and other States; to transact all necessary business with the officers of government, civil and military; to take care that the laws are executed to the best of his ability; and to expedite all such measures as may be resolved upon by the legislature.

The Articles of Confederation

The decision by the Continental Congress to declare independence from Great Britain in the summer of 1776 was accompanied by another decision calling for, as stated in the motion by the Virginian Richard Henry Lee, "a plan of confederation [to] be prepared and transmitted to the respective Colonies for their consideration and approbation." Such a step was militarily necessary. Although the Declaration of Independence made all of the states, in effect, independent nations, they could not fight a common war against the British without some sort of common government.

The states, however, covetous of their independence and reluctant to substitute even a homegrown central government for the British government they had just rejected, surrendered power grudgingly. They stipulated to their members in Congress that the confederation was to be no stronger than was absolutely necessary to wage the war for independence. Reacting against their experience with British rule, the states also made clear that the confederation's executive component must be minimal. Nothing remotely resembling a king would be tolerated.

On June 11, 1776, a Committee of Thirteen (one from each state) was formed in the Continental Congress to draft a plan of confederation. The committee, acting expeditiously, submitted its recommendation on July 12. More than a year later, on November 15, 1777, Congress adopted a revised version of the plan, calling it the Articles of Confederation and Perpetual Union. Ratification by the states came slowly, with the last state not voting its approval until March 1, 1781. But the Articles were so much like the ad hoc arrangement that the states already were using under the Continental Congress that the delay in ratification posed no serious problems.

The Articles of Confederation embodied the states' dread of central government and executive power. Indeed, they hardly created a government at all—more an alliance or, as the Articles themselves put it, "a league of friendship." Each state, regardless of wealth or population, was represented equally in Congress. The president, chosen by Congress, was merely its presiding officer. Eventually, after the task of making all financial, diplomatic, and military decisions and executing all legislative enactments became more than Congress itself could handle, Congress created departments headed by appointed officials. The activities of these departments, however, were closely monitored by Congress. In truth, few laws of consequence were enacted by Congress, because passage required the support of nine of the thirteen states. Amendments to the Articles had to be approved unanimously.

In addition to setting forth a weak institutional structure, the Articles undermined the power of the national government in other ways. Technically, Congress was empowered to declare war, make treaties and enter alliances, raise an army and navy, regulate coinage and borrow money, supervise Indian affairs, establish a post office, and adjudicate disputes between states. Funds and troops were to be supplied by the states according to their wealth and population. But Congress had no power to tax the states or to enforce its decisions. When, as often happened, one or two states balked at meeting an obligation, other states followed suit. "Each state sent what was convenient or appropriate," observed the historians Christopher Collier and James Lincoln Collier, "which usually depended on how close to home the fighting was going on." [8] After the Revolutionary War was won and the common threat from

THEY SHAPED THE PRESIDENCY

Of the fifty-five delegates who attended the Constitutional Convention, fewer than half played important roles in the creation of the presidency. Of those who did, eight stand out. James Wilson and Gouverneur Morris urged the convention to make the presidency the leading institution of the new national government. Wilson and Morris did not accomplish all that they had hoped for, but they were effective in persuading their fellow delegates to create a stronger executive than they originally had been disposed to do. Alexander Hamilton was less effective, George Washington less vocal, and James Madison less certain in their support of a strong executive. But, in various ways, the influence of each was crucial. Roger Sherman and Edmund Randolph were staunch opponents of the presidency as it developed during the convention, but their contributions to the debate helped to shape the delegates' deliberations. Charles Pinckney's suggestions about the presidency and other offices were influential beyond his historical reputation. (See box, The Puzzle of the Pinckney Plan, p. 16.)

the British was ended, states felt even less reason to honor the requests of the national government.

National Problems

For all its weaknesses, the Articles of Confederation did not prevent the United States from winning independence. The Revolutionary War effectively ended on October 17, 1781, when Gen. George Washington's American army and a French fleet, anchored off Yorktown, Virginia, forced the British forces led by Lord Cornwallis to surrender.

The problems of a weak, purely legislative national government became more apparent in the half-decade that followed victory. No longer bound together by the threat of a common foe, the states turned their backs almost completely on Congress and on each other.

Overlapping claims to western lands brought some states into conflict— Connecticut settlers and Pennsylvania troops even clashed violently in a disputed area. The western territory was the nation's most valuable resource, but until the states' rival land claims were settled, it was difficult to develop and profit from it. On the East Coast, some states with port cities, such as New York, Massachusetts, and South Carolina, placed taxes on goods imported from overseas by merchants in neighboring states.

The new nation also was burdened by a crippling debt. Money was owed to soldiers who had fought and merchants who had provided supplies during the Revolutionary War. Threatened in some cases with bankruptcy or foreclosure, many of these soldiers and merchants became angry and sometimes violent. By 1789, foreign creditors held more than $10 million in promissory notes and were owed $1.8 million in unpaid interest. Unless paid, they were unwilling to engage in further trade with the United States. Yet Congress was unable to persuade the states to contribute to the Treasury. The total income of the national government in 1786, for example, was less than one-third of the interest due that year on the national debt.

The United States faced numerous problems on and outside its borders as well. The nation's northern, southern, and western boundaries were under siege, with only an ill-equipped, poorly financed army of seven hundred members

JAMES WILSON

No delegate contributed more to the creation of the presidency than James Wilson of Pennsylvania. Wilson, forty-six years old at the time of the convention, was born in Scotland. The son of a small farmer, he studied law and emigrated to America when he was twenty-four. He became a highly successful lawyer and, in the opinion of many, the preeminent legal scholar of his time. In addition, observed William Pierce, a Georgia delegate who wrote perceptive short profiles of his colleagues at the convention,

Wilson is well acquainted with Man, and understands all the passions that influence him. Government seems to have been his peculiar Study, all the political institutions of the World he knows in detail, and can trace the causes and effects of every revolution from the earliest stages of the Grecian commonwealth down to the present time. No man is more clear, copious, and comprehensive than Mr. Wilson, yet he is no great Orator. He draws the attention not by the charm of his eloquence, but by the force of his reasoning.

Being foreign born, Wilson was much more devoted to the United States as a nation than to any particular state. He signed the Declaration of Independence and helped to write the Articles of Confederation. One of the few lowborn delegates, he had a high regard for the common sense and good instincts of the people. Indeed, he believed that the president should be popularly elected, but, realizing the hopelessness of persuading the convention to adopt that idea, he became the first delegate to propose a scheme of presidential election by electors chosen by the people. Wilson also worked hard and effectively to have the executive power entrusted to a single person, who would be unshackled by a council and eligible for reelection. Wilson spoke as often at the convention as any delegate except Madison, whose support he rallied for a strong presidency.

Wilson's achievements at the Constitutional Convention are all the more remarkable because of the personal travails he was suffering at the time. His beloved wife, Rachel, had died one year earlier, leaving him to care for their six young children, and his personal fortune, built mainly on land speculation, was beginning to unravel. Wilson's financial decline continued and probably caused his early death in 1797— he actually was jailed for debt in New Jersey while serving as a justice of the U.S. Supreme Court.

to defend them. British soldiers continued to occupy two Great Lakes forts that their government had promised to vacate under the Treaty of Paris, which had been concluded in 1783 to settle the Revolutionary War. Similarly, Spain closed the Mississippi River to U.S. ships and made claim to land east of the river that, according to the treaty, rightfully belonged to the United States. Both Spain and Britain encouraged Indian raids on American frontier settlements. (Spain, in particular, roused the Creeks in Florida to harass settlements in Georgia.) Abroad, American ships were preyed on by pirates in the Mediterranean Sea and denied entry by the British to Britain's colonies in Canada and the West Indies, two lucrative markets for U.S. trade.

GOUVERNEUR MORRIS

Gouverneur Morris was one of the more flamboyant delegates at the Constitutional Convention. But his brilliance earned him respect as a strong and effective advocate of executive power. As William Pierce observed:

> Mr. Gouverneur Morris is one of those Genius's in whom every species of talent combine to render him conspicuous and flourishing in public debate:—He winds through all the mazes of rhetoric, and throws around him such a glare that he charms, captivates, and leads away the senses of all who hear him. With an infinite stretch of fancy he brings to view things when he is engaged in deep argumentation, that render all the labor of reasoning easy and pleasing. But with all these powers he is fickle and inconstant,—never pursuing one train of thinking,—nor ever regular. . . . This Gentleman . . . has been unfortunate in losing one of his Legs, and getting all the flesh taken off his right arm by a scald, when a youth.

Morris blended the characters of the successful businessman and the stylish rake. Indeed, he fostered the rumor that his leg had been lost after he injured it leaping from a married woman's second-story window to escape her husband—the truth was that he had hurt it in a carriage accident. At the convention, Morris fought successfully against having the executive be chosen by the legislature, a process that he felt would degenerate into "the work of intrigue, of cabal, and of faction: it will be like the election of a pope by a conclave of cardinals." Morris also urged that the president be permitted to stand for reelection, in order to take advantage of "the great motive to good behavior, the hope of being rewarded with a re-appointment." Aware of his fellow delegates' reluctance to entrust as much power as he would have liked to a single executive, Morris allayed some of their fears by arguing that an impeachment provision be included in the Constitution.

To a large degree, British hostility to the United States was caused, or at least rationalized, by the American failure to comply with two provisions of the Treaty of Paris. One provision compelled the United States to reimburse British loyalists for property that had been seized from them during the war; the other required that prewar debts to British merchants be paid. States actively resisted both of these requirements, and the national government was powerless to enforce them.

In the midst of foreign and domestic difficulties, another problem developed that mixed elements of both. A currency crisis occurred in the United States, partly because Americans had gone on a buying spree after the Revolutionary War ended, importing luxury items such as clocks, glassware, and furniture from Great Britain. As gold and silver (the only American money acceptable to foreign creditors) flowed out of the country to pay for these products, they became scarce at home. Meanwhile, many debtors, especially farmers who had left the land to fight for independence and still had not been paid by the financially destitute national government, faced bankruptcy or foreclosure. In response, they pressured their state legislatures to print vast sums of paper money that they could use to pay off their debts. Creditors, horrified at the prospect of being reimbursed in depreciated currency, fought back politically, but with limited success. State legislatures, being both powerful and democratic, often were more responsive to the greater number of debtors than to the smaller number of creditors among their constituents.

Fear of executive power remained strong among Americans during the decade after independence was declared. But the problems that beset the United States under the strong legislative governments of the states and the weak legislative government of the Articles of Confederation taught certain lessons, particularly to conservatives and people of property. As the political scientist Charles Thach has written, "Experience with the state governments during the period following the cessation of hostilities served . . . to confirm the tendencies toward increasing confidence in the executive and increasing distrust of the legislature." Experience also taught certain lessons about the proper design of an effective executive:

> It taught that executive energy and responsibility are inversely proportional to executive size; that, consequently, the one-man executive is best. It taught the value of integration; the necessity of executive appointments, civil and military; the futility of legislative military control. It demonstrated the necessity of the veto as a protective measure . . . [for] preventing unwise legislation. . . . It demonstrated the value of a fixed executive salary which the legislature could not reduce. It discredited choice by the legislature, though without teaching clearly the lesson of popular choice. . . . And, above all, it assured the acceptance of, if it did not create, a new concept of national government—the fundamental principles of which were the ruling constitution, the limited legislature, and the three equal and coordinate departments.[9]

A Convention Is Called

Of all the problems that plagued the new nation after independence, none seemed more amenable to solution than those involving commerce among the states. Few benefited, and many suffered, from the protectionist walls that several states had built around their economies. The Virginia state assembly, at the petition of James Madison, one of its youngest members, called for a trade conference to be held at Annapolis, Maryland, in September 1786 and urged all the other states to send delegations.

In some ways, the Annapolis Convention was a failure. Only three states (Virginia, New Jersey, and Delaware) sent full delegations, and seven states, suspicious of Virginia's intentions, boycotted the meeting altogether. The convention made no proposals to remedy the nation's trade difficulties.

But the delegates who did come to Annapolis, notably Madison and Alexander Hamilton of New York, George Washington's young aide in the Revolutionary War, rescued the enterprise by issuing a bold call to Congress to convene an even more wide-ranging meeting. They urged that the states be enjoined to choose delegates to "meet at Philadelphia on the second Monday in May next [1787], to take into consideration the situation of the United States, to devise such further provisions as shall appear to them necessary to render the constitution of the Federal Government adequate to the exigencies of the Union."

Congress initially was cool to the summons of the Annapolis Convention, but within weeks an event occurred that lent urgency to the nationalist cause. Mobs of farmers in western Massachusetts, saddled with debts and unable to persuade the state legislature to ease credit, closed down courts and stopped sheriffs' auctions to prevent foreclosure orders from being issued and executed against their lands. Although similar outbreaks had occurred in other states, they had been suppressed easily. This one, dubbed Shays' Rebellion after one of its leaders, the Revolutionary War hero Daniel Shays, threatened for a time to rage out of control. The reaction around the country among people of

ALEXANDER HAMILTON

Alexander Hamilton's role in the framing of the Constitution was enormously important, but his contributions at the Constitutional Convention were less significant.

Before the convention, it was Hamilton and James Madison, more than anyone else, who transformed the failed Annapolis Convention of 1786 into a vehicle to persuade the old Congress of the Articles of Confederation to summon delegates to a more far-reaching convention.

After the Constitutional Convention was over, Hamilton recruited Madison and John Jay to help him write an eighty-five-part newspaper series to urge the ratification of the Constitution. (Hamilton wrote about fifty.) The collection of articles, which were written under the pen name "Publius" and later compiled into a book called *The Federalist Papers*, generally is regarded as the greatest work of political philosophy ever written in the United States. *(See box, The Federalist Papers on Powers of the Presidency, p. 43.)*

At the convention itself, however, Hamilton was not a major figure. This was partly because the three-member New York delegation to which he belonged also included Robert Yates and John Lansing, two opponents of a stronger central government who consistently outvoted Hamilton. Frustrated, Hamilton left Philadelphia early in the convention, returning only after Yates and Lansing themselves decided to leave.

Another reason for Hamilton's middling influence at the convention was his arrogant, impatient manner, which was ill suited to the deliberative, sometimes tedious work of the convention. The thirty-two-year-old Hamilton had always been a man in a hurry. A child of illegitimate birth in the British West Indies, he had made his way to New York as a teenager, fought in the Revolutionary War, and even won a command (at age twenty-one) under Gen. George Washington. According to William Pierce's description,

> [T]here is something too feeble in his voice to be equal to the strains of oratory;—it is my opinion that he is rather a convincing Speaker, [than] a blazing Orator. Colo. Hamilton requires time to think,—he enquires into every part of his subject with the searchings of philosophy, and when he comes forward he comes highly charged with interesting matter, there is no skimming over the surface of a subject with him, he must sink to the bottom to see what foundation it rests on.... He is ... of small stature, and lean. His manners are tinctured with stiffness, and sometimes with a degree of vanity that is highly disagreeable.

A final reason for Hamilton's relatively minor role at the convention is that his ideas were far more radical than either the country or his fellow delegates were willing to accept. As much as possible, Hamilton wanted to transplant the British form of government into American soil. The Senate, like the British House of Lords, would have life tenure. So, like the British monarch, would the "supreme Executive Authority," which he proposed to call "Governor." Only members of the House of Representatives would be elected for brief terms, as was the House of Commons.

For all his disappointment with the convention and his role in it, Hamilton defended the Constitution in *The Federalist Papers* as enthusiastically as if he had written every jot and title of the document. Indeed, in No. 69, he took great pains to persuade his readers not only that the American president was unlike the British king but also that the president was to be preferred for that very reason.

Satisfied with the status quo, these four prominent Americans refused to attend the Constitutional Convention because they were basically satisfied with existing governing arrangements. From left, Patrick Henry and Richard Henry Lee of Virginia, George Clinton of New York, and Samuel Adams of Massachusetts.

property and, more generally, those worried about social disorder was one of shock and horror, both at the class warfare that seemed to be erupting and the inability of the national government to deal with it. On February 21, 1787, Congress decided to act on the request of the Annapolis Convention:

> RESOLVED, That in the opinion of Congress it is expedient that on the second Monday in May next a Convention of delegates who shall have been appointed by the several states be held in Philadelphia for the sole and express purpose of revising the Articles of Confederation and reporting to Congress and the state legislatures such alterations and provisions therein as shall when agreed to in Congress and confirmed by the states render the federal constitution adequate to the exigencies of government & the preservation of the Union.

The states were, of course, no more compelled to obey this summons of Congress than any other—Rhode Island never did send delegates to the convention. But when a sufficient number of states—whether frightened by the prospect of further uprisings similar to Shays' Rebellion, concerned about the nation's growing domestic and international weakness, or inspired by the example of the nationally revered Washington, who decided to attend as a delegate from his native Virginia—selected delegations, other states fell into line for fear of having their interests ignored.

THE CONSTITUTIONAL CONVENTION

The Constitutional Convention has been variously described over the years as an "assembly of demigods" (Jefferson), a "miracle at Philadelphia" (author Catherine Drinker Bowen), and a "nationalist reform caucus" (political scientist John Roche), to cite but three descriptions. The convention may have been all of these things and more. But, mundane-

ly, it also was a gathering of fifty-five individuals (the delegates) in a particular setting (Philadelphia) at a specific moment in history (summer 1787).

The risk was great once the convention was called. As Benjamin Franklin wrote to Jefferson on April 19, 1787, "If it does not do good it will do harm, as it will show that we have not the wisdom among us to govern ourselves." [10] Nor did the work of the convention always proceed smoothly. Near the midway point, Washington wrote, "I almost despair of seeing a favourable issue to the proceedings of the Convention, and do therefore repent having had any agency in the business."[11] Nevertheless, from May to September the delegates used drafts and debates, compromises and committees to work through the many issues that faced them. The design of the presidency not only took a great deal of their time and effort in its own right but also was interwoven with the design of the other institutions and processes of the new government.

The Delegates

Nearly seventy-five delegates were selected by the various states to represent them at the convention in Philadelphia; of these, fifty-five actually attended. Self-selection had much to do with determining who was chosen and who went. Political leaders who were committed to the idea that the political system had to be dramatically improved embraced the opportunity to attend the convention. Most of those who were basically satisfied with the status quo—including such prominent Americans as Patrick Henry and Richard Henry Lee of Virginia, Samuel Adams of Massachusetts, and George Clinton of New York—stayed away. (Henry said he "smelt a rat.") Had they attended and fought stubbornly for their positions, observed the political scientist Clinton Rossiter, the convention "would have been much more perfectly representative of the active citizenry of 1787. It would also, one is bound to point out, have been crippled as a nation-building instrument." [12]

The fifty-five delegates were generally united, then, in their belief that a stronger national government was vital to the health of the new American nation. In part, this was because many of them had shared similar experiences. Forty-two were current or former members of Congress; twenty-one had risked life and livelihood by fighting in the Revolutionary War; and eight had signed the Declaration of Independence.

Other shared characteristics contributed to the delegates' common outlook on many fundamental issues. Almost all were prosperous—around half were lawyers and another quarter owned plantations or large farms. Only two delegates were small farmers, who made up 85 percent of the nation's white population. All had held public office; indeed, more than forty currently occupied positions in their state governments, including ten judges, thirty legislators, and three governors. Several had helped to write their state constitutions. All were well known in their states; about one-fourth had national reputations.

All of the delegates to the convention were white males. All but the two Roman Catholics were Protestant Christians in affiliation, but most were rationalist in outlook. Thirty had attended college, at a time when a college education was rigorous and rare. The College of New Jersey (now Princeton University), the College of William and Mary, and Yale University were the most frequently represented alma maters.

Collectively, the convention was young. Many of the delegates were "the young men of the Revolution" in the phrase of the historians Stanley Elkins and Eric McKitrick— men who had come of age during the revolutionary decade of the 1770s, when the idea of building a nation was more inspiring than traditional state loyalties. [13] Madison, at thirty-six, was older than eleven other delegates, including several who were to play significant roles at the convention, such as Gouverneur Morris of Pennsylvania (thirty-five), Edmund Randolph of Virginia (thirty-three), and Charles Pinckney of South Carolina, who was twenty-nine but said he was twenty-four so that he could claim to be the youngest delegate. (That distinction belonged to Jonathan Dayton of New Jersey, who was twenty-six.) The average age of the delegates—even counting Franklin, who at age eighty-one was sixteen years older than the second-oldest delegate—was forty-three.

Still, differences could be found among those who attended the convention. Some represented small states, some large ones. Some were southerners, some were from the middle Atlantic region, some were from New England. Regardless of region, however, most lived in the long-settled eastern coastal parts of their states; the backcountry was

ROGER SHERMAN

"Mr. Sherman exhibits the oddest shaped character I ever remember to have met with," William Pierce observed. "He is awkward, unmeaning, and unaccountably strange in his manner.... [T]he oddity of his address, the vulgarness that accompany his public speaking, and that strange New England cant which runs through his public as well as his private speaking make everything that is connected with him grotesque and laughable."

For all his strangeness of speech and manner, Sherman was one of the most influential political leaders of his time. He had signed and helped to write both the Articles of Confederation and, along with Thomas Jefferson, John Adams, and Benjamin Franklin, the Declaration of Independence. After the Constitution took effect, Sherman was elected as a representative from Connecticut in the first Congress and a senator in the second. At the Constitutional Convention, Sherman spoke more frequently than anyone other than James Madison and, perhaps, James Wilson and was the author of the Connecticut Compromise on representation in Congress, an issue that had stymied the convention. Even Pierce agreed that Sherman "deserves infinite praise,—no Man has a better Heart or a clearer Head. If he cannot embellish he can furnish thoughts that are wise and useful. He is an able politician, and extremely artful in accomplishing any particular object;—it is remarked that he seldom fails."

Sherman was fifty-six years old in 1787. He was unusual among the delegates in two obvious ways. First (like Wilson), he was lowborn, the son of a small family farmer. The house Sherman grew up in contained nine people and three beds. Second, he was a career politician who, during most of his life, earned his living from holding office.

Sherman was one of the most effective opponents of a strong presidency at the convention. He regarded the ideal executive "as nothing more than an instrument for carrying the will of the Legislature into effect." For that reason, he believed that the legislature should be free to create and revise the executive as it saw fit. Specifically, Sherman wanted the legislature, not the Constitution, to define the executive's powers; "he wished the number might not be fixed, but that the legislature should be at liberty to appoint one or more as experience might dictate"; and he urged that "the national Legislature should have power to remove the Executive at pleasure." To Sherman, in fact, an "independence of the executive on the supreme legislative was in his opinion the very essence of tyranny."

GEORGE WASHINGTON

George Washington spoke hardly a word during the debates at the Constitutional Convention—he thanked his fellow delegates on the first day of the convention for choosing him to preside and urged them on the last day to pass a minor motion involving representation in Congress. But, perhaps as much as any other delegate, Washington's presence was felt at the convention, especially on the subject of the presidency.

Washington's decision to attend the Constitutional Convention gave the proceedings an otherwise unattainable legitimacy among the people. William Pierce wrote:

> Having conducted these states to independence and peace, he now appears to assist in framing a Government to make the People happy. Like Gustavus Vasa, he may be said to be the deliverer of his Country;—like Peter the Great he appears as the politician and the States-man; and like Cincinnatus he returned to his farm perfectly contented with being only a plain Citizen, after enjoying the highest honors of the Confederacy,—and now only seeks for the approbation of his Country-men by being virtuous and useful.

Despite the silence in debate that Washington maintained as president of the convention, he clearly favored a stronger central government and a strong executive within that government. This is attested to not just by his correspondence and one of his few recorded votes at the convention (in favor of a unitary executive rather than a council), but also by the record of his life.

Washington, who was fifty-five at the time of the convention, already had been, as commander in chief of the revolutionary army, the closest thing to a national executive in the young nation's experience. His fears were less of government power than of the disorder that the absence of power invited. These views were made known to his fellow delegates, not in formal debate, but in private and informal discussions.

Washington influenced the creation of the presidency in various ways. His fellow delegates' certain knowledge that he would be the first president increased their willingness to resolve doubts about executive power in favor of the presidency. The constitutional powers of the president "are full great," wrote South Carolina delegate Pierce Butler to a British kinsman after the convention, "and greater than I was disposed to make them. Nor, entre nous, do I believe they would have been so great had not many of the delegates cast their eye on General Washington as President; and shaped their Ideas of the Powers to be given to a President, by their opinions of his Virtue."

---

hardly represented. Temperamentally, wrote the Colliers, they were "as diverse as any group of people is likely to be. Some were bold, some cautious; some shy, some outspoken; some politically adept, some bristly and rancorous." [14]

The wealth of most of the delegates derived from personal property—that is, government securities and investments in manufacturing, shipping, and land speculation. The prosperity of other delegates lay in real property, notably agricultural land and, in the South, slaves. (The historian Charles A. Beard believed that the enactment of the Constitution, more than anything else, was a triumph of the "personalty"—that is, financial and commercial interests— over the "realty," or landed interests.[15]) In the realm of political philosophy, the delegates agreed on basic goals but often differed on the proper means to achieve them.

Delegates also varied in the extent of their participation at the convention. Of the fifty-five who came to Philadelphia, only twenty-nine were there at the beginning and stayed until the end. This number, however, included Madison, Randolph, Washington, and George Mason of Virginia, Wilson and Franklin of Pennsylvania, Elbridge Gerry of Massachusetts, Roger Sherman of Connecticut, Charles Pinckney of South Carolina, and most of the other more able members of the convention.

The other twenty-six delegates were part-timers to varying degrees, although some of them also played important roles, such as Pennsylvania's Gouverneur Morris, Oliver Ellsworth of Connecticut, and William Paterson of New Jersey. These delegates either arrived late at the convention (in some cases because their states had been tardy in choosing them) or left early because of illness, dissatisfaction with the proceedings, or a need to attend to state or personal business. Thus most sessions of the convention were attended by thirty to forty delegates, of whom the majority were regulars and the rest a shifting cast.

The Setting

Philadelphia was the site of the Constitutional Convention. The capital of Pennsylvania at the time the convention took place (Harrisburg replaced it in 1812), Philadelphia was in many ways the nation's capital as well, even though Congress met in New York. Philadelphia was by far the largest American city, with a population of around 45,000. It also was the commercial, cultural, and intellectual center of the United States. Not least among Philadelphia's virtues was its central location. Travel was arduous and time-consuming in the late eighteenth century. Few southerners wanted to travel to New York or Boston and few New Englanders to

Charleston, South Carolina, which were the other leading cities of the day.

One of Philadelphia's least-appealing qualities was its notoriously hot, humid, and insect-ridden summers. The summer of 1787, especially after a heat wave struck on June 11, was no exception. The city sweltered for almost the entire duration of the Constitutional Convention. The delegates found that although closed windows made the heat even more stifling, open windows were invitations to Philadelphia's infamous black flies during the day and its mosquitoes at night. Sometimes they moved up to the second floor to conduct their business.

As in most other cities, much of the social and business life of Philadelphia during the late eighteenth century took place in taverns, which were more like inns than modern bars or saloons. The leading tavern in Philadelphia was the Indian Queen, described by one New England traveler as "a large pile of buildings, with many spacious halls and numerous small apartments," each equipped with a bed, bureau, table, mirror, and one or two chairs. Many of the delegates stayed at the Indian Queen, and even those who did not (Madison and most of the Virginia delegation, for example,

stayed at the boardinghouse of Mrs. Mary House, and Washington was the houseguest of Robert Morris, a Pennsylvania delegate to the convention) helped to make the tavern the convention's after-hours social and, in many cases, business center.

During the convention, the delegates' days settled into a routine. After breakfast and a morning walk or ride, most of them would stroll over to Independence Hall—then called the State House and used as the capitol building for the government of Pennsylvania—where they would meet from nine-thirty or ten o'clock in the morning until three or four in the afternoon. From the street, delegates would enter through the main door into the State House's great hallway. To the right were the chambers of the state supreme court; straight ahead and up the stairs were the offices of Pennsylvania's Supreme Executive Council (Franklin was its president); and to the left was the forty-by-forty-foot room in which the state legislature usually met.

The legislature's room was used by the delegates during the convention, just as it had been used by the Continental Congress from 1775 to 1783. (Among other things, the Declaration of Independence was signed there.)

JAMES MADISON

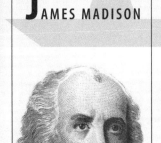

Even as admiring a scholar as the political scientist Charles Thach, who wrote in his book *The Creation of the Presidency* that "Madison has with much justice been called the father of the Constitution," conceded that "the claims for his paternity do not extend to the fundamentals of Article II."

Madison himself claimed no paternity of the presidency. As he wrote George Washington on April 16, 1787, less than a month before the scheduled opening of the convention, "I have scarcely ventured as yet to form my own opinion either of the manner in which [the executive] ought to be constituted or of the authorities with which it ought to be cloathed." Madison's Virginia Plan left the number and term of the executive unspecified and offered only a vague definition of what the executive's powers would be. The plan was more specific in providing that the legislature would select the executive, but James Wilson and Gouverneur Morris soon persuaded Madison to change his mind on this issue. Madison actually argued against legislative selection on July 19 and spoke favorably about election by the people.

Indeed, far from being preoccupied with the design of the executive, Madison's primary concern was for the creation of a government by the people, not the states. This purpose would be achieved, he believed, mainly through the legislature, which he felt should be checked and balanced internally but apportioned according to population and empowered both to pass laws that acted directly on individuals and to veto state laws.

A member of the Virginia aristocracy, Madison was thirty-six years old at the time of the convention; he had been educated at the College of New Jersey in Princeton. Always fearful of power, Madison's main battles as a state legislator in Virginia had been against British tyranny and the established church. In Congress his target became what he regarded as the runaway state governments and the threat they posed to property. Madison's solution was a central government strong enough to curb the power of the states but thoroughly saddled with internal checks and balances so that its own power did not become excessive.

At the Constitutional Convention, which he and Alexander Hamilton had worked so hard to arrange, Madison made a deep and positive impression on his fellow delegates. William Pierce observed:

> [E]very Person seems to acknowledge his greatness. He blends together the profound politician, with the Scholar. In the management of every great question he evidently took the lead in the Convention, and tho' he cannot be called an Orator, he is a most agreeable, eloquent, and convincing Speaker. From a spirit of industry and application which he possesses in a most eminent degree, he always comes forward the best informed Man of any point in debate. The affairs of the United States, he perhaps, has the most correct knowledge of, of any Man in the Union. . . . Mr. Madison is . . . a Gentleman of great modesty,—with a remarkable sweet temper. He is easy and unreserved among his acquaintances, and has a most agreeable style of conversation.

The high-ceilinged room was simple—only the convention's speaker's mahogany chair and inkstand lent any ornamentation. The speaker, or presiding officer, sat behind a table with only a small bell (no gavel) to call meetings to order. Thirteen other tables were scattered about the room, covered, like the speaker's table, with green baize (a thick wool cloth). Each was equipped with inkstands, goose quill pens, sand, and writing paper. (Delegates added their own materials, including papers, books, and snuff and tobacco boxes.) Each table was reserved for a state delegation—the southern tables on one side, the New England tables on the other, and the middle states' tables in between. Washington, after being elected president of the convention, sat in the speaker's chair. Madison, although a Virginia delegate, found a chair near the front and middle of the room so that he could keep thorough notes of the debates. He later claimed, "I was not absent for a single day, nor more than a casual fraction of an hour in any day, so that I could not have lost a single speech, unless a very short one." [16]

Rules and Procedures

Congress had called upon the convention to assemble on Monday, May 14, 1787. But not until Friday, May 25, were the seven state delegations that were needed for a quorum present in Philadelphia. Most of the other delegations arrived within a few days, but some came much later. Rhode Island, whose legislature was fiercely opposed to any effort to strengthen the national government, boycotted the convention entirely.

The first order of business on May 25 was to elect a president, a word that, in the usage of the day, suggested a "presiding officer" more than a "leader" or "chief executive." [17] Not surprisingly, George Washington was the delegates' unanimous choice. Washington spoke on only one minor issue during the convention—he rose on the last day to support a proposal that members of the House of Representatives represent at least thirty thousand people rather than forty thousand. (The delegates agreed unanimously.) But clearly Washington played more than a ceremonial role. According to the Colliers, "During that long, hot summer, this gregarious man was constantly having dinner, tea, supper with people, and one must assume of course that he was actively promoting his position"—namely, a strong national government and a strong executive within that government.[18] Even Washington's last-minute speech on representation was politically meaningful in symbolic terms. As Gordon Woods points out, "It was his way of saying to his colleagues that he favored the Constitution." [19]

After Washington's election as convention president, a secretary was chosen—Maj. William Jackson of Pennsylvania. Jackson kept the convention's official journal, which was little more than a record of motions and votes. Fortunately, Madison decided to keep a more extensive record of the delegates' debates and deliberations. Madison had been frustrated in his studies of other governments by the near-impossibility of determining what their founders had intended when creating them. Although he was acting on his own initiative, the other delegates knew what he was doing. In fairness to them, he decided to keep his notes secret until the last delegate died. This turned out to be himself; he died in 1836, at the age of eighty-five. Along with the rest of Madison's papers, his notes on the Constitutional Convention were purchased by Congress in 1837 and published in 1840.

The only other business of the convention's first day was to accept the credentials of the various state delegations. In doing so, the delegates implicitly agreed that the then-customary procedure of having each state cast an equal vote in any national body would be followed. Wilson of Pennsylvania was displeased by this arrangement (he felt that the more populous states should have a greater voice) but was persuaded by Madison and others that to alienate the small state delegates at such an early stage would abort the entire proceedings.

On Monday, May 28, the delegates adopted additional rules and procedures. None was more important to the success of the convention than the rule of secrecy. The rule was simple: no delegate was to communicate anything to anyone, including members of his family, about the convention's discussions and deliberations.

Thomas Jefferson, then the U.S. ambassador to France, wrote John Adams, the ambassador to Great Britain, that he was appalled by "so abominable a precedent [as secrecy] . . . . Nothing can justify this [decision] but the innocence of their intentions and ignorance of the value of public discussions." But in a letter to Jefferson, Madison explained the delegates' action. "It was thought expedient in order to secure unbiased discussion within doors, and to prevent misconceptions & misconstructions without, to establish some rules of caution which will for no short time restrain even a confidential communication of our proceedings." [20] In other words, secrecy permitted delegates to think through issues and even to change their minds when necessary without appearing weak or vacillating. It also kept opponents of the convention from sensationalizing particular proposals or decisions as a means of discrediting the whole undertaking. Years later, Madison told historian Jared Sparks that "no Constitution would ever have been adopted by the Convention if the debates had been made public." [21]

Another important rule adopted by the convention was to permit its decisions to be reconsidered at the request of even a single delegate. Because issues could always be raised and decided again, those who were on the losing side of a crucial vote were encouraged to stay and try to persuade the other delegates, rather than to walk out and return home in protest and frustration.

An Overview of the Convention

The Constitutional Convention was not a scripted or even an especially orderly proceeding. The delegates' decision to allow issues to be redecided, reinforced by their twin desires to build consensus among themselves and to create a government whose parts would mesh with one another, meant that the convention "could not, and did not, proceed in a straight line, neatly disposing of one issue after the next until all were dealt with. It moved instead in swirls and loops, again and again backtracking to pick up issues previously debated." [22] The historian Jack Rakove has compared the constitution-writing process to "the solution of a complex equation with a large number of dependent variables: change the value of one, and the values shift throughout." [23]

Still, the Constitutional Convention was not a completely chaotic undertaking. Various plans (submitted by delegates) and committees (appointed by the convention) helped to order its deliberations. These plans and committees structured the convention into seven main stages:

- Introduction of the Virginia Plan (May 29)
- The convention's decision to recast itself as a Committee of the Whole, originally for the purpose of considering the Virginia Plan in detail but later to evaluate Alexander Hamilton's plan and New Jersey Plan as well (May 30–June 19)
- Clause-by-clause debate by the delegates of the decisions of the Committee of the Whole (June 20–July 26)
- Work of the five-member Committee of Detail, appointed by the convention to produce a draft of the new Constitution that reflected the delegates' manifold decisions on particular issues (July 24–August 6)
- Consideration by the delegates of each provision of the report of the Committee of Detail (August 7–31)
- Recommendations of the eleven-member Committee on Postponed Matters (or Committee of Eleven), created to propose acceptable solutions to the problems that continued to divide the delegates (August 31–September 8)
- Final adjustments, including the work of the Committee of Style, which was charged to write a complete and polished draft of the Constitution, and last-minute tinkering by the delegates, culminating in the signing of the proposed plan of government (September 9–17).

Virginia Plan (May 29)

The Virginia Plan, introduced on May 29 by Gov. Edmund Randolph but written mainly by Madison, offered a radical departure from the weak, one-branch government of the Articles of Confederation. The plan proposed to create a three-branch national government and to elevate it to clear supremacy over the states, in part by grounding the new government's authority squarely in the sovereignty of the people.

According to the Virginia Plan, the heart of the national government would be a bicameral legislature, with the lower house apportioned according to population and its members selected by the people and the upper house elected by the lower house. The legislature's powers would include broad authority not just to pass laws, but also to conduct foreign policy and to appoint most government officials, including judges.

A national judiciary, organized into one or more "supreme tribunals" and various "inferior tribunals" and appointed (with life tenure) by the legislature, would form a second branch. One of its broad-ranging powers was "impeachments of any National officers."

The government also would have an executive branch, although it was vaguely defined in the Virginia Plan. The "national executive" (the plan left unresolved the question of whether this would be a person or a group) was "to be chosen by the National Legislature for a term of ___ years." Its powers were obscure: "besides a general authority to execute the National laws, it ought to enjoy the Executive rights vested in Congress by the [Articles of] Confederation." No one knew exactly what those "Executive rights" were.

Another element of the proposed new government was a "Council of revision," consisting of "the executive and a convenient number of the National Judiciary," that would be empowered to veto laws passed by the national legislature, subject to override if a vetoed law was repassed by an unspecified legislative majority.

Finally, the new government would have the power to veto state laws that were in conflict with the Constitution or with national laws. For Madison, argues Gordon Wood, the worst thing about the Articles of Confederation was not the weakness of the national government but "the vices within the several states" that had produced an abundance of unjust and inconsistent legislation. Thus, when this provision of the Virginia Plan was rejected by the convention, Madison was for a time "convinced that the Constitution was doomed to fail." [24]

The Virginia Plan was one of two offered to the convention on May 29. Madison recorded in his notes for that day that Charles Pinckney of South Carolina also introduced a plan. But Madison, who had long loathed Pinckney from their days together in Congress, neither described the plan nor included its text. (See box, The Puzzle of the Pinckney Plan, p. 16.)

The delegates' response to the Virginia Plan was remarkably placid, especially considering the radical departure in the direction of a strong national government that the plan proposed. "So sharp a break was Virginia asking the other states to make with the American past that one wonders why at least one stunned delegate . . . did not rise up and cry havoc at the top of his lungs," Rossiter has written. "Instead, the delegates ended this [May 29] session by resolv-

THE PUZZLE OF THE PINCKNEY PLAN

Charles Pinckney

Did James Madison cheat Charles Pinckney of South Carolina out of proper credit for his role in crafting the Constitution?

Madison, the author of the highly significant Virginia Plan and sometimes called the "Father of the Constitution," kept the only set of thorough notes on the debates and resolutions of the Constitutional Convention. Yet when Pinckney presented "the draught of a federal government which he had prepared" to the convention on May 29 (just after Gov. Edmund Randolph of Virginia introduced the Virginia Plan), Madison failed to describe it in his notes. He also omitted any description of Pinckney's June 25 speech about his plan. Yet convention records show that the Pinckney Plan was referred for consideration to the Committee of the Whole and the Committee of Detail.

In 1818, noting these discrepancies while reviewing the convention's records, Secretary of State John Quincy Adams wrote Pinckney to ask for a copy of his plan. Pinckney replied that he had several rough drafts in his papers, but sent Adams "the one I believe it was."

The document that Pinckney sent to Adams resembled Madison's Virginia Plan in some ways—for example, it called for a strong, three-branch national government—but went beyond the Virginia Plan in other ways that seemed to foreshadow the convention's ultimate decisions. Pinckney's president was unitary and vigorous; his Senate was apportioned partly by state and partly by population; his House of Representatives had the duty of impeachment; his enumeration of the powers of the three branches was detailed; and so on.

Pinckney freely admitted that he had borrowed widely in creating his plan, notably from the Articles of Confederation, the Massachusetts constitution, and,

especially, the New York constitution. Still, depending on how one does the counting, somewhere between twenty-one and forty-three specific contributions to the Constitution seem to have been made by Pinckney.[1]

After Adams published the records of the convention, including the Pinckney Plan, Madison and his admirers attempted to discredit Pinckney, and his contemporary admirers continue to do so. Madison biographer Irving Brant has branded Pinckney "a sponger and a plagiarist," accusing him of stealing ideas from the Virginia Plan that Madison had shared with him in preconvention conversations. Clinton Rossiter's account of the convention says that the Pinckney Plan was "at best merely a source of familiar phrases for the members of the Committee of Detail." Madison himself, through the historian Jared Sparks, suggested that Pinckney had sent Adams a bogus draft that made his own role in creating the Constitution seem far more important than it really was. In truth, studies of the ink and paper used for the draft Pinckney sent Adams dated it at 1818, not 1787, but this may only mean that Pinckney kept the original and had a copy made for mailing.[2]

What seems indisputable is that Madison disliked Pinckney intensely. In addition, Pinckney had a personal stake in making his role at the convention seem central. He was, after all, an unlovely character—ambitious, vain, egocentric, aggressive, and not always truthful. Twenty-nine years old at the time of the convention, he told the other delegates that he was twenty-four so that he, not the twenty-six-year-old Jonathan Dayton of New Jersey, would be regarded as the youngest delegate. But Pinckney had been a staunch advocate of a strong central government for years. And the historical record—not just his own writings but documents found in the papers of delegate James Wilson of Pennsylvania and others—seems to accord Pinckney a greater share of the credit for writing the Constitution than Madison and his partisans have allowed.

1. S. Sidney Ulmer, "James Madison and the Pinckney Plan," *South Carolina Law Quarterly* 9 (spring 1957); Ulmer, "Charles Pinckney: Father of the Constitution?" *South Carolina Law Quarterly* 10 (winter 1958); Christopher Collier and James Lincoln Collier, *Decision in Philadelphia: The Constitutional Convention of 1787* (New York: Ballantine, 1986), 97.

2. Irving Brant, *James Madison*, vols. 1–6 (Indianapolis: Bobbs-Merrill, 1941–1961), 3: 28; Clinton Rossiter, *1787: The Grand Convention* (London: MacGibbon and Kee, 1968), 171; Collier and Collier, *Decision in Philadelphia*, chap. 7.

ing to go into a 'committee of the whole house' " on the next day to "consider the state of the American union." [25]

Committee of the Whole (May 30–June 19)

In becoming a Committee of the Whole, the convention was, in a sense, simply giving itself a different name—the same group of delegates made up the committee as made up the convention. But as the Committee of the Whole they could operate more informally. (To symbolize this change, Washington temporarily stepped down as president, and Nathaniel Gorham of Massachusetts was chosen to preside.) In addition, any decision made by the delegates while meet-

ing as the Committee of the Whole would be in the form of a recommendation to the convention and thus would have to be voted on at least one more time.

From May 30 to June 13, the Committee of the Whole spent most of its time going over the Virginia Plan, clause by clause. Much of the plan was accepted. But some of it was altered, and some ambiguous provisions were clarified. For example, the executive was defined as a unitary, or one-person, office. This person would be elected for a single, seven-year term by the legislature and was subject to impeachment and removal on grounds of "malpractice or neglect of duty." The executive alone, not a council of revision, was empowered to veto laws passed by the legislature, subject to override by a two-thirds vote of both houses. The requirement for a super majority, here and elsewhere in the new plan of government, was an American invention, unknown to the British Parliament but widely used in the states.[26]

In deference to the states, members of the upper house of the national legislature (who had to be at least thirty years old) would be chosen by the various state legislatures. They would serve seven-year terms and be eligible for reelection. Members of the lower house, also eligible for reelection, would serve three-year terms. All members of the national legislature would be barred from holding any other government office, mainly to prevent conflicts of interest from arising. As for the courts, there would be a "supreme tribunal," and judges who served on it or on such "inferior tribunals" as the national legislature might create would be appointed by the upper house of the legislature for a lifetime term.

New Jersey Plan

One plank of the Virginia Plan was especially controversial—the provision that both houses of the national legislature be apportioned according to population. Delegates from the states that thought of themselves as large (specifically, those from Virginia, Massachusetts, Pennsylvania, and the three states whose populations were growing most rapidly, Georgia, North Carolina, and South Carolina) favored the idea. They split sharply with the delegates from the other states, who feared that their constituents would be hopelessly outnumbered in the legislature and who favored instead the existing arrangement—namely, equal representation in Congress for each state. A compromise plan, proposed by Roger Sherman of Connecticut on June 11, would have apportioned the lower house of the legislature according to population and the upper house on the basis of one state, one vote, but few delegates were ready yet for compromise. Instead, delegates from the small states responded to the Virginia Plan with a sweeping counterproposal of their own. It was introduced on June 15 by William Paterson of New Jersey.

The New Jersey Plan came in the form of amendments to the Articles of Confederation, rather than as a new constitution. It proposed to add two new branches to the one-branch national government—a plural, or committee-style, executive, to be elected by Congress for a single term and "removeable by Cong[ress] on application by a majority of the Executives of the several States," and a supreme court, with its judges appointed by the executive for lifetime terms. The plan also would declare national laws and treaties to be "the supreme law of the respective States" and would authorize the executive to use force if necessary to implement them. In addition, Congress would be empowered to regulate interstate and international commerce and to impose taxes. But the main purpose of the New Jersey Plan was an unstat-

ed one: to preserve the structure of Congress under the Articles—a single house in which each state, regardless of size, would cast one vote.

Hamilton's Plan

On June 18, Alexander Hamilton delivered a four-to-six-hour-long speech to the delegates in which he urged them to consider his plan for an avowedly British-style government. "[H]e had no scruple in declaring," according to the notes kept by Madison, "supported as he was by the opinions of so many of the wise & good, that the British Government was the best in the world: and that he doubted much whether any thing short of it would do in America."

Specifically, Hamilton proposed that, as in Great Britain, the national government would be supreme. State governors would be appointed by the national legislature and granted the right to veto any laws passed by their own assemblies. Members of the upper house of the national legislature, like members of the British House of Lords, would serve for life. As for the executive, "the English model is the only good one on this subject," Hamilton asserted. Although he did not suggest that the United States create a hereditary monarchy, Hamilton did propose that an executive be chosen by electors and granted lifetime tenure and vast powers, including "a negative on all laws about to be passed, . . . the direction of war when authorized or begun, the sole appointment of the heads of the departments, the power of pardoning all offences except Treason," and, along with the Senate, the treaty-making power. In truth, argues biographer Ron Chernow, Hamilton's proposal was for "a new hybrid form of government that would have the continuity of a monarchy combined with the civil liberties of a republic." [27]

Hamilton's speech was dismissed by the delegates as being far beyond the bounds of what the people or the states would accept. Some scholars have suggested that his real purpose was to offer a plan so extreme that the Virginia Plan would seem moderate by comparison.[28] Several of his specific proposals were adopted later in the convention, notably those concerning the president's powers to grant pardons and to negotiate treaties. As for the New Jersey Plan, it was defeated on June 19 by a vote of seven states to three. Later that day, the Virginia Plan, as modified by the Committee of the Whole, was approved and referred to the convention for further consideration. The conflict between the delegates from the large and from the small states over apportionment in the national legislature, however, was far from resolved.

Convention Debate (June 20–July 26)

On June 20, with Washington again in the chair as president of the convention, the delegates began their clause-by-clause evaluation of the plan of government they had laid out while meeting as the Committee of the Whole.

BENJAMIN FRANKLIN

Benjamin Franklin was eighty-one years old in 1787—old enough to be the father of even the oldest of the other delegates, the grandfather of most of them, and the great-grandfather of some. (He was twenty-six years older than George Washington, forty-five years older than James Madison, and fifty-five years older than the youngest delegate to the Constitutional Convention, Jonathan Dayton.) Franklin's health was very bad. When he was able to attend sessions of the convention, he had to be carried from his home in a sedan chair by prison trusties. Often his speeches were delivered on his behalf by someone else, usually his fellow Pennsylvanian, James Wilson.

Franklin had few clear ideas about what the new government the convention was creating should be like, and most of those he did have were voted down. He favored a unicameral legislature and a plural executive. He opposed salaries for government officials. He urged that a clergyman be brought into the convention to open each of its sessions with a prayer. These suggestions typically were received with respectful tolerance by most of his fellow delegates. Franklin's motion against salaries, for example, "was treated with great respect," wrote James Madison, "but rather for the author of it than from any conviction of its expediency or practicability."

William Pierce of Georgia described Franklin as "the greatest philosopher of the present age.... But what claim he has to the politician, posterity must determine. It is certain that he does not shine much in public council; he is no speaker, nor does he seem to let politics engage his attention."

For all his feebleness, Franklin was one of the most important delegates at the Constitutional Convention. His presence lent luster to the proceedings—no American, other than Washington, enjoyed Franklin's national and international stature as scientist, inventor, author and publisher, diplomat, and statesman. Equally important, Franklin deliberately played the role of conciliator at the convention. Although he lacked clear ideas about government himself, he did his best to calm his colleagues' tempers and assuage their differences so that the convention would stay together to produce a plan.

Among the changes they voted in the plan were these:

- Members of the lower house of the legislature would be elected for a term of two years, not three; they also would be required to be at least twenty-five years old.
- The term for members of the upper house would be six years rather than seven. Their terms would be staggered so that one-third were elected every two years.
- The national legislature would not have the power to veto state laws, much to Madison's dismay. But, borrowing a plank from the New Jersey Plan, national laws and treaties would be "the supreme law of the respective States."
- A property requirement for members of the executive, legislative, and judicial branches would be established. (This idea later was abandoned.)
- Sufficient displeasure was expressed with the provision for legislative election of the president to a single, seven-year term as to guarantee that it would not remain in the final document, but no generally satisfactory alternative was agreed upon.

More than any other issue, legislative apportionment consumed the convention's time, attention, and endurance during these five weeks of debate. Delegates from the small states pressed relentlessly for equal representation of the states in Congress: large state delegates were equally adamant in their insistence on representation according to population.

A special committee, with members from every state, was appointed on July 2 to propose a compromise. On July 5, after a break to celebrate Independence Day, the committee recommended a plan of equal representation for each state in the upper house, apportionment according to population in the lower house (with each slave counted as three-fifths of a person), and, as a sop to delegates from the large states who feared that the upper house would push for spending programs that would impoverish their states, exclusive power in the lower house to originate all legislation dealing with money.

For more than a week the delegates engaged in a complex and sometimes bitter debate over the proposal. New questions were raised, for example, about whether states yet to be admitted to the Union should receive as much representation as the original thirteen, how often a national census should be taken to measure population changes, and whether apportionment in the lower house should reflect wealth as well as population. On July 16, the convention voted narrowly to approve the main points of the special committee's compromise proposal, sometimes called the Connecticut Compromise in honor of its original author, Roger Sherman of Connecticut. On July 23, the delegates undermined the idea that the upper house should represent the states in the new government; by deciding that each state should have two members in the upper house, each of them free to vote independently.

Committee of Detail (July 24–August 6)

On July 24, the convention voted to appoint a Committee of Detail to review all of its decisions and draft a plan of government that incorporated them. The five-member committee included representatives of the three main regions of the country—Nathaniel Gorham of Massachusetts and Oliver Ellsworth of Connecticut (a protégé of Sherman) from New England, James Wilson of Pennsylvania from the middle states, and Edmund Randolph of Virginia and John Rutledge of South Carolina from the South. The committee worked while the rest of the convention adjourned until August 6.

One index of the committee's influence is that it took convention-passed resolutions amounting to 1,200 words and transformed them into a draft of 3,700 words. The committee also drew from a wide range of other sources in compiling its report: the New Jersey Plan, the Articles of Confederation, the rules of Congress, the Pinckney Plan, and some state constitutions, notably those of New York and Massachusetts.

Most of the memorable terms and phrases in the Constitution were written by the Committee of Detail, including "state of the Union" and "We the People." Institutions were named: the executive became the "president"; the national tribunal, the "Supreme Court"; and the legislature, "Congress," with its upper house called the "Senate" and the lower house the "House of Representatives."

For the most part, the committee, in keeping with its name, simply fleshed out the details of earlier convention decisions. It established procedures for the president's veto, defined the jurisdiction of the courts, and adjusted certain relations between the states. In some instances, however, the committee substituted its own judgment for the convention's. It vested the power to impeach, for example, in the House, with only the power to convict remaining in the Supreme Court. The property requirement for officeholders was omitted.

Perhaps the most important decision of the Committee of Detail was to transform general grants of power into specific ones. What had been Congress's broadly stated authority "to legislate in all cases for the general interests of the Union" became instead a list of eighteen enumerated powers, including the power to "lay and collect taxes," regulate interstate commerce, establish post offices, make war, elect a national treasurer, and set up inferior courts—

all culminating in a sweeping grant "to make all laws that shall be necessary and proper for carrying into execution" these and "all other powers vested" in the government. The states were forbidden certain powers—notably, to make treaties with other nations, to print money, and to tax imports.

The committee granted the president the power to recommend legislation to Congress, make executive appointments, receive ambassadors from other nations, issue pardons, "take care" that the laws be executed, and command the armed forces. An oath to "faithfully execute the office" of president also was included, as was a provision that the president of the Senate would exercise the powers and duties of the presidency if the president died, resigned, or became disabled. The judiciary—the Supreme Court and other, "inferior courts" to be created by law—was given jurisdiction in controversies between states or between citizens of different states, as well as in cases arising under the laws of the national government.

Finally, responding to a threat to walk out by Gen. Charles Cotesworth Pinckney of South Carolina (an older cousin of Charles Pinckney), the committee forbade Congress to tax or ban the importation of slaves and the export of goods. In another concession to southern delegates, who feared that Congress might legislate navigation acts requiring that American exports be transported on American ships (a boon to northern shipbuilders, but a burden to southern agricultural exporters), the committee required that such acts would have to pass both houses by a two-thirds vote.

Convention Debate (August 7–31)

As they had with the Virginia Plan and the report of the Committee of the Whole, the delegates reviewed the draft constitution that was proposed by the Committee of Detail clause by clause. Much of the draft was approved. Some parts, however, were modified, and others became matters of serious controversy.

Modifications

The delegates tinkered with several provisions of the Committee of Detail's draft.

- Citizenship requirements for legislators (seven years for members of the House, nine years for senators) were approved, along with a requirement that legislators be inhabitants of the states they represented in Congress.
- The requirement for a two-thirds vote of both houses of Congress to override a president's veto was raised to three-fourths. (Near the end of the convention, the two-thirds figure was restored.)
- Congress's power to "make war" was judged too sweeping to protect the national security during times when

Congress was out of session. It was revised to read: "declare war."

- Congress was forbidden to pass ex post facto laws—that is, retroactive criminal laws—and bills of attainder (laws that declare a person guilty of a crime without a trial).
- The government was barred from granting "any title of nobility" to any person, and government officials were forbidden to receive "any present, emolument, office, or title of any kind whatever from any king, prince, or foreign state."
- Congress was empowered to call forth the militia of any state "to execute the laws of the Union, suppress insurrections, and repel invasions."
- The two-thirds requirement for congressional passage of navigation acts was dropped.
- A procedure was created to amend the Constitution: "on the application of the legislatures of two-thirds of the states in the Union for an amendment of this Constitution, the legislature of the United States shall call a convention for that purpose."
- Religious tests were prohibited as a requirement for holding office.
- The president's oath was expanded to include these words: "and will to the best of my judgment and power preserve, protect, and defend the Constitution of the United States." (Still later, "to the best of my judgment and power" became "to the best of my ability.")
- The Committee of Detail had proposed that the new constitution take effect when ratified by a certain number of state conventions (not state legislatures) but had left the number unspecified. The delegates now voted to set it at nine.

Controversies

The draft constitution's slavery provisions came under fierce assault from several northern delegates, both the three-fifths rule for counting slaves as part of the population and the prohibition against laws banning the importation of new slaves. Much of the North's concern derived from fear of slave rebellions, which might attract foreign invaders and, in any event, probably would require northern arms and money to be subdued. Southern delegates not only defended the provisions protecting slavery but also declared that their states would not ratify any constitution that placed slavery in jeopardy.

As it had with the large state–small state controversy, the convention appointed a special committee on August 22 to seek a compromise solution. Two days later, the committee proposed that Congress be authorized, if it so decided, to end the importation of slaves after 1800. In the meantime, Congress could tax imported slaves at a rate no higher than ten dollars each. (A euphemism—not "slaves," but "such Persons"—was used in the Constitution.)

General Pinckney persuaded the convention to change 1800 to 1808. The committee's recommendation, as amended, was passed.

Controversies over two other matters caused the convention to bog down: the powers of the Senate (which delegates from the large states wanted to minimize and delegates from the small states wanted to maximize) and a cluster of issues regarding presidential selection. On August 31, nearing the end of its labors, the convention appointed a Committee on Postponed Matters, with a member from each state delegation, to propose solutions to these vexing problems.

Committee on Postponed Matters (August 31–September 8)

Beginning on September 4, the Committee on Postponed Matters, chaired by David Brearley of New Jersey, made several recommendations concerning the presidency. The committee, sometimes referred to as the Committee on Unfinished Parts or, because it had one member from each state delegation, the Committee of Eleven, proposed a term of four years rather than seven, with no restriction on the president's eligibility for reelection. The president was to be chosen by an electoral college, not by Congress. To constitute the electoral college, each state would be assigned the right to select, by whatever means it chose, electors equal in number to its representatives and senators in Congress. The candidate who received the greatest number of electoral votes, assuming the support of a majority of electors, would become president. The candidate who finished second would become vice president. (This was the first mention of the vice presidency at the convention.) If no candidate received majority, the Senate would select a president and vice president from among the five candidates who had received the greatest number of electoral votes.

As a corollary to its proposal for an electoral college, the committee recommended that certain responsibilities be assigned to the vice president—namely, to preside over the Senate, with the right to cast tie-breaking votes, and to act as president if the office became vacant before the expiration of the president's term. Finally, the committee recommended that qualifications for president be stated in the Constitution. The president would have to be at least thirty-five years old, a natural born citizen of the United States or a citizen at the time of the Constitution's enactment, and a resident of the United States for at least fourteen years.

For several days, the delegates carefully considered the committee's complex and surprising proposal for presidential selection. On September 7, they passed it after making only one substantial change: the House of Representatives, rather than the Senate, would choose the president in the event of an electoral college deadlock, with each state delegation casting one vote. The Senate still would choose the vice president if the electoral college failed to produce a winner.

Having approved the electoral college, the convention quickly took other actions to reduce the powers of the Senate, mostly in response to the demands of the delegates from the large states. The president was granted the authority to make treaties and to appoint ambassadors, public ministers, consuls, Supreme Court justices, federal judges, and all other officers whose appointments were not otherwise provided for. Senate confirmation was made a requirement for all of these appointments and a two-thirds vote by the Senate was stipulated for ratifying treaties.

On September 8, the convention approved two final proposals of the Committee on Postponed Matters. The president was to be impeached by the House on grounds of "treason or bribery or other high crimes and misdemeanors against the United States," and removed from office on conviction by the Senate. The delegates added the vice president and other civil officers to the roster of officials subject to impeachment but raised the majority needed for Senate conviction from a simple to a two-thirds majority. In addition, the House was empowered to originate "all bills for raising revenue."

Having thus completed (or so they believed) their work on the Constitution, the delegates ended the day's business on September 8 by voting to create a five-member Committee of Style to write a polished, final draft for them to sign. The committee's leading members were Gouverneur Morris (who seems to have done most of its work), Madison, and Hamilton.

Final Adjustments (September 9–17)

Even as the Committee of Style labored, the convention continued to modify its earlier decisions. On September 10, Madison urged that special constitutional conventions not be a part of the process of amending the Constitution. Instead, he argued, amendments should be initiated by a two-thirds vote of Congress or by two-thirds of the state legislatures, with subsequent approval by three-fourths of the states needed for ratification. The Committee of Style incorporated Madison's idea into its draft.

On September 12, Hugh Williamson of North Carolina successfully moved that the requirement for overriding a president's veto be reduced from a three-fourths vote of each house of Congress to a two-thirds vote.

Meanwhile, more fundamental reservations about the Constitution were being expressed by some delegates. Randolph worried that the convention had gone far beyond its original charter from Congress, which was to propose revisions in the Articles of Confederation. He urged that the approval not just of state ratifying conventions but also of Congress and the state legislatures be sought for the proposed constitution, even if this process necessitated a second

constitutional convention. Randolph's fellow Virginian, George Mason, joined Elbridge Gerry of Massachusetts in objecting to the absence of a bill of rights from the Constitution.

The Committee of Style reported to the convention on September 12. Its draft not only reduced the number of articles from twenty-three to seven but also included some significant innovations. The most memorable of these was the preamble:

> We the People of the United States, in Order to form a more perfect Union, establish Justice, insure domestic Tranquility, provide for the common defence, promote the general Welfare, and secure the Blessings of Liberty to ourselves and our Posterity, do ordain and establish this Constitution for the United States of America.[29]

The Committee of Style also added a provision that barred states from passing laws to impair the obligations of contracts. Finally, a pair of vesting clauses for Congress and the president was written that, intentionally or not, suggested that the president might have executive powers beyond those enumerated in the Constitution. (See " 'The Executive Power,' " p. 32.)

The committee's draft met with widespread approval from the delegates, but they continued to tinker. Congress was stripped of its power to choose the national treasurer in favor of the president. A provision was added that the Constitution could not be altered to deprive a state of equal representation in the Senate without the state's consent. And, at the initiative of Gouverneur Morris and Elbridge Gerry, a compromise procedure for amending the Constitution was created that incorporated both the Committee of Detail's recommendation and Madison's plan. As finally agreed, a constitutional amendment could be proposed by either a two-thirds vote of both houses of Congress or a convention that Congress was required to call if two-thirds of the state legislatures requested one. In either case, three-fourths of the states would have to ratify an amendment for it to become part of the Constitution.

Randolph, Gerry, and Mason remained unhappy, expressing doubts about the magnitude of the changes the convention was recommending. But their motion for a subsequent constitutional convention to consider objections and recommendations that might be raised at the state ratifying conventions was defeated by a vote of eleven states to none. From experience, Rakove has noted, the delegates realized that "a second federal convention would assemble encumbered by proposals for amendments of all kinds and bound by instructions that would make it impossible to replicate the process of persuasion, compromise, and bargaining from which the completed Constitution had so laboriously emerged."[30]

The convention's labors completed, the delegates assembled on September 17 to sign an engrossed, or final, copy of the Constitution. (This is the copy on public display at the National Archives in Washington, D.C.) Forty-one of the original fifty-five delegates still were present at the convention, and all but Randolph, Mason, and Gerry signed the document. Even then the delegates could not resist some fine-tuning, unanimously approving a Washington-supported motion to alter slightly the apportionment formula for the House of Representatives.

On the last day of the convention, as the delegates prepared to sign the Constitution, Benjamin Franklin offered his thoughts on the document. Clinton Rossiter has described Franklin's closing speech as "the most remarkable performance of a remarkable life" [31]:

> Mr. President, I confess that there are several parts of this constitution I do not at present approve, but I am not sure that I shall never approve them. For having lived long, I have experienced many instances of being obliged by better information, or fuller consideration, to change opinions even on important subjects, which I once thought right, but found to be otherwise. . . . I doubt too whether any other convention we can obtain may be able to make a better constitution. . . . It therefore astonishes me, Sir, to find this system approaching so near to perfection as it does, and I think it will astonish our enemies. . . . Thus I consent, Sir, to this constitution because I expect no better, and because I am not sure it is not the best. [32]

Later, as the last few delegates waited to affix their signatures to the Constitution, Franklin offered an informal benediction. He gestured to Washington's chair and said to those standing nearby:

> Painters have found it difficult to distinguish in their art a rising from a setting sun. I have often in the course of this session and the vicissitudes of my hopes and fears as to its issue, looked at that sun behind the President without being able to tell whether it was rising or setting. But now, at length, I have the happiness to know that it is a rising and not a setting sun. [33]

CREATING THE PRESIDENCY

During the course of the Constitutional Convention, the presidency developed along two major lines. First, the rather loosely designed executive of the Virginia Plan took on greater clarity and specificity. Second, the weak executive, subordinate to the legislature, that most of the delegates initially seem to have favored was made stronger. These two developments manifested themselves in a variety of specific issues of executive design. The issues included the number of the executive, the method of executive selection, the length and character of the term, the means of removal in extraordinary circumstances, the institutional separation between executive and legislature, and the enumerated powers of the executive.

An Overview of the Creation of the Presidency

The design of the executive was one of the most vexing problems of the Constitutional Convention, and its solution was the convention's most creative act. Other issues were more controversial, but they typically lent themselves to compromise solutions, such as when the small states split the difference with the large states and provided for a bicameral legislature and northern and southern delegates worked out the three-fifths rule for counting slaves. When it came to the nature and powers of the executive, however, the delegates labored in a realm of such intellectual and political uncertainty that the politics of compromise was largely irrelevant. The result, although long in coming, was that "the presidency emerged not from the clash of wills to gain a long-contested point, but from a series of ingenious efforts to design a new institution that would be suitably energetic but safely republican." [34]

One problem the delegates encountered was that their experience offered several models of what they did not want in an executive but few models that they found attractive. The British monarch and the royal colonial governors had been, in their eyes, tramplers of liberty. The state constitutions that were written after independence provided for governors who were unthreatening but also weak to the point of impotence. The national government of the Articles of Confederation, such as it was, had no chief executive at all. The plethora of proposals for an executive that various delegates offered during the convention (listed by the author Fred Barbash) is more a mark of their uncertainty than of any strongly held desires:

> Three executives, each from a different part of the country.
> An executive joined with a council.
> A single executive, with a life term.
> A President, without a life term, chosen by the people.
> A single executive, chosen by the Congress and eligible for reelection.
> A single executive, chosen by the Congress and ineligible for reelection.
> An executive chosen by the governors of the states.
> A President chosen by members of the Congress, to be drawn by lot, or chosen by the Congress the first time and by electors the second time, or chosen by electors all the time. Electors chosen by state legislatures. Electors chosen by the people. [35]

A second problem that stymied the delegates derived from their general ambivalence about executive authority. They wanted an executive branch that was strong enough to check a runaway legislature, but not so strong as to become despotic. This ambivalence was shared by the American people, whose hatred of monarchy existed side by side with their longing to make George Washington king. As the political scientist Seymour Martin Lipset has shown, Washington was a classic example of what Max Weber, the German sociologist, called a charismatic leader, one "treated as endowed with supernatural, superhuman, or at least specifically exceptional powers or qualities." The historian Marcus Cunliffe recorded:

> Babies were being christened after him as early as 1775, and while he was still President, his countrymen paid to see him in waxwork effigy. To his admirers he was "godlike Washington," and his detractors complained to one another that he was looked upon as a "demigod" whom it was treasonous to criticize. "Oh Washington!" declared Ezra Stiles of Yale (in a sermon of 1783). "How I do love thy name! How have I often adored and blessed thy God, for creating and forming thee into the great ornament of humankind!" [36]

But the public's longing for Washington was just that: a longing for Washington, not for a monarchy. As the historians Elkins and McKitrick have pointed out, Washington's wide-ranging responsibilities as commander in chief during the Revolutionary War meant that "he had in a certain sense been acting as President of the United States since 1775." [37] Delegates and citizens alike knew that Washington would wield power responsibly and relinquish it voluntarily—he had already done so once. But would Washington's successors? "The first man at the helm will be a good one," Franklin told the convention. "No body knows what sort may come afterwards." [38]

Despite the delegates' difficulties, the presidency slowly took shape as the convention wore on. For all their intellectual uncertainty, the delegates moved steadily in the direction of a clearly designed executive. For all their ambivalence, they made the executive stronger as well than they were initially inclined to do.

Clarity

Charles Thach noted in his book *The Creation of the Presidency* that James Madison "has with much justice been called the father of the Constitution." But even as admiring a scholar as Thach conceded that "the claims for his paternity do not extend to the fundamentals of Article II." [39]

Madison himself claimed no paternity of the presidency. As he wrote to Washington on April 16, 1787, less than a month before the scheduled opening of the convention, "I have scarcely ventured as yet to form my own opinion either of the manner in which [the executive] ought to be constituted or the authorities with which it ought to be cloathed." Madison's Virginia Plan offered the convention a shadowy and vaguely defined executive. Even the basic structure of the plan's executive—was it to be a single person, a chaired board, or a committee?—was unclear. In addition, the length of the executive's term was unspecified, and its powers were not enumerated.

Madison's fellow delegates seem to have shared his uncertainty. The only issues they resolved to their satisfac-

tion during the convention's first two months were the unitary nature of the executive and its power to veto laws passed by the legislature. Other issues left them floundering, as evidenced by the Colliers' account of the convention's efforts during the week of July 17:

> The delegates appeared to be struggling to create an executive that was strong without being strong. Over the week the Convention reversed itself again and again. On July 17 it constructed a weak executive dominated by Congress. On the nineteenth and twentieth it created a strong executive independent of Congress. On July 24 it went back to the executive chosen by Congress. At various times it was suggested that his term might be eight, fifteen, and, even though the proposal was facetious, thirty years. [40]

The Committee of Detail, which began its work on July 24, helped matters some: it gave the executive the name of president, provided for succession, and enumerated its powers. But the main issues that divided the delegates—selection, term, and reeligibility—were not resolved until September, when the Committee on Postponed Matters proposed selection by an electoral college, a term of four years with no limit on eligibility for reelection, and the creation of the vice presidency.

Strength

For all the vagueness of its conception, the national executive of the Virginia Plan generally accorded with what most delegates at the start of the Constitutional Convention seem to have been looking for—namely, an agent of restraint in a basically legislative government. The executive in Madison's proposed government was weak (it was bound by a council and devoid of enumerated powers), but it certainly was stronger than in the government of the Articles of Confederation. The executive also was subordinate to the legislature, which was empowered to elect it. But it was not subservient, as demonstrated by its fixed term, the veto power, and the bar on legislative reductions of the executive's salary.

Dissatisfied with the convention's early consensus on a subordinate executive, a coterie of committed and talented delegates worked diligently and effectively to strengthen the office's constitutional power. They were led by James Wilson, who envisioned the executive as "the man of the people," and by Gouverneur Morris, who regarded a properly constituted executive as "the great protector of the Mass of people." Interestingly, although Wilson and Morris both favored a strong executive, they did so for different reasons. Wilson thought a strong executive would enhance the influence of public opinion in government. Morris thought such an executive would restrain public opinion. [41]

During the course of the convention, the pro-executive delegates won victory after victory:

- The executive was defined as a unitary, not a committee-style, office and was left unshackled by a council.
- The executive, instead of being chosen by the legislature for a single term, was given its own electoral base and the right to run for reelection. Indispensable to this victory was Wilson's conversion of Madison, who declared on July 19 that "it is essential then that the appointment of the Executive should either be drawn from some source, or held by some tenure, that will give him a free agency with regard to the Legislature. This could not be if he was appointable from time to time by the Legislature."
- The Committee of Detail spelled out an extensive list of executive powers, including those of military command, involvement in the legislative process, pardon, and the execution of the laws.
- After the Connecticut Compromise transformed the Senate into the small states' bastion in Congress, large-state delegates joined forces with pro-executive delegates to transfer some of the Senate's powers to the executive, notably those of appointment and treaty making.

For all their victories, Wilson, Morris, and the other delegates who favored a strong executive did not get everything they wanted, such as an absolute veto and easier procedures for Senate ratification of treaties. But they moved the convention much further in the direction of a strong executive than it initially had been inclined to go.

Number of the Executive

The number of the executive was the first issue to rouse the delegates. The debate on number took two forms. First, should the executive be unitary or plural—that is, a single-person or a committee-style office? Second, should the executive be forced to consult with a council before exercising some or all of its powers?

Unitary or Plural?

The Virginia Plan said nothing about the number of the executive, perhaps because Madison had no clear opinion on the matter or perhaps because, like Roger Sherman of Connecticut, Madison felt that the legislature should be free to define, then redefine the executive's number as it saw fit.

On June 1, the convention, meeting as the Committee of the Whole, heard a motion from James Wilson that the executive be a single person. According to Madison's notes, "a considerable pause ensu[ed]" as the usually talkative delegates lapsed into silence, discomforted by the prospect of discussing the issue in the presence of George Washington, whom everyone assumed would be the leader of whatever executive branch was created.[42] After Franklin admonished

his colleagues that they were obliged to speak freely, however, the debate was joined, and the issue became an early test for the pro-executive forces at the convention.

Edmund Randolph and Sherman led the fight against Wilson's motion. Randolph, arguing that a single executive, by its nature, would be the "foetus of monarchy," proposed instead a three-person executive committee, with one member from each region of the country. Sherman, who regarded the ideal executive "as nothing more than an institution for carrying the will of the Legislature into effect," said he "wished the number might not be fixed, but that the legislature should be at liberty to appoint one or more as experience might dictate." Franklin's reasons for supporting a plural executive were more positive. He argued that the policies pursued by an executive board would be less easily changed, and thus more stable and consistent, than those of an individual.

Wilson defended his motion shrewdly. To be sure, he argued, a single executive would be a source of "energy" and "dispatch"—that is, of leadership and action—in the new government. But Wilson also urged that a single executive was indispensable to control executive power—how could responsibility for incompetence or for abuses of power be assigned to a committee? These arguments were persuasive to most delegates. They feared monarchy but realized how much the national government had suffered under the Articles of Confederation from the diffuseness of executive responsibility. As property owners, they also feared threats to the social order such as Shays' Rebellion and regarded a single executive as more likely to respond quickly and effectively to riot and discord than a committee would be.

On June 4, the convention voted overwhelmingly in favor of a unitary executive. One of Washington's few recorded votes was in favor of this motion. On average, the most vocal opponents of a unitary executive were nearly fifteen years older than the proponents. The reason for this discrepancy, the political scientist Richard Ellis has argued, is that the views of executive power of the older delegates were colored by their battles against the royal governors. The younger delegates, who had come of age during the 1770s and 1780s, were more worried about the weakness of executive power in the state constitutions and the Articles of Confederation.[43]

A Council?

The Virginia Plan provided that a "council of revision" consisting of the executive and "a convenient number of the National Judiciary" would be empowered to veto laws passed by the legislature. All thirteen state constitutions provided for a council of some sort, most of them legislatively select-

---

NUMBER OF THE EXECUTIVE

The executive Power shall be vested in a President of the United States of America.

—*from Article II, Section 2*

ed. Sherman, who voted in the end for the single executive, said he had done so only because he assumed it would be required to share power with a council. Wilson, however, opposed a council because he believed that it would dilute the virtues of the unitary executive—energy, dispatch, and responsibility.

The proposal for a council was tabled on June 4 after two Massachusetts delegates, Elbridge Gerry and Rufus King, injected a new argument into the debate. Gerry and King questioned the wisdom of having judges participate in making laws on which they later would be asked to rule. Confusion also existed among the delegates about what effect a council would have on executive power. Some saw it as a check on the executive, but others, including Madison, thought that a council would buttress the executive with the support of the judiciary, thus strengthening it in its relations with the legislature.

The council idea recurred in various guises and at various times throughout the convention. Morris and others tried to persuade the delegates to accept a purely advisory council, consisting mainly of the heads of the executive departments. As late as September 7, Mason suggested that the House of Representatives or the Senate be charged to appoint an executive council with members drawn from all regions of the country. "The Grand Signor himself had his Divan," Mason noted from Ottoman history. But because no consensus ever formed about either the wisdom of having a council or the form that it should take, the idea simply was abandoned.

Selection and Succession

James Wilson was as much opposed to the part of the Virginia Plan that provided for the executive "to be chosen by the National Legislature" as he was in favor of a unitary executive. Legislative selection would make the executive a creature of (and thus subservient to) the legislature, Wilson believed. On June 1, he proposed instead that the executive be elected by the people. Wilson said he realized that his idea "might appear chimerical," but he could think of no better way to keep the executive and legislative branches "as independent as possible of each other, as well as of the states."

The delegates virtually ignored Wilson's proposal for popular election. In principle, the idea was too democratic. (They thought of democracy as suited only for small com-

ELECTION OF THE PRESIDENT

Each State shall appoint, in such Manner as the Legislature thereof may direct, a Number of Electors, Equal to the whole Number of Senators and Representatives to which the State may be entitled in the Congress: but no Senator or Representative or Person holding an Office of Trust or Profit under the United States, shall be appointed an elector.

The Electors shall meet in their respective States, and vote by Ballot for two Persons, of whom at least one shall not be an Inhabitant of the same State with themselves. And they shall make a List of all the Persons voted for, and the Number of Votes for each; which List they shall sign and certify, and transmit sealed to the Seat of the Government of the United States, directed to the President of the Senate. The President of the Senate shall, in the Presence of the Senate and the House of Representatives, open all the Certificates, and the votes shall then be counted. The Person having the greatest Number of Votes shall be President, if such Number be a Majority of the whole Number of Electors appointed; and if there be more than one who have such Majority, and have an equal Number of Votes, then the House of Representatives shall immediately chuse by Ballot one of them for President; and if no Person have a majority, then from the five highest on the List the said House shall in the like manner chuse the President. But in chusing the President, the Votes shall be taken by States, the Representatives from each State having one Vote. A quorum for this purpose shall consist of a Member or Members from two thirds of the States, and a Majority of all the States shall be necessary to a Choice. In every Case, after the Choice of the President, the Person having the greatest Number of Votes of the Electors shall be the Vice President. But if there should remain two or more who have equal Votes, the Senate shall chuse from them by Ballot the Vice President.

The Congress may determine the Time of chusing the Electors and the Day on which they shall give their Votes; which Day shall be the same throughout the United States.

—from Article II, Section 1*

* Modified by the Twelfth Amendment

munities.) In addition, by requiring voters to pass judgment on candidates from distant states of whom they knew little or nothing, popular election seemed impractical as well. Mason stated both of these objections cogently: "It would be as unnatural to refer the choice of a proper character for chief Magistrate to the people, as it would, to refer a trial of colours to a blind man." On behalf of the southern delegates, Madison added a more overtly political point: in direct elections, candidates from the more populous north almost always would win.

Undiscouraged, Wilson returned to the convention on June 2 with a proposal for an electoral college to select the executive. For purposes of election, each state would be divided into a few districts; the voters in these would choose electors, who in turn would gather at a central location to select an executive. A plan like Wilson's was briefly accepted on July 19 and ultimately was adopted in September, but at this stage of the convention it still seemed too novel. Delegates feared the mischief that might ensue, perhaps at the instigation of foreign agents, when the electors met. They also doubted whether "men of the 1st nor even of the 2d. grade" would be willing to serve as electors." [44] The delegates voted instead to affirm the legislative selection provision of the Virginia Plan.

The convention's decision for legislative selection, although it was reaffirmed in several votes taken in July and August, was not a happy one. The source of the unhappiness was that, in the delegates' minds, a legislatively selected executive could not be allowed to stand for reelection, lest executive power and patronage be used for the purpose of, in effect, bribing legislators for their support. But the delegates also believed that eligibility for reelection was a valuable incentive to good performance in office and regretted that legislative selection of the executive ruled reeligibility out. (See "Term of Office," p. 27.) The result was an ongoing search for a selection process that was desirable in its own right and that allowed for reelection. This was no easy task. In the memorable description of the political scientist Robert Dahl, "The Convention twisted and turned like a man tormented in his sleep by a bad dream as it tried to decide." [45]

Among the ideas the delegates considered and rejected, wrote Clinton Rossiter, were some rather far-fetched ones:

> election by the state governors or by electors chosen by them, neither a scheme that could muster any support; nomination by the people of each state of "its best citizen," and election from this pool of thirteen by the national legislature or electors chosen by it, an unhelpful proposal of John Dickinson; election by the national legislature, with electors chosen by the state legislatures taking over whenever an executive sought reelection, a proposal of [Oliver] Ellsworth that found favor with four states; and, most astounding of all, election by a small group of national legislators chosen "by lot." [46]

The search for an alternative to legislative selection became more urgent after August 24. Until that day, no consideration had been given to how the legislature was to choose the president. Now, by a vote of seven states to four, the convention approved a motion that Congress would elect the president by a "joint ballot" of all the members of the House of Representatives and Senate, following the practice most states used to elect their governors. This decision, by giving the large states a clear majority in the presidential selection process (there would be many more representatives than senators), threatened to reignite the large state–small state controversy that already had split the convention once. To avert this catastrophe, Roger Sherman, the author of the Connecticut Compromise between the large and small states on legislative apportionment, moved on August 31 to refer the whole issue of presidential selection to the Committee on Postponed Matters.

On September 4, the committee proposed the electoral college as a method to elect the president, with no restrictions on the president's right to seek reelection. The president would be selected by a majority vote of the electors, who would be chosen by the states using whatever methods they individually adopted. (The delegates expected that most states would entrust the selection of electors to the people.) Each state would receive a number of electoral votes equal to its representation in Congress. If no presidential candidate received votes from a majority of electors, the Senate would elect the president from among the five highest electoral vote recipients. In addition, to prevent a "cabal" from forming in the electoral college, electors would never meet as a national body—instead, they would vote in their state capitals and then send the results to the Senate for counting. Finally, to ensure that the electors would not simply support a variety of home-state favorites, each was required to vote for two candidates for president from two different states (an idea first proposed by Gouverneur Morris on July 25), with the runner-up in the presidential election filling the newly created office of vice president.

The proposal for an electoral college was generally well received by the delegates. As Fred Barbash has argued, it was the ideal political compromise, "baited" with something for virtually every group at the convention:

> For those in the convention anxious for the President to be allowed reelection, the committee made him eligible without limit.
> For those worried about excessive dependence of the President on the national legislature, the committee determined that electors chosen as each state saw fit would cast ballots for the presidency.
> For the large states and the South, the committee decided that the number of electors would be proportioned according to each state's combined representation in the House and Senate. . . .
> For the small states, the committee determined that when no candidate won a majority of electoral votes, the Senate would choose the president from among the leading contenders.[47]

Only one aspect of the proposed electoral college was controversial among the delegates—Senate selection of the president in the absence of an electoral college majority. Large-state delegates objected because the Senate underrepresented them in favor of the small states. Moreover, not foreseeing the development of a two-party system, some delegates believed that after Washington (the obvious choice as the first president) left office, majorities seldom would form in the electoral college and the Senate would choose most presidents. Mason estimated that the electoral college would fail to reach a majority "nineteen times in twenty."

Once again, Sherman proposed what the historian Carol Berkin has called a "brilliant solution": let the House of Representatives elect the president if the electoral college failed to produce a majority, but assign each state delegation a single vote.[48] The Senate still would choose the vice president. Quickly, on September 6, the convention agreed.

One issue that the creation of the vice presidency resolved, at least partially, was: What happens if the president dies, resigns, becomes disabled, or is impeached and convicted? The Committee of Detail was the first to deal with the matter. It recommended that the president of the Senate "discharge the powers and duties of [the Presidency] . . . until another President of the United States be chosen, or until the disability of the President be ended." When Madison and other delegates objected to this proposal because it might give the Senate an incentive to remove the president in favor of one of its members, the issue was referred to the Committee on Postponed Matters.

The committee proposed that the vice president, not a senator, be president of the Senate; it also designated the vice president as the person to step in if a vacancy occurs in the presidency. The convention agreed, but only after passing an additional motion that seemed to call for a special presidential election before the expiration of the departed president's term. Somehow this intention was lost when the Committee of Style wrote its final draft of the Constitution. No one caught the error. As a result, the convention left the Constitution vague on two important matters. First, in the event of the president's death, resignation, disability, or removal, was the vice president to become president or merely to assume the powers and duties of the presidency? Second, was the vice president to serve out the unexpired balance of the president's term or only fill in temporarily until a special election could be held to pick a new president? (See "The Vice Presidency," p. 39, and Chapter 7, Selection by Succession.)

Term of Office

Questions about length of term, eligibility for reelection, and selection were so interwoven in the minds of the delegates that they could not resolve any of them independently of the others. Indeed, one political scientist has compared the convention's efforts to sort out these questions to a game of "three-dimensional chess."[49]

The Virginia Plan left the length of the executive's term of office blank—literally. ("Resolved, that a National Executive be . . . chosen by the National Legislature for a term of ____ years.") The plan also stipulated that the executive was "to be ineligible a second time." When these provisions came before the Committee of the Whole on June 1, a variety of alternatives were proposed, including a three-year presidential term with no limit on reeligibility, a three-year term with two reelections allowed, and a seven-year term with no reeligibility. Although the delegates approved the single seven-year term, the vote was close, five states to four.

Underlying the delegates' uncertainty was a basic choice between two alternatives concerning the executive that they regarded as incompatible: eligibility for reelection or legislative selection. Mason forcefully stated the reason that, in their view, the Constitution could not include both:

TERM OF OFFICE

He shall hold his Office during the term of four Years, and, together with the Vice President, chosen for the same term, be elected . . .

—from Article II, Section 1*

* Modified by the Twenty-second Amendment

---

if the legislature could reelect the executive, there would be a constant "temptation on the side of the Executive to intrigue with the Legislature for a re-appointment," using political patronage and illegitimate favors in effect to buy votes.

On July 17, the convention voted for both legislative selection and reeligibility, but when James McClurg of Virginia pointed out the contradiction between these two decisions, the one-term limit on the executive was reinstated. McClurg, supported by Gouverneur Morris and by Jacob Broom of Delaware, offered a different way out of the dilemma: election of the executive by the legislature for a life term. But this proposal smacked too much of monarchy to suit the other delegates.

On July 24 and 26, the convention voted again to have the legislature select the executive for a single seven-year term. But the advantages the delegates saw in reeligibility were so powerful that the issue remained alive. Reeligibility not only would give the nation a way of keeping a good executive in office, it also would give the executive what Morris called "the great motive to good behavior, the hope of being rewarded with a re-appointment." As Hamilton later argued in *Federalist* No. 72, even an executive whose behavior was governed by such personal motives as "avarice," "ambition," or "the love of fame" would do a good job in order to hold on to the office that could fulfill those desires. "Shut the Civil road to Glory," warned Morris, more ominously, "& he may be compelled to seek it by the sword."

To complicate their task further, the delegates' decision between legislative selection and reeligibility implied a related decision between a short term for the executive and a longer term. If the executive were to be chosen by the legislature for a single term, the delegates believed, the term should be long. If the executive were eligible for reelection, a shorter term was preferable.

In late August, the convention changed course for the last time. Effectively deciding against legislative selection of the president, the delegates created the Committee on Postponed Matters to propose an alternative. The committee's recommendation, adopted by the convention, was that an electoral college choose the president for a four-year term, with no limit on reeligibility. *(See "Selection and Succession," p. 25.)*

Removal

During the course of the convention, the delegates decided to provide for situations in which the executive needed to be removed from office before the expiration of the term. Serious abuse of power was one such situation—the remedy was the impeachment process. Disability was the other, but, even at the end of the convention, the delegates were less than clear about what ought to be done if the executive became disabled.

Impeachment

Impeachment was a traditional practice of the British political system, with deep roots in British history. During the seventeenth century, as Richard Ellis has written, impeachment of the king's ministers and councilors by the House of Commons, with trial by the House of Lords, "became a vital tool in Parliament's struggle to rein in the power of the monarchy and to make ministers of the Crown accountable to Parliament." [50] In the eighteenth century, when the House of Commons gained the power to force ministers to resign with votes of no confidence, impeachment waned in importance. But the tradition of executive accountability remained.

Although the Virginia Plan made no specific provision for impeaching the executive (it said only that the "supreme tribunal" would "hear and determine . . . impeachments of

any National officers"), most of the delegates agreed from the outset that some mechanism should be included explicitly in the Constitution. Even proponents of a strong executive quickly came to realize that their goal could be achieved only if the other delegates were assured that an out-of-control executive could be removed from office.

The convention's consensus on impeachment was revealed on June 2, when the Committee of the Whole quickly passed North Carolina delegate Hugh Williamson's motion that the executive be "removable on impeachment and conviction of malpractice or neglect of duty." (Impeachment is comparable to indictment by a grand jury; it must be followed by a trial and conviction in order for the impeached official to be removed from office.) The consensus was confirmed and strengthened on July 19, when Morris suggested that if the executive were assigned a short term, there would be no need for impeachment—the passage of time would lead to the executive's removal soon enough. Morris was answered the next day by Gerry, Randolph, Franklin, and Mason, each of whom made clear that he regarded impeachment not only as a vital safeguard against and punishment for abuses of power, but also (at least in Franklin's view) as a way to remove tyrants without having to resort to assassination. Morris quickly retreated, declaring that he was persuaded by his colleagues' arguments.

The Committee of Detail tried to clarify Williamson's definition of the grounds for presidential impeachment, changing it from "malpractice or neglect of duty" to "treason, bribery, or corruption." It also created a mechanism for removal: "impeachment by the House of Representatives and conviction in the Supreme Court." The convention did not take up the impeachment provision of the committee's report until August 27, when Morris asked that it be tabled. He argued that if, as still seemed possible, the convention decided to create a council of revision for the president that included the chief justice of the Supreme Court, the court should not be involved in the impeachment process. The delegates agreed to Morris's motion without objection. Later that week, on August 31, the Committee on Postponed Matters was formed and took charge of the impeachment issue.

The committee made its three-part recommendation on September 4: first, impeachment by the House; second, trial by the Senate, but with the chief justice of the Supreme Court presiding; and third, impeachment on grounds of treason or bribery, but not the vague offense of "corruption." On September 8, Mason com-

---

IMPEACHMENT

The President, Vice President, and all civil Officers of the United States shall be removed from Office on Impeachment for, and Conviction of, Treason, Bribery, or other High Crimes and Misdemeanors.

—*from Article II, Section 4*

The House of Representatives . . . shall have the sole Power of Impeachment.

—*from Article I, Section 1*

The Senate shall have the sole Power to try all Impeachments. When sitting for that Purpose, they shall be on Oath or Affirmation. When the President of the United States is tried, the Chief Justice shall preside: And no Person shall be convicted without the concurrence of two thirds of the Members present.

Judgment in Cases of Impeachment shall not extend further than to removal from Office, and disqualification to hold and enjoy any Office of honor, Trust or Profit under the United States: but the Party convicted shall nevertheless be liable and subject to Indictment, Trial, Judgment and Punishment, according to law.

—*from Article I, Section 3*

plained that to bar only treason and bribery "will not reach many great and dangerous offenses," including certain "attempts to subvert the Constitution." Drawing from the constitutions of six states, including that of his home state of Virginia, he proposed that "maladministration" be added to the list of impeachable offenses. After Madison objected that in practice maladministration would mean nothing more than unpopularity in Congress, Mason substituted "other high crimes and misdemeanors." This phrase was adopted, despite Madison's continuing objection to its breadth.

The delegates made three other modifications to the committee's impeachment proposal on September 8. The majority required for Senate conviction was raised to two-thirds. In addition, the vice president and "all civil officers of the United States" were made subject to impeachment in the same way as the president. Finally, to remind senators that they should vote impartially, a provision that "they shall be on Oath or Affirmation" was added.

Disability

As thorough as the delegates were in considering the grounds for and process of presidential impeachment, they treated cavalierly the situation of a president who is disabled. The matter was first put before the convention on August 1, as part of a provision of the Committee of Detail report that dealt mainly with succession. It read: "In the case of [the president's] . . . disability to discharge the powers and duties of his office, the President of the Senate shall exercise those powers and duties, until another President of the United States be chosen, or until the disability of the President be removed."

On August 27, when this provision of the committee's report came before the convention, John Dickinson of Delaware complained that "it was too vague. What is the extent of the term 'disability' & who is to be the judge of it?" The delegates decided to postpone their discussion of disability until another time, presumably intending to devise answers to these questions. But in a historic case of oversight, that time never came. Disability was left an undefined

---

SUCCESSION AND DISABILITY

In Case of the Removal of the President from Office, or of his Death, Resignation, or Inability to discharge the Powers and Duties of the said Office, the Same shall devolve on the Vice President, and the Congress may by Law provide for the Case of Removal, Death, Resignation, or Inability, both of the President and Vice President, declaring what Officer shall act accordingly, until the Disability be removed, or a President shall be elected.

—from Article II, Section 1*

* Modified by the Twentieth and Twenty-fifth Amendments

---

term in the Constitution; nor was any process created either to determine if a president is disabled or to transfer the powers and duties of the presidency to a temporary successor. Instead, the Committee on Postponed Matters merely named the vice president, rather than the president of the Senate, as the successor to a disabled president and substituted "inability" for "disability" without explaining what difference, if any, this substitution made.

Institutional Separation from Congress

Many of the delegates strongly influenced by the idea that in order to preserve liberty, government should be designed to incorporate the principle of separation of powers. Various political philosophers of the Enlightenment, including John Locke, had articulated this idea, but no version was more familiar to the delegates than that of the

---

INSTITUTIONAL SEPARATION FROM CONGRESS

No Senator or Representative shall, during the Time for which he was elected, be appointed to any civil Office under the Authority of the United States, which shall have been created, or the Emoluments whereof shall have been increased during such time; and no Person holding any Office under the United States, shall be a Member of either House during his Continuance in Office.

—from Article I, Section 6

The President shall, at stated Times, receive for his Services a compensation, which shall neither be encreased nor diminished during the Period for which he shall have been elected, and he shall not receive within that Period any other Emolument from the United States, or any of them.

—from Article II, Section 1

French author, Baron de Montesquieu. As the author of *L'Esprit des Lois* (The Spirit of the Laws) in 1748, Montesquieu was "the oracle who is always consulted and cited" on the subject of separation of powers, wrote Madison in *Federalist* No. 47. In a passage of Montesquieu's book that the delegates knew well and that *Federalist* No. 47 quoted, the philosopher had written:

> When the legislative and executive powers are united in the same person, or in the same body of magistracy, there can be no liberty; because apprehensions may arise lest the same monarch or senate should enact tyrannical laws, to execute them in a tyrannical manner. . . . Were the power of judging joined with the legislative, the life and liberty of the subject would be exposed to arbitrary control, for the judge would then be the legislator.[51]

As applied in the Constitution, the separation of powers principle did not require a strict division of labor, in which each branch of the government was assigned exclusive power to perform certain functions. Indeed, the Constitution assigns few powers to the federal government that are not shared by two or more branches. *(See "Enumerated Powers," p. 31.)* Separation of powers actually meant something more like "separated institutions sharing powers" to the delegates, a separation in which the membership of one branch does not overlap and cannot persecute the membership of the other.[52]

From the beginning, the convention imposed two prohibitions to preserve institutional separation within the government. The first prohibition was against alterations in the incumbent executive's salary. The other was against simultaneous membership in the legislative and executive branches. Both prohibitions were stated in the Virginia Plan and remained substantially unaltered in the final Constitution.

Salary

Immediately after the clause stating that the executive shall be chosen by the legislature, the Virginia Plan provided that the executive shall "receive punctually at stated times, a fixed compensation for the services rendered, in which no increase or diminution shall be made so as to affect the Magistracy existing at the time of increase or diminution." In view of the Virginia Plan's brevity and generality, the detail in this provision is remarkable, as is the priority assigned to it. Clearly, Madison feared that the legislature either might infringe on an executive's independence by lowering or delaying the salary or might reward or entice the executive with an increase in salary.

During the course of the convention, the provision for executive salary was modified only slightly. The delegates eventually added a stipulation that the president "shall not receive within [his term of office] any other Emolument from the United States, or any of them."

On June 2, Franklin wrote and, because of Franklin's frailty, Wilson read aloud a long, almost wistful speech urging that the executive not be compensated at all. To attach a salary to the position, Franklin argued, "united in view of the same object" two "passions which have a powerful influence on the affairs of men. These are ambition and avarice, the love of power, and the love of money. . . . Place before the eyes of men a post of honor that shall be at the same time a place of profit, and they will move heaven and earth to obtain it." The delegates gave Franklin's speech a courteous listening and no more. Their concern was to protect the executive from the legislature, not to create an office that only the rich could afford to occupy.

Membership

As with the ban on altering an incumbent president's salary, the delegates' commitment to separating membership in Congress from membership in the executive branch did not

waver. The Virginia Plan said that legislators were "ineligible to any office established by a particular State, or under the authority of the United States, except those peculiarly belonging to the functions of the first branch [the legislature], during the term of service, and for the space of _____ after its expiration." The final document, although lifting the restriction on legislators holding executive office after they left Congress, included essentially the same provision: "no Person holding any Office under the United States, shall be a Member of either House during his Continuance in Office." The Constitution also prohibited members of Congress from serving as electors in presidential elections.

The delegates wanted to keep the membership of the legislative and executive branches separate to prevent the executive from, in effect, bribing members of Congress with jobs and salaries. On June 22, Pierce Butler of South Carolina, supported by Mason, "appealed to the example of G[reat] B[ritain] where men got into Parl[iamen]t that they might get offices for themselves or their friends. This was the source of corruption that ruined their Govt." On June 23, Butler added: "To some of the opposers he [George III] gave pensions—others offices, and some, to put them out of the house of commons, he made lords. The great Montesquieu says, it is unwise to entrust persons with power, which by being abused operates to the advantage of those entrusted with it."

The office-holding issue was raised again on August 14, when John Mercer of Maryland took the opposite side of the question. He argued that because "[g]overnments can only be maintained by force or influence" and the president lacks force, to "deprive him of influence by rendering members of the Legislature ineligible to Executive offices" was to reduce the president to "a mere phantom of authority." Unpersuaded, the delegates did not alter their earlier decision, either then or on September 3, when Wilson and Charles Pinckney argued that honorable people would be reluctant to serve in government if the official presumption was that they were too corrupt to fulfill faithfully the responsibilities of more than one office.

Nothing was said during the convention about judges holding executive offices. The New Jersey Plan would have prohibited them from doing so, but the subject never was discussed or debated on the convention floor. Indeed, most of the proposals that delegates made for a council of revision included one or more federal judges as members. *(See "Number of the Executive," p. 24.)* The political scientist Robert Scigliano has argued that allowing judges to hold executive office was not an oversight on the delegates' part. Instead, they regarded the executive and judicial powers as joined because both involved carrying out the law. The delegates also believed that Congress would be the most powerful branch in the new government unless the executive and the judiciary could unite when necessary to restrain it.[53]

ENUMERATED POWERS

Every Bill which shall have Passed the House of Representatives and the Senate, shall, before it become a Law, be presented to the President of the United States; If he approve he shall sign it, but if not he shall return it, with his Objections to that House in which it shall have originated, who shall enter the Objections at large on their Journal, and proceed to reconsider it. If after such Reconsideration two thirds of that House shall agree to pass the Bill, it shall be sent, together with the Objections, to the other House, by which it shall likewise be reconsidered, and if approved by two thirds of that House, it shall become a Law. But in all such Cases the Votes of both the Houses shall be determined by Yeas and Nays, and the Names of the Persons voting for and against the Bill shall be entered on the Journal of each House respectively. If any Bill shall not be returned by the President within the ten Days (Sundays excepted) after it shall have been presented to him, the Same shall be a Law, in like Manner as if he had signed it, unless the Congress by their Adjournment prevent its Return, in which Case it shall not be a Law.

Every Order, Resolution, or Vote to which the Concurrence of the Senate and House of Representatives may be necessary (except on a question of Adjournment) shall be presented to the President of the United States; and before the Same shall take Effect, shall be approved by him, or being disapproved by him, shall be repassed by two thirds of the Senate and House of Representatives, according to the Rules and Limitations prescribed in the Case of a Bill.

—from Article I, Section 7

The executive Power shall be vested in a President of the United States of America. . . .

—from Article II, Section 1

The President shall be Commander in Chief of the Army and Navy of the United States, and of the Militia of the several States, when called into the actual Service of the United States; he may require the Opinion, in writing, of the principal Officer in each of the executive Departments, upon any Subject relating to the Duties of their respective Offices, and he shall have power to grant Reprieves and Pardons for Offences against the United States, except in Cases of Impeachment.

He shall have Power, by and with the Advice and Consent of the Senate, to make Treaties, provided two thirds of the Senators present concur: and he shall nominate, and by and with the Advice and Consent of the Senate, shall appoint Ambassadors, other public Ministers and Consuls, Judges of the Supreme Court, and all other Officers of the United States, whose Appointments are not herein otherwise provided for, and which shall be established by Law; but the Congress may by Law vest the Appointment of such inferior Officers, as they think proper, in the President alone, in the Courts of Law, or in the Heads of Departments.

The President shall have Power to fill up all Vacancies that may happen during the Recess of the Senate, by granting commissions which shall expire at the End of their next Session.

—from Article II, Section 2

He shall from time to time give to the Congress Information of the State of the Union, and recommend to their Consideration such Measures as he shall judge necessary and expedient; he may, on extraordinary Occasions, convene both Houses, or either of them, and in Case of Disagreement between them, with Respect to the Time of Adjournment, he may adjourn them to such Time as he shall think proper; he shall take Care that the Laws be faithfully executed, and shall Commission all the Officers of the United States.

—from Article II, Section 3

Enumerated Powers

The delegates were slow to enumerate the powers either of the presidency or of the other branches of the government. Indeed, their initial inclination seems to have been to give each branch a general grant of powers rather than a specific list. The Virginia Plan, for example, empowered the legislature simply "to legislate in all cases to which the separate states are incompetent, or in which the harmony of the United States may be interrupted by the exercise of individual Legislation." The executive, in addition to sharing the veto with a council, was to execute the national laws.

The advantage the delegates saw in a general grant of powers (which they approved both while meeting as the Committee of the Whole and soon afterward in convention) was that the alternative, a specific enumeration, risked limiting the government to a list of powers that the passage of time could render obsolete. But the convention was uneasy with its choice. "Incompetent" was a vague word, easily subject to abuse, but so was any other word or phrase they might invent for a general grant.

Reading the delegates' mood, the Committee of Detail included an enumeration of each branch's powers in the draft constitution that it presented to the convention. The convention's reaction confirmed the committee's judgment. Although the delegates debated each proposed power separately, they never questioned the decision to enumerate.

The powers of the presidency are detailed in Article II of the Constitution (except for the veto power, which is in Article I, Section 7). They are discussed here in the order of their appearance in the Constitution. Three other provisions that are examined in this section—the president's title, oath of office, and qualifications—are also spelled out in Article II.

Veto

The right to veto acts passed by the legislature was the only specific grant of power to the executive proposed in the Virginia Plan. The states' recent experience with weak governors and powerful legislatures was proof enough to the delegates that the veto was indispensable to executive self-defense against legislative encroachments. Even so, they were initially reluctant to cede too much responsibility to the executive.

The Virginia Plan provided that the executive could cast a veto only with the cooperation of a council of judges. Madison believed that the support of a council would buttress the executive's willingness to cast vetoes. He based this belief on the recent experiences of Massachusetts, where the governor alone had the veto power and almost never used it, and New York, where council-supported governors vetoed bills freely.[54] The plan also stipulated that vetoes could be overridden (and the vetoed act become law) by vote of an unspecified majority of both houses of the legislature.

On June 4, Wilson and Hamilton urged the delegates, then meeting as the Committee of the Whole, to grant the executive an absolute veto—that is, a veto not subject to legislative override. Franklin, Sherman, Mason, and others rose in opposition to this suggestion, invoking their own and the public's memories of the British king and the royal governors, who had cast absolute vetoes against the acts of American legislatures in colonial times. "We are not indeed constituting a British monarchy, but a more dangerous monarchy, an elective one," argued Mason, who wanted to empower the executive only to postpone the enactment of an offensive law in the hope that the legislature would revise it. Gerry found a middle ground that was acceptable to the delegates: an executive veto, subject to override by a two-thirds vote of each house of the legislature. The recommendation that the executive share the veto power with a council was tabled.

In its report of August 6, the Committee of Detail, although faithfully reflecting the decisions of the Committee of the Whole regarding the veto, also sought to settle two unresolved issues. First, it assigned the power to cast vetoes to the president alone. Second, it stipulated that after a bill was passed and presented, the president would have seven days in which to respond. If the bill was neither signed nor vetoed by the president in that period, it would become law. An important exception was made, however, to prevent Congress from getting its way by adjourning before the pres-

ident had a chance to cast a veto. If Congress adjourned within the seven-day period, the president had merely to ignore the bill for it to be vetoed. Such vetoes later came to be called "pocket vetoes." *(See "Pocket Veto," p. 655, in Chapter 12.)*

On August 15, the convention voted to modify the Committee of Detail report in ways that strengthened the president's veto power. The two-thirds requirement for congressional override of a veto was raised to three-fourths. In addition, to prevent Congress from evading a veto by passing legislation and calling it something other than a "bill," the veto power was extended to "every order, resolution, or vote" of Congress. Finally, the period in which a president could cast a veto was extended from seven days to ten days, not including Sunday.

Only one further modification was made in the veto power. On September 12, in a gesture to delegates suspicious of presidential power that was designed to win their signatures on the Constitution, the convention voted to restore the two-thirds requirement for a legislative override.

"The Executive Power"

The Virginia Plan introduced the executive article by stating "that a national Executive be instituted." The Committee of the Whole modified this provision of the plan by adding "to consist of a single person." The Committee of Detail, however, proposed "vesting" clauses for all three branches of government:

> The legislative power shall be vested in a Congress. . . .
>
> The Executive Power of the United States shall be vested in a single person. His stile shall be "The President of the United States," and his title shall be, "His Excellency."
>
> The Judicial Power of the United States shall be vested in one Supreme Court, and in such inferior courts as shall, when necessary, from time to time, be constituted by the Legislature of the United States.

The vesting clause that the committee proposed for the president was particularly important because it made clear that the powers of the presidency derived directly from the Constitution, not from discretionary grants by Congress.

But the clause was less instructive on another important aspect of presidential power. As the political scientist Richard Pious has shown, " 'Executive Power' was a general term, sufficiently ambiguous so that no one could say precisely what it meant. It was possible that the words referred to more than the enumerated powers that followed, and might confer a set of unspecified executive powers."[55] First among these would be prerogative power, which had been discussed at length in a book that was widely familiar among the delegates, John Locke's *Second Treatise of Government*. Locke had argued that in times of crisis, laws and constitutional provisions that were inadequate to the challenges at hand might temporarily have to "give way to the executive power, viz., that as much as may be, all the members of society are to be preserved." Prerogative, according to Locke, was "the people's permitting their rulers to do several things of their own free choice, where the law was silent, or sometimes, too, against the direct letter of the law, for the public good, and their acquiescing in it when so done." [56]

The theory that the powers of the presidency extend beyond those listed in the Constitution is supported by the language of the document itself, thanks to a "joker," as Charles Thach has called it, that Gouverneur Morris, the chief drafter for the Committee of Style, tossed into the final version. The committee's charge was merely to put the Constitution into polished language. "Positively with respect to the executive article," noted Thach, Morris "could do nothing." His pro-executive biases were so well known that any substantive changes would have been quickly detected. Morris left the vesting clause for the presidency unaltered ("the executive Power shall be vested in a President of the United States of America") but changed the vesting clause for Congress to read: "All legislative powers *herein granted* shall be vested in a Congress of the United States" (emphasis added).

Thach suspects that Morris did his tinkering "with full realization of the possibilities"—namely, that presidents later could claim that the different phrasing of the branches' vesting clauses implies that there are executive powers beyond those "herein granted." (Otherwise, why would the Constitution not apply those restricting words to the president in the same way it does to Congress?) "At any rate," Thach concluded, "whether intentional or not, it admitted an interpretation of executive power which would give the president a field of activity wider than that outlined by the enumerated powers." [57]

Commander in Chief

Because nothing was said in the Virginia Plan about who would direct the armed forces, the delegates took it for granted during the early stages of the convention that Congress would be the controlling branch, as it had been under the Articles of Confederation. The issue did not come up for debate in the Committee of the Whole. The Committee of Detail, however, included a military role for the president in its enumeration of the suggested powers of each branch.

The committee proposed that the president "shall be commander in chief of the Army and Navy of the United States, and of the Militia of the several States." But it also recommended that Congress be empowered "to make war; to raise armies; to build and equip fleets; to call forth the aid of the militia, in order to execute the laws of the Union; enforce treaties; suppress insurrections, and repel invasions." The meaning of these provisions confused the delegates when

they took them up for consideration on August 17. Clearly, Congress's power to "make" war included directing the actual conduct of the fighting, but so did the president's power as "commander in chief of the Army and the Navy." Which branch, then, would actually order soldiers and sailors into action? Which would tell them where to go and what to do when they got there?

Debate on the convention floor about the powers of war was brief and went only part way toward resolving the ambiguities created by the Committee of Detail. Pierce Butler, doubting that Congress (or even the Senate alone) would be able to act quickly enough on military matters if the need should arise, urged the convention to vest the power to make war in the president, "who will have all the requisite qualities, and will not make war but when the Nation will support it." Madison and Gerry, agreeing that Congress might be unable to respond to foreign invasions promptly (perhaps because it was not in session) but not willing to entrust the president with such vast military powers, "moved to insert 'declare' [war], striking out 'make' war; leaving to the Executive the power to repel sudden attacks." Sherman agreed: "The Executive shd. be able to repel and not to commence war." Madison and Gerry's motion passed.

As for control of the various state militia, on August 27 the convention approved without discussion a motion by Sherman that the president serve as commander in chief of the militia only after explicitly calling those militia "into the actual service of the U. S." Thus the clause as finally written in the Constitution reads: "The President shall be Commander in Chief of the Army and Navy of the United States, and of the Militia of the several States, when called into the actual Service of the United States." *(See "Appointment and Commissioning Power," p. 35.)*

"Require the Opinion"

The Constitution empowers the president to "require the Opinion, in writing, of the principal Officer in each of the executive Departments, upon any Subject relating to the Duties of their respective Offices." This curious provision (Hamilton described it in *Federalist* No. 74 "as a mere redundancy in the plan, as the right for which it provides would result of itself from the office") was proposed by the Committee on Postponed Matters and adopted by a unanimous vote on September 7.[58] But the clause's origin lies in the Virginia Plan's proposal for an executive council, an idea that recurred frequently during the convention.

Although most delegates seem to have favored some sort of council, they never created one because they held such varied opinions about who would be on the council and whether its relationship to the president would be merely advisory or would involve the shared exercise of certain executive powers. *(See "Number of the Executive," p. 24.)* One version of the council idea was included in a sweeping plan for the organization of the executive branch that Gouverneur Morris and Charles Pinckney introduced on August 20. The Morris-Pinckney plan provided that five departments would be created, to be headed by, respectively, a secretary of domestic affairs, of commerce and finance, of foreign affairs, of war, and of marine. All five of these "principal officers" would be appointed by the president and serve at the president's pleasure. Together with the chief justice of the Supreme Court, they would constitute a Council of State whose purpose would be to

> assist the President in conducting the Public affairs. . . . The President may from time to time submit any matter to the discussion of the Council of State, and *he may require the written opinion of any one or more of the members:* But he shall in all cases exercise his own judgment, and either Conform to such opinions or not as he may think proper; and every officer abovementioned shall be responsible for his opinion on the affairs relating to his particular Department (emphasis added).

The Morris-Pinckney plan was not debated by the delegates, but the proposal to empower the president to require written opinions from individual department heads on matters related to their responsibilities seems to have been the basis for the September 4 recommendation of the Committee on Postponed Matters. Although on September 7 Mason, Franklin, Wilson, Dickinson, and Madison again urged that a council be created, their colleagues, frustrated by their inability to agree on a specific proposal and eager to conclude the convention's business, approved the committee's recommendation as written.

Pardon

Hamilton was the first to suggest to the convention that it grant the president the power to pardon criminals. In his long speech to the delegates on June 18 he urged that the executive "have the power of pardoning all offences except Treason; which he shall not pardon without the approbation of the Senate." *(See "Hamilton's Plan," p. 17.)* Perhaps persuaded by Hamilton's proposal, the Committee of Detail recommended that the president "shall have power to grant reprieves and pardons; but his pardon shall not be pleadable in bar of an impeachment" (that is, to prevent an impeachment).

The pardon power is a power of kings. In Great Britain, all crimes were regarded as offenses against the Crown. Accordingly, the power to forgive was a royal prerogative. Crimes in the United States were regarded as offenses against the law, not the executive, which is why no state constitution allowed its governor a unilateral pardon power.[59]

Thus it is remarkable that the delegates resisted efforts to modify the Committee of Detail's recommendation in any substantial way. Sherman's August 25 motion to require the president to gain Senate consent for a pardon was defeated

by a vote of eight states to one. Two days later, Luther Martin of Maryland moved to allow pardons only "after conviction"; he withdrew the motion when Wilson, using the crime of forgery as an example, objected that "pardon before conviction might be necessary in order to obtain the testimony of accomplices." On September 12, the Committee of Style clarified one aspect of the pardon power by limiting it to "offences against the United States"—that is, to violations of national rather than state law. A September 15 motion by Edmund Randolph to disallow pardons for treason ("The President may himself be guilty. The Traytors may be his own instruments.") was defeated by a vote of eight states to two after Wilson argued that if the president "be himself a party to the guilt he can be impeached and prosecuted." The pardon power entered the Constitution as the president's only unchecked power.

Although no thoroughgoing case for granting the pardon power to the president ever was offered at the convention, Hamilton's defense of it in *Federalist* No. 74 may reflect the delegates' thinking. Hamilton began by pleading the need for leeway in the criminal justice system to "make exceptions in favor of unfortunate guilt." As to pardons for treason, he wrote (perhaps with Shays' Rebellion in mind), "The principal argument for reposing the power of pardoning in this case in the Chief Magistrate is this: in seasons of insurrection or rebellion there are often critical moments when a well-timed offer of pardon to the insurgents or rebels may restore the tranquility of the commonwealth; and which, if suffered to pass unimproved, it may never be possible afterwards to recall."

"Make Treaties"

At the start of the convention, most delegates seemed to assume that the power to make treaties with other countries would be vested in Congress. That had been the practice under the Articles of Confederation and, although the Virginia Plan said nothing explicitly about treaties, it did provide that "the National Legislature ought to be impowered to enjoy the Legislative Rights vested in Congress by the Confederation."

The first suggestion that the treaty power should be shared between the legislative and executive branches seems to have been made by Hamilton. One of the specific provisions of the plan of government he proposed on June 18 was that the executive should "have with the approbation and advice of the Senate the power of making all treaties." The delegates did not discuss Hamilton's suggestion on the convention floor, and it appeared to be dead when the August 1 report of the Committee of Detail proposed instead that "the Senate shall have the power to make treaties."

The committee's proposal sparked a heated debate, much of it spawned by changes in the design of the Senate that had occurred during the convention. The conclave of national statesmen envisioned by the Virginia Plan had become a states-dominated body, a smaller and perhaps more easily manipulated version of the Continental Congress.[60] George Mason argued that an exclusive treaty-making power would enable the Senate to "sell the whole country by means of treaties." James Madison thought that the president, who would represent all of the people, should have the power. Regional concerns also were expressed. Southern delegates worried that their states' right to free navigation of the Mississippi River might be surrendered in a future treaty. New Englanders expressed similar fears about their right to fish in the waters near Newfoundland. The delegates, having reached an impasse, referred the treaty issue to the Committee on Postponed Matters.

On September 4, the committee recommended that the president "with the advice and Consent of the Senate" be granted the treaty-making power and that no treaty be approved "without the consent of two-thirds of the members [of the Senate] present." The provision for a two-thirds vote, which was designed to assuage the concerns of the southerners and the New Englanders that they would be outnumbered on issues of regional importance, was highly controversial and provoked numerous motions to revise. One proposal would have deleted the two-thirds requirement for ratification in favor of a simple majority vote. Another would have strengthened the requirement by stipulating two-thirds approval by the entire membership of the Senate, not just those who were present for the vote. Another would have included the House of Representatives in the treaty ratification process. Yet another proposal—which initially passed and then was rejected—would have applied the simple majority rule to treaties whose purpose was to end a war. In the end, however, the committee's recommendation of a two-thirds vote of the senators present was accepted.

The proposal to involve the president with the Senate in treaty making was relatively uncontroversial, reflecting an alliance between pro-executive delegates and small-state delegates that had formed after the convention decided that states would be represented equally in the Senate. Only one motion was made to modify the president's role: Madison moved to allow two-thirds of the Senate, acting alone if it chose to do so, to conclude peace treaties. Madison worried that the president, who inevitably would derive unusual power and prominence from a state of war, might be tempted to "impede a treaty of peace." His motion failed when Nathaniel Gorham of Massachusetts pointed out that Congress could end a war by simply refusing to appropriate funds to continue the fighting.

Appointment and Commissioning Power

Article II, Section 2, of the Constitution, as finally written, provides three methods for appointing federal judges and other unelected government officials: presidential appointment with Senate confirmation (the ordinary method); presidential appointment without Senate confirmation (when the Senate is in recess); and, when Congress so determines by statute, appointment of certain "inferior Officers" (that is, officers subordinate to the heads of the departments or the courts of law) by the department heads or the courts. Clearly, the delegates moved a long way from both the Articles of Confederation, which vested the appointment power entirely in Congress, and the Virginia Plan, which proposed to continue that practice.

The appointment power was one of the first, last, and (in between) most contentious issues at the convention. Although, as Richard Ellis has shown, no delegate doubted that "it was the legislature and not the executive that should have the power to create offices, there the agreement ended." [61] On June 1, meeting as the Committee of the Whole, the delegates approved Madison's motion to modify the Virginia Plan slightly by adding to the then-limited powers of the executive the ambiguous phrase "to appoint to offices in cases not otherwise provided for." But this decision simply opened the door to stronger advocates of executive power, such as Wilson and Hamilton, who wished to make the appointment of judges, ambassadors, and other government officials a purely executive responsibility, with no involvement by the legislature at all.

Heated debate erupted periodically during the months of June and July about issues such as which branch of government would be most prone to favoritism in appointments and which would know best the qualifications of prospective appointees. Many delegates, mindful of how George III and his royal governors in the colonies had used government appointments as patronage plums to curry support among legislators, dreaded giving this power to even a home-grown executive.

On July 21, the delegates voted to confer on the Senate sole responsibility for judicial appointments. The Committee of Detail added the appointment of ambassadors to the Senate's list of powers, then stipulated that Congress as a whole should elect the national treasurer (that is, the secretary of the Treasury). The committee also confirmed the convention's earlier decision that the president "shall appoint officers in all cases not otherwise provided for by this Constitution" and empowered the president to "commission all the officers of the United States." It remained unclear, however, where responsibility would lie for appointing the heads of the departments or other departmental officials and employees.

On August 24, during a period in which the delegates generally were turning away from senatorial power, they passed a motion that, although not altogether clear, seemed to expand the president's power to make appointments, while leaving complete responsibility for choosing judges and ambassadors in the Senate's jurisdiction. The motion, which was offered by John Dickinson, stated that the president "shall appoint to all offices established by this Constitution, except in cases herein otherwise provided for, and to all offices which may hereafter be created by law." But the delegates did not revisit their August 17 rejection of Delaware delegate George Read's motion to allow the president to appoint the treasurer. They still wanted anything to do with money firmly in Congress's hands.

As it had with the treaty-making power, the Committee on Postponed Matters proposed in early September to increase further the president's role in the appointment process. Judges, ambassadors, ministers, and officers that the delegates had not already provided for would be appointed by the president with the advice and consent of the Senate. A simple majority vote of the senators present would suffice to confirm a presidential appointment. Wilson tried again to persuade the delegates to make appointments a unilateral power of the president. To involve the Senate, he argued, had "a dangerous tendency to aristocracy." But Wilson's motion was unsuccessful.

The convention accepted the committee's recommendation after making three additions: the president was given the power to fill vacancies that occurred while the Senate was in recess (September 6), the power to appoint the Treasury secretary was transferred from Congress to the president (September 14), and control over certain forms of patronage was distributed between the two branches by giving the two houses of Congress the power to "vest the appointment of such inferior officers as they think proper" in the president, the courts, or the heads of the departments (September 15).

Advisory Legislative Powers

In enumerating the proposed powers of the presidency, the Committee of Detail specified: "He shall, from time to time, give information to the Legislature, of the state of the Union: he may recommend to their consideration such measures as he shall deem necessary, and expedient." The latter of these two provisions, both of which were uncontroversial, was modified slightly in response to an August 24 motion by Gouverneur Morris. He argued that the Constitution should make it "the duty of the President to recommend [measures to Congress], & thence prevent umbrage or cavil at his doing it." In other words, Congress would be less likely to resent presidential recommendations if the president had no constitutional choice but to offer them.

The convention approved Morris's specific suggestion that the words "he may" be replaced by "and." Thus the Constitution as finally written reads: "He shall from time to time give to the Congress Information of the State of the Union, and recommend to their Consideration such Measures as he shall judge necessary and expedient."

Powers to Convene and Adjourn Congress

The Committee of Detail recommended that the president be empowered to "convene them [the House and Senate] on extraordinary occasions"—that is, to call Congress into special session. Further, "In case of disagreement between the two Houses, with regard to the time of their adjournment, he may adjourn them to such time as he thinks proper."

James McHenry of Maryland, wanting to grant the president the option to call only the Senate back into session, presumably to consider a treaty or presidential appointment, persuaded the delegates to amend the special session clause to that effect on September 8. The Constitution therefore reads: "he may, on extraordinary Occasions, convene both Houses, or either of them."

"Receive Ambassadors"

The president's power to "receive Ambassadors" was proposed by the Committee of Detail. The committee joined this power to another—permission to "correspond with the supreme Executives of the several States" (the state governors)—which the convention rejected on August 25 as being, according to Morris, "unnecessary and implying that he could not correspond with others." As for receiving ambassadors, the absence of debate or discussion by the delegates makes it unclear whether they meant this power to be substantive or merely ceremonial. In practice, the power to receive or, in particular cases, to refuse to receive ambassadors has made the president the sole official recipient of communications from foreign governments and the sole maker of decisions about which governments the United States will recognize diplomatically.

"Take Care"

According to the Virginia Plan, the executive was to have "general authority to execute the National Laws." On June 1, Madison sought to revise this to read: "power to carry into effect the national laws . . . and to execute such other powers not Legislative or Judiciary in their nature as may from time to time be delegated by the national Legislature." The stipulation about legislative and judicial powers reflected Madison's acceptance of a suggestion by Gen. Charles Cotesworth Pinckney, who felt it was important to explicitly prohibit "improper powers" from being delegated to the executive. The other South Carolina Pinckney (Charles) persuaded the delegates to strike the amendment as "unnecessary." No further controversy over the "take care" clause ensued. The Committee of Detail's formulation—"he shall take care that the laws of the United States be duly and faithfully executed"—was adopted without discussion by the convention and survived virtually intact in the final Constitution: "he shall take Care that the Laws be faithfully executed."

Title

During the first two months of their deliberations, the delegates usually referred to the head of the executive branch as the "national executive," "supreme executive," or "governor." On August 6, the Committee of Detail included the term "president" in its report to the convention. The title had been used for the presiding officer of Congress and many other legislative bodies, including the convention itself. It was familiar and unthreatening to those who feared that the delegates might be creating a monarchical or tyrannical office. Once proposed by the committee, "president" was accepted without debate by the convention.

Oath of Office

"Before he enter on the Execution of his Office," the Constitution requires of the president that "he shall take the following Oath or Affirmation:—'I do solemnly swear (or affirm) that I will faithfully execute the Office of President of the United States, and will to the best of my Ability, preserve, protect and defend the Constitution of the United States.' " Although another provision of the Constitution states that all legislators, judges, and other officials of both the national government and the various state governments "shall be bound by Oath or Affirmation, to support this Constitution," the language of only the president's oath is included in the document. Some regard the wording of the presidential oath (it pledges the president to execute "the office" rather than the laws) as further support for the claim that there are implied powers of presidential prerogative in the Constitution. *(See " 'The Executive Power,' " p. 32.)*

Virtually no debate or discussion accompanied the writing of the president's oath by the Constitutional Convention. The first half of the oath was proposed by the Committee of Detail on August 6: "I solemnly swear (or affirm) that I will faithfully execute the office of President of the United States of America." On August 27, Mason and Madison moved that the phrase "and will to the best of my judgment and power, preserve, protect and defend the Constitution of the United States" be added to the oath. Wilson objected that a special presidential oath was unnecessary, but Mason and Madison's motion passed handily. On September 15, the delegates substituted "abilities" for "judgment and power," but no discussion was recorded that explains this alteration.

Departing from the practice that prevailed in most of the states at the time, the convention barred the imposition of religious oaths on the president and other officials of the national government. Some state constitutions required an adherence to Christianity as a condition for serving as governor, others to Protestant Christianity. North Carolina, for example, insisted that its governor affirm the existence of God and the truth of Protestantism and hold no religious beliefs that were inimical to the "peace and safety" of the

---

OATH OF OFFICE

Before he enter on the Execution of his Office, he shall take the following Oath or Affirmation: —"I do solemnly swear (or affirm) that I will faithfully execute the Office of President of the United States, and will to the best of my Ability, preserve, protect and defend the Constitution of the United States."

—*from Article II, Section 1*

---

state. On August 30, Charles Pinckney moved that "no religious test shall ever be required as a qualification to any office or public trust under the authority of the U. States." Sherman said he thought the proposal was "unnecessary, the prevailing liberality being a sufficient security agst. such tests." Nonetheless, Pinckney's motion was approved.

Qualifications

No statement of qualifications for president was included in the Constitution until September 7, when the convention, unanimously and without debate, approved the recommendation of the Committee on Postponed Matters that the president be thirty-five years or older, a natural born citizen

---

QUALIFICATIONS

No person except a natural born Citizen, or a Citizen of the United States, at the time of the Adoption of this Constitution, shall be eligible to the Office of President; neither shall any Person be eligible to the Office who shall not have attained to the Age of thirty five Years, and been fourteen Years a Resident within the United States.

—*from Article II, Section 1*

(or a citizen at the time of the Constitution's adoption), and a resident of the United States for at least fourteen years.

In all likelihood, the lateness of the convention's actions on presidential qualifications was the result of deliberation, not neglect. Throughout their proceedings, the delegates seem to have operated on the principle that qualifications for an office needed to be established only if qualifications for those who choose the person to fill the office were not.[62] Thus as early as the Virginia Plan, qualifications, which were not stated for voters, were included for members of the national legislature. (Ultimately, it was decided that members of the House of Representatives must be at least twenty-five years old, seven years a citizen, and an inhabitant of the state they represented; senators must be at least thirty years old, nine years a citizen, and an inhabitant of the state.)

Conversely, qualifications for judges and other appointed offices never were included in the Constitution because these officers were to be selected by other government officials for whom qualifications were stated.

Through most of the convention's deliberations, the majority of delegates remained wedded to the idea that Congress, a body of constitutionally "qualified" members, would elect the president. *(See "Selection and Succession," p. 25.)* Thus they felt no need to include qualifications for president in the Constitution. By mid-August, however, it was obvious that most of the delegates had changed their minds about legislative selection of the executive. Although they had not yet decided on an alternative, whatever procedure they eventually devised to choose the president clearly would involve selection by an "unqualified" body because members of Congress were the only officials for whom constitutional qualifications were stated. This new election procedure, in turn, would necessitate the writing of qualifications for president. These qualifications would have to be high, because the delegates also seem to have agreed that the greater the powers of an office, the higher the qualifications for it should be.

On August 20, Elbridge Gerry moved that the Committee of Detail be revived for the purpose of proposing a list of qualifications for president. Two days later, the committee did so: the president was to be at least thirty-five years old, a citizen, and an inhabitant of the United States for at least twenty-one years. On September 4, the Committee on Postponed Matters submitted a revised statement of qualifications: thirty-five, a natural born citizen or a citizen at the time of the Constitution's adoption, and fourteen years a resident. The delegates approved the revised recommendation on September 7.

Each element of the presidential qualifications clause was grounded in its own rationale. The age requirement had two justifications. First, the delegates presumed, age would foster maturity. As Mason said in the debate on establishing a minimum age for members of the House of Representatives, "[E]very man carried with him in his own experience a scale for measuring the deficiency of young politicians, since he would if interrogated be obliged to declare that his political opinions at the age of 21 were too crude & erroneous to merit an influence on public measures." Second, the passage of years left in its wake a record for the voters to assess. According to John Jay, the author of *Federalist* No. 64,

> By excluding men under 35 from the first office [president], and those under 30 from the second [senator], it confines the electors to men of whom the people have had time to form a judgment, and with respect to whom they will not be liable to be deceived by those brilliant appearances of genius and patriotism which, like transient meteors, sometimes mislead as well as dazzle.

The residency and citizenship requirements for president were grounded less in principles of good government than in the politics of the moment. The stipulation that the president must be at least fourteen years a resident of the United States was designed to eliminate from consideration both British sympathizers who had fled to England during the Revolutionary War and popular foreign military leaders, notably Baron Frederick von Steuben of Prussia, who had emigrated to the United States to fight in the Revolution. As to the length of the residency requirement, the Committee of Detail's recommendation of twenty-one years probably was reduced to fourteen because the longer requirement—but not the shorter—might have been interpreted as barring three of the convention's delegates from the presidency: Hamilton, Pierce Butler, and James McHenry.

The reason for requiring that the president be a natural born citizen was similarly tied to contemporary politics. Rumors had spread while the convention was meeting that the delegates were plotting to invite a European monarch to rule the United States. Prince Henry of Prussia and Frederick, Duke of York, who was King George III's second son, were the most frequently mentioned names. The practice of importing foreign rulers was not unknown among the European monarchies of the day and would not have seemed preposterous to Americans who heard the rumor. The delegates, aware that the mere existence of an independent executive in the Constitution was going to provoke attacks from opponents who suspected that the presidency was a latent monarchy, seem to have believed that they could squelch at least the foreign king rumor by requiring that the president be a natural born citizen of the United States.[63]

A property qualification for president was not included in the Constitution, even though most state constitutions required that their governors be property owners and the delegates had approved a similar requirement for the president more than a month before they approved the presidential qualifications clause. On July 26, the convention adopted a motion by Mason and the Pinckneys that a property qualification be stated for judges, legislators, and the executive. The Committee of Detail neglected the motion in its proposed draft of the Constitution, which provoked both a complaint and another motion from Charles Pinckney on August 10. John Rutledge of South Carolina, the chair of the committee, apologized and seconded Pinckney's motion. He said the committee members had made no recommendations about property "because they could not agree on any among themselves, being embarrassed by the danger on one side of displeasing the people by making them too high, and on the other of rendering them nugatory by making them low."

In response, Franklin rose to attack the very idea of property qualifications. As Madison summarized Franklin's speech: "Some of the greatest rogues he was ever acquainted with were the richest rogues." Pinckney's motion, Madison noted, quickly "was rejected by so general a no, that the States were not called." In truth, the practical difficulty of establishing an acceptable property requirement, more than any belief that such a requirement should not be included on principle, seems to explain why the Constitution was silent on property ownership by the president.

The Vice Presidency

The idea of an office like the vice presidency was not unknown among the delegates to the Constitutional Convention. During the period of British rule, several colonies had lieutenant governors (known in some states as deputy governors or by another title) whose ongoing duties were minor but who stood by to serve as acting governor if the governor died, was removed from office, was ill, or was absent from the colony.

After independence, five states—New York, Connecticut, Rhode Island, Massachusetts, and South Carolina—included lieutenant governors in their constitutions. Each lieutenant governor was elected in the same manner as the governor and was charged to act as governor when needed. New York's lieutenant governor also was the president of the state senate and was empowered to break tie votes. Other states handled the matter of gubernatorial

---

VICE PRESIDENT

The Vice President of the United States shall be President of the Senate, but shall have no Vote, unless they be equally divided.

The Senate shall chuse . . . a President pro tempore, in the Absence of the Vice President, or when he shall exercise the Office of the President of the United States.

—from Article I, Section 3

(For additional constitutional provisions concerning the vice president, see the boxes on term, election, succession and disability, impeachment, and the Twelfth, Twentieth, and Twenty-fifth Amendments in this chapter.)

---

death, absence, or inability differently. In Virginia and Georgia, for example, the head of the privy council, a cabinet-style body, was the designated gubernatorial successor; in Delaware and North Carolina it was the speaker of the upper house of the legislature; in New Hampshire, the senior member of the state senate.[64]

It is difficult to say whether the experience of the states had much influence on the convention's decision to create the vice presidency. No reference was made to the state lieutenant governors in the debates. Nor was any proposal made to include a vice president in the Constitution until very late in

---

An AMBIGUOUS OFFICE

The haste with which the vice presidency was invented at the Constitutional Convention made the constitutional status of the office a matter of some confusion. A variety of practices and opinions have emerged through the years. Vice President Thomas Jefferson, dwelling on the vice president's role as president of the Senate, said, "I consider my office as constitutionally confined to legislative duties." John Nance Garner, a twentieth-century vice president, placed the vice presidency in "a no man's land somewhere between the executive and legislative branch." Walter F. Mondale said that as vice president he was "a member of both . . . branches."

As part of both (or neither) the executive and legislative branches, the vice presidency has never been fully at home in either one. In this century, the Senate has become steadily less receptive to vice presidents who hoped to play a formal role in that body. Nothing illustrates this better than the rebuff that Senate Democrats handed Lyndon B. Johnson, arguably the most effective Senate majority leader in history, when he asked to be allowed to continue presiding over meetings of the Senate Democratic caucus at the start of his term as vice president in 1961. As Sen. Clinton Anderson, who had been one of Johnson's closest political allies, protested, the office of vice president is not a legislative office.

Neither is the vice presidency fully executive. But a number of recent developments, starting with the establishment by President Franklin D. Roosevelt of the presidential nominee's right to designate the running mate, have moved the vice presidency more clearly into the executive domain—in practice, if not in constitutional theory.

The difference between theory and practice was decorously observed in the working relationship between President Dwight D. Eisenhower and Vice President Richard Nixon. Eisenhower firmly believed that the vice president "is not legally a member of the executive branch and is not subject to direction by the president." Thus the president would never tell his vice president to do anything. Instead, recalled Nixon, Eisenhower would "wonder aloud if I might like to take over this or that project." Nixon, of course, never refused these requests; indeed, he estimated after seven years as vice president that about 90 percent of his time had been spent on executive branch activities and only 10 percent on legislative matters. But, following constitutional form, Eisenhower said that he regarded Nixon's efforts on the administration's behalf as "working voluntarily."

In one very important sense, theory really does guide practice. The vice presidency, being an elective office with a fixed four-year term, is constitutionally independent. However closely the vice president may be associated with the administration, presidents are reluctant to assign certain important tasks to vice presidents, knowing that, unlike department heads and other executive officials, they cannot be removed or held formally accountable for their words and actions. Historically, the two major efforts to assign a vice president supervisory responsibility for an executive agency or staff unit ended in failure and disappointment— when President Franklin Roosevelt named Vice President Henry A. Wallace to chair the three thousand-member Economic Defense Board and when President Gerald R. Ford allowed Vice President Nelson A. Rockefeller to head the White House Domestic Council. *(See Chapter 3, History of the Vice Presidency.)*

the proceedings. Indeed, the invention of the vice presidency seems to have been an afterthought of the convention, a residue of its solution to the problem of presidential selection.

The delegates initially had decided that the legislature should choose the executive, but they eventually replaced legislative selection with the electoral college, in which each state was to pick presidential electors, who in turn would choose the president by majority vote. A possibly fatal defect of this procedure was that the electors simply would vote for a variety of local favorites, preventing the choice of a nationally elected president. But the committee remedied this potential problem by assigning each elector two votes for president, requiring that they cast at least one of these votes for a candidate who "shall not be an Inhabitant of the same State with themselves," and attaching a consequence to both votes: the runner-up in the election for president would be awarded the newly created office of vice president.

Thus as Hugh Williamson, a member of the Committee on Postponed Matters, testified, "Such an office as vice-President was not wanted. It was introduced only for the sake of a valuable mode of election which required two to be chosen at the same time." But, having invented the vice presidency, the committee proposed that the office also be used to solve two other problems that had vexed the convention.

Senate President. The first problem was the role of president of the Senate. Some delegates had fretted that if a senator were chosen for this position, one of two difficulties inevitably would arise. If the senator were barred from voting on legislative matters except in the event of a tie (which was customary for presiding officers because it guaranteed that tie votes would be broken), the senator's state would effectively be denied half its representation on most issues. If the senator were allowed to vote on all matters, the state would be overrepresented in the Senate, occupying two voting seats and the presiding officer's chair. The Committee on Postponed Matters recommended that, as a way around this dilemma, the vice president serve as president of the Senate, voting only to break ties. An exception was made for impeachment trials of the president, when the chief justice of the Supreme Court would preside over the Senate. In an oversight, vice presidents were not barred from presiding over their own impeachment trials.

Succession. The second loose end that the committee used the vice presidency to tie off was presidential succession when the presidency unexpectedly became vacant. This, too, was a matter to which the convention turned rather late. The Virginia Plan and the New Jersey Plan had been silent about succession. On June 18, as part of his sweeping proposal for a national executive chosen by electors to serve for life, Hamilton had suggested that in the event of the executive's death, resignation, impeachment and removal, or absence from the country, the senator who served as president of the Senate should "exercise all the powers by this Constitution

vested in the President, until another shall be appointed, or until he shall return within the United States, if his absence was with the Consent of the Senate and Assembly [House of Representatives]." Sustained attention was first given to the succession question by the Committee of Detail. Knowingly or not, the committee followed Hamilton's lead in its August 6 report to the convention: "In the case of his [the president's] removal as aforesaid, death, resignation, or disability to discharge the powers and duties of his office, the President of the Senate shall exercise those powers and duties, until another President of the United States be chosen, or until the disability of the President be removed." Considerable dissatisfaction was voiced when the delegates discussed this provision of the committee's report on August 27. James Madison, who feared that the Senate would have an incentive to create presidential vacancies if its own president were the designated successor, suggested instead that "the persons composing the Council to the President" fill that role instead. Gouverneur Morris offered the chief justice as successor. Finally, Williamson asked that the question be postponed. The convention agreed, placing the issue in the hands of the Committee on Postponed Matters.

The committee, which reported to the convention on September 4, proposed: "In the case of his [the president's] removal as aforesaid, death, absence, resignation, or inability to discharge the powers or duties of his office the Vice President shall exercise those powers and duties until another President be chosen, or until the inability of the President be removed." Three days later, Edmund Randolph, in an effort to supplement the committee's proposal with one that would provide a method of presidential succession if there were no vice president, moved: "The Legislature may declare by law what officer of the United States shall act as President in the case of the death, resignation, or disability of the President and Vice President; and such Officer shall act accordingly until the time of electing a President shall arrive." Madison moved to replace the last nine words of Randolph's motion with "until such disability be removed, or a President shall be elected." The motion passed, as amended.

Madison's reason for amending Randolph's motion is clear: he wanted to allow Congress to call a special election to replace a departed president or, in his words, to permit "a supply of vacancy by an intermediate election of the President." Other evidence from the records of the convention suggests that most of the delegates intended that the president's successor would serve only as acting president until a special election could be called. But sometime in the period September 8–12, when the Committee of Style was working to fulfill its charge to produce a smooth, final draft of the Constitution, that intention was, probably unwittingly, lost. The committee took the September 4 motion of the Committee on Postponed Matters and Randolph's September 7 motion and merged them into one passage, which, with minor modification, became Clause 6 of Article II, Section 1, of the Constitution:

> In case of the Removal of the President from Office, or of his death, Resignation, or Inability to discharge the Powers and Duties of the said Office, the Same shall devolve on the Vice President, and the Congress may by law provide for the Case of Removal, Death, Resignation, or Inability, both of the President and Vice President, declaring what Officer shall then act as President, and such officer shall act accordingly, until the Disability be removed, or a President shall be elected.[65]

Clearly, the delegates' intentions regarding succession were obscured by the Committee of Style. Grammatically, it is impossible to tell—and in its rush to adjournment, the convention did not notice the ambiguity—whether "the Same" in this provision refers to "the said office" (the presidency) or, as the delegates intended, only to its "powers and duties." Nor can one ascertain if "until . . . a President shall be elected" means until the end of the original four-year term or, again as intended, until a special election is held.[66]

The vice presidency was not a very controversial issue at the Constitutional Convention. On September 4, when the delegates were considering the Committee on Postponed Matters proposal for the electoral college, Nathaniel Gorham worried that "a very obscure man with very few votes" might be elected, because the proposal required only that the vice president be runner-up in the presidential election, not the recipient of a majority of electoral votes. Roger Sherman replied that any of the leading candidates for president would likely be qualified.

The role of the vice president as president of the Senate became a subject of minor controversy on September 7. Elbridge Gerry, seconded by Randolph, complained about the mixing of legislative and executive elements: "We might as well put the President himself at the head of the Legislature. The close intimacy that must subsist between the President & vice-president makes it absolutely improper." Gerry was "agst. having any vice President." Gouverneur Morris responded wryly, "[T]he vice president then will be the first heir apparent that ever loved his father." Sherman added that "if the vice-President were not to be President of the Senate, he would be without employment." He also reminded the convention that for the Senate to elect its president from among its own members probably would deprive that senator of a vote. George Mason ended the brief debate by branding "the office of vice-President an encroachment on the rights of the Senate; . . . it mixed too much the Legislative and Executive, which as well as the Judiciary departments, ought to be kept as separate as possible."

Despite these objections, the convention voted overwhelmingly to approve the vice presidency. Interestingly, the delegates gave no serious attention to the vice president's responsibilities as successor to the president.

RATIFYING THE CONSTITUTION

Congress's original call for a convention in Philadelphia had charged the delegates only to propose amendments to the Articles of Confederation, not to design an entirely new system of government. By itself, the delegates' decision to ignore this charge ensured that controversy would ensue when, having met so long in secret, they published their proposed plan of government in September. In addition, several provisions of the draft constitution, including the enhanced powers of the national government and the design of the legislative branch, were certain to be controversial. But nothing astonished the nation more than the convention's decision to recommend that a strong national executive be established—unitary, independently elected for a fixed term, and entrusted with its own grant of powers.

In the debates that the various state ratifying conventions held on the Constitution, Anti-Federalists (the label that was attached to those who opposed the Constitution) concentrated much of their fire on the presidency. Federalists (those who wanted the Constitution ratified) rose to its defense, their intellectual arsenal well stocked with arguments from a series of newspaper articles that Alexander Hamilton, James Madison, and John Jay published under the name "Publius." In the end, the Federalists prevailed, although the outcome of the battle for ratification was not certain until the very end.

The Anti-Federalist Critique of the Presidency

Anti-Federalists attacked the presidency as a disguised monarchy that, in collaboration with an allegedly aristocratic Senate, eventually would rule the United States much as the British king, assisted by the House of Lords, was said to rule England.

The most strenuous opposition to the presidency was registered by Patrick Henry of Virginia. On June 7, 1788, speaking with unvarnished fervor, Henry voiced the Anti-Federalists' fears of a presidential monarchy to his state's ratifying convention:

> This Constitution is said to have beautiful features, but when I come to examine these features, Sir, they appear to me to be horridly frightful: Among other deformities, it has an awful squinting; it squints towards monarchy: And does this not raise indignation in the breast of every American?
>
> Your President may easily become a King; . . . if your American chief, be a man of ambition, how easy it is for him to render himself absolute: The army is in his hands, and if he be a man of address, it will be attached to him; . . . I would rather infinitely, and I am sure most of these Convention are of the same opinion, have a king, Lords, and Commons, than a Government so replete with such insupportable evils. If we make a King, we may prescribe the rules by which he shall rule his people, and interpose such checks as shall prevent him from infringing them: But

the President, in the field, at the head of his army, can prescribe the terms on which he shall reign master, so far that it will puzzle any American ever to get his neck from under the galling yoke. . . . And what have you to oppose this force? What will then become of you and your rights? Will not absolute despotism ensue?[67]

Other Anti-Federalists directed their polemical fire at the close relationship they thought the Constitution fostered between the "monarchical" president and the "aristocratic" Senate, the two bodies that, without the involvement of the "democratic" House of Representatives, shared the powers of appointment and treaty making. A group of delegates at the Pennsylvania ratifying convention published a report on December 18, 1787, asserting that the Constitution's treaty-making provisions virtually invited foreign meddling. The Senate would consist of twenty-six members, they noted, two from each of the thirteen states. Fourteen senators would constitute a quorum for that body, of whom only ten were needed to provide a two-thirds vote to ratify a treaty proposed by the president. "What an inducement would this [small number] offer to the ministers of foreign powers to compass by bribery such concessions as could not otherwise be obtained," the Pennsylvania dissenters warned.[68]

Although monarchy was the Anti-Federalists' main fear, few features of the presidency were immune from their attack. The Virginia and North Carolina ratifying conventions urged that a constitutional amendment be enacted to limit each president to no more than eight years in office in any sixteen-year period. George Clinton, writing as "Cato" in the *New York Journal* in November 1787, argued that the president's term was too long and cited Montesquieu's prescription for one-year terms. In addition, Clinton charged, the absence of a council meant that the president will "be unsupported by proper information and advice, and will generally be directed by minions and favorites." Instead of direct election by the people (which Clinton said he favored), the president "arrives to this office at the fourth or fifth hand." [69]

Some of the most pointed criticisms of the proposed constitution came from disaffected delegates to the Constitutional Convention. George Mason, for example, told the Virginia ratifying convention that the "mode of [presidential] election is a mere deception . . . on the American people" because, after George Washington, the electoral college almost never would produce a majority for a candidate and the House of Representatives would end up selecting the president.[70] Luther Martin complained to the Maryland convention that the veto power allowed the president's will to prevail over all but a two-thirds majority of both houses of Congress.[71]

Interestingly, the presidency drew criticism from two future presidents. Thomas Jefferson observed archly in a letter to Madison that a president who could be reelected indefinitely and who commanded the armed forces "seems a bad edition of a Polish king." James Monroe fretted about the possibility of a president being reelected into life tenure. The office also was attacked by two future vice presidents—Gerry, one of the three delegates to the Constitutional Convention who refused to sign the document, and Clinton, who was jealous of the presidency's resemblance to his own powerful office, governor of New York. "This government is no more like a true picture of your own than an Angel of Darkness resembles an Angel of Light," Clinton warned his fellow New Yorkers.[72]

The Federalist Defense of the Presidency

Article II posed a political problem to Federalists who were trying to persuade the states to ratify the Constitution. Not only was the presidency the most obvious innovation in the

> The Federalist Papers, *originally published as a series of eighty-five newspaper articles, sought to persuade the American public to adopt the Constitution.*

THE

FEDERALIST:

ADDRESSED TO THE

PEOPLE OF THE STATE OF NEW-YORK.

NUMBER I.

Introduction.

AFTER an unequivocal experience of the inefficacy of the subsisting federal government, you are called upon to deliberate on a new constitution for the United States of America. The subject speaks its own importance; comprehending in its consequences, nothing less than the existence of the UNION, the safety and welfare of the parts of which it is composed, the fate of an empire, in many respects, the most interesting in the world. It has been frequently remarked, that it seems to have been reserved to the people of this country, by their conduct and example, to decide the important question, whether societies of men are really capable or not, of establishing good government from reflection and choice, or whether they are forever destined to depend, for their political constitutions, on accident and force. If there be any truth in the remark, the crisis, at which we are arrived, may with propriety be regarded as the æra in which

A   that

*T*HE FEDERALIST PAPERS ON POWERS OF THE PRESIDENCY

Nos. 69–72 of the *The Federalist Papers* are the best-known defense of the Framers' design of the presidency. They explain the nature of the office and contrast it with that of the British monarchy. In *Federalist* Nos. 73–77, the enumerated powers of the presidency are treated individually, in the order they are stated in Article II of the Constitution. In all cases, the author, Alexander Hamilton, labored to demonstrate to readers that the powers of the presidency, far from being threatening, were modest and essential to the operations of good government. Excerpts from his arguments follow.

Veto. "The propensity of the legislative department to intrude upon the rights, and to absorb the powers, of the other departments has been already more than once suggested. . . . Without [the veto,] . . . he might gradually be stripped of his authorities by successive resolutions or annihilated by a single vote. . . . But the power in question has a further use. It not only serves as a shield to the executive, but it furnishes an additional security against the enaction of improper laws. . . . Nor is this all. The superior weight and influence of the legislative body in a free government and the hazard to the executive in a trial of strength with that body afford a satisfactory security that the negative would generally be employed with great caution; and that there would oftener be room for a charge of timidity than of rashness in the exercise of it."

Commander in Chief. "Even those [constitutions] which have in other respects coupled the Chief Magistrate with a council have for the most part concentrated the military authority in him alone. Of all the cares or concerns of government, the direction of war most peculiarly demands those qualities which distinguish the exercise of power by a single hand."

Require the Opinion of Department Heads. "This I consider as a mere redundancy in the plan, as the right for which it provides would result of itself from the office."

Pardon. "As the sense of responsibility is always strongest in proportion as it is undivided, it may be inferred that a single man would be most ready to attend to the force of those motives which might plead for a mitigation of the rigor of the law, and least apt to yield to considerations which were calculated to shelter a fit object of its vengeance. . . . But the principal argument for reposing the power of pardoning in this case in the Chief Magistrate is this: in seasons of insurrection or rebellion, there are often critical moments when a well-timed offer of pardon to the insurgents or rebels may restore the tranquility of the commonwealth; and which, if suffered to pass unimproved, it may never be possible afterwards to recall. The dilatory process of convening the legislature, or one of its branches, for the purpose of obtaining its sanction to the measure, would frequently be the occasion of letting slip the golden opportunity."

Treaties. "With regard to the intermixture of powers [between the president and the Senate,] . . . the essence of the legislative authority is to enact laws, or, in other words, to prescribe rules for the regulation of the society; while the execution of the laws and the employment of the common strength, either for this purpose or for the common defense, seem to comprise all the functions of the executive magistrate. The power of making treaties is, plainly, neither the one nor the other. . . . It must indeed be clear to a demonstration that the joint possession of the power in question, by the President and Senate, would afford a greater prospect of security than the separate possession of it by either of them."

Appointment. "I proceed to lay it down as a rule that one man of discernment is better fitted to analyze and estimate the peculiar qualities adapted to particular offices than a body of men of equal or perhaps even of superior discernment. The sole and undivided responsibility of one man will naturally beget a livelier sense of duty and a more exact regard to reputation. He will, on this account, feel himself under stronger obligations, and more interested to investigate with care the qualities requisite to the stations to be filled, and to prefer with impartiality the persons who may have the fairest pretensions to them. . . . It is also not very probable that his nomination would often be overruled. The Senate could not be tempted by the preference they might feel to another to reject the one proposed; because they could not assure themselves that the person they might wish would be brought forward by a second or by any subsequent nomination. . . . To what purpose then require the co-operation of the Senate? I answer, that the necessity of their concurrence would have a powerful, though, in general, a silent operation. It would be an excellent check upon a spirit of favoritism in the President, and would tend greatly to prevent the appointment of unfit characters. . . . The possibility of rejection would be a strong motive to care in proposing."

Other Powers. "The only remaining powers of the executive are comprehended in giving information to Congress on the state of the Union; in recommending to their consideration such measures as he shall judge expedient; in convening them, or either branch, upon extraordinary occasions; in adjourning them when they cannot themselves agree upon the time of adjournment; in receiving ambassadors and other public ministers; in faithfully executing the laws; and in commissioning all the officers of the United States. Except some cavils about the power of convening *either* house of the legislature, and that of receiving ambassadors, no objection has been made to this class of authorities; nor could they possibly admit of any."

new plan of government, but its unitary nature roused fears of the most horrifying specter Americans could imagine—a monarchy like the one they had overthrown in the Revolutionary War. Anti-Federalists, as we have seen, inflamed these fears.

Proponents of the Constitution at the state ratifying conventions stressed both the virtues of the presidency and the restraints that the Constitution placed on the office. In doing so, they relied heavily on the explanations and defenses of the Constitution that Hamilton, Madison, and Jay were

putting forth in the series of eighty-five newspaper articles that Hamilton, who conceived the project, had commissioned. These articles, later gathered in a book called *The Federalist Papers*, appeared pseudonymously in several New York newspapers under the name "Publius" (after the Roman republican statesman Publius Valerious). Hamilton wrote about fifty of them, Madison about twenty-five, Jay (who became ill after writing four of the first five papers in the series) five, and Hamilton and Madison jointly wrote the rest. The articles were reprinted and disseminated widely throughout the states. (*See box,* The Federalist Papers *on Powers of the Presidency, p. 42.)*

In March 1788, Hamilton wrote *Federalist* Nos. 69–77, which dealt with the presidency. *Federalist* No. 69 squarely addressed the charge by the Anti-Federalists that the presidency was a latent monarchy. Hamilton argued that, in contrast to the British king, who secured his office by inheritance and served for life, the president was elected for a limited term. The king had an absolute veto on laws passed by Parliament; the president's vetoes could be overridden by Congress. The king could both declare war and raise an army and navy; the president could do neither. The king could prorogue Parliament for any reason at any time; the president could adjourn Congress only when the House of Representatives and the Senate could not agree on an adjournment date. The king could create offices and appoint people to fill them; the president could not create offices and could fill them only with the approval of the Senate. Finally, Hamilton noted that although the king could not be impeached and removed, the president could be. In *Federalist* No. 65, he described impeachable offenses as "the abuse or violation of some public trust. They are of a nature which may with peculiar propriety be denominated POLITICAL, as they relate chiefly to injuries done immediately to the society itself."

Hamilton dissembled to some degree in drawing these contrasts. The powers he ascribed to the British monarch were more characteristic of the seventeenth century than of the eighteenth, during which time the influence of Parliament and the prime minister had grown relative to the king. For example, the last British monarch to veto an act of Parliament was Queen Anne in 1707. But *Federalist* No. 69 was effective in deflating the Anti-Federalists' caricature of the presidency. Indeed, Hamilton deftly argued that in many cases the power of the presidency was less than that wielded by the governor of New York, the staunchly Anti-Federalist Clinton.

Federalist No. 70, less defensive in tone than the first article, described the virtues of the presidency. Its theme was "energy," a quality that, according to Hamilton, is requisite to good government:

> It is essential to the protection of the community against foreign attacks; it is not less essential to the steady administration of the laws; to the protection of property against those irregular and high-handed combinations which sometimes interrupt the ordinary course of justice; to the security of liberty against the enterprises and assaults of ambition, of faction, and of anarchy.

Energy, in the government created by the Constitution, was provided by the presidency, Hamilton argued, mostly because of the office's unitary character. Unity provided the presidency with a whole host of virtues—"decision, activity,

secrecy, and dispatch . . . vigor and expedition." In contrast, a plural, or committee-style executive, would be riven by disagreements that would render it slow to act and prone to develop factions. It also would be hard to hold a plural executive responsible for failure because each member of such an executive could blame the others.

In *Federalist* Nos. 71–73, Hamilton defended the presidency as having additional qualities indispensable to energy. "Duration," the theme of No. 71, was one—the four-year term provided the president with enough time to act with firmness and resolve but was not so long as "to justify any alarm for the public liberty."

Hamilton claimed that eligibility for reelection, which he discussed in No. 72, shrewdly acknowledged that "the desire of reward is one of the strongest incentives of human conduct." Without that incentive, a president would be tempted either to slack off or, at the opposite extreme, to usurp power violently. Presidential reeligibility also allowed the nation to keep a president in office if it so desired.

"Adequate provision for its support" was a third energy-inducing quality of the presidency, according to Hamilton. Interestingly, he attached great importance to the prohibition that the Constitution placed on Congress not to raise or lower an incumbent president's salary. In the first part of No. 73, Hamilton argued that without such a bar, Congress could "reduce him by famine, or tempt him by largesse" and thus "render him as obsequious to their will as they might think proper to make him."

Later in No. 73, and continuing in Nos. 74–77, Hamilton defended the enumerated powers of the presidency, which, along with unity, duration, and adequate support, were the indispensable ingredients of presidential energy. Far from being threatening, he argued, the office's constitutional powers were modest and essential to the operations of good government. (*See box,* The Federalist Papers *on Powers of the Presidency, p. 42.)*

The Vice Presidency in the Ratification Debate

"Post-convention discussion of the vice presidency was not extensive," notes legal scholar John D. Feerick, the author of two books on the vice presidency.[73] The only mention of the office in *The Federalist Papers* is in No. 68, written by Hamilton. Like the delegates' debate at the Constitutional Convention, this passage is concerned mainly with the vice president's role as president of the Senate:

> The appointment of an extraordinary person, as Vice-President, has been objected to as superfluous, if not mischievous. It has been alleged, that it would have been preferable to have authorized the Senate to elect out of their own body an officer answering to that description. But two considerations seem to justify the ideas of the Convention in this respect. One is, that to secure at all times the possibility of a definitive resolution of the body,

it is necessary that the President should have only a casting [tie-breaking] vote. And to take the Senator of any State from his seat as Senator, to place him in that of President of the Senate, would be to exchange, in regard to the State from which he came, a constant for a contingent vote. The other consideration is, that, as the Vice-President may occasionally become a substitute for the President, in the supreme Executive magistracy, all the reasons which recommend the mode of election prescribed for the one, apply with great if not with equal force to the manner of appointing the other.[74]

Hamilton may have been responding in part to concerns raised by the Anti-Federalist Clinton. Clinton was later to serve as vice president in the Jefferson and Madison administrations, but in November 1787, writing as Cato, he argued that the vice presidency was both "unnecessary" and "dangerous." "This officer," warned Clinton, "for want of other employment is made president of the Senate, thereby blending the executive and legislative powers, besides always giving to some one state, from which he is to come, an unjust preeminence."

Luther Martin of Maryland, who opposed ratification, expressed concern that a large state like neighboring Pennsylvania or Virginia typically would benefit from the vice president's Senate role:

After it is decided who is chosen President, that person who has the next greatest number of votes of the electors, is declared to be legally elected to the Vice-Presidency; so that by this system it is very possible, and not improbable, that he may be appointed by the electors of a single large state; and a very undue influence in the Senate is given to that State of which the Vice-President is a citizen, since, in every question where the Senate is divided, that State will have two votes, the President having on that occasion a casting voice.

George Mason, another delegate to the convention who opposed ratification in his state, also complained about the vice president's right to vote in the Senate and the office's mix of legislative and executive responsibilities. His fellow Virginia Anti-Federalist, Richard Henry Lee, worried about the absence of stated qualifications for the vice president.[75]

Defenders of the vice presidency made a virtue of the office's role as Senate president. In their view, the vice president's election by the nation as a whole would be good for the Senate. "There is much more propriety to giving this office to a person chosen by the people at large," urged Madison, "than to one of the Senate, who is only the choice of the legislature of one state." William R. Davie of North Carolina expressed confidence that a nationally elected vice president would cast tie-breaking votes "as impartially as possible." Answering another argument of the Constitution's critics, Connecticut delegates Oliver Ellsworth and Roger Sherman wrote separately that the vice president did not wield a mix of legislative and executive powers, but rather that the vice presidency was a part of the legislative branch except in the event of a succession, at which time it entered the executive branch.[76]

In all, as Feerick has concluded, the vice presidency "received scant attention in the state ratifying conventions. . . . The discussion of the vice-presidency that did occur centered mostly on the fact that the office blended legislative and executive functions."[77] As in the Constitutional Convention, little was said in the state debates about the vice president's duties as successor to the president.

The Politics of Ratification

Most historians agree that a majority of Americans were initially opposed to the Constitution. Certainly there was intense and vocal opposition in many states. But the Federalists had two compelling advantages in the battle for ratification. First, their cause was defended in most of the state ratifying conventions by leaders who had been at the Constitutional Convention and could knowledgeably explain the Constitution's provisions, defend its virtues, and answer any criticisms that might arise. Second, Washington played an active, behind-the-scenes role in helping Hamilton to coordinate the campaign for ratification across state lines. As the historian Joseph Ellis has written, Washington's Mount Vernon home became "the electoral headquarters for plotting strategy and tracking the state-by-state results as they rolled in."[78] Whatever doubts people may have entertained about ratification, no better alternative to the status quo was at hand. "It was clear enough that the old government was finished," noted the Colliers. "If the Constitution was not ratified, the union would dissolve, and with what result nobody could calculate."[79]

Delaware, a small state that expected the new government to protect it against its large-state neighbors, became the first state to ratify, on December 7, 1787. Pennsylvania, by a vote of 41–23, followed five days later, but only after considerable doubts were expressed at the state's ratifying convention about the absence of a bill of rights. Similar complaints were voiced in many states, prompting Federalists to promise that the first Congress would propose such a bill in the form of amendments to the Constitution.

New Jersey, Georgia, and Connecticut were next to ratify, New Jersey and Georgia unanimously and Connecticut by an overwhelming vote of 128–40. Massachusetts, in which opposition to the Constitution was intense, voted to ratify by a narrow margin of 187–168 after the Constitution was endorsed by John Hancock, the state's popular governor. Hancock seems to have believed that if Virginia did not ratify, he, not George Washington, would be elected as the first president. In April 1788, Maryland ratified by a 63–11 vote; South Carolina followed in May by 149–73. New Hampshire, by a close vote of 57–47, became the ninth state to ratify on June 21.

New Hampshire's endorsement meant that the Constitution was enacted. Although ratification by the two remaining large states, Virginia and New York, probably was essential if the new government was to be successful, Virginians and New Yorkers in turn realized that their states would be weakened if they decided to remain isolated. In both states, the Federalists prevailed even though they were initially outnumbered by the Anti-Federalists. On June 25, Virginia voted 89–79 to ratify. Governor Randolph helped to turn the tide when, after defending his refusal to sign the Constitution at the convention, he declared that in light of the decisions of the other states, he would vote to ratify rather than see the union dissolved. New York's July 26 decision to ratify (by a vote of 30–27) was similarly grudging. North Carolina (November 19, 1789) and Rhode Island (May 29, 1790) followed, but not until after the first president and Congress had been elected and the new government had gotten under way.

CONSTITUTIONAL AMENDMENTS

Article V of the Constitution defines several processes—all of them difficult—by which the Constitution may be amended. An amendment may be suggested by one or more members of Congress, by the president in a message to Congress, or by resolutions passed and sent to Congress by two-thirds of the state legislatures.

If the suggested amendment originates with the president or from within Congress, it may then be considered by Congress, which can propose (that is, approve) it only by a two-thirds vote of both the House of Representatives and the Senate. If the suggested amendment originates in the state legislatures, Congress is enjoined to call a national convention to consider and possibly propose it. In either case, Congress must send the proposed amendment to the states for ratification. If three-fourths of the states vote to ratify, the amendment, it becomes part of the Constitution. As part

of its charge to the states, Congress decides whether ratification should be by the state legislatures or by specially called conventions within each state.

Some provision for amending the Constitution was included at every stage of the Constitutional Convention. The Virginia Plan, reflecting the delegates' apprehensions about the accountability of the stronger national government they were designing, said only that a procedure ought to be created to enact constitutional amendments that did not require the consent of the national legislature. The Committee of Detail proposed such a procedure: a convention called by Congress to enact any amendment that was requested by two-thirds of the state legislatures. Although the delegates initially accepted the committee's proposal, disquiet about the nature of such a convention—its composition, rules, powers, and likely biases (some delegates predicted that conventions would be pro-state government power, some that they would be antistate government power)—surfaced on September 10. Madison then suggested that either state or congressional initiative be allowed, followed in every case by state ratification. The delegates accepted his proposal, and the Committee of Style drafted the final language.[80]

In practice, every amendment that has been added to the Constitution since 1789 has been first considered and proposed by Congress, and every amendment but one (the Twenty-first Amendment, which ended Prohibition) has been ratified by the state legislatures.[81] Since 1918, Congress sometimes has required that a proposed amendment be ratified within a seven-year period or expire.[82]

The Constitution does not specify how a constitutional convention would be called if two-thirds of the states asked for one, how its members would be chosen, or what its rules, procedures, and agenda would be. Nor has Congress, jealous of its role in the amendment process and fearing a "runaway convention" that would exceed its charge (like the original constitutional convention in Philadelphia!), been willing to create such procedures. In the 1960s, thirty-three states (just one fewer than the required two-thirds) requested a convention to reconsider the "one person, one vote" rule regarding the apportionment of seats in the state legislatures that the Supreme Court had instituted in *Baker v. Carr* (1962).[83] During the 1970s, thirty-two state legislatures requested a convention to consider a balanced-budget amendment to the Constitution.

Amending the Constitution, although an easier task to accomplish under the Constitution than under the Articles of Confederation (which required ratification by all of the state legislatures for any proposed amendment), is an arduous undertaking. One-third-plus-one of the members of either the House or the Senate can prevent Congress from proposing an amendment. If an amendment is proposed, barely thirteen of the ninety-nine houses of the fifty state legislatures (all but the Nebraska legislature are bicameral)

AMENDING THE CONSTITUTION

The Congress, whenever two thirds of both Houses shall deem it necessary, shall propose Amendments to this Constitution, or, on the Application of the Legislatures of two thirds of the several States, shall call a Convention for proposing Amendments, which, in either Case, shall be valid to all Intents and Purposes, as part of this Constitution, when ratified by the Legislatures of three fourths of the several States, or by Conventions in three fourths thereof, as the one or the other Mode of Ratification may be proposed by the Congress; Provided that . . . no State, without its Consent, shall be deprived of its equal Suffrage in the Senate.

—from Article V

can deny it ratification, because the approval of the full legislatures of thirty-eight (three-fourths) of the states is required.[84] The consequence, according to the constitutional scholar James Sundquist, is that

> [w]ithin the political elite, for an amendment to clear the barriers to passage, its acceptance must come close to unanimity. . . . [A] proposed amendment either must have no measurable adverse effect on anybody—as, say, the amendment that rescheduled inauguration days and congressional sessions—or must distribute its adverse effects so nearly neutrally that no substantial interest is offended.[85]

Since the Bill of Rights (the first ten amendments) was added to the Constitution in 1791, the Constitution has been amended only seventeen times.[86] Seven other amendments have been proposed by Congress but failed to be ratified. Four of the seventeen ratified amendments deal explicitly with the presidency and vice presidency:

- Twelfth Amendment (1804): instituted separate balloting by electors for president and vice president in presidential elections; the House of Representatives to choose the president from among the three highest electoral vote recipients if no candidate wins an electoral vote majority; constitutional qualifications for president applied to the vice president.
- Twentieth Amendment (1933): set January 20 as the inauguration day for the president, January 3 as the beginning of the term for members of Congress; provided the vice president-elect would become president if the president-elect died or was disqualified.
- Twenty-second Amendment (1951): imposed a two-term limit on the president.
- Twenty-fifth Amendment (1967): defined the full successorship rights of the vice president should a presidential vacancy occur; created procedures for responding to presidential disabilities; provided for the filling of vice-presidential vacancies.

Three of the four presidency-related amendments did little more than clarify or correct minor flaws in the original Constitution. The Twelfth Amendment adapted the electoral college to the rise of national political parties. The Twentieth Amendment answered some unresolved procedural questions about presidential succession. The Twenty-fifth Amendment established a process that would satisfy the original Constitution's provision that the vice president should step in during a presidential disability; it also guaranteed that a vice president would always be available to fulfill this responsibility. Only the Twenty-second Amendment's two-term limit altered a fundamental element of the presidency's original design. The Framers had strongly rejected efforts to limit the president's eligibility for reelection.

In addition to the four presidency-related amendments, five other constitutional amendments have expanded the right to vote, which has affected participation in presidential elections. Three of these five amendments—the Fifteenth (1870), Nineteenth (1920), and Twenty-sixth (1971)—extended the suffrage to African Americans, women, and eighteen- to twenty-year-olds, respectively. The Twenty-third Amendment (1961) granted three electoral votes in presidential elections to the District of Columbia. The Twenty-fourth Amendment (1964) banned the poll tax, which some states had required citizens to pay as a prerequisite to voting. Interestingly, the five voting rights amendments took less time to ratify—an average of fewer than twelve months each—than any other category of constitutional amendments.[87]

Numerous other amendments to alter the presidency have been suggested in recent years. Some have been endorsed by the public in opinion surveys, by one or more presidents, and by several members of Congress. None, however, has been approved by Congress and sent to the states for ratification. Some recently discussed amendments would:

- Abolish the electoral college and choose the president by direct vote of the people. This highly popular alteration of the Constitution would bring the presidency into line with virtually all of the nation's other elective offices and remove the possibility of either an electoral college stalemate or the election of a president who had less than a plurality of popular votes. In the aftermath of the much-contested 2000 election, Sen. Hillary Rodham Clinton of New York introduced a direct election amendment. But critics say direct election would be hard to implement and would subvert the principle of federalism that the current, state-centered system upholds.
- Allow all citizens to become eligible to be president, not just "natural born citizens." After the 2000 census revealed that approximately 10 percent of the U.S. population were either naturalized citizens or legal immigrants who were eligible to becomes citizens, Sen. Orrin Hatch (R-Utah) introduced a constitutional amendment to make anyone who has been a citizen for at least twenty years eligible for the presidency. Several recent governors, senators, and cabinet members have been naturalized citizens, including Gov. Arnold Schwarzenegger (R-Calif.), Sen. Mel Martinez (R-Fla.), and former secretary of state Madeleine Albright.[88]
- Limit the president to a single term, but extend the term to six years. Advocates, including presidents Andrew Jackson, Dwight D. Eisenhower, Lyndon B. Johnson, and Jimmy Carter, have claimed that a single, six-year term would free the president from the political pressures of reelection and grant the administration more time to accomplish its long-term goals. Opponents point out that with a single six-year term, an unpopular president

would serve two years more than under the current system and a popular president two years less.

- Repeal the Twenty-second Amendment's two-term limit. President Ronald Reagan, a strong advocate of repeal, argued that the voters should not be denied the opportunity to extend a president's tenure for as long as they like. Critics warn of an overly personalized presidency.

- Empower the president with a line-item veto, which could be used to remove specific items from spending legislation. Presidents Reagan, George H. W. Bush, Bill Clinton, and George W. Bush asserted that the line-item veto would enable the president to control federal spending. Critics have argued that the president already has ample means to influence the budget without upsetting the constitutional balance of power between the president and Congress. In 1996 Congress enacted a statutory version of the line-item veto, but the Supreme Court ruled in the 1998 case of *Clinton v. City of New York* that such a measure would require a constitutional amendment.[89]

- Abolish the vice presidency and fill presidential vacancies by special election. Proponents, such as the historian Arthur M. Schlesinger Jr., differ with critics on the issue of how valuable an institution the vice presidency is and

how politically disruptive succession by special election would be.

As these examples illustrate, most proposals to amend the Constitution stem from ongoing political controversies, such as the threat of electoral college stalemate, the four-term presidency of Franklin D. Roosevelt, and a mutual pointing of fingers by president and Congress on the issue of budget deficits. Because they are mired in partisan politics, it is virtually impossible to pass such proposals through the arduous process of approval by Congress and ratification by the states.

Twelfth Amendment (1804)

Paragraphs 2 through 4 of Article II, Section 1, which created the electoral college method of choosing the president and vice president, were among the least controversial provisions of the Constitution, both during the late stages of the Constitutional Convention and in the state ratification debates that followed. "The mode of appointment of the Chief Magistrate of the United States," wrote Hamilton in *Federalist* No. 68, "is almost the only part of the system of any consequence, which has escaped without severe censure, or which has received the slightest mark of approbation from its opponents." It is all the more ironic, then, that the electoral college was the first institution of the new government to undergo a major constitutional overhaul.

The main effect of the Twelfth Amendment was to change a system in which electors cast two votes for president, with the candidate receiving the largest majority elected as president and the second-place finisher elected as vice president, to a system in which the electors were charged to vote separately for president and vice president, with a majority of electoral votes required to win each office.

The Twelfth Amendment also reduced from the five to the three highest electoral vote recipients the pool of candidates from which the House would elect the president in the event that no candidate received a majority of electoral votes. Authority to select a vice president in the event of an electoral college failure was lodged exclusively in the Senate, not partially, as in the original Constitution. The amendment empowered the Senate to choose from the two highest electoral vote recipients for vice president, with a majority vote of the entire membership of the Senate required for election. The Consti-

TWELFTH AMENDMENT (1804)

The Electors shall meet in their respective states and vote by ballot for President and Vice President, one of whom, at least, shall not be an inhabitant of the same state with themselves; they shall name in their ballots the person voted for as President, and in distinct ballots the person voted for as Vice President, and they shall make distinct lists of all persons voted for as President, and of all persons voted for as Vice President, and of the number of votes for each, which lists they shall sign and certify, and transmit sealed to the seat of the government of the United States, directed to the President of the Senate;—The President of the Senate shall, in the presence of the Senate and House of Representatives, open all the certificates and the votes shall then be counted;—The person having the greatest number of votes for President, shall be elected the President, if such number be a majority of the whole number of Electors appointed; and if no person have such majority, then from the persons having the highest numbers not exceeding three on the list of those voted for as President, the House of Representatives shall choose immediately, by ballot, the President. But in choosing the President, the votes shall be taken by states, the representation from each state having one vote; a quorum for this purpose shall consist of a member or members from two-thirds of the states, and a majority of all the states shall be necessary to a choice. [And if the House of Representatives shall not choose a President whenever the right of the choice shall devolve upon them, before the fourth day of March next following, then the Vice President shall act as President, as in the case of the death or other constitutional disability of the President.]* The person having the greatest number of votes as Vice President, shall be the Vice President, if such number be a majority of the whole number of Electors appointed, and if no person have a majority, then from the two highest numbers on the list, the Senate shall choose the Vice President; a quorum for the purpose shall consist of two thirds of the whole number of Senators, and a majority of the whole number shall be necessary to a choice. But no person constitutionally ineligible to the office of President shall be eligible to that of Vice President of the United States.

*Possibly modified by the Twentieth Amendment

tution's age, residency, and citizenship requirements for president were extended to the vice president. Finally, the amendment stated that if a vice president, but not a president, is chosen by the March 4 following the election, "the Vice President shall act as President as in the case of the death or other constitutional disability of the President."

The Old System Breaks Down

The original electoral college was designed by the Constitutional Convention on the assumption that political parties would not arise and dominate the presidential election process. Instead, the delegates had believed that states and ad hoc groups would nominate candidates for president. The most popular and, presumably, the best-qualified candidate would be elected as president and the second most popular as vice president.

Despite the Framers' intentions, two political parties—the Federalists and the Democratic-Republicans—formed during George Washington's first term as president and, within a few years, began nominating complete national tickets: Federalist and Democratic-Republican candidates for president and Federalist and Democratic-Republican candidates for vice president. In 1800 the inevitable happened. All seventy-three Democratic-Republican electors (a majority of the electoral college) cast one of their votes for Thomas Jefferson and the other for Aaron Burr, the Democratic-Republican candidates. Although these electors wanted Jefferson to be elected as president and Burr to become vice president, the vote was constitutionally recorded as a tie between Jefferson and Burr for the office of president. Under Article II, Section 1, Clause 3, the House of Representatives was then forced to choose between them.

Dominated by a lame-duck Federalist majority, the House, through thirty-five ballots, denied Jefferson the majority of state delegations that was required for election. On the thirty-sixth ballot, prodded by Hamilton to cease its mischief making, the House elected Jefferson as president and Burr as vice president. But some disgruntled Federalists began plotting for the 1804 election. If the Democratic-Republican candidates won, they decided, Federalist electors would cast one of their votes for the Democratic-Republican Party's vice-presidential nominee, thus electing him, not the presidential nominee, as president and the presidential nominee as vice president.

Proposal and Ratification

Aware both of the unsuitability of the original Constitution's presidential election process to the new reality of party politics and of the Federalists' willingness to continue exploiting the process's weaknesses, the Democratic-Republican–controlled Congress voted to propose the Twelfth Amendment in December 1803. All but the most ardent Federalist states quickly ratified the amendment (Massachusetts finally rati-

fied in 1961), and it became part of the Constitution in June 1804, just in time for the presidential election.

Separate Balloting for President and Vice President

The Twelfth Amendment's requirement that electors vote separately for president and vice president completely solved the problem that had occasioned the amendment's enactment. Not since 1800 has there been any real confusion about who was running for president and who for vice president. Also, as the historian David Kyvig points out, the Twelfth Amendment reinforced the unitary character of the executive by eliminating the possibility that the vice president would be the leader of the opposition party.[90]

Less benign, however, were the amendment's effects on the vice presidency. The office, always constitutionally powerless and now stripped of its status as the position awarded to the second most successful presidential candidate, became a political backwater. Even before the Twelfth Amendment was enacted, parties had begun using the vice-presidential nomination mainly to "balance the ticket" with someone from either a different region of the country or a different faction of the party than that of the presidential nominee. But with the office now bereft of prestige as well as power, ambitious and talented political leaders shunned such nominations. The vice presidency sank into a century-long torpor and was occupied frequently by ailing or undistinguished politicians.

At least some members of Congress anticipated the Twelfth Amendment's likely effect on the vice presidency and, during the congressional debate, moved to abolish the office. But they failed to persuade a sufficient number of their colleagues. (See Chapter 3, History of the Vice Presidency.)

One aspect of electoral voting that emerged as an issue only much later was that of the "faithless elector." Whatever the Framers' intentions may have been, in practice electors have always been chosen to vote for the candidate supported by their state, not to exercise independent judgment in deciding whom to support.[91] No constitutional requirement binds electors to do so, however. Twenty-four states and the District of Columbia currently have laws that require electors to support the candidates whom they are pledged to represent, but these laws may well violate the Twelfth Amendment.

Historically, only eleven of the nearly twenty thousand electors who have been chosen since 1789 have been "faithless," and none have been punished for violating their pledges.[92] In no case have their votes affected the outcome of an election. But the frequency of faithless voting has increased from one in every twenty elections from 1789 to 1944 to more than one in every two elections from 1948 to 2004. In 2000 an elector from the District of Columbia abstained rather than vote for Al Gore, who had carried the

District with 85 percent of the vote. She explained that she was protesting the District's lack of representation in Congress. No elector had ever used his or her vote in such a way. Nor had an elector ever voted faithlessly in such a close election.[93] In 2004 a Minnesota elector who was pledged to vote the Democratic ticket of John Kerry for president and John Edwards for vice president instead voted for Edwards for vice president and "John Ewards" for president, the latter an apparent mistake that nonetheless denied Kerry an electoral vote.

House Election of the President

The Twelfth Amendment reduced the number of candidates from which the House of Representatives, in the event of an electoral college deadlock, must choose the president—from the five highest electoral vote recipients to the three highest. The reduction was an acknowledgment that a two-party system had developed, in which even three candidates were unlikely to receive electoral votes in most elections, and that the parties had taken over the presidential nominating process. In 1824 when four presidential candidates received electoral votes, the House's freedom to choose from only three may have eased its difficulties in reaching a decision in time for the inauguration.

The House had to clarify several procedural ambiguities in the Twelfth Amendment before voting for president in 1825. One of the most important rules it adopted required that, in order for the vote of a state delegation to be cast for a candidate, a majority of the state's entire delegation (not just of the members present) was needed. Another stated that "the House shall continue to ballot for a President, without interruption by other business, until a President be chosen." Finally, House members were allowed to vote by secret ballot in individual ballot boxes for each state. These rules were not enacted as law, however, and a future House could readily replace them at its discretion.

The Twelfth Amendment is unclear about yet another potentially important matter, partly because of complications introduced by the subsequent enactment of the Twentieth and Twenty-fifth amendments. *(See "Twentieth Amendment," p. 52, and "Twenty-fifth Amendment," p. 56.)* The Twelfth Amendment states that "if the House of Representatives shall not choose a President whenever the right of choice shall devolve upon them, before the fourth day of March next following, then the Vice President shall act as President, as in the case of the death or other constitutional disability of the President." Harvard University law professors Laurence H. Tribe and Thomas M. Rollins argue that this provision was superseded by the Twentieth Amendment and that the House is obliged to keep balloting until either it elects a president or the president's four-year term expires. Conceivably, then, a Senate-elected vice president could serve as acting president for a full presidential term. Political scientist Allen P. Sindler maintains that not only does the Twelfth Amendment still apply, but also that if the House has not elected a president by March 4, balloting ceases and the vice president becomes president. Under the Twenty-fifth Amendment, the vice-president-turned-president would then nominate a new vice president. This nomination would require congressional confirmation.[94]

Senate Election of the Vice President

Only once since the Twelfth Amendment was enacted has the electoral college failed to choose a vice president. In 1836 the Democratic Party's presidential candidate, Martin Van Buren, received a majority of electoral votes, but his running mate, Richard M. Johnson, fell one vote short of being elected vice president when Virginia's twenty-three Democratic electors, disapproving Johnson's dalliances with a succession of slave mistresses, denied him their support. The Senate, charged to choose a vice president from among the top two electoral vote recipients by a majority vote of all its members, quickly elected Johnson over the Whig Party's vice-presidential nominee, Francis Granger, by a vote of 33–16. The straight party nature of the vote, however, leaves one to wonder what would have happened if the Whigs had controlled the Senate. In view of the amendment's requirement that a quorum of two thirds must exist in order for the Senate to elect a vice president, another open question is what would happen if one party's senators boycotted the Senate election.

These circumstances notwithstanding, the Twelfth Amendment makes it easier for the Senate to elect a vice president than for the House to elect a president. The Senate chooses between two, not three, candidates, and a simple majority of its members, not a majority of state delegations, is all that is required for a decision.

Legislative Elaboration of the Twelfth Amendment

By federal and state law, procedures have been established for the selection, certification, and tabulation of electoral votes beyond the very general provisions offered in the Constitution. Electors are chosen on the first Tuesday after the first Monday in November. Since 1860, every state's laws have provided that electors shall be chosen by popular vote, although each state is free under the Constitution to choose its electors by some other method.[95] All but Maine and Nebraska have decided to employ a "winner-take-all" system in which the candidate who receives a plurality of a state's popular votes wins all of the state's electoral votes.[96] If any dispute arises about the outcome of the presidential election in a state, federal law authorizes the state to resolve the dispute in accordance with its own existing procedures.[97]

The electoral college never meets as a single body. Instead, the electors gather to vote in their states on the first Monday after the second Wednesday in December. The electors then send the results of their vote to Washington, where they are counted on January 6 in front of a joint session of Congress by the vice president, acting in the capacity of president of the Senate. Three recent vice presidents—Richard Nixon in 1961, Hubert H. Humphrey in 1969, and Al Gore in 2001—announced their own defeats for president. In 1989 George H. W. Bush announced his own election.

Proposed Reforms

More suggested constitutional amendments (more than five hundred) have been offered in Congress to alter or abolish the electoral college than any other feature of the Constitution. In recent decades, four proposed amendments have been widely discussed.[98]

The Automatic Plan. Some reformers, including Presidents John F. Kennedy and Lyndon Johnson, have proposed that each state's electoral votes be cast automatically for the candidate who receives the most popular votes in the state. As the political scientist Stephen J. Wayne has observed, the plan "keeps the electoral college intact but eliminates the electors."[99] It also eliminates both the "faithless elector" problem and the possibility that if third party candidates prevent a majority from forming in the electoral college, they could use the votes of electors pledged to them as bargaining chips to negotiate a deal with one of the major party candidates.

Politically, the main problem with the automatic plan is that it has roused little public or congressional interest. The flaws it seeks to remedy are relatively minor. Some oppose the plan because they like the electoral college the way it is, others because they want to overhaul the electoral college in more fundamental ways.

The Proportional and District Plans. Popular in the 1950s, when it was sponsored in Congress by Sen. Henry Cabot Lodge Jr., R-Mass., and Rep. Ed Lee Gossett, D-Texas, the proportional plan would eliminate not just electors, but also the winner-take-all principle of awarding state electoral votes. Instead, electoral votes in each state would be divided among the presidential candidates in proportion to their share of the state's popular vote. The purported advantage of the Lodge-Gossett proposal is that it would encourage candidates to campaign in every state, even those in which they expect to get fewer popular votes than their opponent. The proportional plan also would heighten the incentive for third party candidates to run, however, and would substantially increase the chances that presidential elections would end up in the House and vice-presidential elections in the Senate.[100] Politically, large states regard the proportional plan as a threat to their primacy in presidential politics.

The district plan, under which candidates would receive two electoral votes for each state they carry and one for each congressional district, would extend Maine and Nebraska's arrangement to the entire nation. It has all of the advantages and disadvantages of the proportional plan.[101]

The National Bonus Plan. Proposed by a Twentieth Century Fund task force, the national bonus plan would retain the electoral college but tilt it more heavily in favor of the popular vote winner. The candidate who receives a plurality of popular votes nationally would receive a "bonus" of 102 electoral votes.[102] This would virtually eliminate the possibility of a presidential election being decided in Congress. A problem with the bonus plan, however, is that in an especially close election, like the one in 1960, it might take a long time to decide who had received the most popular votes and thus who should receive the 102-vote bonus and be elected president.[103]

Direct Election. The most popular proposal to reform presidential elections has been to abolish the electoral college and elect the president by direct vote of the people. In most versions of the direct election plan, a minimum plurality of 40 percent would be needed for election; if no candidate received 40 percent, a runoff election would be held between the two highest vote-getters. Several recent presidents, notably Nixon, Gerald R. Ford, and Carter, have endorsed direct election. The House of Representatives approved a direct election amendment to the Constitution in 1969 by a vote of 338–70. The Senate voted 51–48 in favor of direct election in 1979, which was sixteen votes less than the necessary two-thirds majority. The public regularly expresses its approval of direct election in Gallup polls by margins of anywhere from three-to-one to seven-to-one.[104]

The main arguments in favor of direct election are that it would bring presidential elections into line with virtually all other U.S. elections, making the process more comprehensible and legitimate to the public; that it would eliminate the possibility of an electoral college deadlock and a House election; and that it would prevent a candidate who lost the popular vote from winning the election, as happened in 1824, 1876, 1888, and 2000.

Opponents assert that direct election would violate the constitutional principle of federalism on which the electoral college is based; encourage the formation of third parties, whose hope would be to deny any candidate 40 percent, then put their endorsement up for bid in the runoff election; and, as with the national bonus plan, increase the possibility for confusion and delay in a close national election.

In the immediate aftermath of the 2000 election, in which Gore received a national popular vote plurality of more than 500,000 votes but lost the election narrowly in the electoral college, new voices were raised on behalf of reform. For example, Sen. Hillary Rodham Clinton of New York proposed a constitutional amendment to abolish the electoral college in favor of direct election. But concern about constitutional reform was drowned out by the hue and cry over which candidate had won Florida's twenty-five electoral votes.

Politically, direct election amendments have been defeated in Congress by a coalition of small states, which are especially well represented in the Senate and which fear losing what little advantage they have in the electoral college, and liberal interest groups, which argue that minority, union, and urban voters, who are concentrated in the large states, would lose their strategic advantage if these states were no longer as central to the fortunes of presidential candidates as they are in the electoral college.

In 2006 National Popular Vote, an organization led by several former members of Congress, announced that it intended to persuade every state legislature to form a compact agreeing to cast all of their electoral votes for whichever presidential candidate received the most popular votes nationally. The compact would take effect when states with electoral votes totaling at least 270 (that is, a majority of all electoral votes) joined. In effect, the National Popular Vote proposal was a strategy to bring about direct election of the president without changing the language of the Constitution, which already empowers each state to appoint its presidential electors "in such manner as the Legislature thereof may direct."

Senator George W. Norris was the chief proponent of the Twentieth Amendment.

Twentieth Amendment (1933)

The Twentieth Amendment, also known as the "lame-duck" amendment, was written mainly to shorten the time between the election of the president, vice president, and members of Congress and their entry into office. The hiatus for newly elected representatives and senators (unless the president called Congress into special session) had been thirteen months—from the first Tuesday after the first Monday in November (election day) until the first Monday in December of the following year, the date established by Article I, Section 4, Clause 2, of the original Constitution as the initial meeting day for Congress. The delay for presidents and vice presidents had been approximately four months, from election day until the following March 4. The source of this date for presidential inauguration was a decision by the "old Congress" of the Articles of Confederation. After the Constitution was ratified in 1788, Congress had declared March 4, 1789, the date "for commencing proceedings under the said Constitution." A law passed by the House and Senate in 1792 confirmed March 4 as the starting date for future presidential terms.

Sen. George W. Norris, R-Neb., the main author of the Twentieth Amendment, sought to remedy three major flaws in the traditional arrangement, which he regarded as better suited to an age when travel was difficult and time-consuming and the business of the federal government was relatively minor. The first flaw was the biennial lame-duck session of Congress, which typically lasted from the December after the election until the following March and which included many outgoing members of the defeated party. Second, by not having Congress begin its term before the president, existing procedures empowered the lame-duck Congress, not the most recently elected one, to choose the president and vice president in the event of an

TWENTIETH AMENDMENT (1933)

SECTION 1. The terms of the President and Vice President shall end at noon on the 20th day of January, . . . and the terms of their successors shall then begin. . . .

SECTION 3. If, at the time fixed for the beginning of the term of the President, the President elect shall have died, the Vice President elect shall become President. If a President shall not have been chosen before the time fixed for the beginning of his term, or if the President elect shall have failed to qualify, then the Vice President elect shall act as President until a President shall have qualified; and the Congress may by law provide for the case wherein neither a President nor a Vice President elect shall have qualified, declaring who shall then act as President, or the manner in which one who is to act shall be selected, and such person shall act accordingly until a President or Vice President shall have qualified.

SECTION 4. The Congress may by law provide for the case of death of any of the persons from whom the House of Representatives may choose a President whenever the right of choice shall have devolved upon them, and for the case of the death of any of the persons from whom the Senate may choose a Vice President whenever the right of choice shall have devolved upon them.

electoral college deadlock. This had happened in 1801 and 1825. Finally, Norris regarded four months as too long a time for the nation to have, in effect, two presidents—an outgoing incumbent and an incoming president-elect.

Section 1

To remedy the lame-duck and two-presidents problems, Section 1 of the Twentieth Amendment established noon on January 20 as the beginning of the president's and vice president's four-year terms and noon on January 3 as the start of the term for members of Congress. The wisdom of moving up the president's inauguration seemed vindicated when, in the last transition to take place under the old system, a nation gripped by the Great Depression had to endure four months of awkward stalemate between President-elect Franklin Roosevelt and the incumbent president he had defeated in the 1932 election, Herbert C. Hoover. Yet nearly a half-century later, the political scientist Richard E. Neustadt bemoaned one quality of the January inauguration—the "eleven week scramble" between the election and the start of the term that a president-elect now must undergo in order to get people and policies in place for the beginning of the administration.[105] In 1993 many of Bill Clinton's early problems as president were attributed to the haste with which he put together his administration's personnel and policies.

Section 3

Norris also used the Twentieth Amendment as a vehicle to address two other potential problems in the presidential and vice-presidential selection process. Section 3 provides that if the president-elect dies before the start of the term, the vice president-elect would be inaugurated as president.[106] Under Section 2 of the Twenty-fifth Amendment, which became part of the Constitution in 1967, the vice president-elect who thus succeeds to the presidency then would appoint a new vice president, pending congressional approval.

In addition to death, Section 3 also stipulates that if, by inauguration day, no presidential candidate has received the electoral vote majority or, failing that, the majority of state delegations in the House of Representatives that is required for election, the vice president-elect becomes acting president until a president is chosen. The same would be true if a president-elect is found to be unqualified under Article II, Section 1, Clause 5, by virtue of age, citizenship, or residency. The amendment also authorized Congress to legislate for the possibility that a vice president-elect might not be chosen either, whether through failure to secure an electoral vote majority or inability to win a Senate election. Congress passed such a law in 1947, the Presidential Succession

Act. The act stipulated that the Speaker of the House would serve as the acting president until a president or vice president is elected.[107]

Section 4

The possibility that either a winning presidential or vice-presidential candidate might die before officially receiving "elect" status when Congress counts the electoral votes on January 6 underlay the writing of Section 4.[108] The section simply calls on Congress to legislate for these contingencies. Congress never has done so, however, which means that if such a death were to occur, legislators would have to improvise. One of Congress's options, in counting the votes, would be to declare the dead candidate elected, thus triggering (if the presidential candidate died) Section 1 of the amendment, under which the vice president-elect would become president, or (if the winning vice-presidential candidate died) Section 2 of the Twenty-fifth Amendment, under which the vice-president-elect-turned-president would nominate a new vice president after being sworn in as president. Congress's other choice—less absurd than electing a dead person but politically more problematic—would be to allow the House of Representatives to elect one of the defeated presidential candidates as president.[109]

Proposal and Ratification

The Twentieth Amendment passed easily through Congress on March 2, 1932, and was ratified without controversy on February 6, 1933. As David Kyvig points out, it is the only amendment in history to be ratified by every state when initially considered.[110] The wisdom of the amendment seemed confirmed when, nine days later, an assassin shot at President-elect Franklin Roosevelt on a speaker's platform in Miami, Florida.

Twenty-second Amendment (1951)

The Twenty-second Amendment prohibits any person from being elected president more than two times. It also prevents successor presidents from being elected more than once if they have served more than two years of a departed presi-

TWENTY-SECOND AMENDMENT (1951)

No person shall be elected to the office of the President more than twice, and no person who has held the office of President, or acted as President for more than two years of a term to which some other person was elected President shall be elected to the office of the President more than once. But this Article shall not apply to any person holding the office of President when this Article was proposed by the Congress, and shall not prevent any person who may be holding the office of President, or acting as President, during the term within which this Article becomes operative from holding the office of President, or acting as President, during the remainder of the term.

Franklin Roosevelt's candidacy for a third term prompted deep divisions among the electorate. Republicans nominated business leader Wendell Willkie and took up the cry "No third term!"

dent's four-year term. If they serve two years or less of an unexpired term, they may be elected two times on their own, for a maximum tenure of ten years. The amendment was written in such a way as to exempt Harry S. Truman, who was president at the time Congress was considering the matter, from its coverage.

The Two-Term "Tradition"

Thomas Jefferson was the first president to argue that no president should serve more than two terms. Responding on December 10, 1807, to a letter from the Vermont state legislature urging him to run for a third term (six other states had sent similar letters), Jefferson replied:

> If some termination to the services of the Chief Magistrate be not fixed by the Constitution, or supplied by practice, his office, nominally four years, will in fact become for life, and history shows how easily that degenerates into an

inheritance. Believing that a representative Government responsible at short periods of election is that which produces the greatest sum of happiness to mankind, I feel it a duty to do no act which shall essentially impair that principle, and I should unwillingly be the person who, disregarding the sound precedent set by an illustrious predecessor [George Washington], should furnish the first example of prolongation beyond the second term of office.[111]

Jefferson's invocation of Washington was not altogether appropriate: Washington had stepped down voluntarily from the presidency after two terms, but as he explained in his Farewell Address, he had done so not as a matter of principle, but because he longed for "the shade of retirement." [112] Still, Jefferson's defense of a two-term limit took root quickly in presidential politics.[113] Indeed, the Whig Party and many Democrats soon argued for a one-term limit. Andrew Jackson was the last president until Abraham Lincoln to be elected to two terms, and even Jackson said he would prefer a constitutional amendment barring more than one presidential term (albeit a six-year term). Of the first thirty presidents (Washington to Herbert Hoover), twenty served one term or less.

In the late nineteenth and early twentieth centuries, the issue of a third term arose only occasionally. Ulysses S. Grant (in 1876) and Woodrow Wilson (in 1920) would have liked to serve another four years but were too unpopular at the end of their second terms even to be renominated by their parties. Theodore Roosevelt's situation was more complicated. He was elected president only once, in 1904, but, as vice president, he had served all but six months of the term of his assassinated predecessor, William McKinley. In 1908 Roosevelt declined a certain renomination and, considering his great popularity, a probable reelection, calling the two-term limit a "wise custom." Four years later, however, he ran for president again, first as a Republican, then as a third party candidate. That he had declined a "third cup of coffee" in 1908, Roosevelt said, did not mean that he never intended to drink coffee again. "I meant, of course, a third consecutive term." [114]

FDR

The two-term tradition was broken by President Franklin Roosevelt in 1940. In 1937 Roosevelt, although not flatly ruling out a third term, had declared that his "great ambition on January 20, 1941" (the day his second term would expire) was to "turn over this desk and chair in the White House" to a successor. A number of Democrats, including Postmaster General James A. Farley, Vice President John Nance Garner, and former Indiana governor Paul V. McNutt, began preparing their presidential candidacies. But as Roosevelt's second term wore on, he became increasingly frustrated by Congress's resistance to his policies and programs. In 1939 World War II broke out in Europe in response to German,

Three presidents were constrained by the Twenty-second Amendment's two-term limit: Republicans Dwight Eisenhower and Ronald Reagan and Democrat Bill Clinton.

Italian, and Soviet aggression, with little prospect that the United States would be able to remain above the fray. Waiting until the Democratic convention in July 1940, Roosevelt finally signaled his willingness to be renominated. The delegates overwhelmingly approved.[115]

Public opinion polls had shown that the voters were deeply divided about the propriety of Roosevelt's candidacy, and Republicans took up the cry "No third term!" on behalf of their nominee, business leader Wendell Willkie. Roosevelt won the election, but by a much narrower popular vote margin than in 1936—five million votes, compared with eleven million. In 1944, with the United States and its allies nearing victory in World War II, Roosevelt won another term, by three million votes. Ill at the time of his fourth election, he died less than three months after the inauguration.

Proposing the Amendment

Congress had never been fully satisfied with the original Constitution's provision for unrestricted presidential reeligibility: from 1789 to 1947, 270 resolutions to limit the president's tenure had been introduced in the House and Senate, sixty of them—an average of three per year—since 1928.[116] But the Roosevelt years added a partisan dimension to this long-standing concern. In 1932 the Republicans, who had formed the nation's majority party since 1860, were driven from power by Roosevelt's New Deal Democratic coalition. Conservative Democrats, mostly southern, lost control of their party to liberals and northerners at the national level.

In the midterm elections of 1946, the Republicans regained a majority of both houses of Congress. On February 6, 1947, less than five weeks after the opening of the Eightieth Congress, the House passed a strict two-term amendment to the Constitution by a vote of 285–121. The House bill provided that any president who had served one full term and even one day of another would be barred from seeking reelection. Republicans supported the amendment unanimously (238–0); Democrats opposed it by 47 to 121, with most of the Democratic yea votes coming from south-

erners. Five weeks later, on March 12, the Senate passed a slightly different version of the amendment (it allowed a president who had served one full term and less than half of another to seek an additional term) by a vote of 59–23. Republican senators, like their House colleagues, were unanimous in their support (46–0); Democrats opposed the amendment by a vote of 23–13. The differences between the two versions of the amendment were ironed out quickly in favor of the Senate's and final congressional action took place on March 24, 1947.

The debate on the Twenty-second Amendment painted a thin gloss of constitutional philosophy over a highly partisan issue. Republicans contended that a two-term limit would protect Americans against the threat of an overly personal presidency; besides, argued Rep. Leo Allen, R-Ill., "the people should be given the opportunity to set limits on the time an individual can serve as Chief Executive." Democrats like Rep. Estes Kefauver of Tennessee rejoined that the people, "by a mere majority vote, have the opportunity of deciding every four years whether they want to terminate the services of the President if he stands for reelection."[117] Little, if any, consideration was given to the Constitutional Convention's original decision to place no restrictions on presidential reeligibility. Nor did Congress foresee the beneficial political effect of the amendment on the vice presidency. With second-term presidents barred from reelection, vice presidents could openly campaign for their party's presidential nomination without jeopardizing their standing within the administration, as Richard Nixon did in 1960, George H. W. Bush did in 1988, and Al Gore did in 2000.

Ratification

Once proposed, the Twenty-second Amendment received a mixed response from the states. Only one other amendment to the Constitution has taken longer to ratify than the three years, eleven months required for the two-term limit.[118] Eighteen state legislatures—exactly half the needed number—approved the amendment in 1947, all of them in predominantly Republican states. Afterward, ratification proceeded slowly, with most victories coming in the South. Although the South was heavily Democratic, David Kyvig points out, every Truman-sponsored civil rights initiative provoked a few more pro-segregation southern legislatures to ratify.[119] The adoption of the Twenty-second Amendment was certified and declared part of the Constitution by Jess Larson, administrator of the General Services Administration, on February 27, 1951. (Previously, amendments had been certified by the secretary of state.) Five more states later ratified, bringing the total to forty-one.

Conclusion

So few presidents have served two full terms since the Twenty-second Amendment was enacted that its effects on the modern presidency are hard to measure. John Kennedy was assassinated late in the third year of his first term. Because Lyndon Johnson, who succeeded to the presidency on November 22, 1963, served less than half of Kennedy's term, the amendment allowed him to run for two full terms of his own. But Johnson's political unpopularity in 1968 led him to withdraw from the race. Nixon was elected to a second term in 1972 but resigned less than two years later. Gerald Ford served more than half of Nixon's second term, which limited him to only one elected term as president. But Ford failed to win even that. The candidate who defeated him in 1976, Jimmy Carter, was defeated in turn by Ronald Reagan in 1980. Reagan's successor, George H. W. Bush, failed in reelection in 1992.

The constraints of the two-term limit, then, have been felt by only three presidents, two Republicans and one Democrat. Dwight Eisenhower, the first president to whom the Twenty-second Amendment applied, would have liked to run for a third term in 1960, according to John Eisenhower, his son and deputy chief of staff. While president, Eisenhower expressed "deep reservations" about the two-term limit.[120] Reagan was the second president to be denied the opportunity to run for reelection by the Twenty-second Amendment. During his second term, he campaigned for a constitutional amendment that would repeal the two-term limit, although not in a way that would apply to him. In 1993 Bill Clinton, at age fifty-four, became the youngest president to be forced out by the Twenty-second Amendment. George W. Bush's reelection in 2004 meant that his second and final term was scheduled to expire on January 20, 2009, when he would be sixty-two.

The American people show little sign of wanting to abandon the Twenty-second Amendment, despite the popularity of presidents Eisenhower and Reagan, the restriction the two-term limit places on their right to choose, and their general support for a strong presidency. In 1966 the political scientist Roberta Sigel summarized the presidential job description implicit in American political culture: "Wanted is a man who is strong, who has ideas of his own on how to solve problems, and who will make his ideas prevail even if Congress or the public should oppose him. . . . Finally, this powerful man should exit from his office after eight years lest he become too powerful." [121] *Person* may have replaced *man* in this formulation, but the belief endures that presidents should be strong leaders but only for a limited time.

Twenty-fifth Amendment (1967)

The Twenty-fifth Amendment was proposed by Congress and ratified by the states mainly to provide for two separate but related situations: vacancies in the vice presidency and presidential disabilities.[122] According to Section 2 of the amendment, vice-presidential vacancies are to be filled by presidential nomination, pending confirmation by a majority of both houses of Congress. A set of procedures for handling presidential disabilities was created by sections 3 and 4. These sections provide that either the president alone or the vice president and a majority of the cabinet may declare a president disabled and temporarily transfer the powers and duties of the office to the vice president. Congress is charged to resolve disagreements about presidential disability that may arise between the president and the rest of the executive branch leadership.

Presidential Disabilities

The original Constitution stated in Article II, Section 1, Clause 6, that, as with presidential deaths, resignations, and impeachments, "in Case of the . . . Inability [of the president] to discharge the Powers and Duties of the said Office, the Same shall devolve on the Vice President." The Constitution gave no guidance about what a disability was, how the vice president was to step in should the need arise, or even whether the vice president was actually to become president in response to a presidential disability or merely to assume temporarily the powers and duties of the office.

The problems created by the Constitution's vagueness became dramatically apparent during the long disabilities of presidents James A. Garfield and Woodrow Wilson. Garfield lay dying for eighty days after he was shot in 1881. His cabinet met to discuss the situation but concluded that if Vice President Chester A. Arthur were to invoke Clause 1, he would legally become president and thus prevent Garfield from resuming the office should he recover.

Wilson's cabinet and many members of Congress were more disposed to transfer power temporarily to Vice President Thomas R. Marshall during Wilson's long illness in 1919 and 1920, but the Constitution's lack of guidance and a protective White House staff stayed their hands. When Secretary of State Robert Lansing raised the possibility with Joseph Tumulty, Wilson's personal secretary, Tumulty replied, "You may rest assured that while Woodrow Wilson is lying in the White House on the broad of his back I will not be a party to ousting him." The vice president confided to his secretary, "I am not going to seize the place and then have Wilson—recovered—come around and say, 'Get off, you usurper.' " [123] Although Garfield's and Wilson's disabilities were unusual in their length, as many as one-third of the nation's presidents have been disabled for at least brief periods of their terms.[124]

Vice-Presidential Vacancies

The vice presidency becomes vacant when the vice president dies, resigns, or is impeached and removed, or when the vice president succeeds to the presidency after the president dies, resigns, or is impeached and removed. Such circumstances left the nation without a vice president sixteen times between 1789 and 1963: seven times because the vice president died (all of natural causes), eight times because the president died (four of natural causes and four by assassination), and once because the vice president resigned.[125] *(See Chapter 8, Removal of the Vice President.)*

Changing succession laws provided for the possibility of a double vacancy in the presidency and vice presidency by placing the president pro tempore of the Senate and the Speaker of the House, respectively, next in line to the presidency (pending a special presidential election) from 1792 to 1886; the secretary of state and the other department heads next in line (pending an optional special election) from 1886 to 1947; and the Speaker of the House and the Senate president pro tempore, respectively, next in line (with no special election) since 1947. By merest chance, a double vacancy never occurred.

Addressing the Problem

Public and congressional concern about the problems of presidential disability and vice-presidential vacancy was minor and episodic through most of the first century and a half of U.S. history, usually rising for brief periods while a president was disabled, then waning when the crisis passed. From 1945 to 1963, however, a combination of events took place that placed these problems high on the nation's constitutional agenda.

The invention and spread of nuclear weapons and intercontinental ballistic missiles after 1945 heightened con-

TWENTY-FIFTH AMENDMENT (1967)

SECTION 1. In case of the removal of the President from office or of his death or resignation, the Vice President shall become president.

SECTION 2. Whenever there is a vacancy in the office of the Vice President, the President shall nominate a Vice President who shall take office upon confirmation by a majority vote of both Houses of Congress.

SECTION 3. Whenever the President transmits to the President pro tempore of the Senate and the Speaker of the House of Representatives his written declaration that he is unable to discharge the powers and duties of his office, and until he transmits to them a written declaration to the contrary, such powers and duties shall be discharged by the Vice President as Acting President.

SECTION 4. Whenever the Vice President and a majority of either the principal officers of the executive departments or such other body as Congress may by law provide, transmit to the President pro tempore of the Senate and the Speaker of the House of Representatives their written declaration that the President is unable to discharge the powers and duties of his office, the Vice President shall immediately assume the powers and duties of the office as Acting President.

Thereafter, when the President transmits to the President pro tempore of the Senate and the Speaker of the House of Representatives his written declaration that no inability exists, he shall resume the powers and duties of his office unless the Vice President and a majority of either the principal officers of the executive departments or of such other body as Congress may by law provide, transmit within four days to the President pro tempore of the Senate and the Speaker of the House of Representatives their written declaration that the President is unable to discharge the powers and duties of his office. Thereupon Congress shall decide the issue, assembling within forty-eight hours for that purpose if not in session. If the Congress, within twenty-one days after receipt of the latter written declaration, or, if Congress is not in session, within twenty-one days after Congress is required to assemble, determines by two-thirds vote of both Houses that the President is unable to discharge the powers and duties of his office, the Vice President shall continue to discharge the same as Acting President; otherwise, the President shall resume the powers and duties of his office.

cern that an able president be available at all times to wield the powers of the office. Then, in rapid succession, President Eisenhower suffered a series of disabling illnesses—a heart attack in 1955, an ileitis attack and operation in 1956, and a stroke in 1957. Finally, the assassination of President Kennedy in 1963 left the nation with a president, Lyndon Johnson, who had a history of heart trouble and whose legally designated successors, in the absence of a vice president, were an ailing House Speaker, John W. McCormack, D-Mass., and, as Senate president pro tempore, an even more enfeebled Carl Hayden, D-Ariz.

The first tangible result of this series of developments was a letter, released to the public on March 3, 1958, that President Eisenhower sent to Vice President Nixon. The letter stated that if Eisenhower ever were disabled again, he would instruct the vice president to serve as acting president until the disability passed, at which time the president would reclaim his powers. If Eisenhower were disabled but unable to communicate with Nixon for some reason, Nixon could make the decision to assume power himself. Again, Eisenhower would determine when it was time to resume the powers of his office.

The Eisenhower letter was later adopted by President Kennedy and Vice President Johnson, President Johnson and Speaker McCormack, and (after the 1964 election) President Johnson and Vice President Humphrey. But it hardly solved the problem of presidential disability. For one thing, such letters lack the force of law. For another, Eisenhower's letter made no provision to relieve a president who was disabled, perhaps mentally, but who refused to admit it. Finally, the letter did not—nor could it—address the related problem of the vacant vice presidency.

Proposing the Amendment: Disability

In December 1963, less than a month after the Kennedy assassination, Sen. Birch Bayh, D-Ind., the chairman of the Senate Judiciary Committee's Subcommittee on Constitutional Amendments, announced that he would hold hearings in early 1964 to consider constitutional remedies to the disability and vacancy problems. Coordinating his efforts with those of a special committee of the American Bar Association, Bayh drafted the amendment that formed the basis for the subcommittee's hearings and that, with minor modifications, later entered the Constitution as the Twenty-fifth Amendment.

The Senate approved the amendment on September 29, 1964, by a vote of 65–0. The House did not act in 1964, perhaps because to propose an amendment to fill vice-presidential vacancies would be perceived as a slap at Speaker McCormack, who under the existing arrangement was first in line to succeed President Johnson. In 1965 however, after Humphrey's election as vice president in November 1964, the House joined the Senate (which had reaffirmed its support of the amendment by a vote of 72–0 on February 19) and on April 13 voted its approval by a margin of 368–29.

From the beginning, most of Congress's concerns about the Twenty-fifth Amendment were directed at its disability provisions. As drafted by Bayh and enacted by Congress, three very different situations were covered by sections 3 and 4 of the amendment. In the first, the president is "unable to discharge the powers and duties of his office" and recognizes the condition, say, before or after surgery. A simple letter from the president to the Speaker of the House and the president pro tempore of the Senate is sufficient to make the vice president the acting president. A subsequent letter declaring that the disability is ended restores the president's powers.

In the second situation, the president is disabled but, having perhaps lost consciousness, is unable to say so. Should this happen, either the vice president or the head of an executive department may call a meeting of the vice president and cabinet to discuss the situation. If both the vice president and a majority of the heads of the departments declare the president disabled, the vice president becomes acting president—again, until the president

writes to congressional leaders to announce an end to the disability. The rationale for this procedure was explained by attorney John Feerick, who assisted Bayh in writing the amendment:

> The Vice President, it was said, should have a voice in the process because it would be his duty to act as President once the determination had been made. Consequently, he should not be forced to take over under circumstances which he felt to be improper. On the other hand, it was urged that he not have the sole power of determination since he would be an interested party and therefore possibly reluctant to make a determination.[126]

Some critics of Bayh's proposal argued that it vested too much power in the executive branch to make disability determinations. Suggestions were offered to create a disability commission that included members of all three branches, perhaps joined by a number of physicians. Bayh defended his proposal by saying that any move to strip power from the president by officials outside the administration risked violating the constitutional principle of separation of powers. In the end, both to satisfy the critics and to preclude the possibility that a president might fire the cabinet to forestall a declaration of disability, the amendment empowered Congress, at its discretion, to substitute another body for the cabinet.

The third situation covered by the disability portions of the amendment is the most troubling. It involves instances (such as questionable mental health or sudden physical disability) in which the president's ability to fulfill the office is in dispute—the president claims to be able, but the vice president and cabinet judge differently. The amendment provides that should this happen, the vice president would become acting president pending a congressional resolution of the matter. Congress would have a maximum of three weeks to decide whether or not the president is disabled, with a two-thirds vote of both the House and the Senate needed to overturn the president's judgment. The reason for the requirement of an extraordinary majority was the presumption that the president should receive the benefit of any doubt. But because the Twenty-fifth Amendment only transfers power to the vice president for as long as the president is disabled, a subsequent claim of restored health by the president would set the whole process in motion again.

Interestingly, the Twenty-fifth Amendment, although creating an elaborate set of procedures for disability determinations, includes no definition of *disability*. It is clear from the congressional debate that disability does not mean incompetence, laziness, unpopularity, or impeachable conduct. As to what disability is, Congress thought that any definition it might write into the Constitution in 1965 would be rendered obsolete by changes in medical theory and practice.[127]

Proposing the Amendment: Vice-Presidential Vacancies

Widespread agreement existed in Congress about the need to replace the vice president when the office becomes vacant, both to increase the likelihood of a smooth succession to the presidency by a member of the president's party and to ensure that the presidential disability provisions of the Twenty-fifth Amendment would always have a vice president on hand to execute them. Bayh's proposal—that the president nominate a new vice president when the office becomes vacant and that a majority of both houses of Congress, voting separately, confirm the nomination—prevailed and became Section 2 of the amendment. Enactment came after consideration was given to a variety of other suggestions to have, say, Congress or the electoral college from the previous election choose the vice president. Proposals to impose a time limit on Congress either to vote on a president's nominee for vice president or to forfeit its right to reject the nomination also were considered and rejected.

Ratification

No serious opposition to the Twenty-fifth Amendment arose during the ratification process. The needed approval of thirty-eight state legislatures was attained on February 10, 1967, barely a year and a half after Congress proposed the amendment. In the end, all but three states voted to ratify.[128]

part infrequent and grudging. No occasions of disability arose until March 30, 1981, when President Ronald Reagan was wounded by a would-be assassin's bullet. Although conscious and lucid before surgery, he did not sign his powers over to Vice President George H. W. Bush. Meanwhile, presidential aides stifled discussion at the White House about the possibility of a cabinet-voted transfer. In July 1985, before

Under the provisions of the Twenty-fifth Amendment, President Nixon appointed Gerald Ford, left, vice president after the scandal leading to Spiro Agnew's resignation in 1973. When Nixon resigned, Ford himself appointed a vice president, Nelson Rockefeller, right.

Conclusion

Section 2 of the Twenty-fifth Amendment—the vice-presidential vacancy provision—was put to use rather quickly, albeit in surprising circumstances. Vice President Spiro T. Agnew, facing prosecution in federal court on a variety of bribery-related charges, resigned from office as part of a plea bargain on October 10, 1973. President Nixon nominated House Republican leader Gerald Ford to replace Agnew on October 12. After a thorough, nearly two-month-long investigation, the Senate approved Ford's nomination on November 27 by a vote of 92–3, and the House gave its approval on December 6, voting 387–35. Barely eight months later, when President Nixon resigned on August 9, 1974, to avoid being impeached for his involvement in the Watergate cover-up, Ford became president. On August 20, he nominated Gov. Nelson A. Rockefeller of New York to be vice president. Congress investigated and debated the nomination for four months before approving Rockefeller by a vote of 90–7 in the Senate (December 10) and 287–128 in the House (December 19).

Use of the Twenty-fifth Amendment's presidential disability provisions (sections 3 and 4) has been for the most

undergoing cancer surgery, Reagan did sign his powers over to Bush, but only after arguing that the Twenty-fifth Amendment was not meant to apply to such brief episodes of disability.

As president, Bush's approach to the matter of disability was more constructive than his predecessor's. Before entering the hospital in May 1991 because of an irregular heartbeat, Bush announced a plan to turn over power to Vice President Dan Quayle in the event that his condition required electroshock therapy. It did not, so the plan did not need to be implemented.

In 2002 President George W. Bush invoked the Twenty-fifth Amendment just before undergoing light sedation for a colonoscopy. At 7:09 a.m. on January 29, he signed a letter to Speaker of the House J. Dennis Hastert (R-Ill.) and Senate president pro tempore Robert Byrd (D-W.Va.) declaring that "I am unable to discharge the Constitutional powers and duties of the Office of President of the United States" and that Vice President Richard B. Cheney would serve as acting president. At 9:24 a.m. Bush sent a second letter declaring that he was once again able and was resuming the powers and duties of the presidency. Invoking the recent September 11, 2001, terrorist attacks on the World Trade Center and Pentagon, Bush explained to the press that "we're at war and I just want to be super-cautious." [129]

Election Amendments

Three constitutional amendments—the Fifteenth, Nineteenth, and Twenty-sixth—have broadened the suffrage. Two other amendments—the Twenty-third and Twenty-fourth—have changed some of the rules for voting in presidential elections. In all five cases, partisan presidential politics has affected and been affected by the amendments.

Fifteenth Amendment (1870)

Before the Union's victory in the Civil War in 1865, only nine states allowed African Americans to vote: the nine northern-most states of New England and the upper Midwest that had the fewest blacks. After the war, the eleven states of the Confederacy were forced by the Reconstruction Act of 1867, which was passed by the Republican-controlled Congress, to extend the suffrage to African Americans as a condition for readmission to the Union. The votes of southern blacks were indispensable to the popular vote plurality of Ulysses S. Grant, the Republican candidate for president, in 1868.

Fearing that southern blacks might lose their franchise to white politicians in the South, and eager for the support of blacks who lived in the northern and border states that did not practice universal manhood suffrage, Republicans pushed the Fifteenth Amendment through a lame-duck session of Congress in February 1869. The House of Representatives passed a version of the amendment that forbade states to discriminate against African Americans in matters of suffrage. The Senate, anticipating that "the South could circumvent mere protection of impartial suffrage by imposing race-neutral criteria such as education or property holding,[130] passed a version that would bar discrimination on the basis not just of race and color, but also on the basis of property or education. A conference committee voted for the House version, and the amendment as passed provided simply that neither the United States nor any individual state could deprive a citizen of the right to vote "on account of race, color, or previous condition of servitude." The Fifteenth Amendment was ratified on February 3, 1870, by a combination of New England, upper midwestern, and black-controlled southern state legislatures. As one Republican member of Congress said, "[P]arty expediency and exact justice coincide for once."

The amendment secured the Republicans' major short-term political goal by effectively safeguarding the right to vote for northern blacks. But southern states, which once again came under the control of conservative whites after Union troops left in 1876, found extraconstitutional ways to disenfranchise African Americans. These included not just

violence and intimidation, but also legal subterfuges such as literacy tests (illiterate whites were exempted from taking the test if their ancestors had been eligible to vote before 1867—the so-called grandfather clause) and white primaries (political parties, as "private" organizations, were authorized to exclude blacks from membership and participation).

Although the Supreme Court eventually declared both of these practices to be unconstitutional under the Fifteenth Amendment—the grandfather clause in *Guinn and Beall v. United States* (1915) and the white primary in *Smith v. Allwright* (1944)—voter registration among southern blacks remained below 30 percent as late as 1960.[131] Not until the Voting Rights Act was passed in 1965 was the Fifteenth Amendment effectively implemented in the South. The act suspended literacy tests (banned permanently in 1970) and authorized the federal government to take over the voter registration process in any county in which less than 50 percent of the voting-age population was registered or had voted in the most recent presidential election. Since 1960, the registration rate for southern blacks has more than doubled.

Until the 1930s, most enfranchised African Americans, grateful to the party of Abraham Lincoln for freeing the slaves and granting them the vote, supported the Republicans. During the Great Depression of the 1930s, Franklin Roosevelt and the Democratic Party won roughly two-thirds of the black vote with New Deal social and economic relief programs. The Democratic Party–sponsored civil rights laws and Great Society social programs of the 1960s made African American voters into a virtually monolithic Democratic constituency. For example, according to the Gallup poll for the 1984 election, 87 percent of African American voters supported Walter F. Mondale even as he was losing the election to Ronald Reagan by a margin of 59 percent to 41 percent. Bill Clinton won 77 percent of the black vote as the Democratic nominee in 1992, but only 39 percent of the white vote.[132] In 2004 John Kerry won 88 percent of the black vote and 41 percent of the white vote.

Nineteenth Amendment (1920)

Securing the vote was a stated goal of the women's movement from the moment of its birth at the first women's rights convention in Seneca Falls, New York, in 1848. In 1890 women were granted full suffrage by Wyoming. By 1919 women had the franchise in fifteen states and the right to vote only in presidential elections in fourteen others. As time went by, the only significant political opposition to granting women the vote came from the liquor industry, which feared that women would support Prohibition. Even without national women's suffrage, however, Prohibition entered the Constitution when the Eighteenth Amendment was enacted in 1919.

The Nineteenth Amendment passed easily through the House of Representatives on May 21, 1919. The Senate, urged to approve it by President Woodrow Wilson in an unprecedented speech in the Senate chamber, followed suit on June 4, 1919. The amendment was ratified by the required three-fourths of the state legislatures on August 26, 1920, after the governor of Tennessee called the state legislature into special session so that Tennessee could provide the thirty-sixth ratification in time for the 1920 elections. The Nineteenth Amendment followed the form of the Fifteenth Amendment: neither the United States nor any state can deny or abridge the right to vote "on account of sex."

For more than a half-century after the enactment of the Nineteenth Amendment, women and men usually voted very much alike. The only "gender gap" was in voter turnout: fewer women voted. By the 1980s, however, the disparity in turnout rates had closed, and significant differences between men's and women's views on some issues and candidates had emerged. Women tend to be more concerned than men (and have more liberal views) about issues such as social welfare, public policies concerning families and children, and war and peace. For example, although women supported Republicans Reagan in 1980 and 1984 and Bush in 1988, their margin of support was narrower than for men, according to the Gallup poll. In 1992 women gave Democrat Clinton 46 percent of their votes; men gave him only 41 percent of theirs.[133] Similarly, in 2000 Democrat Al Gore won 54 percent of the women's vote and 42 percent of the men's vote.[134]

Twenty-sixth Amendment (1971)

The Fourteenth Amendment (1868) set twenty-one as the highest minimum age that a state could require for voters. By 1970, only four states had exercised their right to establish a voting age lower than twenty-one.

Political pressure to reduce the voting age by constitutional amendment rose during the late 1960s, spurred by the combination of an unusually large number of young people in the population (the post–World War II "baby boom" generation) and the Vietnam War, a controversial undertaking that saw the conscription of hundreds of thousands of eighteen-year-olds into the army. Bowing before the cry "Old enough to fight, old enough to vote," Congress passed a law

In 1869 Susan B. Anthony organized the National Woman Suffrage Association (NWSA), which led the fifty-year fight to secure the right to vote for women. NWSA leaders are shown here, with Anthony in the center.

in 1970 to lower the voting age in all elections to eighteen. The Supreme Court, in *Oregon v. Mitchell* (1970), ruled that the law was constitutional in its application to federal elections—that is, elections for president, vice president, and Congress—but not for state elections.[135] The decision, which would have required states to establish two sets of voting procedures for state and federal elections, threatened to throw the 1972 elections into turmoil.

Responding quickly to *Oregon v. Mitchell*, Congress passed the Twenty-sixth Amendment on March 23, 1971. It followed the form of both the Fifteenth and Nineteenth Amendments: the right to vote for citizens who are eighteen years or older shall not be denied or abridged by the United States or any state "on account of age." Ratification by the states, which was completed on July 1, 1971, took only 107 days, less than half the time required to ratify any other constitutional amendment.

Young voters departed from their elders mainly by registering and voting at a much lower rate—barely one-third of eighteen- to twenty-year-olds have voted in recent elections, compared with roughly two-thirds of people forty-five and older.[136] This upset the pre-amendment forecasts of many political experts, who believed that masses of young

TWENTY-THIRD AMENDMENT (1961)

The District constituting the seat of government of the United States shall appoint in such manner as the Congress may direct:

A number of electors of President and Vice President equal to the whole number of Senators and Representatives in Congress to which the District would be entitled if it were a State, but in no event more than the least populous State; they shall be in addition to those appointed by the States, but they shall be considered for the purposes of the election of President and Vice President, to be electors appointed by a State; and they shall meet in the District and perform such duties as provided by the twelfth article of amendment.

people would turn out in the 1972 elections and move the political system dramatically to the left.[137]

Twenty-third Amendment (1961)

Until the Constitution was written, the location of the capital of the United States was precarious and ever changing. At various times, it moved or was forced to move to Philadelphia, Trenton, New York, and elsewhere. To prevent this migration from happening again, the Constitutional Convention stipulated in Article I, Section 8, Clause 17, that the new capital would be a federal city, governed by Congress and carved out of territory "not exceeding ten miles square" that was ceded to the federal government by the states.[138]

One result of being neither a state nor a part of a state was that the District of Columbia (Washington) was not represented in the federal government. It lacked senators and representatives in Congress and electoral votes in the presidential election. Over the years, this became the source of much resentment among the tax-paying citizens of Washington, whose population by 1950 exceeded 800,000, making it more populous than thirteen states.

The Twenty-third Amendment, proposed by Congress on June 16, 1960, granted the District a "number of electors of President and Vice President . . . in no event more than the least populous state"— that is, three. The amendment passed both houses on voice votes, mostly because Democrats and Republicans each thought they had a chance to win the District. It was ratified quickly, on March 29, 1961, although Tennessee was the only southern state to vote its approval. Overwhelmingly African American and Democratic, the District of Columbia has never given less than 75 percent of its vote to the Democratic candidate for president. In 2004 Sen. John Kerry (D-Mass.) carried the District by 91 percent to 10 percent for Republican president George W. Bush.

In 1978 Congress proposed a constitutional amendment to repeal the Twenty-third Amendment and expand the voting rights of District residents. The proposed amendment would have granted the District some of the electoral rights of states such as power to ratify proposed constitutional amendments, two senators, and a number of representatives and presidential electors commensurate with its population.[139] Mostly for partisan reasons (Republicans now realized that they had little hope of winning elections in the District), the amendment failed. Only sixteen states—fewer than half the number needed—had ratified it by the time the seven-year deadline for state action expired.

Twenty-fourth Amendment (1964)

Proposed by Congress on August 27, 1962, and ratified by the states on February 4, 1964, the Twenty-fourth Amendment bars the United States or any state from requiring citizens to pay a "poll tax" to vote in primary or general elections for president and Congress. Although once used by many southern states as a tool to disenfranchise blacks and poor whites, the poll tax already had been abandoned by all but five states at the time the Twenty-fourth Amendment was passed. Congress's main purpose in proposing the

TWENTY-FOURTH AMENDMENT (1964)

The right of citizens of the United States to vote in any primary or other election for President or Vice President, for electors for President or Vice President, or for Senator or Representative to Congress, shall not be denied or abridged by the United States or any State by reason of failure to pay any poll tax or other tax.

amendment seems to have been to make a positive gesture to the growing civil rights movement.

The Twenty-fourth Amendment says nothing about poll taxes for state and local elections. But in 1966, in the case of *Harper v. Virginia Board of Electors,* the Supreme Court ruled that they too were unconstitutional because they violated the Fourteenth Amendment's guarantee of "equal protection of the laws." [140] In a sense, this ruling rendered the Twenty-fourth Amendment superfluous.

NOTES

1. Quoted in Jack N. Rakove, *Original Meanings: Politics and Ideas in the Making of the Constitution* (New York: Knopf, 1996), 131.

2. Aristotle, *The Politics,* trans. Carnes Lord (Chicago: University of Chicago Press, 1984), books 3.14–3.18 and 4.

3. Jack P. Greene, *Peripheries and Center: Constitutional Development in the Extended Polities of the British Empire and the United States* (Athens: University of Georgia Press, 1969), 27.

4. Quoted in Charles C. Thach Jr., *The Creation of the Presidency, 1775–1789* (Baltimore: Johns Hopkins University Press, 1969), 27.

5. Ibid.

6. Gordon S. Wood, *The Creation of the American Republic, 1776–1787* (Chapel Hill: University of North Carolina Press, 1969), 138.

7. Thomas Jefferson, *Notes on the State of Virginia,* ed. William Peden (Chapel Hill: University of North Carolina Press, 1955).

8. Christopher Collier and James Lincoln Collier, *Decision in Philadelphia: The Constitutional Convention of 1787* (New York: Ballantine, 1986), 5.

9. Thach, *Creation of the Presidency,* 49, 52–53.

10. Walter Isaacson, *Benjamin Franklin: An American Life* (New York: Simon and Schuster, 2003), 445.

11. Quoted in Joseph J. Ellis, *His Excellency, George Washington* (New York: Knopf, 2004), 178.

12. Clinton Rossiter, *1787: The Grand Convention* (London: MacGibbon and Kee, 1968), 141.

13. Stanley Elkins and Eric McKitrick, "The Founding Fathers: Young Men of the Revolution," *Political Science Quarterly* 76 (June 1961): 181–216.

14. Collier and Collier, *Decision in Philadelphia,* 104–105.

15. Charles A. Beard, *An Economic Interpretation of the Constitution* (New York: Macmillan, 1913).

16. Catherine Drinker Bowen, *Miracle at Philadelphia: The Story of the Constitutional Convention* (Boston: Little, Brown, 1966), 30.

17. Unless otherwise noted, the source for these discussions of the Constitutional Convention is Max Farrand, ed., *The Records of the Federal Convention of 1787,* vols. 1–4 (New Haven: Yale University Press, 1913), or James H. Hutson, ed., *Supplement to Max Farrand's The Records of the Federal Convention of 1787* (New Haven: Yale University Press, 1987). An excellent chronological account of the convention may be found in William Peters, *A More Perfect Union: The Making of the United States Constitution* (New York: Crown, 1987).

18. Collier and Collier, *Decision in Philadelphia,* 108.

19. Gordon S. Wood, *Revolutionary Characters: What Made the Founders Different* (New York: Penguin, 2006), 46.

20. Lester Cappon, ed., *The Adams-Jefferson Letters* (Chapel Hill: University of North Carolina Press, 1959), 1:191; and Farrand, *Records,* 3:35.

21. John Roche has argued that the preservation of secrecy by the delegates is great testimony to their sense of shared enterprise: even when they disagreed strongly over particular issues, they were sufficiently committed to the effort to keep their objections within the convention's walls. John P. Roche, "The Founding Fathers: A Reform Caucus in Action," *American Political Science Review* 55 (December 1911): 799–816.

22. Collier and Collier, *Decision in Philadelphia,* 120.

23. Jack N. Rakove, *Original Meanings: Politics and Ideas in the Making of the Constitution* (New York: Knopf, 1996), 14.

24. Wood, *Revolutionary Characters,* 157, 160.

25. Rossiter, *1787,* 171.

26. Richard J. Ellis, ed., *Founding the American Presidency* (Lanham, Md.: Rowman and Littlefield, 1999), 131.

27. Ron Chernow, *Alexander Hamilton* (New York: Penguin, 2004), 232.

28. Clinton Rossiter dismisses this view in *Alexander Hamilton and the Constitution* (New York: Harcourt, Brace and World, 1964).

29. The preamble the committee replaced was blander and more state-centered: "We the people of the states of New Hampshire, Massachusetts," and so forth.

30. Rakove, *Original Meanings,* 107.

31. Rossiter, *1787,* 234.

32. Farrand, *Records,* 2:641–643.

33. Even later that day, according to an oft-repeated story, someone asked Franklin as he left the hall, "Well, Doctor, what have we got? A republic or a monarchy?" "A republic," Franklin replied, "if you can keep it."

34. Rakove, *Original Meanings,* 82.

35. Fred Barbash, *The Founding: A Dramatic Account of the Writing of the Constitution* (New York: Linden Press/Simon and Schuster, 1987), 175.

36. Seymour Martin Lipset, *The First New Nation* (New York: Basic Books, 1963), chap. 1; Max Weber, *The Theory of Social and Economic Organizations* (New York: Oxford University Press, 1947), 358; Marcus Cunliffe, *George Washington: Man and Monument* (New York: New American Library, 1958), 15.

37. Stanley Elkins and Eric McKitrick, *The Age of Federalism: The Early American Republic, 1788–1800* (New York: Oxford University Press, 1993), 34.

38. Contemporaries often compared Washington to Cincinnatus, the ancient Roman who left his plow when called to lead Rome against Carthage, then returned to it as soon as the victory was won. Garry Wills, *Cincinnatus: George Washington and the Enlightenment* (New York: Doubleday, 1984), 36–37.

39. Thach, *Creation of the Presidency,* 81.

40. Collier and Collier, *Decision in Philadelphia,* 300.

41. Ellis, *Founding the American Presidency,* 12–13.

42. Charles L. Mee Jr., *The Genius of the People* (New York: Harper and Row, 1987), 118.

43. Ellis, *Founding the American Presidency.*

44. Indispensable to eventual adoption of the electoral college was Wilson's conversion of Madison, who declared on July 19 that "it is essential then that the appointment of the Executive should either be drawn from some source, or held by some tenure, that will give him a free agency with regard to the Legislature. This could not be if he was appointed from time to time by the Legislature."

45. Robert A. Dahl, *Pluralist Democracy in the United States: Conflict and Change* (Chicago: Rand-McNally, 1967), 84.

46. Rossiter, *1787,* 199. See also Shlomo Slonim, "The Electoral College at Philadelphia: The Evolution of an Ad Hoc Congress for the Selection of a President," *Journal of American History* 73 (1986): 35–58.

47. Barbash, *Founding,* 182.

48. Carol Berkin, *A Brilliant Solution: Inventing the American Constitution* (New York: Harcourt, 2002), 143–144.

49. Roche, "Founding Fathers," 810.

50. Ellis, *Founding the American Presidency,* 233.

51. Alexander Hamilton, James Madison, and John Jay, *The Federalist Papers,* with an introduction by Clinton L. Rossiter (New York: New American Library, 1961), 301, 303. All quotes from *The Federalist Papers* are from this edition.

52. Richard E. Neustadt, *Presidential Power* (New York: Wiley, 1960), 35.

53. Robert Scigliano, "The Presidency and the Judiciary," in *The Presidency and the Political System,* 3d ed., ed. Michael Nelson (Washington, D.C.: CQ Press, 1984), 471–499.

54. Ellis, *Founding the American Presidency,* 130–131.

55. Richard M. Pious, *The American Presidency* (New York: Basic Books, 1978), 29.

56. John Locke, *The Second Treatise on Government* (Indianapolis: Bobbs-Merrill, 1952), 91–96.

57. Thach, *Creation of the Presidency,* 138–139.

58. Political scientist David K. Nichols finds additional meaning in the clause—namely, "a basis for executive privilege, because Congress is nowhere given power to require opinions in writing of department heads or other administrative officers." Nichols, *The Myth of the Modern Presidency* (University Park: Pennsylvania State University Press, 1994), 51–52.

59. Ellis, *Founding the American Presidency,* 220–221.

60. Rakove, *Original Meanings,* 89, 267.

61. Ellis, *Founding the American Presidency,* 190.

62. Michael Nelson, "Constitutional Qualifications for the President," *Presidential Studies Quarterly* 17 (spring 1987): 383–399.

63. Another reason the convention decided to include a requirement of natural born citizenship for the president may be found in a letter that John Jay sent to George Washington on July 25. "Permit me to hint," Jay wrote, "whether it would not be wise and reasonable to provide a strong check on the admission of foreigners into the administration of our National Government, and to declare expressly that the command in chief of the American Army shall not be given to, nor devolve upon, any but a natural born citizen." On September 2, two days before the Committee on Postponed Matters proposed the natural born citizen requirement to the convention, Washington replied to Jay, "I thank you for the hints contained in your letter." (Farrand, *Records,* 4:61, 76)

64. John D. Feerick, *From Failing Hands: The Story of Presidential Succession* (New York: Fordham University Press, 1965), chap. 2.

65. On September 15, 1787, delegates discovered a clerical error in the committee's draft and changed "the period for chusing another president arrive" to "a President shall be elected."

66. For a thorough comparison of the convention's decisions on succession and the Committee of Style's rendering of them, see Feerick, *From Failing Hands,* 48–51. Feerick speculates that the committee may have omitted presidential "absence" from the list of situations requiring a temporary successor because it was covered by the term "inability."

67. Quoted in Ralph Ketcham, ed., *The Anti-Federalist Papers and the Constitutional Convention Debates* (New York: New American Library, 1986), 213–214.

68. Ibid., 251.

69. Quoted in Cecelia M. Kenyon, ed., *The Antifederalists* (Indianapolis: Bobbs-Merrill, 1966), 302–309.

70. Ellis, *Founding the American Presidency,* 117.

71. Ibid., 145.

72. Quoted in Pious, *American Presidency,* 39.

73. Feerick, *From Failing Hands,* 51.

74. Quoted in Kenyon, *Antifederalists,* 305.

75. Feerick, *From Failing Hands,* 52, 53–54.

76. Quotes are drawn from ibid., 52–55.

77. Ibid., 53.

78. Ellis, *His Excellency, George Washington,* 181.

79. Collier and Collier, *Decision in Philadelphia,* 347.

80. Madison, perhaps aware of how far afield the Philadelphia convention had strayed from its original charter, dreaded the prospect of additional amending conventions. In January 1789, he expressed a strong preference that Congress propose a bill of rights rather than convene another convention to do so. In a letter to George Eve, Madison wrote: "The Congress who will be appointed to execute as well as to amend the Government, will probably be careful not to destroy or endanger it. A convention, on the other hand, meeting in the present ferment of parties, and containing perhaps insidious characters from different parts of America, would at least spread a general alarm, and be but too likely to turn everything into confusion and uncertainty." Quoted in Walter E. Dellinger, "The Recurring Question," *Yale Law Journal* (October 1979).

81. Congress feared that Prohibition repeal would not be ratified by a sufficient number of states if the decision were left to rural-dominated legislatures.

82. The Eighteenth (Prohibition), Twentieth (inauguration day), Twenty-first (Prohibition repeal), and Twenty-second (two-term limit for presidents) Amendments included a seven-year ratification deadline. So did the Equal Rights Amendment (ERA), proposed by Congress in 1972, and the amendment proposed in 1978 that would have granted the District of Columbia full representation in Congress and a potentially larger share of electoral votes in presidential elections. Neither of the latter two amendments was ratified by a sufficient number of states, even after Congress, in a move of questionable constitutionality, extended the ERA ratification deadline by three years.

83. *Baker v. Carr,* 319 U.S. 186 (1962).

84. Seven state constitutions require the approval of an extraordinary majority of either two-thirds or three-fifths of the members of both houses of their legislatures in order to ratify.

85. James L. Sundquist, *Constitutional Reform and Effective Government,* rev. ed. (Washington, D.C.: Brookings, 1990), 17.

86. Nothing threatened the ratification of the proposed Constitution more than the absence of a bill of rights. Delegates to the Philadelphia convention believed that individual rights were safeguarded in the Constitution because it created a government of limited powers, none of which permitted any infringement of basic rights. This argument, however, carried little weight politically. Federalist delegates at several state conventions promised that the new Congress would approve a bill of rights to the Constitution in the form of constitutional amendments. When first convened, Congress did so expeditiously.

87. The Bill of Rights took fourteen and a half months to ratify. Even excluding the Twenty-seventh Amendment, which took more than two centuries (!) to ratify, the eleven other nonvoting amendments required an average of twenty-two months.

Two constitutional amendments have affected the presidency strongly but indirectly: the Sixteenth Amendment (1913), which declared a federal income tax constitutionally permissible, and the Seventeenth Amendment (1913), which required that U.S. senators be elected by the people rather than the state legislatures.

88. Michael Nelson, "Constitutional Qualifications for President," in *Understanding the Presidency,* 4th ed., ed. James P. Pfiffner and Roger H. Davidson (New York: Pearson Longman, 2007), 14–22.

89. *Clinton v. City of New York,* 524 U.S. 417 (1998).

90. David E. Kyvig, *Explicit and Authentic Acts: Amending the U.S. Constitution, 1776–1995* (Lawrence: University Press of Kansas, 1996), 115–116.

91. In forty-two states and the District of Columbia, the electors' names do not even appear on the ballot, just the names of the presidential and vice-presidential candidates to whom they are pledged.

92. Of the twenty-four states that legally bind electors, only five—New Mexico, North Carolina, Oklahoma, South Carolina, and Washington—stipulate penalties for violators. The eleven "faithless" votes were cast in 1791, 1820, 1948, 1956, 1960, 1968, 1972, 1976,

1988, 2000, and 2004. The first electoral vote for a woman was cast in 1972 by Roger MacBride, a Virginia elector pledged to the Republican ticket of Richard Nixon and Spiro T. Agnew. He voted for the Libertarian Party ticket of John Hospers for president and Theodora Nathan for vice president.

93. Michael Nelson, "The Election: Ordinary Politics, Extraordinary Outcome," in *The Elections of 2000,* ed. Michael Nelson (Washington, D.C.: CQ Press, 2001), 84.

94. Laurence H. Tribe and Thomas M. Rollins, "Deadlock: What Happens If Nobody Wins," *Atlantic,* October 1980, 49; and Allen P. Sindler, "Presidential Selection and Succession in Special Situations," in *Presidential Selection,* ed. Alexander Heard and Michael Nelson (Durham: Duke University Press, 1987), 393.

95. South Carolina was the last state to allow its legislature to choose electors. All the other states had abandoned the practice by 1828.

96. Maine and Nebraska each use a district plan—two electors are awarded to the candidate who carries the state, with one more added for every congressional district that a candidate carries.

97. In 1876 with no such law on the books, the electoral votes of three southern states were disputed. Congress improvised a solution by creating a special commission. The commission awarded all the votes in question to the Republican candidate, Rutherford B. Hayes. Hayes, who had lost the national popular vote to Democrat Samuel J. Tilden, was thus elected by a margin of one electoral vote (185–184). Charges of corruption and foul play were rampant. In 1887 Congress decided to charge states to resolve similar electoral vote disputes in the future.

98. This discussion draws heavily on Stephen J. Wayne, *The Road to the White House: The Politics of Presidential Elections,* 4th ed. (New York: St. Martin's Press, 1992), 290–297.

99. Ibid., 291.

100. The proportional plan would have denied any candidate a majority in four of the last eleven elections (1960, 1968, 1976, and 1992).

101. Interestingly, Nixon would have defeated Kennedy in 1960 under the district plan, by a vote of 278–245. The district plan would have produced a tie vote (269–269) between Ford and Carter in 1976.

102. The principle underlying the 102 figure is two votes times the fifty states and the District of Columbia.

103. In 1960 one consideration that kept Nixon and the Republicans from challenging alleged vote fraud in Chicago was that even if it had turned out that Nixon had carried Illinois, he still would have lacked an electoral vote majority. With 102 bonus votes in addition to those of Illinois, however, he may have been less reluctant to do so, thus prolonging the election indefinitely.

104. Wayne, *Road to the White House,* 299–300.

105. Richard E. Neustadt, *Presidential Power,* 3d ed. (New York: Wiley, 1980), 219.

106. Section 2 said nothing about the presidency. It merely stated that Congress must assemble at least once a year, convening on January 3 or, if it chooses, some other day.

107. To do so, the Speaker not only would have to meet the constitutional qualifications for president but also would have to resign from Congress. Next after the Speaker in the line of temporary succession is the president pro tempore of the Senate, followed by the secretary of state and the other department heads in the order their departments were created. Because cabinet officers serve until they resign or are replaced by the president, they would of necessity be members of the outgoing president's administration.

108. Section 4 also pertains to the death of a presidential candidate after an election in which no candidate receives an electoral vote majority.

109. Technically, Congress would declare the dead candidate ineligible to be president, then count the electoral votes of the losing candidates and let the House of Representatives choose among the three highest electoral vote recipients who had lost the election. In almost all presidential elections, however, only one rival to the winning candidate wins electoral votes.

110. Kyvig, *Explicit and Authentic Acts,* 274.

111. Quoted in Edward S. Corwin, *The President: Office and Powers, 1787–1984,* 5th rev. ed. (New York: New York University Press, 1984), 378. In 1788 while the Constitution was still awaiting ratification, Jefferson had written to Washington that the "perpetual reeligibility" of the president "will, I fear, make an office for life. I was much the enemy of monarchy before I came to Europe. I am ten thousand times more so since I have seen what they are. . . . I shall hope that before there is danger of this change taking place in the office of President the good sense and free spirit of our countrymen will make the change necessary to prevent it" (378–379).

112. Indeed, Washington wrote in a 1788 letter that "I differ widely myself from Mr. Jefferson . . . as to the necessity or expediency of rotation in that department [the presidency]. . . . I can see no propriety in precluding ourselves from the services of any man who in some great emergency shall be deemed universally most capable of serving the public." Even Jefferson later told the Vermont legislature that "one circumstance could engage my acquiescence in another election; to wit, such a division about a successor, as might bring in a monarchist" (ibid., 379, 378).

113. For example, John Quincy Adams described the two-term tradition as "tacit subsidiary Constitutional law." Quoted in Arthur B. Tourtellot, *The Presidents on the Presidency* (Garden City, N.Y.: Doubleday, 1964), 34–35.

114. Quoted in Corwin, *President,* 42.

115. In his acceptance speech, delivered by radio from the Oval Office to the convention in Chicago by a president "too busy" to leave his "post of duty," Roosevelt said: "I find myself . . . in a conflict between deep personal desire for retirement . . . and that quiet invisible thing called conscience. . . . Lying awake, as I have on many nights, I have asked myself whether I have the right, as Commander-in-Chief of the Army and Navy, to call on men and women to serve their country or to train themselves to serve, and at the same time decline to serve my country in my personal capacity, if I am called upon to do so by the people of my country."

116. Paul G. Willis and George L. Willis, "The Politics of the Twenty-second Amendment," *Western Political Quarterly* 5 (September 1952): 469.

117. Quoted in Willis and Willis, "Politics of the Twenty-second Amendment," 470.

118. The Twenty-seventh Amendment, which restricts Congress's ability to raise its members' salaries, was ratified in 1992, a record 203 years after Congress sent it to the states in 1789.

119. Kyvig, *Explicit and Authentic Acts,* 332–333.

120. Michael R. Beschloss, *Mayday: Eisenhower, Khrushchev, and the U-2 Affair* (New York: Harper and Row, 1986), 3.

121. Roberta S. Sigel, "Image of the American Presidency: Part II of an Exploration into Popular Views of the Presidential Power," *Midwest Journal of Political Science* 10 (February 1966): 125–126. Sigel also reported a public opinion poll that showed six-to-one support for the two-term limit.

122. A third matter—the right of the vice president to succeed to the office, not just assume the powers, of the presidency—also is treated in the Twenty-fifth Amendment. The original Constitution was vague as to whether the vice president was to become president or merely acting president when the president died, resigned, or was removed. John Tyler had asserted the vice president's right of full

successorship when he succeeded President William Henry Harrison in 1841, which set the precedent for future successions. Section 1 of the Twenty-fifth Amendment simply wrote this practice into the Constitution: "In case of the removal of the President from office or of his death or resignation, the Vice President shall become President."

123. John D. Feerick, *The Twenty-fifth Amendment* (New York: Fordham University Press, 1992), 13; Irving G. Williams, *The Rise of the Vice Presidency* (Washington, D.C.: Public Affairs Press, 1956), 112, 114.

124. In addition to Garfield and Wilson, there were James Madison, William Henry Harrison, Chester A. Arthur, Grover Cleveland, William McKinley, Warren G. Harding, Franklin D. Roosevelt, Dwight D. Eisenhower, John F. Kennedy, and Ronald Reagan. Feerick, *Twenty-fifth Amendment,* chap. 1.

125. The seven vice presidents who died in office were George Clinton (1812), Elbridge Gerry (1814), William R. King (1853), Henry Wilson (1875), Thomas A. Hendricks (1885), Garret A. Hobart (1889), and James S. Sherman (1912). The eight presidents who died in office were: William Henry Harrison, who was succeeded by Vice President John Tyler (1841), Zachary Taylor, succeeded by Millard Fillmore (1850), Abraham Lincoln, succeeded by Andrew Johnson (1865), James A. Garfield, succeeded by Chester A. Arthur (1881), William McKinley, succeeded by Theodore Roosevelt (1901), Warren G. Harding, succeeded by Calvin Coolidge (1923), Franklin D. Roosevelt, succeeded by Harry S. Truman (1945), and John F. Kennedy, succeeded by Lyndon B. Johnson (1963). The vice president who resigned was John C. Calhoun (1832).

126. Feerick, *Twenty-fifth Amendment,* 61.

127. Ibid., 200–202.

128. Georgia, North Dakota, and South Carolina voted against ratification.

129. White House, Office of the Press Secretary, "Remarks by the President Upon Departure for Camp David," June 28, 2002.

130. Kyvig, *Explicit and Authentic Acts,* 179.

131. *Guinn and Beall v. United States,* 238 U.S. 347 (1915); and *Smith v. Allwright,* 321 U.S. 649 (1944).

132. Harold W. Stanley and Richard G. Niemi, *Vital Statistics on American Politics,* 5th ed. (Washington, D.C.: CQ Press, 1995), 97–98.

133. Stanley and Niemi, *Vital Statistics on American Politics.*

134. Nelson, "Election: Ordinary Politics, Extraordinary Outcome," 6.

135. *Oregon v. Mitchell,* 400 U.S. 112 (1972).

136. Stanley and Niemi, *Vital Statistics on American Politics,* 79.

137. See, for example, Frederick G. Dutton, *Changing Sources of Power: American Politics in the 1970s* (New York: McGraw-Hill, 1971).

138. Maryland and Virginia contributed the land to build a capital city.

139. Currently, the District's population is about the same as Delaware's, so it would continue to have three electoral votes.

140. *Harper v. Virginia Board of Electors,* 383 U.S. 163 (1966).

SELECTED BIBLIOGRAPHY

Barbash, Fred. *The Founding: A Dramatic Account of the Writing of the Constitution.* New York: Linden Press/Simon and Schuster, 1987.

Beard, Charles A. *An Economic Interpretation of the Constitution.* New York: Macmillan, 1913.

Berkin, Carol. *A Brilliant Solution: Inventing the American Constitution.* New York: Harcourt, 2002.

Bowen, Catherine Drinker. *Miracle at Philadelphia.* Boston: Little, Brown, 1966.

Chernow, Ron. *Alexander Hamilton.* New York: Penguin, 2004.

Collier, Christopher, and James Lincoln Collier. *Decision in Philadelphia: The Constitutional Convention of 1787.* New York: Ballantine, 1986.

Corwin, Edward S. *The President: Office and Powers, 1787–1984.* 5th rev. ed. New York: New York University Press, 1984.

Cronin, Thomas E., ed. *Inventing the American Presidency.* Lawrence: University Press of Kansas, 1989.

Elkins, Stanley, and Eric McKitrick. *The Age of Federalism: The Early American Republic, 1788–1800.* New York: Oxford University Press, 1993.

———. "The Founding Fathers: Young Men of the Revolution." *Political Science Quarterly* 76 (June 1961): 181–216.

Ellis, Joseph J. *His Excellency, George Washington.* New York: Knopf, 2004.

———., ed. *Founding the American Presidency.* Lanham, Md.: Rowan and Littlefield, 1999.

Farrand, Max, ed. *The Records of the Federal Convention of 1787.* New Haven: Yale University Press, 1913.

Hutson, James H., ed. *Supplement to Max Farrand's The Records of the Federal Convention of 1787.* New Haven: Yale University Press, 1987.

Isaacson, Walter. *Benjamin Franklin: An American Life.* New York: Simon and Schuster, 2003.

Kenyon, Cecelia M., ed. *The Antifederalists.* Indianapolis: Bobbs-Merrill, 1966.

Ketcham, Ralph, ed. *The Anti-Federalist Papers and the Constitutional Convention Debates.* New York: New American Library, 1986.

Kyvig, David E. *Explicit and Authentic Acts: Amending the U.S. Constitution, 1776–1995.* Lawrence: University Press of Kansas, 1996.

Locke, John. *Second Treatise on Government.* Indianapolis: Bobbs-Merrill, 1952.

Mee, Charles L., Jr. *The Genius of the People.* New York: Harper and Row, 1987.

Milkis, Sidney M., and Michael Nelson. *The American Presidency: Origins and Development, 1776–1998.* Washington, D.C.: CQ Press, 1999.

Nelson, Michael. "Constitutional Qualifications for the President." *Presidential Studies Quarterly* 17 (spring 1987): 383–399.

Peters, William. *A More Perfect Union: The Making of the United States Constitution.* New York: Crown, 1987.

Rakove, Jack N. *Original Meanings: Politics and Ideas in the Making of the Constitution.* New York: Knopf, 1996.

Roche, John. "The Founding Fathers: A Reform Caucus in Action." *American Political Science Review* 55 (December 1961): 799–816.

Rossiter, Clinton. *1787: The Grand Convention.* London: MacGibbon and Kee, 1968.

Slonim, Schlomo. "The Electoral College at Philadelphia: The Evolution of an Ad Hoc Congress for the Selection of a President." *Journal of American History* 73 (1986): 35–58.

Sundquist, James L. *Constitutional Reform and Effective Government.* Rev. ed. Washington, D.C.: Brookings, 1992.

Thach, Charles C., Jr. *The Creation of the Presidency, 1775–1789.* Baltimore: Johns Hopkins University Press, 1969.

Wood, Gordon S. *The Creation of the American Republic, 1776–1787.* Chapel Hill: University of North Carolina Press, 1969.

———. *Revolutionary Characters: What Made the Founders Different.* New York: Penguin, 2006.

chapter 2

History of the Presidency

by Sidney M. Milkis

The Constitution of 1787 provides only the barest outline of the duties and responsibilities of the president. Article II was loosely drawn and thus left considerable leeway for future presidents and events to shape the executive office. By stating that "the Executive Power shall be vested in a President of the United States" and that "he shall take care that the laws be faithfully executed," without in most cases stipulating what those executive and administrative responsibilities would be, the Constitution has given rise to more than two centuries of conflict over the appropriate extent of presidential authority.

This chapter examines the major developments that have shaped the idea of presidential power in U.S. history, as well as the institutional changes that have followed from the debates and struggles over the proper definition of executive authority.

THE PRESIDENCY OF GEORGE WASHINGTON

The election of George Washington in 1789 as the first president of the United States was never in doubt. Yet, as one historian has written, "Never was the election of a president so much a foregone conclusion and yet so tortuous in consummation." [1]

The electoral college met on February 4, 1789, but its unanimous vote for Washington could not be official until the president of the Senate, temporarily elected for the purpose, opened the ballots in the presence of both houses of Congress. According to the Constitution, Congress was due to convene in New York, the first capital, on March 4 (in 1933 the Twentieth Amendment changed the date to January 3). The newly elected legislators were slow to arrive, however, and a quorum still had not been reached by the

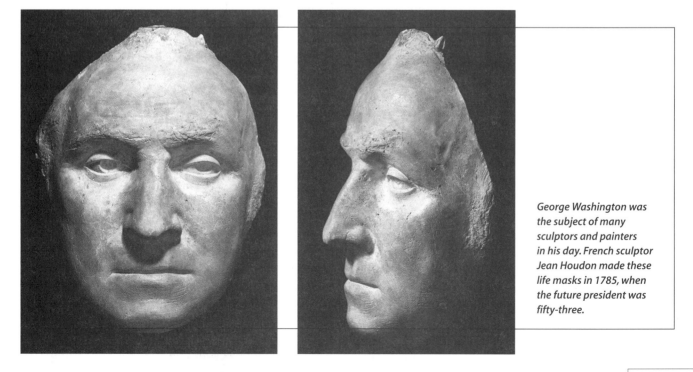

George Washington was the subject of many sculptors and painters in his day. French sculptor Jean Houdon made these life masks in 1785, when the future president was fifty-three.

end of the month. Any candidate other than Washington might have been in the capital in time for the opening of Congress, which finally occurred when the House obtained a bare quorum on April 1 and the Senate on April 6, but Washington wanted to fulfill the strictest requirements of correct behavior. Because he would not be elected officially until a joint session of Congress tallied the votes of the electors, he waited for formal word at his Mount Vernon, Virginia, home and worried over the "stupor or listlessness" being displayed by the members of the newly forming legislative body on whom the success of the Constitution largely would depend.[2]

Ironically, the start of the new government was further delayed by Washington himself who, upon finally receiving notice of his election on April 14 from Secretary of the Congress Charles Thompson, took his time riding from Virginia to New York "lest unseemly haste suggest that he was improperly eager for the office." [3] Because the president-elect believed that the future of the government required its acceptance by the people, he was concerned with how his progress through the states to the capital would be received. The popular adulation that greeted him during the trip made obvious his country's devotion to him. The nation's first president finally arrived in New York in time to be inaugurated on April 30.

The long and complicated business involved both in the election of Washington and his assuming the responsibilities of the chief executive foretold of the major task of his administration: "to make the government which had been adopted, often by the thinnest of majorities, and in only eleven out of thirteen states, happily acceptable to the overwhelming majority of the entire population." [4] This was an ambitious task: it required the construction of a unified and energetic national government on a political landscape that was traditionally inhospitable to strong central authority. That the "more perfect union" framed by the Constitution included a strong executive authority was particularly notable, even radical in the American context, for executive power had been the object of distrust in America for a long time. In most of the state constitutions and in the Articles of Confederation, executive power was weak. The author of the Declaration of Independence, Thomas Jefferson, wrote James Madison in December 1787 to register his opposition to the Constitution's creation of a strong president: "I own that I am not a friend to a very energetic government. It is always oppressive." [5]

In view of this tradition, bringing the presidency to life successfully may have been an impossible task without Washington's great popularity and propriety. Indeed, Washington was, or so James Madison wrote in 1789, the only aspect of the government that had caught the public imagination.[6]

Making the Presidency Safe for Democracy

As America's first "republican monarch," the historian Joanne Freeman has written, "Washington had an exceedingly difficult role: somehow he had to embody the new government's dignity and authority without rising to monarchical excess." [7] Washington's awe-inspiring personality and popularity made him an indispensable source of unity and legitimacy for the newly formed government. At the same time, to those who were suspicious of strong executive power, these qualities made him seem extremely dangerous. The result was that many of the conflicts that arose during Washington's administration and that of his successor, John Adams, involved efforts to make executive power compatible with representative democracy.

For example, Washington's schedule became a subject of controversy at the start of his administration, prompting him to distribute queries to his trusted advisers "on a line of conduct most eligible to be pursued by the President of the United States." The challenge, as Washington understood it, was to establish precedents for the conduct of the presidency that would allow the executive enough privacy to get his work done and sufficient distance to retain the dignity of the office, without giving the impression that he disdained contact with the people. The course that Washington decided on satisfied neither those, such as Vice President John Adams and Treasury secretary Alexander Hamilton, who wanted to insulate the president from excessive popular influence nor zealous republicans who wished to see an open executive office. Nevertheless, he revealed his great sensitivity to the importance of attaining public support and respect for the presidency through activities that, no matter how mundane, were of great symbolic importance:

> Washington established two occasions a week when any respectably dressed person could, without introduction, invitation, or any prearrangement, be ushered into his presence. One was the President's "levee," for men only, every Tuesday from three to four. The other was Martha's tea party, for men and women, held on Friday evenings. Washington would also stage dinners on Thursdays at four o'clock in the afternoon. To avoid any charges of favoritism or any contests for invitations, only officials and their families would be asked to the dinners, and these in an orderly system of rotation.[8]

A more controversial issue of etiquette was the form of address for the new president. A committee of the House of Representatives suggested simply "the President of the United States," as in the Constitution. But the Senate in May 1789, at the behest of Vice President John Adams, rejected the House report. Adams, believing that "titles and politically inspired elegance were essential aspects of strong government," supported the title "His Highness the President of the United States and protector of their Liberties." Washington initially had wanted the president to have a title nearly as grand as Adams suggested: "His High Mightiness, the President of the United States and Protector of Their Liberties." [9] But when he saw how controversial the matter was he threw his support to Madison, even expressing annoyance at Adams's efforts "to bedizen him with a superb but spurious title." On May 27 the Senate agreed that the chief executive should have no fancier title than "the President of the United States."

Forming the Executive Department

During Washington's first term, Congress passed bills setting up three major departments of government: the Departments of State, Treasury, and War. The heads of these departments were nominated by the president and ratified by the Senate.

For secretary of state, Washington chose Jefferson, who as minister to France had shown himself to be an excellent diplomat. Alexander Hamilton, a recognized expert on finance and commerce, became head of Treasury. Gen. Henry Knox, a diligent administrator, who as chief of artillery had served Washington reliably during the Revolutionary War, was selected to be secretary of war. Edmund Randolph of Virginia became the first attorney general. The office of attorney general did not yet possess the status and dignity of a department, but after 1792 its incumbent regularly attended cabinet meetings and served as legal adviser of the president and of the department heads.

In forming the cabinet and the executive branch, the Washington administration employed highly informal procedures. In general, the administration was ad hoc and personal. The notion of a "president's cabinet" did not even take form during the early years of Washington's tenure. Washington did not use the word *cabinet* until April 1793, and he did not call formal meetings of the department heads until close to the end of his first term.

Administrative informality did not mean, however, that the appointments and procedures of Washington's presidency had no purpose. Recognizing the need to invest the national government with talent and moral character that would advance the acceptability of the new government, Washington sought the most brilliant people possible in carrying out its functions. The president's three principal aides—Hamilton, Jefferson, and Madison, a member of the House of Representatives from Virginia—formed a remarkable constellation of advisers; in the generation after Washington, they became the nation's most important political leaders. Washington recognized the varied talents of these three independent-minded leaders and, for a time, was able to yoke them in a "single harness." His ability to do so and the general success that he achieved as an administrator helped "plant in the minds of the American people the model of a government which commanded respect by reason of its integrity, energy, and competence." [10]

Washington's appointments to minor jobs in the government also were made with attention to the need to establish the legitimacy of the fledgling national government. As the various enactments creating the major departments became law during his first term, the president found himself with nearly a thousand offices to fill. Considering these appointments important, Washington devoted an enormous amount of time to them: "no collector of customs, captain of a cutter, keeper of a lighthouse, or surveyor of revenue was appointed except after specific consideration by the President." [11]

Although besieged by applicants, directly or through intermediaries, Washington "scrupulously declined to exploit the opportunity to create a patronage system." His appointments were only partisan in the sense that he chose persons "of known attachment" to the new government.[12] Washington also was less concerned with expertise as such

After Congress established the major executive departments, President George Washington chose well-known figures for his first cabinet. On Washington's left are Henry Knox, secretary of war; Alexander Hamilton, secretary of the Treasury; Thomas Jefferson, secretary of state; and Edmund Randolph, attorney general.

than he was with a strong commitment to the Constitution and the applicants' reputations for "good character." Apart from personal integrity, standing in one's local community was a principal ingredient of fitness, reflecting Washington's desire to cultivate a favorable opinion of the national government in the far flung sections of the Union. As historians Stanley Elkins and Eric McKitrick have observed, Washington routinely referred to his appointees as "first Characters . . . who by virtue of their abilities and records of public service stood first, as it were, in the respect of their neighbors." [13] In sum, Washington's personnel policies manifested his concern for the requirements of building a nation.

Presidential Supremacy and Conduct of the Executive Department

In addition to his hiring policies, Washington established the critical precedent that authority over the executive branch belongs primarily to the president. He subscribed to a theory of administration that viewed members of the cabinet as "assistants or deputies" of the president. As Hamilton had written in *Federalist* No. 72, such persons "ought to derive their offices from his appointment, at least from his nomination, and ought to be subject to his superintendence." Washington's theory of national administration prevailed against competing views that foresaw either the Senate or individual cabinet officers sharing fully in the direction of the executive departments.[14]

The belief that the upper house of the legislature should be involved in the details of administration was especially strong in the American tradition, reaching far back into the colonial era. Indeed, a bill nearly passed Congress during Washington's first term that would have severely restricted the president's administrative authority. The bill, which involved the creation of the State Department, raised the issue of where the power to dismiss an executive official should lie. Significantly, Hamilton's advocacy of the "deputy" theory of administration did not extend to the removal of executive officeholders. In *Federalist* No. 77, he had cited the principle of "steady administration" to contend that the Senate's approval would be needed to remove an official, just as it was to appoint one. Opponents of a strong presidency seized on Hamilton's position to contend that the constitutional provision that presidents can appoint only with Senate approval implies that they can dismiss only with Senate approval.

Washington and Madison, his chief congressional ally in this matter, responded that presidents would be rendered impotent if they were not the master of their own domain. As Madison argued during the House debate on the State Department bill, "Vest [the removal power] in the Senate jointly with the President, and you abolish at once the great principle of unity and responsibility in the executive department, which was intended for the security of liberty and the common good." [15] In other words, how could the president be held accountable for the actions of incompetent or disobedient executive officials if he could not remove them under his own authority?

Madison successfully led the fight in the House against senatorial interference with presidential removals; but the Senate was evenly divided, and the final vote was tied. Vice President Adams, as presiding officer, broke the tie in favor of the president's unilateral power to remove executive appointees from office. From then on, Congress followed Madison's leadership in passing laws establishing the major departments of government that were carefully designed to minimize the legislature's influence on the executive branch.

Congress's eventual acquiescence to presidential supremacy over the executive departments was probably a tribute to Washington's devotion to the separation of powers. The president shared Madison's view that the chief executive should be supreme in matters pertaining to the conduct of the executive branch but restrained in matters that were rightfully the legislature's. Washington did recommend legislation to Congress, albeit sparingly, but he made no special effort to get his program enacted. Nor, the Washington biographer James Thomas Flexner has observed, "did he attempt during his first term to achieve by executive orders any matter which the strictest interpretation of the Constitution could regard as within the legislative domain." [16]

Hamilton had argued in *Federalist* No. 73 that aggressive use of the veto was essential for the president to protect the office from legislative usurpation and to "furnish security against the enaction of improper laws." But Washington adhered to the view that the presidential veto power properly extended only to bills of doubtful constitutionality, not to unwise policy.[17]

Washington's propriety in executive-legislative relations extended even to foreign policy. Washington did not hesitate to assert his primacy in diplomatic affairs, but he worked hard to develop lines of communication between the chief executive and the Senate, which he believed the Constitution required in its stipulation that the president seek the Senate's "advice and consent" on treaties. Washington initially considered this constitutional requirement to mean prior consultation with the Senate, before treaty negotiations began. But his efforts to involve the Senate fully in the making of treaties resulted in an awkward and embarrassing incident that established a precedent contrary to his desire to consult the upper chamber.

Having drafted instructions for a commission he had appointed, with Senate approval, to negotiate a treaty with the Creek Indians, Washington accompanied acting secretary of war Knox to the Senate chamber in August 1789, seeking "advice and consent." After the treaty was read to the Senate by Vice President Adams, however, the president's appeal for consultation was met by a "dead pause," an awkward silence broken reluctantly by the senators, who proceeded to engage in a confused and feeble discussion of the treaty. Finally, Sen. William Maclay of Pennsylvania, sensing that there was "no chance of a fair investigation of subjects while the President of the United States sat there," recommended that the papers of the president be submitted to a committee for study. As the senator sat down after making this recommendation, Washington started up in what Maclay described as a "violent fret" and cried out: "This defeats every purpose of my coming here." [18]

Although in the end Washington achieved his purpose—the treaty was ratified with only minor changes—neither he nor any subsequent president ever again consulted the Senate in person. Most significant, Washington's failure to obtain the active cooperation of the Senate in the preliminary work of making treaties firmly established presidential supremacy in matters of diplomacy. The president did not come into possession of an unhampered power to make treaties, but the Washington administration established a precedent whereby the Senate was relegated to approving or rejecting a treaty that was negotiated by the chief executive without prior consultation.

Presidential Nonpartisanship and the Beginning of Party Conflict

Washington's conduct as president embodied his understanding that the presidency is a nonpartisan office. Like most of the Framers of the Constitution, he disapproved of "factions" and did not see himself as the leader of any political party. Although Washington insisted on being master of the executive branch, trying to influence elections or the legislative process was contrary to his principles. He believed his primary duty was to enforce the laws.

Hamilton and Jefferson

Washington's conception of the presidency, however, did not survive even his own administration. Ultimately, disagreements within his brilliant constellation of advisers led to the early demise of the nonpartisan presidency. Party conflict arose from the sharp differences between Hamilton and Jefferson that emerged during Washington's first term and became irreconcilable during the second term. These differences became obvious in reaction to Hamilton's financial measures for the "adequate support of public credit," which he proposed in a series of reports presented to Congress between 1790 and 1791. In the reports, Hamilton called on Congress to assume the war debts of the states, to create a national bank, and to enact a system of tariffs to protect infant manufacturing industries in the United States.

Jefferson did not oppose all of Hamilton's measures. For example, he approved Hamilton's plan to pay the national government's domestic and foreign debt. But Jefferson, and eventually Madison, opposed Hamilton's program for a national bank, which was contained in the Treasury secretary's report presented to Congress in December 1790. According to Jefferson and Madison, Hamilton's plan would establish national institutions and policies that transcended the powers of Congress. Furthermore, the proposed domestic and international initiatives presupposed a principal role for the president in formulating and carrying out public policy. This necessarily subordinated, Jefferson and Madison believed, the more decentralizing and democratic institutions—Congress and the states—to the executive, thus undermining popular sovereignty and pushing the United States toward a British-style monarchy.

The Neutrality Proclamation of 1793

When war between Great Britain and France broke out in 1793, a difference of opinion regarding the executive's proper role in foreign affairs aggravated the growing rift between Hamilton and Jefferson. The Anglo-French question provoked a bitter exchange of views about the executive's proper role in foreign policy when President Washington issued the Neutrality Proclamation of 1793.

The proclamation declared that the duties and interests of the United States required that it "should with sincerity and good faith adopt and pursue a conduct friendly and impartial to the belligerent powers." To Americans, it prohibited "committing, aiding, or abetting hostilities against any of the said powers, or by carrying to them any of those articles which are deemed contraband by the modern usage of nations." [19]

The great controversy stirred by this policy prompted Hamilton to defend the executive proclamation in a series of newspaper articles under the pseudonym "Pacificus." Madison, at the urging of Jefferson, replied to these articles in the "Helvidius" letters. Supporting the neutrality proclamation, Hamilton put forth a sweeping defense of discretionary presidential power. In doing so, he distinguished between the grants of legislative and executive power. Article I of the Constitution states: "All legislative powers herein granted shall be vested in a Congress of the United States." Article II provides a much more general grant: "The executive power shall be vested in the President of the United States." Hamilton argued that the broad language of Article II, not having the words *herein granted*, meant that the executive power of the nation was both wide ranging and vested exclusively in the presidency, "subject only to the exceptions and qualifications which are expressed in the Constitution."

In foreign affairs, the explicit constitutional restrictions on presidential power extended no further than the right of the Senate to approve treaties and of Congress to declare war. These rights of the legislature, insisted Hamilton, did not hinder the executive in other matters of foreign policy, which "naturally" was the domain of the president.[20] Indeed, Hamilton not only set forth a theory of presidential power that delegated to the chief executive nearly absolute discretion in foreign affairs but also proposed a broad conception of "emergency powers which later Presidents, particularly those in the twentieth century, would generously draw upon." [21]

Madison, replying as Helvidius, denied that foreign policy was "naturally" an executive power. The tasks of foreign policy—the powers to declare war, to conclude peace, and to form alliances—were among "the highest acts of sovereignty; of which the legislative power must at least be an integral and preeminent part." In foreign policy, as in domestic matters, Madison argued, representative government required that the president's power be confined to the execution of laws. To suggest, as Hamilton did, that foreign policy was within the proper definition of executive power, implying in effect that the executive department naturally included a legislative power, was "in theory an absurdity—in practice a tyranny." [22]

Important as it was, the precedent established by Washington that the president can unilaterally enunciate a policy of neutrality was less significant than the larger principle in the debate that took place between Washington's leading advisers—namely, whether the president was to be limited by the letter of the Constitution or was a sovereign head of state, with discretion to act independently, barring where the Constitution specifically "enumerated" exceptions and limitations. The debate between Pacificus and Helvidius was the first of many such struggles about the proper boundaries of executive power. Washington's hope of establishing a presidency above parties proved impractical, thwarted by fundamental conflicts about the constitutional interpretation of presidential power.

Ultimately, this debate caused strains that made open party conflict inevitable. The full implications of this conflict between the Federalists, who shared Hamilton's point of view, and the Democratic-Republicans, who shared Jefferson's, became clear during the presidency of John Adams, who took office in 1797. Still, this party conflict never became as raw and disruptive as the Framers feared factional strife might be. The enduring limits of "factionalism" in the United States were probably attributable largely to Washington's forceful example of nonpartisanship. To some extent Washington sought to deal with the divisive conflict between the Hamiltonians and Jeffersonians by avoiding it, by choosing to continue to "preside" rather than to lead and direct.[23] He thereby exerted a moderating influence at a time when maintaining unity was critical to the survival of the new government. In domestic and foreign policy Washington did take stands, usually tilting to the Hamiltonian point of view. Yet his extraordinary stature and popularity, combined with a commitment to the existence of a strong and independent legislature, restrained partisan strife as long as he presided over the nation. Moreover,

Washington's renunciation of party leadership, clearly articulated in his Farewell Address, left his successors a legacy of presidential "impartiality" that has never been completely eclipsed. *(See "Washington's Farewell Address," p. 1754, in Reference Materials, Vol. II.)* Even after a formal party system emerged, the Washington precedent demanded that the chief executive lead the nation, not just the party that governed the nation.

THE RISE OF PARTY POLITICS AND THE TRIUMPH OF JEFFERSONIANISM

The end of Washington's administration marked an important change in the executive office. This change is best characterized as the transformation of the presidency from a nonpartisan to a partisan institution. This change did not entail a complete metamorphosis. Those who were leaders in the first great party conflicts in the United States—John Adams, Alexander Hamilton, Thomas Jefferson, and James Madison—viewed partisanship with great disfavor. Yet the struggles that followed Washington's tenure made open party conflict a central part of the American presidency. Thereafter, presidents might attempt to rise above party, but partisanship had become an unavoidable condition of effective presidential leadership.

Washington's Retirement and the 1796 Election

As the end of 1795 approached, the paramount question for most public figures in the United States was whether Washington would accept another term as president. The Constitution imposed no limit on presidential reeligibility, and although Washington's political reputation was slightly tarnished by the partisan animosities that had divided his cabinet, he could easily have remained in office had he chosen to do so.

Washington, however, was anxious to return to Mount Vernon. In September 1796 he announced his retirement, an event marked by the release of his Farewell Address, which was published rather than spoken to an audience. Washington's voluntary retirement set a precedent for limiting presidents to two terms, a practice that endured for nearly 150 years. (The two-term limit became part of the Constitution with the ratification of the Twenty-second Amendment in 1951.) His decision eased somewhat the Jeffersonians' concerns about the dangerous use of executive power. Washington's example converted Jefferson from his original belief that the president should serve a single seven-year term.[24]

Washington's retirement cleared the way for a more partisan form of presidential politics. As long as the first president was on the scene, he was able by dint of his prestige to restrain open party conflict. But Vice President Adams, although a distinguished and respected statesman, lacked Washington's stature as well as his reputation for impartiality. In the division between Federalists and Democratic-Republicans, Adams was clearly identified with the Federalists. His role in the controversy over the president's title and his well-known admiration for the British form of government marked him in the eyes of Jeffersonians as a monarchist.

In the campaign of 1796, generally considered one of the most bitter and scurrilous in U.S. history, the appearances of nonpartisanship gave way to competition between national political parties. For the first time in a presidential election, a contest was organized around two party tickets. The Federalists supported John Adams and Thomas Pinckney for president and vice president, respectively. The Democratic-Republicans chose Thomas Jefferson for president and Aaron Burr for vice president.

The issues that divided the Federalists and Democratic-Republicans in the election of 1796 were crystallized by the controversial Jay Treaty, signed in London in November 1794. Through this treaty, the United States secured a promise from Britain to evacuate by 1796 the northwest posts, which had sustained a British presence on U.S. soil since the Revolution, and a limited right of U.S. vessels to trade with the British West Indies. As such, the treaty secured the territorial integrity of the United States and helped to end dangerous conflicts at sea, resulting from Britain's war with France, that had brought the United States and Britain to the brink of war. Yet, when the terms of the treaty were released November 2, 1795, a firestorm of controversy ensued that made the Washington administration and John Jay (the chief justice of the United States who, as a presidential envoy, negotiated the agreement with Great Britain) the target of vicious party attacks.

Democratic-Republican opposition to the Jay Treaty was animated by a strong dislike of the British, which was reinforced by Britain's use of western posts as vantage points for the arming of Indians and rebel slaves to attack settlers in the Northwest Territory. To Democratic-Republicans, the Jay Treaty reflected the Washington administration's preference for the British monarchy over the French Republic. In effect, the Jay Treaty became the issue through which the emerging polarization between Hamiltonians and Jeffersonians was hardened into organized two-party conflict.[25]

In spite of the strong disagreements that divided Federalists and Democratic-Republicans, the contestants in the partisan strife of the 1790s were reluctant warriors. Partisanship was still not considered respectable in U.S. politics, and candidates for president were not expected to seek the office actively. Both Adams and Jefferson made efforts to stay above party conflicts, even as they (Jefferson especially) worked behind the scenes to achieve the triumph of the parties they represented. Neither Adams nor Jefferson made the slightest public effort to influence the outcome of the elec-

tion, as both considered it unethical to campaign on their own or their parties' behalf.

The result of the 1796 election was a narrow Federalist victory. Adams obtained the presidency with seventy-one electoral votes: he swept New England and, except for Pennsylvania, the Middle Atlantic states, while he lost the South. Jefferson's sixty-eight electoral votes made him vice president, as the nonpartisan constitutional mechanism for selecting the president and vice president had not yet been changed to accommodate the outbreak of partisan competition. The Constitution originally directed that every elector vote for two persons for president, with the second place candidate becoming vice president. This mechanism did not easily accommodate the selection of a party ticket, a fact that was not changed until the Twelfth Amendment was ratified in 1804. Hence the election of 1796 yielded a presidential administration shared by the leaders of deeply divided political organizations.

The Embattled Presidency of John Adams

John Adams became president in extraordinarily difficult circumstances. No other chief executive would have the unenviable task of succeeding a leader of Washington's stature. More significant, the foreign situation that Adams faced in 1797 was perilous. The Jay Treaty had greatly worsened U.S. relations with an aggressive French government, which, after Napoleon Bonaparte had beaten Austria in October 1797, was at the height of its power. The French interference with U.S. commerce at sea made Britain's interference in 1793 seem mild in comparison. As Jefferson said of George Washington's retirement, "The President is fortunate to get off just as the bubble is bursting, leaving others to hold the bag."[26]

The virtual naval war with France was severely aggravated when Adams's diplomatic attempts to maintain Washington's policy of neutrality resulted in insulting and humiliating treatment by the French foreign ministry. The French foreign minister, Talleyrand, sent three representatives of the French government (referred to in dispatches as "X, Y, and Z") to confront the U.S. emissaries in Paris and to find out how much the United States was willing to pay in bribes to French officials and loans to the French government to secure a treaty. When the "XYZ affair" became public early in 1798, a furor erupted in the United States that seemed to make war with France inevitable.

Adams's efforts to deal with the domestic and international crises of the late 1790s continued to be hindered as much by members of his own party as by the opposition. Although everyone expected the Democratic-Republicans, led behind the scenes by Vice President Jefferson, to oppose Adams's actions, "the Federalists were often as recalcitrant or bitter toward the president."[27] His most influential critic within the party was Hamilton, who regarded Adams as being too moderate politically and therefore incapable of dealing with the nation's problems.

Adams was a Federalist, but he intended to follow Washington's example of remaining above party as much as possible. The president was willing to accept a war declared by France but hoped to avoid one. His primary objectives were to protect American commerce, through diplomacy and an expanded navy, and to force the French to respect the American flag. Hamilton and his Arch-Federalist allies, however, wanted to exploit the conflict with France, not to contain it. Ultimately, these differences caused an irreconcilable split to occur within the Federalist Party. Jefferson noted in May 1797 that the "Hamiltons" were "only a little less hostile [to Adams] than to me." [28]

Hamilton severely tested the president's authority in several ways. He was determined to guide the policy of the government, even though he was not a part of it. Hamilton had retired from the Treasury at the end of January 1795, but during the latter days of Washington's second term and throughout Adams's tenure he remained the dynamic center of the Federalist Party. Indeed, Hamilton's influence was enhanced after 1797 as a result of Adams's decision to retain Washington's cabinet, a policy the new president pursued both in deference to the stature of his predecessor and because he believed that good government required the presence of able and experienced administrators. [29]

Three members of Washington's cabinet, Secretary of State Timothy Pickering, Secretary of War James McHenry, and Oliver Wolcott, who succeeded Hamilton as head of the Treasury, largely owed their government positions to Hamilton, who had persuaded Washington to appoint them. In all-important questions they looked to Hamilton, and not Adams, to guide their actions. Only Charles Lee, the attorney general and the least powerful cabinet member, and Benjamin Stoddert, who joined the cabinet as head of the newly established Navy Department in 1798, were loyal to Adams. Consequently, unity of executive policy was achieved only when the president agreed with Hamilton. Thus in Adams's administration there emerged "an extraordinary situation in which the control of public policy became the prize of a struggle between a New York lawyer and a president who apparently was not fully aware of the activity of his rival." [30]

The rising conflict between Adams and the Arch-Federalists culminated in 1799. Early that year, Adams prepared to send a second mission to France in an effort to avoid war. In February 1799, without previous consultation with the secretary of state or the cabinet, he nominated William Vans Murray, then minister to the Netherlands, as minister plenipotentiary to the French Republic. Murray was chosen because of his good relations with France. Adams learned through Murray of France's willingness to receive a new U.S. mission and desire to avoid war with the United States. The Senate, which was sympathetic to Hamilton's

views, would have rejected the nomination, but Adams's quick and unilateral action caught its members by surprise. Instead, senators compromised by asking for a commission of three. The president consented.

Thwarting attempts by Secretary of State Pickering and others to postpone the sailing of the second mission, Adams first indicated that he was not opposed to a delay, but then hurried the peace commission aboard an American frigate. The mission arrived in time to take advantage of France's uncertain situation in the aftermath of a series of military defeats by the British. Although Adams's bold course aggravated his problems with the cabinet and the Federalist Party, it achieved a commercial agreement with France that ended the threat of war, thus preserving the principle of neutrality toward Europe that he inherited from the Washington administration.

More significant, Adams rescued the authority of the presidency. Adams's position was shaken by this incident; in all likelihood it cost him his chance for reelection. But as Leonard White, a scholar on the early development of the U.S. presidency, has written:

> the outcome was a resounding affirmation of the authority of the President as chief executive and of the subordination of the department heads to his leadership and direction. Adams confirmed the character of the presidency as the Constitutional Convention had outlined it and as Washington had already formed it—but only after events which stirred grave doubts concerning its future. [31]

Solidifying his leadership in the aftermath of the peace mission, Adams rid the cabinet of the two men who were most disloyal to him. In May 1800, he asked for McHenry's resignation, which he received, and summarily removed Pickering when the latter refused to resign. Pickering thus became the first cabinet officer to be removed by a president.

Although historians frequently have praised John Adams for upholding the authority of the presidency in the face of a badly divided cabinet and party, he has been condemned for his role in the passage and enforcement of the Alien and Sedition Acts in 1798. The Alien Act gave the president authority to expel any foreigner considered dangerous to the public peace; the Sedition Act made it a crime, punishable by fine or imprisonment, to bring "false, scandalous and malicious" accusations against the president, Congress, or the government.

The Alien Act generally was viewed as a defensible measure in support of the national government's right of self-protection, even though it was taken to task severely by the Democratic-Republicans for vesting extraordinary powers in the hands of the president and thus violating the principle of the separation of powers. The sedition law, however, was widely denounced as unconstitutional. To be sure, the act was not as oppressive as similar European statutes: it imposed on the prosecution the burden to prove an "intent to defame" and required a jury trial to convict. But the law was enforced in ways that treated legitimate political opposition as if it were conspiracy against the government. As such, the Sedition Act violated the First Amendment of the Constitution, which had been added in 1791 as part of the Bill of Rights and which, among other things, forbade Congress to pass any law abridging freedom of speech or press.

Adams had little sympathy for the more extreme purposes of the Alien and Sedition Acts. Both acts were the product of war fever, which the Ultra-Federalists in Congress regarded as an opportunity to discredit Democratic-Republicans as anti-American. Adams signed them into law without demurral, but he resisted the intention of Secretary of State Pickering to use the alien laws to deport large numbers of people who were not citizens. He also opposed the Arch-Federalists' proposal to establish a large standing army. Adams's restraint was not unimportant. As historian Richard Hofstadter has written, "If we can imagine a determined High Federalist President in the White House seizing upon the most intense moment of Anti-French feeling to precipitate a war, we can imagine a partisan conflict that would have cracked the Union." [32]

The Revolution of 1800

Although Adams's efforts to rise above party conflict may have avoided civil discord, they did not prevent his defeat at the hands of Thomas Jefferson in the 1800 election. Ironically, Adams's dislike of party politics contributed to the evolution of a formal two-party system, for the avoidance of war with France and the triumph of the more moderate Federalist Party allowed for the first peaceful transition of power to an opposing party in a presidential election. But the coming of the Democratic-Republican Party to power was preceded by an odd set of events that precipitated a constitutional crisis and nearly abrogated the results of the presidential election.

These events were the result of fully developed party competition operating for the first time under constitutional provisions that did not make allowances for a formal party system. *(See "Emergence of Parties," p. 231, in Chapter 5.)* The Constitution, originally written without party tickets in mind, arranged for no separate designation of presidential and vice-presidential candidates. By 1800, however, formal party organizations were fully in place. A caucus of each party's members of Congress was held to choose its nominees for president and vice president. The caucus's decision was then coordinated with party organizations in the various states so that electors were selected as instructed agents of the party and pledged to cast their two ballots for president for its presidential and vice-presidential candidates. The election broke along the same North-South divide as in 1796, but this time the Democratic-Republicans added New York, giving them seventy-three electoral votes to the Federalists' sixty-five. Jefferson expected that one or two of Georgia's electors would cast their votes for him and for someone other than Aaron Burr, the party's vice-presidential candidate.[33] When that did not happen, Jefferson and Burr ended up with the same number of electoral votes for president. Consequently, the election of 1800 resulted in a tie between Thomas Jefferson and his running mate, Aaron Burr, who each received seventy-three votes from the Democratic-Republican electors. One vote was to have been withheld from the vice-presidential candidate, but because of a lapse in party planning, Jefferson and Burr received the same number of electoral votes.

According to the Constitution, it then fell to the lame duck Federalist majority in the House of Representatives to decide which Democratic-Republican—Jefferson or Burr—would become president.[34] Federalist leaders in Congress saw some advantage in making Burr president. Burr was a less principled and, therefore, a more pliable politician than the "fanatic" Jefferson. Burr, for his part, refused to take the honorable steps required to

Thomas Jefferson won the election of 1800, but the contest had to be decided by the House of Representatives after Jefferson and Aaron Burr tied in the electoral college vote.

correct the results of the electoral college, despite a clear understanding by all parties involved that Jefferson was the head of the ticket. Instead, when Burr "fully realized that he had a credible chance to win the presidency," the historian Sean Wilentz has written, "he decided to play out the string, come what may." [35] The result was a deadlock. Under the Constitution a majority of the representatives in nine of the sixteen states was needed to elect the president, and neither party could produce the votes. The stalemate lasted through thirty-five ballots. Not until February 17, 1801, on the thirty-sixth ballot, was Jefferson elected.

The electoral contest of 1800–1801 led to the adoption of the Twelfth Amendment, a decisive step "toward constitutional recognition of the role played by parties in the federal government." [36] The electoral college was changed, allowing for separate ballots for president and vice president. Neither the Democratic-Republicans nor the Federalists were comfortable in recognizing that a two party system had developed, but the experience of 1801 and the desire to avoid such incidents in the future took precedence over the strong dislike of party that characterized partisans during the early history of the presidency.

Jefferson's triumph in the 1800 election marked the beginning of a critical realignment in American politics. Sweeping the congressional elections as well as the presidency in 1800, the Democratic-Republicans became the nation's leading political party and remained so until 1828. During the last decade of his life, in a letter to the eminent lawyer and legal scholar Spencer Roane, Jefferson spoke of the "revolution of 1800," saying that although effected peacefully in the course of a popular election, it was "as real a revolution in the principles of our government as that of 1776 was in its form." [37] As historian Joanne Freeman has pointed out, the peaceful revolution may have forestalled a violent one. If the Federalists in Congress had persisted in their efforts to deny him the presidency, Jefferson wrote, "The certainty is that a legislative usurpation would be resisted by arms." [38]

In Jefferson's view, the principles of the Revolutionary War had been perverted by the Federalists in their ardent commitment to expand the responsibilities of the national government. In effect, the domestic and international initiatives of the Federalists constituted an attempt to establish a monarchy. The task of the Democratic-Republican revolution was to restore republican government by casting off the Federalist institutions and, according to historian Forrest McDonald, by instilling "the people with the historical knowledge and true principles that would prevent them from losing their liberties ever again." [39]

Jefferson's desire to preserve the integrity of majority decisions animated his war with the federal judiciary. In a desperate attempt to maintain a foothold in the national government, the Federalists tried to pack the courts with judges of their own party before Adams left office. The Judiciary Act of 1801, enacted by the Federalist Congress and signed by Adams shortly before Jefferson was inaugurated, created a number of new federal judgeships, which were hurriedly filled through so-called "midnight" appointments by the outgoing Adams administration. To the Jeffersonians, the judiciary constituted "the final barrier to be assaulted in the advance of popular government and political liberty." To the Federalists the courts represented "the last bastion of moderation and sanity arresting the progress of mob rule and anarchy." [40]

More than partisan power was at stake in this dispute. The Democratic-Republicans opposed the doctrine that the Constitution implicitly vests the courts with a broad authority to overturn the actions of elected officials on constitutional grounds. The Federalists supported the judiciary's claim to be the ultimate arbiter of the Constitution. Although Jefferson and his followers did not challenge the courts' right of judicial review, they insisted that each branch of government shares equally the responsibility to decide matters of constitutionality.

These issues of power and principle came to a head in the case of *Marbury v. Madison* (1803). Chief Justice John Marshall decided in favor of Jefferson, but on grounds that claimed powers for the judiciary that Jefferson denied it had. In effect, Marshall gave Jefferson a free hand to dismiss Federalist appointees (while he scolded Jefferson for wishing to do so), but only on condition that the president accept the Court's power to pass upon the constitutionality of acts of Congress.[41] *(See "Statutory Interpretation and Judicial Review," p. 1408, in Chapter 34.)*

Jefferson was reluctant to accept victory on these terms. So adroit was Marshall's ruling, however, that the president had no way to disobey the chief justice and the judiciary, as he had hoped to do. When he failed in a subsequent effort to impeach and remove the highly partisan but indisputably competent Justice Samuel Chase, Jefferson's war with the judiciary came to an end. In any event, developments during his first term seemed to make the war unnecessary. By 1804 much of the Democratic-Republican program that Jefferson had heralded in his first inaugural was completed. Nevertheless, although the judiciary weathered the storm of Jefferson's first term, the question that had given rise to the conflict between Jefferson and the courts was never fully resolved. That question—whether ultimate authority rests with elected representatives in Congress and the White House or in a standard of fixed law as interpreted by the judiciary—has arisen repeatedly in American history.

The Democratic-Republican Program and Adjustment to Power

In important respects, the Democratic-Republican program was negative. A great deal of it aimed at repealing Federalist policies that the Jeffersonians believed had undermined the

Constitution. In 1801, Jefferson and Congress, which the Democratic-Republicans also captured in the elections of 1800, removed the last vestiges of the Sedition Act. The act had expired the day before Jefferson took office. But wanting to underscore his fierce opposition to it, the president pardoned everyone (mostly Democratic-Republican newspaper publishers) convicted under the act. Moreover, at Jefferson's request, Congress voted to repay with interest all the fines that were levied as part of their sentences.[42] During Jefferson's first term, Congress also abolished most of the internal taxes, including the unpopular whiskey and direct property taxes, which the Federalists enacted in 1798 to prepare for a possible war with France. Finally, Congress reduced the size of the already small military establishment, severely cutting army and naval appropriations.

Although Jefferson stressed the need to restrain the role of the national government, he was not narrowly doctrinaire in his conception of the proper limits of government. His main concern was to make the government more responsive to the will of the people. "His faith in the people," as one scholar has remarked, "gave to his views on power a flexibility that permitted the use of power in positive ways to emphasize the freedom from government."[43] In those areas where the national government's responsibility was proper—that is, in matters pertaining to foreign affairs and relations among the states—Jefferson believed that the powers of the central government should be exercised with energy and efficiency.

When circumstances required, Jefferson was even willing to tolerate government action that seemed to contradict his stated principles. Thus, in 1803, Jefferson consented to the purchase of the Louisiana Territory, which doubled the size of the United States, although, as he granted in a letter to Sen. John Breckinridge, he did not feel the Constitution provided "for our holding foreign territory, still less for incorporating foreign nations into our union."[44] In 1807, seeking to preserve the long-standing American commitment to neutrality between Great Britain and France, Jefferson imposed an embargo on all foreign commerce. Enforcing the embargo involved coercion by the federal government on a scale rivaling that of the notorious Alien and Sedition Acts.

Jefferson's actions as president reflected a "duality that was to underlie the whole of the [Democratic-Republican] era and to account for many of its frustrations."[45] Tensions within the party's philosophy of government became evident in the Jeffersonians' conduct of the presidency. Opposing conceptions of executive power had been at the center of the bitter conflict between the Federalists and Democratic-Republicans. In view of these differences, one might have expected important changes to occur in the conduct of the presidency when Jefferson and his party took control in 1801. The Democratic-Republicans soon realized,

however, that a wholesale dismantling of executive power would make governing virtually impossible.

Jefferson, with the able support of his secretary of the Treasury, Albert Gallatin, exercised as much executive control of domestic policy as Hamilton had during the Washington administration. Indeed, Jefferson secured from a Democratic-Republican Congress a grant of authority to enforce the embargo policy that exceeded any grant of executive power undertaken by the Federalists. Moreover, he used those powers with all the energy that the Democratic-Republican partisans in opposition had denounced as a mark of tyranny.

In important respects, then, the revolution of 1800 brought no sweeping alterations in the government's institutional arrangements. Hamilton was among those who recognized that Jefferson was not opposed to the firm exercise of executive power and assured his colleagues in 1801 that "it is not true, as alleged, that he [Jefferson] is for confounding all the powers in the House of Representatives."[46] Hamilton's observations predicted accurately how Jefferson was to act as president.

Nevertheless, Jefferson's presidency marked an important change in the executive's relationship to the people.[47] Jefferson's predecessors, Washington and Adams, believed that presidential power derived from its constitutional authority. Jefferson, while not rejecting this view out of hand, maintained that the strength of the presidency ultimately depended upon the "affections of the people." Jefferson clearly implied in his first inaugural address that the program of the Democratic-Republican Party should be enacted because of its endorsement by a majority of the people in the 1800 election.

Washington and Adams viewed their task as one of maintaining some distance from the people and serving as a moderating force in the clash of parties and interests in Congress. But Jefferson believed that the most effective and responsible way to lead the government was through the institutions that were rooted most firmly in a popular base—the House and, to a lesser extent, the Senate. Instead of standing apart from developments occurring in the legislature, he sought to direct them. Thus, in contrast to Hamilton's concept of a strong presidency, which emphasized the need for independent executive initiatives, Jefferson assumed the mantle of party leader in an effort to yoke together the separate branches of government in the service of his and the Democratic-Republican Party's agenda.

Informed by a clear conception of the presidency, Jefferson's administration wrought other important institutional changes to forge a closer relationship between the president and the people. One such change was to reduce the ceremonial trappings of the executive office. Jefferson stripped away much of the pomp and ceremony to which Washington and Adams had adhered, regarding excessive formality in the conduct of the presidency as incompatible with a popularly based government. Unlike Washington, Jefferson rode around the capital not in a coach attended by liveried outriders, but on his own horse, with only one servant in attendance. His clothing stressed republican simplicity, to the point of offending some who regarded his appearance as unsuitable for a head of state.

Jefferson's interest in removing the "monocratic" features from the executive office also spawned efforts to simplify the president's relationship with Congress. His decision to submit his first annual message to Congress in writing instead of delivering it in person was "a calculated political act, designed to reduce the 'relics' left by the Federalists and to underline the return to sound republican simplicity." [48] (It also reflected his acute discomfort at public speaking.) Jefferson thus inaugurated what turned out to be the century-long practice of presidents' sending their State of the Union messages to Congress to be read aloud by the clerk of the House.

Jefferson's adoption of a simpler presidential etiquette corresponded nicely with the transfer of the capital from Philadelphia to Washington, D.C., in 1800. The move left members of Congress, executive branch officials, and diplomats, who had been accustomed to the well-developed culture and comforts of Philadelphia, "stranded" on the banks of the Potomac. One historian described Washington, D.C., in the early 1800s as "a village pretending to be a capital, a place with a few bad houses, extensive swamps, hanging on the skirts of a too thinly peopled, weak and barren country." [49] Yet Jefferson, who was never fully comfortable in cities, appreciated the change in setting. His informal style was compatible not just with his view of the executive office but also with Washington's rustic surroundings.

The Limits of Popular Leadership

Important as it sometimes was, popular presidential leadership had its limits during the Jeffersonian era. Neither Jefferson nor his Democratic-Republican successors—James Madison (1809–1817), James Monroe (1817–1825), and John Quincy Adams (1825–1829)—tried to enhance their power by bartering patronage or other sorts of favors in return for legislation in Congress. Indeed, until 1829, presidents seldom used the spoils of federal appointments to enhance party unity or to obtain legislation. Nor was it considered respectable during the Jeffersonian era for the president to appeal directly to the public. [50] Until the twentieth century, presidents usually exercised popular leadership indirectly, through their influence on the party mechanisms in Congress and the state governments.

For example, Jefferson was able to get an embargo enacted by using his popularity to exert influence indirectly on Democratic-Republican leaders in Congress. Notwithstanding the controversy over the embargo, Jefferson never took the issue to the people. Although Democratic-Republican leaders received behind-the-scenes directives from the president, Jefferson presented "an imperturbable, almost sphinx-like silence to the nation." [51] To have done otherwise would have violated the custom that prohibited presidents from trying to influence public opinion directly.

After fourteen months of existence, the embargo was repealed by a rebellious Congress. The defeat of Jefferson's embargo policy marked the first striking example of the limits of presidential power. It also marked the beginning of a long decline in the influence of the presidency that affected the administrations of Jefferson's three Democratic-Republican successors. A combination of personal factors and institutional developments caused the presidency after Jefferson to shrink to its limited constitutional role as prescribed by the orthodox Democratic-Republican doctrine.

The Presidency of James Madison

The decline of presidential influence was especially evident during James Madison's two terms in office. While he was president, major institutional developments transferred power from the executive to the legislative branch. One such development was the advent of the congressional nominating caucus as an independent source of power.

The nomination of Jefferson in 1800 and 1804 was a foregone conclusion, but the Democratic-Republican caucus of 1808 had a real decision to make. Secretary of State

President Thomas Jefferson, depicted here as being robbed by King George and Napoleon, found himself in 1805 in the middle of the war between England and France. The cartoon symbolizes the war's effect on U.S. trade.

Madison generally was regarded as Jefferson's heir apparent, but the leader of the small anti-Jefferson faction in the Democratic-Republican Party, Rep. John Randolph of Virginia, tried to secure the nomination for James Monroe. In the end, Madison was nominated with strong support from Jefferson and was elected in a 122–47 electoral vote landslide that reduced his opponent, Charles Cotesworth Pinckney, to the Federalist Party's shrinking New England base. But the promises Madison had to make to his party's members in Congress to win their endorsement suggested that subsequent presidential nominations might well become occasions "to make explicit executive subordination to congressional president-makers." Indeed, some scholars believe that Madison's renomination by the Democratic-Republican Party in 1812 was delayed until he assured "War Hawks" in the congressional caucus that he supported their desire for war with Great Britain.[52]

The emergence of Speaker of the House Henry Clay of Kentucky as an important leader in Congress and his extraordinary use of the office during the Madison administration further reduced executive power in relation to Congress. Until Clay's election as Speaker in 1811, party leadership in the House usually was shared among several designated floor leaders, with the Speaker acting mainly as a moderator. Clay changed this practice dramatically:

> Clay was chosen Speaker on an issue that President Madison was unable to grip, and with the intention of forcing national action despite the President's incapacity to act—war with Great Britain. Clay succeeded in this purpose, and until the last day of Madison's administration the initiative in public affairs remained with Clay and his associates in the House of Representatives.[53]

Under Clay's direction, the House strengthened its capacity to meet its broader legislative obligations by expanding the number and influence of its standing committees, which enabled each representative to specialize in an area of interest. Because the committees' activities were coordinated by the party leaders, the House became an effective legislative instrument. From 1811 to 1825 Clay was arguably the most powerful man in the nation.

The decline of the presidency was demonstrated most dramatically during the War of 1812. Madison's message of June 1, 1812, which urged Congress to declare war against Great Britain, was the first war message by an American president. Later historical developments were to establish formidable wartime powers for the president, but Madison's command of the nation's military effort was singularly undistinguished. He was handicapped not only by his inability to exert influence over Congress but also by personal qualities that were poorly suited for the tasks at hand. Madison's figure was slight, his manner was quiet (even somber), his speaking voice was weak, and the force of his personality was, at best, moderate. As Gaillard Hunt, a generally sympathetic Madison biographer, has written of the president's war leadership:

> The hour had come but the man was wanting. Not a scholar in governments ancient and modern, not an unimpassioned writer of careful messages, but a robust leader to rally the people and unite them to fight was what the time needed, and what it did not find in Madison.[54]

From a military standpoint, the War of 1812 was the most unsuccessful in American history. The low point in the war occurred in August 1814, when President Madison had to evacuate the capital for three days as a British force of fewer than five thousand men moved unchecked up the Chesapeake Bay and marched with little resistance into the heart of Washington, burning the Capitol, the White House, the Navy Yard, and most other public buildings in Washington.

The nation eventually was saved from disaster by Britain's decision not to prosecute the war on a massive scale. Morale was boosted belatedly by Gen. Andrew Jackson's victory at New Orleans on January 8, 1815, even though it had no effect on the outcome of the war. (Peace had been concluded two weeks earlier.) In the wake of Jackson's triumph, the American people greeted the end of the war joyfully, which allowed Madison to retire as president in 1817 with some measure of honor. New Orleans also rendered a fatal political wound to the pro-British Federalists, many of whom opposed the war from the beginning and some of whom had even threatened to secede from the Union. "The confident nationalist party of Washington, Hamilton, and Adams," historian Sean Wilentz has observed, "had shriveled into [a] phobic sectional party."[55]

Federalist defeat, however, did not translate automatically into Democratic-Republican triumph. In important respects, Madison's failures transcended his personal limitations—they were attributable in part to the legacies he inherited from the Jefferson administration and from the Democratic-Republican tradition of which he had been one of the major architects. By opposing the creation of anything more than a minimal army or navy, Madison and Jefferson, preaching economy in government, had undone many of the military preparations that the Adams administration had undertaken. Their foreign policy depended on diplomacy to solve America's problems with France and Britain. When negotiations failed, the Democratic-Republicans were forced to rely on the 1807 embargo, an impractical policy of peaceful coercion that proved disastrous for the U.S. economy without stopping either Britain or France from interfering with American ships. The collapse of his own embargo, enacted in 1812, left Madison no alternative but war when British provocations continued, even though he knew the country was neither prepared nor united for battle.

Years later, Madison recounted that he had hoped to overcome the nation's unpreparedness by "throw[ing] forward the flag of the country, sure that the people would press onward and defend it." [56] Yet the rapid decline in the status of the presidency after Jefferson left Madison in a poor position to rally Congress and the nation. Contrary to his expectations, the traditional Democratic-Republican doctrine of hostility to centralized power was not abandoned during wartime. Congress was willing to declare war but not to provide the revenue required to carry it out. Moreover, the Madison administration's plan to use the state militia was scuttled by the state governments' lack of cooperation. The governors of Massachusetts and Connecticut, for example, refused to release their militia for the purpose of fighting the war, while the president, a strong advocate of states' rights, "offered no suggestion for stopping so grave a defiance of federal authority." [57]

Madison began to face up to the limitations of Democratic-Republican principles in his seventh annual message to Congress in December 1815, in which he recommended a number of policies to solidify the national resolve, including the chartering of the Second Bank of the United States. (The Democratic-Republicans had allowed the first bank charter to expire in 1811.) With no national bank in operation during the War of 1812, the federal government lacked a convenient and stable source of currency, exacerbating a financial crisis that saw the national debt grow from $45 million in 1811 to $127 million by the end of 1815. Believing that a national bank was a necessary evil, Madison signed the bank bill into law in 1816. The severe economic dislocations of the war and the hope of achieving a stable currency persuaded Madison and the Democratic-Republicans to embrace "the ghostly presence of Hamilton's national bank, with all its potential for corrupting the republic." [58]

Madison never ceased to express profound concerns, however, about the potential abuses of executive power that he believed Hamilton had encouraged and committed during the 1790s. In every one of his critical relationships and decisions—in bringing the nation to war, in dealing with Congress, in arranging his cabinet, in overseeing the executive branch, and in enduring near treasonable dissent—Madison sought to uphold Democratic-Republican principles of executive leadership. In the final analysis, these principles simply were not congenial to dynamic presidential leadership.[59]

The Presidencies of James Monroe and John Quincy Adams

James Madison's Democratic-Republican successors, James Monroe and John Quincy Adams, were unable to restore the strength of the presidency that had dissipated after Jefferson's retirement. Monroe, although a forceful statesman and a stronger personality than his predecessor, was stiff and formal in his personal dealings, which made it difficult for him to lead the party effectively. Like Washington

and John Adams, he was more suited to the task of presiding than directing.

Monroe also was hindered by a growing split within his party between "old" Democratic-Republicans, who inclined toward a strict construction of the Constitution, and "new" Democratic-Republicans, or National Republicans, who were more nationalist in outlook. Monroe was identified with the former group; the latter, represented by prominent figures such as Henry Clay, John C. Calhoun, and Monroe's successor, John Quincy Adams, dominated the party after the War of 1812, even when Monroe was president.

One of the major domestic issues of the day, internal improvements, turned on whether it was constitutional for the national government to construct roads and canals. Monroe informed Congress of his belief that an amendment to the Constitution would be required for the national government to undertake such a responsibility. Nevertheless, Congress, under the strong direction of Clay, defied Monroe and passed a bill to repair the main east-west highway, known as the Cumberland Road. The president's veto of this bill signaled a breakdown within the ranks of the Democratic-Republicans that was to plague Monroe throughout his two terms.

This split in the Democratic-Republican ranks reinforced the transfer of power from the executive to the legislative branch. In his battle with Clay and Congress, Monroe, adhering to the prevailing custom, rarely used the veto power. His action in the Cumberland Road controversy was the exception rather than the rule. Following the practice begun under Washington, Monroe vetoed only legislation he deemed unconstitutional.

Monroe's deference to the legislature went beyond custom. More than any of his predecessors, Monroe believed in legislative supremacy. Hence he abstained almost completely from involvement in the greatest issue of the day: the admission of Missouri as a state, which for the first time forced Congress to debate the status of slavery in the Louisiana Territory. Now a private citizen, Jefferson observed the bitter debate about Missouri with great concern. Writing to Rep. John Holmes of Maine, he said: "This momentous question, like a fire-bell in the night, awakened and filled me with terror. I considered it at once the knell of the Union." [60] The Missouri Compromise of 1820 settled the slavery controversy for a time, but President Monroe had virtually no hand in resolving this crisis, save for signing the final bill hammered out in Congress.[61]

The passive character of the Monroe administration prompted Supreme Court Justice Joseph Story to remark in 1818 that "the Executive has no longer a commanding influence. The House of Representatives has absorbed all the popular feeling and all the effective power of the country." [62]

Justice Story's lament was not as pertinent to foreign affairs as to domestic matters. Previous service as secretary of

Henry Clay and John C. Calhoun dominated the National Republicans, the new wing of the Democratic-Republican Party, after the War of 1812.

state made all of the Jeffersonian presidents more confident and more confidence-inspiring in the international arena. Even Madison asserted the powers of the president as the wartime commander in chief, however ineptly he wielded them during the War of 1812.[63]

Monroe reinforced the right of presidents to take the initiative in foreign affairs by issuing the Monroe Doctrine, which became one of the pillars of U.S. foreign policy. The Monroe Doctrine resulted from the president's attempt to respond to the revolt of Spanish colonies in Latin America that nearly liquidated the Spanish empire. The Monroe administration was alarmed at reports that European powers, France in particular, had designs on several Latin American nations. Simultaneously, Czar Alexander I of Russia reportedly was interested in staking out claims to the territory on the northwest coast of the Oregon region. By authority of the maintenance of a trading station at Fort Ross in Bodega Bay, near San Francisco, the czar issued a decree claiming exclusive trading rights to the area north of the fifty-first parallel. In response, the president included in his State of the Union address to Congress on December 2, 1823, a sweeping statement that denounced colonization in the Western Hemisphere and proclaimed the independence of the American nations from interference by the European powers.[64]

The Monroe Doctrine provided an important example, at a time of general executive weakness, that the president was paramount in making foreign policy. Monroe's defiant expression of hemispheric independence committed the United States to more burdensome diplomatic and military responsibilities, most of which would inevitably fall upon the chief executive. For a time, this commitment was without important effect, but its potential to become a guiding influence on foreign policy was realized by the end of the nineteenth century.

The end of the Monroe presidency in 1825 marked the end of a quarter-century long political dynasty. Monroe was the last member of the Virginia triumvirate—Jefferson, Madison, and Monroe—to serve as president. During the 1790s, the country's first decade under the Constitution, each had been a founder of the Democratic-Republican opposition to the Federalists and a leader during its rise as a governing party. Monroe was also the last president from the generation that had won the War of Independence. With the end of the Virginia dynasty, the Democratic-Republicans no longer were led by national figures whose stature as Founders could hold the party together.

Ironically, political unity became all the more difficult to achieve because of the extraordinary electoral success of the Democratic-Republican Party. Mobilizing popular support for a governing party requires a credible opponent. Yet during Monroe's first term as president, the Federalist Party disappeared as a national organization. Monroe was unopposed for reelection in 1820. The so-called Era of Good Feeling followed the second war with England, between 1812 and 1820, when Democratic-Republican dominance over the nation was unassailable. Yet triumph brought dissolution. Even as Monroe was being inaugurated for the second time, his party was being torn apart by the ambitions of the many candidates who wanted to succeed him as president. In fact, as historian Catherine Allgor has pointed out, the 1824 campaign may have begun as early as 1817. In 1818 John Quincy Adams, Monroe's secretary of state, observed that "political, personal and electioneering intrigues are intermingling themselves with increasing heat and violence." As a result, Adams lamented, the government was "assuming daily more and more a character of cabal, and preparation, not for the next presidential election, but for the one after." [65]

With the Federalists vanquished and the Democratic-Republicans fragmented, the 1824 presidential election became a contest of individuals rather than of issues. For the first time no Virginian was in the race, further evidence that an era had passed. Rival leaders from New England, the Deep South, and the West, each supported by his own personal organization and following, ran for the presidency in one of the most bitter and confusing elections ever staged. The results of the election stirred a storm of controversy and led to a revolt against the party procedures that had prevailed for a quarter century. Moreover, John Quincy Adams, the eventual winner, inherited an impossible governing situation, one that ended the Democratic-Republican era amidst bitter conflicts that endured for a generation.

In 1824, for the second time in American history, an election was determined not by the voters, but by the House of Representatives. Sen. Andrew Jackson of Tennessee, the hero of the battle of New Orleans, received the most electoral votes, 99, but fell far short of the 131 necessary for a majority and election. Adams, who felt that as secretary of state he was the logical heir to the presidency, came in second with 84 electoral votes. Monroe's secretary of the Treasury, William Crawford, was the choice of the Democratic-Republican caucus. However, the party machinery had run down badly by 1824, and its support was no longer tantamount to nomination. Crawford finished third with 41 votes. The powerful Speaker of the House, Henry Clay of Kentucky, finished fourth with 37 votes. Jackson also won a strong plurality of popular votes in all but six of the eighteen states that now allowed voters to choose the electors.

According to the Twelfth Amendment, the House was to choose from the top three candidates. This removed Clay as a candidate, and if the fourteen House delegations from the states in which Jackson finished either first or second to Clay in the election had supported Jackson, he would have become president.[66] But Clay used the influence he still had to help secure Adams's election. The new president, in turn, rewarded Clay by naming him secretary of state.

Not surprisingly, Jackson's supporters were furious, charging that Adams and Clay had made a corrupt bargain to violate the will of the people. Although the charge of conspiracy against Adams and Clay was in all likelihood unfounded, the controversial election of 1824 ensured the demise of what had come to be called "King Caucus."

John Quincy Adams, the last president of the Jeffersonian era, was severely constrained by the general view that he was a minority president. But Adams was a statesman of considerable talent and accomplishment. Not content to remain in the shadow of Congress, he undertook to renew the strength of the presidential office. In fact, Adams was the first president in American history to attempt to lead Congress openly in an active program of governmental achievement.

In his first annual message, Adams recommended a broad program of internal improvements, a national university, an observatory, scientific exploration, and voyages of discovery. His three Democratic-Republican predecessors had strong reservations about the constitutional power of Congress to mandate such policies and to appropriate funds for them. Madison and Monroe followed Jefferson in believing that a constitutional amendment was needed before any such programs could be enacted. But Adams rejected this narrow interpretation of the Constitution, as well as the deference of his predecessors to legislative primacy in most domestic affairs. In spite of the reservations of his cabinet members, who believed Adams's ambitious plans were impractical, Adams was determined to go ahead. Recounting the resistance of his cabinet to his program, Adams wrote in his diary, "Thus situated, the perilous experiment must be made. Let me make it with full deliberation, and be prepared for the consequences." [67]

Adams was the first president "to demonstrate the real scope of creative possibilities of the constitutional provision to 'recommend to their [Congress's] consideration such measures as he shall judge necessary and expedient.' " [68] But Adams had no popular mandate—far from it. In addition, his formal and stern manner was ill suited to the task of building a political coalition. A quarter century of Jeffersonian presidents had not prepared the country for the sort of assertive executive leadership that Adams attempted. Thus most of his proposals were ignored or ridiculed.

Adams's influence, never very great, was effectively ended with the congressional elections of 1826. His political opponents, representing Jackson's opposition to the administration, won a majority in both the House and the Senate—the first time that the executive and legislative branches of government were controlled by different parties. The Democratic-Republican era of the presidency ended with Congress, not the president, at the center of government power, but with the strongest president to date poised to take control of Washington at the head of a new democratic army.[69]

THE JACKSONIAN PRESIDENCY

By 1828, the confused situation of the previous presidential campaign, in which four candidates ran for office, had been replaced by a new party alignment. The Democratic-Republicans now were divided into two major factions. John Quincy Adams and Henry Clay, who stood for the more national aspirations of the "new" Republicans (or National Republicans), led one group; and Andrew Jackson and John C. Calhoun, the vice president during Adams's administration, led the opposition, which dedicated itself to the "old"

Democratic-Republican causes of states' rights and a strict interpretation of the national government's powers. By 1832, these factions developed into the Whig and Democratic Parties, which dominated the U.S. political landscape until the eve of the Civil War.

The Jacksonian Democrats had the better of this competition. From 1828 until 1856, the electoral success of the Democrats was interrupted in only two presidential campaigns: the election of Whigs William Henry Harrison in 1840 and Zachary Taylor in 1848. Jackson's victory in 1828 marked the culmination of a trend that began during the Jeffersonian era: the emerging agrarian and frontier interests of the South and West triumphed over the commercial and financial interests of the East. The purchases of Louisiana in 1803 and Florida in 1819 had added millions of acres to the territory of the United States and afforded greater influence to those who formerly had stood outside of the regular channels of political power.

Jackson was the first outsider to become president of the United States. Jackson's predecessors had undergone extensive apprenticeships in national politics and diplomacy. The hero of the battle of New Orleans had less formal education than any of them. Moreover, he had little experience in Congress and none in public administration. He was a self-made man, a powerful symbol of his times, who had risen from a small cabin in the pine woods of South Carolina to a plantation near Nashville, Tennessee, to the White House in Washington. Jackson's principles and presence were to hold sway over the country for nearly three decades. This period in U.S. history is called the "Age of Jackson." [70]

Jacksonian Democracy

The most important political theme of the Age of Jackson was the widespread desire for equality of opportunity, the belief that no one should have special privileges at the expense of anyone else. Jackson followed Jefferson in believing that to eliminate privilege, political leaders must strictly limit the role of the national government. The rapid expansion of the country was accompanied by a dynamic society and economy that seemed to foster unlimited opportunity. Within that expansive environment, Jacksonians believed that the best approach to government was to confine power as much as possible to the less obtrusive state governments.

To be sure, the Jacksonians' concern for expanding equality of opportunity was limited to white males, especially those who previously had been barred from voting because they did not own enough property. But the Jacksonian political philosophy encouraged a much bolder assault on national institutions and programs than the generally more flexible Jeffersonians had undertaken. Jackson withdrew the federal government from the field of internal improvements. Military power, especially the army, was kept to a minimum. Jackson's fiscal policy was to hold down expenditures. The Bank of the United States, which Jeffersonians had learned to live with, was dismantled, and its deposits were reinvested in selected state banks.

Jackson's View of the Presidency

The Age of Jackson had its contradictory and compensating aspects when it came to the authority of the national government. The Jacksonians regarded the president as the "tribune of the people," the true instrument of the people's voice in government, an idea that invested the executive, in an age dominated by democratic aspiration, with tremendous influence. During the Jeffersonian era, the presidency began to develop a closer relationship with the people. But this development took place on the authority of political principles and attendant institutional arrangements that generally supported the supremacy of the legislature and championed Congress as the true voice of the people. Jackson tried to establish a direct relationship between the executive and the people, thus challenging Congress's status as the national government's principal representative institution. The strengthened presidency, especially during Jackson's two terms, "gave voice in a new age to the rising spirit of democratic nationalism," one that sustained and strengthened the Union in the face of serious sectional conflict over the tariff and slavery.[71]

Thus, although Jackson supported states' rights, he also personified and defended the sovereignty of the nation during his presidency, never more so than in the nullification crisis that arose near the end of his first term. Seeking to compel the federal government to accede to its demands for a lower tariff, South Carolina's legislature summoned a convention on November 24, 1832, that declared the existing 1832 tariff law "null and void." South Carolina cited John Calhoun's Nullification Doctrine, which held that a state could declare a federal law null and void within its boundaries whenever it deemed such a law unconstitutional.

In the face of this threat to the Union, Jackson issued a proclamation that vigorously rejected South Carolina's right to disobey a federal statute. The power to annul a law of the United States, assumed by one state, he argued, was "incompatible with the existence of the Union, contradicted expressly by the letter of the Constitution, unauthorized by its spirit, inconsistent with every principle on which it was founded, and destructive of the great object for which it was formed." [72] In 1861, Abraham Lincoln based his own response to southern succession on the same argument.

Jackson placed the responsibility to defend the Union squarely upon the shoulders of the president. It was the people, he believed, acting through the state ratifying conventions, who had formed the Union in 1787–1788, and the president—not Congress or the states—embodied the will of the people. Jackson's concept of the presidency "transcended the older categories of nationalism versus states' rights" and portrayed a new understanding of national sovereignty.[73]

The idea that the president is the direct representative of the people lay at the heart of Jacksonian democracy. Although more supportive of popular rule than were the Federalists, the Democratic-Republican faith in democracy had been restrained. The battle between Democratic-Republicans and Federalists about the meaning of the Constitution hid their basic agreement about the need to moderate democracy through various kinds of formal institutional relationships: among the legislative, executive, and judicial branches; between the state and national governments; and between the people and their representatives. The Jacksonians sought to reverse this equation by making the Constitution and its institutional arrangements the servant of public opinion.

The Jacksonian concept of the people was limited. It did not include African Americans, women, or Native Americans. But the dramatic surge of democratic reform in the 1830s had a profound effect on the presidency. Jackson's election as president coincided with changes in election laws in the various states that replaced legislatures with voters in the selection of presidential electors. In the first three presidential elections, most electors were chosen by the state legislatures. But electors were selected by popular vote in all but six states in 1824, and by 1832, in every state except South Carolina, which retained legislative selection until the Civil War. Jackson was arguably the first popularly elected president of the United States, thus strengthening his and his supporters' conviction that his mandate came directly from the source of all sovereignty.[74]

The president's claim to be the direct representative of the people also gained credence from the expansion of the electorate. The Jacksonians worked successfully to persuade the states to eliminate property qualifications for voting, which meant that universal white manhood suffrage was virtually established by 1832. This development brought into the electorate farmers, mechanics, laborers—those Jackson referred to as "the humble members of society"—who regarded the executive office under "Old Hickory's" superintendence as a rallying point. Their support rescued the executive office from the congressional dominance that characterized presidential administrations from James Madison to John Quincy Adams. Indeed, with the collapse of the congressional nominating caucus in 1824, Jackson became the first president since George Washington to be chosen in an election that did not involve the national legislature. Taking office in 1829, Jackson found himself in the position, therefore, to revitalize the presidency with a new independence and energy.[75]

Party Conventions

The advent of the Jacksonian presidency was associated with important developments in the party system. The decline of King Caucus as a nominating device in presidential campaigns left a vacuum that was filled by the national convention. (See "The Development of Party Nominating Conventions," p. 219, in Chapter 5.) A convention was used by the Democrats to nominate candidates in 1832 and by the Whigs after the presidential campaign of 1836.

National convention delegates were selected by conventions in the states, which consisted in turn of local party members. Implicit in the idea of the national convention was the premise that delegates' authority sprang directly from the rank and file or, as Jackson put it, "fresh from the people." [76] Taken together, the new and elaborate Whig and Democratic organizations reached far beyond the halls of Congress and eventually penetrated every corner of the Union. Sustained by his party's far-reaching political network, Jackson became the first president in U.S. history to appeal to the people over the heads of their legislative representatives.[77]

Jackson's Struggle with Congress

The transformation of the presidency from a congressionally to a popularly based office did not take place without a tremendous political struggle. The Whig Party, although winning only two presidential elections between 1828 and 1856, offered vigorous opposition to the Democrats.

Proclaiming the ideas of Henry Clay and John Quincy Adams, the Whigs took a national approach to the country's problems, advocating a program, known as the "American plan," to recharter the Second Bank of the United States, enact a protective tariff, and foster internal improvements. This program, which rested on a broad Hamiltonian construction of the Constitution, contradicted the states' rights policies of the Democrats. Yet the Whigs, who formed as a party of opposition to Jackson, resisted the expansion of executive power and defended the legislature as the principal instrument of representative democracy. President Jackson and the Democratic Party firmly controlled the House. But the Senate, led by such forceful Whig statesmen as Clay and Daniel Webster, often challenged both Jackson's policies and claims to executive primacy. Although the Whigs were not the majority party in the Senate, they forged a coalition with Calhoun and some other states' rights-oriented Democrats, who resented Jackson's defense of the Union in the nullification crisis of 1832.

Veto of the Bank Bill

The conflict between the president and the Whigs came to a head in July 1832, when Jackson vetoed the bill to recharter the national bank four years before the existing charter

Although President Jackson, left, and the Democratic Party controlled the House, forceful Whig senators such as Henry Clay, right, and Daniel Webster, center, challenged Jackson's policies and use of executive prerogatives.

expired. Jackson's veto of the bank bill and the defense of this action in his message to Congress of July 10, 1832, was, according to historian Robert Remini, "the most important veto ever issued by a president." [78]

The veto established a precedent that significantly strengthened the presidency. Beginning with Washington, Federalist and Democratic-Republican presidents alike had agreed that a veto should be cast only when the president believed that a piece of legislation was unconstitutional. In forty years under the Constitution only nine acts of Congress had been struck down by the chief executive, and only three of those dealt with what could be considered important issues. Yet Jackson successfully vetoed twelve bills in eight years, even putting the pocket veto to use for the first time. He believed, and so stated in the message to Congress that accompanied the bank veto, that a president should reject any bill that he felt would injure the nation. For Jackson, a veto was justified if the president had a policy disagreement with Congress. In demanding the right to be involved in the development of legislation, Jackson "essentially altered the relationship between the executive and legislative branches of government." [79]

Two other aspects of Jackson's famous veto message were significant. First, it contained Jackson's view—one that Jefferson first articulated—that the president, as well as Congress, possessed coordinate power with the courts to determine questions of constitutionality. Jackson argued that the national bank was unconstitutional as well as bad policy, a claim that his Whig opponents considered outrageous in view of Chief Justice John Marshall's decision in *McCulloch v. Maryland* (1819) that Congress had the constitutional power to charter a bank. [80]

Jackson insisted, however, that in matters of constitutional interpretation the executive was no more bound by judicial rulings than by acts of Congress. Congress, the executive, and the Supreme Court, he asserted, "must each for itself be guided by its opinion of the Constitution." [81] Thus Jackson's veto message dramatically reopened the question, which seemingly had been resolved in 1803 by *Marbury v. Madison,* of the appropriate authority of the federal courts. [82] His claim that the president and Congress, the popularly elected branches of government, could reach their own judgments about the Constitution expressed his determination to forge a stronger connection between the people and their government.

The other notable aspect of Jackson's bank veto was the manner in which he laid the controversy before the American people. The last paragraph of the veto message, anticipating the president's impending campaign for reelection, indicated that the final decision rested with the American people. "If sustained by his fellow citizens," said Jackson (speaking of himself), he would be "grateful and happy."

Concerned about the political effects of the bank war, Congress failed to override the president's veto. Jackson's overwhelming defeat of Clay in the 1832 election, which was fought in large measure over the bank issue, convinced even his political opponents, as the weekly *Niles' Register* reluctantly reported after the election, that the president "had cast himself upon the support of the people against the acts of both houses of Congress" and had been sustained. Jackson's victory confirmed his conviction that the president, not Congress, was the people's true representative in Washington. [83]

Aftermath of the Veto

The Jacksonian revolution was extended in the aftermath of the bank veto. Vindicated by his reelection in 1832, Jackson decided to kill off the bank once and for all by withdrawing its public deposits and placing them in selected state banks. Because Congress refused Jackson's request for authority to remove the bank's funds, the authority to do so remained with the secretary of the Treasury, who had been granted this right in the law chartering the second bank. When Secretary of the Treasury Louis McLane opposed removal of deposits, he was transferred to the State Department and replaced by William J. Duane. Duane also resisted the president's efforts to kill the bank and was dismissed within four months of taking the oath of office. His replacement, Roger B. Taney, formerly the attorney general, finally gave Jackson the cooperation he was looking for, which provoked the Senate to pass a censure resolution that accused the president of assuming "authority and power not conferred by the Constitution and laws." [84]

Taken together, Duane's dismissal, Taney's removal of public deposits from the national bank, and the Senate's censure of Jackson raised a fundamental constitutional question: Can the president, using the constitutionally implied dismissal power, dictate how a discretionary power that Congress has vested exclusively in the head of a department shall be exercised?

The Senate censure controversy—one battle in the long-standing war between the president and Congress for control of executive administration—was won decisively by Jackson. Because Jackson's "Protest" to the Senate's resolution of censure became the leading issue in the next round of Senate elections, Jackson's Democratic allies took control of the upper house in 1837. Thus before Jackson left office, he had the satisfaction of seeing the resolution of censure formally expunged on January 16, 1837. The Senate's decision to recant not only signified a personal political triumph for Jackson, but it also confirmed his broad interpretation of the present's power to control the executive branch.

The Limits of the Jacksonian Presidency

According to the Whigs, the main legacy of Jackson's presidency was a dangerous expansion of presidential power. The bank controversy demonstrated, they argued, that the chief executive now possessed powers that dwarfed the influence of Congress as well as the judiciary, thus undermining the separation of powers.

Indeed, it was during this controversy that the Anti-Jackson National Republican Party assumed the party name "Whig." Historically, the label derived from the party in England that was opposed to the power of the king and supported parliamentary—or legislative—supremacy. Whigs in the United States meant by their name to imply that the Jackson wing of the Democratic-Republican Party—the Democrats—had abandoned Jeffersonian principles in favor of an elected monarch, whom Whigs dubbed "King Andrew the First." [85]

In truth, the institutional legacy of Jackson's two terms as president was much more ambiguous than his political opponents believed. Jackson did not simply expand the opportunities for unilateral executive action. His extension of executive power depended on the emergence of the president as popular leader, a role that was mediated in critical ways by his party. Even Jackson's "appeal to the people" in the bank controversy was not entirely direct. Instead, he waged the campaign mainly through his party.

The Party Press

The bank fight and other political struggles during the Jackson presidency were carried on by the party press that emerged during the 1830s. Jackson's close relationship with party journalists such as Amos Kendall and Francis Blair added an important dimension to his leadership. These editors provided the president with a new and acceptable tool for political influence by translating "White House decisions into forceful language and announc[ing] them with persuasive eloquence to the American people." [86] Blair's *Globe*, in fact, became the official organ of both the Jackson and the succeeding Van Buren administrations. The newspaper enjoyed special access to official circles and financial support from printing contracts and other perquisites that were controlled by the government.

Every Democratic president from Jackson to James Buchanan secured the solid support of at least one important newspaper. Yet the "administration press" was also a Democratic press, dedicated to the party's program and organization.[87] Hence a more assertive presidency was bound inextricably to a more aggressive and popular party press.

The "Spoils System"

Jackson also implanted a system of rotation in government personnel practices, using the president's power of appointment and removal to replace federal employees for purely partisan reasons. Until Jackson became president, the prevailing belief was that the government workforce should be stable and politically neutral. Beginning in 1829, however, Jackson and every one of his successors during the nineteenth century rejected this principle and deliberately removed or sanctioned the removal of hundreds, even thousands, of subordinates for partisan reasons. The credo of the new patronage system was, as New York senator William L. Marcy put it, "to the victor belong the spoils of the enemy." [88]

In theory, the "spoils system" expanded the powers of the president enormously. The president was now in a position, as Jackson's dismissal of Duane illustrated, to enforce conformity to administration policies within the executive branch. In practice, however, most patronage was controlled

BORN TO COMMAND.

OF VETO MEMORY.

HAD I BEEN CONSULTED.

KING ANDREW THE FIRST.

In this 1832 cartoon, "King Andrew the First" is depicted as a tyrant trampling the Constitution, a ledger of Supreme Court decisions, and the watchwords Virtue, Liberty, and Independence.

by local party organizations in a manner that actually circumscribed presidential leadership. When party leaders demanded offices as a reward for rallying voters to the national ticket in congressional and presidential elections, even powerful chief executives were not inclined to reject them. Moreover, to keep their jobs, many federal officeholders, particularly those who served in the widely scattered customhouses and postal offices, were required to return part of their salaries to the local party organization that sponsored the office, to do party work at election time, and to "vote right." [89]

The postal system became the primary source of partisan favors. Beginning with the Jackson administration, and continuing well into the twentieth century, it became common practice to appoint as postmaster general an individual who served as the principal agent of patronage, representing the interests of the party to the president.

Presidents who were insensitive to partisanship paid a severe price in loss of political support. James Buchanan, for example, was attacked by many influential Democratic Party leaders when he removed loyal Democratic officeholders who had been appointed by his predecessor, Franklin Pierce.[90]

The powers of the presidency that Jackson brought to life constrained not only the party system but also the fundamental political doctrine he espoused: to limit the responsibilities of the national government. The Democrats' strict construction of the Constitution, historian Richard John has written, "weakened the organizational capabilities of the national government." [91] It exalted states' rights into a national creed that limited both federal and presidential authority. Jacksonian Democrats rejected internal improvements and national banks; and despite their celebration of the "humble members of society," they denied the national government had any authority to prevent the expansion of, let alone abolish slavery. "General Jackson's power is constantly increasing," French author Alexis de Tocqueville wrote, "but that of the president grows less. The federal government is strong in his hands; it will pass to his successor enfeebled." [92]

Martin Van Buren and the Panic of 1837

As Tocqueville anticipated, Jackson's successor, the able and shrewd Martin Van Buren, took office under difficult circumstances. Van Buren became the first president to face a domestic crisis.

No sooner had he assumed office than the economy began a downward spiral, a decline that was at least in part the legacy of Jackson's assault on the national bank. The Panic of 1837 was caused in large measure by speculation. A boom in western land, manufacturing, transportation, banking, and several other business enterprises began in 1825 and brought about an overextension of credit.

By removing the deposits from the conservative Bank of the United States and placing them in selected pet state banks, the Jackson administration contributed to the liberal expansion of credit. Then, conscious of the problems posed by an overextended economy, Jackson issued a Treasury order, the Specie Circular, in July 1836, requiring that hard currency be used in payment for all federal lands. This order aroused concern that Jackson and his successor would do all they could to contract the currency, causing banks to call in loans and consequently helping to bring on the panic.

By early 1837, American mercantile houses began to fall, and riots broke out in New York over the high cost of flour. In short order, almost every bank in the country had suspended specie payments, and the state banking system that Jackson set up to replace the national bank collapsed, costing the Treasury some $9 million.

Van Buren was a more pragmatic statesman than his predecessor, but he was sufficiently wedded to Jacksonian principles to resist government-sponsored solutions to the

This 1840 campaign cartoon shows Andrew Jackson leading Martin Van Buren to the White House for a second term. Van Buren, known as "Old Kinderhook" after his New York home, lost to the "hard cider and log cabin" candidate, William Henry Harrison. But his partisan rallying cry, "OK," entered the language as an expression of agreement or approval.

economic crisis. He rejected any notion of reviving a national institution such as the Bank of the United States to regulate currency. Similarly, he rejected the view that the Treasury ought to provide a paper medium to facilitate domestic exchange. The Treasury was to attend to its own affairs and let business do the same.

Spurning the "constant desire" of the Whigs "to enlarge the power of government," Van Buren's response to the panic was modest. He proposed to establish an independent treasury, which would hold government funds in federal vaults instead of depositing them in state banks. The subtreasury, however, was to have limited power, leaving state banks free from federal regulations. Van Buren's proposal was not implemented until 1840: it was resisted for most of his term by a coalition of conservative Democrats and Whigs, many of whom wanted the national government to become more active in the economy. Thus the presidential election of 1840 took place in the midst of an economic crisis for which many voters held the Democratic Party responsible.

The Jacksonian Presidency Sustained

The triumph of the Whig candidate, William Henry Harrison, in the election of 1840 posed a challenge not only to the Jacksonians' domestic program but also to their institutional achievements. The triumphant Whig Party was united above all else by its opposition to the expansion of executive power that had taken place during the Jackson administration. Accordingly, Whig leaders, such as Henry

Clay and Daniel Webster, saw the Panic of 1837 as an opportunity to reassert the powers of Congress.

Clay was the obvious candidate to head the Whig ticket in 1840. He was both the architect of the anti-Jackson program and the real founder of the Whig coalition. But believing General Harrison to be more electable than Clay, the Whigs nominated the aged (he was sixty-seven years old at the time of his election) hero of the War of 1812's Battle of Tippecanoe. Perhaps it consoled Clay and his allies that the general had proclaimed his support for the Whig assault on the executive in 1838, dedicating himself to a program that would limit the executive to one term, free the Treasury from presidential control, and confine the exercise of the veto to legislation that the president deemed unconstitutional.[93]

Although the 1840 campaign was not distinguished by serious discussion of issues, Harrison did pledge publicly to step down after one term. Harrison's inaugural address, which Webster and Clay helped write, provided further reason to believe that the Whig victory in 1840 would undo Jackson's reconstruction of the presidency. Indeed, when Harrison deemed "preposterous" the idea that the president could "better understand the wants and wishes of the people than their representatives," Jacksonians suspected that designing Whig leaders may have persuaded the politically inexperienced president to accept the status of figurehead, delegating the powers of his office to Congress.[94]

Yet the Jacksonian executive survived the Whig challenge. The importance of the presidency was so firmly established in the popular mind by 1840 that the executive no longer could be restored to the weak position it maintained during the latter stages of the Jeffersonian period.

The Whigs, in fact, unwittingly contributed to the permanent transformation of the presidency by their conduct during the 1840 campaign. Jackson's political enemies had looked with disfavor on the popular campaign tactics that the Democratic Party had employed during the three previous presidential campaigns. But having lost all of them to Jackson and Van Buren, the Whigs did everything in their power to "go to the people" in 1840. They bought up newspapers for party propaganda, held great mass rallies, used popular party spokesmen for speech-making tours, and concentrated on mobilizing the largest possible number of voters.

So intent were the Whigs on outdoing the Democrats' campaign in 1840 that they gave serious attention to elements that they previously subordinated, such as slogans, songs, and symbols. Not only did "Tippecanoe and Tyler too" catch on (an alliterative catchphrase made possible by the nomination of Virginia's John Tyler for vice president), but a great deal of rabble-rousing occurred that for the first time made the log cabin an important symbol in presidential politics. A Democratic journalist had said scornfully of the rough-hewn Harrison: "Give him a barrel of hard cider and . . . a pension of $2000, and . . . he will sit the remainder of his days in his log cabin by the side of a . . . fire and study moral philosophy." [95] Clever Whig propagandists pounced on this remark, turning it to their candidates' advantage. In no time, Harrison became "the log cabin and hard-cider candidate," an image that endeared him to many voters.

The log cabin, hard cider campaign stimulated tremendous interest and enthusiasm in the country. Electoral turnout increased substantially: the 2.4 million voters who cast their ballots represented 80.2 percent of the eligible electorate, a percentage that has been surpassed only twice, in 1860 and 1876. Ironically, by accepting and expanding on the successful campaign techniques of the Democrats, the Whigs unwittingly ratified the Jacksonian concept of the president as a popular leader. The Whig anti-executive doctrine notwithstanding, it no longer was possible for the presidency to be restored to its late Jeffersonian status, however inept a particular president might be.[96]

John Tyler and the Problem of Presidential Succession

This consolidation of the Jacksonian presidency became more pronounced when Harrison died after only a month in office. Vice President John Tyler quickly took the oath as president, thus imposing a solution on the unresolved question of the vice president's right to assume the full status of the presidency when it became prematurely vacant. (The succession clause of Article II was vague, stipulating only that in case of the president's death, resignation, removal, or inability to discharge the powers and duties of the office "the Same" shall "devolve to the Vice President.") Leaving absolutely no doubt that he intended to be his own man as president, Tyler went before an audience assembled in the capital on April 9, 1841, and gave an inaugural address in the manner of an elected president. Tyler's "exposition of the principles" that would govern his administration was a signal to the country that he would not be content to stand in Harrison's shadow. It was also a warning to Whigs that Tyler did not intend to be a compliant servant to Clay, Webster, and other party leaders. By acting boldly and decisively, Tyler established, in the absence of clear constitutional guidance, the firm precedent that an "accidental" president enjoys the same station as an elected president.

A TIPPECANOE PROCESSION.

Supporting candidates William Henry Harrison, known for his victory over the Native Americans at the Battle of Tippecanoe, and John Tyler, Whig partisans rolled a huge paper ball from city to city, singing, "It is the ball a-rolling on for Tippecanoe and Tyler too." Thus the expression "keep the ball rolling" came into the language.

The difficulties that Tyler faced in office went beyond the constitutional doubts that shrouded his succession. His elevation to the presidency also created a political impasse. Tyler represented a faction of the Whig Party that dissented from many of the nationalist views preached by its leaders. Tyler's nomination was a gesture of compromise from the National Republican wing of the Whig Party to the smaller southern states' rights wing. Yet in this case ticket balancing backfired: Tyler decisively seized the reins of office after Harrison's death and proceeded to exercise the powers of the presidency in a way that thwarted the Whig efforts to enact Clay's "American plan" for government-sponsored economic development.[97]

Tyler's opposition to much of the Whig domestic program prompted him to cast more vetoes than any of his predecessors except Jackson. In 1841 he vetoed two successive bills that resembled the old bank legislation that Jackson had killed. The outburst of fury against Tyler after his second veto led every cabinet member except Secretary of State Daniel Webster to resign. Had Webster not resisted pressure from Senator Clay to join this "conspiracy," which included plans to prevent Tyler from reconstructing his cabinet, Tyler himself may have been forced to resign.

The bank battles were only the beginning of the struggle between Tyler and his party. His veto of a tariff measure a year later provoked the first attempt in history to impeach a president of the United States. Tyler's assertive exercise of the veto power could not be reconciled with the Whig theory of executive subordination to Congress. Clay even proposed a constitutional amendment that would permit Congress to override a veto by a simple majority vote.

Tyler, claiming for the president a right to participate in the legislative process that was reminiscent of Jackson, defended his veto of the tariff bill on programmatic, not constitutional, grounds. Like Jackson, too, Tyler argued that when a conflict developed between the president and Congress, the people were to decide who was right. When the Whigs were defeated in the congressional election of 1842, Tyler believed that his defense of the executive had been thoroughly vindicated. Moreover, nothing came of the movement to impeach the president, and the proposal for a constitutional amendment to curb the veto power was greeted with public indifference.

Thus although Tyler lost his party's support and with it any chance to be reelected in 1844, he prevented a potentially damaging setback to the executive office. As one scholar wrote, Tyler "prepared the way for the completion of the movement toward executive leadership started by Andrew Jackson." [98]

The Presidency of James K. Polk

Few would have guessed as John Tyler's term came to an end that his Democratic successor, James K. Polk, would lead a successful administration. Yet if Tyler saved the presidency from a debilitating setback, Polk moved it forward, successfully assuming responsibilities for the office that were either resisted by or denied to his predecessors.

The achievements of the Polk administration did not come easily. He faced militant Whig minorities in both houses of Congress, and he was elected as the head of a Democratic Party that had begun to reveal the first serious signs of breaking apart as a result of the slavery issue. The conflict over slavery, especially its role in the expanding U.S. territories, was the issue that led to Polk's surprising election to the presidency.

Winning the Nomination

The election of 1844 revealed that the Jacksonians' commitment to limiting the role of government in American life could not keep the slavery issue off of the national political agenda. Martin Van Buren was widely expected to receive the 1844 Democratic nomination, but then the issue of Texas, and its annexation to the United States, intervened. Just before the nominating conventions of the Whigs and the Democrats, Calhoun, Tyler's secretary of state, concluded a treaty with the Republic of Texas for its annexation. As a result, the two principal contestants for president, Van Buren and Clay, the leading Whig contender, were forced to announce their views on annexation, an issue that aroused serious disagreements over the desirability of expanding the cotton-growing and slave-holding territory of the United States.

Clay's opposition to annexation caused little controversy, but when Van Buren took the same position, a firestorm erupted in the Democratic Party. The Democrats, and their hero, Andrew Jackson, had long supported territorial expansion, an issue sacred to the emerging frontier interests in the South and the West. To defeat the Whigs, the Democrats needed strong support in the South, where states' rights advocates looked westward to expand slavery. Yet Van Buren, best known as a pragmatic politician, chose to follow what he called "the path of duty" and resist the extension of slavery. His decision cost him his chance to return to the White House. With Van Buren's candidacy seriously wounded, Governor Polk of Tennessee emerged at the deadlocked Democratic convention as a compromise choice between North and South, the first "dark horse" candidate in the history of American presidential elections. [99]

Reasserting Presidential Power

By a combination of shrewd political maneuvering and forceful statesmanship, Polk was able to overcome successfully the centrifugal forces that were beginning to dominate U.S. politics during the late 1840s. After winning the Democratic nomination, he stole one of the Whigs' main issues by disclaiming any intention of seeking a second term. Yet during his four years in office, Polk asserted vigorously and effectively executive functions that reinforced, even expanded, the Jacksonian conception of presidential power. As political scientist Stephen Skowronek has written, Polk was "determined to use his party's power as aggressively as he could to realize great national achievements." [100]

Polk was the first president to exercise close, day-to-day supervision over the executive departments. Until Polk, routine and consistent executive influence had been especially absent from the president's relations with the Treasury Department. Presidents never had been granted legal responsibility to oversee the various departmental budgetary estimates that were submitted annually to Congress. Instead, in the Treasury Act of 1789 Congress had assigned to the secretary of the Treasury the duty to prepare and report estimates of expenditures to the legislature.

George Washington's Treasury secretary, Alexander Hamilton, did not even consult the president in this matter. Hamilton was distinctive, as was Albert Gallatin, who served in the Jefferson and Madison administrations, mainly in the initiative he took in budgetary policy making. Their successors as Treasury secretary only gathered together the departmental estimates and submitted them to Congress in one package. In 1839, for example, Van Buren's secretary of the Treasury, Levi Woodbury, denied any responsibility for a composite budget or for a review of budget items submitted to him by other departments. [101]

One of Polk's major achievements was to begin to coordinate the formulation of budgetary policy. For the first time in the history of the presidency there was an executive budget. Not only did Polk review the budget requests, but he also insisted that the department heads revise their estimates downward. Polk faced the need for tight fiscal control after the Mexican War began in 1846, especially because he was operating under the reduced tariff rates of the Walker Act, which he considered one of the major accomplishments of his administration.[102]

Like his fellow Tennessean Andrew Jackson, Polk displayed a strong commitment to limiting government expenditures and a hatred of public debt. Intent upon establishing a record of sound fiscal economy for his administration and determined to assert aggressively the prerogatives of the chief executive, Polk effectively functioned as the director of the budget. *(See "The Budgeting Power," p. 608, in Chapter 11, and Chapter 15, Chief Economist.)* That Polk was successful in his efforts to control the budget was demonstrated by the tight rein he imposed on fiscal matters after the end of the Mexican War, directing his reluctant secretary of war, William Marcy, to force his bureau chiefs to accept a return to the prewar level of expenditures.

The precedents Polk established were not followed by any of his nineteenth-century successors, with the exception of Abraham Lincoln. But Polk's assertions of the president's right and duty to control the departmental activities of the executive branch implanted the Jacksonian concept of the presidency more deeply in the American constitutional order. He succeeded, wrote historian George Bancroft, who served as Polk's secretary of the navy, "because he insisted on being its [his administration's] center and in overruling and guiding all his secretaries to act as to produce unity and harmony." [103]

Polk's most important contribution to the development of the president's administrative power was his forceful performance as commander in chief during the Mexican War, which broke out in 1846 and was not settled until 1848. According to historian Leonard White, "Polk gave the country its first demonstration of the *administrative* capacities of the presidency as a war agency." [104]

Polk was only the second president to wield power as commander in chief in wartime, and James Madison, who during the War of 1812 became the first to assume this role, had done little to reveal the potential of this grant of constitutional authority. Polk did not push the power of commander in chief to its furthest limits; this task was accomplished by Abraham Lincoln during the Civil War. Unlike Madison during the War of 1812, however, Polk did establish the precedent that a president without previous military experience could control his generals. Polk insisted on being the final authority in all military matters.

Polk's efforts as commander in chief were not without partisan motivation or serious blunders. A loyal Democrat, he was disconcerted that the war was making a hero of Gen. Zachary Taylor, who was a Whig and potentially a formidable opponent for the Democrats in 1848. In a mean and petty partisan action, Polk refused to sign an order requiring the troops to fire a salute in honor of Taylor's victory in Buena Vista.

The president's relations with the army's top commander, Gen. Winfield Scott, also a Whig, were similarly governed by partisanship. Polk attempted, for example, to create a post of lieutenant general for Democratic senator Thomas Hart Benton, so the senator could supersede General Scott as the commanding officer in the field. Benton's military experience was so limited that the Democratic Senate narrowly rejected the president's recommendation.[105]

Polk's problems with his generals could be traced in part to the close relationship between the Jacksonian presidency and the newly institutionalized party system. Partisan practices had become so embedded in presidential politics during the 1830s and 1840s that these practices could not easily be put aside even in wartime.

Notwithstanding the limitations of partisan practices and doctrine, Polk's command of the Mexican War was, on the whole, very able. The general strategy he personally devised and commanded realized a decisive victory by 1848, resulting in the acquisition of New Mexico and California. Thus Polk obtained the major objective of the war and became, except for Jefferson, the president who brought the most territory under the domain of the United States. By demonstrating that the president as commander in chief could plan and oversee the execution of war strategy, Polk effectively asserted the principle that the president is responsible for the military operations of the United States.[106]

Slavery and the Twilight of the Jacksonian Presidency

Polk was the last president of the Jacksonian era who was not consumed by the slavery question. The annexation of Texas and the Mexican War greatly expanded the southwest territory of the United States, making the question of the status of slavery in this area an explosive one. The slavery issue began to split apart the Democratic Party in 1844, a development that was avoided by the compromise choice of Polk. But the spoils of the Mexican War made a similar rapprochement impossible in 1848. Martin Van Buren, the organizational genius who did so much to bring the Democratic coalition together, now split from his party to run as the third party Free Soil candidate.

Although Van Buren managed to win only 10 percent of the vote, his candidacy drew support away from the Democratic candidate Lewis Cass, thereby benefiting the Whig candidate Zachary Taylor. In all likelihood, the Van Buren candidacy did not determine the outcome of the 1848 election—Taylor, the hero of the Mexican War, probably would have been the winner in any case. But the Free Soil Party drew enough votes to affect the outcome in many state elections. Van Buren's campaign also made it more difficult for Democrats and the Whigs to ignore the slavery issue any longer. In less than a decade, the party system that had dominated the Jacksonian era would collapse and a new governing coalition would emerge.

The Presidency of Zachary Taylor

Because of its strong base in the South, the Democratic Party would survive the slavery controversy and the Civil War, although in a greatly weakened state. But the election of Taylor in 1848 was to be the last major political success of the Whig Party, which collapsed soon thereafter. The Whigs stood for national unity, an ideal that was rendered politically irrelevant by the slavery controversy. Moreover, the Whig opposition to executive power was shown decisively to be unworkable by the last Whig to be elected to the executive office. Taylor's inaugural address contained the sort of self-denying declaration regarding executive power that suggested support for Whig principles. But Taylor's brief administration (he died in 1850) was hardly true to his promise of self-denial.

More than anything else, Taylor is remembered for his consistent and unyielding opposition to the Compromise of 1850, a collection of legislative measures designed to achieve temporary peace on the slavery issue. Taylor's opposition to the compromise, which imposed no restrictions on slavery in the formerly Mexican southwest territories and strengthened the national fugitive slave law, angered slaveholders. (The compromise also admitted California to the Union as a free state and ended the slave trade in the District of Columbia.) Yet the president stood firm against the southern threats of disunion. He told southern congressional leaders that he would take the field in person to restore the Union and would hang rebels "with as little mercy as he had hanged deserters and spies in Mexico."

The Presidency of Millard Fillmore

Taylor died before the crisis created by the 1850 debate over slavery matured. His successor, Vice President Millard Fillmore of New York, repeated Whig assurances in favor of restraint over executive power yet proved no more willing than Taylor to leave critical domestic matters to Congress. But Fillmore was as determined to see the Compromise of 1850 passed as his predecessor was committed to preventing its enactment. His support was politically important. One member of the House reported that before Taylor's death between twenty and thirty representatives adamantly opposed the provisions of the compromise legislation that would allow for an expansion of slavery into the territories acquired in the Mexican War, but they did a dramatic turnabout in the face of Fillmore's support of the slavery compromise.[107]

Having seen the Compromise of 1850 through to enactment, Fillmore was determined to enforce the new and stringent Fugitive Slave Act vigorously. When Massachusetts refused to cooperate in the prosecution of its citizens who violated the act, Fillmore declared that his administration would admit "no right of nullification North or South." In practice, however, the president was never able to find a reliable means of securing compliance in those areas of the country where fugitive slaves were protected.[108]

The Presidency of Franklin Pierce

Although Fillmore's tenure demonstrated again that the Jacksonian era had transformed the presidency irrevocably, even the strengthened executive was no match for the crisis engendered by the slavery question. The final two presidents of this era, Franklin Pierce of New Hampshire and James Buchanan of Pennsylvania, were irresolute leaders who sought vainly to hold the northern and southern factions of the Democratic Party together. Each tried to defuse, rather than come to terms with, slavery as a political issue. But it was too late for temporizing. The nation's polarization over slavery was only aggravated by the efforts of Pierce and Buchanan to quell the issue.

The Kansas-Nebraska Act in 1854 was the most telling failure of Pierce's attempt to allay sectional conflict. The brainchild of Stephen Douglas, an influential Democratic senator from Illinois, the act tried to remove slavery from the national political agenda by resting its status in the territories on the principle of "popular sovereignty." According to this principle, the people of the new territory would decide whether or not they would have slavery as soon as they obtained a territorial legislature. Because the Kansas-Nebraska Act would apply popular sovereignty to the Great Plains territory of Kansas and Nebraska, the central ingredient of the 1820 Missouri Compromise, which prohibited slavery north of Missouri's southern boundary, would be repealed.

The debate on Douglas's popular sovereignty bill dragged on for three months. Pierce used all of the powers of his office, including patronage, to ensure its passage. Party discipline among Democrats, buttressed by presidential influence, prevailed. On May 25, 1854, the Kansas-Nebraska bill passed the Senate by a comfortable margin, and Pierce signed it into law. Within six months, however, it became apparent that the repeal of the Missouri Compromise had aggravated, not quelled, the slavery controversy and had divided the Democratic Party irrevocably. Perversely, Pierce's forceful leadership of his party hastened its demise as a governing institution.

The elections of 1856 revealed the emergence of a new political alignment. The Whigs' collapse after 1852 and the northern crusade against slavery in Kansas (Nebraska's vote to become a free territory was never in doubt) prompted a new party to form. Offering a platform that stood squarely against the expansion of slavery, the Republican Party nominated John C. Fremont for president in 1856. Although the

The Kansas-Nebraska Act, 1854

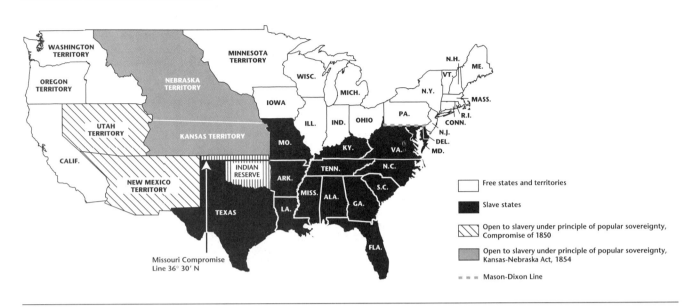

Republicans made a good showing in the election, they received no support in the South and were not yet sufficiently organized in the North to overcome this handicap. Winning Indiana, New Jersey, California, Illinois, his home state of Pennsylvania, and all 112 of the southern electoral votes, the Democratic candidate, James Buchanan, was elected president.

The Presidency of James Buchanan

Buchanan, who was just as anxious as Pierce to defuse the slavery controversy, was determined to avoid the political damage that Pierce had suffered by fighting for a legislative solution. In his inaugural address, Buchanan associated himself with an as yet unannounced Supreme Court decision, arguing that the resolution of the slavery question in the territories rightfully belonged to the federal judiciary. Referring to the pending suit by a sixty-two-year-old slave, Dred Scott, who claimed that residence in free territories had made him a free man, Buchanan pledged that he would "in common with all good citizens . . . cheerfully submit" to the decision of the Supreme Court.[109]

Such a pledge, Wilfred E. Binkley notes, "was a strange abdication of executive claims by a member of the party of Jackson who . . . had emphatically denied the right of the judiciary thus to determine public policies through the medium of court opinions." [110] In truth, Buchanan's avowed deference to the Supreme Court was disingenuous. He had privately urged Justice James Grier, who held a critical swing vote on the Court, to side with colleagues who wanted to deny Congress and the territorial legislatures the right to prohibit slavery.[111]

Buchanan's attempt to settle the agitation over slavery in a surreptitious alliance with the Supreme Court failed miserably. The Court's decision in *Dred Scott v. Sandford*, opened the entire West to slavery, regardless of what the people in the territories might decide.[112] This aggressive foray into the slavery controversy not only damaged the prestige of the Court, it also opened the floodgates to an outpouring of sectional strife that further fractured the Democratic Party and catapulted an obscure Illinois Republican, Abraham Lincoln, to the presidency in the election of 1860.

THE PRESIDENCY OF ABRAHAM LINCOLN

Abraham Lincoln was the last nineteenth-century president to make an important contribution to the theory and practice of the executive. Lincoln's accomplishments were born of a national crisis that threatened to destroy the foundations of constitutional democracy. The leadership he displayed in navigating the uncharted waters of emancipation and civil war won him the esteem of most Americans as their finest president.[113]

Whether Lincoln's talents and achievements strengthened or weakened constitutional democracy is a matter of some dispute. Lincoln's record as president has led some scholars to adjudge him not only a forceful leader but also a dictator, albeit a benevolent one in most accounts.[114] As commander in chief, especially, Lincoln demonstrated the presidency's great potential to assume extraordinary powers during a national emergency.

Conceding that Lincoln went far beyond the normal bounds of presidential power during the Civil War, constitutional scholar James G. Randall nonetheless has argued that the president showed notable restraint and leniency in administering his wartime measures, befitting his high regard for individual liberty. By doing so, Lincoln used his extraordinary powers not to subvert democracy but to save it.[115] Lincoln certainly did not regard his presidency as a dictatorship. He defended his conduct by invoking a conception of the Constitution that, although respectful of procedural regularity and formal legality, was concerned above all with the president's responsibility to uphold the basic principles of the constitutional order. Thus Lincoln's presidency not only marked a critical moment in political history but also raised anew, under conditions of unprecedented urgency, questions about the appropriate place of executive power in the American system of republican government.

It is ironic that Lincoln was the president who so forcefully extended the boundaries of the executive. Until the Kansas-Nebraska Act was passed and the Republican Party founded in 1854, Lincoln had been a Whig whose political career was distinguished by his eloquent and forceful expression of the party's opposition to the Jacksonian Democrats' expansion of presidential power. Significantly, Lincoln's first important speech, delivered in January 1838 before the Springfield Young Men's Lyceum, took the form of an allegory against great political ambition. The Framers of the Constitution were men of ample ambition, he conceded, but their passion for personal achievement proved to be a force for good because it found outlet in a great and constructive enterprise—writing, ratifying, and implementing the Constitution. But what of succeeding generations?

The twenty-nine-year-old Lincoln warned in his speech that the "perpetuity of our free institutions"—the survival of the Constitution—would be threatened by other leaders of great ambition who would not be content simply to uphold the work of the founding generation. Such men would disdain the well-worn path of constitutional government, Lincoln feared. They were members of the "family of the lion, or the tribe of the eagle" who would seek to use public office to remake politics and government in their own image. Then, in words that could be understood clearly as a condemnation of the Jacksonians' aggrandizement of execu-

The Supreme Court's denial of Dred Scott's bid for freedom effectively opened all western territories to slavery and intensified the divisions between the North and South.

tive power, Lincoln foretold of the danger of demagogy, a danger made greater by the rise of the slavery controversy. "It thirsts and burns for distinction," he said of excessive ambition, "and if possible, it will have it, whether at the expense of emancipating the slaves, or enslaving free people." In the conclusion of the Lyceum address, Lincoln urged that "a reverence for the constitution and laws" become the civil religion of the nation, a reverence that might serve as a bulwark against immoderate presidential ambition.[116]

In the mid-1840s, Lincoln's devotion to settled, standing law informed his opposition to Polk's assertive leadership in initiating and prosecuting the war with Mexico. As a Whig member of Congress, Lincoln argued that the Constitution gave the "war making power to Congress" and that "the will of the people should produce its own result without executive influence."[117]

Lincoln's pre-presidential commitment to executive restraint notwithstanding, he appeared to become as president the "towering genius," a member of the "tribe of the eagle," against whom his Lyceum appeal for a reverence of law was ostensibly directed. Lincoln never disavowed the Constitution, but his celebration of the Declaration of Independence, especially its guarantees of equality before the law and the consent of the governed, imparted a new meaning to the Framers' handiwork, a meaning that could no longer abide the principle of states' rights and the institution of slavery. According to Garry Wills, "Lincoln not only put the Declaration in a new light as a matter of founding *law,* but put its central proposition, equality, in a newly favored position as a principle of the Constitution."[118]

Lincoln was, as historian James McPherson has written, a "conservative revolutionary" who wanted to preserve the Union as the revolutionary heritage of the Framers. Preserving this heritage was the purpose of the Civil War. "My paramount object in this struggle," Lincoln wrote to Horace Greeley in the summer of 1862, "*is* to save the Union, and is *not* either to save or destroy slavery." Yet Lincoln believed that to save the Union not just for the moment but enduringly, slavery would have to become anathema to the national creed and be set on the road to extinction in law and policy.[119]

Lincoln and the Slavery Controversy

Lincoln was no abolitionist. His relative moderation on the issue helped him to wrest the 1860 presidential nomination of his party away from the avowedly pro-emancipation William H. Seward, the former governor of New York and the most prominent national Republican leader.[120] Although Lincoln consistently proclaimed himself "naturally antislavery," he believed that the national government lacked the authority to abolish slavery where it already existed. As he wrote to a friend in Kentucky, Joshua A. Speed, in 1855, "I acknowledge *your* rights and my obligations, under the Constitution, in regard to your slaves. I confess I hate to see the poor creatures hunted down, and caught, and carried back to their stripes, and unrewarded toils; but I bite my lip and keep quiet." [121]

At the same time, Lincoln believed that the extension of slavery into the western territories should not be tolerated, for such a policy threatened to perpetuate and expand the vile institution as a "positive good." With the enactment of the Kansas-Nebraska Act in 1854, Congress had violated the Framers' understanding that slavery was a "necessary evil" that must be contained and allowed to die a "natural death." This constitutional impropriety was compounded in 1857 by the *Dred Scott* decision, in which the Supreme Court declared unconstitutional any act to abolish slavery by Congress or the territorial legislatures.

Lincoln was especially distressed because the Kansas-Nebraska Act and *Dred Scott* overturned the Missouri Compromise of 1820, which had prohibited slavery in the northern part of the Louisiana territory. The spirit of the Missouri Compromise, Lincoln claimed, was true to the principles of the Declaration of Independence, as well as to the Constitution. The author of the Declaration, Thomas Jefferson, had first given form to this spirit when he conceived the policy embodied in the Northwest Ordinance of 1787, which banned slavery in the five states—Ohio, Michigan, Indiana, Wisconsin, and Lincoln's own Illinois— that composed the old Northwest Territory. Lincoln wanted to restore the Missouri Compromise not only for the sake of the Union but also for the "sacred right of self government" and the restoration of "the national faith." As he said in his Peoria address of 1854:

> Our republican robe is soiled, and trailed in the dust. Let us repurify it. Let us turn and wash it white, in the spirit, if not in the blood, of the Revolution. Let us turn slavery from its "moral rights" back upon its existing legal rights and its argument of "necessity." Let us return it to the position our fathers gave it, and there let it rest in peace.[122]

Thus although his respect for the limits imposed by the Constitution deterred Lincoln from attacking the existence of slavery in the southern states, he, unlike Stephen Douglas, his opponent in the 1858 Illinois Senate election and the author of the Kansas-Nebraska Act, was unwilling to save the Union at the price of tolerating slavery's extension into the territories. To do so would create a crisis by depriving the Constitution of its moral foundation. Lincoln argued that the South should join the North in restoring the long-standing national compromise on slavery that was embedded in the Northwest Ordinance and the Missouri Compromise.

But the logic of Lincoln's own position on slavery would not be satisfied by political compromise. In portraying his opposition to slavery as an act of statesmanship to restore the country's basic values, Lincoln shifted the terms of debate. His call for a new and explicit connection between the Declaration of Independence and the Constitution made a national struggle over the existence of slavery all but inevitable. As he said in his speech accepting the Illinois Republican Party's nomination to the Senate in 1858:

> A House divided against itself cannot stand.
>
> I believe this government cannot endure, permanently, half *slave* and half *free*.
>
> I do not (expect the Union to) be *dissolved*—I do not expect the House to *fall*—but I do expect it will cease to be divided.
>
> It will become *all* one thing, or *all* the other.[123]

The 1860 Election

The 1860 election did not provide Lincoln with a mandate to resolve the moral crisis created by the slavery controversy. He was a minority president who received almost no votes in the South. With the old Whig and Democratic coalitions supplanted by fiercely sectional politics, the election of 1860 became a fragmented contest among four candidates. The northern vote was split between the Republican Lincoln and Stephen Douglas, the official Democratic nominee; the southern electorate was divided between John C. Breckinridge of Kentucky, the standard-bearer of southern Democrats, and John Bell of Tennessee, who was nominated by the National Constitutional Union, a party that formed from the remnant of southern Whiggery.

Although the balloting yielded a decisive electoral college victory for Lincoln, who carried every northern state but New Jersey, he won slightly less than 40 percent of the popular vote. Even if the Democrats had been united in 1860, Lincoln still would have won the electoral college, but he would have lost the popular vote. As it was, Lincoln received a smaller percentage of the popular vote than any other successful presidential candidate in the nation's history. Lincoln's victory was greeted throughout the South with ominous threats of secession. In bidding farewell to the citizens of Springfield, Illinois, on the eve of his journey to the nation's capital, Lincoln said, "I now leave, not knowing when, or whether ever, I may return, with a task before me greater than that which rested upon Washington." [124]

Lincoln's likening of his task to that faced by the first president bespoke not only the troubles he anticipated but also his hope of igniting a renewed faith in freedom. "Washington fought for National Independence and triumphed," the Republican senator from Massachusetts, Charles Sumner, wrote in an 1865 eulogy for Lincoln. "Lincoln drew his reluctant sword to save those great ideas, essential to the character of the Republic, which unhappily the sword of Washington had failed to place beyond the reach of assault." [125]

Lincoln and Secession

In the face of such dire political circumstances, Lincoln's inaugural address of March 4, 1861, sought to reassure southerners that his policy toward them was one of forbearance, not coercion. Despite the widespread southern fear that the election of a Republican president threatened their property, peace, and personal security, Lincoln observed that there had never been any "reasonable cause for such apprehension." Restating his long-standing position, he renounced any "purpose, directly or indirectly, to interfere with the institution of slavery in the states where it exists." [126]

The "only substantial dispute" that faced the country, Lincoln asserted, was over the extension of slavery. "One section of the country believes slavery is *right* and ought to be extended," he said, "while the other believes it is *wrong* and ought not to be extended." This moral dispute was not, Lincoln maintained, a matter that could be settled by "legal right," as the Supreme Court had claimed when it ruled in the *Dred Scott* case that Congress could not prohibit slavery in the territories. Instead, the new president argued, slavery was an issue to be settled in the court of public opinion, through the regular course of elections. Otherwise, "the people will have ceased to be their own rulers, having to that extent practically resigned their government into the hands of an eminent tribunal." [127]

Lincoln's words fell on deaf ears. Ten weeks earlier, on December 20, 1860, South Carolina had become the first state to take itself out of the Union. Echoing its Ordinance of Nullification, which was issued in 1832 during the tariff controversy, South Carolina claimed that secession was each state's constitutional right and declared itself restored to a "separate and independent place among nations." By the time of Lincoln's inauguration, six other Deep South states—Georgia, Alabama, Mississippi, Florida, Louisiana, and Texas—had also seceded. Lincoln, following Andrew Jackson's example, used his inaugural address to pronounce the secessionist movement as treasonous: "I hold that in contemplation of universal law and of the Constitution the Union of these states is perpetual . . . , that no state upon its own mere notion can lawfully get out of the Union." [128] The new president declared that he intended to defend and maintain the Union and to enforce federal laws in all the states, just as the Constitution enjoined him to do.

Lincoln's appeal for a peaceful resolution of the slavery controversy was quickly rejected by secessionist leaders.[129] Southern whites were unwilling to distinguish his call for a compromise from outright abolitionism. They were more than half right: Lincoln's plea for compromise thinly veiled his own moral indignation against slavery. Lincoln understood slavery to be a matter of right and wrong, as a struggle between two ways of life that could not be satisfied by political compromise. This

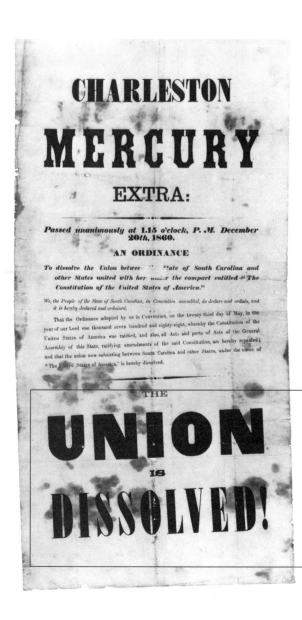

On December 20, 1860, South Carolina became the first state to take itself out of the Union. By Lincoln's inauguration March 4, 1861, six more Southern states had seceded and formed the Confederate States of America.

Alignment of states, 1861

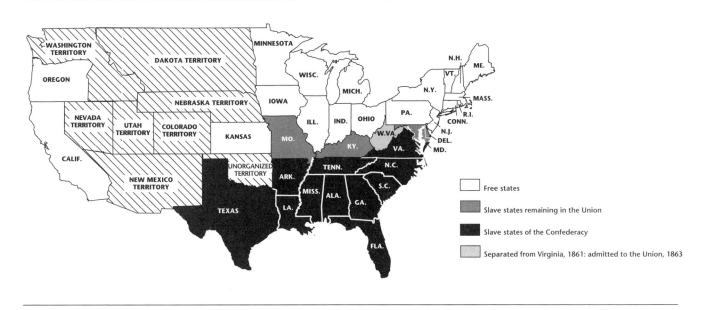

Free states

Slave states remaining in the Union

Slave states of the Confederacy

Separated from Virginia, 1861: admitted to the Union, 1863

proposition was not acceptable to the South. Nor would Lincoln compromise on what he defined as the Republican bedrock – no expansion of slavery in the territories. When word leaked out before Lincoln's inauguration that such a proposal might be offered as part of a negotiated settlement to the secession crisis, the president-elect acted quickly and forcefully. He wrote to several Republican legislators, demanding that they give no quarter: "I will be inflexible in the territorial question . . . Stand firm." [130] Lincoln's unwillingness to compromise on this issue belied the notion that he was willing to save the Union at all costs; indeed, the connection he drew between the ideal of equality and liberty and the constitutional order meant that North and South could be reconciled only on moral grounds that rejected the Southern way of life. His party agreed; despite all talk of settlement, when votes were taken on compromise measures offered by Republican senator John Crittenden of Kentucky, not a single Republican vote was cast in Congress in their favor. [131]

Lincoln's determination to carry out his party's platform and the Republicans' rejection of any compromise on their pledge to prohibit slavery in federal territories only reinforced concern among leaders in the southern states that they were engaged in a struggle to prevent the extinction of slavery. On March 5, 1861, the day after his inauguration, rebel batteries in South Carolina surrounded Fort Sumter in Charleston harbor, making an outbreak of hostilities inevitable. If the southern states' abandonment of the Union became violent and irrevocable, Lincoln believed that his oath to uphold the Constitution allowed him to take extraordinary measures, including the emancipation of the

slaves, if that was what had to be done to restore the Union. As he wrote in an 1864 letter to the Kentuckian A. G. Hodges, domestic rebellion imposed on him an obligation to use "every dispensable means" to preserve "the nation, of which the Constitution was the organic law." It was senseless, Lincoln argued, to obey legal niceties while the very foundation of the law itself—the preservation of the Union—was threatened.

> Was it possible to lose the nation and yet preserve the Constitution? By general law, life and limb must be protected, yet often a limb must be amputated to save a life; but a life is never wisely given to save a limb. I felt that measures otherwise unconstitutional might become lawful by becoming indispensable to the preservation of the nation. [132]

Even more than Lincoln's words, the reaction of southern states to his election dramatically confirmed the transformation of the presidency that had occurred during the Jacksonian era. Although a few southern leaders counseled against secession, arguing that Lincoln's power would be limited, such advice meant nothing to people who had witnessed an important expansion of executive power since 1829. While the president's authority was exaggerated in the popular mind, the myth that the presidency was the all-important organ of the national government was symptomatic of important precedents that, in effect, had made the office so powerful.

Lincoln's Wartime Powers

Lincoln did not hesitate to resort to "otherwise unconstitutional" measures after the rebels bombarded Fort Sumter on

April 12, 1861. From that day until Congress convened on July 4, everything that was done to protect the Union and prosecute the war was done by or upon the authority of the president.

The early stages of the Civil War marked the first dramatic example of a chief executive taking the law into his own hands; to that extent Lincoln waged a "presidential war." [133] Some of his actions, such as the mobilization of seventy-five thousand state militia, were clearly within the proper bounds of presidential authority. Yet Lincoln went well beyond these bounds. Hoping to bring the insurrection to a speedy end, he imposed a naval blockade of the Southern coast, enlarged the army and navy (adding eighteen thousand men to the navy and twenty-two thousand to the army), and suspended the writ of *habeas corpus*. This suspension broadly empowered government officials who were acting under the president's authority. They could make arrests without warrant, for offenses undefined in the laws, without having to answer for their actions before the regular courts.

Many of Lincoln's measures raised grave doubts about the constitutionality of the prosecution of the war. The unauthorized enlargement of the military seemed to disregard Congress's clear constitutional power "to raise and support armies." In referring to his proclamation of May 3, 1861, which called for enlistments in the regular army far beyond the existing legal limits, Lincoln frankly admitted that he had overstepped his authority.

Suspension of the Writ of Habeas Corpus

The president's critics also argued that because the power to suspend the writ of *habeas corpus* during a national emergency is mentioned in Article I of the Constitution, which defines the authority of the legislature, the right to exercise the power belongs to Congress. This was an especially controversial matter—Lincoln's suspension of *habeas corpus* struck at what presidential scholar Edward Corwin has called "the greatest of all muniments of Anglo-American liberty." [134]

Not surprisingly, the severity of Lincoln's war measures prompted charges of "military dictatorship," even from some Republicans. The president's decision not to call a special session of Congress until Independence Day lent support to these charges.

In 1863 the constitutionality of Lincoln's conduct as president became an issue before the Supreme Court in the *Prize Cases*.[135] Ships had been captured by the Union navy for violating the president's proclamations of April 19 and 27, 1861, which imposed the blockade on the Southern coast. In determining whether it was lawful for the navy to obtain these "prizes," the Court in effect decided the whole issue of the war's legality in its early stages. Shipping interests argued that a war begins only when Congress declares

war, which it did not do until July 13, 1861. Accordingly, the argument continued, the actions Lincoln took to suppress the Southern insurrection before convening the legislature, including the blockade order, were not valid.

Not unexpectedly, considering the urgent circumstances that prevailed in 1863, the Court brushed aside the shipping interests' constitutional claims. It upheld the legality of the war from the time of Lincoln's proclamation establishing a blockade, sustaining completely the president's actions taken while Congress was in recess. Curiously, in rendering this decision the Court drew attention to the legislation Congress passed on July 13 to ratify Lincoln's orders, yet refused to declare that the legislation was necessary. "If it were necessary to the technical existence of the war that it should have a legislative sanction," said the Court, "we find it in almost every act passed at the extraordinary session of . . . 1861." [136] The Supreme Court's decision in the *Prize Cases* supported Lincoln's claim that his actions were justified not only by the threat to public safety but also by his expectation that Congress would eventually approve what he had done.[137]

The extraordinary powers that were accorded to Lincoln can be understood only in terms of the extraordinary conditions he confronted. It was of considerable legal significance that, from the standpoint of the government in Washington, the Civil War began as an "insurrection." [138] Constitutionally, the president may not declare war but may proclaim the existence of a domestic rebellion, or insurrection. Lincoln believed, and Congress and the Supreme Court generally agreed, that organized and violent treasonous activity at home required quick and unilateral presidential action of a sort that might not be permissible in a formally declared war against a foreign nation. An internal rebellion, Lincoln proclaimed, may impose a special burden on the legal process because the execution of the laws is "obstructed . . . by combinations too powerful to be suppressed by the ordinary course of judicial proceedings." [139]

Lincoln's conception of the president's responsibility to suppress treasonous activity justified the suspension of the *habeas corpus* privilege and the establishment of martial law in many areas of the country. Thus he claimed sweeping powers to arrest and detain those who were suspected of rebellious activity, and citizens residing in some peaceful regions of the country were tried before military tribunals. Gen. Washington used military tribunals (sometimes called military commissions), during the Revolutionary War; these military courts were created to try members of enemy forces during wartime and operated outside the rules of evidence and other conventional codes of conduct that apply to civilian courts. Lincoln, however, was the first president to authorize their use. As the Civil War progressed, Lincoln claimed even more comprehensive powers for the military authorities, without any apparent thought of seeking authorization from Congress.[140] For example, on September 24, 1862, an executive order declared that all rebels and insurgents and all persons who discouraged enlistment, resisted the draft, or were guilty of any disloyal practice were subject to martial law and to trial by either courts-martial, which use rules of evidence similar to civilian courts, or by military tribunals.[141]

This order provoked sharp controversy in the North. The draft, which was imposed for the first time during the Civil War, was very unpopular. Prominent Republican newspaper editor Horace Greeley warned the administration, "The people have been educated to the idea of individual sovereignty and the principle of conscription is repugnant to their feelings and cannot be carried out except as a great peril to the free states." Greeley's words proved prophetic. In July 1863, draft riots broke out in New York City, sparking the greatest civil disorder in the nation's history, save for the Civil War itself. Yet resistance to the draft convinced the president that military justice and the suspension of *habeas corpus* were necessary not only while the war was being fought but also in peaceful regions of the country.[142]

Abraham Lincoln believed that the extension of his presidential powers, although of questionable constitutionality, was necessary to preserve the Union during the Civil War.

Imposition of Martial Law

The Supreme Court eventually challenged Lincoln's more far-reaching martial law measures, although not until the Civil War was over. In the case of *Ex parte Milligan*, which was decided in 1866, the Supreme Court declared illegal the use of military tribunals for the trials of citizens in districts unaffected by invasion and remote from the presence of armies.[143] *(See "Domestic Trials by Military Authorities," p. 1440, in Chapter 30, Vol. II.)* The Court declared that the constitutional guarantees of a fair trial were violated by the unrestricted exercise of martial law and that these freedoms could not be set aside merely because a state of insurrection existed. Conditions had to be so grave as to close the civil courts and depose the civil administration. Martial law, the Court stated, "could never exist where the Courts are open" but had to be "confined to the locality of actual war."[144]

The *Milligan* case diluted somewhat the legal significance of the wartime precedents that were established by Lincoln's presidency. But the powers and prerogatives that Lincoln assumed during the Civil War demonstrated conclusively, as Corwin has written, "that in meeting the domestic problems that a great war inevitably throws up an indefinite power must be attributed to the president to take emergency measures."[145]

Although Lincoln took extreme measures, neither Congress nor the Court effectively restrained him. Congress did challenge the suspension of *habeas corpus* in an 1863 statute, which directed that prisoners be released unless they were indicted in a civil court. Yet the law did not put an end to extralegal imprisonments, and it did not succeed in shifting the control of punishments from the military to the civilian tribunals. Similarly, while that war was still in progress the Supreme Court refused to interfere with the operation of the military tribunal in a case that was similar to *Milligan*.[146] In legal terms, the Civil War stands out as an exceptional period in U.S. history, "a time when constitutional restraints did not fully operate and the rule of law largely broke down."[147]

Although Lincoln's grasping of the reins of power caused him to be denounced as a dictator, other aspects of his leadership demonstrated his faithfulness to the purposes for which the Union and Constitution were ordained. The powers that Lincoln claimed were far-reaching, offering ample opportunity for abuse. But his exercise of these powers was remarkably restrained. In most cases a short military detention was followed by release or parole. As for martial law, military tribunals almost always were used to try citizens in military areas for military crimes. Cases that, like *Milligan*, involved military trials for nonmilitary crimes in peaceful areas were few.

Thus the Constitution, although stretched severely, was not subverted during the Civil War. It is a "striking fact," as Randall has noted, "that no life was forfeited and no sentence of fine and imprisonment [was] carried out in any judicial prosecution for treason arising out of the 'rebellion.' " [148] Lincoln was driven by circumstances to use more arbitrary power than perhaps any other president. Yet he was criticized for leniency as often as for severity.

The Emancipation Proclamation

Lincoln's concern with maintaining the integrity of the Constitution was revealed most clearly in his cautious handling of emancipation. The president had argued consistently that to abolish slavery where it existed was beyond the constitutional powers of Congress. Yet believing that the president's duties as commander in chief allowed him to grasp in war much that was forbidden in peace, Lincoln issued the celebrated Emancipation Proclamation on January 1, 1863.[149] Presidential proclamations are usually associated with ceremonial pronouncements, the best known example being the Thanksgiving Proclamation, which was first pronounced by Washington, and which has been issued every year since 1863.[150] But some of these decrees, such as Washington's Neutrality Proclamation of 1793, are hard to distinguish from executive orders, the type of measures which Lincoln took after the outbreak of the Civil War, requiring the federal government to take action pertaining to domestic or foreign affairs. Lincoln's 1863 proclamation appeared to establish emancipation, and not just the restoration of the Union, as the objective of the Civil War. Even so, the Emancipation Proclamation was a more limited, cautious measure than Lincoln's cabinet and the so-called Radical Republicans in Congress had hoped it would be. The proclamation did not proclaim a comprehensive and sweeping policy of emancipation. Lincoln earlier had declared unauthorized and void declarations by two of his generals that slaves in captured territory were free. Instead, Lincoln, who based his proclamation solely upon the "war power" and regarded it as "a fit and necessary war measure for suppressing rebellion," abolished slavery only in the unconquered parts of the Confederacy.[151] (See "Emancipation Proclamation," p. 1761, in Reference Materials, Vol. II.) It also declared that the door was open for African Americans "to be received into the armed services of the United States."

As an act based upon "military necessity," the Emancipation Proclamation had an important practical effect. Emancipation struck at the heart of the South's war effort by disrupting its labor force and by converting part of that labor force into a Northern military asset. More than 100,000 former slaves became Union soldiers. "Some of the commanders of our armies in the field who have given us our most important successes, believe the emancipation policy, and the use of colored troops, constitute the heaviest blow yet dealt to the rebellion," Lincoln wrote to the former mayor of Springfield, Illinois, James C. Conkling, in August 1863.[152] To be sure, there was grumbling and dissent by some Northern soldiers, who said they had enlisted to fight for the Union, not for the "nigger." But most soldiers understood and accepted the policy. As a colonel from Indiana put it, whatever their opinion of slavery and blacks, his men "desire to destroy everything that gives the rebels strength." Therefore, "this army will sustain the emancipation proclamation and enforce it with the bayonet." [153]

Although emancipation became a critical part of Union war strategy, the proclamation neither condemned slavery outright nor guaranteed that it would be abolished after the war was over. Lincoln later vetoed the Wade-Davis bill of 1864, which included the sort of sweeping emancipation and reconstruction measures that he still believed the federal government had no constitutional right to impose on the states. Yet the president seems to have realized that it was unthinkable to return blacks to slavery. When urged to do so by some Northern Democrats, who argued that the coupling of emancipation with the Union was the only stumbling block to peace negotiations with the Confederacy, Lincoln countered that "as a matter of policy, to announce such a purpose, would ruin the Union cause itself." Why would black soldiers risk their lives for the Union, he asked, "with the full notice of our purpose to betray them?" The morality of such an act was even more troubling. If he were "to return to slavery the black warriors," Lincoln stated plaintively, "I should be damned in time and eternity for so doing." [154]

In fact, Lincoln had long believed that the Union and slavery were incompatible and that the nation was threaded together by a set of principles that required equality before the law. Those who signed the Declaration of Independence "did not mean to assert the obvious untruth, that all were actually enjoying that equality, nor yet, that they were about to confer it immediately upon them," Lincoln had said in his criticism of the Dred Scott decision. "They meant simply to declare the right, so that enforcement of it might follow as fast as circumstances should permit." [155] The Civil War created the circumstances—indeed, the necessity—to pursue a course of emancipation. Thus Lincoln's presidential reconstruction policy, which he announced in December 1863, offered pardon and amnesty to white southerners who took an oath of allegiance both to the Union and to all wartime policies concerning slavery and emancipation. Reconstructed governments sponsored by Lincoln in Arkansas, Louisiana, and Tennessee abolished slavery in the Union-controlled areas of those states even before the war ended.[156]

Still, Lincoln was too respectful of procedural regularity and formal legality to abolish slavery by executive fiat. Instead, he worked to achieve abolition by constitutional amendment. In 1864 Lincoln took the lead in persuading the Republican convention to adopt a platform calling for an amendment to prohibit slavery anywhere in the United States. Because slavery was "hostile to the principles of republican government, justice, and national safety," declared the platform, Republicans vowed to accomplish its "utter and complete extirpation from the soil of the Republic." Full emancipation had thereby become an end as well as a means of Union victory.[157] But it was accomplished through regular constitutional procedures—in 1864 and 1865 Lincoln pressed the Thirteenth Amendment through a reluctant Congress. The ratification of the amendment in 1865 eliminated slavery "within the United States or any place subject to their protection."

Thus Lincoln's disregard for legal restrictions on the war power went hand in hand with a deep and abiding commitment to the principles and institutions of the U.S. Constitution. His ability to reconcile devotion to the Constitution with the ambition to eliminate slavery played a critical part in focusing the will and resources of the Union on defeating the Confederacy. As historian Phillip Paludan has written:

> Without Lincoln's unmatched ability to integrate egalitarian ends and constitutional means he could not have enlisted the range of supporters and soldiers necessary for victory. His great accomplishment was to energize and mobilize the nation affirming its better angels, by showing the nation at its best: engaged in the imperative, life-preserving conversation between structure and purpose, ideal and institution, means and ends.[158]

Lincoln did not become the tyrant he had warned against a quarter century earlier in the Lyceum speech. Instead, he invested his talent and ambition in strengthening the law by rooting it more firmly in a moral set of beliefs. As Lincoln said in his Gettysburg Address, the great task of the war was that the "nation—under God, shall have a new birth of freedom."[159]

Neither slavery nor involuntary servitude, except as a punishment for crime whereof the party shall have been duly convicted, shall exist within the United States, or any place subject to their jurisdiction.

—*Thirteenth Amendment, Section 1*

The Election of 1864

The free and full party competition that marked the 1864 election further suggests that Lincoln did not conduct the war in a dictatorial manner.[160] The stakes in this contest were great. Democrats charged that the war was hopeless. The Union army lost battles, and the Confederacy persisted in rebellion because Republicans were elevating blacks over whites and the nation over the states and individuals. With enthusiastic support from the entire convention, the 1864 Democratic platform declared that "after four years of failure to restore the Union by the experiment of war[,] . . . justice . . . and the public welfare demand that immediate efforts be made for a cessation of hostilities." [161]

Although the Democratic candidate, Gen. George B. McClellan, eventually disavowed the party's "peace before reunion" plank, he opposed the Emancipation Proclamation and wanted the Union to continue the fight only until the pre-secession status quo was restored. Thus the Republicans held "the reasonable conviction," historian Harold Hyman has written, "that a Democratic triumph would mean Confederate independence, the perpetuation of slavery, and the further fragmentation of the dis-United States." [162]

Lincoln and other Republican leaders believed that a Democratic victory was likely in 1864. There was widespread public opposition to Lincoln's conduct of the war, and the custom of the previous three decades had been for the president to serve only one term. Since Jackson's victory in 1832, no president had been reelected, and with the exception of Martin Van Buren in 1840, none even was nominated by his party for a second term. Six days before the Democratic convention, Lincoln was resigned to defeat, hoping only to defuse pressures for an immediate compromise with the Confederacy. "This morning, as for some days past," he admitted privately, "it seems exceedingly probable that the Administration will not be reelected. Then it will be my duty to so cooperate with the President-elect, as to save the Union between the election and inauguration; as he will have secured his election on such ground that he cannot possibly save it afterwards." [163]

Historian Herman Belz has argued that, in allowing the 1864 election to take place, Lincoln "accepted a risk and permitted his power to be threatened in a way that no dictator, constitutional or not, would have tolerated." [164] Lincoln's commitment to popular sovereignty was evident in the lenient attitude of his administration throughout the war in dealing with the rights of press and speech. Despite some notable and unfortunate exceptions, anti-Lincoln and anti-Union news organs were, as a rule, left undisturbed.[165] Seeing the alternatives clearly, the American people gave Lincoln 55 percent of the popular vote and an overwhelming electoral college majority of 212–21. Some Democrats charged fraud and corruption, but McClellan himself granted that Lincoln's claim to a second term was untainted. "For my country's sake I deplore the result," he reflected in a private statement, "but the people have decided with their eyes open." [166]

The election was characterized by a remarkably spirited, even strident, campaign in the midst of military hostilities, "adding not a little," as Lincoln granted after the election, "to the strain" caused by the civil insurrection. But as the president told a crowd of supporters who gathered at the White House to celebrate his victory on November 10, 1864, the election was necessary: "We cannot have free government without elections; and if rebellion could force us to forgo or postpone a national election, it might fairly claim to have already conquered and ruined us." The free and open presidential campaign, he concluded, "demonstrated that a people's government can sustain a national election in the midst of a great civil war. Until now, it has not been known to the world that this was a possibility." [167]

These were revealing words. The principal task of Lincoln's presidency had been to demonstrate that a democratic republic could survive a national struggle that threatened its survival. As he remarked on one occasion, "It has long been a grave question whether any government, not too strong for the liberties of its people, can be strong enough to maintain its existence in great emergencies." [168] His conduct of the Civil War seemed to answer this question in the affirmative. As Randall wrote:

> In a legal study of the war the two most significant facts are perhaps these: the wide extent of the war powers; and, in contrast to that, the manner in which the men in authority were nevertheless controlled by the American people's sense of constitutional government.[169]

ANDREW JOHNSON AND THE ASSAULT ON EXECUTIVE AUTHORITY

Andrew Johnson, who was elected vice president with Abraham Lincoln in 1864, faced extraordinarily difficult circumstances when he succeeded to the presidency on April 15, 1865, the morning after Lincoln was shot by the Confederate zealot John Wilkes Booth at Ford's Theatre in Washington. The Civil War had established the permanence of the Union and emancipated the slaves, but with the end of hostilities in the spring of 1865 came the enormous problems of Reconstruction. How were the Confederate states to rejoin the Union? What would be the status of the emancipated slaves?

Lincoln and the majority of the Republicans in Congress agreed that the major objectives of Reconstruction were to destroy slavery and to deny political power to the leaders of the Confederacy. They disagreed, however, about how harsh Reconstruction policies had to be to plant liberty in soil tainted by slavery. Lincoln wanted to restore the Union as quickly as possible, without imposing extensive conditions for readmission on the rebellious states. The Radicals of his party, however, led by Massachusetts senator Charles Sumner, believed that high-ranking Confederates should be punished severely for their treason, Southern states should not be granted full membership rights in the Union until they were thoroughly reconstructed and their

loyalty ensured, and blacks should be guaranteed the rights of full citizenship.

The conflict within the Republican Party over Reconstruction remained unresolved as the war drew to an end. In 1863 Lincoln had promulgated a lenient program of reunification for three Confederate states that had been conquered by the Union army—Arkansas, Louisiana, and Tennessee. According to this plan, if even 10 percent of a state's voters took an oath of allegiance to the United States, the state could form a government and elect members of Congress. The Republican-dominated Congress, declaring that reconstruction was a legislative, not an executive, function, rejected these terms as too lenient and refused to seat the newly elected legislators from the Southern states.

Congress's Reconstruction program was embodied in the Wade-Davis bill, which disenfranchised all high-ranking Confederates, stipulated that 50 percent of the voters in a rebel state must take a loyalty oath before elections could be held, and made the abolition of slavery a condition for readmission to the Union. Lincoln's pocket veto of this legislation in July 1864, accompanied by a message in which he argued that reunification should be an executive function, provoked the Republican leaders in Congress to issue the Wade-Davis Manifesto. This manifesto—a bold attack on Lincoln's Reconstruction program and a defense of the "paramount" authority of Congress—was reminiscent of the Whigs' assaults on Andrew Jackson.[170] Lincoln's landslide reelection in November took the wind out of the Radical Republicans' sails, but their strength was restored after he was assassinated. As Wilfred E. Binkley has written:

> To those who had applauded the furious blast of the Wade-Davis Manifesto against Lincoln only to see its effect nullified by the triumphant re-election of the President it must have now seemed as if fate, through the assassin's bullet, had at last delivered the government into their hands. Their glee was but ill concealed.[171]

The Radicals initially had confidence in Johnson. Before Lincoln appointed him military governor of Tennessee in early 1862 (a post he held until his nomination as Lincoln's running mate in 1864), then senator Johnson had been one of them, serving as a member of the Radical-dominated Congressional Joint Committee on the Conduct of the War. This committee criticized Lincoln's wartime initiatives constantly, often charging that the president had usurped the rightful powers of Congress. Only a few hours after Lincoln died, the committee paid a visit to Johnson. Its chair, Sen. Benjamin Wade, the cosponsor of the Wade-Davis bill and manifesto, declared, "Johnson, we have faith in you. By the gods, there will be no trouble now in running the government!" [172]

The Radical Republicans' faith was short-lived. Johnson kept Lincoln's cabinet, spurning the Radicals' advice "to get rid of the last vestige of Lincolnism." Then, without consulting Congress, he proceeded to put Lincoln's Reconstruction policies into effect by executive proclamations during the spring and summer of 1865. With the end of the Civil War, Johnson could have chosen to reconvene Congress for the purpose of establishing a jointly negotiated postwar agenda. He instead chose to preempt congressional participation in reconstruction.[173] Congressional Republicans were furious yet unable to respond. Congress was not scheduled to convene until December, and Johnson refused to call it into a special session before then.

Johnson's bold, unilateral actions no doubt were influenced by the success Lincoln had in executing major policy decisions at the outset of the Civil War while Congress was in recess, leaving the legislature with little choice but to ratify his *faits accomplis* when it returned to Washington.[174] But Johnson lacked Lincoln's political stature and skill and the latitude that the general sense of wartime urgency had allowed him. Congressional Republicans moved to establish their dominance over Reconstruction as soon as the regular session of Congress convened in December 1865.

Johnson's struggle with Congress was aggravated by the sharp differences of principle that distinguished him from most Republicans. In contrast with Lincoln, who wanted to strengthen the national government's authority to secure equality before the law for blacks, Johnson challenged Reconstruction legislation in the interest of preserving the rights of the states. To be sure, Johnson was a strong defender of the Union. During the secession crisis of 1860–1861, Johnson was the only Southern senator not to join the rebels. But in background and belief, he was also a Jacksonian Democrat. Although he gave up that affiliation to join Lincoln's Union ticket in the 1864 presidential campaign, Johnson was never comfortable in the Republican Party.

The new president's Jacksonian commitment to states' rights put him at odds with nearly all Republicans, not just Radicals. As Congress first began to pass Reconstruction legislation, moderate lawmakers repeatedly approached Johnson with strategies designed to build a consensus around modified versions of the president's own policies. But Johnson rejected these efforts.[175] In February 1866 Johnson vetoed a bill, sponsored by the moderate Republican senator Lyman Trumball of Illinois, to continue the Freedman's Bureau. He argued in his message to Congress that in time of peace it would be unconstitutional to sustain the agency, which had been created during the war to promote the welfare of Southern blacks. In vetoing Trumball's bill, Johnson was challenging not just the Radicals but every Republican in Congress.

The ties between Johnson and the Republican Party were severed irrevocably about a month later when he vetoed the Civil Rights Act, which, like the Freedman's Bureau, enjoyed unanimous support from congressional Republicans. This bill, parts of which were included in the Fourteenth Amendment, declared blacks to be citizens and bestowed on all persons born in the United States (except Native Americans) an equal right to make and enforce contracts, to sue and be witnesses in the courts, to own land and other property, and to enjoy equal protection under the law.

Had Johnson supported the Civil Rights Act, he would have satisfied the North's desire to protect blacks in the South. Radical Republicans considered any Reconstruction policy that did not impose some degree of black suffrage on the southern states as a condition for readmission tantamount to the perpetuation of "an Oligarchy of the skin." But moderate Republicans did not insist on immediate black suffrage as long as policies were adopted that recognized, and initiated a movement toward, the fulfillment of African Americans as full citizens.

Johnson's veto of the Civil Rights Act united both the party and public opinion against him. On April 6, the Senate voted 33–15 to override the president's veto of the bill; three days later the House did the same, 122–41. Congress's passage of the Civil Rights Act over Johnson's veto was a landmark in constitutional development—the first time in history that the legislature had overridden a presidential veto on an important issue. The override was equally important as a political event. Congress, not the president, was now the master of Reconstruction.[176]

Congress Assumes Control of Reconstruction

The midterm elections of 1866 were widely regarded as a referendum on the question of whether Johnson or Congress should control Reconstruction. Johnson took an active part in the campaign. In a "Swing Around the Circle" he toured the country attacking his congressional opponents and championing a National Union movement, made up of supporters of his restoration policy. The National Union "party," a coalition of Democrats, conservative Republicans, and sympathetic southerners, gathered in a convention in August. The president also used the executive patronage to punish his adversaries and purged his cabinet of those who did not support the National Union movement (of these, only Secretary of War Stanton, who was sympathetic to Congressional Reconstruction, remained) and in their place appointed conservative Republicans. Johnson's efforts to build an alternative, executive-centered organization failed as the Radical Republicans' won significant victories across the North.[177] Disgusted when all the Southern states that had been reconstructed by presidential proclamation rejected the Fourteenth Amendment, the voters routed Johnson's followers and gave the Radicals firm control over both houses of Congress. Particularly damaging to Johnson was that he had encouraged the Southern states to reject the amendment.

Spurred on by the mandate of the 1866 elections, Congress passed a series of measures in 1867 that not only deprived Johnson of his control over Reconstruction but also stripped the office of the authority to conduct the affairs of the executive departments. The Military Reconstruction Act replaced the Southern state governments that Johnson had approved with military districts led by military commanders who were granted almost total independence from presidential direction. Congress buttressed the commanders' autonomy by tacking on to the 1867 army appropriation bill riders that required the president and secretary of war to transmit their orders through General of the Army Ulysses S. Grant and forbade the president to relieve, suspend, or transfer Grant without the Senate's consent. This direct challenge to the president's authority as commander in chief was instigated and designed by Secretary of War Edwin Stanton, who, along with Grant, conspired with Republican congressional leaders to exclude Johnson from the administration of Congress's Reconstruction program.

Johnson vetoed the Military Reconstruction Act, charging that it would create an absolute despotism in the South, and protested the riders that Congress attached to the army appropriations bill by claiming that these clauses were an assault on his authority as commander in chief. Congress overrode the veto and ignored the protest. Then, to prevent Johnson from reasserting control of Reconstruction, Congress arranged to stay in session permanently. This action both nullified the president's constitutional privilege to pocket veto legislation that was passed with fewer than ten days remaining in a session of Congress and usurped the president's authority to call (or not to call) Congress into special session.[178]

Having stripped Johnson of his ability to influence legislation and the conduct of military government in the South, Congress next divested the president of his control over the personnel of the executive branch. In March 1867 Congress overrode Johnson's veto and passed the Tenure of Office Act, which prohibited the president from removing any Senate-confirmed official without first obtaining the Senate's approval. The act reversed the First Congress's decision in 1789 to uphold the president's authority to remove executive officials, which had prevailed without serious challenge for nearly eight decades. But the struggle against Johnson had reached a point where neither settled precedents nor explicit constitutional proscriptions would deter Radical Republicans any longer from attacking the rights of the executive.

By the spring of 1867, Johnson was nearly bereft of political power. He was helpless to block any legislation that Congress saw fit to pass. His only recourse was to appeal directly to public opinion. (See "The Age of Reform," p. 383, in Chapter 6.) Jefferson and, especially, Jackson had sought to establish closer ties between the presidency and the public, but they had worked through the party organization to do so. But once Johnson's efforts to build an alternative political organization to the Republicans' failed, he no longer had a party. His only recourse was to go over the heads of the congressional leaders, hoping that appeals to public opinion would restore his severely weakened presidency.

Johnson fancied himself a good orator. But especially when goaded by hecklers, his forceful attacks on Congress were prone to excess. On the evening of February 22, 1866, Washington's Birthday, he told a crowd of supporters who had marched on the White House to demonstrate their support for his veto of the Civil Rights Act that new rebels had appeared in the country, this time in the North. These men, the Radical leaders in Congress, "had assumed nearly all the powers of government" and prevented the restoration of the Union. Johnson charged Thaddeus Stevens, the Pennsylvania representative who led the Radicals in the House, and Sumner, Johnson's major opponent in the Senate, with being just as traitorous as the leaders of the Confederacy.[179]

Johnson's rhetoric backfired. Most of Johnson's speeches were delivered during his "Tour" through the North. But the press quickly seized on this expression as an object of derision and a subject of political cartoons. The vast majority of Northerners felt outraged and ashamed as they read, or read about, Johnson's speeches. The public especially resented the attacks on Stevens and Sumner, who, whatever else they might be, were no traitors to the Union. Moreover, during the nineteenth century, the purpose of Johnson's speeches—to rouse public opinion in support of his policies—was considered illegitimate, a form of demagogy that was beneath the dignity of the presidential office.[180]

The Impeachment of Andrew Johnson

Johnson's politically improper rhetoric strengthened his opposition and served as the basis for one of the eleven articles of impeachment brought against the president by the House of Representatives on February 24, 1868. Article X charged that the president ignored the duties of his office in seeking to impugn Congress and by making and delivering "with a loud voice certain intemperate, inflammatory, and scandalous harangues . . . amid cries, jeers, and laughter of the multitude then assembled."[181] The charge of "bad and improper" rhetoric was not the major reason for the impeachment proceeding against Johnson. Many members of Congress doubted that inflammatory speech was an impeachable offense. Yet because custom placed severe limitations on direct popular leadership by nineteenth-century executives, many in Congress did not consider the charge frivolous.[182] Moreover, Johnson's inflammatory speeches sought to defy the expressed will of Congress and were thus widely viewed as part of a strategy of executive usurpation,

In 1868 the House of Representatives impeached President Andrew Johnson. This sketch depicts Johnson's trial in the Senate, where by one vote he was acquitted and allowed to remain in office.

pressure of public opinion to bear upon the Senate's deliberations. Moderate Republicans, who had broken with Johnson but feared that to remove him from office would destroy the constitutional system of checks and balances, were threatened in the party press and by voters at home.[184]

Had Johnson been convicted under such conditions, the presidency might have suffered irreparable damage to its power and prestige. Yet seven Republicans stood up to the pressure of party discipline and public opinion, leaving the Radicals one vote shy of the two-thirds plurality they needed to depose Johnson. (See "Impeachment of Andrew Johnson," p. 482, in Chapter 8.)

the cause that aroused his political enemies to impeach the president. As Massachusetts representative Benjamin Butler, the leading proponent of Article X, argued during the impeachment trial: "It may be taken as an axiom in the affairs of nations that no usurper has ever seized upon the legislature of his country until he has familiarized the people with the possibility of so doing by vituperating and decrying it." [183]

Johnson's dismissal of Secretary of War Stanton was the principal issue in the impeachment proceedings. In unilaterally firing Stanton, who in spite of his position in the cabinet was regularly conspiring with the president's enemies in Congress, Johnson disregarded the requirements for Senate approval that were established by the Tenure of Office Act. His intention was to get the law into the courts to test its constitutionality. The House's 126–47 vote to impeach meant that the constitutional question would be decided, in effect, by the Senate, not the judiciary. Indeed, in the final analysis, Johnson's political enemies in Congress believed that he had to be removed not simply because he violated a law but because his violation of the Tenure of Office Act was part and parcel of a plan to subordinate the will of the legislature to executive power.

Johnson's impeachment trial, which lasted six weeks, threatened not only Johnson's presidency, but also the independence of the executive office. The Senate proceedings resembled less a trial to determine whether Johnson had committed "high crimes and misdemeanors" than a convention of the Radical Republican Party to run Johnson out of office. Republican leaders did all they could to bring the

ULYSSES S. GRANT AND THE ABDICATION OF EXECUTIVE POWER

The failure of the Senate to remove Johnson did not restore to strength either the president or the executive office. The remainder of Johnson's term was characterized by a relatively quiet impasse between the executive and the legislature. Nor did the election of Ulysses S. Grant to the presidency in 1868 revive the power of the executive. If the American people, made uneasy by the subordination of the president to Congress, thought they were electing a forceful leader in Grant, they were sorely mistaken. Although Grant's military career seemed to justify a belief that he had unusual executive ability, he was unable to transfer his talents from the battlefield to the White House. Lacking experience in civil administration, Grant had neither the detailed knowledge of the governmental process required to perform the tasks of chief executive nor the political experience needed to bend other leaders to his purposes.

Grant's shortcomings as a civilian leader were demonstrated almost immediately. The president had let it be known after his election that he favored the repeal of the Tenure of Office Act and that he would not make any appointments beyond his cabinet until such action was taken. The House soon complied with Grant's wishes, but the Senate, under the control of the Radical Republicans, approved a compromise amendment that essentially preserved its role in the removal of executive officials. Had Grant asserted himself in favor of repeal, he probably would have prevailed, considering the popularity and stature he

Gen. Ulysses S. Grant, shown here in 1864 during the Civil War, had no experience in civil administration when he became president. His successful military career suggested unusual executive ability, but he was unable to transfer that success to the presidency.

enjoyed at the time of his election. Instead, not realizing the implications of his decision, Grant capitulated to the Senate, which prompted Republicans in both houses to join ranks in support of the compromise. An advocate of repealing the Tenure of Office Act, former secretary of the navy Gideon Welles, expressed the disappointment of those who hoped Grant would restore the stature of the executive office: "The lawyers duped and cowed him. The poor devil has neither the sagacity and obstinacy for which he has credit, if he assents to this compromise, where the Executive surrenders everything and gets nothing."[185]

Grant's strategic error set the tone for his entire two terms as president. He never recovered the prestige and power he lost in his first showdown with Republican leaders in the Senate.[186] Yet his acquiescence to the Senate on the question of whether to repeal the Tenure of Office Act was no doubt influenced by his concept of the presidency. Grant

considered himself to be purely an "administrative officer"—"except on rare occasions he was, as president, disposed to accept without question the work of Congress as the authoritative expression of the will of the American people."[187] Grant's understanding of executive leadership accorded well with that of the Republican leaders in the Senate. In Grant, unlike Lincoln or Johnson, congressional Republicans had a man who was manageable. As a result, the Senate achieved the peak of its power during the Grant administration. George F. Hoar, a Republican member of the House, described the Senate's attitude toward the president:

> The most eminent Senators—[Charles] Sumner [R-Mass.], [Roscoe] Conkling [R-N.Y.], [John] Sherman [R-Ohio], George F. Edmunds [R-Vt.], [Matthew H.] Carpenter [R-Wis.], [Frederick T.] Frelinghuysen [R-N.J.], Simon Cameron [R-Pa.], [Henry B.] Anthony [R-R.I.], [John A.] Logan [R-Ill.]—would have received as a personal affront a private message from the White House expressing a desire that they should adopt any course in the discharge of their legislative duties that they did not approve. If they visited the White House, it was to give, not to receive advice.... Each of these stars kept his own orbit and shone in his sphere within which he tolerated no intrusion from the President or from anybody else.[188]

Grant did not abdicate presidential responsibilities entirely in the face of congressional dominance. Indeed, he restored the most important power of the nineteenth-century executive: the veto. Johnson had wielded this weapon aggressively, but most of his vetoes were overturned. Grant used the veto ninety-three times—more than all of his predecessors combined—and only four vetoes were overturned.[189] The most important of these vetoes killed the 1874 Inflation Bill, which Congress had passed in response to the Panic of 1873, a serious recession caused by a wave of bank failures throughout the country. The legislation would expand paper money ("greenbacks") in the economy in the hope that increasing the currency would ease the growing debt crisis, one that was especially hard on small farmers in the West. Although Grant was sympathetic to rural hardship (he owned a farm in St. Louis that had become a losing proposition), he was wary of setting lose economic forces that might wreck the government's credit and cause a spiral of inflation, thus turning a recession into a depression. With the support of Republican leadership in the Congress, Grant's veto was sustained. This action, combined with the passage of the Resumption Act at Grant's urging in 1875, made him "the president most responsible for putting the country on the gold standard."[190]

For the most part, however, Grant was uninterested in domestic policy. As a career soldier, his attention was engaged most fully by national security issues. Believing the United States, having formed a Union, should begin to protect its interests abroad, Grant cast an expansionist eye toward Central America. In his first message to Congress, Grant called for the construction of a canal linking the Caribbean and the Pacific. The president also believed the navy needed a large natural harbor. His hope was to follow through on plans initiated by the Johnson administration to purchase San Domingo (now known as the Dominican Republic), the home of Samana Bay, one of the best anchorages in the Caribbean. But the scheme ran into a buzz saw of opposition in the Senate. Charles Sumner, chairman of the Senate Foreign Relations Committee, opposed Grant's expansionist policies, considering them an affront to the high ideals that gave birth to the Republican Party. He and a number of former abolitionists bitterly scorned the attempt to annex one of the few independent black republics in the world. "To the African belongs the equatorial belt," Sumner intoned, "and he should enjoy it undisturbed." [191] Sumner's moral indignation was fueled by resentment. Sorely disappointed at not being named secretary of state, he was determined to control American foreign policy through his committee. In this case, Sumner prevailed. In 1870 the Senate rejected Grant's San Domingo treaty, with support for it falling far short of the two-thirds majority needed for ratification.[192]

Grant did not take Congress's rejection of his Caribbean policy lightly. He prevailed on the Republican leaders in the Senate to strip Sumner of his chairmanship of the Foreign Relations Committee. This measure of revenge did nothing for the president's policy toward San Domingo: the treaty was voted down again in 1871. But it did enable the Grant administration to obtain Senate ratification of the Treaty of Washington, which settled the country's bitter lingering disputes with Great Britain. These negotiations involved damages to the United States resulting from the Alabama and other British-built Confederate commerce raiders. Sumner, decrying British hypocrisy—Great Britain professed to be against slavery, yet it profited from the Civil War by selling blockade runners to the Confederacy—called for an uncompromising stance that would compensate the United States for indirect as well as direct damages. These ships, he insisted, resulted not only in the devastation of the American merchant fleet but also in the prolongation of the war. Although he shared Sumner's disdain for British neutrality, Grant was anxious to settle the dispute. He accepted the British proposal for arbitration. With Sumner deposed as chairman of the Foreign Relations Committee, and a strong Grant supporter, Simon Cameron of Pennsylvania, installed in his place, a treaty committing both sides to submit the issue to arbitration passed the Senate easily. The result was an award of $15 million and the establishment of an important precedent in international law; this was the first major dispute between two world powers to be settled not by force but by an international panel of arbitrators.[193]

Grant was thus a stronger president than most have recognized. But as his biographer Geoffrey Perret has noted, "Grant had no grand vision of his own to guide the country."

He was a transitional figure who wrestled with domestic and international events that signaled a shift from the Civil War era to the so-called Gilded Age, which saw the United States emerge as a commercial and military power. As his stance against the Inflation Bill suggested, Grant tended to view this transition favorably. But he offered no program to oversee its course. Instead, Grant's main concern was to keep "the Republican party in the White House as long as possible in order to keep the Democrats out: Republicans saved the Union; Democrats had threatened its destruction." [194]

The Grant-led Republicans were practical politicians who depended on the spoils system to maintain the vigor of their party's organization. Out of a misplaced faith in the sanctity of party loyalty, Grant exposed his administration to patronage abuses and outright peculation. The most dramatic and probably the most damaging scandal involved the evasion of internal revenue taxes on distilleries—the so-called Whiskey Ring. The Whiskey Ring included Gen. John A. McDonald, collector of internal revenue in St. Louis, who, with the collusion of Treasury officials and the president's private secretary, Gen. Orville E. Babcock, defrauded the government of millions of dollars in taxes. Perhaps the most disconcerting aspect of this scandal was Grant's efforts to protect Babcock, who was acquitted on the strength of a deposition in his favor that was prepared by the president. The honest but hopelessly naive Grant repaid Secretary of the Treasury Benjamin H. Bristow's efforts to break the Whiskey Ring and to bring its perpetrators, including Babcock, to justice by making it clear that he was no longer welcome in the cabinet. (He resigned in 1876.) Babcock, however, received a presidential appointment as inspector of lighthouses.[195]

Despite Grant's unfortunate conduct in the Whiskey Ring scandal, he was concerned about the existing system of public administration. In 1870 he called for civil service reform, declaring that "the present system [of party patronage] does not secure the best men and often not even fit men, for public place." [196] After receiving the necessary authority from Congress in March, Grant set up a board, soon known as the Civil Service Commission, and charged it to devise reformist rules and regulations. George William Curtis, the leader of the civil service reform movement in the United States, was appointed as chairman of the commission, and a competitive examination system was established in each department to conduct agency examinations under the supervision of the commission. Thus did one of the most corrupt presidential administrations in history make the first earnest attempt to reform the civil service system.

Despite this promising beginning, most of what happened during Grant's second term thwarted the cause of civil service reform. The patronage system had long been dominated by individual members of Congress, and they liked it that way. Sen. Roscoe Conkling of New York, the leader of the so-called Stalwart wing of the Republican Party, led an assault on the new commission. He was supported not only by most leaders of his party but by patronage-seeking Democrats as well. Republicans who supported civil service reform in the early 1870s turned to a third party—the Liberal Republicans. But Liberal Republicans never flourished at the grass roots. After nominating the celebrated newspaper editor Horace Greeley to run (unsuccessfully) against Grant in 1872, Liberal Republicans became anathema to the president and unable to work cooperatively with him to fend off the congressional attacks on the Civil Service Commission. Yielding, characteristically, to resistance from Congress, which refused to allocate funds for the Civil Service Commission in 1874, Grant abandoned the reform program. In strict accord with his belief that the legislature was the proper branch to determine policy, the president announced in his annual message of December 7, 1874, that if Congress adjourned without passing a civil service reform law, he would discontinue the system. Congress adjourned without taking action, and on March 9, 1875, Grant ordered that civil service examining boards throughout the country be abolished.[197]

THE FIGHT TO RESTORE PRESIDENTIAL POWER

Grant retired from the presidency in 1877, leaving the office he had occupied for eight years at one of its lowest ebbs. The Senate, its leaders believed, was "secure in its mastery over the executive."[198] Yet Grant's successor, Rutherford B. Hayes, was intent upon emancipating the executive from congressional dominance. During his administration, the prerogatives of presidential power would be defended persistently and effectively for the first time since the Civil War.

Rutherford B. Hayes

Although Hayes eventually brought more than a decade of executive decline to an abrupt end, his administration began in the least auspicious of circumstances. After eight years of Grant, a Republican defeat seemed certain in the election of 1876. Samuel J. Tilden, the Democratic candidate who as governor of New York had exposed the efforts of William Marcy ("Boss") Tweed and various political rings to corrupt the state's canal system, initially appeared to have won the election.[199] But the electoral votes of three Southern states, still subjected to military rule, and of Oregon were doubtful. Without them, Tilden had only 184 electoral votes; if Hayes carried all the uncertain states, he would have 185 votes and would win the election.

The four states—Florida, Louisiana, Oregon, and South Carolina—each sent two sets of electoral votes to Washington to be counted. Congress responded by setting up a fifteen-member electoral commission, eight Republicans and seven Democrats, to sort out the matter. At this point a deal—the Compromise of 1877—was worked out by Republican and southern Democratic leaders: In return for the Democrats' acquiescence to Hayes's election, the Republicans promised to end military rule in the South. Both sides kept their ends of the bargain. On March 2, 1877, the electoral commission by a strict party vote rejected the Democratic returns from the doubtful states and declared Hayes the winner by one electoral vote. Hayes, in turn, removed troops from the South, thus putting an end to virtually all attempts to enforce the Fourteenth Amendment's guarantee of civil rights to every citizen, including the former slaves. Nor, thereafter, did the national government make any serious effort to uphold the Fifteenth Amendment, which since 1870 had affirmed the right of citizens of the United States to vote, regardless of "race, color, or previous condition of servitude." *(See "Compromise: 1876," p. 378, in Chapter 6.)*

It is ironic that such an unsavory bargain brought to power a president who was uncompromisingly dedicated to breaking the Senate's grip on the executive office and to reforming the civil service. In his inaugural address, Hayes proclaimed that civil service reform should be "thorough, radical, and complete."[200] Congress, for its part, was uninterested in reform. By the end of Grant's second term, the influ-

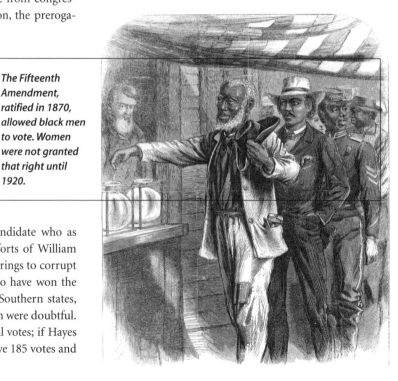

The Fifteenth Amendment, ratified in 1870, allowed black men to vote. Women were not granted that right until 1920.

ence of senators and, to a lesser extent, representatives on executive appointments had become substantial.

Hayes first offended Republican leaders in the Senate by making his choices for the cabinet without consulting them. This disrupted the Stalwarts' plan to dictate the composition of the president's cabinet. With the nomination of former Confederate David M. Key as postmaster general, it also aroused their patriotic wrath. The major insult Hayes perpetrated on the Senate, however, was his choice of civil service reformer Carl Schurz to head the Department of the Interior, a jobs-laden position that members of Congress feared Schurz would use to wage war on patronage.

Even though Hayes's nominees were a distinguished and qualified group, the offended Senate oligarchy took the president's selection as a challenge. When the president submitted his Cabinet nominations to the Senate for confirmation, the entire list was referred to committees for prolonged examination. Hoping that delay would force the president's hand, the Senate did not even exempt Sen. John Sherman, whom Hayes had nominated as secretary of the Treasury, from this process, violating the custom that fellow members, especially those as qualified as Sherman, be confirmed without investigation.

For the Senate to delay the confirmation of an entire cabinet was unprecedented, and a storm of indignation swept the country. The White House was flooded with telegrams and letters urging the president to stand firm. The Senate quickly capitulated to public opinion and, voting almost unanimously, confirmed the whole list of cabinet nominations. "For the first time since the Civil War," Wilfred E. Binkley has written, "the Senate had been vanquished on a clear cut issue between it and the President. The Senate had passed its zenith." [201]

Yet the great battle between Hayes and Congress was still to come. Having installed a cabinet of his choice, the president now set his sights on the patronage system. "Now for Civil Service Reform," Hayes wrote in his diary on April 22, 1877.[202] One of his first acts was to appoint a number of independent commissions to investigate the federal customhouses in New York, San Francisco, New Orleans, and elsewhere. These federal outposts were controlled by local party machines and had fallen into some outrageous practices in the course of collecting federal revenues. Although the investigations led to reforms in many areas of the country, the customhouse in New York, which collected more than two-thirds of all the customs revenues of the federal government, continued to serve the party machine. The independent commission that inquired into the practices of the New York customhouse found that employees were hired in response to political pressure; revealed a system of "assessments," in which employees were expected to contribute a certain percentage of their salaries to the party; and called attention to widespread incompetence and corruption among customhouse personnel.

Upon receiving the report on the New York customhouse, Hayes sought to replace its three top officials, Collector Chester A. Arthur, Surveyor General George H. Sharpe, and naval officer Alonzo B. Cornell—all of whom were prominent members of the New York state Republican organization. Yet the president's intention was impeded both by custom and by law. One obstacle was the practice of senatorial courtesy that had emerged since the Civil War. Under this practice, which still exists, if senators of the president's party object to a nominee for federal office who lives or would serve in their state, they can rely on the support of their fellow senators to reject the nomination. The Stalwart New York senator Roscoe Conkling, for whom the New York customhouse was an important base of political power, invoked senatorial courtesy to deny confirmation to the nominees Hayes selected to replace the Republican spoilsmen.

The president's nominations were referred to the Senate Committee on Commerce. Conkling, who chaired the committee, invoked the Tenure of Office Act, which had been revised in 1869, and the session of Congress ended without the nominations being confirmed. Under the amended terms of this act, the Senate no longer was authorized to confirm a presidential removal, but until it approved the president's choice of a successor, the suspended official remained in office. Thus when Hayes's nominations, which were greeted in the Senate with derisive laughter, were not approved, Arthur, Sharpe, and Cornell retained their federal posts. More important, Conkling and the New York Republican machine maintained control of the federal customhouse.

The stubborn Hayes resolved to continue the fight. On December 12, 1877, he recorded in his diary: "In the language of the press, Senator Conkling has won a great victory over the administration. . . . But the end is not yet. I am right and I shall not give up the contest." [203] After Congress adjourned in 1878, Hayes again dismissed the three officials in question, replaced them temporarily with recess appointments and in December sent to the Senate his nominations for the once-again vacant customhouse positions. Although Conkling was able to delay Senate action for two months, he finally defeated himself by delivering a bitter speech against the president, in which he alienated many senators by reading from the private correspondence of cabinet members.[204] The Senate voted to confirm Hayes's nominations on February 3, 1879.

In his letter of congratulations to Gen. E. A. Merritt, who was Arthur's replacement, the president established principles for a complete overhauling of the personnel system of the New York customhouse. Besides insisting that Merritt's office be conducted "on strictly business principles," Hayes required that the new collector confine patronage to the narrowest possible bounds. "Let no man be put out merely because he is a friend of the late collector," he wrote, "and no man be put in merely because he is our friend." [205]

Hayes's victory over Conkling came at a great cost. During the almost eighteen months it took to remove Arthur, Cornell, and Sharpe, the president was virtually powerless as the administrative head of government. Thus, even though Hayes's triumph restored some of the executive powers that had been lost since the assassination of Lincoln, his administration was to be remembered mainly for "holding its ground, rather than for developing new frontiers." [206] Still, Hayes himself was satisfied with the blows he had struck against the power of the senatorial group that for so long had directed the government. A year after winning his battle for control of the New York customhouse, Hayes wrote in his diary:

> The end I have chiefly aimed at has been to break down congressional patronage. The contest has been a bitter one. It has exposed me to attack, opposition, misconstruction, and the actual hatred of powerful men. But I have had great success. No member of either house now attempts even to dictate appointments. My sole right to make appointments is now tacitly conceded.[207]

James A. Garfield

The struggle between the president and Congress to determine the conduct of the executive office was not ended by Hayes's defeat of Conkling. The battles for appointments that had dominated Hayes's term in office were renewed, with unexpected ferocity, during the first weeks of James A. Garfield's administration.

Intraparty factionalism dominated American politics by the time of the 1880 elections. Garfield was nominated by the Republican Party on the thirty-sixth ballot. He was chosen as a compromise between the Stalwarts, led by Conkling, and the moderate wing of the party (the so-called Half-breeds), led by Sen. James G. Blaine of Maine.[208] The party further bandaged party wounds by selecting Conkling's lieutenant and former head of the New York customhouse, Chester A. Arthur, as the vice-presidential candidate. The Democrats settled on a compromise candidate of their own, the "pallid and unexceptional" Civil War general Winfield Scott Hancock of Pennsylvania, in a convention torn by factional disputes within Indiana, New York, Ohio, and Pennsylvania delegations. Out of the 9,219,467 votes cast in the election, Garfield won the national popular vote by a razor-thin margin—he received just 9,457 more votes than Hancock. Garfield prevailed by 214 to 155 in the electoral college. The closeness of the contest was not the result of a keen struggle over major issues. Instead, it was the product of highly mobilized, closely balanced national parties bringing out their supporters to the polls.

Close elections were the norm throughout the post-Reconstruction era, signifying the public's ambivalence about the parties. The electorate's unwillingness to decisively support either parties or individual candidates reflected the dominance of a highly mobilized, intensely competitive form of intraparty factionalism, in which presidents were frequently ensnared in organizational battles over local issues and spoils.[209]

Garfield seemed well suited to the new game of party politics. Unlike Hayes, the new president was by nature prone to conciliation and compromise. Once in office, he hoped to work cooperatively with both factions of the Republican Party. Yet against his will, Garfield was soon caught up in severe factional conflicts. In the heat of these intraparty squabbles, he was forced to continue the assault against senatorial courtesy that his predecessor had begun.

Garfield's attack on the Senate came in response to the Conklingites' attempt to dictate his choice for secretary of the Treasury. They demanded that the president appoint Levi P. Morton, a New York banker. Garfield resisted, arguing that Morton's Wall Street connections and his extremely conservative views on the economy made him unacceptable to western Republicans. But his conciliatory offer to name Morton as secretary of the navy and to consider other recommendations for the Treasury was scorned. The Stalwarts' answer was unequivocal: Morton must be secretary of the Treasury.

Garfield was not so conciliatory as to yield to such an aggressive challenge to executive authority. After generously recognizing the Conkling wing of the New York Republican Party by placing many of its members in federal positions, he insisted on his choices for the cabinet. He now realized, as clearly as had Hayes, that the constitutional independence of the executive "could be preserved only by a bold challenge of the pretensions of the Senate and a duel to the finish with the most militant champion of senatorial courtesy." [210]

Garfield left no doubt of his intention to challenge the Senate when he nominated William H. Robertson as collector of the port of New York. Robertson was Conkling's political enemy in New York and a friend of Conkling's major rival in national politics, Blaine. Robertson's appointment, then, was a more distinct challenge to Conkling and to the practice of senatorial courtesy than Hayes had ever issued. As Garfield wrote to his longtime friend B. A. Hinsdale, the president of Hiram College:

> This [nomination] brings on the contest at once and will settle the question whether the President is registering a clerk of the Senate or the Executive of the United States. . . . Summed up in a single sentence this is the question: shall the principal port of entry in which more than ninety percent of all our customs duties are collected be under the control of the administration or under the local control of a factional senator? [211]

Conkling marshaled his political machine in an attempt to compel Garfield to withdraw Robertson's nomination. Vice President Arthur participated fully in these maneuvers, despite stiff criticism from the press. But the president refused to budge.

When Conkling and his allies in the Senate attempted to outwit the president by preparing to confirm all the nominations except Robertson, Garfield withdrew every other New York appointment. There would be no further nominations, Garfield insisted, until the issue of who controlled the executive office was settled. The president's bold maneuver left the Stalwarts practically helpless and electrified his supporters. On May 16, 1881, seeing that Robertson's confirmation was inevitable, Conkling and fellow New York senator Thomas C. Platt resigned, hoping that the state legislature would help them to save face by reelecting them. The legislature refused to do so. After a long struggle, two other men were chosen to represent New York in the Senate.

Garfield's victory was complete. The Senate confirmed Robertson's nomination unanimously, and Conkling never was restored to public office. The president's triumph, which ended the long struggle that began with Hayes's attempt to reform the New York customhouse, marked, historian John A. Garraty has written, a "milestone in the revival of the power and prestige of the White House." Although the influence that senators wielded in suggesting persons for presidential appointments and rejecting objectionable nominees remained substantial, their claim to supersede executive discretion was ended.[212]

Chester A. Arthur and the Enactment of Civil Service Reform

Garfield did not have time to pursue a comprehensive program of civil service reform. On July 2, 1881, in a Washington railroad station, a deranged lawyer named Charles J. Guiteau shot the president in the back. Guiteau, who apparently had expected to receive a presidential appointment, blurted out upon being arrested, "I am a Stalwart; now Arthur is president." When Garfield died, after lingering until September 19, Vice President Arthur became the president.

Civil service reformers expected little from the New York Stalwart. Former president Hayes predicted that Arthur's former patron, Conkling, would be "the power behind the throne, superior to the throne."[213] But Garfield's assassination inflamed public opinion against the spoils system, and Arthur quickly realized that for him not to support civil service reform would jeopardize the dominant political position the Republican Party had enjoyed since the Civil War. The new president soon laid to rest the worst fears of those who had predicted that he would "turn the White House into a larger version of the New York customhouse."[214] Intent on strengthening his political position in the country,

Arthur, to the surprise of his critics, expressed support for limited civil service reform in his first annual message to Congress.

Arthur's commitment to reform was strengthened by the results of the 1882 congressional elections, in which the Democrats achieved dramatic gains. In his second annual message, the president called on Congress to pass the Pendleton Act, which had been introduced in 1881 by the Democratic senator from Ohio, George Hunt Pendleton. The civil service reform bill contained measures, such as competitive examinations for government jobs and a ban on political assessments, that Arthur originally had opposed. But when Congress passed the act in early 1883, Arthur signed it. Thus did the president who once had been removed as collector of the port of New York for flagrant partisan abuses launch civil service reform in the United States.

The Pendleton Act was of limited application. Its coverage extended to employees only in Washington and in major customhouses and post offices. The vast majority—all but 14,000 of 131,000 federal officeholders, including many postal workers—still were not covered. Control over the rich supply of remaining patronage jobs would be the primary source of conflict between Congress and Arthur's successor to the presidency, Grover Cleveland.

Nevertheless, the achievement of civil service reform in 1883, political scientist Leonard White has written, "was a fundamental turning point in the history of the federal administrative system." In addition to the support that it provided for merit hiring and its prohibition against on-the-job solicitations of campaign funds from federal employees, the Pendleton Act established a bipartisan, three-member Civil Service Commission, to be appointed by the president and confirmed by the Senate. The commission was vested with two important powers—to control hiring examinations and to investigate whether the new civil service rules were being enforced. Finally, the president was authorized to extend the classified service by executive order. However limited its initial application, then, the Pendleton Act laid a solid foundation on which to build the civil service in succeeding decades.[215]

The First Term of Grover Cleveland

Neither the Republicans' belated support of civil service reform nor their nomination for president of Speaker of the House James G. Blaine, the leader of the moderate, Half-breed faction of the party, could stave off defeat in the 1884 election. The Democrats' standard-bearer, Gov. Grover Cleveland of New York, won a narrow victory. He was the first Democratic president elected in twenty-four years.

Moderates in every section of the country believed that Cleveland's election heralded the true end of the bitter conflicts that had been generated by the Civil War. Cleveland was anxious to prove them correct. As the head of the party that received its greatest support from the South, he appointed many southerners to high office, including two to his cabinet. Nonetheless, Republicans still were not willing to stop waving the "bloody shirt"; they continued to paint the Democrats as unworthy of controlling the councils of power. Indeed, Cleveland's vetoes of military pension bills provided Republicans with political ammunition that became more explosive when the president signed an order returning captured Confederate flags to the South.[216] Yet Cleveland's victory was proof that the post–Civil War political order would not be upset by the election of a Democratic president. The 1884 campaign and its aftermath confirmed that recent elections were more contests to control federal patronage than grand confrontations over national issues. The Democratic victory also indicated that the nation was turning its attention away from the legacy of the Civil War and toward tariffs, currency, and other economic controversies.[217]

Not surprisingly, the 1884 election brought no moratorium in the struggle between the president and Congress to control appointments to the federal government. By winning major victories against the Senate, Hayes and Garfield had restored some prestige to the presidency, which had been so badly tarnished during the Johnson and Grant years. It fell to Cleveland, however, to fight one last battle over appointments that finally brought about the repeal of the Tenure of Office Act.

The battle began when Cleveland attempted to reward with appointments loyal Democrats, who, after being out of office for so long, were hungry to partake of the spoils of patronage. The president was no spoilsman; he had established a reputation for reform as mayor of Buffalo and governor of New York. He enforced the Pendleton Act and devoted an enormous amount of his time to scrutinizing the qualifications of candidates for federal positions that were not covered by the newly established civil service procedures. Cleveland's approach yielded a number of outstanding appointments and won him praise from civil service reformers.

Still, fashioning himself a Jacksonian Democrat, President Cleveland appreciated the benefits of the patronage system. He wanted to place deserving Democrats in jobs that had long been held by Republicans. Operating under the constraints of the amended Tenure of Office Act, however, the president was able merely to suspend, not to remove, federal employees from their jobs. In effect, Cleveland could replace officials only when the Senate was in session and approved his own nominees. The Republican-controlled Senate was loath to cooperate. Of the 643 suspensions (and corresponding appointments) that Cleveland made during the early days of his presidency, the Senate, after being in session for three months, had considered only 17, and confirmed only 15.

The larger controversy between the president and the Senate was joined in a battle for the control of one particular office, the position of United States attorney in Alabama. When Cleveland suspended the incumbent, George M. Duskin, and nominated John D. Burnett as his replacement, the chairman of the Senate Judiciary Committee, George F. Edmunds of Vermont, decided to subject the nomination to intense and protracted scrutiny. He asked Cleveland's attorney general to send to his committee all papers pertaining not just to Burnett's appointment but also to Duskin's dismissal. Cleveland directed his attorney general to comply with the request for information about Burnett. But determined to establish once and for all the president's right to remove federal officials without congressional interference, Cleveland refused to release any information about his decision to suspend Duskin.

Cleveland's refusal stung Senate Republicans, who responded with a resolution to condemn the administration for its unwillingness to cooperate. The president, in turn, sent a message to the Capitol that defended his actions and accused the legislature of infringing on his constitutional responsibilities as chief executive. Of the Senate's demand for information about his suspension of federal officials, Cleveland wrote:

> They [requests for information] assume the right of the Senate to sit in judgment upon the exercise of my exclusive discretion and executive function, for which I am solely responsible to the people from whom I have so lately received the sacred trust of office. My oath to support and defend the Constitution . . . compels me to refuse compliance with these demands.[218]

Cleveland's message to Congress dramatized his conflict with the Senate in a way that quickly caught the nation's attention. As in previous battles of this sort, public opinion supported the president. Recognizing that it was beaten, the Senate found a face-saving avenue of retreat. Someone discovered that, during the controversy, Duskin's term had expired, which made his suspension by the president no longer necessary. Burnett's appointment as U.S. attorney was quickly confirmed.

Cleveland's position on appointments was vindicated when, a few months later, with overwhelming support from both Democrats and Republicans, a bill to repeal the Tenure of Office Act was passed by Congress. "Thus," wrote Cleveland long after the event, "was an unhappy controversy happily followed by an expurgation of the last pretense of statutory sanction to an encroachment upon constitutional Executive prerogatives, and thus was a time-honored interpretation of the Constitution restored to us." [219]

CONGRESSIONAL GOVERNMENT AND THE PRELUDE TO A MORE ACTIVE PRESIDENCY

During the twelve years that passed from the end of the Grant administration in 1877 until the end of Cleveland's first term in 1889, the post–Civil War decline of executive prestige was halted. The Senate's grip on the details of administration, especially the removal power, was loosened in the defeats administered by Hayes, Garfield, and Cleveland. And the struggle to rejuvenate the independence of the presidency was advanced by the enactment of civil service reform, which began the process of insulating federal appointments from the local concerns of party spoilsmen.

The achievements of Grant's immediate successors notwithstanding, the presidency remained small in scale and limited in power during the latter half of the nineteenth century. The president's control of the executive's domain was restored, but the domain itself was still highly constricted. Late-nineteenth-century presidents had little influence on either government expenditures or the policies that were pursued by the bureaus and departments of the executive branch. *(See "The Evolution of Institutions, Laws, and Rules," p. 807, in Chapter 15.)*

In fiscal affairs, the end of the Civil War marked a transition from emergency presidential control over the amounts and purposes of government spending to renewed efforts by Congress to reassert its authority. In response, Hayes and Cleveland had exercised the veto aggressively to ward off Congress's most egregious attempts to use spending bills to impose its will on the executive. For example, in 1879 Hayes successfully vetoed an army appropriations bill because it included riders attached by the Democrats to prohibit federal marshals from employing troops or armed civilians in the southern states to keep the peace at the polls in congressional elections. In so doing, Hayes established a powerful precedent against appropriation riders that encroach on the executive power.[220]

Yet the use of the veto to affect fiscal affairs was strictly a defensive measure. Until the Budget and Accounting Act was passed in 1921, presidential authority for taxing and spending was "almost, if not entirely, lacking." [221] Presidents, at least in peacetime, were never involved when department and agency spending estimates were made and seldom were consulted when those estimates were reviewed by the various congressional committees. The secretary of the Treasury was merely a compiler, not a minister, of finance. The absence of executive leadership in fiscal matters fostered irresponsible and disorderly budgets, made worse by Congress's practice of dispersing its decision-making authority over spending among a number of appropriations committees.

The president's ability to provide guidance in public policy and to enlist Congress's support for an administration program was also limited during the latter half of the nineteenth century. No president of this era advanced a theory of presidential power that supported legislative leadership. Cleveland, for example, fiercely defended executive independence but did not believe that the president's legislative

responsibilities went beyond recommending programs for Congress to consider. Even on an issue such as the tariff, which was central to the conflict between Democrats and Republicans in the 1880s, Cleveland made little effort to bend Congress to his will. After the Democrats fared poorly in the 1886 midterm elections, Cleveland delivered a forceful message that urged Congress, in conformance with Democratic principles, to reduce tariff rates sharply. But having done this much, the president did little more. As historian John A. Garraty has written, "Like a great lethargic bear, Cleveland had bestirred himself . . . and shaken the political hive, but then he slumped back into querulous inactivity." [222]

Benjamin Harrison

The narrow bounds that constrained presidential leadership during the second half of the nineteenth century prompted Woodrow Wilson to declare in 1885, the second year of Cleveland's first term, that "unquestionably, the predominant and controlling force, the center and source of all motive and of all regulative power, is Congress." [223] Cleveland did not challenge the principle of legislative supremacy. His successor, Benjamin Harrison, enthusiastically embraced it.

Harrison, a Republican senator from Indiana, won a close election in 1888. By piling up big margins in the South, Cleveland won a plurality of the popular vote, but he lost the big northern states and thus the electoral college. This unusual development (there would not be another discrepancy between the popular and electoral college votes until the 2000 election) brought to the presidency a man who understood congressional efforts to retain control over the conduct of government. Harrison came from the dominant group of Senate leaders who had clashed with Cleveland over the president's power of dismissal. He, therefore, did not require much urging to accept the advice that Republican senator John Sherman offered him a few weeks after the election about how the office of the presidency should be conducted. "The President," Sherman wrote Harrison, "should have no policy distinct from his party and that is better represented in Congress than in the Executive." Suggesting that "Cleveland made a cardinal mistake in [seeking to dictate] a tariff policy to Congress," Sherman urged the new president to cultivate friendly relations with legislators and to follow the dictates of, rather than seek to lead, the Republicans in the House and Senate.[224]

Thus, in spite of unquestioned industry and dignified supervision of executive affairs, Harrison marked a retreat in the struggle to revive the status of the executive office. Garraty wrote of Harrison's conduct as president: "Cleveland had surrendered to the patronage system after a battle; Harrison embraced it from the start. Cleveland squabbled with Congress, and fumbled [in the tariff controversy] toward presidential leadership at least once;

Cartoonist Joseph Keppler shows President Benjamin Harrison as being too small to wear the hat of his grandfather, President William Henry Harrison. Secretary of State James Blaine, who disagreed with Harrison over an important tariff bill, is depicted here as "The Raven."

Harrison cheerfully submitted to being practically a figure-head."[225]

The absence of presidential leadership during Harrison's term, and the triumph of the doctrine of congressional sovereignty, spawned efforts to reorganize the House and Senate to perform their duties more efficiently. Before the 1880s, Congress had been primarily a deliberative body; by the end of the nineteenth century, it was a complex and well-disciplined institution that was organized to govern.

In the House, especially, lawmaking increasingly came under the control of the congressional leadership—that is, the heads of leading committees and the Speaker. The Republican Speaker during Harrison's tenure, Thomas B.

Reed, imposed rules on the House that greatly streamlined its chaotic proceedings. Confronted with the minority Democrats' use of the disappearing quorum, in which members sat mute during attendance calls to deny the Speaker the quorum he needed to conduct business, Reed counted the recalcitrants whether they signified their presence or not. In 1891 the Supreme Court sanctioned the transformation of the House into a more disciplined body by upholding the constitutionality of this and other "Reed rules," such as the ban on filibusters.[226]

A similar change occurred in the Senate, prompting the distinguished and critical English observer of the American political system James Bryce to write in 1890 that the Senate was "modern, severe, and political."[227] Forceful leaders, such as Finance Committee chair Nelson W. Aldrich of Rhode Island and Appropriations Committee chair William B. Allison of Iowa, imposed controls on the Senate that resembled the ones "Czar" Reed had established in the House. As a result, Republicans were able to bring a previously unknown degree of partisan and procedural discipline to the Senate during Harrison's tenure.

The Harrison administration, then, was one in which Congress and party organization reigned supreme. A burst of important legislation during the first half of Harrison's term, including the protectionist McKinley Tariff of 1890, marked the rise of party discipline and institutional efficiency. As such, the Harrison years offered a striking example of Whiggish, Congress-centered party government, now put into practice for the first time by the Republicans.[228]

Yet developments were under way in the country that soon would render the Whig-Republican model of party government obsolete. Massive social and economic changes were increasing the scale and complexity of American life, producing jarring economic dislocations and intense political conflicts. In the face of change, pressures mounted for a new form of governance, one that would require a more expansive role for the national government and a more systematic administration of public policy. The limited, nineteenth-century polity, which could accommodate decentralized party organizations, political patronage, and a dominant Congress, began to give way to a new order that depended upon consistent and forceful presidential leadership. The rise of a more intensely ideological politics in the 1890s, culminating in the Bryan-McKinley presidential contest of 1896, and the growing role of the United States in world affairs, which began with the Spanish-American War of 1898, set the stage for a significant transformation of the presidency.

The Second Term of Grover Cleveland

The effects of the new political order on the presidency first became apparent during the second term of Grover Cleveland, who defeated Harrison in the 1892 election.

This banner celebrates the return of Grover Cleveland and his wife, Frances, to the White House in March 1893.

Cleveland owed his political comeback to the failure of the probusiness Republican Party to assuage the nation's concerns about the economic dislocations caused by corporate industrialization.

Although the Republican-controlled Fifty-first Congress passed the Sherman Antitrust Act in 1890 to lessen the concentration of economic power in massive corporations and responded to inflationary pressures by expanding the coinage of silver, it proved to be one of the most unpopular Congresses in history. In 1890 the Democrats regained control of the House by a huge margin—the prelude, as it turned out, to Cleveland's victory two years later. Yet when Cleveland and the Democrats were themselves caught by a severe depression in 1893, the Republicans regained control of Congress in the midterm elections of 1894.

Despite Democrats' political defeat, Cleveland responded to the Panic of 1893 by wielding the powers of the presidency more vigorously, albeit no more successfully, than any president since Lincoln.[229] His call of a special session of Congress to secure the repeal of the Sherman Silver Purchase Act represented effective leadership in defense of the gold standard. Yet this dramatic departure from the hands-off approach to legislation that Cleveland had pursued during his first term cost him the support of his party. He not only alienated inflationist Democrats such as Nebraska representative William Jennings Bryan but also insulted congressional leaders who resented the president's aggressive intervention in domestic policy.

The Democratic Party's repudiation of Cleveland was all but guaranteed by his intervention in the Pullman strike against the railroads in 1894. Without consulting John P. Altgeld, the Democratic governor of Illinois, Cleveland dispatched troops to Chicago, supposedly to protect U.S. property and "to remove obstructions to the United States mails." This action infuriated Altgeld, who proclaimed in a telegram to Cleveland that

to absolutely ignore a local government in matters of this kind, when the local government is ready to furnish assistance needed, and is amply able to enforce the law, not only insults the people of this State by imputing to them an inability to govern themselves or an unwillingness to enforce the law, but is in violation of a basic principle of our institutions.[230]

Unimpressed, Cleveland replied that "in this hour of danger and public distress, discussion may well give way to active efforts on the part of all in authority to restore obedience to law and to protect life and property."[231]

Cleveland's intervention in the Pullman strike elaborated on precedents set by Lincoln during the Civil War and expanded the concept of executive emergency powers beyond the contexts of formal war and domestic insurrection. Cleveland's use of federal troops was all the more significant because he possessed neither explicit statutory authority for his actions nor the informal authorization of state and local officials.[232] Nevertheless, the president's conduct was ringingly endorsed by the Supreme Court in the *Debs* case, which upheld the arrest of Eugene V. Debs and other strike leaders for conspiring to obstruct the mails.[233] The Court ruled, in effect, that the president was authorized under his general executive powers, as stated in Article II of the Constitution, to take virtually any measure to protect the peace of the United States.[234]

Politically, Cleveland once again paid a high price for his success. Although the conservative wing of the Democratic Party praised the president, laborers and friends of labor turned against him and his party.[235] The rift between Democrats and workers was widened when the party's national convention nominated Bryan, a rural Nebraskan, for president in 1896 and fought the campaign mainly on the issue of free silver, the proposal to expand the currency by basing it on silver as well as gold. Given that the industrial cities were the fastest growing part of the country, the heavy losses that the Democrats suffered among workers and other urban voters in 1896 precipitated a lasting political realignment in favor of the Republicans.[236]

William McKinley

The dramatic Republican triumph in the 1896 election brought an astute and skilled politician, Gov. William McKinley of Ohio, to the White House. McKinley's presidency often is regarded as an uneventful prelude to the vigorous and energetic administration of Theodore Roosevelt (TR). But continuing the forceful leadership of Cleveland's second term, McKinley inaugurated important changes in the executive during his first four years.

McKinley's tenure was highly traditional in some respects. He, like Benjamin Harrison, was a party professional who came to the presidency after a long apprenticeship in Congress. Consequently, McKinley believed that good government could come only through party organization. He also carried into office a deep and abiding respect for congressional primacy. Unlike Harrison, however, McKinley did not permit the executive to decline on his watch. McKinley was the first post–Civil War president to take the political initiative without arousing the resentment of his party in Congress.[237]

Although McKinley's legislative leadership was active, it was of a kind that did not advance the cause of presidential power in enduring ways. His style of influence in Congress resembled that of Jefferson, who had quietly used the congressional caucus to enact the Democratic-Republican program nearly a century before. Jefferson's successors were unable to match his legislative influence, however, thus demonstrating the limits of party government as an instrument for sustained executive leadership.

The McKinley administration, however, was dominated not by legislation but by war and foreign policy. The president made an enduring mark on the office as commander in chief and chief diplomat.

In 1898 a conflict arose with Spain over the desire of Cuba, its colony, for independence. McKinley favored a peaceful resolution, but he ultimately yielded to public sentiment, which, aroused by sensationalist propaganda in the press, strongly favored war. McKinley carried out a "day by day, and sometimes—an hour by hour" supervision of the war effort that laid the foundation for more intense presidential involvement and greater executive control of foreign policy in the future.[238] The hostilities were so brief, the victory so complete, and, most important, the expansion of U.S. territory in the Caribbean and Pacific so considerable that no postwar reaction set in against executive power, as it had after the Civil War.

The acquisition of the Philippines and the greater influence over Cuba that accompanied victory in the Spanish-American War broadened the international obligations of the United States in ways that subdued partisan differences. For the first time since George Washington, the president attained a status above party politics. Having territory in the Pacific also increased the interest of the United States in the Far East. American participation in China during the Boxer uprising of 1900 and the successful U.S. insistence upon an open door trade policy in Asia reinforced the public's view that the United States now occupied a new and prominent position in world affairs. Thus the Spanish-American War was a landmark in the constitutional development of the executive.[239] As McKinley said to his secretary, "I can no longer be called the President of a party; I am now the President of the whole people."[240]

McKinley's tenure, then, marked an important transformation of the presidency. To be sure, his administration gave only a hint of what soon was to come in the way of vigorous presidential leadership. Committed to a limited role for the national government in the economy, McKinley did not offer or endorse a positive program to deal with trusts, labor, the civil service, race relations or other important issues of the day. Nor did he attempt to influence public opinion except through the regular channels of party politics. Although McKinley did address issues pertaining to foreign trade and America's role in the Philippines in speeches and written messages, he rarely mentioned particular bills or treaties. Following the tradition of the nineteenth-century executive, McKinley said with regard to American policy toward the Philippines, "the whole subject is now with Congress, and Congress is the voice, the conscience, and the judgment of the American people."[241]

Tellingly, however, Congress did not enact legislation to determine the civil rights and political status of America's first colony. Rather, the legislative branch sanctioned the authority of the president to set up a military government in the Philippines. Congress would exercise little oversight of the islands, which fell under the authority of the commander in chief. As a wartime president, then, McKinley capitalized on a wartime crisis and its aftermath to expand the powers of his office beyond the limits that had constrained his predecessors.[242]

THEODORE ROOSEVELT TO WOODROW WILSON

During the last three decades of the nineteenth century, major changes in American life placed increased burdens on the national government, and particularly on the office of the president. The population of the United States doubled between 1870 and 1890. Urbanization and immigration increased at extraordinary rates. These changes were accompanied by a shift in business activity from local, small-scale manufacturing and commerce to large-scale factory production and mammoth national corporations. The technological breakthroughs and frenzied search for new markets and new sources of capital that were associated with rapid industrialization caused unprecedented economic growth. Indeed, from 1863 to 1899 the index of manufacturing production rose by more than 700 percent. But dynamic growth also generated a wide range of problems that seriously challenged the capacity of the American political system to respond.

Industrial development was accomplished at the expense of other social and political values, which were sacrificed in unchecked pursuit of economic progress. The increased concentration of wealth at the turn of the century yielded giant trusts that, according to reformers, constituted uncontrolled and irresponsible units of power within American society. These industrial combinations aroused fears that opportunity would be less equal in the United States, because growing corporate might would jeopardize the ability of individuals to climb the economic ladder. Moreover, many believed that great business interests had captured and corrupted the men and methods of government for their own profit.

The first wave of protest against the financial exploitation and political corruption unleashed by industrial growth was the Populist revolt that culminated in William Jennings Bryan's ill-fated crusade for the presidency in 1896. The Progressive Era emerged after the collapse of populism. It was a period of urban and middle-class protest against many of the same forces of expanding industrialization and unrestrained finance capitalism that caused the agrarian revolts of the late nineteenth century. Because it represented the fastest growing segments of the population, progressivism had a major influence on the nation. As historian Richard Hofstadter noted, it "enlarged and redirected" agrarian discontent, resulting in industrial reform and changes in government institutions that "affected in a striking way . . . the whole tone of American political life." [243]

The progressive movement helped to bring about important changes in the office of president. Although the executive had developed significantly in the hands of strong leaders such as Washington, Jefferson, Jackson, and Lincoln, the roles and powers of the president remained tightly restricted until the twentieth century. Theodore Roosevelt changed the old pattern.

Roosevelt and the Expansion of Executive Power

On September 6, 1901, President McKinley was shot by an anarchist while attending the Pan-American Exposition in Buffalo, New York. *(See "William McKinley," p. 473, in Chapter 8.)* The president died a week later, elevating the vice president, Theodore Roosevelt, to the presidency on September 15, 1901. Disregarding the advice of friends who warned that he would seem but a "pale copy of McKinley," Roosevelt announced his intention to continue unchanged McKinley's policies and cabinet. "If a man is fit to be President," TR wrote, "he will speedily so impress himself in the office that the policies pursued will be his anyhow, and he will not have to bother as to whether he is changing them or not." [244]

The prospect of Theodore Roosevelt "impressing himself" upon the executive office greatly troubled the politicians and other men of affairs who dominated national politics at the beginning of the twentieth century. The conservative leaders of the Republican Party feared that the young president (at only forty-two he was the youngest person ever to assume the office) was not to be trusted. Throughout his political career, including his tenure as governor of New York, Roosevelt had established a reputation as a progressive and impetuous statesman, one who lived uneasily with the patronage practices and probusiness policies that dominated the Republican Party. As governor he was so troublesome to New York party regulars that they took pains to remove him from their midst by securing his nomination for vice president in 1900. "Anything can happen now that that damn cowboy is in the White House," remarked Mark Hanna, chairman of the Republican National Committee, when his friend McKinley died. Conservatives in New York and Washington openly hoped for the best, yet privately they agreed with Hanna.

Roosevelt's plain-speaking and unconventional style of leadership aside, he was not the "madman" Hanna feared. He was no enemy of business interests or party. Like most progressive reformers, he accepted the new industrial order that had grown up since the Civil War, wanting only to curb its worst abuses through government regulation. Without moderate reform, Roosevelt believed, the connection between citizens and their leaders that was the essence of republican government would be dangerously attenuated. He styled himself a conservative reformer who hoped to preserve constitutional government by pursuing a moderate program of change.

Roosevelt's Concept of Presidential Power

Presidential scholars Samuel and Dorothy Rosenman have written that, in both foreign and domestic matters, "Roosevelt extended executive authority to the furthest limit permitted in peacetime by the Constitution—if not further." [245] After leaving office, Roosevelt himself described the extension of executive authority as the principal ingredient of his remarkably successful tenure as president. "The most important factor in getting the right spirit in my administration," he wrote in his *Autobiography*, "was my insistence upon the theory that the executive power was limited only by specific restrictions and prohibitions appearing in the Constitution or imposed by Congress in its constitutional powers." [246] Believing that the delimitation of presidential power during the nineteenth century had rendered the American political system impotent and subject to capture by special interests, Roosevelt proclaimed that the president, and every executive officer in high position, was "a steward of the people bound actively and affirmatively to do all he could for the people, and not to content himself with the negative merit of keeping his talents undamaged in a napkin." [247]

Roosevelt's confidence that the president possessed a special mandate from the people made him a conscious disciple of Andrew Jackson. Unlike Jackson, however, Roosevelt wanted to join popular leadership to a greater sense of national purpose—a "New Nationalism" that foretold of an unprecedented expansion of the government's responsibility to secure the social and economic welfare of the nation.

In important respects, Roosevelt's exposition of executive power drew upon the defense of a broad discretionary authority for the president that Alexander Hamilton had articulated in 1793 under the pen name of "Pacificus." *(See "The Presidency of George Washington," p. 67.)* To justify George Washington's issuance of the Neutrality Proclamation, Hamilton had offered a theory of the presidency that was largely unacceptable until Theodore Roosevelt entered the White House. "The general doctrine of our Constitution," Hamilton argued, "is that the executive power of the nation is vested in the president; subject only to the exceptions and qualifications which are expressed in the instrument." [248] Washington, Jackson, and Lincoln had taken a broad view of the president's authority, especially in a time of national crisis. Roosevelt, however, was the first chief executive to embrace the Hamiltonian position as a recipe for the day-to-day administration of government.

Yet TR's acceptance of Hamiltonian principles certainly was not complete. Hamilton supported an energetic executive because he thought it would curb, not abet, popular influence. In contrast to the Hamiltonian concept of executive nationalism, Roosevelt expressed and embodied the Progressive's aspiration to establish the president as an agent of social and economic reform. He looked with favor on the statesmanship of Lincoln, whose uncompromising defense of the Union served the "high purpose" of achieving equality of opportunity. "Men who understand and practice the deep underlying philosophy of the Lincoln school of American political thought," wrote TR, "are necessarily Hamiltonian in their belief in a strong and efficient National Government and Jeffersonian in their belief in the people as the ultimate authority, and in the welfare of the people as the end of government." [249]

Beginning of the Rhetorical Presidency

Roosevelt's determination to use the executive office to serve the public interest, as he understood it, brought about a number of significant changes in the conduct of the executive office. Arguably, the most important of these changes was to advance the president's role as the leader of public opinion. In doing so, Roosevelt ushered in the "rhetorical presidency," that is, the use of popular rhetoric as a principal technique of presidential leadership.[250] Roosevelt was an irrepressible, if not always eloquent speaker, and is said to have been the first to use the term "bully pulpit."

The rise of the rhetorical presidency signified a dramatic transformation in the founding theory and early history of the executive. The Framers of the Constitution explicitly proscribed popular leadership. During the nineteenth century, presidential efforts to rouse public opinion in support of policy initiatives in Congress were considered illegitimate, a form of demagogy that was beneath the dignity of executive office. Roosevelt's stewardship theory of the executive, however, demanded the forging of stronger, more direct links with the public. Accordingly, on a number of occasions TR appealed directly to the people to bring pressure to bear on members of Congress who were reluctant to support his policies.

Much of Roosevelt's legislative program was designed, as TR put it, to "subordinate the big corporation to the public welfare." [251] But the Republican Party in Congress was led by conservatives—notably, Nelson Aldrich of Rhode Island and Eugene Hale of Maine in the Senate and Speaker Joseph Cannon of Illinois in the House—who distrusted anything progressive. Roosevelt sided with the "stand patters" (they were also called "Old Guard") in their support of the gold standard and in their recognition of the need, after the Spanish-American War, for a strong American presence in world affairs. Domestic policy was different. As TR later wrote of his relationship with the Republican Old Guard, "Gradually I was forced to abandon the effort to persuade them to come my way, and then I achieved results only by appealing over the heads of the Senate and House leaders to the people, who were the masters of both of us." [252]

Perhaps the most important product of Roosevelt's popular appeals was the Hepburn Act in 1906. The act enhanced the power of the Interstate Commerce Commission (ICC) to regulate railroad shipping rates and to enforce compliance with these regulations. The president's proposal was received favorably by the House of Representatives, which quickly passed railroad rate legislation in early 1905. But it ran into trouble in the Senate, where the conservative Committee on Interstate Commerce conducted long public hearings, mostly to receive opposing testimony from railroad executives.

As the Senate hearings proceeded, the president left the capital for a long vacation in the West. Speculation arose that he had given up on rate regulation.[253] In fact, Roosevelt's trip through the Middle West and Southwest in April and May of 1905 turned out to be a campaign for the Hepburn bill. The president fired his first rhetorical blast in Chicago, where, speaking before the Iroquois-Republican Club on May 10, he demanded that the ICC have "ironclad powers" to set rates.[254] This speech and similar addresses in Dallas, San

Antonio, and Denver received extensive and favorable coverage in the press.

The campaign for rate regulation continued in the early fall of 1905 on a swing through the Southwest and culminated in Roosevelt's annual message to Congress in December. Although addressed to Congress, Roosevelt's message had a larger audience in mind, the American people, and the pressure of public opinion eventually overcame the Senate's resistance to the Hepburn Act. Soon after the president's annual message, Secretary of War William Howard Taft told his brother about a confidential talk he had with the president of the Rock Island Railroad. The railroad executive had admitted that the senators he had counted on for "allegiance," while still opposed to the Hepburn bill, were yielding, because the president had so "roused the people that it was impossible for them to stand against the popular demand."[255] When Congress reconvened in 1906, the House, once again, passed the law quickly in early February. This time, however, on May 18, Roosevelt's bill also was passed by the Senate. Only three senators voted against it.

The Hepburn Act, historian George Mowry has written, "was a landmark in the evolution of federal control of private industry."[256] Among other things, it gave the ICC the power to set aside a railroad rate schedule on complaint of a shipper and prescribe a reasonable rate subject to review. This substantial expansion of federal administrative power marked the first important step away from laissez-faire and toward regulation and control of the nation's business practices. Remarkably, considering the previous history of the presidency, the Hepburn Act passed even though it was opposed from beginning to end in the Senate by the leaders of the president's own party.

Roosevelt's remarkable victory in the battle for the Hepburn Act was helped considerably by the press. He was the first president to recognize the value of the press as a medium to communicate with the people and the first to understand that journalistic support had to be pursued actively and continuously. It was TR's good fortune that his presidency coincided with the development of mass-circulation newspapers and popular magazines. Partly by inspiring intimates in the press to write articles, and partly through the force of his personality and ideas, TR "kept the pages of the popular magazines glowing with support" for his crusades.[257] As the journalist Mark Sullivan noted, "Roosevelt, in marshalling public opinion for the railroad rate bill, had, as always, help from the magazine writers."[258] Many of these journalists, including Henry Beech Needham, Ray Stannard Baker, and Walter Hines, were intimates of the president.[259]

Roosevelt also made good use of the "bully pulpit" and press in the struggle over the Pure Food and Drug Act, which made it unlawful to manufacture adulterated or mislabeled food and drugs, and the Meat Inspection Act, a response to the gruesome conditions of the meat-packing houses that were depicted in Upton Sinclair's *The Jungle*. Both of these laws were enacted in 1906. TR's triumph in the matters of rate regulation, food and drug marketing, and meat inspection signaled a change in the executive: The president's most important political relationship soon would be with the public, not with his party or with Congress. But Roosevelt also believed that a balance must exist between presidential initiative and congressional deliberation to maintain the U.S. system of government. Accordingly, even as he insisted that the modern president had to assume a more prominent place in public affairs than in the nineteenth century, TR worked assiduously to win support in Congress by cooperating with his party's leaders in the Senate and the House. In fighting for the Hepburn Act, for example, he feigned interest in a bill to reduce tariffs, which the GOP "Old Guard" regarded as the linchpin of the Republican program for industrial development, but traded his abandonment of that controversial proposal for congressional support of his more important objective, railroad regulation. The president also was willing to compromise with congressional leaders by accepting judicial review of the ICC's findings.

Thus, in leading Congress, Roosevelt artfully deployed the resources of office and person. He succeeded in part because of his remarkable political gifts and his willingness to compromise to attain his objectives. TR's presidency ensured that future presidents would have to be legislative leaders. At the same time, "Roosevelt's dealing with Congress underscored that modern presidents could not simply bend lawmakers to their will."[260]

Roosevelt and Policy Leadership

The rise of the rhetorical presidency that began during the Roosevelt administration went hand in hand with an expansion of the executive's responsibility to guide the formation of public policy. The ability of the president to lead an often factious and defiant Congress in policy matters had been limited during the latter half of the nineteenth century. McKinley's successful party leadership and the executive responsibilities in foreign policy that arose in the aftermath of the Spanish-American War suggested a more active role for the president. But only with the advent of the Progressive Era and the enormously effective stewardship of Theodore Roosevelt was a fundamental challenge posed to the way in which Congress and the party organizations held sway over the affairs of state. Thereafter, government action would be much more likely to bear the president's personal stamp than in the past.

Roosevelt's all-out campaign for the Hepburn Act and the progressive principles that it embodied came to symbolize his whole domestic policy. While in office, Roosevelt called his program the "Square Deal," proclaiming that the proper function of government was to maintain a "just balance" between management and labor, between producer and consumer, and between the extremists on both sides of the political divide.

However defined, the importance of Roosevelt's enunciation of the Square Deal to the development of the modern presidency was that it invoked principles of fairness as he, instead of his party or Congress, understood them.[261] Several presidents would define their administrations in similar terms: Woodrow Wilson's New Freedom, Franklin D. Roosevelt's New Deal, Harry S. Truman's Fair Deal, Lyndon B. Johnson's Great Society, and Ronald Reagan's Opportunity Society. The effort, routine after Roosevelt, to advertise a catchy phrase to symbolize the president's programmatic philosophy was symptomatic of a new style of presidential leadership. In this new style, the executive, not Congress, assumed the major burden of formulating public policy.

Significantly, Roosevelt's first used the term "Square Deal" during the 1904 presidential campaign to describe his vigorous intervention two years before in a nationwide coal strike. Rather than follow the example of Cleveland, who had sent troops to break up the Pullman strike of 1894, Roosevelt called representatives of the coal industry and the miners to ask both sides to agree, in the interests of the health and welfare of the nation and as a matter of patriotism, to accept binding arbitration. John Mitchell, the head of the United Mine Workers, pledged to cooperate fully with the president. But the coal industry balked at Roosevelt's proposal, even lecturing the president about the folly of "negotiating with the fomenters of anarchy." In the face of the coal industry's refusal to participate in arbitration, Roosevelt was prepared to take more drastic action. If he could not persuade management to accept arbitration voluntarily, he would appoint a settlement board without their consent and arrange for the governor of Pennsylvania to request federal assistance to keep the peace. Roosevelt also intended to have federal troops "seize the mines and run them as a receiver for the government." [262]

By previous constitutional interpretation, dating back to the *Debs* decision of 1894, the president had the authority to send soldiers into a state to ensure that the national government could exercise its authorized powers, such as to deliver the mail. Nowhere was the president's right to seize and operate private property even hinted at in the Constitution, much less specified. As it happened, such an action did not prove necessary: An agreement was reached to end the strike in October 1902, and a five member commission, appointed by the president, arbitrated the points of issue between the miners and the coal industry. Yet Roosevelt's avowed willingness to act exemplified his style as the "steward of the people." Dedicated to expanding the national government to guarantee a "just balance" between rival claims in society, Roosevelt became the first president in history to recognize the rights of labor in an industrial

dispute. The government by precedent if not by law had become responsible for managing labor disputes.[263]

Roosevelt also expanded the executive's responsibility to manage the nation's natural resources. Although the practice of setting aside nationally-owned timberlands had begun with Benjamin Harrison and was continued by Grover Cleveland, Roosevelt was the first president to adopt a comprehensive conservation program. Credit for this policy was owed in part to Roosevelt's young Forest Service director, Gifford Pinchot, who inspired the president to make conservation a leading cause of the administration. The president did so with his usual energy. By appealing to public opinion and by setting aside 43 million acres of national forest from excessive commercial exploitation, Roosevelt made conservation a national movement.[264]

In an effort to curtail Roosevelt's zeal for protecting public lands, Congress enacted a law in 1907 that barred the establishment of new national forests in the Northwest. But Roosevelt and Pinchot prepared a "midnight forests" executive proclamation that protected 16 million acres just before the bill went into effect. Roosevelt believed that the steward theory of the presidency, which allowed the president to do whatever was not expressly forbidden in the Constitution, empowered him to act without the explicit authority of the Congress or even in the face of legislative opposition when he deemed such action to be in the public interest. Lincoln's executive orders during the Civil War marked the most powerful historical examples of executive prerogative. But Roosevelt's use of executive orders established important precedents that expanded the opportunities for the routine use of prerogative power. He issued 1,091 executive orders during his two terms, nearly as many as had been issued by all previous presidents over the prior 111 years (1,259).[265]

The President as World Leader

Theodore Roosevelt's innovative and path-breaking activism in domestic politics, important as it was, pales by comparison with his conduct of foreign policy. Although the president's authority to initiate foreign policy and negotiate treaties had become settled practice during the nineteenth century, Roosevelt also asserted primacy in the execution of such policy, even when clear support from the legislature was lacking.

TR's executive theory had a policy purpose. The acquisition of territories from Spain gave the United States a new position in world affairs after 1898. Roosevelt was determined to build on this position. "Whether we desire it or not," he told Congress in his first annual message, "we must henceforth recognize that we have international duties no less than international rights." [266] Just as many progressives believed that laissez-faire must give way to a greater sense of national purpose in domestic affairs, they also urged that the general nineteenth-century commitment to international isolation be abandoned in favor of the doctrine of manifest destiny, which proclaimed for the United States a natural right to expand as much as was necessary for freedom and republican government to prosper. Progressives couched the doctrine in ethical terms, arguing that to extend U.S. territory and influence was not imperialism but its opposite. Roosevelt was in hearty accord with Herbert Croly's assertion that "peace will prevail in international relations, just as order prevails within a nation, because of the righteous use of superior force—because the power which makes for pacific organization is stronger than the power which makes for warlike organization." [267]

Practical considerations also prompted a more active foreign policy. The expansion of U.S. territory in the Caribbean and the Pacific required a dominant military presence in Central and South America, a new emphasis on the Pacific basin, and an isthmus canal so that naval power could move efficiently between the Atlantic and Pacific Oceans.

The Panama Canal. Roosevelt considered the canal to be especially important. On December 3, 1901, in his first annual message to Congress, he said, "No single great material work which remains to be undertaken on this continent is of such consequence to the American people as the building of a canal across the isthmus connecting North and South America." [268] The site eventually chosen for this project, Panama, belonged to Colombia, which to Roosevelt's surprise and embarrassment, was not willing to grant the United States the right to build the canal on the president's terms. A complicated round of diplomacy and intrigue ensued that revealed some of the most important characteristics of the Theodore Roosevelt era in American foreign policy.

On January 22, 1903, Roosevelt's secretary of state, John Hay, negotiated and signed a treaty with the Colombian minister in Washington, Thomas Herran. Under the Hay-Herran Treaty, the New Panama Canal Company, which was to construct the project, would receive $40 million from the United States, $10 million from Colombia, and an annual subsidy of $250,000. Complete sovereignty in the three-mile canal zone, however, would belong to the United States in perpetuity. These conditions were rejected by the Colombian dictator, José Manuel Marroquin.

Instead of negotiating further, Roosevelt formulated a policy to attain by force what he had failed to achieve by diplomacy. He gave tacit support to the efforts of investors in the New Panama Canal Company to foment a secessionist revolution in Panama. Roosevelt also indicated clearly that if a Panamanian revolution occurred and was unsuccessful, he would take possession of the isthmus anyway. Standing on the tenuous legal foundation of an 1846 treaty with Colombia, in which both countries had guaranteed the right of transit across the isthmus, TR was prepared to recommend to Congress that the United States should at once occupy the canal zone without any further negotiation with Colombia. He had drafted a paragraph in early October to be included in his 1903 annual message to Congress recommending this course of action. [269] When the more cautious Mark Hanna, who was now a leading figure in the Senate, was informed of this plan, he counseled patience. The president's answer typified his preference for decisive action: "I think it is well worth considering whether we had not better warn those cat-rabbits that great though our patience has been, it can be exhausted. . . . I feel that we are certainly justified in morals and . . . justified in law under the treaty of 1846, in interfering summarily and saying that the canal is to be built and that they shall not stop it." [270]

A successful revolution in Panama made it unnecessary for Roosevelt to attack Colombia. But the president did aid and protect the revolution when it broke out on November 3, 1903. A U.S. warship, the U.S.S. *Nashville,* conveniently docked in Colon the eve of the uprising and on the following days prevented Colombian troops from reinforcing their outnumbered forces in Panama. On November 6, Panama became a free and independent nation, and within an hour and a half it was recognized by the United States. Shortly after the new republic had been proclaimed, the Panamanian government signed a treaty granting the United States canal rights in return for $10 million, the amount originally offered to Colombia.

Roosevelt's course of action in the canal zone controversy applied his stewardship theory of the presidency to foreign policy. He was not reluctant to act quickly and independently, even when the support of Congress and the legal foundation for his maneuvers seemed uncertain. Roosevelt treated constitutional criticism of his policy with disdain. "At different stages of the affair," he wrote, "believers in a do-nothing policy denounced me as having 'usurped authority'—which meant, that when nobody else could or would exercise efficient authority, I exercised it." [271]

Roosevelt built the canal, proclaiming some years later that having done so was "by far the most important action that I took in foreign affairs during the time I was President." [272] Still, Colombia felt cheated and continued to press its claims for justice. Later, over former president Roosevelt's protest, an apology was extended to Colombia by the Wilson and Harding administrations, along with an indemnity award of $25 million. Yet as historian William Goldsmith has written, "the wounds in this incident were never really eradicated. . . . An unfortunate pattern of overbearing American domination in Latin American affairs was established, and even when they [interventionist policies] were at least partially abandoned in later years, the memory remains to plague future American Presidents." [273]

The taking of the canal zone signified a new policy toward Latin America, one that entailed an expanded U.S.

role in foreign affairs and enlarged presidential powers to support this role. The desire to dominate the Caribbean was buttressed by the concern of Roosevelt and others in Washington that many of the independent republics in Central and South America had weak governments with chaotic finances, thus offering a standing invitation to Europe to intervene.

In 1903 an incident in Santo Domingo prompted Roosevelt to modify significantly the Monroe Doctrine. *(See "The Presidencies of James Monroe and John Quincy Adams," p. 80.)* A corrupt dictatorship had left Santo Domingo bankrupt and unable to meet its obligations, and a revolution had left the island in chaos. In the early winter of 1903, France, Germany, and Italy were threatening intervention, and by the end of the year there were rumors that a German naval squadron was heading across the Atlantic to protect the German interests in the Caribbean. Roosevelt began to articulate a policy that proclaimed the duty of the United States to intervene in the affairs of Latin American countries that acted wrongfully or were rendered impotent by a mismanagement of their economic and political affairs. The president pronounced this policy in 1904 in his annual message to Congress. The Roosevelt Corollary to the Monroe Doctrine was a bold statement of future policy toward the debt-ridden, unstable governments of Latin America:

> If a nation shows that it knows how to act with reasonable efficiency and decency in social and political matters, if it keeps order and pays its obligations, it need fear no interference by the United States. Chronic wrongdoing, or an impotence which results in a general loosening of the ties of civilized society may in America, as elsewhere, ultimately require intervention by some civilized nation, and in the western hemisphere the adherence of the United States to the Monroe Doctrine may force the United States, however reluctantly, in flagrant cases of such wrongdoing or impotence, to the exercise of an international police power.[274]

The Roosevelt Corollary altered the Monroe Doctrine, which had denied to Europeans the right to intervene in the Americas, by sanctioning United States intervention. Less than a month after Roosevelt announced the new policy, worsening conditions in Santo Domingo led him to translate his words into action. In early 1905, confronted on the one side with a nation that faced bankruptcy and on the other with European powers demanding satisfaction for their accounts, Roosevelt forced an agreement on Santo Domingo to establish a U.S. financial protectorate over the island. When the Senate, resentful of the president's acting unilaterally to develop a novel foreign policy, failed to ratify the treaty, Roosevelt implemented the protectorate anyway, considering it an executive agreement, which further antagonized his congressional critics. The executive agreement was two years old before the Senate finally acquiesced and approved it with minor modifications in 1907.

The eventual success of Roosevelt's Caribbean policy strengthened both his personal political position and, ultimately, the institutional status of the president in foreign affairs. In the past, it had not been uncommon for Congress, especially the Senate, to intervene in foreign policy. The role that Theodore Roosevelt staked out for the president was not bounded by specific provisions of the Constitution, statutes passed by Congress, or, as his resort to an executive agreement with Santo Domingo illustrated, even the Senate's power to ratify treaties. "The Constitution did not explicitly give me power to bring about the necessary agreement with Santo Domingo," Roosevelt wrote in 1913. "But the Constitution did not forbid my doing what I did."[275]

The Russian-Japanese War. The departure from the nineteenth-century doctrine of isolation that Roosevelt's Latin American policy signified was revealed even more clearly by TR's initiatives in Asia, especially his unprecedented intervention in a conflict between Russia and Japan over China in 1905.

After Russia moved troops into China in 1902—an action that, among other things, threatened the U.S. Open Door Policy of free trade in China—Japan staged a devastating surprise attack on the Russian fleet anchored at Port Arthur. Because Roosevelt considered Russia a greater imperialistic threat in Asia, his sympathies lay with Japan. Indeed, the president fortified the Japanese with secret verbal assurances that the United States would support Japan if any of the European powers came to the aid of the Russians. This extraordinary commitment also included an agreement by Japan to recognize U.S. jurisdiction in the Philippines in return for U.S. recognition of Japan's claim to Korea. Thus, for the first time, a president had committed the United States to possible future military action, as well as to the recognition of one nation's claim on another nation's territory and sovereignty, without consulting the Senate.

Roosevelt's audacious diplomacy ended in triumph. Although the president favored Japan as a counterweight to Russia's designs on China, he feared that too great a Japanese victory might endanger the peace of the entire Pacific area. When fighting in the Russo-Japanese War tilted dramatically in Japan's favor, Roosevelt arranged, without the knowledge of the cabinet, Congress, or even most of the State Department, for Russia and Japan to meet in a peace conference at Portsmouth, New Hampshire. There the president managed, through what Mowry has called "patient, tactful and brilliant diplomacy," to bring about the Peace of Portsmouth in September 1905. The agreement achieved a balance of power in Asia that satisfied the interests not only of the warring nations but also, because the open door policy was maintained, of the United States.[276] Roosevelt's policy was further advanced in 1907, when, again without consulting Congress or the cabinet, he sent the U.S. battle fleet on a tour around the world. This daring and brilliant maneuver won public support for an expanded navy and demonstrated to the Japanese the intention and ability of the United States to protect its interests in Asia.

Roosevelt's approach to foreign policy, although successful, did not complete the recently begun task of establishing the United States as a world power. His effort to expand both America's role in the world and the executive responsibility in foreign affairs took place without sustained and serious discussion by either the American people or their representatives in Congress. As Goldsmith has written, "Theodore Roosevelt set the stage for the American President to play a world historical role that in many instances successive Presidents were neither capable of nor inclined to follow, nor were the American people prepared to support it." [277]

The Troubled Presidency of William Howard Taft

Roosevelt was a remarkably popular and influential president. Had TR decided to stand for another term in 1908, he almost certainly would have been renominated and most likely would have been reelected. [278] But he had promised in November 1904 that he would not run again. The three and a half years he had already served, Roosevelt stated at the time, constituted his first term. Because he considered the custom that limited presidents to two terms a wise one, on election night he issued a statement declaring that he would not be "a candidate for or accept another nomination." [279]

Although Roosevelt was clearly tempted to go back on this promise in 1908, the fact that he did not do so revealed his commitment to the traditions and institutions of constitutional government. Roosevelt believed strongly that the powers of the president needed to be expanded for the good, indeed the survival, of the nation. But he was also acutely aware that representative government would be poorly served by the concentration of too much power in its first citizen.

Self-denial, however, did not prevent Roosevelt from selecting William Howard Taft, his secretary of war and closest adviser during the second term, as his successor. Nor did it stop him from "throwing his hat in the ring" in 1912 and challenging Taft's renomination, charging that his friend and fellow Republican had betrayed the progressive principles he was elected to uphold. Taft sincerely intended to carry on the policies of his predecessor, and he had some success in doing so. But he was ill suited, by philosophy and personality, to match TR's stewardship of the executive office.

In the wake of Roosevelt's presidency, Taft seemed an anachronism. Although never saying so publicly, Taft disap-

proved of TR's theory that it is the president's duty "to do anything that the needs of the nation demand, unless such action is forbidden by the Constitution or the law." Taft's view of executive power, like the understanding that had prevailed during the latter half of the nineteenth century, eschewed a broad interpretation of the executive's discretionary powers. As he wrote some years after leaving office:

> The true view of the executive function ... is that the President can exercise no power which cannot be reasonably or fairly traced to some specific grant of power or justly implied or included within such express grant as necessary and proper to exercise. Such specific grant must be either in the Constitution or in an act of Congress passed in pursuance thereof. There is no undefined residuum of power which he can exercise because it seems to be in the public interest. [280]

Because he construed the executive power narrowly, Taft denied that to be president required him to exercise either popular or policy leadership. He rejected the notion that he bore a special mandate from the people and refused to make any serious effort to court public opinion or the press. Taft also rejected Roosevelt-style "swings around the circle" as a device either to publicize his program or to bring public pressure to bear upon Congress. Such speaking tours as Taft undertook came at the urging of his aides and were made with considerable reluctance. "The Taft administra-

Theodore Roosevelt (left) stands with his hand-picked successor, William Howard Taft.

tion," political scientist Elmer Cornwell has noted, "represented a hiatus in the presidential leadership of opinion, if not actually a retrograde step." [281]

Taft dedicated himself to an ambitious legislative program that would institutionalize in law the reforms that Roosevelt's vigorous and independent executive action had begun. For example, in an effort to make conservation policy a matter of settled law, Taft prepared a special message in 1909 that asked Congress to pass a bill to codify Roosevelt's "midnight forests" executive order. As he wrote to California conservationist William Kent, "we have a government of limited power under the Constitution, and we have got to work out our problems on the basis of law." [282] But Taft's passive view of presidential power shaped his pursuit of the bill in Congress. He has serious misgivings about interfering in the legislative process. "I have no disposition," Taft told Senate majority leader Aldrich, "to exert any other influence than that which it is my function under the Constitution to exercise." [283]

Although Taft's position on conservation prevailed, his broader policy of forbearance in legislative matters cost him dearly, especially during the early days of his presidency. Indeed, his passivity led people to think that he agreed with the conservative Republican leadership in Congress, which caused an irrevocable split between Taft and the Roosevelt administration alumni whom he had allowed to stay in office. Pinchot felt that Taft's unwillingness to act in the absence of explicit authority crippled progressive policies. "After TR came Taft," Pinchot later wrote. "It was as though a sharp sword had been succeeded by a roll of paper, legal size." [284]

Taft's modest definition of executive power governed his relations with Congress even on those policies that were closest to his heart. Of all the campaign promises he made in 1908, Taft was probably the most serious about wanting to reduce tariff rates. Yet the president stood by passively in 1910 as Congress watered down his proposal to alter the nation's protectionist policies. Senate Republicans added more than eight hundred amendments to the strong tariff reform bill that had been passed by the House. Taft simply signed the version that came out of the House-Senate conference committee, even though it closely resembled the Senate bill. [285]

Public deference to Congress, by itself, did not necessarily foreclose an impressive legislative record. Jefferson and McKinley had worked quietly within party councils to exercise considerable influence over Congress. But Taft lacked the political skill to provide this kind of party leadership. His pre-presidential experience was confined to judicial and administrative offices. Like Herbert Hoover in 1929, Taft came to the White House relatively unversed in public and legislative politics. [286]

Taft also suffered from changing political conditions. The Republican Party was badly divided between an increasingly stubborn conservative, probusiness majority and a large and growing progressive minority that was bent on reform. By force of personality and popular support, Roosevelt held the party together, even when his progressivism, which grew stronger during his presidency, made the cleavage between the Old Guard and the insurgent Republicans more distinct. In contrast, Taft's feeble efforts to mediate the differences between conservatives and reformers only aggravated the situation.

The outbreak of virtual civil war in the Republican Party began with a progressive revolt in the House of Representatives. Unwilling to tolerate any longer the conservative policies and arbitrary leadership of Speaker Cannon, Republican insurgents, led by Rep. George Norris of Nebraska, united with the Democrats in March 1910 to strip the speakership of most of its power. Although Cannon was not removed as Speaker, his influence was limited substantially. No longer would the Speaker control the members' committee assignments or the all-important Rules Committee, which set the House's legislative agenda. Even the Speaker's constitutional role of presiding officer was narrowed by new rules that limited his discretionary parliamentary prerogatives. [287]

The weakening of party leadership, long a bulwark of congressional government, ultimately hastened the fundamental transfer of power from Congress to the White House that first had became noticeable during Roosevelt's presidency. The same progressive revolt that toppled the speakership in the House also undermined the foundation of party government in the Senate, depriving the leaders of their control of legislative deliberations. Power in both houses of Congress devolved to committees, especially the committee chairs, who became specialized masters of legislation. Congress grew steadily less able to meet the growing responsibilities of the national government.

Taft, his narrow construction of executive power notwithstanding, was sensitive to the new public demands. Late in his term he suggested that the presidential and legislative branches be brought closer together by giving cabinet members nonvoting seats in Congress. He also endorsed a presidential commission's call for the president to hold various departments and agencies to a comprehensive budgetary program. Taft submitted the first executive budget in 1913 just before he went out of office.

Taft's proposals to strengthen the executive were ignored by Congress. But they revealed that even he had come to recognize that Roosevelt's dynamic leadership and the changing character of the country had placed more responsibility in the presidency than during the nineteenth century.

Woodrow Wilson and the Defense of Popular Leadership

After the Republicans lost control of the House of Representatives in the 1910 midterm elections, it became apparent that Taft probably would not be reelected as president. This election, Mowry has written, was "one of those significant divides in American history which signalize a reversal in trends before a complete transfer of power occurs." [288] For the first time in sixteen years the Democratic Party controlled the House of Representatives, and although the Republicans kept their majority in the Senate, it was a purely nominal one. The insurgent Republicans, who strengthened their position in the primary and general elections of that year, held the balance of power between the almost evenly divided regular Republican and Democratic forces. The 1910 election also went far to rehabilitate the Democratic Party because it furnished it with a number of progressives, most of whom were unattached to William Jennings Bryan, the fiery rural populist who had led the party to defeat in three of the past four presidential campaigns.

Among the newly elected progressive Democrats was Woodrow Wilson, who had been a political science professor and was the president of Princeton University. In 1910 Wilson was elected governor of New Jersey. Two years later, after a long deadlock, the Democratic national convention nominated Wilson for president on the forty-sixth ballot. The nomination was secured when former Democratic presidential nominee William Jennings Bryan, in a symbolic passing of the torch, threw his full support to Wilson in hopes of thwarting the Democratic Party's conservative eastern business interests. Thus, after failing for two decades to offer a program that addressed the challenges of the Progressive Era, the Democrats suddenly found themselves led by an articulate and forward-looking scholar-politician. Wilson's victory in 1912 was only the third by a Democrat since the Civil War. Enough Democrats were swept into Congress to give the party solid majorities in both the Senate and House for the first time in more than fifty years.

The Democratic opportunity to govern might not have been realized had the Republicans not self-destructed in 1912. An intraparty progressive revolt against Taft gave rise to the insurgent candidacy of Wisconsin senator Robert La Follette, who challenged the president's bid for renomination. When La Follette failed to draw much support outside the Midwest, progressives turned to Theodore Roosevelt, who on February 21 announced, "My hat is in the ring." Persuaded that his candidacy was indispensable to the progressive cause and bored by four years of inactivity, TR abandoned his pledge not to run again for president.

For the first time, direct primaries would contribute significantly to the selection of delegates to the party conventions. The Republican rank and file supported Roosevelt in these contests. In the thirteen states that selected convention delegates by primary, Roosevelt won 276 delegates; Taft, 46; and La Follette, 36. But in 1912 most delegates still were selected at state conventions dominated by regular party leaders, who much preferred Taft's stolidity to the frenetic progressivism of Roosevelt.

When it became clear at the Republican national convention that Roosevelt would not be nominated, he and his followers walked out, reconvening in Chicago on August 5, 1912, as the Progressive Party. In a speech that advanced the cause of New Nationalism, Roosevelt called for "strong national regulation" of interstate corporations; social insurance in times of injury, sickness, unemployment, and old age; and constitutional reforms to establish a "pure democracy." The progressives' vision of democratic government was to be realized by enacting an easier method to amend the Constitution, universal use of the direct primary, voter initiatives, referenda on laws that the state courts declared unconstitutional, women's suffrage, and limits on the judicial power to issue labor injunctions.

The 1912 presidential election was a triumph for progressivism, but it sent Wilson, not Roosevelt, to the White House. Although, like Lincoln, Wilson polled a minority of popular votes, he won the election easily. The final tally awarded 6.3 million popular votes and 435 electoral votes to Wilson, 4.1 million popular votes and 88 electoral votes to Roosevelt, and 3.5 million popular votes and 8 electoral votes to Taft. Eugene V. Debs collected 900,000 votes, the highest total ever for a Socialist Party candidate in a presidential election, but no electoral votes.

Above all, the 1912 election was a decisive rejection of the Republican Old Guard. Its candidate, the incumbent Taft, was able to carry only two states, Vermont and Utah. The combined popular vote of Wilson, Roosevelt, and Debs, all three advocates of progressive policies, was more than 75 percent.[289] The results enabled Wilson, although he was a minority president, to reap the benefits of a reform movement that was cresting just as he entered the White House. The new president seized the opportunity not just to advance progressive social and economic policies but also to extend further the restructuring of executive leadership that Roosevelt had begun.

Wilson's Theory of Executive Leadership

Woodrow Wilson had long wanted to reform the principles and institutions that governed the U.S. political system to ameliorate what he regarded as a disconcerting lack of energy and consistency. In 1879, as a student of twenty-three, he published an article that called for major institutional reforms to establish closer ties between the executive and the legislature. At the time, Wilson believed this connection could be forged best by enhancing the power of Congress, which dominated politics during the second half of the nineteenth century. Wilson urged the United States to adopt a British-style cabinet system, which concentrated power in an executive board that was responsible to the legislature (or Parliament, as it was called in Britain). Specifically, he proposed that the Constitution be amended "to give the heads of the Executive departments—the members of the Cabinet—seats in Congress, with the privilege of the initiative in legislation and some part in the unbounded privileges now commanded by the Standing Committees."[290] The president, who, in Wilson's view, had been rendered virtually useless in the aftermath of the Civil War, would become a figurehead like the British monarch.

Although Wilson never abandoned the idea that checks and balances should be replaced by an American version of Parliament, his views about presidential leadership changed dramatically. In the early 1900s, he argued that the best hope for leadership in the United States lay in a strong presidency.[291] No doubt Wilson was influenced by Theodore Roosevelt, whose vigorous and independent stewardship demonstrated the potential power of the executive. Wilson disagreed strongly with TR about certain institutional and policy matters, but he credited him for charting a new path of presidential leadership. "Whatever else we may think or say of Theodore Roosevelt," Wilson said in 1909, "we must admit he was an aggressive leader. He led Congress—he was not driven by Congress. We may not approve of his methods but we must concede that he made Congress follow him."[292]

Wilson's theory of presidential power required a more comprehensive rethinking of the American constitutional order than did Roosevelt's stewardship model. As president, TR had accepted the constitutional system of checks and balances, seeking only to revive and modify Hamiltonian nationalism so that the government could address the problems of an industrial society. Even when Roosevelt roused the people to bring pressure to bear upon Congress, he did so in a way that was intended to preserve the independence of both branches.

Wilson agreed with TR that the president must direct more attention to national problems. But he also believed that executive leadership would be ineffective or dangerous unless it was accompanied by a fundamental change in the government's working arrangements. Such a change would unite the usually separated branches of government.[293] Most significant, the president's role as party leader would be strengthened. Instead of limiting executive power, as it had during much of the nineteenth century, the party system would be modified to enable the president to command Congress's support.

Wilson's Presidency and the Art of Popular Leadership

As president, Wilson tried to perfect Roosevelt's methods of popular leadership and to apply them in a way that would establish him as the leader of Congress and the Democratic Party. He was not completely successful in this endeavor, but Wilson's two terms in office brought about major changes in the presidency. According to Wilson biographer Arthur Link, "historians a century hence will probably rate the expansion and perfection of the powers of the presidency as his most lasting contribution."[294]

In contrast to Roosevelt, who regarded popular rhetoric and "swings around the circle" as methods to be used infrequently and in defense of specific pieces of legislation, Wilson believed that an ongoing effort to inspire the American people was the main ingredient of executive leadership. His effective use of oratory and public messages established a new rhetorical standard: The president now was required to articulate a vision of the future and to guide the nation toward it. As Wilson announced in his first inaugural address:

> This is the high enterprise of the new day: to lift everything that concerns our life as a nation to the light that shines from the hearthfire of every man's conscience and vision of the right. . . . We know our task to be no mere task of politics but a task which shall search us through and through, whether we be able to understand our time and the need of our people, whether we be indeed their spokesmen and interpreters, whether we have the pure heart to comprehend and the rectified will to choose our high course of action.[295]

At his best, Wilson was a spellbinder. He not only understood the popular aspirations of his day but also was able to translate them into words. In the course of doing so he consciously defended and, by example, established the legitimacy of public rhetoric as a principal tool of presidential leadership.

Wilson's desire to be in close touch with the people led him to make enduring innovations in the executive's relationship with the press and Congress. Unlike Roosevelt, Wilson distrusted reporters. He was by temperament and philosophy unable to cultivate reporters personally. He was, however, the first president to have formal press conferences, which he held frequently during his first two years in office. In a sense, Wilson started regular press conferences because he distrusted the Fourth Estate. Less gregarious than Roosevelt, yet certain that regular contact with the press was an essential part of his effort to take the people fully into his confidence, Wilson employed formal and restricted press conferences as an effective forum for his relations with journalists.[296]

Nevertheless, Wilson did not rely on the press to communicate his views. The president's preferred devices for public leadership were speeches and formal messages. Wilson began his presidency by reviving the practice of appearing in person before Congress to deliver the State of the Union address and other important public messages. Thomas Jefferson had abandoned the custom (established by George Washington and carried on by John Adams) of appearing before Congress because it resembled too much the British monarch's speech from the throne. The White House's announcement on April 6, 1913, that Wilson himself would speak on tariff reform to the two houses of Congress on April 8 shocked some legislators. Especially concerned were certain of the president's fellow Democrats, who revered the Jeffersonian custom. Sen. Sharpe Williams of Mississippi, an original Wilson supporter, led the attack, concluding hopefully that the tariff message "would be the only instance of the breach of the perfectly simple, democratic and American custom of messages in writing which Thomas Jefferson instituted." [297] Williams's hope was disappointed. Wilson addressed Congress in person frequently. "As he no doubt foresaw," Cornwell has written, "this forum would so concentrate public attention as to eliminate the likelihood that the newspapers would either slight or distort his message." [298]

Wilson's Relations with Congress

Appearances before Congress also served Wilson's desire to break down the wall that so long divided the executive from the legislature. Although part of his purpose was to guide public opinion, it was equally important to establish customs and make symbolic gestures that would strengthen the president's ties to Congress. Wilson began his tariff address to the somewhat tense legislators by speaking directly to the symbolic purpose of his appearance:

> I am very glad indeed to have this opportunity to address the two houses directly and to verify for myself the impression that the President of the United States is a person, not a mere department of government hailing Congress from some isolated island of jealous power, sending messages, not speaking naturally with his own voice—that he is a human being trying to cooperate with other human beings in a common service. After this pleasant experience I shall feel quite normal in all our dealings with one another.[299]

Wilson's precedent-shattering speech was well received by most members of Congress. It launched the first successful campaign for tariff reform since before the Civil War. Some of the other innovations also were significant, such as the practice of visiting Capitol Hill to meet personally with members of Congress while deliberations proceeded on an important bill. Wilson followed his dramatic tariff address by appearing the next day in the president's room of the Senate to confer with the Finance Committee, which was responsible for tariff legislation. No president since Grant had met with members of a congressional committee at the Capitol.

Nothing contributed more to Wilson's leadership of Congress than the control he asserted over the House and the Senate Democrats. The Democrats were at least as divided between conservative and progressive as the Republicans. Nevertheless, Wilson decided to work with his party in Congress instead of governing with a coalition of progressive Democrats and progressive Republicans, as he might have done. He labored assiduously to formulate a comprehensive policy program and to establish it as the party plan. He even persuaded the House Democratic caucus to adopt a rule that bound its members to support the administration's policies. Similar discipline was obtained in the traditionally more individualistic Senate, where the party caucus declared important pieces of legislation such as the tariff bill to be party measures and urged all Democrats to support them.

Owing to his effective leadership, Wilson was able to drive through Congress the major policies of his 1912 electoral platform, heralded by him as the New Freedom. The catchphrase expressed Wilson's own understanding of progressivism, which he believed was rooted deeply in the traditions of the Democratic Party.

Roosevelt's New Nationalism had accepted the evolution of great corporations as both inevitable and, with strict public regulation of their activities by a powerful federal government, desirable. In contrast, Wilson wanted to free business from the plague of monopoly and special privilege, thus making unnecessary a correspondingly dangerous centralization of administrative power. "As to monopolies, which Mr. Roosevelt proposes to legalize and welcome," Wilson remarked during the 1912 campaign, "I know that they are so many cars of juggernaut, and I do not look forward with pleasure to the time when the juggernauts are licensed and driven by commissioners of the United States." [300] As the leader of the Democratic Party, Wilson promised tariff reform, an overhaul of the banking and currency system, and a vigorous antitrust program that would "disentangle" the "colossal community of interest" in the United States and restore fair competition to the economy.[301]

To the astonishment of both Wilson's friends and enemies, Congress approved most elements of the New Freedom agenda in 1913 and 1914. The Underwood Tariff Act became law in October 1913. The Federal Reserve Act, which reconstructed the national banking and currency system, followed in late December. Finally, two statutes passed in 1914, the Clayton Anti-Trust Act and the Federal Trade Commission Act, whch strengthened the government's authority to prevent unfair competition.

Taken as a whole, Wilson's legislative achievements were remarkable. In contrast to Roosevelt, Wilson had turned his fractious party into a disciplined body. In the course of doing so, he enacted programs that progressives had been demanding for two decades. Still, the New Freedom program soon was compromised severely by weak administration and a conservative judiciary, which still adhered to a restrictive view of the federal government's constitutional powers in the economy. The New Freedom program was narrowly conceived. Given the strength of laissez-faire doctrine in the United States, it was a notable achievement. However, Wilson's concept of reform sought to restore competition in the business world, not to provide government support for the impoverished or to enact laws for the benefit of the laborer.

Wilson's New Freedom also failed to address the problem of racial discrimination. Indeed, the Democratic victory in 1912 brought southerners into government who strengthened the grip of Jim Crow laws in the South and extended their reach to the nation's capital. "The South," a reporter for *Harper's Weekly* observed, "is in the Saddle." [302] A Virginia native, Wilson supported cabinet officials such as Treasury Secretary William McAdoo and Postmaster General Albert S. Burleson, who solidified racial segregation of federal government workers, especially those in Washington, D.C. To be sure, neither Roosevelt nor Taft had been champions of racial justice. But Wilson and the Democratic Party actively pursued a policy that segregated the departments and agencies of the federal government.

Although his commitment to reform was bounded by his beliefs and party, Wilson did transform the presidency substantially. The office that only two decades before had seemed so unimpressive to Wilson the political scientist had been elevated to a position of unrivaled influence in the American political system. As the *New Republic* proclaimed in 1914: "Under Mr. Wilson the prestige of the presidency has been fully restored. He has not only expressly acknowledged and acted on this obligation of leadership, as did Mr. Roosevelt, but he has sought to embody it in constitutional form." [303]

Wilson as World Leader

From 1901 to 1909, Roosevelt expanded the president's influence and reduced the effectiveness of Congress in foreign affairs. Wilson's approach to foreign affairs, although just as ambitious as Roosevelt's, was somewhat more idealistic. TR's diplomatic initiatives were rooted in a mixture of progressive philosophy and *realpolitik* that sustained his administration's vigorous pursuit of American strategic and economic interests. Wilson and his secretary of state, William Jennings Bryan, charted a more high-minded course, assuming somewhat naively, as Link has written, "that moral force controlled the relations of peace, that reason would prevail over ignorance and passion in the formation of public opinion, and that men and nations everywhere were automatically progressing toward an orderly and righteous international society." [304] Wilson was determined to pursue a foreign policy that was as energetic as TR's but that was based more on altruism and less on narrow considerations of the national interest than Roosevelt's had been.

Wilson's most severe test in foreign affairs came during and after World War I, when, for the first time, the president was required to exercise executive power in conditions of global conflict. The United States formally entered World War I on April 6, 1917, when Wilson signed a proclamation that a state of war existed with Germany. Congress voted to declare war four days after hearing the president's moving and eloquent appeal, in which he called on the United States to end its traditional position of neutrality in the face of European conflicts. "It is a fearful thing to lead this great peaceful people into war, into the most terrible and disastrous of all wars," said Wilson on this solemn occasion. "But the right is more precious than the peace, and we shall fight for . . . a universal domination of right by such a concert of free peoples as shall bring peace and safety to all nations, and make the world at last free." [305]

The fight to make the "world safe for democracy," as Wilson called it, placed new demands on the war powers of the president. To wage a "total war" successfully required the mass production of complex weapons. It also entailed the mobilization and, at a great distance from the United States, the deployment of troops on a grand scale. The president became responsible for organizing and controlling the industrial economy and for coordinating the transportation and communications industries so that they could meet the requirements of a large-scale military commitment. All of this was in addition to the president's traditional duties as commander in chief of the armed forces.

The need to impose wartime economic and social controls on American society strained the settled procedures of U.S. constitutional government to an extent not seen since the Civil War. Perhaps conscious of the postbellum reaction against presidential authority, Wilson, whenever possible, sought explicit delegations of power from Congress. But he did not rely on statutory power for everything. For example, when Congress failed to pass a bill that authorized the president to arm merchant vessels, Wilson armed them anyway, knowing that he had the constitutional power to do so. But Wilson had believed from the start of his presidency that the full flowering of presidential authority required legislative support, even in wartime, when the expansive character of executive authority was well established by constitutional doctrine and historical precedents.

Of the many congressional delegations of power to the president that followed Congress's declaration of war, the most striking was the Lever Food and Fuel Control Act of 1917. The Lever Act granted authority to the president "to regulate by license the importation, manufacture, storage, mining or distribution of necessaries"—meaning, in effect, to regulate the entire national economy. Because such a grant of power was without precedent, many legislators assailed it as a precursor to dictatorship. To allay such concerns, the Senate added a provision that created a bipartisan committee to oversee the conduct of war.

Wilson attacked the Senate amendment vehemently. Hoping to kill it in the House-Senate conference committee, he fired off a letter to the bill's sponsor, Rep. A. F. Lever, protesting that the proposed oversight committee would "amount to nothing less than the assumption on the part of the legislative body of the executive work of the administration." Wilson invoked the "ominous precedent" of the

Committee on the Conduct of War, which Congress had constituted during the Lincoln administration. That committee, he argued, "was the cause of constant and distressing harassment and rendered [Lincoln's] task all but impossible."[306] By standing firm and by convincing legislative leaders such as Lever to do the same, Wilson managed to have the amendment removed. The president signed the Lever Act on August 10, 1917, establishing once more his claim to congressional leadership.

The emergency powers that Wilson assumed during World War I were extraordinary. As Corwin has noted, the contrast between Wilson's and Lincoln's "dictatorship" was not one of "tenderness for customary constitutional restraints"; instead, it was one of "method."[307] Once having obtained his extraordinary authority, however, Wilson appointed competent aides—such as Bernard Baruch, who chaired the powerful War Industries Board; Herbert Hoover, who served as food administrator; and Secretary of the Treasury William Gibbs McAdoo, who managed the railroads—to handle the details of administration. Similarly, Wilson left the management of military affairs to his European commander, Gen. John J. Pershing. The president intervened only when large political and diplomatic considerations were involved.

Wilson's style of delegating detailed tasks to trusted members of the administration, while he assumed responsibility for the overall direction of the war effort, suited his approach to government. It also was an understandable adaptation to the exigencies of modern warfare. By the twentieth century, the conduct of war was far too massive and complex for the president to contribute directly to the development of strategy and tactics as Polk, Lincoln, and McKinley had done. It was by providing moral leadership to arouse and administrative appointments to sustain the nation's engagement in total war that Wilson contributed to the development of the president as the commander in chief.[308]

The Defeat of the League of Nations

Ironically, defeat greeted Wilson's effort to accomplish the task for which he believed his influence and talents were best suited: the building of a lasting structure of peace. One reason Wilson had been cautious in asserting his powers as commander in chief during the war was that he did not want to jeopardize the opportunity to take charge at the peace table. As historian Ernest R. May has argued, "From the first day of the war to the last, all that Wilson sought was a peace that could be secured by the League of Nations, a peace that would make the world safe for democracy."[309]

Wilson's plan for an international peacekeeping association was the most controversial of his Fourteen Points, the peace program that he formulated in early 1918. *(See "Wilson's 'Fourteen Points' Speech," p. 1767, in Reference Materials, Vol. II.)* He hoped to persuade the Allies and the

Senate to accept the program, which also included lenient terms for the defeated Central powers. The president had to compromise on some points in the postwar peace negotiations, particularly on those pertaining to the conditions that were to be imposed on Germany. But the League of Nations was included in the Treaty of Versailles, which was signed by the major powers in June 1919.

Wilson began the treaty fight with little doubt that he would prevail. He had displayed throughout his presidency an almost unsurpassed ability to enlist public support for the causes he championed. Yet in the fight for the League, he disdained to employ the methods that had succeeded magnificently in passing his New Freedom program.

In domestic affairs, Wilson carefully cultivated support in Congress, collaborating closely with the House and Senate Democratic leadership. In foreign affairs, however, Wilson felt justified in acting alone. Whatever the president's formal constitutional responsibilities and informal obligations as party leader, Wilson believed that the initiative in foreign policy belonged to the executive "without any restriction." Wilson's views on foreign policy making, like Roosevelt's, resembled those Alexander Hamilton had expressed in the Pacificus letters. Like Hamilton, Wilson believed in the functional superiority of the executive in matters of diplomacy, claiming "virtually the power to control them absolutely."[310]

The conflict between Wilson and the Senate over the League of Nations may have been inevitable, rooted deeply in the country's traditional fear of "entangling alliances." But the conflict was greatly exacerbated by Wilson's expansive understanding of the president's foreign policy prerogatives. The limits of Wilson's influence first became evident in the 1918 midterm elections, even before the Versailles treaty was signed. No sooner had the Fourteen Points been pronounced and peace negotiations started than Congress, tiring of Wilson's independent course in seeking a settlement, began to challenge the president's conduct of foreign affairs. Former president Theodore Roosevelt, who had returned to the Republican Party, abetted this opposition by urging the Senate to repudiate Wilson's Fourteen Points. On October 25, 1918, TR sent a telegram to Republican leaders: "Let us dictate peace by hammering guns and not chat about peace to the accompaniment of clicking typewriters."[311]

Flustered by the Republican efforts to discredit him with the public before the November congressional elections, Wilson sought to rally the nation in support of his war policy. The day after Roosevelt's telegram was released, he appealed to the voters to return a Democratic majority to Congress in the upcoming elections. "If you have approved of my leadership and wish me to be your unembarrassed spokesman in affairs at home and abroad," his announcement to the press read, "I earnestly beg that you will express yourself unmistakably to that effect by returning a

Democratic majority to both the Senate and the House of Representatives." [312]

Wilson's unwillingness to tolerate opposition reached beyond the halls of Congress. The president signed the Espionage Act of 1917, which imposed fines of up to $10,000 and jail sentences ranging to twenty years for persons convicted of aiding the enemy or obstructing the recruitment of soldiers. He also authorized the postmaster general to ban from the mails material that seemed treasonable or seditious. In May 1918, at Wilson's urging, Congress passed the Sedition Act, which made "saying anything" to discourage the purchase of war bonds a crime. The act also made it illegal to "utter, print, write, or publish any disloyal, profane, scurrilous, or abusive language" about the government, the Constitution, or the uniforms worn by soldiers and sailors.

The 1918 campaign, occurring as it did in the midst of a war, seemed an inappropriate occasion for a president to appeal to party loyalty. When the Republicans made substantial gains in 1918 and, for the first time in eight years, took control of both houses of Congress, the *New Republic* scolded Wilson for having discouraged public debate on foreign affairs, even on the League of Nations: "In allowing the mind of the country to stagnate, he had played into the hands of the incorrigible enemy of his own policy." Americans had "voted in the dark" and remained "wholly unprepared to deal with the new responsibilities to which [the nation] is committed as the consequence of its own acts and the convulsions of the world." [313] Roosevelt declared soon after the election that "our allies and our enemies and Mr. Wilson himself should all understand that Mr. Wilson has no authority whatever to speak for the American people at this time. His leadership has just been emphatically repudiated by them." [314]

The 1918 election diminished the president's prestige abroad and in Congress, adding immeasurably to the difficulties he was to encounter at the postwar peace conference and, especially, with Congress. Although Wilson managed to salvage much of his program at Versailles, he failed in Washington. The opposition to the treaty was led by an implacable Wilson foe, Massachusetts Republican Henry Cabot Lodge, who, as a result of the elections, chaired the Senate Foreign Relations Committee. Unwilling to compromise with Lodge, Wilson left Washington on September 3, 1919, on a month-long speaking tour of the western states. He hoped to create, as he had in the past, a groundswell in favor of his policies that would force the Senate to ratify the treaty.

Instead, Wilson's speaking tour further reduced his influence. Conceivably, but not likely, the campaign would have succeeded had his failed health not broken toward the end of the grueling tour. But the tide of public opinion had been moving against the president since the 1918 elections. Repeating its criticism of Wilson's participation in the campaign, the *New Republic* lamented that the president "preferred the lone hand to the effort of building an informed and energetic public opinion in America to back him up." [315]

Wilson's abortive campaign for the league offered dramatic evidence that although the presidency had gained considerable influence since the turn of the century, the office still was constrained by a powerful, if no longer dominant, Congress and the vagaries of public opinion. Because of Roosevelt and Wilson, Americans no longer considered it inappropriate for the president to try to rouse public support with rhetorical appeals. But no guarantee existed that every campaign of persuasion would succeed. The 1920 presidential election, which the conservative, anti-League of Nations, Republican senator Warren G. Harding won in a landslide was a major setback for progressivism but also for Wilson's theory of presidential power. Soon after election day, the Senate issued the final defeat of the League of Nations Treaty.

WARREN HARDING TO HERBERT HOOVER

The election of Warren G. Harding by a huge majority in 1920 marked the end of the Progressive Era. In May 1920, Harding told the Home Market Club in Boston, "America's present need is not heroics, but healing; not nostrums but normalcy; not revolution but restoration . . . not surgery but serenity." [316]

The word *normalcy* captured the temper of the times concerning not just public policy but the presidency as well. The Republicans resumed power in March 1921, militant in their determination to restore Congress and the party organization to their former stature. Leading the official committee that notified Harding of his nomination by the 1920 Republican convention, Senator Lodge presented the candidate with something of an ultimatum. Alluding to the transfer of power from Congress to the White House that had occurred during Wilson's administration, Lodge reminded Harding that the "makers of the Constitution intended to coordinate the three great elements of government and strove to guard against either usurpation or trespass by one branch at the expense of the other." "In that spirit," the senator added, "*we all know well*, you will enter upon your great responsibility." [317]

Neither Harding nor his two Republican successors, Calvin Coolidge (1923–1929) and Herbert C. Hoover (1929–1933), took exception to the sentiment expressed by Lodge. As before in American history, strong executive leadership was followed by passivity and drift.

The Harding Era

True to his promise as a candidate, President Harding made little effort to lead Congress. His model was McKinley, whose influence on Capitol Hill was achieved through quiet consultation and compromise with his party's congressional leadership.[318]

But McKinley-style legislative leadership was no longer possible in the 1920s. The congressional revolt of 1910, which dethroned the Speaker, had weakened party ties in the House. The Senate, too, had been affected by the insurgent revolt against party leadership. Moreover, the enactment in 1913 of the Seventeenth Amendment, providing that the people, not the state legislatures, would elect senators, further undermined party discipline in the upper chamber. The senator, one observer wrote in 1922, "came to think more in terms of himself and his own reelection, nearly always an impelling motive, and less in terms of party." [319] Wilson's bold methods of party leadership had forged, at least for a time, new connections between the president and Congress. Harding's passivity guaranteed deadlock and confusion.

One consequence of the new president's forbearance was that his program to address the postwar economic problems, notably through higher tariffs and lower taxes, made little headway in the legislature. Instead, Congress became bogged down in disagreements about what to do. As his policies foundered in Congress, Harding began to regret his pledge to defer to the legislative branch. Yet regret was unaccompanied by reform. Even when, to the astonishment of many, Harding went before Congress personally on July 12, 1921, to chide the House and, especially, the Senate for inaction, he did not follow through with the sort of forceful and painstaking efforts at public or personal persuasion that might have moved his fractious party to action. Harding did not bow down to Congress, but neither did he have the energy or the ability to lead it forward.[320]

Fresh from its defeat of the League of Nations, Congress was determined to direct foreign affairs during Harding's term. Most significant, the Senate took the initiative in curbing the naval race that had preoccupied the major powers since the beginning of World War I. Progressive Republican senator William E. Borah amended the 1921 naval appropriations bill by calling on the president to invite Great Britain and Japan to a naval disarmament conference

President Woodrow Wilson rides with President-elect Warren G. Harding to Harding's inauguration March 4, 1921. Harding promised a "return to normalcy" after the Progressive Era and the tumultuous war years.

to reduce naval expenditures. This rider passed Congress in spite of Harding's efforts to replace it with a weaker resolution. Harding was not opposed to having a conference, but he felt it prudent to build up the American fleet first.

Still, Harding was not one to engage Congress in a bitter and protracted struggle. Bowing to congressional and popular pressure, he called an international disarmament conference, which took place in Washington from the end of 1921 to early 1922. The Washington Naval Disarmament Conference successfully worked out an agreement not only on naval armaments but also on relations between the major Pacific powers. Ironically, the accord reached at the Washington Naval Disarmament Conference, the result of a Senate initiative, proved to be Harding's most significant foreign policy achievement.

Teapot Dome and Other Scandals

Harding's presidency began slowly and ended disastrously. By 1923, it became clear that a heavy price was to be paid for his passive leadership and deference to the regular party apparatus. The president's pledge to restore "normalcy" included a renewed enthusiasm for patronage practices. The steady extension of the merit civil service that had begun with the passage of the Pendleton Act in 1883 and had continued ever since, especially during Roosevelt's presidency, went no further in the Harding administration. "By the middle of the summer of 1921 the spoils efforts of the Republicans began to assume the proportions of a sizable if not full scale raid," historian Paul Van Riper has written.[321]

Nor was the Harding administration reluctant to manipulate the remaining unclassified service, which now constituted about one-fourth of the federal workforce. Some of Harding's appointments were excellent, notably his selection of Herbert C. Hoover as secretary of commerce and Charles Evans Hughes as secretary of state. Many others, however, were characteristic of the Grant era and resulted in the worst fraud and corruption since the advent of civil service reform.

The first disturbing situation to come to light involved Charles Forbes, the director of the Veterans' Bureau. In March 1923, Harding was told that Forbes had been selling items from the government's medical supply base in Perryville, Maryland, to private contractors at low prices. He was also making undercover deals relating to hospital building contracts and site selections. Forbes had to resign, and on March 14, 1923, his principal legal adviser, Charles F. Cramer, committed suicide.

When the Veterans' Bureau scandal was followed soon after by another in the attorney general's office, Harding became convinced that his administration was deeply tainted with corruption. Fearing for his reputation and the fortunes of his party, he is reported to have remarked to the journalist William Allen White, "My God, this is a hell of a job! I have no trouble with my enemies. . . . But my damned friends, my God-damned friends, White, they're the ones that keep me walking the floor nights."[322]

Despondent and in poor health, the president decided to escape Washington on a cross-country speaking tour that would culminate in Alaska. In the course of his return trip, Harding fell ill of ptomaine poisoning, then pneumonia, and died of an embolism in San Francisco on August 2, 1923. Vice President Calvin Coolidge became president.

Harding's death preceded by a few months the uncovering of a complicated and subtle plot to defraud the government, known as the Teapot Dome scandal. Albert B. Fall, secretary of the interior, entered into a corrupt bargain with the oil companies of Edward L. Doheny and Harry F. Sinclair to turn over to them valuable petroleum deposits, which President Wilson had reserved for the navy. The Elk Hill oil reserve in California was leased to Doheny, and the Teapot Dome oil reserve in Wyoming to Sinclair. Fall personally received at least $100,000 from Doheny and $300,000 from Sinclair.

Armed with these facts, and other damaging revelations unearthed by a Senate investigation, a special commission appointed by President Coolidge initiated prosecutions in early June 1924. The resultant trials and legal maneuver-

ing went on for almost six years, after which Fall was sentenced to a year in jail and a $100,000 fine and Sinclair was sentenced to six months in jail. But Doheny was acquitted, a ridiculous verdict in view of the fact that Fall had been convicted of taking a bribe from him. The acquittal provoked the progressive Republican senator from Nebraska, George Norris, to remark, with reference to Doheny's expensive legal fees, that it is "very difficult, if not impossible to convict one hundred million dollars."[323]

The Budget and Accounting Act of 1921

Harding's public reputation, which remained high while he was alive, suffered tremendously from the scandalous revelations that rocked the government after he died. But the Harding administration was not without its achievements. During his tenure, for example, the first national budget system was created, enhancing significantly the president's authority to oversee the expenditures of the executive departments and agencies. This authority was achieved by the enactment of the Budget and Accounting Act of 1921.

The budget act required an annual, comprehensive executive budget, assigning to the president the responsibility to estimate both the government's financial needs and the revenues it expected to collect during the coming fiscal year. The act also established a Bureau of the Budget (BOB) to support presidential use of this new budget authority. Although formally assigned to the Treasury Department, the budget office was intended to serve as a presidential staff agency. Finally, the budget act created the General Accounting Office as an auditing arm of Congress.

With the passage of the budget act, the president finally obtained legal authority to influence the allocation of expenditures in the executive branch. Thus the practitioner-scholar Herbert Emmerich judged the budget act to be "the greatest landmark of our administrative history except for the Constitution itself."[324]

Harding and the first director of the budget bureau, the capable Charles G. Dawes, made effective use of the powers that the new law had placed in the president's hands. Harding's 1920 call for a return to "normalcy" had included a pledge to reduce government spending. Dedicated as he was to fulfilling this pledge, Harding, acting somewhat out of character, managed to hold his cabinet to a stern fiscal program that by 1923 had achieved almost $2 billion in savings.[325]

Public Relations during the Harding Era

Although neither Harding nor his successor, the taciturn Calvin Coolidge, regarded himself as a lawgiver or a tribune of the people in the sense that Roosevelt and Wilson had, each found that he could not serve the laissez-faire economic policies that he embraced without taking a strong hand in administering the executive departments and agencies.

Harding's promise of economy in government could not have been fulfilled without the expanded fiscal powers that the president was granted by the Budget and Accounting Act. Moreover, the national government's involvement in domestic affairs could not have been reduced without public support. In the wake of TR and Wilson, public relations had become a critical ingredient of successful presidential leadership.

Although Harding's presidency ended disastrously, he did manage to add to the arsenal of presidential techniques for leading public opinion. Having been the editor-publisher of the *Marion Star* in Ohio before entering politics, Harding had a good sense of how the press worked. He developed an intimacy with journalists that greatly benefited his presidential campaign and, until the scandals of 1923, his image as president. Harding was the first president to recognize that public opinion could be courted through leisurely as well as through formal and ceremonial activities, even to the extent of playing golf with particular correspondents.

As president, Harding revived the practice of holding regular press conferences, open to all accredited correspondents, which Wilson had begun but had allowed to taper off after 1915. In addition, it was under Harding that the "White House spokesman" device was invented to convey information from the administration to the public without attributing it to the president. Harding recognized that to hang this veil between himself and newspaper readers gave him room to maneuver that he otherwise would not have had. Finally, Harding was the first president to benefit from "photo opportunities." He willingly posed for photographers several times a week.

Harding's conscious innovations in press relations helped to amplify the effects of his warm and engaging personality and to win support for his administration's policies. He also decided to retain Wilson's practice of delivering messages to Congress in person. Harding immensely enjoyed speech-making tours. The mounting burden of the rhetorical presidency led Harding to appoint the first presidential speechwriter, newspaper journalist Judson Welliver.

Harding died before the American people realized his shortcomings. Although he enjoyed the glamour and attention that recently had become part of the presidency, he found the responsibilities that accompanied the office's new stature to be unbearable. Poring over an immense stack of correspondence, he is reported to have lamented to an aide, "I am not fit for this office and should never have been here." [326]

Nevertheless, the death of Harding, who had served barely two years and whom history would number as one of the least successful presidents, caused an extraordinary outpouring of national emotion. The public reaction to Harding's death reflected the growing importance of the presidency. Because of the minute, journalistic surveillance of the president's activities that began during his administration, the stature of the office did not shrink but, to a surprising degree, continued to grow during the Harding era. "More than ever before," one scholar has remarked about the reaction to Harding's death, "thanks to the media and use made of them on the President's behalf, the presidency was destined to blow up the man to heroic proportions and project this image constantly on the national screen." [327]

The Silent Politics of Calvin Coolidge

Calvin Coolidge was an unlikely heir to the increasingly public presidency. Plain in appearance and so sparing in words that he was dubbed "Silent Cal," Coolidge's public persona was ordinary at a time when the executive office seemed to require individuals of heroic demeanor. Yet in spite of his limitations, or perhaps in part because of them, Coolidge was one of the most popular presidents in history.

Coolidge raised inactivity to an art. When it came to exerting his will on matters of public policy, Coolidge felt even less responsible to act than had Harding. He made little effort to join the Republican leaders in Congress to advance a legislative program. "I have never felt it was my duty," Coolidge wrote in his autobiography, "to attempt to coerce Senators or Representatives, or to take reprisals." [328]

Restraint in legislative relations comported with Coolidge's general disdain for programmatic initiatives. "The key to an understanding of the presidential career of Calvin Coolidge is to be found in the fact that he had a distaste for legislation," historian Wilfred E. Binkley has written.[329] Like Harding, Coolidge believed that there were too many federal programs and that his energies should be spent administering the government economically and efficiently. One of the few legislative measures that Coolidge promoted vigorously was the Mellon tax reduction plan of 1923, which took its name from Andrew Mellon, the conservative Treasury secretary who served during the Harding and Coolidge administrations.

Aside from a bill that, like the tax cut, reduced the national government's involvement in the economy, Coolidge maintained a public silence about legislation that would have befitted a nineteenth-century executive. Even in the matter of the protocol of the World Court, a treaty that Coolidge sent to the Senate for ratification, he gave neither encouragement nor direction to Republican senators. Instead, the president spoke barely a word as his supporters fought a valiant but, in the face of the isolationist mood that gripped the nation after World War I, a losing battle.

Despite Coolidge's lack of success with Congress, he formed a strong bond with the American people. To some degree, Coolidge had the virtue of his defects. His stern Yankee demeanor and businesslike administrative style were a welcome respite from the scandals that had rocked the government in 1923. He also benefited from the apparent prosperity of the postwar economy. The Harding-Coolidge economic program, emphasizing free markets at home and protection from competition abroad, put "business in the saddle," as *Harper's* magazine described it in 1925.[330] For a time, business was up to the job. Throughout the spring of 1924, disclosures of the Harding administration's scandals competed for attention on the front pages of the newspapers with dramatic evidence of increasing dividends, profits, and spiraling sales.[331]

Coolidge's enormous popularity was grounded not just in his commitment to business but also in his ability to express that commitment in words that exalted the governing principles of the era. "The genius of this day was not altogether material," Coolidge said of the ascendant Republican Party's faith in commerce. "It had its spiritual side, deep and significant. . . . Prosperity came to the people that they might have the resources for more of the refinements of life, more for the needs of education and religion, more to minister to the things of the soul. Power came to the nation that it might the better serve its own citizens and bear its share of the burden of civilization." Coolidge inspired the people by persuading them, as he put it in his 1925 inaugural address, that his program reflected "idealism in its most practical form." [332]

Coolidge's popularity was reinforced by his shrewd sense of public relations. Extraordinarily faithful in discharging what he felt to be his obligations to reporters, Coolidge held 520 press conferences during his five years in office, more per month than the gregarious Franklin D. Roosevelt (FDR). Not surprisingly, concern for the press corps won him a considerable measure of good will with reporters.

On rare occasions, the president used his exceedingly cordial relations with reporters to exert legislative leadership. For example, in ten press conferences between December 1923 and June 1924, Coolidge urged Congress to enact the Mellon tax reduction package. But much of Coolidge's public relations effort was designed to sell himself, not his policies. Characteristically, while Republican senators, without an encouraging word from the president, fought a losing battle for the administration's World Court treaty, Coolidge used a White House lunch with prominent editors and authors to disseminate benign personal impressions.[333]

Coolidge had a keen understanding of the public's interest in the human side of the presidency. Harding was the first to exploit human interest stories in the press, but Coolidge displayed an even greater readiness to benefit from the nation's growing fascination with the personal lives of those who resided in the White House. Convinced that news about his personal activities would pave the way for popular acceptance of his more serious pronouncements, the shy Coolidge threw open his private life to unprecedented public gaze. One contemporary reporter

suggested that "Mr. Coolidge would don any attire or assume any pose that would produce an interesting picture. He was never too busy." [334]

Important as the newspapers were to Coolidge, his most substantial contribution to the development of White House communications was the use of the radio. Lacking the barnstorming ability of his recent predecessors, Coolidge was blessed with a new medium, which he used effectively to enhance his image. "I am fortunate I came in with the radio," he told Sen. James Watson of Indiana. "I can't make an engaging, rousing, or oratorical speech to a crowd as you can, . . . but I have a good radio voice, and now I can get my messages across to them without acquainting them with my lack of oratorical ability." [335]

As with his courting of reporters, Coolidge used the radio less to rouse public opinion in support of his policies than to enhance his personal popularity. Had he not formed a strong bond with the public in this way, Coolidge might not have been nominated by his party in 1924 and elected president in his own right. Before the Republican convention in June, Coolidge made sure that he entered the homes of the American people at least once a month with carefully staged broadcasts that conveyed an impression of his own personality and ideas.

Coolidge was nominated overwhelmingly on the first ballot, which signified an important step, as Coolidge himself recognized, in the emergence of the president as "the sole repository of party responsibility." [336] The conservative Republican senators who controlled their party after 1912 had little regard for Coolidge. Unlike Harding, this taciturn New Englander, the former governor of Massachusetts, was not one of them. As William Allen White wrote in 1925, "the reason why the senatorial group ceased hoping to defeat Coolidge for the Republican nomination was the obvious fact that Coolidge was getting stronger and stronger with the American people." [337] Noting that the radio in no small measure had made this possible, Cornwell has written: "Here was the first President in history whom more than a tiny fraction of the populace could come to know at first hand. Small wonder that the man developed a tangible meaning for millions—more so perhaps than any of his predecessors." [338]

Herbert Hoover and the Great Depression

When Herbert Hoover, capitalizing on Coolidge's popularity, defeated the Democrat Al Smith in the 1928 election, he was expected to be an able—even a brilliant—leader. "The Great Engineer," as Hoover was called, brought to the White House a tremendous reputation for accomplishment and public service earned in his service as food administrator during the Wilson administration and as secretary of commerce under Harding and Coolidge. Dedicated to the probusiness program of Harding and Coolidge, yet confident that knowledgeable and efficient administration of the nation's affairs could build a stronger foundation for prosperity, Hoover seemed the perfect man to consolidate the gains of the postwar economic recovery.

Yet the same president who entered office with such great expectations left four years later as the object of scorn and derision. This startling political reversal could be attributed in part to the Great Depression, the worst economic crisis in the nation's history. The Depression struck when the stock market crashed in October 1929, only seven months after Hoover was inaugurated. But the Hoover administration was in trouble even before the crash.

Much of Hoover's difficulty as president stemmed from the contrast between his desire to effect important changes in the economy and society and his unwillingness or inability to undertake the tasks of leadership that could have made these changes possible. Like Harding and Coolidge, Hoover subscribed to a political philosophy that confined the national government to the few activities for which it has clear constitutional authority. But Hoover's fear of big government coexisted with his faith, born of the Progressive Era, in the government's ability to improve social and economic conditions.[339]

This Charles Dunn caricature of Herbert Hoover is said to have been the president's favorite. Hoover kept twenty thousand cartoons of himself in a White House room he called his "Chamber of Horrors."

Early in his presidency, Hoover called a special session of Congress to recommend a significant program of reform. The new president sought major changes in tariffs, taxes, conservation, and government organization. Hoover also believed his administration should play a leading role in mobilizing industrial and civic organizations to facilitate better economic coordination and enhanced opportunity. He was concerned that the nation's prosperity was marred by several problems: an imbalance between production and consumption; a weak agricultural sector; the lack of orderly, rational, and bureaucratic procedures in industrial organizations; feverish speculation that was fueled by unsound currency and lending policies; and the weak condition of labor, which allowed for a disproportionate share of profits to go to owners and managers. The solution to these problems,

Hoover believed, lay not in expanding the role of the national government but in using the powers of the presidency and the rest of the executive branch to encourage the development of more rational and just economic arrangements.

Hoover's philosophy and personality, however, rendered him incapable of providing the brand of leadership he advocated, especially after the hammer blow of the Depression fell. Sharing Coolidge's respect for the autonomy of Congress, Hoover failed to provide legislative leadership during the special session of Congress that he called in 1929. After leaving office, Hoover explained his reticence:

The encroachments upon our liberties may not be overt—by repeal of any of the Constitutional guarantees—but they may be insidious and no less potent through encroachment upon the checks and balances which make its security. More particularly does the weakening of the legislative arm lead to encroachment by the executive upon the legislative and judicial functions, and inevitably that encroachment is upon individual liberty.[340]

Despite the president's unassertiveness, a farm bill, at least, was enacted. The Agricultural Marketing Act created the Federal Farm Board to administer loans so that agricultural cooperatives could help farmers to produce and market their crops. Before a bill that was acceptable to Hoover could pass, however, Republican leaders in the Senate had to quell a revolt by party insurgents. Against the president's wishes, western progressives had moved to subsidize farmers who were exporting commodities abroad at a price lower than the domestic rate. After weeks of deadlock, Congress approved the president's version of the agricultural measure, but with little help from Hoover.

Congress was not so accommodating when the issue was tariffs. The president favored a limited revision of tariff schedules to aid stricken farmers. Without his active engagement in the legislative process, however, Congress, particularly the Senate, increased tariffs on nonfarm as well as farm commodities, resulting in a bill that raised schedules to the highest levels in history. Hoover signed the protectionist Smoot-Hawley tariff, which he privately characterized as "vicious, extortionate, and obnoxious," in the face of ardent pleas from all parts of the country to veto it.[341]

Hoover's passivity seemed inappropriate to his ambitions for the nation. As historian Martin Fausold has remarked, "No activist president in this century has kept the distance from Congress as did Hoover."[342] By the fall of 1929, even Republican leaders in Congress were criticizing Hoover's nonpolitical approach to the presidency. The press, although not yet willing to dismiss Hoover as a weak executive, was mystified. Assessing the president's aloofness from the special session of Congress, one commentator concluded that "a strange paralysis seemed to rest upon Mr. Hoover during the first year after Congress met."[343]

Hoover's "strange paralysis," which caused only concern and confusion during the early days of his presidency, provoked bitter jest and withering scorn after the onslaught of the Depression. Dignified silence in the face of congressional indifference to his program was one thing, but for the president to remain above the fray when unemployment reached 25 percent of the workforce seemed appalling and heartless. Yet Hoover resisted the growing demands that he assume the mantle of legislative leader and work to produce a body of law that would authorize the executive departments and agencies to take more responsibility for economic coordination and social services.

The president's aloof stance became especially disabling after the Republicans lost control of Congress in the 1930 midterm elections. When congressional Democrats refused to cooperate with him, Hoover chose to suffer in silence, bewailing their intransigence in the intimacy of his White House study but declining to go over their heads to the people. As he later wrote in his memoirs:

> I had felt deeply that no President should undermine the independence of the legislative and judicial branches by seeking to discredit them. The constitutional division of powers is the bastion of our liberties and was not designed as a battleground to display the prowess of Presidents. They just have to work with the material that God—and the voters—have given them.[344]

The struggling president's constitutional principles, which kept him from exerting public leadership, were reinforced by personal qualities that ill suited him for the tasks of legislative, party, and popular leadership. Like Grant, Hoover came to the presidency with no background in elected office. His experience had been as a builder and manager of organizations, not as a politician working to forge legislative coalitions or a popular following. He was comfortable

dealing with facts, which he could marshal to support a given course of action. But as the journalist Walter Lippmann wrote, Hoover was "diffident in the presence of the normal irrationality of democracy."[345] He fought losing battles to keep both his private life and his negotiations on public policy screened from view. His administration "served to make painfully plain," Cornwell has observed, "that no future President could hope to emerge from his White House ordeal unless he was prepared in talent and temperament to cope with and master the demands of an age of mass communications."[346]

Hoover was hardly the do-nothing president that Franklin D. Roosevelt and the Democrats made him out to be in the 1932 election. He called for programs, such as the Reconstruction Finance Corporation, that would provide federal loans to banks, railroads, and certain agricultural organizations. But he would not offer bold political leadership to rouse popular support for these programs or to ensure their energetic operation. Similarly, Hoover marshaled the entire executive branch to encourage private and local groups to provide the needy with relief from the depression but he rigidly refused to offer direct government aid. Seeking to come to terms with the great drought of 1930 and 1931, Hoover admonished the Red Cross to feed the people, instead of having the federal government do it. When the Red Cross balked and Congress demanded a relief package, Hoover still demurred, stating simply that direct federal assistance was unconstitutional. It was a sorry spectacle: the president standing on a supposed constitutional prohibition, while Congress pleaded for basic human relief.[347]

In a sense, Hoover put traditional, nineteenth-century American political practices and principles to their greatest test. But his unalterable commitment to preserving these traditions even in the face of national calamity served only to discredit them. In this way, Hoover unwittingly laid the groundwork for a fundamental break with the politics and policies of the past.

FRANKLIN D. ROOSEVELT TO GEORGE H. W. BUSH

The 1932 election marked the beginning of a new political era. Franklin D. Roosevelt became the first Democratic candidate to be elected president with a majority of the national popular vote since Franklin Pierce in 1852. Roosevelt won a 472–59 electoral vote landslide, carrying forty-two states to six for the incumbent, Herbert C. Hoover. In the new Congress, Democrats outnumbered Republicans by 60 to 35 in the Senate and 310 to 117 in the House.

FDR's victory indicated, in the opinion of the progressive Republican journalist William Allen White, "a firm desire on the part of the American people to use government as an agency for human welfare."[348] Roosevelt did not disappoint this desire. He not only accepted the progressive reformers' commitment to regulate business, so as to curb its worst abuses, but also believed it was the responsibility of the federal government to guarantee the economic security of the American people.

Franklin Roosevelt's extraordinary leadership in expanding the role of the state to meet the demands of a national crisis, the Great Depression, and later an international one—World War II—had a profound effect on the presidency. The modern presidency, especially the executive office that took shape during the first half of the twentieth century, was advanced by his long tenure in the White House.[349]

What marked the twentieth-century transformation of the executive was the emergence of the president, not Congress or party organizations, as the leading instrument of popular rule, the "steward of the public welfare." Acting on this concept of presidential power, Theodore Roosevelt and Woodrow Wilson inaugurated the practices that strengthened the president as popular and legislative leader. It fell to FDR, however, to consolidate, or institutionalize, the changes in the executive office that were initiated during the Progressive Era. Roosevelt's leadership was the principal ingredient in a full-scale partisan realignment of the political parties, the first in history that placed executive leadership at the heart of its approach to politics and government. After Roosevelt's long tenure, the new understanding of presidential responsibilities would lead even conservative Republican presidents to wield executive power according to the vision of the office that was celebrated by their progressive forebears.

FDR and the Breakthrough to the Modern Presidency

So great an impression did FDR make on the American political system that in the most recent surveys of historians he has ranked as the second greatest president in history, surpassed only by Abraham Lincoln.[350] Above all, FDR's high ranking is owed to his efforts to lead the American people through the Great Depression.

In the 1932 presidential election, Franklin D. Roosevelt's image of strength and optimism provided a dramatic contrast to his 1932 Republican opponent, President Hoover.

Roosevelt came to office in the fourth year of a persistent world economic crisis that raised grave doubts about the viability of republican government—indeed, about the future of the Western world. As Roosevelt prepared to take the oath of office, fifteen million Americans were unemployed. Every bank in thirty-two states had been closed by state government edict. On the morning of FDR's inauguration, March 4, 1933, the New York Stock Exchange had shut down, causing the editor of *Nation's Business* to describe the national mood as one of "fear, bordering on panic, loss of faith in everything, our fellowman, our institutions, private and government." [351]

In this atmosphere of national despair, Roosevelt's arrival in Washington was greeted with hope. Everyone who watched and waited, wrote *New York Times* columnist Arthur Krock, was "ready to be enthusiastic over any display of leadership," eager to be convinced that the new president would exhibit the kind of bold and energetic initiative that the American people had demanded but not received from Hoover.[352]

Unlike Hoover, Roosevelt was admirably suited to lead by virtue of his personality and background. "The essence of Roosevelt's presidency," Clinton Rossiter has written, "was his airy eagerness to meet the age head on." [353] His confidence stemmed not only from a privileged, albeit challenging, upbringing in Hyde Park, New York, but also from an admirable political education: state senator, assistant secretary of the navy in the Wilson administration, vice-presidential nominee in 1920, and two-term governor of New York (then the largest state in the Union). Roosevelt's faith in his abilities was matched by a willingness to experiment, which he displayed throughout his presidency.

The Critical Early Days

Roosevelt began his presidency with a solemn, compelling inaugural address that spelled out in clear and uncompromising language both his indictment of the practices that he believed should be abandoned and his intention to act boldly to deal with the crisis at hand. *(See "Franklin D. Roosevelt's First Inaugural Address," p. 1769, in Reference Materials, Vol. II.)* Laying the blame for the Depression squarely on the laissez-faire doctrines and halting leadership of his Republican predecessors, Roosevelt summoned the nation to a higher purpose: "The money changers have fled from their high seats in the temple of our civilization. We may now restore that temple to ancient truths. The measure of that restoration lies in the extent to which we apply social values more noble than mere monetary profit." [354]

Just as boldly, the new president stated his determination to lead the nation and the government:

> It is to be hoped that the normal balance of executive and legislative authority may be wholly adequate to meet the unprecedented task before us.... But in the event that Congress shall fail to take [action] ... and in the event that the national emergency is still critical ... I shall ask the Congress for one remaining instrument to meet the crisis—broad executive power to wage a war against the emergency, as great as the power that would be given to me if we were in fact invaded by a foreign foe. [355]

Roosevelt lost no time translating his intentions into action. On March 5, one day after taking the oath of office, he issued the "Bank Holiday Proclamation," which suspended "the heavy and unwarranted withdrawals of gold and currency from our banking institutions." The bank edict, an unprecedented exercise of executive power in peacetime, declared that from March 6 to March 9, 1933, banks in the United States would be required to suspend all transactions. [356]

During the final days of the Hoover administration, Secretary of Commerce Ogden Mills had urged the president to call a bank holiday, arguing that the authority to do so had been granted to the executive by the Trading with the Enemy Act of 1917. But Hoover was reluctant to act on his own initiative, especially when the attorney general questioned whether a wartime measure could be applied to a domestic situation, no matter how grave. Hoover may have been willing to close the banks if the president-elect had offered his public support, but Roosevelt refused to assume responsibility for any action before becoming president. [357]

Once sworn in, however, FDR did not hesitate to use the full powers of his office to address the national emergency. He felt no reluctance to attack the banking crisis with a World War I measure. Four days after issuing the bank edict, on March 9, he introduced the Emergency Banking Bill, which marshaled the full resources of the Federal Reserve Board to support the faltering banks and to restore the confidence of the people in the banking system. The bill was the first to be passed during the extraordinary "One Hundred Days" (from noon on March 9, to 1 a.m. on June 15, 1933), when Congress passed a relentless succession of Roosevelt-sponsored laws. *(See box, The First Hundred Days of Franklin D. Roosevelt, p. 667, in Chapter 12.)* Remarkably, the bank bill was enacted in fewer than eight hours; forty-five minutes later, with photographers recording the scene, Roosevelt signed it into law.

FDR promptly announced that he would go directly to the people on Sunday evening, March 12, to explain in a radio address what he had done and why he had done it. This was the first of Roosevelt's "fireside chats," which were a revolutionary advance in the presidential use of the mass media. [358] Coolidge and, less successfully, Hoover had spoken on the radio, but only to broadcast fixed, formal policy pronouncements such as the State of the Union message. The fireside chats were more relaxed. Their purpose was either to shape public opinion in support of a specific piece of legislation or, as in the first talk, to enlist popular support for a course of action.

Of all the fireside chats Roosevelt was to give (he delivered two or three during each year of his presidency), none was more successful than the banking crisis address. Both Roosevelt's unmatched radio style and the phrasing of the talk were ideally suited to his purpose of reassuring the people and restoring hope and confidence in the U.S. financial system:

> It was the government's job to straighten out the situation and do it as quickly as possible. And the job is being performed.... Confidence and courage are the essentials of success in carrying out our plan. You people must have faith; you must not be stampeded by rumors or guesses. Let us unite in banishing fear. We have provided the machinery to restore our financial system; it is up to you to support it and make it work. [359]

The bank bill and the fireside chat ended the banking crisis. There were no runs on the banks when they reopened on Monday morning, March 13. On the contrary, deposits far exceeded withdrawals as hoarded currency poured back into the vaults. A few days later, the New York Stock Exchange, closed since March 4, opened with the greatest single-day rise in memory. "Capitalism was saved ... in eight days," Roosevelt's aide Raymond Moley declared dramatically. [360]

The first two weeks of Roosevelt's presidency lifted the spirit of the country. In place of the despair and political paralysis of the Hoover years was an ebullient national mood and a refashioned executive, which forged a vital link between the government and the people. In the past, one thousand pieces of mail a day had arrived at the White House during peak periods. FDR's inauguration was greeted by 460,000 letters. One person had been able to handle Hoover's mail. A staff of fifty had to be hired to take care of Roosevelt's, which averaged five thousand letters a day.

The New Deal

The advent of the welfare state, which entailed a massive transfer of the responsibility to help those in need from the states and the private sector to the national government, created new responsibilities for the president. Roosevelt initiated this transfer, carefully preparing the nation for the revolutionary departures in public policy that took place during the 1930s.

Ffte centerpiece of Roosevelt's program was the Social Security Act, which proposed to create a comprehensive federal system of old-age and unemployment insurance. To sell social security was no easy task. Remarking on the unusually strong American commitment to self-reliance, Sen. Hugo Black of Alabama wrote to a member of the Roosevelt administration on June 19, 1934: "The public in our country has little conception of the possibilities of social insurance," and "there are few people in this country who realize such systems of social insurance have been adopted in most of the civilized countries in the world." [361]

Fourteen months after Black's letter, the Social Security Act of 1935 sailed through Congress and was signed into law ceremoniously by the president. In the interim, FDR had nurtured public opinion carefully. He saw his task as one of civic education, teaching the American people that social insurance was not alien to their values. Roosevelt argued that the development of a national industrial society made it impossible for most individuals to achieve financial security within the familiar bonds of the small community and the family. Instead, the complexities of great cities and of organized industry required that the federal government help people to secure their welfare in time of need. To bring this lesson home, the president's fireside chat of June 28, 1934, included a folksy yet effective illustration: the remodeling of the White House office building (the West Wing), which he likened to the adoption of social insurance. After describing the wiring and plumbing of the modern means of keeping offices cool in the hot Washington summers that were being installed, Roosevelt noted: "It is this combination of the old and new that marks orderly peaceful progress, not only in building buildings, but in building government itself. Our new structure is part of and a fulfillment of the old. . . . All that we do seeks to fulfill the historic traditions of the American people." [362]

Roosevelt's leadership involved, as one presidential scholar has written, "a careful process of grafting social secu-

rity onto the stalk of traditional American values." [363] By the end of this process, Roosevelt had moved the nation beyond the traditional idea that "rights" embody only guarantees against government oppression to the new understanding that government also has an obligation to ensure economic security. It was just such a new understanding of rights that Roosevelt had in mind when, at the 1932 Democratic convention, he pledged himself to "a new deal for the American people." [364]

The New Deal was a series of legislative acts, executive orders, and proclamations that sought not only to secure the economic welfare of the individual but also to remedy the broader economic problems of the Great Depression. During Roosevelt's tenure as president, programs were established to aid the aged, the unemployed, the disabled, and families with dependent children. Work projects were financed by the greatest single peacetime appropriation in history. For the first time the national government fostered unionization. When Roosevelt took office, almost no factory worker belonged to a union. By the time he left office, industrial unionism was firmly established, largely because of the National Labor Relations Act (the Wagner Act) of 1935, which empowered the government to enter factories to conduct elections so that workers could decide whether to join a union.

Not every major innovation in public policy during the 1930s originated in the White House. Some of the New Deal programs, such as the Tennessee Valley Authority, had long been on the public agenda but needed the impetus of a national crisis to move forward.[365] Other parts of what Roosevelt called the new "economic constitutional order," such as the Wagner Act, redounded to the president's credit, even though he backed such measures haltingly. That FDR was hailed for the initiatives of Robert F. Wagner and others signified the American people's growing tendency to think of the president as the government.

The Institutionalization of the Modern Presidency

The 1936 election ensured that the important political changes that had taken place in the country since 1932 would endure. FDR's 1932 victory had expressed the public's rejection of Hoover more than its approval of Roosevelt or his party. But sweeping confirmation of Roosevelt's leadership and of the New Deal came in 1936, when FDR won 60 percent of the popular vote—the largest majority ever by a presidential candidate—and carried all but two small states—Maine and Vermont. The 1936 elections also strengthened the Democratic hold on both houses of Congress, marking the Democrats' emergence as the nation's new majority party.

As Americans increasingly came to regard the presidency as their country's preeminent source of moral leadership, legislative guidance, and policy innovation, pressures mounted to increase the size and professionalism of the president's staff. A modest office since the time of its creation, the presidency developed after the 1930s into a full-blown institution.

Roosevelt hastened this development when he named three of the country's foremost scholars of public administration—Louis Brownlow, Charles Merriam, and Luther Gulick—to a President's Committee on Administrative Management. Concluding that "the President needs help," the Brownlow Committee, as it came to be called after its chair, proposed that the Executive Office of the President (EOP) be established. The EOP would include the Bureau of the Budget and a new White House Office and would be staffed by loyal and energetic presidential aides whose public influence was to be limited by their "passion for anonymity." In contrast to the regular cabinet departments and independent agencies, which were extensively influenced by Congress, the EOP would be a *presidential* institution that would be responsible for tasks closely linked to the presidents' priorities and staffed with individuals who would share their political and policy objectives.[366] For example, most individuals who filled important positions in the EOP would be selected exclusively by the president and did not have to be confirmed by the Senate. The committee proposed to enhance the president's control of the expanding activities of the executive branch. It recommended that all of the more than one hundred government agencies then in existence be integrated into twelve major departments, each of them under the virtually complete authority of the president.

Roosevelt supported the Brownlow Committee's recommendations wholeheartedly. Congress, for its part, had little quarrel with the new EOP. But the proposal to overhaul the departments and agencies, which was embodied in the 1937 executive reorganization bill, provoked one of the most intense controversies of FDR's presidency. His two-year battle for comprehensive administrative reform wrote a new chapter in the long-standing struggle between the executive and the legislature for the control of administration. What gave the battle special intensity was that it occurred just as administration was becoming an important arena of public policy. The expansion of welfare and regulatory programs during the New Deal meant that the complex responsibilities of government increasingly were set forth in discretionary statutes that left the principal task of shaping programs to the bureaucracy. Thus the struggle between the White House and Congress for control of the departments and agencies was no longer simply a squabble about patronage and prestige. The right to shape the direction and character of American public life also was at stake.

When Congress finally did enact the Executive Reorganization Act of 1939, it granted the president new administrative powers, but set them within serious limits.

For example, it placed a two-year limit on FDR's authority to overhaul the bureaucracy and exempted twenty-one of the more important government agencies from reorganization. Nevertheless, the implementation of the 1939 statute by Executive Order 8248 affected many of the Brownlow recommendations. The order created the Executive Office of the President and moved many agencies under its umbrella. In addition to the White House Office, the first Executive Office of the President included the National Resources Planning Board (a long-term planning agency) and a strengthened Bureau of the Budget, which was moved from the Treasury Department. Newly housed, the budget bureau began to acquire much greater powers, eventually attaining the responsibility to oversee the formation of the president's domestic program.

Most significant, the 1939 reforms hastened the development of the "administrative presidency," which exercised extensive domestic power on behalf of the president through rule making and policy implementation.[367] The absence of detail in Article II of the Constitution had always left the door open for independent presidential action, but the institutionalization of the presidency established an organizational structure that presidents and their appointees could use to short circuit the separation of powers, accelerating the transfer of authority from Congress to the executive.

Constitutional Crisis

The New Deal provoked a serious constitutional crisis toward the end of Roosevelt's first term. Roosevelt argued that the modern presidency, like the welfare state, was not a departure from sound constitutional principles. "The only thing that has been happening," he told the nation in his fireside chat of May 7, 1933, "has been to designate the President as the agency to carry out certain of the purposes of Congress. This was constitutional and in keeping with past American traditions."[368] Such was not the view, however, of the New Deal's opponents. As they saw it, the constitutional system of checks and balances was being destroyed by an ambitious president, determined to usurp power that properly belonged to Congress and the states.

The ranks of New Deal critics included not just Roosevelt's enemies in Congress and business, but also a majority of the Supreme Court. In 1935 and 1936 the Court struck down more important national legislation than in any other comparable period of U.S. history. Roosevelt responded in February 1937 with the most controversial action of his presidency, the so-called Court-packing plan: For every justice who failed to retire within six months after reaching the age of seventy, the president could appoint a new justice. Six of the nine justices were already seventy or older, which meant that Roosevelt would be able to enlarge the court to fifteen members by making new appointments. Presumably, these new judges would overcome the Court's resistance to the New Deal. *(See "Franklin D. Roosevelt and the Court-packing Plan," p. 1420, in Chapter 30, Vol. II.)*

Roosevelt's plan sought to eliminate the final constitutional barrier to a vast expansion of government activity and, thereby, to ratify the president's power to direct the affairs of state. Significantly, the two Supreme Court decisions that enraged FDR the most were *Humphrey's Executor v. United States* and *Schechter Poultry Corp. v. United States,* both of which imposed constraints on the president's personal authority.[369] The decisions were handed down on May 27, 1935, soon known to New Dealers as "Black Monday." In different ways, each of them threatened to derail the institutional changes that Roosevelt believed were necessary to solve the underlying problems of the Depression.

The Humphrey case denied the president the right to remove appointees from the independent regulatory commissions, a legal power that Roosevelt and his advisers thought had been established by tradition and affirmed by precedent in the *Myers* case of 1926.[370] The *Schechter* ruling was a direct challenge to the modern administrative state. It declared that the discretionary authority that Congress had granted, at Roosevelt's request, to the National Recovery Administration, the leading economic agency of the early New Deal, was an unconstitutional delegation of legislative power to the executive.

Although the Court-packing plan failed in Congress, Roosevelt claimed that in losing the battle he had won the war: The Court never again struck down a New Deal law. In fact, since 1937, the Supreme Court has not invalidated any significant federal statute to regulate the economy, nor has the Court judged any law (with the exception of the line-item veto of 1996) to be an unconstitutional delegation of authority to the president.[371] Most of the judicial barriers to national and presidential power had fallen.

But the bitter fight over Court-packing entailed a considerable political cost. The Court issue effectively brought Roosevelt's mastery of Congress and the Democratic Party to an end. Moreover, it served as a lightning rod, sparking a resurgence of congressional independence and the formation of a bipartisan "conservative coalition." The new alliance of conservative Democrats and Republicans blocked nearly every presidential reform initiatives from 1937 until the mid-1960s.

Foreign Policy

The economic crisis that dominated Roosevelt's first two terms as president was displaced in the late 1930s by the approach and then the outbreak of World War II. Even before the United States declared war in December 1941, the growing U.S. involvement in the European and Asian conflicts intensified the concentration of power in the national government, its administrative apparatus, and the president. Significantly, it was the international crisis that led Roosevelt

to stand for reelection in 1940. His victory made him the only president in history to break the two-term tradition. In 1944, during the latter stages of the war, he also won a fourth term. Only death in April 1945 cut short Roosevelt's protracted reign.

In 1937 Roosevelt began to confront the isolationist mood that had dominated the polity since the end of World War I.[372] Ironically, FDR's efforts were fortified by the same Court that had been such an obstacle to his domestic program. In late 1936, in the case of *U.S. v. Curtiss-Wright Export Corp.,* the Supreme Court upheld a 1934 law that authorized the president to place an embargo on the sale of U.S.-made weapons to countries that were engaged in armed conflict. The law had been passed with the so-called Chaco War between Bolivia and Paraguay in mind, and Roosevelt quickly forbade the sale of arms to both countries. Weapons merchants challenged the measure as an unlawful delegation of authority to the president. A federal district court agreed. But in a somewhat surprising opinion, written by conservative justice George Sutherland, a near unanimous Court laid down a sweeping doctrine of presidential authority in foreign affairs.

The Court held that the president's constitutional powers in domestic and foreign matters are fundamentally different. "The broad statement that the federal government can exercise no power except those specifically stated in the Constitution, and such implied powers as are necessary and proper to carry into effect the enumerated powers," Justice Sutherland wrote, "is categorically true only in respect to internal affairs." In foreign affairs, the actions of the president as the government's "sole organ" in international relations depend neither on a specific grant of power from the Constitution nor on authorization from Congress. Because the executive's authority in foreign policy is "plenary and exclusive," the president enjoys a freedom from statutory restriction that "would not be admissible were domestic affairs alone involved." [373]

The *Curtiss-Wright* case established as constitutional doctrine the sweeping defense of the executive's prerogatives in foreign affairs that Alexander Hamilton had offered in 1793 to defend President's Washington's Neutrality Proclamation. Along with the 1937 *Belmont* case, which justified the president's right to reach executive agreements with other countries (that is, quasi-treaties that are forged without the participation of the Senate), *Curtiss-Wright* made it virtually impossible to challenge Roosevelt's increasingly internationalist policies on constitutional grounds.[374]

Relying on his broad, Court-sanctioned understanding of the president's foreign policy authority, Roosevelt concluded the controversial destroyer-for-bases deal with Great Britain in 1940. The agreement, which paved the way for the United States to send fifty naval destroyers to help England in its desperate battle with Nazi Germany, marked a departure from the official U.S. policy of neutrality. In contrast, Roosevelt's Lend-Lease program to aid Great Britain required congressional action because it involved an initial appropriation of around $7 billion. The debate over Lend-Lease and its eventual enactment by Congress produced a rough consensus of the sort Roosevelt had not been able to achieve through unilateral executive action. Before Lend-Lease "the most Americans would commit themselves to was aid to the democracies short of war," historian David Kennedy has written. Now Roosevelt had "edged them closer to a commitment to aid the democracies even at the risk of war." [375]

As the New Deal prepared the country for war, Roosevelt spoke not only of the government's obligation to guarantee freedom from want, but also its responsibility to guarantee freedom from fear—to protect the American people, and the world, against foreign aggression. The obligation to uphold "human rights" became a new guarantee of security, which presupposed a further expansion of national administrative power.[376] (See "Franklin D. Roosevelt's 'Four Freedoms' Speech," p. 1771, in Reference Materials, Vol. II.)

Once under way, World War II greatly accelerated the flow of power to the executive, allowing Roosevelt to assert an inherent executive prerogative more aggressively than he could have before the attack on Pearl Harbor. Under the conditions of total war, Roosevelt believed, the president is empowered not only to direct military operations abroad but also to manage affairs at home. In a bold—his critics claimed brazen—expression of such power, the president demanded that an effective program of price and wage controls be created. "I ask the Congress," FDR said in his Labor Day message of September 7, 1942, "to take ... action by the first of October." In the event that Congress did not act, Roosevelt warned, "I shall accept the responsibility, and I will act." [377]

Congress enacted the economic controls the president demanded, and Roosevelt never had to follow through on his threat. But the legislature's reluctant acquiescence in this matter indicated that as Depression gave way to war, another expansion of presidential authority was under way, linked chiefly now to the creation of a national security state.[378]

The Court's acquiescence to presidential power also peaked during World War II.[379] Its 1944 Yakus v. U.S. decision upheld the Roosevelt administration's national price and wage controls, issued in pursuance of the congressional legislation that Roosevelt demanded in 1942. With its justification of these regulations, which relied on the vaguest of legislative standards, the Court all but abandoned the nondelegation principles announced in the 1935 Schechter decision.[380] In Ex Parte Quirin, the Court sanctioned Roosevelt's use of military tribunals to try those accused of sabotage on American soil. This case dealt with the White House's actions during the capture, trial, and punishment of eight Germans who came to the United States during World War II to commit acts of sabotage. After the saboteurs were cap-

tured in June 1942, Roosevelt convened a secret military tribunal on July 2, 1942, which sentenced the eight men to death. The president later commuted the death sentences of two of the prisoners of war, as they had both confessed and assisted in capturing the others. The remaining six were executed on the electric chair on August 8, 1942, in Washington, D.C. The Court had issued its opinion on July 31, 1942, but did not release a full opinion until October 29, 1942. In his opinion for the Court, Chief Justice Stone distinguished this case from Ex Parte Milligan (see above), decided soon after the Civil War, because the defendant in that case was not "part of or associated with the armed forces of the enemy." Moreover, the conditions of modern warfare made acts of sabotage on American soil more likely and insidious—the sort of egregious crimes that justified military commissions:

> Modern warfare is directed at the destruction of enemy war supplies and the implements of their production and transportation, quite as much as at the armed forces. Every consideration which makes the unlawful belligerent punishable is equally applicable whether his objective is the one or the other. The law of war cannot rightly treat those agents of enemy armies who enter our territory, armed with explosives intended for the destruction of war industries and supplies, as any the less belligerent enemies than are agents similarly entering for the purpose of destroying fortified places or our Armed Forces. By passing our boundaries for such purposes without uniform or other emblem signifying their belligerent status, or by discarding that means of identification after entry, such enemies become unlawful belligerents subject to trial and punishment.[381]

Although the Roosevelt administration's treatment of Nazi saboteurs was strongly supported by the public, a large part of the academic and legal community argued that the Quirin case set a dangerous precedent. Indeed, the criticism of Roosevelt's order led the White House to modify it when a second set of saboteurs was captured in 1944. In truth, the legacy of Roosevelt's use of military tribunals and the Quirin decision was of little consequence until the events of September 11, 2001. As discussed below, President George W. Bush's authorization of military tribunals to punish those who provided assistance to the terrorist attacks against the United States followed closely Roosevelt's 1942 executive order concerning the Quirin saboteurs.[382]

The most controversial Court decision during World War II was its ruling in the 1944 case of Koramatsu v. U.S., which condoned the Roosevelt administration's use of racial classification to imprison a large number of Japanese Americans.[383] On February 8, 1942, Roosevelt signed an executive order authorizing the removal of one hundred thousand Americans of Japanese descent from their homes on the West Coast and authorizing their placement in desolate and isolated relocation camps. These Americans had committed no crime, and, although FDR's order was justified on the grounds of "military necessity," no real evidence was offered to demonstrate that these individuals posed a security risk. Indeed, to prove their American patriotism, many of the young men who had been sent to the camps volunteered for service in the American armed forces and served with distinction.

This egregious affront to American ideals of justice was not FDR's idea. It originated with California politicians, most notably Attorney General Earl Warren, who would later serve as chief justice of the Supreme Court. The politicians were reacting to widespread fears that arose in the wake of Japan's stealth attack on Pearl Harbor and the racism that led to falsely equating Japanese Americans with Japanese nationals. Some members of the administration opposed the internment order, but like FDR, they were preoccupied with the military crisis and were unwilling to spend political capital to help such politically vulnerable victims. One such victim, Fred Korematsu, of Japanese ancestry, was a twenty-three-year-old American-born citizen of the United States who had a good job and an Italian-American fiancée, and no wish to leave either. After his arrest for violating the military's evacuation order, Korematsu agreed to allow the American Civil Liberties Union to use his case as a test of the Japanese internment policy.

Clearly queasy about the *Korematsu* case, the Court acknowledged that "all legal restrictions which curtail the civil rights groups of a single racial group are immediately suspect." Nonetheless, Justice Hugo Black's majority opinion concluded that military necessity provided sufficient grounds to believe that the internment of Japanese Americans was justified: "Compulsory exclusion of large groups of citizens from their homes, except under circumstances of direct emergency and peril, is inconsistent with our basic governmental institutions. But when under conditions of modern warfare our shores are threatened by hostile forces, the power to protect must be commensurate with the threatened danger. . . ." In a haunting dissenting opinion, Justice Robert Jackson objected that such extreme judicial deference to executive power during wartime posed a dire threat to constitutional rights: "[O]nce a judicial opinion rationalizes . . . an order [such as the Civilian Exclusion Order] to show that it conforms to the Constitution, or rather rationalizes the Constitution to show that the Constitution sanctions such an order, the Court for all time has validated the principle of racial discrimination in criminal procedure and of transplanting American citizens. The principle then lies about like a loaded weapon ready for the hand of any authority that can bring forward a plausible claim of an urgent need." [384]

As it was, no racially restrictive law has every since passed the test of military necessity prescribed in *Korematsu*. In truth, no sooner had the Court pronounced on this case than it came to be viewed as a judicial travesty. Congress in 1948 provided $37 million in reparations for the victims of Japanese internment. In another burst of conscience forty years later, Congress awarded $20,000 to each surviving detainee. President Bill Clinton further atoned for a contrite nation in 1998 when he awarded the nation's highest civilian honor, the Presidential Medal of Freedom, to Fred Korematsu. [385] Yet these officials acts of atonement have never completely erased the deeply troubling failure of the Congress and judiciary to strike a balance between enabling the president to have enough prerogative power to keep the nation safe while simultaneously preventing the president from abusing that discretion.

Harry S. Truman and Dwight D. Eisenhower

FDR dominated American political life for more than twelve years. His legacy included a more powerful and prominent presidency. But Roosevelt's long tenure also aroused serious concern about concentrating too much power in the White House.

Truman and the Roosevelt Inheritance

When the Senate adjourned at about five o'clock on April 12, 1945, Harry S. Truman, vice president of the United States and president of the Senate, made his way over to the office of Speaker Sam Rayburn to join his friends for their afternoon round of bourbon and tap water. No sooner had his drink been poured than the vice president received a call from White House press secretary Steve Early, who told him to come to the executive mansion as soon as possible. Upon his arrival, Mrs. Roosevelt came up to him, put her arm around his shoulders, and said softly, "Harry, the president is dead." After a moment of shock, Truman asked Mrs. Roosevelt, "Is there anything I can do for you?" She replied, "Is there anything we can do for you? For you are the one in trouble now." [386]

Eleanor Roosevelt was not the only one who felt that Truman was in trouble. With the country still at war, it seemed incomprehensible that anyone, let alone this "little man" from Missouri, as some of Truman's contemporaries disdainfully referred to him, could take Roosevelt's place as president of the United States. As the journalist William White wrote, "For a time he walked, as completely as the smallest laborer who had been a 'Roosevelt man,' in the long shadow of the dead President." [387]

That Truman eventually was able to emerge from FDR's shadow had little to do with his ability to rouse the public. A poor speaker who was awkward in the presence of the press and microphones, Truman was uncomfortable in the limelight of the modern presidency, especially in comparison with the self-command and bonhomie displayed by Roosevelt. Truman's personal and rhetorical shortcomings contributed to his low popularity. His public approval was

In his 1948 whistle-stop campaign Harry S. Truman traveled more than 31,500 miles across the country and delivered 356 speeches to win a surprising reelection.

lower than 50 percent for much of his time in office, including the entire final three years of his second term.[388]

In other respects, however, Truman was a solid successor to Roosevelt. He believed deeply in the changes that the New Deal had made in the United States. Although he was all too aware of his personal limitations, Truman also recognized that FDR's legacy required active leadership from the late president's successors. Truman liked to say that "being a president is like riding a tiger. You have to keep on riding or be swallowed." [389]

Truman's Fair Deal. Truman's twenty-one-point message to Congress on September 6, 1945, made clear that he would not be to Roosevelt what Harding had been to Wilson. The message, which introduced the "Fair Deal" agenda, called for extension of Social Security, increases in the minimum wage, national health insurance, urban development, and a full employment bill.

Truman achieved little of his domestic program, however, and the 1946 congressional election appeared to be a dramatic rejection of the Fair Deal. That campaign was organized around the theme that the country had had enough of Roosevelt-Truman liberalism. When, for the first time in sixteen years, the Democrats lost control of Congress, many concluded that the party could not survive the passing of FDR.[390]

Truman fought every attempt by the Republican Eightieth Congress (1947–1949) to dismantle the New Deal. The president cast more than two hundred vetoes during his presidency, mostly on matters of tax and labor policy. Truman's most significant veto was of the 1947 Taft-Hartley bill, legislation widely viewed as an attack on labor unions. The veto, although overridden, caused labor and middle-class liberals to line up solidly behind Truman.

Shrewdly taking the political initiative, Truman turned the 1948 presidential campaign into a referendum on the Roosevelt era. When he surprised nearly everyone by winning a come-from-behind victory over his Republican opponent, New York governor Thomas Dewey, Truman stepped at least partially out of FDR's shadow. Not only had the president saved the New Deal and revived the Democratic coalition, but the assertiveness he displayed in his battles with Congress confirmed the preeminence of the modern presidency in legislative affairs.

Although Truman was never able to shatter the legislative stalemate in domestic policy that had prevailed from the beginning of his presidency, he could claim some success. His Social Security, minimum wage, and public housing proposals were enacted during the Eighty first Congress (1949–1951), which, as a result of the 1948 election, was again controlled by the Democrats. Most important, his administration was successful in assembling a bipartisan foreign policy coalition in Congress. Postwar tensions between the United States and the Soviet Union, who had been allies against Nazi Germany, brought the world into an era of cold war. Democrats and internationalist Republicans voted to authorize the Truman Doctrine to contain communist expansion, the Marshall Plan to rebuild Europe, and other postwar policy initiatives that were designed to maintain the international commitments of the United States after World War II.

Truman's Use of Executive Power. Neither the limited success that Truman had with Congress in domestic matters nor the effective bipartisan coalition he assembled in foreign affairs discouraged him from staking out a substantial sphere for independent executive action. On December 6, 1946, Truman established by executive order the President's Committee on Civil Rights (PCCR), which was authorized "to determine whether and in what respect current law enforcement measures and the authority and means possessed by Federal, State, and local governments may be strengthened and improved to safeguard the civil rights of the people." [391] He recommended legislative action based on the PCCR's report. When Congress proved unresponsive, the president did what he could on his own authority as chief executive. In 1948, for example, Truman issued an executive order to establish equal opportunity for all races in the armed services.

Truman's most daring and politically costly initiatives came in the realm of international security. These included his decisions to use atomic weapons against Japan near the end of World War II and, in 1950, to commit troops to Korea. The Korean intervention, which followed communist North Korea's invasion of South Korea in June 1950, was an important extension of the president's power as commander in chief. For the first time in history, U.S. troops were deployed in a full-scale war without a congressional declaration.

In part, Truman's intervention in Korea was a logical consequence of the postwar emergence of the United States as a superpower, actively and constantly engaged in international affairs. In 1945 the Senate overwhelmingly ratified the United Nations (UN) charter, and Congress passed the United States Participation Act, which would subject the United States to certain UN decisions. Truman invoked this act as the primary justification for his deployment of troops in Korea. Once the UN Security Council decided to help South Korea, the president argued, he had a duty to respond under Articles 39 and 42 of the UN charter.

But Truman also defended his actions in Korea by claiming to have a sweeping presidential power to use U.S. armed forces without consulting Congress. He believed that the cold war against communism and the president's new responsibilities as leader of the free world had greatly diminished the role of Congress in foreign policy. As he said in March 1951, "the congressional power to declare war has fallen into abeyance because wars are no longer declared in advance." [392]

Limits still existed on the powers of the modern presidency, however, even in foreign policy. Truman paid dearly in the coin of public and congressional criticism as the war in Korea dragged on inconclusively. Most important, his claim that the Korean conflict endowed the president with emergency economic powers was rebuffed by the Supreme Court in its 1952 decision in *Youngstown Sheet and Tube Co. v. Sawyer. (See "Other Domestic Powers Related to National Security," p. 1443, in Chapter 30, Vol. II.)*

Truman and the Modern Presidency. Truman's tenure as president reaffirmed the modern presidency. He demonstrated that a president without extraordinary political gifts or popularity could achieve important objectives, define the terms of national political debate, and control at least the main lines of domestic and foreign policy.

But Truman also made an independent contribution to the development of the presidency by formalizing and expanding the presidency as an institution. Although Franklin Roosevelt had created the Executive Office of the President, his own staff was unstructured, reflecting his penchant for improvised, ad hoc arrangements. Truman, in contrast, was a systematic administrator. During his presidency, responsibilities within the White House Office became more clearly defined. Truman also used the Bureau of the Budget more extensively than Roosevelt, relying heavily on it to carry out his executive and legislative duties. Truman assigned responsibility to the BOB to clear and coordinate all legislative requests that originated within the federal departments and to draft White House–sponsored legislation and executive orders.[393] As a result, Truman developed an advisory process in which political issues came to him only for decision, not, as with FDR, for development.

Congress helped Truman to institutionalize the presidency, sometimes unintentionally. Congressionally initiated statutes, for example, established the Council of Economic Advisers (CEA) in 1946 and the National Security Council (NSC) in 1947 to help the president formulate fiscal and foreign policy, respectively. Although many legislators had hoped that the CEA and NSC would serve as checks on the president's autonomy in fiscal and security matters, Truman acted effectively to make these agencies part of the president's team.

The law that established the NSC—the National Security Act—created two more executive bodies that strengthened the president's capacity to influence world affairs. One was the Central Intelligence Agency (CIA), which constituted a powerful new tool for diplomacy and military strategy in the cold war era. Although Truman feared that he might be creating a "Gestapo," the unification of the government's previously far-flung intelligence activities appealed to his desire for centralization and clear lines of responsibility.

The other new agency was the Department of Defense, which housed under one roof the previously separate branches of the armed forces. By the end of World War II, most members of Congress were convinced that some sort of consolidation of the chaotic, antagonistic bureaucracies responsible for the national defense was needed. Truman, characteristically, favored any effort to make administration more orderly. The 1947 statute created the National Military Establishment, headed by a secretary of defense, who was charged to coordinate the operations of the army, navy, and air force. This proved to be a Herculean task; indeed, it drove the first secretary, James Forrestal, to nervous collapse and suicide. Forrestal and Truman suggested amendments to the act that were enacted in 1949. These amendments strengthened the authority of the secretary and replaced the National Military Establishment with a full-blown Department of Defense. To further centralize military planning, the 1949 amendments created the position of chairman of the Joint Chiefs of Staff (JCS) to denote the officer who was to serve as the principal military adviser to the defense secretary and the president. Although these changes did not eliminate interservice rivalry, the new cabinet-level department, along with the NSC and CIA, greatly increased the president's resources for directing foreign and military policy.[394]

Truman's effort to strengthen the institutional presidency received surprising help from former president Herbert Hoover. The Republican-controlled Eightieth Congress had appointed Hoover to head the Commission on the Organization of the Executive Branch of the Government. The task of the commission, as Republican leaders understood it, was to lay the groundwork for an assault on New Deal programs and to circumscribe the executive by foreclosing the possibility of another personalized, FDR-style administration. Yet Hoover, who as president had grappled with the problems of the executive branch, saw the need to fortify the modern presidency.[395]

Thus, after much study, the Hoover Commission submitted a report that was very similar to the one that Brownlow and his colleagues had submitted in 1937 to support FDR's program of administrative reform. The president still needed help, the Hoover Commission argued, especially to supervise the far-flung activities of the enlarged executive branch. Its recommendations formed the basis of the 1949 executive reorganization act, which authorized Truman (who enthusiastically embraced the commission's report) to make important changes in many of the departments, agencies, and independent regulatory commissions.

Especially significant was Truman's Reorganization Plan No. 8, which he issued in 1950. Truman included provisions in the plan that eroded the regulatory commissions' autonomy from presidential influence and thereby reduced the effect of the Court's ruling in *Humphrey's Executor v. United States* that the president may not remove a commissioner. The reorganization plan provided that the chairs of the regulatory commissions would be "appointed by the president and serve at his pleasure." The chairs in turn were granted considerable authority to oversee the daily business of their commissions and to appoint and supervise commission staff. Consequently, presidents were better able to give direction to regulatory agencies than in the past.[396]

Hoover's endorsement of executive reorganization suggested that a political consensus was forming in support of the modern presidency. Republicans had "historically been against Presidents," one Truman aide noted, but Hoover's interest in the problems of administrative management offered bipartisan support for "the kind of Chief Executive office that will have enough authority and the right kind of organization to do the most difficult jobs." [397]

Dwight D. Eisenhower: The Reluctant Modern President

Dwight D. Eisenhower fostered bipartisan acceptance of the modern presidency, albeit with some reluctance. Although the Republican president had no intention of dismantling the "Roosevelt revolution," he came to the White House in 1953 with a different perception of the executive office from Roosevelt's and with different aspirations. Eisenhower had served as supreme Allied commander in Europe, a position to which FDR appointed him, and was the most celebrated of the World War II generals. "Ike" brought to the presidency a soldier's sense of duty. He was resolved not to lead the federal government into the new and untried but instead to restore a sense of national calm after the controversial and frenetic activism of Roosevelt and Truman. One of the political aftershocks of the New Deal and Fair Deal was the Twenty-second Amendment, prohibiting any person from being elected president more than two times, which was proposed by the Republican-dominated Eightieth Congress in 1947 and ratified by the states in 1951. In many ways Eisenhower was like Coolidge—he wanted to preside over a postwar healing process.

Eisenhower's concern for duty initially inclined him to accept the argument of some members of his party that balance should be restored to the relationship between the president and Congress. He was no partisan Republican. Some Democrats had tried to draft him to run for president in 1948, only to discover that he considered it so much his duty to remain above politics that he had never voted. But Eisenhower did accept the prevailing Republican doctrine that the proper relationship between Congress and the White House had been upset by his immediate Democratic predecessors. For example, as the first Republican president since 1933, Eisenhower decided not to submit a legislative program to Congress during his first year in office.

Some Americans regarded Eisenhower's constant professions of respect for Congress as refreshing evidence that the hallowed traditions of legislative government were being restored. Others, however, especially in the press, looked disdainfully upon Eisenhower's ostentatious display of reverence for balanced government. Reporters graded Eisenhower at the end of his First Hundred Days, and he did not fare well when measured by FDR's standard.

The Hidden Hand. Appearances to the contrary, Eisenhower did not simply sit and watch history pass by. He exercised power with much more relish and shrewdness than his contemporaries realized. His was a "hidden-hand" presidency, as political scientist Fred Greenstein has put it, in which Ike exercised power behind the scenes, while presenting to the public the image of detachment from Washington's political machinations.[398] Ultimately, Eisenhower believed, the dignity and influence of the office were lost when the president not only led politically, but also appeared to lead politically, as Truman had.

Ike's solution to the dilemma of modern executive leadership was not to abdicate responsibility for policy. Although Eisenhower was a domestic political conservative who had no desire to innovate except in modest, incremental ways, he believed that the New Deal had become a permanent part of the U.S. government. When his conservative brother Edgar criticized him for carrying on liberal politics, the president bluntly replied, "Should any political party attempt to abolish social security and eliminate labor laws and farm programs, you should not hear of that party again in our political history."[399] Moreover, unlike many Republicans, Eisenhower had long shared the international-ist aspirations of FDR and Truman.

Eisenhower realized, then, that because of the New Deal legacy and the emergence of the United States as leader of the free world, the president could no longer simply pre-side. Instead, the task, as he understood it, was to lead active-ly without seeming to lead, to remain quietly and persistent-ly involved in political affairs while maintaining the public face of the congenial war hero.

The most instructive example of Eisenhower's hidden-hand approach to government was his handling of Sen. Joseph McCarthy. The nation was traumatized by the Wisconsin Republican's charges that communists had infil-trated the federal government. Eisenhower refused publicly to attack McCarthy, who chaired the Senate Committee on Government Operations and its Permanent Subcommittee on Investigations, although he regarded McCarthy's red-baiting as demagogy of the worst kind. The president's crit-ics claimed that by not upbraiding McCarthy, he abetted the senator in unjustly ruining many lives and careers. "Unopposed by the one public leader who could have dis-credited him," wrote historian Alonzo Hamby, "McCarthy ran amok."[400]

But Eisenhower's public silence did not indicate timid-ity or tacit approval. He feared that taking McCarthy on publicly would undermine the dignity of the presidency and the unity of the Republican Party, thereby jeopardizing his chances of pursuing an internationalist foreign policy. "I will not," Eisenhower told his brother Milton, "get into a pissing contest with that skunk."[401]

What the president did instead, working closely with his press secretary, James Hagerty, was to use the media and his congressional allies to ruin McCarthy's political effective-ness.[402] Through Hagerty, Eisenhower helped manage the congressional hearings that culminated in McCarthy's cen-sure in December 1954. In addition, Eisenhower and Vice President Richard M. Nixon, although carefully avoiding any direct mention of McCarthy, condemned the kind of actions in which the senator engaged.

As his handling of McCarthy indicates, Eisenhower did not reject the modern presidency. Instead, he tried to manage its responsibilities in a way that suited his own strengths and political objectives. Despite criticism in the press, Eisenhower remained extraordinarily popular with the American people. Coolidge had shown thirty years ear-lier that presidential leadership of public opinion need not be exercised solely to achieve reform or innovation. Eisenhower's popularity indicated that, at least at times, the

The supreme commander of all Allied forces in Europe, Dwight D. Eisenhower, walks with Winston Churchill. "Ike," the most celebrated military officer of World War II, was elected president in 1952.

public still appreciated quiet leadership to preserve the sta-tus quo.

Eisenhower's Legacy. Eisenhower has been condemned frequently by presidential scholars for the work he left undone. "No president in history," wrote political scientist Clinton Rossiter, "was ever more powerfully armed to per-suade the minds of men and face up to the inevitable and then failed more poignantly to use his power."[403] For all his popularity, critics have charged, Eisenhower failed as presi-dent by not rousing the country politically to redress prob-lems of civil rights, education, and social justice.

Critics have charged, in particular, that Eisenhower's approach to civil rights revealed a troubling deficiency in his understanding of presidential responsibility. In 1954 the Supreme Court decision in *Brown v. Board of Education of Topeka,* which struck down the "separate but equal" doctrine that allowed racially segregated public schools, raised the hopes of civil rights reformers that segregation had finally been routed.[404] But Eisenhower dampened those hopes by refusing to say whether he approved or disapproved of the decision. His equivocation probably slowed progress toward racial equality; certainly it helped set the stage for the ugly racial incident that occurred in Little Rock, Arkansas, in 1957. On September 23, nine African American students were turned away from Central High School by a howling, hate-filled mob of segregationists from Arkansas and other states. Eisenhower was reluctant to interfere, believing that to use federal troops to enforce desegregation might cause the violence to spread. But when neither state nor local authorities dispersed the mob, the president could avoid responsibility no longer. On September 24, a contingent of regular army paratroopers was dispatched to Little Rock.

Many have found it difficult to understand Eisenhower's reluctance to act in the Little Rock crisis. To Eisenhower's credit, however, he eventually did act firmly, thus establishing a precedent that would make it difficult for future presidents to deny the federal interest in racial matters, which until then had been regarded as essentially state and local concerns.[405]

Eisenhower also contributed to the institutionalization of the modern presidency. Drawing on his long experience with military staffs, the president enlarged and formally organized the White House Office. This is not to say that Eisenhower organized the White House along military lines, as many Washington observers erroneously concluded during his tenure. Instead, the enthusiasm that Ike had gained for careful organization as an army general predisposed him to entertain seriously the recommendation of the Brownlow Committee to establish a clearer and more formal line of command between the White House and the rest of the executive branch.[406] He established a line of command and communication that ran from the president through a chief of staff (who reported directly to him) to the rest of the president's team and back again. Sherman Adams, who was the first chief of staff, worked zealously to free the president from the everyday demands of the White House and the rest of the executive branch.[407] (See "Eisenhower: The Formalized Staff," p. 1067, in Chapter 22, Vol. II.)

Eisenhower's modest programmatic ambitions notwithstanding, he also created the first White House office of legislative liaison. The task of the liaison office was to promote the president's policies on Capitol Hill. Although Eisenhower offered no program to Congress during his first year, pressure from several quarters soon forced him to become more actively involved in legislative affairs. Eisenhower himself, having talked of "restoring the balance" between the branches, soon realized that even a conservative president who wanted mostly to curb policy innovation needed to have his views represented effectively to Congress. Thus a presidential program accompanied the State of the Union message in January 1954, and Eisenhower and his legislative liaison office worked systematically to enact it. During his eight years as president, Ike became increasingly involved in legislative issues, such as the effort to create the interstate highway system and the space program. He even

managed to work well with a Congress that, after 1954, was controlled by the Democrats.

Eisenhower's "special triumph" in congressional relations, as historian Stephen Ambrose has noted, was to hold down defense spending.[408] The former military commander wanted to avoid an arms race with the Soviet Union, fearing that a military buildup would trigger uncontrollable inflation and eventually would bankrupt the United States, all without providing additional security. During his second term, the Democrats in Congress, led by Sen. John F. Kennedy, criticized the president for putting a balanced budget ahead of national defense. But Eisenhower, confident of his own military judgment, was unmoved. Inheriting a $50 billion annual defense budget from Truman, he reduced it to $40 billion.

The importance of controlling defense spending was the principal theme of Eisenhower's farewell address, the first of its kind to be delivered on television. The president's speech did not downplay the threat of communism—"it commands our whole attention, absorbs our whole being." At the same time, he warned, the country had "to guard against the acquisition of unwarranted influence, whether sought or not, by the military-industrial complex." The conjunction of an immense military establishment and a large arms industry—"a new American experience"—held "the potential for the disastrous rise of misplaced power." The task of statesmanship, Eisenhower insisted, was not to rouse the people to "emotional and transitory sacrifice of crisis," but to constrain the national security state, to "compel the proper meshing of the huge industrial and military machinery of defense with our peaceful methods and goals, so that security and liberty may prosper together." (See "Eisenhower's Farewell Address," p. 1775, in Reference Materials, Vol. II.)

After a doubtful start, then, Eisenhower upheld the modern presidency. His defense of the twentieth-century executive was never more apparent than in his active involvement in the campaign to defeat the Bricker Amendment, which would have curtailed the president's authority to conduct foreign policy. By the terms of the amendment, executive agreements with other nations would take effect only if they were approved by Congress and did not conflict with state laws. The amendment's author, the Republican senator John Bricker of Ohio, and its adherents in Congress endorsed isolationist sentiments that, according to Eisenhower, threatened the future of both the United States and the Republican Party.

In the Senate, mainly because of the president's personal influence, the Bricker Amendment fell one vote short of passage. The close vote indicated that many Americans still believed that the modern executive's exercise of initiative in foreign affairs was excessive. It was the reluctant modern president—"Dwight D. Eisenhower—nobody

John F. Kennedy delivers perhaps the most memorable and eloquent of inaugural addresses, January 20, 1961.

them the sacrifices that will be necessary." [410]

On November 22, 1963, less than three years after Kennedy took the oath of office, he was assassinated by Lee Harvey Oswald in Dallas, Texas. At age forty-three, Kennedy had been the country's youngest elected president. Yet despite his truncated term, or perhaps because of it, Kennedy has found a lasting place in American culture. As one historian has observed, Kennedy is "part not of history but of myth," much as the warrior Achilles was in ancient Greece.[411] Kennedy's popularity persists not only because of his tragic death but also because of certain qualities that he displayed as president. Kennedy sought to inspire the nation to meet the challenges of the post–World War II era. During the 1960 campaign, JFK summoned the American people to a "New Frontier" that appealed "to their pride, not their pocketbook," that held "out the promise of more sacrifice instead of security." [412]

Kennedy's inaugural address, the most important speech of his presidency, placed this challenge before the nation with eloquence and grace. *(See "Kennedy's Inaugural Address," p. 1776, in Reference Materials, Vol. II.)* Uplifting and optimistic in tone, it articulated a vision that greatly augmented the fragile base of support Kennedy had received from the election (Kennedy's margin of victory was only 120,000 votes out of the nearly 69 million cast). Both liberals and conservatives found something to applaud in the new president's celebration of nationalism, spirit of sacrifice, and sense of mission. The best remembered passage from the address emphasized these themes.

> In the long history of the world, only a few generations have been granted the role of defending freedom in its hours of maximum danger. . . . The energy, the faith, the devotion which we bring to this endeavor will light our country and those who serve it—and the glow from that fire can truly light the world. And so, my fellow Americans: ask not what your country can do for you—ask what you can do for your country.

else," an embittered Senator Bricker claimed—who preserved the executive's right to make international agreements unilaterally.[409]

JFK and the Personalization of the Modern Presidency

John F. Kennedy (JFK) was elected president in 1960 to get the country moving again by lifting the United States out of the complacency that seemed to have settled on it during the Eisenhower years. The combination of a sluggish economy, a simmering civil rights problem, and the Soviet threat abroad had created doubts about the country's future that led a slim plurality of voters back to the Democratic Party.

Running against Vice President Richard Nixon, Kennedy campaigned on a theme of change, tying that theme to the presidency itself. The United States could no longer afford a president, he declared, "who is praised primarily for what he did not do, the disasters he prevented, the bills he vetoed—a President wishing his subordinates would produce more missiles or build more schools." Instead, Kennedy insisted, the nation "needs a Chief Executive who is the vital center of action in our whole scheme of government." The president must be "willing and able to summon his national constituency to its finest hour—to alert the people to our dangers and our opportunities—to demand of

Kennedy's call for self-sacrifice and national glory resonated with the historical experience of postwar America. The giftedness, or charisma, of the young president—handsome, graceful, and celebrated as a hero for his courageous actions as commander of PT-109 during World War II—fit America's feeling that it could solve the world's problems and break through the ancient barriers that previously had limited humankind, even, as Kennedy pledged, land a man on the moon and return him safely to the earth.[413]

The First Television President

It was not just Kennedy's words that stirred the nation but also the vibrant and reassuring image he conveyed when delivering them. His administration marked a revolutionary advance in the use of television in politics. Although Eisenhower had been the first president to appear on television regularly, "it was under and because of Kennedy that television became an essential determinant—probably the essential determinant—of a president's ability to lead the nation."[414] As political scientist Bruce Miroff has written, Kennedy and other members of his administration staged "spectacles," or message-laden symbolic displays, that "projected youth, vigor, and a novelty, that recast the [presidency] itself as a headquarters for intelligence and masterful will."[415]

Kennedy's televised speeches were one element of his strategy of public communication. But after his inauguration, the president went before the cameras only nine times to deliver a prepared address. Convinced that citizens would tire quickly of formal speech making, JFK relied on the press conference as his principal forum for reaching the public. Kennedy was the first president to allow press conferences to be televised without restriction, recognizing that live, unedited broadcasts of his give and take with reporters would be a superb means of addressing the nation. Eisenhower's press conferences had been televised, but they were taped and the White House retained the power to revise them for broadcast. Eisenhower's press secretary, James C. Hagerty, believed that live television was dangerous—the president might misspeak on a sensitive matter, jeopardizing the national security. But Kennedy, who benefited greatly from his television debates with Nixon in 1960, regarded television as an ally.

Previous presidents, notably Theodore Roosevelt and Franklin Roosevelt, had used press conferences to cultivate the journalistic fraternity, which in turn had helped them to convey their purposes to the American people. But the live, televised press conference relegated reporters to the reluctant role of stage props. Under Kennedy's auspices, the press conference became the functional equivalent of the fireside chat—that is, it afforded the president a relatively informal and personal way to reach the public, over the heads of the members of Congress and the proprietors of the media. Kennedy held sixty-four press conferences, and

his pleasing personality, quick wit, and impressive knowledge of government set a standard that his successors have struggled to meet.[416]

The Personal Presidency

Woodrow Wilson believed that the "extraordinary isolation" of the presidency, if used effectively, allowed the president both to inspire and to benefit from public opinion. Wilson himself and, later, FDR did much to advance the president's relationship with the people. But with Kennedy and the advent of television, what political scientist Theodore Lowi has called the personal presidency came into its own.[417]

Kennedy's effective use of the media was part of his personalization of the presidency. His presidential campaign and his governing style also established significant precedents that amplified the power of the executive and set its activities apart from those of party politics, the cabinet, the executive departments, and Congress.

All of Kennedy's campaigns for office, including his run for the presidency, were highly personal undertakings. They were managed by members of his family, with his brother Robert playing a prominent role. The success of Kennedy's organization, the "Kennedy Machine," diminished the importance of the regular party organization. Henceforth, campaigns for president would be directed by each candidate's advisers and strategists. Coordination and liaison with the party would frequently be of secondary importance.[418]

The Kennedy organization also made its mark on government. Most members of JFK's campaign staff were appointed to similar positions in the White House Office, which contributed to the personalization of the president's staff. To reinforce this development, more responsibility for policy making was concentrated in the executive office than had been the practice in past administrations. For example, Kennedy's White House assistant for national security, McGeorge Bundy, carried out many of the duties that traditionally had been reserved for the secretary of state.

The Kennedy Legacy

Although John Kennedy was a popular president during his brief stay in the White House and, in the public mind, has passed from life into enshrinement as the best of the modern presidents, many aspects of his presidency were unsuccessful. For example, his administration was responsible for the disastrous invasion of Cuba on April 17, 1961, by a brigade of some 1,400 anticommunist exiles from the regime of Fidel Castro. The rebels were crushed three days after landing in Zapata Swamp at Cuba's Bay of Pigs. Their failure to overthrow Castro was a humiliating defeat for Kennedy, who had been in office for less than one hundred days.

The Bay of Pigs would not be Kennedy's final attempt to overthrow Castro. Kennedy's militant anti-Communism and strong animus against Cuba's ruler led to a series of failed plots to assassinate Castro. "Although the defenders of the president have asserted that these schemes went forward without his knowledge," presidential historian Lewis Gould has written, "it is clear that John and Robert Kennedy created a climate in the White House where such covert ventures received implicit sanction at the highest levels." Moreover, such covert activity advanced the dangerous creed that presidents could work outside of the law to accomplish their foreign policy objectives.[419]

Kennedy also can be faulted for initiating the ill-fated U.S. involvement in Vietnam. Eisenhower was criticized by the military when the French colonial government collapsed in July 1954. But Eisenhower had determined to avoid involvement in the region, certain that victory on the battlefield was impossible. Kennedy also doubted the wisdom of direct involvement in Vietnam, but he sent more than sixteen thousand military advisers to assist the South Vietnamese army in counterinsurgency warfare, and then encouraged a military coup against the government of Ngo Dinh Diem in Saigon. Diem's death profoundly destabilized South Vietnam. In the view of Kennedy's successor, Lyndon B. Johnson, it also obligated the United States to support any subsequent regime. "Though [Kennedy] privately thought the United States 'overcommitted' in Southeast Asia," Arthur Schlesinger Jr., a historian who served on Kennedy's staff, has written, "he permitted the commitment to grow. It was the fatal error of his presidency."[420]

Yet Kennedy did not lack for notable accomplishments as president. During the Cuban Missile Crisis, in particular, he led brilliantly under the most difficult of circumstances. For seven days in October 1962, after the United States discovered Soviet nuclear missile bases in Cuba, the world seemed poised on the brink of a nuclear war. Kennedy and Soviet Premier Nikita Khrushchev engaged in what Secretary of State Dean Rusk later called an eyeball-to-eyeball confrontation. The impasse was resolved only when, in response to a U.S. naval quarantine of Cuba, the Soviets agreed to dismantle the missiles. In return, the United States pledged not to attack Cuba, and Kennedy privately assured Khrushchev that, after the crisis was settled, he would remove American missiles from Turkey, which shared a border with the Soviet Union. Throughout the crisis, Kennedy joined firmness to restraint, a course that allowed Khrushchev to yield to the president's demands without being humiliated.[421]

Kennedy's triumph in the missile crisis demonstrated that he had matured considerably since the Bay of Pigs fiasco. His growth in office also was apparent when he took measures to make another such crisis less likely. On August 5, 1963, the United States and the Soviet Union signed the nuclear test ban treaty, their first bilateral arms control agreement. The treaty was a small step forward (it did not ban underground tests, for example), but it raised hopes for more substantial progress in the future.

To supporters of the president, the test ban treaty and the missile crisis triumph were signs of developing greatness. "But Kennedy's greatness," as the journalist Theodore White observed, "was to be cut off at the promise, not after the performance."[422] One of the most frequent criticisms of Kennedy, both when he was president and after his death, was that he promised much more in the way of domestic reform than he delivered.

In particular, JFK was faulted for his failures as a legislative leader. Kennedy's New Frontier program embodied the high expectations he had articulated in his inaugural address. For example, in advocating medical insurance (Medicare) and federal aid to education, he sought to consolidate and extend the accomplishments of Roosevelt and Truman, his most recent Democratic predecessors. In other ways, however, Kennedy sought to reshape his party's liberal tradition by offering initiatives, such as the Peace Corps and civil rights legislation, that reflected the themes of social justice and national service he had injected into the 1960 presidential campaign. Some of Kennedy's legislative initiatives, including the Peace Corps, became law. But most of his important bills—those representing the heart and soul of the New Frontier—were spurned by Congress while he was in office.

It is impossible to know whether Kennedy would have accomplished his domestic goals and avoided the travail of Vietnam had he lived. But the inability to deliver on promises was to become a recurring trait of the modern presidency.

Partly because of Kennedy, the evolution of the presidency had given rise to a more powerful, prominent, and yet politically isolated president. The modern presidency has been the object of expanding public expectations about government. It has been transformed into an elaborate and far-reaching institution with considerable autonomous power. At the same time, however, the president has been increasingly cut off from Congress and the party, which has made it difficult to satisfy public demands by enacting lasting reforms. Kennedy did not create most of these conditions. But his legacy to his successors was a significant personalization of the presidency that greatly accentuated its separation from the other centers of political power in the United States.

Lyndon B. Johnson and Presidential Government

The tragedy in Dallas placed the presidency in the hands of Lyndon Johnson, a Texan whom Kennedy selected as his vice-presidential running mate in 1960 to balance the ticket geographically. LBJ's effective campaigning in the South, especially in Texas and Louisiana, was crucial to the Democrats' narrow victory against Nixon. Before becoming vice president, Johnson was known as a consummate politi-

Lyndon Johnson takes the presidential oath aboard Air Force One en route to Washington after John F. Kennedy's assassination.

cal operator in the Senate, where as majority leader he exercised enormous influence during the Eisenhower years.[423]

It remained to be seen, however, whether the quintessential legislative insider could adapt successfully to the requirements of the presidency.

Johnson's challenges as a successor president were compounded by the bitterness that many liberals felt about a southern power broker taking the place of their fallen leader. African Americans, especially, whose hopes for equality and justice had been raised by Kennedy, were disconcerted, as Johnson put it, to awake "one morning to discover that their future was in the hands of a President born in the South."[424] After all, it was southern Democrats in Congress who had blocked Kennedy's civil rights legislation.

Despite these obstacles, Johnson quickly grasped the reins of power. Indeed, he did more than reassure the nation and build confidence in his leadership. He continued—even accelerated—developments of the Kennedy era that accentuated the power and independence of the executive. Arguably, his administration marked the height of "presidential government." Regrettably, LBJ's failings also brought into serious question—for the first time since the 1930s—the widespread assumption that the public interest is served whenever the president dominates the affairs of state.

LBJ's Great Society

Johnson defined his first task as the enactment of Kennedy's New Frontier, including civil rights, a tax cut, and Medicare. He succeeded. Congress passed all of these controversial measures in short order. Especially notable was the Civil Rights Act of 1964. When Kennedy died, the bill was bogged down in the Senate. But, invoking the memory of a fallen leader and bringing to bear his own extraordinary skill and experience in legislative politics, Johnson prevailed. Johnson's greatest strength as majority leader in the Senate had been personal persuasion, a talent he used as president to convince the Senate Republican leader, Everett Dirksen, to support the bill and to enlist moderate Republicans in the cause. This support did not come without a price. Dirksen insisted on compromises that reduced the power of the Equal Employment Opportunity Commission and limited the authority of the Justice Department to bring suits against businesses to those situations in which a clear "pattern and practice" of discrimination existed.[425] These compromises responded to moderate Republicans' distaste for overlapping bureaucracies and excessive litigation, as well as their desire to protect northern and western businesses from intrusive federal agencies, without emasculating the Civil Rights bill's principal objective of eliminating entrenched segregation in the South.

The bipartisan alliance that Johnson and Dirksen formed sounded the death knell for the conservative coalition against civil rights. For the first time, the Senate voted cloture against a southern filibuster designed to thwart a civil rights bill and did so by a considerable margin of seventy-one to twenty-nine. Once the filibuster ended, Congress passed the bill quickly, and Johnson signed it on July 2, 1964.

The enactment of the Civil Rights Act of 1964 signaled a dramatic reinvigoration of the president's preeminence as legislative leader. Even more important, the act enlisted the president and several executive agencies in the ongoing effort to ban racial discrimination. It empowered the federal bureaucracy—especially the Department of Justice; the Department of Health, Education, and Welfare; and the newly formed Equal Employment Opportunity

Commission—to assist the courts by creating parallel enforcement mechanisms for civil rights. These proved to be effective. For example, within four years the executive branch under Johnson accomplished more desegregation in the southern schools than the courts had during the previous fourteen years.[426]

Johnson's successful battle for civil rights dazzled liberals in his party. But civil rights was only the beginning. Johnson's desire to move beyond Kennedy's agenda toward what he called the "Great Society" made him impatient to push on. The 1964 election, in which he and the Democrats won a resounding victory over the Republicans and their candidate, the archconservative senator Barry Goldwater of Arizona, provided the opportunity to do so. The election gave LBJ the most convincing popular mandate in history—more decisive, even, than FDR's triumph in 1936. Johnson won more than 60 percent of the national popular vote, and the Democrats gained thirty-seven seats in the House and one in the Senate, which gave them two-to-one majorities in both houses of Congress.

Johnson had first unveiled his hopes for the Great Society on May 22, 1964, in a commencement speech at the University of Michigan. His bold vision took the reform aspirations of the past only as a point of departure:

> The Great Society rests on abundance and liberty for all. It demands an end of poverty and racial injustice, to which we are totally committed in our time. But this is just the beginning.

> The Great Society is a place where every child can find knowledge to enrich his mind and to enlarge his talents. It is a place where leisure is a welcome chance to build and reflect, not a feared cause of boredom and restlessness. It is a place where the city of man serves not only the needs of the body and the demands of commerce but the desire for beauty and the hunger of the community.[427]

Johnson's vision gave rise to a legislative program of extraordinary breadth, which was placed before the Eighty-ninth Congress when it convened in January 1965. *(See "Lyndon B. Johnson's 'Great Society' Speech," p. 1778, in Reference Materials, Vol. II.)* Congress responded enthusiastically. In 1965 alone, Congress passed eighty of Johnson's legislative proposals, denying him only three. These new laws included important policy departures such as Medicaid, the Voting Rights Act of 1965, the Older Americans Act, the Elementary and Secondary Education Act, the War on Poverty, the Air Pollution and Control Act, and legislation to create the Department of Transportation and the Department of Housing and Urban Development.

LBJ and the Institution of the Presidency

Johnson's domination of the political process had enduring effects on the presidency, some of which extended developments that had begun with Kennedy. The programs of the Great Society gave new meaning to the idea of a president's program. More and more, policies began to be invented by the White House staff, which was committed to moving quickly on the president's agenda. Concomitantly, career staff in the departments and agencies and professional policy analysts in the budget bureau became less influential. Moreover, Johnson established a personal governing coalition that reached beyond his party. As the columnist David Broder wrote in 1966, more than was true of any of his predecessors, LBJ's leadership and program depended "for its success largely on the skill, negotiating ability, and maneuvering of the president." [428]

The personalization of presidential policy making was not only extended during the Johnson years, it also was institutionalized. Joseph Califano, the chief White House aide for domestic affairs, supervised the creation of several task forces, composed of government officials and prominent academics, which were charged with formulating innovative proposals for the president's domestic agenda. By placing policy development under White House supervision, free from traditional institutional restraints, the task force approach evaded what Johnson and his advisers regarded as the timidity and conservatism of the old system. Califano's group was the precursor of the Domestic Policy Council, established by Johnson's successor, Richard Nixon, and of the domestic policy staffs that have been a part of subsequent administrations.[429]

Soon, however, Johnson overextended himself. Ironically, the personalization of his presidency contributed to his undoing. Although LBJ was a gifted government insider, he could not rouse the public in the way that was required by the office he had helped to create. As his aide Harry MacPherson noted, Johnson was incapable of "rising above the dirt of 'political governing,' so that he could inspire the nation." [430] His best words and teachings were laws and policies, but he was unable to cultivate the stable basis of popular support that his domestic program ultimately required to be implemented effectively. Even Johnson realized that his most serious weakness as president was "a general inability to stimulate, inspire, and unite all the public in the country." [431]

LBJ's Downfall

The war in Southeast Asia clearly demonstrated both Johnson's shortcomings and the more troubling aspects of presidential government. In 1965 the president concluded that a communist takeover in South Vietnam could be prevented only by committing a large contingent of U.S. forces to combat. Johnson's extraordinary ability to build a governing coalition helped to sustain the Americanization of the war. With little resistance from either Congress or, at the beginning, the public, U.S. forces rose from 23,000 at the end

This famous caricature shows LBJ displaying his gall bladder scar, drawn by the artist in the shape of South Vietnam.

of 1964 to 181,000 a year later, to 389,000 a year after that, and 500,000 by the end of 1967.

The war in Southeast Asia became, in an unprecedented way, the president's war. Harry Truman at least had been able to claim that the United States was "carrying out an obligation for the United Nations" when he sent troops to fight in Korea. But in Vietnam, as political scientist Richard Pious has written, "no treaty obligations or other commitments required the United States to intervene." [432] Nor did Congress ever declare war. It passed only the Gulf of Tonkin resolution, which was rushed through Congress on August 7, 1964, after an alleged attack on U.S. destroyers off the coast of North Vietnam. The resolution stated that Congress "approves and supports the determination of the President, as Commander-in-Chief, to take all necessary measures to repel any armed attack against the forces of the United States and to prevent further aggression." The Gulf of Tonkin resolution was hardly the functional equivalent of a declaration of war, as Under Secretary of State Nicholas Katzenbach claimed at a Senate hearing in 1967.[433] Johnson believed that although the resolution was a useful device to protect his political flank, he already had all the authority he needed to deploy troops in Vietnam.

By early 1968, however, the military situation in Vietnam had deteriorated and Johnson's political consensus at home had crumbled. On March 31, 1968, he announced, "I shall not seek, and I will not accept, the nomination of my party for another term as your President." But Johnson never lost his faith in the extraordinary powers of the presidency. Nor, even under the stress of war, did he ever give up his dream of the Great Society. Indeed, Johnson's insistence on trying to have "guns and butter"—the Vietnam War and the Great Society—subjected the economy to strains of inflation that were aggravated by his reluctance to ask Congress to enact a tax increase.

Richard Nixon and the Twilight of the Modern Presidency

The legacy of the Johnson years for the presidency was mixed: more legal authority but less political influence. Soon after LBJ left the White House, one of his assistants, George Reedy, wrote, "We may well be witnessing the first lengthening shadows that will become the twilight of the presidency." [434] The failure in Vietnam had fostered public cynicism about the merits of presidential policies, opposition to the unilateral use of presidential power, and a greater inclination in the news media to challenge the wisdom and even the veracity of presidential statements and proposals.[435] Yet much was still demanded of presidents. They remained at the center of citizens' ever-expanding expectations of government.

The 1968 presidential elections dramatized the political disarray in which Johnson had left the country. The Democratic nominee for president, Vice President Hubert Humphrey, led a bitterly divided party. The party's convention in Chicago was ravaged by controversy, both within the hall and on the streets, where antiwar demonstrators clashed violently with the Chicago police. Without contesting a single primary, Humphrey was nominated by the regular party leaders, who still controlled a majority of the delegates and who preferred him to the antiwar candidate, Sen. Eugene McCarthy. Humphrey's more powerful opponent, Sen. Robert F. Kennedy, had been assassinated on June 4, the night of his triumph in the California primary.

Politically, Humphrey was damaged goods. As Johnson's vice president, he found it difficult to distance himself from "Johnson's war." Unwilling to embrace the war, unable to make a clean break, he looked merely weak. Humphrey was rejected not only by the antiwar wing of his party but also by conservative Democrats, many of whom looked with favor on the third-party candidacy of the segregationist governor of Alabama, George C. Wallace.

Humphrey's controversial nomination and the failure of his general election campaign against the Republican candidate, former vice president Richard Nixon, gave rise to important institutional reforms. The rules of the Democratic Party were revised in 1971 by the party-appointed

McGovern-Fraser Commission in an effort to make presidential nominating conventions more representative of the party's rank and file.[436] The new rules caused most states to change from selecting delegates in closed councils of party regulars to electing them in direct primaries. Although the Democrats initiated these changes, many were codified in state laws that affected the Republican Party almost as much.

The declining influence of the traditional party organizations was apparent not only in the new nominating rules but also in the perceptions and habits of voters. The 1968 elections marked the beginning of an increased tendency for voters to split their tickets—that is, to divide their votes between the parties. Since then, the mile of Pennsylvania Avenue that separates the White House and Congress has rarely been bridged by a common partisan affiliation.

Divided government profoundly affected the course of the Nixon administration, exacerbating the problems of modern presidential government that had become so obvious during the Johnson years. Despite the Democratic disarray in 1968, Nixon did not win a decisive mandate to govern. The Democrats retained clear control of both houses of Congress, making Nixon the first new president since Zachary Taylor in 1848 to be elected without a majority for his party in either the House or the Senate.

Congress was not the only rival for power that the new president faced. Because the country had elected only one other Republican president since 1932, the departments and agencies of the executive branch included a large number of Democrats. Most of them were protected by civil service procedures, which had been extended "upward, outward and downward" since the New Deal to encompass almost all of the federal workforce. In his memoirs Nixon explained that "one of our most important tasks would be to place our stamp on the federal bureaucracy as quickly and firmly as we possibly could." [437]

Nixon's New Federalism

The first Republican president of the New Deal era, Dwight Eisenhower, often spoke of "restoring the balance" between the branches of government by returning authority from the president to the Congress. To be sure, Eisenhower eventually accepted the responsibilities of the modern executive, especially as he came to realize that even a politically moderate president had to exert strong leadership if he wanted to delimit the boundaries of the federal government's activities. But Eisenhower was a reluctant modern president. His "hidden-hand" approach emphasized both flexible accommodation to the New Deal and respect for the other institutions of American government.

Nixon, in contrast, aggressively sought to expand presidential power. Indeed, he was the first Republican president since Theodore Roosevelt to embrace an expansive understanding of executive authority. But in contrast to TR, who

also was the first chief executive of either party to regard the presidency as the stewardship of the public welfare, Nixon sought to recast the office as the center of growing skepticism about social reform.

Even Nixon, however, was not rigidly opposed to the welfare state.[438] The main purpose of his major domestic initiative, the New Federalism, was to sort out the responsibilities of government so that national problems would be handled by the national government and problems that were more suited to decentralized solutions would be handled by state and local authorities. Welfare, which Nixon believed required a single set of standards, was an example of the former; job training, which he thought would benefit from a more flexible approach, typified the latter.

Nixon's New Federalism was conservative mainly in its challenge to the New Deal presumption that social problems invariably are addressed most effectively at the national level. This challenge was enough, however, to provoke powerful opposition in the Democratic Congress and, especially, in the specialized bureaucracies of the executive branch, which would have lost power to the states and localities if the New Federalism had been enacted.[439]

Interestingly, Nixon's commitment to decentralization in the federal system went hand in hand with his desire to centralize power in the White House. He was convinced that the federal government and its special interests had grown so powerful that only a very strong president could reverse the flow of power from the states and communities to Washington. Leonard Garment, a member of the president's legal staff, observed that the "central paradox of the Nixon administration was that to reduce *federal* power, it was first necessary to increase *presidential* power." Or, as Nixon himself said, "Bringing power to the White House was necessary to dish it out." [440]

Nixon and Vietnam

Nixon's aggrandizement of presidential power was especially pronounced in matters that pertained to foreign policy. Certainly it was in his political interest to end the war in Vietnam as soon as possible. "I am not going to end up like LBJ," Nixon once said, "holed up in the White House afraid to show my face on the street. I'm going to stop that war. Fast." [441] But Nixon was no more successful than Johnson in obtaining what he called "peace with honor" in Vietnam—that is, a way to withdraw U.S. troops without losing South Vietnam to the communists. Vietnam consumed Nixon's first term, from January 20, 1969, until the war was formally concluded on January 2, 1973. In the interim, Nixon escalated the U.S. involvement by secretly bombing North Vietnamese military enclaves in Cambodia, a neighboring neutral country. When bombing failed to do the job, Nixon told the nation on April 30, 1970, that he was sending troops to Cambodia, a militarily futile venture that provoked mas-

Bidding farewell to his staff and the presidency, Richard Nixon departs the White House on August 9, 1974, after submitting his resignation.

sive demonstrations in the United States and an unprecedented hostile reaction in Congress.

Nixon's policies in Vietnam not only reinforced but also made more rigid and controversial his aggressive use of presidential power. Like Truman, Kennedy, and Johnson, he believed that in time of war the president may assume extralegal powers. Although Nixon was a wartime president for all but twenty months of his five and a half years in the White House, he was to find, as Truman and Johnson had before him, that public acceptance of a claim to sweeping executive power does not flow automatically to a president who prosecutes an unpopular, undeclared war.

Nixon's determination to expand the boundaries of presidential power in the face of growing political resistance encouraged him to pursue his domestic and foreign policies by executive fiat. In doing so, he effected significant changes in the organization and conduct of the presidency. But he also planted the seeds of his own disgrace and resignation in 1974.[442]

The Administrative Presidency

Nixon's "administrative presidency" was born of his inability to persuade Congress to enact the New Federalism. Although Nixon took a legislative approach during his first two years as president, most of his proposals bogged down on Capitol Hill. In response, he shifted to a strategy that would achieve his objectives through administrative action.

The first phase of Nixon's administrative strategy was to expand and reorganize the Executive Office of the President (EOP) so that it could preempt the traditional responsibilities of the departments and agencies. The staff of the White House Office was doubled from 292 under Johnson to 583 by the end of Nixon's first term. With size came power. Nixon loyalists in the White House and in the other agencies of the EOP not only formulated policy, as had been the case in the Johnson administration, but tried to carry out policy as well.

In foreign affairs, Nixon's assistant for national security affairs, Henry Kissinger, created the first completely White House–dominated system of policy making. Since Kennedy, the president's national security adviser and his aides had taken on an increasing share of the responsibilities of the State Department. But Nixon and Kissinger built a foreign policy staff of unprecedented size and power. So marginal was the State Department that Secretary William P. Rogers was not even informed in advance of the administration's most innovative diplomatic initiative the opening to China, which Nixon visited in February 1972 after nearly a quarter century of fierce hostility between the United States and the Communist Chinese government that had taken power in 1949.[443]

The staff of the newly formed Domestic Policy Council, which was headed by White House assistant John Ehrlichman, took charge of domestic policy making. In addition, the Bureau of the Budget was reorganized and expanded to strengthen the president's influence in domestic affairs. On July 1, 1970, by executive order, BOB became OMB, the Office of Management and Budget, with a new supervisory layer of presidentially appointed assistant directors for policy inserted between the OMB director and the office's senior civil servants. Consequently, the budget office assumed additional responsibility for administrative management and became more responsive to the president.

By itself, the swelling of the Executive Office of the President did not bring full presidential control of public policy. Recalcitrant bureaucrats and their allies in Congress still were able to resist many of Nixon's efforts to seize the levers of administrative power. Two weeks before the 1968 election, former president Eisenhower had written that he hoped for, and expected, an electoral victory so sweeping that it would give Nixon "a strong clear mandate and a Republican Congress." Eisenhower noted that such a victory would help Nixon to "change the ingrained power structure of the federal government (the heritage of the years of Democratic control), placing more responsibility at the state and local levels." [444] But befitting Nixon's four-year-long emphasis on an autonomous presidency, even his 1972 landslide reelection did little to help his party. The Republicans failed to make inroads in the House, Senate, or state legislatures.

Still lacking the support he needed from Congress to become an effective legislative leader, Nixon resolved to carry the administrative presidency one step further. Early in his second term he undertook a reorganization to re-create the bureaucracy. Making massive changes in personnel, the president moved proven loyalists into the departments and agencies, then consolidated the leadership of the bureaucracy into a "supercabinet" of four secretaries whose job was to implement all of the administration's policies. One of these "supersecretaries" was Kissinger, who became secretary of state while retaining his position as the assistant to the president for national security affairs. As such, Kissinger became responsible, in a formal as well as an informal sense, for foreign policy, second only to Nixon himself.

Nixon and the Imperial Presidency

The Watergate affair was the principal cause of Nixon's becoming the first president in U.S. history to resign his office. The president's political fortunes were badly damaged by the Supreme Court decision in *United States v. Nixon,* which rejected Nixon's sweeping claim of executive privilege and forced the release of certain secret White House tape recordings. The Nixon presidency came to an end shortly after the House Judiciary Committee, acting on the heels of the Court's decision in the tapes case, voted to impeach him on August 4, 1974. Nixon's chances of surviving a Senate trial were dealt a blow when he admitted that among tapes he had been ordered to produce was one that clearly implicated him in the Watergate cover-up.[445] *(See "The Case of Richard Nixon," p. 487, in Chapter 8, and "Richard Nixon and Executive Privilege," p. 1422, in Chapter 30, Vol. II.)*

After witnessing the indiscretions of the Johnson and Nixon years, historian Arthur Schlesinger Jr., until then an eloquent defender of strong presidential leadership, wrote in 1973, "In the last years presidential primacy, so indispensable to the political order, has turned into presidential supremacy. The constitutional presidency—as events so apparently disparate as the Indochina War and the Watergate affair showed—has become the imperial presidency and threatens to be the revolutionary presidency." [446]

In truth, as Nixon learned to his regret, the federal government could not be remade by executive fiat. The modern presidency was never truly imperial; its power depended on agreement among Congress, the bureaucracy, and the courts that responsibilities should be delegated to the executive. By the time Johnson left office, the political environment had become less supportive of strong presidential leadership. Nixon only strengthened opposition to the unilateral use of executive power by further attenuating the bonds that tied the president to the Congress, the party system, and the American people.

More than anything else, perhaps, Nixon's bitter relations with Congress led to his downfall. His early inability to win support on Capitol Hill led him to construe the powers of his office much too broadly, which only aggravated the relationship. Nixon's use of his power of commander in chief to bomb and invade Cambodia provoked a major legislative protest. So did his sweeping application of the president's traditional right to impound—that is, not spend—funds that had been appropriated by Congress. Nixon's impoundment of funds, unlike the use of this power by several of his predecessors, was not for the purpose of economy and efficiency; it was an attempt to contravene the policies of the Democratic Congress by undoing the legislative process. Nixon defended his challenge to Congress's power of the purse as inherent and nonnegotiable. Although Caspar Weinberger, Nixon's deputy budget director, conceded in a 1971 appearance before a Senate panel that Congress had the power to *appropriate,* he insisted that it "did not follow from this . . . that the *expenditure* of government funds" involved "an exclusively legislative function." A Congressional appropriation of funds, Weinberger boldly asserted, was "permissive and not mandatory in nature." [447]

Joining aggressive action to his administration's grandiose constitutional claims, Nixon used impoundments to eliminate entire programs he opposed. For example, the Office of Economic Opportunity (OEO), the cornerstone of Johnson's War on Poverty and a symbol of the Great Society, was eliminated in Nixon's budget. Congress had appropriated funds to continue the OEO, but Nixon had the agency's acting director, Howard Phillips, issued orders to dismantle it. At the same time, Nixon refused to nominate Phillips as the permanent OEO director because he knew that the nomination would be rejected by the Senate.[448] According to former vice president and now Senator Hubert Humphrey (D-Minn.), the Nixon administration's assault on the OEO amounted to a "policy impoundment," the modification or even elimination of laws passed by Congress.[449]

Thus Watergate or no Watergate, there still would have been a war between Nixon and Congress. Both sides had geared themselves up for a constitutional struggle before anything was known about the Watergate affair. As political scientist Fred I. Greenstein has noted, "the willingness of Congress to take the extraordinary step of removing a president was in part a response to Nixon's continuing failure to use persuasion to win Congressional support and to his repeated efforts to circumvent Congress." [450]

An Imperiled Presidency: Gerald Ford and Jimmy Carter

The Watergate scandal shattered the recent consensus in American politics—already undermined by the controversies of the Johnson administration—that strong executive leadership embodied the public interest. When asked in 1959 whether the president or Congress should have "the most say in government," a representative sample of Americans had favored the president by 65 percent to 17 percent. A similar survey in 1977 indicated a striking reversal: 58 percent believed that Congress should have the most say in government; only 26 percent supported presidential primacy.[451]

Rallying to this change in public opinion, Congress passed a multitude of new laws to curb the powers of the presidency. One important law that Congress passed to restrict the unilateral exercise of presidential power was the Congressional Budget and Impoundment Control Act of 1974, which required the president to obtain congressional approval before impounding any funds and which established budget committees in the House and Senate to coordinate and strengthen the legislature's involvement in fiscal matters. *(See "The Impoundment Control Act of 1974," p. 810, in Chapter 15.)* The law also created the Congressional Budget Office (CBO), a legislative staff agency that would make available to Congress the same sort of expertise on fiscal matters that the OMB provided to the executive branch.

Congress also reasserted its influence on foreign affairs. The War Powers Resolution, which Congress enacted over Nixon's veto in 1973, was intended to prevent a recurrence of Vietnam—that is, a prolonged period of presidential war making without formal authorization from Congress. The resolution required the president to consult Congress "in every possible instance" before committing troops to combat, then to submit a report within forty-eight hours of doing so. After sixty days, the troops were to be removed unless Congress voted to declare war or to authorize their continued deployment. *(See "War Powers Resolution," p. 753, in Chapter 14.)*

In and of themselves, these laws did not restrict the modern presidency severely. But their enactment expressed Congress's broader determination to reestablish itself as an equal, if not the dominant, partner in the governance of the nation. In effect, "executive stewardship was replaced by interbranch cooperation in order to accommodate the merging reality of divided government and diverse policy commitments." [452] Congressional procedures were reformed to produce a more aggressive legislature. Decentralized since its rebellion against Speaker Joseph Cannon in the early twentieth century, Congress became even more so. In effect, the power of the standing committees devolved to subcommittees, whose numbers, staff, and autonomy grew rapidly. The rise of subcommittee government posed a severe challenge to the modern president's preeminence in legislative and administrative affairs. As political scientist Shep Melnick has written:

> Using subcommittee resources, members initiated new programs and revised old ones, challenging the president for the title of "Chief Legislator." No longer would Congress respond to calls for action by passing vague legislation telling the executive to do something. Now Congress was writing detailed statutes which not infrequently deviated from the president's program. Subcommittees were also using oversight hearings to make sure that administrators paid heed not just to the letter of legislation, but to its spirit as well.[453]

Gerald Ford and the Post-Watergate Era

Vice President Gerald R. Ford succeeded to the presidency on August 9, 1974, under some of the most difficult circumstances that any president has ever faced. Ford had never run for national or even statewide office; his electoral experience was confined to Michigan's fifth congressional district. He was representing this district in the House, where he served as the Republican leader, when, on October 10, 1973, Spiro T. Agnew was forced to resign as vice president in response to the revelation that he had been taking bribes ever since he was the county executive of Baltimore County, Maryland. Under the Twenty-fifth Amendment, which was enacted in 1967, Nixon nominated Ford to replace Agnew. The new vice president took office on December 6, after having been confirmed by both houses of Congress. Thus when the Watergate scandal later forced Nixon to resign, Ford became the first, and to date the only, president not to have been elected either as president or vice president.[454]

Ford was a unique president in one other respect—never before had a vice president succeeded to the presidency because his predecessor had resigned. That Nixon left office in disgrace made the start of Ford's presidency especially difficult. Ford lacked an electoral mandate, and he took office when the country was still deeply scarred and divided by the Vietnam War, when respect for the institution of the presidency was greatly diminished, and when the nation's economy and foreign relations were in disarray.

Both with symbolic actions and with changes in public policy and political style, Ford made an earnest effort to restore the integrity of the presidency and purge the nation of the effects of Watergate.[455] Invoking the Twenty-fifth Amendment to choose his own successor as vice president, Ford nominated Nelson A. Rockefeller, the long-respected former governor of New York. Many of the trappings of the so-called imperial presidency were removed. Ford had reduced the White House staff by 10 percent, from 540 to 485. In addition, for certain kinds of occasions the Marine band was instructed to replace "Hail to the Chief" with the University of Michigan's fight song. Finally, the living quarters in the White House now were referred to as "the residence" instead of "the mansion."

Symbolic changes were accompanied by new policies and a new presidential style. After three days in office Ford accepted the recommendation of a Senate resolution that he convene a White House summit on the economy. The Conference on Inflation, which included business and labor leaders and a bipartisan group of economists, and other events, such as numerous meetings between the new president and groups of governors, mayors, and county officials, were all part of Ford's attempt to open the doors of the recently isolated and insulated White House.

Ford's innovations in symbols, style, and policy initially earned considerable goodwill for the administration. His self-effacing manner seemed less to diminish the presidency than to endow it with an endearing folksiness, which the press celebrated in favorable accounts of how the new president toasted his own muffins in the morning and took a healthy swim at the end of the day. In his first week in office Ford received a 71 percent approval rating; only 3 percent disapproved of his performance, and 26 percent were undecided.[456]

Almost overnight, however, Ford's standing with the public and the press crumbled. On September 8, 1974, only four weeks after he became president, Ford granted Nixon a full and unconditional pardon. The Nixon pardon expressed Ford's desire to put the nation's recent past behind it. Instead, the pardon turned him into Watergate's final victim. By the end of September, Ford's approval rating had dropped to 50 percent.

Few challenged Ford's personal integrity and, the outcry over the Nixon pardon notwithstanding, his plain, forthright manner did much, as his successor Jimmy Carter said in his inaugural address, "to heal our land." But Ford was unable to restore the power of the modern presidency. The limits of executive influence were revealed most clearly by his inability to work his will with an aggressive and sometimes hostile Democratic Congress. The 1974 congressional election, which swelled the Democratic majority by fifty-two seats in the House and four in the Senate, made the task of legislative leadership still more difficult.

Ford did not wilt in the face of partisan opposition. He had some success with Congress in tax cutting and deregulation. But for the most part, Ford's influence was greatest in preventing action. He cast sixty-six vetoes, mostly against spending bills, during his twenty-nine months in office, and he was overridden only twelve times. As such, the Ford administration was more like the energetic nineteenth-century executive than the modern presidency.

Ford's difficulties with Congress did not stop at the water's edge. Congress refused to respond to a number of Ford's most urgent foreign policy proposals: his request for emergency assistance for the disintegrating government of South Vietnam, his plea to lift an embargo on aid to Turkey, and his plan to help the anti-Marxist guerrillas in Angola. More than anything, the lack of support in foreign affairs caused Ford to complain in March 1976 that "there had been a swing of the 'historic pendulum' toward Congress, raising the possibility of a disruptive erosion of the president's ability to govern." [457]

When Ford lost the 1976 presidential election to former Georgia governor Jimmy Carter, a man whom he viewed as an outsider with little more to recommend him than a winning smile, he felt he had every reason to believe that the presidency was slipping into receivership.

A President Named Jimmy

James Earl Carter Jr.—he preferred "Jimmy"—embodied the extremes of promise and disappointment to which the contemporary executive office is prone. His elevation to the White House was a remarkable personal triumph, as was his initial popularity as president. Yet so far did Carter fall politically, that, as one presidential scholar has noted, "at the time he left office his reputation had nowhere to go but up." [458]

A one-term governor who was virtually unknown outside of Georgia before running for the presidency, Carter won the 1976 Democratic nomination with little support from the leaders of his party. To emphasize his personal relationship with the people, Carter went further than Ford to try to eliminate imperial trappings from the presidency. "Hail to the Chief" was banned temporarily from presidential appearances; Carter sometimes carried his own luggage; and at his inaugural parade he and his family stepped from their black limousines and walked the mile from the Capitol to the White House.

Carter's informality, which had appealed to many voters during the campaign, worked to his detriment once he became president. As with Ford, the iconoclastic White House press corps quickly began to treat the president's unpretentious manner as an expression of his modest talents. Carter's attempt to provide the televised equivalent of a fireside chat, for example, is remembered less for its content (the energy crisis) than for the unfavorable reviews that his appearance in a cardigan sweater received. Carter failed to recognize that presidential authority requires a certain measure of dignity.

But Carter's problems went beyond style and symbolism. Before the end of his first year as president, he clearly was having a terrible time with Congress. Nixon and Ford had experienced similar problems, but they had confronted a legislature that was controlled by the opposition party. Carter's presidency revealed that the tensions between the White House and Congress were not simply an artifact of divided partisan rule. Presidents and legislators had become, in effect, independent entrepreneurs, each establishing their

President Carter, center, grasps hands with Egyptian president Anwar Sadat and Israeli prime minister Menachem Begin at the signing of the Camp David peace accords on March 26, 1979.

own constituencies. As a result, the two branches were even less likely than in the past to regard each other as partners in a shared endeavor—namely, to promote a party program. The Congressional Budget and Impoundment Control Act of 1974 institutionalized disagreements between the president and Congress. Although less conservative than his Republican predecessors, Carter tried to hold budget costs down, especially as inflationary pressures mounted during the later part of his term. He was no more successful than Nixon or Ford, however, in getting the liberal Democratic Congress to respond to his call for fiscal restraint.[459]

Carter was able to learn from his mistakes and, after his first year in office, to establish better relations with Congress. The president's record with the Ninety-fifth Congress (1977–1979) was quite respectable. In 1978 Congress ratified the controversial Panama Canal treaties and enacted airline deregulation, civil service reform, and natural gas pricing legislation. It also eliminated some of the most egregious pork-barrel public works projects from the budget.

The improvements in Carter's performance as chief legislator can be explained in part by his effective White House Office of Public Liaison (OPL). Nixon had created the OPL in 1970 as an organizational home within the White House for the increasing number of aides who cultivated the support of particular groups. Carter expanded and formalized the OPL's

activities. By the time he left office in 1981, special staff members were assigned not only to such traditional constituencies as African Americans, labor, and business, but also to such diverse groups as consumers, women, the elderly, Jews, Hispanics, white ethnic Catholics, Vietnam veterans, and gays.[460] Headed by Anne Wexler, Carter's OPL represented a significant contribution to the institution of the presidency, making it possible for a president who lacked great rhetorical ability to form a link with the public. As political scientist Erwin Hargrove has written "The Wexler office compensated for Carter's limitations as a presidential persuader by institutionalizing the persuasion function, not with Congress, but by bringing groups of citizens to the White House for briefings by the president and others on current legislative issues." [461]

In addition to his occasional legislative achievements, Carter scored a personal diplomatic triumph with the March 26, 1979, signing of the Camp David accords by Egyptian president Anwar Sadat and Israeli prime minister Menachem Begin. Frustrated with the difficulty of persuading Begin and Sadat to negotiate solutions to the conflicts of the Middle East, Carter invited both of them to the presidential retreat at Camp David. Carter's unwavering determination to reach an agreement and his keen mind for detail, which he displayed throughout the thirteen days of diplomacy between the two Middle East leaders, were crucial to their bringing about the first rapprochement between Israel and an Arab nation.[462]

But despite the accomplishments of his last three years in office, Carter never recovered fully from the confusion and ineptness of his early days as president. His poor start colored his relations with Congress and the public for the rest of his term.

Much of Carter's problem was that his outsider's approach to the presidency required effective popular leadership to appeal directly to the people. Yet rousing the American people was not Carter's strong suit.[463] He was an effective campaigner in 1976, presenting himself to the voters as a moral, trustworthy leader and a competent manager in time of widespread disillusionment with dishonesty and inefficiency in Washington. But Carter lacked a unifying vision that would enable him to lead the nation in a particular direction. Having offered, during his first few months in office, a bewildering array of legislative proposals concerning energy, welfare, education, urban decay, and much more, Carter failed to provide any integrating themes that the public or his party could use to make sense of these measures. "I came to think," wrote his speechwriter James Fallows, "that Carter believes fifty things, but not one thing."[464]

Even when some of Carter's proposals were enacted, the public seldom believed that he deserved the credit. Yet perversely, when Carter was overcome by setbacks that were beyond his control—notably, the wildly inflationary OPEC (Organization of Petroleum Exporting Countries) oil price increases and the Iranian hostage crisis—he was roundly blamed. His tendency to personalize the problems of state was especially damaging during the hostage crisis. Any president, no matter how gifted, would have had trouble dealing with these problems. But Carter's style of leadership brought down on him the full brunt of adversity. Regarding the hostage situation, "As the problem failed to go away," Hargrove has noted, "Carter became a prisoner in the White House, and the initial public favor that he had received by personalizing the issue turned sour."[465]

The consuming crises of Carter's presidency did not prevent him from fending off a serious challenge from Massachusetts senator Edward M. Kennedy for the 1980 Democratic nomination. But Carter entered the fall campaign burdened with a public image as a weak and indecisive leader. He was trounced by Ronald Reagan in the general election, the first time that a president had been denied reelection since Herbert Hoover lost to Franklin Roosevelt in 1932.

A Restoration of Presidential Power? Ronald Reagan and George H. W. Bush

"Among the consequences of Reagan's election to the presidency," political scientist Jeffrey Tulis wrote in 1987, "was the rewriting of textbooks on American government." It was no longer possible to claim, he noted, that the fragmented and demoralized conditions in U.S. politics "would frustrate the efforts of any president to accomplish substantial policy objectives, to maintain popularity, and to avoid blame for activities beyond his control."[466] In contrast to Ford and Carter, Reagan successfully advanced an ambitious legislative program in 1981 and 1982. He was renominated without opposition and reelected handily in 1984. He retired from the White House as the most popular president since Franklin D. Roosevelt.

The Reagan Revolution

Reagan's political success prompted considerable speculation that the 1980 election, like the election of 1932, had begun a partisan realignment in American politics. Although the liberal consensus had been unraveling since 1968, Reagan was the first president to envision and work for an enduring national conservative Republican majority. Richard Nixon, Gerald Ford, and Jimmy Carter were relatively conservative presidents, and each challenged certain policies of the New Deal and the Great Society. But they generally accommodated themselves to liberalism, seeking mainly to curb its excesses and to administer its programs more economically. Because Reagan, in contrast, had been outspokenly conservative for many years, some pundits dubbed his landslide victory in 1980 the "Reagan revolution."

In truth, the meaning of the 1980 election was somewhat ambiguous. In a three-candidate race among Reagan, Carter, and an independent, Rep. John Anderson of Illinois, Reagan won by a landslide in the electoral college, sweeping forty-four states with 489 electoral votes. Although Reagan captured 10 percent more popular votes than Carter, his closest rival, his tally of 51 percent was only three percentage points more than Ford's tally in 1976. The results of the congressional races were more impressive. For the first time since 1952, the Republicans won a majority in the Senate, and several prominent liberal senators were defeated. Nevertheless, although the ranks of the House Republicans rose by thirty-three seats, the Democrats retained clear numerical control of the lower chamber.

Reagan's ability to transform his ambiguous mandate into concrete legislative achievements testified to his considerable rhetorical gifts. Critics dismissed his ability to communicate effectively as a former actor's trick of the trade—namely, to learn and deliver his lines. But Reagan's supporters maintained that there was logic and substance to his message, that he was not the "Great Communicator" but the "Great Rhetorician," who, like Wilson, the two Roosevelts, and Kennedy before him, articulated a vision that inspired the nation.[467] In his inaugural address (see "Reagan's First Inaugural Address," p. 1790, in Reference Materials, Vol. II)—the first by a president in more than fifty years to appeal for limited government—Reagan sounded his intention to preside over a fundamental transformation of the American political landscape:

> In this present crisis, government is not the solution to our problem; government is the problem. From time to time we've been tempted to believe that society has become too complex to be managed by self-rule, that government by an elite group is superior to government for, by, and of the people. Well, if no one among us is capable of governing himself, then who among us has the capacity to govern someone else?[468]

Reagan's rhetoric was matched by his skill as a legislative leader. In contrast to Carter's array of legislative proposals, Reagan concentrated on one domestic theme: shrinking the welfare state.[469] His administration embodied this theme in two proposals: a large income tax cut and a major reduction in domestic spending. The president's enormous popular appeal, his willingness to lobby Congress for his program, and the political skill of his staff enabled the administration to mount a legislative campaign in 1981 that rivaled the early breakthroughs of the New Freedom, the New Deal, and the Great Society. Reagan persuaded Congress to approve a dramatic departure in fiscal policy: more than $35 billion in domestic program reductions, a multiyear package of nearly $750 billion in tax cuts, and a three-year, 27 percent increase in defense spending.

Reagan's first year as president seemed to restore the executive's preeminence as chief legislator. Like Lyndon Johnson's Great Society, this public policy was conceived in the White House and hastened through Congress by the legislative talent of the president and his sophisticated congressional liaison team. Consequently, Reagan's hastily conceived package suffered from some of the same defects as the Great Society. The substantial tax cuts exceeded by far the reductions in domestic spending and were accompanied by large increases in defense spending. Conservative such as New York representative Jack Kemp had argued that the tax cut would not increase the budget deficit. They were persuaded by supply-side economists such as Arthur Laffer and Paul Craig Roberts that a large tax cut would so stimulate productivity that rising tax revenues would balance the budget by 1984. Inflation also would fall, along with interest rates. Savings, in turn, would increase because investors' fears of inflation would be allayed.[470] Yet as OMB director David Stockman privately admitted at the time, "None of us really understand what's going on with all these numbers."[471] As things turned out, the Reagan administration, contrary to the supply-side projections, saddled the country with the largest increase in the national debt in history, which increased from $1 trillion in 1981 to $3 trillion in 1989.

Yet the unanticipated consequences of Reagan's fiscal program did not harm the president's standing with the public. Even when he faced political adversity, as during the severe recession of 1982, Reagan remained confident and on the march, vowing to "stay the course." That the economy began to perform well in 1983 seemed to justify the president's self-assurance.

Reagan as Party Leader

Reagan's hopes that his principles would animate a national partisan realignment never flagged, even after the Democrats rebounded in the 1982 congressional elections. His own reelection in 1984, in which he won 59 percent of the popular vote and all but thirteen electoral votes, convinced the president that events were moving in the right direction.

Reagan's efforts to inaugurate a new political era benefited from, and in turn helped to galvanize, the renewal of party politics. The development of the modern presidency had fostered a serious decline in the traditional, patronage-based parties. Yet institutional developments during the late 1970s and 1980s suggested that a new form of party politics had emerged. In effect, the erosion of old-style partisan politics had allowed a more national and issue-oriented party system to take shape, forging new links between presidents and their parties. Because the reconstituted party system was associated less with patronage than with political issues and sophisticated fund-raising techniques, it did not seem to pose as much of an obstacle to the personal and programmatic ambitions of presidents as did the traditional system. Indeed, by 1984 the Republican Party had become a solidly right-of-center party, made over in Ronald Reagan's image.

Reagan abetted this transformation by breaking with the tradition of the modern presidency and identifying closely with his party. The president worked hard to strengthen the Republicans' organizational and popular base, surprising his own White House political director with his "total readiness" to make fund-raising and other appearances for the party and its candidates.[472] The close ties between Reagan and his party proved to be mutually beneficial. Republican support solidified both the president's personal popularity and the political foundation for his program in Congress. In turn, the president served his fellow Republicans by strengthening their fund-raising efforts and by encouraging voters to extend their loyalties not just to him but also to his party. Surveys taken after the 1984 election showed that the Republicans had attained virtual parity with the Democrats in partisan loyalties for the first time since the 1940s.

It appeared, then, that the 1980s perhaps marked a watershed of renewed and strengthened ties between presidents and the party system. Unwilling to fall permanently behind the Republicans, the Democrats also became a more national and programmatic party, with an ideological center that was decidedly liberal. The playing out of the New Deal and the Great Society, and the conservative Republican response, had sharply reduced the presence of traditional southern Democrats in Congress. In the Seventy-fifth Congress (1937–1939), which balked at FDR's Court-packing plan, the thirteen southern states (the old Confederacy, plus Kentucky and Oklahoma) held 120 House seats, 117 of which were in Democratic hands. In the One Hundredth Congress, near the end of the Reagan era, those same states had 124 seats. But only 85 of them were Democratic; nearly a third had migrated to the Republican side of the aisle. Moreover, the 1965 Voting Rights Act had substantially increased the number of African American voters in the South, thereby transforming the voting behavior of southern Democrats in Congress. "It was the sign of the times in 1983," *Congressional Quarterly*'s Alan Ehrenhalt wrote in 1987, "when Southern Democrats voted 78–12 in favor of the holiday honoring the Rev. Martin Luther King."[473]

Reagan and the Administrative Presidency

Despite the transformation of the party system, the Reagan revolution was hardly the dawn of a new era of disciplined party government. Reagan's never converted his personal popularity into Republican control of Congress. His landslide in 1984 did not prevent the Democrats from maintaining a strong majority in the House of Representatives, and despite his plea to the voters to elect Republicans in the 1986 congressional elections, the Democrats held the House and recaptured the Senate.

Reagan enjoyed considerably more support in the country and in Congress than had his two Republican predecessors, Nixon and Ford. Still, the president suffered a number of reversals on important matters. After 1982, Congress refused to cut domestic spending any further. It also required the administration to slow the pace of its rearmament program and restricted the president's ability to aid the anti-Marxist contra rebels in Nicaragua by enacting a series of amendments—the Boland Amendments—to foreign military assistance bills.

In the face of mounting legislative opposition, the Reagan White House resorted to some of the same tactics of "institutional combat" that Nixon and his staff had employed.[474] To support the Nicaraguan contras, it secretly built an alternative intelligence apparatus within the staff of the National Security Council. This covert apparatus was able to conduct operations that Congress either had refused to approve (such as continued military aid to the contras) or almost certainly would not have countenanced (such as the sale of weapons to Iran). Its efforts exposed the administration to severe political risks and, eventually, to a damaging scandal, the Iran-contra affair. In November 1986, the nation learned that, with the president's approval, the United States had sold weapons to Iran and that, with or without the president's knowledge, some of the proceeds had been used by National Security Council staff members to assist the contras. Public reaction to the Iran-contra affair was swift and dramatic—Reagan's approval rating fell from 67 percent to 46 percent in one month.

Responding to strong political pressure from Congress, the news media, and the American people, the president appointed former Texas Republican senator John Tower to chair a bipartisan review board. The Tower Commission roundly criticized Reagan's management style, even suggesting that the president was blithely out of touch with the affairs of state, a figurehead who reigned at the mercy of his staff. But the Iran-contra affair was not simply a matter of the president being asleep on his watch. It also revealed the Reagan administration's determination to carry out its foreign policy without interference from Congress or any other source. As political scientist Richard Pious has argued, "Iran-contra was not due to a weak and uninvolved president mismanaging the national-security decision making process," as

the Tower Commission claimed. It was symptomatic of the restoration of presidential prerogative in foreign policy—the excesses of what Pious calls the "National Security Constitution." [475]

The Reagan administration's use the administrative presidency in foreign policy was hardly an aberration. As a matter of course, when the president and his advisers confronted legislative resistance on an issue, they charted administrative avenues to advance their goals unilaterally. Indeed, often they did not even try to modify the statutory basis of a liberal program, relying instead on administrative discretion as a first resort.

Reagan's most controversial administrative action targeted Social Security.[476] In May 1981, the president proposed deep and immediate cuts in benefits for early retirees—that is, persons who chose to retire with reduced benefits between the ages of 62 and 64 rather than wait for full benefits at the normal retirement age of 65. The administration also proposed to eliminate a statutory provision that guaranteed retirees a minimum benefit. The attempt to cut Social Security benefits sparked a furious reaction in Congress. Members of both parties repudiated the administration overwhelmingly, with the Senate voting 96 to 0 against the cut in early retirement benefits and the House voting 405 to 13 against the minimum benefit proposal. Although Congress's opposition was bipartisan, Speaker Thomas P. O'Neill turned the Reagan administration's mistake into a partisan issue that Democrats exploited in the 1982 midterm election and for years to come.

OMB director David Stockman, the leading proponent of the president's Social Security proposals, conceded that the punishing defeat in Congress marked the end of the effort to arrest the growth of Social Security. "The centerpiece of the American welfare state had now been overwhelmingly ratified and affirmed in the white heat of political confrontation," he wrote after leaving office.[477] Nevertheless, the defeat did not discourage Reagan appointees in the Social Security Administration (SSA) from trying to cut Social Security through administrative action. Claiming authority from a 1980 law that mandated a review of the disability program, they engaged in a large-scale effort to purge the rolls of those whom they considered ineligible. Between 1981 and 1984, the SSA informed nearly a half million individuals that they no longer qualified for disability benefits.

Both the federal courts and congressional Democrats maintained that the Reagan administration's action violated the intent of the 1980 legislation. The SSA reviewed cases over-zealously, they charged, with budget savings, not administrative reform, as the real goal. Courts overturned the agency's rulings against more than two hundred thousand claimants and interpreted the disability statute to require the SSA to prove that a recipient's medical condition had improved before it could cut off benefits. The SSA refused to apply this standard, arguing that the statute itself made no mention of a "medical improvement standard." Although the agency restored benefits to the specific individuals who had won in court, it refused to change its general policy to conform to the predominant judicial interpretation of the law. This led a number of judges to threaten the agency with contempt of court. After a two-year struggle to resolve the dispute, Congress passed the Disability Benefits Reform Act of 1984, which codified the medical improvement standard. The protracted battle over disability insurance testified dramatically to the Reagan administration's fervent commitment to challenge the social welfare policies of the past, with or without authorization from Congress or the courts.[478]

In the area of social regulation, the Reagan administration's attempt to weaken environmental, consumer, and civil rights regulations also came not through legislative change but through administrative action, delay, and repeal. Reagan's Executive Orders 12291 and 12498 mandated a comprehensive review of proposed agency regulations by the OMB. Reagan also appointed a Task Force on Regulatory Relief, headed by Vice President George H. W. Bush, to apply cost-benefit analysis to existing rules. The task force's review included a reconsideration of the so-called midnight regulations issued in the last days of the Carter administration. Reagan imposed a sixty-day freeze on the regulations on January 29, 1981.[479]

In sum, Reagan advanced the development of the administrative presidency by resuming the long-standing trend toward concentrating power in the White House that had been suspended briefly in the aftermath of Vietnam and Watergate. He also confirmed for conservatives that centralizing power in the presidency was essential to carry out their objectives. As Greenstein has written, "Nixon and Reagan had the courage to act on what once were the convictions of liberals, taking it for granted that the president should use whatever power he can muster, including power to administer programs, to shape policy." [480]

Except for the Iran-Contra affair, the administrative presidency served Reagan's interests well. After the televised Iran-contra congressional hearings were concluded in the summer of 1987, Reagan recaptured a large measure of public approval. By the end of the year, with the signing of the Intermediate Nuclear Forces (INF) treaty in Washington, Reagan had fully resumed the political high ground. The treaty, which eliminated U.S. and Soviet intermediate-range nuclear missiles from Europe, enshrined him as a peacemaker on the great stage of East-West relations.[481] Throughout 1988, Reagan's approval rating improved steadily, eventually reaching 63 percent.

Reagan's politically successful tenure notwithstanding, the modern presidency of the 1980s did not command the political system, as it had during the early years of the Johnson administration. Instead, the executive was challenged forcefully by a modern Congress that had developed its own tools of influence. Members of Congress, acting in partnership with the courts, bureaucratic agencies, interest groups, and the press, were able to modify the Reagan administration's program of regulatory relief for corporations and other private institutions.

The embarrassing revelations of the Iran-contra affair also helped the Democratic Congress to weaken the Reagan administration during its final two years, although more in matters of personnel and policy than of politics. Among other things, the president was compelled to appoint a national security adviser, a director of the Central Intelligence Agency, and a White House chief of staff who were acceptable to Congress. In the realm of policy, the president was unable to advance a conservative agenda. Indeed, he found it possible to take on only those initiatives—most notably arms control—that coincided with the agenda of the liberal opposition.[482]

A Reagan Court?

Reagan's effect on the federal judiciary is perhaps the best example of both the force and limitations of the Reagan Revolution. In keeping with its effort to transform the terms of national political discourse, the Reagan administration, as political scientists Benjamin Ginsberg and Martin Shefter have observed, "sought not simply to ensure that conservative judges would replace liberals on the federal bench, but sought also to stage an intellectual revolution by enhancing the impact of conservative ideas on American jurisprudence." [483] Prominent conservative legal scholars, such as Ralph K. Winter and Robert H. Bork of Yale University and Richard Posner of the University of Chicago, were appointed to the federal appeals courts. In 1986, when Chief Justice Warren Burger announced his retirement from the Supreme Court, Reagan promoted Justice William H. Rehnquist to chief justice and filled the vacancy on the Court with Judge Antonin Scalia. Rehnquist and Scalia were especially supportive of and had indirectly helped to shape the administration's legal agenda. The administration had based many of its positions on separation of powers, federalism, and the competing claims of majority rule and minority rights on Rehnquist's and Scalia's legal writings and judicial opinions.[484]

The culmination of Reagan's effort to reconstitute the federal judiciary came in 1987, when he nominated Judge Bork to the Supreme Court. Bork was perhaps the leading conservative legal scholar in the country, a brilliant and outspoken critic of the liberals' recent procedural and programmatic judicial innovations. His appointment almost certainly would have tilted a closely divided Court decisively to the right on controversial issues such as abortion, affirmative action, and the death penalty.[485]

President Ronald Reagan, pictured here in 1985 with the entire Supreme Court, sought to extend his conservative revolution through his appointments to the federal judiciary.

The controversy that greeted Bork's nomination was extraordinary. A public debate ensued that was without parallel in the history of judicial nominations for its partisanship and vitriol. The debate was stoked in part by extensive media and direct-mail campaigns by liberal and conservative interest groups. Equally incendiary were the Senate confirmation hearings, which were broadcast on national television. In five days of questioning before the mostly Democratic Judiciary Committee, Bork abandoned the practice of previous controversial nominees, such as Louis Brandeis in 1916, of letting their records speak for them. Instead, as political scientist David O'Brien has noted, "Bork sought to explain, clarify, and amend his twenty-five year record as a Yale Law School professor, as a solicitor general, and as a judge. That broke with tradition and gave the appearance of a public relations campaign." [486]

In a resounding defeat for the Reagan administration, Bork became the twenty-eighth Supreme Court nominee in history— but only the fourth in the twentieth century—to fail to be confirmed by the Senate. No previous nominee had been battered so badly as Bork during his nearly thirty hours of testimony before the Judiciary Committee. The Senate vote to reject him was 58–42, the widest margin of disapproval in the history of Supreme Court nominations.

In part, Bork's rejection testified to the widespread public resistance to the Reagan administration's social agenda. Although most voters supported cutting taxes and strengthening the nation's defenses, the administration's plan to restore "traditional" American values by retreating from liberal policies on civil rights, abortion, and prayer in the public schools was much more controversial. The breadth of the opposition to Reagan's social agenda was apparent in the vote against Bork, which included thirteen southern Democratic senators and six moderate Republicans.

Bork's rejection also testified to the heightened level of conflict over judicial nominations that marked the era of divided government. From 1900 to 1968, a period in which the same party usually controlled both the presidency and the Senate, the president's nominees almost always were confirmed. The approval rate was forty-two of forty-five, or 93 percent. Since then, however, institutional combat between the Republican executive and the Democratic legislature and the expanding policy activism of the judiciary have combined to politicize the judicial appointment process in blatant ways. The battle over Bork was only the latest and most visible confrontation in the struggle between the Democrats and the Republicans to control the federal courts. [487]

Still, eight years of judicial appointments by Reagan left behind an important and enduring legacy. Eventually, the administration nominated a moderate conservative jurist who was acceptable to the Senate, Judge Anthony M. Kennedy. Soon after, the Court, with Kennedy providing the decisive vote, moved to reconsider a 1976 pro–civil rights decision—rapid confirmation that Reagan had moved the Court in at least a slightly more conservative direction. [488]

Moreover, because Reagan was the first two-term president since Dwight D. Eisenhower, he was able to select 78 appeals court judges and 290 district court judges, nearly one-half of the federal judiciary. In the course of making these appointments, Reagan successfully challenged the tradition that lower court judgeships are mostly a matter of senatorial patronage. By strengthening the president's control over judicial selection, he ensured that the federal courts would issue more conservative rulings than in the past.

INS v. Chadha

The most important Supreme Court decision concerning the presidency during the Reagan years was *Immigration and Naturalization Service (INS) v. Chadha,* the so-called legislative veto case. [489] In the half century since the New Deal had dramatically expanded the scope of federal activity,

Congress increasingly dealt with complex problems of public policy by writing laws in broad language and granting wide discretion to the executive branch about how to implement them. To prevent federal agencies (or even the president) from exercising this discretion in ways that legislators disapproved, a provision was made for the legislative veto, which permitted Congress to overturn an executive regulation or action within a prescribed length of time. In all cases, legislative vetoes were final. The president, who has the power to veto ordinary bills that are passed by Congress, had no power to overturn a legislative veto.

On June 23, 1983, the Supreme Court ruled 7–2 that the legislative veto was unconstitutional. Writing for the majority, Chief Justice Burger argued that the legislative veto violated the separation of powers, in particular the Presentment Clause of Article I, Section 7 of the Constitution, which says that binding actions emanating from Congress must be presented to the president for signature or veto. The *Chadha* decision turned out to be a less decisive victory for the executive than it seemed at the time. Numerous laws contain legislative veto provisions, most of which require the prior approval of the House and Senate appropriations committees. A number of de facto legislative vetoes also have been implemented through informal agreements between Congress and the executive. *(See "The Legislative Veto," p. 593, Chapter 11, and "A Special Case— The Legislative Veto," p. 1434, in Chapter 30, Vol. II.)* For example, the 1996 Contract with America Advancement Act established a "report and wait" provision that requires a regulatory agency to submit a report to each house of Congress on significant rules that it issues. For such "major rules," Congress has a minimum of sixty days to review the rule, during which time it may pass a joint disapproval resolution rejecting the measure. Although some have argued that the availability of "report and wait" provisions and other measures that allow Congress to scrutinize executive action have rendered *Chadha* largely irrelevant, congressional oversight has decreased significantly since the mid-1970s. "Vigorous hearings on matters of policy" the political scientist Andrew Rudalevige has written, "have dropped off sharply." [490]

The Accession of George H. W. Bush

Reagan never did transform Washington completely. Instead, he strengthened the Republican beachhead in the federal government, solidifying his party's recent dominance of the presidency and providing better opportunities for conservatives in Washington. Concomitantly, his two terms witnessed an intensification of the struggle between the executive and legislature.

A major forum for partisan conflict during the Reagan years was a sequence of investigations in which the Democrats and the Republicans sought to discredit one another. For example, from the early 1970s to the mid-1980s

a tenfold increase occurred in the number of indictments brought by federal prosecutors against national, state, and local officials, including more than a dozen members of Congress, several federal judges, and a substantial number of high-ranking executive officials. Increased legal scrutiny of public officials was in part a logical response to the Watergate scandal. Congress passed the Ethics in Government Act of 1978, which provided for the appointment of independent counsels to investigate allegations of criminal activity by executive officials. But divided government encouraged the exploitation of the act for partisan purposes. Political disagreements were readily transformed into criminal charges. Moreover, investigations under the special prosecutor statute tended to deflect attention from legitimate constitutional and policy differences and to focus the attention of Congress, the press, and citizens on scandals. Thus disgrace and imprisonment joined electoral defeat as a risk of political combat in the United States. [491]

The era of divided government that began in 1968 did not end with Reagan's retirement in 1989. On November 8, 1988, when the voters elected a Democratic Congress and George H. W. Bush, a Republican president, it was the fifth time in the last six presidential elections that they had divided control of the government between the parties. Vice President Bush's easy victory over his Democratic opponent, Massachusetts governor Michael S. Dukakis, was in one sense a triumph for Reagan. Bush won the support of almost 80 percent of the voters who approved of Reagan's performance as president. Like Andrew Jackson, who in 1836 aided the last incumbent vice president to be elected president, Martin Van Buren, Reagan proved to be unusually helpful to his vice president, both in his popularity and in his active support during the campaign. [492]

Yet Bush's (and thus Reagan's) triumph was incomplete. Never before had a president been elected—by a landslide, no less—while the other party gained ground in the House, the Senate, the state governorships, and the state legislatures. [493] Never before had the voters given a newly elected president fewer fellow partisans in Congress than they gave Bush. Never, in short, had the American constitutional system of checks and balances been characterized by such partisan segmentation. The incompleteness of the Reagan revolution—and the major policy problems that Reagan left behind for his successor—suggested that Bush might face a severe crisis of governance.

Bush and Congress. In his 1988 presidential campaign, Bush had portrayed himself as the true heir to Reagan in domestic policy, albeit a "kinder and gentler" version, as he put it in his acceptance speech to the Republican national convention. His "Read my lips: no new taxes" campaign pledge was joined to a promise to be the "education president" and the "environmental president." Bush carried the theme of consolidation past the election. His inaugural address thanked Reagan "for the wonderful things that you have done for America," even as he urged that the harsh ideological and partisan conflict that had characterized divided government during the past two decades give way to a new spirit of cooperation:

> We've seen the harsh looks and heard the statements in which not each other's ideas are challenged, but each other's motives. And our great parties have too often been far apart and untrusting of each other.
>   A new breeze is blowing—and old bipartisanship must be made new again.[494]

Bush's conciliatory approach to governance partly reflected his more eclectic vision of Republicanism. Just as significant were strategic considerations. Facing a Democratic Congress and lacking Reagan's rhetorical ability, Bush had little choice but to reach across party lines to accomplish his goals.

The president's "kinder, gentler" approach to Congress was often reciprocated during his first year. After intensive negotiations, Bush was able to work out an agreement with the Democratic leaders of Congress concerning Nicaragua, the most acrimonious issue that had divided Reagan from Congress. Although Bush and Secretary of State James A. Baker were contra supporters, they understood that Congress could not be persuaded to approve new military assistance to the anti-Marxist Nicaraguan rebels. Determined to find a bipartisan solution that would end the long and enervating interbranch conflict over contra aid, Baker and the congressional leaders struck a deal to provide $4.5 million a month in nonlethal assistance to the contras for a limited period. The administration then elicited sufficient pressure from Europe, the Soviet Union, Latin America, and Democratic members of Congress to persuade the Marxist Sandinista government of Nicaragua to conduct a fair election in February 1990, which the Sandinistas lost.

The Bush administration also was able to negotiate an agreement with Congress to bail out the ailing savings and loan associations. The Federal Home Loan Bank Board had reported in 1988 that hundreds of federally insured savings and loan industries had recently become insolvent, threatening both the savings of tens of thousands of depositors and public confidence in the entire savings and loan industry. When it became clear that to replenish the federal deposit insurance fund would cost more than $100 billion, Reagan and Congress decided to postpone the matter.

The savings and loan crisis awaited the new president on his first day in office. As with contra aid, Bush achieved a bipartisan agreement by inviting influential members of Congress to the White House for conferences. The administration agreed to abandon its own proposal to finance the bailout, in which the cost would be borne by both taxpayers and still-healthy savings institutions, in favor of a plan that relied more heavily on taxpayers. The compromise overcame strong congressional resistance to the original bill, which was led by delegations from California, Texas, and Florida—the states with the most permissive thrift regulations and the largest savings and loan failures.

Initially, Bush won high marks from many legislators for his give-and-take approach to domestic and foreign policy, as well as for the personal attention that he paid to the political needs of Democrats and Republicans alike. But several Republicans, especially the party's more conservative members, grew restless at Bush's disinclination to lead in a more partisan style. The Republican Party would never gain control of Congress, they feared, so long as the president continued to submerge the differences between the parties.

In fall 1990 a serious intraparty struggle emerged over the 1991 budget. Seeking to work out an agreement with the Democratic congressional leadership on a deficit reduction plan, Bush accepted a fiscal package that included excise tax hikes on gasoline and home heating oil. In turn, the Democratic leadership agreed to cut Medicare spending. The deal left liberal Democrats and conservative Republicans furious. Especially strong resistance arose in the House, where the Democratic opposition abhorred the Medicare cuts and the regressive nature of the new taxes while many Republicans, led by Minority Whip Newt Gingrich of Georgia, felt betrayed by Bush's willingness to abandon his celebrated "no new taxes" pledge. At the urging of Democratic and Republican supporters of the tax agreement, Bush went on television to try to sell the package to the American people. This was the president's first attempt to rouse public opinion in support of his legislative program. The effort ended in dismal failure. Despite Bush's rhetorical appeal and feverish administration lobbying efforts on Capitol Hill, a majority of Republicans followed Gingrich in opposing the compromise, dooming it to defeat. The subsequent budget agreement that passed the House and Senate included a hike in the tax rate on high-income taxpayers, a proposal that Bush had earlier opposed. A month later, inundated by criticism from conservative, anti-tax Republicans and from voters who were outraged that he had violated his main campaign promise, Bush told reporters that the agreement made him "gag," a sentiment that he maintained through the end of the 1992 election campaign.[495] Meanwhile, a stubborn recession caused the deficit to continue to rise. The budget shortfalls of Bush's four years as president added another $1 trillion in debt to the $3 trillion accumulated under Reagan.

The Renewal of Institutional Confrontation

During the early days of his presidency, George H. W. Bush showed little interest in attacking what his predecessor called the "Washington Colony." He seemed content to join the old order, to reach out to Democrats in Congress, and to restore the badly frayed consensus of American politics. But he gave

George H. W. Bush was skillful in maintaining close relationships with world leaders and achieved his greatest success in foreign policy. Here Bush walks with Israeli prime minister Yitzhak Shamir.

no reasonable defense for his pragmatism, and the defiant sound bites and images of his 1988 campaign promised a continuation of the divisiveness of the Reagan years. Once he abandoned his antitax pledge, Bush's presidency seemed to float adrift—his search for agreement with Congress in the absence of any clear principles threatened the modern presidency with the same sort of isolation and weakness that characterized the Ford and Carter years.

Yet Bush revealed unexpected strengths as a leader, especially in foreign affairs. In contrast to Reagan, Bush gave almost all of his attention as president to his constitutional roles as chief diplomat and commander in chief. Although international affairs had not been a prominent theme of his election campaign in 1988, it was in a sense the theme of his life. Before becoming president, Bush had served as a U.S. ambassador to the United Nations, the director of the Central Intelligence Agency, the U.S. emissary to China, and the most active diplomatic traveler of any vice president in history. In these positions, he had cultivated a wide personal acquaintance among world leaders. As president he spent hours at a time touching base with his fellow presidents and prime ministers by telephone.

Bush's accomplishments in foreign policy nearly spanned the globe. In 1990 he sent twelve thousand troops to Panama to capture the anti-American dictator, Gen. Manuel Noriega, and return him to American soil to stand trial for drug trafficking. (Noriega had been indicted by a federal grand jury in Miami in 1988.) Guillermo Endara, the winner of a presidential election that Noriega had annulled,

was sworn in as president. "Operation Just Cause," as Bush dubbed the Panama invasion, not only was the largest U.S. military effort since Vietnam, but it also was considerably more successful.

In Europe, Bush oversaw the collapse of the Soviet Empire and, soon after, of the Soviet Union itself. He was encouraging but not intrusive in 1989 and 1990 when first Poland, then East Germany and the other Soviet-dominated governments in Eastern Europe collapsed, followed in 1991 by the dissolution of the Soviet Union. Bush's public stature was not enhanced by the death of communism in Europe, however. Ronald Reagan's words and policies had done much to set the stage for the collapse of what he called the "Evil Empire," but victory abroad left America without a compelling mission in world affairs and intensified demands for renewed attention to intractable problems at home.

For a time, Bush's command was restored by a crisis in the Middle East. Iraq's invasion of Kuwait in August 1990 created a situation that challenged the president's deepest commitments and allowed him to display considerable skills of crisis leadership. Bush showed a deft and steady hand in diplomacy and military strategy, and the U.S.-led allied forces rapidly triumphed over the troops led by Iraqi dictator Saddam Hussein, forcing Iraq to withdraw from Kuwait. Amid a national celebration that seemed to dispel the agonizing memory of Vietnam, Bush's popularity reached a historic peak, with 89 percent of the American public approving of his performance as president.[496]

Substantively and politically, the victory over Iraq was the high-water mark of the Bush presidency—it was all downhill from there. The patriotic fervor aroused by the Gulf War served only to conceal fundamental differences about foreign policy between the president and Congress that foreshadowed a renewal of institutional conflict. The vote authorizing Bush to use troops against Iraq revealed a Congress that was deeply divided along partisan lines. Not since the War of 1812 had Congress so narrowly approved the use of military action. Although Republicans lined up solidly for Bush (by 42–2 in the Senate and 165–3 in the House), Democrats voted against authorizing military action by large margins (45–10 in the Senate and 179–86 in the House). After the vote, the Democrats closed ranks behind Bush as the nation prepared for war. However, a broader dispute about constitutional powers lingered in a reference in the Gulf War resolution to the War Powers Resolution, the statute passed in the wake of the Vietnam War that granted Congress a specific role in approving the use of force.

Although Bush had concluded that the deep divisions in the country required him to seek Congress's approval, he reasserted the claim of every president since the War Powers Resolution was passed in 1973 that it was unconstitutional. The administration's pronouncements that it would welcome congressional support for the Gulf War were followed by a statement, released after Congress passed the war resolution, explicitly denying that the president needed legislative support to implement the UN resolution authorizing force against Iraq. Viewing this conflict between Bush and Congress as another sorry episode of the "National Security Constitution," Pious criticized the administration's disavowal of the War Powers Resolution as the most recent example of "presidents ... playing a shell game, claiming to act according to law yet dispensing with statutory law at their convenience in national security matters." [497]

The "National Security Constitution" was but one element, albeit an extremely important one, of the institutional conflict spawned by the post-1968 era of divided government. This conflict would survive, even undermine, Bush's modest efforts to establish a new spirit of cooperation between the president and Congress. Consequently, far from creating the conditions for the restoration of consensus, the Gulf War set the stage for bitter conflicts in domestic affairs during the final two years of the Bush presidency that rivaled the ideological and institutional clashes of the Reagan years.

The most bitter of these fights occurred in 1991, when Bush nominated Clarence Thomas, an African American appellate judge with impeccable conservative credentials, to the Supreme Court. The Bush administration steered Thomas's nomination through the Democratic Senate, but not before Thomas was required to respond in televised hearings to claims by a former employee, Anita F. Hill, that he had sexually harassed her.

Although the White House boasted of securing a conservative majority on the Court, the fierce battle waged over the Thomas nomination left the nation in a state of profound unease. The Senate voted in favor of Thomas by a margin of 52–48, the closest Supreme Court confirmation in more than a century and one that reflected the same sort of bitter partisan division that had characterized the Bork hearings. Thomas was spared Bork's fate by the votes he received from eleven Democratic senators, most of them southerners, whose support was encouraged by the strong base that the judge, a Georgia native, had among southern African Americans. Yet, as one journalist reported, the televised hearings that investigated Hill's charges "marked one of the wildest spectacles in modern congressional history, a subject for satire and scorn that rocked the Senate." [498]

Bork's rejection, the Thomas debacle, and other nomination battles during the Reagan and Bush presidencies signaled a heightened level of conflict over judicial nomination in an era of divided government. This conflict extended to legal battles over court rulings. The Democratic Congress did not hesitate to reverse rulings it did not like, even as the Republican White House sought to uphold the judiciary's retreat on certain social provisions. The most controversial conflict over the court's statutory interpretation during Bush's presidency took place over the Civil Rights Act of 1991. This legislation nullified nine Supreme Court rulings, thus restoring legal standards that placed the burden of proof in antidiscrimination lawsuits on employers. Bush had vetoed a similar bill 1990, arguing that it would lead to quotas for minorities and women in hiring practices. But in the wake of the explosive Thomas hearings, he decided to sign a modified version of the bill. At the same time, the president issued a "signing statement" that gave a more narrow interpretation of the legislation than Democratic members of Congress were willing to accept. [499]

Bush's signing statement that accompanied the 1991 Civil Rights bill was the most controversial example of a tactic he regularly employed to shape legislation during his presidency. As the president described this practice in an address delivered at Princeton University, "[On] many occasions during my presidency, I have stated that statutory provisions violating the Constitution have no binding legal force." [500]

Unlike the constitutional power of the veto, these presidential signing statements declared certain features of congressional statutes null and void by executive fiat. Although previous presidents had used signing statements, Bush issued many more of them, with far greater policy consequences, than had any of his predecessors. He thus significantly expanded a method by which presidents could avoid a direct confrontation with Congress over controversial legislation and still pursue their legislative objectives. "Taken overall," a former general counsel of the House of Representatives has written, "the 1989–1992 outpouring of signing statements that purposed to strike down or revise new laws staked a major presidential claim to personal power. . . ." [501]

It soon became clear that institutional conflict between the president and Congress would not be confined to legislation and nominations. As the 1992 elections approached in the midst of a serious recession, the Bush administration turned its attention to "liberating the economy" from new regulatory initiatives spawned by legislative measures—related to the environment, consumer protection, and discrimination against the disabled—that Bush himself had approved. [502] The Council on Competitiveness, a regulatory review board chaired by Vice President Dan Quayle, assumed increasing importance in executive deliberations, putting regulatory agencies on notice that the administration expected them to justify the cost of existing and proposed regulations. Bush also imposed a ninety-day moratorium on new regulations. One liberal public interest group complained that the president was "waging war" on his own agencies. "It is almost as if the President is choosing to run in this year's election as an outsider campaigning against the bureaucracy." [503]

Bush planned to run against Congress as well. Some Republican leaders hoped that the president would duplicate Truman's feat in 1948, when the beleaguered heir to the Roosevelt revolution ran a spirited campaign against an opposition-controlled Congress and won a personal and party triumph. But Bush's attempt to mimic and repeat his Democratic predecessor's success by blaming Congress for all the nation's problems made a mockery of Truman's adage that "the buck stops here." Neither his leadership of his party nor his struggles with Congress gave the impression that Bush was resolutely committed to a program or a set of principles.

In the elections of 1992, the Democrats, with Arkansas governor Bill Clinton as their presidential candidate, not only captured the White House, but the Democrats also retained control of both houses of Congress, ending twelve years of divided rule in American politics. In his 1989 inaugural address, Bush had urged that the harsh ideological and partisan conflict that had characterized divided government during the past two decades give way to a new spirit of cooperation. Yet serious substantive disagreements between the president and Congress defied Bush's efforts to make "the old bipartisanship . . . new again." Some political analysts had regarded divided partisan control of the presidency and Congress as the healthy consequence of the voters' desire to mute the ideological polarization that characterizes modern party politics. Yet the Bush years dramatically revealed how thoroughly divided government obscures political responsibility and mires government in petty, virulent clashes that undermine respect for the nation's political institutions. Clinton's victory, then, seemed to represent more than a rejection of the incumbent president. In part, it expressed the voters' hope that the institutional combat they had witnessed during the era of divided government would now come to an end.

BILL CLINTON AND THE AMERICAN PRESIDENCY

The 1992 elections contained both optimistic and pessimistic portents for the modern presidency. Although the Democrats ran an effective campaign and Clinton skillfully, if not always boldly, addressed the party's liabilities, the election results showed that fundamental conflicts continued to divide Americans, even as they seemed united in their dissatisfaction with the way government worked.

Clinton, in a three-way race, won 43 percent of the popular vote. Bush's losing share of the popular vote in 1992, 37.7 percent, was the lowest of an incumbent president since

William Howard Taft finished third in 1912. Like Taft, whose reelection effort was plagued by the presence in the race of former Republican president Theodore Roosevelt, Bush was beset by a strong third candidate, Texas billionaire H. Ross Perot. Perot's 19 percent of the popular vote posed the most serious electoral challenge to the two-party system since Roosevelt's Progressive Party campaign.

The Perot campaign underscored just how much presidential politics had been emancipated from the constraints of party. Perot had never held political office of any kind, and his campaign, dominated by thirty-minute commercials and hour-long appearances on talk shows, set a new standard for direct, plebiscitary appeals to the voters. Disdaining pleas to form a third party from those interested in party renewal, Perot required no nominating convention to launch his candidacy. Instead, he called his supporters to arms on the popular Cable News Network (CNN) talk show *Larry King Live*.[504]

Perot suggested a novel forum in which to link the presidency to public opinion. He proposed instituting "electronic town halls" as a means of governing. Public opinion would be used as a supplement to, or a substitute for, the deliberations of constitutional government, in a manner that Perot never explained. In late spring, with Perot leading both Bush and Clinton in the polls, his concept of presidential leadership seemed destined to play an important and disconcerting part in American politics.[505] "Perot hints broadly at an even bolder new order," historian Alan Brinkley wrote in July 1992, "in which Congress, the courts, the media, and the 'establishment' are essentially stripped of their legitimacy; in which the president, checked only by direct expressions of popular desire, will roll up his sleeves and solve the nation's problems." [506]

The New Covenant

In the end, however, the American people invested their hopes for constructive change more cautiously, in the possibility that Bill Clinton represented a new form of Democratic politics that would cure the ills brought on by the ideological and institutional conflicts of the 1970s and 1980s. Clinton dedicated his campaign to principles and policies that "transcended," he claimed, the exhausted left-right debate that had immobilized the nation for two decades. In the mid-1980s, Clinton was a leader of the Democratic Leadership Council (DLC), a moderate group in the Democratic Party that developed many of the ideas that became the central themes of his run for the presidency. As Clinton declared frequently during the campaign, these ideas represented a new philosophy of government that would "honor middle class values, restore public trust, create a new sense of community and make America work again." He heralded "a new social contract," a "new covenant"—one that in the name of community and responsibility would seek to constrain the demands for economic rights that had been unleashed by the New Deal. The essence of Clinton's message was that the liberal commitment to guaranteeing economic welfare through entitlement programs such as Social Security, Medicare, Medicaid, and Aid to Families with Dependent Children had gone too far. The objective of the New Covenant was to correct the tendency of Americans to celebrate individual rights and government entitlements without any sense of the mutual obligations they had to each other and their country.[507] Clinton was a great admirer of John F. Kennedy, and his philosophy of government elaborated on Kennedy's call for a renewed dedication to national community and service, as exemplified by the Peace Corps.

Clinton's Unsteady Beginning

Clinton's first hundred days as president "diminished public expectations," the *Washington Post* reported, "that he—or anyone else—can do much to turn around a country that seven out of ten voters think is going in the wrong direction." [508] Hoping to be a dominating Democratic president in the FDR tradition, Clinton found himself the victim of the same sort of ridicule that had plagued his most recent Democratic predecessor, Jimmy Carter. Like Carter, Clinton was a former governor of a small southern state whom many believed to be in over his head. As political scientist Walter Dean Burnham observed during the summer of 1993, "there has been no successful transition yet from the very small and parochial world of Little Rock to Big Time Washington." [509]

The most hostile White House press corps faced by any president since Nixon amplified Clinton's weaknesses. Because the advent of cable television and the proliferation of talk shows allowed the new president to go directly to the American people, Washington correspondents often felt left out of the picture. Indeed, Clinton held only one White House press conference during the first three months of his presidency.[510] Frustrated by its diminishing influence, the national press corps eagerly pounced on the administration's gaffes. News accounts of serious White House lapses in judgment, ranging from a $200 haircut in the Los Angeles airport to the trashing of Cinton's first two choices for attorney general, corporate attorney, Zöe Baird and Kimba Wood, for employing illegal aliens as nannies, left the country incredulous and angry.[511]

The transition from governor to president was made all the more difficult by Clinton's assembling of a White House staff headed by close associates from Arkansas, such as Chief of Staff Thomas F. "Mack" McLarty, who appeared to be unprepared for the complexity and toughness of Washington politics. Clinton did name some impressive figures to the cabinet, including Sen. Lloyd Bentsen of Texas as secretary of the Treasury, Wisconsin representative Les Aspin as secretary of defense, and former Arizona governor Bruce Babbitt as secretary of the interior. But he centered political

and policy decisions in the White House staff. The staff in turn manifested the virtues and flaws of the president, who, much more than his recent Republican predecessors, assumed the daily burden of decision making.[512]

Still, the White House staff was only part of the problem. Most of Clinton's political difficulties originated with the president himself. Clinton seemed desperate to please all sides—a leadership flaw that was magnified by a Democratic Party fashioned from a demanding constellation of sometimes competing interest groups.[513] During the campaign, Clinton had professed to be a New Democrat who would challenge these groups and ignore their demands for more entitlement programs. But his commitment to control government spending and to recast the welfare state was obscured during his first hundred days by a number of traditional liberal actions. No sooner had he been inaugurated than Clinton announced his intention to issue an executive order to lift the long-standing ban on homosexuals in the military. This policy could be carried out instantly, "with a stroke of the pen," Clinton believed, leaving him free to focus "like a laser" on the economy.[514]

It was unrealistic, however, to expect that such a divisive social issue could be resolved through executive order. To be sure, the development of the administrative presidency had given presidents more power to conduct domestic policy autonomously. But as Reagan and Bush had discovered, the use of this power provoked powerful opposition from Congress, interest groups, and the bureaucracy when it affected the direction and character of American political life. Intense opposition from the head of the Joint Chiefs of Staff, Gen. Colin Powell, and the chair of the Senate Armed Services Committee, Sam Nunn of Georgia, forced Clinton to defer his executive order on gays and lesbians for six months while he sought a compromise solution, thus arousing the ire of gay and lesbian activists who had given him strong financial and organizational support during the election.[515] Most damaging for Clinton was that the issue became a glaring benchmark of his inability to revitalize progressive politics to redress the economic insecurity and political alienation of the middle class.[516]

The bitter partisan fight in the summer of 1993 over the administration's budgetary program served only to reinforce doubts about Clinton's ability to lead the nation in a new, more harmonious direction. Clinton's plan, even though it promised to reduce the deficit, did not clearly distinguish him from "tax and spend" Democrats, a charge that congressional Republicans leveled at the president with alacrity. In August 1993, Clinton successfully faced the challenge of forging a budget deal in a congressional conference committee without any support from the Republicans, who voted unanimously in both houses against the package. (The House adopted the conference report by 218–216, and the Senate cleared the bill 50–50, with Vice President Al Gore casting the deciding vote.) To win support for the plan, Clinton promised moderate Democrats that he would put together another package of spending cuts in the fall. Clinton won this narrow, bruising victory only after promising moderate Democrats that he would offer another package of spending cuts in the fall.

The Clinton administration linked the prospects for achieving such savings to its "reinventing government" (REGO) program. This initiative was originally championed by journalist David Osborne and former Visalia, California, city manager Ted Gabler, who argued that the fall of communism and the failure of traditional bureaucracies in the free world to solve basic social and economic problems called for an alternative to standard centralized administration.[517] A prominent feature of Clinton's New Democratic agenda, REGO was the centerpiece of the National Performance Review (NPR), which was commissioned by Clinton and chaired by Vice President Gore. Beyond promising budgetary savings of $108 billion in five years, Gore's report, issued in September 1993, called for "a new customer service contract with the American people, a new guarantee of effective, efficient, and responsive government." REGO would trim 252,000 federal jobs, overhaul federal procurement laws, update government's information systems, eliminate a few programs and subsidies, and cut bureaucratic red tape.[518]

Critics dismissed the promises of government reinvention as hollow rhetoric, and Congress failed to enact Gore's most important recommendations. Nevertheless, as Donald Kettl, a prominent scholar of the American bureaucracy, has written, the NPR accomplished far more than critics anticipated: "It energized employees, . . . attracted citizens, . . . drew media attention to government management, . . . and made the point that management matters."[519]

In November 1993 Clinton achieved a more important victory, winning the battle for passage of the North American Free Trade Agreement (NAFTA)

President Bill Clinton successfully mobilized popular support to win passage of the North American Free Trade Agreement (NAFTA) in 1993.

with Canada and Mexico. This time he knew that a partisan approach would not work. Indeed, Democratic support for free trade was so weak that Clinton had to rely on winning more Republican than Democratic votes in Congress. Reviving his identity as an outsider, the president launched a successful campaign for the treaty by reaching beyond Congress to the American people. The turning point in the struggle came when the administration challenged Perot, the leading opponent of NAFTA, to debate Vice President Gore on *Larry King Live*. Gore's forceful and optimistic defense of open markets was well received by the large television audience, rousing enough support for the treaty to persuade a majority of legislators in both houses of Congress to approve the trade agreement.[520]

NAFTA was one of the few foreign policy issues in which Clinton initially took much interest. In a post–cold war world, his primary objective was to extend free markets in a global setting, in the hope that they would advance both economic and strategic interests for the United States. "No president in the last fifty years has tried to do what Bill Clinton has done in foreign policy," observed presidential historian Michael Beschloss, "which is essentially to keep it away from the Oval Office as much as possible during the first six months."[521] Nonetheless, when he took office, Clinton found the international arena overflowing with actual and potential crises that demanded his attention. He faced a challenge from Saddam Hussein, whose alleged assassination plot against former president Bush provoked the new president to order air strikes against an Iraqi intelligence installation in June 1993. Saber rattling by the Iraqi leader would recur throughout the Clinton presidency.

The Clinton administration faced its most troubling foreign policy predicament in Somalia, where Clinton had allowed

American troops deployed for humanitarian purposes to become part of a dangerous and controversial United Nations peacekeeping mission. Operating under the authority of Security Council resolutions that ordered the capture of warlord Mohammed Aidid, the mostly American UN forces became the target of "Black Hawk Down"-style attacks in which American soldiers were wounded, captured, and killed. In October, despite strong pressure from Congress to withdraw from Somalia, Clinton sent reinforcements. Finally, with Congress threatening to cut off funding for the mission by February 1, 1994, two months earlier than the president intended, the Clinton administration agreed to limit its goals to protecting American forces and securing supply lines for relief aid.[522] Somalia seemed to underscore Clinton's lack of resolve in international affairs.

The 1994 Elections and the Restoration of Divided Government

With the successful November 1993 fight for NAFTA, moderate Democrats began to hope that Clinton had finally begun the task of dedicating his party to the principles and policies that he had espoused during the 1992 campaign. But the Clinton administration's next major legislative battle was for its health care program, which promised "to guarantee all Americans a comprehensive package of benefits over the course of an entire lifetime." [523] The plan was announced with much fanfare in September 1993, with Clinton brandishing a red, white, and blue "health security card," a symbol of his ambition to carry out the most important extension of welfare policy since the enactment of Social Security in 1935. The program would create a new government entitlement, funded by a new payroll tax on workers and businesses. It would be administered by a massively complex bureaucratic apparatus.[524] This was hardly the leaner, more efficient government that Clinton's National Performance Review envisioned. With its complexity (the bill was 1,342 pages long), cost (an estimated $50 to 100 billion per year), and obtrusive bureaucracy, the Clinton proposal was an easy target for Republicans and hostile interest groups.[525] Although the public at first welcomed the plan, support soon eroded in the onslaught of negative ads sponsored by the Health Insurance Association of America, representing smaller firms that were most threatened by the legislation. These ads (the "Harry and Louise" spots) effectively countered the promise of a new right to universal health care with an opposing one—the right to choose one's own doctor.[526]

Although the administration made conciliatory overtures to the plan's opponents, hoping to forge bipartisan cooperation on Capitol Hill and a broad consensus among the general public, the possibilities for comprehensive reform hinged on settling fundamental disagreements about the appropriate role of government that had divided the parties and the country for the previous six decades. This

task proved impractical. Health care reform died in 1994 when a compromise measure, negotiated by Senate Democratic leader George Mitchell of Maine and Republican senator John Chafee of Rhode Island, could not win enough Republican support to break a threatened filibuster.[527] In the end, by proposing such an ambitious bill, Clinton enraged conservatives. By failing to deliver on his promise to provide a major overhaul of the health care system, he dismayed liberals.

Clinton and his party paid dearly for the health care debacle in the 1994 midterm elections. In taking control of Congress for the first time in forty-two years, the Republicans gained fifty-two seats in the House and eight in the Senate. The GOP also made substantial gains at the state and local levels of government, picking up fourteen governorships and eight state legislative houses.

The Republicans achieved their victory in a midterm campaign that was unusually partisan and ideological. The charged atmosphere of the elections owed largely to the efforts of House Republican leader Newt Gingrich of Georgia. Gingrich persuaded more than 300 of his party's House candidates to sign a "Republican Contract with America," which promised to restore limited government by eliminating programs, reducing regulatory burdens, and cutting taxes. Although surveys showed that most voters had little, if any, knowledge of the contract's provisions, the Republicans were seen as more inclined than the Democrats to challenge the "liberal state." [528] Clinton's decision to attack the contract during the campaign clarified what was at stake. The president's strategy served only to abet Republicans in their effort to highlight the president's failure to reinvent government.[529]

The dramatic Republican triumph in the 1994 elections led political pundits to suggest that Clinton was, for all intents and purposes, a lame duck president. As Gingrich seized control of the legislative process during the early months of the 104th Congress, Clinton was left to assert plaintively in April 1995, "The president is relevant here." [530]

THE COMEBACK PRESIDENT

Ironically, the seeds of Clinton's reelection were sown in the aftermath of the 1994 elections. The president's initial response to the decisive defeat the Democrats suffered in the midterm elections was conciliatory, almost contrite. Hoping to revive the impression, created during the 1992 campaign, that he stood for a new philosophy of government, Clinton resurrected the New Covenant message for his 1995 State of the Union address. In translating these words into government action Clinton embraced adviser Dick Morris's goal of triangulation. Morris, along with the polling team of Mark Penn and Dick Schoen, thought it was important for the president not only to stake out a position at the political center, midway between liberal congressional Democrats and conservative congressional Republicans, but also to find new issues that would allow Clinton to rise above the conventional left-right political spectrum. The three points of the new political triangle would then be occupied by orthodox Democrats and Republicans at opposite ends of the baseline, with Clinton hovering at a point above and between them. As Morris urged Clinton to embrace, and thereby neutralize, Republican issues such as crime, taxes, welfare, and the budget, the president displayed a renewed commitment to middle class concerns. "[I] had discovered the middle class in [my] presidential campaign," the president conceded, "and forsaken them as president." [531]

Clinton's adoption of the triangulation strategy clearly accounts for his approach to the defining controversy of his third year as president—the fiscal year 1996 budget battle with Congress. Fresh from their triumph in the midterm elections, the Gingrich-led Republicans committed themselves to cutting taxes and domestic spending dramatically. The most controversial part of their proposal, which called for a balanced budget by 2002, was an initiative to scale back the growth of Medicare by encouraging beneficiaries to enroll in health maintenance organizations and other private, managed health care systems. Congressional Democrats launched a full-scale attack, aiming most of their fire at the spending reductions. In mid-1995 Clinton angered Democrats by embracing the goal of a balanced budget but infuriated Republicans by insisting that popular Democratic programs such as Medicare, Medicaid, support for education, and environmental enforcement must be left substantially unaltered.

The public, roused by millions of dollars' worth of television commercials sponsored by the Democratic National Committee, supported the president on both counts. When the Republicans tried to impose their own budget on Clinton, he refused to yield. The president then pointed out to voters that Gingrich, Senate Republican leader Robert Dole, and the Republican Congress were responsible for two federal government shutdowns that occurred in late 1995 in the absence of a budget agreement.

In his third State of the Union address, Clinton co-opted the Republican Congress's most popular theme, declaring that "the era of big government is over." [532] Despite predictions to the contrary, the National Performance Review Board had said in its second annual report, issued in September 1995, that the REGO-spawned budgetary savings and personnel cutbacks promised by Vice President Gore two years earlier would be achieved.[533] More significant, Clinton withstood severe criticism from liberal members of his party and signed welfare reform legislation in August 1996 that replaced the sixty-year-old entitlement to cash payments for low-income mothers and their dependent children with temporary assistance and a strict work require-

ment. Clinton conceded that the Welfare Reform Act of 1996 was flawed, cutting too deeply into nutritional programs for the working poor and unfairly denying support to legal immigrants. Nevertheless, by forcing welfare recipients to take jobs, the new act advanced a fundamental principle that Clinton had championed in the 1992 campaign, "recreating the Nation's social bargain with the poor." [534]

Acting Presidential

Hoping to strengthen his credentials as an effective independent executive, Clinton began to present himself to the voters as statesmanlike, rather than as a partisan or political figure. The terrorist bombing of the Oklahoma City federal building on April 19, 1995, gave him his first opportunity to do so. His effort was successful. As one observer recorded, in the aftermath of the traumatic bombing Clinton "exhibited the take-charge determination as well as the on-key rhetoric that Americans expect of their president in times of trouble." [535] Clinton's presidential sure-footedness in Oklahoma City was not an isolated event. His White House staff began to function more effectively after he appointed longtime Washington insider Leon Panetta as chief of staff and Mike McCurry as press secretary in 1994. After many years in which his only experience was with the part-time legislature of his state, Clinton also learned how to deal with an active, independent-minded Congress.

In foreign policy, the president gained confidence as commander in chief when he discovered during the latter two years of his first term that the American people respected him for having the courage to make unpopular decisions to extend assistance to Bosnia, Haiti, and Mexico. For example, in November 1995, after Clinton overruled public opinion and strong congressional opposition by sending twenty thousand troops to a peacekeeping mission in Bosnia, the voters' approval of his handling of foreign policy went up. Clinton initially was reluctant to intervene in Yugoslavia, but the cause of the Bosnian Muslims, who were the target of Serbian leader Slobodan Milošević's ethnic-cleansing, and pressure from America's European allies persuaded the president to employ military forces as peacekeepers in the Balkans. Clinton's resolve to uphold American responsibilities in the world, coming on the heels of his eyeball-to-eyeball confrontation with Congress over the budget, appeared to belie his reputation as a waffler who lacked a clear set of principles.

The Election of 1996

In the 1996 presidential election, Clinton held firmly to the centrist ground that he had staked out after the 1994 elections, campaigning on the same New Democratic themes of "opportunity, responsibility, and community" that had served him well during his first run for the White House. In dozens of appearances around the country, Clinton emphasized that he and Gore represented a proven, moderate alternative to the extremism of Gingrich and the 104th Congress. He pointed with pride to the economic progress that had flowed from the initially unpopular tax increases and spending reductions of his first term: four consecutive years of low inflation, a drop in the unemployment rate from 7 percent in 1992 to 5 percent in 1996, steady economic growth, and a reduction in the annual budget deficit from $209 billion the year he became president to $106 billion in the fourth year of his term. He celebrated the enactment of welfare reform and the establishment of the service-based AmeriCorps program, along with his successful defense of "Medicare, Medicaid, education, and the environment" (a litany that frequent hearers recast as M2E2) against alleged Republican assaults. Finally, to buttress his stature as a unifying rather than a partisan leader, Clinton signed environmental legislation at the Grand Canyon and presided over an emergency Arab-Israeli conference at the White House.

Still, Clinton's discussion of the future during the campaign was hardly the stuff of which mandates are made. Standing under banners that proclaimed "Building America's Bridge to the 21st Century," Clinton repeatedly offered empty "bridge" rhetoric to the voters in lieu of substantive discussion of his plans for a second term. In addition, even when his lead in the polls stretched to fifteen points, Clinton avoided tying his campaign to the fortunes of congressional Democrats. The president's remarkable political comeback in 1995 had been fueled by soft money donations that were designed for party-building activities and thus were not limited by federal campaign finance laws.[536] But these expenditures were used instead to mount television advertising campaigns, such as the media blast at the Republican Congress during the 1995 budget battle, that championed the president's independence from partisan squabbles. Finally, media exposure of the administration's legally questionable fund-raising methods during the final days of the election helped to push Clinton's share of the popular vote below 50 percent and undermined the Democrats' effort to retake the House.[537] In 1996, in contrast to 1992, a plurality of voters told election day exit pollsters that they preferred divided government to unified party government.

Bland as it was, Clinton's campaign was visionary when compared with that of his Republican opponent, Bob Dole.[538] The seventy-three-year-old Senate veteran, who in three previous runs for national office had never displayed strong gifts as a campaigner, showed little improvement in 1996. Although his quirky personality did not wear as well as in 1992, Perot, as the Reform Party candidate, continued to draw support, revealing the fragility of the two-party system. Four of the eight presidential elections that took place between 1968 and 1996 (including three of the last five) included independent or third party candidates: the 1968

election, when George Wallace received 14 percent of the popular vote and forty-six electoral votes; the 1980 election, when John Anderson received 7 percent of the popular vote; and the elections of 1992 and 1996, when Perot received 19 percent and 8 percent, respectively. Extended periods of third party activity have occurred before, notably the twelve years from 1848 to 1860 and the thirty-two years from 1892 to 1924. But the contemporary era has witnessed the emergence of independent candidates who champion a direct, plebiscitary form of politics and who are indifferent, if not hostile, to the idea of political parties.[539]

In truth, Clinton openly imitated Perot's personalistic politics. Triangulation was conceived as a campaign strategy that would portray the president as an outsider, an insurgent leader who disdained the petty and mean-spirited skirmishes that had dominated party politics since the late 1960s. On election day, Clinton won 49 percent of the popular vote to Dole's 41 percent, along with 379 electoral votes to Doles's 159—to that extent, the president's reelection strategy, supported by a strong economy, was effective. Clinton thus became the first Democratic president to be elected to a second term since Franklin Roosevelt. But the candidate-centered campaign that Clinton conducted, although the safest strategy he could have pursued, denied him any chance of winning a mandate based on a change-oriented policy agenda and long congressional coattails. The Democrats lost two seats in the Senate, nearly outweighing their modest gain of nine seats in the House.

More ominously, in 1996 only 49 percent of the eligible electorate voted, the lowest turnout since 1924, when many women, newly enfranchised by the Nineteenth Amendment, did not take the opportunity to vote and many states had registration laws that discriminated against recent immigrants and African Americans. Just as strong party attachments increase voters' psychological involvement in politics and make the act of voting meaningful, so do weak attachments tend to distance them from politics and undermine their sense of political efficacy. With the decline of partisanship and the rise of candidate-centered campaigns, fewer voters were seeing a connection between what they do on election day and what the government does afterward.

BALANCED BUDGETS, IMPEACHMENT POLITICS, AND THE LIMITS OF THE THIRD WAY

Clinton staked his success as president on forging a "third way" between Republican conservatism and Democratic liberalism. The disjunction between bitter partisanship in Washington and weakening partisan loyalties in the country gave Clinton, with his skill in combining political doctrines, a certain appeal.[540] His gift for forging compromise was displayed in May 1997, when he and the Republican leadership in Congress agreed on a plan to balance the budget by 2002. Arguably, this deal was struck on Republican terms. The most dramatic measures in the budget—the first net tax cut in sixteen years, the largest Medicare savings ever enacted, and constraints on discretionary spending below the expected rate of inflation over five years—shifted priorities in a Republican direction.[541]

Nevertheless, Clinton exacted some important concessions from the Republicans, enough so that he was able to persuade a majority of Democrats in Congress to support the plan. Most significant, the 1997 Balanced Budget Act smoothed the rough edges of the Welfare Reform Act of 1996. It provided substantial additional funding for immigrant benefits and a bit more for food stamps. It also included $16 billion in spending to cover a new children's health program for low-income working families who were not eligible for Medicaid. These concessions allowed Clinton to claim that he had fulfilled his promise to renegotiate a fair new social contract with the poor.[542]

To be sure, the budget agreement between the White House and the Republican-controlled Congress was made possible because of a revenue windfall caused by the robust economy, which enabled Clinton and GOP leaders to avoid the sort of hard choices over program cuts and taxes that had animated the bitter struggles of the first term.[543] Those hard choices, especially concerning entitlement programs like Social Security, Medicare, and Medicaid, would still have to be made if the nation's long term fiscal health was to be assumed. Even so, the rapprochement, which brought about in fiscal year 1998 the first balanced budget in three decades, testifies to the ability of modern presidents to advance principles and pursue policies that defy the sharp cleavages of the national party system.

Yet as the 1998 House impeachment and the 1999 Senate trial of Clinton dramatically revealed, the "extraordinary isolation" of the modern presidency is riddled with problems.[544] Just as Reagan and Bush had been plagued by independent counsels who investigated alleged abuses in their administrations, so, too, were Clinton and members of his cabinet subjected to intense legal scrutiny. Republicans had long opposed reauthorization of the 1978 Ethics in Government Act, which provided for fixed terms and judicial appointments of independent counsels. But their resistance to Democratic efforts to reauthorize the statute came to an end in 1993, when the president and first lady were accused of shady dealings in an Arkansas real estate investment during the 1980s—the so-called "Whitewater" scandal.

In January 1998, independent counsel Kenneth Starr was authorized to expand the scope of the Whitewater inquiry to pursue allegations that the president had had an affair with a White House intern, Monica Lewinsky, and that he and his friend Vernon Jordan had encouraged her to lie

about it under oath. The Clinton administration's response was to accuse Starr, a prominent Republican, and his supporters in Congress of orchestrating a slanderous, partisan attack on the president. Clinton's rapid counterattack proved effective in the court of public opinion. The president's popular support remained high in the face of the scandal, as voters remained focused on his record of "peace, prosperity, and moderation."[545]

But the administration's reluctance to cooperate with Starr's investigation led Clinton to make broad claims of executive privilege that, as the *New York Times* observed, were "freighted with echoes of Watergate and President Nixon's efforts to keep his White House tapes secret."[546] Clinton's assertion of an executive privilege to keep aides Sidney Blumenthal and Bruce Lindsey, as well as Secret Service agents, from testifying before the grand jury convened by Starr was rebuffed by a federal district court judge and eventually dropped by the White House. The president, however, continued to press a claim of lawyer-client privilege in an effort to limit the questioning of Lindsey, his closest confidant. This claim, too, was rejected, not only by the court but also by Clinton's attorney general, Janet Reno, who contended that in a criminal inquiry the president's attorney-client privilege can be pierced by a federal judge's finding that the evidence being sought is essential.[547]

Reno was not the only Democrat who was reluctant to rally to Clinton's defense. Most Democratic legislators, still smarting from the president's seeming indifference to their programmatic commitments and election prospects, initially maintained a deafening silence as the Republicans sought to exploit the allegations against Clinton.[548] The president's uneasy relationship with congressional Democrats also threatened his legislative program. For example, the majority of House Democrats refused to support legislation to give Clinton fast-track authority to negotiate international trade agreements, a power that previous Democratic Congresses had readily conferred on Republican presidents Ford, Reagan, and Bush.

Democrats also challenged the line-item veto, a power that a Republican Congress had granted the president in a 1996 act (albeit in hopes that a Republican would be wielding it after the election). The new law, which was passed with Clinton's strong support, allowed the president to cancel, within five days of signing an appropriations bill, any new spending projects, narrowly targeted tax breaks, and entitlement programs. The president's action would be subject to an override by a two-thirds vote of both the House and Senate. In 1998 the Supreme Court in *Clinton v. City of New York* declared the line item veto unconstitutional, relying on the Presentment Clause of Article I, Section 7 (every bill "shall be presented to the President of the United States" for either approval or veto) for its reasoning.[549] *(See "Line-Item Veto," p. 810, Chapter 15.)* Fifteen years earlier, the Court had relied heavily on the same constitutional clause in *Immigration and Naturalization Service v. Chadha,* which declared unconstitutional Congress's long-standing use of the legislative veto to second-guess the executive branch after delegating it authority to make discretionary decisions about how laws should be implemented.

With the decline of Clinton's personal stature and the historical pattern of substantial losses for the parties of second-term presidents at midterm, nearly every political expert predicted that the Republicans would emerge from the 1998 elections with a tighter grip on Congress and, by implication, on the president's political fate.[550] But the Republicans had been preoccupied by the Lewinsky scandal for the entire year and lacked an appealing campaign message. They were unable to increase their 55–45 margin in the Senate and lost five seats in the House, leaving them a slim 223–211 majority. Clinton thus became the first president since Franklin D. Roosevelt to see his party gain seats in the midterm elections. Bitterly disappointed by the results, the Republicans fell into soul-searching and recriminations. Ironically, it was the hero of their 1994 ascent to power, Speaker Newt Gingrich, and not Clinton, who was forced from office. After the elections, Gingrich announced that he was resigning not only his leadership position but also his seat in Congress.

The 1998 elections seemed likely to take the steam out of the House impeachment inquiry. But as the president gathered with friends and aides to celebrate what appeared to be another remarkable political comeback, the Republicans prepared to move forward with impeachment. A centrist, poll-driven politician, Clinton underestimated the willingness of congressional Republicans to defy the survey-tested will of the people.[551] In truth, the hands of Republican legislators were tied. Their core constituencies—Republican voters and, especially, party activists—strongly favored impeachment.[552]

In December, after a year of dramatic and tawdry politics on both sides, Clinton was impeached on separate counts of perjury and obstruction of justice by a bitterly divided House of Representatives. The House voted virtually along party lines to recommend that the Senate remove the president from office. Article I, the perjury count, was approved by a vote of 226–206, with Republicans providing all but five of the aye votes and Democrats providing all but five of the nays. The 221–212 vote in favor of Article II, which charged Clinton with obstruction of justice, was almost as close and partisan. Only five Democrats voted for the article, and only thirteen Republicans voted against it.[553]

But even impeachment did not undermine Clinton's popular support. Soon after the House's historic action, large majorities of Americans expressed approval of Clinton's handling of his job, opposed a Senate trial, and proclaimed that Republican members of Congress were "out

of touch with most Americans." [554] Still, Republican leaders were determined not to abort the constitutional process. After a five-week Senate trial, the president's accusers failed to gain a simple majority, much less the constitutionally mandated two-thirds, for either charge against Clinton. On February 12, 1999, the Senate rejected the perjury article, 55–45, with ten Republicans voting against conviction. Just six minutes later, with five Republicans breaking ranks, the Senate split 50–50 on the article that accused the president of obstruction of justice. Clinton's job was safe. The most obvious casualty of the impeachment process was the Ethics in Government Act, which Congress did not reauthorize when it lapsed in summer 1999.

Clinton's problems with Congress, however, continued. Virtually every item in his legislative agenda—each of them popular in its own right—failed to be enacted, including campaign finance reform, tobacco regulation, school construction, a minimum wage increase, and a patients' bill of rights. But the perception that Clinton was an enfeebled president, thwarted at every turn by fierce Republican opposition and unsteady Democratic support, was belied by his aggressive use of the administrative presidency. Beginning in 1995, Clinton had issued a blizzard of executive orders, regulations, proclamations, and other decrees on matters such as tobacco regulation and environmental protection to achieve his goals, with or without the blessing of Congress.[555]

Moreover, Clinton once again withstood congressional opposition to the use of military force in the Balkans. This time it was in Kosovo, a province of Serbia, where Milošević's ruthless and repressive domination of the majority Muslim population renewed ethnic cleansing. Although the House defeated a resolution in May 1999 endorsing an air campaign in Kosovo, Clinton's stubborn pursuit of a NATO (North Atlantic Treaty Organization) victory in Yugoslavia forced Milošević to accept a peace settlement.

The cost to civilians in Yugoslavia during the air campaign, in comparison to no allied casualties, may have sent an unsettling message to the rest of the world, namely that the United States is willing to fight, but only when it can be sure it will not have to pay the ultimate cost. On June 10, the president declared that "we have achieved a victory for a safer world, for our democratic values and for a stronger America." Once criticized for his lack of experience and interest in military affairs, Clinton now readily embraced the president's power as commander in chief.[556]

Still, whatever moral authority Clinton may have had at the beginning of his administration to establish a new covenant of rights and responsibilities between citizens and their government was shattered by the public's disrespect for his personal morality. The virulent partisanship that characterized the impeachment process forced Clinton to seek refuge once again among his fellow Democrats in Congress, thus short-circuiting his plans to pursue entitlement reform as the capstone of his presidency.[557] In the wake of the impeachment debacle, Clinton positioned himself as the champion of Social Security and Medicare, urging Congress to invest a significant share of the mounting budget surplus in these traditional liberal programs.[558]

Clinton's efforts to avoid litigation and impeachment also led to a series of court decisions that weakened the authority of the presidency. In May 1997, in the case of *Clinton v. Jones,* the Supreme Court rejected the president's claim of immunity against a sexual harassment lawsuit brought by a former Arkansas employee, Paula Jones.[559] The ruling established that even sitting presidents are subject to civil suits. It also set the stage for the sworn testimony by Lewinsky and Clinton in the *Jones* case that provoked the independent counsel to charge the president with perjury and obstruction of justice. Moreover, Starr's investigation established legal precedents by producing appeals court rulings that neither the president's security agents nor the government lawyers he consulted could invoke executive privilege and refuse to testify in a criminal investigation.[560] The main effect of Clinton's efforts to forestall investigations of his conduct as governor and president, then, was to corrode the constitutional safeguards of presidential immunity and executive privilege and codify the declining prestige of the post-Watergate presidency.

GEORGE W. BUSH AND BEYOND

The 2000 campaign testified to the fragility of the modern presidency. Neither the Democratic nominee, Vice President Al Gore, nor the Republican nominee, Texas governor George W. Bush, took positions that suggested a way out of the fractious state of American politics that had corroded the foundations of presidential authority for the past three decades. Instead, both candidates took centrist positions that were designed to shore up the principal programs of the welfare state such as Social Security and Medicare. Gore sought to distance himself from Clinton's personal failings, making it difficult for him to embrace the president's record and achievements. But the vice president defended the Clinton administration's support for welfare reform and free trade, and the policy positions Gore took, although tinged with populist symbolism, gave no indication that he contemplated a significant departure from Clinton's New Democrat course. Bush, distancing himself from the antigovernment rhetoric of the Reagan years, fashioned a new kind of Republicanism based on the theme of "compassionate conservatism." He spoke of the need for a government role in reducing poverty and improving education that signaled he was breaking from the reigning image of conservatism that was associated with the congressional Republicans.[561]

Bush v. Gore

After the polls closed on election night 2000, Gore clearly had defeated Bush in the popular vote, but the electoral vote count, which determined who would become president, was undecided. Neither Bush nor Gore had garnered enough electoral votes to claim victory. The outcome of the election would be determined by the twenty-five electoral votes of the state of Florida, whose popular vote tally was in dispute.[562]

As required by Florida law in a close election, an automatic statewide machine recount took place, on November 10, which resulted in a minuscule lead for Bush. Claiming that machines had failed to count all his votes, and thus thwarted the will of the people, Gore called for a hand count in four counties that had voted strongly Democratic and that were controlled by Democratic election commissions. The core of Gore's legal challenge, supported by the state supreme court, was that Florida's voting machines, and therefore its official ballots, were flawed, especially in Democratic counties. Meanwhile, Bush's lawyers appealed to the Supreme Court to stop the recount. They argued that the Florida court decision violated both the Constitution's provision that the state legislature must determine how a state's electors will be chosen and the 1887 Electoral Count Act's requirement (passed in the wake of the disputed 1876 Hayes-Tilden election) that electors be chosen according to state laws enacted by the legislature before election day. Bush's lawyers also claimed that the recount violated the Equal Protection Clause of the Fourteenth Amendment. As he pursued legal channels, Bush had the comfort of knowing that the state legislature, which arguably had the power to appoint a slate of electors if all other approaches failed, was heavily Republican. Furthermore, the Republican governor of Florida was his brother Jeb, who was responsible for informing the National Archives which slate of electors had been chosen by the state.[563]

The Supreme Court in *Bush v. Gore* on December 12 ruled 7–2 that the recounting process ordered by the Florida court, which required manual recounts of every undervote in Florida (that is, every ballot in the state for which a machine failed to register a vote for president), was unconstitutional. Failing to establish a standard by which counties across the state would judge the voters' intention, the Florida court violated the Fourteenth Amendment's requirement that states protect the right of individuals to equal protection and due process under the law. The Court divided more closely and bitterly in the second, decisive part of its ruling. In a 5-4 vote, the Court ruled that the Florida court had also violated the Constitution by overruling the state legislature, which had indicated its intention to take advantage of an Electoral College Act provision that insulates a state's electors from challenge so long as they are certified by December 12. "Because it is evident that any recount" that would meet Fourteenth Amendment standards would frustrate the constitutional prerogative of the state legislature to determine how electors are chosen, the Court argued, "we reverse the judgment of the Supreme Court of Florida ordering the recount to proceed." [564]

Gore conceded the election the next day, but his surrender did not take place without considerable protest. Gore's supporters were emboldened by Justice John Paul Stevens's dissent, in which he decried the Court's majority for emphasizing the state's need to certify its electoral votes by December 12 rather than enforcing Florida's obligation to determine the intention of its voters. In the interest of "finality," Stevens charged, "the majority effectively orders the disenfranchisement of an unknown number of voters whose ballots reveal their intent—and are therefore legal votes under state law—but were for some reason rejected by ballot-counting machines." The Court's position, Stevens concluded, privileged the will of the state legislature over that of the voters, a stance that could only arouse the cynicism, if not the anger, of the American people. "Although we may never know with complete certainty the identity of the winner of this year's Presidential election," he wrote, "the identity of the loser is perfectly clear. It is the Nation's confidence in the judge as an impartial guardian of the rule of law." [565]

Stevens's dark forebodings about the judiciary losing the confidence of the American people were not fulfilled. The Court's decision bitterly divided political activists, but not the public, many of whom, following the recent pattern of low turnout elections, had stayed away from the polls. Less than half of the eligible voters had cast ballots in 1996, the lowest share of the electorate to vote since 1924. Although the 2000 election was a closely fought campaign and guaranteed the choice of a new president, the turnout rate increased only to 51 percent. [566]

The Early Days of the George W. Bush Presidency

After winning the election, Bush revived the theme of bipartisan cooperation that had marked his tenure as governor of Texas and his campaign for the presidency. Like Clinton and the elder Bush, the new president faced the conflicting tides of bitter partisanship within the Capitol and an indifferent public outside of it. Bush started out with Republicans in control of Congress, albeit by the narrowest of margins. The Senate was evenly split between Democrats and Republicans, with Vice President Richard Cheney, as president of the Senate, available to break a tie in the Republicans' favor. Like Clinton at the beginning of his administration, Bush chose to cooperate with his party's strongly ideological leaders in Congress. Like Clinton, too, Bush may have preferred to solidify the support of his party before reaching out to independent voters. The president's emphasis on traditional conservative issues such as tax cuts, regulatory relief, energy production, and missile defense risked alienating moderate Republicans, a dwindling, but pivotal group in the closely

divided House and Senate. The president and his party paid dearly for this emphasis in May 2001, when Republican senator James Jeffords of Vermont announced that he was becoming an independent, thus giving control of the Senate to the Democrats. [567]

Bush reaped both the benefits and the costs of his early strategy of partisan conservatism. The president persuaded Congress to enact the leading conservative plank in his 2000 platform, a ten-year, $1.5 trillion tax cut. But the Republicans lost control of the Senate in May 2001 when Sen. James Jeffords of Vermont announced that he was changing his allegiance from the Republican to the Democratic caucus. [568] Within days, every Senate committee and subcommittee chairmanship was transferred into Democratic hands.

Facing the prospect of ongoing partisan obstruction in the Senate, the Bush administration intensified its efforts to consolidate authority within the White House. The president assigned his top political adviser, Karl Rove, to take the lead in recruiting candidates and devising Republican campaign strategies for the 2002 state and congressional elections. In doing so, Bush undercut the authority of Republican National Committee chair James S. Gilmore III, the governor of Virginia. Politics was joined to policy when, midway into 2001, Rove began positioning the president as a centrist, nontraditional Republican. By the end of his first summer in the White House, Bush was beginning to stress education and "faith-based" social services, not taxes and defense. [569]

Bush's compassionate conservatism bore a striking resemblance to Clinton's New Covenant. Indeed, conservatives roundly attacked Bush for advocating "Clintonism without Clinton." Bush's speeches, which proclaimed the values of "responsibility," "community," and "education," bore a striking resemblance to Clinton's rhetoric during the 1992 and 1996 elections. The programs that embodied these values, especially Bush's proposals for education and welfare reform, invoked many of the ideas incubated in the Democratic Leadership Council that gave rise to Clinton's policy initiatives. [570]

To be sure, Bush differed from his Democratic predecessor in important ways. Clinton never made clear how his "third way" politics served the core principles of the Democratic Party. He and the DLC were highly ambivalent about partisanship. But Bush embraced Republican conservatism. His rhetoric and policy proposals, White House aides argued, were a deliberate attempt to play to conservative values, but not in a fashion that was reflexively antigovernment. [571] Bush's call for substantial tax cuts appealed to conservatives' hostility to government, but the president acknowledged, columnist E. J. Dionne observed, "that most people do not draw meaning from the marketplace alone, and that the marketplace is not the sole test or most important source of virtue." [572] "The invisible hand works many miracles," Bush said in July 1999. "But it cannot touch the human heart. . . . We are a nation of rugged individuals. But we are also the country of the second chance—tied together by bonds of friendship and community and solidarity." [573]

In part, the moral commitment Bush endorsed would be supporting nonprofit organizations that worked outside of government. Bush proposed changes in federal and state regulations that would allow private faith-based organizations, such as churches, synagogues, temples, and mosques, to play a larger role in providing government social services to the poor, the addicted, the illiterate, and others in need. But the federal government would take an important part in securing the general welfare as well. Although conservatives had once wanted to eliminate the Department of Education, Bush proposed that the department make public schools more accountable by linking federal aid to national standards and measurements of student learning. Social conservatives had long sought to advance morality by opposing abortion. Bush professed to be staunchly pro-life, but he called for a more incremental attack on abortion. More important, he proposed to associate conservative religious values with an affirmative government responsibility to help the poor and to ensure that "every child will be educated." [574]

Bush-style compassionate conservatism promised to soften the Republican Party's harsh anti-government edge. It also gave the president a platform to act independently of his party. Programs such as faith-based initiatives and educational reform were not pursued within Republican councils. Rather, as has been the custom since the development of the modern presidency, the White House pursued these objectives through executive orders and bipartisan cooperation.[575] The education bill in particular seemed less a use of government to serve conservative principles than an uneasy compromise between liberal demands for more spending and conservative insistence on standards.[576] Bush trumpeted his alliance with the liberal Democratic icon, Sen. Edward M. Kennedy, in passing education reform legislation in 2001.

September 11 and the War on Terrorism

Bush's agenda changed dramatically when the United States was attacked by terrorists of the al Qaeda network on September 11, 2001. In the aftermath of the first attack on the American continent since the War of 1812, and the most deadly in the nation's history, the country appeared to unite overnight. Citizens gave generously to relief funds to aid the families of those who lost their lives. The American flag was unfurled everywhere, and patriotic hymns, especially, "God Bless America," were sung repeatedly. Polls showed a remarkable jump in public support for Bush, from 51 percent approval of the job he was doing as president to 90 per-

cent approval, within days of the September 11 attack. A strong consensus quickly formed in support of his military response to the terrorist assault.

In the short term, the war on terrorism strengthened the modern presidency and greatly tempered the polarized partisanship that had held it hostage during the previous three decades. Hardly a discouraging word was heard when the Bush administration created an Office of Homeland Security, imposed tighter restrictions on airport security, and embraced deficit spending to help the economy and to fight a war in Afghanistan, which harbored the leaders of the al Qaeda network that carried out the terrorist attacks. Highlighting the need for bipartisanship in a time of national crisis, Bush justified the war on terrorism in words that echoed Franklin Roosevelt. "Freedom and fear are at war," he told a joint session of Congress on September 20. "The advance of human freedom—the great achievement of our time, and great hope of every time—now depends on us. Our nation—this generation—will lift a dark threat of violence from our people and our future. We will rally the world to this cause by our efforts, by our courage. We will not tire, we will not falter, and we will not fail." [577]

In February 2002, in his first State of the Union address, Bush warned the nation that "our war against terrorism is only beginning." Beyond Afghanistan, America's goal was "to prevent regimes that sponsor terror from threatening America or our friends and allies with weapons of mass destruction." Bush called on the nation to stand vigilant against states such as North Korea, Iran, and Iraq, identifying them as part of "an axis of evil." He stressed that the struggle against state-sponsored terror may last for generations: "This campaign may not be finished on our watch—yet it must be and it will be waged on our watch." [578]

As the president prepared the nation for new responsibilities at home and abroad, the imperiled presidency seemed a faint whisper and presidential scholars and public officials once again sounded warnings of an imperial presidency. Already executive-centered in its approach to politics and policy, the Bush White House became even more insulated from Congress and the Republican Party as it planned and fought the war against terrorism. Both Democrats and Republicans complained when Office of Homeland Security director Tom Ridge refused to testify before Congress about the president's homeland defense budget. The administration claimed that Ridge's office was akin to the National Security Council, a presidential agency whose officials did not have to appear before Congress. Similarly, bipartisan criticism of Attorney General John Ashcroft emerged when the administration unilaterally put some measures in place to crack down on terrorism at home, including military tribunals to try suspected foreign terrorists.[579] According to an executive order issued by President Bush on November 13, 2001, "Unlawful enemy combatants" were to be brought to trial not through the regular court system but, rather, through a system of military commissions. Although some American citizens would be designated as "enemy combatants," the order targeted non-citizens who were determined by the president to be a present or former member of al Qaeda; be "engaged in, aided or abetted, or conspired to commit acts of international terrorism or acts in preparation thereof" that would have "adverse effects" on the "United States, its citizens, national security, foreign policy, or economy"; or have "knowingly harbored" someone who had. The wording of the 2001 order, defending the president's power to establish military tribunals without congressional authorization, invoked Franklin Roosevelt's proclamation in 1942 concerning the *Quirin* saboteurs. But as critics of the Bush order pointed out, the 1942 order was drafted retrospectively to apply to a specific case, not prospectively to those individuals whom the president determined to be enemies of the United States.[580]

For a time, these complaints paled against the aura of invincibility that Bush had enjoyed since September 11. But the roots of congressional resentment of executive slights ran deep. Beginning in spring 2002, Bush administration officials, and then the president himself, openly pursued the possibility of another military venture: an invasion of Iraq that, unlike the 1991 Persian Gulf War, would have as its mission the removal of Saddam Hussein from power. In October 2002, Congress passed a resolution authorizing the president to use military force against Iraq "as he determines to be necessary." In doing so, it sustained the Bush administration's revival of the cold war–era belief that an overriding cause—the containment of communism then, the war against terrorism now—justifies the expansive use of presidential power around the globe.

The Bush administration's determination to fight the war against terrorism outside the bounds of conventional legal constraints was a constant source of tension between the White House and Congress. Indeed, bipartisan resistance stiffened further toward the end of 2005, buttressed by revelations that the Bush administration had used the highly secret National Security Agency to monitor some domestic communications without judicial review or consultation with Congress. This inter-branch struggle was roiled not only by Bush's policy to use military tribunals to try enemy combatants and the White House's justification for surveillance of overseas phone calls but also by the administration's expansive rules permitting tough interrogation of suspected terrorists. A series of memos from the CIA's general counsel and from the Justice Department's Office of Legal Counsel claimed for the agency wide imprisonment and interrogation powers that in some cases overrode the Geneva Convention, international rules that had governed the treatment of prisoners and civilians during wartime and occupation for half a century. Since terrorists were not fighting on

behalf of an established state or in uniform, the Bush administration argued, they were not covered by the law of war. President Bush approved a permissive set of rules governing interrogation, which allowed the CIA to set up secret detention centers abroad; high level terrorist suspects were reportedly subject to treatment that approached (or were considered to be) torture—for example, techniques like "water-boarding," where a bound prisoner is held underwater to the brink of drowning.

Withstanding vigorous White House opposition, Congress, led by Republican senator John McCain, himself a victim of torture as a prisoner of war in Vietnam, enacted the Detainee Treatment Act of 2005. Bush signed this legislation, which prohibited interrogation techniques that subjected persons under U.S. control or custody to "cruel, inhuman, or degrading treatment or punishment," but not without appending a statement objecting to some of its provisions and explicitly reserving the right to interpret them "in a manner consistent" with his constitutional authority as president and commander in chief. Following, indeed surpassing, the practice of his father, Bush used this sort of signing statement—one of more than five hundred that the president added to laws during his first six years in office—to insulate executive power from congressional and judicial oversight, especially in matters pertaining to national and homeland security.

Bush's defense of a "unitary executive" did not go unchallenged. In June 2006, the Supreme Court ruling of *Hamdan v. Rumsfield* strongly limited the power of the executive to conduct military tribunals for, and employ aggressive interrogation techniques against, suspected terrorists imprisoned at the U.S. Navy's base in Guantanamo Bay, Cuba.[581] Brushing aside administration pleas not to second-guess the commander in chief during wartime, a five justice majority ruled that the commissions were neither authorized by federal law nor required by military necessity, and violated the Geneva Convention. Consequently, the court ruled, no military commission could try either Salam Ahmed Hamdan, the former aide to Usama bin Ladin captured in Afghanistan, whose case was before the justices, or anyone else, unless the president did one of two things he had refused to do for four years: operate the commissions by the laws of regular military court marshal or ask Congress for specific permission to proceed differently.

President Bush thus had little choice but to press for legislation endorsing his leadership against terrorism. The White House's efforts to get Congress to narrowly define U.S. obligations under the Geneva Convention met strong resistance in the Senate, however, where three respected Republicans—McCain, Lindsay Graham of South Carolina, and John Warner of Virginia, chairman of the Armed Services Committee—rejected the administration's approach as not only unbefitting a free nation but also as an invitation to other countries, including Iran, Syria, and North Korea, to reinterpret international rules regarding the treatment of prisoners as they saw fit if they ever held U.S. soldiers. Anxious to resolve this dispute within his party before the 2006 elections, Bush and dissident Republicans reached a compromise in September 2006, on legislation that did not formally alter the United States' compliance with the Geneva Convention but recognized the president's special constitutional responsibilities as commander in chief. The White House, for its part, gave up its desire to secure congressional approval for a restricted obligation under Common Article 3 of the Geneva accords. Article 3 requires humane treatment of detainees and prohibits "violence to life and person," including death and mutilation as well as cruel treatment and "outrages upon personal dignity." In turn, Congress delegated to the president a dominant role in deciding which interrogation methods are permitted by Article 3 along with some discretion to withhold information about sources of evidence. The Military Commissions Act, which Bush signed into law on October 18, 2006, authorized the use of military tribunals and denied defendants the right of *habeas corpus*, a hallowed legal protection that would compel the government to allow them to appear before a civilian judge.[582]

The war on terrorism affirmed the preeminence of the modern presidency in other ways as well. The new responsibilities the war thrust on the executive office led Bush, urged by many members of Congress, to pursue major institutional reforms. In June 2002, he called for the creation of a Department of Homeland Security, outlining the most ambitious reorganization of the government's national security apparatus in a half century. Likening his plan to the 1947 National Security Act, which authorized President Harry S. Truman to create the National Security Council and the Department of Defense, Bush asked Congress to create "a single, permanent department with an overriding and urgent mission: securing the homeland of America, and protecting the American people." [583]

Bush initially had resisted the idea of creating another government department. The small Office of Homeland Security, which the president created by executive order in the frantic days after September 11 and which was headed by former Pennsylvania governor Tom Ridge, was conceived as part of the White House staff, a domestic counterpart to the National Security Council. With an office in the West Wing and a close personal relationship with Bush, Ridge appeared well positioned to "lead, oversee, and coordinate" a national crusade against terrorism.[584] The administration changed course, however, when faced with criticism about whether it had done everything possible to avoid the September 11 attacks and had taken adequate measures to forestall future ones. Ridge's office, critics claimed, appeared to have inadequate authority over the budgets and activities of the many

executive agencies whose actions he was responsible for coordinating.

Once Bush was persuaded to transform the homeland security office into a full-scale Department of Homeland Security, he urged Congress to enact legislation to relocate by law a huge swath of the executive branch, including the Customs Service, the Secret Service, the Immigration and Naturalization Service, and the Federal Emergency Management Agency, in the new department.[585] Democrats and Republicans on Capitol Hill looked favorably on Bush's proposal, in part because Congress has much more authority over departments than over a White House office. The president's plan promised to end the protracted struggle about whether Ridge was obligated to testify before Congress concerning his budget and programs. (As head of a department, he was.) At the same time, the creation of a cabinet department would signify that homeland security had become an ongoing responsibility of the national government. In accepting the idea of a department and urging Congress to authorize it by statute, Bush paved the way for an important expansion of the extraordinary yet fragile authority of the modern presidency.

Bush and Congress also placed new responsibilities on the executive for regulating the economy. In the early 2000s, the collapse of Enron, a large energy trading corporation, and WorldCom, a leading telecommunications company, amid revelations of fraudulent accounting practices and unethical boardroom scheming, caused the stock market and consumer confidence to plummet. Bush lacked the credibility on economic issues that he enjoyed regarding homeland security and the war on terror. Few presidents have been more closely associated with support for corporate America than Bush.

Facing criticism from members of his party, who feared that business scandals would hurt Republicans in the November 2002 midterm elections, Bush rushed to take charge of efforts, already well advanced in Congress, to reform corporate behavior. Sounding more like Theodore Roosevelt than like his party's more recent conservative icons, the president gave a tough speech on Wall Street in July 2002, proclaiming that America's "greatest economic need is higher ethical standards—standards enforced by strict laws and upheld by responsible business leaders." He announced the creation of a Corporate Fraud Task Force to coordinate federal, state, and local efforts to investigate and prosecute financial crimes.[586]

A few weeks later, Bush signed the Sarbanes-Oxley Act, celebrated as "the most far-reaching reform of American business practices since the time of Franklin Delano Roosevelt." Among other provisions, the act strengthened the Securities and Exchange Commission, which has been created as part of FDR's New Deal, and formed a Public Accounting and Oversight Board "to enforce professional standards, ethics, and competence for the accounting profession." [587] Clearly the prevailing wisdom of the 1980s and 1990s, supported by an extraordinary stock market boom, that Washington should interfere as little as possible with securities trading and corporate practices had lost influence in the nation's capital. In trying to shore up his administration's credibility on the economy, Bush had upheld Theodore Roosevelt's admonition that the president must serve as the steward of the public welfare.

Bush and the Republican Party

For much of the history of the modern presidency, executive power and partisanship have appeared to be at odds. The forging of direct ties between the White House and public opinion, combined with aggressive executive administration, has tended to subordinate partisan loyalty to the personal and programmatic ambitions of the president. According to some scholars, Bush's presidency defied collective partisan responsibility. As the controversies over spying on terrorist suspects and detention of enemy combatants reveal, the Bush administration sought to expand the powers of the modern executive office.

At the same time, however, Bush and his top political advisor, Karl Rove, were unusually committed to building an enduring governing party and partisan coalition. In fact, since the flowering of the modern presidency, no White House has been so committed to party building. Bush's presidency thus suggests how a strongly partisan president can use the expanded powers of the White House for party purposes. Indeed, with the steadfast support of Republican leaders in Congress, Bush exploited his party's beliefs and organization to advance a conservative, executive-centered administrative state. This started in the Reagan administration, but Bush trumped Reagan in his commitment to what might be termed "big government conservatism." The most dramatic example was the Bush administration's foreign policy, especially its controversial "preemption doctrine," used to justify the war in Iraq. The preemption doctrine states that because terrorists may strike anywhere and at any time with no warning, it is impossible to wait for evidence of a clear and present danger before taking military action against them. Therefore, offensive measures provide the only prudent defense against terrorist aggression.

Bush's big government conservatism had extended far beyond homeland security into domestic policy. Rather than try to curtail New Deal and Great Society entitlements, as the Reagan administration and the Gingrich-led 104th Congress attempted to do, Bush sought to recast these programs in a conservative form. His hope was to cement ties between the Republican Party and groups that had conservative beliefs but whose members needed government help. For example, Bush's "faith based" initiative was, in part, a response to religious organizations feeling that they have

President George W. Bush shakes hands with Sen. Paul Sarbanes, D-Md., right, as Rep. Mike Oxley, R-Ohio, applauds prior to signing the Sarbanes-Oxley Act in the East Room of the White House on July 30, 2002.

been unfairly disadvantaged in obtaining federal funds to help those in need. Moreover, with his commitment to the No Child Left Behind Act, Bush sought to rally conservatives around the idea of making schools better by having the federal government make them more demanding. Finally, in response to pressure from the elderly, Bush fought for the enactment of an extremely costly expansion to Medicare, the 2003 addition of prescription drug coverage.

Even Bush's most spectacular policy failure, the doomed effort during his second term to reform Social Security, reflected his commitment to big government conservatism. Unlike Reagan, Bush proposed not to cut social security benefits, but rather to "privatize" them by allowing workers under age fifty-five to divert some of their Social Security payroll taxes into personal retirement accounts. This reform, the White House claimed, would yield beneficiaries a better rate of return on funds dedicated to Social Security benefits and would recast the core New Deal entitlement as a vehicle by which individuals would assume greater responsibility to plan for their own retirement. Significantly, although Bush's plan to reform Social Security would transfer a substantial portion of tax revenues from the control of government to individual accounts, government would still force people to save, control the investment choices they made, and regulate the rate of withdrawals.[588]

The Bush administration's party building activities complemented its agenda of big government conservatism. The president's active recruitment of Republican candidates and diligent fundraising considerably strengthened the national party organization; and his public displays of religious faith and use of strong moral language served to consolidate the Republican identity of moral and religious conservatism that has energized Republican partisans. During most of his presidency, these efforts yielded handsome political returns.

Risking the bipartisan support that he accrued in the aftermath of the September 11 attacks, Bush threw himself into the 2002 midterm election campaign earlier and more energetically than any president in history. He and advisor Karl Rove recruited strong Republican challengers to incumbent Democratic senators, even to the point of intervening in state party politics to do so. The president was the featured attraction at sixty-seven fundraising events that raised a record $141 million in campaign contributions for the Republican Party and its candidates. Throughout the fall, Bush campaigned ardently for Republican nominees. For example, in the five days leading up to the election, he traveled ten thousand miles to speak at Republican rallies in seventeen cities in fifteen states. Several of these appearances were in states where the Republican candidate was trailing and where, if the Democrat had won, Bush risked being blamed for the defeat.

The results of the election vindicated Bush's decision to become actively involved in the campaign. The Republicans gained two seats in the Senate, transforming them from minority to majority status, while increasing their majority in the House of Representatives. Political analysts were quick to describe the historic nature of the Republican victory. It marked the first time in more than a century that the president's party had regained control of the Senate in a midterm election. It was the first election since 1934—and the first ever for a Republican president—in which the president's party gained seats in both houses of Congress in a first-term midterm election.

Analysts also were quick to credit Bush with his party's success. An election-eve CBS News poll indicated that 50 percent of the voters were basing their decision on their opinion of the president, many more than the 34 percent who had done so in 1990 or the 37 percent who had done so in 1998. Of these 50 percent, 31 percent were pro-Bush and only 19 percent opposed him.[589]

Bush could not take all of the credit for the Republican gains. Since the late 1970s, the Republican Party had been developing into a formidable national organization in which the Republican National Committee, rather than state and local organizations, became the principal agent of party building activities. This top-down approach to party building appeared to many critics to be too centralized and too dependant on television advertising to perform the parties' traditional role of mobilizing voters and popular support; but the Republican Party, believing that it had been out organized "on the ground" by Democrats in the 2000 election, began to put together a massive grassroots mobilizing strategy in 2002. Democrats since the New Deal had relied on auxiliary party organizations like labor unions to get out the vote. But the GOP created its own national organizations to mobilize supporters. Indeed, one could argue that they built the first "national party machine" in American history—an elaborate network of campaign volunteers concentrated in the sixteen most competitive states, which was credited as a key to Bush's narrow but decisive victory over the Democratic nominee, Senator John Kerry of Massachusetts, in the 2004 presidential election, and with helping to increase Republicans' command of the Senate and House in 2002 and 2004.[590] Bush thus surpassed Reagan, whose party leadership never led to Republican majorities in both the House of Representatives and the Senate. Indeed, Bush's reelection made him the first president since Franklin Roosevelt to be reelected while his party also gained seats in both the House and the Senate.

Bush not only benefited from the development of what might be considered the first national party machine in history, he also played a critical role in strengthening it. Throughout his presidency the White House recruited candidates, raised money to fund their campaigns, and helped to attract volunteers to identify Republican voters and get them out to vote. Just as Ronald Reagan played a critical part in laying the philosophical and political foundation that enabled the Republican Party to become a solidly conservative and electorally competitive party by 1984, so did Bush make an important contribution in enlarging and energizing the party's base of core supporters. In 2004, instead of focusing on so-called "swing" voters—voters who were still on the fence between the two candidates—the Bush-Cheney grassroots organization reached out to "lazy Republicans." These were people predisposed to vote for Republicans at all levels but who needed to be prodded and reminded to go to the polls.[591]

In fact, the 2004 campaign may have marked a culmination of sorts in the development of a "new" national party system. Prior to 2004, the new party system had strengthened partisan discipline in Washington, D.C., most notably in Congress, and had been a valuable source of campaign services—especially campaign funds—for candidates. But it had failed to stir the passions and allegiance of the American people, as attested by anemic voting rates. In contrast, the 2004 campaign was passionate, polarizing, and participatory. Thus the Republican grass roots mobilization—and earnest Democratic efforts to match it—represent the best evidence that a new party system has come of age. Significantly, both the Republican grassroots organization and the Get-Out-the-Vote campaign of Americans Coming Together (ACT), the 527 ("shadow party") group that assumed principal responsibility for the Kerry campaign's voter mobilization efforts, were organized outside of the regular state and local party organizations.[592] Both campaigns sought to recruit new insurgent leaders in the states and localities to serve as company commanders in a national party offensive. Beyond its immediate electoral effectiveness, then, the Bush White House's mobilization efforts in 2004 may provide a plausible blueprint for a revitalized party politics that draws more people into the political process and renews linkages between citizens and elected officials.

Although Bush's partisan leadership marks the most systematic effort by a modern president to create a strong national party, the prospects that the new party system can hold the modern presidency accountable are still very uncertain. In fact, the new party system may turn out to be nothing more than a tool of the modern presidency. As Rove put it, the national parties that have emerged since the 1980s are "of great importance in the tactical and mechanical aspects of electing a president." But they are "less important in developing a political and policy strategy for the White House." In effect, Rove said, parties served as a critical "means to the president's end." [593]

The Bush-Cheney 2004 campaign sought to frame the choice the voters faced as one between two individuals, George W. Bush and John Kerry, not one between Republican and Democratic principles. Voters were urged to focus on the questions of character and temperament. Which candidate, in the aftermath of 9/11, was more likely to manage the imposing tasks of economic and homeland security? The Bush campaign's emphasis on wartime leadership was skillfully tied to national security and traditional values that appealed to Republican partisans, but it also tended to emphasize loyalty to Bush rather than to a political party with a past and a future. As Matthew Dowd, the top strategist for the 2004 Bush-Cheney campaign, suggested, "Leadership is a window into the soul—people want someone they can count on in tough times, and [after 9-11] Bush filled this paternalistic role." [594] Given the president's campaign message, the impressive grassroots operation may have been less a means for mobilizing support for shared values and partisan goals than for mobilizing public approval for the president's personal leadership in the war on terrorism.

The Kerry campaign, too, emphasized personal competence and strength of character. A central theme of the Democratic National Convention was Kerry's military service. He accepted the nomination with a salute and an emphatic pronouncement that he was, "Reporting for duty!" The Convention did not emphasize party principles, but focused instead on presenting the Democratic senator as a "plausible alternative" to the incumbent president, one who displayed the "strength required of a leader in post–9-11 America." [595]

Kerry's electoral chances suffered from his "flip-flopping" on the question of whether he supported the war in Iraq, which appeared to defy his campaign's emphasis on his strength of character. But the deciding factor in the election was not his personal indecisiveness but the unwillingness of his party to resist Bush's use of his prerogative power. Like many Democrats in the Congress, Kerry justified his vote for the Iraq-war resolution in 2002 by claiming that it did not declare war, but, instead, delegated to the president authority to go to war and determine its scope and duration. He maintained during the 2004 campaign that he would have cast the same vote even after knowing what subsequently happened in Iraq; after all, he said, "I believe it's the right authority for the president to have." [596] This acceptance of executive aggrandizement badly hamstrung Kerry's effort to challenge Bush on the central issue of the 2004 presidential election.

Consequently, although both the Republicans and Democrats engaged in innovative and effective practices in raising campaign funds, getting their message out, and mobilizing voters during the 2004 elections, it remains unclear whether these protonational machines (or popular allegiance to them) will endure beyond the election. Ultimately, as Dowd acknowledged, "both parties' organizing force has focused on President Bush—the Republicans in defense of his leadership; the Democrats in opposition—hostilely—to it. After the election, both parties will be challenged to sustain a collective commitment independently of their devotion to, or hatred of Bush." The question remains, therefore, whether the profound revival of the modern executive's governing authority in the wake of 9/11 has brought a national party system to fruition or continued the long-term development of a modern presidency that undermines collective partisanship.[597]

THE MODERN PRESIDENCY AT THE NEW CENTURY

The war on terrorism reestablished the modern presidency's place at the center of politics and government in the United States. Given the domestic and international challenges posed by the twentieth and twenty-first centuries, the development of the modern presidency in that era as the principal agent of American democracy seems justified. A new sense of executive responsibility was needed, one that the contemporary presidency fulfills admirably. Indeed, without the emancipation of the executive from previous institutional and partisan constraints, the two greatest moral triumphs of recent American history—ending racial segregation in the South and the triumphant conclusion to the cold war—might not have occurred.

In the absence of vital party politics, however, both Johnson and Reagan failed in their hope of becoming great democratic leaders in the tradition of Franklin Roosevelt. The tragedy of Vietnam, which deflected Johnson's attempt to build a Great Society, might have been forestalled by a vigilant Democratic Party, just as the debacle of Iran-contra might have been prevented by an alert Republican Party. As these disasters illustrate, modern presidents navigate a treacherous and lonely path, subject to a volatile political process that makes responsible democratic leadership very difficult to achieve.

Caught between the Scylla of bureaucratic indifference and the Charybdis of the public's demand for new rights, the modern presidency has evolved or degenerated into a plebiscitary form of politics that mocks the New Deal concept of "enlightened administration" and exposes citizens to the sort of public figures who will exploit their impatience with the difficult tasks of sustaining a healthy constitutional democracy. As the shifting fortunes of the Clinton and Bush presidencies dramatically illustrated, the New Deal freed the executive from the local party politics of the nineteenth century polity, but at the cost of subjecting it to the fractious politics within the Washington beltway and a volatile public opinion outside of it.

Perhaps the reinvigorated national parties that have arisen during the past two decades will rebind the modern presidency to America's democratic tradition. The current Republican Party and the president seem more committed and better equipped to coordinate campaigns and collaborate on policy than were the Democrats and Bill Clinton. Just as Bush played a critical part in drawing campaign funds and loyalists to his party, so he benefited from the steadfast backing of his party members in Congress and party loyalists in the electorate. Without this rock-solid support of his fellow Republicans, Bush's pursuit of a polarizing war in Iraq would have been far more treacherous politically in 2004. In turn, popular disaffection with the Iraq war, which led to a dramatic decline in support for Bush among independents and moderate Republicans, reenergized Democrats and enabled them to capture the House and Senate in the 2006 elections.

If the political center continues to reassert itself in years to come, as it did in the 2006 election according to exit polls, then partisan rancor might recede for a time. Roughly nine in ten Republicans and Democrats cast votes for their parties' candidates, just as they did in the 2004 elections. But the Democrats gained a far greater advantage among independents in 2006 than they did in 2004, which proved crucial to their success in picking up thirty seats in the House and six in the Senate. Several post–election surveys, moreover, suggested that the American people expected President Bush and the Democratic Congress to work together, especially in finding a resolution to the Iraq quagmire. Claiming to have heard the voices of the people, both Bush and congressional Democrats have expressed a willingness to avoid the rancorous partisanship that has dominated the past two decades of American politics.

Some post–election developments, however, suggested that the White House and congressional Democrats might honor this pledge more in the breach than the observance. Notably, both the White House and Democratic Party leaders reacted coldly to the report of the bipartisan Iraq Study Group, co-chaired by Republican James Baker and Democrat Lee Hamilton, that sought to hammer out a compromise between the Bush administration, intent on staying the course in Iraq, and Democratic leaders in Congress, who believed that the 2006 election gave them a mandate to pose hard challenges to the White House's conduct of the war. Bush supporters labeled the report, which called for a gradual reduction of America's military presence, a plan for surrender, while liberals criticized it for not proposing a firm timetable for withdrawal.

The prospect for a full-blown partisan debate over foreign policy is not eagerly anticipated by most Americans. "Sharpened debate is arguably helpful with respect to domestic issues," political scientist James Q. Wilson has acknowledged, "but not for the management of important foreign and military matters. . . . Denmark or Luxembourg can afford to exhibit domestic anguish and uncertainty over military policy; the United States cannot. A divided America encourages our enemies, disheartens our allies, and saps our resolve—potentially to fatal effect." [598]

★

NOTES

1. James Thomas Flexner, *George Washington and the New Nation: 1783–1793* (Boston: Little, Brown, 1970), 171.

2. Ibid.

3. Forrest McDonald, *The Presidency of George Washington* (Lawrence: University Press of Kansas, 1974), 24.

4. Flexner, *George Washington*, 398.

5. Letter, Thomas Jefferson to James Madison, December 20, 1787, in *The Portable Thomas Jefferson*, ed. Merrill D. Peterson (New York: Viking Press, 1975), 431.

6. Flexner, *George Washington*, 193.

7. Joanne B. Freeman, *Affairs of Honor: National Politics in the New Republic* (New Haven, Conn.: Yale University Press, 2001), 43.

8. Ibid., 196.

9. Gordon S. Wood, *Revolutionary Characters: What Made the Founders Different* (New York: Penguin Press), 54.

10. Leonard White, *The Federalists: A Study in Administrative History, 1789–1801* (New York: Macmillan, 1948), 101.

11. Ibid., 106.

12. McDonald, *Presidency of George Washington*, 38.

13. Stanley Elkins and Eric McKitrick, *The Age of Federalism: The Early American Republic, 1788–1800* (New York: Oxford University Press, 1993), 54.

14. McDonald, *Presidency of George Washington*, 39.

15. "James Madison's Defense of the President's Removal Power," in *The Evolving Presidency*, ed. Nelson (Washington, D.C.: CQ Press, 1994), 38–39.

16. Flexner, *George Washington*, 221.

17. Washington made one important exception to the rule that the presidential veto power should extend only to bills of doubtful constitutionality. He vetoed legislation that would reduce the size of the army by dismissing two specific companies serving at outposts on the western frontier. Washington's explanation to Congress was based not on constitutional grounds but on the position that the legislation was bad military policy. The frontier, he believed, was the last place to turn for troop reductions. Moreover, the bill would stop the troops' pay immediately, although weeks would pass before the soldiers could be notified and sent home. In casting this veto, Washington implied that presidential deference to the legislature was more appropriate in domestic matters than in foreign affairs and military policy. See Glen A. Phelps, "George Washington: Precedent Setter," in *Inventing the American Presidency*, ed. Thomas Cronin (Lawrence: University Press of Kansas, 1989), 268–269.

18. "Account by William Maclay of President George Washington's First Attempt to Obtain the Advice and Consent of the Senate to a Treaty," August 22, 24, 1789, in *The Growth of Presidential Power: A Documented History*, ed. William M. Goldsmith (New York and London: Chelsea House, 1974), 1:392–396.

19. In *Letters of Pacificus and Helvidius on the Proclamation of Neutrality of 1793* (Washington, D.C.: Gideon, 1845), 3.

20. Ibid., 5–15.

21. Goldsmith, *Growth of Presidential Power*, 1:398.

22. *Letters of Pacificus and Helvidius*, 53–64.

23. McDonald, *Presidency of George Washington*, 114.

24. Leonard White, *The Jeffersonians: A Study in Administrative History, 1801–1829* (New York: Macmillan, 1951), 30.

25. Forrest McDonald, *The Presidency of George Washington* (Lawrence: University Press of Kansas, 1974), 160.

26. Letter, Thomas Jefferson to James Madison, January 8, 1797, *The Writings of Thomas Jefferson*, ed. Paul Leicester Ford (New York: Putnam, 1895), 7:39–40.

27. Ralph Adams Brown, *The Presidency of John Adams* (Lawrence: University Press of Kansas, 1975), 25.

28. Letter, Jefferson to Elbridge Gerry, May 13, 1797, in *The Portable Thomas Jefferson*, ed. Merrill D. Peterson (New York: Viking Press, 1975), 471–474.

29. Brown, *The Presidency of John Adams*, 26–27.

30. White, *The Federalists*, 241.

31. Ibid., 237.

32. Richard Hofstadter, *The Idea of a Party System* (Berkeley: University of California Press, 1969), 110.

33. John Ferling, *Adams vs. Jefferson: The Tumultuous Election of 1800* (New York: Oxford University Press, 2004), 161.

34. The method of voting added to the uncertainty of the House election. The Federalists controlled the House but did not control the congressional delegations from a majority of states. Of the sixteen states, eight could be counted on to support Jefferson, while six were controlled by the Federalists. The remaining two states were evenly divided. For a full account of the national trauma caused by the electoral gridlock of 1801, see Ferling, *Adams vs. Jefferson*; and James Roger Sharp, *American Politics in the Early Republic* (New Haven, Conn.: Yale University Press, 1993), 250–275.

35. Sean Wilentz, *The Rise of American Democracy: Jefferson to Lincoln* (New York: W. W. Norton, 2005), 93.

36. Hofstadter, *The Idea of a Party System*, 139.

37. Thomas Jefferson to Spencer Roane, September 6, 1819, in *The Writings of Thomas Jefferson*, ed. Albert Ellery Bergh (Washington, D.C.: Thomas Jefferson Memorial Association, 1903), 15:212–216.

38. Joanne B. Freeman, *Affairs of Honor: National Politics in the New Republic* (New Haven, Conn.: Yale University Press, 2001), 243.

39. Forrest McDonald, *The Presidency of Thomas Jefferson* (Lawrence: University Press of Kansas, 1976), 34.

40. Robert M. Johnstone Jr., *Jefferson and the Presidency* (Ithaca: Cornell University Press, 1978), 162.

41. McDonald, *Presidency of Thomas Jefferson*, 50–51.

42. Forrest McDonald, *The American Presidency: An Intellectual History* (Lawrence: University Press of Kansas, 1994), 268.

43. Johnstone, *Jefferson and the Presidency*, 46.

44. Letter, Thomas Jefferson to John Breckinridge, August 12, 1803, in Peterson, *The Portable Thomas Jefferson*, 494–497.

45. White, *The Jeffersonians*, 3.

46. Quoted in Johnstone, *Jefferson and the Presidency*, 53.

47. The discussion of the change in the presidency during the Jeffersonian era is derived from James Ceaser, *Presidential Selection: Theory and Development* (Princeton: Princeton University Press, 1979), 88–122; and Johnstone, *Jefferson and the Presidency*, 52–75.

48. Johnstone, *Jefferson and the Presidency*, 58–59.

49. Merrill D. Peterson, *Thomas Jefferson and the New Nation: A Biography* (New York: Oxford University Press, 1970), 653.

50. Jeffrey Tulis, *The Rhetorical Presidency* (Princeton: Princeton University Press, 1987).

51. Leonard W. Levy, *Jefferson and Civil Liberties: The Darker Side* (Cambridge: Harvard University Press, 1963), 95.

52. White, *The Jeffersonians*, 53–54. See also Gaillard Hunt, *The Life of James Madison* (New York: Russell and Russell, 1902), 316–319.

53. White, *The Jeffersonians*, 55.

54. Hunt, *Life of James Madison*, 325.

55. Wilentz, *Rise of American Democracy*, 165.

56. Ibid., 318–319.

57. Ibid., 329–330.

58. James D. Savage, *Balanced Budgets and American Politics* (Ithaca and London: Cornell University Press, 1988), 98–99; see also Robert Allen Rutland, *The Presidency of James Madison* (Lawrence: University Press of Kansas, 1990), 68–70, 95–203.

59. Ralph Ketcham, "James Madison and the Presidency," in *Inventing the American Presidency*, ed. Thomas Cronin (Lawrence: University Press of Kansas, 1989), 360–361.

60. Letter, Thomas Jefferson to John Holmes, April 22, 1820, in Peterson, *The Portable Thomas Jefferson,* 567–569.

61. The Missouri Compromise admitted Missouri to the Union without restricting slavery, allowed Maine to enter as a free state, and banned slavery from all western territories north of Missouri's southern border (latitude 36°30').

62. Quoted in White, *The Jeffersonians*, 39.

63. Goldsmith, *Growth of Presidential Power* 1:378–386.

64. James Monroe, "State of the Union Address," December 2, 1823, in *Messages and Papers of the Presidents*, ed. James D. Richardson (New York: Bureau of National Literature, 1897), 1:778.

65. Catherine Allgor, *Parlor Politics: In Which the Ladies of Washington Help Build a City and a Government* (Charlottesville: University Press of Virginia, 2000), chap. 4.

66. Wilentz, *Rise of American Democracy,* 250.

67. John Quincy Adams, "Diary Account of Cabinet Discussions of His First State of the Union Message," November 25–26, 1825, in *The Growth of Presidential Power: A Documented History*, ed. William M. Goldsmith (New York and London: Chelsea House, 1974), 1:325.

68. Ibid.

69. White, *Jeffersonians*, 42.

70. Robert V. Remini, *Andrew Jackson and the Course of American Democracy, 1833–1845* (New York: Harper and Row, 1984), 7.

71. Major L. Wilson, *The Presidency of Martin Van Buren* (Lawrence: University Press of Kansas, 1984), 13.

72. Richardson, *Messages and Papers of the Presidents*, 3:1206.

73. Wilson, *Presidency of Martin Van Buren*, 13.

74. Wilfred E. Binkley, *President and Congress* (New York: Knopf, 1947), 67.

75. Edward S. Corwin, *The President: Office and Powers, 1787–1957*, 4th ed. (New York: New York University Press, 1957), 20–21.

76. Letter, Andrew Jackson to James Gwin, February 23, 1835, cited in *Niles' Register*, April 4, 1835:80.

77. Ibid.; see also Leonard D. White, *The Jacksonians: A Study in Administrative History, 1829–1861* (New York: Macmillan, 1954), 24–25.

78. Robert V. Remini, *Andrew Jackson and the Course of American Freedom, 1822–1832* (New York: Harper and Row, 1981), 369.

79. Richardson, *Messages and Papers of the Presidents*, 3:1152; Remini, *Andrew Jackson and the Course of American Freedom*, 370.

80. *McCulloch v. Maryland*, 4 L.Ed. 579 (1819).

81. Richardson, *Messages and Papers of the Presidents*, 3:1144–1145.

82. *Marbury v. Madison*, 1 Cranch 138 (1803).

83. *Niles' Register*, November 17, 1832, quoted in White, *The Jacksonians*, 23; Remini, *Andrew Jackson and the Course of American Freedom*, 373.

84. Quoted in Binkley, *President and Congress*, 79.

85. Ibid., 80.

86. Remini, *Andrew Jackson and the Course of American Freedom*, 325.

87. On the development of the "administration press," see White, *The Jacksonians*, chap. 15.

88. Quoted in ibid., 320.

89. Ibid., 332–343.

90. Ibid., 313. The deleterious effects of the system of rotation on public administration often have been exaggerated (ibid., 308, 343).

91. Richard R. John, "Affairs of Office: The Executive Departments, the Election of 1828, and the Making of the Democratic Party," in *The Democratic Experiment*, Meg Jacobs, William J.Novak, and Julian Zelizer, eds. (Princeton, N.J.: Princeton University Press, 2003), 65.

92. Alexis de Tocqueville, *Democracy in America*, ed. J. P. Mayer (Garden City, N.Y.: Doubleday, 1969), 394.

93. Letter, Gen. William Henry Harrison to Rep. Harmer Denny, December 2, 1838, in *The Growth of Presidential Power: A Documented History*, ed. William M. Goldsmith (New York and London: Chelsea House, 1974), 2:637–641.

94. Binkley, *President and Congress*, 89.

95. John de Ziska, the Baltimore Republican, December 11, 1839.

96. Ibid., 108.

97. Robert J. Morgan, *A Whig Embattled: The Presidency under John Tyler* (Lincoln: University of Nebraska Press, 1954), chap. 2; Binkley, *President and Congress*, 92–99.

98. Binkley, *President and Congress*, 99.

99. On the nomination of Polk as the first "dark horse," see Charles A. McCoy, *Polk and the Presidency* (Austin: University of Texas Press, 1960), chap. 2; on Van Buren's actions in 1844, see Donald B. Cole, *Martin Van Buren and the American Political System* (Princeton: Princeton University Press, 1984), chap. 13.

100. Stephen Skowronek, *The Politics Presidents Make: Leadership from John Adams to Bill Clinton* (Cambridge, Mass: Harvard University Press, 1997), 157.

101. McCoy, *Polk and the Presidency*, 74–75; White, *The Jacksonians*, 77–79.

102. Polk and the Democrats had long been committed to the passage of a low tariff act. "Just as [Jacksonians] interpreted territorial expansion as a way to diminish the threat of industrialization and urbanization," historian Paul Bergeron has written, "so they also perceived protective tariffs as beneficial only to manufacturers and therefore detrimental to the working classes and to the vision of an agrarian America." Paul H. Bergeron, *The Presidency of James K. Polk* (Lawrence: University Press of Kansas, 1987), 185–186. As Speaker of the House, Polk had supported Presidents Andrew Jackson and Martin Van Buren in their attempts to enact a low tariff law. And he devoted several pages of his first State of the Union address to a proposal that advocated a general lowering of tariff rates and the placing of rates on an *ad valorem* basis. Polk's dedication to a revision of the tariff did not falter as war with Mexico approached. Instead, he pressured Congress to pass the Walker Act in 1846, considering this assault on protectionism his most important domestic accomplishment—a vital measure for codifying the Jacksonian idea of economic justice.

103. Quoted in Binkley, *President and Congress*, 100–101.

104. White, *The Jacksonians*, 50.

105. Ibid., 51.

106. McCoy, *Polk and the Presidency*, 119–120; White, *The Jacksonians*, 66.

107. Binkley, *President and Congress*, 106.

108. White, *The Jacksonians*, 522, 529.

109. Richardson, *Messages and Papers of the Presidents*, 7:2962.

110. Binkley, *President and Congress*, 107.

111. Elbert B. Smith, *The Presidency of James Buchanan* (Lawrence: University Press of Kansas, 1975), 23–29.

112. *Dred Scott v. Sandford*, 19 Howard 1393 (1857).

113. Robert K. Murray and Tim H. Blessing, "The Presidential Performance Study: A Progress Report," *Journal of American History* 70:4 (December 1983): 535–555. This ranking was confirmed in a 1996 poll. Arthur M. Schlesinger Jr., "Rating the Presidents: Washington to Clinton," *Political Science Quarterly* 112:2 (summer 1997): 179–190.

114. For a critical examination of the view that Lincoln's presidency was one of constitutional dictatorship, see Herman Belz, *Lincoln and the Constitution: The Dictatorship Question Reconsidered* (Fort Wayne, Ind.: Louis A. Warren Lincoln Library and Museum, 1984).

115. James G. Randall, *Constitutional Problems under Lincoln*, rev. ed. (Urbana: University of Illinois Press, 1951), 30–47; and James G. Randall, "Lincoln in the Role of Dictator," *South Atlantic Quarterly* 28 (July 1929): 236–252. See also Belz, *Lincoln and the Constitution*, 5–6.

116. J. B. McClure, ed., *Abraham Lincoln's Speeches* (Chicago: Rhodes and McClure, 1891), 21, 22.

117. Corwin, *The President: Office and Powers*, 451; Binkley, *President and Congress*, 110.

118. Garry Wills, *Lincoln at Gettysburg: The Words That Remade America* (New York: Simon and Schuster, 1992), 145 (Wills's emphasis).

119. James M. McPherson, *Abraham Lincoln and the Second American Revolution* (New York: Oxford University Press, 1991), 41;

Letter, Lincoln to Greeley, August 22, 1862, in *The Collected Works of Abraham Lincoln,* ed. Roy P. Basler (New Brunswick, N.J.: Rutgers University Press, 1953), 5:388 (Lincoln's emphasis).

120. Allan Nevins, *The Emergence of Lincoln: Prologue to Civil War, 1859–1861* (New York: Scribner's, 1950), 233–239.

121. Abraham Lincoln to Joshua A. Speed, August 24, 1855, in *The Political Thought of Abraham Lincoln,* ed. Richard N. Current (Indianapolis, Ind.: Bobbs-Merrill, 1967), 80.

122. McClure, *Abraham Lincoln's Speeches,* 127.

123. Current, *Political Thought of Abraham Lincoln,* 95 (Lincoln's emphasis).

124. Basler, *Collected Works of Abraham Lincoln,* 4:191.

125. Charles Sumner, *The Promises of the Declaration of Independence: Eulogy on Abraham Lincoln* (Boston: Ticknor and Fields, 1865), 9.

126. Richardson, *Messages and Papers of the Presidents,* 7:3206.

127. Ibid., 7:3211 (Lincoln's emphasis), 3210.

128. Ibid., 7:3208.

129. For an account of Lincoln's views on slavery and the Constitution, see Robert K. Faulkner, "Lincoln and the Constitution," in *Revival of Constitutionalism,* ed. James Muller (Lincoln: University of Nebraska Press, 1988).

130. Roy Basler, ed., *The Collected Works of Abraham Lincoln* (New Brunswick, N.J.: Rutgers University Press, 1953), vol. 4: 149–151, 154, 155, 172, 183.

131. Phillip Shaw Paludan, *The Presidency of Abraham Lincoln* (Lawrence: University Press of Kansas, 1994), 33.

132. John G. Nicolay and John Hay, eds., *Complete Works of Abraham Lincoln* (Harrogate, Tenn.: Lincoln Memorial University, 1894), 10:66.

133. Randall, *Constitutional Problems under Lincoln,* 51.

134. Corwin, *The President: Office and Powers,* 62.

135. *Prize Cases,* 2 Black 635 (1863). For a discussion of these cases, see Randall, *Constitutional Problems under Lincoln,* 52–59.

136. *Prize Cases,* 67 U.S. 635 at 670.

137. Richardson, *Messages and Papers of the Presidents,* 7:3225.

138. For a discussion of the importance of the legal distinction between an insurrection and a war against an independent nation, see Randall, *Constitutional Problems under Lincoln,* 59–73.

139. "Proclamation of April 15, 1861," in *Messages and Papers of the Presidents,* ed. James D. Richardson (New York: Bureau of National Literature, 1897), 7:3299.

140. Corwin, *The President: Office and Powers,* 145–147.

141. Richardson, *Messages and Papers of the Presidents,* 7:3299.

142. Greeley cited in Mark E. Neeley, *The Last Best Hope on Earth: Abraham Lincoln and the Promise of America* (Cambridge: Harvard University Press, 1993), 129.

143. *Ex parte Milligan,* 4 Wall. 2 (1866). For a discussion of this case, see Randall, *Constitutional Problems under Lincoln,* 180–186.

144. *Ex parte Milligan,* 4 Wall. 2 at 127.

145. Corwin, *The President: Office and Powers,* 234.

146. See the *Vallandigham* case (1 Wall. 243), decided in 1864, which found acceptable the arrest and sentencing of a prominent antiwar agitator, who was detained for a speech that he gave in Mount Vernon, Ohio.

147. Randall, *Constitutional Problems under Lincoln,* 521.

148. Ibid., 91.

149. For a discussion of Lincoln's policy of emancipation, see Faulkner, "Lincoln and the Constitution."

150. Kenneth R. Mayer, *With the Stroke of a Pen: Executive Orders and Presidential Power* (Princeton, N.J.: Princeton University Press, 2001, 34–35.

151. Richardson, *Messages and Papers of the Presidents,* 7:3359.

152. Letter, Abraham Lincoln to James C. Conkling, August 26, 1863, in Basler, *Collected Works of Abraham Lincoln,* 6:408–409.

153. Cited in McPherson, *Abraham Lincoln and the Second American Revolution,* 34–35.

154. Letter, Abraham Lincoln to Charles D. Robinson, August 17, 1864, and Lincoln interview with Alexander W. Randall and Joseph T. Mills, August 19, 1864, in Basler, *Collected Works of Abraham Lincoln,* 7:499–500 and 7:506–507.

155. Current, *Political Thought of Abraham Lincoln,* 88–89 (Lincoln's emphasis).

156. McPherson, *Abraham Lincoln and the Second American Revolution,* 86.

157. Ibid.

158. Phillip Shaw Paludan, *The Presidency of Abraham Lincoln* (Lawrence: University Press of Kansas, 1994), 319.

159. Basler, *Collected Works of Abraham Lincoln,* 7:23.

160. Belz, *Lincoln and the Constitution,* 15.

161. "Democratic Platform of 1864," in *History of American Presidential Elections,* ed. Arthur Schlesinger Jr. and Fred I. Israel (New York: Chelsea, 1971), 2:1179–1180.

162. Harold M. Hyman, "Election of 1864," in *History of American Presidential Elections,* ed. Arthur Schlesinger Jr. and Fred I. Israel (New York: Chelsea, 1971), 2:1167; see also Lord Charnwood, *Abraham Lincoln* (Garden City, N.Y.: Garden City Publishing Company, 1917), 414–415.

163. Quoted in Hyman, "Election of 1864," 1170.

164. Belz, *Lincoln and the Constitution,* 16.

165. Randall, *Constitutional Problems under Lincoln,* chap. 9.

166. Quoted in Hyman, "Election of 1864," 1175.

167. Nicolay and Hay, *Complete Works of Abraham Lincoln,* 10:263–264.

168. Ibid., 10:263.

169. Randall, *Constitutional Problems under Lincoln,* 522.

170. Benjamin Wade and Henry Winter Davis, "The Wade-Davis Manifesto," in *History of American Presidential Elections,* ed. Arthur Schlesinger Jr. and Fred I. Israel (New York: Chelsea, 1971), 2:1195–1196.

171. Binkley, *President and Congress,* 128. For a discussion of the Reconstruction controversy inherited by Andrew Johnson, see Albert Castel, *The Presidency of Andrew Johnson* (Lawrence: University Press of Kansas, 1979), 17–20.

172. Quoted in Castel, *Presidency of Andrew Johnson,* 20.

173. Nicole Mellow and Jeffrey Tulis, "Andrew Johnson and the Politics of Failure," in Stephen Skowronek and Matthew Glassman, eds., *Formative Acts: Reckoning with Agency in American Politics* (Philadelphia: University of Pennsylvania Press, 2007).

174. Ibid., 31.

175. Mellow and Tulis, "Andrew Johnson and the Politics of Failure."

176. On the struggle between Johnson and Congress over civil rights legislation, see ibid., 68–76; and Binkley, *President and Congress,* 136–137.

177. Mellow and Tulis, "Andrew Johnson and the Politics of Failure" in Keith Whittington, *Constitutional Construction: Divide Powers and Constitutional Meaning* (Cambridge, Mass.: Harvard University Press, 1999), 114–115, 125.

178. Binkley, *President and Congress,* 138.

179. Castel, *Presidency of Andrew Johnson,* 68–70.

180. For a discussion of how the constitutional and political constraints on popular rhetoric during the nineteenth century contributed to Johnson's problems with Congress, see Tulis, *The Rhetorical Presidency,* 87–93.

181. "The House of Representatives, Articles of Impeachment against President Andrew Johnson," March 2–3, 1868, in *Growth of Presidential Power: A Documented History,* ed. William M. Goldsmith (New York and London: Chelsea House, 1974), 2:1068–1069.

182. The improper rhetoric charge had strong support in the House, passing by a vote of 87–41. *New York Times,* March 4, 1868, 1.

183. *New York Times,* March 4, 1861, 1.

184. David Miller Dewitt, *The Impeachment and Trial of Andrew Johnson* (Madison: State Historical Society of Wisconsin, 1967), 517–518.

185. Gideon Welles, *Diary of Gideon Welles* (Boston: Houghton Mifflin, 1911), 3:560.

186. Goldsmith, *Growth of Presidential Power,* 2:1102.

187. Binkley, *President and Congress,* 147.

188. George F. Hoar, *Autobiography of Seventy Years* (New York: Scribner's, 1903), 2:46.

189. Frank Scaturro, *President Grant: Reconsidered* (Lanham, Md.: University Press of America, 1998), 60.

190. Ibid.

191. Morton Keller, *Affairs of State: Public Life in the Late Nineteenth Century* (Cambridge: Harvard University Press, 1977), 95.

192. Geoffrey Perret, *Ulysses S. Grant: Soldier and President* (New York: Random House, 1997), 393–400.

193. Ibid., 409–410; Keller, *Affairs of State,* 96–97.

194. Perret, *Ulysses S. Grant,* 416.

195. Leonard D. White, *The Republican Era: 1869–1901: A Study in Administrative History* (New York: Macmillan, 1958), 372–376.

196. Ulysses S. Grant, "First Statement to Congress on Civil Service Reform," December 5, 1870, in *Growth of Presidential Power: A Documented History,* ed. William M. Goldsmith (New York and London: Chelsea House, 1974), 2:986.

197. Richardson, *Messages and Papers of the Presidents,* 9:4254–4255; White, *Republican Era,* 281–287.

198. Binkley, *President and Congress,* 161.

199. The scandals that afflicted the federal government during the Grant administration were, as historian Samuel Eliot Morison has written, merely "the summit of a pyramid of corruption in the Northern states." In New York City, William Marcy ("Boss") Tweed built a Democratic machine, known as Tammany Hall, that stole $100 million from the city treasury. A similar ring, which operated at the state level under the auspices of the Republican Party (but included some Democrats as well), perpetrated systematic fraud in canal construction, which caused estimated losses to the state of nearly $1 million. See Samuel Eliot Morison, *The Oxford History of the American People* (New York: New American Library, 1972), 3:36.

200. Rutherford B. Hayes, "Inaugural Address," March 5, 1877, in *Messages and Papers of the Presidents,* ed. James D. Richardson (New York: Bureau of National Literature, 1897), 6:4396.

201. Binkley, *President and Congress,* 155.

202. Charles Richard Williams, ed., *Diary and Letters of Rutherford B. Hayes,* 5 vols. (Columbus: Ohio State Archeological and Historical Society, 1924), April 22, 1877, 3:430.

203. Ibid., December 12, 1877, 3:454.

204. Binkley, *President and Congress,* 157.

205. Rutherford B. Hayes, "Letter to General E. A. Merritt Defining Criteria for Appointments to the New York Custom House," February 4, 1879, in *Growth of Presidential Power: A Documented History,* ed. William M. Goldsmith (New York and London: Chelsea House, 1974), 2:1112.

206. Ibid., 2:1113.

207. Williams, *Diary and Letters of Rutherford B. Hayes,* July 4, 1880, 3:612–613.

208. The Stalwarts had dubbed Sen. James G. Blaine's followers "Half-breeds," implying that they were deficient in Republican loyalty. In reality, however, the partisanship of the Blaine wing, although it paid lip service to civil service reform, was just as strong.

209. Morton Keller, *Affairs of State Life in Late Nineteenth Century America* (Cambridge, Mass: Harvard University Press, 1977), 266–268.

210. Binkley, *President and Congress,* 158–159.

211. Quoted in Theodore Clark Smith, *James Abram Garfield: Life and Letters* (New Haven: Yale University Press, 1925), 2:1109.

212. John A. Garraty, *The New Commonwealth: 1877–1890* (New York: Harper and Row, 1968), 273; White, *Republican Era,* 34–35; Binkley, *President and Congress,* 159–160.

213. Williams, *Diary and Letters of Rutherford B. Hayes,* 4:23.

214. Garraty, *New Commonwealth,* 276.

215. White, *Republican Era,* 393; see also 301–302.

216. Matthew Crenson and Benjamin Ginsberg, *Presidential Power: Unchecked and Unbalanced* (New York: W.W. Norton, 2007).

217. Garraty, *New Commonwealth,* 287; Keller, *Affairs of State,* 546.

218. Grover Cleveland, "Message to the Senate on the President's Power of Removal and Suspension, March 1, 1886," in *The Growth of Presidential Power: A Documented History,* ed. William M. Goldsmith (New York and London: Chelsea House, 1974), 2:1121.

219. Grover Cleveland, *Presidential Problems* (New York: Century, 1904), 76.

220. White, *Republican Era,* 38.

221. Ibid., 66.

222. Garraty, *New Commonwealth,* 295.

223. Woodrow Wilson, *Congressional Government* (Boston: Houghton Mifflin, 1885; New York: Meridian Books, 1956), 31.

224. John Sherman, *Recollections of Forty Years in the House, Senate, and Cabinet* (Chicago: Werner Company, 1895), 2:1032.

225. Garraty, *New Commonwealth,* 305.

226. Keller, *Affairs of State,* 302–303.

227. James Bryce, *The American Commonwealth* (London: Macmillan, 1891), 1:115.

228. Binkley, *President and Congress,* 182.

229. Garraty, *New Commonwealth,* 306–308.

230. John P. Altgeld, "Telegram to President Grover Cleveland on the Use of Federal Troops in Illinois," July 5, 1894, in *The Growth of Presidential Power: A Documented History,* ed. William M. Goldsmith (New York and London: Chelsea House, 1974), 2:1155.

231. Grover Cleveland, "Telegram to Governor John P. Altgeld on the Use of Federal Troops in Illinois," July 6, 1894, in *The Growth of Presidential Power: A Documented History,* ed. William M. Goldsmith (New York and London: Chelsea House, 1974), 2:1157.

232. Scott C. James, "The Evolution of the Presidency: Between the Promise and the Fear," in Joel D. Aberbach and Mark Peterson, eds., *The Executive Branch* (New York: Oxford University Press, 2005), 16–17.

233. *In re Debs,* 158 U.S. 564 (1895).

234. Corwin, *The President: Office and Powers,* 134.

235. J. Rogers Hollingsworth, *The Whirligig of Politics: The Democracy of Cleveland and Bryan* (Chicago: University of Chicago Press, 1963), 24–25.

236. Garraty, *New Commonwealth,* 306.

237. Binkley, *President and Congress,* 189.

238. Lewis L. Gould, *The Presidency of William McKinley* (Lawrence: University Press of Kansas, 1980), 93.

239. Binkley, *President and Congress,* 191.

240. Charles S. Olcott, *William McKinley* (Boston: Houghton Mifflin, 1916), 2:296.

241. William McKinley, speech in Chariton, Iowa, October 13, 1898, McKinley Papers, Library of Congress, Washington, D.C. See also Tulis, *The Rhetorical Presidency*, 87.

242. Lewis L. Gould, *The Modern American Presidency* (Lawrence: University Press of Kansas, 2003), 13.

243. Richard Hofstadter, *The Age of Reform: From Bryan to F. D. R.* (New York: Knopf, 1955), 5.

244. Theodore Roosevelt, *The Works of Theodore Roosevelt* (New York: Scribner's, 1926), 20:340.

245. Samuel and Dorothy Rosenman, *Presidential Style: Some Giants and a Pygmy in the White House* (New York: Harper and Row, 1976), 123.

246. Roosevelt, *Works*, 20:347.

247. Ibid., 347.

248. Hamilton and Madison, *Letters of Pacificus and Helvidius*, 10.

249. Roosevelt, *Works*, 20:414. Abraham Lincoln's defense of the Union and audacious use of executive power occurred under the stress of a domestic rebellion. His understanding of the national government's powers in less dire circumstances was far more circumspect than Theodore Roosevelt's.

250. Tulis, *The Rhetorical Presidency*, 97–116.

251. Roosevelt, *Works*, 20:416.

252. Ibid., 20:342.

253. George Mowry, *The Era of Theodore Roosevelt: 1900–1912* (New York: Harper and Brothers, 1958), 201.

254. "Address Delivered before the Iroquois Club at a Banquet in Chicago, May 10, 1905," in *The Roosevelt Policy*, ed. William Griffith (New York: Current Literature, 1919), i:266–273; see also Mowry, *Era of Theodore Roosevelt*, 201.

255. Mowry, *Era of Theodore Roosevelt*, 203.

256. Ibid., 205.

257. Mark Sullivan, *Our Times: Pre-War America* (New York: Scribner's, 1930), 3:80.

258. Ibid., 3:240.

259. Mowry, *Era of Theodore Roosevelt*, 203.

260. Gould, *The Modern American Presidency*, 24.

261. Tulis, *The Rhetorical Presidency*, 96.

262. A full account of Roosevelt's activities during the strike appears in a letter he wrote to Gov. Winthrop Murray Crane of Massachusetts, who was a concerned and apprehensive observer. See Roosevelt to Crane, October 22, 1902, in *Letters of Theodore Roosevelt*, ed. Elting Morrison (Cambridge, Mass.: Harvard University Press, 1951), 3:359–360.

263. Mowry, *Era of Theodore Roosevelt*, 140.

264. Ibid, 214–216.

265. Mayer, *With the Stroke of a Pen*, 51–52; 75.

266. Roosevelt, *Works*, 15:117.

267. Herbert Croly, *The Promise of American Life* (New York: Dutton, 1963; New York: Macmillan, 1909), 313.

268. Roosevelt, *Works*, 15:114.

269. Ibid., 20:549–550.

270. Letter, Theodore Roosevelt to Marcus Alonzo Hanna, October 5, 1903, in *The Letters of Theodore Roosevelt*, ed. Elting E. Morrison (Cambridge: Harvard University Press, 1951), 3:625.

271. Roosevelt, *Works*, 20:501.

272. Ibid., 501.

273. Goldsmith, *Growth of Presidential Power*, 2:1233.

274. Roosevelt, *Works*, 15:256–257.

275. Ibid., 20:490.

276. Mowry, *Era of Theodore Roosevelt*, 185.

277. Goldsmith, *Growth of Presidential Power*, 2:1269.

278. Mowry, *Era of Theodore Roosevelt*, 226.

279. Ibid., 180; Roosevelt, *Works*, 20:378.

280. William Howard Taft, *Our Chief Magistrate and His Powers* (New York: Columbia University Press, 1916), 139–140.

281. Elmer E. Cornwell Jr., *Presidential Leadership of Public Opinion* (Bloomington: Indiana University Press, 1965), 27.

282. Goldsmith, *Growth of Presidential Power* 2:1269.

283. Quoted in Mowry, *Era of Theodore Roosevelt*, 245.

284. Taft cited in William Henry Harbaugh, *Power and Responsibility: The Life and Times of Theodore Roosevelt* (New York: Farrar, Straus, and Cudahy, 1961), 384.

285. Ibid., 246, 232.

286. Binkley, *President and Congress*, 200. The only office that William Howard Taft ever ran for, except the presidency, was that of justice of the State Superior Court in Ohio.

287. For a discussion of the revolt in Congress against the regular party leadership, see Lawrence C. Dodd and Richard L. Schott, *Congress and the Administrative State* (New York: Wiley, 1979), 58–100.

288. Mowry, *Era of Theodore Roosevelt*, 272.

289. Goldsmith, *Growth of Presidential Power*, 3:1343.

290. Woodrow Wilson, "Cabinet Government in the United States," *International Review* 7 (August 1879): 150–151.

291. Woodrow Wilson's revised thoughts on presidential power were first expressed in 1900, in the preface to the fifteenth printing of *Congressional Government*. The growing role of the United States in world affairs and other developments, he had come to believe, were likely to place the president at the center of national politics and government. See Woodrow Wilson, *Congressional Government* (New York: Meridian Books, 1956; Boston: Houghton Mifflin, 1885), 19–23. Subsequently, Theodore Roosevelt's dynamic leadership convinced Wilson that this likelihood had become a reality. Wilson's mature views on presidential leadership and constitutional change are expressed in his *Constitutional Government in the United States* (New York: Columbia University Press, 1908).

292. Quoted in David Lawrence, *The True Story of Woodrow Wilson* (New York: Doran, 1924), 39.

293. Wilson, *Constitutional Government*, 68–69. For a comprehensive treatment of Wilson's understanding of constitutional government, see Daniel D. Stid, *The President as Statesman: Woodrow Wilson and the Constitution* (Lawrence: University Press of Kansas, 1998).

294. Arthur S. Link, *Wilson and the New Freedom* (Princeton: Princeton University Press, 1956), 145.

295. Woodrow Wilson, *The Papers of Woodrow Wilson*, ed. Arthur S. Link (Princeton: Princeton University Press, 1966–1985), 27:151. On Wilson's contribution to the expansion of popular leadership in the United States, see Tulis, *The Rhetorical Presidency*, 117–144.

296. Cornwell, *Presidential Leadership of Public Opinion*, 32–44.

297. *New York Times*, April 8, 1913, 8.

298. Cornwell, *Presidential Leadership of Public Opinion*, 46.

299. Wilson, *Papers*, 27:269–270.

300. Quoted in Arthur S. Link, *Woodrow Wilson and the Progressive Era: 1910–1917* (New York: Harper and Row, 1954), 21.

301. Woodrow Wilson, "Monopoly or Opportunity," in *The Growth of Presidential Power: A Documented History*, ed. William M. Goldsmith (New York and London: Chelsea House, 1974), 3:1334–1342.

302. A. Maurice Low, "The South in the Saddle," *Harper's Weekly* 57 (February 8, 1913): 20; Gould, *The Modern American Presidency*, 48.

303. *New Republic*, December 5, 1914, 11–12.

304. Link, *The New Freedom*, 277.

305. Wilson, *Papers*, 41:526.

306. Quoted in Baker, *Woodrow Wilson: Life and Letters,* 7:185–186.

307. Corwin, *The President: Office and Powers,* 237.

308. Goldsmith, *Growth of Presidential Power,* 3:1705, 1711.

309. Ernest R. May, "Wilson (1917–1918)," in *The Ultimate Decision: The President as Commander in Chief,* ed. Ernest R. May (New York: Braziller, 1960), 131.

310. Wilson, *Constitutional Government in the United States,* 77–79. On Wilson's dual conception of the presidency, see Daniel Stid, "Rhetorical Leadership and 'Common Counsel' in the Presidency of Woodrow Wilson," in Ellis, *Speaking to the People.*

311. Quoted in Rosenman and Rosenman, *Presidential Style,* 241.

312. Wilson, *Papers,* 51:381.

313. *New Republic,* November 9, 1918, cited in Thomas J. Knock, *To End All Wars: Woodrow Wilson and the Quest for a New World Order* (New York: Oxford University Press, 1992), 186.

314. Quoted in Warren, *President as World Leader,* 108. The Republicans outnumbered the Democrats in the Sixty-sixth Congress by 240 to 190 in the House and 49 to 47 in the Senate.

315. *New Republic,* May 24, 1919, 103, cited in Knock, *To End All Wars,* 262.

316. Quoted in Robert K. Murray, *The Harding Era: Warren G. Harding and His Administration* (Minneapolis: University of Minnesota Press, 1969), 70. Confusion still exists about how the word *normalcy* originated. The best guess is that President Warren G. Harding meant *normality* but said *normalcy.*

317. Henry Cabot Lodge cited in Andrew Sinclair, *The Available Man: The Life behind the Masks of Warren Gamaliel Harding* (New York: Macmillan, 1965), 152 (Lodge's emphasis).

318. Binkley, *President and Congress,* 217.

319. George Rothwell Brown, *The Leadership of Congress* (New York: Arno Press, 1974; Indianapolis, Ind.: Bobbs-Merrill, 1922), 258.

320. Murray, *The Harding Era,* 128.

321. Paul P. Van Riper, *History of the United States Civil Service* (Evanston, Ill.: Row, Peterson, 1958), 287.

322. William Allen White, *The Autobiography of William Allen White* (New York: Macmillan, 1946), 619.

323. Quoted in Murray, *The Harding Era,* 418.

324. Herbert Emmerich, *Federal Organization and Administrative Management* (Tuscaloosa: University of Alabama Press, 1971), 40–41. For a discussion of the enactment and early history of the Budget and Accounting Act, see Goldsmith, *Growth of Presidential Power,* 3:1478–1495.

325. Murray, *The Harding Era,* 178.

326. Quoted in ibid., 418.

327. Cornwell, *Presidential Leadership of Public Opinion,* 73.

328. Calvin Coolidge, *The Autobiography of Calvin Coolidge* (New York: Cosmopolitan, 1929), 232.

329. Binkley, *President and Congress,* 223.

330. Edward S. Martin, "Shall Business Run the World?" *Harper's Magazine,* February 1925, 381.

331. Murray, *The Harding Era,* 505.

332. "The Destiny of America," delivered at Memorial Day services, Northampton, Mass., May 30, 1923, in Calvin Coolidge, *The Price of Freedom: Speeches and Addresses* (New York: Scribner's, 1924), 342; and Calvin Coolidge, "Inaugural Address," March 4, 1925, in *Calvin Coolidge, 1872–1933,* ed. Philip R. Moran (Dobbs Ferry, N.Y.: Oceana, 1970), 65.

333. TRB, "Washington Notes," *New Republic,* February 10, 1926, 326.

334. The reporter quoted is Jay C. Hayden of the *Detroit News,* who covered the White House for sixteen years. Hayden considered Calvin Coolidge to be as masterful as Theodore Roosevelt at the "human interest" game, "although the Coolidge process was more subtle" (*Literary Digest,* July 25, 1931, 8).

335. Quoted in Cornwell, *Presidential Leadership of Public Opinion,* 90.

336. Coolidge, *Autobiography,* 231.

337. William Allen White, *Calvin Coolidge: The Man Who Is President* (New York: Macmillan, 1925), 137.

338. Cornwell, *Presidential Leadership of Public Opinion,* 92.

339. Ellis Hawley, "The Constitution of the Hoover and F. Roosevelt Presidency during the Depression Era: 1930–1939," in *The Constitution and the American Presidency,* ed. Martin L. Fausold and Alan Shank (Albany: State University of New York Press, 1991), 89–91.

340. Herbert Hoover, *The Challenge to Liberty* (New York: Scribner's, 1934), 125–126.

341. Robert Allen and Drew Pearson, *Washington Merry-Go-Round* (New York: Horace Liveright, 1931), 66.

342. Martin L. Fausold, *The Presidency of Herbert C. Hoover* (Lawrence: University Press of Kansas, 1985), 49.

343. Quoted in Binkley, *President and Congress,* 229.

344. Herbert Hoover, *The Memoirs of Herbert Hoover: The Great Depression, 1929–1941* (New York: Macmillan, 1952), 3:104.

345. Walter Lippmann, "The Peculiar Weakness of Mr. Hoover," *Harper's Magazine,* June 1930, 5.

346. Cornwell, *Presidential Leadership of Public Opinion,* 113.

347. Fausold, *The Presidency of Herbert C. Hoover,* 111.

348. Quoted in Stefan Lorant, *The Presidency: A Pictorial History of Presidential Elections from Washington to Truman* (New York: Macmillan, 1951), 594.

349. Many political scientists, most notably Fred I. Greenstein, consider Franklin D. Roosevelt to be the first modern president. For example, see Fred I. Greenstein, "Introduction: Toward a Modern Presidency," in *Leadership in the Modern Presidency,* ed. Fred I. Greenstein (Cambridge: Harvard University Press, 1988). As Jeffrey Tulis argues, however, many of the characteristics of the executive that Greenstein identifies as distinctly modern, such as legislative leadership, found practical expression in the nineteenth century if not earlier. See Tulis, *The Rhetorical Presidency,* especially chap. 1. See also Stephen Skowronek, *The Politics Presidents Make: Leadership from John Adams to George Bush* (Cambridge: Harvard University Press, 1993).

350. Robert K. Murray and Tim H. Blessing, "The Presidential Performance Study: A Progress Report," *Journal of American History* 70:3 (December 1983): 542; Arthur M. Schlesinger Jr., "Rating the Presidents: Washington to Clinton," *Political Science Quarterly* 112:2 (summer, 1997): 179–190. A 2005 poll conducted by the *Wall Street Journal,* with James Lindgren of Northwestern Law School and the Federalist Society, in which the editors adjusted the results to give Democratic and Republican leaning scholars equal weight, rated Roosevelt third, behind George Washington and Abraham Lincoln. http://www.opinionjournal.com/extra/?id=110007243.

351. Quoted in Robert M. Collins, *The Business Response to Keynes* (New York: Columbia University Press, 1981), 28.

352. *New York Times,* March 4, 1933, 1.

353. Clinton Rossiter, *The American Presidency,* 2d ed. (New York: Harcourt Brace, 1960), 145.

354. Franklin D. Roosevelt, *Public Papers and Addresses,* 13 vols. (New York: Random House, 1938–1950), 1:12.

355. Ibid., 1:15.

356. Ibid., 2:24–26.

357. Roosevelt was the last president to be inaugurated on March 4. The Twentieth Amendment, added to the Constitution in 1933, established noon on January 20 as the beginning of the president's

and the vice president's four-year term and noon on January 3 as the start of the new term for representatives and senators. The long and awkward interregnum that the nation endured between Herbert Hoover and Franklin D. Roosevelt, in the midst of the Great Depression, lent dramatic testimony to the amendment's wisdom.

358. The term *fireside chat* originated with Robert Trout of the Columbia Broadcasting System's Washington station, who introduced Roosevelt on the occasion of his first radio address. At ten o'clock on the evening of March 12, 1933, Trout told sixty million people, seated before twenty million radios, that "the President wants to come into your home and sit at your fireside for a little fireside chat" (Kenneth S. Davis, *FDR: The New Deal Years, 1933–1937* [New York: Random House, 1986], 60).

359. Roosevelt, *Public Papers and Addresses,* 2:65.

360. Raymond Moley, *After Seven Years* (New York: Harper and Brothers, 1939), 155.

361. Letter, Hugo Black to James Farley, June 19, 1934, box 34, folder "Roosevelt, Franklin D., 1934," James Farley Papers, Manuscript Division, Library of Congress.

362. Roosevelt, *Public Papers and Addresses,* 3:317–318.

363. Cornwell, *Presidential Leadership of Public Opinion,* 131.

364. Roosevelt, *Public Papers and Addresses,* 1:659.

365. Fred I. Greenstein, "Nine Presidents in Search of a Modern Presidency," in *Leadership in the Modern Presidency,* ed. Fred I. Greenstein (Cambridge: Harvard University Press, 1988), 299.

366. Matthew Dickinson, "The Executive Office of the President: The Paradox of Politicization," in Joel D. Aberbach and Mark A. Peterson, eds., *The Executive Branch* (New York: Oxford University Press, 2005).

367. The term *administrative presidency* is drawn from Richard Nathan's book on the use of administrative strategies by modern presidents to pursue their policy objectives. See Richard Nathan, *The Administrative Presidency* (New York: Wiley, 1983).

368. Roosevelt, *Public Papers and Addresses,* 2:161.

369. *Humphrey's Executor v. United States,* 295 U.S. 602 (1935); *Schechter Poultry Corp. v. United States,* 295 U.S. 495 (1935).

370. *Myers v. United States,* 272 U.S. 53 (1926).

371. William E. Leuchtenburg, *The Supreme Court Reborn: The Constituional Revolution in the Age of Roosevelt* (New York: Oxford University Press, 1995), 236.

372. Hawley, "The Constitution of the Hoover and F. Roosevelt Presidency," 99–100.

373. *United States v. Curtiss-Wright Export Corporation,* 299 U.S. 304 (1936).

374. *United States v. Belmont,* 301 U.S. 324 (1937).

375. David M. Kennedy, *Freedom from Fear: The American People in Depression and War, 1929–1945* (New York: Oxford University Press, 1999), 474.

376. Roosevelt, *Public Papers and Addresses,* vol. 9, 671–672.

377. *Congressional Record,* 77th Cong., 2d sess., 1942, 7044.

378. Hawley, "The Constitution of the Hoover and F. Roosevelt Presidency," 101.

379. R. Shep Melnick, "The Courts, Jurisprudence, and the Executive Branch," in Aberbach and Peterson, *The Executive Branch,* 458.

380. *Yakus v. U.S.* 321 U.S. 414 (1944).

381. *Ex Parte Quirin* 317 U.S. 1 (1942).

382. Andrew Rudalevige, *The New Imperial Presidency: Renewing Presidential Power after Watergate* (Ann Arbor: University of Michigan Press, 2005), 230.

383. *Korematsu v. U.S.* 323 U.S. 214 (1944).

384. Ibid., 245-46.

385. David M. Kennedy, *Freedom from Fear: The American People in Depression and War, 1929–1945* (New York: Oxford University Press, 1999), 756–759.

386. Harry Truman, *Memoirs,* 2 vols. (Garden City, N.Y.: Doubleday, 1955), 1:4–5; and William E. Leuchtenburg, *In the Shadow of FDR: From Harry Truman to Ronald Reagan,* rev. ed. (Ithaca and London: Cornell University Press, 1985), 1.

387. William S. White, "The Memoirs of Harry S. Truman," *New Republic,* November 7, 1955, 16.

388. Alonzo L. Hamby, "Harry S. Truman: Insecurity and Responsibility," in *Leadership in the Modern Presidency,* ed. Fred I. Greenstein (Cambridge: Harvard University Press, 1988), 42–43.

389. Quoted in Larry Berman, *The New American Presidency* (Boston: Little, Brown, 1987), 212.

390. Leuchtenburg, *Shadow of FDR,* 23.

391. Harry S. Truman, "Executive Order 9308 Establishing the President's Committee on Civil Rights," December 5, 1946, in *The Growth of Presidential Power: A Documented History,* William M. Goldsmith (New York and London: Chelsea House, 1974), 3:1568–1569.

392. *Public Papers of the Presidents of the United States: Harry S. Truman* (Washington, D.C.: Government Printing Office, 1961–1966), March 1, 1951, 176.

393. Greenstein, "Nine Presidents," 334.

394. Hamby, *Man of the People,* 309–311. With the enactment of the Goldwater-Nichols Act in 1986, the president's authority over the military was further strengthened. It authorized the president, rather than the Joint Chiefs of Staff, to select a chairman to communicate with the civilian government. Goldwater-Nichols thus clearly established the Chairman of the Joint Chiefs of Staff to be the principal military advisor to the president.

395. Peri E. Arnold, *Making the Managerial Presidency: Comprehensive Reorganization Planning, 1905–1980* (Princeton: Princeton University Press, 1986), 127.

396. Martha Derthick and Paul J. Quirk, *The Politics of Deregulation* (Washington, D.C.: Brookings, 1985), 61–74.

397. Truman's budget director James Webb, as quoted in Arnold, *Making the Managerial Presidency,* 142.

398. Fred I. Greenstein, *The Hidden-Hand Presidency: Eisenhower as Leader* (New York: Basic Books, 1982).

399. Quoted in Leuchtenburg, *Shadow of FDR,* 49.

400. Alonzo L. Hamby, *Liberalism and Its Challengers: FDR to Reagan* (New York: Oxford University Press, 1985), 126.

401. Quoted in Stephen E. Ambrose, "The Eisenhower Revival," in *Rethinking the Presidency,* ed. Thomas E. Cronin (Boston: Little, Brown, 1982), 107.

402. Greenstein, *The Hidden-Hand Presidency,* chap. 5.

403. Rossiter, *American Presidency,* 163.

404. *Brown v. Board of Education of Topeka,* 347 U.S. 483 (1954).

405. "Dwight D. Eisenhower's Little Rock Executive Order," in *The Evolving Presidency: Addresses, Cases, Letters, Reports, Resolutions, Transcripts, and Other Landmark Documents, 1787–1998,* ed. Michael Nelson (Washington, D.C: CQ Press, 1999), 145–149.

406. Philip G. Henderson, *Managing the Presidency: The Eisenhower Legacy—From Kennedy to Reagan* (Boulder: Westview Press, 1988), 17–24.

407. Greenstein, "Nine Presidents," 307–311.

408. Ambrose, "The Eisenhower Revival," 108.

409. Quoted in Elmo Richardson, *The Presidency of Dwight D. Eisenhower* (Lawrence: University Press of Kansas, 1979), 53.

410. John F. Kennedy, speech to the National Press Club, Washington, D.C., January 14, 1960, in *"Let the Word Go Forth": The*

Speeches, Statements and Writings of John F. Kennedy, ed. Theodore C. Sorensen (New York: Delacorte, 1988), 17–23.

411. Leuchtenburg, *Shadow of FDR,* 119 See also Michael Nelson, "Kennedy and Achilles: A Classical Approach to Political Science," *PS: Political Science and Politics* 29:3 (September 1996): 505–510.

412. John F. Kennedy, "Acceptance of Presidential Nomination," Democratic National Convention, Los Angeles, California, in *"Let the Word Go Forth": The Speeches, Statements, and Writings of John F. Kennedy,* ed. Theodore C. Sorenson (New York: Delacorte, 1988), 101. On Kennedy's legacy, see Carl M. Brauer, "John F. Kennedy: The Endurance of Inspirational Leadership," in *Leadership in the Modern Presidency,* ed. Fred I. Greenstein, (Cambridge: Harvard University Press, 1988), 119.

413. Nelson, "Kennedy and Achilles."

414. Brauer, "John F. Kennedy," 119.

415. Bruce Miroff, "The Presidency and the Public: Leadership as Spectacle," in *The Presidency and the Political System,* 5th ed., ed. Michael Nelson (Washington, D.C.: CQ Press, 1998), 305.

416. Brauer, "John F. Kennedy," 118.

417. Theodore Lowi, *The Personal President: Power Invested, Promise Unfulfilled* (Ithaca and London: Cornell University Press, 1985).

418. Ibid., 75–76; Harold F. Bass, "The President and the National Party Organization," in *Presidents and Their Parties: Leadership or Neglect?* ed. Robert Harmel (New York: Praeger, 1984), 62.

419. Gould, *The Modern American Presidency,* 133.

420. Arthur M. Schlesinger Jr., *The Cycles of American History* (Boston: Houghton Mifflin, 1986), 414.

421. Recent findings, based on tapes of President John F. Kennedy's meetings with the Executive Committee of the National Security Council (ExComm), the group convened to manage the Cuban missile crisis, support the proposition that this was Kennedy's finest hour. See Ernest R. May and Philip Zelikow, eds., *The Kennedy Tapes: Inside the White House during the Cuban Missile Crisis* (Cambridge: Harvard University Press, 1997), 663–701.

422. Theodore H. White, *In Search of History: A Personal Adventure* (New York: Harper and Row, 1986), 518.

423. Robert A. Caro, *Master of the Senate: The Years of Lyndon Johnson* (New York: Random House, 2002); Rowland Evans and Robert Novak, *Lyndon B. Johnson: The Exercise of Power* (New York: New American Library, 1966).

424. Lyndon Baines Johnson, *The Vantage Point: Perspectives on the Presidency, 1963–1969* (New York: Holt, Rinehart, and Winston, 1971), 18.

425. The Equal Employment Opportunity Commission, charged with preventing racial and sexual discriminatory practices in employment was stripped of its authority to file suit in the Courts. The Commission had the power to make recommendations, but only the Justice Department had the power to initiate a suit. The Justice Department, in turn, could file suits only under conditions where obvious discriminatory practices, which characterized Jim Crow laws in the South, prevailed. On Dirksen's relationship with Johnson and the role that the Republican Senate leader played in enacting civil rights legislation, see Byron C. Hulsey, *Everett C. Dirksen and His Presidents: How a Senate Giant Shaped American Politics* (Lawrence: University Press of Kansas, 2000), 183–204.

426. R. Shep Melnick, "The Courts, Congress, and Programmatic Rights," in *Remaking American Politics,* eds. Richard A. Harris and Sidney M. Milkis (Boulder: Westview Press, 1989), 192–195. In 1954 in *Brown v. Board of Education of Topeka* (347 U.S. 483), the Supreme Court declared segregated public schools unconstitutional.

427. *Public Papers of the Presidents of the United States: Lyndon Baines Johnson, 1963–1964* (Washington, D.C.: Government Printing Office, 1965), 1704.

428. David Broder, "Consensus Politics: End of an Experiment," *Atlantic Monthly,* October 1966, 62.

429. Greenstein, "Nine Presidents," 329.

430. Author interview with Harry MacPherson, aide to President Lyndon B. Johnson, July 30, 1985.

431. Walter Cronkite interview with Lyndon B. Johnson, no. 1, December 27, 1969: "Why I Chose Not to Run," 5 (Austin, Texas: Lyndon Baines Johnson Library).

432. Richard M. Pious, *The American Presidency* (New York: Basic Books, 1979), 399.

433. Senate Foreign Relations Committee, "National Commitments," Senate Report 797, 90th Cong., 1st sess., 1967, 19–22.

434. George E. Reedy, *The Twilight of the Presidency* (New York: New American Library, 1970), xv.

435. Greenstein, "Nine Presidents," 330.

436. "The McGovern-Fraser Commission Report," in Nelson, *The Evolving Presidency,* 177–183.

437. Richard Nixon, *RN: The Memoirs of Richard Nixon* (New York: Warner, 1978), 1:440–441.

438. "The President as Potentate," *American Prospect,* November 5, 2001, 42–46.

439. Nathan, *The Administrative Presidency,* 27.

440. Leonard Garment quoted in A. James Reichley, *Conservatives in an Age of Change: The Nixon and Ford Administrations* (Washington, D.C.: Brookings, 1985), 259. Richard M. Nixon quoted in Joan Hoff-Wilson, "Richard M. Nixon: The Corporate Presidency," in *Leadership in the Modern Presidency,* ed. Fred I. Greenstein (Cambridge: Harvard University Press, 1988), 177.

441. Quoted in George C. Herring, *America's Longest War: The United States and Vietnam* (New York: Wiley, 1979), 219.

442. Hoff-Wilson, "Richard M. Nixon," 165.

443. Greenstein, "Nine Presidents," 332. For a balanced account of Nixon's administrative presidency, see Nathan, *The Administrative Presidency,* 43–56. On Henry Kissinger's National Security Council, see John D. Leecacos, "Kissinger's Apparat," *Foreign Policy,* no. 5 (winter 1971–1972): 3–27.

444. Cited in Stephen E. Ambrose, *Eisenhower the President* (New York: Simon and Schuster, 1984), 10.

445. *United States v. Nixon,* 418 U.S. 683 (1974).

446. Arthur M. Schlesinger Jr., *The Imperial Presidency* (New York: Popular Library, 1973), 10.

447. Weinberger cited in Rudalevige, *The New Imperial Presidency* (Ann Arbor: University of Michigan Press, 2005), 89.

448. Berman, *New American Presidency,* 263.

449. Humbrey cited in Rudalevige, *The New Imperial Presidency,* 90.

450. Greenstein, "Nine Presidents," 334.

451. These surveys are discussed in James MacGregor Burns, J. W. Peltason, and Thomas Cronin, *Government by the People,* 11th ed. (Englewood Cliffs, N.J.: Prentice Hall, 1981), 359.

452. Whittington, *Constitutional Construction,* 206.

453. R. Shep Melnick, "The Politics of Partnership," *Public Administration Review,* vol. 45 (November 1985): 655.

454. The Twenty-fifth Amendment was added to the Constitution in response to a series of events that highlighted the problem of presidential succession. The immediate catalyst was the assassination of President Kennedy in 1963. Kennedy's death left the nation with a president, Lyndon Johnson, who had a history of heart trouble and whose legally designated successors, in the absence of a

vice president, were an old and ailing House Speaker, John W. McCormick, and, as the Senate president pro tempore, an even older and less energetic Carl Hayden. The Twenty-fifth Amendment provided for two separate but related situations: vacancies in the vice presidency and presidential disabilities. According to section 2 of the amendment, vice-presidential vacancies are to be filled by presidential nomination, pending confirmation by both houses of Congress. Procedures for handling presidential disabilities were established by sections 3 and 4. Either the president alone or the vice president and a majority of the cabinet may declare the president to be disabled and may transfer temporarily the powers of the office to the vice president. Congress is charged with resolving any disagreements about presidential disabilities that may arise between the president and the rest of the executive branch.

455. These changes are discussed in Roger Porter, "Gerald Ford: A Healing Presidency," in *Leadership in the Modern Presidency,* ed. Fred I. Greenstein (Cambridge: Harvard University Press, 1988), 206–213.

456. Berman, *New American Presidency,* 293–294.

457. Philip Shabecoff, "Presidency Is Found Weaker under Ford," *New York Times,* March 28, 1976, 1.

458. Greenstein, "Nine Presidents," 340.

459. Political scientist John Coleman has argued that Jimmy Carter successfully defied Congress to pursue a policy of restraint during the recession of 1980. See John Coleman, *Party Decline in America: Policy, Politics, and the Fiscal State* (Princeton: Princeton University Press, 1996), 174–175. Still, Carter's control of fiscal policy was severely challenged by Sen. Edward M. Kennedy, D.-Mass., the champion of liberal Democrats in Congress, who came close to denying the incumbent president the Democratic nomination in 1980. Kennedy's insurgency forced Carter to run on a party platform that repudiated his own economic program. See Stephen Skowronek, *The Politics Presidents Make: Leadership from John Adams to Bill Clinton* (Cambridge: Harvard University Press, 1997), 405.

460. John P. Burke, "The Institutional Presidency," in *The Presidency and the Political System,* 4th ed., ed. Michael Nelson (Washington, D.C.: Congressional Quarterly, 1995), 389.

461. Erwin C. Hargrove, "Jimmy Carter: The Politics of Public Goods," in *Leadership in the Modern Presidency,* ed. Fred I. Greenstein (Cambridge: Harvard University Press, 1988), 251.

462. William B. Quandt, *Camp David: Peacemaking and Politics* (Washington, D.C.: Brookings, 1986).

463. Hargrove, "Jimmy Carter," 233.

464. James Fallows, "The Passionless Presidency," *Atlantic Monthly,* May 1979, 42.

465. Hargrove, "Jimmy Carter," 254.

466. Tulis, *The Rhetorical Presidency,* 189.

467. On Ronald Reagan's use of rhetoric, see William K. Muir Jr., *The Bully Pulpit: The Presidential Leadership of Ronald Reagan* (San Francisco: Institute for Contemporary Studies, 1992).

468. "Inaugural Address of President Ronald Reagan," January 20, 1981, in Richard Nathan, *The Administrative Presidency* (New York: Wiley, 1983), 159.

469. Marc Landy and Martin A. Levin, "The Hedgehog and the Fox," *Brandeis Review* 7:1 (fall 1987): 17–19.

470. James P. Pfiffner, *The President and Economic Policy* (Philadelphia: Institute for the Study of Human Issues, 1986), 122.

471. William Greider, *The Education of David Stockman and Other Americans* (New York: Dutton, 1982), 33. See also David A. Stockman, *The Triumph of Politics: Why the Reagan Revolution Failed* (New York: Harper and Row, 1986), 79–99.

472. David S. Broder, "A Party Leader Who Works at It," *Boston Globe,* October 21, 1985, 14; author interview with Mitchell Daniels,

assistant to the president for political and governmental affairs, June 5, 1986.

473. Alan Ehrenhalt, "Changing South Perils Conservative Coalition," *Congressional Quarterly Weekly Report,* August 1, 1987, 1704.

474. Benjamin Ginsberg and Martin Shefter, *Politics by Other Means: The Declining Importance of Elections in America* (New York: Basic Books, 1990).

475. Richard M. Pious, "Prerogative Power and the Reagan Presidency: A Review Essay," *Political Science Quarterly* 106:3 (fall 1991): 499–510.

476. On the Reagan administration's efforts to reform Social Security, see Martha Derthick and Steven M. Teles, "Riding the Third Rail: Reagan and Social Security," paper delivered at Conference on the Reagan Presidency, Santa Barbara, California, March 27–30, 2002.

477. Stockman, *The Triumph of Politics,* 193.

478. Pamela Fessler, "Disability Measure Wins Unanimous Approval," *Congressional Quarterly Weekly Report,* September 22, 1984, 2332–2334. For a comprehensive discussion of the running battle between the Reagan administration and the federal courts over statutory interpretation, see R. Shep Melnick, *Between the Lines: Interpreting Welfare Rights* (Washington, D.C.: Brookings, 1994).

479. Richard A. Harris and Sidney M. Milkis, *The Politics of Regulatory Change: A Tale of Two Agencies,* 2d ed. (New York: Oxford University Press, 1996). The "midnight rules" were issued by the Carter administration between December 29, 1980, and January 23, 1981. The strong disagreement in regulatory philosophy between Carter's appointees and the incoming conservative Republican administration intensified the traditional last-minute attempt by departing officials to push through favored policies. Carter's regulators essentially cleared their desks of all rules pending at the end of 1980, producing more than 200 new regulations in both proposed and final form. The rules, which represented a wide range of social causes for which Reagan and his regulatory task force had little sympathy, fell largely within the purviews of the Environmental Protection Agency and the Occupational Safety and Health Administration. See Edward Paul Fuchs, *Presidents, Management, and Regulation* (Englewood Cliffs, N.J.: Prentice-Hall, 1988), 85–90.

480. Greenstein, "Nine Presidents," 345.

481. I. M. Destler, "Reagan and the World: An Awesome Stubbornness," in *The Reagan Legacy,* ed. Charles O. Jones (Chatham, N.J.: Chatham House, 1988), 249–253.

482. Ginsberg and Shefter, *Politics by Other Means,* 148.

483. Ibid., 154–156.

484. David M. O'Brien, "The Reagan Justices: His Most Enduring Legacy?" in Jones, *Reagan Legacy,* 86–87.

485. Ibid., 90.

486. Ibid., 91.

487. The Democrats controlled both the executive and Congress between 1976 and 1980, but President Carter did not have the opportunity to make any appointments to the Supreme Court. Carter faced little opposition to his nominations for the lower federal courts until the end of his presidency, when Republicans managed to block seventeen of his nominations to the district courts to allow incoming GOP president Ronald Reagan to fill the posts. See *CQ Almanac, 1980,* 16-a. For a discussion of the politics of judicial appointments under the conditions of divided rule, see Michael Nelson, "Constitutional Aspects of the Elections," in *The Elections of 1988,* ed. Michael Nelson (Washington, D.C.: Congressional Quarterly Inc., 1989), 201–205.

488. *Runyon v. McCrary,* 427 U.S. 160 (1976); see also Walter Dean Burnham, "The Reagan Heritage," in *The Election of 1988:*

Report and Interpretations, ed. Gerald M. Pomper (Chatham, N.J.: Chatham House, 1989), 12–13.

489. *Immigration and Naturalization Service v. Chadha,* 103 S. Ct. 2764 (1983).

490. Rudalevige, *The New Imperial Presidency,* 178.

491. Benjamin Ginsberg and Martin Shefter, *Politics by Other Means: Politicians, Prosecutors, and the Press from Watergate to Whitewater* (New York: W. W. Norton, 1998); Cass Sunstein, "Unchecked, Unbalanced: The Independent Counsel Act," *American Prospect* (May/June 1998): 20–27.

492. Nelson, "Constitutional Aspects of the Elections," 191–192.

493. The Democrats gained two seats in the House, one in the Senate, one governorship, and more than a dozen seats in the state legislatures.

494. "Inaugural Address of George Herbert Walker Bush," in *The Elections of 1988: Report and Interpretations,* ed. Gerald M. Pomper (Chatham, N.J.: Chatham House, 1989), 209–210.

495. Michael Duffy and Dan Goodgame, *Marching in Place: The Status Quo Presidency of George Bush* (New York: Simon and Schuster, 1992), 83, 285.

496. George C. Edwards III, "George Bush and the Public Presidency: The Politics of Inclusion," in *The Bush Presidency: First Appraisals,* ed. Colin Campbell and Bert Rockman (Chatham, N.J.: Chatham House, 1991), 138.

497. Pious, "Prerogative Power and the Reagan Presidency," 510, n. 27.

498. Joan Biskupic, "Thomas Victory Puts Icing on Reagan-Bush Court," *Congressional Quarterly Weekly Report,* October 19, 1991, 3026.

499. The Civil Rights Act of 1991 restored the legal standard established by the Supreme Court's ruling in *Griggs v. Duke Power Company,* 401 U.S. 424 (1971), which held employers responsible for justifying employment practices that wree seemingly fair but had an "adverse impact" on women and minorities. A 1989 ruling *Wards Cove Packing Company v. Antonio,* 490 U.S. 642 (1989) had shifted the burden, saying workers had to show that companies had no legitimate need for the challenged practices. The new legislation instructed the courts to follow the standard of *Grigg* and related rulings prior to *Wards Cove.* Bush agreed to sign the bill, but he proclaimed the documents introduced by Senate Minority Leader Robert Dole (R.-Kansas), which offered a narrow interpretation of the statute would "be treated as authoritative guidance by all officials in the executive branch with respect to the law of disparate impact as well as other matters covered in the document." Joan Biskupic, "Bush Signs Anti-Job Bias Bill amid Furor over Preferences," *Congressional Quarterly Weekly Report,* November 23, 1991, 3463.

500. Bush cited in Charles Tiefer, *The Semi-Sovereign Presidency: The Bush Administration's Strategy for Governing Without Congress* (Boulder, Colorado: Westview Press, 1994), 3.

501. Ibid.

502. Jonathan Rauh, "The Regulatory President," *National Journal,* November 30, 1991, 2902–2906.

503. OMB Watch, "President Bush's Regulatory Moratorium," *OMB Watch Alert,* January 24, 1992.

504. See, for example, Theodore Lowi, "The Party Crasher," *New York Times Magazine,* August 23, 1992, 28, 33.

505. Paul Starobin, "President Perot?" *National Journal,* July 4, 1992, 1567–1572.

506. Alan Brinkley, "Roots," *New Republic,* July 27, 1992, 45.

507. Bill Clinton, "The New Covenant: Responsibility and Rebuilding the American Community," speech delivered at Georgetown University, Washington, D.C., October 23, 1991.

508. Dan Balz and David Broder, "President Clinton's First Hundred Days," *Washington Post,* April 29, 1993.

509. Walter Dean Burnham, "On the Shoals, Nearing the Rocks," *American Prospect* 14 (summer 1993): 10–11.

510. Sidney Blumenthal, "The Syndicated Presidency," *New Yorker,* April 5, 1993, 42–47.

511. Kimba Wood was never nominated for attorney general. Burned once by his pick of Zöe Baird, President Bill Clinton awaited results of a full background check before announcing his near-certain choice of Wood, a New York federal judge. When it was discovered that Wood, like Baird, had hired an illegal immigrant to babysit, she withdrew herself from consideration.

512. "From what one can tell," presidential scholar Joel D. Aberbach has written, "real responsibility for most [of the early political and policy difficulties] lies primarily in the White House [and White House staff] . . . , not in the agencies or their appointed or career personnel." Joel D. Aberbach, "The Federal Executive under Clinton," in *The Clinton Presidency: First Appraisals,* ed. Colin Campbell and Bert A. Rockman (Chatham, N.J.: Chatham House, 1996), 176.

513. Burt Solomon, "Musical Chairs in the West Wing May Bring Order from Cacophony," *National Journal,* April 24, 1993, 1661.

514. On President Clinton's use of executive orders, see Thomas L. Friedman, "Ready or Not Clinton Is Rattling the Country," *New York Times,* January 31, 1993, IV, 1. Candidate Clinton's promise to focus on the economy "like a laser" is quoted in Ann Devroy and Ruth Marcus, "President Clinton's First Hundred Days: Ambitious Agenda and Interruptions Frustrate Efforts to Maintain Focus," *Washington Post,* April 29, 1993, A1.

515. Friedman, "Ready or Not," IV, 1.

516. Richard L. Berke, "Clinton in Crossfire," *New York Times,* July 20, 1993, A16. Clinton arrived at a compromise plan in July 1993. It permitted homosexuals to serve in the military if they would not engage in homosexual behavior on or off base and would remain quiet about their sexual identity. It also made it difficult for commanders to initiate investigations without clear evidence of homosexual behavior. Thomas L. Friedman, "President Admits Revised Policy Isn't Perfect," *New York Times,* July 20, 1993, A1, A16.

517. David Osborne and Ted Gabler, *Reinventing Government: How the Entrepreneurial Spirit Is Transforming the Public Sector* (Reading, Mass.: Addison-Wesley, 1992).

518. Al Gore, *Creating a Government That Works Better and Costs Less: Report of the National Performance Review, September 7, 1993* (Washington, D.C.: Government Printing Office, 1993).

519. Donald F. Kettl, *Reinventing Government: Appraising the National Performance Review* (Washington, D.C.: Brookings, 1994), ix.

520. David Shribman, "A New Brand of D.C. Politics," *Boston Globe,* November 18, 1993, 15; Gwen Ifill, "56 Long Days of Coordinated Persuasion," *New York Times,* November 19, 1993, A27.

521. CNN transcripts, July 5, 1993.

522. Clifford Krause, "White House Reaches a Deal with Byrd on Role in Somalia," *New York Times,* October 15, 1993, A12.

523. William Clinton, "Address to Congress on Health Care Plan," in *Congressional Quarterly Weekly Report,* September 25, 1993, 2582–2586; Robin Toner, "Alliance to Buy Health Care: Bureaucrat or Public Servant?" *New York Times,* December 5, 1993, 11, 38.

524. Address to Congress on Health Care Plan, in *Congressional Quarterly Weekly Report,* September 25, 1993, 2582–2586; Robin Toner, "Alliance to Buy Health Care: Bureaucrat or Public Servant," *New York Times,* December 5, 1993, 1, 38.

525. For a fuller account of the health care reform battle, see Haynes Johnson and David S. Broder, *The System: The American Way of Politics at the Breaking Point* (Boston: Little, Brown, 1996);

and Theda Skocpol, *Boomerang: Clinton's Health Security Effort and the Turn Against Government* (New York: Norton, 1996).

526. The Harry and Louise ads showed a middle-class couple, portrayed by two actors, discussing their doubts about the Health Security Act. It focused on the theme that polls revealed voters to be most concerned about distrust of bureaucrats. The effectiveness of the ads caught the attention of the nightly news, which provided 324 seconds of free airtime. For a fuller account of the health care reform battle, see Haynes Johnson and David S. Broder, *The System: The American Way of Politics at the Breaking Point* (Boston: Little, Brown, 1996); Theda Skocpol, *Boomerang: Clinton's Health Security Effort and the Turn against Government* (New York: Norton, 1996); and Cathie Jo Martin, "Dead on Arrival? New Politics, Old Politics, and the Case of National Health Reform," in *Seeking the Center: Politics and Policymaking at the New Century,* ed. Martin A. Levin, Marc K. Landy, and Martin Shapiro (Washington, D.C.: Georgetown University Press, 2001).

527. Adam Clymer, "National Health Program, President's Greatest Goal, Declared Dead in Congress," *New York Times,* September 27, 1994, A1, B10.

528. Everett Carll Ladd, "The 1994 Congressional Elections: The Post-Industrial Realignment Continues," *Political Science Quarterly* 110:1 (spring 1995): 10–14.

529. William Schneider, "Clinton: The Reason Why," *National Journal,* November 12, 1994, 2630–2632. Schneider cites a nationwide poll by Voter News Service revealing that voters who approved of the job Clinton was doing as president (44 percent of all those who voted) cast their ballots for Democrats in House elections by 82 to 18 percent. Those who disapproved of his performance (51 percent of all who voted) chose Republicans by 83 to 17 percent.

530. Rupert Cornwell, "Clinton Proves No Match for Home Improvement," *Independent,* April 20, 1995.

531. Bob Woodward, *The Choice* (New York: Simon and Schuster, 1996), 25.

532. William Clinton, "Address before a Joint Session of Congress on the State of the Union," January 23, 1996, in *Congressional Quarterly Weekly Report,* January 27, 1996, 258–262.

533. Al Gore, *Commonsense Government* (New York: Random House, 1995), 7.

534. William Clinton, "Remarks on Signing the Personal Responsibility and Opportunity Reconciliation Act," in *Weekly Compilation of Presidential Documents* (Government Printing Office, August 22, 1996), 1484–1489.

535. "Victory March," *Newsweek,* November 18, 1996, 48.

536. Anthony Corrado, "Financing the 1996 Elections," in *The Elections of 1996,* ed. Gerald Pomper (Chatham, N.J.: Chatham House, 1997).

537. Michael Nelson, "The Election: Turbulence and Tranquility in Contemporary American Politics," in *The Elections of 1996,* ed. Michael Nelson (Washington, D.C.: CQ Presss, 1997), 52; and Gary Jacobson, "The 105th Congress: Unprecedented and Unsurprising," in *The Elections of 1996,* ed. Michael Nelson (Washington, D.C.: CQ Presss, 1997), 161.

538. Almost one in five voters identified a "vision for the future" as the most important quality driving the presidential vote; Clinton received 77 percent of their votes. See James W. Ceaser and Andrew E. Busch, *Losing to Win: The 1996 Elections and American Politics* (Lanham, Md.: Rowman and Littlefield, 1997), 166.

539. The distinction between third party candidates and independent candidates is nicely drawn in Steven J. Rosenstone, Roy L. Behr, and Edward H. Lazarus, *Third Parties in America,* 2d ed. (Princeton: Princeton University Press, 1996), 48, 81.

540. Clinton's "third way" politics is placed in historical perspective and carefully analyzed in Skowronek, *The Politics Presidents Make,* 447–464.

541. Daniel J. Palazzolo, *Done Deal? The Politics of the 1997 Budget Agreement* (Chatham, N.J.: Chatham House, 1999), 189.

542. R. Kent Weaver, "Ending Welfare as We Know It," in *The Social Divide: Political Parties and the Future of Activist Government,* ed. Margaret Weir (Washington, D.C.: Brookings, 1998), 397.

543. Richard Stevenson, "After Year of Wrangling, Accord Is Reached on Plan to Balance the Budget by 2002," *New York Times,* May 3, 1997, 1.

544. The term *extraordinary isolation* is Woodrow Wilson's. See Wilson, *Constitutional Government,* 69.

545. John R. Zaller, "Monica Lewinsky's Contribution to Political Science," *PS: Political Science and Politics* 31: 2 (June 1998): 182–189.

546. John M. Broder, "In Aide's Claim, Echoes of Watergate," *New York Times,* May 12, 1998.

547. Stephen Labaton, "White House and Reno at Odds on Privilege," *New York Times,* June 28, 1998, A14.

548. Adam Clymer, "Under Attack, Clinton Gets No Cover from His Party," *New York Times,* March 16, 1997, 1; Todd S. Purdum, "Clinton Most Charming at a Distance," *New York Times,* September 17, 1998, 18.

549. *Clinton v. City of New York,* No. 97-1374 (June 25, 1998), 9–10.

550. Janny Scott, "Talking Heads Post-Mortem: All Wrong, All the Time," *New York Times,* November 8, 1998, A22.

551. Richard L. Berke, John M. Broder, and Don Van Natta Jr., "How Republican Determination Upset Clinton's Backing at the Polls," *New York Times,* December 28, 1998.

552. Gary C. Jacobson, *The Politics of Congressional Elections,* 5th ed. (New York: Longman, 2000), 258–259.

553. Two other proposed articles were defeated in the House: one dealing with perjury by 205–229 and the other dealing with abuse of power by 148–285. Only the latter vote, which included eighty-one Republican nays, was anything close to bipartisan.

554. "Early Views after Impeachment: The Public Supports Clinton," *New York Times,* December 21, 1998.

555. Robert Pear, "The Presidential Pen Is Still Mighty," *New York Times,* June 28, 1998.

556. Emily O. Goldman and Larry Berman, "Engaging the World: First Impressions of the Clinton Foreign Policy Legacy," in *The Clinton Legacy,* ed. Colin Campbell and Bert A. Rockman (New York: Chatham House, 2000), 246–249; Paul Starobin, "The Liberal Hawk Soars," *National Journal,* May 14, 1999.

557. Author interview with Will Marshall, president, Progressive Policy Institute, June 14, 1999.

558. David E. Rosenbaum, "Surplus a Salve for Clinton and Congress," *New York Times,* June 29, 1999.

559. *Clinton v. Jones,* 117 S. Ct. 1636 (1997).

560. See *In re: Sealed Case,* No. 98-3069 (D.C. Cir.), July 7, 1998; and *In re: Bruce Lindsey (Grand Jury Testimony),* No. 98-3060 (D.C. Cir.), July 27, 1998.

561. James W. Ceaser and Andrew Busch, *The Perfect Tie: The True Story of the Presidential Election* (Lanham, Md.: Rowman and Littlefield, 2001), 37–46; also see Wilson Carey McWilliams, "The Meaning of the Election," in *The Election of 2000,* ed. Gerald Pomper (New York: Chatham House, 2000), 179–185.

562. Michael Nelson, "The Postelection Election: Politics by Other Means," in *The Elections of 2000,* ed. Michael Nelson (Washington: CQ Press, 2001), 211–224.

563. Ibid., 220–221.

564. *George W. Bush et al., Petitioners v. Albert Gore Jr. et al.,* No. 00–949 (United States Supreme Court), December 12, 2000, 12.

565. Ibid., Justice Stevens, with whom Justice Ginsberg and Justice Breyer join, dissenting, 5, 7.

566. Nelson, "The Election," 78–80.

567. Tish Durkin, "The Scene: The Jeffords Defection and the Risk of Snap Judgments," *National Journal,* May 26, 2001.

568. Ibid.

569. Fred Barnes, "The Impresario: Karl Rove, Orchestrator of the Bush White House," *Weekly Standard,* August 20, 2001; Carl M. Cannon and Alexi Simendinger, "The Evolution of Karl Rove," *National Journal,* April 27, 2002, 1210–1216.

570. New Democrats accused George W. Bush of trying to steal their politics. As Democratic Leadership Council president Al From wrote in the spring of 1999, Bush's effort to call himself a "compassionate conservative" appeared to be an effort by Republicans "to do for their party what New Democrats did for ours in 1992—to redefine and capture the political center." Al From, "Political Memo," *New Democrat,* vol. 11, no. 3 (May/June, 1999), 35. Many Republicans agreed. One skeptical conservative revealed that if he wanted to know the Bush campaign's position on a particular issue, he would consult the Democratic Leadership Council's magazine, *New Democratic Blueprint.* Author interview with Bush campaign adviser, not for attribution, November 13, 2001.

571. Author interview with Karl C. Rove, senior adviser to the president, November 15, 2001; Michael Gerson, Bush's principal speechwriter, noted that the president's rhetoric did not try to "split the difference" between liberalism and conservatism. Instead, Bush's speeches sought to convey how "activist government could be used for conservative ends." Author interview with Michael Gerson, deputy assistant to the president and director of speechwriting, November 15, 2001.

572. E. J. Dionne Jr., "Conservatism Recast," *Washington Post,* January 27, 2002.

573. George W. Bush, "Duty of Hope," remarks at Indianapolis, Indiana, July 22, 1999, www.georgewbush.com.

574. Rove interview; George W. Bush, remarks at Cedar Rapids, Iowa, June 12, 1999, www.georgewbush.com.

575. On January 29, 2001, Bush created a faith-based office to "eliminate unnecessary legislative, regulatory, and other bureaucratic barriers that impede faith-based and other community efforts to solve social problems." Executive Order 13199, "Establishment of Faith-Based and Community Initiatives." Furthermore, he ordered the Departments of Labor, Education, Health and Human Services, and Housing and Urban Development, as well as the Attorney General's Office, to establish Centers for Faith-Based and Community Initiatives within their departments. These centers must perform internal audits, to identify barriers to the participation of faith-based organizations in providing social services and to form plans to remove these barriers. Executive Order 13198, "Agency Responsibilities with Respect to Faith-Based and Community Initiatives," January 29, 2001. The education bill involved a compromise between the White House, and its commitment to accountability, and liberal Democrats in the Senate, who pushed for increased spending. The president referred to this rapprochement with Senator Kennedy in his State of the Union Address, joking about how the folks back in the Crawford, Texas, coffee house would be shocked at his praise for the leading liberal senator. Bush and his advisers viewed education as the central issue in distinguishing Bush as a different kind of Republican. George W. Bush, "State of the Union Address," January 29, 2001, www.whitehouse.gov; and Rove interview.

576. David S. Broder, "Long Road to Reform: Negotiators Force Education Legislation," *Washington Post,* December 17, 2001.

577. George W. Bush, address to a joint session of Congress and the nation, September 20, 2001, www.whitehouse.gov.

578. Ibid.

579. David Nather and Jill Barshay, "Hill Warning: Respect Level from White House Too Low," *CQ Weekly,* March 9, 2002.

580. Rudalevige, *The New Imperial Presidency,* 229–231.

581. *Hamdan v. Rumsfeld,* 126 S.Ct. 2749 (2006).

582. Michael A. Fletcher, "Bush Signs Terrorism Measure," *Washington Post,* October 18, 2006.

583. George W. Bush, Address to the Nation, June 6, 2002, www.whitehouse.gov.

584. Eric Pianan and Bill Miller, "For Ridge, Ambition and Realities Clash; Homeland Security Chief May Lack Means to Implement Major Initiatives," *Washington Post,* January 23, 2002.

585. Mike Allen and Bill Miller, "Bush Seeks Security Department; Cabinet-Level Agency would Coordinate Anti-Terrorism Effort," *Washington Post,* June 6, 2002.

586. George W. Bush, Executive Order, Establishing the Corporate Fraud Task Force, July 9, 2002, www.whitehouse.gov; Bush, statement at signing the Corporate Corruption Bill, July 30, 2002, www.whitehouse.gov.

587. Bush, Executive Order.

588. Stephen Mufson, "FDR's Deal in Bush's Terms," *Washington Post,* February 20, 2005.

589. Adam Nagourney and Janet Elder, "In Poll, Americans Say Both Parties Lack Vision," *New York Times,* November 3, 2002. An election-eve Gallup Poll reported that 53 percent would be using their vote "in order to send a message that you support [or oppose] George W. Bush." Of these, 35 percent said they would vote to support him and 18 percent said they would vote to express their opposition. In 1998, the last election in which the president's party gained seats, the split was 23 percent to 23 percent among the 46 percent who said they were using their vote to express their attitude toward President Clinton. David W. Moore and Jeffrey M. Jones, "Late Shift Toward Republicans in Congressional Vote," www.gallup.com/poll/releases/pro21104.asp?Version=p, November 4, 2002.

590. Author interview with Matthew Dowd, political strategist for the Bush-Cheney campaign, July 8, 2004; see also, Matt Bai, "The Multilevel Marketing of the President," *New York Times Magazine,* April 25, 2004, 43.

591. Author interview with Terry Nelson, Political Director, George W. Bush-Richard Cheney '04. August 19, 2005.

592. The tendency of the Democratic party to rely on auxiliary organizations such as labor unions was accentuated by the enactment of the Bipartisan Campaign Finance Reform Act in 2002, which proscribed party organizations, but not independent issue groups, from raising and spending "soft" money. The "527 groups," named for a section of the tax code that regulated them, were formed outside of the regular party organization, in part, to circumvent campaign finance regulations. No less important, however, was the view of some leaders of the 527 organizations that the Democratic National Committee and state parties were not capable of mobilizing the base support of liberal causes (author interview with ACT official, not for attribution, August 19, 2005). These groups formed an alliance to build an impressive media and ground campaign to match the efforts of the Republican Party.

593. Author interview with Karl Rove, November 15, 2001.

594. Author Interview with Matthew Dowd, July 20, 2005.

595. Author Interview with Tad Devine, Political Strategist, John Kerry-John Edwards '04. July 2004.

596. Comment of John Kerry on CNN's *Inside Politics,* August 9, 2004.

597. Author interview with Matthew Dowd, July 26, 2004.

598. Wilson, "How Divided Are We?" *Commentary* (February 2006).

SELECTED BIBLIOGRAPHY

Arnold, Peri E. *Making the Managerial Presidency.* Princeton: Princeton University Press, 1986.

Aberbach, Joel D. and Mark A. Peterson, editors. *The Executive Branch.* New York: Oxford University Press, 2005.

Binkley, Wilfred E. *The President and Congress.* New York: Alfred A. Knopf, 1947.

Ceaser, James. *Presidential Selection: Theory and Development.* Princeton: Princeton University Press, 1979.

Cornwell, Elmer E., Jr. *Presidential Leadership of Public Opinion.* Bloomington: Indiana University Press, 1965.

Corwin, Edward. *The President: Office and Powers, 1787–1984.* 5th rev. ed. New York: New York University Press, 1984.

Cronin, Thomas E., ed. *Inventing the American Presidency.* Lawrence: University Press of Kansas, 1989.

Ellis, Richard, ed. *Founding the American Presidency.* Lanham, Md.: Rowman and Littlefield, 1999.

Hargrove, Erwin. *The President as Leader: Appealing to the Better Angels of Our Nature.* Lawrence: University Press of Kansas, 1998.

Letters of Pacificus and Helvidius on the Proclamation of Neutrality of 1793. Washington, D.C.: Gideon, 1845.

Lowi, Theodore. *The Personal President.* Ithaca: Cornell University Press, 1995.

Mayer, Kenneth R. *With The Stroke of a Pen: Executive Orders and Presidential Power.* Princeton: Princeton University Press, 2001.

Milkis, Sidney M., and Michael Nelson. *The American Presidency: Origins and Development, 1776–1998,* 3d ed. Washington, D.C.: CQ Press, 2000.

Nelson, Michael, ed. *The Presidency and the Political System,* 7th ed. Washington, D.C.: CQ Press, 2002.

Paludan, Philip Shaw. *The Presidency of Abraham Lincoln.* Lawrence: University Press of Kansas, 1995.

Rudalevige, Andrew. *The New Imperial Presidency: Renewing Presidential Power After Watergate.* Ann Arbor: University of Michigan Press, 2005.

Skowronek, Stephen. *The Politics Presidents Make: Leadership from John Adams to Bill Clinton.* Cambridge: Harvard University Press, 1997.

Tulis, Jeffrey. *The Rhetorical Presidency.* Princeton: Princeton University Press, 1987.

Urofsky, Melvin, ed. *The American Presidents: Critical Essays.* New York: Garland Press, 2000.

White, Leonard. *The Federalists: A Study in Administrative History.* New York: Macmillan, 1948.

———. *The Jacksonians: A Study in Administrative History, 1829–1861.* New York: Macmillan, 1954.

———. *The Jeffersonians: A Study in Administrative History, 1801–1829.* New York: Macmillan, 1951.

———. *The Republican Era: A Study in Administrative History, 1869–1901.* New York: Macmillan, 1958.

Wilson, Woodrow. *Constitutional Government in the United States.* New York: Columbia University Press, 1908.

chapter 3

History of the Vice Presidency

by Michael Nelson

Almost since its creation, the vice presidency has been an easy and frequent target of political humor. Benjamin Franklin quipped that the vice president should be addressed as "Your Superfluous Excellency." Mr. Dooley, the invented character of the writer Finley Peter Dunne, described the office as "not a crime exactly. Ye can't be sint to jail f'r it, but it's kind iv a disgrace. It's like writin' anonymous letters." The popular 1930s musical *Of Thee I Sing* featured a fictitious vice president whose name (which no one in the play could remember) was Alexander Throttlebottom. Vice President Throttlebottom spent most of his time feeding pigeons in a park and trying to find two people willing to serve as references so that he could get a library card.

Even some vice presidents have poked fun at the office. Thomas R. Marshall, who occupied the vice presidency during Woodrow Wilson's two terms as president, said that the vice president is like "a man in a cataleptic fit; he cannot speak; he cannot move; he suffers no pain; he is perfectly conscious of all that goes on, but has no part in it." Marshall also told the story of the two brothers: "One ran away to sea; the other was elected vice president. And nothing was heard of either of them again." John Nance Garner was a fairly active vice president during the first two terms of Franklin D. Roosevelt's administration, but his pithy assessment of the office is probably the most frequently quoted of all: "The vice presidency isn't worth a bucket of warm spit." [1] (That is the G-rated version of what Garner said.)

Another vice president, Dan Quayle, was himself the object of a relentless barrage of jokes and gibes from comedians and editorial cartoonists. Quayle inadvertently invited some of these—on one occasion, he told a student who had spelled "potato" correctly to add an "e" to the end of the word; on another, he seemed to suggest that the water in Mars's canals would make human exploration of the planet feasible. But Quayle was also the victim of entirely apocryphal humor. A joke by Rep. Claudine Schneider, R-R.I., that had Quayle saying, "I was recently on a tour of Latin America, and the only regret I have is that I didn't study Latin harder in school so that I could converse with those people," was widely repeated as if it were real. [2] All vice presidents have been ridiculed to some extent (Quayle's successor, Al Gore, quipped at his own expense that the only way people could pick him out of a crowd of Secret Service agents was to look for the stiff one), but Quayle jokes were taken to the extreme.

Many a truth—about the vice presidency as well as about other things—has been spoken in jest. Constitutionally, the vice presidency was born weak and has not grown much stronger. But lost in all the laughter is an appreciation of the importance—ongoing in the twentieth century and growing in recent years—of the position the vice presidency occupies in the American political system. *(See Chapter 23, Office of the Vice President, Vol. II.)*

The vice presidency is most significant when, cocoonlike, it empties itself to provide a successor to the presidency. "I am vice president," said John Adams, the first person to hold the office. "In this I am nothing, but I may be everything." [3] Nine vice presidents, almost 20 percent of those who have served in the office, became president when the incumbent chief executive died or resigned. Collectively, they led the nation for forty-two years. Each of the five twentieth-century vice presidents who succeeded to the presidency—Theodore Roosevelt, Calvin Coolidge, Harry S. Truman, Lyndon B. Johnson, and Gerald R. Ford—subsequently was nominated by his party for a full term as president, and all but Ford were elected. In 1965 Congress determined that the advisability of having the vice presidency occupied at all times was so strong that it passed the Twenty-fifth Amendment, which established a procedure for filling vice-presidential vacancies. In addition, the amendment, which was ratified by the states in 1967, stated unequivocally the right of the vice president, in the event of the president's death, resignation, or impeachment, to serve as president for the balance of the term and created a mechanism by which the vice president could assume the powers and duties of the presidency if the president became disabled.

Besides its long-standing role as presidential successor, the vice presidency also has become an important electoral springboard to the presidency. The modern vice president is not only a presumptive candidate for president but the presumptive front-runner as well. Seventeen of twenty-two twentieth-century vice presidents went on to seek the presidency. Death or ill health accounts for four of the exceptions—James S. Sherman, Charles Curtis, Alben W. Barkley, and Nelson A. Rockefeller—and criminal conviction for the fifth, Spiro T. Agnew. Richard B. Cheney, who became George W. Bush's vice president in 2001, is the rare vice president who took office with no intention of seeking the presidency. In addition to Cheney's age and history of heart problems, his preference for backstage politics and government accounts for his lack of ambition for higher office.

In the history of the Gallup poll, which extends back to 1936, Garner and every vice president who turned presidential candidate since Richard Nixon (except Quayle) have led in a majority of surveys that measure the voters' preferences for their party's presidential nomination.[4] In all four of the elections since 1956 in which the president did not or could not run for reelection, the incumbent party has nominated the vice president as its presidential candidate. Seven of the ten most recent vice presidents later were nominated for president in their own right: Nixon, Johnson, Hubert H. Humphrey, Ford, Walter F. Mondale, George H. W. Bush, and Al Gore.

Finally, recent changes in the vice presidency have made the office itself increasingly substantial. The vice presidency has become "institutionalized" to some degree. This is true both in the narrow sense that it is organizationally larger and more complex than in the past (the vice president's staff, for example, has grown from sixteen in 1960 to around seventy today) and in the broader sense that certain kinds of vice-presidential activities now are taken for granted. These include regular private meetings with the president (usually a weekly lunch), a wide-ranging role as senior presidential adviser, attendance at many important presidential meetings, membership on the National Security Council, full intelligence briefings, access to the Oval Office paper flow, frequent and sometimes sensitive diplomatic missions, public advocacy of the president's leadership and programs, liaison with congressional leaders and interest groups, and a role in the party second only to the president's. Modern vice presidents have a lot more to do than, in Vice President Marshall's gibe, "to ring the White House bell every morning and ask what is the state of health of the president." [5]

The vice presidency, then, both as successor and springboard to the presidency and as an institution in its own right, has become an important office. But its history is a problematic one, and not all of those problems have been solved.

THE FOUNDING PERIOD

The vice presidency was invented late in the Constitutional Convention of 1787, not because the delegates saw any need for such an office, but rather as a means of perfecting the arrangements they had made for presidential election and succession and, to some degree, for leadership of the Senate. The original Constitution provided that the vice presidency was to be awarded to the person who received the second highest number of electoral votes in the presidential election. If two or more candidates finished in a second-place tie in the presidential election, the Senate would choose among them. The office's only ongoing responsibility was to preside over the Senate, casting tie-breaking votes. The most important duty of the vice president was to stand by as successor to the president in the event of the president's death, impeachment and removal, resignation, or "inability to discharge the Powers and Duties" of the office. But the Constitution was vague about whether the vice president was to assume the office of president or only its powers and duties, as well as about whether the succession was to last until the end of the departed president's four-year term or until a special election could be held to choose a new president. The Constitution also left the term *inability* undefined and provided no procedure for the vice president to take power in the event the president became disabled. Finally, by giving the vice presidency both legislative and executive responsibilities, it deprived the office of solid moorings in either Congress or the presidency. *(See "The Constitutional Convention," p. 10, in Chapter 1.)*

Thus, although the vice presidency solved several problems related to the presidency and the Senate, it was plagued from birth by problems of its own. The office's hybrid status was bound to arouse suspicion in legislative councils because it was partly executive and in executive councils because it was partly legislative. The single ongoing responsibility of the vice president, to preside over the Senate, was not very important. The poorly defined successor role was to be an inevitable source of confusion and, perhaps, of tension between the president and the vice president. The fabled "heartbeat away" that separates the vice president from the presidency is, after all, the president's. Finally, more than any other institution of the new government, the vice presidency required the realization of the Framers' hope that political parties would not develop. The office would seem less a brilliant than a rash improvisation of the Constitutional Convention if it were occupied as a matter of course by the president's leading partisan foe.

John Adams was the first person to be elected vice president. *(See "Washingtons First Election: 1789," p. 353, in Chapter 6.)* Midway through his tenure, Adams lamented to his wife, Abigail, that "my country has in its wisdom contrived for me the most insignificant office that ever the invention of man contrived or his imagination conceived." [6] Little did Adams realize that the vice presidency was at an early peak of influence during the period he served. Because the Senate was small and still relatively unorganized, Adams was able to cast twenty-nine tie-breaking votes (still the record), guide the upper house's agenda, and intervene in debate. Adams also was respected and sometimes consulted on diplomatic and other matters by President George Washington, who invited him to meet with the cabinet in the president's absence. Moreover, having won the vice presidency by receiving the second largest number of electoral votes for president in 1789 and 1792, it is not surprising that Adams was elected as president in 1796 after Washington left office.

Adams's election was different from Washington's, however. The Framers' hopes notwithstanding, two political parties, the Federalists and the Democratic-Republicans, emerged during the Washington administration. The result in 1796 was the election of Adams, the Federalist, as president, and Thomas Jefferson, the Democratic-Republicans' presidential nominee, as vice president. Adams tried to lure Jefferson into the administration's fold by urging him to undertake a diplomatic mission to France, but Jefferson, eager to build up his own party and win the presidency away from Adams, would have no part of it. He justified his refusal by claiming that, constitutionally, the vice presidency was a legislative office. By Jefferson's own testimony, that was the end of his dealings with President Adams, except on formal occasions. He did make a mark as Senate president, writing a book—*Manual of Parliamentary Practice*—that, although never formally adopted by the Senate, became its working procedural guide. But most of Jefferson's congressional activities involved behind-the-scenes opposition to President Adams and the Federalists.

Dissatisfied with the divided partisan result of the 1796 election, each party nominated a complete ticket in 1800, instructing its electors to cast their two votes for its presidential and vice-presidential candidates. The intention was that both candidates would be elected; the result was that neither was. After the electors voted as instructed, Jefferson and his vice-presidential running mate, Aaron Burr, ended up with an equal number of votes for president. This outcome was doubly vexing: not only was Jefferson the party's clear presidential choice, but there was little love lost between him and Burr, who had been placed on the ticket to balance the Virginia wing of the party with a New Yorker. Under the Constitution, the House of Representatives was required to choose between them. It eventually did so, picking Jefferson, but not before Federalist mischief-makers kept the result uncertain through thirty-six ballots. Burr became vice president.

The Burr vice presidency was marked not only by bad relations between Burr and Jefferson, but also by various misdeeds, including a duel in which Burr shot and killed former Treasury secretary Alexander Hamilton. The election itself produced the widespread realization that something had to be done about the electoral college so that it could accommodate the emergence of party competition. Vice-presidential selection was the problem. An obvious solution was to require electors to vote separately for president and vice president.

In opposing the proposal for a separate ballot, some members of Congress argued that it would create a worse problem than it solved. Because "the vice president will not stand on such high ground in the method proposed as he does in the present mode of a double ballot" for president, predicted Rep. Samuel Taggart of Massachusetts, the nation could expect that "great care will not be taken in the selection of a character to fill that office." Sen. William Plumer of New Hampshire warned that such care as was taken would be "to procure votes for the president." [7] But Taggart and Plumer, who were leaders of the rapidly declining Federalist party, also shared the widespread Federalist belief that finishing second in presidential elections offered their party its only hope of securing even a toehold in the executive branch.[8] In truth, as the nomination of Burr indicated, the parties already had begun to degrade the vice presidency into a device for balancing the ticket in the election.

In 1804 motions were made in Congress to abolish the vice presidency rather than continue it in a form diminished from its original constitutional status as the position awarded to the second-most-qualified person to be president. These motions failed by votes of 12–19 in the Senate and 27–85 in the House. Instead, the Twelfth Amendment was enacted. The amendment provided that electors "shall name in their ballots the person voted for as President, and in distinct ballots the person voted for as Vice President." It also stipulated that if no one received a majority of electoral votes for vice president, then "from the two highest numbers on the list, the Senate shall choose the Vice President; a quorum for the purpose shall consist of two-thirds of the whole number of Senators, and a majority of the whole number shall be necessary to a choice." The amendment's final provision regarding the vice presidency extended the Constitution's original age, citizenship, and residency qualifications for president to the vice president. (*See "Constitutional Amendments," p. 46, in Chapter 1.*)

THE VICE PRESIDENCY IN THE NINETEENTH CENTURY

The development of political parties and the enactment of the Twelfth Amendment sent the constitutionally weak vice presidency into a tailspin that lasted until the end of the nineteenth century. Party leaders, not presidential candidates (who usually were not even present at national nominating conventions and who, if present, were expected to be seen and not heard), chose the nominees for vice president, which certainly did not foster trust or respect between the president and the vice president once in office. Aggravating the tension were the main criteria that party leaders applied to vice-presidential selection. One criterion was that the nominee placate the region or faction of the party that had been most dissatisfied with the presidential nomination, which led to numerous New York–Virginia, North–South, Stalwart–Progressive, and hard money–soft money pairings. Another criterion was that the nominee be able to carry a swing

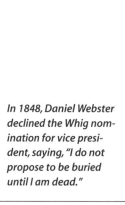

In 1848, Daniel Webster declined the Whig nomination for vice president, saying, "I do not propose to be buried until I am dead."

state in the general election where the presidential candidate was not sufficiently popular. Ironically, only 45 percent of presidential candidates in the nineteenth century carried their vice-presidential running mate's home state.[9]

In addition to fostering tension within the government, ticket balancing as the main basis for vice-presidential selection also placed such a stigma on the office that many politicians were unwilling to accept a nomination. (Daniel Webster, declining the vice-presidential place on the Whig Party ticket in 1848, said, "I do not propose to be buried until I am dead."[10]) Those who were nominated and elected found that fresh political problems four years after their nomination invariably led party leaders to balance the ticket differently: no first-term vice president in the nineteenth century was renominated for a second term by a party convention. Nor, after Vice President Martin Van Buren in 1836,

John Tyler was the first vice president to succeed to the presidency. When William Henry Harrison died in 1841, Tyler set a precedent by assuming the office of president, not just its powers and duties, and by serving out his predecessor's full term, rather than calling a special election.

was any nineteenth-century vice president elected or even nominated for president. Finally, the vice president's role as Senate president (which most vice presidents, following Jefferson's lead and for want of anything else to do, spent considerable time performing) became more ceremonial as the Senate took greater charge of its own affairs. John C. Calhoun, for example, who served from 1825 to 1832, was the last vice president whom the Senate allowed to appoint its committees.

Not surprisingly, the nineteenth-century vice presidents make up a veritable rogues' gallery of personal and political failures. Because the office was so unappealing, an unusual number of the politicians who could be enticed to run for vice president were old or in bad health. Six died in office, all of natural causes: George Clinton, Elbridge Gerry, William R. King (who took his oath of office in Cuba and died the next month), Henry Wilson, Thomas A. Hendricks, and Garret A. Hobart. Some vice presidents became embroiled in financial scandals. Daniel D. Tompkins was charged with keeping inadequate financial records while serving as governor of New York during the War of 1812, and Schuyler Colfax and Henry Wilson were implicated in the notorious Crédit Mobilier stock scandal of the 1870s.

Other vice presidents fell prey to personal weaknesses or political jealousies. Tompkins and Andrew Johnson were heavy drinkers. (Johnson's first address to the Senate sounded to listeners like a drunken harangue.) Richard M. Johnson kept a series of slave mistresses, educating the children of one but selling another when she lost interest in him. Clinton, Calhoun, and Chester A. Arthur each publicly expressed his dislike for the president. Clinton refused to attend President James Madison's inauguration and openly attacked the administration's foreign and domestic policies.

Calhoun alienated two presidents, John Quincy Adams and Andrew Jackson, by using his role as Senate president to subvert their policies and appointments, then resigned in 1832 to accept South Carolina's election as senator. Arthur attacked President James A. Garfield over a patronage quarrel. "Garfield has not been square, nor honorable, nor truthful. . . ," he told the *New York Herald*. "It's a hard thing to say of a president of the United States, but it's only the truth." [11] Finally, some vice presidents did not even live in Washington. Richard Johnson left his post to run a tavern.[12]

The history of the nineteenth-century vice presidency is not entirely bleak. A certain measure of comity existed between a few presidents and vice presidents, notably Andrew Jackson and Van Buren, James K. Polk and George M. Dallas, Abraham Lincoln and Hannibal Hamlin, Rutherford B. Hayes and William A. Wheeler, and William McKinley and Hobart. But even in these administrations, the vice president was not invited to cabinet meetings or entrusted with important tasks. What strengthened most such relationships was the president's respect for the vice president's advice, which was sought informally, and the vice president's effectiveness as an advocate of the administration's policies in the Senate. More important, in one area of vice-presidential responsibility—presidential succession—the nineteenth-century vice presidency witnessed a giant step forward. *(See Chapter 7, Selection by Succession.)*

The succession question did not arise until 1841, when William Henry Harrison became the first president to die in office. The language of the Constitution provided little guidance about whether the vice president, John Tyler, was to become president for the remainder of Harrison's term or merely acting president until a special election could be held. All of the delegates to the Constitutional Convention were dead, and the most complete record of the convention, which could have clarified the Framers' intentions (they had wanted a special election), still was not widely available. In this uncertain situation, Tyler's claim to both the office and the balance of Harrison's term was accepted grudgingly, but with little debate, setting a precedent that the next successor president, Vice President Millard Fillmore, was able to follow without any controversy at all. Fillmore succeeded to the presidency in 1850, after President Zachary Taylor died.

But even this bright moment in the history of the vice presidency was tarnished. Because Tyler came from a different wing of the party than Harrison, his presidency was marred by debilitating disagreements both with party leaders, especially in Congress, and with the late president's cabinet, all but one of whom resigned within five months. Fillmore and the other two nineteenth-century successor presidents, Andrew Johnson and Arthur, encountered similar problems for similar reasons. They too had been chosen to run for vice president because they represented a different faction of the party than the presidential nominee, and

they too lost or discharged all or most of the cabinet they had inherited within two (Fillmore) to six (Arthur) months. Johnson was impeached by the House and came within one vote of being removed from office by the Senate. In hindsight, none of the four has been regarded as a successful president. In the most thorough round of historians' rankings, Johnson was rated a failure, Tyler and Fillmore as below average, and Arthur as average.[13] *(See Chapter 4, Rating the Presidents.)* Nor was any nineteenth-century successor president nominated for a full term as president in his own right.

Unresolved issues of succession and disability also vexed the vice presidency during the nineteenth century. Taken together, six vice-presidential deaths, one vice-presidential resignation, and four presidential deaths left the nation without a vice president during eleven of the century's twenty-five presidential terms. President Taylor's death in July 1850 and Vice President King's death in April 1853 meant that, with the exception of the month King spent in Cuba for treatment of tuberculosis after taking the oath of office there in March 1853, the vice presidency was vacant for seven consecutive years, until March 1857. Fortunately, no president has died while the vice presidency has been vacant.

The issue of vice-presidential responsibility in periods of presidential disability also remained unresolved. Five nineteenth-century presidents seem to have been disabled for measurable lengths of time.[14] In 1881, during the eighty days that President Garfield lay comatose before dying from an assassin's bullet, Vice President Arthur could only stand by helplessly, lest he be branded a usurper.

Perhaps the unkindest epitaph for the nineteenth-century vice presidency was written by the political scientist Woodrow Wilson in his 1885 book, *Congressional Government*. After spending less than a page on the vice presidency (in the chapter on "The Senate," not in the chapter on "The Executive"), Wilson concluded that "the chief embarrassment in discussing this office is that in explaining how little there is to be said about it one has evidently said all there is to say." [15]

THEODORE ROOSEVELT TO TRUMAN

The rise of national mass-circulation magazines and newspaper wire services, a new style of active presidential campaigning, and alterations in the vice-presidential nominating process enhanced the status of the vice presidency during the first half of the twentieth century. In 1900 the Republican nominee, Theodore Roosevelt, became the first vice-presidential candidate (and, other than William Jennings Bryan, the Democratic nominee for president in 1896, the first member of a national party ticket) to campaign vigorously nationwide. While President William McKinley waged a sedate "front porch" reelection campaign,

Roosevelt gave 673 speeches to three million listeners in twenty-four states.

The national reputation that Roosevelt gained through travel and the media stood him in good stead when he succeeded to the presidency after McKinley was assassinated in 1901. Roosevelt was able to reverse the earlier pattern of successor presidents and establish a new one: unlike Tyler, Fillmore, Johnson, and Arthur, Roosevelt was nominated by his party to run for a full term as president in 1904. This set the precedent for Coolidge in 1924, Truman in 1948, Lyndon Johnson in 1964, and Ford in 1976. Roosevelt's success may also help to explain another new pattern that contrasts sharply with nineteenth-century practice. Starting with Sherman in 1912, ten of the eleven vice presidents who have wanted a second term have been nominated for reelection.[16] Finally, Roosevelt helped to lay the intellectual groundwork for an enhanced role for the vice president in office. In an 1896 article, he argued that the president and vice president should share the same "views and principles" and that the vice president "should always be . . . consulted by the president on every great party question. It would be very well if he were given a seat in the Cabinet . . . a vote [in the Senate], on ordinary occasions, and perchance on occasion a voice in the debates." [17]

Roosevelt was unable as vice president and unwilling as president to practice what he preached about the vice presidency. Just as party leaders imposed the vice-presidential nomination of Charles W. Fairbanks on him to balance the ticket in 1904 (Roosevelt was from the progressive wing of the party, Fairbanks from the Old Guard), so had Roosevelt's nomination as vice president been forced on McKinley in 1900, and for the same reason. Neither McKinley nor Roosevelt liked or trusted his vice president, much less assigned him responsibilities. President Roosevelt often repeated the humorist Dunne's response when the president said that he was thinking of going down in a submarine: "Well, you really shouldn't do it—unless you take Fairbanks with you." [18]

Still, the enhanced political status of the vice presidency soon began to make it a more attractive office to at least some able and experienced political leaders, including Charles G. Dawes, who had served in three administrations

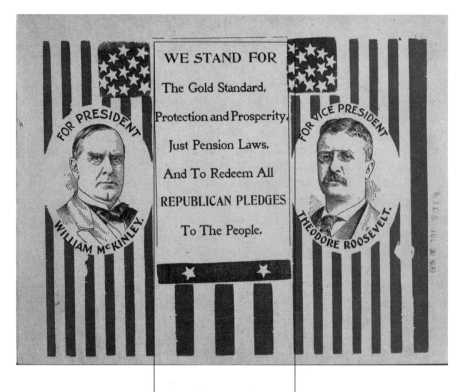

Campaign poster for William McKinley and Theodore Roosevelt.

and won a Nobel Prize; Curtis, the Senate majority leader; and Garner, the Speaker of the House. With somewhat more talent to offer, some vice presidents were given more responsibilities by the presidents they served. John Adams had been the last vice president to meet with the cabinet, for example, but when President Woodrow Wilson went to Europe in 1918 to negotiate the treaty that ended World War I, he asked Vice President Marshall to preside in his absence. Wilson's successor as president, Warren G. Harding, invited Vice President Coolidge to meet with the cabinet as a matter of course, as has every president since Franklin Roosevelt.[19]

Roosevelt, like his cousin Theodore, had both run for vice president before becoming president (TR lost in 1920) and written an article urging that the responsibilities of the vice presidency be expanded. In the article, Roosevelt had identified four roles that the vice president could perform helpfully: cabinet member, presidential adviser, liaison to Congress, and policy maker in areas "that do not belong in the province" of any particular department or agency.[20]

As president, Roosevelt initially had so much respect for Vice President John Nance Garner that even though the conservative Texan's nomination had been imposed on him at the 1932 Democratic convention, the president relied on

VICE PRESIDENTS OFTEN ATTAIN TOP SPOT

Fourteen of the forty-three men who have served as president of the United States were vice presidents first, but only five of them got to the Oval Office by being elected to it. The others made it because of the death or resignation of the president.

Of the five vice presidents elevated by election, two—John Adams and Thomas Jefferson—were elected when there was no public participation in the presidential nominating process and little participation in the general election. Martin Van Buren was elected directly to the presidency in 1836, as was George H. W. Bush in 1988. Richard Nixon narrowly lost his bid to move up from the vice presidency in 1960 but was elected president eight years later.

A few other vice presidents have come close to attaining the Oval Office. Hubert H. Humphrey lost narrowly to Nixon in 1968. Walter F. Mondale won the Democratic presidential nomination in 1984, four years after his term as vice president ended, but lost to Ronald Reagan. Al Gore was defeated by Republican George W. Bush in 2000, even though Gore won a plurality of the national popular vote.

Two other vice presidents ran unsuccessfully as third party presidential candidates. John C. Breckinridge, Democrat James Buchanan's vice president (1857–1861), was the nominee of the Southern Democrats in 1860. Henry A. Wallace, Franklin D. Roosevelt's second vice president (1941<en>1945), was the candidate of the Progressive Party in 1948.

Vice presidents who became president and those who won a major party presidential nomination are listed below. The party affiliation of the vice presidents and the names of the presidents under whom they served are noted.

Assumed Presidency on Death or Resignation	Year Assumed Presidency
John Tyler, Whig (W. H. Harrison)	1841
Millard Fillmore, Whig (Taylor)	1850
Andrew Johnson, D (Lincoln)	1865
Chester A. Arthur, R (Garfield)	1881
Theodore Roosevelt, R (McKinley)	1901
Calvin Coolidge, R (Harding)	1923
Harry S. Truman, D (F. Roosevelt)	1945
Lyndon B. Johnson, D (Kennedy)	1963
Gerald R. Ford, R (Nixon)	1974

Elected President Directly from Vice Presidency	Year Elected President
John Adams, Federalist (Washington)	1796
Thomas Jefferson, D-R (J. Adams)	1800
Martin Van Buren, D (Jackson)	1836
George H. W. Bush, R (Reagan)	1988

Elected President Later	Year Elected President
Richard Nixon, R (Eisenhower)	1968

Nominated for President but Lost	Year Sought Presidency
Richard Nixon, R (Eisenhower)	1960
Hubert H. Humphrey, D (L. Johnson)	1968
Walter F. Mondale, D (Carter)	1984
Al Gore, D (Clinton)	2000

Garner during the first term as "a combination presiding officer, cabinet officer, personal counselor, legislative tactician, Cassandra, and sounding board.[21] Most significant, the vice president served as an important liaison from Roosevelt to Congress—it was Garner's suggestion that led to Roosevelt's practice, which presidents continue to follow, of meeting regularly with congressional leaders. Garner also undertook a goodwill mission to Mexico at the president's behest, another innovation that practically all administrations have continued.

During the second term, Roosevelt and Garner fell out over the president's plan to pack the Supreme Court, support for organized labor, and other liberal policies. Garner even challenged Roosevelt for the party's 1940 presidential nomination. This rupture between the president and the vice president set the stage for an important modification of the vice-presidential selection process that was designed to foster greater harmony between presidents and vice presidents. In 1936, at Roosevelt's insistence, the Democrats had abolished their two-thirds rule for presidential nominations, which meant that candidates for president no longer had to tolerate as much horse trading of vice-presidential nominations and other administration posts in order to win at the convention. (The party also abolished the two-thirds rule for

vice-presidential nominations, reducing the degree of consensus needed for that decision as well.) In 1940 Roosevelt completed his coup by seizing the party leaders' traditional prerogative to determine nominations for vice president and making it his own. Roosevelt's tactic was simple: he threatened that unless the convention nominated Secretary of Agriculture Henry A. Wallace for vice president (which it was loath to do), he would not accept the Democratic nomination for president.

Unlike Garner and many of his other predecessors, Wallace had never been a member of Congress and, while serving as vice president, he spent little time on Capitol Hill. But he did become the first vice president to be appointed as head of a government agency. In July 1941 Roosevelt named Wallace to chair the new Economic Defense Board, a three-thousand-member wartime preparation agency, which, after World War II was declared in December, was renamed the Board of Economic Warfare and assigned major procurement responsibilities. Unfortunately, the powers and duties of Wallace's agency overlapped with those of several cabinet departments, notably State and Commerce. These overlaps generated interagency conflicts about jurisdiction and policy that weakened the war effort and undermined Wallace's authority. But because the vice president is a constitutionally independent official whom the president cannot command or remove, Roosevelt felt compelled to abolish the warfare board, which left Wallace embarrassed and devoid of function. In the end, then, what seemed to be a new birth of vice-presidential power turned out to be false labor. No president since FDR has ever asked the vice president to head an executive agency.

Nonetheless, the steadily growing involvement of the vice presidency in executive branch activities persisted under Wallace. The vice president continued to sit with the cabinet, advise the president, and travel abroad as an administration emissary. Even Wallace's lack of involvement with Congress exemplified, although to an unusual degree, a developing characteristic of the twentieth-century vice presidency—namely, the atrophy of the office's role as president of the Senate. To some degree, the first development explains the second. To the extent that vice presidents became more involved with the presidency, they had less time to spend on the floor of the Senate and less ability to win its members' trust. But changes in the Senate also help to account for the decline of the vice president's constitutional responsibilities in that institution. For one thing, the admission of many new states over the years caused the Senate to grow larger, making tie votes statistically less probable. The Senate also became ever more institutionalized, developing a body of rules and procedural precedents, which the president of the Senate was expected merely to announce, on the advice of the parliamentarian.

Advances in the visibility, stature, and extraconstitutional responsibilities of the vice presidency may help to explain the office's improved performance of its main constitutional duty: to provide an able successor to the presidency. Historians rate two of the five twentieth-century successor presidents (Theodore Roosevelt and Truman) as near-great, one as above average (Lyndon Johnson), and only Coolidge as below average.[22] But for all its gains, the vice presidency on the eve of midcentury remained a fundamentally weak office. Its constitutional status was substantially unaltered, although the Twentieth Amendment (1933) established the full successorship of the vice president–elect in the event of the president-elect's death. All the ambiguities of the vice president's rights and duties in times of presidential disability still were unresolved, as dramatized by the passive role Marshall felt compelled to play during the prolonged illness of Woodrow Wilson. *(See "Presidential Disability," p. 499, in Chapter 8.)* Tension continued to mark some presidential–vice-presidential pairings, although less frequently after Franklin Roosevelt won for presidential candidates the right to choose their running mates.

Even the glimmerings of enhanced vice-presidential influence sometimes seemed to be no more than that. When he ran for a fourth term in 1944, Roosevelt replaced the unpopular Wallace with Senator Harry Truman. On inaugu-ration day in 1945, the president was ill, and World War II was coming to a close. Yet Truman later was to say that in his eighty-two days as vice president, "I don't think I saw Roosevelt but twice . . . except at cabinet meetings."[23] He was at most dimly aware of the existence of the atomic bomb, the contents of the Allies' plans for the postwar world, and the serious deterioration of the president's health. In this woeful state of ignorance and unpreparedness, Truman succeeded to the office of president and to its full range of powers and duties when Roosevelt died on April 12, 1945. He told a friend later that day, "I feel like I have been struck by a bolt of lightning."[24]

THE MODERN VICE PRESIDENCY

Truman's lack of preparation in 1945, along with the subsequent development of an ongoing cold war between the United States and the Soviet Union and the proliferation of intercontinental ballistic missiles armed with nuclear warheads, heightened public concern that the vice president be a leader not just willing but also ready and able to step into the presidency at a moment's notice if the need should arise. This concern has had important consequences for vice-presidential selection, activities, succession and disability, and political status.

Selection

To meet the new public expectations about vice-presidential quality, most modern presidential candidates have paid considerable attention to experience, ability, and political compatibility in selecting their running mates. Winning votes on election day is as much the goal as in the days of old-style ticket balancing, but presidential nominees realize that voters now care more about competence and loyalty—a vice-presidential candidate's ability to succeed to the presidency ably and to carry on the departed president's policies faithfully—than they do about having all regions of the country or factions of the party represented on the ticket.[25] This realization has helped to create a climate for a more influential vice presidency. As the legal scholar Joel Goldstein has shown, the president is most likely to assign responsibilities to the vice president when the two are personally and politically compatible and when the president believes that the vice president has talents the administration needs.[26] These conditions now are likely to be met (and have been, in every administration since 1974) as a consequence of the new selection criteria.

Little is left to chance in modern vice-presidential selection, at least when the presidential nominating contest is settled, as has been typical since 1952, well in advance of the nominating convention. Jimmy Carter set a precedent in 1976 when he conducted a careful, organized preconvention search for a running mate. A list of four hundred

Democratic officeholders was compiled and scrutinized by aides, then winnowed down to seven finalists who were investigated and, ultimately, interviewed by Carter. (He tapped Walter Mondale at the convention.) Carter also leaked the names of the candidates he was considering to the news media both to gauge the public reaction to each of them and to ensure that any scandalous or embarrassing behavior they had engaged in would be revealed before he made his decision rather than afterward.

The "Carter model" of vice-presidential selection caught on: Mondale in 1984, Michael S. Dukakis in 1988, Bill Clinton in 1992, and both Al Gore and George W. Bush in 2000 followed similar procedures. Ronald Reagan did nothing so elaborate in 1980 because he hoped to lure former president Gerald Ford onto the ticket, but he and his aides did give considerable thought to the kind of running mate they wanted. George H. W. Bush searched widely before choosing Dan Quayle in 1988, as did Robert J. Dole before choosing former Housing and Urban Development secretary Jack Kemp in 1996.

The fruit of both the new emphasis on loyalty and competence and the new care that is invested in the selection process can be seen in the roster of postwar vice-presidential nominees. The modern era has been marked by an almost complete absence of ideologically opposed running mates, and those vice-presidential candidates who have differed even slightly on the issues with the heads of their tickets have hastened to gloss over past disagreements and to deny that any exist in the present. The record is even more compelling with regard to competence. From 1948 to 2004, the vice-presidential candidate was as often as not the more experienced member of the ticket in high government office, including John Sparkman in 1952, Estes Kefauver in 1956, Lyndon Johnson and Henry Cabot Lodge in 1960, Walter Mondale in 1976, George H. W. Bush in 1980, Lloyd Bentsen in 1988, Al Gore in 1992, and Richard B. Cheney in 2000.[27]

To be sure, nothing guarantees that reasoned, responsible vice-presidential nominations will emerge on every occasion. Politicians do not always see their interests clearly. Nixon, the Republican presidential nominee in 1968, was too clever by half when, acting on the theory that a relatively unknown running mate would have few enemies and cost the ticket few votes, he chose Agnew as his candidate for vice president. In 1984 many observers thought Mondale seemed too eager to placate feminist groups within the party when he selected Geraldine Ferraro, a three-term member of the House of Representatives with no notable foreign affairs experience. Similarly, George McGovern may have been overly concerned about satisfying organized labor in picking Thomas F. Eagleton in 1972. (It was revealed soon after Eagleton's nomination for vice president that he had concealed from McGovern the electroshock treatment he underwent for a nervous breakdown, which led to his being

dropped from the ticket.) Bush miscalculated when he chose Quayle in 1988, thinking (erroneously) that the Indiana senator's youth and good looks would attract votes from baby boomers and women, respectively.[28]

What seems certain, however, is that the presidential candidate who pays insufficient attention to competence and loyalty in choosing the vice-presidential nominee will suffer for it in the election: the news media will run critical stories, the other party will air harsh commercials, and the now traditional vice-presidential debate, which is nationally televised in prime time, may reveal the nominee as an unworthy presidential successor.[29] Vice-presidential candidates dominate the news during at least two periods: at the time the presidential candidates announce their names and during the week surrounding the vice-presidential debate. A candidate for president who chooses badly not only forfeits an opportunity for good news coverage but invites bad news coverage.[30]

In the 1988 election, Bush's selection of Quayle may have reduced his margin of victory in the popular vote by as much as four to eight percentage points.[31] In contrast, the nomination of Gore successfully defied all the conventions of ticket balancing. Like Clinton, Gore was a southerner, a Baptist, a moderate, and a baby boomer. But Gore's obvious intelligence and ability appealed to many voters.[32] A *Time-CNN* poll found in July 1992 that when asked, "Who do you think is more qualified to be president—Quayle or Gore?" 63 percent of respondents said Gore and 21 percent the incumbent vice president, Quayle.[33]

Because the Republican convention preceded the Democratic convention in 2000, George W. Bush had to choose his running mate before Gore did. To screen potential nominees, Bush established a vetting process headed by Cheney, a veteran Washington politician with experience in the House of Representatives and in several Republican administrations, including prominent service as secretary of defense under Bush's father. In the end, Bush chose Cheney himself. The selection was surprising in one way—most of the speculation had centered on Bush's fellow big-state Republican governors, such as Tom Ridge of Pennsylvania and John Engler of Michigan. (Bush was governor of Texas.) But in a more important way, Bush's selection of Cheney was not surprising at all. Governors who are nominated for president—FDR in 1932, Alfred M. Landon in 1936, Thomas E. Dewey in 1944, Adlai Stevenson in 1952 and 1956, Carter in 1976, Reagan in 1980, Dukakis in 1988, and Clinton in 1992—almost always choose experienced Washington figures for vice president. They do so to reassure the voters that their own inexperience in national government, especially in foreign policy, will be offset by the vice president's experience and expertise. Bush underlined this virtue of the Cheney nomination by declaring that he had chosen him less to help win the election than to help him govern "as a

Saudi crown prince Sultan bin Abdulaziz greets Vice President Dick Cheney as he arrives at King Faisal Airbase in Saudi Arabia, May 12, 2007. President George W. Bush has frequently drawn on the foreign policy experience the vice president gained as defense secretary under the first President Bush. In that role, Cheney traveled to the Middle East in 1990 to offer U.S. assistance days after Iraq invaded Kuwait.

valuable partner"—a shrewd tactic for helping Bush to win the election.[34]

Gore enlisted Warren Christopher to screen potential Democratic running mates, persuaded of the former secretary of state's skill at this assignment by Christopher's direction of the process that had led to Gore's own selection in 1992. Between February and July 2000, Christopher and Gore whittled a list of around forty names down to four, all of them senators: John Edwards of North Carolina, John F. Kerry of Massachusetts, Bob Kerrey of Nebraska, and Joseph Lieberman of Connecticut, who was added at Gore's insistence. (The Republican Party's domination of the nation's statehouses—in 2000 they had thirty governors and the Democrats had twenty, only one of whom was in a large state—meant that Gore had few governors to choose from.) Gore wanted to make a bold choice that would help to establish him in the voters' minds as a leader in his own right, not just as President Clinton's loyal lieutenant. When the time came, no one doubted the boldness of Gore's decision to choose Lieberman, a deeply religious Jew who had publicly criticized Clinton's behavior during the Monica Lewinsky affair as "immoral."[35]

In the end, Bush's selection of Cheney and Gore's of Lieberman were helpful to their tickets in offsetting ways. In the election day exit poll, 72 percent of all voters said that Lieberman's religion would make him neither a better nor a worse vice president, but of the remaining 28 percent, twice as many said they thought it would make him a better one. Asked whom they would prefer as vice president, 46 percent of the voters said Lieberman and 48 percent said Cheney, a statistical wash.[36] Cheney's main contribution to Bush was

indirect. His extensive experience in foreign affairs helps to explain why most of the voters who regarded foreign policy as the most important issue in the election supported Bush, even though Bush's background in this area was considerably weaker than Gore's.

In 2004 Democratic presidential candidate John Kerry chose his chief rival for the nomination, Sen. John Edwards, as his vice-presidential running mate. Kerry's choice of someone he had just defeated was not unusual: eight of the twenty vice-presidential nominees from 1960 to 2004 had already run for president at least once. But Kerry and Edwards often seemed uncomfortable together in joint appearances, and the Kerry campaign made no effort to carry Edwards's home state of North Carolina.

A concern for competence and loyalty in the vice presidency characterized the solution Congress invented in the 1960s to a recurring problem of the executive that the challenges of the postwar era had made urgent: vice-presidential vacancies. The Twenty-fifth Amendment, which was ratified in 1967, established a procedure for selecting vice presidents in unusual circumstances. Before then, the vice presidency had been vacant for parts of sixteen administrations, leaving the presidency without a constitutionally designated successor.[37] The new amendment stated that "whenever there is a vacancy in the office of the Vice President, the President shall nominate a Vice President who shall take office upon confirmation by a majority vote of both Houses of Congress," with each house voting separately. This procedure came in handy, albeit in circumstances its authors scarcely had imagined, in 1973 when Vice President Agnew resigned as part of a plea bargain and was replaced by Ford, and in 1974 when Ford became president after President Nixon resigned to avert impeachment proceedings and appointed Rockefeller to fill the vacated vice presidency. *(See "Filling Vice-Presidential Vacancies," p. 450, in Chapter 7.)*

Activity

One thing modern presidents do to reassure the nation that the vice president is prepared to succeed to the presidency is to keep their vice presidents informed about matters of state. As President Dwight D. Eisenhower's remark at a news conference indicates, to do otherwise would invite public criticism: "Even if Mr. Nixon and I were not good friends, I would still have him in every important conference of government, so that if the grim reaper would find it time to remove me from the scene, he is ready to step in without any interruption." [38] In 1949, at President Truman's behest, the vice president was made a statutory member of the National Security Council. (The only other task assigned to the vice president by law is membership on the board of regents of the Smithsonian Institution.) Vice presidents also receive full national security briefings as a matter of course.

As a further means of reassurance, most presidents now encourage the vice president to stay active and in the public eye. Since Garner began the practice, vice presidents have traveled abroad on the president's behalf with growing frequency and in pursuit of a variety of diplomatic missions, ranging from simple expressions of American goodwill to actual negotiations. Vice presidents since Garner also have met regularly with the cabinet and served, to some degree, as legislative liaison from the president to Congress—counting votes on Capitol Hill, lobbying discreetly, and listening to complaints and suggestions.

Alben W. Barkley, who served as vice president in the second Truman administration, elevated the ceremonial duties of the vice presidency to center stage. Some of these, such as crowning beauty queens (a Barkley favorite), are inconsequential. Others, such as commencement addresses and appearances at events that symbolize the administration's goals, need not be. Nixon, serving a president who did not enjoy partisan politics, carved out new vice-presidential roles that were as insignificant as chair of a minor study commission and as important as public advocate of the administration's policies, leadership, and party. The advocacy role exposed the vice president frequently to a wide range of audiences, including interest groups, party activists, journalists, and the general public.

During the 1960s and 1970s, vice presidents began to accumulate greater institutional resources to help them fulfill their more extensive duties. Lyndon Johnson, the vice president to President John F. Kennedy, gained for the vice presidency an impressive suite of offices in the Executive Office Building, adjacent to the White House. Agnew won a line item in the executive budget. The result was to free vice presidents from their earlier dependence on Congress for office space and operating funds.

Franklin Roosevelt's vice president, John Nance Garner, began the practice of traveling abroad on the president's behalf. He is perhaps best remembered, however, for his pithy assessment of the office: "The vice presidency isn't worth a pitcher of warm spit."

Even more significant institutional gains were registered by Ford and Rockefeller, the two vice presidents who were appointed under the Twenty-fifth Amendment and whose agreements to serve were urgently required by their presidents, for political reasons. Ford, who feared becoming too dependent on a president who might well be impeached and removed from office, persuaded Nixon to increase dramatically his budget for staff. The new personnel included support staff for press relations, speech-writing, scheduling, and administration (which meant vice presidents no longer had to depend on the often preoccupied White House staff for these functions), policy staff (enabling vice presidents to develop useful advice on matters of presidential concern), and political staff (to help vice presidents protect their interests and further their ambitions). Rockefeller secured a weekly place on the president's calendar for a private meeting.[39] He also enhanced the perquisites of the vice presidency—everything from a better airplane to serve as *Air Force Two* to an official residence (the old Admiral's House at the Naval Observatory) and a redesigned seal for the office. The old seal showed an eagle at rest; the new one, an eagle with wings spread, a claw full of arrows, and a starburst at its head.

The vice presidency came into full flower during Mondale's tenure in the Carter administration. As a candidate in 1976, Mondale participated in the first nationally televised debate between the vice-presidential candidates. His most tangible contributions to the institution during his term as vice president, building on earlier gains, were the authorization he won to attend all presidential meetings, full access to the flow of papers to and from the president, and an office in the West Wing of the White House. More important, perhaps, Mondale demonstrated that the vice president

As President Jimmy Carter's vice president, Walter Mondale was one of the most influential vice presidents. Unlike his predecessors, Mondale had an office in the West Wing of the White House.

could serve the president (who, as noted earlier, had selected him with unprecedented care and attention) as a valued adviser on virtually all matters of politics and public policy. Some vice presidents in each of the earlier eras of the office's history, and most vice presidents in the modern era, had been consulted by their presidents on at least some important matters—Johnson on space exploration issues, Humphrey on civil rights, Rockefeller on domestic policy. But no vice president had ever attained Mondale's status as a general adviser to the president.

George H. W. Bush, as vice president to President Reagan, was heir to all the institutional gains in both roles and resources that his recent predecessors had won. Although he did not enter office enjoying the same sort of personal relationship with Reagan that Mondale had with Carter, Bush worked hard and, for the most part, successfully to win the president's confidence. As president, Bush fostered an even stronger relationship with Quayle, whom he appointed to chair the new White House Council on Competitiveness, a de facto board of regulatory review that was empowered to overturn regulations issuing from the federal bureaucracy.

From the beginning, Clinton's relationship with Gore rivaled Carter's with Mondale in terms of trust and responsibility. Until strains developed when Gore ran for president in 2000, the relationship exceeded any previous one between a president and a vice president in terms of personal friendship. Gore was the administration's star player in September 1993 when he issued the fat-trimming "reinventing government" report of the National Performance Review Commission.

Two months later, he soundly defeated administration critic and businessman H. Ross Perot in a widely watched, nationally televised debate about the proposed North American Free Trade Agreement (NAFTA) on CNN's *Larry King Live.*

More generally, Gore was one of the three or four people whose advice Clinton sought on virtually every important matter of presidential politics and policy. On one occasion in 1993, when Clinton was immobilized with doubt about how to proceed with his economic program in Congress, he asked Gore, "What can I do?" "You can get with the goddamn program!" Gore replied, with considerable exasperation. After a pause, Clinton said, "Okay." [40] According to the veteran reporter Elizabeth Drew, "Gore was in large measure responsible for the boldness of Clinton's [first-year] economic program." [41] In 1998 a Clinton adviser listed the areas in which Al Gore, at Clinton's request, made decisions that the president rubber-stamped: "science, technology, NASA, telecommunications, the environment, family leave, tobacco, nuclear dealings with the Russians, media violence, the Internet, privacy issues and, of course, reinventing government." [42]

Cheney's responsibilities in the administration of George W. Bush may surpass those of any vice president in history, including Mondale and Gore. Bush asked Cheney to direct the transition between election and inauguration, the first time a vice president–elect had been assigned this responsibility. Cheney also was charged to develop the administration's energy policy initiatives in spring 2001. After the terrorist bombings of New York City's World Trade Center and the Pentagon on September 11, 2001, Cheney was kept in a secret location while Bush remained in the White House, for fear that a terrorist attack might kill them both if they were in the same place. Nevertheless, Cheney, building on his experience as secretary of defense during the U.S. war with Iraq some ten years earlier, was Bush's primary adviser in the war against terrorism, participating through teleconferencing and other electronic means in every important meeting of the president and his war cabinet.

Cheney's role in the war to topple the Saddam Hussein regime in Iraq, which was launched in 2003, was more controversial. He relentlessly pressed the argument, both in speeches and in private administration councils, that Hussein had stockpiled weapons of mass destruction and was cooperating with the al Qaeda terrorist network that was responsible for the 2001 attacks. Although U.S. and allied forces easily defeated Hussein, neither of these arguments proved valid. Still worse, anti-American insurgents in Iraq waged ongoing guerilla warfare against the occupying forces, undermining the stability of the elected Iraqi government that succeeded the Hussein regime. [43]

Every vice president realizes that the degree to which the new activities of the vice presidency translate into real influence within the White House still depends in large part on the president's perception of the vice president's ability, energy, and, perhaps most important, loyalty. But because of the new vice-presidential selection criteria, this perception is more likely to be favorable now than at any time in history. And because of the institutionalization of numerous roles and resources in the vice presidency, the vice president has a greater opportunity than ever to be of real service to the president.

Succession and Disability

In addition to creating a procedure to fill vice-presidential vacancies, the Twenty-fifth Amendment accomplished two other purposes. One was to state explicitly the right of the vice president to assume the office of president and to serve for the remainder of the departed president's term, an uncontroversial measure that conferred constitutional sanction on the tradition that Tyler had established after President Harrison died in 1841. The other was to create a set of procedures to handle situations of presidential disability. Disability had been a recurring problem of the presidency, but President Eisenhower's heart attack and other ailments during the 1950s brought matters to a head. In an age of nuclear confrontation, he and many others felt, the nation could not run the risk of being leaderless even briefly. Eisenhower's short-term solution was to write Vice President Nixon a letter in 1958 stating that if he were ever disabled again, he would instruct the vice president to serve as acting president for as long as the disability lasted. If Eisenhower were unable to communicate for some reason, Nixon could make the decision himself.

Presidents Kennedy and Johnson endorsed this arrangement when they took office, but it hardly solved the disability problem. The Eisenhower letter lacked the force of law and made no provision to relieve a president who was disabled but, like President Wilson, refused to admit it. The Twenty-fifth Amendment provided a constitutional method for the president, by means of a letter to the leaders of Congress, to name the vice president as acting president during a time of disability, as well as for the vice president and a majority of the heads of the departments to make that decision if the president were unable to do so. The amendment even created a procedure to be followed if the vice president and cabinet believed the president to be disabled and the president disagreed. The vice president would become acting president, but the president would be restored to power within twenty-one days unless two-thirds of both the House of Representatives and the Senate voted against the president.

Few clear situations of presidential disability have arisen since the Twenty-fifth Amendment was passed, both during the Reagan administration. The first occurred when Reagan was shot on March 30, 1981. Some thought was given to naming Vice President George H. W. Bush as acting president, but White House aides discouraged any such action for fear that it might make Reagan appear weak or confuse the nation.[44]

Criticism of the administration's failure to act in 1981 shaped its preparation for the second instance of presidential disability, Reagan's cancer surgery on July 13, 1985. This time the president did relinquish his powers and duties to Bush before undergoing anesthesia. Curiously, however, he did not explicitly invoke the Twenty-fifth Amendment in doing so, saying instead that he was not convinced that the amendment was meant to apply to "such brief and temporary periods of incapacity." Still, a precedent was established, raising expectations that the Twenty-fifth Amendment would work as intended in future administrations. This precedent was followed in May 1991 when President Bush announced a plan to turn power over to Vice President Quayle in the event that his irregular heartbeat required electroshock therapy. (It did not.)

On January 29, 2002, President George W. Bush explicitly invoked the Twenty-fifth Amendment just before undergoing light sedation for a colonoscopy. For approximately two hours Cheney was acting president. Although Cheney was not called upon to do anything, Bush explained to the press that in light of the recent September 11, 2001, terrorist attacks on New York and Washington, "we're at war and I just want to be super-cautious."[45]

Political Status

The vice president enjoys a curious political status. Until George H. W. Bush's 1988 victory, no incumbent vice president had been elected president since 1836, when Van Buren accomplished the feat. Yet in a marked departure from previous political history, the modern vice presidency has been an effective steppingstone to a major party presidential nomination. Of the other recent vice presidents, Nixon, Humphrey, Mondale, and Gore were nominated directly for president; and Truman, Johnson, and Ford were nominated for full terms after succeeding to the presidency. Agnew and Rockefeller did not actively seek a presidential nomination, and Cheney made clear from the start that he would not seek the presidency.

What accounts for the recent ascendancy of the vice presidency in the politics of presidential nominations? First, the two-term limit that was imposed on presidents by the Twenty-second Amendment (1951) makes it possible for the vice president to step forward as a presidential candidate during the president's second term without alienating the president, as Nixon did in 1960, Bush did in 1988, and Gore did in 2000. (This effect of the amendment was wholly unanticipated when it was enacted.) Second, the roles that Vice President Nixon developed, with Eisenhower's encour-

In 1988 George H. W. Bush became the first incumbent vice president to be elected to the presidency since Martin Van Buren in 1836.

a 1998 postimpeachment rally of Democratic House members that Clinton "will be regarded in the history books as one of our greatest presidents" doubtless roused the spirits of his fellow partisans, but it seemed wildly excessive to almost everyone else.[49] As for the woodenness that many people attributed to Gore, it was partly a long-standing personal trait but mostly an artifact of the hundreds of vice-presidential moments he spent standing motionless and silent in the background while Clinton spoke animatedly to the television cameras.

agement, as party builder (campaigning during election years, raising funds between elections) and as public advocate of the administration and its policies uniquely situate the vice president to win friends among the political activists who influence presidential nominations. Finally, the recent growth in vice-presidential activities has made the vice presidency a more prestigious office and thus a more plausible steppingstone to the presidency. Foreign travel and the trappings of the office—the airplane, mansion, seal, West Wing office, and so on—are tangible symbols of prestige.[46]

Perhaps more important, in their efforts to assure the nation that they are fulfilling their responsibility to prepare for a possible emergency succession, presidents may make inflated claims about the role of the vice president in the administration. Thus the typical modern vice president can plausibly argue, as Mondale frequently did, that the vice presidency "may be the best training of all" for the presidency:

> I'm privy to all the same secret information as the president. I have unlimited access to the president. I'm usually with him when all the central decisions are being made. I've been through several of those crises that a president inevitably confronts, and I see how they work. I've been through the budget process. I've been through the diplomatic ventures. I've been through a host of congressional fights as seen from the presidential perspective.[47]

Yet vice presidents who are nominated by their party for president carry certain disadvantages into the fall campaign that are as surely grounded in the office as are the advantages they bring to the nominating contest.[48] Indeed, some of the activities of the modern vice presidency that are most appealing to the party activists who influence nominations may repel other voters. Days and nights spent fertilizing the party's grassroots with fervent, sometimes slashing rhetoric can alienate those who look to the presidency for leadership that unifies rather than divides. Gore's remark to

Certain institutional qualities of the modern vice presidency also handicap the vice-president-turned-presidential candidate. Vice presidents must work hard to gain a share of the credit for the successes of the administration. But they can count on being attacked by the other party's presidential nominee for all of the administration's shortcomings. Such attacks allow no effective response. A vice president who tries to stand apart from the White House may alienate the president and cause voters to wonder why the criticisms were not voiced earlier. Gore did himself no good, for example, when he spent the evening of his official announcement for president telling the *20/20* television audience that Clinton's behavior in the Monica Lewinsky affair was "inexcusable."[50]

The vice president's difficulties are only compounded when it comes to matters of substantive public policy. For example, every time during the 2000 campaign that Gore tried to identify a problem he wanted to solve as president, George W. Bush would step forward to chastise him for not having already persuaded Clinton to solve it. During their first debate, when Gore mentioned his proposal to extend prescription drug benefits to seniors, Bush replied, "Four years ago they campaigned on getting prescription drugs for seniors. And now they're campaigning on getting prescription drugs for seniors. It seems like they can't get it done."[51]

Vice presidents can always say that loyalty to the president forecloses public disagreement, but that course is no less perilous politically. The public that values loyalty in a vice president values different qualities in a potential president. Strength, vision, and independence are what they look for then—the very qualities that vice presidents almost never get to display.[52] Polls that through much of the election year showed Gore trailing Bush in the category of leadership were less about Bush and Gore than about the vice presidency. So was the election day exit poll showing that voters who regarded strong leadership as the personal quality they most wanted in a president supported Bush by 64–34 percent.[53]

The political handicaps that vice presidents carry into the general election are considerable. They need not be insurmountable. As with all things vice-presidential, much depends on their relationship with presidents they serve. One of the main reasons that Nixon and Humphrey lost, for example, is that their presidents were so unhelpful. When a reporter asked Eisenhower to name a single "major idea of [Nixon's] you had adopted" as president, he replied, "If you give me a week, I might think of one." [54] Johnson treated Vice President Humphrey spitefully as soon as it became clear that the 1968 Democratic convention was not going to draft the president for another term despite his earlier withdrawal from the race.

In contrast, more than a century earlier Van Buren benefited enormously from his association with President Andrew Jackson, who regarded his vice president's election to the presidency as validation of the transformation he had wrought in American politics. Reagan was equally committed to Bush's success in 1988, putting ego aside to praise the vice president's contributions to what the president began calling the "Reagan-Bush administration." Reagan's popularity was of still greater benefit to his vice president. Bush won the votes of 80 percent of those who approved of Reagan's performance as president.[55]

Although Clinton said in 2000 that he wished he could run for a third term (and identified Gore only as "the next best thing"),[56] he combined Jackson's belief that his legacy was closely tied to his vice president's political success with Reaganesque approval ratings and a strong economy. Gore, however, chose to distance himself from Clinton, rejecting the president's repeated offers to campaign for him, which party leaders pleaded with Gore to accept.[57] Instead of emphasizing the national prosperity that had marked the Clinton-Gore years, Gore ran a populist-style campaign more appropriate for a candidate challenging an incumbent in economic hard times than for a vice president seeking to extend his party's control of the presidency in good times. In the three nationally televised debates with Bush, Gore never mentioned Clinton. "We might have blown it," a Gore aide said near the end of the campaign. "We didn't remind people of how well off they are." [58]

To be sure, vice presidents are not destined to lose general elections any more than they are destined to win presidential nominations. Before Bush's election in 1988, Nixon in 1960 and Humphrey in 1968 came within less than two percentage points of victory. In 2000 Gore won the national popular vote, and only lost the electoral vote narrowly. But the electoral tensions vice presidents face are inherent in the office. As President Eisenhower once said, "To promise and pledge *new* effort, *new* programs, and *new* ideas without appearing to criticize the current party and administration—that is indeed an exercise in tightrope walking." [59]

CONCLUSION

In selection, activity, succession and disability, and political status, the vice presidency has come a long way over the last century, especially since 1945. But the curious political status of the vice presidency is a reminder that, for all its progress as an institution, some weaknesses of the office endure. Although new selection criteria make the nomination of vice-presidential candidates who are qualified to be president more likely, the recent examples of Agnew in 1968, Eagleton in 1972, Ferraro in 1984, and Quayle in 1988 indicate that older forms of ticket balancing are not yet extinct. New selection criteria may foster greater harmony in office between presidents and vice presidents, but they do not guarantee it. (Perhaps it is not surprising that the two modern presidents who inflicted the greatest pain on their vice presidents, Johnson and Nixon, once were vice presidents themselves.[60]) Finally, although vice presidents enjoy more resources, responsibilities, and influence than ever before, they do so mainly at the sufferance of the president. The price of power for a vice president can be high—unflagging loyalty, sublimation of one's views and ambitions, and willing receptiveness to the president's beck and call. But in view of the inherent constitutional weakness of the office, no other path to influence exists.

NOTES

1. These familiar quotations about the vice presidency may be found in Michael Dorman, *The Second Man: The Changing Role of the Vice Presidency* (New York: Delacorte Press, 1968), 6–7.

2. Joseph A. Pika, "The Vice Presidency: New Opportunities, Old Constraints," in *The Presidency and the Political System*, 6th ed., ed. Michael Nelson (Washington, D.C.: CQ Press, 2000), 533–569.

3. Quoted in Paul C. Light, *Vice-Presidential Power: Advice and Influence in the White House* (Baltimore: Johns Hopkins University Press, 1984), 13.

4. Joel K. Goldstein, *The Modern American Vice Presidency* (Princeton: Princeton University Press, 1982); various editions of *The Gallup Poll* (Wilmington, Del.: Scholarly Resources, 1982–1987).

5. Thomas R. Marshall, *Recollections* (Indianapolis: Bobbs-Merrill, 1925), 368.

6. Quoted in David McCullough, *John Adams* (New York: Simon and Schuster, 2001), 447.

7. Quoted in Goldstein, *Modern American Vice Presidency*, 6.

8. David E. Kyvig, *Explicit and Authentic Acts: Amending the U.S. Constitution, 1776–1995* (Lawrence: University Press of Kansas, 1996), 116.

9. Jody C. Baumgartner, *The American Vice Presidency Reconsidered* (Westport, Conn.: Praeger, 2006), 19.

10. Quoted in Thomas E. Cronin, "Rethinking the Vice Presidency," in *Rethinking the Presidency,* ed. Thomas E. Cronin (Boston: Little, Brown, 1982), 326. Rather than being buried, of course, Webster would have succeeded to the presidency when Zachary Taylor died in 1850.

11. Quoted in Irving G. Williams, *The Rise of the Vice Presidency* (Washington, D.C.: Public Affairs Press, 1956), 66.

12. Johnson was the protagonist in two other unique events in the history of the vice presidency. In the election of 1836, Virginia's Democratic electors refused to vote for Johnson because they objected to his interracial sexual extravagances. This left Johnson one vote short of the required electoral vote majority, so the Senate elected him by 33–16. Four years later, Johnson refused to withdraw as a candidate for the Democratic nomination for vice president, dividing the party convention to such an extent that it selected no vice-presidential candidate at all. (The Democrats lost the election.) For additional information about the history of the vice presidency, see Jules Witcover, *Crapshoot: Rolling the Dice on the Vice Presidency* (New York: Crown, 1992).

13. Robert K. Murray and Tim H. Blessing, "The Presidential Performance Study: A Progress Report," *Journal of American History* 70 (December 1983): 535–555.

14. The five nineteenth-century presidents who were disabled for a measurable period of time were Madison, William Henry Harrison, Arthur, Garfield, and Grover Cleveland. John D. Feerick, *The Twenty-fifth Amendment* (New York: Fordham University Press, 1992), chap. 1.

15. Woodrow Wilson, *Congressional Government* (New York: Meridian Books, 1956), 162.

16. The exception was Henry A. Wallace in 1944. For a detailed historical perspective on the growing political security of vice presidents, see George S. Sergiovanni, "Dumping the Vice President: A Historical Overview and Analysis," *Presidential Studies Quarterly* 24 (fall 1994): 765–782.

17. Theodore Roosevelt, "The Three Vice-Presidential Candidates and What They Represent," *Review of Reviews,* September 1896, 289.

18. Quoted in Williams, *Rise of the Vice Presidency,* 89.

19. Marshall's decision to accept Wilson's invitation to meet with the cabinet was made with some misgivings. Although he once had described the president as "my commander-in-chief" whose "orders would be obeyed," Marshall believed that, constitutionally, the vice president, as president of the Senate, was a "member of the legislative branch," ill-suited to executive responsibilities. Thus he told the cabinet that he wanted it clearly understood that he was present only "informally and personally" and would "preside in an unofficial and informal way." Before his inauguration in 1925, Vice President Dawes said publicly that he would not accept an invitation from President Coolidge to meet with the cabinet, if, as seemed likely, one was forthcoming. "The cabinet and those who sit with it should always do so at the discretion and inclination of the president. . . ," Dawes told reporters, neglecting the possibility that Coolidge might wish to exercise his discretion to have the vice president present. "No precedent should be established which creates a different and arbitrary method of selection." Quoted in Williams, *Rise of the Vice Presidency,* 108–110, 134.

20. Franklin D. Roosevelt, "Can the Vice President Be Useful?" *Saturday Evening Post,* October 6, 1920, 8.

21. Williams, *Rise of the Vice Presidency,* 158–159.

22. Murray and Blessing, "Presidential Performance Study."

23. Quoted in Williams, *Rise of the Vice Presidency,* 219.

24. Quoted in Robert J. Donovan, *Conflict and Crisis: The Presidency of Harry S. Truman, 1945–1948* (New York: Norton, 1977), 15.

25. Ticket balancing is of little explanatory value in accounting for vice-presidential nominations since 1940. Lee Sigelman and Paul J. Wahlbeck, "The 'Veepstakes': Strategic Choice in Presidential Running Mate Selection," *American Political Science Review* 91 (December 1997): 62.

26. Goldstein, *Modern American Vice Presidency,* 147–148. Updated by author.

27. Ibid., 85.

28. Michael Nelson, "Choosing the Vice President," *PS: Political Science and Politics* 21 (fall 1988): 858–868.

29. The debates appear to have a short-term effect on voters' intentions. Thomas M. Holbrook, "The Behavioral Consequences of Vice Presidential Debates," *American Politics Quarterly* 22 (October 1994): 469–482.

30. Baumgartner, *American Vice Presidency Reconsidered,* chap. 5.

31. Michael Nelson, "Constitutional Aspects of the Elections," in *The Elections of 1988,* ed. Michael Nelson (Washington, D.C.: CQ Press, 1989), 181–210.

32. Michael Nelson, "Conclusion: Some Things Old, Some Things New," in *The Elections of 1992,* ed. Michael Nelson (Washington, D.C.: CQ Press, 1993), 183–192. Gore's selection may have been ticket balancing of a different sort: "Clinton's potential vulnerabilities as a foreign policy novice, prodevelopment governor, skirt chaser, and draft avoider were buttressed by Gore's Senate experience, environmentalist credentials, stable family life, and service in the Vietnam War" (190).

33. *National Journal,* August 8, 1992, 1862.

34. David Von Drehle, " 'First, Do No Harm' Rule," *Washington Post National Weekly Edition,* July 31, 2000, 9.

35. Bob Woodward, *Shadow: Five Presidents and the Legacy of Watergate* (New York: Simon and Schuster, 1999), 454.

36. CNN, "Exit Polls" *(www.cnn.com/ELECTION/2000/ RESULTS/index.epolls.html),* accessed November 10, 2000.

37. Vice-presidential vacancies occurred seven times because the vice president died, once because the vice president resigned, and eight times because the president died.

38. *Public Papers of the Presidents* (Washington, D.C.: Government Printing Office, 1957), 132.

39. Rockefeller also headed the White House Domestic Council, an assignment that, like Henry Wallace's, ended in failure.

40. Bob Woodward, *The Agenda: Inside the Clinton White House* (New York: Simon and Schuster, 1994), 281. Gore's influence on the president is a major theme of this insider's account of the early Clinton presidency.

41. Elizabeth Drew, *On the Edge: The Clinton Presidency* (New York: Simon and Schuster, 1994), 228.

42. Richard L. Berke, "A Gore Guide to the Future," *New York Times Magazine,* February 22, 1998, 47.

43. Cheney's influence in the Bush administration and, especially, his role in the war on Iraq are chronicled in Bob Woodward, *Bush at War* (New York: Simon and Schuster, 2002); Woodward, *Plan of Attack* (New York: Simon and Schuster, 2004); and Woodward, *State of Denial* (New York: Simon and Schuster, 2006).

44. Lawrence I. Barrett, *Gambling with History: Ronald Reagan in the White House* (Garden City, N.Y.: Doubleday, 1983), chap. 7.

45. White House, Office of the Press Secretary, "Remarks by the President Upon Departure for Camp David," June 28, 2002.

46. As Vice President Ford remarked in 1974, "I am now surrounded by a clutch of Secret Service agents, reporters and cameramen, and assorted well-wishers. When I travel I am greeted by bands playing 'Hail Columbia' and introduced to audiences with great solemnity instead of just as 'my good friend, Jerry Ford.' " Quoted in Light, *Vice-Presidential Power*, 10.

47. Quoted in Cronin, "Rethinking the Vice Presidency," 338.

48. The following discussion is drawn from Michael Nelson, "The Election: Ordinary Politics, Extraordinary Outcome," in *The Elections of 2000*, ed. Michael Nelson (Washington, D.C.: CQ Press, 2001), 55–92; and Michael Nelson, "The Curse of the Vice Presidency," *American Prospect*, July 31, 2000, 20–24.

49. Bill Turque, *Inventing Al Gore* (Boston: Houghton Mifflin, 2000), 356.

50. Ibid., 361.

51. "Transcript of Debate between Vice President Gore and Governor Bush," *New York Times*, October 4, 2000.

52. Michael Nelson, "Evaluating the Presidency," in *The Presidency and the Political System*, 6th ed., ed. Michael Nelson (Washington, D.C.: CQ Press, 2000), 3–28.

53. CNN, "Exit Polls."

54. Witcover, *Crapshoot*, 138.

55. Nelson, "Constitutional Aspects of the Elections," 190.

56. David E. Sanger, "After 'Next Best Thing,' Clinton Carefully Praises Gore," *New York Times*, November 4, 2000.

57. David S. Broder, "Gore's Clinton Problem," *Washington Post National Weekly Edition*, October 30, 2000, 4.

58. "What a Long, Strange Trip," *Newsweek*, November 20, 2000, 126.

59. Dwight D. Eisenhower, *Waging Peace* (Garden City, N.Y.: Doubleday, 1965), 596.

60. Paul Light calls this the "abused child syndrome" in *Vice-Presidential Power*, 108.

SELECTED BIBLIOGRAPHY

Baumgartner, Jody C. *The American Vice Presidency Reconsidered.* Westport, Conn.: Praeger, 2006.

Cronin, Thomas E., ed. *Rethinking the Presidency.* Boston: Little, Brown, 1982.

Dorman, Michael. *The Second Man: The Changing Role of the Vice Presidency.* New York: Delacorte Press, 1968.

Goldstein, Joel K. *The Modern American Vice Presidency.* Princeton: Princeton University Press, 1982.

Holbrook, Thomas M. "The Behavioral Consequences of Vice Presidential Debates." *American Politics Quarterly* 22 (October 1994): 469–482.

Light, Paul C. *Vice-Presidential Power: Advice and Influence in the White House.* Baltimore: Johns Hopkins University Press, 1984.

McCullough, David. *John Adams.* New York: Simon and Schuster, 2001.

Milkis, Sidney M., and Michael Nelson. *The American Presidency: Origins and Development,* 1776–2002. 3d ed. Washington, D.C.: CQ Press, 2003.

Nelson, Michael. *A Heartbeat Away.* New York: Unwin Hyman, 1988.

———. "Choosing the Vice President." *PS: Political Science and Politics* 21 (fall 1988): 858–868.

———. "The Curse of the Vice Presidency." *American Prospect,* July 31, 2000, 20–24.

———. "The Election: Ordinary Politics, Extraordinary Outcome." In *The Elections of 2000,* ed. Michael Nelson. Washington, D.C.: CQ Press, 2001.

Pika, Joseph A. "A New Vice Presidency?" In *The Presidency and the Political System,* ed. Michael Nelson. 2d ed. Washington, D.C.: CQ Press, 1987.

———. "The Vice Presidency: New Opportunities, Old Constraints." In *The Presidency and the Political System,* ed. Michael Nelson. 6th ed. Washington, D.C.: CQ Press, 2000.

Sergiovanni, George S. "Dumping the Vice President: A Historical Overview and Analysis." *Presidential Studies Quarterly* 24 (fall 1994): 765–782.

Sigelman, Lee, and Paul J. Wahlbeck. "The 'Veepstakes': Strategic Choice in Presidential Running Mate Selection." *American Political Science Review* 91 (December 1997): 62.

Turque, Bill. *Inventing Al Gore.* Boston: Houghton Mifflin, 2000.

Williams, Irving G. *The Rise of the Vice Presidency.* Washington, D.C.: Public Affairs Press, 1956.

Witcover, Jules. *Crapshoot: Rolling the Dice on the Vice Presidency.* New York: Crown, 1992.

chapter 4

Rating the Presidents

by Michael Nelson

One approach that historians have taken to the history of the presidency is to rate the presidents' performances in office, then rank them in relation to one another. In doing so, historians participate in the great American pastime of listing and ranking almost everything, from the ten best movies to the top forty songs. But historians also hope to learn from their rankings. What makes a president great, average, or a failure? Have different eras been marked by notable differences in presidential quality?

Presidential ratings also try to shed light on a larger historical issue, namely, has the American presidency been a generally successful institution? James Bryce, the distinguished nineteenth-century British observer of American politics, took one position on this question in a chapter titled "Why Great Men Are Not Chosen Presidents" from his book *The American Commonwealth*. The answer, according to Bryce, was that the political party bosses who controlled the selection of candidates for president preferred "safe," or mediocre, nominees to brilliant ones. Harold J. Laski, another British student of the American presidency, rejoined that the United States had a remarkable record of finding great presidents when they were needed to lead the nation in times of crisis, such as the Civil War and the Great Depression.[1]

THE SCHLESINGER POLLS

Arthur M. Schlesinger, the Harvard University historian, conducted the first presidential ratings surveys in 1948. He wrote to fifty-five distinguished historians and asked them to evaluate each president as either great, near great, average, below average, or a failure.[2] The only yardstick Schlesinger offered his colleagues was that their evaluations must be based solely on "performance in office, omitting anything done before or after." Schlesinger reported the results of his survey in the November 1, 1948, issue of *Life* magazine.[3]

"Those who believe that in a democracy people generally get the kind of government they deserve will be heartened by the results of [my survey]," Schlesinger wrote. "Only

two of our past Presidents were labeled 'failure'; four were judged 'near great'; and six received the accolade 'great.' "[4] He noted a high degree of consensus among the participants in the poll about which presidents belonged in each of these categories. The six presidents judged as great were Abraham Lincoln (the only president to be named as great on all fifty-five ballots), George Washington, Franklin D. Roosevelt, Woodrow Wilson, Thomas Jefferson, and Andrew Jackson, in that order. The four near-great presidents, ranked seven through ten among the twenty-nine presidents evaluated in the poll, were Theodore Roosevelt, Grover Cleveland, John Adams, and James K. Polk. Only Ulysses S. Grant and Warren G. Harding were judged to have been failures. All the other presidents scored as average or below average, with less consensus among the experts about exactly how they should be ranked. *(See Table 4-1, p. 220.)*

Schlesinger repeated his poll in 1962, this time drawing on the judgments of seventy-five participants, including, in addition to the historians, several political scientists, journalists, and Supreme Court Justice Felix Frankfurter. The results, which appeared in the July 29, 1962, issue of the *New York Times Magazine*, were similar to those of the first survey.[5] Lincoln, Washington, Franklin Roosevelt, Wilson, and Jefferson again were judged great presidents, in the same order as in 1948. Jackson remained sixth, but slipped to near-great status, along with Theodore Roosevelt, Polk, Harry S. Truman (a new addition), John Adams, and Cleveland. Grant and Harding still were the sole occupants of the failure category. Dwight D. Eisenhower, whose presidency occurred between the dates of the two polls, ranked twenty-second, near the bottom of the average presidents.

John F. Kennedy, the incumbent president in 1962, was not evaluated, but as the Pulitzer Prize–winning author of the book *Profiles in Courage*, was invited by Schlesinger to fill out a ballot. Kennedy declined. "A year ago I would have responded with confidence . . ." he wrote, "but now I am not so sure."[6]

Assessing the results of his two polls, Schlesinger drew some conclusions about the perceived qualities that cause a

TABLE 4-1 **The Schlesinger Polls, 1948 and 1962**

1948 Poll (N = 55)	1962 Poll (N = 75)
Great	**Great**
Lincoln	Lincoln
Washington	Washington
F. Roosevelt	F. Roosevelt
Wilson	Wilson
Jefferson	Jefferson
Jackson	
	Near great
	Jackson
Near great	T. Roosevelt
T. Roosevelt	Polk
Cleveland	Truman
J. Adams	J. Adams
Polk	Cleveland
Average	
J. Q. Adams	**Average**
Monroe	Madison
Hayes	J. Q. Adams
Madison	Hayes
Van Buren	McKinley
Taft	Taft
Arthur	Van Buren
McKinley	Monroe
A. Johnson	Hoover
Hoover	B. Harrison
B. Harrison	Arthur
	Eisenhower
	A. Johnson
Below average	
Tyler	
Coolidge	**Below average**
Fillmore	Taylor
Taylor	Tyler
Buchanan	Fillmore
Pierce	Coolidge
	Pierce
Failure	Buchanan
Grant	
Harding	**Failure**
	Grant
	Harding

SOURCE: Arthur M. Schlesinger, "The U.S. Presidents," *Life*, November 1, 1948; Schlesinger, "Our Presidents: A Rating by 75 Historians," *New York Times Magazine*, July 29, 1962, 12ff.

NOTE: The Schlesinger polls asked historians, political scientists, and journalists to rate a list of U.S. presidents based on their performance in office. N = number of respondents to the survey.

president to be ranked high, low, or somewhere in between. The great presidents were, among other things, "lucky in their times: they are all identified with some crucial turning point in our history."[7] Washington and the birth of the republic, Jefferson and the opportunity for national expansion, Jackson and the rise of agrarian democracy, Lincoln and the Civil War, Wilson and the progressive movement and World War I, Franklin Roosevelt and the depression and World War II—each served at a time when the opportunity for presidential leadership was unusually large.

The great presidents shared some personal and political qualities as well, according to Schlesinger. Notable among these were strength and the desire for power. "Washington apart," Schlesinger wrote, "none of [the great presidents] waited for the office to seek the man; they pursued it with all their might and main." Once in office, their greatness was established by the fact that "every one of [them] left the Executive branch stronger and more influential than he found it." When dealing with Congress, they knew "when to reason and to browbeat, to bargain and stand firm . . . and when all else failed, they appealed over the heads of the lawmakers to the people." Nor did the great presidents shy away from confrontations with the Supreme Court. They were, to be sure, inattentive to their duty to administer the departments and agencies, but this freed them, according to Schlesinger, for the more important task of "moral leadership." All the great presidents were castigated by the press and by powerful political opponents. Finally, each "took the side of liberalism and the general welfare against the status quo."[8]

The near-great presidents shared the great presidents' desire to set the nation's political course but were less fortunate in their times, less skillful as leaders, or both. The average and below-average presidents were marked by a belief in "negative government, in self-subordination to the legislative power," Schlesinger observed. The failure category was reserved for presidents "who, by their moral obtuseness, promoted a low tone in official life, conducting administrations scarred with shame and corruption."[9]

Schlesinger was heartened by the results of his polls. He regarded the generally positive ratings of the presidents as "favorable not only to them, but also the political system which made it possible for them to rise to power." Even the average presidents "rendered useful services according to their gifts," he suggested; besides, "there are moments indeed when the general welfare may call for rest and recuperation." Ultimately, however, "what endows a country with greatness is the ability to produce greatness when greatness is needed. Measured by such a standard, America has been served well by her Presidents."[10]

LATER SURVEYS

Schlesinger's surveys spawned a number of successors. Gary Maranell, a sociologist at the University of Kansas, tried to improve on the earlier polls by including a broader array of historians in his sample and asking them to rate the presidents not only according to their overall prestige but also according to their strength, activeness, idealism, flexibility, and accomplishments. Of the 1,095 members of the Organization of American Historians whom Maranell asked to participate in March 1968, 571 returned questionnaires.

The results of the Maranell poll were generally similar to those obtained by Schlesinger, but with some interesting differences. Respondents ranked Jefferson higher than Wilson, and Truman higher than Jackson and Polk. Eisenhower, Herbert C. Hoover, James Monroe, and Andrew Johnson each moved up the list. William McKinley, among others, moved down. Of the presidents who were rated for the first time, Kennedy ranked ninth and Lyndon B. Johnson sixteenth.[11] (*See Table 4-2, below.*)

Maranell also ascertained, through statistical analysis of his results, which criteria were important to historians in assessing the presidents' prestige. His findings confirmed Schlesinger's insights. The significance of a president's accomplishments, the strength of the role he played in directing the government and shaping the events of his day, and the activeness of his approach toward governing were all closely tied to the historians' overall assessment of his presidency. In contrast, the idealism that underlay a president's actions and the flexibility with which he implemented his programs and policies mattered little.

The largest effort to measure how historians rate the presidents, in terms of the number of scholars canvassed and the number of questions asked, was conducted in 1981 by Robert K. Murray and Tim H. Blessing, two historians at Pennsylvania State University. They sent questionnaires to every American historian with a doctoral degree who held the rank of assistant professor or above, a total of 1,997. Of that group, 953 filled out their questionnaires in full, answering detailed queries about the presidential office in general and various presidential actions in particular, as well as queries about themselves.[12]

The overall rankings obtained by Murray and Blessing differed somewhat from those of previous polls. Lincoln, Washington, and Franklin Roosevelt remained the three most highly rated presidents, but Roosevelt moved past Washington into second place. Eisenhower's standing rose dramatically from twenty-second in the second Schlesinger poll to eleventh. In contrast, the reputations of Cleveland, Rutherford B. Hayes, and Andrew Johnson fell steeply. Murray and Blessing found that the historians in their poll differed widely in their assessments of Nixon, Lyndon Johnson, Hoover, and Jackson but were virtually unanimous in their praise for Lincoln, Franklin Roosevelt, and Washington. Finally, certain kinds of historians—those who

DWIGHT EISENHOWER AND ANDREW JOHNSON

With two exceptions, the rankings of presidents have not changed much since Arthur M. Schlesinger conducted his first survey of historians in 1948.

The first exception is Dwight D. Eisenhower, who rose from twenty-second in 1962 to ninth in 2000. How did he do it? Part of the explanation is that previously secret papers and documents from his administration were released. After studying the Eisenhower papers in the 1970s, political scientist Fred Greenstein wrote that he felt compelled to abandon the then-common scholarly view of Eisenhower as "an aging hero who reigned more than he ruled and who lacked the energy, motivation, and political skill to have a significant impact on events." Greenstein's book *The Hidden-Hand Presidency* instead portrayed Eisenhower as a president who was "politically astute and informed, actively engaged in putting his personal stamp on public policy, applied a carefully thought-out conception of leadership to the conduct of his presidency." [1] Events of the 1960s and 1970s also made Eisenhower's presidency seem more successful in hindsight. His personal integrity and the restraint he showed in withholding U.S. troops from the war in Indochina stood in sharp contrast to the later record of Vietnam and the Watergate scandal.

The second exception is Andrew Johnson, whose reputation has gone in the opposite direction in recent decades. An average president in the opinion of historians in 1948 (he ranked nineteenth), Johnson was deemed a failure in 2000. For years historians had treated Johnson kindly because they believed he had been impeached unjustly. But more recent studies have argued that Johnson was a reckless and incompetent president who may have deserved to be stripped of his office.[2]

1. Fred I. Greenstein, *The Hidden-Hand Presidency: Eisenhower as Leader* (Baltimore: Johns Hopkins University Press, 1994).
2. James David Barber, "Adult Identity and Presidential Style: The Rhetorical Emphasis," *Daedalus* 97 (summer 1968): 938–968; Michael L. Benedict, *The Impeachment and Trial of Andrew Johnson* (New York: Norton, 1973).

TABLE 4-2 **The Maranell Poll, 1968**

Presidential Rating (N = 571)

1. Lincoln	18. Hoover
2. Washington	19. Eisenhower
3. F. Roosevelt	20. A. Johnson
4. Jefferson	21. Van Buren
5. T. Roosevelt	22. McKinley
6. Wilson	23. Arthur
7. Truman	24. Hayes
8. Jackson	25. Tyler
9. Kennedy	26. B. Harrison
10. J. Adams	27. Taylor
11. Polk	28. Coolidge
12. Cleveland	29. Fillmore
13. Madison	30. Buchanan
14. Monroe	31. Pierce
15. J. Q. Adams	32. Grant
16. L. Johnson	33. Harding
17. Taft	

NOTE: The Maranell poll asked members of the Organization of American Historians to rate the U.S. presidents according to their overall prestige, strength, activeness, idealism, flexibility, and accomplishments. N = number of respondents to the survey.

TABLE 4-3 **The Murray-Blessing Rating, 1981**

Presidential Rating (N = 953)

Great	Near great	Above average	Average	Below average	Failure
Lincoln	T. Roosevelt	J. Adams	McKinley	Taylor	A. Johnson
F. Roosevelt	Wilson	L. Johnson	Taft	Tyler	Buchanan
Washington	Jackson	Eisenhower	Van Buren	Fillmore	Nixon
Jefferson	Truman	Polk	Hoover	Coolidge	Grant
		Kennedy	Hayes	Pierce	Harding
		Madison	Arthur		
		Monroe	Ford		
		J. Q. Adams	Carter		
		Cleveland	B. Harrison		

NOTE: N = number of respondents to the survey.

were older, male, and specialized in the era of the president they rated—tended to be less severe in their judgments of the presidents than were their colleagues. *(See Table 4-3, above.)*

In 1996 the *New York Times* commissioned Schlesinger's son, the historian Arthur M. Schlesinger Jr., to replicate his father's polls. He found that "[t]he choice of best and worst presidents has remained relatively stable through the years." So had historians' emphasis on strong leadership and the desire for power. In the eyes of presidential scholars, Schlesinger wrote, a great president was one who "took risks ... provoked controversy ... st[ood] in Theodore Roosevelt's 'bully pulpit.'" [13]

Schlesinger himself disagreed with one of main findings of presidential rankings surveys, including his own. "Most polls," he noted, "inevitably end up with Grant and Harding as the two conspicuous failures among American presidents ... because of the scandal and corruption that disgraced their administrations." Yet in Schlesinger's view, "James Buchanan, Andrew Johnson, Herbert Hoover, and Richard Nixon damaged the republic a good deal more than did the hapless Grant and the feckless Harding" because their failures were of policy more than probity.[14]

Among the most recent polls is one conducted in late 2000 for the *Wall Street Journal* by Northwestern University law professors James Lindgren and Steven G. Calabresi.[15] Hoping to assemble a broad group of scholarly evaluators, Lindgren and Calabresi surveyed thirty historians, twenty-five political scientists, and twenty-three law professors. The results were strikingly similar to those obtained over the years in other polls, with two important differences: Washington was for the first time judged as the greatest of the great presidents, and Reagan was ranked eighth, sandwiched between Truman and Eisenhower in the near-great category. Lindgren and Calabresi found that Reagan, who had finished twenty-fifth in Schlesinger's 1996 survey, generated the most controversy among the evaluators: he was named the most underrated president as well as the second most overrated president. First among the overrated presidents, according to the evaluators, was Kennedy, whom they ranked eighteenth.

CRITICS OF THE RATINGS

Historians' efforts to rate and rank the presidents have drawn fire from critics, including at least two presidents. When a reporter asked former president Truman about the second Schlesinger survey, in which he was rated near great and ranked ninth, Truman said, "Nobody will be able to assess my administration until about thirty years after I'm dead." Kennedy, after declining to participate in Schlesinger's 1962 poll, told Arthur M. Schlesinger Jr., then a White House aide, "How the hell can you tell? Only the President himself can know what his real pressures and his real alternatives are. If you don't know that, how can you judge performance?" [16]

Some scholars also have taken the polls to task. The historian Thomas A. Bailey, in his book *Presidential Greatness,* argued that bias clouds historians' judgments when they rate the presidents. Like all Americans, the historian "is in some degree brainwashed before he reaches maturity." Surrounded by parks, memorials, cities, airports, and other places named after presidents such as Lincoln, Washington, Jefferson, and Jackson; culturally imprinted with the monumental granite images on Mt. Rushmore; and used to seeing certain presidents' faces on coins and currency, how can one grow up in the United States without taking for granted that these presidents are great?[17]

In addition to bias, Bailey found a more fundamental flaw in the ratings. "Judging presidents is not like judging those who play duplicate bridge," he argued; "no two incumbents were ever dealt the same hand." Nineteenth-century presidents served in an era when strong presidential leadership generally was not desired, which may explain why so many of them rate as average or below average. The great presidents, in contrast, each were "'lucky' enough to serve in a time of great crisis" when extraordinary presidential power was encouraged.[18]

THE PUBLIC RATES THE PRESIDENTS

Since the early 1970s the Gallup Poll has occasionally surveyed the public's views of the presidents. Poll results reveal that average citizens have a somewhat different set of presidential heroes than do scholars.

From 1975 to 1991, Gallup occasionally asked Americans, "Which three U.S. presidents do you regard as the greatest?" In 2000 Gallup changed its question to: "Whom do you regard as the greatest U.S. president?" The results of all these polls have been dominated by recent presidents. In 2005, for example, Ronald Reagan (one year after his death) ranked first and Bill Clinton ranked second. Almost all of the other presidents mentioned by citizens came from the roster of those rated great by scholars, including Abraham Lincoln (third), Franklin D. Roosevelt (tied for fourth), and George Washington (sixth).

PRESIDENT	1975	1985	1991	2000	2005
Reagan	—	21	19	11	22
Clinton	—	—	—	—	15
Lincoln	49	48	40	18	14
F. Roosevelt	45	41	29	12	12
Kennedy	52	56	39	22	12
Washington	25	25	21	5	5
G. W. Bush	—	—	—	—	5
Carter	—	9	10	3	3
Truman	37	26	17	3	2
T. Roosevelt	9	7	8	3	2
Jefferson	8	7	6	3	2
Eisenhower	24	16	14	3	1
Nixon	5	11	10	2	1
G. H. W. Bush	—	—	18	3	1
L. Johnson	9	5	3	0	0
Wilson	5	1	3	0	0
Hoover	0	1	0	0	0
All others	9	3	—	3	3
Don't know	3	2	—	4	2

SOURCE: Compiled by the author from Gallup Poll data.

NOTE: Figures from 1975, 1985, and 1991 represent percentage who chose the president as one of three greatest presidents; 2000 and 2005 figures represent percentage who chose the president as the single greatest.

Nelson Polsby, a political scientist, criticized the presidential ratings game from a different perspective, namely, its effect on current and future presidents. Presidents know they will someday be rated and hope to rank highly. But Polsby has argued, "the aspiration to presidential greatness . . . leads to a variety of difficulties. For fear of being found out and downgraded, there is the temptation to deny failure, to refuse to readjust course when a program or a proposal doesn't work out. There is the temptation to hoard credit rather than share it. . . . There is the temptation to offer false hopes and to proclaim spurious accomplishments to the public at large." [19]

ERAS OF PRESIDENTIAL SUCCESS AND FAILURE

As critics of the historians' polls suggest, surveys that rate the presidents may reveal as much about the scholars who do the rating as about the presidents themselves. At the very least, such surveys indicate the criteria by which historians evaluate presidents, notably political strength (if untainted by corruption) and the desire to be strong.[20]

To the extent that the presidential ratings surveys are valid, however, one of the most interesting insights they offer is that different historical eras have been marked by widely different levels of presidential quality. The nation's first half century (1789–1837) produced, according to the *Wall Street Journal* poll, six presidents who were above average or better, one who was average, and none who was below average. *(See Table 4-4, below.)* The next century stood in sharp contrast. Only six of the twenty-one rated presidents who served between 1837 and 1933 were great (one), near great (three), or above average (two). Of the fifteen others, five were judged average, six below average, and four as failures. Perhaps, then, it is encouraging to see

TABLE 4-4 **The Wall Street Journal Poll**

Great	Near great	Above average	Average	Below average	Failure
1. Washington	4. Jefferson	12. Cleveland	19. Taft	27. B. Harrison	36. A. Johnson
2. Lincoln	5. T. Roosevelt	13. J. Adams	20. J. Q. Adams	28. Ford	37. Pierce
3. F. Roosevelt	6. Jackson	14. McKinley	21. G. H. W. Bush	29. Hoover	38. Harding
	7. Truman	15. Madison	22. Hayes	30. Carter	39. Buchanan
	8. Reagan	16. Monroe	23. Van Buren	31. Taylor	
	9. Eisenhower	17. L. Johnson	24. Clinton	32. Grant	
	10. Polk	18. Kennedy	25. Coolidge	33. Nixon	
	11. Wilson		26. Arthur	34. Tyler	
			25. Fillmore		

SOURCE: James Lindgren and Steven G. Calabresi, "Ranking the Presidents," Wall Street Journal, November 16, 2000.

NOTE: This poll surveyed thirty historians, twenty-five political scientists, and twenty-three law professors. William Henry Harrison and James A. Garfield, whose terms were very brief, are not ranked.

that the modern era more closely resembles the distant past than the recent past. From 1933 to 2001 the nation boasted six presidents who rated above average or better in the *Wall Street Journal* poll (including one great and three near-great presidents), and only four who rated average (two) or below average (two).

★

NOTES

1. James Bryce, *The American Commonwealth* (1888; reprint, New York: Macmillan, 1924), 1: 77. Harold J. Laski, *The American Presidency: An Interpretation* (New York: Harper and Row, 1940), 49–53.

2. William Henry Harrison and James Garfield were left off the list because they died so soon after taking office; Harry S. Truman was not included because he was the incumbent president.

3. Arthur M. Schlesinger, "The U.S. Presidents," *Life,* November 1, 1948; Schlesinger, *Paths to the Present* (New York: Macmillan, 1949), chap. 5.

4. Schlesinger, "The U.S. Presidents."

5. Arthur M. Schlesinger, "Our Presidents: A Rating by 75 Historians," *New York Times Magazine,* July 29, 1962, 12ff.

6. Thomas A. Bailey, *Presidential Greatness* (New York: Appleton-Century, 1966), 43.

7. Schlesinger, "The U.S. Presidents," 68.

8. Schlesinger, "Our Presidents."

9. Ibid.

10. Schlesinger, *Paths to the Present,* 110–111.

11. Gary Maranell, "The Evaluation of Presidents: An Extension of the Schlesinger Polls," *Journal of American History* (June 1970): 104–113.

12. Robert K. Murray and Tim H. Blessing, "The Presidential Performance Study: A Progress Report," *Journal of American History* 70:4 (December 1983): 535–555. The results of all the polls discussed in this chapter are listed in this article.

13. Arthur M. Schlesinger Jr., "The Ultimate Approval Rating," *New York Times Magazine,* December 15, 1996, 47–51.

14. Arthur M. Schlesinger Jr., "Commentary," in *The Uses and Misuses of Presidential Ratings,* ed. Meena Bose and Mark Landis (New York: Nova Science, 2003), 96–99.

15. James Lindgren and Steven G. Calabresi, "Ranking the Presidents," *Wall Street Journal,* November 15, 2000.

16. Bailey, *Presidential Greatness,* 40–41, 43.

17. Ibid., chaps. 4–5.

18. Ibid.

19. Nelson Polsby, "Against Presidential Greatness," *Commentary,* January 1977, 61–64.

20. Michael Nelson, "Evaluating the Presidency," in *The Presidency and the Political System,* 7th ed. (Washington, D.C.: CQ Press, 2003), 1–26.

chapter 5

The Electoral Process and Taking Office

by Michael Nelson, Charles C. Euchner, and John Anthony Maltese

Against a twenty-first-century backdrop, the early days of presidential politics seem almost quaint. The original system aspired to create a republic, in which sovereign power resided in the people but was exercised by their elected representatives. Democracy, in the sense of direct popular rule, was considered a pejorative term. The Framers premised their insulated system of presidential selection on the ability of an "electoral college" of the nation's most virtuous and learned men to rise above petty factions and select leaders with national vision.

Since the election of the first president, George Washington, in 1789, the franchise, or right to vote, in American presidential elections has expanded by class, race, sex, and age. Only property-owning men could participate in the nation's early elections. By 1971 virtually every adult citizen eighteen years or older was eligible to vote.

Over the years the process for electing the president not only has shifted political power from the few to the many but also has become longer, more complex, and more subject to the unintended consequences of reform and the changing technologies of business and everyday life. A vast array of interlocking elements now makes up the campaign to elect one person as president. The people involved in a campaign include the candidate and his or her family, a vice-presidential running mate and his or her family, political allies, campaign strategists, lawyers and accountants, television producers and consultants, schedulers and advance people, advertising experts, issues experts, fund-raisers, pollsters, computer analysts, Web site designers, and sometimes the incumbent president. The private organizations that affect the campaign include corporations, labor unions, interest groups, political action committees, the national party, state parties, and third parties. Constitutional requirements for candidates and complex national and state campaign laws establish rules that the campaign must follow. The campaign must direct itself toward state primaries and caucuses, conventions, televised debates, and the vote of the electoral college (and possibly Congress or, as in 2000, the Supreme Court). Not least among these diverse elements are the substantive and symbolic issues of the day.

HISTORY OF PRESIDENTIAL ELECTIONS

Presidential elections are perhaps the most important events in national politics, giving shape to dominant issues, the makeup of national parties and interest groups, regional economic and political alignments, and the way citizens understand and talk about their society.

Campaigns for the White House have shaped American politics in several stages. Historically, presidential elections have been at the center of political controversies involving federalism, banking, tariffs and other taxes, economic change, corporate power, unions, war, international affairs, social welfare programs, moral values, consumer issues, and disputes among the branches of government. Presidential elections have articulated the changing moods of the nation since the first election.

Original Constitutional Provisions

The method of choosing the president proved to be one of many vexing problems for the fifty-five men who assembled in Philadelphia in May 1787 to draft the Constitution. The Articles of Confederation, which the Constitution was designed to replace, were riddled with weaknesses. *(See "Articles of Confederation," p. 1741, in the Reference Materials, Vol. II.)* Adopted in 1781, the Articles established an impotent federal government consisting of a weak Congress and no executive branch. By the time the Constitutional Convention convened, the confederation was but a "cobweb." [1]

From the start of the convention, it was clear that the federal government would be strengthened and that there would be some sort of executive branch. The convention was split, however, between those who wanted a strong executive (the "presidentialists") and those who were wary of executive authority and wanted instead to increase the power of the national legislature (the "congressionalists"). [2]

There also was the question of whether the national executive should consist of several persons or just one. Congressionalists wanted a plural executive with minimal power. Presidentialists wanted a strong executive with power vested in the hands of one individual. *(See "Number of the Executive," p. 24, in Chapter 1.)*

As it became clear that the executive would be unitary, the tension between the two camps shifted to the question of presidential selection. Congressionalists, intent on having the executive remain subordinate to the legislature, wanted the president to be elected by Congress. Presidentialists, however, wanted the president to be chosen independently.

This issue remained unresolved for most of the summer. By the end of August, there still was no consensus on how to select the president. Therefore, that issue—along with other "questions not settled"—was sent to the convention's Committee on Postponed Matters for resolution. Because the committee was dominated by presidentialists, it pushed for a proposal that would avoid legislative appointment. The result was a compromise that was reported to the convention on September 4, 1787, and that served, with little alteration, as the basis for the actual constitutional provision.

The compromise, as finally approved, provided for election of the president by what soon would be known as the electoral college.[3] This system allowed each state to appoint, in the manner directed by its legislature, the same number of electors as it had senators and representatives in Congress. Virginia, for example, had two senators and ten representatives and so could choose twelve electors. Every state was able to choose at least three electors. Those electors would then meet in their respective states and vote by ballot for two persons for president from two different states. When the ballots of all the electors from all the states were tallied, the candidate with the greatest number of votes would become president (assuming it was a majority), and the second-place candidate would become vice president. In case of a tie, or if no candidate received a majority, the House of Representatives would choose the president from among the top five electoral vote recipients.[4]

The compromise won the support of the convention because it was broadly appealing. First, the provision that the president be selected by electors satisfied the presidentialists, who were opposed to appointment by Congress. It also satisfied those who were wary of direct election by the people. Electors, it was thought, would infuse an element of judgment into the selection process, thereby offsetting the whims of mass opinion.

Second, individual state legislatures were allowed to determine how electors would be chosen in their respective states. As a result, the convention did not have to agree on one method of appointing electors for all the states.

Third, if no candidate received a majority, the outcome of the election would be decided by the House of Representatives. Because it was widely assumed that few candidates after George Washington would receive a majority of electoral votes, many thought that selection by the House would become the norm. Thus congressionalists believed that they had lost the battle but won the war. From their perspective, electors usually would nominate candidates, and the House would select the president.

Finally, because each elector voted for two persons for president—one of whom could not be from the elector's own state—"favorite-son" candidates would tend to cancel each other out. This helped to dispel the fear that large states would consistently elect large-state presidents. But because the number of electors from each state would equal the state's total number of senators and representatives in Congress, the relative weight of the more populous states would not be discounted.

Despite the Framers' good intentions, numerous flaws emerged in the electoral system in the nation's early years. A constitutional crisis developed in 1800, for example, when the Democratic-Republican Party's presidential and vice-presidential candidates both received the same number of electoral votes. As a result, the Twelfth Amendment soon was adopted to prevent a repeat of that crisis. But however flawed the early electoral system, it met the needs of the moment and its basic form has endured for more than two centuries. The electoral college was an acceptable compromise among the diverse positions within the Constitutional Convention.

The Framers' Views of Political Parties

The Framers were proponents of moderation. They also held a quite different understanding of the presidential selection process than is generally accepted today. Most notably, the Framers envisaged a nonpartisan process. They viewed political parties as selfish "factions," a political evil. The goal of the selection process was to choose men of civic virtue who would be able to exercise unbiased judgment.

The Framers' views of political parties were a natural outgrowth of the Anglo-American tradition. Opposition parties are now considered an essential part of representative democracy, but the Framers believed they would cause tumult and discord. Historian Richard Hofstadter has argued that in eighteenth-century British political thought there were three archetypal views of party that may have influenced the Framers.[5]

The first, which Hofstadter called "the Hamiltonian view" because it was associated with Alexander Hamilton, was based on the antiparty doctrine of Bolingbroke, an English statesman who wrote two important pamphlets on politics in the 1730s. For Bolingbroke, the best sort of state would be led by a "patriot king"—a benign monarch who would subdue factions through good statecraft. To him, parties were by definition antithetical to the common good. Nevertheless, Bolingbroke conceived of instances when a unifying "country party," speaking for the nation as a whole rather than for particular interests, could be used to restore stability in a society.

The second view, which Hofstadter termed "Madisonian" after James Madison, was based on the writings of the eighteenth-century Scottish philosopher David Hume. Like Bolingbroke, Hume thought that parties were evil, but unlike Bolingbroke he thought that their existence was inevitable in a free state. Champions of liberty could check and limit the excesses of parties, but they could not abolish them. Madison expressed this view in *Federalist* No. 10, concluding that the only satisfactory method of "curing the mischiefs of faction" was to control their effects. To remove the causes of faction would be to destroy liberty.

Finally, Hofstadter pointed to the views of the British statesman Edmund Burke, who felt that parties were not only inevitable but for the most part good. But Burke's writing, published in 1770, came too late to influence the Framers at the Constitutional Convention.

Voting Requirements

The electorate of the eighteenth century was quite different from the electorate of today. The Constitution left it to the states to determine who could vote, and all states agreed on one requirement: only men could cast a ballot. Property ownership was another requisite for the right to vote, although the exact qualifications differed among states. Colonial restrictions had tended to be harsher than those adopted by the states and often were based on extensive land ownership. Some colonies, such as Massachusetts, even had religious qualifications for voting.[6]

In Virginia, the home of some of the most important members of the Constitutional Convention, property ownership had been a prerequisite for voting since 1677. From 1705 until 1736, the laws were quite liberal: any male tenant who rented or owned land for life (his own or that of another person, such as his wife or child) was considered a freeholder and could vote. In other words, as a qualification to vote, leasing property was the equivalent of owning property. From 1736 onward, Virginia's definition of freeholder was more restrictive. To vote, a man living in the country had to hold twenty-five acres of cultivated land with a house, or one hundred acres (changed to fifty in 1762) of uncleared land. A man living in town had to own a house with a lot.[7] By the standards of the time, those requirements were not excessive.[8]

Although the American Revolution brought no suffrage reform to Virginia, it did to other states. The Virginia constitution of 1776 stated that voting requirements "shall remain as exercised at present." [9] Even those who paid taxes or fought in the militia could not vote unless they held the requisite amount of land. By 1800 Virginia was one of five states that retained real estate property qualifications. At the other extreme, four states had established universal male suffrage by 1800, and various other states allowed the ownership of personal property or the payment of taxes to substitute for holding real estate.[10]

Property requirements of one kind or another were not abandoned by all the states until 1856. It is not clear how much of the electorate was excluded by property requirements; historians differ on this point, sometimes quite markedly.[11] But the effect of property qualifications can be overstated. The United States was predominantly a middle-class society with fairly widespread ownership of property.

Early Experience, 1789–1828

The years 1789–1828 saw a tremendous change in many of the ideas and institutions that the Framers had envisaged. Nonpartisan elections for president did not last even a decade. Deadlock in the election of 1800 forced the young nation to modify the method of choosing the president and vice president. A system of nominating presidential candidates by congressional caucus was developed, then overturned. And the original understanding of the function of electors was significantly altered.

Role of the Electoral College and the Selection of Electors

The Constitution provided that each state appoint electors "in such manner as the legislature thereof may direct." As a result, diverse methods for choosing electors were used throughout the country. In some states, the legislature appointed the electors, either by joint ballot (both houses voting together) or by concurrent vote (each house voting separately). Others allowed popular election of electors on a statewide general ticket; still others, popular election by districts. There also were mixed systems in which electors were chosen partly by the people in districts and partly by the state legislature, or by the legislature from nominees voted by the people, or by the legislature from among the top candidates for elector if none received a majority in the popular vote.[12]

The electors in the first presidential election were chosen on the first Wednesday of January 1789. Only four states (Delaware, Maryland, Pennsylvania, and Virginia) used direct popular election. New Hampshire also called for popular election but required that an elector receive a majority vote to win. When a majority was not forthcoming, the election was thrown to the legislature. Likewise, Massachusetts preferred a mixed system. Five states (Connecticut, Georgia, New Jersey, New York, and South Carolina) used legislative appointment to choose electors, but New York's Federalist Senate and Anti-Federalist House deadlocked and the state chose no electors. North Carolina and Rhode Island had not yet ratified the Constitution and therefore did not participate in the 1789 election.

Congress apparently had assumed that state legislatures would appoint the electors, at least for the first election,

A war hero from Virginia and presiding officer of the Constitutional Convention, George Washington, more than six feet tall, was the very symbol of legitimacy for the new republic.

because it allowed less than four months (from September 13, 1788, to the first Wednesday in January 1789) for the electoral system to be implemented—not much time given the slowness of communication and the amount of work to be done. Distant states did not learn of Congress's directive for two weeks or more. The states then had to call their legislatures into session (itself a time-consuming process), pass laws providing for the selection of electors (which often entailed lengthy debate), canvass and choose the electors, and arrange for the electors to meet and vote. In some cases, there was not enough time to prepare for a popular election, even if that were the preferred method of selection.[13]

The appointment of electors by state legislatures continued to be the norm in the 1792 election. Nine states—Connecticut, Delaware, Georgia, New Jersey, New York, North Carolina, Rhode Island, South Carolina, and Vermont—used that method. Electors were chosen by popular election on a general ticket in Maryland and Pennsylvania, and by popular election by district in Virginia and Kentucky. Massachusetts also called for popular election by district but required a majority of votes to win. In five Massachusetts districts, majorities were achieved; in the other nine, the General Court (the state legislative body) chose the electors. New Hampshire had a mixed system in which both the people and the legislature chose the electors.[14]

By 1792 Congress had changed the dates for elections. Electors were required to cast their votes on the first Wednesday in December, with electors to be chosen in each state within the thirty-four days preceding that date.[15] This

change caused a problem for North Carolina, which had undergone legislative reapportionment after the 1790 census. The reapportionment became law on April 13, 1792, but North Carolina's legislature was out of session and was not scheduled to meet again until November 15. Because electors had to be chosen by December 5, there was not enough time to provide for popular election. To respond to the situation, the state government divided the state into four districts. The members of the state legislature who resided in each district then met on November 25 and chose three electors. That unusual arrangement, however, was never used again by any state. Before adjourning, the North Carolina legislature provided for electors to be chosen by popular election in districts in future years.[16]

After the first three presidential elections (1789, 1792, and 1796), popular election increasingly became the preferred method of choosing electors. By 1824 only six of twenty-four states—Delaware, Georgia, Louisiana, New York, South Carolina, and Vermont—still used legislative appointment.[17] From 1832 until 1860, every state but South Carolina chose electors by popular vote. Since 1860, only Florida in 1868 and Colorado in 1876 have used legislative appointment.[18]

After 1832 the statewide "winner-take-all" popular vote system largely prevailed—that is, electors were chosen by the people of the state in at-large, or statewide, elections as opposed to district elections. In addition, under the so-called unit rule, electors for each party were grouped together on a general ticket and were elected as a bloc. In this way, a vote for one elector on a general ticket was equivalent to a vote for all the electors on that ticket. In time, electors' names were removed from the ballot in most states. People voted for the presidential and vice-presidential ticket of a particular party, and the ticket with the most votes won—"winner takes all." The winning ticket, then, consisted of all the electors representing the state.

Because under the general ticket system voters selected a party rather than individual electors, general tickets were closely associated with the rise of partisan presidential elections. As a result, the nature of the electoral college changed. The Framers of the Constitution had expected electors to act as free agents, exercising individual and nonpartisan judgment in their selection of the president. Instead, the electoral college was transformed into a contingent of party proxies. As Supreme Court Justice Robert Jackson wrote in *Ray v. Blair* in 1952: "Electors, although often personally eminent, independent, and respectable, officially became voluntary party lackeys and intellectual nonentities. . . . As an institution the electoral college suffered atrophy almost indistinguishable from *rigor mortis*." [19]

In addition to increasing the power of political parties, the general ticket system allowed states to maximize their influence in the election. Instead of scattering a state's electors among several candidates, the system consolidated them behind the candidate who received the most votes.

In 1801 former Treasury secretary Alexander Hamilton drafted a constitutional amendment that would have prohibited the selection of electors by general ticket or by state legislatures, but it was rejected.[20] The selection of electors by general ticket soon became so much the norm that when Michigan passed a law in 1891 providing for the election of presidential electors by congressional districts instead of by general ticket, the law was contested and ultimately made its way to the Supreme Court. In the case, *McPherson v. Blacker* (1892), the Court stated that the Constitution had clearly provided state legislatures with plenary, or full, power to prescribe the method of choosing electors; the fact that states had all adopted the same method of selection did not in any way reduce that power.[21] Today, only Maine and Nebraska use the district system. All other states (including Michigan, which voluntarily returned to its former system) choose their electors by general ticket.

Emergence of Parties

Although the early electoral system was undemocratic by modern standards, Washington's unanimous election as president in 1789 and 1792 has been described as "a triumph of popular will." [22] Washington was the living symbol of national unity, a hero who held the confidence of virtually all the people. As the presiding officer of the Constitutional Convention he had lent legitimacy to the enterprise. Now he would lend legitimacy to the new government.

In the election of 1789, there is no record of any elector expressing opposition to the election of Washington. Each elector had to vote for two persons, however, with the candidate having the second highest number of votes becoming vice president. In the days before the electors met, a consensus formed that the vice president should be a person who complemented Washington: he should be a civilian from a northern state. Some also suggested that he should not have to vacate an office in which his services were already needed. John Adams of Massachusetts fit all of those qualifications, and he soon came to be regarded as the leading candidate for vice president.

Because there was no separate ballot for the office of vice president, some electors began to worry: Adams con-

A civilian and former minister to France and Great Britain, John Adams was considered an excellent complement to Washington in 1789. The short, stocky, bald New Englander soon came to be regarded as the candidate for the vice presidency.

ceivably could get the same number of votes as Washington. At best, such a situation would be an embarrassment. At worst, it could degenerate into a divisive power struggle between supporters of the two men. To avoid this situation, Hamilton maneuvered to siphon votes away from Adams. In the end, all the electors cast one of their votes for Washington, giving him a total of sixty-nine electoral votes. Adams received thirty-four electoral votes, and the thirty-five other votes were divided among ten other candidates.[23] Adams was appalled by his low vote, and a lasting enmity developed between him and Hamilton.[24]

After two terms in office Washington decided not to run for reelection. Much has been made of Washington's precedent of serving only two terms, but his decision to retire was mainly personal. (He had wanted to retire after one term, but he felt unable to do so without adversely affecting the young nation.)[25] He informed his closest associates of his decision early in 1796, and by autumn it was public knowledge. The first two presidential elections had been nonpartisan. This would never be the case again.

Students of the American electoral system disagree about when and why political parties emerged.[26] Although Washington was avowedly nonpartisan, he did not appoint former Anti-Federalists (or opponents to ratifying the Constitution) to positions in his administration. To do so, he thought, would put the Constitution at risk. *(See box, When and Why Did Parties Begin?, p. 232.)*

Nonetheless, divisions formed within the Washington administration. For example, when Secretary of the Treasury Hamilton lobbied Congress to pass administration pro-

WHEN AND WHY DID PARTIES BEGIN?

Although there is no precise date for the beginning of political parties, both Alexander Hamilton (a Federalist) and Thomas Jefferson (a Democratic-Republican) referred to the existence of a Jeffersonian republican "faction" in Congress as early as 1792.

The two competing parties had their roots in the division of public sentiment for and against adoption of the Constitution. The Federalist Party, a loose coalition of merchants, shippers, financiers, and other commercial interests, favored the strong central government provided by the Constitution. Their opponents during the ratification process were intent on preserving state sovereignty. But not all of those who became Democratic-Republicans began as opponents of the Constitution. James Madison, for example, was both a leading supporter of ratification and a founding member of the Democratic-Republican Party.

Although party organizations became more formalized in the 1790s and early 1800s, the Federalists thought of themselves not as a political party but rather as a gentlemanly coalition of interests representing respectable society. What party management there was, they kept clandestine, a reflection of their own fundamental suspicion of parties. The Jeffersonians achieved a high degree of organization but never acquired a nationally accepted name. Their most common name for themselves was "Republican." (In his conciliatory inaugural address of 1801, Jefferson said, "We are all Republicans, we are all Federalists.") Their opponents labeled them "Anti-Federalists," "disorganizers," "Jacobins," and "Democrats"— the latter an unflattering term in the early years of the Republic. To many Americans in the late eighteenth century, a democrat was a supporter of mob rule.

The designation "Democrat-Republican" was used by the Jeffersonians in several states but was never widely accepted as a party label. Historians often refer to the Jeffersonians as the "Democratic-Republicans," however, to avoid confusion with the later and unrelated Republican Party founded in 1854.

Although early American political leaders acknowledged the development of parties, they did not foresee the emergence of a two-party system. Rather, they often justified the existence of their own party as a just reaction to an unacceptable opposition. Jefferson defended his party involvement as a struggle between good and evil: "[When] the principle of difference is as substantial and as strongly pronounced as between the republicans and the Monocrats of our country, I hold it as honorable to take a firm and decided part, and as immoral to pursue a middle line, as between the parties of Honest men, and Rogues, into which every country is divided."

grams such as an excise tax and the establishment of a national bank, opposition arose from James Madison, then a member of the House of Representatives, and others. In the cabinet, Hamilton and Secretary of State Thomas Jefferson often disagreed. Federalists, such as Hamilton, believed in an active central government led by a vigorous executive. Democratic-Republicans, such as Jefferson and Madison, were more concerned with states' rights and the will of the people as expressed through the legislature.

Newspapers both reflected and widened these divisions. In 1789 Hamilton established the *Gazette of the United States* to serve as the unofficial mouthpiece of the administration and, not coincidentally, of the Federalist position.[27] In return, the newspaper was awarded government patronage in the form of printing orders from the Treasury Department and, for a time, the contract to print the laws.[28]

In 1791 Jefferson was instrumental in establishing a rival newspaper—the *National Gazette*—to express the Democratic-Republican position. When Jefferson left Washington's cabinet in 1793, the *Gazette* was replaced by the rabidly pro–Democratic-Republican *Aurora*. The polarized positions of the rival papers and their exchanges of editorial attacks attracted attention throughout the country. Such exchanges went to extremes in both personal and policy-oriented attacks. The *Aurora*, for example, deemed most of President Washington's acts unconstitutional, accused the president of overdrawing his salary, and labeled him "a frail mortal, whose passions and weaknesses are like those of other men, a spoiled child, a despot, an anemic imitation of the English kings."[29] On another occasion, the *Aurora* proclaimed: "If ever a nation was debauched by a man, the American nation has been debauched by Washington. If ever a nation has suffered from the improper influence of a man, the American nation has suffered from the influence of Washington. If ever a nation was deceived by a man, the American nation has been deceived by Washington."[30]

Events abroad served only to widen the divisions in the new government. The French Revolution was under way, and in 1793 France declared war on England. Although the United States remained officially neutral, passions ran high and American political debate was affected by the European conflict. Likening them to the Jacobins of the French uprising, Federalists denounced the Democratic-Republicans as populist radicals who wanted to undermine the authority of the executive through a powerful legislature. Democratic-Republicans condemned the Federalists as being a pseudo-British party of aristocratic monarchists.[31]

The 1796 Election. Although there was no formal party machinery, the election of 1796 was a de facto contest between the Federalists and the Democratic-Republicans. The Democratic-Republicans had formed a congressional caucus, in which the party's members of Congress gathered to plan strategy, but it was not convened to choose the party's candidates for president and vice president. That

Jefferson would be chosen as the presidential nominee was obvious, and although there was no clear agreement on a vice-presidential candidate, the problem was not considered important enough to call the caucus into session.[32] By the time the campaign was in full swing, however, it was understood in Democratic-Republican circles that the party's vice-presidential candidate was Aaron Burr of New York.

Federalist members of Congress appear to have discussed their choice of presidential and vice-presidential candidates in the summer of 1796. Hamilton was considered but rejected because he had made many enemies during the Washington administration. John Jay also was rejected, primarily because he had negotiated a controversial treaty with England at Washington's request. The Federalists finally placed their support behind Vice President Adams. Thomas Pinckney of South Carolina was the party's choice for vice president because it was thought that he would take votes away from Jefferson (a Virginian) in the South.

In September 1796 Washington published his famous Farewell Address. *(See "Washington's Farewell Address," p. 0000, in Reference Materials, Vol. II.)* The address, written with Madison and Hamilton's help, warned against the dangers of political parties. Although the address was largely a response to the divisiveness of recent events, it is likely that his denunciation of parties was a veiled attack on the Democratic-Republicans.[33] Washington cited "the common and continual mischiefs of the spirit of Party" and said that this was "sufficient to make it the interest and the duty of wise people to discourage and restrain it." Elaborating on the spirit of parties and its baneful effects, Washington wrote:

> It serves always to distract the public councils and enfeeble the public administration. It agitates the community with ill founded jealousies and false alarms, kindles the animosity of one part against another, foments occasionally riot and insurrection. It opens the door to foreign influence and corruption, which find a facilitated access to the government itself through the channels of party passions. . . . A fire not to be quenched; it demands a uniform vigilance to prevent its bursting into flame, lest instead of warming it should consume.[34]

Despite Washington's warning, the election of 1796 became an intensely partisan contest. Newspapers fanned the flames as the Federalist press attacked Jefferson and the pro–Democratic-Republican *Aurora* attacked Adams.[35]

When the electors met to choose the president and vice president, the weakness of the selection process became apparent. As designed by the Constitutional Convention, the system did not take into account partisan contests—that is, it made no provision for candidates from the same party to be elected as a ticket. In South Carolina, the electors did not follow party lines in their choice. Instead, they voted for an all-southern ticket, with the Democratic-Republican Jefferson and the Federalist

Pinckney splitting the state's votes equally. In the North, some electors slighted Pinckney because they feared that his vote might exceed that of Adams. Hamilton urged northern electors to give equal support to the two Federalist candidates, but only because he actually hoped that Pinckney would upset Adams.

Because there was no separate ballot for vice president, the candidate with the second highest number of electoral votes was elected to that office. Thus Adams was elected president with seventy-one electoral votes, and his rival from the Democratic-Republican Party, Jefferson, was elected vice president with sixty-eight electoral votes. Pinckney came in third with fifty-nine electoral votes, and Burr trailed a distant fourth with thirty.

The 1800 Election. The election of 1796 was a portent of the problems of the presidential selection process. The election of 1800 demonstrated them. In the spring of 1800, Adams (for president) and Gen. Charles Cotesworth Pinckney of South Carolina (for vice president) were nominated as the Federalist candidates by a caucus of Federalist senators and representatives. About the same time, a caucus of forty-three Democratic-Republican senators and representatives convened. Once again there was no question that Jefferson would be the party's candidate for president. The caucus met to designate a candidate for vice president and unanimously nominated Burr.[36]

When the electors voted in December 1800, every Democratic-Republican elector cast his two votes for Jefferson and Burr, which meant they tied for first place with seventy-three electoral votes each. As specified in the Constitution, the election was thrown into the House of Representatives, which was dominated by Federalists. A majority of the sixteen state delegations was required to elect a president. Although it was common knowledge that Jefferson was the presidential candidate and Burr was the vice-presidential candidate, some Federalists considered Burr the lesser evil and plotted to elect him president. Hamilton, cognizant of the new nation's fragile unity, roundly discouraged the idea. In a letter to New York senator Gouverneur Morris he wrote: "I trust the Federalists will not finally be so mad as to vote for Burr. . . . If there be a man in the world I ought to hate, it is Jefferson. With Burr I have always been personally well. But the public good must be paramount to every private consideration." [37] Nevertheless, many Federalists continued to support Burr.

On Wednesday, February 11, 1801, the House met to vote. On the first ballot, Jefferson received the votes of eight states and Burr the votes of six. Because the other two states were divided, there was no majority. The House balloted eighteen more times that day with no change in the outcome. The balloting continued through Saturday, February 14, and resumed on Monday. The tide finally turned on the thirty-sixth ballot on Tuesday, February 17. Jefferson received a majority, with the votes of ten states. On March 4 he became president and Burr became vice president.

The Twelfth Amendment

It was evident from the problems of 1796 and 1800 that the constitutional process for presidential selection was flawed. When the Eighth Congress convened in October 1803, the matter of a constitutional amendment was considered at great length. After much debate, the resolution for an amendment was passed on December 8, 1803. The amendment was ratified by the states with unusual speed. It was officially adopted as the Twelfth Amendment to the Constitution on September 25, 1804. Thirteen states voted for ratification; three (Connecticut, Delaware, and Massachusetts) dissented.[38] *(See box, Twelfth Amendment (1804), p. 48, in Chapter 1.)*

The Twelfth Amendment required each elector to vote for president and vice president on separate ballots. If none of the candidates for president had a majority, the House of Representatives would choose the winner from the top three vote getters. As before, a majority of the states in the House was needed to elect. If none of the candidates for vice presi-

dent had a majority, the winner would be chosen from the top two vice-presidential candidates by a majority of the Senate. The vice presidency would no longer be awarded to the runner-up in the presidential election. *(See "Twelfth Amendment (1804)," p. 48, in Chapter 1.)*

Congressional Caucus Nominating System

By 1800 caucuses in Congress were nominating the major presidential and vice-presidential candidates. To some degree, this approximated what the congressionalists had wanted at the Constitutional Convention: selection of the executive by the legislature. The Democratic-Republican caucus nominated Jefferson in 1800 and 1804, although the real reason the caucus met in those two years was to select a candidate for vice president. In 1808 the Democratic-Republican caucus nominated James Madison for president and George Clinton of New York (the incumbent vice president under Jefferson) as his running mate. Madison was renominated by a near unanimous vote of the caucus in 1812. Initially, John Langdon of New Hampshire was chosen as his running mate, but he declined the nomination because of his age. (He turned seventy-one in 1812.) At a

How Primaries Work

Presidential primaries are of two kinds. One is the presidential preference primary, in which voters vote directly for the person they wish to be nominated for president. In the other, voters elect delegates to the national party conventions.

States use various combinations of these methods:

- A state may have a preference vote but choose delegates at party conventions. The preference vote may or may not bind the delegates.
- A state may combine the preference and delegate-selection primaries by electing delegates pledged or favorable to a candidate named on the ballot. Under this system, however, state party organizations may run unpledged slates of delegates. Most states use this system or a variation of it.
- A state may have an advisory preference vote and a separate delegate-selection vote in which delegates may be listed as pledged to a candidate, favorable to a candidate, or unpledged.
- A state may have a mandatory preference vote with a separate delegate-selection vote. In these cases, the delegates are required to reflect the preference primary vote.

For those primaries in which the preference vote is binding on the delegates, state laws vary as to the number of ballots through which delegates at the convention must remain committed.

Most primary states hold presidential preference votes, in which voters choose among the candidates who have qualified for the ballot in their states. In most states the vote is binding on the delegates, who either are elected in the primary itself or are chosen outside of it by a caucus process, by a state committee, or by the candidates who have qualified to win delegates.

Delegates may be bound for as little as one ballot or for as long as a candidate remains in the race. National Democratic Party rules in effect in 1980 required delegates to be bound for one ballot unless released by the candidate they were elected to support. The rule was repealed for 1984.

Delegates from primary states are allocated among the presidential candidates in various ways. Most of the methods are based on the preference vote—proportional representation, statewide winner-take-all (in which the candidate winning the most votes statewide wins all the delegates), congressional district and statewide winner-take-all (in which the high vote-getter in a district wins that district's delegates and the high vote-getter statewide wins all the at-large delegates), or some combination of the three.

In the proportional representation system, the qualifying threshold for candidates to win delegates can vary. After a decade of intensive debate, Democratic leaders voted to require proportional representation in all primary and caucus states in 1980. But by 1984, after more rules changes, states were given the right to retain proportional representation only if they wished, awarding delegates to any candidate who drew a minimum of roughly 20 percent of the vote. This threshold was changed for the 1988 election to 15 percent of the vote. The Republicans allow the primary states to set their own thresholds.

In nearly half the primary states, major candidates are placed on the ballot by the secretary of state or a special nominating committee. Elsewhere, candidates must take the initiative to get on the ballot. The filing requirements range from sending a letter of candidacy to election officials to filing petitions signed by a specified number of registered voters and paying a filing fee.

On many primary ballots, voters have the opportunity to mark a line labeled "uncommitted" if they do not prefer any of the candidates.

second caucus, Massachusetts governor Elbridge Gerry was nominated for vice president. In 1816 Secretary of War James Monroe was nominated for president by a vote of 65–54 over Secretary of War William H. Crawford of Georgia, with New York governor Daniel D. Tompkins chosen as Monroe's running mate.

By 1820 the Federalist Party was dead. The Federalists had performed dismally in presidential elections since their narrow loss in 1800 and had been discredited politically by their unpopular opposition to the War of 1812. No record has been found of how they selected their candidates in 1804. In 1808 and 1812, the candidates were chosen at secret meetings of Federalist leaders in New York. By 1816 the party had given up nominating candidates for president and vice president. According to historian Edward Stanwood, "Nothing whatever was done to nominate candidates in opposition to Monroe and Tompkins. On December 3, the day before the electors were to vote, the *Boston Daily Advertiser,* published in one of the three states that had chosen Federalist electors, remarked: 'We do not know, nor is it very material, for whom the Federal electors will vote.' " [39] (They voted for New York senator Rufus King.) In 1820 Democratic-Republican Monroe ran for president unopposed. With virtual one-party rule, nomination by the Democratic-Republican caucus was tantamount to election.

In 1824, however, "King Caucus," as its critics called it, was dethroned. Some had objected to the caucus system from the start. In 1808, when Sen. Stephen Bradley of Vermont had sent notice to the Democratic-Republican members of the House and Senate that the caucus would meet, a representative from Virginia published a response that said, in part: "I cannot . . . countenance, by my presence, the midnight intrigues of any set of men who may arrogate to themselves the right, which belongs only to the people, of selecting proper persons to fill the important offices of president and vice president." [40] After Madison's nomination by the caucus in 1808, seventeen Democratic-Republican members of Congress signed a protest against the system. Even Vice President Clinton, who was nominated by the caucus, expressed disapproval of it. They did so because they felt the caucus system was undemocratic. Voters had no say in the nomination, and those states and districts not represented by the party in Congress were effectively disenfranchised.

At the 1824 Democratic-Republican caucus, only 66 of 261 members of Congress were present. Three-quarters of them were from just four states. By the time the caucus met, five serious presidential candidates had emerged, all with roughly equal strength: Secretary of State John Quincy Adams of Massachusetts, Secretary of War John C. Calhoun of South Carolina, House Speaker Henry Clay of Kentucky, Secretary of the Treasury William Crawford, and Sen. Andrew Jackson of Tennessee. Crawford won the caucus nomination, and Albert Gallatin of Pennsylvania was chosen

as his running mate. The other candidates, however, refused to abide by the caucus's decision. In his home state of Tennessee, Jackson was nominated by the state legislature, which also passed a resolution condemning the caucus system. Kentucky did the same for Clay. Of the original five candidates, Calhoun was the only one to withdraw.

At the polls, Jackson got the most popular votes. He also got the most electoral votes—ninety-nine to Adams's eighty-four—but not the constitutionally required majority. Crawford came in third with forty-one electoral votes. Clay finished fourth with thirty-seven. Thus the race was thrown into the House of Representatives where Adams—despite Jackson's plurality of the popular and electoral vote—was elected.

The caucus system died because presidential candidates no longer acquiesced to the choice of the caucus. But the demise of the caucus also reflected the growing democratization of the political system. By 1824 only six states were still choosing electors by legislative appointment; all the other states were doing so by popular election. Mass participation in presidential elections was increasing dramatically. In 1791 Vermont had instituted universal manhood suffrage. Kentucky and New Hampshire followed suit in 1792, as did Indiana in 1816. By 1824 most states had dropped property restrictions on voting, although several still retained tax-paying restrictions. Mississippi, which entered the Union in 1817, was the last state to institute tax-paying restrictions, and it dropped them in 1832.[41] The caucus system was a holdover from an age that distrusted democracy. That age was dying.

But it was the caucus's selection of the staid Crawford over the frontier hero Jackson, as well as the subsequent House election in 1824 of Adams, that was the kiss of death for the caucus system. Adams's election also hastened the decline of the Democratic-Republican Party by encouraging Jackson's supporters to form a party of their own, the Democrats.

Major Electoral Developments, 1828–2004

After the election of 1828, the United States began to develop what would become the most stable two-party system in the history of the world. National party conventions were held regularly beginning in 1831, and presidential primaries took place in party politics in the early 1900s. Throughout the nineteenth and twentieth centuries, the electorate continued to expand as African Americans, women, and young adults won the right to vote.

The Two-Party System

In 1828 Andrew Jackson swept into the presidency as the head of the newly formed Democratic Party. The Democratic-Republicans had split earlier in the decade over the tariff issue. Under the "American system" of Henry Clay,

Andrew Jackson was greeted by enthusiastic crowds as he traveled from Tennessee to Washington for his Inauguration In 1829. Capturing the spirit of America's expanding frontier, "Old Hickory" established the age of popular politics.

the United States would use high, or protective, tariffs both to nurture nascent domestic industries and to fund internal improvements such as canals and highways. After his election as president in 1824, Adams adopted much of Clay's program. But agrarian interests resisted the high tariffs because they raised the prices of finished products (imported goods were still cheaper), and Jackson emerged as the farmers' champion. Under Jackson, the geographic and economic expansion of the nation and the development of broader-based national party organizations advanced rapidly.

The Democrats and the Whigs. Jackson, who inaugurated an age of popular politics, was an activist president throughout his two terms. His programs for repealing the Bank of the United States and controlling the federal bureaucracy were landmarks in American history. *(See "The Jacksonian Presidency," p. 82, in Chapter 2.)*

In reaction to Jackson's populism, a collection of aggrieved interests pulled together under the Whig Party label. The Whigs aimed to end what they considered to be an era of "mob rule" that gave the president excessive authority. Two military heroes, William Henry Harrison (1840) and Zachary Taylor (1848), won presidential elections under the

Whig banner. But the Whigs suffered from their lack of a strong national organization and from geographic, economic, and cultural divisions within the party that could not be overcome. The rise of industrialism and a Protestant-based abolition movement in the North made Whig Party unity impossible to maintain by midcentury.

In the 1836 election, the Whigs fielded a set of regional candidates for president against Jackson's vice president, Democrat Martin Van Buren. By running several regional candidates rather than one national candidate, the Whigs hoped to send the election to the House. Van Buren won easily, however. The fact that they could only win presidential elections by nominating military heroes, like Harrison and Taylor, pointed to the organizational weakness of the Whig party. It took personally popular leaders to temporarily overcome the Whigs' internal schisms and lack of organization.

Slavery split the Whigs badly. As the abolitionist movement grew in the northern states, the Whigs had difficulty appealing to southerners. By 1856 the Whigs had been replaced by the Republican Party. The founding of the Republican Party stemmed from public anger over the Kansas-Nebraska Act of 1854, which allowed territories in the West to decide whether to enter the Union as slave states or as free states. In the debate over the act, the Republicans emerged to represent all those who opposed extending slavery to any new state. By supporting the extension of slavery into new territories and opposing high tariffs, the Democrats lost any hope of building an alliance with northern industrialists, who were becoming a greater force in American politics. The Republicans won these industrialists' support by adding the protective tariff to their platform.

The Republicans conducted their first national campaign in 1856, when John Charles Frémont ran against Democrat James Buchanan. They lost that election but won the next one in 1860 when a former Whig, Abraham Lincoln, defeated the divided Democratic Party.

Republican Dominance. For seven decades after Lincoln's election in 1860, the Republicans largely dominated American politics. Between 1860 and 1932, the

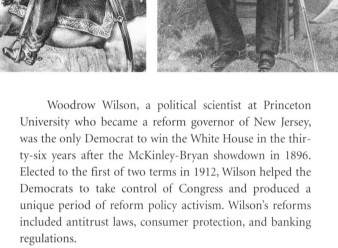

The Whigs nominated two military heroes for president: William Henry Harrison in 1840, left, and Zachary Taylor in 1848, right. The party picked such charismatic figures for leadership to compensate for deep schisms and poor organization.

Democrats won the presidency only in 1884 and 1892 (with Grover Cleveland on the ticket) and in 1912 and 1916 (with Woodrow Wilson).

The political bargain that settled the election of 1876—in which Republican Rutherford B. Hayes won the presidency even though Democrat Samuel Tilden won the national popular vote—created an electoral crisis that eventually led to a new party alignment. After long negotiations between Republicans and Democrats over which candidate had carried Oregon and three disputed southern states, a deal was reached that declared Hayes the winner. But as part of the election deal the Republicans agreed to pull federal troops out of the South. After the troops left the old Confederacy, the Democrats took over and began disenfranchising blacks through an elaborate set of racially discriminatory "Jim Crow" laws. The Republicans maintained their national majority by vigorously pursuing an economic policy based on high tariffs, funding of exploration and transportation, limitations on labor unions, and tight-money policies. When the Democrats won the presidency under Cleveland, the nation continued to follow these policies. Especially in the areas of labor relations and monetary policy, Cleveland pursued a basically Republican agenda.

The Democrats became particularly vulnerable toward the end of the nineteenth century when discontent among the nation's farmers reached fever pitch. Farmers had been hurt by the high-tariff and tight-money policies that Republican and Democratic presidents had promoted, which depressed crop prices and inflated the costs of the manufactured and imported goods that farmers needed, such as plows and other farm implements. The farmers' solution to their problem was unlimited coinage of silver to expand the money supply.

The Democratic Party not only divided over the populist uprising in the western states but also faced a Republican Party with better financing and organization. The 1896 election, in which Republican William McKinley defeated the farmers' champion, the pro-silver Democrat William Jennings Bryan, solidified Republican dominance of American politics.

Woodrow Wilson, a political scientist at Princeton University who became a reform governor of New Jersey, was the only Democrat to win the White House in the thirty-six years after the McKinley-Bryan showdown in 1896. Elected to the first of two terms in 1912, Wilson helped the Democrats to take control of Congress and produced a unique period of reform policy activism. Wilson's reforms included antitrust laws, consumer protection, and banking regulations.

But the Democrats' ascendance in national politics was short-lived, largely because of the public bitterness that accompanied the end of World War I. President Wilson's failed attempt to win Senate approval of the Treaty of Versailles, which would have brought the United States into the newly formed League of Nations, shattered his career and split his party badly. Able to exploit the national mood of cynicism about liberal activism abroad and at home, the Republicans won the presidency in the elections of 1920, 1924, and 1928.

The New Deal Era. Republican dominance ended in the aftermath of the stock market crash of October 29, 1929, which occurred when Herbert C. Hoover occupied the White House. Hoover took a number of measures to provide relief for victims of the nation's greatest economic catastrophe, but his lack of empathy for the poor and unemployed and his failure to understand the fundamental nature of the crisis made him into a political pariah. For most of his four-year term, many Americans hated Hoover. Any Democrat promoting change in 1932 was practically guaranteed victory.

Franklin D. Roosevelt, the governor of New York and a former assistant secretary of the navy, not only won the presidency in 1932 but also changed the face of American politics. Supported by the coalition that Roosevelt built, the Democrats dominated national politics for the next three decades. The New Deal coalition included southerners, African Americans, organized labor, urban dwellers, Catholics, Jews, and liberals. Beginning in 1932, Democrats won seven of the next nine presidential elections. The only Republican victor between 1932 and 1964 was World War II hero Dwight D. Eisenhower (in 1952 and 1956).

The issue of race and a variety of economic developments began to pull the Democratic Party apart in the post–World War II years. When the party adopted a strong civil rights platform in 1948, a group of southerners led by Gov. J. Strom Thurmond of South Carolina bolted the Democratic National Convention and formed their own party. *(See "Third Parties," p. 324.)* Despite the defection that same year of the liberal former vice president Henry Wallace, President Harry Truman retained the support of most elements of the New Deal coalition and was returned to the White House. But the party's once-strong hold on the South was beginning to erode. In 1948 Thurmond won more than 22 percent of the popular vote in the South, as well as the electoral votes of Alabama, Louisiana, Mississippi, and South Carolina.

The Republicans suffered divisions of their own during this period. The party's isolationist, high-tariff wing was still strong under the leadership of Sen. Robert A. Taft of Ohio. But other party leaders, such as Eisenhower, New York governor Thomas E. Dewey, former State Department official Nelson A. Rockefeller, and Sen. Richard M. Nixon of California, wanted the United States to be a bulwark against the Soviet Union in world politics and an engine of economic expansion at home and abroad.

The Postwar Party System. In the years after World War II, two major economic changes and a variety of racial issues shifted the balance of power in American politics. First, the locus of economic activity in the United States shifted from the Northeast to the South and the West and from the cities to the suburbs. The loosening of old economic ties led to the loosening of social and political ties. Second, the United States faced growing competition in world markets from European and Asian countries that had rebuilt their economies after the war. By the late 1960s, the U.S. share of world markets had been cut in half, the position of the dollar in international finance was in decline, and inflation was threatening domestic prosperity. An explosion in federal social spending created resentment among some middle- and working-class voters. The American economy was not growing fast enough to satisfy all the elements of the New Deal Democratic coalition, which began to compete with one another.[42]

A number of social movements also helped to undermine the Democratic majority in the post–World War II years. One of the most dramatic, the civil rights movement, shattered the Democratic Party's dominance of the South. President Lyndon B. Johnson ruefully remarked that when he signed major civil rights legislation in 1964 he was delivering the South to the Republican Party. Other liberal movements, such as feminism, environmentalism, and gay rights, also initiated basic changes in public policy. But by doing so, these movements upset a wide range of relationships that had been the foundation of the New Deal Democratic coalition. Conservative movements arose to challenge government policies on taxes, busing, abortion rights, and secularism in schools. The Democratic Party was especially torn by the new factionalism of the 1970s and 1980s.[43] Indeed, the Democratic coalition split not only over racial and economic issues but also over the proper U.S. role in international affairs. The Vietnam War divided the party into "hawk" and "dove" factions.

The Republicans won control (albeit narrowly) of Congress during some of the Truman and Eisenhower years and of the Senate for the first six years of the Reagan administration. The party regained control of both houses of Congress, by healthy margins, in the 1994 midterm elections during the administration of Bill Clinton. They held on to the House by narrow majorities in the next several elections, but briefly lost control of the Senate in 2001 when Sen. James Jeffords of Vermont, previously a Republican, began voting with the Democrats, giving them a 51–49 majority.

In contests for the presidency, the Republicans won seven of ten elections from 1968 to 2004, four by landslides. The only Democrats to win presidential elections in this period were southern governors: the Georgian Jimmy Carter in 1976 and Bill Clinton of Arkansas in 1992 and 1996. The Republicans had a strong hold on the Rocky Mountain West, the Plains states, and the South and made inroads into the blue-collar vote in the Northeast and industrial Midwest. The party also became dominant in the South at the state and congressional levels.

Although public resistance to some of the increasingly liberal policies of the Democrats created an opening for the GOP, the Democrats still had strong natural bases. Since 1964, for example, no Democratic presidential candidate has won less than 84 percent of the African American vote. In the 1986 Democratic takeover of the Senate, black support was crucial to the victories in five southern states. Clinton's victory in 1992 suggested that the Democratic Party had a chance to bring parts of the South back into its coalition. The Arkansan Clinton built a measurable base with help from Sen. Al Gore of Tennessee, his running mate. With Arkansas and Tennessee in the Democratic camp, the Clinton-Gore ticket appealed to other states in the region with traditions of moderation. The ticket won the nearby border states of Missouri and Kentucky, and the southern states of Georgia and Louisiana. Combined, these states provided Clinton with fifty-eight electoral votes. He held on to all of these southern and border states except Georgia when he ran for reelection in 1996, and more than made up for the loss by carrying Florida—a net gain of twelve electoral votes. In both elections, Clinton swept the Northeast, the industrial Midwest, and the Pacific West.

Gore did well as the Democratic nominee for president in 2000 in the northeastern quadrant of the country and in the Pacific West. His Republican opponent, Texas governor George W. Bush, carried all the other regions overwhelmingly. Unlike Clinton, Gore lost every southern and border state, including his home state of Tennessee. The South's electoral votes gave Bush a 271–266 electoral college victory. In 2004, running for reelection against Sen. John F. Kerry of Massachusetts, Bush again swept the South. Although Kerry carried the rest of the country by 252 to 133 electoral votes, Bush's 153–0 victory in the South was enough to elect him by a margin of 286 to 251.

The Development of Party Nominating Conventions

The first method political parties used to select their candidates for president and vice president was the congressional caucus—separate meetings of each party's members of Congress. In 1824, however, a popular reaction against the closed nature of the caucus system paved the way for the birth of the national convention system in 1831. Since then, nominating conventions of party leaders and activists from all the states have been held to choose their presidential and vice-presidential candidates. Conventions also produce platforms, or statements of party principles and promises. Present-day national conventions are more media events than deliberative gatherings. Long before the convention meets, the party usually knows whom it will nominate based on how many delegates each candidate won in state primaries and caucuses.

The Anti-Masonic Party held the first national party convention in September 1831. Delegates from thirteen states nominated William Wirt of Maryland for president. The National Republican, or Whig, Party held a convention in December 1831 and nominated Henry Clay for president. In May 1832 the Democrats convened to renominate President Andrew Jackson and choose Martin Van Buren for vice president.

Although they represented a repudiation of the Framers' dislike for parti-

When conventions were still deliberative events, the Democrats, in the summer of 1924, went through seventeen days, 103 ballots, and sixteen candidates before choosing John W. Davis as the presidential nominee. Davis lost to Republican Calvin Coolidge.

sanship, conventions were in tune with the nation's federal ideals. State parties chose their own delegates, but once a state's delegates met with the delegates from the other states, they had to consider national concerns.

National party conventions have gone through three eras since their invention in the 1830s.[44] From 1832 to 1952 conventions were the arena in which presidential nominations usually were fought and won. Party leaders from around the country assembled, wheeled and dealed, and decided on a nominee. As one measure of their contentiousness, twenty-eight of the sixty-one Democratic, Whig, and Republican conventions that took place in this 120-year period were multiballot affairs. The 1924 Democratic convention needed seventeen days and 103 ballots to choose its nominee, John W. Davis. Eight other conventions required ten or more ballots. The Democrats took an especially long time because, until 1936, their rules required two-thirds support for any nominee.

The second era began with the 1956 election and lasted through 1980. None of the fourteen major-party conventions in this period took more than one ballot to nominate its candidate. The flowering of presidential primaries, which advanced the beginning of the nominating contest to much earlier in the election year, and the presence of live television cameras at the conventions, which rendered closed-door dealing in smoke-filled rooms impossible, invariably led to the emergence of a nominee sometime before the convention met. But the legacy of the convention as an important decision-making body was not entirely lost. Conventions in this quarter-century period were frequently marked by open battles about the party platform, the convention rules, delegate credentials, and other matters. In 1964, for example, conservative supporters of Sen. Barry Goldwater shouted down Nelson A. Rockefeller, the liberal governor of New York, during a platform debate. In 1980 Sen. Edward M. Kennedy battled President Carter fiercely over a rule that bound the delegates to vote for the candidate they had been elected to support in their state's primary or caucus.

Beginning in 1984, conventions entered a third era, which has lasted to the present. Not only are modern con-

TABLE 5-1 **Voter Turnout in 2004 Elections**

State	2004 Voting age population	Registration: 2004 general election	Percentage voting age registered	Presidential vote	Presidential Vote as Percentage of Voting age population	Presidential Vote as Percentage of Registered voters
Alabama	3,419,000	2,842,985	83.2%	1,883,449	55.1%	66.2%
Alaska	447,000	473,927	106.0%	312,598	69.9%	66.0%
Arizona	3,768,000	2,643,331	70.2%	2,012,585	53.4%	76.1%
Arkansas	2,057,000	1,684,684	81.9%	1,054,945	51.3%	62.6%
California	20,754,000	16,557,273	79.8%	12,421,852	59.9%	75.0%
Colorado	3,275,000	3,114,566	95.1%	2,130,330	65.0%	68.4%
Connecticut	2,390,000	2,044,181	85.5%	1,578,769	66.1%	77.2%
Delaware	601,000	553,885	92.2%	375,190	62.4%	67.7%
Florida	11,904,000	10,301,290	86.5%	7,609,810	63.9%	73.9%
Georgia	6,135,000	4,951,955	80.7%	3,301,875	53.8%	66.7%
Hawaii	877,000	647,238	73.8%	429,013	48.9%	66.3%
Idaho	985,000	798,015	81.0%	598,447	60.8%	75.0%
Illinois	8,544,000	7,499,488	87.8%	5,274,322	61.7%	70.3%
Indiana	4,572,000	4,296,602	94.0%	2,468,002	54.0%	57.4%
Iowa	2,190,000	2,106,658	96.2%	1,506,908	68.8%	71.5%
Kansas	1,954,000	1,591,428	81.4%	1,187,756	60.8%	74.6%
Kentucky	3,134,000	2,794,286	89.2%	1,795,882	57.3%	64.3%
Louisiana	3,310,000	2,923,395	88.3%	1,943,106	58.7%	66.5%
Maine	984,000	1,023,956	104.1%	740,752	75.3%	72.3%
Maryland	3,804,000	3,074,889	80.8%	2,386,678	62.7%	77.6%
Massachusetts	4,501,000	4,098,634	91.1%	2,912,388	64.7%	71.1%
Michigan	7,289,000	7,164,047	98.3%	4,839,252	66.4%	67.5%
Minnesota	3,658,000	3,559,400	97.3%	2,828,387	77.3%	79.5%
Mississippi	2,155,000	1,791,666	83.1%	1,152,145	53.5%	64.3%
Missouri	4,242,000	4,194,146	98.9%	2,731,364	64.4%	65.1%
Montana	709,000	638,474	90.1%	450,445	63.5%	70.6%
Nebraska	1,256,000	1,160,199	92.4%	778,186	62.0%	67.1%
Nevada	1,528,000	1,071,101	70.1%	829,587	54.3%	77.5%
New Hampshire	942,000	855,861	90.9%	677,738	71.9%	79.2%
New Jersey	5,702,000	5,005,959	87.8%	3,611,691	63.3%	72.1%
New Mexico	1,322,000	1,105,372	83.6%	756,304	57.2%	68.4%
New York	12,496,000	11,837,068	94.7%	7,391,036	59.1%	62.4%
North Carolina	6,208,000	5,519,992	88.9%	3,501,007	56.4%	63.4%
North Dakota	483,000	—		312,833	64.8%	—
Ohio	8,486,000	7,972,826	94.0%	5,627,908	66.3%	70.6%
Oklahoma	2,581,000	2,143,978	83.1%	1,463,758	56.7%	68.3%
Oregon	2,581,000	2,141,243	83.0%	1,836,782	71.2%	85.8%
Pennsylvania	9,230,000	8,366,663	90.6%	5,769,590	62.5%	69.0%
Rhode Island	752,000	651,950	86.7%	437,134	58.1%	67.1%
South Carolina	3,120,000	2,315,462	74.2%	1,617,730	51.9%	69.9%
South Dakota	569,000	552,441	97.1%	388,215	68.2%	70.3%
Tennessee	4,462,000	3,742,829	83.9%	2,437,319	54.6%	65.1%
Texas	14,197,000	13,098,329	92.3%	7,410,765	52.2%	56.6%
Utah	1,587,000	1,278,251	80.5%	927,844	58.5%	72.6%
Vermont	470,000	444,077	94.5%	312,309	66.4%	70.3%
Virginia	5,290,000	4,517,980	85.4%	3,198,367	60.5%	70.8%
Washington	4,370,000	3,508,208	80.3%	2,859,084	65.4%	81.5%
West Virginia	1,423,000	1,168,694	82.1%	755,887	53.1%	64.7%
Wisconsin	4,057,000	—		2,997,007	73.9%	—
Wyoming	380,000	232,396	61.2%	243,428	64.1%	104.7%
District of Columbia	391,000	383,919	98.2%	227,586	58.2%	59.3%
Total	**201,541,000**	**172,445,197**	**85.6%**	**122,295,345**	**60.7%**	**70.9%**

SOURCE: Richard M. Scammon, Alice V. McGillivray, and Rhodes Cook, *America Votes 26* (Washington, D.C.: CQ Press, 2006), 1.

ventions one-ballot events, but they also are planned and even scripted by the nominee's campaign staff. Such choreography is politically desirable because, as political scientist Martin P. Wattenberg has shown, parties that present a united front to the country gain an advantage over parties that place their divisions on display.[45] It is politically possible because the recent "frontloading" of the delegate-selection process toward the first three months of the election year almost invariably produces an early winner in the fight for the party's nomination. In 1976, after New Hampshire voted in February, only five states held primaries in March. By 2000 twenty-seven states voted by the end of March, including nearly all of the large states with the richest delegate prizes. To ensure that a nominee emerges from this blizzard of winter primaries and that the party can unite long before the convention, party leaders and fund-raisers rally to the candidate who takes the early lead, rendering effective opposition to the front-runner nearly impossible.

At the convention itself, platform, credentials, and rules fights in the modern era are either suppressed (under recently adopted party rules, no challenge to a convention committee's decision is allowed on the convention floor unless at least 25 percent of the delegates demand it) or shunted into off-hours sessions, outside the gaze of television network programming. Prime time is devoted to speeches, celebrity appearances, and videos whose content is strictly controlled by the nominee. The delegates are little more than a studio audience. In sum, the modern convention is "a huge pep rally, replete with ritual, pomp, and entertainment—a made-for-TV production. From the perspective of the party and its nominee, the convention now serves primarily as a launching pad for the general election." [46] Some of those launches have been spectacular. Clinton, for example, went from trailing Bush by eight percentage points before the 1992 Democratic convention to leading him by twenty-two points afterward.[47] Bush seized the lead from Kerry in 2004 with a convention that featured powerful speeches from former New York mayor Rudolph Giuliani, movie star and California governor Arnold Schwarzenegger, and former Democratic governor of Georgia Zell Miller.

The 2000 Republican convention was focused on rousing support for George W. Bush's candidacy, and centrist swing voters were the intended audience. Other than Bush and his vice-presidential running mate, Richard B. Cheney, nearly all of the speakers who were featured in prime time during the convention were African Americans, Latinos, women or, in one case, a gay Republican member of Congress. Bush surely hoped to win more support than Republicans usually do among the groups of voters these speakers represented, as he had done during his successful gubernatorial campaigns in Texas. But his greater purpose was to assure moderate, independent voters that he was not a conservative extremist. Bush underscored this purpose in

his acceptance speech at the Republican convention and throughout the general election campaign by emphasizing issues such as education and social security reform and by promising that he would seek to govern in a bipartisan spirit. "I have no stake in the bitter arguments of the last few years," Bush told the delegates and, more important, the large television audience. "I want to change the tone of Washington to one of civility and respect."

Bush's postconvention five-percentage-point bounce in the polls gave him his biggest lead of the campaign. Two weeks later, Gore closed the gap with a ten-point bounce after a Democratic convention in Los Angeles that was at least as appealing to the voters as the Republican convention had been. (Gore, trailing in the preconvention polls, had more room to gain ground than Bush did.) Gore dispelled his reputation for woodenness not only by giving a fighting acceptance speech, but also by passionately kissing his wife on camera just before delivering it.

History of the Primary System

One of the Progressive movement's greatest contributions to presidential politics was its introduction of the primary election to the nominating process at the start of the twentieth century. Progressives persistently complained about the undemocratic way in which local and state political machines chose candidates for public office. Their solution was to put the decision in the hands of the voters. Similarly, the quest for a purer democracy animated reforms such as the Seventeenth Amendment (which provides for direct election of U.S. senators, previously selected by state legislatures), referendums and recall votes in state constitutions, and voter initiatives (which are similar to referendums but are instigated by citizen petitions rather than legislative action).

The logical extension of pure democracy to presidential politics was the direct primary. The idea was to bypass completely the vested interests that controlled nominations and thereby limited the people's choices in the general election. Proponents of the primary wanted to abolish completely the deal making that had been characteristic of the nominating process throughout American history. Primaries would provide for the direct election of the delegates from each state, a vote in which voters expressed their preferences for the presidential candidates themselves, or some combination of the two.

Early Days. Florida passed the first presidential primary law in 1901, but the primary got its biggest boost when the 1904 Republican convention refused to seat the backers of Progressive Party leader Robert M. La Follette. As a result, in 1905 La Follette successfully promoted legislation in Wisconsin that provided for primary election of delegates to national party conventions. In 1906 Pennsylvania also established a primary.

In 1912 former president Theodore Roosevelt won nine out of twelve GOP primaries but was out-maneuvered by William Howard Taft at the Republican convention. In reaction, Roosevelt ran on his own "Bull Moose" ticket, calling for national primaries to decide the nomination.

In 1910 Oregon established the first primary election in which voters expressed a preference among the candidates themselves. Convention delegates were legally bound to vote for candidates according to the results of the primary.

By 1916 twenty-five states had passed laws for presidential primaries. The greatest surge of support for primaries, and the primary system's greatest disappointment, came with the 1912 Republican nomination struggle. Former president Theodore Roosevelt used the primaries to battle President William Howard Taft for the nomination. But despite his nine primary victories, compared with La Follette's two and Taft's one, Roosevelt lost the nomination to Taft. After declaring that Taft had "stolen" the nomination, Roosevelt ran on his own "Bull Moose" party ticket and called for national primaries to decide presidential nominations.[48]

But resistance to primaries persisted for years. Party leaders in state legislatures, courts, and local election boards worked against the new system.

Time accomplished what the opponents of primaries could not manage. The arrival of World War I, the political apathy of the 1920s, and the struggle for economic survival during the Great Depression brought about the collapse of the primary system. The high costs of primaries, the low voter turnout, and the avoidance of the contests by presidential candidates turned them into vestiges of the Progressive movement.

Eight of the twenty-five states that adopted primaries during the Progressive surge abolished them by 1935. Only a three-way Republican race in 1920 created any voter interest or candidate activity in primaries—and even then the biggest vote-getter, Hiram Johnson, was denied the nomination. The disaster that befell Republican Wendell Willkie in 1944 when he tried to use the Wisconsin primary as a springboard to a second consecutive nomination—he won only 4.6 percent of the vote—seemed to indicate that primaries offered candidates great risk and little potential for gain.

But a comeback for primaries was not far away. Former Minnesota governor Harold E. Stassen almost captured the Republican nomination in 1948 when he won the Wisconsin, Nebraska, and Pennsylvania primaries. Stassen saw his chance for the nomination slip away when he took on Sen. Robert Taft in Taft's home state of Ohio and lost. New York governor Thomas Dewey, the eventual nominee, then beat Stassen in the critical Oregon primary after campaigning there for three weeks.

After the dramatic events of 1948, interest in primary elections surged. A number of states, including Indiana, Minnesota, and Montana, reinstated primaries in time for the 1952 election. Voter participation in primaries jumped from 4.8 million in 1948 to 12.7 million in 1952. Thus, although enthusiasm for primaries did not run as high as it had during the Progressive Era, and some states even repealed their primary laws during the 1950s, primaries had found an important niche. *(See Table 5-2, below.)*

The Mixed System. Presidential nomination politics evolved into a "mixed system" in the 1950s and 1960s. Under the mixed system, candidates could restrict their public campaigns to a few primaries that would supplement other strengths, such as fund-raising ability, endorsements, support from state and local machines, regional and ideological loyalties, and skill at negotiating with other political leaders.

The major function of primaries under the mixed system was to allow the candidate to demonstrate an ability to campaign and to appeal to voters. As a rough test of "electability," primaries served to supplement—not replace—the need for other political strengths. In 1960 Massachusetts senator John Kennedy used West Virginia's Democratic primary to demonstrate to skeptical party leaders that he could overcome Protestant resistance to a Catholic candidacy. Later, in 1968, Richard Nixon used a string of primary victories to demonstrate that he was not a "loser" with the voters,

despite earlier defeats in the 1960 presidential and 1962 California gubernatorial campaigns.

Entering primaries under the mixed system was considered a risk. Performing below expectations could be fatal to a campaign, as Lyndon Johnson learned in 1968 when he barely defeated long-shot challenger Eugene McCarthy. Good primary showings, moreover, did not ensure a nomination, as Estes Kefauver learned in 1952 and McCarthy discovered when he failed to win the nomination in 1968.

Primaries always have been vehicles for long-shot candidates. McCarthy's second-place finish to President Johnson in the 1968 New Hampshire primary and his big victory in Wisconsin established him as a serious candidate for the Democratic nomination even though he lost it to Vice President Hubert H. Humphrey after Johnson withdrew from the election and Sen. Robert F. Kennedy was assassinated. Other dark-horse candidates who became instant contenders after important primary showings included Estes Kefauver (1952), George S. McGovern (1972), Jimmy Carter (1976), George Bush (1980), Gary Hart (1984), Pat Buchanan (1992), and John McCain (2000).

Under the mixed system, a candidate who dominated the primary season could lose the nomination if enough

TABLE 5-2 **Votes Cast and Delegates Selected in Presidential Primaries, 1912–2004**

Year	Democratic Party			Republican Party			Total		
	Number of primaries	Votes cast	Delegates selected through primaries (%)	Number of primaries	Votes cast	Delegates selected through primaries (%)		Votes cast	Delegates selected through primaries (%)
1912	12	974,775	32.9	13	2,261,240	41.7		3,236,015	37.3
1916	20	1,187,691	53.5	20	1,923,374	58.9		3,111,065	56.2
1920	16	571,671	44.6	20	3,186,248	57.8		3,757,919	51.2
1924	14	763,858	35.5	17	3,525,185	45.3		4,289,043	40.4
1928	16	1,264,220	42.2	15	4,110,288	44.9		5,374,508	43.5
1932	16	2,952,933	40.0	14	2,346,996	37.7		5,299,929	38.8
1936	14	5,181,808	36.5	12	3,319,810	37.5		8,501,618	37.0
1940	13	4,468,631	35.8	13	3,227,875	38.8		7,696,506	37.3
1944	14	1,867,609	36.7	13	2,271,605	38.7		4,139,214	37.7
1948	14	2,151,865	36.3	12	2,653,255	36.0		4,805,120	36.1
1952	16	4,928,006	38.7	13	7,801,413	39.0		12,729,419	38.8
1956	19	5,832,592	42.7	19	5,828,272	44.8		11,660,864	43.7
1960	16	5,687,742	38.3	15	5,537,967	38.6		11,224,631	38.5
1964	16	6,247,435	45.7	16	5,935,339	45.6		12,182,774	45.6
1968	15	7,535,069	40.2	15	4,473,551	38.1		12,008,620	39.1
1972	21	15,993,965	65.3	20	6,188,281	56.8		22,182,246	61.0
1976	27	16,052,652	76.0	26	10,374,125	71.0		26,426,777	73.5
1980	34	18,747,825	71.8	34	12,690,451	76.0		31,438,276	73.7
1984	29	18,009,192	52.4	25	6,575,651	71.0		24,584,843	59.6
1988	36	22,961,936	66.6	36	12,165,115	76.9		35,127,051	70.2
1992	39	20,239,385	66.9	38	12,696,547	83.9		32,935,932	72.7
1996	35	10,947,364	65.3	42	13,991,649	84.6		24,939,013	69.2
2000	40	14,048,951	64.6	43	17,157,075	83.8		31,206,026	70.8
2004	36	16,182,439	83.2	27	7,940,331	56.9		24,122,770	70.0

SOURCE: Rhodes Cook, *United States Presidential Primary Elections, 2000–2004* (Washington, D.C.: CQ Press, 2007).

state party organizations rallied behind another candidate—a highly unlikely event today. For example, Kefauver lost the 1952 Democratic nomination to Adlai E. Stevenson despite attracting 64.5 percent of the total primary vote to Stevenson's 1.6 percent. In 1968 McCarthy had 38.7 percent of the total primary vote, yet Humphrey won the nomination without entering any primaries.

The candidacies of Lyndon Johnson in 1960 and Barry Goldwater in 1964 illustrate the possibilities for waging a campaign under the mixed system without depending on the primaries. Although Johnson did not announce his candidacy formally until just before the Democratic convention (he said that his duties as Senate majority leader had been too pressing), he managed to build a strong base of support in the months leading up to the convention. By delivering a series of weekend speeches before state conventions, attending fund-raisers, and appearing before other party groups, Johnson won high visibility for his "noncandidacy" and gained the support of about four hundred southern and Rocky Mountain delegates. But LBJ was painted by rivals as a regional candidate, and his strength going into the convention was limited to a possible vice-presidential nomination.

Before the 1964 primary season even began, Goldwater's supporters lined up enough delegates to make him the front-runner for the Republican nomination. To gain the support of state party organizations, however, he needed some primary wins to persuade party leaders of his popular appeal. Goldwater's California primary victory sealed his nomination.

Selective participation in primaries no longer appears to be a viable option for a presidential campaign. Humphrey hoped that the Democratic Party would turn to him in a deadlocked convention in 1976, but Jimmy Carter had already secured a majority of delegates in the primaries.

Recent Years. Since 1968 primaries, which nearly tripled in number between 1968 and 2004, have been at the center of the nominating process. *(See box, How Primaries Work, p. 243.)* Today, early contests, especially the Iowa caucus and New Hampshire primary, are vital to any campaign because the media and campaign professionals use those tests to determine a front-runner. In advance of the 2008 election, the Democratic National Committee added Nevada and South Carolina to the list of early contests.

Candidates now routinely campaign for at least two years before the first electoral test. The early primaries and caucuses eliminate all but a few candidates, and the survivors battle until one wins enough delegates for a first-ballot nomination at the convention. In recent years, the eventual nominee has emerged well before the convention. Not since Walter F. Mondale and Gary Hart battled for the Democratic

HOW CAUCUSES WORK

Compared with a primary, the caucus system is complicated. Instead of focusing on a single primary election ballot, the caucus is a multitiered system that involves meetings scheduled over several weeks, sometimes even months. Mass participation occurs only at the first level, with meetings often lasting several hours and, in most cases, attracting only the most enthusiastic and dedicated party members.

Caucuses are operated differently from state to state, and each party has its own set of rules. Most begin with precinct caucuses or some other type of local mass meeting open to all party voters. Participants publicly declare their votes, then elect delegates to the next stage in the process, usually the county convention.

Voter participation, even at the first level of the caucus process, is much lower than in the primaries. Most caucus participants are local party activists. Many rank-and-file voters find a caucus complex, confusing, burdensome, or intimidating.

In a caucus state the focus is on one-on-one campaigning. Thus time, not money, is the most valuable resource for a candidate, as well as an early start, which is far more crucial in a caucus state than in most primaries. Because only a small segment of the electorate is targeted in most caucus states, candidates usually use media advertising sparingly.

Although the basic steps in the caucus process are the same for both parties, the rules that govern them are vastly different. Democratic rules have been revamped substantially since 1968, establishing national standards for grassroots participation. Republican rules have remained largely unchanged, with the states given wide latitude in deciding how to select their delegates. Most Democratic caucuses are open to Democrats only. Republicans generally allow independents

or voters who are willing to switch parties to participate where state law permits.

The first step of the Democratic caucus process is open, well-publicized local meetings. In most states Republicans do the same.

MODERN INFLUENCE

Caucuses in Iowa have dramatically changed the dynamics of presidential nominating campaigns in the modern era.

An obscure former governor of Georgia, Jimmy Carter, spent months wooing the voters of Iowa and gained national attention with his victory in that state's Democratic caucuses, the nation's first formal balloting. The favorable publicity Carter received for his Iowa upset helped him to win the New Hampshire primary and march to his party's nomination in 1976.

Carter's victory in the Iowa caucuses transformed caucuses into means of attracting national publicity. In subsequent elections, dark-horse candidates, such as Republicans George Bush in 1980 and Pat Robertson in 1988 and Democrat Gary Hart in 1984, attracted national attention because of their victories or surprisingly strong showings in the Iowa contests.

Iowa's influence on the nominating process declines when a candidate from Iowa or a neighboring state runs for president. For example, in 1988 Richard Gephardt and Paul Simon from the neighboring states of Missouri and Illinois finished a close first and second in the first round of the Democratic caucuses. Pundits dismissed their strong finishes as signs of midwestern provincialism rather than as evidence of national vote-getting ability.

nomination in 1984 has either party had a contest that continued into the final week of the primary season.[49] In most cases, the identity of that nominee is known in March.

Caucuses. Since the passage of Democratic reforms after the 1968 election, the nominating process has been dominated not just by primaries, but also by caucuses. Caucuses occupy a middle ground between primary elections, dominated by the voters, and state conventions, dominated by the party professionals. *(See box, How Caucuses Work, p. 244.)*

Caucuses are neighborhood or precinct meetings at which party members debate the merits of the candidates before voting. Backers of each candidate try to persuade other caucus-goers to join their side. At the end of as many as three hours of debate, each local meeting in a state votes on which delegates it will send to county, congressional district, and state conventions.

The media usually cover the outcomes of early caucus maneuverings as if they were straightforward primary elections. The Iowa caucus receives more media attention than most other state contests because it comes first on the election calendar.

The Franchise and the Electorate

The history of American elections has been an ongoing effort to break down legal barriers to voting and to expand the size of the electorate. *(See Table 5-3, above.)* Of the seventeen amendments added to the Constitution since the Bill of Rights was enacted, nine address the way citizens participate in elections.[50] The Supreme Court also has been active in this area. For example, in *Smith v. Allwright* (1944), the Court held that all-white primaries are unconstitutional. *Harman v. Forssenius* (1965) struck down the poll tax for federal elections, and *Harper v. Virginia State Board of Elections* (1966) ruled the poll tax unconstitutional for state and local elections as well.[51] On the legislative front, some of the nation's most storied political battles have been fought over the regulation of elections. Voting rights have been a continuing source of contention in American politics.

The vast majority of citizens who are at least eighteen years old are now entitled to vote, subject no longer to restrictions based on wealth and property, sex, and race. One important restriction that remains in effect is the bar on voting by convicted criminals that applies in varying forms in the states. In all but four New England states, felons may not vote while they are incarcerated. Thirty-two states prohibit those on parole from voting, and twenty-nine prohibit those on probation. Fourteen states impose lifetime denials of voting rights on ex-convicts as well. This burden has fallen disproportionately on African American men, of whom around 15 percent are ineligible to vote.[52]

The Framers of the Constitution left the regulation of voting rights to the states. These rights have been expanded

TABLE 5-3 **Franchise in the United States, 1932–2004**

Presidential election year	Estimated population of voting age	Vote cast for presidential electors	
		Number	Percent
1932	75,768,000	39,758,759	52.5
1936	80,174,000	45,654,763	56.9
1940	84,728,000	49,900,418	58.9
1944	85,654,000	47,976,670	56.0
1948	95,573,000	48,793,826	51.1
1952	99,929,000	61,550,918	61.6
1956	104,515,000	62,026,908	59.3
1960	109,672,000	68,838,219	62.8
1964	114,090,000	70,644,592	61.9
1968	120,285,000	73,211,875	60.9
1972	140,777,000	77,718,554	55.2
1976	152,308,000	81,555,889	53.5
1980	164,595,000	86,515,221	52.6
1984	174,468,000	92,652,842	53.1
1988	182,779,000	91,594,809	50.1
1992	189,044,000	104,425,014	55.2
1996	196,507,000	96,277,872	49.0
2000	205,814,000	105,396,627	51.2
2004	201,541,000	122,295,345	60.7

SOURCES: Bureau of the Census, *Statistical Abstract of the United States 2007* (Washington, D.C.: Government Printing Office, 2007); Richard M. Scammon, Alice V. McGillivray, and Rhodes Cook, America Votes series. (Washington, D.C.: CQ Press, 2006).

at two levels. First, many states have moved to liberalize voting requirements. Second, the federal government has intervened to prohibit the states from excluding certain classes of voters from the franchise. Over the years, the nationalization of economic and political life has been accompanied by the nationalization of election laws. In the first few decades after the United States won independence from Great Britain, the thirteen states allowed only male property-holders or taxpayers to vote. Several of those states required ownership of land; the others required a certain value of possessions or evidence of having paid taxes. As a result, about half of all white males were not eligible to vote in the Republic's early days. Religious restrictions on voting, which were prevalent in the colonial period, no longer were the norm. Still, in 1790 women, blacks, Native Americans, and indentured servants could not vote. Tax-paying requirements gradually replaced property-holding requirements for men, and by 1850 most states had eliminated the tax-paying restriction as well.[53]

African Americans and the Right to Vote. The group that has faced the most persistent discrimination has been African Americans. The Constitution sanctioned slavery, and in the infamous 1857 *Dred Scott* case the Supreme Court held that slaves are property. The constitutional provision that declared a slave to be three-fifths of a person for purposes of allocating seats in the House of Representatives was perhaps the most convoluted expression of early American

The first African American to serve in Congress was Republican Hiram R. Revels of Mississippi, left, who served in the Senate from 1870 to 1871. In 1874 Mississippi Republican Blanche K. Bruce, right, was elected to the Senate. He was the first black member to serve a full term in that chamber.

disregard for blacks. By the outbreak of the Civil War, all but six of the thirty-three states barred African Americans from voting at any time, solely because of their race.

Although the Civil War was not fought primarily about the morality of slavery, it led to the constitutional extension of the right to vote to African Americans. In response to the passage of "black codes" right after the war ended in many southern states, which barred blacks from voting and holding office, the Radical Republicans who controlled Congress passed a number of measures to bring blacks into American political life. The most important was the Reconstruction Act of 1867, which set up military governments in the Confederate states and tied each state's readmission to the Union to ratification of the Fourteenth Amendment.

The Fourteenth Amendment is the most important constitutional amendment since the Bill of Rights. The amendment bars states from limiting the "privileges and immunities" of citizens and orders states to respect all citizens' rights to "due process" and the "equal protection of the laws." It was ratified in 1868. The Fifteenth Amendment, which grants the franchise to all adult males regardless of race or "previous condition of servitude," entered the Constitution in 1870.

The addition of African Americans to the electorate was crucial in Ulysses S. Grant's slim 300,000-vote margin of victory over Horatio Seymour in the 1868 presidential election. In that election, blacks for the first time also were elected to state and federal offices. Between 1870 and 1900, twenty-two southern blacks won election to Congress. Two blacks, Mississippi Republicans Hiram R. Revels and Blanche K. Bruce, served in the Senate. Federal troops enforced voting rights.

Federal resolve to guarantee civil rights to African Americans died during the maneuvering over the 1876 presidential election results. As part of a deal that gave the disputed election to Republican nominee Rutherford B. Hayes, the Republicans agreed to pull federal troops out of the South and, by implication, to allow southern states to pass laws restricting blacks' ability to participate in politics and in mainstream economic and social life.

Southern states kept blacks from the polls with a variety of racially discriminatory measures: poll taxes, literacy tests, "grandfather clauses" (which exempted whites from the other measures by guaranteeing the franchise to citizens whose ancestors had voted or served in the state militia), property requirements, and tests of "morality." The "white primary" banned blacks from the Democratic Party with the legal reasoning that the party was a private organization not subject to the Fourteenth Amendment. When these devices did not block black political activity, violence and intimidation did. By the turn of the century, southern politics was almost entirely a white man's vocation.

In response to the wide range of voter registration requirements that restricted ballot access to African Americans and vulnerable groups of whites, such as illiterates, voter turnout in southern states fell by as much as 60 percent between 1884 and 1904.[54] The whites, most of them poor, were excluded for fear that they would support populist, antiestablishment candidates in southern state elections.

Shortly after the turn of the century, Congress and the federal courts began to chip away at voting discrimination against African Americans. In 1915 the Supreme Court struck down the use of grandfather clauses. It banned all-white primaries in 1944.[55]

The Civil Rights Act of 1957 established the Civil Rights Commission, which was empowered to study voter discrimination, and granted the attorney general authority to bring federal lawsuits against anyone restricting blacks' right to vote. The Civil Rights Act of 1960 empowered the attorney general to bring further action in suits that disclosed patterns of discrimination. It also authorized the appointment of federal officials to monitor elections. The Civil Rights Act of 1964 required states to adopt uniform election procedures for all citizens, as well as to show sufficient cause for rejecting voters who had completed the sixth grade or demonstrated an equivalent level of intellectual competence. The 1964 act further eased procedures for federal consideration of voting rights cases.

The Voting Rights Act of 1965 was the most effective of all. It suspended literacy tests in seven southern states and parts of another. It also required federal supervision of voter registration in states and counties that on November 1, 1964, still had literacy tests or other qualifying tests and where less than 50 percent of all voting-age citizens had voted in the 1964 presidential election. Jurisdictions under federal supervision needed to receive Justice Department approval for any changes in election procedures. This act quickly led to the addition of millions of African Americans to the voting rolls.

A 1970 amendment to the Voting Rights Act suspended for five years all literacy tests, whether they were discriminatory or not. In 1970 the Supreme Court upheld the law's constitutionality, and the tests were banned by law permanently in 1975. The "trigger" for federal involvement was applied to additional states and jurisdictions by amendments passed by Congress in 1970, 1975, and 1982. The 1982 law extended for twenty-five years the provisions requiring nine states and parts of thirteen others to get Justice Department approval for election law changes. The law also included: "bail-out" procedures for states that had demonstrated a clean ten-year record on voting rights; tests for discrimination based on results rather than intent; and provisions for bilingual ballots. In 2006, with support from President George W. Bush, Congress renewed the Voting Right Act for another twenty-five years.

Women and the Vote. Women won the right to vote with passage of the Nineteenth Amendment in 1920 after a battle for the suffrage that lasted for nearly a century.

Several states granted women the vote in school board elections in the nineteenth century, but the push for suffrage

Supporters of the Nineteenth Amendment—giving women the right to vote—picket the White House in 1916.

for women did not end there. The 1848 Women's Rights Convention in Seneca Falls, New York, marked the unofficial beginning of the feminist movement in the United States. Susan B. Anthony of Massachusetts led a suffragist campaign that claimed for women the right to vote under the Fourteenth Amendment while seeking a women's suffrage amendment to the Constitution. In 1887 Congress defeated the proposed amendment. Soon afterward, however, full voting rights were granted to women in Wyoming in 1890; Colorado in 1893; Utah and Idaho in 1896; Washington in 1910; California in 1911; Arizona, Kansas, and Oregon in 1912; Montana and Nevada in 1914; and New York in 1917.

The movement for women's suffrage accelerated in 1914 when a more militant group led a campaign against congressional candidates who opposed the amendment. President Woodrow Wilson initially opposed a constitutional amendment, arguing that continued state action was more appropriate. But in 1918 when protests escalated to hunger strikes, Wilson announced his support for the amendment. The western states formed the foundation of the suffrage movement and helped to secure quick ratification of the Nineteenth Amendment after Congress sent the amendment to the states in 1919. Tennessee provided the necessary thirty-sixth vote for ratification in 1920.

The debate over women's suffrage was not always enlightened. Assertions that women's suffrage would usher in a utopian era of compassionate government and respect among all citizens were countered with the argument that the amendment would wipe away all distinctions between the sexes.[56]

Other Issues Related to Voting and Voting Rights. Residency laws have long posed difficulties for millions of geographically mobile citizens. Until the 1970s most states required one year of residency in the state (some required two years), as well as shorter periods of residency in the county and election district. The 1970 voting rights legislation guaranteed the vote in presidential elections to citizens who had lived in the voting district for at least thirty days before the election. This measure made an additional five million people eligible to vote in the 1972 election.

In 1972 the Supreme Court ruled in *Dunn v. Blumstein* that states could not deny the full franchise to people who had lived in a state for a year and in a county for three months.[57] By 2000, twenty-four states had no minimum residency requirement, and none of the other states required more than thirty days of residency.

Congress passed legislation in 1976 guaranteeing the right to vote by absentee ballot to Americans living abroad. The states have made it easier for citizens at home to vote absentee without having to claim illness or absence as a reason. More than twenty states now have an "early voting" option that allows voters to cast ballots in person as much as three weeks before the election. In 1998 Oregon eliminated in-person voting entirely and now conducts all of its elections by mail. Recently the Defense Department has developed an Internet-based voting system for military personnel.

The most recent constitutional change affecting the right to vote was the lowering of the voting age to eighteen. Before World War II no state allowed citizens to vote before age twenty-one. Led by Georgia's World War II–inspired change in the voting age to eighteen in 1943, after a campaign marked by the slogan "Fight at 18, Vote at 18," a few states passed the more liberal requirement. President Eisenhower proposed a constitutional amendment in 1954, but it died in a Senate committee. The Voting Rights Act of 1970 set a minimum voting age of eighteen for all federal, state, and local elections, but the act was declared unconstitutional for state and local elections. The Court said Congress exceeded its authority because states have the right to set the voting age for their own elections. In 1971, however, the eighteen-year voting age was guaranteed by the Twenty-sixth Amendment for all elections.

Low voter participation in the United States has been an ongoing source of concern among democratic theorists and leaders of movements for poor people. No state or federal laws ban any significant class of people from voting, but only around half of the voting-age population votes in presidential elections, and only about a third vote in midterm congressional elections. Explanations for the disappointing turnout range from a lack of meaningful choices to satisfaction with the current policies of the government. The highest percentage of voter participation in recent years was in 1960, when 62.8 percent of all eligible citizens voted in the presidential race. By 1980 the participation rate had fallen to 52.8 percent; in 1992 it rose to 55.1 percent. In 1996 voter turnout dipped below 50 percent, to 49.0 percent. In 2000 turnout rose slightly to 51.2 percent. In 2004 it rose to 55.3 percent, the highest level in nearly forty years *(See Figure 5-1, p. 249.)*

The United States and the Western nations with high turnout—such as Great Britain, Germany, Canada, and Australia—differ in how they register citizens to vote. The United States is one of only a few nations that place the burden of qualifying for electoral participation on the citizen. In other nations, government agencies sign up voters. Registration is inconvenient in many American jurisdictions, although much less so than in the past.

For years, political activists have tried to simplify the process for registering to vote. President Carter backed bills to allow voters to register on election day. By the late 1980s, the majority of American citizens lived in states that allowed registration by mail. Oregon, Wisconsin, North Dakota, and Minnesota currently allow registration on the day of the election.

In 1993 President Clinton signed the "motor-voter" bill into law. The measure requires all states to provide voter registration forms in government offices such as motor vehicle bureaus and public assistance agencies. It also requires states to allow voters to send in registration forms by mail.

Campaign Practices and Technology

In the early days of partisan politics, newspapers conveyed most campaign messages—and they were unabashedly partisan. Alexander Hamilton started the pro-Federalist *Gazette of the United States,* and his rival Thomas Jefferson founded the *National Gazette* as the mouthpiece of the Democratic-Republican Party. *(See "Origins of Press Coverage: 1789–1860," p. 941, in Chapter 18.)*

As popular participation in presidential selection grew in the early nineteenth century, parties began to organize get-out-the-vote drives. Concurrently, they were building the party structures needed to carry out their campaign activities. The two major parties at the time, the Democrats and Whigs, developed hierarchical party organizations. One Whig supporter described a prevalent model:

> The fundamental idea is borrowed from the religious organizations of the day. The model of my primary local association is the Christian Church. The officers, the exercises, the exhortations, the singing, the weekly meetings (on Wednesday night), the enrollment of members, the contributions, and all are to be on the primitive apostolic model. . . . These little unit associations are to be mutually fraternized and affiliated to County, District—and state central associations, with regular and definite means of communication.[58]

FIGURE 5-1 **Percentage of Voting-Age Population that Voted for President, 1920–2004**

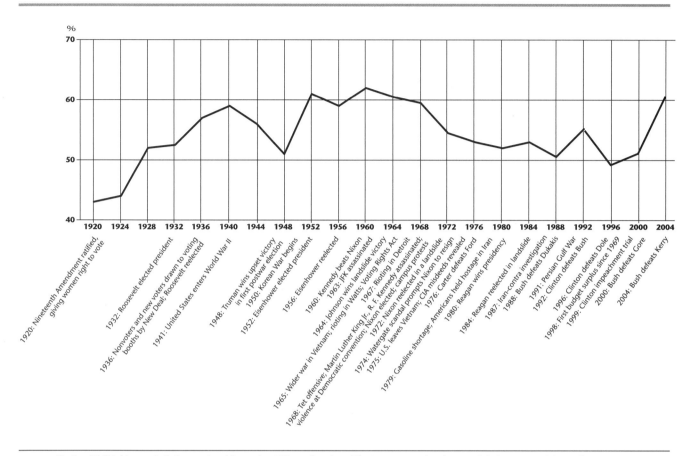

SOURCES: *Elections '88* (Washington, D.C.: Congressional Quarterly, 1988), 141; *Presidential Elections, 1789–1992* (Washington, D.C.: Congressional Quarterly, 1995), 5; *America Votes 26* (Washington, D.C.: CQ Press, 2006).

Tammany Hall, the most famous party organization in American political history, began as a fraternal society in New York City in the late 1700s. Tammany came to typify the party organizations of the nation's states and cities. These "machines" were marked by a pyramidal organization with top-down control, door-to-door voter recruitment, extensive use of patronage, close relations with businesses and utilities seeking government protection, and recreational activities. As sociologist Robert Merton has argued, party organizations dominated politics not only because of their discipline but also because they fulfilled many social needs that governments did not address.[59] In fact, state and local party organizations were central to American politics for more than a century.

With the coming of the New Deal in the 1930s, government at all levels assumed a vast number of citizen-aid functions and special interest groups took the lead in making demands on the political establishment. As a result, instead of going to a party leader for action, citizens began to approach government agencies and interest groups, as well as their legislative representatives. In addition, organizations loyal to specific candidates rather than to the party as a whole began to take over the presidential selection process.

It was not until the early 1900s that candidates for president felt compelled to tour the country making campaign speeches in their own behalf. In the nineteenth century, candidates had struck the pose of disinterested statesmen who stood for the presidency rather than ran for it. The harbinger of future campaign practices was the 1896 underdog campaign of Democratic nominee William Jennings Bryan. Bryan traveled eighteen thousand miles and delivered around six hundred speeches to approximately five million people. In 1900 Bryan ran again, and this time GOP vice presidential nominee Theodore Roosevelt shadowed him with a speaking tour on behalf of President William McKinley. The development of presidential primaries in the first decade of the twentieth century, and of advanced transportation and communications systems later on, contributed to the tendency of candidates to set out on the hustings.

Primaries demanded that candidates make public appeals for support. Theodore Roosevelt's participation in the 1912 Republican primaries against his handpicked successor as president from four years earlier, William Howard Taft, set the standard for political barnstorming that continues to this day. In tandem, TR and the primary system institutionalized the kind of public campaign that Bryan inaugurated.

Until the 1970s, primaries were just part of the presidential nominating process. But since the Democratic Party put a series of reforms in place before the 1972 election, primaries have dominated the process. *(See "History of the Primary System," p. 241.)* Today, a candidate cannot win the nomination without undertaking a long public campaign.

The rise of the mass media contributed to the need to make public appeals. A century ago, some cities had as many as a dozen daily newspapers. In addition, dozens of mass-circulation magazines helped to shape political debate. Citizens began to demand more information about the candidates' personal backgrounds and demeanors as well as their policy positions. Radio spread throughout the country during the 1920s. Franklin Roosevelt excelled in making campaign talks and, as president, "fireside chats" on radio, setting a new standard for mass political communication.

The acquisition of television sets by nearly all American families during the 1950s ushered in a new age of political discourse. The first presidential candidate to use television advertising was Dwight Eisenhower in 1952. By the 1960s television advertising was an integral element in political campaigning. Virtually every aspect of today's presidential campaign is shaped by considerations of television coverage.

Sophisticated polling methods based on computer analysis and random sampling techniques were developed after World War II. Princeton University professor Hadley Cantril's assessments of wartime consumer demands were among the first polls to move beyond simple snapshots of candidate strength.[60] Today, news organizations, campaign staffs, and parties use polls to determine the viability of candidates and campaign strategies. Privately conducted polls have become central to the strategy of the candidates by helping them to understand the importance of certain issues and even phrases to voters. In 1952 Eisenhower used polling data to develop themes for television advertising and to target specific socioeconomic blocs of voters for appeals. John Kennedy used polling extensively in his 1960 campaign. Kennedy's strategy for dealing forthrightly with public resistance to his Catholicism was developed partly with such data.

Today's candidates demand information about how voting groups with specific economic, ethnic, religious, geographic, educational, occupational, gender, lifestyle, and residential characteristics approach issues. Polling data were especially crucial to the political victories of Jimmy Carter in 1976, Ronald Reagan in 1980, Bill Clinton in 1992, and George W. Bush in 2000 and 2004.

In 1984 campaigns began to use instant polling procedures to determine the effects of specific candidate perform-

ances. Selected voters would watch candidates in debates and other appearances and register their reactions at intervals of several seconds on a handheld computer device. The device indicates whether they are feeling positive or negative toward the candidate's specific statements and general demeanor.

More recent campaigns have used videotapes and DVDs, faxes, email, Web sites, telephone calling technology, text messages, and targeted radio and cable television appeals to get their messages to the voters. In 1992 the Bush and Clinton campaigns "blast-faxed" attacks and responses to major news outlets. New telephone technology in 1992 allowed automatic dialing and sophisticated routing of calls. By 2000 every candidate had a well-designed, interactive campaign Web site. Republican John McCain was even able to use his Web site as a successful fund-raising tool. Donors simply logged on and made their contributions by credit card. In 2004 Democrats Howard Dean and John Kerry made even more effective use of Web sites as fund-raising devices.

Some democratic theorists have expressed concern about the effects of certain technologies—such as sophisticated polling techniques—and media-related tactics, including negative advertising. These critics contend that the new technologies are creating a pervasive process of manipulation. Others maintain that technology offers new possibilities for involving citizens in important electoral and governmental decisions. *(See Chapter 20, Public Support and Opinion.)*

Rules Changes in the Democratic Party

Since 1968 many efforts have been made to reform the presidential nominating process. The most notable of these took place within the Democratic Party, although once the Democrats made changes, the Republicans followed suit. *(See Tables 5-4 and 5-5, pp. 252–253.)* The roots of such reform can be traced in part to the tumultuous political climate of 1968, a year of widespread violence and public disillusionment with politics.[61]

The Tet offensive, launched by North Vietnam against South Vietnam in January 1968, provoked strong domestic opposition to the Vietnam War. In the March 12 New Hampshire Democratic primary, Sen. Eugene McCarthy of Minnesota campaigned against President Johnson's Vietnam policies. In response, Democratic Party regulars waged a write-in campaign for the president. They managed to beat McCarthy by 49.6 to 41.9 percent, but the news media—impressed by McCarthy's showing against the president in a conservative state—portrayed Johnson as the loser.

McCarthy's "victory" underscored the lack of popular support for Johnson's policies and prompted Sen. Robert F. Kennedy of New York to enter the race against the president on March 16. Two weeks later, on March 31, with a McCarthy victory predicted in the Wisconsin primary, Johnson withdrew his candidacy. Nevertheless, the

Democratic Party remained deeply divided. Vice President Hubert Humphrey entered the race as Johnson's heir apparent on April 27, having purposely delayed his formal entry into the campaign to avoid participating in the Democratic primaries. With the support of state party regulars, who commanded most delegate votes, Humphrey banked on a victory at the Democratic national convention. His victory was ensured when Robert Kennedy was assassinated on the night he won the California primary, June 5. But it was a hollow victory for the vice president, won at a bitterly divided convention that was shaken by violent confrontations between the police and antiwar demonstrators in the streets of Chicago. Humphrey, who had campaigned on the theme of the "politics of joy," accepted the nomination amid the politics of anger.

But the anger was felt not merely on the streets. Beyond the rancor of the demonstrators, the hurling of rocks and debris, and the clubbings and gassing by the police, there was anger on the convention floor. State delegations who opposed Humphrey's nomination felt excluded from the process, and they let their bitterness be known. McCarthy's supporters were particularly angry. During the campaign, they had formed the ad hoc Commission on Democratic Selection of Presidential Nominees, chaired by Iowa governor Harold Hughes. Just before the start of the convention the commission issued its report, which argued that party leaders had cheated McCarthy of support during the delegate-selection process. In fact, the nominating process afforded little influence to rank-and-file Democratic voters. Nearly one-third of the convention delegates already had been chosen by the time McCarthy announced his candidacy.[62] As political scientist William Crotty has written: "Presidential selection [in the Democratic Party] was controlled from the top down. The rules governing the process, to the extent that they existed, were made and enforced by those in power, the party regulars in charge of party operations. Such things as primary victories and popular support among grass-roots party elements had little effect on the choice of a presidential nominee." [63] In short, the Hughes Commission report concluded, the Democratic Party's delegate-selection process displayed "considerably less fidelity to basic democratic principles than a nation which claims to govern itself can safely tolerate." [64]

The McGovern-Fraser Commission. At the 1968 Democratic convention, many elements of the Democratic Party were determined to change the rules of the game to make them more fair. The report of the convention's Credentials Committee alleged that unfair and exclusionary practices had been used in the delegate-selection process and proposed that a party committee be established to examine the problem and offer recommendations. As a result, in February 1969 the party formed the Commission on Party Structure and Delegate Selection, chaired by Sen. George

McGovern of South Dakota and, later, by Rep. Donald M. Fraser of Minnesota. The commission came to be known as the McGovern-Fraser Commission. Its report, issued in 1970, set forth eighteen detailed "guidelines" for the state-by-state delegate-selection processes.

The commission's guidelines were designed to counteract rules and practices that either inhibited voter access to the delegate-selection process or diluted the voters' influence. The guidelines condemned discrimination because of race, color, creed, sex, or age and required that affirmative steps be taken to represent minorities, women, and young people in state convention delegations in proportion to their population in each state. The guidelines further required that restrictive fees (defined as those exceeding $10) and petition requirements for delegate candidates be eliminated. To help prevent individual delegates' influence from being diluted, the guidelines banned the "unit rule," in which a majority of delegates in a state delegation bound the rest to their will, and "proxy voting" (which allowed votes to be cast by someone who was absent from a meeting) at every level of the delegate-selection process. The guidelines also disallowed ex officio delegates (those who were automatically appointed because of their public office or party position).

Stressing that its guidelines were mandatory, the McGovern-Fraser Commission finished its work early. Thus by the time the 1972 Democratic national convention met, the commission was able to claim that virtually all the states were in full or substantial compliance with the guidelines, that only 1.1 percent of the convention delegates were still elected by state party committees, and that the number of black, female, and young delegates had increased three to four times since 1968.[65]

The guidelines' effects were considerable. Compliance substantially democratized the system by opening avenues for citizen participation. It also reduced the power of party leaders, prompting some observers to say that the reforms had "dismantled" the party.[66] In the process, delegate-selection systems were fundamentally altered. For example, "party caucuses" and "delegate primaries" were abolished in favor of "participatory conventions" and "candidate primaries." In the party caucus system, national convention delegates had been chosen by delegates appointed by low-level party officers. In the participatory convention, selection of the delegates was open to any party member. In the delegate-primary system, the names of delegates to the national convention, not the names of presidential candidates, had appeared on the ballot. The candidate primary required that the presidential candidates be listed on the ballot.[67]

The McGovern-Fraser guidelines also urged the party to move toward the proportional representation system commonly found in European electoral systems. Under proportional representation, delegates were awarded to candidates in proportion to the percentage of the total vote that

TABLE 5-4 **Democratic Party's Reform Commissions on Presidential Selection**

Known as	Formal name	Years in operation	Chair	Size	Mandatingbody
McGovern-Fraser Commission	Commission on Party Structure and Delegate Selection	1969–1972	Sen. George McGovern (S.Dak.), 1969–1970; Rep. Donald M. Fraser (Minn.), 1971–1972[a]	28	1968 national convention
Mikulski Commission	Commission on Delegate Selection and Party Structure	1972–1973	Barbara A. Mikulski, Baltimore city councilwoman	81	1972 national convention
Winograd Commission	Commission on Presidential Nomination and Party Structure	1975–1976 1976–1980[b]	Morley Winograd, former chairman of Michigan Democratic Party	58	1976 national convention
Hunt Commission	Commission on Presidential Nominations	1980–1982	Gov. James B. Hunt Jr. of North Carolina	70	1980 national convention
Fairness Commission	Fairness Commission	1984–1986	Donald Fowler, chairman of South Carolina Democratic Party	53	1984 national convention
Commission on Nomination Timing and Scheduling	Commission on Nomination Timing and Scheduling	2004–2005	Alexis Herman, former U.S. secretary of labor; Rep. David Price (N.C.)	40	2004 national convention

SOURCE: Reprinted by permission from William J. Crotty, *Party Reform* (New York: Longman, 1983), 40–43. Updated by the authors.

NOTES: a. Fraser assumed chair January 7, 1971 b. The original Winograd Commission was not authorized by the national convention. It was created by the national chairman, Robert Strauss. The post-1976 committee membership was expanded.

TABLE 5-5 **Republican Party's Reform Committees on Presidential Selection**

Known as	Formal name	Years in operation	Chair	Size	Mandatingbody
DO Committee	Committee on Delegates and Organization	1969–1971	Rosemary Ginn, member, Republican National Committee, from Missouri	16	1968 national convention
Rule 29 Committee	Rule 29 Committee	1973–1975	Rep. William A. Steiger (Wis.)	57	1972 national convention

SOURCE: Compiled by the authors.

Major recommendations	Distinctive features	Principal report
"Quotas"; rules for opening delegate selection to 1972 national convention	First, most ambitious, and most important of reform groups. Completely rewrote rules for presidential selection; made them mandatory for state parties and state practices; within Democratic Party, set model other reform commissions attempted to follow.	*Mandate for Change* (1970)
Modified McGovern-Fraser rules; revised quotas; provided for proportional representation of presidential candidates' strength; increased role of party regulars in delegate selection	Commission had a stormy, if brief, life. Its principal recommendations were intended to placate regulars and modify most controversial aspects of McGovern-Fraser rules. Its major achievement, however, was in *not* seriously revising the McGovern-Fraser provisions. With the work of this commission, the assumption underlying the reforms became generally accepted within the party.	*Democrats All* (1973)
10% "add-on" delegates for party officials; steps to close system at top	Vehicle of party regulars and Carter administration to tighten system, increase role of party regulars, and adopt rules expected to help Carter's renomination. Developed complicated procedures that are heavily dependent on national party interpretation.	*Openness, Participation and Party Building: Reforms for a Stronger Democratic Party* (1978)
25% quota for party officials	Expanded role of party and elected officials in national conventions.	*Report of the Commission on Presidential Nomination* (1982)
Loosened restrictions on "open primaries"; lowered the threshold for "fair representation" to 15%; increased number of "superdelegates."	Tried to satisfy both wings of the party by simultaneously increasing the power of party leaders (by increasing the number of superdelegates) and by lowering the threshold for fair representation.	No formal report.
Preserving the first-in-the-nation status of Iowa and New Hampshire but adding other states in the pre-window period; adding 1 or 2 new first-tier caucuses between Iowa and New Hampshire, and 1 or 2 new primaries between New Hampshire open window for all other states on February 5, 2008; DNC Rules and Bylaws Committee to determine which states added, using criteria: racial and ethnic diversity; geographic diversity; and economic diversity, including union density.	Tried to increase diversity of states early in selection process while respecting traditional first-in-nation status of Iowa and New Hampshire contests. In 2006 DNC Rules and Bylaws Committee voted for Nevada caucus to follow Iowa and precede New Hampshire primary and the South Carolina primary to follow New Hampshire.	*Report of the Commission on Nomination Timing and Scheduling* (2005)

Major recommendations	Distinctive features	Principal report
Proposals for increasing participation in delegate selection process.	The committee's recommendations were not binding; designed "to implement the Republican Party's Open Door policy."	No formal report.
Implement "positive action" to open delegate selection process; institute RNC review of such actions.	Most ambitious reform effort by the Republican Party. The committee's major recommendations, however, were rejected by the RNC and by the 1976 national convention.	No formal report.

each candidate received. (The usual alternative was a "winner-take-all" system, in which the candidate who won a plurality of the popular vote received all of the delegates.) Furthermore, the guidelines were interpreted as requiring mandatory "quotas" for the minority groups in proportion to their share of each state's population.

Although all the state Democratic parties were in full or substantial compliance with the guidelines by the time of the 1972 Democratic convention, criticism of the reforms increased after the Democratic Party's massive defeat in that year's presidential election. Some observers argued that the new rules contributed to McGovern's overwhelming loss to Nixon. They argued that a demographically balanced slate of delegates did not necessarily represent the political views of Democratic voters. More to the point, the rules produced a slate of delegates that was significantly more liberal than the party's rank and file. Political scientist Jeane J. Kirkpatrick found that in 1972 the policy preferences of the average Democratic voter were better represented by delegates to the Republican national convention than by Democratic delegates.[68]

The Mikulski Commission. The 1972 Democratic convention called for the establishment of another delegate-selection commission. The call was issued largely in response to the controversy over some of the McGovern-Fraser reforms. By the time it was actually appointed, the new Commission on Delegate Selection and Party Structure, chaired by Baltimore city councilmember Barbara Mikulski, was facing a Democratic Party even more badly divided than in 1968 between those who wanted to return to traditional delegate-selection procedures and those advocating further reforms. The commission responded by trying to appease both sides.[69]

Since the strongest reaction against the McGovern-Fraser Commission had concerned quotas, the Mikulski Commission sought to placate critics by making it clear that quotas were not required, although they were permitted. The Mikulski Commission dictated, however, that if quotas were abandoned "affirmative action programs" must be adopted to expand the participation of women and minorities in party affairs.[70] As further concessions to the critics of McGovern-Fraser, the Mikulski Commission allowed party regulars to appoint up to 25 (instead of 10) percent of a state's delegation; partly removed the ban on proxy voting; and extended convention privileges (not including voting rights) to public officials and party regulars.

Nevertheless, advocates of reform won a major victory in the Mikulski Commission's decision to require proportional representation of all candidates receiving a minimum of 10 percent of the vote in state contests (later changed to "from 10 to 15 percent," to be decided by the individual state parties)—something that McGovern-Fraser had urged but not required. In short, the Mikulski Commission advanced

the main goals of the McGovern-Fraser Commission. To the extent that it loosened the McGovern-Fraser requirements, it did so not to eliminate them but to make the reforms less controversial.[71]

In the wake of the Democratic Party's reforms, the number of presidential primaries mushroomed from seventeen in 1968 to thirty in 1976. Most state party leaders felt that adopting a presidential primary was the easiest way to conform to the new rules and thereby prevent a challenge to their delegates at the next national convention. Party regulars also feared that reformed caucuses would bring ideological activists into local party decision making, a consequence that they felt was worse than turning to a primary system.

Members of the McGovern-Fraser Commission had not intended such an increase in primaries. As Austin Ranney, a political scientist and member of the commission, has written:

> I well remember that the first thing we members of the [commission] agreed on—and about the only thing on which we approached unanimity—was that we did not want a national presidential primary or any great increase in the number of state primaries. Indeed, we hoped to prevent any such development by reforming the delegate-selection rules so that the party's nonprimary processes would be open and fair, participation in them would greatly increase, and consequently the demand for more primaries would fade away. . . .
>
> But we got a rude shock. After our guidelines were promulgated in 1969 no fewer than eight states newly adopted presidential primaries, and by 1972 well over two-thirds of all the delegates were chosen or bound by them. . . . So here was a case in which we had a clear objective in mind; we designed our new rules to achieve it; we got them fully accepted and enforced; and we achieved the opposite of what we intended.[72]

The Winograd Commission. The proliferation of presidential primaries weakened the role of state party organizations in selecting candidates. Their dissatisfaction led to the formation of yet another Democratic Party commission in 1975: the Commission on the Role and Future of Presidential Primaries (later changed to the Commission on Presidential Nomination and Party Structure), headed by former Michigan Democratic chairman Morley Winograd. Despite its founding purpose, the Winograd Commission ultimately skirted the question of primaries. With the election of Jimmy Carter in 1976, the commission was recast to reflect at least partially the interests of the incumbent president, which included securing his renomination in 1980. When it produced its final report, the commission stated that it could not reach a consensus on the issue of primaries, and it offered no recommendations in that area.

Unlike its earlier counterparts, the Winograd Commission worked outside the spotlight of publicity—the media had largely lost interest in the reform process. The commission's recommendations mirrored President Carter's preferences. First, the nominating season was shortened to three months, lasting from the second Tuesday in March to the second Tuesday in June (although exemptions to begin earlier were soon given to several states, including Iowa and New Hampshire). This change tended to favor the incumbent president because in a compressed time frame, the effect of early primaries and caucuses in which long shots can be thrust onto center stage is diminished, with less time available for unknown candidates to gain name recognition and money.

Second, the Winograd Commission proposed that the filing deadline for a candidate to enter a primary or a caucus be at least fifty-five days before the event. This, too, favored an incumbent by discouraging last-minute challengers from entering the race. The Democratic National Committee (DNC) later amended the proposal and allowed deadlines to fall within a more flexible thirty-to-ninety-day range, according to each state.

Third, the commission proposed that the threshold for a candidate to be eligible for a proportional share of delegates be based on a scale that increased from 15 to 25 percent as the nominating season progressed. This proposal made it extremely difficult for a candidate to wage a successful challenge to a front-runner or incumbent over the entire course of the primary season. Again, the DNC modified the proposal and set the threshold range at 15 to 20 percent.

Finally, the commission proposed the "bound-delegate" rule, which required that a delegate who was elected in behalf of a particular candidate be bound to vote for that candidate at the national convention. This became a major point of contention at the 1980 Democratic convention when Sen. Edward Kennedy of Massachusetts, hoping to win the nomination from Carter, forced a floor fight over the rule. Kennedy argued that the bound-delegate rule prevented delegates from taking into account events that occurred after they were selected, such as the growing unpopularity of the front-runner.

Other proposals of the Winograd Commission included a ban on open primaries (meaning that a registered Republican could no longer vote in a Democratic primary); a suggestion that state party committees be able to appoint an additional 10 percent of the delegates to the national convention; continued support of affirmative action programs to represent women and minorities; and a rejection of the idea that state delegations must be equally divided between men and women. The Democratic National Committee later overturned this last recommendation in its call to the 1980 convention.

Finally, the commission eliminated so-called loophole primaries, which had served to undermine proportional representation. In such primaries, citizens voted directly for individual delegates rather than the delegates being distrib-uted in proportion to the relative vote tallies of the presidential candidates. Because such primaries generally produced winner-take-all results, they were a "loophole" to the proportional representation requirement of the party rules.[73]

Democratic Rules Changes Since the 1980s

In June 1982 the Democratic National Committee (DNC) adopted several additional changes in the presidential nominating process that were recommended by the party's Commission on Presidential Nominations, chaired by Gov. James B. Hunt Jr. of North Carolina. The Hunt Commission, as it came to be known, wanted to increase the power of party leaders and to give the convention more freedom to act on its own. It was the fourth time in twelve years that the Democrats, struggling to repair their nominating process without repudiating earlier reforms, had rewritten their party rules.

One major change in the Democrats' rules was the creation of a new group of "superdelegates." These were party and elected officials who would go to the 1984 convention as delegates unbound to vote for any candidate and would cast about 14 percent of the ballots. The DNC also adopted a Hunt Commission proposal to weaken the rule binding delegates to vote for their original presidential preference on the first convention ballot.

One of the most significant Hunt Commission recommendations was to relax proportional representation by lifting the ban on the "loophole" primary, which provided for winner-take-all by district. Proportional representation was blamed by some Democrats for protracting the primary fight between President Jimmy Carter and Sen. Edward M. Kennedy of Massachusetts in 1980. Because candidates needed only about 20 percent of the vote in most states to qualify for a share of the delegates, Kennedy was able to remain in contention even when it was clear he could not win.

The DNC retained the delegate-selection season it had adopted in 1978, a three-month period stretching from the second Tuesday in March to the second Tuesday in June. But in an effort to reduce the growing influence of early states in the nominating process, the Democrats required Iowa and New Hampshire to move their highly publicized elections to late winter, only eight days apart from each other. Five weeks had intervened between the Iowa caucuses and New Hampshire primary in 1980.

The Democratic Party's presidential nominating process remained basically the same in 1988 as in 1984. The rules adopted by the national committee included only minor modifications suggested by the party's latest rules review panel, the Fairness Commission.

At the urging of the Fairness Commission, the bloc of uncommitted superdelegates was expanded slightly from 14 percent to 16 percent and rearranged to reserve more convention seats for members of Congress, governors, and the

Democratic National Committee. The rules restricting participation in the Democratic primaries and caucuses to Democratic voters was relaxed slightly to accommodate the open primaries mandated by state law in Wisconsin and Montana. Finally, the share of the vote a candidate needed to receive in a primary or caucus to qualify for delegates was lowered from the 20 percent level used in most states in 1984 to 15 percent.

Only the rule regarding the 15 percent "threshold" spawned much debate during the rules-writing process. Most party leaders, including DNC Chairman Paul G. Kirk Jr., wanted a threshold of at least 15 percent because they thought it would help steadily shrink the field of presidential candidates during the primary and caucus season and ensure that the convention would be a "ratifying" body that confirmed the choice of the party's voters.

But civil rights leader and presidential candidate Jesse Jackson saw the issue differently, as did a cadre of liberal activists. They wanted a convention that was more "deliberative," and they complained that getting one was virtually impossible under the existing system because it discriminated against long-shot candidates and produced an artificial consensus behind one candidate.

At the DNC meeting where the new rules were approved, some African American committee members joined with a few white liberal activists in proposing to eliminate the 15 percent threshold altogether. The proposal was rejected by voice vote. A second proposal, to lower the threshold to 10 percent, was defeated 92 to 178.

In 1990 the DNC moved forward the officially sanctioned start of the 1992 presidential primary season by one week, from the second to the first Tuesday in March, once again making an exception for Iowa and New Hampshire to continue holding earlier contests. Both parties wanted to speed up the nominating contest and settle it by no later than April or early May, so that united parties could organize their conventions with an eye on the November election.

By the mid-2000s, the prominent role assigned to Iowa and New Hampshire had become controversial among Democrats. In practice no candidate had a realistic chance to win the Democratic nomination without a victory in one of these two small, rural, overwhelmingly white states. In 2006 the DNC voted to insert Nevada between Iowa and New Hampshire on the 2008 primary calendar and to follow New Hampshire with South Carolina. The idea was to mirror the party's regional and ethnic diversity by granting privileged positions on the calendar to a western state with a substantial Latino population and a southern state with a substantial African American population.

Rules Changes in the Republican Party

Although the proliferation of primaries that accompanied the reforms of the Democratic Party also affected the Republicans, the GOP did not experience the same kind of internal pressures to reform that the Democrats did.[74] To a large degree, this was because the Republicans were a more ideologically cohesive party than the Democrats. The Republicans also had far fewer minority members, which meant that there was less demand from within its ranks for equal representation.

To the extent that ideological factions did exist within the Republican Party, they did not find the rules of the nominating process problematic. Conservative insurgents had been quite successful in 1964. In short, a grass-roots takeover of the party (an "amateur" movement to overturn politically moderate party professionals, to use the terminology of James Q. Wilson) was apparently more feasible among the Republicans than among the Democrats. It was the failure of a similar amateur movement against party professionals within the Democratic ranks that spawned that party's reforms.[75]

Differences also existed in the structures of the two parties. Unlike the Democrats' previously loose and uncodified rules, Republican rules were strictly codified and could be changed only with the approval of the national convention. Finally, the Republicans already had achieved several of the reforms sought by Democrats. Use of the unit rule at the Republican national conventions had been banned since the nineteenth century. A similar ban on proxy voting at the national convention had long been in force. Republican leaders were quick to point out that some of the reforms the Democrats were getting around to in 1968 had been accomplished by their party years before.

To the extent that the Democrats' reforms went beyond the existing rules of the Republican Party, rank-and-file Republicans were not overly anxious to keep up the pace. A number of the Democrats' farther-reaching efforts—such as quotas or strictly enforced affirmative action programs—did not comport with the more conservative ideology of the Republican Party. Indeed, after the Democrats made their initial reforms, the Republicans warned against the effects that "McGovernizing" their party could bring about.

Nonetheless, the Republicans did institute some reforms in the post-1968 era, often along the same lines as the Democrats. *(See Table 5-5, p. 252.)* David Price, a political scientist and U.S. representative from North Carolina who served as staff director of the Hunt Commission, has written that the Republicans' efforts were partly "imitative," often "reactive," and to a degree "defensive." [76]

The reforms were *imitative* in the sense that the Republicans were eager to garner some of the favorable publicity that the Democrats had engendered from their early reforms. The Republicans also were eager to reduce discrimination and to broaden their demographic base—especially among the millions of young voters who were enfranchised in 1971 by the Twenty-sixth Amendment.

Republican reforms were *reactive* in that Republicans did not want to adopt what they perceived to be the debilitating aspects of the Democrats' reforms—this is what they feared when they warned against "McGovernizing." In an effort to prevent "run-away" commissions, the Republican national convention amended its rules in 1976 so that a subcommittee of the Republican National Committee (RNC) would undertake all future rules review.

Finally, the Republican reforms were *defensive* in the sense that reforms by the Democratic Party often prompted changes in state laws that also affected the Republicans, including the creation of state primaries. Republicans had to accommodate those changes, whatever their own preferences may have been.

In 1968 the Republican national convention called for the establishment of a committee to consider party rules changes. All sixteen members of the Committee on Delegates and Organization (DO Committee), which was chaired by Rosemary Ginn of Missouri, came from the RNC. Unlike the recommendations of the McGovern-Fraser Commission, the DO Committee's recommendations did not bind the state parties. Indeed, the report contained no enforcement or compliance mechanism at all, which reflected the states' rights orientation of the Republican Party.

Among the DO Committee's recommendations were proposals to ban ex officio delegates, to eliminate proxy voting from meetings on delegate selection, and to encourage each state party to have an equal number of men and women in its delegation to the national convention. The 1972 national convention approved these recommendations but rejected a DO Committee proposal that delegations try to include delegates under the age of twenty-five in proportion to their population in each state. Nevertheless, the convention strengthened the rule to end discrimination and increase participation. It also established a new reform committee under Rule 29 of its bylaws.

The Rule 29 Committee was chaired by Rep. William A. Steiger of Wisconsin. Its fifty-eight members included not only members of the RNC but also state party leaders, governors, members of Congress, and young people. Among its recommendations was a proposal that state parties be required to take "positive action" to broaden participation and, most important, that their actions be reviewed by the RNC. Although no sanctions were attached to the review procedure, and quotas were not a part of the Rule 29 Committee's recommendation, the RNC objected to the proposal on the grounds that it interfered with the party's states' rights philosophy. The 1976 national convention rejected the establishment of any compliance procedures.

Between 1976 and 1996 the Republicans made no major changes in their rules for presidential selection. But consecutive defeats in the 1992 and 1996 elections made the GOP regret the quickness with which the early primaries were settling their nomination contests. Thus, in preparation for the 2000 campaign, Republicans offered bonus delegates to states that waited until after mid-March to choose their national convention delegations. After few states took them up on the bonus-delegate offer, the RNC decided in 2000 to propose an even more drastic solution to frontloading. The so-called "Delaware Plan" would have allowed smaller states to choose their delegates early in 2004, but required larger states to choose later. The proposal was rejected by the 2000 Republican convention at the request of party nominee George W. Bush, who preferred the system under which he had just been nominated. The convention decided instead to abolish the new bonus delegates and add automatic superdelegate slots at the 2004 convention for all RNC members.

Constitutional Change

After Franklin Roosevelt won four consecutive presidential elections, Republicans and conservative Democrats in Congress succeeded in initiating a constitutional amendment to limit future presidents to two terms. In 1951 the Twenty-second Amendment, which bars third terms, became part of the Constitution. The incumbent president, Harry Truman, was exempted from the limit, which took effect with the election of Dwight Eisenhower in 1952.

The Twenty-second Amendment has changed the dynamics of national elections. To the extent that a president derives bargaining strength in Congress or in international relations from the prospect of heading the ticket in another national election, a second-term president is less powerful than in the first term. *(See "Twenty-second Amendment," p. 53, in Chapter 1.)*

The two-term limit had been followed as a matter of tradition before FDR. The precedent George Washington unintentionally set when he refused to seek a third term held until 1940. An effort to pass a two-term amendment in 1876, to prevent President Ulysses Grant from seeking a third term, failed. (He was denied renomination by his party anyway.) Other presidents, such as Woodrow Wilson, indicated that they would like a third term, but they did not receive their party's nomination. Yet even if a third term was in practice improbable, the mere possibility that a president always could seek reelection affected the power maneuverings between the president and Congress.

Franklin Roosevelt was the only president to be nominated for a third term. Two members of his administration who had become candidates on their own in 1940, Vice President John Nance Garner and Postmaster General James Farley, found themselves undercut by their boss's maneuverings. After months of speculation about who the president would tap as his successor, Roosevelt willingly accepted a "draft" for renomination at the 1940 Democratic convention.

Since the amendment's passage, second-term presidents such as Eisenhower, Ronald Reagan, and Bill Clinton have questioned the wisdom of the two-term limit. In the mid-1980s, with President Reagan's popularity high and no other Republican developing a similarly loyal following, a movement to repeal the Twenty-second Amendment briefly developed. The movement died in 1986 when Reagan became embroiled in the Iran-contra affair, the controversy over an arms-for-hostages deal with Iran and the secret use of profits from the arms sales to support Nicaraguan rebels.

Turning Points in the Alignment of the Electorate

Several elections since 1828 have fundamentally altered the nation's voting habits. Scholars differ over the proper definition of terms such as *critical election* and *realignment.* Nevertheless, a number of elections stand out as turning points. *(See Chapter 6, Chronology of Presidential Elections.)*

The Rise of Andrew Jackson: 1828. The hold of the so-called Virginia dynasty on American politics was shattered by the ascension of Andrew Jackson, a hero of the War of 1812. The rough-hewn Tennessean lost the 1824 election to John Quincy Adams after the electoral college deadlocked and sent the contest to the House of Representatives. Jackson's supporters asserted that Adams had stolen the election by making a corrupt deal with House Speaker Henry Clay, and Jackson plotted revenge. In 1828 Jackson won easily with broad support from farmers and laborers, especially in the rapidly growing South and West. As the nation expanded, Jackson's appeal for local democratic processes to replace centralized elite maneuverings struck a powerful chord with the voters.

Under the tutelage of Vice President Martin Van Buren of New York, Jackson developed a strong grass-roots national Democratic Party organization based on patronage—that is, rewarding supporters with government jobs. Disciplined party organization soon became a prerequisite for competition in national politics. Van Buren easily defeated the Whigs in 1836.

Preservation of the Union: 1860 and 1864. After Congress passed the Kansas-Nebraska Act of 1854, which reopened the slavery question by allowing territories to decide the issue when they applied for statehood, the nation became irreparably divided over whether slavery should be extended or confined to its existing borders. The 1854 legislation threatened to undermine the delicate balance of power between slave and free states.

In the 1860 presidential race, Republican nominee Abraham Lincoln of Illinois defeated two candidates from the divided Democratic Party and one from the Constitutional Union Party on a platform of containing slavery within its existing borders. After Lincoln was elected, several Southern states seceded and in February 1861 formed the Confederate States of America. For the next four years, the Union and the Confederacy fought the Civil War.

Lincoln was reelected in 1864 under the banner of the National Union Party. His running mate was Sen. Andrew Johnson of Tennessee, a pro-Union Jacksonian Democrat.

Radical Reconstruction: 1868. Northern Republicans were bent on victory in 1868, particularly because the Democrat Andrew Johnson had succeeded to the presidency after Lincoln's assassination in April 1865. The Republicans nominated Gen. Ulysses Grant of Illinois, who narrowly defeated New York Democrat Horatio Seymour. With the Republicans in control of Congress and the presidency, the South was placed under a set of severe Reconstruction policies. The Republicans controlled the South through military governors and, aided by high tariffs, proceeded with industrial expansion in the North and West. Republican Reconstruction policies were motivated in part by humanitarian concern for the recently freed slaves and in part by a desire for revenge and political power. Reconstruction embittered the South even more than the war had.

Electoral Legitimacy and the Rise of Jim Crow: 1876. Disputed election results in the 1876 contest between Republican Rutherford B. Hayes of Ohio and Democrat Samuel Tilden of New York created a constitutional crisis and aroused fears that another civil war was imminent. The crisis was resolved through backroom bargaining that gave the Republicans the presidency in exchange for a pledge to pull federal troops out of the South and commit federal money to internal improvements in the region. The deal left southern politics in the hands of many of the same figures who had led the Confederacy. In the years that followed, the Democrats took control of the political apparatus and passed a series of racially discriminatory measures—known as "Jim Crow" laws. One effect of these laws was to disenfranchise most African Americans, more than 90 percent of whom lived in the South.

Defeat of Populism: 1896. After decades of falling agricultural prices, debt, and bankruptcy, farmers took over the Democratic Party and in 1896 nominated one of their own, William Jennings Bryan of Nebraska, for president. Bryan called for unlimited coinage of silver to expand the money supply and to lighten the financial burden on farmers. But his opponent, Republican William McKinley, who spent ten times as much as Bryan and ran on a pro-business platform, won the election, which saw the voter turnout rate approach the all-time high. As it turned out, Bryan had failed to bring urban workers into his "common man" coalition, probably because his criticism of high tariffs was perceived as threatening the jobs of protected American industries.

In the aftermath of the 1896 election, the competitive two-party system that existed in most parts of the United States shifted to Republican domination in the North and West and Democratic domination in the South. One-party politics developed in nearly all regions of the country.

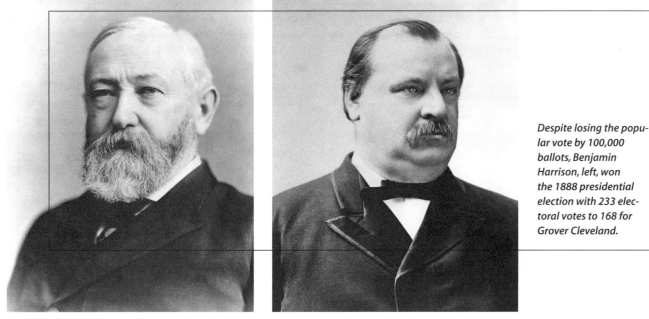

Despite losing the popular vote by 100,000 ballots, Benjamin Harrison, left, won the 1888 presidential election with 233 electoral votes to 168 for Grover Cleveland.

Sectional rhetoric undermined populist appeals for a more competitive class-oriented politics.

The Republicans Self-destruct: 1912. Between 1860 and 1932 only two Democrats won the presidency—Grover Cleveland in 1884 and 1892 and Woodrow Wilson in 1912 and 1916. Cleveland, the governor of New York, actually won a plurality of the national popular vote in three consecutive elections but lost the 1888 contest when Republican Benjamin Harrison was able to convert his 100,000 vote popular vote deficit into a sixty-five vote electoral college majority. Cleveland's two elections carried no ideological significance. He was as conservative as any of his Republican opponents.

In Wilson, a former university professor and governor of New Jersey, the Democrats nominated a progressive on economic and foreign policy issues. But Wilson probably would not have won the general election without the bitter battle in the Republican Party that pitted the incumbent president, William Howard Taft, against the popular former president, Theodore Roosevelt.

The Taft-Roosevelt feud stemmed largely from Roosevelt's feeling that Taft had betrayed the trust-busting, environmental, and foreign policies that Roosevelt pursued as president between 1901 and 1909. Roosevelt was a proud advocate of the presidential "bully pulpit," and Taft was ill suited to the rough-and-tumble of public controversies with Congress.

While Roosevelt fought Taft in the GOP primaries— the first-ever public campaign for a presidential nomination—Wilson plodded to the Democratic nomination. He was nominated on the forty-sixth ballot, after unsuccessful maneuvering by William Jennings Bryan, House Speaker

Champ Clark, and a cast of governors, favorite sons, and other contenders.

Wilson took to the hustings in the fall campaign, urging Americans to seek a moral awakening and to approve a program of liberal reforms involving labor relations, regulation of corporations and financial institutions, agriculture, and relations with other nations. He won the November election when Roosevelt bolted the Republican Party to run his own Progressive ("Bull Moose") Party campaign. The politically inexperienced Wilson won the presidency with 41.8 percent of the popular vote, while the upstart Roosevelt finished second with 27.4 percent and the incumbent, Taft, finished third with 23.2 percent (less than half of the 51.6 percent he had won in 1908). Wilson received 435 electoral votes to Roosevelt's 88 and Taft's 8. It was the most unusual of presidential election results, with a third party nominee outpolling the incumbent president and both of them losing to a candidate with little political experience.

Dawn of the New Deal: 1932. Republican Herbert Hoover's uncertain leadership following the stock market crash of 1929 enabled Democrat Franklin Roosevelt to win the presidency in 1932 and oversee one of the greatest shifts in political alignments in American history. The diverse New Deal Democratic coalition included city dwellers, blacks, Jews, Catholics, laborers, farmers, and white southerners. The New Deal, by involving the federal government for the first time in almost every aspect of the nation's economic life, changed the American political system dramatically. By the time Roosevelt's tenure came to an end in 1945, most Republicans no longer opposed the basic structure of the New Deal, only the Democrats' implementation of its programs.

The Coming of the Great Society: 1964. After John Kennedy's assassination in 1963, his successor, Lyndon Johnson, moved to enact Kennedy's unfinished New Frontier agenda of tax cuts, civil rights legislation, and Medicare. In 1964 Johnson needed a landslide against Republican nominee Barry Goldwater in order to move out from Kennedy's shadow and accomplish his own Great Society reforms. Johnson got his landslide and oversaw one of the most prolific sessions of Congress in history. The Eighty-ninth Congress passed ambitious programs affecting voting rights, medical care for the poor, education, welfare, urban development, and housing. But some of those programs created a backlash against federal social planning, especially after riots occurred in Los Angeles in 1965 and other cities in 1967 and 1968. Johnson also increased American involvement in the Vietnam War, which eventually gave rise to a widespread antiwar protest movement. As a result of his policies, the Democratic Party divided between "hawks" and "doves" on the war, and some traditional groups in the Democratic coalition, especially white southerners and blue-collar workers, broke away and in 1968 helped to elect Richard Nixon as president.

The Reagan Revolution: 1980 and 1984. Ronald Reagan, a former movie star and television personality, won the hearts of America's conservatives with a nationally televised speech for Goldwater in 1964 that fervently attacked government involvement in the economy and called for an aggressive foreign policy toward the Soviet Union. After serving two terms as governor of California, Reagan almost defeated Republican president Gerald R. Ford for the Republican nomination in 1976.

Reagan won landslide elections over President Jimmy Carter in 1980 and former vice president Walter Mondale in 1984. He shepherded dramatic cuts in both taxes and domestic spending through Congress in 1981 and promoted the largest peacetime military buildup in American history. Reagan put a conservative stamp on a wide range of policies: the environment, federalism, welfare, education, intervention against the communist side in civil wars from Afghanistan to Nicaragua, civil rights, and energy. He also appointed more than half of the federal judiciary, most of them relatively young conservatives. Reagan's policy successes and relaxed but dignified demeanor helped to rekindle Americans' awe of the presidency, which had been diminished under recent presidencies. Scholars had wondered whether anyone could handle the pressures of the modern office until Reagan came along.

The Cold War Ends, the War on Terrorism Begins: 1988–2004. Soon after Reagan left office in 1989 it became clear that the world had changed, and so had America's political landscape. With the gradual collapse of communism and the triumphant American victory in the cold war, the United States was left as the world's lone superpower.

Voters' concerns shifted from the threat of nuclear attack to the economy, crime, pollution, and other serious domestic problems. In this changed atmosphere, the battle to succeed Reagan produced an election between two moderates, Republican George Bush and Democrat Michael S. Dukakis. Bush became the first sitting vice president since Martin Van Buren in 1836 to be elected as president. But Bush's forty-state landslide did not ratify a clear direction for either foreign or domestic policy. His campaign was dominated by patriotic appeals and attacks on Dukakis, not a plan of action.[77] In addition, the Democrats increased their majorities in both houses of Congress.

Once in office, Bush became deadlocked with Congress on virtually every major domestic issue—civil rights, taxes, the budget, the environment, school reform, banking regulation, economic and trade strategy, abortion, and judicial appointments. Although Bush dominated foreign affairs, especially during the collapse of the Soviet empire and then the Soviet Union itself in 1990 and the successful Persian Gulf War in 1991, his only achievements in domestic policy came when he capitulated to congressional Democrats.

Bill Clinton defeated Bush in 1992 by focusing on "the economy, stupid," the issue that a sign in Clinton headquarters exhorted staffers to highlight in the campaign. A founder of the Democratic Leadership Council, which sought to push the Democratic Party toward the political center, Clinton appealed to voters who thought the Democratic Party had drifted too far to the left, as well as to voters hurt by the 1991–1992 economic recession. As a result, he was able to put together a coalition that was diverse enough to beat Bush and independent candidate H. Ross Perot.

Clinton's leadership foundered during his first two years as president, especially in 1994 when his health care reform proposal was defeated and the Republicans gained control of both houses of Congress for the first time in forty years. But Clinton moved adroitly to reclaim the political center, portraying the Republican Speaker of the House, Newt Gingrich of Georgia, as a right-wing extremist. In 1996 Clinton handily defeated Robert J. Dole, who resigned as Senate majority leader in midyear to devote all his time to campaigning for president. Clinton's victory made him the first Democrat since FDR to win reelection to a second term.

Clinton's hold on the presidency was challenged in 1998 when it was revealed that he had conducted an affair with a young White House intern, Monica Lewinsky, and lied about the relationship in a sworn deposition in a legal proceeding. In a nearly straight party-line vote, the Republican House of Representatives voted to impeach the president. But Clinton's job approval rating in the polls remained high, mostly because of the booming economy, which many Americans attributed to his balanced-budget economic policies. Clinton easily survived the Senate trial in early 1999 and served out the remainder of his second term.

Clinton's vice president, Al Gore, seemed likely to ride the tide of prosperity to election as president in 2000, much as Vice President Bush had after Reagan's second term came to an end in 1988. But instead of promising more of the same, Gore ran a "people-against-the-powerful" populist campaign more appropriate to an outsider than to an incumbent. He also performed badly in the debates and neglected his home state of Tennessee, which he lost in the election. Gore was defeated by Gov. George W. Bush of Texas, the son of the former president, in an election so close that its outcome was uncertain until December, when the U.S. Supreme Court brought to an end the postelection controversy over whether Florida's twenty-five electoral votes should be moved from Bush's column to Gore's.

No one realized until September 11, 2001, that the Bush presidency would be dominated by a global war against terrorism, in particular the al Qaeda organization that planned and executed that day's attacks on the World Trade Center in New York City and the Pentagon near Washington, D.C. Although Bush had several domestic policy victories during his first term, such as large tax cuts and education reform, most voters regarded him as a wartime president when he ran for reelection in 2004. Bush's Democratic opponent, Sen. John F. Kerry of Massachusetts, argued that Bush had diluted the war on terrorism by waging a different war, initiated in 2003, to depose Iraqi dictator Saddam Hussein and, less successfully, to help Iraq become a democratic nation. But in an election in which turnout soared to nearly 60 percent, Bush won a majority of popular votes and electoral votes.

THE CAMPAIGN FINANCE SYSTEM

The Beatles sang in the 1960s that "money can't buy you love." Money cannot buy electoral success either—but it can help.

To say that money matters to campaigns is an understatement. The total cost of general election campaigns for the four presidential candidates in 1948 was $4.86 million. In 2000 the three main contenders spent $140.80 million in the general election. The amount of money spent per voter in 1948 had doubled in real terms by 1988. The cost per voter in 1948 was 42 cents in constant 1982–1984 dollars; by 1988 it was 85 cents.[78] These figures do not include money spent on vote-getting and other efforts conducted independently of the candidates' official campaign organizations.

In modern elections, money is an essential ingredient of successful campaigns because it can be converted quickly into other resources, such as polls, Web sites, computer-generated direct-mail and telephone operations, get-out-the-vote drives, and especially television commercials.[79] Thus a campaign with ample funds can develop a wide range of strategies.

Money has been called both the ultimate corrupter of the American political system and a major source of vigorous political debate and competition. Journalist Elizabeth Drew argues that "Politicians who . . . do not have great wealth of their own to spend, are signed up on a systematic basis by interests who wish to enjoy influence over their official conduct. Until the problem of money is dealt with, it is unrealistic to expect the political process to improve in any other respect." [80]

Taking a different point of view, another journalist, Robert J. Samuelson, wrote, "Groups need to feel they can express themselves and participate without colliding with obtuse rules intended to shut them out. Our politics is open and freewheeling. Its occasional excesses are preferable to arbitrary restraints." [81] Nevertheless, in 2002 Congress enacted and President George W. Bush signed major legislation intended to reduce the influence of money in national politics.

Much of the debate about money in politics can be traced to the explosion in campaign spending after World War II, much of it for advertising on the new medium of television. But all along, Congress has attempted to limit the influence of private donors on the political process. In the early 1970s Congress passed major reform legislation—the Federal Election Campaign Act (FECA)—and then amendments to that act. Reform has been limited, however, by the political interests of members of Congress. For example, Congress has moved slowly on the issue of political action committees (PACs) formed by business, labor, and other special interest and ideological groups, arguably because far more PAC contributions go to incumbents than to challengers. PACs have grown in importance because FECA permits them to receive $5,000 a year from each contributor, while individual candidates may receive no more than $2,000 per election from any one source.[82]

The campaign finance debate turns on the extent to which private money affects a candidate's behavior before and after the election and on whether electoral competition is stifled by private money. Money arguably made the difference in the 1968 election of Richard Nixon and was a factor in the 1980 election of Ronald Reagan. With estimated expenditures of $25.4 million, Nixon spent more than twice as much as Hubert Humphrey in 1968. In 1980, even with the FECA limitations in place, $191.3 million was spent in behalf of Reagan and other Republican presidential candidates, compared with $107.8 million for the defeated Democratic incumbent, Jimmy Carter.[83]

The independent presidential campaign of Texas business executive H. Ross Perot in 1992 was a testament to the possibilities of money. Perot spent $68.3 million of his own fortune on his 1992 bid. The money enabled Perot to bypass the news media and deliver his message directly to the American public. Perot's strongest surge of support in the fall campaign came when he delivered a series of half-hour, prime-time "infomercials" on network television in which he used charts and plain talk to explain the perils facing the American economy. Some of his programs attracted larger television audiences than prime-time sports and entertainment programming. When Perot ran again in 1996, he relied on public funds to finance his campaign.

Understanding the link between contributions and the positions candidates take on issues can be difficult because of the circularity and subtlety of candidate-donor relations. Contributors usually eschew a hard sell and insist only that their views on relevant issues be heard. But if their concerns are ignored frequently, contributors probably will abandon a politician—a prospect likely to enter the calculations of reelection-conscious officials.

Supporters of unlimited campaign spending maintain that even if the wealthiest and most influential groups and individuals contribute the most money, so many factions exist among these elites that they tend to check the influence of one another. In the language of economist John Kenneth Galbraith, the goals of one interest serve as a "countervailing force" against the goals of another interest.[84]

Many studies of campaign finance explain American politics in economic terms: the political system is an "economy" with a "demand" side and a "supply" side. By forming interest groups to express their concerns and by casting ballots on election day, voters send signals to politicians. These signals are the demand side of the political economy. They force the suppliers of political goods—the politicians—to be responsive to the wishes of the electorate. Such studies emphasize the voters' ability to shape the political environment by making independent choices—their demand is presumed to shape the supply of political goods.

Political scientists Thomas Ferguson and Joel Rogers take a different view, however. They have argued that the American citizenry is disorganized and fragmented. "The real market for political parties," they write, "is defined by major 'investors'—groups of business firms, industrial sectors, or, in some (rare) cases, groups of voters organized collectively." [85] Ferguson and Rogers argue that campaign contributions constitute a form of political participation that is more important than voting.

Business, which has the resources and unity to form wealthy and effective interest groups, tends to support the Republicans—a tendency that has become more pronounced in recent years. Labor unions traditionally have been the cornerstone of the Democratic Party alliance. The labor movement peaked during the Great Depression when the economic crisis aroused workers to engage in hundreds of spontaneous protests and strikes. Later, New Deal legislation such as the National Industrial Recovery Act and the Wagner Act encouraged workers to form unions. Since the 1950s, however, the labor movement has declined. By 2000

unions represented only 13.5 percent of the national workforce. Labor still exerts power in Rust Belt states and in Democratic primaries, but nationally it is at its lowest ebb since the early days of the Great Depression.[86] Only public employee unions such as the American Federation of State, County, and Municipal Employees have grown substantially in recent years. In 2000 37.5 percent of government employees—but only 9.0 percent of private-sector employees—were union members.[87]

History of Campaign Finance

The importance of money in politics can be traced to the requirements of the American party system. When Federalist John Adams was elected president in 1796, for example, Thomas Jefferson channeled funding to newspapers that promoted Democratic-Republican opposition views. But only with the expansion of the electorate in the 1820s did money become a central element in presidential campaigns. Reaching an expanded pool of voters required national publicity, which, in turn, required money.

Campaign Finance in the Nineteenth Century

In 1828 Andrew Jackson challenged John Quincy Adams in a fierce battle for the presidency. Jackson decried the "corrupt bargain" of the 1824 election, in which the House of Representatives had decided the deadlocked contest in Adams's favor even though Jackson had won a plurality of popular and electoral votes. Adams's supporters, meanwhile, spread gossip about Jackson's character and urged Adams to use his own money to support newspapers critical of Jackson. Adams recalled the dilemma:

> To pay money [in an election] directly or indirectly, was in my opinion incorrect in principle. This was my first and decisive reason for declining such a contribution. A second reason was that I could not command such a sum as $5,000 without involving myself in debt for it; and the third was, that if I once departed from my principle and gave money, there was no rule, either of expediency or of morality, which would enable me to limit the amount of expenditure which I ought to incur.[88]

Henry Clay, who took up the opposition in Congress to the victorious Jackson, did not share Adams's reservations about money's influence in politics. President Jackson's opposition to the Bank of the United States stirred urban financiers to action. Between 1830 and 1832, the bank spent $42,000 on pamphleteering. Clay wrote: "It seems to me that our friends who have ability should contribute a fund for aiding the cause; and if that be deemed advisable, the appeal should be made in the large cities where alone the Capital is to be found." [89]

Both the Democratic and Whig parties attracted large donors. Whig sponsors included the Weed and du Pont families, and Democratic sponsors included the Rothschild family, August Belmont, and Samuel Tilden. The parties attempted to build fund-raising systems to extract regular contributions from supporters at all levels, including party activists who were hired for government jobs

By the time of Republican Abraham Lincoln's election in 1860, a presidential campaign cost around $100,000. Industrialism further fed the campaign cost spiral. Wealthy entrepreneurs who donated money to Ulysses Grant in the 1868 election included Jay Cooke, Cornelius Vanderbilt, A. T. Stewart, Henry Hilton, and John Astor. As one historian wrote, "Never before was a candidate placed under such great obligation to men of wealth as was Grant." [90] In 1896 expenses grew to $16 million—mostly because of increased spending on advertising for William McKinley's winning campaign.[91]

The first major effort to reform the campaign finance system stemmed from concern about the power of trusts and the role of campaign professionals such as Mark Hanna. Hanna, an Ohio mining magnate and McKinley's main political strategist, raised money for the Republican Party through a systematic assessment of banks and corporations. He used the money to make McKinley financially solvent, to influence convention delegates, and to pay for the kind of campaign that would change the face of national electioneering forever.[92]

McKinley's successor as president, Theodore Roosevelt, accepted large gifts in his 1904 campaign. Roosevelt argued that "the wrong lies not in receiving the contribution" but in exercising improper pressure or making promises to get it.[93]

Campaign Finance in the Twentieth Century

After revelations by "muckraking" journalists about campaign finance and agitation by progressive reformer Robert La Follette, a senator from Wisconsin, Congress passed the Tillman Act of 1907. The act banned bank and corporate gifts to candidates seeking federal office. The legislation was ineffective, however, because it contained no formal mechanism for monitoring the far-flung activities of the various campaigns.

Although the earliest campaign finance laws dealt with congressional campaigns, they helped to pave the way for later attempts to regulate the raising and spending of money for presidential elections. The Federal Corrupt Practices Act of 1910 established disclosure requirements for candidates for the House of Representatives. The law required committees and individuals "which shall in two or more states . . . attempt to influence the result" of House races to provide a complete record of their campaign transactions. The record was to include the names and addresses of donors giving $100 or more and of candidates receiving $10 or more. But voters were unable to use the information because disclosure did not take place until after the election.

The next year, Congress extended the requirements to Senate candidates and campaign contributors. The 1911 law also required House and Senate candidates to submit campaign expense reports. The legislation contained a provision that would be controversial throughout the rest of the century: a limitation on spending by candidates.

Mining magnate and financier Mark Hanna (standing at the far right between President and Mrs. McKinley) raised millions of dollars for McKinley's 1896 and 1900 campaigns. His fund-raising practices sparked the first major effort toward campaign finance reform.

Senate candidates could spend no more than $10,000 per election, and House candidates were limited to $5,000. Congressional candidates also were made subject to any additional restrictions that might be imposed by state laws.

The Federal Corrupt Practices Act of 1925 required campaigns to report receipts and expenditures. But neither the 1910 nor the 1925 legislation contained enforcement mechanisms to monitor the activities of political campaigns. Spending limits were avoided by breaking up party and campaign committees into smaller units and by selling advertising in party publications, then selling copies of the publications at inflated prices.

The Hatch Act, which Congress passed in 1939, was designed to eliminate the last vestiges of the federal patronage system that had long been prominent in American elections.

The law stemmed from a series of newspaper reports that Franklin Roosevelt's administration was improperly using the Works Progress Administration to bolster the reelection campaign of a Senate ally. Democratic senator Carl Hatch of New Mexico led a coalition of Republican and anti–New Deal Democrats to pass the act. *(See box, Hatch Act Restrictions on Federal Employees, p. 1309, in Chapter 28, Vol. II.)*

The Hatch Act barred federal employees from taking part in organized national political activity. It also banned solicitations from anyone receiving federal relief funds. President Roosevelt considered a veto but instead signed the bill and led a successful effort the next year to extend the restrictions to employees of state agencies receiving federal funds.

Other amendments to the Hatch Act that were passed in 1940 banned federal contractors from contributing to the campaigns of candidates for federal office, asserted Congress's authority to regulate the nominating process, limited contributions to a federal candidate or committee to $5,000 a year (contributions to a "state or local committee" were exempt), and limited the spending of committees operating in two or more states to $3 million. The last provision underscored the toothless nature of the law. A single campaign could evade the spending limits by simply breaking up into many legally distinct but coordinated committees.

In 1942 Congress passed the War Labor Disputes Act, which included labor unions along with national banks and corporations in the 1907 ban on contributions to political campaigns. That provision was made permanent in the Taft-Hartley Labor-Management Relations Act of 1947.

By 1952 both parties were well financed. In the race for the Republican nomination, supporters of Dwight Eisenhower spent $65,000 to Sen. Robert A. Taft's $50,000 in New Hampshire; and Eisenhower outspent Taft in South Dakota by $44,000 to $40,000. Eisenhower, the eventual Republican nominee, was the first presidential candidate to make television commercials a central part of his campaign. He spent $500,000 on television in 1952, and his Democratic opponent, Adlai Stevenson, spent $77,000.[94]

From 1952 to 1968, campaign spending climbed steadily with the rise of television advertising, professional campaign consultants, and polling. Concern about campaign spending rose in response to developments such as John Kennedy's extensive use of his family fortune to campaign for the 1960 Democratic nomination and Richard Nixon's two-to-one spending advantage over Hubert Humphrey in 1968.

Congress considered several campaign finance reforms in the 1950s and 1960s but passed none of them. In 1962 President Kennedy's Commission on Campaign Costs made a number of recommendations, including tax credits for campaign donors, the removal of limits on interstate political committees, reporting requirements for presidential campaigns, and a new federal agency to enforce campaign regulations. In May 1962 Kennedy proposed five bills pertaining to election finance reform, but none was passed.

The 1971 Legislation

In 1971 Congress passed two major reform laws: the Federal Election Campaign Act (FECA) and the Revenue Act. President Nixon signed the 1971 legislation only after congressional leaders agreed to delay implementation until after Nixon's reelection campaign in 1972.

The Federal Election Campaign Act of 1971. The FECA attacked the growing influence of media advertising and private contributors with blunt instruments: a limit on the amount of money that could be spent on media campaigns (repealed in 1974), per-voter spending limits on campaign spending during the nominating process, and a requirement for periodic disclosure of spending and of funds received from private sources.

The legislation was passed by a bipartisan majority, with both Republicans and Democrats concerned about appearing to limit private influence on legislative decision making while protecting their sources of financial support. Republicans were determined to protect their business support, and Democrats were determined to maintain their alliance with labor unions.

The idea behind FECA was that the excessive political influence of private money could be reduced by bringing it into the light of day. As with many "sunshine" ordinances of the era, the law's premise was that illicit influence thrives in secret and healthy political contests flourish in public view.

The new media spending limits would be based on a formula of 10 cents per voter and pegged to the inflation rate. For presidential candidates, the overall media limit for 1976, the first election that took place under the new limits, was $14.3 million per candidate, of which no more than $8.5 million could be used for television and radio. In the 1968 election, Nixon had spent $12.6 million of his general election treasury of $24.9 million on media advertising, and Humphrey had spent $6.1 million of his $10.3 million.[95] The legislation also required that broadcasters charge the candidates the same unit cost that other advertisers would be charged.

The FECA disclosure provisions called for federal candidates to file quarterly reports on campaign spending and receipts listing donors who contributed $100 or more. Candidates also were required to file additional reports fifteen days and then five days before the election. Donations of $5,000 or more had to be disclosed publicly within forty-eight hours of receiving them.

Congress required that the disclosures be made during primary, caucus, convention, and runoff campaigns as well as during the general election. Any political committee with assets greater than $1,000 had to disclose its financial activities, thereby partly closing a loophole in which campaigns hid expenses by creating many separate campaign organizations that were technically independent of the main campaign committee.

But the law still had weaknesses. True disclosure required a thorough examination and dissemination of the information that candidates filed, but listings of contributions were often so bulky and complex that no one could adequately determine the sources of support. Moreover, a flood of contributions late in a campaign could not be examined before the election took place. Newspapers generally reported on the top donors to the campaigns and listed other donors. But the effects of the donations were rarely explored.

The Income Tax Checkoff. Congress passed the Revenue Act of 1971 after a long and bitter struggle between congressional Democrats and the Nixon administration. The legislation, now a centerpiece of federal financing of presidential elections, created the Presidential Election Campaign Fund to finance both the nomination and general election campaigns of participating presidential candidates. The act specified that the amount of money candidates would receive during the nominating process would be determined by a per-voter spending formula. A candidate would qualify to receive federal matching funds by raising at least $100,000 in twenty or more states, with at least $5,000 from each of these states coming in the form of individual contributions of $250 or less.

Candidates who chose to accept federal funds for their general election campaigns would not be allowed to accept private contributions. The act's sponsors hoped that federal campaign funding would level the playing field for candidates who qualified for the matching funds.

Presidential candidates of minor parties could receive partial funding based on the share of popular votes they received in the general election. Major parties were defined as those that received 25 percent or more of the vote in the previous election. Minor parties were those receiving between 5 and 25 percent. Candidates of new parties could obtain funding retroactively if they received 5 percent or more of the vote. No provision was made for independent candidates, but a 1980 Federal Election Commission (FEC) ruling enabled John Anderson of Illinois to receive partial funding after his independent candidacy drew 6.6 percent of the presidential vote.

The federal government raised the money to fund presidential campaigns through a "checkoff" option for taxpayers. When filling out their income tax forms, taxpayers could designate that $1 of their tax payment ($2 for couples) be put into the presidential election campaign fund. Because the campaign fund faced a shortage of money in the early 1990s, Congress authorized an increase in the taxpayer checkoff from $1 to $3 in 1993. The number of Americans opting to earmark tax money for the fund fell from a high of 28.7 percent in 1980 to a low of 12.4 percent in 1996.[96]

The Watergate Election

The last privately financed presidential election was the 1972 race. President Nixon's campaign organization spent $61.4 million, while the Democratic campaign of George McGovern spent $21.2 million.

The Committee to Re-elect the President (or "CREEP," as it became known) relied mostly on large contributions. Nixon's chief fund-raiser, Maurice Stans, got the campaign off to a fast start by raising $20 million before April 7, the date after which, under the FECA, contributions were required to be made public. Approximately $5 million came into the Nixon coffers on April 5 and 6 alone. It later was disclosed that the leading contributors were insurance magnate W. Clement Stone, who gave $2 million, and Richard Scaife, an heir to the Mellon oil and banking fortune, who gave $1 million.[97] The Nixon campaign troubled reformers because of some large donors' apparent expectation that they would receive government favors in return for their generosity. Stans reportedly informed wealthy individuals and corporations that they had to contribute 1 percent of their net worth or gross annual sales to the campaign if they wished to have a good working relationship with the Nixon administration.[98]

Perhaps the most blatant example of influence seeking in 1972 was the offer by International Telephone and Telegraph (ITT) to donate $400,000 in services at the Republican national convention, which was scheduled to be held in San Diego. ITT later had an important antitrust case settled favorably by the Nixon Justice Department. Eventually the Nixon campaign turned down the ITT offer and even asked that the convention be moved to Miami Beach to avoid the further appearance of impropriety.[99] Other large contributors with an interest in influencing government policy included Robert Vesco, who was under investigation by the Securities and Exchange Commission; Dwayne Andreas, who was seeking a federal bank charter; the dairy industry, which was seeking higher milk price supports; and the Seafarers International Union, which wanted the Justice Department to dismiss an indictment.[100]

Besides access to important administration officials, the rewards for hefty donations sometimes included positions in the administration. Nine of Nixon's appointees as ambassadors or heads of foreign missions each contributed more than $20,000 to the 1972 campaign. But the Nixon campaign did not rely solely on large donors. It also continued the party's successful efforts, begun in 1964, to raise money from small donors.

Post-Watergate Finance Laws

Congress passed the most sweeping campaign finance legislation ever in the climate of electoral reform produced by the

Watergate scandal. *(See "The Case of Richard Nixon," p. 487, in Chapter 8.)* Gerald Ford, who succeeded to the presidency when Nixon resigned, signed into law the Federal Election Campaign Act (FECA) amendments in October 1974.

Congress was not the only body to get involved in campaign finance reform. By August 1974, when political scandal forced Nixon out of the White House, seventeen states had imposed limitations on the amount of money that individuals could donate to campaigns for state and local office. New Jersey's contribution limit of $600, which was eligible for state matching funds, was the lowest in the nation.[101]

The new federal law was to prove most important for presidential politics. Technically just an amendment to the 1971 FECA, the new statute superseded some of the previous law's provisions and expanded others. The FECA amendments provided for the following:

- Establishment of a federal election commission. The six-member bipartisan commission's job was to oversee the enforcement of the FECA and its amendments. The makeup of the commission was later ruled unconstitutional by the Supreme Court because the method of members' appointment (some by the president and some by Congress) violated the separation of powers, which entrusts appointments to the president and confirmation to the Senate. The Federal Election Commission was reconstituted as a body whose members are appointed by the president and confirmed by the Senate.
- A limit of $1,000 per election on an individual's donation to a candidate for a federal (presidential or congressional) office. Gifts made in nonelection years would be counted toward the gifts for the following election year.
- A limit of $25,000 per election year on each individual's total contributions to federal candidates.
- Candidate spending limits of $10 million for the presidential nominating process and $20 million for the general election. Spending in the nominating process would also be limited in each state according to the size of the state's voting-age population. In future elections, these sums would rise according to the inflation rate. In 2004, for example, the limits for each presidential candidate in the nominating and general election phases were $37.3 million and $74.6 million, respectively.
- A system of federal matching funds for candidates in presidential nominating campaigns. Candidates who raised $100,000 on their own initiative—including $5,000 in each of twenty states in individual donations of $250 or less—could collect federal matching funds. Some candidates—Republicans John Connally in 1980, Steve Forbes in 1996 and 2000, and George W. Bush in 2000 and 2004, as well as Democrats Howard Dean and John Kerry in 2004—rejected federal matching funds

for their nomination campaigns. As a result, these candidates were able to spend as much money as they could raise, although they were bound by the $1,000 ceiling on individual contributions (raised to $2,000 in time for the 2004 election) and the $5,000 ceiling on PAC contributions.

- A limit of $5,000 per election (presidential and congressional) on the contributions of independent political committees (usually PACs). To qualify as an independent committee, a group must register six months before making the donation, receive contributions from at least fifty persons, and make gifts to five or more candidates for federal office. Any group not qualifying is bound by the $1,000 individual contribution limit.
- Inclusion of indirect donations in tallies of donations. Gifts made to ancillary committees that end up in a candidate's campaign treasury would be considered a direct contribution to the campaign.
- A requirement that no gifts greater than $100 be made in cash. Any combination of cash gifts exceeding $100 to a single recipient would be illegal. This provision was intended to help track donations and make money-laundering difficult.
- A limit of $50,000 on a candidate's contributions to his or her own campaign and a limit of $1,000 per person on contributions from members of a candidate's family. The Supreme Court later struck down the limitation on candidates' use of their own money.
- A federal grant of $2 million to each major party for staging its quadrennial national convention. That amount would be increased in later elections according to the inflation rate. The Republican and Democratic Parties each received $13.5 million for their 2000 conventions, a figure that rose to $14.6 million in 2004. The Reform Party received $2.5 million in 2000, the first-ever convention grant to a third party.
- A ban on contributions by foreign nationals.
- A requirement that candidates establish a single organization through which all campaign spending would flow and which would submit regular reports.

Court Cases and Constitutional Issues

The 1974 FECA amendments faced an important federal court challenge, *Buckley v. Valeo,* soon after they took effect.[102] The Supreme Court's 1976 ruling in the case reduced congressional authority over campaign activity.

A broad ideological coalition challenged the 1974 law on a wide range of constitutional grounds. The main argument was that limits on campaign contributions amounted to restrictions on political expression and association. Another argument was that the financial disclosure requirement violated the donors' right to privacy. The anti-FECA coalition also argued that the law posed unreasonable barriers to minor political parties and violated the separation of powers. In all, the plaintiffs said, the law violated the First, Fourth, Fifth, Sixth, and Ninth Amendments to the Constitution. The ideologically diverse coalition opposing the law included James Buckley, a Conservative senator from New York; former Democratic senator Eugene McCarthy of Minnesota, a prospective third party presidential candidate in 1976; the New York Civil Liberties Union; the American Conservative Union; and *Human Events*, a conservative periodical.

When the U.S. Court of Appeals for the District of Columbia upheld the FECA amendments on August 14, 1975, the coalition appealed the decision to the Supreme Court. On January 30, 1976, the high court issued a 137-page unsigned opinion in *Buckley v. Valeo* that upheld some of the law's provisions and struck down others. In five separate opinions, different justices concurred with and dissented from various parts of the Court's main ruling. Congress responded to the Court's decision the same year with amendments that answered many of the justices' objections.

The Court approved the FECA's disclosure provisions as well as its limitations on how much individuals and organizations could contribute to national candidates. The Court also approved the federal financing of presidential election campaigns. But one of the most controversial elements of the reform—limits on individuals' independent spending—was overturned. The Court agreed with the plaintiffs' First Amendment argument that restrictions on spending amounted to an abridgment of free speech. The Court ruled, however, that campaign organizations could be required to honor spending limits if they accepted federal money. The Court stated:

> A restriction on the amount of money a person or group can spend on political communication during a campaign necessarily reduces the quantity of expression by restricting the number of issues discussed, the depth of their exploration, and the size of the audience reached. This is because every means of communicating ideas in today's mass society requires the expenditure of money.

Only Justice Byron White rejected the Court's reasoning. White pointed to the "many expensive campaign activities that are not themselves communicative or remotely related to speech." [103]

One important aspect of the Supreme Court's ruling, overlooked at the time, was that the $25,000 limitation on personal donations to federal candidates could not be extended to political action committees. This opened the way for PACs to spend as much as they could gather in behalf of a candidate so long as they did not have a formal connection with the candidate's campaign. Later legislation that allowed individuals to donate $5,000 to PACs, compared with $1,000 to candidate committees, also promoted the growth of PACs.

The Court struck down the FECA limit of $50,000 on how much presidential candidates could spend of their own money on their own campaigns. The Court, however, accepted limits on contributions to others' campaigns. The rationale for the apparent double standard was that allowing candidates to spend unlimited amounts in their own behalf would free them from the same outside influences that limits on outside contributions were intended to curb. The majority opinion read: "The use of personal funds reduces the candidate's dependence on outside contributions and thereby counteracts the coercive pressures and attendant risks of abuse to which the act's contribution limits are directed." Justice Thurgood Marshall, in a dissenting opinion, wrote, "It would appear to follow that the candidate with a substantial personal fortune at his disposal is off to a significant 'head start.'" Marshall added that the Court's reasoning on this issue could encourage more wealthy candidates to enter the political process. [104]

The Supreme Court also struck down the provision creating a federal election commission because the makeup of the panel violated the separation of powers and appointment provisions of the Constitution. The Court maintained that members of the commission appointed by Congress could not be permitted to exercise executive authority.

More FECA Amendments

Rather than simply rework the FECA legislation to meet the Court's immediate concerns, Congress in 1976 passed a completely new set of amendments to the law. [105]

The Federal Election Commission created by the 1976 amendments was a six-member panel appointed by the president and confirmed by the Senate. The commission was granted both authority to prosecute civil violations of campaign finance law and jurisdiction over violations previously covered in the criminal code.

In response to a different part of the Court ruling, Congress passed an amendment limiting independent spending. The Court had declared unconstitutional the 1974 law's limitations on independent political expenditures. In 1976 Congress required individuals and committees making independent expenditures greater than $100 in support of a candidate to swear that the expenditures were not made in collusion with the candidate or the candidate's agent.

The 1976 amendments also set new contribution limits. An individual could give no more than $5,000 to an independent committee, including a PAC, or more than $20,000 to the national committees of a political party. The new amendments also set a total limit of $50,000 on donations from the families of candidates who were receiving federal funds.

In 1979 Congress passed new FECA amendments designed to strengthen state and local parties and reduce red tape. The legislation did not trigger any major partisan controversies.

The 1979 legislation's most important provisions addressed complaints that federal regulation strangled state and local party organizations. The bill allowed unlimited spending by state and local organizations on voter registration and get-out-the-vote drives. These party organizations also were permitted to buy unlimited campaign materials for volunteer activities. The items included buttons, bumper stickers, yard signs, posters, and hand bills. Mere mention of a presidential candidate in local campaign literature no longer counted as a contribution to that candidate under the 1979 amendments. Determining the monetary value of such mentions had been the source of bookkeeping nightmares.

Volunteer activities were encouraged by doubling to $1,000 the amount of money a person could spend on housing, food, and personal travel in behalf of a candidate without reporting the amount to the FEC. A person could spend $2,000 on such expenses in behalf of a party.

The amendments reduced the number of reports required of federal candidates from twenty-four to nine in each two-year election cycle, reduced the amount of detail in financial disclosure reports, and eliminated disclosure requirements for candidates who spent less than $5,000.

McCain-Feingold

Complaints about the influence of money on presidential campaigns continued into the 1990s. But reform proposals foundered whenever Republicans and Democrats feared losing fund-raising advantages. During the first Bush administration, Republicans favored proposals to eliminate campaign contributions from political action committees, which were a major Democratic source of funding. Democrats favored proposals that targeted independent money, an important Republican source of support. Rep. Richard Cheney of Wyoming, later the vice president, summed up the reform stalemate: "If you think this Congress, or any other, is going to set up a system where someone can run against them on equal terms at government expense, you're smoking something that you can't buy at the corner drugstore." [106]

In 1995 Sen. John McCain (R-Ariz.) and Sen. Russ Feingold (D-Wis.) combined efforts with two members of the House of Representatives—Christopher Shays (R-Conn.) and Martin T. Meehan (D-Mass.)—to promote a federal ban on "soft money," that is, unlimited donations of money to political parties. McCain based his campaign for the 2000 Republican presidential nomination on campaign finance reform, and although he did not win, he roused strong public support for his proposal. Soft money donations to both political parties had peaked at $495 million in 2000. Nearly two-thirds of that amount came from around 800 corporate, union, and individual contributors who gave at least $120,000 each.

On April 2, 2001, the Senate passed McCain-Feingold by a vote of 59 to 41, despite the opposition of President George W. Bush, who favored capping rather than banning such donations. The bill also raised the amount an individual could donate to a candidate for federal office from $1,000 to $2,000; the figure was indexed to rise with the inflation rate. It further banned "issues advertisements" by corporations, unions, or interest groups that criticized a particular candidate for federal office within thirty days of a primary election or sixty days of a general election.

The Republican-controlled House seemed disinclined to pass its own version of McCain-Feingold, the Shays-Meehan bill, until a scandal broke in early 2002 involving the collapse of the Enron Corp., an energy-trading company that had contributed money to around three-fourths of all senators, more than half of all House members, and the 2000 Bush campaign. Bush withdrew his opposition to the bill, and on February 14, 2002, the House approved it by a vote of 240 to 189. Five weeks later, on March 20, the Senate endorsed the House version on a 60–40 vote, and Bush signed the bill into law on March 27.

Although the official name of the bill was the Bipartisan Campaign Reform Act, more than 95 percent of Democrats in both the House and Senate voted for the bill while around 80 percent of Republicans voted against it. Republican senator Mitch McConnell of Kentucky immediately challenged the law in court, claiming that it placed unconstitutional restrictions on freedom of speech. Yet political observers noted that the only way the Democrats had been able to remain financially competitive with the Republicans in recent elections had been through soft money, which both parties raised in roughly equal amounts. They also noted that the law would not take effect until after the 2002 elections.

The 2002 act

- Banned soft money donations to national party organizations.
- Capped soft money donations to state political parties at $10,000 per year and restricted the use of these funds to voter outreach and registration drives.
- Raised the ceiling on individual donations to particular candidates for federal office from $1,000 to $2,000. The ceiling on individual donations to political parties per two-year election cycle increased from $20,000 to $25,000, and the limit on all political donations by an individual increased from $25,000 to $47,500. All of the ceilings on these donations of "hard money" (that is, money that can be used to urge the election of specific candidates) will be adjusted to reflect changes in the rate of inflation.
- Restricted unions, corporations, and interest groups from running issues ads that praise or criticize a candi-

THE BIPARTISAN CAMPAIGN REFORM ACT

The first major overhaul of federal campaign finance laws since 1974—more than 90 pages long—is aimed principally at banning "soft money" and regulating election-time issue advertising on radio and television by corporations, unions and interest groups. Here are the major provisions of the law, also known as McCain-Feingold:

- Soft money—National party committees cannot accept or spend soft money—unregulated contributions from corporations, labor unions and wealthy individuals ostensibly intended for "party-building" activities, such as voter registration, but often used for campaign-related purposes.
- State and local parties—Non-national political parties cannot spend soft money on federal election activities. They may spend soft money on voter registration and mobilization under certain conditions.
- Tax-exempt organizations—National, state and local parties may neither solicit money from nor contribute to any nonprofit that spends money on federal elections. They also may not contribute to or solicit money from so-called 527 organizations that intervene in campaigns but do not expressly advocate any candidate's election or directly subsidize federal campaigns.
- Hard-money contribution limits—Effective Jan. 1, 2003, individual contribution limits for House and Senate candidates will be doubled to $2,000 per election, indexed to grow with inflation; aggregate contribution limits for individuals will be $95,000: $37,500 to candidates and $57,500 to parties and political action committees (PACs). Contribution limits for PACs are unchanged: $5,000 per can-

didate per election, plus $15,000 to a national party committee and $5,000 combined to state and local party committees.

- Electioneering communications—Broadcast, cable, or satellite communications that name candidates for federal office or show their likeness and are targeted at candidates' states or districts—known as "electioneering communications"—may not be issued within 60 days of a general election or 30 days of a primary.
- Unions and corporations—Labor unions and corporations are prohibited from directly funding "electioneering communications" and can pay for such advertising only through political action committees (PACs) with regulated hard money.
- Nonprofits and 527s—One contingent provision bars "electioneering communications" by nonprofit organizations except through PACs. If that provision is ruled unconstitutional, an alternative provision would allow nonprofits to pay for such ads only with individual contributions, not from corporations or unions.
- Independent and coordinated expenditures—The Federal Election Commission (FEC) must issue new rules regulating coordination between candidates or parties and outside groups. The regulation cannot require formal evidence of coordination to treat spending by outside groups as a regulated "contribution" instead of an unregulated "independent expenditure."

SOURCE: Jost, K. (2002, November 22). Campaign finance showdown. *The CQ Researcher Online*, 12, 969–992

date for federal office within thirty days of a primary or sixty days of a general election.
- Allowed the remainder of the law to remain in effect if the Supreme Court found one or more parts of it unconstitutional—the so-called "severability" provision.

Money in Presidential Primaries

Pursuing a presidential nomination has always been expensive. In 1920 Gen. Leonard Wood spent $1.8 million—a vast amount of money at the time—in thirteen primaries on his unsuccessful campaign for the Republican nomination. Other big spenders in the nominating process have included Herbert Hoover, Franklin Roosevelt, Robert Taft, John Kennedy, Robert J. Dole, Steve Forbes, John F. Kerry, and George W. Bush.

From 1928 to 1948, the average cost of competing in a single contested presidential primary rose from $50,000 to $100,000. The costs increased much faster in the postwar years. By 1960 the average cost of a single contested primary had risen to $200,000; in 1964 the figure was $400,000. The costs of primary campaigns in more recent presidential elections have varied so much that an average figure is not

meaningful. But it is clear that campaign costs have soared. In 1972, for example, Democrat George McGovern spent $316,000 in Massachusetts; $182,000 in Pennsylvania; $231,000 in Ohio; $159,000 in Oregon; and $4.2 million in California.[107]

Bill Clinton, the governor of a small and generally poor state, seemed an unlikely fund-raiser when he launched his campaign for president in 1991. But Clinton's home state of Arkansas included some big businesses—Wal-Mart, the nationwide discount store chain; Arkla, a *Fortune* 500 natural gas company run by a boyhood friend; Tyson Foods, the nation's leading producer of poultry; and a number of banks and savings and loan institutions. As a leader of the Democratic Leadership Council and the National Governors Association during the 1980s, Clinton also developed a national network of supporters. Clinton told friends that he would not run unless he had $1 million in contributions by the time of his announcement. He aided his cause by attracting some leading party fund-raisers such as Robert Farmer of Massachusetts, who had raised money successfully for Michael Dukakis in 1988.

In 2000 George W. Bush decided to forego federal matching funds, a decision that freed him from any limitation on the amount of money he could raise and spend. By July 31, 2000, Bush had raised $94.5 million (almost all of it from individual donors) and spent $89.1 million. As governor of Texas, Bush drew heavily on home state donors. As the son of former president George Bush, he tapped into his father's national network of friends and supporters. Bush outspent his nearest rival for the nomination, Sen. John McCain, by a two-to-one margin.[108]

Four years later, Bush faced no opposition for the GOP nomination, but he raised $258.9 million anyway. Like Bush, leading Democratic contenders Howard Dean and John Kerry rejected federal funding and raised $51.0 million and $234.0 million, respectively. (Much of Kerry's money came in after he had clinched the nomination from contributors who wanted him to be able to match Bush's spending.)[109]

Altogether, in the nominating phase of the 2000 presidential race the eighteen candidates spent a total of $326.4 million through July 31. Of the $343.0 million those candidates raised, $233.6 million came from individual contributions, $57.7 million from federal matching funds, and $2.9 million from PACs. An additional $43.2 million came from candidates' donations to their own campaigns (almost all of it from Republican contender Steve Forbes), and $5.6 million from other sources.[110] In 2004 the candidates raised $606.6 million from individual contributions, $27.4 million from federal matching funds, $3.6 million from PACs, and $24.4 million from other sources by August 31, for a total of $661.9 million.[111] The dramatic increase in individual contributions was due in part to a change in federal law that raised the ceiling on individual donations from $1,000 to $2,000.

Money does not ensure success. The record for futile big spending belongs to former Texas senator Phil Gramm, who spent $28.0 million, raised mostly from the business community, in the 1996 Republican primaries and won no delegates. In 2000 George W. Bush and Steve Forbes both outspent John McCain heavily in the New Hampshire primary, but McCain beat them by margins of 18 and 36 percentage points, respectively.

Congress first encouraged small political donations with the Revenue Act of 1971. The 1974 Federal Election Campaign Act then offered matching funds to contenders for party nominations and encouraged campaigns to seek small donations. Before the 1974 FECA amendments were passed, a small number of "sugar daddies" underwrote many nomination campaigns. General Motors heir Stewart Mott, for example, gave liberals Eugene McCarthy $300,000 in 1968 and George McGovern $400,000 in 1972. Mott also made a practice of making large loans to candidates—such as $200,000 to McGovern in 1972. Some $31.3 million in federal money was disbursed to candidates meeting matching-fund requirements in 1980, $30.9 million in 1984, $66.7 million in 1988, $42.1 million in 1992, $56.0 million in 1996, $57.7 million in 2000, and $27.4 million in 2004. But George

W. Bush won the 2000 and 2004 Republican nomination and John Kerry won the 2004 Democratic nomination without accepting any federal funds at all.

In recent elections, the need to raise money has spurred presidential candidates to begin their campaigns early. Early fund raising can be crucial to a campaign because of the high costs of building and maintaining a campaign organization and the need to demonstrate political viability. Because of individual donor limits, a presidential campaign must have access to fund-raisers with lots of generous friends. The best states for fund raising have been California, New York, Florida, and Texas, which supply about one-half of all campaign donations to presidential candidates. As one observer has put it, "A modern presidential campaign is designed to suck money out of New York and California and spend it in Iowa and New Hampshire." [112]

Candidates sometimes have a special fund-raising entree with certain groups. Democratic candidate Michael Dukakis raised millions in 1988 from Greek Americans who were proud to see one of their own seek the White House. In 1988 Jesse Jackson had the support of well-heeled African Americans across the country. Clinton's forthright support for gay rights spurred activists such as David Mixner to raise more than $2 million for the Arkansas governor in 1992. Clinton also built bridges to Hollywood figures, who have become prominent fund-raisers for both parties (but especially the Democrats) in recent years.

Because matching funds are cut off from candidates who receive less than 10 percent of the vote in two consecutive state primaries, candidates seeking delegates face a dilemma in states where they may not perform well: risk missing out on the delegate hunt by not entering a primary or risk losing matching-fund eligibility by finishing poorly. The 10 percent threshold is a crucial factor in the campaign's high dropout rate after the first couple of primaries. Poor primary performances—and the fund-raising drought and loss of federal matching funds that ensued—forced all but Bill Clinton and Jerry Brown out of the Democratic race by late March 1992. In previous years, candidates had stayed in the race much longer. The first dropout in the 1972 presidential race was Mayor John V. Lindsay of New York, in April.

Spending limits do not apply to candidates who decline federal assistance, such as Connally in 1980, Forbes in 1996 and 2000, Bush in 2000, and Bush, Kerry, and Dean in 2004.

An important element of campaign momentum is fund-raising ability. Carter's early fund raising and electoral victories in 1976 enabled him to increase his campaign's total monthly receipts from $125,000 in January to $400,000 in February, $612,000 in March, and $732,000 in April. Carter built on a strong foundation of regional pride: almost half of his primary treasury came from his home state of Georgia.[113] Incumbent governors who run for president often benefit from the contributions of companies and individuals that do business with their state government, including Dukakis (Massachusetts) in 1988, Clinton (Arkansas) in 1992, and Bush (Texas) in 2000.

Spending is heaviest in the early stages of the nominating campaign. In the early primary states, campaigns spent about 85 percent of their state limits in recent campaigns. The FECA assigns each state contest its own spending limit according to its voting-age population.

But early spending is not always wise spending. Gary Hart's 1984 campaign spent most of its reserves in the campaign's early stages, neglecting the need for costly organizing in later states that could have earned him more than one hundred additional delegates. The major candidates in 1976 displayed the same inability to save money for the important battles. In preparing for the 1976 race, eleven Democratic and Republican candidates spent in 1975 $13 million of the $13.3 million they had raised that year. In contrast, a frugal Carter paid his 1976 campaign staffers one-third the salaries of staffers working for Sen. Henry Jackson, ensuring that the Carter campaign never faced a cash-flow crisis.[114] In 1980 Sen. Edward Kennedy "spen[t] himself virtually out of existence" on high staff salaries, first-class travel, and extravagant headquarters—$2.4 million in two months compared with the Carter campaign's expenses of $2.8 million in ten months.[115]

Campaigns have been ingenious in getting around the state-by-state spending limits, especially in the early contests. In New Hampshire, for example, campaign workers typically rent cars and set up lodging in neighboring Massachusetts. They advertise heavily on Boston television and radio stations to reach voters in populous southern New Hampshire.

The 1984 Mondale campaign deliberately violated state spending limits. Mondale spent $2.85 million in the New Hampshire primary (and lost), despite a legal limit of $404,000; he later accepted a $400,000 fine as a cost of doing business. "It [the fine] wasn't a lot, and that's the whole point," said Mondale aide Robert Beckel. "The FEC is not one of the great enforcement agencies of modern politics." [116]

One effect of the state spending limits is that campaigns are forced to shut down their headquarters in a state right after the caucus or primary takes place. Efforts to organize volunteers and educate voters are abandoned until the general election. If the headquarters could remain in operation, the state organizations could build strong links between state and national party officials and keep the campaign atmosphere alive all year.

Even though campaigns pump millions of dollars into television and radio outlets, the stations often are wary of doing business with them. Campaigns provide only a short burst of business that may endanger the stations' arrangements with regular advertisers. Furthermore, the ad hoc nature of many campaigns makes doing business with them

TABLE 5-6 **Funds Raised by Democratic and Republican National Committees, 1983–2004 (millions of dollars)**

Election cycle	Democratic Party	Republican Party
1983–1984	98.5	297.9
1985–1986	64.8	255.2
1987–1988	116.1	257.5
1989–1990	78.5	202.0
1991–1992	163.3	264.9
1993–1994	132.8	244.1
1995–1996	221.6	416.5
1997–1998	160.0	285.0
1999–2000	275.2	465.8
2001–2002	217.2	424.1
2003–2004	678.8	782.4

SOURCES: Harold W. Stanley and Richard G. Niemi, *Vital Statistics on American Politics, 2005–2006* (Washington, D.C.: CQ Press, 2006), 98; Federal Election Commission, www.fec.gov.

difficult. Broadcast outlets therefore set stringent standards for campaign advertising. Candidates often must contract for broadcast spots weeks ahead of time, and they must pay in advance.

Money in the General Election Campaign

Under the FECA, the campaigns of the major party nominees for president are financed entirely by the federal government. But private money and nominally independent organizations have continued to play an important role in the general election.

The first campaign underwritten by public money was the 1976 race. In that election, each candidate was given $22 million. Funding rose in later years because of automatic inflation adjustments—to $29.4 million in 1980, $40.4 million in 1984, $46.1 million in 1988, $55.2 million in 1992, $61.8 million in 1996, $67.6 million in 2000, and $74.6 million in 2004. The federal funding goes directly to each presidential candidate's campaign organization. Direct candidate support reduces the role of the political parties in the fall campaign.

Federal funding of presidential campaigns has not eliminated special interests from the election. Instead, it has redirected their money into other channels. In 2000 pro-Gore liberal groups such as Planned Parenthood, the Sierra Club, and Handgun Control Inc. outspent pro-Bush groups by $14 million to $2 million in funding issues ads. This nonetheless paled in comparison with the $100 million-plus advantage that Republicans regularly have over Democrats in spending on election campaigns.[117]

Major Donors in American Politics

Perpetual fund raising is the electoral equivalent of an arms race. Candidates are so concerned with survival that they spend ever more time and use ever more sophisticated technology to gain an advantage. They raise money not according to objective standards of need but out of a fear other candidates are raising more. The arms race mentality, argues Elizabeth Drew, affects every aspect of politics. "It is not relevant whether every candidate who spends more than his opponent wins. What matters is what the chasing of money does to the candidates, and to the victors' subsequent behavior. The point is what raising money, not simply spending it, does to the political process."[118] Hubert Humphrey, who sought the presidency in 1960, 1968, and 1972, described the ways that fund raising affects the tenor of the campaign:

> Campaign financing is a curse. It's the most disgusting, demeaning, disenchanting, debilitating experience of a politician's life. It's stinky, it's lousy. I just can't tell you how much I hate it. I've had to break off in the middle of trying to make a decent, honorable campaign and go up to somebody's parlor or to a room and say, 'Gentlemen, and ladies, I'm desperate. You've got to help me.' . . . And you see the people there—a lot of them you don't want to see. And they look at you, and you sit there and you talk to them and tell them what you're for and you need help and, out of the twenty-five who have gathered, four will contribute. And most likely one of them is in trouble and is someone you shouldn't have had a contribution from.[119]

Fund-raisers in both parties have been drawn to large donors because of the quicker returns on their efforts. But critics of the large-donor approach point out that the parties risk being perceived as beholden to the wealthy.

A campaign that depends on small donations is not necessarily a grass-roots insurgency. To the contrary, both parties—especially the Republicans—have developed extensive telephone, direct-mail, and Internet operations for securing thousands of small donors. In 1992 independent candidate Ross Perot created sophisticated computer systems at his Dallas headquarters to parlay telephone calls into fund-raising data that might be used to get other donations. The telephone numbers of incoming calls were recorded and sent for analysis, thereby revealing which communities seemed to be fertile territory for Perot's fund raising.

Political Action Committees

Political action committees have been controversial in recent years because of their explosive growth, negative campaign tactics, special-interest messages, and limited accountability. Potential presidential candidates often form their own "leadership" PACs to make political contacts and explore the possibility of running. But for the most part, PAC influence is limited to congressional and state campaigns. PACs account for a tiny fraction of all spending in presidential elections.

A PAC is a committee created to raise and distribute money for political purposes. Many PACs are affiliated with corporations, trade and professional associations, or labor unions. Others are based on a political cause or issue.

Between 1974 and 1988 the number of PACs grew from 608 to a high of 4,268. Since then the number has never varied by more then a few hundred organizations from year to year, with 4,184 registered in 2004. *(See Table 5-7, p. 273.)* But PAC contributions to or independent spending for federal candidates has continued to grow—from $77.4 million in 1978 to $842.9 million in 2004, with a substantial percentage going to congressional campaigns.

The PAC that provided the most money to federal candidates in 2004 was the National Association of Realtors Political Action Committee. Other leading donors were PACs for the National Automobile Dealers Association, the International Brotherhood of Electrical Workers, and the National Beer Wholesalers Association.[120]

Much more important than PAC spending on presidential campaigns are the leadership PACs that would-be candidates create before the election year. These PACs ostensibly are designed to promote a wide range of congressional and state campaigns across the country; by law, a PAC must contribute to at least five federal candidates. But in reality most of these PAC dollars are used to support the presidential aspirations of the PACs' founders. Because PACs do not have the legal status of campaign organizations, they escape many of the spending and reporting requirements of formal campaign structures.

Among the advantages of leadership PACs over presidential campaign organizations, donors may contribute $5,000 annually to a multicandidate PAC but only $2,000 to a presidential campaign, and PACs are not subject to the campaign spending ceilings and other regulations that formal campaign organizations must heed.

As recently as 1976, none of the prospective candidates set up their own PACs. But before the 1980 election, four of the ten candidates established PACs. Five of nine did so before the 1984 election. By the start of the 1988 election, nine of fourteen candidates had set up PACs, and three others had set up similar organizations.

Political scientist Anthony Corrado argues that the preelection-year PAC "fosters inequities" by favoring well-known potential candidates with an ability to raise money early in the election cycle. In this way, candidates with sophisticated fund-raising operations can become prohibitive favorites for the nomination, leaving behind long-shot candidates. Two examples of the latter, McGovern and Carter, may not have been able to compete seriously for the nomination if their well-heeled opponents had been able to establish PACs early in the election cycle.[121]

THE NOMINATING PROCESS

Americans vote at two stages of the electoral process. In the first stage, they help select the nominees of the two major parties. In the second, general election stage, they choose

TABLE 5-7 **Number of Political Action Committees (PACs), by Type, 1974–2005**

Date	Corporate	Labor	Trade/membership/health	Cooperative	Corporation without stock	Nonconnected[b]	Total
December 31, 1974	89	201	318	—	—	—	608
November 24, 1975	139	226	357	—	—	—	722
December 31, 1976	433	224	489	—	—	—	1,146
December 31, 1977	550	234	438	8	20	110	1,360
December 31, 1978	785	217	453	12	24	162	1,653
December 31, 1979	950	240	514	17	32	247	2,000
December 31, 1980	1,206	297	576	42	56	374	2,551
December 31, 1981	1,329	318	614	41	68	531	2,901
December 31, 1982	1,469	380	649	47	103	723	3,371
December 31, 1983	1,538	378	643	51	122	793	3,525
December 31, 1984	1,682	394	698	52	130	1,053	4,009
December 31, 1985	1,710	388	695	54	142	1,003	3,992
December 31, 1986	1,744	384	745	56	151	1,077	4,157
December 31, 1987	1,775	364	865	59	145	957	4,165
December 31, 1988	1,816	354	786	59	138	1,115	4,268
December 31, 1989	1,796	349	777	59	137	1,060	4,178
December 31, 1990	1,795	346	774	59	136	1,062	4,172
December 31, 1991	1,738	338	742	57	136	1,083	4,094
December 31, 1992	1,735	347	770	56	142	1,145	4,195
December 31, 1993	1,789	337	761	56	146	1,121	4,210
December 31, 1994	1,660	333	792	53	136	980	3,954
December 31, 1995	1,674	334	815	44	129	1,020	4,016
December 31, 1996	1,642	332	838	41	123	1,103	4,079
December 31, 1997	1,597	332	825	42	117	931	3,844
December 31, 1998	1,567	321	821	39	115	935	3,798"
January 1, 2000	1,548	318	844	38	115	972	3,835
January 1, 2001	1,545	317	860	41	118	1,026	3,907
July 1, 2001	1,525	314	872	41	118	1,007	3,877
January 1, 2002	1,508	316	891	41	116	1,019	3,891
July 1, 2002	1,514	313	882	40	110	1,006	3,865
January 1, 2003	1,528	320	975	39	110	1,055	4,027
July 1, 2003	1,534	320	902	39	110	1,040	3,945
January 1, 2004	1,538	310	884	35	102	999	3,868
July 1, 2004	1,555	306	877	34	97	1,174	4,040
January 1, 2005	1,622	306	900	34	99	1,223	4,184

NOTES: "—" indicates not available. The counts above reflect federally registered PACs. Registration does not necessarily imply financial activity. Trade/membership/health category for 1974–1976 includes all PACs except corporate and labor; no further breakdown available. Midyear counts for additional years can be found in earlier editions of *Vital Statistics on American Politics* (Washington, D.C.: CQ Press). a. Connected PACs are associated with a sponsoring organization that may pay operating and fundraising expenses. They are typically subdivided by the type of sponsor: corporate (with stockholders), labor (unions), membership/trade/health (professional groups and associations of corporations), cooperatives (primarily agricultural), and corporations without stock. b. Nonconnected PACs do not have a sponsoring organization.

SOURCES: Harold W. Stanley and Richard G. Niemi, *Vital Statistics on American Politics 2005–2006* (Washington, D.C.: CQ Press, 2006), 101–102; Federal Election Commission, ""FEC Issues Semi-Annual Federal PAC Count," press release, January 25, 2005 (http://www.fec.gov), accessed March 18, 2005.

between those two candidates (and possibly one or more third party or independent candidates).

The nominating process usually attracts less public interest than the general election. But, in many ways, nominations represent the more important phase of the process. The nominating process reduces a vast field of possible candidates down to two serious contenders, the Republican and Democratic nominees.

Eligibility

Prospective presidential candidates must meet a few constitutional requirements, but much more important are the unwritten, informal requirements for eligibility. The habits, preferences, and in some cases the prejudices of the American people demand that their chief executive meet several career and social background criteria.

Constitutional Requirements

Article II of the Constitution stipulates that the president must be a "natural born citizen" who has "been 14 years a Resident within the United States" and is at least thirty-five years old. In 1804 the Twelfth Amendment extended the age, citizenship, and residency requirements to the vice president as well. These requirements were intended to ensure that candidates have absolute fidelity to the United States and, in the case of the age requirement, maturity. The Founders were wary of the new nation coming under foreign influence.

In 1951 the Twenty-second Amendment placed a further limit on eligibility. By forbidding presidents to seek a third term, it disqualified all two-term presidents.[122] *(See "Twenty-second Amendment," p. 53, in Chapter 1.)*

The Constitution does not include property qualifications and it explicitly forbids religious qualifications, both of which were common in state constitutions at the time the Constitution was enacted. The delegates to the Constitutional Convention explicitly forbade "religious tests" as a qualification for office. Most of them wanted to require candidates to own a certain amount of property to be eligible to run for president, but they could not agree on a minimum amount or on a definition of what kinds of property counted.[123]

Unwritten Requirements

More important for screening potential presidential candidates are cultural norms. Political scientist Clinton Rossiter's classic 1960 study of the American presidency described a limited pool of candidates: middle-aged, white, Protestant males who embody small-town family values, have state government experience, are lawyers, and come from large northern states.[124] Since Rossiter's study, however, five southerners (Lyndon Johnson in 1964, Jimmy Carter in 1976, George Bush in 1988, Bill Clinton in 1992, and George W. Bush in 2000), one older man (Ronald Reagan in 1980 and 1984), one younger man (John Kennedy in 1960), one Roman Catholic (Kennedy), and five who were not lawyers (Johnson, Carter, Reagan, and both Bushes) have been elected president.

Celebrity status can overcome a lack of the traditional qualifications. Celebrity presidential hopefuls—actors (Reagan), athletes (Jack Kemp, Bill Bradley), astronauts (John Glenn), media personalities (Pat Buchanan, Pat Robertson), and military heroes (Bob Dole, John McCain, Wesley Clark)—enjoy the critical advantage of widespread name recognition.[125] Politicians without celebrity status must make names for themselves through public service and years of campaigning in primary and caucus states. "The

PRESIDENTIAL NOMINATING PROCESS

BEFORE 1968

Party-dominated

The nomination decision is largely in the hands of party leaders. Candidates win by enlisting support of state and local party machines.

Few primaries

Most delegates are selected by state party establishments, with little or no public participation. Some primaries are held, but their results do not necessarily determine nominee. Primaries are used to indicate candidate's "electability."

Short campaigns

Candidates usually begin their public campaign early in the election year.

Easy money

Candidates frequently raise large amounts of money quickly by tapping a handful of wealthy contributors. No federal limits on spending by candidates.

Limited media coverage

Campaigns are followed by print journalists and, in later years, by television. But press coverage of campaigns is not intensive and generally does not play a major role in influencing the process.

Late decisions

Events early in the campaign year, such as the New Hampshire primary, are not decisive. States that pick delegates late in the year, such as California, frequently are important in selecting nominee. Many states enter convention without making final decisions about candidates.

Open conventions

National party conventions sometimes begin with nomination still undecided. Outcome determined by maneuvering and negotiations among party factions, often stretching over multiple ballots.

SINCE 1968

Candidate-dominated

Campaigns are independent of party establishments. Endorsements by party leaders have little effect on nomination choice.

Many primaries

Most delegates are selected by the voters in primaries and caucuses. Nominations are determined largely by voters' decisions at these contests.

Long campaigns

Candidates begin laying groundwork for campaigns three or four years before the election. Candidates who are not well organized at least eighteen months before the election may have little chance of winning.

Difficult fund raising

Campaign contributions are limited to $2,000 per person ($1,000 before 2004), so candidates must work endlessly to raise money from thousands of small contributors.

Media-focused

Campaigns are covered intensively by the media, particularly television. Media treatment of candidates plays crucial role in determining the nominee.

"Front-loaded"

Early events, such as the Iowa caucuses and New Hampshire primary, are important. The nomination may be decided even before many major states vote. Early victories attract great media attention, which gives winners free publicity and greater fund-raising ability.

Closed conventions

Nominee is determined before convention, which does little more than ratify decision made in primaries and caucuses. Convention activities focus on creating favorable media image of candidate for general election campaign.

barriers have changed . . . ," journalist Alan Ehrenhalt has argued. "The aspiring candidate no longer needs to worry much about what important people think of him. He needs to worry whether he has the stamina and desire to make it through the grueling work that lies ahead."[126]

Geraldine Ferraro's Democratic vice-presidential nomination in 1984 broke the barrier that excluded women from serious consideration for high office. Ferraro's nomination followed a long period of public lobbying by organizations such as the National Organization for Women. Republican Elizabeth Dole sought her party's nomination for president in 2000. The percentage of the electorate professing an unwillingness to vote for a woman for president declined from 64 percent in 1941 to 41 percent in 1958 to 19 percent in 1978 and 7 percent in 1999.[127] The number of women holding high elective office has grown dramatically in recent years, increasing the pool of women who might pursue more ambitious political goals. For example, the 109th Congress (2005–2007) included thirteen women senators and sixty-eight women representatives.

Jesse Jackson's pursuit of the Democratic nomination in 1984 and 1988 may have weakened the race barrier to the presidency. Jackson, the leader of the civil rights group Operation PUSH, attracted 18 percent of the vote in the 1984 primaries. In 1988 Jackson won the near-unanimous support of African American leaders—many of whom had been wary of him four years earlier—and made small inroads into white farm and industrial votes. In that year Jackson finished second out of the eight Democratic candidates who began the primary and caucus season. In 1996 Colin Powell seriously considered seeking the Republican nomination but decided not to for family and personal reasons.

Rossiter's portrait of what Americans want in a president may be obsolete, but it still captures their desire for a leader who combines the often contradictory qualities of political involvement and nonpartisanship, majesty and simplicity, experience and freshness, friendliness and detachment. The electorate seeks candidates who can fill the symbolic functions of the chief of state as well as the policy-oriented functions of the chief of government.[128]

Moral Values and Character. Americans look for moral leadership in their presidents. Lacking a royal family to symbolize the nation, Americans also look for a president who will personify the nation's values and spirit.

Bill Clinton struggled against charges of character flaws, including draft-dodging and adultery, throughout his 1992 campaign. Although Clinton's compelling personal story—son of a widow, popular small-town boy, Rhodes scholar, energetic reform governor—helped him to overcome these charges, the voters remained uncertain about their young president throughout his two terms in office.

Former democratic vice-presidential candidate Geraldine Ferraro addresses an annual Ultimate Women's Power Lunch for U.S. Rep. Jan Schakowsky, D-Ill., in Chicago, Friday, May 4, 2007.

"Toughness" is another character trait sought by the electorate and the media. Gov. George Romney of Michigan, a strong contender for the 1968 Republican nomination, dropped out after he said that he had been "brainwashed" by generals about the American role in the Vietnam War. Sen. Edmund S. Muskie's 1972 Democratic campaign faltered when he appeared to cry as he lashed out against the attacks being made against his outspoken wife by the *Manchester Union Leader.*[129]

Political Experience. The preferred political experience of presidential nominees has gone through three distinct phases since the start of the twentieth century. Until 1960, governors predominated among the major party nominees. William McKinley, Theodore Roosevelt, Woodrow Wilson, James Cox, Calvin Coolidge, Alfred E. Smith, Franklin Roosevelt, Alfred M. Landon, Thomas E. Dewey, and Adlai Stevenson were all former governors. *(See box, Governors Who Became President, p. 277.)* Other major party nominees in this period included members of Congress, judges, cabinet members, a business leader, and a military hero.

From 1960 to 1972, the nominees were all current or recent senators: John Kennedy, Nixon, Johnson, Goldwater, Humphrey, and McGovern. *(See box, Members of Congress Who Became President, p. 277.)* In this period, the electorate was preoccupied with international concerns, especially the Cold War with the Soviet Union. As Washington figures with distinct constitutional responsibilities in foreign affairs, senators were thought to have relevant experience that governors lacked.

Former governors William McKinley, left, and Theodore Roosevelt, right, were the first two twentieth-century presidents. Six other twentieth-century presidents also held governorships before becoming president.

Since 1976, governors once again have dominated the nominating process. An anti-Washington mood in the country brought nomination victories to current or former governors Carter, Reagan, Dukakis, Clinton, and George W. Bush. Also throughout each of the two most recent periods, vice presidents usually were able to win their party's nomination: Nixon in 1960, Humphrey in 1968, Mondale in 1984 (four years after his term as vice president), George Bush in 1988, and Al Gore in 2000.

Candidates with no experience in elective politics have boasted having other relevant experience. Wendell Willkie and Dwight Eisenhower, the Republican nominees in 1940 and 1952, respectively, claimed executive experience as a business leader (Willkie) and a general (Eisenhower). Democrat Carter in 1976 augmented his short political résumé—two years as a state legislator and four years as governor of Georgia—by highlighting his experience as a nuclear engineer, farmer, and businessman. Reagan often mentioned his term as the head of the Screen Actors Guild to augment his political experience as governor of California. In his 1984 and 1988 campaigns, Democrat Jesse Jackson stressed his civil rights activities and leadership of Operation PUSH. Republican Pat Robertson, a television evangelist, introduced himself as a businessman and lawyer in 1988. Publisher Steve Forbes sought the Republican nomination as a business leader in 1996 and 2000.

Foreign Policy Experience. Voters regularly list foreign policy as an important consideration in choosing a president. Senators who seek the White House regularly invoke their experience on issues such as arms control, the North Atlantic Treaty Organization, international trade, military oversight, antiterrorism campaigns, and intelligence activities as reasons they should be elected.

In the nuclear age and, more recently, the era of international terrorism, a perceived inability to manage foreign affairs can cripple a campaign. Carter, Reagan, Dukakis, Clinton, and George W. Bush all were criticized for their relative lack of foreign policy experience. In 2000 a Boston radio interviewer embarrassed Bush by administering an on-air quiz about the names of world leaders, none of whom Bush could identify offhand.

Clinton had no foreign policy experience in 1992, but he compensated for this shortcoming by showcasing members of the foreign policy establishment who supported his candidacy. The former chairman of the Joint Chiefs of Staff, Adm. William J. Crowe Jr., was Clinton's most visible military backer. Bush did the same in 2000, consulting frequently and publicly with a host of foreign policy advisers from his father's administration.

In recent years, several candidates with negligible foreign policy experience have been elected president. Carter, Reagan, Clinton, and George W. Bush could cite only their efforts to attract foreign trade as governors and, in Carter's case, membership in the Trilateral Commission. Inexperience was countered with vows to shift the foreign policy goals of the nation. In 1976 and 1980, for example, Reagan punctuated his campaigns with strong denunciations of the Soviet Union, arms-control initiatives, treaty negotiations with Panama, and American "abandonment" of Taiwan, a longtime ally.

Age. A candidate's age occasionally has been an issue, but it has not prevented some older and some younger candidates from running. John Kennedy—who asked headline writers to call him "JFK" rather than the youthful-sounding "Jack"—became the youngest elected president in 1960 at age forty-three. His opponent, Nixon, was forty-seven. Jerry

Governors who Became President

When George W. Bush was elected president in 2000, he continued the recent trend of governors advancing to the White House. Between 1976 and 2000, former or sitting governors won six out of seven presidential elections. In all, seventeen presidents have served previously as state governors.

Following is a list of these presidents and the states they served as governor. Two additional presidents served as governors of territories: Andrew Jackson was the territorial governor of Florida and William Henry Harrison was the territorial governor of Indiana.

President	State
Thomas Jefferson	Virginia
James Monroe	Virginia
Martin Van Buren	New York
John Tyler	Virginia
James K. Polk	Tennessee
Andrew Johnson	Tennessee
Rutherford B. Hayes	Ohio
Grover Cleveland	New York
William McKinley	Ohio
Theodore Roosevelt	New York
Woodrow Wilson	New Jersey
Calvin Coolidge	Massachusetts
Franklin D. Roosevelt	New York
Jimmy Carter	Georgia
Ronald Reagan	California
Bill Clinton	Arkansas
George W. Bush	Texas

SOURCE: *American Political Leaders 1789–2005* (Washington, D.C.: CQ Press, 2005); *America Votes 26* (Washington, D.C.: CQ Press, 2006).

Members of Congress who Became President

Twenty-four presidents have served previously in the House of Representatives, the Senate, or both.

Following is a list of these presidents and the houses in which they served. In addition, three other presidents—George Washington, John Adams, and Thomas Jefferson—served in the Continental Congress, as did James Madison and James Monroe.

James A. Garfield was elected to the Senate in January 1880 for a term beginning March 4, 1881, but declined to accept in December 1880 because he had been elected president. John Quincy Adams served in the House for seventeen years after his term as president, and Andrew Johnson returned to the Senate five months before he died.

House Only	Senate Only	Both House and Senate
James Madison	James Monroe	Andrew Jackson
James K. Polk	John Quincy Adams	William Henry Harrison
Millard Fillmore	Martin Van Buren	John Tyler
Abraham Lincoln	Benjamin Harrison	Franklin Pierce
Rutherford B. Hayes	Warren G. Harding	James Buchanan
James A. Garfield	Harry S. Truman	Andrew Johnson
William McKinley		John F. Kennedy
Gerald R. Ford		Lyndon B. Johnson
George Bush		Richard M. Nixon

SOURCE: *Biographical Directory of the United States Congress, 1774–1989* (Washington, D.C.: Government Printing Office, 1989); *American Political Leaders 1789–2005* (Washington, D.C.: CQ Press, 2005).

Brown (1976) and Al Gore (1988) ran for the presidency when they were still in their thirties. In contrast, Reagan was elected in 1980 at the age of sixty-nine, the oldest person ever to become president. His vigorous campaigning in the primaries eliminated questions about his ability to meet the job's physical demands. In 1984, when asked about his age in a debate, Reagan deflected the question with a quip: he did not, he said, intend to exploit his opponent's "youth and inexperience."

Social Class. Almost by definition, presidential candidates are prosperous and high-status individuals by the time they are nominated. But if one measures social class in terms of the family status in which an individual is born and raised, the class backgrounds of presidential candidates have broadened in recent decades. Of the eight presidents who served between 1897 and 1945, a majority came from upper-class families: Theodore Roosevelt, William Howard Taft, Warren G. Harding, and Franklin Roosevelt. Three were raised in middle-class families (William McKinley, Woodrow Wilson, and Calvin Coolidge) and just one in a working-class family (Herbert Hoover).

In contrast, the eleven presidents who have served since 1945 have been spread almost evenly among the classes. Four grew up in working-class families: Dwight Eisenhower, Richard Nixon, Ronald Reagan, and Bill Clinton. Another four had modest but middle-class origins: Harry Truman, Lyndon Johnson, Gerald Ford, and Jimmy Carter. Only three—John Kennedy, George Bush, and George W. Bush—were from the upper class.

The Decision to Compete

The decision to seek the presidency is serious and difficult. Running for president requires one to master a complex set of policy issues, to attract endorsements, to recruit a competent and enthusiastic staff, to raise a great deal of money, and to develop an image suitable for media campaigning. The prospective candidate also must consider the effect a national campaign will have on his or her family—not just the stress of publicity and frequent travel but also possible revelations about personal or professional "skeletons in the closet."

In other ways, the decision to run is as idiosyncratic as the character of the potential candidates. Some candidates

VICE PRESIDENTS WHO BECAME PRESIDENT

Fourteen vice presidents have become president. Nine succeeded to the presidency when the president died or resigned. Of these, four went on to win a presidential election in their own right and five did not.

Five vice presidents were elected president on their own. Of these, only Richard Nixon (1968) was not serving as vice president at the time of his election.

Following is a list of vice presidents and the presidents (in parentheses) with whom they served before becoming president themselves.

Succeeded to the presidency but never elected president
John Tyler (William Henry Harrison)
Millard Fillmore (Zachary Taylor)
Andrew Johnson (Abraham Lincoln)
Chester A. Arthur (James Garfield)
Gerald R. Ford (Richard M. Nixon)

Succeeded to the presidency and then elected president
Theodore Roosevelt (William McKinley)
Calvin Coolidge (Warren Harding)
Harry S. Truman (Franklin D. Roosevelt)
Lyndon B. Johnson (John F. Kennedy)

Elected president on their own
John Adams (George Washington)
Thomas Jefferson (John Adams)
Martin Van Buren (Andrew Jackson)
Richard M. Nixon (Dwight D. Eisenhower)
George Bush (Ronald Reagan)

are instilled with high political ambition from their youth. John Quincy Adams, Benjamin Harrison, John Kennedy, Lyndon Johnson, and both Roosevelts were such presidents. When his son was inaugurated as vice president in 1993, former senator Albert Gore Sr. said he had groomed his son for the White House since he was a boy. Bill Clinton recalled that he was inspired to pursue a political career as a teenager when he shook President Kennedy's hand at a White House ceremony. Others acquire the ambition late in life. Reagan did not run for political office until he was fifty-five.

Some presidents come to the White House fueled by ambitions that many consider unhealthy and perhaps even dangerous. Richard Nixon and Lyndon Johnson are examples of presidents who seemed driven by deep-seated psychological urges to dominate others.[130]

Still others seem to have been uninterested in the presidency until it came to them. Calvin Coolidge was the little-known governor of Massachusetts when he was tapped as the Republican nominee for vice president in 1920. He became president when President Warren Harding died in

1923. Rep. Gerald Ford of Michigan never aspired to any office higher than Speaker of the House of Representatives until President Nixon appointed him vice president after Vice President Spiro T. Agnew resigned in 1973.

Prospective candidates gradually develop confidence that they can handle the office's demands. Carter decided to run for president soon after being elected governor of Georgia. Carter says he first considered the idea after meeting several presidential candidates who, he said, did not impress him as possessing any more raw intelligence or energy than he had.[131]

Some presidential campaigns have been undertaken as crusades, designed not to win the White House but to publicize certain causes. Many observers considered Barry Goldwater's 1964 campaign to be primarily cause-motivated because Goldwater did not think he had much chance of defeating President Johnson. In his Republican primary battles with New York governor Nelson Rockefeller, Goldwater stressed the party's need to change its ideology rather than to win the election. Goldwater's campaign is credited with moving the party in a conservative direction and thus enabling Reagan to be elected president in 1980.

Jesse Jackson's 1984 Democratic campaign followed months of deliberation among African American leaders about how to counter the perceived rightward drift of American politics. But many of these leaders opposed his candidacy and instead supported former vice president Mondale. The Jackson candidacy, with its religious fervor and cries of "Our time has come," was seen as a mostly symbolic effort from the start. Partly because he did not expect to win, Jackson was not forced to moderate his liberal positions.

Incumbency and Its Implications

Despite the real advantages of incumbency for a presidential candidate, recent years have shown that renomination is not inevitable. Ford, Carter, and the elder Bush all faced strong challenges when they sought a second term. Truman and Johnson decided not to run rather than risk defeat.

If the incumbent president appears at all vulnerable, another strong candidate may emerge to contend for the party's nomination. An incumbent is ripe for a challenge if economic or foreign policy failures occur during the first term. But even unpopular presidents are not politically helpless. When several Democratic members of Congress considered challenging President Clinton for renomination after the Republican sweep in the 1994 midterm elections, Clinton embarked on a massive political fund-raising campaign to deter them from running. His success in this effort made him the first Democratic presidential candidate since Johnson in 1964 not to have to fight for his party's nomination.

Although challenges are more likely today than in the past, the president still can command media attention, oversee the government's budgetary and regulatory operations, and take foreign policy initiatives—advantages that help to defeat any rivals. In addition, the prestige of the office is so great that most party members are reluctant to reject an incumbent. Fears that a prolonged intraparty battle could cripple the eventual nominee in the fall campaign are a major consideration. No president has lost a serious renomination effort since 1884, when the Republican Party replaced Chester A. Arthur as its nominee with James G. Blaine.

When President Carter confronted the challenge of Massachusetts senator Edward Kennedy for the 1980 Democratic nomination, the unemployment and inflation rates were both high, and the country had experienced foreign policy setbacks with Iran and the Soviet Union. The administration's relations with the Democratic Congress also were bad. Kennedy entered the race when polls showed him leading Carter by a margin of more than two-to-one.

But President Carter defeated Senator Kennedy by using the powers of incumbency. His chief advantage was his ability to use a strategy that only presidents can use. Instead of campaigning, Carter displayed his preoccupation with governmental affairs, especially the hostage crisis in Iran, by staying at the White House. When Kennedy criticized his performance in the hostage crisis, Carter intimated that his opponent was being unpatriotic. On the morning of the Wisconsin primary, Carter announced an imminent breakthrough in the crisis. The breakthrough fizzled, but he won the primary.

Drawing further on the power of the presidency, Carter wooed voters in primary states with promises of federal funds. He was by no means the first president to use this advantage of incumbency. In 1976, for example, while campaigning against Ronald Reagan in the Florida primary, President Ford promised the state a Veterans Administration hospital in St. Petersburg, an interstate highway in Fort Myers, and an aerospace contract and mass transit funds in Miami. Referring to the president's campaign promises, Reagan quipped to a crowd of supporters in North Carolina, "If he comes here with the same bag of goodies to hand out that he's been giving away elsewhere, the band won't know whether to play 'Hail to the Chief' or 'Santa Claus Is Coming to Town.' "[132]

The Exploratory Stage

Candidates always have maneuvered for position long before the election year. Until recently, however, the maneuvering usually took place behind the scenes and was designed to impress state and local party leaders rather than gain a high public profile. Kennedy's polling of many primary states in advance of the 1960 election, for example, helped him to establish credibility with party leaders who doubted that a Catholic could be elected president. Sen. Goldwater's success at building an organization of conservative activists at the local level starting in 1961 was a crucial element in his strategy for gaining the 1964 Republican nomination.

Some of the most important victories of the nomination struggle occur even before any primaries or caucuses have taken place. In the year before the election, reporters and campaign professionals watch a number of events to see which candidates are likely to be viable. In the so-called "invisible primary" of 1991, Arkansas governor Clinton performed well. He delivered well-received addresses at Georgetown University and to the Association of Democratic State Chairs. He also won media praise for his interviews, established a strong campaign staff, and raised more money than other candidates. Most important, several prominent Democrats with stronger national followings decided to stay out of the race. Unlike Clinton, they were convinced that President George Bush was unbeatable in the afterglow of the American triumph in the Persian Gulf War.

In the past, candidates delayed announcing their candidacy until the year of the election. Even when they knew they would run, they wanted to avoid the disadvantages of candidacy, especially strong media scrutiny. In recent years, however, politicians have not considered an early announcement to be a sign of political weakness. Carter's surprise election in 1976, after a two-year public campaign, prompted Republican candidates in the 1980 election to get started right after the 1978 congressional elections.[133] *(See Figure 5-2, p. 280–281.)*

Just a year into the George W. Bush administration, Democratic senators John Edwards of North Carolina, John Kerry of Massachusetts, and Joseph Lieberman of Connecticut and former vice president Al Gore were among those visiting the sites of early primary and caucus contests to take soundings. All but Gore eventually entered the 2004 race. Bush himself had used the year before the 2000 election to raise $67 (of an eventual $94) million for his campaign and to secure the support of most of the Republican governors.

Political Action Committees

It has been customary in recent elections for potential presidential candidates to create political action committees to broaden their visibility and to test their appeal and fundraising ability. These PACs enable prospective candidates to raise money, to assess their strength with interest groups and local party leaders, to undertake polling and other marketing operations, to recruit political professionals, and to travel around the country making speeches, forging contacts, and giving interviews.

PACs also allow the candidate to pick up some important political IOUs. Since Nixon's successful barnstorming in behalf of Republican state and congressional candidates in the 1966 midterm election, when the GOP made major gains in both houses of Congress, presidential hopefuls have broadened their base of support by making campaign appearances for other politicians. A candidate's PAC funds his or her political travel. Mondale's 1984 Democratic nomination can be

FIGURE 5-2 **Presidential Nominating Campaign Lengths, 1968–2004**

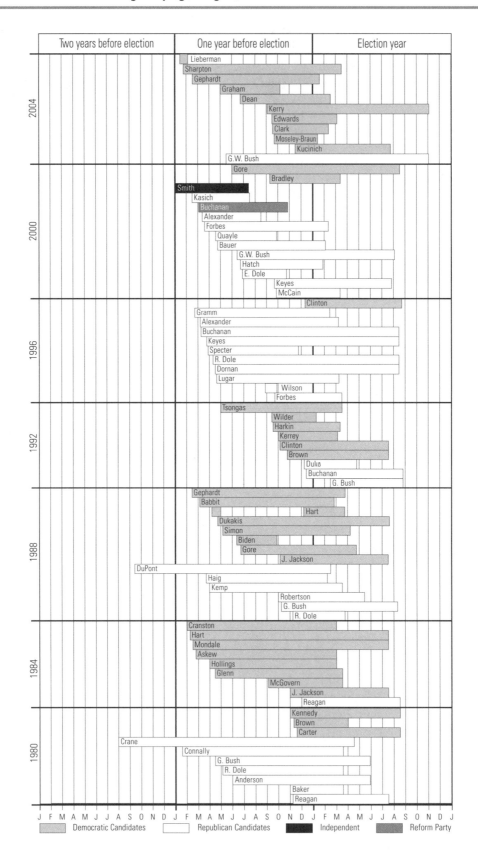

FIGURE 5-2 *(Continued)*

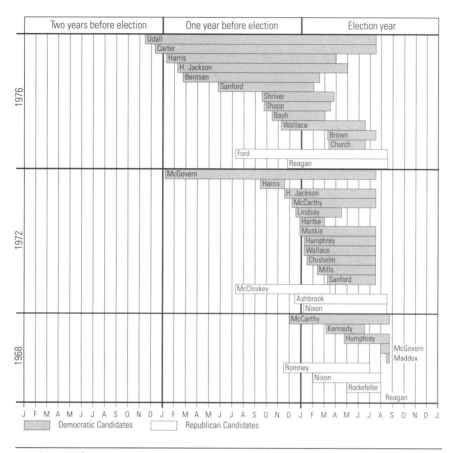

NOTE: Begining of campaigns is determined by date of the formal announcement.

SOURCES: 1968–1984: Congressional Quarterly, *Elections '80* (Washington, D.C.: Congressional Quarterly, 1980), and Congressional Quarterly, *Congressional Quarterly's Guide to U.S. Elections,* 2d ed. (Washington, D.C.: Congressional Quarterly, 1985), 387; 1988–1996: *Congressional Quarterly Weekly Report* (1987), 2732; (1988), 1894, 1896, 1899; (1991), 3735; (1992), 66, 361, 556, 633, 1086; (1995), 2, 13, 15, 3025, 3606; (1996), 641, 716; 2000, 2004: compiled by the editors from news reports, various sources.

attributed in part to the endorsements he garnered after extensive campaigning for other candidates. Mondale enjoyed a particularly strong base among the "superdelegates"—that is, the Democratic elected and party officials who made up almost 15 percent of the party convention.

Reagan was one of the first major political figures to organize his national candidacy around a PAC. One year after losing his 1976 bid for the Republican presidential nomination, Reagan used $1.6 million in leftover funds to form Citizens for the Republic in preparation for his eventual 1980 run. By 1986 PACs created by several candidates were paying for their early travel and office expenses in the lead-up to the 1988 campaign, a practice that is now standard among would-be presidential candidates.

Fund Raising

Success in fund raising is one of the few tangible ways to assess a candidate's early strength. Without adequate funds, it is

impossible to become a serious contender. Vice presidents have an advantage because of the experience their position gives them raising funds at the national level. So do governors, who are able to raise a great deal of money from home-state businesses that rely on contracts with the state government.

Public Opinion Polls

Candidates use public opinion polling extensively to help them determine their chances. Modern polling techniques indicate the candidate's potential on a number of issues and with a variety of constituencies. Besides polling broad demographic groups, campaigns also intensively interview smaller gatherings of people with selected demographic characteristics in "focus groups."

Exploratory Committees

When prospective candidates form an "exploratory committee," they are in effect announcing their presidential ambitions. Although his or her PAC is crucial in giving a candidate a base for a national campaign, the exploratory committee undertakes a sober analysis of the candidate's prospects for a presidential run. The members of the committee consider possible campaign themes and strategies, give advice on speeches and position papers, line up major endorsements, recruit professionals and volunteers, assemble campaign organizations in important primary and caucus states, hire pollsters and campaign consultants, and develop media appeals.

Straw Polls

Candidates' primary and caucus successes often are presaged by preelection-year skirmishes. Straw polls—that is, informal tallies of candidate preference at gatherings of party activists—provide the first numerical measures of candidate support. Because they attract media coverage and impress campaign professionals, these mock elections often influence the early stages of the nominating process.

Long shots try to use straw polls to increase their visibility. In October 1975 Carter gained national press attention by winning 23 percent of the vote in a straw poll conducted at the annual Jefferson-Jackson Day dinner in Iowa. Four years later, supporters of both President Carter and Senator Kennedy spent $1 million on a Florida straw poll in November 1979. (Carter won handily.) Sen. Howard H. Baker Jr. of Tennessee damaged his Republican presidential prospects in November 1979 with a poor performance at a similar contest in Maine.[134] In 1987 Pat Robertson made headlines with his displays of organizational strength in the Michigan and Iowa skirmishes.

State and regional party organizations sometimes use straw polls as a way of pressuring candidates to come to their events. In March 2006, more than two years before the 2008 Republican convention, the Southern Republican Leadership Conference held a straw poll at its meeting in Memphis. Among the would-be presidential candidates who spoke at the event were Gov. Mitt Romney of Massachusetts, Sen. John McCain of Arizona, Sen. George Allen of Virginia, and Sen. Bill Frist of Tennessee. Although Frist won the straw poll, political pundits discounted his victory because the group was meeting in Tennessee.

The Primary and Caucus Schedule

The sequence of election year primaries and caucuses provides the basic strategic setting for presidential nominating contests. Early contests are important because they weed out the weaker candidates and increase the early winners' visibility and fund-raising strength.

In 1980 concerns about the length and divisiveness of nominating campaigns prompted the Democratic Party to shorten the campaign calendar and push many contests to the early months of the year. Party reformers hoped to limit the campaign to three months in order to sustain voter interest, give an advantage to candidates with nationwide support, and allow plenty of time for the defeated candidates to reconcile with the winner. The Democratic National Committee adopted a rule restricting delegate selection to the period from the second Tuesday in March until the second Tuesday in June. But this "window" exempted Iowa and New Hampshire, which conduct the nation's first caucuses and primary, respectively. By state law and historical tradition, New Hampshire initiates the primary season and attracts nearly every candidate seeking the nomination. Since 1976, the Iowa caucuses also have influenced the nominating process by testing the organizational strength of the candidates. Iowa also is important because it votes before New Hampshire.

Although Iowa has maintained its place as the first binding nominating contest, the Democratic National Committee voted in 2006 to insert a Nevada contest between Iowa and New Hampshire in 2008, and to follow the New Hampshire primary with a contest in South Carolina just four days later. The idea was to force Iowa and New Hampshire to share the spotlight with a western state with a large Latino population and a southern state with a large African American population.

Even before 2008, however, the trend had been toward "front-loading"—that is, concentrating nominating contests in the early months of the election year—as a result of states' jockeying for national media attention.

In 1992 more than 700 delegates were selected by eleven states on March 10. This 1992 version of Super Tuesday—a 1988 creation of southern Democratic leaders that led most southern states to hold their primaries on the second Tuesday in March—was preceded by an event known as "Junior Tuesday"—a set of primaries held one week before. Delegates were selected in five states on March 3. Clinton's strong performance in Georgia offset setbacks in Colorado and Maryland, thus setting up his Super Tuesday victories the following week.

The biggest change in 1996 was the shift of the California primary from June to March. The change increased the importance of early fund raising because of the need to conduct a mass-media campaign in the nation's most populous state. By 2000 more primaries were held on the first Tuesday in March than on any other day. Junior Tuesday, previously the lead-up to Super Tuesday, was renamed "Titanic Tuesday" to reflect its new prominence on the nomination calendar.

Before party reforms expanded the number of primaries in 1972, the spacing of primary contests was fairly even across the calendar. No states held primaries in February 1968, and only New Hampshire held a primary in March; the bulk of the contests took place in May and

June. In contrast, in 2004 twenty-four states held primaries in January, February, and March, and several more held caucuses.

But whatever the order of the nominating contests, less than 20 percent of all eligible voters participate in them. In 2000 14.05 million Democratic voters participated in forty primaries. Some 17.16 million Republicans participated in forty-three primaries. In 2004 the Republican nomination went to President Bush without a contest, but 16.70 million voters participated in thirty-six Democratic primaries.

The Early Contests

The early stages of the presidential nominating campaign have become important because the focus of the nominating process has shifted from party bosses meeting at the convention in smoke-filled rooms to rank-and-file voters participating in primaries and caucuses. In most recent elections, the early contests have all but determined the nominees.

After a small number of early tests, the field of candidates shrinks considerably. Within a month and a half after the 1972 New Hampshire primary, four major candidates had left the Democratic field.[135] Four years later, all the original Democratic candidates except Carter and Morris Udall withdrew within nine weeks.[136] The "winnowing" process was more evident in the 1984 Democratic contest, when five candidates withdrew less than three weeks after the New Hampshire primary. In 1988 all but two Republican candidates— George Bush and Bob Dole—lost their public profile after New Hampshire and were soon out of the race. In 2000 the starting field of nearly a dozen contenders for the Republican nomination was again winnowed down to two—George W. Bush and John McCain—after New Hampshire voted. Iowa and New Hampshire undid the candidacy of front-runner and former governor Howard Dean of Vermont in 2004, leaving John Kerry and Sen. John Edwards of North Carolina to battle for the Democratic nomination.

The media pay far more attention to Iowa and New Hampshire (and perhaps will, starting in 2008, to the new early contests in Nevada and South Carolina) than to other states with larger, more representative populations. An analysis of 1984 media coverage found that the New Hampshire primary received 19.2 percent of the total nomination coverage, and the Iowa caucuses received 12.8 percent, even though together the states made up only 2.9 percent of the national population.[137] An important reason for the attention to New Hampshire is that it is the first state where voters actually go to the polls. But "to put matters in perspective," wrote political scientist William Adams, it is as "if one-third of all European media coverage were about Luxembourg and Portugal." [138]

The early primaries and caucuses also are important because they indicate to financial contributors which candidates have a chance to win the nomination. Because making a contribution is in many ways an effort to invest in the next administration, it makes greater sense to give money to someone with a good chance of heading that administration than to someone who is unlikely to win. Money flows to some candidates but not to others once the contributors are able to identify the most viable candidates.

Many experts have criticized the role of New Hampshire and Iowa in the nominating process. Both states are predominantly rural with largely white, Anglo-Saxon, Protestant populations. Candidates therefore pay almost no attention to major problems such as the decline of American heavy industry and of the cities. The Democratic National Committee's decision to add other early contests in Nevada and South Carolina in 2008 was intended to test the candidates' ability to appeal to all races and ethnic groups and to all regions of the country.

For several weeks after the early contests, the goal of the remaining candidates is to attract media attention by winning, or doing "better than expected," in the subsequent caucuses and primaries. The small number of delegates at stake in the first contests does not matter nearly as much as the media attention those states receive.

Ultimately, candidates seek to develop enough momentum to carry them to the nomination. In 1988 the Republican Bush and the Democrat Dukakis benefited from the perception among primary voters that they were the candidates who had the best chance to win in the fall. Political scientist Alan I. Abramowitz argues that Bush's margin of support in Republican primaries and caucuses "would have been substantially smaller" without the perception that Bush had a better chance than any other Republican contender to beat a Democrat in the general election.[139]

In 1984 Democrats Mondale and Hart competed hard in the Super Tuesday electoral sweepstakes, paying less attention to delegate counts than to their ability to show momentum and broad vote-getting ability. Hart won more primaries, but Mondale was able to portray his handful of victories as a comeback from his upset loss in New Hampshire.

Carter's 1980 campaign turned on scheduling changes that the president himself initiated. Using a "sequence as strategy" approach, he arranged to move up the dates of a number of southern primaries so that states favorable to him chose delegates on the same days as states favorable to his rival, Senator Kennedy.

In 1992 Clinton gained momentum when he finished second in New Hampshire and won a decisive primary in Georgia the following week. Clinton performed so well in the next week's eleven Super Tuesday primaries and caucuses that the nomination was his. Dole (victorious in Iowa) and television commentator Pat Buchanan (the winner in New Hampshire) split the first two major delegate-selection events in 1996, which had the effect of eliminating all of the

Sen. John Kerry, D-Mass., celebrates his Democratic presidential nomination with his wife Teresa Heinz Kerry at a rally in Charleston, W.V., on March 16, 2004. Kerry's primary victory in Illinois put him over the top in the delegate count.

ies and caucuses as to accumulate a clear majority of convention delegates. In recent nominating contests, this stage of the process has been a mopping-up operation for the winner of the early primaries and caucuses.

The candidates also woo the delegates of candidates who have dropped out, delegates pledged to "favorite-son" candidates, and, for Democrats, the bloc of superdelegates (elected and party officials) that constitutes 15–20 percent of the party's convention.

In 1976 Carter managed to accumulate enough delegates for a first-ballot Democratic nomination by finishing in second or third place in many late primaries. Carter had a commanding delegate lead that enabled proportional delegate allocations to clinch the nomination.[140] Mondale, the eventual 1984 Democratic nominee, followed a similar strategy. He also dominated the new superdelegate competition.[141]

In 1992 Democrat Clinton eliminated most of his competitors early but still faced opposition from his remaining rival, former California governor Jerry Brown, until the convention. Brown's shoestring campaign did not require much money, so he could afford to stay in the race. Clinton could not get complacent in case Brown was able to rouse the opposition of restless voters in the later primary and caucus states. Clinton's main job in the later contests was to rebut Brown's charges of character flaws and corruption. If Brown's charges had registered with a majority of voters, the Democrats might have been tempted to search for an alternative to Clinton.

All of the major party nominees in the three most recent elections—Dole in 1996, Bush and Gore in 2000, and Kerry in 2004—were able to lock up their nominations early in the year. This allowed them ample time to unite their parties in preparation for the general election campaign.

other contenders from the race. Dole then swept to victory in the remaining primaries.

Both parties experienced hard-fought nomination campaigns in 2000, but once again the outcomes were clear by mid-March. Gore defeated former New Jersey senator Bill Bradley handily in Iowa and narrowly in New Hampshire. He then breezed to the nomination, not losing a single primary or caucus all year. When George W. Bush won the January 24 Iowa Republican caucuses and Sen. John McCain won the New Hampshire primary on February 1, the February 19 South Carolina primary became the crucial test. Bush won the state by 12 percentage points, propelling him into a decisive string of victories in early and mid-March. In 2004 Kerry traded on Democratic voters' strong desire to unite behind the candidate who had the best chance of defeating Bush's bid for reelection. Many Democrats regarded Kerry's status as a decorated Vietnam War veteran as a surefire defense against the charge that a Democrat would pursue the war on terrorism less effectively than a Republican.

The Late Contests

After most of the primaries have been held, attention turns to the question of which candidate leads in the delegate race and how many delegates are needed for a first-ballot convention victory. Candidates try not so much to win later primar-

Campaign Strategies

Every would-be president must have a detailed strategy for attracting voter support and winning delegates before announcing his or her candidacy. Such a plan incorporates analyses of the rival candidates and the rules of the nominating process. It also attempts to forecast likely high and low points of the campaign.

Types of Strategy

The approaches a candidate may pursue are: the insider strategy, the outsider strategy, the early knockout, trench warfare, the slow buildup, and the wait-and-see strategy.

- Insider strategy. This approach, which depends heavily on the endorsements and resources of major party and government leaders, was dominant in the period before the party reforms of 1969 and still offers the best strategy for some candidates. Franklin Roosevelt (1932, 1936, 1940, 1944), Harry Truman (1948), Robert A. Taft (1952), Adlai Stevenson (1952 and 1956), Richard Nixon in 1960, and Hubert Humphrey in 1968 all used the insider strategy. George Bush's 1988 and 1992 campaigns called for continuing the status quo and were backed by powerful party leaders. Gore, as the incumbent vice president, pursued an insider strategy in 2000, as did George W. Bush, the well-connected son of the former president.

  Since the delegate-selection reforms of the early 1970s, even candidates pursuing an insider strategy have had to compete successfully in the primaries and caucuses. Being the favorite of party insiders, however, enables them to raise money, attract talented campaign staffers, and secure endorsements from prominent state and local party leaders.

Patrick J. Buchanan, from the conservative wing of the Republican Party, mounted a serious challenge of incumbent George Bush in 1992 and GOP front-runner Robert J. Dole in 1996.

- Outsider strategy. The outsider candidate offers a "fresh face" to voters weary of politics as usual. Barry Goldwater in 1964, Eugene McCarthy and Robert Kennedy in 1968, Jimmy Carter in 1976, and Ronald Reagan in 1976 and 1980 based their campaigns on opposition to the Washington establishment. Jesse Jackson in 1984 and 1988, Jerry Brown in 1992, and Pat Buchanan in 1992 and 1996 gave voice to disaffected outsiders but never posed a real threat to the front-runners. John McCain ran a well-executed outsider campaign in 2000. He rose from the pack to become Bush's main opponent and came close to winning the nomination. Howard Dean's outsider candidacy in 2004 followed a similar arc of early success followed by eventual defeat.
- Early knockout. Front-runners almost always try to parlay their early strength in polls, fund raising, and endorsements into decisive victories at the beginning of the primary season. Their hope is to build such an impressive early lead that the competition will quickly drop out. Mondale in 1984 sought an early knockout but

was forced to adopt a more gradual approach after Gary Hart defeated him in New Hampshire. George Bush won swift victories in 1988 and 1992.

- Trench warfare. No candidate's favorite strategy, this approach requires candidates to struggle through the long primary season with the hope of barely outpacing their opponents. The danger lies in sapping the party's resources to such an extent that the eventual nominee is weakened in the general election. The races between McCarthy, Kennedy, and Humphrey in 1968; McGovern, Humphrey, and Wallace in 1972; Ford and Reagan in 1976; Carter and Kennedy in 1980; and Mondale and Hart in 1984 were examples of trench warfare.
- Slow buildup. The idea here is to build support for the campaign slowly so that the candidate can avoid early traps and criticism and gain the aura of party savior when all the other candidates look weak. This strategy may be obsolete today since early losses are almost fatal to a candidacy. When Gore sought the Democratic presidential nomination the first time, in 1988, he dropped out of the Iowa and New Hampshire contests in hopes of jump-starting his campaign in the southern primaries.
- Wait and see. Even though all modern nominations have been decided in the primaries and caucuses, a number of politicians have tried to sit on the sidelines in hopes of emerging as the consensus candidate after an indecisive primary season. Humphrey won the 1968 Democratic nomination after a divisive primary season without entering a single contest. The same strategy did not work for him in 1976.

As Carter's successful nomination campaigns in 1976 and 1980 illustrate, candidates may choose different strategies for different circumstances. Carter's 1976 victory was the product of a classic outsider strategy. In an astute 1972 memo, Carter aide Hamilton Jordan had urged the candidate to travel abroad extensively to build up foreign policy "experience," to get involved in national party politics, and to stress the fiscally austere programs of his governorship as a way of supplementing his "good guy brand of populism." Jordan wrote, "It will take more than the hand-shaking and the projection of the 'I understand the problems of the average man' image to put Carter over. This is still his greatest asset and it must still be projected but he will also have to convince the press, public, and politicians that he knows how to run a government." [142] Carter conducted an anti-Washington campaign based on his reputation as a leader of the "New South" and his appeals for the nation to heal the wounds of the Watergate scandal and the Vietnam War. By the time the media began scrutinizing his record as governor of Georgia, Carter had become a strong front-runner. The party's new proportional representation system for awarding delegates meant that Carter needed to win just ten of the last twenty-one primaries to secure a majority at the convention.

In contrast, Carter's 1980 nomination campaign followed a classic insider strategy. Carter consciously used the advantages of incumbency to line up the support of party and business leaders. He also successfully manipulated the primary and caucus calendar to his advantage. Carter staffers arranged for three southern states where Carter was strong—Alabama, Florida, and Georgia—to hold their primaries on March 11, which ensured a big sweep for the president. They also arranged to switch the date of Connecticut's primary from March 4 to March 25 to avoid a possible Kennedy sweep on March 4, the day Massachusetts—Kennedy's home state—was holding its primary.

Strategic Considerations

The campaign strategy a candidate selects will depend on a wide variety of considerations. These include the nature of the competition, the primary schedule, the candidate's fund-raising ability and endorsements, media requirements, and the mood of the electorate.

The Competition. A candidate who is successful in a one-on-one contest may find it difficult to play off a number of other candidates against each other. A liberal candidate may run well against a single conservative opponent in a Democratic primary but struggle to prevail in a field dominated by other liberals.

Going into the 1976 Democratic primaries, some experts rated Indiana senator Birch Bayh and Arizona representative Mo Udall as the top prospects for the nomination because they had strong liberal support. The candidates' combined 37.9 percent (Udall, 22.7 percent; Bayh, 15.2 percent) share of the New Hampshire primary vote was impressive, but the centrist Carter's 28.4 percent was enough to win the primary. Udall, Bayh, former Oklahoma senator Fred R. Harris, former Peace Corps director Sargent Shriver, Idaho senator Frank Church, and Gov. Jerry Brown of California split the liberal vote throughout the primaries. Carter received only 39 percent of the total primary vote, but he won the nomination because his opposition among liberals was fragmented. If Carter had faced a single liberal opponent with national political experience, he might have lost.

Bill Clinton became the favorite for the 1992 Democratic nomination when better-known candidates decided to stay out of the race. President George Bush's high approval ratings in 1991 discouraged nationally known figures such as New York governor Mario Cuomo, House Democratic leader Richard Gephardt, and senators Bill Bradley and Al Gore from entering the race.

The Stages of the Campaign. Candidates must compete in the early stages of the nomination campaign to gain the national visibility they need to continue their campaigns. For example, Colorado senator Gary Hart's nearly successful bid for the 1984 Democratic nomination was sustained in the later stages of the process by the burst of success he had at the beginning. But to actually win the nomination, candidates must have the funds to stay in the race long enough, despite defeats along the way, so that they can participate in the later primaries and caucuses.

Whatever strategy a candidate pursues, the early primary contests have a disproportionate influence on the shape of the campaign. Successes in Iowa and New Hampshire have transformed candidates from dark horses to front-runners in a matter of weeks, as measured in poll standings, endorsements, financial backing, and media coverage. If a leading candidate fails in these contests, his or her campaign faces a crisis.

In every recent election, all but two or three candidates have been forced to drop out after a few early contests because they could not finance a sustained drive. Gov. George Romney in 1968, Sen. Henry Jackson in 1976, and Sen. Phil Gramm in 1996 are among those who did not have the opportunity to bring their campaigns to more favorable turf because of early losses.

Once the early contests winnow out most candidates, the delegate count becomes the major focus of attention. A big victory can breathe new life into a moribund campaign, as Reagan's 1976 North Carolina victory over President Ford and Kennedy's 1980 Pennsylvania and New York victories over President Carter attest. But it is the delegate race that ultimately is important. Late surges of support are unlikely to undo the mathematics of cumulative delegate counts.

Fund-Raising Ability and Spending Strategies. One of the few measures of candidate strength in the preprimary stage of the campaign is fund raising. Financial disclosure reports to the Federal Election Commission are reported in the media as indicators of campaign progress.

Candidates face important decisions about how to allocate money—for example, whether to spend most of their funds early in the hope of making an electoral breakthrough (which in turn could bring a windfall of new contributions), or to spend frugally and extend the time in which they can make their case to the primary voters.

Generally, established candidates can afford to husband some of their resources for later primaries and caucuses. But newcomers to national politics can only gain political credibility with good showings in the early contests, and so they invest most of their resources in Iowa and New Hampshire. Such candidates do not focus on accumulating delegates for the national convention until they have established themselves with the media and financial contributors. Fred Harris, a long shot for the Democratic nomination in 1976, said: "If we could raise the money and we could do well in those early contests, then the delegates would take care of themselves as we got into the later contests. . . . Then you're going for delegates; the first [contests] you're not, you're just going for staying in it." [143]

Fund-raising success carries political risks, however. One is a false sense of security. Senator Kennedy's 1980 campaign was marked by profligate staff spending and poor planning that undercut the early momentum he derived from the fame of his family. Spending mistakes early in the race reduced the amount of money the campaign was legally permitted to use in the later stages. Similarly, Howard Dean's race to the front of the fund-raising pack in 2003 did not protect him against inefficient spending. Dean spent a great deal of money building organizations in states he never competed in, because his candidacy had collapsed before their contests rolled around.

Another risk is getting tagged as the candidate of special interests. In 1980 the lavish spending of former Treasury secretary John Connally aggravated voters' uneasiness about his independence from big business. Multimillionaire Steve Forbes's largely self-financed campaigns for the Republican nomination in 1996 and 2000 enjoyed sufficient resources to command the voters' attention but not to win their support.

Economic and Political Makeup of the States. Candidates are famous for donning hats and tee shirts and eating foods native to the region in which they campaign. But more important is the way the candidates fashion their rhetoric to each region.

Candidates, it is guaranteed, will discuss farm problems, energy costs, gun control, and trade issues in Iowa and New Hampshire. But the prevalence of farm and small-town concerns in those two states may bore or even alienate the rest of the electorate. Some observers have attributed widespread voter apathy during the early stages of the contest to the candidates' emphasis on the concerns of the smaller states. [144] The Democrats' decision to add early contests in 2008 in two more small states, Nevada and South Carolina, still leaves out the large states where most voters live.

Jimmy Carter forged a bond with the voters of Iowa and New Hampshire in 1976 based partly on the background he shared with them as farmers and rural dwellers. In contrast, Tennessee senator Al Gore developed problems in the 1988 New York primary when he became embroiled in the bitter racial politics of New York City. Gore was embraced by Mayor Edward I. Koch, who offended many

voters with his attacks on African American candidate Jesse Jackson.

As the primary calendar unfolds, the candidates' attention turns to industrial issues in the northern Rust Belt states and to defense and social issues in the southern states. Senator Kennedy's populist rhetoric on unemployment in New York and Pennsylvania produced important primary victories during his otherwise troubled bid for the 1980 Democratic nomination. [145] One of the reasons California advanced its primary from June to March was to force candidates to address the issues that concerned its voters.

Media Requirements. When Democratic senator Paul Simon of Illinois began his 1988 presidential campaign, analysts argued that his chances were poor not just because he was an old-fashioned New Deal liberal but also because of his frumpy appearance. A bookish man who wore horn-rimmed glasses and a bow tie, it was said, was not what media-saturated Democratic voters were seeking.

The conventional wisdom of contemporary presidential politics stresses cosmetic requirements in the media age. Citing John Kennedy and Ronald Reagan, some pundits argue that candidates need good looks to have a chance of creating widespread appeal. Others reason that a candidate must simply appear to be "presidential"—calm, sincere, knowledgeable, firm, gentle, and commanding.

Some analysts assert that Kennedy prevailed over Vice President Nixon in 1960 because of his appearance in the first presidential debate. On the black and white television screens of the time, Nixon looked pale and ill at ease, while Kennedy looked tan and serene. Polls showed that most people who heard the debate on radio thought that Nixon had won it. After President Reagan's landslide victory in the 1984 election, Democratic candidate Mondale complained that television required candidates to be masters of "the 20-second snip, the angle, the shtick, whatever it is." [146]

At a minimum, to compete in the primary process candidates require access to the media. Carter's foresight in making himself available in New York City for morning television programs like *Today* and *Good Morning America* after his 1976 Iowa caucus victory was a good example of a candidate recognizing the importance of the media in modern politics. In 1992 Clinton made a point of appearing on nontraditional television such as *The Arsenio Hall Show* and MTV. Spending on television commercials is the main reason for the tremendous increase in campaign costs in recent years. [147]

Strength of State Parties and Other Institutions. Until the 1970s state party organizations dominated the presidential nominating process. But in recent years the state parties have been overshadowed by candidate organizations and interest groups.

The leaders of state parties often are political executives—usually the governor or a big-city mayor. Executives control many of the patronage jobs and contracts that bind state and local parties together. Political parties tend to be organized hierarchically, with state leaders playing important roles in national party organizations. But because of the media-based nature of political campaigns, the rising power of interest groups, and changes in the rules for selecting presidential candidates, state party organizations have lost some of their influence on national politics.

State parties still play major roles in recruiting people for political activity, in organizing elections and government institutions, in providing cues for voters, and in clarifying and resolving some important policy issues. Because its main goal is to win elections for its candidates, the party is likely to compromise on specific issues. State parties also are concerned about the coattail effects of national campaigns. In some elections a strong presidential candidate can add as much as 5 percent to the vote of state candidates.[148]

In 1964 Goldwater recruited conservative loyalists to join and take over local and state party organizations. To the extent that he was successful, political amateurs replaced political professionals. Nelson Polsby and Aaron Wildavsky wrote: "The absence of central leadership on a state-by-state basis meant that delegates were freer to follow their personal preferences and also free to weigh ideological considerations more heavily than if they had been responsible to a leader who would suffer badly if Republicans were defeated for state offices. Similar considerations have affected Democrats in recent years." [149]

Endorsements. Voters sometimes judge candidates by the company they keep. Endorsements by prominent politicians, business and labor leaders, celebrities such as actors and athletes, and citizens organizations can lend credibility to a presidential candidate. But endorsements also can cause

trouble if they make the candidate appear beholden to narrow or unusually controversial interests.

The campaigns of Walter Mondale in 1984, Richard Gephardt in 1988, and Howard Dean in 2004 underscore the plusses and minuses of endorsement-based candidacies. Mondale secured the endorsements of labor unions, women's groups, and civil rights organizations.[150] These endorsements—and the volunteers and fund-raising capabilities that they brought—made him the front- runner and sustained his candidacy in a difficult race against Gary Hart. But they also gave Hart a line of attack against Mondale, whom Hart tagged as the candidate of the special interests.

Gephardt built his early viability in 1988 on his insider ties. He appeared on the steps of Capitol Hill to accept the endorsements of dozens of fellow House members. He also lined up support from several Democratic interest groups. Gephardt's rivals and the media called him a creature of "the system" who was beholden to special interests. After a victory in the Iowa caucuses, his campaign faltered.

Dean's candidacy was more complicated. He began his campaign for the 2004 Democratic nomination as a political outsider, championing his opposition to the Iraq war at a time when few other Democratic candidates were willing to take such a position. But after his candidacy caught fire at the grass-roots level in summer 2003, Dean sought and won endorsements from prominent party leaders such as defeated 2000 presidential nominee Al Gore. In doing so, however, he diluted his insurgent appeal, and he lost badly in the 2004 Iowa caucuses and New Hampshire primary.

"Covert endorsements" also can affect the nominating campaign. Strategists in the opposite party sometimes try to promote the candidate they regard as their easiest opponent. President Herbert Hoover maneuvered behind the scenes in 1932 to promote the Democratic candidacy of Franklin Roosevelt, whom he considered unprincipled and politically weak. But Hoover's calculation turned out to be spectacularly wrong.[151] Forty years later, the Nixon campaign ordered "dirty tricks" to damage Edmund Muskie's campaign and boost George McGovern's effort. Nixon's strategy helped to produce the desired effect: Muskie was driven out of the race early and McGovern won the nomination and proved a weak opponent to Nixon.

Grass-roots Organizations. In early 1975 Carter gained an advantage on his rivals for the 1976 Democratic nomination by campaigning extensively in Iowa almost a year before the caucuses. His surprise Iowa victory gave him the credibility he needed to win a string of primaries. George Bush pursued the same strategy in seeking the 1980 Republican nomination. His victory in Iowa made him Ronald Reagan's main competitor.

Intense organizing in Iowa did not work in 1988. A dozen presidential candidates concentrated early on the Iowa caucuses, spending more than a combined eight hun-

TABLE 5-8   **Party Identification, 1940–2004 (percent)**

Year	Republican	Democratic	Other
1940	38	42	20
1950	33	45	22
1960	30	47	23
1964	25	53	22
1968	27	46	27
1972	28	43	29
1976	22	45	33
1980	26	43	31
1984	31	40	29
1988	29	43	28
1992	29	36	35
1996	31	37	33
2001	32	34	34
2004	36	35	29

SOURCES: Gallup Polling Organization; Harold W. Stanley and Richard G. Niemi, *Vital Statistics on American Politics,* various editions (Washington, D.C.: CQ Press).

On the campaign trail in 1948, Republican presidential candidate Thomas Dewey lets himself be "kidnapped" by members of the Oregon Cavemen Club.

dred days in the state. Democratic representative Richard Gephardt of Missouri typified the candidates' concern with Iowa: he actually rented an apartment in the state and kept his family there to campaign when he was not able to be on hand. Gephardt won, but derived little momentum from his victory because political pundits attributed it to his being from a neighboring state.

In Iowa and New Hampshire, the candidates need local political operatives who know the political makeup of the state down to the precinct level. When Gary Hart and Joseph Biden dropped out of the Democratic race in 1987, other candidates scrambled to sign up their local organizers.

In the later primary states, where campaigns are dominated by media appeals instead of face-to-face campaigning, other aspects of grass-roots organizing become important. In particular, the candidates must develop ties to newspaper and broadcast journalists. The move from the intimate, "retail" politics of the early small-state contests to broad-based, "wholesale" politics requires a campaign organization to target its appeals to large blocs of voters, such as residents of nursing homes, religious organizations, and veterans groups.

The Tenor of the Electorate. A number of scholars have asserted that American history follows distinct cycles and that candidates must fashion appeals that correspond with the dominant mood of the electorate.

Political scientist Stephen Skowronek has presented his notion of "political time" in a sophisticated cyclical theory. Skowronek argues that presidential politics moves through three stages over an extended period of time: from "order-creating" to "order-affirming" to "order-shattering" before starting over with another period of "order-creating." Each stage contains the makings of the next. All presidents, then, must respond to the durable policies and ideas that their predecessors established and shape their initiatives in response to what went before.[152]

Another cyclical theorist is historian Arthur M. Schlesinger Jr., who has argued that politics swing from periods of government activism to periods of preoccupation with private interests and back again. Intervals of minimalist government include the late nineteenth century, the 1920s, the 1950s, and the years beginning with Nixon's election in 1968. Periods of activism include the Progressive Era of the early twentieth century, the New Deal Era, and the Kennedy and Johnson years.[153] Schlesinger's prediction that the 1990s would be an age of liberalism appeared to be refuted by massive distrust of government.[154]

Erwin C. Hargrove and Michael Nelson have argued that presidency-centered cycles of politics and policy move along three stages of policy change and implementation.[155] Government activism waxes and wanes depending on where the country is in the cycle of preparation, achievement, and consolidation.

Presidents of achievement include Woodrow Wilson, Franklin Roosevelt, Lyndon Johnson, and Ronald Reagan. Their activist administrations were ushered in by election victories in which the winning candidate promised great changes, won a landslide victory, and brought in many new members of Congress on his coattails. Once in office, these presidents spurred dramatic alterations in the role of the federal government in American society.

The presidents of achievement build on the groundwork laid by the presidents of preparation, who also campaign for political change but are elected with more modest mandates. During these administrations, policy proposals that have been percolating in the bureaucracy and in academic and political circles are raised to the top of the national political agenda by the president. The nation is not yet ready to accept broad-based policy changes but is being prepared by the president for an era of activism. Preparation presidents included Theodore Roosevelt, John Kennedy, and Jimmy Carter.

A president of consolidation weaves the president of achievement's innovations into the fabric of government. Even presidents who originally may have opposed programs for philosophical reasons will accept their political popularity and work to implement them well. The Republican presidents of the 1920s along with Dwight Eisenhower and Richard Nixon were in this category.

Past Electoral Performances and Electability. More than ever, candidates must demonstrate widespread voter appeal whether they are considered front-runners or underdogs. Candidates who enter the race with little national reputation need to perform better than their more famous rivals just to receive serious consideration by politicians, campaign professionals, political reporters, and financial donors.

In 1968 Nixon needed a series of primary victories to shed the loser image he had developed in his unsuccessful 1960 presidential and 1962 California gubernatorial campaigns. Because he had been out of office for almost eight years, Nixon faced widespread doubts about his electability. He eliminated those doubts with primary victories in New Hampshire, Wisconsin, Pennsylvania, Oregon, and New Jersey. Other strong contenders who had weak past political performances to overcome were Walter Mondale (who had dropped out of the 1976 campaign early) in 1984, George Bush (who lost the 1980 nomination campaign to Reagan) in 1988, Bob Dole (who lost to Reagan in 1980 and Bush in 1988) in 1996, and Al Gore (who lost to Dukakis in 1988) in 2000.

Running a good race, even in a losing effort, can set the stage for future success. For example, Reagan's string of primary victories in 1976 established him as a proven vote-getter in 1980. Arizona senator John McCain's strong run for the 2000 Republican nomination was unsuccessful, but it positioned him as an early front-runner to succeed George W. Bush—the candidate who had defeated him—in 2008.

Studies have indicated that some voters are so concerned about "wasting" their vote that electability is a major aspect of their decision making. Assertions about which candidate has the best chance of winning in November reverberate throughout the nominating process. Kerry's main appeal to anti-Bush Democratic voters in 2004 was that he was the most electable candidate in the race. The electability issue is most prominent toward the end of the primary season. The candidates each try to show the public, the media, and political professionals that they would do best against the likely nominee of the other party.

President Ford used the electability issue effectively against Reagan in 1976, and President Carter used it well against Senator Kennedy in 1980. Ford and Carter stressed polls that showed them leading the other party's possible nominees. They also argued that their party would suffer if it denied the nomination to a sitting president. As it turned out, both Ford and Carter were defeated in the general election.

The Complexity of Primary and Caucus Rules

The states have a wide variety of rules for ballot qualifications and allocation of delegates. When Colorado representative Patricia Schroeder announced that she would not seek the Democratic nomination in 1988, she cited the complexity of state rules as a major consideration. Because of these rules, which require lengthy study and early action by the candidates, a late-starting campaign is practically impossible, even for a longtime national figure. Candidates not only must meet all the legal requirements to qualify for state contests, but they also must adapt their campaigns to the state's strategic imperatives.

The states' rules differ on many aspects of the contest, including eligibility of nonparty members to vote in the primary or caucus, filing requirements and entry deadlines, allocation of delegates, stages in the selection of delegates, timing of the contests, and the choice of superdelegates.

Eligibility of Nonparty Members

Most states limit participation in primary and caucus voting to registered party members, but many welcome independents and members of the other party. When nonparty members participate, they usually sign a form stating that they would like to affiliate with the party.

"Open" primaries can have an important effect on the campaign. John Kennedy won the 1960 Democratic primary in Wisconsin largely on the basis of crossover Catholic Republican voters. Kennedy's victory dealt his opponent, Sen. Hubert Humphrey of Minnesota, a severe defeat because it came in a neighboring state. Alabama governor George Wallace won the 1972 Wisconsin Democratic primary with as many Republican as Democratic votes. Four years later, Reagan won a North Carolina primary victory over President Ford with the help of Democratic crossover voters. Open primary victories often are termed illegitimate by the losers because nonparty members are involved. The victors' response is that winning a broad base of support is essential to success in the general election.

Filing Requirements and Deadlines

The first step in the competition for delegates is to get on the ballot. Most states require petitions, filing fees, or both to get on the primary ballot. Other states leave the makeup of the ballot to state or party officials and committees.

The range of legal requirements that candidates must meet to put delegates on the ballot at the congressional district and state levels requires extensive planning. In 1984 Hart neglected to recruit delegate candidates in all states;

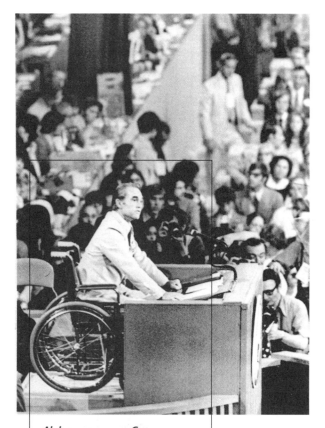

Alabama governor George Wallace explains his views of the Democratic platform to the party's delegates at the 1972 national convention.

allocated to the candidates in a number of ways. "Beauty contest" states use the vote simply as a measure of popular preferences for the candidates; the selection of delegates takes place later. A candidate who lacks strong support among party activists in the state could lose the majority of delegates after winning the primary.

Delegates are allocated at different levels. Some states require candidates to recruit delegates to run in each congressional district. Other states allow delegates to be recruited from anywhere in the state.

In some states, delegates are allocated proportionally according to each candidate's share of the popular vote. In 1976, 80 percent of Idaho's delegates were distributed proportionally to candidates who received at least 5 percent of the vote. In Kentucky, only the top four finishers with at least 15 percent of the vote received any delegates.[156] A number of other states use "bonus proportional representation" systems in which candidates receive delegate bonuses for winning congressional districts, in addition to a proportional allocation of delegates based on their overall share of the vote.

Winner-take-all primaries are now largely obsolete. Reformist Democrats were the first to do away with them, and Republicans eventually were compelled to follow suit because the law governing their primaries were enacted by Democrat-dominated state legislatures. In the past, winner-take-all contests sometimes provided big boosts for candidates. For example, Reagan's 1976 campaign against Ford was energized by winner-take-all victories in his home state of California and in Georgia, Montana, and Texas.[157] McGovern was boosted by a winner-take-all primary victory in California in 1972.

Candidates in some states compete at the congressional district level under a "loophole" winner-take-all system—so called because it avoids the bans on statewide winner-take-all primaries. In these states, a candidate who wins a plurality in every congressional district ends up winning all of the delegates in the state.

Stages of the Delegate-Selection Process

Caucus states select their delegates in several stages. Although the media sometimes convey the impression that party members select delegates when they vote in neighborhood caucuses, this stage of balloting is often just the start of the process.

In some caucus systems, successively smaller groups of party members meet several times before deciding which presidential candidates to support. This explains why candidates who appear to do well in the precinct caucuses sometimes end up with a smaller number of delegates than was first projected.

The multistage system is sensitive to fluctuations in candidate strength throughout the nominating process. In the 1988 Iowa precinct caucuses, for example, Rep. Richard

consequently, he received few delegates in later Democratic primaries in which he polled well. Hart's failure to field full slates of delegates was the price he paid for allocating his scarce political resources to the early stages of the campaign on the grounds that it would have been foolish to save them for the later primaries if his candidacy did not survive until then.

Allocation of Delegates

The various ways in which states allocate their delegates to the national convention constitute a major organizational concern for candidates. Systems for determining the number of delegates that a candidate receives in a primary or caucus are complicated and, if neglected, can deal major setbacks to a strong candidate. Moreover, understanding the different systems is crucial to allocating scarce campaign time and resources. If a candidate spends a lot of time in a state with a delegate-allocation system that favors his or her competitor, the results can be disastrous.

Party members in states with binding presidential preference systems vote directly for candidates, and delegates are

Gephardt of Missouri and Sen. Paul Simon of Illinois led a Democratic field of seven candidates. But before the delegate-selection process moved up to the county, congressional district, and state levels, Gephardt and Simon dropped out of the race. Massachusetts governor Michael Dukakis, who had finished third in the Iowa precinct caucuses, won most of Iowa's delegates.

Timing of State Nominating Contests

States follow various practices for scheduling state and presidential nominating contests. Some states schedule primaries for other offices to coincide with the presidential primary. Depending on the importance of the state and local contests, such a move could tilt the presidential campaign toward parochial concerns. The candidate's grasp of state politics becomes more important when the presidential and state primaries coincide.

Holding presidential and state primaries on the same day can cause trouble for some state politicians. Because the national conventions are held in the summer, a state's presidential primary or caucus must take place in the late winter or spring. Many state officials, however, favor an August or September primary for state offices. But the effect of separating the statewide and local contests from the presidential primaries usually is to reduce voter turnout in both selection processes.

Superdelegates

In 1984 the Democratic Party adopted a rule to include at its conventions a large bloc of uncommitted superdelegates—delegate positions reserved for elected officials and party officials. The purpose of the rule was to create a stronger link between the party's leaders and its presidential selection process.

The superdelegates were integral to former vice president Mondale's strategy in 1984. Mondale won the support of 450 of the 568 superdelegates—about 80 percent—compared with Hart's 62.[158] Mondale and his delegate-tracking team spent hours on the telephone courting the superdelegates, most of whom Mondale had known personally for years. Without their support, he may have fallen short of a majority at the convention. Gore's success in the 2000 primaries meant that he did not need the superdelegates to win the Democratic nomination, but they would have tried to deliver him the nomination if the need had arisen.

Who Votes in Primaries?

American presidential elections suffer from low turnout in both the nominating process and the general election. Less than one-fourth of all party members typically vote in primaries. Less than one-tenth participate in most caucuses. In the general election, only around half of the electorate turns out to vote.

Austin Ranney found in a study of competitive presidential primaries between 1948 and 1968 that the mean voter turnout was 39 percent. Ranney defined competitive primaries as those with two or more candidates in which no candidate got more than 80 percent of the vote. The mean turnout in such states was 28 percent in 1976—an eleven-point drop from the earlier average.[159]

Low turnout rates for nominating contests give the advantage to well-organized and well-staffed campaigns. Especially in caucuses—which demand more of party members than the simple act of voting in a primary—each candidate's ability to get supporters to the meetings takes on great importance. With a low overall turnout, strong support from certain blocs of voters—for example, seniors in Florida—could be tantamount to victory.

The unpredictability that low turnouts bring to primaries and caucuses can undo the best-laid plans of campaign strategists. Bad weather in Iowa and New Hampshire, for example, can undermine the efforts of candidates to get supporters to the polls. The controversy over the Vietnam War spurred antiwar students from around the country to become active in the 1968 New Hampshire primary.

Political scientist James Q. Wilson's study of the amateur political club movement of the 1950s suggests the kinds of party members whom presidential contenders must attract. The "amateur" is a political activist devoted to an issues-oriented, clean style of politics. Modern-day examples of amateurs include environmentalists, antiwar activists, and Christian conservatives. Amateurs are different from "professionals," party members who are concerned less with ideology and issues than with winning elections.[160]

The tug-of-war between amateurs and professionals shapes the nominating process from election to election. The strong performances of Barry Goldwater (1964), Eugene McCarthy (1968), George McGovern (1972), and Ronald Reagan (1976 and 1980) can be attributed to their appeal to the amateurs. The strong performances of Hubert Humphrey (1968), Gerald Ford (1976), Walter Mondale (1984), Bob Dole (1996), Al Gore (2000), George W. Bush (2000), and John F. Kerry (2004) can be attributed to their appeal to professionals.

Political scientists have found that primary and caucus participants tend to be more ideological than the rest of the party's supporters. To win the nomination, candidates must package their messages to make them acceptable to these activists, who tend to be very liberal in the Democratic Party and very conservative in the Republican Party. In recent years, for example, the Democratic Party has adopted liberal positions on civil rights, abortion, gay rights, and the environment in order to satisfy party activists. The Republican Party has taken conservative positions on these issues, as well as on taxes and military spending.

Besides appealing to the activists, candidates often stake out distinctive positions on one or two issues to distinguish themselves from their competitors. Tennessee senator Al Gore assumed a stronger posture on defense issues than his Democratic rivals in 1988. John McCain promoted campaign finance reform in his battle for the Republican nomination in 2000.

Centrist candidates, however, sometimes succeed in primary contests. In 1976 Carter won the nomination when several opponents split the liberal vote among themselves. On the Republican side, President Ford withstood a strong challenge from former California governor Reagan to win the nomination. Reagan's campaign was based on conservative complaints about détente with the Soviet Union and the negotiation of a treaty to cede control of the Panama Canal to Panama.

Nominating Campaign Issues, Polls, and Organizations

Modern presidential nominating campaigns are built on a three-legged stool of issues, polls, and organizations. Issues are what set the candidates apart from each other. Polls help a candidate to define the issues and identify the groups of voters most receptive to the candidate's positions. Organizations hold the campaign together and give continuity to the candidate's efforts to gather the most votes by addressing the issues most effectively.

Issues

The "spatial model" of politics helps explain the way presidential candidates approach issues. Economist Anthony Downs and others have argued that the nominating process pulls candidates away from the political center and toward the ideological extremes. The general election battle between the two parties then pulls the candidates back toward the center.

According to this model, candidates search for their party's ideological midpoint during the nominating contest. Each party's midpoint is off-center from that of the entire electorate—to the right for Republicans, to the left for Democrats. In the general election, candidates have to move away from their party's midpoint and toward the national midpoint to attract wide support. Presumably, the candidates will retain the support of the more ideological party members when moving to the center because these party members have no better choice.[161]

In 1976 Democrat Jimmy Carter staved off late challenges by liberals Frank Church and Jerry Brown by moving to the left. Carter's proposals for a national health system and full employment allayed suspicions among his party's liberals. But once the fall campaign began, Carter shifted back to more conservative themes, such as government reorganization and federal deficit reduction. Even so,

Democratic voters stood behind Carter because his views were more compatible with theirs than those of the more conservative Republican candidate, Gerald Ford.

Ronald Reagan moderated many of his emphases in the 1980 general election campaign after winning the Republican nomination with a strongly conservative appeal. Reagan rebutted President Carter's charges that he would dismantle important social welfare programs such as Social Security and Medicare. He also reframed his call for a military buildup, saying that it would make arms negotiations more productive rather than simply enable the United States to be more assertive in world affairs.

The spatial model, however, obscures a number of elements of the general election campaign dynamic. Often it is more important to keep appealing to activists in the party than to abandon them for centrist voters. In 1960, for example, the efforts of Massachusetts senator John Kennedy in behalf of jailed civil rights leader Martin Luther King Jr. solidified Kennedy's support among African Americans and liberals. In 1980 Republican Reagan found he was able to broaden his overall support by making strongly conservative statements on selected issues. Christian conservative groups such as the Moral Majority—which called for a constitutional ban on abortion, reinstatement of prayer in public schools, and policies to restore the traditional family—brought to the polls people who had never voted. These groups' efforts did not alienate centrist voters who were more concerned about the economy and foreign policy.[162] Bill Clinton's appeal to social conservatives in 1992 on issues such as the death penalty and welfare reform undermined President Bush's hold on those centrist voters who had voted Republican in recent elections.

Whenever possible, a candidate will try to appeal both to party activists and to the general public with ambiguous statements. Clinton's stance on abortion in 1992—he personally opposed abortion but believed it should be "safe, legal, and rare"—was designed to appeal to all sides of the divisive issue. In 2000 George W. Bush appealed both to the center and the right with his theme of "compassionate conservatism."

Polls

Polling data are used extensively during the nominating campaign. Journalists, campaign professionals, and financial contributors use polls to assess the political viability of the various campaigns. Candidate-conducted polls are central to the internal strategies of campaigns, helping candidates to understand which issues and personal qualities are important to voters and which ways of phrasing their positions are most effective.

During the 1930s and 1940s, campaign polling consisted of simple snapshots showing which candidate was ahead and which was behind. In 1952 Republican presidential can-

Pollster Patrick Caddell, left, worked closely with Carter in campaigns and in the White House.

paign on university towns, blue-collar workers, and the young professionals living near the southern border of the state. In 1976 Jimmy Carter followed Caddell's advice and concentrated on the southern and middle parts of Florida in his important primary win over George Wallace.

In the 1984 election, campaigns began using a process pioneered by the advertising industry: instant polling to determine the effect on voters of specific candidate performances. Selected groups of voters watched the candidates' debate and registered their feelings from moment to moment by adjusting knobs on a handheld device. The knobs indicated whether their response was "positive" or "negative" toward each of a candidate's specific statements or actions. Campaign analysts could then tabulate and analyze the reactions.

didate Dwight Eisenhower used polling data to develop themes for television advertising and to target specific socioeconomic groups for appeals. In 1958 John Kennedy hired Louis Harris to conduct polls in several important presidential primary states to help him prepare for a possible presidential candidacy in 1960. Kennedy's concern that his Catholicism would be a political liability and his decision to treat mostly Protestant West Virginia as an important primary state both stemmed from Harris's polls.

President Lyndon Johnson and several other candidates in 1964 used extensive "image" polling to determine that Sen. Barry Goldwater's chief liability was the widespread perception that he was an ideological extremist with a dangerous tendency to act without thinking. After New York governor Nelson Rockefeller hammered away at this perception in his primary campaign against Goldwater, Johnson picked up the theme in the general election.

In more recent years, polling has moved beyond broad-brush portraits of the electorate to sophisticated geographic, ethnic, and lifestyle breakdowns. Polling is one of the most expensive elements of a modern campaign because campaigns now receive information on the economic, ethnic, religious, geographic, educational, occupational, behavioral, lifestyle, purchasing, and residential characteristics of many groups and how those characteristics affect attitudes about a wide range of issues.

In attaining his surprising second-place finish in the 1972 New Hampshire primary, George McGovern followed pollster Patrick Caddell's advice and concentrated his cam-

Nominating Campaign Organizations

The modern campaign is dominated by professional, technically proficient staffs with loyalties more to the candidate and to their own careers than to the party as a whole. Because presidential candidates are able to appeal to activist voters in primaries and caucuses, they no longer need to rely on state party leaders. The nomination campaign turns on how successfully candidates fashion and transmit their messages to blocs of likely voters and how well the candidates' organizations get those voters to the polls or to caucus meetings.

Perhaps the most important stage of any campaign is the early recruitment of campaign professionals, such as fund-raisers, strategists, pollsters, speechwriters, media advisers, Web site designers, issues experts, delegate rules experts, and volunteer coordinators. Political reporters carefully monitor the shaping of each candidate's staff, treating it as the first indication of the campaign's viability.

Clinton became a viable contender for the 1992 Democratic nomination when he attracted renowned fundraiser Robert Farmer and strategists such as James Carville, Paul Begala, George Stephanopoulos, and Stanley Greenberg. Having worked in several national campaigns, these individuals offered technical prowess as well as a populist orientation in a year when voter dissatisfaction with Washington was boiling over.

Almost every aspect of a campaign is now scripted by professionals. Aides determine the "theme of the day" for the nonstop campaign and brief the candidate between stops about the day's events and issues. Not since Adlai Stevenson in 1956 have major candidates written their own speeches.[163]

Campaign professionals are a well-defined, if transient, lot. Most rise to the top by working in congressional or gubernatorial elections and then, after a period of "candidate shopping," hitch up with a presidential effort. William Henkel, the head of President Reagan's advance team in 1984, had done similar work for Nixon and Ford in previous elections. Howard Druckman, the head of Mondale's 1984 advance team, began working on presidential campaigns with Edmund Muskie's 1972 effort.

Many political professionals have become legendary figures because of their ability to shape a campaign. Among the more prominent campaign strategists of recent years are John Sears (Nixon, 1968), Gary Hart (McGovern, 1972), Hamilton Jordan (Carter, 1976), Patrick Caddell (McGovern, 1972; Carter, 1976), Oliver Henkel (Hart, 1984), Ed Rollins (Reagan, 1984), Lee Atwater (Bush, 1988), James Carville (Clinton, 1992), and Karl Rove (Bush, 2000 and 2004).

The importance of campaign professionals is underscored by the campaigns that fail to organize adequately. After victories in Florida and Michigan, George Wallace was ineligible to compete in the 1972 winner-take-all California primary because he had missed the state's filing deadline. Four years later, Rep. Mo Udall was left off the Indiana Democratic ballot because he fell fifteen signatures short of the petition requirement in one congressional district. In 1984 Hart did not receive all the delegates that his electoral performance entitled him to in several states because he had failed to recruit slates of delegates. Because Jesse Jackson made the same mistake that year, Walter Mondale's well-organized campaign won more delegates than it ordinarily would have been entitled to.

Candidate Debates

Because of the central importance of primaries in the nominating process, and the tendency of the parties to have large fields of contenders, voters and political pundits have come to rely on debates to help sort out the candidates. Especially in the early stages of a campaign, debates are important because they offer the only events at which the candidates can be compared.

Debates among each party's presidential contenders have been significant events in most of the nominating campaigns since 1980. The 1980 debates in Iowa and New Hampshire were crucial turning points in the Republican nominating process. Reagan became vulnerable in Iowa when he refused to debate his opponents: he fell from 50 percent to 26 percent in the polls between December and the day after the January 5 debate that he ducked. In contrast, Reagan's assertiveness in the 1980 Nashua, New Hampshire, debate gave his campaign an important lift. Reagan invited all the other Republican candidates to join a scheduled one-on-one debate between him and Bush. When Bush resisted including the others and debate moderator Jon Breen ordered Reagan's microphone cut off, Reagan, misstating

Breen's name, declared angrily, "I paid for this microphone, Mr. Green." The righteous declaration won applause for Reagan and made Bush appear stiff and unyielding. Reagan, who had lost the Iowa caucuses, won the New Hampshire primary.

The 1984 Democratic debates first chipped away at Mondale's status as front-runner, then dealt a devastating blow to Hart. Mondale's mocking of Hart's "new ideas" campaign with an allusion to the punchline of a popular television commercial—"Where's the beef?"—left Hart on the defensive in a major Atlanta debate. In 1992 Clinton showed his mastery of policy minutiae in his debate appearances. Clinton's performance in a face-to-face, unmoderated debate with Brown on the *Donahue* television show helped to dispel the notion that his experience as a small-state governor did not qualify him to be president. In 2000 Gore showed unexpected vitality in a debate with rival Sen. Bill Bradley before a largely African American audience. His performance helped allay Democratic fears that Gore was too stiff and formal to wear well with the voters.

National Party Conventions

The first national party nominating convention was held by the Anti-Masons, a short-lived third party, in Baltimore, Maryland, in September 1831. (*See "Third Parties," p. 324.*) With 116 delegates attending from thirteen states, the convention nominated William Wirt for president and Amos Ellmaker for vice president. During the next eight months, the two major parties followed suit with conventions of their own. In December the National Republicans held a convention and nominated Henry Clay and John Sergeant, and in May 1832 the Democrats convened to renominate President Andrew Jackson and to add Martin Van Buren to the ticket. With that election, the convention system was born. It has remained in place ever since, even though conventions have changed in function and declined in importance in recent years

Convention Sites

Baltimore proved to be a popular spot for the first conventions. From 1831 to 1852, ten conventions (including the Democratic Party's first six) were held there, partly because of the city's relatively central location. Most other popular convention cities of this era (such as Harrisburg, Philadelphia, and Pittsburgh, all in Pennsylvania) met that criterion as well, although Buffalo, New York, hosted the northern-based Liberty Party in 1843 and Free Soil Party in 1848.

The choice of convention sites after 1856 reflected the country's expansion westward. For the past century and a half, Chicago has been the most popular choice: it had hosted twenty-five major party conventions by 2004. Cincinnati and St. Louis were two other popular sites in the latter 1800s.

At the Republican convention in Chicago in May 1860, Abraham Lincoln won the nomination and went on to become the first Republican president. From 1856 to 2004 Chicago hosted twenty-five conventions, the most of any city.

Corporate underwriting of national conventions ended in 1972 when it was discovered that an antitrust suit against International Telephone and Telegraph (ITT) had been settled in ITT's favor by the Justice Department shortly after the Sheraton Corporation (an ITT subsidiary) offered to supply $400,000 worth of services to the Republicans if they held their 1972 convention in San Diego. The revelation forced the party to move its convention to Miami Beach.

Campaign finance legislation passed in the wake of the Nixon administration's Watergate scandal prohibited corporate funding of conventions and provided for each national party to receive $2.2 million from the government to finance its convention. Although that amount has increased to reflect inflation ($14.6 million for each major party in 2004), it is still far less than is needed to fund a convention. As a result, the Federal Election Commission has loosened its restrictions by allowing private businesses to offer services, such as free hotel accommodations, as long as the other party receives comparable benefits. The FEC also allowed state and local governments to offer a number of services free of charge, including security and the use of a convention hall.

The choice of a convention city also depends on the facilities that are available. Conventions require 20,000 or more hotel and motel rooms to house delegates, party officials, journalists, television crews, and the candidates' staffs. The city also needs a convention hall large enough to seat delegates and accommodate the media, including space for overhead booths for the television networks.

Security considerations play a major role in the choice of a convention site. New York hosted Democratic conventions in 1976, 1980, and 1992 and the Republican convention in 2004 only after state and city officials offered to provide extraordinary security measures. President Nixon approved Miami Beach for the Republican convention in 1972 when he was assured that antiwar protesters would be kept at bay.

Political strategy is an important factor in convention planning. Republicans portrayed the 1984 Democratic convention in San Francisco as a radical and un-American spectacle. San Francisco's liberal social environment, said convention orator Jeane Kirkpatrick, was emblematic of the "blame America first" mentality of the Democratic Party. Democrats selected Atlanta as their 1988 convention site as part of a strategy to appeal to moderate voters and get away from the liberal image of San Francisco. In 1992 the GOP selected Houston in an appeal for the state's thirty-two elec-

Until recently, the South seldom was chosen to host a convention. In 1860 the Democrats held a tumultuous convention in Charleston, South Carolina, that ultimately deadlocked, forcing a second convention to be held in Baltimore. The Democrats did not hold another southern convention until 1928, when Houston, Texas, was chosen as a gesture to appease southerners who, party leaders knew, would be unhappy with the nomination of Al Smith, an anti-Prohibition Catholic from New York. The Republicans did not hold their first southern convention until 1968. In 1988, however, both parties held their conventions in the South—the Democrats in Atlanta and the Republicans in New Orleans. California has also become a popular convention setting. The Republicans met in San Diego in 1996, and the Democrats held their 2000 convention in Los Angeles.

At some point, the desire for a central location gave way to a more pressing need: money. For a time, the major consideration in choosing a convention site was the amount of money that cities offered to the national party committee in cash and services. By 1968 contributions from cities were approaching $1 million. Local economies get a significant boost from the influx of thousands of conventioneers and journalists into their cities. Illinois officials estimated that the 1996 Democratic convention in Chicago would provide a $100 million boost to the local economy. Chicago won the right to host the event by offering Democrats a package of incentives worth $32 million.[164]

toral votes and as a tribute to its adopted son, President George Bush. The Democrats selected Chicago for the 1996 convention partly to appeal to the party's base in the industrial heartland.

The choice of a site often serves as a gesture to a particular part of the country or reflects the personal preference of an incumbent president running for reelection. Ronald Reagan, for example, wanted to have Dallas selected as the site of the 1984 Republican convention because of the support he had received from Texas conservatives in 1976 and 1980. An unwritten rule holds that when the race for the party nomination is wide open, states with candidates cannot host the convention. An exception was the 2004 Democratic convention, which was held in Boston, the capital of John Kerry's home state of Massachusetts.

The choice of a site may symbolize a theme that the party wishes to convey. The Republicans met in Detroit in 1980 to counteract the party's image of being unconcerned about the nation's inner cities. The selection also was intended to depict Detroit as "a back-from-trouble renaissance city, much as the GOP sees itself as a party restored to health." [165] In 2004 the GOP not only selected New York to remind voters of President Bush's strong response to the September 11, 2001, attack on the World Trade Center, but also held its convention in early September—weeks later than conventions are usually scheduled—to underscore the reminder.

A city usually is chosen more than a year before the convention by a committee of a dozen or so party members appointed by the national chair, although incumbent presidents have as large a say in choosing the site as they want. The national party committee officially announces the convention's dates and site, and then appoints its officers and committees.

Delegates

Setting the number of votes that each state delegation will have at the national convention is one of the most important parts of the formal call to the convention. This apportionment of votes originally coincided with the number of votes each state had in the electoral college, which in turn was determined by the size of the state's congressional delegation. From the beginning, however, states often sent more delegates to the convention than the number of their electoral votes allowed. In 1848 the Democrats tried without success to limit the actual voting power of each state delegation to its electoral college vote, regardless of the number of delegates sent by the state. In an effort to deal with the problem of extra delegates, the Democrats passed a rule in 1852 giving every state twice as many delegates as it had electoral votes, with each delegate receiving a half vote. To do away with fractional votes, the total number of votes was doubled in 1872, giving each delegate a whole vote. [166]

From its first convention in 1856, the Republican Party also followed a system of apportionment that roughly corresponded to the electoral college. The GOP gave each state six at-large delegates, plus three delegates for each congressional district. This was changed in 1860 to four at-large delegates, plus two delegates for each congressional district.

Both parties, then, followed a system that allocated convention delegates mainly according to population rather than their voting strength in each state. That system of apportionment came under attack after the Civil War with the rise of one-party states. In such states, a minority party, such as the Republicans in the post-Reconstruction South, would be overrepresented at the GOP convention. Since 1972 the Republicans have followed a complicated formula that gives each state six at-large delegates, three delegates for each congressional district, a number of delegates equal to 60 percent of the state's electoral vote total (rounded up), four-and-a-half bonus delegates if the Republican ticket carried the state in the last presidential election, one bonus delegate for each Republican senator, one bonus delegate for a House delegation that is at least one-half Republican, and one bonus delegate for states with a Republican governor. In addition, the party awards fourteen delegates to the District of Columbia, eight to Puerto Rico, and four each to Guam and the Virgin Islands. The GOP rule also ensures states that they will receive at least as many convention votes as they had in the previous election. [167]

The Democrats did not institute a bonus system until 1944. For that year's convention they simply awarded two bonus delegates to each state that the party had carried in the last presidential election. The number of bonus delegates was increased to four in 1948. Since then, the Democrats have used a variety of delegate allocation formulas. Beginning in 1972, they used a formula that based nearly half of a state's voting strength at the convention on its Democratic vote in the last three presidential elections. The other measure of voting strength was based on the state's electoral votes. [168]

The number of delegates attending national conventions has increased dramatically. The first convention, held by the Anti-Masons in 1831, boasted 116 delegates. The Democratic convention the next year had 283. In 1856 the first Republican convention was attended by 567 delegates. By the early 1900s, both major party conventions had approximately 1,000 delegates. That number remained fairly stable until the 1950s, when the Democratic Party began to increase participation in its national convention.

In 1956 the Democrats allowed states to send delegates on a "half-vote" basis. Under that system, states could send twice as many delegates to cast the same number of votes. Between 1952 and 1956, the number of Democratic delegates increased from 1,642 to 2,477. At the same time, the number of delegate votes began increasing as well. This

With a national party's presidential nominee determined by primaries, modern conventions have become carefully choreographed television productions aimed at the successful marketing of the presidential ticket.

increase initially reflected the use of bonus delegates but later was spurred by the Democrats' greater democratization of their conventions in the aftermath of the party's post-1968 reforms. Thus the number of delegate votes at Democratic conventions increased to 3,331 in 1980. In 2004, 3,520 regular delegates and 802 superdelegates—a total of 4,322—cast votes at the Democratic convention.

The size of the Republican conventions has not increased quite so dramatically. Nevertheless, party reforms in the early 1970s provided for a 60 percent increase in delegate strength. As a result, the number of delegates at the Republican convention rose from 1,348 in 1972 to 2,259 in 1976.[169] By 2000 the number of Republican delegates had fallen slightly to 2,066. The number of delegates in 2004, however, was a record-high 2,509.

Preconvention Committees

Three major committees carry out the preparatory work of the national convention: credentials, rules, and platform. These committees traditionally meet before the start of the national convention, usually during the week before it begins. More recently, the Democrats have begun holding committee sessions several weeks before the convention.

The Credentials Committee reviews all disputes concerning the credentials of delegates to the convention. Before the convention begins, the committee receives a list of the delegates from each state. It then holds hearings on any challenges to those delegates (usually based on the procedures by which they were chosen) and offers its recommendation about which delegates should be seated to the convention, which makes the final decision on the matter. Such disputes usually involve rival delegations for the same seats. If a challenge is found valid, the committee may seat the competing delegation.

When there is a close presidential nominating contest, the Credentials Committee can influence which candidate is nominated. A notable instance was the 1912 Republican convention when President William Howard Taft was locked in a bitter nomination battle with former president Theodore Roosevelt. Roosevelt's forces contested 254 pro-Taft delegates, but the Credentials Committee recommended that all but nineteen of them be seated. The convention upheld that recommendation, virtually guaranteeing Taft's renomination.

A similar battle occurred in 1952 in the contest between Dwight Eisenhower and Ohio senator Robert A. Taft (the son of William Howard Taft) for the Republican nomination. Like his father in 1912, Taft controlled the party machinery. In the Credentials Committee, Eisenhower supporters contested sixty-eight pro-Taft delegates from Georgia, Louisiana, and Texas. The committee recommended that they be seated, but the convention overturned the recommendation. Eisenhower went on to win the nomination.

The credentials challenge with the greatest long-term consequences occurred at the 1964 Democratic convention in Atlantic City. The Mississippi Freedom Democratic Party (MFDP), a new and racially integrated organization formed at a time when African Americans were not allowed to vote in the state's presidential primary, demanded to be seated at the convention. MFDP's delegates had been selected in a state convention that was open to all Mississippians. Civil rights leaders Martin Luther King Jr. and James Farmer, among others, testified for the insurgents in nationally televised hearings of the Credentials Committee. After nervous negotiations involving President Johnson, Minnesota senator Hubert Humphrey, civil rights lawyer Joseph Rauh, and MFDP members, convention officials agreed to give the MFDP two "at-large" seats and require that Mississippi send integrated convention delegations in the future. The MFDP contingent rejected the compromise and went home. The drama, which enlivened an otherwise placid convention, attracted national attention to the growing voting rights movement. By the time of the 1968 convention, Mississippi and other Deep South states had opened their delegations to African Americans.

The Rules Committee is responsible for proposing the operating rules of the convention. Until 1972 the Democratic Party did not have a formal set of rules that it retained from convention to convention. Instead, the party's rules evolved in an ad hoc fashion, although many rules from the previous convention invariably were readopted. In contrast, Republican rules were strictly codified.

Among the most controversial rules used in the past by the Democrats were the "two-thirds" rule and the "unit" rule. The two-thirds rule required that any nominee for president or vice president receive a two-thirds majority of the convention vote. Because the two-thirds rule made it harder to win the nomination, protracted balloting was commonplace. The Republican Party, which has always nominated by simple majority, has had just one convention in its entire history that required more than 10 ballots. (They needed 36 ballots in 1880.) In contrast, the Democratic Party had seven such conventions during the life of the two-thirds rule: 49 ballots in 1852, 17 in 1856, 59—spread over two conventions—in 1860, 22 in 1868, 46 in 1912, 43 in 1920, and 103 in 1924.

Proposals were introduced to abolish the two-thirds rule in the wake of the 103-ballot 1924 marathon convention and again in 1932 by supporters of Franklin Roosevelt, who feared that he might not be able to gather all the votes necessary to win the nomination. At Roosevelt's urging, and despite considerable opposition, the Democrats finally eliminated the two-thirds rule at their 1936 convention. The South, in particular, objected to the change because the two-thirds rule had given that region a virtual veto over any nominee at a time when southerners found it politically impossible to nominate presidential candidates from their region. To make up for that loss, southern state delegations were granted more votes at later conventions.

The unit rule allowed the majority of a state delegation at the Democratic convention to cast all of the delegation's votes for the candidate or position supported by a majority of the state's delegates. (This rule was never used by the Republicans.) Proponents of the unit rule argued that it muted conflict within the party by overriding dissident minorities, and therefore strengthened state party organizations. Opponents argued that the rule was undemocratic. Conceivably, a candidate with a minority of the delegates could win the nomination by controlling the votes of a narrow majority of the dozen or so largest state delegations. In 1968 the Democratic Rules Committee recommended that the unit rule be repealed, and the convention adopted its recommendation.

Actions by the Rules Committee can influence the outcome of a convention. In 1976 Reagan announced his intention to nominate Pennsylvania senator Richard Schweiker as his running mate if he won the Republican presidential nomination, then proposed a rules change to force his opponent, Ford, to offer his own nominee. Reagan, who entered the convention trailing Ford slightly, hoped he might be able to win enough delegates alienated by Ford's choice for vice president to secure the nomination. But Ford supporters voted down the rules change, and Ford went on to become the Republican nominee.

The so-called "bound delegate" rule required delegates to vote according to their pledge at the time they were selected. The rule was the subject of a major fight at the 1980 Democratic convention. President Carter supported the rule because it bound the majority of delegates who had been chosen to support him. Carter's rival, Senator Kennedy, fought to overturn the rule in the hope that some of those delegates would transfer their support to him if they could. The Carter forces won the rules fight and the nomination.

The Platform Committee is responsible for presenting a proposed platform, or statement of party principles and promises, to the convention for its approval. Because party leaders want to mute conflict within the party and appeal to as wide a range of voters as possible, platforms seldom have much punch. Wendell Willkie, the Republican nominee in 1940, called them "fusions of ambiguity." Nevertheless, platforms sometimes cause bitter fights. The addition of a strong civil rights plank to the 1948 Democratic platform provoked opposition from southern states and prompted the Mississippi delegation and thirteen members of the Alabama delegation to walk out. Some of the disgruntled southerners and their supporters then formed their own party—the States' Rights Democratic Party, or the Dixiecrats—who held a convention in Birmingham, Alabama, and nominated South Carolina governor J. Strom Thurmond for president and Mississippi governor Fielding L. Wright for vice president.

Platforms offer interest groups a welcome opportunity to influence the parties. Dozens of groups typically appear before each party's platform committee. Most groups focus their appeal on the party that offers them greater access and a friendlier ear. They especially want the support of the party's likely nominee, except in circumstances when working with the underdog candidate enables them to make a splash at the convention. About one-fifth of all interest groups who testify before platform committees take the "even money approach" and appeal to both parties.[170]

Since 1852 most conventions have adopted the platform before nominating their candidates. As a result, platform fights can serve as another indicator of the relative strength of rival candidates, especially when those candidates hold different ideological positions. Platform fights also can signal divisions within the party that may prove fatal in the general election. Such was the case for the Democrats in 1968, when the convention fought bitterly over the party's platform plank on Vietnam. In recent years, the parties have made it more difficult to challenge the platform committee's recommendations.

Convention Officers

A national party convention is called to order by the party's national committee chair, who presides until a temporary convention chair is appointed. The temporary chair then wields the gavel until the convention approves the recommended slate of candidates for permanent officers. During the first half of the twentieth century, the temporary chair served as the keynote speaker at the convention. It also was traditional that the temporary chair be a senator. Since 1952, when Gen. Douglas MacArthur delivered the keynote address at the Republican convention, the keynote speaker usually has been someone other than the temporary chair. And in recent years, the tradition of appointing a senator to be temporary chair has been less frequently observed.

The permanent chair usually is appointed on the second day of the convention, but the national committee's choice for the post is announced before the convention begins. He or she invariably is approved by the convention with no contest. The permanent chair presides while the platform is adopted and during the actual nominating procedure. Thus the permanent chair may be in a position to make strategic rulings that can help or hinder particular candidates. Indeed, the permanent chair is often described as the most important officer of the convention.[171]

In the late 1800s and early 1900s, prominent state and local political leaders usually filled the post of permanent chair. Beginning in the 1930s, however, it became customary for the party's leader in the House of Representatives to serve as permanent chair. In 1972 the Democrats undermined that custom by requiring that the position alternate every four years between men and women.

Prenomination Oratory and Films

H. L. Mencken once wrote that convention orators are "plainly on furlough from some home for extinct volcanoes."[172] Oratory—and lots of it—plays a major role at national party conventions. During much of the behind-the-scenes maneuvering and unfinished committee work that takes place during the early phase of the convention, speeches are a way of filling time. They also are a means of staking out positions on important rules or platform planks, rallying support for candidates, or reestablishing unity at the end of a bitter convention.

During most recent conventions, at which the identity of the nominee has been known for weeks or even months, the main purpose of the speeches has been to persuade the television audience of the nominee's virtues. A secondary

Cartoonist Rube Goldberg's view of convention speeches reflects the popular opinion.

purpose has been to present an appealing image of the party to the voters.

One of the major speeches at every convention is the keynote address, usually delivered on the first day. This address is preceded and followed by many other words: the call to order; the invocation; addresses by party notables, including former presidents; the reading of committee reports; entertainment; nominating speeches; and acceptance speeches.

Keynote speakers typically are chosen for their oratorical skills since they are there to whip up enthusiasm among the delegates. Before the age of television, keynote addresses often lasted well over an hour.

Until the 1950s, the temporary chair of the convention customarily delivered the keynote address, but in recent years that honor has fallen to someone else. In both parties, current or former governors have been popular choices as keynoters (Reubin Askew, Frank Clement, Mario Cuomo, Paul Dever, Daniel Evans, Thomas Kean, Zell Miller, Harold Stassen, Earl Warren). Others have been current or former senators (Howard Baker, Evan Bayh, Bill Bradley, Frank Church, Phil Gramm, Mark Hatfield, Daniel Inouye, Richard Lugar, John Pastore), military and space heroes (John Glenn, Douglas MacArthur, Colin Powell), or women

(Anne Armstrong, Barbara Jordan twice, Katherine Ortega, Ann Richards). In 2000, for the first time, both parties chose African Americans as their keynoters, Colin Powell for the Republicans and Rep. Harold E. Ford Jr. for the Democrats.

Keynote addresses offer well-known political figures an opportunity to set the tone for the upcoming campaign, and for emerging political figures an opportunity to distinguish themselves. Ann Richards, the Texas state treasurer, delivered a memorable keynote at the 1988 Democratic convention. "Poor George," Richards thundered in a twangy Texan accent, "he can't help it. He was born with a silver foot in his mouth." [173] The delegates roared approval at her mockery of Bush's privileged background. Two years later, Richards was elected governor of Texas. But in 1994 the Bush family had the last laugh. Bush's son, George W. Bush, defeated Richards in her bid for reelection.

Much convention oratory is neither riveting nor profound. More often than not, the delegates pay scant attention to the speakers. But in the millions of words that have poured forth from national conventions, a few have struck a chord and galvanized a convention. Often the phrases live on, such as Franklin Roosevelt's promise of a "new deal" in his 1932 acceptance speech and the coinage of the term "G. I. Joe" by Clare Booth Luce in an address to the Republican convention in 1944. George Bush's acceptance speech promise, "Read my lips: No new taxes," helped him to win the 1988 election, but it came back to haunt him when he raised taxes in 1990.

Perhaps the greatest convention speech of all occurred in 1896 when William Jennings Bryan, a young leader of the Nebraska delegation, stunned the Democratic national convention with what has become known as his "Cross of Gold" speech. By the end of the convention Bryan was the party's nominee for president. The speech evolved out of the platform fight over whether the United States should maintain the gold standard or allow the unlimited coinage of silver. Bryan's speech was instrumental in leading the convention to a prosilver stance. Throughout the speech, which was delivered before the days of microphones, Bryan held some twenty thousand spectators spellbound. He later recalled that the vast crowd would "rise and sit down as one man" as it responded to his oratory.[174]

Couching his appeal for the free coinage of silver as a fight for "the struggling masses," Bryan intoned, "We have petitioned, and our petitions have been scorned. We have entreated, and our entreaties have been disregarded. We have begged, and they mocked when our calamity came. We beg no longer, we entreat no more, we petition no more. We defy them." And from the floor of the convention hall, the thousands echoed: "We defy them." In the hush that fell back over the hall as Bryan spoke, he concluded, "We will answer their demand for a gold standard by saying to them: You shall not press down upon the brow of labor this crown of thorns, you shall not crucify mankind upon a cross of gold." [175]

In recent years, both parties have supplemented convention oratory with films, most of them devoted to introducing the candidates in carefully produced packages of propaganda. Like other aspects of modern campaigns, the films have become more professional in recent years. For example, the biographical films of Bush in 1988 and Clinton in 1992 spun tales of the American dream. Bush's film highlighted his World War II heroism, independent oil business in Texas, and marriage to Barbara Bush. Clinton's film, put together by television producers Harry Thomason and Linda Bloodworth-Thomason, told the story of Clinton's mother's sacrifice after the death of his father, his popularity as a boy growing up in Hot Springs, Arkansas, and his growth as a young politician. The film also showed footage subtly implying that John Kennedy had passed the torch to Clinton. As a member of a youth organization, Clinton had gone to the White House and shaken Kennedy's hand. The film showed the encounter in slow motion.

The great appeal of films for convention planners is that they are virtual campaign commercials beamed free of charge across cable and often network television. Such films can reach tens of millions of voters. Convention organizers

As a high school youth and member of Boys Nation, Bill Clinton shakes President John F. Kennedy's hand at the Rose Garden ceremony in 1963.

are careful to slot the films in the prime-time viewing hours, often scheduling them just before the presidential nominee's acceptance speech. Because the lights are turned off in the convention hall when a film is shown, television is unable to cover other events from the floor. But since the 1980s the networks have been more restrictive in their coverage. In 1988 the Republican film introducing Bush caused problems. NBC, for example, had aired the seven-minute films introducing Michael Dukakis and Jesse Jackson at the Democratic convention but said that the Republican film, which lasted twenty minutes, was too long. NBC agreed to show it only after Bush aides desperately trimmed it down to seven minutes and seven seconds.[176]

Presidential Nomination

In recent years national conventions have been transformed into mere ratifying assemblies. Since 1952 all the nominees of the two major parties have been chosen on the first ballot. Candidates now use the conventions as a form of extended advertising, a way to introduce themselves and their themes to the millions watching the proceedings on television.

Several factors account for the decline of conventions as deliberative assemblies. The abolition of the unit rule and the two-thirds rule by the Democrats helped to reduce the protracted balloting that was common in that party. Even more important was the changing nature of the political landscape: the rise of primaries (which bind delegates to candidates before the convention), the increased cost of campaigning (which has accelerated the winnowing of candidates because losers in early primaries quickly find themselves without the financial resources to continue their campaigns), and the televising of conventions (in which appearing unified before the nation is the party's main concern).

The democratization of the selection process makes an old-style brokered convention, at which party bosses choose the nominee behind closed doors, all but impossible. In recent years, political enthusiasts have imagined scenarios in which deadlocks occur among the candidates that restore the suspense of old-time conventions. But for such an event to happen, the primaries and caucuses would have to end in stalemate, a highly unlikely occurrence.

To corral votes at the convention, campaign managers keep in close contact with the state delegations. Candidates have floor leaders to direct their supporters' voting and to deal with any problems that may arise among state delegations. In addition, "floaters" wander around the floor in search of trouble. All of these people have access to virtually instant communication with their candidate's command post via cell phones and wireless connections from handheld computers. Floor leaders and floaters often wear specially colored clothing or baseball caps so they can be spotted easily.[177] Candidates go to these lengths because they are eager to please the delegates and to ensure their enthusiastic support, not just at the convention but afterward. In 1976 Carter met and shook hands with each of the more than 1,800 delegates pledged to him.[178]

Nominating speeches mark the beginning of the formal selection process. The convention of the National Republican Party (which met in Baltimore in December 1831, three months after the Anti-Masons held the first national party convention) is said to have had the first nominating speech.[179] In the early years, such speeches were short. In 1860 Abraham Lincoln's name was placed into nomination with only twenty-seven words. The name of his chief rival for the nomination, William H. Seward of New York, was put forward with only twenty-six.[180] Over the years, the length of nominating speeches increased. It also became customary to schedule a series of shorter seconding speeches after the nominating speech. The seconding speeches were interspersed with floor demonstrations in support of the nominee.

Television has reshaped nominating and seconding speeches, just as it has reshaped the rest of the activity at national conventions. Eager for coverage of their event to be streamlined to entertain viewers, convention managers have encouraged a return to shorter nominating speeches and fewer seconding speeches. (In 1936 Franklin Roosevelt was seconded fifty-six times.) But things can still go awry. At the 1988 Democratic convention, Arkansas governor Bill Clinton was allotted fifteen minutes to nominate Michael Dukakis, and seconding speeches were eliminated altogether. To the dismay of Dukakis organizers, Clinton spoke for more than half an hour, despite constant signals to stop. Dukakis later joked that Clinton was available "to do the same fine job at the Republican convention as he did for me at the Democratic convention." [181]

The best nominating speeches underscore common themes that unify the party. When Gov. Mario Cuomo of New York nominated Clinton at the 1992 Democratic convention in New York, he spoke of the United States as a "family" and extolled Clinton's embrace of "the politics of inclusion, the solemn obligation to create opportunity for all our people, not just the fit and the fortunate." [182]

Sometimes the persons who nominate candidates or second their nominations are strategically chosen to display party unity. New York governor Nelson Rockefeller, a longtime foe of Richard Nixon, was selected for this reason to nominate Nixon in 1972. Similarly, after an unsuccessful effort by Harold Stassen to dump Vice President Nixon from the 1956 ticket and replace him with Massachusetts governor Christian Herter, Nixon was renominated for vice president by Herter and seconded by Stassen.

Each nominating speech is followed by a floor demonstration in which delegates and other supporters march around the convention hall chanting support for their candidate. At conventions where the outcome is in doubt, the length and enthusiasm of these demonstrations are gauged as indicators of candidate strength. In the modern era of conventions as ratifying assemblies seeking a large prime-time television audience, these demonstrations are mere rituals, abbreviated so as not to bore the viewing audience.

Once the nominating and seconding speeches are over, the roll call of the states begins. When the name of each state is called, the chair of the state's delegation rises to announce the vote of that delegation.[183] At early conventions, the order of the roll call was determined partly by geographical location and partly by the order in which states had entered the Union. Since the late 1800s, however, both parties have called the roll of states in alphabetical order, with one exception. In 1972 the Democrats determined the order of the roll call by lottery, thereby giving each state, including those that came early in the alphabet, the chance to have the honor of pushing the nominee over the top. By luck of the draw, the roll call in 1972 started with California and ended with Oklahoma. Despite these good intentions, the change was a disaster because delegation chairs were not familiar with the new order and seldom were ready to announce their delegations' votes when they were called on.

Before the modern era, many ballots often were required to nominate candidates. Of the deadlocked Democratic conventions, those of 1860 and 1924 were the most famous. The 1860 convention in Charleston, South Carolina, was turbulent from the start because of major divisions between northern and southern delegates. When the convention adopted a platform plank that took a northern-supported stance on slavery, forty-five delegates from nine states, including a majority of six southern delegations, walked out. The convention's chairman, Caleb Cushing of Massachusetts, ruled that the presidential and vice-presidential nominees would require the votes of two-thirds of the total number of delegates rather than two-thirds of the delegates still in attendance. As a result, it was almost impossible for any candidate to receive the nomination. After fifty-seven ballots, the convention disbanded and reconvened in Baltimore the next month. Stephen A. Douglas of Illinois then won the nomination on the second—or fifty-ninth—ballot.

The 1924 Democratic convention at New York's Madison Square Garden needed 103 roll calls to choose its nominee and lasted for an unprecedented seventeen days. The main division at that convention was between urban and rural delegates. The leading contenders were New York governor Alfred E. Smith and William Gibbs McAdoo of California, but fourteen other names were also placed in nomination. With so many candidates, the Democrats' two-thirds rule prevented anyone from being chosen. The balloting went on and on. During the thirty-eighth ballot, William Jennings Bryan, who was serving as a delegate from Florida, stood and spoke in opposition to Smith. Unlike his triumphant "Cross of Gold" speech twenty-eight years before, Bryan's last convention speech was drowned out in a chorus of boos from urban delegates.

As the balloting continued, McAdoo consistently came out ahead of the other candidates but short of the two-thirds majority required for nomination. After the eighty-second ballot, a resolution was passed that released all delegates from their commitments to candidates. On the eighty-sixth ballot, Smith outpolled McAdoo, but without the required two-thirds. It eventually became clear that neither of the two major candidates could win. On the ninth day of balloting and the one-hundred-and-third ballot, the Democrats nominated John W. Davis for president. That was the first Democratic convention to be broadcast live on radio, and listeners got an earful.

Long conventions have occurred less frequently among Republicans because the GOP never required more than a simple majority for nomination. The most notable deadlock at a Republican convention came in 1880, when former president Ulysses S. Grant sought renomination for a third term. After thirty-six ballots, James A. Garfield was nominated for president.

More recently, Thomas Dewey entered the 1940 Republican convention the clear front-runner, with Ohio senator Robert Taft close behind. But there was growing support at the convention for Wendell Willkie, a business leader and former Democrat. On the first ballot, Dewey received 360 votes to 189 for Taft, 105 for Willkie, and 76 for Sen. Arthur Vandenberg of Michigan. As the balloting continued, an outpouring of public sentiment for Willkie came in the form of thousands of letters and telegrams to the delegates urging his nomination. The convention hall's balconies were packed with spectators chanting "We want Willkie!" Willkie was nominated on the sixth ballot.

A genuine draft of a reluctant candidate is very rare. The first was of New York governor Horatio Seymour, who was nominated by the Democrats in 1868. The chief contenders for the nomination were President Andrew Johnson, George H. Pendleton of Ohio, and Gen. Winfield Scott Hancock of Pennsylvania. On the fourth ballot, North Carolina voted for Seymour, who promptly declared, "I must not be nominated by this convention. I could not accept the nomination if tendered."

The Johnson and Pendleton candidacies eventually collapsed, leaving General Hancock as the front-runner. Opponents of Hancock introduced a new candidate, Sen. Thomas A. Hendricks of Indiana. Determined that an easterner be nominated, the Ohio delegation voted for Seymour on the twenty-second ballot, and suddenly the tide turned toward him. Seymour rushed to the rostrum shouting, "Your candidate I cannot be!" Friends pulled him from the platform and hustled him to the Manhattan Club, where he later learned he had been nominated. Seymour's response, with

In 1868 New York governor Horatio Seymour did not want the Democratic presidential nomination, declaring "Your candidate I cannot be!" He was drafted anyway.

Choosing the Vice-Presidential Nominee

After nominating the presidential candidate, the convention chooses a vice-presidential candidate. Until recently, presidential candidates had little role in selecting their running mate. The 1920 Republican convention ignored Warren Harding's recommendation of Sen. Irwin L. Lenroot of Wisconsin and chose Massachusetts governor Calvin Coolidge instead. The choice was the prerogative of the party leaders.

This practice changed in 1940 when Franklin Roosevelt threatened not to run unless the convention accepted his vice-presidential choice: Secretary of Agriculture Henry A. Wallace. The convention reluctantly acquiesced, but Wallace was prevailed on not to deliver an acceptance speech.[186]

The method of nominating the vice-presidential candidates mirrors the procedure for presidential nominations: nominating and seconding speeches, floor demonstrations, and balloting. In recent years, likely nominees have selected their running mates before the convention begins.

The actual choice of the vice-presidential candidate sometimes is motivated by geographical considerations in an effort to balance the ticket. For years, a balanced ticket was one that boasted an easterner and a midwesterner. More recently, the balance usually has been between a northerner and a southerner. In 2004, for example, Democratic nominee John Kerry from Massachusetts chose Sen. John Edwards of North Carolina for vice president. Ideological considerations sometimes play a part in ticket balancing. Thus a liberal presidential candidate may pair himself with a more conservative running mate in hopes of attracting a broader base of votes. The choice of the vice-presidential candidate also may be used to appease factions within the party that are unhappy with the presidential candidate.

Because an increasing number of vice presidents go on to be president, greater public attention is now given to the abilities of the person who is chosen as running mate. In addition, more prominent figures are willing to accept a vice-presidential nomination.[187] In 1972 the Democrats' vice-presidential nominee, Missouri senator Thomas F. Eagleton, was forced to withdraw from the ticket when it was disclosed that he had concealed his hospitalizations for "nervous exhaustion and fatigue" during the 1960s. The Democratic National Committee subsequently ratified presidential nominee George McGovern's choice of R. Sargent Shriver to replace him.

Candidates seldom campaign openly for the vice-presidential nomination, but Jesse Jackson made it clear in the days before the 1988 Democratic convention that he wanted to be offered the number-two spot. Dukakis ultimately chose conservative Texas senator Lloyd Bentsen as his running

tears streaming down his face, was "Pity me! Pity me!"[184] Since then there have been two other drafts of reluctant candidates: Supreme Court Justice Charles Evans Hughes by the Republicans in 1916 and Illinois governor Adlai Stevenson by the Democrats in 1952.

In the age of brokered conventions, nominations often were decided by powerful party bosses meeting behind closed doors in smoke-filled rooms. Mark Hanna, who was instrumental in achieving William McKinley's nomination by the Republicans in 1896, was one of the most famous of these bosses. The reforms instituted by the parties after 1968 were largely an effort to end the influence of such people and increase rank-and-file participation in the nominating process.

For many years, a good deal of convention time was taken up by the nomination of favorite-son candidates put forth by their own state delegations. Such nominations were seldom taken seriously by the convention as a whole. Since 1972 the Democrats have required that every name placed into nomination have the written support of at least fifty delegates from three or more state delegations, with no more than twenty of these signatures coming from any one delegation. That action streamlined the proceedings and effectively ended favorite-son nominations.[185]

mate in an effort to forge a Democratic ticket with a balance of ideology, experience, and geography and to evoke images of the Boston-to-Austin team of John Kennedy and Lyndon Johnson in 1960.

At the 1988 Republican convention, sixty-four-year-old George Bush chose forty-one-year-old senator Dan Quayle of Indiana to balance age with youth. Quayle was the first presidential or vice-presidential candidate to be born after World War II. Almost immediately, reports surfaced that Quayle's wealthy family had secured for him a spot in the National Guard in 1969 to help him avoid combat duty in Vietnam. The allegations embarrassed the Republicans, who took pride in asserting their patriotism and military service.

In 1992 Clinton selected Al Gore for vice president after a quiet search conducted by Vernon Jordan, a corporate lawyer and former head of the National Urban League. The pick was considered unconventional because Clinton and Gore were from the neighboring states of Arkansas and Tennessee. In addition, both were Southern Baptists, both represented the same centrist wing of the party, and both were about the same age. But Gore, a senator, helped Clinton, a governor, compensate for his lack of Washington and foreign policy experience. As a Vietnam veteran and a strong family man, Gore also helped offset Clinton's avoidance of military service and some questions that had arisen about his personal morality. Finally, Gore's strong credentials reassured environmental groups that were unimpressed by Governor Clinton's record on the environment.

Robert Dole's selection of former representative, cabinet member, and presidential candidate Jack Kemp as his running mate in 1996 balanced the GOP ticket also in unconventional ways. Kemp was energetic and visionary where Dole was laconic and pragmatic, buoyant and articulate where Dole was dour and cryptic, and youthful where Dole was older. Kemp balanced the ticket in traditional terms as well. Dole was from Kansas, Kemp from New York. Dole embodied the traditional Republican concern for fiscal austerity. Kemp was a champion of major tax cuts.

Because the Republican convention preceded the Democratic convention in 2000, Bush had to choose his running mate before Gore did. To screen potential nominees, Bush established a vetting process headed by Richard Cheney, a veteran Washington politician with experience in the House of Representatives and in several Republican administrations, including prominent service as secretary of defense under Bush's father. In the end, Bush chose Cheney himself.

The selection was surprising in one way—most of the speculation had centered on Bush's fellow big-state Republican governors, such as Tom Ridge of Pennsylvania and John Engler of Michigan. But in a more important way, Bush's selection of Cheney was not surprising at all.

Governors who are nominated for president—FDR in 1932, Alfred M. Landon in 1936, Thomas E. Dewey in 1944 (but not 1948), Adlai Stevenson in 1952 and 1956, Carter in 1976, Reagan in 1980, Dukakis in 1988, and Clinton in 1992—almost always choose experienced Washington figures for vice president. They do so to reassure the voters that their own inexperience in national government, especially in foreign policy, will be offset by the vice president's experience. Bush underlined this virtue of the Cheney nomination by declaring that he had chosen him less to help win the election than to help him govern "as a valuable partner." This turned out to be a shrewd tactic for helping Bush win the election.[188]

Gore enlisted former secretary of state Warren Christopher to screen potential Democratic running mates, impressed by Christopher's skillful direction of the process that had led to Gore's own selection by Clinton in 1992. Between February and July 2000, Christopher and Gore whittled a list of around forty names down to four, all of them senators: John Edwards of North Carolina, John Kerry of Massachusetts, Bob Kerrey of Nebraska, and Joseph Lieberman of Connecticut, who was added at Gore's own insistence. The Republican Party's domination of the nation's statehouses—in 2000 they had thirty governors and the Democrats had twenty, including only one governor from a large state—meant that Gore had few governors to choose from.

Gore wanted to make a bold choice that would help to establish him in the voters' minds as a leader in his own right, not just as Clinton's loyal lieutenant. "This choice says everything about you," Christopher reportedly told Gore in their final meeting, "what's in your heart, what's in your soul, what's in your mind." No one doubted the boldness of Gore's decision to choose Lieberman, a deeply religious Jew who had publicly criticized Clinton's behavior during the Monica Lewinsky affair as "immoral" and "harmful." [189]

In 2004 Kerry took a page out of John Kennedy and Ronald Reagan's playbook and selected Edwards for vice president. Both Kennedy and Reagan had chosen their chief rivals as their running mates—Lyndon Johnson ran against Kennedy for the Democratic presidential nomination in 1960, George Bush ran against Reagan for the 1980 GOP nomination, and both ended up on the ticket with the candidate who bested them. Similarly, Edwards rose from the pack in 2004 to become Kerry's main challenger. Respecting Edwards's gifts as a campaigner, Kerry added him to the ticket. Remarkably, however, the Kerry campaign made no effort to win Edwards's home state of North Carolina against President Bush in the fall.

Acceptance Speeches

In recent times, the acceptance speeches of the candidates for president and vice president have been the main events of the convention. Acceptance speeches became a part of conventions in 1932, when Franklin Roosevelt broke precedent. Eager to show that his physical disability would not keep him from acting vigorously, Roosevelt made a dramatic flight from Albany to Chicago to address the Democratic convention that had nominated him for president. Noting that he was the first candidate ever to deliver an acceptance speech to a national convention, Roosevelt said: "I am here to thank you for the honor [of nominating me]. Let it be symbolic that in so doing, I broke traditions. Let it be from now on the task of our party to break foolish traditions." [190] In 1944 New York governor Thomas Dewey became the first Republican nominee to deliver an acceptance speech.

The drafting of acceptance speeches is a major undertaking, often involving the work of many writers. Strategic lines are inserted to satisfy specific voting blocs and interest groups, and the overall structure and delivery of the speech are designed to capture the interest of the millions of television viewers. Candidates rehearse their acceptance speeches extensively. They realize that the speech marks not just the end of the nominating process, but also the beginning of the general election campaign. No other speech they give during the campaign will be seen or heard by nearly as many people.

Television and Other Press Coverage

Modern national party conventions are media events. They offer a flamboyant setting with cheering crowds, passionate speakers, poignant appearances by party elders, and limitless opportunities for on-the-spot interviews and human-interest stories. Of course, there are times when conventions are hard on both "the cerebral centers and the *gluteus maximus*," [191] as H. L. Mencken wrote. But, on the whole, conventions are the breeding ground of drama, and drama is the grist for news.

The convention system originated before the telegraph or telephone, in an age when newspapers were highly partisan mouthpieces of political parties. Communication and transportation were slow, so conventions took place in relative isolation. Today, all that has changed. Thousands of reporters and camera operators attend conventions, making millions of Americans privy to the action.

The 1924 conventions were the first to be broadcast on the radio. The 1940 Republican convention was televised on an experimental basis, but it was seen by only a tiny audience. The televised 1948 Democratic convention reached about 400,000 viewers along the eastern seaboard. The Democrats also used closed-circuit television that year so that an overflow crowd of 6,000 could watch the proceedings in an auditorium adjacent to the convention hall. [192]

The advent of the television age had a tremendous effect on national party conventions. Television brought the 1952 conventions—the first to be nationally televised—into the living rooms of several million Americans. All three networks offered gavel-to-gavel coverage of the conventions themselves, as well as considerable coverage of the Credentials Committee hearings that took place before the conventions gathered. [193] It soon became apparent that under the close scrutiny of the television eye, the use of unfair tactics against the opposition could have disastrous political consequences.

Credentials fights between the Taft and Eisenhower forces at the 1952 Republican convention were played out for all the world to see. Eisenhower supporters introduced the "Fair Play" amendment and won the fight after emotional "Thou shalt not steal" speeches by Eisenhower's floor leaders. As ABC commentator Elmer Davis said, it was "no longer possible to commit grand larceny in broad daylight." [194] Steamroller tactics, such as blatantly unfair rulings by the convention chair or forced recesses during roll calls to deflate enthusiasm for a candidate or mobilize the opposition, largely became a thing of the past.

The era of one-ballot conventions coincides almost perfectly with the era of televised conventions. Conventions are now almost completely choreographed for television by the party's nominee. Convention planners are careful to prevent boring lulls in the action, to keep potentially divisive rules or platform fights out of prime-time viewing hours, and to orchestrate "spontaneous" demonstrations and telegenic events such as the release of thousands of colorful balloons from the ceiling down to the convention floor. Consultants coach speakers on makeup, wardrobe, and how to read the TelePrompTer. The convention chair is even coached on how many times to bang the gavel. Eric Lieber, a television consultant for the Democrats in 1976, said that gavel banging was a sign of disorder. Subsequently, use of the gavel was restricted to three bangs per session, regardless of what was happening on the floor. [195]

But attempts at image management do not always succeed. The 1968 Chicago convention was a disaster for the Democrats. Bloody confrontations between unruly antiwar demonstrators and helmeted police in the streets outside the hall, along with anger and divisiveness among delegates inside the hall, set the tone for television coverage. In 1972 George McGovern, the Democratic nominee for president, had the ignominious distinction of delivering his acceptance speech at almost three o'clock in the morning eastern daylight time because of a long string of symbolic vice-presidential nominations brought about by the open politics of the new Democratic Party rules. On the first day of their 1976 convention in New York's Madison Square Garden, Democrats were aghast to see television cameras pointing to some three thousand empty seats. Harried convention aides were instructed to hand out tickets along Seventh Avenue to anyone who walked by.

The media age has changed conventions substantively as well. The parties have passed rules that effectively eliminate lengthy favorite-son nominations. Severe limits have been imposed on the number and length of seconding speeches. Roll calls have been streamlined—the old practice of state chairs delivering a short speech before announcing their delegations' votes is gone.[196]

News organizations that cover the convention also are concerned with image. Officials of each television network are anxious to win higher ratings than their competitors, and they assign their best-known reporters and anchors to cover the event. Indeed, many Americans are more familiar with the network journalists than with the politicians. Anchors and analysts cover the convention from overhead booths, while scores of reporters roam the floor in search of fast-breaking stories. The networks also hire spotters to scan the floor for possibly interesting interviews.

Television often produces images just as misleading as those that media consultants conjure up for the political parties. In particular, television tries to create an illusion of action to maintain viewer interest. This is accomplished by switching cameras back and forth between events and interviews. As a result, television sometimes conveys a false sense of confusion and disorder at conventions.[197] As Theodore H. White observed, television "displays events, action, motion, arrival, departure; it cannot show thought, silence, mood or decision. And so [television catches] the carnival outer husk of the convention in all its pageantry."[198]

Although the broadcast networks have reduced their coverage of conventions in recent elections, overall coverage has expanded. Cable news networks, syndicated talk shows, Web logs (blogs), and video Web sites have increased their convention coverage. In addition, outlets such as MTV and *Comedy Central* offer untraditional broadcasts.

Whatever the format, both parties treat their conventions as extended television infomercials beamed at a large prime-time audience. Recognizing this, networks frequently cut away from the proceedings and offer their own commentary or interviews. In 1988 Republican efforts to shape the image of the convention were thwarted by the networks' emphasis on the vice-presidential selection process. Coverage of the convention's first two days centered on speculation about whom Bush would choose. Coverage of the last two days centered on controversy surrounding his choice of Dan Quayle.[199]

Other Functions of National Party Conventions

A national party convention serves as the forum for officially selecting candidates and determining party policy and rules. But the ultimate aim of a national convention is to fos-

The 1952 conventions were the first to be broadcast to a coast-to-coast television audience. Republican nominees Dwight D. Eisenhower and Richard Nixon were seen by approximately seventy million television viewers.

ter party unity and launch the general election campaign by closing ranks enthusiastically behind the nominees.

Ideally, the convention introduces the ticket to the public so positively that voters from the other party will consider supporting it. Polls showed that Bush in 2004, Gore in 2000, Clinton in 1992, Reagan in 1980, Carter in 1976 and 1980, and Nixon in 1968 received double-digit "bounces" in voter support from the conventions that nominated them. The biggest bounces often come from conventions in which all the factions within the party come together in a unified front for the fall campaign. The challenge for the candidates is to follow up the convention with events that reinforce whatever positive impressions the convention has produced. In 1988 Dukakis squandered a 6 percentage point convention bounce by suspending his campaign while the Republicans attacked him.[200]

Death or Resignation of a Convention Nominee

If a nominee dies or resigns from the ticket before election day, Democratic and Republican rules call for the national party committee to meet and choose a replacement. If it is the vice-presidential nomination that becomes vacant, the committee will take its cue from the presidential nominee. Thus in 1972, at George McGovern's recommendation, the Democratic National Committee chose Sargent Shriver as the party's vice-presidential nominee after Thomas Eagleton resigned from the ticket. Because no presidential nominee has ever had to be replaced, it is not clear how the national party committees would decide on a new candidate.

Proposals to Reform the Nominating Process

Does the current presidential nominating process foster the selection of the candidates who are most likely to win in the general election and most qualified to serve as president? Does the process weaken the power of political parties? Does it give too much influence to particular states or regions of the country? Is it deliberative enough? Is it sufficiently responsive to voter preferences? Is it too long? Too oriented to the media?

These are some of the questions raised by observers of the nominating process. Many are unhappy with the current system and have suggested various changes, depending on which purposes they think the process should achieve.[201]

The post-1968 reforms served to open the system, making it more responsive to rank-and-file party members and less responsive to party leaders. The reformers wanted to produce a more participatory process. But some argue that the reforms went too far. The antireform group wants to restore the influence and involvement of party leaders in the nominating process. Such critics argue that the post-1968 reforms explicitly weakened the parties. Nonetheless, as political scientist Michael Nelson has pointed out, the parties were already in a state of decline in the 1950s and 1960s. Indeed, he has argued that the decline has been halted and in many cases reversed since the mid-1970s, partly because the reforms helped the parties adapt "to the changed social and political environment that underlay their decline." [202]

Those who want to strengthen the power of party leaders adhere to an organizational (or "party regular") model of presidential selection. Those favoring a more open system adhere to a participatory (or "reform") model.[203] There is, of course, a range of positions between the two extremes. Most proposals to increase the power of party leaders have been far from radical. Usually such proposals have called for increased participation by party officials at the national convention by reserving delegate slots for them (the so-called superdelegates) and for increased flexibility for state parties to design their own delegate selection systems.[204] Both of these proposals were incorporated in the recommendations of the Democratic Party's 1984 Hunt Commission. *(See "Democratic Rules Changes in the 1980s and 1990s," p. 000.)* More radical proposals, such as the suggestion that Congress eliminate primaries and require that nominating conventions consist only of party leaders and elected officials, are seldom taken seriously. As political scientist Thomas E. Mann has written, most proposals "move in the direction of increasing or channeling, not eliminating, participation by rank-and-file party identifiers." [205]

The National Primary

If democracy on a small scale is good, then democracy on a large scale is even better. Such is the logic of the frequent call to expand the scope of primary voting from the state to the national level.

A national primary was proposed in Congress as early as 1911, and quickly won the endorsement of President Woodrow Wilson.[206] Since then, several versions of the idea have been presented. One would require each party to conduct a single national primary on a designated day. To appear on the ballot, a candidate would have to file a petition containing signatures equivalent to 1 percent of the votes cast in the previous presidential election. This primary (with a runoff election, if no candidate received 40 percent of the vote) would determine the party's presidential nominee, although a convention could still be held to choose a vice-presidential candidate, adopt a platform, and conduct other party business.

Another version of the national primary would have the primary select two-thirds of the delegates to the national convention, with each candidate receiving a percentage of delegates equal to his or her percentage of the national primary vote. The other one-third of the delegates would be party leaders. When a national primary was not decisive, this system could allow for a deliberative convention with party leaders in the driver's seat.[207] Yet another proposal would authorize the national convention to develop a party platform and select several candidates who would then compete in a national primary.[208]

Those who support a national primary argue that it would simplify the process. They further argue that it would make the system more democratic: votes would count equally, the candidate would be chosen by the rank and file, and voter participation would increase. In the process, the campaign season would be shortened, small states like Iowa and New Hampshire would no longer be accorded special weight, issues of national concern would be addressed by the candidates, and the influence of the media's interpretation of early primaries and caucuses would be reduced.[209]

Opponents argue that a national primary would weaken, if not destroy, the party organizations and would all but eliminate grass-roots campaigning. They further argue that it would accelerate candidates' use of the media and allow for no winnowing of the field of candidates through the multistage campaign season.[210] Finally, opponents contend that the system would be biased against little-known but able candidates who, in the existing system, can make a name for themselves in the early primaries and then contend seriously for the nomination. They regret that candidates would not have to survive a string of contests and continually prove themselves over an extended period.[211]

Other Proposals

Another frequently mentioned suggestion to reform the nominating process is the idea of regional primaries. Proposals for such a system were introduced in the 1970s by two senators, Democrat Walter Mondale of Minnesota and Republican Bob Packwood of Oregon. Under each of their proposals, the country would be divided into regions (six in Mondale's proposal, five in Packwood's). Each state within a region would be required to hold its primary or caucuses on the date assigned by law. These dates would fall at intervals of two weeks (Mondale) or one month (Packwood). The order in which the regions vote would be determined by lot, changing from one election to the next.[212] As in the current system, the primaries would be used to select delegates to the national nominating convention.

The regional primary plan is an attempt to correct a system that critics say is too fragmented. By requiring that all states within a particular region hold their primary on a designated day, the undue influence of individual states that hold early primaries (such as New Hampshire) would be eliminated. That advantage would be transferred to a region as a whole, but the shifting order of the primaries would prevent any one region from enjoying an advantage for long. As political scientists William Crotty and John S. Jackson III have written, such plans attempt "to resolve some of the difficulties of the current system of scattered primaries, while retaining the strengths both of the party system and of reform era democratization."[213]

Critics say that regional primaries would severely weaken the importance of federalism in the presidential selection process because candidates would devote less attention to the needs of individual states. They see such plans as merely a modified version of the national primary. Like the national primary, they say, regional primaries would reduce grass-roots campaigning, be biased against little-known candidates (unless they were from the region that voted first), and increase the candidates' reliance on media campaigning.

In 2000 the Republican Party seriously considered adopting a plan proposed by a commission chaired by former national party chair Bill Brock. The so-called "Delaware Plan" was designed to prevent any candidate from locking up the presidential nomination early by postponing the large states' primaries until late in the process. Depending on their size, states would hold their primaries in an assigned month, with the smallest states voting in February and the largest states in May. By "backloading" the process so that more than half the delegates would be chosen in the final round of primaries, the plan would have made it impossible for any candidate to amass a convention majority until every state had its say.

The Delaware Plan was approved by the Republican National Committee (RNC) on the eve of the party's 2000 convention, but it was buried in the convention's rules committee after presidential nominee George W. Bush's campaign organization announced that it opposed the plan. Some of the large states had expressed concern that their influence over presidential nominations would decline if they were required to vote en masse so late in the process, and Bush supporters did not want a convention floor fight to mar the unity of the gathering. An important practical objection also was raised: the difficulty of persuading dozens of state legislatures to change the dates of their primaries to conform to Republican rules.

In advance of the 2008 election, the Democratic Party changed its rules in a way that accepted the importance of the early nominating contests but sought to increase the number and variety of such contests. Iowa and New Hampshire were perceived as being too white, too rural, and too northern to play such a dominant role in winnowing the field of presidential candidates and sometimes all but determining the party's nominee for president. The Democrats decided that Nevada, a western state with a large Latino population, should vote after Iowa but before New Hampshire, and that South Carolina, a southern state with a large African American population, should vote a few days after New Hampshire.

GENERAL ELECTION CAMPAIGN

Even before they have their party's nomination, presidential candidates start to focus on winning the general election. They must choose the strategy they think will propel them to victory against the other party's nominee and pursue it in a complex political environment that includes the news media, the opposition party, and interest groups. Not least among their problems are those of expanding and organizing their own staffs—pollsters, media consultants, strategists, and other senior advisers—and coordinating their campaigns with their party's state and national organizations.

Types of Strategy

Presidential elections are fought state by state, with each candidate trying to win a combination of states that has enough electoral votes to constitute the majority required for victory. Thus, most strategies begin with geographic considerations. Democratic candidates usually are strongest in the Northeast, upper Midwest, and along the Pacific Coast (the so-called "blue states" because of the color the television networks usually use on election night broadcasts to show which states' electoral votes have been won by the Democratic candidate). Until the 1950s, the South was a Democratic stronghold, but the white conservative voters who dominate southern politics increasingly have been attracted to Republican candidates in presidential elections. In 2000 Democrat Al Gore lost every southern state to George W. Bush, a pattern that was repeated when Bush ran for reelection against John Kerry in 2004. The Republicans also dominate the Rocky Mountain West and the Plains states.

To appeal to a large geographic constituency, most tickets consist of presidential and vice-presidential candidates from different parts of the country. When Minnesotan Walter Mondale chose Geraldine Ferraro of New York as his running mate in 1984, Ronald Reagan's strategist, Lee Atwater, was elated. He predicted that the Democrats' choice of a "North-North" ticket would give the South to the Republicans and guarantee victory for Reagan.[214] In 1992 Bill Clinton of Arkansas formed a "South-South" ticket by choosing Al Gore of Tennessee as his running mate. It became the first successful all-southern ticket since Andrew Jackson (Tennessee) and John C. Calhoun (South Carolina) in 1828.

Regional strength does not tell all, however. Because states do not count equally in the electoral college, candidates often concentrate their efforts on states across the country with large electoral vote counts. As a result of the 2000 census, the electoral votes of just eleven states—California, New York, Texas, Florida, Pennsylvania, Illinois, Ohio, Michigan, New Jersey, North Carolina, and Georgia—are enough to secure victory in the general election.

For a candidate to devote time and money to all fifty states is a waste of scarce campaign resources. Richard Nixon promised to campaign personally in every state when he ran for president in 1960, but he later regretted that pledge when he was forced to waste valuable time visiting states with few electoral votes while his rival, John Kennedy, was targeting the large states. This point was driven home with particular force on the last weekend before the election. As Nixon flew to Alaska to fulfill his promise, Kennedy campaigned in New York, New Jersey, and Massachusetts. When Nixon ran again in 1968 he was careful to target particular states. For example, he did not visit small and heavily Republican Kansas that year. As Robert Ellsworth, a Nixon campaign aide and a Kansan, said: "If you have to worry about Kansas, you don't have a campaign anyway." [215]

Aside from deciding what kind of geographic strategy to pursue, candidates are faced with other strategic choices. Should they stress their party affiliation or their individual merit? Should they run an ideological campaign or emphasize moderation and consensus? Should they concentrate on style or on substance? Should the thrust of their campaign be positive (vote for me) or negative (vote against my opponent)?

Party labels provide important cues to voters. Nelson Polsby and Aaron Wildavsky have noted that even most independents have party preferences: "About two-thirds of all independents have leanings; scratch an independent and underneath you are likely to find an almost-Republican or a near-Democrat, and those who are left are least likely to turn out." [216]

Since the New Deal, the Democrats consistently have had more registered voters than the Republicans, although by a steadily decreasing margin in recent years. As a result, it traditionally has been more advantageous for the Democrats to follow an overtly partisan campaign than it is for the Republicans. It also has behooved the Democrats to encourage a large voter turnout, either by stressing the civic obligation to vote or through more tangible efforts, such as providing telephone reminders or even baby sitters and transportation to the polls.[217] Efforts of both kinds appear to have secured Kennedy's victory in 1960.[218]

Because Republican presidential candidates could be hurt by a large voter turnout or by running an intensely partisan campaign, Republican candidates sometimes have de-emphasized their party label. In 1976 Gerald Ford's official campaign poster featured his picture but gave no indication that he was a Republican.[219] Likewise, Nixon's campaign organization in 1972—the Committee to Re-elect the President—intentionally bypassed the Republican Party.

In 2004, however, Republicans made a massive effort to identify their supporters and get them registered and to the polls. The GOP's goal was higher voter turnout, but only among Republicans. The strategy succeeded. Democratic nominee John Kerry got all the votes his campaign thought he needed to be elected, based on voter turnout rates in previous elections. But Bush won many more votes in 2004 than he had in 2000, especially in crucial states like Ohio and Florida. Bush's national popular vote increased from 47.9 percent in 2000 to 50.7 percent in 2004, and the overall voter turnout rate jumped from 51.2 percent to 55.3 percent.

Unlike partisan campaigns, which stress party loyalty, ideological campaigns stress the candidate's devotion to a particular political ideology. In doing so, these campaigns excite and energize the candidate's core supporters. But they can alienate moderate voters, including members of the candidate's own party.[220]

Yet another strategy is a consensual campaign, which makes broad appeals outside the confines of either partisanship or ideology. When Republican Barry Goldwater in 1964 and Democrat George McGovern in 1972 ran strongly ideological campaigns, their opponents, Lyndon Johnson and Nixon, respectively, responded successfully with consensual campaigns whose theme was that even loyalists of the other party had more in common with them than with their ideologically extreme opponents. George Bush's failed 1992 reelection bid suffered when the Republican convention in Houston struck many observers as ideologically extreme, particularly in its strident attacks on liberals by speakers from the religious right. In contrast, Bush's son, George W. Bush, offered "compassionate conservatism" and an array of minority, female, and gay speakers at the 2000 Republican convention.

Bill Clinton's 1992 campaign stressed themes designed to appeal to moderate Republicans as well as traditional Democrats. His self-designation as a "new Democrat" was calculated to distance him from the more ideologically liberal Democratic candidates of the past. Clinton insisted that the Democratic platform state, "We reject both the do-nothing government of the last twelve years and the big government theory that says we can hamstring business and tax and spend our way to prosperity." The Clinton-approved platform offered a "third way" that combined economic growth, family vitality, personal responsibility, and law and order—all of them themes usually espoused by Republican candidates.

Candidates also must decide how specific they will be on the issues. Fearful of antagonizing groups of voters with strong stands, many candidates couch their positions in generalities. They repeat the same phrases in speech after speech in an effort to tell audiences what they want to hear. A few candidates, such as Adlai Stevenson in 1952, took pride in crafting new speeches for every occasion, but this is not the norm. In fact, the tactic ultimately hurt Stevenson. Because he was not repeating a well-worn text, his delivery suffered and his message never took root in the minds of most voters.[221]

In 1984 Democrat Walter Mondale tried to appear honest and straightforward by taking specific stands on controversial issues. He promised, for example, to raise taxes. He also lost. Most candidates—Democrat and Republican alike—are cautious and repetitive, at least in public. At the same time, their campaign organizations send email and other targeted communications to members of various groups to underscore the candidate's support for these groups' pet causes.

Advantages and Disadvantages of Incumbency

Presidential incumbents enjoy advantages that their opponents lack, many of which stem from the simple fact that they already occupy an office that lends them credibility, respect, and visibility. More important, they are in a position to use the resources of the federal government to influence events and benefit important constituencies. As part of the job, presidents can cut active campaigning to a minimum, make official appearances in carefully controlled settings (such as greeting heads of state and signing legislation), and wrap themselves in the symbols and setting of the office.

Incumbency can have drawbacks, however. Presidents are blamed for failures as well as credited with successes. Even events over which presidents have little control may be blamed on them. For example, oil shortages and adverse economic conditions may arise through no fault of the president. And sticking too closely to the job in times of trouble

Unlike most candidates, Adlai Stevenson crafted new speeches for every occasion—a tactic that ultimately hurt him. By not repeating a well-worn text, his delivery suffered, and he was accused of speaking over people's heads.

may open the president to criticism that he is hiding in the White House rather than facing the people. Carter was accused of this in 1980, when there was widespread public displeasure over his handling of the Iranian hostage crisis.

In 1976 Ford's strategy included challenging his opponent, Carter, to the first series of televised debates since 1960. The plan was suggested in a memorandum from two White House aides to Richard Cheney, Ford's chief of staff.[222] As Cheney later observed, the debate option was "part of a 'no campaign' campaign strategy," with the debates serving as "a means of de-emphasizing traditional campaigning, maximizing the advantages of incumbency, and forcing Governor Carter to deal substantively with the issues." [223] Journalist Martin Schram noted that the debates also were "a chance for the President to dispel the notions that he was not intelligent and not capable of running the country." [224]

Ford adopted the debate strategy because he was far behind in the polls. He generally was regarded as a poor campaigner but, because of his years in Congress, a competent debater. Ford and his advisers calculated that he had little to lose and much to gain by debating. In challenging Carter, he also would seize the initiative in the campaign.

As a rule, incumbents have more to lose than their opponents in face-to-face debates. Debates allow challengers to prove their mettle by placing them on an equal footing

Behind in the polls, President Gerald R. Ford chose a campaign strategy that included televised debates with former Georgia governor Jimmy Carter.

with the president. Because incumbents are tied to their records and their policies, they can easily be placed on the defensive.

President Bush obviously was reluctant to debate Clinton and Ross Perot in 1992. When a heckler dressed as a chicken started taunting Bush at his rallies, the president finally agreed to "get it on" with his opponents. By most accounts, Bush performed poorly in the debates. His misunderstanding of a voter's question about the recession reinforced his image of being out of touch. Clinton and Perot, meanwhile, were comfortable with the informal debate format and performed well.

The advantage challengers derive from debates still are outweighed by the advantage of already being in office. The president not only already enjoys the stature of the office but is able both to influence media coverage with official actions and to use pork-barrel politics to appeal to specific constituencies. International crises that place the president at center stage or announcements of favorable government statistics on the economy can also help the incumbent. Not least, the president benefits from the public's reluctance to reject a tested national leader.

The emotional bond of the people with the president offers an additional advantage. Perhaps the greatest examples in recent years are Lyndon Johnson's 1964 reelection, which benefited from the nation's deep desire for continuity in the wake of the Kennedy assassination, and Ronald Reagan's evocation of patriotic themes in his 1984 campaign for reelection. President George W. Bush benefited in 2004 from the nation's memory of him as a resolute leader in the aftermath of the September 11, 2001, attacks on the United States.

The president's control of foreign relations probably provides the greatest opportunity for an incumbent to enhance the chances for reelection. In 1972 President Nixon orchestrated a number of major foreign policy initiatives that guaranteed him continuing and favorable media coverage, including election-year visits to both of the nation's leading foes, the Soviet Union and the People's Republic of China. As the campaign neared its end, the Nixon administration expressed confidence about the prospects of a peace settlement of the Vietnam War. In late October, Secretary of State Henry Kissinger announced that "peace is at hand." The administration's public pronouncements on Vietnam undercut the antiwar campaign of Nixon's Democratic rival, Sen. McGovern of South Dakota.

Even foreign policy difficulties can be advantageous for an incumbent. Initially at least, Carter's popularity got a boost from the November 1979 seizure of American citizens as hostages in Iran. After invading Grenada in October 1983 Reagan benefited politically from the nation's willingness to "rally 'round the flag." In 2004 many voters seem to have decided that even though they had concerns about the war in Iraq, the country would be safer staying the course with Bush than going with his untested opponent, John Kerry.

In times of economic or foreign policy crisis, the president's prominence also can have a negative effect on the campaign. President Carter's bid for reelection in 1980 was doomed by "stagflation"—a combination of high unemployment and high inflation—and Iran's refusal to release its American hostages. Carter's credibility on foreign policy was damaged by his apparent surprise at the Soviet invasion of Afghanistan in 1979 and the unpopular retaliatory actions he took—an embargo of grain sales to the Soviets and a U.S. boycott of the 1980 Moscow Olympics.

Despite his reputation as a foreign policy expert, President Bush struggled in his 1992 reelection campaign. Bush's leadership in the American-led victory in the 1991 Persian Gulf War actually undermined his campaign because he seemed to voters to be more preoccupied with foreign affairs than with the weakening economy.

On the economic front, most first-term presidents seem intent on managing the economy so that if a recession must occur, it will be early in the administration. The idea is that by the time the reelection campaign begins, the economy will rebound and voters will gain confidence in the administration's economic management. President Reagan presided over the highest unemployment rate since the Great Depression early in his first term, but by the time he sought reelection in 1984 both the unemployment and inflation rates had declined significantly. Bush benefited in 2004 from an economy that had begun to rebound from a previously sluggish performance.

As the defeats of Ford, Carter, and George Bush demonstrate, the advantages of being president do not guarantee victory. Poor performance or unfortunate circumstances can doom an incumbent. And all three recently defeated presidents suffered from bitter struggles for their party nominations.

Role of the Campaign Staff and Advisers

Presidential campaigns in the media age are elaborate, multimillion-dollar operations. Within these operations, important strategic and tactical decisions are made by the professional campaign consultants who form the core of a candidate's personal campaign organization. Consultants usually are engaged for highly specialized tasks such as public opinion sampling, data processing, policy formulation, fund raising, accounting, Web site design, voter turnout drives, and the production of television commercials. The rise of professional campaign consultants is, in part, an attempt to provide the expertise needed to compete in increasingly complex modern elections. Such consultants also help to fill the void left by the now weakened party organizations that used to coordinate campaigns.[225]

Pollsters

Candidates always have relied on advisers to guide them through the campaign. But technological advances, especially in telecommunications and information management, have spawned a new breed of consultants. Among them, pollsters have risen to the higher echelons of presidential campaigns because they are able to gather and decipher strategic information.

Polls tell the candidates where their bases of support lie, what the voters think of them, which issues are important to the electorate, and which words and phrases most effectively convey the candidates' ideas.[226] Thus polls can be used by candidates to decide whether or not to run, to improve their image, to identify the opposition's weaknesses, to formulate mass media advertising, and to allocate scarce campaign resources with maximum efficiency.[227] Candidates also find polls helpful in deciding how to appeal to specific blocs of voters.

Pollster Louis Harris maintains that polls can shift the outcome of an election by as much as 4 percentage points if one candidate uses polling data to target resources more efficiently than the other.[228] Since 1960, when John Kennedy hired Harris, every presidential candidate has made extensive use of polls. Presidents also have kept close tabs on survey data once they are in office. For example, Jimmy Carter's close association with pollster Patrick Caddell strongly influenced his decisions both on the campaign trail and in the White House.[229]

Polling played a central role in Bill Clinton's winning 1992 campaign. Pollster Stanley B. Greenberg conducted surveys that helped Clinton develop almost instantaneous responses to charges made by his opponents, Bush and Perot. Polls were especially important—and volatile—in 1992 because of the presence of a strong independent candidate. The two major parties struggled to navigate political waters roiled by the maverick Perot, who was cutting into President Bush's conservative and suburban constituencies while also challenging Clinton for the anti-incumbent vote.

Polls, however, are not infallible. There is room for error both in the polls themselves and in their interpretation.[230] The most famous example is from 1948, when virtually every pollster predicted that Republican Thomas Dewey would defeat the Democratic incumbent, Harry Truman. For a variety of reasons—including poor sampling techniques and mistaken assumptions about how the undecided would vote—the pollsters were wrong. Most pollsters also substantially underestimated the size of Ronald Reagan's victory in 1980.[231]

According to sociologists James R. Beniger and Robert J. Giuffra Jr., polls that forecast the outcome of elections are only one of many kinds of polls that candidates use. Early *baseline* surveys provide basic information about a candidate's initial appeal and the political mood of the nation. These polls can be useful to candidates in deciding whether to run. *Follow-up surveys* are used to gather more extensive data bearing on concerns raised in the initial baseline surveys. These are used in planning campaign strategy.

Panel surveys are used to refine strategy further by reinterviewing previous respondents to see what the campaign is doing well and what it needs to work on. These surveys are supplemented by continual tracking polls, which measure fluctuations in general voter support for the candidate on a frequent basis.

Focus groups—small groups of voters whose views on candidates, issues, and other campaign-related matters are probed through extensive discussion—help strategists to supplement the statistical data gathered in polls. And continuing developments in computer technology have allowed candidates to use new techniques such as the geodemographic targeting system, in which census data and specially programmed voter registration lists pinpoint swing voters.[232]

Used together, all of these surveys provide information that candidates are convinced they cannot do without.

Media and Other Consultants

Image building has become especially important since the development of television. In 1976, urging Carter to take symbolic actions that would play well on television, pollster Caddell warned the candidate that "too many good people have been beaten because they tried to substitute substance for style." [233] He encouraged Carter to hold folksy town meetings and carry his own luggage. Increasingly, candidates rely on media consultants to help them cultivate an appealing style.

Media savvy was a vital part of Clinton's successful 1992 campaign. Political strategists James Carville and Mandy Grunwald, among others, helped the Arkansas governor to keep his campaign focused. The famed "War Room"—a crisis-control center at Clinton's headquarters in Little Rock—coordinated rapid responses to media criticisms and to charges from the Bush campaign. Occasional bus tours of small towns helped foster an appealing image for Clinton, vice-presidential nominee Gore, and their wives.

Dwight Eisenhower was the first presidential candidate to make extensive use of television commercials and an advertising agency when he ran as the Republican nominee in 1952. Nixon shunned the use of an advertising agency and most modern media techniques in the 1960 campaign. Nixon's performance in the first televised debate with Kennedy was marred by his poor makeup, haggard appearance, and lack of attention to his wardrobe. Nixon lost the election. His next campaign for president (he won in 1968) was a pure case of campaigning as media marketing.[234] Since then, media consultants have become an integral part of presidential campaigns, coordinating everything from the personal appearance of the candidates to the color of their bumper stickers and the look of their Web sites.

Media consultants also have fine-tuned their production and distribution of television advertisements. For example, Nixon's commercials stressed his foreign policy experience in 1968 after polls showed that viewers thought such experience was especially important that year. In the

Political strategist James Carville, left, managed Bill Clinton's 1992 campaign for president from the "War Room" in Little Rock, Arkansas.

aftermath of Vietnam and Watergate, Carter's commercials displayed him as an honest, folksy candidate. Even the color of his campaign posters (green) stressed how Carter was different from mainstream politicians, most of whom used red, white, and blue.[235]

Technological advances also have led to the use of direct mail. Using computers, campaign organizations send "personalized" mailings to targeted individuals whose names are culled from lists of contributors to the candidate's party, from the mailing lists of conservative (Republican) or liberal (Democratic) magazines, from membership lists of various organizations, and even from lists of the users of products that tend to mark them as disposed to vote Republican (pickup trucks) or Democratic (Volvos).

Direct mail often is used as a fund-raising device. It was first employed in 1952 by Eisenhower, who compiled a donor list with the aid of the publisher of *Reader's Digest*. But it was not until the 1970s that vigorous use of direct mail was spurred by campaign finance legislation that limited individual contributions to $1,000 ($2,100 as of 2006) per candidate. Under the new rules, direct mail served as a grassroots approach to reaching a wide base of small contributors. With a well-coordinated program that contacts both potential contributors ("prospective mailings") and those who have given money in the past ("in-house" or "contributor mailings"), a relatively small investment can reap a tremendous return.[236]

The goal of such mailings is to create an illusion of intimacy with each recipient. In 1980 mailings for Bush's nomination campaign included reprints of newspaper articles with "personal notes" laser-printed in the margin: "To [recipient's name]— I thought you might be interested in these recent clippings— G. B." [237] The illusion of intimacy, coupled with careful packaging and emotional pleas, is designed to draw the recipient into the campaign by giving money.

Perhaps the most famous direct-mail consultant was conservative activist Richard Viguerie. Viguerie came to prominence in 1976 when he managed a highly successful direct-mail operation for George Wallace, who was seeking the Democratic nomination for president. In 1980 Viguerie helped the Republican Party broaden its financial base and usher in the presidency of Reagan and the first Republican Senate in twenty-six years. By 1982 the Viguerie Company was employing more than three hundred people.[238] Viguerie maintained that his operation had amassed an "in-house list of eleven million proven contributors." [239]

In addition to direct mail, candidates use telephone banks and email to recruit volunteers and to target potential voters. Contacting households by phone or email offers a means of reaching more voters with less effort than door-to-door canvassing.[240] Campaigns also use telephones and computers in their fund-raising drives. In an effort to generate contributions, some media ads encourage voters to call a toll-free number or access a Web site where they can make a donation by credit card.[241]

Recognizing that presidential campaigns are increasingly shaped by the mass media, political strategists work hard to develop memorable appeals. A large proportion of political advertising is negative. Cognitive studies have shown that voters absorb negative information more deeply than positive information. Jill Buckley, a Democratic consultant, has observed, "People say they hate negative advertising, but it works. They hate it and remember it at the same time. . . . With negative [advertising], the poll numbers will move in three or four days."

The effect of media consultants on the outcome of political campaigns is debatable, especially because both candidates in a general election are able to hire experienced and talented professionals. Their effect on the process itself, however, is clear. Professionals drive up the costs of competing and elevate the importance of style and image.[242] The danger, as political scientist Larry Sabato has concluded, lies in the possibility that candidates and voters will confuse the style of campaigning with the substance of governing.[243] A candidate may be well suited to win a presidential election but ill prepared to handle the rigors of the presidency.

Roles of Parties and Interest Groups

Winning elections entails giving voters a reason to go to the polls and vote. Traditionally, state party organizations have organized party appeals, but since World War II interest groups and the media have played a growing role.

State Party Organizations

State and local party organizations offer an important supplement to the efforts of the national campaign.

In recent years, state parties have become better at recruiting and training candidates for lower office, using modern campaign technology, raising money, and coordinating their activities with national party organizations. State parties also undertake grass-roots efforts to register likely supporters and get them to the polls. Party organizations own extensive lists of reliable and potential supporters. As election day approaches, the organization sends these voters letters and cards urging them to vote, and volunteers phone them to reinforce the message.

Coordination between a party's national, state, and local campaign efforts is informal. The receipt of federal funds requires a presidential candidate to limit campaign spending, so the efforts of other groups must be legally separate. By setting campaign priorities, however, the candidate's organization gives important cues to its state and local allies.

Under the 1979 amendments to the Federal Election Campaign Act, state and local organizations may spend unlimited amounts of money on get-out-the-vote drives and political paraphernalia such as bumper stickers, buttons, and lawn signs. The organizations also can produce and distribute media appeals that promote the whole party. Such appeals usually follow the national campaign themes set by the presidential candidate. The 2002 McCain-Feingold act left these spending limits unaltered but placed an annual $10,000 ceiling on the amount that a donor can contribute to a state party organization.

Many state party organizations influence the awarding of patronage jobs and construction and service contracts, as well as routine political and governmental operations. Many also control the mechanics of the electoral process. Ohio law, for example, requires that voter registration officials be approved by county party leaders. In addition, nearly half the states allow single-ticket voting, in which voters can cast their ballot for all of a party's candidates by pulling a single lever or using one ballot. By creating strong party competition in all races simultaneously, single-ticket voting increases the importance of intraparty cooperation.

Issues activists have become more involved in many state parties in recent years. In Iowa, for example, Christian conservatives play a large role in Republican politics. In New York, feminists and civil rights activists are important players in Democratic politics.

Political scientist Kay Lawson argues that national party rules and state legislation have undermined the organizational integrity of state parties. But even if parties do not enjoy the autonomy they once did, they remain an independent and important force in state and national politics.[244]

National Party Organizations

In addition to their important organizing function in presidential campaigns, committees of the national parties raise large sums of money and develop long-range political strategies. The efforts of some party chairs, notably Republicans Ray Bliss and William E. Brock and Democrats Charles T. Manatt and Paul G. Kirk Jr., have been especially significant. During the mid-to-late twentieth century, these chairs developed wide-ranging strategies for coordinating presidential campaigns and reaching out to important political groups. Bliss was central in developing the GOP as a reenergized party after Goldwater's massive defeat in 1964, and Brock was equally important after Watergate. Manatt developed ties to influential business leaders long neglected by the Democrats, and Kirk worked to diminish the Democrats' "special-interest" reputation.

The fund-raising abilities of the Republican Party committees have outstripped those of their Democratic counterparts in recent years. In the 2000 election cycle, the Republican Party raised $294.9 million in "hard money"—that is, money that can be used to support individual candidates—compared with the Democrats' $172.7 million. The GOP outraised the Democrats more narrowly ($210.7 million to $199.0 million) in "soft money," which can be used to undertake party-building activities such as funding congressional and state candidates, supporting advertising campaigns, organizing get-out-the-vote drives, polling, lobbying state legislatures on redistricting, making direct-mail appeals, and hiring consultants.[245]

Although soft money contributions to national political parties were banned with the enactment of the McCain-Feingold act in 2002, more money than ever before flowed into national party treasuries in 2004. National Republican organizations—the Republican National Committee, the National Republican Senatorial Committee, and the National Republican Congressional Committee—raised $554.7 million in hard money from individuals and PACs. Their Democratic equivalents raised $451.8 million in hard money, for a record two-party total of more than $1 billion.[246]

Interest Groups

The United States includes many social, economic, and ethnic groups with distinctive identities. Successful candidates must make separate appeals to these groups within the framework of their broader appeals. Groups with distinctive political interests and voting habits include Catholics, Jews, African Americans, Latinos, Asians, Irish, Greeks, feminists, gays and lesbians, bankers, trial lawyers, real estate developers, laborers, farmers, environmentalists, senior citizens, urbanites, southerners, evangelical Christians, and many others.

Candidates are sensitive to the turnout rates of different groups—that is, what percentage of each group votes.

Because voter turnout often is low, state and local organizations work to register voters and get them to the polls on election day.

Robert Axelrod has estimated that the proportion of the poor in Democratic vote totals fell from 28 percent to 5 percent between 1952 and 1980.[247] It is probably no accident, therefore, that Democratic appeals to the poor have declined in recent years. Similarly, both parties try much harder to win the support of old people, who turn out at a very high rate, than young people, who do not.

In recent years, political action committees—organizations designed to promote the concerns of ideological or social groups, business, and labor mainly by funding election campaigns—have played an important role in supplementing the direct-mail and mass-media appeals of the two major presidential candidates, who may spend only the money they receive from the federal government on their campaigns. The number of PACs has grown tremendously since the 1970s, and PAC spending has increased along with that growth. PAC expenditures increased from $19.2 million in 1972 to $394.9 million in 1992 and $579.4 million in 2000.[248] PACs enjoy an advantage over the candidates' campaign organizations because individuals are permitted to donate $5,000 to a PAC and only $2,000 to a campaign under federal law. *(See "The Campaign Finance System," p. 261.)* One effect of political action committees is to increase the number of narrow or single-issue appeals by candidates and parties at the expense of the broader concerns of the nation as a whole.

The major group spending on the 2004 election was by "527" groups, named after the section of the tax code that allows groups independent of the political parties or their candidates to raise unlimited amounts of money to spend on election-related television commercials, voter registration drives, and other activities. For example, the pro-Democratic 527 group America Coming Together had total receipts of almost $80 million in 2004, with 91 percent of its contributions coming in amounts of $100,000 or more. The pro-Republican group Progress for America had receipts of nearly $45 million that year. In all, 527 groups spent more than $435 million in 2004.[249]

Role of the Media

The mass media—television, radio, newspapers and magazines, and political Web sites of various kinds—play an increasingly important role in presidential elections. This is because the media serve as the dominant source of information about candidates and elections for most Americans—more than family, friends, associates, or direct contacts with political parties and candidate organizations.[250] The media also have taken over many of the intermediary functions of party organizations, linking voters with the larger political system.[251] News sources appear to be most influential early in the nominating process. At that stage of the process the media help to form voters' impressions of the large field of candidates, many of whom may be unfamiliar. By the time of the general election, most voters have clear impressions of the candidates, which makes it more difficult for additional media coverage to influence them.

The pervasive influence of the media has given rise to a new kind of campaign and candidate. An appealing style and image, joined with an ability to speak succinctly and warmly before cameras, have become basic ingredients of a successful candidacy. A candidate with a colorless, low-key personality, such as Calvin Coolidge, or one with a controversial past, such as Grover Cleveland, who fathered a child out of wedlock, probably could not be elected today. In addition, careful debate and deliberation on complex issues tend to be foreclosed by the rapid fire campaign coverage offered by the news media.

News values influence the campaign. News is drama, and drama thrives on conflict.[252] As a result, the media often emphasize the competitive game-like characteristics of presidential campaigns. Strategy, momentum, and error are often featured at the expense of the candidates' records and policy pronouncements. Journalists covering presidential debates, for example, are more concerned with who wins than with the issues the candidates discuss. In the process, news coverage is personalized—that is, issues are subordinated to personalities.[253]

By exposing a flaw in a candidate's personal history the media can derail a campaign long before the first vote is cast. This happened to Democrats Gary Hart and Joseph Biden, who in 1987 abandoned fledgling presidential bids after receiving adverse publicity. Hart was caught in an extramarital relationship; Biden had engaged in plagiarism.

Yet the modern media also provide candidates with an unprecedented ability to take their message directly to the people. Television, in particular, is often said to have transformed electoral politics. Cutting across all socioeconomic divisions, television reaches nearly 98 percent of all households in the continental United States.[254] One study shows that as recently as 1982, more Americans had televisions than refrigerators or indoor plumbing.[255]

In analyzing the media context of candidate appeals, political scientists David Paletz and Robert Entman have identified three types of messages: unmediated messages, partially mediated messages, and mostly mediated messages.[256]

Unmediated Messages

Unmediated messages are those in which the candidate's message is passed to the people directly and unfettered by commentary or criticism, such as paid political advertisements and campaign Web sites. Since they were first used by Dwight Eisenhower in 1952, television advertisements have played a prominent role in presidential elections. Between them, George W. Bush and Al Gore spent $67.1 million on television advertising in the 2000 general election campaign. Their parties spent $79.8 million on issues ads in the same period.[257]

The precise effects of campaign commercials are difficult to determine.[258] In trying to assess the influence of the media on public attitudes, many analysts have echoed the wry observation of sociologist Bernard Berelson, who concluded that "some kinds of communications on some kinds of issues, brought to the attention of some kinds of people under some kinds of conditions, have some kinds of effects." [259] Paletz and Entman have argued that unmediated messages such as television commercials are of limited effectiveness in swaying voters because many people realize that commercials are self-serving. In addition, such messages are "vulnerable to the Gorgons of selective exposure, selective perception, and selective retention." [260] As political scientist Doris Graber has concluded, "Commercials are perceiver-determined. People see in them pretty much what they want to see—attractive images for their favorite candidate and unattractive ones for the opponent." [261]

In 1992 Ross Perot's half-hour television infomercials, videos, and books were the basis of one of the least mediated campaigns in modern history. Perot never hesitated to express his disdain for the working press. Rather than talk to voters through print and broadcast news reports, he tried to set up his own information system. Perot dropped out of the presidential race in July when reporters began investigating his past business and political activities. After Perot reentered the race in early October, the media at first did not pay much attention to him, giving him a grace period to present his views to the voters the way he wanted. Ultimately, Perot's credibility was damaged when he told the CBS news program *60 Minutes* that he had been driven out of the race by Republican plans to disrupt his daughter's wedding.

An even newer and more direct way than commercials to reach the voters is by computer. In 1996 the two major parties and most presidential candidates provided sites on the Internet where online users could obtain schedules, speech texts, and other information from the various campaigns. Sen. John McCain turned his campaign Web site into a major fund-raising tool in his campaign for the 2000 Republican nomination. McCain raised around $5 million through the Web site, including a rapid infusion of much-needed cash immediately after his victory in the New Hampshire primary.[262] In 2003 Howard Dean went from being the relatively obscure former governor of Vermont to the leading candidate (at least for a time) for the 2004 Democratic nomination by using the Web to promulgate his strongly antiwar views and to raise money from small donors.

Partially Mediated Messages

Partially mediated messages are those passed along to voters through such vehicles as televised press conferences, debates, talk shows, and interviews. Here candidates have an opportunity to air their views and repeat well-worn phrases, but their ability to do so is constrained by the questioning of media representatives and, in debates, by the responses of opposing candidates.

First held in 1960, televised debates have been part of every presidential campaign since 1976. Although they provide a setting in which candidates can discuss their policy positions, viewers often seem more impressed by the style of the debaters than by their stands on specific issues. Richard Nixon was widely considered to have lost his first debate with John Kennedy in 1960 on the basis of manner and appearance, not because his arguments were weak. Ronald Reagan succeeded against Jimmy Carter in the 1980 debate largely because he was more engaging. The warm image that Reagan conveyed through his folksy anecdotes, his rejoinders to the president ("There you go again."), and the simple rhetorical terms in which he structured his answers all helped to belie some voters' fears that he was too extreme or too shallow to be president.

The 1992 campaign debates, which involved three candidates, saw the introduction of a new format. The first and third debates used the traditional format in which a panel of reporters asks questions, although the candidates were given unusual leeway to respond to each other. But the second debate used a television talk-show format, with a moderator eliciting questions from a studio audience. This format best suited Clinton, a candidate who enjoyed empathetic face-to-face encounters with voters.

The effect of debates is hard to measure, especially because they are quickly followed by a barrage of media commentary and speculation over who won. Surveys taken immediately after the second debate between Ford and Carter in 1976, for example, indicated that viewers, by almost two to one, felt that Ford had won. But the media's next-day focus on Ford's misstatement that Eastern Europe was not dominated by the Soviet Union dramatically reversed public opinion within three days.[263] Debates have the greatest potential to change minds when the voters are undecided or only weakly committed to the candidates.[264]

Debates can also make a difference when they depart from expectations. Gore carried a reputation into the 2000 campaign as an aggressive, experienced, and skillful debater, a reputation that Bush did not have.[265] But it was Bush, who entered the debates trailing Gore by around five percentage points in the polls, who benefited politically, coming out of them with about a five-point lead. In the first debate, a formal affair in which both candidates stood before a podium, Gore treated his opponent in an unattractively disdainful way, often speaking condescendingly when it was his turn and sighing and grimacing while Bush spoke. Chastened by the adverse public response to his behavior, Gore was deferential to the point of seeming obsequious during the second debate, a more loosely structured event at which the two candidates sat around a table with a moderator. Gore hit his stride in the town meeting–style third debate, but the inconsistency of his approach and manner from one debate to the next fed voters' doubts about who Gore really was. Bush was not strongly impressive in any of the debates, but voters saw the same Bush in all three of them. They also heard Bush discuss foreign policy during the second debate with apparent poise and competence, easing some of their doubts about how well he would perform as president on diplomatic and security matters.

The 2000 vice-presidential debate between Lieberman and Cheney, which took place between the first and second presidential debates, also redounded to Bush's benefit. Lieberman and Cheney discussed the issues reasonably and amicably, and were equally impressive in doing so. But Cheney, a rusty campaigner who had gotten off to a slow start after he was nominated for vice president, had much more to gain in the minds of voters than did Lieberman, who had already demonstrated his appeal in a number of highly successful joint appearances with Gore.

The 2004 election demonstrated that simply winning debates was not enough to win the election. Many pundits and voters thought that challenger John F. Kerry had bested President George W. Bush in one or more of their three televised encounters. But Bush was the winner on election day.

Talk shows provide one of the best settings for partially unmediated messages in presidential campaigns. By the end of the 1992 election, for example, the three major candidates had appeared ninety-seven times on talk shows such as *Donahue, Larry King Live,* and *Today.* Clinton appeared on these shows forty-eight times, Perot thirty-three times, and Bush sixteen times. Bush rejected the talk-show format early in the year as unpresidential but sought invitations later in the campaign.[266]

Mostly Mediated Messages

Mostly mediated messages are those that the candidates control the least, such as news stories that are constructed by reporters about the candidate. Paletz and Entman contend that mostly mediated messages have the greatest effect on public opinion precisely because the candidates do not control their content. Candidates' campaign staffs therefore use a wide variety of techniques to try to influence such messages, including staging events, rationing reporters' access to the candidate, and controlling the flow of information from the campaign organization.[267] Incumbents are particularly able to attract favorable coverage through official presidential actions. Only an incumbent, for example, can schedule an event in the Rose Garden or the East Room of the White House, or participate in dramatic international summit meetings as Nixon did in China and the Soviet Union in 1972.

The Vice-Presidential Campaign

In the Republic's early years, before the Twelfth Amendment was enacted in 1804, the vice presidency was awarded to the candidate who finished second in the presidential election. Thus early vice presidents, including Thomas Jefferson, actually were defeated presidential candidates. With the ratification of the Twelfth Amendment in 1804, presidential and vice-presidential candidates were elected as part of the same party ticket.

Since Jimmy Carter's tenure in the White House (1977–1981), vice presidents have played important advisory roles in shaping administration policy. And, of course, the vice president is just a heartbeat away from the presidency. The assassination and resignation of two recent presidents—John Kennedy and Richard Nixon, respectively—increased the public's awareness that the vice president could someday become president. Nine vice presidents have succeeded to the presidency after the president died in office or (in the most recent case) resigned the office: John Tyler (1841), Millard Fillmore (1850), Andrew Johnson (1865), Chester A. Arthur (1881), Theodore Roosevelt (1901), Calvin Coolidge (1923), Harry Truman (1945), Lyndon Johnson (1963), and Gerald Ford (1974).

Presidential nominees insist that their running mates fully endorse their approaches to government. But, especially in tight elections, the vice-presidential candidate is selected to broaden the presidential candidate's appeal in terms of geography, religion, ideology, government experience, personal background, and political style.

Defying traditional ticket balancing, Bill Clinton of Arkansas selected Al Gore of Tennessee as his running mate in 1992. Clinton-Gore was the only major party ticket in American history with candidates from neighboring states. But what the ticket lacked in geographic balance it made up for in balancing the candidates' other attributes. Clinton, who had state-level experience as a governor, lacked foreign policy experience and had a mixed environmental record. Gore had a strong foreign policy and environmental record in Congress. Clinton, who had avoided military service in the Vietnam War, also was strengthened by Gore's status as a veteran.

One of the most successful modern ticket-balancing maneuvers was Massachusetts senator John Kennedy's selection in 1960 of Senate Majority Leader Lyndon Johnson of Texas as his running mate. Kennedy's Catholic faith and northern urban appeal required some sort of gesture to conservative southern Democrats. As the candidate's father, former ambassador Joseph P. Kennedy, remarked, choosing Johnson was the shrewdest move of the campaign.

The 1988 Democratic nominee, Michael Dukakis, tried to duplicate Kennedy's "Boston-to-Austin" formula. The Massachusetts governor selected Texas senator Lloyd Bentsen as his running mate. But the gambit failed to lure Texas or the rest of the South to the Democratic fold. Texans voted overwhelmingly for Republican George Bush, a native New Englander who had long made Texas his home.

Carter picked Sen. Walter Mondale of Minnesota as his running mate in 1976 to counteract his inexperience in Washington and to appeal to certain traditional Democratic constituencies, especially organized labor. President Ford had announced the previous year that he was abandoning his vice president, Nelson Rockefeller, whose liberal New York credentials made him anathema to party conservatives. Ford later admitted he had treated Rockefeller badly.

Dole chose Kemp in 1996 in hopes of rousing the enthusiasm of the Republican Party's tax-cutting wing. When both men served in Congress, Kemp was a leading champion of sweeping tax cuts and Dole was a skeptic, fearing that runaway budget deficits would ensue. Bush's selection of Cheney in 2000 was intended to assure the voters that although Bush was a newcomer to foreign policy, a veteran policy maker would be at his side.

The vice-presidential nomination sometimes provides a point of entry to groups traditionally excluded from the political process. Ferraro's selection as Mondale's Democratic running mate in 1984—the first woman to run on a major party national ticket—is perhaps the most notable example of this breakthrough phenomenon. Its historical significance is closely matched by Gore's choice of Lieberman, the first Jewish major party nominee for national office, in 2000.

How vice-presidential candidates fashion their appeal to the voters depends on the presidential nominee's overall strategy. As a rule, presidential candidates appeal to the broad electorate while their running mates appeal to specific groups and try to rouse the party faithful. In 1968, for example, Republican Nixon took the high road by campaigning for a negotiated end to the Vietnam War while his running mate, Maryland governor Spiro T. Agnew, invoked conservatives' resistance to the civil rights and antiwar movements. In 1976 GOP standard-bearer Ford stressed his role as a national conciliator after the Watergate scandal while Dole, his vice-presidential running mate, took "the lead in implementing the Attack Carter plan." [268]

Vice-presidential candidates must take part in the televised debate that has become a mainstay of general election campaigns. Some voters watch the debate closely because the vice president will be president if anything happens to the president.

The 1988 vice-presidential debate reinforced Republican Dan Quayle's poor image. Quayle, trying to rebut critics who questioned his suitability for national office, argued that his government experience was greater than John Kennedy's at the time Kennedy ran for president in 1960. The grandfatherly Bentsen scolded Quayle, "Senator, I served with Jack Kennedy. I knew Jack Kennedy. Jack Kennedy was a friend of mine. Senator, you are no Jack Kennedy." [269] The moment undermined Quayle's search for respect.

In general, the vice-presidential candidate serves to shore up weak points that the electorate perceives in the presidential candidate. If a presidential candidate has little foreign policy or Washington experience, as was true of Reagan, Carter, Clinton, and George W. Bush, a running mate with experience in those areas can reassure the voters.

Personal Campaigning by Presidential Candidates

It now is taken for granted that presidential candidates will actively campaign in their own behalf. But for many years candidates avoided personal appearances, claiming it was unsavory to ask voters for the opportunity to serve. They "stood" rather than "ran" for office. As Stephen Wayne has written: "Personal solicitation was [once] viewed as demeaning and unbecoming of the dignity and status of the Presidency." [270] Thus, while their supporters engaged in propaganda, public relations, mass rallies, and other sorts of hoopla, the candidates themselves sat quietly on the sidelines.

The first major party candidate to break that tradition was Stephen A. Douglas in his 1860 race against Abraham Lincoln. The two had held seven public debates in 1858 when they were running for the same Senate seat from Illinois, but in the presidential race Lincoln vowed not to

In the 1896 election William Jennings Bryan, left, traveled over eighteen thousand miles and delivered more than six hundred speeches.

"write or speak anything upon doctrinal points." [271] Instead, he remained in Springfield, Illinois, receiving visitors and shunning rallies and political meetings.

Douglas, in contrast, set out on a personal campaign to try to mend the divisions in the Democratic Party caused by the slavery issue. Southern Democrats had nominated their own candidate, John C. Breckinridge, on a proslavery platform. When Douglas realized that he would not win the election, he transformed his campaign into an effort to save the Union. A speaking tour took him from New England to the South, and then to the Midwest where he heard some initial electoral vote returns. Aware that Lincoln would be the next president, Douglas returned to the South in a last-ditch effort "to lift the voice of reason in behalf of Union." [272]

The circumstances of 1860, however, were unique. Thus it was thirty-six years before another presidential candidate actively campaigned in his own behalf. In the election of 1896, William Jennings Bryan, whose stunning "Cross of Gold" speech at the Democratic convention had secured his nomination, traveled eighteen thousand miles and delivered more than six hundred speeches. [273] His opponent, William McKinley, followed a more traditional approach. Although he was an excellent public speaker and campaigned for the Republican nomination, McKinley felt that pleading his own cause once he was his party's nominee was unbecoming to the dignity of the presidency. Instead, McKinley stayed home and waged a "front porch" campaign in which the people came to him—and they came in droves. Historian Eugene H. Roseboom has referred to these excursions to McKinley's home as "mass pilgrimages." [274] From his front porch,

McKinley greeted his visitors and occasionally delivered a formal speech. McKinley won the election.

In 1900 Bryan challenged McKinley for reelection. As he had in 1896, Bryan embarked on a lengthy speaking tour. Although McKinley stayed in the White House, he sent his vice-presidential running mate, Theodore Roosevelt, to campaign. Outspoken in his views, flamboyant on the podium, and vigorous in his rhetoric, Roosevelt was an immediate success with his audiences. "Buffalo Bill" Cody referred to Roosevelt as the "American cyclone." [275] Roosevelt appeared in many of the same places as Bryan, and the campaign quickly developed into a contest between the two orators. [276]

In the election of 1904, the candidates reverted to a more traditional approach. Roosevelt, who had been elevated to the presidency when McKinley was assassinated in 1901, did not embark on a speaking tour, although his running mate, Charles Fairbanks, campaigned for the Republican ticket. The Democratic nominee, Alton B. Parker—cautious, colorless, largely unknown, and politically conservative—stayed above the fray. So did his running mate, the eighty-one-year-old West Virginia millionaire Henry G. Davis. Democrats had hoped that Davis would use his millions to help fund the campaign, but he did not. The Republicans won. [277]

The norms of campaigning soon began to change more permanently. Bryan, nominated for a third time in 1908, hit the campaign trail, as did his Republican opponent, William Howard Taft. In 1912 both Democratic candidate Woodrow Wilson and "Bull Moose" candidate Roosevelt campaigned strenuously. *(See Chapter 6, Chronology of Presidential Elections.)* By 1932 personal campaigning had become the norm. In that election, Herbert Hoover became the first incumbent to campaign actively for his own reelection. [278]

Modern Campaigning

In modern times, direct appeals to the people are an integral part of presidential campaigning. Indeed, with the development of jet travel, candidates are now able to crisscross the country extensively.

At the height of the campaign, it is common for candidates to visit several states in one day. Nearing the end of the 1988 election, Democrat Michael Dukakis campaigned around the clock. In the final two days, Dukakis traveled 8,500 miles to make appearances in eleven cities, crossing all four time zones three times. His last stop was Detroit at seven o'clock in the morning of election day.

In the 1896 campaign Bryan's opponent, William McKinley, took a more traditional approach by staying at home and waging a "front porch" campaign. People traveled to McKinley's home to hear him speak.

Personal campaigning has also been revolutionized by developments in communications technology, which have made new forms of direct mass appeal available. Televised debates, campaign commercials, Web-based bulletin boards and discussion groups, talk shows, and direct-mail operations are all relatively new ways for candidates to take their messages straight to the people. Even campaign appearances are now designed more for the media than for those actually attending the event. Enthusiastic crowds, colorful backdrops, and telegenic campaign symbols are carefully coordinated at every stop. Candidates hopscotch from airport to airport, often not venturing beyond the tarmac, to appear in as many media markets as possible. Sometimes the only event at each campaign stop is a brief press conference.

Family Appearances

Personal appearances by members of presidential candidates' families, especially their spouses, have grown in importance since the advent of television and jet travel. Although wives once were seldom seen until the election was won, today many accompany their husbands and share in the shaking of hands and making of speeches. Whether the husbands of female presidential candidates would be equally devoted remains to be seen.

The 1992 election witnessed an unusually strong and outspoken woman at the side of each major party nominee. Barbara Bush and Hillary Clinton, although strikingly different, were similar in their high visibility and active participation in their husbands' campaigns. President Bush's wife, motherly and white-haired, was genteel yet firm in denouncing her husband's detractors. Hillary Clinton, a lawyer, was more controversial, drawing criticism that she was in effect running for "co-president." After Bill Clinton won, he placed his wife, who for a time began using her maiden name of Rodham as her middle name, in charge of his ill-fated overhaul of the nation's health care system. During the final year of Clinton's presidency, Hillary Clinton sought and won a U.S. Senate seat from New York, which sent her to the top of the list of political leaders who were widely expected to run for president someday.

The personal life of a presidential candidate's spouse can be a sensitive matter for the campaign. In 1988 Kitty Dukakis, the wife of Democratic nominee Michael Dukakis, won praise for admitting that she was fighting a sometimes losing battle against alcohol addiction.

The Journey Toward the General Election

For years, the traditional opening day of the presidential election campaign was the first Monday in September, Labor Day. The period before Labor Day was reserved at least partly for the candidates to develop strategy in conjunction with their close aides.

In recent years, candidates have been unwilling to wait that long to launch their campaigns. In summer 1980, for example, Republican Ronald Reagan gave a number of speeches to groups to test and develop campaign themes. In fact, Reagan used the month before Labor Day as a learning period. He was able to try out several themes during the period when the media and the voters were least attentive. In 1992 Bill Clinton, running mate Al Gore, and their wives boarded a bus for a trip through the Northeast right after the Democratic convention. After the Republican convention in August, George Bush made campaign appearances in Florida.

The questions that the nominees consider as they head into the fall campaign include whether to concentrate their appeals on certain sections of the country, which themes and issues to stress, what kind of television commercials to air, what kind of collaboration to undertake with their party's congressional candidates, and how to organize state and local campaign efforts. The candidates also try to anticipate the opposition's strategy.

Nominees often must undertake fence-mending efforts with rivals in their own party. In 2000 Republican nominee George W. Bush made overtures to his main opponent in the primary, Sen. John McCain of Arizona, whose support he needed in the fall. Some presidential candidates, such as Kennedy in 1960, Reagan in 1980, and Kerry in 2004, have reunited the party by placing their main defeated rival on the ticket as the vice presidential nominee.

The presidential nominee's own campaign organization for the general election is usually an extension of the nomination organization, separate from the national and state party organizations. By tradition, nominees name their party's national committee chair, who will help to coordinate the party's efforts in the campaign.

The candidate's campaign committee receives its funding from the Federal Election Commission (FEC). In exchange for federal funding, the campaign must agree to limit spending to the amount received from the FEC. Since 1976, when federal funding of elections began, all major party nominees have chosen to accept the government funds rather than raise their own money. In 2000 Gore and Bush each received $67.56 million from the FEC. Four years later Bush and Kerry each received $74.6 million.

Although presidential campaigns that accept federal funding are limited in their expenditures, allied organizations can supplement the campaigns with more or less independent efforts. State and local party organizations, political action committees, independent committees established to help specific candidates, and labor unions contribute time, money, and volunteers to assist the candidate of their choice.

Even though the candidates and their advisers map out a campaign strategy before Labor Day, the campaign inevitably shifts its tactics according to polls, events, the opponent's activities, and the candidate's instincts about which approaches will succeed. For example, the Reagan-Carter race in 1980 shifted with developments in the Iran hostage crisis.

The winner-take-all electoral college system, in which the leading vote-getter in a state wins all of that state's electoral votes, encourages candidates to campaign in the large and competitive states rather than in states where they are especially weak or strong. Most smaller states also are slighted in the candidates' quest for large blocs of electoral votes. But if the election is close and a small state is competitive, that may change. In 2000 Bush made a major effort to win West Virginia, a traditionally Democratic state with only five electoral votes. Carrying West Virginia turned out to be crucial to his one-vote margin over Democrat Al Gore in the electoral college.

The 1992 Clinton-Gore campaign used a sophisticated computer program to guide its decisions about where to focus the candidates' time and other resources. The program identified the major media markets on an electronic map and each week assessed which markets had the most persuadable voters. A color-coded system based on eight sets of data helped to decide the best way to deploy the candidates and other major party speakers, media advertising, voter canvassing, and get-out-the-vote operations. Clinton won all but one of the thirty-two states his campaign targeted. The campaign also pumped significant resources into two other states that Clinton had little chance of winning—Texas and Florida—in order to force the George Bush campaign to spend resources there.

Competing in every part of the country can be difficult. In 1960 Richard Nixon gave speeches in all fifty states but lost the election to John Kennedy. Had he spent less time in states that heavily favored Kennedy or himself and more time in close states such as Illinois and Missouri, he might have won the election. In 2000 Democrat Al Gore neglected his home state of Tennessee and lost it to Bush. If Gore had carried Tennessee, he would have become president.

The ideological tone of the presidential campaign usually moderates once the parties have chosen the nominees. After winning the nomination by appealing to the ideological core of their respective parties, the nominees must try to attract independents and voters from the other party. Because the candidates usually can depend on the support of the most ideological members of their own party, they are able to shift their emphases in the fall.

The exception to this rule occurs when a candidate has suffered a bruising nomination battle and must persuade the backers of his defeated rival to go to the polls. In 1980, after President Carter defeated Sen. Edward Kennedy for the Democratic nomination, Carter had to make continued liberal appeals to satisfy the disappointed Kennedy supporters. Barry Goldwater in 1964 and Hubert Humphrey in 1968 faced similar challenges.

Deciding which issue stances to highlight is a major question for every campaign. Campaign consultants often advise against being too specific. Mondale's pledge in 1984 to raise taxes showed both the opportunity and the risk of being specific. For a while, the proposal put President Reagan, who had presided over historic budget deficits, on the defensive. But the proposal backfired when Reagan reminded voters that Mondale intended to take money out of their pockets.

Candidates also must bear in mind the effects of campaign promises on their ability to govern if they win. During the 1992 campaign, Clinton vowed to end the ban on gays serving in the military, to allow Haitian refugees into the United States, to end genocide in Bosnia, to cut taxes for the middle class, and to hold China responsible for human rights violations. Those promises helped Clinton get elected, but as president he reversed or modified all of them.

Daily campaign activities are geared toward getting impressive visual "bites" on national and local television news programs. The ill fortunes of the 1984 Mondale campaign were underscored on Labor Day, when the television networks contrasted the poor turnout at a rainy parade Mondale attended in New York City with President Reagan's campaign opener, a sunny, balloon-filled rally in southern California.

George Bush's campaign in 1988 was masterful at getting attractive visuals onto television news programs. Most of the visuals served the dual purpose of showing Bush in a picturesque setting and bashing Michael Dukakis, his Democratic rival. For example, Bush appeared in a sea of uniformed police officers to challenge the Massachusetts governor's record on crime, in flag factories to criticize Dukakis's veto of a bill directing schoolchildren to recite the Pledge of Allegiance, on a boat in Boston Harbor to attack Dukakis's failure to clean up the harbor, and on the shore of Lake Erie to identify himself as an environmentalist. Some of Bush's appearances used backdrops designed to reinforce the color schemes of his television advertisements.

Depending on their standing in the polls, and on whether they are running for or against the party in power, the candidates switch back and forth between appeals to bolster their own image and attacks to undermine their opponent's credibility. In 1984 Mondale faced a twofold and, as it turned out, impossible challenge: first, to break down the positive image of the popular President Reagan, and, second, to portray himself as a worthy replacement. If a candidate already has an unfavorable image, as President Carter did in 1980, the opponent only needs to persuade voters that he or she is a trustworthy alternative. Reagan succeeded at that task.

In 1992 Clinton got an assist from independent candidate Ross Perot. While Perot persistently attacked Bush's record, Clinton was able to present himself as above the fray. Eventually, Perot's attacks on Bush's economic record softened up the president to the point that voters began to look for an alternative. Perot also attacked Clinton, but not as frequently or personally.

Although the candidates use television and radio throughout the fall to advertise their campaigns, the pace quickens at the end of October when many voters are just beginning to pay close attention to the race. Whether the broadcast spots address specific issues or confine themselves to positive images of the candidate (and negative ones of the opponent) depends on the target audience, the salience of the issues, and the closeness of the race. In 1984 the Reagan campaign used feel-good commercials with gauzy images of Americana because it needed to reinforce a positive mood in the nation rather than sway many voters. Mondale used issues-oriented spots that year in an attempt to break up Reagan's coalition of support. In 1988 George Bush used the "good cop–bad cop" approach. Some of his commercials presented warm images of the candidate in family and patriotic settings. Others hammered relentlessly at Dukakis as an unreliable and elitist liberal. The "Willie Horton" spots, which criticized Dukakis for a Massachusetts program that allowed prisoners to earn weekend furloughs from prison for good behavior, were especially effective. Horton was a convicted murderer who raped a woman while on a furlough.

Televised debates by presidential and vice-presidential candidates have become a fixture of campaigns. Until 1976 the candidate leading in the polls resisted debates because he had little reason to give his opponent the opportunity to outshine him. Front-runners also feared making "gaffes"—

politically damaging offhand remarks—that might attract negative press coverage and give the opposition ammunition for the campaign trail.

In recent years, front-runners have been obliged to take part in debates to avoid the charge that they are hiding from the opponent. Candidates reluctant to debate try to put off the encounters by complaining about the proposed debates' timing and formats. In 1980, for example, Democratic president Carter avoided a debate that included both his Republican and independent opponents. He eventually faced Republican Reagan one-on-one, but only after suffering widespread criticism for his stance. In 2000 George W. Bush proposed joint appearances with rival Al Gore on the television programs *Larry King Live* and *Meet the Press*. Bush eventually agreed to participate in three conventional debates.

The effect of debates goes beyond the words the candidates speak. Voters also can be swayed by nonverbal messages. The first 1960 debate between Kennedy and Nixon gave Kennedy a boost because of his forceful, mature presentation of himself, especially in contrast to the tired-looking Nixon. Gore's sighs and grimaces while Bush was speaking during their first debate in 2000 proved unattractive to voters watching at home. Similarly, Bush's grimaces during his first debate with Kerry in 2004, joined with a too-high podium that accentuated his comparatively short stature, did little to enhance his performance.

Presidential candidates take different stances toward the campaigns of fellow party members in state and congressional elections. Nixon and Clinton were not willing to use their reelection campaigns to help other candidates. In contrast, in 1980, running against President Carter, Reagan was determined to spur a realignment of voters' party loyalties toward the Republicans and devoted much time and atten-

tion to campaigning for his party's other candidates.[279] In 2004 Bush told his campaign strategists that he did not want a "lonely victory," that is, a landslide without coattails in the congressional elections.[280] No other president seeking reelection has shown greater concern for his party's other candidates. Bush's approach was rewarded when the GOP gained four Senate seats.

Third Parties

The American system of elections favors a two-party competition for national offices. The electoral college, the first-past-the-post method of congressional elections, campaign finance laws, and state rules governing parties and campaigns all give a distinct advantage to the Republican and Democratic Parties.

But the party system is not static. Third parties often enter the electoral fray. Such parties, however, usually garner little support and die quickly. Since 1832, third parties have received more than 10 percent of the popular vote in only eight presidential elections, and more than 20 percent in only two elections. *(See Table 5-9, below.)* Nevertheless, recent elections have seen a resurgence of third party activity.

What Makes Third Parties Significant?

Over the years, more than forty political parties have run candidates for president.[281] Some scholars have defined significant third parties as those that have received more than 5.6 percent of the national popular vote, which is the average third party vote historically cast for president.[282] By that criterion, thirteen parties or independents qualify as significant.[283] *(See Table 5-9.)*

Popular support does not reveal everything, however. The States' Rights Democratic (Dixiecrat) Party, for example,

TABLE 5-9 **Top Vote-Winning Third Parties, 1832–2004**

Party	Election year	Candidate	Popular vote (percent)	No. electoral votes
Anti-Masonic	1832	William Wirt	7.8	7
Free Soil	1848	Martin Van Buren	10.1	0
American ("Know-Nothing")	1856	Millard Fillmore	21.5	8
Southern Democrats	1860	John C. Breckinridge	18.1	72
Constitutional Union	1860	John Bell	12.6	39
Populist	1892	James B. Weaver	8.5	22
Socialist	1912	Eugene V. Debs	6.0	0
Progressive (Bull Moose)	1912	Theodore Roosevelt	27.4	88
Progressive	1924	Robert M. La Follette	16.6	13
American Independent	1968	George C. Wallace	13.5	46
Independent	1980	John B. Anderson	6.6	0
Independent	1992	H. Ross Perot	18.9	0
Reform	1996	H. Ross Perot	8.5	0

SOURCE: *Guide to U.S. Elections,* 5th ed. (Washington, D.C.: CQ Press, 2005), 446.

NOTE: These parties (or independents) received more than 5.6 percent of the popular vote, the average third party vote historically cast for president. Daniel A. Mazmanian, *Third Parties in Presidential Elections* (Washington, D.C.: Brookings, 1974), 4–5.

received 7.3 percent of the electoral vote in 1948 even though its candidate, Strom Thurmond, won only 2.4 percent of the popular vote. Conversely, John Anderson (1980) and Ross Perot (1992 and 1996), whose campaigns are deemed significant if judged by popular votes, did not receive a single electoral vote.[284]

Even parties that receive only a small share of the popular or electoral vote can influence an election significantly. For example, the Liberty Party, an organization dedicated to the abolition of slavery, received only 2.3 percent of the popular vote and no electoral votes in 1844, yet Liberty candidate James G. Birney drained enough votes from the Whig Party to guarantee the election of the Democratic candidate, James K. Polk. The thirty-six electoral votes that Polk narrowly won in New York were particularly important. As James L. Sundquist has written, "The New York *Tribune* estimated that 90 percent of the Liberty party vote in New York came from Whigs."[285] Thus the outcome of the election almost certainly would have been different had the Liberty Party not run. Similarly, the 97,000 votes that Ralph Nader received in Florida in 2000 kept Al Gore, who lost the state by less than one thousand votes, from receiving Florida's twenty-five electoral votes and winning the election.

Third parties that do not garner many votes in the general election may also exercise influence by publicizing important issues that the major parties have ignored.[286] Because the major parties do not want third parties to siphon away their votes, they may even adopt positions they otherwise would not adopt to keep from losing votes to their third party rivals.

Some third parties are most notable for the long periods of time they have survived, even if they have never captured a significant portion of the popular or electoral vote. The Prohibition Party is an example. Formed in 1869, it is the longest-lasting third party in American history. In 2004 the party nominated Earl F. Dodge for president for the sixth consecutive time. Dodge received 140 popular votes nationwide.

In the nineteenth century, third parties tended to mirror the organization of the major parties. They ran slates of

When former Minnesota senator Eugene J. McCarthy waged his independent campaign in 1976, he chose no running mate and purposely refrained from establishing any party machinery.

candidates for offices in addition to president, held nominating conventions, drew up platforms, and existed for more than one election. In the mid-1850s the American, or "Know-Nothing," Party elected seven governors, five senators, and forty-three members of the House of Representatives and controlled several state legislatures.

In contrast, third parties in the twentieth century usually were ephemeral and personality-centered. The Progressive Party of 1912 was more a platform for Theodore Roosevelt's candidacy than an enduring political party. Once Roosevelt ceased to be a candidate, the party died. The candidacies of George Wallace in 1968, Eugene McCarthy in 1976, and John Anderson in 1980 functioned with little or no party organization. Ross Perot's personality and business background attracted followers to his 1992 and 1996 campaigns, but his Reform Party won less than 1 percent of the national popular vote in 2000.

Each of these men sought the presidency more as an independent candidate than as a part of a broader-based third party effort. To a large extent, they found that technological innovations in transportation and communication reduced the need for an established party organization to rally voter support.[287]

Varieties of Third Parties

Political scientist James Q. Wilson has identified four varieties of third parties: ideological parties, one-issue parties, economic protest parties, and factional parties.

Ideological Parties. Ideological parties include parties at both ends of the political spectrum, such as the Socialist and Libertarian Parties. They possess a "comprehensive view of American society and government that is radically different from that of the established parties."[288] Although ideological parties appeal to a narrow base of support, they have proven to be the most enduring type of third party, largely because their members are committed to ideas rather than individual candidates.

The longest established ideological parties are those that embraced Marxism. The Socialist Party, for example, formed in 1901 with Eugene V. Debs as leader. In 1912, running with vice-presidential candidate Emil Seidel, Debs received 6.0 percent of the popular vote for president. During World War I, Debs was convicted of sedition for making a speech espousing the Socialist Party's antiwar stance. In 1920 he ran for president from the federal penitentiary in Atlanta, Georgia, and won 3.4 percent of the popular vote. (Seymour Stedman was his running mate that year.) The party has run national candidates in most presidential elections since then.

The most recent variant of the socialist movement is the Socialist Workers Party, formed in 1938 by followers of Soviet communist Leon Trotsky who were expelled from the U.S. Communist Party. The Socialist Workers have run candidates for president in every election since 1938. The Communist Party, from which the Socialist Workers split, formed in the early 1920s and ran presidential candidates from 1924 through 1940. Throughout the 1950s, the party was outlawed by restrictive legislation passed by Congress. In the late 1960s, however, the party was reconstituted. It ran a presidential candidate (Gus Hall) in every election from 1972 to 1984. Since then, there have been no Communist Party candidates for president.

At the opposite end of the political spectrum is the Libertarian Party, formed in 1971. Libertarians are dedicated to the concept of individual freedom, and they oppose government intervention in both personal and economic life. They have run candidates in every presidential election since 1972, when Roger MacBride, as a "faithless" Republican elector from Virginia, cast the only electoral vote the Libertarians have ever received. In 1976 the Libertarians chose MacBride as their presidential candidate and David Bergland as his running mate. They appeared on the ballot in thirty-two states and won 173,000 popular votes—0.2 percent of the national vote.

In 1980 the Libertarian Party was on the ballot in all fifty states and the District of Columbia. Presidential nominee Ed Clark of California and vice-presidential nominee David Koch of New York garnered 921,000 votes, or 1.1 percent of the national popular vote. Although it has continued to appear on nearly all state ballots, the party has not attained that level of support in subsequent elections. In 2004 software engineer Michael Badnarik of Texas and his running mate, Richard Campagna of Iowa, received 397,367 votes (0.3 percent of the national popular vote).

The Green Party made an impressive debut in presidential politics in 1996 when consumer activist Ralph Nader agreed to head its ticket. Nader received 685,040 popular votes (0.7 percent). In 2000 he made an even more impressive showing, winning 2.9 million votes (2.7 percent). Nader finished third, well behind the major party nominees but well ahead of all the other third party contenders. Nader drew votes mostly at the expense of the Democrats, which threw Florida and perhaps one or two other states into the Republican column. Nader and his running mate, Native American activist Winona LaDuke of Minnesota, were on the ballot in forty-seven states, up from twenty-two states in 1996. In 2004, however, Nader ran as an independent candidate and appeared on only thirty-four state ballots.

One-Issue Parties. Dissatisfaction with the major parties often centers on their stances toward important and controversial issues. Many third parties have arisen to address a single policy concern, such as slavery, states' rights, currency, opposition to immigration ("nativism"), abortion, and even hostility to lawyers.[289] But once such an issue ceases to be salient, the basis for the party's existence disappears. Because most issues provoke intense feelings for a relatively brief period—or, if they persist, eventually are dealt with by the major parties—one-issue parties tend to be short-lived.

Many of the earliest third parties were formed in response to the slavery issue. The best known of these was the Free Soil Party, which was formed in 1848 as a coalition of three antislavery movements: the Liberty Party, the Barnburners, and the Conscience Whigs. At its convention in Buffalo, New York, in 1848, the Free Soil Party nominated former Democratic president Martin Van Buren as its presidential candidate and Charles F. Adams, the son of former president John Quincy Adams, as his running mate. Although it lost the presidential election, the Free Soil Party succeeded in winning thirteen seats in Congress.[290]

The American Party, better known as the "Know-Nothings" because its members told outsiders they knew nothing about its secret rituals and greetings, was another notable single-issue party of the 1800s. The Know-Nothings emerged in the 1850s in opposition to European immigration, which was at a pre–Civil War peak because of severe economic conditions abroad. The party was particularly hostile to Catholics. In 1854 and 1855 the Know-Nothings were extremely successful. They elected five senators, forty-three members of the House of Representatives, and seven governors and won control of six state legislatures. In 1856 the Know-Nothings nominated former Whig president Millard Fillmore for president and Andrew Jackson Donelson for vice president. The party divided, however, over slavery. Most northern Know-Nothings turned to the Republican Party. Southern and border state Know-Nothings joined with former Whigs to form the Constitutional Union Party in 1860.

One party that persists despite the apparently final resolution of its issue is the Prohibition Party. Dedicated to banning the sale of alcohol, the Prohibition Party has run a presidential candidate in every election since 1872. Although primarily dedicated to the temperance issue, the Prohibition Party strongly supported the early feminist movement.

Economic Protest Parties. Economic protest parties evolve in opposition to depressed economic conditions. The Greenback Party, for example, was an outgrowth of the

Panic of 1873, a post–Civil War economic depression. Farmers who wanted the government to issue "greenbacks" (paper money) to stem the shortage of available capital organized the party. Because paper money was inflationary, farmers also hoped that the use of greenbacks would make it easier to pay their debts.

The Greenback Party held its first national convention in 1876. With Peter Cooper, an eighty-five-year-old New York philanthropist, as their presidential candidate and Samuel F. Cary as the vice-presidential nominee, the Greenbacks won less than 1 percent of the popular vote. But as hard times continued, they mobilized more support. Most important, the Greenbacks joined forces with labor groups. In 1877 and 1878 they won fourteen House seats and showed strength in state and local elections. By 1880, however, economic conditions were improving. Although the Greenbacks held conventions and nominated candidates in the presidential elections of 1880 and 1884, they saw their support dwindle. By 1888 the party was effectively dead.

Prompted by the return of bad economic conditions, the People's Party, or "Populists," formed and held a national convention in Cincinnati, Ohio, in 1891. Currency was again a prime concern, although the new cry was for the free coinage of silver. The Populists, with James B. Weaver as their presidential candidate and James G. Field as his running mate, won 8.5 percent of the popular vote in the 1892 presidential election. Four years later, however, the Democrats embraced the Populists' main issue and nominated William Jennings Bryan on a free-silver platform. The Populists ran candidates in presidential elections through 1908 but with little success.

Factional Parties. Factional parties develop from splits in one of the major parties. They usually form to protest "the identity and philosophy of the major party's presidential candidate." [291] In the twentieth century, factional parties have been the most successful third parties at winning votes.

The Progressive Party was first formed to support the candidacy of former president Theodore Roosevelt after the raucous Republican convention of 1912, in which President William Howard Taft defeated Roosevelt for the nomination. Dubbed the "Bull Moose" Party, the Progressives held a convention in Chicago to nominate Roosevelt for president and Hiram Johnson for vice president and to draw up a party platform. Although defeated by Woodrow Wilson, Roosevelt outpolled Taft, winning 27.4 percent of the national popular vote to Taft's 23.2 percent and eighty-eight electoral votes to Taft's eight. *(See "Wilson and the Divided Republicans: 1912 and 1916," p. 386, in Chapter 6.)* In that same election the Bull Moosers also ran candidates in state and local races and won thirteen seats in the House of Representatives. But their appeal to the voters was based on Roosevelt's involvement, and when he later withdrew the party disintegrated. Wilson's Democratic administration

South Carolina governor J. Strom Thurmond raises his hands over his head in response to a tumultuous ovation accorded him by delegates to the Dixiecrats' States' Rights Convention in Birmingham, Ala., on July 17, 1948. Thurmond had just been nominated by the Dixiecrats for the presidency of the United States. At left is Walter Sillers, convention chairman.

then incorporated many of the Progressives' reform proposals and drew much of their support.

Like Theodore Roosevelt, Sen. Robert M. La Follette of Wisconsin represented the liberal wing of the Republican Party. In 1924 he split from the Republicans and revived the Progressive Party label. The Progressives then held a convention in Cleveland, where they nominated La Follette for president and Burton K. Wheeler for vice president. La Follette went on to receive an impressive 16.6 percent of the popular vote but only thirteen electoral votes. The party relied primarily on La Follette's personal appeal. When he died in 1925, the party collapsed.

In 1948 the Progressive Party label was revived yet again. This time, however, it split off from the liberal wing of the Democratic Party. At a convention in Philadelphia, former vice president Henry A. Wallace was nominated as the Progressives' presidential candidate and Glen H. Taylor as his running mate. That same year, southern conservatives split off from the Democratic Party over a dispute about a platform plank endorsing President Truman's civil rights program. They walked out of the Democratic convention, formed the States' Rights Democratic ("Dixiecrat") Party, and convened in Birmingham, Alabama, where they nominated South Carolina governor Strom Thurmond for president and Mississippi governor Fielding Wright for vice president.

Although both the Progressives and the Dixiecrats received nearly the same number of popular votes (Wallace received 1.157 million votes and Thurmond 1.169 million), the Dixiecrats carried four states in the Deep South with thirty-nine electoral votes and the Progressives carried none. The Dixiecrats' success illustrates the electoral college's bias toward third parties with a regional base. Despite the fracturing of his party, Harry Truman managed to defeat his Republican challenger, Thomas Dewey.

In 1968 Alabama governor George Wallace bolted from the Democratic Party and formed the American Independent Party. He did not hold a convention and chose as his running mate the retired Air Force general Curtis E. LeMay. Wallace had come to national attention in 1963 when he stood in the doorway of the University of Alabama to block the court-ordered admission of two African American students. The next year he ran strongly in three Democratic presidential primaries in protest against the 1964 Civil Rights Act.

Wallace's third party candidacy in 1968 gained support from white blue-collar workers who were fed up with civil rights activism, antiwar demonstrations, urban riots, and the national Democratic Party's embrace of liberalism. In the general election Wallace received 13.5 percent of the popular vote and carried five Deep South states with forty-six electoral votes. Some feared at the time that he would win enough support to throw the election into the House of Representatives, but the Republican candidate, Richard Nixon, managed to outpoll Wallace in enough southern states to win an electoral vote majority. Wallace returned to the Democratic Party to seek its presidential nomination in 1972 and 1976, and the American Independent Party soon died.

Illinois representative John Anderson formed the National Unity Campaign as the vehicle for his independent candidacy in 1980 when he failed to win the Republican nomination. He chose former Wisconsin governor Patrick J. Lucey, a Democrat, as his running mate. In a year when many voters were dissatisfied with the candidates of the two major parties, Anderson received widespread publicity for his willingness to take controversial stands on issues, including proposing a steep tax on gasoline. Despite considerable support in early polls and a well-received performance in a presidential debate, he ultimately captured only 6.6 percent of the popular vote and no electoral votes.

The Perot Phenomenon

In 1992 and 1996, billionaire H. Ross Perot led a factional third party that, unlike most previous factional parties, drew evenly from discontented members of both major parties. A business executive with no experience in government might seem a peculiar spokesman for populist anger against elites. Yet Perot, who made a $4 billion fortune in the computer industry, became one of the most successful third party candidates in history when he tapped popular disillusionment with politics in the 1992 presidential race.

Perot had a long association with Republican presidents and causes, but he never contemplated a political career until early 1992, when President George Bush fell in the public opinion surveys and the Democrats running to replace him failed to capture the voters' imagination. At the prodding of a television talk-show host, Perot said he would consider a race for the presidency.

Perot's campaign unofficially began when he appeared on the cable talk show *Larry King Live* on February 20, 1992. When King asked Perot whether he would seek the presidency, Perot at first demurred but then said he would run if supporters could get his name on the ballot in all fifty states. Within weeks, volunteers had gotten his name on the ballot in dozens of states. In June a Harris poll showed Perot leading the race with 37 percent of those surveyed to Bush's 33 percent and Clinton's 25 percent.

In response to these developments, Perot vowed to spend $100 million or more of his own money to run a "world-class campaign." (He actually spent around $70 million.) Perot hired two of the nation's leading campaign strategists—Democrat Hamilton Jordan, who ran Carter's 1976 and 1980 campaigns, and Republican Ed Rollins, who ran Reagan's 1984 campaign—but they soon quit, complaining that he ignored their advice.

Perot's appeal stemmed from neither a strong ideology nor a bold stance on a major issue. Instead, voters seemed attracted to his business background and folksy manner. Perot had amassed his fortune by starting his own company, Electronic Data Systems. His pithy statements on complicated issues—he vowed to "take back the country" and "clean out the barn"—contrasted with Bush and Clinton's measured and sometimes convoluted pronouncements.

But as volunteers continued to circulate petitions to put him on the ballot, Perot came under growing scrutiny from the media. Reporters investigated his business practices and personal foibles. Pundits criticized his authoritarian management style.

In response, just as the Democrats were concluding their July convention Perot stunned followers by announcing that he would not run. Perot's stated reason for dropping out was that his campaign might deadlock the election and send it to the House of Representatives. He also praised Clinton, the Democratic nominee, for revitalizing his party.

After a brief hiatus, during which Perot's book *United We Stand: How We Can Take Back Our Country* climbed onto paperback bestseller lists, Perot announced on October 1 that he would run after all. He appeared at several rallies but mostly delivered his message in television advertisements. In a series of half-hour infomercials that aired in prime time, Perot offered straightforward explanations of the economic and social ills facing the nation. Perot also appeared in three presidential debates with Bush and Clinton. He hit Bush the hardest but also jabbed Clinton. The issue Perot focused on most was the need for a balanced budget.

Except for the brief period when he was advised by Jordan and Rollins, Perot did not employ any high-priced political talent. He used his money to air television and radio commercials, to print and distribute campaign literature and other materials, and to maintain a Dallas headquarters where volunteers ran telephone banks.

Perot's running mate, retired Navy vice-admiral James Stockdale, was a renowned scholar and decorated former prisoner of war in Vietnam, but he had no experience in politics. In the televised vice-presidential debate, Stockdale sometimes looked befuddled and performed poorly. As a result, he became an object of parody and undermined Perot's claim to be a serious candidate.

Like many third party candidates, Perot forced the major parties to address important issues, especially the budget deficit and corruption in politics. But in the end, he could not attract enough support to win any states. Perot ended up with 19 percent of the popular vote and no electoral votes.

Unlike many third party candidates, Perot won support from a broad demographic base. He ran best among self-described independents, men under thirty, and voters who viewed their family's financial situation as getting worse.[292] His influence on the election's outcome, however, was a matter of dispute. Exit polls showed that if Perot had not been on the ballot, one-third of his supporters would have voted for Bush, one-third would have voted for Clinton, and the remaining third would not have voted at all.

After the election, Perot sniped at Clinton's policies on free trade, welfare reform, campaign finance reform, and various foreign policy problems. In September 1995 he announced that he was forming the Reform Party. He ran again in 1996 and received 8 percent of the popular vote and no electoral votes. In contrast to his self-financed 1992 campaign, Perot paid for his 1996 effort with $29 million in federal funds. In 2000 the Reform Party nominated conservative activist Pat Buchanan for president. Buchanan received $12.6 million in federal campaign funds but won less than 1 percent of the national popular vote. Because campaign finance laws stipulate that a party must receive at least 5 percent of the popular vote in an election in order to receive federal funding four years later, Buchanan's lack of success caused the demise of the Reform Party.

Obstacles and Opportunities

Third parties face considerable legal, political, cultural, and psychological barriers. Many voters will not cast their ballot for a third party because they are loyal to one of the two major parties. Instead, if they are unhappy with their party they will work to promote change from within or simply not vote.[293] That explains why when third parties prosper, voter turnout often declines.[294] People with weak party allegiances, including many new voters, are more likely to vote for third parties.

The fact that third parties have little chance of winning further diminishes their support. People often feel that a vote for a third party is a wasted vote. Some also have the sense that third parties are somehow illegitimate, that they disrupt the normal two-party system.[295] Of particular concern is the fear that a third party will carry enough states to cause a deadlock in the electoral college and throw the election to the House of Representatives. Major parties benefit from and therefore encourage the feeling that third parties are illegitimate.

These psychological barriers are accompanied by legal ones. Most notable are statutory obstacles. Since the 1890s, states have used the so-called Australian ballot, which lists the candidates for each office, usually by party. These ballots are provided to voters, who mark them in secret. Before that time, parties prepared the ballots themselves. Voters then chose the ballot of the party they wished to vote for and simply dropped it in the ballot box.[296]

Most states that adopted the Australian ballot also enacted a ballot access law to keep their official ballots from being too long. The two major parties automatically appear on the ballot, but minor parties have to clear a series of hurdles that are different in each state, including petition requirements, filing deadlines, and fees. Meeting these requirements is time-consuming, costly, and complicated. Since the late 1960s, a series of court cases have modified ballot access laws to prevent rules that are blatantly unfair to third parties. Nevertheless, such laws continue to differ from state to state and serve as a considerable hurdle for third parties.

The 1974 FECA amendments also have served as a barrier to third parties. The act allows major party candidates to receive $74.6 million each (the figure in 2004) in public funds during the general election campaign, but third parties are allotted public funds only after the election is over and only if they appear on the ballot in at least ten states and receive at least 5 percent of the national popular vote. Receiving public funds after the fact, rather than during the campaign when money is needed, puts third parties at a significant disadvantage. Not only is the money not in hand, but valuable time must be spent on fund raising instead of other campaign activities.

Winning 5 percent of the popular vote not only guarantees a third party reimbursement, it also guarantees funding for the party in the next election. This can lead to strange outcomes. In 2000 Reform Party nominee Pat Buchanan received $12.6 million in funding because Perot had received more than 5 percent in 1996. Buchanan's heavily funded campaign received less than 1 percent of the popular vote.

Initially, FECA discriminated against independent candidates as opposed to third parties. Eugene McCarthy would not have been eligible to receive public funding in 1976 even if he had received more than 5 percent of the popular vote because he was technically an independent candidate, not a "minor party" nominee. The rule was changed for Anderson's benefit in 1980. In making the change, the Federal Election Commission said that Anderson was the functional equivalent of a third party.[297]

The electoral college poses another legal barrier to most third parties because the candidate with the most popular votes in each state wins all of the state's electors. This winner-take-all arrangement hurts third parties with a broad geographical appeal because their popular votes seldom are concentrated enough to carry any states. But the electoral college can magnify the support of third parties that have a regional base. Thurmond, for example, won a disproportionate share of electoral votes in 1948 by carrying four southern states.

The rise of party primaries also has helped to maintain the two-party system. Through primaries, dissident groups within a major party have an opportunity to air their views, vent their frustrations, and resolve their differences within the party. Without this opportunity, such groups might be more inclined to leave the party.[298]

In addition to psychological and legal barriers, third parties also face political barriers. Because third parties tend to be short-lived, they lack the foundation of lasting voter loyalty that the Republicans and Democrats enjoy. Compared with the major parties, third party organizations tend to be weaker and less experienced, their candidates usually are less well known, and they have less money to publicize their causes and fund their activities.

To compound their problems, third parties usually receive less free media coverage than the major parties. Their candidates often are excluded from televised debates between the two major party candidates. Their nominating conventions (if they hold any) are not beamed into American homes by the major television networks. Even in 1980, when Anderson received considerable media attention, the two major party candidates received ten times more coverage than he and all ten of the other third party candidates combined.[299]

Whether a two-party system is good or bad is open to debate. Some see third parties as a threat to the stability of democratic politics in the United States. Others see them as a vital element in expressing minority sentiments and as a breeding ground for new or neglected issues and innovations.[300] Whatever their merits, and despite the obstacles to their success, third parties persist. In the course of doing so,

they often perform important functions. Third parties focus attention on issues that might otherwise be ignored and provide a testing ground for the presentation of new ideas and policies. As a result, they may force the major parties to innovate in important and beneficial ways.

Certainly third parties occupy a more prominent part of the political landscape than they have in many decades. The average share of the national popular vote that was won by all third party candidates in elections from 1932 to 1964 was 1.6 percent. That figure quadrupled to 6.7 percent for elections in the period 1968–2000.[301] What is more, the Libertarian Party and Green Party have sunk roots in state and local politics, running candidates for office at all levels of the federal system. In 2000, for example, the Green Party fielded 270 candidates in races ranging from town council to U.S. senator to president of the United States.

THE ELECTION

The general election in the fall is a less complicated undertaking than the nominating process in the first half of the year. Not only has the field been limited to two or occasionally three nominees, but the rules of voting are virtually identical throughout the nation. The general election, however, has the potential to become complicated. Once the people vote, the selection of the president could move from the electoral college to the House of Representatives or even, as happened in 2000, to the Supreme Court. Eighteen presidents have been elected with less than a majority of the national popular vote. (See Table 5-10, right.) Four presidents have been elected despite receiving fewer popular votes than their opponent, including George W. Bush in 2000.

Election Day

More than 100 million people go to the polls each presidential election day, the first Tuesday after the first Monday in November in years divisible by four. Among other things, the day triggers aggressive competition among the media.

In recent years, the media have been criticized for approaching their election-day competition for audiences too aggressively. Some observers have suggested that broadcasters undermine the democratic process in their eagerness to report the winners early. The major television networks have developed a variety of ways to make their own projections of the election outcomes in all the states. They project winners based on their analyses of both exit polls (that is, surveys of voters as they leave the voting booths) and actual returns from a representative sample of each state's precincts. Exit polls allow the networks to prepare their projections even before the polls close.

The networks' practice of declaring winners on the basis of incomplete information caused major controversies in 1980 and, especially, in 2000. All three networks declared

TABLE 5-10 **"Minority" Presidents**

Under the U.S. electoral system, there have been eighteen presidential elections (decided by either the electoral college itself or by the House of Representatives) where the victor did not receive a majority of the popular votes cast in the election. Four of these presidents—John Quincy Adams in 1824, Rutherford B. Hayes in 1876, Benjamin Harrison in 1888, and George W. Bush in 2000—actually trailed their opponents in the popular vote.

The following table shows the percentage of the popular vote received by candidates in the eighteen elections in which a "minority" president (designated by boldface type) was elected:

Year Elected	Candidate	Percentage of Popular Vote	Candidate	Percentage of Popular Vote	Candidate	Percentage of Popular Vote	Candidate	Percentage of Popular Vote
1824	Jackson	41.34	**Adams**	30.92	Clay	12.99	Crawford	11.17
1844	**Polk**	49.54	Clay	48.08	Birney	2.30		
1848	**Taylor**	47.28	Cass	42.49	Van Buren	10.12		
1856	**Buchanan**	45.28	Fremont	33.11	Fillmore	21.53		
1860	**Lincoln**	39.82	Douglas	29.46	Breckenridge	18.09	Bell	12.61
1876	Tilden	50.97	**Hayes**	47.95	Cooper	.97		
1880	**Garfield**	48.27	Hancock	48.25	Weaver	3.32	Others	.15
1884	**Cleveland**	48.50	Blaine	48.25	Butler	1.74	St. John	1.47
1888	Cleveland	48.62	**Harrison**	47.82	Fisk	2.19	Streeter	1.29
1892	**Cleveland**	46.05	Harrison	42.96	Weaver	8.50	Others	2.25
1912	**Wilson**	41.84	T. Roosevelt	27.39	Taft	23.18	Debs	5.99
1916	**Wilson**	49.24	Hughes	46.11	Benson	3.18	Others	1.46
1948	**Truman**	49.52	Dewey	45.12	Thurmond	2.40	Wallace	2.38
1960	**Kennedy**	49.72	Nixon	49.55	Others	.72		
1968	**Nixon**	43.42	Humphrey	42.72	Wallace	13.53	Others	.33
1992	**Clinton**	43.01	G. Bush	37.45	Perot	18.91	Others	.64
1996	**Clinton**	49.24	Dole	40.71	Perot	8.4	Others	1.65
2000	Gore	48.38	**G. W. Bush**	47.87	Nader	2.74	Others	1.01

SOURCE: *Guide to U.S. Elections*, 5th ed. (Washington, D.C.: CQ Press, 2005), 229.

Republican Ronald Reagan the winner of the 1980 election over President Jimmy Carter before the polls closed in the western states, and Carter conceded the election at 8:45 p.m. eastern standard time (EST). Media critics argued that the early projection discouraged people in the West, where the polls still were open, from going to vote because the national election was apparently a foregone conclusion. Although the scholarly evidence is mixed, it is likely that a higher turnout in the West would have changed the outcome of some close state and congressional races there.[302]

In 2000, at about 2:00 a.m. EST on election night, all of the networks declared that Bush had carried Florida and thus attained the 271 electoral votes he needed to become president. Across the country, newspapers went to press with headlines reading "Bush!" and "Bush Wins!" Although the networks realized within a couple of hours that their declaration was premature, the five-week struggle that ensued over which candidate had won the election was shadowed by the presumption that Bush was the victor unless Gore could prove otherwise.

Although Congress has considered action to restrict network pronouncements on election day and the networks have pledged to withhold the results in each state until its polls close, the basic problem of news outracing events is likely to remain. Some have suggested that a longer balloting period—a full twenty-four hours; a full weekend, as was the case in some states in the nineteenth century; or (a growing practice in several states) an early voting period of two to three weeks—would modify the media's imperative to report news instantly.

Whether the presidential election is close or not, cable and broadcast networks stay on the air with special election coverage into the wee hours of the next morning. The candidates watch the returns on television in their homes or hotel suites before going to election headquarters either to celebrate or commiserate with their supporters.

Few elections are stolen nowadays through corrupt tampering with ballots. In 1960 Richard Nixon considered demanding a recount of his losing contest with John Kennedy after ballot tampering was reported in Texas, Illinois, and other closely contested states. But almost two weeks after the election, Nixon decided not to do so. He later wrote in his memoir *Six Crises* that he made that decision because of the constitutional crisis in presidential succession that a recount might have provoked.

But the 2000 election showed that even honest voting systems are subject to breakdown. Fierce controversy over the results in Florida revealed that ballot design and voting technology affect the likelihood that voters who show up at the polls will have their votes counted. Nationally, 2.1 million ballots—around 2 percent of all ballots cast—were marked either for more than one presidential candidate or for none, sometimes intentionally but often as a consequence of voter confusion.

These errors were especially widespread among the 36 percent of voters whose states and counties used the old-style punch-card system, in which a voter must punch through a pre-perforated square, or "chad," next to the name of the candidate of his or her choice. The 27 percent of voters whose ballots must be marked (SAT- or ACT-style) in pencil, then read by an optical scanning device encountered fewer problems, as did the 9 percent who voted on ATM-like electronic touch screens and the 18 percent who voted by pulling a small lever next to their candidate's name in a manual voting machine.[303]

The postelection furor over the outcome of the voting in Florida augured a national effort to ensure that voters can easily and accurately express their intentions in the voting booth.[304] Civil rights groups were especially incensed that the less expensive, more error-prone punch-card system is more prevalent in poor and minority precincts than in affluent jurisdictions.

In the wake of the 2000 elections, numerous states passed laws to improve the fairness and accuracy of their voting systems. Congress also acted: the House passed the Help America Vote Act on December 12, 2001, by a 362–63 margin, and, on April 11, 2002, the Senate passed the Equal Protection of Voting Rights Act by a vote of 99 to 1. Both bills set national standards for the conduct of elections and both authorized federal grants to help states comply with the new standards. Punch-card systems were banned by the act, and most states moved toward optical scanning devices or electronic touch screens.

The Electoral Vote

The Framers of the Constitution intended that the "electoral college"—which they hoped would consist of the nation's most learned and public-spirited citizens—would select the president. The electors were to be chosen by the states as each state legislature saw fit. Some time after their selection the electors would meet in their separate state capitals to vote for the next president.

As the electoral system operates today, electors gather in their state capitals on the first Monday after the second Wednesday in December, cast their ballots, and prepare a statement of their vote to send to Washington. Congress counts the votes on January 6. States receive one elector for each representative and senator they have in Congress.

In theory, the electoral college system favors the smallest and, especially, the largest states. The smallest states are favored because, regardless of their population, they are awarded two electors to represent the state's two Senate seats plus one elector for the state's seat in the House of Representatives. (The Twenty-third Amendment also allots three electoral votes to the District of Columbia.) The largest states are favored because their large blocs of electoral votes ensure that the candidates will pay close attention to their interests.

In practice, however, the electoral college favors states that are neither reliably "red," or Republican, nor dependably "blue," or Democratic. (The color scheme is based on the television networks' election night maps showing which states have gone for which party.) Thus in 2004 Bush and Kerry ignored California, Texas, and New York, the three largest states in the country, because both campaigns were convinced that Texas was solidly for Bush and New York and California were solidly for Kerry. Meanwhile, the candidates worked very hard to win votes in smaller but less politically predictable states such as New Mexico and Iowa.

Since 1836, all the states except Maine and Nebraska have allocated electors to candidates on a winner-take-all basis. (Maine and Nebraska allocate two votes based on who carries the state and one vote for carrying each congressional district.) The state-by-state system of allocating electors encourages candidates to identify a geographical base of strength and attempt to build on that base. Modern Democrats usually can count on the Pacific Coast, the industrial Northeast, and the upper Midwest to serve as a strong base of support. Modern Republicans have a strong hold on the Rocky Mountain West, the Plains states, and the South.

The Framers expected a plethora of state "favorite-son" candidates to keep all but a few candidates from winning a majority of electoral votes in any election, thus sending most presidential elections to the House of Representatives. If they had been right, the United States might have developed a variant of a parliamentary system in which the legislature chooses the executive.

Numerous reforms have been proposed to alter either the fundamental concept of the electoral college or some of its odder aspects. One reform would eliminate "faithless" electors—those who vote for a different candidate than they were elected to support—by automatically casting a state's electoral votes for the candidate receiving the most popular votes. Historically, only eleven electors have broken faith with the voters, and in no case has the outcome of an election been affected by their actions. But the frequency of faithless voting has increased from once in every twenty elections from 1789 to 1944 to more than once in every two elections from 1948 to 2004. Around half the states outlaw faithless voting by electors, but because the Constitution imposes no such constraint, these laws are of doubtful constitutionality.

In 2000 an elector from the District of Columbia abstained rather than vote for Gore, who had carried the district by 85 percent to 9 percent. She withheld her vote to

Only two presidential elections—those of 1800 and 1824—have been decided by the House of Representatives. In 1800 Thomas Jefferson, left, and the intended vice-presidential candidate, Aaron Burr, right, tied in the electoral college vote.

protest the District's lack of representation in Congress. No elector had ever used his or her vote in such a way.

A second proposed reform of the electoral college would allocate electoral votes by congressional district rather than by state and would award each state's two Senate-based votes to the presidential candidate who carries the state as a whole. A third proposal would provide for each state's electoral votes to be allocated proportionally—for example, if a candidate carried a state with 60 percent of the popular vote, he or she would receive 60 percent of the state's electoral votes. A fourth proposal, and the one that enjoys the most popular support, would replace the electoral college with a system of direct election.

When the Electoral College Is Deadlocked

When no presidential candidate receives a majority of electoral votes, the Constitution directs that the president be chosen by the House of Representatives and the vice president by the Senate.

The Framers of the Constitution thought that most presidential elections would be deadlocked. George Mason, for example, predicted that nineteen out of twenty elections would be decided by the House.[305] In fact, only two presidential elections—those of 1800 and 1824—have been decided that way.

Procedure

If an election is thrown into the House, the newly elected representatives elect the president from among the three candidates with the most electoral votes. Before the Twentieth Amendment to the Constitution was ratified in 1933, both the new Congress and the new presidential term began on March 4. Thus the old lame duck Congress was

responsible for electing the president. Under the amendment, the new Congress convenes on January 3 and the president's term begins on January 20.

The changes brought about by the Twentieth Amendment mean that if the electoral college were deadlocked, Congress would have considerably less time than before to choose a president. Originally, the House had until March 4 to elect someone. Because of the amendment, the House has only seventeen days to make a choice before the president's term begins on January 20. If the House is deadlocked and cannot make a choice by that date, the Twentieth Amendment directs that the vice president–elect "shall act as president until a president shall have qualified." [306]

The language surrounding that provision can be read in different ways. For example, legal scholars Laurence H. Tribe and Thomas M. Rollins have argued that the House, if deadlocked, "could go on voting, with interruptions for other business and indeed with an infusion of members in midterm, for four full years." They point out that this would transform the government into a "quasi-parliamentary system," since the acting president would be "subject to termination at any time until the House deadlock is finally broken." [307] Political scientist Allan P. Sindler has argued, however, that the old March 4 deadline was not superseded by the Twentieth Amendment. As such, the House can replace the acting president only until that time. If the House acts before March 4, the acting president becomes vice president. If it fails to act by March 4, the acting president becomes president.[308]

When selecting the president, each state delegation in the House has one vote, but a state casts no vote if its delegation is evenly divided. Members of each delegation vote by secret ballot, and an absolute majority of the delegations (twenty-six of the fifty states) is necessary for election.[309]

In the election of 1824, none of the candidates won an electoral majority. Although Andrew Jackson, right, outpolled his competitors, John Quincy Adams, left, was chosen by the House of Representatives.

If no vice-presidential candidate receives a majority of votes in the electoral college, the Senate elects the vice president from the two candidates with the most electoral votes. Unlike the House procedure, each senator votes as an individual. Again, an absolute majority—fifty-one votes—is needed for election. Because the Senate chooses between only two candidates and is not beset with the potential problems of split delegations, the vice-presidential selection process is less likely to deadlock than the presidential selection process. By statute, the newly elected Senate makes the decision.

The Presidential Succession Act of 1947 prescribes what happens in the absence of both a president and a vice president. The act calls for the Speaker of the House to serve as acting president until a candidate qualifies. But to do so the Speaker must resign from Congress.[310] If the Speaker refuses, the president pro tempore of the Senate is next in the line of succession and also required to resign from Congress. If neither congressional leader is willing to serve, the line of succession reverts to members of the cabinet from the previous administration in the order their departments were established, starting with the secretary of state.

Neither the Constitution nor the Presidential Succession Act specifies what criteria House members should use in choosing among the candidates. As many commentators have pointed out, this raises several problems. Should legislators vote for the candidate who received the most electoral votes or the most popular votes? If they base their decision on the popular vote, should they look at the popular vote in their district, in their state, or in the nation as a whole? Or should they simply vote for the candidate of their party or of their conscience? Could they use their votes to wring concessions from the candidates?[311] Although there is little to guide legislators in making such decisions, undoubtedly there would be considerable public pressure to act in a way that would foster an orderly and legitimate transfer of power.

The selection process is further complicated if neither a president nor a vice president is chosen by January 20, the date set for the inauguration. In such an event, the Twentieth Amendment empowers Congress to decide by law "who shall then act as President, or the manner in which one who is to act shall be selected, and such person shall act accordingly until a President or Vice President shall have qualified." [312]

Precedents: 1800 and 1824

Presidential elections have been thrown into the House of Representatives only twice in American history: in 1800 and 1824. In the first case, the deadlock was brought on by the old method of electors voting for two candidates for president, with the second-place candidate becoming vice president. The Federalist ticket consisted of John Adams for president and Charles Cotesworth Pinckney for vice president. The Democratic-Republican ticket consisted of Thomas Jefferson for president with Aaron Burr as his running mate. When the electors voted in December 1800, the two Democratic-Republican candidates tied for first place with seventy electoral votes each.

Under the constitutional provisions then in effect, the lame-duck House, which had a Federalist majority, elected the president. Many Federalists considered Aaron Burr less politically repugnant than Thomas Jefferson and therefore plotted to elect him president, even though it was clear that Jefferson was the Democratic-Republican presidential candidate and Burr was their vice-presidential candidate.

Although Federalist leader Alexander Hamilton strongly discouraged the idea, the majority of Federalists in the House backed Burr in ballot after ballot. Indeed, if the Constitution had provided that the decision be made by the votes of individual members rather than by the votes of state delegations, Burr would have won. Instead, the situation remained deadlocked because some state delegations were divided evenly between Jefferson and Burr. From the time the balloting began on February 11, 1801, it was clear that

After finishing last in the election of 1824, Henry Clay threw his support to John Quincy Adams, making him president. Adams subsequently appointed Clay secretary of state.

the House was in for a long fight. As one observer recalled: "Many [congressmen] sent home for night caps and pillows, and wrapped in shawls and great-coats, lay about the floor of the committee rooms or sat sleeping in their seats. At one, two, and half-past two, the tellers roused the members from their slumbers, and took the same ballot as before." [313]

Seven days and thirty-six ballots later, the tide turned. The day before, Federalist representative James Bayard of Delaware had told a party caucus that the balloting had gone on long enough. To delay the process any longer would endanger the Constitution. After receiving word from Maryland Democratic-Republican leader Samuel Smith that Jefferson would agree to preserve the Hamiltonian financial system, respect the integrity of the navy, and not dismiss Federalists from lower-level government jobs simply on the basis of politics, Bayard was convinced that the Federalists must relent. On the thirty-sixth ballot, Bayard and several other Burr supporters from Maryland, South Carolina, and Vermont cast blank ballots, giving the presidency to Jefferson. [314]

The election of 1824 is the only one to be thrown into the House since the adoption in 1804 of the Twelfth Amendment, which requires electors to cast one ballot for president and a separate ballot for vice president. No candidate received a majority of electoral votes in 1824, largely because the field of candidates was so crowded. The Democratic-Republican congressional caucus nominated William H. Crawford, who had served as secretary of the Treasury under President James Monroe. But others balked at the choice for two reasons. First, Crawford had suffered a paralytic stroke the year before that left him greatly impaired. Second, democratic sentiment was rising, and outside Washington Crawford's selection by a small group of legislators smacked of political manipulation. The Federalist Party was dead, but different state legislatures promptly nominated John Quincy Adams, John C. Calhoun, Henry Clay, and Andrew Jackson for president.

Attempts were made to limit the field of candidates, to little avail. Crawford's supporters dropped his running mate, Albert Gallatin, in the hope that they could persuade Clay to take his place. Their plan was that Clay supporters, recognizing that Crawford might not live out his term, would push Crawford to victory. Clay, hoping to win on his own, refused. [315] Among the candidates, only Calhoun withdrew from the race.

When all the electoral votes were tallied, no candidate had a majority. Jackson led with ninety-nine electoral votes, followed by Adams with eighty-four, Crawford with forty-one, and Clay with thirty-seven. In accordance with the Twelfth Amendment, the names of Jackson, Adams, and Crawford were placed before the House. It immediately became apparent that Clay's supporters would tip the balance between the two front-runners.

Clay was not fond of either candidate, but he clearly felt that Adams was the lesser of two evils. In early January, Clay and Adams conferred, and Clay let it be known that he would support Adams in the House election. Soon afterward, a letter in a Philadelphia newspaper alleged that Adams had offered Clay the post of secretary of state in return for his support. Jackson was furious, and his rage only grew when Adams won the House election with a bare majority of thirteen out of twenty-four state delegations and proceeded to name Clay as secretary of state.

The Senate has chosen a vice president only once, in 1837. Martin Van Buren had been elected president with 170 of 294 electoral votes. But his running mate, Richard M. Johnson of Kentucky, received only 147 electoral votes, one less than a majority. The twenty-three Virginia electors who had been chosen to support Van Buren boycotted Johnson because of his long-term romantic entanglement with a black woman. [316] The remaining electoral votes were split among three other vice-presidential candidates: Francis Granger of New York, who received seventy-seven electoral votes; John Tyler of Virginia, who received forty-seven; and William Smith of Alabama, who received twenty-three.

The names of the top two candidates, Johnson and Granger, were sent to the Senate. In making its selection, the Senate adopted a resolution that required all senators to vote by voice as the roll was called in alphabetical order. [317] The Senate elected Johnson by a vote of 33–16.

Close Calls

Although no presidential election has been thrown to the House since 1824, several have come close. The elections of

Abraham Lincoln in 1860, John Kennedy in 1960, and Richard Nixon in 1968, for example, would have gone to the House with a shift of only a few thousand votes.[318] A relatively small shift of votes also could have sent the elections of 1836, 1856, 1892, and 1948 to the House. *(See Chapter 6, Chronology of Presidential Elections.)*

In 1968, for example, Alabama governor George Wallace ran as a strong third party candidate on the American Independent Party ticket. There was widespread fear that Wallace would deadlock the election and throw it to the House. Republican Richard Nixon and Democrat Hubert Humphrey ran one of the closest races in history. Despite his earlier hopes of sweeping the South, Wallace won only five states and forty-six electoral votes. If Nixon had lost either California or two or three smaller states that were close, he would have been denied an electoral vote majority. Well aware of his strategic position, Wallace elicited written affidavits from his electors promising that they would vote as he instructed them. Wallace took a hard line on the concessions he would require for delivering his votes to another candidate. Among other things, he called for the repeal of all civil rights legislation, the repeal of the federal antipoverty program, and the criminal indictment of anyone advocating a North Vietnamese victory in the Vietnam War.[319]

Death or Resignation after Election Day

If a president-elect or vice president–elect were to die or resign after election day but before the date in mid-December when the electors cast their ballots, the national party committee would choose a replacement in an effort to guide the vote of the electors. Although Republican vice president James S. Sherman died on October 30, 1912, just before the election, his name remained on the ballot in all the states. After the election, the Republican National Committee nominated Columbia University president Nicholas Murray Butler to receive Sherman's electoral votes.

If the death or resignation takes place during the two weeks after the electoral votes are counted and announced by Congress (January 6) but before the inauguration (January 20), the selection process is governed by the Twentieth Amendment. That amendment specifies that if the president-elect dies or resigns, the vice president–elect will become president. If both of them die or resign during that period, the Presidential Succession Act would take effect, and the Speaker of the House would become president.

The procedure is less clear if the death or resignation takes place between the time when the electors cast their votes in December and the time when the votes are counted by Congress. Since the electoral votes are technically not valid until counted by Congress, no president-elect or vice president–elect would exist, and the Presidential Succession Act could not be used. If the candidate who died or resigned during that period did not have a majority of the electoral votes, the majority candidate simply would win. If, however, the candidate who died or resigned did have a majority of the electoral votes, the choice of a president would be thrown to the House of Representatives, and the choice of a vice president to the Senate.[320]

THE TRANSITION PERIOD

In the time between the election and the inauguration of a president, the nation's capital bustles with speculation and intrigue. To ensure a smooth transition, the incumbent president invites the president-elect to the White House, and the new chief executive and incoming staff receive a battery of briefings on matters ranging from budget deficits to U.S. military alliances. All the while, the new president's transition team pores over resumes and considers legislative strategy.

Media and academic accounts stress the cooperative nature of the transition period. Only in the United States, political analysts say, can the government be turned over to political opponents with such good cheer and cooperation. Transitions rarely involve active recrimination, and seldom is there a struggle over the legitimacy of the electoral outcome like the disputed Bush-Gore contest in 2000. The transition is a rare celebration of a stable democracy based on political parties that differ on specific policies but achieve consensus on the most important matters of state.

Until recently, presidents-elect financed their own transitions. Then in 1964 Congress passed the Presidential Transitions Act, which granted the newly elected president $450,000 and the outgoing president $450,000 to help cover their transition expenses. In 1988 Congress revised the act to grant $3.5 million to each incoming administration and $1.5 million to each outgoing administration, with these amounts to be adjusted for inflation. The revised act also authorized the president-elect to raise money from private donors to cover any additional costs of the transition, provided that donations did not exceed $5,000 per donor and the names of the donors were disclosed publicly. Bill Clinton's 1992–1993 transition spent a total of $8.3 million, $4.8 million from private sources. In 2000–2001 George W. Bush spent slightly more, $8.5 million, $4.3 million from private sources. *(See Table 5-11, right.)* The money is used for staff salaries, travel expenses, talent searches, policy deliberations, and public relations activities. Separate federal funds are used for the inaugural ceremonies.

In many ways, the presidential transition is the most important phase of the new president's term. The transition period offers incoming presidents a chance to forge a governing strategy, aided by thorough analyses of national security and economic issues. The incoming administration of Bill Clinton was especially active during the transition period. For example, the president-elect convened an economic conference in Little Rock, Arkansas, in December 1992 to

TABLE 5-11   **Growth of Transition Teams and Expenditures, 1952–2001**

President	Size of transition team	Expenditure dollars (millions)		
		Public funds	Public funds	Public funds
Eisenhower (1952–1953)	100	0	0.4	0.4
Kennedy (1960–1961)	50[a]	0	1.3	1.3
Nixon (1968–1969)	125–150	0.5	1.0	1.5
Carter (1976–1977)	300	1.7	0.2	1.9
Reagan (1980–1981)	1,550	2.0	1.0	3.0
G. Bush (1988–1989)	150[b]	3.5	0	3.5
Clinton (1992–1993)	450	3.5	4.8	8.3
G. W. Bush (2000–2001)	800[c]	4.2	4.3	8.5

SOURCES: Laurin L. Henry, *Presidential Transitions* (Washington, D.C.: Brookings, 1960); Frederick C. Mosher, W. David Clinton, and Daniel G. Lang, *Presidential Transitions and Foreign Affairs* (Baton Rouge: Louisiana State University Press, 1987); Herbert E. Alexander, *Financing the 1968 Election* (Lexington, Mass.: Lexington Books, 1971); *Financing the 1976 Election* (Washington, D.C.: CQ Press, 1979); *Financing the 1980 Election* (Lexington, Mass.: Lexington Books, 1983); Herbert E. Alexander and Monica Bauer, *Financing the 1988 Election* (Boulder: Westview Press, 1991); Herbert E. Alexander and Anthony Corrado, *Financing the 1992 Election* (New York: Sharpe, 1995); General Services Administration; White House Press Office.

NOTES: a. Estimate based on statement by Richard Neustadt that Carter's transition staff was six times the size of Kennedy's (Richard Neustadt, Presidential Power [New York: Macmillan, 1980], 218). b. Plus 100–150 volunteers. c. Includes an unspecified number of volunteers.

address the economic and budgetary problems facing the nation. During the five weeks it took to resolve the outcome of the disputed 2000 election, George W. Bush began transition planning on the assumption that he would win. Bush appointed Richard B. Cheney, his vice-presidential running mate, to oversee the transition.

New presidents often are so confident in the wake of winning the election that they pay little attention to the perils awaiting them at the White House. Presidents-elect have their own agendas and sometimes are unwilling to listen to the counsel of others. Moreover, they may underestimate the challenge. As one former transition aide warned, "A transition is like assembling and then tearing down a multimillion dollar corporation in a span of ninety days. It doesn't exist November 5 and then it is destroyed January 20. So there's a lot of chaos. You're going to make mistakes." [321] An additional problem, observed political scientist Charles O. Jones, is that "[p]residents-elect enter the critical transition period in a physically and mentally exhausted state, typically dependent on an equally fatigued staff." [322]

The time that a president-elect has to accomplish the transition from campaigning to governing is brief. Political scientist Richard E. Neustadt calls the transition the "eleven-week scramble." [323] But the stakes in accomplishing a successful transition are high. Historian Carl M. Brauer notes:

> Transitions are filled with peril and opportunity. . . . Newly elected presidents have ended wars or prolonged them. They have demonstrated acumen or ineptitude on national security and foreign policy issues. They have maximized their mandates and led Congress, or squandered their mandates and failed to lead Congress. They have inspired or failed to inspire the public through their statements and actions. They have established economic and social policies with widely varying results. They have wisely or imprudently adopted or discarded inherited policies. They

have appointed people who helped them achieve their goals and who graced public service and others whom they came to regard as liabilities and mistakes. [324]

The extent of the new president's electoral "mandate" is central to the transition period. Yet John F. Kennedy's slim victory in 1960 did not stop him from taking an aggressive approach to leading the nation. Kennedy stated after the election: "The margin is narrow, but the responsibility is clear. There may be difficulties with Congress, but a margin of only one vote would still be a mandate." [325] As foreseen, Kennedy had many problems with Congress. Ronald Reagan's 1980 landslide election led to more policy victories than a slimmer electoral triumph would have allowed.

Sometimes the most important transition moves are made behind the scenes. In 1992 President-elect Clinton met with Alan Greenspan, the chairman of the Federal Reserve Board, to confer about what policies would reassure financial markets enough to justify keeping interest rates low—a vital condition for economic growth. Indeed, Clinton and his wife, Hillary Rodham Clinton, nurtured a relationship with Greenspan, a Republican, to help push the president's economic plans through Congress. At the same time, Vice President–elect Al Gore sounded out Republican leaders on Capitol Hill about various deficit-cutting measures. Gore learned from these meetings that the GOP would not provide any support on budgetary and tax issues. That moved the Clinton White House toward a partisan approach to congressional relations.

Finally, the transition period can be crucial in determining what kind of "honeymoon" the new president is likely to have with Congress and the public. The length of the honeymoon, in turn, has a big effect on whether the new president can be a decisive and strong leader in the first term.

Management Style

Transition watchers pay especially close attention to the incoming president's management style. Although presidents-elect usually promise to involve cabinet members in the decision-making process, a strong White House staff can reduce the influence of the cabinet in that process. Eisenhower was the last president to have anything approaching a true "cabinet government." Recent presidents, determined to control the bureaucracy, have relied more on a White House staff with a strong chief of staff. Nixon found the hundreds of cabinet meetings under Eisenhower "unnecessary and boring." [326] Much like Franklin Roosevelt and Eisenhower before him, Kennedy insisted on playing advisers off one another. "I can't afford to confine myself to one set of advisers," he said. "If I did that I would be on their leading strings." [327]

Largely because of the important roles that Nixon White House staff members played in the Watergate scandal, Carter was reluctant to appoint a chief of staff; he maintained that the position encouraged overzealous aides to insulate the president. Instead, Carter acted at first as his own chief of staff (Hamilton Jordan later filled this role), providing several advisers with direct access. Reagan, who always espoused delegation of authority on a wide range of issues, appointed a chief of staff at the beginning of his administration. So did each of his successors: Bush, Clinton, and Bush.

Presidents sometimes allow their cabinet secretaries to choose their own assistant secretaries. Nixon in his first term and Carter did not exert control over mid-level appointments, as many other presidents have done. Both soon found that the departments were "captured" by career bureaucrats and the interest groups connected with the agencies. Recognizing that the lack of central coordination of appointments had reduced Carter's ability to control his administration, Clinton insisted on his right to make sub-cabinet appointments. By placing loyal supporters in key department posts, he hoped to ensure that the policies carried out within the bureaucracy were those of his administration. Although Clinton was criticized for the slow pace at which he filled policy-making positions, this strategy effectively centralized political power within the White House.

The administration's congressional liaison is an especially important member of the administration. Carter's liaison, Frank Moore, lacked experience on Capitol Hill and was ineffective as the president's lobbyist. Reagan's liaisons, Max Friedersdorf and Kenneth Duberstein, won high marks, especially for their efforts in behalf of the administration's tax- and budget-cutting initiatives.

Early Advice

Incoming presidents have outside allies who offer advice on appointments and policy options. For example, the Democratic Leadership Council, a politically moderate think tank that Clinton had chaired in the 1980s, prepared a set of proposals for President-elect Clinton in 1992. Earlier, in 1980, the Heritage Foundation had provided Reagan's transition team with a three-thousand-page report urging a quick selection of top aides and several policy initiatives.

The outgoing administration's briefings of the president-elect and the incoming team could be helpful, but the different styles of the two groups often block meaningful exchanges. The most important briefing deals with the nuclear capacities of other nations—a briefing that never fails to sober the new president from the intoxication of the recent electoral success.

The meeting between the incoming and outgoing president is usually cordial, but the new executive is reluctant to take much advice. In 1952, after providing President-elect Eisenhower with advice on staff operations, Harry S. Truman remarked, "I think all this went into one ear and out the other." [328] Carter reported that Reagan was inattentive during their Oval Office meeting. The Reagan transition team's cooperation with agencies such as the Office of Management and Budget was more sustained.

Early Considerations

A president's early signals to the bureaucracy are an important factor in relations between the White House and the rest of the executive branch. Nixon encouraged

Bowing Out

From John Adams's "midnight" judge appointments to Jimmy Carter's unsuccessful efforts to free American hostages from Iran, the outgoing president's last days have been fateful moments. The outgoing administration prepares a budget for the next fiscal year and issues administrative regulations. President George Bush also pardoned key figures in the Iran-contra scandal before leaving office. And, one month after he lost reelection, he ordered U.S. troops to strife-torn Somalia to ensure famine relief, initiating what became a controversial fifteen-month mission for the Clinton administration. Among the pardons issued by President Clinton, that of billionaire fugitive Marc Rich proved especially controversial partly because Rich's former wife, Denise, had ties to the Democratic Party.

The outgoing president often delivers a "farewell address" to draw attention to the major problems of the nation. George Washington's call for limited foreign engagements remains the most famous farewell address. Recent prominent addresses include Dwight D. Eisenhower's warning about the "military-industrial complex" and Carter's plea for recognition of environmental and economic limits. *See "Washington's Farewell Address," p. 1754, and "Eisenhower's Farewell Address," p. 1775, in Reference Materials, Vol. II.)*

On April 30, 1789, at Federal Hall in New York City, George Washington took the oath of office. The practice of adding the words "so help me God" at the end of the oath was begun by Washington at this first inaugural ceremony. Only Franklin Pierce, in 1853, affirmed (rather than swore) to faithfully execute the office that he was about to enter.

the bureaucratic resistance he feared with his repeated statements about the Democratic and liberal bias of civil servants.[329] Reagan appointed lower-level administrators only after a thorough screening by his transition team to ensure ideological purity and loyalty to the administration.

The size of the legislative agenda is another important consideration for the new administration. Clinton's initiatives—federal deficit reduction, economic stimulus, health care reform, "reinventing government," campaign finance reform, better relations with Russia—were so wide-ranging that the president was not able to muster the influence needed to prevail in all areas. Even when his efforts succeeded, Clinton did not receive much credit because of other failures along the way. Carter had had the same difficulty. Reagan, by contrast, emphasized issues directly pertaining to the budget—taxes, cuts in domestic spending, and increases in military spending. The work of incoming budget director David Stockman was crucial to Reagan's ability to "hit the ground running." George W. Bush confined his early legislative agenda to the issues he had stressed in the election: tax cuts, education reform, and support for faith-based groups in the provision of social services.

THE INAUGURATION

Ritual acts pervade politics in recognition that the symbolism of public rites reassures and binds together diverse peoples. In keeping with this understanding, each presidential election is capped by a ceremony of grand proportions: the inauguration of the new president. This ceremony is an overt political ritual intended to instill patriotism, unite the nation behind its leader, and provide for an orderly transfer of power. It does so through a combination of pageantry and rhetoric.[330] Yet almost nothing of that ceremony is required by law. Most of it has evolved by way of tradition.

The four-year presidential and vice-presidential terms expire at noon on the January 20 that follows a presidential election. Before the 1933 enactment of the Twentieth Amendment, the Constitution was silent on when terms began and ended. Presidential inaugurations were held on March 4 as required by a 1792 act of Congress.

Oath of Office

The only part of the inaugural ceremony that is required by the Constitution is the taking of the oath of office. Article II, Section 1, Clause 8, states the words that every president has repeated: "I do solemnly swear (or affirm) that I will faithfully execute the Office of President of the United States, and will to the best of my Ability, preserve, protect, and defend the Constitution of the United States." Only Franklin Pierce in 1853 affirmed (rather than swore) to faithfully execute the office that he was about to enter. The practice of adding the words "so help me God" at the conclusion of the oath is said to have been initiated by George Washington at the first inaugural ceremony. The vice president recites the same oath taken by all other federal officers except the president. It is prescribed by Congress in the *United States Code*.

Washington also was the first president to take the oath of office with his left hand placed on the Bible and his right hand raised toward heaven. Although not required by the Constitution, the practice of taking oaths on the Bible was deeply ingrained in English and colonial history. For centuries, the kings and queens of Britain had taken their coronation oaths on Bibles, and the use of a Bible was an established practice in the administration of oaths in civil and ecclesiastical courts.[331]

Nevertheless, no one thought to secure a Bible for Washington's inauguration until shortly before the general arrived at Federal Hall in New York City for his swearing in. The chief justice of the New York state judiciary, Chancellor Robert R. Livingston, who was to administer the oath, feared that the oath would lack legitimacy without a Bible, but none could be found in the building. One was finally borrowed from St. John's Masonic Lodge No. 1, a few blocks away on Wall Street.[332]

After being sworn in as the forty-third president of the United States, George W. Bush sings the national anthem with former president Bill Clinton and former vice president Al Gore on inauguration day, January 20, 2001.

There is no definite record of a Bible being used again at a swearing-in ceremony until James K. Polk's inauguration in 1845 (although it is believed that Andrew Jackson used one in 1829 and again in 1833). Since James Buchanan in 1857, every president has taken the oath on a Bible except for Theodore Roosevelt in 1901, when he was hastily sworn in after the assassination of William McKinley. Indeed, several modern presidents have used the same Bible as Washington, including Dwight Eisenhower, Jimmy Carter, and both George Bushes. The oldest inaugural Bible was the one used by Franklin Roosevelt in all four of his inaugurations. It was printed in Amsterdam around 1686 (in Dutch) and contained the Roosevelt family records—the earliest of which was the birth of Jacob Roosevelt in "1691/92." [333]

The page to which the Bible is opened during the administration of the oath is sometimes a random choice and sometimes a deliberate one. During Washington's first inauguration, it was randomly opened to Genesis 49–50. Rutherford B. Hayes placed his hand on Psalm 118:11–13, which reads in part: "Thou hast thrust sore at me that I might fall: but the Lord helped me." These words were significant, given the circumstances of Hayes's fiercely contested election. Franklin Roosevelt's Bible was opened to I Corinthians 13 for all four of his inaugurals ("Though I speak with the tongues of men and of angels, and have not charity, I am become as sounding brass . . ."). Nixon, who entered office in the midst of the Vietnam War in 1969, placed his hand on Isaiah 2:4—"and they shall beat their swords into plowshares, and their spears into pruning hooks: nation shall not lift up sword against nation, neither shall they learn war any more." [334]

After Washington's first inauguration, the oath of office was administered indoors until 1817. Washington's second inauguration, as well as that of John Adams, was held in Philadelphia in the Senate chamber of Independence Hall. Thomas Jefferson was the first president to be inaugurated in the District of Columbia, where in 1801 he took his oath in the new Senate chamber. In later years, the ceremony was moved to the House chamber. It was not until James Monroe's inauguration in 1817 that the ceremony was moved outdoors to a platform erected in front of the east portico of the Capitol. In 1981 Reagan moved the site of the ceremony from the East to the West Front of the Capitol.

With rare exceptions, the presidential oath of office has been administered by the chief justice of the United States, although the Constitution makes no provision for this. An associate justice of the Supreme Court usually swears in the vice president. The first vice president sworn in by a woman was Dan Quayle, who took the oath in 1989 from the first female justice, Sandra Day O'Connor.

At Washington's first inauguration, the Supreme Court had not yet been appointed, and at his second inauguration Associate Justice William Cushing filled in for Chief Justice John Jay. Thus John Adams was the first president to take the oath of office from the chief justice (who was then Oliver Ellsworth).

Other judges have administered the oath in times of unexpected presidential succession. But such occasions raise questions. For example, can a person assume the presidency without having taken the oath of office? The first president to die in office was William Henry Harrison in 1841. His vice president, John Tyler, initially thought that he did not need to take the presidential oath. In his mind, the vice-presidential oath sufficed. Nevertheless, Tyler took the presidential oath on April 6, 1841 (two days after Harrison's death) for "greater caution"—a practice that continues in similar circumstances.[335]

Still, the period between the death of a president and the swearing in of the successor to that office remains a gray area. As recently as the assassination of Kennedy in 1963, there was some question whether Lyndon Johnson should take the oath immediately in Dallas or wait until his return to Washington. Attorney General Robert F. Kennedy advised that the oath be administered immediately, and it was, by federal district judge Sarah T. Hughes aboard *Air Force One*.[336]

Ceremony and Celebration

From the beginning, inaugurations have included much more than just the swearing in. When Washington set out from his home at Mount Vernon on his journey to New York City (then the seat of government) he only recently had recovered from a severe bout of rheumatism, and he was sad about leaving the home he loved. On April 16, 1789, he wrote in his diary: "About ten o'clock I bade adieu to Mt. Vernon, to private life, to domestic felicity, and with a mind oppressed with more anxious and painful sensations than I have words to express, set out for New York." [337]

Along the way, Washington was met by crowds, celebrations, speeches, ringing bells, cavalry troops, and cannon fire. In Philadelphia, thousands turned out to watch him ride down Market and Second Streets. By the time he finally reached New York, the crowds had worked themselves into a frenzy. Indeed, they were so loud when Washington stepped off the barge at Murray's Wharf that even the ringing church bells were drowned out.

On April 30, 1789—the morning of his inauguration—Washington traveled from his quarters at Franklin House to Federal Hall in an ornate horse-drawn carriage. Upon his arrival at Federal Hall, he was escorted to the balcony where he took the oath of office in front of a huge crowd. After yet more pandemonium, he moved inside the Senate chamber to deliver a brief speech, thus establishing the precedent for inaugural addresses. That night the celebration was capped by a fireworks display. Since then, inaugurations have usually been a time for much pomp and circumstance.

Customarily, when the presidency changes hands, the president-elect and the incumbent president ride together from the White House to the Capitol for the inauguration ceremony. On occasion, however, this has been an awkward journey. In 1869 President-elect Ulysses S. Grant refused to ride in the same carriage with Andrew Johnson, prompting President Johnson to boycott the inauguration, as had John Adams in 1801, John Quincy Adams in 1829, and Martin Van Buren in 1841 (although Van Buren had made a point of meeting President-elect William Henry Harrison during the interregnum). Herbert Hoover and Franklin Roosevelt barely exchanged glances during the trip in 1933. Most presidents, however, have made the trip. Even Woodrow Wilson, partially paralyzed, drove with Warren G. Harding to the Capitol in 1921, although the bitter cold prevented him from witnessing the ceremony.[338]

In the early days, inaugural parades were held before the swearing in and proceeded to the Capitol. Initially, these were relatively simple events with small presidential escorts and spontaneous crowds. James Madison was the first president to wrap the parade in military formality when he was escorted by cavalry in 1809. With the exception of Andrew Jackson—who vetoed the idea of any kind of parade and simply walked to the Capitol on the sidewalk—successive presidents saw larger and larger parades.

With William Henry Harrison in 1841 came a parade filled with bands, loyal supporters, and militia units, and James Buchanan's parade in 1857 added a huge float representing the goddess of liberty. It was not until Benjamin Harrison's inauguration in 1889 that parades came from the Capitol after the swearing in. Harrison also was the first president to watch the parade from a reviewing stand rather than participate in it.[339]

Today, inaugural parades are elaborate events that are broadcast live on television. President Reagan's 1985 inaugural parade—canceled because of extremely cold weather—was scheduled to include 12,000 people, 730 horses, 66 floats, and 57 marching bands. Just the cost of building the reviewing stand and bleachers and housing the horses reached nearly $1 million. All told, the estimated cost of the 1985 inauguration was $12 million, with some $800,000 to have been raised from the selling of 25,000 parade tickets (ranging in price from $12.50 to $100 each).[340]

Only eight years later, the total cost of a presidential inauguration had grown tremendously. The direct costs of the inauguration of Bill Clinton and Al Gore were estimated to have been more than $25 million, with additional government costs—such as police and public safety expenses—bumping the figure to more than $36 million. However, the government was able to recoup two-thirds of the cost through ticket and souvenir sales ($17 million) and television broadcast rights to the inaugural events ($7 million).[341] The 1993 inauguration also demonstrated how much the spectacle of Americans embracing their new president had grown. Beginning with a preinaugural bus ride by the presidential party from Jefferson's Monticello home in Virginia to Washington, D.C., festivities crowded an entire week in January

Gestures during inaugural ceremonies range from the mundane to the highly symbolic. To the horror of Secret Service agents, President Carter walked back to the White House from his swearing in at the Capitol in 1977 with his wife and children at his side. Most presidents and first ladies since Carter have walked part of the way as well. Yet the ease with which presidents can mingle with the public has changed markedly over the years. In 1789 Washington thought nothing of walking home through crowds of people in New York after watching the evening fireworks display with friends. In 1829 Jackson's swearing in was followed by an open reception at the White House for anyone who cared to attend. Refreshments were prepared for twenty thousand people, but organizers did not anticipate the full force of a hungry throng anxious to greet "Old Hickory." The crowd soon became unruly—surging toward Jackson and the food, destroying furniture, tracking in mud, breaking windows, and ultimately forcing the president to flee.[342] After Abraham Lincoln's second inauguration in 1865, the crowd romped through the White House, stealing food, silver, and even parts of draperies.[343] Yet despite the mayhem of those inaugural festivities, many presidents continued to greet virtually anyone who stood in line to meet them at the White House after the inauguration.

In the evening, the festivities traditionally have ended with an inaugural ball. The first such ball was held by James and Dolley Madison in 1809, and, with a few exceptions, the tradition has continued. There was no ball after Jackson's first inauguration because of the recent death of his wife. Wilson—appalled at the idea of being paraded in front of hundreds of gawking people—scuttled plans for balls in 1913 and 1917. Harding wanted a ball in 1921, but after complaints that his plans were too extravagant, he reluctantly canceled all postinaugural festivities. Calvin Coolidge simply went to bed in 1925 (even though there was an unofficial ball held at the Mayflower Hotel), and Franklin Roosevelt suspended the practice of balls after his first inauguration because of the crises of the Great Depression and World War II.[344]

Since then, however, balls have been a prominent part of the inaugural day landscape. In recent years, to accommodate the throngs of people who have wanted to attend, several balls have taken place throughout the city with the president and his wife making appearances at all the official

ones. In 1977 Carter had inaugural "parties" rather than "balls" to symbolize a new era of simplicity in government. In 1981 and 1985 Ronald and Nancy Reagan restored the grandeur of inaugural celebrations. As part of Reagan's second inauguration, they visited nine balls attended by some 50,000 people who had paid $125 each.[345]

Inaugural Addresses

When Washington entered Federal Hall after taking the oath of office in New York City on April 30, 1789, he proceeded to the Senate chamber and gave a brief speech. That was the first inaugural address, and every inaugural ceremony since then has included one—even though giving a speech is not a constitutional requirement.

Initially, such speeches were made to a joint session of Congress and were held in either the House or Senate chamber. But beginning with James Monroe in 1817, inaugural

Extremely cold weather forced the swearing-in ceremony for the second term of President Ronald Reagan and Vice President George Bush to be held indoors underneath the Capitol Rotunda.

addresses have been delivered outdoors to the general public. Inclement weather sometimes has made this tradition uncomfortable. The most tragic example was the inauguration of 1841. Although the day was damp and extremely cold, Gen. William Henry Harrison insisted on delivering his inaugural address—the longest in history, taking over an hour and forty minutes to read—without an overcoat or hat. To make matters worse, he had traveled to the Capitol on horseback (again with no coat or hat) in a very slow procession, even though he was sixty-eight years old and exhausted from a long journey to Washington. The exposure brought on pneumonia, and Harrison died exactly one month after his inauguration. In 1985, when the wind chill plummeted well below zero, seventy-three-year-old Reagan (the oldest president to be sworn in) moved the ceremony indoors to the Capitol Rotunda and canceled the parade. Four years earlier, Reagan had enjoyed one of the warmest January inaugurations, when temperatures soared close to sixty degrees. The average high temperature for a January 20 in Washington is forty-four degrees.

Every inaugural address since Truman's in 1949 has been carried live on television. Today such instant communication is taken for granted, but early in the nation's history the distribution of the president's remarks to all parts of the country took a long time. In 1841 a record was set when the text of Harrison's address was rushed by train from Washington to New York in only ten hours.[346] Four years later, Samuel F. B. Morse stood on the inaugural platform and transmitted an account of the proceedings to Baltimore via his telegraph machine as Polk was sworn in.[347] Coolidge's 1925 inaugural address was the first to be broadcast by radio. The earliest known photograph of an inauguration was taken at Buchanan's swearing in on March 4, 1857. *(For the inaugural addresses of Jefferson, Lincoln, Franklin Roosevelt, Kennedy, Ford, and Reagan, see the Documents and Texts section of Reference Materials in Vol. II.)*

After the divisiveness of a presidential election, inaugural addresses usually stress unity and nonpartisanship. Jefferson reminded the joint session of Congress listening to his inaugural address that "every difference of opinion is not a difference of principle. We have called by different names brethren of the same principle. We are all Republicans, we are all Federalists." When Wilson entered the White House in 1913, he said: "This is not a day of triumph; it is a day of dedication. Here muster, not the forces of party, but the forces of humanity." After the unusually divisive election of 2000, George W. Bush offered his inaugural address as a hymn to national consensus. With his defeated rival, outgoing vice president Al Gore, seated behind him on the inaugural platform, Bush organized his remarks around themes of "civility, courage, compassion, and character."

In troubled times, an inaugural address is an opportunity for reassurance and supplication. Franklin Roosevelt,

This is the earliest known photograph of an inauguration, taken at James Buchanan's swearing in on March 4, 1857.

entering office in the midst of economic crisis, recognized that "only a foolish optimist can deny the dark realities of the moment." But he preached the gospel of restoration and entreated his audience with memorable words: "the only thing we have to fear is fear itself—nameless, unreasoning, unjustified terror which paralyzes needed efforts to convert retreat into advance."

Lincoln, who began his second term in 1865 as the Civil War was winding to a close, told a hushed crowd: "Fondly do we hope, fervently do we pray, that this mighty scourge of war may speedily pass away. . . . With malice toward none, with charity for all, with firmness in the right as God gives us to see the right, let us strive on to . . . bind up the nation's wounds."

When Ford became the first unelected president after Nixon resigned in 1974, he addressed a crowd in the East Room of the White House, saying:

I assume the Presidency under extraordinary circumstances never before experienced by Americans. This is an hour of history that troubles our minds and hurts our hearts. . . . We must go forward now together. . . . [O]ur long national nightmare is over. Our Constitution works;

our great Republic is a Government of laws and not of men. Here the people rule.

Optimism is probably the most common theme of inaugural addresses. That theme was perhaps best represented by Kennedy's inauguration in 1961. As the nation's youngest elected president, he set the tone for an era of change:

> Let the word go forth from this time and place, to friend and foe alike, that the torch has been passed to a new generation of Americans—born in this century, tempered by war, disciplined by a hard and bitter peace, proud of our ancient heritage—and unwilling to witness or permit the slow undoing of those human rights to which this nation has always been committed. . . . So let us begin anew.

Most new presidents echo the theme of new challenges and old responsibilities. As George Bush remarked in 1989: "The new breeze blows, a page turns, the story unfolds—and so today a chapter begins: a small and stately story of unity, diversity and generosity—shared and written together."

Clinton's 1993 inauguration was billed as a "people's" celebration. In his address, Clinton asked the American public to restore their faith in government.

> And so I say to all of you here: Let us resolve to reform our politics so that power and privilege no longer shout down the voice of the people. Let us put aside personal advantage so that we can feel the pain and see the promise of America. Let us resolve to make our Government a place for what Franklin Roosevelt called bold, persistent experimentation, a Government for our tomorrows, not our yesterdays.

The "poetry" of politics, as New York governor Mario Cuomo described political rhetoric, is difficult yet important. But it is simple compared to the "prose" of governing. Every president discovers that when finally seated in the Oval Office for the first day of business.

★

NOTES

1. Richard M. Pious, *The American Presidency* (New York: Basic Books, 1979), 22.

2. Ibid., 25–29.

3. The term *electoral college* does not appear in the text of the Constitution. Citing Andrew C. McLaughlin, Edward Corwin wrote that the term "was used by Abraham Baldwin in 1800 and by John Randolph in 1809, and 'officially' in 1845" (Edward S. Corwin, *The President: Office and Powers,* 5th ed. [New York: New York University Press, 1984], 385 n. 21).

4. The original compromise called for the Senate to make the final decision in such circumstances.

5. Richard Hofstadter, *The Idea of a Party System* (Berkeley: University of California Press, 1969), 16–39.

6. John F. Hoadley, *Origins of American Political Parties* (Lexington: University Press of Kentucky, 1986), 34.

7. Ibid.; A. E. Dick Howard, *Commentaries on the Constitution of Virginia,* vol. 1 (Charlottesville: University Press of Virginia, 1974), 318–319.

8. Howard, *Commentaries,* 320.

9. Quoted in ibid., 323.

10. Ibid., 325–326.

11. See, for example, Hoadley, *Origins,* 34–35; Robert E. Brown, *Charles Beard and the Constitution* (Princeton: Princeton University Press, 1956), 61–72; and Alexander Keyssar, *The Right to Vote: The Contested History of Democracy in the United States* (New York: Basic Books, 2000).

12. *McPherson v. Blacker,* 146 U.S. 1 (1892) at 29; Eugene H. Roseboom, *A History of Presidential Elections,* 2d ed. (New York: Macmillan, 1964), 15.

13. Edward Stanwood, *A History of the Presidency from 1788 to 1897,* revised by Charles Knowles Bolton (Boston: Houghton Mifflin, 1928), 21–22.

14. Ibid., 38–39.

15. Roseboom, *History of Presidential Elections,* 28.

16. Stanwood, *History of the Presidency,* 38–39.

17. Ibid., 136.

18. Corwin, *The President,* 45–46.

19. *Ray v. Blair,* 343 U.S. 214 (1952), quoted in Harold W. Chase and Craig R. Ducat, *Edward S. Corwin's The Constitution and What It Means Today,* 13th ed. (Princeton: Princeton University Press, 1973), 380.

20. Stanwood, *History of the Presidency,* 78.

21. *McPherson v. Blacker,* 146 U.S. 1 (1892).

22. Roseboom, *History of Presidential Elections,* 17.

23. Stanwood, *History of the Presidency,* 27. According to Stanwood: "Although in all the newspaper references to the coming election . . . Mr. Adams was spoken of as a candidate for Vice-President, that gentleman did not so regard himself, but rather as a candidate for the presidency. If he received more votes than Washington, he would be President; if the votes were equal, the House of Representatives would choose one of the two. He showed plainly that he regarded his own merits as equal to those of Washington" (p. 26).

24. David McCullough, *John Adams* (New York: Simon and Schuster, 2001), 393–394.

25. Roseboom, *History of Presidential Elections,* 33.

26. James S. Chase, *Emergence of the Presidential Nominating Convention: 1789–1832* (Urbana: University of Illinois Press, 1973), 8.

27. Richard L. Rubin, *Press, Party, and Presidency* (New York: Norton, 1981), 11.

28. Culver H. Smith, *The Press, Politics, and Patronage* (Athens: University of Georgia Press, 1977), 13.

29. John Tebbel, *The Compact History of the American Newspaper* (New York: Hawthorn Books, 1963), 64, 65.

30. From the December 23, 1796, issue of the *Aurora,* quoted in Willard Grosvenor Bleyer, *Main Currents in the History of American Journalism* (Boston: Houghton Mifflin, 1927), 116.

31. James MacGregor Burns, *The Deadlock of Democracy: Four-Party Politics in America* (Englewood Cliffs, N.J.: Prentice-Hall, 1963), 29.

32. Chase, *Presidential Nominating Convention,* 11. But see others who say that the caucus did meet: Congressional Quarterly, *Guide to U.S. Elections,* 3d ed. (Washington, D.C.: CQ Press, 1994), 9; Noble

E. Cunningham Jr., *The Jeffersonian Republicans: The Formation of Party Organization, 1798–1801* (Chapel Hill: University of North Carolina Press, 1957), 91. Austin Ranney, in *Curing the Mischiefs of Faction* (Berkeley: University of California Press, 1975), notes that it is not clear when the first caucuses were, but that most historians agree that both parties held caucuses in 1800 (p. 64).

33. Noble E. Cunningham Jr., ed., *The Making of the American Party System: 1789–1809* (Englewood Cliffs, N.J.: Prentice-Hall, 1965), 14.

34. From text of the speech in ibid., 16–17.

35. Stanwood, *History of the Presidency,* 45–46.

36. Chase, *Presidential Nominating Convention,* 12.

37. Quoted in Stanwood, *History of the Presidency,* 70.

38. The history of the amendment is covered in some detail in ibid., 77–82.

39. Ibid., 111.

40. Quoted in ibid., 90.

41. William J. Crotty, *Political Reform and the American Experiment* (New York: Crowell, 1977), 11.

42. Thomas Byrne Edsall and Mary D. Edsall, *Chain Reaction: The Impact of Race, Rights, and Taxes on American Politics* (New York: Norton, 1991).

43. See ibid.

44. Michael Nelson, "The Elections: Ordinary Politics, Extraordinary Outcome," in *The Elections of 2000* (Washington, D.C.: CQ Press, 2001), 65–69.

45. Martin P. Wattenberg, *The Rise of Candidate-Centered Politics: Presidential Elections in the 1980s* (Cambridge: Harvard University Press, 1991), chap. 3.

46. Stephen J. Wayne, *The Road to the White House 1996: The Politics of Presidential Elections* (New York: St. Martin's Press, 1996), 150.

47. Ibid., 178.

48. Woodrow Wilson also called for national primaries in his first message to Congress as president in 1913, but the initiative died of neglect. Polls since World War II have found steady majorities favoring national primaries, but there has never been a serious effort to bring about such a system.

49. Rhodes Cook, *Congressional Quarterly Weekly Report,* August 19, 1995, 2484.

50. The nine amendments are: Twelfth (1804), placing the presidential and vice-presidential candidates on a single ticket; Fourteenth (1868), providing for equal protection under the law and for a decrease in the number of House members of any state that denied citizens the vote; Fifteenth (1870), specifying that the right to vote cannot be denied because of race; Seventeenth (1913), providing for direct election of senators; Nineteenth (1920), giving women the right to vote; Twenty-second (1951), limiting presidents to two terms; Twenty-third (1961), giving the District of Columbia electoral votes; Twenty-fourth (1964), eliminating the poll tax; and Twenty-sixth (1971), giving eighteen-year-olds the right to vote.

51. *Smith v. Allwright,* 321 U.S. 649 (1944); *Harman v. Forssenius,* 380 U.S. 528 (1965); *Harper v. Virginia State Board of Elections,* 383 U.S. 663 (1966).

52. Stephen J. Wayne, *The Road to the White House 2000: The Politics of Presidential Elections* (New York: Bedford/St. Martin's Press, 2000), 70–71.

53. Some jurisdictions below the state level retained tax-paying requirements into the twentieth century.

54. E. E. Schattschneider, *The Semisovereign People* (Hinsdale, Ill.: Dryden, 1975), 82.

55. *Guinn v. United States,* 238 U.S. 347 (1915); *Smith v. Allwright,* 321 U.S. 649 (1944).

56. See Delores Hayden, *The Grand Domestic Revolution* (Cambridge: MIT Press, 1981).

57. *Dunn v. Blumstein,* 405 U.S. 330 (1972).

58. Jasper B. Shannon, *Money and Politics* (New York: Random House, 1959), 19–20.

59. Robert Merton, *Social Theory and Social Structure* (New York: Free Press, 1957), 71–82.

60. Professor Hadley Cantril's department of psychology at Princeton University conducted a wide variety of polls both about domestic production and consumption during the war and about the attitudes and needs of troops on the front. See James R. Beniger and Robert J. Giuffra Jr., "Public Opinion Polling: Command and Control in Presidential Campaigns," in *Presidential Selection,* ed. Alexander E. Heard and Michael Nelson (Durham, N.C.: Duke University Press, 1987), 190.

61. This account draws on William J. Crotty, *Party Reform* (New York: Longman, 1983); Nelson W. Polsby, *Consequences of Party Reform* (New York: Oxford University Press, 1983); and David E. Price, *Bringing Back the Parties* (Washington, D.C.: CQ Press, 1984), chap. 6.

62. From the McGovern-Fraser Commission Report, quoted in Crotty, *Party Reform,* 25.

63. Ibid., 26.

64. Quoted in Price, *Bringing Back the Parties,* 146.

65. Crotty, *Party Reform,* 62.

66. For an overview of the literature on this point, see Austin Ranney, "The Political Parties: Reform and Decline," in *The New American Political System,* ed. Anthony King (Washington, D.C.: AEI Press, 1978), 214–215.

67. Polsby, *Consequences of Party Reform,* 34–35, quoting Byron Shafer.

68. Terry Sanford, *A Danger of Democracy: The Presidential Nominating Process* (Boulder: Westview, 1981), 20–21.

69. James W. Ceaser, *Presidential Selection: Theory and Development* (Princeton: Princeton University Press, 1979), 284.

70. Price, *Bringing Back the Parties,* 151.

71. Crotty, *Political Reform and the American Experiment,* 246.

72. Austin Ranney, "Changing the Rules of the Nominating Game," in *Choosing the President,* ed. James David Barber (Englewood Cliffs, N.J.: Prentice-Hall, 1974), 73–74.

73. Ibid., 151; and James W. Davis, *Presidential Primaries: Road to the White House* (Westport, Conn.: Greenwood Press, 1980), 66.

74. This account of the Republican Party's reform efforts is based on Crotty, *Party Reform,* chaps. 17 and 18; Robert J. Huckshorn and John F. Bibby, "National Party Rules and Delegate Selection in the Republican Party," *PS* 16, no. 4 (fall 1983): 656–666; and Price, *Bringing Back the Parties,* 156–159.

75. For a discussion of this, see Ceaser, *Presidential Selection,* 265–271.

76. Price, *Bringing Back the Parties,* 156.

77. Jean Bethke Elshtain, "Issues and Themes in the 1988 Campaign," in *The Elections of 1988,* ed. Michael Nelson (Washington, D.C.: CQ Press, 1989), 111–126.

78. Howard L. Reiter, *Parties and Elections in Corporate America* (New York: Longman, 1993), 163.

79. Robert L. Heilbroner, *The Nature and Logic of Capitalism* (New York: Norton, 1985), 55.

80. Elizabeth Drew, *Politics and Money: The New Road to Corruption* (New York: Macmillan, 1983), 2, 4.

81. Robert J. Samuelson, "The Campaign Reform Fraud," *Newsweek,* July 13, 1987, 43.

82. Jeffrey Berry, *The Interest Group Society* (Boston: Little, Brown, 1984), 168.

83. Herbert E. Alexander, *Financing Politics: Money, Elections, and Political Reform,* 3d ed. (Washington, D.C.: CQ Press, 1984), 7, 123.

84. John Kenneth Galbraith, *American Capitalism: The Concept of Countervailing Power* (Boston: Houghton Mifflin, 1952), esp. chap. 2.

85. Thomas Ferguson and Joel Rogers, *Right Turn: The Decline of the Democrats and the Future of American Politics* (New York: Hill and Wang, 1986), 45.

86. Thomas Geoghegan, *Which Side Are You On? Trying to Be for Labor When It's Flat on Its Back* (New York: Farrar, Straus, and Giroux, 1991).

87. U.S. Census Bureau, *Statistical Abstract of the United States: 2001* (Washington, D.C., 2001).

88. Shannon, *Money and Politics,* 15.

89. Ibid., 17–18.

90. Ibid., 25.

91. Ibid., 31.

92. By the time of McKinley's reelection drive in 1900, Hanna had refined his fund-raising system to the point where it was "unofficial taxation." Corporations were expected to contribute "according to [their] stake in the general prosperity of the country." Hanna returned $50,000 of the Standard Oil Company's $250,000 donation because it was considered more than the company's "fair share" for the campaign. See Michael E. McGerr, *The Decline of Popular Politics: The American North, 1865–1928* (New York: Oxford University Press, 1986), 44–45; and Shannon, *Money and Politics,* 33.

93. Shannon, *Money and Politics,* 37.

94. Samuel Kernell, *Going Public: New Strategies of Presidential Leadership,* 2d ed.(Washington, D.C.: CQ Press, 1993), 109, 118.

95. Herbert E. Alexander, *Money in Politics* (Washington, D.C.: Public Affairs Press, 1972), 10.

96. Herbert E. Alexander, "Spending in the 1996 Elections," in *Financing the 1996 Election,* ed. John C. Green (Armonk, N.Y.: M. E. Sharpe, 1999), 31.

97. Ibid., 32. Of the money raised before the disclosure requirement took effect, eighty-seven contributors of $50,000 or more gave a total of $12.4 million. Some $4.4 million of the $43.3 million raised after that point came from thirty-seven contributors of $50,000 or more.

98. Adamany and Agree, *Political Money,* 39.

99. Nelson W. Polsby and Aaron Wildavsky, *Presidential Elections: Strategies of American Electoral Politics,* 9th ed. (Chatham, N.J.: Chatham House, 1995), 66. As might be expected, the sequence of events is as disputed as it is crucial. From 1969 to 1971, the Nixon administration negotiated with International Telephone and Telegraph (ITT) over the suit. President Nixon was involved personally. Tapes revealed that, at the same time, administration officials knew of ITT's offers for campaign and convention assistance. See Herbert E. Alexander, *Financing the 1972 Election* (Lexington, Mass.: Lexington Books, 1976), 263–268.

100. Stephen Hess, *The Presidential Campaign* (Washington, D.C.: Brookings, 1974), 82.

101. Ibid., 48.

102. *Buckley v. Valeo,* 424 U.S. 1 (1976).

103. From *Buckley v. Valeo.* Cited in *Guide to Congress,* 5th ed. (Washington, D.C.: Congressional Quarterly, 2000), 881.

104. Ibid.

105. The delays in revamping the FEC had an immediate effect on the 1976 presidential nomination contests. Arizona representative Morris Udall and former California governor Ronald Reagan did not receive federal funds they had planned to use, and they had to trim their primary efforts in several states. It is conceivable that both candidates could have won their party nominations if they had had the money at the critical periods. See Jules Witcover, *Marathon: The Pursuit of the Presidency, 1972–1976* (New York: Viking Press, 1977), 219–221.

106. Dan Clawson, Alan Neustadt, and Denise Scott, *Money Talks: Corporate PACs and Political Influence* (New York: Basic Books, 1992), 213.

107. Davis, *Presidential Primaries,* 217–218; Alexander, *Financing the 1972 Election,* 110–159.

108. Anthony Corrado, "Financing the 2000 Elections," in *The Election of 2000,* ed. Gerald M. Pomper (New York: Chatham House Publishers, 2001), 92–124.

109. Marian Currinder, "Campaign Finance: Funding the Presidential and Congressional Elections," in *The Elections of 2004,* ed. Michael Nelson (Washington, D.C.: CQ Press, 2005), 108–132.

110. Harold W. Stanley and Richard G. Niemi, *Vital Statistics on American Politics, 2001–2002* (Washington, D.C.: CQ Press, 2001), 90.

111 Currinder, "Campaign Finance," 108–132.

112. Davis, *Presidential Primaries,* 206. Committees to draft reluctant candidates are not automatically subject to campaign spending limits. The money spent by the 1979 draft committees for Massachusetts senator Edward Kennedy did not count against Kennedy's overall spending limits.

113. Davis, *Presidential Primaries,* 207.

114. Davis, *Presidential Primaries,* 206–207.

115. Richard Harwood, ed., *The Pursuit of the Presidency 1980* (New York: Berkley, 1980), 102–103.

116. "Manufacturing the Next President," *Harper's,* December 1987, 49.

117. Corrado, "Financing the 2000 Elections."

118. Quoted in Kayden, "Regulating Campaign Finance," 276.

119. Quoted in Herbert Asher, *Presidential Elections and American Politics* (Homewood, Ill.: Dorsey Press, 1980), 279–280.

120. Stanley and Niemi, *Vital Statistics on American Politics, 2005–2006* (Washington, D.C.: CQ Press, 2006), 85–111.

121. Corrado, *Creative Campaigning,* 185.

122. For recent examinations of the president's need to make public appeals for support of policy initiatives, see Jeffrey K. Tulis, *The Rhetorical Presidency* (Princeton: Princeton University Press, 1987); and Kernell, *Going Public.*

123. Sidney M. Milkis and Michael Nelson, *The American Presidency: Origins and Development, 1776–1998* (Washington, D.C.: CQ Press, 1999), 51–52.

124. Rossiter's portrait of the president reads in part: "He must be, according to unwritten law: a man, a white, a Christian. He almost certainly must be: a Northerner or Westerner, less than 65 years old, of Northern European stock, experienced in politics and public service, healthy. He ought to be: from a state larger than Kentucky, more than forty-five years old, a family man, of British stock, a veteran, a Protestant, a lawyer, a state governor, a Mason, a Legionaire, or Rotarian—preferably all three, a small-town boy, self-made man, especially if a Republican, experienced in international affairs, a cultural middle-brow who likes baseball, detective stories, fishing, pop concerts, picnics, and seascapes. It really makes no difference whether he is: a college graduate, a small businessman, a member of Congress, a member of the Cabinet, a defeated candidate for the Presidency, providing that he emerged from his defeat the very image of the happy warrior. . . . He almost certainly cannot be: a Southerner . . . , of Polish, Italian, or Slavic stock, a union official, an ordained minister. He cannot be, according to unwritten law: a Negro, a Jew, an Oriental, a woman, an atheist, a freak. . . ." See Clinton Rossiter, *The American Presidency* (New York: Harcourt Brace, 1960), 193–194.

125. David Canon, *Actors, Athletes, and Astronauts* (Chicago: University of Chicago Press, 1990).

126. Alan Ehrenhalt, *The United States of Ambition: Politicians, Power, and the Pursuit of Office* (New York: Times Books, 1992), 256.

127. Wayne, *Road to the White House 2000,* 171.

128. Edwin C. Hargrove and Michael Nelson, *Presidents, Politics, and Policy* (Baltimore, Md.: Johns Hopkins University Press, 1984), 20–24.

129. David S. Broder, "The Story That Still Nags at Me," *Washington Monthly,* February 1987, 29–32.

130. A variety of psychological studies of political leadership have argued that a candidate's insecurities can be an important part of his or her energy but also an unhealthy distraction from rational political behavior. See James David Barber, *The Presidential Character* (Englewood Cliffs, N.J.: Prentice-Hall, 1972), for portraits of Wilson, Johnson, and Nixon. Among the most prominent "psychobiographies" are those by Alexander George and Juliette George, *Woodrow Wilson and Colonel House* (New York: John Day, 1956); and Bruce Mazlish, *In Search of Nixon* (New York: Basic Books, 1972).

131. Jimmy Carter, *Why Not the Best?* (New York: Bantam Books, 1976), 158–159.

132. Davis, *Presidential Primaries,* 159.

133. Polsby and Wildavsky, *Presidential Elections,* 95.

134. Elaine Ciulla Kamarck, "Structure as Strategy: Presidential Nominating Politics since Reform" (Ph.D. diss., University of California, Berkeley, 1986), 46–47.

135. William G. Mayer, "The New Hampshire Primary: A Historical Overview," in *Media and Momentum: The New Hampshire Primary and Nomination Politics,* ed. Gary Orren and Nelson W. Polsby (Chatham, N.J.: Chatham House, 1987), 24.

136. Two others, Jerry Brown and Frank Church, entered the campaign late.

137. William C. Adams, "As New Hampshire Goes . . . ," in Orren and Polsby, *Media and Momentum,* 45.

138. Ibid., 49.

139. Alan I. Abramowitz, "Viability, Electability, and Candidate Choice in a Presidential Primary Election: A Test of Competing Models," *Journal of Politics* 51 (November 1989): 989.

140. Witcover, *Marathon: The Pursuit of the Presidency,* 327–354.

141. Jack Germond and Jules Witcover, *Wake Us When It's Over: Presidential Politics of 1984* (New York: Macmillan, 1985).

142. Martin Schram, *Running for President: A Journal of the Carter Campaign* (New York: Pocket Books, 1976), 64.

143. Paul-Henri Gurian, "The Influence of Nomination Rules on the Financial Allocations of Presidential Candidates," *Western Political Quarterly* 43 (September 1990): 668.

144. New York governor Mario Cuomo argued that the "stature problem" of the 1988 Democratic candidates would fade as soon as one or two candidates emerged from the field in the Iowa caucuses and New Hampshire primary.

145. Norman H. Nie, Sidney Verba, and John R. Petrocik, *The Changing American Voter* (Cambridge: Harvard University Press, 1979), 210–242.

146. Stephen Hess, "Why Great Men Are Not Chosen Presidents: Lord Bryce Revisited," in *Elections American Style,* ed. A. James Reichley (Washington, D.C.: Brookings, 1987), 81.

147. Davis, *Presidential Primaries,* 213–219, 224–239.

148. The effect of presidential coattails should not be overstated. More important may be the "drag" effect that an unpopular president may have on the party's candidates. See Warren E. Miller, "A Study in Political Myth and Mythology," *Public Opinion Quarterly* 19 (winter 1955–1956): 26–39.

149. Polsby and Wildavsky, *Presidential Elections,* 49.

150. The organizations backing Mondale included the American Federation of Labor-Congress of Industrial Organizations, the United Auto Workers, the National Education Association, the National Organization for Women, and a number of members of Congress and other politicians such as Atlanta mayor Andrew Young.

151. William G. Thiemann, "President Hoover's Efforts on Behalf of FDR's 1932 Nomination," *Presidential Studies Quarterly* 24 (winter 1994): 87–91.

152. Stephen Skowronek, *The Politics Presidents Make: Leadership from John Adams to George Bush* (Cambridge: Harvard University Press, 1993).

153. Arthur M. Schlesinger Jr., *The Cycles of American History* (Boston: Houghton Mifflin, 1986).

154. Fred Barnes, "Earthquake," *New Republic,* October 17, 1994, 18.

155. Hargrove and Nelson, *Presidents, Politics, and Policy.*

156. Davis, *Presidential Primaries,* 65.

157. Ibid., 67–68.

158. Paul R. Abramson, John H. Aldrich, and David W. Rohde, *Change and Continuity in the 1984 Elections,* rev. ed. (Washington, D.C.: CQ Press, 1986), 25.

159. Davis, *Presidential Primaries,* 139.

160. James Q. Wilson, *The Amateur Democrat* (Chicago: University of Chicago Press, 1962).

161. See Anthony Downs, *An Economic Theory of Democracy* (New York: Harper and Row, 1957).

162. Theodore H. White, *America in Search of Itself: The Making of the President, 1956–1980* (New York: Harper and Row, 1982), 318–319.

163. See Kathleen Hall Jamieson, *Eloquence in an Electronic Age* (New York: Oxford University Press, 1988).

164. James W. Davis, *National Conventions in an Age of Party Reform* (Westport, Conn.: Greenwood Press, 1983), 45.

165. Morton Krondracke, quoted in Davis, *National Conventions,* 47; see also Polsby and Wildavsky, *Presidential Elections,* 115–116.

166. Paul T. David, Ralph M. Goldman, and Richard C. Bain, *The Politics of National Party Conventions* (Washington, D.C.: Brookings, 1960), 165.

167. Davis, *National Conventions,* 58–59.

168. Ibid., 54.

169. Ibid., 42–44.

170. Terri Susan Fine, "Interest Groups and the Framing of the 1988 Democratic and Republican Party Platforms," *Polity* 26 (spring 1994): 517–530.

171. David et al., *Politics of National Party Conventions,* 66.

172. Quoted in Malcolm Moos and Stephen Hess, *Hats in the Ring* (New York: Random House, 1960), 119.

173. Jack W. Germond and Jules Witcover, *Whose Broad Stripes and Bright Stars? The Trivial Pursuit of the Presidency 1988* (New York: Warner Books, 1989), 352.

174. Quoted in Roseboom, *History of Presidential Elections,* 309.

175. Quoted in Stefan Lorant, *The Glorious Burden* (New York: Harper and Row, 1968), 440.

176. "Rift Over Campaign Films," *New York Times,* August 11, 1988, D19; Maureen Dowd, "A Man Is Chosen, but a Verb Is Born," *New York Times,* August 18, 1988, A23.

177. Witcover, *Marathon: The Pursuit of the Presidency,* 487.

178. Richard Reeves, *Convention* (New York: Harcourt Brace Jovanovich, 1977), 19.

179. Sanford, *Danger of Democracy,* 31.

180. Moos and Hess, *Hats in the Ring,* 124.

181. "We Point with Pride," *New York Times,* August 10, 1988, A14.

182. *Congressional Quarterly Weekly Report,* July 18, 1992, 2125.

183. Moos and Hess, *Hats in the Ring,* 130–131.

184. Ibid., 302–304; see also Roseboom, *History of Presidential Elections,* 215.

185. Davis, *National Conventions,* 203.

186. Joel K. Goldstein, *The Modern American Vice Presidency* (Princeton: Princeton University Press, 1982), 47.

187. Moos and Hess, *Hats in the Ring,* 144–158.

188. David Von Drehle, "First, 'Do No Harm' Rule," *Washington Post National Weekly Edition* (July 31, 2000), 9.

189. Bob Woodward, *Shadow: Five Presidents and the Legacy of Watergate* (New York: Simon and Schuster, 1999), 454.

190. Quoted in Lorant, *Glorious Burden,* 592–594.

191. H. L. Mencken, quoted in Moos and Hess, *Hats in the Ring,* 15.

192. Irwin Ross, *The Loneliest Campaign: The Truman Victory of 1948* (New York: New American Library, 1968), 93–94.

193. Kurt Lang and Gladys Engel Lang, *Politics and Television* (Chicago: Quadrangle, 1968), 78–79.

194. Quoted in ibid., 24.

195. Reeves, *Convention,* 35–36.

196. Davis, *National Conventions,* 202–203; Moos and Hess, *Hats in the Ring,* 131.

197. David L. Paletz and Martha Elson, "Television Coverage of Presidential Conventions: Now You See It, Now You Don't," *Political Science Quarterly* 91 (spring 1976), discussed in Davis, *National Conventions,* 206–207.

198. Theodore H. White, *The Making of the President 1960* (New York: Atheneum, 1961), 151–152.

199. Michael Oreskes, "Convention Message Is Garbled by Quayle Static," *New York Times,* August 19, 1988, A16.

200. James E. Campbell, Lynna L. Cherry, and Kenneth A. Wink, "The Convention Bump," *American Politics Quarterly* 20 (July 1992): 287–307.

201. For an overview, see William Crotty and John S. Jackson, *Presidential Primaries and Nominations* (Washington, D.C.: CQ Press, 1985), 213–220.

202. Michael Nelson, "The Case for the Current Presidential Nominating Process," in *Before Nomination: Our Primary Problems,* ed. George Grassmuck (Washington, D.C.: AEI Press, 1985), 24.

203. Ibid., 217 (citing Robert T. Nakamura and Denis G. Sullivan, "Party Democracy and Democratic Control," in *American Politics and Public Policy,* ed. Walter Dean Burnham and Martha Wagner Weinberg [Cambridge: MIT Press, 1978], 26–40).

204. Thomas E. Mann, "Should the Presidential Nominating System Be Changed (Again)?" in *Before Nomination,* 39.

205. Ibid., 40–41.

206. Michael Nelson, "Two Cheers for the National Primary," in *Rethinking the Presidency,* ed. Thomas E. Cronin (Boston: Little, Brown, 1982), 55.

207. Mann, "Should the Presidential Nominating System Be Changed (Again)?" 44–45.

208. Gerald Pomper, *Passions and Interests* (Lawrence: University Press of Kansas, 1992).

209. Nelson, "Two Cheers," 55–58.

210. Crotty and Jackson, *Presidential Primaries and Nominations,* 222.

211. Mann, "Should the Presidential Nominating System Be Changed (Again)?" 43. For a further discussion of the costs and benefits of such a system, see Austin Ranney, *The Federalization of Presidential Primaries* (Washington, D.C.: AEI Press, 1978), chap. 5.

212. Crotty and Jackson, *Presidential Primaries and Nominations,* 225–227.

213. Ibid., 227.

214. Abramson et al., *Change and Continuity in the 1984 Elections,* 51.

215. Lewis Chester, Godfrey Hodgson, and Bruce Page, *The American Melodrama: The Presidential Campaign of 1968* (New York: Viking, 1969), 620.

216. Polsby and Wildavsky, *Presidential Elections,* 149.

217. Ibid., 148.

218. Pious, *American Presidency,* 104.

219. Stephen J. Wayne, *The Road to the White House,* 3d ed. (New York: St. Martin's Press, 1988), 182.

220. Richard M. Pious and Robert C. Weaver, "Presidential Campaigns: Strategies and Tactics," in *Selection/Election: A Forum on the American Presidency,* ed. Robert S. Hirschfield (New York: Aldine, 1982), 118.

221. Polsby and Wildavsky, *Presidential Elections,* 170, 182.

222. The complete text of the memorandum, prepared by Mike Duval and Foster Channock of the White House staff and dated June 11, 1976, is included in: Martin Schram, *Running for President: A Journal of the Carter Campaign,* expanded edition (New York: Pocket Books, 1978), 320–324.

223. Richard B. Cheney, "The 1976 Presidential Debates: A Republican Perspective," in *The Past and Future of Presidential Debates,* ed. Austin Ranney (Washington, D.C.: AEI Press, 1979), 110.

224. Schram, *Running for President,* 326.

225. Richard Joslyn, *Mass Media and Elections* (Reading, Mass.: Addison-Wesley, 1984), 32.

226. Howard L. Reiter, *Parties and Elections in Corporate America* (New York: St. Martin's Press, 1987), 159–160 (based on a 1984 memorandum from Stuart Spencer to Ronald Reagan).

227. Beniger and Giuffra, "Public Opinion Polling," in *Presidential Selection,* 189–215.

228. Bruce E. Altschuler, *Keeping a Finger on the Public Pulse: Private Polling and Presidential Elections* (Westport, Conn.: Greenwood Press, 1982), 7.

229. Larry J. Sabato, *The Rise of Political Consultants* (New York: Basic Books, 1981), 70.

230. Ibid., 92–104.

231. Wayne, *Road to the White House,* 243–244.

232. Beniger and Giuffra, "Public Opinion Polling," 194–196.

233. Altschuler, *Public Pulse,* 3.

234. Sabato, *Political Consultants,* 113–115. For an account of Nixon's 1968 campaign, see Joe McGinniss, *The Selling of the President: 1968* (New York: Trident Press, 1969).

235. Beniger and Giuffra, "Public Opinion Polling," 192; Wayne, *Road to the White House,* 215–216.

236. Sabato, *Political Consultants,* 224–229.

237. Ibid., 238.

238. Dom Bonafede, "Part Science, Part Art, Part Hokum, Direct Mail Now a Key Campaign Tool," *National Journal,* July 31, 1982, 1334–1335.

239. Reiter, *Parties and Elections,* 189 n. 13.

240. Sabato, *Political Consultants,* 201.

241. Ibid., 254.

242. Reiter, *Parties and Elections,* 162–168.

243. Sabato, *Political Consultants,* 337.

244. Kay Lawson, "How State Laws Undermine Parties," in *Elections American Style,* ed. A. James Reichley (Washington, D.C.: Brookings, 1987).

245. Corrado, "Financing the 2000 Elections," 117, 119. These figures extend through October 18, 2000.

246. Currinder, "Campaign Finance," 108–132.

247. Robert Axelrod, "Where the Votes Come from: An Analysis of Electoral Coalitions, 1952–1968," *American Political Science Review* 66 (March 1972).

248. Stanley and Niemi, *Vital Statistics on American Politics, 2001–2002,* 101.

249. Currinder, "Campaign Finance," 108–132.

250. F. Christopher Arterton, *Media Politics: The News Strategies of Presidential Campaigns* (Lexington, Mass.: Lexington Books, 1984), 1.

251. See, for example: Nelson W. Polsby, "The News Media as an Alternative to Party in the Presidential Selection Process," in *Political Parties in the Eighties,* ed. Robert A. Goldwin (Washington, D.C.: AEI Press, 1980), 50ff; and Donald R. Matthews, "Winnowing," in *Race for the Presidency,* ed. James David Barber (Englewood Cliffs, N.J.: Prentice-Hall, 1978), 55ff.

252. David L. Paletz and Robert M. Entman, *Media Power Politics* (New York: Free Press, 1981), 16.

253. W. Lance Bennett, *News: The Politics of Illusion* (New York: Longman, 1983), 7–8; Paletz and Entman, *Media Power Politics,* 52.

254. Barry Cole, ed., *Television Today: A Close-up View* (New York: Oxford University Press, 1981), 183.

255. National Institute of Mental Health, *Television and Behavior,* vol. 1 (Washington, D.C.: Government Printing Office, 1982), 1.

256. Paletz and Entman, *Media Power Politics,* 45–49.

257. Corrado, "Financing the 2000 Elections," 107. The figure for spending by the parties covers the nation's seventy-five largest media markets.

258. See Joslyn, *Mass Media and Elections,* chap. 7, for an overview of this question.

259. Bernard Berelson, quoted in Joseph T. Klapper, *The Effects of Mass Communication* (Glencoe, Ill.: Free Press, 1960), 4.

260. Paletz and Entman, *Media Power Politics,* 45.

261. Doris Graber, *Mass Media and American Politics,* 4th ed. (Washington, D.C.: CQ Press, 1993), 248–249.

262. Corrado, "Financing the 2000 Elections," 101–102.

263. Wayne, *Road to the White House,* 223.

264. Joslyn, *Mass Media and Elections,* 210 (see 203–214 generally for a discussion of the effects of presidential debates).

265. James Fallows, "An Acquired Taste," *Atlantic Monthly* (July 2000), 33–53.

266. Paul J. Quirk and Jon K. Dalager, "The Election: A 'New Democrat' and a New Kind of Presidential Campaign," in *Elections of 1992,* ed. Michael Nelson (Washington, D.C.: CQ Press, 1993), 62.

267. Wayne, *Road to the White House,* 227.

268. Witcover, *Marathon: Pursuit of the Presidency,* 535.

269. "Quayle and Bentsen, Running Mates Under Fire," *Congressional Quarterly Weekly Report,* October 8, 1988, 2838–2839.

270. Wayne, *Road to the White House,* 171.

271. Quoted in Lorant, *Glorious Burden,* 246.

272. Ibid., 249.

273. Wayne, *Road to the White House,* 172.

274. Roseboom, *History of Presidential Elections,* 313–314.

275. Lorant, *Glorious Burden,* 466.

276. Roseboom, *History of Presidential Elections,* 331.

277. Lorant, *Glorious Burden,* 486.

278. Wayne, *Road to the White House,* 173.

279. Larry J. Sabato, *The Party's Just Begun* (Reading, Mass.: Addison-Wesley, 1996), 59–61.

280. Michael Nelson, "The Setting: George W. Bush: Majority President," in *The Elections of 2004,* ed. Michael Nelson (Washington, D.C.: CQ Press, 2005), 1–17.

281. This number, based on Appendix A in Steven J. Rosenstone, Roy L. Behr, and Edward H. Lazarus, *Third Parties in America*

(Princeton: Princeton University Press, 1984), includes only those parties and candidates that received popular votes in more than one state in any given election.

282. Daniel A. Mazmanian, *Third Parties in Presidential Elections* (Washington, D.C.: Brookings, 1974), 4–5 (drawing on William Nisbet Chambers).

283. Some would discount the Anti-Masons in 1832 since two-party competition was not yet firmly established throughout the country. See Rosenstone, Behr, and Lazarus, *Third Parties in America,* 10–11.

284. Ibid., 17.

285. James L. Sundquist, *Dynamics of the Party System,* rev. ed. (Washington, D.C.: Brookings, 1983), 58 (notes omitted). Sundquist notes that analysis of the election returns also supports this view (p. 58 n. 23).

286. Rosenstone, Behr, Lazarus, *Third Parties in America,* 8.

287. Ibid., chaps. 3 and 4 (esp. pp. 78–79, 119–121).

288. James Q. Wilson, *American Government: Institutions and Policies* (Lexington, Mass.: D.C. Heath, 1980), 155.

289. Rosenstone, Behr, Lazarus, *Third Parties in America,* 5.

290. Sundquist, *Dynamics of the Party System,* 60–65.

291. Wilson, *American Government,* 155.

292. Rhodes Cook, "Clinton Picks the GOP Lock on the Electoral College," *Congressional Quarterly Weekly Report,* November 7, 1992, 3553.

293. For a full discussion of the dynamics of the use of "exit" versus "voice" by members of organizations, see Albert O. Hirschman, *Exit, Voice, and Loyalty: Responses to Decline in Firms, Organizations, and States* (Cambridge: Harvard University Press, 1970).

294. Mazmanian, *Third Parties in Presidential Elections,* 77.

295. Rosenstone, Behr, Lazarus, *Third Parties in America,* 40.

296. This discussion of legal constraints is based on ibid., 19–27.

297. Ibid., 26.

298. Mazmanian, *Third Parties in Presidential Elections,* 3.

299. Rosenstone, Behr, and Lazarus, *Third Parties in America,* 33.

300. Mazmanian, *Third Parties in Presidential Elections,* 67.

301. Nelson, "The Election: Ordinary Politics, Extraordinary Outcome," 69.

302. John E. Jackson, "Election Night Reporting and Voter Turnout," *American Journal of Political Science* 27 (November 1983): 615–635.

303. Richard Lacayo, "Is This Any Way to Vote?" *Time,* November 27, 2000, 54–56.

304. *Bush v. Gore* 69, U.S.L.W. 4029.

305. Laurence H. Tribe and Thomas M. Rollins, "Deadlock: What Happens if Nobody Wins," *Atlantic Monthly,* October 1980, 49.

306. U.S. Constitution, Amendment XX, Section 3.

307. Tribe and Rollins, "Deadlock," 60–61.

308. Allan P. Sindler, "Presidential Selection and Succession in Special Situations," in *Presidential Selection,* ed. Alexander Heard and Michael Nelson (Durham, N.C.: Duke University Press, 1987), 355.

309. Ibid.

310. Ibid., 356.

311. Ibid., 355; Tribe and Rollins, "Deadlock," 58–60.

312. U.S. Constitution, Amendment XX, Section 3.

313. Quoted in Tribe and Rollins, "Deadlock," 60.

314. Milton Lomask, *Aaron Burr: The Years from Princeton to Vice President (1756–1805)* (New York: Farrar, Straus, Giroux, 1979), 291–294.

315. Eugene H. Roseboom and Alfred E. Eckes Jr., *A History of Presidential Elections,* 4th ed. (New York: Macmillan, 1979), 38.

316. Tribe and Rollins, "Deadlock," 60.

317. Stanwood, *History of the Presidency,* 187.

318. Tribe and Rollins, "Deadlock," 50.

319. Ibid., 56. Wallace's terms were delivered in a press conference on February 19, 1968.

320. Walter Berns, ed., *After the People Vote: Steps in Choosing the President* (Washington, D.C.: AEI Press, 1983), 18–20.

321. Quoted in Charles O. Jones, *Passages to the Presidency: From Campaigning to Governing* (Washington, D.C.: Brookings, 1998), 173.

322. Ibid., 13.

323. Richard E. Neustadt, *Presidential Power: The Politics of Leadership* (New York: Wiley, 1960), 219.

324. Carl M. Brauer, *Presidential Transitions: Eisenhower through Reagan* (New York: Oxford University Press, 1986), xiv.

325. Quoted in ibid., 62.

326. Brauer, *Presidential Transitions,* 127.

327. Ibid., 65.

328. Quoted in ibid., 16.

329. Ibid., 177.

330. For a more thorough discussion of rituals and symbols in politics, see Murray Edelman, *The Symbolic Uses of Politics* (Urbana: University of Illinois Press, 1985).

331. *Presidential Inaugural Bibles: Catalogue of an Exhibition (November 17, 1968–February 23, 1969)* (Washington, D.C.: Washington Cathedral, 1969), 6–7.

332. Ibid., 12.

333. Ibid., 43.

334. Ibid., 12, 29, 43; 1969 Inaugural Committee, *The Inaugural Story: 1789–1969* (New York: American Heritage, 1969), 67.

335. Edward S. Corwin, *The President: Office and Powers, 1787–1957,* 4th rev. ed. (New York: New York University Press, 1957), 54.

336. Harold W. Chase and Craig R. Ducat, *Edward S. Corwin's The Constitution and What It Means Today,* 13th ed. (Princeton: Princeton University Press, 1973), 119.

337. Quoted in Edna M. Colman, *Seventy-five Years of White House Gossip: From Washington to Lincoln* (Garden City, N.J.: Doubleday, Page, 1925), 4.

338. 1969 Inaugural Committee, *Inaugural Story,* 42–45.

339. Ibid., 86–87.

340. Phil Gailey, "The Cold Bottom Line: No Parade and No Profit," *New York Times,* January 22, 1985, A19. Ticket holders could receive a refund if they made their request before February 10, 1985.

341. Herbert E. Alexander and Anthony Corrado, *Financing the 1992 Election* (New York: Sharpe, 1995), 290–291.

342. Colman, *Seventy-five Years of White House Gossip,* 155.

343. 1969 Inaugural Committee, *Inaugural Story,* 103.

344. Ibid., 97–107.

345. Irvin Molotsky, "Nine Grand Balls: The Reagans and Thousands of Well-Wishers Go Dancing," *New York Times,* January 22, 1985, A19.

346. Colman, *Seventy-five Years of White House Gossip,* 186.

347. 1969 Inaugural Committee, *Inaugural Story* 56.

SELECTED BIBLIOGRAPHY

Abramson, Paul R., John H. Aldrich, and David W. Rohde. *Change and Continuity in the 1984 Elections.* Rev. ed. Washington, D.C.: CQ Press, 1987.

——-. *Change and Continuity in the 1992 Elections.* Rev. ed. Washington, D.C.: CQ Press, 1995.

Alexander, Herbert E., and Monica Bauer. *Financing the 1988 Election.* Boulder, Colo.: Westview, 1991.

Alexander, Herbert E., and Anthony Corrado. *Financing the 1992 Election.* New York: Sharpe, 1995.

Alexander, Herbert E., and Brian A. Haggerty. *Financing the 1984 Election.* Lexington, Mass.: Lexington Books, 1987.

Arterton, F. Christopher. *Media Politics: The News Strategies of Presidential Campaigns.* Lexington, Mass.: Lexington Books, 1984.

Barber, James David, ed. *Choosing the President.* Englewood Cliffs, N.J.: Prentice-Hall, 1974.

——-. *The Presidential Character.* Englewood Cliffs, N.J.: Prentice Hall, 1972.

Bennett, W. Lance. *News: The Politics of Illusion.* 4th ed. White Plains, N.Y.: Longman, 2000.

Berkman, Ronald, and Laura W. Kitch. *Politics in the Media Age.* New York: McGraw-Hill, 1986.

Brauer, Carl M. *Presidential Transitions: Eisenhower through Reagan.* New York: Oxford University Press, 1988.

Burden, Barry C. "United States Senators as Presidential Candidates." *Political Science Quarterly* 117 (spring 2002).

Ceaser, James W. *Presidential Selection: Theory and Development.* Princeton: Princeton University Press, 1979.

——-. *Reforming the Reforms.* Cambridge: Ballinger, 1982.

Chambers, William Nisbet, and Walter Dean Burnham, eds. *The American Party Systems: Stages of Development.* New York: Oxford University Press, 1967.

Chase, James S. *Emergence of the Presidential Nominating Convention: 1789–1832.* Urbana: University of Illinois Press, 1973.

Clinton, W. David, ed. *Presidential Transitions: The Reagan to Bush Experience.* Lanham, Md.: University Press of America, 1992.

Clinton, W. David, and Daniel G. Lang. *What Makes a Successful Transition?* Lanham, Md.: University Press of America, 1993.

Cole, Barry, ed. *Television Today: A Close-Up View.* New York: Oxford University Press, 1981.

Colman, Edna M. *Seventy-five Years of White House Gossip: From Washington to Lincoln.* Garden City, N.J.: Doubleday, Page, 1925.

CQ Press. *Guide to U.S. Elections.* 5th ed. Washington, D.C.: CQ Press, 2005.

Corwin, Edward S. *The President: Office and Powers.* 5th ed. New York: New York University Press, 1984.

Crotty, William J. *Political Reform and the American Experiment.* New York: Crowell, 1977.

Crotty, William J., and John S. Jackson III. *Presidential Primaries and Nominations.* Washington, D.C.: CQ Press, 1985.

Cunningham, Noble E., Jr., ed. *The Making of the American Party System: 1789–1809.* Englewood Cliffs, N.J.: Prentice-Hall, 1965.

Davis, James W. *National Conventions in an Age of Party Reform.* Westport, Conn.: Greenwood Press, 1983.

——. *Presidential Primaries: Road to the White House.* Westport, Conn.: Greenwood Press, 1980.

Drew, Elizabeth. *Politics and Money: The New Road to Corruption.* New York: Macmillan, 1983.

Edelman, Murray. *The Symbolic Uses of Politics.* Urbana: University of Illinois Press, 1985.

Edsall, Thomas Byrne. *The New Politics of Inequality.* New York: Norton, 1984.

Ferguson, Thomas, and Joel Rogers, eds. *The Hidden Election: Politics and Economics in the 1980 Presidential Campaign.* New York: Random House, 1981.

——. *Right Turn: The Decline of the Democrats and the Future of American Politics.* New York: Hill and Wang, 1986.

Fiorina, Morris P. *Retrospective Voting in American National Elections.* New Haven: Yale University Press, 1981.

Graber, Doris A. *Mass Media and American Politics.* 6th ed. Washington, D.C.: CQ Press, 2000.

Germond, Jack W., and Jules Witcover. *Mad as Hell: Revolt at the Ballot Box, 1992.* New York: Warner, 1993.

——. *Wake Us When It's Over: Presidential Politics of 1984.* New York: Macmillan, 1985.

——. *Whose Broad Stripes and Bright Stars: The Trivial Pursuit of the Presidency 1988.* New York: Warner, 1989.

Hanson, Russell L. *The Democratic Imagination in America: Conversations with Our Past.* Princeton: Princeton University Press, 1985.

Harmel, Robert, ed. *Presidents and Their Parties.* New York: Praeger, 1984.

Heard, Alexander, and Michael Nelson, eds. *Presidential Selection.* Durham, N.C.: Duke University Press, 1987.

Hess, Stephen. *Organizing the Presidency.* Washington, D.C.: Brookings, 1988.

Hirschman, Albert O. *Exit, Voice, and Loyalty: Responses to Decline in Firms, Organizations, and States.* Cambridge: Harvard University Press, 1970.

Hofstadter, Richard. *The Idea of a Party System.* Berkeley: University of California Press, 1969.

Jackson, John S., and William Crotty. *The Politics of Presidential Selection.* 2d ed. New York: Longman, 2000.

Jones, Charles O. *Passages to the Presidency: From Campaigning to Governing.* Washington, D.C.: Brookings, 1998.

Joslyn, Richard. *Mass Media and Elections.* Reading, Mass.: Addison-Wesley, 1984.

Ladd, Everett Carll, Jr., and Charles D. Hadley. *Transformations of the American Party System.* New York: Norton, 1978.

Lang, Kurt, and Gladys Engel Lang. *Politics and Television.* Chicago: Quadrangle, 1968.

Lowi, Theodore J. *The Personal President.* Ithaca: Cornell University Press, 1994.

McGinniss, Joe. *The Selling of the President: 1968.* New York: Trident Press, 1969.

Macy, John W., Bruce Adams, and J. Jackson Walter. *America's Unelected Government: Appointing the President's Team.* Cambridge: Ballinger, 1983.

Mann, Thomas E. "Should the Presidential Nominating System Be Changed (Again)?" In *Before Nomination: Our Primary Problems,* ed. George Grassmuck. Washington, D.C.: AEI Press, 1985.

Marshall, Thomas R. *Presidential Nominations in a Reform Age.* New York: Praeger, 1981.

Matthews, Donald R. "Winnowing." In *Race for the Presidency,* ed. James David Barber. Englewood Cliffs, N.J.: Prentice-Hall, 1978.

Mazmanian, Daniel A. *Third Parties in Presidential Elections.* Washington, D.C.: Brookings, 1974.

Moos, Malcolm, and Stephen Hess. *Hats in the Ring.* New York: Random House, 1960.

Mosher, Frederick C., W. David Clinton, and Daniel G. Lang. *Presidential Transitions and Foreign Affairs.* Baton Rouge: Louisiana State University Press, 1987.

Nelson, Michael. "Two Cheers for the National Primary." In *Rethinking the Presidency,* ed. Thomas E. Cronin. Boston: Little, Brown, 1982.

Orren, Gary R., and Nelson W. Polsby. *Media and Momentum: The New Hampshire Primary and Nomination Politics.* Chatham, N.J.: Chatham House, 1987.

Paletz, David L., and Martha Elson. "Television Coverage of Presidential Conventions: Now You See It, Now You Don't." *Political Science Quarterly* 91 (spring 1976).

Paletz, David L., and Robert M. Entman. *Media Power Politics.* New York: Free Press, 1981.

Patterson, Thomas E. *The Mass Media Election.* New York: Praeger, 1980.

Pfiffner, James P. *The Strategic Presidency: Hitting the Ground Running.* Chicago: Dorsey Press, 1988.

Pika, Joseph A., and Richard A. Watson. *The Presidential Contest.* 5th ed. Washington, D.C.: CQ Press, 1995.

Pious, Richard M. *The American Presidency.* New York: Basic Books, 1979.

Pious, Richard M., and Robert C. Weaver. "Presidential Campaigns: Strategies and Tactics." In *Selection/Election: A Forum on the American Presidency,* ed. Robert S. Hirschfield. New York: Aldine, 1982.

Piven, Frances Fox, and Richard A. Cloward. *Why Americans Don't Vote.* Boston: Beacon Press, 2000.

Polsby, Nelson W. "The News Media as an Alternative to Party in the Presidential Selection Process." In *Political Parties in the Eighties,* ed. Robert A. Goldwin. Washington, D.C.: AEI Press, 1980.

Polsby, Nelson W., and Aaron Wildavsky. *Presidential Elections: Strategies of American Electoral Politics.* 9th ed. Chatham, N.J.: Chatham House, 1995.

Ranney, Austin. *The Federalization of Presidential Primaries.* Washington, D.C.: AEI Press, 1978.

Roseboom, Eugene H. *A History of Presidential Elections.* 2d ed. New York: Macmillan, 1964.

Rosenstone, Steven J., Roy L. Behr, and Edward H. Lazarus. *Third Parties in America.* 2d ed. Princeton: Princeton University Press, 1996.

Sabato, Larry J. *The Party's Just Begun.* Reading, Mass.: Addison-Wesley, 1996.

——. *The Rise of Political Consultants.* New York: Basic Books, 1981.

Sanford, Terry. *A Danger of Democracy.* Boulder, Colo.: Westview, 1981.

Schlesinger, Arthur M., Jr., ed. *The Cycles of American History.* Boston: Houghton Mifflin, 1986.

Schram, Martin. *Running for President: A Journal of the Carter Campaign.* Exp. ed. New York: Pocket Books, 1978.

Stanley, Harold W., and Richard G. Niemi. *Vital Statistics on American Politics, 2005–2006.* Washington, D.C.: CQ Press, 2006.

Sundquist, James L. *Dynamics of the Party System.* Rev. ed. Washington, D.C.: Brookings, 1983.

Wayne, Stephen J. *The Road to the White House, 2000: The Politics of Presidential Elections.* New York: St. Martin's Press, 2001.

White, Theodore H. *The Making of the President 1960.* New York: Atheneum, 1961.

——. *The Making of the President 1972.* New York: Atheneum, 1973.

Witcover, Jules. *Marathon—The Pursuit of the Presidency: 1972–1976.* New York: Viking, 1977.

Wolfinger, Raymond, and Stephen Rosenstone. *Who Votes?* New Haven: Yale University Press, 1980.

chapter 6

Chronology of Presidential Elections

by Charles C. Euchner, John L. Moore, and Deborah Kalb

In the early years of the Republic, the American colonists and their leaders were ambivalent about the concept of democracy. On the one hand, Americans searched for ways to prevent the kind of tyranny they had experienced at the hand of elite rulers such as King George of England. On the other hand, political elites feared the instability that might result from mass participation in politics. This ambivalence was evident in the compromise for presidential selection worked out at the Constitutional Convention in 1787 and in the halting steps the nation took toward party competition.

The presidential selection process has changed significantly since George Washington was elected to his first term in 1789. The electoral college is still the center of the system, but all of the related institutions and processes are dramatically different, in part because the constitutional provisions for presidential selection are so vague.

The major features of the electoral system have developed over time as a process of trial and error. The Constitution contains no provisions for organizing political parties, nominating candidates, or campaigning for office. The Framers assumed, incorrectly, that the selection process would be a reasoned one that would transcend petty partisanship. The original provision for balloting by the electoral college was flawed and had to be superseded by the Twelfth Amendment in 1804.

Until the eighteenth century, competitive elections were rare. The nation's first legislative body, the Virginia House of Burgesses, had largely single-candidate elections until the 1700s, and later, even when the elections for state legislatures attracted more than one candidate, there was little active campaigning. It was only with the decline of homogeneous communities and the end of elite control over politics that election contests began to occur.

The very concept of the political party—a way to organize electoral coalitions—was viewed with distrust by the nation's earliest leaders. As George Washington described the dangers of parties in a letter: "A fire not to be quenched; it demands a uniform vigilance to prevent its bursting into a flame, lest instead of warming it should consume." [1] Only after the experience of factional debate in Congress, where bitter strife developed over issues such as banking, tariffs, and slavery, did the idea of parties seem necessary and capable of control.

THE EMERGENCE OF THE ELECTORAL PROCESS

The method of choosing presidential and vice-presidential candidates has moved through four distinct phases, according to political scientist Richard P. McCormick. [2] The first phase was a period marked by uncertain and hazardous rules that lasted until the Twelfth Amendment was ratified in 1804. The second phase, continuing through 1820, saw the decline of the Federalists as a national force and the dominance of the Democratic-Republicans. This phase is associated with "King Caucus"—the nomination of candidates by congressional caucuses. In the third phase, King Caucus was replaced by factional politics and unsettled rules for selecting candidates. The fourth phase—still in effect today—evolved between 1832 and 1844. It is characterized by a two-party system that nominates candidates by national conventions. In recent years, however, the conventions have been rendered obsolete by mass politics, which takes the form of mass media presentations of candidates to the public and mass participation of party members in primary elections.

Washington's First Election: 1789

Establishment of the rules for democratic decision making in the United States occurred inauspiciously. The states completed their separate ratifications of the Constitution in July 1788—nearly nine months after the close of the Constitutional Convention in Philadelphia. The Continental Congress then decided that New York City would serve as the seat of government. There, on September 13, 1788, Congress passed a resolution requiring the states to appoint electors on the first Wednesday in January, the electors to assemble and vote in their respective states on the first

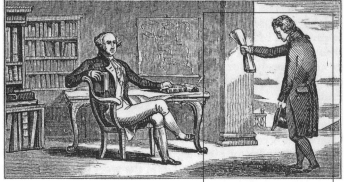

After riding his horse for a full week, Charles Thomson, secretary of the Continental Congress, arrived at Mt. Vernon on April 14, 1789, with the official news of George Washington's election as the first president of the United States.

Wednesday in February, and the new government to convene on the first Wednesday in March.

Under the Constitution, the method of choosing electors was left up to the individual state legislatures. The requirement that all electors be chosen on the same day proved to be troublesome for the states. Some did not have time to call elections. In New York, for example, where electors were to have been chosen by the legislature, dissension between the two houses led to a stalemate and prevented the state from participating in the election.

No formal nomination of candidates took place in 1788. Nevertheless, it had been widely anticipated since the Constitutional Convention the previous year that George Washington of Virginia, the reluctant hero of the Revolutionary War, would be president. The only real question was who would be the vice president. Leaders of the Federalists, a group organized in the fall of 1787 to achieve ratification of the Constitution, ultimately decided to support John Adams of Massachusetts.

The inherent flaws of the electoral system became evident quickly. Under the Constitution, each elector was to cast two votes for president. The two votes had to be for different persons, and the two candidates could not both receive votes from a common home state. The individual receiving the votes of a majority of the electors was to be named president, and the person receiving the second highest total was to be named vice president. Because no distinction was made between balloting for president and vice president, it was possible for more than one candidate to receive an equal number of votes, thereby throwing the election into the House of Representatives. It also was possible that a candidate for vice president—through fluke or machination—actually could end up with the most votes and become president.

The Federalist leader Alexander Hamilton recognized the danger, and his personal animosity toward Adams aggra-

vated his concern. In response, he plotted to siphon away votes from Adams. In a letter to James Wilson of Pennsylvania, Hamilton wrote: "Everybody is aware of that defect in the constitution which renders it possible that the man intended for vice president may in fact turn up president." To prevent such a crisis, Hamilton recommended that several votes that would otherwise have gone to Adams be thrown away on other candidates: "I have proposed to friends in Connecticut to throw away 2 [votes], to others in New Jersey to throw away an equal number and I submit to you whether it would not be well to lose three or four in Pennsylvania." [3]

Hamilton's efforts were successful. Washington was unanimously elected president with sixty-nine electoral votes. Adams, however, won the vice presidency with only thirty-four electoral votes. Just two states—New Hampshire and his own Massachusetts—voted solidly for him. Because in other states Federalist leaders withheld support from Adams and sometimes worked against him, he did not receive any votes from Delaware, Georgia, Maryland, and South Carolina, and he received only one vote from New Jersey. The remaining votes were spread among ten other candidates, including John Jay, John Hancock, Robert Harrison, John Rutledge, and George Clinton.

Although the new government was supposed to open its doors on March 4, 1789, not enough members of Congress had arrived in New York City by that date to achieve a quorum. When the Senate finally convened on April 6 and counted the electoral votes, a messenger was dispatched on horseback to deliver the news to President-elect Washington at his home in Mount Vernon, Virginia. He received the news on April 14. Washington then set out for New York where he was sworn in on April 30.

Before the end of Washington's first term as president, political divisions developed that would lead to a party system. James Madison emerged as the de facto opposition leader in Congress. Seventeen members of the House of Representatives regularly sided with Madison, and a bloc of fifteen supported the administration. The other dozen or so members of the House switched back and forth between the administration's and Madison's faction.[4]

The election of 1789 demonstrated the potential for partisanship and intrigue in presidential contests. It also revealed the weaknesses of the existing election calendar (which had made it difficult for New York to participate in the election) and reminded participants of the danger of the constitutional "defect" in the selection process that made it possible for the person intended to be vice president to become president.

Washington's Reelection: 1792

Washington remained first in the hearts of his countrymen when his first term as president drew to a close in 1792. But the facade of national unity was showing signs of crumbling as bitter oppositional factions began to develop. From this arose a system of electoral competition.

Washington won a second unanimous term as president in 1792, but the election did produce competition for vice president. An overtly partisan contest broke out when the Democratic-Republicans, as one faction was now known, decided to challenge the Federalist Adams. Some of Adams's approving statements about the British angered populists, who campaigned behind the scenes against him. Adams managed to win, but not before bitter partisan identities had developed in response to the nation's only unanimous administration.

The election was different from the 1789 one in another way as well. The election calendar was changed and made more flexible by an act of Congress that allowed states to choose electors within a thirty-four-day span before the first Wednesday in December when the electors met to vote. The new law remained in effect until 1845.

Thomas Jefferson, the leader of the Democratic-Republicans, chose not to run for vice president in 1792, in part because he came from the same state as President Washington. Because electors could vote for only one candidate from their own state, Jefferson was tacitly precluded from receiving the large electoral vote of Virginia. Besides, a "balanced ticket" required regional diversity. Instead, Democratic-Republican leaders from New York, Pennsylvania, Virginia, and South Carolina chose New York governor George Clinton as their candidate at a meeting in Philadelphia in October 1792. The endorsement of Clinton was a milestone in the evolution of the presidential nominating process and a step away from the Framers' original understanding of the selection process.

Both Washington and Adams were reelected, but Clinton scored well in the electoral college. Adams received 77 electoral votes to Clinton's 50 (with four votes going to Jefferson and one to Sen. Aaron Burr of New York), and Washington was reelected president by a unanimous electoral vote of 132.

The political tensions brought out by the Adams-Clinton contest became even tauter as policy controversies arose. Jefferson resigned as secretary of state in 1793 in protest over Secretary of the Treasury Hamilton's growing influence in foreign affairs. Jefferson complained: "In place of that noble love of liberty and Republican government which carried us triumphantly through the war, an

Thomas Pinckney, the Federalist choice for vice president, was not elected in 1796, although Federalist presidential candidate John Adams won the election. Democratic-Republican Thomas Jefferson won the vice presidency. The Twelfth Amendment (1804) precluded future split-ticket administrations.

Anglican, Monarchical, and Aristocratical party has sprung up, whose avowed subject is to draw over us the substance as they have already done the forms of the British government." Even Washington was subject to attacks. A Pennsylvania politician wondered aloud if Washington had not "become the tyrant instead of the saviour of his country." [5]

News of the French Revolution's period of terror divided the nation's political leaders. Federalists recoiled in horror with the news of a democratic revolution gone awry, while democrats such as Jefferson expressed sympathy for France's struggle. The U.S. government's use of troops to suppress the Whiskey Rebellion of 1794, approval of the Jay Treaty of 1794, and maneuvering between the warring French and British also polarized the young nation into factions. State-level Democratic-Republican societies formed during this period in opposition to the Federalists.

The First Succession: 1796

Washington decided not to run for president again in 1796, even though the Constitution did not bar a third term and public sentiment supported it. With Washington out of the race, the United States witnessed its first partisan contest for president. Washington's Farewell Address, published in the summer of 1796, was "a signal, like dropping a hat, for the party racers to start." [6]

On the Democratic-Republican side, Jefferson faced no opposition as the presidential candidate; a consensus of party leaders selected him to run in 1796. But a caucus of Democratic-Republican senators was unable to agree on a running mate, producing a tie vote for Burr of New York and Sen. Pierce Butler of South Carolina that ended with a walk-out by Butler's supporters. As a result, there was no formal Democratic-Republican candidate to run with Jefferson.

The Federalists, by contrast, held what historian Roy F. Nichols has described as a "quasi caucus" of the party's members of Congress in Philadelphia in May 1796.[7] The gathering chose Vice President Adams and Minister to Great Britain Thomas Pinckney of South Carolina as the Federalist presidential and vice-presidential candidates. The choice of Adams was not surprising because he was Washington's vice president. Nevertheless, Adams was unpopular in the South, and he continued to be disliked by Hamilton. As a result, Hamilton tried to use the "defect" in the Constitution to make Pinckney president instead of Adams. He urged northern electors to give equal support to Adams and Pinckney in the hopes that the South would not vote for Adams and that Pinckney would therefore win the most votes.

Had the northern electors followed Hamilton's advice, Pinckney might have won the presidency. Instead, eighteen votes were thrown to other Federalists (thereby preventing a Pinckney claim to the presidency), giving Adams the presidency with seventy-one electoral votes. Pinckney—with fifty-nine votes—was not even able to win the vice presidency. Jefferson—the candidate of the opposing Democratic-Republican ticket—came in second with sixty-eight votes and became Adams's vice president. Although the results again played up the defects in the constitutional procedure for electing presidents, Federalists and Democratic-Republicans did not seem unduly concerned that the president and vice president were of opposing parties. Both sides felt that they had prevented the opposition from gaining total victory.

For the first and last time, a foreign figure played an active and public role in the election. French ambassador Pierre Adet promoted Jefferson's campaign in appearances and in written statements. Whether the Adet effort helped or hurt Jefferson is uncertain. The effort aroused supporters of France but angered others who favored Great Britain or resented outside interference.

Jefferson's Revenge: 1800

The election of 1800 was the first in which both parties used congressional caucuses to nominate candidates for their tickets. Such caucuses were an important innovation in the presidential selection process because they formalized partisan alignments in Congress and demonstrated the emergence of organized political parties.

President Adams was hated bitterly by farmers, populists, and states' rights advocates. In one of the nation's first professionally run smear campaigns, Adams was denounced as a "hideous hermaphroditical character which has neither the force and firmness of a man, nor the gentleness and sensibility of a woman." [8]

Federalist members of Congress met in the Senate chamber in Philadelphia on May 3, 1800, to choose their candidates. As in previous presidential election years, Federalists were divided in their support of Adams, yet they felt they had to nominate him because he was the incumbent president. Their ambivalence toward Adams was revealed, however, when they nominated both Adams and Maj. Gen. Charles Cotesworth Pinckney of South Carolina without giving preference to one or the other for president. Pinckney was the elder brother of the Federalist vice-presidential candidate in 1796.

The choice of Pinckney was made at Hamilton's insistence. Once again Hamilton was plotting to use the constitutional defect against Adams. In 1796 South Carolina had voted for an all-southern ticket—Jefferson and Thomas Pinckney—even though the two were of opposing parties. Hamilton hoped that South Carolina would vote the same way in 1800, and that all other Federalist electors could be persuaded to vote for Adams and Charles Pinckney. That would give Pinckney more votes than Adams, thus making him president.

Although the deliberations of the Federalist caucus were secret, the existence of the meeting was not. It was described by the local Democratic-Republican paper, the Philadelphia *Aurora*, as a "Jacobinical conclave." Further denunciations by the paper's editor, Benjamin F. Bache, earned him a personal rebuke from the U.S. Senate.

The Democratic-Republicans once again chose Jefferson as the presidential candidate by consensus. On May 11 a caucus of Democratic-Republican members of Congress met at Marache's boarding house in Philadelphia to choose a running mate. Their unanimous choice was Burr.

Although there was no such thing as a formal party platform in 1800, Jefferson wrote fairly detailed statements of principle in letters to various correspondents. Among other things, the Democratic-Republicans believed in states' rights, a small national government, and a relatively weak executive. They opposed standing armies in peacetime, a large naval force, and alliances with other countries. They also denounced the Alien and Sedition Acts, which had been passed by the Federalists in 1798, ostensibly to protect the nation from subversives given the threat of war with France.

The presidential election in 1800 witnessed other signs of formal public campaigning. Tickets listing the names of Democratic-Republican electors were printed and distributed in a number of states, including New York, Massachusetts, Pennsylvania, and Delaware. Speeches in behalf of the candidates increased markedly. Partisan newspapers also helped to spread the party positions—the number of newspapers in the United States had grown dramatically in the last decade of the century, from 91 to 234.[9] Despite attempts by the Federalist Party to muzzle the opposition press with the passage of the Sedition Act of 1798, partisan newspapers on both sides actively defamed the opposition. Ultimately, the Sedition Act worked against the Federalists by turning the Democratic-Republicans into public champions of a free press.

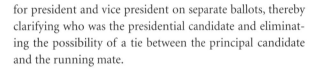

This 1807 anti-Jefferson cartoon compares Washington and Jefferson in contrasting images of good and evil.

Increased partisan activity spurred voter participation. Because electors still were chosen indirectly in twelve of the sixteen states, voters often expressed themselves through state legislative elections as a means of influencing future presidential elections.[10] The seeds were being sown for a new phase in the development of the presidential election process.

A harbinger of Democratic-Republican success came in May when the New York state party won state legislative elections. Burr managed the campaign in the state, building a machine with ward and precinct organizations. Burr's efforts showed the importance of large-scale mobilization—a lesson that would not be lost on the party in future years.

When the electors voted in December, the constitutional defect did not work as Hamilton had hoped. Instead of resulting in a Pinckney victory, the defect produced an unexpected tie vote between the two Democratic-Republican candidates, Jefferson and Burr—each of whom had seventy-three electoral votes. Adams came in third with sixty-five, and Pinckney followed with sixty-four. In accord with the Constitution, the election was thrown into the Federalist-controlled House of Representatives.

Some Federalists felt that Burr was the lesser of the two evils and plotted to elect him president instead of Jefferson, even though Jefferson was clearly the presidential candidate. Hamilton helped to squelch the idea as he preferred Jefferson over Burr. After thirty-six ballots, Jefferson carried a majority in the House of Representatives. The crisis—which could have fatally wounded the nation by calling into question the legitimacy of the new president—was over. Jefferson was elected president and Burr, vice president.

The near disaster brought about by the constitutional defect led to the passage of the Twelfth Amendment to the Constitution in September 1804. It called for electors to vote

for president and vice president on separate ballots, thereby clarifying who was the presidential candidate and eliminating the possibility of a tie between the principal candidate and the running mate.

Jefferson's Reelection: 1804

By the 1804 election, President Jefferson had grudgingly accepted the emergence of a party system. Indeed, the president wrote that year: "The party division in this country is certainly not among its pleasant features. To a certain degree it will always exist." [11]

Jefferson's record—lower taxes, a reduced national debt, repeal of the Alien and Sedition Acts, and purchase of the Louisiana Territory from France—assured him of a second term. Particularly important was Jefferson's willingness to expand the nation's reach and power with the Louisiana Purchase, which compromised his philosophical preference for a small republic. The opposition's case against Jefferson was personal. But the voters were not convinced of the need to make a change.

The 1804 election was the first one held after the Twelfth Amendment went into effect, requiring electors to cast separate votes for president and vice president. Therefore as of that election parties always specifically designated their presidential and vice-presidential candidates.

The Democratic-Republicans retained the caucus system of nomination in 1804, as they did for the next two decades, and for the first time they publicly reported their deliberations. When the party caucus met on February 25, 1804, it attracted 108 of the party's senators and representatives.

President Jefferson was renominated by acclamation, but Vice President Burr, who had fallen out with his party, was not considered for a second term. On the first nominating roll call publicly reported in U.S. political history, New York governor George Clinton was chosen by the caucus to run for vice president. He received sixty-seven votes and easily defeated Sen. John Breckinridge of Kentucky, who collected twenty votes. To "avoid unpleasant discussions" no names were placed in nomination and the vote was conducted by secret ballot.

Before adjourning, the caucus appointed a thirteen-member committee to conduct the campaign and promote the success of Democratic-Republican candidates. A forerunner of party national committees, the new campaign group included mem-bers of both the House and Senate, but with no two persons from the same state. Because the Twelfth Amendment had not yet been passed when the caucus met, the committee was designed to "manage" the vote of Democratic-Republican elec-tors to make sure that the events of 1800 were not repeated. In fact, that precaution was not necessary because the Twelfth Amendment was ratified in September—well before the electors voted.

By 1804 the Federalist Party had deteriorated badly. The new era of dominance by the Virginia-led Democratic-Republicans had begun. The Federalists did not even hold a congressional caucus to elect their nominees. Instead, Federalist leaders informally chose Charles Cotesworth Pinckney for president and Rufus King of New York for vice president. How the Federalists formulated this ticket is not clear. There is no record in 1804 of any formal meeting to nominate Federalist candidates.

The Federalists then mounted a disorganized and dispirited national campaign. Despite concerted efforts to win at least the votes of New England, the Federalists failed miserably. Pinckney received only 14 electoral votes—those of Connecticut and Delaware, plus 2 from Maryland. Jefferson, the Democratic-Republican candidate, was the overwhelming victor with 162 electoral votes.

Madison's Victory: 1808

Following Washington's precedent, Jefferson refused to seek a third term of office. The nation was bitterly divided over Jefferson's policy toward France and Britain. In an attempt to stay out of their war, Jefferson had supported a trade embargo so that neither country would seize American ships. But the embargo only undermined American business interests. Under attack, Jefferson decided to return to his beloved home of Monticello near Charlottesville, Virginia.

Despite the unpopularity of the administration's European policy, Jefferson's secretary of state and chosen successor, Madison, won the presidency in 1808. Jefferson's retirement provided a serious test to the authority of the Democratic-Republican congressional caucus to select presidential candidates. The caucus met on January 23, 1808, after, for the first time, a formal call was issued. Sen. Stephen R. Bradley of Vermont, chairman of the 1804 caucus, issued the call to all 146 Democratic-Republicans in Congress and several Federalists sympathetic to the Democratic-Republican cause. A few party leaders questioned Bradley's authority to call the caucus, but various reports indicate that between eighty-nine and ninety-four members of Congress attended.

As in 1804, the balloting took place without names being formally placed in nomination. Madison easily won the presidential nomination with eighty-three votes. Despite earlier support for future secretary of state James Monroe among Democratic-Republicans in Virginia, and Vice President Clinton's desire to be president, each won only three votes at the caucus. But the caucus overwhelmingly renominated Clinton as vice president, giving him seventy-nine votes; runner-up John Langdon of New Hampshire collected five votes.

The Democratic-Republican caucus also repeated its practice of appointing a committee to conduct the campaign. Membership was expanded from thirteen to fifteen House and Senate members, and it was formally called the "committee of correspondence and arrangement." The committee was authorized to fill vacancies on the national ticket, should any occur. Before the caucus adjourned, it passed a resolution defending the caucus system as "the most practicable mode of consulting and respecting the interest and wishes of all." Later caucuses adopted similar resolutions throughout the history of the system.

Still, the Democratic-Republicans suffered divisions. Forty percent of the Democratic-Republican members of Congress had refused to attend the nominating caucus. Monroe refused to withdraw from the presidential race even after his defeat in the caucus. Clinton, although nominated for vice presidency, was angry at not being nominated for president—so much so that he publicly denounced the caucus, as did Monroe's supporters. Pro-Clinton newspapers in New York launched harsh attacks on Madison and even suggested a Clinton-Monroe ticket. Some Clinton supporters went so far as to hope that Federalists would nominate Clinton for president later in the year. But such a thought was unpalatable to the Federalists, who ultimately nominated Charles Cotesworth Pinckney.

The Federalists chose their ticket at a secret meeting of party leaders in New York City in August 1808. Initially, the meeting was called by the Federalist members of the Massachusetts legislature. Twenty-five to thirty party leaders from seven states, all north of the Potomac River except South Carolina, attended the national meeting. Despite the suggestion from Massachusetts representatives that Clinton be nominated, the gathering decided to run the same ticket they had chosen in 1804: Pinckney and King.

The Federalists did not actively publicize their ticket. The party itself was divided and devoid of leadership. Indeed, many Virginia Federalists formally endorsed Monroe, even though he was a Democratic-Republican. Others preferred to align themselves with Clinton.

In the end, Madison achieved a wide margin of victory with 122 electoral votes; Pinckney came in second with 47 votes. Monroe received no electoral votes. For the sake of future party unity, Democratic-Republicans had retained Clinton as their vice-presidential nominee even though he had tried to subvert Madison's candidacy. Clinton won, receiving 113 electoral votes for vice president. He even received 6 electoral votes from New York for president.

Madison's Reelection: 1812

The winds of war were sweeping through presidential politics when Madison sought a second term in 1812. In response to constant agitation by "war hawks," the president asked Congress on June 1 for a declaration of war against Great Britain. Madison, benefiting from the public's willingness to rally in times of national emergency, swept to a second term. The Federalists did not field a candidate but supported a dissident from Madison's party.

The possibility of war had long hung over the United States. Great Britain had taken American ships captive for years—boarding the vessels, taking cargo, and intimidating seamen. Anti-British political forces also charged that the British had encouraged American Indians in their attacks against settlers in the North and West.

The Democratic-Republican Party held its quadrennial nominating caucus on May 18, 1812. Only eighty-three of the 178 Democratic-Republicans in Congress participated. The New England and New York delegations in particular were poorly represented. Many of the New Yorkers supported the candidacy of their state's lieutenant governor, DeWitt Clinton (George Clinton's nephew), who also was maneuvering for the Federalist nomination. New England was noticeably upset with Madison's foreign policy, which was leading to war with England. Others did not attend the caucus because they opposed the system in principle.

Madison won a near-unanimous renomination in the caucus, receiving eighty-two votes. John Langdon of New Hampshire got the vice-presidential nomination by a wide margin, collecting sixty-four votes to sixteen for Gov. Elbridge Gerry of Massachusetts. But Langdon declined the nomination, citing his age (seventy) as the reason. The Democratic-Republicans held a second caucus on June 8 to select another vice-presidential candidate. Gerry was the clear winner with seventy-four votes, and he responded with a formal letter of acceptance. Ten members of Congress who

had not been present at the first caucus also took the opportunity to endorse Madison's presidential candidacy.

Democratic-Republicans from New York were unwilling to accept the choice of Madison. They held their own caucus, composed of nearly all party members from the New York state legislature, where they unanimously nominated Clinton, who responded with a written "Address" that was a precursor to party platforms. Clinton won the endorsement of the Federalists as well.

As they had four years earlier, the Federalists convened a three-day secret meeting in New York City. The September meeting was more than twice the size of the 1808 gathering, with seventy representatives from eleven states attending. Delegates were sent to the conference by Federalist general committees, with all but nine of the delegates coming from the New England and Middle Atlantic states.

Debate centered on whether to run a separate Federalist ticket or to endorse Clinton. After much debate, they decided to endorse Clinton, and they nominated Jared Ingersoll of Pennsylvania for vice president. Originally, the caucus's decision was meant to be kept a secret, but leaks eventually were reported by Democratic-Republican newspapers.

The presidential election of 1812 was the first wartime contest for power in the United States. The Federalists, calling Madison a dupe of French emperor Napoleon Bonaparte, aligned themselves with the cause of peace and unimpeded commerce. In some northern states the Federalists even adopted the Peace Party label.

Despite all the opposition, President Madison beat Clinton by an electoral vote count of 128–89. The vote reflected the growing split between southern agricultural states, which supported Madison, and northern commercial states, which supported Clinton. Indeed, the common bond that held the Clinton coalition together was a hatred of Virginia—the kingmaker of the Democratic-Republican Party.

The 1812 race was the last real campaign by the Federalists. Disgraced by their obstructionist tactics during the war, isolated by their talk of secession from the Union, and unable to coordinate a national campaign, the Federalists faded from a system increasingly marked by permanent party competition.

Monroe's Victory: 1816

Monroe, President Madison's old foe who had left the Democratic-Republican Party in 1808, seemed like an unlikely presidential candidate for the party in 1816. But not only did Monroe return to the Democratic-Republican fold, he also won the White House without any opposition.

The inconclusive War of 1812 colored American politics for years. The United States and Great Britain fought to a stalemate, and then both sides offered conditions for ending the war that the other would not accept. The British, for example, demanded control over the Great Lakes and

Mississippi River for commerce, as well as the creation of an American Indian state in the Northwest. In the end, both parties simply accepted the end of hostilities. An American representative said the treaty was "a truce rather than a peace." [12] Inconclusive or not, the war sparked a generation of nationalism. Rufus King revived the Federalist Party in 1816 with his race for the governorship of New York. But he lost the race and afterward found the job of maintaining the party a "fruitless struggle." Efforts were made to convene another secret meeting in Philadelphia to nominate candidates for president and vice president, yet the party held no such meeting. With the Federalists not running candidates, nomination by the Democratic-Republican caucus was tantamount to election.

Despite his opposition to Madison in 1808, Monroe had been accepted back into the Democratic-Republican fold in the years that followed. In 1811 Madison had named him secretary of state; by 1816 he was Madison's heir apparent. But many states were increasingly jealous of the Virginia dynasty that had held a grip on the presidency since 1804. Democratic-Republicans in such states opposed Monroe (himself a Virginian) and favored Secretary of War William H. Crawford of Georgia.

A Democratic-Republican caucus met in the House chamber on March 12, 1816, but only fifty-eight members of Congress—mostly Crawford supporters—attended. With the expectation of better attendance, a second caucus was held on March 16. It drew 119 of the 141 Democratic-Republicans in Congress. There, Monroe narrowly defeated Crawford by a vote of 65–54. Forty of Crawford's votes came from five states: Georgia, Kentucky, New Jersey, New York, and North Carolina. The vice-presidential nomination went to New York governor Daniel D. Tompkins, who easily outdistanced Pennsylvania governor Simon Snyder, 85–30.

The nominations of Monroe and Tompkins revived a Virginia-New York alliance that extended back to the late eighteenth century. With the lone exception of 1812, every Democratic-Republican ticket from 1800 to 1820 was composed of a presidential candidate from Virginia and a vice-presidential candidate from New York.

With the Federalist Party still in disarray, the Democratic-Republican ticket won easily. Monroe received 183 electoral votes. The three states that had chosen Federalist electors—Connecticut, Delaware, and Massachusetts—cast their 34 electoral votes for King.

Although the collapse of the Federalists ensured Democratic-Republican rule, it also increased intraparty friction and spurred further attacks on the caucus system. Twenty-two Democratic-Republican members of Congress had not attended the second party caucus, and at least fifteen were known to be opposed to the system. Mass meetings around the country protested the caucus system. [13] Opponents asserted that the writers of the Constitution did

not envision the caucus, that presidential nominating should not be a function of Congress, and that the caucus system encouraged candidates to curry the favor of Congress.

Monroe's Reelection: 1820

The 1820 election took place during the "Era of Good Feeling," a phrase coined by a Boston publication, the *Columbian Centinel,* to describe a brief period of virtual one-party rule in the United States. But that phrase glosses over serious sectional divisions that were growing during Monroe's presidency. The divisions, however, did not prevent Monroe from winning another term.

Sectional strife was on the brink of eruption during Monroe's first term over the admission of Missouri as a new state. Tensions between northern and southern states had simmered for years. The emotional core of the struggle was slavery. Therefore whichever region controlled Congress might decide whether slavery was extended into new territories—and the shape of the nation's economy and culture—for years to come.

In the Senate, there was a tenuous balance between the two regions—eleven free states and eleven slave states—but the admission of Missouri threatened that balance. The two sides finally agreed to a compromise in which both Missouri and Maine would apply for statehood at the same time, Maine as a free state and Missouri as a slave state. Monroe remained neutral in the debate leading up to the compromise. Despite a financial panic in 1819, he retained overwhelming popular support, bolstered by peace and a wave of nationalistic feeling that overshadowed any partisan divisions.

While the United States struggled over the slavery issue, President Monroe embarked on a bold new foreign policy. Still smarting over the British presence in North America that had resulted in the War of 1812, the president declared that the United States would view any European attempts to colonize the Western Hemisphere as acts of hostility. The Monroe Doctrine claimed the hemisphere as the preserve of the United States. It was the boldest venture yet of the nation into foreign policy and permanently defined America's role in world affairs.

Although several rival Democratic-Republican candidates aspired to win the presidency when Monroe retired in 1824, none wanted to challenge his reelection in 1820. A nominating caucus was called for early March, but fewer than fifty of the Democratic-Republican Party's 191 members of Congress showed up. The caucus voted unanimously to make no nominations and passed a resolution explaining that it was inexpedient to do so because so few of the party's members were in attendance. Although Monroe and Tompkins were not formally renominated, electoral slates were filed in their behalf.

Because the Federalist Party was finally dead, Monroe ran virtually unopposed. Even John Adams, the last

Federalist president, voted for Monroe as an elector from Massachusetts. Only one elector, a Democratic-Republican from New Hampshire, cast a vote against Monroe, supporting instead John Quincy Adams, son of the former president.

Last of the Old Order: 1824

The 1824 election, in an odd way, represented everything that the Framers of the Constitution had hoped to see. Without a permanent party system, a number of candidates vied for the presidency. Unable to win an electoral majority, the top three finishers saw their names submitted to the House of Representatives for a final decision. The candidate representative of elite interests and sensibilities and who had House ties won.

But if the 1824 election of John Quincy Adams represented something old, it also represented something new. The popular vote winner and House loser, Andrew Jackson, protested loudly that the election had been stolen from the people. In fact, soon he would mobilize the Democratic Party around a populist rallying cry. American politics would never be the same.

In 1824, as in 1820, only one working party existed in the United States: the Democratic-Republican. But that party had an abundance of candidates competing for the presidency: Secretary of State Adams of Massachusetts, Senator Jackson of Tennessee, Secretary of War John C. Calhoun of South Carolina, House Speaker Henry Clay of Kentucky, and Secretary of the Treasury William H. Crawford. The number of candidates, coupled with the growing democratization of the U.S. political system, led to the demise of King Caucus in 1824.

Early on, Crawford was the leading candidate. He had strong southern support and appeared likely to win the support of New York's Democratic-Republicans. Because it was assumed that he would win a caucus if one were held, Crawford's opponents joined the growing list of caucus opponents. But Crawford's apparent invincibility suddenly ended in September 1823 when he suffered a paralytic stroke. Nearly blind and unable even to sign his name, he was incapacitated and stayed in seclusion for months.

In early February 1824, eleven Democratic-Republican members of Congress issued a call for a caucus to be held in the middle of the month. Their call was countered by twenty-four other members of Congress from fifteen states who deemed it "inexpedient under existing circumstances" to hold a caucus. They claimed that 181 members of Congress were resolved not to attend if a caucus were held.

The caucus convened in mid-February, but only sixty-six members of Congress showed up. Three-quarters of those attending came from just four states—Georgia, New York, North Carolina, and Virginia. Despite his illness, Crawford won the caucus nomination with sixty-four votes. Albert Gallatin of Pennsylvania was selected for vice presi-

dent with fifty-seven votes. The caucus adopted a resolution defending its actions as "the best means of collecting and concentrating the feelings and wishes of the people of the Union upon this important subject." The caucus also appointed a committee to write an address to the people. As written, the text of the address viewed with alarm the "dismemberment" of the Democratic-Republican Party.

In fact, the action of the caucus just aggravated splits in the party. Because so few members of Congress attended the caucus—almost all of them Crawford supporters—opponents could argue that the choice was not even representative of the Democratic-Republicans serving in Congress. Crawford was roundly criticized as being an illegitimate candidate. His opponents derided King Caucus, and his physical condition made it even easier for them to reject his nomination. As it stood, other candidates simply refused to follow the caucus's decision. Never again were candidates chosen by the caucus system.

With the caucus devoid of power and the party lacking unity or leadership, there was no chance of rallying behind a single ticket. In addition, many political issues proved to be divisive. Western expansion and protective tariffs, for example, benefited some parts of the country but hurt others. Thus the various candidates came to represent sectional interests.

The candidates themselves recognized that such a crowded field was dangerous. The election would be thrown into the House of Representatives if no candidate received a majority. The candidates therefore made efforts to join forces. Adams tried to lure Jackson as his running mate. Adams was a short, stocky, aloof, well-educated New Englander who came from a family of Federalists, while Jackson was a tall, thin, hot-tempered war hero with little formal education who came to epitomize a new brand of populist democracy. In trying to recruit Jackson onto their team, Adams's supporters envisaged a ticket of "the writer and the fighter." Jackson would have nothing of it.

In the meantime, Crawford dropped Gallatin as his vice-presidential running mate. His supporters then tried to persuade Clay to drop his quest for the presidency and join the Crawford team. They hinted that Crawford's physical condition was such that he would probably not finish out a term of office if elected (in fact, he lived ten more years). But Clay was not swayed. Calhoun then dropped his race for the presidency and joined efforts with Jackson.

Four candidates remained in the field, and each collected electoral votes. None, however, received a majority. Jackson received the most with ninety-nine, followed by Adams with eighty-four, Crawford with forty-one, and Clay with thirty-seven. Therefore the election was thrown into the House of Representatives.

In accordance with the Twelfth Amendment, the names of the top three candidates—Jackson, Adams, and

This 1836 cartoon depicts Jackson attacking the Bank of the United States with his veto stick. Vice President Van Buren, center, helps to kill the monster, whose heads represent Nicholas Biddle, president of the bank, and directors of the state branches.

set for a rematch between Adams and Jackson in 1828.

THE AGE OF JACKSON

Andrew Jackson was in many ways the perfect man to usher in an age of popular politics, although his rhetoric was more populist than his style of governing. The textbook version of U.S. history depicts Jackson as a coarse man of the frontier, a war hero, a battler of banks and moneyed interests, and a leader of the unschooled and exploited men who built a mass party on patronage and charismatic leadership. Jackson was the first politician to break the Virginia dynasty that had governed the country since the Revolution. After his bitter defeat in the 1824 election, Jackson fought back and grabbed the reins of government in the turbulent election of 1828. These two elections signaled the passing of elite politics and the rise of popular politics. In 1828 Jackson roused the people to turn Adams and his aristocratic clique out of office.

But the Jacksonian folklore has serious flaws. Jackson traveled in elite business circles, for example, and one of his greatest contributions as president was the creation of a more rationally organized bureaucracy.[14] Still, the textbook depiction of Jackson suffices to show some trends in U.S. politics, including the development of a stable mass party system, sectionalism, urbanization, and shifts in the debate about U.S. expansionism.

While President John Quincy Adams was struggling with warring factions in Washington, an opposition force was gathering strength and, in fact, was able to deal the president a num-ber of humiliating defeats. Adams's desire for a national program of roads and canals, education, and research in the arts and sciences antagonized even the most nationalistic groups in the country. U.S. participation in a conference of countries from the Western Hemisphere and the imposition of a tariff (a tax on imported goods designed either to raise revenues or to protect domestic industries from foreign competition) also were divisive issues. But even though Adams was under constant personal attack, the opposition was divided on the same issues. The opposition was united, however, behind "Old Hickory." [15]

Jackson, hero of the Battle of New Orleans in the War of 1812, had a strong appeal to the common man even

Crawford—were placed before the House. Clay, who had come in fourth and was Speaker of the House, would play a major role in tipping the balance in favor of one of the candidates.

In contrast to Jackson, Adams actively lobbied for support, and Washington rocked with rumors of corruption. Clay informed Adams in January that he would support the New Englander in the House election—a major blow to Jackson. Shortly thereafter, a letter in a Philadelphia newspaper alleged that Adams had offered Clay the post of secretary of state in return for his support. Adams went on to win the House election narrowly by carrying thirteen out of twenty-four state delegations. Jackson came in second with seven, and Crawford third with the remaining four. Consequently, the candidate who won the most electoral votes and the most popular votes did not win the presidency.

Jackson was furious at what he considered to be unfair bargaining between Adams and Clay. He felt that the will of the people had been thwarted, and he seethed when President Adams proceeded to name Clay secretary of state as rumor had indicated he would. In this way, the events of 1824 kindled the flame of popular democracy. The stage was though he traveled in the circles of southern gentlemen. People who met with Jackson talked of his unerring "intuition" about people and politics. Jackson's decision to push for reforms of the punishment of debtors was an important gesture to small businesspeople and workers who were held to a kind of indentured servitude to their creditors. Sen. Martin Van Buren of New York, Jackson's strongest supporter in the Northeast, said the people "were his blood relations—the only blood relations he had." [16]

Jackson's First Victory: 1828

Jackson and his running mate, John C. Calhoun, easily beat Adams in their 1828 rematch; Jackson won 178 electoral votes, and Adams won 83. (Calhoun also had been vice president under John Quincy Adams.) Of the popular vote, Jackson received 643,000 votes (56.0 percent) to Adams's 501,000 (43.6 percent). Sectional splits showed in the vote distribution. Adams held all but 1 of New England's electoral votes, all of Delaware's and New Jersey's, 16 of New York's 36 votes, and 6 of Maryland's 11 votes. Jackson took all the rest—the South and the West. The election, then, was decided by the newly enfranchised voters in the burgeoning regions of the country. The U.S. electorate, however, was expanding not only in the West but also in the original states. Between 1824 and 1856 voter participation grew from 3.8 percent to 16.7 percent of the total population.[17]

Jackson had only begun to exert electoral influence with his revenge victory over Adams. The expanded pool of politically involved citizens that had brought Jackson victory also brought him demands for patronage jobs with the federal government. Van Buren, a master machine politician from New York State, tutored the beleaguered new president in dealing with the office seekers. Jackson replaced fewer than one-fifth of the government's employees, which he defended as a perfectly reasonable "rotation in office" that would keep the ranks of the bureaucracy fresh. But the effect of his system was greater. Appointees of previous administrations were able to retain their jobs only when they expressed loyalty to Jackson and his party. Far more important than any government turnover, Jackson's spoils system inaugurated an age in which mass party loyalty was a paramount concern in politics.

The increased importance of loyalty, to the president and to the party, became clear with Jackson's dispute with Vice President Calhoun and the subsequent purging of the cabinet. A growing feud between Jackson and Calhoun came to a head when a personal letter in which Calhoun criticized Jackson's conduct of the Seminole Indian campaign and the 1818 invasion of Florida became public. In a letter to Calhoun during the cabinet crisis, Jackson wrote: "Et tu, Brute." A purge of Calhoun men in the cabinet followed the incident. Secretary of State Van Buren enabled the president to make the purge when he and Secretary of War John Eaton, both Jackson allies, resigned their posts; the president then called on the whole cabinet to quit.

The central element of the Jacksonian program was expansion. Much like twentieth-century politicians who would talk about economic growth as the key to opportunity, Jackson maintained that movement West "enlarg[ed] the area of freedom." [18] The administration fought to decentralize the management of expansion. Jackson railed against the "corrupt bargain" between the government and banks, joint-stock companies, and monopolies, which, he said, were squeezing out the average person seeking opportunity.

Indeed, Jackson opposed the Bank of the United States and promoted state banks because of his desire to free finance capital from central control. In his first term, the president carried on a long-running battle with Nicholas Biddle, the head of the Bank of the United States, and with Congress over the status of the bank. Alexander Hamilton had created the bank to manage the nation's monetary policy and investment, but Jackson opposed it as a tool of the eastern financial establishment. Jackson may have failed to close the bank, but he did manage to strip it of much of its basic authority and functions by placing its deposits in a number of regional institutions.

Jackson's presidency was activist from the beginning. His administration negotiated treaties with France, the Ottoman Empire, Russia, and Mexico. Jackson himself established a distinctive interpretation of federalism when he vetoed a number of public improvement bills as unconstitutional infringements of local affairs. He also called for a tariff that would yield revenues for dispersal to the states for their public projects—an early form of "revenue sharing." Jackson also signed the Indian Removal Act of 1830, which provided for settlement of the territory west of the Mississippi River. Late in his first term, Jackson's strong stand defeated the South Carolina legislature's claim that it could "nullify," or declare "null and void," federal tariff legislation that the state disliked.

Jackson's Reelection: 1832

There was never any doubt that Jackson would be renominated in 1832; in fact, several state legislatures endorsed him before the convention. Jackson's political strength was further underscored with the introduction of a quintessentially party-oriented institution: the national party convention. Jacksonians from New Hampshire proposed the Democratic convention of 1832, and the president and his advisers jumped at the opportunity. The only previous national convention had been held by the Anti-Masonic Party in 1831. Conventions had been the principal means of selecting candidates for local offices since the early part of the century. Especially when compared with the caucus system that preceded it, the convention system was a democratic leap forward.

The convention system enabled the parties to gather partisans from all geographic areas, and it welded them together as a cohesive unit that ultimately was accountable to the electorate, if only in a plebiscitary way. Voters had the opportunity to give approval or disapproval to a party program with one vote. Historian Eugene H. Roseboom has written: "It was representative in character; it divorced nominations from congressional control and added to the independence of the executive; it permitted an authoritative formulation of a party program; and it concentrated the party's strength behind a single ticket, the product of compromise of personal rivalries and group or sectional interests." [19]

Given Jackson's popularity in 1832, the purpose of the convention was to rally behind the president and select a new vice-presidential candidate. Van Buren got the nomination, despite lingering resistance from Calhoun supporters and various "favorite sons" (prominent state and local leaders of state party organizations).

As in 1828, Jackson's political opposition was fragmented. The Whigs—the opposition party that had developed from grassroots protests in the North and West against Jackson's tariff and development policies—held their national convention in Baltimore in December 1831 and unanimously nominated Henry Clay of Kentucky for president. Eighteen states used a variety of selection procedures to determine who would be their convention delegates. The party's platform sharply criticized the Jackson administration's patronage practices, relations with Great Britain, and ill-tempered congressional relations, as well as Supreme Court decisions.

In the election, the incumbent easily dispatched the opposition. "The news from the voting states blows over us like a great cold storm," wrote Rufus Choate, a prominent lawyer, to a friend.[20] Despite last-minute maneuvering to unite the opposition to Jackson and a well-financed campaign by the Bank of the United States, the president won 219 electoral votes to Clay's 49, Independent John Floyd's 11, and Anti-Mason William Wirt's 7. Jackson won all but seven states. Clay won Kentucky, Massachusetts, Rhode Island, Connecticut, and Delaware, plus five electors from Maryland. Jackson won 702,000 popular votes to Clay's 484,000 and Wirt's 101,000.[21]

Jackson, who finally left the political stage in 1837, changed the face of U.S. politics. Even if his pretensions to being an everyman were overstated, he did open up the system to mass participation, and he forced politicians to listen to popular demands. He developed the notion of a strong party organization. He fought, and eventually defeated, the national bank by withdrawing its funds and placing them in state banks. He strongly opposed two forces that could have torn the nation apart—the nullification principle of state sovereignty and the Supreme Court's bid for broader discretion over political issues (that is, to review legislation and state actions)—by simply proclaiming the law to be "unauthorized by the Constitution" and "therefore null and void."

Van Buren's Win: 1836

Many historians consider the election of 1836 to be the most important event in the development of the party system. Van Buren, a Democratic follower of Jackson and a theorist on the role of political parties in a democratic system, easily won the election against an uncoordinated Whig Party. The defeat eventually persuaded Whig leaders of the need for a permanent organization for political competition. The emergence of two permanent parties extinguished the American suspicion of the morality of a party system based on unabashed competition for the levers of power.

Van Buren, who had allied with Jackson during the cabinet controversies and promoted his philosophy of parties and patronage, received the Democratic nomination in 1836 at a convention packed with Jackson administration appointees. The vice-presidential nomination of Richard M. Johnson of Kentucky, whose earlier relationship with a mulatto woman caused controversy, damaged the ticket in the South, but the Democrats won anyway.

The Whigs' campaign strategy was to run several favorite sons to prevent any candidate from getting a majority of the electoral votes, thereby throwing the election into the House of Representatives. As one Whig put it: "The disease [Democratic rule] is to be treated as a local disorder—apply local remedies." [22] The Whig expectation was that one of two favorite sons—Gen. William Henry Harrison of Ohio or Hugh Lawson White of Tennessee—would be selected by the House after the electoral college vote proved inconclusive.

Van Buren, however, had Jackson's machine and his personal backing and was able to overcome the Whigs' local strategy. Thus in this race, the last for the White House before presidential elections became dominated by two national parties, Van Buren took 170 electoral votes—22 more than he needed for election. Of the Whig candidates, Harrison received 73 electoral votes; White, 26; and Daniel Webster of Massachusetts, 14. Willie Mangum, an Independent Democrat from North Carolina, received 11 electoral votes from the South Carolina legislature, which was hostile to White because of his role in nullification politics. Van Buren won 764,000 popular votes (50.8 percent); Harrison, 551,000 (36.6 percent); White, 146,000 (9.7 percent); and Webster, 41,000 (2.7 percent). For the only time in history, the Senate selected the vice president, Van Buren's running mate Johnson, who had fallen one vote shy of election by the electoral college. In the Senate, Johnson defeated Francis Granger by a 33–16 vote.

Van Buren was besieged with problems practically from the minute he took the oath of office in March 1837. About midway through his term, the economy crashed after years of feverish business growth, overspeculation in land

and business, huge private debt accumulation, and unregulated financial and trade practices. Van Buren's approach to the economic crisis alternated between stubborn refusal to fix a mess that he had not created and action that was guaranteed to antagonize key interest groups.

When Van Buren moved to create an independent treasury to insulate the federal government from state financial institutions, he was opposed by conservative Democrats who were supporters of the state financial institutions that Jackson had promoted in his legendary national bank battles. When Van Buren was not hit from the right, he was hit from the left. The nascent labor movement called for protection of jobs and wages and made protests against monopoly and privilege.

THE IDEA OF A PARTY SYSTEM

Whatever problems Martin Van Buren had in governing, he should receive credit at least for helping to establish the principle of party government in the United States. That principle, much derided in the early days of the nation's history, now enjoys widespread allegiance.

Van Buren's arguments for a party system—contained in his book, *An Inquiry into the Origin and Course of Political Parties in the United States*—were similar to the economic principle of Adam Smith, which had held that the pursuit of selfish ends redounded to the good of the entire community. American leaders from George Washington through John Quincy Adams had believed that self-interested factions endangered the functioning and virtue of the Republic. These leaders also had warned against the dangers of democracy, which they often called "mob rule." In the worst possible scenario, permanent parties with strong ideological stances appealed to the mass public for support, undermining the ability of national leaders to guide public virtue.[23]

The basic tension that Van Buren had to resolve was the system's need for stability and responsible leadership and the parties' imperative to gain office. How could a party's selfish desire to run the government and award patronage and contracts to political allies benefit the whole system?

Van Buren argued that the absence of parties—that is, collections of people from disparate backgrounds—resulted in a system of personal politics that fueled demagogy, perpetual campaigns, and a lack of accountability. Personal presidential politics was more polarizing than the politics of consensus or of coalition building. Presidents should be able to do their job without constant carping from outsiders who fancied themselves prospective presidents. Mass parties with certain partisan principles would enable presidents to get the backing they needed to do their work.

Moreover, the existence of two parties would enable the nation to move beyond its many cleavages—that is, toward the general interest and away from simple clashes of particular interests. Competition among parties, like competition among economic enterprises, would bring about a situation in which disparate demands would be promoted by a party. The key was to achieve a balance of competing forces. Summarizing Van Buren, political scientist James W. Ceaser has written:

> Established parties . . . may stand "over" the raw electoral cleavages, possessing some leeway or discretion about which potential issues and electoral divisions will be emphasized and which will be suppressed or kept at the fringes. This discretion is exercised according to the interests of the organizations and the judgement of their leaders. But it is important to keep in mind that the degree of this discretion is limited. . . . Their discretion is always threatened or held in check by the possibility that they might be displaced by a new party having as its goal the advancement of a certain policy. . . . When a sufficiently powerful and enduring issue exists, an impartial reading of American party history suggests that the party system in the end will have to respond to it, regardless of how the established parties initially react.[24]

The Age of Jackson brought a fundamental shift from republican to democratic values as the nation's territory and activities expanded. Republicanism was the product of a variety of strains of thought—from the Romans Cicero and Tacitus and the Greek Polybius to the Frenchman Charles Montesquieu—that stressed the need for a balancing of interests to produce public virtue. Republicans worried about excess in any single form of governance, particularly "mob rule." For them, *democracy* was a term of derision. That is why the Constitution contained many buffers against this and other forms of excess.

Republicanism declined in many stages. A greater stress on the individual's role in society, embodied in the work of Adam Smith and David Hume, restricted the kinds of issues open to public deliberation. At the same time, the pace of economic change undermined established patterns. As the nation demanded large-scale projects (such as canals and railways), and as rival factions looked to the mobilization of larger and larger parts of the electorate to augment their strength, democratic rhetoric gained respectability. Mass party participation became a vehicle for pursuing civic virtue and balance, and the notion of a constant opposition party gained strength. If the democratic process had enough constitutional "checks," political thinkers now reasoned, the harmful "mob" aspects of democracy could be tempered. The development of the Jacksonian party as a way of arbitrating interests was the final stage in republican decline and democratic ascendance.

Political scientist Russell Hanson has noted that the new democratic ethos sprang from one of the same goals as the old republican ethos: development of a public spirit by rising above particular restraints. "Support for popular sovereignty became the lowest common denominator for a

Democratic Party composed of interests seeking liberation from a variety of sectionally specific restraints on the 'will of the people.' " [25]

A two-party system persisted as the nation drifted toward civil war, but it was not a simple two-party system. The Democrats and Whigs competed for the presidency and other political offices until 1856, when the Republican Party fielded its first national ticket and made the Whigs obsolete. But the parties were so unstable that their many elements were constantly forming and breaking up coalitions—and threatening to bolt from the system itself. Moreover, a series of third parties entered the national electoral arena for short periods, applying or relieving pressures on the two major parties.[26]

Only by examining the parties and their various factions and struggles can one understand the presidential contests in the two decades before the Civil War, and the way that the Civil War revealed the basic fault lines of U.S. politics.

The Whigs' Victory: 1840

The Whigs developed to fill the role of their British namesake, which had been to mount a republican opposition to the royal ruling power. When the rise of Andrew Jackson and his supposedly imperial presidency threatened the "balance" of the United States, the Whigs rose to restore that balance. The Whigs saw Jackson's Democrats as a faction of the most dangerous variety—a majority faction that had the ability to trample liberties in its mad scramble for spoils.

The key to Whiggery was the notion of balanced development. The Whigs opposed the war with Mexico and other expansionist programs because they feared the perils of overextending the nation's abilities and getting entangled with foreign powers. They favored internal improvements, but only as a way of maintaining balance and staving off the corruption of the Jackson era. The protective tariff was central to the Whigs' program of internal development and protection from outsiders. According to Hanson,

> Even in America, which was uniquely blessed by an abundance of natural resources and a citizenry of hardy stock, there was need for informed guidance and direction of progress. For the Whigs, government was the primary agent of this progress. Government represented a strong and positive force to be used in calling forth a richer society from the unsettled possibilities of America. In the economic realm this meant that government was responsible for providing the essential conditions for a sound economy, namely, a reliable currency, ample credit, and the impetus for internal improvements. In the social realm, the government was responsible for promoting virtue in its citizenry through education and exhortation.[27]

The Whigs' desire for balance and compromise was intended to give the party a national rather than a sectional identity. Moreover, their tendency to nominate widely popular military heroes helped to create at least the illusion of a party of national dimensions. A series of Senate battles with President Jackson, especially the tariff battles of 1833, which resulted in an unsatisfying compromise, gave impetus to grassroots organizations in the North and West and to Southern Democratic opponents. In fact, the Whigs developed first in the South where voters were dissatisfied with Jackson's selection of Van Buren as his running mate. There, loose coalitions elected candidates in the 1834 and 1835 state and congressional elections. Westerners also organized to oppose the Democratic Party, which was headed by a New Yorker.

The first serious Whig presidential contest was a loss, but an encouraging one. In 1836 the Whig tickets headed by William Henry Harrison and others had shown surprising appeal in the loss to the Democrat Van Buren. The Whigs had won Jackson's home state of Tennessee and neighboring Georgia, as well as three border slave states, and were strong competitors elsewhere. Harrison had carried the old Northwest (now the Midwest) and had come close in northern states such as Pennsylvania.

Because of the rise of the antislavery "conscience Whigs," the Whigs eventually moved to a completely different base of support—the North rather than the South and West—but their early organizing at least broke the Democratic stranglehold on the latter two regions. The Whigs nominated Harrison in 1840 after a nomination struggle with Henry Clay. A Clay supporter, John Tyler of Virginia, was the vice-presidential nominee. This time, the popular if politically inexperienced hero of the War of 1812 won his ticket to the White House. Harrison defeated the incumbent Van Buren in an electoral vote landslide, receiving 234 of the 294 electoral votes—all the states except Alabama, Arkansas, Illinois, Missouri, New Hampshire, South Carolina, and Virginia. For the popular vote, Harrison won 1.3 million (52.9 percent) to Van Buren's 1.1 million (46.8 percent).

According to political scientist Richard P. McCormick,

> The campaign of 1840 brought the American party system at last to fruition. In every region of the country, and indeed in every state, politics was conducted within the framework of a two-party system, and in all but a handful of states the parties were so closely balanced as to be competitive. In broad terms, it was the contest for the presidency that shaped this party system and defined its essential purpose.[28]

Harrison's campaign was as vague as his government experience was unimpressive. The image of Harrison as a sort of frontier everyman—which received its popular expression when a Baltimore newspaper mocked him as a sedentary man who would sit in a log cabin and drink cider rather than perform great deeds of leadership—was the theme of numerous parades and mass meetings. On issues from banking and currency to slavery, Harrison spoke in generalities. Harrison's strategist acknowledged that he advised the candidate to "say not a single word about his principles or creed. Let him say nothing—promise nothing." [29]

As it happened, Harrison did not have an opportunity to do much as president besides discipline the aggressive Clay. Clay had assumed that he and the rest of the congressional leadership would play the leading role in the government, but Harrison quickly dispelled that notion in a note rebuking him. But one month after his inauguration, the sixty-eight-year-old Harrison developed pneumonia and died. On April 6, 1841, the burdens of the presidency fell on Vice President Tyler.

The rift between the White House and Congress widened under Tyler. Clay acted as if he were prime minister during a special session of Congress, pushing through a legislative program that included a recharter of the long-controversial Bank of the United States, higher import taxes, and distribution of proceeds from land sales to the states. Tyler, a lifetime states' rights advocate, vetoed two bills for a national bank, and the Whigs in Congress and his cabinet began a bitter feud with the president. In 1842 Clay left the Senate to promote his presidential aspirations, and everyone in the cabinet except Secretary of State Daniel Webster quit. Tyler was all alone, but he did manage to defeat the Whig program in his four years as president.

Polk's Dark-Horse Victory: 1844

The Democrats were transformed into a well-organized party by Jackson and Van Buren between 1828 and 1836. But, like the Whigs, the Democratic Party became vulnerable because of the irreconcilable differences among many of its parts.

From the beginning, the Democratic Party had contained contradictory elements. According to political scientist James L. Sundquist: "The party had been formed originally as an alliance between Southern planters and New Yorkers and had always spanned both regions. Northern men of abolitionist sympathies were accustomed to sitting with slaveholders in presidential cabinets and collaborating with them in the halls of Congress." [30] But northern Democrats went so far as to organize antiabolitionist rallies in their cities and towns, and newspapers and churches also defended slavery.

The deepest Democratic divisions—which eventually would lead to the failure not only of the party but also of the nation—were the regional differences based on slavery. But other, more complex divisions also affected the operation of the Democratic Party. When the party was able to reconcile or even delay action on the divisive issues, it won. When the divisions burst into the open, the party was in trouble.

James K. Polk of Tennessee, the first "dark-horse" candidate in history, defeated the Whig Henry Clay in 1844 by supporting an expansionist program and winning the support of the solid South. One of the key issues in the campaign was whether Texas should be admitted to the Union and, if so, whether it should be a slave or free state. President Van Buren in 1840 had opposed annexation—opposition that may have cost him the presidency—and the Democrats and Whigs hedged on the issue for the next eight years. In 1844 Polk endorsed the annexation of Texas as a slave state; that was enough for him to lock up the South.

During the 1844 nominating convention, the Democrats finessed the sectional dangers of the Texas issue by combining it with a call for occupying Oregon and eventually bringing that state into the Union. The Democrats also appealed to Pennsylvania and the rest of the Northeast by supporting a high tariff. Both parties spoke out against the growing foreign elements in the cities, but the Whigs were more effective because of the Democrats' swelling immigrant ranks.

In the election, the Democrat Polk defeated the Whig Clay, winning 1.34 million votes (49.5 percent) to Clay's 1.30 million (48.1 percent) and 170 electoral votes to Clay's 105. Clay received his strongest support from five northeastern states and five border slave states. Of the expansionist Northwest, only Ohio fell in the Clay column.

The Liberty Party—an abolitionist party formed out of more than two hundred antislavery societies in time for the 1840 election—may have been the deciding factor in the 1844 race. Although the party received only 2.3 percent of the popular vote and no electoral votes, it was strong enough in New York to prevent the Whigs from winning that state's crucial thirty-six electoral votes. Those votes went to the Democrat Polk rather than to the Whig Clay.

The depth of the Democrats' divisions were agonizingly evident even when the party won elections and started to pass out spoils and make policy. Like Harrison, the Whig who had won the presidency four years before, President Polk faced the antagonisms of party factions when he began making appointments after his 1844 win. Westerners were angry when they were shut out of the cabinet and Polk vetoed a rivers and harbors bill. Supporters of both Van Buren and John Calhoun were angry that their faction did not win more prominent positions. Northeasterners were upset at tariff cuts. The New York split between the reformist "Barnburners" and the party-regular "Hunkers"—who disagreed on every issue, including banks, currency, internal improvements, and political reforms—also disrupted the administration.

Creating still more dissension was the war with Mexico (1846–1848), fought because of the dispute over the Texas border and the possible annexation of California. Northerners resented the country's fighting Mexico over a slave state.

Whig Success under Taylor: 1848

In 1848 the Whigs recaptured the White House behind another military hero, Gen. Zachary Taylor, who was vague on most political issues. Hailing from Louisiana, where he was a slave owner, Taylor defeated the irrepressible Clay and Gen. Winfield Scott for the nomination on the fourth convention ballot. His running mate was New Yorker Millard Fillmore. Clay mounted an impressive public campaign that drew large crowds, but the Whigs had lost too many times with Clay.

The Whigs were so determined to avoid sectional and other splits that they not only nominated the popular Taylor but also eschewed writing a platform. Despite such extreme measures to maintain unity, the convention was disturbed by squabbles between pro- and antislavery forces on the question of the Wilmot Proviso, which would ban slavery in any territory the United States obtained from Mexico.

At the Democratic national convention, Sen. Lewis Cass of Michigan defeated Sen. James Buchanan of Pennsylvania and Supreme Court Justice Levi Woodbury for the presidential nomination, and Gen. William Butler was picked as his running mate. (The Democratic incumbent Polk had declared after taking his office that he would not seek a second term.) But the convention experienced splits between two New York factions: the Barnburners, who were part of the antislavery movement, and the more conservative Hunkers, who had ties to Southerners. The Barnburners finally defected from the party to become part of the Free Soil Party.

The Democrats behind Cass praised the administration of the beleaguered Polk, defended the war with Mexico, congratulated the French Republic that emerged from the wave of revolution in Europe, and did everything it could to avoid the nasty slavery issue. The nomination of Cass—a "doughface," or northerner with southern principles—was expected to appeal to both sides of the simmering issue.

But Taylor defeated Cass, winning 1.4 million popular votes (47.3 percent) to Cass's 1.2 million (42.5 percent). New York Democrat Van Buren, the former president, running on the Free Soil ticket, won 291,500 votes (10 percent) but no electoral votes. Taylor received 163 electoral votes to Cass's 127, with a strong showing in the North. Taylor won Connecticut, Massachusetts, New Jersey, New York, Pennsylvania, Rhode Island, and Vermont in the North; Delaware, Kentucky, Maryland, North Carolina, and Tennessee in the border states; and Florida, Georgia, and Louisiana in the Deep South. This combination was enough to beat Cass's coalition of seven slave states, six northwestern states, and two New England states.

On July 10, 1850, Fillmore succeeded to the presidency when Taylor died suddenly. After consuming too many refreshments at a Fourth of July celebration, Taylor had developed cramps and then a fatal illness, probably typhoid fever.

Despite this turn of events, Fillmore was unable to secure the party nomination two years later, in 1852, although he had an early lead in convention polling. Gen.

Scott won the nomination, and the Whigs entered into permanent decline.

SLAVERY DIVIDES THE NATION

Try as they might by selecting military heroes as candidates and taking vague stances on issues, the Whigs could not delay facing the nation's disagreements forever. When divisive issues erupted, the party suffered.

The tariff issue and their mildly probusiness stance gave the Whigs strength in the North. But, like the Democrats, they also needed to attract support in the South—a goal they sought by trying to keep the slavery question out of their rhetoric. The Whigs could count on being competitive in the border slave states but not in the rest of Dixie. In 1844 Henry Clay had won only the northern rim of slave states (Delaware, Kentucky, Maryland, North Carolina, and Tennessee).

The abolitionist movement, which may be dated to the founding of William Lloyd Garrison's newspaper, the Liberator, in 1831, posed problems for the Whigs that eventually proved fatal. The antislavery belt developed in the Whigs' strongest territory—New England—and westward into the modern-day Midwest. Abolitionism was largely an upper- or middle-class and religious cause. But it also became a partisan issue: the Whigs, the party out of power for years, needed an issue with which to confront the Democrats, and slavery was a useful one, even if the Whigs' antislavery stance in the North contradicted their accommodating stance in the South.

As Sundquist has noted, both the Whig and Democratic parties in the pre–Civil War era attempted to ignore the slavery issue, but the Whigs had less room to maneuver. The Democrats' agrarian and populist position gave them the solid South as a foundation, and they could make a variety of antiabolitionist appeals to the rest of the electorate. Democrats could argue that their support for slavery in the South was compatible with their many "moderate" positions. The appeal of Senators Stephen A. Douglas of Illinois and James Buchanan rested on such a coalition-building strategy. The Whigs, however, included vociferous opponents of slavery who could not be reconciled easily with "moderate" positions. Abolitionism had upper-class and religious roots that were difficult to use as a foundation. The support the Whigs were able to retain in the South was based on their positions on local issues. In sum, the Whigs did not have the same potential to build a national party organization as the Democrats.

Because both parties contained slavery sympathizers and opponents, neither was willing to take a principled stand against the institution, particularly where it already existed. This was not the case, however, for issues such as westward expansion, banking questions, public improvements, the tariff, and foreign relations, where their differences were more evident. But third parties such as the Liberty and Free Soil parties had no such hesitations about pressing the slavery issue. In fact, sectional cleavages were so strong that in 1836 Congress passed a "gag rule" that forbade the reading of antislavery statements in Congress. Such attempts to silence abolitionist fervor were in vain, however, because politics was entering an age of mass communication and organization. The slavery issue would become irrepressible.

The slavery issue split the Whigs badly with the controversy over the admission of Texas to the Union in 1845. A splinter group of young party members calling themselves the "Conscience Whigs" argued for a straightforward statement of principle against slavery. An opposition group, "Cotton Whigs," wanted to defuse the slavery issue by ignoring moral arguments and simply calling for a halt to annexation. The party split became complete with Clay's Compromise of 1850, which admitted California as a free state, ended slave trade in the District of Columbia, and admitted Texas but reduced its size by splitting off the New Mexico territory. After agitation from Conscience Whigs and General Winfield Scott's nomination in 1852, the party was irreparably rent by the slavery issue.

The 1852 Whig convention platform contained several statements supporting states' rights and the principles behind Clay's compromise[31]—concessions made by northern Whigs to win southern support for their presidential favorite, General Scott. But when no Whigs voted for the Kansas-Nebraska Act in 1854, which permitted new states to determine individually the slavery question, the Whigs' remaining ties to Dixie were severed.

The Whigs' strength in the Northwest was almost nonexistent. Only Ohio, in 1844, went for the Whigs even once over the course of the 1844, 1848, and 1852 presidential elections. Previously strong ties between the "lake region" and the South deteriorated as immigrants and others moved from the Northeast to the Northwest and, after the completion of railroad links, the two regions developed strong economic ties.

The Whigs' last gasp came in 1852, when Scott was demolished by Democrat Franklin Pierce, who won all thirty-one states except two in New England (Massachusetts and Vermont) and two border states (Kentucky and Tennessee). In 1856 the Whigs split their votes among Democrat Buchanan, former Whig Millard Fillmore, and Republican John C. Fremont. At that time, not all Whigs were ready yet to join the nascent Republican Party because of the extremism of some of the party's abolitionists. But the majority of Whigs folded into the Republicans in 1860 when Republican presidential candidate Abraham Lincoln avoided a white "backlash" by insisting that he supported slavery where it existed and opposed its spread only because of how it would affect the economic fortunes of poor northern whites.

The Democrats suffered a North-South cleavage that Lincoln exploited in the 1860 election against Douglas. Southern Democrats were intent on protecting slavery, and control of Congress was necessary to their strategy. They believed that extension of slavery to the new states joining the Union was needed to maintain their congressional strength. In short, the extension of slavery was the issue that most divided the Democratic Party.

Northern Democrats were willing to allow Dixie to maintain its peculiar institution but were scared about their electoral prospects if slavery should expand. At first they rallied to Douglas's doctrine of "popular sovereignty" (under which the people of new states could decide whether to adopt slavery), but they became nervous when Lincoln hammered away at his argument that any unchecked slavery threatened the freedom of whites as well as blacks. Lincoln argued that Democrats such as Douglas wanted to make slavery a national, rather than an individual state, institution.

Lincoln planted seeds of doubt about partial solutions to the slavery extension question by asserting that slavery could extend to whites if it were nationalized: "If free negroes should be made *things,* how long, think you, before they will begin to make *things* out of poor white men?" [32] Lincoln also maintained that the extension of slavery into new territories would close off those areas for whites seeking upward mobility: "The whole nation is interested that the best use be made of these Territories. We want them for homes of free white people. This they cannot be, to any considerable extent, if slavery shall be planted within them." [33]

Following Lincoln's lead, the growing movement against the extension of slavery was based on a concern for the upward mobility of labor. Rather than stressing the common interests of blacks and poor, northern, white laborers, the antiextension movement played up the competition between the two groups. Horace Greeley's vision of the frontier as "the great regulator of the relations of Labor and Capital, the safety valve of our industrial and social engine" left little room for the extension of slavery into the new territories.[34]

Democrat Pierce's Victory: 1852

Clay's congressional compromise on slavery in the territories, known as the Compromise of 1850, turned out to be the major reason for the Democrats' 1852 victory. The compromise addressed the slavery question in all of the new U.S. territories by making concessions to both sides of the struggle. For the North, California would be admitted as a free state, and the slave trade (but not slavery itself) would be abolished in the District of Columbia. For the South, fugitive slave laws would be strengthened, and the New Mexico territory would be divided into two states where the voters, exercising popular sovereignty, would decide the slave issue.

The compromise was designed to settle the issue of slavery in new territories once and for all. But the slavery issue could not be contained by region; it had an increasingly important "spillover" effect. Because of concerns about the congressional balance of power and the difficulties of enforcing slavery provisions such as the fugitive slave law in states that opposed slavery, it was impossible to isolate the slavery question into particular regions as Clay intended.

President Zachary Taylor had stalled action on the compromise for months and even suggested that California and New Mexico might become independent nations. But his successor, Fillmore, had thrown his support behind the compromise. The Whigs were divided on the proposal.

General Scott won the Whig nomination in 1852 after platform concessions to the party's southern delegation. Scott's appeal was always limited to the North, while Fillmore appealed to the South and Daniel Webster appealed to New England. Scott won on the fifty-third ballot.

Pierce, governor of New Hampshire, a dark-horse candidate who gained fame with his Mexican War record, won the Democratic nomination in 1852. His vice-presidential running mate was Sen. William Rufus de Vane King of Alabama. The party held together a coalition of groups with contradictory positions on the slavery issue and regional affairs. The convention, meeting in Baltimore, pledged to "abide by, and adhere to" Clay's compromise and to do what it could to smother the slavery issue.

Attempts to inject issues of economics and foreign affairs into the election failed, and the campaign degenerated into squabbles over personalities. Pierce easily won with 1.6 million popular votes (50.8 percent) to Scott's 1.4 million (43.9 percent). Pierce carried twenty-seven states and 254 electoral votes to Scott's four states and 42 electoral votes. Free-Soil candidate John P. Hale took 4.9 percent of the popular vote and won no electoral votes.

The Democrats' Bruising Victory: 1856

By 1856 the national parties were coming apart. The North-South split had eliminated the Whigs as a national party and was rendering the Democrats into two camps, damaging the party's chances for winning national elections in the decades ahead. A new national party, the Republican Party, emerged from the remnants of the Whigs and dissatisfied members of other factions.

Congress had opened the slavery issue by passing the Kansas-Nebraska Act of 1854. The act declared "null and void" the Missouri Compromise of 1820, which had prohibited slavery in new territories north of the 360309 parallel except in Missouri. The 1854 legislation created two territories (Kansas and Nebraska) from the original Nebraska territory and left the slavery issue to be determined by popular sovereignty there and in the Utah and New Mexico territories.

The Kansas-Nebraska Act was a vehicle to spur the development of the West. Such development was part of a long-standing American approach to creating opportunity and freedom via growth. Senator Douglas of Illinois—the promoter of the law and the main advocate of popular sovereignty—held that the law was necessary if the country was to be bound together by rail and telegraph lines and was to drive Great Britain from the continent. The latter goal was based on the widely held suspicion that Britain was exploiting the slavery issue to distract American politics and stunt American growth.

Whatever the economic motives for unification, the Kansas-Nebraska Act was bitterly divisive. Northern state legislatures passed resolutions denouncing the law. The development of sectional parties continued. A flood of new settlers into Kansas, and the violence that accompanied balloting over whether Kansas was to be a free or a slave state, further inflamed passions. Neighboring Missourians took part in the controversy, arguing that their status as slave owners would be undermined if Kansas voted to be free.

After an 1854 meeting in Ripon, Wisconsin, where the party was first proposed, the Republican Party developed quickly. The Republicans had developed a strong grassroots organization in the Northwest after the Kansas-Nebraska Act passed in 1854 and attracted disgruntled abolitionists, Whigs, Know-Nothings, Northern Democrats, and members of the Liberty and Free Soil parties who were troubled by the possible extension of slavery. Uncertainty about how the extension of slavery would affect laborers who sought opportunity in the territories also helped to unite the new coalition.

The first Republican nominating convention met in Philadelphia in 1856 with delegates from all of the free states, four border states, three territories, and the District of Columbia. The party's opposition to slavery was far from unanimous, but its willingness to address rather than suppress the issue enabled it to redefine the political dialogue. Besides strong antislavery statements, the party platform contained proposals for several internal improvements advantageous to the North. The party did not offer anything to the solidly Democratic South. To win a national election, it would have to sweep the North. Col. John Charles Fremont was named the Republicans' first presidential candidate. Former Whig senator William Dayton of New Jersey received the vice-presidential nomination.

The Democrats, in endorsing the Kansas-Nebraska Act in 1856, continued rapidly on the path of becoming a southern party. Meeting in Cincinnati, Ohio, after seventeen roll-call votes, the party nominated the pro-South Buchanan as presidential candidate. John Breckinridge of Kentucky, who later served as a Confederate general, was Buchanan's running mate. The Democrats' platform stressed limited federal government and sought compromises on slavery. Benefiting from close wins in Buchanan's home state of Pennsylvania and in New Jersey, and in western states such as Illinois, Indiana, and California, the Democrats won the White

House. But the only strong region for the Democrats was the South. Buchanan won all the slave states except Maryland. Overall, Buchanan won 1.8 million popular votes (45.3 percent) to Fremont's 1.3 million (33.1 percent). The electoral college gave Buchanan a 174–114 victory.

The nativist American Party—or the "Know-Nothings," as they were called—nominated former Whig president Fillmore, but the party was never able to move beyond an urban strength based on parochial resistance to immigration and Catholicism. Fillmore won only the state of Maryland; overall, he got 873,000 popular votes (21.5 percent) and 8 electoral votes.

The Fateful Election: 1860

When the time came for the 1860 presidential campaign, the Democrats had become hopelessly split over slavery. The biggest sticking point was the Supreme Court's infamous 1857 *Dred Scott* decision, which, by decreeing that Congress had no power to prohibit slavery in a territory, was just what Southerners favoring popular sovereignty wanted. Yet it also created uncertainty about any legislature's authority over slavery. If Congress could not regulate slavery, could state legislatures? Illinois senator Douglas insisted on state resolution of the slavery issue. However, the Democratic administration of President Buchanan had waged war on Douglas earlier by ousting his allies from the federal bureaucracy for opposing the administration's prosouthern stance on the Kansas issue. Jefferson Davis of Mississippi, who later became president of the Confederate States of America, led Southern Democrats in Congress who argued that Congress had the right to promote and protect slavery in new territories.

At the Democratic convention in Charleston, South Carolina, Douglas managed several moderate platform victories, defeating resolutions that called for acceptance of the *Dred Scott* decision and protection of slavery in the territories. But Douglas's success prompted delegates from ten southern states to bolt the convention. After disputes over quorum rules and fifty-seven ballots, the Democrats were unable to muster the necessary two-thirds majority for Douglas. The convention therefore adjourned, reassembled in Baltimore in June, and faced disputes about the seating of delegates that caused further defections from the South. With southern radicals effectively eliminated from the convention, Douglas swept to a unanimous nomination victory.

Meanwhile, the southern defectors held their own Democratic convention in June and nominated Vice President Breckinridge for the presidency. The Southern Democrats insisted that they were the backbone of the party and could win the White House as they had been strong enough to elect Buchanan four years before. The Constitutional Union Party, which developed as a futile attempt to repair the nation's geographic divisions, nominated moderate John Bell of Tennessee.

With the *Dred Scott* decision as a rallying point for popular control of government, and the Democrats in disarray, the Republicans held a frenzied convention in Chicago. After the convention blocked several radical candidates, Lincoln, the former U.S. representative of Illinois, emerged as the compromise choice. Although Lincoln had lost the 1858 Senate race to Douglas two years earlier, his stance against the expansion of slavery into the territories had made him a national figure. The fact that Lincoln was widely supported throughout Illinois also had improved his chances at the Chicago convention.

None of the four major candidates seeking the presidency, however, could compete seriously throughout the nation. The two Southerners, Breckinridge and Bell, were doomed from the start, because the South's electoral vote total was significantly below that of the North. The presidential winner was likely to be a candidate from the North, the region with the most electoral votes—that is, either Lincoln, a Republican, or Douglas, a Democrat.

Lincoln won easily with a total of 180 electoral votes to Breckinridge's 72, Bell's 39, and Douglas's 12. Lincoln's closest competitor in the popular vote was Douglas. Lincoln had 1.9 million northern popular votes (40.0 percent); Douglas had 1.4 million (29.5 percent) spread out geographically. The two other principal candidates received much less support, which was concentrated in the South: Breckinridge won 848,000 popular votes (18.1 percent); Bell, 591,000 (12.6 percent).

Thanks to the wide-ranging Republican coalition— one that eluded the Whigs in their last years of existence— Lincoln was able to count on strength in the areas that Fremont had won in 1856: New England and the upper Northwest, as well as New York and Ohio. Lincoln's political ties to Illinois, where he practiced law and began his public career, would help in Illinois and Indiana, and his background as a former Whig was a plus in the Ohio valley. The coal and iron regions of Pennsylvania and Ohio were attracted to the party's high-tariff policy. Urban immigrants, particularly Germans, were attracted by the Republican support of homestead (frontier settlement) legislation and the Lincoln campaign's "Vote Yourself a Farm" appeal.[35] The vice-presidential selection of Hannibal Hamlin of Maine, a former Democrat, broadened the coalition beyond partisan lines. Lincoln's oft-stated desire not to challenge slavery where it then existed was an appeal to border states.

The Republicans succeeded in 1860 because they were able to pull together a variety of potentially warring factions. But above all else the Republicans stood against the extension of slavery into new territories. By accepting slavery where it already existed but warning against the spread of the system, the Republicans divided the Democrats and picked up support from a diverse array of otherwise contentious factions—abolitionists, moderate abolitionists, and

Stephen Douglas, at five feet and four inches, was the 1860 Democratic candidate for president.

whites who feared for their position in the economy. Moreover, the *Dred Scott* decision enabled the Republicans to rail publicly against the high court in the tradition of Jefferson and Jackson. While opposing the Democratic doctrine of popular sovereignty, the Republicans picked up some states' rights sympathizers by having a middle-ground slavery stance.

Because some Southerners had vowed to secede from the Union if Lincoln won the election, in the period before Lincoln's inauguration congressional committees sought to put together a compromise that would save the nation from civil war. They failed, however, because of Lincoln's refusal to abandon his policy of containing slavery. He rejected proposals for popular sovereignty or a slave-free geographic division of western states, and he would not comment on proposals for constitutional amendments or popular referenda on the issue.

After Lincoln was elected, South Carolina, Louisiana, Mississippi, Alabama, Georgia, Texas, and Florida seceded from the Union and on February 7, 1861, adopted a constitution forming the Confederate States of America. After a protracted standoff between Union soldiers who held Fort Sumter and the Confederate soldiers who controlled South Carolina, the Confederates fired on the fort. Virginia, Arkansas, North Carolina, and Tennessee then joined the Confederacy on April 13, 1861, and the Civil War was under way.

The Civil War Election: 1864

The Union's military difficulties in 1861 and 1862 created resentment against and impatience with President Lincoln. The splits that developed in the Republican Party seemed to imperil his chances for renomination and reelection.

From the very beginning of his administration, Lincoln suffered because of the difficulty he had finding a general who could successfully prosecute the war. Repeated military setbacks and stalemates—such as the Battles of Fredericksburg and Chancellorsville, Confederate general Robert E. Lee's escape after the battle of Antietam (Sharpsburg), and heavy casualties in the drive to Richmond—hurt the Republicans. Publicized conflicts with Union generals such as George McClellan caused further damage. In addition to the military problems, the president's announcement in September 1862 of the emancipation of slaves in rebellious states (the Emancipation Proclamation) created legal and political controversy.

In the 1862 midterm elections, the Republicans experienced widespread losses in congressional and state elections. Among the more bitter defeats for Lincoln was Democrat John Stuart's victory in the president's old congressional district in Illinois. By the time of the presidential election, Stuart, a former law partner of the president, was an ardent political foe.

The military frustrations gave rise to deep divisions within Lincoln's cabinet. Treasury Secretary Salmon P. Chase was a constant critic of Lincoln's capacity to serve as commander in chief, and the Philadelphia banker Jay Gould briefly led a movement for Chase's nomination for president in 1864. Chase withdrew only after the Lincoln forces dealt him a severe blow at the party caucus in his home state of Ohio. Other radicals met in Cleveland in May 1864 and named John Fremont to run against Lincoln in the fall. Fremont withdrew only after a series of Union military victories strengthened Lincoln's political standing.

The president manipulated the Republican convention in Baltimore brilliantly, ensuring not only his renomination but also the selection of pro-Union governor Andrew Johnson of Union-occupied Tennessee—a lifelong Democrat—as the vice-presidential candidate. Lincoln professed indifference about a possible running mate. "Wish not to interfere about V.P. Cannot interfere about platform," he said in a letter. "Convention must judge for itself." [36] Nevertheless, he maneuvered to build support for Johnson. Johnson's selection was in accord with the desire of the party, which also called itself the Union Party as a way to attract Democrats and to develop nationwide unity. Yet Lincoln's reelection drive was so uncertain that he obliged his cabinet in August 1864 to sign a statement pledging an orderly transition of power if he lost. The statement read: "This morning, as for some days past, it seems exceedingly probable that this Administration will not be reelected. Then it will be my duty to so cooperate with the President-elect, as to save the Union between the election and the inauguration; as he will have secured his election on such ground that he cannot possibly save it afterwards." [37]

The man for whom Lincoln anticipated arranging a wartime transition was Democratic nominee George McClellan, whom Lincoln had fired as general in January 1863. McClellan had won the Democratic nomination with the strong backing of "peace Democrats" such as Clement L. Vallandigham of Ohio, who was arrested by Union general Ambrose E. Burnside after making a series of antiwar speeches. (Vallandigham later took up exile in Canada.) McClellan's running mate was Rep. George Pendleton of Ohio, who after the war would sponsor landmark civil service reform legislation.

Although popular with his soldiers, General McClellan had not won a single major battle of the war despite many infusions of extra troops. Yet he blamed Lincoln for the losses. Indeed, he was a vocal critic of the administration. McClellan's presidential campaign was built around a call for a cease-fire and a convention to restore the Union. He and his fellow peace Democrats also criticized the administration's violation of civil liberties and other unconstitutional actions.

Republican presidential candidate Abraham Lincoln stood tall at six feet and four inches.

PRESIDENT OF THE CONFEDERACY

In 1861, two weeks before Abraham Lincoln was inaugurated in Washington, D.C., as the sixteenth president of the United States, another president was inaugurated in Montgomery, Alabama. On February 18, 1861, Jefferson Davis became the first and only president of the Confederate States of America.

Davis was born in Christian (now Todd) County, Kentucky, on June 3, 1808. He was the youngest of the ten children of Samuel and Jane Davis, who moved their family to a small Mississippi plantation when Jefferson was a boy. He attended private schools and Transylvania University in Lexington, Kentucky, before his oldest brother, Joseph, secured his appointment to West Point in 1824.

After graduating from the academy, Davis was stationed in Wisconsin under Col. Zachary Taylor. There he saw action in the Black Hawk War during the early 1830s and fell in love with Taylor's daughter, Sarah Knox. In 1835 he left the army, married Sarah, and settled on a one-thousand-acre plantation in Mississippi, which was given to him by his brother Joseph. Tragically, Sarah died from malaria three months after the wedding, and for several years Davis devoted himself to developing his land and wealth.

Jefferson Davis

In 1845 Davis married Varina Howell, a member of the Mississippi aristocracy, and was elected to the U.S. House of Representatives. He served in Washington less than a year before the Mexican War began, and he gave up his seat to accept a commission as a colonel. He became a national hero when his company made a stand at the Battle of Buena Vista that was said to have saved Gen. Zachary Taylor's army from defeat.

In 1847 he left the army and was elected to the Senate. He served there until 1851, when he ran unsuccessfully for governor of Mississippi. He returned to Washington in 1853 after being appointed secretary of war by President Franklin Pierce. Davis was credited with strengthening the armed forces during his time in office. He also was influential in bringing about the Gadsden Purchase from Mexico in 1853, which added southern areas of present-day Arizona and New Mexico to the United States.

In 1857 Davis was reelected to the Senate. Although he became a leading spokesperson for the South, he did not advocate secession until 1860 when it had become inevitable. Davis hoped to be appointed commanding general of the South's army, but instead he was chosen as president by a convention of the seceding states.

Davis believed his first priority as president was to preserve Southern independence. He tried to secure French and British assistance for the Confederacy, but he was largely unsuccessful. Like Lincoln he helped develop military strategy and on occasion interfered with the plans of his generals. In managing the war effort, Davis was hampered by his paradoxical position. The South could fight most effectively as a unified nation run by the central government in Richmond, but the Southern states had succeeded in part to preserve their rights as independent states. Davis took actions, including the suspension of habeas corpus and the establishment of conscription, that were regarded as despotic by many Southerners.

When the Union's victory appeared imminent in early 1865, Davis fled south from Richmond and was captured by federal troops. He was indicted for treason and imprisoned for two years, but he never stood trial. He lived in Canada and Europe for several years before retiring to Mississippi. There he wrote his Rise and Fall of the Confederate Government, which was published in 1881. He died in New Orleans on December 6, 1889.

Lincoln's fortunes improved in the two months before the election. When Gen. William Tecumseh Sherman took Atlanta after a scorched-earth march through the South, the Confederacy was left badly divided geographically. The military victory cut off the Gulf states from the Confederate capital of Richmond. Gen. Philip Sheridan had had important successes in the Shenandoah Valley, and Gen. Ulysses S. Grant had fared well in Virginia.

Not only did the Democrats face a Republican Party reconstituted for the war election as the Union Party and united by recent military victories, but McClellan also had a difficult time developing consistent campaign themes. He was at var-ious times conciliatory toward the Confederacy and solicitous of the soldiers who fought for the Union. The balancing problem was underscored by the inclusion of both war and peace songs in the *McClellan Campaign Songster*, a piece of campaign literature.[38] McClellan also had a difficult time selling his message to northern industrialists who were profiting from munitions procurement.

Not until the arrival of election results from three state elections on October 11 were Lincoln and the Unionists confident that they would win the national election in November. Republican victories in Indiana, Ohio, and Pennsylvania were the first concrete indications that Lincoln's fortunes had turned around.

Lincoln overwhelmed McClellan by winning all of the loyal states except Delaware, Kentucky, and New Jersey for a 212–21 electoral vote victory. Lincoln garnered 2.2 million popular votes (55.0 percent) to McClellan's 1.8 million (45.0 percent). The electoral votes of Louisiana and Tennessee, the first Confederate states to return to the Union, were not accepted by Congress.

POSTWAR RADICALISM

The end of the Civil War left the nation almost as divided as it had been in the antebellum years. Concerns about punishment of the rebel states, the status of the freedmen, and economic development replaced slavery as the principal sources of disagreement.

The nation undoubtedly would have experienced bitter splits no matter who had served as chief executive, but the assassination of President Abraham Lincoln on April 14, 1865, shortly after the Confederate surrender, created a crisis of leadership. Lincoln's vice president, Andrew Johnson, ascended to the presidency and quickly came into conflict with the radical Northern Republicans who controlled Congress. Johnson, a Democrat from Tennessee, was stubborn, which only aggravated the troubles that were inevitable anyway because of his party and regional background.

Johnson intended to continue Lincoln's plans for the reconstruction of the North and South "with malice toward none"; he chafed at the notion of the South as a conquered territory. A states' rights politician, Johnson attempted to put together a coalition of moderates from all parts of the country that would bring about a quick reconciliation between his administration and Congress.

But Congress was intent on establishing political institutions that would respect the rights of former slaves and promote economic growth and vowed to use military occupation to destroy the South's old political elite.[39] Thus Johnson and Congress fought over bills that would extend the life of the Freedmen's Bureau (an agency established to help blacks make the transition from slavery to citizenship) and guarantee the franchise and equal protection to blacks, with the result that Johnson vetoed both bills. Johnson also opposed the Fourteenth Amendment, which guaranteed equal protection, as well as the stipulation that Confederate states approve the amendment as a condition of their readmission to the Union.

When the Radical Republicans took over Congress in the 1866 midterm elections, the war with Johnson began in earnest. In March 1867 Congress established limited military rule in recalcitrant Southern states and in May passed the Tenure of Office Act limiting the president's right to dismiss his appointees. Johnson contemptuously disregarded the tenure act and fired Edwin Stanton, his secretary of war. For this action Johnson was impeached by the House and tried by the Senate. When the Senate voted in May 1868, he avoided the two-thirds total needed for conviction by a single vote (35–19).

The Grant Victories: 1868 and 1872

Ulysses S. Grant was more than a concerned citizen during the dispute between Johnson and Congress. Despite its portrayal in many history books as a clear instance of congres-

The 1872 Republican campaign called voters' attention to the humble backgrounds of presidential candidate Ulysses S. Grant and his running mate, Henry Wilson.

sional abuse of power, the affair was more complicated. All of the players in the drama negotiated their way with care, and almost none of them escaped without major scars. Grant was a central figure, and his style of maneuvering was dictated by his ambition to succeed Johnson as president.

Radical Republicans in Congress achieved a lasting victory when they secured passage of the Civil Rights Act of 1866 over President Johnson's veto, but they were increasingly disturbed by reports that the statute was not being enforced. A congressional investigation of violence against blacks in Memphis concluded that the Freedmen's Bureau could not enforce civil rights without help. Radicals began to look to Secretary of War Stanton to enforce the law that the president clearly disliked and repeatedly subverted. When Stanton indicated that he would carry out the law in the Confederacy as Congress intended, Johnson began to think about replacing him. At this point Congress passed the

Tenure of Office Act over Johnson's veto in May 1867, reasoning that its constitutional "advise and consent" powers over appointments could be extended to removal as well. Johnson, however, decided to test the law's constitutionality.

In replacing Stanton, Johnson's concern—and indeed the concern of all involved—was who could assume the secretary of war post with minimal threat to Johnson's position. The president first considered General Sherman but decided to appoint Grant on a temporary basis. Originally a Democrat and supporter of moderate policies toward the South, Grant worried about appearing too close to the unpopular president. As a result, after vaguely assuring Johnson that he would accept a temporary appointment, Grant hedged. He increasingly expressed support for the notion that appointees should interpret and obey laws according to congressional intent. Eventually Grant told the president in a letter that he could not accept the appointment.

After the drama of Johnson's impeachment in 1868, Grant was in a good position to seek the White House. He had avoided allying himself with controversy during both Johnson's search for a replacement for Stanton and the ensuing impeachment battle. In fact, he and Chief Justice Salmon Chase were the only ones not tainted by the affair. Grant even managed to maintain his public posture of disinterested duty. Thus during one of the nation's ugliest political episodes, Grant looked clean. He was ready for a presidential campaign.

As Johnson endured his Senate impeachment trial in March, Grant won his first electoral victory. A New Hampshire congressional campaign, which normally would favor the Democrat, became an early Grant referendum when Republican candidate Donald Sickles told voters that a vote for a Republican was a vote for Grant; Sickles won. Just before the Republican convention in May, a Soldiers and Sailors Convention "nominated" Grant. Yet he avoided an excessively military image when he vowed to reduce the size of the standing army. Grant was on his way.

Grant won the presidential nomination without opposition. The real battle at the 1868 Republican convention was for the vice-presidential nomination. Schuyler Colfax of Indiana, the Speaker of the House, won on the sixth ballot; eleven candidates received votes on the initial roll call.

The Democrats had a difficult time finding a nominee. Johnson sought the Democratic nomination, but his appeal was to the South. (Because many Southern states were still outside the Union, Northern politicians were selecting the nominee.) Chief Justice Chase, highly regarded for his fairness during Johnson's Senate trial, was a possibility, but his strong stand for black suffrage was a barrier. Sen. Thomas A. Hendricks of Indiana was strong in the East, and George Pendleton of Ohio, the party's vice-presidential candidate four years earlier, was strong in the West. Gen. Winfield Scott Hancock of Pennsylvania presented the opportunity of running one military hero against another.

After twenty-three bitter ballots in a sweltering New York City, Horatio Seymour, the national party chair and popular war governor of New York, accepted the Democratic nomination against his will. Gen. Francis P. Blair Jr. of Missouri was the vice-presidential nominee. The party platform called for the rapid reentry of Confederate states to the Union, state authority over suffrage questions, and the "Ohio Idea," which promised an inflationary money supply that would help the indebted South.

Both sides were well financed in the election, but the Republicans had the edge. The Republican Party's probusiness positions on the tariff, railroad grants, and the currency attracted millions of dollars. Newspapers and magazines tended to be pro-Republican because of their urban business orientations.

Grant, who ran his campaign from his home in Galena, Illinois, was vague about issues ranging from the currency to voting rights. Appearances in Colorado with fellow generals Sherman and Sheridan were taken to be endorsements. Everything seemed to go Grant's way. Even the traditional campaign gossip about the sexual activities of candidates did not hurt him. Charges that Grant was excessively problack—"I am Captain Grant of the Black Marines, the stupidest man that was ever seen" were the lyrics of one ditty[40]—helped him with the recently enfranchised citizens. Without the black vote, Grant probably would have lost the popular vote and perhaps the electoral vote. Results from October state elections that favored the Republicans created a brief movement for Seymour and Blair to quit the contest so that the Democrats could name a new ticket. Instead, Seymour took the October results as an incentive to get on the campaign stump. Seymour was a good speaker, but he still came up short.

Grant defeated Seymour by 3.0 million (52.7 percent) to 2.7 million votes (47.3 percent). The electoral vote tally was 214 for Grant and 80 for Seymour. Finally, Grant won all but eight of the thirty-four states taking part in the election. He benefited from Radical Republican reconstructionist sentiment in the North and newly enfranchised blacks in the South.

With Grant's ascension to the presidency in 1869, the Republican Party entered a new era—what the German sociologist Max Weber would have called a shift from "charismatic" to "rational" institutional authority. In other words, the party shifted its devotion from a great moral cause to its own survival as an organization. It had begun as a coalition of activists fervently opposed to the expansion of slavery (many opposed slavery itself) and to the rebellion of Southern states from the Union. The Republicans' 1868 victory under Grant was the first not dominated wholly by crisis conditions.

The Republicans had a strong base of support: eastern bankers, manufacturers, railroad tycoons, and land speculators. With the old Confederacy under the control of military governments and with blacks given the franchise, the Republicans had strength in the South. The West was restive, however, because of depressed farm prices, high taxes, and debt. The industrial-agrarian split between North and South before the Civil War would be resumed as an East-West split in the years after the war.

The Republican leadership itself was changing. Age was claiming a number of the early Republican leaders, such as Thaddeus Stevens, William Seward, Benjamin Wade, Charles Sumner, James Grimes, Stanton, and Chase. New party leaders included Senators Roscoe Conkling of New York, Oliver Morton of Indiana, Simon Cameron of Pennsylvania, and Zachariah Chandler of Michigan, and Representatives Benjamin Butler of Massachusetts, John Logan of Illinois, James A. Garfield of Ohio, and James G. Blaine of Maine.

As for the new Grant administration, it was undistinguished. The new president's inaugural address—spoken without the traditional company of the outgoing president because Grant had neglected to respond to Johnson's polite letters—was decent but uninspiring. Grant vowed that "all laws will be faithfully executed, whether they meet my approval or not," that debtors would not be tolerated, and that blacks should get the vote throughout the country and Indians should be offered "civilization and ultimate citizenship." [41] With a few important exceptions, cabinet positions went to old Grant cronies.

In 1869 the nation experienced a financial panic when financiers Jay Gould and Jim Fisk attempted to corner the world's gold market. Their scheme led to "Black Friday," September 24, 1869. Gould and Fisk had met with President Grant and had urged him not to sell government gold, therefore keeping the price of gold high. At the last minute, however, Grant decided to reject their advice and dumped $4 million worth of gold on the market. That dumping caused a severe drop in gold prices, breaking up the Gould-Fisk conspiracy but also causing tremendous losses for thousands of speculators. It was the worst disaster on Wall Street up to that time. Although it did not cause a depression, the South and West were hard hit by the financial retrenchment program that followed. Tariff rates remained high on most manufactured goods, despite tentative efforts to reform the system.

The spoils system was in full swing during the Grant years. Grant himself was not involved in the scramble for booty, but his family and aides were often shameless in their greed. When Grant learned that liberal Republicans were planning an independent presidential campaign against him in 1872, he took the edge off the spoils issue by creating the Civil Service Reform Commission, but his neglect of the commission made it ineffective.

Before the 1872 election, the *New York Sun* exposed the Crédit Mobilier scandal. The newspaper reported that the firm's board of directors had many of the same members as the Union Pacific Railroad Company, which hired it to build a transcontinental route, and that Crédit Mobilier had paid its board exorbitant profits. To avoid a public investigation, Crédit Mobilier offered stock to Vice President Colfax and Representative (later president) Garfield. Colfax lost his place on the Republican ticket for his role in the scandal; Sen. Henry Wilson of New Hampshire took his position as the vice-presidential candidate in 1872.

Liberal Republicans, unhappy with protective tariffs, spoils, and the uneven administration of the Southern states, bolted the party in 1872. The group was interested in policies such as civil service and free trade that would promote individual virtue in a laissez-faire economic system. The reformers thought they had a chance to win. The German-born senator Carl Schurz of Missouri wrote to a friend that "the administration with its train of offices and officemongers [is] the great incubus pressing upon the party. . . . The superstition that Grant is the necessary man is rapidly giving way. The spell is broken, and we have only to push through the breach." [42]

Candidates for the nomination from this group of Republicans included former ambassador to Great Britain Charles Francis Adams, son of President John Quincy Adams and grandson of President John Adams; Supreme Court Justice David Davis; Chief Justice Salmon Chase; Sen. Lyman Trumbull of Illinois; and Horace Greeley, editor of the *New York Tribune.* Greeley won the nomination on the sixth ballot and ran as a Democrat and Liberal Republican. The Democrats were so weak that they did not field a candidate of their own. They endorsed the Greeley ticket. (Charles O'Conor of New York was nominated by a group of "Noncoalition Democrats" for president. He did not accept the nomination.)

Since his early days as a newspaper reporter, when he described President Van Buren as an effeminate failure, Greeley had won fame as a pungent social critic. He was a crusading, abolitionist editor and a dedicated reformer, but his rumpled appearance and unpolished speaking style made him appear "unpresidential." Greeley was unable to parlay an amalgam of promises to various interest groups—blacks, soldiers, immigrants, and laborers—into a victory over Grant. Groups that Greeley actively courted found him wanting for a variety of reasons, and even though Greeley advocated the tariff favored by the North, he could not cut into Grant's northeastern strength. One Republican cartoon that revealed Greeley's difficult task showed a fence on which sat a laborer, skeptical because of Greeley's stand against strikes, and a black, concerned because of Greeley's advocacy of amnesty for Confederates. Sitting on the sidelines was a German, upset with Greeley's prohibitionist stance: "Oh! Yaw! You would take my Lager away, den you must get widout me along!" [43]

Even though he went on the stump and delivered a series of impressive speeches, Greeley never had a chance. Republican gubernatorial victories in North Carolina in August and in Pennsylvania, Ohio, and Indiana in October were clear harbingers that the Republican Party would do well in November. Grant took the entire North and the newly admitted South with 3.6 million popular votes (55.6 percent). Greeley won three border states, as well as Tennessee, Texas, and Georgia, with 2.8 million popular votes (43.9 percent). Less than a month after the election, Greeley died. Of the electoral votes, which were cast after Greeley's death, Grant received 286; the Democrats' 63 electoral votes were scattered among various candidates, and 17 Democratic electoral votes were not cast.

Compromise: 1876

The pattern of Republican, northern, and business domination of presidential politics was institutionalized in the 1876 election. Republican Rutherford B. Hayes, the three-time governor of Ohio, lost the popular vote and had a questionable hold on the electoral college vote, but he managed to beat Democrat Samuel J. Tilden for the presidency when the election was settled by a special commission created by Congress. (Hayes won 4.0 million votes to Tilden's 4.3 million—48.0 and 51.0 percent of the popular vote, respectively.) Perhaps the most controversial election outcome in history, some feared it would set off a second civil war.

The problem arose when the vote tallies in Florida, South Carolina, and Louisiana were called into question. Violence had accompanied the voting in all three states, but President Grant had not sent in federal troops to ensure fair balloting. On those states hung the electoral outcome. There was good reason to be suspicious of any vote count in those and other Southern states. While the Republicans had controlled the balloting places and mounted vigorous drives to get blacks to the polls, the Democrats had used physical intimidation and bribery to keep blacks away. The bitterness between northern interests and southern whites was apparent in the violence that often took place at polls.

When state election board recounts and investigations did not settle the question of the vote tallies, Congress took up the matter. An electoral commission made up of five senators (three majority-party Republicans, two minority Democrats), five representatives (three majority-party Democrats, two minority Republicans), and five Supreme Court justices (two from each party, one independent) assembled to hear complaints about the disputed states. At the last minute the independent justice disqualified himself, and his place was taken by a Republican who was accepted by Democrats because they considered him to be the most independent of the Republican justices. Weeks of bargaining followed, during which the Republican vote totals of the disputed states were confirmed and the Southern Democrats extracted promises of financial aid and political independence from the federal government.

When the validity of the Florida vote count for Hayes was challenged, the commission responded that it did not have the capacity to judge the actual conduct of the balloting, only the validity of the certificates presented to Congress. That decision gave the state to Hayes. Challenges to the vote counts of Louisiana, South Carolina, and Oregon were dismissed in a similar way, so Hayes was awarded the presidency by a single electoral vote, 185 to 184.

The compromise not only settled the partisan dispute between Hayes and Tilden but also established a rigid alignment of political interests that would dominate U.S. politics for the next half-century. Although Democrats won occasional victories, the Republican, eastern, conservative, business-oriented establishment held sway over the system until Franklin Roosevelt's election in 1932.

The institutional form of the regional splits created by the compromise remained much longer. Historian C. Vann Woodward has argued that secret wheeling and dealing among congressional and party leaders institutionally divided the political system by party, region, economic interest, and governmental branches. Northern Republican industrial interests were given control of the presidential election process, and southern Democratic agricultural interests were given autonomy over their regional politics, which led to domination of Congress.[44] This alignment was not completely dislodged until the passage of important civil rights legislation in the 1960s.

To reward Southern Democrats for throwing the 1876 election to the Republican Hayes, northern politicians agreed to pull federal troops out of the South and to allow southern whites to take over the system. Within months Southern states were erecting a powerful edifice of racial discrimination that would last until the 1960s. Former South Carolina governor Daniel H. Chamberlain, a Republican, later summed up the deal:

> What is the president's Southern policy? [I]t consists in the abandonment of Southern Republicans and especially the colored race, to the control and rule not only of the Democratic Party, but of that class of the South which regarded slavery as a Divine Institution, which waged four years of destructive war for its perpetuation, which steadily opposed citizenship and suffrage for the negro—in a word, a class whose traditions, principles, and history are opposed to every step and feature of what Republicans call our national progress since 1860.[45]

THE AGE OF REPUBLICANISM

From 1860 to 1908, the Republicans won eleven elections; the Democrats won only two. Only Grover Cleveland could put together Democratic wins, and he was as conservative on most issues as the Republicans of the period. Presidential election winners after the Great Compromise were Rutherford B. Hayes (1876), James A. Garfield (1880), Cleveland (1884), Benjamin Harrison (1888), Cleveland (1892), William McKinley (1896 and 1900), Theodore Roosevelt (1904), and William Howard Taft (1908).

The political aspirants of the day were required to adhere to the creed of high tariffs, laissez-faire economics, and tight money. Tight money policies—the restricted issuance of currency, which favored bankers and other established interests but hurt debtors and those seeking more rapid expansion of some kinds of investment and spending—provided rare openings for effective Democratic resistance to Republican hegemony. Resistance did develop, however, when the scramble for tariff protections created obvious inequities among businesses and hardships for the consumer. Yet populist uprisings, such as Democrat William Jennings Bryan's 1896 campaign, faltered because of strong mobilization by the Republicans and divisions within the Democratic ranks. Bryan failed to bring a likely Democratic constituency—the worker—into the fold. Eastern business owners were able to portray their interest in industrial growth as a common concern with labor and Bryan's western agrarian alliance as a danger to that growth.

Although the Republican Party dominated presidential politics, the parties were well balanced in Congress and in state governments until the class and sectional cleavages of the 1890s. The Senate was split evenly in 1881, 37–37, and two years later the Republicans had a 38–36 edge. The Democrats had made gains in northern congressional races, and Republicans were making smaller gains in the South. The House tended to provide a majority for whichever party held the White House.

Garfield Carries the Republican Banner: 1880

Hayes honored his pledge to serve only one term, setting off a scramble for both parties' nominations in 1880. When the early momentum for a third term for Grant faltered, the Republican contest became a battle between Grant, Sen. James G. Blaine of Maine, and Treasury secretary John Sherman of Ohio. Grant was able to muster a first-ballot plurality but could not attract new supporters as the balloting proceeded. A stalemate between Blaine and Sherman ensued.

Rep. Garfield of Ohio, a former preacher who was impressive in his oratory and organization for Sherman, was the compromise choice for the nomination. He selected as his running mate Chester A. Arthur, the collector of the Port of New York, an important patronage job.

The Democrats named Gen. Winfield Hancock of Pennsylvania and former Indiana representative William English to head their ticket. The Democratic platform advocated the gold standard, a low tariff designed to raise revenue, civil service reform, restrictions on Chinese immigra-

tion, and a belated criticism of the 1876 deal that gave the presidency to Hayes. Except for the tariff and 1876 questions, the Democrats' platform was close to the Republicans' statement of principles.

The regional breakdown of support, with most of the North and West falling in Garfield's camp and the South lining up behind Hancock, gave the presidency to Garfield. The popular vote was close—4.45 million (48.27 percent) to 4.44 million (48.25 percent)—but Garfield won a 214–155 electoral vote victory.

The festering issue of patronage and civil service came to a head shortly after Garfield's inauguration. On July 2, 1881, Charles Guiteau, a man later described as a "disappointed office-seeker," shot Garfield while he was en route to Williams College to deliver a commencement address. Garfield died in September, and Arthur became president.

The outstanding feature of Arthur's presidency was the easy passage of the Pendleton Act—legislation that set up a commission to regulate the provision of federal jobs and the behavior of civil servants. The number of federal workers removed from the patronage system was at first small, but successive presidents widened the coverage of nonpartisan workers so that today less than 1 percent of all federal workers are appointed by the president.[46]

The tariff question also emerged as crucial during the Arthur presidency. The Tariff Act of 1883 "gave little or no relief to the consumer and took care of every important industrial interest." [47] The Democrats opposed the bill and later worked for the gradual lowering of rates, but they failed. The tariff would be a major issue in later elections.

Democrat Cleveland Wins: 1884

Arthur wanted the Republican nomination in 1884, and his record as stand-in for the assassinated Garfield arguably should have earned him the nod—even though no successor president during the nineteenth century had been nominated by his party. Not only was he an important player in civil service reform and the tariff issue, but he initiated modernization of the navy and vetoed the Chinese Exclusion Act of 1882, which prohibited Chinese laborers from entering the United States for ten years. His veto of the $19 million rivers and harbors bill was a model of fiscal probity.

Blaine of Maine—secretary of state in Arthur's administration—stood in the president's way. After months of public appeals by old-line Republicans interested in stronger leadership and more generous patronage from their party, Blaine quit his administration position and opposed Arthur for the nomination.

Blaine was the most charismatic figure of the period. A former teacher, editor, state legislator, and member of Congress, Blaine's fiery oratory captured the imagination of the political establishment. He had made a national name for himself when he opposed an 1876 congressional resolution expressing forgiveness to Civil War rebels including the Confederate president, Jefferson Davis. Col. Robert G. Ingersoll, a rising political figure in the Republican Party, said of Blaine: "Like an armed warrior, like a plumed knight, James G. Blaine marched down the halls of the American Congress and threw his shining lance full and fair against the brazen forehead of every traitor to his country." [48] The sobriquet "Plumed Knight" caught on.

The Republican convention in Chicago praised Arthur's administration and fudged the tariff issue. The tariff that passed in 1883 was the product of the efforts of swarms of lobbyists for private interests. The Republican platform promised better protection for raw wool interests, angered by their treatment in 1883, and a generally protective stance for domestic industry. The platform also called for an international currency conference, railway regulation, a national agency for labor affairs, and further improvements in the navy.

At a frenzied convention, Blaine took the lead over Arthur on the first ballot. Old-line party leaders quickly united behind Blaine, while Arthur was unable to consolidate the support of reform Republicans still skeptical of his leadership abilities from his days as a patronage politician and collector of the Port of New York. Blaine won the nomination on the fourth ballot. Gen. John Logan of Illinois received the vice-presidential nomination.

The Democrats nominated Cleveland after skirmishes with Sen. Thomas F. Bayard Jr. of Delaware and Sen. Thomas A. Hendricks of Indiana. Hendricks, whose liberal expansionist currency stance would balance the more conservative stance of Cleveland, was named the vice-presidential candidate. The Democratic platform vaguely promised reform of the tariff laws to make them fairer and, even more vaguely, promised a more honest and efficient administration.

Cleveland was a former teacher, lawyer, assistant district attorney, and reform mayor of Buffalo who had won the governorship of New York only two years before. Members

The fiery oratory of 1884 Republican candidate James G. Blaine captured the imagination of the political establishment, but it was not enough to win him the election over Democrat Grover Cleveland.

of both parties consistently underestimated Cleveland's intellect and resolve. As governor, he had made enemies through his vetoes of low public transit fares and aid to sectarian schools. He also had defied Tammany Hall, the Democratic Party organization that dominated New York politics, especially in New York City.

Cleveland's nomination signaled a triumph for the "educational politics" characteristic of urban progressivism. (Progressives took a patriarchal view of politics in which elites assumed an obligation to better their social underlings through education and various social services.) In a move away from the highly partisan and vitriolic campaigns of the post–Civil War era, Cleveland and other disciples of former New York governor Samuel Tilden promoted their program through a "literary bureau" that distributed pamphlets describing the party's policy positions. Campaign themes were developed at the national level and disseminated via the mails and meetings with the many professional and community organizations. The educational style was adopted by Republican candidate Harrison in 1888.[49]

In contrast, Blaine's campaign was one of the dirtiest in U.S. history. He first attempted to spark sectional antagonisms with his "bloody shirt" warnings that the South was trying to reassert its rebel ways through Cleveland. Blaine also tried to rouse the fears of business with claims that Cleveland would institute free trade policies damaging to domestic industries. But that appeal failed because the Democratic platform's plank on the tariff laws specifically supported protection of those interests. Finally, Blaine tried to make a scandal of Cleveland's admission that he had fathered a child out of wedlock years before. Cleveland was charged, among other things, with kidnapping and immuring both the mother and child to cover up the story.

The campaign eventually turned on Cleveland's victory in New York, which resulted from a number of blunders by Blaine. One blunder had occurred years before, when Blaine mocked New York party boss Roscoe Conkling: "The contempt of that large-minded gentleman is so wilted, his haughty disdain, his grandiloquent swell, his majestic, supereminent, overpowering, turkey-gobbler strut, has been so crushing to myself that I know it was an act of the greatest temerity to venture upon a controversy with him." [50] Conkling was so peeved by the turkey image that he spent his whole career battling Blaine, including the presidential campaign of 1884. Even Blaine's running mate, Logan, sympathized with Conkling in the dispute.

The other Blaine faux pas occurred a week before the election when a Protestant minister praised Blaine and proclaimed, "We are Republicans, and do not propose to leave our party and identify ourselves with the party whose antecedents have been rum, Romanism, and rebellion." Blaine did not divorce himself from the remark, which angered New York Democrats—and ethnic voters everywhere—and cost him many votes. Later the same day Blaine attended a formal dinner with a number of wealthy persons that became known as "the millionaires dinner." That event belied Blaine's claim to speak for ordinary people.

Of Irish background, Blaine appealed to Irish immigrants in New York for their votes. But Cleveland countered Blaine's Irish tactic by obtaining the last-minute endorsement of the powerful Tammany leader Edward Kelly. On the Saturday before the election, he attended a parade in New York City that attracted 40,000 people chanting: "Blaine, Blaine, James G. Blaine, the Monumental Liar from the State of Maine!" With the help of an economic downturn and the "Mugwumps"—independents and liberal Republicans offended by Blaine—Cleveland won the presidency.

The race, however, was close. Cleveland received 4.9 million votes (48.5 percent) to Blaine's 4.8 million (48.3 percent). He won the solid South, Indiana, Connecticut, New Jersey, and, most important, New York (although by only 1,047 out of 1.13 million votes cast). Still, the election controversy did not end with the balloting. The New York Tribune reported that Blaine had won the race, fueling fears about an election deadlock similar to the Hayes-Tilden contest of 1876. But Cleveland received 219 electoral votes to Blaine's 182, making the Democrat the clear winner.

Cleveland's first two years in the White House were pro- ductive. His inaugural address and cabinet selections elicited wide praise. His style of leadership—examined closely in the newspapers—appeared refreshingly unassuming. The Cleveland agenda included issues such as tariff reform (cutting rates on the "necessaries of life"), modernization of the navy, civil service, expansion, and land law reform. The president oversaw passage of the Presidential Succession Act and the Electoral Count Act, changes in currency policy, and labor controversies.

Just as he had done during his terms as mayor of Buffalo and governor of New York, Cleveland icily refused to compromise his values. This steadfastness proved to be a problem, however, when Cleveland entered the White House. Thousands of Democratic Party workers went to Washington seeking jobs in the new administration only to be disappointed. "Ah, I suppose you mean that I should appoint two horse thieves a day instead of one," Cleveland said in response to one party leader.[51] In vetoing pension bills, Cleveland called their sponsors "blood-suckers," "coffee-boilers," "pension leeches," and "bums." [52] The president appeared just as aloof to labor when a record number of strikes and disturbances swept the nation in 1886; the federal troops that Cleveland sent to the Haymarket riot in Chicago killed thirty people.

When Cleveland did bend to political realities, his timing was off. After standing firm against patronage when party enthusiasm for reform was at its height, Cleveland disappointed reformers when he allowed lieutenants such as First Assistant Postmaster Adlai E. Stevenson to distribute favors.

The biggest controversy of the Cleveland administration involved tariffs. Concerned about federal budget surpluses that threatened to stall economic activity, Cleveland prodded the House of Representatives to pass tariff reductions. The Senate responded with a protective (high) tariff measure.

The Republican Recovery: 1888

The tariff issue propelled the two parties into the 1888 election. At their national convention the Democrats nominated Cleveland by acclamation and chose seventy-five-year-old judge Allen G. Thurman of Ohio for the vice presidency. The Democrats tried to soften their low-tariff image by promising that open trade would open world markets to domestic industries. Lower tariffs were said to be necessary for avoiding disastrous federal budget surpluses, preventing the development of monopolies, and ensuring consumers reasonable prices for basic goods.

As for the Republicans, a politics-weary Blaine sent word from Florence and Paris that he would not be a candidate in 1888, leaving the race open to some lesser political lights, including Sen. John Sherman of Ohio, Gov. Russell Alger of Michigan, Sen. William Allison of Iowa, and Sen. Harrison of Indiana. At the Republican national convention Sherman led the early balloting but quickly lost ground to Alger and Harrison. After extensive backroom maneuvering, including a last-minute plea by party members to Blaine to accept the nomination, Harrison, who had the backing of state party bosses, won on the ninth ballot. Levi Morton, a banker, got the vice-presidential nomination.

Harrison, a senator from Indiana, was a former Civil War brigadier and the grandson of President William Henry Harrison. Characterized by a scandal-free if colorless demeanor, Harrison was a good speaker, but he often appeared aloof. One historian wrote: "Those who talked

Captioned "Another Voice for Cleveland," this 1884 cartoon played on Cleveland's admission that he had fathered an illegitimate son.

with him were met with a frigid look from two expressionless steel grey eyes, and their remarks were sometimes answered in a few chill monosyllables devoid of the slightest note of interest." [53] Harrison pledged a modernized navy, civil service reforms, and the traditional Republican policies to protect trusts and restrict U.S. markets.

The election turned, as in 1884, on New York and Indiana—both states with extensive evidence of voter intimidation and manipulation of vote counts. Harrison won the two states narrowly—New York by only 14,373 votes out of the 1.3 million cast—and captured the White House. Except for Connecticut and New Jersey, Harrison swept the North and West. Cleveland won the South. Overall, Harrison won 5.4 million popular votes (47.8 percent) and 233 electoral votes; Cleveland won 5.5 million popular votes (48.6 percent) and 168 electoral votes.

Cleveland left the White House with an unusual amount of good will among the public because of his honest tariff campaign. His popularity increased during the next four years as the economy hit slumps and as the former president, while practicing law, delivered speeches calling for a more egalitarian brand of politics. Cleveland would be back in 1892 for vindication.

With a majority in Congress and a president in the White House—the first time the party had accomplished such a feat in a dozen years—the Republicans went about

their business briskly after the election. Postmaster General John Wanamaker dispensed patronage with zeal. President Harrison signed into law the McKinley Tariff Act and the Sherman Silver Purchase Act. The former raised duties on manufactured goods to their highest level ever but also included provisions for negotiating with other countries to bring the rates down. The silver act loosened the money supply, which stimulated economic activity but angered creditors and bankers (money, when it is more readily available, is worth less).

Cleveland's Comeback: 1892

The 1890 midterm elections brought huge Democratic gains. Voters all over the country—but especially in the depressed farm belt—rebelled against the inflation that high tariffs brought. The Republicans held on to the Senate, but the new House of Representatives had 235 Democrats, 88 Republicans, and 9 Farmers' Alliance members. The brief experiment with party government ended with two years of stalemate.

President Harrison evoked widespread discontent in 1892 for both his demeanor and his policies, but no Republican could mount an effective challenge. Through their strong party government, Republicans had cast their lot with Harrison and had few places to turn for an alternative. Political wizard Mark Hanna, a wealthy coal magnate who had become a powerful behind-the-scenes Republican strategist, promoted Ohio governor William McKinley, and Secretary of State Blaine became an alternative when he abruptly quit the administration just before the Republican convention. But Harrison received a first-ballot nomination. Former minister to France Whitelaw Reid of New York got the vice-presidential nomination.

In the battle for the Democratic nomination, Cleveland enjoyed widespread backing among rank-and-file voters, but party leaders were suspicious. New York governor David B. Hill got a head start when he called a "snap" state convention and won the delegation. An "anti-snapper" convention from New York sent a rival delegation to the national party convention. Democrats across the country rebelled at Hill's move and rapidly switched their support to Cleveland.

Another problem for Cleveland was the rising sentiment in agrarian states for free and unlimited coinage of silver—a way of boosting sagging farm prices by inducing inflation in the overall economy. Cleveland always had opposed this solution. The former president's consistent, principled stance on the issue not only added to his reputation for integrity but also kept business- and finance-dominated northeastern states in the Democratic camp. Cleveland defeated Hill for the nomination on the first ballot and selected his former first assistant postmaster Adlai Stevenson of Illinois as his running mate.

The fall campaign was uneventful. Historian Eugene Roseboom wrote: "Honest bearded Benjamin Harrison confronting honest mustached Grover Cleveland in a tariff debate was a repeat performance that did not inspire parades with torches or the chanting of campaign ditties. . . . Democrats, out of power, could assail Republican tariff policy without clarifying their own position." [54]

Cleveland won easily. He received 5.6 million popular votes (46.1 percent) to Harrison's 5.2 million (43.0 percent) and 277 electoral votes to Harrison's 145. Populist general James B. Weaver, advocating expansion of currency and limits on interest rates, won 1.0 million popular votes (8.5 percent) and 22 electoral votes.

THE AGE OF REFORM

Throughout the period dominated by Republican conservatism—from Ulysses S. Grant's election in 1868 to William McKinley's 1896 win—movements for the reform of political and economic institutions gathered strength at all levels of the American political system. The so-called populists and progressives did not overturn the system, as their rhetoric sometimes suggested, but over time they made major changes in the operation and discourse of U.S. politics.

Depending on the time and place, people who called themselves "populists" and "progressives" promoted such contradictory notions as strict morals and free spirits, tight money and loose money, redistribution to the masses and control of the economy by elites, federal intervention and local control of politics, the opening and closing of electoral participation, technological progress and a return to a long-gone pastoral ideal, individualism and community action, ethnic celebration and immigration barriers, scientific investigation and religion, and internationalism and isolationism.

Reformism was the response to the pressures of national expansion, urban development, and growth. Both major parties had adopted probusiness, laissez-faire policies in the latter part of the nineteenth century; indeed, the parties seemed to exist mainly to ensure the terrain was suitable for economic expansion. But the lack of any program to deal with the undesired consequences of explosive growth led to an accumulation of problems that demanded attention. The most obvious problems evolved on the opposite ends of the rural-urban continuum: on the farms and in the cities.

The farm problem developed as the United States became a major economic power in the world. Agriculture expanded on a vast scale to feed the booming cities and, with international trade, to bring foreign capital to the United States. By 1880 the value of U.S. wheat and flour exports nearly equaled that of cotton exports.[55] As agriculture became part of the international market, farmers became dependent not only on the vagaries of the weather but also on the fluctuations of currency in the larger economy.

Grover Cleveland is welcomed back on board the "Ship of State" in this 1893 cartoon. Having served as president from 1885 to 1889, he lost the 1888 election but regained the White House in the 1892 contest. Cleveland remains the only president to serve two nonconsecutive terms.

In the thirty years after the Civil War, prices for farm staples fell steadily. A debt that could have been paid by producing one thousand bushels of grain immediately after the war required three thousand bushels in 1895. The more farmers produced to meet their obligations, the more prices fell to exacerbate their problems. A solution to the problem required confronting a wide array of issues, including tight money, bankers who charged 20 percent interest for loans, monopolies among farm equipment producers, high tariffs, railroad price gouging, shipping inflation, warehouse monopolies, and land speculation. Throughout the farm belt, particularly in the West, tens of thousands of farmers developed an "intense class consciousness." [56]

All these issues received attention from a variety of third parties and independent organizations, but the two major parties usually were inattentive. The Granger Movement of the 1870s, for example, took hold in several farm states and elected new legislatures and high state officials. The Greenback Party attempted to merge a labor-farmer alliance with a doctrine of silver use for public debts. Later, the Farmers' Alliance politicized the same issues. In 1892 the Populist Party had won 8.5 percent of the vote on a platform calling for free coinage of silver.

Another site of growing reformist strength was the city. The dominance of machines of both parties in the cities established an electoral system based on patronage but stubbornly opposed to any coherent program for addressing urban ills such as poverty, poor housing, unsanitary conditions, transportation, education, and unfair workplace practices. Electoral fraud spurred mostly middle-class reformers to devise new electoral and city government machinery, while social problems incited some insurgent class politics.[57] The labor movement developed strength during this period.[58]

Other parts of the progressive agenda developed with a greater understanding of the nationalization of the economic and political systems. The wider sphere of economic activities created calls for regulation of corporations, railroads, and banks, as well as attention to health and environmental concerns and product safety.

Until the ascendance of William Jennings Bryan, the Democratic presidential nominee in 1896, 1900, and 1908, the reformers had been unable to capture a major party. Partly because political activism was based at the state and local level, neither national party had adopted the reformers' widely variegated program as its own. But the depression of 1888 caused the populist forces to pull together more than they had during previous economic downturns, probably because of the accumulated effects of inaction. The earlier panic of 1873 had created a sectional rather than a party split, with the Democrats eventually adopting a more conservative stance on the debate over whether the currency should be expanded to spur economic activity and redistribute social burdens.[59]

The Republican presidential candidates in the post–Civil War years steadfastly opposed the class-oriented proposals of the progressive movement, especially the loose-money demands. The only Democrat to win the presidency since the Civil War was Cleveland, a stubborn advocate of hard money and other conservative economic policies, in 1884 and 1892. President Cleveland vetoed dozens of private pension bills, only grudgingly accepted railroad regulation, and did not address domestic problems in any comprehensive way. Cleveland's public statements on the currency question were especially strong. He called the use of silver "a dangerous and reckless experiment" that was "unpatriotic."[60] On the question of labor, Cleveland was just as conservative: he called out federal troops to put down the Pullman strike of 1894 and regularly preached about the evils of disorder that the labor movement seemed to foster.

Despite the complexity of the agriculture issue, the most concerted populist action concentrated on the currency question. The drive to overturn the prevailing conventional economic thought by moving from a gold (tight) to a gold and silver (loose) money standard captured the imagination of the entire farm belt stretching from the Southeast to the prairie and silver-producing states of the West. The silver standard was a very simple answer to the problem of farm prices: "If money was scarce, the farmer reasoned, then the logical thing was to increase the money supply."[61]

Republican McKinley Triumphs: 1896 and 1900

Gold runs on banks, manipulation of the gold crisis by J. P. Morgan and other leading financiers, procorporation Supreme Court decisions, and antilabor actions all stirred up resentment in the South and West. The silver sentiment escalated. The Democratic convention in 1896 called for the issuance of silver and rejected a resolution praising President Cleveland.[62] The movement for a silver currency found an eloquent advocate in Bryan, a member of the House of Representatives from Nebraska, who defeated Richard P. Bland of Missouri for the 1896 Democratic presidential nomination on the strength of his fiery "Cross of Gold" speech.

The speech was one of the most emotional and successful in U.S. history. Bryan attacked eastern financiers and businessmen who exploited farmers. Using a theme to which his fall campaign would return, Bryan sought to expand the traditional Democratic conception of the independent working man to include farmers and factory workers.[63] In his speech's fortissimo, Bryan declared: "You shall not press down upon the brow of labor this crown of thorns, you shall not crucify mankind upon a cross of gold."[64]

In 1896 the Republicans nominated Ohio governor McKinley after brilliant maneuvering by his manager, Mark Hanna. Hanna's chief strengths were fund-raising and his mastery over state party organizations.

McKinley had little difficulty defeating Bryan. McKinley outspent the prairie populist by as much as ten-to-one, and he attracted the disaffected progold wing of the Democratic Party.[65] The Grand Old Party (or GOP as it was by then called) platform called for retention of the gold standard unless international negotiations could produce a bimetallic (silver and gold) currency system. The platform also called for restored tariff protections and an aggressive foreign policy in the Western Hemisphere.

Bryan's campaign was a political hurricane. He spent just $650,000, most of it donated by silver interests, compared with the millions McKinley spent. But Bryan traveled 18,000 miles and gave 600 speeches, and his campaign staffers put out an impressive quantity of literature. Several million copies of *Coin's Financial School,* a prosilver pamphlet, were distributed during the fall of 1896. Other silverites also maintained busy speaking schedules in the fall.

Bryan's appeal to industrial workers to join his coalition of independent businesspeople failed, largely because they depended for their livelihoods on the very eastern interests that Bryan attacked. McKinley won not only the East but also the small cities and towns in Bryan's southern and western belt of support. Bryan was unable to win rural areas in the East. McKinley won the popular vote 7.1 million (51.0 percent) to 6.5 million (46.7 percent) and the electoral vote 271–176.

The effect of the 1896 presidential election was lasting. James Sundquist wrote: "For 20 years the two-party system had been based on dead issues of the past. It had offered the voters no means of expressing a choice on the crucial issues of domestic policy around which the country had been polarizing. . . . Then suddenly, with the nomination of Bryan in 1896, the party system took on meaning once again." [66]

The new Republican coalition included residents of cities, where capital and labor were both reasonably content with the economic growth that the GOP tariff policy promoted; farmers in the East and Midwest, who had strong ties to the "party of Lincoln" and who had come to favor high tariffs; Catholic, German Lutheran, and other liturgical Christian denominations; and some border states. Sundquist noted: "It was the persistence of the Civil War attachments that made the realignment of the North so largely a one-way movement—pro-Republican." [67]

After 1896 the competitive party balance that had prevailed for years gave way to lopsided party strength according to region—Democrats in the South, Republicans in the North. Strong opposition parties disappeared in all regions of the country, vesting political power in the hands of those already part of the system.

As political scientist E. E. Schattschneider has observed:

> The 1896 party cleavage resulted from the tremendous reaction of conservatives in both major parties to the Populist movement. . . . [S]outhern conservatives reacted so strongly that they were willing to revive the tensions and animosities of the Civil War and the Reconstruction in order to set up a one-party sectional southern political monopoly in which nearly all Negroes and many poor whites were disenfranchised. One of the most important consequences of the creation of the Solid South was that it severed permanently the connection between the western and the southern wings of the Populist movement. [68]

Conservative Republicans won the White House in all but two (1912 and 1916) of the nine elections from 1896 to 1928. During this period the country experienced economic prosperity that blunted the possible activism of workers and the previous activism of farmers. With good harvests and rising commodity prices, the agrarian revolt fizzled. The development of new ore extraction methods and discovery of new gold deposits made calls for silver to expand the currency supply superfluous. The Spanish-American War in 1898, which McKinley reluctantly entered and the burgeoning mass media publicized, created a patriotic fervor.

McKinley's reelection in 1900 was even stronger than his 1896 election. He won 7.2 million popular votes (51.7 percent) to Bryan's 6.4 million (45.5 percent), and 292 electoral votes to Bryan's 155. McKinley swept to victory with all states except the South and the silver states of the West (Colorado, Montana, Idaho, and Nevada).

The Rise of Theodore Roosevelt: 1904

Because Vice President Garret A. Hobart died in office in 1899, the Republicans selected New York's progressive governor, Theodore Roosevelt, to share the ticket with McKinley in the 1900 election. Roosevelt, an independent-minded environmentalist and trust-buster, was promoted for vice president by New York GOP boss Thomas Platt, who wanted to rid the state of him and his progressive politics. Roosevelt was reluctant to take the job: "I am a comparatively young man yet and I like to work. . . . It would not entertain me to preside in the Senate." [69] He accepted, however, when a convention movement and McKinley prevailed on him.

When McKinley was assassinated in 1901 and Roosevelt became president, presidential politics came under the influence of a variant of the progressive movement. As Gabriel Kolko and other historians have demonstrated, Roosevelt's administration was friendly to many of the GOP's traditional conservative allies. But Roosevelt's rhetoric and his legacy of regulation and conservation had strong progressive or reformist elements. [70]

Roosevelt's leadership of the progressives was an example of generational politics. (As each generation assumes control over political and social structures, it stamps those institutions with its distinctive style and ethos.) The new president grew up in an era in which economic expansion was straining the nation's fabric, causing political figures to seek idealistic but pragmatic solutions to a wide variety of problems. The previous generation had grown up in a simpler age when "politics were devoid of substance, built around appeals to tradition and old loyalties and aimed at patronage." [71]

Roosevelt steered his party toward conservation of natural resources, enforcement of antitrust laws, promotion of the concerns of labor, and railroad regulation. The government's suit to dissolve the Northern Securities Company under the Sherman Anti-Trust Act and Roosevelt's intervention in the anthracite coal miners' strike, both in 1902, established the tenor for an activist presidency. TR (the first president identified by his initials) also used his office as a "bully pulpit" to promote his progressive ideology.

Roosevelt had no trouble winning the nomination for election as president in his own right in 1904. The Republican convention, arranged in advance at the White House, unanimously voted for Roosevelt and his platform of trust-busting, tariffs, labor relations, and activist foreign

The Democrats selected sober-visaged judge Alton B. Parker to run against the outgoing Theodore Roosevelt in the 1904 election. Roosevelt won by a wide margin.

Taft had impressive governmental experience. Before joining Roosevelt's cabinet, he had been a Cincinnati judge, U.S. solicitor general, federal circuit judge, head of the U.S. Commission on the Philippines, and the first civil governor of the Philippines.

Roosevelt's only problem in pushing Taft at the convention was avoiding a stampede in his own favor. Despite a highly disciplined convention, the galleries demonstrated wildly for Roosevelt. But Taft—a newcomer to electoral politics—easily won the nomination on the first ballot. He had 702 votes to the runner-up Philander C. Knox's 68. Rep. James S. Sherman of New York was selected as his running mate.

The Democrats nominated William Jennings Bryan for the third time. The electoral disaster that befell Judge Parker in 1904 was said to be evidence that the party needed an aggressive challenger to the Republicans rather than another conservative candidate. The Democrats were bereft of new talent, especially in competitive states in the East and Midwest, and turned to Bryan despite his disastrous campaign record and the warnings of former president Cleveland.

Taft campaigned on the Roosevelt record. Bryan called for government ownership of railroads and other liberal measures—such as a lower tariff, campaign finance reform, a graduated income tax, labor reforms, and greater enforcement of antitrust and other business regulations.

With Roosevelt and Taft promoting much of the progressive agenda, Bryan's message was no longer distinctive, and Taft won easily. He gathered 7.7 million popular votes (51.6 percent) to Bryan's 6.4 million (43.1 percent), and 321 electoral votes to Bryan's 162. The North, most of the West, and the border states went into the Republican column.

Wilson and the Divided Republicans: 1912 and 1916

Taft was not, by temperament, an ideal executive. His lifelong ambition had been to serve on the Supreme Court, and his disciplined legal mind and collegial nature eventually would enable him to become one of the high court's most able chief justices. (He was appointed to the Court by President Warren G. Harding in 1921.) But Taft foundered in the presidency. He carried out Roosevelt's program of business regulation and conservation, yet Roosevelt responded not with gratitude but with a series of nasty statements and plans for a campaign against Taft.

The tariff issue proved to be Taft's early trouble spot. Taft was committed to reducing tariffs, but he was less cau-

policy. Sen. Charles W. Fairbanks of Indiana was the GOP vice-presidential nominee.

To oppose the rambunctious Roosevelt, the Democrats selected a sober-visaged judge. Alton Parker, the chief justice of the New York State Court of Appeals, received the backing of the Democratic Party's conservative establishment when former president Cleveland turned down entreaties to make a fourth presidential run. Parker was opposed by William Randolph Hearst, a member of Congress and newspaper magnate. Bryan forced the party to adopt a liberal platform, as a balance to the conservative judge.

The Roosevelt victory was a landslide. He won 7.6 million votes (56.4 percent) to Parker's 5.1 million (37.6 percent) and carried all but the southern states. Roosevelt won 336 electoral votes to Parker's 140. Both houses of Congress were overwhelmingly Republican. President Roosevelt pledged not to seek another term because he had already served most of McKinley's second term. He occupied himself with his progressive agenda and groomed his secretary of war, William Howard Taft, as his successor.

Roosevelt Picks Taft: 1908

Roosevelt appeared to be genuinely dismayed by talk in 1907 of a possible third term, so he made public shows of his support for Taft. Because he also was able to line up state delegations for Taft, the nomination was never in doubt. Taft, through Roosevelt, was particularly strong among Republicans in the South. Attempts to restrict southern representation and pass a more liberal party platform were defeated.

tious than Roosevelt, who had fudged the divisive issue. As a result, Taft quickly became embroiled in a fight with Congress, which wanted to raise tariffs. The Senate remolded House legislation to push up various duties, and Taft publicly promoted the legislation after he managed to secure new corporate taxes and tariff reductions for raw materials. Overall, then, Taft proved ineffective and indecisive on the tariff issue and, as a consequence, began losing his party.

The Glavis-Ballinger affair further muddied the image of the administration. The scandal broke when the chief forester of the Interior Department, Gifford Pinchot, charged that Secretary Richard A. Ballinger had betrayed the cause of conservation and had even engaged in corrupt practices regarding minerals and water power. Pinchot also charged that Ballinger had wrongly fired another Interior official, Louis Glavis, for trying to expose the scandal. Pinchot took his complaints directly to Taft, but Taft sided with Ballinger and urged Pinchot to drop the matter. After an indignant Pinchot went public with the issue, Taft fired him, fueling suspicion of a cover-up at Interior. The incident was a major embarrassment to Taft because of the priority that conservation had received under Roosevelt and because of the inevitable complaints that Taft was betraying his mentor on the issue.[72]

Divisions within the Republican Party eventually created rival Taft and Roosevelt factions. Tariffs, Arizona's new state constitution (which included a provision for recall of the governor which Taft opposed), treaties, and antitrust issues split the former president and the sitting president. In many ways, the dispute was over personalities. Taft carried out Roosevelt's program but lacked his fervor and decisiveness. In a still conservative age, progressives felt they needed more aggressive leadership than the judicially tempered Taft would ever give them.

Roosevelt spent more than a year of Taft's term hunting in Africa, but he was an active speaker and campaigner when he returned to the United States. He gave a detailed accounting of his philosophy of government in a 1912 speech in Columbus, Ohio, calling for binding votes on public issues, recall of elected officials, and curbs on judicial power. When a dump-Taft movement decided in 1911 that Wisconsin senator Robert La Follette had no chance to defeat the president for the GOP nomination, party discontents turned to the energetic and still young (fifty-two years) Roosevelt.

Roosevelt made an all-out effort for the Republican nomination, entering twelve primaries and winning all but three. More specifically, Roosevelt won 278 delegates in states with primaries to Taft's 48 and La Follette's 36. In today's system, Roosevelt probably would have marched to a first-ballot nomination. (Today, more delegates are allocated by popular votes than by the party organizations, which then dominated the process.) Three crucial Republican states—

Pennsylvania, Illinois, and Ohio—went for Roosevelt. He clearly, then, had great popular appeal and vote-getting ability—perhaps more than ever.

But Taft won the nomination. The president controlled the party machinery, and most of the convention's delegates were sent by the state party machines. Roosevelt challenged the credentials of Taft delegates at the Chicago convention, and the nomination's outcome turned on battles over almost one-fourth of the delegates. The fight went to the floor of the convention, but Taft's smooth operation defeated Roosevelt. Roosevelt appeared at the convention to buoy his forces and cry foul.

After the defeat, Roosevelt urged his supporters to continue their fight, which motivated some bolting progressive delegates to organize a convention in August to mount a third-party effort. The bolters formed the Progressive Party. When Roosevelt remarked to a reporter during the GOP convention, "I'm feeling like a bull moose," his vigorous campaign had a symbol.

With the Republicans divided, the Democrats saw their first opportunity to win the presidency since Cleveland in 1892. As the 1912 Democratic convention in Baltimore neared, several national candidates and favorite sons were vying for the nomination. The front-runner was House Speaker James Beauchamp "Champ" Clark of Missouri, a party regular who had party organization support and years of experience to recommend him.

Gov. Woodrow Wilson of New Jersey—who held a doctorate in political science and who had moved into politics after a distinguished career as professor and president at Princeton University—was another strong candidate. Wilson's virtues were the opposite of Clark's. He did not have an extensive political record for opponents to attack, and he was supported enthusiastically because of his dynamic presence and reformist rhetoric. Although the New Jersey machine had brought Wilson into politics, he quickly asserted his independence and became something of a crusader.

As a newcomer to national politics, Wilson both refreshed and alienated Democratic crowds in speeches before the convention. He came out strongly for the "radical" platform of referendum, initiative, and recall, prompting a newspaper to report: "The boldness, the directness, the incisiveness, the fearlessness, and the force of the 'Virginian-Jerseyan's' words crashed at times through the throng like a series of thunderbolt jolts." [73] But Wilson's embrace of the progressive agenda and attacks on business alienated many southerners; even the delegates from Wilson's home state of Virginia opposed him at the convention.

Other Democratic candidates were the conservative representative Oscar Underwood of Alabama, author of a historic tariff act; another conservative, Gov. Judson Harmon of Ohio; and four favorite-son governors. Clark appeared to have won the nomination when a Tammany

Woodrow Wilson traveled widely in the 1912 election campaign. His dynamic presence and reformist rhetoric appealed to the crowds who came to hear.

bloc of delegates moved to support him after he won a tenth-ballot majority. The requirement for a two-thirds majority, however, gave other candidates time to maneuver. Wilson almost dropped out of the race, but Bryan's late transfer of his support from Clark to Wilson created a bandwagon effect for Wilson. On the forty-sixth ballot, Wilson accumulated the necessary two-thirds of delegates for the nomination. Gov. Thomas Marshall of Indiana, one of the favorite-son candidates, was picked to be the vice-presidential nominee because Underwood, Wilson's choice, would not accept it.

The Democratic platform was progressive. It called for tariff reduction, utility regulation, banking reforms, legislation to curb monopolies, a national income tax, direct election of senators, campaign finance reforms, and a national presidential primary. Roosevelt actually praised Wilson as "an able man" in the early fall and said he might not have started a third-party effort if he had known Wilson would be the Democrats' candidate. But Wilson and Roosevelt eventually criticized each other's approach to government, especially after Wilson expressed reservations about government activism.[74]

Wilson easily won the election, receiving 435 electoral votes to Roosevelt's 88 and Taft's 8. The Republican split obviously helped Wilson; if Roosevelt and Taft had combined their totals of 4.1 million votes (27.4 percent) and 3.5 million votes (23.2 percent), they would have topped Wilson's 6.3 million (41.8 percent). Yet even though Wilson was a minority president, there was a clear Democratic trend since the Democrats had taken over the House and replaced several Republican governors in the 1910 midterm elections. It was the worst showing ever for an incumbent president—third place with only two states.

Whatever the strength of Wilson's "mandate," he acted as though he had won by a landslide. His first term was one of the most productive in U.S. history. With the Democrats in control of Congress, and with a shrewd political adviser in Col. Edward M. House, Wilson adopted a reform agenda that had been percolating at various levels of government for years. He broke precedent by delivering his first State of the Union message to Congress in person. At the center of the message was a call for reductions in tariff rates. After a bitter fight that raged for a month, Wilson went public with a demand that members of Congress reveal their property holdings. The revelations, in response to public pressure, showed close links between their holdings and the kinds of tariff protections on the books. Congress soon was shamed into passing tariff cuts of 15 percent. More than 100 items were placed on a free-trade list for the first time.

Wilson also addressed other areas successfully: taxes (institution of a graduated income tax in 1913, which replaced reliance on tariffs and various excise and user taxes); banking regulation (the Glass-Owen Act of 1913, which created the Federal Reserve system); antitrust legislation (the Clayton Anti-Trust Act of 1914, creation of the Federal Trade Commission in 1914); labor relations (Section 6 of the Sherman Anti-Trust Act, which exempted unions from antitrust strictures); agriculture (the Smith-Lever Act of 1914, the Federal Farm Loan Act of 1916); conservation (creation of the National Park Service in 1916); and the judiciary (the appointment of Louis Brandeis to the Supreme Court).

Despite his strong leadership—highlighted by his stirring oratory—Wilson still faced the prospect in 1916 of a tough reelection. He had won the presidency in 1912 with only 41.8 percent of the popular vote, and the escalating war in Europe was be-ginning to disturb the American process of steady economic growth.

Public opinion on the Great War was volatile, largely because more than a third of the U.S. population was either foreign born or the offspring of foreign-born parents. Some 11 million Americans surveyed in the 1910 census were of direct German or Austrian descent, and another five million were from Ireland. Many other immigrants were Russian, Italian, Hungarian, British, and French. Wilson sought to diffuse feelings for the immigrants' native lands when he denounced "hyphenism"—the tendency of many citizens to identify themselves with appellations that linked their ethnic origins and American status—but politicians at lower levels tailored their campaigns to specific nationality voting blocs.[75]

Wilson and Vice President Marshall won renomination without any opposition. The most significant event of the Democratic convention was the passage of the platform, which indicated the party's main campaign theme. By calling for national universal suffrage, Wilson helped himself in the eleven western states where women already had won the vote. The platform praised "the splendid diplomatic victories of our great president, who has preserved the vital interests of our government and its citizens, and kept us out of war." The latter phrase would be repeated endlessly during the fall.[76]

The Republicans gave the presidential nomination to Supreme Court Justice Charles Evans Hughes. Hughes was silent in the months before the convention, but a number of party leaders lined up enough delegates for him to win a third-ballot nomination. Other potential candidates in 1916 included former president Roosevelt, former senator Elihu Root of New York, former vice president Fairbanks, and Senators John Weeks, Albert Cummins, and Lawrence Sherman. Fairbanks won the vice-presidential nomination.

Prosperity and reformism limited the campaign themes available to the Republicans. The GOP railed against Wilson's foreign policy as "shifty expedients" and "phrase-making" that put the United States in danger of entering the war. Hughes turned out to be a bad campaigner, but he bridged the gap between conservative and progressive Republicans that had cost the party the 1912 election. Wilson was occupied with Congress throughout the summer of 1916, but he emerged to give a series of speeches in the fall. Democratic strategists, meanwhile, conceived and executed a masterful strategy to return Wilson to the White House. The Democrats concentrated all their resources on "swing states" and ignored states they thought Wilson was sure to lose. Illinois, for example, was ignored since it was a certain Republican state. Bryan, Wilson's secretary of state, toured the West.

Wilson won one of the closest elections in history. California, an uncertain state, ensured Wilson's victory when, because of the urban vote, it went the president's way late in the campaign. The margin of victory was 3,420 votes in that state. The president defeated Hughes by a margin of 9.1 million (49.2 percent) to 8.5 million popular votes (46.1 percent). The electoral college gave Wilson 277 votes and Hughes 254.

Even though Wilson's campaign in 1916 was based on his determination to stay out of the Great War, the United States was in the war by 1917. Wilson's conduct of the war won him the status of war hero, but his diplomatic efforts after the war failed. Wilson was the architect of the Treaty of Versailles, which created a League of Nations to prevent future wars. But Wilson was unable to induce the Senate to approve the treaty, and he left office in 1921 a broken and dispirited man.

THE "RETURN TO NORMALCY" AND THE ROARING TWENTIES

After the tumult of Woodrow Wilson's domestic reforms, World War I, and the divisive battle over the Versailles treaty, the time was ripe for a period of conservatism and Republican government. Deep resentment had developed toward Wilson and the Democratic Party, and the Democrats themselves were divided over many issues, including economic regulation, Prohibition, and race relations.

Blessed with good luck, substantial financial backing, and a strong trend toward split-ticket voting, beginning in the 1920s the Republicans were able to resume their dominance over national politics with three successful presidential campaigns: Warren G. Harding in 1920, Calvin Coolidge in 1924, and Herbert C. Hoover in 1928.

The 1920s are usually pictured as a time of steady, unexciting politics. The conservatives dominated the federal government, and occupying the White House were men who spoke of "normalcy" and a noninterventionist brand of politics in both domestic and foreign affairs. One of the symbols of the age was President Coolidge's program of tax cuts, which reduced the rates on the wealthy. The wartime Revenue Act of 1918 had driven tax rates to the highest point in U.S. history—77 percent in the highest brackets. In 1921, 1923, and 1926, Secretary of the Treasury Andrew Mellon presented to Congress proposals to cut taxes, the most controversial being the reduction in the maximum surtax from 77 to 25 percent. Congress eventually cut the surtax to 40 percent in 1924 and 20 percent in 1926.[77]

But the sober men who filled the presidency in the twenties met challenges from progressives of both parties in Congress and in the state governments. On a wide range of issues—including relief of the poor, subsidies for the depressed farm sector, regulation of utilities, immigration, race relations, states' rights, tax cuts, and Prohibition—the conservative presidents encountered strong challenges. They frequently responded by vetoing legislation, but such an expedient would not prevent the pressures for a more activist government from developing.

Harding and "Normalcy": 1920

Harding, a product of the GOP machine of Ohio, emerged from a crowded and largely unknown pack to win the Republican nomination in 1920 at a convention dominated by economic interests such as oil, railroads, and steel. The early candidates were Gen. Leonard Wood, an old Roosevelt ally; Gov. Frank Lowden of Illinois, who married into the Pullman family and therefore had ample financing for a

Democratic presidential candidate James M. Cox of Ohio, left, and vice-presidential candidate Franklin D. Roosevelt (one year before he was stricken with polio) campaign in the 1920 election. They lost to Republican presidential candidate Warren G. Harding and his running mate, Gov. Calvin Coolidge of Massachusetts.

York, the assistant secretary of the navy, was rapidly selected to be Cox's running mate.

The image of Wilson hung over the convention and would hang over the fall campaign. The Democratic platform praised Wilson's conduct of the war and his domestic reform program. But the results in the November election indicated deep unease over the Democratic administration.

Harding amassed 16.1 million popular votes (60.3 percent) to Cox's 9.1 million (34.2 percent), and 404 electoral votes to Cox's 127. Harding carried the North and West including Oklahoma and all of the southern and border states except Tennessee and Kentucky.

Harding's landslide victory was termed "election by disgust" by political analysts. The wartime sacrifices demanded under Wilson were widely perceived as the cause of Harding's victory rather than a desire for the ideology or policy proposals that Harding was offering. The New York Post editorialized: "We are in the backwash from the mighty spiritual and physical effort to which America girded herself when she won the war for the Allies. . . . The war has not been repudiated, though the administration that fought it has been overwhelmed. We are now in the chill that comes with the doctor's bills." [78]

The electorate's ability to shift allegiances from the Republicans to the Democrats and back again—from one period to the next, and from one level of government to the next—suggested a dissolution of partisan alignments. The addition of women to the electorate after passage of the Nineteenth Amendment in 1920 and the increasing independence among all voters induced uncertainty. National exhaustion from the war and the lack of sharp ideological differences between the candidates produced apathy. The electorate's instability was suggested by the divisions within both parties on high-profile issues such as Prohibition, the League of Nations, agricultural policies, and other social and economic matters—among them, technical assistance and trust busting. The appearance of numerous "blocs" in both parties represented "little if anything more than a transitory alignment upon a particular vote or issue." [79]

The shifts in control of congressional and state offices also indicated electoral instability. The Democrats had had comfortable control of Congress under Wilson, but in 1920 the Republicans gained a majority of 301 to 131 in the House

campaign; and Sen. Hiram Johnson of California, whose progressive and isolationist stances put him in good stead with voters in many states. A dozen favorite sons hoped that a deadlocked convention might bring the nomination their way. All of the candidates were on hand in Chicago to maneuver for the nomination.

While Wood, Johnson, and Lowden performed reasonably well in the primaries, Harding won only his home state of Ohio and did not arouse much popular enthusiasm. But under the direction of a shrewd campaign manager, Harry Daugherty, Harding gained the support of the party's bosses and won the nomination on the tenth ballot after a brief interview with them in the "smoke-filled room" that was synonymous with boss control. Governor Coolidge of Massachusetts, a favorite-son contender for president, became Harding's vice-presidential candidate.

The Democrats selected Gov. James Cox, also from Ohio, after lengthy platform battles and balloting for the nomination. Early ballots put former Treasury secretary William G. McAdoo and Attorney General Mitchell Palmer in the lead, but Cox gained steadily and had the nomination by the forty-fourth roll call. Franklin D. Roosevelt of New and 59 to 37 in the Senate. Impressive liberal gains in congressional and state elections in the midterm election of 1922 appeared to be a slap at the Harding administration. The high turnover of votes also indicated unstable party affiliations: the 14.2 percentage point increase in the Republican vote between the 1916 and 1920 presidential elections was the largest since the Civil War, another time of turmoil.[80]

President Harding died on August 2, 1923, of a heart attack, just as revelations of kickbacks and favoritism in the administration began to surface and several members of the administration quit and two committed suicide. The investigation into the so-called Teapot Dome scandal—so named after the site of naval oil reserves that were transferred to private hands in exchange for bribes—would last five years. The Democrats hoped to make the scandal a major issue in the 1924 election, but Democratic complicity in the wrongdoing and the personal integrity of Harding's successor, Calvin Coolidge, defused the issue.

Coolidge Cleans Up: 1924

President Coolidge fired Attorney General Harry M. Daugherty and other members of Harding's clique and projected an image of puritan cleanliness. Coolidge—a taciturn man who had slowly climbed the political ladder in Massachusetts from city council member to city solicitor, mayor, state legislator, lieutenant governor, and governor before he became vice president—expounded a deeply individualistic Yankee philosophy that helped to separate him from the corrupt men in the Harding White House.

Except for appointing as attorney general Harlan Fiske Stone, former dean of the Columbia University School of Law, Coolidge allowed others to finish cleaning up the mess left behind by Harding. The new president was concerned about unnecessarily alienating himself from party leaders.

By the time Coolidge sought the presidency on his own in 1924, the economy had rebounded. One of the most conservative presidents ever, Coolidge's platform called for additional tax cuts but said nothing substantive about increasingly salient agriculture and labor issues. Coolidge also pushed an isolationist foreign policy plank. He won the nomination on the first ballot.

While the Republicans were able to "Keep Cool with Coolidge," the Democrats spent sixteen days in a seemingly endless attempt to pick a nominee in New York's sweltering Madison Square Garden. A fight developed because the party was badly split between its northeastern urban bloc and its more conservative southern and western rural bloc. New York governor Alfred E. Smith and former Treasury secretary William McAdoo of California were the key combatants at the convention until the delegates were freed from the instructions of party bosses on the one-hundredth ballot.

Suspicions between the two regional blocs were intense. A platform plank denouncing the Ku Klux Klan created the most controversy. Northerners wanted an explicit repudiation of the society that preached hatred of blacks, Catholics, and Jews; in the end, southerners would settle only for a vaguely worded rebuke. (The Klan had infiltrated the party in many rural areas.) Another divisive issue was Prohibition, with northerners attacking the initiative and southerners supporting it. These sectional splits would cripple the Democrats in the 1924 and 1928 elections.

After the delegates were freed from instructions, a stampede developed for John W. Davis of West Virginia, a lawyer with Wall Street connections. The ticket was balanced with the vice-presidential selection of Charles W. Bryan of Nebraska, the younger brother of three-time presidential candidate William Jennings Bryan.

The Progressive candidacy of Robert La Follette complicated the calculations of voters, particularly those on the liberal end of the political spectrum. Because the Democrats had a nearly impenetrable hold on the South, La Follette was not given a reasonable chance of winning. But the conservatism of both Coolidge and Davis meant that La Follette was the only liberal in the race. Still, many liberals voted for Davis or even Coolidge because of the fear of an inconclusive election that would have to be resolved in the House of Representatives.

Coolidge won the election easily, with the Democrats poll-ing their smallest percentage ever. Coolidge won 54.1 percent of the vote, Davis won 28.8 percent, and La Follette won 16.6 percent. Coolidge attracted 15.7 million popular votes and 382 electoral votes; Davis, 8.4 million and 136; and La Follette, 4.8 million and 13.

"Keep Cool with Coolidge" was the Republican incumbent's 1924 campaign slogan, used on posters, banners, buttons, and decorative stamps such as this one from Wisconsin.

On August 2, 1927, when Coolidge announced his decision not to seek reelection by passing out a brief note to reporters and then refusing further comment, the Republicans began jockeying for the nomination for the 1928 election.

The Hoover Succession: 1928

Secretary of Commerce Hoover was the obvious choice to replace Coolidge at the head of the GOP ticket. A native of Iowa who learned mining engineering at Stanford University, Hoover was immensely popular with most of the party. Hoover's administration of Belgian relief and food distribution programs during World War I had earned him the status of statesman and humanitarian.

Hoover began working for the nomination soon after Coolidge dropped out, spending $400,000 in the nominating phase of the election. He won the nomination on the first ballot over Governors Frank Lowden of Illinois and Charles Curtis of Kansas. Curtis was named Hoover's running mate.

Hoover was religious in his zeal for what he called "the American system" of free enterprise and individualism. He did not see any inconsistency in having the government vigorously support businesses with tax breaks, tariffs, public provision of infrastructures, and police protection, while at the same time denying relief to people in need. Hoover appeared to be less rigid than Coolidge, however. He proposed creation of a special farm board and said he would consider legislation to protect labor unions from abuses in the use of court injunctions.

Al Smith, the Tammany-schooled governor of New York, was the Democratic nominee. Smith had the support of all the party's northern states, and he won a first-ballot nomination. Sen. Joseph T. Robinson of Arkansas was the vice-presidential candidate.

Smith's candidacy polarized the electorate, particularly the South. He was the first Catholic to be nominated for president by a major party, and he endured religious slurs throughout the fall. Moreover, he favored repeal of Prohibition, still a divisive issue, and he was an urbanite, a problem for a nation that had nurtured a rural ideal since Thomas Jefferson. Because he also was a machine politician, he presented a problem for anyone outside (and many people inside) the nation's great cities. He also was a strong opponent of the Klan, which put him in trouble in the South. Finally, he was an unabashed liberal who proposed public works, farm relief programs, stronger protection of workers, and regulation of banking and industry.

During the fall campaign, Hoover acted like the incumbent and Smith barnstormed the country, trying in vain to pick up support in the South and West. The 1928 campaign was the first with extensive radio coverage, and Hoover generally fared better than Smith on the airwaves. Hoover, the small-town boy who made good, represented fulfillment of the American Dream; Smith, the inner-city boy who made good, also embodied that ideal, but he had too many ethnic traits for much of the nation to realize it.

The November election produced another Republican landslide. Hoover carried forty states with 21.4 million popular votes (58.2 percent) and 444 electoral votes, while Smith carried only eight states with 15.0 million popular votes (40.8 percent) and 87 electoral votes. As disastrous as the election appeared to be for the Democrats, it put them in position to build a wide-ranging coalition in future years.

Smith carried only six southern states, but the defection of the others was temporary. More important to the Democrats' long-range fortunes was the movement of cities into the Democratic column, where they would stay for the rest of the century. Immigrants in cities were expanding

In 1932 World War I veterans, seeking early receipt of their service bonuses, staged a protest by setting up camps near the Capitol. President Herbert C. Hoover ordered federal troops, headed by Gen. Douglas MacArthur, to disperse the veterans with tear gas.

their vision from local politics to the national stage for the first time. In all, Smith diverted 122 northern counties from the GOP to the Democratic Party. Catholics, whose turnout previously had been low, turned out in record numbers. Smith also seemed to pick up some of the Progressive farm vote that La Follette had tapped before; in Wisconsin, for example, the Democratic vote jumped from 68,000 to 450,000 from 1924 to 1928. Finally, Smith's candidacy put the Democrats solidly in the "wet" column, just as the national temper began to resent Prohibition.

President Hoover impressed political observers with his managerial skills and "coordinating mind." With passage of the Agricultural Marketing Act in June 1929, the administration appeared to address the most pressing economic problem for the business-minded president. He met some legislative setbacks, but, overall, the Great Engineer appeared to be in good political condition as the nation looked back over his record when Congress began its recess in the summer of 1929.

The national economic and social fiesta that had begun at the close of World War I came to an abrupt end on October 29, 1929. After climbing to dizzying new heights for months, the stock market crashed. First described by economists and politicians as a temporary interruption of the good times, the crash quickly led to a wave of business and bank failures, mortgage foreclosures, wage cuts, layoffs, and a crisis of political leadership. By the end of Hoover's term in 1933, more than 12 million workers had lost their jobs; the unemployment rate was approximately 25 percent. An October 1931 advertisement for 6,000 jobs in the Soviet Union brought 100,000 American applications.[81]

President Hoover, who had celebrated his inauguration with a prediction that poverty and hunger were near an end, did not know how to cope with the crisis. In a special session that Hoover called, Congress created the Federal Farm Board to coordinate marketing of agricultural products, but Hoover steadfastly opposed further moves, especially subsidies. In 1930 Hoover signed the Smoot-Hawley Tariff Act to protect manufacturers, but, true to the predictions of economists and bankers, the tariff only aggravated economic conditions by hurting foreign trade.

Hoover later approved agricultural relief and public works programs and established the Reconstruction Finance Corporation. The president refused to approve direct relief to the unemployed and businesses, but he did approve some loans and aid to specific sectors of the economy.

Despite his earnest and tireless efforts, Hoover became a figure of widespread enmity. The low point of his distinguished career came when World War I veterans petitioned for early receipt of their service bonuses, which, by contract, were not to be paid until 1945. They set up camp in Washington, singing old war songs and carrying placards that bore their pleas. The "Bonus Army" numbered 20,000 at its height. When Hoover feared a protracted protest, he ordered federal troops to take over buildings where some veterans were camping. In two skirmishes, two veterans were killed. The president then sent in Gen. Douglas MacArthur with tanks, infantry, and cavalry soldiers. (MacArthur's junior officers included Dwight D. Eisenhower and George Patton.) After successfully removing the veterans, the military forces overran nearby veterans' camps in a rain of fire and tear gas. Thousands of veterans and their families fled the burning district.

The administration's tough stance against a defeated, ragtag band of former war heroes shocked and embittered the nation. The barricaded White House and administration statements about "insurrectionists" symbolized a dangerous gulf between the government and the people.

Partly because of the economic crisis he did not create, but also because of his dour and unimaginative demeanor, Hoover probably never had a chance to win reelection. The 1930 midterm elections indicated a loss of confidence in the administration. The House went Democratic, 219 to 214, and the Senate came within a seat of going Democratic as well.

Those election results did not convey the bitterness and despair that the Depression would aggravate before the next presidential campaign. Hoover was mercilessly ridiculed in newspapers and in Democratic speeches. The Democratic Party coordinated a comprehensive anti-Hoover campaign that made the president politically impotent.

"The New Deal" Election: 1932

Franklin D. Roosevelt, fifth cousin to Theodore Roosevelt, was the perfect candidate to oppose Hoover. The New York governor had been an activist in state politics, first opposing the state's Tammany machine and then pioneering many relief and reconstruction programs that Hoover refused to expand to the national scale. Roosevelt had been the party's vice-presidential candidate twelve years earlier, and he had served in the federal government as assistant secretary of the navy.

Perhaps more important than any of his political accomplishments were FDR's image of strength and optimism and his deft handling of hot issues and disparate members of the potential Democratic coalition. Although he was a polio victim, Roosevelt often smiled—a devastating contrast to Hoover. (Gutzon Borglum, the sculptor, wrote: "If you put a rose in Hoover's hand, it would wilt."[82]) Roosevelt was able to campaign for the presidency without putting forth a comprehensive program: the simple promise of a change in leadership was enough.

Some observers found the man from Hyde Park wanting. Journalist Walter Lippmann, for example, complained that Roosevelt was "a pleasant man who, without any important qualifications for the office, would like very much to be president."[83] But those detractors and a large field of

Franklin D. Roosevelt campaigns by car in West Virginia, October 19, 1932.

Democratic candidates were not able to keep Roosevelt from his "rendezvous with destiny." [84]

The Democratic field included the 1928 Democratic standard-bearer, Smith; John Nance Garner, the Speaker of the House; Gov. Albert Ritchie of Maryland; Gov. George White of Ohio; Gov. Harry Byrd of Virginia; and former senator James Reed of Missouri. Most considered Smith more of a "stalking horse" for the anti-FDR forces than a serious candidate on his own. Garner had impressive backing from the newspaper magnate William Randolph Hearst and former Democratic candidate William McAdoo.

The many favorite sons in the race threatened to deadlock the convention and deny the nomination to the frontrunner, as they had done so often in the past. Roosevelt had difficulty with his region of the country because of his opposition to the Tammany machine in New York. Acquiring the required two-thirds vote of delegates for the nomination was difficult for Roosevelt or any other candidate, but FDR eventually won on the fourth ballot when he promised the vice-presidential slot to Garner.

In U.S. political history, Franklin Roosevelt was the first candidate to appear before the convention that nominated him. In an acceptance speech to the conventioneers who had staged wild rallies in his support, Roosevelt made passing reference to the "new deal" that his administration would offer Americans. That phrase, picked up in a newspaper cartoon the next day, came to symbolize the renewal for which Americans yearned as riots and radicalism seemed to threaten the nation's spirit and the legitimacy of its institutions.

Roosevelt conducted an active fall campaign, traveling 23,000 miles in forty-one states to quell suspicions that his physical handicaps would deter him from performing his job. Besides barnstorming the nation, Roosevelt took to the radio airwaves—he was the first sophisticated electronic media candidate—where he conveyed a sense of warmth and confidence. He also showed an intellectual bent and an open mind when he called on academics and professionals—the famed "brain trust"—for their expert advice on the issues.

Roosevelt won 22.8 million votes (57.4 percent) to Hoover's 15.8 million (39.6 percent). Forty-two of the forty-eight states and 472 of the 531 electoral votes went for Roosevelt. The election was a landslide and a realignment of the major forces in U.S. politics.

THE NEW DEAL COALITION

The profound effect of Franklin D. Roosevelt's victory on U.S. politics can hardly be overstated. The New Deal coalition that Roosevelt assembled shaped the political discourse and electoral competition of the United States until the late 1960s. In many respects, that coalition is a central element of politics today.

The new Democratic coalition brought together a disparate group of interests: southerners, African Americans, immigrants, farmers, capital-intensive producers, international businessmen, financiers, urbanites, trade unions, intellectuals, Catholics, and Jews. Rexford Tugwell called it "the most miscellaneous coalition in history." [85] These blocs were not always in perfect harmony—for example, the Democrats juggled the demands of blacks and white southerners with great difficulty—but they were solid building blocks for national political dominance.

The dominance was impressive. Between 1932 and 1964, the Democrats won seven of nine presidential elections. The only successful Republican, Dwight D. Eisenhower, could just as easily have run as a Democrat. Party leaders in fact asked him to run as a Democrat in 1948 and 1952, and his name was entered in some Democratic primaries in 1952.

The strength of Roosevelt's rule was attributable partly to the president's personality. He could be soothing. When he gave his first "fireside chat" about the banking crisis, the nation responded with cooperation; the raids and violence at banks ended in a matter of weeks. More important than his soothing nature was his ability to experiment and shift gears. Professor James David Barber described Roosevelt's many public postures:

> Founder of the New Deal, modern American democracy's closest approximation to a common political philosophy, Roosevelt came on the scene as the least philosophical of men—"a chameleon in plaid," Hoover called him. Firm fighter of yet another Great War, Roosevelt appeared to H. L. Mencken in 1932 as "far too feeble and wishy-washy a fellow to make a really effective fight." Architect of world organization, he introduced himself as totally concerned with America's domestic drama. His name is inseparable from his generation's great social revolution; in 1932, nearly all the heavy thinkers scoffed at him as just another placebo politician—a "pill to cure an earthquake," said Professor [Harold] Laski.[86]

More important than personality was what Roosevelt had to offer the many groups in his coalition. As historian Richard Hofstadter has noted, the New Deal was "a series of improvisations, many adopted very suddenly, many contradictory." [87] The Roosevelt credo was: "Save the people and the nation, and if we have to change our minds twice a day to accomplish that end, we should do it." [88]

Until the vast expenditures of World War II, there was not enough pump-priming to end the Depression, but Roosevelt's initiatives touched almost everyone affected by the slump.[89] For the jobless, there were unemployment insurance and public works programs such as the Works Progress Administration and the Civilian Conservation Corps. For the poor, there were categorical aid programs. For westerners, there were conservation measures. For the banks, there was the famous holiday that stopped runs on holdings, and there were currency and securities reforms. For farmers, there were incentives and price supports and cooperatives.

For the aged, there was Social Security. For southeasterners, there was the Tennessee Valley Authority. For southern whites, there was a hands-off policy on race matters. For blacks, there were sympathy and jobs programs. For those living in rural areas, there was electrification. For families, there were home loans. For the weary worker eager for a few rounds at the local tavern, there was the repeal of Prohibition. For laborers, there was acknowledgment of the right to negotiate for their share of the national wealth. For business, there were the Federal Emergency Relief Act and the National Industrial Recovery Act, as well as diplomatic negotiation to reduce trade barriers.

The remarkably divergent interests in the coalition were underscored by the politics of race. Blacks moved en masse to the Democratic Party from their traditional position in the "Party of Lincoln," partly because of Hoover's failure but also because of the inclusive rhetoric of the New Deal. Yet Roosevelt was too concerned about his bloc of southern support to accept even antilynching legislation.

Scholars have argued that the New Deal coalition did not indicate a wholesale shift in existing political loyalties, but rather that new groups such as urbanites and blacks had joined an already stable alliance to tip the competitive balance of U.S. parties. The political discourse in the United States changed not because all or even most groups changed their behavior but because new groups and issues became involved.[90]

The core of Roosevelt's winning coalition was easy to describe: "Southern white Protestants, Catholics, and non-Southern white Protestants of the lowest socioeconomic stratum together accounted for roughly three-fourths of all Americans of voting age in 1940 who thought of themselves as Democrats. By way of contrast, these three groups provided only about 40 percent of the smaller cadre of Republican identifiers." [91] Within the Democratic coalition, there were both new and old elements.

Although the Democratic Party encompassed new constituencies and addressed new issues, it retained many of its traditional supporters. The segregated "Jim Crow" South had consistently been in the Democratic column; in 1896, for example, the South's percentage support for Democrat William Jennings Bryan exceeded that of the rest of the nation by 15.3 points. Even in 1928, when Al Smith's Catholicism reduced support for the Democrats to under 50 percent for the first time, the Deep South supported the Democrats more than the border South did.[92] To the South, the Democrats were reliably the party of white supremacy and agricultural interests, while Republicans favored the industrial interests of the North.

Outside the South, the Democratic Party was the party of immigrants and Catholics. Since Andrew Jackson's day, the overwhelmingly Democratic voting patterns of Catholics had contrasted with the split vote of Protestants in the

United States. The Catholic-Protestant divisions represented "not so much religious as more general ethnocultural traditions." [93] The Democratic hold on the Catholic vote was reinforced by the heavy immigration into northern cities in the last half of the nineteenth century. While the anti-Catholic Ku Klux Klan received Democratic backing in the South, it received Republican backing in the North, pushing northern Catholics decisively into the Democratic Party.

A steady base in the Democratic Party consisted of laborers and the poor. From the first party machines in the early nineteenth century to Bryan's campaign on behalf of the depressed farm belt in 1896 to Woodrow Wilson's acceptance of labor bargaining in 1914, the Democrats had shown sympathy for the less-privileged classes. Such sympathies often were constricted by prejudice or conservatism, but the Democrats offered more hope of representation than the business-oriented Republicans. Roosevelt solidified the support of the poor and laboring classes.[94] Sundquist has written: "The party system undoubtedly reflected some degree of class before the realignment, but there can be little doubt that it was accentuated by the event. It was in the New Deal era that tight bonds were formed between organized labor and the Democratic Party, that ties equally close if less formal and overt were formed between business and the GOP, and that politics for the first time since 1896 sharply accented class is-sues." [95] Roosevelt consistently received the support of more than two-thirds of the voters of low socioeconomic status.[96]

New converts to the Democratic Party included blacks and Jews. The inclusion of blacks into the New Deal coalition underscored a "multiplier effect" at work within thriving interest group politics. The Republicans received the black vote in the seventeen elections from Reconstruction to 1932. That year, Roosevelt received 35 percent of the black vote, but his black support was as low as 23 percent in Chicago and 29 percent in Cincinnati.[97] Even though Roosevelt did little to promote black interests in the South, where most blacks lived but could not vote, the black vote for him increased to 70 percent in 1936 and 1940. Migration of blacks to the North and the spillover effects of Roosevelt's many domestic programs brought blacks to the Democratic Party.

Jews, who had voted Republican since their numbers swelled during immigration around the turn of the century, turned to the Democrats as they became the more liberal party. Roosevelt got 85 percent of the Jewish vote in 1936 and 84 percent in 1940. New Deal assistance programs and Roosevelt's efforts to fight Nazism appealed to Jews, but perhaps more important was "the historic pattern of discrimination which forced or disposed Jews to oppose conservative parties." [98] The class division that split other social groups was absent in the Jewish population.

In many ways, the whole of the New Deal was greater than the sum of its parts. Political scientist Samuel Beer has argued that two long-competing visions of U.S. politics—the national idea and the democratic idea—at last came together during Roosevelt's administration. With the New Deal, the Democratic Party was able to combine its traditional concern for local, individualistic interests with a national vision. By bringing "locked-out" groups into the system, the Democrats enhanced both nation building and individual freedoms. The parts, put together, created a stronger whole. Beer quotes the French sociologist Emile Durkheim: "The image of the one who completes us becomes inseparable from ours. . . . It thus becomes an integral and permanent part of our conscience. . . ." [99]

The political genius of "interest-group liberalism" [100] was not just that it offered something to everyone, but that it created a new age of consumerism in which everyone's interest was in economic growth rather than structural change. The general good was defined as growth. The potentially divisive competition over restricted and unequally distributed resources was avoided with a general acceptance of growth as the common goal. When there was growth, everyone could get a little more. That public philosophy became a permanent part of American political discourse.

Roosevelt's First Reelection: 1936

Roosevelt's coalition and leadership were so strong that he became the only president to win more than two elections. He won four elections and served a little more than twelve years in the White House before dying in office at the start of his fourth term.

Roosevelt's four electoral triumphs caused Republicans to fume about his "imperial" presidency; all they could do in response to FDR was to promote a constitutional amendment to limit presidents to two terms. But more important than this perception was the way Roosevelt shaped the U.S. political agenda. For many people of the time, it was difficult to imagine the United States under any other leader.

It is possible that Roosevelt could have forged an even stronger liberal coalition than he did. But Roosevelt was a pragmatist above all else and alternately angered and wooed such groups as business, labor, farmers, and the military. For example, Roosevelt kept his distance from Upton Sinclair's populist campaign for governor of California in 1934. Because he threatened business interests, Sinclair was the target of a sustained personal attack by business and other conservative forces in the state in what one authority has called the first media campaign in American history. Sinclair's losing effort, the historian Greg Mitchell argued, undermined the power of reformers nationally.[101]

Roosevelt's three successful reelection drives evoked a changing response from Republicans. Roosevelt's first reelection opponent, in 1936, was Gov. Alfred M. Landon of Kansas, who strongly criticized every aspect of the New Deal. After 1936, Republican candidates did not criticize federal intervention in economic and social affairs but rather the speed and the skill of Democratic intervention. In the third election the Republicans argued that Roosevelt was a "warmonger" because he tilted toward Great Britain in World War II. The GOP also argued in the third and fourth elections that Roosevelt threatened to become a "dictator" by exceeding the traditional two-term limit.

Landon was the early favorite for the Republican nomination in 1936. Sen. Charles McNary of Oregon, Sen. Arthur Vandenberg of Michigan, and *Chicago Daily News* publisher Frank Knox provided weak opposition. A Republican bolter for Theodore Roosevelt's "Bull Moose" candidacy in 1912, Landon was consistently to the left of the GOP. Historian James MacGregor Burns observed: "Landon had just the qualities of common sense, homely competence, cautious liberalism and rocklike 'soundness' that the Republicans hoped would appeal to a people tiring, it was hoped, of the antics and heroics in the White House." [102]

In 1936 the Republicans could not have stated their opposition to the popular New Deal in any stronger terms. The platform read: "America is in peril. The welfare of American men and women and the future of our youth are at stake. We dedicate ourselves to the preservation of their political liberty, their individual opportunity, and their character as free citizens, which today for the first time are threatened by government itself." [103]

The Republicans called for ending a wide range of government regulations, returning relief to state and local governments, replacing Social Security, balancing the budget, and changing tariff and currency policies. Landon's only innovation was to call for a constitutional amendment allowing the states to regulate the labor of women and children; the Supreme Court had struck down a New York minimum wage law in 1935. After Landon won the nomination on the first ballot, he selected Knox as his running mate.

The only time the two presidential candidates met was at a meeting Roosevelt called with state governors in Des Moines to discuss farm relief and a recent drought. FDR hoped to put Landon on the spot about farm relief. But Landon turned out to be the aggressor, demanding that FDR address the dire situation of 100,000 starving farmers in Oklahoma. FDR responded that he had some federal agencies working on programs "just as fast as the Lord will let them." When Landon said that such an answer was small consolation, Roosevelt retorted: "What more can you say to the hungry farmer, governor? The machinery will be put in gear just as fast as the Lord will let you?" [104]

Landon's campaign possessed a lavish war chest of $9 million, benefited from the defections of Democratic stalwarts such as John Davis and Al Smith (the party's presidential nominees in 1924 and 1928) and well-coordinated campaign work by business lobbies, and engaged in smear campaigns that portrayed Social Security as a simple "pay reduc-

tion" measure and Roosevelt as physically and mentally ill. Landon also argued that New Deal spending was just another form of spoils politics, a charge Roosevelt addressed by folding postmasters into the civil service system.

The only important innovation at the Democratic convention was the repeal of the party's requirement that a candidate receive two-thirds of the delegates to win the nomination. After some arm twisting, southern delegates backed the change, but the governor of Texas wondered aloud if the change was designed for a third Roosevelt run in 1940. Roosevelt was renominated without opposition. He asked Garner to run with him a second time.

In response to Landon's GOP nomination and agitation by leaders of the left and right—including Huey Long of Louisiana, Father Charles E. Coughlin of Detroit, Dr. Francis Townsend of California (who espoused a federal pension plan for senior citizens), and the Socialist Norman Thomas of New York—President Roosevelt in his acceptance speech launched a rhetorical war against "economic royalists" who opposed his programs. He dropped the idea of a "unity" campaign in favor of a partisan ideological attack intended to gain a mandate for a variety of stalled programs rather than a personal vote of confidence.[105]

At first, Roosevelt had planned a low-key campaign of "conciliation," but when Landon got the GOP nomination he decided to wage the more aggressive campaign. After all, Landon had run an impressive nominating campaign and was thought to appeal to American pinings for governmental stability. In the early stages of the fall campaign, Roosevelt pretended not to be a partisan politician. He crisscrossed the country making "official" inspections of drought states and public works programs and delivering speeches on electrical power, conservation, and social welfare programs, among other topics. Roosevelt assigned Postmaster General James Farley the task of addressing party rifts and Republican charges of spoils.

At the end of September, Roosevelt assumed the role of partisan leader. The president answered Republican charges point by point, then lashed out at the Republicans in biting, sarcastic terms. As the campaign progressed and Roosevelt sensed a strong response from the large crowds to his attacks, the attacks became stronger. At the close of the campaign, he said:

> We have not come this far without a struggle and I assure you that we cannot go further without a struggle. For twelve years, our nation was afflicted with a hear-nothing, see-nothing, do-nothing government. The nation looked to the government but the government looked away. Nine mocking years with the golden calf and three long years of the scourge! Nine crazy years at the ticker and three long years at the breadlines! Nine mad years of mirage and three long years of despair! And, my friends, powerful influences strive today to restore that kind of government with its doctrine that that government is best which is most indif-

President Franklin D. Roosevelt's Republican opponents during his three successful reelection campaigns were, from left: Gov. Alfred M. Landon of Kansas in 1936; former Democrat and business executive Wendell L. Willkie in 1940; and Gov. Thomas E. Dewey of New York in 1944. Dewey ran again and lost against President Truman in 1948.

ferent to mankind. . . . Never before in all of our history have these forces been so united against one candidate as they stand today. They are unanimous in their hate for me—and I welcome their hatred.[106]

Especially to sophisticated campaign technicians of the modern age, a poll that predicted a big Landon victory provides some amusement. The *Literary Digest,* which had predicted past elections with accuracy, conducted a postcard poll of its readers that pointed toward a Landon landslide. But the heavy middle- and upper-class bias of the magazine's readership meant that the views of the voters on the lower rungs of the economic ladder were left out of the sample. To this day, the poll is cited as the prime example of bad survey group selection.

The failure of the *Literary Digest*'s survey pointed to the most salient aspect of the election results: the heavy class divisions among the voters. Polls showed that class divisions widened starting around the midpoint of Roosevelt's first term. The broad support Roosevelt had enjoyed because of a common economic disaster had hardened along class lines by the time of the 1936 election.

In the 1936 election, Roosevelt won 27.7 million popular votes (60.8 percent) to Landon's 16.7 million (36.5 percent). Roosevelt carried all but two of the forty-eight states, and he took 523 of the 531 electoral votes. In addition, the Senate's Democratic majority increased to 75 of 96 seats, and the House majority increased to 333 of 435 seats. Roosevelt even ran ahead of candidates—such as gubernatorial candidate Herbert Lehman of New York—who had been recruited to boost his vote totals in various states. In fact, the Democratic victory was almost too overwhelming, Roosevelt suggested, because it would encourage Democrats to fight among themselves rather than with Republicans.

Roosevelt's Third Term: 1940

Soon after his 1936 landslide, Roosevelt tempted fate with a proposal that would have increased the size of the Supreme Court from nine to fifteen members in order to "pack" the Court with justices closer to the president's political philosophy. In 1935 and 1936 the high court had struck down important New Deal initiatives such as the Agriculture Adjustment Act, the National Recovery Administration, and the tax on food processing.

Roosevelt shrouded his proposal in statements of concern about the capacities of some of the Court's older justices. In a fireside speech, Roosevelt said the Court's failure to keep pace with the other "horses" in the "three-horse team" of the federal government constituted a "quiet crisis." [107] The elderly chief justice, Charles Evans Hughes, belied that charge with the energy he brought to the tribunal. But Roosevelt refused to compromise on the bill, and it became an executive-legislative dispute. The proposal was widely seen as a brazen power play, and Congress defeated it by the summer of 1937.

Nevertheless, President Roosevelt eventually got the judicial approval he wanted for his initiatives—what wags called "the switch in time that saved nine." The Court appeared to shift its philosophy during the court-packing affair, and, before long, enough justices had retired so that Roosevelt could put his own stamp on the Court.

Other problems awaited Roosevelt in the second term. Splits in the labor movement gave rise to violence during organizing drives, and the president responded haltingly. After his rift with business over the full range of New Deal policies, Roosevelt appeared to be drifting. Conservatives in Congress were more assertive than ever in opposing the "socialist" measures of the Roosevelt years. The only major New Deal legislation in the second term was the Fair Labor Standards Act of 1938, which abolished child labor and set a minimum wage and an official rate of time-and-a-half for overtime.

As Roosevelt looked toward a third term in 1940, the widening war in Europe posed a difficult problem. Nazi Germany had invaded the Rhineland, Poland, France, Norway, Denmark, Holland, Belgium, and Luxembourg and had made alliances with Italy and the Soviet Union. Japan had invaded China. Adolf Hitler launched the Battle of Britain in the summer of 1940; all-night air raids of London came soon afterward.

British prime minister Winston Churchill desperately petitioned Roosevelt to provide fifty naval destroyers. Britain's need for the destroyers was so great that Roosevelt balked at asking Congress for help. He reasoned that congressional action probably would take three months, and isolationists might even block action, dealing a crippling blow to Britain. After lengthy debate within the administration, Roosevelt agreed to send Churchill the destroyers as part of a "lend-lease" agreement. The United States would receive British bases in the Caribbean as part of the deal.

A favorite parlor game as the 1940 election approached was guessing whom Roosevelt might tap as his successor. Roosevelt publicly maintained that he did not want another term, but he refused to issue a definitive statement begging off the race. Despite the historic precedent against third terms, Roosevelt wanted to remain president. To avoid the appearance of overzealousness, however, Roosevelt wanted the Democrats to draft him in 1940.

While the nation waited for Roosevelt to act, Vice President Garner announced his candidacy. Postmaster General Farley and Secretary of State Cordell Hull also wanted to be president, and Roosevelt gave both vague assurances of support. Roosevelt, whose relations with Garner had soured since the court-packing episode (which Garner opposed), simply watched the vice president struggle to gain a respectable public profile. The Farley and Hull prospects withered without the help of the old master.

From a distance, Roosevelt watched state Democratic delegations declare their support. Polls showed Roosevelt's fortunes rising with the deepening European crisis. Just before the GOP convention, Roosevelt appointed Republicans Henry Stimson and Frank Knox to his cabinet. But Roosevelt did not reveal his plans for 1940, even to his closest aides. The president did not forbid aides such as

Harry Hopkins to work on a draft, but he did not get involved because he wanted the Democrats to call on him and not the other way around.

At the Chicago convention, Sen. Alben Barkley told the delegates: "The president has never had, and has not today, any desire or purpose to continue in the office of president. . . . He wishes in all earnestness and sincerity to make it clear that all the delegates of this convention are free to vote for any candidate." [108] The statement was followed by an hour-long demonstration and Roosevelt's first-ballot nomination.

The convention mood turned sour, however, when Roosevelt announced that he wanted the liberal secretary of agriculture, Henry Wallace, as his running mate. The announcement disgruntled delegates who already had lined up behind other candidates. But Wallace eventually beat Alabama representative William Bankhead, his strongest opponent for the nomination.

The Republicans mounted their strongest challenge to Roosevelt in 1940, largely based on the charge that Roosevelt was moving the United States toward involvement in the world war. Several moves toward military preparedness had failed at the hands of isolationists in Congress. When Roosevelt asked for increases in defense spending after Gen. Francisco Franco's victory in Spain and Germany's annexing of Austria in 1938, critics asserted that the president was attempting to cover up domestic failures with foreign adventures. Roosevelt pressed on, however, and Congress passed the Selective Service Act and increases in military spending in 1940.

The Republican field in 1940 included several fresh faces: Sen. Robert A. Taft of Ohio, son of the former president; District Attorney Thomas E. Dewey of New York City; and Sen. Charles L. McNary of Oregon and Sen. Arthur H. Vandenberg of Michigan who had been considered long shots for the Republican nomination in 1936. The freshest face of all was Wendell L. Willkie, a utility executive who had never run for political office. A large, affable man, former Democrat Willkie had barnstormed the country for seven years speaking in opposition to the New Deal.[109] Hundreds of "Willkie clubs" sprang up in the summer of 1940, and a number of publications, including Henry Luce's *Time* magazine, chronicled Willkie's career and encouraged the Willkie groundswell. Despite concern about Willkie's lack of political experience, which led to a "stop Willkie" movement, the Indianan won a sixth-ballot nomination by acclamation. Senator McNary, the Republicans' Senate floor leader, reluctantly accepted the vice-presidential nomination.

Traveling 30,000 miles in thirty-four states, Willkie gave some 540 speeches. By the time his campaign ended, his already husky voice had turned hoarse. The Republicans spent lavishly and organized grassroots clubs for Willkie across the country. Charges against Roosevelt of managerial incompetence, "warmongering," and imperial ambitions punctuated the Willkie effort. A dramatic moment came when labor leader John L. Lewis called on workers to back Willkie.

After a period of strictly "presidential" behavior, Roosevelt took to the campaign trail with partisan vigor. He answered Willkie's warmongering charges with a promise never to involve the United States in "foreign wars" (which left Roosevelt free to respond to a direct attack).

The alienation of some Democratic and independent voters was symbolized by Vice President Garner, who did not even vote. Roosevelt won, but by the slimmest popular vote margin of any race since 1912. He received 27.3 million popular votes (54.7 percent) to Willkie's 22.3 million (44.8 percent). The electoral vote tally was 449–82.

The War and Its Legacy: 1944

Roosevelt's third term and fourth election were dominated by World War II. Japan attacked U.S. bases at Pearl Harbor, Hawaii, on December 7, 1941. The president, speaking before Congress, declared the date of the surprise attack "a day that will live in infamy." Congress shook off its isolationist inclinations and declared war. A few days after Pearl Harbor, Germany and Italy declared war on the United States, confronting the nation with a two-front war.

The war did for the economy what the New Deal, by itself, could not: it brought economic prosperity. The number of unemployed workers fell from eight million to one million between 1940 and 1944. The boom brought seven million more people, half of them women, into the job market. Inflation, worker shortages, and occasional shortages in raw materials posed problems for wartime agencies. The number of U.S. families paying taxes quadrupled, and by 1945 tax revenues were twenty times their 1940 level. Budget deficits reached new heights.[110]

The fighting in Europe and Asia was grim for the first two years of the president's new term. Isolationist sentiment again built up in Congress, with the Midwest proving the region most resistant to Roosevelt's foreign policy. Criticism of how the Roosevelt administration was managing U.S. participation in the wars on both fronts was rampant. The administration won key congressional votes on the war but faced stubborn resistance on domestic measures. In the 1942 midterm elections, the Republicans gained ten seats in the Senate and forty-seven seats in the House—a major repudiation of Roosevelt.

After several setbacks, the Allied forces won impressive victories. Roosevelt and Churchill worked closely together. Allied forces, led by General Eisenhower, routed the Axis powers in North Africa in 1942. The Soviet Union beat back a Nazi assault on Stalingrad in the winter of 1942–1943. The Allies invaded and occupied Italy in 1943 before crossing the English Channel to confront the Nazis in France in 1944. In September 1944 British and American troops entered Germany. In the Pacific war, American offensives protected Australia in 1942 and secured the Philippines in 1944.

Despite the bitter opposition that prevailed through much of his third term, Roosevelt had no trouble winning a fourth term in 1944. The Allies found greater success on the battlefield and on the sea, and the nation did not appear willing to risk untested leadership to prosecute the war. The Republicans turned to the governor of New York, Thomas Dewey. Willkie wanted another shot at the White House, and his best-selling book *One World* put him in the public eye, but old-line conservatives blamed him for the 1940 election defeat. Governors John Bricker of Ohio and Harold Stassen of Minnesota and Gen. Douglas MacArthur were the other hopefuls.

Dewey's primary victories over Willkie in the Wisconsin, Nebraska, and Oregon primaries ended Willkie's public career. Dewey was too far in front to stop. At the convention he won a nearly unanimous first-ballot nomination after Bricker and Stassen dropped out. After Gov. Earl Warren of California refused the vice-presidential nomination, Bricker accepted it.

The party platform extolled the virtues of free enterprise but did not criticize the concept of the New Deal and even made bids for the votes of blacks and women. In his acceptance speech Dewey criticized "stubborn men grown old and tired and quarrelsome in office."[111]

The 1944 election marked the early resistance of the South to the modern Democratic Party. Roosevelt was a shoo-in for the nomination, but southerners wanted a replacement for Wallace as vice president, restoration of the two-thirds nominating rule, and a platform declaration of white supremacy. Dissatisfied southerners threatened to bolt the party in November, but when the party adopted only a vague civil rights plank in its platform, southern discontent dissipated. The rest of the platform called for an internationalist thrust in foreign policy and further New Deal–style reforms domestically.

Roosevelt expressed support for Wallace but said he would allow the convention to pick his running mate. Wallace gave a stirring convention speech but disturbed conservatives with his stand against the poll tax and for equal opportunity for all "regardless of race or sex." Sen. Harry S. Truman of Missouri, who had won fame as a critic of defense spending, beat Wallace for the vice-presidential nomination on the second ballot.

The Democratic campaign was dominated by references to the need for wartime unity and reminders of the Republican rule under Hoover. One leaflet bore the words "Lest We Forget" and a photograph of an unemployed man selling apples in front of a "Hoover Club"; an inset photograph showed Dewey conferring with former president Hoover. The Republicans spent nearly as much money in 1944 as they had in the record-setting 1936 election.

Roosevelt won with 25.6 million popular votes (53.4 percent) to Dewey's 22.0 million (45.9 percent). The electoral vote was 432 to 99. But President Roosevelt, who reshaped U.S. politics at all levels, did not have the opportunity to see the end of the war or to participate in the making of the postwar world. On April 12, 1945, less than three months after his fourth inauguration, he collapsed while sitting for a portrait in Warm Springs, Georgia, and died a few hours later.

The Truman Presidency: 1948

The shock of President Roosevelt's death was perhaps greatest for the former haberdasher and machine politician who succeeded him. Truman had been a last-minute choice as FDR's running mate the previous year, and he never became a part of Roosevelt's inner circle. Truman did not know about the most important military program of the age—the Manhattan Project, which, in a race with the Nazis, was developing a nuclear bomb in the secrecy of the brand-new town of Oak Ridge, Tennessee.

Truman also faced a problem of stature. Roosevelt had done nothing less than redefine the presidency in his twelve years in office. He not only effected a partisan realignment in U.S. politics, but he changed the very scope of government activity. As would become clear during the Eisenhower presidency, even Republicans had come to accept, grudgingly, the notion that the government ought to play an active role in stimulating the economy and addressing the needs of specific constituency groups.

Another problem facing Truman: many people could not fathom a presidency without Roosevelt. One member of the White House staff said later: "It was all so sudden, I had completely forgotten about Mr. Truman. Stunned, I realized that I simply couldn't comprehend the presidency as something separate from Roosevelt. The presidency, the White House, the war, our lives—they were all Roosevelt." [112] Other aides could not bring themselves to call Truman "Mr. President," as if so doing would dishonor the late president.

Truman's personality could not have presented a greater contrast to that of Roosevelt. Plain-speaking, blunt, middle-class, midwestern, high school educated, wheeling-and-dealing, and surrounded by old pals from the Pendergast machine of Missouri (the Democratic organization that dominated politics in the state), Truman offended people who had been accustomed to the charisma of Roosevelt. The new first lady, Bess Truman, also paled in comparison to her predecessor, the dynamic, more public Eleanor Roosevelt. Nevertheless, Truman showed absolute loyalty to the New Deal, but that would never be enough for many old Roosevelt hands and a nation entering a difficult period of postwar readjustment.

By the time the 1948 election neared, Truman was in grave political shape. He brought former president Hoover back from exile for special projects—one of the many ways he rankled the sensibilities of former Roosevelt aides and Eleanor Roosevelt. Truman also professed a desire to "keep my feet on the ground" and avoid the "crackpots and lunatic fringe" that had surrounded FDR. [113] Toward that end he got rid of Commerce Secretary Henry Wallace and others. The independent journalist I. F. Stone wrote of Truman's personnel moves: "The little nameplates outside the little doors . . . began to change. In Justice, Treasury, Commerce and elsewhere, the New Dealers began to be replaced by the kind of men one was accustomed to meeting in county court-houses." [114]

The politics of postwar adjustment was difficult. The Republican 80th Congress, elected in 1946, sought to dismantle many New Deal programs, and it frustrated anti-inflation efforts. Truman, then, had to duel with Congress, vetoing 250 bills (eleven vetoes were overridden). Tentative civil rights initiatives disgruntled the South. Labor unrest was on the rise. Truman's efforts to "contain" Soviet geopolitical ambitions not only created splits among Democrats but also brought attacks from Republican isolationists. To make matters worse, Truman was said to have performed inadequately at Potsdam, the conference of World War II victors held in the summer of 1945 that established many geographic borders in Europe.

The situation was so bad that Roosevelt's own son promoted General Eisenhower and Supreme Court Justice William O. Douglas for a 1948 run for the Democratic nomination against Truman. Truman, in other words, was doing a good job antagonizing both the left and the right. In August 1948 the Democratic convention appeared to reflect a dangerously polarized nation. The convention began with a feeling of desperation when Eisenhower and Douglas refused to run. Then a "states' rights" plank offered by southern delegates was defeated, and, after strong speeches by Minneapolis mayor Hubert H. Humphrey and others, a strong northern civil rights plank passed. The party's New Deal and northern machine elements decided that southern defection would be less damaging than northern defection.

Defect is just what some southerners did. The "Dixiecrats," under the leadership of South Carolina's governor J. Strom Thurmond, left the convention to conduct their fall campaign. Thurmond's candidacy ran under the Democratic Party label in four states (Alabama, Louisiana, Mississippi, and South Carolina) and under the States' Rights Democratic Party elsewhere in the South. Meanwhile, the party's left wing, behind Henry Wallace, protested Truman's Marshall Plan (a multimillion-dollar program to rebuild the economies of western Europe), military buildup, and confrontational stance toward the Soviet Union. It, too, ran its own fall campaign under the banner of the Progressive Citizens of America (the Progressive Party).

In 1948 pollsters and the media fed Republican candidate Thomas E. Dewey's overconfidence in his campaign to unseat President Harry S. Truman. Truman had the last laugh on the press and his opponent.

The seeds of Dixie defection were planted long before the convention. In 1947 the President's Committee on Civil Rights issued a report calling for the protection of the rights of all minorities. It was just the kind of spark southern segregationists needed to begin a dump-Truman drive and to organize their own campaign in 1948. The Southern Governors Conference in March 1948 recommended that southern states send delegates to the Democratic convention and electors to the electoral college who would refuse to back a pro–civil rights candidate.

As political scientist V. O. Key Jr. has shown, the degree of resistance to civil rights in southern states depended on two basic factors: the proportion of blacks in the population and the strength of the two-party system. Key argued that the existence of a large black population led to stronger Democratic measures against black enfranchisement and led whites to support the Democratic Party in greater numbers. "To them [the whites in such districts], a single Negro vote threatened the whole caste system." [115] Alabama, Louisiana, Mississippi, and South Carolina ended up voting for the Thurmond ticket. Other southern states found broader economic and political issues more compelling than race and voted for Truman.[116]

Many of FDR's old political allies eventually got behind Truman, but the president's election prospects looked bleak. Some support was grudging—Eleanor Roosevelt offered a straightforward endorsement only to rebut newspaper reports that she favored the Republicans. While the Democratic Party was badly fractured, the Republican Party united behind Dewey.

Dewey, who had been the 1944 GOP candidate, survived a large field in 1948 to become the nominee once again. Senator Taft of Ohio was the main threat, but his isolationism and dull public demeanor were liabilities. The most spirited opposition came from Governor Stassen of Minnesota, who appealed to the more liberal and internationalist wing of the party. An anathema to party bosses, Stassen proved his strength in a series of primary victories. Other candidates or potential convention contenders included Generals Eisenhower and MacArthur, Governor Warren, and Senator Vandenberg. Polls showed all of the Republicans but Taft beating Truman.[117]

Dewey gained the preconvention momentum he needed with an impressive primary victory over Stassen in Oregon. He spent three weeks in the state, while Stassen frittered away his time and resources with a hopeless challenge to Taft in the Ohio primary. Dewey was especially tough in a primary debate with Stassen about communism. With these successes, as well as his impressive organizational strength and mastery over convention mechanics, Dewey won the presidential nomination on the third ballot. Warren was selected as the vice-presidential nominee.

Dewey was part of a new breed of Republican leaders—pragmatic and accepting of the New Deal and the international role that the United States would play in the postwar era. He expressed support for the basic tenets of postwar liberalism, including Social Security, civil rights, and the United Nations. In the 1948 campaign, Dewey planned to put himself above the slashing attack style of President Truman. His constant calls for national unity—spoken in a baritone voice and perfect English—expressed broad public acceptance of the vast changes in U.S. politics over the previous twenty years.

From the beginning of the campaign, the media and professional politicians gave Truman little chance of retaining the White House. Early polls showed Dewey with such a strong lead that pollsters simply stopped surveying voters. But the polls failed because of a bias in the way the questions were asked and a presumption that the large undecided vote would cast their ballots in the same way as the rest of the population, when it in fact heavily favored Truman.[118]

Dewey was so certain of victory that he ran as if he were the incumbent. He made a series of bland, almost diplomatic statements rather than energetic campaign speeches. Dewey appeared confident that his advice to one audience—"Vote your own interests"—would attract an amalgam of disaffected groups. Never even mentioning the president's name, Dewey calmly canvassed the country and just smiled when people called him "President Dewey." Dewey was careful to avoid the overaggressive posture that he thought had ruined his 1944 campaign against Roosevelt. He even made some initial cabinet and policy decisions.

Truman's strategy from the beginning was simply to mobilize the New Deal coalition. The biggest danger was apathy, he and campaign aide Clark Clifford reasoned, so the best strategy was to give the voters a reason to go to the polling booths. Because the Democrats were the majority party, they had to concentrate mainly on getting their long-time supporters to the polls.

Truman ran a scrappy and blunt underdog campaign that could have been mistaken for an outsider's effort. Truman was the president, but he ran against the Washington establishment. Crisscrossing the nation on a whistle-stop train tour, Truman traveled some 31,000 miles and spoke before six million people. He turned his record of vetoes into an asset, claiming that the "do-nothing" Republican 80th Congress made him do it. He assailed the conservative Republican record on inflation, housing, labor, farm issues, and foreign affairs. The president drew large crowds—sometimes many times the size of Dewey's crowds—but he was virtually the only political professional who thought he would win.

Truman himself predicted in October that he had 229 solid electoral votes to Dewey's 109 and Thurmond's 9; 189 votes, he said, could go either way. The best anyone would say about the Truman campaign was that its fighting spirit improved the Democrats' chances to win the Senate. Truman answered the Republicans' claims of liberalism and reformism by criticizing the GOP for obstructing his policies. Truman's outsider taunt was constant: "that no-account, do-nothing, Republican 80th Congress!"[119]

Despite the *Chicago Tribune*'s now-famous headline—"Dewey Defeats Truman"—President Truman prevailed. Early returns put Truman in front, but it was expected that the later-reporting western states would give Dewey the win. When California and Ohio went into the Truman column midmorning on Wednesday, Dewey conceded defeat.

Considering the Democratic defections, Truman's appeal was widespread. He won twenty-eight states with 24.11 million votes (49.51 percent) and might have won more in the South and North with a united party—as it was, Thurmond won 22 percent of the vote in the South. Dewey

won 21.97 million votes (45.12 percent), and Thurmond polled 1.17 million votes (2.40 percent). Henry Wallace won some 1.16 million votes (2.38 percent) but no electoral votes. Wallace's candidacy may have cost Truman New York, Michigan, and Maryland. Yet Wallace may have done Truman a favor by freeing him from the taint of being the most liberal candidate in a time when the electorate was weary of liberalism. Particularly because the Republicans did not have a midwesterner on their ticket and talked about cutting back agricultural subsidies, farmers felt safer with Truman. In all, Truman won 303 electoral votes, Dewey, 189, and Thurmond, 39.

The Democratic defections may have helped Truman by making him the candidate of the center. The Wallace campaign freed the president from suspicions on the right, and the Thurmond defection strengthened Truman's more liberal northern constituency. In addition, the defections may have inspired Democratic voters to turn out in larger numbers than they would have had victory seemed certain.

In the end the election mostly confirmed long-held partisan allegiances. In the words of political scientist Angus Campbell and his colleagues, it was a "maintaining" election: "The electorate responded to current elements in politics very much in terms of its existing partisan loyalties. Apparently very little of the political landscape attracted strong feeling in that year. But what feeling there was seemed to be governed largely by antecedent attachments to one of the two major parties."[120]

"I Like Ike": 1952

Truman's political fortunes worsened during his second term to the extent that he decided belatedly against making a bid for the Democratic nomination. In 1952, for the first time in twenty-four years, neither party had an incumbent president as its nominee.

The Democrats suffered from a weariness that is bound to affect any party that has been in power for twenty years. Problems and opponents' frustrated ambitions were piling up, and in General Eisenhower the Republicans were able to recruit a candidate with universal appeal who was coveted by both parties. The national mood in the years before the 1952 election was sour. The nation was tiring of price controls, recurring scandals among members of the White House staff, and the Korean War, which the Truman administration had begun in 1950 but did not appear interested in either winning or pulling U.S. troops out of. The Republicans asked for a chance to "clean up the mess" in Washington and punctuated their appeals with the question: "Had enough?"

The Truman administration had met with repeated frustration in dealing with Congress. On civil rights, tariffs, taxes, labor reform, and the sensationalized question of communist sympathizers in the government, Truman had had to cope with a stubborn Democratic Congress, which, in turn, became more stubborn after Republican gains in the 1950 midterm elections. When Truman seized control of the steel mills because he said the steelworkers' strike threatened the nation's security, he was rebuffed by the Supreme Court.[121]

Truman's biggest problems, however, had concerned cronyism and war. Republicans in congressional investigations and on the stump had hammered away at conflict-of-interest scandals in Truman's administration, creating nationwide sentiment to "clean up" Washington with a new administration. Meanwhile, the United States was mired in a stalemate in Korea—a distant war that was being fought inconclusively under the aegis of the United Nations, with uncertain goals (was it to protect South Korea or to defeat North Korea as well?) and uncertain enemies (was the People's Republic of China an opponent as well as North Korea?). Truman evoked ire with his firing of General MacArthur, who wanted to take the war into China, and with the slow movement toward a settlement. Just as the nation had tired of sacrifices in World War I under Woodrow Wilson, it had tired of sacrifices under Truman.

General Eisenhower—who had just left the presidency of Columbia University to take charge of the forces of the North Atlantic Treaty Organization (NATO)—was recruited by Republicans to run when it appeared that other GOP candidates lacked the national appeal to win the White House. Senator Taft was running again, but his isolationism was considered a liability in the postwar age of internationalism. Stassen, MacArthur, and Warren were other likely Republican candidates.

Eisenhower's popular appeal was revealed when he attracted 50.4 percent of the vote in the New Hampshire primary to Taft's 38.7 percent and Stassen's 7.1 percent. Eisenhower performed well in the northeast area primaries, and Taft generally performed well in the Midwest. A write-in campaign for Eisenhower almost upset Stassen in his home state of Minnesota.

When the GOP convention finally met in Chicago, Taft had the lead in convention delegates. In crucial delegate-seating contests, many of them played out on national television, Eisenhower defeated Taft and won the right to seat pro-Eisenhower insurgents from the South. Taft had relied on the old strategy of mobilizing state machines, but such tactics looked unsavory on television. Eisenhower had undisputed popular appeal, and he won on the first ballot after his early lead turned into a stampede.

Eisenhower selected Sen. Richard Nixon of California as his running mate. The thirty-nine-year-old conservative had won national recognition with his activities on the controversial House Committee on Un-American Activities, which investigated the alleged Soviet ties of Alger Hiss, a former State Department official. Hiss would serve time for a perjury conviction.

The Democrats moved haltingly toward putting together a ticket. Truman did not announce his decision to stay out of the race until April, after two primary losses. Sen. Estes Kefauver of Tennessee, who had gained fame with his televised hearings on organized crime, ran an aggressive primary campaign and entered the convention with the lead in delegates. Other candidates included Gov. Averell Harriman of New York, Vice President Alben Barkley, Sen. Robert Kerr of Oklahoma, and Sen. Richard Russell of Georgia.

The eventual nominee was Gov. Adlai Stevenson of Illinois, grandson of Grover Cleveland's second vice president. Stevenson had had experience in the navy and State departments before running for governor. President Truman had privately recruited Stevenson for the race—at first unsuccessfully. Then Truman and Illinois backers set up a draft movement for Stevenson, which the governor disavowed until the last minute. Kefauver was the early leader in convention balloting, but Stevenson, always close, pulled into the lead on the third ballot.

Stevenson's campaign was an eloquent call to arms for liberals and reformers. Years later Democrats would recall that the campaign had inspired the generation that would take the reins of power under John F. Kennedy in 1960. Democratic politics at all levels in the 1950s and 1960s would revolve around battles between party regulars and reformers.

Stevenson did not have a chance, however, against the popular Eisenhower. Some southern states bolted the Democratic Party, and the Republicans hammered away at the misdeeds of the Democratic administration under Truman. Such issues as the 1949 communist revolution in China ("Who lost China?"), the protracted Korean War, administration corruption, and the alleged communist infiltration of the government captured the nation's attention more than Stevenson's oratory.

More than anything, however, the desire for party change rather than policy change determined the election. The Republican evocation of the theme of "Corruption, Korea, and Communism" did not challenge the policies that the Democrats offered the nation as much as the way they executed those policies. Eisenhower was a proven administrator and was free of the taint of everyday U.S. politics. Stevenson was a reformer himself, but his campaign had the conspicuous backing of President Truman. Stevenson's divorce and his public support of Hiss were constant if only vaguely stated issues.

The campaign's biggest controversy developed when newspaper reports alleged that Nixon had used a "secret fund" provided by California millionaires to pay for travel and other expenses. To a Democratic Party weary of charges of impropriety, the revelation offered an opportunity to accuse Nixon of being beholden to special interests. Nixon admitted the existence of the fund but maintained that he used the money solely for travel and that his family did not accept personal gifts.

Nixon originally reacted to the story by asserting that it was a communist smear. When Eisenhower would not publicly back his running mate, speculation developed that Ike would ask Nixon to leave the ticket—and the Republican *New York Herald Tribune* openly called for him to drop out. When Nixon decided to confront his accusers with a television speech, campaign aides told him he would be dropped if the public reaction was not favorable.

Nixon's speech was remarkable. He denied any impropriety and stated that the Stevenson campaign was hypocritical in its criticisms because it had similar funds. More specifically, Nixon denied that he had accepted such gifts as a mink coat for his wife, Pat; he said that his wife wore a "Republican cloth coat." He acknowledged, however, receiving a pet dog named Checkers from a Texas admirer: "And you know, the kids love that dog, and I just want to say this right now, that regardless of what they say about it, we're going to keep it." [122] His folksy message and appeal for telegrams created a wave of sympathy, which Eisenhower rewarded with a pledge of support. The crisis was over.

In a personal victory—surveys showed that the nation still favored the programs of the New Deal but simply wanted to put the cronyism, sacrifices, and Korean War behind it—Eisenhower swept to the White House. Ike won the entire North and West, parts of the South, and some border states—a total of thirty-nine states to Stevenson's nine. His 442 electoral votes and 33.9 million popular votes (55.1 percent) overwhelmed Stevenson's 89 electoral votes and 27.3 million popular votes (44.4 percent). The election of 1956 would bring more of the same.

Eisenhower's Reelection: 1956

Despite his age (sixty-six) and having had a heart attack in 1955, Eisenhower was the strong favorite to be the GOP nominee for another term. Close cooperation with the Democratic congressional leadership and a "hidden-hand" leadership style seemed to comport with the electorate's wishes for normalcy.[123] The White House staff was ably run by the chief of staff, Sherman Adams, and foreign policy was supervised by Secretary of State John Foster Dulles. The genius of Eisenhower's management style was his use of aides as "lightning rods" for unpopular policies.

Even without lightning rods, Eisenhower probably would have fared well. The economy was booming, and Eisenhower had quickly brought the Korean War to a close. His nuclear policy gave the nation a "bigger bang for the buck" in defense spending and kept the troop requirements low. Federal housing and highway programs gave impetus to suburbanization, now considered part of the middle-class American Dream. Issues that would in the future become divisive, such as civil rights, were muffled.

The only unsettled Republican issue was whether Nixon would again be the vice-presidential candidate. Eisenhower offered him a cabinet post, and Stassen mounted a campaign to replace Nixon with Massachusetts governor Christian Herter. After some hesitation, however, Eisenhower stood by his controversial running mate.

In the Democratic camp, Kefauver challenged Stevenson for the right to face Eisenhower in the fall. After impressive primary victories in New Hampshire and Minnesota for Kefauver, the Stevenson campaign fought back with a string of primary wins in states as varied as California, Florida, and Oregon.

Former president Truman endorsed New York governor Harriman—not Stevenson—at the opening of the Democratic convention. A variety of other favorite sons entered the race. But with the help of Eleanor Roosevelt, Stevenson was able to win the nomination for a second time. Stevenson won on the first ballot.

Stevenson left the vice-presidential slot open to the convention delegates. Kefauver eventually won, after battling Senators John Kennedy, Albert A. Gore, and Hubert Humphrey and New York mayor Robert Wagner. The open contest highlighted the future national political potential of Kennedy, who, according to later accounts, mainly intended not to win the second spot on the ticket but to gain visibility for a 1960 presidential run.

The campaign was bereft of real issues. Eisenhower's campaigning was a tempered appeal to American values and bipartisan consensus. Nixon was left the job of hacking away at the opposition; he called Stevenson "Adlai the Appeaser" and a "Ph.D. graduate of Dean Acheson's cowardly College of Communist Containment." [124] Overall, however, the campaign was an example of what James David Barber has called "the politics of conciliation," with little conflict or desire for change.

Whether or not the electorate was "asleep," as frustrated critics charged, Eisenhower nailed down another strong victory. He won forty-two states, 457 electoral votes, and 35.6 million popular votes (57.4 percent), compared with Stevenson's six states, 73 electoral votes, and 26.0 million popular votes (42.0 percent). In an unprecedented development, however, both houses of Congress went to the opposition.

Kennedy and the Politics of Change: 1960

The periodic national desire for change came at the expense of the Republicans in 1960, when Massachusetts senator Kennedy became the youngest person ever elected president by defeating Vice President Nixon. The presidential election was foreshadowed by the 1958 midterm election, when the Democrats made impressive gains in Congress. An economic recession and generational politics created the first major shift toward liberalism since the administration of Franklin D. Roosevelt. The "Class of '58" decisively changed the dis-

In the 1960 presidential campaign John F. Kennedy worked hard to win the West Virginia primary. His victory in this overwhelmingly Protestant state blunted the issue of his Catholicism and set him on the way to a first-ballot nomination.

Former Illinois governor Adlai Stevenson, the party's nominee in 1952 and 1956, stood on the sidelines, hoping that a convention deadlock or draft movement would finally bring him a ticket to the White House. Early speculation was that the convention would be deadlocked and a compromise candidate would have to emerge. It appeared likely that the nomination would go to Symington, Johnson, Humphrey, or to one of the two senior candidates, Stevenson and Kefauver; the other candidates were good bets for the vice-presidential slot.

Kennedy presented the most intriguing candidacy. He was the son of Joseph P. Kennedy, the millionaire who had been Roosevelt's ambassador to Britain before their bitter break over U.S. involvement in World War II. John Kennedy also was an Ivy League graduate (of Harvard University), a war hero (described in the book *P.T. 109*), and a Pulitzer Prize winner (for *Profiles in Courage*). With an experienced campaign staff, he had won an overwhelming reelection to the Senate in 1958. Moreover, he had been planning a run for the White House for years.

There were Kennedy skeptics, however. No Catholic except Alfred Smith had been a major party nominee, and Smith's bitter loss and the anti-Catholic sentiments he aroused in 1928 made political professionals wary of naming another Catholic. Some considered Kennedy, at age forty-three, to be too young. Others focused on the influence of Joseph Kennedy, who had bankrolled his son's political career.[126] Truman's comment captured the crux of Kennedy's liabilities: "It's not the Pope I'm afraid of, it's the Pop."[127]

course of U.S. politics. After the election the Democrats held 64 of 98 Senate seats and 283 of 436 House seats, and thirty-five states had Democratic governors. The time appeared ripe for reopening issues that had long been stifled such as civil rights, urban problems, and education.[125]

The 1960 Democratic field was dominated by senators—Kennedy, Lyndon B. Johnson of Texas, Humphrey of Minnesota, and Stuart Symington of Missouri. Each had important advantages and disadvantages. Kennedy was from a wealthy and politically minded family, but his Catholicism and undistinguished Senate record were liabilities. Johnson was a masterful majority leader, but no southerner had won the White House since James K. Polk in 1844. Humphrey was popular in the Midwest, but he lacked financial backing and was considered too loquacious and liberal. Symington had a strong Senate record and Truman's backing, but he was considered colorless, and Truman's backing carried liabilities.

To address the doubts, Kennedy entered political primaries that would enable him to demonstrate vote-getting ability and to confront the religion problem. The two key primaries were Wisconsin and West Virginia. In Wisconsin, Kennedy would answer the charge that he was too conservative. But the Kennedy strategists were divided about whether he should oppose Senator Humphrey of neighboring Minnesota. Wisconsin's growing independence in party politics eventually convinced them, however, that it would present a low risk in return for the possibility of beating Humphrey in his native region. In West Virginia, Kennedy would attempt to blunt the religion issue by attracting the votes of an overwhelmingly Protestant electorate.

In the end, Kennedy defeated Humphrey in Wisconsin. Kennedy's impressive campaign treasury enabled him to staff offices in eight of the ten congressional districts in the state; Humphrey had only two offices. Humphrey maintained that the defeat stemmed from crossover Republican Catholic votes and was therefore illegitimate. (Most of the state's Catholics, who made up 31 percent of the population, belonged to the GOP.) But to Kennedy and many political observers, it was still an important victory.

Humphrey wanted to even the score in West Virginia. If Humphrey had quit the campaign and left Kennedy with no opponents, as many advised him to do, a Kennedy victory would have attracted little attention.[128] But Kennedy was able to use the Appalachian state as a way to deflect the religion issue as well as the "can't win" problem. Kennedy had a thorough organization in West Virginia, and he worked hard. He had commissioned polls in the state as far back as 1958 in anticipation of the presidential race.

Kennedy's handling of the religion question in the primaries was shrewd and would be repeated in the fall campaign. He framed the question as one of tolerance—which put Humphrey on the defensive because he had never tried to exploit the religion issue. Kennedy had his campaign workers plant questions about how his religious beliefs would affect his loyalty to the nation, to which the candidate replied with a stock answer: "When any man stands on the steps of the Capitol and takes the oath of office as president, he is swearing to uphold the separation of church and state; he puts one hand on the Bible and raises the other hand to God as he takes the oath. And if he breaks the oath, he is not only committing a crime against the Constitution, for which the Congress can impeach him—but he is committing a sin against God." [129]

Kennedy's direct confrontation of the religion issue worked to his benefit. Kennedy had the money to get his message across: his television expenditures alone in the state totaled $34,000, while Humphrey had only $25,000 for the whole primary campaign in West Virginia.[130] Early polls gave Humphrey wide leads, and interviews elicited strong reservations about Kennedy's Catholicism. As the commercials aired and the primary neared, the lead became smaller, and voters privately said they would vote for Kennedy.

JFK, as he asked headline writers to call him instead of the youthful-sounding "Jack," easily won the primary, taking 61 percent of the vote to Humphrey's 39 percent. He was on his way to a first-ballot nomination.

The Kennedy campaign staffers managed the Democratic convention with consummate skill. Had they failed to gain a majority on the first ballot, pressure might have developed for another candidate. But the Kennedy team efficiently lobbied delegations to augment support; the vice-presidential slot was vaguely offered to several politicians. In the end, Lyndon Johnson was the surprise choice for running mate. Even Kennedy supporters had doubts about Johnson, but the selection of the southerner was a classic ticket-balancing move.[131]

Central to Kennedy's winning campaign was his younger brother Robert F. Kennedy. A former counsel to Republican senator Joseph McCarthy, Robert developed into the consummate political operative. He was JFK's confidant, chief strategist, delegate counter, fund-raiser, taskmaster, and persuader. Biographer Arthur M. Schlesinger Jr. wrote that Robert Kennedy's strength "lay in his capacity to address a specific situation, to assemble an able staff, to inspire and flog them into exceptional deeds, and to prevail through sheer force of momentum." [132]

Vice President Nixon was the overwhelming choice for the Republican nomination. Nelson A. Rockefeller, elected governor of New York in 1958, was a liberal alternative, but he announced in 1959 that he would not run. There was a brief surge for Rockefeller when he criticized the party and its "leading candidate," but meetings with Nixon settled the differences. Some conservatives were disgruntled with Nixon, but their efforts for Sen. Barry Goldwater of Arizona would have to wait until 1964.

Nixon selected United Nations Ambassador Henry Cabot Lodge as his running mate, and the party platform and rhetoric stressed the need for experience in a dangerous world. Nixon promised to continue President Eisenhower's policies. He attempted to portray Kennedy as an inexperienced upstart, even though he was Kennedy's senior by only four years and the two had entered Congress the same year. Nixon led in the polls at the traditional Labor Day start of the fall campaign.

Kennedy's campaign was based on a promise to "get the nation moving again" after eight years of calm Republican rule. Specifically, he assured voters that he would lead the nation out of a recession. The gross national product increased at a rate of only 2.25 percent annually between 1955 and 1959. Economists puzzled over the simultaneously high unemployment and high inflation rates.[133] Kennedy repeatedly called for two related changes in national policy: pump up the economy and increase defense spending dramatically.

The Democrat faced up to the religion issue again with an eloquent speech before the Greater Houston Ministerial Association, and he attracted attention from civil rights leaders when he offered moral and legal support to the Reverend Martin Luther King Jr. after King was arrested for taking part in a sit-in at an Atlanta restaurant. While Kennedy appealed to the party's more liberal and moderate wing, Johnson toured the South to appeal to regional pride and to assuage fears about an activist government.

The high point of the campaign came on September 26, 1960, when the candidates debated on national television before 70 million viewers. Kennedy was well rested and tanned; he had spent the week before the debate with friends and associates. Nixon was tired from two solid weeks of campaigning; he had spent the preparation period by himself. Their appearances alone greatly influenced the outcome of the debates.

Kennedy's main objective had been simply to look relaxed and "up to" the presidency. He had little to lose. Nixon was always confident of his debating skills, and he performed well in the give-and-take of the debate. But the rules of debating—the way "points" are allocated—are not the same for formal debating and televised encounters. Kennedy's managers prepared their candidate better for the staging of the debate. Nixon's five-o'clock shadow reinforced the cartoon image of him as darkly sinister. As a result of all these factors, polls of radio listeners found that Nixon had "won" the debate, but polls of the more numerous television viewers found that Kennedy had "won." Historian Theodore H. White wrote: "It was the picture image that had done it—and in 1960 it was television that had won the nation away from sound to images, and that was that." [134]

While Kennedy called for a more activist and imaginative approach to world problems, Nixon stressed the candidates' similarities so much that their differences paled into insignificance. Kennedy called for a crusade to eliminate want and to confront tyranny. Nixon responded: "I can subscribe completely to the spirit that Senator Kennedy has expressed tonight." [135] With ideology an unimportant part of the debate, the images of personal character the candidates were able to project gained in importance.

The candidates held three more debates, addressing issues such as Fidel Castro's Cuba, whether the United States should defend the Chinese offshore islands of Quemoy and Matsu in the event of a military strike by China, and relations with Nikita Khrushchev's Soviet Union. None of the debates had the effect of the first, which neutralized Nixon's quasi-incumbency advantage. Nor was Nixon greatly helped by President Eisenhower, who did not campaign for his protégé until late in the campaign.

The election results were so close that Nixon did not concede his defeat until the afternoon of the day after the election. After a vacation in Florida and Nassau, Nixon returned to Washington on November 19 to consider a series of charges that voter fraud had cost him the election. A shift of between 11,000 and 13,000 votes in a total of five or six states could have given Nixon the electoral vote triumph. Nixon said he decided against demanding a recount because it would take "at least a year and a half" and would throw the federal government into turmoil.[136] Other commentators have pointed out that had Nixon, for instance, challenged voting irregularities in Illinois in Democratic precincts in Chicago, irregularities in Republican rural areas of the state could have been challenged by Kennedy.

When the electoral college voted, Kennedy won 303 electoral votes to Nixon's 219. Democratic senator Harry F. Byrd of Virginia attracted 15 electoral votes. Kennedy won twenty-three states to Nixon's twenty-six. (Six Alabama electors and all eight Mississippi electors, elected as "unpledged Democrats," as well as one Republican elector from Oklahoma cast their votes for Byrd.) The overall popular vote went 34.2 million for Kennedy and 34.1 million for Nixon. The margin was about two-tenths of 1 percent, or 118,574 votes. Moreover, the margins in many states were close. Kennedy won Illinois by 8,858 votes and Texas by 46,242 votes. Despite statements that the religion question would hurt Kennedy, it probably helped him by mobilizing Catholics on his behalf. Gallup polls showed that 78 percent of Catholics voted for JFK. Although Catholics were a traditional Democratic constituent group—supporting the party by margins of three or four to one—they had shown support for Republicans Eisenhower and Senator McCarthy.[137] In addition, Kennedy put together a predictable coalition: he won the support of voters in the Northeast, in most of the South, and in cities, plus blacks and union workers. Upper New England, the Midwest, and the West went primarily to Nixon.

After the election, Kennedy and Goldwater discussed, in an informal way, how they would conduct their campaigns for the presidency in 1964. The two expected to win their parties' nominations easily, and they talked about crisscrossing the nation in head-to-head debates, which would set a new standard for national campaigns.[138]

The Kennedy-Goldwater campaign never came to be, however. On November 22, 1963, while riding in a motorcade in Dallas, Texas, President Kennedy was assassinated by a gunman named Lee Harvey Oswald.[139] Vice President Johnson assumed the presidency.[140]

In his brief administration, Kennedy had compiled a record disappointing even to many of his supporters. The Bay of Pigs fiasco in which a Central Intelligence Agency plan—begun under Eisenhower—to overthrow the Cuban government failed miserably, the inability to obtain passage of landmark civil rights legislation, budget deficits and a drain of gold supplies from the United States, confrontations with the Soviet Union in Cuba, Hungary, and Berlin, and the nascent U.S. involvement in the Vietnam War created doubts about the young president's control of the government.

Kennedy had, however, made a start on many important issues. Arms control initiatives such as the test ban treaty, economic growth through tax cuts, modernization of the military, the successful management of the Cuban Missile Crisis, civil rights and other domestic initiatives, the Peace Corps and Alliance for Progress, and growing world stature all offered hope for the second term. It would fall to

Johnson, the legendary former Senate majority leader, to bring the Kennedy plans to fruition. First acting as the loyal servant of the slain president, then on his own, Johnson was able to bring to legislative enactment many of the initiatives long cherished by liberals—most notably the Civil Rights Act of 1964, which was considerably stronger than the Kennedy bill that had stalled in Congress.

"All the Way with LBJ": 1964

From the time of his sad but graceful ascension to the White House, Johnson was never in doubt as the Democrats' 1964 nominee. He was expected to select an eastern or midwestern liberal as his running mate, and he did so when he tapped Senator Humphrey of Minnesota at the convention, which his campaign organization stage-managed down to the last detail. The only dissent from Democratic unity was provided by Gov. George C. Wallace of Alabama, whose segregationist campaign took advantage of a backlash against the civil rights movement. Wallace entered three primaries against Johnson-allied favorite sons, and he polled 43 percent of the vote in Maryland. Wallace talked about mounting a third-party bid in the fall, but he backed off.

The Republicans were divided into two bitter camps led by Senator Goldwater of Arizona, the eventual nominee, and by Governor Rockefeller of New York. The nomination contest was a struggle for the soul of the party. Other active and inactive candidates included Ambassador to Vietnam Henry Cabot Lodge, former vice president Nixon, and Gov. William Scranton of Pennsylvania. After a New Hampshire primary victory by Lodge, achieved through a well-organized write-in drive while he was still ambassador to Vietnam, Goldwater and Rockefeller scrapped through a series of primaries. The moderate Lodge later helped Scranton in a late effort to recruit uncommitted delegates to stop Goldwater, but by then it was too late. Goldwater lined up strong delegate support to get the nomination before the primary season even began, but he needed to use the primaries to show that he had vote-getting ability. The state organizations that backed him also needed evidence that his conservative message would find popular acceptance.

In the "mixed" nominating system then in place, candidates were able to pick and choose the primaries that best suited their strategies. Front-runners avoided risks, and long shots entered high-visibility and often risky contests as a way to attract the attention of party professionals. As expected, Goldwater won widespread support in the southern state conventions and had strong primary showings in Illinois and Indiana. Rockefeller beat Lodge in Oregon, but the decisive test came when Goldwater narrowly upset Rockefeller in California.

More important than the confusing preconvention contests was the rhetoric. Both the conservative Goldwater and the liberal Rockefeller vowed to save the party from the other's ideology. Goldwater, who rode the bestseller success of his *Conscience of a Conservative* to hero worship among conservatives, made a vigorous case against New Deal politics and for American sway in world politics: "I don't give a tinker's damn what the rest of the world thinks about the United States, as long as we keep strong militarily." [141] Rockefeller implied that Goldwater would risk nuclear war and would recklessly dismantle basic social programs.

The nominating contest was a regional as well as an ideological struggle. The westerner Goldwater—backed by labor-intensive manufacturers, small business and agricultural enterprises, and domestic oil producers—opposed internationalist banking and commercial interests.[142] Goldwater made eastern media the objects of scorn. Rockefeller and his family, of course, represented the apex of the eastern establishment. Because of his strategy, Goldwater isolated his campaign from the manufacturing and financial interests that had been at the center of American economic growth for a generation.

Bitter battles over the party platform and unseemly heckling of Rockefeller displayed the party's divisions at the convention. When the conservatives won the nomination and the platform, there was no reconciliation. Goldwater selected Rep. William Miller of New York, another conservative, as his running mate and vowed to purge the party of liberal and moderate elements.

In a defiant acceptance speech, Goldwater painted a picture of the United States as inept in international affairs and morally corrupt in domestic pursuits, and he vowed an all-out crusade to change the situation: "Tonight there is violence in our streets, corruption in our highest offices, aimlessness among our youth, anxiety among our elderly, and there's a virtual despair among the many who look beyond the material successes toward the inner meaning of their lives. . . . Extremism in defense of liberty is no vice; moderation in pursuit of justice is no virtue." [143]

To a nation experiencing prosperity and unaware of the true proportions of its involvement in Vietnam, the "choice, not an echo" that Goldwater offered was a moral crusade. But the American consensus was built on material, consumer foundations, and an "outsider" appeal would have to wait until the system's foundations became unstable.

The divided GOP made for easy pickings for Johnson. The fall campaign was dominated by Goldwater's gaffes, which started long before the campaign began. He said, for example, that troops committed to NATO in Europe probably could be cut by at least one-third if NATO "commanders" had the authority to use tactical nuclear weapons in an emergency.[144] Goldwater also proposed a number of changes in the Social Security system, called for selling off the Tennessee Valley Authority, criticized the civil rights movement, and denounced the Supreme Court, the National Labor Relations Board, and the federal bureaucracy. Except for the use of nuclear weapons and changes in Social Security, most of Goldwater's proposals when taken alone were not shocking. But the sum of his proposals—and his sometimes halting explanations— scared many voters.

President Johnson campaigned actively to win a mandate for an activist new term. He traveled throughout the country making speeches to build a consensus for his domestic programs as well as his reelection. Johnson resisted Goldwater's frequent calls for televised debates. The nation's prosperity was probably enough to keep the president in the White House.[145]

Johnson desperately wanted a personal mandate to pursue a variety of domestic programs that fell under the rubric of the "Great Society"—a term that Johnson used in a 1964 commencement address (borrowed from a book of the same title by British socialist Graham Wallas). The desired landslide—underscored by his campaign slogan, "All the Way with LBJ"—was essential to initiatives in civil rights, health care, community action, education, welfare, housing, and jobs creation. Central to the landslide was not only economic prosperity but also peace in the world's trouble spots. Johnson therefore ran as a "peace" candidate.

But while he was trying to build a coalition that would sustain his domestic initiatives, Johnson faced an increasingly difficult dilemma about the U.S. role in Vietnam. The United States had been involved in opposing Ho Chi Minh's revolution against French colonial rule in the 1940s and 1950s, and under Presidents Eisenhower and Kennedy the United States had made a commitment to the leaders of South Vietnam (created after the failure of the 1954 Geneva accord) as a bastion against communist expansion in Asia. But talk of war would likely imperil the domestic initiatives of the Great Society.

So while Johnson was campaigning as the peace candidate in 1964, he also was preparing for a major increase in U.S. involvement in Vietnam. As early as February 1964, the administration began elaborate covert operations in Southeast Asia and prepared a resolution to give the president a "blank check" in Vietnam.[146] By June the resolution was ready, and the Pentagon had chosen ninety-four bombing targets in North Vietnam and made provisions for

In accepting the 1964 Republican nomination, Sen. Barry Goldwater called for a moral crusade, declaring, "Extremism in defense of liberty is no vice; moderation in pursuit of justice is no virtue."

bombing support systems on the ground. But on June 15, Johnson decided to delay major offensives until after the election.[147] In August Johnson sent to Congress what would be known as the Tonkin Gulf resolution, which granted the president broad authority to wage war in Vietnam. The resolution passed quickly and nearly unanimously—after all, the president had instructed congressional leaders to get an overwhelming majority so his policy would be bipartisan.

Johnson also seized on Rockefeller's use of the peace issue during the Republican primaries against Goldwater. He alluded to some of Goldwater's scarier statements about war, and he pledged that "we are not about to send American boys nine or ten thousand miles away from home to do what Asian boys ought to be doing for themselves."[148] A week before the election Johnson said: "The only real issue in this campaign, the only one you ought to get concerned about, is who can best keep the peace."[149]

Johnson's popular vote landslide was the largest in U.S. history. He won 61 percent of the popular vote to Goldwater's 38 percent (or 43.1 million to 27.2 million votes). In the electoral college Johnson received 486 votes to Goldwater's 52, and he carried forty-four states—all but Goldwater's home state of Arizona and five deep South states. In addition, the Democratic Party amassed huge majorities in both the Senate (67–33) and the House of Representatives (295–140).

On election day, Johnson created a working group to study "immediately and intensively" the U.S. options in Southeast Asia.[150] The war was increasing far beyond what most supporters of the Tonkin Gulf resolution or "peace" supporters of the president imagined. In 1965 alone the number of U.S. troops in Vietnam increased from 15,000 to nearly 200,000.[151]

THE BREAKUP OF CONSENSUS

A long period of uncertainty in American politics began sometime after Lyndon B. Johnson's landslide victory over Barry Goldwater in 1964. By 1968 some 30,000 Americans had been killed in action in Vietnam, and television was bringing the war into the living rooms of American families.

Despite repeated assertions that the United States was defeating the North Vietnamese enemy, U.S. bombing efforts and ground troops did not break the resolve of the communists in the North or their sympathizers who had infiltrated the South. The corrupt South Vietnamese government and army appeared to lack the will to fight the war on their own.

In the United States, the opposition to the war developed as the casualties mounted, and the administration experienced a "credibility gap" because of its statements about the war. Before the United States left Vietnam in 1975, 55,000 Americans had died in combat. Perhaps more important than the number of casualties—about the same as in the Korean War—was the long-term commitment that the United States appeared to have made with little evidence of progress. The "quagmire," as *New York Times* reporter David Halberstam called the war, was perhaps typified by the program of intense U.S. bombing raids that were judged by many experts to be ineffectual against the North's guerrilla warfare strategy.[152]

As opposition to the war grew among an increasingly vocal and well-organized minority, strains developed in Johnson's economic and domestic programs. Starting with the riots in the Watts section of Los Angeles in 1965, urban areas sizzled with resentment of the mainstream liberal establishment. Detroit, Newark, and many major U.S. cities erupted in other riots that burned miles of city streets and caused millions of dollars in damage. The assassination of civil rights leader Martin Luther King Jr. in Memphis in April 1968 led to riots throughout the nation. Even before the riots, however, a conservative reaction against the Great Society had developed.

The activities of the Great Society were many and varied: the Civil Rights Act of 1964, the Voting Rights Act of 1965, Head Start, Model Cities, mass transit legislation, food stamps, Medicaid, the Elementary and Secondary Education Act, college loans, and housing programs that included subsidies for the poor, to name just the most prominent programs.

The conservative backlash was apparent before many programs had time to do their work. Efforts such as the Model Cities program and the Community Action Program, which mandated that poverty programs promote "maximum feasible participation" by the poor themselves, often were badly organized. The programs also created new struggles over jurisdiction in cities that already were notorious for divisive politics. Liberal efforts that predated the Great Society, such as school desegregation, only added to the tensions in cities.

One of the greatest sources of backlash in the late 1960s was an alarming increase in street crime. Even though African Americans and the poor were the chief victims of the increase, the issue was most salient for conservative whites. Many tied the breakdown in order to the growth of the welfare state caused by the Great Society. The crime rate seemed

to many to be nothing less than ingratitude on the part of the poor. James Sundquist wrote: "While increasing millions were supported by welfare, rising state and local taxes made the citizen more and more aware of who paid the bill. And while he armed himself for protection against thieves or militants, the liberals were trying to pass legislation to take away his guns." [153]

The crime problem was an important element in both national and metropolitan politics. Polls taken in the late 1960s showed that half the women and a fifth of the men in the country were afraid to walk alone in their own neighborhoods at night.[154] In Alabama, Gov. George Wallace was whipping up his supporters in a frenzy of prejudice and resentment. The fear of crime also would be an important element in Richard Nixon's 1968 campaign.

"Nixon Now": 1968

With the nation divided over the war and domestic policy, the Democrats entered the 1968 campaign in an increasingly perilous state. In December 1967 Sen. Eugene McCarthy of Minnesota challenged President Johnson for the Democratic nomination, a move based almost entirely on McCarthy's antiwar stance. McCarthy did unexpectedly well against Johnson's write-in candidacy in the New Hampshire primary on March 12, 1968, drawing 42.4 percent of the vote to Johnson's 49.5 percent. Anticipating a devastating defeat in the Wisconsin primary on April 2, Johnson dramatically announced his withdrawal from the campaign in a televised address March 31.

After the New Hampshire primary, Sen. Robert F. Kennedy of New York declared his antiwar candidacy, which put in place all the elements for a Democratic fight of historic proportions. Vice President Hubert Humphrey took Johnson's place as the administration's candidate. McCarthy and Kennedy fought each other in the primaries, and Kennedy appeared to have the upper hand when he closed the primary season with a victory in California on June 5. But after making his acceptance speech, he was assassinated, and the party was in greater turmoil than ever.

At the party convention in Chicago, a site Johnson had chosen for what he thought would be his renomination, Humphrey became the Democratic Party's candidate. He had eschewed the primaries; he won the nomination on the strength of endorsements from state party organizations. The vice president took the nomination on the first ballot after Mayor Richard Daley of Chicago committed the Illinois delegation to his effort. Humphrey won with support from the traditional elements of the Democratic coalition—labor, African Americans, urban voters—plus the backers of President Johnson. Humphrey appealed to many of the party's "moderates" on the issue of the Vietnam War.

Preliminary battles over rules and delegate seating, the representativeness of the party, and the Vietnam War caused

Former vice president Richard Nixon tapped into widespread discontent over the Vietnam War and domestic turmoil to win the 1968 presidential election, one of the closest in U.S. history.

ugly skirmishes on the convention floor. The party's platform eventually endorsed the administration's war policy, including bombing, but strong opposition to this plank left the Democrats divided.[155]

Outside the convention halls, demonstrations for civil rights and an end to the war met brutal rejection from the police. After three days of sometimes harsh verbal and physical battles with antiwar demonstrators in city parks, the police charged a group of protesters who planned a march on the convention. Theodore H. White described the scene that played on national television:

> Like a fist jolting, like a piston exploding from its chamber, comes a hurtling column of police from off Balbo into the intersection, and all things happen too fast: first the charge as the police wedge cleaves through the mob; then screams, whistles, confusion, people running off into Grant Park, across bridges, into hotel lobbies. And as the scene clears, there are little knots in the open clearing—police clubbing youngsters, police dragging youngsters, police rushing them by their elbows, their heels dragging, to patrol wagons, prodding recalcitrants who refuse to enter quietly.[156]

Humphrey and his running mate, Sen. Edmund S. Muskie of Maine, faced an uphill fight.

The Republicans united behind Richard Nixon, the 1960 nominee whose political career had seemed at an end after he lost in the 1962 California gubernatorial election. The GOP did not have to deal with any of the divisiveness of the 1964 Goldwater-Rockefeller battle.

Nixon outspent Humphrey two-to-one. He also followed a carefully devised script that avoided the exhausting schedule of his 1960 campaign and capitalized on the national discontent created by the Vietnam War, urban riots, political assassinations, and general concern about the speed of change wrought by the Great Society. Nixon traveled the high road in his own campaign by calling for the nation to unite and heal its wounds. Promising an "open administration," Nixon's main offer was change. "I must say the man who helped us get into trouble is not the man to get us out."[157] To avoid scrutiny by the national media, Nixon gave few major addresses, preferring instead a series of interviews with local newspapers and broadcasters.

As President Johnson resisted calls for a halt in the bombing of North Vietnam, Nixon said he had a "secret plan" to end the war. He appealed to weary Democrats with his pledge of an activist administration and alternative approaches to dealing with some of the problems the Great Society addressed. Nixon promised to give African Americans, in his words, "a piece of the action with a program to encourage entrepreneurial activity in cities." The "new Nixon" appeared willing to deal with the Soviet Union, which he had scorned earlier in his career. Meanwhile, his vice-presidential nominee, Gov. Spiro T. Agnew of Maryland, offered a slashing critique of the Democrats to middle-class and blue-collar Americans who resented the civil rights laws, government bureaucracy, Vietnam War protesters, and the young protest generation.

Alabama governor Wallace, heading up one of the strongest third-party campaigns in U.S. history, ran as an antiestablishment conservative, railing away at desegregation, crime, taxes, opponents of the war in Vietnam, social programs, and "pointy-head" bureaucrats and "intellectual morons." His American Independent Party was the strongest effort since Robert La Follette's Progressive run in 1924. As did the earlier third-party campaigns, the Wallace run caused concern about the soundness of the electoral college system. Because the race was so close, it was conceivable that no candidate would win an electoral college victory. In that event, Wallace could have held the balance of power.[158]

Despite his early disadvantage, Humphrey made steady inroads into Nixon's support by disassociating himself from Johnson's Vietnam policies. When Johnson on November 1 ordered a halt to all bombing of North Vietnam, Humphrey appeared to be free at last from the stigma of the administration. But this change in policy was not enough to win the election for Humphrey.

The 1968 election was one of the closest in U.S. history. Nixon's victory was not confirmed until the day after the election when California, Ohio, and Illinois—each with close counts—finally went into the Nixon column. Nixon attracted 31.8 million votes (43.4 percent of all votes cast); Humphrey, 31.3 million votes (42.7 percent); and Wallace, 9.9 million votes (13.5 percent). Nixon won thirty-two states and 301 electoral votes, compared with Humphrey's thirteen states and 191 electoral votes. Nixon won six southern states (Wallace won five others), all of the West except Texas, Washington, and Hawaii, and all the midwestern states except Michigan and Minnesota. Humphrey won all of the East except New Hampshire, Vermont, New Jersey, and Delaware, plus West Virginia, Maryland, and the District of Columbia.

One long-lasting effect of 1968 was a transformation of the nominating process. In response to the bitter complaints about their 1968 convention, the Democratic Party adopted rules that would make the primaries the center of the nominating process. The Chicago convention, dominated by party professionals at the expense of many important constituencies—African Americans, women, youth—had nominated a candidate who did not compete in any primaries. The key reform was a limit on the number of delegates that state committees could choose—after 1968, no more than 10 percent of the delegation.

Nixon's Reelection: 1972

Sen. George S. McGovern of South Dakota was the miracle candidate of 1972, but his miracle did not last long enough. Muskie, a veteran of the U.S. Senate and the vice-presidential nominee in 1968, was the early favorite to win the Democratic nomination. But because of party reforms enacted in response to the disastrous 1968 convention, the nominating process was bound to create surprises and confusion.

No fewer than fifteen contenders announced their candidacy, twelve with serious hopes of winning or influencing the final selection. Some twenty-two primaries to choose 60 percent of the party's delegates—a third more than in 1968—were to take place over four months. The marathon would be decided by accidents, media strategy, and a confusing array of voter choices that changed with each new development.

Muskie was badly damaged before the New Hampshire primary when he appeared to cry while lashing back at the *Manchester Union Leader*'s vicious and unrelenting attacks on his campaign and on his outspoken wife, Jane. The *Union Leader* had printed a series of attacks on Jane and then falsely reported that Muskie had laughed at a derogatory joke about French Canadians. Muskie later said of the incident: "It changed people's minds about me, of what kind of a guy I was. They were looking for a strong, steady man, and here I was weak." [159]

Muskie won the first-in-the-nation New Hampshire primary, but his 46.4 percent of the vote was considered a "disappointing" showing. Senator McGovern, the antiwar candidate who won 37.1 percent of the vote, was pronounced the real winner by media and pundits. He had attracted a corps of youthful volunteers, and his strong showing—engineered by imaginative young political operatives led by Gary Hart—was a surprise.

After New Hampshire, the Democrats battled through the summer. Wallace parlayed his antibusing rhetoric into an impressive victory in the Florida primary (41.6 percent). Better organized than the others, McGovern won the Wisconsin delegation by winning 29.6 percent of the state vote. McGovern then won an easy Massachusetts victory with 52.7 percent of the vote to Muskie's 21.3 percent. Humphrey edged McGovern in Ohio by 41.2 to 39.6 percent, but McGovern claimed a moral victory.

In the popular primary vote before the late summer California primary, McGovern actually stood in third place behind Wallace and Humphrey. But the delegate allocation rules gave the edge to the candidate who could squeeze out narrow victories in congressional districts, and that was McGovern. McGovern had 560 delegates to Humphrey's 311. Wallace had 324 delegates, but he was paralyzed after being shot in a Maryland shopping center on May 15, 1972, and therefore no longer appeared to have a chance at the nomination.

The big McGovern-Humphrey showdown was California, which offered 271 delegates to the winner. It was a spirited campaign that included a head-to-head debate and strong Humphrey assaults on McGovern's positions on welfare and defense spending. McGovern went on to beat Humphrey by five percentage points in the winner-take-all primary. McGovern also won a majority of the delegates in New Jersey, South Dakota, and New Mexico on the last day of the primary season. [160]

After platform battles over welfare, busing, and the Vietnam War, McGovern won the nomination handily. He then selected Sen. Thomas Eagleton of Missouri as his running mate after several others declined. McGovern did not get to deliver his acceptance speech—perhaps the best speech of his career—until almost three o'clock in the morning, when most television viewers already were in bed.

President Nixon and Vice President Agnew were renominated with barely a peep out of other Republicans. Rep. Paul N. "Pete" McCloskey Jr. of California opposed Nixon in the primaries but won only one delegate (from New Mexico). Rep. John M. Ashbrook of Ohio also ran in the primaries.

McGovern would have been an underdog in the best of circumstances, but his chances were badly damaged by what came to be known as the "Eagleton affair." As the McGovernites celebrated their hard-won nomination,

rumors circulated that Eagleton had been hospitalized for exhaustion in the early 1960s. Eagleton finally told McGovern operatives that he had been hospitalized three times for nervous exhaustion and fatigue, and his treatment included electroshock therapy. Despite McGovern's public statement that he was "1,000 percent for Tom Eagleton, and I have no intention of dropping him," Eagleton left the ticket less than two weeks after his nomination.

McGovern eventually replaced Eagleton with his sixth choice, R. Sargent Shriver, former executive of the Peace Corps and Office of Economic Opportunity. But the aura of confusion that surrounded the Eagleton affair and the search for a new vice-presidential candidate hurt the campaign badly. The columnist Tom Braden likened it to a school teacher who could not control the class: "Nice people, too. One looks back with sympathy and a sense of shame. But at the time—was it that they were too nice?— their classes were a shambles. The erasers flew when they turned their backs." [161]

Nixon was in command of the fall campaign. He paraded a litany of accomplishments—the Paris peace talks over the Vietnam War, the diplomatic opening to China, the arms limitation treaty with the Soviet Union, and a number of domestic initiatives. Most of all, he was a strong figure. If he still aroused suspicion, he was at least a known commodity.

Nixon won all but Massachusetts and the District of Columbia in the fall election. His popular vote margin was 47.2 million to McGovern's 29.2 million; the electoral college cast 520 votes for Nixon and only 17 for McGovern. Nixon's 60.7 percent share of the popular vote stood second only to Johnson's 61.1 percent in 1964.

On the surface, it appeared in 1972 that American politics was entering an age of calm consensus. At the time of the election, the economy was temporarily strong. Moreover, opposition to the Vietnam War had faded as the two sides negotiated in Paris for an end to the war, and the United States had signed an important nuclear arms treaty with the Soviet Union and had made important diplomatic moves with that country and the People's Republic of China. Nixon's landslide victory appeared to be a mandate and a vote of confidence.

But trouble loomed behind the apparent stability and consensus. The war in Vietnam continued, as did the antiwar protests, and generational cleavages remained. The economy experienced the first of many "shocks" in 1973 when the Organization of Petroleum Exporting Countries agreed to ban oil exports to the United States. The economic turmoil that resulted in the United States was topped off with a wage and price freeze. In addition, a warlike atmosphere between the White House and the media (as well as other perceived enemies of the administration who appeared on Nixon's "enemies list") and the mushrooming Watergate scandal combined to create a dark side to U.S. politics in the 1970s.[162]

The Watergate affair was perhaps the greatest political scandal in U.S. history. For the first time, a president was forced to leave office before his term expired. President Nixon resigned on August 9, 1974, when it became apparent that the House of Representatives would impeach him for "high crimes and misdemeanors" and the Senate would convict him. In addition, a number of Nixon aides, including his first attorney general and campaign manager, John Mitchell, would spend time in jail because of the scandal.

At its simplest, the Watergate affair was "a third-rate burglary," followed by a cover-up by President Nixon and his aides. In the summer of 1972, several employees of the Committee to Re-elect the President (dubbed "CREEP") were arrested after they were discovered breaking into and bugging the Democratic National Committee's offices at the posh Watergate complex in Washington. The break-in was not a major issue in the 1972 election, but the next year a Senate committee began an investigation of the entire affair.

During the investigation, a presidential aide revealed that Nixon had secretly taped Oval Office conversations with aides. When the Watergate special prosecutor, Archibald Cox, ordered Nixon to surrender the tapes in October 1973, Nixon ordered Cox fired. But because Nixon's attorney general, Elliot Richardson, and assistant attorney general, William D. Ruckelshaus, refused to fire Cox, the task was carried out by Solicitor General Robert Bork, igniting a constitutional crisis dubbed the "Saturday night massacre."

Nixon soon handed over the tapes Cox had sought. In the summer of 1974, the Supreme Court ruled that Nixon had to surrender even more tapes, which indicated that he had played an active role in covering up the Watergate scandal. Nixon resigned the presidency when his impeachment and conviction appeared certain. The impeachment articles charged him with obstruction of justice, abuse of presidential powers, and contempt of Congress.

Many scholars of the Watergate affair maintain that the illegal campaign activities were just part of a tapestry of illegal activities in the Nixon administration—including secretly bombing Cambodia, accepting millions of dollars in illegal campaign contributions, offering government favors in return for contributions, "laundering" money through third parties, wiretapping and burglarizing a wide variety of people thought to be unsupportive of the president, offering executive clemency to convicted campaign workers, engaging in "dirty tricks" to discredit other political figures, compromising criminal investigations by giving information to the people under scrutiny, and using government funds to renovate the president's private residence.[163]

In 1973 Nixon's vice president, Spiro Agnew, resigned after pleading "no contest" to charges of taking bribes while he was governor of Maryland. After Agnew's resignation on October 10, 1973, Nixon named House Minority Leader Gerald Ford, a longtime GOP stalwart, to become vice president under the Twenty-fifth Amendment. Ford, who had never entered a national election, then became president after Nixon's resignation and quickly attracted the support of the American public with his modest, earnest disposition. He responded to the widespread feeling that Nixon's isolation in the Oval Office had contributed to his downfall by promising to work closely with Congress and to meet with the press regularly.

One month after becoming president, however, Ford ignited a firestorm of criticism with his full pardon of Nixon for all crimes he may have committed while president. Ford testified before Congress that he believed Nixon had suffered enough and that the nation would have been badly torn if a former president were brought to court to face criminal charges. Critics asserted that Ford had made a "deal" in which Nixon resigned the presidency in exchange for the pardon.[164]

Ford selected former New York governor Nelson Rockefeller to be his vice president. Rockefeller received Senate and House confirmation on December 10 and 19, respectively, after long, difficult hearings that centered on his financial dealings.

The Election of "Jimmy Who?": 1976

With the benefit of the Watergate scandal and Ford's pardon of Nixon, the Democrats won resounding victories in the 1974 midterm elections. The Democrats' gains of fifty-two House seats and four Senate seats not only created stronger majorities but also reduced the number of members with allegiance to the old system of organizing congressional business.

The moralistic zeal of the "Watergate class" forced major changes on Congress as well as on the presidency and the nation's process of pluralistic political bargaining. The new crop of legislators was so large that it was able to undermine the seniority system that had ordered the way Congress had operated for years. The new system of committee assignments led to a proliferation of subcommittees on which most members had prominent roles. That, in turn, created a fragmented policy-making process—less susceptible to coercion by presidents and party leaders but more susceptible to interest group politics.[165]

The 1976 campaign was the first governed by campaign finance reform legislation enacted in 1971 and 1974. The Federal Election Campaign Act (FECA) of 1971 limited campaign expenditures and required disclosure of campaign receipts and expenditures. The Revenue Act of 1971 created a tax check-off that enabled taxpayers to allocate $1 of their taxes for public financing of elections. The FECA amendments of 1974 limited spending and donations for both primary and general election campaigns, established a system of partial public funding of elections, and created the Federal Election Commission to monitor campaign activities.

The Democrats and their eventual nominee, Jimmy Carter, continued to exploit the nation's discontent through the 1976 election. Ronald Reagan, a former movie actor and California governor, added to the Republican Party's vulnerability by waging a stubborn primary campaign against President Ford.

The Democrats appeared headed for a long and bitter nomination struggle for the third time in a row. A few candidates—such as Senators Henry Jackson of Washington and Birch Bayh of Indiana and Governor Wallace of Alabama—had greater stature than others, but their appeal was limited to specific factions of the Democratic coalition. Other candidates included Rep. Morris Udall of Arizona, Sen. Fred Harris of Oklahoma, Sen. Frank Church of Idaho, and Gov. Edmund G. "Jerry" Brown Jr. of California. Church and Brown entered the race late, and Senators Humphrey of Minnesota and Edward M. Kennedy of Massachusetts awaited a draft in the event of a deadlocked convention.

The moderate Carter, whose name recognition in polls stood in single figures when the campaign began, executed a brilliant campaign strategy to win the nomination on the first ballot. Constructing strong organizations for the Iowa caucuses and the New Hampshire primary, Carter won both contests by slim margins. Although liberal candidates Udall and Bayh together polled more votes than Carter, it was Carter who received cover billings on national magazines and live interviews on morning television talk shows.[166] Within a matter of days, Carter went from long shot to front-runner.

Udall performed well in the primaries but never won a single state; he and other liberals were splitting the liberal vote. Udall's chance for a Wisconsin primary win fizzled when Harris refused to back out to create a one-on-one matchup of a liberal with Carter.[167] Carter ran into strong challenges from Church and Brown in later primaries, but Carter had the delegates and endorsements by the time of the Democratic convention in New York for a first-ballot nomination. The convention itself was a "love fest" with the Democrats united behind Carter and his running mate, Sen. Walter F. Mondale of Minnesota.

The GOP was divided between Ford and Reagan. Ford won the early contests, but Reagan scored big wins in the North Carolina and Texas primaries. Reagan was put on the defensive with his proposals for transferring welfare obligations to the states, but when he focused on foreign policy he had success. For example, he attacked Ford for his policy of détente with the Soviet Union and his negotiation of a treaty that would forfeit U.S. control of the Panama Canal.

In the late summer, with Ford and Reagan locked in a close contest for delegates, Reagan tried to gain the advantage by breaking precedent and naming his vice-presidential candidate before the convention. Reagan's choice—Sen. Richard S. Schweiker of Pennsylvania, a moderate—widened

Virtually unknown to the country at the outset of the campaign, former Georgia governor Jimmy Carter emerged from a field of candidates to win the Democratic nomination and the presidency. His casual and honest approach appealed to many voters.

Reagan's ideological appeal but angered many of his conservative supporters. When Reagan tried to force Ford to name a vice-presidential candidate in advance as well, the convention vote on the issue became a crucial test of the candidates' delegate strength. But Ford won that test and the nomination. He selected the acerbic senator Robert J. "Bob" Dole of Kansas as his running mate as a consolation prize for disappointed conservatives.

Carter emerged from the Democratic convention with a wide lead over Ford, but the race was too close to call by election day. A number of gaffes—such as Carter's interview with *Playboy* magazine, his ambiguous statements about abortion, and his confused observations on tax reform—hurt the Democratic contender.[168] Ford also gained in the polls when he began to use the patronage powers of the presidency and effectively contrasted his twenty-seven years of

Washington experience to Carter's four years as governor of Georgia.

For the first time since 1960, the major candidates took part in televised debates. As the outsider, Carter helped himself by demonstrating a good grasp of national issues and by appealing to Democrats to vote the party line. Ford hurt himself with a claim that Eastern European nations did not consider themselves to be under the control of the Soviet Union.[169] The remark was intended to be testimony to the Europeans' sense of national identity, but it was interpreted as evidence of the president's naiveté.

Carter's main advantage was regional pride. The Democrats had long since lost their hold over the South, but Carter gained widespread support as the first candidate nominated from the region on his own in more than a century. The Democratic Party's many factions—including such big city mayors as Richard Daley of Chicago and Abraham Beame of New York, civil rights activists, and organized labor—put on a rare display of unity.

Carter defeated Ford by a slim margin, winning 40.8 million votes (50.1 percent) to Ford's 39.1 million (48.0 percent). In the electoral college, 297 votes went to Carter, 240 to Ford. Carter won by pulling together the frazzled New Deal coalition of industrial and urban voters, African Americans, Jews, and southerners. Ford won the West, and Carter won the South, except Virginia. Ford won all the states from the Mississippi River westward except Texas and Hawaii, plus states in his native Midwest like Iowa, Illinois, Michigan, and Indiana. Ford also won Connecticut and the three northernmost New England states—New Hampshire, Vermont, and Maine.

Carter's Uncertain Leadership: 1980

After his election, President Carter's ability to hold the coalition together was limited. The growing influence of the mass media, the fragmenting effects of interest groups, poor relations with Congress, and difficult issues that cut across many different sectors—inflation and unemployment, oil shocks and the more general energy crisis, the Iran hostage crisis, relations with the Soviet Union, and budget austerity moves such as proposed cutbacks in water projects and social welfare—all damaged Carter's governing ability.

As the 1980 election approached, voters were poised to reject a president for the fourth time in a row (if one counts Ford's loss in 1976, Nixon's resignation in 1974, and Johnson's withdrawal from the primaries in 1968). Carter appeared to have lost all but his institutional strength: he controlled party processes, such as the primary schedule; he had access to key financial support and skilled political operatives; and he shaped much of the political agenda. But Kennedy was hitting him hard from the left, and Reagan and others were hitting him hard from the right. As a result, Carter was unable to forge a lasting consensus on important issues. Kennedy was leading Carter in the polls by a two-to-one margin when he announced his challenge to the incumbent president in November 1979. But Carter overcame that lead by the start of the nominating season when the seizure of American hostages in Iran rallied the nation around the president and Kennedy made a series of political mistakes. Kennedy was unable to develop campaign themes or answer questions about his personal conduct in the 1969 Chappaquiddick incident in which a woman died after a car he was driving went off a bridge. Other "character" issues, such as Kennedy's alleged "womanizing," and more substantive issues, such as his liberal voting record, also hurt him in a year dominated by conservative themes. Finally, Kennedy's campaign was in financial jeopardy early because of lavish spending on transportation, headquarters, and other expenses.

The campaign of Gov. Jerry Brown of California was unable to find much support for his appeal for recognition of economic and environmental limits. He dropped out of the race in April.

The president was able to manipulate the primary and caucus schedule to bunch together states favorable to him and to match pro-Kennedy states with pro-Carter states. The result was an early, strong Carter lead in delegates. Kennedy came back with some solid primary wins in New York and Pennsylvania, but his campaign by then had been reduced to a vehicle for anti-Carter expressions. Many Kennedy voters hoped for a deadlocked convention at which a third candidate would win the nomination.

Carter won the nomination on the first ballot despite a variety of stop-Carter efforts and Kennedy's attempt to free delegates to vote for any candidate. When Carter won the crucial floor vote on the "open convention" question, Kennedy did not have a chance. The Carter-Mondale ticket entered the fall campaign as a wounded army unable to generate much enthusiasm from the troops.

The Republicans united early behind Reagan. By April 22, 1980, less than two months after the New Hampshire primary, six candidates had dropped out of the race, and George H. W. Bush, Reagan's only surviving competitor, was desperately behind in the delegate count. Reagan's campaign experienced an early scare when Bush beat Reagan in the Iowa caucuses, but Reagan rebounded, changed campaign managers and tactics, and won a string of primaries and caucuses. By the time of the convention, Reagan was the consensus candidate, and he improved party unity by adding Bush to the fall ticket.

Reagan called on the electorate to replace politics that he said was marked by "pastels," or compromising and uncertain policies, with "bold colors." Reagan's proposed bold strokes included a 30 percent reduction in marginal income tax rates based on a "supply-side" economic theory—which even Bush had said was a dangerous kind of "voodoo

economics"—and massive increases in military expenditures. At the same time Reagan criticized Carter's alleged vacillation and his commitment to liberal policies.

President Carter, who was vulnerable as the hostage crisis neared its first anniversary (on November 4, election day) and high inflation and unemployment rates persisted, attempted to portray Reagan as a dangerous, heartless, and inexperienced amateur. Reagan managed to use Carter's attacks to his advantage by assuming a posture of hurt feelings at the unfair criticism. When in a televised debate Carter attacked Reagan's previous opposition to social welfare programs, Reagan cut him off with a line, "There you go again," that suggested Carter was unfairly and relentlessly distorting Reagan's record.

The greatest controversy of the campaign did not emerge until years later. Books published after the Reagan years charged that the Reagan-Bush campaign negotiated a deal with Iran to delay release of the hostages until after the campaign to embarrass President Carter. Gary Sick, a national security aide for Carter, charged that Reagan campaign officials met with Iranian officials in Europe in the summer of 1980 to arrange weapons sales in exchange for holding the hostages. If true—and many disputed the charges—the deal could have cost Carter the presidency.[170]

Carter strategists also were concerned about the independent candidacy of Rep. John B. Anderson of Illinois, a moderate who dropped out of the Republican race when it became clear that conservatives would dominate that party. After some stronger support in the polls, Anderson stood at about 10 percent for the final two months of the campaign. Carter was concerned that Anderson would take more votes from him than from Reagan, even though analysis of Anderson support suggested otherwise.[171]

Private money almost doubled the amount that Reagan was legally entitled to spend under the federal campaign financing system. Well-organized groups from the "new right," which opposed abortion, gun control, détente, and many social welfare programs, spent lavishly on television commercials and efforts to register like-minded voters. These groups also made a "hit list" of leading liberals in Congress. These candidates were so weakened by the new right's attacks that they put a local and regional drag on an already dragging Democratic ticket.[172]

Polls before election day predicted a close race. Reagan, however, won all but six states and took the White House in an electoral landslide, 489 electoral votes to 49. Reagan won 51 percent of the vote, while Carter managed 41 percent and Anderson 7 percent. Carter ran tight races in ten additional states that could have gone his way with a shift of less than one and a half percentage points. In twenty-one states, Anderson's vote totals made up most or all of the difference between Reagan and Carter. Despite these factors and polls that regularly showed preference for Carter's policy positions, Reagan's victory was impressive. He beat Carter by a better than two-to-one margin in nine states.

Even more surprising than Reagan's electoral landslide was the Republican takeover of the Senate. The new right's targeting of several Senate liberals—such as McGovern, Bayh, Gaylord Nelson of Wisconsin, and John Culver of Iowa—created the biggest Senate turnover since 1958. The Republicans now held the Senate by a 53–46 margin.

President Reagan was able to parlay his claims of an electoral mandate into wide-ranging changes in tax, budget, and military policies. Among other things, he won passage of a three-year, 25 percent cut in tax rates that would reduce federal revenues by $196 billion annually by the time the three-stage program was in place. He also secured omnibus legislation that cut the domestic budget by $140 billion over four years and increased defense spending by $181 billion over the same period. The media hailed Reagan as the most successful handler of Congress since Lyndon Johnson.

THE NEW CONSERVATIVE DISCOURSE

Ronald Reagan's rise ushered in a new age of conservatism in the American political discourse. The vigorous conservative campaigns for the presidency and Congress were accompanied by a host of new "think tanks" and publications with a restyled set of philosophical and policy pronouncements.

The most celebrated event of the conservative revival was the publication in 1980 of George Gilder's *Wealth and Poverty*, a far-reaching attack on welfare state policies that rested on supply-side economic theory. Gilder argued that free markets and low taxes promoted not only economic efficiency and growth but also other benefits such as family strength and artistic creativity. Gilder's book was a central element of Reagan's campaign for major tax cuts.[173] But the supply-side tracts of Gilder and others were only the most visible signs of the conservative movement. Reagan's criticism of the Supreme Court decisions on abortion and school prayer helped to bring evangelical Christians into the political process. Businesses and conservative philanthropists, meanwhile, sponsored an unprecedented level of public policy research that shaped the debate of elections and government policy.[174]

Reagan's political appeal, according to scholar Garry Wills, turned on his ability to blend contradictory elements of American culture such as capitalism, conservatism, and individualism. While Reagan decried the decline of "traditional American values," for example, he extolled the dynamic economic system that demanded constant change. Wills wrote: "There are so many contradictions in this larger construct that one cannot risk entertaining serious challenge to any of its details. In Reagan, luckily, all these clashes are resolved. He is the ideal past, the successful present, the hopeful future all in one."[175]

Using the "bully pulpit" of the presidency, Reagan was able to overwhelm his opponents with his vision. When Democrats criticized specific Reagan policies, Reagan deflated them with expressions of disdain for "little men with loud voices [that] cry doom."[176] Jeane Kirkpatrick's depiction of Democrats as the "blame America first crowd" neatly expressed the way the Reagan rhetoric foreclosed debate on major policy issues such as the budget and trade deficits, military spending, the U.S. role in the third world, and U.S.-Soviet relations.

By the time the 1984 campaign took place, much of the nation had adopted Reagan's terms of debate. Walter F. Mondale's strongest performance, in fact, was in the first debate when he congratulated Reagan for restoring national pride and suggested not that Reagan should be ousted but rather that he be given a graceful retirement. Mondale's campaign was basically conservative: he did not propose a single new social program and called the federal budget deficit the nation's top problem.

Reagan's Landslide: 1984

Reagan's popularity dipped to 44 percent in 1983—about the average for modern presidents—but it rebounded when the economy later picked up.[177] As the 1984 election approached, Reagan faced no opposition from Republicans, but a large field of Democrats sought the right to oppose him in the fall.

The Democrats' early front-runner was former vice president Mondale, who had accumulated a wide range of endorsements (AFL-CIO, National Education Association, United Mine Workers, and the National Organization for Women) and an impressive campaign treasury. The more conservative senator John Glenn of Ohio, the first American to orbit the earth, was considered a strong challenger. Other candidates included Senators Gary Hart of Colorado, Alan Cranston of California, and Ernest Hollings of South Carolina, civil rights leader Jesse Jackson, former presidential candidate George McGovern, and former governor Reubin Askew of Florida.

The early results eliminated all but Mondale, Hart, and Jackson just sixteen days after the New Hampshire primary. Hart became the serious challenger to Mondale when he finished second in Iowa and first in New Hampshire, creating an explosion of media coverage. After Mondale recovered, the two fought head-to-head until the convention. Jackson, the second African American to run for the presidency, stayed in the race to promote his liberal party agenda.[178]

After interviewing a wide range of candidates, Mondale selected Rep. Geraldine A. Ferraro of New York as his running mate—the first woman ever to receive a major party nomination for national office. Representative Ferraro's vice-presidential candidacy probably was a drag on the ticket, not so much because she was a woman but

Democratic presidential candidate Walter F. Mondale and his running mate, Geraldine Ferraro, the first woman to receive a major party nomination for national office, campaign in the 1984 presidential race.

because of the controversy created by her husband's finances and her stand on the abortion question. The controversies hindered the Democratic campaign's effort to articulate its vision for the nation.[179]

Ferraro appeared knowledgeable and strong in her debate with Vice President Bush, and she often drew large and enthusiastic crowds. But she was stuck in controversy when details of her husband's questionable real estate, trusteeship, and tax practices became public. Opponents of abortion held prominent and often loud protests at the sites of her speeches, and she got involved in a lengthy public dispute over abortion with Catholic archbishop John O'Connor. Ferraro also did not help the ticket in regions where the Democrats were weak, such as the South and West.

Mondale ran a generally conservative campaign, concentrating on a proposed tax increase to address the unprecedented budget deficit of more than $200 billion and proposing no new social programs. Mondale criticized Reagan's record on the arms race, but he did not outline basic disagreements on other foreign affairs issues. He charged that Reagan, the oldest president in history, was lazy and out of touch. Only late in the campaign, when his speeches became unabashedly liberal and combative, did Mondale create any excitement.

Just once—in the period after the first presidential debate—did Mondale appear to have a chance to defeat President Reagan. Political pundits had marked Mondale as a poor television performer, but the challenger outfoxed Reagan in the debate and afterward appeared to be gaining ground for a few days. Before the debate, Mondale aides had

leaked erroneous information that suggested he would make a slashing attack. But Mondale surprised Reagan by adopting a "gold-watch approach" suitable to a family business retiring an old-timer—"sort of embracing a grandfather, and gently pushing him aside." [180]

Mondale gave the president credit for helping to restore national patriotism and beginning a national debate on education reform, but he said it was time for new leadership. Reagan appeared confused and, in the rush to demonstrate statistical knowledge of policies, he failed to outline broad themes.

Although the first debate boosted the Mondale campaign's morale, it never brought Mondale within striking range of Reagan—he never came within ten percentage points of Reagan in the polls. Reagan's campaign was a series of rallies with masses of colorful balloons and confident talk about the United States "standing tall" in domestic and world affairs. Reagan was so sure of victory that he made a last-minute trip to Mondale's home state of Minnesota with the hope of completing a fifty-state sweep of the nation.

As it was, Reagan won forty-nine states, with 2-to-1 margins in eight states. Idaho, Nebraska, and Utah each gave Reagan more than 70 percent of the vote. Mondale won only the District of Columbia and his home state of Minnesota, where he beat Reagan by only two-tenths of a percentage point. As for the popular vote, Reagan won 54.5 million votes (58.8 percent) to Mondale's 37.6 million (40.6 percent). In the electoral college, he received 525 votes to Mondale's 13 votes.

Reagan's two landslides and the conservative discourse of his administration led many experts to wonder if they were witnessing a "realignment"—a major shift in political alliances among a variety of social, economic, and ethnic groups.[181] The trend during the 1970s and 1980s appeared to be one of a Democratic hold on congressional and state elections and Republican dominance of presidential elections. Some experts pointed to the electorate's ticket-splitting tendencies as evidence of "dealignment"—a breakdown of the old system without development of an entirely new system.[182]

Perhaps the most noteworthy development of recent years, which fits the dealignment thesis, has been the convergence of the appeal of the two parties. Michael Barone, in *The Almanac of American Politics*, wrote:

> Political preferences in the America of the 1940's correlated to a fair degree with income. Republican strength was greater than average in high income states ... while Roosevelt and Truman carried virtually every state with incomes below the national average. But today there is virtually no correlation between income level and political preference. Utah, with one of the lowest per capita incomes, was one of the nation's most Republican states in 1980.... In the Midwest, high income Illinois is more Democratic than low income Indiana.[183]

Bush's Ascendancy: 1988

The election of 1988 was the first after 1968 in which an incumbent president did not run. With no major figure and no major issues, the campaign was a tumultuous affair. Fourteen candidates struggled to develop an identity with the voters, and the campaign lurched from one symbolic issue to the next, never developing the overarching themes of previous campaigns.

In the absence of any major new issues, and in a time of general peace and prosperity, Republican vice president George H. W. Bush won the presidency. Bush defeated Democratic Massachusetts governor Michael S. Dukakis by a margin of 54 percent to 46 percent—48.9 million votes to 41.8 million votes. Bush's electoral vote margin was more impressive, 426–111. A negative campaign and limited voter registration efforts resulted in the lowest voter turnout rate since the 1920 and 1924 race percentages of 49 percent of all eligible voters. Just a little more than 50 percent of all eligible citizens voted for president in 1988.

Bush, benefiting from the Nixon-Reagan presidential coalition, won all the states of the old Confederacy, the entire West except Oregon and Washington, and several northern industrial states. Dukakis originally had hoped to crack the South by selecting a favorite son, Sen. Lloyd M. Bentsen Jr. of Texas, as his running mate, but that tactic failed. Dukakis lost crucial states that he had fought for to the end, such as California, Pennsylvania, Illinois, Ohio, and Missouri. He won New York, Massachusetts, Wisconsin, Minnesota, Oregon, Washington, West Virginia, Iowa, Rhode Island, Hawaii, and the District of Columbia.

President Ronald Reagan's retirement after two full terms created a political void. By most accounts, Reagan was the most popular president since Dwight Eisenhower. His dominance of national politics left little room for other figures to establish presidential stature.

Reagan's fiscal and social policies reduced the possibility for candidates to offer ambitious new programs. The national government's huge budget deficits—which exceeded $200 billion, compared with about $73 billion in the last year of the Carter administration—checked any grandiose new spending plans. The Reagan debt had exceeded the debt of the previous thirty-eight presidents.

President Reagan also had reshaped the dialogue on foreign affairs. He maintained strong opposition to the Soviet Union and other "Marxist" nations with his policies in Nicaragua, Afghanistan, and Angola. He also had projected an image of strength with military action in Libya and Grenada. At the same time, however, he had co-opted his critics by meeting with Soviet leader Mikhail Gorbachev several times and signing a nuclear arms control agreement. Reagan even asserted that the Gorbachev regime was fundamentally different from previous Soviet regimes, which he had called the "evil empire."

The early Republican front-runners were Bush and Sen. Robert J. "Bob" Dole of Kansas; former senator Hart of Colorado was considered the early Democratic leader. The campaign got scrambled before it began, however. Hart left the race in 1987 when the *Miami Herald* augmented rumors of Hart's infidelity with a report that he had spent the night with a young model. The newspaper had staked out Hart's Washington townhouse with two reporters, two editors, and a photographer. The investigators sat in a rental car, loitered nearby, and jogged down the street. Hart, considered by many to be the brightest and most issue-oriented candidate, had long faced criticism about his "character."

The Hart story dominated the political news in 1987. Network news programs devoted 132 minutes to Hart, mostly in the first half of the year, and, on the GOP side, 32 minutes to the long-shot television evangelist Marion G. "Pat" Robertson. The two front-runners and eventual nominees, Bush and Dukakis, got 28 and 20 minutes, respectively.[184]

Sen. Joseph R. Biden Jr. of Delaware was the next casualty of the media's 1987 concern with character issues.[185] Media reports that he had committed plagiarism on a law school paper and in campaign speeches led to Biden's early exit from the campaign. Biden had been considered a leading candidate because of his experience and strong speaking style.

With Hart and Biden out of the race, the Democrats were in disarray. Dubbed "dwarfs," the remaining candidates—Rev. Jackson of Illinois, Dukakis, Rep. Richard A. Gephardt of Missouri, Sen. Albert A. "Al" Gore Jr. of Tennessee, Sen. Paul M. Simon of Illinois, and former

Arizona governor Bruce Babbitt—lacked the combination of extensive government experience and strong national bases many observers thought necessary to win the presidency.

The Republicans had problems of their own. Vice President Bush was the early favorite, and he benefited from his association with President Reagan. But Bush's public fealty to Reagan also created a problem: he was considered a "wimp," unable to stand on his own. Almost every major position Bush had held in his political career was the result of an appointment: ambassador to the United Nations, chair of the Republican National Committee, envoy to China, director of the Central Intelligence Agency, and vice president. Bush had represented Texas for two terms in the House of Representatives and lost two Senate races.

At the outset of the race, Dole was considered a strong contender. As Republican leader in the Senate, he had a high profile in national politics and proven fund-raising abilities. His wife, Elizabeth, was prominent as secretary of transportation. Dole also had a biting wit, which gave spark to his campaigning style but irritated some voters. Other GOP candidates were Rep. Jack Kemp of New York, former secretary of state Alexander M. Haig Jr. of Pennsylvania, former Delaware governor Pierre S. "Pete" du Pont IV, and television evangelist Pat Robertson of Virginia.

The marathon campaign for the nomination began with the Iowa caucuses, a significant event only because of intense media attention. Gephardt barely edged Simon in the Democratic contests, and Dole won the Republican race. The big story was how badly Bush performed: he finished third behind Dole and Robertson.

The Iowa loss caused Bush to emerge from his isolation and confront his rivals for the nomination. (Bush had been the most restrained and cautious candidate as he tried to benefit from the prestige of the White House.) Bush also became more animated on the campaign trail. As a result of these changes—and a series of television advertisements charging that Dole would raise taxes—Bush beat Dole in the New Hampshire primary. Dole had failed to respond quickly to the Bush offensive, and when he snapped on national television about Bush's "lying about my record," he reinforced his image as a mean-spirited candidate.

Among the Democrats, Governor Dukakis easily won the New Hampshire primary, capitalizing on his regional popularity. Most of the Democratic fire in that race took place between the two runners-up, Gephardt and Simon.

After two popular terms as president, Ronald Reagan and wife Nancy pass leadership of the "Reagan Revolution" to newly inaugurated President George H. W. Bush and wife Barbara in 1989.

Dukakis escaped without any major criticism, and his already strong fund-raising machine went into high gear.

The decisive stage of the GOP campaign was Super Tuesday—March 8—when twenty-two states held presidential primaries or caucuses. Benefiting from a well-organized campaign and his new aggressiveness on the campaign trail, Bush won seventeen of the eighteen GOP contests. Dole staked his campaign on the ensuing Illinois primary, but he lost badly, and Bush was virtually ensured the Republican nomination.

The one issue that threatened Bush throughout 1988 was the Iran-contra scandal. Revelations that the Reagan administration had traded arms to Iran in exchange for the release of hostages held in Lebanon, then used the proceeds illegally to fund the war in Nicaragua, raised questions about Bush's role in the matter. Administration officials admitted lying to Congress, destroying evidence, and operating outside normal government channels; one top official even attempted suicide. The question of Bush's involvement in the affair, however, fizzled after months of inconclusive questioning.

On Super Tuesday, Democratic front-runner Dukakis won Texas and Florida and five northern states, thereby confirming his shaky front-runner status. Civil rights leader Jesse Jackson was the big surprise, however, winning five southern states. Gore won seven states. Even though it was designed to help conservative candidates, Super Tuesday fit Jackson's strengths. Six of the nine states in which Jackson had scored best in 1984 held their contests on Super Tuesday in 1988.

Super Tuesday also was supposed to put the South in the national spotlight, but the region received only a few more candidate visits in 1988 (149) than it had in 1976 (145).[186]

The Democratic marathon continued into Illinois, Michigan, and New York. Dukakis took and maintained the lead in delegates with steady wins over Jackson and Gore. Gore finally dropped out after finishing third in a divisive New York primary, and the rest of the campaign was a one-on-one race between Dukakis and Jackson. Only once—after his victory over Dukakis in the Michigan caucuses—did Jackson appear to have a chance to win the Democratic nomination. But in their next encounter, the Wisconsin primary, Dukakis defeated Jackson.

Jackson was a mixed blessing for the party. An energetic campaigner, he attracted support from blacks and from farmers and blue-collar workers who were disgruntled by the uneven rewards of economic growth. But Jackson was considerably to the left of the rest of the party and never had held any government office. Race also was a factor: no political professional believed that a liberal black could be elected president.

Dukakis practically clinched the nomination with his victory over Jackson in the New York primary. The issue of race was at the center of the campaign. New York City mayor Edward I. Koch, a Gore supporter, called Jackson a "radical" and said Jews would be "crazy" to vote for him. Such remarks aggravated tensions between blacks and Jews that had festered since the 1960s. Dukakis avoided the race issue and won the primary.

As the summer conventions approached, Bush and Dukakis each had the full support of his party. The parties' internal divisions were on display as the prospective nominees considered possible vice-presidential candidates. Blacks lobbied for Jackson's selection by Dukakis, while "new right" GOP leaders lobbied against a "moderate" running mate for Bush.

Dukakis selected conservative senator Lloyd Bentsen of Texas as his running mate before the Atlanta Democratic convention. Jackson complained publicly and privately about the decision, but he eventually embraced Bentsen for the sake of party unity. Dukakis hoped Bentsen would be able to help carry Texas: no Democrat had won the presidency without winning Texas since the state became part of the nation in 1845.

The July convention was a success for the Democrats. After a week of Bush-bashing and Democratic conciliation, Dukakis gave an effective acceptance speech peppered with statements in Spanish and Greek. Dukakis left the convention with a double-digit lead over Bush in the polls.

The Republican convention in August did not start out as well. Bush announced his vice-presidential selection, Sen. James Danforth "Dan" Quayle of Indiana, when he arrived in New Orleans. After revelations that Quayle had avoided military service in the Vietnam War by enlisting in the Indiana National Guard, many Republicans criticized Bush's choice. Some even said that Quayle might have to be dropped from the ticket.[187] By the end of the convention, however, the Republicans had weathered the storm. Bush delivered a crisp address, which provided the appealing self-portrait the vice president needed, and moved into the fall campaign for a close battle with Dukakis.

Bush took the offensive immediately after the August GOP convention and hit Dukakis as a "liberal" out of touch with American "values." More specifically, Bush attacked Dukakis for his membership in the American Civil Liberties Union, his veto of a bill requiring Massachusetts teachers to lead children in the Pledge of Allegiance, and a Massachusetts program allowing prisoners time off for weekends. The Bush campaign's "Willie Horton" commercial—which told of a black prisoner raping a woman while out on a weekend release program—was particularly controversial. As Bush pounded away at these symbolic issues (effectively drowning out other major issues such as the national debt, trade deficit, housing, education, U.S.-Soviet relations, the environment, and ethics in government), Dukakis's "negative" ratings with voters soared. Roger Ailes, Bush's media adviser, admitted that the Bush camp knew it would have to define Dukakis. The media themselves had no interest in substance, Ailes pointed out, leaving candidates "three ways to get on the air: pictures, attacks, and mistakes." Thus the Bush campaign spent its time "avoiding mistakes, staying on the attack, and giving them pictures."[188]

Not believing the attacks would affect his standing with undecided voters—and believing they might even hurt Bush—Dukakis did not respond forcefully to the frontal assault until October. By then, however, Bush had effectively defined Dukakis as a newcomer to national politics. Dukakis's counteroffensive in the last two weeks of the campaign came too late. As Dukakis fell behind Bush, his campaign pinned its hopes on two nationally televised debates. Dukakis performed well in the first debate, but Bush appeared to "win" the second debate. Dukakis failed to gain on Bush.

The only major problem for Bush was Quayle. Most political professionals considered Quayle a "lightweight." The forty-one-year-old Quayle had been a poor student and was a marginal member of Congress.[189] Dukakis said Bush's selection of Quayle amounted to failure in his "first presidential decision." Dukakis compared Quayle to the more experienced Bentsen, who performed much better in a vice-presidential debate. Indeed, in that debate Bentsen gave the campaign perhaps its most memorable moment. Responding to Quayle's assertion that he had as much congressional experience as Jack Kennedy had when he sought the presidency, Bentsen said, "Senator, I served with Jack

Kennedy. I knew Jack Kennedy. Jack Kennedy was a friend of mine. Senator, you're no Jack Kennedy." [190]

Public polls revealed that most voters thought that Quayle was a bad choice. The Bush campaign tried to minimize the damage by limiting Quayle's public exposure and carefully scripting his statements. Quayle rarely spoke in major media markets; many of his campaign stops were accessible only by bus. While Bush delivered speeches in several states each day, Quayle often made just one speech before schoolchildren or partisan audiences.

After months of inconsistent and confusing strategy, Dukakis finally developed a strong appeal in the last two weeks of the campaign. He told voters he was on their side and portrayed Bush as a toady to the wealthy. Dukakis said the middle class had been "squeezed" by the policies of the Reagan administration and that the Democrats would provide good jobs, affordable housing and health care, and tough enforcement of environmental protection laws.

But it was not enough. Bush, who had made a fortune in the oil business before entering politics and was the son of a former U.S. senator, persuaded more voters that his experience and values were what they wanted in the very personal choice of a president.

THE CLINTON ERA

In March 1991, in the aftermath of the U.S.-led victory over Iraq in the Persian Gulf War, President George H. W. Bush received the highest approval ratings since opinion polling began: around 90 percent of respondents said they approved of his performance as president. But just a year later, Bush was struggling to keep his job—and he failed.

Bill Clinton's victory over Bush in 1992 could have been viewed, on the one hand, as a dramatic shift in American politics. Touting his campaign slogan of "change," the forty-six-year-old Arkansas governor repeatedly blasted the Republican White House for its inattention to domestic problems such as the budget deficit, health care, welfare, civil rights, crime, trade, and economic investment. President Bush, Clinton said, was too obsessed with foreign policy and unconcerned with domestic affairs.

On the other hand, Clinton's election could have been viewed as an aberration. Only the second Democrat elected president since 1968, Clinton got only 43 percent of the vote in a three-candidate race. Voters said they voted against Bush, not for Clinton. The independent candidacy of Texas billionaire H. Ross Perot may have cost Bush the election, as much by tarnishing his reputation as by taking away the votes of the angry middle class. Even people who supported Clinton expressed reservations about his character. Voters reacted warily to reports of Clinton's avoidance of military service in Vietnam, marital infidelity, and conflicts of interest while governor, and to his evasiveness about smoking

marijuana as a student. On policy questions, Clinton was well informed, but sometimes he appeared insincere. A label pinned on Clinton in Arkansas—"Slick Willie"—stuck.

President Bush began the election cycle looking unbeatable. Coasting on the apparent success of his leadership during the Gulf War, Bush appeared to have the strength to lead the United States into what he called the "new world order." In 1989 the countries of the so-called Soviet bloc—East Germany, Poland, Czechoslovakia, Romania, Hungary—had broken from communist rule in a series of nonviolent revolutions. In August 1991 an attempted coup against Mikhail Gorbachev's "perestroika" government in the Soviet Union had failed. Afterward, the Soviet regime—Communist Party and all—had collapsed. The Bush presidency had overseen the most remarkable realignment of world politics since World War II.

Indeed, Bush took credit for presiding over the dramatic changes, but those American "victories" also undermined his position. The Republican Party had dominated recent presidential politics at least partly because of its hawkish policies during the cold war. With the end of the Soviet threat, the GOP no longer had a "gut" issue to use against the Democrats. According to journalist Sidney Blumenthal, "The Cold War's end was not a photo opportunity, a sound bite, a revelation of 'character,' a political consultant's tactic, or even a theme. It was a global sea change as profound as the Cold War's beginning." [191] Bush had a hard time adjusting.

For a while, President Bush looked so strong that many Democrats were reluctant to take him on. The party's leading figures—Gov. Mario Cuomo of New York; Senators Bill Bradley of New Jersey, Al Gore of Tennessee, and Jay Rockefeller of West Virginia; and Rep. Richard Gephardt of Missouri—announced they would not run. Only former senator Paul E. Tsongas of Massachusetts, recently recovered from a bout with cancer, announced his candidacy in spring 1991.

Despite high polling numbers, President Bush might have been doomed from the start. Despite three decades in public life, Bush had never conveyed a coherent identity or campaign theme. His advisers planned to "narrowcast" messages to selected groups until the summer, when Bush would deliver his big "what-I-stand-for" speech. But by that time, Bush's opponent had defined him as weak and unprincipled. His attempt to divert attention to Clinton's foibles only intensified Bush's image as uncertain of his own values and goals.[192]

By spring 1992 Bush's base had crumbled. The president had decided to "sit" on his high popularity ratings and win reelection by avoiding mistakes. Bush's chief of staff, John Sununu, summed up the strategy: "There's not another single piece of legislation that needs to be passed in the next two years for this president. In fact, if Congress wants to come together, adjourn, and leave, it's all right with us." [193] The results of this strategy were devastating. In May 1992 a poll found that 76 percent of the public disapproved of the way Bush was handling the economy.[194] His overall approval rating dropped an unprecedented 57 percentage points from the end of the Gulf War to the beginning of the 1992 GOP convention.

A bitter anti-incumbent mood dominated the new campaign year. Nationwide, reformers promoted the idea of term limits for elected officials as a way to sweep out career politicians.[195] Perot, who had parlayed his wealth into a number of headline-grabbing exploits over the years, became a viable independent candidate.[196] His pithy statements about how to "fix" government captured the imagination of the public.

Pennsylvania voters sent a warning shot to the White House when they rejected the 1991 Senate candidacy of Bush's friend and first attorney general, Richard Thornburgh. Democrat Harris Wofford, appointed to the seat that had opened with the death of Sen. John Heinz in April 1991, won on a platform of national health care and a return to domestic priorities—themes that Clinton reprised in 1992. Wofford, a former college president and Kennedy administration official, came from 30 points behind in the polls to win with 55 percent of the vote. It was the highest percentage that any Democrat had received in Pennsylvania senatorial elections. Wofford's campaign was run by a young operative named James Carville.

Bush's major domestic initiative—the budget law passed in October 1990—angered the Republican Party's right wing. Conservatives had long distrusted Bush because of his past moderate positions on taxes, abortion, civil rights, and social programs. The budget act, which increased taxes by $150 billion, broke the pledge of "no new taxes" that Bush had taken in the 1988 presidential campaign.

As the recession and other domestic crises deepened, the president seemed increasingly out of touch. Bush's reported confusion over the use of bar codes at a grocery store symbolized his elite background and isolation. After race riots in Los Angeles drew the nation's attention to the severity of poverty, Bush was photographed teaching baffled-looking urban youths how to use a fishing pole. In a

Democratic presidential candidate Bill Clinton talks with young people on a program hosted by the MTV cable channel. The 1992 campaign was revolutionary in the way candidates used nontraditional media to reach voters.

political environment couched in symbolism, these images were ruinous.

Bush had begun his term with less party support than any president in history—the Democrats controlled the Senate by ten seats and the House by eighty-five seats. As a result, Bush's legislative initiatives were routinely labeled "dead on arrival." In 1989, for the first time, the Senate rejected an incoming president's cabinet nominee when it voted down former senator John G. Tower's bid to be secretary of defense. In his dealings with Capitol Hill, Bush had vacillated between confrontation and compromise. In fact, Bush regularly tussled with Congress, vetoing forty-four bills between 1989 and 1992.

Three-way Race: 1992

The Democratic field grew slowly. Besides Clinton and Tsongas, the field included former governor Edmund G. "Jerry" Brown Jr. of California, Senators Thomas Harkin of Iowa and Robert Kerrey of Nebraska, and Gov. L. Douglas Wilder of Virginia. Wilder dropped out, however, before the first contest. Clinton won the "invisible primaries" before the formal balloting began; he attracted $3.3 million in contributions by the end of 1991. Harkin was second best with a little more than $2 million.[197] The Clinton campaign then organized supporters in most states holding early contests.

By calling himself a "new Democrat," Clinton hoped to separate himself from some of the rejected Democratic candidates of the past: Jimmy Carter, Walter Mondale, and Michael Dukakis. In keeping with this strategy, Clinton promised to move beyond liberal orthodoxy and "reinvent government." [198] His record in Arkansas suggested a willingness to oppose liberal nostrums on issues such as the death penalty, economic growth, and public education.

The centerpiece of Clinton's strategy was to appeal to the "forgotten middle class." Suburbanites, the working class, and southerners and westerners had abandoned the Democratic Party since the late 1960s. Unfortunately for the Democrats, these groups composed a growing part of the electorate. In fact, many pundits argued that these groups gave the Republicans a "lock" on the presidency.[199] Clinton's goal, then, was to forge a new ideological center and "pick" the lock.

As expected, "favorite-son" Harkin easily won the Iowa caucuses in February. Clinton led the polling before the New Hampshire primary until he ran into trouble when the media questioned his character. A woman claimed that she and Clinton had had an affair, and Clinton was reported to have misled an Army Reserves recruiter as part of a scheme to avoid service in Vietnam. But Clinton hit back. Appearing on the television news magazine *60 Minutes* after the January 1992 Super Bowl game, Clinton admitted he had "caused pain" in his marriage but said he and his wife had solved their problems. Hillary Clinton's appearance with her husband seemed to close the matter. Skeptics should vote against Clinton, she said, but they also should drop the character charges.

Tsongas won the New Hampshire primary on February 18 with 33.2 percent of the vote to Clinton's 24.7 percent. Tsongas offered the policy equivalent of castor oil. He said the nation needed to make difficult economic choices such as higher taxes and program cutbacks. He called Clinton, who spoke in favor of a tax cut and the costly Connecticut-built Polaris Navy submarine, a "pander bear." Clinton exuberantly called his second-place finish a victory by noting Tsongas's regional ties and declaring himself the "Comeback Kid." His campaign, however, was out of money and had to be rescued by a $3.5 million line of credit from an Arkansas bank.

Tsongas and Brown won the occasional contest after New Hampshire, but Clinton rolled to the nomination starting with his March 3 victory in the Georgia primary. Kerrey and Harkin dropped out in early March. Clinton's sweep of southern states on "Super Tuesday," March 10, and his decisive wins in Michigan and Illinois on March 17 practically clinched the nomination. But he had a scare when Brown beat him in Connecticut on March 24. He then beat Brown decisively in New York on April 7. Tsongas, by that time an inactive candidate, finished ahead of Brown in New York.

Clinton won thirty-one state primaries with 51.8 percent of the vote; Tsongas, four states with 18.1 percent; and Brown, two states with 20.1 percent.[200] Even as Clinton won state after state and Bush plummeted in the polls, Democratic leaders searched for an alternative; they had grown nervous about Clinton's ability to confront the char-

Independent H. Ross Perot mounted his 1992 campaign for the presidency by relying on his own money and appearing on television talk shows, such as here with Larry King.

acter issue. In March almost half the Democratic voters in Connecticut's primary said Clinton lacked the "honesty or integrity" to be president.[201] Former governor Brown fed the uncertainty with his relentless attacks on Clinton's ties to special interests. Talk of drafting another candidate continued, but party professionals became resigned to Clinton's nomination.

President George H. W. Bush faced an unusually pointed challenge from conservative columnist and former White House aide Patrick J. Buchanan, who charged that Bush had betrayed the conservative faith. His main point of attack was the 1990 tax increase. Although in the end Bush won New Hampshire, the media focused on the 37 percent of the vote that the underdog Buchanan received. Buchanan then made a vigorous effort to win some of the southern contests in early March, but he never matched his New Hampshire numbers. Buchanan continued his campaign until June, assured of media attention by virtue of his quixotic quest and uncompromising rhetoric. In the final analysis, however, he did not win any states with his 22 percent of the total primary vote.[202]

Ironically, in taking his hard hits at Bush, Buchanan may have helped to neutralize another protest candidate, former Ku Klux Klan leader David Duke, who had finished second in the Louisiana gubernatorial contest in 1991. Republican leaders were embarrassed by Duke's GOP membership, but he disappeared after a poor showing in New Hampshire.

Perot's on-and-off campaign unsettled Republicans' plans to build on their base in the South and West. Perot's folksy antigovernment rhetoric appealed to voters in the suburbs and high-growth areas of the 1980s—the heart of the GOP base since Richard Nixon's 1968 campaign. Perot's campaign began where much of the 1992 campaign was waged: on the television talk show circuit. On the cable TV show *Larry King Live,* Perot said in February that he would run for president if volunteers put him on the ballot in all fifty states. He also said he would spend up to $100 million of his own money to fund a "world-class campaign." At one point, Perot appeared to have a chance to win the presidency. Polls in May showed him in second place nationally behind President Bush and winning some southern and western states outright.

As Perot's unofficial campaign progressed, the media raised doubts about his background and grasp of government. For example, Perot had made his fortune by gaining rights to a computer accounting system for government health programs, and it was only his behind-the-scenes lobbying that prompted the Nixon administration to halt a government battle for control of the computer system. On a more personal level, Perot's conspiracy theories about issues such as prisoners of war in Vietnam and political opponents led to speculation about possible paranoia. When asked about the details for his plans to address the budget deficit, improve government efficiency, improve U.S. trade, and address foreign affairs, Perot appeared ill-informed and irritable. Thus by summer more people viewed Perot unfavorably than favorably.

Perot dropped out of the campaign before he had a chance to announce his entry formally. He pointed out that Clinton's selection of well-respected Gore as his running mate indicated that the Democrats were "getting their act together." He also recognized that his campaign might split the vote badly and send the election into the House of Representatives.

Perot resumed his campaign in the fall, blaming his temporary exit on a Republican "dirty tricks" effort to smear his family. By then the critical reporting had faded. But it was too late for Perot because his erratic behavior had driven away supporters and curious voters alike. Perot also had difficulty finding a credible running mate. His selection of retired admiral James Stockdale became the subject of parody when Stockdale appeared confused and poorly informed during the debate of the vice-presidential candidates.

Even though Perot had no real chance to win, his campaign was significant. He spent $60 million of his money, mostly to purchase half-hour television advertisements. Some of the ads, dubbed "infomercials," won critical acclaim for their plain talk about the dangers of the federal budget deficit. Perot's bluntness lent credibility to his relentless attacks on Bush.

The communications revolution changed the way the candidates reached voters. For example, candidates appeared in settings once considered undignified for potential presidents. Television talk shows, such as *Larry King Live,* as well as radio programs, such as *Imus in the Morning,* provided a way for candidates to bypass the establishment media. The blurred lines between news and entertainment were perhaps most evident on cable television in the rock music MTV channel's ongoing coverage of the presidential campaign. New outlets were especially important for candidates facing credibility problems in mainstream media (Clinton) and for the insurgents (Perot and Brown).

Bush's campaign was on the defensive early for using "dirty" campaign tactics. Democrats cited Bush's 1988 "Willie Horton" commercials as evidence of a Republican willingness to appeal to racism and fear. Newspaper citations of the Horton campaign were greater in 1992 than 1988, suggesting that the Democrats eventually got more from the ad's backlash than Republicans got from the original campaign.

Clinton parroted Perot's rhetoric about the evils of special-interest influence in Washington and promised reforms of the campaign finance system. Clinton, however, also raised money aggressively. The Democrats raised $71 million in 1992, $9 million more than the Republicans.[203] Clinton's selection of moderate senator Gore of Tennessee as a running mate was central to his fall strategy. Gore's service in Vietnam and military expertise countered Clinton's suspect status in foreign policy. Moreover, Gore's Washington experience going back to 1976 helped Clinton to compensate for his lack of federal government experience. Finally, Gore's reputation as an intellectual—he wrote an acclaimed book about the environment in 1992[204]—contrasted with Vice President Quayle's lightweight reputation.

In his campaign, Clinton benefited from the "year of the woman." Women had supported Democratic candidates in greater numbers than men since the Republican Party dropped its support for the Equal Rights Amendment and abortion rights in 1980. But the Democrats were not able to exploit the "gender gap" until 1992. The galvanizing issue was the allegation that Clarence Thomas, a Bush appointee to the Supreme Court, had sexually harassed a former colleague named Anita Hill. Women were outraged with the Senate Judiciary Committee's handling of the matter, and feminist groups mobilized to increase female representation in politics. The issue put President Bush on the defensive, while Clinton rallied liberals and libertarians alike with his calls for equal opportunity and abortion rights.

The Republican convention in Houston was a turning point in the campaign. Strategists decided to shore up Bush's right-wing support and raise doubts about Clinton's character. The party's platform committee was dominated by the right-wing Christian Coalition. Speeches by Patrick Buchanan, Pat Robertson, and Marilyn Quayle, questioning the Democrats' patriotism and arguing for a rollback of civil liberties, played badly. Bush's lost convention opportunity was apparent in the meager 3 percentage point "bounce" in poll support, compared with Clinton's 17 to 20 percent increase after the Democratic convention.[205]

Clinton ran a sophisticated general election campaign, coordinated from the "war room" in Little Rock by strategists, led by James Carville, who choreographed every aspect of the campaign, from television commercials to talk show appearances to speechwriting to the bus tours of small towns. The campaign professionals were especially adept at answering charges from the opposition. When Bush attacked, Clintonites issued instant, detailed responses. The quick response prevented Bush's charges from dominating the news cycle.

The Bush-Quayle fall campaign was erratic. Early on, it focused on "family values," critiquing the Democrats as elitists out of touch with ordinary people. Then Bush used the powers of incumbency by announcing billions of dollars in grants to different states. All along, Bush criticized Clinton's character and experience. But the personal attacks often appeared shrill; at one point, he called Clinton and Gore "bozos" and said "my dog Millie" would be better at foreign policy than they. Bush criticized Clinton's visit to the Soviet Union as a student and suggested that he wanted to import British-style socialism to the United States.

Bush's credibility came under fire in the campaign's final days when a special prosecutor indicted former defense secretary Caspar Weinberger and released a memorandum that indicated Bush had participated in the Iran-contra scandal much more actively than he had acknowledged.

The Clinton-Gore ticket gave the Democrats a solid base in the border states to build on. With Arkansas and Tennessee in the Democratic camp, the Democrats could build outward into the old Confederacy (Georgia, Louisiana, Kentucky), north into the industrial states (Illinois, Michigan, Ohio), and west and north into the farm states (Iowa, Minnesota, Wisconsin). The Democrats had consistently lost those states in presidential elections in the past generation, despite strong support in congressional and statewide races.

The Democrats also built on their core of support in the Northeast (winning all the states from Maine to West Virginia) and capitalized on disgruntlement with Bush in the West (California, Colorado, Hawaii, Montana, Nevada, New Mexico, Oregon, and Washington went for Clinton). That was enough to "pick" the Republican "lock" on the electoral college.

Clinton took only 43 percent of the popular vote but garnered 370 electoral votes. This compared with Bush's 38 percent of the popular vote and 168 electoral votes. Perot's 19 percent share of the vote was the largest percentage a third party had won since 1912, but he did not win any electoral votes.

The hard anti-incumbent mood of the electorate, stoked by Perot, helped to produce the highest voter turnout rate since 1960. Some 55 percent of eligible voters participated in the election. That participation rate was far below rates of other countries and earlier periods in U.S. history. But it seemed to stem, momentarily, the apathy and resignation of American politics.

Clinton's Reelection: 1996

In 1994 many voters sent a strong message of disapproval with President Clinton's record by electing a Republican Congress. That dramatic event led many political analysts to conclude that Clinton would be a one-term president. But what many had not anticipated was that the new GOP Congress, led prominently by controversial House Speaker Newt Gingrich of Georgia, would incorrectly interpret the 1994 election results as a mandate for their conservative ideological agenda and then push for substantial—and unpopular—policy reform. This miscalculation provided President Clinton with a new opportunity to redefine himself and to rehabilitate his political future.

While the Republicans strove hard for conservative policy change, Clinton adopted more moderate positions and portrayed himself as a check against the "extremism" of the GOP agenda. That tack proved successful by the end of 1995. With the president and Republican legislators feuding over spending priorities, Congress failed to pass a budget in time to avoid two temporary government shutdowns. As the impasse persisted, the Republican Congress began to appear unreasonable in the public's eye, and the president benefited from the comparison. This budgetary standoff against Congress was perhaps the single most important event to Clinton's political rehabilitation.

The president entered the 1996 election season with renewed political strength and high approval ratings. In addition to the political miscalculations of the majority in Congress, Clinton benefited from a strengthening economy. A third factor also began to weigh in the president's favor: he lacked an intraparty challenge for renomination, while the GOP nomination contest was an expensive, highly negative, and divisive process.

From the beginning Senate Majority Leader Bob Dole of Kansas was the clear front-runner for the Republican Party's nomination. He had the broadest party support of any announced candidate, the most prominent endorsements, and the best grassroots campaign organization. Although there never was any serious doubt that he would be the Republican nominee, for several months Dole had to fight off a large group of presidential aspirants including television commentator Buchanan, former Tennessee governor and Education secretary Lamar Alexander, Texas senator Phil Gramm, Indiana senator Richard Lugar, California representative Robert Dornan, and multimillionaire publisher Malcolm S. "Steve" Forbes Jr.

Of these candidates, initially Gramm appeared to be the most formidable because of his status in the Senate and ability to raise huge sums of money for a campaign. Yet

President Bill Clinton and Vice President Al Gore accept their renomination at the Democratic National Convention in August 1996. In the general election Clinton became the first Democratic president reelected to a second term since Franklin Roosevelt in 1936.

Gramm lacked grassroots support, and his campaign faded quickly. Colleague Lugar was highly regarded by party moderates and many opinion leaders, but he ran a bland campaign that dwelt on foreign policy issues that were not driving the Republican electorate. Buchanan had support among many of the dedicated antiabortion conservatives in the party, and he fared surprisingly well in some of the early caucuses and primaries, but most in the GOP considered him too extreme and his campaign too faltered.

The most important opponent to Dole ultimately was the publishing tycoon Forbes, who spent an extraordinary sum of his personal fortune to challenge the front-runner with extensive negative television ads. Although Forbes's campaign failed to dislodge Dole from the front of the pack, it succeeded at raising serious doubts about the senator's ability to beat Clinton. The negative ads also hurt Dole's standing with the wider public and forced him to spend his campaign resources on the nomination battle as Clinton amassed campaign funds for the general election.

Dole's eventual nomination—even after losing the traditionally crucial battleground primary in New Hampshire to Buchanan—did not ensure a united Republican Party to challenge the president. Although Dole had long supported the antiabortion stance of many in his party, social conservatives who made up a crucial bloc of the Republican vote were not convinced of his commitment to their cause. Many considered him too moderate in temperament and too willing to compromise principles. Party moderates worried that Dole would allow the Christian right to force his campaign to adopt positions that would enable the Democrats to once again capitalize on the "extremism" charge.[206]

Even after his nomination was ensured, Dole's campaign failed for weeks to capture the public's attention. In part he appeared too much a part of the GOP agenda in Congress that Democrats had successfully defined as harshly conservative. As senate majority leader Dole had found himself in the difficult position of having to manage his official duties while campaigning for president. This involved promoting the GOP agenda in Congress while at the same time trying to distance himself from its less popular elements. Dole made a bold strategic gamble when he decided to resign from the Senate altogether to campaign full time for the presidency. His emotional departure from the Senate on June 11 temporarily energized his campaign.

At his nominating convention in San Diego, Dole performed a tough balancing act in keeping warring moderates and social conservatives from dividing the party. Dole especially sought to avoid the kind of negative publicity that had surrounded "family values night" at the 1992 GOP convention in Houston.[207] The Republicans struck an awkward compromise: although the party platform was conservative and kept the antiabortion plank, the convention that the country saw on television was moderate in tone and did not feature prime-time addresses by controversial figures such as Buchanan and television evangelist Robertson.

Dole surprised many with two bold campaign moves. First, he selected as his running mate former New York representative and secretary of Housing and Urban Development Jack Kemp, who earlier had endorsed Forbes. Second, Dole proposed an across-the-board 15 percent income tax cut. This proposal was especially surprising because Dole had cultivated a well-deserved reputation as a "deficit hawk" who opposed supply-side economic theory. Yet to energize his lagging campaign, Dole abandoned his lifelong approach to economic policy. Although Dole succeeded in attracting attention with this move, not all of it was positive as many political analysts focused on the contradictions between his tax cut proposal and earlier statements.

Although polls throughout 1996 showed Clinton with a commanding lead against Dole, those same polls pointed to voter uneasiness with the president's character. Because of continued negative media coverage resulting from Whitewater-related charges, the badly handled White House firing of its travel office staff, and a sexual harassment lawsuit against Clinton, most of the public believed that their president was an individual of unsatisfactory personal character. Yet the polls also indicated that Americans would reelect a flawed president because of their uneasiness with the Republican nominee, their low opinion of the Republican majority in Congress, and their general satisfaction with the state of the economy.

Throughout the campaign season, Clinton often seemed to be running against the unpopular Gingrich and the Republican Congress more than he was taking on Dole.

What made Clinton's campaign so strong, in part, was his governing strategy of what one key aide called "triangulation": that is, separating himself from the unpopular elements of both political parties and establishing a less partisan identity at the center of the political spectrum. To achieve that end, Clinton adopted a number of policy initiatives that were conservative, but also largely popular. He signed a welfare reform bill that liberals in his party opposed, pushed for imposition of a V-chip in televisions to allow parents to screen program content for children and for a television program rating system, proposed a balanced budget by the year 2002, and extolled his record in reducing the federal budget deficit. Clinton also stayed true to his Democratic roots by opposing congressional efforts to reduce Medicare spending and weaken environmental regulation and by proposing new government programs to make college education more affordable.

Clinton's strategy was brilliant. He effectively took away from Dole's campaign a number of issues that usually help Republican presidential candidates, such as welfare reform, deficit reduction, and family values. He kept his Democratic base by positioning himself as the only viable check against the "extremism" of the Republican Congress.

From a stylistic standpoint, the Clinton and Dole campaigns could not have been more different. Admirers and critics alike agree that Clinton was an effective campaigner and a strong communicator. By contrast, despite protestations by those who know him to be a warm and humorous person, Dole projected the image of a threatening and humorless politician. Despite a vigorous campaign, Dole never overcame the uneasiness that most voters felt about him personally. In past campaigns he had acquired the negative persona of a political "hatchet man" and that image stuck with him throughout the 1996 race. Indeed, Dole tried so hard to change that image that he spent months refusing to attack Clinton's most serious political weakness: his character. When implored by partisan Republicans to attack the president, Dole would reply that he considered Clinton "my opponent, not my enemy." In his two debates with Clinton, Dole did little to improve his public image, as his presentational style was stiff and somewhat harsh—in large contrast to Clinton who projected a much more assuring image.

In the last weeks of the campaign, when it was clear that Dole had no realistic chance of winning, the Republican candidate made a final gamble: he decided finally to attack the president's character and to make it an overriding theme of the campaign. Dole's attacks on the president made a difference in the campaign polls when the news media began to report on questionable fund-raising practices by the Democratic National Committee (DNC) and meetings between foreign lobbyists and Clinton. Stories of unethical and possibly illegal Democratic campaign contributions dovetailed with the Dole message that Clinton lacked good character—and that such a fault was unsuitable for the person serving as president.

Clinton perhaps further hurt himself when he avoided directly confronting the negative stories about the fund-raising practices of his party. Instead, he protested that candidates had no choice but to raise funds and campaign under a flawed system and that, if reelected, he would propose fundamental campaign finance reform. Although this negative publicity and the Dole charges were not enough to deny Clinton's victory, just days before the election one major poll by the Zogby Group for Reuters News Agency placed Clinton's lead at only 7 percent, significantly below the double-digit margins he had maintained throughout the race.[208]

Billionaire Perot, who was running again under the Reform Party banner, also benefited somewhat from the negative Clinton press. Although he had never been a serious factor in 1996 as he had been as an independent candidate in 1992—and as a result was excluded from the presidential debates—Perot's support increased by several percentage points in the late polls. But in the end, Perot had little impact on the elections. Because of a perceived strong economy and a substantial reduction in the federal debt, the public frustration with the two major parties that had given growth to Perot's candidacy in 1992 simply did not exist in 1996.

As the Dole campaign emphasized the character issue, his senior staff were aware that the *Washington Post* was investigating a story about a past marital indiscretion by their candidate. In a controversial decision, the *Post* decided not to publish the information it had gathered about an extramarital affair Dole had in 1969. The newspaper's decision to not publish even after confirming beyond any doubt all the facts angered Clinton partisans who felt that the Post had displayed a double standard. Clinton, of course, had been subjected to unrelenting coverage of allegations of extramarital affairs, and these stories had always played a key role in the president's reputation for poor character. Had the newspaper published the story late in the campaign there is little doubt that it would have had an adverse impact on Dole's late surge in the polls that had largely been driven by the character issue. The *Post*'s editor concluded that the story had no relevance to the issue of Dole's qualification to be president—a decision that most journalists thought should have been left to an informed electorate.[209]

Clinton easily won reelection with 49.2 percent of the popular vote and 379 electoral votes to Dole's 40.7 percent and 159 electoral votes. Reform Party candidate Perot polled 8.4 percent of the vote, less than half of his 1992 total, and once again received no electoral votes.[210] Clinton's victory made him the first Democrat to win reelection since Franklin D. Roosevelt won his second term in 1936. He became the first Democrat to be elected to the presidency along with a Republican-controlled Congress. Clinton won every state he had captured in 1992, except for Georgia,

Montana, and Colorado. However, he picked up Florida and Arizona—becoming the first Democratic presidential candidate to win Florida since 1976 and first to win Arizona since 1948. The so-called gender gap was key to Clinton's victory: while the male vote was evenly split between the two candidates, Clinton won the female vote by 16 percent, the largest margin ever. Clinton also beat Dole among every age group and was the clear choice of minorities: he received 80 percent of the black vote and 70 percent of the Hispanic vote.[211]

Yet three facts remained discouraging for Clinton. First, for the second straight election he had failed to win a majority of the popular vote. Second, voter turnout was less than 50 percent, the lowest since 1924. Third, Democrats failed to regain control of Congress, despite the unpopularity of Gingrich and many of his Republican colleagues. Given this scenario, it was difficult for the president to credibly claim that he had achieved any kind of mandate from the American people.

Exit polling data suggested that the incumbent Clinton indeed benefited from positive public feelings about the economy. In one voter poll conducted by numerous news organizations about 60 percent of the respondents said that the economy was doing well. Those respondents heavily favored Clinton. In 1992 the exit polls found that less than 20 percent said the economy was doing well, a situation that had benefited the challenger Clinton.[212]

Perhaps what was most remarkable about the 1996 national elections was just how little had actually changed, despite the two major parties having spent about $500 million on campaign activities. Political analysts have aptly referred to the 1996 elections as reaffirming the status quo, a dramatic difference from both the 1992 and 1994 elections in which voters expressed frustration with the existing political arrangement and sought substantial changes in their government.

REPUBLICANS RETAKE THE PRESIDENCY

The last presidential election of the twentieth century, the closest in forty years, brought the nation to the brink of a constitutional crisis that was narrowly averted only after an unprecedented thirty-six days of rancorous arguing and litigation over who won, Democrat Al Gore or Republican George W. Bush. The eventual outcome, with Texas governor Bush the official winner, did little to unite the electorate, which had split a hundred million votes almost evenly between the two major party candidates.

Although Gore, the departing vice president, clearly won the national popular vote in the 2000 race by more than a half-million votes, Bush claimed the 25 electoral votes of Florida, where the election had been extremely close. Ultimately the state's Republican administration, headed by

Gov. Jeb Bush, certified his brother as the popular vote winner in Florida, raising the GOP candidate's nationwide electoral vote total to 271—one more than he needed to win. Gore unsuccessfully contested the election on grounds that the state had stopped the recounts prematurely, leaving thousands of machine-processed ballots not subjected to the scrutiny of human eyes in a hand recount.

In the end, a sharply divided U.S. Supreme Court halted the Florida count, effectively deciding the election in Bush's favor. It was the first time the Court had taken up a disputed presidential election, let alone the first time it had gone against its traditional states' rights principles to overturn a state judiciary in such a matter. In a historic election studded with anomalies, "firsts," and ironies, the Court for the first time immediately released audio tapes of its hearings on the suit.

The tumult focused new attention on proposals to abolish or reform the electoral college system. It brought to light the need to modernize the problem-prone voting systems still in use in many states besides Florida. It also exposed serious flaws in the technology that broadcast media rely on to project election results minutes after the polls have closed. Repercussions of the event would be felt for many years to come.

Bush's victory marked the fourth time in U.S. history that the popular vote loser gained the presidency. The first such election, in 1824, was won by John Quincy Adams, who, like Bush (son of former president George H. W. Bush), was the son of a president, John Adams. Although Andrew Jackson won the 1824 popular vote, none of the four candidates received the required electoral vote majority and the House of Representatives decided the election in Adams's favor. All four candidates represented factions of the Democratic-Republican Party. In an 1828 rematch with Adams, Jackson won the presidency and changed his party's name to Democratic. (See "Last of the Old Order: 1824," p. 361.)

The second contested presidential election, in 1876, was more analogous to the Bush-Gore dispute in that it too involved charges of irregularities in the election process. New York Democrat Samuel J. Tilden won the national vote against Ohio Republican Rutherford B. Hayes, but controversies over the popular votes in three southern states, including Florida, led to rival sets of electoral vote results being sent to Congress from the three states. Lacking a procedure for resolving the dispute, Congress formed a bipartisan special commission, including Supreme Court justices, that gave the votes to Hayes in return for concessions to the South. Hayes thereby won the presidency by a single electoral vote, a margin only one vote lower than Bush's. (See "Compromise: 1876," p. 378.)

In 1887 Congress enacted the Electoral Vote Count Act, specifying procedures for settling electoral vote disputes. One year later Republican Benjamin Harrison won the 1888 presidential election even though Democrat Grover Cleveland received more popular votes. The 1887 act did not come into play, however, because Harrison decisively won the electoral college vote, 233 to 168. *(See "The Republican Recovery: 1888," p. 381)*

Had the Supreme Court not intervened in 2000, it was conceivable that Florida might have sent competing sets of electors' votes to Congress. Although that did not happen, the rules of the 1887 act thwarted efforts by some House members to challenge Florida's electoral votes. In one of the ironies of the election, it fell to Gore as Senate president to reject his supporters' objections.

Favorites Win Nomination

From the outset, the election was Gore's to lose. It is almost axiomatic that the party in power retains the White House in times of peace and prosperity. With President Clinton ineligible to succeed himself, Gore stood to inherit the advantage of running on Clinton's successes, especially an economy that had gone from record federal deficits to record surpluses, which opened the prospect of retiring the $3.7 trillion national debt while safeguarding Social Security, Medicare, and other popular but expensive social programs. Clinton could also claim legislative successes in welfare reform and the North American Free Trade Agreement (NAFTA) as well as foreign policy efforts in Bosnia, Kosovo, Northern Ireland, and the Middle East. On the other hand, Republicans controlled Congress for six of Clinton's eight years in office.

Despite his high job approval ratings, Clinton himself was perhaps Gore's biggest handicap. Bush and other Republican candidates tried to saddle Gore with the sins of the Clinton administration, particularly Clinton's December 1998 impeachment for lying under oath about his affair with Monica Lewinsky when she was a White House intern. The Republicans' strategy was to run against "Clinton-Gore" rather than against Gore alone—even though Gore's marital fidelity was not at issue.

Conservative congressional Republicans were still angry at Clinton for escaping removal from office through the impeachment process. In November 1998, with impeachment looming, Clinton became the first president since Franklin D. Roosevelt in 1934 to gain House seats at a midterm election. He made a net gain of five seats and got rid of his nemesis, Speaker Newt Gingrich, who resigned from Congress in reaction to the GOP setback. Then, in a political twist of the knife, Clinton handily won acquittal from the Senate in his impeachment trial.

The 2000 primary season was rather lackluster, dominated throughout by Gore on the Democratic side and Bush on the GOP's. Both locked up their nominations early. Gore had to face a strong nomination challenge from former New Jersey senator Bill Bradley. Bradley, failing to win a single

George W. Bush and Al Gore compete for moderator Jim Lehrer's attention during the final presidential debate held October 17 in St. Louis. Although Gore was given a slight edge in most disinterested postdebate analyses of who won or lost, Bush did better than expected, and, presenting a more likable persona, improved his standing with voters over the course of the three debates.

primary in the opening round, dropped out of the race in early March. In a speech to the Democratic convention at Los Angeles, he expressed his support for Gore.

Gore's need to distance himself from Clinton's indiscretions was implicit in his choice of Joseph I. Lieberman as his running mate. An Orthodox Jew, the first of his faith to run on a major party ticket, Lieberman was known for speaking out on moral issues and family values. Although he voted in the Senate to acquit Clinton, Lieberman had publicly taken the president to task for his dalliance with Lewinsky. In the 2000 campaign, however, neither the Republicans nor the Democrats openly raised the "character issue." The *Washington Post* called impeachment the 2000 election's "stealth issue." [213] On the Republican side, Bush's frequent pledges to "restore the honor and dignity" of the presidency also were a thinly veiled reference to Clinton's impeachment.

Bush entered the race in early 1999 and quickly established himself as the favorite of the Republican establishment and its campaign donors. Without a sitting Democratic president to compete against, the contest attracted a dozen hopefuls for the GOP nomination. But even before the kickoff Iowa caucuses in January 2000 half of the field dropped out, including former vice president Dan Quayle, former Tennessee governor Lamar Alexander, and Elizabeth Dole, head of the Red Cross and wife of 1996 nominee Bob Dole, who said she was unable to compete with Bush's fund-raising prowess. Conservative commentator Pat Buchanan, a past contender, decided instead to seek the Reform Party nomination.

By early February, Bush, publisher Malcolm S. "Steve" Forbes Jr., and Senator John McCain of Arizona remained the only serious contenders. Forbes, who finished third in New Hampshire, ended his campaign after a less impressive showing in Delaware. McCain, a former Vietnam prisoner of war and cosponsor with Sen. Russell Feingold of Wisconsin of the bipartisan campaign finance reform legislation, was perceived as a moderate despite his solid conservative voting record in the Senate. This, and his penchant for bluntness, appealed to many non-Republicans, who could vote in the growing number of open or semi-open GOP primaries. McCain upset Bush in the New Hampshire and Michigan primaries, but Bush went on to win a cluster of March 7 primaries. In all, McCain defeated Bush in seven of the eighteen primaries he entered, but Bush won enough convention delegates to clinch the nomination in March.

McCain eventually endorsed Bush and was the only member of Congress accorded a prime-time speaker's slot at the party's nominating convention in Philadelphia. Bush chose Richard B. Cheney, the former representative from Wyoming and defense secretary under Bush's father, for his running mate.

After the conventions Gore, more so than Bush, faced a vote-siphoning threat from the Green Party candidate, consumer advocate Ralph Nader, who received almost 1 percent of the presidential vote in 1996 and was aiming for 5 percent in 2000—a level that would ensure federal campaign funding for the Greens in the 2004 election. Although Republican swing voters were unlikely to switch to corporation-basher Nader, disaffected liberals who supported Bradley found Nader an attractive alternative.

With polls continuing to show the electorate almost evenly divided, the major party race settled down to basically a personality contest between two Ivy Leaguers—Gore (Harvard) and Bush (Yale). The public perceived Bush as personable but perhaps not so intelligent as Gore, despite Bush's master's degree from Harvard's business school. Although known privately as humorous, Gore was seen publicly as somewhat wooden. In the first of their three debates, Gore came off as smart-alecky against Bush, the self-styled "compassionate conservative." In their subsequent debates, Gore toned down his grimacing and head-shaking at Bush's remarks.

Gore's greatest asset was his experience, sixteen years in Congress and eight years in the vice presidency, against Bush's six years as Texas governor. But being vice president was no guarantee of success. Only four sitting vice presidents, including Bush's father in 1988, had been elected president. The vice presidency also was not a compelling qualification for promotion. As political scientist George O. Jones observed, "Most of them couldn't win the nomination on their own without being the vice president." [214]

Both candidates took a lot of negative press and ribbing from late-night comedians about their speaking habits—Bush for malapropisms and Gore for exaggerations. Bush, for example, in one off-hand statement derided people who regard Social Security as "some kind of federal program," which of course it was. Gore's most ridiculed statement was about his purported claim of "inventing" the Internet. What he actually said on a CNN program, however, was: "During my service in Congress I took the initiative in creating the Internet"—referring to his sponsorship of legislation that funded the early development of the technology. Despite the alleged "liberal bias" of the news media, a preconvention study by the Pew Research Center and the Project for Excellence in Journalism found that most news coverage portrayed Gore as an exaggerator or as scandal tainted (for his role in the Democrats' 1996 fund-raising practices), while Bush was usually referred to more positively as "a different kind of Republican." [215]

With the cold war over and most people better off than they were eight years earlier, traditionally Democratic pocketbook and social issues dominated the campaign—Social Security, education, health care, abortion rights, and gun control. The huge federal surpluses fueled the money issues, with Bush pushing for tax cuts and heavier outlays for antimissile research and development. Gore pledged a "lockbox" for Social Security and criticized Bush's concept of allowing workers to divert part of their trust fund contributions to private investment accounts. Bush's conservative stance on gun control brought him $1.7 million in support from the National Rifle Association (NRA), which was more than the lobby's independent expenditures for all candidates in 1996. In all, the Bush campaign raised almost $100 million, mostly from individuals, allowing it to decline federal grants and the spending limits that go with them. The Gore campaign accepted federal funding.

Some Gore supporters felt that the vice president distanced himself too much from Clinton, thereby sacrificing the opportunity to take his share of the credit for the booming economy and other positive aspects of the Clinton legacy. Clinton himself was said to feel "underused" by the Gore campaign. By the final weeks of the campaign Gore became less reluctant to run on Clinton's record, but it was too late to make much of an impression on undecided voters.

Cliff-Hanger Election: 2000

The election had been expected to be close. Bush and Gore ran neck-and-neck in public opinion polls, right up to election day. Problems with the crucial Florida vote erupted almost immediately on election day November 7, 2000. Voters in Palm Beach County reported difficulties with an unusual "butterfly" punch-card ballot. Some Democratic voters there thought that they had inadvertently voted for Reform Party nominee Pat Buchanan instead of for Gore. In some of the other twenty-four counties using outmoded punch-card systems, but with regular ballot forms, voters said they were unable to punch out the hole for the candidate of their choice.

Within hours, as news of the problems spread, people around the world became familiar with the obscure noun *chad,* singular or plural, meaning the tiny piece of paper that is pushed out in a punch-card system. If the chad is only dented (dimpled) or partially dislodged, the voting machine may not register the punch as a vote. Therein lay the basis for much of the contention in the days and weeks that were to follow.

Another serious problem emerged shortly after the polls closed, this one having to do with the system—based on exit polling—devised by the news media to project election winners before the votes are counted. The system is uncannily accurate, but its worst and most embarrassing mistake happened at 7:47 p.m. eastern standard time when the broadcast networks, using Voter News Service (VNS) data, projected Gore as the winner in Florida. People were

Countdown in Florida

The following is a day-by-day chronology of the events surrounding the disputed presidential election results from Florida in the 2000 race between Republican candidate George W. Bush and Democrat Al Gore.

November 7, 2000. Election in Florida too close to call, with Bush holding narrow lead. TV networks retract premature reports declaring Gore winner of state's twenty-five electoral votes.

November 8–10. Gore calls Bush to concede early November 8, then calls back to withdraw concession. Gore seeks hand recounts in four largely Democratic counties. Bush has unofficial 1,784-vote lead November 9. After all but one of Florida's sixty-seven counties complete machine recount required by state law, Bush lead falls to 327 votes.

November 11–14. Broward, Miami-Dade, Palm Beach, and Volusia Counties undertake manual recounts requested by Gore; federal court on November 13 rejects Bush bid to block hand counts; Volusia finishes recount November 14.

November 13. Florida secretary of state Katherine Harris says she will enforce state law deadline of November 14 for counties to submit returns and will not include manual recounts; election boards in Volusia and Palm Beach Counties ask state court judge to overturn deadline.

November 14–16. Leon County Circuit Judge Terry P. Lewis says Harris must justify her position on deadline; Harris reaffirms decision November 15; Lewis hears new round of arguments November 16.

November 17. Lewis upholds Harris's decision to disregard manual recounts, but Florida supreme court bars certification of state results pending oral arguments on November 20; federal appeals court rejects Bush suit over manual recounts.

November 18. Bush lead grows to 930 votes with absentee ballots; Bush campaign criticizes Democrats for challenging absentee votes from military.

November 21. Florida supreme court rules manual recounts must be included in presidential race if submitted to Harris by 5:00 p.m. Sunday, November 26.

November 22–24. Bush running mate Richard Cheney has heart attack, leaves Washington hospital two days later after surgery to insert stent in artery. Shouting, fist-waving crowd, including Republican congressional aides, tries to enter private room where recounts resume in Miami-Dade. County stops recount, pleading too little time and denying intimidation by the demonstrators. State supreme court on November 23 rejects Gore suit to force Miami-Dade to resume counting. U.S. Supreme Court agrees to hear Bush appeal of Florida supreme court action allowing extended deadline for certifying presidential race.

November 25–26. Manual recounts: Broward finishes November 25; Palm Beach falls just short of completion November 26. Harris announces November 26

that state elections canvassing board certifies Bush as winner by 537-vote margin; Bush claims victory, says he and Cheney are "honored and humbled" to have won Florida's electoral votes.

November 27–29. Gore formally contests the Florida election on November 27. He sues in Leon County Circuit Court, in Tallahassee, claiming the number of legal votes "improperly rejected" and illegal votes counted in Nassau, Palm Beach, and Miami-Dade Counties is enough to change outcome. Judge N. Sanders Sauls orders ballots brought to Tallahassee for possible counting. More than one million ballots are trucked with police escort to the state capital.

December 1. U.S. Supreme Court hears Bush appeal of deadline extension. Florida justices refuse to order revote requested in Palm Beach County because of controversial "butterfly ballot" used there.

December 2–3. Judge Sauls hears testimony on whether 13,000 ballots from Miami-Dade and Palm Beach Counties should be manually counted. Both sides call witnesses on reliability of punch-card voting systems.

December 4. Sauls rejects Gore's request for manual recount and refuses to decertify Bush as winner. U.S. Supreme Court asks state high court to explain its November 21 action allowing manual recounting and extending deadlines.

December 8–9. Florida justices order hand count of ballots on which machines found no vote for president. U.S. Supreme Court unexpectedly halts the hand counts the next day.

December 10–11. U.S. Supreme Court receives briefs and hears arguments in Bush v. Gore.

December 12. U.S. Supreme Court splits 5–4 in ruling for Bush against further hand counts. Florida legislature convenes special session to meet the federal deadline for designating presidential electors. Twenty states miss the deadline by a few days.

December 13. Gore concedes election, congratulates Bush and jokingly adds "and I promised him that this time I wouldn't call him back."

December 18. Presidential electors meet in state capitals to cast votes.

January 6, 2001. Congress meets in joint session to count electoral votes. As Senate president, Vice President Gore presides over his own defeat. Twenty Gore supporters, mostly Congressional Black Caucus members, try to block Florida's votes but Gore rejects each representative's objection because none has also been signed by a senator as the 1887 Electoral Vote Count Act requires. One District of Columbia elector, Barbara Lett-Simmons, withholds her vote from Gore in protest of the District's lack of representation in Congress. Final electoral vote tally is 271 for Bush, 266 for Gore with one abstention.

January 20. Inauguration of Bush as president and Cheney as vice president. Protests, largely nonviolent, mar—but do not disrupt—the inaugural parade.

(REPUBLICAN)		
GEORGE W. BUSH · PRESIDENT	3➤	
DICK CHENEY · VICE PRESIDENT		

(REFORM)
◄ 4   PAT BUCHANAN · PRESIDENT
          EZOLA FOSTER · VICE PRESIDENT

(DEMOCRATIC)		
AL GORE · PRESIDENT	5➤	
JOE LIEBERMAN · VICE PRESIDENT		

(SOCIALIST)
◄ 6   DAVID McREYNOLDS · PRESIDENT
          MARY CAL HOLLIS · VICE PRESIDENT

(LIBERTARIAN)		
HARRY BROWNE · PRESIDENT	7➤	
ART OLIVIER · VICE PRESIDENT		

(CONSTITUTION)
◄ 8   HOWARD PHILLIPS · PRESIDENT
          J. CURTIS FRAZIER · VICE PRESIDENT

(GREEN)		
RALPH NADER · PRESIDENT	9➤	
WINONA LaDUKE · VICE PRESIDENT		

(WORKERS WORLD)
◄ 10   MONICA MOOREHEAD · PRESIDENT
            GLORIA La RIVA · VICE PRESIDENT

(SOCIALIST WORKERS)		
JAMES HARRIS · PRESIDENT	11➤	
MARGARET TROWE · VICE PRESIDENT		

WRITE-IN CANDIDATE
To vote for a write-in candidate, follow the
directions on the long stub of your ballot card.

(NATURAL LAW)		
JOHN HAGELIN · PRESIDENT	13➤	
NAT GOLDHABER · VICE PRESIDENT		

The "butterfly" ballot used in Palm Beach, Florida, confused some voters who, intent on voting for Al Gore, punched out the second hole from the top, recording a vote instead for Reform Party candidate Patrick J. Buchanan (listed on the right side). The confusion probably cost Gore enough votes to swing the state, and thus the electoral college majority to Bush.

still voting in Florida's western panhandle, in the central time zone, when the election was called for Gore. A short time later, the networks retracted and said Florida was too close to call. *(See box, "Countdown in Florida," p. 433.)*

In the early hours of November 8 the news reports put Bush ahead. Gore called Bush from Nashville and told him he was prepared to concede. Later, after being advised that there might be a recount in Florida, Gore called again to Bush in Austin. "You mean you're retracting your concession?" a surprised Bush reportedly asked. "You don't have to get snippy about it," Gore is said to have replied.

Weary television journalists apologized repeatedly for confusing their viewers during the long election night, which finally extended into weeks. "We don't just have egg on our face," said NBC's Tom Brokaw, "we have an omelet." CBS's Dan Rather said, "If you're disgusted with us, frankly I don't blame you."

Besides leading nationwide in the popular vote, Gore outside of Florida led in the electoral college vote, 267 to 246 (after the counting of the absentee vote in Oregon and New Mexico concluded several days later). The entire 2000 presidential election therefore hung on the final results of the popular vote in Florida, which would determine the winner of the state's twenty-five electoral votes.

The close election triggered an automatic machine recount, showing Bush ahead by about 300 votes in Florida. But the Gore camp focused on the thousands of votes that the machines rejected as undervoted, showing no vote for president, or overvoted, showing more than one vote for presidential candidates. Only a manual count of those ballots could discern votes that the machines could not detect, Gore lawyers argued. The Democrats' war cry became, "Every vote counts; count every vote."

In what may have been a tactical mistake, Gore did not request an immediate statewide revote or recount. Instead his lawyers fought to keep hand counts going where Gore was picking up votes, in mostly Democratic counties such as Broward, Miami-Dade, and Volusia, and in Palm Beach County where the butterfly-ballot had recorded an unlikely 3,407 votes for Pat Buchanan, three times more than he received elsewhere in the state. Buchanan himself said it appeared he received votes meant for Gore. Just as fiercely, the Bush forces fought to stop the hand counts. They argued that the votes had been legally counted and recounted, including military and other absentee ballots that favored Bush, and that the canvassers had no uniform standards for gauging the difference between a vote and a nonvote on a punch-card ballot. Allowing more time for recounts, they said, would be changing the rules after the game started.

Both sides assembled high-powered legal teams, each headed by a former secretary of state, James A. Baker III for Bush and Warren Christopher for Gore. Both served as above-the-fray spokespeople while the trench warfare fell chiefly to lawyers Barry Richard for Bush and David Boies for Gore. U.S. Supreme Court arguments for Bush were presented by Ted Olson and for Gore initially by Laurence Tribe of Harvard Law School and later by Boies.

During the weeks of contentious legal maneuvering over the Florida vote, partisan tempers flared throughout the United States. Large groups of demonstrators in Florida and Washington, D.C., shouted at the television cameras and waved signs supporting Bush and his vice-presidential choice, Cheney, or Gore and his running mate, Lieberman. In the midst of the uproar, Cheney experienced his fourth (an apparently mild) heart attack. Doctors at George Washington University Hospital in Washington used angioplasty to install a stent, an expandable metal tube, in Cheney's heart to open a blocked artery. Within a few days Cheney was back on the job as head of Bush's transition team.

But it was a race against the calendar, and Katherine Harris was the timekeeper. Harris, Florida's secretary of state and former cochair of Bush's campaign in the state, announced November 13 that counties had until the following day, the date set in state law, to submit their returns, without any manual recount figures. Lawsuits stayed Harris's hand, however, and the manual counts proceeded by fits and starts until Sunday, November 26, under an extension granted by the seven-member Florida supreme court, made up mostly of Democratic appointees. That evening Harris ceremoniously "certified" Bush as the Florida winner by 537 votes out of six million cast.

The battle was by no means over, however. Gore formally contested the election and Bush meanwhile protested the deadline extension to the U.S. Supreme Court, which heard the arguments December 1. In Tallahassee, after hearing two days of televised testimony, Leon County Circuit Judge N. Sanders Sauls ruled that Gore failed to prove the need for manual recounts. Gore's witnesses had testified that "chad buildup" and poorly maintained equipment could prevent voters from cleanly punching out a machine-read ballot. Gore received another setback the same day, December 4, when the U.S. Supreme Court returned the deadline-extension case to the Florida high court for clarification.

Gore scored a short-lived victory December 8 when the Florida court by a 4–3 vote ordered a resumption of the hand counts, only to have the U.S. Supreme Court quickly halt them the following day, pending its decision in Bush v. Gore. In its 5–4 decision, handed down December 12, the Court majority ruled for Bush that the lack of uniform standards for manual recounts denied "equal protection of the laws" to Florida voters. The Court split along ideological lines in the unsigned decision. In the majority were conservatives William Rehnquist, Antonin Scalia, Clarence Thomas, Anthony Kennedy, and Sandra Day O'Connor. Dissenting were liberals or moderates Stephen Breyer, Ruth Bader Ginsburg, David Souter, and John Paul Stevens.

The Court action left 42,000 Florida undervotes unexamined, including 35,000 from the punch-card counties, but it effectively resolved the 2000 presidential race and possibly averted a constitutional crisis that might have arisen had the dispute resulted in Florida's sending two sets of electoral votes to Congress. The state legislature had already designated a slate of electors committed to Bush. Faced with a hopeless situation, Gore folded his campaign and conceded December 13.

When the presidential electors met in their states December 18 to cast their ballots, one District of Columbia elector, Barbara Lett-Simmons, withheld her vote from Gore in protest of the District's lack of representation in Congress. This reduced Gore's electoral vote total to 266 against 271 for Bush. Gore received 51.0 million votes (48.4 percent) to 50.5 million (47.9 percent) for Bush. Gore's lead in the popular vote was 539,947. Nader's 2.8 million votes amounted to 2.7 percent of the total. Buchanan received less than 1 percent with 447,798 votes.

An embarrassing loss to Gore was his home state of Tennessee and its eleven electoral votes. Had he won there he would have had an electoral vote majority and the Florida

vote would have been irrelevant. Likewise, had Gore received a fraction of the Nader vote in several close states, including Florida, he would have been over the top in electoral votes. Cook, however, pointed out while Nader may have siphoned off Gore voters in Florida and elsewhere, Reform Party candidate Pat Buchanan, whose supporters traditionally lean Republican, may have prevented Bush from winning a few states that went closely for Gore. "[T]here were 30 additional electoral votes that Bush may have won if Buchanan had not been in the race, compared to 29 more electoral votes that may have gone to Gore if Nader had not run. In short, the effect of the two third-party candidates on the electoral vote was essentially a wash."[216]

Nationwide, African Americans voted 9 to 1 for Gore. On January 6, 2001, twenty House members, mostly members of the Congressional Black Caucus, tried to disqualify Florida's electoral votes as Congress met in joint session to count the electoral votes. As Senate president by virtue of his being U.S. vice president, Gore one by one ruled the objections out of order because they had not been signed by a senator as required by law. None of the 100 members of the new Senate, evenly divided between Republicans and Democrats, including presidential spouse Hillary Rodham Clinton of New York, had signed a challenge to the Florida votes. Gore in his concession had asked his supporters to accept the Court verdict and the "finality of the outcome."

The lingering bitterness put a damper on the inauguration of Bush as the forty-third U.S. president on January 20, 2001. On the cold, rainy Saturday, thousands of protesters, under tight security, lined the Pennsylvania Avenue parade route to the White House. They were noisy and visible, but there were relatively few arrests and clashes with the police. Long and bitter as it was, the thirty-six-day 2000 election "night" was shorter and perhaps less vitriolic than its 1876 counterpart, which extended from November 7 to two days before inauguration, then in March. Because March 4, 1877, fell on a Sunday, President Hayes was sworn in privately at the White House and the public ceremonies took place quietly on Monday.

Similarly, the nation witnessed another peaceful transfer of power with the Bush-Cheney inauguration. As historian David McCullough phrased it, the peacefulness was typical of past inaugurations but perhaps for a different reason. "As close as it was, this election was not about visceral issues like slavery or war—things people are really passionate about," McCullough said. "The nation is closely divided, certainly, but we seem to be divided over which party controls the middle of the political spectrum. I'm not sure it's happened quite like that before."[217]

Effect of 2001 Terrorist Attacks

Entering the White House in January 2001, George W. Bush moved rapidly on his priorities and managed to push through a $1.35 billion tax cut—a key campaign pledge; additional tax cuts followed in subsequent years. Despite his pledge to be "a uniter, not a divider," education reform was the only major bipartisan legislation the president passed in 2001. The new administration faced a sharply divided Congress. Although Democrats had made some gains, Republicans retained a narrow majority in the House. The 2000 elections had caused a 50–50 split in the Senate as the Democrats had picked up five seats. Because Cheney, as vice president, could cast tie-breaking votes, the chamber was still under effective Republican control. But in May, after Republican James Jeffords of Vermont opted to leave his party and become an independent who caucused with the Democrats, the Democrats took control of the Senate.

Vice President Cheney played a key role in the Bush White House. Cheney added gravitas and a seasoned foreign policy background to the inner circle of a president regarded by many as lacking in international experience. Cheney had a history of heart trouble, and in June 2001, after tests that showed occasional irregular heartbeats, he had a pacemaker implanted.

The events of September 11, 2001, altered the course of Bush's first term in office. A presidency that had seemed more focused on domestic issues suddenly was faced with the worst terrorist attack on U.S. soil in the country's history. That morning, terrorists hijacked four U.S. planes, crashing two of them into the Twin Towers of the World Trade Center, a Manhattan landmark, and one of them into the Pentagon, just outside Washington, D.C., in Virginia. The fourth plane crashed in Pennsylvania. Everyone aboard the planes was killed; several thousand more died on the ground; the towers collapsed.

The unprecedented, massive attacks on U.S. soil shifted the Bush administration's focus to a "war on terrorism." The president, whose popularity ratings had been dropping before the attacks, saw it rocket upwards to a historic 90 percent as the country rallied behind him. His visit to Ground Zero in New York several days after the attacks, where he spoke with rescue workers, was seen as a high point of his first year in office.

One impact of September 11 was a heightened sense of security affecting the entire country and the way the government functioned. For example, although Cheney remained an important part of the president's circle of advisers, for security reasons, he often traveled to what was called an "undisclosed location." Public tours of the White House were suspended temporarily and a part of E Street, close to the building, was shut down.

Another change involved the shape of the federal government bureaucracy. Bush called for a White House Office of Homeland Security, to be headed by former Pennsylvania governor Thomas Ridge. While Bush originally opposed the idea of a new federal Department of Homeland Security, he changed his mind and joined in calls for its creation. Bush signed a bill in late 2002 creating the department, which officially came into existence on March 1, 2003. The reorganization was the largest in the federal government since the late 1940s and involved the merging of a variety of agencies, including the Secret Service, the Coast Guard, and the Immigration and Naturalization Service.

A third outgrowth of the terrorist attacks was the actual "war on terror" itself. The United States that had basked in a post– Cold War hiatus in which international concerns took a back seat found itself in the midst of a full-fledged war. A strongly supportive Congress approved a $40 billion emergency appropriation, as well as a resolution that authorized using force against terrorist groups and countries that backed them. U.S. forces attacked Afghanistan, toppling the Taliban government that had supported September 11 mastermind Osama bin Laden and his al Qaeda terrorist network, and began to prepare for a possible invasion of Iraq.

In 2002 and into 2003, the Bush administration pushed for military action against the Iraqi regime of Saddam Hussein. Bush's father had fought a war against Iraq more than a decade earlier, but Saddam remained in power. The George W. Bush administration sought to link Saddam to Osama bin Laden and al Qaeda. In addition, the White House focused on what it called Saddam's "weapons of mass destruction." In fall 2002 Congress approved military action against Iraq. The U.N. Security Council unanimously backed a resolution seeking stringent weapons inspections in Iraq by the international body and granting Saddam a final chance to disarm. In February 2003 Secretary of State Colin Powell delivered a forceful slide presentation to the United Nations, laying out the administration's case for war.

The war began on March 19, 2003, with a "coalition of the willing"—its most prominent member was Great Britain—joining the United States in its attack on Iraq. However, many other countries that had joined Bush's father in the first Gulf War, including France, opted out of this one. Saddam's regime fell within several weeks, and on May 1 Bush triumphantly spoke on the U.S.S. *Abraham Lincoln,* behind a sign reading "Mission Accomplished," to declare the end of large-scale combat operations in Iraq.

The terrorist attacks also affected the U.S. economy, which already had been faltering. The budget surplus in effect when Bush came into office, $86 billion in fiscal year 2000, turned into a deficit. By fiscal year 2004, the deficit had reached $412 billion.[218]

In addition to his foreign policy concerns, the president devoted much of 2002 to campaigning for Republican candidates around the country. Generally, midterm elections had resulted in losses for the president's party, the only twentieth-century exceptions being in 1934 and 1998. Also incumbent presidents usually do not throw themselves into off-year elections. But Bush's hard work paid off, and the Republicans picked up seats in both the House and Senate, maintaining control of the House and—even more important—winning back control of the Senate. Still, the Republican margin in both chambers was narrow, and Congress continued to be bitterly divided during the next two years.

No sooner were the 2002 midterm elections over than attention shifted to the 2004 presidential contest, in which Bush was seeking election to a second term. Unlike his father, who in his 1992 reelection bid had seen a tough primary challenge from the right, from commentator Pat Buchanan, Bush faced no primary opposition. His father also had seen a third-party candidate, H. Ross Perot, affect the balance in the November election. Independent Ralph Nader, who had run on the Green Party ticket in 2000, had been a factor in parts of the country that year, with many Democrats saying his vote totals in such closely contested states as Florida took the election away from Gore. Nader, much to Democrats' dismay, chose to run again, as an independent, in 2004. But this time, the longtime consumer advocate turned out to be far less of a factor, despite worried Democrats filing suits in a number of states to prevent him from appearing on the ballot.

During Bush's 2004 reelection campaign, issues of terrorism and the new term "homeland security" were at the forefront. Bush successfully used his incumbency to portray an image of strength in the face of the terrorist enemy, despite a lackluster economy and the growing unpopularity of his venture into Iraq.

Bush's Reelection: 2004

For much of 2001 and 2002, many political observers had assumed that Gore would run for president again in 2004, forcing a rematch with Bush after their 2000 showdown. After all, they reckoned, Gore had won the popular vote, he had a strong base of support, and he would easily have become the front-runner in the Democratic field. After the 2000 election, Gore had taken some time out of the public spotlight, co-writing two books with his wife, Mary Elizabeth "Tipper" Gore, and teaching at a number of universities. But in December 2002, Gore declared that he would not run for president in 2004, leaving the Democratic field wide open.

A large crop of candidates jumped into the Democratic race, including Senator Lieberman of Connecticut, who had been Gore's vice-presidential running mate in 2000; John F. Kerry, a long-serving senator from Massachusetts who had made his name in the early 1970s as a decorated Vietnam veteran who turned against the war; and Sen. John Edwards, the charismatic first-term senator from North Carolina who had been a successful trial lawyer. Former House minority leader Richard Gephardt of Missouri, a favorite of organized labor, also was in the mix, as were Rep. Dennis Kucinich of Ohio, retired general Wesley Clark, the Reverend Al Sharpton, former senator from Illinois and ambassador Carol Moseley Braun, and former Vermont governor Howard Dean. Sen. Bob Graham of Florida also entered the race but exited before the first contest.

The sputtering economy at home and, in particular, the war in Iraq quickly became the major issues in the primary campaign. Lieberman was a hawk on Iraq, while Kerry had voted for the congressional authorization for the use of force against Iraq. Kerry later voted against an $87 billion supplemental authorization, which laid the foundation for Bush's later criticism of the senator as a "flip-flopper." Although Bush had declared an end to major combat activities in Iraq, violence continued there, and U.S. military forces were to extend their tours amid increasing casualties. Kucinich and Dean carved out strong antiwar positions, and as 2003 wound on, Dean's antiwar stance—in addition to his innovative use of the Internet as a tool for garnering financial support through "meet-up" sessions—propelled him to the front of the pack. The 2004 election marked the first time the Internet became a primary source of fund-raising for political campaigns. In addition, campaign fund-raising was affected by the adoption in 2002 of the McCain-Feingold campaign finance reform bill. The measure limited private funding to campaigns and indirectly led to the prominence in 2004 of so-called "527" groups, which serve as outside surrogates of funding to skirt the new law. Dean carved out an image as an outsider challenging the political establishment, but he also won endorsements from mainstream figures, such as Gore and Gore's 2000 primary opponent, Bradley of New Jersey.

While Dean had been the front-runner at the end of 2003, the momentum began to shift by the Iowa caucuses, the first major test for the primary candidates. In recent years, the key Iowa and New Hampshire contests were moved earlier and earlier, and 2004 was no exception, with the Iowa caucuses scheduled for January 19 and the New Hampshire primary for January 27. In Iowa, Kerry's background as a war hero began to help him, as voters pondered choosing someone with military experience as violence continued in Iraq.

When the votes in Iowa were counted, Kerry—who referred to himself as the "comeback Kerry"—had emerged on top, with Edwards a surprising second. In a major blow to a former front-runner, Dean found himself in third place. Gephardt, who had been hoping his labor friends would come through for him, came in fourth and dropped out of the race. In fact, Iowa would prove disastrous for Dean as well; in a speech after the results were known, the former governor appeared somewhat out-of-control, shouting about all the states in which he still planned to compete and ending the rendition with a loud scream. The

Dean scream became fodder for comedians and a liability for the candidate.

Iowa's momentum helped Kerry win the New Hampshire primary, where Dean had been ahead, confirming Kerry's new status as leader of the Democratic pack. Gradually, most of the other candidates dropped out, including Dean (who ended up winning only his home state of Vermont), Clark (who won Oklahoma), and Edwards (who won the primary in South Carolina, the state where he was born). Still hanging on for months was Kucinich, whose antiwar message appealed to some more activist Democrats, despite his lack of fund-raising success and his dismal poll numbers.

Kerry's choice for a vice-presidential running mate surprised few: he selected Edwards, who had performed well in the primaries and attracted a popular following. On the campaign trail, Edwards had developed a "two Americas" theme, in which he focused on the existence of one America for the rich and one for everyone else, and in which he expressed optimism that everyone could join together in one America. The son of a millworker and the first in his family to graduate from college, Edwards played up his working-class southern roots. Although Kerry and Edwards got a boost of good publicity following Kerry's July 6 announcement of Edwards's selection, the ticket did not have history on its side. The last sitting senator elected to the White House was John F. Kennedy—Kerry's hero as a young man—in 1960.

The Kerry campaign, as did the Bush campaign, decided against taking federal matching funds during the primaries. Kerry raised $234.6 million during that period. After their conventions, each candidate was given $74.6 million in public financing for the general election. The Democrats were quick to exploit the 527 loophole; the Republicans were not far behind. Democrats, for the first time in recent history, found themselves with enough money to compete with the GOP in ad purchases and other campaign costs.

The Democrats held their convention in late July, in Kerry's home town of Boston—the first time the city had hosted a convention. Kerry focused on his Vietnam-era service, rather than his Senate record. As he appeared before the applauding crowd on July 29, Kerry saluted, declaring, "I'm John Kerry, and I'm reporting for duty." While Kerry's speech harkened back to the Vietnam era, Edwards's address was similar to the "two Americas" speech he had successfully delivered on the campaign trail. Another Democratic family loomed at the convention—former president Bill Clinton and Sen. Hillary Clinton, who both spoke on the first night of the convention. Many pundits already were predicting a future showdown, in 2008 or 2012, depending on the success of the Kerry-Edwards team, between Edwards and Senator Clinton for the presidential nomination. The keynote address was delivered by Barack Obama, a "rising star" within the Democratic party who would go on to win his Illinois Senate race to become the third African-American senator since Reconstruction.

Kerry emerged from his convention without much of a "bounce," or rise in the polls; the race was still close. But throughout the month of August, a new foe was on the attack: a 527 group called Swift Boat Veterans for Truth, which began airing anti-Kerry ads attacking the candidate's service in Vietnam. Kerry was slow to respond to the ads; the Bush campaign, meanwhile, while saying it had nothing to do with the ads, was equally slow to condemn them. In addition, the Bush campaign was having success with its portrayal of Kerry as a "flip-flopper" who switched positions at will on the Iraq war and would not provide a steady hand in the White House at a time of national crisis.

Bush chose to keep Cheney on the ticket for the 2004 campaign, although some observers had speculated that Bush might dump the vice president—whose poll ratings were low—for someone more popular. Cheney had been out of the public eye for much of the time since the September 11 attacks. In addition, his former company, Halliburton, was involved in controversy, including an investigation by the Securities and Exchange Commission (SEC). Halliburton eventually agreed to pay a penalty of $7.5 million in a settlement with the SEC. Cheney's history of heart trouble also was a factor. But Bush relied on Cheney, and the vice president was an enthusiastic campaigner on the trail, focusing much of his attention on what he described as Kerry's weakness regarding the terrorist threat.

The president opted to forego federal matching funds during the primary phase of the campaign, which allowed him to raise as much money as he could. In total, he raised $269.6 million during the primaries. The Republicans held their convention from August 30 to September 2, later than usual, in New York City, the site of the September 11, 2001, attack. At the convention, the focus was on the president's success in fighting global terrorism. Among the speakers was Democratic senator Zell Miller, a Georgia conservative who had endorsed President Bush. In his keynote address, Miller ripped into the Democrats and into his Senate colleague Kerry for what Miller described as misguided, waffling weakness. Bush emerged from the convention with an average bounce of six percentage points.

The three major networks chose not to broadcast much of either convention in 2004. Network coverage of conventions had been decreasing in recent years, and ABC, CBS and NBC planned only three hours of coverage over each four-day convention. But various cable-news outlets, such as CNN, C-SPAN, MSNBC, and Fox News Channel, covered the events, as did public broadcasting.

Kerry's service in Vietnam continued to be an issue, as press reports focused on additional Swift Boat ads. But Bush's Vietnam-era career also hit the headlines, as news

The nine contenders for the 2004 Democratic presidential nomination stand assembled prior to their debate in Durham, N.H., December 2003. Seen from left to right are: Rep. Richard Gephardt, D-Mo.; Sen. Joseph Lieberman, D-Conn.; Rev. Al Sharpton; Carol Moseley Braun; Rep. Dennis Kucinich, D-Ohio; Sen. John Edwards, D-N.C.; Howard Dean; and Sen. John Kerry, D-Mass. Kerry would go on to become the Democratic candidate with Edwards as his running mate.

organizations examined his National Guard service and tried to pin down whether the future president had performed his duty adequately or had received preferential treatment. In the end, one of these reports, by CBS News anchor Dan Rather on the *60 Minutes Wednesday* broadcast, got CBS into far more trouble than it got Bush. The report, which aired September 8, turned out to have included falsified documents, and several top CBS executives ended up losing their jobs the following January.

In the wake of the Republican convention, Bush held his lead in many polls, and some pundits were predicting an easier-than-expected win for the president. The Democratic challenger seemed unable to capitalize on either the worsening situation in Iraq or the less-than-robust economy. In Iraq, insurgents continued to mount a terror campaign, and the weapons of mass destruction—a key rationale for the Bush administration's invasion of Iraq—had not been located. In addition, the U.S. military was suffering the fallout from a scandal uncovered that spring involving U.S. soldiers abusing Iraqi prisoners at Iraq's Abu Ghraib prison.

In the first of three presidential debates on September 30 in Miami, Kerry came through as poised and intelligent, greatly improving his image. Bush, meanwhile, seemed to grimace and scowl as his opponent spoke, and the president

often appeared less focused in his answers than did the Democrat. Kerry received a postdebate "bounce" that turned the contest back into a horse race. The next debate, the vice-presidential event between Cheney and Edwards, turned feisty with the candidates disagreeing on issues including the economy, the war in Iraq, and their records. Edwards stressed Cheney's past connections with Halliburton, while Cheney said Edwards had been an undistinguished senator. The debate was generally viewed as a tie, and the next two presidential debates, held October 8 and 13, also did not shift the close contest in either candidate's favor.

In the days leading up to November 2, 2004, polls showed a tight race between Bush and Kerry, and many pundits predicted a result similar to that of the extremely close 2000 election. The election hinged on a handful of states that were neither Republican "red" nor Democratic "blue"— about a dozen "purple" states where the candidates spent most of their time and money, including television advertisements. These states included New Hampshire; the midwestern states of Ohio, Michigan, Wisconsin, Minnesota, and Iowa; New Mexico and Nevada; and the 2000 cliff-hanger, Florida. Florida, in particular, received attention from both sides. That fall, the state had suffered through four hurricanes, and President Bush had visited the disaster areas along with his brother Jeb Bush, Florida's governor, and provided immediate federal assistance. Democrats, meanwhile, were determined to avoid a repeat of their 2000 fiasco and dispatched teams of lawyers to the state to prepare for whatever battles might emerge.[219]

Election Day was marked by exceptionally high turnout and high expectations on both sides—especially in the battleground states. People stood in line for hours outside polling places in such hotspots as Ohio. As the afternoon progressed, some exit poll results were leaked, showing Kerry doing well in a variety of battleground states, leaving Democrats ecstatic and Republicans deflated. But in the evening and into the night, it became clear that the exit polls were wrong—as they had been in 2000—and that it was the president who seemed the likely victor.

Still, the vote was close, as most of the states lined up the same way they had in 2000. Bush carried Florida, the state that had proved so troublesome four years earlier. But Ohio—a Bush state in 2000—was harder to predict, although Bush appeared to be holding a narrow lead, and most of the networks declined to call a winner overnight. The next day, November 3, Kerry, convinced that Bush's margin of more than 100,000 votes in Ohio could not be overcome, conceded the election to Bush. The concession came as a blow to many Democrats, who had hoped for victory, and a relief to many Republicans, who had dreaded a rerun of the drawn-out 2000 process. Republicans also welcomed the news that they had, for the second election in a row, picked up seats in the House and Senate, solidifying their control on Washington.

Across the nation Bush won 51 percent of the vote to Kerry's 48 percent and an electoral college majority of 286–252. (One elector from Minnesota ended up voting for Edwards, so the final total was 286–251.) The election of 2004 involved more fund-raising and spending than any other presidential contest in U.S. history. According to the Federal Election Commission, private and public spending during 2004 on presidential candidates and national conventions totaled a little more than $1 billion, "56 percent more than comparable activity during the 2000 campaign."[220]

On January 6, 2005, Congress met in joint session to certify the electoral vote. Unlike four years earlier when no senator agreed to back the House members' effort to protest voting irregularities in Florida, Sen. Barbara Boxer of California backed Rep. Stephanie Tubbs Jones and other House members who were protesting voting conditions in Tubbs Jones's home state of Ohio. Under the rules, Boxer's gesture forced separate debates that day by members of the House and the Senate before the process—generally a pro forma matter—could continue. It was the first time since 1969 that this type of challenge had been used, and it gave discouraged Democrats a little bit of solace.

Bush was sworn in for his second term on January 20, 2005, by ailing Supreme Court Chief Justice William Rehnquist. The inauguration's cost was estimated at $40 million. Because it was the first presidential inauguration since September 11, 2001, the central area of Washington, D.C., was locked down under unprecedented security. Access to the parade route along Pennsylvania Avenue was limited; the blocks close to the route were cordoned off with high metal barriers. Two thousand out-of-town police officers united with about 4,000 local officers in the effort.[221] In his inaugural address, Bush called for an expansion of freedom across the world. As befitted a president known for his early-to-bed routines, Bush attended the inaugural balls that night but still managed to get home to the White House by 10:00 p.m., an hour and 22 minutes ahead of schedule.[222]

★

NOTES

1. A. James Reichley, *The Life of the Parties: A History of American Political Parties* (New York: Free Press, 1992), 17.

2. Richard P. McCormick, *The Presidential Game: The Origins of American Presidential Politics* (New York: Oxford University Press, 1982), chap. 1.

3. Ibid., 33–34.

4. Reichley, *Life of the Parties,* 42.

5. Ibid., 49.

6. Robert J. Dinkin, *Campaigning in America: A History of Election Practices* (New York: Greenwood Press, 1989), 18.

7. Roy F. Nichols, *The Invention of the American Political Parties* (New York: Macmillan, 1967), 192.

8. Bruce L. Felkner, *Political Mischief: Smear, Sabotage, and Reform in U.S. Elections* (New York: Praeger, 1992), 31.

9. Dinkin, *Campaigning in America,* 15, 18.

10. Edward Stanwood, *A History of the Presidency* (Boston: Houghton Mifflin, 1898), 63.

11. John F. Hoadley, *Origins of American Party Politics, 1789–1803* (Lexington: University Press of Kentucky, 1986), 191.

12. T. Harry Williams, *The History of American Wars: From Colonial Times to World War I* (New York: Knopf, 1981), 134.

13. Stanwood, *History of the Presidency,* 110.

14. Matthew A. Crenson, *The Federal Machine* (Baltimore, Md.: Johns Hopkins University Press, 1971), 11–30.

15. Jackson biographer Robert V. Remini explains the nickname "Old Hickory." In an arduous five-hundred-mile march, Jackson gave his three horses to wounded soldiers and marched on foot with his troops to give them moral support. The soldiers serving under him agreed that their general was as tough as hickory. "Not much later," Remini writes, "they started calling him 'Hickory' as a sign of their respect and regard; then the affectionate 'Old' was added to give Jackson a nickname . . . that admirably served him thereafter throughout his military and political wars." Robert V. Remini, *Andrew Jackson* (New York: Harper and Row, 1969), 54.

16. Arthur M. Schlesinger Jr., *The Age of Jackson* (New York: New American Library, 1945), 34.

17. *Guide to Congress,* 5th ed. (Washington, D.C.: CQ Press, 2000), 807.

18. Russell L. Hanson, *The Democratic Imagination in America: Conversations with Our Past* (Princeton, N.J.: Princeton University Press, 1985), 125.

19. Eugene H. Roseboom, *A History of Presidential Elections* (New York: Macmillan, 1970), 106.

20. Schlesinger, *Age of Jackson,* 55.

21. Estimates of vote totals vary, especially in the years before standardized methods of balloting. Discrepancies developed because of disputes about stuffing ballot boxes, the eligibility of some voters, absentee ballots, and simple counting and reporting difficulties in the premedia age.

22. Roseboom, *History of Presidential Elections,* 112.

23. Hanson, *Democratic Imagination,* 54–120.

24. Ibid., 140–141.

25. Ibid., 136.

26. See Albert O. Hirschman, *Exit, Voice, and Loyalty* (Cambridge, Mass.: Harvard University Press, 1970).

27. Hanson, *Democratic Imagination,* 138.

28. Richard P. McCormick, "Political Development and the Second Party System," in *The American Party Systems: Stages of Development,* ed. William Nisbet Chambers and Walter Dean Burnham (New York: Oxford University Press, 1967), 102.

29. Paul Taylor, *See How They Run: Electing a President in the Age of Mediaocracy* (New York: Knopf, 1991), 4.

30. James L. Sundquist, *Dynamics of the Party System,* rev. ed. (Washington, D.C.: Brookings, 1983), 51.

31. Roseboom, *History of Presidential Elections,* 143.

32. Richard Hofstadter, *The American Political Tradition* (New York: Vintage, 1948), 113.

33. Ibid.

34. Hanson, *Democratic Imagination,* 176.

35. Roseboom, *History of Presidential Elections,* 177–181.

36. Paul N. Angle, ed., *The Lincoln Reader* (New York: Pocket Books, 1954), 523.

37. Ibid., 531.

38. Roseboom, *History of Presidential Elections,* 201.

39. Eric Foner, *Reconstruction: America's Unfinished Revolution, 1863–1877* (New York: Harper and Row, 1988).

40. William S. McFeely, *Grant* (New York: Norton, 1981), 283.

41. Ibid., 288–289.

42. Ibid., 381.

43. Bernhard Bailyn et al., *The Great Republic: A History of the American People* (Boston: Little, Brown, 1977), 802.

44. C. Vann Woodward, *Reunion and Reaction* (New York: Doubleday Anchor Books, 1951).

45. Kenneth M. Stampp, *The Era of Reconstruction, 1865–1877* (New York: Vintage, 1965), 210–211.

46. Michael Nelson, "A Short, Ironic History of American National Bureaucracy," *Journal of Politics* 44 (winter 1982): 747–777.

47. Roseboom, *History of Presidential Elections,* 264.

48. Harry Thurston Peck, *Twenty Years of the Republic, 1885–1905* (New York: Dodd, Mead, 1906), 20.

49. Michael E. McGerr, *The Decline of Popular Politics: The American North, 1865–1928* (New York: Oxford University Press, 1986), 82–106.

50. Peck, *Twenty Years of the Republic,* 41.

51. Ibid., 78.

52. Ibid., 144.

53. Ibid., 169.

54. Roseboom, *History of Presidential Elections,* 290.

55. Bailyn et al., *Great Republic,* 786.

56. Sundquist, *Dynamics of the Party System,* 107.

57. For a concise account of the machine reform struggle, see Dennis R. Judd, *The Politics of American Cities* (Boston: Little, Brown, 1984), 50–110.

58. See David Montgomery, *The Fall of the House of Labor* (New York: Cambridge University Press, 1987).

59. Sundquist, *Dynamics of the Party System,* 116–118.

60. Ibid., 143, 152.

61. Hofstadter, *American Political Tradition,* 187.

62. Sundquist, *Dynamics of the Party System,* 149–152.

63. Hofstadter, *American Political Tradition,* 192–193.

64. See "William Jennings Bryan, Cross of Gold Speech," in *Great Issues in American History: From Reconstruction to the Present Day, 1864–1969,* ed. Richard Hofstadter (New York: Vintage, 1969), 166–173.

65. Jasper B. Shannon, *Money and Politics* (New York: Random House, 1959), 30–32.

66. Sundquist, *Dynamics of the Party System,* 158.

67. Ibid., 169; for a general discussion of the 1896 election's resulting realignment, see pages 160–169.

68. E. E. Schattschneider, *The Semisovereign People* (Hinsdale, Ill.: Dryden Press, 1975), 76–77.

69. Edmund Morris, *The Rise of Theodore Roosevelt* (New York: Ballantine, 1979), 718.

70. See Gabriel Kolko, *The Triumph of Conservatism* (New York: Free Press, 1963).

71. Sundquist, *Dynamics of the Party System,* 176.

72. See Alpheus I. Mason, *Bureaucracy Convicts Itself* (New York: Viking Press, 1941); and James Penick Jr., *Progressive Politics and Conservation* (Chicago: University of Chicago Press, 1968).

73. August Heckscher, *Woodrow Wilson* (New York: Scribner's, 1991), 231–232.

74. Ibid., 259.

75. J. Leonard Bates, *The United States, 1898–1928* (New York: McGraw-Hill, 1976), 187.

76. Roseboom, *History of Presidential Elections,* 384.

77. John L. Shover, ed., *Politics of the Nineteen Twenties* (Waltham, Mass.: Ginn-Blaisdell, 1970), 148.

78. Ibid., 4.

79. Ibid., 12.

80. Ibid., 10.

81. James David Barber, *The Pulse of Politics: Electing Presidents in the Media Age* (New York: Norton, 1980), 239.

82. William E. Leuchtenberg, *Franklin D. Roosevelt and the New Deal* (New York: Harper and Row, 1963), 13.

83. Frank Friedel, *Franklin D. Roosevelt: The Triumph* (Boston: Little, Brown, 1956), 248–249.

84. Barber, *Pulse of Politics,* 243.

85. Ibid., 244.

86. Ibid., 238.

87. Hofstadter, *American Political Tradition,* 332.

88. Barber, *Pulse of Politics,* 244.

89. See Robert Lekachman, *The Age of Keynes* (New York: Random House, 1966).

90. Schattschneider argues in *The Semisovereign People* that the key element of any conflict is the extent to which the protagonists are able to control how many people get involved. Every "scope of conflict" has a bias. The size of the group involved in the conflict is almost always open to change. Schattschneider writes: "A look at political literature shows that there has indeed been a long-standing struggle between the conflicting tendencies toward the privatization

and socialization of conflict" (p. 7). The New Deal was a stage of socialization of conflict.

91. Everett Carll Ladd Jr. and Charles D. Hadley, *Transformations of the American Party System* (New York: Norton, 1978), 86.

92. Ibid., 43.

93. Ibid., 46.

94. Ibid., 64–74, 112; Sundquist, *Dynamics of the Party System,* 214–224.

95. Sundquist, *Dynamics of the Party System,* 217.

96. Ladd and Hadley, *Transformations,* 82.

97. Ibid., 58–59.

98. Ibid., 63.

99. Samuel H. Beer, "Liberalism and the National Interest," *Public Interest,* no. 1 (fall 1966): 81.

100. Theodore J. Lowi, *The End of Liberalism* (New York: Norton, 1969). See also Hanson, *Democratic Imagination,* 257–292.

101. Greg Mitchell, *The Campaign of the Century: Upton Sinclair's Race for Governor of California and the Birth of Modern Media Politics* (New York: Random House, 1992).

102. James MacGregor Burns, *Roosevelt: The Lion and the Fox* (New York: Harcourt Brace and World, 1956), 282–283.

103. Roseboom, *History of Presidential Elections,* 447.

104. Burns, *Roosevelt,* 277–278.

105. Ibid., 269–271.

106. Ibid., 282–283.

107. Ibid., 300.

108. Ibid., 427.

109. Barber, *Pulse of Politics.* This book tells the story behind the Willkie movement and the role played by Henry R. Luce, the founder of Time Inc.

110. See Lekachman, *Age of Keynes,* especially chaps. 5 and 6.

111. Roseboom, *History of Presidential Elections,* 483.

112. William E. Leuchtenberg, *In the Shadow of F.D.R.: From Harry Truman to Ronald Reagan* (Ithaca, N.Y.: Cornell University Press, 1983), 1–2.

113. Ibid., 15.

114. Ibid., 21.

115. V. O. Key Jr., *Southern Politics in State and Nation* (Knoxville: University of Tennessee Press, 1984), 649.

116. Ibid., 330–344.

117. Barber, *Pulse of Politics,* 50.

118. Nelson W. Polsby and Aaron Wildavsky, *Presidential Elections* (New York: Scribner's, 1984), 205–206.

119. Barber, *Pulse of Politics,* 61.

120. Angus Campbell, Philip E. Convers, Warren E. Miller, and Donald E. Stokes, *The American Voter* (New York: Wiley, 1960), 532.

121. Richard Neustadt, *Presidential Power* (New York: Wiley, 1980), 10, 12–14, 16, 18, 19, 22–25, 43, 67–68, 178.

122. Garry Wills, *Nixon Agonistes* (New York: New American Library, 1969), 91.

123. Fred Greenstein, *The Hidden-Hand Presidency* (New York: Basic Books, 1982).

124. Barber, *Pulse of Politics,* 269.

125. Eric F. Goldman quipped, "The returns, as the gangsters said, made even Alf Landon look good," in *The Crucial Decade* (New York: Vintage, 1960), 326.

126. The elder Kennedy always had planned for his sons to enter national politics. He originally pushed his eldest son, Joseph Jr., but the son died in combat in World War II. John was next; he ran for Congress in 1946. Robert, the third Kennedy son, served as an aide to Sen. Joseph McCarthy before managing John's 1960 presidential campaign and serving as his attorney general. Edward, the youngest, worked on the 1960 campaign and won his first Senate race in 1962.

127. Merle Miller, *Plain Speaking* (New York: Berkeley, 1974), 199.

128. Theodore H. White, *The Making of the President 1960* (New York: Atheneum, 1961), 114–116.

129. Ibid., 128.

130. Ibid., 130.

131. Ibid., 198–204.

132. Arthur M. Schlesinger Jr., *Robert F. Kennedy and His Times* (Boston: Houghton Mifflin, 1978), 193.

133. Henry Fairlie, *The Kennedy Promise* (New York: Dell, 1972), 30–31.

134. White, *Making of the President 1960,* 329.

135. Ibid., 327.

136. Richard M. Nixon, *Six Crises* (Garden City, N.Y.: Doubleday, 1962), 412.

137. White, *Making of the President 1960,* 397–401.

138. Sen. Barry Goldwater, letter to the author, January 25, 1988.

139. The Warren Commission, appointed by Johnson, concluded that Oswald acted alone, but Oswald himself was killed before he had a chance to give full testimony. Many experts dispute the Warren Commission conclusion.

140. The Kennedy assassination fomented passage of the Twenty-fifth Amendment, which provides for a more orderly system of replacement. Previously, when a vice president ascended to the White House after the death or removal of a president, the vice presidency was left vacant. The amendment provides for presidential appointment of a vice president to fill the vacant spot. It also provides for at least temporary replacement of the president in the case of disability. The latter provision developed out of a concern that the country could have become leaderless had Kennedy been physically or mentally impaired but not killed.

141. Barber, *Pulse of Politics,* 167.

142. Thomas Ferguson and Joel Rogers, *Right Turn: The Decline of the Democrats and the Future of American Politics* (New York: Hill and Wang, 1986), 53.

143. Theodore H. White, *The Making of the President 1964* (New York: New American Library, 1965), 261.

144. Ibid., 353.

145. The central importance of economic conditions to electoral politics is widely documented. See, for example, Stanley Kelley Jr., *Interpreting Elections* (Princeton, N.J.: Princeton University Press, 1983); Edward R. Tufte, *Political Control of the Economy* (Princeton, N.J.: Princeton University Press, 1978); and Campbell, et al., *The American Voter.* On the link between economic conditions and the 1964 election, see Kelley, *Interpreting Elections,* 194.

146. Stanley Karnow, *Vietnam: A History* (New York: Viking, 1983), 358.

147. Ibid., 362.

148. Ibid., 395.

149. James David Barber, *The Presidential Character* (Englewood Cliffs, N.J.: Prentice Hall, 1972), 34.

150. Karnow, *Vietnam,* 403.

151. Ibid., 479.

152. David Halberstam, *The Best and the Brightest* (New York: Random House, 1969).

153. Sundquist, *Dynamics of the Party System,* 384.

154. Ibid., 383.

155. The administration plank supported a bombing halt only when it "would not endanger the lives of our troops in the field," did not call for a reduction in search-and-destroy missions or a withdrawal of troops until the end of the war, and advocated a new government in Saigon only after the war had ended. The minority plank, drafted by McCarthy and McGovern, called for an immediate

halt to the bombing, reduction of offensive operations in the South Vietnamese countryside, a negotiated troop withdrawal, and encouragement of the South Vietnamese government to negotiate with communist insurgents. After nearly three hours of debate, the minority plank was defeated, 1,5673/4 to 1,0411/4.

156. Theodore H. White, *The Making of the President 1968* (New York, Atheneum, 1969), 371.

157. Roseboom, *History of Presidential Elections,* 603.

158. See Russell Baker, *The Next President* (New York: Dell, 1968).

159. David Broder, "The Story That Still Nags at Me," *Washington Monthly,* February 1987, 29–32. See also Theodore H. White, *Making of the President 1972* (New York: New American Library, 1973), 82.

160. White, *Making of the President 1972,* 129.

161. Ibid., 207.

162. On the politics of the period, see Sundquist, *Dynamics of the Party System,* 393–411; and Theodore H. White, *America in Search of Itself* (New York: Harper and Row, 1981). Good accounts of the Watergate scandal include those by Theodore H. White, *Breach of Faith* (New York: Atheneum, 1975); Jonathan Schell, *The Time of Illusion* (New York: Knopf, 1976); and Lewis Chester et al., *Watergate* (New York: Ballantine, 1973).

163. See Bruce Odes, ed., *From the President: Richard Nixon's Secret Files* (New York: Harper and Row, 1989).

164. Seymour Hersh, "The Pardon," *Atlantic,* August 1983, 55–78.

165. David J. Vogler, *The Politics of Congress* (Boston: Allyn and Bacon, 1977), 15–20, 25–26, 34, 147–155, 243–245.

166. For a good account of Carter's 1976 Iowa victory, see Hugh Winebrenner, *The Iowa Precinct Caucuses* (Ames: University of Iowa Press, 1987), 67–93.

167. Jules Witcover, *Marathon* (New York: Viking, 1977), 274–288.

168. Ibid., 545–560.

169. Responding to a question during a debate, Ford said: "There is no Soviet domination of Eastern Europe, and there never will be under a Ford administration. . . . I don't believe . . . that the Yugoslavians consider themselves dominated by the Soviet Union. I don't believe that the Romanians consider themselves dominated by the Soviet Union. I don't believe that the Poles consider themselves dominated by the Soviet Union." Ibid., 597, 598.

170. See Gary Sick, *October Surprise: America's Hostages in Iran and the Election of Ronald Reagan* (New York: Times Books, 1992).

171. Richard Harwood, ed., *The Pursuit of the Presidency 1980* (New York: Berkeley, 1980), 305–307.

172. Thomas Byrne Edsall, *The New Politics of Inequality* (New York: Norton, 1984), 77–78.

173. George Gilder, *Wealth and Poverty* (New York: Basic Books, 1980). Another prominent supply-side tract is that by Jude Wanniski, *The Way the World Works* (New York: Basic Books, 1978). A sympathetic summary of the whole movement can be found in Robert Craig Paul, *The Supply-Side Revolution* (Cambridge, Mass.: Harvard University Press, 1984).

174. Ferguson and Rogers, *Right Turn,* 86–88, n. 245.

175. Garry Wills, *Reagan's America: Innocents at Home* (Garden City, N.Y.: Doubleday, 1987), 387.

176. Ibid., 385.

177. Ferguson and Rogers, *Right Turn.*

178. Rep. Shirley Chisholm of Brooklyn, New York, was the first African American to seek a major party nomination. Her participation in the 1972 Democratic primaries won 151 delegates.

179. Geraldine Ferraro, with Linda Bird Francke, *Ferraro: My Story* (New York: Bantam, 1985), 164.

180. Paul R. Abramson, John H. Aldrich, and David W. Rohde, *Change and Continuity in the 1984 Elections,* rev. ed. (Washington, D.C.: CQ Press, 1986), 58.

181. V. O. Key Jr., "A Theory of Critical Elections," *Journal of Politics* 17 (February 1955): 3–18.

182. Abramson et al., *Change and Continuity,* 286–287.

183. Michael Barone and Grant Ujifusa, *The Almanac of American Politics: 1984* (Washington, D.C.: National Journal, 1983), xiv. See also Ladd and Hadley, *Transformations,* 237–249.

184. Taylor, *See How They Run,* 76.

185. Also that year, two Supreme Court nominees, Robert H. Bork and Douglas H. Ginsburg, failed to win Senate confirmation. Bork lost because of his views on a wide variety of social issues, but many criticisms focused on his personality. Ginsburg withdrew from consideration after revelations that he had smoked marijuana as a student and law school professor.

186. Barbara Norrander, *Super Tuesday: Regional Politics and Presidential Primaries* (Lexington: University Press of Kentucky, 1992), 101.

187. In the twelve days after Bush picked Quayle, ABC, CBS, and NBC aired ninety-three stories about him—more than Dukakis received during the whole primary season. Two-thirds of the stories were negative. See Taylor, *See How They Run,* 162.

188. Nelson W. Polsby and Aaron Wildavsky, *Presidential Elections: Contemporary Strategies of American Electoral Politics,* 8th ed. (New York: Basic Books, 1991), 248.

189. Quayle did not meet the requirements set for political science majors and failed the first general examination at DePauw University in Indiana. He also failed to gain admission to law school under the usual application procedure. A study of Quayle's congressional career concludes that Quayle had no policy achievements in the House of Representatives but mastered some policy issues in the Senate. See Anthony Lewis, "The Intimidated Press," *New York Times,* January 19, 1989, 27; and Richard F. Fenno Jr., *The Making of a Senator: Dan Quayle* (Washington, D.C.: CQ Press, 1988).

190. *The Presidency A to Z* (Washington, D.C.: Congressional Quarterly, 1992), 29.

191. Sidney Blumenthal, *Pledging Allegiance: The Last Campaign of the Cold War* (New York: HarperCollins, 1990), 317.

192. Michael Duffy and Dan Goodgame, *Marching in Place: The Status Quo Presidency of George Bush* (New York: Simon and Schuster, 1992), 267–268.

193. Quoted in Michael Nelson, "The Presidency: Clinton and the Cycle of Politics and Policy," in *The Elections of 1992,* ed. Michael Nelson (Washington, D.C.: CQ Press, 1993), 144.

194. Paul J. Quirk and Jon K. Dalager, "The Election: A 'New Democrat' and a New Kind of Presidential Campaign," in Nelson, *Elections of 1992,* 61.

195. The unofficial manifesto of this movement is that by George F. Will, *Restoration: Congress, Term Limits, and the Recovery of Deliberative Democracy* (New York: Free Press, 1993).

196. Perot's rescue of his employees from Tehran during the 1979 Iranian revolution, for example, resulted in a best-selling book—Ken Follett's *On Wings of Eagles* (New York: Morrow, 1983)—and a made-for-TV movie. Earlier, he had founded a national organization to support President Nixon's Vietnam policy. Later, his company's merger with General Motors provoked a public dispute that cast him as the problem solver and GM officials as entrenched bureaucrats.

197. Ryan J. Barilleaux and Randall E. Adkins, "The Nominations: Process and Patterns," in Nelson, *Elections of 1992,* 38–39.

198. See David Osborne and Ted Gaebler, *Reinventing Government: How the Entrepreneurial Spirit Is Transforming the*

Public Sector (Reading, Mass.: Addison-Wesley, 1992), for a manifesto of Clinton's approach to government reform.

199. For an excellent treatment of the importance of the middle class and suburbanism on modern American politics, see Thomas Byrne Edsall and Mary D. Edsall, *Chain Reaction: The Impact of Race, Rights, and Taxes on American Politics* (New York: Norton, 1991).

200. Barilleaux and Adkins, "The Nominations," 48–49.

201. Duffy and Goodgame, *Marching in Place.*

202. *Congressional Quarterly Weekly Report,* supplements, July 4, 1992, 71, and August 8, 1992, 67.

203. Daniel Hellinger and Dennis R. Judd, *The Democratic Facade* (Belmont, Calif.: Wadsworth, 1994), 180.

204. Al Gore, *Earth in the Balance: Ecology and the Human Spirit* (Boston: Houghton Mifflin, 1992).

205. Ross K. Barker, "Sorting Out and Suiting Up: The Presidential Nominations," in *The Election of 1992,* ed. Gerald M. Pomper (Chatham, N.J.: Chatham House, 1993), 67.

206. See Mark J. Rozell and Clyde Wilcox, "It Isn't the Old Christian Right Anymore," *Los Angeles Times,* April 29, 1996, B5.

207. See Clyde Wilcox and Mark J. Rozell, "Dole's Delicate Balancing Act," *Christian Science Monitor,* June 4, 1996, 20.

208. "Polls and the Election," *The Public Perspective,* December 1996/ January 1997, 58.

209. Howard Kurtz, "A Big Story: But Only Behind the Scenes; Media Fretted Over Reporting Dole Affair," *Washington Post,* November 13, 1996, D1.

210. Green Party candidate Ralph Nader polled 0.7 percent and Libertarian Harry Browne polled 0.5 percent. Rhodes Cook, "Even with Higher Vote, Clinton Remains Minority President," *Congressional Quarterly Weekly Report,* January 18, 1997, 185–188.

211. Howard Fineman, "Clinton's Big Win," *Newsweek,* November 18, 1996, 8–13; Rhodes Cook, "Clinton's Easy Second-Term Win Riddles GOP Electoral Map," *Congressional Quarterly Weekly Report,* November 9, 1996, 3189–3194.

212. See Richard L. Berke, "Clinton Wins Second Term by Solid Margin," *New York Times,* November 6, 1996.

213. Matthew Vita, "2000's Stealth Issue: Impeachment's Effects Are Playing Out in Races from National to District Level," *Washington Post,* November 1, 2000, A1.

214. See Gregory L. Giroux, "In His Own Right," *Congressional Quarterly Democratic Convention Guide,* August 12, 2000, 9.

215. Jane Hall, "Gore Media Coverage: Playing Hardball," Columbia Journalism Review, September/October 2000, 30.

216. Rhodes Cook, "The Nader Factor: Overrated?" *Rhodes Cook Letter,* January 2001, 7.

217. See Ken Ringle, "For Jan. 20, a Peaceful Precedent," *Washington Post,* January 10, 2001, C9.

218. John F. Harris, "Deficit Worries Threaten Bush Agenda," *Washington Post,* February 7, 2005, A5.

219. Josephine Hearn, "John Kerry's Lawyers Wear Smiles, Ties," *The Hill,* November 2, 2004.

220. Federal Election Commission.

221. Del Quentin Wilber, "From Across U.S., 2,000 Police Officers Volunteer for Duty," *Washington Post,* January 18, 2005, B1.

222. Roxanne Roberts, "On Inaugural Night, ISO an After-Party with a Pulse," *Washington Post,* January 22, 2005, C1.

chapter 7

Selection by Succession

by Michael Nelson

The original Constitution—supplemented by the Twentieth Amendment (1933), the Twenty-fifth Amendment (1967), the succession acts of 1792, 1886, and 1947, the rules of the Republican and Democratic Parties, and various informal precedents and practices—provides that under certain circumstances the president may be selected not by election, but by succession.

Historically, nine presidents have reached the White House through succession—four of them when the incumbent president died of natural causes, four when the president was assassinated, and one when the president resigned. Four succeeded to the presidency in the nineteenth century, five in the twentieth century. None of the nineteenth-century vice presidents was subsequently nominated by his party for a term as president in his own right. All five twentieth-century successors were nominated, and four were elected.

Each of the nine successor presidents was vice president at the time he succeeded to the presidency.

- Vice President John Tyler became president when President William Henry Harrison died of an illness just one month after his inauguration in 1841.
- Vice President Millard Fillmore succeeded to the presidency in 1850 when President Zachary Taylor died of natural causes during the second year of his term.
- President Abraham Lincoln, who was assassinated six weeks after the start of his second term in 1865, was succeeded by Vice President Andrew Johnson.
- Vice President Chester A. Arthur became president in 1881 after the death of President James A. Garfield, who also was assassinated near the start of his term.
- Vice President Theodore Roosevelt succeeded to the presidency in 1901 after an assassin killed President William McKinley. Roosevelt served out the remaining three and one-half years of McKinley's term and was elected president in 1904.
- President Warren G. Harding died of natural causes with nineteen months left in his term in 1923. He was succeeded by Vice President Calvin Coolidge, who ran for president and was elected in 1924.

- President Franklin D. Roosevelt died of natural causes three months after the start of his fourth term in 1945 and was succeeded by Vice President Harry S. Truman. Truman was elected president in 1948.
- Vice President Lyndon B. Johnson succeeded to the presidency in 1963 after President John F. Kennedy was assassinated with fourteen months remaining in his term. Johnson was elected to a full term as president in 1964.
- Under threat of imminent impeachment and removal, President Richard M. Nixon resigned in 1974, after serving less than two years of his second term. Vice President Gerald R. Ford became president. Ford was nominated for a full presidential term by his party in 1976 but was narrowly defeated in the general election.

Two vice presidents have served briefly as acting president: George H. W. Bush, who assumed the powers and duties of the presidency when Ronald Reagan was disabled because of cancer surgery in 1985, and Richard B. Cheney, who stepped in during George W. Bush's colonoscopy in 2002. In each case, the vice president took the president's place for only a few hours.

Assassination attempts, impeachment proceedings, and illness elevated concerns about succession to national prominence during twenty of the nation's first forty-two presidencies (George Washington through Bill Clinton).[1] With the exception of Walter F. Mondale, every vice president since 1945 has become the focus of public attention because of some event of presidential health or safety that raised the possibility that he would succeed to the presidency.

Vacancies also have occurred in the vice presidency on eighteen occasions. The vice presidency became vacant each of the nine times the vice president succeeded to the presidency. In addition, seven vice presidents died in office: George Clinton (1812), Elbridge Gerry (1814), William R. King (1853), Henry Wilson (1875), Thomas A. Hendricks (1885), Garret A. Hobart (1899), and James S. Sherman (1912). Two vice presidents—John C. Calhoun (1832) and Spiro T. Agnew (1973)—resigned.

The original Constitution provided, but not fully, for presidential selection through succession by the vice president. It said nothing about filling vacancies in the vice presidency. Presidential succession practices had to be clarified and supplemented over the years: by precedent (Tyler's succession to the office of the president, not just to its powers and duties, and for the full balance of the president's unexpired term, not just until a special election could be called), by law (Succession Acts passed by Congress in 1792, 1886, and 1947 to extend the line of succession beyond the vice president), and by constitutional amendment (the Twentieth Amendment, enacted in 1933 to provide for succession during the period between the election and the start of the president's term, and the Twenty-fifth Amendment, which became part of the Constitution in 1967, to provide for both presidential disabilities and vice-presidential vacancies).

THE CONSTITUTIONAL CONVENTION

The Framers of the Constitution were aware that merely to elect a president to a four-year term was no guarantee that the president would be able, willing, or worthy to fulfill the term. At the Constitutional Convention of 1787, they provided for four circumstances that might require presidential selection not by election but by succession: the president's resignation from office; the president's death, whether by assassination or natural causes; the temporary or permanent inability of the president to meet the responsibilities of the office, and the impeachment and removal of the president by Congress for "Treason, Bribery, or other high Crimes and Misdemeanors."

As prudent as the delegates were in anticipating that circumstances might arise that would require a president to be chosen by succession, they were less than thorough in addressing six related issues.

First, who would be the successor? In August the Committee of Detail suggested the president of the Senate, but this idea ultimately was rejected for fear that it would create an incentive for senators to convict a president who had been impeached by the House of Representatives to replace the president with one of their own. Individual delegates proposed the chief justice of the United States (Gouverneur Morris of Pennsylvania was the author of this idea) or a council of state (James Madison of Virginia offered this one) as the designated presidential successor. When, late in the convention, the vice presidency was invented by the Committee on Postponed Matters as a way of making the electoral college work, the vice president—almost offhandedly—was made successor to the president. *(See "The Vice Presidency," p. 39, in Chapter 1.)*

Second, if the presidency did become vacant, would the vice president serve out the unexpired balance of the president's four-year term, or would succession to the presidency be temporary, pending a special presidential election? Although history's answer has been full succession to the balance of the term, the convention almost certainly intended that succession be partial and temporary.

The delegates' intentions about succession and a special election were obscured because of what can only be called a clerical error. The Committee of Style, created at the end of the convention to put the delegates' myriad decisions into a final, polished draft of the Constitution, was given two succession resolutions to incorporate: one from a report by the Committee on Postponed Matters that was submitted to the convention on September 4, and the other from a motion that was made on the floor by Edmund Randolph of Virginia on September 7.

The first resolution stated: "In the case of his [the president's] removal as aforesaid, death, absence, resignation, or inability to discharge the powers or duties of his office the Vice President shall exercise those powers and duties until another President be chosen, or until the inability of the President be removed."

The second resolution, which was intended to supplement the first by providing a method for presidential succession if there were no vice president, read: "The Legislature may declare by law what officer of the United States shall act as President in the case of the death, resignation, or disability of the President and Vice President; and such Officer shall act accordingly, until such disability be removed, or a President shall be elected." The last eleven words of this resolution—"until such disability be removed, or a President shall be elected"—were Madison's amendment to Randolph's motion. They were inserted, Madison told the delegates, expressly to permit "a supply of vacancy by an intermediate election of the President"—that is, a special election.

What appeared in the final draft of the Committee of Style, which was mildly modified by the convention, was the product of the committee's effort to compress the two resolutions into one—Clause 6 of Article II, Section 1, of the Constitution:

> In case of the Removal of the President from Office, or of his Death, Resignation, or Inability to discharge the Powers and Duties of the said Office, the Same shall devolve on the Vice President, and the Congress may by law provide for the case of Removal, Death, Resignation, or Inability, both of the President and Vice President, declaring what Officer shall then act as President, and such Officer shall act accordingly, until the Disability be removed, or a President shall be elected.

Clearly, the delegates' intentions about succession were obscured, no doubt unwittingly, by the Committee of Style.[2] Grammatically, it is impossible to tell—and in their rush to adjournment the delegates did not notice the ambiguity—whether "the Same" in the constitutional provision refers to "the said Office" (the presidency) or, as the convention intended, to its "Powers and Duties." Nor can one ascertain whether "until . . . a President shall be elected" means until the end of the original four-year term or, again as intended, until a special election is held.

Third, the delegates left Congress to legislate on the matter of presidential selection by succession when the vice presidency was vacant, either because the vice president had died, resigned, or been impeached and removed or because the vice president had succeeded to the presidency.

Fourth, the original Constitution was silent as to what would happen if a person whom the electoral college had chosen to be president or vice president died, withdrew, or was found to be constitutionally unqualified by virtue of age, residence, or citizenship before being inaugurated.

Fifth, the delegates made no provision for succession to the vice presidency or replacement of the vice president when the office became vacant.

Finally, the delegates did not deal comprehensively with presidential inability. Death, resignation, impeachment and removal—these were well-defined events. Little doubt could exist as to when succession was needed. But inability, whether mental or physical, was a more subjective matter and would not always be so readily apparent. Nor did the

delegates create a procedure for determining whether a presidential disability existed. "What is the extent of the term 'disability'," John Dickinson of Delaware asked the convention on August 27, "& who is to be the judge of it?" No one answered him.

THE VICE PRESIDENT AS FULL SUCCESSOR

Fifty-two years elapsed between the ratification of the Constitution in 1789 and the first vacancy in the presidency in 1841, when William Henry Harrison died shortly after his inauguration. Since 1841, the nation has never gone nearly this long without the presidency becoming prematurely vacant. Because the language of the Constitution was vague, the official and unofficial records of the Constitutional Convention had not yet been published, and no delegates to the convention were still alive, it was impossible to say authoritatively what was supposed to happen next.

Initially, some members of Congress and of Harrison's cabinet seemed to think that the president's death made Vice President John Tyler only the acting president. Tyler believed differently. He quickly took the oath of office as president, delivered a sort of inaugural address, declared his intention

LINE OF SUCCESSION

On March 30, 1981, President Ronald Reagan was shot by would-be assassin John Hinckley outside a Washington, D.C., hotel and rushed to a nearby hospital for surgery. Vice President George H. W. Bush was on a plane returning to Washington from Texas. Meanwhile, presidential aides and cabinet members gathered at the White House, where questions arose among them and in the press corps about who was "in charge."[1] Secretary of State Alexander M. Haig Jr. rushed to the press briefing room and, before an audience of reporters and live television cameras, said, "As of now, I am in control here in the White House, pending the return of the vice president. . . . Constitutionally, gentlemen, you have the president, the vice president, and the secretary of state."

Haig was, as many critics later pointed out, wrong. The Constitution says nothing about who follows the vice president in the line of succession. The Succession Act of 1947 (later modified to reflect the creation of new departments) establishes first the congressional leaders and then the heads of the departments, in the order the departments were created, in the line of succession that follows the vice president. [Legislation has been proposed, but not yet passed, to insert the secretary of the Department of Homeland Security into the line of succession.]

The line of succession is:

    vice president
    Speaker of the House of Representatives
    president pro tempore of the Senate
    secretary of state
    secretary of the Treasury

    secretary of defense
    attorney general
    secretary of the interior
    secretary of agriculture
    secretary of commerce
    secretary of labor
    secretary of health and human services
    secretary of housing and urban development
    secretary of transportation
    secretary of energy
    secretary of education
    secretary of veterans affairs

The full import of the succession act becomes apparent to the American people every year when one department secretary does not attend the president's nationally televised State of the Union address before Congress so that the secretary will be available to succeed to the presidency if the president, vice president, and the other members of the line of succession are assassinated simultaneously. Of note, the Constitution stipulates that the president must be a natural born citizen of the United States. This provision makes George W. Bush administration Secretary of Commerce Carlos Gutierrez (born in Cuba) and Secretary of Labor Elaine Chao (born in Taiwan) ineligible to assume the presidency.

1. "Confusion Over Who Was in Charge Arose Following Reagan Shooting," *Wall Street Journal*, April 1, 1981.

to serve out the remainder of Harrison's term, and moved into the White House. One reason Tyler's claims were accepted was that he acted decisively in a constitutionally and politically uncertain situation. Another is that members of Congress and the cabinet knew that whether Tyler was declared president or acting president, he would wield the powers of the office in ways that might be detrimental to those who opposed him. An effort in Congress to address Tyler officially in correspondence as "Vice President, on whom, by the death of the late President, the powers and duties of the office of President have devolved" was defeated overwhelmingly.[3]

Tyler's action set a precedent that Millard Fillmore (nine years later) and future vice presidents were able to follow without controversy. Not until the Twenty-fifth Amendment was enacted in 1967, however, did the Constitution explicitly codify the vice president's right, when the presidency becomes prematurely vacant, to succeed to the office and serve for the balance of the unexpired term.[4] Section 1 of the amendment states: "In case of the removal of the President from office or of his death or resignation, the Vice President shall become President."

OTHER OFFICIALS IN THE LINE OF SUCCESSION

Article II, Section 2, Clause 6, of the original Constitution did not delineate a line of succession extending past the vice president. Instead, it charged Congress to provide by law for situations in which the vice presidency was vacant when a successor to the president was needed.

The Second Congress passed the Succession Act of 1792. The act stipulated that a double vacancy in the presidency and vice presidency would be remedied by a special election to a full four-year term the following November unless the vacancy occurred during the last six months of the departed president's term. During that period, the president pro tempore of the Senate or, if there were none, the Speaker of the House of Representatives would "act as President." Madison, then a representative from Virginia, objected to this provision of the act, mostly because he thought that the presence of legislators in the line of succession violated the principle of separation of powers, and partly because the line bypassed the leader of his party, Secretary of State Thomas Jefferson.

Although the double vacancy provided for in the 1792 Succession Act never has occurred, the nation has frequent-

ly been at risk. Sixteen of the first thirty-six presidents (Washington to Lyndon Johnson) served without a vice president for part of their terms. A particular problem arose in 1881. President Garfield was assassinated at a time when there was neither a president pro tempore of the Senate nor a House Speaker. If anything had happened to Vice President Arthur, Garfield's successor, the nation would have been without a president.[5] Congress did nothing to correct this problem, and it arose again in 1885, when President Grover Cleveland, a Democrat, was president. Republicans controlled the Senate that year, which drew attention to another problem with the 1792 act: a successor drawn from Congress might be of a different political party than the president.

Responding at last to the double vacancy problem, Congress passed the Succession Act of 1886. The new law located the line of succession in the president's cabinet in the order the departments were created, beginning with the secretary of state. Some members of Congress (including a future president, Rep. William McKinley of Ohio) opposed the measure on the grounds that it violated democratic principles by allowing the president to appoint the successors. Moreover, the statute was unclear about whether succession would be temporary (pending a special election) or permanent in the event of a double vacancy.

The issue of selection by succession was reopened by President Truman, who succeeded to the presidency when President Roosevelt died near the beginning of his fourth term in 1945. Rejecting the idea that, in the absence of a vice president, the secretary of state should be next in line to the presidency, Truman said: "It now lies within my power to nominate the person who would be my immediate successor in the event of my own death or inability to act. I do not believe that in a democracy this power should rest with the Chief Executive." In 1945 Truman called for a return to the 1792 act, but with the Speaker of the House first in the line of succession and the president pro tempore of the Senate (now largely an honorific office awarded to the most senior senator of the majority party) second. Truman also wanted the old act's special election provision restored.[6]

On April 12, 1945, Vice President Harry S. Truman succeeded Franklin Roosevelt to the presidency when FDR died three months into his fourth term. Bess Truman, the vice president's wife, watches her husband take the oath of office.

After the 1946 midterm elections, in which the Republicans regained control of both legislative houses, Congress mostly accepted Truman's recommendation by passing the Succession Act of 1947. Although Congress rejected special elections for fear that they would produce an excessive discontinuity of leadership within a four-year term, it did rearrange the line of succession as follows: Speaker of the House, president pro tempore of the Senate, then cabinet members in the order their departments were created. *(See box, Line of Succession, p. 447.)* In the absence of a vice president, this placed Republican Speaker Joseph Martin, not Secretary of State George C. Marshall, next in line to the presidency until after the 1948 election.

The Twenty-fifth Amendment did not repeal the 1947 Succession Act. But by providing for the filling of a vacant vice presidency, the amendment reduced the possibility that a lengthy double vacancy would occur. *(See "Filling Vice-Presidential Vacancies," p. 450.)*

PREINAUGURATION SELECTION BY SUCCESSION

A combination of legislation, constitutional amendments, and political party rules covers, albeit incompletely, the variety of circumstances under which a president-elect or presidential candidate would have to be replaced before being inaugurated as president.

The possibility that a president-elect might die before taking office was dramatized less than three weeks before the inauguration of Franklin Roosevelt in 1933. An anarchist named Joseph Zangara shot at Roosevelt on a speaker's platform in Miami, Florida. The bullet missed Roosevelt but killed Chicago mayor Anton J. Cermak, who was nearby. Later that year, the Twentieth Amendment became part of the Constitution. *(See "Twentieth Amendment," p. 52, in Chapter 1.)* Section 3 of the amendment deals in various ways with the problem of preinaugural presidential succession.

One clause of Section 3 states clearly that if the president-elect dies, the vice president-elect becomes president at the beginning of the term. Another clause provides that if neither the electoral college nor the House of Representatives is able to fulfill its responsibility under the Twelfth Amendment to elect a constitutionally qualified president by inauguration day, the vice president-elect shall serve as acting president until a president is elected. Finally, Section 3 states that Congress may provide by law for the situation in which neither a president nor a vice president who is constitutionally qualified has been chosen by inauguration day. Congress did so by designating the Speaker of the House, followed by the president pro tempore of the Senate and the other presidential successors listed in the 1947 Succession Act.

As clear as Section 3 is, it covers at most the period from January 6 (the day that, by law, Congress counts the electoral votes for president and vice president and, assuming one pair of candidates has received a majority, declares who is president-elect and vice president-elect) to January 20, the day fixed by Section 1 of the Twentieth Amendment as the start of the president's term.[7] The Constitution provides no guidance, however, about what would happen if a presidential candidate died, withdrew, or was found to be unqualified before Congress certified the victory of the president-elect on January 6.

The Republican and Democratic Parties have filled in part of the preinaugural succession puzzle, the piece that fits between the national nominating conventions in July or August and the first Monday after the second Wednesday in December, which is when the electors who are chosen by the people on election day in November meet in their state capitals to cast the electoral votes that constitutionally elect the president and vice president. The rules of both national parties provide that vacancies on the ticket will be filled by the national committee. Presumably, a party ordinarily would nominate the vice-presidential candidate for president should the need arise.[8]

What would happen if the presidential candidate who had won a majority of electoral votes died, withdrew, or was found to be constitutionally unqualified in the period between the first Monday after the second Wednesday in December (when the electoral votes are cast) and January 6 (when the electoral votes are counted by Congress)? Section 4 of the Twentieth Amendment calls on Congress to legislate for this possibility. But Congress never has done so.

Without a law to guide it, Congress would have to improvise in counting the electoral votes on January 6. One course of action would be for Congress to declare that no qualified candidate for president had received a majority, in which case the House of Representatives would have to choose the president under the Twelfth Amendment. Because the House's choice is constitutionally confined to the three highest electoral vote recipients in the presidential election, its only alternatives would be to elect a defeated candidate or to elect no one at all. In the latter case, the Twelfth Amendment's provision that the vice president would serve as acting president for the entire four-year term would apply.

Alternatively, Congress could count all the electoral votes and declare the departed presidential candidate elected. That would produce a more pleasing result, because the vice president-elect would be inaugurated as president under Section 3 of the Twentieth Amendment. But as a procedure, such an action would mock both common sense and the Constitution's requirement that to be eligible for president, a person must be at least thirty-five years old and, presumably, alive.

SHOULD PRESIDENTIAL VACANCIES BE FILLED BY SPECIAL ELECTION?

The constitutional process of selection by succession is not bereft of critics, most of whom regard it as inadequate to the task of ensuring the nation effective leadership and would prefer that vacancies in the presidency be filled by special election. Proponents of a special election argue that vice presidents are not likely to be of presidential caliber. As former Democratic representative James G. O'Hara of Michigan put it, presidential candidates will not choose running mates "to succeed them. They will choose them to succeed." Nor, they add, is the experience of being vice president helpful preparation for the presidency. Historian Arthur M. Schlesinger Jr. frequently has called service as vice president "a maiming, not a making, experience."

ARGUMENTS FOR SPECIAL ELECTION

The critics of vice-presidential succession are as convinced of the virtues of special election as they are of the weaknesses of the vice presidency. One line of argument is avowedly idealistic: American practice should conform to the original constitutional intent that the president "be elected," an ideal later enshrined, at least in part, in the 1792 Succession Act, which provided for a special election in the event of a double vacancy in the presidency and vice presidency. The other main argument for a special election, practical in nature, draws attention to the experience of the French Fifth Republic. The constitution of France—which, like that of the United States, established a presidential system—provides that in the event of a vacancy in the presidency, the president of the Senate shall serve as the government's caretaker until a special election is held within five weeks to choose a new president for a full term of office. In 1974, when President Georges Pompidou died, the special election took place thirty-three days afterward, followed by a runoff two weeks later and the inauguration of a new president eight days after that.

Schlesinger suggests some American variations on the French practice. Because any designated caretaker from Congress could well be a leader of a party different from the late president's, the acting president should be a member of the administration, preferably the secretary of state. Because American political parties are large and decentralized, the special election should not take place until ninety days after the vacancy, with the parties' national committees choosing the candidates. Finally, to allow the usual presidential selection process to run its course, no special election should be held if a vacancy occurs during the final year of a president's term. Instead, the caretaker should serve out the term.[1]

What of the vice presidency in this new scheme? To be sure, the office need not be abolished in the course of instituting special elections. The vice president still would be the Senate president and the vital figure in situations of presidential disability. But as Schlesinger realizes, the office would best be eliminated under the special election proposal. It would be difficult to attract competent people to the vice presidency if its successor role were stripped from it, in which case even the office's limited powers would be exercised poorly. Also, after the special election brought in a new president, the vice presidency might well be occupied by a member of the opposition party, a problem best headed off by abolishing it.

ARGUMENTS AGAINST SPECIAL ELECTION

The special election idea has attracted a variety of critics. Some identify problems in the proposal itself. Unlike France, the United States is a superpower. It cannot afford the uncertainty that would attend caretaker leadership, especially in view of the frequency with which presidential vacancies have occurred during the past two centuries.

FILLING VICE-PRESIDENTIAL VACANCIES

In contrast to their treatment of the presidency, the Framers made no provision in the Constitution to fill vacancies in the vice presidency. As it happened, vacancies in the vice presidency occurred sixteen times between 1789 and 1963, an average of once every eleven years. Seven vacancies occurred in this period because the vice president died, one because the vice president resigned, and eight because the president died and the vice president succeeded to the presidency. In 1965 Congress passed the Twenty-fifth Amendment, part of which established a mechanism to replace departed vice presidents by presidential appointment and congressional confirmation. The amendment was ratified and became part of the Constitution in 1967. Since then, it has been invoked on two occasions: when Vice President Agnew resigned in 1973 and was replaced by House minority leader Gerald Ford, and when Vice President Ford succeeded to the presidency after President Nixon resigned in 1974 and was replaced as vice president by former New York governor Nelson A. Rockefeller.

Vice-Presidential Vacancies, 1789–1963

The vice presidency can become vacant when either the vice president dies, resigns, or is removed after conviction for impeachment or the president dies, resigns, or is removed after conviction for impeachment. (In the latter cases, the vice presidency becomes vacant because the vice president succeeds to the presidency.) Taken together, the sixteen occasions on which these situations arose during the nation's first thirty-six vice presidencies—that is, before the passage of the Twenty-fifth Amendment—left the office vacant for thirty-seven years.

From 1789 to 1912, presidential deaths left the vice presidency vacant on five occasions: William Henry Harrison (1841), Taylor (1850), Lincoln (1865), Garfield (1881), and McKinley (1901). But the most frequent cause of a vacancy in the vice presidency was a vice-presidential death. Seven vice presidents died during this period, all of natural causes. Most were old, and some were in ill health when elected. One vice president resigned. The nineteenth-century vice presidency was a weak, even despised office, and

Also unlike in France, presidential selection in the United States is an inherently lengthy undertaking. The nominating process is diffuse, the pool from which presidents are drawn is broad, and a considerable amount of time is required for voters and political activists to sort through all the alternatives. Staffing a new president's administration and developing its policies also is time-consuming. In practice, the proposed ninety-day interregnum, itself long, might last thirty to sixty days longer, with the added time serving as a de facto transition period for the new president.

Other criticisms of the special election proposal concern its operation. For example, would the caretaker president be allowed to run in the special election? If not, the nation would be guaranteed a lack of continuity in leadership and, perhaps, deprived of an able president. If so, how would the caretaker's candidacy influence the conduct of the temporary administration? And how would the selection of people to fill the office that provides the caretaker be affected? The qualifications of a good acting president and those of, say, a good secretary of state may be quite different. Still other questions come to mind. Could the parties' national committees do an adequate job of nominating the presidential candidates, an assignment to which they would bring little experience? Would presidential and congressional elections remain forever unsynchronized? Would the caretaker be granted the full range of presidential powers and duties?

In addition to attacking the special election idea, some critics have defended the virtues of vice-presidential succession. Above all, they argue, the traditional procedure of instant, certain, and full succession by the vice president is a source of stability in the political system. Presidential deaths are, in a literal sense, traumatic events for many citizens, triggering feelings not only of personal grief but also of fear for the Republic.[2] In this uncertain and emotional setting, Americans historically have accepted the vice president's succession as legitimate. Survey data for the last three successions show the public rallying to support each new president to an extent unrivaled by even the most popular newly elected president.[3] Legitimacy and stability are qualities of the historic system of vice-presidential succession. They are not qualities that a polity can take for granted on occasions of leadership change.

Beyond the virtues of vice-presidential succession as a procedure in its own right, some argue that the system also works well in practice, providing able presidents when needed. In the twentieth century, voters elected four of the five successors to full terms while rejecting the reelection bids of four of the ten elected presidents who ran for reelection.

Changing electoral incentives meant that vice presidents in the late twentieth century were chosen more with their successor role in mind, and were better prepared for it while in office, than at any time in history. In a real sense, critics say, proponents of a special election are prescribing a cure for an ailment that is healing of its own accord.

1. Arthur M. Schlesinger Jr., *Cycles of American History* (Boston: Houghton Mifflin, 1986), chap. 12.

2. Paul B. Sheatsley and Jacob J. Feldman, "The Assassination of President Kennedy: Public Reactions," *Public Opinion Quarterly* 28, no. 2 (summer 1964): 189–215.

3. See the data reported in Erwin C. Hargrove and Michael Nelson, *Presidents, Politics, and Policy* (Baltimore: Johns Hopkins University Press, 1984), 21–22.

vigorous, ambitious political leaders typically shunned vice-presidential nominations. *(See Chapter 3, History of the Vice Presidency.)*

The first vice president to die in office was George Clinton, who served under Presidents Thomas Jefferson and James Madison. Clinton died in 1812, with ten months remaining in his term. Madison's second vice president, Elbridge Gerry, died two years later, with two years and three months left in his term. (John C. Calhoun, the vice president to Presidents John Quincy Adams and Andrew Jackson, resigned in 1832, with three months left in his term, to accept South Carolina's election as U.S. senator.) President Franklin Pierce's vice president, William R. King, died less than four weeks after taking the oath of office in 1853. Henry Wilson, the vice president during the second term of President Ulysses S. Grant, died in 1875, with fifteen months remaining in his term. Thomas A. Hendricks died in 1885, nine months after his inauguration as vice president in the first Grover Cleveland administration. Garret Hobart, who served under William McKinley, died in 1899 after less than three years in office. Finally, President William Howard Taft's vice president, James S. Sherman, died in 1912, with four months left in his term. Although Sherman died days before the 1912 election, his name remained on the ballot and three million citizens voted for electors pledged to him and Taft. After the election, the Republican National Committee nominated Nicholas Murray Butler, the president of Columbia University, to replace Sherman as the party's nominee for vice president and receive Sherman's eight electoral votes.

From 1913 to 1963, the vice presidency became vacant three times, in each case because the president died: Harding (1923), Franklin Roosevelt (1945), and Kennedy (1963).

Because the vice president's ongoing constitutional duties are minimal—to preside over the Senate and to cast tie-breaking votes—the absence of a vice president seldom created serious problems before 1963. Still, each time the vice presidency became vacant the nation lacked a constitutionally designated successor to the president. The original Constitution had simply called on Congress to legislate a line of presidential succession that extended past the vice president. Congress did so in 1792, 1886, and 1947.

Remarkably, the nation has never experienced a presidential term in which both the president and vice president died; as a result, the statutory line of succession has never had to be invoked. Still there were some periods of high risk. The deaths of President Taylor and Vice President King left the vice presidency vacant for all but four weeks from July 9, 1850, until March 4, 1857, a seven-year period. From September 19, 1881, when President Garfield died, until March 4, 1889, when Vice President Levi P. Morton was inaugurated, the vice presidency was vacant for all but the nine months that Vice President Hendricks served in 1885 before dying. The vice presidency also lay vacant during parts of President Madison's two terms and for more than three years of the terms of Presidents Tyler, Andrew Johnson, Arthur, Cleveland, Theodore Roosevelt, and Truman.

The Twenty-fifth Amendment

The possibility that a vice president would not be available to succeed to the presidency was not regarded as intolerable until after President Kennedy was assassinated on November 22, 1963. To be sure, the importance of having an able and informed successor standing ready to become president had become dramatically clear when Vice President Truman, unaware of the nation's postwar plans and of the existence of the atomic bomb, succeeded to the presidency in 1945. But the absence of a vice president during the first fourteen months of Lyndon Johnson's presidency seemed especially distressing because the next two offices in the 1947 line of succession were occupied by weak and unwell members of Congress, Speaker of the House John W. McCormack of Massachusetts and President Pro Tempore of the Senate Carl Hayden of Arizona. As the legal scholar John D. Feerick wrote in *The Twenty-fifth Amendment,* "Neither had been chosen for his position with an eye toward possible succession to the presidency, and neither was viewed by the public as a person of presidential stature."[9]

On December 12, 1963, less than three weeks after the Kennedy assassination, Democratic senator Birch Bayh of Indiana, who chaired the Subcommittee on Constitutional Amendments of the Senate Committee on the Judiciary, proposed a constitutional amendment that, in addition to addressing the issue of presidential disability, empowered the president to nominate a vice president when the office became vacant, pending confirmation by a majority of both houses of Congress. In presenting his amendment, Bayh argued:

> The accelerated pace of international affairs, plus the overwhelming problems of modern military security, make it almost imperative that we change our system to provide for not only a president but a vice president at all times. The modern concept of the vice presidency is that of a man

"standing in the wings"—even if reluctantly—ready at all times to take the burden. He must know the job of president. He must be current on all national and international developments. He must, in fact, be something of an "assistant president."[10]

The hearings that were held by the constitutional amendments subcommittee in early 1964 revealed near-unanimous support for finding a solution to the problem of the vacant vice presidency. Witnesses differed, however, about the best method to fill such vacancies. Senator Bayh's proposal that the president nominate and both houses of Congress confirm the new vice president—a procedure supported by the American Bar Association and numerous scholars—was grounded in the idea that, as Harvard law professor Paul Freund stated at the hearings, "the vice presidency should have a popular base and at the same time be in harmony with the presidency. These objectives can best be achieved by associating the Congress and the president in the selection, with the opportunity for informal consultation to be expected in such a process." Even those who supported Bayh's proposal, however, wondered whether a time limit should be placed on the congressional confirmation process and whether confirmation should come from a joint meeting of the House and Senate or from each house voting separately. Democratic senator Frank Church urged that the president be required to submit a list of several names to the Senate and that those ratified by the Senate be passed on to the House for a final selection.

Other proposals emerged during the hearings. Democratic senator Sam Ervin of North Carolina, arguing that "the potential president should be democratically elected," wanted to entrust the selection of a new vice president to Congress alone. New York Republican senator Jacob K. Javits worried that such a vice president might be unacceptable to the president and urged that the president be empowered to veto Congress's choice. Democrat Frank Moss of Utah rejoined that presidents should not be forced to rebuke Congress to get the vice presidents they wanted. Former vice president Richard Nixon proposed that the president submit the vice-presidential nomination to the electoral college from the previous election, which had formally elected the departed vice president and which was, almost by definition, controlled by the president's party. But, as Bayh argued, "the electoral college is not chosen, as is Congress, to exercise any considered judgment or reasoning"—because it meets simultaneously in all the states, it is not a body at all.

After tinkering slightly with Bayh's original proposal, the constitutional amendments subcommittee voted on May 27, 1964, to recommend a new amendment to the Constitution that stated in part: "Whenever there is a vacancy in the office of the Vice President, the President shall nominate a Vice President who shall take office upon confir-

On February 23, 1967, Lyndon B. Johnson signed the Twenty-fifth Amendment, which addresses the issue of presidential disability and empowers the president to nominate a vice president when that office becomes vacant.

cies, remained unchanged from the version that had been in the original Senate Judiciary Committee recommendation.

On June 30, the House voted final passage of the Twenty-fifth Amendment by voice vote. The Senate followed on July 6 with a 68–5 vote. Ratification by the states proceeded quickly and without controversy. The amendment was approved by the necessary three-fourths of the state legislatures (thirty-eight) on February 19, 1967, and was formally proclaimed the Twenty-fifth Amendment to the Constitution at a White House ceremony on February 23, 1967. Although the process of amending the Constitution does not involve the presidency, President Johnson had supported the amendment in press conferences and speeches and took special pleasure in its enactment.

The smooth passage of the Twenty-fifth Amendment belied the numerous concerns that were raised along the way by critics, some of whom would later seem prescient. One was the absence of a time limit on the president to nominate a vice president and, especially, on Congress to confirm. Clearly, a long delay would thwart a major purpose of the amendment: to ensure that the nation would always have a vice president standing at the ready to succeed to the presidency if the need arose. A second concern was that the amendment allowed for not only the vice presidency but also the presidency to be transformed into an appointed office in the event that an appointed vice president were to succeed to the presidency. If that happened, the next vice president to be appointed would be chosen by a president who originally had been appointed, and so on, until the end of the term. Finally, there was the matter of vice-presidential disability, which the amendment did not address. Specifically, if the vice president were disabled, the nation still would lack a qualified successor to the presidency.

In all cases, these concerns were considered by Congress but not addressed in the amendment for fear that it would grow too cumbersome and complex and that any attempted solutions would create problems of their own.

mation by a majority vote of both Houses of Congress." The full Judiciary Committee approved the amendment on August 4. The Senate then passed it both by voice vote on September 28 and, at the request of Democratic senator John Stennis of Mississippi, by a roll call vote of 65–0 on September 29.

The House of Representatives took no action on vice-presidential succession in 1964, partly because the Senate did not act until late in the second year of the Eighty-eighth Congress, but mostly out of institutional pride. One effect of the proposed amendment would have been to remove Speaker McCormack from his statutory place in the line of succession. After a new vice president was elected in 1964, however, the House moved swiftly. After commencing hearings on February 9, the House Judiciary Committee approved the amendment on March 24. One week later, on March 31, the Rules Committee cleared it for floor consideration by a 6–4 vote; and on April 13 the full House passed the amendment by a vote of 368–29. (The Senate, having already considered and passed the amendment in 1964, whisked it through by a 72–0 vote on February 19, 1965.) Minor differences in the versions of the amendment that were passed by the House and Senate required the calling of a conference committee, which eventually agreed on a common version and brought it back to both houses for final passage. Section 2 of the amendment, the part that dealt with vice-presidential vacan-

TWO VICE-PRESIDENTIAL VACANCIES

The authors of the Twenty-fifth Amendment assumed both that vacancies in the vice presidency would occur fairly frequently and that death, either the president's or the vice president's, would be the usual cause. These were reasonable assumptions: from 1789 to 1963 there had been sixteen vice-presidential vacancies and all but one had come about because the vice president died or the president died and was succeeded by the vice president.

The assumption about frequent vice-presidential vacancies was borne out quickly: the vice presidency became vacant in both 1973 and 1974. But in each case it was a resignation in the face of impeachment, not a death, that left the nation without a vice president.

The Nomination of Gerald R. Ford

On October 10, 1973, Vice President Spiro Agnew resigned as part of a plea bargain with the Justice Department that allowed him to avoid prosecution on most of the bribery and income tax evasion charges that the government was preparing to bring. *(See Chapter 8, Removal of the Vice President.)* Later that day, Ronald L. Ziegler, the president's press secretary, told reporters that "President Nixon intends to move expeditiously in selecting a nominee and he trusts the Congress will then act promptly to consider the nomination."

Nixon's first choice for vice president was former Treasury secretary John B. Connally, a Democrat-turned-Republican who had supported the president in the 1972 election and whom Nixon greatly admired. But Democrats in Congress, joined by some Republicans, resisted the idea of naming a turncoat Democrat and potential candidate for president in the 1976 election as vice president. At the same time, a groundswell began to form among members of both congressional parties in favor of the House Republican leader, Gerald Ford, who was widely liked and respected but was not regarded as ambitious to be president. Wishing to avoid a prolonged confirmation battle and possible defeat, Nixon announced Ford's nomination in a televised speech from the East Room of the White House on the evening of October 12, 1973. He told the nation that Ford met all three of the criteria he had set for a vice president: Ford was qualified to be president, able to work with Congress, and in harmony with the president's views on domestic and foreign policy. It was widely reported that Nixon privately expressed the opinion (which turned out to be errant in the extreme) that Congress would be reluctant to impeach and remove him if to do so meant that Ford would become president.

Hearings on the Ford nomination began promptly in both houses of Congress. Although there was some disagreement about which committee should conduct the Senate hearings, the nomination eventually was referred to the Committee on Rules and Administration because of its tra-

ditional jurisdiction in matters relating to presidential succession and presidential and vice-presidential elections. (The Judiciary and Government Operations Committees also had claimed jurisdiction; others had suggested that a special committee be formed.) The House referred the nomination to its Judiciary Committee.

Ford's nomination prompted the most extensive investigation ever conducted into the background of a nominee for government office. At Congress's request, approximately 350 agents of the Federal Bureau of Investigation (FBI) conducted more than one thousand interviews of people who had known Ford. When the FBI was done, it issued a seventeen-hundred-page report. The Library of Congress, the Internal Revenue Service, and staff members detailed from the General Accounting Office and various congressional committees pored over Ford's public career, tax returns, medical records, campaign finance reports, bank accounts, and payroll records. Nothing seriously detrimental was uncovered.

The ongoing investigation of President Nixon's involvement in the Watergate affair, which coincided with Congress's consideration of the Ford nomination, colored the confirmation process. As Senate Rules Committee chair Howard W. Cannon, D-Nev., said at the beginning of his committee's hearings, the "committee should view its obligations as no less important than the selection of a potential president of the United States." For his part, Ford assured the committee that "I have no intention to run [for president in 1976], and I can foresee no circumstances where I would change my mind." (Ford, however, would run.)

On the House side, Judiciary Committee chair Peter Rodino, D-N.J., later recalled, "There was pressure, heavy pressure [from some liberal Democrats] to get me to delay the confirmation so that if we went ahead with impeaching Nixon there would be a vacancy, and the Democratic Speaker would take over." [11] But Rodino and Speaker Carl Albert, D-Okla., who was first in the line of succession for as long as the vice presidency was vacant, firmly resisted such pressure.

One concern shared by both congressional committees was the proper criteria to use in evaluating a president's nominee for vice president. Democratic representative Robert F. Drinan of Massachusetts, a member of the Judiciary Committee, argued that "this is really an election by the House, that it doesn't really compare with the 'advice and consent' [standard for other presidential nominations]. ... [P]olitical ideology is relevant and to some extent partisan concepts may be employed, and compatibility [with the president] is not the sole consideration." Representative Drinan's view differed from that expressed by Senator Bayh, who noted that the intent of the Twenty-fifth Amendment "was to get a vice president who would be compatible and could work harmoniously with the president." Congress's

On December 6, 1973, Gerald R. Ford was sworn in as vice president by Chief Justice Warren Burger before a joint session of Congress, with President Nixon in attendance. Ford replaced Spiro T. Agnew, who resigned.

responsibility was to determine whether the nominee had "honesty, integrity, [and] no skeletons in the closet."

Because of the confusion and disagreement about the appropriate bounds of Congress's investigation of a vice-presidential nomination, the questions put to Ford in the House and Senate committee hearings ranged widely. According to calculations by attorney Joel Goldstein, Senate committee members asked 50 percent of their questions about "institutional" matters (the proper operations of the institutions of government, including executive privilege, openness, and the government's right to lie), 33 percent about "personal" matters (tax returns, associations, past political conduct), and 17 percent about "issues" (welfare, civil rights, foreign policy). In the House, 50 percent of the questions asked of Ford were personal, 35 percent were institutional, and 15 percent concerned issues. In both houses, questions about issues were asked almost exclusively by Democrats.[12]

Ford patiently answered all the questions that committee members asked. In responding to Watergate-related questions, Ford was careful not to contradict positions that had been stated by Nixon. But he did emphasize his respect and concern for good relations with Congress. "I believe I can be a ready conciliator and calm communicator between the White House and Capitol Hill," Ford told one questioner, "between the reelection mandate of the Republican president and the equally emphatic mandate of the Democratic 93rd Congress."

When the hearings were over, most members of Congress seemed to have accepted Senator Bayh's argument that Congress's proper role in reviewing vice-presidential nominations is to defer to the president except when defects of character, competence, or integrity make a nominee unacceptable. On November 20, 1973, the Senate Rules Committee voted 9–0 to approve Ford's nomination. After brief floor debate on November 27, the Senate confirmed the nomination by 92–3. Two days later, the House Judiciary Committee recommended Ford's nomination by a vote of 29–8, and on December 6, the full House followed suit,

387–35. Although all of the votes against Ford came from Democrats, the vast majority of Democrats voted to confirm him. As Democratic representative James G. O'Hara of Michigan argued, "I submit that to allow ourselves to be caught up in measuring Mr. Ford's qualifications for office against the subjective yardstick of our own philosophies would be to disserve the American people who expect Congress, at this critical moment in history, to rise above partisanship."

On December 6, 1973, immediately after the House vote, Ford was administered the oath as vice president by Chief Justice Warren Burger before a joint session of Congress, with President Nixon in attendance. With precedent for the future in mind, Speaker Albert had insisted, over White House objections, that the swearing-in ceremony take place at the Capitol. The entire confirmation process, from nomination to swearing in, took seven weeks.

The Nomination of Nelson A. Rockefeller

Gerald Ford served only eight months as vice president. When President Nixon resigned on August 9, 1974, Ford became president and the vice presidency was once again vacant. Ford's succession posed an early test for the legitimacy of the vice-presidential appointment process that had been created by the Twenty-fifth Amendment. Not only was Ford the handpicked choice of his discredited predecessor, but his own nomination of a new vice president would mean that for the first time in history the nation would be led by an unelected president and an unelected vice president.

Hours after he took the oath as president, Ford told congressional leaders that he considered the nomination of a new vice president to be his first important decision as president and that he planned to make a selection within ten days. On August 11, Ford decided privately that he would nominate former governor Nelson Rockefeller of New York for vice president.[13] Rockefeller was a national leader of demonstrated competence in the fields of urban and foreign policy. Although he had declined offers to run for vice president in 1960 and 1968 (he dismissed the office as "standby equipment"), Rockefeller now expressed to Ford his willingness to serve. Out of office at age sixty-six, his own ambitions for the presidency largely extinguished, Rockefeller regarded the vice presidency as a crown to his career.

On August 20, after soliciting the views of Republicans in Congress and around the country, President Ford announced his selection to wide press and public acclaim. Ford had worried that prominent Republican Party conservatives, such as Sen. Barry Goldwater of Arizona and Sen. John G. Tower of Texas, might oppose a Rockefeller nomination and was pleased to find that they did not. Shortly afterward, Rockefeller declared that he would not campaign in the fall congressional elections until after his nomination as vice president was confirmed. This may have been a tactical error. Congress, controlled by Democrats who had no desire to see Rockefeller on the campaign trail, responded by dragging its feet in considering his nomination. The Senate Rules Committee did not begin its hearings until September 23, and the House Judiciary Committee waited until November 21. Meanwhile, the FBI, at Congress's request, conducted an even more extensive investigation into Rockefeller's background than it had into Ford's. More than three hundred agents interviewed more than fourteen hundred sources.

For all the delay, there seemed little doubt at the outset of the congressional confirmation process that Rockefeller's nomination to be vice president would be approved. But two political bombshells exploded during the course of the Senate hearings that clouded his prospects. First, Rockefeller disclosed that during the previous seventeen years he had given $1.97 million in gifts to twenty staff members, including $625,000 to William Ronan, the chairman of the Port Authority of New York and New Jersey, and $50,000 to Henry A. Kissinger, a former Rockefeller aide who currently was President Ford's secretary of state. Second, the FBI suggested to the House Judiciary Committee that Rockefeller, through intermediaries, may have financed the writing of a critical biography of his Democratic opponent in the 1970 New York gubernatorial election. The book, written by Victor J. Lasky, was called *Arthur J. Goldberg: The Old and the New.* The fundamental question that both incidents seemed to raise was whether Rockefeller had used his wealth to buy political power.

Rockefeller defended the practice of giving financial gifts to aides on the grounds that it had enabled him to keep them in public service despite their relatively low salaries. He claimed that his long record in government demonstrated his commitment to the public interest instead of to personal gain. He also offered a "sincere and unqualified apology" to Goldberg.

Both congressional committees probed deeply into the issue of Rockefeller's wealth. In contrast to the Ford hearings, 77 percent of the questions asked by members of the Senate Rules Committee and 63 percent of those asked by members of the House Judiciary Committee concerned "personal" matters. (Seven percent of the Senate committee's questions and 13 percent of the House committee's questions dealt with institutional matters; 16 percent of the Senate committee's questions and 24 percent of the House committee's questions involved issues.)[14] Annoyed by the amount of time that Congress was taking to probe into Rockefeller's background, President Ford stated in a news conference on November 14 that it was time for Congress to "fish or cut bait." He further urged that the Twenty-fifth Amendment be altered to impose a time limit on congressional confirmation of vice-presidential nominations. The nation "needs a vice president at all times," Ford argued.

Prodded by Ford and persuaded by Rockefeller's testimony, the Senate Rules Committee approved the nomination on November 22, by a 9–0 vote. On December 10, the full Senate voted 90–7 for confirmation. Approval by the House Judiciary Committee came on December 12, by a vote of 26–12. On December 19, the full House voted 287–128 in Rockefeller's favor, completing the four-month confirmation process. Immediately after the House voted, President Ford and Rockefeller went to the Senate chamber, where Rockefeller was sworn in as vice president by Chief Justice Warren Burger.

Some commentators marked the irony that on July 4, 1976, the bicentennial of the nation's birth, the government was presided over by an unelected president and an unelected vice president. That no question was raised about the legitimate right to rule of either President Ford or Vice President Rockefeller seemed powerful testimony to the confidence Americans have in the Constitution. Nonetheless, both men were only in office a short time. In response to pressure from conservatives in the Republican Party, Ford encouraged Rockefeller to withdraw as a possible candidate for renomination in the 1976 election. Rockefeller complied, making him only the second vice president in the twentieth century to be dropped from the ticket after one term. Ford ran for president in 1976, but he was barely renominated by his party and narrowly lost in the general election. Ford thus became the century's only successor president not to be elected to a full presidential term.

TEMPORARY SUCCESSION WHEN THE PRESIDENT IS DISABLED

Presidential disability was a minor concern at the Constitutional Convention and a recurring inconvenience during much of American history. It became a potentially grave crisis in the nuclear age. *(See "Twenty-fifth Amendment," p. 56, in Chapter 1.)*

The original Constitution provided that, as in the case of a president's death, resignation, or impeachment and removal, "in Case of the . . . Inability [of the president] to discharge the Powers and Duties of the said Office, the Same shall devolve on the Vice President . . . until the Disability be removed, or a President shall be elected." No debate accompanied the enactment of this clause, so it is impossible to determine what the delegates meant by "Inability" or "Disability." Nor was any procedure created to determine whether a president was disabled.

By one estimate, eleven presidents who served in the period 1789–1967 were disabled during at least part of their administrations, including Garfield, who hovered near death for eighty days after being shot in 1881, and Woodrow Wilson, who in 1919 was felled by a stroke that largely incapacitated him during his final seventeen months in office.[15] Discussions took place within both presidents' cabinets about transferring power to the vice president, but the absence of constitutional guidance made them reluctant to act.

Presidential disability became a pressing issue after World War II, with the invention of nuclear weapons launched by intercontinental ballistic missiles. Awareness spread that the nation no longer could afford to be leaderless even for brief periods—the president might be called on at a moment's notice to make a decision that could destroy the world. After a series of severe health problems in the mid-1950s, President Dwight D. Eisenhower improvised an arrangement with Vice President Nixon under which Eisenhower, by letter, would temporarily transfer the powers and duties of the presidency to Nixon if he were again disabled. The arrangement also provided that Nixon could take those powers (again, it was hoped, temporarily) if the president were unable to transfer them voluntarily. Presidents Kennedy and Lyndon Johnson made similar arrangements with their vice presidents.

In 1965 a constitutional answer was offered to the disability question when Congress proposed the Twenty-fifth Amendment. (It was ratified by the states in 1967.) Although the amendment did not define disability, it created procedures for determining when the president is disabled and for transferring the powers and duties of the presidency to the vice president until the disability is ended.

The amendment authorizes a disabled president to make the vice president acting president simply by sending a letter to the Speaker of the House of Representatives and the president pro tempore of the Senate. The president, when once again able, can regain the powers and duties of the office by writing another letter. Should the president be unable or unwilling to declare that a disability exists, the vice president and a majority of the heads of the departments may declare the vice president to be acting president. Again, a letter from the president to the leaders of Congress would restore the president to power. But if the vice president and a majority of the cabinet were to disagree with the president's claim of restored capacity, Congress would have to decide who was right. In the meantime, to prevent the president from simply firing the cabinet, Congress could substitute another body for it. Unless two-thirds of both the House and Senate sided with the vice president and the cabinet, the president's claim would prevail.

George H. W. Bush, who served with President Ronald Reagan, was the first vice president to become acting president under the Twenty-fifth Amendment. Criticism of Reagan and his aides for not transferring the powers and duties of the presidency to the vice president when Reagan was shot in 1981 prompted the president, albeit grudgingly, to send the constitutionally required letter to congressional leaders before undergoing cancer surgery in 1985. Bush spent his eight hours as acting president at home, playing tennis and chatting with friends. President George W. Bush activated the amendment's disability provision more willingly in 2002, during the two hours he was sedated for a colonoscopy. Vice President Richard Cheney worked in the White House and led the president's regularly scheduled national security meetings.

NOTES

1. Joel K. Goldstein, *The Modern American Vice Presidency*, 2d ed. (Princeton: Princeton University Press, 1982), 207–208.

2. See, for example, Ruth C. Silva, *Presidential Succession* (New York: Greenwood Press, 1968); Edward S. Corwin, *The President: Office and Powers*, 5th rev. ed. (New York: New York University Press, 1984), chap. 2; and John D. Feerick, *From Failing Hands: The Story of Presidential Succession* (New York: Fordham University Press, 1965), chap. 1.

3. Leonard Dinnerstein, "The Accession of John Tyler to the Presidency," *Virginia Magazine of History and Biography* 70, no. 4 (October 1962): 447–458; and Stephen W. Stathis, "John Tyler's Presidential Succession: A Reappraisal," *Prologue* 8, no. 4 (winter 1976): 223–236.

4. Amendments to the Constitution only clouded the issue. The Twelfth Amendment (1804) seemed to suggest, albeit offhandedly and not by clear congressional intent, that the vice president was to be acting president. In providing for the failure of both the electoral college and the House of Representatives to elect a president by the scheduled start of the term, the amendment stated that "the Vice President shall act as President, as in the case of the death or other constitutional disability of the President." The provision was replaced in 1933 by the Twentieth Amendment, which stated more blandly that if a president had not been elected by inauguration day, "the Vice President shall act as President until a President shall have qualified." The Twenty-second Amendment (1951) left the matter explicitly unresolved, stating that "no person who has held the office of President, or acted as President, for more than two years of a term to which some other person was elected President shall be elected to the office of the President more than once."

5. Nor had the 1792 act provided for the possibility that there might not be a constitutionally qualified Senate president or House

Speaker should the need arise. Yet congressional leaders, unlike presidents, need not be natural born citizens or thirty-five years old. Henry Clay, for example, was elected Speaker at age thirty-four in 1811.

6. Arthur M. Schlesinger Jr., *The Cycles of American History* (Boston: Houghton Mifflin, 1986), 351.

7. Not until January 6 does Congress count the electoral votes and declare who is elected, after an opportunity is provided to consider objections to any of the votes. Walter Berns, ed., *After the People Vote: A Guide to the Electoral College* (Washington, D.C.: American Enterprise Institute, 1992), 17–19.

8. No presidential nominee has ever failed either to live until or to qualify for election. In 1912 Vice President James S. Sherman, the Republican nominee for reelection as vice president, died on October 30. The Republican National Committee replaced him with Nicholas Murray Butler, the president of Columbia University. In 1972 the Democratic vice-presidential nominee, Thomas F. Eagleton, withdrew from the ticket when it was revealed shortly after the convention that he had undergone treatments for mental illness. The Democratic National Committee, which was responsible for filling vacancies on the ticket, approved presidential nominee George McGovern's nomination of former Peace Corps director Sargent Shriver for vice president.

9. John D. Feerick, *The Twenty-fifth Amendment: Its Complete History and Earliest Applications* (New York: Fordham University Press, 1992), 59.

10. Quotations from the debate about the proposed Twenty-fifth Amendment and from the Ford and Rockefeller confirmations are drawn from ibid.

11. James Cannon, *Time and Chance: Gerald Ford's Appointment with History* (New York: HarperCollins, 1994), 220.

12. Goldstein, *Modern American Vice Presidency,* 242–243.

13. This account of the Rockefeller confirmation is drawn from Michael Nelson, "Nelson A. Rockefeller and the American Vice Presidency," in *Gerald R. Ford and the Politics of Post-Watergate America,* vol. I, ed. Bernard J. Firestone and Alexej Ugrinsky (Westport, Conn.: Greenwood Press, 1993), 143–147.

14. Ibid., 245.

15. The other temporarily disabled presidents, according to John Feerick, *Twenty-fifth Amendment,* chap. 1, were James Madison, William Henry Harrison, Chester Arthur, Grover Cleveland, William McKinley, Warren Harding, Franklin Roosevelt, Dwight Eisenhower, and John Kennedy.

SELECTED BIBLIOGRAPHY

Berns, Walter, ed. *After the People Vote: A Guide to the Electoral College.* Washington, D.C.: American Enterprise Institute, 1992.

Cannon, James. *Time and Chance: Gerald Ford's Appointment with History.* New York: HarperCollins, 1994.

Corwin, Edward S. *The President: Office and Powers, 1787–1984.* 5th rev. ed. New York: New York University Press, 1984.

Feerick, John D. *From Failing Hands: The Story of Presidential Succession.* New York: Fordham University Press, 1965.

———. *The Twenty-fifth Amendment: Its Complete History and Earliest Applications.* New York: Fordham University Press, 1992.

Goldstein, Joel K. *The Modern Vice Presidency.* 2d ed. Princeton: Princeton University Press, 1982.

Nelson, Michael. "Nelson A. Rockefeller and the American Vice Presidency." In *Gerald R. Ford and the Politics of Post-Watergate America,* edited by Bernard J. Firestone and Alexej Ugrinsky. Vol. I. Westport, Conn.: Greenwood Press, 1993.

Silva, Ruth C. *Presidential Succession.* New York: Greenwood Press, 1968.

chapter 8

Removal of the President and the Vice President

by Margaret Jane Wyszomirski and Michael Nelson

The four-year presidential term specified in the Constitution may be cut short by one of three events: death from either natural causes or assassination, impeachment and removal, or resignation. As of 2007, nine of the thirty-eight men who have been elected president have failed to serve out the term of office for which they were chosen.

During the first fifty-two years of the Republic, no deaths, impeachments, or resignations occurred—the longest stretch in American history in which none of these eventualities arose. Not until the death of President William Henry Harrison in 1841 were the succession provisions of the Constitution activated. Since that time, three other presidents have died, like Harrison, of natural causes: Zachary Taylor in 1850, Warren G. Harding in 1923, and Franklin D. Roosevelt in 1945. Four other presidents have been assassinated: Abraham Lincoln in 1865, James A. Garfield in 1881, William McKinley in 1901, and John F. Kennedy in 1963. Three presidents—Andrew Johnson in 1868, Richard M. Nixon in 1974, and Bill Clinton in 1999—faced the serious possibility of being removed from office through impeachment. Johnson narrowly survived the impeachment process and completed his term. So did Clinton, but with considerably less difficulty. Nixon short-circuited the process by becoming the first president in history to resign.

ISSUES IN PRESIDENTIAL SUCCESSION

Article II, Section 1, of the Constitution requires that the president and vice president "be elected" and provides for succession as follows:

> In Case of the Removal of the President from Office, or of his Death, Resignation, or Inability to discharge the Powers and Duties of the said Office, the Same shall devolve on the Vice President, and the Congress may by Law provide for the Case of Removal, Death, Resignation or Inability, both of the President and Vice President, declaring what Officer shall then act as President, and such Officer shall act accordingly, until the Disability be removed, or a President shall be elected.

This section gave rise to three issues during the century after ratification. The first concerned the status of the vice president who succeeded upon a disability or vacancy in the presidency. The Framers seem to have intended "a Vice President or an officer designated by Congress merely to *act* as president" until a special election could be held, not to become president until the end of the departed president's term.[1] This intention was lost when Vice President John Tyler succeeded Harrison in 1841. Tyler became president instead of remaining vice president while serving temporarily as acting president, and he stayed in office for the last three years and eleven months of Harrison's term. When Zachary Taylor died in office less than ten years later, no one questioned Vice President Millard Fillmore's decision to follow Tyler's precedent. In 1967 the Twenty-fifth Amendment settled any remaining doubts about the succession: "In case of the removal of the President from office or of his death or resignation, the Vice President shall become President."

The second issue was the congressional practice of providing a line of succession for occasions when unexpected vacancies occurred in both the presidency and the vice presidency. Congress has passed succession acts three times. Each act set a different order of succession from its predecessor and had a different provision concerning special elections. The Succession Act of 1792 established a two-person line after the vice president: first, the president pro tempore of the Senate, then the Speaker of the House of Representatives. Either of these officials would have become acting president until a special election could be held to choose a new president. In 1886 Congress passed a law that moved the line of succession from Congress to the cabinet, starting with the secretary of state and running down through the list of secretaries in the order in which their departments were created. The act also gave Congress discretion to decide in each case whether and when a special election should be called. Finally in 1947, at the behest of Harry S. Truman (himself a successor president), Congress again changed the order of succession to begin with the Speaker of the House, followed by the president pro tempore of the Senate and the cabinet secretaries in their departments' order of creation.[2] *(See box, Line of Succession, p. 447, in Chapter 7.)* In addition, the 1947 act barred the use of special elections. The successor president would serve "until the expiration of the then current presidential term."

The third issue—hinted at but not dealt with explicitly in the original Constitution—was presidential disability. Although the Constitution refers to situations of "Inability," it says nothing about what the word means or what process should be used to determine whether a president is disabled. Throughout American history, several presidents have been disabled for parts of their terms. But not until the Twenty-fifth Amendment was any formal attempt made to provide for such situations. Although the amendment offers no definition of disability, Sections 3 and 4 empower the president, the vice president and the cabinet, or Congress (depending on the circumstances) to determine whether a president is disabled. The amendment also states that until the disability is ended, the vice president will serve as acting president. *(See "Twenty-fifth Amendment," p. 56, in Chapter 1.)*

During the history of the presidency, three conditions have been vital to workable and legitimate presidential succession arrangements. First, the succession must be certain. No question should exist about who will succeed to the presidency if the office becomes vacant or its incumbent is disabled.

Second, the succession must be immediate. A time lag may have been acceptable in earlier years when the pace and magnitude of national affairs were less. But in the age of nuclear weapons and terrorism, it is now imperative that there be a president at all times to respond immediately to sudden major crises.

Third, the provisions for presidential succession must promote political continuity. Although each successor president has pledged to maintain the policies of his predecessor, the transition has not always worked out that way in practice. To be sure, the vice president usually has been of the same political party as the president. But often he was placed on the ticket to balance the president's ideological wing of the party with someone from a different wing, with different programmatic preferences. The more profound these differences, the more difficulties the successors have faced in maintaining their political support and effectively exercising presidential leadership. Similar problems might afflict congressional leaders of the departed president's party or, especially, of the opposite party.

In recent years, the threats to political continuity from the succession process have lessened. Because of changes in the vice-presidential nominating process, presidents and vice presidents are more likely to agree on programs and policies than in the past. In addition, Section 2 of the Twenty-fifth Amendment reduces the likelihood that the line of succession will reach to congressional leaders by pro-viding that, when a vacancy occurs in the vice presidency, the president shall appoint a new vice president, subject to confirmation by a majority of both houses of Congress. Until the amendment was enacted, vice-presidential vacancies remained unfilled until the next election.

The 1787 Constitutional Convention showed little concern for the vice presidency in general and for vice-presidential removal in particular. No provision was made for the death, resignation, or disability of the vice president, and no discussion was devoted to these contingencies by the delegates. The reason may have been that the convention thought it had provided in other ways for the fulfilling of the only two constitutional responsibilities of the vice presidency—as Senate president and presidential successor—in the event that there was no vice president. Article I stipulates that the Senate shall elect a president pro tempore to preside "in the absence of the Vice President." Article II calls on Congress to "by Law provide for the Case of Removal, Death, Resignation, or Inability, both of the President and Vice President, declaring what Officer shall then act as President."

The convention did vote on September 8, 1787, to include the vice president and "other civil officers of the United States" in the roster of officials who may be impeached and removed from office for "Treason, Bribery, or other high Crimes and Misdemeanors" by a majority vote of the House of Representatives and a two-thirds vote of the Senate. The decision, which came after no discussion, was unanimous.

Historically, seven vice presidents have died in office, two have resigned, and nine have become president by succession. These eighteen vice-presidential vacancies have left the nation without a vice president for a little more than one-sixth of its history.

In 2001 serious questions were raised about the health of Vice President Richard B. Cheney, who had a history of heart attacks and experienced a series of heart ailments after taking office. An additional set of Cheney-related concerns arose after the September 11, 2001, terrorist attacks on New York and Washington, D.C. The safety of both the president and the vice president from future terrorist attacks was in doubt, leading President George W. Bush to order Cheney to spend his days working in a variety of undisclosed locations.

DEATH FROM NATURAL CAUSES

Four presidents have died in office from natural causes: two in the nineteenth century (William Henry Harrison in 1841 and Zachary Taylor in 1850) and two in the twentieth century (Warren G. Harding in 1923 and Franklin D. Roosevelt in 1945). The natural death of a president, if preceded by a period of illness, is less traumatic than an assassination, because both the people and the government usually have been able to prepare themselves for a change of leadership.

Also, a natural death is less likely than an assassination to provoke fears of national peril. In the wake of President John F. Kennedy's assassination in 1963, in the midst of the cold war, for example, many Americans feared for the safety of the Republic. Nonetheless, the death of a president is always an occasion of profound public loss.

This sense of loss seems particularly acute in two circumstances. One is when a president dies soon after taking office—for example, Harrison's death one month after his inauguration—leaving a sense of unfulfilled promise and unrealized expectations. The other circumstance is when a long-serving and popular president dies in office, thereby closing an era of familiar and effective leadership. For example, the death of Franklin Roosevelt, who had served more than twelve years as president, left behind an entire generation that had never known any other leader.

William Henry Harrison

William Henry Harrison, a frontier general and war hero who became famous in the 1811 Battle of Tippecanoe and later fought as commander in chief of the Army of the Northwest in the War of 1812, was one of the first presidential candidates to be selected by a national party convention. The 1840 Whig convention that nominated Harrison of Ohio as its presidential standard-bearer also chose John Tyler of Virginia as his running mate. Tyler was a former Democrat who opposed several important Whig programs, including protective tariffs, internal improvements, and a national bank. He was nominated to balance the northern Harrison with a southerner.[3] The convention adopted no party platform, and the campaign generally avoided serious discussion of public issues. Thus the policy differences between Harrison and Tyler remained muted.

The Whig ticket of "Tippecanoe and Tyler too" easily defeated its Democratic opponents, and, at the age of sixty-eight, Harrison became the oldest president ever to be inaugurated. (He held that record until 1981, when the sixty-nine-year-old Ronald Reagan was inaugurated.) Although Harrison came to office without a clearly defined program, he was, as his biographer James A. Green has noted, "a President around whom more high hopes were centered, from whom more

Within a mere month of his inauguration, William Henry Harrison became the first president to die in office. In memoriam, many Americans wore armbands like this one.

was expected and who enjoyed a greater degree of the love and affection of the people than any of his fellows since the days of Washington."[4]

Harrison launched his administration with great promise. On March 4, 1841, after being sworn in as president on the east portico of the Capitol by U.S. Supreme Court chief justice Roger B. Taney, the hatless and coatless Harrison proceeded to speak in cold and wet weather for the better part of two hours, easily the longest inaugural address that any president has ever given. The text of the address was printed immediately by Horace Greeley's *Daily National Intelligencer* and was distributed as far away as New York City in record time, less than ten hours.[5]

Harrison assembled a distinguished cabinet composed of leaders with national reputations, including Daniel Webster as secretary of state, Thomas Ewing as secretary of the Treasury, and John J. Crittenden as attorney general. With the core of his administration in place, the president summoned Congress into a special session, to begin on May 31, 1841, for the purpose of considering the nation's revenue and finance policies.[6]

Because Harrison's Whig administration had displaced the twelve-year Democratic rule of Andrew Jackson and Martin Van Buren, the president was besieged with Whig office seekers and pressed by the attendant problems of staffing a new government and rewarding partisan supporters. During his first week in office Harrison found himself nearly overwhelmed by daily cabinet meetings, an incessant stream of job-seeking visitors, and numerous social events.

Weakened by his inauguration and fatigued by his schedule, Harrison was caught in a rainstorm during his morning walk on March 27. In any event, he subsequently took to his bed. Initially, the president was diagnosed as having pneumonia, but consulting physicians later found his condition to be complicated by congestion of the liver and neuralgia, and they changed their diagnosis to bilious pleurisy. In all the confusion, Harrison was subjected to a host of different, and at times contradictory, remedies, only to have his condition worsen.[7] On April 4, 1841, a week after taking sick and a month after his inauguration, William Henry Harrison became the first American president to die in office.

As soon as Harrison died, Secretary of State Webster dispatched his son Fletcher, who was the chief clerk in the State Department, to notify Vice President Tyler at his home in Williamsburg, Virginia. Tyler immediately set out for Washington, arriving on April 6. Meeting informally with members of the cabinet, Tyler asked them all to continue to serve and indicated that he would remain faithful to Harrison's policies. Tyler then took the presidential oath of office. Some officials, including Tyler himself, believed that the vice president did not need to take the oath because his vice-presidential oath already required him to discharge his duties as successor to the president. But according to Chief Judge William Cranch of the Circuit Court of the District of Columbia, who administered the presidential oath, Tyler nonetheless took it "for greater caution" and to allay any doubts that he had acted appropriately.[8] Although the Constitution did not make his status clear, Tyler also declared that he regarded himself as president until Harrison's term expired on March 4, 1845, not as acting president until a special election could be called. He then moved into the White House.

In claiming to be president, Tyler established what came to be called the "Tyler Precedent," in which the vice president succeeds fully to the office of the president when a vacancy occurs in the presidency. At the time, some opposition was expressed to this interpretation, including that of former president John Quincy Adams, who was then a Whig member of the House of Representatives from Massachusetts. Adams maintained that Tyler had only succeeded, temporarily, to the powers and duties of the presidency, not to the office itself. Webster countered that the office was inseparable from its powers and duties. Similarly, the leading Whig newspaper of the day, the *Daily National Intelligencer*, argued: "By his original election as Vice President, he was provisionally elected President; that is, elected to the office of President upon the happening of any one of the conditions provided in the Constitution." [9]

Although Adams chose not to make an issue of Tyler's constitutional status, others in Congress did. On May 31, 1841, Rep. Henry Wise of Virginia moved that a committee be formed "to wait on the President of the United States." John McKeon of New York proposed an amendment to strike "President of the United States" from the motion and substitute "Vice President, now exercising the office of President." The House rejected McKeon's amendment, passed Wise's motion, and sent it to the Senate, where a more extensive debate over Tyler's status ensued.

Sen. William Allen of Ohio opened the debate by pointing out that, because the language of the Constitution was the same for disability as for death, Tyler's claim that he was president meant that a president who stepped aside because of disability would not be allowed to resume the office even if he recovered. "What would become of the office?" Allen asked. "Was it to vibrate between the two claimants?"

Sen. Robert J. Walker of Mississippi made a similar argument for the opposing position. If Tyler were judged merely to be the vice president acting as president, Walker noted, he could come to the Senate in the vice president's constitutional capacity as president of the Senate and cast tie-breaking votes. In the end, the Senate joined the House in affirming Tyler's status as president for the remainder of Harrison's four-year-term.

The uncertainty surrounding presidential succession and the initial conflict that accompanied Tyler's bold claim to the office drew attention away from Harrison's death. Nonetheless, the custom of having the late president's body lie in state in the White House was begun with Harrison. He had been the first president-elect to arrive for his inauguration in Washington by train; his body now became the first to depart the city by train. He was buried in his adopted home town of North Bend, Ohio.

Although the Tyler Precedent established the status of the "accidental president," two other problems would trouble future successor presidents. One was the line of succession beyond the vice president. The issue arose in February 1844 when a naval gun on board the first propeller-driven warship, the U.S.S. *Princeton,* exploded during a demonstration while the ship was on a presidential inspection cruise. The explosion killed the secretaries of state and navy, as well as five other people on board. President Tyler escaped harm, but only because he happened to be below deck. Since his succession to the presidency, Tyler had served without a vice president. Thus, according to the Succession Act of 1792, if Tyler had been killed in the explosion, the powers and duties of the presidency would have passed, at least temporarily, to a legislative officer, Senate President Pro Tempore Willie P. Mangum of North Carolina.[10] Mangum was a Whig, but the prospect that a successor president from Congress would be of a different party from the departed president was a real one.

The second problem—and one of more immediate political significance—was the continuity of personnel and policy between an elected president and his successor. Tyler originally had pledged to maintain Harrison's policies, but he also let the cabinet know that "I can never consent to being dictated to as to what I shall or shall not do. I, as president, will be responsible for my administration." In time, Tyler began to assert his own views, and his administration became known for its opposition to various Whig programs. Tyler's September 1841 veto of a bill to establish a national bank prompted the wholesale resignation of his cabinet, except for Webster. Two days later, President Tyler was "officially" expelled from the Whig Party by a caucus of congressional Whigs. Although he remained politically ambitious to the end of his life (at age seventy he actively sought the 1860 Democratic presidential nomination and in 1861 was elected to the Confederate congress), Tyler was not considered seriously by either the Whig or the Democratic national convention in 1844.

Despite Tyler's problems with the Whig Party, his administration could claim a number of achievements, including reorganization of the navy, establishment of a weather bureau, negotiation of a trade treaty with China, termination of the Seminole War, and annexation of Texas.[11] But certainly his most lasting legacy was the Tyler Precedent.

Zachary Taylor

The power of the Tyler Precedent soon was demonstrated. Less than a decade after President William Henry Harrison died in office, President Zachary Taylor died a little more than sixteen months into his term. Upon his death Vice President Millard Fillmore succeeded to the presidency. No one questioned Fillmore's status or suggested that he was merely acting temporarily as president.

Zachary Taylor was the first member of the regular army to become president. During his more than forty years of army service, he advanced rapidly, winning acclaim first as an Indian fighter and then as the hero of the Mexican American War. "Old Rough and Ready" (as some of his troops called him) was a man of meager formal schooling. He knew little of law and government, and he seems to have been uninterested in politics until he was nominated for president in 1848. (Reportedly, Taylor had never voted in an election.) As with Harrison, the Whig Party nominated Taylor knowing little about where he stood on the issues; it was more interested in trading on his popularity as a war hero. Millard Fillmore of New York was the party's compromise choice as Taylor's running mate.[12]

After defeating Lewis Cass, the Democratic presidential candidate, in the 1848 election, Taylor delayed his arrival in Washington to begin assembling his administration. His resignation from the army did not become effective until February 28, 1849, less than a week before the inauguration. Without political experience, Taylor came to the presidency possessed of a "naive assumption that good intentions and a genuine dedication to the common good would triumph." [13]

Taylor's election did little to unite or strengthen the Whig Party, which was held together mostly by its opposition to the Jacksonian Democrats. Whig leaders Daniel Webster and Henry Clay declined invitations to join Taylor's cabinet, as did the architect of Taylor's successful presidential campaign, John Crittenden. Taylor was thus able to assemble only a relatively weak cabinet of secondary party leaders. By the time Taylor died, six of his seven cabinet members were under heavy attack for corruption, incompetence, and patronage abuses. Shortly before his death Taylor had decided to replace his entire cabinet. Thus his successor, Millard Fillmore, did not inherit a strong administration on which he could rely during his early months in office.[14]

In 1850, even before Taylor's death, Congress and the country were embroiled in a fierce debate about California's admission to the Union, which would have tipped the even balance in the Senate between slave and free states in favor of the latter. The underlying, and thornier, questions concerned the conditions for admitting new states from the southwest territories, the retention of slavery in the South, and the problem of fugitive slaves. In the midst of this intense controversy, President Taylor suddenly took ill.

The circumstances of Taylor's illness were unusual, so much so that rumors that he had been poisoned endured for more than a century. (The rumors were laid to rest only after Taylor's body was exhumed from its Louisville, Kentucky, grave and autopsied in 1991.) While attending a long, hot Fourth of July celebration in Washington the president consumed large quantities of ice water, chilled milk, and fresh cherries—all items that Washingtonians had been warned away from for fear of an Asiatic cholera epidemic that was sweeping the city. During the next two days Taylor began to develop various ailments, which were diagnosed by army surgeon Alexander Witherspoon as cholera morbus, a catchall nineteenth-century term for several intestinal maladies (but not the Asiatic cholera). At first, Taylor seemed to respond to treatment, but then he began to weaken, to develop intermittent fevers, and eventually to suffer intense dysentery and vomiting. On July 8 the president predicted (overoptimistically, it turned out) that "in two days I shall be a dead man." Late in the evening of July 9 he bade farewell to his wife, Margaret Smith Taylor, beseeching her not to grieve and saying: "I have always done my duty. I am ready to die. My only regret is for the friends I leave behind me." Soon afterward, the president lost consciousness and died. He was sixty-five.

Vice President Fillmore was notified immediately, as was the cabinet, which formally announced the president's death. At noon the next day, July 10, 1850, Fillmore took the oath of office in the House of Representatives chamber and became the thirteenth president of the United States. The oath was administered by William Cranch, the same federal judge who had sworn in John Tyler as the first successor president in 1841. Congress appointed a joint committee to make funeral arrangements for the late president and members delivered a round of eulogies. On Friday, July 12, a public viewing of Taylor's body was held in the East Room of the White House, and a funeral was scheduled for the next day. An estimated ten thousand people congregated along the funeral route.

It had often been said by contemporaries that Vice President Fillmore looked more "presidential" than President Taylor.[15] Despite appearances, however, the vice president had played only a minor role in the Taylor administration. Although Fillmore was a national political figure at the time of his nomination, he lacked a strong political base in his home state of New York because he opposed the dominant faction of the New York Whig Party, which was headed by Sen. William H. Seward.[16] Prior to the 1849 inauguration, Fillmore had called on the president-elect to discuss possible cabinet appointments, only to be told that Taylor had already made those decisions after consulting Crittenden. As Seward steadily won Taylor's confidence and friendship during the course of the administration, Taylor froze out Fillmore even from patronage in New York.[17]

Thus Fillmore succeeded to the presidency after having only a distant relationship with the president in whose administration he had served. When the discredited cabinet members he inherited tendered what they thought were pro forma resignations, the new president accepted them all, but with a request that they stay on for a month to help him make a smooth transition. Miffed, the cabinet agreed to remain only one week, thus plunging the new president into feverish activity to establish a new administration.[18]

Fillmore also inherited the smoldering tension between North and South that had been raging in Congress since the start of the year. President Taylor had indicated that he would veto any omnibus compromise bill on California statehood and other slavery-related issues, thereby limiting the possibilities for successfully defusing the crisis. In contrast, Fillmore, an experienced legislator from his days in the House of Representatives, took a more flexible stance, seeking regional harmony as his primary goal. In September 1850, his tactical political maneuvering, complemented by the herculean efforts of Whig senators Henry Clay of Kentucky and Daniel Webster of Massachusetts and Democratic senator Stephen A. Douglas of Illinois, helped to bring about congressional enactment of the Compromise of 1850.[19] Although the compromise averted civil war for a decade, it aroused ire against Fillmore in both the North and South. As angry as Northerners were about, for example, the strengthened fugitive slave law, Southerners were equally enraged about the abolition of the slave trade in the District of Columbia.

Increasingly, Fillmore found himself in a lame-duck position as president, confronting divisive national issues without a strong base in his own party. From the very start of his presidency Fillmore had been ambivalent about seeking the Whig nomination for a full presidential term. When he finally decided to let his name go forward, it was too late. In June 1852, the national party convention nominated Winfield Scott, like Taylor a popular general of Mexican War fame. Four years later Fillmore ran for president as the candidate of the American, or Know-Nothing, Party. Although he finished a strong third in the popular vote with 21.5 percent, he carried only one state (Maryland) with eight electoral votes.

Thus, like Tyler, Fillmore inherited the office, powers, and responsibilities of his predecessor, but not his popularity or political support. Consequently, both Tyler and Fillmore experienced an erosion of their leadership, culminating in their rejection for renomination in the next election.

Warren G. Harding

Warren G. Harding's editorials in the *Marion Star* in Marion County, Ohio, provided the springboard for his entry into politics. He was elected to the state senate, ran unsuccessfully for lieutenant governor, and eventually won a seat in the Senate. His 1914 Senate campaign demonstrated that he was a strong vote-getter in a changing electoral system. In the past, senators had been chosen by state legislatures. Now, as a result of the Seventeenth Amendment (1913), senators were elected officials. Harding secured the Republican Senate nomination in the first statewide primary in Ohio history. He then won by 100,000 votes in the first popular election of senators.[20]

In Washington, Harding proved to be an affable Senate insider but an unimpressive legislator. Nevertheless, he rose in the ranks of the Republican Party, which selected him to deliver the keynote address at its 1916 national convention. As a member of the powerful Senate Foreign Relations Committee, Harding was immersed in the controversy over the League of Nations treaty. His decision to stand with the antileague reservationists provided a useful platform from which to launch his presidential bid in 1920. Conducting a masterful and gentlemanly campaign, Harding seemed to personify the "normalcy" that he promised to restore to the country. As the historian Robert K. Murray has noted, to the voters "Harding represented solid ground, stability, a return to national tranquility." [21] They responded overwhelmingly, electing Harding in a landslide that at the time constituted the largest popular vote majority in history. In addition, the Republicans expanded their control of the House of Representatives to 303–131 and acquired a twenty-two-seat majority in the Senate.[22]

At first, Harding enjoyed the presidency, especially its public roles, but later he began to feel overwhelmed by the scope of his responsibilities. Labor strikes, recurring controversies about patronage, and the difficulties of enforcing Prohibition combined to make Harding feel inadequate and unhappy as president. By the fall of 1922 he had begun to lapse into a general mental depression that was only compounded by the illness of his wife, Florence Kling De Wolfe Harding, whose kidney ailment brought her close to death for six weeks in September and October. Then in 1923, as the scandal that would become known as Teapot Dome began to unfold, Harding's worry and anxiety mounted and his own health suffered. An attack of influenza in January triggered a rapid deterioration of his condition. Harding's blood pressure rose precipitously, and he was generally listless and tired.

In the midst of these travails, the president launched a much-publicized cross-country trip to Alaska in mid-June.

Intended in part to resolve administration infighting over the management of the Alaska territory and in part to shore up Harding's popular support, the trip included arduous travel and a heavy speaking schedule. After reaching Tacoma, Washington (with speaking stops along the way), by rail, the president was to sail to Alaska, remain there for a time, and then return to Washington, D.C., via the Panama Canal and Puerto Rico—in all, a two-month-long trip. As Harding progressed along the route, he delivered speeches, often in searing heat, that outlined his political and economic beliefs and elaborated on the themes of his December 1922 State of the Union message.[23]

The first part of Harding's journey went well, but by late July the president was tiring noticeably and experiencing nausea, abdominal pains, and a rapid heartbeat. By July 29 it was clear that Harding was suffering from cardiac problems and bronchopneumonia. On August 1 he appeared to rally, and it was announced that the crisis had passed and the presidential party would soon return to Washington, D.C. On the night of August 2, however, as Mrs. Harding was reading to her husband in his San Francisco hotel room bed, he twisted convulsively. She immediately ran from the room to call for the doctors. They administered stimulants to the president's heart, but to no avail—Harding was dead. The official cause of death was "apoplexy," but the actual cause remains uncertain. It may have been a cerebral hemorrhage caused by a burst sclerotic blood vessel in the brain or a ruptured wall of the heart—in either case, a cause related to the president's high blood pressure.

A cross-country funeral procession followed the president's death, and throughout the nation people turned out to mourn his passing. The crowds were immense. In Chicago alone an estimated million and a half people lined the rails as the funeral train passed. Pennies were placed on the tracks to be flattened by the train and retrieved as historic souvenirs. Upon its arrival in Washington on August 7, the president's casket was taken to the East Room of the White House, where Mrs. Harding maintained a solitary vigil. The next morning the coffin was carried to the Capitol and placed in the rotunda, where ten truckloads of flowers banked the walls. After a brief service and a viewing by more than thirty-five thousand mourners, the casket was borne to Union Station for the final train trip to Marion, Ohio, for burial.

Between August 4 and President Harding's burial on August 10 the nation was in an official period of mourning. The world press lamented the loss of "a man of peace," and many observers remarked that Harding's devotion to his job had made him a martyr for the presidency.[24] Secretary of Commerce Herbert C. Hoover captured the public sentiment by saying: "When he came into responsibility as President he faced unprecedented problems of domestic rehabilitation. It was a time when war-stirred emotions had created bitter prejudices and conflict in thought. Kindly and genial, but inflexible in his devotion to duty, he was strong in his determination to restore confidence and secure progress." [25]

When Harding died, the mantle of office fell on Vice President Calvin Coolidge. Coolidge's father, a notary public, administered the oath of office to his son, who was vacationing at the family home in Plymouth, Vermont. As governor of Massachusetts, Coolidge had won national recognition during the 1919 Boston police strike when he declared, "There is no right to strike against the public safety by anybody, anywhere, any time." [26]

President Harding had seldom relied on Vice President Coolidge for advice. The vice president did not participate in either political or administrative decisions, although, at the president's invitation, he did sit with the cabinet at its Tuesday and Friday meetings as an ex officio member, the first vice president to do so regularly.[27] Instead, Coolidge was assigned many social responsibilities, becoming the "official diner-out of the administration." [28] He also spent considerable time at the Capitol, where he enjoyed performing his constitutional duty of presiding over the Senate.

Part of Coolidge's problem as vice president was that Harding did not find him congenial. Taciturn and somewhat somber and aloof, Coolidge was temperamentally different from the gregarious and affable Harding. Yet these characteristics stood Coolidge in good stead during his presidency, because they set him apart from the poker-playing, carousing, and scandalous image that tarnished the reputation of the Harding administration when the Teapot Dome scandal was uncovered a few months after Harding's death. *(See "Teapot Dome and Other Scandals," p. 131, in Chapter 2.)*

In many ways, the change from Harding to Coolidge was more of style and probity than of substance. Coolidge retained Harding's cabinet until public and congressional pressure forced out two members, Secretary of the Navy Edwin Denby and Attorney General Harry M. Daugherty, who were implicated in Teapot Dome. Not until Coolidge was elected to a full term as president in 1924 did he make significant changes in cabinet, ambassadorial, and regulatory personnel.

As for policies, Coolidge declared when he announced Harding's death that he would stay the course. Consequently, in foreign affairs Coolidge supported the collection of all war debts, U.S. participation in the World Court, and improved relations with Latin America. In domestic and economic affairs, he promised to continue seeking restrictions on immigration, economy in government, protective tariffs, and increased aid for farmers. Like Harding, Coolidge refused to recognize the new communist government in Russia or pay a soldier's bonus to World War I veterans.[29] In all, unlike earlier successor presidents who failed to honor their initial pledges of continuity, Coolidge remained remarkably faithful to the legacy of his predecessor for the balance of his term.

Also unlike most earlier successor presidents, Coolidge retained the support of his party and of the general public. He was fortunate that Harding had bequeathed him an economic and political philosophy that suited the public mood of the day.[30] From the moment in December 1923 when Coolidge formally announced that he would seek a full term, he had little serious opposition within the Republican Party. With the Democrats in disarray (they required 103 ballots to choose their presidential nominee) and the economy apparently in good shape, Coolidge had no difficulty winning the 1924 election. In 1927, convinced that to run again would be punished by the party and the voters as a violation of the two-term tradition, Coolidge announced that he would not seek another term.

Franklin D. Roosevelt

Franklin Roosevelt served as president longer than any other person. Although his death was sudden, rumors about his health had circulated for a long time. Some even said that he had suffered a series of small strokes beginning in 1938. But the president's health was not a serious concern until 1943, midway through World War II and his third term in office. By then, not only were his long years of service and the pace of the wartime presidency taking their toll on Roosevelt, but the need to consult personally with British prime minister Winston Churchill and Soviet leader Joseph Stalin demanded that the president undertake several difficult trips abroad to engage in extensive, exhausting negotiations. Late in 1943, after a wartime conference in Teheran, Roosevelt experienced a pronounced deterioration in health and vigor, and the strain of leadership began to show. During the next few months, he suffered an alarming loss of weight, appetite, and strength. His face became haggard and gaunt, the circles under his eyes darkened, he developed a persistent cough, and his concentration began to wander. Roosevelt's staff became so concerned that in March 1944 they prevailed on him to undergo a thorough physical examination at nearby Bethesda Naval Hospital. The results were not encouraging.

Dr. Howard Bruenn, a heart specialist, reported that Roosevelt was suffering from hypertension, a general deterioration of the cardiovascular system, and an enlarged heart. In short, the diagnosis was that Roosevelt, at age sixty-two, was a seriously ill man who might, at best, live for another year or two.[31] Bruenn prescribed a program of rest and restricted diet, along with codeine to control Roosevelt's cough and digitalis for his heart. Bruenn was brought into the White House to serve as the president's physician-in-residence. But he was not permitted to discuss the president's condition with anyone (including the president and his family) except Adm. Ross McIntire, the navy surgeon general and White House physician. Thus the state of the president's health was a closely guarded secret.

Although Roosevelt was nominated unanimously for a fourth term by the 1944 Democratic national convention, questions were asked persistently about his health. These questions were answered in medical reports that claimed to certify Roosevelt's physical vitality and in occasional campaign appearances by the president. In October, riding in an open limousine on a cold and rainy day, Roosevelt waved to massive and cheering New York City crowds during a four-hour motorcade. Exhilarated by the experience, the president seemed to recapture something of his old buoyancy and energy. It was a masterful performance that reassured the public and temporarily silenced doubts about his health.

In November 1944, Roosevelt won his fourth election as president by a wide electoral vote margin (432–99) but by the smallest percentage of the popular vote (53.4 percent) of any of his victories. The weeks after the election were intensely busy, leaving little time for rest. Political activities

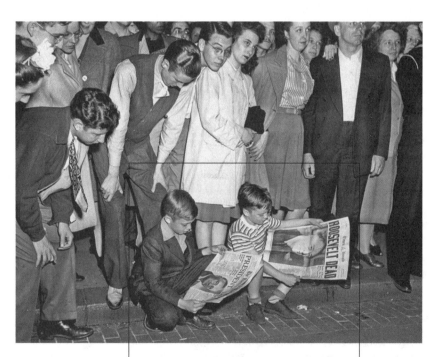

On hearing the news of President Franklin D. Roosevelt's death, crowds keep vigil on Pennsylvania Avenue in front of the White House, April 12, 1945.

at home, the war effort abroad, and planning for the forth-coming Yalta Conference, which was intended to secure Soviet entry into the war against Japan and to begin drawing the map of postwar Europe, preoccupied Roosevelt and left him exhausted. His 1945 inauguration was brief and somber. On a raw, overcast day the president, looking pained and haggard, delivered the shortest inaugural address of any elected president in history.[32] Two days later, on January 22, he began the arduous trip to Yalta to meet with Churchill and Stalin.

Roosevelt's spirits seemed refreshed when he returned from Yalta to the United States at the end of February, but his physical condition was strained. Symptomatic of the president's decline was his delivery of a report on the conference to a joint session of Congress on March 1, 1945. For the first time, Roosevelt spoke from his wheelchair, which had been brought into the well of the House of Representatives. His speech was halting and imprecise, renewing speculation about his health. Pale, tired, sometimes listless and depressed, the circles under his eyes deepening and darkening, his hands often trembling, Roosevelt complained to confidants of sleeplessness and a poor appetite. Finally, confident that victory in the war was well in hand, he was persuaded to leave Washington and go to Warm Springs, Georgia, for a long rest that would help him to regain strength before hosting the upcoming United Nations Conference on International Organization. Delegates from fifty nations would be meeting in San Francisco to draft the United Nations charter.

After arriving in Warm Springs on March 30, 1945, Roosevelt seemed to improve, regaining color, appetite, and good spirits. On the morning of April 12, the president awoke rested but with a slight headache. After a productive morning, and while sitting for a portrait, he suddenly complained, "I have a terrific headache," and lapsed into unconsciousness. A little after three-thirty in the afternoon Roosevelt was dead from a massive cerebral hemorrhage.

In Washington the president's wife, Eleanor Roosevelt, was notified, and she calmly began the process of telling the children of their father's death. She also asked that Vice President Harry Truman be called to the White House. Before being chosen as vice president at the 1944 Democratic convention, Truman had been a senator from Missouri, unknown to most of the public but well respected by his fellow senators. No evidence exists that Roosevelt chose Truman as his running mate with possible succession in mind, and certainly he did little to prepare the vice president to become president after the election. Of his eighty-two days as vice president, Truman later said, "I don't think I saw Roosevelt but twice."[33] He was at most dimly aware of the existence of the atomic bomb and the Allies' postwar plans.

Word that he was wanted at the White House reached Truman while he was enjoying a late afternoon drink at the Capitol with House Speaker Sam Rayburn. When the vice president arrived he was escorted to Mrs. Roosevelt's study. The new widow put her arm around Truman's shoulder and said, "Harry, the president is dead." For a few moments Truman stood stunned and speechless as he tried to comprehend what had happened and what it would mean for himself and the country. When he finally found words he asked Mrs. Roosevelt, "Is there anything I can do for you?" She replied, "Is there anything we can do for you? For you are the one in trouble now."[34]

By dinnertime, reports of President Roosevelt's death were on the wire services and the radio; the tragic news spread more quickly and widely than the news of any previous presidential death. The public seemed to feel a strong sense of personal loss, bereavement, and bewilderment. Roosevelt had dominated the nation's public life for so long that it was stunning to contemplate his passing. On hearing of his death many wept and prayed. Quietly that evening several hundred people gathered in Lafayette Square, across the street from the White House, to keep a hushed vigil.

By seven o'clock in the evening, Truman, members of the cabinet, Truman's wife, Bess, and daughter, Margaret, and Supreme Court chief justice Harlan Fiske Stone had assembled in the cabinet room of the White House. At 7:05 p.m. Truman was sworn in as the thirty-third president of the United States. Ten minutes later he convened his first cabinet meeting and made his first decision: The United Nations conference would go on as planned.[35] Truman asked all the cabinet members to remain at their posts and told them that he intended to continue the foreign and domestic policies of the Roosevelt administration. When the meeting adjourned, Secretary of War Henry L. Stimson remained to speak privately to the new president about a matter of great urgency. He then told Truman about the Manhattan Project, which had nearly completed the atomic bomb.[36]

On the brink of the nuclear age, with the nation still at war, and with the remaining three years and nine months of Roosevelt's term stretching before him, Truman faced the prospect of replacing a president who to many seemed irreplaceable. The historian Cabell Phillips has written that Truman's "tenure was one of the most torturous of any President in history . . . marked by intense and sometimes paralyzing political strife, by personal denigration such as no President since Andrew Johnson has had to endure."[37] The president's party lost control of Congress in the midterm elections of 1946, and his own popularity was so low in the months leading up to the 1948 presidential election that several Democratic leaders urged him to step aside. When Truman was nominated at the Democratic national convention, his party splintered. Dissident Democrats on the right (represented by South Carolina governor J. Strom Thurmond of the newly formed States' Rights, or Dixiecrat, Party) and the left (former vice president Henry A. Wallace of the Progressive Party) each fielded a third party candidate in the general election, draining the president of electoral support from normally Democratic voters.

Despite these trials, Truman won the 1948 election in one of the greatest political upsets in American history, vindicating his performance as Roosevelt's successor. In recent years, historians have come to value Truman's courage, determination, and common sense and to rank him as a "near great" president. *(See Chapter 4, Rating the Presidents.)*

PRESIDENTIAL ASSASSINATIONS

Half of the presidents who have died in office were felled by assassins' bullets: Abraham Lincoln in 1865, James A. Garfield in 1881, William McKinley in 1901, and John F. Kennedy in 1963. All except Kennedy were killed early in their terms (Lincoln and McKinley in their second term and Garfield in his first term), leaving their successors to serve out nearly full terms of office. Lincoln is the only president who is known to have been killed as part of a political conspiracy.

Although William Henry Harrison was the first president to die in office and Lincoln the first president to be assassinated, Andrew Jackson came close to being the first in both categories. On January 30, 1835, while Jackson was attending the funeral of South Carolina representative Warren Davis in the rotunda of the Capitol, a house painter named Richard Lawrence tried to shoot him. Aiming from a distance of only seven feet, Lawrence fired two pistols at the president. Both guns misfired, however, and the president was spared. Lawrence was captured and later was judged to be insane.[38]

Abraham Lincoln

The death of a president is always a shock to the body politic. Lincoln's death was probably the greatest shock of all, however, for three reasons: It was the third in a twenty-five-year series of presidential deaths (Harrison had died in 1841 and Zachary Taylor in 1850, both of natural causes); it came just when the nation was beginning to see an end to the terrible bloodshed of the Civil War; and, especially, it was the first instance of a presidential assassination. The unprecedented murder of a president was shocking to a people who had come to pride themselves on their country's record of peaceful and orderly transfers of executive power, which had been uninterrupted even by war since the first presidential election in 1789.

Throughout his first term Abraham Lincoln had been a controversial president. The demands of leadership during the nation's only civil war had led him to exercise expansive presidential powers, which in turn had prompted congressional and partisan criticism. Early in 1864 it seemed that Lincoln would have a hard time winning reelection to a second term. In August he told the cabinet that defeat was likely and instructed its members to prepare for a peaceful transfer of power to the Democratic nominee, former Union general George B. McClellan. Nonetheless, the Republicans, temporarily calling themselves the National Union Party in hopes of broadening their political appeal, renominated Lincoln and chose Tennessee senator Andrew Johnson, a southern Democrat but a Union loyalist, as his running mate. On the strength of some timely Union victories on the battlefield, Lincoln and Johnson won a resounding victory with 212 of 234 electoral votes.[39]

Lincoln's second term began auspiciously. Within a month of his March 4, 1865, inauguration, the capital of the Confederacy, Richmond, Virginia, fell to Union forces. A few days later, on April 9, Gen. Robert E. Lee surrendered to Gen. Ulysses S. Grant at Appomattox, Virginia. Curiously, victory came shortly after the president was said to have had an ominous dream. In it, Lincoln awakened to the sound of people weeping in the White House. He made his way to the East Room, only to find himself lying in a coffin on a catafalque, while mourners wailed, "The president is dead."[40] In the wake of Lee's surrender, however, Lincoln brushed aside the

John Wilkes Booth, a Confederate sympathizer, shot Abraham Lincoln on April 14, 1865, while the president was watching a play at Ford's Theatre. Lincoln died the following morning.

TABLE 8-1 **Assassinations of and Major Assaults on Presidents, Presidents-Elect, and Presidential Candidates**

Date	Victim	Length of administration at time of attack/ president-elect/candidate	Location	Type of weapon and result	Assailant, outcome, professed or alleged reason for assaults
Jan. 30, 1835	Andrew Jackson (D)	Six years	Washington, D.C.	Pistol, misfired	Richard Lawrence, declared insane. Said Jackson was preventing him from obtaining money.
April 14, 1865	Abraham Lincoln (R)	Four years, one month	Washington, D.C.	Pistol, fatal	John Wilkes Booth, killed by Union soldiers. Loyalty to the Confederacy, revenge for defeat, slavery issue.
July 2, 1881	James A. Garfield (R)	Four months	Washington, D.C.	Pistol, fatal	Charles J. Guiteau, convicted. Disgruntled office seeker, supporter of opposite faction of Republican Party.
Sept. 6, 1901	William McKinley (R)	Four years, six months	Buffalo, N.Y.	Pistol, fatal	Leon F. Czolgosz, convicted. Anarchist.
Oct. 14, 1912	Theodore Roosevelt (Progressive-Bull Moose)	Candidate	Milwaukee, Wis.	Pistol, wounded	John Schrank, declared insane. Had vision that McKinley wanted Schrank to avenge his death.
Feb. 15, 1933	Franklin D. Roosevelt (D)	President-elect, three weeks before first inauguration	Miami, Fla.	Pistol, bullets missed FDR, killed Chicago mayor Anton J. Cermak	Joseph Zangara, convicted of murdering Chicago mayor. Hated rulers and capitalists.
Nov. 1, 1950	Harry S. Truman (D)	Five years	Washington, D.C.	Automatic weapons, prevented from shooting at president	Oscar Collazo, convicted of murdering guard; Giselio Torresola, killed. Puerto Rican independence.
Nov. 22, 1963	John F. Kennedy (D)	Three years	Dallas, Texas	Rifle, fatal	Lee Harvey Oswald, murdered by Jack Ruby. Motive unknown.
June 4, 1968	Robert F. Kennedy (D)	Candidate	Los Angeles, Calif.	Pistol, fatal	Sirhan Sirhan, convicted. Opposed candidate's stand on Israeli-Arab conflict.
May 15, 1972	George C. Wallace (D)	Candidate	Laurel, Md.	Pistol, wounded	Arthur Bremer, convicted. Motive unknown.
Sept. 5, 1975	Gerald R. Ford (R)	One year	Sacramento, Calif.	Pistol, misfired	Lynette A. Fromme, convicted. Follower of Charles Manson "Family."
Sept. 22, 1975	Gerald R. Ford (R)	One year	San Francisco, Calif.	Pistol, missed target	Sara Jane Moore, convicted. To bring about "the upheaval of needed change," revolutionary ideology.
March 30, 1981	Ronald Reagan (R)	Ten weeks	Washington, D.C.	Pistol, wounded	John W. Hinckley Jr., arrested, indicted, found not guilty by reason of insanity, confined to a psychiatric hospital. To attract the attention of actress Jodie Foster.

SOURCES: Derived from Frederick M. Kaiser, *Presidential Protection: Assassinations, Assaults and Secret Service Procedures* (Washington, D.C.: Congressional Research Service, 1981). Data for the incidents through 1968 were drawn from James E. Kirkham, Sheldon G. Levy, and William J. Crotty, *Assassination and Political Violence: A Report to the National Commission on the Causes and Prevention of Violence* (Washington, D.C.: Government Printing Office, 1969), 8:22.

dream and decided to celebrate the end of the war by taking his wife, Mary Todd Lincoln, to see the comic play *Our American Friend* at Ford's Theatre in Washington. They went on Good Friday, April 14.

While watching the play from a box, President Lincoln was shot by John Wilkes Booth, an actor and a Confederate sympathizer. Booth knew the play well and timed his shot to coincide with a laugh line that would drown out the sound of him entering the president's box. He had been plotting for months to kidnap or kill the president. Once he learned that the president would be in the theater that evening, he quickly set in motion an assassination plan. The defeat of the South had led Booth to believe that "our cause being almost lost, something decisive and great must be done." [41] Not only Lincoln, but also Vice President Johnson and Secretary of State William Seward, would be assassinated. Booth's target was the president. His co-conspirator George Azerodt was to kill Johnson at his lodgings in the Kirkwood House, and Lewis Thornton Powell was to kill Seward as he lay at home in bed recovering from a recent carriage accident.

As a celebrated actor, Booth was well known at Ford's Theatre and had no trouble gaining access to either the building or the president's box. Lincoln's bodyguard had left his post to watch the play. Standing less than four feet behind the president, Booth fired. The single bullet struck Lincoln behind the left ear, drove through his skull and brain, and came to rest behind his right eye. A guest of the president, Major Henry R. Rathbone, tried to seize the assassin, but Booth dropped his pistol, drew a dagger, and slashed at the major. Booth then vaulted the railing of the box, shouting, "Sic semper tyrannis! [Ever thus to tyrants!]" He landed on the stage, breaking a bone in his leg, and ran out a rear exit, where he mounted his horse and escaped.

While Booth was carrying out his end of the plan, Powell went to Secretary of State Seward's house. Forcing his way in, Powell beat one of Seward's sons senseless. Then he stabbed at Seward's face and neck several times, cutting the secretary's right cheek so severely that his tongue could be seen through the gaping and bloody hole in his face. [42] A second son, a nurse, and a State Department messenger also were wounded before the would-be assassin escaped. Vice President Johnson was more fortunate. He was spared when Azerodt changed his mind and fled to Maryland. Azerodt, Powell, and two other conspirators, David Herold and Mary Surratt, later were tried, found guilty, and executed by hanging. Booth was shot to death while being apprehended in Virginia.

Immediately after Lincoln's shooting, three doctors who happened to be in the theater ran to the president's side to render such aid as they could. They managed, through artificial respiration, to restore the president's breathing, then directed that he be taken to the nearest bed. Unconscious, Lincoln was carried across the street to a pri-

vate home, where the doctors tried to make him comfortable. Because the president's six-foot-four-inch frame was too long for the bed, he was arranged diagonally, with his head settled on two oversized pillows propped against a door. Hour after hour these pillows soaked up the president's blood as it drained from his wound. Eventually they were so saturated that a crimson pool began to form on the carpet.

Nothing could be done for the president except to keep vigil over his final hours. [43] During the night members of the cabinet, the vice president, members of the president's family, the surgeon general, the president's pastor, and others visited, waiting for the inevitable. At 7:22 on the morning of Saturday, April 15, Lincoln breathed his last at the age of fifty-six. As a brief requiem prayer was pronounced, Secretary of War Edwin M. Stanton said, "Now he belongs to the ages."

The outpouring of national grief at Lincoln's death was unprecedented. [44] The funeral services, held in Washington, lasted for nearly a week. On Tuesday, April 18, the president's body lay in the East Room atop a four-foot high catafalque called the "Temple of Death." Special trains brought sixty thousand people into the city. All day a long line of mourners filed past the catafalque.

Services at the White House on Wednesday morning were followed by a solemn procession to the Capitol, where the president's body lay on display in the rotunda. The procession included officer contingents from the army, navy, and Marine Corps, a detachment of African American soldiers, twenty-two pallbearers, marshals, clergy, attending doctors, government officials, and family members. Just behind the hearse was Lincoln's favorite horse, now riderless, with his master's boots reversed in the stirrups. In tribute to the fallen commander in chief, many convalescent soldiers left their hospital beds to hobble in the funeral march. Four thousand African Americans—holding hands, marching in lines of forty across, and wearing high silk hats and white gloves—also joined the procession.

On Friday the president's coffin began a circuitous journey back to Lincoln's home in Springfield, Illinois, where it was buried on May 4, 1865. For twenty days and more than sixteen hundred miles the funeral train crept through Baltimore, Harrisburg, Philadelphia, New York City, Albany, Buffalo, Cleveland, Columbus, Indianapolis, Michigan City, and Chicago on its way to Springfield. At each stop the coffin was removed from the train to lie in state on a prominent catafalque in a public square, allowing the people to bid Lincoln farewell. A million Americans walked past his coffin; thirty million more attended church services or watched the train or the hearse pass by. On April 26, as Lincoln's funeral train made its way west, Booth was found in Virginia and shot to death by Union soldiers when he tried to escape a burning barn.

Vice President Andrew Johnson, who succeeded Lincoln, became president under inauspicious circumstances. The Civil War had established the permanence of the Union and had emancipated the slaves, but now the enormous problems of Reconstruction had to be faced. How were the Confederate states to rejoin the Union? How were the rights of citizenship to be restored to the rebels? What would be the status of the emancipated slaves?

Johnson, a Unionist but also a Southerner and a Democrat, favored policies that were lenient to the South, although not much more so than Lincoln's. But having been chosen as Lincoln's running mate in 1864 to balance the ticket, Johnson had little support in the Republican Congress, which favored much sterner measures. In addition, Johnson was handicapped by an aggressive personal style, which alienated even many of his friends. After a series of angry confrontations with Congress, Johnson was impeached by the House of Representatives in 1868. He barely survived a trial in the Senate when thirty-five of fifty-four senators, one short of the required two-thirds, voted to remove him from office. Johnson's entire presidency was consumed in acrimony between him and Congress. *(See "Impeachment of Andrew Johnson," p. 482.)*

James A. Garfield

A scholar, a soldier, and a politician, James Garfield was nominated for president as a dark-horse compromise candidate on the thirty-sixth ballot of the 1880 Republican national convention. The forty-eight-year-old senator-elect from Ohio had been a member of the Electoral Commission that was formed to resolve the disputed election between Rutherford B. Hayes and Samuel J. Tilden in 1876. Garfield also had served as the Republican floor leader in the House of Representatives.

Chester A. Arthur, a product of the New York Republican political machine (the "Stalwarts"), was nominated as Garfield's running mate. In the fall campaign, Arthur played a crucial role, acting as perhaps the first advance man in American political history. Arthur coordinated rallies, meetings, and the campaign tours of former president Grant and New York Republican boss Roscoe Conkling.[45] In the close election that followed, the Garfield-Arthur ticket won by less than one-tenth of one percentage point in the popular vote. The margin in the electoral college was more comfortable (214–155), but only because of Arthur's ability to help carry his home state of New York with its thirty-five electoral votes.[46]

After the election, Garfield confronted a host of political and administrative problems related to political patronage. Assembling a cabinet from a Republican Party that was deeply divided between Stalwart and "Half-breed" (or moderate reformist) wings was a complex task that consumed much of the president-elect's time and energy during the transition period. In fact, Garfield did not succeed in completing his cabinet until March 5, 1881, the day after his inauguration.[47]

But this was only the first of the new president's problems with government appointments. The line of job applicants that awaited him after he took the oath of office stretched down Pennsylvania Avenue. Meanwhile, the expectations of civil service reformers were at odds with those of Republican activists of all stripes, who felt entitled to patronage positions in return for their support during the campaign.

Garfield's problems extended beyond appointments and into administration. Soon after he took office, a scandal erupted in the Post Office Department involving the awarding of contracts for mail routes (it became known as the Star Route affair). After a full-scale investigation a general overhaul of the department was ordered in April 1881, and grand jury indictments were prepared carrying charges of fraud.

Wearied by patronage woes and increasingly committed to reform, Garfield decided to undertake a two-week tour of New England, including Massachusetts, where he planned to attend commencement exercises at Williams College, his alma mater. On the morning of July 2, 1881, as the president and Secretary of State James G. Blaine walked through the Washington depot of the Baltimore and Potomac Railroad, shots rang out and Garfield fell to the floor, bleeding. He had been hit by two bullets, one grazing his arm and the other lodging in his spinal column. The assassin, who was captured immediately, was identified as Charles J. Guiteau. Guiteau, a disturbed man who imagined that he had played a role in Garfield's election, had previously visited the White House where he fruitlessly demanded that Garfield appoint him U.S. ambassador to France.

While being arrested, Guiteau declared: "I did it and will go to jail for it. I am a Stalwart; now Arthur is president!" In his pocket were two letters. The first, addressed to the American people, maintained that "the President's tragic death was a sad necessity, but it will unite the Republican party and save the Republic. . . . His death was a political necessity." The second, addressed to Vice President Arthur, informed him of the assassination and his succession to the presidency. The letter went on to recommend names for cabinet appointments.

At first, these letters led investigators to suspect that Guiteau was part of a conspiracy, perhaps involving Arthur or other Stalwarts. This theory was quickly rejected, however, and on January 25, 1882, Guiteau was found guilty of murder despite his lawyer's, almost certainly correct, argument that he was insane. He was hanged at the jail in Washington, D.C., on June 30, 1882. But Guiteau's rejoicing that Arthur was president diminished Arthur's popularity and placed him in a difficult political position during the long period of Garfield's disability.[48] Nor did it help Arthur that in recent months he had publicly criticized the president on several occasions.

Initially, little hope was held out for Garfield's recovery. Then the president rallied for a time and the doctors became optimistic. During the first three weeks of July, Garfield seemed to make steady progress and a day of national thanksgiving was declared for July 18. August, however, was a roller coaster ride of gains and setbacks, recovery and relapse. Finally, after another rally, the president asked to be moved from the White House to a cottage on the New Jersey shore at Elberon. On September 19, less than two weeks after making the trip, Garfield complained of a sudden pain in his chest, then died. An autopsy revealed that the immediate cause of death was a rupture of the peritoneum caused by a hemorrhage of the mesenteric artery in the chest. It also was discovered that several abscesses had formed along the path of the bullet that had lodged in the president's spine. Since being shot, he had lost eighty pounds.

During the eighty days that President Garfield was disabled, the nation lacked a leader and almost no executive functions were carried out. Throughout this period, writes Sarah Vowell, "the people were obsessed, transfixed, following the daily, sometimes hourly dispatches on the president's condition." [49] Immediately after the president was shot, the doctors announced that his only chance for survival was to be "kept perfectly quiet." Fortunately, Congress was not in session at the time, minimizing the press of legislative business. During his entire disability Garfield signed only one official document.

For almost the whole month of July only the president's wife, Lucretia Rudolph Garfield, and attendants were allowed in the president's sickroom. When a member of the cabinet, Secretary of State James Blaine, finally was permitted to see Garfield on July 21, his visit was limited to ten minutes. Other members of the cabinet were not allowed to visit until the president had been moved to Elberon in September. Vice President Arthur never saw or spoke with President Garfield during the entire eighty-day period.

In late August, a time when the president's condition seemed to be worsening, the cabinet weighed its constitutional responsibilities and considered asking the vice president to assume the powers and duties of the presidency. But the Constitution offered little guidance: Article II, Section 1, mentioned disability but did not define it, did not describe a process for determining whether a president was disabled, and could be interpreted to mean that once executive responsibilities were transferred to the vice president they could not be transferred back, even if the president recovered. When consulted, Arthur indicated that he had no intention of doing anything that might make it appear he was trying to supplant the president. Arthur spent the entire period of Garfield's disability away from Washington, at his New York home. [50] After Garfield rallied for what turned out to be the last time, the cabinet decided not to pursue the matter.

Arthur received word of the president's death by telegram on September 20, 1881. Later that day he took the oath of office from Judge John R. Brady of the New York

Supreme Court and, joined by Secretary of State Blaine and Secretary of War Robert Todd Lincoln, traveled to Elberon to pay his respects to the dead president's widow. Lincoln was the son of Abraham Lincoln, the first president to be assassinated.

The same special train, now swathed in black crepe, that had brought Garfield to Elberon carried his body to Washington, where it lay in state for two days in the rotunda of the Capitol. More than seventy thousand people filed pass the coffin in tribute to the slain president. A train then carried Garfield's body to Cleveland, Ohio, where another 150,000 people (equivalent to the city's entire population) passed by the hundred-foot high pavilion on which the body lay. Garfield was buried in Cleveland on September 26, 1881, just a few weeks shy of what would have been his fiftieth birthday. [51]

Upon arriving in Washington on September 22, Arthur retook the oath of office to establish a federal record of the act, delivered a brief inaugural address, and convened a formal meeting of Garfield's cabinet. The next day the new president issued a proclamation calling the Senate into special session on October 10 so that it could elect a president pro tempore.

The need for a president pro tempore was urgent because, under the Succession Act of 1792, that senator was first in the line of presidential succession whenever the vice presidency became vacant. (The Speaker of the House was next.) For months the Senate had been unable to choose a president pro tempore because it was evenly divided between Republicans and Democrats. But while the Senate was in recess, two Republican senators resigned, leaving the Democrats with a majority. They chose Sen. Thomas F. Bayard of Delaware as president pro tempore. The price of having a presidential successor in place was to put a member of the opposition party next in line to the presidency.

Because the House of Representatives chosen in the 1880 election was not scheduled to convene until December 1881, there also was no House Speaker when Arthur became president. (At that time the Speaker's term coincided with the time the House actually was in session.) Thus when Arthur succeeded Garfield, the first three positions in the line of succession were vacant: there was no vice president, Senate president pro tempore, or Speaker of the House. Aghast at this situation, Arthur tried three times during his presidency to prod Congress to deal with the issues of presidential succession and disability. But with the immediate crisis past, Congress failed to act. [52]

Arthur assumed the presidency encumbered by a number of disadvantages. A machine politician who had obtained the Republican vice-presidential nomination through sharp dealing and who hailed from a different faction of the party than Garfield, Arthur had little national experience and inspired scant public confidence.

Furthermore, he inherited a divided party in which other leading figures already were jockeying for position in the race for the 1884 presidential nomination.

To his credit, however, Arthur conducted himself with dignity and diplomacy during President Garfield's disability, thereby winning a certain measure of public support. After becoming president, he stopped acting like a state political boss and began acting in what he saw as the best interests of the country. Arthur took particular care to appoint talented, capable officials to his administration, while embracing Garfield's commitment to civil service reform. In 1883 Arthur signed the Pendleton Act, which created the merit-based civil service system for hiring federal employees. In doing so, the president lost considerable political support among his old Stalwart allies and thus became "virtually a President without a party." [53] Like the other nineteenth-century successor presidents, Arthur was not nominated by his party to run for a full term as president. After leaving office in March 1885, he retired from public life and resumed practicing law in New York City. Arthur died in 1886.

William McKinley

William McKinley was chosen as president in 1896, in an election that established the Republicans as the nation's majority party for the next third of a century. A former member of Congress and a two-term governor of Ohio, McKinley was a champion of the protective tariff and a nationalist in world affairs. During his first term as president he worked to restore prosperity to an economically troubled nation; by the time of his second inauguration on March 4, 1901, McKinley was able to declare, "Now every avenue of production is crowded with activity, labor is well employed, and American products find good markets at home and abroad." [54] McKinley's successful conduct of the Spanish-American War of 1898 was crowned by U.S. acquisition of the Philippine islands, Puerto Rico, and Guam. That same year he annexed the Hawaiian islands.

Theodore Roosevelt initially joined the McKinley administration as assistant secretary of the navy, a position he left at the outbreak of the fighting in Cuba to organize the Rough Riders. Roosevelt's celebrated heroics in leading the Rough Riders on a charge up San Juan Hill helped to catapult him into the governorship of New York in 1898. From that position he was selected by the 1900 Republican national convention to become McKinley's running mate in his bid

for a second term. [55] Roosevelt was chosen despite the ardent opposition of Republican National Committee chair Mark Hanna, who was McKinley's chief supporter. "Don't you realize that there's only one life between that madman and the White House?" the exasperated Hanna complained. [56] The one life was McKinley's.

Five months after his second inauguration, President McKinley traveled to the Pan-American Exposition in Buffalo, New York. On September 5, President's Day at the exposition, McKinley delivered a speech that outlined his goals for the second term and trumpeted the historic accomplishments of the Republican Party. [57] The next day, the president attended an afternoon public reception at the Temple of Music.

Although he was accompanied by a newly assigned contingent of Secret Service agents, as well as by four special guards and several soldiers, McKinley was shot as he stood in the receiving line and greeted people. Leon Czolgosz (pronounced "chol-gosh"), an anarchist, fired two bullets at McKinley. One bounced off a coat button and the other hit the fifty-eight-year-old president in the stomach. The assassin was subdued quickly and, in the span of less than two months, was tried, convicted, and executed. "I killed President McKinley because I done my duty," Czolgosz said. "I don't believe in one man having so much service and another man having none." [58] The wounded president said he thought that his assailant was "some poor misguided fellow" and worried how his wife, Ida Saxton

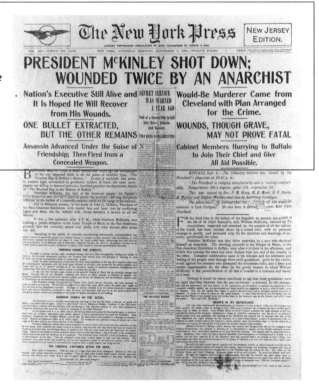

Despite the protection of Secret Service agents, special guards, and soldiers, President William McKinley was shot as he greeted people at the Pan-American Exposition in Buffalo, New York. The headlines of September 7, 1901, held out hope that the president would recover, but he died eight days later.

McKinley, who was in poor health, would respond to the news of the shooting.[59]

An operation was performed immediately on President McKinley, but the bullet could not be found. The wounds were then bathed, and the president seemed to be on the road to recovery. On September 10, Vice President Roosevelt and most of the cabinet members, who had come to Buffalo, were told that the president's condition had improved so much that they could safely disperse. Roosevelt departed for a vacation with his family in the Adirondack Mountains.

During the next three days, however, McKinley experienced fever, gangrene, and infection, weakening him severely. Once again the vice president and the cabinet were summoned to Buffalo. President McKinley died in the early morning hours of Friday, September 14, 1901. After the by now traditional lying-in-state in Washington, McKinley's body was transported home by train and buried adjacent to Westlawn Cemetery in Canton, Ohio. Illinois senator Shelby M. Cullom paid tribute to McKinley: "He looked and acted the ideal President. He was always thoroughly self-poised and deliberate; nothing ever seemed to excite him and he always maintained a proper dignity." Theodore Roosevelt described McKinley as "the most widely loved man in all the United States." [60]

Mark Hanna, now a senator from Ohio, did not repay the compliment. "I told William McKinley it was a mistake to nominate that wild man," said Hanna, referring to Roosevelt. "Now look, that damned cowboy is President of the United States." [61] Roosevelt, at age forty-two, was the youngest person ever to become president. (His record still stands.) He took the oath of office in Buffalo on September 15, the day after McKinley died, from federal district court judge John R. Hazel. The new president then returned to Washington and held his first cabinet meeting, at which he asked the cabinet to stay and help him to carry out McKinley's program. In his first message to Congress, Roosevelt denounced anarchists as "ordinary murderer[s]" and called for legislation to prevent anarchists from emigrating to the United States. In 1903 Congress responded by passing the Anarchist Exclusion Act, "the first law allowing potential immigrants to be questioned about their political views." [62]

Not much time passed before the energetic, strong-willed Roosevelt began putting his own stamp on the presidency. During the remaining three and a half years of the late president's term, Roosevelt proved to be a forceful leader.[63] He embarked on a "Square Deal" program of social reform, supported the organization of trade unions and greater social and industrial justice for laborers, and launched a trust-busting campaign. He also won passage of the Reclamation Act of 1902 for western lands, and in 1903 he oversaw the creation of the Department of Commerce and Labor and signed a treaty for the construction of the Panama Canal. In foreign affairs, the president announced the "Roosevelt Corollary" to the Monroe Doctrine and did much to enhance American prestige abroad.

In all, Roosevelt was twice blessed as an accidental president: He inherited a legacy of prosperity, successful policies, and a strong political party from his predecessor, and he was able to build his own political record as a forceful and popular president. So effective was Roosevelt's successor presidency that he was nominated for a full term by acclamation at the 1904 Republican national convention and went on to win the general election by a margin of more than 2.5 million votes. In doing so, Roosevelt ended the pattern of political futility that had plagued previous successor presidents. Neither Tyler, Fillmore, Johnson, nor Arthur had even been nominated by his party, much less elected as president. Beginning with Roosevelt, however, every successor president has been nominated, and most have been elected president in their own right.

John F. Kennedy

When he entered office in January 1961, forty-three-year-old John F. Kennedy was the youngest person ever elected as president, a distinction that he still owns. Succeeding as he did the oldest (to that date) person ever to be president, Dwight D. Eisenhower, Kennedy and his administration seemed to inject new energy into government. Nevertheless, Kennedy had won an extremely close election in 1960, and he faced considerable conservative opposition from Republicans and southern Democrats in Congress. Thus the president invested his hopes in a strong reelection victory in 1964 that would enable him to capitalize on the political and policy foundations he had laid during his first term.

In November 1963, as part of his preparations for the 1964 election, the president traveled to Dallas, Texas. Kennedy was concerned about retaining his support in the South, especially Texas. To that end, and with the help of Vice President Lyndon B. Johnson, a Texan, the president hoped to persuade the Texas Democratic Party's quarreling liberal and conservative factions to put their differences aside and unite behind him in 1964.[64]

Texas, especially the strongly conservative city of Dallas, did not promise to be particularly hospitable to President Kennedy. Even Johnson had been spat on while campaigning for the Kennedy-Johnson ticket in Dallas in 1960. And just four weeks before the president's planned trip the U.S. ambassador to the United Nations, Adlai E. Stevenson, had been heckled in Dallas while speaking at a United Nations Day event. On the way to his car after the speech an angry crowd of picketers had closed in on Stevenson; one woman hit him on the head with a sign. Stevenson had been so shaken by the experience that he told the president the atmosphere in Dallas was "ugly and frightening" and urged him to reconsider his scheduled trip.[65]

Kennedy, who regarded courage as a supreme virtue and thought Stevenson was soft, went to Dallas anyway.

On the morning of November 22, 1963, a motorcade was formed at Love Field outside the city to bring the presidential party through downtown Dallas. Kennedy and first lady Jacqueline Bouvier Kennedy were in the lead car, along with Texas governor John B. Connally and his wife, Nell. Vice President Johnson, his wife, Lady Bird Johnson, and Sen. Ralph W. Yarborough, D-Texas, were in the next car. Just as the motorcade, which had been greeted by cheering crowds, began its final stretch, Mrs. Connally was pleased to comment, "You can't say Dallas doesn't love you, Mr. President," to which Kennedy replied, "No, you can't." [66]

As the motorcade turned off Main Street onto Elm and rolled passed the Texas School Book Depository, a brief series of short, sharp noises startled everyone. Some thought they were firecrackers; others thought a car engine was backfiring. Hunters instantly recognized the sound of rifle fire.

Suddenly the lead car was awash in blood—the president had been shot two times. One of the bullets also struck Governor Connally. As Mrs. Kennedy cradled her husband's shattered head, the motorcade dissolved and the lead car raced for the nearest hospital. Secret Service agents near the vice president's car pushed Johnson down in his seat and rushed him to the hospital, too.

Instantly, word of Kennedy's shooting went out over the television and radio networks and the newspaper wire services. Military forces in the Washington, D.C., area were placed on special alert. A plane with half the cabinet aboard, including Secretary of State Dean Rusk, was in midflight to Japan. The plane immediately turned around and returned to Washington.

Medical efforts to save President Kennedy were futile; the wounds were too severe. In another hospital room security personnel and staff urged Vice President Johnson, who was uninjured, to leave Dallas as soon as possible. In the absence of information to the contrary, they feared that a larger conspiracy might exist and wanted the new president to return to the more secure environs of Washington.[67]

At two o'clock in the afternoon the television networks interrupted regular programming to bring word to a stunned nation that President Kennedy had died. In truth, Kennedy had been pronounced dead at 1:15, but the announcement was delayed until Johnson was safely at the Dallas airfield. In no other instance of presidential assassina-

As millions watched on national television, Jack Ruby, a Dallas club owner, shot and killed Lee Harvey Oswald as the accused assassin of President Kennedy was being transferred to another jail.

tion had death come so quickly. Before many Americans knew that the president had been hurt, he was dead.

Johnson, on board *Air Force One*, now awaited the arrival of Mrs. Kennedy and the late president's casket. Meanwhile, the Dallas police had identified and apprehended the suspected assassin, Lee Harvey Oswald, a worker at the book depository who had lived in the Soviet Union and been involved in pro-communist causes. Before the plane took off, a brief swearing-in ceremony was held. Federal district court judge Sarah T. Hughes administered the oath of office to Johnson, with Mrs. Johnson and Mrs. Kennedy present.

Upon its return to Washington, President Kennedy's body lay in state in the East Room of the White House, where a steady stream of family, friends, Washington officials, diplomats, and heads of state came to pay their final respects. On Sunday, November 24, shortly before the funeral procession to the Capitol was scheduled to begin, Oswald was shot and killed in Dallas as he was being transferred from one jail to another. Jack Ruby, a local nightclub owner, was the killer. He had elbowed through the crowd of police and reporters, shouting, "You killed the president, you rat!" The shooting was caught on national television and rebroadcast repeatedly in the days that followed. Although retribution against presidential assassins usually had been swift, never before had an assassin been killed so quickly, publicly, and illegally.

At one o'clock in the afternoon on November 24, the funeral procession began its solemn journey from the White House to the Capitol. The presidential caisson, followed by a riderless black horse in the manner of Lincoln's funeral, passed by silent, mournful crowds along Pennsylvania Avenue. The late president's toddler son, John Jr., saluted as the caisson passed. The casket was then placed in the Capitol rotunda for public viewing. Thousands of people lined up to file past the closed casket; many millions more—an estimated 95 percent of the American adult population—joined the proceedings via television or radio. The networks canceled all other programming, including commercials. Domestic broadcasts were relayed to Europe and parts of Asia; the funeral was even telecast in the Soviet Union.[68]

On Monday morning, November 25, the caisson reclaimed the president's casket and carried it first to St. Matthew's Roman Catholic Cathedral for a requiem mass and then to Arlington National Cemetery, where President Kennedy's body was interred. Afterward the nation, and in particular President Johnson, turned to the business of trying to carry on. Within days of the funeral the new president, speaking of Kennedy's policies and programs, pledged "Let us continue" in a nationally televised speech to Congress. Johnson also persuaded Supreme Court chief justice Earl Warren to head an independent commission to investigate the assassination. Ten months later the Warren Commission reported its finding that Oswald was the lone assassin and dismissed the possibility that he was part of a wider conspiracy. Conspiracy theories have abounded ever since, however.

Less than a year away from the 1964 election, President Johnson succeeded in advancing the legislative agenda of his slain predecessor while establishing a record of his own. Johnson was unanimously nominated for president at the 1964 Democratic national convention and won the November election by one of the largest majorities in history, carrying many new liberal Democrats into Congress on his coattails. In 1965 and 1966, Johnson proposed and Congress enacted the largest agenda of domestic legislation since the New Deal. Some of the bills were part of Kennedy's "New Frontier" program; the rest were part of Johnson's "Great Society."

Jacqueline Kennedy and her children, Caroline and John Jr., follow the flag-draped coffin of President John F. Kennedy out of St. Matthew's Roman Catholic Cathedral. After the requiem mass, the presidential caisson carried the casket to Arlington National Cemetery, where Kennedy's body was interred.

Another important but indirect consequence of the Kennedy assassination was a renewed concern for both the presidential line of succession and the problem of presidential disability. Johnson's succession to the presidency meant that for the sixteenth time in history, the nation had no vice president. Under the Presidential Succession Act of 1947, the first two officials in line to become president if Johnson died, resigned, became disabled, or was impeached and removed were Speaker of the House John W. McCormack, D-Mass., and Senate President Pro Tempore Carl T. Hayden, D-Ariz. Both lawmakers were advanced in age—McCormack was in his seventies and Hayden in his eighties—and both were in ill health. From November 22, 1963, until January 20, 1965, when Minnesota senator Hubert H. Humphrey was sworn in as the newly elected vice president, many Americans dreaded what would happen if Johnson were killed or suffered a heart attack similar to those he had experienced during the 1950s.

The nature of President Kennedy's wounds reinforced concern about the problem of presidential disability. As Sen. Kenneth B. Keating, R-N.Y., noted, "A matter of inches spelled the difference between the painless death of John F. Kennedy and the possibility of his permanent incapacity to exercise the duties of the highest office in the land." [69]

Alarmed by these problems of succession and disability, Congress passed the Twenty-fifth Amendment, which created a procedure for determining whether a president is disabled and provided a means to fill vacancies in the vice presidency. A joint resolution proposing the amendment was approved by Congress virtually without opposition in July 1965. Ratification by the states proceeded swiftly and was completed by February 1967. (See "Passage of the Twenty-fifth Amendment," p. 503.)

VICE-PRESIDENTIAL DEATHS

Seven vice presidents have died in office, all of them during the century-long period 1812–1912 and all of natural causes. (The political weakness of the vice presidency seems to have made it an unappealing target for assassins, in contrast to the presidency.) This concentration of vice-presidential deaths in one period is probably not coincidental. Until the Twelfth Amendment was ratified in 1804, the vice presidency was awarded to the runner-up in the presidential election. The vice presidents elected before 1804—John Adams, Thomas Jefferson, and Aaron Burr—were, not surprisingly, vigorous political leaders. The Twelfth Amendment, which enjoined electors to vote separately for president and vice president, diminished the vice presidency by stripping it of its status as the office held by the person who, presumably, was the second most qualified individual in the country to be president. As a result, a large share of the political leaders who could be persuaded to run for vice president were long past their political prime. Later, in the twentieth century, the vice presidency regained some of its luster as a stepping-stone to the presidency and more energetic political leaders, who were less likely to fall prey to fatal diseases, once more were attracted to the office. (See Chapter 3, History of the Vice Presidency.)

George Clinton, who served in the administrations of Presidents Jefferson and James Madison, was the first vice president to be elected under the Twelfth Amendment and the first to die in office. Clinton's death came three years into his second term on April 20, 1812, at age seventy-two. Clinton had been renominated unanimously for vice president in 1808 despite his bad health. (Sen. Stephen Bradley described him to John Quincy Adams in January 1808 as "too old [to be president]; and we are all witnesses that his faculties are failing.") Clinton's successor as vice president under President Madison, Elbridge Gerry, was in bad health throughout his term and died of a hemorrhage on November 23, 1814, after twenty months in office. Gerry was seventy.

William R. King, who was elected as vice president with Franklin Pierce in 1852 at age sixty-six, was in Cuba on inauguration day and took his oath of office there. He died shortly after his return to the United States, barely four weeks later, on April 18, 1853.

Henry Wilson was the fourth vice president to die in office. Elected with President Ulysses S. Grant in 1872, he served almost three years before dying, at age sixty-three, on November 22, 1875. Ten years later, Vice President Thomas A. Hendricks died on November 25, 1885, at age sixty-six, after serving nine months under President Grover Cleveland. Garret A. Hobart, who was both vice president and a close adviser to President William McKinley, died on November 21, 1899, at age fifty-five, almost three years into his term.

The last vice president to die in office was the fifty-seven-year-old James S. Sherman. Sherman had been renominated for a second term on the ticket headed by President William Howard Taft in 1912 (the first vice president ever to be renominated by a party convention). He died on October 30, 1912, just before the election. The Taft-Sherman ticket lost, and the Republican National Committee chose Nicholas Murray Butler, the president of Columbia University, to receive Sherman's electoral votes.

Taken together, vice-presidential deaths have left the office unoccupied for thirteen years. For another twenty-six years, the vice presidency has been vacant because presidents died and vice presidents succeeded to the presidency. Thus, the nation has been without a vice president for thirty-nine years. This includes a seven-year stretch—interrupted only by Vice President King's four-week stint in the office—that lasted from July 9, 1850, when Vice President Millard Fillmore succeeded to the presidency after President Zachary Taylor died, until March 4, 1857, when John C. Breckinridge was inaugurated as vice president in the administration of President James Buchanan.

Until recently, a vacant vice presidency was not regarded as a serious problem. The president pro tempore of the Senate took the place of the vice president as Senate president. In accordance with the Constitution, Congress passed a succession act in 1792 that placed the president pro tempore next in line to succeed to the presidency. In 1886 Congress replaced the Senate president with the secretary of state in the line of succession. In 1947, it replaced the secretary with the Speaker of the House of Representatives.

In 1965, however, Congress passed the Twenty-fifth Amendment. One of its sections provided that, when the vice presidency became vacant, the president would nominate a new vice president, subject to confirmation by both houses of Congress. The amendment was ratified in 1967.

OTHER ASSAULTS AND ISSUES OF PRESIDENTIAL SECURITY

In addition to the four presidents who died at the hands of assassins, five other presidents have withstood assassination attempts: Andrew Jackson in 1835, Franklin D. Roosevelt in 1933, Harry S. Truman in 1950, Gerald R. Ford (twice) in 1975, and Ronald Reagan in 1981.

Threatening situations have plagued still other presidents, dating back to John Quincy Adams, who was accosted by a court-martialed army sergeant demanding reinstatement. President John Tyler once was the target of rocks thrown by an intoxicated painter. During the Nixon administration a would-be assailant tried to hijack an airplane and crash it into the White House. Nixon's successor, Gerald Ford, was the target of a man who wired himself with explosives in hopes of ramming his car through the White House gates, while another intruder scaled the White House security fence armed with what appeared to be a bomb. The intruder was fatally shot by security officers.[70]

President Bill Clinton experienced a series of strange and threatening events during the fall of 1994.[71] On September 12, Frank Corder, a Maryland truck driver, crashed a small Cessna plane into a large magnolia tree just outside the president's White House bedroom. Corder was killed in the crash but the president and his family, who were staying across the street at Blair House while renovations were being made on the executive mansion, were unaffected. On October 29, while Clinton was watching a basketball game on television in the second-floor family quarters of the White House, a Colorado hotel worker named Francisco Duran fired a spray of bullets at the mansion's north facade from Pennsylvania Avenue, only fifty yards away. A few weeks later, in the early morning hours of December 17, several bullets were fired by an unknown gunman at the south facade of the White House from the Ellipse. Several days later, on December 20, a knife-wielding homeless man, Marcelino Corniel, was shot to death by police on the Pennsylvania Avenue sidewalk in front of the White House.

After the late 1994 attacks on the White House, together with the massively destructive car bombing of an Oklahoma City federal office building on April 19, 1995, Clinton accepted a Secret Service recommendation that the two blocks of Pennsylvania Avenue on which the White House is situated be closed to vehicles and converted to a more easily secured pedestrian mall. The new policy took effect May 21, 1995.

Most of the early, serious assassination attempts on presidents were successful, and the attempt on Andrew Jackson probably would have been if the gunman's weapons had not misfired from point-blank range. In the years after President Garfield's assassination in 1881, the need for greater protection of the president finally was recognized. During Grover Cleveland's two terms in office (1885–1889, 1893–1897), Secret Service agents accompanied him to his summer home in Buzzards Bay, Massachusetts. Such protection was used more regularly during the McKinley administration (1897–1901), when the president, responding to assassination threats, requested that agents accompany him on formal outings. Even the presence of three agents and

other guards failed to protect McKinley from an assassin's bullet at a public reception in Buffalo, New York, however.

Secret Service protection for presidents was formally authorized by Congress in 1906, with two agents at a time normally assigned to presidential guard duty. Eight agents provided round- the-clock coverage when the president was traveling or on vacation. In 1908 similar protection was extended to the president-elect and in 1945 to the vice president. In 1950, after an attempted attack on President Truman by terrorists advocating Puerto Rican independence, the Secret Service instituted procedures to limit public access to the president by varying the time and place of his leisure activities (for example, Truman's morning walks) and by restricting access to the White House and its environs.

In addition to the fatal McKinley and Kennedy shootings, serious attempts were made on the lives of five other presidents during the twentieth century.[72] The first occurred on February 15, 1933, in Miami, Florida's Bayfront Park. Less than a month before his inauguration, President-elect Franklin Roosevelt narrowly escaped death from shots fired by Joseph Zangara, an anarchist who said he hated all rulers and capitalists. Roosevelt was seated at the time in an automobile that had been brought onto a speaker's platform. The man with whom he was speaking, Chicago mayor Anton J. Cermak, was fatally wounded.

On November 1, 1950, Leslie Coffelt, a White House police officer, and Giselio Torresola, one of the two Puerto Rico nationalists who were trying to kill President Truman, were shot to death during their assault on Blair House, where Truman was staying because renovations were being made on the Executive Mansion.

The Kennedy assassination in 1963 prompted extensive changes in Secret Service protection procedures. These were made in response to the findings and recommendations of the Warren Commission. A new protection strategy was devised that involved closer liaison between the Secret Service and other government agencies, especially the Federal Bureau of Investigation (FBI). The Warren Commission had discovered that although the FBI was aware that Lee Harvey Oswald was a communist supporter with revolutionary views who lived in Dallas, this information had not been transmitted to the Secret Service before or during President Kennedy's fateful trip. As a reform measure, the Secret Service and FBI drew up guidelines for the regular dissemination of FBI reports to the Secret Service. In 1976 this procedure was modified so that FBI reports were passed on only at the specific written request of the director of the Secret Service.

In September 1975, two attempts were made on President Gerald Ford's life, both while he was traveling in California. In each instance protective actions by Secret Service agents and others succeeded in deflecting the attacker. On September 5, 1975, as President Ford visited

On March 30, 1981, a psychiatric patient shot Ronald Reagan as the president was leaving a Washington, D.C., hotel. Reagan quickly recovered, making his next public appearance less than one month later.

serious chest wound from a bullet lodged in his left lung. The operation to remove the bullet lasted two hours, and the president remained hospitalized until April 11. Reagan made his first major public appearance after the shooting on April 28, when he delivered a nationally televised speech on the economy to a joint session of Congress.[73] The dramatic appearance galvanized support for his economic programs, which were passed into law that summer. Thus Reagan became the only president in history to recover from injuries sustained in an attempted assassination.

Sacramento to speak to the California General Assembly, Lynette A. "Squeaky" Fromme, a young associate of mass murderer Charles Manson, emerged from the crowd and pointed a gun at the president from two feet away. A Secret Service agent walking behind Ford saw the gun, grabbed it, and wrestled the would-be assassin to the ground. Less than three weeks later, on September 22, a single gunshot rang out as the president walked from a San Francisco hotel to his car at the end of another trip to California. Two Secret Service agents and presidential assistant Donald H. Rumsfeld pushed the president down, then shoved him onto the floor of the car's backseat and shielded him with their bodies until the car could make a hasty departure for the airport. The woman who had fired the gun, Sara Jane Moore, was quickly identified and apprehended. Both assailants attributed their assassination attempts to vaguely articulated nihilist or revolutionary ideologies.

On March 30, 1981, twenty-five-year-old John W. Hinckley Jr. shot and wounded President Ronald Reagan outside a Washington, D.C., hotel. Presidential press secretary James Brady, a Secret Service agent, and a District of Columbia police officer also were wounded. Hinckley was arrested at the scene of the shooting and, less than a month later, was indicted by a grand jury for trying to assassinate the president and on twelve additional counts related to the injuries he inflicted on the others. Hinckley, who had been under psychiatric care, claimed that he had shot the president to impress Jodie Foster, a young movie actress with whom he was infatuated. At his trial he was found not guilty by reason of insanity and confined for an indefinite period to St. Elizabeth's Hospital in Washington, an institution for the mentally ill.

After the shooting the seventy-year-old president was rushed to George Washington University hospital with a

IMPEACHMENT

Within the American constitutional system, impeachment is an extraordinary legislative check on both executive and judicial power. As such it is one of the most potent, yet least exercised, powers of Congress. Since 1789 impeachment proceedings have been initiated in the House of Representatives just sixty-two times. Only seventeen of these proceedings led the House, by simple majority vote, to lodge impeachment charges of "Treason, Bribery, or other high Crimes and Misdemeanors." Impeached were thirteen federal judges, two presidents, one senator, and one cabinet member. Three of these individuals resigned from office before a Senate trial could be held. The remaining fourteen were tried in the Senate, resulting in seven convictions and seven acquittals. (Convictions require a two-thirds vote of the senators present.) The three most significant impeachment cases, each of which ended in an acquittal, involved Supreme Court justice Samuel P. Chase in 1805, President Andrew Johnson in 1867–1868, and President Bill Clinton in 1998–1999. In all three instances the proceedings were animated largely by political conflicts between the political parties. In 1974 the House Judiciary Committee voted to recommend impeachment charges against President Richard Nixon to the full House, but Nixon's resignation ended the process, which almost certainly would have led to his impeachment and removal.

Although impeachment is a political act whose penalty is removal from office and possible disqualification from subsequent officeholding, not criminal conviction or the imposition of civil damages, it often is discussed in legal-sounding terminology.[74] The House of Representatives acts first as a kind of grand jury by considering and adopting impeachment charges and then as prosecutor by appointing a group of its members (called managers) to present the charges to the Senate. The Senate chamber becomes the courtroom, with the Senate acting as jury. Although the chief justice of the United States presides when the Senate tries a president, the Senate also acts as judge in many ways, because it decides procedural issues by majority vote. Since 1935, the Senate has routinely authorized a twelve-member Senate committee to try judicial impeachments. Such committees report, without recommendation, to the Senate, and the senators vote whether to convict.[75]

Origins and Purposes of Impeachment

In *Federalist* No. 65 Alexander Hamilton called impeachment "a method of national inquest into the conduct of public men." [76] The Constitution stipulates that impeachment proceedings may be brought against "the President, Vice President and all Civil Officers of the United States." It is not specific, however, about who is and is not a civil officer. In practice, most impeachment efforts have been directed at federal judges, who under the Constitution hold lifetime appointments "during good Behaviour" and thus cannot otherwise be removed from office. One early impeachment case raised the possibility that members of Congress could be impeached, but this idea was rejected by the Senate in favor of its less formal equivalent, expulsion. In other instances, impeachment has been sought against executive officials such as cabinet members, diplomats, customs collectors, and a United States attorney. Of all these cases, only one cabinet member ever was impeached. The reason that removal of executive officials almost never requires full impeachment proceedings is that they can be dismissed from office by the president.

English Origins: Constraining the Executive

The impeachment process dates from fourteenth-century England, where the fledgling Parliament used it as a device to make the king's officers accountable. Although the monarch was immune from such oversight, ministers and judges who were believed guilty of criminal offenses or of abusing executive power were liable to impeachment by Parliament. As described by Supreme Court justice and constitutional historian Joseph Story, impeachment offenses included not only "bribery and acting grossly contrary to the duties of their office," but also "misleading the sovereign by unconstitutional opinions and . . . attempts to subvert the fundamental laws and introduce arbitrary power." [77]

By the mid-fifteenth century impeachment had fallen into disuse, largely because the strong Tudor monarchs of the era succeeded in forcing Parliament to remove contentious officials by using bills of attainder or imposing pains and penalties. Later, during the early-seventeenth-century reigns of the Stuart kings, Parliament revived the impeachment power as a means of curbing the absolutist tendencies of monarchs.

In 1642 the power struggle between the executive and the legislature—that is, between king and Parliament—peaked with the impeachment of the Earl of Strafford, a minister of Charles I. According to some historians, the success of this effort was critical in preventing "the English monarchy from hardening into an absolutism of the type then becoming general in Europe." [78]

During the seventeenth and eighteenth centuries more than fifty impeachment trials were held in the House of Lords on charges brought by the House of Commons. Even as the U.S. Constitution was being drafted, the long impeachment and trial of Warren Hastings, the first governor general of India, was under way in London. By the time Hastings was acquitted in 1795, parliamentary impeachments were no longer considered necessary because the responsibility of government ministers had been redefined as being primarily to Parliament, not the monarch. The last British impeachment trial occurred in 1806.

Constitutional Convention

American colonial governments adopted the English process of impeachment, under which charges are brought by the lower house of the legislature and the upper house sits in judgment. Although the early state constitutions preserved this process, the Constitutional Convention debated whether the Senate was the appropriate body to conduct impeachment trials. (No one questioned that the House of Representatives should be responsible for bringing impeachment charges.) Framers James Madison and Charles Pinckney opposed assigning that role to the Senate, arguing that it would make presidents too dependent on the legislative branch for their tenure in office. Suggested alternatives included the Supreme Court and a convocation of the chief justices of the state supreme courts. In the end, however, tradition was followed and the Senate was selected to conduct impeachment trials.

The convention also debated the definition of an impeachable offense. Initially, it was proposed that the president be subject to impeachment for "malpractice or neglect of duty." Later, this definition was changed to "treason, bribery, or corruption," then simply to "treason or bribery." George Mason argued that the latter grounds were "too narrow" and proposed adding "maladministration," which Madison in turn opposed as being too broad. In the end, impeachable offenses were defined in the Constitution as "Treason, Bribery, or other high Crimes and Misdemeanors."

The constitutional provisions related to impeachment are scattered among the first two articles of the Constitution. In Article I the House is given "sole Power of Impeachment" and the Senate is accorded "the sole Power to try all Impeachments," with the chief justice of the United States presiding at presidential impeachment trials. Article II subjects "The President, Vice President and all Civil Officers of the United States" to impeachment for "Treason, Bribery, or other high Crimes and Misdemeanors." It also states that the consequences of a conviction by the Senate shall extend no further "than to removal from Office, and disqualification to hold and enjoy any Office of honor, Trust or Profit under the United States."

Impeachment Procedures

The impeachment process has been used so seldom that no standard practice for initiating impeachment has been established. Instead, impeachment proceedings have been initiated in several ways: by the introduction of a resolution by a member of the House, by a letter or message from the president, by a grand jury action forwarded to the House from a territorial legislature, by a resolution authorizing a general investigation, and by a resolution reported by the House Judiciary Committee. In the cases that have reached the Senate since 1900, the latter method of initiating impeachment proceedings has been preferred.

After a resolution to impeach has made its way to the House floor, the House decides whether to adopt the resolution by majority vote. In making this decision the House may choose to amend, delete, or add to the articles that make up the resolution before voting to adopt it.[79]

If the House adopts the resolution, its next task is to select managers to serve as prosecutors at the Senate trial. The managers—usually an odd number ranging from five to eleven—have been selected in various ways: by adopting a resolution that fixes the number of managers and empowers the Speaker to appoint them, by adopting a resolution that fixes both the number and names of the managers, or by adopting a resolution that fixes the number but empowers the House to elect the managers. Once selected, the House managers deliver the articles of impeachment to the Senate and inform it of the need to hold a trial. Any House member may attend the trial, but only the managers may actively represent and speak for the House.

The Senate trial is similar to a legal proceeding. Both sides may present evidence and witnesses, and the defendant is allowed counsel and has the right to testify and conduct cross-examinations. If the president is on trial, the chief justice presides. The Constitution is silent, however, about who is to preside in other impeachment trials. In the past either the vice president or the president pro tempore of the Senate has done so.

The chief justice (or other presiding officer) rules on all questions of evidence, but any ruling may be overturned by a majority vote of the Senate. The chief justice may ask the Senate to make a ruling by majority vote instead of making the ruling himself. The chief justice also questions witnesses and asks any questions submitted in writing by senators, who are not permitted to question witnesses directly.

At the conclusion of the testimony the Senate goes into closed session to debate the question of conviction or acquittal. During this session each senator may speak no longer than fifteen minutes. The articles of impeachment are voted on separately. If any article receives two-thirds approval from the senators present, the impeached official is convicted. The Senate may also vote to disqualify the convicted official from ever holding another federal office.

Controversial Questions

The constitutional grounds for impeachment and the character of the impeachment process have long been debated. Clearly, treason and bribery are grounds for impeachment, and their definitions have been well established. Treason and the requirements for its proof are defined in the Constitution, and bribery is defined in statutory laws that bar the giving, offering, or accepting of rewards in return for official favors. The meaning of the remaining grounds for impeachment—"other high Crimes and Misdemeanors"— however, is anything but clear and has been the subject of much contention.

Most interpreters of the Constitution have advocated a definition of the phrase that includes not only criminal offenses but also actions that constitute a serious abuse of office. As a 1974 staff report of the House Judiciary Committee proposed:

> Impeachment conduct . . . may include the serious failure to discharge the affirmative duties imposed on the president by the Constitution. Unlike a criminal case, the cause for removal . . . may be based on his entire course of conduct in office. . . . It may be a course of conduct more than individual acts that has a tendency to subvert constitutional government. . . . Impeachment was evolved to cope with both the inadequacy of criminal statutes and the impotence of the courts to deal with the conduct of great public figures.[80]

Perhaps the most extreme example of how loosely "high Crimes and Misdemeanors" can be construed is a statement made by House Republican leader Gerald Ford when he was attempting to impeach Supreme Court justice William O. Douglas in 1970. "An impeachable offense," Ford declared, "is whatever a majority of the House of Representatives considers it to be at a given moment in history; conviction results from whatever offense or offenses two-thirds of the other body considers to be sufficiently serious to require removal of the accused from office."[81]

Conversely, narrow constructionists contend that "other high Crimes and Misdemeanors" refers only to indictable criminal offenses. As the lawyers for Richard Nixon argued in 1974, for example, "Impeachment of a president should be resorted to only for causes of the gravest kind—the commission of a crime named in the Constitution or a criminal offense against the laws of the United States." [82]

The debates at the Constitutional Convention seem to indicate that impeachable offenses were not meant to be limited to indictable crimes, but included serious abuses of office. Conversely, the criminal code defines as crimes many actions of insufficient seriousness to warrant impeachment. [83] Thus neither the broad nor the narrow construction of "other high Crimes and Misdemeanors" is fully acceptable. Not all indictable crimes constitute valid grounds for impeachment, yet neither are indictable crimes the only valid grounds for impeachment.

The character of the impeachment process has engendered considerable debate as well—is it a political process or a judicial one? [84] The view that impeachment is a judicial proceeding is grounded in part in the language of the Constitution. Article II provides for the impeached official's removal from office upon "conviction," and Article III guarantees Americans a jury trial for "all Crimes, except in cases of Impeachment." This view has implications for the due process protections that should be accorded any officials who are impeached, as well as for their right to judicial review and their vulnerability to double jeopardy.

The opposing interpretation regards impeachment as a political process in which the Constitution assigns the leading roles to elected legislators. In this view, the purpose of impeachment is not to punish crimes but to protect the government and the people against gross official misconduct by divesting offenders of public office. A guilty verdict does not punish the accused through any deprivation of life, liberty, or property; it merely removes an official from office. As a political process, impeachment proceedings may adopt some judicial procedures, but they are not bound to conform to all legal requirements, such as a jury trial or judicial review.

In 1993 the Supreme Court came down squarely on the political side of this debate. In the case of *Nixon v. United States,* the Court voted 9–0 to uphold the Senate's conviction of federal district court judge Walter L. Nixon Jr. on impeachment charges. Chief Justice William H. Rehnquist's majority opinion, which was joined in full by five other justices, declared that the courts have no standing to review impeachment proceedings because the Constitution grants the Senate the "sole power" to try impeachments. "Judicial involvement in impeachment proceedings, even if only for purposes of judicial review, is counter-intuitive because it would eviscerate the 'important constitutional check' placed on the Judiciary by the Framers," Rehnquist wrote. [85]

Impeachment of Andrew Johnson

Andrew Johnson was the first president against whom impeachment charges were brought by the House and tried in the Senate. Formally, the primary reason Congress

attempted to remove him from office in 1867–1868 was the charge that Johnson, in violating a federal statute, the Tenure of Office Act of 1867, had failed to fulfill his oath to "take Care that the Laws be faithfully executed." But this charge was brought against a backdrop of broader political issues: control of the Republican Party, the character of post–Civil War Reconstruction policy, the treatment and protection of the freed slaves, and various monetary and other economic policy matters.

Beyond these political issues, the Johnson impeachment also had significant implications for the constitutional separation of powers. One school of historians has regarded Johnson as the victim of a resurgent Congress seeking to reassert its prerogatives after the wartime "constitutional dictatorship" of President Abraham Lincoln. [86] Arthur M. Schlesinger Jr. has carried this argument even further, speculating that if Johnson had been removed from office, "the constitutional separation of powers would have been radically altered . . . and . . . the presidential system might have become a quasi-parliamentary regime." [87] Another school of historical thought, led by Michael L. Benedict, has argued that "Johnson had usurped the rightful legislative powers of Congress by inaugurating his own system of Reconstruction." [88] From this perspective, Congress undertook impeachment proceedings to preserve the separation of powers against presidential encroachment.

Johnson's Leadership Style

Benedict also has argued that the attempt to impeach Johnson was precipitated by the president's "inept" political leadership and "stubborn refusal to accommodate." [89] Similarly, the political scientist James David Barber, who developed four categories of presidential character types, has explained Johnson's behavior as typical of the "active-negative" president. [90] Active-negatives often turn political controversies into personal crusades and stubbornly refuse to accommodate valid political differences. Thus, Barber argues, Johnson came to regard his own cause as that of "the battling champion of the common man, valiantly resisting cynical radicals bent on the vindictive destruction of southern society and the subjugation of southern whites before ignorant and venal blacks led by corrupt white Carpetbaggers." [91]

In describing President Johnson's stubborn leadership style, the historian William Goldsmith observed: "Once he finally made up his mind, he was unprepared to change it; his record of failure only stimulated him to fight for his policy all the harder. He resented criticism of any kind. . . . [H]e refused to admit . . . mistakes and frequently compounded his error(s) by continuing rigidly along his chosen path." [92]

Certainly, character flaws were not the main cause of Andrew Johnson's impeachment. But they were an element in the dramatic events of 1867–1868 that led to his impeachment. As Benedict wrote, "[I]f the critical importance of Reconstruction for the security of the nation provided the kindling for the impeachment crisis, it was the torch of Andrew Johnson's personality that ignited the flame." [93]

The Political Situation of a Successor President

Andrew Johnson rose from humble origins that resembled in many ways those of Abraham Lincoln, the president with whom he briefly served as vice president. Like Lincoln, Johnson was born in a log cabin—but in North Carolina, not Kentucky. Both men lacked formal schooling and were essentially self-taught. Both had earned an early political reputation as a skillful debater. Unlike Lincoln, however, Johnson was left fatherless at age four and was apprenticed to a tailor at age ten. With the help of a shop supervisor, he taught himself to read; later his young wife taught him to write.

The similarities in background between Johnson and Lincoln affected them differently. Lincoln felt no stigma because of his lack of formal education. He enjoyed matching wits with all comers, had an open mind, and was a consummate politician. Johnson, in contrast, was embarrassed by the deficiencies of his education. He developed a rigid cast of mind that sought refuge from complex problems in unwavering adherence to principles. Heedless of the political or personal cost, Johnson would maintain his position in any argument tenaciously.[94]

Johnson rose quickly in politics. Upon moving to Greeneville, Tennessee, in 1827 to open his own tailor shop, he joined the local debating society and hosted a Democratic political club. Elected as a city alderman before he was twenty-one, Johnson was soon chosen by the voters to be mayor of Greeneville. During the next thirty years he ascended the political ladder, climbing from mayor to state representative to state senator to member of Congress to governor of Tennessee. In 1857 Johnson was elected U.S. senator by the Tennessee state legislature. When the Civil War broke out, he was the only senator from a seceding state to remain loyal to the Union and to support President Lincoln's use of military force to restore it. During the war Lincoln appointed Johnson as military governor of Tennessee, where he served courageously and with considerable success despite the hostile political climate in his state.

On the basis of Johnson's record of loyalty to the Union, and in an attempt to strengthen the appeal of the wartime National Union Party to War Democrats, the Republican national convention chose Johnson as Lincoln's running mate in the 1864 election. Although Lincoln's reelection looked uncertain for a time, his prospects were improved by news of an impressive string of Union military victories in the fall. Lincoln was reelected handily in November, with Johnson as his vice president. But the president's assassination only a few weeks after his second inauguration left behind an awkward governing situation for his successor.

Johnson was a Southerner at a time when the South had just rebelled against the Union and former officeholders in the South were automatically suspected of disloyalty. He was a Jacksonian Democrat who believed in states' rights, hard money, and minimal activity by the federal government.[95] He also adhered rigidly to his own strict interpretation of the Constitution.[96] Yet Johnson was the successor to a Northern Republican president who had exercised broad executive power to an unprecedented extent and who had pursued expansive policies for both the money supply and the role of the federal government.

Because he served as vice president for only six weeks before Lincoln's assassination catapulted him into the White House, Johnson had little time after his return from Tennessee to become reacquainted with the mood in Congress or to build a relationship with the Republican congressional leaders. Johnson's initial Reconstruction policies were generous to the South, as were those Lincoln had pursued during the final phases of the rebellion. But Johnson did not appreciate that the late president had sustained his moderating efforts only by expansive use of his war powers. Once the war ended, these powers lost much of their usefulness, making it necessary to reach an accommodation with Congress.[97]

Controversy over Reconstruction

Reconstruction placed three central issues before Washington policy makers: the status of the insurrectionist states, the status of the individuals who had participated in the insurrection, and the status of the newly freed slaves. On each point President Johnson's ideas clashed with the wishes of the Republican majority in Congress, especially the Radical Republicans.

Both Lincoln and Johnson favored reconstructing the Southern states as quickly and as simply as possible. Before his death Lincoln had begun the Reconstruction process in Arkansas, Louisiana, and Tennessee, three states that the Union army controlled completely. Using his war powers, the commander in chief had imposed military rule on the recaptured states and established provisional governments. Under Lincoln's Reconstruction policy, a state could rejoin the Union fully only by having a substantial proportion of its former voters swear allegiance to the United States and by having the new state government ratify the Thirteenth Amendment, thereby nullifying its previous secession, repudiating the debts of its Confederate government, and abolishing slavery.[98]

Lincoln encountered considerable opposition to what some in Congress regarded as too lenient an approach to Reconstruction. An alternative and harsher plan was embodied in the Wade-Davis Bill of 1864. Lincoln pocket-vetoed the bill, clearly indicating that differing executive and congressional positions were being formulated. By the time

Johnson succeeded to the presidency, it was evident that, although compromises might be worked out on the status of insurrectionist states and individuals, the status of the freed slaves was a much more contentious issue.

By the war's end, protecting the new freedom of the ex-slaves had become a minimal condition of Reconstruction for most Northerners and for the majority of congressional Republicans, both moderate and radical. Thus Congress's Reconstruction plans emphasized the far-reaching restructuring of Southern economic and social institutions and imposed difficult conditions on insurrectionist states and individuals wanting to reclaim their political rights and privileges in the Union. These conditions were intended to guarantee that control of the new South would not revert to those who had led the old South into secession and rebellion as well as that slavery and its vestiges would be eliminated. In pursuing these goals, congressional Republicans wanted a Freedman's Bureau to protect and provide services for ex-slaves and a civil rights bill to defend their rights and privileges as citizens.

In 1865 Congress passed a Freedman's Bureau bill and a civil rights bill. President Johnson vetoed both of them. A lack of consensus between moderate and Radical Republicans in Congress prevented them from overriding the Freedman's Bureau veto. But the president's veto of the civil rights bill drove the moderate Republicans into alliance with the Radicals, and together they were able to repass the bill by the required two-thirds majority. After they overrode Johnson's veto, most legislators began to believe that the president intended to disregard Congress and attempt to thwart its effort to play a significant role in Reconstruction policy making.

In 1866, during the midterm election campaign, Congress and the president battled over Reconstruction in Washington and around the country. The election was a landslide for the Radical Republicans, thereby increasing their numbers as well as their resolve to confront the president and control Reconstruction. As the historian David Miller DeWitt has written:

> The Congressional majority came back to their seats . . . flushed with triumph and bent on vengeance. They meant to strip the President of the prerogatives and functions of his office, as far as they could do by statute, and, if he struggled against the process of emasculation, as they had every reason to believe he would, to impeach and remove him out of the way.[99]

When Congress returned to Washington after the midterm elections, it quickly enacted legislation designed to limit presidential power and impose its own design on Reconstruction. The Tenure of Office Act was enacted speedily, in February 1867. The act stripped the president of the power to remove appointed officials from the executive branch without the Senate's approval, thus allowing officials who were responsive to congressional instead of presidential Reconstruction policies to remain in office.

Congress also enacted other measures to establish new Reconstruction policies and procedures, and in the process to further constrain the president's administrative discretion. The new Reconstruction Act, which was passed in the spring of 1867, marked the end of President Johnson's unsuccessful attempt to reconcile North and South. Instead, the act imposed Northern control on the vanquished states of the former Confederacy. It abolished the provisional governments that presidents Lincoln and Johnson had established in some Southern states and divided the South into five military districts, each under the command of a high-ranking military officer. New conditions for the readmission of insurrectionist states to the Union were established, including ratification of the Fourteenth Amendment, which, among other things, granted equal protection of the full privileges and immunities of citizenship to all Americans regardless of race. In addition, Congress barred federal and state government officials who had repudiated their allegiance to the United States during the Civil War from holding any civil or military office in the reconstructed Southern state governments.[100]

A third bill, attached as a rider to an army appropriations bill, deprived President Johnson of any real authority as commander in chief and thus prevented him from controlling how the military implemented the congressionally mandated Reconstruction program. The rider required that all orders to the five military governors be channeled through the general of the army, Ulysses S. Grant. Under this arrangement General Grant, who because of the Tenure of Office Act could not be removed from office by the president without Senate approval, was largely responsible to Congress for carrying out Reconstruction. Concomitantly, Congress barred Johnson from issuing his own orders to either countermand or bypass the general.

Taken together, the Tenure of Office Act, the Reconstruction Act, and the army appropriations rider emasculated the presidency and established congressional control of Reconstruction policy. Johnson believed that the Tenure of Office Act and the army appropriations rider were unconstitutional. Although he vetoed both the Tenure of Office Act and the Reconstruction Act, both vetoes were easily overridden. In all, Congress overrode thirteen of Johnson's fifteen vetoes during the final two years of his presidency, rendering his use of the veto power the least effective of any president in history.[101]

Meanwhile, by early 1867 relations between President Johnson and Secretary of War Edwin M. Stanton had deteriorated beyond repair. According to DeWitt, although the president had never liked or trusted Stanton (Johnson suspected the secretary of underhanded dealings with his adversaries in Congress), he initially had been reluctant to dismiss any of the cabinet members appointed by Lincoln.[102] As the controversy over Reconstruction policy raged between the president and Congress, however, Stanton's support from the Radical Republicans increased and the president's willingness to tolerate him declined. It was Congress's desire to protect the cabinet, and especially Secretary Stanton, from presidential removal that had led it to pass the Tenure of Office Act.[103]

The first moves toward impeachment were made in early 1867. Rep. James M. Ashley, R-Ohio, called for the president's impeachment by charging him, under the rubric of "other high Crimes and Misdemeanors," with usurping congressional power and corruptly using the presidential powers of appointment, pardon, and the veto. Although these general charges were widely recognized as political grievances and not serious abuses of office, Ashley's resolution prompted an inquiry by the House Judiciary Committee. Just before the end of the Thirty-ninth Congress the committee reported that it had reached no conclusion on impeachment.

On March 7, 1867, as the Fortieth Congress convened, Representative Ashley reintroduced his resolution, which was referred again to the Judiciary Committee. On November 25, after a long investigation, the committee reported an impeachment resolution. But on December 6, the House refused, by a resounding vote of 108–57, to impeach Johnson, mostly because many lawmakers did not believe that he had violated any law.[104]

The House Moves to Impeach

Buoyed by the defeat of the impeachment resolution in the House, Johnson moved quickly to remove Secretary Stanton from the cabinet. On December 12, six days after the House vote, the president suspended Stanton. Johnson also convinced General Grant both to accept an interim appointment as secretary of war and to promise that he would remain as secretary even if the Senate supported Stanton, thereby forcing Stanton to take the matter to court. If Stanton did so, Johnson was certain that the Tenure of Office Act would be declared unconstitutional. On January 13, 1868, the Senate, as expected, refused to concur in Stanton's removal, which according to the act (but not the president) meant that Stanton was once again the secretary of war.

At this point Grant broke his promise to President Johnson and vacated the office, which Stanton promptly reoccupied. On February 21, 1868, Johnson directed the army adjutant general, Maj. Gen. Lorenzo Thomas, to assume the duties of the secretary of war until a formal appointment could be made. Thomas presented a letter from the president containing this order, along with one removing Stanton from office, to the secretary at the War Department. Feigning compliance, Stanton asked Thomas for time to gather and remove his personal effects before

leaving. Thomas agreed, then left to spend the evening celebrating his new appointment. As soon as Thomas left, Stanton alerted his supporters in Congress and had a warrant sworn out for the general's arrest for violating the Tenure of Office Act. Thomas was arrested before breakfast the next morning. Released on bond, he returned to the War Department later in the day to confront Stanton and demand that he surrender the office. Stanton, surrounded by several members of Congress, refused and instead ordered Thomas to leave. After some cordial discussion and a round of drinks, Thomas departed and Stanton barricaded himself in his office. On each of the next two days Thomas returned and renewed his claim, but both times he was rebuffed and withdrew.[105] The situation at the War Department was at an impasse.

Congress's response to the Stanton controversy was swift and decisive. When the House met on February 21, 1868, it immediately reopened the question of impeachment. Moderate Republicans and Democrats, who had supported Johnson and voted against impeachment in December 1867 because they thought the charges were too general, now were confronted with what seemed to be incontrovertible evidence of illegal conduct by the president. Johnson's dismissal of Stanton and appointment of Thomas not only violated the Tenure of Office Act, House members believed, but also, under the terms of the act itself, constituted a "high misdemeanor" and therefore an impeachable offense.

The February 21 resolution of impeachment was referred to the Committee on Reconstruction, which was headed by Rep. Thaddeus Stevens of Pennsylvania, a leader of the Radical Republicans. The resolution was reported out of committee the next day with a strong recommendation in favor of impeachment. Two days later, on February 24, 1868, the House adopted the resolution by a vote of 126–47. On March 2 and 3, it approved eleven specific articles of impeachment and appointed seven managers, all of them Republicans, to argue the case against the president at the Senate trial: George S. Boutwell of Massachusetts, Benjamin F. Butler of Massachusetts, James F. Wilson of Iowa, Thomas Williams of Pennsylvania, John A. Bingham of Ohio, John A. Logan of Illinois, and Stevens.

The Senate Trial

The first eight articles of impeachment, which dealt with President Johnson's removal of Secretary of War Stanton, charged the president with intent to violate the Tenure of Office Act and the Constitution of the United States. Article I referred specifically to Johnson's allegedly illegal and unconstitutional attempt to remove Stanton, while the next seven articles concerned various aspects of the president's action, including conspiracy. Article IX contended that Johnson had violated the army appropriations bill by

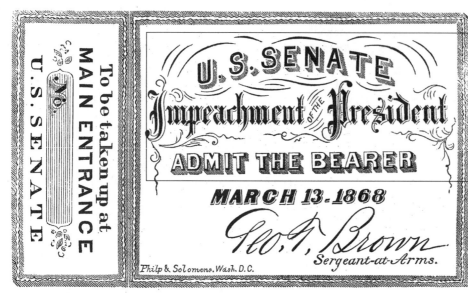

FAC-SIMILE OF TICKET OF ADMISSION TO THE IMPEACHMENT TRIAL.

Admission to the Senate galleries for the March 1868 impeachment trial of President Andrew Johnson required a ticket.

attempting to bypass General Grant and issue an order directly to another general. Finally, Articles X and XI accused the president of seditious libel against Congress in speeches he had made during the 1866 midterm campaign. In those speeches Johnson allegedly had sought to bring Congress into "disgrace, ridicule, hatred, contempt, and reproach" and had questioned the authority and legitimacy of the Thirty-ninth Congress because its membership did not represent all of the states.

The president's lawyers argued his case in the Senate, led by Henry Stanbery, who had resigned as attorney general in order to do so. The defense's case rested on three major points.[106] First, it sought to demonstrate that in removing Secretary Stanton from his cabinet position, the president had acted within his constitutional authority and in accordance with the practice of every president since George Washington. In raising this defense, Stanbery and his colleagues questioned the constitutionality of the Tenure of Office Act. They also argued that violating the act was essential to bringing it before the courts so that its constitutionality could be determined. Thus in firing Stanton, Johnson had upheld his oath to "preserve, protect and defend" the Constitution.

Second, the defense contended that the president had not violated the Tenure of Office Act. The relevant part of the act, Johnson's lawyers pointed out, read as follows:

> That the Secretaries of State, of the Treasury, of War, of the Navy, and of the Interior, the Postmaster-General and the Attorney-General shall hold their offices, respectively, for and during the term of the President by whom they may have been appointed and one month thereafter, subject to removal by and with the advice and consent of the Senate.[107]

Under this provision, the defense claimed, President Johnson was not constrained from removing Stanton because Stanton had been appointed by Lincoln during the late president's first term. At most, Stanton was legally entitled to serve for one month after Lincoln died and Johnson succeeded to the presidency. Thereafter, Stanton and all others like him served at the pleasure of the new president and thus—under the act itself—could be removed without the Senate's approval. By this argument, even if the Tenure of Office Act was constitutional, President Johnson was innocent of having violated it.

Third, the defense argued that, whether the Tenure of Office Act was constitutional or not and had been violated or not, the president personally had done nothing to violate the law, because he had not, in fact, removed Stanton from office. Stanton had remained physically barricaded in his office at the War Department. As for the charges contained in Articles X and XI, Johnson's lawyers dismissed them as mere complaints "that the President made speeches against the Congress," speeches that surely were protected by the First Amendment. Further, the charges were inaccurate: Johnson had attacked "not the entire constitutional body . . . [but] the dominant majority" in Congress.[108]

The Senate trial of Johnson was marred by serious violations of procedural fairness and inappropriate political passion. One of the House managers exhorted the Senate to be "bound by no law" because in this matter it was a law unto itself.[109] The defense was denied adequate time to prepare its case, important evidence that it tried to present was ruled inadmissible, and the normal rights and courtesies accorded to the defense were denied.[110]

After weeks of argument and testimony the Senate took a test vote on Article XI, the article Johnson's foes thought was most likely to attract a two-thirds majority. The Senate had fifty-four members, with the votes of thirty-six needed for conviction and removal. Twelve senators—nine Democrats and three conservative Republicans—were certain to support the president. Equally certain were the guilty votes of thirty of the remaining senators. That left twelve senators, all of them Republicans, whose opinions were unknown. Many of these undecided senators had serious reservations about at least one consequence of removing Johnson: In the absence of a vice president and in accordance with the 1792 succession law, Senate President Pro Tempore Benjamin Wade of Ohio, perhaps the most radical of the Radical Republicans, would become president.[111] The vote to remove one president was, in effect, a vote to choose another.

The partisan pressure that was placed on the undecided senators was unprecedented and unremitting. According to DeWitt, once the trial was over and the Senate went into closed session to deliberate its verdict, Republican leaders

> went into caucus and organized a far-reaching combination to coerce the suspected judges into submission to their party's decree. . . . The [undecided senators] were threatened in the party press; their constituents were stirred up to threaten them from home; letters were sent to them from all quarters filled with threats of political ostracism and even of assassination, in the event of their treason.[112]

On May 16, 1868, the Senate voted on Article XI. Seven of the twelve undecided senators joined Johnson's twelve supporters, giving him nineteen votes and his opponents thirty-five—one vote shy of the two-thirds majority needed to convict. Identical votes on Articles II and III, taken on May 26, demonstrated that the impeachment effort had failed. The Senate abandoned the remaining articles and adjourned, thus ending the Johnson impeachment case abruptly.

Epilogue

Although the political passions that had prompted the effort to impeach and remove Andrew Johnson from the presidency had been thwarted by the Senate, they continued to cloud the remainder of his term. Within months the president was repudiated by the Republican national convention, which chose Grant as its presidential candidate in the 1868 election. After finishing out his term as perhaps the lamest of lame-duck presidents, Johnson returned to Tennessee, where eventually he succeeded in making a political comeback. In 1874 Johnson was elected as a U.S. senator, and upon his return to the Senate he was greeted by the applause of the gallery and the congratulations of his colleagues.[113] He died on July 31, 1875, five months into his Senate term.

The seven undecided Republican senators who in the end voted for Johnson were vilified by both the party press and their constituents and were ostracized by their Senate colleagues. Two left politics because of illness, and two retired at the end of their term.

As for the Tenure of Office Act, it was amended, at President Grant's insistence, to be somewhat less constraining of the president's removal power. In 1885 the act was repealed.[114]

The Case of Richard Nixon

Not until Congress tried to impeach President Richard Nixon did it seriously consider again removing a president from office. The move toward impeachment stemmed mostly from the revelations of official misconduct, corruption, and abuse of power that arose in the aftermath of the June 17, 1972, burglary of the Democratic National Headquarters in the Watergate building in Washington, D.C. The burglary was perpetrated by individuals associated with the Committee to Re-elect the President and later was covered up by President Nixon and members of his White House staff.

It took the "Saturday Night Massacre" of October 20, 1973, when President Nixon fired Archibald Cox, the special prosecutor appointed by the attorney general to investigate the break-in and its cover-up, to spur the House of Representatives to take up the question of impeachment. The event that made impeachment and removal certain, had Nixon chosen to fight on, was a July 24, 1974, Supreme Court decision ordering the president to surrender certain subpoenaed tape recordings of White House conversations that took place after the Watergate break-in. These recordings, especially the tape of a June 23, 1972, conversation in which Nixon had plotted to obstruct justice, provided Congress with the "smoking gun" that some members had been demanding—incontrovertible proof that the president had participated in the Watergate cover-up. On August 8, 1974, President Nixon announced his resignation, effective at noon the next day.

Political Situation

Richard Nixon staged a remarkable political comeback in winning his second bid for the presidency in 1968. Yet he came to office at a time when the country was seriously divided over the Vietnam War and Congress was controlled by the opposition Democratic Party. During much of his first term President Nixon sought to build a record that would help him win a solid reelection. In 1972 he won such a victory, carrying forty-nine states and 60.7 percent of the popular vote. As soon would be revealed, however, Nixon and his supporters resorted to extraordinary and illegal measures in waging the campaign that helped to secure his victory. One of these measures was the break-in at the Democratic National Headquarters by five agents associated with Nixon's re-election committee, which was followed in turn by ongoing attempts by Nixon and his staff to cover up the administration's involvement in the break-in. Thus, in seeking the landslide reelection that he felt he needed to govern boldly and effectively, Nixon destroyed the legitimacy of his presidency.

Watergate Investigations

During the first year of Nixon's second term, the lid began to come off Watergate and other administration scandals. By early 1973 a series of investigative articles begun the previous fall by *Washington Post* reporters Bob Woodward and Carl Bernstein was focusing public attention on the origins and aftermath of the Watergate burglary. It soon was revealed at the confirmation hearings for L. Patrick Gray, the new director of the Federal Bureau of Investigation, that presidential counsel John W. Dean III had been inappropriately involved in an FBI investigation of the Watergate break-in. This revelation turned the corruption and cover-up trail toward the White House. Although presidential press secretary Ronald L. Ziegler initially did his best to dismiss the Watergate incident as a "third-rate burglary attempt," the hunt for evidence of administration involvement was on.[115]

Pursuing the hints of a White House cover-up that had emerged during Gray's confirmation hearing, the Senate launched its own inquiry into Watergate. On February 7, 1973, the Senate voted 77–0 to establish the Select Committee on Presidential Campaign Activities. The committee was charged to investigate "the extent . . . to which illegal, improper or unethical activities" occurred in the 1972 election. It instantly became known as the Senate Watergate committee.

During the first phase of the Watergate committee's hearings numerous employees of the Committee to Re-elect the President and former White House aides testified. The hearings revealed the existence of a special White House investigative unit called the "Plumbers." The Plumbers used unorthodox and sometimes illegal methods to "plug leaks" in the administration—that is, to keep unauthorized information from being passed on to reporters and members of Congress. In late June 1973 former White House counsel Dean charged that Nixon himself had been actively engaged in the cover-up and that Nixon's two closest aides, H. R. Haldeman and John D. Ehrlichman, and several other administration officials, including Attorney General John Mitchell, had been involved in planning the break-in or covering it up, or both. Nixon had fired Dean and, under intense political pressure, had requested the resignations of Haldeman and Ehrlichman on April 30, 1973. Haldeman, Ehrlichman, and Mitchell also testified before the Watergate committee, but none of them confirmed Dean's charges of wrongdoing by the president. In speeches and press conferences Nixon proclaimed his innocence.

Throughout the summer of 1973 the nationally televised Watergate hearings brought the sordid details of administration misconduct to the American people, whose support for the president began to erode. The Watergate committee's live audience in the committee room made its feelings about each day's testimony known, which influenced the television audience. For example, committee chair Samuel J. Ervin Jr., a courtly but prosecutorial Democratic senator from North Carolina, received a standing ovation whenever he entered the hearing room, and the crowd's reaction to the testimony of many witnesses was vocally anti-Nixon. By midsummer the word "Watergate" had come to encompass not just a range of illegal activities, but everything else that seemed wrong about the president and about politics.[116]

The Senate Watergate hearings also damaged the presidency and sparked efforts to reclaim congressional power. In the midst of the hearings Congress passed the War Powers Resolution of 1973, which was designed to limit the president's ability to exercise war-making powers unilaterally. When President Nixon vetoed the bill, Congress overrode the veto. In 1974 Congress passed (again over Nixon's veto) the Budget and Impoundment Control Act, which reasserted congressional influence in the budgetary process.

For a time the Watergate hearings seemed likely to bog down in a morass of unresolvable charges and countercharges about who was lying—Dean or the president. The president contended that he had never approved clemency offers to the Watergate burglars, that he was unaware of payoffs to them, and that he had played no part in any attempted cover-up. Then, in mid-July 1973, came the surprise revelation by former White House aide Alexander P. Butterfield that in 1971 Nixon had installed an elaborate, voice-activated audiotaping system in several presidential offices, including the Oval Office. Suddenly the way to determine who was telling the truth seemed clear: subpoena the tapes.[117] But the president refused to hand over any tapes to the committee, citing his executive privilege to withhold information from Congress and the courts that would jeopardize either the national security or the confidentiality of executive communications.

Meanwhile, Special Prosecutor Cox decided to seek the tapes to use in his investigation of possible criminal wrongdoing by various White House aides and administration officials. Late in August 1973 Judge John Sirica of the U.S. District Court for Washington, D.C., ruled that the president must turn over the tapes that the special prosecutor had subpoenaed. The administration appealed the decision to the U.S. Court of Appeals, also in Washington. The Senate committee was less successful in its own legal effort to get the tapes.

In October Vice President Spiro T. Agnew, although untouched by the Watergate scandal, added to the travails of the Nixon administration. Under investigation for taking bribes while serving as Baltimore County executive, governor of Maryland, and even as vice president, Agnew resigned on October 10, 1973. Agnew's resignation was part of a plea bargain that required him to resign and plead nolo contendere to a charge of income tax evasion in return for no prison sentence. Agnew maintained that he had resigned because "the American people deserve to have a vice president who commands their unimpaired confidence and trust" and because he did not want to "subject the country to a further agonizing period of months without an unclouded successor to the presidency."[118]

On October 12, two days after Agnew resigned, President Nixon nominated House Republican leader Gerald Ford to fill the vacant vice presidency under the provisions of the Twenty-fifth Amendment, which had become part of the Constitution only six years earlier. Ford's confirmation hearings moved deliberately through both Democratic-controlled houses of Congress—he was approved by the Senate on November 29 and by the House on December 6, 1973.

Ford's confirmation process was shadowed by the widely shared belief that a president, not just a vice president, was being chosen. When Ford became vice president, he replaced House speaker Carl Albert of Oklahoma as first in the line of presidential succession. Instead of a decision to remove Nixon that would result in replacing a Republican with a Democrat in the White House, it would replace one Republican with another. This made it harder for opponents of impeachment to brand the move as a partisan takeover by the party that had lost the 1972 election.

On the same day that Ford's nomination was announced, the appeals court, by a 5–2 vote, upheld Judge Sirica's earlier ruling that President Nixon must surrender the Watergate-related tapes to the special prosecutor. The president then offered Cox a compromise: transcripts of certain tapes in return for Cox's promise not to subpoena additional tapes or documents. Cox rejected the offer. Arguing that the special prosecutor had now exceeded his authority by deliberately challenging the president, Nixon decided to fire him. Attorney General Elliot L. Richardson, whom Nixon directed to carry out the firing, refused, reminding the president that he had publicly pledged to uphold the independence of the special prosecutor. Richardson then resigned, as did Deputy Attorney General William Ruckelshaus, who also refused to carry out the president's order. Finally, the third-ranking member of the Justice Department, Solicitor General Robert H. Bork, acting as attorney general, fired Cox.

This sequence of events, which instantly became known as the "Saturday Night Massacre," prompted such a firestorm of swift and overwhelming adverse public reaction that House Democratic leaders decided to file impeachment resolutions against the president. The resolutions were referred to the House Judiciary Committee. For his part, Nixon succumbed to public pressure by naming a new special prosecutor, Leon Jaworski, and promising him the very independence that he had denied to Cox. Jaworksi promptly demanded that Nixon turn over the subpoenaed tapes as soon as the appeals process had run its course.

The Move to Impeach

In February 1974, the House Judiciary Committee began holding hearings on possible impeachment charges against President Nixon. Conscious of the highly politicized Johnson impeachment proceedings of the 1860s, the committee took particular care to dampen partisanship and proceed in as evenhanded a manner as possible. Meanwhile, Special Prosecutor Jaworski filed criminal charges against a host of Nixon administration officials. In March former attorney general Mitchell and several former White House aides, including Haldeman and Ehrlichman, were indicted for conspiracy to cover up the Watergate burglary. The president was named as an unindicted coconspirator. In April the Internal Revenue Service (IRS) reported that Nixon owed nearly half a million dollars in back taxes and interest on income tax returns he had improperly filed during his first term as president. The issue of possibly illegal conduct was being brought very close to President Nixon himself. But as long as he was serving as chief executive, most legal scholars and officials believed, the president could not be prosecuted in a criminal court.

In May 1974, the House Judiciary Committee began closed hearings to consider possible grounds for impeachment. Its subpoenas for White House tapes and documents carried more legal weight than the Senate Watergate committee's because the House was engaged in the fundamental constitutional process of impeachment. In response to the Judiciary Committee's subpoenas, the special prosecutor's subpoenas, and, more generally, intense public pressure, Nixon released more than thirteen hundred pages of edited transcripts of White House tape recordings. But he retained the actual tapes and other materials under the claim of executive privilege. Simultaneously, Special Prosecutor Jaworski, citing an urgent need for a prompt and final judicial ruling on the tapes and the executive privilege issue, asked the Supreme Court to take up the controversy before it recessed for the summer. As the Supreme Court hearing proceeded, President Nixon repeatedly implied in private that he might not abide by an adverse ruling, especially if the justices were not unanimous.

On July 24, 1974, Chief Justice Warren E. Burger announced an 8–0 decision of the Court in the case of *United States v. Nixon.* The decision acknowledged for the first time in history that constitutional underpinnings existed for a presidential claim of executive privilege. But the Court also found that the privilege was superseded in the Watergate case by the "demands of due process of law in the fair administration of criminal justice." [119] The president responded through his attorney, James D. St. Clair, that he would turn over the tapes.

On the same day that the Supreme Court announced its decision, the House Judiciary Committee began its debates on the adoption of articles of impeachment against the president. As each member of the committee made an opening statement, it became apparent that, even without the evidence of the soon-to-be-released tapes, seven of the seventeen Republican members were inclined to vote for impeachment, as were all twenty-one of the committee's Democrats—an overwhelming majority.

Within a week the Judiciary Committee approved three articles of impeachment. Article I charged the president with obstructing justice, which violated his oath to faithfully execute the office of president and to take care that the laws be faithfully executed. These charges referred primarily to deeds undertaken in conjunction with the Watergate cover-up and included: withholding evidence, condoning perjury, approving the payment of "hush money" to the Watergate burglars, interfering with lawful investigations, and making false and misleading statements to investigators and to the public. Article II contended that in conducting the cover-up the president had abused executive authority and misused the resources of various executive agencies, including the FBI, the IRS, and the Central Intelligence Agency (CIA). Finally, Article III charged the president with contempt of Congress for, among other things, failing to honor subpoenas issued by the Judiciary Committee.

On July 27, 1974, Article I was approved by the Judiciary Committee by a vote of 27–11, Article II by 28–10, and Article III, more narrowly, by 21–17. The generally bipartisan character of the committee's votes on Articles I and II belied the White House's contention that the inquiry was a Democratic "witch hunt" conducted by a "kangaroo court" that was trying to overturn the results of the 1972 election. The vote also served notice that the full House probably would adopt most of the impeachment charges overwhelmingly and send them to the Senate for trial.

Each of the impeachment articles included elements of both indictable criminal offenses and serious abuses of the public trust "to the manifest injury of the people of the United States." Two additional articles that were debated and rejected confirmed the compound nature of what the committee considered to be an impeachable offense. An article that faulted the president for secretly expanding the Vietnam War into Cambodia was rejected. Clearly, the committee regarded issues of war making as political questions with substantial partisan overtones, not as impeachable offenses. Conversely, a second rejected article, which concerned the president's admission of income tax evasion, also failed to satisfy the dual definition of an impeachable offense. Although an indictable crime, income tax evasion was not a serious abuse of official power.

On August 5, 1974, President Nixon, in compliance with the Supreme Court ruling, turned over the tapes that had been subpoenaed by Special Prosecutor Jaworski. Included in these recordings was the so-called smoking gun tape of June 23, 1972, made just six days after the Watergate break-in. In it White House chief of staff Haldeman told Nixon that campaign manager John Mitchell had approved the illegal operation against the Democratic National Headquarters. Nixon then ordered that the FBI be told not to look any further into the case at the request of the CIA. Public release of this taped conversation made it clear that, contrary to the president's repeated public statements, he had been involved in the cover-up virtually from the beginning. One measure of how much the release of the tapes damaged Nixon's case in Congress was that all ten of his Republican supporters on the Judiciary Committee shifted from opposition to support of impeachment. His defenders had argued that the case against the president lacked conclusive evidence. The released tapes provided just such evidence.

A President Resigns

As support for President Nixon dwindled in Congress, he asked congressional Republican leaders to meet with him at the White House to assess the situation. House Minority Leader John J. Rhodes of Arizona and Senate Minority Leader Hugh Scott of Pennsylvania painted a gloomy but realistic picture: Nixon had no more than ten supporters in the House and fifteen in the Senate.

On Wednesday night, August 7, Nixon decided to resign. On Thursday the public was told that the president would meet with congressional leaders that evening and then address the nation. In his televised speech Nixon announced his resignation, effective noon the following day. He made no reference to the impending impeachment proceedings. Instead, he attributed his decision to the lack of a "strong enough political base in Congress to justify continuing" in office.

Although Nixon's resignation obviated the need for an impeachment, the process nonetheless had to be brought to a formal conclusion. Furthermore, the work of the House Judiciary Committee had historical and precedential value that needed to be preserved for future generations that might face similar crises. Thus the committee persevered in the preparation of its report, explaining carefully the basis for its decision to recommend impeachment. The 528-page report was accepted by a 412–3 vote of the House. As Rep. Charles B. Rangel, D-N.Y., noted, the House's acceptance of the report made "it abundantly clear ... that he [Nixon] committed impeachable crimes and that on the available evidence he would have been impeached by the House of Representatives." [120] Little doubt exists that the president also would have been convicted and removed by the Senate.

On the morning of August 9, 1974, Nixon bade an emotional farewell to his cabinet and staff and left the White House for his residence in San Clemente, California. Nixon's terse letter of resignation reached the appropriate official— Secretary of State Henry A. Kissinger—shortly after 11:30 the same morning. [121] Less than thirty minutes later, at noon, Vice President Gerald Ford was sworn in as the thirty-eighth president of the United States.

With the near certainty of a House vote for impeachment, President Richard Nixon announces his resignation in an emotional television address on August 8, 1974. His wife, Pat, and daughter, Tricia, are at right.

Ford's second far-reaching act as president was to grant former president Nixon a "full, free and absolute pardon . . . for all offenses against the United States which he . . . has committed or may have committed." Although Ford offered the pardon on September 8, 1974, in the hope of ending the bitter and divisive national debate that had raged for the past year and a half, public and congressional reaction was overwhelmingly negative, ending the new president's brief "honeymoon" period. Critics argued that to pardon Nixon before he was indicted, tried, and convicted was to short-circuit the judicial process, and the House Judiciary Committee's Subcommittee on Criminal Justice held hearings to investigate why the pardon was granted. In an unprecedented appearance Ford became the first incumbent president in history to testify formally before a congressional committee. He vigorously denied that he had made any secret arrangement with Nixon to grant a pardon in exchange for his resignation.

By 1999, twenty-five years after the Nixon pardon, polls indicated that most Americans agreed that Ford had done the right thing under the circumstances. But at the time, the pardon tainted Ford and his administration with suspicions of deception and political corruption. Moreover, the public reaction to the pardon, along with the time-consuming Rockefeller confirmation battle, distracted the new president from his efforts to assume control of the government quickly. During the remaining two years of his presidency, Ford found that strong differences between Congress and the executive persisted. When he changed his mind about seeking the 1976 Republican presidential nomination, Ford confronted serious opposition within his own party. His liabilities in seeking the nomination of his increasingly conservative party included his moderate political approach to most issues and the perception of him as a caretaker president who had never in his long political career been regarded as "presidential timber." Strongly challenged for the nomination by former California governor Ronald Reagan, a hero to Republican conservatives, Ford prevailed only narrowly. In the general election against Democrat Jimmy Carter, Ford was burdened by the disrepute that Nixon had brought to the Republican Party and by his own modest record of accomplishment as president. Although the elec-

The new president declared to a waiting nation, "Our long national nightmare is over. Our Constitution works." Congress and the American people rallied to Ford's support. Because Ford had been well liked as a member of Congress and well respected for his conduct of the vice presidency, it was widely hoped that relations between the executive and the legislature would improve. Addressing a joint session of Congress, Ford called for an "era of good feeling" and expressed confidence that Congress would be both his "working partner" and his "constructive critic."

President Ford acted quickly to secure the line of succession by nominating former New York governor Nelson A. Rockefeller as vice president, who earlier in his career had unsuccessfully sought the Republican nomination for president two times and twice turned down vice-presidential nominations. Despite the initially favorable reaction to his nomination, Rockefeller's substantial personal wealth generated considerable controversy and concern during the confirmation process. In four months of grueling congressional hearings, senators and representatives questioned Rockefeller's practice of making loans and gifts to former members of his New York State administration. Eventually, Rockefeller was confirmed and, on December 19, 1974, was sworn in as vice president. For the first time in history both the president and the vice president were appointed, not elected, officials, chosen under the provisions of the recently enacted Twenty-fifth Amendment.

tion was close, Ford became the first incumbent president since Herbert Hoover in 1932 to be defeated for reelection.

The Clinton Impeachment

President Bill Clinton was impeached by the House in 1998 and acquitted by the Senate in 1999 of charges that he committed perjury and obstructed justice in an effort to cover up his relationship with a young White House intern, Monica Lewinsky. Clinton was never in any real danger of being removed from office, in part because his job approval rating in public opinion polls remained high. But the historical record will forever note prominently the president's adamant denials of wrongdoing; his grudging apologies; and, finally, on his last full day in office, his admission that he had lied under oath.

The Scandal Unfolds

The Lewinsky scandal was pursued by Kenneth W. Starr, who had been appointed as independent counsel in August 1994 to investigate Clinton and his wife, Hillary Rodham Clinton, in connection with their involvement in a complicated Arkansas land deal known as Whitewater. A former solicitor general with close ties to conservative Republicans, Starr soon expanded his operation to look into several other events: the abrupt firing of White House Travel Office personnel in 1993; the subsequent suicide of Vincent W. Foster Jr., the close friend and aide of the first family who played a role in the firings; and administration requests in 1993 and 1994 for hundreds of confidential FBI files, including those of former Republican White House officials.

Clinton was also the defendant in a sexual harassment suit brought against him in February 1994 by Paula Corbin Jones. Jones had accused the president of requesting oral sex from her in a Little Rock hotel room when he was governor of Arkansas and she was a low-level state employee. Clinton's attorneys had fought off the case until May 1997, when the Supreme Court ruled in the case of *Clinton v. Jones* that a sitting president is not immune to a civil suit for a personal action that allegedly occurred before he took office.[122] Hoping to demonstrate at the trial that Clinton's alleged conduct with Jones was part of an established pattern of sexual harassment, Jones's attorneys compiled a list of women whose names had been linked publicly and privately with Clinton's over the years. One name on that list was Monica Lewinsky.

Lewinsky filed a sworn affidavit on January 7, 1998, in which she denied ever having sexual relations with Clinton. Lewinsky, however, had told several friends about her relationship with the president while it was taking place. Their encounters had begun in November 1995, when Lewinsky was twenty-two and working in the White House Legislative Affairs Office, and continued sporadically through 1996 and early 1997. One of Lewinsky's confidantes was Linda R. Tripp, a former White House employee whom Lewinsky had met at the Pentagon, where they both worked after leaving the White House. Unknown to Lewinsky, Tripp had taped several conversations in which Lewinsky described her sexual relations with Clinton and said that Clinton had urged her to lie about their relationship. Lewinsky was recorded urging Tripp, herself a witness in the Jones case, to lie to the court about her knowledge of Lewinsky's affair with the president.

Starr's investigation and the Jones case became linked when Tripp turned the tapes over to the independent counsel's office on January 12, 1998. Tripp later agreed to wear a body-wire recorder during the January 16 meeting that she had arranged with Lewinsky at a suburban Virginia hotel. With FBI agents monitoring the conversation, Tripp got Lewinsky to say once again that the president had urged her to lie about their relationship and to ask Tripp to lie about it.

Later the same day, prosecutors from Starr's office confronted Lewinsky with the tapes and sought her cooperation in their investigation of the president. Starr also used the tapes to persuade Attorney General Janet Reno to recommend to the three-judge special division that oversaw the jurisdiction of independent counsels that Starr be permitted to investigate the Lewinsky affair. The judges granted Starr the permission he sought.

Unaware that Starr had confronted Lewinsky, President Clinton told Jones's attorneys in a sworn deposition on January 17 that he had never had sexual relations with Lewinsky—a denial that he repeated publicly after the *Washington Post* broke the news of the alleged affair and the president's possible perjury on July 21. On January 26, the day before he was scheduled to give the annual State of the Union address, Clinton looked directly into the television cameras, wagged his finger, and said, "I want to say one thing to the American people. I want you to listen to me. I'm going to say this again. I did not have sexual relations with that woman, Miss Lewinsky. I never told anyone to lie. Not a single time. Never. These allegations are false."

The Clintons also mounted a rhetorical counterattack against Starr. Appearing on NBC's *Today* show, first lady Hillary Clinton referred to the independent counsel as a "politically motivated prosecutor" allied with "right-wing opponents of my husband." At an April 30 news conference the president said that he believed it was obvious to Americans that the Starr investigation was "a hard, well-financed, vigorous effort over a long period of time" to discredit him by any means possible.

Throughout the spring and summer Starr called a steady stream of Clinton's aides and Lewinsky's friends before a federal grand jury in Washington. Several White House efforts to block Starr from taking testimony from administration officials failed when federal courts rejected claims of executive privilege and attorney-client privilege.

Starr subpoenaed Clinton himself on July 17, 1998. It was the first time a sitting president had been subpoenaed to appear before a federal grand jury. Clinton's lawyers immediately began stalling for time, but on July 29 Clinton agreed to testify voluntarily. His decision came a day after Starr and Lewinsky concluded months of negotiations on a deal granting her immunity in return for her grand jury testimony.

Starr then withdrew his subpoena of Clinton, thus averting any potential clash over whether a sitting president could be forced to testify. In another unprecedented move, Clinton also agreed to a blood test, which determined that his DNA matched that of semen stains left on a blue dress that Lewinsky wore at one of their encounters. Appearing before the grand jury on August 6, Lewinsky acknowledged that she and the president had had a sexual relationship but insisted that he had never told her to lie about it under oath.

Clinton's turn before the grand jury came on August 17, when he testified from the White House Map Room on closed-circuit television. Previous presidents had given sworn testimony in legal proceedings, but Clinton was the first to give evidence to a grand jury investigating his own alleged criminal conduct. Clinton was questioned for four hours by attorneys from the independent counsel's office; the president's private attorney David E. Kendall was also present. The grand jurors watched Clinton testify on two large television screens that had been set up in a nearby federal courthouse. Jurors were able to call in with questions, which were then relayed to the president.

After giving his grand jury testimony on August 17, Clinton appeared on national television that evening and admitted to the American people that he had misled them. "I did have a relationship with Miss Lewinsky that was not appropriate. In fact it was wrong," the president said. But Clinton denied that he had done anything illegal, and he lashed out at Starr for pursuing a politically motivated investigation into what were essentially private matters.

Any hope in the White House that a confrontation with Congress over Clinton's misconduct could be avoided was dashed on September 9, 1998, when Starr delivered a report to Congress containing what he described as "substantial and credible evidence" that the president had committed impeachable offenses in trying to cover up his relationship with Lewinsky.[123] The eleven charges Starr outlined included perjury, obstruction of justice, witness tampering, and abuse of power. Nearly overshadowing these charges, however, were Starr's graphic and detailed descriptions of the sexual encounters between Clinton and Lewinsky. The explicit descriptions were regrettable but necessary, Starr said, to show that the president had lied under oath when he said that he had never had sexual relations with Lewinsky.

Although Democratic and Republican congressional leaders had pledged to consider any charges Starr might level in a spirit of bipartisanship, that resolve evaporated in the debate about when and how to release the report. Republican leaders announced on September 10 that they would post the report on the Internet the next day, before anyone in Congress had an opportunity to read it. Although Democrats argued that the president's attorneys should be given at least forty-eight hours to review the report before it was made public, the Republican-controlled House voted 363–63 to release it immediately.

The referral, as it was formally called—or Starr Report, as it was more commonly known—leveled charges against Clinton in four areas.

First, the referral said that Clinton had committed perjury by lying numerous times, both in his civil deposition in the Jones sexual harassment case and in his August 17 grand jury testimony, about the nature of his relationship with Lewinsky and his efforts to conceal it. In his deposition Clinton had denied that he had ever had a sexual relationship with Lewinsky. In his grand jury testimony, he had said that his statements in the Jones case deposition, although misleading, were accurate because he had not engaged in sex with Lewinsky as defined by Jones's lawyers. In an attempt to show that Clinton had lied, the Starr Report detailed several encounters between Clinton and Lewinsky that occurred between November 15, 1995, and December 28, 1997.

According to Lewinsky's testimony, the two never had sexual intercourse, but she performed oral sex on the president nine times, and he touched her breasts and genitals during some of these encounters. Although a narrow interpretation of the definition used by the Jones lawyers might not cover oral sex, some thought Clinton's fondling of Lewinsky fell within the scope of the definition. The referral further charged that Clinton was untruthful during his deposition when he said he could not recall if he had ever been alone with Lewinsky or exchanged gifts with her.

Second, the referral said Clinton had obstructed justice by urging Lewinsky to lie under oath in the Jones case about their relationship. Lewinsky originally had signed an affidavit denying her affair with Clinton, but she changed her story when she received a grant of immunity from Starr. According to the referral, Clinton and Lewinsky also had agreed to conceal gifts they had given each other instead of turning them over to lawyers in the Jones suit. The referral further said that Clinton attempted to impede investigators by helping Lewinsky find a job in New York to forestall her from testifying truthfully in the Jones case.

Third, the report charged that Clinton had improperly tampered with a potential witness by attempting to influence his secretary, Betty Currie, to testify falsely before the grand jury, as well as by lying to White House staff members, knowing that they would probably repeat those lies in good faith in their subsequent grand jury testimony.

Finally, the Starr Report said that Clinton's actions in the Lewinsky matter were inconsistent with his constitutional duty to faithfully execute the laws. Specifically, the president had promised to cooperate with the investigation but then refused six invitations to testify voluntarily; he had deliberately misled his senior aides, his cabinet, and the American people about the affair; and he had asserted executive privilege "all as part of an effort to hinder, impede and deflect possibly inquiry by the Congress of the United States."

In their rebuttal, Clinton's attorneys declared that, as a matter of law, Clinton had not done any of the things of which he was accused. Regarding the perjury charges, the rebuttal said that Starr had not shown that Clinton had willfully misinterpreted the definition of sex presented by Jones's attorneys at his deposition. The rebuttal also said that Clinton had acknowledged in his deposition that he and Lewinsky had exchanged gifts and denied that he had ever tried to conceal the gifts. Nor did Clinton ever try to get Lewinsky a job for the purpose of influencing her testimony, the rebuttal said. Clinton's attorneys quoted the Starr Report's own acknowledgment that there was "no evidence" of any "arrangement . . . explicitly spelled out."

Clinton's attorneys were blistering in their remarks about Starr's motives. "Any fair reader of the Referral," they argued, "will easily discern that many of the lurid allegations . . . have no justification at all, even in terms of any OIC [Office of Independent Counsel] legal theory. . . . They are simply part of a hit-and-run smear campaign and their inclusion says volumes about the OIC's tactics and objectives." [124]

Public reaction to the referral was immediate. By late afternoon on September 11 people across the country were reading the Starr Report on the Internet. Some television reporters were visibly embarrassed by the explicit sexual descriptions they were reporting. People expressed a range of emotions, from embarrassment to outrage. Some of the outrage was aimed at the president; some was directed at Starr and Republican members of Congress.

On Capitol Hill, legislators in both parties expressed anger, shock, and deep disappointment with the president's behavior as described in the report. The two Democratic leaders of Congress, House Minority Leader Richard A. Gephardt of Missouri and Senate Minority Leader Tom Daschle of South Dakota, asked Congress to move quickly to determine whether and how to punish Clinton. Some legislators had already begun to explore the possibility of censuring and perhaps fining the president for his misconduct as an alternative to impeachment.

Republican leaders, however, were eager to press ahead with a full-scale impeachment inquiry that examined not only Clinton's conduct with Lewinsky, but also several other allegations against the president. Clinton had long been the object of political animosity from many Republican legislators, in part because he had co-opted several popular items from their political agenda and then become the first Democratic president since Franklin Roosevelt to win reelection. Moreover, some Republicans had not forgiven the Democrats for mounting a lengthy investigation of Ronald Reagan and several White House aides for their actions in the Iran-contra scandal in the 1980s.

The House Impeaches

Even before the formal debate on impeachment began, the partisan gulf on the issue was evident. By a party-line vote, the House Judiciary Committee decided on September 21 to release the videotape of Clinton's August 17 grand jury testimony. The tape was immediately aired on all the major television networks. As he had in his deposition in the Jones case, Clinton gave narrow, literal, and legalistic answers to most of the questions. He began with a prepared statement in which he acknowledged "inappropriate intimate contact" with Lewinsky but said that it "did not constitute sexual relations as I understood that term to be defined" at his January deposition. He refused to provide any specific details about the intimate contact, and he avoided directly answering many questions. "It depends on what the meaning of the word 'is' is," he said in response to a question about his January denial that he was having an affair with Lewinsky. "If . . . 'is' means is and never has been . . . that is one thing. If it means there is none, that was a completely true statement."

But if the Republicans had hoped to embarrass Clinton further with the videotape, the move backfired. Polls taken the day after the tape was released showed that although a majority of those surveyed believed that Clinton had lied under oath, the president's approval rating had gone up six to nine percentage points since the tape was aired. Moreover, according to a *New York Times*/CBS News Poll conducted September 22–23, 65 percent of those surveyed did not want Congress to hold impeachment hearings and 78 percent said Starr's investigation was not worth the time and money it was taking.

Nevertheless, the House Judiciary Committee began its formal public deliberations on impeachment on October 8. A round of opening statements from each of the panel's twenty-one Republicans and sixteen Democrats laid out the arguments for and against impeachment that would be heard repeatedly in the months to come. Republicans argued that Clinton had committed perjury and obstructed justice in dereliction of his duty as president to take care that the laws be faithfully executed. Clinton's alleged lies under oath constituted "an assault on the rule of the law" that threatened "our system of government," argued Rep. Henry Hyde, R-Ill., the committee chair.

Democrats countered that Clinton's efforts to cover up his actions were the understandable reactions of a man trying to avoid personal and public embarrassment over a tawdry affair and that they did not rise to the level of impeachable "high Crimes and Misdemeanors." Rep. John Conyers Jr. of Michigan, the ranking Democratic member of the Judiciary Committee, summarized his party's argument: "Under our constitutional system of government, if the president misbehaves in a way that does not impact on his official duties, the remedy still lies in the voting booth and not in a legislative takeover of the executive branch." After hearing these opening statements, the committee put the inquiry on the back burner as Congress rushed to complete an omnibus appropriations bill before going home to campaign in the 1998 midterm election.

When the committee returned to Washington after the elections, the political situation surrounding impeachment had changed dramatically. Instead of gaining twenty House seats, as they had hoped, the Republicans lost five seats, reducing their majority to only six in the 106th Congress. Speaker Newt Gingrich of Georgia, who had been credited with helping the Republicans win control of Congress in 1994, was blamed for taking positions unpopular with the voters, including his pursuit of impeachment. Instead of facing a certain challenge to his leadership from within the Republican Party, Gingrich announced that he was resigning as Speaker and leaving the House.

The Judiciary Committee seemed unfocused, even erratic, as committee Republicans struggled with competing pressures from the general public to abandon impeachment and from Republican activists in their districts to pursue it. In an effort to avoid a soap opera–like atmosphere, the committee sought no testimony from Lewinsky and others with firsthand information about the president's behavior. At the same time, it voted to extend its inquiry into campaign finance issues and other allegations of sexual misconduct against Clinton. Although the committee voted to subpoena witnesses in these side inquiries, it never called them.

The inquiry's public hearings ranged from thoughtful discourses by judges and scholars on the definition of impeachable offenses to testimony from two convicted perjurers whose cases involved deceptions related to sex. But the most significant event in the committee's deliberations, and certainly the most damaging to Clinton, was the president's response to a series of eighty-one questions posed by the committee. Clinton's responses, carefully phrased in the same legalese that had marked his grand jury testimony, disappointed many legislators, including moderate Democrats, who wanted the president to admit openly that he had lied under oath, even though such an admission might place him in greater jeopardy of criminal prosecution after he left the White House.

The inquiry ended December 11–12 when the Judiciary Committee approved four articles of impeachment against Clinton, charging him with two counts of perjury, obstruction of justice, and abuse of power. *(See "Articles of Impeachment against Clinton," p. 1805, in Reference Materials, Vol. II.).*

On December 12 the committee also voted down a resolution offered by the Democrats that would have censured Clinton for "making false statements" as an alternative to impeachment. The proposed censure resolution said that by his conduct Clinton had "violated the trust of the people, lessened their esteem for the office of the President, and dishonored the presidency." All twenty-one Republicans on the committee and one Democrat, Robert C. Scott of Virginia, voted against censure. Many other Republicans who had been known to favor censure then announced that they would vote to impeach.

Republican leaders in the House (and during the subsequent trial, the Senate) objected to a censure resolution on two principal grounds. First, they argued that the Constitution did not provide for congressional censure of the president. Unpleasant and tortuous as it might be, impeachment was the only route constitutionally open to Congress in cases of extreme presidential misbehavior. Second, and perhaps more important in political terms, Republican leaders viewed censure as providing a politically easy out for Democratic members who did not want to vote to remove the president but did want to rebuke him.

Formal debate on the proposed articles of impeachment began on the House floor on December 18. A nearly full House of Representatives sat quietly as the clerk read the four articles of impeachment. Members of the House Judiciary Committee began the debate with short statements summarizing the charges against the president. "The president was obliged, under his sacred oath, to faithfully execute our nation's laws," said James E. Rogan, R-Calif. "Yet he repeatedly perjured himself and obstructed justice."

The mood on the House floor darkened on December 19 when Rep. Robert L. Livingston of Louisiana, whom House Republicans had chosen to succeed Gingrich as Speaker, announced that he was resigning from Congress after confirming a news story that he had engaged in extramarital affairs. The voting on Clinton then began.

By a vote of 228–206, with only five Republicans and five Democrats crossing party lines, the House adopted the first article, which accused Clinton of committing perjury in his August 17 grand jury testimony. This article had always been considered the most likely to be approved, legislators said, because Clinton's testimony was clearly material to Starr's investigation.

By a vote of 205–229, the House then rejected the second article, which charged the president with committing perjury in his deposition in the sexual harassment suit brought by Paula Corbin Jones. On this article, twenty-eight Republicans and five Democrats broke ranks with their party.

The House voted 221–212 to adopt the third article, which charged Clinton with obstruction of justice for his efforts to find Lewinsky a job in New York, possibly in return for her silence, and for alleged witness tampering directed at his personal secretary, Betty Currie. Five Democrats voted for this article; twelve Republicans voted against it.

Finally, by a vote of 148–285, the House rejected the fourth article, which accused the president of abuse of power. Among other things, this article charged Clinton with "a pattern of deceit and obstruction" in providing misleading statements to the eighty-one questions posed by the Judiciary Committee. Only one Democrat voted for this article, and eighty-one Republicans voted against it.

After approving two impeachment articles, the House authorized the appointment of thirteen Republican members of the Judiciary Committee to prosecute the case in the Senate. Democrats had refused to serve as managers, in large part to highlight the essentially partisan nature of the case against Clinton. The "managers," as they were called, then walked across the Capitol, where Hyde presented a leather-bound book containing the approved articles of impeachment to the secretary of the Senate.

At about the same time, several dozen loyal House Democrats arrived at the White House for a show of solidarity with President Clinton. Accompanied by first lady Hillary Clinton and Vice President Al Gore, the president appeared somber but determined. "I will continue to do the work of the American people," the president vowed. "It's what I've tried to do for six years. It's what I intend to do for two more until the last hour of the last day of my term."

The Senate Sits in Judgment

When the Senate convened in January 1999 its first order of business was to deal with the two articles of impeachment that the House of Representatives had approved three weeks earlier. With the Senate closely divided (fifty-five Republicans and forty-five Democrats), there was never any serious prospect that the pro-impeachment side would muster the two-thirds vote of sixty-seven needed to remove Clinton from office. As one scholar found, despite the public's clear disgust with Clinton's personal behavior, "peace, prosperity, and moderation" enabled the president to continue to enjoy extraordinarily high job approval ratings in the polls.[125] In that political atmosphere, the Senate trial became an exercise in damage control for Republicans in the Senate, with members of both parties eager to be seen as handling the case fairly and with dignity.

The Senate formally opened the Clinton trial on January 7, with Chief Justice William Rehnquist presiding, as mandated by the Constitution. The next day all one hundred senators met privately in the Capitol's Old Senate Chamber for an extraordinary "bipartisan caucus" that produced an agreement on how the trial would be conducted. The overwhelming majority of senators appeared to want the trial to be as short as possible but long enough to assure the public that the Senate had taken its constitutional responsibilities seriously.

Despite occasional efforts by both sides to portray the trial as a nonpartisan affair, partisan politics played as important a role in the Senate deliberations as they had in the House proceedings. Two crucial votes on January 27 demonstrated the deep divide between the parties. First, the Senate rejected by 44–56 a motion by senior Democrat Robert C. Byrd of West Virginia to dismiss the charges against Clinton. Then the Senate voted 56–44 to subpoena Lewinsky and two other witnesses for closed-door depositions. In both votes, Democrat Russell D. Feingold of Wisconsin was the only senator to break ranks and vote with the other party.

As the trial progressed, the major procedural issues involved the number of witnesses the House managers could call and the format of their testimony. The managers wanted to bolster their case by calling several dozen witnesses, most of whom had not testified during the House Judiciary Committee hearings in the fall of 1998. Senate Democrats, and even many Republicans, objected to the House managers' proposal, arguing that it would prolong the trial unnecessarily.

The witness issue was resolved on February 4, when senators voted 70–30 not to require Lewinsky to testify in person before the full Senate. Instead, the Senate approved a procedure in which the videotaped testimony that Lewinsky had given to the House managers on February 1 would be available for use by either side during the presentation of arguments in the Senate. Senators agreed to a similar procedure for the videotaped testimony of two other witnesses: Vernon Jordan, the Washington lawyer whom Republicans suspected of trying to silence Lewinsky at Clinton's request by finding her a job in New York; and Sidney Blumenthal, a Clinton aide who was deeply involved in the White House public relations offensive against the Republicans.

Led by Hyde, the thirteen House managers began presenting their case against Clinton on January 14. Perhaps because the outcome was a foregone conclusion, they devoted much of their effort to a public campaign countering Clinton's defense. Hyde and other managers held numerous press conferences just outside the Senate chamber, to the annoyance of many senators.

For senators and other observers, the House managers' strongest argument was that Clinton should be made to face the consequences of his actions, even though he was president. Several House managers noted that the Senate had repeatedly removed federal judges from office for offenses similar to the president's and that military officers had suffered serious penalties for lying about adulterous relationships.

One of the highlights of the House case came on February 6, when prosecutors showed senators a videotape of Lewinsky's testimony, contrasting statements by the former White House intern with videotape of Clinton denying a sexual relationship between the two of them. It was the first time the public had a chance to hear Lewinsky speak directly about her relationship with the president. Lewinsky said that Clinton had never asked her to lie about their relationship. However, she said she had known she would deny her involvement with the president because "it was part of the pattern of the relationship."

The president's lawyers began their defense by accusing the Republican House managers of constructing a flimsy case against the president. Led by White House counsel Charles F. C. Ruff, the lawyers responded to the charges contained in the two impeachment articles point by point, at several stages ridiculing the allegations as lacking any basis in fact. At one point, Ruff summarized a key part of the Republican case as consisting of "sealing wax and strings and spiders' webs."

From the outset, Clinton's lawyers acknowledged that the president's behavior with Lewinsky had been inexcusable and wrong. The lawyers also admitted that Clinton had misled the public about the relationship and had been "evasive" and "misleading" in his grand jury testimony, But, the lawyers insisted, the president had not committed perjury or obstructed justice and, therefore, should not be removed from office. White House lawyer Gregory B. Craig said, "If you convict and remove President Clinton on the basis of these allegations, no president of the United States will ever be safe from impeachment again."

The president's lawyers also sought to focus attention on the conduct of those who had investigated Clinton, primarily Starr and the House Republicans. In the midst of the trial, the independent counsel's office leaked word to the *New York Times* that Starr was considering seeking an indictment against Clinton after he left office. The newspaper's report, on January 31, set off a flurry of charges and countercharges about Starr's handling of his investigation, in particular his apparent use of news leaks to try to shape public opinion. All this played into the hands of the president's defenders.

Senators voted on February 9 to conduct their final deliberations in private. After three days of closed-door speeches to each other—speeches that many senators later delivered in public—the Senate opened the doors to its chamber for a public reckoning on February 12. "Senators, how say you? Is the respondent, William Jefferson Clinton, guilty or not guilty?" Chief Justice Rehnquist asked. One by one senators stood at their desks as their names were called and responded "guilty" or "not guilty" to each of the two articles of impeachment.

On the first article, which accused Clinton of perjury, the Senate voted 45–55 against conviction, twenty-two votes short of the two-thirds vote necessary for conviction. Ten Republicans joined all forty-five Democrats in voting "not guilty." All ten were moderates who said they strongly disapproved of Clinton's behavior but did not believe his denials in the Lewinsky case amounted to "high Crimes and Misdemeanors" for which he should be removed from office. On the second article, which accused Clinton of obstruction of justice, the Senate divided 50–50, with five Republicans joining all the Democrats in voting "not guilty."

After the Senate voted, Clinton offered his most direct apology yet for his actions. "I want to say again to the American people how profoundly sorry I am for what I said and did to trigger these events and the great burden they have imposed on the Congress and on the American people," he said in a televised address from the White House Rose Garden. "Now, I ask all Americans, and I hope all Americans here in Washington and throughout our land, will rededicate ourselves to the work of serving our nation and building our future together."

Postimpeachment Developments

The not-guilty verdict in the Senate trial did not end Clinton's legal troubles. Two months later, on April 12, 1999, Judge Susan Webber Wright, the federal district court judge in Arkansas who was overseeing the Jones case, held Clinton in contempt of court for providing false testimony in his January 17, 1998, deposition in that case. Judge Wright said in her finding, "The record demonstrates by clear and convincing evidence that the president responded to plaintiff's questions by giving false, misleading, and evasive answers that were designed to obstruct the judicial process." She ordered Clinton to pay "any reasonable expenses" incurred by Jones as a result of his testimony. Jones's lawyers sought $496,000 from the president, but Judge Wright on July 29 reduced the award to $89,483, which Clinton later paid.

With less fanfare, Congress in 1999 allowed the law under which Starr's investigation was authorized to lapse. The Independent Counsel Act had been controversial since it was enacted in the wake of the Watergate scandal that forced President Richard Nixon from office in 1974. But never did an independent counsel investigation cause as much controversy as Starr's five-year probe of Clinton, which the president and his supporters characterized as a nasty partisan vendetta aimed at driving Clinton out of office.

In September 2000, the six-year-long investigation into the failed Arkansas land deal known as Whitewater came to a formal close when Independent Counsel Robert W. Ray announced that the evidence gathered was insufficient to bring criminal charges against either President Clinton or his wife, Hillary Rodham Clinton. (Ray became the independent counsel after Starr resigned on October 18, 1999.) Earlier in the year, Ray also had closed related investigations into allegations of misconduct related to the firing of several White House Travel Office employees and the acquisition by the Clinton White House of confidential FBI files.

Still pending, however, was a grand jury investigation into whether President Clinton had lied under oath to cover up his relationship with Lewinsky. Ray said he still might indict Clinton for perjury or obstruction of justice after he left the White House on January 20, 2001.

On January 19, 2001, Clinton's last full day as president, the White House announced that he had agreed to a settlement with Ray. In return for avoiding the possibility of indictment, Clinton admitted that he had given false testimony under oath and agreed to give up his right to practice law for five years. Clinton also agreed to pay a fine of $25,000 to the Arkansas Committee on Professional Conduct, which had been considering whether to disbar him. In his statement released on January 19, Clinton said that in his January 17, 1998, deposition in the Jones case, he "tried to walk a fine line between acting lawfully and testifying falsely, but I now recognize that I did not fully accomplish this goal and certain of my responses to questions about Ms. Lewinsky were false." Clinton's attorney David Kendall said that the president was glad to have "closure" in the matter.

VICE-PRESIDENTIAL IMPEACHMENT AND RESIGNATIONS

The only procedure for vice-presidential removal that was provided for in the original Constitution—impeachment—has never been used. Impeachment proceedings, which require investigation and debate by the House to bring an indictment, then a full-scale trial and a two-thirds vote to convict in the Senate, are inherently lengthy and controversial undertakings whose only effect is to remove the impeached and convicted official from office. This may explain why two vice presidents who arguably committed impeachable offenses—Aaron Burr and Schuyler Colfax—were allowed to complete their terms without undergoing impeachment and why Congress preferred that Vice President Agnew resign rather than be impeached.

Vice President Burr's offense was to shoot and kill Alexander Hamilton in a duel on July 11, 1804. Burr was indicted for murder in New York and New Jersey but was never arrested and prosecuted. Sen. William Plumer, a Federalist opponent of President Jefferson, reacted to Congress's unwillingness to impeach the vice president by writing, "We are indeed fallen on evil times. . . . The high office of president is filled by an infidel, that of the vice president by a murderer."

In the case of Vice President Colfax, evidence against him did not surface until he already had been dropped from the Republican ticket in 1872 and was in the last months of his term. Colfax was found to have received, while still in Congress, twenty shares of the notorious Crédit Mobilier, a dummy construction company that the Union Pacific Railroad had created to receive the proceeds of government contracts. The *New York World* called for Colfax's impeachment, and a House committee investigated him in December 1872. But the committee concluded that, constitutionally,

impeachment was intended to remove a person from an office only for offenses committed while occupying it.

On September 25, 1973, after Vice President Agnew learned that the Justice Department was about to seek an indictment for bribery, corruption, and income tax evasion, he met with Speaker Carl Albert and other House leaders to ask them to begin impeachment proceedings against him. Agnew's strategy seems to have been to preempt the criminal investigation. The next day, Albert declined, explaining that Agnew's request "relates to matters before the courts." Albert also was concerned that Congress not be tied up with a vice-presidential impeachment when impeachment proceedings against President Nixon seemed possible. The vice president resigned two weeks later.

Only two vice presidents—John C. Calhoun and Spiro T. Agnew—have resigned from the vice presidency. In some ways, this low number is surprising, especially for the period before 1940. Until that year's Democratic national convention, when President Franklin D. Roosevelt threatened not to run for reelection unless the party accepted his choice of Henry A. Wallace as his running mate, vice-presidential nominees were placed on the ticket by party leaders. Not only was the presidential nominee largely excluded from this decision, the vice president often was chosen to balance the ticket with someone from a different, sometimes hostile wing of the party. Consequently, discord was almost built into the relationship between the president and vice president. Most vice presidents were frozen out of the policy and patronage processes. Some responded by leaving Washington for long periods; others by actively undermining the president's policies and leadership; still others by suffering in silence.

During this nineteenth- to early-twentieth-century period of ticket balancing, the one vice president who resigned did so because he had a better offer. In December 1832, near the end of his second term as vice president, South Carolina offered Vice President Calhoun a U.S. Senate seat, and he accepted. Calhoun had first been elected vice president in 1824 after convincing supporters of both of the leading presidential candidates, John Quincy Adams and Andrew Jackson, that he was in their camp. Calhoun, whose real ambition was to be president, accepted the second office in the hope that both the electoral college and the House of Representatives would deadlock in the presidential election, leaving him as acting president for four years. Although the electoral college did fail to elect a president, the House did not, choosing Adams. *(See "Congressional Caucus Nominating System," p. 234, in Chapter 5.)*

Vice President Calhoun used his position as president of the Senate to undermine President Adams by stacking committees with Adams's opponents, delaying presidential appointments, and allowing vicious speeches to be made against the president by certain senators. These activities endeared Calhoun to Jackson, who made the vice president his running mate in 1828 and did nothing to discourage Calhoun's hope of becoming his elected successor. But Calhoun feuded bitterly after the election with the president's other protégé, Martin Van Buren, and broke with President Jackson over his strongly pro-Union policies. When Jackson learned that Calhoun, as secretary of war in the administration of President James Monroe, had criticized his activities as an army general in 1818, the break became irreparable. "I never expected to say to you . . . Et tu, Brute," Jackson wrote Calhoun.

Calhoun's method of resigning—no procedure was provided in the Constitution—set the precedent for future presidents and vice presidents. He sent a one-sentence letter to the secretary of state: "Having concluded to accept of a seat in the United States Senate, I herewith resign the office of Vice-President of the United States."

Vice President Agnew's resignation in 1973 was the product of an entirely different set of circumstances. The vice president's relationship with President Richard Nixon was reasonably harmonious, and his popularity with rank-and-file Republicans made him an early favorite for the party's 1976 presidential nomination. What undid Agnew was a federal criminal investigation into bribes he had received from contractors, architects, and engineers while serving as county executive of Baltimore County, Maryland, governor of Maryland, and vice president. The bribes totaled more than $100,000. Agnew had received the last of them in his White House office.

Agnew revealed and denied the bribery charges at a televised news conference on August 8, 1973. Despite White House pressure to resign, he vowed as late as September 29 that "I will not resign if indicted." (Agnew also claimed that, constitutionally, a vice president could not be indicted while in office.) White House pressure on Agnew intensified. Presidential chief of staff Alexander Haig Jr. told Agnew that his choice was to resign or face a "no holds barred[,] . . . nasty and dirty" prosecution.

On October 10 Agnew pleaded nolo contendere (no contest) to one count of income tax evasion, in return for a Justice Department agreement not to prosecute him on other charges and to seek a lenient sentence for the tax evasion conviction. Agnew resigned as vice president that same day. Attorney General Elliot Richardson believed that, with Watergate threatening Nixon's removal as president, the highest priority was to get Agnew out of the line of succession. Agnew's resignation letter to Secretary of State Henry Kissinger read: "I hereby resign the Office of Vice President of the United States, effective immediately." U.S. District

After pleading no contest to income tax evasion, Spiro T. Agnew resigned from the vice presidency on October 10, 1973.

Court Judge Walter E. Hoffman sentenced Agnew to three years of unsupervised probation and ordered him to pay a $10,000 fine and $150,000 in back taxes.

PRESIDENTIAL DISABILITY

Presidential impeachment and presidential death are relatively straightforward matters compared with presidential disability. One knows when a president is dead or has been impeached and convicted, but questions of disability are often subjective. Whether a president is able or unable "to discharge the Powers and Duties" of the office is a matter subject to honest disagreement. Yet disabilities do occur. According to one scholar's calculations, periods of presidential disability, taken together, have left the country without a functioning president for nearly a full year.[126] Others argue that Woodrow Wilson alone was disabled during the final year and a half of his second term as president.

For most of the nation's history the issue of disability was covered entirely by a provision of Article II of the Constitution:

> In Case of . . . Inability to discharge the Powers and Duties of the said Office, the Same shall devolve on the Vice President, and the Congress may by Law provide for the case of . . . Inability, both of the President and Vice President, declaring what Officer shall then act as President, and such Officer shall act accordingly, until the Disability be removed, or a President shall be elected.

As presidential scholar Louis W. Koenig has noted, this provision is a "quagmire of ambiguity" that leaves many important questions unanswered.[127] What does *disability* mean—does it include both mental and physical impairments? What about other disabling situations, such as a presidential kidnapping by a terrorist group? Who is authorized to declare that the president is disabled—Congress, the vice president, the cabinet, some combination of the three, or only the president? To what position does the vice president succeed in the case of a presidential disability—acting president with the "Powers and Duties of the said Office" or the presidency itself? Is the succession temporary or permanent? During the country's first century under the Constitution, these questions seemed remote. President James Garfield's lengthy disability in 1881 made them real.

Although section 2 of the Twenty-fifth Amendment provides for the filling of vice-presidential vacancies that are caused by the death, resignation, or impeachment of the vice president, it is silent on the matter of vice-presidential disabilities. This is a curious omission. Other sections of the amendment create procedures for handling presidential disabilities. What is more, some of these procedures make the vice president the main figure in determining whether a presidential disability exists, and all of them stipulate that the vice president will serve as acting president for as long as the president remains disabled. Clearly, the presidential disability provisions of the Twenty-fifth Amendment assume that a vice president will always be both available—that was one of the reasons for including section 2 in the amendment—and able. Yet neither the amendment nor any other provision of the law or the Constitution offers the nation any protection against a disabled vice president.

The First Lengthy Presidential Disability

The bullet that pierced President Garfield's spinal column left him incapacitated and generally unable to fulfill the powers and duties of his office during the eighty-day period between his shooting on July 2, 1881, and his death on September 19, 1881. During those months the problem of presidential disability was discussed widely.

According to one opinion that was offered at the time, the term *disability* applied only to permanent mental incapacity. As former senator William W. Eaton, D-Conn., maintained, "There could be no disability that the President can be conscious of." [128] Others took the broader position that a disability could be mental or physical and either temporary or permanent. Still others adopted a more situational approach. Former senator Lyman Trumbull, R-Ill., for example, argued that a presidential disability should be declared only when an incapacity that was generally known was joined to an urgent need for executive action.

The consequences of the vice president assuming presidential authority in the event of a presidential disability also were debated. The predominant view was that the vice president would act as president only temporarily, until the disabled president had recovered. Some believed, however, that once the duties of the presidency "devolved," the vice president became the president for the remainder of the term, thereby dispossessing the disabled president of the office to which he had been elected.

Opinion about who could declare a president disabled was similarly divided, in this case between those who thought it was a legislative function and those who thought it was up to the vice president. At one point, Garfield's cabinet decided unanimously that Vice President Chester Arthur should assume presidential responsibilities. But when they proposed this course of action to Arthur, he adamantly refused. To assume power while Garfield was alive and without Garfield's blessing, the vice president believed, would be politically reckless and constitutionally uncertain.

All of the questions that plagued Garfield's contemporaries during his period of disability were traceable to the vagueness of the Constitution itself. After Arthur became president, he repeatedly expressed concern about the ambiguities of the succession provision of the Constitution, especially the proper response to a presidential disability. Arthur's concern did not stem solely from his experience during the Garfield disability. During the summer of 1882 Arthur learned that he was suffering from a fatal kidney disease. Thus he faced the possibility that his own disability or death might occur at a time when the nation lacked a vice president. A year later the illness forced President Arthur to reduce his schedule to half a day, and the work of the government slowed noticeably. Nonetheless, for political reasons Arthur did not disclose the full extent of his illness, and he did not succeed in persuading Congress to address the succession and disability issue.[129]

The Secret Disability

Shortly after Grover Cleveland became president for the second time a financial panic struck the country. Major industries went bankrupt, banks closed their doors, businesses shut down, and millions of people were thrown out of work. President Cleveland believed that a primary cause of the depression was the Sherman Silver Purchase Act of 1890. On June 30, 1893, he called Congress into special session to consider repealing the act.

The night Cleveland called the special session, he boarded the yacht *Oneida* in New York City and embarked on a five-day cruise of Long Island Sound. For the next month the president alternated between visits to his summer home at Buzzards Bay in Massachusetts and cruises on the yacht. On August 5 he returned to Washington, where two days later he addressed the special session of Congress.

Unknown to the public and virtually all members of the government, including Vice President Adlai E.

Stevenson, Cleveland had undergone surgery during the initial five-day cruise and had spent the subsequent weeks recuperating.[130] A surgeon had removed a cancerous growth from the roof of Cleveland's mouth as well as a major portion of his upper jaw. The entire operation, which had taken place while the unconscious president was strapped to a chair propped against the yacht's mast, had taken less than ninety minutes. Later, at his summer home, Cleveland was fitted with an artificial jaw so that he could speak intelligibly. In late July, during another cruise, the president underwent a second operation to remove suspicious tissue that had been noticed during the first operation.

On August 7, 1893, Cleveland was sufficiently recovered to address the special session of Congress with his customary vigor and coherence. At the end of the summer the *Philadelphia Press* published an account of the operations that was officially denounced as a hoax. Others put out a story that the president had simply suffered a toothache that required the extraction of some teeth. Because Cleveland seemed to be in fine health, with no noticeable changes in his facial structure or speech, the story faded.

Not until twenty-four years later, with the publication in 1917 of a story in the *Saturday Evening Post* by one of Cleveland's doctors, were the facts revealed. Cleveland had insisted on complete secrecy because he did not want to risk further unsettling a public that was already in the throes of a financial panic. As the doctor-author commented, "What the consequences would have been had it become known at the time we can only surmise and shudder!"[131]

The Wilson Disability

On September 25, 1919, in the midst of a speaking tour of the country to rouse support for the League of Nations, President Woodrow Wilson fell ill. The public was told that the president had suffered a complete nervous breakdown brought on by overwork and the effects of an earlier attack of influenza. The rest of the tour was canceled, and Wilson returned to Washington. On October 2 he suffered a stroke that paralyzed the left side of his body.

After Wilson's stroke, the White House was turned into a nursing ward under the direction of Dr. Cary Grayson, the president's close friend and physician, and Edith Galt Wilson, the president's wife. They were assisted by presidential secretary Joseph P. Tumulty. Vague and ambiguous health bulletins sparked wild rumors about Wilson's condition. Nevertheless, Mrs. Wilson's first concern was to save her husband, and if that meant shielding him from the responsibilities and burdens of the presidency, then she was determined to do so.[132]

For more than six months after his stroke, President Wilson was bedridden and saw very few people. Meanwhile, the country was in the midst of a difficult transition from war to peace, with the attendant challenges of shifting the economy to a peacetime footing, demobilizing the armed forces, and considering the Versailles peace treaty with its controversial provision for a League of Nations.

Clearly, presidential leadership was necessary in such circumstances. Mrs. Wilson and Tumulty did what they could to marshal and focus the president's meager energies for occasional demonstrations of competency and for official tasks such as approving papers and dictating instructions for the treaty fight. Secretary of State Robert Lansing, however, was concerned about the potential drift in government affairs. The day after Wilson's stroke, Lansing spoke to Tumulty about the possibility of asking Vice President Thomas R. Marshall to serve as acting president. At that meeting Lansing read the succession and disability provision of the Constitution to Tumulty, who replied that he needed no tutoring on the subject. Tumulty then declared, "You may rest assured that while Woodrow Wilson is lying in the White House on the broad of his back I will not be a party to ousting him."[133] At a cabinet meeting on October 6, 1919, called at Lansing's initiative, a discussion of presidential disability ended abruptly when Tumulty and Grayson arrived. They informed the assembled heads of the departments that they, the president's secretary and physician, would repudiate any effort to declare Wilson disabled.

As months passed, repeated calls were made for Vice President Marshall to step in as acting president. But in the face of ambiguous constitutional guidelines, an absence of historical precedents, a hostile presidential staff, and a reluctant vice president, the affairs of state continued to drift. Marshall carefully avoided any appearance of attempting to usurp presidential authority, and he certainly was loath to incur the wrath of Mrs. Wilson. The vice president reportedly said, "I am not going to get myself entangled with Mrs. Wilson. No politician ever exposes himself to the hatred of a woman, particularly if she's the wife of the President of the United States."[134]

As the senior member of the cabinet, Secretary of State Lansing continued to try to coordinate government affairs by convening informal cabinet meetings. Between October 1919 and February 1920 he called more than twenty such meetings. But because the United States has never had a system of cabinet government, many matters arose that the cabinet simply could not handle. For example, it could not respond to legislation—nearly thirty bills became law when they were neither signed nor vetoed by the president during this period. Because the cabinet could not make presidential appointments, many vacancies in government went unfilled. Needless to say, the cabinet also could not manage the League of Nations controversy in the Senate or accept the credentials of foreign ambassadors.

Perhaps it was a sign of Wilson's partial recovery that in February 1920 he wrote to Lansing to voice his objections to the secretary's initiative in convening the cabinet. In replying to the president's letter, Lansing declared that his actions betrayed no intention to assume or exercise presidential powers. Wilson responded with the blunt suggestion that Lansing resign as secretary of state, which he did on February 12, 1920. Wilson reportedly told Tumulty, "It is never the wrong time to spike disloyalty. When Lansing sought to oust me, I was upon my back. I am on my feet now and I will not have disloyalty about me." [135] Despite his claim to be "on my feet," Wilson remained seriously impaired by his illness.

In the aftermath of Lansing's dismissal, two disability proposals were considered by Congress. One plan sought to empower the Supreme Court to declare a president disabled in response to a congressional resolution authorizing it to do so. The other plan would have allowed the cabinet to certify a presidential disability by majority vote. Hearings were held on these proposals, but no action was taken. On April 13, 1920, President Wilson held his first cabinet meeting in six months. Although he never fully recovered from his illness, the president became a bit more active and finished out the remaining months of his second term.

The Wilson disability reinforced at least two important lessons of the earlier Garfield disability. First, a president could be disabled for weeks, even months, without the situation being addressed in any satisfactory way. Second, a formal constitutional mechanism was needed to declare a president disabled. Clearly, informal attempts to draft the vice president to step in as acting president or to encourage the cabinet to provide executive leadership in the president's stead were bound to prove inadequate and appear disloyal. Still, as was the case in the years after Garfield died, once Wilson's term ended and the crisis was past, these two lessons faded from memory.

The Eisenhower Disabilities

The presidency of Dwight Eisenhower brought the disability issue into vivid and recurring focus. Between 1955 and 1957 President Eisenhower suffered three illnesses that each left him disabled for several days or weeks. This series of illnesses prompted Eisenhower to create a set of informal precedents and procedures for dealing with presidential disabilities.

Eisenhower's first disability, a moderate heart attack that required complete rest for about a month, occurred while he was vacationing in Colorado in September 1955. Fortunately, the illness struck when the press of public business was light—the international situation was calm and Congress was out of session. In addition, throughout his presidency Eisenhower had made extensive use of the National Security Council and the cabinet, which meant that Vice President Richard Nixon, who was a council and cabinet member, was well versed in the domestic and international issues that the administration was facing. Moreover,

because Eisenhower had put in place an extensive staff structure in the White House, the conduct of the presidency did not depend on him alone.

Finally, Eisenhower and Secretary of State John Foster Dulles were fully aware of the problems presented by the Wilson disability (they had both been young men at the time) and were determined to avoid similar problems. Eisenhower remembered how the vague official reports about President Wilson's illness had led to rampant speculation about his true condition, and so he was determined to keep the press and public fully informed about his medical condition and progress.[136] Dulles recalled how the apprehensions and misunderstandings stemming from the cabinet meetings called by Secretary of State Robert Lansing (Dulles's uncle) had led to Lansing's dismissal by the president.[137] Dulles therefore was determined to avoid even the appearance of impropriety or disloyalty. But more than that, he and Eisenhower encouraged the vice president to preside at cabinet meetings in the president's absence.

As a result, Eisenhower's first illness was handled relatively smoothly. By the end of the president's first week in the hospital both the National Security Council and the cabinet had met at their usual time, with Vice President Nixon presiding. At its meeting the cabinet agreed on a set of administrative operating principles, including the assignment of Sherman Adams, a presidential assistant and the de facto chief of staff, to act as the primary liaison with the president.[138] A rough and workable division of labor emerged: Adams oversaw the day-to-day business of the executive branch, and Nixon carried on the established public functions of the presidency.

The president's recuperation progressed well. He began receiving visitors after the second week and was discharged from the hospital in six weeks. Eisenhower met with the cabinet in late November and returned to the White House, completely recovered, in mid-January 1956. The president's rapid and full recovery not only defused the disability issue, but also put to rest speculation about his ability to run for reelection in November.

Less than nine months after his heart attack, however, President Eisenhower was struck by another illness, an attack of ileitis, or inflammation of the ileum, which is part of the small intestine. The president underwent successful exploratory surgery on June 9, 1956. Within two days he was ambulatory and able to meet with staff. Although Eisenhower needed to rest, he was capable of performing official acts. On July 21, for example, he embarked on a trip to Panama to attend a meeting with South American presidents. But despite his rapid recovery, Eisenhower was disturbed that in the nuclear age the country had been without a functioning president while he was on the operating table.

The president's third illness, a mild stroke, occurred a year and a half later, on November 25, 1957, a time of con-

One of the physicians attending Dwight D. Eisenhower explains the president's surgery to the press. Concerns about presidential disability in the nuclear era spurred passage of the Twenty-fifth Amendment.

1963, and by President Johnson and Vice President Hubert H. Humphrey in January 1965.

Passage of the Twenty-fifth Amendment

Although presidential illnesses had sparked periodic discussions about how to deal with disability and succession throughout U.S. history, in each case the passing of the immediate crisis had removed the incentive for formal action. The 1963 assassination of President Kennedy, however, helped to generate an irresistible momentum toward dealing with both disability and the related issue of vice-presidential vacancies. In the mid-1960s a consensus formed that in the nuclear age the United States should not find itself without executive leadership, even briefly.

siderable international tension. The United States was still reeling from the Soviet Union's launch in October of the space ship *Sputnik I,* the first manmade object to orbit the Earth. At the same time, warning signs were emerging of what would turn out to be the severe economic recession of 1958, and a meeting of heads of state organized by the North Atlantic Treaty Organization (NATO) was just three weeks off. Fortunately, the president's mild stroke caused him only some brief difficulty in speaking, and by December 2 he was back to his normal routine.

In the aftermath of his third illness, President Eisenhower asked the Justice Department to recommend a procedure for dealing with presidential disabilities. The department proposed a constitutional amendment that would describe how to declare and terminate a disability. When, once again, Congress seemed uninterested in acting, Eisenhower and Nixon worked out their own informal arrangement through a letter of agreement that was made public on March 3, 1958. The arrangement was simple: Either the president or, if the president were unable, the vice president could decide when the vice president should step in to act as president until such time as the president declared himself restored. In the absence of a constitutional amendment addressing presidential disability, this agreement also was adopted by President John Kennedy and Vice President Lyndon Johnson in August 1961, by President Johnson and House Speaker John McCormack in December

Sustained awareness of the disability and succession issues came at the very end of a series of troubling experiences. After the death of Franklin Roosevelt in 1945 each postwar president had confronted these issues in one form or another. Harry Truman served as president for nearly four years without a vice president. Dwight Eisenhower was temporarily disabled by a succession of illnesses during the mid-1950s. After Eisenhower's 1955 heart attack the House Judiciary Committee set up a special subcommittee chaired by Rep. Emanuel Celler, D-N.Y., to study the problems of presidential disability. The subcommittee could not agree on a remedy, however. Then, after Eisenhower's 1957 stroke, Sen. Estes Kefauver, D-Tenn., chair of the Subcommittee on Constitutional Amendments of the Senate Judiciary Committee, held hearings on the issue in January and February 1958. But these proceedings, too, failed to produce procedures for determining when a disability begins and ends.

In the early 1960s, during the Kennedy administration, Senators Kefauver and Kenneth B. Keating, R-N.Y., joined forces to promote reconsideration of the matter. Convening hearings in June 1963, Kefauver noted that the incumbency of a young and healthy president was an opportunity for Congress to explore the topic of disability "without any implication that the present holder of that high office is not in good health" and thus would allow the nation "to prepare now for the possible crises of the future." [139] But a double tragedy first delayed and then spurred action: Senator Kefauver's unexpected death in August 1963 brought the committee's proceedings to a halt, and the Kennedy assassination in November emphasized anew the need to prepare for the unexpected.

Kennedy's assassination also triggered concern about vacancies in the vice presidency. When Lyndon Johnson succeeded to the presidency in November 1963, more than a year loomed ahead in which there would be no vice president—the sixteenth time the office had been vacant in the previous thirty-six presidencies, sometimes for three years or more. This was especially troubling because of the advanced age and poor health of the next two officials in the line of succession: House Speaker John McCormack, who was seventy-one, and Senate President Pro Tempore Carl Hayden, who was eighty-six. The Speaker's constitutional status if the president became disabled created another complication. Because the Constitution bars anyone from serving simultaneously in the executive and legislative branches, the Speaker would have to resign from the House to act even temporarily as president. A Speaker's understandable reluctance to fill a temporary presidential vacancy could thwart efforts to ensure that the country would always have a functioning chief executive.[140] Further, the Speaker might be of a different political party from the president, undermining prospects for continuity in policy on a variety of important issues.

Kefauver's successor as chair of the Subcommittee on Constitutional Amendments, Sen. Birch Bayh, D-Ind., brought considerable energy and interest to the issues of presidential disability and vice-presidential vacancy. Bayh mobilized the American Bar Association to assist Congress in writing a constitutional amendment to address these issues. During hearings in early 1964, he forged a consensus on acceptable procedures for declaring and terminating a period of presidential disability, as well as on procedures for filling any vacancy in the vice presidency. In July 1965, the proposed Twenty-fifth Amendment to the Constitution was approved by both houses of Congress with virtually no opposition. Ratification by the states proceeded expeditiously, and the amendment took effect on February 10, 1967.

According to the Twenty-fifth Amendment, the vice president becomes acting president under either of two circumstances: if the president informs Congress that he is unable to perform the powers and duties of the presidency,

or if both the vice president and a majority of the cabinet (or some other body designated by Congress) find the president to be disabled. In either case the vice president becomes acting president until the disability ends. If the president claims to be able, Congress is given twenty-one days to resolve the dispute. A two-thirds vote of both houses is required to deny the president's claim. Finally, when a vacancy occurs in the vice presidency, whether because of the death, resignation, or impeachment and removal of the vice president or because the vice president has succeeded to the presidency, the president must appoint a new vice president, subject to confirmation by a majority of both houses of Congress.

Application of the Twenty-fifth Amendment

Since the Twenty-fifth Amendment became part of the Constitution, it has been invoked several times. Two vacancies have occurred in the vice presidency, one when Vice President Spiro Agnew resigned in October 1973 and the other when Gerald Ford, the vice president whom President Nixon appointed to replace Agnew, succeeded to the presidency after Nixon resigned in August 1974. Ford then nominated Nelson Rockefeller as vice president.

The disability provision of the amendment has been invoked twice, first when President Ronald Reagan was hospitalized for colon cancer surgery in July 1985 and the second time when President George W. Bush underwent a colonoscopy in 2002.[141] Although Reagan was aware of the Twenty-fifth Amendment, he did not think it applied to a situation in which he would be unconscious during surgery. Stating that he did not want to set a precedent that would bind future presidents, Reagan nonetheless wrote a letter to Congress in which he passed "to the vice president his powers and duties . . . commencing with the administration of anesthesia . . . in this instance."[142] In the second instance, Bush explicitly invoked the amendment.

Thus in passing the Twenty-fifth Amendment, lawmakers sought to embody the lessons gained from previous experience. Although the amendment could not resolve every problem and ambiguity, it was, as the columnist Walter Lippmann observed, "a great deal better than an endless search . . . for the absolutely perfect solution[,] . . . which will never be found, and . . . is not necessary."[143]

★

NOTES

1. Ruth C. Silva, *Presidential Succession* (Ann Arbor: University of Michigan Press, 1951), 8.

2. For a discussion of the lines of succession, see John D. Feerick, *From Failing Hands: The Story of Presidential Succession* (New York: Fordham University Press, 1965), 264–269.

3. Ibid., 87–88.

4. James A. Green, *William Henry Harrison: His Life and Times* (Richmond, Va.: Garrett and Massie, 1941), 393.

5. Ibid.

6. James D. Richardson, *Messages and Papers of the Presidents, 1789–1897* (Washington, D.C.: Bureau of National Literature, 1897), 4:21.

7. For details of what Green considers Harrison's mistreatment by physicians, see *William Henry Harrison*, 398–399.

8. Richardson, *Messages and Papers,* 4:31–32.

9. *Daily National Intelligencer,* April 15, 1841, 3.

10. Robert Seager II, *And Tyler Too: A Biography of John and Julia Gardiner Tyler* (New York: McGraw-Hill, 1963), 149.

11. Feerick, *From Failing Hands,* 98.

12. For more on the campaign, see K. Jack Bauer, *Zachary Taylor: Soldier, Planter, Statesman of the Old Southwest* (Baton Rouge: Louisiana State University Press, 1985), 239–247.

13. Ibid., 254–255.

14. For further discussion of the disunity of the Whig Party and the disarray of the Taylor cabinet, see Benson Lee Grayson, *The Unknown President: The Administration of Millard Fillmore* (Washington, D.C.: University Press of America, 1981), 2–5.

15. John Durant and Alice Durant, *Pictorial History of American Presidents* (New York: Barnes, 1955), 94.

16. Bauer, *Zachary Taylor,* 237. William H. Seward was the senior U.S. senator from the state of New York and a major figure in the Whig Party there. Thurlow Weed was Whig Party boss in the state of New York.

17. Ibid., 308.

18. Robert J. Rayback, *Millard Fillmore, Biography of a President* (Buffalo, N.Y.: Henry Stewart, 1959), 242.

19. For more on the legislative and executive tactics used to achieve the Great Compromise, see ibid., 246–253.

20. Robert K. Murray, *The Harding Era* (Minneapolis: University of Minnesota Press, 1969), 13–14.

21. Ibid., 69.

22. Ibid., 66–67.

23. For the details of this final trip, see ibid., 439–445.

24. Ibid., 456–457.

25. Quoted in ibid., 457–458.

26. Durant and Durant, *Pictorial History,* 243.

27. Michael Nelson, *A Heartbeat Away* (Washington, D.C.: Brookings, 1988), 31–34.

28. Murray, *The Harding Era,* 499.

29. Ibid., 500–501.

30. For an assessment of the Harding-Coolidge transition and legacy, see ibid., 498–514.

31. See Jim Bishop, *FDR's Last Year* (New York: Morrow, 1974), 3–12. For general accounts of Roosevelt's declining health, see Kenneth R. Crispell and Carlos F. Gomez, *Hidden Illness in the White House* (Durham: Duke University Press, 1988), chap. 3; and Doris Kearns Goodwin, *No Ordinary Time: Franklin and Eleanor Roosevelt, The Home Front in World War II* (New York: Simon and Schuster, 1994).

32. Cabell Phillips, *The 1940's: Decade of Triumph and Trouble* (New York: Macmillan, 1975), 242–243.

33. Sidney M. Milkis and Michael Nelson, *The American Presidency: Origins and Development, 1776–1993* (Washington, D.C.: CQ Press, 1994), 421.

34. Bishop, *FDR's Last Year,* 596–598.

35. Ibid., 609–610.

36. Harry S. Truman, *Memoirs* (Garden City, N.Y.: Doubleday, 1955), 1:9–10.

37. Phillips, *The 1940's,* 252.

38. Marquis James, *Andrew Jackson* (New York: Bobbs-Merrill, 1937), 390–391.

39. Durant and Durant, *Pictorial History,* 128.

40. Recounted in Dorothy Meserve Kunhardt and Philip B. Kunhardt Jr., *Twenty Days* (North Hollywood, Calif.: Newcastle, 1985), 12.

41. Quoted in Feerick, *From Failing Hands,* 109.

42. For more on the attack on Seward, see Kunhardt and Kunhardt, *Twenty Days,* 50–53.

43. Physician A. R. Fraser has argued that Lincoln's wound was not necessarily fatal and that unsanitary handling of the wound by the attending physicians may have killed him. Fraser is similarly critical of the medical care that Presidents Garfield and McKinley received. See Fraser, "How Did Lincoln Die?" *American Heritage* 46 (February–March 1995): 63–70.

44. For more on the funeral arrangements in Washington, D.C., and on the trip back to Springfield, Illinois, for burial, see Kunhardt and Kunhardt, *Twenty Days,* 119–302.

45. Justus D. Doenecke, *The Presidencies of James A. Garfield and Chester A. Arthur* (Lawrence: Regents Press of Kansas, 1981), 27.

46. Ibid., 29.

47. For more on the negotiations and maneuvering in forming the Garfield cabinet, see ibid., 30–35.

48. Feerick, *From Failing Hands,* 118–120.

49. Sarah Vowell, *Assassination Vacation* (New York: Simon and Schuster, 2005), 124.

50. Ibid., 127–128.

51. Allen Peskin, *Garfield* (Kent, Ohio: Kent State University Press, 1978), 608–609.

52. For more on the problems in the line of succession that followed Arthur, see Birch Bayh, *One Heartbeat Away: Presidential Disability and Succession* (Indianapolis, Ind.: Bobbs-Merrill, 1968), 17–18.

53. Quoted in Doenecke, *The Presidencies,* 181.

54. Inaugural address quoted in Lewis L. Gould, *The Presidency of William McKinley* (Lawrence: Regents Press of Kansas, 1981), 240.

55. McKinley's first vice president, Garret A. Hobart, died of a heart attack in November 1899. For more on the Hobart vice presidency and the Roosevelt nomination, see Feerick, *From Failing Hands,* 152–155.

56. Milkis and Nelson, *American Presidency,* 207.

57. See Gould, *Presidency of William McKinley,* 250–251.

58. Eric Rauchway, *Murdering McKinley: The Making of Theodore Roosevelt's America* (New York: Hill and Wang, 2003), 19.

59. Ibid., 251.

60. James Ford Jones, *The McKinley and Roosevelt Administrations, 1897–1909* (New York: Macmillan, 1922), 172.

61. Rauchway, *Murdering McKinley,* 38.

62. Vowell, *Assassination Vacation,* 220.

63. Edmund Morris, *Theodore Rex* (New York: Random House, 2001).

64. For more on the purpose of Kennedy's visit to Texas, see Arthur M. Schlesinger Jr., *A Thousand Days* (New York: Fawcett, 1977), 1017–1019.

65. Ibid., 1021.

66. William Manchester, *The Death of a President* (New York: Harper and Row, 1967), 153.

67. Ibid., 233.

68. Ibid., 530.

69. Quoted in Feerick, *From Failing Hands,* 243–244.

70. For further information about the various assaults on and assassinations of presidents as well as their effects on protective services and practices and on politics, see Frederick M. Kaiser, "Presidential Assassinations and Assaults: Characteristics and Impact on Protective Procedures," *Presidential Studies Quarterly* 11 (fall 1981): 545–558; and William C. Spragens, "Political Impact of Presidential Assassinations and Attempted Assassinations," *Presidential Studies Quarterly* 10 (summer 1980): 336–347.

71. Arguably some of these incidents, especially the plane crash and the Duran shooting, were assassination attempts.

72. In 1912 an attempt was made to assassinate former president Theodore Roosevelt, who was then a presidential candidate after being out of office for almost four years. Although the assailant, John Schrank, wounded Roosevelt, the wound was not fatal. Attempts also have been made on two other presidential candidates, Sen. Robert F. Kennedy, D-N.Y., in 1968 and Alabama governor George C. Wallace in 1972. Kennedy died, and Wallace was severely injured.

73. For more details on the Reagan assassination attempt, see *Reagan's First Year* (Washington, D.C.: Congressional Quarterly, 1982), 3–9.

74. In 1989 U.S. District Judge Alcee L. Hastings was impeached and convicted on bribery charges, but he was not barred from subsequent officeholding. In 1992 Hastings was elected to the U.S. House of Representatives from Florida, taking his seat alongside members who had voted to impeach him.

75. All three federal judges impeached by the House since 1935 have been tried by the Senate in this manner. All three were then convicted by vote of the full Senate.

76. Alexander Hamilton, *Federalist* No. 65, in Alexander Hamilton, James Madison, and John Jay, *The Federalist Papers,* with an introduction by Clinton Rossiter (New York: Mentor, 1961), 397.

77. Joseph Story, *Commentaries on the Constitution of the United States* (Boston: Hilliard Gray, 1833), vol. 2, sec. 798.

78. Raoul Berger, *Impeachment: The Constitutional Problems* (Cambridge: Harvard University Press, 1973), 31, in which he quotes G. M. Trevelyan's *Illustrated History of England* (London: Longmans Green, 1956), 391.

79. For more on House impeachment procedures, see U.S. Congress, House, Committee on the Judiciary, *Impeachment: Selected Materials on Procedure,* 93d Cong., 1st sess., 1973, and 93d Cong., 2d sess., 1974.

80. See U.S. Congress, House Committee on the Judiciary, *Constitutional Grounds for Presidential Impeachment,* 93d Cong., 2d sess., January 1974.

81. Quoted from the *Congressional Record* in Louis Fisher, *Constitutional Conflicts between Congress and the President* (Princeton: Princeton University Press, 1985), 200–201.

82. "An Analysis of the Constitutional Standards for Presidential Impeachment," February 1974, prepared by James D. St. Clair, John J. Chester, Michael A. Sterlacci, Jerome Murphy, and Loren A. Smith (attorneys for the president).

83. Fisher, *Constitutional Conflicts,* 202.

84. For a discussion of this debate, see Berger, *Impeachment,* 78–85.

85. Holly Idelson, "Senate Impeachment Powers Upheld by Justices," *Congressional Quarterly Weekly Report,* January 16, 1993, 129–130.

86. The concept was proposed by Edward S. Corwin in *The President: Office and Powers, 1787–1948* (New York: New York University Press, 1948), 369. He wrote that initially Lincoln claimed an interim war power that was operative only until Congress could ratify his actions. Later the Supreme Court's decision in the *Prize Cases* (2 Black 635, 1863) led to a more expansive claim, which in turn "led him to break over constitutional bounds and become a dictator even exceeding the Roman model." Clinton Rossiter used the term *constitutional dictator* to describe Lincoln's expansive use of presidential powers during a time of national emergency. See Clinton Rossiter, *The American Presidency,* rev. ed. (New York: New American Library, 1960), 142.

87. Arthur M. Schlesinger Jr., *The Imperial Presidency* (Boston: Houghton Mifflin, 1973), 74.

88. Michael L. Benedict, *The Impeachment and Trial of Andrew Johnson* (New York: Norton, 1973), 21.

89. In a historiographical essay discussing changing interpretations of the Johnson presidency, his impeachment, and histories of the Reconstruction period, Benedict noted that the earliest historians of the period placed much of the blame for Johnson's political troubles on the president himself. See ibid., 202.

90. James David Barber, "Adult Identity and Presidential Style: The Rhetorical Emphasis," *Daedalus* 97 (summer 1968): 938–968.

91. According to Benedict (*Impeachment and Trial of Andrew Johnson,* 202), historians of the 1920s had come to develop a new appreciation for President Johnson and had begun to cast him as something of a heroic figure attempting to curb the excesses of the Reconstruction Congress.

92. William M. Goldsmith, *The Growth of Presidential Power* (New York: Chelsea House, 1974), 2:1036.

93. Benedict, *Impeachment and Trial of Andrew Johnson,* 3.

94. See commentary in ibid., 3.

95. *Guide to Congress,* 4th ed. (Washington, D.C.: Congressional Quarterly, 1991), 304.

96. Benedict, *Impeachment and Trial of Andrew Johnson,* 3.

97. Goldsmith, *Growth of Presidential Power,* 2:1033–1035.

98. Abraham Lincoln, "Last Public Address on Reconstruction, April 11, 1985," in ibid., 2:1020–1023.

99. David Miller DeWitt, *The Impeachment and Trial of Andrew Johnson* (New York: Macmillan, 1903), 135.

100. Goldsmith, *Growth of Presidential Power,* 2:1054.

101. Compiled from *Presidential Vetoes, 1789–1988* (Washington, D.C.: Government Printing Office, 1992).

102. DeWitt, *Impeachment and Trial of Andrew Johnson,* 269.

103. DeWitt quotes a private letter from General Grant to the president about the possible removal of Secretary of War Stanton. In the letter of August 1, 1867, Grant comments that Stanton's "removal cannot be effected against his will without the consent of the Senate. . . . It certainly was the intention of the legislative branch of the Government to place cabinet ministers beyond the power of Executive removal and it is pretty well understood that . . . [the Tenure of Office Act] was intended specifically to protect the Secretary of War" (ibid., 272).

104. Benedict, *Impeachment and Trial of Andrew Johnson,* 102.

105. For more on the attempt to remove Stanton from office and on the interchanges between Stanton and Thomas, see DeWitt, *Impeachment and Trial of Andrew Johnson,* 339–356.

106. For more on the trial, see ibid., chap. 6; on Johnson's defense, see 422–514.

107. See the text of the Tenure of Office Act reprinted in Goldsmith, *Growth of Presidential Power,* 2:1045–1047, particularly sec. 1.

108. DeWitt, *Impeachment and Trial of Andrew Johnson,* 436.

109. Berger, *Impeachment,* 264.

110. Ibid., 267–269.

111. In *The Impeachment and Trial of Andrew Johnson,* Benedict wrote that a number of Republicans feared that a Wade administration would be disastrous for both the country and the party. Benedict quoted a May 1868 letter from Garfield to James Harrison Rhodes in which Garfield wrote that Wade is "a man of violent passions, extreme opinions, and narrow views; . . . a grossly profane coarse nature who is surrounded by the worst and most violent elements in the Republican Party" (134–135).

112. DeWitt, *Impeachment and Trial of Andrew Johnson,* 517–518.

113. Ibid., 623–624.

114. The opinion written by former president and Chief Justice William Howard Taft in *Myers v. United States,* 272 U.S. 52 (1926),

enunciated a broad interpretation of the president's removal power, declaring it unrestricted, even in the presence of statutory limits.

115. For a full account of the Watergate investigations and their political impact, see *Watergate: Chronology of a Crisis,* 2 vols. (Washington, D.C.: Congressional Quarterly, 1974); and Theodore H. White, *Breach of Faith: The Fall of Richard Nixon* (New York: Dell, 1975).

116. George A. Nikolaieff, *The President and the Constitution* (New York: H. W. Wilson, 1974), 38.

117. "Judge John Sirica: Standing Firm for the Primacy of Law," *Time,* January 7, 1974, as reprinted in ibid., 64–65.

118. Eleanora W. Schoenebaum, ed., *Profiles of an Era: The Nixon-Ford Years* (New York: Harcourt Brace Jovanovich, 1979), xvi.

119. Quoted by Nikolaieff from "A Very Definitive Decision," *Newsweek,* August 5, 1974, 23–26.

120. As reported from the committee report in *Presidency, 1974* (Washington, D.C.: Congressional Quarterly, 1975), 32.

121. For the text of Nixon's televised address as well as his farewell remarks the following day, see Richard M. Nixon, *The Public Papers of the President, 1974* (Washington, D.C.: Government Printing Office, 1975), 626–633. According to 62 Stat. 678, dated June 25, 1948, the secretary of state is the designated recipient of any resignation letters by presidents and vice presidents.

122. *Clinton v. Jones,* 117 S.Ct. 1646 (1997).

123. *The Starr Report: The Findings of Independent Counsel Kenneth W. Starr on President Clinton and the Lewinsky Affair* (New York: Public Affairs, 1998).

124. "White House's Extended Rebuttal," *USA Today,* September 13, 1998.

125. John R. Zaller, "Monica Lewinsky's Contribution to Political Science," *P.S.: Political Science and Politics* 32 (June 1998): 182–189.

126. Richard Hansen, *The Year We Had No President* (Lincoln: University of Nebraska Press, 1962), cited in Louis W. Koenig, *The Chief Executive,* 4th ed. (New York: Harcourt Brace Jovanovich, 1981), 79.

127. Koenig, *Chief Executive,* 114.

128. Quoted by Feerick in his discussion of the Garfield disability. See *From Failing Hands,* 133–139, especially 133.

129. John D. Feerick, *The Twenty-fifth Amendment* (New York: Fordham University Press, 1992), 10–11.

130. On the Cleveland case, see Feerick, *From Failing Hands,* 147–151; and *The Twenty-fifth Amendment,* 11–12.

131. Quoted in Feerick, *From Failing Hands,* 151.

132. In her memoirs Mrs. Wilson said that "Woodrow Wilson was first my beloved husband whose life I was trying to save, fighting with my back to the wall—after that he was the President of the United States." Quoted in a discussion of the Wilson disability in ibid., 173.

133. Joseph P. Tumulty, *Woodrow Wilson as I Know Him* (Garden City, N.Y.: Doubleday, 1921), as quoted in Feerick, *The Twenty-fifth Amendment,* 13.

134. Quoted in Feerick, *Twenty-fifth Amendment,* 14.

135. For more on the exchange of letters between Wilson and Lansing, see Feerick, *From Failing Hands,* 176–177. Wilson's comments on Lansing's disloyalty are quoted on p. 179.

136. Ibid., 215–216.

137. For more on Dulles's awareness of the Lansing experiences, see Feerick, *Twenty-fifth Amendment,* 18.

138. Koenig, *Chief Executive,* 83.

139. Quoted in Feerick, *From Failing Hands,* 243.

140. Many of these arguments were summarized in a *Washington Post* article of December 2, 1963, which is reprinted in Bayh, *One Heartbeat Away,* 9–10.

141. Arguably the Twenty-fifth Amendment should have been invoked when Reagan was shot in 1981. See Herbert L. Abrams, *"The President Has Been Shot": Confusion, Disability, and the 25th Amendment in the Aftermath of the Attempted Assassination of Ronald Reagan* (New York: Norton, 1992).

142. Letter from President Reagan to the Speaker of the House of Representatives, dated July 13, 1985, summarized and quoted in White Burkett Miller Center of Public Affairs, *Miller Center Commission Report* (Lanham, Md.: University Press of America, 1988), 6.

143. Quoted in Koenig, *Chief Executive,* 86.

SELECTED BIBLIOGRAPHY

Abrams, Herbert L. *"The President Has Been Shot": Confusion, Disability, and the 25th Amendment in the Aftermath of the Attempted Assassination of Ronald Reagan.* New York: Norton, 1992.

Bauer, K. Jack. *Zachary Taylor: Soldier, Planter, Statesman of the Old Southwest.* Baton Rouge: Louisiana State University Press, 1985.

Bayh, Birch. *One Heartbeat Away: Presidential Disability and Succession.* Indianapolis, Ind.: Bobbs-Merrill, 1968.

Benedict, Michael L. *The Impeachment and Trial of Andrew Johnson.* New York: Norton, 1973.

Berger, Raoul. *Impeachment: The Constitutional Problems.* Cambridge: Harvard University Press, 1973.

Corwin, Edward S. *The President: Office and Powers, 1787–1984.* 5th rev. ed. New York: New York University Press, 1984.

Crispell, Kenneth R., and Carlos F. Gomez. *Hidden Illness in the White House.* Durham: Duke University Press, 1988.

DeWitt, David Miller. *The Impeachment and Trial of Andrew Johnson.* New York: Macmillan, 1903.

Doenecke, Justus D. *The Presidencies of James A. Garfield and Chester A. Arthur.* Lawrence: Regents Press of Kansas, 1981.

Donald, David. "Why They Impeached Andrew Johnson." *American Heritage* 8 (December 1956): 20–25.

Feerick, John D. *From Failing Hands: The Story of Presidential Succession.* New York: Fordham University Press, 1965.

———. *The Twenty-fifth Amendment: Its Complete History and Earliest Applications.* New York: Fordham University Press, 1992.

Fisher, Louis. *Constitutional Conflicts between Congress and the President.* 3d rev. ed. Lawrence: University Press of Kansas, 1991.

Goldsmith, William M. *The Growth of Presidential Power.* Vol. 2. New York: Chelsea House, 1983.

Goodwin, Doris Kearns. *No Ordinary Time: Franklin and Eleanor Roosevelt, The Home Front in World War II.* New York: Simon and Schuster, 1994.

Grayson, Benson Lee. *The Unknown President: The Administration of Millard Fillmore.* Washington, D.C.: University Press of America, 1981.

Green, James A. *William Henry Harrison, His Life and Times.* Richmond, Va.: Garrett and Massie, 1941.

Hansen, Richard. *The Year We Had No President.* Lincoln: University of Nebraska Press, 1962.

Kaiser, Frederick M. *Presidential Protection: Assassinations, Assaults, and Secret Service Protective Procedures.* Washington, D.C.: Congressional Research Service, 1981.

Manchester, William. *The Death of a President.* New York: Harper and Row, 1967.

McKitrick, Eric. *Andrew Johnson: President on Trial.* New York: Farrar, Straus, and Giroux, 1960.

Moe, Ronald C. *Presidential Succession.* Washington, D.C.: Congressional Research Service, 1979.

Murray, Robert K. *The Harding Era.* Minneapolis: University of Minnesota Press, 1969.

Posner, Richard A. *An Affair of State: The Investigation, Impeachment, and Trial of President Clinton.* Cambridge: Harvard University Press, 1999.

Rayback, Robert J. *Millard Fillmore, Biography of a President.* Buffalo, N.Y.: Henry Stewart, 1959.

Report of the Miller Center Commission on Presidential Disability and the Twenty-fifth Amendment. Lanham, Md.: University Press of America, 1988.

Rossiter, Clinton. *The American Presidency.* Rev. ed. New York: New American Library, 1960.

Seager, Robert, II. *And Tyler Too: A Biography of John and Julia Gardiner Tyler.* New York: McGraw-Hill, 1963.

Silva, Ruth C. *Presidential Succession.* New York: Greenwood Press, 1968.

Sindler, Allan P. *Unchosen Presidents.* Berkeley: University of California Press, 1976.

U.S. Congress. House. Committee on the Judiciary. *Impeachment: Selected Materials.* Washington, D.C.: Government Printing Office, October 1973.

U.S. Congress. House. Committee on the Judiciary. *Impeachment: Selected Materials on Procedure.* Washington, D.C.: Government Printing Office, January 1974.

U.S. Congress. House. Committee on the Judiciary. *Constitutional Grounds for Presidential Impeachment.* Washington, D.C.: Government Printing Office, February 1974.

Watergate: Chronology of a Crisis. Vol. 2. Washington, D.C.: Congressional Quarterly, 1974.

White, Theodore H. *Breach of Faith: The Fall of Richard Nixon.* New York: Dell, 1975.

PART III ★ POWERS OF THE PRESIDENCY

chapter 9

Unilateral Powers of the Presidency

by Andrew Rudalevige

The Constitution won ratification in part by being vague. But Article II wins out, as Edward Corwin once commented, as its "most loosely drawn chapter."[1] Its very first sentence provides one of the document's least specific but potentially most far-reaching grants of power: that "the executive power shall be vested in a President of the United States of America." By contrast, the parallel language pertaining to Congress in Article I's vesting clause includes a key qualifier, that "all legislative powers *herein granted* shall be vested in a Congress." Does the discrepancy imply that "the executive power" goes beyond the list of powers delineated in the rest of Article II, as claimed by proponents of presidential power as early as the George Washington administration? Even if so, what is that power, exactly? What unilateral actions might it allow the president to take? On this point the document is silent. The answer has been crafted instead by history, worked out in practice and through interbranch contestation.

THE EXECUTIVE POWER

The American government under the Articles of Confederation, of course, had no executive branch at all. And most of the state constitutions at the time sharply limited executive authority: the Virginia constitution of 1776, for example, required that the governor work within the constraints of an independent Council of State, forbade claims of prerogative, and limited executive powers to those specifically granted by the assembly. With these models before them, and concerned that legislative dominance could itself lead to mob-fueled tyranny, the drafters of the Constitution shied away from having Congress dictate the boundaries of presidential action.[2] Instead they left the range of executive powers undefined and ripe for reinterpretation by later presidents.

To be sure, the other executive example fresh in the Framers' minds was that of King George III. Thus the Constitution actually grants to presidents a limited array of explicit powers. Presidents were given the ability to grant reprieves and pardons, which the Framers believed might be useful in resolving domestic insurrections such as Shays' Rebellion of 1786 (which in many ways had prompted the Constitutional Convention in the first place). Consistent with the fundamental constitutional principle of checked authority, though, many of the other powers in Article II come with an asterisk of sorts. Presidents' treaties must be ratified by two-thirds of the Senate, and their appointments confirmed by a Senate majority. Presidents may suggest laws, but Congress must pass them (and can override presidential vetoes); presidents may conduct wars, but Congress has the power to declare them. Presidents have control of their department heads, but Congress decides what departments exist in the first place, as well as how much the departments have to spend each year. As defenders of the Constitution sparred with antifederalist writers like the pseudonymous "Cato," they did not dispute his contention that "to live by one man's will [becomes] the cause of all men's misery." Instead, they sought to show that presidents' powers were hemmed in by institutional checks ranging from their inability to impose taxes or appointees to Congress's power to impeach and remove them from office.[3]

At the same time, as Alexander Hamilton pointed out in *Federalist* No. 70, only some of the "energy" of the executive branch comes from a president's formal powers and ability to resist legislative encroachment. The crucial choice to create a single executive, rather than the plural presidency favored by some at the Constitutional Convention, gives its occupant a leg up on its rivals for power. The fact that Congress is a divided body run by collective choices gives presidents inherent advantages of "decision, activity, secrecy, and dispatch." Presidents can make decisions quickly and discreetly and can often act on them alone. Even if they do not get the last say, presidents often get to make the first move—which itself may shape the landscape over which subsequent decisions are taken. "The executive, in the exercise of its constitutional powers," Hamilton noted, "may establish an antecedent state of things, which ought to weigh in the legislative decision."[4]

To these advantages were added powers that Article II was taken to imply. The divergent wording of the vesting clauses that introduced Articles I and II has already been noted; Hamilton called this clear evidence that the subsequent discussion of presidential powers in Article II merely specified limits on various aspects of that "more comprehensive grant contained in the general clause." If so, the president's ability to control what would later be termed the "unitary executive branch" is absolute. Others suggested that inherent powers were also implied by the president's duty to "take care that the laws be faithfully executed" (President Grover Cleveland called this "a grant of all the power necessary to the performance of his duty in the faithful execution of the laws"); in the presidential oath of office to "preserve, protect, and defend the Constitution"; or by the office of commander-in-chief, even in peacetime.[5]

Are presidents, then, limited to the specific powers affirmatively listed in the Constitution? Or can they take whatever actions they deem in the public interest so long as those actions are not actually prohibited by the Constitution? President Theodore Roosevelt argued the latter: that "it was not only [the President's] right but his duty to do anything that the needs of the Nation required unless such action was forbidden by the Constitution or by the laws." Here are the seeds of what one scholar recently termed "venture constitutionalism."[6]

The argument held special force in times of national emergency. English philosopher John Locke, in his *Second Treatise of Government* (1690), defended "prerogative," defined as the power of the executive "to act according to discretion, for the publick good, without the prescription of the Law, and sometimes even against it." Legislatures were slow, Locke argued, and the law could not foresee all "accidents and necessities" that might arise. Indeed, even where statutes were in place, their rigid implementation might sometimes do more harm than good. Thus the executive needed discretion to set a policy course even in normal times; in dire crisis, "it is fit that the laws themselves should give way to the executive power, or rather to this fundamental law of nature and government, [namely] that, as much as may be, all the members of society are to be preserved."[7] Abraham Lincoln would later put the point this way: "often a limb must be amputated to save a life; but a life is never wisely given to save a limb. . . . [M]easures, otherwise unconstitutional, might become lawful, by becoming indispensable to the preservation of the constitution, through the preservation of the nation."[8]

James Madison, however, argued that presidential action, to be "properly executive, must pre-suppose the existence of the laws to be executed"—and "to see the laws faithfully executed constitutes the essence of the executive authority." From this might be deduced the power to remove subordinate officers responsible for executing the law (itself a question at issue in the first Congress in 1789), but little else. Madison charged Hamilton with arguing for an expansive theory of presidential power not from the Constitution's text but from "*royal prerogatives* in the *British government*."[9] President William Howard Taft likewise took strong issue with his one-time mentor, Theodore Roosevelt. "The President can exercise no power which cannot be fairly and reasonably traced to some specific grant of power or justly implied within such express grant as proper and necessary to its exercise," Taft wrote. "There is no undefined residuum of power which he can exercise because it seems to him to be in the public interest."[10] Even James Wilson, the most persuasive advocate of a strong new executive branch at the Constitutional Convention, assured delegates that the only strictly executive powers under the Constitution should be to carry out the laws and choose personnel. Indeed, if presidents were vested with vast executive authority, why bother to point out in Article II that they could require written opinions from their department heads?[11]

This struggle, between presidents claiming the power to act without clear constitutional mandates and critics arguing to the contrary, underlines much of U.S. history. While the evidence from the Framers' debates probably favors the critics, in practice, Hamilton's view has decisively won out.[12] Congress may be the first branch of government, leaving presidential power as the residual authority left over from other actors in the system. Yet those leavings have hardly been meager; silence (in the constitutional text) has not proven golden for advocates of a limited executive. The powers it implies, however tacitly, have instead been given substance by years of continuous reinterpretation by presidents, courts, and even legislators. As such they have served as sources of the president's ability to act alone, even absent specific congressional delegation of power, in ways whose extent and potency have grown beyond anything the Founders could have foreseen. On its face, for example, the "take care" clause directs the president to administer statutes in a manner faithful to legislative language and intent. But in an 1890 case, the Supreme Court ruled that executing the laws could not be "limited to the enforcement of acts of Congress or of treaties . . . according to their *express terms*" but rather included "the rights, duties and obligations growing out of the Constitution itself, our international relations, and all the protection implied by the nature of the government under the Constitution."[13]

By this reasoning, presidents could in theory undertake any action deemed necessary to carry out their constitutional duties, to provide for the nation's defense, or to protect the common good. Still, what are those duties, and where do they leave off? What does that defense require? For that matter, who gets to decide the substance of the "common good"? To the extent those answers are the president's to give, the potential of unilateral powers is both awesome and rightly controversial.

The remainder of this chapter traces the growth and tools of executive discretion, as well as its limits. As legislators realized after Watergate, these methods have the potential for abuse. Most recently, the renewed claims to unilateral executive authority of the George W. Bush administration, especially after the terrorist attacks of September 11, 2001, led to renewed debate over what presidential powers are necessary and appropriate.

THE GROWTH OF EXECUTIVE DISCRETION

Federalists such as Hamilton wanted a national government that "left substantial freedom of action to high officials and kept Congress out of most administrative details." [14] And, in fact, Congress generally trusted the revered first president to get the new nation on its feet. However, in 1793 Washington unilaterally declared U.S. neutrality in the war between France and England. Washington argued that his constitutional responsibility to represent the nation included the implied power to keep the United States out of war. This rationale did not convince James Madison, who retorted that the proclamation was invalid because only Congress could decide issues of war and peace. "Those who are to conduct a war cannot in the nature of things, be proper or safe judges, whether a war ought to be commenced, continued, or concluded," he argued.[15]

But even Thomas Jefferson, who urged Madison to attack the Neutrality Proclamation, adopted a broad view of the executive powers upon attaining them. He purchased the Louisiana Territory without prior congressional approval, ordered offensive naval action against Mediterranean piracy, and spent unappropriated funds to restock military stores after the U.S. frigate *Chesapeake* was seized by Britain in 1807. In an 1810 letter he argued that "to lose our country by a scrupulous adherence to written law, would be to lose the law itself, with life, liberty, property and all those who are enjoying them with us; thus absurdly sacrificing the end to the means." [16]

That logic took its strongest tangible form during the Civil War, when Abraham Lincoln took an array of unilateral actions beyond his constitutional authority—blockading Southern ports, spending unbudgeted funds on weapons and ships, expanding the armed services, censoring the mail, suspending the right of *habeas corpus* to hold prisoners without charges or trial, and even instituting military tribunals in place of the civilian judiciary. When Supreme Court chief justice Roger Taney ruled that Lincoln had usurped the sole power of Congress to suspend writs of *habeas corpus* during an emergency, Lincoln ignored the decision.[17] Later, by executive proclamation, he ordered that slaves be emancipated without compensation to their owners.

Lincoln claimed such an extensive array of emergency war powers to preserve the Union that he became, in the words of presidential scholar Clinton Rossiter, a "constitutional dictator." Yet Lincoln did ask Congress for retroactive approval of his actions (for instance, in the Habeas Corpus Act of 1863), and ran for reelection in 1864.[18] In the end, legal nuances paled before the emergency at hand. In the *Prize Cases* (1863), shipowners whose vessels were seized trying to run the Union lines sued on the grounds that the

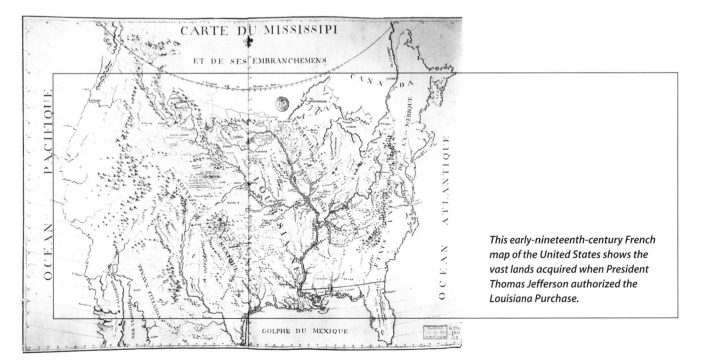

This early-nineteenth-century French map of the United States shows the vast lands acquired when President Thomas Jefferson authorized the Louisiana Purchase.

blockade itself was unconstitutional because Congress had not declared war. This was technically true, but, the Court ruled, war was simply a fact and Lincoln was required to defend the nation.[19]

To be sure, for most of the nineteenth century Congress took an assertive view of the legislative role in governance. Even Jefferson and his allies, notes historian Leonard White, "emphasized the responsibility of the executive branch and the administrative system to Congress." Congress held tight reins over executive branch actions through highly detailed statutes, strict budget controls, and reviews of even the most mundane administrative matters.[20] Though the Supreme Court ruled in1827 that Madison was right during the War of 1812 to overrule governors and activate state militias—arguing that the president alone defines emergencies when the nation is at war or is faced with imminent hostilities[21]—this was an exception to pre–Civil War claims of presidential emergency powers. In most instances, presidents deployed U.S. forces against pirates abroad or Native American uprisings at home to protect U.S. citizens and their property. Their actions usually were based on a specific congressional grant of authority, such as the power that Congress gave James Monroe to protect American merchant ships against pirates, or the congressional declaration of war on Mexico in 1846. In general, early presidents—even the headstrong Andrew Jackson—exhibited restraint in exercising their commander-in-chief responsibilities. And during Reconstruction, legislative dominance seemed to bounce back from Lincoln's exertions; for a time, as legislator George Hoar wrote, if senators "visited the White House, it was to give, not to receive, advice." [22] The Supreme Court, which had upheld Lincoln's naval blockade and subsequent seizure of foreign merchant ships, decided in 1866 that the president had not possessed the power to bypass civilian courts and institute military trials in Union territory. The idea that the Constitution could be suspended by some "theory of necessity" was "pernicious" and "false," Justice Davis wrote in *Ex parte Milligan*. Indeed, "it could be well said that a country, preserved at the sacrifice of all the cardinal provisions of liberty, is not worth the cost of preservation." [23]

Still, that Supreme Court decision came down safely after the war was over. Even during this subsequent period some historians' shorthand convention of presidential torpor is not fully accurate. Presidents Rutherford B. Hayes, James A. Garfield, Chester A. Arthur, and Grover Cleveland, for example, strongly defended presidential appointment and administrative powers against congressional incursion, to popular acclaim. In *In re Neagle* (1890), as noted above, the Court agreed with the attorney general's contention that the presidential oath must, "by necessary implication," be read to "invest the President with self-executing powers; that is, powers independent of statute." [24] In like fashion, the Court held in 1895 that the federal government's powers

could not be limited to legislation punishing interference with those processes after the fact. That extra power—the residual between the power utilized by congressional legislation and "the entire strength of the nation"—could be used by the president proactively, in the absence of contrary law, when federal functions were threatened. *U.S. v. Midwest Oil*, a third decision, in 1915, held that when presidential assertions of power in an area had been accepted frequently over time by Congress, such historical precedent might govern executive-legislative relations as much as constitutional doctrine in "determining the meaning of a statute or the existence of a power." [25]

By the early 1900s Americans expressed a growing acceptance of federal (and presidential) responsibility in the United States and abroad. Theodore Roosevelt, as already described, made clear his belief that as "steward of the people" the president enjoyed a range of residual executive powers implied in the Constitution. Such powers, Roosevelt argued, were neither enumerated in the Constitution nor assigned broadly to a specific branch; instead, they resided in basic concepts such as national sovereignty and the public good. The president, then, was to represent the nation as a whole, distinct from the parochialism of locally elected legislators. Woodrow Wilson turned this into a grand version of popular stewardship, viewing the party system not as a constraining force but as a nearly parliamentary means for translating the president's program into policy change.[26]

But the Constitution says very little about what powers might be available to a stewardship presidency. Political scientist Richard Pious suggests that "like Excalibur's sword, [the president] must wrest his powers from the Constitution before he can wield them." In those terms the image of a truly discretionary presidency did not begin to take shape until World War I.

In part this was because by the twentieth century, "total war" was at hand, blurring the lines between combatants and civilians and involving the entire social, economic, and industrial capacities of nations. It thus required swift, massive, and sustained national organization and mobilization, the capacities for which lay mostly in the executive branch. In 1917 Congress passed a spate of laws granting Wilson broad powers along these lines: he was empowered to nationalize defense-related facilities; to regulate food production, manufacturing, and mining; to fix prices on commodities; to raise an army; to restrict exports; and to regulate and censor external communications. Wilson also was granted broad authority to monitor actions by resident aliens, to regulate or operate transportation and communications facilities, and to reorganize executive branch agencies where necessary. In effect, then, he was granted almost free rein to conduct the war and to direct the domestic economy.[27] Even so, Wilson did not shy away from asserting inherent prerogatives as commander in chief. Issuing two thousand executive orders along the way, he claimed the right to go beyond the scope of congressional authorization in creating wartime agencies, enforcing "voluntary" press censorship, and coordinating private industry. Nor did the powers Wilson asserted in wartime vanish once hostilities ceased—in the postwar 1918–1921 "Palmer Raids," for example, supposed communist subversives were searched, detained, and even deported without warrant. The precedents set would endure for later presidents in a ratchet-like expansion of executive power.

The New Deal and World War II

By the twentieth century, in Wilson's phrase, "the President [was] at liberty both in law and conscience to be as big a man as he can." [28] From Franklin D. Roosevelt's time forward, these tools became expectations rather than possibilities. The Great Depression, World War II, the cold war, and the "War on Terror," dramatically raised Americans' demands on their presidents as well as the size, scope, and reach of the federal government. Richard E. Neustadt, in a play on Wilson's observation, noted that the president could certainly still be big; "but nowadays he cannot be as small as he might like." [29]

Franklin Roosevelt gave permanence to Theodore Roosevelt's stewardship view of the presidency and made it part of the very definition of the "modern presidency." [30] Elected as depression raged, and given wide latitude by Congress and the American people, Roosevelt relied heavily on executive initiatives to attack the economic crisis and rally the nation. He issued 654 executive orders in 1933 alone. These included his inauguration day proclamation closing all banks for four days to restructure the crumbling banking system (the authority for which was grounded in a law left over from World War I) and the creation of mechanisms for implementing New Deal programs. In most cases, Roosevelt received quick and sometimes retroactive congressional approval. In 1933, for example, legislators approved a law granting Roosevelt emergency powers to alleviate the bank crisis after only eight hours of debate. Congress also uncharacteristically appropriated discretionary funds so that the executive branch could develop programs more quickly and perhaps more effectively than might be possible via normal legislative procedures.[31] The crisis prompted support for decisive action and enabled Roosevelt to stretch the boundaries of his constitutional powers to the limit. "In the event Congress shall fail to act, and act adequately, I shall accept the responsibility, and I will act," FDR proclaimed in 1942. "The President has the powers, under the Constitution, and under Congressional acts, to take measures necessary to avert a disaster. . . ." [32]

Roosevelt was seeking a law governing wage and price controls, and he got one. But the 1942 speech highlights his willingness to use executive authority, broadly defined, with

or without congressional approval. This highly muscular view of presidential discretion was buttressed by the sheer growth in the federal government during the 1930s and 1940s that brought with it an explosion in executive branch responsibility. Congress found it increasingly difficult to grapple with the size and complexity of new national programs and began the widespread delegation of authority that marks contemporary government.

After World War I, Congress had reasserted itself in foreign policy, and its powerful isolationist wing resisted Roosevelt's efforts to link the United States to the European nations facing Nazi expansionism. Still, even before Pearl Harbor, Roosevelt made broad claims of authority to prosecute the war. The 1936 *Curtiss-Wright* decision—still cherished by presidents, if not by scholars of constitutional law—affirmed the "very delicate, plenary, and exclusive power of the President as the sole organ of the federal government in the field of international relations—a power which does not require as a basis for its exercise an act of Congress." [33] Roosevelt moved unilaterally in many instances, basing his actions on powers that he claimed derived from his constitutional duties as commander in chief and chief executive. Seeking to sidestep congressional declarations of neutrality as Europe fell into war, for instance, in 1939 he declared a "limited" state of emergency, which allowed him to invoke existing statutes (many of which had been enacted in Wilson's day) to prepare the nation militarily. After the fall of France, Roosevelt declared an "unlimited national emergency," under which he reorganized the executive branch and prepared to deal with the domestic economy once the United States entered into hostilities, spending more than $15 billion appropriated for military preparedness measures. In neither instance did Roosevelt seek prior congressional authorization for his actions, although he usually cited existing statutory powers.

As the war approached, Roosevelt also concluded a series of executive agreements, thus evading the Senate ratification needed for treaties, most famously transferring fifty destroyers to Britain in return for eight Caribbean naval bases. Such a transaction violated a 1917 statute prohibiting the transfer of warships to a belligerent nation, and also the 1940 Neutrality Act, since the ships were usable military equipment; however, the attorney general's opinion justifying the agreement grounded it in various principles including the "plenary powers of the President as Commander-in-Chief of the Army and Navy and as head of state in its relations with foreign countries." In January 1941, months before lend-lease legislation finally passed, FDR began to arrange $3 billion in supplies for the Soviet Union. An executive agreement with Denmark in April 1941 allowed U.S. forces to occupy Greenland, followed in July by an agreement to defend Iceland as well; by October the navy was told to provide "neutrality patrols" near merchant ships and sink

Japanese citizens and Japanese Americans wait in line for their assigned homes at an alien reception center in Manzanar, Calif., on March 24, 1942, after being forced from their homes in Los Angeles by the U.S. Army.

Axis ships even if they were not near the convoys. Once Congress declared war in December 1941, Roosevelt dropped even the pretense of delegated powers. His seizure of defense plants immediately after Pearl Harbor, for example, was based on claims of authority given to him by the Constitution and "the laws," although he never made clear which ones.[34]

Domestically, FDR worried about sabotage of the war effort. Even though the Supreme Court had sought to limit the use of evidence obtained through wiretapping, and Roosevelt failed to receive legislative authorization overriding that decision, he pressed on, directing Attorney General Robert H. Jackson in 1940 to surveil "persons suspected of subversive activities against the Government of the United States." Had large scale domestic sabotage broken out during World War II, Jackson later wrote, "there is no doubt in my mind that President Roosevelt would have taken most ruthless methods to suppress it. . . . [H]e did not share the extreme position about civil rights that some of his followers have taken."[35]

Executive Order 9066, issued in 1942, made that point clear. The order spurred the detention of 112,000 Japanese Americans on the West Coast in internment camps for the duration of the war, justified by the need to prevent espionage and sabotage. Though endorsed by Congress and (at least tacitly) by the Supreme Court, this decision later came to be viewed as a gross violation of the civil liberties of U.S. citizens. In 1988 Congress appropriated reparations for those interned.[36]

The Permanent Emergency

As noted above and detailed further below, crises empower the executive branch: a menacing world requires the swift

decision-making capacity of centralized leadership. And the postwar period, marked by wars cold and hot, ushered in a seemingly perpetual period of crisis. "Emergencies in policy," by prewar standards, Richard Neustadt wrote in 1960, became business as usual, "a way of life."[37] With the threat of nuclear Armageddon as backdrop, national security became the primary justification for unilateral executive action in the years after World War II. The bipolar standoff between the United States and the Soviet Union expanded U.S. commitments around the world, and a consensus on the need for assertive executive leadership prompted Congress to accede to presidential dictates across a wide spectrum of domestic and international policy domains.[38]

Many scholars characterize the period between the late 1940s and early 1970s as one of relative congressional decline in which legislators appeared to surrender many of their traditional prerogatives. On this subject, Allen Schick noted that "when Congress controls, it legislates the particulars; when Congress withdraws, it legislates in general terms."[39] Indeed, statutes in both domestic and foreign policy areas became far less detailed and constraining compared to those passed before Roosevelt.

This development was generally applauded. Scholars began to tout "presidential government," openly supporting the idea that broad executive discretion would lead to more efficient and effective administration. Constitutional constants such as separation of powers and federalism, long defended as essential for safeguarding citizens' rights and liberties, now appeared to be impediments to progressive government. Strong presidential leadership was needed to overcome the fragmentation and delays inherent in the nation's structure of governance. If, as Corwin concluded long before Watergate, "the history of the presidency has been a history of aggrandizement," that aggrandizement was generally well received.[40]

The presidency that evolved from the New Deal through the Vietnam War was thus the presidency at its least constrained—leading to a state of affairs ultimately and enduringly dubbed by historian Arthur Schlesinger Jr., as the "imperial presidency." [41] The tools of that presidency are described in the next section.

TOOLS OF UNILATERALISM: THE MODERN PRESIDENCY

Changes in the presidency starting from the time of the New Deal have "added up to so thorough a transformation that a modifier such as 'modern' is needed to characterize the post-1932 manifestations of the institution that had evolved from the far more circumscribed traditional presidency." [42] Modern presidents have immense visibility and thus agenda-setting powers; and they have creatively used their formal and informal powers to carve out influence over policy formulation and implementation. The tools of contemporary executive unilateralism are tallied briefly below.

Agenda Setting

The rise of radio, and then television, meant that presidents could seize the public's agenda through what John F. Kennedy's aide Ted Sorensen called "direct communication" without "alteration or omission." [43] The mechanics of the industry helped too. It was far easier for the mass media to focus on one person than on the inchoate multitudes in Congress, far easier to follow a personal narrative than an institutional collective. To be sure, television also shaped presidential agendas—Kennedy's civil rights program in 1963, for example, was decisively prompted by the televised brutality against peaceful marchers in Birmingham, Alabama. But generally, the stewardship presidency was reinforced by moving Theodore Roosevelt's "bully pulpit" to the broadcast age. *(See Chapter 20, Public Support and Opinion.)*

The power of agenda setting also links closely with the expanded role of the president in the legislative arena. *(See Chapter 29, The President and Congress, Vol. II.)* Into the 1920s, the constitutional invitation to provide Congress with measures the president deemed "necessary and expedient" was rarely treated as an open one. But Franklin Roosevelt's famous "hundred days," marked new boundaries. During this time a flood of proposals rolled out of the executive branch and into law, receiving remarkable legislative deference. In the House temporary rules even prevented members from amending administration proposals on the floor. By the time Dwight Eisenhower took office, legislators not only accepted but demanded a presidential agenda. Despite his reluctance to do so, Eisenhower complied and even created a White House staff devoted to congressional liaison.

Even as divided government became a regular feature of American governance, the presidential program remained an important part of the legislative agenda. After his party lost control of Congress in the 2006 midterms, for example, George W. Bush denied that he was "out of the policy business"—to the contrary, he said, "the microphone of the president has never been louder. . . . Without presidential involvement, nothing will happen." [44]

Once bills reached the president's desk, they faced a newly aggressive veto pen. The earliest presidents used the veto only on bills they thought unconstitutional; FDR, by contrast, reportedly told his cabinet to "find me something I can veto." Even the supposedly passive Eisenhower vetoed nearly two hundred bills in eight years. But veto bargaining was as important as the act itself. Though he did not issue a single veto in his first five years in office, George W. Bush would later comment that "the best tool I have besides persuasion is to veto." As had his predecessors, he pointed out that the veto made him part of the legislative process. Presidents came to take full advantage of that leverage.[45]

Controlling the Bureaucracy: People and Process

One of the modern presidency's greatest tasks is to control the federal establishment itself. The president may be chief executive, but this does not ensure prompt bureaucratic execution of White House dictates. Close to four million people work for the executive branch, spread across fifteen cabinet departments and nearly sixty independent agencies.[46] They report to the president, true, but are suspended between the branches, buffeted in the battles between president, Congress, and courts; between interest groups and the national interest; between presidential directives and their own statutory duties and organizational cultures. Presidents may be vexed most by the tenacity of linkages forged between the professional bureaucracy and Congress. The power of Congress over lawmaking and budgets, the tenure offered by civil service rules, and the relatively temporary nature of presidential terms of office make it incredibly hard for presidents to force their preferences upon the permanent government. Presidents have used two major strategies for seeking bureaucratic control: centralization and politicization.[47]

Centralization

Centralization refers to the shift of functions from the wider executive branch to the Executive Office of the President (EOP), which was created in 1939. *(See Chapter 22, Executive Office of the President: White House Office, Vol. II.)* The most obvious ramification is the growth of the White House staff over time, from a handful of personal aides under Franklin Roosevelt to perhaps several thousand employees with substantive duties in the early twenty-first century. Presidents have used their White House and EOP staffs as an alternate mechanism for coordinating and formulating policy. The EOP now houses aides, and aides to aides, devoted to policymaking (domestic, economic, and national security), communications (with the public, the bureaucracy, Congress, and interest groups), and its own internal administration. New staff units spring up to reflect salient presidential and societal concerns, from energy (under Richard Nixon) to the drug czar (under Reagan) to an AIDS outreach office (under Bill Clinton) to one (under George W. Bush) implementing faith-based initiatives.[48] In many cases Congress has provided the requisite statutory authority afterward. But there have sometimes been limits to congressional acquiescence. For example, FDR's tendency to use executive orders to create wartime agencies and fund them with funds appropriated for other purposes eventually provoked a backlash. In 1944 Congress barred use of any appropriations for an agency created through executive order unless the funds were authorized specifically for that agency.[49]

One recent work on presidential power calls the president "chief budgeter," [50] despite the vesting of the power of the purse in Congress, and thus a division of EOP worth special mention is the Office of Management and Budget (OMB). From its position astride the annual budget process, OMB gives the president particular leverage over bureaucratic behavior. Prior to 1921, presidents had little centralized control over agency requests for funding, but the passage of the Budget and Accounting Act that year required a unified executive budget and thus gave presidents a new mechanism for managing their agenda. In 1933 Franklin Roosevelt transferred all executive branch budget-making authority from department heads to the Bureau of the Budget (OMB's forerunner, itself created by the 1921 law.) In 1939 Roosevelt moved the bureau from the Treasury Department to the newly created EOP, making it a truly presidential agency rather than simply a departmental coordinator.[51]

Upon arriving in the EOP, the Budget Bureau organized not only the president's budget but the president's legislative program as well. That included efforts to control monies after funds were appropriated, through allotment and impoundment, and the "central clearance" of agency testimony and legislative proposals. In 1970 Richard Nixon sought to enhance the Bureau's ability to influence agency management practices as well, reorganizing it into the Office of Management and Budget. Ronald Reagan added regulatory review functions to the mix. (See "Rulemaking and Regulatory Review," p. 519.) Though presidents have never been entirely satisfied with OMB's management reach, the agency continues to be a centerpiece of their efforts to shape bureaucratic outputs and outcomes, housing offices overseeing procurement, financial management, and government technology efforts. President Clinton reorganized OMB in 1994 to merge managerial and budgetary staff into "Resource Management Offices." George W. Bush's long-term "President's Management Agenda" empowered OMB to develop the Program Assessment Rating Tool (PART) system, intended to grade programmatic effectiveness and ultimately link it to funding decisions.

Congress in particular criticizes this tendency toward staff growth and the creation of a "presidential branch," though most complaints seem to come from those opposing the policies of particular presidents. Future presidents are unlikely to reverse this trend, because the desire to control the bureaucracy is common to Democratic and Republican presidents alike. Presumably, though, the battle over the bureaucracy will remain a major source of conflict between the branches.[52]

Politicization

Another front of that battle concerns presidential efforts at politicization—their efforts to structure and staff the bureaucracy in ways that make bureaus more responsive to their will. (See Chapter 31, The President and the Bureaucracy, Vol. II.) There are some six thousand executive branch political appointments, ranging from the cabinet secretaries down to lower level "Schedule C" posts deep within the bureaucracy. If, as the Reagan administration felt, "Personnel is Policy," presidents pay close attention to those personnel, even where (as in the inspectors general corps) they are ostensibly nonpartisan. Through appointing personal loyalists across the executive branch, presidents have sought, in the words of one George W. Bush aide, to "implant their DNA throughout the government." To be sure that DNA is faithfully replicated, they have developed aggressive personnel recruitment and vetting operations, a process that extends to candidates for the federal judiciary. In 2001 Bush required that the White House Office of Personnel interview and approve every candidate, even for subcabinet appointments often delegated to cabinet officers.[53]

These efforts can be controversial—loyalty that trumps competence, after all, can lead to performance in office that reflects badly on the president, as the aftermath of Hurricane Katrina in the fall of 2005 proved.

Even more contested are efforts to control the personal views or behavior of executive branch employees via oath or test. Woodrow Wilson, for example, sought to dismiss government employees alleged to hold socialist or other "un-American" views in the lead up to World War I by issuing a 1917 executive order giving agency heads the power to fire any employee judged "inimical to the public welfare." Later, as the nation became caught in the grip of the cold war with the Soviet Union, Truman's Executive Order 9835 in 1947 instituted loyalty oaths for all federal employees to root out possible communist sympathizers.[54] On another front, Reagan ordered in 1986 all executive branch agencies to establish random drug-testing programs for personnel in "sensitive" positions. Civil libertarians asserted that random tests violated the privacy rights of public employees, but in 1989 the Supreme Court ruled that mandatory drug tests were constitutional under certain conditions.[55]

To be sure, high-level appointees must receive Senate confirmation. However, the Civil Service Reform Act of 1978 gave presidents more leeway over appointments just below those requiring confirmation (in what was now called the Senior Executive Service): Reagan used this tool to remove numerous career officials from key positions and replace them with his own partisans, while using staffing cuts to eliminate entire offices of civil servants.

Presidents also use "recess appointments" to circumvent the confirmation process. Article II, Section 2, allows presidents to fill vacancies while the Senate is in recess, until the end of the next Senate session. In the 1790s, of course, logistics dictated long breaks from the Capitol. While these days legislators are in near-continuous session, recess appointments remain a way of installing contested nominees without Senate interference. After Reagan failed to abolish the Legal Services Corporation statutorily, for example, he used recess appointments to install an entirely new board hostile to the agency's mandate. In all he made nearly 250 recess appointments in eight years, a figure that dropped off under George H. W. Bush (he made seventy-five such appointments in four years) and Bill Clinton (139 in eight years), though in late 2000 Clinton made a rare recess appointment to the federal judiciary. George W. Bush embraced this strategy; through 2006 he had made 161 recess appointments in six years, including two federal judges and the ambassador to the United Nations, John Bolton.[56] Recess appointments attract dissent and may serve only as a temporary fix for a president seeking responsiveness—Bolton, for instance, was not confirmed by the Senate at the end of his recess appointment in December 2006 and submitted his resignation.

POLICY IMPLEMENTATION

Article II requires presidents to "take care that the laws be faithfully executed." It is less clear what constitutes fidelity to this charge when the laws themselves are vaguely drafted or even (to presidents' minds at least) unconstitutional. Thus presidents have sought to increase their influence over policy implementation by mechanisms ranging from control over agency rulemaking to executive command.

Rulemaking and Regulatory Review

Congress frequently finds itself unable or unwilling to respond to complex national problems with highly specific statutory language. Instead, legislative language sets goals, timetables, and standards, delegating to the executive branch the power to hammer out the frequently arcane technical matters that carry out a statute's intent.

Thus the substance of any law is in many ways determined by the regulations issued in its name; rule making by executive agencies can serve as a relatively low-salience mechanism for effecting tangible policy change, sometimes in ways not anticipated by a statute's legislative authors.[57] The "No Child Left Behind" education reforms passed in 2001 provide a good example: how increased testing and accountability requirements would actually affect schools and students was not clear until the Department of Education had issued rules governing what kind of tests were required and how state standards for measuring pupil performance could be defined. Part of the appeal to presidents of the politicization process noted above, therefore, is that it helps ensure that even lower-level appointees are in tune with administration policy preferences. It is no accident, to continue the example above, that the Department of Education is one of the most politicized agencies in the federal government. In recent years the Environmental Protection Agency and Food and Drug Administration have also been targeted by presidents seeking to reduce the regulatory burden on business.

The importance of the rulemaking process rose with the growth of the American federal establishment and the administrative state. By the 1970s, federal regulation reached into most corners of the U.S. economy, from consumer protection to workplace safety. President Nixon thus sought to give OMB the power to approve regulations, and Presidents Gerald R. Ford and Jimmy Carter directed agencies to consider the inflationary impact and cost-benefit ratio of new regulations. However, it was left to Ronald Reagan to move regulatory review into OMB's extant process of central clearance. In February 1981, he issued an executive order stating flatly that "regulatory action shall not be undertaken unless the potential benefits to society for the regulation outweigh the potential costs to society." OMB—in particular, its Office of Information and Regulatory Affairs (OIRA)—had the power to recommend that regulations be withdrawn if they could not "be reformulated to meet its objections." In 1985 another order extended OMB's reach to agency "prerulemaking activities," defined as almost any activity that could lead to consideration of the need for a regulation. This order also required OMB to approve an annual "regulatory program" submitted by each agency and prohibited actions not in that program unless cleared by OMB observers. The process as it developed was largely off-the-record—over the phone or via confidential comments—which served to shield it from legislative or judicial review. Despite congressional grumbling, there was little legislative reaction; and regulatory review remained in place through the presidencies of George H. W. Bush, Bill Clinton, and George W. Bush. The latter Bush strengthened OIRA's focus on cost-benefit analysis and expanded OMB's review power to include even "guidance documents" short of formal regulation. His desire for regulatory responsiveness in environmental policy attracted perhaps the most attention, as scientists charged that technical review procedures were being shunted aside in favor of political considerations, usually favoring development over preservation. Nonetheless, regulatory review has become a fixture of the administrative presidency, if not one with any statutory basis.[58]

Signing Statement and Item Vetoes

Another means of directing policy implementation is the use of "signing statements" issued upon the signing of a bill into law. These statements provide constitutional commentary on aspects of the new statute to influence its judicial interpretation, guide rule making, and announce the mechanisms by which the executive branch will enforce the disputed provisions—if at all. While examples can be found dating to the Monroe administration, Reagan and his successors—especially George W. Bush—were more self-conscious and systematic about the strategy. Indeed, Bush's use of signing statements has been markedly aggressive—by one count, he issued more than all other presidents combined, recording 116 separate objections to the Consolidated Appropriations Act of 2005 alone.[59]

Presidents have argued that Congress cannot interfere with any processes leading to the utilization of Article II powers such as the proposal of legislation or the selection of nominees to office. In 1999, for instance, Clinton filled a newly created National Nuclear Security Administration with extant Energy Department staff in defiance of statutory dictate, while in 2001 George W. Bush said that a section of a statute directing the administration to submit a bill addressing bovine disease control would be interpreted instead as a suggestion.

Claims about foreign affairs powers have, perhaps, been more notable. For example, after Reagan issued a national security directive with strict enforcement provisions governing the disclosure of information deemed sensitive, Congress passed a bill forbidding the administration from enforcing those provisions. Reagan signed it—but stated that since it "impermissibly interfered with my ability to prevent unauthorized disclosures of our most sensitive diplomatic, military, and intelligence activities. . . , in accordance with my sworn obligation to preserve, protect, and defend the Constitution, [it] will be considered of no force or effect. . . ." Along similar lines, the younger Bush, like other presidents, routinely included language in signing statements rejecting provisions that would in his view "unconstitutionally constrain my authority regarding the conduct of diplomacy and my authority as Commander-in-Chief."[60] In late 2005 that position brought the signing statement into the public eye when he asserted that he would construe the Detainee Treatment Act's ban against the "cruel, inhuman, or degrading treatment or punishment" of pris-

oners "in a manner consistent with the constitutional authority of the President to supervise the unitary executive branch and as Commander in Chief and consistent with the constitutional limitations on the judicial power." In late 2006 a signing statement to the U.S.-India Peaceful Atomic Energy Cooperation Act claimed Congress could not "purpor[t] to establish U.S. policy with respect to various international affairs matters." Bush would take legislative direction, including a ban on the transfer to India of certain nuclear materials, only as "advisory." [61]

In these cases and others, then, presidents claimed the right to determine how—and whether—the law would be implemented. The formulaic nature of the language used in asserting these executive claims tended to conceal their extraordinarily broad affirmations of presidential power. While their practical impact on policy implementation is unclear, they have been largely unchecked thus far. Though a circuit court once scolded the Reagan administration's effort to avoid parts of a contracting act by saying "this claim of right for the President to declare statutes unconstitutional and to declare his refusal to execute them . . . is dubious at best," courts have usually ignored the practice. At the least, such presidential assertions have proven hard to overturn; and more often than not, Congress has not tried.[62]

Signing statements, if taken literally, constitute a form of line-item veto. The Constitution does of course provide that presidents may disapprove bills passed by Congress, subject to override by two-thirds of each chamber. But unlike more than forty state governors, presidents may not pick out specific provisions in legislation for the veto pen. Despite this, they have long claimed the right to refuse to spend appropriated funds when, as in Ulysses S. Grant's declaration, they were "of purely private or local interest"; at times Congress itself has given presidents discretionary impoundment power in order to limit expenditures. By 1950, in fact, statutory language authorized President Truman to impound funds if spending became unnecessary due to "changes in requirements" or "other developments." [63]

President Nixon upped the ante, arguing that while Congress had the power to appropriate funds, the executive power covered their actual expenditure. "The Constitutional right of the President of the United States to impound funds," he claimed, "is absolutely clear." His impoundments subsequently encompassed as much as a fifth of the federal government's discretionary spending, aimed largely at programs whose passage he had opposed. In 1975 the Supreme Court ruled against such impoundments in *Train v. City of New York*; by then, Congress had already made them illegal in the Budget and Impoundment Control Act of 1974.[64]

However, as the 1980s and early 1990s produced record budget deficits, presidents revived pressure for some form of line-item veto power. "I'll make the cuts, I'll take the heat," Reagan asserted in his 1986 State of the Union address. In

1996 Congress passed the Line-Item Veto Act. It provided the president with "enhanced rescission" power that allowed the president's proposed vetoes of specific spending or revenue items to go into effect unless Congress passed a bill that reinstated the spending. That bill would, in turn, be subject to presidential veto. As a result, the president could rescind spending with the support of just one-third plus one member of either the House or the Senate. Senate Appropriations chair Ted Stevens (R-Alaska) called this "the most significant delegation of authority by the Congress to the President since the Constitution was ratified." Clinton used the power to propose cancellation of about forty items in 1997, but the law was struck down by the Supreme Court in 1998. The item veto procedure, the Court held, did not follow the Constitution's presentment clause, which only a constitutional amendment could change. Notably, though, when persistent deficits returned in the mid-2000s, George W. Bush again proposed legislation providing a form of item veto authority, and the House (but not the Senate) passed one version of this in 2006.[65]

Executive Orders

A key instrument of presidential power is the executive order. Though defined nowhere in the Constitution, executive orders in various forms—including proclamations, national security directives, presidential decision memoranda, and the like[66]—are generally construed as presidential directives intended to carry out other executive powers. As such, an executive order's legal authority derives either from existing statutes or from the president's constitutional responsibilities, not from any specific congressional approval. Executive orders usually pertain directly to government agencies and officials. They are used most frequently to issue binding directives to members of the executive branch; to shape regulatory action; to reorganize agencies or decision-making procedures; to control the military; or even to make new policy, especially in areas where Congress has not acted or where presidential initiative is generally accepted. The Louisiana Purchase was consummated by proclamation, as was emancipation of the slaves during the Civil War; and presidents have used executive orders to create Native American reservations, grazing areas, lighthouses, military reservations, and millions of acres of conservation land. More recently, presidents have kicked off their administrations by issuing multiple orders designed to set the tone for their administration. One of the first actions by President Clinton in January 1993 was to reverse a "gag rule" that had, under the Reagan and George H. W. Bush administrations, prohibited abortion counseling and referrals at family planning clinics that received federal funding. In his turn, President George W. Bush reversed Clinton's order in January 2001—and also put a sixty-day hold on all regulations approved in the last days of his predecessor's term.[67]

As this sequence suggests, executive orders are hardly unfettered. Not only can subsequent administrations change them, Congress or the courts can also overturn them. In late 2006, for example, a district court judge overturned George W. Bush's September 2001 executive order naming various

PROCESSING EXECUTIVE ORDERS

Proposed executive orders can originate from almost anywhere in the executive branch. A few are drafted directly in the White House, but most originate from within the various executive departments and agencies. Some orders, such as those imposing trade sanctions on another nation, may be drafted at the express instruction of the president. Most, however, are devised by career personnel in the departments and agencies to implement federal regulations, propose new rules or procedures, or to add technical language to congressional statutes. In any case, and because executive orders have the force of law, they are crafted largely by professional legal counsel at the instruction of the president's appointees. Rarely does a president take a direct hand in writing an order.

Because it has the force of law, each proposed executive order is composed and submitted according to precise procedures laid out in the *U.S. Code.* It must be prepared in a specific format and style (for example, on certain types of paper, in certain language) and must contain language explaining its nature, purpose, background, and effects, along with an assessment of how it relates to existing law. The proposed order is then sent, with seven copies, to the director of the Office of Management and Budget (OMB), where it is examined for adherence to the current administration's overall policy and budgetary goals. If approved, the order and its copies are sent next to the attorney general, whose office scrutinizes it for potential legal problems. Because both the attorney general and the director of OMB typically are among the president's closest personal advisers, clearance by these offices normally can be assumed to signify presidential approval.

After these steps, the proposed order is transmitted to the director of the Office of the Federal Register, a part of the National Archives and Records Services that is itself part of the General Services Administration, the federal government's housekeeping arm. The order is reviewed once more for stylistic and typographical errors, after which it and three copies are submitted to the president for final approval. If signed by the president, the order and two copies go back to the director of the Federal Register for publication in the *Federal Register,* the official publication of the executive branch. It is only upon the moment of publication in the *Federal Register* that an executive order takes force.

Not all executive orders follow these precise steps. Those relating to some natural emergency or international crisis may bypass much of the lengthy review process and go directly to the president for final approval. Moreover, the text of an order dealing with some aspect of national security may be treated as confidential, in which case only the order's number is published in the *Federal Register.* Most executive orders do not fit into these categories, however, so the process for creating and implementing an order typically follows a pattern set by law.

TABLE 9-1   **Executive Orders, by President, 1789–2006**

President	Years in office	Number of orders	Average per year
Washington	8.00	8	1.00
J. Adams	4.00	1	0.25
Jefferson	8.00	4	0.50
Madison	8.00	1	0.13
Monroe	8.00	1	0.13
J. Q. Adams	4.00	4	1.00
Jackson	8.00	11	1.38
Van Buren	4.00	10	2.50
W. H. Harrison	0.08[a]	0	—
Tyler	4.00	17	4.25
Polk	4.00	19	4.75
Taylor	1.25	4	3.20
Fillmore	2.75	13	4.73
Pierce	4.00	35	8.75
Buchanan	4.00	15	3.75
Lincoln	4.00	48	12.00
A. Johnson	4.00	79	19.75
Grant	8.00	223	27.88
Hayes	4.00	92	23.00
Garfield	0.50	9	—[b]
Arthur	3.25	100	30.77
Cleveland (1st term)	4.00	113	28.25
B. Harrison	4.00	135	33.75
Cleveland (2d term)	4.00	142	35.50
McKinley	4.75	178	37.47
T. Roosevelt	7.25	1139	157.10
Taft	4.00	752	188.00
Wilson	8.00	1841	230.13
Harding	2.60	487	187.31
Coolidge	5.40	1259	233.15
Hoover	4.00	1011	252.75
F. Roosevelt	12.33	3728	302.35
Truman	7.67	896	116.82
Eisenhower	8.00	486	60.75
Kennedy	2.92	214	73.29
L. Johnson	5.08	324	63.78
Nixon	5.60	346	61.79
Ford	2.40	169	70.42
Carter	4.00	320	80.00
Reagan	8.00	381	51.13
G. H. W. Bush	4.00	166	41.50
Clinton	8.00	364	45.50
G. W. Bush	6.00[c]	224	37.33

SOURCE: Calculated by the authors from Lyn Ragsdale, *Vital Statistics on the Presidency: Washington to Clinton,* rev. ed. (Washington, D.C.: Congressional Quarterly, 1998), 346–352, and the Federal Register (www.archives.gov/federal-register/executive-orders/).

NOTES: Includes both numbered and unnumbered executive orders.
a. W. H. Harrison died after only one month in office.   b. Garfield was assassinated after six months in office, during which he issued nine executive orders. At that rate his average would have been eighteen per year.
c. Through 2006.

groups and individuals as "specially designated global terrorists," objecting to the president's claim to "unfettered discretion." [68] But outright negation is relatively rare. And in the interim, executive orders can give the president power to model or remodel the policy landscape, often under the political radar—they "hide in plain sight." If nothing else, they have dramatically reshaped the government's organization chart: unilateral orders in various guises have created a majority of the federal administrative agencies catalogued in the *U.S. Government Manual.*[69]

During the nation's first hundred or so years, executive orders were issued without any system of publication or recording. They were not formally tracked until 1895, and their numbering began only in 1907, with numbers assigned retroactively to the time of Abraham Lincoln. In January 2007 President Bush issued Executive Order 13422. However, haphazard record-keeping throughout much of history—even after 1907—leads scholars to estimate that between 15,000 and 50,000 directives were never recorded. To respond to growing concerns that such lax procedures undermined democratic accountability, Congress in the Administrative Procedures Act (APA) of 1946 mandated that the number and text of all executive orders, executive branch announcements, proposals, and regulations must be published in the *Federal Register,* the official U.S. government record. Exceptions to this rule are the "classified" executive orders pertaining directly to sensitive national security matters, which are entered into the *Federal Register* by number only. Furthermore, in 1994 the Supreme Court held that the development of presidential executive orders was not subject to the APA's requirements for public comment or a balanced research process.

While the total number of executive orders issued by presidents has dropped since the early 1940s, the number of significant orders has risen dramatically over time. One exhaustive survey of the executive orders issued between 1936 and 1999 found that after a surge in usage during World War II the proportion of substantively significant orders tripled from the 1950s to the 1990s. Another study similarly concluded that the number and scope of substantive orders has risen impressively since the Reagan administration. Recent examples include the Clinton set-aside of nearly two million acres of land in Utah as a national monument, as well as the creation of George W. Bush's Office of Faith-Based and Community Initiatives, department-based centers thereof, and his 2002 mandate that faith-based organizations receive the "equal protection of the laws" in federal procurement efforts. As Bush told a gathering of representatives from such organizations, "I got a little frustrated in Washington because I couldn't get the bill passed out of the Congress. They were arguing process. . . . Congress wouldn't act, so I signed an executive order—that means I did it on my own." [70]

Such orders are supposed to be grounded in statutory authority. As such they often show the unintended consequences of congressional delegation. Clinton's Utah proclamation, for example, rested on a 1906 statute long forgotten by Congress, but not by presidents. The accumulation of a large body of administrative law replaced the need for unilateral presidential action in routine matters, such as personnel administration and regulatory procedures. Of the almost two thousand executive orders issued between 1945 and 1965, more than 80 percent were based on existing statutory authority, indicating in part the breadth of the statutory web woven after World War II.[71] Even congressional efforts to constrain executive authority sometimes legitimated it. A good example is the International Emergency Economic Powers Act (IEEPA). The IEEPA was passed in 1977 to rein in the use of its titular powers. But by providing a statutory process for declaring emergencies as a means of preventing economic transactions with disfavored regimes, Congress formalized a previously shadowy claim to power, and presidents declared thirty "national emergencies" between 1979 and 2000. In some cases these were vehicles for overriding legislative preferences, as when President Reagan applied IEEPA sanctions against Nicaragua in 1985 as a substitute for those Congress had refused to enact.[72]

Some scholars argue that it is unwise or illegitimate for Congress to delegate broad discretionary authority to the president, and executive orders can certainly arouse animosity when they are used to bypass or confront Congress. In 1963, for example, John Kennedy used Executive Order 11063 to bar racial discrimination in federally subsidized housing after finding the legislative route blocked by southern conservatives. Lyndon B. Johnson later issued an executive order to create minority hiring guidelines for federal contracts after Congress failed to embody affirmative action in the Civil Rights Act of 1964.

As these examples suggest, safeguarding or promoting civil rights has been a persistent rationale of executive orders, beginning with Franklin Roosevelt, who eased racial segregation of defense plants during World War II. Many orders were applied to operating procedures and rules within executive branch agencies, while others reshaped the implementation of entire federal programs when Congress proved unable or unwilling to act. For example, in 1948 Harry Truman used Executive Order 9981 to integrate the armed forces, an action that, combined with calls within the Democratic Party for stronger civil rights protection, split Democrats and sparked the creation of a separate "Dixiecrat" party during the 1948 election. Johnson's creation of "affirmative action" noted above was followed, somewhat rede-

fined, by Nixon's "Philadelphia Plan," a 1969 executive order instituting racial hiring quotas on federal projects. Nixon's action ran contrary to the 1964 Civil Rights Act, which forbade quotas of any kind, but his order was upheld by a federal court of appeals based partly on the implied power of the president to set federal procurement policies.[73]

A telling example of the controversy created when presidents use executive orders to bypass Congress on issues involving discrimination is an order never actually signed: President Clinton's 1993 promise to lift a long-standing ban on homosexuals serving in the military. The proposal, coming early in Clinton's term, erupted into a major political firestorm that threatened to overtake the rest of his nascent domestic agenda. He abandoned the idea of an executive order and sought an unofficial compromise with congressional and military leaders that eventually took the form of a "don't ask, don't tell" directive issued by the military.[74] Clinton's experience highlights the limits of the discretionary presidency, at least in peacetime.

As with the use of the veto, unilateral strategies are most pronounced among presidents facing a Congress controlled by the other party. Nixon used executive orders to restructure and gain tighter presidential control over the executive branch after Congress turned down his reorganization proposals. Reagan used an executive order to preempt congressional action mandating drug testing for federal employees. George H. W. Bush sidestepped Congress to give a new White House Council on Competitiveness the power

EXECUTIVE ORDER 12836

FEBRUARY 1, 1993
REVOCATION OF CERTAIN EXECUTIVE ORDERS
CONCERNING FEDERAL CONTRACTING

By the authority vested in me as President by the Constitution and the laws of the United States of America, and in order to eliminate Executive orders that do not serve the public interest, it is hereby ordered as follows:

SECTION 1. Executive Order No. 12818 of October 23, 1992 (prohibiting the use of project agreements on Federal construction contracts), and Executive Order No. 12800 of April 13, 1992 (requiring Federal contractors to post a notice that workers are not required to join unions), are revoked.

SECTION 2. The heads of executive agencies shall promptly revoke any orders, rules, or regulations implementing Executive Order No. 12818 of October 23, 1992 or Executive Order No. 12800 of April 13, 1992, to the extent consistent with law.

William J. Clinton
The White House,
February 1, 1993

SOURCE: Office of the Federal Register, *Weekly Compilation of Presidential Documents,* February 8, 1993 (Washington, D.C.: Government Printing Office, 1993), 120.

to assess the economic consequences of new regulations. Clinton's use of executive orders became more strategic after the Republican Party took over control of Congress in 1995. As Clinton aide Rahm Emanuel explained in 1998, "sometimes we use [an executive order] in reaction to legislative delay or setbacks. Obviously, you'd rather pass legislation that can do X, but you're willing to make whatever progress you can on an agenda item." [75]

Executive orders are less controversial when based clearly on existing statutory authority. But they may spark dispute when they rely instead on the happily vague "executive power" of the Constitution or implied powers. Presidents frequently maintain that they have the constitutional authority to act unilaterally because they possess inherent war or emergency powers during periods of apparent crisis. They may also claim implied authority to act in the absence of legislative action in a given area. Federal courts tend to judge each case individually, but usually give presidents the benefit of the doubt when Congress has failed to decide an issue over a prolonged period. Making matters still more complex, Congress often gives presidents retroactive authority for their unilateral actions, particularly during emergencies. In the 1793 dispute, Congress reluctantly approved Washington's proclamation of neutrality a year after he made it, a pattern repeated enough that presidents often proceed on the assumption that Congress will acquiesce eventually.

Checking presidential power requires that the other branches know what power is being exercised, and this has not always been the case. As noted above, federal law mandates the publication of executive orders and proclamations, but it also allows for secret orders to protect the public interest, when they deal with military or intelligence matters. For example, Truman's 1952 executive order creating the National Security Agency, the largest and most secretive of the nation's intelligence organizations, remained officially classified for more than forty years after he issued it. Beyond this presidents also use classified executive directives drafted through the National Security Council staffing process.[76] In the mid-1980s, such national security directives underlay policies in Iran and Nicaragua that ran afoul of the statutory bans on arms sales to terrorists and aid to the contras, respectively.[77] They provided negotiation instructions to diplomats working on nuclear arms control and shaped the Strategic Defense Initiative. They even implemented the "Plan for Economic Warfare against the USSR," which laid out aggressive plans for hindering Soviet commerce. Needless to say, this plan did not receive congressional review or approval. While the penchant for executive secrecy and, particularly, for excluding Congress from foreign policy decision making briefly lessened a bit with the end of the cold war and the dissolution of the former Soviet Union, the September 11, 2001, terrorist attacks reactivated the trend (See "The 'New' Imperial Presidency?" p. 530.).

Secrecy and Executive Privilege

Executive orders may also be used to create secrecy—that is, to create a system for classifying government documents or other information in the name of national security. Governments always have pursued secrecy in sensitive diplomatic or military matters, but the idea that the United States should maintain a formal classification system did not take hold until the eve of World War II, when Franklin Roosevelt authorized in March 1940 the classification of military intelligence information. The test of what constituted secrets worth classifying, Roosevelt said, was "what the Commander in Chief of the Army and Navy thinks would be harmful to the defense of this country to give out." [78]

As the war progressed, subsequent executive orders extended classification beyond its original confines, and the trend did not end once hostilities ceased. Instead, the exigencies of the cold war led presidents to expand the categories of information deemed essential to national security. Truman used two executive orders to extend classification authority to any executive branch agency when secrecy was deemed essential. Where Roosevelt extrapolated his 1940 executive order from authority provided by a 1938 statute classifying military charts, Truman's expansion of secrecy was based simply on an assertion that inherent executive powers gave him the responsibility to do whatever was necessary to protect national security.[79] Constitutional scholars debated the legality of Truman's claim but worried even more about the effects of pervasive secrecy on democratic accountability if Congress was kept under- or misinformed.[80] The government could now classify virtually anything, and there were few mechanisms to guard against the tendency toward the overclassification that is inevitable when agencies hoard information as a valuable resource, when they skirt the law in pursuit of other ends, or when they simply wish to hide their mistakes. By the Kennedy administration, the classification system itself was classified. Under President Nixon's 1972 order, "national security" encompassed any information in "the interest of the national defense or foreign relations of the United States," including information about domestic intelligence activities. President Reagan extended the standard classification period for documents and suspended automatic declassification.[81]

Issues of secrecy seemed to change with the end of the cold war and the collapse of the Soviet Union, with greater declassification of documents dating back to World War II. A highly charged twist to this effort concerned documents related to military personnel missing in action or held as prisoners of war during the Vietnam War. In 1992 President George H. W. Bush issued an executive order expediting the declassification of Vietnam-era materials, and President Clinton expanded this effort with his order dated Veterans' Day 1993.

A 1995 Clinton executive order streamlined declassification procedures for archival material more than twenty-five years old and reversed extant policy by providing that in unclear cases the government's basic stance should be against classification. However, in March 2003 George W. Bush issued an executive order that removed the default stance toward declassification, exempted additional information (such as that pertaining to "current vulnerabilities" in security) from the automatic declassification process, enhanced the ability of the vice president to classify documents, and gave the Central Intelligence Agency (CIA) new power to resist declassification decisions. (The CIA also worked with the National Archives to reclassify previously public information.) Future classification was abetted by complementary low-profile administrative orders that gave three new cabinet officers—the secretaries of Agriculture and Health and Human Services and the director of the Environmental Protection Agency—the right to designate documents as "secret." [82]

A November 2001 executive order may also substantially expand governmental secrecy. Executive Order 13233 was entitled "Further Implementation of the Presidential Records Act." But in practical terms it rewrote that act to give presidents enhanced latitude to deny access to public records in the presidential libraries starting with Ronald Reagan's. Under the terms of the order, a current president can assert privilege even if the former president objected, and vice versa; vice presidents—and even presidents' and vice presidents' estates—could also make binding claims of privilege. And whereas the Presidential Records Act placed the burden on past and current presidents to establish a need for secrecy and thereby deny requests for documents, the Bush executive order reversed this requirement to require researchers to prove a "demonstrated, specific need" for a given record.

More generally, the exercise of executive privilege to prevent the release of information has been claimed by presidents as part of the broader "executive power," which limits the ability of other branches of government to define the boundaries of that power. Nixon, indeed, argued that "the manner in which the president exercises his assigned executive powers is not subject to questioning by another branch of the government." His attorney general, Richard Kleindienst, told the Senate in 1973 that the president could direct any member of the executive branch to refuse information in response to congressional request: "your power to get what the President knows," he said, "is in the President's hands." [83]

It was Eisenhower's attorney general, William P. Rogers, who came up with the phrase "executive privilege." But the practice it described goes back to the Washington administration, which concluded it had the right to withhold information from Congress concerning military operations and diplomatic negotiations. Over time most presidents claimed the right to determine what, in President James K. Polk's phrase, was "compatible with the public interest to communicate." Largely these claims concerned sensitive issues of foreign relations. Later, as the Executive Office of the President grew, the claim expanded to provide for the confidentiality of advice to presidents from their staffs, using the model of lawyer-client privilege. [84]

Nixon's efforts to withhold incriminating tape recordings from the criminal trial of his subordinates led to a unanimous Supreme Court decision in 1974 overturning his assertion of executive privilege. But if Nixon lost that battle, presidents arguably won the war—since the Court also held that, while inapplicable in this case, some sort of communications "privilege is . . . inextricably rooted in the separation of powers under the Constitution." When "military, diplomatic, or sensitive national security secrets" were at stake, the Court owed the president "great deference." [85] In 1994 a circuit court divided executive privilege into "deliberative process privilege" and "presidential communications privilege." Both could sometimes be valid grounds for denying information to other branches, but the latter, when invoked, made the relevant documents "presumptively privileged." [86]

Thus even after Watergate, whether called by its name or disguised as "deliberative process privilege," "attorney work product" and "attorney-client privilege," "internal departmental deliberations," "secret opinions policy," "deliberations of another agency," and the like, executive privilege was alive and well. Refusing a congressional request for documents concerning the administration's policies in Haiti, for instance, Clinton administration Attorney General Janet Reno made the startling claim that Congress had no power to conduct oversight of foreign affairs, due in part to the "sole organ" doctrine of the 1936 *Curtiss-Wright case*; the investigating committee backed down. George W. Bush likewise refused to turn over documents relating to Federal Bureau of Investigation (FBI) investigations into organized crime or allegations of campaign finance violations in the 1996 campaign. He also resisted allowing national security advisor Condoleezza Rice to testify before the 9/11 Commission, and he only relented after extracting written assurances from House and Senate leaders that her appearance "does not set, and should not be cited as, a precedent for future requests" for any White House official to testify before a legislative body. [87]

In general, then, as one scholar recently noted, "With a nontrivial amount of freedom to craft new kinds of unilateral directives, citing national security concerns and executive privilege as justifications for concealing their actions, presidents have obstructed the efforts of members of Congress to keep pace." [88]

EMERGENCY POWERS

Secrecy is, of course, most critical to foreign affairs. But in times of crisis, whether foreign or domestic, Congress has endorsed or allowed enhanced presidential discretion.

Foreign Affairs

The United States has entered into five declared wars, one civil war, and numerous undeclared hostilities in its history. In each instance presidents have asserted claims to some type of emergency powers to deal with the threat, but the justifications put forth have differed starkly. In some cases presidents assert an aggressively broad view of the president's inherent war powers, based largely on wedding the presidential oath of office with the vesting and commander-in-chief clauses. When President Reagan sent marines to Lebanon in 1982, he said the troops had been deployed under his "constitutional authority with respect to the conduct of foreign relations and as Commander-in-Chief." [89]

That sort of assertion can be justified by the existence of an obvious crisis, as in the Civil War. Ironically, it can also be justified by a situation's relative lack of severity, that is by its supposed standing as a police action rather than as a "real" use of force that would require a declaration of war. William McKinley, Theodore Roosevelt, William Howard Taft, Woodrow Wilson, and Calvin Coolidge, for example, used U.S. troops to rule Cuba, Nicaragua, Haiti, and the Dominican Republic, and even to occupy Veracruz, Mexico. The decision by President George H. W. Bush in 1989 to send troops into Panama to capture Gen. Manuel Noriega,

Panama's leader and a reputed leader in the international drug trade, also falls into this category; likewise Bill Clinton used force in Haiti, Sudan, Afghanistan, and, most aggressively, in Kosovo, without requesting or receiving legislative sanction. Most dramatically, Harry Truman never sought legislative approval for his extended "police action" on the Korean peninsula (and later sought to use the fact of conflict to justify his seizure of the nation's steel mills when a strike loomed.)[90]

In other cases presidents have received broad congressional grants of executive authority to prosecute a war. Wilson and Franklin Roosevelt, during World Wars I and II, respectively, benefited from this pattern. And, as detailed below, Congress authorized George H. W. Bush to repel Iraqi forces from Kuwait in 1991 and George W. Bush to retaliate against the perpetrators of the September 11, 2001, terrorist attacks, and to renew the fight with Iraqi president Saddam Hussein.

But every president exercises a mix of inherent and delegated war powers simultaneously. Lyndon Johnson asked for discretionary authorization to ramp up hostilities in Vietnam via the Gulf of Tonkin Resolution in 1964, but did not feel bound in turn to draw down forces when Congress soured on the war; Richard Nixon, in fact, simply ignored the resolution's repeal by Congress in 1971. While George H. W. Bush requested approval for armed action against Iraq during the Gulf War, he never claimed to need it—and, indeed, would later assert that "I didn't have to get permission from some old goat in the United States

CATEGORIES AND EXAMPLES OF EMERGENCY POWERS

When emergencies are declared, or during times of crisis, the president has at hand a broad array of potential powers. These emergency powers can be grouped into three categories of actions the president may take:

Powers over Individuals

Confine individuals seen to be threats to national security

Restrict travel of Americans to other nations (such as Cuba) or travel of some foreigners to the United States

Restrict movement of citizens within the United States

Require persons, because of their backgrounds, associations with certain groups, or ownership of particular articles (such as weapons), to register with government officials

Restrict certain persons from working in industries critical to national security

Remove federal employees regarded as threats to national security

Suspend writs of *habeas corpus*

Declare martial law

Assign armed forces to conflicts in foreign nations

Powers over Property

Order stockpiling of strategic materials (such as uranium)

Impose restrictions on exports (such as computer equipment)

Allocate materials in ways necessary to aid national defense

Require industries to give priority to government contracts and seize industries failing to comply with such orders

Fix wages and prices

Powers over Communications

Withhold information from Congress and the public deemed potentially sensitive to national security

Monitor and censor communications between the United States and other nations

Require foreign representatives to register with U.S. government.

SOURCES: U.S. Congress, House of Representatives, Committee on the Judiciary, Subcommittee on Administrative Law and Governmental Relations, *Hearings on H.R. 3884, National Emergencies Act*, 94th Cong., 1st sess., March 6–April 9, 1975, 22–23; Robert E. DiClerico, *The American President* (Englewood Cliffs, N.J.: Prentice-Hall, 1979), chap. 8.

Congress to kick Saddam Hussein out of Kuwait." An interesting twist in the first Gulf War and later in Kosovo was presidents' reliance on United Nations and NATO obligations, respectively, as a substitute for congressional action in activating presidential war powers.[91]

Presidents do not always inform legislators about their actions abroad. The use of "executive agreements" with foreign leaders is one mechanism whereby presidents can institute policy change without going through the arduous process of receiving Senate ratification of a formal treaty. President Reagan concluded 3,000 such agreements between 1981 and 1988, compared to only 125 treaties. Agreements likewise outnumbered treaties by more than nine to one under Presidents George H. W. Bush and Clinton.[92]

Other covert operations involve espionage and, frequently, the use of force. The CIA and its cousin organizations over time have long constituted a "secret arm of the executive, with a secret budget."[93] "Black ops'" high-water mark was perhaps in the 1950s when the United States quietly helped guide the overthrow of governments in Iran, Guatemala, and Laos. Still, despite some high-profile failures, as at the 1961 Bay of Pigs invasion of Cuba and with contra operations in 1980s Nicaragua (the high profile being one definition of failure, perhaps), covert operations remain important weapons in the foreign affairs arsenal. In the early 2000s, CIA operatives were among the first in Afghanistan and Iraq, and espionage will have continuing value in the battle against terrorism.

Although Congress has sought to require consultation about and notification of intelligence operations (for example, in the 1975 Church Committee hearings and the subsequent Intelligence Oversight Act), presidents have been reluctant to fully comply. In part, they correctly fear the difficulty Congress has in keeping secrets; sometimes, though, secrecy is simply a useful means to fend off legislative interference. It is difficult to balance the need for confidentiality with the need for accountability, as suggested by an extraordinary handwritten 2003 letter from Senator John D. Rockefeller IV (D-W.V.), ranking member of the Senate

The Civilian Conservation Corps, part of President Franklin D. Roosevelt's New Deal program, not only provided relief for jobless young men during the Great Depression but helped protect and conserve the nation's natural resources. Roosevelt visited one of the camps in Big Meadows, Virginia, in August 1933. Seated with Roosevelt are, from left, Gen. Paul B. Malone, Col. Louis Howe, Secretary of the Interior Harold I. Ickes, Director of the Civilian Conservation Corps Robert Fechner, Secretary of Agriculture Henry A. Wallace, and Assistant Secretary of Agriculture Rexford G. Tugwell.

Select Committee on Intelligence, to Vice President Richard B. Cheney. "The activities we discussed [dealing with domestic surveillance] raise profound oversight issues. . . ." Rockefeller wrote. "Given the security restrictions associated with this information, and my inability to consult staff or counsel on my own, I feel unable to fully evaluate, much less endorse these activities."[94]

Even congressionally approved war powers often lead to states of emergency that long outlive the war itself. Recall that FDR closed the banks in 1933 under authority granted Wilson in World War I. As noted above, multiple stand-by powers were available to presidents through the mid-1970s, when a special Senate Committee on National Emergencies and Delegated Powers found 470 statutes on the books that combined to give presidents the right to seize private property and regulate private enterprise, restrict travel, organize and control all means of production and transportation, assign military forces overseas, and institute martial law. But some claims are even more remote. When members of the Senate Foreign Relations Committee asked Nixon's secretary of defense Melvin R. Laird what would happen if Congress cut off all funds for continued U.S. involvement in

Indochina, they were informed that the president could bypass Congress entirely and spend unappropriated funds through authority granted in a 1799 "feed and forage" statute. This law, enacted during a time when Congress met only half a year at a time, allowed the secretary of war to obtain advance funding to provide supplies to American soldiers in remote outposts without having to await congressional appropriation. It was still on the books more than 170 years later.[95]

Presidents have also sometimes sought to win domestic political advantage under the cover of national security claims. For example, Nixon's use of intelligence agencies to investigate Americans and determine whether they were threats to national security entailed domestic surveillance aimed at groups opposed to U.S. action in Vietnam and included secret wiretapping, breaking into offices, and infiltrating groups with government informers. Details of past activities came to light when Congress held investigative hearings in the mid-1970s, and the ensuing controversies forced Ford and Carter to narrow the range of permissible domestic surveillance actions and to impose stricter control over federal agents. In 1981, however, Ronald Reagan issued an executive order loosening considerably extant restrictions. Revelations in 1988 that the FBI had relied on this broad authority to conduct an extensive covert surveillance program against groups opposed to U.S. policy in Central America sparked tremendous controversy. Critics charged that the investigatory and surveillance tools granted law enforcement in the October 2001 USA PATRIOT Act, while necessary in some cases, could likewise be used to persecute political dissidents rather than prosecute terrorists.[96]

Economic Crisis

Presidents also wield emergency powers during periods of serious economic instability. During such times, presidential power appears to emanate exclusively from statutes, although presidents have shown ingenuity in stretching the boundaries of that authority. For example, the Trading with the Enemy Act of 1917 gave the president the authority to impose an array of economic measures in times of war or national emergency. This law was intended as a wartime measure, but it was not repealed at war's end. Subsequent presidents, such as Franklin Roosevelt, delightedly discovered the apparent statutory justification for emergency actions to manage a faltering economy.

Roosevelt's actions had been taken in response to a stark crisis, but Nixon's August 1971 declaration of an emergency in response to a growing imbalance in the U.S. balance of payments struck many observers as overly dramatic. Here, too, however, Nixon had legislative sanction from the Economic Stabilization Act of 1970. The law authorized the president to "issue such orders as he may deem appropriate to stabilize prices, rents, wages and salaries." Nixon announced he was disconnecting the value of the dollar from the gold standard, levying a 10 percent surtax on imports, and freezing domestic prices for ninety days. The overall effect was to devalue the dollar, drive down the prices of U.S. goods overseas, and temporarily halt inflation.[97]

PROCEDURES FOR EMERGENCY ORDERS

The National Emergencies Act of 1976 (PL 94–412) terminated all states of emergency legally in effect until that time, including some dating as far back as the 1930s. The act also set in place procedures for declaring and, equally important, terminating future states of emergency. As this brief overview suggests, the provisions of the National Emergencies Act were intended to force Congress and the president, acting singly or together, to ensure that any state of emergency does not outlive the conditions on which it was based.

The president by law cannot declare a state of national emergency without also specifying the provisions of existing law or constitutional provisions under which the proposed action falls. Furthermore, any proclamation of a national emergency must be transmitted immediately to Congress and published in the *Federal Register*.

During a declared national emergency the president and all relevant executive branch agencies or departments must maintain files on all rules, regulations, executive orders, or any other activities carried out to address the emergency. This information must be transmitted promptly to Congress. Matters requiring confidentiality are to be handled in a prescribed manner (for example, restricted to members of congressional intelligence committees and those staff members with security clearances). All expenditures made by the executive branch to address the emergency also must be reported to Congress within ninety days after each six-month period following the declaration of the emergency.

The law also specifies how states of emergency are to be terminated. No later than six months after an emergency is declared, the two houses of Congress must meet to consider a concurrent resolution to determine whether the emergency should be terminated. The resolution must go through the normal congressional procedures, but according to a specific schedule to avoid delays. Should Congress be unable or unwilling to terminate the emergency (perhaps because of some disagreement between the House and the Senate), it must consider another such resolution within the next six-month period.

The president can terminate unilaterally a declared state of emergency when it is deemed that the conditions mandating the emergency have passed. But, to avoid another situation where states of emergency endure legally for decades, the law calls for automatic termination of an emergency upon the anniversary of its declaration, unless the president previously notifies Congress (and publishes in the *Federal Register*) of the need to continue the emergency. One way or another, states of emergency are to be terminated.

Domestic Unrest and Natural Disaster

Presidential emergency powers include the authority to call out federal troops or to take control of state national guards (descendants of the state militias) to quell domestic unrest or to deter violence. Such authority has been used in the United States to put down illegal labor strikes, ensure delivery of the mail, impose order during natural disasters and urban riots, and prevent volatile situations from exploding.

Before the 1940s, and particularly during the late nineteenth century, presidents became involved in domestic disorders most frequently during labor strikes. Until passage of the Wagner Act of 1935 ensuring the right to collective bargaining and establishing procedures for labor negotiations, strikes usually were considered illegal and often resulted in violence between strikers and company security forces. President Grover Cleveland's use of troops to break the 1894 Pullman strike in Chicago was the most famous example of a practice that had virtually ended by the 1950s. However, in March 1970 President Nixon responded to a postal strike by declaring a state of emergency and calling out federal troops to take over the postal system and keep mail deliveries flowing. Nixon's use of troops to sort and deliver the mail was unusual, but it showed how presidents can react to potential disturbances.

In the 1950s and 1960s presidents relied on federal troops or state national guards to ensure calm during efforts to enforce racial desegregation. The first and perhaps most notable instance was in 1957 when Dwight Eisenhower sent troops into Little Rock, Arkansas, to enforce desegregation of Central High School in the face of resistance from state officials and angry mobs. In 1962 John Kennedy federalized the Mississippi National Guard to ensure the integration of the University of Mississippi, and in 1963 he confronted Alabama governor George Wallace by sending federal troops to enforce the integration of the University of Alabama. Kennedy, and Lyndon Johnson after him, also on occasion used troops to protect civil rights marchers.

During the late 1960s soldiers were used frequently to quell urban riots or to maintain order during demonstrations against U.S. involvement in Vietnam. For example, the April 1968 assassination of civil rights leader Martin Luther King Jr. sparked widespread rioting throughout more than one hundred cities and forced Johnson and various governors to call out 55,000 troops. In May 1970 President Nixon directed troops to maintain order on some college campuses after the deaths of some college students during protests

President Grover Cleveland's suppression of the Pullman Strike of 1894 is an example of presidential enforcement authority. Here, a meat train leaves the Chicago stockyards under escort of U.S. Cavalry.

against the U.S. incursion into Cambodia. In 1992 George H. W. Bush sent marines to help quell the riots and looting that followed the acquittal of Los Angeles police officers accused in the severe beating of an African American suspect.

Finally, presidential emergency powers are frequently used during natural disasters such as hurricanes, floods, or earthquakes. By declaring a state of emergency in a given locale, the president sets in motion the government machinery that can provide immediate aid, such as food, shelter, and police protection, not to mention longer-term assistance such as federally guaranteed, low-interest home and business loans. This enables the federal government to soften the economic effects of the disaster; not surprisingly, even federalism-minded governors are quick to request such a presidential designation when natural disasters strike. President Clinton made disaster relief a mechanism for building political support after the massive floods along the Mississippi River in 1993 and the Northridge earthquake in southern California the next year. However, local reliance on the national government can be a double-edged sword for a president. In 1992 Floridians criticized the tardy response by federal aid agencies to the massive damage caused by Hurricane Andrew that August. In August 2005 Hurricane Katrina devastated the Gulf Coast and especially the city of New Orleans—killing perhaps 2,000, causing $80 billion in damage, and forcing tens of thousands of residents to evacuate their homes. President George W. Bush declared states of emergency in the affected states (covering 90,000 square miles) even before the storm made landfall. But federal officials' slow reaction to, and even apparent denial of, suffering on the ground, all of it broadcast around the clock on television and Internet outlets, prompted widespread anger at the administration's perceived incompetence.[98] In this area, as in others, expectations for presidential action may be inflated—but they are real.

THE RESURGENCE REGIME

The question of accountability for the unilateral exercise of presidential power emerged with renewed force in the 1970s. The war in Vietnam and Nixon's "incursion" into Cambodia, his excessive use of impoundment, domestic surveillance and other abuses of civil liberties, and, finally, Watergate suggested to many observers an out-of-control "imperial presidency." Congress began to seek ways to limit what was perceived widely as a gradual but systematic aggregation of expansive executive power and its apparent abuses in both the domestic and foreign policy spheres. Throughout the decade legislators erected a "resurgence regime" that aimed to rein in the discretion enjoyed by the chief executive and create a much greater role for congressional advice and consent in interbranch relations.[99] Congress intended to play a key role in authorizing and overseeing America's military deployments and covert adventures; and to keep a close eye on executive corruption.

Even a partial list of enactments gives a sense of the scope of that ambition. For example, the Congressional Budget and Impoundment Control Act of 1974 prohibited unilateral presidential spending decisions and created important centralizing structures (the Budget Committees, the Congressional Budget Office [CBO]) to guide the legislative budget process. In foreign policy, the War Powers Resolution (1973) was enacted to ensure that Congress had a say in the use of U.S. forces. The Case Act of 1972, tightened in 1977, was meant to force the president to reveal the executive agreements with foreign nations negotiated outside of legislative view; the Hughes-Ryan amendment (1974) and the Intelligence Oversight Act (1980) were passed to keep legislators informed of covert operations. The Non-Detention Act (1971), the Justice Department's own Domestic Intelligence Guidelines (1976), and the 1972 *Keith* decision[100] and 1978 Foreign Intelligence Surveillance Act (FISA) all limited presidents' security powers at home. The National Emergencies Act of 1976 terminated ongoing states of emergency as well as the attendant emergency presidential powers and mandated that future states of emergency would lapse after six months unless renewed.

The executive branch's workings were to be made more transparent through an expanded Freedom of Information Act (1974), various "government in the sunshine" laws, and the timely release of presidential documents mandated by the 1974 Presidential Materials and Presidential Records Act of 1978. In 1974 the Supreme Court ruled in *U.S. v. Nixon* that the president's power to assert "executive privilege" was not absolute and was reviewable by the courts. The role of money in politics was to be diminished by a new Federal Election Commission established by the Federal Election Campaign Act of 1974; and should all this fail, investigations of executive malfeasance would be conducted under a new independent counsel operation created by the Ethics in Government Act (1978).

Meanwhile, the use of legislative vetoes increased even as federal programs received shorter-term authorizations to ensure more frequent congressional reviews of executive agencies. Congress also dramatically expanded its own institutional capacities for overseeing the executive branch by hiring thousands of additional staff and by creating or expanding congressional support agencies such as the General Accounting Office (renamed the Government Accountability Office in 2004) and CBO.

The "New" Imperial Presidency?

In the late 1970s Congress appeared to have successfully limited presidential discretion. Ex-president Gerald Ford complained that "We have not an imperial presidency but an imperiled presidency. Under today's rules . . . the presidency does not operate effectively."[101]

But the resurgence regime was itself built on fragile foundations. Even in the decade following Nixon's resignation, the office of the presidency retained a solid base of authority grounded in the powers and strategies traced throughout this chapter. Especially after Ronald Reagan's election in 1980, presidents aggressively used many of these unilateral tools—from regulatory review to signing statements to recess appointments—to enhance their influence over bureaucratic agencies and avoid legislative dictation.

The statutory side of the resurgence regime also crumbled. In some cases, as in the IEEPA example above, efforts to specify the limits of presidential powers gave statutory status to powers earlier exercised only informally. In other cases Congress itself backed away from using the processes it had created to challenge the president, or failed to make them work. Most dramatically, the War Powers Resolution did not rein in presidents' use of force, as myriad post-1973 unilateral military deployments, from Grenada to Kosovo, suggest. In the latter example, although 800 U.S. aircraft flew more than 20,000 air sorties against 2,000 Serbian targets, President Bill Clinton did not deem that troops had, in the language of the War Powers Resolution, been "introduced into hostilities or into situation where imminent involvement in hostilities is clearly indicated by the circumstances."[102]

The Congressional Budget Act, likewise, failed to bring discipline to federal spending; deficits veered upward in the 1980s, and again in the 2000s after a brief blip into surplus ended in fiscal 2001. Perhaps more important, the deliberative process laid out in 1974 was often honored in the breach: though thirteen budget bills each year required passage, in the six fiscal years 2002 through 2007, a total of ten such bills were passed by the October 1 deadline. The outcome of late budgets and the massive omnibus bills that resulted was to increase the president's veto leverage, especially after Clinton's successful showdown with the Republican Congress in 1995–1996.[103]

To be sure, not every element of the resurgence receded at once, or for all time. Most obviously, Clinton's impeachment and trial in 1998–1999 was the first since 1868 and the first ever of an elected president. Yet while it seems strange to talk about congressional deference in that context, even this period highlighted the potential powers of the president and renewed legislative acquiescence to their use. Clinton himself set the tone after the Democrats lost Congress in 1994: "I think now we have a better balance of both using the Presidency as a bully pulpit and the President's power of the Presidency to do things, actually accomplish things, and . . . not permitting the presidency to be defined only by relations with the Congress." [104] In 1998 cruise missiles were fired at the Sudan and Afghanistan at the president's order even as the House debated his fate. The very process of impeachment—in the face of hostile public opinion—helped to discredit it, and to encourage the expiration of the independent counsel statute in 1999.[105]

But it was the George W. Bush administration, beginning in 2001, that expended the most effort in rebuilding, and aggressively justifying, the post-Watergate unilateral infrastructure. "I have an obligation to make sure that the Presidency remains robust. I'm not going to let Congress erode the power of the executive branch," Bush noted in 2002. Vice President Richard Cheney, who got started in political life as a staffer in the Nixon White House, argued that he had "repeatedly seen an erosion of the powers and the ability of the president . . . to do his job," thanks to the resurgence regime.[106]

In some areas, that attitude was translated into action even before the 2001 terrorist attacks. As noted above, the Bush administration cracked down on Freedom of Information Act releases, increased federal executives' ability to withhold information from public view, and issued an executive order to expand past administrations' capacity to delay or bar the opening of historical records. Legislative requests for information were also routinely denied or delayed. The administration went to court, successfully, to defend its ability to withhold—even without formally claiming executive privilege—documents from congressional auditors or others

seeking information about the energy task force headed by Vice President Cheney.[107]

The brutal September 11, 2001, attacks on New York and Washington, D.C., however, brought tremendous renewed visibility and leverage to the presidential office. President Bush acted aggressively to move the country onto a war footing, and on a variety of fronts legislators hastened to expand his authority. A $40 billion Emergency Response Fund was immediately appropriated for the president to use as he saw fit in assisting victims of the attack and strengthening national security. And with just one dissenting vote in either chamber—most Senate discussion of the bill actually took place after the vote—Congress passed a resolution three days after the attacks, stating that "the president has authority under the Constitution to take action to deter and prevent acts of international terrorism against the United States" and granting him the power to use "all necessary and appropriate force against those nations, organizations, or persons he determines planned, authorized, committed, or aided the terrorist attacks that occurred on September 11, 2001, or harbored such organizations or persons, in order to prevent any future acts of international terrorism against the United States. . . ." [108] This Authorization for the Use of Military Force (the AUMF), used first in the overthrow of the Taliban regime in Afghanistan, would become critical to justifying far-flung executive action. On the domestic front, the USA PATRIOT Act, which Congress passed rapidly to administration specifications in October 2001, enhanced the executive's prosecutorial tools and power to conduct criminal investigations by relaxing limits on surveillance and softening the barrier between domestic law enforcement and foreign intelligence gathering. The Patriot Act was renewed, largely unchanged, in spring 2006.[109]

In the fall of 2002 Congress passed another broad delegation of authority to use force against Iraq. This came after the administration's September 2002 *National Security Strategy of the United States* urged preemptive (and thus, executive-driven) action against potential threats.[110] Despite the 1991 Gulf war and a decade of sanctions, Saddam Hussein remained in control of Iraq, and most U.S. policymakers believed he retained weapons of mass destruction of some sort. Soon after the 2001 attacks, the president ordered that invasion options be prepared. In early 2002 he signed a secret order giving the CIA authority to assassinate Saddam Hussein. By summer military planning was well under way.[111]

The White House counsel's office advised the president that war with Iraq would not require legislative approval. The argument was (1) that the president's commander-in-chief powers were themselves sufficient; (2) that the AUMF already encompassed it; and (3) that the congressional resolution from the first Gulf War granted any necessary authority, since Iraq had violated the terms of the 1991 cease-fire. However, this was not a question of repelling a sudden attack on the United States or an ally; nor could it be argued there was no time for congressional deliberation. There was little evidence to tie the Iraqi regime to the September 11 attacks, and the 1991 resolution spoke only to the liberation of Kuwait.[112] Thus, given that legislators seemed willing and even eager to authorize war, the Bush administration asked in October 2002 for discretionary power to use force against Iraq. Legislators removed sweeping language from the president's draft that would have allowed him to use "all means" to "restore international peace and security in the region," and invoked the reporting requirements of the War Powers Resolution. Nonetheless, the final wording was broad: the president was "authorized to use the Armed Forces of the United States as he determines to be necessary and appropriate in order to defend the national security of the United States against the continuing threat posed by Iraq." After UN weapons inspectors were unsuccessful in locating weapons of mass destruction (WMDs), American airstrikes began in March 2003, followed quickly by ground forces. By late 2006 Congress had approved more than $500 billion in spending, largely in supplemental appropriations bills outside the normal budget process, for military and reconstruction operations in Afghanistan and Iraq. WMDs were never found, leading to questions about the efficacy of the U.S. intelligence operations and whether the administration had overstated the threat posed by the Iraqi regime.[113]

Despite the legislative deference he received after the attacks on September 11, 2001, President Bush often preferred to act alone rather than ask for congressional sanction. The administration's interpretation of the commander-in-chief power was perhaps broadest, and certainly most controversial. In October 2001, for instance, President Bush issued a secret executive order authorizing the National Security Agency (NSA) to track communications between individuals abroad with suspected terrorist connections and Americans within the United States. On its face this action seemed to violate the 1978 Foreign Intelligence Surveillance Act (FISA), which required issuance of a warrant by a special surveillance court in such cases. FISA did allow for wiretapping for fifteen days after the declaration of war, and for emergency wiretaps for up to seventy-two hours (increased from twenty-four hours after September 11) before issuance of a warrant.

When the initiative was revealed by the media in late 2005, the administration dubbed it the "Terrorist Surveillance Program" and argued that the president had both inherent and statutory power to order such wiretaps. "My legal authority is derived from the Constitution, as well as the [September 2001] authorization of force by the United States Congress," President Bush told a news conference.[114] A January 2006 Justice Department white paper defending the NSA program argued that far from violating FISA, the president was following its letter, since the September 2001 congressional resolution authorizing military force should be read as direct statutory approval for the wiretapping program. In this reading, wiretapping was a "fundamental incident" of warfare similar to the detention of enemy combatants approved by the Supreme Court elsewhere (see the *Hamdi* case, below.) In addition, the Justice Department argued,

> the NSA activities are supported by the President's well-recognized inherent constitutional authority as Commander in Chief and sole organ for the Nation in foreign affairs to conduct warrantless surveillance of enemy forces for intelligence purposes to detect and disrupt armed attacks on the United States. The President has the chief responsibility under the Constitution to protect America from attack, and the Constitution gives the President the authority necessary to fulfill that solemn responsibility.[115]

Because neither FISA nor Congress generally could limit the president's "core exercise of Commander in Chief control"; any statute that sought to do so was simply unconstitutional and did not need to be enforced.

The idea that the executive power is indivisible (and that, for example, the commander in chief power is separable from Congress's overlapping powers to declare war and to provide for the regulation of armed forces and hostilities) stems from a relatively recently enunciated theory termed the "unitary executive." In its mildest iteration, that theory—drawn from Article II's vesting clause—simply holds that all of the executive powers under the Constitution are exercised by the president, but does not dictate what the "executive power" might mean in substance. In more extreme versions, as endorsed by the George W. Bush administration, the theory holds not only that Congress cannot infringe on the executive power but that only the president himself can determine the boundaries of that power.[116]

Such "unitarian" logic underlay the administration's expansive claims to confidentiality, as noted above, and its consistent claim in signing statements that legislatively imposed reporting requirements would be treated as advisory requests. It was also prominent in the administration's treatment of prisoners captured during various antiterror operations after 2001, a policy largely devised via executive order.[117] Some detainees were kept at so-called "black sites" run secretly by the CIA around the world. Hundreds more were imprisoned at the custom-built prison at the U.S. naval base in Guantánamo Bay, Cuba. Those captured in Afghanistan were given a blanket designation by the president not as prisoners-of-war (POW) but rather as "unlawful enemy combatants," without the rights POW status confers. "[P]ursuant to my authority as Commander in Chief and Chief Executive of the United States," Bush declared in February 2002, "I . . . determine that none of the provisions of Geneva apply to our conflict with al Qaeda in Afghanistan or elsewhere throughout the world." He added that "our values as a Nation . . . call for us to treat detainees humanely" and "consistent with the principles of Geneva."[118] However, Secretary of Defense Donald Rumsfeld said this would be implemented so that those detained "would be treated in "a manner that is reasonably consistent" with the Conventions—"for the most part."[119]

In practice this meant that previous army regulations constraining interrogation methods were superseded, setting off an extended controversy over the definition of torture and the relationship of extreme interrogation methods to U.S. law. Techniques employed at Guantánamo Bay were apparently transferred to other military facilities, often in tragically embellished form. The most notorious example was at the Abu Ghraib prison outside Baghdad in 2004. By 2005 CIA personnel had been implicated in the deaths of at least four prisoners in agency custody. Late that year the president conceded the existence of the "black sites"; around the same time, the practice of "extraordinary rendition," which involved sending prisoners abroad for interrogation in countries unencumbered by due process of law, also came to light.[120] The president repeatedly insisted that "we do not torture," but at the same time his Office of Legal Counsel (OLC) issued legal definitions of torture that many observers criticized as overly narrow.[121]

In any case, as a memo constructed by a working group of administration attorneys concluded, "in order to respect the President's inherent constitutional authority to manage a military campaign, [the prohibition against torture] as well as any other potentially applicable statute must be construed as inapplicable to interrogations undertaken pursuant to his Commander-in-Chief authority."[122] Congress could not encroach on the exercise of that authority. Thus, as noted above in the discussion of signing statements, when legislators did overwhelmingly approve limits on interrogation procedures the president asserted his right to implement it "consistent with the constitutional authority of the President to oversee the unitary executive branch and as Commander in Chief." The message, as with the NSA program, was that the president would determine the limits of his power, and of the law itself.

A third example of that principle reflected efforts by the administration to bypass the civilian justice system. President Bush asserted that in time of war he was empowered to detain indefinitely without charge or counsel even American citizens arrested within the United States. The designation of this sort of "enemy combatant" was, according to the president, entirely up to him; judges and legislators had no power even to review that status. (So long as the executive could provide "some evidence" of wrongdoing by the detainee, "the court may not secondguess the military's enemy combatant determination," the Justice Department

told the Circuit Court.)[123] Under this principle U.S. citizens Yaser Hamdi, captured on the Afghan battlefield, and José Padilla, arrested at Chicago's O'Hare Airport, were held in isolation in a military brig for as long as three and a half years. In its 2004 decision in *Hamdi v. Rumsfeld,* the Supreme Court rejected the notion that the executive had sole discretion over the designation of combatants and required that they receive at least some procedural safeguards: "A state of war is not a blank check for the President when it comes to the rights of the Nation's citizens. Whatever power the United States Constitution envisions for the Executive in its exchanges with other nations or with enemy organizations in times of conflict, it most assuredly envisions a role for all three branches when individual liberties are at stake."[124]

However, a plurality of the court held that the AUMF did constitute affirmative legislative delegation to the president sufficient to name enemy combatants in the first place. The 1971 Non-Detention Act was held inapplicable to Hamdi's case since taking prisoners was so central to armed conflict that "it is of no moment" that the AUMF did not specifically override it. As a result, a circuit court panel upheld José Padilla's detention as well, though in late 2005 the administration formally charged Padilla with conspiracy and moved him to the criminal court system.[125]

The Padilla criminal case was soon bogged down in controversy over his treatment by military interrogators, raising questions about the utility of the criminal courts in such cases.[126] Questions arose as well over how the other, noncitizen, detainees noted above were to be tried—if at all. President Bush proposed using a system of military tribunals created by presidential "military order" in November 2001. In drafting the order the administration relied heavily on World War II–era precedents stemming from the case of German saboteurs captured within the United States. While the use of tribunals goes back to the American Revolution, critics charged that they were inappropriate in this case; that Congress had the power to regulate the detention regime; and that the president had in any case tailored tribunal procedures in ways that limited the rights of the accused. While regulations were to be established by the Pentagon, the record of any trial, including the conviction and sentence, was to be sent directly to the president "for review and final decision."[127]

Though the order stated that individuals bound over for the tribunals had no right to "seek any remedy" in state or federal court, prisoners did challenge the legality of their detention (asserting *habeas corpus* rights despite their status as noncitizens) and the process by which their status was to be determined. In *Hamdan v. Rumsfeld,* decided in June 2006, the Supreme Court held that the structure and procedures of the tribunal system as established—particularly its rules of evidence—violated both the Geneva

Conventions and the Uniform Code of Military Justice (UCMJ). The justices did not address the president's power to detain Hamdan or others for the duration of hostilities. But they held that the AUMF was insufficient grounds for the president to establish tribunals that deviated from standard court-martials and that doing so required legislative sanction.[128]

The various enemy combatant cases combined when President Bush responded to the *Hamdan* decision by proposing the Military Commissions Act of 2006. As passed by Congress in October of that year, the act amended the UCMJ to provide legal authority for the tribunals at Guantanamo Bay, allowing for amended evidentiary standards and immunizing U.S. personnel against criminal prosecution for interrogation tactics short of torture occurring before passage of the 2005 Detainee Treatment Act. The act also retroactively stripped detainees of the right to file *habeas corpus* petitions in federal court; it allowed for some court review of tribunal decisions, but largely limited that review to whether the tribunal had followed its prescribed process rather than to the results of that process. The definition of "unlawful enemy combatant" was put in statute but also left wide room for executive discretion: it could include any "person who has engaged in hostilities or who has purposefully and materially supported hostilities against the United States or its co-belligerents who is not a lawful enemy combatant." The president was also authorized to issue executive orders interpreting "the meaning and application of the Geneva Conventions." [129]

As this suggests, in the Military Commissions Act legislators followed an old pattern in regularizing many of the powers previously claimed unilaterally by the president. Certainly by its passage the resurgence regime of the 1970s no longer bound, or even guided, legislative-executive interaction. President Bush, given the extraordinary circumstances after the terrorist strikes of 2001, was a particular beneficiary of this practice. He received historically high levels of legislative support throughout his first six years in office; indeed, his five-year streak without a veto was the longest since Thomas Jefferson's administration, and through 2006 he had vetoed only one bill. Congressional oversight over executive behavior was largely absent, prompting bipartisan accusation that the legislature had become a "broken branch." [130]

Oversight seemed likely to increase after the 2006 midterm elections returned Democrats to majority status in both House and Senate. However, the precedents already set suggested that future presidents would rely upon a "normal" balance of presidential-congressional power far more tilted toward the "imperial" end of the spectrum than could have been foreseen by the post-Watergate generation of legislators—or, for that matter, by the Framers of the Constitution.

Unitary Executives in the Constitutional Framework

As noted at the outset of this chapter, the Framers sought to build interlocking institutions that would provide "those who administer each department the necessary constitutional means and personal motives to resist encroachments of the others." [131] The goal was to separate institutions rather than to separate powers; in fact, powers would necessarily overlap to the extent required to give each branch some ability to prevent unilateral action by the others. American government is therefore prone to tremendous inertia, even stalemate. Despite the consistent, and often successful, efforts of presidents over two centuries and more to expand their institutional resources past the sparse grants of Article II, they ultimately remain subject to its constraints.

Unilateral presidential power, then, is a real temptation for presidents, legislators, and the public alike. But as Supreme Court Justice Robert Jackson explained in 1952, such power suggests "both practical advantages and grave dangers for the country." [132]

The practical advantages are clear. After all, how can one provide direction to an enormous nation, with an enormous national executive establishment and enormous public expectations, and still hope to limit the authority necessary to meet those needs? Congress—even a Congress suspicious of executive power—will not abolish the discretionary presidency. During a crisis, especially, quick and forceful response is required; while the structural constraints imposed by "separate institutions sharing powers" [133] might be maddening to participants in normal times, they could be fatal to the republic when crisis or war intrudes. The problems of administration that arose during the Articles of Confederation period in a much smaller country, with a much smaller Congress, in what seemed a much larger world, were sufficient to drive the Framers to submerge their fear of monarchy and empower a single person as president; a globalized, polarized world seems to call out for endowing leadership sufficient to match its powers to the tasks at hand. Abraham Lincoln, in defending his remarkable usurpation of power during the early months of the Civil War, asked simply, "Must a government of necessity be too strong for the liberties of its people, or too weak to maintain its own existence?" [134]

Lincoln's experiences during the Civil War were unique, but history is dotted with other moments when this dilemma emerged powerfully. Yet while few doubt the need for presidents to wield extraordinary powers in times when the crisis is apparent to all, debates rage when claims to emergency powers seem overstated. Indeed, the dangers of unilateral authority are indeed "grave," because once those claims are asserted they logically admit no limits. And a crisis model of presidential leadership may foster in the White House itself a view of the office that should exist only during crises: the quick response to problems with little delib-

JUSTICE JACKSON'S TEST OF PRESIDENTIAL EMERGENCY POWERS

Justice Robert Jackson's concurring opinion in *Youngstown Sheet and Tube Co. v. Sawyer* (1952) remains a classic analysis of the conditions under which a president may in fact possess extraordinary powers.[1] More important, Jackson's dispassionate examination suggests when those emergency powers may not exist.

Mr. Justice Jackson, concurring:

The actual art of governing under our Constitution does not and cannot conform to judicial definitions of the power of any of its branches based on isolated clauses or even single Articles torn from context. While the Constitution diffuses power the better to secure liberty, it also contemplates that practice will integrate the dispersed powers into a workable government. It enjoins upon its branches separateness but interdependence, autonomy but reciprocity. Presidential powers are not fixed but fluctuate, depending upon their disjunction or conjunction with those of Congress. We may well begin by a somewhat oversimplified grouping of practical situations in which a President may doubt, or others may challenge, his powers, and by distinguishing roughly the legal consequences of this factor of relativity.

1. When the President acts pursuant to an express or implied authorization of Congress, his authority is at its maximum, for it includes all that he possesses in his own right plus all that Congress can delegate. In these circumstances, and in these only, may he be said (for what it may be worth) to personify the federal sovereignty. If his act is held unconstitutional under these circumstances, it usually means that the Federal Government as an undivided whole lacks power. A seizure executed by the President pursuant to an Act of Congress would be supported by the strongest of presumptions and the widest latitude of judicial interpretation, and the burden of persuasion would rest heavily upon any who might attack it.

2. When the President acts in absence of either a congressional grant or denial of authority, he can only rely upon his own independent powers, but there is a zone of twilight in which he and Congress may have concurrent authority, or in which its distribution is uncertain. Therefore, congressional inertia, indifference or quiescence may sometimes, at least as a practical matter, enable, if not invite, measures on independent presidential responsibility. In this area, any actual test of power is likely to depend on the imperatives of events and contemporary imponderables rather than on abstract theories of law.

3. When the President takes measures incompatible with the expressed or implied will of Congress, his power is at its lowest ebb, for then he can rely only upon his own constitutional powers minus any constitutional powers of Congress over the matter. Courts can sustain exclusive presidential control in such a case only by disabling the Congress from acting upon the subject. Presidential claim to a power at once so conclusive and preclusive must be scrutinized with caution, for what is at stake is the equilibrium established by our constitutional system.

Into which of these classifications does this executive seizure of the steel industry fit? It is eliminated from the first by admission, for it is conceded that no congressional authorization exists for this seizure. That takes away also the support of the many precedents and declarations which were made in relation, and must be confined, to this category.

Can it then be defended under flexible tests available to the second category? It seems clearly eliminated from that class because Congress has not left seizure of private property an open field but has covered it by three statutory policies inconsistent with this seizure. In cases where the purpose is to supply needs of the Government itself, two courses are provided: one, seizure of a plant which fails to comply with obligatory orders placed by the Government; another condemnation of facilities, including temporary use under the power of eminent domain. The third is applicable where it is the general economy of the country that is to be protected rather than exclusive governmental interests. None of these were invoked. In choosing a different and inconsistent way of his own, the President cannot claim that it is necessitated or invited by failure of Congress to legislate upon the occasions, grounds, and methods for seizure of industrial properties.

This leaves the current seizure to be justified only by the severe tests under the third grouping, where it can be supported only by any remainder of executive power after subtraction of such powers as Congress may have over the subject. In short, we can sustain the President only by holding that seizure of such strike-bound industries is within his domain and beyond control of Congress. Thus, this court's first review of such seizures occurs under circumstances which leave presidential power most vulnerable to attack and in the least favorable of possible constitutional postures.

1. *Youngstown Sheet and Tube Co. v. Sawyer,* 343 U.S. 579 (1952).

---

eration or consultation with Congress, the temptation to resort to extraconstitutional (even unconstitutional) means to achieve important ends, and the tendency to function as if the president were above the law. Such attitudes—which some observers saw in Nixon's 1970 decision to invade Cambodia, Reagan's efforts to support rebels in Nicaragua, Clinton's tussle with the independent counsel's office, or George W. Bush's broadest claims of commander-in-chief authority—ultimately may do the institution of the presidency more harm than good, if they invite congressional and public backlash. Even Locke's version of prerogative had

crucial checks; it was only legitimate as it reflected the public commonweal, and could only be temporary: executive control in the absence of legislative direction stood only until "the Legislature can be conveniently assembled to provide for it." [135] Laws can be amended; but in a government under the law, they cannot be long ignored. In that very American context the constraints on prerogative are even stronger.

The long struggle between presidential claims to extraordinary powers and the right of Congress to impose its constitutional will probably never be resolved entirely. Nor is there any one right resolution. In our separated system, legitimating large-scale change requires bridging its divisions by persuasion and coalition. While executive discretion is, in fact, increasingly important, the framework within which that discretion may be exercised—the beating of the bounds between the branches—is not a matter for decree but deliberation. While presidents' arguments have been distinctly unitarian, the Constitution is in turn devoutly trinitarian. Ambition, Americans should hope, will continue to counteract ambition.

★

NOTES

1. Edward S. Corwin, *The President: Office and Powers,* 5th rev. ed., with Randall W. Bland, Theodore Hinson, and Jack W. Peltason (New York: New York University Press, 1984), 3.

2. Willi Paul Adams, "The State Constitutions as Analogy and Precedent: The American Experience with Constituent Power before 1787," in *The United States Constitution: Roots, Rights, and Responsibilities,* ed. A. E. Howard (Washington, D.C.: Smithsonian Institution Press, 1992); James Madison, *Federalist* No. 48, in Alexander Hamilton, James Madison, and John Jay, *The Federalist Papers,* with an introduction by Clinton L. Rossiter (New York: New American Library, 1961). All citations to *The Federalist Papers* are to this edition.

3. "Cato," Letter V of November 22, 1787, in *The Anti-Federalist Papers and the Constitutional Convention Debates,* ed. Ralph Ketcham (New York: Mentor, 1986), 317; in response, see especially Alexander Hamilton, *Federalist* No. 69.

4. Alexander Hamilton, *Federalist* No. 70; and see John Jay, *Federalist* No. 64; "The Pacificus-Helvidius Letters," in *The Evolving Presidency,* 2d ed., ed. Michael Nelson (Washington, D.C.: CQ Press, 2004), 39–47.

5. "Pacificus-Helvidius Letters"; Grover Cleveland, *The Independence of the Executive* (Princeton: Princeton University Press, 1913), 14–15.

6. Theodore Roosevelt, *An Autobiography* (New York: Da Capo Press, 1985), 372; Ryan J. Barilleaux, "Venture Constitutionalism and the Enlargement of the Presidency," in Christopher S. Kelly, ed., *Executing the Constitution: Putting the President Back into the Constitution* (Albany: State University of New York Press, 2005).

7. John Locke, *Second Treatise of Government,* ed. C. B. Macpherson (Indianapolis: Hackett, 1980 [1690]), 84.

8. Lincoln letter to Albert G. Hodges, April 4, 1864, reprinted in *The President, Congress, and the Constitution: Power and Legitimacy in American Politics,* ed. Christopher H. Pyle and Richard M. Pious (New York: Free Press, 1984), 65; see, too, his Message to Congress, July 4, 1861.

9. "Pacificus-Helvidius Letters," emphases in original. However, see Madison's argument in *Federalist* No. 41 regarding the extra-constitutional demands of national self-preservation.

10. William Howard Taft, "Our Chief Magistrate and His Powers" (1916), in Pyle and Pious, *President, Congress, and the Constitution* 70–71.

11. See, for example, David Gray Adler and Michael A. Genovese, "Introduction," in *The Presidency and the Law: The Clinton Legacy,* ed. David Gray Adler and Michael A. Genovese (Lawrence: University Press of Kansas, 2002).

12. For a detailed recounting, see Andrew Rudalevige, *The New Imperial Presidency: Renewing Presidential Power after Watergate* (Ann Arbor: University of Michigan Press, 2005), which informs much of this chapter.

13. *In re Neagle,* 135 U.S. 1 (1890); see also Corwin, *President: Office and Powers,* 170–171. A dissenting opinion sardonically noted that the presidential oath of office might perhaps pledge presidential fealty to Article I ("the Congress shall have powers . . . to make all laws. . . .").

14. Leonard White, *The Federalists* (New York: Macmillan, 1948), 512.

15. "Pacificus-Helvidius Letters"; Stanley Elkins and Eric McKitrick, *The Age of Federalism: The Early American Republic, 1788–1800* (New York: Oxford University Press, 1993), 336–365.

16. Jefferson to John V. Colvin, September 10, 1810, reprinted in Pyle and Pious, *President, Congress, and the Constitution,* 62.

17. *Ex parte Merryman,* 17 Fed. Cas. 9487 (1861). Note that while the Constitution anticipates the possibility of suspending the writ in times of "rebellion or invasion," this is enumerated in Article I.

18. Clinton Rossiter, *Constitutional Dictatorship* (Princeton: Princeton University Press, 1948); and see Richard M. Pious, *The American Presidency* (New York: Basic Books, 1979), 55–60.

19. *Prize Cases,* 67 U.S. (2 Black) 635 (1863). However, as Arthur M. Schlesinger Jr., points out, the justices endorsed such executive power only in cases of domestic rebellions or invasions, and not, as some later presidents asserted, for use against other sovereign nations. See Schlesinger, *The Imperial Presidency* (Boston: Houghton Mifflin, 1973), 64–66.

20. Leonard White, *The Jeffersonians* (New York: Macmillan, 1951), 552.

21. *Martin v. Mott,* 12 Wheat. 19, 23–33 (1827).

22. Hoar quoted in Wilfred E. Binkley, *President and Congress,* 3d rev. ed. (New York: Vintage, 1962), 185.

23. *Ex parte Milligan,* 71 U.S. (4 Wall.) 2 (1866).

24. Binkley, *President and Congress,* chaps. 8–9; *In re Neagle,* 135 U.S. 1 (1890).

25. *In re Debs,* 158 U.S. 564 (1895); *U.S. v. Midwest Oil Co.,* 236 U.S. 459 (1915).

26. Pious, *American Presidency,* 49; James Ceaser, *Presidential Selection* (Princeton: Princeton University Press, 1979), 170 and chap. 4.

27. Corwin, *President: Office and Powers,* 269–270.

28. From his 1908 book *Constitutional Government in the United States,* quoted in Binkley, *President and Congress,* 215.

29. Richard E. Neustadt, *Presidential Power: The Politics of Leadership* (New York: Wiley, 1960), 5.

30. Fred I. Greenstein, "Toward a Modern Presidency," in Greenstein, ed., *Leadership in the Modern Presidency* (Cambridge, Mass.: Harvard University Press, 1988), 3; William E. Leuchtenburg, *In the Shadow of FDR: From Harry Truman to Ronald Reagan* (Ithaca, N.Y.: Cornell University Press, 1983).

31. Louis Fisher, *Presidential Spending Power* (Princeton: Princeton University Press, 1975), 61–64.

32. Franklin D. Roosevelt, "Message to Congress on Stabilizing the Economy," September 7, 1942; much of the text was repeated in FDR's radio address that evening, see (www.fdrlibrary.marist.edu /090742.html).

33. *United States v. Curtiss-Wright Export Corp.,* 299 U.S. 304 (1936).

34. See ibid.; Pious, *American Presidency*; John Roche, "Executive Power and the Domestic Presidency: The Quest for Prerogative," *Western Political Quarterly* 5 (December 1952); Barton J. Bernstein, "The Road to Watergate and Beyond: The Growth and Abuse of Executive Authority Since 1940," *Law and Contemporary Problems* 40 (spring 1976).

35. Bernstein, "Road to Watergate," 64; Robert H. Jackson, *That Man: An Insider's Portrait of Franklin D. Roosevelt* (New York: Oxford University Press, 2003), 68–73.

36. *Korematsu v. United States,* 323 U.S. 214 (1944); Civil Liberties Act of 1988 (P.L. 100-383).

37. Neustadt, *Presidential Power,* 3.

38. It is worth noting that the postwar crisis was not just de facto but de jure. The United States officially lived under a state of declared national emergency from 1933 to 1975: Roosevelt's bank emergency (1933), Truman's mobilization after North Korea's invasion of South Korea (1950), Nixon's use of troops to maintain mail deliveries (1970), and Nixon's response to international economic conditions (1971), all remained in force until passage of the National Emergencies Act in 1976.

39. Allen Schick, "Politics Through Law: Congressional Limitations on Executive Discretion," in *Both Ends of the Avenue,* ed. Anthony King (Washington, D.C.: AEI Press, 1983), 161; James Lindsay, "Deference and Defiance: The Shifting Rhythms of Executive-Legislative Relations in Foreign Policy," *Presidential Studies Quarterly* 33 (September 2003): 530–546.

40. Corwin, *President: Office and Powers,* 4. See, for example, James MacGregor Burns, *Presidential Government: The Crucible of Leadership* (Boston: Houghton Mifflin, 1965). A contemporary version of this argument can be found in James Sundquist, *Constitutional Reform and Effective Government* (Washington, D.C.: Brookings, 1986); and, as regards foreign affairs, in John Yoo, *The Powers of War and Peace* (Chicago: University of Chicago Press, 2005).

41. Schlesinger, *Imperial Presidency*; Rudalevige, *New Imperial Presidency,* chap. 2.

42. Greenstein, "Toward a Modern Presidency," 3.

43. Sorensen quoted in Samuel Kernell, *Going Public: New Strategies of Presidential Leadership,* 3d ed. (Washington, D.C.: CQ Press, 1997), 86.

44. Andrew Rudalevige, *Managing the President's Program: Presidential Leadership and Legislative Policy Formulation* (Princeton: Princeton University Press, 2002), chap. 3; "President Bush on Iraq, Immigration, and Elections" (interview transcript), *Washington Post,* December 20, 2006, A16.

45. Charles M. Cameron, *Veto Bargaining: Presidents and the Politics of Negative Power* (New York: Cambridge University Press, 2000); *Weekly Compilation of Presidential Documents* (April 26, 2002), 692.

46. This figure includes approximately 700,000 postal employees and 1.4 million military personnel.

47. Terry Moe, "The Politicized Presidency," in *The New Direction in American Politics,* ed. John E. Chubb and Paul E. Peterson (Washington, D.C.: Brookings, 1985); Scott C. James, "The Evolution of the Presidency: Between the Promise and the Fear," in *The Executive Branch,* ed. Joel D. Aberbach and Mark A. Peterson (New York: Oxford University Press, 2005), 27–30.

48. See John Burke, *The Institutional Presidency,* 2d ed. (Baltimore: Johns Hopkins University Press, 2000); Matthew J. Dickinson, *Bitter Harvest: FDR, Presidential Power, and the Growth of the Presidential Branch* (New York: Cambridge University Press, 1997); Karen M. Hult and Charles E. Walcott, *Empowering the White House: Governance under Nixon, Ford, and Carter* (Lawrence:

University Press of Kansas, 2003); David E. Lewis, "Staffing Alone: Unilateral Action and the Politicization of the Executive Office of the President," *Presidential Studies Quarterly* 35 (September 2005): 496–514.

49. Fisher, *Presidential Spending Power,* 36.

50. Steven A. Shull, *Policy by Other Means: Alternative Adoption by Presidents* (College Station: Texas A&M Press, 2006), 73.

51. Executive Order 8248.

52. John Hart, *The Presidential Branch,* 2d ed. (Chatham, N.J.: Chatham House, 1995). On the tensions between Congress and the presidency over the direction of public policy, see Charles O. Jones, *The Presidency in a Separated System,* 2d ed. (Washington, D.C.: Brookings, 2005); Joel Aberbach and Mark Peterson, eds., *The Executive Branch* (New York: Oxford University Press, 2005), especially chap. 13; and Jon Bond and Richard Fleisher, eds., *Polarized Politics: Congress and the President in a Polarized Era* (Washington, D.C.: CQ Press, 2000).

53. Thomas J. Weko, *The Politicizing Presidency: The White House Personnel Office, 1948–1994* (Lawrence: University Press of Kansas, 1994), 89 and generally; Mike Allen, "Bush to Change Economic Team," *Washington Post,* November 29, 2004, A1; Richard Nathan, *The Administrative Presidency* (New York: Macmillan, 1983); Alexis Simendinger, "Help Wanted," *National Journal* (December 16, 2006): 26–29; David A. Yalof, *Pursuit of Justices: Presidential Politics and the Selection of Supreme Court Nominees* (Chicago: University of Chicago Press, 1999); Martha Kumar and Terry Sullivan, eds., *The White House World* (College Station: Texas A&M Press, 2003).

54. Corwin, *President: Office and Powers,* 115–125.

55. *Skinner v. Railway Labor Executives Association,* 489 U.S. 602 (1989); *National Treasury Employees Union v. Von Raab,* 489 U.S. 656 (1989).

56. Simendinger, "Help Wanted," 29; Henry Hogue, *Recess Appointments: Frequently Asked Questions,* Report RS21308 (Washington, D.C.: Congressional Research Service, August 25, 2006).

57. Cornelius Kerwin, *Rulemaking: How Government Agencies Write Law and Make Policy,* 3d ed. (Washington, D.C.: CQ Press, 2003).

58. See Executive Order 12291 (1981), 12498 (1985), and 13422 (2007); Kenneth R. Mayer, *With the Stroke of a Pen: Executive Orders and Presidential Power* (Princeton: Princeton University Press, 2001), 125–134; Cindy Skrzycki, "Tiny OIRA Still Exercises its Real Influence Invisibly," *Washington Post,* November 11, 2003, E1; Philipp Steger, "Bringing Science into Politics: The Debate on Scientific Integrity in U.S. Policymaking," *Bridges* 5 (April 14, 2005), available at www.ostina.org/content/blogsection/7/149/.

59. *Weekly Compilation of Presidential Documents* (December 8, 2004), 2924; and see Christopher Kelley, "Rethinking Presidential Power: The Unitary Executive and the George W. Bush Presidency," (paper presented at the annual meeting of the Midwest Political Science Association, Chicago, April 2005).

60. Phillip J. Cooper, *By Order of the President: The Use and Abuse of Executive Direct Action* (Lawrence: University Press of Kansas, 2002), 204–210; the Reagan statement is cited on p. 205. For George W. Bush, see *Public Papers of the Presidents, 2001,* May 24 (p. 575), November 28 (p. 1459), and December 28 (p. 1554). See also Christopher Kelley, "The Unitary Executive and the Presidential Signing Statement," (Ph.D. diss., Miami University of Ohio, 2003); Phillip J. Cooper, "George W. Bush, Edgar Allen Poe, and the Use and Abuse of the Presidential Signing Statement," *Presidential Studies Quarterly* 35 (September 2005): 515–532.

61. See Section 1003 of the Detainee Treatment Act (P.L. 109-148); "President's Statement on Signing of H.R. 2863," Office of the

White House Press Secretary, December 30, 2005; "President's Statement on H.R. 5682," Office of the White House Press Secretary, December 18, 2006.

62. See *Ameron, Inc. v. U.S. Army Corps of Engineers, et al.,* 787 F.2d 875 (3d Cir. 1986); on the difficulty of overturning signing statements, see Cooper, *By Order of the President,* 222; see also 18 *Opinions of the Office of Legal Counsel* 199 (1994), listing Supreme Court decisions that purportedly condoned signing statements, from *Myers v. U.S.* in 1926 to *Freytag v. Commissioner* in 1991.

63. James Sundquist, *The Decline and Resurgence of Congress* (Washington, D.C: Brookings, 1981), 202.

64. Fisher, *Presidential Spending Power,* 165; Schlesinger, *Imperial Presidency,* 239; *Train v. City of New York,* 420 U.S. 35 (1975).

65. Rudalevige, *New Imperial Presidency,* 141–149; Peter Baker, "Bush Calls on Senate to Pass Line-Item Veto," *Washington Post,* June 28, 2006, A3.

66. Proclamations generally encompass such hortatory matters as Thanksgiving Day or National Black History Month, but some—the 1793 Neutrality Proclamation, the 1863 Emancipation Proclamation, etc.—involve substantive issues that carry the force of law. The Supreme Court, in *Wolsey v. Chapman,* 101 U.S. 755 (1879), ruled that there is no material difference between proclamations and executive orders; nor is there much practical difference between executive orders and the other forms of presidential orders described most comprehensively by Cooper, *By Order of the President.* See also Mayer, *With the Stroke of a Pen*; William G. Howell, *Power without Persuasion: The Politics of Direct Presidential Action* (Princeton: Princeton University Press, 2003).

67. Mayer, *With the Stroke of a Pen,* 66f; Cooper, *By Order of the President.*

68. Adam Liptak, "Judge Rules 2001 Listing of Terrorists Violated Law," *New York Times,* November 29, 2006, A24.

69. Cooper, *By Order of the President,* 70; David E. Lewis, *Presidents and the Politics of Agency Design* (Stanford, Calif.: Stanford University Press, 2003). For an extended discussion of the "first mover" advantage orders grant, see Howell, *Power without Persuasion.*

70. Mayer, *With the Stroke of a Pen,* 79–87; Howell, *Power without Persuasion,* 83–85; Executive Order 13279.

71. Ruth Morgan, *The President and Civil Rights* (New York: St. Martin's Press, 1970), 5.

72. Harold Hongju Koh, *The National Security Constitution: Sharing Power After the Iran-Contra Affair* (New Haven: Yale University Press, 1990), 46–48; Harold C. Relyea, "National Emergency Powers," Report 98-505-GOV, Congressional Research Service (June 28, 2001).

73. Executive Order 11246. See Mayer, *With the Stroke of a Pen,* 203–206.

74. See Elizabeth Drew, *On the Edge* (New York: Touchstone, 1994).

75. Emanuel quoted in Alexis Simendinger, "The Paper Wars," *National Journal,* July 25, 1998, 1737.

76. George H. W. Bush called these National Security Directives, Bill Clinton called them Presidential Decision Directives, and George W. Bush called them National Security Presidential Directives. Legislative efforts in the late 1980s to obtain a list of national security directives failed; Rep. Lee Hamilton (D-Ind.) complained in 1988 that such directives "are revealed to Congress only under irregular, arbitrary, or even accidental circumstances, if at all." See Cooper, *By Order of the President,* 144, 165, 194–195.

77. On the Iran-contra controversy see, among many works, Jane Mayer and Doyle McManus, *Landslide: The Unmaking of the President, 1984–1988* (Boston: Houghton Mifflin, 1988); Lawrence E. Walsh, *Final Report of the Independent Counsel for Iran/contra Matters, Vol. I: Investigations and Prosecutions* (Washington, D.C.: United States Court of Appeals, District of Columbia Circuit, August 4, 1993).

78. Schlesinger, *Imperial Presidency,* 339.

79. Ibid., 340.

80. Pious, *American Presidency,* 348; more broadly, see Daniel Patrick Moynihan, *Secrecy* (New Haven: Yale University Press, 1998).

81. The Nixon and Reagan orders are Executive Order 11652 and Executive Order 12356, respectively.

82. The Clinton and Bush orders are Executive Order 12598 and Executive Order 13292, respectively. The orders granting HHS, EPA, and Agriculture the right to classify documents were issued on December 10, 2001; May 6, 2002; and September 26, 2002, respectively; they may be found in the *Federal Register.*

83. Nixon, "Statement on Executive Privilege," *Public Papers of the President,* March 12, 1973; Richard Kleindienst, Hearings before the Senate Subcommittee on Intergovernmental Relations, "Executive Privilege, Secrecy in Government, Freedom of Information," 93d Cong., 1st sess., April 10, 1973, Vol. I, 20, 45, 51.

84. Schlesinger, *Imperial Presidency,* 156–159; Mark J. Rozell, *Executive Privilege: Presidential Power, Secrecy, and Accountability,* 2d rev. ed. (Lawrence: University Press of Kansas, 2002); Louis Fisher, *The Politics of Executive Privilege* (Durham, N.C.: Carolina Academic Press, 2004).

85. *U.S. v. Nixon,* 418 U.S. 683 (1974).

86. *In re Sealed Case,* 121 F. 3d 729 (D.C. Cir. 1998).

87. Rozell, *Executive Privilege,* 106–107; "Excerpts from White House Letter on Rice's Testimony," *New York Times,* March 31, 2004, A14.

88. William Howell, "Unilateral Powers: A Brief Overview," *Presidential Studies Quarterly* 35 (September 2005): 425.

89. Ronald Reagan, "Letter to the Speaker of the House and the President Pro Tempore of the Senate on the Deployment of United States Forces in Beirut, Lebanon," August 24, 1982.

90. Schlesinger, *Imperial Presidency,* chap. 6; Ryan C. Hendrickson, *The Clinton Wars* (Nashville, Tenn.: Vanderbilt University Press, 2002).

91. Louis Fisher, "War Power," in *The American Congress: The Building of Democracy,* ed. Julian E. Zelizer (Boston: Houghton Mifflin, 2004), 696. Note that the War Powers Resolution specifically prohibits use of treaty obligations as an approval mechanism.

92. Kiki Caruson, "International Agreement-making and the Executive-Legislative Relationship," *Presidency Research Group Report* 25 (fall 2002): 21–28; Shull, *Policy by Other Means,* chap. 6.

93. Bernstein, "Road to Watergate," 81; on the Afghan war, see Bob Woodward, *Bush at War* (New York: Simon and Schuster, 2002). More generally, see John Prados, *Safe for Democracy: The CIA's Secret Wars* (Chicago: Ivan Dee, 2006).

94. The letter was dated July 17, 2003, and is available at (*http://www.talkingpointsmemo.com/docs/rock-cheney1.html*).

95. See Fisher, *Presidential Spending Power,* 240.

96. See Rudalevige, *New Imperial Presidency,* 65–74, 109–113, 180–181, 241–248; Geoffrey R. Stone, "The Reagan Amendment, the First Amendment, and FBI Domestic Security Investigations," in *Freedom at Risk,* ed. Richard O. Curry (Philadelphia: Temple University Press, 1988); William C. Banks and M. E. Bowman, "Executive Authority for National Security Surveillance," *American University Law Review* 50 (October 2000): 1–130; Stephen J. Schulhofer, *Rethinking the Patriot Act* (New York: Century Foundation Press, 2005); "Abuse of Authority: The FBI's Gross Misuse of a Counterterrorism Device," *Washington Post* (March 11, 2007), B6.

97. Allen J. Matusow, *Nixon's Economy* (Lawrence: University Press of Kansas, 1998).

98. Douglas Brinkley, *The Great Deluge: Hurricane Katrina, New Orleans, and the Mississippi Gulf Coast* (New York: William Morrow, 2006).

99. Rudalevige, *New Imperial Presidency,* chap.4.

100. *U.S. v. U.S. District Court,* 407 U.S. 297 (1972).

101. Ford interview in *Time* (November 10, 1980), 30.

102. Louis Fisher and David Gray Adler, "The War Powers Resolution: Time to Say Goodbye," *Political Science Quarterly* 113 (spring 1998): 1–20; Shull, *Policy by Other Means,* chap. 7.

103. Elizabeth Drew, *Showdown: The Struggle Between the Gingrich Congress and the Clinton White House,* paperback ed. (New York: Touchstone, 1997); Victoria Allred, "Versatility with the Veto," *CQ Weekly* (January 20, 2001), 176.

104. *Public Papers of the Presidents, 1995,* 1475.

105. David Gray Adler, "Clinton in Context," in David Gray Adler and Michael A. Genovese, eds., *The Presidency and the Law: The Clinton Legacy* (Lawrence: University Press of Kansas, 2002).

106. *Weekly Compilation of Presidential Documents* (March 13, 2002), 411; Cheney quoted in Dana Milbank, "In Cheney's Shadow," *Washington Post,* October 11, 2004, A21; and see Bob Woodward, "Cheney Upholds Power of the Presidency," *Washington Post,* January 20, 2005, A7.

107. See *In re Cheney* (02-5354), U.S. Circuit Court for the District of Columbia, May 10, 2005.

108. The AUMF is P.L. 107-140.

109. The Patriot Act is P.L. 107-56, as renewed and amended by P.L. 109-177.

110. See George W. Bush, 2002 State of the Union Address; *National Security Strategy of the United States of America* (September 17, 2002), Part V. The classified version of the document evidently discussed the use of preemptive nuclear strikes to halt the transfer of weapons of mass destruction. See Mike Allen and Barton Gellman, "Preemptive Strikes Part of U.S. Strategic Doctrine," *Washington Post,* December 11, 2002, A1.

111. Ron Suskind, *The Price of Loyalty* (New York: Simon & Schuster, 2004), 70–76; Glenn Kessler, "U.S. Decision on Iraq has Puzzling Past," *Washington Post,* January 12, 2003, A1; Bob Woodward, *Plan of Attack* (New York: Simon & Schuster, 2004); Thomas E. Ricks, *Fiasco* (New York: Penguin Press, 2006).

112. Mike Allen and Juliet Eilperin, "Bush Aides Say Iraq War Needs No Hill Vote," *Washington Post,* August 26, 2002, A1.

113. P.L. 107-243; for a timeline, see Michael R. Gordon and Bernard Trainor, *Cobra II: The Inside Story of the Invasion and Occupation of Iraq* (New York: Random House, 2006). For cost information, see the Congressional Research Service figures quoted in Carl Hulse, "Democrats Plan to Take Control of Iraq Spending," *New York Times,* December 14, 2006, A1. For critical assessments of the use of intelligence, see Ricks, *Fiasco*; Mark Danner, *The Secret Way to War* (New York: New York Review Books, 2006).

114. "Press Conference of the President," Office of the White House Press Secretary, December 19, 2005.

115. U.S. Department of Justice, *Legal Authorities Supporting the Activities of the National Security Agency Described by the President,* January 19, 2006, 1–2, 10–11, 17, 30–31.

116. See especially John Yoo, *War by Other Means* (New York: Atlantic, 2005), and the series of law review articles by Steven G. Calabresi, Christopher S. Yoo, and Anthony Colangelo culminating in "The Unitary Executive During the Modern Era: 1945–2004," *Iowa Law Review* 90 (2004): 601ff; and Justice Antonin Scalia's dissenting opinion in *Morrison v. Olson* (1988). A useful journalistic treatment is Jess Bravin, "Judge Alito's View of the Presidency: Expansive Powers," *Wall Street Journal,* January 5, 2006, A1.

117. David Johnston, "CIA Tells of Bush's Directive on the Handling of Detainees," *New York Times,* November 15, 2006.

118. Katherine Q. Seelye, "First 'Unlawful Combatants' Seized in Afghanistan Arrive at U.S. Base in Cuba," *New York Times,* January 12, 2002, A7.

119. Joseph Margulies, *Guantanamo and the Abuse of Presidential Power* (New York: Simon & Schuster, 2005).

120. Michael Fletcher, "Bush Defends CIA's Clandestine Prisons," *Washington Post,* November 8, 2005, A15; Jane Mayer, "A Deadly Interrogation," *New Yorker,* November 14, 2005; Dana Priest, "Covert CIA Program Withstands New Furor," *Washington Post,* December 30, 2005, A1.

121. The term "torture," the Justice Department argued, was legally limited to acts sufficient to cause pain equivalent to, for example, "organ failure . . . or even death," and then only if inflicting such pain (and not, say, gaining information) was the "precise objective" of the interrogator. In late 2004 the administration ostensibly toned down this definition but continued to argue that any previously approved techniques did not constitute torture. For contrasting views of this analysis, see Margulies, *Guantanamo* and Yoo, *War by Other Means.* The original documentation may be found in Karen Greenberg and Joshua Dratel, eds., *The Torture Papers* (New York: Cambridge University Press, 2005) as Memo 14, 172–217.

122. See the *Working Group Report on Detainee Interrogations in the Global War on Terrorism: Assessment of Legal, Historical, Policy, and Operational Considerations,* U.S. Department of Defense, April 4, 2003, 21 and Section III generally; reprinted in Greenberg and Dratel as Memo 26; see especially 286, 302–307.

123. Brief for Respondents-Appellants, June 2002, *Hamdi v. Rumsfeld* (Fourth Circuit Court of Appeals, 02-6895); Government's Brief and Motion, August 27, 2002, *Padilla v. Bush* (U.S. Dist. Court, Southern Dist. of New York, 02-4445); Jennifer Elsea, "Presidential Authority to Detain 'Enemy Combatants,' " *Presidential Studies Quarterly* 33 (September 2003): 568–601.

124. *Hamdi v. Rumsfeld,* 542 U.S. 507 (2004).

125. *Padilla v. Hanft,* 05-6396, 4th Circuit Court of Appeals, September 9, 2005.

126. Dan Eggen, "Padilla Case Raises Questions about Anti-Terror Tactics," *Washington Post,* November 19, 2006, A3.

127. The November 13, 2001, order is printed at 66 *Federal Register* 57833. For a critique and general history of tribunals see Louis Fisher, *Military Tribunals and Presidential Power* (Lawrence: University Press of Kansas, 2005). Key court cases include *Ex parte Quirin,* 317 U.S. 1 (1942) and *Johnson v. Eisentrager,* 339 U.S. 763 (1950).

128. *Hamdan v. Rumsfeld,* 05-184 (June 29, 2006). The Court also held that the charge against Hamdan, conspiracy, could not be tried by military commission since it was not a violation of the laws of war. An earlier question, affirming that U.S. courts' jurisdiction reached to prisoners held in Guantanamo Bay, was settled in *Rasul v. Bush,* 542 U.S. 466 (2004).

129. P.L. 109-366 (October 17, 2006).

130. See Andrew Rudalevige, "George W. Bush and Congress: New Term, New Problems—Same Results?" in *The Second Term of George W. Bush: Prospects and Perils,* ed. Robert Maranto, Douglas M. Brattebo, and Tom Lansford (New York: Palgrave Macmillan, 2006); Thomas Mann and Norman Ornstein, *The Broken Branch* (New York: Oxford University Press, 2006).

131. Madison, *Federalist* No. 48 and No. 51.

132. Concurring opinion to *Youngstown Sheet and Tube Co. v. Sawyer,* 343 U.S. 579 (1952).

133. Neustadt, *Presidential Power,* 33.

134. Quoted in Schlesinger, *Imperial Presidency,* 59; see also Rossiter, *Constitutional Dictatorship,* and Benjamin Kleinerman, "Lincoln's Example: Executive Power and the Survival of Constitutionalism," *Perspectives on Politics* 3 (December 2005): 801–816.

135. Locke, *Second Treatise,* 84.

SELECTED BIBLIOGRAPHY

Cooper, Phillip J. *By Order of the President: The Use and Abuse of Executive Direct Action.* Lawrence: University Press of Kansas, 2002.

Corwin, Edward S. *The President: Office and Powers.* 5th rev. ed., with Randall W. Bland, Theodore Hinson, and Jack W. Peltason. New York: New York University Press, 1984.

Fisher, Louis. *Presidential War Power.* 2d rev. ed. Lawrence: University Press of Kansas, 2004.

Howell, William G. *Power without Persuasion.* Princeton: Princeton University Press, 2003.

Kelley, Christopher S., ed. *Executing the Constitution: Putting the President Back into the Constitution.* Albany: State University of New York Press, 2005.

Mayer, Kenneth R. *With the Stroke of a Pen: Executive Orders and Presidential Power.* Princeton: Princeton University Press, 2001.

Nelson, Michael, ed. *The Presidency and the Political System.* 8th ed. Washington, D.C.: CQ Press, 2006.

Neustadt, Richard E. *Presidential Power and the Modern Presidents: The Politics of Leadership from Roosevelt to Reagan.* New York: Free Press, 1990.

Rozell, Mark J. *Executive Privilege: Presidential Power, Secrecy, and Accountability.* 2d rev. ed. Lawrence: University Press of Kansas, 2002.

Rudalevige, Andrew. *The New Imperial Presidency: Renewing Presidential Power after Watergate.* Ann Arbor: University of Michigan Press, 2005.

Schlesinger, Arthur M., Jr. *The Imperial Presidency.* Boston: Houghton Mifflin, 1973.

Shull, Steven A. *Policy by Other Means: Alternative Adoption by Presidents.* College Station: Texas A&M Press, 2006.

chapter 10

Chief of State

by Mary Stuckey and Daniel C. Diller

Every government must have a chief of state who symbolizes the nation and presides over ceremonial functions.[1] French statesman Charles De Gaulle, for instance, famously argued that the chief of state "embodies the spirit of the nation," meaning that in his or her policies as well as in his or her more symbolic actions, the chief of state personifies the essence of the people he or she represents. And the chief of state tries to embody the best of the people being represented. He or she seeks to appear strong, compassionate, tough, gentle, and worldly, while possessing the common touch. In many countries the function of chief of state is fulfilled by a monarch with little governmental authority or an official whose post was created to shelter the chief executive from ceremonial drudgery. In the United States the chief executive is the chief of state.

The ceremonial activities for which presidents are responsible are as diverse as those that monarchs must perform, but presidents also must perform their duties as chief executive, commander in chief, chief diplomat, chief legislator, and head of their political party. Presidents, therefore, can devote only a fraction of their time to ceremonial activities. During the small amount of time allotted to these ceremonial activities, presidents must show qualities citizens understand as exemplifying good leadership. As political scientists Thomas E. Cronin and Michael A. Genovese note, the presidency is thus the repository of complicated paradoxes in public attitudes. While Americans are suspicious of power, they want a strong president; they want an exemplary person who is a man of the people; they want a hero who is just like them.[2] These paradoxes cannot be resolved without recourse to the ceremonial functions of the presidency. When the president acts as chief of state, he can be all of these different things at different times without appearing inconsistent.

Like a monarch, a U.S. president is the embodiment of the American people and a focal point for national unity. Citizens seem to elect presidents whose characteristics reflect the political and historical times in which they govern, searching for strength in times of war and compassion in

times of peace, for instance. Jimmy Carter, for example, wanted to simplify the office in the wake of the imperial presidencies of Lyndon B. Johnson and Richard M. Nixon. Carter walked from the Capitol to the White House following his inauguration, curtailed the playing of "Hail to the Chief," carried his own suit bag on and off *Air Force One,* and did numerous other things to show that he was a "man of the people." Initially, these moves were popular. But after a while, Carter was criticized for not being presidential enough.

Contrast that with the example of Ronald Reagan, who was good at communicating the common touch. Like Carter, he would often wear blue jeans, told folksy stories, and was frequently photographed chopping wood at his California ranch. But Reagan also looked comfortable in a tuxedo and excelled at performing the more formal aspects of the office. Reagan could convey both images: he could be both a man of the people and a leader of those people.

Other presidents have struggled as they sought to find a balance between these two important aspects of the presidency. George Bush, for instance, was seen as out of touch and aloof, and he was sharply criticized for his perceived inability to recognize the scanners used in grocery stores (he was in fact aware of the technology) and for his failure to articulate how hard economic times had affected him personally. Early in his administration, Bill Clinton was often thought to err in the opposite direction, having as a candidate answered a question about his underwear preferences on national television. The George W. Bush was equally uneven, especially in his first few months in office, although, like Clinton, he found an appropriate balance later in his presidency.

Especially in times of crisis, a president's demeanor has a profound effect on the confidence of the nation. Many citizens were reassured and inspired by George W. Bush's visit to Ground Zero following the tragic events of September 11, 2001, and by his claim to the gathered firefighters and police officers that "I can hear you, the rest of the world can hear you, and the people who knocked these buildings down will hear all of us soon." Bush displayed both his empathy with those who perished in the Twin Towers and the rescue workers who were still there and his toughness.

As chief of state then, presidents symbolize the country's history, liberty, and strength. They can delegate ceremonial functions to their representatives, but while they are in office they cannot escape their chief of state role. At every moment they represent the United States to the international community and to the American people. This representative function continues even after presidents have left office, when their libraries and museums become repositories for an often idealized understanding of national political and cultural history. History is often understood and remembered through the lens offered by the representative function of the president as chief of state.

CEREMONIAL DUTIES AND FUNCTIONS

As chief of state, presidents preside over an endless series of ceremonies that range in tone from the solemnity of the inauguration to the informality of a White House barbecue. They greet foreign ambassadors, dedicate monuments, pin medals on war heroes, buy Girl Scout cookies, visit schools, throw out the first ball on opening day of the baseball season, and hold state dinners for foreign chiefs of state. National ceremonies have much the same purpose for the country as religious rituals have for a church. Ceremonies create shared symbols and sentiments that comfort, motivate, and unify the people.

Such events provide opportunities to dramatize and personalize the presidency. On ceremonial occasions, presidents campaign for their reelection, make policy proposals, articulate their political philosophies, underscore the need for unity, create an atmosphere of confidence, and promote patriotism and national pride. Presidents who neglect ceremonial duties may have more time to develop policy and run the government, but they are sacrificing a tool of leadership that can be used not only to inspire the nation to greater accomplishments, but also to improve their own popularity.

Constitutional Ceremonial Duties

The Constitution obliges presidents to perform several ceremonial duties. They are required to take an oath of office, periodically inform Congress about the state of the Union, and receive "Ambassadors and other public Ministers." Because these constitutional ceremonial duties firmly designate the president as leader of the whole nation, the nation's first president, George Washington, and his successors could safely assume the role of chief of state. Both the oath of office ceremony and State of the Union address physically place the president out in front of other government officials and focus the nation's attention on the president's opinions and recommendations. The president's duty to receive ambassa-

dors implies that foreign governments are to regard the president as the official representative of the United States. Because the international community sees the president as chief of state, domestic chief of state responsibilities could not be assumed gracefully by anyone but the president.

Oath of Office and Inauguration

Article II, Section 1, Clause 8, of the Constitution requires the president-elect to recite the following thirty-five-word oath before assuming the presidency: "I do solemnly swear (or affirm) that I will faithfully execute the Office of President of the United States, and will to the best of my Ability preserve, protect, and defend the Constitution of the United States." The occasion for this oath taking is not described in the Constitution, but the inaugural ceremony at which it is administered has become one of the U.S. government's most important traditions and the president's first chief of state function. *(See "The Inauguration," p. 339, in Chapter 5.)*

Like a coronation, the inaugural ceremony symbolically invests presidents with the power of their office. At the inauguration the president appears before the people not as the manager of one of the three coequal branches of government but as the preeminent leader of the nation who swears to "preserve, protect, and defend" the Constitution.

The oath of office conjures up heroic images of the nation's heritage. The new president's recitation of the same oath that George Washington, Thomas Jefferson, Abraham Lincoln, Woodrow Wilson, Franklin D. Roosevelt, and every other president has repeated conveys a sense of historic continuity and links the incumbent to the glories of past presidencies.

George Washington established the tradition that presidents should deliver an inaugural address after taking the oath of office. Inaugurals help unify the public around a specific vision of citizenship, and they place the president at the center of the nation. Because of this, it is important that presidents also explicitly recognize the limits of their power by acknowledging the supremacy of the Constitution. In his second inaugural address, for instance, George W. Bush said, "On this day, prescribed by law and marked by ceremony, we celebrate the durable wisdom of our Constitution, and recall the deep commitments that unite our country. I am grateful for the honor of this hour, mindful of the consequential times in which we live, and determined to fulfill the oath that I have sworn and you have witnessed."

Just as the inaugural address is the first opportunity for a new president to assume the role of chief of state, the inauguration and the parades and parties that have usually followed it also provide the first glimpse of the new chief of state's ceremonial style. Some presidents (Washington, John Adams, John F. Kennedy) have preferred formal events while others (Jefferson, Carter) have favored more informality.

CONSTITUTIONAL BASIS OF PRESIDENTIAL CHIEF OF STATE ROLE

The Framers of the Constitution did not specifically designate the president as the nation's chief of state, but they created no other office that reasonably could claim the chief of state power. Presidents are the logical possessors of the title of chief of state under the Constitution because they are chosen by a national electorate, are never out of session, and are recognized as the voice of U.S. foreign policy. Consequently, the president can be said to represent the entire nation, is always available to provide ceremonial leadership, and is positioned to perform both international and domestic ceremonial functions.

The Framers never considered establishing a chief of state office separate from the presidency. The creation of a single office that would be filled by one person serving as both the ceremonial and executive leader of the nation, however, was not their only option. The continuing transfer of executive power from the monarch to the prime minister in Great Britain provided the Framers with a model of a political system in which the ceremonial and executive functions were separated.[1] Given the objections of many members of the convention to any pretense of royalty in the presidency and the unanimous concern that no president would have the means to become a despot, it is somewhat surprising that the Framers accepted the fusion of the two roles without debate.

One can imagine the convention designating a member of Congress such as the Speaker of the House or president pro tempore of the Senate as chief of state, especially because most of the delegates considered the legislature to be the most important branch of government. Such an arrangement would have augmented Congress's power by making it the ceremonial focus of the government, while diminishing the symbolic resources available to any president who sought dictatorial power.

The Framers also could have created an executive council composed of several persons instead of a unitary presidency. They seriously considered this option, but the focus of their debate was on the safety of lodging enormous executive powers in the hands of one person, not on dividing presidential functions between executive officials. The original proposal for a single executive, made by James Wilson of Virginia, was strongly opposed by Benjamin Franklin, Edmund Randolph, George Mason, Roger Sherman, and other prominent members of the convention who feared that having a single executive would lead to despotism or the subordination of the country's interests to the interests of the executive's home region. After several days of debate, however, the Framers decided to reject proposals for a plural executive or an executive advisory committee attached to the presidency in favor of a single executive.[2] Presumably, had the convention opted for an executive committee instead of a single president, the chief of state power would have resided in the entire committee, not in one specified member.

According to political scientist Rexford G. Tugwell, an executive committee would not have captured the imagination of the American people the way individual presidents have:

> Since he [the president] would not have been alone in the White House in semi-royal state, with relatives and associates of consuming interest to all his fellow citizens, it would not have been a matter of such consequence whether or not he had an invalid wife and irresponsible children, . . . or whether he possessed social graces as well as wisdom and political talent. He would not, in other words, have been the focus of interest and the symbol of Union for the whole American people, watched with avid curiosity and criticized inevitably by those with standards of conduct differing from his own.[3]

By creating a single executive, the Framers guaranteed that public attention and therefore symbolic power would flow to the president.

1. Erwin C. Hargrove and Michael Nelson, *Presidents, Politics, and Policy* (Baltimore: Johns Hopkins University Press, 1984), 20.
2. Donald L. Robinson, *To the Best of My Ability* (New York: Norton, 1987), 69–76.
3. Rexford G. Tugwell, *The Enlargement of the Presidency* (Garden City, N.Y.: Doubleday, 1960), 481.

Increasingly, inaugurals are major political events, with balls and receptions in several locations around the nation's capital and in the candidate's home state, many of which are televised. This also means that they are increasingly expensive. Ronald Reagan's 1981 inaugural festivities—the most expensive in history up to that time—included a parade with eight thousand marchers, eight $100-a-ticket balls, and a nationally televised inaugural "gala" that featured many Hollywood celebrities. The cost of the festivities was estimated at $16 million, compared with just $3.5 million spent for the Carter inaugural in 1977.

George Bush, Bill Clinton, and George W. Bush followed Reagan's lead in choosing to host elaborate inaugural celebrations. George Bush's 1989 inaugural cost $30 million and included a parade with 214 marching bands. Clinton's 1993 inaugural cost about $25 million and featured eleven inaugural balls; in 1997, however, he spent about $42 million on the festivities, which included a record twelve balls.[3]

George W. Bush's 2001 inaugural committee raised nearly $40 million to pay for elaborate celebrations that drew tens of thousands of his supporters to Washington, D.C. Although Bush did not spend more the second time around in 2005, he received considerable criticism for entertaining lavishly in wartime.[4]

In sum, the president's choices in planning the inauguration reveal his political principles, his style of governance, and his understanding of the connection between the substance and the ceremony of the new administration.

State of the Union Address

The Constitution also states that the president "shall from time to time give to the Congress information of the State of the Union, and recommend to their Consideration such Measures as he shall judge necessary and expedient." From this clause developed the ritual of the president's annual message, or "State of the Union address," as it has been

Rutherford B. Hayes was the first president to use an eagle as the official presidential seal. In 1903 Theodore Roosevelt added a circular seal around it, bearing the words, and in 1945 Harry Truman changed the eagle's head from one side to the other. The ring of fifty stars represents the fifty states.

of his effort to "put the ship of state back on its republican tack," he submitted his report to Congress in writing.[5] Presidents continued to send, not deliver, the Annual Message, as it was then known, until Woodrow Wilson revived the custom of presenting the message as a speech in 1913.

The Constitution does not mandate the scheduling of the address, but by tradition, it is given in late January or early February. At the president's request, Congress sends an invitation to the White House, which the president accepts, and the speech is then scheduled. It is always given in the House chamber, reflecting its symbolic importance as a message given simultaneously to Congress and to the American people. Besides the vice president (as president of the Senate), most cabinet officials, and members of the Joint Chiefs of Staff, the audience in the chamber includes justices of the U.S. Supreme Court. An international audience now listens in as well. The speech is televised live and receives considerable media attention both before and after it is given. It is considered a major test of the president's political abilities.

Because all three branches of the federal government are represented in the House chamber, the State of the Union Address gives the president an important opportunity to enact his unique role as the sole voice of the nation. In characterizing the state of the union, the president becomes, in effect, the national historian, reflecting on the past as a frame for the actions he desires in the future. As rhetoricians Karlyn Kohrs Campell and Kathleen Hall Jamieson put it, "[T]he annual message has been, from the outset, one symbolic moment in which the head of state has woven the cloth of common national history, character, and identity."[6] Presidents thus perform the role of chief of state throughout the State of the Union Address, reflecting on national values and enacting national democracy. By applauding (or refusing to do so) members of Congress show their approval (or disapproval) of the president's symbolic and political representation of the nation.

known since 1945. *(See "The State of the Union Address," p. 669, in Chapter 12.)*

George Washington delivered the first annual message to Congress on January 8, 1790. John Adams, who enjoyed royal formalities, followed Washington's precedent, but Thomas Jefferson objected to having presidents deliver their annual messages in person. Like many of his Democratic-Republican colleagues, he thought the custom, which had derived from the British monarch's speech from the throne at the opening of Parliament, had royal pretensions. As part

▌NAUGURAL POEMS

Presidents have sometimes attempted to use the celebrity and visibility of their office to promote changes in the lifestyle of the nation. John F. Kennedy intended to use his position to encourage interest in the fine arts and U.S. culture. He and his wife, Jacqueline, set an example for the nation by frequently patronizing the work of artists, musicians, and writers.

Kennedy began his patronage of the fine arts the day he became president. He asked the venerable poet Robert Frost to recite a poem at his inauguration ceremony on January 20, 1961. The eighty-six-year-old Frost planned to read a short introductory verse he had composed for the occasion followed by his poem "The Gift Outright." After Boston's Cardinal Cushing delivered a long invocation, the chair of the Inaugural Committee, Sen. John Sparkman, introduced Frost. The poet began reading his introductory verse, but the bright sunlight magnified by the glare from the snow that had fallen the day before blinded him. Frost read only three lines before stopping.

He said, "I'm not having a good light here at all. I can't see in this light." He tried to continue with the help of Vice President–elect Lyndon B. Johnson, who shaded the poet's manuscript with a top hat, but Frost still could not see. He gave up on the introductory verse, saying, "This was to have been a preface to a poem which I do not have to read." He then recited "The Gift Outright" from memory in a clear voice, changing the last phrase at Kennedy's request from "such as she *would* become" to "such as she *will* become."

In 1993, Bill Clinton, who cherished his connections to John Kennedy, also included a poem as part of his inaugural. Poet Maya Angelou's "On The Pulse of Morning" testified to the changes the nation had encountered since 1960. At Clinton's second inaugural in 1997 fellow Arkansas native Miller Williams recited his poem "Of History and Hope."

Reception of Ambassadors

The Constitution gives the president the duty to "receive Ambassadors and other public Ministers." The authors of the Constitution regarded the reception of foreign visitors as a purely ceremonial responsibility. It was to be given to the president, according to Alexander Hamilton, because Congress could not conveniently perform this function. He wrote in the *Federalist* No. 69 that presidential reception of ambassadors "is more a matter of dignity than of authority. It is a circumstance which will be without consequence in the administration of the government; and it was far more convenient that it should be arranged in this manner than that there should be a necessity of convening the legislature, or one of its branches, upon every arrival of a foreign minister." [7] Subsequently, however, the presidential responsibility to receive ambassadors was used by chief executives as a constitutional justification of their authority to recognize or deny recognition to foreign governments. *(See "The Recognition Power," p. 719, in Chapter 13.)*

In the spirit of this constitutional provision, presidents have customarily received the official ambassador of every recognized foreign government. The growth of the Washington diplomatic corps during the twentieth century and the overcrowded presidential schedule have forced presidents to receive most ambassadors, especially those from smaller countries, in groups at the White House to save time.

Customary Ceremonial Functions

Presidents and their representatives also perform numerous chief of state functions that do not have their origins in the Constitution and are not based on a specific legal sanction. Some of these activities have been established as annual events by a succession of presidents. Others are performed by individual presidents for their public relations value. Presidents can choose to de-emphasize their chief of state role by delegating ceremonial functions to the vice president and others, but they cannot escape many events and practices that the American people have come to regard as part of the president's job. A president who claims to be too busy to light the national Christmas tree or to congratulate the World Series champions would waste valuable opportunities to score political points and would risk being perceived as indifferent to American life. Like the three ceremonial functions based on the Constitution, these informal chief of state activities emphasize the president's role as the leader of the nation, but many of them also serve to humanize the president and symbolically bridge the gap between the president and the people.

National Endorser

A presidential proclamation or dedication is a national stamp of approval for cultural events, national monuments, public works projects, charity drives, and special weeks and days. Such proclamations promote national concern and awareness of worthy organizations and causes by indicating that the president thinks the object of the proclamation is important enough to recognize. Often presidents highlight their recognition of a charity, organization, or movement by inviting its leaders to the White House. Such an invitation is a further measure of the group's importance, because time is made in the president's schedule to accommodate the visit.

Presidential recognition of an event, cause, group, or monument can inspire patriotic sentiments. A new hydroelectric dam is said to be not just a source of power for a particular region, but an engineering feat and a symbol of American industrial might and technological ingenuity. The work of a charitable organization such as the American Red Cross is praised as an example of the nation's caring spirit.

Presidential endorsements are constantly in demand by organizations and charities, and the president's staff must choose which will receive presidential time. Many of the causes presidents endorse from year to year are determined by precedent. The United Way, Easter Seals, American Cancer Society, and many others receive annual presidential endorsements. Yet the type of causes that receive presidential recognition also may reflect the incumbent's political interests or philosophy. However, presidents now do so much of this that the effect can be somewhat diminished. Bill Clinton signed some one hundred special proclamations in 1996 alone, including proclamations delineating Education and Sharing Day (March 29), National Pay Inequity Awareness Day (April 11), and National Farm Safety and Health Week (September 13). George W. Bush also signs about one hundred proclamations a year. In 2005, for example, he commemorated National Mentoring Month (January 12), Save Your Vision Week (March 4), and Leif Erickson Day (October 7).[8] Presidents who wish to recognize worthy causes run the risk of trivializing that recognition by overusing proclamations.

Moreover, this aspect of the chief of state role can cause problems for a president. When George Bush publicly announced his dislike of broccoli, for example, farmers whose livelihoods depended on it were vociferous in their protests. Just as signs of presidential favor can bring much-needed attention to worthy causes, presidents have to be careful. Too much exposure can cheapen presidential endorsements, enmity can be earned by denying endorsements, and the wrong endorsement can create negative attention.

Conveyor of Awards and Congratulations

In accordance with their role as national spokesperson, presidents are expected to be the conveyors of national awards and congratulations. Presidents routinely invite citizens to the White House, where they are congratulated on their accomplishments and presented with an award or

PRESIDENTIAL MEDAL OF FREEDOM

Created by President John F. Kennedy in 1963 as a civilian honor, the Presidential Medal of Freedom remains the nation's highest award for civilian achievement. Only the president can award the lustrous red, white, and blue enameled medal, which recognizes significant contributions to American life, the country's national security, or even to world peace. Only about four hundred people have received the medal to date. The winners have come from nearly every imaginable background—scientists, writers, government officials, artists, movie stars, and even sports legends. Among past winners are astronaut Neil Armstrong, comedienne Lucille Ball, Civil War historian Bruce Catton, labor leader Cesar Chavez, former first lady Betty Ford, longtime senator J. William Fulbright, industrialist Edgar Kaiser, and baseball great Jackie Robinson.[1]

Early in 1963 President Kennedy issued the executive order renaming the Medal of Freedom and establishing new, broad-based criteria for awarding the Presidential Medal of Freedom to individuals "who had made especially meritorious contributions to (1) the security or national interests of the United States, or (2) world peace, or (3) cultural or other significant public or private endeavors."

President Lyndon B. Johnson and every president who followed him have awarded additional medals during their terms of office. Presidents have sole discretion to decide who gets the award, or even whether it will be given at all residents have tended to select medal winners who have had long and distinguished careers. However, a few highly publicized specific accomplishments have garnered awards. President Richard Nixon, for example, gave medals to the astronauts of the history-making *Apollo 11* moon mission in 1969 as well as to the astronauts and Mission Operations Team of the near-tragic *Apollo 13* mission in 1970).

Government service is a persistent theme among the recipients. President Johnson made a point of rewarding key figures in his administration with the president's medal, and other presidents followed suit. For example, President Gerald R. Ford named his secretary of state, Henry Kissinger, and President Jimmy Carter his national security assistant, Zbigniew Brzezinski. Five former presidents—John Kennedy (from Johnson), Lyndon Johnson (from Carter), Ronald Reagan (from George Bush), Gerald R. Ford (from Bill Clinton), and Jimmy Carter (also from Clinton)—and two former vice presidents—Hubert H. Humphrey (from Carter) and Nelson A. Rockefeller (from Ford)—have been given the award. In all, about a third of the president's medals have gone to government officials.

Although Presidential Medal of Freedom winners are usually Americans, presidents also have selected a few foreign recipients over the years. Bill Clinton honored Simon Wiesenthal.

1. Bruce Wetterau, *The Presidential Medal of Freedom: Winners and Their Achievements* (Washington, D.C.: Congressional Quarterly, 1996) is available online at http://medaloffreedom.com/Recipiene (accessed August).

---

memento of their visit. Presidents also bestow a variety of official awards, the most prominent of which is the Presidential Medal of Freedom, the highest civilian honor bestowed by the government. *(See box, Presidential Medal of Freedom, above.)*

Presidents have used this role as a tool of moral and patriotic leadership. In congratulating popular American heroes, presidents make a moral statement by holding up those individuals to the nation as examples to emulate. Presidential congratulations encourage citizens to be as dedicated as a spelling bee champion, as brave as a war hero, as creative as a great artist, or as resilient as a person celebrating a hundredth birthday. For example, on June 12, 1995, President Clinton joined the national accolades for air force captain Scott F. O'Grady by inviting him to a well-publicized White House lunch. O'Grady had become a heroic figure by evading capture by Serbian military units after his jet was downed over Bosnia-Herzegovina. He had been rescued on June 8 by a helicopter commando mission ordered by the president

President Reagan developed presidential congratulations into a political art. He made a practice of weaving the introduction of carefully selected heroic Americans into his upbeat State of the Union addresses. His heroes included an infantry medic who rescued wounded soldiers in Grenada, a twelve-year-old prodigy of gospel music, a woman about to

graduate from West Point despite having escaped to the United States from Vietnam only ten years before with no possessions or knowledge of English, and a seventy-nine-year-old Harlem woman who cared for infants born of mothers addicted to heroin.

Every president since Reagan has used this device when addressing Congress. George W. Bush opened his historic speech to Congress on September 20, 2001, with the emotionally powerful introduction of Lisa Beamer, the widow of Todd Beamer, who had participated in the effort by passengers of the hijacked United Flight 93 to retake the plane from terrorists on September 11. Apparently because the passengers resisted the hijackers, the plane crashed to the ground in Pennsylvania before it could strike an intended target in Washington, D.C.

Congratulating a hero brings obvious political benefits to presidents. Members of championship sports teams are now routinely invited to the White House where they joke with the president and present the chief executive with a jersey, game ball, or other memento of their victory. The president can become identified with their sport, demonstrate good humor, and be photographed with America's current sports idols.[9] Presidents gain similar public relations benefits from congratulating artists, scientists, heroic members of the armed forces, and others who have performed feats of skill, intelligence, or courage. . Presidents can bask in the reflected

President Clinton, left, stands with former president Jimmy Carter, right, and former first lady Rosalynn Carter after Clinton awarded the couple the Presidential Medal of Freedom, the nation's highest civilian honor, during a ceremony at the Carter Center in August 1999. Carter is one of five former presidents to receive the award.

glory of those they honor, and they can also hope to earn support for their policies by associating those policies with heroic or otherwise admirable Americans.

First Average American

Alexis de Tocqueville, a French aristocrat and author who traveled widely in the United States during the first half of the nineteenth century, observed that "public officers themselves are well aware that the superiority over their fellow citizens which they derive from their authority they enjoy only on condition of putting themselves on a level with the whole community by their manners." [10] Most presidents have understood that although Americans want their president to be an exceptional person who is intelligent, decisive, and inspiring, they also want a leader with common tastes and experiences. Americans want to believe that their president rose to the top through hard work, moral integrity, and a little ambition.

Despite the bromide that "anyone can grow up to be president," until recently, few chief executives came from humble, much less disadvantaged, backgrounds, and the "log cabin presidency" is more myth than reality. [11] Between Dwight D. Eisenhower (1953–1961) and George W. Bush (2001–), half of the presidents were from comfortable to wealthy homes (Eisenhower, Kennedy, Carter, and the two Bushes), while the other half were from much less affluent families (Johnson, Nixon, Ford, Reagan, and Clinton). That is a much higher percentage of nonwealthy presidents than during any other comparable period of time.

The public values common sense as much as an Ivy League education. The ability to understand the needs and desires of the average American is as important as understanding the most complicated foreign policy or economic problems. In short, people want their president to be an exceptional example of an average American.

Presidents have realized that while the regal trappings of the presidency fortify their power and prestige, they also must project a populist image to satisfy the democratic ideals of the American people. Presidents who appear too urbane or who flaunt the privileges of their office risk alienating many citizens who are attracted to politicians with folksy images, and presidents work hard to combine their presidential images with evidence that they share tastes in common with the people. They may eat jelly beans (Reagan) or pork rinds (George Bush) or watch football (Nixon), basketball (Clinton), or NASCAR (George W. Bush). They may make their own breakfast (Ford) or carry their own bags (Carter). They may rope steers (Johnson), chop wood (Reagan), or clear brush (George W. Bush). But all this behavior is geared toward accomplishing the same end: establishing commonality with the American people.

Presidential appearances at cultural events also can reinforce the image of a president as an average person. Presidents attend historical and artistic exhibits, ethnic festivals, and other events where they can display their interest in American life. They have been especially fond of attending sporting contests. Since William Howard Taft threw out the first baseball of the 1910 major league season on April 14 in Washington, most presidents have observed the tradition. Kennedy wanted to make such a good appearance at the yearly event that he secretly practiced his throwing on the

Throwing out the first baseball of the 1910 major league season, President William Howard Taft began a tradition that most succeeding presidents have followed.

White House grounds.[12] George W. Bush traveled to Yankee Stadium in New York City to throw out the first ball in the third game of the 2001 World Series. The appearance was meant to underscore not only Bush's identification with baseball fans, but also his solidarity with New York after the terrorist destruction of the World Trade Center.

Both George Bush and Bill Clinton projected inconsistent portraits of a first average American. Bush possessed a personable and accessible manner, demonstrated in his penchant for writing personal thank-you notes. He talked frequently of his all-American experiences, including his college baseball career, his service during World War II, and raising a family in Texas. He relished such common pastimes as horseshoe pitching and fishing. Yet Bush also was a Yale-educated millionaire and the son of a Connecticut senator. During his long vacations at his summer home in Maine, he made little effort to disguise his wealthy lifestyle, playing multiple rounds of golf and piloting his twenty-eight-foot powerboat in the ocean.

Bill Clinton's biography as a self-made man who rose from a difficult childhood in tiny Hope, Arkansas, provided a solid base on which to build an image as the first average American. Clinton skillfully used his small-town origins to his advantage during the 1992 campaign. But after becoming president his early failure to project a common image contributed to his sharp drop in popularity. The initial impression some Americans developed of their new president was of a cerebral, but unfocused, Ivy League "policy wonk" with Hollywood pretensions. One damaging incident occurred on May 18, 1993, when it was reported that *Air Force One* was delayed at the Los Angeles airport, keeping two runways closed because of standard security procedures, so that the president could get a $200 haircut from a Beverly Hills hairdresser noted for his work on movie stars. While subsequent investigation suggested that the haircut in fact caused no delays, the damage was done from a public relations standpoint.

Political scientist Fred I. Greenstein wrote that during Clinton's first months in office he tended "to confine himself to impersonal and distinctly noninspirational messages on such themes as the need to 'grow the economy.' He and his associates did little to humanize his presidency: Hillary Clinton became the all-business Hillary Rodham Clinton; daughter Chelsea dropped from sight; and the campaign bus was garaged." [13]

Clinton responded to his sliding poll numbers by bringing David Gergen, a Republican media strategist, into his administration. Among other adjustments, Clinton agreed to allow more news coverage of his family life and scheduled an increasing number of media opportunities that allowed him to display his considerable talent at interacting with ordinary Americans. Clinton particularly excelled at events that called for the expression of sympathy

or identification with the downtrodden. He became so adept at personalizing his speeches and projecting concern that many observers dubbed him "the Great Empathizer," a modification of Ronald Reagan's moniker, the "Great Communicator." Clinton's phrase, "I feel your pain," uttered during the 1992 presidential campaign, was often cited derisively by critics as evidence that his talent for empathy was shallow or manipulative. But Clinton recognized that his ability to project compassion was one of his premier political assets.

Despite his privileged upbringing and his Ivy League degrees, George W. Bush proved equally adept at connecting with the American people. Voters in 2004, for instance, declared that they preferred Bush to his Democratic opponent, John Kerry, as a potential guest in their homes.[14] Bush's somewhat erratic grammar and lack of facility with some words may provide late-night comedians with much of their material, but they also convey the image of Bush as a regular guy.

Presidents who can position themselves as "regular" in this sense without sacrificing their ability to appear presidential have found the right balance between the formal demands of the office and the need to affirm democracy by displaying the common touch.

Observer of Holidays

National holidays reduce societal divisions by emphasizing universal patriotic themes and common traditions. Millions of Americans of all races, religions, and regions share the common experience of watching fireworks on the Fourth of July or preparing a banquet on Thanksgiving. On Veterans Day most American citizens will recall someone who served in the military, and on Memorial Day many will remember someone who died in a war. Holidays, therefore, can draw a nation together and enhance citizens' sense of belonging to a single national culture.

As chief of state, presidents lead the nation's observation of annual holidays. They light the national Christmas tree, deliver a patriotic address on the Fourth of July, and lay a wreath at the Tomb of the Unknown Soldier on Memorial Day. Presidents also commemorate milestone holidays of importance to the nation. Gerald Ford addressed many events associated with the U.S. Bicentennial in 1976, and Bill Clinton delivered a nationally televised speech from the Lincoln Memorial to a crowd of millennium revelers just after the clock struck midnight on January 1, 2000.

Presidents traditionally have issued statements celebrating official holidays such as Memorial Day and Thanksgiving and unofficial holidays such as St. Patrick's Day. They cannot, however, proclaim an official federal holiday without an act of Congress. George Washington was the first president to proclaim a national holiday. In response to a congressional recommendation, he declared that a national day of thanksgiving should be observed on Thursday, November 26, 1789.[15] This proclamation contributed to the development of the Thanksgiving holiday now observed in the United States. The most recent holiday established by the government commemorates the birthday of Martin Luther King Jr. After initial opposition, Ronald Reagan signed legislation on November 2, 1983, declaring the third Monday in January beginning in 1986 to be a legal federal holiday honoring the civil rights leader.

Holidays can also prove divisive and alienating, however. The fight to add a holiday in honor of Dr. King was long and difficult. When presidents light the annual Christmas tree, they can also be understood as relegating other religions to second-class status. Some Native Americans object to celebrations of Thanksgiving and Columbus Day.

As with endorsements, presidents have to be aware of the complicated nature of celebrating holidays. When a president selects certain holidays to celebrate, he is also celebrating a specific version of the national identity, one that usually is endorsed by a majority of citizens, but that can also underline the minority status of others.[16]

Mourner and Eulogizer

When a disaster occurs at home or abroad, or when a prominent American dies, the president is expected to lead the nation in mourning. The president routinely issues statements eulogizing Americans who have died. Presidential statements concerning death come in three main forms: brief statements announcing a death or disaster, more extended statements following the death of a specific person or persons, and still lengthier, formal eulogies given at funerals or memorial services.[17] The president's attendance at funerals, however, generally is reserved for former presidents, high government officials, close presidential friends and relatives, or people who died in national tragedies. In all cases, the president, as chief of state, finds a connection between the decedent and the polity, usually holding up the recently deceased as an exemplar of citizenship and, in the case of foreign leaders, of more generalized democratic values.[18]

When presidents do attend funerals in the United States in their role as chief of state, they usually address the mourners. President Nixon delivered the eulogy at Eisenhower's state funeral at the U.S. Capitol on March 30, 1969. President Clinton delivered a eulogy at Nixon's funeral in California on April 27, 1994. Both President Bush and Vice President Richard B. Cheney eulogized Ronald Reagan when he died in June 2004.

Presidents also must respond to the deaths of Americans who died while serving their country. Perhaps the most famous of all presidential speeches, Lincoln's

Gettysburg Address, was delivered during Lincoln's visit to the site of the great battle where thousands of Union and Confederate troops lost their lives. *(See box, The Gettysburg Address, p. 1761, in Reference Materials, Vol. II.)* During a war presidents rarely have time to memorialize individual members of the armed services. In peacetime, however, presidents often honor Americans whose deaths capture the attention of the nation. For example, President Reagan addressed the nation on January 31, 1986, at the memorial service for the seven astronauts killed in the *Challenger* space shuttle disaster, and President Clinton spoke at the April 23, 1995, memorial service for the victims of the Oklahoma City bombing. President George W. Bush proclaimed September 14, 2001, a national day of "prayer and remembrance" for the victims of the World Trade Center and Pentagon terrorist attacks. He eulogized the dead at a nationally televised, multifaith service held at Washington's National Cathedral on that day.

As head of state, presidents receive invitations to the funerals of foreign leaders. Johnson attended Konrad Adenauer's funeral in Cologne in April 1967, and Nixon traveled to Paris to attend Charles de Gaulle's funeral in November 1970. Presidents rarely go to funerals overseas because of the difficulty of postponing other business and arranging security measures on short notice.

If the president does not go to the funeral, a representative is sent in the president's place. The decision of whom to send to a foreign funeral depends on the importance of the country to the United States, the current state of diplo-

Five years after a bomb destroyed the Alfred P. Murrah Federal Building in Oklahoma City, President Bill Clinton helped dedicate the Oklahoma City National Memorial in April 2000. Where the nine-story building once stood, 168 bronze and stone chairs memorialize each victim of the bombing.

President Ronald Reagan and staff grimly watch television reports on the Challenger disaster that killed seven astronauts. Americans often look to the president to lead them in dealing with national tragedy.

matic relations between the two nations, and the deceased leader's political relationship with the United States. The vice president or secretary of state usually represents the president and the nation at the funerals of prominent world leaders. Former presidents who worked closely with a fallen leader also sometimes attend. President Reagan and Vice President Bush did not attend Egyptian president Anwar Sadat's funeral in October 1981 for security reasons, but Reagan asked former presidents Nixon, Ford, and Carter to represent the United States. At the funerals of leaders of countries that have a strained or minimal relationship with the United States, the U.S. ambassador to that country often will represent the president.

American Tourist

George Washington established the precedent that presidents should travel among the American people. He made two regional tours as president: New England in 1789 and the South in 1791. For Washington, the purpose of these tours of the states was "to become better acquainted with their principle Characters and internal Circumstances, as well as to be more accessible to numbers of well-informed persons." [19] Since then, presidents have been expected to leave the capital occasionally to reacquaint themselves with the nation's prob-

lems and listen to the public's needs and complaints. Franklin Roosevelt explained his own need for such travels: "I have always thought it was part of the duty of the Presidency to keep in touch, personal touch, with the Nation. . . . [N]ow I am going to the Coast . . . to have a 'look-see,' to try to tie together in my own mind the problems of the Nation, in order that I may, at first hand, know as much about the questions that affect all the forty-eight states as possible." [20]

Citizens may become apathetic toward politics and government if they perceive that leaders in the capital are playing a game and that they do not care what happens in the rest of the country. By traveling out to the people in the "provinces," presidents can show their interest in the culture of particular regions. They can reawaken public interest in their administration's programs and in government in general. Presidents consequently now engage in multiple town meetings during their administrations, when they visit small towns and meet with carefully selected members of the public, who are allowed to ask questions (sometimes approved in advance). Such events allow presidents to offer the appearance of keeping in touch with all of their constituents.

Presidents who neglect this aspect of the chief of state role may find themselves in trouble with the public. George Bush was perceived as neglecting California following riots in Los Angeles in 1992, especially when Democratic presidential candidate Bill Clinton made a point of going to the city. As president, Clinton was equally quick to respond, visit, or speak out on events such as the murder of Matthew Shepard, a gay man, in 1998 and the shooting at Columbine High School in Littleton, Colorado, in 1999.

Simply speaking out or even visiting may not be enough. George W. Bush was heavily criticized for a general lack of concern immediately following Hurricane Katrina, for instance. Critics complained that it took him far too long to visit the area, although he appeared within days of the disaster and visited twice more within the month. Failure to appear among the people will make matters worse for a president, but appearing is a necessary, not a sufficient, condition for political success as chief of state.

CHIEF OF STATE ROLE AND PRESIDENTIAL POWER

The ceremonial and symbolic aspects of the presidency appear less important than the responsibilities that come with the president's other powers. When presidents veto bills, sign treaties, nominate Supreme Court justices, issue pardons, or order military actions, they obviously have exercised presidential power. As chief of state, however, the president acts neither as a commander nor as an administrator. The effects of ceremonial leadership are less observable and impossible to quantify. Consequently, the chief of state duties are seldom described as a power and are sometimes denounced as a waste of the president's time.

Although the president's authority to dedicate a monument or congratulate an astronaut may mean little, the symbolism of the chief of state role does constitute a real power, because it enhances presidential authority and legitimizes and magnifies other presidential powers. As political scientist Clinton Rossiter explained, "No President can fail to realize that all his powers are invigorated, indeed are given a new dimension of authority, because he is the symbol of our sovereignty, continuity, and grandeur." [21]

The presidency, therefore, is elevated above other offices and institutions not just by its legal authority, but by its symbolic mystique. This mystique has been built up by two centuries of veneration for an office that has been occupied by many of the nation's greatest heroes. Rossiter also said, "The final greatness of the Presidency lies in the truth that it is not just an office of incredible power but a breeding ground of indestructible myth." [22] Astute chief executives wield that mythic power in the service of their more concrete ones.

Symbolic Leadership

The symbolic power of the chief of state role is both immense and important. Presidents can use their ceremonial duties to underline their other powers (George W. Bush announcing "mission accomplished" on the deck of an aircraft carrier during the war on Iraq), to buttress their political position when those other powers may be faltering (Bill Clinton's triumphant State of the Union Address in the midst of his impeachment scandal), and to gain support that they may have lacked previously (through invitations to the White House, signatures on photographs, and speeches given to select audiences or in specific cities).

Presidents also use their symbolic power when they engage in ceremonies for the people. They can provide uplift in times of crisis (Franklin Roosevelt's jaunty cigarette holder became a symbol of hope during the Great Depression), calm in times of trouble (Reagan's address in the wake of the *Challenger* disaster), strength in time of war (Woodrow Wilson's principled stand in the war "to make the world safe

for democracy" and George W. Bush's comments at Ground Zero), and compassion in time of peace (Lyndon Johnson's address following the march in Selma, Alabama). Presidents acting symbolically as chief of state also let citizens know what is important culturally by inviting performers and artists to the White House and by attending events outside of it. They reflect national identity by representing the people at those events.

The chief of state role equips presidents with several symbolic assets through which they can reinforce their executive leadership. Presidents are seen as the symbol of national unity, the symbol of national continuity, and the symbol of the federal government. Although presidents may have varying success at using these assets to further their policies, all presidents possess them by virtue of holding office and exercising presidential powers.

Symbol of National Unity

The Constitution provided for three independent branches of government, but the president, not Congress or the courts, has become the symbol of national unity. The presidency's emergence as a unifying symbol was predictable. George Washington, who was a national symbol even before he became president, saw his presidential role primarily as that of a national unifier who would draw together the citizens of the thirteen states and the followers of various political philosophies into one nation. Although no president since has been able to remain as nonpartisan as Washington, few presidents have been slaves to their parties, and most have worked in some way to reduce national divisions. In addition, presidents are the most identifiable national leaders and the only elected officials (with the exception of vice presidents) who have a national constituency. As such they are seen as the guardian of the interests of the whole nation against the narrow demands of partisan and sectional groups.

The president's status as a symbol of national unity is an especially valuable political asset because much of what the president does as chief executive and party leader divides the nation. Political scientist Thomas E. Cronin has observed that presidents

> necessarily divide when they act as the leaders of their political parties, when they set priorities that advantage certain goals and groups at the expense of others, when they forge and lead political coalitions, when they move out ahead of public opinion and assume the role of national educators, and when they choose one set of advisers over another. A President, as a creative executive leader, cannot help but offend certain interests. [23]

Being a symbol of national unity allows presidents to heal some of the wounds they open while acting in their other roles and to maintain the public's confidence in them as leader of the entire nation. Eisenhower was particularly adept at projecting an image of an amiable unifier while hiding his political side, thereby maximizing the unifying potential of his chief of state role.[24] George W. Bush claimed that he was "a uniter, not a divider," but he had considerably less success than Eisenhower in fostering that image. Bush has presided over one of the most politically polarized peri-

GEORGE WASHINGTON AS THE FIRST CHIEF OF STATE

When George Washington became president, it was inevitable that the chief of state role would become a prominent aspect of the presidency. His status as a military hero and the leader most identified with the American Revolution both in the United States and abroad made him a national symbol even before he became president. Because he had embodied the higher purposes of the revolution, his acceptance of the presidency brought legitimacy to the Constitution. Presidents since Washington have derived respect and authority from their presidential office and powers. With Washington, however, the flow of benefits was reversed. It was he who brought legitimacy and prominence to an office that had no tradition or established operating procedures and would have been distrusted by the people had he not held it.[1]

Washington believed his primary task as president was to unify the country and establish strong political institutions. In no other presidency were ceremony and symbolism more important to the fulfillment of the president's goals. John Adams saw George Washington as a master of dramatic, symbolic leadership. Many years after Washington's death he commented: "We may say of him, if he was not the greatest President he was the best Actor of the Presidency we have ever had. His address to The States when he left the Army: His solemn Leave taken of Congress when he resigned his Commission: his Farewell Address to the People when he resigned his Presidency. These were all in a strain of Shakespearean and Garrickal excellence in Dramatic Exhibitions."[2]

Washington understood that everything he did as president would set a precedent for future presidents and that even small matters of ceremony could affect the reputation and success of the new government and his office. He wrote:

> Many things which appear of little importance in themselves and at the beginning, may have great and durable consequences from their having been established at the commencement of a new and general government. It will be much easier to commence the administration, upon a well adjusted system, built on tenable grounds, than to correct errors or alter inconveniences after they shall have been confirmed by habit.[3]

Washington, therefore, carefully performed ceremonial functions so as to strike a balance between the dignity and accessibility of the presidency. He traveled to his New York inauguration in a carriage, acknowledging the cheers of crowds, but gave a highly formal speech at his inauguration and did not participate in the public revelry surrounding the occasion. Early in his presidency he established a system of formal receptions known as "levees," which allowed him to frequently receive members of government and the public but also to maintain a solemnity that preserved his aura of authority. He also accepted the formal title of "President of the United States" granted by Congress but did not endorse or participate in Vice President John Adams's campaign to have Congress establish the ostentatious presidential title "His Highness the President of the United States and Protector of the Rights of the Same."[4]

Washington's attention to the details of his chief of state role had significance beyond establishing the proprieties of his office. Washington was also determined to strengthen the common identity of Americans and the primacy of the federal government over the states. The weakness of the federal government and its dependence on the states under the Articles of Confederation had greatly disturbed Washington and had been the motivation behind the establishment of the new government.

Convincing the nation of the primacy of the federal government and inspiring in the American people a sense of common identity were difficult tasks. The Constitution clearly gave the federal government legal preeminence over the states. Nevertheless, most Americans felt a greater allegiance to their state than to the Union, and state officials naturally tended to resist federal authority as an intrusion into their jurisdictions. The fledgling government lacked the tools to implement government policy. In particular, the federal government had no army or navy and only a few federal marshals who could gather information and enforce federal laws. Consequently, Washington had to rely on state governors to provide militia and law enforcement officers to deal with violations of federal statutes.

Washington used his chief of state role to counter impressions that the federal government lacked authority and did not deserve the primary loyalties of the people. He traveled to every state to underscore national unity, taking trips to the northern states in 1789 and to the southern states in 1791. He also insisted that foreign governments deal with him, the representative of all the people, instead of with Congress, which was chosen by local constituencies. When Congress voted for a day of thanksgiving in November 1789, Washington issued the proclamation instead of having Congress ask the states to issue it, as had been done with similar declarations under the Articles of Confederation.[5]

Even when seemingly trivial matters of protocol were concerned, Washington was careful to assert the primacy of the presidency and the federal government. During his tour of New England in 1789 he asked to dine with John Hancock, the governor of Massachusetts, but indicated that Hancock should call on him first. When Hancock claimed to be too ill to visit the president, Washington canceled dinner and wrote a stiff note to the governor: "The president of the United States presents his best respects to the Governor, and has the honor to inform him that he shall be at home 'till 2 o'clock. The President of the United States need not express the pleasure it will give him to see the Governor; but at the same time, he most earnestly begs that the Governor will not hazard his health on the occasion."[6] Washington scored an important symbolic victory for the presidency and the Constitution when Hancock relented after a two-day standoff. The governor, who continued to profess an illness, was carried to the president's lodgings by several servants.[7]

1. Glenn Phelps, "George Washington and the Founding of the Presidency," *Presidential Studies Quarterly* 17 (spring 1987): 352.

2. Quoted in Clinton Rossiter, *The American Presidency,* 2d ed. (New York: Harcourt, Brace, and World, 1960), 92.

3. Quoted in James Hart, *The American Presidency in Action, 1789* (New York: Macmillan, 1948), 12.

4. Joseph E. Kallenbach, *The American Chief Executive: The Presidency and the Governorship* (New York: Harper and Row, 1966), 274.

5. Phelps, "George Washington and the Founding of the Presidency," 351.

6. Quoted in ibid., 351–352.

7. Hart, *American Presidency in Action, 1789,* 20.

ods in recent American history, and many consider him responsible for that polarization.[25] Even making adept use of his chief of state role has not been enough to heal the divisions in the nation, but it has helped to keep those divisions from becoming even more serious. When Americans do not like the president as an individual, they generally continue to respect the office.

The power of the presidency as a unifying symbol is demonstrated by the public's reaction to an international crisis. Even when Americans disagree with the president's policies, they have tended to rally around the president when the nation's interests are threatened by a foreign power. Public opinion polls have shown that presidential approval ratings usually improve when the nation becomes involved in a war or other international crisis. For example, President Kennedy's public approval rating jumped thirteen percentage points in 1962 after the Cuban missile crisis. In 1975 Ford's public approval rating shot up eleven points after he ordered marines to rescue the crew of the merchant ship *Mayaguez,* which had been seized by Cambodian forces. George Bush's approval rating briefly reached 89 percent after the swift defeat of Iraq by a U.S.-led coalition in the 1991 Persian Gulf War.

But even this record score was topped by George W. Bush, who received the approval of 90 percent of Americans polled ten days after the September 11, 2001, terrorist attacks against the World Trade Center and the Pentagon. That rating represented an amazing jump of thirty-nine percentage points over the rating he held the week before the attack. As the nation continued to fight a war against terrorism in Afghanistan amid the possibility of additional terrorist attacks on the U.S. homeland, Bush's approval rating remained near record levels until plummeting in 2005. The sustained support for President Bush reflected the gravity of the threat to the United States and the public's desire for a unified and vigorous response to the attacks.

Although presidential approval ratings will improve the most when the public perceives that the president has acted skillfully or boldly to meet an international crisis, even clear foreign policy failures can add to a president's popularity. In May 1960, the Soviets shot down an American U-2 spy plane over Soviet territory. President Eisenhower denied the United States was conducting intelligence flights over the Soviet Union, but when Moscow produced the captured pilot, Eisenhower took responsibility for the missions. Eisenhower's approval rating jumped six percentage points after the incident, despite heightened East-West tensions and the collapse of a summit meeting in Paris later in the month. Similarly, after the U.S.-sponsored Bay of Pigs invasion of Cuba by exiled Cuban nationals in 1961, President Kennedy's approval rating improved eleven points, to 83 percent, even though the invasion was considered a disaster.[26]

The public rallied around Eisenhower and Kennedy in these situations not because they achieved anything, but because they were the symbols of the United States during a time of international confrontation.

These effects, however, tend to be short-lived. Extended crises and protracted armed conflicts can severely strain a president's relationship with the public. At the height of the Vietnam War, for example, Lyndon Johnson was so besieged by protestors that he drastically reduced his public speaking. The war in Iraq has damaged George W. Bush's standing in the polls. All the major polling organizations listed his public approval numbers as hovering between the high 30 percent approval and low 40 percent approval range for most of the summer of 2006.[27] A president's ability to serve as a symbol of national unity in time of crisis is inversely related to the length of the crisis.

Symbol of Continuity

Presidents also benefit from occupying an office that is identified with the continuity of the United States and the stability of its political institutions. The American people see the president not only as the current national leader but also as the latest in a long line of presidents who have guarded the freedom and laws of the United States. Lincoln, perhaps the most celebrated U.S. president, is remembered primarily for preserving the Union. When political rivals challenge the president, they are in the position of confronting the defender of the Constitution and the heir of Washington, Jefferson, Lincoln, and the Roosevelts.

Presidents work hard to fortify their symbolic power by emphasizing past associations. In particular, they often cite and quote the founders, Lincoln, and both Roosevelts to justify their policy and political preferences. Contemporary Republicans often add Reagan to that list. George W. Bush does less of this than most of his predecessors, preferring scriptural to political references, although he, too, has rmentioned the country's shared political past, noting in his first inaugural, for instance, a letter written by John Page to Thomas Jefferson. Such references are usually liberally sprinkled throughout presidential speeches, as they seek to connect themselves to the nation's history.

Yet special links to the past need not be present for a president to take advantage of the inherent continuity symbolized by the office. When Bill Clinton went to Normandy in June 1994 to commemorate the fiftieth anniversary of the Allies' D-Day invasion, he could not claim to have a personal link to the heroics he would honor. He was the first president born after World War II, and he had avoided service in the military during the Vietnam War. As chief of state, however, he was inherently linked to American history, the survival of the nation, and the succession of generations. His speeches on the occasion emphasized the victory of the

World War II generation and the obligation of his own generation to build on their sacrifice.

The history of the presidency itself demonstrates the stability of the nation's political institutions. Power has always been transferred peacefully from one president to the next. The unbroken chain of presidents has survived assassinations, civil war, impeachment proceedings, election fraud, and a presidential resignation. Even before the presidency faced any of these trials its continuity impressed Martin Van Buren, president from 1837 to 1841, who wrote: "The President under our system, like the king in a monarchy, never dies." [28]

When presidents leave office they continue to symbolize the United States of a past era and the continuity of the nation's democratic institutions. Although there have been exceptions, retiring presidents customarily attend the inaugural ceremonies of their successors, thereby symbolically demonstrating the strength of the Constitution, which provides for the peaceful and orderly transfer of presidential power[29] Former presidents also can contribute to an image of stability during crises. At John Kennedy's funeral, Herbert C. Hoover, Harry S. Truman, and Dwight Eisenhower sat with Lyndon Johnson in a show of nonpartisan support. Together they constituted a powerful symbol of continuity that reassured a nation not yet recovered from the shock of Kennedy's assassination.[30]

Similarly, all the living ex-presidents appeared together at ceremonies honoring Richard Nixon and Ronald Reagan upon their deaths. Political differences, political animosities, and even political failures are subsumed by the importance of honoring the presidency as a symbol of service to the nation.

Symbol of Government

As chief of state the president symbolizes not only the nation but also its government. Because the presidency is occupied by a single familiar individual who has broad executive powers, including the prerogative to initiate policy, it is the most dynamic and understandable element of the federal government.

For many Americans, presidential actions become synonymous with governmental action. For example, a president unveiling a tax reform proposal to a national television audience is more easily understood than the bargaining and consultations within the executive branch that produced the proposal or the complex political and procedural battles that will be fought over the tax reform issue in Congress. The proposal is seen as emanating not from the Treasury Department or the executive branch, but from the president. Historians and journalists frequently organize American history according to presidential administrations. Policy programs, military conflicts, and economic conditions all become identified with the president who was serving at the

time they came into existence, even if that president was not primarily responsible for them. The presidency, therefore, is used by many Americans as a "cognitive handle" that personalizes and simplifies the detailed processes of governing the nation.[31]

George W. Bush recognized the link between the image he projected after the September 11, 2001, terrorist attacks and public confidence in the U.S. government. The attacks occurred while Bush was making an appearance at a grade school in Florida. Initially, he was transported by *Air Force One* to secure military bases in Louisiana and then Nebraska. Later in the day, he returned to Washington to demonstrate that the government was operating and that he was in charge. That night he delivered a televised address to the American people from the Oval Office in which he declared: "Our country is strong. A great people has been moved to defend a great nation. Terrorist attacks can shake the foundations of our biggest buildings, but they cannot touch the foundation of America. These acts shatter steel, but they cannot dent the steel of American resolve."

Over the next several weeks, Bush made numerous high-profile public appearances to bolster public morale, even though these appearances required extraordinary security arrangements. Like Franklin Roosevelt after Pearl Harbor, Bush recognized that public optimism was essential to fostering the recovery of a shaken nation and affirming its confidence that the government was doing everything possible to prevent further attacks.

Being the most visible symbol of government can work against presidents as well as for them. Public expectations of the president are often unreasonable. Because it is easier to blame an individual for society's problems than to understand all the complicated factors contributing to them, presidents receive much unjust criticism. Public dissatisfaction with federal government policies or local conditions over which the president has little control may be translated into disapproval of the president.

The precipitous drop in George Bush's approval ratings during the year and a half that preceded the 1992 election stemmed in part from his abdication of the symbolic power he had accrued as the victor of the Persian Gulf War. Bush failed to seize on the opportunity provided by his 89 percent approval rating to put forward a bold domestic program or explain his economic policies, especially his assent to a tax increase in 1990.[32] He was able to unite the country against a foreign enemy, but he failed to offer a vision of how to respond to domestic troubles. As a result, Bush became identified with a stagnant economy and a government in gridlock.

For better or for worse, presidents symbolize the government as a whole. Their status can rise and fall with public perceptions of the performance of that government. Similarly, presidents can, through judicious use of the role of chief of state, influence those perceptions. This is true both at home and abroad.

Tool of Foreign Policy

As chief of state, the president is the ceremonial representative of the United States to the international community. Presidents make ceremonial visits to foreign countries and greet foreign dignitaries who visit the United States. Whether presidents are receiving visitors in the White House or touring the world, they are expected to fulfill both their diplomatic and ceremonial responsibilities. When U.S. presidents visit Great Britain, for example, they usually have a ceremonial meeting with the reigning monarch and a policy meeting with the prime minister.

The international chief of state role, however, cannot be neatly separated from the president's activities as the architect of U.S. foreign relations. State visits and other international ceremonies and spectacles that the president undertakes as chief of state are tools of foreign policy. They are a means of communicating the intentions and attitudes of the administration and improving the relationships of the United States with foreign governments.

Presidents and their representatives also use international ceremonial appearances and events to lobby for the support of foreign peoples and leaders. The foreign public observes U.S. presidents most often in their chief of state role. When presidents admire landmarks, make speeches, and attend state dinners on their foreign trips, they are trying to increase their popularity overseas and establish a reservoir of good will to benefit U.S. interests. International respect for a president will enhance the image of the United States, the confidence of the U.S. public, and the president's ability to exert leadership in the international arena. In these globalized and increasingly interdependent times, even the world's lone superpower is loath to act entirely alone, and the necessity of international coalition building has led to an increased reliance on international good will. Henry A. Kissinger is credited with creating "shuttle diplomacy" between foreign capitals during his service in the Nixon and Ford administrations, but it is now a fact of life for presidents, their secretaries of state, and other high-ranking administration officials.

Greeting Foreign Leaders

Presidents must entertain many visiting chiefs of state, prime ministers, and other foreign dignitaries every year. These visits often include a photo session and a state dinner attended by selected members of Congress, administration officials, and national celebrities.

The manner in which presidents receive a foreign chief of state sends a signal to that leader and other nations about U.S. policy. President Carter's friendly greeting of Chinese vice premier Deng Xiaoping in January 1979 was a ceremo-

nial act with profound diplomatic implications. Before, during, and after Deng's visit to the United States, the vice premier had pointedly attacked the leaders of the Soviet Union for pursuing an aggressive foreign policy. The Carter administration's warm reception of Deng and its refusal to condemn his belligerent rhetoric signaled tolerance for the vice premier's views and a clear tilt toward the Chinese in the trilateral relationship. When George W. Bush received Russian president Vladimir Putin in November 2001, he wanted to emphasize not only the warmer relations developing between the two countries, but also the warmer personal relationship he was developing with the Russian president. Symbolically, the Bush White House achieved this goal by scheduling, after the formal meetings in Washington, a two-

In May 1860 President James Buchanan greets Japan's first envoys to the United States.

day visit to Bush's ranch in Crawford, Texas, where Bush treated Putin to a Texas barbecue.

Presidents also can make a statement about their foreign policy priorities through their invitations to visit the United States. In 1977, for example, Carter wished to emphasize the importance of U.S. relations with its North American neighbors. Consequently, the first two foreign leaders he invited to the White House were President Josè López Portillo of Mexico and Prime Minister Pierre Trudeau of Canada.

FOREIGN CHIEFS OF STATE

The division of the head of state and head of government roles between two or more individuals in most European governments demonstrates that a nation's chief executive does not also need to be its figurehead, as is the case in the United States. In many nations, including Belgium, Denmark, Great Britain, the Netherlands, Norway, and Sweden, a king or queen serves as chief of state even though the monarchy has lost executive powers. In these countries the monarchs have become integrative figures who embody the history and ideals of their nations.

In other countries such as France, Germany, Israel, and Italy, the chief of state role is assigned to an elected official who serves alongside the head of the government.[1] Many democracies in Latin America have followed the model of the United States, lodging both the chief of state and chief executive powers in a single president.

Significantly, no democratic nation has both a monarch and a president, perhaps because the symbol of a nation cannot be divisible.[2] Yet no chief executive can be entirely insulated from ceremonial duties. Even when a chief of state's office is a cherished part of the national culture grounded in centuries of tradition, such as the British monarchy, the person who wields power will be expected to preside at some symbolic functions. In particular, chief executives must greet important foreign visitors who want to meet with the most powerful person in the country, not just the reigning figurehead.

1. Merlin Gustafson, "Our Part-Time Chief of State," *Presidential Studies Quarterly* 9 (spring 1979): 164.
2. David F. Prindle, "Head of State and Head of Government in Comparative Perspective," *Presidential Studies Quarterly* 21 (winter 1991): 57.

Chief of State in Wartime

Presidents want to maintain good relations with foreign leaders because they can become important sources of support. When presidents go to war, for instance, increasingly they do so as part of a multinational force. Presidents prefer, when possible, to have the support of U.S. allies and of the United Nations when committing troops abroad. Such support is facilitated by firm personal relationships and the kind of mutual trust that can come only from knowing a person individually. Winston Churchill and Franklin Roosevelt, for example, had a warm personal relationship, which eased their negotiations during the Second World War. British prime minister Tony Blair and President George W. Bush share an equally close relationship, which has contributed to their ability to work together during the Iraqi war.

Another important function of the chief of state in wartime is to bolster the morale of the troops themselves. As national symbol, the president can be a powerful reminder of the purpose of an armed conflict, and the presence of the commander in chief can help the troops to remain focused and committed to the tasks at hand. The president can also wield his role as chief of state to help maintain public support for a war. He can present medals, talk with the families of service personnel, bring those who serve to State of the Union addresses as important symbols of the war effort, and

he can use of his ceremonial function to make implicit arguments justifying the need for war.

In general, the American people defer to the president, especially in times of war. Because his ability to function as commander in chief includes the unilateral exercise of power, it is important that the president act in ways that reaffirm his commitment to democratic values. The chief of state role allows him to do this by giving him a forum in which it is appropriate to discuss such values, and his commitment to them. It also allows him to be seen speaking and interacting with the troops, foreign leaders, and the American public in ways that look democratic and can thus counteract any criticism that he is assuming too much power.

Partisan Politics

When a political system separates the chief of state role from that of the chief executive, the chief of state can transcend partisanship. The British monarch takes no official position in the political struggles between British political parties. Such nonpartisanship is impossible for the U.S. president, who must function as the leader of a political party as well as chief of state.

Virtually everything the president does in public as chief of state has political significance. Political scientist David F. Prindle observed that skillful presidents can take advantage of the ambiguity of their office for partisan purposes:

> A dominant president, that is, one that both functions as a symbol and has pre-eminent policy-making authority, is an ambiguous sort of figure. Ordinary citizens are liable to confuse the two roles, seeing the partisan utterances of the politician as the disinterested pronouncements of the symbol. The Head of State role can thus be used by clever presidents to overawe opposition to the programs they advocate as Head of Government.[33]

Partisanship can provide both an opportunity and a challenge for a president. Both Bill Clinton and George W. Bush, for instance, faced a nation that was sharply divided along partisan lines, giving them both implacable enemies and fervent supporters. Clinton seemed to prefer a confrontational strategy in coping with this situation, using the ceremonial stature of his office to his advantage.[34]

Bush has also used the chief of state role to partisan advantage, although he has done so differently than his predecessor. According to political scientist Peri Arnold, by acting as if he not only won the 2000 election outright but also achieved a popular mandate, Bush used the divided nature of Congress and the public to create the perception of a country unified under his administration. He did not dwell on the differences the election magnified, but claimed the fact of his election as a justification of his policy proposals.[35]

The dignity and status conferred on presidents as the nation's ceremonial and symbolic leader increase their popularity with the American public and their bargaining advantages over other government officials. The chief of state role also provides presidents with a justification to preside over events that have obvious public relations appeal. Chief of state activities can be staged to make presidents look patriotic, amiable, concerned, skilled, and noble. Because chief of state activities are built into the president's job description, the role allows presidents to campaign subtly throughout their term without having to appear overly political or self-serving.

Presidential Popularity

One of the most important factors affecting presidents' domestic political power is the public support they receive. When a solid majority of Americans backs the president on a particular issue, other political institutions, including Congress, rarely will launch a challenge. he chief of state role is a political asset primarily because it fortifies the president's popularity. Some Americans will support the office of the presidency even when they disagree with the incumbent's policies. They believe the office symbolizes the nation and the government.

Popular support for the presidency may be sustained even when the occupant of the office is mired in scandal.

JIMMY CARTER'S ATTEMPTS TO "DEPOMP" THE PRESIDENCY

During Jimmy Carter's presidential campaign leading up to his 1976 election, he perceived that the American people were still disturbed by the Watergate scandal and wanted the next president to restore their trust in government. Carter's emphasis on establishing an honest and unpretentious administration helped to propel him to the White House past several better-known Democratic candidates and the Republican incumbent, Gerald R. Ford. As president, Carter was determined to eliminate barriers between the presidency and the people.

Carter began his campaign to "depomp" the presidency on his first day as president. After his inauguration ceremony, he and his wife got out of their limousine and walked up Pennsylvania Avenue to the White House. This gesture symbolized his intention to cut back on the privileges surrounding his office. After Carter's term was over, he wrote about his decision to walk back to the White House:

> I began to realize that the symbolism of our leaving the armored car would be much more far-reaching than simply to promote exercise. I remembered the angry demonstrators who had habitually confronted recent Presidents and Vice Presidents, furious over the Vietnam war and later the revelations of Watergate. I wanted to provide a vivid demonstration of my confidence in the people as far as security was concerned, and I felt a simple walk would be a tangible indication of some reduction in the imperial status of the President and his family.[1]

Thereafter Carter continued his efforts to undo the imperial presidency. He sold the presidential yacht, carried his own garment bag, donated blood, and ordered the White House thermostat to be set at sixty-five degrees in the winter.[2] In addition, he stopped the practice of having "Hail to the Chief" played when he entered the scene of an official event, delivered a Franklin D. Roosevelt-style fireside chat, and was often photographed in informal clothing.

Carter also attempted to dispel the imperial atmosphere surrounding the presidency by emphasizing his accessibility. During the first several months of his presidency, he held frequent press conferences and question-and-answer sessions with federal employees. He also attended town meetings in rural communities, conducted a phone-in talk show in which members of the public could ask him direct questions, and, when traveling within the country, lodged in the homes of American families.[3] Carter even invited John B. Shanklin, a Washington, D.C., hotel worker, to the White House, just as he had promised during a 1974 encounter with Shanklin at the outset of Carter's campaign for the Democratic nomination.

During his first months in office, Carter's openness appealed to the American people, and he enjoyed high public approval ratings. As time passed, however, Carter and his aides suspected that they had gone too far in eliminating pomp from the presidency. As the president's popularity dropped throughout most of his first year and a half in office, it appeared that Carter's populist style had made him seem less presidential than past chief executives and had muted the patriotic message contained in presidential symbols. For some people, Carter's actions also seemed to be weakening the office of the president.[4] Carter recalled: "I overreacted at first. We began to receive many complaints that I had gone too far in cutting back the pomp and ceremony, so after a few months I authorized the band to play 'Hail to the Chief' on special occasions. I found it to be impressive and enjoyed it." [5] As his term progressed, Carter tried to establish a balance between the regal symbols that contributed to an image of himself as a powerful, decisive president and the populist symbols that had helped him to get elected.

Carter had initially misinterpreted what the public wanted after the Watergate scandal. Undoubtedly, the people desired honesty and openness in the White House, but not at the expense of the symbolism that contributed to the presidency's historic and paternal image. The imperial presidency of Richard Nixon did not end in disgrace because he enjoyed the ceremonial display of his office, but rather because he had broken the law, cut himself off from everyone but a handful of advisers, and betrayed the trust of the American people. Carter learned that the symbols of the presidency contribute to presidential power, and no president can reject them without risking an erosion in popular support.

1. Jimmy Carter, *Keeping Faith* (New York: Bantam Books, 1982), 17–18.

2. Larry Berman, *The New American Presidency* (Boston: Little, Brown, 1987), 314.

3. Harold M. Barger, *The Impossible Presidency: Illusions and Realities of Executive Power* (Glenview, Ill.: Scott, Foresman, 1984), 378.

4. Thomas E. Cronin, *The State of the Presidency,* 2d ed. (Boston: Little, Brown, 1980), 159.

5. Carter, *Keeping Faith,* 27.

During congressional impeachment proceedings in late 1998 and early 1999, President Clinton's weekly Gallup poll approval ratings never fell below 62 percent. The poll taken immediately after his impeachment by the House of Representatives on December 19, 1998, showed his approval rating had jumped ten points, to 73 percent. And Clinton's approval ratings remained high despite the public's low regard for his honesty. The Gallup polls taken January 15 through January 17 (during the Senate trial) found that 69 percent of those polled approved of the job Clinton was doing, even though only 24 percent regarded him as "honest and trustworthy" and only 35 percent believed he shared their values. Congress's attempt to remove Clinton for lying about sexual indiscretions caused the public to rally around the president, even if many saw him as deeply flawed. In the public's view, the reversal of an election and the removal of the leader and symbol of the country required more substantial transgressions than Clinton had committed.

Presidents benefit from chief of state activities because such activities make them appear presidential. Formal ceremonies such as the State of the Union address and a state dinner for a foreign head of state feature the president in the role of the nation's leader and guardian and underscore the president's links with the past glories of the office and its revered former occupants. Conversely, chief of state activities also personalize the president. Less formal ceremonies such as a trip to a sporting event or a White House reception for a civic group make the president appear as an average, friendly person who shares the everyday interests and concerns of Americans.

Finally, many Americans will support an incumbent's foreign policies because the president is the representative and symbol of the United States before the world. Few events make a president look more like a world leader than a summit meeting with a prominent head of state or a glittering reception in a foreign country. Presidents attempt to maximize the public relations benefits of their chief of state role by dramatizing their foreign tours and staging them for television. President Nixon timed his historic arrival in Beijing in 1972 to coincide with Sunday night prime-time television viewing hours. The president's return to Washington also was timed to coincide with prime time, even though this required a nine-hour "refueling stop" in Alaska.[36]

Intragovernmental Relations

Although the public often thinks of presidents as leaders who run the country, they are far from omnipotent. Congress can block most presidential initiatives, and the courts can declare a presidential action unconstitutional. Cabinet officers and other members of the executive branch can check presidential power by withholding information, slowing down implementation of presidential directives, leaking details of controversial policies to the media, publicly announcing their opposition to a policy, or resigning to protest a presidential decision. Consequently, presidential power depends on the authority of presidents to issue orders and make proposals as well as on their ability to persuade others that those orders and proposals are correct.

The president's status as chief of state strengthens the president's ability to influence other members of the government. Political scientist Richard E. Neustadt observed:

> Presidential "powers" may be inconclusive when a President commands, but always remain relevant as he persuades. The status and authority inherent in his office reinforce his logic and his charm. . . . [F]ew men—and exceedingly few Cabinet officers—are immune to the impulse to say "yes" to the President of the United States. It grows harder to say "no" when they are seated in his oval office at the White House, or in his office on the second floor, where almost tangibly he partakes of the aura of his physical surroundings.[37]

Such presidential lobbying is hard to resist, especially for members of the president's own party who risk political isolation if they do not have a good record of supporting the chief executive. Presidents, therefore, can exploit the symbolic power of their office to pressure an official or member of Congress for support.

Presidents also can use the glamour and social prestige of the White House to influence members of Congress and other public leaders by granting or denying them access to White House meetings and social functions. Officials want to be close to the president not just because they benefit from having access to the chief executive's authority, but also because they wish to bask in the glow of presidential celebrity. An invitation to a White House dinner or reception can be one of the most sought after tickets in Washington. It allows the lucky invitee to rub elbows with the most powerful and famous people in the country, and it is a confirmation of that person's importance to the president. Although presidents and their staffs will invite members of the other party to White House events in the name of bipartisanship, political allies of the president receive more invitations than political enemies. Politicians who engage the president in a particularly bitter political battle or become enmeshed in a scandal may be cut off from the president's presence entirely.[38]

Furthermore, when presidents are faced with a stubborn Congress, their status as chief of state bolsters their ability to appeal to the people over the head of the legislative branch. In a strategy known as "going public," presidents have presented their case to the people on an issue and hope that favorable popular opinion and active public pressure on individual legislators will force Congress to back presidential policy.[39] Franklin Roosevelt had great success with this tactic. His popularity with the American people weakened resistance in Congress to his New Deal programs. Reagan also used this strategy successfully. During his first year in office, he asked the public to pressure Congress to support his efforts to change dramatically the federal government's taxing and spending policies. Despite a solid Democratic majority in the House of Representatives, he was able to pass a large tax cut and bolster spending on defense.

Other presidents have been less successful at using public opinion. In September 1919, President Wilson undertook a cross-country crusade to promote U.S. entry into the League of Nations. After making dozens of speeches in twenty-nine cities across the Midwest and West, he became ill and returned to Washington, D.C., where he suffered a stroke on October 2. Despite Wilson's efforts, the public remained skeptical of an activist foreign policy, and the Republican-controlled Senate refused to ratify the Treaty of Versailles, which established the league.

President Clinton hoped that public pressure would push a skeptical Congress to adopt his comprehensive health care reform bill in 1994. On August 3, he held a news conference to implore action by Congress on the legislation. He also spoke to pro–health care reform rallies and endorsed a bus caravan touring the nation to drum up support. But opponents of the Clinton plan countered with their own campaign that portrayed Clinton's complex approach as an expensive, overly bureaucratic one that would limit choice of doctors and erode the quality of care. Despite the president's efforts, public support for his plan sank during August and September. The bill died without coming to a final vote in either house of Congress.

Some evidence exists that speeches help the president persuade members of the executive branch and the bureaucracy in general. These speeches serve as signals to those who do not normally interact with the president about what he is thinking and how he understands the priorities of the administration. Thus, the primary audience may not be the mass public at all, but other members of the Washington community of policy makers.[40]

However, some scholars, most notably George C. Edwards III, argue that presidential speech making is largely ineffective as a tool of pressuring Congress and thus is a waste of valuable presidential time. He notes that the public pays little attention to presidential speeches and is generally uninterested in policy. Edwards suggests that presidents are better off "staying private" than "going public," if they want to influence members of Congress.[41]

Presidents continue to try to persuade the public of the merits of their policies even though their success in doing so is decidedly mixed. Even if they are unable to garner public support for specific policies, such speech making is an important part of the institution. If nothing else, it allows the president to play his role as chief of state and connect to the mass public.

Extragovernmental Power

The president is indisputably the nation's first celebrity. One 1969–1970 survey found that 98 percent of adult Americans knew who was president, a much higher percentage of recognition than for any other public figure except the vice president, who was known by 87 percent. In contrast, only 57 percent knew the name of one senator from their state, and only 39 percent could identify their representative in the House. A 1995 national survey found even less recognition of public figures other than the president: only 60 percent could identify the vice president, 46 percent could name one senator from their state, and 33 percent could name their representative.[42] Majorities among Americans polled in 2003 could not name any of the cabinet departments of the executive branch or any of the justices of the Supreme Court.[43] In this political environment, the president has a clear advantage over other members of the federal government.

The president, the first lady, and former occupants of the White House frequently head the list in "most admired person" polls. In 2005, for instance, the three most admired men in America, according to a Gallup poll, were George Bush, Bill Clinton, and Jimmy Carter. Hillary Rodham Clinton was the most admired woman, followed by Oprah Winfrey, Condoleeza Rice, and Laura Bush.[44] Most national radio and television news broadcasts will discuss the president's major activity of the day, and few adult Americans would not be able to recite some basic details about the president's personal and political background. More than nine million people tried to telephone the White House during President Carter's call-in radio press conference in 1977. In just the first five months of the Clinton administration, the first family received 3.5 million pieces of mail. By 2006 the White House had so much difficulty handling e-mail that people were sent responses explicitly stating that the administration could not hope to answer even a small fraction of the messages received. Constant attention contributes to the president's political power and gives presidents and their families influence over national culture and attitudes.

But it can also constrain the president, whose every move—and every mistake—is magnified, and presidents are often held responsible for the problems of their family members. Richard Nixon, Jimmy Carter, and Bill Clinton had difficulties because of their brothers' various antics. More recently, George W. Bush had to contend with headlines caused by his daughters' underage drinking and by the arrest of one of his nieces on drug-related charges. No presidential relative has caused serious political difficulties for a chief executive, but most presidents have had to worry that they might.

The Electronic Chief of State

With the advent of the Internet, electronic communication has become increasingly important to politics in general and to the president's ability to communicate with the American public through his role as chief of state.

On the main presidential web page, at www.white-house.gov, visitors can take a virtual tour of the White House and find transcripts of the president's major speeches, press conferences, proclamations, and news releases. The president's positions on most issues are available through this searchable site as well. Moreover, the George W. Bush administration sponsors "Ask the White House," which is an "online interactive forum" allowing visitors to participate in real-time conversations with administration officials. Transcripts of previous discussions are also available. Visitors to the site can also ask a question of a particular official. There is even a link to barney.gov, featuring the Bush family's pet Scottish terrier. The Bush administration thus uses its official government-sponsored web page to communicate with citizens, to interact with them, to provide them with information, and to offer a humanized portrait of the president and his family.

Such communication can be important in a world that is characterized by fragmentation and diversity. It is difficult for a president, or for anyone else, to break through the noise of the contemporary world. Stiff competition for people's attention makes it is hard for a president to be sure of being heard when he speaks. Having an electronic presence online allows a president to reach people he may not be able to get to in any other way.

The Internet is increasingly important as a source for voters to learn about politics.[45] As a result, candidates use their web sites and blogs to communicate with those voters and potential voters.[46] Candidates increasingly send out e-mail messages to voters, just as they send campaign fliers through the mail.[47]

The Internet can be a powerful tool for candidates, but it can also pose a serious threat. In 2004, for instance, primary candidate Howard Dean shattered previous fund-raising records, garnering more than $25 million through his astute use of the Internet to broadcast his antiwar message to Democrats. Despite his success in garnering a large war chest via the Internet, he would bow out of the race for the Democratic nomination after his "scream" following the Iowa caucuses was widely replayed and discussed, to his detriment, on television and the internet. However, he was able to parlay his achievements into winning the chairmanship of the Democratic National Committee.

The Internet allows presidents to broadcast their view of things of issues and events and to reveal certain aspects of their personalities, but it does so in a way that minimizes the authority of the presidency. On the Internet, a government web page is perhaps more authoritative than a blog, but there is no guarantee that Internet users will find the government site when doing a web search or that they will access it. The days when the president could monopolize conversations by monopolizing air space or time are gone. The Internet allows for more voices to enter any conversation and for voices that do not belong to the administration to be heard.

Presidents are also increasingly sophisticated about using more traditional means of electronic communication, such as radio and television. President Reagan began the practice of reaching his conservative Republican base by broadcasting a weekly Saturday radio address, something that all his successors have continued. By taking the time to offer a brief speech that is geared toward their supporters, presidents can keep them happy, reassure them that the administration is keeping them in mind, and explain their policy preferences in a forum where they have the listeners' attention.

As chief of state, presidents can also use cable and even network television to their advantage. George W. Bush's staff carefully selects and screens audiences for his town hall meetings. He consequently gets asked questions such as "How can I help you accomplish your goals?" Such screening and selection is ridiculed by the president's opponents, but it makes for better television for the president than the protests that accompanied Lyndon Johnson's public speeches and allows the chief executive to appear more presidential.

Through well-managed use of the electronic media—television, radio, and the Internet—presidents can connect with the American people in ways that are otherwise difficult. They can foster images of themselves as competent leaders, and they can raise money and bolster support for their policies and for themselves. Presidents sometimes encounter difficulties because they cannot control what is said over the Internet or by late-night television hosts, but the electronic chief of state is likely to be among the most important aspects of the role in the twenty-first century.

Spiritual Leadership

Although one of the most cherished and accepted principles embodied in American law and tradition is the separation between church and state, many Americans look upon presidents as moral and spiritual leaders. Presidents attend church services and national prayer breakfasts, address religious groups, discuss issues with religious leaders, and frequently invoke God in their speeches. Religious influence flows to presidents, because they are the nation's foremost celebrities and the symbols of traditional American values. The moral and religious example they set affects the religious climate of the nation during their term.

The president's role as an unofficial spiritual leader was first exercised by George Washington, who said in his first inaugural address that

> it would be improper to omit in this first official act, my fervent supplications to that Almighty Being who rules over the Universe. . . . No people can be bound to acknowl-

edge and adore the invisible hand, which conducts the Affairs of men, more than the People of the United States. Every step, by which they have advanced to the character of an independent nation, seems to have been distinguished by some token of providential agency.

Since then, all presidents have mentioned God in their inaugural addresses.[48] Washington also added the words "so help me God" after the oath of office. Every president has followed Washington's example, thereby making an acknowledgment of God part of the president's first official act

During the modern era, the tendency of presidents to make religious and moral references has been more prevalent. Political scientist Barbara Hinckley found that religious and moral references in inaugural addresses occurred with greater frequency during the post–World War II period than before. The inaugural addresses of Presidents Truman through Reagan contained fourteen times as many religious and moral references as partisan political references. Even in the economic addresses of these presidents, moral and religious references were twice as common as partisan political references.[49] This phenomenon was encouraged by the cold war, when American presidents frequently and explicitly pitted the "god-fearing United States" against the "godless communists." For example, at Eisenhower's urging the phrase "Under God" was added to the Pledge of Allegiance in 1954 and in 1956, Congress passed legislation (PL 84–140) declaring "In God We Trust" the national motto.

Although Americans expect their president to profess a belief in God and occasionally participate in religious ceremonies and rituals, they are ambivalent about the president's religious role. The majority of Americans want their president to be a religious person, affirm religious values, and set a moral example, but they do not want the president to govern the country according to a private conception of God's will or use the presidency to promote a specific religious faith. Carter, who considered himself a "born again" Christian, understood this ambivalence. He openly professed a deep faith in God but denied that he considered himself to be a religious leader.[50]

In general, instead of promoting a particular faith, presidents have generally promoted the concept of religion and the basic values common to most religions. Above all, presidents are expected to take an ecumenical approach to religion that does not offend any faith with significant numbers of adherents. As the first Roman Catholic to become president, Kennedy made a point of scheduling meetings with Protestant and Jewish groups during the first months of his presidency. Eisenhower often professed his faith in God and spoke of the importance of religion in American society, but he was careful not to define God narrowly. In a 1959 speech to the National Council of Churches, he stated that the spiritual unity of the West included not only Judeo-Christian traditions but also "the Mohammedans, the

Buddhists and the rest; because they[,] too, strongly believe that they achieve a right to human dignity because of their relationship to the Supreme Being."[51]

The 2001 inaugural ceremony of George W. Bush appeared to cross the traditional ecumenical boundaries of presidential religious symbolism when two invited clergy prayed during the ceremony in the name of Jesus Christ instead of using broader references to God. One of the clergy, the Rev. Kirbyjon Caldwell, closed his prayer by saying, "We respectfully submit this humble prayer in the name that's above all other names, Jesus, the Christ. Let all who agree say, 'Amen.' " Responding to criticism of the prayer the following week, Caldwell said, "If I had to do it over again, I probably would not say, 'All who agree, say Amen.' Additionally, I probably would not say 'Jesus, the name that's above all other names.' That truly could be interpreted as inflammatory or offensive."[52]

Since becoming president, Bush has been both praised and criticized for his frequent and explicit use of specifically Christian religious language, but it is also true that even before September 11, 2001, and certainly since, he has been careful to include other faiths as well. His Faith-based Initiative, for instance, created by Executive Order in January 2001, encompassed charity work by synagogues and mosques as well as by Christian churches, and he was carefully ecumenical in memorializing the victims of September 11. Bush has consistently argued that the war in Iraq is not a religious war and has opposed discrimination against Arabs and American Muslims, though his critics have argued that the tone of his rhetoric has not always been consistent with these stated positions.

Cultural Leadership

Details about the lives of presidents and their families are sought eagerly by the U.S. media outlets. Just as the British scan their newspapers and magazines for information about the royal family, the American public avidly follows the private lives of the first family, the closest American equivalent to royalty.

Under the national spotlight, presidents and their families are well positioned to influence the lifestyles, habits, and cultural activities of Americans. Presidents will often spark new trends in clothing, foods, hobbies, or athletics even if they do not try to do so. Ronald Reagan's fondness for jelly beans and Clinton's penchant for Big Macs led to increased attention for both products.

First ladies can have an equally dramatic effect on national trends. Uncounted women, fascinated by the glamorous Jacqueline Kennedy, adopted her hairstyle and clothing tastes. Many Americans disapproved of Nancy Reagan's consultations with an astrologer, but popular interest in astrology increased after knowledge of her hobby was made public.

PUBLIC REACTION TO THE DEATH OF A PRESIDENT

The reaction of Americans to the death of a president provides dramatic evidence of the public's emotional attachment to the presidency. Americans regard the death of an incumbent president not just as the death of their elected leader, but also as the death of the symbol of the government, the guarantor of the nation's security and stability, and a person almost as familiar as a family member.

Although no systematic studies were done of public reactions to the deaths of incumbent presidents before John F. Kennedy, anecdotal evidence suggests that Americans have often experienced a traumatizing grief when an incumbent president has died. Hundreds of thousands of people lined the railways to view the train carrying Abraham Lincoln's body from Washington, D.C., to Albany, New York, and west to the grave site in Springfield, Illinois. The massive outpouring of grief for Franklin D. Roosevelt, who had led the nation through the Great Depression and World War II, demonstrated that an incumbent's death by natural causes also could produce a national spasm of emotion.

Nor was it necessary for the president to have been perceived as a great historical figure. After the shooting of James A. Garfield in 1881, large crowds took to the streets of major cities seeking news of the president's condition. The attack was the main topic of church sermons the next Sunday, and Garfield, who had entered office only four months before as a dark-horse candidate from Ohio, was lionized in the press as a great statesman.[1] Similarly, William McKinley and Warren G. Harding were mourned deeply by the public despite their relative lack of historical prominence.

After the assassination of President Kennedy on November 22, 1963, social scientists at the National Opinion Research Center at the University of Chicago hastily constructed a survey designed to probe the American people's feelings in the aftermath of the tragedy. The survey showed that the death of President Kennedy produced a response in the American people usually associated with the death of a relative or close friend.

The interviewers asked 1,384 persons a series of questions about their reactions to the assassination. Only 19 percent of the respondents said they were able to continue their day "pretty much as usual" after hearing of the assassination. Sixty-eight percent of the respondents reported that at some time during the four-day period between the assassination and the president's funeral they "felt very nervous and tense." Fifty-seven percent said they "felt sort of dazed and numb." Fifty-three percent said they had cried. Seventy-nine percent said when they first heard about the assassination, they "felt deeply the loss of someone very close and dear." Seventy-three percent felt anger, and 92 percent felt sorry for Kennedy's wife and children.[2]

1. Charles E. Rosenberg, *The Trial of the Assassin Guiteau* (Chicago: University of Chicago Press, 1968), 7.
2. Paul B. Sheatsley and Jacob J. Feldman, "The Assassination of President Kennedy: A Preliminary Report on Public Reactions and Behavior," *Public Opinion Quarterly* (summer 1964): 189–215.

Some presidents have deliberately tried to influence the lifestyle of the nation. Theodore Roosevelt not only urged Americans to live an active life full of outdoor pursuits, but he also set an example for his fellow citizens to emulate. He climbed trees on the White House grounds, swam in the Potomac, played marathon tennis matches, and went for obstacle walks in which he would go over or through anything that stood in his way. Roosevelt also promoted vigorous activity by inviting athletes, explorers, cowboys, and other citizens who led strenuous lives to the White House. In addition, Roosevelt waged a campaign to make simplified phonetic spelling acceptable, but he found such a controversial cultural reform beyond even his powers.[53]

Decades later, the Kennedys, with their patronage of cultural events and recognition of the achievements of writers, artists, and performers, awakened American interest in the fine arts. The president and first lady also promoted interest in science and history. At one famous dinner in 1962 honoring American Nobel Prize winners, the president declared: "This is the most extraordinary collection of talent . . . that has ever been gathered together at the White House—with the possible exception of when Thomas Jefferson dined alone."[54] Mrs. Kennedy, dismayed by the meager White House library, stocked it with 1,780 great works of literature selected by James T. Babb, Yale University's librarian. She also recovered many historical pieces from museums, private collections, and White House storage areas and had the executive mansion redecorated in authentic early-nineteenth-century style.

However, not all presidential interests catch on as national trends. George Bush played horseshoes and ate pork rinds, and neither became popular with the mass public. Nor is there evidence that Clinton's jogging or that of George W. Bush has led to an increase in the number of the nation's runners. Even though they cannot always influence American behavior, presidents remain important national icons. They are treated as national exemplars, their behavior serving as a barometer of the nation's cultural and even moral health.

CHIEF OF STATE BURDENS

One of the justifications of the British monarchy offered by its contemporary proponents is that it shelters the prime minister from many ceremonial duties. Prime ministers can devote their time and energies to formulating policy and dealing with Parliament and foreign governments while the royal family presides at ceremonial functions and absorbs

This candid photo of JFK in the Oval Office has come to signify the heavy burden of the presidency.

media and public attention. Presidents have no shield against ceremonial activities equivalent to that represented by the British monarchy. Although family members, vice presidents, cabinet secretaries, and other presidential associates can lighten the president's ceremonial burden, the president is responsible for innumerable ceremonial functions and never ceases to be chief of state. Between lobbying a member of Congress to support a bill and meeting with the National Security Council to discuss an international hot spot, the president may be scheduled to greet Olympic athletes or Miss America. The president's chief of state duties, therefore, may interrupt or even interfere with the president's duties as chief executive.

Calvin Coolidge, who as president refused to overcrowd his schedule, warned:

> The duties of the Presidency are exceedingly heavy. The responsibilities are overwhelming. But it is my opinion that a man of ordinary strength can carry them if he will confine himself very strictly to a performance of the duties that are imposed upon him by the Constitution and the law. If he permits himself to be engaged in all kinds of outside enterprises, in furnishing entertainment and amusement to great numbers of public gatherings, undertaking to be the source of inspiration for every worthy public movement, for all of which he will be earnestly besought with the inference that unless he responds civilization will break down and the sole responsibility will be on him, he will last in office about 90 days.[55]

Few presidents, however, have been able or have wanted to limit their activities the way Coolidge said he did, and several have driven themselves to exhaustion. Because the chief of state duties increase the presidential workload, one can argue that they are an onerous burden. In addition to the drain on a president's time and energy, the chief of state role can make the president more vulnerable to assassination attempts, reinforce unreasonable public expectations of the president, and contribute to an atmosphere of deference that may warp the president's judgment. In response to these problems, some observers of the presidency have suggested that the office be reformed so that the president, like the British prime minister, is free of ceremonial responsibilities.

Demands on Time

Presidential time is a scarce resource. Presidents are ultimately responsible for everything that the executive branch does. They must have time to preside over policy meetings, review the work of their staff and cabinet, establish working relationships with members of Congress, read intelligence reports, study new policy proposals, hold press conferences, and perform numerous other functions necessary to the operation of the government and their administration. In addition, they must find time for political campaigning, personal relaxation, and ceremonial functions.

No chief executive can begin to satisfy all the requests for presidential attention. Woodrow Wilson and Franklin Roosevelt, two presidents with a hands-on managerial style, complained of the burdens of their office. Wilson called the presidential workload "preposterous," and Roosevelt claimed to work fifteen-hour days.[56] Lyndon Johnson related in his memoirs: "Of all the 1,886 nights I was President, there were not many when I got to sleep before 1 or 2 a.m., and there were few mornings when I didn't wake up by 6 or 6:30." [57] Even presidents such as Eisenhower and Reagan, who were noted for their willingness to delegate responsibility and authority to their subordinates, faced daily decisions about which activities would have to be sacrificed to the pressures of time.

Although presidential responsibilities expanded greatly in the twentieth century, eighteenth- and nineteenth-century presidents also had more work than time in which to do it. George Washington found himself overwhelmed by the number of visitors he had to receive and civic functions he had to attend. He complained: "From the time I had done breakfast and thence till dinner and afterwards till bedtime I could not get relieved from ceremony of one visit before I had to attend to another." [58] Washington approached the problem in his typical manner—by asking the advice of colleagues he trusted. He solicited the opinions of Alexander Hamilton, John Jay, James Madison, and John Adams. After hearing their recommendations, Washington decided to limit his public entertaining to a dinner every Thursday at four o'clock for government officials and their families, a public levee on Tuesday afternoons for men, and a public tea party on Friday evenings for men and women.[59]

The enormousness of presidential responsibilities received a judicial validation in 1807. Chief Justice John Marshall subpoenaed President Jefferson to appear before the grand jury in Richmond considering former vice president Aaron Burr's indictment for treason. Jefferson refused to appear. He justified his decision in part by explaining that a president's duties as chief executive should not be set aside for an appearance at a trial: "The Constitution enjoins his constant agency in the concerns of six millions of people. Is the law paramount to this, which calls on him on behalf of a single one?" [60] The court accepted Jefferson's refusal to appear and withdrew its request for his testimony. The president cooperated fully with the investigation and offered to give a deposition, but the court never asked him for one.

Of all presidential activities, ceremonial functions are usually regarded as the most expendable and are frequently delegated to other individuals. Each year the White House turns down hundreds of requests for the president's time from groups and organizations seeking to publicize their causes through an appointment with the president. Many ceremonies over which presidents have presided are trivial when compared with the weighty affairs of state. For example, appearing at the annual White House Easter egg roll is a questionable use of the president's time, considering the unending procession of problems that require the president's attention. Yet public expectations, historic traditions, and opportunities for favorable media coverage combine to perpetuate White House ceremonies and events that are unrelated to policy making or the president's constitutional roles.

Risks to the President's Health

Scholars and presidents have generally agreed that the presidency is a tremendous physical burden.[61] The pressures of the presidency can weaken the health of even the strongest person. Presidents usually work long hours, must occasionally take extended trips that require physical and mental stamina, and must endure enormous emotional stress arising out of the responsibilities of their job. Presidents seldom look as vigorous when they leave office as when they entered it.

One study of presidential longevity has shown that most presidents have failed to reach the age to which they were expected to live at the time of their election. Excluding the four presidents who were assassinated, twenty-one of the thirty-two presidents who died of natural causes failed to reach their individual life expectancy. As the nation and presidential responsibilities have expanded, so has the tendency of presidents to die prematurely. From 1841 to 1991 only five of twenty-eight deceased chief executives reached their individual life expectancies.[62] This occurred despite advances in medicine and the excellent medical care available to presidents.

Illnesses can and have inhibited the execution of presidential duties. Four presidents—William Henry Harrison, Zachary Taylor, Warren G. Harding, and Franklin Roosevelt—died of natural causes before their terms expired. Several other presidents, including Wilson and Eisenhower, were incapacitated by illness during their incumbency.[63] Ronald Reagan temporarily assigned his executive functions to Vice President Bush when he underwent surgery for cancer.

George E. Reedy, who served as press secretary under Lyndon Johnson, has argued that even if ceremonial functions do take up valuable presidential time, the primary source of strain on presidents is not long workdays but the knowledge of the consequences of their actions.[64] From war to welfare reform, presidential policies can have life and death consequences. For presidents who have served during the atomic age, the knowledge of their responsibility as the person who must decide to use nuclear weapons can be particularly stressful. Lyndon Johnson wrote that he felt relief after hearing Richard Nixon complete the oath of office in part because "I would not have to face the decision any more of taking any step, in the Middle East or elsewhere, that might lead to world conflagration—the nightmare of my having to be the man who pressed the button to start World War III was passing." [65]

Reedy maintains, as others have, that chief of state duties can provide presidents with a psychological release from the overwhelming responsibilities of their office.[66] These ceremonial events allow presidents to get away from the strains of decision making, and because ceremonies are an accepted presidential responsibility, presidents are unlikely to feel as if they are neglecting their duties.

The effect of the chief of state role on a president's mental and physical health may depend on that individual's personality. For those presidents who revel in the spotlight of national attention or are stimulated by an affirmation of public affection, such as Theodore Roosevelt, Franklin

Roosevelt, Ronald Reagan, Bill Clinton, and George W. Bush, chief of state duties can be the most enjoyable and rejuvenating aspect of the presidency. Those presidents, however, who are uncomfortable with the public attention showered on them, such as William Howard Taft and Herbert Hoover, or who feel that they are wasting time when they divert their attention from policy matters, such as James Polk or George Bush, will likely regard chief of state duties as a burden, not a release.

Presidential Vacations

Perhaps because of the pressures associated with the office, presidents frequently leave the White House for vacation. While the duties of the presidency travel with the chief executive, presidents take the opportunities afforded by such travel to hike, fish, and otherwise enjoy themselves. Richard Nixon was a frequent visitor to his retreats in Key Biscayne, Florida, and San Clemente, California. Clinton was more peripatetic, visiting almost every state in the nation. George W. Bush set a record for presidential vacation days. By August 2003, he had spent a reported 27% of his time on vacation. His father spent a total of 543 days on vacation, while Reagan took 335 vacation days, and Clinton some 152. Jimmy Carter took the fewest number of days off at 79.[67]

So important is presidential relaxation that presidents used to have the services of a yacht, first the *Williamsburg* (decommissioned by Eisenhower) and then the *Sequoia* (sold by Carter), and still have a compound in the Catoctin Mountains of Maryland, Camp David. A favorite retreat for weekends and working vacations, Camp David began as a Works Progress Administration project in 1935, serving as an example of creating parks out of worn-out agricultural land. It was originally designed as a retreat for federal employees and their families but was redesigned for Franklin Roosevelt, who needed a safe place for recreation during the Second World War. He named his compound Shangri-La. It subsequently was renamed Camp David in honor of Eisenhower's grandson.

While presidents often weekend at Camp David, much presidential work also goes on there. Winston Churchill is among the British prime ministers who have spent time at Camp David, Nikita Khrushchev visited during the Eisenhower administration, and most, famously, the Camp David Accords between Israel and Egypt were signed there in 1978. Camp David has also been the site of other kinds of ceremonies. For example, Dorothy Bush, daughter of one president and sister of another, was married there in 1992.

Presidential vacations both allow the president to escape some of the pressure of Washington and facilitate his role as chief of state by allowing him to relax in ways that further his identification with the American public, display his diplomatic skills, and enact his role as First American. Presidents are never completely on vacation, but they appear to need—and certainly enjoy—even brief respites from official Washington.

Risks to the President's Safety

The assassination of a president is an even greater national disaster than the death of a president by natural causes. There may be time to prepare for the transfer of power to the vice president when a president dies from an illness, but an assassination usually does not allow for a period of administrative or emotional preparation. Not only can an assassination cause governmental confusion, but it also can send the country into shock, because people perceive an attack on the president, the symbol of the United States, as an attack on the nation itself.

Assassination attempts against presidents have not been uncommon. Lincoln, James A. Garfield, William McKinley, and Kennedy were killed by their assailants. Andrew Jackson, Truman, Ford (twice), and Reagan (who was wounded) survived attempts on their lives. In addition, President-elect Franklin Roosevelt was attacked three weeks before his first inauguration; and three presidential candidates, Theodore Roosevelt, Robert F. Kennedy, and George Wallace, all were shot—with Kennedy being killed. In all, presidents, presidents-elect, and presidential candidates have been attacked thirteen times. All but three of these attacks occurred in the twentieth century.

In 1995 concerns about security led to the closure of Pennsylvania Avenue in front of the White House. Security analysts judged that a truck bomb of the type used in the devastating attack on the Oklahoma City federal building in April of that year posed a threat to the White House. The September 11, 2001, terrorist attacks led to even tighter presidential security. The attacks made clear that the United States and its government were a target for well-organized terrorist groups. So great was the concern for the protection of the White House that public tours were stopped for a while after the attacks (*See Chapter 27, Housing of the Executive Branch, Vol. II.*). The closing of "America's main street" and the suspension of White House tours symbolized the difficulty of reconciling the need to protect presidents with the tradition that they should be accessible to the people.

The most dangerous presidential activities are those that require the president to appear before a large crowd.[68] Because the chief of state role often involves such appearances, it contributes to the danger of assassination. The symbolic goal of many chief of state events is to bridge the gap between the government and the people. This goal is difficult to accomplish from inside a bullet-proof limousine or behind a wall of Secret Service agents. Consequently, presidents, especially those running for reelection, still seek personal contact with gatherings of voters while nervous Secret Service agents scan the crowd for possible danger. Yet the benefits of a ceremonial event or symbolic gesture in a location where the president's safety cannot be absolutely guaranteed must always be weighed against the risk of an assassination attempt.

The threat of assassination and the cumbersome security measures necessary to ensure the president's safety have forced changes in the way presidents perform their chief of state role. The days when presidents were expected to wade unprotected into a crowd of citizens to shake hands are gone. Just before leaving office Ronald Reagan commented that he would have liked to have gone to see the Army-Navy football game as many other presidents had done, but he did not because "nobody wants to run 75,000 people through a magnetometer." Reagan even justified his lack of church attendance, a traditional activity of the president, on the grounds that the security measures needed to ensure his safety would disrupt the congregation.

In today's extraordinarily security-conscious world, the president, likely for security, as well as political, reasons, is largely confined to communicating with the American people via orchestrated events in front of carefully screened groups and televised speeches and press conferences. As a result, presidents are increasingly isolated from their constituents. When presidents place themselves before a crowd, as George W. Bush did when he addressed rescue workers at the World Trade Center site three days after the September 11 attacks, it is often considered a brave and confident gesture.

Excessive Public Expectations

For better or worse, the presidency is an idealized and romanticized office that elicits high expectations from the American people. With each election the public hopes for a president who will combine the best qualities of past presidents and achieve a range of contradictory goals.

Godfrey Hodgson has agreed that the expectations of the American people are not easily reconciled:

> The things "the people" want are mutually inconsistent. They want lower taxes and higher benefits. They want to be sure of the supply of gasoline, *and* they do not want to pay higher prices for it. They want national security and disarmament. They do not want American boys to be sent abroad to be killed, and they want the United States to be respected and feared.[69]

The chief of state role contributes to high public expectations of the presidency by creating the public perception that presidents have more power than they actually do. Political scientist Merlin Gustafson wrote: "When one person exercises both symbolic and political authority his public image tends to become distorted. A substantial portion of the public may be led to identify the presidential person with the governmental process, and assume that he alone determines national policy or 'runs the country.' "[70]

The public tends to blame and praise presidents for virtually everything that occurs during their terms regardless of their actual level of responsibility for conditions. For example, the public holds presidents responsible for economic prosperity even though the natural swings of the business cycle, foreign economic conditions, and economic shocks such as droughts and oil embargoes guarantee that even the best presidential economic policies will not yield economic growth all the time.

When judging presidents, the public often ignores the fact that the Constitution was designed to prevent any one person from completely dominating the government. Presidents must work with a Congress that may be controlled by the opposing party and is always composed of members primarily concerned with serving their home states and districts. Presidents also must avoid unconstitutional actions and must motivate executive branch subordinates who are capable of undermining presidential policies and initiatives. Yet presidents who cannot get their legislative proposals passed into law or their programs implemented often are accused of being weak leaders or poor compromisers. In short, even though presidents are constrained by the Constitution, they are often expected to be as effective as if they were absolute monarchs.

High public expectations and their often negative effect on presidential approval ratings can cause presidents to take actions that are popular but that are not in the public interest. In the worst case, presidents may be tempted to skirt legal constraints in pursuit of effective leadership. Cronin has commented: "Our expectations of, and demands on, the office are frequently so paradoxical as to invite two-faced behavior by our presidents. We seem to want so much so fast that a president, whose powers are often simply not as great as many of us believe, gets condemned as ineffectual. Or a president often will overreach or resort to unfair play while trying to live up to our demands."[71]

Dangers of Deference

Because presidents are partisan political leaders they are routinely attacked by their political opponents and scrutinized by a combative press. Yet because they are the chief of state, a symbol of the unity and power of the United States, they also are treated with deference.

Presidents are provided with a mansion, guards, aircraft, and custom-made automobiles and have every need attended to by a host of servants. They are addressed as "Mr. President" even by close friends they have known for many years. The strains of "Hail to the Chief" greet them when they enter the scene of an important occasion. An omnipresent contingent of reporters seeks their thoughts on any subject, no matter how mundane or irrelevant to national policy. Despite the democratic origins of the presidency, the president enjoys the luxury and veneration usually reserved for monarchs.

The intoxicating effects of the deference given to presidents are reinforced by the historic significance of the presidency and the White House. Newly elected presidents become members of an elite and celebrated club. They know historians will rate themagainst Lincoln, Washington, and other "great" presidents. Election to the presidency ensures that many books will be written about their lives. When they have left office, politicians and journalists will continue to seek their opinions as elder statesmen. Presidential libraries will be constructed to hold their official papers, and when they die their graves will become national landmarks. Presidents are reminded daily of their place in history as they live in a house that is one of the nation's most cherished monuments and that was occupied by every president except George Washington. In the White House they are surrounded by the artifacts of past administrations. They can view the portrait of George Washington that was rescued by first lady Dolley Madison in 1814 when the British burned the capital, or they can write at the desk given to President Rutherford B. Hayes by Queen Victoria in 1880 and used by many presidents since.

Outside the White House presidents can take a walk through the gardens past the magnolia tree planted by Andrew Jackson in memory of his wife, Rachel, or the Rose Garden originally planted by Ellen Wilson and redesigned under John Kennedy. George Reedy has observed that an "aura of history" can envelop a president:

> He lives in a museum, a structure dedicated to preserving the greatness of the American past. He walks the same halls paced by Lincoln waiting feverishly for news from Gettysburg or Richmond. He dines with silver used by Woodrow Wilson as he pondered the proper response to the German declaration of unrestricted submarine warfare. He has staring at him constantly portraits of the heroic men who faced the same excruciating problems in the past that he is facing in the present. It is only a matter of time until he feels himself a member of an exclusive community whose inhabitants never finally leave the mansion.[72]

The deference shown presidents because they are chief of state and the mythic atmosphere created by presidential privileges and the regal White House environment may ennoble some presidents by giving them a sense of destiny or historic duty, but the royal trappings of the office also can have damaging effects. During the Nixon administration, the well-being of the president and the presidency became more important than the law. The respect given to Nixon as chief of state and the privileges of the presidency, which he relished, undoubtedly enabled Nixon and his staff to justify more easily to themselves violations of the law and unethical political tactics.

In addition, if the deference shown presidents causes them to believe they are always right and above criticism, meaningful debate on presidential policies may be squelched. Presidents who become overconfident of their own judgment may feel resentment toward staff members who disagree with their opinions. Such an attitude will likely cause subordinates to avoid expressing negative opinions to preserve their own influence with the president. Political scientist Robert DiClerico has written:

> Presidents have a tendency to become intoxicated by the deference and veneration shown to the Office they hold. They begin to see themselves as deserving of praise and come to view challenge and disagreement as an affront. . . . The isolation of presidents from the disquieting advice of staff members was especially pronounced in the Johnson and Nixon administrations. Both men were lacking in a sense of security, and consequently they were especially susceptible to the arrogance generated by the intoxicating atmosphere of the Presidency.[73]

Presidents accustomed to being treated like monarchs inside the White House grounds may also develop a deep resentment of criticism coming from outside the White House. This may cause a president to rely exclusively on a small group of loyal advisers. Even if the president permits disagreement and frank discussion within this group, an isolated decision-making process will deprive the president of valuable sources of insight and information.

Proposals for Change

Given the problems inherent in having a president who is both the nation's chief executive and chief of state, observers of the presidency have occasionally put forward proposals to reform the chief of state role. Change could be accomplished through executive orders or practices that formalize the delegation of most chief of state duties away from the president or through a constitutional amendment that assigns ceremonial duties to a new or existing office. More sweeping reforms of the presidency, such as the creation of a plural executive or the incorporation of parliamentary elements into the American political system, also would affect the chief of state role.

Altering the president's chief of state role has not been a major concern of presidents and their advisers. The most prominent executive branch study of the issue was done by Eisenhower's Advisory Committee on Government Organization, also known as the Rockefeller Committee. The committee, which functioned throughout Eisenhower's tenure in office and studied the organization of the entire executive branch, recommended merely that the vice president perform many ceremonial duties to lighten the president's chief of state burden.[74] Presidents have commonly delegated ceremonial duties to the vice president and other individuals, but no president has set up formal rules about which officials should preside at which events.

Most proposals for changing the president's chief of state power by amending the Constitution have come from scholars and public officials who have speculated on ways to make the presidency more efficient while acknowledging the difficulty of convincing the American people that such reforms are desirable.

One such proposal was a constitutional amendment introduced by Rep. Henry S. Reuss, D-Wis., in 1975. It would have created an office of "Chief of State of the United States" separate from the presidency. The office as conceived by Reuss would be a purely ceremonial position. The president would nominate a candidate for chief of state who would be confirmed by a majority vote of both houses of Congress. To promote the office's nonpartisanship, the chief of state's four-year term would begin two years into the president's term and last two years into the next administration. There would be no limit on the number of terms a chief of state could serve. The amendment designated the chief of state as "the ceremonial head of the United States" and "the sole officer of the United States to receive ambassadors and other public ministers." In addition, the chief of state would carry out ceremonial duties "as recommended by the president." The chief of state was to be paid a salary identical to that of the president and to be subject to the same impeachment provisions.

When introducing the amendment, Reuss acknowledged that tinkering with the Constitution was controversial. He maintained, however, that the demands of the chief of state role on the president's time and the dangers of the "symbolic deification of the president" warranted amending the Constitution.[75] Besides, having a chief of state who lacked both power and tradition would be little more than an empty symbol.

Consequently, neither Congress nor the American people showed much interest in Reuss's amendment. Most Americans are not eager to alter an institution to which they are accustomed and with which they associate many of the nation's foremost heroes. Given that Abraham Lincoln, Franklin Roosevelt, and other great presidents were able to use the power of the presidency to meet the nation's great crises, they reason, the solution to the nation's problems will not be found by changing the presidency but by electing leaders who can make it work.

Political scientist Thomas S. Langston has suggested that even if dramatic constitutional changes in the presidency are unlikely, some reduction in deference for the president might be achieved if presidents were given "competition" for historical honors:

> We celebrate Presidents' Day. Why not celebrate Speakers' Day? How about a Speakers' Memorial in Washington, D.C.? And if Andrew Jackson, the archene-

my of paper money, can be made to grace the twenty-dollar bill, surely we should not be timid about proposing that famous Speakers of the House, or senators, also ennoble our currency.[76]

At the turn of the millennium, however, neither the American public nor the American political establishment appeared interested in departing from the memorialization of presidents. In 1997 an elaborate federal memorial to Franklin Roosevelt was dedicated near the Mall in Washington, D.C. In 1998 Congress passed bills renaming Washington National Airport and the Central Intelligence Agency complex after Ronald Reagan and George Bush, respectively. In 1999 it renamed the venerable Old Executive Office Building next to the White House after Dwight Eisenhower. In 2001, motivated by public interest in a popular biography of John Adams, Congress passed a bill authorizing construction of a new monument to the second president on federal land in the District of Columbia.

DELEGATION OF CHIEF OF STATE FUNCTIONS

Starting with George Washington, presidents have sought ways to control the number of ceremonial events over which they must preside. Presidents have delegated ceremonial tasks to family members, vice presidents, cabinet officers, close associates, and staff members. Like representatives sent to negotiate with foreign governments, these substitute chiefs of state have authority because they either occupy an important office within the administration or have a personal relationship with the president. Because they do not possess the power of the presidency, their presence does not have the symbolic force of a presidential appearance, but they are substitutes that most groups readily accept.

First Lady and Family

Presidents have often delegated ceremonial functions to their wives. First ladies are fitting presidential representatives because they are nearly as well known as the president and are themselves recognized symbols of American history and culture. When a first lady addresses an organization or presides over a ceremonial event, the audience understands that the president is being represented by an intimate confidante and adviser.

Eleanor Roosevelt's ceremonial activism set the standard for modern first ladies. Franklin Roosevelt frequently sent his wife to the scene of strikes, disasters, and centers of poverty as his personal representative. She also traveled to England, South America, and the South Pacific during World War II to encourage U.S. troops and allies. Most succeeding first ladies also performed chief of state duties. Rosalynn Carter made an ambitious good-will tour of Latin America in 1977 in which she carried out diplomatic as well

Laura Bush, on her first solo international diplomatic trip as first lady, addresses the Organisation for Economic Co-operation and Development in Paris, May 2002. The former teacher and librarian focused on the importance of education in overcoming hopelessness and poverty, which she called the root causes of terrorism.

as ceremonial missions. Nancy Reagan visited several foreign countries as her husband's representative, including Great Britain in 1981 for the wedding of Prince Charles and Lady Diana, Monaco in 1982 for the funeral of Princess Grace, and Mexico in 1985 to express concern for the victims of an earthquake. In the summer of 1995 Hillary Clinton and her daughter, Chelsea, made a five-nation tour of South Asia that focused on issues related to women and children. Mrs. Clinton also attended a United Nations conference on women's issues in China in September 1995 as chair of the U.S. delegation. Laura Bush became the first first lady to deliver the weekly presidential radio address on November 17, 2001. She spoke against the repression of women by the Taliban regime in Afghanistan.

The first lady, because she is presumed to have the president's ear, can serve as an important delegate. But because she has no political power in her own right, she is not suited for all occasions. For those events, the president may send another of his political partners, the vice president.

Vice Presidents

The Constitution gives the vice president no formal policy-making or administrative powers other than to preside over the Senate and break tie votes in that body. As a result, few vice presidents of the nineteenth and early twentieth centuries had a significant role in their administrations. Modern vice presidents have become more involved in policy making, but they continue to perform many ceremonial functions. *(See Chapter 3, History of the Vice Presidency, and Chapter 23, Office of the Vice President, Vol. II.)*

Vice presidents are well positioned to act as substitute chiefs of state because their office is associated with the presidency. Vice presidents run on the same ticket as their presidential running mates and are the only officials besides presidents who are elected by the entire nation. In addition, although their office may at times seem trivial, vice presidents are first in line for the presidency. Fourteen vice presidents have become president, including eight who succeeded to the presidency when the incumbent died in office and one when the incumbent resigned. The political and historic link between the two offices makes the vice president an appropriate stand-in for the president at ceremonial functions.

Since the advent of the airplane, presidents have frequently sent their vice presidents on ceremonial missions overseas. Sometimes these missions have included serious negotiations with leaders of important nations, but often their purposes have been more symbolic than substantive. Hubert H. Humphrey, who served as Lyndon Johnson's vice president, explained the vice president's diplomatic role: "He can perform assignments that the President feels would be unwise for him to take on himself, but for which an official lower than Vice President would be unsuitable." [77]

These assignments have included representing the United States and the president at inaugurations, coronations, and funerals of foreign leaders and major world figures. George Bush, who traveled more than one million miles and visited more than seventy countries as vice president, frequently took President Reagan's place at ceremonial functions overseas. Bush's attendance at the funerals of foreign dignitaries became so common that he joked that his motto should be: "I'm George Bush. You die, I fly." [78]

Presidents can enhance the symbolic effect of a vice-presidential trip by demonstrating their interest in it and designating the vice president as their personal envoy. John Kennedy would usually hold a publicized meeting with Lyndon Johnson before the vice president left on a foreign mission. Immediately after entering office, Jimmy Carter sent Vice President Walter F. Mondale on a tour of Europe and Japan to demonstrate the importance of close allied cooperation with the Carter administration. In a South Lawn ceremony, President Carter bolstered his vice president's status by declaring: "Vice President Mondale has my complete confidence. He is a personal representative of mine, and I'm sure that his consultation with the leaders of these nations will make it much easier for our country to deal directly with them on substantive matters in the future." [79]

In the aftermath of the September 11, 2001, terrorist attacks, Vice President Richard B. Cheney facilitated the president's chief of state role in an unusual manner. The attacks had raised grave concerns that assassination plots or further attacks on Washington could result in both Bush and Cheney being killed. To ensure that the Bush-Cheney administration would survive, the vice president was assigned to stay out of harm's way so that he could lead the government if an attack succeeded in killing the president. Thus instead of replacing President George W. Bush at ceremonial functions, Cheney remained in a secure, and often undisclosed, location while the president kept a busy public schedule to reassure the nation. It was vital that the president, not a replacement, bolster the nation's confidence through ceremonial and patriotic appearances.

Cabinet Members and Personal Advisers

Cabinet members often operate as assistant chiefs of state within the area of their department's concern. For example, the education secretary makes ceremonial visits to public schools; the housing and urban development secretary tours inner-city housing projects; the commerce secretary speaks to business groups; the interior secretary addresses environmentalist groups; and the defense secretary inspects military installations and presides at ceremonies honoring war heroes and veterans. In addition, cabinet members often use ceremonial occasions or symbolic settings to make speeches that unveil a new program or announce a policy decision affecting their department.

Henry Kissinger became the most recognized symbol of President Richard Nixon's foreign policy. Originally national security adviser, he became secretary of state in 1973.

The secretary of state has a special ceremonial role. After the president and vice president, the secretary of state is the nation's highest diplomatic and ceremonial representative. The secretary meets with foreign ministers who visit the United States and often heads U.S. delegations at funerals, inaugurations, and other special ceremonies overseas that are not attended by the president or vice president. In matters of protocol the secretary of state also is considered to be the highest-ranking cabinet officer. This unofficial rank is reinforced by the Succession Act of 1947, which designates the secretary of state as the first cabinet officer in line for the presidency and the fourth government official after the vice president, Speaker of the House, and president pro tempore of the Senate.

During the Nixon administration, National Security Adviser Henry Kissinger transformed his post from that of a behind-the-scenes presidential aide into a rival of the secretary of state for the diplomatic spotlight. The force of Kissinger's personality, his close relationship to President Nixon, and his celebrated diplomatic missions to the People's Republic of China and the Soviet Union made him the most recognized symbol of Nixon's foreign policy. During Kissinger's second trip to China in October 1971, he participated in ceremonial activities, including visits to the Great Wall of China and other Chinese landmarks. Kissinger also was constantly at the president's side during the historic 1972 summit meetings in Beijing and Moscow. Kissinger's activities resembled those of the secretary of state so much that he was criticized by some defenders of the State Department for having usurped the role of the secretary. After Secretary of State William Rogers resigned, Kissinger assumed the post in September 1973.

While Bill Clinton traveled a great deal overseas , George W. Bush relies on his advisers to do most of his traveling for him. As secretary of state, first Colin Powell and then Condoleeza Rice each took between fourteen and eighteen trips abroad a year. *(See box, Presidential Travel, right.)*

PRESIDENTIAL TRAVEL

Presidential travel is an important part of the president's role as chief of state. The development of air travel has expanded his ability to travel overseas. According to John Berthoud and Demian Brady, Bill Clinton set a record for presidential travel.[1] They found that,

- Bill Clinton made 133 visits to foreign nations.
- These 133 visits break down into an average of 16.6 nations visited per year.
- In his eight years in office, Clinton made more foreign visits than Presidents Dwight D. Eisenhower, John F. Kennedy, Lyndon B. Johnson, and Richard M. Nixon combined (over the years 1953–1974).
- In his eight years in office, Clinton visited almost as many nations as Presidents Jimmy Carter, Ronald Reagan, and George Bush combined (over the years 1977–1993).

- While Clinton was president for one-sixth of the period analyzed (eight of the forty-eight years between 1953 and 2001), he accounted for almost one-third of all presidential visits.
- Clinton's closest competitor was President George Bush, who made sixty visits to foreign nations during his four years in office. While Bush was arguably more focused on foreign policy than almost any other president of this forty-eight-year period, Clinton still managed to have an annual average 11 percent higher than Bush's.
- Clinton visited seventy-four different countries or entities.

PRESIDENTIAL VISITS, 1953–2001

President	Years in office	Visits	Visits per year
Dwight D. Eisenhower	8	37	4.6
John F. Kennedy	2.84	16	5.6
Lyndon B. Johnson	5.16	27	5.2
Richard M. Nixon	5.55	42	7.6
Gerald R. Ford	2.45	19	7.8
Jimmy Carter	4	31	7.8
Ronald Reagan	8	49	6.1
George Bush	4	60	15
Total, 1953–1993	40	281	—
Four-year average	—	28.1	—
Eight-year average	—	56.2	—
Bill Clinton	8	133	16.6

SOURCE: State Department data, the media, and other reports on presidential activities.
NOTE: Visits are the number of countries visited (that is, if the president leaves the United States and visits six countries before returning, that counts as six).

PRESIDENTIAL DAYS TRAVELING ABROAD, 1953–2001

President	Years in office	Days abroad	Days abroad per year
Dwight D. Eisenhower	8	98	12.3
John F. Kennedy	2.84	33	11.6
Lyndon B. Johnson	5.16	37	7.2
Richard M. Nixon	5.55	82	14.7
Gerald R. Ford	2.45	37	15.1
Jimmy Carter	4	67	16.8
Ronald Reagan	8	118	14.8
George Bush	4	102	25.5
Total, 1953–1993	40	574	—
Four-year average	—	57.4	—
Eight-year average	—	114.8	—
Bill Clinton	8	229	28.6

SOURCE: State Department data, the media, and other reports on presidential activities.

1. John Berthoud and Demian Brady, "Bill Clinton: America's Best-Traveled President—A Study of Presidential Travel, 1953–2001," National Taxpayer's Union policy paper, http://www.ntu.org/main/press.php?PressID=218&org_name=NTU.

CONCLUSION

When the president acts as chief of state, the role both offers strong advantages and imposes important constraints upon him. The most important constraint is on his time. Presidential ceremonial duties require a significant investment of time and energy on the part of the chief executive. But, in exchange, the president receives the benefit of reinforcing the public perception of him as a leader, the person who represents the nation at all of its most important ceremonial occasions, who speaks for the nation, and who in a sense embodies the nation. That can be a powerful resource for him in times of political trouble.

Because the role of chief of state allows the president to rely on the public's respect for the institution, and to conflate that respect with public attitudes toward the individual, it reflects the president's public image, not his private one. When acting as chief of state, presidents are expected to be "presidential" and behavior that strikes the public as being unsuitable for a president can undermine their faith in his ability to perform the other roles required by the office. Success as chief of state, however, can lead the public to have more faith in the president's capacity in his other roles. On balance, then, the president gains much more than he loses when acting as the nation's symbolic and ceremonial leader.

NOTES

1. Mary Stuckey would like to thank Michael Nelson for his suggestions, which improved the chapter, and Kristina Curry for her help in researching the finer points of the chief of state role.

2. Thomas E. Cronin and Michael A. Genovese, *The Paradoxes of the American Presidency* (New York: Oxford University Press, 2003).

3. There is some dispute over the cost of Clinton's inaugural. The low estimates are around $23 million, the high ones claim $42 million. See Kevin Anderson, "No Expense Spared at Inauguration," BBC News, January 20, 2005, http://news.bbc.co.uk/2/hi/americas/4187023.stm (accessed August 26, 2005); Joseph Curl, "Inaugural Price Tag in Line with History," *Washington Times,* January 20, 2005, http://washingtontimes.com/national/20050119-103531-1062r.htm (accessed August 26, 2006); and Hauenstein Center for Presidential Studies, "Cost for Inaugurations," January 21, 2005, http://washingtontimes.com/national/20050119-103531-1062r.htm (accessed August 26, 2006).

4. Curl, "Inaugural Price Tag in Line with History"

5. Arthur M. Schlesinger Jr., "Annual Messages of the Presidents: Major Themes of American History," in *The State of the Union Messages of the Presidents 1790–1966,* vol. 1 (New York: Chelsea House, 1966), xiv.

6. Karlyn Kohrs Campbell and Kathleen Hall Jamieson, *Deeds Done in Words: Presidential Rhetoric and the Genres of Governance* (Chicago: University of Chicago Press, 1990), 55.

7. Alexander Hamilton, *Federalist* No. 69, in Alexander Hamilton, James Madison, and John Jay, *The Federalist Papers* (New York: New American Library, 1961), 420.

8. For details on presidential proclamations, see American Presidency Project, "Proclamations," 2005. 26 August 2006 http://www.presidency.ucsb.edu/proclamations (accessed September 15, 2006).

9. For more discussion of this point, see Michael Hester, "America's #1 Fan: A Rhetorical Analysis of Presidential Sports Encomia and the Symbolic Power of Sports in the Articulation of Civil Religion in the United States," dissertation, Georgia State University, Department of Communication, 2005.

10. Quoted in Richard Pious, *The American Presidency* (New York: Basic Books, 1979), 5.

11. Edward Pessen, *The Log Cabin Presidency: The Social Backgrounds of the Presidents* (New Haven: Yale University Press, 1986).

12. Theodore C. Sorensen, *Kennedy* (New York: Harper and Row, 1965), 368.

13. Fred I. Greenstein, "The Presidential Leadership Style of Bill Clinton: An Early Appraisal," *Political Science Quarterly* 108, no. 4 (1993–1994): 598.

14. See the poll published in July 2004, http://www.casachia.org/Strategems/Archived/July04.html (accessed August 18, 2006).

15. James Hart, *The American Presidency in Action, 1789* (New York: Macmillan, 1948), 24–25.

16. For a further discussion of this point, see Vanessa Beasley, *You the People: American National Identity in Presidential Rhetoric* (College Station: Texas A&M University Press, 2004); and Mary E. Stuckey, *Defining Americans: The Presidency and National Identity* (Lawrence: University Press of Kansas, 2004).

17. In 2005, for instance, the president announced some fifty disasters (not counting Hurricane Katrina), the deaths of fifteen individuals, and gave two eulogies. See *Weekly Compilation of Presidential Documents,* http://www.gpo.gov/nara/nara003.html (accessed September 14, 2006).

18. For a more extended discussion, see Mary E. Stuckey, *Slipping the Surly Bonds: Reagan's Challenger Address* (College Station: Texas A&M University Press, 2006).

19. Ibid., 17.

20. *Public Papers of the Presidents of the United States, Franklin Roosevelt, Containing the Public Messages, Speeches, and Statements of the President, 1937* (Washington, D.C.: Government Printing Office, 1938), 379.

21. Clinton Rossiter, *The American Presidency,* 2d ed. (New York: Harcourt, Brace and World, 1960), 18.

22. Ibid., 102–103. See also David K. Nichols, *The Myth of the Modern Presidency* (University Park: Pennsylvania State University Press, 1994), 22–23.

23. Thomas E. Cronin, "The Presidency and Its Paradoxes," in *The Presidency Reappraised,* 2d ed., ed. Thomas E. Cronin and Rexford G. Tugwell (New York: Praeger, 1977), 79; and David F. Prindle, "Head of State and Head of Government in Comparative Perspective," *Presidential Studies Quarterly* 21 (winter 1991): 56–57.

24. Fred I. Greenstein, *The Hidden-Hand Presidency: Eisenhower as Leader* (New York: Basic Books, 1982), 5.

25. See, for example, Alan I. Abramowitz and Walter J. Stone, "The Bush Effect: Polarization, Turnout, and Activism in the 2004 Presidential Election," *Presidential Studies Quarterly* 36 (2006): 141–155; Carl M. Cannon, "A New Era of Partisan War," *National Journal,* 2006, 43–44; Juan Enriquez, *The United States of America: Polarization, Fracturing, and Our Future* (New York: Crown, 2005); and Gary C. Jacobsen, "Polarized Politics and the 2004 Congressional and Presidential Elections," *Political Science Quarterly* 120 (2005): 199–218. See especially Philip A. Klinkner, "Mr. Bush's War: Foreign Policy in the 2004 Election," *Presidential Studies Quarterly* 36 (2006): 281–296.

26. Erwin C. Hargrove and Michael Nelson, *Presidents, Politics, and Policy* (Baltimore: Johns Hopkins University Press, 1984), 23.

27. Polling data on President Bush's overall job rating can be found at http://www.pollingreport.com/BushJob.htm (accessed August 20, 2006).

28. Quoted in Arthur Bernon Tourtellot, *The Presidents on the Presidency* (Garden City, N.Y.: Doubleday, 1964), 36.

29. Four presidents who finished their terms chose not to attend the inaugural ceremonies of their successors: John Adams, John Quincy Adams, Martin Van Buren, and Andrew Johnson.

30. Pious, *American Presidency,* 7.

31. Dale Vinyard, *The Presidency* (New York: Scribner's, 1971), 5.

32. Craig Allen Smith and Kathy B. Smith, *The White House Speaks: Presidential Leadership as Persuasion* (Westport, Conn.: Praeger, 1994), 236–238.

33. Prindle, "Head of State and Head of Government in Comparative Perspective," 58–59.

34. "The Emperor's New Polls," Editor's Note, *Mother Jones* (September/October 1995), 10 September 2006 http://www.motherjones.com/commentary/ednote/1995/09/klein.html (accessed September 14, 2006).

35. Peri Arnold, "One President, Two Presidencies: George W. Bush in Peace and War," in *High Stakes and Big Ambition: The Presidency of George W. Bush,* ed. Steven E. Schier (Pittsburgh: University of Pittsburgh Press, 2004), 147.

36. Robert E. DiClerico, *The American President,* 4th ed. (Englewood Cliffs, N.J.: Prentice Hall, 1995), 135–136.

37. Richard E. Neustadt, *Presidential Power and the Modern Presidents: The Politics of Leadership from Roosevelt to Reagan,* 3d ed. (New York: Free Press, 1990), 30.

38. Herman Finer, *The Presidency: Crisis and Regeneration, an Essay in Possibilities* (Chicago: University of Chicago Press, 1960), 103.

39. Samuel Kernell, *Going Public: New Strategies of Presidential Leadership* 3d ed. (Washington, D.C.: CQ Press, 1997).

40. Matthew Eshbaugh-Soha, *The President's Speeches: Beyond Going Public* (New York: Lynne Reinner, 2006).

41. George C. Edwards, III, *On Deaf Ears: The Limits of the Bully Pulpit* (New Haven: Yale University Press, 2003).

42. Fred Greenstein, "What the President Means to Americans," in *Choosing the President,* ed. James David Barber (Englewood Cliffs, N.J.: Prentice Hall, 1974), 125; and Richard Morin, "Who's in Control? Many Don't Know or Care," *Washington Post,* January 29, 1996, A6.

43. See http://www.informationclearinghouse.info/article5158.htm (accessed September 15, 2006).

44. Polling data can be found at http://pollingreport.com/news.htm(accessed August 15, 2006).

45. See, for instance, Dan Drew and David Weaver, "Voter Learning in the 2004 Presidential Election: Did the Media Matter?" *Journalism and Mass Communication Quarterly* 83 (2006): 25–42.

46. Kaye D. Trammel, Andrew Paul Williams, Monica Postelnicu, and Kristen D. landreville, "Evolution of Online Campaigning: Increasing Activity in Candidate Web Sites and Blogs Through Text and Technical Features," *Mass Communication and Society* 9 (2006): 21–44.

47. Andrew Paul Williams and Kaye D. Trammel, "Candidate Campaign E-Mail Messages in the 2004 Presidential Election," *American Behavioral Scientist* 49 (2005): 560–574.

48. James David Fairbanks, "The Priestly Functions of the Presidency: A Discussion of the Literature on Civil Religion and Its Implications for the Study of Presidential Leadership," *Presidential Studies Quarterly* 11 (spring 1981): 225.

49. Barbara Hinckley, *The Symbolic Presidency: How Presidents Portray Themselves* (New York: Routledge, 1990), 73–79.

50. Arthur J. Hughes, " 'Amazin' Jimmy' and 'A Mighty Fortress Was Our Teddy': Theodore Roosevelt and Jimmy Carter, the Religious Link," *Presidential Studies Quarterly* 9 (winter 1979): 80–81.

51. Quoted in James David Fairbanks, "Religious Dimensions of Presidential Leadership: The Case of Dwight Eisenhower," *Presidential Studies Quarterly* 12 (spring 1982): 264.

52. Bill Broadway, "God's Place on the Dias," *Washington Post,* January 27, 2001, B9.

53. Joseph E. Kallenbach, *The American Chief Executive: The Presidency and the Governorship* (New York: Harper and Row, 1966), 280.

54. Sorensen, *Kennedy,* 384.

55. Quoted in Tourtellot, *Presidents on the Presidency,* 366.

56. Ibid., 365 and 369.

57. Lyndon B. Johnson, *The Vantage Point* (New York: Holt, Rinehart, and Winston, 1971), 425.

58. Michael P. Riccards, *A Republic, If You Can Keep It: The Foundation of the American Presidency, 1700–1800* (New York: Greenwood Press, 1987), 87.

59. Ibid., 88.

60. Hart, *American Presidency in Action, 1789,* 46.

61. Robert E. Gilbert, *The Mortal Presidency: Illness and Anguish in the White House,* 2d ed. (New York: Fordham University Press, 1998), 1–18.

62. Ibid., 2–6.

63. Louis W. Koenig, *The Chief Executive,* 6th ed. (New York: Harcourt Brace College Publishers, 1996), 80–85.

64. George E. Reedy, *The Twilight of the Presidency: From Johnson to Reagan,* rev. ed. (New York: New American Library, 1987), 45.

65. Johnson, *Vantage Point,* 566.

66. Reedy, *Twilight of the Presidency,* 46. See also Gustafson, "Our Part-Time Chief of State," 167; and Thomas E. Cronin, *The State of the Presidency,* 2d ed. (Boston: Little, Brown, 1980), 158.

67. For information, on presidential vacations, see http://ask.yahoo.com/20031001.html.

68. In seven of the nine attacks on incumbent presidents, the assailants assaulted the chief executive with a handgun while he was near a crowd. The exceptions were the 1950 attack by two men with automatic weapons on the Blair House in Washington, D.C., where Harry Truman was staying while the White House was being renovated, and the 1963 fatal shooting of John Kennedy by Lee Harvey Oswald, who used a high-powered rifle to kill the president as he traveled through Dallas in a motorcade.

69. Godfrey Hodgson, *All Things to All Men: The False Promise of the Modern American Presidency* (New York: Simon and Schuster, 1980), 241.

70. Gustafson, "Our Part-Time Chief of State," 169.

71. Cronin, "Presidency and Its Paradoxes," 69.

72. Reedy, *Twilight of the Presidency,* 21.

73. DiClerico, *American President,* 225.

74. Gustafson, "Our Part-Time Chief of State," 164.

75. U.S. Congress, House, *Congressional Record,* daily ed., 94th Cong., 1st sess., July 21, 1975, 23716–23719.

76. Thomas S. Langston, *With Reverence and Contempt: How Americans Think about Their President* (Baltimore: Johns Hopkins University Press, 1995), 143.

77. Cited in Joel K. Goldstein, *The Modern American Vice Presidency* (Princeton: Princeton University Press, 1982), 160.

78. David S. Cloud, "Loyal Lieutenant Bush Seeks Job at the Top," *Congressional Quarterly Weekly Report,* August 6, 1988, 2176.

79. *Public Papers of the Presidents of the United States, Jimmy Carter, Containing the Public Messages, Speeches, and Statements of the President, 1977,* Book 1 (Washington, D.C.: Government Printing Office, 1978), 11.

SELECTED BIBLIOGRAPHY

Barger, Harold M. *The Impossible Presidency: Illusions and Realities of Executive Power.* Glenview, Ill.: Scott, Foresman, 1984.

Beschloss, Michael. *The President: Every Leader from Washington to Bush.* New York: ibooks Inc., 2005.

Bunch, Lonnie G., Spencer R. Crew, and Mark G. Hirsch. *The American Presidency: A Glorious Burden.* New York: HarperCollins, 2000.

Campbell, Karlyn Kohrs, and Kathleen Hall Jamieson. *Deeds Done in Words: Presidential Rhetoric and the Genres of Governance.* Chicago: University of Chicago Press, 1990.

Cronin, Thomas E., and Rexford G. Tugwell, eds. *The Presidency Reappraised.* 2d ed. New York: Praeger, 1977.

Dallek, Robert. *Hail to the Chief: The Making and Unmaking of American Presidents.* New York: Oxford University Press, 2001.

Edwards, George C., III. *On Deaf Ears: The Limits of the Bully Pulpit.* New Haven: Yale University Press, 2003.

Eshbaugh-Soha, Matthew. *The President's Speeches: Beyond Going Public.* New York: Lynne Reinner, 2006.

Gilbert, Robert E. *The Mortal Presidency: Illness and Anguish in the White House.* 2d ed. New York: Fordham University Press, 1998.

Greenstein, Fred I. *The Hidden-Hand Presidency: Eisenhower as Leader.* New York: Basic Books, 1982.

Gustafson, Merlin. "Our Part-Time Chief of State." *Presidential Studies Quarterly* 9 (spring 1979): 163–171.

Han, Lori Cox. *Governing from Center Stage: White House Communication Strategies in the Television Age of Politics.* Cresskill, N.J.: Hampton Press, 2001.

Hargrove, Erwin C. *The President as Leader: Appealing to the Better Angels of Our Nature.* Lawrence: University Press of Kansas, 1999.

Hargrove, Erwin C., and Michael Nelson. *Presidents, Politics, and Policy.* Baltimore: Johns Hopkins University Press, 1984.

Hart, James. *The American Presidency in Action, 1789.* New York: Macmillan, 1948.

Hinckley, Barbara. *The Symbolic Presidency: How Presidents Portray Themselves.* New York: Routledge, 1990.

Kallenbach, Joseph E. *The American Chief Executive: The Presidency and the Governorship.* New York: Harper and Row, 1966.

Langston, Thomas S. *With Reverence and Contempt: How Americans Think About Their President.* Baltimore: Johns Hopkins University Press, 1995.

Medhurst, Martin J., ed. *Beyond the Rhetorical Presidency.* College Stattion: Texas A&M University Press, 1996.

Neustadt, Richard. *Presidential Power and the Modern Presidents: The Politics of Leadership from Roosevelt to Reagan* New York: Free Press, 1991.

Nichols, David K. *The Myth of the Modern Presidency.* University Park: Pennsylvania State University Press, 1994.

Novak, Michael. *Choosing Presidents: Symbols of Political Leadership.* 2d ed. New Brunswick: Transaction Publishers, 1992.

Phelps, Glenn. "George Washington and the Founding of the Presidency." *Presidential Studies Quarterly* 17 (spring 1987): 345–363.

Pious, Richard. *The American Presidency.* New York: Basic Books, 1979.

Prindle, David F. "Head of State and Head of Government in Comparative Perspective." *Presidential Studies Quarterly* 21 (winter 1991): 55–71.

Reedy, George E. *The Twilight of the Presidency: From Johnson to Reagan.* New York: New American Library, 1987.

Riccards, Michael P. *A Republic, If You Can Keep It: The Foundation of the American Presidency, 1700–1800.* New York: Greenwood Press, 1987.

Rossiter, Clinton. *The American Presidency.* 2d ed. New York: Harcourt, Brace and World, 1960.

Ryfe, Donald. *Presidents in Culture: The Meaning of Presidential Communication.* New York: Peter Lang, 2005.

Shogun, Colleen. *The Moral Rhetoric of American Presidents.* College Station: Texas A&M Press, 2005.

chapter 11

Chief Administrator

by Shirley Anne Warshaw, W. Craig Bledsoe, James Brian Watts, and Mark J. Rozell

rticle II of the Constitution lists the president's powers. Section 1 of the article clearly grants executive power to the president: "the executive Power shall be vested in a President." Section 3 makes the president responsible for the execution of federal laws: the president "shall take Care that the Laws be faithfully executed."

In theory, these directives make the president responsible for carrying out or executing the laws of the federal government. In practice, however, the ambiguity of this mandate often has increased the power of the presidency. For example, by broadly interpreting the authority to execute the law, Grover Cleveland used federal troops to break a labor strike in the 1890s and Dwight D. Eisenhower sent troops to help integrate a public school in Little Rock, Arkansas, in 1957.

At the beginning of the Constitutional Convention, the Framers expressed uncertainty about the exact nature of the executive. They derived many of their political ideals from seventeenth- and eighteenth-century European writers such as John Locke, Jean Jacques Rousseau, and Baron de Montesquieu, whose theories emphasized both popular sovereignty and individual liberty. If the Framers had fully adopted the political beliefs of these writers, the chief executive would be a directly elected public official responsible only to the people and representing the popular will.

Still, the Framers feared the effects of an unrestrained democracy. They were afraid that the chief executive might be too inclined to accede to popular demands in ways harmful to minority rights. Consequently, they attempted to insulate the office of president by having the public participate in presidential selection only indirectly through the electoral college.

The debate over the strength of the executive spilled over into the effort to define the exact nature of the president's administrative duties. Influenced by classical liberal writers, such as Montesquieu, the Framers dispersed power by structuring an executive branch separate and independent from the legislature. In doing so, they gave the presidency sweeping administrative responsibilities to "faithfully execute" the laws. But to keep the presidency from becoming too powerful, they subjected it to certain constraints by giving Congress immense powers of its own. The president has the power to appoint officials of the executive branch, but the Senate must confirm many of the appointments. And the president is in charge of administering the federal laws and programs, but Congress creates them, and it may change them at any time. Specifically, Congress can create and destroy agencies, and it determines whether they are going to be located in the executive branch or outside it. In other words, if it chooses, Congress can make an agency completely independent of the president.

The legislature also has the power of appropriation, which gives it ultimate control over federal agencies. Congress can define exactly what an agency has the power to do and not do. Consequently, as political scientist Peter Woll has observed, "Congress has virtually complete authority to structure the administrative branch and determine where formal lines of accountability shall be placed. It may or may not decide to let the President exercise various types of control." [1]

In *The Federalist Papers,* Alexander Hamilton defined the president's administrative activities as "mere execution" of "executive details." His was a narrow interpretation, for he in no way understood what would develop later. Hamilton, however, saw the president as the person solely responsible for administrative action. In *Federalist* No. 72 he wrote,

> The persons, therefore to whose immediate management these different [administrative] matters are committed, ought to be considered as the assistants or deputies of the chief magistrate, and on this account they ought to derive their offices from his appointment, at least from his nomination, and ought to be subject to his superintendence. This view of the subject will at once suggest to us the intimate connection between the duration of the executive magistrate in office and the stability of the system of administration. [2]

Since the 1930s Congress has delegated to the president the broad authority to achieve several general goals. Congress will often pass laws, leaving to the president and the executive branch the discretion to define the regulations and programs to be put into effect. This practice has come into being through political events, not by design. Americans increasingly look to the president for leadership in times of crisis and in everyday affairs, making the chief executive responsible for a growing portion of the nation's successes and failures. Consequently, the administrative responsibilities of the presidency have grown tremendously. As the presidency evolved, presidents found themselves serving as chief administrators, chief personnel officers, chief financial officers, and chief law enforcers—all part of the job of "chief executive."

The executive power shall be vested in a president of the United States of America.

—*from Article II, Section 1*

The President shall be Commander in Chief of the Army and the Navy of the United States, and of the Militia of the several States, when called into the actual Service of the United States.

—*from Article II, Section 2*

Political scientist Clinton Rossiter was so impressed with the demands on the presidency that he introduced his classic book, *The American Presidency,* with a quotation from Shakespeare's *Macbeth:* "Methought I heard a voice cry 'Sleep no more!' "[3] A few days before he was assassinated on November 22, 1963, President John F. Kennedy wrote Rossiter to comment on the use of the quote from *Macbeth.* Kennedy believed the quote to be apt but thought an even more appropriate one could be found in Shakespeare's *King Henry IV, Part I,* in which Glendower boasts, "I can call spirits from the vasty deep," and Hotspur replies, "Why so can I, or so can any man; but will they come when you do call for them?" Kennedy pointed to the difference between presidents' calling for action and actually accomplishing their desired goals. After almost three years in office, he understood the paradoxical nature of presidential power and its limitations.

THE PRESIDENT AS CHIEF ADMINISTRATOR

Although the Founders placed a high priority on the presidency's executive duties, the Constitution provides very few instructions about the president's tasks as head of the executive branch. Specific presidential administrative powers have evolved as the presidency has matured.

The Constitution does not make direct provisions for the vast administrative structure that the president must oversee. It does, however, authorize the president to demand written reports from the "principal Officer in each of the executive Departments, upon any Subject, relating to the Duties of their respective Offices" (Article II, Section 2). This clause implies a division of labor within the executive branch and clearly establishes an administrative hierarchy with the president as the chief administrative officer.

Similar to chief executives in private corporations, the chief executive in the White House tries to persuade subordinates in government to conform to presidential objectives. In other words, the chief executive tries to give direction to the administration. Presidents do not have time to follow through on every action taken by the bureaucratic departments and agencies directly under their control. After all, they sit atop a federal executive structure that has approximately three million civilian employees. They must, then, develop techniques that give them control over this vast administrative organization. Because this organization has grown tremendously since the early days of the Republic, analysis of the president's power as chief executive entails discussion of the structure of the executive branch.

Structure of the Executive Branch

Often the term *bureaucracy* is considered pejorative, because to many it suggests red tape, inflexibility, and confusion. Opposition to "big government" has become almost synonymous with opposition to bureaucracy. Political candidates from both major political parties usually decry the evils of the burgeoning U.S. bureaucracy, denouncing it for removing Americans from the decision-making process of their federal government.

Those who work in the federal bureaucratic structure—"bureaucrats"—are often criticized for being unproductive and obstinate. Political scientist Charles T. Goodsell has written that "the employee of bureaucracy, that 'lowly bureaucrat,' is seen as lazy or snarling, or both. The office occupied by this pariah is viewed as bungling or inhuman, or both. The overall edifice of bureaucracy is pictured as overstaffed, inflexible, unresponsive, and power-hungry, all at once."[4]

Bureaucracy, however, has a technical meaning. The German sociologist Max Weber saw the bureaucratic model of organization as one distinguished by its large size, its formulation of rules and procedures, the presence of a clear hierarchy, the systematic maintenance of records, and the employment of a full-time appointed staff who perform specific duties using technical knowledge.[5]

By this definition, a large corporation or university is a bureaucracy, and so is the federal government. The departments, agencies, bureaus, commissions, and offices of the executive branch make up most of the federal bureaucracy. Although not as large and usually not as visible as the executive branch, Congress and the courts have their own bureaucracies.

Despite the negative connotations of the term, a *bureaucrat* is simply an administrator who carries out the policies of the elected officials of government. The structure of the federal bureaucracy under the president's control can be broken down into the Executive Office of the President (EOP), the cabinet departments, the executive agencies, and the regulatory commissions.

Executive Office of the President

In 1939 Executive Order 8248 created the Executive Office of the President to advise the president and to help manage the growing bureaucracy. The EOP includes a variety of offices, including the White House Office, the Council of Economic Advisers, the National Security Council (NSC), and the Office of Management and Budget (OMB)—agencies conceived to help the president control the expanding executive branch.

Since then the EOP has grown tremendously, employing 1,850 staff in 2005 with a budget of $341 million. Its most important components are the White House Office, the NSC, and OMB.

The White House Office consists of the president's closest assistants. Their roles and titles vary from one administration to another, but under each new president it is this group that oversees the political and policy interests of the administration. Serving as a direct extension of the president, these people do not require Senate confirmation. The creation of the White House Office has allowed the president to centralize executive power within the White House at the expense of the cabinet secretaries.

In 1947, early in the cold war, Congress passed the National Security Act, which created the NSC to help coordinate military and foreign policies. Responsible for coordinating activities between the State Department and the Defense Department, the NSC has four statutory members: the president, the vice president (added in 1949), the secretary of state, and the secretary of defense. The act further names the chairman of the Joint Chiefs of Staff and the director of the Central Intelligence Agency (CIA) as advisers to the NSC. In addition to the NSC but distinct from its formal membership is the NSC staff. Made up of foreign policy advisers and headed by the national security adviser, the NSC staff has evolved into an apparatus used by many presidents to implement their own foreign policy goals. Because the role of the NSC and its staff is purely advisory, presidents have used it to varying degrees. President Kennedy, preferring his own close advisers, used the NSC infrequently. President Richard M. Nixon, however, gave the NSC formal authority in formulating and executing foreign policy. *(See "National Security Council," p. 1121, in Chapter 24, Vol. II.)*

The role of the NSC as an advisory structure is largely dependent on the influence of the national security adviser (NSA), who is both assistant to the president for national security affairs and staff director of the National Security Council. Zbigniew Brzezinski, President Jimmy Carter's NSA, often was the dominant player in advising the president on foreign policy issues, as the Iranian hostage crisis showed. In contrast, Ronald Reagan's six national security advisers were less influential with the president, eclipsed by his secretaries of defense and state. Presidents Bill Clinton and George W. Bush had a strong relationship with their national security advisers, who were integrated into their national security and foreign policy advisory teams.

In 1970 President Nixon created the Office of Management and Budget to replace the Bureau of the Budget (BOB), established in 1927. OMB is the largest of the EOP agencies—in 2005 it operated with about 478 employees. Its staff members help presidents achieve their policy objectives by formulating and administering the federal budget. Departments and agencies of the executive branch must submit annual budget requests to OMB. Besides preparing the budget, OMB serves as an important managerial tool of the president by reviewing the organizational structure and management procedures of the executive branch, assessing program objectives, and developing reform proposals. In the early 1980s, President Ronald Reagan relied heavily on OMB director David Stockman for the technical expertise necessary to implement his political objectives concerning the budget. *(See "Office of Management and Budget," p. 1112, in Chapter 24, Vol. II.)*

Recent presidents have considered the director of OMB among their closest advisers. Both Presidents Clinton and George W. Bush gave their OMB directors cabinet status and both eventually moved their OMB directors into the White House as chief of staff. Leon Panetta, Clinton's OMB director, replaced Thomas "Mack" McLarty as chief of staff in 1994, and Joshua Bolten replaced Andrew Card as chief of staff in 2006.

Cabinet Departments

The cabinet is made up of the heads, or "secretaries," of the major departments of the government. Originally, there were only three cabinet departments—State, War, and Treasury. By 2002 the number had grown to fifteen with the creation of the Department of Homeland Security. Lacking any constitutional or statutory base, the cabinet is primarily an advisory group. Although presidents may work closely with individual cabinet officers, they rarely use the collective cabinet for advice. Once President Abraham Lincoln, opposed by his entire cabinet on an issue, remarked, "Seven nays, one aye; the ayes have it." President Eisenhower, who held regular cabinet meetings and listened to opinions of others, came closer than any other modern president to making the cabinet a truly deliberative body.

Each cabinet secretary is appointed to head a specific department with a specific constituency. Although presi-

President George W. Bush, right, meets with the Homeland Security Council, Vice President Dick Cheney, and members of his Cabinet, Friday, June 1, 2007, to discuss the federal government's preparedness for the year's hurricane season in the White House Situation Room.

dents make the appointments, with Senate confirmation, the power they have over a specific department is limited. One reason is that the president can appoint only a limited number of a department's employees. When President Bill Clinton came into office in 1993, for example, he could appoint only about one hundred people to positions in the Department of Transportation—less than 1 percent of its employees. *(See Chapter 25, The Cabinet and Executive Departments, Vol. II.)*

Executive Agencies

Executive agencies are agencies or commissions that are not considered to be a part of the cabinet and that often have quasi-independent status by law. Examples of these executive agencies include the National Aeronautics and Space Administration (NASA), the Small Business Administration (SBA), and the Environmental Protection Agency (EPA).

The difference between a "presidential" agency and an "independent" agency often is vague. Generally, heads of presidential agencies and commissioners serve at the discretion of, and may be removed by, the president. Independent agency heads and commissioners are appointed for fixed terms of office and have some independence from the president in their operations.

Government corporations, such as the Tennessee Valley Authority (TVA), also fall into the category of executive agencies. Similar to private corporations, these organizations perform business activities such as operating a transportation system (Amtrak) or selling electricity (TVA). Government corporations are generally controlled by boards of directors and are run like businesses. Because the president appoints these boards and their chairs, they have come increasingly under the control of the presidency.

Regulatory Commissions

Regulatory commissions are responsible for regulating certain segments of the economy. Many of them, such as the Food and Drug Administration (FDA) and the Occupational Safety and Health Administration (OSHA), are located within cabinet departments. FDA is a part of the Department of Health and Human Services, and OSHA is in the Labor Department. Other regulatory agencies, such as the Consumer Product Safety Commission and the Federal Trade Commission, are independent in their relationship to the executive branch and so are insulated from regular presidential control and policy direction.

By statutory law each independent regulatory agency is governed by a bipartisan board of commissioners, who serve overlapping terms of five years or more. Although presidents have the power to appoint board members, they do not have the power to remove these appointees from office unless they can prove incompetence. This ensures a certain amount of independence from executive control—that is, presidents cannot fire commission members simply because they do not like the policy direction of the agency, and they cannot veto agency actions.

Still, presidents influence regulatory commission policies by choosing the commissioners and the chairs. Bipartisanship rarely means much in the composition of these boards, for presidents always have been able to name board members who share their views regardless of political party affiliation. Many conservative Democrats share the same policy beliefs as Republicans, and many liberal Republicans share the same policy beliefs as Democrats. Although commissioners serve long, overlapping terms, presidents still have the opportunity to place a majority of their appointees in any given agency.

Bureaucratic Growth and Reform

In 1789 President George Washington's administration consisted primarily of the three cabinet departments (State, Treasury, and War) and employed only a few hundred people. By 1816 the number of federal civilian employees had grown to a little more than 4,800. Only about 500 of these worked in Washington, D.C. Most of the rest were scattered throughout the country providing mail service as employees of the Post Office Department. By 1931, however, the number of federal civilian employees had reached slightly more than 600,000, and by 1953 the number had expanded to about 2.5 million. By 2005 the number of federal civilian employees had only risen to 2.7 million, after topping out at 3.2 million in 2000.

Although the number of federal employees has remained relatively constant since the 1950s , federal expenditures have continued to increase. Between 1965 and 2001, annual federal expenditures jumped from $118 billion to more than $1.8 trillion. This period also saw an increase in the number of people working for the federal government as either contractors or consultants or through grant-in-aid programs administered by state or local governments. Federal employment figures usually overlook the large and growing number of people who work indirectly for the federal government as employees of private firms and state and local governments that are largely, or entirely, funded by U.S. taxpayers. In 1978 Secretary of Health, Education and Welfare Joseph A. Califano observed that although his department employed almost 144,000 people, it indirectly paid the salaries of about 980,000 more in state and local governments through numerous grant-in-aid programs.[6]

Every president, eventually frustrated by the large and often unresponsive bureaucracy, talks of bureaucratic reform. Reform-minded presidents must move carefully, however. They must convince key members of the bureaucracy that proposed changes are worth making for the country as a whole and that they will not hurt individual bureaucrats. In addition, and far more important, presidents are subject to the same private interest pressures that afflict an individual agency. By the time they reach office, presidents have become indebted to people who have contributed to their campaigns and helped them achieve their political stature. Presidents therefore are reluctant to undermine an agency that might serve one of their clientele groups.

As a result of these factors, few presidents are successful in achieving the reforms they seek. When President Jimmy Carter came into office, he vowed to make a wholesale overhaul of the ninety-five-year-old civil service system, but the Civil Service Reform Act (1978) that finally passed Congress in Carter's second year in office had little effect. Campaigning for office, Carter had promised to reduce the nineteen hundred existing federal agencies to two hundred. After he took office, however, the campaign promise was quickly forgotten and never appeared in the civil service reform law. In fact, in attempting to win their support for the reform measure, Carter promised civil service employees, "No one will be demoted, have their salaries decreased, or be fired as a result of reorganization. You need not fear that." [7]

President Reagan entered office after pledging during the 1980 election campaign to dismantle the newly created Department of Education. Although Reagan and his White House staff urged the secretary of education, first Terrel H. Bell (1981–1984) and then William J. Bennett (1985–1988), to dismantle the department, each sought to protect the department.[8]

Some presidential reforms have been more successful. In 1993 President Clinton promised to reduce the number of federal employees, cut bureaucratic waste, and, in the process, improve the efficiency and effectiveness of the workforce by "reinventing government." After a six-month study, the National Performance Review, under the direction of Vice President Al Gore, offered several recommendations to save $108 billion and cut 252,000 jobs, mostly managerial, from the 2.9 million-person federal workforce. The final annual report of Gore's commission noted that the reforms resulted in a reduction of the federal workforce by 426,000 and savings of $136 billion. Thirteen of the fourteen departments were reduced in size; only the Department of Justice grew larger. Commission recommendations also resulted in the elimination of 640,000 pages of internal agency rules and of some 250 programs and agencies, including the Tea-Tasters Board and the Bureau of Mines. The Clinton initiative enjoyed widespread support from the public and from both Republicans and Democrats in Congress. Because the initial cuts were achieved through attrition, early retirements, and buyouts, and by cutting paperwork, the National Performance Review proposals also had widespread support among government employees' unions.

Carter's and Clinton's efforts are typical—in fact, the evolution of the federal bureaucracy has been largely a history of presidential attempts at reform. Although these efforts were aimed at reducing the power of the bureaucracy, instead they gradually increased it. In examining these recurring efforts, presidential scholar Michael Nelson has pointed out the irony in bureaucratic reform: the disparity between what reforms have intended and the actual results has led to increases instead of reductions in the power and scope of bureaucracy.[9]

The Founders were ambivalent about the exact nature of the government's administrative structure and about who was to control it. And because the subject was not mentioned in convention debates, it was not mentioned in the Constitution. Nelson argues that this ambivalence helped to create the rapid growth that later characterized the American bureaucracy. By not spelling out the exact nature of the government's administrative structure, the Founders created a situation that allowed the bureaucracy to come under the simultaneous control of both the president and Congress in the nineteenth century. The system of dual control allowed administrators to increase their own independence by playing one institution off the other. Nelson observed:

> The Constitutional Convention, in loosing the agencies from their old legislative moorings (politically necessary if the support of executive power adherents was to be won) without tying them securely to the presidency (equally politic if anti-federalist support was to be kept), forced agencies to find and exercise relatively independent power. Agencies began to learn to play one branch off of another; if neither president nor Congress was supreme, then law was, and the agencies interpreted and implemented the law.[10]

Nelson concludes that the power of bureaucracy has grown in part because of the attempts to control it. For example, early reformers, intent on controlling the bureaucracy by making it less susceptible to corruption, actually made it less efficient and responsible. To make it harder for public employees to defraud the government, agencies developed elaborate systems of internal checks and balances. These checks and balances took time to operate. Efficiency, responsiveness, or some other value often was sacrificed for the sake of preventing official cheating.

Nelson's historical account of bureaucratic reform points out that bureaucratic power usually endures even throughout the most challenging of reforms. Although the historical record indicates that reformers have unintentionally increased the power and scope of bureaucracy, attempts at reform will undoubtedly continue. Future presidents, like their predecessors, will become frustrated with the sluggishness and unresponsiveness of their administrations. Efforts at deregulation, civil service reform, and cutbacks in government expenditures that aim at removing the financial support for various bureaucratic agencies therefore will continue. Political scientist Robert Sherrill has outlined the problem: "Because so many portions of the bureaucracy are no longer responsive to the needs of the general public, and because they do their narrowly selfish work without fear of reprisal from the public, it may seem useless to talk of reform. But it isn't useless to talk of reform; it is only naive to expect much."[11]

Control of the Bureaucracy

Presidents often complain that they lack sufficient control over the executive branch bureaucracy. They are quick to blame the bureaucracy for the many problems that hinder the implementation of presidential programs. Franklin D. Roosevelt, in one of the best-known illustrations of a president's lack of control over the bureaucracy, reportedly had the following exchange with one of his aides:

"When I woke up this morning, the first thing I saw was a headline in the *New York Times* to the effect that our Navy was going to spend two billion dollars on a shipbuilding program. Here I am, the Commander in Chief of the Navy having to read about that for the first time in the press. Do you know what I said to that?"

"No, Mr. President."

"I said: 'Jesus Chr-rist!' "[12]

Other presidents faced similar frustrations later. Contemplating what it would be like for Eisenhower to be president instead of a general, Harry S. Truman once said, "He will sit here and he will say, 'Do this! Do that!' And nothing will happen. Poor Ike—it won't be at all like the Army! He'll find it very frustrating."[13] In office nineteen months, Clinton was surprised to find that a $310 million spy complex was being built without his administration's knowledge. The budget for the National Reconnaissance Office was buried in the budget for intelligence discretionary funds, known as the "black budget." Cost overruns brought the building to the attention of the Senate Intelligence Committee, which eventually disclosed the project to the Clinton administration.

Chief executives expect to have their orders obeyed and their programs set in motion. Yet upon assuming office, they often find that their programs rarely are implemented as promptly or as efficiently as they would like. They must face, and learn how to manage, an obstinate and unruly bureaucracy. Controlling the bureaucracy has become a major priority for most presidents. All presidents after Franklin Roosevelt, whether liberal or conservative, have shared the desire to make the bureaucracy more responsive to their program objectives. Historian Arthur M. Schlesinger Jr. commented: "As any sensible person should have known, the permanent government has turned out to be, at least against innovating presidents, a conservatizing rather than a liberalizing force."[14]

Presidents face a tremendous task when they try to manage the bureaucracy and make it work for them. To control a specific agency, the chief executive must know what the agency does now and did in the past, the preferences and inclinations of its members, and the pressures being put on the agency by clientele groups. In addition, the president must anticipate the political implications of the agency's actions. Ideally, the chief executive should be able to do this for the hundreds of departments, bureaus, boards, commissions, independent commissions, and public corporations under White House supervision. But even with the help of the Executive Office of the President, it is an almost impossible task. Presidential scholar Richard M. Pious wrote: "It takes a few weeks for a new administration to learn how to intervene in the affairs of a bureau; it may take a few years for the president to know enough to stay out of them."[15] Instead of being intimately involved in every little detail of an agency's affairs, a president must learn to delegate—that is, the president must be a manager. According to presidential scholar Thomas E. Cronin:

> He must constantly delegate, he must be most precise about what he is delegating, and he must know whether and for what reasons the agencies to which he is delegating share his general outlook. He must be sensitive to bureaucratic politics, to the incentives that motivate bureaucrats, and to the intricacies of their standard operating procedures. He must have some assurance (and hence an adequate intelligence system) that what he is delegating will be carried out properly.[16]

Unfortunately, most presidents have not done well in this respect. They often have misunderstood the bureaucracy and have concentrated on the goals instead of the implementation of policy. Political scientist Richard Rose has argued that "once in office, a president is much more concerned with choosing what to do than he is with how these decisions are implemented (that is, how choices are turned into routine government activities) or the conduct of program activities on a continuing basis."[17]

In addition to the problems of understanding the exact nature of the bureaucracy, presidents must face problems inherent in the political process itself that make it difficult to control their administrations. Upon entering office, presidents find that most bureaucratic institutions are already fixed. If they want to reorganize, as did Nixon, they run the risk of a confrontation with Congress. Few presidents want to risk an outcry of disapproval from a Congress that tries to protect the interests of its constituencies, who are often the clients of the existing bureaucratic agencies. Instead, newly elected presidents attempt to do the best they can with the bureaucratic structures already at their disposal. Constitutional inhibitions also make it difficult for the chief executive to fashion the bureaucracy into a more responsive institution. Presidential programs require legislative approval and appropriations, and they are subject to review, and possible nullification, by the courts. Even with statutory and constitutional authority, the president often faces untold difficulty in making the bureaucracy more responsive. Although the Constitution charges presidents with the execution of the laws, the formal authority to take that action is often statutorily vested in a cabinet secretary or the head of a specific agency. In theory, such presidential appointees will carry out the president's objectives. In practice, however, heads of departments and agencies often operate independently of the president and are more attuned to their clientele groups than to the administration's goals.

Instruments of Presidential Control

Although the obstacles to effective management of the bureaucracy are great, presidents do have two tools that afford them at least a small measure of influence: their authority to appoint top officials and their own centralized management staff—the Executive Office of the President.

Appointments. Presidents appoint fifteen cabinet heads and some six thousand other executive officials, including all members of the independent and regulatory agencies. In other words, presidents may hire or fire almost all of their top officials at will, except the board members of independent regulatory commissions. This authority gives them great control over their immediate aides and department and agency heads, but not over the vast majority of the executive branch.

In addition to the power of removal, presidents may also attempt to make appointments that are ideologically compatible with their policies. President Reagan attempted to transform departments and agencies by appointing officials who shared his desire to curb the size and influence of the federal establishment. For example, Reagan appointed Thorne Auchter, an opponent of "unnecessary" federal rules, to head the Occupational Safety and Health Administration and Robert F. Burford, who helped to lead a movement to return greater control of federal lands to the states, as director of the Interior Department's Bureau of Land Management. Similarly, President Clinton attempted to place his stamp on the bureaucracy by keeping control of appointments firmly within the White House. George W. Bush continued this practice and kept all subcabinet appointments under the control of the White House, ensuring ideological consistency throughout the administration.[18]

Centralized Executive Power. In 1933 Franklin Roosevelt found himself facing a bureaucracy staffed by holdovers from preceding conservative Republican administrations. He feared that his New Deal programs, if left to the discretion of these bureaucrats, would never be put into effect, at least not in the way they were intended. To ensure compliance with the intent of the New Deal legislation, he established numerous new agencies, such as the short-lived National Emergency Council, to coordinate directives through new and old agencies committed to his liberal programs. By adding on to the existing bureaucracy, Roosevelt created an organizational monster.

Roosevelt also found it difficult to get the information he needed to implement his policies. Frustrated by the bureaucratic mess of his administration, he asked Congress to expand his supervisory staff. Congress agreed, and on September 8, 1939, Roosevelt issued Executive Order 8248, which established the Executive Office of the President. In so doing, Roosevelt created a miniature bureaucracy to help him control the vast executive apparatus and thus expanded the modern presidency. Clinton Rossiter described the creation of the EOP as a "nearly unnoticed but nonetheless epoch-making event in the history of American institutions."[19]

Roosevelt maintained that only a strong, well-staffed presidency could provide unity and direction to the federal government. Later presidents agreed and continued trying to centralize power within the White House to control the bureaucracy. More often than not, however, such attempts overloaded the White House staff and undermined the effectiveness of the presidency. By the early 1970s, the presidency was attempting to centralize all policy at the White House by using White House staff to oversee programs of high presidential priority.[20] In attempting to centralize power within the White House, Nixon structured his staff in a way that limited his associates to those over whom he had the most control. This attempt at centralization isolated him and put him out of touch with the rest of the government.

However interested these presidents might have been in centralizing power, it did not work. The White House staff was simply not large enough to control the massive executive branch, which in the early 1970s was made up of nearly five million military and civilian employees and spent more than $300 billion annually. This observation points to the reality that no presidential mechanism has ever been large enough or powerful enough to control the bureaucracy. Some scholars maintain that presidents should not be in complete control of the bureaucracy.[21] They contend that the president's role in overseeing the success or failure of federal programs should be relinquished to the executive departments. Most federal laws, they argue, deliberately provide for discretion to be given to top departmental and agency officials. Richard Rose has pointed out that the work of the executive branch is carried out by operating departments granted specific powers and responsibilities by acts of Congress, and not by presidential delegation.[22] Therefore, both appointed and career executives should have the liberty to apply standards, revise regulations, and interpret legislative intent to fit specific situations, and the president and the EOP should not be involved in most situations. These scholars hold the view that Congress is as much in charge of administration as the president, for it is Congress that creates the laws, funds the programs, and confirms the executive branch appointments.

Most presidents oppose this view. They argue that only the president can provide the coordination necessary to master the complexity of the federal bureaucracy. Cronin summarized the presidential perspective: "Only the president should have discretion over budget choices and the administration of federal policies. He is the one charged with faithfully executing the laws. . . . [A] strong presidency makes a major difference in the way government works, and . . . this difference will be in the direction of a more constructive (desirable) set of policy outcomes."[23]

This is the position that Alexander Hamilton advocated in *Federalist* No. 70: "A feeble Executive implies a feeble execution of the government. A feeble execution is but another phrase for a bad execution; and a government ill-executed, whatever it may be in theory, must be, in practice,

bad government." [24] *(See* The Federalist, *No. 70, p. 1753, in Reference Materials, Vol. II.)*

At the heart of this argument is the idea that the government bureaucracy has become so large and diverse that the White House itself spends more time reacting to the whims of the bureaucracy than controlling it. Former presidential adviser McGeorge Bundy maintained that the executive branch often "more nearly resembles a collection of badly separated principalities than a single instrument of executive action." [25] The answer, according to this logic, is more hierarchy. An accountable president must be able to control the bureaucracy.

Information Management

Part of the problem of management is the control of information. The maxim "Knowledge is power" is never truer than in the executive branch. Presidents must deal with a highly specialized and expert bureaucracy.

Obtaining Information. How does a president gather the information necessary to make informed decisions? One way is to rely on information supplied by bureaucratic agencies themselves. But if this is the chief executive's only source of information, then the presidency runs the risk of being dominated by, or dependent on, the bureaucracy. To a large extent this dependence on the bureaucracy is unavoidable. Compared with the rest of the executive branch, the president's management staff—the Executive Office of the President—is small, usually about sixteen hundred employees. Thus the president and the EOP must make decisions on the facts and opinions supplied by the agencies themselves. But even if the EOP were enlarged to give the presidency greater information-gathering capability, it could never become large enough to provide the president with relevant information for all policy decisions for every agency. As Peter Woll has written, "The scope and technical complexity of administrative legislation and adjudication alone precludes this, even if there were no legal and political obstacles to presidential control. What is of greater importance is the fact that the president alone cannot personally comprehend these areas." [26]

Those who insist on expansion of the EOP argue that presidents need larger staffs to channel information from the multitude of agencies for which they are responsible. Because the offices within the EOP, such as the Office of Management and Budget, are not dependent on any clientele or constituency group but serve as the president's staff, they are viewed as being independent of the political pressures that other agencies endure. But the EOP suffers from political tensions just like any other executive bureaucracy. In examining the effects of information within the EOP, Woll described the need for presidents to be sensitive also to other major departments and agencies, such as the Department of Agriculture, which have powerful support from Congress.

According to Woll, "Such political support has a way of showing up in the White House sooner or later, and if OMB were continually at odds with the agencies it supposedly supervises, its job would be made impossible both politically and practically." [27] Not only do agencies outside the EOP constantly seek to channel their points of view to the White House, but EOP offices also inevitably become advocates of particular viewpoints of their own. Such advocacy within the president's own management staff poses a serious problem for chief executives who attempt to remain detached from many of their top advisers in the EOP. This detachment allows key EOP staffers to make decisions based on their own particular interests and without presidential supervision. Thus it becomes increasingly difficult for presidents to maintain the type of information surveillance necessary to remain knowledgeable and up-to-date. According to the *Tower Commission Report,* the involvement of Reagan aides Lt. Col. Oliver L. North and John M. Poindexter in the Iran-contra scandal was the result of a lack of presidential control of key advisers. Their strong advocacy of support for the Nicaraguan contras coupled with the president's lack of direction in the activities of his aides resulted in a policy disaster for the Reagan administration. [28]

Transmitting Information. Not only the gathering of information but also its transmission can be a big obstacle for presidents. The transmission of information from one level of the administrative hierarchy to another provides those who receive it with the opportunity to screen out a portion of the information before sending it on. Screening out information may be deliberate on the part of those who wish to frustrate the efforts of a president, or it may be unintentional. Economist Anthony Downs estimated that as much as 98 percent of information can be lost or distorted in this way. [29] With as large a bureaucratic structure as the president must attempt to control, the task of disseminating information is particularly formidable. Presidents cannot simply assume that their instructions, statements of policy, or program directives are traveling down the bureaucratic hierarchy as they intended. To ensure that presidential communications from the EOP have been received and accurately understood, presidents must do follow-up—that is, they must check for agency compliance and require regular feedback. Because administrative agencies resist supplying feedback in the same way that they resist sending information through regular channels, presidents must conscientiously monitor bureaucratic activity to maintain control at the top of the bureaucracy. This monitoring requires extra person-

Lt. Col. Oliver North testifies, in July 1987, before the joint House-Senate panels investigating the Iran-contra affair. North said that he and President Ronald Reagan never discussed the diversion of Iranian arms sales profits to the contra rebels.

nel; it is one reason that most presidents have called for a larger Executive Office of the President.

Building on the experience of previous administrations, President George W. Bush sought to centralize information management in the Office of Management and Budget. In mid-2001 the Bush administration established the President's Management Agenda, which was developed to ensure that the president's policy goals were transmitted throughout the administrative hierarchy of each department. Political appointees were rewarded for successfully meeting the goals of the President's Management Agenda, which often focused on budgeting issues such as privatization and outsourcing. [30] The President's Management Agenda became one of the prime vehicles that the Bush administration used in an effort to reduce federal spending, which had been a stated goal of the 2000 campaign. By fiscal year 2002, however, the Bush administration began running a budget deficit. [31] Agencies were scored on color-coded scorecards for how well the administration's management and budgeting goals had been addressed. Political executives and members of the senior executive service (SES) were rewarded personally for moving their agencies' scorecard from a red, which meant unsatisfactory, to a green, which meant satisfactory.

Permanent versus Presidential Government

Beneath this desire to manage the transmission of information throughout the federal bureaucracy more deliberately is an equally important motivation for greater presidential control of the bureaucracy—an antipathy toward, and a contempt for, the bureaucracy because of its ability to frustrate presidential policy. Most presidents never completely trust civil servants and are not completely at ease with their own political appointees. They fear that bureaucrats and department appointees develop loyalties that may obstruct presidential policy objectives. With this view comes a widely accepted belief among presidential scholars that an administration's failures result from ineffective management of the bureaucracy. Or, more specifically, an administration's failures result from the attempts of careerists (career civil servants who have made their careers in a particular department or agency) to supplant the policies of the president with those of their own.

Arthur Schlesinger Jr., a former Kennedy staffer, said of the Kennedy administration:

> Our real trouble was that we had capitulated too much to the existing bureaucracy. Wherever we have gone wrong . . . has been because we have not had sufficient confidence in the New Frontier approach to impose it on the government. Every important mistake has been the consequence of excessive deference to the permanent government. . . . The problem of moving forward seemed in great part the problem of making the permanent government responsive to the policies of the presidential government.[32]

Consequently, many presidents have sought to reform the executive branch to make the bureaucracy more responsive to their policy initiatives. They want to provide the EOP with a larger staff and greater resources for coordination of the various departments and agencies and their programs. According to Cronin, these presidents see themselves as "the recipients of endless special-interest pleas and narrowminded agitation, even from many of their own cabinet members. In its crudest form, their goal is to presidentialize the executive branch."[33] To gain control over what they perceive to be hostile environments, they push for strong bureaucratic reform measures.

Presidential scholar Louis W. Koenig has argued for reforms that would give presidents powerful administrative control over the bureaucracy:

> The strong presidency will depend on the chief executive's capacity to control and direct the vast bureaucracy of national administration. Ideally, the president should possess administrative powers comparable to those of business executives. What the president needs most can be simply formulated: a power over personnel policy, planning, accounting, and the administration of the executive branch that approaches his power over the executive budget.[34]

Nixon stands out among recent presidents for the depth of his animosity toward the bureaucracy and his suspicion that it was seeking to sabotage his administration. In line with his view of a hostile bureaucracy, Nixon attempted to adopt strategies of governance designed to decrease the role of bureaucracy and increase the power of the White House staff. After abandoning a legislative strategy to put his stamp on domestic policy, Nixon turned to an administrative strategy that called for taking over the bureaucracy and concentrating on achieving policy objectives through administrative action.

Public administration scholar Richard P. Nathan referred to the Nixon administration as the "anti-bureaucracy administration." He noted that over the course of Nixon's tenure in office "there was no reduction in mistrust of the bureaucracy. On the contrary, these attitudes hardened to the point where unprecedented reorganizational steps were planned for the second term to take control of the machinery of domestic government."[35] Hostility toward the bureaucracy could be found in several statements of Nixon's aides. One staff member referred to the "White House surrounded"—apparently by a bureaucracy more attuned to the policies of interest groups than to those of the president. In June 1972 another Nixon aide, former White House staff assistant Michael P. Balzano, described the federal bureaucracy in the following terms: "President Nixon doesn't run the bureaucracy; the civil service and the unions do. It took him three years to find out what was going on in the bureaucracy. And God forbid if any president is defeated after the first term, because then the bureaucracy has another three years to play games with the next president."[36] This view of a hostile bureaucracy probably contributed greatly to some of Nixon's later difficulties in the Watergate affair.

Nathan also pointed out that Nixon's 1973 decision to develop an administrative strategy for his second term brought up an important question. What should be the role of the elected chief executive in influencing the career professionals of the executive branch agencies? Should Congress, the courts, interest groups, the press, and the public be as powerful as the president in controlling the executive branch, or even more so? Nathan argued that the president "should have the most important role in this area of modern government. Purely as a practical matter, the chief executive is in a much better position than a large group of people in a legislative body or the courts to give cohesive policy direction and guidance to the work of large public bureaucracies."[37]

The President's Administrative Style

How the chief executive organizes the EOP affects the success of any administration. Eisenhower, pointing to the need for a president to give considerable thought to administrative organization, wrote: "Organization cannot make a genius out of an incompetent. On the other hand, disorganization can scarcely fail to result in inefficiency and can easily lead to disaster."[38]

Presidents have used different styles in running their administrations. Some are comfortable with a system that is tidy and neat; others prefer a chaotic system that allows them to be innovative. In choosing their administrative styles, they determine how much advice and information they want to receive from within government and how much they want to receive from outside. Their decisions on administrative style determine whether they will give competing assignments and have overlapping jurisdictions or rely on aides with specific and narrowly defined responsibilities. Presidential scholars have traditionally divided these patterns of presidential organization and management into two systems: circular and hierarchical.

The Circular System

Some presidents, such as Franklin Roosevelt and John Kennedy, did not adopt a system with rigid lines of responsibility. They gave staffers different jobs over time and nurtured a competitive spirit. In this way they hoped to find the best person for any given task. Political scientist Stephen Hess described this style of staff organization as "circular," with the president at the hub of the wheel.[39] With no chief of staff to filter out less important information or decide who can and cannot see the president, this system permits large numbers of people—staffers, cabinet secretaries, members of Congress—to have relatively easy access to the Oval Office. Top staffers report directly to the chief executive.

Roosevelt is the clearest example of a hub-of-the-wheel president. Choosing a wide-open, free-wheeling, conflict-loaded system, Roosevelt delighted in encouraging and cultivating chaos in his staff. Although it was seldom clear either to outsiders or insiders where the lines of authority ran, there was never the slightest doubt that Roosevelt was in charge. It was not unusual for Roosevelt to assign two of his top assistants to work on the same problem without informing either of them that the other had the same task. For example, Roosevelt pitted Secretary of State Cordell Hull against Assistant Secretary of State Raymond Moley at the International Monetary and Economic Conference held in London in 1933. The two men, both assigned the responsibility of working out a policy on protective tariffs, had widely differing views. Hull considered protective tariffs a terrible mistake, and Moley was convinced that they were indispensable to industrial recovery at home during the New Deal. Hull, who was chairing the U.S. delegation at the conference, was surprised when Roosevelt sent Moley as his personal liaison when the conference stalled. Who had more authority? Which view was closer to Roosevelt's? No one knew until Roosevelt sided with Hull. Infuriated by the whole episode, Moley resigned.

At whatever cost, Roosevelt had no intention of being isolated in the White House. He was determined to get as much information from as many people as he could, even if doing so meant duplicating assignments or bruising egos. Political scientist Frank Kessler described the Roosevelt system:

One hundred or so persons could get to him directly by telephone without being diverted by a secretary. He employed no chief of staff and permitted few of his staffers to become subject matter specialists. Except for Harry Hopkins, to whom he turned almost exclusively for foreign policy assignments, staffers were assigned problems in a variety of areas. He wanted to be sure that no staffer would become so steeped in an issue area that he would be forced to lean on that person for advice. Everyone but FDR had to be expendable.[40]

The Hierarchical System

Other presidents, such as Dwight Eisenhower and Richard Nixon, valued formal, hierarchical relationships. They felt more comfortable with an arrangement that placed greater coordinating and integrating responsibilities on a chief of staff. According to Hess, these presidents designed a highly structured pyramid system with themselves at the pinnacle.[41]

Leaning heavily on his experience in the army, Eisenhower delegated as much responsibility to his staff as possible. The key to Eisenhower's pyramid operation was Chief of Staff Sherman Adams, who served, in effect, as a deputy president. As a former member of Congress and governor of New Hampshire, Adams came to the Eisenhower administration with a great deal of government experience. Eisenhower placed much confidence in Adams and would not read memos or reports coming across his desk unless his chief of staff had seen them first. Adams wrote: "Eisenhower simply expected me to man a staff that would boil down, simplify and expedite the urgent business that had to be brought to his attention and keep . . . work of secondary importance off of his desk." [42]

The Nixon administration epitomized the pyramid staffing pattern. Similar to the Eisenhower system, Nixon constructed a highly stratified organization with himself at the top and a chief of staff standing between him and the rest of the executive branch. Because he preferred to make decisions from option papers rather than through face-to-face communications, Nixon allowed papers to get through to him more easily than people. Nixon's chief of staff (before the Watergate scandal forced his resignation), H. R. Haldeman, became known as the "Berlin Wall" because he jealously guarded the entrance to the Oval Office—even from passage by other high-level staff members. According to Kessler, "Once Federal Reserve Board Chairman Arthur Burns met Nixon for his allotted ten minutes but, on his way out, he remembered something else he wanted to tell the president. Haldeman reportedly thrust his arm across the doorway telling Burns to make another appointment." [43]

Although Nixon's operation was successful in freeing the president to think out broad policy initiatives, Haldeman often was criticized for controlling access to the president too tightly. Critics also argued that Haldeman took too much responsibility upon himself. But two other chief Nixon aides,

Chief of Staff H. R. Haldeman, left, was called the "Berlin Wall" because he jealously guarded the entrance to the Oval Office. He is shown here meeting with President Nixon and aide C. Stanley Blair.

speechwriter William Safire and national security adviser Henry A. Kissinger, contended that Haldeman was performing the very role that the president assigned him. Nixon wanted to be protected from the "unnecessary" intrusions of his lower staff.[44] Haldeman himself reportedly once insisted, "Every president needs an S.O.B., and I'm Nixon's."

Patterns of Organizational Change

Not all presidential organizational styles fit neatly into the circular or hierarchical systems exemplified by Roosevelt and Nixon, respectively. Political scientist Charles O. Jones, in *The Presidency in a Separated System,* reports that neither the circular nor the hierarchical system adequately reflects how presidents do their work.[45] Relying on these systems to explain the ways in which presidents organize their administrations may oversimplify the vast differences in presidential organization and management. Presidents face different concerns and obstacles when it comes to organizing their administrations. Jones writes: "The process of designing a presidency at the top is allowed to be quite personal, suited to the perception of needs and responsibilities of the occupant. As a consequence, there is an astonishing lack of accepted wisdom as to how it should be done." [46] Consequently, presidents often resort to trial and error when organizing and staffing their administrations.

Instead of relying on the circular or hierarchical system to describe presidential organization and management, Jones looks at organizational changes that take place within individual administrations. These changing patterns of management better portray how presidents go about their work. Jones identifies four organizational patterns of change that describe presidential administrative styles: stable, adjustable, renewable, and transitional. A stable pattern reflects a high degree of continuity in the organizational structure of a president and a high degree of continuity in the personnel serving throughout a president's term. An adjustable pattern reflects ordinary organizational adaptation and ordinary personnel changes through a president's term. A renewable pattern reflects major organizational

restructuring and substantial personnel changes during a presidency. A transitional pattern occurs when one president succeeds another.

Presidents reflect more than one organizational pattern throughout their tenure in office. For example, the administrative styles of Jimmy Carter, Ronald Reagan, George Bush, Bill Clinton, and George W. Bush do not fit neatly into the hub-of-the-wheel or the pyramid administrative system. Instead, their administrations reflect changing patterns of management.

The Carter Administration

The first two and one-half years of the Carter administration were stable, but shortly after midterm the Carter presidency undertook a renewal. This renewal reflected a change in Carter's administrative philosophy. When Carter entered office, he put in place a cabinet government and a decentralized system of administration, one in which substantial authority was to be delegated to the department secretaries. He proclaimed: "I believe in cabinet administration. There will never be an instance while I am president where members of the White House staff dominate or act in a superior position to the Cabinet." [47]

Carter originally organized his staff along functional lines instead of strict lines of command. He devised three administrative levels: the president at the top, nine key aides on the next level, and the rest of the staff below. He envisioned no pecking order. All of his aides, especially those on the level right below him, would have equal access to the president. As Carter's term progressed, the role of the White House staff increased at the expense of the various departments and agencies in the executive branch.

Part of the reason Carter's commitment to cabinet government did not last can be found in a personal work style that proved cumbersome in the White House. Carter had a passion for details that often obscured larger policy goals. Kessler wrote: "Often he overlooked the big picture because he was bogged down in particulars. Memos that crossed his desk in the Oval Office were often returned to the sender with Carter's comments penciled in the margin. He went so far as to correct his young staffer's grammar." [48] Because of his predilection for immersing himself in detail, Carter spent much of his time consuming large amounts of factual information. Early in his administration, senior career civil servants from OMB were astounded to learn that they were to brief Carter personally instead of his top aides on the defense budget. Once, in a meeting that lasted from three o'clock in the afternoon to eleven o'clock at night, the president devoured every piece of information that OMB could feed him. This commitment to detail pushed the administration away from a hub-of-the-wheel approach to a more structured pattern. Political scientist Colin Campbell has suggested that "every fiber of Carter's personal makeup had actually been conspiring all along to run a highly centralized administration. Here the president's tendency to engross himself in details served as the fifth column." [49]

In 1979, after thirty months in office, Carter, in an unusual Camp David retreat with some of his most trusted political advisers, restructured his senior staff and cabinet as his public approval ratings plummeted. The recommended personnel changes led to the resignation of six cabinet secretaries and to the appointment of Hamilton Jordan as chief of staff.

Under Jordan's direction, the White House began to solidify its control over bureaucratic operations. In the first few months of the Carter administration, cabinet secretaries and the heads of many other agencies had enjoyed great latitude in appointing people to fill vacancies. Personnel officers in each of the departments eventually were told, however, that the White House wanted to be consulted on all appointments to high government positions. This announcement was a major blow to the departments, because they had been promised great flexibility and control over their own affairs.

The Reagan and George Bush Administrations

The twelve years of the Reagan and Bush administrations represent a "transitional" presidency, moving through periods of adjustment, renewal, and, finally, transition. The Reagan administration itself moved from an early period of normal adjustment with several changes in cabinet secretaries to a period of renewal as political events unfolded during Reagan's eight years in office. As a vice president elected to follow his own party's immensely popular president, Bush faced some special problems in setting up his administration during the transition period.

Reagan cared little for the details of the presidency. Throughout his administration, he conveyed almost a nonchalance about the specifics of presidential organization and management. Preferring one-page mini-memos that boiled down even the most complex issues to the bare essentials, Reagan operated largely through massive delegation of duties. He maintained a "nine-to-five" schedule characteristic of pyramid presidents who prefer delegation to detail.

Although Reagan had certain broad policy goals he wanted accomplished, he left it to others to organize his administration to achieve these goals. The responsibility for organizing the Reagan presidency fell to James A. Baker III, Michael K. Deaver, and Edwin Meese III, all key Reagan political advisers in the 1980 presidential campaign. The result was a modified pyramid form of staffing in which authority was divided between Baker, who served as chief of staff, and Meese, who served as counselor to the president. Baker was charged with handling political matters and selling the president's programs to the public, the press, Congress, and interest groups. Meese was charged with policy formulation. Deaver's responsibilities included scheduling, appointments, and travel.

Dividing power among Baker, Meese, and Deaver, Reagan gave these three aides almost unlimited access to him in his first term. This arrangement kept Reagan from becoming completely isolated, as Nixon had become by having only a single chief of staff in Haldeman. Meese served as Reagan's political conscience, keeping him true to his conservative policy goals in domestic policy. Baker focused on legislative issues and foreign policy, and Deaver managed the day-to-day operations of the White House. It was a system that suited Reagan's personality and one with which he was comfortable.

Once in office, Reagan exercised great control over the appointment process in the departments and agencies, thereby imposing exceptional discipline on his administration. By ensuring the ideological compatibility of his nominees, Reagan could delegate and not worry about subordinates sabotaging his programs. Reagan's most effective source of discipline early in his administration, however, was OMB under the direction of David Stockman (1981–1985). By mastering the intricacies of the budget process and controlling the budgets of the various departments and agencies, Stockman was able to impose a stringent regimen on the departments and agencies and bring them under the policy directions of the Reagan administration.

The Reagan administration's pattern of renewal roughly corresponded with a changing White House staff and cabinet and events relating to the Iran-contra affair. Although Reagan had one chief of staff during his first administration, he had three during his second: Donald T. Regan, Howard H. Baker Jr., and Kenneth Duberstein. In addition, after the 1984 election Reagan's cabinet underwent five changes. There were no mass firings, but the changes after the election represented a natural point for renewal. The initial Reagan appointments drew heavily from those outside the Washington circles of power. At the point of renewal, Reagan's new appointees often reflected more experience in federal government.

Reagan attempted to maintain a modified pyramid with a tight system of discipline in formulating and implementing presidential initiatives throughout most of his administration. The success of this kind of system depends on a president knowing when to become involved in details and which issues merit concentrated attention. Many who served in the Reagan administration give the president credit for involving himself energetically in important issues such as tax reform and contra funding. One aide stated: "He [Reagan] has a ruthless sense of priorities. He really knows that he can accomplish a few things. He's going to pick some good people and let them handle the rest." [50]

Yet the success of the type of system Reagan used requires that the president have some knowledge of all issues to eliminate those issues that will not receive priority. In several instances, Reagan lacked the depth of knowledge in a specific policy area to make this determination. Political scientist Paul Quirk argues that presidents, such as Reagan, who adopt a "minimalist" approach that relies heavily on the advice of subordinates often have difficulties making intelligent decisions. He writes: "By never paying attention to the complexities of careful policy arguments, one never comes to understand the importance of thorough analysis." [51] In 1987 the *Tower Commission Report* charged that President Reagan relied too much on a bottom-up administrative system. The report noted that Reagan, by delegating too much responsibility to the NSC, did not give enough attention to important details of security policy. His inattention resulted in the secret sale of military equipment to Iran and the diversion of funds to assist U.S.-backed forces in Nicaragua during 1985 and 1986. This ill-fated undertaking became the subject of much public attention and embarrassment to the Reagan administration. The *Tower Commission Report* concluded that Reagan's management style put too much responsibility for policy review and implementation on the shoulders of his advisers: "The president should have ensured that the NSC system did not fail him. He did not force his policy to undergo the most critical review of which the NSC participants and the process were capable. . . . Had the president chosen to drive the NSC system, the outcome could well have been different." [52]

The George Bush presidency reflected a period of transition from one administration to another within the same political party. Although Bush had to live up to expectations arising from the legacy of the popular Reagan administration, he attempted to put his own stamp on his administration by appointing staffers and cabinet members who embodied his priorities. Some of those appointees, however, were holdovers from the Reagan administration. Several cabinet appointments made in the waning months of the Reagan administration appeared to be transitional appointments. Bush called on three members of the last Reagan cabinet and two others who had served in earlier Reagan cabinets to serve in his administration.

Many of those appointed to the Bush administration were longtime political associates and friends of George Bush. One of those longtime political friends proved to be an embarrassment in the early days of the Bush presidency. Former senator John G. Tower, R-Texas, was not confirmed by the Senate as secretary of defense because of problems with alcohol and women. Most Bush appointees, however, were highly regarded. Their competence allowed the president a certain amount of confidence to grant his staff and cabinet the freedom to provide direction to and control over his administration.

There was never any question about the type of management system Bush would use. He chose a chief-of-staff system similar to Reagan's. His years of service in the Reagan administration and his close association with James Baker, Reagan's former chief of staff, contributed to Bush's understanding of presidential management and the ways in which he desired to organize his presidency.

Bush modified the pyramid system, however. Unlike Reagan, Bush wanted to be somewhat involved in the day-to-day operations of his staff. With many friends and close associates on his cabinet and staff, Bush had no desire to be isolated. Although his personality and close friendships among his appointees might point to an administration organized along a hub-of-the-wheel model, Bush saw the need for a chief of staff who would keep the administration in line. For that position, he chose John H. Sununu, a former governor of New Hampshire and a Washington outsider who was not afraid to offend those who disagreed with him. Although vigorous in his pursuit of Bush's objectives, Sununu was not able to stand between Bush and his close associates within the administration. Too many staffers retained access to the president.

After the transition period, most of the Bush presidency was stable, with few adjustments and no wholesale firing of cabinet members that had characterized other administrations. Sununu met a premature demise as chief of staff—partly because of accusations that he had used air force jets for personal reasons at taxpayers' expense. Otherwise, many staffers and cabinet members remained in their positions until the end of the administration. Six of Bush's fourteen cabinet secretaries served until the next administration. Four of those who left took other jobs in the administration. The Bush presidency was one of few traumas in personnel and organization. In particular, the foreign policy team, which included national security adviser Brent Scowcroft, Secretary of Defense Richard B. Cheney, Secretary of State James Baker, and Chairman of the Joint Chiefs of Staff Colin L. Powell, brought new cohesion to the White House–cabinet relationship and added overall stability to the Bush administration.

The Clinton Administration

The way in which President Clinton set up his administration exemplified another organizational pattern not found within traditional geometric models. As is the case with all presidents, the organization of the Clinton administration directly reflects the president's personality. Clinton had run a "hands-on" campaign and wanted to extend that approach to the organization and governing of his presidency. Thus the staffing and organizing of the Clinton presidency took place in Little Rock, Arkansas, the headquarters of the Clinton campaign, under the watchful eye of the president-elect and his wife, Hillary Rodham Clinton. The result of their efforts was a loosely structured and accessible presidency, staffed largely with inexperienced Washington outsiders.

Initially, the Clinton White House was largely unstructured. Elizabeth Drew, in *On the Edge: The Clinton Presidency,* describes Clinton's governing style in the early months of his administration:

> The unhierarchical structure and the collegial style of the Clinton White House seemed, at first, wonderful. Clinton himself contributed to the informality, often wandering the halls and dropping in on aides or on the Vice President. Aides felt fairly free to drop in on him. In March, Bruce Lindsay said, "More people tend to walk in on him than probably any of his predecessors." A peephole in the door leading from the back corridor to his office enabled an aide to see if he was on the phone, or talking with people, before going in.[53]

Clinton enjoyed the informal structure. He encouraged a large number of meetings with a large number of people attending. His desire was to get as much information from as many people as possible. This allowed him to place

himself in the middle of his administration, participating directly in the formulation of policy.

Clinton initially had no desire for either a strong chief of staff, such as Sununu, or the highly structured White House organization that a strong chief of staff would necessitate. During the transition, Clinton chose Thomas F. "Mack" McLarty III as his chief of staff. McLarty, a business executive and Clinton boyhood friend, had limited Washington experience. He was to serve as an "honest broker" instead of a strong chief of staff who had unchallenged control over access to the president. The honest broker structure was designed by both McLarty and Clinton during the transition period after they had carefully studied the organizational structures of previous administrations.[54] Because McLarty did not impose a specific view or try to take charge, Clinton had the freedom he wanted to circulate among his staff in search of different views.

This nonhierarchical system with a weak chief of staff was complicated by the informal policy role assigned to Hillary Clinton. She participated in many of President Clinton's policy decisions, although her influence waned during the second term. She was heavily involved in the staffing and organization of the Clinton administration, and she continued her involvement through key policy-making roles in the administration. Drew reports that, for some Clinton aides, Mrs. Clinton appeared to serve in the first term as a de facto chief of staff, because White House staffers had to make their policy arguments to the president through her. One White House aide reportedly said: "[Mrs. Clinton] concerns herself with the overall management of the White House and what she feels is a failure to integrate the president's politics into the workings of the White House. She expresses frustration about the loose management of the White House and the inability to hold some people accountable."[55] The strong influence of Mrs. Clinton, coupled with the weak chief of staff system under McLarty, proved to be troublesome for the administration.

The Clinton White House made its first significant adjustment five months after the inauguration. In an effort to improve the management of the White House, and thus Clinton's approval rating, which had fallen steadily since he had taken office, McLarty was vested with more authority. McLarty in turn brought David Gergen into the administration as director of communications to give the Clinton presidency a more mature and moderate image. Gergen, who had served in the Nixon and Reagan White Houses, was experienced in Washington and was generally known as a political centrist. In addition, McLarty attempted to shore up lines of responsibility and to limit access to the president. The purpose was to structure the president's time better, freeing him to work more on larger policies instead of the details of policy. Despite McLarty's attempts to tighten control within the administration, it was not apparent that any real organizational change took place. There was little coordination of policy making among various groups within the White House and little clear responsibility. One Clinton aide said, "It's a floating crap game about who runs what around here. The last person who has an idea can often get it done, whether it's part of the strategy or not. The situation hasn't improved." [56]

By mid-1994 the public approval rating of Clinton's presidency and his ability to govern reached another low. Realizing that his presidency was in serious trouble, Clinton once again made significant changes in his White House staff. Acquiescing to advice from his closest advisers, Mrs. Clinton, and Vice President Gore, Clinton replaced his longtime friend McLarty as chief of staff with Leon Panetta, the budget director. Panetta was given great latitude to rearrange the White House staff. He attempted to tighten the White House organization. He controlled access to Clinton much more closely by reducing the number of meetings staffers had with the president and drastically reducing walk-in privileges to the Oval Office. He also tightened lines of authority and generally attempted to return management of the White House to a more traditional, strong chief-of-staff model. McLarty stayed on the White House staff as a counselor to the president. Because his main ally no longer held a position of significant power, Gergen was sent to the State Department. Both men eventually left the administration. Panetta, too, later left the administration and was replaced by Erskine Bowles.

With few exceptions, the Clinton cabinet was chosen for its diversity, not for experience or loyalty to Clinton. Most cabinet members had little Washington experience. One of the ways Clinton attempted to ensure loyalty, and thus control, over his cabinet was to have the White House approve subcabinet appointments. His transition team concluded that the Carter administration made a fatal organizational mistake in not ensuring the loyalty of those holding subcabinet positions. For Clinton, not ensuring loyalty from

his cabinet secretaries may have been a mistake. A few cabinet members, such as Attorney General Janet Reno, often took public positions that differed from Clinton's. This created a public perception of lack of respect for the president among some of his cabinet members.

The George W. Bush Administration

Although George W. Bush spoke disparagingly about Washington politics in his presidential campaign, once elected he set about appointing an administration of experienced Washington insiders. Many of Bush's key appointments were people who had substantial experience in past Republican administrations. Early assessments of Bush's appointments marveled at the return of the Ford administration, because of the large number of key appointees who had served President Gerald R. Ford, including most prominently Donald H. Rumsfeld. But in fact Bush also drew heavily from the ranks of those who had served in his father's administration and in the Reagan administration.

As did Clinton, Bush favored a close family associate for the position of chief of staff. But unlike Clinton's first appointee, Andrew Card came to the Bush administration with vast Washington experience. He first served in the Reagan White House and then in the George Bush administration as deputy to the chief of staff and as secretary of transportation. Card also had run the 2000 Republican national convention on behalf of George W. Bush. In the early months of the George W. Bush presidency, Card received high marks from observers for running a tightly focused and efficient staff system that enabled Bush to maintain discipline in the White House. And he did so in large part by avoiding the kind of heavy-handed leadership approach of his former boss, Bush senior's chief of staff, John Sununu.

Bush gave substantial independent authority to his vice president, Dick Cheney. Cheney was an experienced Washington politician. He had served in the Nixon, Ford, and George Bush administrations, as well as in Congress. A former White House chief of staff and defense secretary, Cheney had substantial executive branch and departmental leadership experience. In the early months of the George W. Bush presidency, some observers criticized Bush for relying on his vice president too heavily. In some Washington circles, there was speculation that Cheney was almost a co-president, effectively running the details of foreign and defense policy while Bush merely established the broad direction of his own administration. In the first year of the Bush administration, the president appointed Cheney to head two task forces: one to reduce U.S. dependence on foreign oil and the other to design a national energy policy.

Two other key Bush confidants were political strategist Karl Rove and White House counselor Karen Hughes. Rove had served as Bush's lead strategist during his 2000 cam-

President Bush and Chief of Staff Andrew Card leave the White House, Feb. 10, 2006, to speak to the House Republican Conference in Cambridge, Md.

paign. In the White House Rove directed the Offices of Public Liaison and Political Affairs. Part of his role was to oversee the development of the administration's political strategy and domestic policy agenda. Rove also informally served the role as the administration's key link to conservative constituency groups. Karen Hughes was Bush's closest adviser during his tenure as governor of Texas. Bush included Hughes in all major policy discussions in the White House and placed her in charge of the White House communications operation, including the Press Office. In the early months of the Bush administration, Hughes was one of the most visible members of the White House staff, and she was directly involved in cultivating a positive public image for the president. Nevertheless, in mid-2002 she announced that she was leaving the Bush White House and returning to private life in Texas. Another major White House appointment was Condoleezza Rice as national security adviser. Rice had served as a chief adviser to the senior Bush's national security adviser, Brent Scowcroft, and then as chief national security adviser to George W. Bush's 2000 presidential campaign.

On the cabinet side, Bush appointed experienced Washington insider Donald Rumsfeld as secretary of defense. Rumsfeld, the oldest defense secretary in history, had held the same post in the Ford administration when he was the youngest. Another familiar face, Colin L. Powell, was tapped to be secretary of state. Powell had served in both the Reagan and George Bush administrations, most prominently as chairman of the Joint Chiefs of Staff during the 1991 Persian Gulf War.

Although Bush drew heavily from past GOP administrations for his top staff, he assembled a diverse group. After the first year of the Bush presidency, a Brookings Institution study found that Bush had appointed the highest percentage

of minorities of any president to the Executive Office of the President (11 percent) and the second highest percentage of women (28 percent, just below Clinton's 29 percent). Another distinctive feature of Bush's appointments was the large proportion (29 percent) from the president's home state of Texas.[57]

Early in his term the president established two new White House units: the Office of Strategic Initiatives (OSI) and the Office of Faith-Based and Community Initiatives.[58] The OSI, headed by Karl Rove, was intended to develop long-term administration policy. The Office of Faith-Based and Community Initiatives was first headed by a Democrat and university professor, John J. DiIulio Jr. After Bush created the latter office by means of executive order, the role of the office immediately attracted criticism from constituencies concerned about the effort to develop policies that would provide government funding for religious organizations involved in charitable and other public services. DiIulio left the office in late 2001 after political battles within the White House.

In the aftermath of the September 11, 2001, terrorist attacks on the United States, the Bush administration made some important staffing decisions. Most important was the creation of a White House office, the Office of Homeland Security (OHS), headed by former Pennsylvania governor Tom Ridge. The OHS coordinated the activities of more than forty federal agencies and departments aimed at protecting the nation from terrorist activities. The OHS was led by a new Homeland Security Council composed of the OHS director, the attorney general, the directors of the Federal Bureau of Investigation (FBI), CIA, OMB, and the Federal Emergency Management Agency (FEMA); the secretaries of defense, Treasury, agriculture, transportation, and health

Condoleezza Rice and Ari Fleischer are sworn in as national security adviser and press secretary on January 22, 2001.

and human services; and the president's and vice president's chiefs of staff. However, when the Department of Homeland Security was created by Congress in 2002, the White House Office of Homeland Security lost its preeminent role.

The duties of aides in various White House offices also were shifted toward dealing with the consequences of the attacks. The administration created a Domestic Consequences Principals Committee, headed by Deputy Chief of Staff Joshua Bolten, to meet regularly and evaluate the effects of the terrorist attacks on domestic policies, although once the Department of Homeland Security was created, this committee lost its value.[59]

During the second term, Bush continued to maintain a strong chief of staff system. In 2006 first-term chief of staff Andrew Card was replaced by Joshua Bolten, who had been appointed OMB director in 2003. Bolten was viewed as having even firmer control over White House and cabinet personnel than Card had. Soon after becoming chief of staff, Bolten suggested that there would be staff changes at all levels of the administration. Within months of Bolten's statement, Secretary of the Treasury John Snow was replaced by Henry Paulson, a former partner of Bolten's at the Goldman Sachs investment firm.

Congressional Oversight

Article I, Section 1, of the Constitution states that "all legislative powers herein granted shall be vested in a Congress of the United States, which shall consist of a Senate and a House of Representatives." Section 8 lists specific congressional powers and gives Congress all powers "necessary and proper" to implement them. Over the years these provisions have been used to establish administrative agencies such as the General Accounting Office to implement congressional policies. The constitutional grants of authority have given Congress the power of life and death over these administrative agencies.

Because Congress has the power to enact laws and create and abolish executive branch agencies without presidential consent, members of Congress have significant opportunities to tell the bureaucracy what to do and how to do it. Most programs enacted into law by Congress are technical and complex, however. In an ideal world, statutes are precise and the legislature's intent is clear. But Congress, starting especially in the 1920s, began to use broader statutory language that, in the process, often delegated substantial discretionary authority to executive branch departments and agencies. Congress did so for several reasons: it did not possess the technical capacity for greater precision, it could not reach consensus on the minutiae of increasingly complex policy questions, or it concluded that the fluidity of circumstances required a degree of executive flexibility in policy implementation. As a result, Congress usually states general goals to be achieved by programs administered through bureaucratic agencies.

The Economic Opportunity Act of 1964, for example, states that the poor should have "maximum feasible participation" in the administration of the programs of the Office of Economic Opportunity (OEO). The interpretation of the act was left entirely to OEO and its local branches. Occasionally, Congress specifies precise standards that eliminate bureaucratic discretionary power, as it did in the Securities Act of 1933, which requires that investors receive financial and other significant information about securities being offered for public sale.

The very size of the *Federal Register*, a journal published each weekday in which agencies announce and publicize all the new rules and regulations used in administering programs, indicates the amount of freedom agencies have in interpreting congressional intent. Delegating this authority to the bureaucracy allows Congress to keep its workload manageable. Otherwise the volume and complexity of its work would allow Congress to accomplish little.

By giving agencies considerable leeway in realizing their objectives, however, Congress abrogates a certain amount of control over the bureaucracy. Thus a great deal of public policy is made by the bureaucracy, without any specific direction from Congress. Because administrative agencies have wide latitude in promulgating regulations and establishing policies, the burden of reconciling conflicts among competing interest groups often falls on the bureaucracy instead of on Congress. Peter Woll has written: "Theoretically, Congress still retains the primary legislative power, and is merely appointing an agent to act for it; in fact, however, virtually complete legislative discretion is given to the designated agency or to the President." [60]

Although Congress delegates to executive branch agencies much of its authority to make and implement policy, it retains considerable influence through a variety of activities known collectively as *congressional oversight.* Through laws and precedents, Congress has developed procedures that allow it to monitor the way the bureaucracy exercises its delegated authority.

The Legislative Reorganization Act of 1946 requires congressional committees to oversee those agencies that they create or that fall under their jurisdiction. For many years after passage of this act, members of Congress were more interested in creating new laws than in monitoring ones they had already made. Oversight, therefore, was not a major concern of the committees. With the growth in the 1960s and 1970s of grant-in-aid programs, which gave state and local governments federal funds to administer specific programs in areas such as highways, hospitals, and welfare services, interest groups and state and local officials encouraged legislative oversight of agencies providing goods and services to constituents.

The Legislative Reorganization Act of 1970 increased the capability of Congress to oversee federal programs by giving committees additional staffing and funds to retain outside experts. In addition, the 1970 legislation increased the resources of the General Accounting Office (GAO)—created by Congress in 1921 to oversee the expenditures of the executive branch—and gave it power to review and analyze government programs whenever a congressional committee ordered it to do so. As a consequence, the GAO hired economists, systems analysts, engineers, and management consultants to help monitor and analyze programs as requested by Congress. Despite the Pentagon's objections, during the 1970s about twelve hundred of the GAO's twenty-seven hundred professional staff audited and evaluated Department of Defense programs.[61]

Because legislation often gives an agency considerable latitude in interpreting congressional intent, the tools provided by the GAO improve committees' capacities to monitor agency actions. Committees also can hold either regular hearings or special investigations on specific aspects of a program. And they can monitor an agency's actions through informal means, such as phone calls and visits with bureaucrats, lobbyists, and constituents. Program evaluations, conducted by either the committee's staff or the GAO, often provide ways in which the agency's actions can be changed to bring it into line with what Congress intended.

Legislative oversight has become increasingly important in recent decades. According to Joel D. Aberbach, the number of days of oversight hearings conducted by House and Senate committees increased almost fourfold from 1961 to 1983.[62] One reason for the increase in oversight hearings is the tension arising from divided party control of Congress and the presidency. As divided government has tended to dominate the political landscape since the early 1950s, Congress has become more assertive in its oversight function. In 1987 a Democratic Congress formed a joint committee to investigate the Reagan administration's secret sales of military equipment to Iran and its policy of using the proceeds from these sales to aid the rebel forces in Nicaragua. In the mid-1990s, a Republican Congress exerted its oversight power to investigate the investment activities of the Clintons, known as the Whitewater affair.

Significant congressional oversight by the president's own party is, not surprisingly, far less likely, but it does occur. During the George W. Bush presidency, the Republican-controlled House of Representatives held hearings and investigated the administration's expansive use of executive privilege to conceal certain Department of Justice deliberative materials. Similarly, the Republican-controlled Senate held hearings on the president's use of signing statements as a way of changing the meaning of bills without vetoing them. The hearings led to no significant action, but Democrats obtained full control of Congress in the 2006 mid-term election, raising the possibility of more aggressive congressional oversight during the remainder of the Bush administration.

The Legislative Veto

Fearing that federal bureaucrats—or the president—might abuse the authority delegated by Congress, congressional committees frequently attach to new statutes provisions that allow the committees to pass preemptive judgment on new regulations or other bureaucratic actions. Such provisions are known as *legislative vetoes.* These provisions typically require that no regulatory action can go into effect for a prescribed length of time (such as ninety days), during which Congress can vote to disallow the regulation or action through a simple resolution of both houses, one house singly, or even one congressional committee, depending on the provision in question. These requirements give committees both a formal veto over executive actions and the authority to approve or disapprove the specific actions of an agency.

The legislative veto was first written into legislation used by President Herbert C. Hoover in his attempt to reorganize the executive branch. In 1932 Congress passed a joint resolution that allowed Hoover to reorganize executive agencies but specified that his changes could not take effect for ninety days. During this time either house of Congress by a simple resolution could veto his reorganizations, but neither did.

Perhaps the best example of the use of a legislative veto involved Congress's Joint Committee on Atomic Energy (JCAE) in the 1950s. In setting up the Atomic Energy Commission, Congress required that agency to keep the JCAE informed on the development of its nuclear reactor programs. As Richard M. Pious concluded, "In effect that provision made the committee a 'board of directors' that supervised the peaceful development of atomic energy. The committee determined what technology would be advanced, the location of experimental facilities, and policies relating to the private development of commercial power plants." [63]

The controversy over legislative vetoes grew through the 1970s as use of the device mushroomed. Notable congressional attempts to rein in the executive branch by use of the legislative veto include provisions of the War Powers Resolution of 1973, which restricted the president's power to deploy troops without a formal declaration of war, and the Budget and Impoundment Control Act of 1974, which allowed the president to rescind expenditures only if both houses of Congress approved. Congress resorted increasingly to legislative veto provisions at that time in no small part because of the partisan, ideological, and political conflicts between Richard Nixon and a Congress dominated by Democrats. Simply put, Congress and the executive were locked in a state of mutual distrust, with Congress particularly loath to allow the president more discretion than necessary in carrying out the legislature's will. Describing the effects of legislative control over the bureaucracy, political scientist Allen Schick noted that by 1983 "Congress had adopted more than 250 veto provisions; of these, more than half were enacted during the 1970s." [64]

If Congress saw the legislative veto as the most effective tool possible to ensure that the president and the bureaucracy conformed to the intent of legislation, many presidents viewed the legislative veto as a violation of the doctrine of the separation of powers and as an unconstitutional encroachment on the powers of the presidency. Worse, at least from a presidential perspective, there was no formal way for a president to respond to legislative vetoes because simple resolutions do not go to the president for approval. Legislative vetoes could not themselves be vetoed.

Although the legislative veto has been challenged by various presidents and their attorneys general, not until June 1983 did the Supreme Court rule on this congressional power. In *Immigration and Naturalization Service v. Chadha*, the Supreme Court held the legislative veto to be unconstitutional. It found that the Constitution requires in Article I that "every order, resolution, or vote to which the concurrence of the Senate and House of Representatives may be necessary . . . shall be presented to the president of the United States" who must either approve it or veto it. [65] In other words, the president must concur in any action that Congress takes that has the force of law, including the leg-

islative veto. If Congress wishes to prevent the executive branch from undertaking some action, the Court's majority ruled, Congress must either legislate in greater detail to begin with or pass a regular bill—subject to presidential review—to redress an action it deems unacceptable.

The decision in *Chadha* left unanswered the question of whether the laws to which the veto provisions were attached also were unconstitutional. To date, the Court has been reluctant to go that far. Congress for its part has adapted to life after *Chadha* in two ways. On the one hand, Congress has gone back to using more explicit statutory language, which raises complaints about congressional micromanagement. On the other hand, Congress has resorted to adding even more language in appropriations bills forbidding funding for some specific bureaucratic or presidential actions. This language provides the functional equivalent of a legislative veto if the president accepts the appropriations bill as a whole. The Court has yet to rule on this strategy. Critics of congressional oversight and the legislative veto argue that instead of allowing committees to oversee agencies effectively, the legislative veto gives too much influence to interest groups. They contend that alliances between an agency, its constituent group, and its congressional committee compromise the ability of the committee to monitor agency activities objectively. According to this theory, because the congressional committee is "captured" by the interest groups it serves, its oversight of agencies and programs will be biased to benefit the constituent groups.

Since the *Chadha* decision, Congress has passed numerous laws containing legislative vetoes. Thus presidential expert Louis Fisher argues that the legislative veto continues to survive "by open defiance and subtle evasions" of *Chadha*.[66] For example, in 1989 President George Bush entered into an informal agreement with Congress, known as the Baker Accord, that restricted the executive branch in its efforts to aid the contras in Nicaragua by requiring that four congressional committees agree to the aid.

Problems of Presidential Control

Congressional oversight and the legislative veto make it much more difficult for the president to control the bureaucracy. Through a variety of oversight techniques, Congress has made significant gains in controlling both foreign and domestic bureaucratic agencies. For example, congressional oversight helped thwart the efforts of the executive branch in its bombing of Cambodia in 1973 and inhibited various other covert intelligence activities during the Nixon years. Political scientists Thomas Franck and Edward Weisband argued that executive dominance in foreign policy has been replaced by a system of policy codetermination in which power is shared by the president and Congress.[67]

As a result, presidents have learned to live with congressional efforts at bureaucratic control, often signing bills that include oversight and veto provisions not completely to their liking. Franklin Roosevelt signed the Lend-Lease Act, under which he lent American destroyers to Great Britain before the United States officially entered World War II, and other wartime measures that gave him extensive war powers, despite the constraints that Congress put on him. Nixon signed the 1974 Impoundment Control Act granting him authority to defer the spending of funds already appropriated by Congress, although either house could veto his actions. Almost any statute that delegates congressional authority to the executive branch will contain provisions for legislative review.

Presidential control of the bureaucracy, however, has not been replaced by congressional control. Congress is much too large and much too overworked to provide effective control of the bureaucracy. According to Pious, "Although Congress' oversight role has increased in recent years, it should not be exaggerated. It is still intermittent, especially in the Senate, where members are spread too thin, serving on too many committees and subcommittees to develop expertise in agency operations." [68]

Reorganization Power

Because the president and Congress often find themselves opposing each other for control of the bureaucracy, presidents frequently look to reorganization as a means of gaining the upper hand and increasing their ability to manage their administrations. In pursuing their reorganization plans, however, presidents find that the affected agencies are strongly protected by their sponsoring congressional committees. Without the cooperation of Congress, it is extremely difficult for presidents to effect any reorganization plan for making the bureaucracy more efficient.

Every president wants to coordinate policy-making efforts as much as possible, but because the number of federal programs has increased rapidly, coordination of the many agencies and departments is difficult. In the area of transportation policy alone, the president must work not only with the Department of Transportation but also with the National Transportation Safety Board and the Federal Maritime Administration, as well as other agencies. This overlap among the agencies means that the executive branch often wastes time and effort trying to manage the development and implementation of public policy.

Brownlow Committee

The first real effort at administrative reorganization recognized these problems of inefficiency in the executive branch. Franklin Roosevelt wanted to establish a line of command that ran directly from the White House through the department secretaries to their subordinates. In March 1936, he created the Committee on Administrative Management and gave it the task of planning the overhaul of the executive branch. With Louis D. Brownlow as its chairman and political scientists Charles E. Merriam and Luther Gulick as the other members, the Brownlow Committee concluded in 1937 that the executive branch under Roosevelt had become so complex that "the president needs help." [69]

The Brownlow Committee specifically recommended that the president receive increased administrative support. It proposed the creation of six new presidential assistants, "possessed of high competence, great physical vigor, and a passion for anonymity," who would be assigned at the president's discretion. In addition, it recommended that discretionary funds be put at the president's disposal to allow him to acquire more help as needed. Finally, the committee proposed a major organizational addition to the presidency, consisting of the Executive Office of the President, with the Bureau of the Budget as its centerpiece. [70]

Roosevelt won approval from Congress in 1939 for some of the Brownlow Committee's recommendations, including placing the Civil Service Commission under the control of the White House. He was given reorganization authority for a two-year period. In addition, Roosevelt was permitted to hire the six assistants that the Brownlow Committee recommended.

In Reorganization Plan No. 1, the president moved three EOP offices—the Bureau of the Budget, the Central Statistical Board, and the National Resources Planning Committee—into the State, War, and Navy Building next door to the White House. Soon after Reorganization Plan No. 1, Roosevelt issued an executive order that delineated the organization and responsibilities of the newly expanded presidency. This order detailed the formal relationships in the EOP among the White House Office, the BOB, and the remaining agencies of the executive branch.

Although Roosevelt got much of what the Brownlow Committee had recommended, the reorganization bill that finally passed Congress in 1939 was less than what he had hoped. The original bill was introduced in 1937 and became embroiled in Roosevelt's attempt to modify the composition of the Supreme Court. The final bill was a compromise and lacked most of Roosevelt's initial proposals. According to Peri E. Arnold, "It [the Reorganization Act of 1939] was on its face a congressional product, drafted under the guidance of Representative Lindsay Warren (D-N.C.) as a way of short-circuiting the intense, negative connection between presidential strength and the reorganization program." [71] Even so, the main thrust of the Brownlow Committee's recommendations was preserved, with regard to both structural changes and the intent to strengthen the president's control over the administration. Although Congress has been reluctant to go along completely with presidential recommendations to extend top-level management, it has allowed presidents to gradually centralize control over the bureaucracy in the EOP.

First Hoover Commission

The next major effort at centralizing presidential control occurred during the Truman administration. After large gains in the congressional elections of 1946, Republicans anticipated the end of the Truman presidency in 1948. The Republican-controlled Congress approved legislation to help a new president grapple with the problems of executive branch organization by setting up the Commission on the Organization of the Executive Branch of the Government. In 1947 Truman appointed former president Herbert Hoover as chairman.

Hoover set about the task of evaluating the effectiveness of executive branch organization with much enthusiasm. Truman, who could have viewed the commission as a means of criticizing his administration, also was enthusiastic about the project and gave it his full cooperation. It is one of the ironies of the U.S. presidency that Truman was the one to benefit from the Hoover Commission's efforts when the Republicans failed to capture the presidency in 1948.

The Hoover Commission report recommended 277 specific measures that would institute "a clear line of control from the president to these departments and agency heads and from them to their subordinates . . . cutting through the barriers that have in many cases made bureaus and agencies practically independent of the chief executive." [72] The commission's report charged that the executive branch was unmanageable; its lines of communication and authority were confusing; and too few tools existed at the top for the development of effective policy.

The commission suggested three major areas of reform. First, department heads should assume the major authority within their departments instead of allowing it to reside in the bureau chiefs. This recommendation was aimed at overcoming the congressional practice of vesting statutory powers directly in agency chiefs. With department heads more easily held responsible to the president, the lines of authority and responsibility would be more distinct. Second, the commission wanted to achieve greater clarity of direction and greater control by grouping the executive branch agencies into departments "as nearly as possible by major purposes in order to give a coherent mission to each department." [73] Third, the commission recommended that the EOP be strengthened by giving the president a stronger staff, including a staff secretariat in the White House. The president should have absolute freedom in dealing with this staff, giving it shape, and appointing its members.

Truman enthusiastically supported the commission's recommendations, and both Congress and the public gave their support to most of the report's proposals. Eventually, the most important recommendations were realized. The recommendations calling for a larger presidential staff and discretion in the use and organization of the EOP were implemented. And, after the commission's proposals, the Post Office and the Departments of Interior, Commerce, and Labor were reorganized. The NSC and some independent agencies, including the Civil Service Commission and the Federal Trade Commission, also were reorganized.

By and large, the success of the reforms reflected the nonpolitical nature of the report. Hoover and his commission approached the presidency solely in managerial terms without engaging in political ideology. Arnold has observed, "At one and the same time, reorganization planning aimed at strengthening the presidency while presenting the issue of enhanced presidential capacity as merely managerial and irrelevant to politics. Herbert Hoover and his commission of 1947–1948 present perhaps the most successful application of that logic within reorganization planning's history." [74]

Second Hoover Commission

When Dwight Eisenhower came to office in 1953, he faced a bureaucracy that had grown tremendously since Hoover, the last Republican president, had left office in 1933. After twenty years of Democratic control of the presidency, few Republicans had experience in running the federal government. In fact, after years of opposing big government and big spending, Republicans now found themselves in charge of the same government they had criticized. Further complicating things for Eisenhower was a bureaucracy composed mostly of Democrats appointed under Democratic presidents. Searching for a way to make the executive branch more responsive to his leadership, Eisenhower in 1953 called once more on Hoover—at that time seventy-nine years old—to head the Commission on the Organization of the Executive Branch of Government (the Second Hoover Commission).

The First Hoover Commission had been interested primarily in improving the administrative management of the executive branch; the Second Hoover Commission focused on issues of policy and function. At the heart of its recommendations was the idea that the executive branch should reduce its scope—saving money, reducing taxes, and eliminating competition with the private sector. The Second Hoover Commission had a specific conservative ideological agenda that aimed at reducing the growth of the government since the New Deal. It argued that many of the Roosevelt-era programs and agencies had become counterproductive. [75] The commission was more concerned with prescribing what government should do rather than how it should be organized and managed.

Most of the commission's recommendations were of only indirect value to the Eisenhower administration as it wrestled with the problems of a massive executive bureaucracy. Yet for the first time a major reorganization report dealt with the relations between political appointees and career public servants. Among its specific recommendations was the creation of a Senior Civil Service made up of approximately three thousand upper-level career executives serving in administrative positions. The commission proposed that these senior civil servants be able to transfer from one agency to another if their particular skills and competencies suited those agencies. These senior civil servants would constitute a personnel pool that would be rotated regularly to improve management quality. The idea finally became incorporated into general personnel practices in the executive branch with the establishment of the Senior Executive Service in 1978.

Ash Council

In April 1969 Richard Nixon sought to simplify the domestic side of policy making in the executive branch by creating the Advisory Council on Executive Organization. Intending to use private sector strategies in reorganization planning for his administration, Nixon appointed industrialist Roy Ash, president of Litton Industries, as chair and named four other private citizens to the council. Known as the Ash Council, the reorganization group set out to address three problems: the executive branch's response to increasing demands on the federal government; the organizational problems of the more than 150 executive branch departments, offices, and agencies; and the organizational complications arising from intergovernmental relations.[76]

The Ash Council recommended that the executive branch's domestic programs be directed by a small number of major-purpose superdepartments. The council believed that this reorganization not only would save the government money but also would increase the effectiveness of executive branch management. Specifically, the council proposed that the secretaries of the superdepartments would be assisted by a small number of secretarial officers who would hold department-wide responsibilities. Secretarial officers would include a deputy secretary who would serve as an alter ego and department manager for the secretary, two undersecretaries, several assistant secretaries, and a general counsel. The recommendations pointed to a desire to "facilitate decentralized management while simultaneously providing for effective secretarial control and department cohesion." [77]

President Nixon sent four departmental reorganization proposals to Congress on March 25, 1971. These proposals would have abolished seven existing departments and replaced them with four new superdepartments. The new Department of Natural Resources would have merged the Interior Department with parts of Agriculture, Defense, and Commerce. The Department of Health, Education, and Welfare would have become the Department of Human Resources. The Department of Community Development would have combined Housing and Urban Development with some of the remaining parts of Agriculture. And the Department of Economic Affairs would have combined Labor with parts of Commerce. But none of the departmental bills ever got out of their congressional committees, and Nixon eventually lost interest in the superdepartments.

Some of the Ash Council's recommendations did become important to executive branch reorganization, however. In its recommendations on the EOP, the council proposed the creation of a Domestic Council and the conversion of the Bureau of the Budget into the Office of Management and Budget. Nixon incorporated these proposals into his Reorganization Plan No. 2, which he submitted to Congress on March 12, 1970.

The Ash Council intended for the Domestic Council to serve as a domestic counterpart to the NSC. It would be a cabinet-level advisory group composed of the president, the vice president, the attorney general, and the secretaries of the Treasury, interior, agriculture, commerce, labor, transportation, housing and urban development, and health, education, and welfare. The important changes to the Bureau of the Budget included expanding its managerial, policy coordination, and program information functions in its reincarnation in the OMB. Both President Nixon's reorganization efforts and the Ash Council's recommendations sought through reorganization to centralize executive branch policy formation in the EOP.

Under the authority granted by Congress through the periodic extension of the Reorganization Act of 1949, presidents could reorganize executive branch entities as they pleased. Congress retained oversight of such reorganizations through a legislative veto provision in the reorganization act.

President Carter used this method several times while in office. In 1978, for example, he ordered four thousand workers involved in border inspection to move their operations from the Justice Department to the Treasury Department. He also shifted thirty-five hundred people from the firearms and explosives division of the Treasury Department to the Justice Department. In 1977 Carter exerted his reorganization powers to their fullest when he established a whole new Energy Department, absorbing two independent agencies—the Federal Power Commission and the Atomic Energy Commission. In 1979 he divided the Department of Health, Education, and Welfare into two new departments, the Department of Education and the Department of Health and Human Services. Congress, however, refused to renew the reorganization act after the Supreme Court declared legislative vetoes unconstitutional in 1983. As a result, executive branch reorganizations must now be achieved through normal legislative procedures. As part of Vice President Gore's National Performance Review to "reinvent government" by making it more efficient, President Clinton reorganized the Department of Agriculture by legislation. In 1994 Congress passed his proposal to merge or eliminate a number of the department's forty-three agencies and reduce staff and personnel.

In 2005 the Bush administration sent Congress the proposed Government and Program Performance Improvement Act of 2005, which would grant the president wide-ranging powers to reorganize the federal government. The key provision in the bill was to provide fast-track authority for specific reorganization proposals. Congress would not be allowed to amend the president's reorganization requests, only vote them up or down. The legislation never reached a floor vote as the 2006 midterm elections neared and the president's approval ratings dipped low, into the mid-30 percent range.

THE APPOINTMENT POWER

As the size of the federal government has grown, presidents have been forced to delegate more and more of their administrative responsibilities to an increasing number of political executives. No single chief executive can make all the important policy and administrative decisions necessary to carry out the functions of the U.S. government. Consequently, one of the most important administrative powers that presidents have is their ability to recruit and appoint people to fill high-level positions in their administrations.[78]

Article II, Section 2, of the Constitution gives the president the power to appoint top political executives. The language of the Constitution separates the appointment process of major executive officers into a two-step procedure shared by the president and the Senate. The president recruits and nominates potential appointees, and the Senate either confirms or rejects the president's appointments. The Constitution also gives Congress the ability to place other appointments within the prerogative of the president (such as the White House staff) or of the department heads without Senate confirmation.

Although the Constitution gives the chief executive the responsibility for selecting the approximately 2.7 million civilian employees (as of 2005) of the executive branch, over the years the chief executive has given up much direct participation in the process to the federal civil service system. Until the 1880s most executive branch jobs were apportioned through *patronage,* the system of granting favors and filling jobs as political rewards. Under such a system, nineteenth-century presidents were able to place their friends and allies in federal government positions. Since 1883 and passage of the Pendleton Act, which created the Civil Service Commission, most agencies must now choose their employees according to their qualifications and ability to do the job. *(See "The Federal Civil Service System," p. 1299, in Chapter 28, Vol. II.)*

Because more than 90 percent of executive branch positions are covered by the civil service, only the most senior executive positions are filled by presidential appointees. For example, the Clinton administration could appoint only

222 (less than 1 percent) of the 37,485 employees of the Department of Commerce. By choosing personnel for these positions, presidents articulate their political goals to the bureaucracy.

[H]e shall nominate, and by and with the Advice and Consent of the Senate shall appoint Ambassadors, other public Ministers and Consuls, Judges of the supreme Court, and all other Officers of the United States, whose Appointments are not herein otherwise provided for and which shall be established by Law; but the Congress may by Law vest the Appointment of such inferior Officers as they think proper in the President alone, in the Courts of Law, or in the Heads of Departments.

—from Article II, Section 2

At the beginning of a new administration, Congress publishes *Policy and Supporting Positions*—known as the "plum book"—which lists the top executive branch positions available for direct presidential appointment, many of which require Senate confirmation. Each new presidential administration must appoint approximately 200 members of the White House staff, 15 department heads, 400–500 members of the subcabinet, 93 U.S. attorneys, and approximately 150 ambassadors. In addition, agency and department heads appoint 600–800 members of the Senior Executive Service and about 1,800 special aides in Schedule C positions, which are exempted from the testing and qualification requirements of the civil service merit system. Altogether, presidents and their subordinates must appoint about 5,200 people to the executive branch.[79] Of these, political scientist Hugh Heclo estimates that presidents are most interested in approximately 300 top political executive posts—cabinet secretaries, undersecretaries, assistant secretaries, and bureau chiefs.[80]

Because executive appointees link the president to the vast organizational components of the executive branch, the right to make such appointments is extremely important to the chief executive's ability to control the disparate components of the federal government. To ensure effective leadership, presidents look for competence and loyalty in their appointees.

The sixteenth-century political theorist Niccolo Machiavelli observed, "The first opinion that is formed of a ruler's intelligence is based on the quality of men he has around him."[81] This observation suggests that an administration is only as good as the people the president appoints to fill it. The immense size of the executive branch makes it impossible, however, for presidents to know most of the people they appoint, much less to make personal assessments of their quality. Upon winning the presidency after several months of campaigning, John Kennedy complained about trying to fill many of his top positions: "People, people, people! I don't know any people. All I know is voters! How am I going to fill these 1,200 jobs?" [82] Kennedy knew fewer than half of his final cabinet appointments.

Some new appointees come to their positions well qualified, but others do not. What occupational and educational characteristics do presidential appointees have? Between 1982 and 1985 a National Academy of Public Administration survey found that 40 percent of federal appointees are transferred or promoted from other positions in the government. Sixty percent, however, come from occupations outside the federal government: 24 percent from business, 16 percent from academic and research communities, 12 percent from the legal profession, 7 percent from state and local governments, and 1 percent from other organizations. The educational level of presidential appointees is relatively high: 19 percent hold bachelor's degrees, 21 percent hold master's degrees, 17 percent hold Ph.D.s, and 34 percent hold law degrees.[83]

In addition to competence and loyalty, presidents consider other factors when making their selections. Most presidents have accumulated many political debts, including money and votes, on their way to the White House, and so they look for ways to reward their chief supporters with major political appointments. Although these selections usually do not constitute the majority of a president's appointments, they are an important consideration. President Truman, for example, appointed banker John Snyder and Democratic National Committee chair Robert Hannegan, both old friends from Missouri, to the positions of Treasury secretary and postmaster general, respectively. Early in his administration, President Clinton appointed Thomas F. "Mack" McLarty III as chief of staff and Mickey Kantor as U.S. trade representative. Both were friends and longtime supporters.

Presidents also make many appointments for purely political reasons. The first presidential personnel selections are the most important politically—they set the tone and priorities of a presidency and so are subject to close public scrutiny. In his study of presidential cabinets, political scientist Richard F. Fenno Jr. commented: "The presidential decisions leading to the composition of a new 'official family' are taken during the peak period of public interest which attends the national election campaign. As executive decisions go, they are pre-eminently concrete and visible. Among the earliest of presidential moves, they are treated as symbolic acts of considerable significance." [84] In addition, presidents consider in what ways future political relationships will be affected by their early choices. An administration's success often depends on the ability of the president to forge political alliances and broaden the presidency's base of support. The president's circle of political allies frequently can be expanded through the appointment process. Finally, presidents often use appointments to get on the good side of members of their own political party, interest groups whose support they seek, and, often, members of Congress.

This strategy can backfire, however. William Howard Taft, quoting Thomas Jefferson, used to lament, "Every time I make an appointment I create nine enemies and one ingrate." As political scientist Calvin Mackenzie wrote: "The selection process, particularly in the early stages of a new administration is governed by scarce resources and multiple, competing demands. Opportunities exist for gaining some political advantage from these early personnel choices, but, if used unwisely, those opportunities are easily squandered." [85]

Another important consideration in presidential appointments is the presidency's managerial needs. As the bureaucracy has become more technologically complex, presidents have had to choose appointees who bring with them managerial and administrative capabilities Recent studies have indicated that presidential appointees may lack the expertise and management skills necessary to oversee complex federal programs because presidents increasingly appoint political loyalists instead of policy experts. Presidential scholar David Lewis examined whether presidential appointees or career staff members in the George W. Bush administration had a stronger record of managing programs effectively. His study concluded that career managers tended to be better program administrators than political appointees. As Lewis noted, his findings "confirm the underlying logic for the creation of the merit system which was to provide a competent, stable, and expert administration of government through the creation of a career civil service." [86]

Although many presidents desperately seek better management, rarely are appointments made on the basis of objective consideration such as management ability. Most jobs are filled immediately after the presidential election, when presidents have the largest number of appointments to make and the least amount of time to consider them. Ironically, at this point in their administrations, when they are best able to lure potential appointees, presidents often are unable to take full advantage of one of their greatest administrative powers. The ability to manage may be one of the last considerations applied to a potential appointee, both because the administration is unable to judge its management needs and because political considerations outweigh managerial skill. Characteristics such as an appointee's geographic or ethnic background are often much more obvious and easy to consider than administrative ability.

No matter how well intentioned they may be in trying to fill their appointments, most presidents rarely succeed in accomplishing their objectives in the appointment process. For example, President Clinton started the staffing process during his campaign. Wishing to instill loyalty and new ideas in his administration, he developed an appointment strategy that emphasized centralizing power in the White House by appointing loyal but qualified individuals. This philosophy of controlling all appointments from the White House, which reflected Clinton's tendency to micromanage, resulted in serious problems for his administration. For one thing, the White House transition team was slow filling positions below the secretary rank. Because subcabinet positions had to be either filled or approved by the White House to ensure loyalty, the process was cumbersome. Clinton would sometimes question a cabinet member's entire slate of nominations because it was not diverse enough or because a single nominee's credentials looked suspect. This had the effect of sending the entire slate back to the secretary. As a result, secretaries often complained that they were understaffed and overworked in the first year or so of the administration. In addition, the emphasis on personal loyalty to Clinton meant that few appointees had any Washington experience. In fact, many appointees felt hostile to Washington and were determined to keep the Clintons out from under its spell.[87]

As a result of the contested results of the 2000 presidential election, President George W. Bush had an unprecedented short election transition period to make his appointments. Given this truncated period, Bush set about making his key appointments at a quicker pace than that of his predecessors. As a result of that effort and a somewhat quickened pace of Senate confirmations, in the first year of the Bush administration confirmation of presidential appointees required an average 7.9 months, compared with 8.3 months during the first year of the George Bush and Clinton administrations.

Bush's appointees in both his first and second terms tended to be experienced in political Washington and were drawn heavily from his home state of Texas. Consequently, early in Bush's tenure the staff worked together in a collegial fashion and were able to avoid the kind of infighting that has characterized some recent presidential staffs. In addition to experience, Bush placed enormous priority on a history of loyalty to the president as a criterion for choosing staff members. Later, as the country declared a "war on terrorism," the experience and compatibility of Bush's staff appeared to pay off for the administration. As former presidential adviser and scholar Bradley H. Patterson Jr. writes: "No one, but no one, will have to remind Dick Cheney, Colin Powell, Don Rumsfeld, Condoleezza Rice, Paul O'Neill, Andy Card, or Nick Calio who is president, or will need to remonstrate them about not fighting their policy differences in public and not undermining their colleagues by leaking [stories] to their favorite columnists."[88]

Constraints on the Appointment Process

The postelection rush to fill vacancies in the new administration places constraints on the appointment process. Between the election and the inauguration, the president works to establish the policy objectives of the administration. While still forming their policy objectives, presidents or their subordinates must make the vast majority of their most important appointments. Cronin has noted: "Too frequently appointees are not carefully related to policy. Many subcabinet appointments, for example, are made by subordinates, with the president hardly aware of whether the appointee is matched with the position."[89] Once in office many appointees adopt new attitudes as a result of their new institutional responsibilities, or some, perhaps ill-suited for institutional management, may become rigidly wedded to the views of the interest groups with which they most frequently interact.

Presidents often find it difficult to persuade their potential nominees to give up high-paying positions in the private sector and move to Washington, D.C. Since the early 1970s, the gap between the salaries paid to private executives and the salaries paid to those in the federal government who perform equivalent work has grown wider. In 1980 the Commission on Executive, Legislative, and Judicial Salaries concluded: "There is growing evidence that low salaries are a major reason for highly talented people declining appointment to key positions in the federal government."[90]

The question of whether salary was a significant obstacle in recruiting staff for senior administration positions was raised again by a 2002 Brookings Institution study. The study concluded that the gap between private sector and public sector salaries was growing. While the private sector may provide greater financial incentives than the public sector, however, the study concluded that "no one can be sure whether these trends in pay inside and outside the government have affected the caliber of people who serve in top federal positions."[91] Although salary may influence the decision of some candidates for senior positions, it does not seem to be a major factor for many others. Some view public service as an important civic contribution, and others view their government connections as a stepping-stone to future earning power when they return to the private sector.

Sometimes presidents have found it difficult to persuade potential nominees to disclose their financial background and income. Because the American public expects executive branch officials to perform their duties without undue regard for special interests, Congress passed strict financial disclosure laws in 1965. Certain top executive branch employees were required to report information about their personal finances to the head of the Civil Service

Commission, who could report this information to the president if there seemed to be a conflict of interest. Title II of the Ethics in Government Act of 1978 broadened disclosure provisions by requiring all presidential appointees to complete the Executive Personal Financial Disclosure Report, which publicly discloses their personal financial information. These provisions have been a source of great concern for many potential appointees. E. Pendleton James, President Reagan's assistant for personnel, stated that "literally hundreds" of potential presidential nominees lost interest as a result of demanding disclosure provisions.[92]

Similarly, presidents must sometimes pass up potential nominees because of the person's involvement with a past administration, a scandal, or even the appearance of wrongdoing. For example, in 1989 former senator John Tower was nominated by George Bush as secretary of defense but was forced to withdraw under opposition from Congress over charges of womanizing and excessive drinking. In *The Confirmation Mess,* law professor Stephen L. Carter argues that the current system for approving presidential nominations demands that more attention be paid to the "disqualifications" than to the qualifications of a nominee. He writes: "We presume the nominees to be entitled to confirmation absent smoking guns, and then we look for the smoke in order to disqualify them." [93] In short, presidents face enormous difficulties in finding appropriate candidates in a shrinking pool of potential nominees who are willing to go to Washington. The difficulties in finding those willing to serve are exacerbated by the fact that appointees must face intense, and often excessive, public scrutiny.

The Role of the Senate

The Senate is an integral part of the appointment process and serves as one of the most important limits to the presidential appointment privilege. The Constitution bestows on the Senate the power to confirm most of the president's major appointments. As a result, the Senate views the appointment procedure as a process in which its members should have a considerable say. As Calvin Mackenzie has observed, "For Senators and Senate committees, the confirmation process is both a responsibility and an opportunity." [94] It is both a constitutional responsibility and a political opportunity. Senators view the appointment process as a way to influence government policy. Cronin has noted that senators even try to influence presidential policy by getting the president to nominate their choices: "They . . . often have candidates of their own. This is especially the case in recent years, for as the staffs of Congress have expanded . . . there are more and more aides to Congress who seek top executive branch appointments." [95]

The number of presidential nominations sent to the Senate for confirmation is staggering. The Senate must process between 90,000 and 170,000 nominations during each Congress (two-year period). Usually, the vast majority of these nominations are routine military commissions and promotions that require little of the Senate's time. Although the number of civilian appointments is much lower, the Senate must still spend a great deal of time and energy processing them. In 1989, the first year of the George Bush administration, the Senate received more than forty-eight thousand nominations, forty-five thousand of which were routine military commissions and promotions. Most of the rest were routine nominations to such civilian organizations as the Foreign Service, the Public Health Service, and the National Oceanic and Atmospheric Administration. Nominations to top-level policy-making positions in the executive branch—which average only about six hundred a session—require far more attention from the Senate than the routine appointments.

Like most other matters before Congress, the nomination process is handled almost entirely by standing (ongoing) committees. Although each committee has different sets of procedures for managing the appointments referred to them, most committees have developed their own standard procedures. Usually, these procedures require additional background checks and financial disclosures, other than those already required by the president's personnel director and the Ethics in Government Act of 1978, and extensive hearings. The result of this rigorous and lengthy investigative process has been an increase in demands on potential appointees. In his study of the Senate's role in the presidential appointment process, political scientist Christopher J. Deering pointed out that this demanding investigatory process has made the Senate's role in the nomination process not only more thorough but also more demanding: "Unfortunately, the process has . . . become more tedious, time-consuming, and intrusive for the nominees. For some the price is too high." [96] The process is made all the more tedious by the fact that from 1981 to 2001 Congress added more than a hundred new and reclassified positions in the cabinet departments that require Senate confirmation.[97]

The Founders intended the Senate's constitutional role in the presidential appointment process to serve as a check on executive power. But to what extent has the Senate checked presidential power through its confirmation power? All presidents have been successful in getting the majority of their nominees confirmed. For example, more than 92 percent of all civilian presidential nominations were confirmed by the Ninety-eighth Congress (1983–1985). *(See Table 29-1, p. 1345, Vol. II.)* Most nominations that are defeated are defeated in committees. Since 1960 only six nominees have been defeated on the floor of the Senate.

Many presidents have had a few of their potential appointees rejected. The Senate regularly thwarted the efforts of James Madison and Ulysses S. Grant to nominate their choices for executive branch positions freely. John Tyler perhaps had the most difficulty with the Senate in attempting to fill vacancies. His appointees were frequently rejected by the Senate, including four cabinet and four Supreme Court appointees. In one day in 1843, the Senate rejected Tyler's nomination of Caleb Cushing as secretary of the Treasury three times. In 1984 President Reagan's nominee for associate attorney general, William Bradford Reynolds, was turned down by the Senate Judiciary Committee. His opponents argued that Reynolds had been negligent in enforcing antidiscrimination laws during his tenure as chief of the Justice Department's Civil Rights Division.

Nominations are often withdrawn it if becomes apparent that the Senate opposes a particular candidate. For example, in the early months of the Clinton administration two nominations to the Justice Department were withdrawn when it became obvious that the Senate would not confirm the president's nominees. Although the Senate does not often reject a presidential nominee, the thoroughness of its investigations of those who are confirmed and its occasional threats of rejection indicate that the Senate does exert some control over the president's prerogative to appoint key members of the administration. George W. Bush often resorted to recess appointments when the Senate failed to confirm his nominees. John Bolton, nominated as ambassador to the United Nations, was given a recess appointment in January 2005 after strong Senate opposition emerged among Democrats and some Republicans. A recess appointee, however, may remain in office only until the last recess of the two-year session of Congress.

Sometimes the Senate uses its confirmation power more as a political bargaining chip than anything else. It will often hold the nominee in limbo until the president agrees to support a particular political position. For example, President Reagan's nomination of Edwin Meese as attorney general was used by the majority leader as leverage to exact a promise to support farm aid legislation. During the periods in which the Republicans controlled the Senate in the 1980s and 1990s, Sen. Jesse Helms, R-N.C., repeatedly held up nominations because he found them politically unacceptable or because he wished to force political opponents to compromise on policy issues. Deering has written: "On numerous occasions in recent years, members of the Senate of both parties have placed holds on particular individuals. In some cases, the nominee is the target, in other cases merely a pawn, but in either case the use of nominees as, in effect, hostages has undermined the integrity of the system." [98]

The Presidential Personnel System

The process by which presidents select their top political appointees remained relatively unchanged throughout the first 150 years of U.S. history. Presidents had little, if any, staff to help them make their appointments; political parties usually controlled personnel selection for the president. *(See*

"Presidential Party Leadership within the Executive Branch," p. 900, in Chapter 17.) Even when chief executives did become actively involved in the selection process, they often used the existing political party structure. Other nominees were usually suggested to the president by party leaders or members of Congress from the president's party. Too often this dependence on the party resulted in administrations filled with top-level appointees with little loyalty to presidential objectives.

Roosevelt and Truman Administrations

Since Franklin Roosevelt entered the White House, newly elected presidents have needed significant staff support and a centralized procedure for choosing personnel because of the vast number of appointments that must be made in a short period of time. Perhaps more important, a centralized appointment process under the president's control ensures faithfulness to White House policies and objectives.

Until the 1940s, the selection of presidential appointees was haphazard and unfocused. Presidential personnel operations relied heavily on chance to place the right people in the right positions. During the 1940s, however, President Roosevelt attempted to alleviate much of the problem by introducing governmental reforms that removed presidential patronage from the national political parties. For example, he appointed an assistant to handle personnel matters in an effort to improve presidential control over the appointment process. In the decades that followed the presidency's administrative powers increased, allowing it more discretion in personnel selection.

Dom Bonafede attributed the growth of a more centralized selection procedure within the White House after 1940 to three factors. First, political reforms that increased the number of state primaries and emphasized grass-roots politics "hastened the decline of the national parties and minimized their brokerage role as conduit and clearinghouse for appointments." Presidents were no longer obligated to party leaders for their election and therefore had less need to reward them with government jobs. Second, the movement toward a strong administrative presidency, which centralized power in the White House, further strengthened the president's hand vis-à-vis Congress and the bureaucracy. Third, "the complexity of domestic and foreign issues, such as arms control, tax reform, federal deficits, and trade imbalances, necessitated elaborate institutional support, placing a premium on substantive knowledge and managerial competence." [99]

Specific recommendations by the Committee on Administrative Management, headed by Louis D. Brownlow, and the two Hoover Commissions helped centralize more power in the presidency. *(See "Reorganization Power," p. 595.)* In 1939, acting on Brownlow Committee recommendations, Congress created the Executive Office of the President and brought the Bureau of the Budget under the control of the president within the EOP. These measures began what has become known as the "institutional presidency." [100] The first and second Hoover Commissions further increased the administrative power of the presidency by giving it more control over the vast federal bureaucracy and substantial authority over the appointment process.

President Truman appointed the first full-time staff member responsible only for personnel matters. Although this aide, Donald Dawson, addressed mostly routine concerns and spent a good deal of time in contact with the Democratic National Committee, the new position signaled the growing importance of staffing issues.

Eisenhower Administration

Dwight Eisenhower came to office in 1953 with a strong desire to improve the management of the executive branch but with a dislike for personnel matters. He frequently wrote in his diary that patronage was one of the great banes of his administration and one of the things most likely to cause him to lose his temper. Consequently, he delegated personnel concerns to members of his staff, primarily to Sherman Adams, his chief of staff. Adams, however, soon found the job of personnel director too demanding when added to his other responsibilities. The president then approved the position of special assistant for executive appointments, which several people held during the eight years Eisenhower was in office. These special assistants did not choose the president's appointees. Instead, they managed the appointment process by narrowing the president's choices to candidates with the best qualifications and the fewest political liabilities. More than anything else, Eisenhower sought appointees who were loyal to his political philosophy and his programs.

Kennedy and Johnson Administrations

Shortly after his election, President-elect Kennedy put together a personnel selection staff called "Talent Hunt." Composed of some of the best people from the campaign, Talent Hunt was a loosely organized operation with two objectives. First, it tried to determine the president-elect's political obligations—supporters who helped him win the election—and

Dan Fenn, President John F. Kennedy's personnel aide, created a White House appointment process that gave the president recruiting ability independent of the political parties.

find appropriate jobs to pay off those debts. Second, it attempted to identify the most important jobs the president would have to fill and to find the best people for those positions. After the inauguration, Talent Hunt broke up, and its members went to their own jobs in the administration.

In mid-1961 Kennedy appointed Dan Fenn of the Harvard Business School faculty to take over the day-to-day personnel responsibilities of the White House. Asked to recommend changes in the traditional method of filling executive positions, Fenn concluded that the procedure was too limited. The most important jobs in the federal government were being filled by an unsophisticated "Whom do you know?" system—a process he called "BOGSAT," or a "bunch of guys sitting around a table."

Fenn attempted to correct this problem by creating a systematic White House appointment operation with three major stages. First, he and his staff developed reliable job descriptions that allowed them to match candidates with positions, something most administrations had not been able to do. Second, Fenn offered the president a wider selection of candidates from whom to choose. He believed that the range of people with whom presidents normally came into contact was too narrow to provide the talent necessary for a successful administration. Third, because he could offer a wider range of choices only by reaching beyond traditional political sources for appointments, Fenn established a network of well-positioned people throughout the country whose opinions the president trusted and who could provide Kennedy with candid information about potential nominees. Although prevailing partisan considerations kept the system Fenn established from working as well as it might have, Fenn's efforts nonetheless marked the first time a president had significant independent recruiting ability, separate from the influence of the political parties.

During Lyndon B. Johnson's administration, the centralization of presidential personnel selection took a giant leap forward. Although Kennedy had put together a significant staff for selecting nominees, he would often bypass the process by selecting appointees without using the system Fenn had established. Johnson, too, would sometimes circumvent his personnel staff, but he always maintained the appearance that the selection had been made through the White House personnel system. The authors of one study of the presidential selection process concluded:

> Those who wanted to influence Johnson's appointment decisions quickly got the message that their contact point for this was the personnel staff and that efforts to evade the established personnel selection procedures would be difficult to pull off. This focused more attention on the White House and significantly strengthened its role at the hub of the appointment process.[101]

The Kennedy and Johnson presidencies therefore brought about three important long-term changes in presidential personnel management. First, a full-time personnel staff became a regular component of the White House Office. Second, presidents began to attempt to maintain their independence from traditional political party pressures by recruiting their own candidates. Third, succeeding administrations have developed and followed routine procedures for scrutinizing the background, competence, integrity, and political loyalty of each potential appointee.

Nixon Administration

When Richard Nixon took office in 1969, he at first failed to incorporate in his presidency many of the advances made in personnel selection in preceding administrations. He had little interest in personnel matters and delegated most of the responsibility for filling offices to his staff. His initial appointment process was slow and cumbersome, and too many times the White House appointed people who had little loyalty to the president's programs. As a result, in 1970 Nixon appointed Frederic V. Malek to study the personnel selection process and recommend improvements. Malek called for a personnel system similar to those of Nixon's predecessors: centralization of the recruiting process in the White House, recruitment outreach beyond traditional political party sources of potential nominees, and a more rigorous clearance process.

In 1971 Nixon appointed Malek director of his personnel operation. Malek, acting on his own recommendations, set up the White House Personnel Office (WHPO). Following the examples of the organizations set up by Fenn and John W. Macy, personnel assistant to President Johnson, Malek made the WHPO a tightly organized operation that

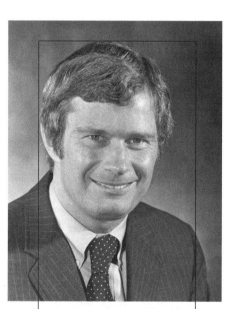

Frederic V. Malek, President Richard Nixon's personnel director, established the White House Personnel Office in 1971.

employed a highly professional staff. The WHPO employed professional headhunters whose sole responsibility was to find the right person for the right job in the administration. In addition, the WHPO developed a much more sophisticated evaluation system than had ever been used in the White House. Thus after two years of haphazard personnel selection the Nixon White House emerged with a firm commitment to centralized personnel decision making for almost all noncareer positions in the federal government. Yet eventually the WHPO lost much of its professionalism, and some of its members went beyond the limits of propriety in attempting to control the appointment process. The WHPO began to manipulate the civil service to benefit the administration. One way was to write job descriptions to fit specific applicants loyal to Nixon. Those unsympathetic were to be transferred to undesirable locations or assignments requiring a great deal of travel. The press and Congress finally intervened, forcing the WHPO to retreat from its continued efforts at centralization.

Ford and Carter Administrations

Gerald Ford's personnel staff spent much of its time trying to clean up the image of the aggressive WHPO under Nixon. The first thing that Ford changed was the name. The WHPO became the Presidential Personnel Office. In addition, Ford reduced the size of the personnel operation and narrowed the focus of its activities to positions traditionally viewed as presidential appointments instead of most noncareer appointments.

Jimmy Carter was the first president to begin planning for his presidency while still running for election. In the summer of 1976, he set up a small staff in Atlanta to begin working on the staffing of his administration. Carter chose Jack Watson to head the operation, which became known as the Talent Inventory Program (TIP). After Carter won the election, Watson moved his operation to Washington. Once there he became locked in a power struggle with Carter's campaign manager, Hamilton Jordan, over who would control the appointment process. As a result of this struggle, the Presidential Personnel Office floundered for almost two years, and the appointment process was hampered. In fact, throughout the Carter administration there was no central coordination of appointments in the White House, and much of the early work of TIP was ignored.

Carter contributed to the disorder in the appointment process by insisting that cabinet heads be given almost total discretion in choosing their subordinates. As part of his commitment to "cabinet government," Carter had proclaimed during the campaign: "There will never be an instance while I am president where members of the White House staff dominate or act in a superior position to the members of our Cabinet." [102] This promise made good campaign rhetoric, but, by decentralizing the decision-making process outside of the White House, it diminished Carter's ability to control his administration. Some departments made appointments after a rigorous search procedure. Others resorted to "politics as usual" and used political networks to select potential nominees whose main qualifications were friendship and loyalty to department secretaries. As Dom Bonafede described the results, "In an unseemly brief period it became clear to the president's top lieutenants—and only later to Carter himself—that he had made a major mistake in giving secretaries carte blanche authority to hand-pick their assistants." [103]

Reagan and George Bush Administrations

Reagan viewed the appointment process as an integral part of his plans for changing the direction of the federal government. Determined to avoid the mistakes of the Carter administration, he centralized the appointment process within the White House.

Reagan also made a determined effort to appoint only persons who shared his political philosophy. E. Pendleton James, Reagan's postelection talent search manager and eventual assistant to the president for personnel, declared, "You can't separate personnel from policy." [104] This outlook pervaded the administration's appointment efforts. From the "kitchen cabinet" made up of Reagan's elite, conservative California advisers who chose politically acceptable potential nominees before his election, to the personnel office, which managed appointments during the administration, the strategy was to choose nominees whose political philosophy matched the president's.

The Reagan appointment process benefited from some of Carter's mistakes. James gave the process a consistency it lacked under Carter. During the transition and throughout the first eighteen months of the Reagan administration, James, working with Lyn Nofziger, presided over the day-to-day operation of the administration's personnel selection. As a result, little confusion arose about the process itself or who was in charge. Also, Reagan visibly involved himself in the appointment process. He made the final decision on all of the important appointments during the transition and the first year. The authors of one study noted:

> This proved to be an effective deterrent to those in the departments and agencies and in Congress who might try and wrest control of appointment decisions away from the

White House. It is one thing to attempt that when low-level White House staff members are making appointment decisions; it is quite another when those decisions are being made in the Oval Office.[105]

E. Pendleton James, Ronald Reagan's assistant to the president for personnel, saw to it that all appointees shared Reagan's political philosophy.

Like Carter, Vice President George Bush began planning for staffing his administration while running for the presidency. Early in his 1988 campaign, Bush named Charles Untermeyer to begin organizing his personnel operation. But because Bush wished to avoid appearing overconfident, Untermeyer was not allowed to establish a formal office or recruit any nominees until after the election. When Bush won the presidential election, his personnel management team moved rapidly into action. Although Bush anticipated no major policy shifts from his Republican predecessor, he did insist that his administration have his stamp on it, promising to replace 90 percent of Reagan's political appointees.

Bush played a much less visible role than Reagan in selecting appointees for his administration. Those charged with making most of the staffing decisions were given two major criteria by the president-elect: loyalty and experience. Where Reagan had sought ideological loyalty, Bush sought personal loyalty in his appointments. Personal friends of the president and those who had played a major role in Bush's campaign were given priority in the new administration. As one who had been around Washington a long time, Bush also sought experience. The resulting appointments made his administration one of the most experienced and thus one of the most competent in recent history.

Clinton and George W. Bush Administrations

During the 1992 fall presidential campaign, Mickey Kantor, Bill Clinton's campaign chair, set up a formal organization—the Clinton-Gore Presidential Transition Planning Foundation—for staffing the hoped-for administration. This early attempt at centralization promised a disciplined staffing process. After the election, however, Kantor ran afoul of other campaign officials and was blocked from heading the transition. The formal responsibility for finding personnel for the new administration fell largely to Harold Ickes, a New York attorney and close friend of Hillary Clinton.

President-elect Clinton, however, abandoned a highly centralized transition operation. Instead, he opted for a kitchen table approach to staffing his administration. Ickes, Mrs. Clinton, Susan Thomases, an attorney and close friend of Mrs. Clinton, and Bruce Lindsey, an attorney and a long-time Clinton loyalist, made most of the actual decisions about staffing the new presidency around a six-foot table at Clinton headquarters in Little Rock, Arkansas. Operating under the dictum that they had been voted to go to Washington to change things, the personnel team chose executive branch staffers who were largely inexperienced in Washington politics. In addition, appointees were young and geographically, ethnically, and racially diverse, as compared with those of previous administrations.

Although Clinton abandoned his early attempt at a centralized transition, he clearly wanted to keep personnel functions within the White House. Clinton based his personnel appointment system on a memo, "Transition Workplan for Reviewing the Staffing and Organization of the White House and Executive Office of the President," written at the direction of Harrison Wellford, a former Carter budget official. The memo urged that appointments to the White House, the Executive Office of the President, the cabinet, and the subcabinet be controlled squarely by the president. This approach contrasted with the Carter system, in which the absence of central coordination of appointments reduced Carter's ability to effectively control his administration.

One of the most distinctive features of the Clinton personnel system was the slowness with which it filled positions in the new administration, stemming in part from his desire for diversity and in part from his system that required White House approval for executive branch appointments. After eight months in office, Clinton still had not nominated political appointees for more than 40 percent of policy-making positions, and about one-third of the posts in independent agencies, on regulatory boards, and on commissions remained unfilled. Clinton was well behind the pace of nominations set by both Carter and Reagan. He was ahead of

George Bush, but as a Republican succeeding another Republican, Bush was in no real hurry to replace personnel.

President George W. Bush was somewhat more successful than his predecessors in getting personnel appointments made in a timely fashion. Even so, by the end of his first year in office one-third of the senior-level posts in the administration had not been filled, either because the president had not named nominees or because those already named had not been approved by the Senate. George W. Bush did appoint more minorities to senior-level posts than former presidents Clinton, Bush, and Reagan. And he appointed more women to these high-level posts than either George Bush or Reagan, and nearly as many as Clinton.

Since Franklin Roosevelt's administration, presidents have relied on increasingly sophisticated methods of centralizing the appointment power in the White House in their attempts to strengthen control over their administrations. The personnel office is now a permanent part of the White House organizational structure. Succeeding presidents have significantly increased the number of staff assigned to find loyal political executives. Most recent presidents have considered the director of the White House Personnel Office a senior staff member with the title "assistant to the president."

The Removal Power

The ability of presidents to control their administrations often depends on their authority to remove subordinates from office. This issue lies at the very heart of the chief executive's power over the bureaucracy. The power of presidents to remove officials who are not doing their jobs properly or who disagree with presidential goals and programs is, however, controversial and has been significantly limited by the Supreme Court. Because the Constitution does not explicitly grant presidents power to remove officials from office, the legitimacy of the power often has rested on court interpretations of specific presidential removal actions.

The Tenure of Office Act of 1867 provided much debate about whether a president could remove executive branch officials. On the suspicion that President Andrew Johnson intended to fire Secretary of War Edwin M. Stanton, Congress passed the act that made it a high misdemeanor to remove without the Senate's approval any government official whose nomination had been confirmed by the Senate. Congress's intention was to protect incumbent Republican officeholders from retaliation if they did not support Johnson. President Johnson vetoed the bill on the grounds that it was unconstitutional to restrict the president's power of removal, but Congress overrode the veto. When Johnson immediately tested the Tenure of Office Act by attempting to remove Stanton, the House voted 126–47 to impeach him. Tried by the Senate, Johnson was acquitted by one vote. The Tenure of Office Act was virtually repealed early in the Grant administration, once Republicans regained control of the appointment power. It was entirely repealed in 1887 when public opinion forced Congress to introduce legislation to repeal it.

Preferring to avoid the issue as long as possible, the Supreme Court refused to make a definitive ruling on the issue of presidential removal of public officeholders until 1926. In *Myers v. United States* the Court ruled that an 1876 law that limited the president's removal power over postmasters was unconstitutional. In 1917 President Woodrow Wilson had appointed Frank S. Myers to be a postmaster in Portland, Oregon, for a term of four years. Attempting to make his administration responsive to his policy goals, Wilson removed Myers from office in 1920 without the consent of the Senate, although the 1876 statute provided that postmasters should be appointed and removed by the president by and with the advice and consent of the Senate. Myers sued for his salary in the U.S. Court of Claims. When he received an adverse judgment, he took his case to the Supreme Court.

In delivering the opinion of the Court, Chief Justice William Howard Taft, a former president, strongly argued that presidents cannot effectively administer the executive branch unless they can control their subordinates with the threat of removal for political and other reasons. He stated that the power of removal was implied in Article II of the Constitution, which gives the president the responsibility to see that the laws are faithfully executed. Furthermore, Congress could not constitutionally restrain or limit that power. Taft, referring to the Tenure of Office Act and declaring it had been unconstitutional, contended that presidents cannot carry out their constitutional responsibilities if Congress interferes with their ability to control the executive branch.[106]

The *Myers* case gave presidents sweeping authority to remove not only immediate executive subordinates but also members of independent regulatory commissions, such as the Interstate Commerce Commission and the Federal Trade Commission. Independent regulatory commissioners are appointed under the provisions of statutes that confer upon them a certain amount of independence and freedom from the political control of the president. In creating these agencies, Congress had carefully outlined the provisions by which a commissioner could be removed in an attempt to free these executives from political control. If the *Myers* case applied to all political executives, then the regulatory commissions would lose their political independence. Sooner or later the question of unlimited presidential power of removal would be challenged.

The question of the president's ability to remove independent regulatory commissioners arose early in Franklin Roosevelt's first term in office and was settled in 1935 by the Supreme Court in *Humphrey's Executor v. United States.* President Herbert Hoover had nominated William E.

Humphrey to the Federal Trade Commission (FTC) in 1931. Under the terms outlined by Congress in the Federal Trade Commission Act of 1914, FTC commissioners were supposed to serve a term of seven years. The act stated that commissioners could be removed by the president only for "inefficiency, neglect of duty, or malfeasance in office." After his election to office in 1933, Roosevelt wrote Humphrey and requested his resignation from the FTC so that "the aims and purposes of the administration with respect to the work of the Commission can be carried out most effectively with personnel of my own selection." After Humphrey's initial reluctance to resign, Roosevelt again wrote him, this time stating: "You will, I know, realize that I do not feel that your mind and my mind go along together on either the policies or the administering of the Federal Trade Commission, and frankly, I think it is best for the people of the country that I should have full confidence." [107] When Humphrey refused to resign, Roosevelt notified him that he had been removed. Humphrey died in 1934, never having agreed to his removal. The executor of Humphrey's estate decided to sue for salary he believed was due Humphrey but never paid him.

The court of claims asked the Supreme Court to answer two questions before it could render a judgment. First, did the Federal Trade Commission Act limit the president's power to remove commissioners except for reasons stated in the act? Second, if the act did indeed limit the president's power to remove commissioners, was it constitutional?

Roosevelt had made clear that the removal of Humphrey was for political reasons. Justice George Sutherland delivered the Court's opinion that the *Myers* case did not apply to Humphrey because the FTC was "an administrative body created by Congress to carry into effect legislative policies." Therefore, it could not "in any sense be characterized as an arm or an eye of the Executive." Sutherland continued:

> Whether the power of the president to remove an officer shall prevail over the authority of Congress to condition the power by fixing a definite term and precluding the removal except for cause will depend upon the character of the office; the Myers decision, affirming the power of the president alone to make the removal, is confined to purely executive officers.[108]

The *Humphrey* decision not only invalidated Roosevelt's removal of Humphrey but also generally limited presidential removal power to officials who could be classified as "purely executive officers." Except for appointees immediately responsible to the president and those exercising nondiscretionary or ministerial functions, such as White House aides, the president's power of removal could be limited by Congress.

The Supreme Court attempted to make a distinction between "executive" and "administrative" functions within the federal bureaucracy. Presidents have complete control over executive functions, or those that deal with the execution of the policy of the administration and are under the direction of the president, such as the functions of the EOP staff and cabinet members. The Court ruled that presidents do not, however, have complete control over administrative functions or those that have quasi-judicial or quasi-legislative roles, such as the functions of the independent regulatory commissions. Only when Congress chooses specifically to give presidents control over these agencies can they remove officials for merely political reasons.

In 1958 the Supreme Court further clarified the removal power of presidents. In *Wiener v. United States* the Court held that if officials are engaged in adjudicative functions presidents may not remove them for political reasons. In 1950 President Truman had appointed Myron Wiener to serve on the War Claims Commission. When Eisenhower assumed office, he requested Wiener's resignation. When Wiener refused, Eisenhower removed him from office. Similar to Roosevelt's removal of Humphrey, Eisenhower's removal of Wiener was based on purely political reasons. Congress had created the War Claims Commission to adjudicate damage claims arising from World War II, and it had made no provisions for removing commissioners. Wiener sued for his lost salary.

Noting the similarity between the *Wiener* and *Humphrey* cases, the Supreme Court ruled in favor of Wiener. The Court argued that in both cases presidents had removed persons from quasi-judicial agencies for political purposes. Calling the War Claims Commission a clearly adjudicative body, Justice Felix Frankfurter concluded for the Court:

> Judging the matter in all the nakedness in which it is presented, namely, the claim that the President could remove a member of an adjudicative body like the War Claims Commission merely because he wanted his own appointees on such a Commission, we are compelled to conclude that no such power is given to the President directly by the Constitution, and none is impliedly conferred upon him by statute simply because Congress said nothing about it. The philosophy of Humphrey's Executor, in its explicit language as well as its implications, precludes such a claim.[109]

In 1988 the Supreme Court further limited the president's removal power in *Morrison v. Olson* by upholding the independent counsel provisions of the Ethics in Government Act of 1978. In the aftermath of the Watergate scandal, Congress created the independent counsel system to investigate and possibly prosecute high-level executive officers accused of serious crimes. Arguing for the majority, Chief Justice William H. Rehnquist defended the creation of an independent counsel within the executive branch who would not be responsible to the president. Rehnquist asserted that the president's inability to remove an independent counsel in no way damaged the president's ability to govern.[110] Justice Antonin Scalia offered a stinging dissent and argued that the position of independent counsel would lead to political vendettas being fought through legal means.[111] A decade later, many considered this lone dissent prescient when President Bill Clinton was the target of a probe by independent counsel Kenneth W. Starr that many Americans believed to be partisan-motivated. After the completion of this unpopular investigation, which led to Clinton's impeachment, there was little public support for the independent counsel law. On June 30, 1999, Congress allowed the statute that authorized the independent counsel position to expire.

Generally, presidents may remove all heads of cabinet departments and all political executives in the Executive Office of the President. In addition, they may remove at any time the directors of the following agencies: the Arms Control and Disarmament Agency, the Commission on Civil Rights, the Environmental Protection Agency, the Federal Mediation and Conciliation Service, the General Services Administration, the National Aeronautics and Space Administration, the Postal Service, and the Small Business Administration.

THE BUDGETING POWER

The power to control the budget process is one of the most important administrative prerogatives of the presidency. The chief executive is an important participant in the budget process, for often it is the president who decides how and on what money is spent. As presidential scholar Richard Pious has noted, "To budget is to govern. In a system of separated institutions that share power, the question is which institution, and by what authority, determines spending levels for the departments?"[112] In the last part of the twentieth century, the presidency assumed an increasingly important role in determining federal spending and thus more responsibility in governing. Although Congress constitutionally controls the purse strings, the president oversees the formulation and development of the budget.

The Constitution does not clearly establish a budgetary process or spell out the president's role in such a process. Because of this ambiguity, presidents have been able to bring much of the process under their control. Article I of the Constitution gives Congress the powers to tax and spend. Article II, Section 3, gives presidents the power to recommend to Congress such measures as they deem appropriate. ("He shall from time to time give to the Congress Information of the State of the Union, and recommend to their Consideration such Measures as he shall judge necessary and expedient.") Implicit in this power is the idea that presidents may present to Congress a financial program.

Historically, presidents have not taken part in budget planning. Even in modern times, presidential involvement in the process has varied from one administration to another. For many presidents, preparing a budget is a tedious and time-consuming job. President Lyndon Johnson once wrote: "The federal budget is a dry, unfathomable maze of figures and statistics—thicker than a Sears-Roebuck catalogue and duller than a telephone directory." [113] Some presidents have been able to maintain consistent interest in the budget's complexities throughout their terms in office; others have not. Political scientist Lance T. LeLoup examined the roles that past presidents played in the budget process and found that shortly after the first year in office, Dwight Eisenhower and Richard Nixon tired of the tedious budget process. Harry Truman and Gerald Ford, however, were able to maintain their enthusiasm throughout their administrations. [114]

Budgeting gives the presidency a tremendous amount of administrative power, and most presidents have recognized the importance of the budget in controlling their administrations. They usually approach their first budget optimistically, excited about the potential power to eliminate or cut back programs that they feel have outlived their usefulness. Describing his involvement in his first budget, Lyndon Johnson wrote: "I worked as hard on that budget as I have ever worked on anything. . . . Day after day I went over that budget with the Cabinet officers, my economic advisers, and the Budget Director. I studied almost every line, nearly every page, until I was dreaming about the budget at night." [115]

Although their enthusiasm may fade, presidents continue to seek to control the budget process. They see their participation in the process as a way of doing things that can benefit the national economy and their own political fortunes. In the words of President Ford, "The budget is the president's blueprint for the operation of government in the year ahead." [116] According to Dennis S. Ippolito in his study of the budget process, presidents become involved in the budget process to achieve a means of administrative management and control: "By affecting the resources available for agencies and programs, the president can seek to promote better planning of what is done, more effective supervision of how it is done, and more systematic evaluation of how well various objectives are accomplished." In addition, Ippolito has pointed out that budget decisions can affect political support: "By emphasizing particular programs or criticizing others, by challenging Congress' spending preferences, by trumpeting the need for fiscal responsibility, or by reiterating commitments to greater economy and efficiency, a president can attempt to dramatize his leadership role and to generate public support for his economic policies and program preferences." [117]

Attempts to control the budget process often force presidents to play a public relations game. Most presidents want to be considered fiscal conservatives. The overwhelming majority of Americans want a balanced budget and want

the president to curtail the growth of federal expenditures. Yet presidents must continue to fund existing programs for various groups and for the American public in general. In addition, presidents are expected to present new initiatives, some of which benefit groups to whom presidents have political obligations. The dilemma is one of holding down public expenditures while trying to solve public problems. It is not an easy task, and it makes presidential participation in the budget process much more demanding and important. For example, the 1995 budget battle between President Clinton and a Republican Congress proved to be more than a public relations game. It became a marathon discussion about the size and role of government in American life. The stalemate that resulted came about from fundamental disagreements about overhauling such programs as health and welfare entitlements.

The President's Role in the Budget Process

Presidents had little influence in managing executive branch funds before passage of the Budget and Accounting Act of 1921. Previously, budget requests went directly from each department to the House of Representatives without much interference from the White House. Congress believed it could handle the budget without much help from the president or the White House staff. By the end of World War I, however, both the executive and legislative branches had realized that the massive growth of the federal government needed better fiscal management.

The Budget and Accounting Act of 1921

The Budget and Accounting Act of 1921 gave presidents important managerial controls over the budgeting process and made them the dominant participants in budgetary politics. Ironically, Congress passed this act in an attempt to bring order into its own chaotic budget process. An earlier House committee had pointed to the haphazard nature of a budget process that lacked a coherent review of the executive branch's budget request. But in attempting to alleviate the problem, the act placed the presidency squarely in the budgetary process by requiring presidents to submit to Congress annual estimates of how much money it would take to run the federal government during the next fiscal year. (A fiscal year is the twelve-month span over which financial accounting is conducted. The federal government's fiscal year runs from October 1 to September 30.)

The annual budget message delivered by the president each February recommends how much money should be appropriated by Congress for each department of the federal government. The White House first evaluates all agency budget requests and decides which to accept or alter before submitting the annual budget message. Consequently, presidents become very much involved in the process. They receive more information about the budget than most members of Congress, allowing them to initiate budget discussions on their own terms.

In addition, the Budget and Accounting Act created the Bureau of the Budget (BOB) and placed it under the control of the Treasury Department. Its role was to "assemble, correlate, revise, reduce, or increase the estimates of the several departments or establishments." [118] In 1939, in response to the growing need to coordinate New Deal programs and recommendations from the Committee on Administrative Management (the Brownlow Committee), President Roosevelt moved BOB into the Executive Office of the President.

BOB began instituting a form of "budget clearance" so that the departments could not bypass its budget review process either for statutory authorizations or for annual appropriations. No longer were the departments on their own in requesting funds from Congress. Bureaus and agencies made requests for funds to their departments, and the departments sent their budgets through BOB for consideration by the president. From 1939 to 1969, BOB evolved into a highly influential component of the EOP.

Office of Management and Budget

In 1970 President Richard Nixon changed the name and modified the function of BOB. Emphasizing the management roles of the budget agency, Nixon renamed it the Office of Management and Budget (OMB). As the word *management* implies, new emphasis was placed on providing departments with advice on ways to improve their efficiency to reduce the costs of their operations.

Nixon specifically assigned four major roles to OMB. First, it was to continue many of BOB's functions, especially writing the federal budget. Second, it was to serve as a clearinghouse for new programs and legislation. Third, Nixon wanted some part of the Executive Office of the President to have the ability to track legislation as it moved through Congress. OMB was vested with this capacity. Fourth, OMB was given the specific authority to provide management advice to the various departments and agencies. Since its inception, OMB has served as the centerpiece of presidential budgeting.

Although the president's budget is not submitted to Congress until the February before the first day of the new fiscal year (October 1), the presidential budget process begins at least nineteen months before submission of the finished budget proposal. *(See Table 11-1.)* The budget cycle begins in early spring with OMB informing the departments of the fiscal outlook and the spending priorities of the president. During the summer, the OMB director issues specific revenue projections and imposes specific guidelines for departmental spending. On September 1, agencies submit their initial budget requests to OMB. OMB then holds formal hearings on these requests at which departmental officials justify their proposed budgets before OMB examiners.

OMB's director examines the entire budget from November 1 to December 1. Often the director will invite the National Security Council, the Council of Economic Advisers, and several White House aides to participate in the review. The OMB director makes final decisions subject to the economic forecast for the coming fiscal year and communicates these decisions to the departments. The departments may appeal the decisions directly to the president. Usually, however, each department will revise its formal budget to coincide with the budget director's wishes, for presidents rarely reverse their budget directors' decisions.

Congress receives the first official hint of what the president wants in the State of the Union address at the end of January, and specifics are then spelled out in the president's budget message in February. Pending approval by Congress, the budget goes into effect with the new fiscal year, October 1.

Not all agency requests are treated equally. Until the Nixon administration, the Defense Department's budget requests were exempt from control by the president's budgeting organization. During the Kennedy and Johnson administrations, the Pentagon submitted its budget directly to the president without review by the Bureau of the Budget. If BOB believed budget items to be too high, it could appeal to the president. This practice, a reversal of the traditional procedure, placed the burden of proof on the budget office instead of on the department. President Nixon changed the procedure for the Pentagon by leaving final decisions with the NSC and OMB and giving the Defense Department the right of appeal. Since then, presidents have continued to use OMB as a counterbalance to the Pentagon's budget requests.

Current Services Budget

Under the provisions of the 1974 Congressional Budget and Impoundment Control Act (PL 93–344), presidents must submit two budget proposals. When they submit their budget for the upcoming fiscal year, they must also submit, through the supervision of OMB, a *current services budget.* The current services budget provides Congress with an indication of the cost of existing budget obligations and a guide for evaluating additional budget proposals. Specifically, the current services budget includes the "proposed budget authority and estimated outlays that would be included in the budget for the ensuing fiscal year . . . if all programs were carried on at the same level as the fiscal year in progress . . . without policy changes." [119]

Although this procedure was intended to provide Congress with a basis for determining the overall size and direction of existing budget commitments and for assessing and evaluating the president's budget proposals, it has never lived up to its potential. Political scientist Howard E.

TABLE 11–1   **Budget Timetable in the Executive Branch and Congress**

Executive branch	Timing	Congress
Agencies subject to executive branch review submit initial budget request materials.	September 1	
Fiscal year begins.	October 1	Fiscal year begins.
President's initial appropriation order takes effect (amounts are withheld from obligation pending issuance of final order).	October 1	
	October 10	Congressional Budget Office (CBO) issues revised report to Office of Management and Budget (OMB) and Congress.
OMB reports on changes in initial estimates and determinations resulting from legislation enacted and regulations promulgated after its initial report to Congress.	October 15	
President issues final sequester order, which is effective immediately, and transmits message to Congress within fifteen days of final order.	October 15	
Agencies not subject to executive branch review submit budget request materials.	October 15	
	November 15	Comptroller general issues compliance report.
Legislative branch and the judiciary submit budget request materials.	November–December	
President transmits the budget to Congress.	1st Monday in February	Congress receives the president's budget.
OMB sends allowance letters to agencies.	January–February	
	February 15	CBO reports to the budget committees on the president's budget.
	February 25	Committees submit views and estimates to budget committees.
OMB and the president conduct reviews to establish presidential policy to guide agencies in developing the next budget.	April–June	
	April 1	Senate Budget Committee reports concurrent resolution on the budget.
	April 15	Congress completes action on concurrent resolution.
	May 15	House may consider appropriations bills in the absence of a concurrent resolution on the budget.
	June 10	House Appropriations Committee reports last appropriations bill.
	June 15	Congress completes action on reconciliation legislation.
	June 30	House completes action on annual appropriations bills.
President transmits the midsession review, updating the budget estimates.	July 15	Congress receives midsession review of the budget.
OMB provides agencies with policy guidance for the upcoming budget.	July–August	
Date of "snapshot" of projected deficits for the upcoming fiscal year for initial OMB and CBO reports.	August 15	
	August 20	CBO issues its initial report to OMB and Congress.
OMB issues its initial report providing estimates and determinations to the president and Congress.	August 25	
President issues initial sequester order and sends message to Congress within fifteen days.	August 25	

SOURCE: Office of Management and Budget, Circular No. A-11 (1988).

Shuman has noted that the current services budget has little significance or meaning: "Only budget buffs and perennial budget watchers pay much attention to it. It is, however, a useful document in assessing whether any or how much fundamental change has been made in the old budget to produce the new one." [120]

Uncontrollable Spending

In any given year, much of OMB's current service estimates can be classified as *uncontrollable spending*—that is, expenditures mandated by current law or some previous obligation. Any changes to the spending on these mandated programs require congressional action. By 1995, 64 percent of

The mammoth U.S. budget for fiscal 1981 rolls off the presses.

the federal budget could be classified as uncontrollable spending. These expenditures can be broken down into three major categories.

The first category, fixed costs, consists of legal commitments made by the federal government in previous years. These commitments require the government to spend whatever is necessary to meet these expenses. The largest and most important component of this category is interest on the national debt. Another fixed-cost expenditure is public housing loans. Fixed costs are "uncontrollable" because they can be eliminated only by extreme measures such as default.

The second category is large-scale government projects that require long-term financing. These multiyear contracts and obligations include the building of dams, weapons systems, aircraft, and the space shuttle. Many of these projects are reviewed annually, and expenditure levels are occasionally modified. For example, in 1994 funding was curtailed for the space program and eliminated for the supercollider. Historically, however, most are not.

The third category of expenditures officially designated as uncontrollable is the largest. These programs, called "entitlements," commit the federal government to pay benefits to all eligible individuals. Any attempt to control these expenditures would require changing the laws that created them. Entitlements include Social Security, Medicare, Medicaid, Supplemental Security Income, food stamps, public assistance, and federal retirement. *(See Table 11-2.)* In some cases, the federal government pays individuals directly; in other cases, the states determine eligibility and administer the programs. Most of these programs have no limit on the amount of spending they may entail. As more people become eligible for benefits, expenditures increase.

As entitlement spending has pushed federal budget deficits higher, presidents have tried to reduce such expenditures. Nixon and Ford, for example, attempted to decrease entitlement expenditures by restricting eligibility and establishing a limit on benefit increases for several programs. In his first full budget year, Reagan proposed an entitlement cut of $11.7 billion. His budget proposal reflected the frustration that many presidents have felt in attempting to deal with uncontrollable expenditures. It said in part, "The explosion of entitlement expenditures has forced a careful reexamination of the entitlement or automatic spending programs. . . . When one looks behind the good intentions of these programs, one finds tremendous problems of fraud, waste, and mismanagement. Worse than this, the truly needy have not been well served." [121]

In 1996 Congress reduced entitlement expenditures for public assistance programs by enacting welfare reform legislation that imposed certain work-related rules on beneficiaries. However, Congress usually finds it difficult to change entitlement programs because of the enormous resistance offered by the groups who would be affected. When President George W. Bush urged Congress to change the Social Security laws in 2005 to allow for personal accounts, he faced insurmountable opposition from interest groups such as the AARP.

Controllable Spending

The president does have some control over several categories of expenditures. Expenditures that can be classified as controllable are used for salaries and fringe benefits for both civilian and military personnel. Although these expenses technically fit the category of controllable expenditures, the practical problems surrounding spending on salaries and fringe benefits make it difficult for a president to control them completely. Seniority and civil service rules protect so many federal employees that it is futile to attempt real cutbacks in expenditures going to salaries.

A second category of controllable federal expenditures is the general operating expenses of the various departments and agencies. Although conservation measures can be

TABLE 11-2 **Entitlement Spending, 1975–2007 (billions of dollars)**

Category	1975	1985	1995	2000	2004	2007[a]
Social Security and railroad retirement	67.3	190.3	337.0	410.5	496.4	571.7
Federal employees' retirement and insurance	18.4	49.8	82.2	100.3	117.4	136.3
Unemployment assistance	12.8	16.2	21.9	21.1	43.1	39.0
Medical care, including Medicare and Medicaid	26.2	104.2	289.7	363.0	515.4	697.8
Assistance to students	6.2	9.2	14.8	13.8	25.7	20.8
Housing assistance	2.1	11.2	25.5	23.9	30.6	31.0
Food and nutrition assistance	6.6	18.5	37.5	32.4	45.9	57.0
Public assistance and related programs	12.2	24.6	61.8	85.3	111.5	120.8
All other payments for individuals	2.0	3.3	4.2	7.2	11.5	5.3
TOTAL PAYMENTS FOR INDIVIDUALS	**153.8**	**427.3**	**874.6**	**1,057.5**	**1,397.6**	**1,679.7**

SOURCE: *Budget of the United States Government: Fiscal Year 2006,* Historical Tables, www.gpoaccess.gov/usbudget/fy06/sheets/hist11z3.xls (accessed Dec. 28, 2006).

NOTE: a. Estimate.

applied to such things as heating, cooling, electricity, transportation, and supplies, expenses will always continue if operations continue. And operating expenses usually increase as inflation increases.

The third category of controllable expenditures is research and development. Medical research, weapons research, and grants to state and local governments make up a large proportion of this category. Again, budget cuts can be made in this category, but only within limits. As a result, even the controllable categories of the federal budget give the president little latitude in budget decisions.

Congressional Response to the President's Budget

Because the presidency traditionally has controlled the compilation of the budget, Congress became dependent on OMB and the presidency for all its budgetary information and complained frequently that it lacked the professional staff it needed to evaluate independently the details, proposals, and estimates of the president's budget. In recent years, however, Congress has become increasingly aggressive in its desire to function equally with the executive branch in its budgetary role.

Congressional Budget Office

To improve its ability to evaluate the budget after constant battles with the Nixon administration, Congress passed in 1974 the Congressional Budget and Impoundment Control Act. The act created the Congressional Budget Office (CBO) and congressional budget committees. CBO was a major innovation for Congress and a major challenge for the presidency. Designed to provide congressional budget committees with a variety of budget and policy information, CBO incorporates several functions performed in the executive branch by OMB.

CBO activities fall into five categories. First, it prepares an annual report on budget alternatives, including fiscal policy options, levels of tax revenues, and budget priorities. Second, it issues five-year budget projections for spending and taxation. Third, CBO projects the long-term costs of bills approved by House and Senate committees and sent to the full Congress for consideration. Fourth, CBO performs a "scorekeeping" function by comparing pending and enacted legislation with targets and ceilings specified by Congress. Fifth, CBO provides Congress with special reports on economic and budgetary issues.

CBO's independent database allows Congress to evaluate presidential budget proposals more effectively. In measuring the success of CBO after its first five years of operation, political scientist Aaron Wildavsky wrote: "The Congressional Budget Office has improved the accuracy of budget numbers by providing a competitive source of expertise, and it has made competent analysis more widely available to those that want it." [122] CBO has allowed Congress to become more independent from the executive branch in its budget-making powers. In his book *The Power Game* political journalist Hedrick Smith wrote: "CBO represents the most important shift of power on domestic issues between the executive branch and Congress in several decades." [123]

This competition in the budget process, however, has irritated more than one president. CBO's economic forecasts usually counter OMB's optimistic and more moderate projections, leading to numerous congressional-presidential confrontations over budget proposals. Shuman notes that in the past CBO "angered President Carter because it disputed his energy program savings and angered President Reagan by saying that his economic assumptions about inflation, interest rates, and unemployment were unrealistic, overly optimistic, and wrong." [124] President George Bush disagreed with various CBO projections on his administration's budget proposals, including the affordability of proposed weapon systems and estimates of the likely effect on economic growth of capital gains tax reductions. Part of the 1995 budget battle between President Clinton and Congress centered around different economic forecasting data produced by OMB and CBO. OMB's numbers were more optimistic than CBO's. After several weeks of negotiations, the White House and Congress agreed that CBO's economic forecast (after consultation with OMB) would serve as a basis for fiscal projections for any budget agreement. CBO then revised its figures slightly upward, but Congress and the White House still remained apart on other budget issues.

Gramm-Rudman-Hollings

With budget deficits growing throughout the 1980s and President Reagan's refusal to support tax increases, Congress believed that additional budget reform was necessary to control spending. In 1985 Congress passed the Balanced Budget and Emergency Deficit Control Act of 1985, also known as Gramm-Rudman-Hollings for its primary sponsors: Sens. Phil Gramm, R-Texas, Warren B. Rudman, R-N.H., and Ernest F. Hollings, D-S.C. Although several budget control measures were discussed, including a line-item veto for the

BUDGETING THEORIES

One of the most important functions served by the budget is to increase presidential administrative control and management of federal agencies and programs. However, the budget process has always been the subject of criticism aimed at improving the efficiency of government management. Over the years, critics, both within the presidency and outside it, have complained about the lack of coordination and centralization in the executive branch's efforts to control the federal administration. Consequently, since the early 1960s various presidents have introduced reforms aimed at making budgeting more efficient, rational, and comprehensive. Rarely, however, have they been as successful as they have hoped.

PLANNING-PROGRAMMING-BUDGETING

In 1961 Secretary of Defense Robert S. McNamara introduced a planning-programming-budgeting (PPB) system into the Pentagon. McNamara brought PPB from the private sector and used it to improve the quality of decision making and budget planning for national security policy. In 1965 President Lyndon B. Johnson announced that PPB also would be applied to domestic operations.

PPB was designed to allow budget decisions to be made by focusing on program goals and on quantitative comparisons of costs and benefits. Once budget officials established priorities among their objectives, they then determined the best expenditure mix in the annual budget to achieve the largest future benefits.

By 1971 PPB had fallen into disfavor with executive budget makers. Although many people had looked to PPB to reform budgeting in the executive branch by making it more rational and less political, PPB failed to gain a permanent place in the budget process for a variety of reasons. It never achieved any great degree of popularity within the departments and agencies in part because it required a formal structure.

In addition, PPB suffered major resistance from Congress. Advocates of PPB apparently forgot that Congress had an important and jealously guarded role in the budget process. Members of Congress who had spent years building up their contacts and knowledge of agency budgets resented a new budget system that disrupted their channels of influence and information in an effort to make budgeting more rational and less political.

MANAGEMENT BY OBJECTIVE

In the late 1950s, economist Peter Drucker developed a management technique for business called management by objective (MBO). In the early 1970s, OMB adopted the system. Similar to PPB, it was an attempt to make budget decisions more rational. Not as ambitious in its comprehensiveness as PPB, MBO simply stated that agencies should specify goals and alternative means of achieving those goals. It was a system much less centralized than PPB, with less emphasis on long-range planning, but it still was based on agencies making rational choices about their policy goals.

Despite its simplification, MBO also had a short life in the federal government. By the beginning of Jimmy Carter's administration, it had passed from use. Lance T. LeLoup pointed out that many of the problems with PPB remained with MBO. He wrote: "It was difficult to specify and agree on objectives, and to quantify benefits. MBO was not supported at middle and lower levels of agency management because it was still perceived as a system that increased control at the upper levels."[1]

ZERO-BASE BUDGETING

An attempt at presidential control over the national budgeting process was zero-base budgeting (ZBB). Developed in the private sector (like PPB and MBO) by Peter Pyhrr of Texas Instruments Inc., ZBB was first applied to state governments.

Under Pyhrr's direction, Jimmy Carter first implemented it in Georgia while he was governor. In 1977, several months after he became president, Carter instructed OMB to implement ZBB. Carter promised that "by working together under a ZBB system, we can reduce costs and make the federal government more efficient and effective." [2] ZBB was primarily designed to avoid incremental budgeting in which some arbitrary percentage is more or less blindly added to the preceding year's budget. Instead, ZBB aims to force agencies to identify and analyze goals and objectives, making them an integral part of the budget process.[3]

Like PPB and MBO, the appeal of a comprehensive budgeting program such as ZBB is tremendous, but its success has been limited. Budget scholar Allen Schick concluded that the effect of ZBB on the budgeting activities of the executive branch had been almost negligible. Under ZBB, most budget items have been funded at or slightly above past current services levels.[4]

1. Lance T. LeLoup, *Budgetary Politics,* 2d ed. (Brunswick, Ohio: King's Court, 1980), 271.
2. Quoted in Joel Haveman, "Zero-Base Budgeting," *National Journal,* April 2, 1977, 514.
3. Peter A. Pyhrr, *Zero-Base Budgeting: A Practical Management Tool for Evaluating Expenses* (New York: Wiley, 1973), 10.
4. Allen Schick, "The Road from ZBB," in *Contemporary Approaches to Public Budgeting,* ed. Fred A. Kramer (Cambridge: Winthrop, 1979), 216.

president and a constitutional amendment to balance the budget, a strategy of mandatory spending cuts was the alternative chosen by Congress.

Gramm-Rudman-Hollings represented a major revision in the budgetary process by providing for deficit-reduction targets over six years. By imposing declining deficit ceilings, it would bring the budget into balance by 1991. If the budget process exceeded these guidelines, the president could order across-the-board spending cuts, or sequestration. (Some programs, such as Social Security and veterans' benefits, were exempt from these mandatory cuts.) The act failed to live up to its billing, however. In the 1986 budget process, Gramm-Rudman-Hollings achieved some modest success. In early 1987, when the CBO announced that the deficit for fiscal 1988 would be well above the target for that year, Congress changed the targets. It moved back the budget deficit targets two years so that the federal budget would be balanced in 1993.

In 1987 President Reagan invoked a $23 billion sequestration under Gramm-Rudman-Hollings. On October 19, one day before Reagan was to begin the procedure for automatic spending cuts, the stock market suffered its worst single-day loss ever. In a deal reached between Congress and the president, the sequestration order was repealed and a budget agreement was reached that was supposed to save $75 billion during the next two years. This agreement included spending cuts and some tax increases to ensure compliance with Gramm-Rudman-Hollings targets. But the actual deficit reduction was less than the proposed targets, and by 1990 deficits stood at record levels. Facing a widening deficit gap, President George Bush and Congress made a budget control agreement for fiscal years 1991–1995 that abandoned the Gramm-Rudman-Hollings deficit-reduction timetable. In doing so, Bush broke his 1988 campaign promise of "Read my lips, no new taxes" by agreeing to some tax increases to help bring down the budget deficit.

The 1990 budget agreement, known as the Budget Enforcement Act (BEA), was amended in 1993 to run through 1998. The BEA sought to lower budget deficits by imposing limits on annual appropriations for discretionary spending in three broad areas: defense, domestic programs, and foreign aid. Under the BEA, OMB determines whether the annual caps have been exceeded and, if so, by how much. It then reports those amounts to the president, who may issue sequestration orders that prevent agencies from spending in excess of the limits set by Congress. In addition, the BEA requires Congress to either raise taxes or reduce other entitlements if it creates any new entitlement programs.

Early in his administration President Clinton had to deal with the accumulated deficits of the Reagan and Bush administrations and the new caps on spending imposed by the BEA. The promise to cut the budget deficit was an important part of Clinton's presidential campaign. As a result of governmental fiscal discipline and the huge economic growth of the mid-late 1990s, the budget was brought into balance and eventually achieved annual surpluses in fiscal years 1998 through 2001. Both President Clinton and the Republican Congress elected in 1994 took credit for this achievement. By fiscal year 2002, with the economy slowing down dramatically and the Bush administration having enacted tax cuts, the federal government once again was running annual budget deficits. After the war in Iraq was launched in March 2003, the federal deficit dramatically climbed to meet the costs of the war. By fiscal year 2005, the federal deficit had reached over $300 billion before dropping to $248 billion in fiscal year 2006.[125]

Congress and Presidential Lobbying

Because an almost adversarial relationship exists between Congress and the president over development of the budget, presidents must actively lobby Congress for their budget recommendations to become public policy. This difficult task is complicated by the dispersal of congressional budget authority among the House and Senate Appropriations Committees and the various standing committees. After the president submits the budget plan, Congress gives different committees jurisdiction over different aspects of it. The House Ways and Means and Senate Finance Committees consider revenue proposals. The various standing committees consider proposals for changes in laws that affect the uncontrollable expenses. The Joint Economic Committee studies the fiscal implications of the president's proposals. The House and Senate Budget Committees obtain budget information and prepare the budget resolution. The House and Senate Appropriations Committees consider expenditure requests. Presidents must exert influence on these different committees if their proposals are to become grants of spending authority for their departments and agencies.

Probably the most important committees with which presidents have to deal are the Appropriations Committees. These are also the most difficult for presidents to influence, because they are among the most powerful and the most isolated from White House control. The Appropriations Committees work with several independent sources of information when they consider presidential budget requests. They have the figures prepared by OMB, estimates from the substantive committees of possible expenditures of programs under their jurisdiction, program estimates and options prepared by CBO, and tentative spending guidelines prepared by the various budget committees.

In addition to their many sources of information outside OMB, the Appropriations Committees are free from the political control of the president. Their members enjoy tremendous electoral stability, especially those in the House. Since the 1980s, more than 90 percent of House incumbents have been reelected at each election cycle. Although the percentages are not as large in the Senate, the number of Senate incumbents reelected has been well above the 80 percent mark in recent years. According to Richard Pious, "Each committee member can maintain his position in his district through delivery of goods and services and patronage, from agencies eager to please him. The president cannot oust these members from his party, the committee, or the House by purging them if they cross him." [126]

Still, the initiative usually remains with the president. A determined president, who exerts the full force of the presidency, can overcome many congressional objections. The momentum in the budget proceedings belongs to the president, whose administration usually speaks with unanimity. By contrast, Congress often speaks with many confused and chaotic partisan voices and so finds it difficult to defeat presidential budget initiatives. As Shuman has pointed out, because of the consensus it represents the White House can control the debate: the president's "budget and . . . views are the subjects of the lead paragraphs in the early budget stories. Congressional criticism trails as an afterthought at the end of the article." [127] For example, after introducing his first budget in Congress, President Reagan went on the offensive by explaining his budget to friendly audiences. Before a joint session of the Iowa legislature he said, "The budget we have proposed is a line drawn in the dirt. Those who are concerned about the deficits will cross it and work with us on our proposals or their alternatives. Those who are not . . . will stay on the other side and simply continue their theatrics." [128]

In 1995 Congress seized the initiative from President Clinton in attempting to balance the budget. Under the energized leadership of newly elected House Speaker Newt Gingrich, R-Ga., the Republican-controlled Congress tried to deliver on its 1994 campaign promise of a balanced budget. In the early stages of the budget negotiations, Republicans were united behind plans to force President Clinton to side with their proposals to downsize the federal government. But as government shutdowns occurred and public opinion turned toward the White House, Congress became less unified in its budget strategy and goals, and President Clinton remained firm in his refusal to capitulate to congressional demands for sharper cuts in programs such as Medicare and Medicaid. As a result, by early 1996 the budgeting initiative had returned to the president. For the next several years the Republicans proved reluctant to challenge the president's budget leadership. Consequently, when the budget achieved balance and then surpluses by 1998, the White House received most of the political credit. In late 2000 the economy began to slow down dramatically, and in 2001 President George W. Bush responded by convincing Congress to pass a substantial tax cut. Budget deficits returned in fiscal year 2002 and were projected once again to begin growing at a fast rate.

Sometimes presidents can use the advantages of their office to pressure recalcitrant members of Congress to go along with their budget proposals. And often these tactics are not so subtle. When Vice President Gore telephoned Sen. Richard Shelby, then a conservative Democrat from Alabama, to urge his support of the Clinton administration's first budget, Shelby had television cameras present and publicly challenged the Clinton budget as being too high on taxes and too low on spending cuts. The Clinton White House did not think this rebuff to the vice president and the president's budget should go unchallenged. Clinton promptly retaliated by moving a NASA project worth $380 million a year and ninety jobs from Huntsville, Alabama, to Houston, Texas. The administration then leaked the story to the media to send a message to other Democrats who might be thinking of abandoning Clinton's budget proposal. [129] The president's strategy, however, eventually backfired. A year later, Shelby became a Republican.

Presidential Spending

Although Congress has power over the appropriations process, presidents always have a certain amount of *discretionary power* over spending—that is, they may spend certain funds as they please within broad areas of responsibility. Often Congress delegates discretionary power to the president. In a crisis, for example, especially during wartime, Congress may give the president "lump sum" (that is, very broadly defined) appropriations so that the president and executive branch officials who represent presidential wishes may devote funds as they deem appropriate within the congressional limit. Although the discretionary power does not give presidents unlimited spending authority, it does give them some budget flexibility and some latitude in the actual spending of funds as well as a final opportunity to make policy. As political scientist Louis Fisher has observed, "What is done by legislators at the appropriations stage can be undone by administrators during budget execution." [130]

Sometimes presidents exercise discretionary spending power that Congress has not delegated specifically by interpreting spending authorizations and appropriations as permissive instead of mandatory. In 1959, for example, President Eisenhower simply did not establish a food stamp program that Congress had passed into law. Presidents also can delay setting up appropriated programs in their efforts to frustrate congressional initiatives. In 1975, after Congress had developed a summer employment program, the Ford administration successfully stymied the program by setting it up so slowly that the appropriated funds could not be spent during the fiscal year. Similarly, OMB can delay funding from the Treasury to an agency in an attempt to eliminate the agency or its programs. In 1975 the Ford administration undermined the Community Services Administration by delaying the agency's funds until after the agency's authority expired. [131]

Confidential Funding

Occasionally, Congress grants the president confidential funding for urgent, highly sensitive, or secretive matters. Presidents have complete discretion over such annually funded budget items. For example, during his 1974 visit to Egypt, President Nixon used a presidential contingency fund to give Egyptian president Anwar Sadat a $3 million helicopter as a gift.

Fisher has reported that several confidential accounts are noted in the public record but are not audited by Congress, including four in the White House, six for diplomatic agencies, and one each for atomic energy, space, the Federal Bureau of Investigation, and the Central Intelligence Agency.[132] One of the most notorious confidential funds was President Nixon's Special Projects Fund, which was used to finance a massive spying and sabotage campaign against Nixon's "political enemies."

Secret Funding

In addition to the various confidential funds, presidents may ask Congress for a general appropriation for secret projects. Secret funds do not require either the appropriation (the amount of money granted by Congress) or the expenditure (the amount of money spent by the executive branch) to be a matter of public record.

Secret funding was used for the Manhattan Project during World War II. The development of the atomic bomb required more than $2 billion, which Congress approved with little scrutiny of the purpose of the appropriation.

Secret funding also is used for intelligence organizations such as the CIA. The CIA's expenditures are drawn on requests from the agency's director and are not made public or audited by Congress. CIA activities are financed by secret transfers of funds from the appropriations accounts of other agencies, primarily the Defense Department. This process keeps the CIA budget hidden not only from the public, but also from many members of Congress.

In recent years Congress has attempted to restrict the use of confidential and secret funds and bring existing funds under greater congressional scrutiny. In 1974, after revelations of covert operations overseas, Congress prohibited the CIA from funding operations other than activities intended solely for obtaining necessary intelligence.[133] More recently, there has been a move to make the funding of the CIA and other intelligence agencies a matter of public record. Congress has the power either to control or to limit this type of discretionary power, but so far it has chosen to impose only moderate limitations.

Transfers

Another method of bypassing the congressional appropriations process is to transfer funds. Such transfers occur when Congress permits the executive to shift funds from one appropriation account to another and therefore use appropriated funds for purposes different from those originally intended. In 1970 the Nixon administration used transfer authority to finance the Cambodian intervention with a $108.9 million transfer from military aid accounts for Greece, the Philippines, South Vietnam, Taiwan, and Turkey. In 1972 Congress prohibited transfers of military aid from one nation to another unless the president gave Congress notice. Yet, despite the Nixon administration's agreements to submit transfers to Congress for approval, the war in Cambodia in 1972 and 1973 was financed by more than $750 million in transfer authority already given the president.

Reprogramming

Presidents also may reprogram funds—that is, move funds within an appropriation account from one budget item to another. By shifting funds for projects that had been approved to projects that had not been approved, some presidents have used reprogramming to frustrate congressional intent.

Presidents most frequently reprogram funds within the defense budget. For example, the Pentagon may reprogram funds in an attempt to develop new weapons systems after the House and Senate Appropriations Committees have cut the defense budget. In the 1960s, as many as one hundred reprogramming actions moved several billion dollars in a single year. And between 1956 and 1972, average annual reprogramming in the Pentagon totaled $2.6 billion. Congressional committees once allowed departments to reprogram first and inform them afterward, but because some departments maneuvered around the intent of appropriations measures, Congress now requires at least semiannual notification and, in some instances, prior clearance with the committees.

Impoundment Powers

Until 1974, the most powerful presidential tool in overcoming the congressional funding prerogative was the power of impoundment—the president's refusal to spend funds that Congress had appropriated for a particular purpose. Historically, presidents have claimed both constitutional and statutory authority to impound funds either by treating the funding as permissive (optional) instead of mandatory and then rescinding spending authority or by deferring spending to future years. The impoundment power is similar to the veto power in that both are attempts to block or thwart congressional actions.

One of the most famous early examples of a president's use of the impoundment power was Thomas Jefferson's refusal in 1803 to spend a $50,000 appropriation for gunboats on the Mississippi River to protect the western frontier. Jefferson carefully informed Congress that the money should be used for the purchase of more advanced boats the next year. Similarly, President Ulysses S. Grant refused to spend funds that Congress had appropriated for public works projects, arguing that they could be completed for less money than had been appropriated. In both cases, Congress eventually accepted the president's power to refuse to spend congressionally appropriated money.

Congress eventually gave impoundment authority a statutory basis by passing the Anti-Deficiency Acts of 1905 and 1906. These laws allowed presidents to withhold funds for a period of time to prevent deficiencies or overspending in an agency. In 1921 the Bureau of the Budget established impoundment authority when its director, Charles G. Dawes, announced that "the president does not assume . . . that the minimum of government expenditures is the amount fixed by Congress in its appropriations." [134]

Under the New Deal, President Roosevelt occasionally used impoundments for budgetary or policy purposes. In some cases, the president acted with at least the implied consent of Congress. During the Great Depression, for example, spending bills were sometimes treated as ceilings, allowing Roosevelt to refuse to spend money that he believed to be unnecessary. During World War II, Roosevelt argued that his war powers gave him the power to cut spending that was not essential to national security. Presidents Truman, Eisenhower, and Kennedy all used impoundments to cut military spending.

President Johnson, however, used impoundments to curtail domestic spending during the Vietnam War. As the war progressed and inflation rose, Johnson impounded funds designated for agriculture, conservation, education, housing, and transportation. These impoundments were usually temporary, and the funds eventually were released. Although Johnson did not use the power of impoundment to cripple congressionally appropriated programs (many of them were his own), his actions did set an example of impoundment power being used to combat inflation—a power later adopted and expanded by Nixon.

Both Johnson and Nixon used impoundment to control spending, but Nixon's use was unprecedented in its scope and effects. Whereas Johnson relied on temporary deferrals instead of permanent cuts and worked personally with Congress to soothe tempers, the Nixon administration's impoundments seemed designed to eliminate or to curtail particular programs favored by the Democratic Congress. Between 1969 and 1974, the administration made a determined effort to redistribute the emphasis of government services. When Congress overrode Nixon's veto of the Federal Water Pollution Control Act Amendments of 1972, for example, the Nixon administration impounded half of the $18 billion that had been allotted for fiscal years 1973–1975, thereby handicapping the program. In addition, the Nixon administration undertook major impoundment

reductions in low-rent housing construction, mass transit, food stamps, and medical research programs.

By 1973 Nixon had impounded more than $20 billion, and his budget for fiscal 1974 contained a list of 109 reductions he wanted to make, 101 of which he said would require no congressional approval. Ippolito concluded, "While administration spokesmen advanced a variety of justifications in support of these impoundments—including precedent, statutory responsibilities, and general executive authority—it was apparent that impoundment was being used to enforce the president's policy preferences and budgetary priorities." [135] More than thirty lower-court cases overturned Nixon impoundments. The Supreme Court eventually tackled Nixon's impoundment of funds for water pollution control. In *Train v. City of New York,* the Court ruled that once water pollution control funds had been appropriated by an act of Congress, funds could not be withheld at a later stage by impoundment. [136]

Eventually, public pressure began to build for Congress to do something about Nixon's use of the impoundment power. At first, individual members attempted to intervene personally with the president in an effort to restore funds to certain projects. By 1972 many subcommittees had become concerned about the impoundment pattern that was beginning to emerge—a pattern that threatened their control of the policy-making process. In 1973 the House and Senate Appropriations Committees began holding hearings on the impoundment of funds for low-income housing, and Congress began inserting mandatory language in certain spending bills to eliminate the discretionary authority that had allowed presidential impoundment.

In 1974 Congress adopted the Congressional Budget and Impoundment Control Act. Besides setting up the Congressional Budget Office to improve congressional monitoring of, and deliberation on, the budget, the act sought to control presidential impoundment. It stipulated two new procedures, *rescissions* and *deferrals,* by which presidents could temporarily override or delay congressional appropriations decisions. If presidents wish to rescind (that is, cancel) all or part of the appropriated funds, they must inform Congress. Unless Congress passes a rescission bill within forty-five days permitting the cancellation of funding, presidents must spend the funds. As the Congressional Budget and Impoundment Control Act was originally written, either house of Congress could block a deferral (that is, delay) of spending. But in 1983 the Supreme Court, in *Immigration and Naturalization Service v. Chadha,* ruled the one-house legislative veto unconstitutional. [137] The effect of *Chadha* was to require a resolution by a majority vote of both houses directing that appropriated funds be spent immediately.

Because Nixon resigned in 1974, a few months before the implementation of the impoundment control provisions of the budget act, he never felt the force of the act. The first administration to be confronted with these statutory impoundment limitations was the Ford administration. Of the $9 billion in rescissions requested by President Ford during his term in office, 86 percent were denied by Congress. Only 24 percent of his deferral requests were rejected, however. This pattern has been followed fairly consistently since the Ford administration. Congress usually grants deferrals; in most years, it allows 90 percent of them. But rescissions are a different matter. In recent years, congressional approvals have ranged from 80 percent in 1979 to none in 1990. Usually, Congress approves fewer than half of presidential rescissions.[138] Both the Reagan and Bush administrations called for increased rescission authority in their efforts to reduce the deficit. In March 1996 the Republican-controlled Congress ended months of negotiation to grant to the president "enhanced rescission" authority—a type of line-item veto. *(See "Line-Item Veto, p. 1352, in Chapter 29, Vol. II.)* President Clinton signed the bill on April 9, 1996. The law gave the president (beginning in 1997) the power to "cancel" individual items in spending and tax bills unless overturned by a two-thirds vote of both houses of Congress. But the president did not possess this authority for long, because the Supreme Court struck down the line-item veto as an unconstitutional violation of separation of powers in 1998 in *Clinton v. City of New York,* 524 U.S. 417.

The line-item veto was revisited when President George W. Bush, in his 2006 State of the Union address, asked Congress to provide him such authority. No action was taken on his request. President Bush had frequently used signing statements as a form of de facto veto of objectionable provisions of authorization bills but sought line-item veto authority for appropriations bills to control rapidly escalating federal spending.

THE PRESIDENT AS CHIEF LAW ENFORCEMENT OFFICER

"All is gloom in the eastern states," wrote John Marshall in January 1787.[139] Farmers, many of them veterans of the American Revolution, sought and were denied legislative or judicial relief from their debts. Under the leadership of Daniel Shays, a former officer of George Washington's army, farmers had revolted in Massachusetts. Would, as Marshall plainly worried, the American experiment in democracy survive?

It did survive. Shays' Rebellion was suppressed by Massachusetts militia, though not without considerable effort. The national government, such as it existed at the time, was powerless to assist. The debtors, however, remained resentful, and property owners had become apprehensive. The political leadership of the United States sought a more durable remedy, and a more durable remedy was found.

In February 1787, the thirteen states of the United States were invited by Congress to send delegates to a May convention in Philadelphia for the purpose of amending the Articles of Confederation. But at the urging of leaders such as James Madison and Alexander Hamilton, the convention ended up summarily rejecting the Articles as a basis for continued political union among the thirteen states. The convention's new formula for government was proposed by Congress on September 17, 1787, and ratified by the requisite nine states the next year. On June 21, 1788, the U.S. Constitution became the supreme law of the land.

It would be excessive to say that Shays' Rebellion was the single or even the most significant event leading to the adoption of the Constitution. Serious defects in the Articles had been generally known well before the Massachusetts farmers revolted. The contribution of Shays to the Constitution, rather, was to force the political leadership of the various states to do what they already knew had to be done. Shays aroused "an emotional surge" in favor of a new constitution.[140]

"We the People of the United States" sought in the Constitution to, among other things, "form a more perfect Union, establish Justice, [and] insure domestic Tranquility" (Preamble). They would not repeat the mistake of the Confederation. Americans would not render the national government powerless to promote domestic tranquility and justice.

The Constitution instructed the president to "take Care that the Laws be faithfully executed" and to preside as chief executive over what would become a vast law enforcement apparatus. The president could invoke the authority of "commander in chief" and deploy the armed forces, including units of state militia, to enforce the law. And, because mercy may be a more effective means of promoting domestic tranquility than the sword, the president would be given extensive clemency authority—the power to grant pardons and reprieves. In other words, the president was to be the chief law enforcement officer of the United States.[141]

The president's law enforcement power has grown in rough proportion to the expansion of the responsibilities and power of the national government itself. In 1789, the year Washington was inaugurated as the nation's first president, the national government generally restricted itself to activities such as collecting customs duties, suppressing domestic insurrections, enforcing federal court orders, and regulating American Indian tribes, the mails, and the army and navy. The law enforcement responsibility and power of the national government was potentially great, but actually weak.

Throughout most of the nineteenth century, direct federal enforcement of the law remained limited in scope. Congress generally left enforcement to state and local authorities. As a result, the states had great discretion in deciding whether to enforce a federal statute. The move toward greater federal enforcement of the law picked up speed in the final two decades of the nineteenth century and during the presidential administrations of Theodore Roosevelt, William Howard Taft, and Woodrow Wilson. Later, increased federal regulatory power was a fundamental element of Franklin Roosevelt's New Deal. And with the post–World War II era came novel and renewed demands for national regulation, demands that have been largely met.

As Congress added to the "police power" of the national government—that is, the power to regulate the health, safety, morals, and general welfare of the nation—it also increased the enforcement power of the executive branch. It supplemented the authority already vested directly in the president by the Constitution, or prior congressional act, and it gave the president additional resources to exercise these grants more effectively and with more power.

Yet Congress has not relinquished its own considerable power over law enforcement. To the contrary, it has insisted that power in law enforcement be shared between the president and Congress. The role of each actor, and the relationship of each to the other, must be understood. So must the unique contribution of the judicial branch to the power of the president in law enforcement.

Law Enforcement by the U.S. Government

The Constitution delegates limited power to the national government, which means, essentially, that the national government possesses only those powers that are specifically granted to it by the Constitution, or those that can be fairly implied from specific grants and that are not limited by any other constitutional provision.

The Constitution does not give any branch of the national government explicit authority to regulate the health, safety, morals, or general welfare of the community.[142] Nonetheless, that result has been obtained. Although the Constitution does not make a grant of general police power to the national government, it does grant or enumerate a variety of powers that have been shaped, constitutionally and politically, into what now resembles a general national police power.

Article I, Section 8, of the Constitution enumerates a variety of powers that may be exercised by Congress. For example, Congress may impose and collect taxes, regulate immigration, print currency and punish counterfeiters, provide postal service, and regulate the armed forces and military bases of the United States. Congress may also regulate commerce "among the several States" (the "commerce clause" of the Constitution). These powers constitute just a portion of the significant law enforcement authority of the national government. The basis for an expansive federal law enforcement power is found in the final clause of Article I, Section 8, known as the "necessary and proper clause" of the Constitution: "The Congress shall have Power . . . To make

all Laws which shall be necessary and proper for carrying into Execution the foregoing Powers, and all other Powers vested by this Constitution in the Government of the United States, or in any Department or Officer thereof." The Supreme Court has interpreted the "necessary and proper clause" of the Constitution to enlarge the enumerated powers of Congress so that it can exercise expansive police or regulatory powers.

In the 1819 case of *McCulloch v. Maryland,* the Court was asked to determine whether the Constitution gave Congress authority to charter a national bank when such a power was not among those specifically granted the legislative branch.[143] If the national government was to be a government of limited, enumerated powers, the state of Maryland argued, then the Court must find that Congress had exceeded its authority.

Writing on behalf of a unanimous Court, Chief Justice John Marshall agreed completely with Maryland's contention that Congress is granted only limited regulatory power by the Constitution. He also conceded that chartering a national bank is not listed in Article I, Section 8. Marshall was too clever a legal logician, however, and too ardent a supporter of national power to allow congressional regulatory authority to be curbed by such a restrictive interpretation of the Constitution.

The constitutional authority of Congress, Marshall wrote, consists of those powers that are expressly granted by the Constitution, plus (here is where he tied the "necessary and proper clause" to the enumerated powers of Congress) those powers that are necessary and proper to the exercise of its expressly granted powers. If the end (for example, collecting taxes or supporting an army) is legitimate (that is, authorized by an enumerated power), then the means chosen by Congress to promote that end (chartering a national bank) will be upheld judicially, so long as those means are not prohibited by some other constitutional provision.

The attention of the Court then shifted to giving meaning to the enumerated powers. Granted, Congress is authorized to enact any law that helps it, for example, to promote the regulation of interstate commerce, but what exactly does "commerce among the several States" mean? Is the Constitution referring to the actual transportation of goods between two or more states? Or does the commerce clause imply more?

On these questions, once again the antecedents of modern constitutional doctrine were established during the tenure of Marshall.[144] But more than a century of judicial review was required before the modern rule became established: Congress has constitutional authority to regulate anything that *affects* interstate commerce, no matter how slight the effect.[145] Little imagination is required to find an affecting relationship between a specified activity and interstate commerce.[146]

The Supreme Court's expansive interpretation of the Constitution did not mandate a particular national role in law enforcement, and it did not in any sense require Congress to exercise its police power to the fullest lawful extent. Instead, the Court conferred constitutional legitimacy on an expansive national police power. It was up to Congress to exercise that power.

Periodically responding to the perceived need and popular demand for national regulation, Congress has added incrementally to the police power of the federal government. The Interstate Commerce Commission Act of 1887 provided for federal regulation of the railroads. This was followed by the Sherman Antitrust Act of 1890, Pure Food and Drug Act of 1906, Federal Reserve Act of 1913, and Federal Trade Commission Act of 1914. The basis for an extensive federal police power was firmly in place by the time Franklin Roosevelt was inaugurated as president in 1933.

The Great Depression was the singular fact faced by Roosevelt and Congress. Congress deferred to the president, and Roosevelt responded with the New Deal, a collection of programs adding directly to the regulatory authority of the federal government. The banking industry became more thoroughly regulated with the enactment of the Banking Act of 1933. Enactment of the Securities Acts of 1933 and 1934 placed the sale of stocks under direct federal supervision. The National Labor Relations Act of 1935 did the same for labor-management relations; and the Civil Aeronautics Act of 1938, for civilian aviation. Wages and hours of employment became the subject of extensive federal regulation with the passage of the Fair Labor Standards Act of 1938.

Roosevelt and Congress had inherited the rudiments of a federal police power in 1933. By the time the New Deal ended, upon the entry in 1941 of the United States into World War II, the regulatory jurisdiction and power of the federal government had become even more inclusive, intensive, and extensive. Regulating the health, safety, morals, and general welfare of the nation had become a major preoccupation of the federal government.

This role expanded in the post–World War II years. The Federal Housing Act of 1949, and multiple amendments, made Washington the principal source of money for financing inner-city public housing construction and urban renewal. Money received from the federal government, whether in the form of loans, grants, or payments for goods and services, is accompanied by a plethora of regulations and contractual obligations. Various pieces of legislation—the most important being the employment, housing, and public accommodations provisions of the Civil Rights Act of 1964—banned discrimination based on race, color, religion, sex, and national origin. In response to nine Supreme Court decisions from 1986 to 1991 that had made it difficult for workers charging discrimination to win lawsuits, Congress enacted, and President George Bush signed, the Civil Rights

Act of 1991.[147] The law reaffirmed and strengthened the antidiscrimination provisions of the 1964 Civil Rights Act and also amended Title VII to allow for monetary damages for victims of discrimination.

Examples of other federal measures enacted during this period are the Federal Aviation Act of 1958, Consumer Credit Policy Act of 1968, National Environmental Protection Act of 1969, Occupational Safety and Health Act of 1970, Consumer Product Safety Act of 1972, Endangered Species Act of 1973, Americans with Disabilities Act of 1990, and Freedom of Access to Clinic Entrances Act of 1993.

Critics of federal law enforcement often charge that the implementation standards enacted by Congress are too vague, leading to abuses. A frequently cited example is the 1970 Racketeer Influenced and Corrupt Organizations Act (RICO). Congress intended this law to be used as a tool against the activities of organized crime. But its provision for triple damage awards—intended as a deterrent to organized crime and an incentive to plaintiffs—gave private businesses an incentive to sue competitors using RICO. The law is broad enough to allow them to do so. The broad language of the law also has resulted in charges against nonviolent demonstrators—for example, antiabortion groups—for engaging in "racketeering activity." The Supreme Court has refused to narrow the scope of RICO, maintaining that only Congress can rewrite the law. Several efforts to do so have not succeeded.

This summary reveals that the police power of the national government has expanded greatly in the past century. Still, only some of the ways in which power has grown are described here. Not mentioned, for example, are the many and frequent amendments to the Internal Revenue Code (annual amendments that are sometimes mockingly called "Lawyers and Accountants Relief Acts") or to the criminal code. Nor have the more "traditional" exercises of federal police power been noted, such as those dealing with immigration, national security, regulation of Native American tribes, imposition of ethical standards on government employees, import restrictions and taxes, and operation of the postal system.

A policy of selective business "deregulation" initiated by President Jimmy Carter and supported and furthered by his successors—Ronald Reagan, George Bush, and to a lesser extent Bill Clinton—deserves special mention. Supporters of deregulation argued that it would reduce consumer costs by fostering competition among businesses and by reducing the costs of regulation (that is, the costs of record keeping, administrative monitoring, and legal advice) borne by businesses and passed on to consumers.

Congress has directed deregulation efforts at a limited number of industries—primarily transportation, communications, and commercial credit—and only at selected business practices. Deregulation has thus reduced but not eliminated the national police power over economic activity. American businesses remain thoroughly regulated by the national government.

After enacting laws, members of Congress do not pin badges on their chests and act as enforcement officers. Instead, Congress makes the laws of the United States and then delegates enforcement jurisdiction and power to agencies and personnel of the executive branch. These agencies are also the creation of Congress.

Development of the federal civilian bureaucracy, and its power, has almost paralleled these diverse bursts of congressional energy. Civilian personnel employed by the federal government in nondefense capacities numbered 4,279 in 1816. Almost 80 percent of these were postal workers. By 1901 the number of such employees had increased to 186,532. In 1993 civilian personnel of the national government employed by nondefense agencies totaled 2.09 million.[148] By 2005, the civilian employment of the federal government had grown to 2.7 million.[149]

Not all of these increases can be attributed to the growth of the police power of the national government. The workforce has grown in areas that have little to do with law enforcement, such as space exploration, agricultural advice, and maintenance of national parks. Nonetheless, most of the expansion of the federal civilian workforce is associated with the increased law enforcement role of the national government.

As chief executive and chief law enforcement officer of the United States, the president has been the most direct and most frequent beneficiary of this expansion of the national government.

Presidential Law Enforcement Authority and Power

John Kennedy exercised the legal power of the president when, in September 1962, he deployed first U.S. marshals (and various other federal civilian law enforcement officers) and then regular army troops to Oxford, Mississippi. Kennedy was acting as chief law enforcement officer of the United States. He was, as Article II, Section 3, of the U.S. Constitution requires, "tak[ing] Care that the Laws be faithfully executed."

Enforcing the law, in this case, meant backing a federal court order. In 1961 James Meredith applied for admission to the University of Mississippi ("Ole Miss"). Meredith was a Mississippi citizen, a veteran of the air force, and an African American. Ole Miss did not admit blacks at the time.

Denied admission by the university, Meredith appealed to the federal courts for assistance. His complaint was initially dismissed by a federal district court, but this decision was reversed by the U.S. Court of Appeals for the Fifth Circuit. A panel of Fifth Circuit judges found that Meredith had been denied admission to the university solely because of his race, and they ordered his enrollment.

Prolonged negotiations between Ross Barnett, the governor of Mississippi, and Kennedy and his lieutenants, principally Attorney General Robert F. Kennedy, failed to produce an agreement for the orderly admission of Meredith. Mississippi, it became clear, would not use its own force to protect Meredith and maintain order on the campus. Protection and the maintenance of law and order, if they were to be supplied at all, would have to come from Washington.

Federal protection was provided initially by a contingent of U.S. marshals. A mob formed, however, and the original federal force had to be reinforced. Additional marshals were sent to Oxford, as were almost any federal law enforcement officers who could be spared—game wardens, border patrol personnel, and prison guards. Even this augmented force was threatened by the persistent and violent mob attacks.

On September 30, 1962, President Kennedy ordered the mob to disperse. He backed his order (and the original court order) with the deployment of regular army troops to the Ole Miss campus. Meredith was registered. *(See box, John F. Kennedy, the Law, and the "Ole Miss" Campaign, pp. 624–625.)*[150]

Kennedy enforced the laws of the United States when he ordered U.S. marshals and troops onto the Ole Miss campus. In doing so, however, he—as the president of the United States—was also acting according to law. In other words, he was acting according to and within the limitations set by the U.S. Constitution and Congress.

Presidential law enforcement power may be defined by either or both sources. Article II, Section 1, of the Constitution vests in the president the "executive Power" of the United States. Section 2 of Article II designates the president as commander in chief of the armed forces, including, when ordered into national service, the National Guard of the various states. It also gives the president authority to appoint the principal officers of the executive and judicial branches, with Senate confirmation. Finally, Section 3 lays responsibility on the president to "take Care that the Laws be faithfully executed."

The Constitution also confers on Congress authority to delegate to the president and executive branch officers extensive enforcement powers. Article I, Section 8, of the Constitution gives Congress authority to make all laws "necessary and proper" to execute its own enumerated authority as well as any other authority conferred by the Constitution on the government or any branch of the government of the United States.

Consequently, Congress has the authority "necessary and proper" to "provide for the Punishment of counterfeiting" the currency of the United States. Congress has used this authority to make counterfeiting a crime, to create the Secret Service of the Treasury Department, and to give the Secret Service authority to arrest suspected violators.

Although the Constitution and Congress vest considerable law enforcement authority in the president, both also limit that authority. The Constitution provides generally for shared decision making in many aspects of law enforcement. For example, presidential appointees with major law enforcement responsibilities—such as the U.S. attorney general, the deputy and various assistant attorneys general, the director of the FBI, and the U.S. attorney for each judicial district—are subject to Senate approval. Moreover, Article I, Section 9, of the Constitution prohibits the president from spending money for law enforcement unless Congress first authorizes an appropriation for that expenditure. Congress has limited the authority of the president to use military force for law enforcement.

Generally, presidential power falls into two categories: *discretionary* authority and *ministerial* authority. Discretionary authority involves the exercise of judgment and choice (such as that required to fill a vacancy on the Supreme Court). Ministerial authority involves the faithful implementation of decisions made by others (such as that required to pay the salary of the person eventually appointed).

Much of the law enforcement authority of the president is discretionary—setting law enforcement priorities and appointing senior law enforcement officials of the executive branch to implement those priorities. These officials, in turn, are delegated considerable discretion by Congress and the president to set additional law enforcement policies—what types of offenses merit the greatest attention, what resources will be allocated, and what cases will be prosecuted.

In exercising their discretionary authority, presidents are often subjected to external political pressures. A sufficiently aroused public can force the president to be more or less aggressive in enforcing a particular law, as can a sufficiently aroused Congress. Congressional and public dissatisfaction with enforcement of the nation's environmental laws in the early years of the Reagan administration, for example, led eventually to the almost wholesale replacement of the top management of the Environmental Protection Agency and therefore to more aggressive enforcement efforts. The Constitution reveals four general categories of presidential authority in law enforcement. The first category stems from the "take care clause" of the Constitution. The other three categories are the executive, military, and clemency powers of the president.

The "Take Care" Power of the President

The U.S. Constitution provides in Article II, Section 3, that the president "shall take Care that the Laws be faithfully executed." Two principal interpretations of that clause often are asserted.

One interpretation holds that the "take care clause" imposes an obligation on the president. The text itself is imperative in mood. It is a command to the president to obey and enforce the law. No separate and independent grant of authority to the president is stated, and none can be implied.

Supreme Court Justice Oliver Wendell Holmes Jr. urged this interpretation in his dissent in *Myers v. United States:* "The duty of the President to see that the laws be executed is a duty that does not go beyond the law or require him to achieve more than Congress sees fit to leave within his power." [151]

No one disputes that presidents are obligated to obey the law and to enforce the law with the authority they are granted. Such a view certainly has been supported by the Supreme Court.[152] The Court, however, has gone further. It has fashioned a power-granting interpretation of the "take care clause," one that does not conform to Holmes's more restrictive interpretation.

The primary ruling resulted from an appeal to the Supreme Court in the case of *In re Neagle.*[153] A deputy U.S. marshal was assigned by the attorney general to guard an associate justice of the Supreme Court, Stephen J. Field. The marshal shot and killed an assailant and was prosecuted for murder by the state of California. The marshal argued that inasmuch as he was performing official law enforcement duties as an officer of the United States at the time the assailant was shot, he was cloaked with immunity from state prosecution.

California did not dispute that U.S. marshals generally are not answerable in state courts for their official actions. It contended, however, that the marshal could not have been acting officially when he was guarding Field, because Congress had not expressly given marshals that authority. Without congressional authorization, the marshal was acting merely in the capacity of a private citizen. He was, therefore, subject to the jurisdiction of the California courts.

The Court rejected California's argument and rendered an expansive interpretation of the "take care clause" in the process. The president's power to enforce the law, wrote Justice Samuel Miller, is not limited to enforcing specific acts of Congress. It also involves enforcing the Constitution and the general peace of the land. The Court ordered California to release its prisoner.

Another notable Supreme Court interpretation of presidential enforcement authority arose in response to President Grover Cleveland's suppression of the Pullman strike of 1894.[154] Arguing that the strike, which spread to twenty-seven states and territories, was interfering with interstate commerce and delivery of the mails, two activities assigned by the Constitution to the national government, the president sought and obtained a federal court injunction ordering the strikers to desist. Cleveland then dispatched federal troops to Chicago to enforce the injunction, and anyone resisting was prosecuted for contempt of court.

The defendants challenged both the injunction and the use of military force to enforce the court order. Congress,

JOHN F. KENNEDY, THE LAW, AND THE "OLE MISS" CAMPAIGN

U.S. CONSTITUTION

The 1962 confrontation between President John F. Kennedy and Mississippi governor Ross Barnett is remembered today as an instance in which federal power overwhelmed state resistance to a judicial order. Because Kennedy faithfully executed the laws of the United States, James Meredith enrolled as a freshman at the University of Mississippi.

But the judicial branch did not just order Meredith's admission to "Ole Miss," and the president did not just enforce that order. The courts and the president acted according to the laws of the United States. Certain of these laws are reproduced here to illustrate how law is connected with the exercise of presidential power.

Various constitutional provisions also were involved in the Ole Miss controversy. These pertained to individual rights, the powers of the president, the powers of Congress, and the power of the national government in general.

Individual Rights. The Fourteenth Amendment, Section 1, of the Constitution provides that no state may "deny to any person within its jurisdiction the equal protection of the laws." In 1954 the Supreme Court interpreted this passage to mean that segregated public educational facilities were constitutionally impermissible.[1] The U.S. Court of Appeals for the Fifth Circuit applied this rule when it ordered the University of Mississippi to admit James Meredith.[2]

Presidential Power. Article II, Section 1, of the Constitution vests the "executive Power" of the United States in the president. Section 2 of this article designates the president "Commander in Chief" of the armed forces of the United States and, when called into federal service, of the several state militias. Finally, Section 3 of Article II says that the president "shall take Care that the Laws be faithfully executed."

Congressional Power. Congress, under Article I, Section 8, of the Constitution, is given the power to "make all Laws which shall be necessary and proper for carrying into Execution" its own enumerated constitutional powers "and all other Powers vested by this Constitution in the Government of the United States, or in any Department or Officer thereof." Among the enumerated powers of Congress are the power "[t]o raise and support Armies," "[t]o make Rules for the Government and Regulation of the land and naval Forces," "[t]o provide for calling forth the Militia to execute the Laws of the Union, suppress Insurrection[,]" and

"[t]o provide for organizing, arming, and disciplining the Militia, and for governing such Part of them as may be employed in the Service of the United States."

National Power. The "supremacy clause" of the Constitution provides that the "Constitution, and the Laws of the United States which shall be made in Pursuance thereof . . . shall be the supreme Law of the Land." State and local officials are bound by interpretations of the Constitution made by federal courts.[3]

CONGRESSIONALLY ENACTED LEGISLATION

According to its constitutional authority to make all laws "necessary and proper" to carry out the powers of Congress and of the president that are enumerated above, Congress enacted the following laws.

Section 332. Use of Militia and Armed Forces to Enforce Federal Authority. "Whenever the President considers that unlawful obstructions, combinations, or assemblages, or rebellion against the authority of the United States, make it impracticable to enforce the laws of the United States in any State or Territory by the ordinary course of judicial proceedings, he may call into Federal service such of the militia of any State, and use such of the armed forces, as he considers necessary to enforce those laws or to suppress the rebellion."[4]

Section 333. Interference with State and Federal Law. "The President, by using the militia, the armed forces, or both, or by any other means, shall take such measures as he considers necessary to suppress, in a State, any insurrection, domestic violence, unlawful combination, or conspiracy, if it—(1) so hinders the execution of the laws of that State, and of the United States within the State, that any part or class of its people is deprived of a right, privilege, immunity, or protection named in the Constitution and secured by law, and the constituted authorities of that State are unable, fail, or refuse to protect that right, privilege, or immunity or to give that protection; or (2) opposes or obstructs the execution of the laws of the United States or impedes the course of justice under those laws. In any situation covered by clause (1), the State shall be considered to have denied the equal protection of the laws secured by the Constitution."[5]

Section 334. Proclamation to Disperse. "Whenever the President considers it necessary to use the militia, or the armed forces under this chapter, he shall, by proclamation, immediately order the insurgents to disperse and retire peaceably to their abodes within a limited time."[6]

---

they argued, had not given the federal court the authority to issue the injunction, and it had not authorized the use of military force by the president to enforce the injunction. The Court rebuffed both challenges.[155]

Neither Supreme Court decision should be read as giving the president power to override or ignore Congress. Instead, the Court invoked the "take care clause" in both instances when Congress had been silent.

Executive Powers of the President

Presidents are elected by the people, presumably to make policy and supervise its implementation. They are not expected to involve themselves in the details of implementation—and, with a few exceptions, they do not.

The same might be said of the attorney general, the Treasury secretary, or even the director of the Federal Bureau of Investigation or the commissioner of the Internal Revenue Service (IRS). Considerable discretion to act is and must be delegated to the men and women who enforce the law: special agents of the FBI who witness a violation of federal law, IRS auditors who discover irregularities in tax filings, and assistant U.S. attorneys who uncover evidence of criminal activity in the files of investigative reports.

PRESIDENTIAL PROCLAMATION AND EXECUTIVE ORDER

Acting on his constitutional and congressionally delegated authority, President Kennedy ordered federal enforcement of the court desegregation order. First, a force of U.S. marshals and other federal law enforcement personnel were dispatched to the Ole Miss campus. Next, when a mob threatened to overwhelm this force, and when it became apparent that state law enforcement personnel would not assist the beleaguered federal force, the president commanded the secretary of defense to deploy regular army troops to the campus. The following excerpts are from Kennedy's September 30, 1962, proclamation ordering the mob to disperse and from his executive order of the same day, mobilizing the army to enforce the law:

PROCLAMATION 3497
Obstructions of Justice in the State of Mississippi
By the President of the United States of America
A Proclamation

WHEREAS, the Governor of the State of Mississippi and certain law enforcement officers and other officials of that State, and other persons, individually and in unlawful assemblies, combinations and conspiracies, have been and are willfully opposing and obstructing the enforcement of orders entered by the United States District Court for the Southern District of Mississippi and the United States Court of Appeals for the Fifth Circuit; and

WHEREAS, such unlawful assemblies, combinations and conspiracies oppose and obstruct the execution of the laws of the United States, impede the course of justice under those laws and make it impracticable to enforce those laws in the State of Mississippi by the ordinary course of judicial proceedings; and

WHEREAS, I have expressly called attention of the Governor of Mississippi to the perilous situation that exists and to his duties in the premises, and have requested but have not received from him adequate assurances that the orders of the courts of the United States will be obeyed and that law and order will be maintained:

NOW, THEREFORE, I, JOHN F. KENNEDY, President of the United States, under and by virtue of the authority vested in me by the Constitution and laws of the United States, . . . do command all persons engaged in such obstructions of justice to cease and desist therefrom and to disperse and retire peacefully forthwith.[7]

EXECUTIVE ORDER 11053
Providing Assistance for the Removal of Unlawful Obstructions
of Justice in the State of Mississippi

WHEREAS, on September 30, 1962, I issued Proclamation No. 3497 reading in part as follows:

[The portions of the proclamation quoted above are reprinted.] and

WHEREAS, the commands contained in that proclamation have not been obeyed and obstruction of enforcement of those court orders still exists and threatens to continue:

NOW, THEREFORE, by virtue of the authority vested in me by the Constitution and laws of the United States, . . . it is hereby ordered as follows:

SECTION 1. The Secretary of Defense is authorized and directed to take all appropriate steps to enforce all orders of the United States District Court for the Southern District of Mississippi and the United States Court of Appeals for the Fifth Circuit and to remove all obstructions of justice in the State of Mississippi.

SECTION 2. In furtherance of the enforcement of the aforementioned orders of the [specified courts], the Secretary of Defense is authorized to use such of the armed forces of the United States as he may deem necessary.

SECTION 3. I hereby authorize the Secretary of Defense to call into the active military service of the United States, as he may deem appropriate to carry out the purposes of this order, any or all units of the [National Guard] of the State of Mississippi to serve in the active military service of the United States for an indefinite period and until relieved by appropriate orders. In carrying out the provisions of Section 1, the Secretary of Defense is authorized to use the units, and members thereof, ordered into the active military service of the United States pursuant to this section.[8]

1. *Brown v. Board of Education,* 347 U.S. 483 (1954).
2. *Meredith v. Fair,* 306 F.2d 374 (5th Cir. 1962).
3. *Cooper v. Aaron,* 358 U.S. 1 (1958).
4. *U.S. Code,* vol. 10 sec. 332.
5. *U.S. Code,* vol. 10 sec. 333.
6. *U.S. Code,* vol. 10 sec. 334.
7. Proclamation 3497, *Code of Federal Regulations,* vol. 3, 225–226 (1959–1963 compilation).
8. Executive Order 11053, *Code of Federal Regulations,* vol. 3, 645–646 (1959–1963 compilation).

The law enforcement power of the president, therefore, depends substantially on the president's ability to affect the behavior of subordinates within the executive branch. And the ability of the president to affect the behavior of these subordinates depends in part on the president's legal authority.

The Constitution says little about presidential authority over officers of the executive branch. The first sentence of Article II, Section 1, states that the "executive Power shall be vested in a President of the United States of America." This appears to give the president great power. However, the Constitution does not define "executive Power." A narrow reading of this provision means that the Constitution merely confers on the president those powers contained in Article II. A more liberal interpretation is that Article II confers authority on the president that is not explicitly defined in the Constitution.

Appointment and Removal of Law Enforcement Officers. The executive power of the president embraces the authority to appoint senior law enforcement officers of the executive branch and judges of the federal judiciary. *(See also "The Appointment Power," p. 598.)* That authority is conferred by the "appointments clause" of Article II, Section 2, of the Constitution. *(See text from Article II, Section 2, p. 1748, and "Instruments of Presidential Control," p. 581.)*

The appointment power of the president applies generally to the senior officers of the executive branch charged with law enforcement responsibility. All cabinet members serve by virtue of presidential appointment, as do agency heads and members of the subcabinet—that is, policy-making officers immediately subordinate to a cabinet officer and at the level of undersecretary, deputy secretary, and assistant secretary. The president, then, appoints not only the attorney general and the principal officers of the Department of Justice, for example, but also the principal political officers of all federal departments and agencies involved in law enforcement.

These appointees generally serve at the pleasure of the president, which means simply that they may be fired by the president—for good reason, bad reason, or no reason at all. Such a move may be costly politically, but it lies within the legal discretion (authority) of the president, and this discretion may not be curbed by Congress.[156]

Some less senior but still high-ranking law enforcement officers also are subject to presidential appointment. The director of the FBI, the commissioner of the IRS, and the administrator of the Drug Enforcement Administration (DEA) are examples. Other examples are the U.S. attorney for each judicial district of the United States, the chief U.S. marshal, and the commissioner of the U.S. Customs and Border Protection.

Presidential authority to fire these officers varies. U.S. attorneys may be removed at the will of the president. Since 1973 the director of the FBI has been appointed to a ten-year term and may not be fired without cause. In July 1993, President Clinton removed FBI director William S. Sessions because of revelations in a Justice Department investigation of improper use of office. Sessions was the first FBI director in the department's history to be fired by the president.

Two other classes of presidential appointees deserve special note: board members and other high-ranking officers of independent regulatory boards and commissions, and federal judges.

Independent regulatory boards and commissions are largely the product of the "good government" movement of the late nineteenth and early twentieth centuries and the belief that certain aspects of policy implementation could and should be separated from ordinary partisan politics. If the organization implementing policy is legally separated from politics, then the decision makers in that organization will faithfully implement policy created by Congress and will not act to promote the partisan advantage of the incumbent president.

Congress created the Interstate Commerce Commission (ICC) in 1887 to regulate the nation's growing railroad industry and later assigned it jurisdiction over trucking as well. (Congress eliminated the ICC in 1996 but transferred some of its regulatory authority to the Department of Transportation.) After establishment of the ICC, Congress created other independent boards and commissions to regulate business trade practices (Federal Trade Commission, or FTC), labor-management relations (National Labor Relations Board, or NLRB), television and radio broadcasting (Federal Communications Commission, or FCC), sales of stocks and bonds (Securities and Exchange Commission, or SEC), banking (Federal Reserve Board, or FRB), and the nuclear power industry (Nuclear Regulatory Commission, or NRC).

The exact authority of these agencies varies. They generally possess power to make law through what is called "rule making" and to adjudicate disputes about the application of the law through quasi-judicial methods. They also have the authority to investigate unlawful conduct and, in some cases, to prosecute civil violations. (Criminal violations are prosecuted only by the Justice Department.) Their authority may extend to rate setting and licensing of businesses and individuals.

Congress has given the president the authority to appoint the principal officers of these agencies. The president's authority to fire them, however, has been limited to reasons specified by law, and these limitations have been upheld by the Supreme Court.[157] *(See "The Removal Power," p. 606.)* Federal judges, including justices of the Supreme Court, also are appointed by the president, but the president's formal authority over the judicial branch ends there. By explicit constitutional provision (Article III, Section 1), federal judges have life tenure and may not be removed from office except by the impeachment process.

Presidential Authority to Command. In addition to the appointment and removal authority, the president possesses the authority to control the official behavior of certain officers of the government who are charged with law enforcement duties.

Federal judges are an exception in that they enjoy independent status from the chief executive. Similarly, presidents lack command authority in most instances over officers of independent regulatory boards and commissions. *(See "Regulatory Commissions," p. 578.)* The president's command authority over officers of the executive branch who do not enjoy independent status is greater, although still not absolute. If the presidential command is lawful, then failure of a subordinate to obey could constitute neglect or insubordination. The president could remove such an officer and justify the decision to do so. Presidents themselves, however, must obey the law, and they have no authority to command their subordinates to commit a violation.

Occasionally disagreement arises over what the law requires or prohibits. Laws are often stated ambiguously and are subject to different interpretations. The president may fire a subordinate for insubordination when such a disagreement arises.

The great majority of federal law enforcement personnel are not appointed by the president. Instead, they are career civil servants, who obtain their positions through a competitive and nonpartisan selection process. *(See also Chapter 31, The President and the Bureaucracy, Vol. II.)* These personnel may be fired only for causes specified by statute or administrative regulation and only after a neutral and procedurally rigorous judicial-type hearing.

Special agents of the FBI, Secret Service, and Bureau of Alcohol, Tobacco, Firearms, and Explosives belong in this category. So do deputy U.S. marshals, assistant U.S. attorneys, IRS auditors, and customs inspectors. In fact, just about all investigating and enforcement officers, supporting staff, and many policy-making officers of the executive branch belong to the civil service.

Civil servants are not obliged to share the same law enforcement goals and priorities with the president. Their goals and priorities are shaped by their personal values and perceptions of what will promote their own interests. The official behavior of civil servants, therefore, should not be expected to conform in all cases with the goals and priorities of the president.

That said, civil servants are obliged to obey all lawful commands of the president and of their own bureaucratic superiors. Willful failure to comply will normally constitute legal cause for discipline, including dismissal. Any bureaucratic resistance to the president must, therefore, be displayed in a less direct, more subtle way to prove successful. More than a century of accumulated experience has provided civil servants with a variety of such methods.

Seasoned bureaucrats know well, for example, the difference between complying with lawful orders and going through the motions of complying. Suppose a president directs federal law enforcement agents to be especially aggressive in investigating members of Congress for corruption. Such an order lies within the discretionary power of the president and is entirely lawful. Most federal agents would comply; that is their job. Other agents, however, may not share the president's enthusiasm for such an investigation. An angry Congress would slice their agency's budget, or particularly powerful members of Congress might retaliate in the future by blocking their appointments to high-level agency positions. In such a case, agents may examine documents (but not too thoroughly) and follow leads (but not too many). They will then document their efforts and pronounce the absence of evidence justifying further investigations, thereby "complying" with the president's order.

The executive power of the president in law enforcement therefore depends substantially on the president's ability to choose trusted appointees who are able to influence the behavior of subordinates. Ideally, subordinates will share the president's values pertaining to law enforcement. Experience shows, however, that at least a degree of bureaucratic resistance may be expected.

Military Power

The Constitution states in Article II, Section 2, that the "President shall be Commander in Chief of the Army and the Navy of the United States, and of the Militia of the several States, when called into the actual Service of the United States." Article IV, Section 4, provides that the United States, "on Application of the [state] Legislature, or of the Executive [governor] (when the Legislature cannot be convened)," shall guarantee "against domestic Violence."

The president's authority to command the armed forces is, however, itself shaped by law. The president and Congress share authority over the armed forces of the United States.

Congress, according to its authority to enact laws "necessary and proper" to "make Rules for . . . Regulation of the land and naval Forces" and "[t]o provide for calling forth the Militia to execute the Laws of the Union, suppress Insurrections and repel Invasions" (Article I, Section 8), has enacted legislation that both authorizes and places limitations on presidential use of the military to enforce the law. *(See box, John F. Kennedy, the Law, and the "Ole Miss" Campaign, pp. 624–625, for a reprinting of these laws.)*

The Constitution does not seriously impede the ability of the president to use military force to assist civil authorities in enforcing the law. To the contrary, wrote Justice David Brewer in 1895: "There is no such impotency in the national government. . . . If the emergency arises, the army of the nation, and all its militia, are at the service of the nation to compel obedience to the laws." [158]

> The President shall be Commander in Chief of the Army and the Navy of the United States, and of the Militia of the several States, when called into the actual Service of the United States.
> —*from Article II, Section 2*

Nor does Congress impede the president in law enforcement. Although Congress has specified the conditions in which such force may be deployed, it leaves to the president considerable discretion in deciding if those conditions have been met.

A different situation arises, however, should the president attempt to declare martial law and supplant civil with military authority within the boundaries of the United States. The Supreme Court has ruled that for such an action to be maintained constitutionally, the situation must be so desperate that the civil courts are closed. [159] The military might of the United States must support, not supplant, the law.

Presidents have used military power to enforce the law in several notable instances. George Washington used military force to quell the Whiskey Rebellion. His precedent was followed by Abraham Lincoln, who used a more powerful military force to suppress the Southern rebellion. Both presidents were, legally speaking, enforcing the law.

Defiance of court injunctions against labor strikes in the nineteenth century prompted both Rutherford B. Hayes and Grover Cleveland to deploy troops to enforce the law. In the twentieth century, Dwight Eisenhower and John Kennedy used force when court desegregation orders were met by local resistance. Lyndon Johnson used his military power in 1968 to put down rioting in Detroit. In December 1989 George Bush ordered the deployment of U.S. forces abroad to enforce federal drug laws. The U.S. military invaded Panama, ousted its drug-trafficking president, Manuel Noriega, and brought him to Florida to stand trial, where he eventually was convicted on drug and racketeering counts. During his second term, George W. Bush used the National Guard to patrol the U.S.–Mexican border to enforce the immigration laws.

Clemency Power

Article II, Section 2, of the Constitution delegates to the president the "[p]ower to grant Reprieves and Pardons for Offenses against the United States, except in Cases of Impeachment." In other words, it gives the president the ability to be merciful as well as vengeful.

But mercy was not necessarily what the Framers had in mind when they included clemency in the enumerated powers of the president. Alexander Hamilton explained in *Federalist* No. 74: "But the principal argument for reposing the power of pardoning . . . in the Chief Magistrate [president] is this: in seasons of insurrection or rebellion, there are often critical moments when a well-timed offer of pardon to the insurgents or rebels may restore the tranquility of the commonwealth." [160] Hamilton urged that the president—"a single man of prudence and good sense"—alone be given the authority to exercise this power, because the legislature was not well suited to both weighing the national interest against other considerations and acting quickly. [161]

The pardon power was first used in 1792 when President George Washington "most earnestly admonish[ed] and exhort[ed]" the whiskey manufacturers of western Pennsylvania to cease their disobedience and obstruction of the law. They were, the president's proclamation continued, not only refusing to pay taxes on the whiskey produced, but also resisting enforcement of the tax law with violence. [162]

Washington tried issuing demands to end the "Whiskey Rebellion," and he tried applying force. Law and order in the western counties of Pennsylvania, however, were not restored until the president promised and granted the offenders a full and absolute pardon. [163]

A reprieve reduces a sentence already imposed by a tribunal. A person sentenced to death by a U.S. district court or military court martial, for example, may have his or her sentence reduced to a long term of imprisonment by presidential reprieve. The guilt is not wiped out, but the severity of the punishment inflicted on the guilty person is reduced.

Presidential pardons wipe out both guilt and punishment. They restore the person pardoned to his or her full civil rights, as if the offense had never been committed. President Gerald Ford, for example, granted a full and unconditional pardon to his predecessor, Richard Nixon, and relieved the former president of the possibility of being prosecuted for any involvement he may have had in the crimes associated with Watergate. In late December 1992, President George Bush issued controversial pardons to several key figures who had been implicated in the Iran-contra scandal during the Reagan administration. *(See box, Presidential Pardons, p. 629.)*

Reprieves and pardons may be granted to individuals or to classes of people in the form of "amnesties." For example, Presidents Abraham Lincoln and Andrew Johnson signed amnesties for Confederate soldiers and political leaders, as did Presidents Gerald Ford and Jimmy Carter for draft evaders during the Vietnam War.

The president may attach conditions to either form of clemency. President Nixon, for example, pardoned labor leader Jimmy Hoffa on the condition that Hoffa never again become involved in union activities.

The clemency authority of the president is extensive. It applies to any federal process or offender except, by express constitutional language, those persons tried (or being tried) and convicted through congressional impeachment. Moreover, it is one of the few constitutional powers of the president that does not require legislative assent. Congress, in fact, may not interfere with presidential clemency authority in any manner, including, the Supreme Court has held, the imposition of restrictions on those pardoned. [164]

Hamilton's argument in favor of extensive presidential clemency authority received its strongest validation in the aftermath of the Civil War. The successful reintegration of Southerners into the American political process, by means of clemency, nourished the healing process. Not only did white Southerners regain the right to vote, but they also ascended to high political office. And although no former Confederate soldier or political officer was ever elected president, many later served in the legislative, executive, and judicial branches of the United States.

The pardon process today is handled by the Office of the Pardon Attorney, created by Congress in 1891. [165] The pardon attorney reviews petitions for clemency and makes a recommendation to the attorney general, who then considers the petition and advises the president. Many presidents have not been reluctant to use this authority. Truman pardoned more than 1,500 people who had violated the Selective Service Act during World War II; Gerald Ford issued 404 pardons in just under two and a half years in office; Jimmy Carter issued 563 pardons and commutations in four years; and Ronald Reagan issued 406 pardons during his two terms in office.[166] George H. W. Bush issued only 77 pardons in his one term, but his post–election defeat pardons of six Iran-contra scandal figures, including Secretary of Defense Caspar Weinberger, were controversial. Bill Clinton issued 457 pardons over his two terms in office. Like his father, George W. Bush has made relatively few pardons. As of mid-2006, Bush had issued a scant 82 pardons. This number was in stark contrast to Franklin D. Roosevelt, who, during his tenure, granted 3,687 pardons.

Perhaps the most controversial gestures of clemency in the modern era were some of the 140 pardons and 36 commutations that Bill Clinton issued on January 20, 2001, his last day in office. Among those, none was more questioned than the pardon of fugitive financier Marc Rich, whose former wife had made appeals for the pardon after she contributed generously to the Democratic Party, the Clinton reelection campaign, and the Clinton presidential library. That Clinton ignored the normal pardon process in the Office of Pardon Attorney in the Department of Justice angered many of his political foes who believed that the president had acted improperly. The timing of the pardon, in the last moments of Clinton's presidency, added to the sense of suspicion about Clinton's motives. Calls for a congressional inquiry and legal challenge to the pardon were heard, but the fact remained that Clinton had the right under the presidential pardon power to do what he did, and his angry critics had no recourse other than to complain.

The Law Enforcement Bureaucracy

The president commands a vast law enforcement bureaucracy, made up of scores of departments and agencies. Perhaps the most familiar element of this bureaucracy is the Federal Bureau of Investigation. But the FBI is not the national police force of the United States, because, in fact, the country has no such force. Instead, the law enforcement power of the United States is distributed throughout the executive branch.

The FBI is part of the Department of Justice, itself the repository of several other important law enforcement agencies, including the Bureau of U.S. Citizenship and Immigration Services (INS), the U.S. Marshals Service, the Drug Enforcement Administration, and the Criminal Division.

PRESIDENTIAL PARDONS

The presidential power to pardon is an absolute one granted by the Constitution. When President Gerald R. Ford granted a full and unconditional pardon to his predecessor, Richard Nixon, controversy arose not over Ford's authority but his timing. Was it wise to circumvent the judicial processes already at work by pardoning someone before he had been charged with a crime? Ford was never able to shake criticism of the Nixon pardon, which contributed to his electoral defeat to Jimmy Carter in 1976. The following is an excerpt from Ford's pardon on September 8, 1974:

It is believed that a trial of Richard Nixon, if it became necessary, could not fairly begin until a year or more has elapsed. In the meantime, the tranquility to which this nation has been restored by the events of recent weeks could be irreparably lost by the prospects of bringing to trial a former President of the United States. The prospects of such trial will cause prolonged and divisive debate over the propriety of exposing to further punishment and degradation a man who has already paid the unprecedented penalty of relinquishing the highest elective office in the United States.

Now, therefore, I, Gerald R. Ford, President of the United States, pursuant to the pardon power conferred upon me by Article II, Section 2, of the Constitution, have granted and by these presents do grant a full, free and absolute pardon unto Richard Nixon for all offenses against the United States which he, Richard Nixon, has committed or may have committed or taken part in during the period from January 20, 1969 through August 9, 1974.

The Justice Department is the lead law enforcement agency at the disposal of the president. The attorney general is the statutory head of the department. Initially, the attorney general served as a part-time legal adviser to the president and the department heads. For example, from 1817 to 1829 William Wirt served in that capacity while maintaining a private law practice. Wirt represented the U.S. government to trial courts as a private counselor and charged a fee for his services, as he would for private clients. The enforcement activities of the federal government were then not extensive enough to require a full-time attorney general.[167]

Today the attorney general commands a variety of important investigatory and enforcement agencies, of which the FBI is only one. The attorney general also commands the principal prosecutorial agencies of the national government, the various U.S. attorneys across the United States, and the centralized prosecutorial divisions in Washington. Finally, the attorney general traditionally serves as the principal legal adviser to the president and supervises for the president clemency and the selection of nominees for federal judicial posts. The attorney general often works closely with the White House counsel in making these decisions, particularly in the selection of judicial nominees. *(See box, Attorneys General of the United States, p. 630.)* Law enforcement responsibility and power are further allocated among the Treasury Department, the Department of Homeland Security, and the Department of Defense.

In one respect, it is misleading to apply the term "chief law enforcement officer of the United States" to the president. Beginning with the Interstate Commerce Commission in 1887, and continuing with the creation of agencies such as

ATTORNEYS GENERAL OF THE UNITED STATES

The attorney general of the United States is the chief legal adviser to the president and is the head of the Department of Justice. Because virtually every official decision made by the president is governed by law, and such a large percentage of the work of the federal government is devoted to enforcing the law, the nature of the attorney general's job almost ensures influence with the president. The attorney general usually is considered one of the inside members of the president's cabinet. The position is one of considerable power.

President George Washington turned to a fellow Virginian, Edmund Jennings Randolph, as his (and the nation's) first attorney general. Randolph had two qualities that have often characterized the individuals who have held that office ever since: talent and controversy.

Before serving with Thomas Jefferson, Alexander Hamilton, and Henry Knox in Washington's first cabinet, Randolph had distinguished himself through his service as a military aide to General Washington, as an attorney general and governor of Virginia, as a delegate to the Virginia constitutional convention of 1776, as a delegate from Virginia to the Continental Congress, and as a delegate to the Constitutional Convention of 1787. Although Randolph refused to sign the convention's final product, the U.S. Constitution, because, among other reasons, he opposed vesting the executive power in a single president, he did urge its ratification by Virginia.

When Thomas Jefferson resigned in 1794 as Washington's first secretary of state, Washington picked Randolph to succeed him. Randolph resigned the following year, however, amid false charges of soliciting bribes and giving secret information to the French government. Although stripped of his public standing by the charges, the capable Randolph led the successful legal defense in the treason trial of Aaron Burr.

Talent and controversy have followed the successors of Randolph. Roger B. Taney, attorney general to President Andrew Jackson, and Harlan Fiske Stone, attorney general to President Calvin Coolidge, became chief justices of the United States (in Stone's case, after serving sixteen years as an associate justice). Other former attorneys general who became Supreme Court justices were Nathan Clifford, Joseph McKenna, James C. McReynolds, Francis W. Murphy, Robert H. Jackson, and Thomas C. Clark.

Harry M. Daugherty was attorney general to President Warren G. Harding and was implicated in the Teapot Dome Scandal. *(See "Teapot Dome and Other Scandals," p. 131, in Chapter 2.)* Many people thought that Ramsey Clark, the last attorney general to President Lyndon B. Johnson, should have been indicted for treason, but he was not. Clark remains controversial for visiting Hanoi during the Vietnam War after he left office. Two of President Richard Nixon's attorneys general, John N. Mitchell and Richard G. Kleindienst, went to prison after leaving office and being convicted of crimes. President Reagan's controversial attorney general, Edwin Meese, spent much of his tenure fighting ethics charges stemming from inconsistencies and omissions in his financial disclosure forms.

One attorney general, Charles Joseph Bonaparte, had an unusual family history for an American leader. Bonaparte was the grandson of Jerome Bonaparte, king of Westphalia and marshal of France. Jerome, in turn, was the younger brother of Napoleon I, emperor of France. The American Bonaparte first distinguished himself as a leader of the good-government movement of the late nineteenth and early twentieth centuries, serving consecutively as president of the National Civil Service Reform League in 1904 and as president of the National Municipal League in 1905. This commitment appealed to President Theodore Roosevelt, who rewarded Bonaparte with appointments first as secretary of the navy and then as attorney general. *(See Cabinet Members and Other Officials, p. 1872, in the Reference Materials, Vol. II.)*

In 1993 President Bill Clinton wanted to appoint the nation's first woman attorney general. His first two choices for the position, Zöe Baird and Kimba Wood, had to withdraw from consideration because of revelations that they had employed illegal immigrants as nannies. Clinton's next choice for the job, Florida prosecutor Janet Reno, was confirmed by the Senate in March 1993. The selection of Reno was symbolically important and enormously popular. Her reputation for integrity was untarnished, and she was known as a straight-speaking, law-and-order prosecutor.

Although she initially was the most celebrated and highly regarded Clinton appointee, Reno soon became mired in controversy. After a lengthy standoff between federal law enforcement officials and members of a religious cult, who had refused to surrender to the authorities, Reno authorized the FBI to inject non-lethal tear gas into the cult's Waco, Texas, compound. The effort failed to drive out the cult members, and a fire erupted at the compound leading to the deaths of eighty-five people, many of whom were children. Reno testified to Congress that she was responsible for the disaster. Reno's candor earned her immediate praise, but many continued to question her handling of the situation.

Reno continued to serve through Clinton's second term and continued to draw controversy to herself and the Justice Department. But the criticism came from both the left and right wings of American politics and involved many high-profile social issues in the 1990s, including gun control, campaign financing, the return of the young Cuban refugee Elián González to his father in Cuba, and even an investigation of alleged wrongdoing by President Clinton himself. Her eight-year term in office was one of the most tumultuous of any recent attorney general.

In 2001 President George W. Bush turned to former U.S. senator John Ashcroft, R-Mo., for attorney general. (Ashcroft had lost a reelection bid in 2000.) Because of his strong ties to the religious conservative movement, Ashcroft was a controversial choice. Civil liberties and other liberal interest groups mounted a vigorous campaign against his confirmation, yet Bush had the advantage of a Republican majority in the Senate where Ashcroft had been well regarded among his former colleagues. In the most contentious debates of all of the Bush nominees, Ashcroft was eventually confirmed by a 58–42 vote.

During his four years as attorney general, Ashcroft remained a staunch supporter of an expansive interpretation of presidential powers in the war on terrorism. In addition, Ashcroft maintained a high profile for his religious views. A Pentecostal, Ashcroft ordered the partially clad female "Spirit of Justice" statue in the Department of Justice to be covered in 2002 at a cost to the department of $8,000. He also held regular prayer meetings with his staff. Ashcroft resigned at the end of the first term and was replaced by Alberto Gonzales, the White House counsel and former Texas judge. Gonzales continued to support sweeping interpretations of presidential authority for the president as commander in chief in the war on terrorism. As White House counsel, Gonzales had authored memos giving President Bush constitutional justification as commander in chief for determining who was an enemy combatant and how an enemy combatant could be detained. These memos became a focus of Gonzales' contentious confirmation hearings. When a vacancy opened on the U.S. Supreme Court during the second term of the Bush administration, speculation emerged in the press that Gonzales would be nominated as the first Hispanic on the Court. However, his memos on enemy combatants sidelined his nomination.

the Federal Trade Commission, the National Labor Relations Board, and the Securities and Exchange Commission, Congress has periodically allocated various law enforcement powers to independent boards and commissions within the executive branch but outside the supervisory authority of the president. The power of the president over these agencies generally is limited to appointing board members and other important agency officers when vacancies occur. These officials may not be fired by the president except for cause, which is defined by Congress.[168]

Categories of Federal Law Enforcement

Agencies of the executive branch undertake law enforcement activities that fall into at least eight categories. These categories overlap in many instances and oversimplify a highly complex regulatory scheme, but they do provide an overview of the law enforcement activities of the executive branch.

Economic. Agencies of the executive branch implement a variety of laws seeking to foster economic growth, stability, and competition. Also included in this category are laws designed to advance fairness in business practices and harmonious labor-management relations. The Antitrust Division of the Justice Department enforces laws promoting fair trade practices and proscribing monopolies. Financial institutions are subjected to regulation by the comptroller of currency and by the Internal Revenue Service in the Treasury Department. Employment is subject to enforcement actions by the Occupational Safety and Health Administration and by the Employment Standards Administration of the Department of Labor. Despite deregulation, substantial regulation of the transportation industry is still administered by the Federal Aviation Administration of the Department of Transportation. Energy, a relative newcomer to the federal regulatory scheme, is under the jurisdiction of the Departments of Energy and Interior.

Social. Congress has enacted laws that promote a mélange of social goals: equality, fairness, and material comfort. Antidiscrimination laws, such as the equal employment and fair housing provisions of the Civil Rights Act of 1964, the Age Discrimination in Employment Act, the Civil Rights Restoration Act of 1988, the Americans with Disabilities Act of 1990, the Civil Rights Law of 1991, and the Family and Medical Leave Act of 1993, belong in this category. Their enforcement generally is accomplished by the combined efforts of the Civil Rights Division of the Justice Department, the Equal Employment Opportunity Commission, and the Department of Education. Each agency of the federal government also has an office charged with enforcing internal compliance with these laws, as well as compliance by firms contracting with the agency. A multitude of retirement, medical care, and educational assistance acts are administered by the Social Security

Administration of the Department of Health and Human Services, the Department of Veterans Affairs, and the Department of Education.

Political. Political decisions are made according to a complex system of procedural laws. The often-stated purpose of these laws is to promote fairness and integrity in government. The Voting Rights Act of 1965, for example, forbids racial discrimination in voting and is enforced by the FBI and the Civil Rights Division of the Department of Justice. Bribery of and extortion by federal government officials of all branches also fall under the jurisdiction of the FBI. Violations that the FBI uncovers are prosecuted by the Criminal Division of the Justice Department.

Judicial. Most judicial orders are complied with voluntarily. Judgment is entered against the defendant, and the defendant complies—that is, the defendant makes payment, stops the unlawful activity, or turns himself or herself over to authorities for completion of a jail sentence. Behind every instance of voluntary compliance, however, is at least the implicit backing of armed force. Armed force also may be necessary on occasion to enforce judicial orders and to protect judges, jurors, witnesses, and other participants in a trial. The U.S. Marshals Service of the Justice Department is the agency that usually enforces the authority of the judicial branch. Its power may, in extreme circumstances, be backed by the armed forces of the United States, principally by the army and by Army National Guard units nationalized by presidential order.

Public Health and Safety. The national government oversees many issues of public health and safety. They include transportation safety, a concern of the Federal Aviation Administration (FAA) of the Department of Transportation; occupational safety and health, consigned by Congress to the aptly named Occupational Safety and Health Administration of the Department of Labor; and food purity, which falls under the jurisdiction of the Food and Drug Administration of the Department of Health and Human Services, the Environmental Protection Agency, and the Food Safety and Inspection Service of the Department of Agriculture.

The public health and safety activities of the executive branch also entail enforcement of more commonly known criminal laws, such as those prohibiting interstate kidnapping, prostitution, and transportation of stolen property. Finally, federal laws attempting to stem drug and alcohol abuse in the United States are enforced by the FBI, DEA, FDA, Coast Guard, U.S. Customs and Border Protection, and Bureau of Alcohol, Tobacco, Firearms, and Explosives. Prosecutions are the responsibility of the Criminal Division of the Justice Department and local U.S. attorneys.

In 1984 Congress passed an anticrime bill that revamped federal sentencing procedures to reduce disparities in the sentencing of criminals. The law reduced judicial discretion by creating a ranking system for crimes and requiring judges to follow sentencing guidelines adopted by a presidential commission. The law also eliminated parole for certain federal offenses, increased penalties for drug trafficking, provided expanded government authority to seize the assets of drug traffickers, and made it more difficult to use the insanity defense.

National Security. Treason and espionage are crimes, as are assorted other activities that jeopardize the military and diplomatic interests of the United States. Protection of national security is associated most often with the FBI, but the efforts of the FBI constitute only a part of the whole. Agencies of the Department of Defense—such as the Defense Investigative Service, the Naval Investigative Service, the Office of Special Investigations (air force), and the Intelligence and Security Command (army)—have law enforcement duties to protect national security, as do the Coast Guard, U.S. Customs and Border Protection, and Bureau of U.S. Citizenship and Immigration Services of the Department of Homeland Security and the Office of Security within the Department of State. The Central Intelligence Agency is not given domestic law enforcement authority by Congress, but it may pass to the FBI intelligence it gathers abroad about American national security breaches.

Public Resources. The public resources of the national government consist of money, property, and people. Almost every law enforcement agency of the national government is involved in protecting one or all of these resources. The better known of these agencies are the FBI and the Secret Service. Others include the Postal Inspection Service, Park Police of the Department of the Interior, U.S. Marshals Service, and Federal Protective Service of the General Services Administration. Each department and agency of the executive branch investigates theft, fraud, and personal security through an office of the inspector general.

Public Revenue. Enforcing the nation's tax laws falls primarily under the jurisdiction of the Department of the Treasury. The Tax Division of the Justice Department prosecutes violations of the various tax laws. The 1994 anticrime bill gave the Customs Service authority to stop and search, without warrant, anyone entering or leaving the United States who appears to be violating a currency transaction law. The Customs Service became part of the Department of Homeland Security in 2002 and was renamed U.S. Customs and Border Protection.

Law Enforcement Functions of the Bureaucracy

The bureaucracy performs four general law enforcement functions: investigation, enforcement, prosecution, and custody.

Investigation. Investigation entails fact finding—that is, searching for facts that may help an agency discharge its assigned law enforcement responsibilities. The search for facts may be directed toward enactment of new laws or the enforcement of existing laws with more effective strategies, policies, and priorities. Most agencies of the executive branch conduct fact-finding activities.

For an assortment of reasons—the need for impartiality, prestige, or outside expertise—the president may prefer on occasion that a particular issue in law enforcement be investigated by persons not affiliated with existing agencies. In such instances, the president may appoint a presidential investigatory commission.

The presidential commission normally is a bipartisan panel of Americans who may or may not be employed by the federal government but who have distinguished themselves publicly. The commission receives a presidential mandate to answer a question, or a series of questions, and is supported by a professional staff paid for by the president.

The National Advisory Commission on Civil Disorders, better known as the "Kerner Commission," is a good example. In July 1967 Detroit, Michigan, was torn by urban rioting. Unable to control the rioting with state and local forces, including the Michigan National Guard, George W. Romney, the governor of Michigan, requested the assistance of the president.

President Lyndon Johnson responded by sending troops, and order soon was restored. But the president wanted to know the causes of the rioting and he wanted to know what could be done to prevent similar disturbances.

To answer these questions, Johnson established on July 29, 1967, the Kerner Commission.[169] He appointed Otto Kerner, then governor of Illinois, to chair a panel composed of four members of Congress, one mayor, a state official, a local police chief, and one representative each from labor, business, and civil rights.[170] Two advisory panels, a large investigative staff, and outside consultants and witnesses assisted the panel.

The commission's findings followed months of public hearings, statistical analyses, and review of programs, policies, and procedures.[171] Some of the recommendations found their way into national policy; others were considered but never implemented. The timing of the Detroit riot, and the timing of the resulting report, was not good because President Johnson devoted much of his remaining and limited time in the White House to managing the Vietnam War. Richard Nixon, his successor in 1969, was not receptive to the proposals contained in the report.

More routinely, a law enforcement investigation is directed at enforcing, not changing, policy. The fact finding is aimed at determining whether an unlawful act has been committed, identifying the perpetrators, and gathering evidence that is both admissible in court and sufficient to obtain a favorable verdict.

Most enforcement agencies of the executive branch are involved in this kind of law enforcement. Other investigations take more time, more effort, and considerably more resources. Investigation by the FBI of a national security breach, for example, may require months of investigative work, including surveillance of potential suspects, installation and monitoring of wiretaps, and rigorous background checks.

Certain investigations involve crimes so complex that the resources of multiple agencies from different departments may be mobilized into single task forces. Organized crime falls in this category; agents from the FBI, IRS, and DEA often join with their counterparts from state and local police forces and with federal and state prosecutors to deal with this persistent problem.

Enforcement. Law enforcement involves more than the arrest and conviction of criminal suspects. It also involves the protection of federal resources and execution of judicial orders. Among the many federal agencies participating in enforcement (most often the same ones that conduct investigations), some of the most prominent are the following:

Food Safety and Inspection Service (Agriculture Department). President Theodore Roosevelt is reputed to have been reading Upton Sinclair's *The Jungle* while eating breakfast one morning in the White House. Disturbed by Sinclair's description of the meat-packing industry in Chicago, the president threw his sausage out of the White House window and began working toward enactment of the Pure Food and Drug Act of 1906. Conditions have improved considerably since Roosevelt's day. Meat-packing and other food production and processing industries are now subjected to standards adopted and enforced by the Department of Agriculture. The job of the Food Safety and Inspection Service is to enforce these standards.

In fiscal year 2005, this agency employed an estimated eleven thousand persons and administered a budget of $817 million. In October 1994 President Clinton signed legislation to reorganize the Department of Agriculture. The reorganization plan called for the elimination of thousands of staff positions over a five-year period. President Clinton and Congress undertook this reorganization as part of a broader mission to downsize the bureaucracy.

U.S. Department of Defense. By order of the president, units of the armed forces of the United States may be used to suppress domestic violence and to remove obstructions to the enforcement of the law. National Guard units of the states may be nationalized for this purpose by presidential order. When they are, they are placed under the operational command of the secretary of defense. The Defense Department and its component Departments of the Army, Navy, and Air Force include internal agencies that have law enforcement responsibilities and authority, such as the Defense Criminal Investigative Service. These agencies,

staffed by both civilian and military personnel, provide protective services to the property and personnel of the department. They also enforce laws pertaining to fraud, corruption, and national security. For example, in 1988 investigations conducted by the Naval Investigative Service uncovered a Pentagon procurement scandal. The Naval Investigative Service was renamed in 1992 as the Naval Criminal Investigative Service and staffed by primarily civilian personnel.

Federal Bureau of Investigation (Justice Department). In almost fifty years of leadership, J. Edgar Hoover, the consummate bureaucratic chief, shaped the FBI into a modern, professional, and semiautonomous law enforcement agency. The bureau gained notoriety in the 1930s by apprehending or killing marauding and overly romanticized criminals, such as John Dillinger. The favorable image Hoover and his agents enjoyed was only enhanced by the agency's successful apprehension of enemy spies during World War II and the ensuing cold war. Always sensitive to public opinion, Hoover insisted that his agents conform to rigid dress and behavioral standards. He also initiated programs cultivating the bureau's reputation for effectiveness—the FBI's "ten most wanted list" is one example.

The mystique surrounding and protecting the FBI began to decay somewhat in the 1960s. Critics charged that Hoover was insensitive to civil rights issues and had refused to commit sufficient resources to the investigation of organized crime. Additional blows to the agency came in the wake of Watergate, when its acting director, L. Patrick Gray, admitted to destroying documents important to the initial investigation and when high bureau officers were convicted and imprisoned for illegal activities. In 2001 it was revealed that in the 1960s the FBI, with the full knowledge and consent of Hoover, had fabricated a legal case against an innocent man for alleged organized crime activity. Reacting to criticism that the agency had been lax to combat such activities, the FBI was overly zealous in its quest to land a high-profile conviction in an organized crime investigation. A congressional investigation of this scandal led to widespread criticism of the agency, and one prominent member of Congress, Rep. Dan Burton, R-Ind., called for the removal of Hoover's name from the FBI building in Washington, D.C.

The FBI is the closest thing the United States has to a general police agency in the national government. Its jurisdiction includes investigation and enforcement of laws pertaining to national security, fraud, corruption, civil rights, elections, kidnapping, and robbery of federally insured banks. In fiscal year 2005, the FBI employed an estimated 30,400 persons and had a budget of $5.9 billion.

Drug Enforcement Administration (Justice Department). Agents of the DEA have perhaps the most dangerous law enforcement job in the federal government: they enforce national drug laws. Most of the work of the DEA is conducted within the boundaries of the United States. Yet agents may and often do extend their investigations to the drug production, refinement, and transportation centers in Latin America, Europe, Asia, and the Middle East. Here they may advise and exchange intelligence information with their foreign counterparts and, depending on arrangements with the host countries, conduct their own investigations. The $2.1 billion budget and 10,984 employees authorized by Congress for the DEA in fiscal year 2005 reflect the agency's importance to federal law enforcement policy.

U.S. Customs and Border Protection (Homeland Security Department).

The Border Patrol, which had been part of the Justice Department, and the Customs Service, which had been part of the Treasury Department, were collapsed into a single agency in the Department of Homeland Security in 2002. With forty-one thousand employees, the agency's fiscal year 2005 budget was $6.5 billion.

U.S. Marshals Service (Justice Department).

U.S. marshals have been a law enforcement resource of the president since the administration of George Washington. In the nineteenth century, marshals acted as the general police force for much of the American West. Large sections of the West had not yet achieved statehood and were organized by Congress as territories of the United States. Television and films have depicted U.S. marshals of this period, of whom Wyatt Earp and Matt Dillon were only two, single-handedly standing between the ordinary law-abiding citizen and a host of predators—gunslingers, horse thieves, and the local cattle baron, all aided, apparently, by corrupt local sheriffs, mayors, and judges.

The job of the marshal in contemporary American society is less romantic but still important. Marshals enforce court orders, serve court papers, maintain security and order in courtrooms, protect witnesses, escort federal prisoners, and suppress domestic disturbances. Marshals possess general law enforcement power and are an all-purpose force at the disposal of the president and attorney general. In fiscal year 2005 the budget for the U.S. Marshals Service was comparatively small—$792 million. The service employed an estimated forty-five hundred persons.

Secret Service (Treasury Department).

The men and women wearing business suits, sunglasses, and earpieces who surround the president on every occasion are the best-known component of the Secret Service. But guarding the president is just one of the duties of this agency of the Treasury Department. It also provides security for the vice president, former presidents, immediate family members of current and former presidents, the president– and vice president–elect, presidential and vice-presidential candidates, and visiting heads of state. A uniformed branch of the Secret Service guards foreign embassies and missions and assists in guarding the White House. The Secret Service also has primary jurisdiction in enforcing laws pertaining to counterfeiting, credit card fraud, and defrauding of federally insured banks with 125 offices in the United States and abroad. Congress appropriated $1.4 billion for the Secret Service in fiscal year 2005, a large portion of which was used to pay the salaries of the estimated five thousand men and women it employs.

Secret Service agents surround President Gerald R. Ford as he works the crowd on a 1976 campaign swing through Louisiana. The Secret Service provides security for the president and the first family as well as for the vice president and past presidents and their families.

Internal Revenue Service (Treasury Department). The IRS not only collects the taxes owed the federal government from individuals and corporations but also processes tax returns from almost every American adult, corporation, partnership, and nonprofit organization. Certain of these returns are selected for audit (usually by computer), a process designed to detect tax fraud and to deter intentional understatement of future tax liabilities. The IRS includes a criminal investigative division, whose agents are authorized to carry firearms, investigate possible criminal violations of the tax code, make arrests, and serve search warrants. In fiscal year 2005, the IRS employed an estimated 101,000 persons and was appropriated a budget of $10.6 billion for operating expenses.

Bureau of Alcohol, Tobacco, Firearms, and Explosives (Homeland Security Department). The bureau has authority to combat illegal firearms use as well as illegal trade practices involving alcoholic beverages and tobacco products. A spate of controversy and bad publicity attended the bureau's disastrous February 1993 raid on the compound of a religious cult in Waco, Texas. Critics charged that the bureau had acted improperly in the raid, which resulted in the deaths of four bureau officers and several cult members. The FBI was called in and the resulting standoff ended two months later in a fire that killed many of the remaining cult members and their children. Later that year, President Clinton proposed that the bureau be merged into the Justice Department. Congress opposed the idea and the Clinton administration dropped it. In 2002, however, the former Bureau of Alcohol, Tobacco, and Firearms was moved from the Treasury Department to the Department of Homeland Security and renamed adding "and Explosives" to its title to reflect homeland security issues. In fiscal year 2005, the bureau had an estimated five thousand employees and a budget of $869 million.

Employment Standards Administration (Labor Department). The Employment Standards Administration enforces laws that cover child labor, minimum wage, overtime, and family and medical leave. It also enforces all laws governing employment standards and practices. In fiscal year 2005, the ESA employed an estimated forty-one hundred persons and had a budget of $392 million.

Occupational Safety and Health Administration (Labor Department). Health and safety in the workplace are the concerns of OSHA. In accordance with legislation passed by Congress, OSHA has put into effect detailed regulations governing matters such as the protective clothing for workers, the handling of hazardous substances, and the protective shields on industrial equipment. Inspectors from local OSHA offices inspect work sites and have authority to cite employers who violate or permit violations of the regulations. OSHA employed an estimated twenty-two hundred persons in fiscal year 2005 and administered a budget of $470 million.

Federal Aviation Administration (Transportation Department). The FAA administers and enforces laws pertaining to commercial air travel. Its jurisdiction includes pilot licensing, airport safety and security (with the exception of baggage and passenger screening, which is handled by the Transportation Security Administration of the Department of Homeland Security), air traffic control, and airplane safety. It employed an estimated forty-seven thousand persons in fiscal year 2005 and administered a budget of nearly $14 billion.

Coast Guard (Homeland Security Department). The Coast Guard traces its origins to the nation's first secretary of the Treasury, Alexander Hamilton, who created a service of revenue cutters (small armed ships) to help prevent smuggling and the resulting evasion of customs taxes. The Coast Guard still performs this function. It also enforces regulations pertaining to maritime safety, licenses boat captains; patrols waterways for hazards (such as icebergs); and rescues people from sunken or disabled vessels. The Coast Guard has an important role in efforts to suppress drug smuggling and to intercept persons attempting to enter the United States illegally by sea. The Coast Guard was transferred from the Transportation Department to the Department of Homeland Security in 2002 and refocused many of its resources to combating terrorism. In fiscal year 2005, Congress gave the Coast Guard a budget of $5 billion, part of which was used to pay its estimated thirty-nine thousand active duty and seven thousand civilian personnel.

Offices of the Inspector General. All federal departments and most federal agencies contain an office of the inspector general. The functions vary somewhat by agency but generally include investigations of fraud, abuse, bribery, waste, and personal misconduct within the agency.

Prosecution. U.S. attorneys filed an estimated 118,700 civil and criminal actions during fiscal 1995. This added to their existing workload of an estimated 146,000 docketed cases.[172]

The U.S. attorney is the workhorse of the federal prosecutorial system. Appointed by the president and located within the Department of Justice, the U.S. attorney assumes the lead responsibility for representing the government in court. One U.S. attorney is appointed for each of the ninety-four judicial districts in the United States. Each is supported by a professional legal staff.

Although the U.S. attorney represents the government in most cases, other prosecutorial resources are found in the executive branch. The Department of Justice itself has divisions that may, at times, be involved in litigation. Each division is headed by an assistant attorney general. The jurisdiction of these officials is indicated by their division title: Antitrust Division, Civil Division, Civil Rights Division, Criminal Division, Environment and Natural Resources Division, and Tax Division.

One other component of the Justice Department involved in the prosecution phase of law enforcement is the Office of the Solicitor General. The solicitor general determines which federal or state appellate court decisions will be appealed by the United States to the Supreme Court and then represents the government in the appeal. Because of the considerable influence the Supreme Court has in interpreting the law, including laws allocating power to the president and presidential agencies, this function is particularly critical to the president. For 2005, the Office of the Solicitor General had fifty employees and a budget of $8,538,000.

Occasionally Congress gives limited prosecutorial authority and resources to departments and agencies outside of the Justice Department. The solicitor of labor, for example, has authority to initiate civil actions in federal court to enforce wage-and-hour and occupational health and safety laws.

Custody. Conviction of a crime in federal court may lead to a sentence of imprisonment. When it does, the prisoner is usually remanded to the custody of the Bureau of Prisons for punishment. The Bureau of Prisons, which is an agency of the Department of Justice, has responsibility for administering the federal prison system. This responsibility includes guarding the inmates (often from one another) and supplying them with housing, food, recreation, medical care, and rehabilitation services such as education and counseling. The Bureau of Prisons employed an estimated forty-one thousand people in fiscal year 2005 with a budget of $4.7 billion.

Law Enforcement within the U.S. Political System

Law enforcement responsibility and power are shared in the U.S. political system, by the national government and the fifty states and their units of local government. They also are shared by the three branches of the national government. With the notable exception of the president's constitutional authority to grant reprieves and pardons, all incidents of presidential law enforcement power may be checked by at least one of the two other branches.

Sharing within the Federal System

Federalism refers to a form of constitutional structure whereby at least two levels of government exercise sovereign power over geographically defined and overlapping jurisdictions. The two levels of sovereign government in the United States are the national government and the fifty independent state governments.

Allocation of law enforcement responsibility and power within the U.S. federal system has evolved significantly since George Washington and members of the First Congress took office in 1789. This evolution generally has increased the power and responsibility of the national government at the expense of state power and independence.

National law enforcement responsibility and power were slight in 1789 and remained so until the Civil War. The states, however, had significant law enforcement responsibility and power during this period. Legislating to promote the public's health, safety, morals, and general welfare was the business of the state legislatures, and it was the business of the local sheriffs, state militia, and state judges to enforce those laws.

This balance gradually shifted, however, in favor of the national government. Led by Chief Justice John Marshall, the Supreme Court handed down rulings in the first decades of the nineteenth century that interpreted expansively the constitutional grants of power to the national government. Congress, the Court ruled, has ample constitutional power to enact any law necessary and proper to carry out its enumerated powers, so long as that law is not proscribed by the Constitution itself.[173] Contrary provisions of state law must yield to laws enacted by Congress in accordance with its constitutional power.[174] State court interpretations of federal law are susceptible to review and possible reversal by federal courts.[175]

Although Marshall and the Supreme Court legitimized an extensive and pervasive national role in law enforcement, a workable consensus among the American people and their elected representatives in Congress that such a role ought to be exercised was not achieved until the latter part of the nineteenth century. Business in the early decades of the American Republic was largely a local activity that was regulated primarily by state and local governments. By the late nineteenth century, however, it had become apparent that many business activities either could not or would not be regulated effectively by state and local governments. The public eventually pressured Washington to assume the burden. Interstate rail transportation came under federal regulatory jurisdiction with enactment of the Interstate Commerce Act of 1887. Today, virtually no business activity is untouched by federal regulation.

The current relationship between the national government and the fifty state governments in law enforcement is complex. Some activities are regulated extensively and simultaneously by both levels of government. Retail sales, occupational health and safety, and banking, for example, are subject to a host of national and state laws and regulations.

Other activities tend to be regulated predominantly by either one or the other level of government. The national government regulates interstate and international airline travel, radio and television broadcasting, and nuclear power production. Most automobile speed limits, assault and battery, marriage and divorce, and medical licensing are principally matters for state regulation.

The current breakdown of state-national law enforcement responsibility reflects the will of Congress. Although Congress is empowered to exert a far-ranging regulatory reach, it leaves the regulation of most activities and the definition and enforcement of most crimes to state governments. Yet Congress may exercise its enforcement authority directly when a special federal connection exists, such as when the crime is committed by a member of the armed forces and on the premises of a military base. Or it may exercise its authority indirectly by mandating that the states adopt national enforcement standards.

When Congress enters a new regulatory field, the reason for such a move can usually be traced to the support of politically powerful interest groups or to the American public, or both. Conversely, lack of congressional interest in a regulatory field is understandable when such a move is supported neither by powerful interest groups nor by a significant segment of the American public. This is especially true when a contemplated law is actively opposed.

Substantial public interest in enacting handgun control led to congressional passage in 1993 of the Brady Bill (named for Reagan press secretary James Brady, who was seriously wounded in the 1981 assassination attempt on President Reagan). President Bill Clinton had strongly backed the measure, which was the most significant gun control law enacted in the United States since 1968. The Brady Bill instituted a five-day waiting period for the purchase of handguns, raised licensing fees for gun dealers, and stipulated that the police be informed of multiple gun purchases.

Little public interest is aroused by the notion of professional licensing by the national government. But the idea arouses strong opposition from well-organized and assertive interest groups such as national and state bar and medical associations. Attorneys and physicians are licensed by state government.

One way in which Congress has sought to ensure that states adopt certain regulatory and enforcement actions has been through the use of unfunded mandates. The 1994 anticrime bill, for example, requires states to take certain law enforcement actions, although the federal government provides no money.

The use of unfunded mandates became pervasive in the late 1980s and early 1990s when the federal government, in response to budgetary restraints, sought to pass on to the states the costs of enforcement activities. State governments protested these federal impositions, and in 1995 the Republican-controlled Congress passed restrictions on the use of unfunded mandates. In so doing, Congress sought to reduce the federal government's regulatory role and to give more autonomy to states and localities.

The relationship between the national law enforcement agencies of the executive branch and their counterparts in state and local governments can be characterized most aptly as competitive but cooperative. Federal law enforcement agencies may request, and often receive, investigatory and enforcement assistance from state and local police forces. Such assistance, for example, may be given to locate and arrest a military deserter, an armed robber of a post office, or a counterfeiter, or it may be given in the form of security for a visiting president or foreign dignitary.

The president and the principal law enforcement officers of the national government are reluctant to deny a reasonable request from a state governor for law enforcement assistance. The request may be for troops to put down a riot, as occurred when President Lyndon Johnson sent troops to Detroit in the summer of 1967. More commonly, though, it will involve special federal attention to local problems that either are beyond the competence of state and local resources to resolve or can be resolved more effectively and efficiently with federal assistance.

In April 1995, after the bombing of a federal office building in Oklahoma City, the FBI coordinated a massive effort involving other government departments as well as state and local authorities to identify and apprehend those responsible for the disaster. The FBI received assistance from the Secret Service, Department of Defense, Drug Enforcement Administration, Bureau of Alcohol, Tobacco, and Firearms, Oklahoma National Guard, Oklahoma Department of Public Safety, and Oklahoma City Police Department.[176] Following the 2001 terrorist attacks, the responsibility for coordinating the federal government's response to terrorism was placed in the Department of Homeland Security, created in 2002.

State and local agencies also receive routine assistance from federal law enforcement agencies. Federal agencies distribute law enforcement assistance grants to state and local governments, offer training in modern law enforcement techniques and technology to state and local enforcement officials, and provide intelligence about local criminal activity.

The federal government also may provide assistance to states and localities to carry out extensive crime-fighting programs. The landmark 1994 anticrime bill, signed into law by President Clinton, provided $30.2 billion in federal assistance to states and localities to hire new police officers, build prisons and boot camps, and initiate crime prevention programs, among other measures. *(See box, Presidential Response to Crime, p. 638.)*

In 2001–2002, the federal government provided substantial assistance to states and localities to assist with efforts to combat the threat of terrorism. President George W. Bush proposed increasing such spending by more than tenfold for fiscal year 2003. Among the plans were grants of $2 billion to states and localities to purchase the equipment needed to respond to any terrorist attack, such as chemical and biological detection systems and protective equipment for citizens; $105 million to enable states and localities to develop terrorist attack response plans; and $245 million to support training exercises for providing aid to victims and responding to attacks.

Sharing within the National Government

High school students learn in civics classes that laws are made by Congress, enforced by the president, and applied by the courts. It is by this means that tyranny in the United States is averted: political power in the national government is divided and allocated to separate and independent branches. Each branch, therefore, has some check on the goings-on (and possible abuses) of the others.

Article I, Section 1, of the Constitution assigns the legislative power to Congress. And Article II vests the executive power of the United States in the president and imposes on the president the obligation to "take Care that the Laws be faithfully executed." Finally, Article III, Section 1, delegates the judicial power of the United States to the Supreme Court and to such other courts as Congress chooses to create.

Still, there is more to this arrangement than the division and allocation of power to separate and independent branches. Power is also shared. Congress, the legislative arm of the national government, makes law according to its constitutional grant of power, but it does so subject to presidential approval or veto, and often at the president's urging. Congress also delegates practical lawmaking power—the authority to promulgate binding administrative rules and

PRESIDENTIAL RESPONSE TO CRIME

The president occasionally sets about to bolster the federal government's law enforcement activities in response to public pressures—usually resulting from highly publicized events or persisting problems with crime. For example, in the 1980s public opinion polls frequently identified the drug scourge as one of the nation's leading problems. First lady Nancy Reagan led a national campaign to stigmatize drug use among the youth. In 1988, with the national elections looming, Congress authorized $2.7 billion for antidrug law enforcement. President Ronald Reagan signed the bill on November 18, 1988. Among the law's provisions were:

1988 ANTIDRUG BILL

- Creation of a cabinet-level position for coordinating a national antidrug strategy
- Harsher penalties for drug dealers
- Federal death penalty for major drug traffickers
- Increased funding for drug interdiction
- Denial of federal benefits to repeat drug-use offenders
- Increased funding for drug treatment, prevention, and education.

In the 1990s, numerous highly publicized incidents of violence outside abortion clinics, some resulting in the murders of abortion providers, emboldened pro-abortion activists to pressure a sympathetic Democratic Congress and President Bill Clinton to enact the Freedom of Access to Clinic Entrances (FACE) Act of 1993. This law made it a federal crime to block access to an abortion clinic; it prohibited intimidation of either women seeking abortions or clinic employees; and it gave similar protections to pregnancy counseling centers and places of worship. Violators became subject to both criminal and civil penalties.

Supporters of the measure framed the issue as one of law and order. They maintained that local authorities were unable to provide adequate protection, thereby requiring a federal response. Abortion protesters objected that the law constituted an infringement on their freedom of speech rights. In *Madsen v. Women's Health Center, Inc.*, a Supreme Court majority came down in favor of FACE, ruling that the government's interest in preserving order and protecting the constitutional right of abortion permits restrictions on protest activities outside of abortion clinics.

With the reported increase in all types of crime in the 1990s, especially the most violent type, opinion polls continually identified crime as one of the nation's leading problems. In his 1994 State of the Union address, President Clinton brought the issue to the national forefront as he endorsed a substantial increase in the reach of the federal law enforcement authority. This presidential attention to the issue helped to mobilize public support and prod Congress to pass a far-reaching anticrime bill that established a $30.2 billion trust fund to pay for various anticrime programs. Among the initiatives funded were:

1994 CRIME BILL

- Hiring 100,000 new police officers
- Constructing new prisons and boot camps
- Providing formula grants for local crime reduction programs
- Banning manufacture and possession of nineteen assault weapons
- Authorizing the death penalty for federal crimes that result in death or murder of federal law enforcement officials
- Allowing juveniles thirteen and older accused of certain crimes to be tried as adults in federal court
- Mandating life imprisonment for conviction of a third violent felony (popularly referred to as "three strikes and you're out").

With terrorism having become the focus of the United States in 2001, President George W. Bush proposed a tenfold increase in spending on domestic efforts to combat that threat. Among the initiatives that Bush proposed were:

- Funding to train firefighters, police, and medical personnel to respond to biological and chemical attacks
- Funding for a program to train personnel to respond to attacks and provide aid and assistance to civilians
- Funding for states and localities to develop their own comprehensive plans to respond to terrorist attacks
- Substantial funding for equipment to enable states and localities to respond to terrorist attacks (protective equipment, chemical and biological detection systems).

regulations—to the president and officers of the executive branch who may or may not report to the president.

Furthermore, although presidents have the authority to enter into treaties with other countries, they share veto power with the Senate, which must ratify the agreements. The president similarly possesses the authority to appoint federal judges and high executive branch officers, but only with the advice and consent of the Senate.

Congress and the President's Law Enforcement Power

Article I, Section 1, of the Constitution states that "[a]ll legislative Powers" of the United States belong to Congress. This power bears directly, extensively, and frequently on the law enforcement obligations and powers of the president. Four categories of power are available to Congress, which, when exercised, may either increase or restrict the law enforcement power of the president. These are lawmaking, investigation, review of presidential appointments, and impeachment.

Lawmaking. Under its lawmaking power, Congress decided that railroads, airlines, and television ought to be regulated by the national government, and Congress determined that national standards ought to apply to the production of food and drugs. The expansion of the national police power is the product of congressional action.

The legislative work of Congress does not end with asserting the regulatory power of the national government. A system and a process must be set in place for enforcing the law. Agencies must be created and empowered. Then they must employ men and women to enforce the law. Finally, law enforcement officers of the executive branch must be granted specific law enforcement authority.

Congress provides the people necessary to staff the president's law enforcement agencies through authorizing legislation, and it provides for payment of their salaries through separate appropriations bills. Through a similar process, it provides enforcement officers with the personnel and material support necessary to do a satisfactory job.

Federal law enforcement agencies and personnel receive two principal forms of authority from Congress: jurisdictional and enforcement. Jurisdictional authority determines the types of laws a given agency is supposed to enforce; enforcement authority provides enforcement officers with the specific powers to make their enforcement effective.

One agency's jurisdiction occasionally overlaps with another's. For example, the Drug Enforcement Administration has primary jurisdiction over enforcement of the nation's narcotics laws. But that jurisdiction overlaps considerably with the jurisdiction given the FBI, the U.S. Customs and Border Protection, the Coast Guard, and the Food and Drug Administration. In an effort to coordinate a federal antidrug strategy, the Office of National Drug Control Policy (ONDCP) was established by Congress as part of the Anti-Drug Control Act of 1988. Congress also created a cabinet-level position to coordinate the nation's antidrug effort. The Office of National Drug Control Policy is required by law to submit a national drug control strategy to Congress annually. The ONDCP is part of the Executive Office of the President *(See box, Presidential Response to Crime, p. 638.)*

As for enforcement authority, special agents and other FBI personnel have congressional authority to "carry firearms [and] serve warrants and subpoenas issued under the authority of the United States." Congress has also given them authority to "make arrests without warrant for any offense against the United States committed in their presence, or for any felony cognizable under the laws of the United States if they have reasonable grounds to believe that the person to be arrested has committed or is committing such felony." [177]

Congress has made similar grants of authority to U.S. marshals, agents of the Secret Service and Drug Enforcement Administration, and a host of other federal law enforcement personnel.[178]

Congress also may limit the authority that it confers on federal law enforcement agencies and personnel. Postal inspectors, for example, have authority to "make arrests without warrant for offenses against the United States committed in their presence." [179] However, they can do this only if the offense is related to the property or use of the Postal Service.[180]

Investigations. Congress may affect the law enforcement power of the president through the exercise of its inherent authority to investigate. Investigations may be conducted for the purpose of determining whether new laws are needed or to determine whether existing laws are being properly enforced.

Congressional investigations frequently are conducted by means of committee hearings. Witnesses give their views on the issue before the committee and subject themselves to questions from committee members and counsel. The testimony may be given voluntarily or under compulsion (subpoena). In most instances, a witness will be placed under oath, which allows prosecution of anyone giving false testimony intentionally.

Impressive resources are available to Congress to assist in these investigations. These may include personal and committee staff, researchers of the Library of Congress, economists of the Congressional Budget Office, auditors of the Government Accountability Office, and analysts of the Office of Technology Assessment. The staffs of each of these congressional agencies have established reputations for objective and competent work.

Television has enhanced the significance of congressional investigations. The specter of organized crime in the United States was revealed starkly in the televised investigations of the Kefauver Committee (Special Committee to

Investigate Organized Crime in Interstate Commerce) in the 1950s. The American people heard, for the first time, mention of the "mafia" and "la cosa nostra" from witnesses who testified to the power and pervasiveness of these organizations in American society.

Separate Senate and House committees investigated alleged criminal activities committed during the Nixon administration, after burglars traced to the White House were arrested during a break-in of the Democratic National Committee headquarters at the Watergate complex in Washington, D.C. In 1987 a joint committee of Congress investigated the circumstances surrounding the Iran-contra affair. In 1998 the House Judiciary Committee investigated allegations that President Bill Clinton had committed perjury and obstruction of justice in the course of a sexual harassment lawsuit brought against him. After extremely contentious hearings, the committee, voting along party lines, recommended articles of impeachment against the president.

Most congressional investigations are not nearly so spectacular, but they are important nevertheless. For example, in 1987 a subcommittee of the House Committee on Interior and Insular Affairs conducted an investigation into the enforcement of federal law by the Nuclear Regulatory Commission. Its findings were critical, as is indicated by the title of its report: *NRC Coziness with Industry: Nuclear Regulatory Commission Fails to Maintain Arms' Length Relationship with the Nuclear Industry.*[181] In 2005 the Senate held hearings on the extraordinary profits being made by oil companies, compelling the chief executive officers of the major oil companies to explain why windfall profit taxes should not be imposed. The hearings, which were closely followed in the news media, appeared to be primarily a public relations tool instead of an in-depth investigation. Members of Congress were eager to show that they were sensitive to the public's outcries about high energy prices. Windfall profit taxes were not imposed on the oil companies.

Review of Presidential Appointments. The president's appointment authority is important to the president's law enforcement power. Congress exercises a considerable restraint on the president's law enforcement power by saying (within constitutional limitations) which offices are subject to presidential appointment and what limitations are imposed on the presidential authority to remove commissioned appointees.

Congress also influences the president's appointment authority by specifying the appointments that must receive Senate confirmation before the appointees may take office. Although most presidential appointees to law enforcement and judicial positions are approved by the Senate, there is less deference to the president in this area today than there used to be. Refusal to confirm is usually based on judgments about the candidate's professional or ethical fitness.

Nonetheless, partisan and ideological considerations often play an important role in considering whether to confirm presidential appointees. President Clinton's 1993 nominee to the Civil Rights Division of the Justice Department, Lani Guinier, withdrew her name after it was clear she would not be confirmed because of her views on affirmative action and quotas.

The effect of Senate approval on the presidential appointment power, however, cannot be measured solely by reference to the number of times the Senate refuses to confirm. Knowing that appointees must be examined and confirmed by the Senate may well cause presidents to make their selections carefully. Moreover, knowing that nominees will be subjected to Senate scrutiny should cause the president to insist that backgrounds be subjected to searching investigation before names are announced and submitted.

Impeachment. The ultimate congressional check on executive law enforcement power is removal from office through the impeachment process. *(See "Impeachment," p. 479, in Chapter 8.)* Article II, Section 4, of the Constitution gives Congress the power to remove from office the president, vice president, "and all civil Officers of the United States," upon impeachment for and conviction of "Treason, Bribery, or other high Crimes and Misdemeanors."

The removal process is conducted in two stages: impeachment and trial. In the first stage, the House of Representatives determines whether probable cause exists to believe that misconduct warranting removal has occurred and that the accused is culpable.[182] Acting much like a grand jury in a criminal case, the House considers charges of misconduct, hears evidence about the alleged acts of misconduct, and makes a preliminary determination of whether the alleged misconduct, if true, warrants removal, and whether the evidence supports the charges. If the House, by a majority vote, considers the allegations of misconduct sufficiently serious to warrant removal and they are supported by the evidence, it reports one or more articles of impeachment to the Senate for trial.

In its proceedings, the Senate acts much like a trial jury in a criminal case. With the chief justice of the United States presiding, its function is to convict or acquit for each article of impeachment, based on evidence heard in a trial conducted in the Senate chambers. Guilt or innocence is determined by a two-thirds vote of the senators present.[183]

No consensus exists on the meaning of "Treason, Bribery, or other high Crimes and Misdemeanors," the constitutionally stated grounds for removal by impeachment. Alexander Hamilton described the impeachment power as political, for it would be applied to persons committing "injuries done immediately to society itself."[184] Such injuries would include not only treason and bribery, but also such criminal acts as murder, rape, and mayhem. It is not clear that "high Crimes and Misdemeanors" include a violation of

Andrew Johnson was the first of only two U.S. presidents to be impeached to date. In 1868 Congress failed by one vote to remove Johnson from office. In December 1998 President Bill Clinton was impeached by the House of Representatives, but the Senate vote fell far short of the two-thirds majority needed to convict him.

Tenure of Office Act, a legislative measure of dubious constitutional validity, did not constitute a sufficient basis for removal of the president.[186] A broader reading of the Senate's action would find significant the failure of the Senate to remove a president for what was really political incompatibility.

In 1998 the House of Representatives impeached President Bill Clinton on charges that he had committed perjury and obstructed justice in a lawsuit brought against him by Paula Jones for sexual harassment while he was governor of Arkansas. Clinton thus became the first elected president in history to be impeached. After a Senate trial, the upper chamber voted not to remove Clinton from office.

The Clinton impeachment was highly controversial because of the circumstances surrounding the charges of perjury and obstruction of justice. Clinton had lied in a legal deposition in the sexual harassment suit when he claimed that he had never had a sexual relationship with White House intern Monica Lewinsky. The president's defenders asserted that his indiscretion was merely a personal one and did not deserve the ultimate constitutional punishment of an impeachment. Advocates of impeachment argued that the president was the nation's top law enforcement official and that the crimes of perjury and obstruction of justice were therefore serious enough to merit impeachment, regardless of the circumstances that led to the president's actions.

Another contemporary example of the impeachment power being used against a president is furnished by the events leading to the resignation of President Nixon in 1974. In 1972 employees of the Committee to Re-elect the President, Nixon's personal campaign organization, were arrested by District of Columbia police during a burglary of the Democratic Party headquarters in Washington's Watergate complex.

Investigations by local and federal law enforcement agencies, a federal grand jury, a Senate investigative committee, and a special prosecutor, as well as newspaper and broadcast journalists, revealed evidence not only of involvement by high- and mid-level members and former members of the Nixon administration in the burglary but also of various other allegedly unlawful activities. An impeachment bill was introduced on the House floor and referred to the House Committee on the Judiciary.

After televised hearings, the committee voted to recommend three articles of impeachment to the House. Each one of the three articles charged the president with violat-

the Constitution, a statute not providing criminal penalties, or a failure to enforce the law.

Only two presidents have been impeached (that is, charged) to date. In 1868 the House charged President Andrew Johnson with violating the Tenure of Office Act of 1867.[185] Specifically, the House charged the president with violating his constitutional obligation to take care that the laws are executed faithfully by firing Edwin M. Stanton, his secretary of war, without cause and without prior Senate consent. The Senate, however, failed by one vote to muster the two-thirds majority necessary to convict Johnson.

The precedent furnished by Johnson's ordeal is primarily negative. A narrow interpretation of the precedent would hold that the Senate merely confirmed that violation of the ing his oath of office and his constitutional obligation to take care that the laws be faithfully executed. The three articles then enumerated specific allegations of misconduct, which, a majority of the committee believed, warranted Nixon's removal: obstruction of justice, abuse of power, abuse of individual rights, misprision (concealment) of a felony, and failure to comply with congressional subpoenas. The House never voted on the three articles because of Nixon's resignation.

Instead of facing certain impeachment, Nixon resigned from office on August 9, 1974. Still, the committee action remains a powerful reminder that the removal power of Congress is not entirely dormant. The circumstances warranting its use must be serious, and the charges must be backed by compelling evidence—a "smoking gun" was the phrase often used by some committee members.

The Judiciary and the President. The judiciary arbitrates and resolves legal disputes according to the law. In doing so, it both supports and checks presidential law enforcement authority. It also creates law enforcement opportunities and burdens for the president and makes law through the process of interpreting law.

The judiciary supports the president's law enforcement power by holding that presidential claims of authority are in accord with the Constitution and laws of the United States. Such pronouncements usually settle any immediate disputes between the president and Congress or the states over the existence and extent of specific presidential law enforcement powers, and they offer reassurance to the American people that their president acted within the law.

The judiciary also supports the president's law enforcement power by invalidating efforts by other political actors, usually Congress and the states, to restrict the president's authority unduly.

Americans witnessed the first type of support for presidential power when the Supreme Court upheld in 1863 assertions of presidential power to deploy military forces to suppress a domestic insurrection (the Civil War) and in 1895 assertions of presidential power to quell strikes inhibiting interstate movement of railroads and delivery of the U.S. mail.[187] Similarly, the Supreme Court upheld in 1890 presidential discretion to use U.S. marshals to maintain peace in situations neither contemplated nor prohibited by legislation.[188] The Court also has protected the president from congressional interference with the power to grant pardons, reprieves, and amnesties.[189]

American judges, however, are an independent lot, constitutionally and in fact. They are not appointed to be mere supporters of the president, and they do not define their own roles in that manner. They have authority to check presidential claims of law enforcement power, and they have the power to make their own authority felt.

The judiciary most often checks the president's law enforcement authority when judges rule against the government in civil or criminal cases. The ruling may be on an important interpretation of law, on the admissibility in a trial of a critical piece of evidence, or on the facts of the case.

When the rulings involve an interpretation of constitutionally or legislatively delegated authority of the president, then the effect may limit the executive law enforcement capability in future cases as well as in the immediate case. Federal law enforcement agents know, for example, that a confession obtained through coercion cannot be used as evidence in a trial.

⭐

NOTES

1. Peter Woll, *American Bureaucracy,* 2d ed. (New York: Norton, 1977), 63.

2. Alexander Hamilton, *Federalist* No. 72, in Alexander Hamilton, James Madison, and John Jay, *The Federalist Papers* (New York: Tudor, 1937), 64.

3. Clinton Rossiter, *The American Presidency,* 3d ed. (New York: Harcourt Brace Jovanovich, 1963).

4. Charles T. Goodsell, *The Case for Bureaucracy* (Chatham, N.J.: Chatham House, 1983), 2.

5. H. H. Gerth and C. Wright Mills, *From Max Weber* (New York: Oxford University Press, 1946), 196–199.

6. George J. Gordon, *Public Administration in America,* 2d ed. (New York: St. Martin's Press, 1982), 297.

7. Quoted in Robert Sherrill, *Why They Call It Politics,* 4th ed. (New York: Harcourt Brace Jovanovich, 1984), 260.

8. Kenneth Dodge et al., "Coming of Age: The Department of Education," Phi Delta Kappan, Papers from the Duke University Education Leadership Summit, May 2002.

9. Michael Nelson, "The Irony of American Bureaucracy," in *Bureaucratic Power in National Policy Making,* 4th ed., ed. Francis E. Rourke (Boston: Little, Brown, 1986), 163–187.

10. Ibid., 169.

11. Sherrill, *Why They Call It Politics,* 259.

12. Quoted in ibid.

13. Quoted in Richard E. Neustadt, *Presidential Power* (New York: Wiley, 1960), 22.

14. Arthur M. Schlesinger Jr., *The Crisis of Confidence* (Boston: Houghton Mifflin, 1969), 291.

15. Richard M. Pious, *The American Presidency* (New York: Basic Books, 1979), 212.

16. Thomas E. Cronin, *The State of the Presidency,* 2d ed. (Boston: Little, Brown, 1980), 333.

17. Richard Rose, *Managing Presidential Objectives* (New York: Free Press, 1976), 23.

18. Shirley Anne Warshaw, "Ideological Conflict in the President's Cabinet," in *Transforming the American Polity: The Presidency of George W. Bush and the War on Terrorism,* ed. Richard S. Conley. (Indianapolis, Ind.: Prentice Hall, 2005).

19. Rossiter, *American Presidency,* 129.

20. Stephen Hess, *Organizing the Presidency* (Washington, D.C.: Brookings, 1988), 6.

21. David Truman, *The Governmental Process* (New York: Knopf, 1951); Hess, *Organizing the Presidency;* and George Reedy, *The Twilight of the Presidency* (New York: World, 1970).

22. Rose, *Managing Presidential Objectives,* 147.

23. Cronin, *State of the Presidency,* 225.

24. Alexander Hamilton, *Federalist* No. 70, in Alexander Hamilton, James Madison, and John Jay, *The Federalist Papers* (New York: Tudor, 1937), 49–50.

25. McGeorge Bundy, *The Strength of Government* (Cambridge: Harvard University Press, 1968), 37.

26. Woll, *American Bureaucracy,* 241.

27. Ibid., 240.

28. Executive Office of the President, President's Special Review Board 1987, *Report of the President's Special Review Board (Tower Commission Report)* (Washington, D.C.: Government Printing Office, 1987).

29. Anthony Downs, *Inside Bureaucracy* (Boston: Little, Brown, 1967), 116–118.

30. Office of Management and Budget, *President's Management Agenda, FY 2002* (Washington, D.C.: Government Printing Office, 2001).

31. *Mandate for Leadership* (Washington, D.C.: Heritage Foundation, 2000).

32. Arthur M. Schlesinger Jr., *A Thousand Days: John F. Kennedy in the White House* (Boston: Houghton Mifflin, 1965), 683.

33. Cronin, *State of the Presidency,* 226.

34. Louis W. Koenig, *The Chief Executive* (New York: Harcourt Brace and World, 1968), 417.

35. Richard P. Nathan, *The Plot That Failed: Nixon and the Administrative Presidency* (New York: Wiley, 1975), 82.

36. "President Nixon Finds a Real Garbageman to Woo Garbagemen," *Wall Street Journal,* June 21, 1972, 1, 25.

37. Richard P. Nathan, "The Administrative Presidency," in *Bureaucratic Power in National Policy Making,* 4th ed., ed. Francis E. Rourke (Boston: Little, Brown, 1986), 216. See also Richard P. Nathan, *The Administrative Presidency* (New York: Macmillan, 1986).

38. Dwight D. Eisenhower, *The White House Years: Mandate for Change, 1953–1956* (Garden City, N.Y.: Doubleday, 1963), 114.

39. Hess, *Organizing the Presidency,* 2.

40. Frank Kessler, *The Dilemmas of Presidential Leadership: Of Caretakers and Kings* (Englewood Cliffs, N.J.: Prentice Hall, 1982), 60.

41. Hess, *Organizing the Presidency,* 3–4.

42. Quoted in Koenig, *Chief Executive,* 193.

43. Kessler, *Dilemmas of Presidential Leadership,* 72.

44. William Safire, *Before the Fall* (Garden City, N.Y.: Doubleday, 1975); and Henry Kissinger, *The White House Years* (Boston: Little, Brown, 1979).

45. Charles O. Jones, *The Presidency in a Separated System* (Washington, D.C.: Brookings, 1994).

46. Ibid., 103.

47. *Congressional Quarterly Weekly Report,* July 21, 1979, 1432.

48. Kessler, *Dilemmas of Presidential Leadership,* 68.

49. Colin Campbell, *Managing the Presidency: Carter, Reagan, and the Search for Executive Harmony* (Pittsburgh: University of Pittsburgh Press, 1986), 61.

50. Quoted in ibid., 71.

51. Paul Quirk, "Presidential Competence," in *The Presidency and the Political System,* 2d ed., ed. Michael Nelson (Washington, D.C.: CQ Press, 1988).

52. *Tower Commission Report,* IV–10.

53. Elizabeth Drew, *On the Edge: The Clinton Presidency* (New York: Simon and Schuster, 1994), 98.

54. Shirley Anne Warshaw, "Clashing Ideologies in the Clinton White House," paper presented at the Clinton Presidential Conference, Hofstra University, November 2005.

55. Ibid., 102.

56. Ibid., 241.

57. See Kathryn Dunn Tenpas and Stephen Hess, "The Bush White House: First Appraisals," background paper, Brookings, Washington, D.C., January 30, 2002.

58. Ibid.

59. Kathryn Dunn Tenpas and Stephen Hess, "The President's Stealth Missile," Businessweekonline.com, December 3, 2001.

60. Woll, *American Bureaucracy,* 11.

61. Pious, *American Presidency,* 222.

62. Joel D. Aberbach, *Keeping a Watchful Eye: The Politics of Congressional Oversight* (Washington, D.C.: Brookings, 1990), 35.

63. Pious, *American Presidency,* 224.

64. Allen Schick, "Politics through Law: Congressional Limitations on Executive Discretion," in *Both Ends of the Avenue: The Presidency, the Executive Branch, and the Congress in the 1980s,* ed. Anthony King (Washington, D.C.: American Enterprise Institute, 1983), 176.

65. *Immigration and Naturalization Service v. Chadha,* 462 U.S. 919 (1983).

66. Quoted in Martin Tolchin, "The Legislative Veto: An Accommodation That Goes On and On," *New York Times,* March 31, 1989, 8.

67. Thomas Franck and Edward Weisband, *Foreign Policy by Congress* (New York: Oxford University Press, 1979).

68. Pious, *American Presidency,* 229.

69. Executive Office of the President, President's Committee on Administrative Management, *Brownlow Commission Report* (Washington, D.C.: Government Printing Office, 1937), 5.

70. Ibid., 6–7.

71. Peri E. Arnold, *Making the Managerial President: Comprehensive Reorganization Planning, 1905–1980* (Princeton: Princeton University Press, 1986), 114–115.

72. Commission on the Organization of the Executive Branch of Government, *General Management of the Executive Branch* (Washington, D.C.: Government Printing Office, 1949).

73. Ibid., 34.

74. Arnold, *Making the Managerial President,* 159.

75. Ibid., 177–193.

76. Ibid., 277.

77. Tyrus G. Fain, ed., *Federal Reorganization: The Executive Branch,* Public Document Series (New York: Bowker, 1977), xxxi.

78. See, for example, Koenig, *Chief Executive,* chap. 8.

79. James P. Pfiffner, "Strangers in a Strange Land: Orienting New Presidential Appointees," in *The In-and-Outers: Presidential Appointees and Transient Government in Washington,* ed. G. Calvin Mackenzie (Baltimore: Johns Hopkins University Press, 1987), 141. The total number of appointees is based on data from the Center for Excellence in Government, February 1989.

80. Hugh Heclo, *A Government of Strangers: Executive Politics in Washington* (Washington, D.C.: Brookings, 1977), 94.

81. Niccolo Machiavelli, *The Prince* (Harmondsworth, Middlesex, England: Penguin, 1961), 124.

82. Quoted in Schlesinger, *Thousand Days,* 127.

83. Pfiffner, "Strangers in a Strange Land," 142.

84. Richard F. Fenno Jr., *The President's Cabinet* (New York: Vintage, 1958), 51.

85. G. Calvin Mackenzie, *The Politics of Presidential Appointments* (New York: Free Press, 1981), 6.

86. David E. Lewis, "Political Appointments and Federal Management Performance," Princeton University, Woodrow Wilson School, September 2005.

87. Drew, *On the Edge,* 33–34, 99–101.

88. Bradley H. Patterson Jr., "The New Bush White House Staff: Choices Being Made," *White House Studies* 1, no. 2 (2001): 235.

89. Cronin, *State of the Presidency,* 164.

90. U.S. Commission on Executive, Legislative, and Judicial Salaries, *Report of the Commission on Executive, Legislative, and Judicial Salaries* (Washington, D.C.: Government Printing Office, 1980), ix, 1.

91. Gary Burtless, *How Much Is Enough?: Setting Pay for Presidential Appointees,* report commissioned by Brookings, Presidential Appointee Initiative, Washington, D.C., March 22, 2002.

92. Quoted in Dick Kirschten, "Why Not the Best?" *National Journal,* June 12, 1982, 1064.

93. Stephen L. Carter, *The Confirmation Mess* (New York: Basic Books, 1994), 7.

94. Mackenzie, *Politics of Presidential Appointments,* 95.

95. Cronin, *State of the Presidency,* 165.

96. Christopher J. Deering, "Damned If You Do and Damned If You Don't: The Senate's Role in the Appointments Process," in *The In-and-Outers: Presidential Appointees and Transient Government in Washington,* ed. G. Calvin Mackenzie (Baltimore: Johns Hopkins University Press, 1987), 119.

97. "Critical Posts in the Bush Administration Remain Vacant as Congressional Session Nears End," *Brookings Institution Report,* December 18, 2001.

98. Deering, "Damned If You Do," 117.

99. Dom Bonafede, "The White House Personnel Office from Roosevelt to Reagan," in *The In-and-Outers: Presidential Appointees and Transient Government in Washington,* ed. G. Calvin Mackenzie (Baltimore: Johns Hopkins University Press, 1987), 32.

100. See John P. Burke, *The Institutional Presidency* (Baltimore: Johns Hopkins University Press, 1992), chap. 4.

101. John W. Macy, Bruce Adams, and J. Jackson Walter, *America's Unelected Government: Appointing the President's Team* (Cambridge: Ballinger, 1983), 32.

102. Quoted in Edward D. Feigenbaum, "Staffing, Organization, and Decision-Making in the Ford and Carter White Houses," *Presidential Studies Quarterly* (summer 1980): 371.

103. Bonafede, "White House Personnel Office."

104. Quoted in ibid., 48.

105. Macy, Adams, and Walter, *America's Unelected Government,* 39.

106. *Myers v. United States,* 272 U.S. 52 (1926).

107. Quoted in Woll, *American Bureaucracy,* 224.

108. *Humphrey's Executor v. United States,* 295 U.S. 602 (1935).

109. *Wiener v. United States,* 357 U.S. 349 (1958).

110. *Morrison v. Olson,* 487 U.S. 654 (1988).

111. Ibid.

112. Pious, *American Presidency,* 256.

113. Lyndon Baines Johnson, *The Vantage Point* (New York: Holt, Rinehart, and Winston, 1971), 34.

114. Lance T. LeLoup, "Fiscal Chief: Presidents and the Budget," in *The Presidency: Studies in Policy Making,* ed. Stephen A. Shull and Lance T. LeLoup (Brunswick, Ohio: King's Court, 1979), 211.

115. Johnson, *Vantage Point,* 36.

116. Gerald Ford, "Budget Message of the President," *The Budget of the United States Government, Fiscal Year 1978* (Washington, D.C.: Government Printing Office, 1977), M–3.

117. Dennis S. Ippolito, *The Budget and National Politics* (San Francisco: Freeman, 1978), 40.

118. *U.S. Statutes at Large* 42 (1921): 20, sec. 206.

119. Office of Management and Budget, *Preparation and Submission of 1977 "Current Services" Budget Estimates,* Bulletin No. 76–4 (Washington, D.C.: Government Printing Office, 1975), 1.

120. Howard E. Shuman, *Politics and the Budget: The Struggle between the President and the Congress* (Englewood Cliffs, N.J.: Prentice Hall, 1984), 225.

121. *Budget of the United States, Fiscal Year 1983: Major Themes and Additional Budget Details* (Washington, D.C.: Government Printing Office, 1982), 37.

122. Aaron Wildavsky, "Constitutional Expenditure Limitation and Congressional Budget Reform," in *The Congressional Budget Process After Five Years,* ed. Rudolph G. Penner (Washington, D.C.: American Enterprise Institute, 1981), 99.

123. Hedrick Smith, *The Power Game* (New York: Random House, 1988), 290.

124. Shuman, *Politics and the Budget,* 287.

125. Richard Wolf, "Federal Deficit Estimate Down to $296B," *USA TODAY,* July 11, 2006; Andrew Taylor, "Budget Deficit Estimates See Contraction," *Associated Press,* January 24, 2007.

126. Pious, *American Presidency,* 272.

127. Shuman, *Politics and the Budget,* 60.

128. *New York Times,* February 10, 1982, A1.

129. Drew, *On the Edge,* 109.

130. Louis Fisher, *Presidential Spending Power* (Princeton: Princeton University Press, 1975), 7.

131. Pious, *American Presidency,* 278.

132. Fisher, *Presidential Spending Power,* 207.

133. *U.S. Statutes at Large* 88 (1974): 1804, sec. 32.

134. Quoted in Pious, *American Presidency,* 278.

135. Ippolito, *Budget and National Politics,* 138–139.

136. *Train v. City of New York,* 420 U.S. 35 (1975).

137. *Immigration and Naturalization Service v. Chadha,* 462 U.S. 919 (1983).

138. John Ellwood and James Thurber, "The Congressional Budget Process Re-examined," in *Congress Reconsidered,* 2d ed., ed. Lawrence C. Dodd and Bruce I. Oppenheimer (Washington, D.C.: CQ Press, 1981), 266.

139. Letter of John Marshall to James Wilkinson, January 5, 1787, reprinted in *The Papers of John Marshall, 1775–1788,* vol. 1, ed. Herbert A. Johnson (Chapel Hill: University of North Carolina Press, 1974), 200.

140. Samuel Eliot Morison, Henry Steele Commager, and William E. Leuchtenburg, *The Growth of the American Republic,* vol. 1 (New York: Oxford University Press, 1969), 242. Pages 227–261 of this volume describe the events immediately preceding and during the Constitutional Convention.

141. Article II of the Constitution enumerates presidential powers.

142. Article I, Section 8, of the Constitution gives Congress authority to "pay the Debts and provide for . . . the general Welfare of the United States." This is interpreted as a grant of authority for Congress to spend money to promote the general welfare of the nation. It is not interpreted as a grant of authority to enact any regulatory scheme that Congress believes will promote the general welfare.

143. *McCulloch v. Maryland,* 17 U.S. (4 Wheat.) 316 (1819).

144. *Gibbons v. Ogden,* 22 U.S. (9 Wheat.) 1 (1824).

145. *Wickard v. Filburn,* 317 U.S. 111 (1942).

146. What, for example, is the relationship between home-grown food for purely household consumption and interstate commerce?

The Supreme Court gave its answer in *Wickard v. Filburn*: If a household grows and harvests food on its own land, and for its own use, then it will be less likely to purchase food products on the commercial market. The effects of this isolated instance of self-sufficiency will eventually be felt across state lines.

147. The most controversial of the nine cases was *Wards Cove Packing Co. v. Antonio*, 109 S.Ct. (1989).

148. U.S. Department of Commerce, Bureau of the Census, *Historical Statistics of the United States: Colonial Times to 1970*, vol. 2 (Washington, D.C.: Government Printing Office, 1975), table Y 308–317, 1102–1103; and U.S. Department of Commerce, Bureau of the Census, *Statistical Abstract of the United States*, 115th ed. (Washington, D.C.: Government Printing Office, 1995), table 527, "Federal Civilian Employment by Branch, Agency, and Area."

149. Office of Personnel Management, *Total Civilian Employment, 2005* (Washington, D.C.: Government Printing Office, 2005).

150. Accounts of the Ole Miss incident may be found in Schlesinger, *Thousand Days*, and in Theodore C. Sorensen, *Kennedy* (New York: Harper and Row, 1965).

151. *Myers v. United States*, 272 U.S. 52, 177 (1926).

152. See, for example, *Kendall v. United States*, 37 U.S. (12 Pet.) 524 (1838); *Youngstown Sheet and Tube Co. v. Sawyer*, 343 U.S. 579 (1952) (also known as the *Steel Seizure Case*); and *United States v. Nixon*, 418 U.S. 683 (1974).

153. *In re Neagle*, 135 U.S. 1 (1890).

154. The strike began when the Pullman Palace Car Company cut the wages of its workers and the company refused an offer of arbitration by the American Railway Union.

155. *In re Debs*, 158 U.S. 564 (1895).

156. *Myers v. United States*.

157. *Wiener v. United States*; and *Humphrey's Executor v. United States*.

158. *In re Debs*.

159. *Ex parte Milligan*.

160. Alexander Hamilton, *Federalist* No. 74, in Alexander Hamilton, James Madison, and John Jay, *The Federalist Papers* (New York: Mentor, 1961), 449.

161. Ibid., 448.

162. Proclamation of September 15, 1792, George Washington, *Messages and Papers of the Presidents, 1789–1897*, vol. I, ed. James D. Richardson (Washington, D.C.: Government Printing Office, 1897), 124–125.

163. See Proclamation of July 10, 1795, George Washington, *Messages and Papers of the Presidents, 1789–1897*, vol. I, ed. James D. Richardson (Washington, D.C.: Government Printing Office, 1897), 181.

164. *Ex parte Garland*, 71 U.S. (4 Wall.) 333 (1866). See generally *Schick v. Reed*, 419 U.S. 256 (1974).

165. *U.S. Statutes at Large* 26 (1891): 946.

166. David G. Adler, "The President's Pardon Power," in *Inventing the American Presidency*, ed. Thomas E. Cronin (Lawrence: University Press of Kansas, 1989), 212, 218–219.

167. Forrest McDonald, *The American Presidency* (Lawrence: University Press of Kansas, 1994), 282.

168. *Wiener v. United States; Humphrey's Executor v. United States*.

169. Executive Order 11365, July 29, 1967.

170. Kerner was later rewarded by the president with appointment to the U.S. Court of Appeals for the Seventh Circuit, but he eventually resigned after being indicted and convicted of a felony.

171. Office of the President, National Advisory Commission on Civil Disorders, *Report of the National Advisory Commission on Civil Disorders* (Washington, D.C.: Government Printing Office, 1968).

172. Ibid., A–631.

173. *McCulloch v. Maryland*.

174. *Gibbons v. Ogden*.

175. *Martin v. Hunter's Lessee*, 14 U.S. (1 Wheat.) 304 (1816); and *Cohens v. Virginia*, 19 U.S. (6 Wheat.) 264 (1821).

176. David Johnston, "Just Before He Was to Be Freed, Prime Bombing Suspect Is Identified in Jail," *New York Times*, April 22, 1995, 10.

177. *U.S. Code*, vol. 18, sec. 3052.

178. See *U.S. Code*, vol. 18, secs. 3053 (U.S. marshals) and 3056 (Secret Service); and *U.S. Code*, vol. 21, sec. 878 (Drug Enforcement Administration).

179. *U.S. Code*, vol. 18, sec. 3061 (a) (2).

180. *U.S. Code*, vol. 18, sec. 3061 (b).

181. U.S. Congress, House, Committee on Interior and Insular Affairs, Subcommittee on General Oversight and Investigations, *NRC Coziness with Industry: Nuclear Regulatory Commission Fails to Maintain Arms' Length Relationship with the Nuclear Industry*, Committee Print No. 5, 100th Cong., 1st sess., 1987.

182. U.S. Constitution, Article I, Section 2.

183. U.S. Constitution, Article I, Section 3.

184. Alexander Hamilton, *Federalist* No. 65, in Alexander Hamilton, James Madison, and John Jay, *The Federalist Papers* (New York: Mentor, 1961), 396.

185. *U.S. Statutes at Large* 14 (1867): 430.

186. Compare *Myers v. United States*.

187. *Prize Cases*; and *In re Debs*.

188. *In re Neagle*.

189. *Ex parte Garland*.

SELECTED BIBLIOGRAPHY

Aberbach, Joel D. *Keeping a Watchful Eye: The Politics of Congressional Oversight.* Washington, D.C.: Brookings, 1990.

Arnold, Peri E. *Making the Managerial President: Comprehensive Reorganization Planning, 1905–1980.* Princeton: Princeton University Press, 1986.

Baker, Nancy V. *Conflicting Loyalties: Law and Politics in the Attorney General's Office, 1789–1990.* Lawrence: University Press of Kansas, 1992.

Bundy, McGeorge. *The Strength of Government.* Cambridge: Harvard University Press, 1968.

Burke, John P. "The Institutional Presidency." In *The Presidency and the Political System*, 4th ed., edited by Michael Nelson. Washington, D.C.: CQ Press, 1995.

Campbell, Colin. *Managing the Presidency: Carter, Reagan, and the Search for Executive Harmony.* Pittsburgh: University of Pittsburgh Press, 1986.

Carter, Stephen L. *The Confirmation Mess: Cleaning Up the Federal Appointments Process.* New York: Basic Books, 1994.

Cronin, Thomas E. *The State of the Presidency.* 2d ed. Boston: Little, Brown, 1980.

Dodd, Lawrence C., and Richard L. Schott. *Congress and the Administrative State.* New York: Macmillan, 1986.

Drew, Elizabeth. *On The Edge: The Clinton Presidency.* New York: Simon and Schuster, 1994.

Fain, Tyrus G., ed. *Federal Reorganization: The Executive Branch.* Public Document Series. New York: Bowker, 1977.

Fenno, Richard F., Jr. *The President's Cabinet.* New York: Vintage, 1958.

Fisher, Louis. *The Politics of Shared Power: Congress and the Executive.* 4th ed. College Station: Texas A&M Press, 2000.

Heclo, Hugh. *A Government of Strangers: Executive Politics in Washington.* Washington, D.C.: Brookings, 1977.

Hess, Stephen. *Organizing the Presidency.* Washington, D.C.: Brookings, 1988.

Ippolito, Dennis S. *The Budget and National Politics.* San Francisco: Freeman, 1978.

Jones, Charles O. *The Presidency in a Separated System.* Washington, D.C.: Brookings, 1994.

Koenig, Louis W. *The Chief Executive.* 5th ed. New York: Harcourt Brace Jovanovich, 1986.

Kramer, Fred A. *Contemporary Approaches to Public Budgeting.* Cambridge: Winthrop, 1979.

LeLoup, Lance T. *Budgetary Politics.* 2d ed. Brunswick, Ohio: King's Court, 1980.

Mackenzie, G. Calvin. *The Politics of Presidential Appointments.* New York: Free Press, 1981.

Mackenzie, G. Calvin, ed. *The In-and-Outers: Presidential Appointees and Transient Government in Washington.* Baltimore: Johns Hopkins University Press, 1987.

Macy, John W., Bruce Adams, and J. Jackson Walter. *America's Unelected Government: Appointing the President's Team.* Cambridge: Ballinger, 1983.

McDonald, Forrest. *The American Presidency: An Intellectual History.* Lawrence: University Press of Kansas, 1994.

Nathan, Richard P. *The Administrative Presidency.* New York: Macmillan, 1986.

Nelson, Michael. *The Presidency and the Political System.* 4th ed. Washington, D.C.: CQ Press, 1995.

Nichols, David K. *The Myth of the Modern Presidency.* University Park: Pennsylvania State University Press, 1994.

Rossiter, Clinton L. *The American Presidency.* 3d ed. New York: Harcourt Brace Jovanovich, 1963.

Rourke, Francis E., ed. *Bureaucratic Power in National Policy Making.* 4th ed. Boston: Little, Brown, 1986.

Rozell, Mark J. *Executive Privilege: Presidential Power, Secrecy, and Accountability.* 2d ed. Lawrence: University Press of Kansas, 2002.

Smith, Hedrick. *The Power Game: How Washington Works.* New York: Random House, 1988.

Spitzer, Robert J. *President and Congress: Executive Hegemony at the Crossroads of American Government.* New York: McGraw-Hill, 1993.

Warshaw, Shirley Anne. *The Keys to Power: Managing the Presidency,* 2d ed. New York: Longman, 2005.

chapter 12

Legislative Leader

by Matthew J. Dickinson and Christopher J. Bosso

The U.S. Constitution, political scientist Richard Neustadt reminds us, did not establish a government marked by "separation of powers"; it created a system of "separated institutions sharing powers."[1] Perhaps nowhere is this more evident than in the constitutional provisions describing the lawmaking process. Although the first sentence in Article I of the Constitution grants "all legislative Powers" to Congress, Article II, Section 3 authorizes the president to recommend to Congress measures deemed "necessary and expedient," and Article I, Section 7 gives the president the power to sign or veto legislation passed by Congress. In addition, the president has the authority "with the Advice and Consent of the Senate" to negotiate treaties with other nations, although treaties gain the force of law only when "two-thirds of the Senators present concur" (Article II, Section 2). The president also has the formal power to convene "emergency" sessions of Congress (Article II, Section 3). But it is the veto power, and the invitation to recommend legislation to Congress, that together provide the most significant constitutional basis for the president to participate in the legislative process.

Although these provisions have remained unchanged since the Constitution was ratified in 1789, the president's legislative role has grown significantly during the ensuing two-and-a-quarter centuries. This reflects changing economic and social conditions that have compelled the national government, including the president, to embrace new responsibilities. In addition, technological innovations, particularly radio and television, helped elevate the president's policy agenda-setting role. New international responsibilities during the cold war and in the fight against terrorism in the wake of the attacks on New York City and Washington, D.C., on September 11, 2001, also contributed to an expansion in presidential responsibilities. The brevity and static nature of the constitutional clauses dealing with the lawmaking process, then, mask a considerable increase in presidents' ability to influence the legislative agenda and the direction of public policy.

Even so, the constitutionally mandated sharing of powers continues to constrain the president's legislative influence; it ensures that the president's relationship with Congress remains fluid, ambiguous, and frequently frustrating. Much of what presidents desire or need, especially in the domestic sphere, still demands congressional cooperation, whether to enact new laws, appropriate funds, or, in the case of the Senate, approve treaties and executive and judicial branch appointments. Congress, however, usually approaches lawmaking from its own unique perspective, due to its members' different electoral constituencies, terms of office, and responsibilities. The result is that the president rarely can take Congress's support for granted, even when Congress is controlled by the president's own political party.[2] In the modern era, then, presidents loom much larger in the lawmaking process, but the elevated vantage point is no guarantee that Congress will do their legislative bidding.

THE VETO

The veto is the primary formal tool presidents use to influence congressional lawmaking. All other means of shaping and directing the legislative process must be understood with reference to this formal power, because only the president's legal capacity to stop legislation gives the other instruments for influencing public policy their teeth. *(See also "Veto Power," p. 1348, in Chapter 29, Vol. II.)*

Constitutional Foundations

The president's authority to block acts passed by Congress has its origins in the 1787 debate over the Constitution, in particular the Framers' efforts to prevent any single branch—and, by extension, any individual or group—from gaining tyrannical political power. These concerns go back to the very roots of the colonial rebellion against England.

Anyone who has studied the Declaration of Independence and the events surrounding it is well aware of the colonists' complaints against England's King George III and their eventual fear of a powerful national executive. Yet often overlooked is their equal dread of unchecked legislative power. Thomas Jefferson's second villain in the Declaration of Independence was the English Parliament, a legislature unobstructed by written constitutional limits and loathed widely in the colonies for its apparent disregard for due process of law. These general fears about an overly strong national government were reflected in the Articles of Confederation, the Republic's first constitution. The Articles, which went into effect in 1781, essentially created a league of friendship among the thirteen newly independent states that made the national government a creature of the states and dependent on them for its powers and funds. (See "Articles of Confederation," p. 1741, in Reference Materials, Vol. II.)

Ultimately, however, the national government under the Articles proved unable to promote either national unity or effective government. One problem, at least for those who had agitated for major changes in the Articles, was the absence of any independent national executive authority to administer the laws and resist legislative tyranny.[3] Not only had Congress under the Articles proven unable to govern by itself, but the political and fiscal excesses of state legislatures during the 1780s led to the perception that such bodies were as dangerous to liberty as an unrestrained monarch. Jefferson, reflecting on his experiences as governor of Virginia, wrote, "All the powers of government . . . result to the legislative body. The concentrating of these in the same hands is precisely the definition of despotic government."[4] These sentiments were shared by many of the delegates to the Constitutional Convention, even those who otherwise feared an overly strong national government.

He shall from time to time give to the Congress Information of the State of the Union, and recommend to their Consideration such Measures as he shall judge necessary and expedient. . . .

—from Article II, Section 3

The concept of a *veto* (Latin for "I forbid") was well known to the Framers. Indeed, in ancient Rome the veto was used by the plebeians to protect the common people from the excesses of a senate dominated by aristocrats. It later surfaced in medieval Europe as a royal check on newly developing legislatures. In England before the seventeenth century, the monarch had the *absolute* power to deny acts by Parliament, a weapon that Queen Elizabeth I for one used quite frequently.[5] Closer to home, by 1787 a few state constitutions (such as that of Massachusetts) contained a form of executive veto.[6]

Every Bill which shall have passed the House of Representatives and the Senate, shall, before it become a Law, be presented to the President of the United States; If he approve he shall sign it, but if not he shall return it, with his Objections to that House in which it shall have originated, who shall . . . proceed to reconsider it.

—from Article I, Section 7

Not surprisingly, then, virtually every plan put forth for revisions in the Articles included some form of an executive check on laws passed by Congress. The Virginia Plan called for a "council of revision" of members from both the executive and the judicial branches that would keep the legislature from drawing "all power into its impetuous vortex."[7] But critics of this idea argued that such a "plural" veto would be too weak, because disputes within the council would undermine decisive executive action. Furthermore, as George Mason of Virginia argued, the veto should be more than a check against legislative intrusion; it also was needed to discourage demagogy and prevent "unjust and pernicious" laws.[8] Other delegates expressed discomfort with having judges act on bills before they came up as legal cases, so the convention eventually granted the veto to the president alone.

Some proponents of a strong executive initially supported an absolute veto, giving Congress no opportunity to respond, but this idea found no support among delegates who were concerned about unresponsive and capricious executives. After some debate, the Framers gave the new executive a "partial negative." The president could reject bills or joint resolutions passed by Congress, but Congress in response could *override* a veto by extraordinary majorities of two-thirds of the members present in each chamber. Presidents could not veto constitutional amendments, concurrent resolutions, or resolutions passed by only one chamber.[9]

The veto would emerge as the constitutional core of executive independence. "The primary inducement to conferring this power in question upon the executive," wrote Alexander Hamilton in *Federalist* No. 73, "is to enable him to defend himself; the second one is to increase the chances in favor of the community against the passing of bad laws, through haste, inadvertence, or design."[10] The legislature is not infallible, Hamilton argued, and, unless checked, its love of power would ultimately betray both it and the ability of government to function effectively. In *Federalist* No. 48, James Madison pointed out that only by giving each branch some control over the others could power be restrained and rights and liberties be protected—a theme he continued in

Federalist No. 51 with his famous line "Ambition must be made to counteract ambition." [11]

Opponents of the veto, even those worried about unrestrained legislative power, argued that Congress alone represented the people. The veto might undermine democratic values by allowing the president to block "good" laws or simply to thwart majority rule. But, Hamilton retorted in *Federalist* No. 73, unrestrained majorities are just as dangerous as an unchecked elite, and "the injury which might possibly be done by defeating a few good laws will be amply compensated by the advantage of preventing a number of bad ones." [12] Moreover, allowing the executive to threaten a veto might induce legislative moderation, making actual use of the veto unnecessary.

The Constitution gives the president three choices after being formally presented with a bill passed by Congress: sign the bill into law; veto the bill and return it to the chamber where it originated within ten legislative days after presentation (Sundays excluded); or, finally, do nothing. [13] If the president does nothing, the bill becomes law automatically after ten legislative days. This provision prevents presidents from thwarting the majority will of Congress through simple inaction. The exception to this rule occurs when Congress passes a bill and then adjourns before ten legislative days have elapsed. Any bill not signed by the president when Congress so adjourns dies automatically—that is, it cannot become law. This condition is called a *pocket veto,* which is discussed later in this section.

Several things can happen once a president vetoes a bill and returns it to Congress. If the legislature fails to act at all, the bill dies. If two-thirds of the members present in each chamber pass the bill once again, it becomes law automatically despite presidential disapproval. [14] Such "supermajorities" in each chamber combine to produce a veto *override.* Overrides are rare—only 106 of 2,551 presidential vetoes issued between 1789 and 2006 were overridden—because to sustain a veto the president needs to gain only one-third plus one of the votes of those present in one chamber. *(See Table 12-1.)* Barring an override, Congress can either rewrite the legislation to meet the president's demands (as Hamilton foresaw) or simply give up and start from scratch.

Bills vetoed by the president normally are returned to Congress accompanied by a message that states reasons for the president's opposition. *(See box, A Veto Message, p. 653.)* Sometimes the president will cite constitutional concerns, at other times political or policy disagreements, but veto messages are always aimed at advancing the president's views on the bill in question. Whatever their other purposes, veto messages ultimately are political statements directed not only at Congress but also at the public at large. In this sense, the veto message is an additional resource presidents can use in their efforts to influence public policy.

TABLE 12-1   **Vetoes and Vetoes Overridden, All Bills, 1789–2006**

President	All bills vetoed	Regular vetoes	Pocket vetoes	Vetoes overridden
Washington	2	2	0	0
J. Adams	0	0	0	0
Jefferson	0	0	0	0
Madison	7	5	2	0
Monroe	1	1	0	0
J. Q. Adams	0	0	0	0
Jackson	12	5	7	0
Van Buren	1	0	1	0
W. H. Harrison	0	0	0	0
Tyler	10	6	4	1
Polk	3	2	1	0
Taylor	0	0	0	0
Fillmore	0	0	0	0
Pierce	9	9	0	5
Buchanan	7	4	3	0
Lincoln	7	2	5	0
A. Johnson	29	21	8	15
Grant	93[a]	45	48[a]	4
Hayes	13	12	1	1
Garfield	0	0	0	0
Arthur	12	4	8	1
Cleveland (1st term)	414	304	110	2
B. Harrison	44	19	25	1
Cleveland (2d term)	170	42	128	5
McKinley	42	6	36	0
T. Roosevelt	82	42	40	1
Taft	39	30	9	1
Wilson	44	33	11	6
Harding	6	5	1	0
Coolidge	50	20	30	4
Hoover	37	21	16	3
F. Roosevelt	635	372	263	9
Truman	250	180	70	12
Eisenhower	181	73	108	2
Kennedy	21	12	9	0
L. Johnson	30	16	14	0
Nixon	43	26[b]	17	7
Ford	66	48	18	12
Carter	31	13	18	2
Reagan	78	39	39	9
G. Bush[c]	44	29	15	1
Clinton	37	36	1	2
G. W. Bush[d]	1	1	0	0
TOTAL	**2,551**	**1,486**	**1,066**	**106**

SOURCE: U.S. House of Representatives, Office of the Clerk, "Historical Highlights, Presidential Vetoes, (1789–2006)" *(clerk.house.gov/art_history/house_history/vetoes.html),* accessed February 1, 2007.

NOTES: a. Veto total listed for Grant does not include a pocket veto of a bill that apparently never was placed before him for his signature. b. Two pocket vetoes, later overturned in court, are counted as regular vetoes. c. Two pocket vetoes, attempted by Bush during intrasession periods, are not counted since Congress considered the two bills enacted into law because of Bush's failure to return them to legislation. d. Through 2006.

Historical Development

Early presidents, whatever their other political beliefs, conformed to the Framers' view that Congress best represented the public will. The idea that a president should veto a bill simply because it was "bad" politics or policy was not yet widely accepted, and so the relatively few vetoes issued between 1790 and 1830 were confined to bills deemed unconstitutional.

This narrow interpretation of the president's right (and perhaps duty) to use the veto was expanded significantly during the presidency of Andrew Jackson (1829–1837) of Tennessee—hero of the War of 1812, foe of eastern business and banking interests, and self-styled "Tribune of the People." Jackson actively engaged in intense partisan warfare with Congress and, as political scientist Clinton Rossiter suggests, "revived the veto and purified it of the niceties that had grown up around it" by making it an overtly political instrument.[15] Indeed, in eight years Jackson issued twelve vetoes, more than all previous presidents combined. None of his vetoes was overridden, despite the controversies they created. Perhaps most controversial of all was Jackson's rejection of an 1832 bill to recharter the Bank of the United States, an institution bitterly despised by Jackson's supporters among the frontier settlers and farmers because of its high interest rates.

Although Jackson's immediate successors professed renewed allegiance to the traditional doctrine of congressional supremacy, they too proved surprisingly resolute when challenged by the legislature. John Tyler (1841–1845) vetoed two major bank bills supported by his party, and his 1842 veto of a controversial tariff measure sparked the first formal attempt in Congress to impeach a president. The effort failed, and Tyler's successors continued to display the independence pioneered by Jackson. Indeed, of the fifty-nine bills vetoed between 1789 and 1865, more than half were by Jackson, Tyler, and Franklin Pierce (1853–1857).

Post–Civil War Era

The period between the Civil War and the late 1890s saw some of history's most acrid partisan battles, which often spilled over into conflict between the branches of government. Presidents routinely clashed with Congress within a national political arena rife with sharp regional and partisan antagonisms, deep social and economic changes, and sharp disputes over the fundamental role of government. This era, although marked generally by congressional dominance, nonetheless saw surges in the use of the veto as successive presidents attempted to grapple with massive numbers of bills spawned by an often antagonistic Congress.

Andrew Johnson (1865–1869), who succeeded the assassinated Abraham Lincoln (1861–1865), suffered most, in no small part because he was a former Democrat from Tennessee confronting a Congress controlled by "Radical Republicans" seeking to punish the states of the defeated Confederacy. Johnson was the first president to have Congress override a veto of an important bill, and, among all presidents, he had the greatest percentage of regular vetoes overridden (fifteen out of twenty-one, or 71 percent). Furthermore, Johnson's refusal to abide by the Tenure of Office Act, a law passed over his veto that prohibited presidents from firing political appointees without congressional approval, led directly to his impeachment by the House. Johnson was acquitted in the Senate by one vote. Congress repealed the Tenure of Office Act, which most scholars viewed as unconstitutional, in 1887.[16]

The visibility of and drama surrounding Johnson's veto battles were more the exception than the rule. Most vetoes issued during the late nineteenth century were directed at "private" bills, legislation that benefited specific individuals, companies, or municipalities. *(See Table 12-2.)* Private bills in the late 1800s usually provided pensions for Civil War veterans, but many of them were fraudulent or excessive claims and often rushed through late in the congressional session. Grover Cleveland (1885–1889, 1893–1897) vetoed 482 private bills during his eight years in office—43 during one three-day period in 1886 alone.[17] Many of these were pocket vetoes, and only three of Cleveland's vetoes of private bills were overridden.

The Veto in the Contemporary Presidency

Franklin D. Roosevelt (1933–1945) used the veto more vigorously and strategically than all presidents to that time, and probably thereafter. He was the first to veto major tax legislation and openly used the threat of the veto in his legislative strategy, even though his own party controlled both houses of Congress throughout his presidency. "Give me something to veto," he reportedly told his aides, so that he could remind members of Congress that he was part of the lawmaking process.[18] Roosevelt's veto strategy helped establish the modern presidency, with the veto becoming but one instrument of executive influence within an environment of expansive federal government action and power.

Contemporary presidents have adopted Roosevelt's strategic use of the veto to shape legislation, particularly because they so frequently find themselves facing a Congress in which the other major political party controls one or both chambers. *(See table, Party Affiliations in Congress and the Presidency, 1789–2006, p. 1869, in Reference Materials, Vol. II.)* Indeed, vetoes are used most frequently when such partisan splits occur. Since the end of World War II, 290 of the 354 presidential vetoes (82 percent of all vetoes) occurred during periods of divided government. A classic example of this strategy took place in 1947, when Harry S. Truman (1945–1953) vetoed the controversial Taft-Hartley Labor-Management Relations Act, a bill passed by a Republican-controlled House and Senate that limited the political activity of federal workers and labor unions.[19] Although the Republican-led Congress overruled Truman's veto, he capitalized on their action to great political effect by rallying labor voters to the Democrats in the 1948 election.

Republican Dwight D. Eisenhower (1953–1961) worked with a Congress dominated by Democrats during all but two of his eight years in office, yet he could rely on a "conservative coalition" of Republicans and southern Democrats to support his agenda and prevent overrides of his vetoes. One notable illustration of this dynamic came in 1959, after liberal northern Democrats had made large gains in the 1958 congressional elections. These Democrats ignored Eisenhower's warnings and tried to push a vigorous domestic agenda, leading Eisenhower to veto a succession of bills authorizing new spending for urban housing, rural electrification, and other domestic programs. These vetoes were upheld by the conservative coalition, and threats of additional vetoes persuaded Democrats to cut back on their efforts.[20]

Democrats John F. Kennedy (1961–1963) and Lyndon B. Johnson (1963–1969), blessed with friendlier partisan majorities in Congress, seldom used the veto, but Republicans Richard Nixon (1969–1974) and Gerald R. Ford (1974–1977) fared differently. Both Nixon and Ford faced off against a Congress dominated by Democrats, so the veto became central to their legislative strategies. Nixon vetoed several major bills he deemed inflationary, and once even appeared on national television to sign a veto of a major appropriations bill. As with Eisenhower, a bipartisan conservative coalition in Congress often proved large enough to sustain Nixon's vetoes.

However, the ultimate success of the veto as a tool for shaping legislation is tied inextricably to a president's overall political "strength." Nixon's deepening legal and political troubles eventually weakened his popular support and, by extension, his influence in Congress. In 1973 Congress soundly overrode his veto of the War Powers Resolution, which aimed at limiting a president's ability to commit U.S. armed forces abroad without congressional approval. Congress also overrode Nixon's veto of the 1974 Budget Impoundment and Control Act, which Nixon opposed because it limited the president's ability to avoid spending funds appropriated by Congress. (*See "Line-item Veto," p. 656.*)

Gerald Ford became president upon Nixon's resignation in August 1974 and, faced with a Congress dominated even more by liberal Democrats after the midterm congressional elections, used the veto frequently and to great effect. Ford was sustained on all but four of the seventeen vetoes he issued in 1975 alone, and used the threat of a veto to stop a popular consumer protection bill from ever passing. Ford's short tenure in office showed how the veto could be used to

compensate partially for the severe political handicaps that came with being an unelected chief executive succeeding a disgraced president.

TABLE 12-2 **Private Bills Vetoed, 1789–2006**

President	Regular vetoes	Pocket vetoes	Vetoes overridden
Washington	0	0	0
J. Adams	0	0	0
Jefferson	0	0	0
Madison	2	0	0
Monroe	0	0	0
J. Q. Adams	0	0	0
Jackson	0	0	0
Van Buren	0	1	0
W. H. Harrison	0	0	0
Tyler	0	0	0
Polk	0	0	0
Taylor	0	0	0
Fillmore	0	0	0
Pierce	0	0	0
Buchanan	2	0	0
Lincoln	0	1	0
A. Johnson	0	2	0
Grant	29	37	3
Hayes	1	0	0
Garfield	0	0	0
Arthur	1	8	0
Cleveland (1st term)	271	82	1
B. Harrison	5	23	0
Cleveland (2d term)	30	99	2
McKinley	4	32	0
T. Roosevelt	27	31	0
Taft	10	7	0
Wilson	7	2	0
Harding	3	0	0
Coolidge	3	17	0
Hoover	4	6	0
F. Roosevelt	317	180	0
Truman	137	38	1
Eisenhower	43	64	0
Kennedy	8	4	0
L. Johnson	12	4	0
Nixon	0	3	0
Ford	3	2	0
Carter	0	2	0
Reagan	2	6	0
G. Bush	0	1	0
Clinton	0	0	0
G. W. Bush[a]	0	0	0
TOTAL	**921**	**652**	**7**

SOURCES: *Guide to Congress,* 5th ed. (Washington, D.C.: CQ Press, 2000); *CQ Weekly,* various issues.

NOTES: The official distinction between public and private bills was rather hazy through the 1930s, although private bills generally were classified as those benefiting a single individual rather than a large segment of society (for example, a private pension bill). Beginning in 1936, however, a Library of Congress publication has listed all private bills.   a. Through 2006.

Jimmy Carter (1977–1981), like Kennedy and Johnson, relied on the veto less frequently than his Republican predecessors because fellow Democrats controlled Congress. A notable exception was his veto of a 1977 energy bill that included funds for a nuclear reactor he thought dangerous and expensive.[21] Congress chose not to challenge Carter on that veto, because many in his party also opposed the reactor. On the other hand, in 1980 Carter became the first president since Truman to suffer a veto override at the hands of a Congress controlled by his party after he vetoed a bill limiting the national debt because it contained a provision eliminating import fees on foreign oil.[22] Congress overrode this veto in part because the fees were unpopular with many Democrats and in part because of an apparent weakening in Carter's general public support as the Iran hostage situation dragged on.

The role of the veto during the presidency of Ronald Reagan (1981–1989) was even more telling, since during Reagan's first term Congress was split between a Republican Senate and a Democratic House. Such partisan divisions made it unlikely that Congress would override a veto, which enabled Reagan to veto spending bills contrary to his priorities. So crucial was the veto to Reagan's strategy that he often warned, "My veto pen is inked up and ready to go," when Congress was about to pass legislation he opposed.[23] His veto of a 1981 appropriations bill was so politically effective that Congress reworked the measure to his satisfaction. However, Reagan found it harder to make veto threats work to his advantage in the later years of his presidency, especially after Democrats regained full control over both chambers of Congress following the 1986 midterm elections. Indeed, in 1987 bipartisan majorities in Congress easily overrode Reagan's vetoes of major water pollution and highway bills, signaling a palpable shift in the president's influence with Congress as his presidency entered its final stages.

The two presidents to follow Reagan offered an especially useful contrast in the use of the veto as a means for influencing legislation. George Bush (1989–1993) issued forty-four vetoes but had only one overridden by the Democrat-controlled Congress. His successor, Bill Clinton (1993–2001), passed his first two years in office without issuing a veto, relying instead on Democratic leaders in Congress to forestall legislative challenges. But in 1994 Republicans gained control over both chambers of Congress for the first time in forty years. It thus seemed only a matter of time before Clinton, faced with a particularly assertive Republican congressional leadership, finally made use of the veto power. Clinton's first veto came on June 7, 1995, twenty-nine months after taking office, when he returned to Congress with his disapproval a major bill that cut spending of funds already appropriated for that fiscal year. This veto, which was not overridden, foreshadowed a struggle between Clinton and congressional Republicans for control over the direction of federal policy. Indeed, Clinton was to use the veto another thirty-five times during the remainder of his presidency, with only two overrides, thus repeating a veto pattern characteristic of presidents facing a Congress dominated by the other party.

President George W. Bush's (2001–) veto strategy represents a return to the pattern of Clinton's first two years in office. Except for a twenty-month period from May 2001 through January 2003 when Democrats narrowly controlled the Senate, Bush enjoyed majority-party support in both chambers of Congress during his first six years as president. In this period Bush vetoed only one bill—a controversial initiative passed by Congress in 2006 to loosen restrictions on federal funding for embryonic stem cell research. His veto was sustained. Bush's lack of vetoes partly reflected the effectiveness of his legislative strategy, particularly on tax and spending bills, which capitalized on the cohesive Republican majority in the House. Bush used this majority to stake out a relatively extreme initial legislative position, and then moderated his stance as necessary to accommodate the more centrist Senate, where the opposition Democratic Party, although in the minority, exercised greater influence. By splitting the difference between the conservative wing of the Republican Party in the House and the more moderate Senate, Bush was able to achieve acceptable legislative outcomes without exercising a veto.

History suggests, however, that with the loss of Congress to the Democrats in the 2006 midterm elections, Bush almost certainly would wield the veto more frequently during his final two years in office. How often he does so may depend on whether the *threat* of a veto is effective at moving legislation closer to his preferences.

An Instrument of Presidential Power

James Bryce, the nineteenth-century English observer of American government, argued that the veto "conveys the impression of firmness." [24] Given the rarity of vetoes, one is tempted to conclude that the impression is fleeting. Between 1945 and 1992, Congress presented more than 17,000 public bills for the president's signature. Presidents vetoed only 434 of these bills, a veto rate of 2.5 percent.[25] Moreover, on the rare occasions when presidents did veto bills, they often did so from positions of political weakness; the veto was a last-ditch effort to prevent legislation the president opposed from becoming law.[26] From this perspective, the veto does not appear to suggest firmness so much as political impotence.

In this regard, consider the experience of Gerald Ford, who may have been dealt the weakest political hand of any contemporary president. After succeeding the disgraced Nixon, Ford faced a fiercely independent Congress dominated by liberal Democrats in a post-Vietnam atmosphere infused with hostility to presidential power. Such political

A VETO MESSAGE

A bill passed by Congress is formally vetoed when the president returns it to Capitol Hill unsigned and accompanied by a message stating the reasons for disapproval. Presidents today rarely write their own veto messages. Instead, the messages typically are composed by professional staff in the Executive Office of the President with input from experts in the Office of Management and Budget (OMB) and other executive branch agencies. The president may scan the final draft and on occasion may pen major parts of controversial veto messages, but the overall process of opposing Congress on a piece of legislation largely is a collective one.

Whether the reasons given for a veto are constitutional, fiscal, substantive, or "merely" political—or a combination of reasons—a veto message is designed with more than Congress in mind. In today's media-saturated political atmosphere any message from the White House to Congress is scrutinized closely for its potential political ramifications. Veto messages thus are crafted carefully, designed above all to sell the president's views on a bill to national opinion makers and to the public, not simply to Congress.

Most veto messages are signed in the relative privacy of the Oval Office and sent by courier to Capitol Hill. They then are delivered to the chamber from whence the bills in question originated, which normally takes the lead in any efforts to override the veto. On vetoes of major bills, however, a president may use the opportunity to convene a public ceremony, complete with supporters and members of the national press, to attack the bill and to generate public sentiment against Congress.

In the following excerpt, President Bill Clinton explains his objections to legislation cutting $16.5 billion in monies already appropriated for the 1995 fiscal year. The legislation also would have provided $7.3 billion for additional spending, some of it to provide funds for natural disaster relief. HR 1158 was Clinton's first veto. Congress made no attempt to override it, since the bill had passed by small majorities in either chamber.

TO THE HOUSE OF REPRESENTATIVES:

I am returning herewith without my approval HR 1158, a bill providing for emergency supplemental appropriations and rescissions for fiscal year 1995.

This disagreement is about priorities, not deficit reduction. In fact, I want to increase the deficit reduction in this bill.

HR 1158 slashes needed investments for education, national service, and the environment, in order to avoid cutting wasteful projects and other unnecessary expenditures. There are billions of dollars in pork—unnecessary highway demonstration projects, courthouses, and other Federal buildings—that could have been cut instead of these critical investments. Indeed, the Senate bill made such cuts in order to maintain productive investments, but the House-Senate conference rejected those cuts. . . .

In the end, the Congress chose courthouses over education, pork-barrel highway projects over national service, Government travel over clean water.

At my instruction, the Administration has provided alternatives to the Congress that would produce greater deficit reduction than HR 1158, cutting even more in fiscal year 1995 spending than is included in HR 1158. But the spending reductions would come out of unnecessary projects and other spending, not investments in working families. . . .

My Administration has provided the Congress with changes that would enable me to sign revised legislation. I urge the Congress to approve a bill that contains the supplemental funding included in HR 1158—for disaster relief activities of the Federal Emergency Management Agency, for the Federal response to the bombing in Oklahoma City, for increased anti-terrorism efforts, and for providing debt relief to Jordan in order to contribute to further progress toward a Middle East peace settlement—along with my Administration's alternative restorations and offsets.

I will sign legislation that provides these needed supplemental appropriations and that reduces the deficit by at least as much as this bill. However, the legislation must reflect the priorities of the American people. HR 1158, as passed, clearly does not.

Bill Clinton
The White House
June 7, 1995

---

circumstances gave Ford little option but to rely heavily on the veto, which he issued more frequently against public bills than any other president during the twentieth century. The fact that most of Ford's vetoes were sustained underscores the veto's utility as a blunt instrument for stopping legislation. Nonetheless, his need to rely on the veto indicates his overall lack of influence during the legislative process.

That weakness is telegraphed even more strongly if the veto is overridden, something that historically has occurred to about 4 percent of presidential vetoes. Truman's crafty use of the veto against congressional Republicans should not obscure the fact that his vetoes were overridden twelve times. Reagan's defeat on successive overrides in early 1987 resulted from his weakened political leverage in light of renewed Democratic dominance in Congress, his own troubles con-

cerning secret arms sales to Iran, and the reality that Reagan was in the "lame duck" phase of his second term of office. For that matter, the only override battle that George Bush (1989–1993) lost came in the last months of his presidency on a bill regulating the cable television industry that was popular with both Democrats and Republicans. Congressional Republicans in this case were more concerned with their reelection prospects than with upholding a veto issued by a president on the verge of suffering a defeat in his bid for reelection.[27]

But if the exercise of the veto often reflects presidential weakness, a veto *threat* can be a potent bargaining tool. Viewed from this perspective, the rarity with which the veto has been used masks its actual utility to presidents as a means for shaping legislative outcomes. Thus although George W.

Bush vetoed only one bill during his first six years as president, he issued by one count more than 140 veto threats during that period.[28] By threatening to veto, presidents signal to Congress what is and is not acceptable legislation. Such threats often are effective at moving legislation closer to the president's preferred outcome. Moreover, political scientist Charles Cameron's research shows that the production of "landmark" legislation is comparatively lower under divided than unified party government, suggesting that the presidential veto threats—which are more likely under divided government—do alter congressional behavior.[29]

Two distinct eras in the Clinton presidency offer particularly good insights into this dynamic. Clinton issued no vetoes in his first two years in office, the longest such stretch since 1850, largely because his party controlled both chambers of Congress.[30] Clinton worked closely with congressional Democrats on legislative compromises that avoided the need for vetoes, yet by late 1994 he was widely seen as having failed to deliver on some of his major campaign promises. Clinton's troubles came about in no small part because his party's majorities in Congress were not large enough to overcome sharp internal partisan and ideological divisions as well as unified opposition by Republicans. Particularly telling was the fate of Clinton's plan for major reform of the nation's health care system, the only piece of legislation in 1993–1994 that he publicly threatened to veto if it did not contain key elements of his own plan. But Clinton's threat was to no avail: congressional Democrats were unable to satisfy enough members of their own party, much less get past almost unanimous Republican opposition. The failure on health care reform contributed to massive losses by Democrats in the 1994 midterm elections, and Republicans took control of both chambers for the first time in forty years.

Clinton now faced a particularly assertive Republican congressional leadership, spearheaded by House Speaker Newt Gingrich, R-Ga., and the veto quickly became the cornerstone of his legislative strategy. This was never more true than in 1995–1996, when Republicans dared him to veto omnibus appropriations bills that made major cuts in his programs and, in the process, risk shutting down most federal government operations. Clinton essentially called their bluff, and congressional Republicans—who apparently had forgotten how Ronald Reagan had outmaneuvered Democrats when the shoe was on the other foot in the 1980s—found that they, not Clinton, were being blamed for the subsequent government shutdowns. Faced with strong public blame for the shutdowns, congressional Republicans backed down each time, and Clinton's political strength grew accordingly. Indeed, thereafter Clinton used the veto as the linchpin of a defensive strategy to force Republicans to accede to his spending and policy priorities at the risk of even more public disapproval. So effective was Clinton in

this regard—even when he was entangled in impeachment proceedings related to his sexual relationship with a White House intern—that scholar George Edwards called his use of the veto "nearly unprecedented" in its strategic role and effectiveness.[31]

Even though Clinton succeeded in his veto strategy, Congress still finds ways to dilute the potency of a veto or veto threat. Members often load up major spending bills with "riders," legislative instructions that may change specific policies, or with pet spending programs that the president may be obliged to swallow to ensure passage of the bill. Clinton, for one, had to decide which of many Republican budget riders he could live with and those he would oppose each time he considered spending bills. Congress also tends to wait until late in each session to pass critical spending bills and to rely increasingly on massive omnibus (or "catch-all") bills to pass the budget, appropriate funds, and levy new taxes simultaneously, all in an effort to narrow the president's range of possible responses. Reagan, for example, had to swallow the Boland Amendment restricting U.S. aid to rebels opposing the Nicaraguan government because it was tacked onto a 1984 appropriations bill. The administration's subsequent efforts to get around the Boland Amendment got it into deep political and legal trouble. George Bush, to gain passage of the 1990 budget act, accepted new taxes, a compromise that angered many in his party and contributed to his defeat in 1992.

Finally, no president can assume automatic support from fellow party members in Congress on veto threats, or even during override battles. Most members of Congress resist being seen by constituents as mere rubber stamps for the president's wishes, especially when the bill in question benefits a member's district or state. This reality was well illustrated in 1987 when Congress overrode Reagan's vetoes of water treatment and highway bills and in 1992 when it overrode a veto by George Bush of a bill that promised to lower cable television rates. In each case, Republicans abandoned their own president in droves, sacrificing a presidential agenda for their constituents' interests. For their part, fellow Democrats deserted Clinton in two instances, most tellingly in 1997 when Congress overrode Clinton's initial (and only) use of the "line-item veto" provision it created in 1996. (See "Line-Item Veto," p. 656.)

The threat of a veto can be a positive tool for shaping policy. Its efficacy depends in part on a president's overall popularity, whether and to what extent the president's party controls Congress, the nature of the issue at hand, broad external political conditions, timing, and even luck. But as FDR understood, it also depends on the president's prior record in carrying through on those threats—hence his charge to aides to find something he could veto. Viewed in this way, the power of the veto is gauged not only by its immediate effect on pending legislation, but also on how it affects a president's reputation for using the veto in subsequent legislative bargaining sessions.

Pocket Veto

The Constitution specifically mentions the veto, as well as the method to be used for congressional override. But, like much of the Framers' handiwork, minor provisions have evolved over time into major constitutional battles between Congress and the presidency. One of the most heated of these battles has been over what is now known as the *pocket veto.*

Constitutional Provision

The Constitution gives the president ten legislative days (excluding Sundays) to sign a bill into law or return it to Congress with a veto message. A bill not approved or vetoed by the president becomes law after ten days "unless the Congress by their Adjournment prevent its Return, in which Case it shall not be a Law" (Article I, Section 7). This provision apparently was meant to make it possible to ward off last-minute actions by Congress that might prove dangerous or foolhardy. The president cannot possibly veto and return bills to Congress as prescribed in the Constitution if Congress already has left for home after adjournment, so the Framers determined that under such circumstances it was better that any bill left unapproved at adjournment simply die.

A *pocket veto* results from executive inaction, not anything the president does actively, and the term reflects the notion that the president "pocketed" a bill rather than acted on it.[32] A president technically cannot "issue" a pocket veto: the entire situation occurs simply because Congress has adjourned and the bill cannot be returned with a regular veto message. Even so, many presidents have asserted a "right" to use the pocket veto as if it were an active power of the office.

The first president to rely on a pocket veto was James Madison, in 1812, and only twice more before 1830 did a president pocket a bill. The incidence of pocket vetoes increased thereafter, especially against the many private pension bills passed by Congress in the second half of the nineteenth century. The champion of the pocket veto in absolute numbers is Franklin Roosevelt (263), but Grover Cleveland used the device more frequently (averaging 30 a year in office, compared with Roosevelt's 22), largely against the private pension bills for Civil War veterans. All told, presidents through 2006 issued 1,066 pocket vetoes, as opposed to 1,484 "regular" vetoes.[33]

Constitutional Issues

The pocket veto is controversial because Congress and the president often disagree over what constitutes congressional adjournment. The Constitution, as so often is the case, is not clear on this point except for adjournment *sine die* (Latin for

> If any Bill shall not be returned by the President within ten Days (Sundays excepted) after it shall have been presented to him, the Same shall be a Law, in like Manner as if he had signed it, unless the Congress by their Adjournment prevent its Return, in which Case it shall not be a Law.
>
> —*from Article I, Section 7*

"without a day," meaning "without a day being set for meeting again"). Adjournment *sine die* marks the end of a two-year Congress, which itself runs the course of the two-year term of the House of Representatives.

That the pocket veto is constitutional upon adjournment *sine die* is undisputed; the controversy concerns whether its use is constitutional with other types of recesses or adjournments. Any interpretation narrowing its use to adjournment *sine die* alone tends to benefit Congress. A more expansive definition magnifies executive power over legislation, because presidents might be able to defeat bills through inaction whenever Congress takes a recess, such as between sessions of the same Congress or during holidays occurring within any single session.

This question was not an issue during the nineteenth century, because Congress sat in session, on average, only half a year, and calling members back to Washington to override vetoes could take weeks of travel. But as Congress began to stay in session almost full time and as new technology made communications to and recall of Congress far easier than the Framers ever envisioned, the issue of when the president can legally use the pocket veto grew in importance.

The first real shot in this battle came with the 1929 *Pocket Veto Case,* in which the Supreme Court ruled that President Calvin Coolidge could pocket veto an Indian claims bill passed just before a four-month congressional recess.[34] The justices ruled that the term *adjournment* applied to any break in the congressional calendar that prevented the return of a bill within the required ten-day period, in this case adjournment between sessions. The ruling, as historian Arthur M. Schlesinger Jr. noted, "was based in part on the idea that, if Congress was in adjournment, no officer or agent was authorized to receive on behalf of Congress a bill rejected by the President."[35] To close this apparent loophole both chambers began to appoint "agents"—usually the clerk of the House and secretary of the Senate—to receive presidential veto messages while members were away, thus theoretically negating a president's rationale for a pocket veto. After all, once Congress returned it could deliberate and perhaps override a presidential veto at any time before adjournment *sine die.*

Franklin Roosevelt asserted that this strategy was unconstitutional when he declared a pocket veto of a bill passed before Congress went on a three-day recess, but the Supreme Court ruled in 1938 that pocket vetoes could not occur during such brief recesses if the appropriate agents had been so named.[36] Regular veto procedures, the justices argued, gave the president enough time to consider a bill *and* gave Congress the opportunity to respond, so the use of agents to receive veto messages was deemed constitutional. Congress, not surprisingly, made this practice commonplace thereafter.

The issue lay dormant until the early 1970s, when Richard Nixon's application of the pocket veto again sparked controversy about what kind of congressional adjournment "prevents" regular veto procedures. Despite the 1938 ruling, Nixon declared in 1970 that he would use a six-day holiday recess to pocket the Family Practice of Medicine Act, which provided funds for medical training. Congress had passed the bill unanimously, had appointed agents to receive presidential messages, and arguably would have overridden a regular veto, but Nixon did not give Congress the chance to respond. Nixon created a furor when he asserted that the short recess was analogous to adjournment *sine die*. Members of Congress countered that the bill had indeed become law because Nixon could not pocket a bill during the recess, and Sen. Edward M. Kennedy, D-Mass., subsequently brought suit against the administration.[37] Kennedy's case was upheld by a U.S. court of appeals, which essentially reaffirmed the 1938 Supreme Court decision.[38] The Nixon administration chose not to appeal this ruling to the Supreme Court.

Senator Kennedy figured in a similar lawsuit after President Ford declared a pocket veto against a bill passed just before the intersession break of the Ninety-third Congress. Once again, a federal court of appeals overturned a lower court decision and ruled that the pocket veto cannot be used except after adjournment *sine die* so long as both chambers appoint agents.[39] The Ford administration announced that it would abide by the ruling.[40]

Despite these precedents, in 1983 Ronald Reagan reasserted a more expansive view when he declared a pocket veto of a bill barring U.S. aid to El Salvador. The legislation had been passed just before the end of the first session of the Ninety-eighth Congress. Like Nixon and Ford, Reagan administration officials argued that the pocket veto applied to any congressional recess longer than three days. And, just as before, many in Congress declared that the device applied only to adjournment *sine die*. Thirty-three House Democrats sued the administration, and a U.S. court of appeals in 1984 again reversed a lower-court decision and reaffirmed the standard set in 1976.[41] The administration appealed the decision to the Supreme Court, which in January 1987 declared the particulars of the case moot (since the dispute over aid to El Salvador had long passed) and upheld the decision of the court of appeals.[42] Both sides

voiced disappointment that the high court had not settled the matter conclusively.

President George Bush confused the issue further. In August 1989, with Congress out on a summer recess, Bush declared a pocket veto of a minor bill that would have expedited the signing of legislation to bail out the nation's failing savings and loan industry. In doing so, Bush became the first president since Nixon to pocket a bill during a legislative session. In November 1989, Bush declared a pocket veto of a bill to allow dissident Chinese students to remain in the United States, but nonetheless returned the bill with a "memorandum of disapproval" outlining his objections. The Senate failed to override this "veto."

The Bush administration defended its actions on the basis of the *Pocket Veto Case* of 1929, which had upheld the use of the pocket veto during short congressional recesses. However, many in Congress—especially Democrats—looked instead to the series of more recent federal appeals court cases that had limited the pocket veto to adjournment *sine die*, and in 1990 they responded to Bush's actions with legislation that would codify these rulings. This bill (HR 849) was approved along party line votes by the House Judiciary Committee and the House Rules Committee, but the legislation failed to get to the floor of either chamber because of sharp partisan disagreements over "codifying" rules governing the pocket veto's use.[43]

To add to this legal confusion, in 1991 Bush declared a pocket veto of a bill passed prior to a holiday recess. The legislation honored retiring House member Morris K. Udall, D-Ariz., by setting up a foundation to promote environmental education. Although Bush said that he supported the thrust of the legislation, he disagreed about how members of the foundation board were to be appointed. This bill was not returned to Congress, but it was not formally vetoed, so legal scholars argued that the bill should be considered a law. However, the Bush administration did nothing to publish or otherwise implement the law, so its legal status was in dispute. Congress, meanwhile, passed another version of the same bill that revised the appointment procedures, which Bush signed into law, leaving the issue of the pocket veto unsettled.[44]

What constitutes constitutional application of the pocket veto thus remains a point of contention between a Congress eager to protect legislative prerogatives and presidents equally keen to find ways to kill unwanted legislation. The issue of the pocket veto may not be settled until the Supreme Court acts.

Line-item Veto

Under the Constitution, the veto is an all or nothing bargaining tool; presidents may not, for example, excise items deemed wasteful from an otherwise acceptable spending bill. Those who have supported greater presidential control over

When Republicans gained control over both chambers of Congress in 1994 for the first time in forty years, Democratic president Bill Clinton was forced to rely on the veto power as a means of influencing legislation. Here Clinton talks with Nevada legislators after vetoing a bill on the storage of nuclear waste in Nevada.

federal spending have considered this a major flaw in the veto process, particularly during the era of large federal budget deficits in the late 1980s through early 1990s, and again after 2001. Proposals to give presidents the capacity to pick and choose among specific appropriations, called a *line-item veto* (or *item veto*), have emerged periodically throughout history; but the effort has been continually thwarted by legislators fearful of even greater executive leverage within their constitutionally prescribed domain.

The Framers appear to have given no attention to a line-item veto during the drafting or ratification of the Constitution, which seems surprising until we recall that even the regular veto proved highly contentious. Moreover, the Framers showed their bias by granting to Congress full power over appropriations and revenues. However, the idea that the president should be able to veto parts of spending bills has enjoyed some popularity throughout American history. The states of the Confederacy included in their constitution a clause that enabled its president to "approve any appropriation and disapprove any other appropriation in the same bill" (Article 1, Section 7, Clause 2). Efforts to pass a constitutional amendment granting such executive power have popped up since the 1870s, but without success. Yet by the 1990s governors in forty-three states had some form of line-item veto. Most of these provisions pertain primarily to spending bills, but others also allow governors to modify substantive laws. At least ten states allow their governors to actually amend spending bills and send them back to the legislature for reconsideration.[45]

Some mid-twentieth-century presidents expressed strong support for a line-item veto, most notably Franklin Roosevelt and Eisenhower. Roosevelt came closest to realizing his wish when the House voted in 1938 to give the president that power: the effort died in the Senate, however.[46] The issue was set aside through the 1970s, but arose again in the 1980s as the federal budget deficit became a major problem. Like the budget, however, the line-item veto quickly became enmeshed in partisan politics, with Republican presidents Reagan and George H. W. Bush in favor and congressional Democrats generally opposed. Supporters argued that the line-item veto would give presidents greater control over federal spending, especially on programs and projects for which Congress may lack the political will to make cuts. Opponents expressed fears that a line-item veto would give the president excessive power over an area in which Congress traditionally—and constitutionally—took the lead.

This clash of partisan and institutional perspectives prevented proposals for the line-item veto from getting very far during the 1980s. In 1985 Reagan and congressional Republicans pushed for a two-year trial run, but the proposal was rebuffed both then and a year later. Even if the Senate had approved the line-item veto in 1986, it was unlikely that the House, which jealously guards its constitutional power of the purse, would have gone along. President George H. W. Bush also pushed publicly for a line-item veto, but he too had little success.

By the mid-1990s, however, the political dynamics surrounding the line-item veto had changed dramatically. President Clinton, who had possessed a line-item veto as governor of Arkansas, openly supported one for the president. Yet key congressional Democrats continued to fight any action that might infringe on Congress's control over the budget. As it turned out, Clinton found an ally on this issue in congressional Republicans, who in 1994 gained control of both chambers of Congress for the first time since 1952. The line-item veto was included in the Republicans' "Contract with America," in part because they anticipated the election of a Republican president in 1996, and thus the prospects for passing some kind of line-item veto improved dramatically. However, efforts to pass a constitutional amendment creating a line-item veto soon fell victim to resistance in the Senate—where even some Republicans opposed it—so proponents took another tack. After months of negotiations, a bipartisan majority voted to grant to the president "enhanced rescission" authority, the power to "cancel" automatically individual items in spending and tax bills unless overturned by a two-thirds vote of both houses of Congress. President Clinton signed this bill into law on April 9, 1996.[47]

Clinton used this new statutory authority for the first—and only—time in 1997, when he cut items in eleven spending bills, ranging from $15,000 allocated for a police training center in Alabama to $30 million for a military program to intercept asteroids in space. Members of Congress who supported the new authority suddenly were faced with actual cuts in pet projects, and Clinton suffered one of his only two veto overrides when Congress restored funding he had struck out in a military construction spending bill. Officials of both parties in New York, upset over some of Clinton's cuts, supported a lawsuit against the president over the new authority. A six-member majority of the Supreme Court, in *City of New York v. Clinton* (1998), struck down the Line Item Veto Act as unconstitutional, ruling that, as constituted, the line-item veto violated the "presentment clause" in Article I, Section 7 of the Constitution.[48]

Despite the Supreme Court's ruling, President Bush proposed legislation in 2006 that would give the president a modified form of the rescission authority exercised by Clinton. Bush's proposal came in the wake of a growing budget deficit and increased public scrutiny of the practice of legislative "earmarks"—provisions members of Congress insert into legislation in order to fund programs that often benefit their constituents, campaign contributors, or pet projects. Under Bush's proposal, the president could eliminate portions of spending bills, as well as tax cuts targeting fewer than one hundred people, and return the excised items to Congress, which would then have ten days to decide whether to repass them by a simple majority vote in each house. Bush argued that this legislation would pass constitutional muster because it was not, constitutionally speaking, a true veto since Congress did not need a two-thirds vote to override the president's action. But with the Democratic takeover of Congress beginning in January 2007, the prospects for Bush's proposal appeared bleak.

"Quasi-item Vetoes"

Presidents have compensated for the lack of formal line-item veto power through other means. For one thing, they have "impounded"—or *not* spent—money appropriated by Congress for fiscal or administrative reasons. The concept of impoundment has not been controversial when presidents could show that the expenditure was no longer needed—such as when Thomas Jefferson impounded funds earmarked for new naval ships because the hostilities that had prompted the appropriation had halted—or when unforeseen circumstances delayed spending. But when presidents try to use impoundment to thwart the intent of Congress for fiscal or policy reasons, a sharp conflict is guaranteed.

Presidents rarely resorted to impoundment until the 1970s, largely because they sought to avoid major fights with Congress over control of the purse.[49] In 1973–1974, however, Richard Nixon—concerned about the amount of government spending against the backdrop of rising inflation—impounded nearly $12 billion of congressional appropriations, or more than 4 percent of the money appropriated for the coming fiscal year. Nixon's attempt proved so controversial that the Democrat-controlled Congress passed in 1974 (over Nixon's veto) the Budget and Impoundment Control Act. This legislation restricted the president's impoundment authority by dividing impoundments into two categories: rescissions, or permanent cancellations of budget authority that required congressional approval, and temporary deferrals of expenditures, which remained in force unless rejected by Congress. Jurisdiction over both categories was assigned to the Appropriations Committees of the House and Senate.

Since then, presidents have continued to "defer" or "rescind" funds under the auspices of the law, although the actions deemed the most controversial have encountered congressional resistance. In 1986, for example, President Reagan attempted to defer $5 billion for housing and urban development programs because Congress had appropriated more money than he had requested, but a federal appeals court ruled that his actions violated the intent of the 1974 law.[50]

Presidents also on occasion refuse to abide by specific provisions in laws they sign, or they issue their own interpretations of the law when they think Congress has acted unconstitutionally. In 1959, for example, President Eisenhower announced that he would disregard a provision for congressional access to secret documents because it would violate the president's need to protect national security. In 1971 Nixon insisted that he was not bound by a provision requiring the president to state a specific time period for withdrawal from Vietnam.[51] In both cases, the president effectively undermined the force of the provision in question, yet the constitutionality of these actions has not been tested in court.[52] President George Bush likewise objected to provisions in appropriations bills that he nevertheless signed into law. In particular, Bush complained about what he saw as unconstitutional congressional interference in executive branch prerogatives, and he expressed his desire for a line-item veto.[53]

Bush's son, President George W. Bush, however, made the most significant use of these presidential "signing statements" as a means of signaling his dissatisfaction with the details of bills even as he signed them into law. During his first six years in office, Bush used these written statements to assert his authority to ignore portions of more than 750 statutes contained in 125 bills that, in his interpretation, conflict with presidential prerogatives under the Constitution. Many of these dealt with national security issues. On at least four occasions Congress passed laws forbidding U.S. troops who are supporting the Colombian government in its drug interdiction efforts from engaging in military combat against leftist guerrilla groups. Although Bush signed these laws, he also claimed the right as commander in chief to ignore the restrictions on U.S. military involvement in Colombia.

In defending this practice, Bush's advisers argue that his actions are consistent with those of previous presidents, and that he has an obligation not to enforce laws that he believes encroach on presidential authority or that are otherwise unconstitutional. Moreover, they assert that just because he reserves the right to disobey a law does not necessarily mean he will not enforce it. Many signing statements, supporters say, are designed to give direction to those responsible for implementing the measure by clarifying the law's intent. But critics suggest that Bush's strategy is tantamount to selectively vetoing portions of a bill without giving Congress the opportunity to override his objections. They point out that many of these bills pass Congress after Bush agreed to compromise on legislative details, only to see Bush then unilaterally assert the right to ignore those compromises.[54] This helps explain Bush's lack of vetoes, they claim; rather than give Congress the opportunity to override his veto, Bush prefers to sign legislation into law even as he announces his intent to ignore those portions he opposes.

Line-item Veto Debate

Bush's expansive use of signing statements is but one part of a concerted effort by members of his administration to reclaim presidential powers that they believe began slipping away as far back as Nixon's presidency. Critics respond that Bush's effort to aggrandize power in the executive branch raises the specter of a new imperialist presidency. In truth, however, the struggle between the president and Congress to stake out and defend their respective roles in the legislative process is ongoing, its origins dating back to the writing of the Constitution. This is because—whether the issue is pocket vetoes, impoundments, or signing statements—the Constitution is open to different interpretations on these matters. This ambiguity invites "ambition to counteract ambition," as members of both branches assert their institutional prerogatives. The courts may step in to temporarily quell the dispute, but they rarely end it; the institutional clash regarding legislative roles merely erupts at a later date, and often in another form.

Thus it was not surprising that, as the budget surpluses of the late 1990s turned once again into massive deficits as a consequence of spending on the war on terror, increased domestic expenditures, a series of tax cuts that reduced revenue, and an economic recession, President Bush once again called for the authority to exercise a line-item veto. Its proponents continue to suggest that such an instrument will help presidents to limit federal spending, excise "wasteful" congressional appropriations, and promote their budget priorities. Political commentator George Will has called the line-item veto an "effective instrument of allocation" that helps presidents carry out their electoral "mandates" to shape the overall direction of the federal government.[55]

Those opposing the line-item veto argue that it would not materially affect federal spending, because it could not be applied to the massive "entitlement" programs such as Social Security and Medicare that make up the bulk of federal spending and that can be reduced only by changing the laws that mandate these programs.[56] Critics also contend that presidents are no less responsible than Congress for the federal budget deficit, because they can use the regular veto to force legislative compliance if they have the political will to do so, as Clinton proved. Still others point out that any reference to line-item veto provisions in state constitutions ignores fundamental differences between federal and state government responsibilities and authority.[57] Above all, however, the debate over the line-item veto is but one part of the ongoing struggle between the president and Congress over how to share the legislative power in practice.

THE PRESIDENT'S PROGRAM

The president's second express constitutional duty in the legislative process is to "from time to time give to the Congress Information of the State of the Union, and recommend to their Consideration such Measures as he shall judge necessary and expedient" (Article II, Section 3). At first blush, this authority to "recommend . . . Measures" seems rather minor, but over time it has become the primary mechanism used by presidents to shape the nation's political agenda, particularly when the nation is not in crisis. To shape the agenda of government—to decide what is or is not a priority—is to decide what government will or will not do.[58] As the political scientist E. E. Schattschneider concluded: "He who determines what politics is all about runs the country, because the definition of the alternatives is the

Vice President Dick Cheney and House Speaker Nancy Pelosi, D-Calif., look on as President Bush delivers his annual State of the Union address to a joint session of Congress on January 23, 2007.

choice of conflicts, and the choice of conflicts allocates power."[59]

Presidents naturally would love to have complete control over the agenda of government, especially at the very start of their terms in office. But in reality a president's control over the agenda is tenuous. At times it is overwhelmed by unforeseen crises such as natural disasters, war, or sudden shifts in the economy. When a crisis occurs, the existing agenda is thrown aside, and a president's "success" is judged solely by the pace and suitability of the response. In the short run, such crises typically magnify a president's agenda-setting power. Franklin Roosevelt's reaction to the virtual collapse of the banking system on the eve of his inauguration in 1933 often is cited as an example of strong presidential leadership. Within days of taking office, Roosevelt called the Democrat-controlled Congress into special session to pass legislation reorganizing the entire federal banking system. Even more important, he went on national radio to persuade citizens to return their savings to the banks, instilling renewed faith in the financial system and taking the first steps toward economic recovery. This marked the start of the celebrated "First Hundred Days" during which Roosevelt worked with Congress to produce fifteen major bills that collectively reshaped every aspect of the economy, from banking and industry to agriculture and social welfare.[60]

The effect of a crisis on a president's agenda-setting power, however, is typically short-lived. George W. Bush's presidency was fundamentally transformed by the need to respond to the terrorist attacks of September 11, 2001. Prior to the attacks, Bush experienced some legislative success on tax cuts and education reform. But on other issues, including his energy plan and grants of federal aid to religious charities, his legislative initiatives seemed stalled. After the attacks, however, Bush refocused his legislative priorities on war-related issues both at home and abroad. His efforts to do so, at least initially, found strong support within Congress and among the public. But when in 2003 Bush sought to expand the definition of the war on terror to include invading Iraq, support for his antiterror foreign policy agenda—which was already weakening—began to ebb. As violence continued unabated in Iraq, Democrats capitalized on the growing opposition to U.S. involvement to regain control of Congress in the 2006 midterm elections.

Crises aside, the presidency has always had a singularly unique *institutional* capacity to shape the nation's agenda of debate and action. As the only political office (along with the vice presidency) with a national constituency, the presidency serves as a public focal point, uniquely suited to address issues of national priority. But this unique vantage point assumed greater importance in the second half of the twentieth century, due to the growth in the scope and influence of the federal government, the emergence of the United States as a superpower—which amplifies the president's role as commander in chief—and the emergence of modern telecommunications.

Today the president, political scientist Bruce Miroff suggests, commands the most area within the "public space" of U.S. politics, largely forcing other participants in the political process to respond to issues as the president defines them.[61] That reality powerfully influences success or failure on policy initiatives, particularly in issue areas in which Americans have no direct experience. For example, most Americans, including members of Congress, had little means for independently evaluating the Bush administration claims that Saddam Hussein's Iraqi government possessed weapons of mass destruction, or that it was actively involved in supporting terrorist actions against the United States. This made it difficult to oppose Bush's decision to invade Iraq in 2003.

Yet the president's institutional capacity to define the national agenda is a largely modern phenomenon; it proved less potent throughout most of the nineteenth century. The federal government was small, and responsible for few national issues, including territorial expansion, tariffs, and foreign policy. Congress, often led by leaders of national reputation, dominated policy debate. Presidents, on the other hand, were not expected to formulate legislative agendas, prepare and present executive budgets, or do much else except oversee the rather modest executive branch, conduct foreign policy (such as it was when the United States was relatively isolated), and keep a check on Congress whenever necessary and possible. Nor did the dominant public view of government hold that presidents should actively initiate or influence public policy, something that would be difficult in any case without technologies of mass communication. Not until Franklin Roosevelt did the presidency become a strong institution, one that remained potent regardless of the person sitting in the Oval Office.

Congress and the Presidency: Separate Branches

Any discussion of the president's influence over legislation must first recognize the essential differences between the branches. Above all, the Constitution grants to Congress the preponderance of power over national policy. Only Congress has the power to make the law, generate revenues, and appropriate funds. The Constitution also establishes governing roles and creates policy-making dynamics that set Congress fundamentally far apart from the presidency. These structural factors have remained remarkably constant throughout history and are important to understanding why presidents succeed or fail in achieving their legislative goals.[62]

Presidents and members of Congress reach office through entirely separate and distinct paths. The national electorate inevitably gives the president a broader perspective on issues. Members of Congress, by contrast, come to national government out of localized constituencies, whether House districts or states, which by itself ensures that for members of Congress "all politics is local," as Speaker of the House Thomas P. "Tip" O'Neill was fond of saying.[63] Members of Congress can and do think broadly about policy questions, but their constitutionally assigned roles as representatives of a specific set of citizens require that they tend to their constituents' needs first.

Presidents and members of Congress also serve for different terms of office. A president serves for four years, but members of the House must run for election every two years, which, as the Framers intended, maintains their sensitivity to the momentary needs and opinions of the people. House members' tendency to focus more on short-term concerns can cause problems for a president's agenda. And, because all House members (and one-third of all senators, who serve six-year terms) are up for reelection in the second year of the president's term, midterm elections frequently are construed as public judgments on presidential performance. The president's party almost invariably loses House and Senate seats in midterm elections, and members of Congress from the president's party are keenly aware that public disenchantment with their leader may cause them serious electoral problems. *(See table, "Party Affiliations in Congress and the Presidency, 1789–2006," p. 1869, in Reference Materials, Vol. II.)* The opposition party, for its part, naturally tries to use these contests to its advantage.

The 2006 midterm election is a case in point; it saw the Democrats pick up 6 Senate and 31 House seats to sweep up control of Congress for the first time since 1994. Pundits proclaimed it an especially stinging defeat for the president's party. Judged by the number of Republican seats lost, however, the outcome was not atypical for a midterm election. Since the end of World War II, the average loss for the party of a second-term presidency in its sixth year has been 29 House seats and 6 Senate seats, almost exactly what took place in 2006. However, the 2006 results took on greater significance in light of more recent midterm elections, especially 1998 and 2002, which exhibited much smaller shifts in party seats, and because they led to the loss of Republican control in Congress. Exit polls suggested that much of the blame for the Republicans' setback could be traced to voter discontent with the Bush administration's handling of the Iraq war, as well as their dissatisfaction with the ethics of the Republican-controlled Congress.

Similarly, the 1994 midterm election results are viewed as a rebuke to President Clinton. His party lost 54 House and 8 Senate seats, and the opposition Republicans gained control of both chambers of Congress for the first time since 1952. From 1993 to 1994, President Clinton had been able to count on Democratic control of the House and Senate to help him pass much of his legislative program, but Republican control of Congress in 1995 altered the political equation for both Congress and the president by temporarily shifting control over the legislative agenda from the White House to the new and assertive congressional majority.

As time went on, however, House Republicans encountered the reality that an institution made up of 435 semiautonomous individuals is hard-pressed to maintain control over the agenda in the face of the presidency's institutional capacity to dominate the nation's attention. Clinton, as noted earlier, used his institutional powers and his overall political skills to great effect in forcing House Republicans onto the defensive throughout the rest of his presidency, even during the period surrounding his impeachment and trial. Indeed, that Republicans actually *lost* House seats in the 1998 midterm elections, a nearly unprecedented occurrence for the party not in the White House, attested to the degree to which they no longer controlled the terms of debate.

The problem posed for presidents by the Senate is a bit different. Members of the Senate serve for six years, with only one-third of the body up for reelection every two years. Thus most senators are not affected directly by a presidential election, and they have much greater freedom to oppose presidential initiatives without as much concern about short-term constituent pressures. The Senate also retains constitutional leverage over the executive through its power to approve presidential nominees to the federal judiciary and to high-level executive branch positions, and through its power to approve or reject treaties with other nations. Moreover, the supermajority decision-making procedures in the Senate are designed to protect the minority party to a far greater degree than in the House, which is typically dominated by the majority party.

These characteristics of the Senate guarantee problems for presidents, even with senators of the same party. Jimmy Carter failed to obtain Senate approval for the 1978 Strategic Arms Limitation Treaty despite Democratic dominance of the chamber, and Ronald Reagan faced the greatest opposition on the 1987 Intermediate Nuclear Forces Treaty from conservative Republicans. In June 2001, the decision by Sen. James Jeffords of Vermont to become an independent cost Republicans control of the then evenly divided Senate and forced the George W. Bush administration to alter its legislative strategy accordingly. Even after Republicans regained control of the Senate in 2002, Bush was forced to moderate many of his policies, such as reducing the size of his second round of tax cuts, in order to ensure Senate support.

The two branches also have distinct decision-making cultures and processes that emerge from their fundamentally different governing responsibilities. The president, whose primary constitutional responsibilities are to implement the laws and act as commander in chief of the armed forces, is ultimately responsible for all policies enacted in his name. It goes too far to say that the executive branch speaks with one voice; even within the president's White House staff, aides are quite adept at courting Congress and enlisting the media as allies in their effort to persuade the president to adopt their policy preferences. Officials working in the outlying departments and agencies, moreover, are at least as responsive to congressional preferences as they are to the president's. Nonetheless, final policy decisions emanating from the executive branch do usually reflect the president's overall ideology and political agenda. Loyalty to the president's program is a paramount virtue among all executive branch appointees, particularly those working closely with the president; those who openly dissent find access to the president severely limited, if not cut off completely.[64]

Congress, by contrast, speaks with many voices simultaneously, one for each of the 535 members of the House and Senate—not to mention the territorial delegates, staff members, and professionals in the congressional agencies. Congress as an institution rarely (if ever) projects a coherent sense of direction. Members both represent their constituents and make national policy—that is, they play often conflicting roles, because what is good for any member's constituents (such as new services or public facilities) may bode ill for the nation as a whole (in the form of budget deficits, for example). Each member wields one vote, regardless of seniority or party position, and no member can be expelled from the legislature simply because of voting behavior or personal opinion. Only constituents have the right to "fire" their representatives.

This constitutionally generated egalitarianism forces Congress as an institution to adhere to relatively nonhierarchical decision-making processes. To do otherwise would appear antidemocratic. Decisions, whether in the form of new pieces of legislation or agreements on appropriations bills, among other things, are achieved only by building coalitions of members large enough to win a succession of committee and floor votes. Successful legislating depends on knitting together enough diverse interests and demands to overcome opposition, even among members of the same party, using whatever tactics seem reasonable or necessary. This is especially true in the even less hierarchical Senate, where traditional voting rules allow a single member to obstruct the majority—or the president—until agreement surfaces.

This clash of cultures powerfully shapes the way in which the branches interact. Presidents always want to move quickly to make the most of their limited opportunities through comprehensive and often dramatic policy initiatives. This is true particularly in the first year, as every president knows that the personal popularity so critical to overcoming the normal inertia of the political system inevitably fades. But, assuming the absence of acknowledged crisis, Congress generally prefers a more cautious weighing of the consequences. Each member's constituency must be treated fairly, and coalitions of support must be constructed. Such considerations usually are more important to Congress, particularly to the Senate, than speed or ideological purity. Many a president has chastised Congress for its glacial pace of deliberation, but the legislature by design marches to its own drummer.

These fundamental differences invariably produce clashes between presidents, who must act on behalf of a national constituency, and members of Congress, who promote their more local constituents' needs. Presidents routinely accuse Congress of waste or inertia, but they also find that cumulative local and state interests often overcome any supposed national good. For example, in 1987 Reagan vetoed a popular reauthorization of the Clean Water Act because he felt that its $20 billion appropriation for water and sewage treatment projects was wasteful, but Congress overrode his veto by overwhelming bipartisan margins. Clinton's effort to push a comprehensive overhaul of the nation's health care system ultimately fell prey in part to the tug of special interests, with members of his party unable— and often unwilling—to push the president's plan through determined Republican opposition. George W. Bush's effort to rein in Social Security costs, in part by allowing taxpayers to reduce their Social Security contributions and instead invest that money in individual investment accounts, met with considerable skepticism, even from members of his own party, who feared a political backlash from voters opposed to tinkering with such a sacrosanct program.[65]

Compare these dynamics with those of a parliamentary system, where the prime minister is selected by the majority party (or party coalition) in the legislature. There is no separation of institutions in the American sense, and strong party cohesion is essential to maintaining control over government. In 1997, for example, Labour Party leader Tony Blair gained his position as British prime minister after his party won control of the British House of Commons. A solid party majority allowed him to push through major legislation far more easily and quickly than any American president could imagine—at least so long as he maintained his party's majority. In the United States, by contrast, members of Congress can openly go against their party and president when constituent interests are on the line. What the Constitution splits apart, party loyalty cannot easily bind together.[66]

The relationship between the president and Congress is shaped powerfully by the Constitution. The Framers were far more concerned with checking the potential abuses of power than with speedy or easy legislating. They wanted Congress and the president to compete for power and to protect their own institutional prerogatives, and they endowed Congress with the capacity to withstand executive pressure and to dictate policy if it so willed. Even when dom-

inated by the president's party, Congress as an institution insists on playing its independent constitutional role according to its own needs and internal dynamics. No president can forget those realities.

Historical Development

"Whether legislator, opinion-maker, commander, or administrator," noted presidential scholar Clinton Rossiter, "the President molds lasting policy in every sector of American life." [67] Presidents recognize as much; early in his presidential term George W. Bush promised to propose "creative ways to tackle some of the toughest problems in our society." [68] Indeed, as political scientist Bertram Gross wrote in 1953: "Except in wartime, Presidents are now judged more by the quality of the legislation they propose or succeed in getting enacted than by their records as executive." [69] Today the presidency appears to be almost another house of Congress, with presidents involved deeply in all aspects of the legislative process and judged by how well they mobilize support for their programs.

The contrast between these contemporary analyses and the experiences of early presidents is noteworthy. Rather than expecting the president to formulate a legislative program and lobby for its enactment, Congress through the 1800s usually resisted presidential involvement in lawmaking as an unwarranted intrusion.[70] Textbook notions that Congress alone makes law, which the president then simply administers, were taken seriously, and presidents who forgot this constitutional nicety were quickly reminded of it by members of Congress always on guard against such presumptuousness.

Whether the Framers meant the president to play so passive a role is hotly debated. Certainly they viewed the presidency chiefly as a bulwark against congressional mischief or tyranny. Yet Alexander Hamilton argued in *Federalist* No. 70 that "energy in the executive is a leading character of good government." [71] *(See "Federalist No. 70," p. 1753, in Reference Materials, Vol. II.)* The Framers rejected the more monarchical schemes for the executive proposed early on by Hamilton and others, but they also rejected making the president entirely subordinate to or separate from Congress. The legislature makes the law, but the Framers did give the president a limited number of instruments for influencing legislation. How effectively the president could bring those resources to bear, however, would be another question.

Early Presidents

George Washington discovered rather quickly how difficult it would be for a president to influence legislation when he became the first—and the last—president ever to sit with Congress during actual floor debate. Washington believed that oral communications were essential to fruitful relations between the branches, so on August 22, 1789, he personally presented to the Senate the particulars of an Indian treaty—the very first to be considered under the procedures prescribed by the Constitution—and requested the Senate's immediate advice and consent. But, to his surprise, the Senate did not automatically approve the treaty. Its main points were read aloud—twice, because some senators could not hear for the noise coming in off the street—after which time an awkward silence descended on the chamber. Sen. William Maclay of Pennsylvania then called for a reading of the treaty itself, and of its accompanying papers, and supported a move to refer the entire matter to a committee for further study. Maclay, as he later wrote in his journal, "saw no chance of fair investigation of subjects if the President of the United States sat there, with his Secretary of War, to support his opinions and over-awe the timid and neutral part of the Senate." Washington, wrote Maclay, "started up in a violent fret" at the proposal to refer the matter to committee, exclaiming, "This defeats every purpose of my coming here." The president eventually calmed down and agreed to a two-day delay, but on his return he found many senators still uneasy about his presence. After completing the business at hand, Washington vowed that he would not repeat the experience.[72]

Washington nonetheless actively sought more indirect influence over legislation. He used cabinet members to lobby members of Congress, a task taken up with particular enthusiasm by Secretary of the Treasury Hamilton, whose ardent belief in an energetic presidency and tireless use of his department to initiate and lobby for legislation soon sparked a backlash—and not just in Congress. In a letter to the president, Secretary of State Thomas Jefferson, despite his overall support for Washington, objected strenuously that Hamilton's "system flowed from principles adverse to liberty, and was calculated to undermine and demolish the republic, by creating an influence of his department over the members of the legislature."[73]

Jefferson, whose Democratic-Republican Party in principle glorified the concept of congressional supremacy, also eschewed personal lobbying when he became president. He went so far as to suspend the fledgling tradition of personally delivering an annual State of the Union message. *(See box, "The State of the Union Address as Political Theater," p. 672.)* But Jefferson was no passive chief executive. He carefully maintained the forms of separated branches and congressional supremacy but relied heavily on cabinet members and the strong congressional caucus of his party, which held the majority in Congress, to initiate and dominate legislative activity. Secretary of the Treasury Albert Gallatin acted as his primary liaison to the party caucus, but Jefferson personally picked the party's floor leaders, who then became known as the president's chief congressional representatives. The strength of the party caucus, held together in many ways by Jefferson's own political skills (and his widely acclaimed dinner parties), produced a style of governing that in many ways paralleled parliamentary systems.

After Jefferson, however, "King Caucus" gave way to congressional supremacy. Jefferson's model of party government decayed as regional and ideological splits within the Democratic-Republican Party eroded its usefulness as a mechanism for executive leverage. Power flowed back to Congress as an institution, and strong congressional leaders such as Henry Clay and John C. Calhoun actively set the agenda of government through the 1820s. House Speaker Clay in particular dominated tariff and public works matters and with his allies even forced a reluctant James Madison to confront the British in the War of 1812. Congress also began to develop its own institutional expertise in policy making, in particular through the standing committees, which during the mid-1800s evolved into power centers in their own right as presidents came and went.

In the 1830s, Andrew Jackson momentarily reinvigorated the role of the (now) Democratic Party and its national convention as a means of setting the national agenda. More notably, the breadth and strength of his party organization allowed Jackson to become the first president to appeal directly to the public over the heads of Congress on issues such as the National Bank and the tariff.[74] However, Jackson's overall legislative strategy was largely reactive, and he relied heavily on his veto power to check hostile congressional initiatives. The idea that the president should actively propose and shepherd legislation through Congress was still controversial, and the increasing power of the congressional standing committees limited Jackson's capacity to dominate Congress through the party.[75]

Aside from these few relatively active presidents, and not including Lincoln's emergency actions during the Civil War, nineteenth-century legislating generally was a congressional affair. The president's constitutional responsibilities over foreign policy and the armed forces did not matter much, since the United States during most of this century kept resolutely out of international politics and maintained a minimal peacetime defense and foreign policy apparatus. On the domestic side, the federal government concerned itself largely with matters like post offices, setting tariff rates, and other public works projects. Except in times of crisis, then, the national government did relatively little through the 1800s, and the presidency played a secondary role in policy formation. Congress never shied away from reminding presidents of their "proper" role, and even Abraham Lincoln, toward the end of the Civil War, was admonished by House leaders that the president "must confine himself to executive duties—to obey and execute, not make the laws."[76]

Shift Toward Presidential Leadership

The legislative role of the presidency began to change toward the end of the nineteenth century as powerful economic, technological, and social forces reshaped the American landscape, and as the United States began to play a greater role in the world. The industrial revolution brought about a transition from a self-sufficient farm economy to an urban manufacturing economy, from largely localized business concerns to huge national corporations, and, as a result, a shift from a minimalist view of federal government action to calls for it to do more. Issues such as interstate commerce, corporate monopoly, child labor, food and drug purity, monetary policy, agricultural research, and rail transportation became more national in scope and often overlapped with the international trade and diplomacy issues that were growing in importance as the United States became more active in the world.

These trends altered prevailing views about the role of the national government and, by extension, of the presidency. Calls for more active executive leadership on legislation began to be heard as Congress found itself institutionally ill-equipped to handle broad national questions. The legislature by nature is better able to deal with issues that can be broken down by congressional districts or state lines, such as allocation of funds for post offices, than with issues having no clear constituency boundaries. Moreover, popular perceptions that Congress was not attentive to emerging national and international problems legitimized the notion of an energetic president. As the nation entered the new era, the constitutional forms of the two branches in most respects stayed the same, but their dynamics were to change subtly.

Theodore Roosevelt, who once said the president "can be as big a man as he can," signaled the development of the legislatively active "modern" president.[77] Keenly aware that he possessed the only purely national voice, Roosevelt saw the presidency as a "bully pulpit" for shaping public opinion and pushing legislation through Congress. "In theory the Executive has nothing to do with legislation," Roosevelt wrote in his *Autobiography*.

> In practice, as things are now, the Executive is or ought to be peculiarly representative as a whole. As often as not the action of the Executive offers the only means by which the people can get the legislation they demand and ought to have. Therefore a good executive under the present conditions of American political life must take a very active interest in getting the right kind of legislation, in addition to performing his executive duties with an eye single to the public welfare.[78]

Roosevelt practiced what he preached. The Pure Food and Drug Act of 1906, a landmark consumer law that established the Food and Drug Administration, was pushed

President Theodore Roosevelt was an energetic legislative leader, but his cousin Franklin D. Roosevelt went still further. FDR redefined the role of the national government through his New Deal legislation and vastly expanded the size of the executive branch.

through a Congress dominated by agriculture and business interests largely on the strength of the president's advocacy, aided by widespread newspaper coverage. Roosevelt also established the national park system, attacked monopolies, and negotiated the end to a war between Japan and Russia, for which he was awarded the Nobel Peace Prize. Even more instructive was Roosevelt's decision to send an American naval squadron on a global tour in a show of strength intended mainly to impress other naval powers. A Congress suffused with isolationism refused to appropriate money simply to "show the flag," but Roosevelt scraped together funds from other navy accounts to send the fleet, with a few newspaper reporters conveniently aboard, halfway around the world. He then challenged Congress to provide enough money to bring the ships home. Public opinion so strongly supported Roosevelt that Congress did as requested.

Theodore Roosevelt was unique in many ways—boundless in energy, aggressively intellectual, eager for public acclaim—but his legacy did not disappear. The nation and Congress had been given a taste of energetic presidential leadership, and succeeding chief executives found both the public and Congress more receptive to their initiatives.

William Howard Taft, Roosevelt's immediate successor, advocated a far less grandiose view of the office. Nonetheless, as political scientist James Sundquist points out, Taft went against the tradition of official presidential noninterference in the legislative process by being the first president since Washington to formally present draft legislation to

Congress.[79] In 1913 Woodrow Wilson became the first president since John Adams to deliver his State of the Union message personally to a joint session of Congress. He thereafter used the address as a statement of his legislative agenda and to put into practice his belief that the president should lead government more actively.[80] Wilson also asserted his right to guide legislation and in a special address to Congress argued, "I have come to you as the head of the government and the responsible leader of the party in power to urge action now, while there is time to serve the country deliberately, and as we should, in a clear air of common counsel."[81] The legislation that Wilson wanted Congress to pass, the Federal Reserve Act of 1913, was drafted largely in conferences at the White House, with Wilson personally in charge.

The Franklin Roosevelt Model

Despite these gradual changes in the presidency during the first third of the twentieth century, the office of the presidency remained, legislatively speaking, a largely reactive force against a dominant Congress, not the source of initiative and leadership that Americans expect today. Although Theodore Roosevelt and Woodrow Wilson in selected instances had taken the lead with legislation, particularly when conditions for presidential initiative were most favorable, the office had only rudimentary institutional mechanisms for sustained legislative influence.

In the 1930s, however, the presidency underwent a major expansion and took on new responsibilities, entering what scholars call its modern era. The architect of these changes was Franklin Roosevelt, who stepped into the presidency in 1933 during the Great Depression that saw one quarter of the workforce unemployed, public faith in government diminished, and the nation's economic and social fabric threatening to unravel. Roosevelt's predecessor, Herbert C. Hoover (1929–1933), had relied largely on the market system to resolve the crisis, but the voters, who thought Hoover's confidence was misplaced, had blamed him for the country's hardships and subjected him to a humiliating defeat in the 1932 presidential election. The emergency worsened dramatically in early 1933, just prior to Roosevelt's inauguration, giving Roosevelt an unparalleled peacetime opportunity to lead the country. Congress, unable to resolve the crisis on its own, awaited strong direction.

Roosevelt's immediate attack on the depression was the beginning of a sweeping and sustained rearrangement of national domestic policies, a legacy that dominated national politics through the mid-1960s, and whose aftereffects endure to some degree to this day. The famous and archetypal "First Hundred Days" of Roosevelt's first term saw Congress, convened in special session, gave the new president a blank check to remold the federal government, introduce new programs, and do almost anything necessary to turn the economy around. Roosevelt and his battalions of energetic "New Dealers" took on the task with joyful gusto, pushing major legislation through a willing Congress with unprecedented speed. *(See box, The First Hundred Days of Franklin D. Roosevelt, 667.)* As presidential scholar Clinton Rossiter said of Roosevelt, "In the first Hundred Days he gave Congress a kind of leadership it had not known before and still does not care to have repeated."[82]

Central to Roosevelt's strategy in 1933 was strengthening the direct link between the presidency and the American people, in large part by capitalizing on his ability to commu-

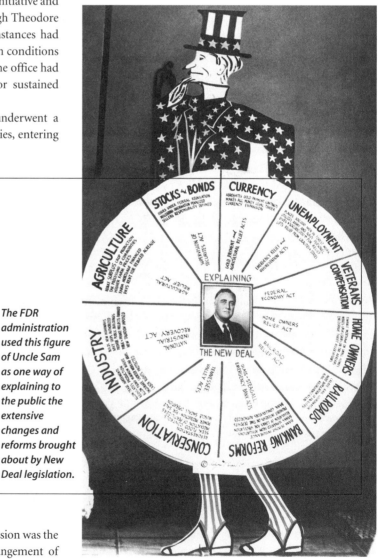

The FDR administration used this figure of Uncle Sam as one way of explaining to the public the extensive changes and reforms brought about by New Deal legislation.

nicate directly to citizens via radio. "This nation asks for action, and action now," he said simply in his first inaugural address, which sparked nearly half a million letters of support. "We must act, and act quickly." [83] (See "Franklin D. Roosevelt's First Inaugural Address," p. 1769, in Reference Materials, Vol. II.) Roosevelt's speeches, radio "fireside chats," and twice-weekly meetings with reporters all spoke directly to the American people and indirectly to Congress about his dreams and priorities. In the process, Roosevelt focused sustained public attention on the presidency.

Roosevelt's actions during the New Deal era and World War II combined to redefine the role of national government and the presidency as an institution. By the time FDR died in office in 1945, the executive branch had exploded in size and in the scope of its responsibilities, and the presidency itself had gained a wider array of resources for influencing legislation, making budgets, and implementing programs. The presidency no longer was a single person but an institution, one growing in size and potency as Congress gave the president more staff and more resources to manage the federal bureaucracy, initiate public policy, and lead the nation's defense. Congress delegated these responsibilities to the presidency because legislators realized that the president was better situated to lead during times of perceived crisis and, more important, because Americans demanded an energetic presidency.

When Harry Truman took up Roosevelt's mantle in April 1945, he sat at the center of an office much transformed during the course of FDR's twelve years in office. By capitalizing on developments in mass-communications technology Roosevelt had greatly expanded the president's traditional role as a symbol of national sovereignty, one that would be further magnified during the next several decades with the growth of television. At the same time, the burgeoning number and complexity of government programs and agencies elevated the president's role as policy coordinator and agenda-setter, while also greatly complicating the president's responsibility as chief executive officer charged with managing the federal bureaucracy. Perhaps most important for his legislative role, the United States' movement from isolationism to front and center on the world stage gave new significance to the president's commander in chief and head diplomat responsibilities. Collectively, these developments heightened expectations for presidential leadership. The

THE FIRST HUNDRED DAYS OF FRANKLIN D. ROOSEVELT

Franklin D. Roosevelt, sworn into office on March 4, 1933, convened the Seventy-third Congress into special session on March 9 to consider the Emergency Banking Act, which it passed after eight hours of debate. Roosevelt at first considered sending Congress back home after passage of the act, but the window of opportunity for even more action presented by the crisis seemed too valuable to waste. As historian Arthur M. Schlesinger Jr. later wrote, "In the three months after Roosevelt's inauguration, Congress and the country were subjected to a presidential barrage of ideas and programs unlike anything known to American history." [1]

Below are the major accomplishments of the now legendary "First Hundred Days":

March 9	Emergency Banking Act: reformed the national banking system
March 20	Economy Act: authorized cuts in federal spending
March 22	Beer and Wine Revenue Act: legalized sale of beer and wine
March 31	Civilian Conservation Corps: created employment for youths in a wide range of conservation efforts
April 19	Abandonment of gold standard: detached value of currency from gold
May 12	Federal Emergency Relief Act: created a national relief system
May 12	Agricultural Adjustment Act: established a national agricultural policy
May 12	Emergency Farm Mortgage Act: refinanced farm mortgages
May 18	Tennessee Valley Authority Act: provided for the unified development of the Tennessee Valley
May 27	Truth in Securities Act: required full disclosure of a firm's financial shape when it issued new securities
June 13	Home Owners' Loan Act: refinanced home mortgages
June 16	National Industrial Recovery Act: created a system of federally supervised industrial self-regulation and a $3.3 billion public works program
June 16	Glass-Steagall Banking Act: separated commercial and investment banking; guaranteed bank deposits
June 16	Farm Credit Act: reorganized federal farm credit programs
June 16	Emergency Railroad Transportation Act: created greater coordination in national railroad system

1. Arthur M. Schlesinger Jr., The Age of Roosevelt: The Coming of the New Deal (Boston: Houghton Mifflin, 1959), 20.

president, Wilson had once boasted, possessed the freedom "to be as big a man as he can." After FDR, however, it was no longer possible to be as small as one might like.[84]

The Roosevelt Legacy

In important respects, Roosevelt's successors have stood in his historical shadow. The office has grown in power and prestige, but perhaps not proportionately with expectations about what presidents must deliver. This is in large part because the relative distribution of power between Congress and the presidency has not fundamentally shifted, despite the acquisition of new presidential responsibilities. Since the emergence of the United States as a world power after World War II, presidents have had to more fully exercise their roles as commander in chief and chief diplomat, but the foreign responsibilities frequently clash with public demands that domestic matters be given top priority. Moreover, the world is smaller—television and the Internet have brought the world more intimately into every home—

and the pace of events has quickened demonstrably. But coalitions of support also seem more fleeting, governing seems all the more difficult, and public expectations about government are greater, creating for the presidency a burden of leadership that may prove too much to bear.[85] And developments that have augmented presidential power, including new communications technology, larger staffs, and heightened visibility, have also benefited Congress.

This is not to argue that presidents have no control over their own destinies, but the extent of their control seems at times to depend less on personal intellect or social skills than on the social, economic, and political contexts within which they govern. Their control also depends on the willingness of other governing institutions, particularly Congress, to cooperate, which is by no means guaranteed. Lyndon Johnson, for example, was a master of the legislative process, having had a long career in Congress as House member, senator, and Senate majority leader. Even so, Johnson's achievement in enacting the Great Society—the most sweeping social agenda since Roosevelt's Hundred Days—depended at least as much on the trauma of John Kennedy's assassination, a national mood supporting broad social change, and an unusually cooperative congressional majority after his landslide 1964 election victory. Johnson's successes in 1965, when Congress approved some 69 percent of his legislative requests, were tempered by the knowledge that times would soon change.[86] "I have watched the Congress from either the inside or the outside, man and boy, for more than 40 years," Johnson commented early in 1965, "and I've never seen a Congress that didn't eventually take the measure of the president it was dealing with." [87]

Jimmy Carter discovered that harsh reality very early in his administration when a Congress dominated by his party proved skeptical of his comprehensive energy plan. Carter's problems in 1977 and later stemmed not only from his lack of experience in and distaste for Washington politics, but also from the changes in Congress, and in American politics generally, during the preceding decade. Congress had become more open, more fragmented, and more independent, thereby forcing presidents to devise new ways of influencing the legislature. Johnson was able to push through his Great Society programs largely because of his ability to rally a few key committee chairs and other congressional leaders, but Carter found it necessary to lobby virtually every member, a more difficult and frustrating task.

Even Reagan, whose rhetorical skills helped him to translate his 1980 election victory into early legislative success, found his later efforts frustrated by his inability to induce Congress to follow his lead. By the end of his presidency, moreover, the constituencies of the two major parties in Congress had been substantially altered due to the transformation of the once Democratic South into an increasingly Republican voting bloc. This trend led to a growing ideo-logical rift between the two parties, due to a decrease in the number of southern conservative Democrats and northeastern moderate Republicans who once formed the basis of cross-party coalitions. Within the more polarized Congress, an increasing number of votes broke along nearly straight party lines, and partisan affiliation became an increasingly important predictor of roll call voting by legislators.[88] The development of more ideologically cohesive parties in Congress did not necessarily help presidents' legislative prospects, particularly during periods of divided government, as George Bush and Clinton discovered. But even under unified government, as experienced by George W. Bush, a president's legislative agenda was often stymied, particularly in the Senate, due to opposition from a cohesive minority party.

The question of context thus is essential to analyzing a president's ability to set the agenda of government and to persuade Congress to enact those priorities. According to presidential scholar Louis Koenig, Congress most consistently follows presidential leadership in three situations.[89] The first is during perceived crises, when Congress and the nation invariably turn to the president for leadership. Roosevelt and the First Hundred Days is the most-cited example, for it is almost impossible to conceive that the New Deal could have been passed under "normal" political conditions. Likewise, it is hard to imagine that the substantial new "antiterrorism" powers that Congress granted to federal authorities shortly after the September 11, 2001, attacks on the Pentagon and New York City's World Trade Center would ever have been approved in the absence of such a crisis.[90]

Second, in matters of national security and foreign affairs, an area in which the Constitution gives the presidency primacy, Congress is generally more amenable to presidential initiatives. This was particularly true between World War II and the end of the Vietnam War, when a general view that partisan "politics ended at the water's edge" gave postwar presidents an unparalleled range of flexibility. Even with the end of the cold war, and as liberals and conservatives disagreed strongly over the U.S. role in the world, Congress continued to give presidents the benefit of the doubt on issues of national defense. For example, in 1990 President George Bush committed U.S. troops to the Persian Gulf soon after Iraqi forces invaded neighboring Kuwait, and he declared that he was prepared to proceed militarily against Iraq even in the absence of congressional support. Shortly thereafter, Congress, after some debate, passed a joint resolution in support of ousting Iraq from Kuwait. Legislators leery about the use of U.S. combat soldiers in the Gulf wanted to avoid being seen as not supporting troops who were already in harm's way.[91]

The tendency for Congress to accede to presidential demands in national security and foreign policy issues had led more than one president to cloak purely domestic programs in the mantle of national security to obtain easier passage. During the cold war, successive presidents defined the interstate highway system, federal education programs, and the space program as essential to national security or pride—highways for easier movement of defense forces, greater education spending to "catch up" to the Soviets after the launch of *Sputnik,* and the Mercury, Gemini, and Apollo programs to win the "space race." These programs thus gained far greater national support than they might have otherwise.

Third, presidents reap benefits from "abnormal" contexts—the combined effects of skilled political leaders, superior partisan dominance in Congress, changing societal values, and, especially, historical timing. Virtually every new president enjoys a postelection "honeymoon" with Congress, a period during which the new occupant of the White House can push priorities within an atmosphere of general cooperation. Presidents usually have their greatest legislative successes during their first six months in office. But as Stephen Skowronek points out, some presidents take office when the existing political "regime" is ripe for reconstruction due to prevailing dissatisfaction with existing policies and political commitments. Historically, these windows of opportunity to change policy direction come on the heels of realigning elections characterized by deep and enduring shifts in voters' partisan allegiances. It is these moments in "political time," Skowronek suggests, that help explain the legislative effectiveness of the nation's greatest presidents, including Jefferson, Jackson, Lincoln, FDR, and Reagan. Conversely, presidents unfortunate enough to take office when their party regime is weakening are dealt a much poorer hand. Such was the case with Pierce, Hoover, and Carter, among others.[92]

Within these broader historical sweeps, a president's legislative success will vary, depending on the general political context and particular events, the strength of congressional majorities, and, of course, the president's personal abilities. However, the ability of any president to dominate the agenda of government, to plan and propose new initiatives, and to lobby successfully for these initiatives depends on more than personal skills or intellect. The character of the U.S. political system, the nature of the times, and the types of issues under debate all affect the extent to which any president can influence the national agenda and the legislative process. Regardless of the powers and prestige of the office, presidents are not entirely in control of their own destinies.

The State of the Union Address

Today, the annual State of the Union address plays an essential and potent role in presidents' efforts to influence the national agenda; they use the address to review their accomplishments and outline their goals. Yet the constitutional requirement that presidents give Congress information on the state of the Union has not always played so central a role in presidential strategies. Although both George Washington and John Adams appeared personally before Congress to deliver their annual messages, Jefferson submitted his report in writing in 1801, because he felt a personal appearance aped the practice whereby the king personally opened each new session of the British Parliament. By eliminating a quasi-monarchical rite, notes Arthur M. Schlesinger Jr., Jefferson hoped to instill stronger values of republicanism (that is, representative government) in the young American system.[93]

Jefferson's precedent lasted more than a century. Not until Woodrow Wilson in 1913 did a president appear again before Congress to deliver the address. Wilson revived the earlier tradition set by Washington because he believed that presidents should make personal appeals to the nation and to Congress. Wilson expressed his view in his first personal appearance before Congress for a special message on finance:

> I am very glad indeed to have the opportunity to address the two houses directly, and to verify for myself the impression that the president of the United States is a person, not a mere department of the government hailing Congress from some isolated island of jealous power, sending messages, and not speaking naturally and with his own voice, that he is a human being trying to cooperate with other human beings in a common service. After this experience I shall feel quite normal in all our dealings with one another.[94]

Wilson also changed the content of the annual message. Before his time the State of the Union message usually was a laborious recitation of department and agency activities; it seldom contained substantive legislative proposals. This orientation reflected the view that Congress made law, and suggestions made by presidents were to be given no greater weight than those offered by average citizens. The single nineteenth-century exception to this informal but ironclad rule only underscored prevailing views. Grover Cleveland deviated from tradition and devoted his entire 1887 message to ideas about tariff reform, but his temerity at openly suggesting ideas to Congress sparked a tremendous debate in the press, divided his Democratic Party, and apparently contributed to his defeat in 1888.[95]

Since Wilson, the State of the Union address has become the major vehicle for expounding the president's legislative agenda and priorities, a tendency magnified by the onset of television. Today the president's annual appearance before a joint session of Congress is a major national event. Indeed, it is the kind of quasi-monarchical rite that Jefferson would have abhorred. It is a moment of high ceremony, a pageant duly attended by the members of Congress, the cabinet, the joint chiefs of staff of the armed forces, justices of the Supreme Court, foreign dignitaries, and invited guests.

TABLE 12-3   **Presidential Appearances before Congress, 1789–2006**

President	Number of appearances	Occasions
Washington	10	8 annual messages (1789–1796); 2 inaugural addresses (1789, 1793—second inaugural before Senate only)
J. Adams	6	4 annual messages (1797–1800); inaugural address (1797); relations with France (1797)
Wilson	26	6 annual messages (1913–1918); tariff reform, bank reform, relations with Mexico (1913); antitrust laws; Panama Canal tolls; relations with Mexico; new tax revenue (1914); impending rail strike (1916); "Peace without Victory" (Senate only); breaking relations with Germany; arming of merchant ships; request for war declaration against Germany (1917); federal takeover of railroads; "14 points" for peace; peace outlook; need for new revenue; request for ratification of women's suffrage amendment (Senate only); armistice (1918); request for approval of Versailles treaty (Senate only); high cost of living (1919)
Harding	7	2 annual messages (1921–1922); federal problems (1921); 2 on the Merchant Marine (1922); coal and railroads (1922); debt (1923)
Coolidge	2	1 annual message (1923); George Washington's birthday (1927)
F. Roosevelt	16	10 annual messages (1934–1943); 100th anniversary of Lafayette's death (1934); 150th anniversary of First Congress (1939); neutrality address (1939); national defense (1940); declaration of war (1941); Yalta conference report (1945)
Truman	17	6 State of the Union messages (1947–1952); prosecution of the war (1945); submission of UN charter (Senate only, 1945); Congressional Medal of Honor ceremony (1945); universal military training (1945); railroad strike (1946); Greek-Turkish aid policy (1947); aid to Europe (1947); national security and conditions in Europe (1948); fiftieth anniversary of the liberation of Cuba (1948); inflation, housing, and civil rights (1948); steel industry dispute (1952)
Eisenhower	7	6 State of the Union messages (1953–1954; 1957–1960); Middle East (1957)
Kennedy	3	3 State of the Union messages (1961–1963)
L. Johnson	8	6 State of the Union messages (1964–1969); assumption of office (1963); Voting Rights Act (1965)
Nixon	7	4 State of the Union messages (1970–1972, 1974); Vietnam policy (1969—separate addresses to House and Senate); economic policy (1971); Soviet Union trip (1972)
Ford[a]	6	3 State of the Union messages (1975–1977); assumption of office (1974); inflation (1974); state of the world (1975)
Carter	6	3 State of the Union messages (1978–1980); energy program (1977); Middle East talks at Camp David (1978); SALT II arms control treaty (1979)
Reagan	11	7 State of the Union messages (1982–1988); 2 budget addresses (1981); Central America (1983); U.S.-Soviet summit (1985)
G. Bush	5	3 State of the Union messages (1990–1992); budget address (1989); Persian Gulf crisis (1991)
Clinton	9	7 State of the Union messages (1994–2000); budget address (1993); health policy reform (1993)
G. W. Bush[b]	8	6 State of the Union messages (2002–2007); budget address; September 11 terrorist attacks (2001)

SOURCE: *Guide to Congress,* 5th ed. (Washington, D.C.: CQ Press, 2000); *CQ Weekly,* various issues; John Woolley and Gerhard Peters, The American Presidency Project (online) (presidency.ucsb.edu/ws/?pid=29643), accessed February 2, 2007."

NOTES: a. On October 17, 1974, President Gerald R. Ford testified before the Subcommittee on Criminal Justice of the House Judiciary Committee on his pardon of former president Richard Nixon for crimes possibly committed during the Watergate affair.   b. Through 2006. Note also that incoming presidents now give a "budget speech" to Congress within weeks of the inauguration. This speech, while not technically a State of the Union address, serves to outline the new president's overall legislative agenda.

Television cameras pan the House chamber as the president speaks, recording the reactions of particular members of the audience to specific presidential statements or proposals. Media commentators and other political experts routinely begin to judge the presidential "performance" before the president's limousine even leaves the Capitol. The issues raised by the president receive serious consideration in the press, if not always in Congress, and the opposition party usually feels compelled to ask for equal time to state its views. *(See Table 12-3.)*

Despite, or perhaps because of, its symbolism, the power of the annual address to shape public opinion and spur on Congress should not be underestimated. Kennedy, for example, used it to launch a national effort to land American astronauts on the moon before the end of the 1960s. Johnson passionately promoted his civil rights and Great Society social programs, and Nixon used the opportunity to propose a sweeping reorganization of the federal establishment and to defend U.S. actions in Vietnam.

Reagan, a master of television, used the annual address to spark national and congressional debate on tax reform, on aid to the rebels in Nicaragua, and on his Strategic Defense Initiative weapons program. Bill Clinton, even when dogged by his self-inflicted sex scandal, effectively used the address to stake out the rhetorical high ground on issues such as Social Security and overall federal spending priorities. George W. Bush's singling out Iraq, Iran, and Korea as an "axis of evil" in his first State of the Union address after 9/11 left an indelible mark on the public psyche by effectively linking them with the war on terror, and helped lay the groundwork for the subsequent invasion of Iraq. The nation discusses whatever presidents discuss, if only for a while.

The State of the Union address is an important part of the "conversation" between presidents and Congress, an ongoing dialogue that may be as formal as the address or as informal as the daily contact among presidents, presidential aides, members of Congress, and Capitol Hill staff.[96] The subjects of this dialogue are revealed in part by the major themes expressed in the State of the Union messages of Presidents Kennedy through George W. Bush. *(See Table 12-4.)* During the 1970s, for example, the emphasis shifted from foreign to domestic policy concerns, particularly the economy. As political scientist Charles O. Jones notes, "Many of the domestic requests by Nixon, Ford, and Carter were reform measures seeking to reshape the structure and substance of programs enacted in the 1960s—a shift from issues requiring expansion of government to those demanding consolidation or even contraction of government." [97] The emphasis shifted back somewhat to foreign policy in the 1980s, reflecting the focus of the Reagan administration, and then returned largely to domestic concerns during the 1990s. Since September 11, 2001, however, the focus has again been on foreign affairs, particularly the war on terror and the ongoing conflicts in Afghanistan and Iraq.

The address also is a moment for presidents to proclaim successes, express their grand desires for the future, and engage in a little political theater. Reagan was particularly adept at using his time to praise American "heroes" and to chastise Congress for the way it prepares budgets. *(See box, The State of the Union Address as Political Theater, p. 672.)* In addition to the theater and symbolism, however, the speech also serves as a vehicle by which to itemize the president's legislative priorities. This can often take the form of what political scientist Andrew Rudalevige describes as a "rhetorical logroll," as presidents seek to reward or appease various factions within their administration by publicly recognizing their policy goals and proposals.[98]

The highly visible nature of the address also has its dangers, however, particularly when events cast doubt on or seem to contradict the president's words. In his January 2003 State of the Union address, President George W. Bush asserted that Iraq had tried to acquire "yellowcake" uranium from Niger, a precursor to developing a nuclear weapon. This became one justification for the subsequent invasion of Iraq. Administration officials later retracted the yellowcake claim, citing insufficient proof and contradictory evidence. But the damage had been done, particularly after it was revealed that Joseph Wilson, a former U.S. ambassador, had been sent to investigate whether Iraq had actually tried to acquire the uranium, only to report that the charge was unequivocally wrong. Later, officials in the Bush administration sought to discredit Wilson, allegedly even going so far as to "out" his wife's status as a covert CIA employee. Vice presidential aide I. Lewis "Scooter" Libby resigned his position in the Bush administration after he was indicted in relation to the case in 2005. In March 2007 he was found guilty of perjury, obstruction of justice, and making false statements.

With its high profile and constitutional underpinnings, the State of the Union message is the most visible

TABLE 12-4 Major Themes in State of the Union Addresses, 1961–2007

President	Year	Major themes
Kennedy	1961	Economy; social programs
	1962	Getting America moving; economy; military strength
	1963	Cuba; economy; tax reduction
L. Johnson	1964	JFK legacy; budget
	1965	Great Society domestic programs
	1966	Vietnam, foreign and defense policy
	1967	Maintaining previous momentum
	1968	Vietnam, foreign and defense policy
	1969	Review of achievements
Nixon	1970	Vietnam, foreign and defense policy
	1971	Vietnam; economic and social policy
	1972	Foreign and defense policy; plea for action on previous requests
	1973[a]	Natural resources; economy; social policy
	1974	Energy; economic issues
Ford	1975	Economy; taxes; energy
	1976	Economic and energy issues
	1977	Energy; achievements
Carter	1978	Economic and energy issues
	1979	Inflation; SALT II
	1980	Foreign and defense policy
	1981[a]	Record of progress; budget priorities
Reagan	1982	Economic and budget issues
	1983	Economic and budget issues
	1984	Federal deficit; foreign policy
	1985	Tax reform; government spending
	1986	Foreign policy; welfare reform
	1987	Foreign policy
	1988	Economic and budget issues
G. Bush	1990	Broad domestic and foreign policy issues
	1991	Support for Persian Gulf mission
	1992	Economic and budget issues
Clinton	1994	Domestic policy; jobs; crime; health reform
	1995	"Reinventing government"; domestic policy issues
	1996	Broad domestic policy issues
	1997	Balancing the federal budget; building communities; education
	1998	Spending future surpluses wisely; Social Security
	1999	Education; Social Security; health care; racial divisions
	2000	Social Security; health care; education; minimum wage
G. W. Bush	2002	War on terror; homeland defense; tax cuts; economic growth
	2003	Iraq; war on terror; tax cuts; Medicare reform
	2004	Iraq; homeland security; economic growth; tax cuts
	2005	Iraq; Social Security reform; homeland security; war on terror
	2006	Iraq; homeland security; entitlement program reform
	2007	War on terror; Iraq; energy; economic growth; health insurance

SOURCES: Charles O. Jones, "Presidential Negotiation with Congress," in *Both Ends of the Avenue: The Presidency, the Executive Branch, and Congress in the 1980s,* ed. Anthony King (Washington, D.C.: American Enterprise Institute, 1983), 103; *CQ Weekly,* various issues; Deborah Kalb, Gerhard Peters, and John Woolley, *State of the Union: Presidential Rhetoric from Woodrow Wilson to George W. Bush* (Washington, D.C.: CQ Press, 2007); John Woolley and Gerhard Peters, The American Presidency Project (online) (presidency.ucsb.edu/ws/?pid=29643), accessed February 2, 2007."

NOTE: a. Written message to Congress.

THE STATE OF THE UNION ADDRESS AS POLITICAL THEATER

Woodrow Wilson's "Annual Message," delivered to Congress in person on December 2, 1913, revived a precedent set by George Washington—but discontinued between 1801 and 1913, when presidents submitted only written messages—of the president personally addressing Congress on the condition of the nation. It was not until the advent of radio and, later, television that the annual speech, known today as the "State of the Union" address, took on powerful symbolic meaning. Widespread public access to radio allowed Franklin D. Roosevelt, for example, to speak directly to the American people and rally the nation out of the depression of the 1930s. But television, with its particular capacity to present emotional visual images, has elevated the State of the Union address to true public theater, complete with an audience (members of Congress assembled) and critics (network commentators). Televised annual addresses have become less a litany of dry statistics than a panorama of past accomplishments, current endeavors, and future dreams. Increasingly, the State of the Union address has become the primary vehicle in setting the nation's annual agenda, with presidents judged on how *well* they delivered their messages. The medium and the message have indeed coalesced.

John F. Kennedy inaugurated the use of television to breathe vibrancy into the annual message, but it was Ronald Reagan, the acknowledged master of visual media, who used the address to its greatest effect thus far. Whether he used it to needle Congress, praise heroes, or express his dreams for America, the State of the Union address in Reagan's hands became an eagerly awaited and heavily analyzed event. Reagan may not have written his own words or dreamed up the various symbolic appeals used—such matters were left to professional speechwriters—but he was the deliverer of the message to the people. The following excerpt from President Reagan's 1988 State of the Union address shows how one president transformed this once banal annual accounting into the preeminent national political event.

. . . Now, it is also time for some plain talk about the most immediate obstacle to controlling federal deficits. The simple but frustrating problem of making expenses match revenues—something American families do and the federal government can't—has caused crisis after crisis in this city. . . . I will say to you tonight what I have said before—and will continue to say: The budget process has broken down; it needs a drastic overhaul. With each ensuing year, the spectacle before the American people is the same as it was this Christmas—budget deadlines delayed or missed completely, monstrous continuing resolutions that pack hundreds of billions of dollars' worth of spending into one bill—and a federal government on the brink of default.

I know I'm echoing what you here in the Congress have said because you suffered so directly—but let's recall that in seven years, of 91 appropriations bills scheduled to arrive on my desk by a certain date, only 10 made it on time. Last year, of the 13 appropriations bills due by October 1st, none of them made it. Instead, we had four continuing resolutions lasting 41 days, then 36 days, and two days, and three days, respectively. And then, along came these behemoths. This is the conference report—1,053-page report weighing 14 pounds. Then this—a reconciliation bill six months late, that was 1,186 pages long, weighing 15 pounds; and the long-term continuing resolution—this one was two months late and it's 1,057 pages long, weighing 14 pounds. That was a total of 43 pounds of paper and ink. You had three hours—yes, three hours, to consider each, and it took 300 people at my Office of Management just to read the bill so the government wouldn't shut down.

Congress shouldn't send another one of these. No—and if you do, I will not sign it. Let's change all this; instead of a presidential budget that gets discarded and a congressional budget resolution that is not enforced, why not a simple partnership, a joint agreement that sets out the spending priorities within the available revenues? And let's remember our deadline is October 1st, not Christmas; let's get the people's work done in time to avoid a footrace with Santa Claus. And yes, this year—to coin a phrase—a new beginning. Thirteen individual bills, on time and fully reviewed by Congress. . . .

SOURCES: *Congressional Quarterly Weekly Report,* January 3, 1988, 221; Deborah Kalb, Gerhard Peters, and John T. Woolley, *State of the Union: Presidential Rhetoric from Woodrow Wilson to George W. Bush* (Washington, D.C.: CQ Press, 2007).

---

means by which presidents seek to set their legislative agenda. But it is not the only means. Congress through statute has required the president to make other annual reports. The Budget Act of 1921 requires the president to submit an annual budget message, and the Employment Act of 1946 mandates an annual report on the economy. Hundreds of other reports, messages, and legislative proposals are submitted to Congress annually, all bearing the president's imprint and expressing White House views on important policy matters. Presidents also use public speeches in other contexts to influence the policy agenda. In his examination of the public papers of the presidents during 1949 to 1996, a period spanning ten presidential administrations, Rudalevige counted 2,769 presidential messages containing 6,296 policy proposals.[99] This total ranged from an average high of almost 300 policy proposals per year by Lyndon

Johnson to an average low of 81 per year by Reagan. Of course these proposals varied in scope, significance, and level of presidential commitment, but each one had potential political influence.

Preparing Legislation

A president's priorities generally require formal congressional approval. Setting the national agenda is only the first stage in successful presidential leadership, if *leadership* is defined simply as getting proposals approved by Congress. In this process, presidents throughout history have relied on a wide array of personnel and resources. (*See* "The President as Chief Legislator," p. 1354, in Chapter 29, Vol. II.)

Drafting legislation is the first *formal* phase of the process. Although members of Congress have often resisted presidential participation in drafting bills, arguing that it violates the constitutional blueprint for separated institutions, presidents always have done so. Early presidents were circumspect about their roles and usually tried to avoid any appearance of interposing their views in a realm zealously guarded by Congress. George Washington, for example, quietly discussed ideas for new measures with cabinet officials and members of Congress. He even secretly helped to compose the odd bill, but he studiously avoided open and direct roles in forming legislation. Instead he assigned cabinet members to consult formally with Congress, an activity deemed more legitimate because department heads appeared regularly before congressional committees on routine business. Congress itself validated this strategy by directing Secretary of the Treasury Hamilton to draft and submit recommendations for a new national bank, a resolution of state debts, and the promotion of manufacturing— tasks Hamilton took on with such relish that he sparked severe criticism of his dominance over the legislative process.[100]

Hamilton's chief critic, Secretary of State Thomas Jefferson, proved no less energetic once he became president. Although his party stressed congressional supremacy, Jefferson secretly composed bills, which he transmitted through his department secretaries to party loyalists in the legislature, and used his cabinet secretaries for maximum influence on legislating. Jefferson's party caucus enjoyed a solid congressional majority, enabling him to maintain the fiction of his complete separateness from lawmaking even as he wielded a strong hand behind the scenes.

Other nineteenth-century presidents continued this pattern of using cabinet officials to lobby for legislation. They had few alternatives. Presidents had few personal staff members, and Congress did not appropriate funds for even clerical assistance until 1857. Nor did they have extensive networks of personal advisers and assistants.[101] Cabinet officials gave presidents valuable access to congressional committees, acted as the president's eyes and ears, and, as political scientist James Young noted, "allowed Presidents to maintain, for what it was worth, the outward appearance of conformity to community norms which decreed social distance between the President and Congress."[102]

But this system had its disadvantages, chief among them the reality that department heads frequently were selected to pay off political favors or to accommodate rival factions within the president's party. Presidents never were entirely sure of their own cabinet's primary loyalties and had to guard against the tendency of strong cabinet officials to cultivate their own power bases in Congress. Lincoln, for example, had to maneuver continually around such formidable political figures as Secretary of State William H. Seward and Secretary of the Treasury Salmon P. Chase, who led their factions within the Republican Party and regularly clashed with Lincoln over Civil War policies.

The Institutional Presidency

The image of the nineteenth-century presidency is one of a lone figure with little reliable assistance. Contemporary presidents, by contrast, reside at the heart of an immense executive institution, aided in their tasks by about seventeen hundred special assistants, personal aides, policy experts, and clerical staffers distributed among several specialized agencies that collectively comprise the Executive Office of the Presidency (EOP). *(See Table 12-5.)* The EOP is, in theory, the president's personal bureaucracy, created expressly to help the chief executive oversee cabinet department and agency activities, formulate budgets and monitor spending, craft legislation, lobby Congress, and, above all, promote the president's priorities. *(See Chapter 22, Executive Office of the President: White House Office, Vol. II, and Chapter 24, Executive Office of the President: Supporting Organizations, Vol. II.)*

Although the EOP was not formally established until 1939, the presidential bureaucracy dates from 1921, when Congress, recognizing the need for a more centralized budgeting process, passed the Budget and Accounting Act. This legislation required the president to coordinate all executive branch spending proposals and present a unified annual budget. To assist presidents in this task, the law also created the Bureau of the Budget (BOB). Thus arose the notion of "central clearance," the use of the BOB to monitor all executive branch spending, to judge new funding requests before they went to Capitol Hill, and, especially, to quash budget proposals not in line with the president's agenda. The pres-

TABLE 12-5 **Employees of the Executive Office of the President, Various Offices, 1941–2005**

Year	White House Office	Office of Management and Budget[a]	National Security Council
1941	53	305	—
1945	61	565	—
1950	295	520	17
1955	290	444	28
1960	446	434	65
1965	292	506	39
1970	491	636	82
1975	525	664	85
1980	426	631	74
1985	362	569	61
1990	391	568	60
1995[b]	400	553	57
2000	398	510	45
2005	406	477	63

SOURCE: Bureau of the Census, *Statistical Abstract of the United States* (Washington, D.C.: Government Printing Office, various editions); U.S. Office of Personnel Management, *Federal Manpower Statistics, Federal Civilian Workforce Statistics*, bimonthly.

NOTES: a. Known until 1970 as the Bureau of the Budget.   b. Estimate.

HOW A BILL BECOMES A LAW

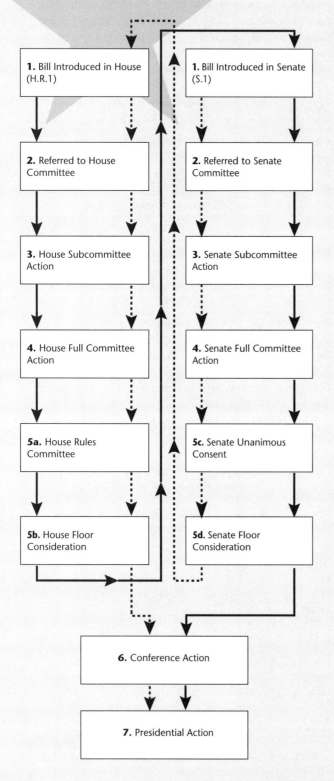

1. Bill Introduced in House (H.R.1)

1. Bill Introduced in Senate (S.1)

2. Referred to House Committee

2. Referred to Senate Committee

3. House Subcommittee Action

3. Senate Subcommittee Action

4. House Full Committee Action

4. Senate Full Committee Action

5a. House Rules Committee

5c. Senate Unanimous Consent

5b. House Floor Consideration

5d. Senate Floor Consideration

6. Conference Action

7. Presidential Action

1. INTRODUCTION OF A BILL IN HOUSE OR SENATE.

A proposal that will eventually become law must be introduced by a member of Congress. Often when a member introduces a bill, he or she will find someone in the other chamber to introduce a "companion bill." Each bill is given a number as it is introduced, and numbering is sequential. House bill numbers start with *HR*, Senate bill numbers start with *S*.

A bill written in the executive branch and proposed as an administration measure usually is introduced "by request" by the chair of the congressional committee that has jurisdiction.

2. REFERRAL TO COMMITTEE.

After a bill is introduced it is referred by the parliamentarian to a standing committee. The committee chair then decides which subcommittee will consider the measure.

3. SUBCOMMITTEE ACTION.

The subcommittee holds hearings on the bill. Testimony may be taken from invited witnesses only, or the committee may issue an open call and hear from anyone who wishes to speak. At this point administration representatives have a chance to urge support for a bill. Subcommittee hearings also provide an opportunity for them to oppose a bill they do not like.

When hearings are completed, the bill is "marked up," that is, rewritten to incorporate the subcommittee's changes. These changes may be designed to strengthen (or weaken) the provisions or they may be politically inspired to improve (or reduce) a bill's chance of passage. If the president has objections, it is at this point that friendly committee members and White House lobbyists attempt to amend the bill to meet presidential approval. When the subcommittee has finished its work, the bill is sent to the full committee.

4. FULL COMMITTEE ACTION.

The full committee may ratify the subcommittee's actions, or it may repeat the subcommittee's steps by holding more hearings and marking up the bill a second time. This second markup gives the administration another chance to alter the bill if its effort to make changes at the subcommittee level failed. Whether or not the subcommittee steps are repeated, only the full committee formally reports the bill back to the chamber for floor action; a subcommittee cannot report a measure directly.

5A. HOUSE RULES COMMITTEE.

After the full committee reports the bill, it is placed on a "calendar" and is ready for floor consideration. In the House, controversial or complicated bills are referred to the Rules Committee, which determines the framework for debate and amendment. A special rule written by the Rules Committee specifies how long debate will last, who will control the time, and how many and what type of amendments may be offered.

After the Rules Committee has recommended a rule, the full House votes on whether to accept it. If the rule does not allow amendments that the president favors, or if the legislation contains provisions the president would like to see deleted, the White House may lobby House members to defeat the rule. The White House is seldom successful in defeating a rule; but when it is, that success is a major victory for the president.

5B. HOUSE FLOOR CONSIDERATION.

If, as usually happens, the House accepts the rule, the next step is debate on the bill. Normal House rules limit each member to one hour during general debate, but often the rule imposes more rigid time limits. Roll call votes may be requested if a certain number of members agree to the request. Roll call votes are taken electronically in the House and usually last fifteen minutes.

If the bill originated in the House, it is referred to the Senate for action after passage (see solid line). If the House is completing consideration of a measure referred from the Senate and the bill has not been amended, it is cleared for presidential action. If the bill is a referral from the Senate and has been substantially amended, it may be referred to a conference committee *(see No. 6)*.

5C. SENATE UNANIMOUS CONSENT.

To expedite floor consideration, the Senate has developed a procedure, known as the "unanimous consent agreement," similar to the special rules written by the House Rules Committee. A unanimous consent agreement is worked out informally by the majority and minority leaders and by any senator with an interest in the bill under consideration. The agreement specifies how much time will be allotted for debate, what amendments will be considered, and how the time will be divided. Unlike a House rule, however, which needs a simple majority to pass, a unanimous consent agreement must be accepted by all senators on the floor at the time it is proposed. A single objection defeats the agreement.

5D. SENATE FLOOR CONSIDERATION.

Floor consideration under a unanimous consent agreement in the Senate is similar to action under a rule in the House. If a unanimous consent agreement cannot be worked out, however, the Senate operates under its normal rules, which are much less restrictive than House rules. There is no time limit on debate. Members opposed to a bill under consideration sometimes "filibuster"—that is, hold the floor by speaking for an extended period of time—to delay or kill a bill. A filibuster can be ended only if sixty senators agree to a "cloture" petition to limit debate. As a result, floor proceedings in the Senate usually take much longer than in the House. Voting in the Senate is not electronic. The roll is called by a clerk who records each senator's vote.

If the bill under consideration originated in the Senate, it is then referred to the House for action after passage (see broken line). If the Senate is completing consideration of a measure referred from the House and the bill has not been amended, it is cleared for presidential action. If the bill is a referral from the House and has been substantially amended, it may be referred to a conference committee *(see No. 6)*.

6. CONFERENCE ACTION.

A bill must be approved by both chambers in identical form before it can be sent to the president. If there are major differences between the versions passed by the House and the Senate, the bill may go to a conference committee, which works out a compromise. The committee usually consists of senior members of the committees that reported the bill. If the president has reservations or objections or prefers the bill passed by one chamber to the version passed by the other, it is in the conference that the White House attempts to influence members to adopt a final version that is acceptable to the administration.

When the conference is completed, the committee files a conference report to which both the House and the Senate must agree. If either rejects the conference agreement, the bill dies. If both agree to the conference report, the measure then goes to the president for final action.

A conference often can be avoided, however. Even if one chamber has amended a bill substantially, it can refer the measure back to the originating chamber, which may accept all the amendments (clearing the bill for the president), accept some and reject others, or even add some amendments of its own (in which case the bill then bounces back to the other chamber a second time). This back-and-forth process can continue until both chambers have agreed to the measure in identical form, thus clearing it for presidential action. In reality, most bills are cleared in this manner, avoiding an official conference.

7. PRESIDENTIAL ACTION.

The president has several options once a bill is received from Congress. If the president approves the bill, he signs it, dates it, and usually writes the word "approved" on the document. If the president disapproves, he vetoes the bill by refusing to sign it and returns it to Congress within ten legislative days of its presentation (Sundays excluded) with a message stating his reasons. The message is sent to the chamber that originated the bill. If no action is taken on the message, the bill dies.

Congress, however, may vote to overturn a veto. Debate can precede this vote, with motions permitted to lay the message on the table, postpone action on it, or refer it to committee. If both chambers vote by a two-thirds majority (of those present and voting) to "override" the veto, the bill becomes law. Otherwise the bill is dead.

Normally if the president does not sign the bill within the ten-day period and Congress is in session, the bill becomes law without his signature. However, should Congress adjourn before the ten days expire and the president has failed to sign the measure, it does not become law. This procedure is called the pocket veto.

When bills are passed finally and signed, or passed over a veto, they are given law numbers in numerical order as they become law. There are two series of numbers, one for public and one for private laws, starting at the number "1" for each two-year term of Congress. They are then identified by law number and by Congress—for example, Private Law 21, 104th Congress; Public Law 250, 104th Congress (or PL 104–250).

ident for the first time had a mechanism to coordinate and perhaps control executive branch activities.[103]

Franklin Roosevelt's New Deal spawned a staggering growth in executive branch responsibilities, which in turn strained the capacity of the presidency to coordinate and control government expenditures and actions. At the same time, the outpouring of new policy proposals during the New Deal compelled Roosevelt to expand the BOB's clearance functions to include screening nonbudgetary legislative proposals and enrolled bills passed by Congress and sent to him for his signature. In 1939, in recognition of its expanding functions, the Bureau of the Budget was moved from the Treasury Department to the newly formed EOP. The EOP, comprised initially of the White House Office, the BOB, and three other staff agencies, was created to help the president bring greater unity of purpose and consistency of action to the executive branch.

Today the EOP includes about a dozen agencies. The most important are the White House Office and related domestic, economic, and homeland security policy staffs; the Office of Management and Budget (formerly the BOB); the National Security Council staff; and the Council of Economic Advisers. Roosevelt intended the EOP agencies (except for the White House Office) to consist primarily of career-based, "neutrally competent" aides who could provide continuity and historical memory. Through time, however, the most important EOP agencies have tended to adopt a more political orientation in which their activities are conducted primarily to serve the interests of the incumbent president. The BOB is a case in point; in 1970 Congress, acting at Richard Nixon's behest, transformed the agency into the Office of Management and Budget (OMB) and later made its director subject to Senate confirmation in recognition of his politicized status. Under Nixon, the OMB became more nearly an instrument of domestic and budgetary policy advocacy, a role that continues to this day. Reagan extended the OMB's clearance power to include regulatory review, and more than any of his predecessors used the agency to ensure that the budgeting process reflected the president's policy objectives. From its origins as a small and even neutral accounting department, the OMB today is a powerful, partisan, and often controversial defender of the president's agenda.

Similarly, the National Security Council (NSC), consisting of the president, vice president, secretaries of defense and state, and others the president may appoint, was established by Congress during the Truman administration to ensure that presidents consulted with the relevant military and diplomatic experts when making foreign policy. The NSC staff, however, has gradually eclipsed the statutory council as the primary source of foreign policy advice to the president. Headed by a special assistant working in the White House, this staff, typically numbering more than fifty specialists, provides information and advice geared to the president's interests and perspective rather than the various foreign policy bureaucracies sitting on the full NSC.

At the apex of the EOP sits the White House Office (WHO), home to the president's closest personal aides and special assistants. Now numbering more than four hundred aides, it was formally established by FDR to house the president's personal staff who handled the president's daily administrative activities: appointments, correspondence, and scheduling. Through the years, however, it has taken on a greater role in policy development and political outreach. Today it works closely with the president in putting together a legislative program, lobbying Congress for its passage, and overseeing policy implementation.

Other EOP agencies come and go, depending on the president's policy interests and desire to use EOP status to showcase their commitment to a particular policy goal. Thus Lyndon Johnson established the Office of Economic Opportunity within the EOP to dramatize his antipoverty efforts. President George W. Bush appointed a White House aide to oversee an Office of Faith-based Initiatives. Unless the agency serves an interest common to subsequent presidents, however, it is likely to have a short existence.

As this overview demonstrates, the contemporary presidency is an *institution* with resources and powers that remain potent regardless of the personal traits of individual chief executives. Ironically, the institutional capacity to carry out all these tasks furnishes presidents with a different dilemma: how to ensure that the Executive Office of the President itself responds to the president's needs and wishes. Presidents cannot be involved personally in every action that occurs below them. They must rely on subordinates to monitor and guide the behavior of an institution that is itself designed to monitor and guide the behavior of the executive branch as a whole. Nineteenth-century presidents bemoaned their lack of staff resources; presidents today wonder how they can make their own vast organization run loyally and well.

The President's Agenda

Much of the legislation Congress ponders originates within the executive branch. No longer do presidents maintain a fiction of separation from the legislative process. Indeed, contemporary presidents more often than not are judged by the quality and timing of their annual policy agendas. Congress and the public alike demand that presidents initiate legislation and criticize severely those who do not. Eisenhower, for example, did not propose a formal legislative agenda in his first year in office, only to receive sharp rebukes from members of both parties. "Don't expect us to start from scratch on what you people want," said one angry House member to an administration official. "That's not the way we do things here. You draft the bills and we work them over." [104]

A multiplicity of sources provides the ideas that form the intellectual foundation of the president's program. Before Franklin Roosevelt's administration, presidents were able to base their agendas on their personal views and experiences, because the role of the executive branch was limited and the problems requiring presidential attention relatively few. Theodore Roosevelt's aggressive national park and wildlife conservation policies stemmed at least in part from his background as a western rancher and big-game hunter. Herbert Hoover's experiences as secretary of commerce under Calvin Coolidge (1923–1929) guided his priorities, at least until the Great Depression overtook his presidency.

Recently, however, a surprising proportion of a chief executive's domestic program may come from "outside" sources—Congress, national and international events, the departments and agencies of the executive branch, and public opinion. Congress, with its hundreds of members and thousands of staff, is fertile ground for legislative ideas. Many of the formal legislative proposals that come officially from the White House actually stem from ideas and proposals that have bounced around Capitol Hill for years, waiting to be adopted as political circumstances permit.[105] One such example of policy adoption was Kennedy's domestic program, a large portion of which was based on ideas and options promoted to no avail by liberal congressional Democrats during the Eisenhower years. What Kennedy could not get through Congress, Lyndon Johnson later incorporated into his Great Society program. Reagan's vaunted tax reduction bill of 1981 was the "offspring" of a Republican tax plan pushed by New York representative Jack Kemp and Delaware senator William Roth beginning in the late 1970s. Likewise, Clinton's signature national service initiative, known as AmeriCorps, in many ways grew out of a proposal developed by Northwestern University sociologist Charles Moskos over a decade earlier.[106] George W. Bush's "No Child Left Behind" educational act draws heavily on the findings of several high-powered commissions dating back to the Reagan administration charged with reforming America's educational system. Hundreds of proposed policies float about at all times, each awaiting the power of a president to lift it out of the mass of proposals and give it life.[107]

Crises or other major events also structure the domestic agenda, probably more than presidents desire or care to admit. In fact, Americans now expect government to respond forcefully to new or sudden problems. There is no question, for example, that Hoover's inability to rein in the depression led to his defeat in 1932 and that Franklin Roosevelt attained mythical status for his innovative ("try anything") attack on the economic crisis.[108] The 1957 Soviet launch of *Sputnik* startled Eisenhower into major spending for science education and the space program. The energy crisis of the 1970s, sparked largely by huge hikes in oil prices by producing nations, dominated the fiscal and budgetary agendas of both Ford and Carter. National concern about the AIDS (acquired immune deficiency syndrome) epidemic forced the Reagan administration to increase research funding to combat the disease, while the ominous signs of global warming combined with rising energy costs have compelled the George W. Bush administration to fund research into alternative energy sources.[109] The demands that presidents respond to issues or events beyond their control probably will intensify as global economic and political conditions become increasingly intertwined with domestic politics.[110]

Executive branch bureaucrats are another wellspring of policy ideas or options, despite the propensity of presidential candidates to attack the bureaucracy during their election campaigns. In his analysis of the sources of presidential legislative initiatives, Rudalevige calculated that more than a fifth of them originated in the executive branch departments and agencies.[111] Career civil servants are deeply dedicated to particular policy areas and possess the technical expertise and perspectives that come from long tenure. A new president wishing to initiate policies or simply avoid repeating the mistakes of the past may find their experience helpful.

The degree to which any president adopts ideas generated from within the professional bureaucracy depends in part on personal ideology and style. The White House staffs of Republicans Nixon and Reagan, for example, were highly suspicious of the motives and political leanings of career civil servants and tried whenever possible to draw policy making directly into the White House.[112] Democrats Jimmy Carter and Bill Clinton, by contrast, tended to share civil servants' fundamental beliefs in the positive role of government and thus showed a greater willingness to tap bureaucratic ideas. Nonetheless, Rudalevige's data show that regardless of ideology or partisan background, presidents dating back to Truman on average do not vary considerably in where they find legislative ideas. More than 50 percent of presidents' legislative initiatives have "mixed" parentage, reflecting the combined influence of the executive branch and the president's own EOP or White House staff. Only about 22 percent, in contrast, are "purely presidential" initiatives originating in the White House or EOP.[113]

Whatever the source of any agenda item, presidents must test its technical, economic, and especially, political soundness before sending it off to Congress. Proposals that fail to take politics into account are ripe for disaster. The degree to which this is true is probably proportionate to the degree of change intended. Incremental changes do not as a rule generate massive political resistance, but plans that seek comprehensive change almost guarantee strong reactions from a wide array of affected interests.[114] Carter's massive effort to reform national energy policy, for example, was hammered out by a panel of experts but suffered embarrassing political defeats once it was sent to Congress. The same fate befell Clinton's plan for health care reform, despite the administration's efforts to include as many perspectives as possible before sending it to Congress. The sheer size of the intended plan may have sparked the flames of its own demise.[115] Similarly, George W. Bush has been singularly unsuccessful in convincing Congress to support Social Security reform that involves allowing taxpayers to place some of their retirement money into individual investment accounts.

Presidents seek out a wide range of expertise in an effort to avoid such fates, but, as they find out, no source is perfect. For example, the professionals who staff the EOP are valuable sources of technical expertise or economic analysis, but they may not be attuned to the political climate or understand well the vagaries of Capitol Hill. Every president has aides and close friends who are valued for their political acumen and who can offer frank advice to the president in ways that others would not dare, be they Franklin Roosevelt's "brain trust," Carter's "Georgia Mafia," or the Californians making up Reagan's "kitchen cabinet." But such people also may be new to Washington or blinded to political reality by their loyalty to the president when controversial decisions must be made. The failure of Clinton's health care reform effort has been attributed in part to the relative inexperience of his White House staff, particularly those placed in charge of developing the policy.

Cabinet secretaries, in contrast to the days when they were the president's primary advisers (and sometimes competitors), today play a secondary role in judging policy proposals unless they also have close personal ties to the president or preside over a department particularly important to presidential priorities. Presidents frequently fill the position of attorney general, for example, with a close friend or political ally who then enjoys ready access to the Oval Office. Kennedy appointed his brother Robert; Nixon looked to his friend and former law partner John Mitchell; and Reagan appointed his longtime aide Edwin Meese. Each of these was more than a department head; they also were close friends.

By contrast, some cabinet members rarely see the president in private, even on issues central to their departments, and complain that their phone calls are routed to presidential aides whom they technically outrank. Samuel Pierce, for example, was secretary of housing and urban development throughout the Reagan presidency, yet he rarely played a central role in policy development because his department was peripheral to the president's agenda. (In fact, as one famous story goes, Reagan even failed to recognize Pierce at a reception for city mayors.) Clinton's labor secretary, Robert Reich, entitled his memoirs of the Clinton years *Locked in the Cabinet,* a reflection of his frustration at his lack of policy influence and access to the president.[116] On occasion, cabinet members are regarded with deep suspicion

because they have succumbed to the tendency of cabinet secretaries to promote departmental interests over the president's agenda, particularly after they have been in office for some time. Cabinet secretaries who "go native" find their access cut off and advice ignored, even when it could prove valuable.

Members of Congress of either political party may be keenly attuned to the political feasibility of new proposals but, as elected officials in their own right, they usually have their own agendas to promote. And, given their distinct electoral and governing roles, their perspectives may differ dramatically from the president's. Carter, for one, deeply distrusted members of Congress; he felt they were too parochial. Indeed, to his dismay he witnessed firsthand the tenacity of local interests in Congress once his proposals went to Capitol Hill. All presidents find this out eventually, and most realize that members of Congress must be heard, if only so that they can warn of the obstacles that may lie ahead.

Career federal bureaucrats know what is feasible technically and economically, but they may have their own policy and institutional goals to consider. Loyalty to their agencies, programs, or own policy ideals may supersede any loyalty to a particular president. In 2006 the Bush administration asked James Hansen, a longtime NASA scientist and specialist on climate change, to clear all public statements with his White House–appointed superiors first. Hansen then publicly accused the Bush administration of trying to prevent him from discussing the causes of global warming.[117] Hansen likely understood that career bureaucrats usually will be in their positions long after any one president has left the White House. They generally can wait out an administration hostile to their views until the political winds change or new leaders come to office.

Outside experts such as academics sometimes offer new ideas and perhaps lend an aura of expertise and legitimacy to controversial issues, but, like many experts, they may not have enough insight into what is feasible politically. Moreover, there is no guarantee that any recommendations made by panels of experts will ever amount to more than reams of paper sitting in a file cabinet. In December 2006, after much anticipation, a commission headed by former secretary of state James Baker and former congressman Lee Hamilton released its congressionally sponsored Iraq Study Group report. Almost immediately, President George W. Bush began distancing himself from the report's most important recommendations, which included negotiating with the governments of Iran and Syria to control the influx of terrorists into Iraq and a reduction in U.S. troop levels there. What experts propose often goes far beyond what politicians are willing to use at a particular time.

In short, many sources for ideas and expertise are available to a president, but only the occupant of the Oval Office can decide which sources will be tapped. Presidents like

Franklin Roosevelt, Lyndon Johnson, and Bill Clinton were voracious consumers of advice from a great number of sources. To get a broad spectrum of opinion, Roosevelt surrounded himself with assistants who were known to disagree violently on major issues. Johnson was famous for his midnight telephone calls to sleepy senators, demanding the latest scoop on a piece of legislation. Both had keen political instincts, and for them information was a resource to be used wisely in political battles. Clinton, an avowed "policy wonk,"

Presidents frequently place a trusted friend or political ally in the position of attorney general. John F. Kennedy appointed his brother Robert.

reveled in seemingly endless discussions on policy matters with virtually anyone who would take part.[118] This style requires, above all, tremendous personal energy and intellect, but it can easily overwhelm a president who does not place some limits on the vast amounts of information headed for the Oval Office daily. Presidents who do not adequately delegate tasks to subordinates risk overload.

Other presidents prefer to let information and policy options "bubble up" through the ranks of advisers and experts, using their closest aides to synthesize advice and present a short list of alternative courses of action. Eisenhower, Reagan, and both Bushes—all Republicans—operated in this manner. Reagan was notably content to let his aides parse out competing choices and to withhold his own views until presented with one or two options. The president's role in this approach is relatively passive, but it can work well when those who actually weigh the alternatives keep the president's values and priorities firmly in mind. Problems arise when a president's aides fail to do so, or when they keep the president in the dark about their activities.

Presidential styles hinge most on personal views and skills, overall goals, and perspectives on the job itself. Carter saw the president's job as one of problem solving, and insisted on being informed of or involved in almost every decision—including, as one story goes, the schedule for the White House tennis courts. His problem, critics charged, was that he was too immersed in the minutiae of policy to discern or convey to the public the broader goals of public policy or of his office. Reagan, by contrast, apparently viewed himself as chairman of the board. He was content to dictate broad goals and directions while allowing his aides to work

out specific policy options. His tendency to remain aloof from the particulars of policy often made him appear uninformed in press conferences, but even Reagan's critics admitted that the passion of his ideals provided his subordinates with clear guidelines by which to judge and select policies.

Lobbying Congress

After legislation is drafted, presidents must persuade Congress to go along with it. Presidential scholar Richard E. Neustadt argues that the primary power of the presidency is the power to persuade others to follow the presidential agenda, but the Constitution is silent on just how presidents are to do so.[119] And that silence is convenient. Presidents seeking little in the way of change can claim that separation of the branches gives them little capacity to influence Congress directly; assertive presidents can use this constitutional silence to justify almost any means of persuasion not expressly forbidden by law or accepted practice. Generally, the way in which presidents organize their lobbying activities and the styles they employ to influence Congress reflect their particular ideology, specific policy goals, knowledge about how government works, and overall personal skills. They also reflect whether—or how much—Congress is willing to be influenced, a state of receptiveness that always is in doubt. *(See "Presidential Lobbyists," p. 1371, in Chapter 29, Vol. II.)*

Presidents through the early 1900s were careful to obey the forms of separation of the branches. They had few instruments for influencing legislation, and their activities generally were constrained by prevailing beliefs in congres-

President George W. Bush meets with Sens. Edward M. Kennedy, D-Mass., Bill Frist, R-Tenn., and James M. Jeffords, I-Vt., in the White House Cabinet room to answer questions from the press regarding Jeffords's defection from the Republican Party in June 2001. Jeffords cited the increasing conservatism of the president and GOP leadership as the reason for becoming an independent, a decision that caused the first-ever midsession power shift to occur in the Senate. His switch marked the end of the Republicans' Senate reign, which began in 1995, and gave the Democrats a 50–49 majority over the GOP. Sen. Tom Daschle, D-S.D., replaced Trent Lott, R-Miss., as majority leader, inheriting that post's power to set the agenda for the Senate.

sional supremacy. Party loyalty, favorable newspaper coverage, and politically connected cabinet members were a nineteenth-century president's primary resources, and presidential lobbying tended to be loosely organized and discreet. This picture had changed dramatically by the 1940s because both government and public attitudes about the nature of presidential leadership had undergone a fundamental reordering. But the evolution of presidential lobbying from the indirect and passive styles of earlier presidents to the open and well-organized practices of today took decades.

Theodore Roosevelt may have cut a more dramatic public figure, but Woodrow Wilson stands out among early twentieth-century presidents for pursuing a strongly personal approach to congressional relations. Although Wilson shied away from open and "direct" lobbying, he vigorously pulled party strings to ensure Democratic support for his agenda and went so far as to sit in on congressional committee deliberations on trade legislation. His chief congressional lobbyist, Postmaster General Albert Burleson, used postal positions as inducements for loyalty to the president's program. Wilson also relied on John Nance Garner, a House Democrat from Texas, to act as his confidential lobbyist within the House. Garner, who sat on the influential Ways and Means Committee, would enter the White House once a week through a side door to consult with Wilson privately on current congressional news and prospects for the president's legislation.

Less than two decades later, Franklin Roosevelt abandoned any pretense of regal noninvolvement and employed an open and direct lobbying strategy. Roosevelt is considered the father of contemporary presidential lobbying styles, beginning with his own sustained and overt role in policy formation. He effectively goaded Congress into action through radio appeals to the public and through a careful cultivation of friendly relations with the press. His personal assistants—James Rowe, Thomas Corcoran, and Benjamin Cohen—wrote bills and lobbied legislators openly. Like Wilson, Roosevelt relied on patronage to reward loyalty and to punish deserters, using Postmaster General James A. Farley, who also served as chair of the national Democratic Party, as his chief enforcer. Inducements included preferential treatment on public works projects and other New Deal spending programs, funds critical to hard-pressed Democrats during election years, and promises for personal campaign appearances by the popular president.[120] At the same time, however, Roosevelt was careful to limit his personal lobbying efforts to his administration's most important initiatives. As he told his cabinet members: "If I make every bill that the government is interested in must legislation, it is going to complicate things. . . . Where I clear legislation with a notation that says 'no objection,' that means you are at perfect liberty to try and get the thing through, but I am not going to send a special message. It is all your trouble, not mine."[121]

Formalizing the Process

Although Roosevelt's overall influence in Congress waxed and waned with changes in the immediate political conditions, he constructed a more vigorous and more central role for the presidency in the legislative process. Indeed, Roosevelt inaugurated or perfected many of the lobbying techniques employed by contemporary presidents, but he did not make lobbying a formal process. Roosevelt would assign a presidential aide to lobby for a program or bill only if it got into trouble. Legislative liaison—the practice of having aides constantly cultivate a receptive environment in Congress—remained an informal affair, in many ways reflecting Roosevelt's more personal approach to politics and his dislike of rigid organizations.[122]

Dwight Eisenhower, the former general, adopted the antithesis of Roosevelt's highly personal and avowedly disorganized approach. Eisenhower was the first president to formalize the executive lobbying process by creating the Office of Congressional Relations (OCR), a specialized structure reflecting his own hierarchical orientation and general dislike of direct lobbying. Eisenhower, who was less comfortable than Roosevelt in the rambunctious world of politics, also wanted the OCR to act as a buffer between himself and members of Congress, even those from his party.[123] Heading the OCR was Bryce Harlow, a veteran House committee staff member who had no other responsibilities than to cultivate cordial relations with Congress and, especially, to keep House and Senate Republicans happy. But Harlow's office seldom took an active role in legislative development, largely because Eisenhower spent more time opposing congressional Democratic proposals than in pushing his agenda.

John Kennedy, by contrast, planned an aggressive legislative agenda and strengthened the liaison office by appointing longtime political ally Lawrence F. O'Brien as chief lobbyist. O'Brien wanted the congressional liaison staff to "create a general climate in favor and receptivity toward the president and the administration among members of Congress, and . . . use these positive perceptions as a resource when attempting to obtain support for particular pieces of legislation."[124] He organized the OCR along lines that paralleled the political makeup of Congress itself, assigning a staff member to interact with nearly every faction and bloc in the legislature, and constructed cooperative relationships with agency personnel, party leaders, and interest groups—whoever might be useful or necessary to the president's success. Many scholars consider O'Brien to be the architect of modern legislative liaison, and the specific system he established continued through the Carter administration.

Even with O'Brien's efforts, Kennedy generally was unable to push an expansive legislative agenda because conservative Democrats in Congress opposed new social programs and civil rights legislation. Kennedy's narrow victory over Richard Nixon in 1960 did not give him enough per-

President John F. Kennedy appointed longtime political ally Lawrence F. O'Brien to head the Office of Congressional Relations in order to strengthen his expansive legislative agenda.

sonal political clout to pressure even fellow Democrats to go along with his agenda. Although Kennedy's liaison office was credited with a handful of notable victories on trade and tax matters, the political climate in Congress was such that no organized lobbying could readily control it. Later presidents would discover that a good liaison office could not overcome a weak political hand.

Lyndon Johnson fared quite differently. Kennedy's assassination had created in the nation and in Congress a desire to pass some of the slain president's legislation, and Johnson's own decisive 1964 election victory over Barry M. Goldwater gave him the kind of public "mandate" that crafty politicians like Johnson can capitalize on with Congress.[125] The 1964 election also brought into Congress many new liberal Democrats, giving Johnson added congressional support for his domestic policy agenda. Johnson retained the liaison office built by Kennedy to augment his own considerable personal political skills, and he insisted that O'Brien and his liaison staff be consulted closely before initiatives were taken. So closely did Johnson work with Congress that political scientist Charles Jones characterizes Johnson's legislative style as akin to that of a majority leader—which Johnson had been in the Senate before becoming vice president under Kennedy.[126] Johnson, always a creature of Congress, believed that legislators should be consulted regularly on policy initiatives. He knew how to include members of Congress in decision making, he was careful not to overload the system, and he was sensitive to the importance of making loyal supporters look good. Above all, Johnson sought out compromise behind the scenes, going directly to the American public only as a last resort, and his liaison staff worked hard to develop and maintain cooperative relationships all over Capitol Hill.[127]

Richard Nixon cared little about domestic political issues and perhaps even less about Congress. He preferred to focus on foreign policy, which required far less congressional involvement. He seldom engaged personally in lobbying and rebelled against the sort of bargaining that Johnson relished. Where Johnson integrated the liaison office into his overall congressional strategy, Nixon removed it from the process and relied heavily instead on a close circle of personal aides for legislative advice and strategy. Where Johnson was accessible to many views and members of Congress, Nixon shielded himself behind a wall of assistants. And where Johnson relied on compromise, Nixon tended to confront and to stick with his course regardless of political considerations.

Nixon's legislative style was not particularly conducive to pushing a legislative program, but in many ways it was well suited to forcing a hostile Congress to accede to his demands or risk a veto, particularly when the politically astute president knew he had public support. Nixon's early successes attest to the degree to which presidents can confront Congress and get their way when they enjoy a high degree of popularity. The opposite also was true: as Nixon's public support fell, so did his capacity to stop Congress from overriding his opposition to major pieces of legislation, such as the 1973 War Powers Resolution.

Gerald Ford in many ways operated more like the Democrat Lyndon Johnson than like fellow Republican Nixon, probably because Ford and Johnson shared longer careers in Congress and believed in the institution more than did Nixon. Like Johnson, Ford committed himself to working with all members of Congress and deployed his legislative liaison team to cultivate friendly relations with both parties. Unlike Johnson, Ford was a minority president, with Democrats in control of both houses of Congress. He, like Nixon, had to rely on the veto as a central part of his overall legislative strategy, using his liaison staff to build coalitions to support his vetoes. In this sense, at least, Ford was effective.

Jimmy Carter was an outsider who had less interest in the process of consensus building than in the substance of policy, and he had a dim view of traditional Washington politics. "Legislative liaison for Carter," Eric Davis suggests, "simply was a matter of convincing members of Congress of the correctness of his positions on the issues."[128] His liaison team as a result was organized initially along issue lines, as opposed to the geographical and voting bloc patterns employed since O'Brien. No single staff assistant could discuss a wide array of issues—or make deals across issues— with any single member of Congress. Also, the Carter White House initially turned its back on the O'Brien method of continually courting members and doling out favors to loyalists and party leaders. Carter's aides so disdained the norms of Washington that even House Speaker Thomas P. "Tip" O'Neill, whose help Carter would need to push through his

legislative agenda, could not get good seats for his guests at the inaugural gala—a slight that an old-school politician like O'Neill would never entirely forget or forgive.[129]

Carter's legislative strategy in many ways reflected his arguably accurate reading of the new political realities of the post-Watergate, post-Vietnam era. Johnson's style looked tawdry to a public increasingly wary of "smoke-filled rooms" and insistent that presidents speak directly to them on major issues. Public faith in government and a willingness to follow political leaders were at a nadir after Watergate and Vietnam, and Congress itself had changed dramatically in the interim. Johnson was able to rely heavily on congressional leaders to carry his banner, because the congressional hierarchy was still strong enough to keep party members in line. But that hierarchy had all but dissolved by the time Carter was elected in 1976, and, to succeed, he had to construct temporary coalitions among as many members as possible. Carter thus tended to present his case to the public first, believing that his primary task was to persuade citizens to adopt his view of an issue and thereby create a political climate favorable to congressional action.

But Carter may have erred too much on the side of first gaining the public's support. Congressional leaders often were not consulted in advance of Carter's statements, and legislative liaison tended toward the exchange of information rather than the still-critical building of legislative coalitions of support.[130] But so fluid had American politics become by the late 1970s that one political scientist likened it to building coalitions out of sand—hard to work with and never quite permanent.[131] Given these realities, Carter's strategy of going directly to the public on important issues is understandable.

Ronald Reagan used Carter's general strategy to better effect, although a great deal of credit also went to an experienced and well-organized legislative liaison staff laden with former Nixon and Ford officials. House Speaker O'Neill called Reagan's victory on the 1981 budget package "the greatest selling job I've ever seen." Reagan's success came about through a mixture of dramatic public appeals by the president, the work of administration officials sent to generate support in key Democratic constituencies, and a good deal of old-fashioned bargaining.[132] Jones has likened Reagan's lobbying style to that of Franklin Roosevelt, with emphasis placed on communicating views and ideals to the public and generating pressure on Congress to go along.[133]

Even for Reagan, however, the strategy had its limits. Appeals to the public can work only so often and only on particularly dramatic issues. Going public tends to have diminishing returns the longer and more frequently a president relies on that strategy, which Reagan discovered during his second term in office. Reagan's immediate successors, regardless of political party, were to discover the difficulty of relying on the public route without having Reagan's unique persona. Neither George Bush nor Bill Clinton—very different personalities facing different legislative terrain—could translate their personal appeals into significant legislative victories. For Bush, the stalemate with a Democrat-controlled Congress was both partisan and ideological, and even his high public approval rating after the Persian Gulf War did not produce action from Congress.[134] For Clinton, the legislative victories of his first two years in office depended almost entirely on remarkably strong party support, with the occasional coalition with Republicans on crime and trade matters. But such an "inside" strategy failed Clinton miserably on health care, largely because his party was fragmented badly on the issue and because Republicans were united in their opposition to Clinton's agenda. After the 1994 midterm election Clinton's legislative posture shifted toward a more centrist strategy, in which he portrayed himself as a moderate bulwark against right-wing Republican extremism. He co-opted a number of Republican positions—supporting welfare reform, balancing the federal budget—but cast them as consistent with "new" Democratic Party principles. Clinton's ability to capture the rhetorical high ground in his political skirmishes with congressional Republicans would serve as the foundation of his legislative strategy for the remainder of his presidency, but his was a defensive posture in an atmosphere marked by tremendous partisan and even personal rancor.

The increased party polarization in Congress also influenced George W. Bush's legislative effectiveness to a far greater degree than did his particular lobbying strategy. For the most part, prior to the 9/11 terrorist attacks Bush's congressional relations can best be characterized as what Charles O. Jones calls "competitive partisanship," in which leaders of both parties moved aggressively to unite their followers in support of their party objectives.[135] For Bush this meant focusing his legislative agenda on a few key issues, including tax cuts, education standards, Social Security and Medicare reform, and federal support for faith-based charities. His lobbying strategy generally involved using campaign-style techniques that focused on mobilizing public support for his agenda. This included emphasizing policy-related symbols in public comments rather than policy details, using public meetings with hand-picked groups to generate favorable publicity, and making sure that all administrative spokespersons stayed "on message." But Bush generally avoided taking a personal role in negotiating legislative details with members of Congress until it became necessary to close a deal.[136] This strategy proved highly successful in pushing a ten-year, $1.35 trillion tax cut through Congress, but less effective on more controversial issues lacking widespread congressional support, such as Medicare reform or aid to faith-based charities. On other issues, such as education reform and agricultural subsidies, Bush was forced to work with leading Democrats to enact his policies.

After 9/11 Bush's congressional orientation changed, and he moved aggressively to capitalize on his commander-in-chief status to dominate the legislative agenda. For their part, congressional Democrats were more willing to work with Bush and congressional Republicans in bipartisan negotiations on terrorist-related policies, including airport security, creation of the Homeland Security Department, and bioterrorist defense. But on other matters, competitive partisanship based on unified parties continued to rule the day. Bush attempted to pressure Democrats by publicly linking as many of his objectives as possible to the war on terror, including his energy policy, trade promotion authority, and economic stimulus proposals, but with only partial success.[137] Indeed, some critics argue that Bush's strategy further divided the two parties.[138] True or not, within a year of the terrorist attacks, the bipartisan consensus on Bush's foreign policy began eroding, as reflected in the divided party vote on the October 2002 resolution authorizing Bush to go to war in Iraq.[139] Although he successfully positioned himself to win reelection in 2004, and the election results slightly strengthened the Republicans' margin of control in both congressional chambers, they did not appreciably increase Bush's bargaining leverage in the highly polarized environment.[140] He continued to find his greatest congressional support on war-related measures, such as renewal of the USA Patriot Act in 2005. But Democratic opposition stymied progress on most of his domestic priorities, such as Social Security and Medicare reform. After the Democratic takeover of Congress in the 2006 elections, Bush hinted that he would return to a more bipartisan legislative approach for the remaining two years of his presidency. At the same time, however, he appeared unwilling to reverse course in Iraq, setting up a potential showdown with the Democrat-controlled Congress.

Styles of Presidential Lobbying

There is no single best way for presidents to lobby Congress, but certain means—such as favors, consultation, and personal phone calls—are always useful. Each president's particular style and way of organizing lobbying activities reflect personal skills, interests, and views about the relationship among the branches of government. Presidents who see themselves as partners with Congress, such as Johnson, operate far differently than those like Nixon, who see the presidency as independent of and generally in competition with the legislature.[141] Each style has its strengths, but neither guarantees success. After all, pushing a legislative agenda also means having to deal with a Congress that sees itself as the energetic center of U.S. government.

Still, even "failed" presidents enjoy a modicum of success in Congress, if success is measured by the percentage of bills supported by the president that Congress passes into law.[142] By some measures, Carter, despite his apparent weaknesses, enjoyed overall success in Congress, while Reagan, for all his mass popularity and rhetorical skills, on average fared much worse. Clinton's generally low public support during his first two years in office also masked a highly productive legislative record. The reason for this disparity may simply be that Carter and Clinton each enjoyed generally supportive Democratic majorities in Congress, while Reagan encountered at least one house dominated by his political foes. Reagan's successes came not on the quantity of bills supported in Congress, but on their scope and importance. *(See "Presidential Support in Congress, 1953–2004," p. 1888, in Reference Materials, Vol. II.)*

Also noteworthy is the inverse relationship over time between the improvement in any administration's lobbying and organizational skills and congressional support for that same administration. In other words, virtually all presidents have found it more difficult to gain congressional approval for major proposals late in their terms in office, even after years of experience, than when they were new on the job. It is tempting to explain this paradox by comparing presidential success in Congress with the president's popularity. Both scores drop over time, suggesting that broad presidential popularity affects legislative success. Members of Congress, George Edwards points out, "respond to the president's current popularity among their supporters," and thus are reluctant to oppose a popular president.[143] However, they are less reluctant to vote against a president whose public support has weakened, particularly if the president is from the opposing party and the president's term in office is nearing its end. However, efforts to tie presidents' legislative success to their approval ratings have found a marginal relationship at best.[144] It may be that a president's legislative success decreases through time because most of the major issues on which there is broad political support are passed early in the president's term; as time goes on, the legislative agenda is increasingly populated by more controversial issues that are inherently more difficult to pass. If so, it reinforces the fact that systemic factors, rather than the behavior of individual presidents, largely determine their legislative effectiveness.

Despite the tendency of the mass media to focus on personalities, whether a president succeeds or fails probably has less to do with personal attributes or styles than with the political conditions at the time. Presidents certainly can influence political conditions, but they cannot control them. Presidents must play the political cards dealt them by the broader political system and by the world at large. Successful presidents may be those who had strengths or values that meshed well with the tenor of the times or with current congressional majorities. Or they may simply have been lucky.

Public Appeals

As suggested earlier, every president has had on occasion to go directly to the people to exert pressure on a recalcitrant

Congress. Be it through speeches to the nation on television, leaks of information to favored journalists, or orchestrated public demonstrations of support, presidents find some way to recruit public opinion in their fights with Congress when they believe conditions and issues warrant it. *(See Table 12-6.)*

Going directly to the people has become easier, and thus more desirable, because modern telecommunications technology, particularly television, has enabled presidents to speak their minds with less worry that intermediaries will garble their messages. The rise of television as the primary means by which most Americans receive their news was a primary factor in the emergence of the contemporary presidency and its power to influence the national agenda. Nonetheless, going directly to the people has its risks, for success hinges largely on the issue in question, a president's own rhetorical skills, the ability of the president's opponents to utilize the same communication tools, and the mood of the public at the moment. None of these factors is predictable. *(See also Chapter 20, Public Support and Opinion, and "The Public Presidency," p. 1378, in Chapter 29, Vol. II.)*

Early Use of Public Appeals

Presidents before the twentieth century neither had the technologies to speak directly to the people nor did they generally conceive of their roles in exactly the same manner as do their contemporary counterparts. The Founders' fear of demagogues, which fed their efforts to insulate the selection of the president from the mass public, influenced the earliest presidents profoundly. Congress, not the president, was meant to represent the people, and Congress generally considered it illegitimate and intrusive for a president to try to pressure its members on legislation.

From the earliest days of the presidency, however, some presidents did attempt to influence public opinion through indirect, often subtle means. Thomas Jefferson relied heavily on his popular dinner parties to influence key legislators, newspaper reporters, and other important political figures. But it was Andrew Jackson among earlier presidents who began the practice of appealing to the common people for support. Jackson, after all, had entered the office as an outsider—he was the first president not to come from one of the original thirteen colonies—and was a foe of the established ways of doing business. He presaged the contemporary presidency by artfully arranging for official documents to be leaked to supportive newspapers, used friendly journalists to convey his views and desires, and relied on his party organization to stir up public support and put pressure on Congress. "King Andrew," as his enemies came to call him, reaped a great deal of criticism for his unorthodox practices, and most pre–Civil War presidents did not follow his pattern. None had Jackson's popularity or his activist philosophy about the role of the presidency.

Abraham Lincoln was usually on the defensive with Congress over his war policies, but he overcame its opposition by winning public support through the newspapers. Lincoln wrote numerous letters and opinion columns, which received favorable coverage from friendly publishers such as Horace Greeley. Lincoln generated other supportive stories through leaks to reporters. It also was said that Lincoln grew his beard after a supporter remarked that his bare face (and lack of chin) did not look "presidential" enough, and inexpensive lithographs (a new technology) of the newly bearded commander in chief soon graced many a Union household.

Theodore Roosevelt thrived on publicity and made himself easily available to favorite reporters. His love of the press was reciprocated, for the flamboyant and erudite Roosevelt made for good copy.[145] Roosevelt is credited with creating the official White House press release, which he often issued on Sundays—traditionally the slowest news day—to give newspapers something to print the next day. He also devised off-the-record "background" press briefings, which he frequently used to float "trial balloons" as one way to assess public and congressional opinion on issues.

Woodrow Wilson outdid Roosevelt in going directly to the public by resuming the practice of delivering the State of the Union address personally and by instituting regular and formal press conferences. He was most effective, however, in making direct appeals to the public usually through the newspapers or speeches before Congress. The notable exception was his grueling nationwide tour in 1919 to generate support for the Treaty of Versailles, an effort that ultimately ruined his health. Wilson's efforts to go to the people went for naught, for the Senate failed to ratify the treaty.

Franklin Roosevelt and Radio

Although Theodore Roosevelt and Wilson were masters at generating favorable public opinion through the press, they lacked easy access to technology that could enable them to go directly into every citizen's home. But Franklin Roosevelt entered the White House just as radio entered its heyday, and the ebullient New Yorker made superb use of the medium. His public speeches, twenty-seven "fireside" radio chats, hundreds of formal press conferences, countless informal background sessions with selected reporters, and shrewd use of the newsreels, all constructed a public persona that millions of Americans would recall fondly for decades. The response to Roosevelt's first inaugural address, in which he averred that "the only thing we have to fear is fear itself," was so great that humorist Will Rogers wrote: "If he burned down the Capitol, we would cheer and say, 'Well, we at least got a fire started somehow.'" [146]

Roosevelt used radio directly to educate and persuade, and there was no greater example than his first "fireside chat" to the nation, which centered on the banking crisis that

TABLE 12-6   **Television Addresses by Presidents, 1961–2007**

President	Year	Topic
Kennedy	1961	Urgent national needs; Berlin Wall
	1962	Racial unrest; quarantine of Cuba
	1963	Civil rights bill; test ban treaty
L. Johnson	1963	Kennedy assassination
	1965	Voting rights bill
	1968	Bombing halt/withdrawal from election
Nixon	1969	National unity in Vietnam; Vietnam peace proposals; Vietnam troop reductions
	1970	Vietnam; Cambodia incursion (2); peace in Indochina
	1971	Withdrawal of troops; economic policy
	1972	Report of trip to People's Republic of China
	1973	Watergate; national energy policy
	1974	White House tapes; resignation
Ford	1974	Post–Nixon resignation speech; inflation
	1975	State of the world
Carter	1977	Energy crisis; energy policy
	1979	Energy crisis; national morale; Soviet troops in Cuba; military spending
	1980	Failure of Iran rescue mission; anti-inflation
	1981	Farewell speech
Reagan	1981	Economic policies and proposals (4)
	1982	Federal budget; Middle East; Lebanon; arms control
	1983	Strategic Defense Initiative and Central America; Grenada; Lebanon
	1985	Tax reform; U.S.-Soviet summit (Geneva)
	1986	Military spending; aid to contras (2); U.S.-Soviet summit (Iceland); Iran arms sales
	1987	Iran arms sales; economic summit; Iran-contra affair; Bork nomination; U.S.-Soviet summit (Washington)
	1988	Contra aid
	1989	Farewell address
G. Bush	1989	Drug war; invasion of Panama
	1990	Deployment of forces to Persian Gulf; budget agreement
	1991	Commencement of attack on Iraq; cease-fire announcement
	1992	Deployment of relief forces to Somalia
Clinton	1993	Economic plan; air raid on Iraq
	1994	Situation in Somalia; "middle class bill of rights"
	1995	U.S. peacekeeping mission in Bosnia
	1998	Sexual affair with White House intern
	2001	Farewell address
G. W. Bush	2001	Stem cell research; September 11 attacks; response to terrorism; start of Afghan military campaign; homeland security
	2002	proposed Department of Homeland Security; anniversary of terrorist attacks; Iraq update
	2003	Loss of space shuttle; Iraq update; start of Iraq war; end of combat operations; progress in war on terror; Hussein captured
	2004	Health care costs
	2005	Iraq elections; war on terror; Justice Roberts nomination; Hurricane Katrina recovery
	2007	Update on Iraq, war on terror

SOURCES: *Congressional Quarterly Almanac,* various issues; *CQ Weekly,* various issues; John Woolley and Gerhard Peters, The American Presidency Project (online) (www.presidency.ucsb.edu/ws/), accessed February 2, 2007.

NOTE: Table does not include State of the Union and inaugural addresses, which also are televised; it only includes those addresses that are not part of a ceremonial occasion.

had worsened on the eve of his inauguration. Roosevelt explained how the banking system worked and why it was important that people take their money out of their mattresses and put it back into their savings accounts. They did, and Roosevelt was credited with ending the crisis. As Arthur M. Schlesinger Jr. wrote, the fireside chats "conveyed Roosevelt's conception of himself as a man at ease in his own house talking frankly and intimately to neighbors as they sat in their living rooms." [147]

But the radio speeches and chats were intended for more than soothing the public: they were meant to move Congress into action on Roosevelt's agenda. According to political scientist Wilfred E. Binkley, Roosevelt "had only to glance toward a microphone or suggest that he might go on the air again and a whole congressional delegation would surrender. They had no relish for the flood of mail and telegrams they knew would swamp them after another fireside chat to the nation." [148] Roosevelt, particularly after the first year, did not always win when he went to the airwaves, but those in opposition never took for granted his power to move the public.

The Television Presidency

Roosevelt proved successful with radio in no small part because the medium forces listeners to use their imaginations to visualize both the speaker and the topic under discussion. He had a powerful voice, which offered to the listener an image of strength and determination. The radio image of Roosevelt belied the physical reality: stricken with polio at the age of thirty-nine, Roosevelt could not walk. Americans may have known of Roosevelt's disability in the abstract—it certainly was no secret—but they were not reminded of it continually because, thanks to a tacit agreement with the press, he rarely was photographed head to toe. But if Roosevelt had run for the presidency in the age of television—a visual medium—he would not have been able to control his public image so masterfully. Whether he could have been elected in the first place, since so many people equate physical strength with strong "leadership"—much less rally a nation through a depression and a war—is one of the tantalizing "what ifs" of history.

The contemporary presidency in many ways lives and sometimes dies by television. Eisenhower was the first president to permit press conferences to be filmed for television, but it was Kennedy, arguably the first president of the television age, who allowed *live* telecasts of his press conferences. The public for the first time watched the press question a president live, with no chance for the White House to edit the president's comments. Kennedy's ease with television, his intellect, and his humor made television a potent tool for communicating with the American people. His persuasive television appearance was not enough, however, to ensure congressional approval of his legislative programs.

Lyndon Johnson, superb as he was in the art of personal lobbying, proved uneasy with television, although his live address urging the passage of the 1965 Voting Rights Act did move the nation and Congress. Johnson was probably the first president to discover television's double-edged sword as Americans absorbed televised images of urban riots and antiwar demonstrations, and for the first time witnessed the horrors of war by watching the evening news. Frequently, these televised images appeared to contradict Johnson's assertions about the pace of social progress at home and the success of the war in Indochina, contradictions that shook the nation's confidence in its government. Johnson was particularly wounded by public reaction to the massive North Vietnamese Tet offensive in early 1968, a coordinated assault on South Vietnamese cities that undercut his declarations that the war was winding down. For the North Vietnamese the attack, although a military disaster, was a psychological victory. Johnson's public support plummeted, and he decided not to run for reelection. Johnson's experience was but an early example of how television-magnified events can influence a president's agenda and popularity.

Richard Nixon, who felt that the official press had been hostile to his candidacy in 1960 and who saw how Johnson had fared with the media, used television directly and extensively to re-tailor his image with the public. Distrustful of the Washington press corps, which often proved unwilling to rally around the administration's Vietnam policy, the president spoke directly to the American people far more often than had his predecessors. In his November 1969 address to the nation on Vietnam, for example, Nixon asserted that a "silent majority" of citizens supported his actions despite what members of the press wrote.[149] Nixon also held few Washington press conferences, which he felt only offered opportunities for his critics to attack him, and instead began to hold press conferences in parts of the country where journalists might be more deferential to his office.

Nixon used Vice President Spiro Agnew to make vigorous attacks on the news media, a tactic that produced one of the most memorable phrases in American political lore. In a September 1970 speech in San Diego, Agnew railed that the Washington press corps was filled with "nattering nabobs of negativism. They have formed their own 4-H Club—the 'hopeless, hysterical hypochondriacs of history.' " [150] The tactic was clear: discredit the news media and connect the president more directly to the American people.

Nixon also used television successfully to pressure Congress in selected instances, such as his televised veto of a 1970 appropriations bill. Thousands of supportive telegrams subsequently poured into both the White House and Capitol Hill, giving the impression of massive popular support for Nixon's position. Whether this reaction was spontaneous or orchestrated by Nixon's supporters was irrelevant to many members of the House, which upheld the veto.

As with Johnson, however, television played a major part in Nixon's downfall. The nation watched in fascination as the daily drama of the 1973 Senate Watergate hearings played out on television. Nixon's own performances during televised press conferences, and even in speeches to the nation, seemed to many viewers to be the picture of a president trying to deceive the public. After evidence pointing to Nixon's complicity in the Watergate cover-up emerged, the president resigned in disgrace on August 9, 1974.

His successor, Gerald Ford, worked to diminish the distrust between the White House and the media that had built up during the Nixon years. Where Nixon basked in the formal trappings of the office, Ford worked to convey a more down-to-earth image; for example, he allowed himself to be photographed making his own breakfast. Where Nixon rarely held press

To reverse the mutual distrust between the White House and the media built up during the Nixon administration, Ford worked to convey a simpler image to the press. Here he allows photographers to take pictures as he makes his breakfast.

conferences, Ford held many—and earned high praise from the media for his openness and honesty. Ford did not escape unscathed, however: his every stumble and slip were grist for the humor mill—an irony, no doubt, for a former college football star. In trying to humanize the office, Ford risked being seen as "unpresidential," an image that all presidents try to avoid.

Jimmy Carter, acting on his populist background and belief that Americans had tired of the "imperial presidency," early on cultivated an image as an outsider by holding televised "town meetings" to which citizens called in questions. Carter also tried his own televised version of Roosevelt's fireside chats; wearing a cardigan sweater, he spoke to the public as he sat before a fire. But what had worked for Roosevelt in the days of the depression and radio did not work for Carter on television in the post-Watergate era. Too many Americans regarded Carter's approach as superficial symbolism, and his efforts to use television to stir the public generally failed. His talk to the nation on the energy crisis, which he called "the moral equivalent of war," evoked no widespread support and even spawned jokes that the acronym for "moral equivalent of war" was MEOW.

But Carter had some successes as well, most notably the televised signing of the 1979 Camp David peace accords, a moment of high drama when Egyptian president Anwar Sadat signed a peace treaty with Israeli prime minister

Menachem Begin. Carter, who had been personally instrumental in bringing these longtime adversaries together, used the signing to rally congressional support for significant American aid to both Israel and Egypt. Generally, however, Carter proved more a victim than a manipulator of television, particularly after Iranian revolutionaries seized and held fifty-three American hostages for more than a year. Each night Americans witnessed on their television sets the humiliation of the hostage situation—a long "crisis" that actually spawned the popular daily ABC news show *Nightline*. Carter's inability to free the hostages contributed to his electoral loss to Ronald Reagan in 1980.

Reagan, who had been a movie and television actor before becoming governor of California, quickly proved a powerful contrast to Carter in his ability to use the media to his political advantage. As radio had been to Franklin Roosevelt, television was to Reagan, and the president relied heavily on his rhetorical talents to whip up support for his dramatic budget and tax policy victories in 1981. Of particular potency was Reagan's May 1981 appeal to a joint session of Congress for support on his budget package, his first public appearance after he was badly wounded in a March 1981 assassination attempt. So powerful was the moment, and so massive the outpouring of public support for the president, that the Democrat-dominated House passed a resolution supporting the outlines of Reagan's budget package a few days later. Reagan also used television to establish intimacy with the American people. Few could resist the emotional pull of his 1984 speech on the cliffs overlooking France's Omaha Beach on the fortieth anniversary of the Normandy invasion, or of his eulogy for the astronauts who died in the 1986 space shuttle *Challenger* disaster.[151]

Reagan's extensive use of mass media to appeal directly to the public even revived the use of a more traditional vehicle—radio. His administration, as if to hearken back to Franklin Roosevelt's fireside chats, began the practice of recording weekly five-minute presidential radio addresses, to be aired each Saturday morning. Democrats subsequently invoked federal rules on political use of the airwaves and got the right to air their own five-minute radio segments. This pattern of weekly presidential radio addresses and opposition "rebuttals" has endured to this day. Relatively few Americans may actually hear the addresses on the radio, but their contents are usually covered in evening television news reports, so the addresses remain part of an overall presidential communications strategy.

But even for Reagan mass media appeals had a double-edged effect. Public responsiveness to media appeals almost inevitably wanes the more frequently a president relies on them, as Reagan discovered during his second term. Startling revelations about secret arms sales to the Iranian government and their possibly illegal use to fund the supply of arms to American-backed rebels fighting the government of Nicaragua eroded public confidence in Reagan's leadership. Televised congressional hearings on the affair raised broad public concern about the president's overall command of his office. By 1988, when the three major networks refused to carry another appeal for aid for the Nicaraguan rebels because it "was not news," it was apparent that the skills so integral to Reagan's early successes no longer were potent enough to prevail.

Even with Reagan's later woes, his immediate successors would discover painfully that Reagan had a rare gift for using the mass media to connect to the public. They also discovered, as Reagan did, that popular approval does not always translate into better prospects for legislative success. As Charles O. Jones argues, popularity is "sometimes a recognition or reward for an action deemed successful or an acknowledgment that things are going well." [152] Even though George Bush enjoyed a stunningly high level of popularity at the end of the Persian Gulf War, he nonetheless was a one-term president. Bush's inability to capitalize on his popularity in part grew out of his apparent discomfort with the demands of the media presidency, an institution that favors high visibility, adeptness at verbal communication, and a nuanced understanding of the symbolic power of the office. The national economic recession and broad public perception that the nation was heading in the wrong direction also contributed to his defeat in the 1992 election, but his presidential style certainly played a role.

But recent presidents' ineffectiveness at "going public" as a means of pressuring Congress to support their legislative priorities reflects more than simply a deficient media style or lack of rhetorical skills; it points to the limits of the strategy itself, particularly in the post-Reagan era. Despite a full-fledged media campaign spearheaded by his own formidable communications skills, Bill Clinton could not translate diffuse public support for health care reform into solid congressional support of his health security legislative proposal. Similarly, George W. Bush failed to mobilize enough public support to pressure Congress into backing his plan to reform Social Security. These cases reveal that presidents' "communications wars" often fail because they stimulate opposing groups to engage in their own media strategies designed to block the presidents' initiatives. Because of the mainstream press' desire for "balanced" coverage, and its tendency to focus on disagreement and controversy, the concerns raised by these opposition groups get extensive media coverage, often leading to a drop in popular support for presidential initiatives.[153] In addition, the Internet provides a medium for the president's opponents to air their views.

This is not to say that the president's voice is indistinguishable from that of any other political actor. George W. Bush's public speeches in the days and weeks after 9/11 demonstrate that, under certain conditions, the president of the United States still has an unparalleled capacity to dominate the national airwaves. Beginning with his nationwide address on the evening of the attacks through his widely publicized tour of the World Trade Center ruins—during which he memorably proclaimed to the gathered first responders who complained they couldn't hear, "I can hear you. The rest of the world hears you. And the people who knocked these buildings down will hear all of us soon"—to his address to a joint session of Congress on September 20, Bush dominated the nation's airwaves. His approval rating during this period shot to 90 percent, the highest ever recorded. Bush capitalized on this support to push several initiatives through Congress, including an open-ended declaration of war on terror and a $40 billion emergency spending bill to fund that war. In the next several weeks Congress passed a $7 billion airline bailout bill and the controversial USA Patriot Act that gave law enforcement agencies more power to prevent further attacks.

Even though congressional support for Bush's policies, particularly those not directly related to national security issues, began to erode soon afterwards, in October 2002 he was still able to use public backing for the war on terror to pressure Congress to pass a resolution authorizing him to invade Iraq. Terrorism also played a significant role in the Republican takeover of Congress in the 2002 midterm elections, and in Bush's reelection in 2004. But these electoral campaigns, although ending successfully for Bush and the Republicans, also revealed the hardening of the partisan fissures in Congress, particularly as 9/11 receded in the public's memory.

As Bush's approval ratings underwent a seemingly inexorable decline during the five years after the terrorist attacks, so too did his ability to monopolize the public airwaves. Indeed, the growing criticisms of Bush's policies vividly demonstrated the increasingly fragmented and partisan sources of information and political coverage in the Internet age, in which a growing number of people receive their news from a computer terminal. While John Kennedy could command almost universal public attention because there were few alternatives to the three major television networks, contemporary presidents no longer have access to a media outlet commanding that type of viewership. Instead, they must compete for attention not just on the hundreds of cable and satellite television channels and talk radio shows, but within the Internet-based "blogosphere" as well. Even the "mainstream" media has fractured into smaller outlets, each tailored to attract a particular segment of its audience. At its worst, this produces an echo-chamber effect where people tune into the media service that produces the message they find most compatible with their own ideological views. For many citizens, the president's voice is heard only through this increasingly partisan-driven and controversy-oriented filter.

Barring a widely perceived crisis, then, the increasingly fragmented media environment means that no one person, not even the president, may be able to "monopolize" the public space—indeed, it is no longer clear that there is a single space to monopolize. Instead, presidents seeking to build

After Democrats took control of both houses of Congress in the November, 2006, mid-term elections, Republican president George W. Bush held a press conference to reflect on the outcome for his party. He said, "If you look at race by race it was close. The cumulative effect, however, was not too close. It was a thumpin."

political coalitions and mobilize support for their legislative initiatives are forced to work even harder to individually tailor their appeals to smaller segments of the polity—and to make those appeals heard in an increasingly cacophonous and partisan atmosphere.

The presidency today may still be a "bully pulpit," but it no longer commands the heights it once did.

NOTES

1. Richard E. Neustadt, *Presidential Power and the Modern Presidents* (New York: The Free Press, 1990), 29.

2. See Charles O. Jones, *The Presidency in a Separated System,* 2d ed. (Washington, D.C.: Brookings, 2005); and David Mayhew, *Divided We Govern: Party Control, Lawmaking, and Investigations, 1946–1990* (New Haven: Yale University Press, 1991).

3. Louis Fisher, *The President and Congress* (New York: Free Press, 1972), 18–21. See also A. E. Howard, ed., *The United States Constitution: Roots, Rights, and Responsibilities* (Washington, D.C.: Smithsonian Institution Press, 1992).

4. Thomas Jefferson, "Notes on Virginia," in *The Life and Selected Writings of Thomas Jefferson,* ed. Adrienne Koch and William Peden (New York: Random House, Modern Library, 1944), 237.

5. *Guide to Congress,* 4th ed. (Washington, D.C.: Congressional Quarterly, 1991), 552.

6. John Adams, "The State Constitutions as Analogy and Precedent," in *The United States Constitution: Roots, Rights, and Responsibilities,* ed. A. E. Howard (Washington, D.C.: Smithsonian Institution Press, 1992), 3–22.

7. James Sundquist, *Constitutional Reform and Effective Government* (Washington, D.C.: Brookings, 1986), 30.

8. Ibid., 30–31.

9. The exemption of constitutional amendments from the veto was established by the Supreme Court in *Hollingsworth v. Virginia,* 3 Dall. 378 (1798).

10. Alexander Hamilton, James Madison, and John Jay, *The Federalist Papers,* ed. Clinton Rossiter (New York: New American Library, 1961), 443.

11. Ibid., 322.

12. Ibid., 444.

13. The Constitution gives presidents the authority to approve or veto legislation within ten days after a bill is *presented* to the White House, as opposed to after it is *passed* by Congress. Bills passed by Congress cannot be presented to the president until they have been signed by the Speaker of the House and the president of the Senate (that is, the vice president, although this function is performed normally by the president pro tempore). Thus an indefinite gap can occur between passage and presentation. At times, Congress has delayed presentation of bills because the president has been out of the country. Presidents also have maneuvered to delay presentation of bills to create opportunities for pocket vetoes. In 1970, Richard Nixon had Vice President Spiro Agnew exercise his authority to sign legislation, which Agnew then delayed doing so that several bills would not be presented to Nixon until just a few days before adjournment. On this, see

Eric Redman, *The Dance of Legislation* (New York: Touchstone Books, 1973).

14. As upheld by the Supreme Court in *Missouri Pacific Railway Co. v. United States,* 248 U.S. 277 (1919).

15. Clinton Rossiter, *The American Presidency,* 2d ed. (New York: Harcourt, Brace, 1960), 91.

16. See James Bryce, *The American Commonwealth,* vol. 1, 2d ed. (New York: Macmillan, 1911), 64. The Supreme Court in 1926 ruled that the power to remove political appointees resided with the president alone. See *Myers v. United States,* 272 U.S. 52 (1926).

17. Louis Fisher, *Presidential Spending Power* (Princeton: Princeton University Press, 1975), 25.

18. Neustadt, *Presidential Power,* 71.

19. Jones, *Presidency in a Separated System,* 270–271.

20. See Neil MacNeil, *Forge of Democracy: The House of Representatives* (New York: David McKay, 1963), 244–245.

21. Jimmy Carter, *Keeping Faith: The Memoirs of a President* (New York: Bantam Books, 1982), 101.

22. *Guide to Congress,* 554.

23. Robert Pear, "Court Is Asked to Define Power of the Pocket Veto," *New York Times,* November 9, 1986, E1.

24. Bryce, *American Commonwealth,* 59.

25. Charles M. Cameron, *Veto Bargaining Presidents and the Politics of Negative Power* (New York: Cambridge University Press, 2000), 8–9.

26. George C. Edwards III, *Presidential Influence in Congress* (San Francisco: Freeman, 1980), 24.

27. *CQ Almanac, 1992* (Washington, D.C.: Congressional Quarterly, 1993), 6.

28. Tom Raum, "Bush's Dusty Veto Pen May Soon Get Busy," *washingtonpost.com,* January 6, 2007 *(www.washingtonpost.com/wp-dyn/content/article/2007/01/06/AR2007010600507.html),* accessed January 6, 2007.

29. Cameron, *Veto Bargaining Presidents,* 152–177.

30. Victoria Alldred, "Versatility with the Veto," *CQ Weekly,* January 20, 2001, 175.

31. Ibid., 175. See also Elizabeth Drew, *Showdown: The Struggle between the Gingrich Congress and the Clinton White House* (New York: Simon and Schuster, 1996).

32. See, for example, Redman, *Dance of Legislation,* 243.

33. Mitchel A. Sollenberger, "The Presidential Veto and Congressional Procedure" CRS Report for Congress, February 27, 2004 *(www.rules.house.gov/archives/RS21750.pdf),* accessed December 17, 2006.

34. *Pocket Veto Case,* 279 U.S. 644 (1929).

35. Arthur M. Schlesinger Jr., *The Imperial Presidency* (New York: Popular Library, 1974), 237.

36. *Wright v. United States,* 302 U.S. 583 (1938).

37. See Redman, *Dance of Legislation,* 275–277.

38. *Kennedy v. Sampson,* 511 F. 2d 430 (D.C. Cir. 1974).

39. *Kennedy v. Jones,* Civil Action no. 74–194 (D.D.C.).

40. Pear, "Power of the Pocket Veto," 4.

41. *Barnes v. Carmen,* 582 F. Supp. 163 (D.D.C. 1984); *Barnes v. Kline,* 759 F. 2d 21 (D.C. Cir. 1985). The lone dissenter was Judge Robert Bork, who argued that members of Congress had no right to sue the president in the first place and that the court had no jurisdiction over such issues. Lawyers for Congress argued that the courts have every right to adjudicate disputes between Congress and the executive.

42. *Burke v. Barnes,* 479 U.S. 361 (1987).

43. *CQ Almanac, 1990* (Washington, D.C.: Congressional Quarterly, 1991), 21–22.

44. *CQ Almanac, 1991* (Washington, D.C.: Congressional Quarterly, 1992), 235.

45. See Louis Fisher, *The Politics of Shared Power,* 3d ed. (Washington, D.C.: CQ Press, 1993), 199.

46. Ibid., 198.

47. Andrew Taylor, "Congress Hands President a Budgetary Scalpel," *Congressional Quarterly Weekly Report,* March 30, 1996, 864–867.

48. Allred, "Versatility with the Veto," 177.

49. Edwards, *Presidential Influence in Congress,* 20.

50. Stuart Taylor Jr., "Court Rebuffs Reagan on Deferral of Spending Ordered by Congress," *New York Times,* January 21, 1987, A1.

51. Edwards, *Presidential Influence in Congress,* 21.

52. Fisher, *Politics of Shared Power,* 21.

53. *CQ Almanac, 1990,* 16.

54. Charles Savage, "Bush Challenges Hundreds of Laws," *Boston Globe,* April 30, 2006 *(www.boston.com/news/nation/articles/2006/04/30/bush_challenges_hundreds_of_laws/),* accessed December 19, 2006.

55. George Will, "Power to the President," *Newsweek,* October 12, 1981, 120.

56. Sundquist, *Constitutional Reform and Effective Government,* 209–215.

57. See Fisher, *Politics of Shared Power,* 198–202.

58. On problem definition and agenda setting, see Frank R. Baumgartner and Bryan D. Jones, *Agendas and Instability in American Politics* (Chicago: University of Chicago Press, 1993); and David A. Rochefort and Roger W. Cobb, eds., *The Politics of Problem Definition: Shaping the Policy Agenda* (Lawrence: University Press of Kansas, 1994).

59. E. E. Schattschneider, *The Semi-Sovereign People: A Realist's View of Democracy in America* (Hinsdale, Ill.: Dryden, 1960), 66.

60. See Arthur M. Schlesinger Jr., *The Age of Roosevelt: The Coming of the New Deal* (Boston: Houghton Mifflin, 1959).

61. Bruce Miroff, "Monopolizing the Public Space: The President as a Problem for Democratic Space," in *Rethinking the Presidency,* ed. Thomas E. Cronin (Boston: Little, Brown, 1982), 218–252.

62. For a cogent discussion of the constants of American governance and their effects on presidential leadership, see Bert A. Rockman, *The Leadership Question: The Presidency and the American System* (New York: Praeger, 1984), chap. 3. See also R. Kent Weaver and Bert A. Rockman, eds., *Do Institutions Matter? Government Capabilities in the United States and Abroad* (Washington, D.C.: Brookings, 1993); and Jones, *Presidency in a Separated System.*

63. Thomas P. O'Neill Jr., with William Novak, *Man of the House: The Life and Political Memoirs of Speaker Tip O'Neill* (New York: Random House, 1987).

64. Stories of battles for the president's ear are legion. See Hugh Heclo, *A Government of Strangers: Executive Politics in Washington* (Washington, D.C.: Brookings, 1977).

65. Craig Gordon, "His Social Aims," April 29, 2005, Newsday.com *(www.newsday.com/news/nationworld/nation/ny-usbush294237838apr29,0,3535649.story),* accessed January 8, 2007.

66. Neustadt, *Presidential Power,* 33; for a critique of the American system, see Sundquist, *Constitutional Reform and Effective Government.*

67. Rossiter, *American Presidency,* 140.

68. Quoted in Andrew Rudalevige, "The Executive Branch and the Legislative Process," in *The Executive Branch,* ed. Joel D. Aberach and Mark A. Peterson (New York: Oxford University Press, 2005), 420.

69. Bertram Gross, *The Legislative Struggle: A Study of Social Combat* (New York: McGraw-Hill, 1953), 101.

70. See James Sundquist, *The Decline and Resurgence of Congress* (Washington, D.C.: Brookings, 1981).

71. Hamilton, Madison, and Jay, *Federalist Papers*, 423.

72. See George M. Haynes, *The Senate of the United States: Its History and Practice*, vol. 1 (Boston: Houghton Mifflin, 1938), 62–63.

73. Quoted in George B. Galloway, *History of the House of Representatives* (New York: Thomas Crowell, 1969), 12.

74. Edward S. Corwin, *The President: Office and Powers, 1789–1957*, 4th ed. (New York: New York University Press, 1957), 21.

75. Ibid., 23.

76. Quoted in Galloway, *History of the House*, 245–246.

77. Corwin, *President: Office and Powers*, 28.

78. Theodore Roosevelt, *Theodore Roosevelt: An Autobiography* (New York: Macmillan, 1913), 282.

79. Sundquist, *Decline and Resurgence of Congress*, 130.

80. Corwin, *President: Office and Powers*, 269.

81. Special address to a joint session of Congress, June 23, 1913; cited in Corwin, *President: Office and Powers*, 269.

82. Rossiter, *American Presidency*, 140.

83. Schlesinger, *Age of Roosevelt*, 1.

84. Neustadt, *Presidential Power*, 6.

85. See, for example, Rockman, *Leadership Question*.

86. *Guide to Congress*, 3d ed. (Washington, D.C.: Congressional Quarterly, 1982), 761.

87. Quoted in Rowland Evans and Robert Novak, *Lyndon B. Johnson: The Exercise of Power* (New York: New American Library, 1966), 490.

88. See Gary Jacobson, "Party Polarization in National Politics: The Electoral Connection," in *Polarized Politics*, ed. Jon Bond and Richard Fleisher (Washington, DC: CQ Press, 2000), 13, 27; and Roger H. Davidson and Walter J. Oleszek, *Congress and Its Members*, 9th ed. (Washington, DC: CQ Press, 2004), 272–273.

89. Louis Koenig, *The Chief Executive*, 5th ed. (New York: Harcourt Brace Jovanovich, 1986), 145–146.

90. Jennifer Dlouhy and Keith Perine, "Deal Clears Way for Final Passage of Anti-Terrorism Legislation," *CQ Weekly*, October 20, 2001, 2475–2476.

91. See Paul E. Peterson, ed., *The President, Congress, and the Making of Foreign Policy* (Norman: University of Oklahoma Press, 1994).

92. Stephen Skowronek, *The Politics Presidents Make: Leadership from John Adams to George Bush* (Cambridge: Harvard University Press, 1994).

93. "Annual Messages of the Presidents: Major Themes of American History," in *The State of the Union Messages of the Presidents, 1790–1966*, ed. Fred L. Israel (New York: Chelsea House, 1966), xiv.

94. *Public Papers of Woodrow Wilson*, 1: 32; cited in Corwin, *President: Office and Powers*, 269.

95. Fisher, *Shared Power*, 18; see also H. Wayne Morgan, *From Hayes to McKinley* (Syracuse: Syracuse University Press, 1969), 274–319.

96. Charles O. Jones, "Presidential Negotiation with Congress," in *Both Ends of the Avenue: The Presidency, the Executive Branch, and Congress in the 1980s*, ed. Anthony King (Washington, D.C.: American Enterprise Institute, 1983), 99.

97. Ibid., 102.

98. Rudalevige, *Managing the President's Program*, 65.

99. Ibid., 71.

100. Fisher, *President and Congress*, 52–53.

101. Cronin, *State of the Presidency*, 118.

102. James S. Young, *The Washington Community* (New York: Columbia University Press, 1966), 167.

103. On the evolution of "central clearance," see Fisher, *Presidential Spending Power*.

104. Richard E. Neustadt, "The Presidency and Legislation: Planning the President's Program," *American Political Science Review* 49 (December 1955): 1015; see also Stephen J. Wayne, *The Legislative Presidency* (New York: Harper and Row, 1978), 19.

105. Paul C. Light, "Presidents as Domestic Policymakers," in *Rethinking the Presidency*, ed. Thomas E. Cronin (Boston: Little, Brown, 1982), 360. See also Paul C. Light, *The President's Agenda: Domestic Policy Choice from Kennedy to Clinton* (Baltimore: Johns Hopkins University Press, 1999); and Mark A. Peterson, *Legislating Together: The White House and Capitol Hill from Eisenhower to Reagan* (Cambridge: Harvard University Press, 1990).

106. Steven Waldman, *The Bill: How the Adventures of Clinton's National Service Bill Reveal What Is Corrupt, Comic, Cynical—and Noble—about Washington* (New York: Viking, 1995), 3.

107. See John W. Kingdon, *Agendas, Alternatives, and Public Policy* (Boston: Little, Brown, 1984). On the intellectual genesis of the 1986 tax reform act, see Jeffrey Birnbaum and Alan Murray, *Showdown at Gucci Gulch: Lawmakers, Lobbyists, and the Unlikely Triumph of Tax Reform* (New York: Random House, 1987).

108. See *History of America, 1932–1972* (Boston: Little, Brown, 1974), 95.

109. Julia Eilperin, "White House Outlines Global Warming Fight," *Washington Post*, September 21, 2006 *(www.washingtonpost.com/wp-dyn/content/article/2006/09/20/AR2006092001697_pf.html)*, (accessed January 8, 2007).

110. See Christopher J. Bosso, "Setting the Public Agenda: Mass Media and the Ethiopian Famine," in *Manipulating Public Opinion: Essays on Public Opinion as a Dependent Variable*, ed. Michael Margolis and Gary Mauser (Monterey, Calif.: Brooks-Cole, 1989), 153–174. On the interconnectedness of "foreign" and "domestic" issues, see James Rosenau, *Turbulence in World Politics: A Theory of Change and Continuity* (Princeton: Princeton University Press, 1990).

111. Rudalevige, *Managing the President's Program*, 81.

112. See Joel D. Aberbach and Bert A. Rockman, "Clashing Beliefs within the Executive Branch: The Nixon Administration Bureaucracy," *American Political Science Review* 70 (June 1975): 456–468.

113. Rudalevige, *Managing the President's Program*, 81.

1114. On the relative merits and pitfalls of incremental versus comprehensive policy change, see Charles O. Jones, *Introduction to the Study of Public Policy*, 3d ed. (Monterey, Calif.: Brooks-Cole, 1984), especially chaps. 2 and 6.

115. See, for example, Haynes Johnson and David S. Broder, *The System: The American Way of Politics at the Breaking Point* (Boston: Little, Brown, 1996).

116. Robert Reich, *Locked in the Cabinet* (New York: Knopf, 1997).

117. CBS News, "Rewriting the Science," July 30, 2006 *(www.cbsnews.com/stories/2006/03/17/60minutes/main1415985.shtml)*, accessed January 9, 2007.

118. See Woodward, *Agenda*.

119. Neustadt, *Presidential Power*.

120. The election of Lyndon Johnson to the House of Representatives in 1937 offers a good case in point about Roosevelt's potency as a campaign resource. See Robert Caro, *The Years of Lyndon Johnson: The Path to Power* (New York: Random House, 1981).

121. Matthew J. Dickinson, *Bitter Harvest: FDR, Presidential Power, and the Growth of the Presidential Branch* (New York: Cambridge University Press, 1997), 221.

122. Eric L. Davis, "Congressional Liaison: The People and the Institutions," in *Both Ends of the Avenue: The Presidency, the Executive Branch, and Congress in the 1980s,* ed. Anthony King (Washington, D.C.: American Enterprise Institute, 1983), 60.

123. Ibid., 61.

124. Ibid., 62.

125. On this notion of electoral "mandates," see Patricia H. Conley, *Presidential Mandates: How Elections Shape the National Agenda* (Chicago: University of Chicago Press, 2001).

126. Jones, "Presidential Negotiation with Congress," 106.

127. See Davis, "Congressional Liaison," 78–79.

128. Ibid., 65.

129. O'Neill, *Man of the House,* 310–311.

130. Davis, "Congressional Liaison," 65.

131. Anthony King, "The American Polity in the Late 1970s: Building Coalitions in the Sand," in *The New American Political System,* ed. Anthony King (Washington, D.C.: American Enterprise Institute, 1979), 371–395.

132. Roger H. Davidson and Walter J. Oleszek, *Congress and Its Members,* 5th ed. (Washington, D.C.: CQ Press, 1996), 308. For an insider's view of the 1981 tax and budget battles, see David Stockman, *The Triumph of Politics: The Inside Story of the Reagan Revolution* (New York: Harper and Row, 1986).

133. Jones, "Presidential Negotiation," 126.

134. See Richard Rose, *The Postmodern President: George H. W. Bush Meets the World,* 2d ed. (Chatham, N.J.: Chatham House, 1991).

135. Jones, *The Presidency in a Separated Party System,* 27.

136. George C. Edwards, *Governing by Campaigning* (New York: Pearson Longman, 2007), 155–166.

137. Congress granted Bush trade promotion authority and a modified energy bill, but he achieved only a stripped-down economic stimulus bill shorn of the tax cuts he sought.

138. See, for example, Gary C. Jacobson, *A Divider, Not a Uniter: George W. Bush and the American People* (New York: Pearson Education, 2007).

139. Joint Resolution 114 passed the Senate by a vote of 77–23, with 22 Democrats and 1 independent voting no, and the House of Representatives by a vote of 296–133, with 126 Democrats and 1 independent voting no.

140. The Republicans gained 4 seats in the Senate, for a 55–44 advantage, and 3 in the House, for a 232–202 margin.

141. Jones, "Presidential Negotiation," 123–125.

142. See Mayhew, *Divided We Govern*; and Jones, *Presidency in a Separated System.*

143. Edwards, *Presidential Influence in Congress,* 110.

144. Jones, *The Presidency in a Separated System,* 134.

145. See Edmund Morris, *The Rise of Theodore Roosevelt* (New York: Ballantine, 1979).

146. Quoted in William Manchester, *The Glory and the Dream: A Narrative History of America, 1932–1972* (Boston: Little, Brown, 1974), 91.

147. Schlesinger, *Age of Roosevelt,* 559.

148. Wilfred E. Binkley, *President and Congress* (New York: Vintage, 1962), 305.

149. Cited in William Safire, *Safire's Political Dictionary* (New York: Ballantine, 1978), 649.

150. Ibid., 444. The phrase "nattering nabobs" was penned by speechwriter William Safire, who later became a popular newspaper columnist and, alternately, a writer on the English language. The term *nabob* is Hindi in origin and has come to mean in English a self-important person.

151. On Reagan's use of television, see, among others, Mark Hertsgaard, *On Bended Knee: The Press and the Reagan Presidency* (New York: Farrar, Straus, Giroux, 1988); and Sam Donaldson, *Hold on, Mr. President!* (New York: Random House, 1987).

152. Jones, *Presidency in a Separated System,* 133.

153. See, for example, Lawrence R. Jacobs and Robert Y. Shapiro, *Politicians Don't Pander: Political Manipulation and the Loss of Democratic Responsiveness* (Chicago: University of Chicago Press, 2000).

SELECTED BIBLIOGRAPHY

Aberbach, Joel D. *Keeping a Watchful Eye: The Politics of Congressional Oversight.* Washington, D.C.: Brookings, 1990.

Bryce, James. *The American Commonwealth.* Vol. 1. 2d ed. New York: Macmillan, 1911.

Corwin, Edward S. *The President: Office and Powers, 1787–1984.* 5th rev. ed. New York: New York University Press, 1984.

Cronin, Thomas E., ed. *Rethinking the Presidency.* Boston: Little, Brown, 1982.

Dodd, Lawrence C., and Bruce I. Oppenheimer, eds. *Congress Reconsidered.* 7th ed. Washington, D.C.: CQ Press, 2001.

Edwards, George C., III. *At the Margins: Presidential Leadership of Congress.* New Haven: Yale University Press, 1989.

Fenno, Richard F. *The President's Cabinet.* Cambridge: Harvard University Press, 1963.

Fisher, Louis. *Presidential Spending Power.* Princeton: Princeton University Press, 1975.

Greenstein, Fred. *Leadership in the Modern Presidency.* Cambridge: Harvard University Press, 1988.

Hargrove, Erwin C., and Michael Nelson. *Presidents, Politics, and Policy.* Baltimore: Johns Hopkins University Press, 1984.

Hart, John. *The Presidential Branch: From Washington to Clinton.* 2d ed. Chatham, N.J.: Chatham House, 1995.

Heclo, Hugh. *A Government of Strangers: Executive Politics in Washington.* Washington, D.C.: Brookings, 1977.

Hess, Stephen. *Organizing the Presidency.* Rev. ed. Washington, D.C.: Brookings, 1988.

Jones, Charles O. *The Presidency in a Separated System.* Washington, D.C.: Brookings, 1994.

King, Anthony, ed. *Both Ends of the Avenue: The Presidency, the Executive Branch, and Congress in the 1980s.* Washington, D.C.: American Enterprise Institute, 1983.

Mansfield, Harvey C., Sr., ed. *Congress against the President.* New York: Academy of Political Science, 1975.

Mayhew, David. *Divided We Govern: Party Control, Lawmaking, and Investigations, 1946–1990.* New Haven: Yale University Press, 1991.

Nelson, Michael. *The Presidency and the Political System.* 6th ed. Washington, D.C.: CQ Press, 2000.

Neustadt, Richard E. *Presidential Power: The Politics of Leadership from FDR to Carter.* New York: Wiley, 1980.

Peterson, Mark A. *Legislating Together: The White House and Capitol Hill from Eisenhower to Reagan.* Cambridge: Harvard University Press, 1990.

Polsby, Nelson W. *Congress and the Presidency.* 4th ed. Englewood Cliffs, N.J.: Prentice Hall, 1986.

Reedy, George E. *The Twilight of the Presidency: From Johnson to Reagan.* New York: New American Library, 1987.

Rockman, Bert A. *The Leadership Question: The Presidency and the American System.* New York: Praeger, 1984.

Rose, Richard. *The Postmodern President: The White House Meets the World.* Chatham, N.J.: Chatham House, 1988.

Rossiter, Clinton. *The American Presidency.* 2d ed. New York: Harcourt, Brace, 1960.

Rudalevige, Andrew. *Managing the President's Program: Presidential Leadership and Legislative Policy Formulation.* Princeton: Princeton University Press, 2002.

Schlesinger, Arthur M., Jr. *The Imperial Presidency.* New York: Popular Library, 1974.

Skowronek, Stephen. *The Politics Presidents Make: Leadership from John Adams to George Bush.* Cambridge: Harvard University Press, 1994.

Sundquist, James. *Constitutional Reform and Effective Government.* Rev. ed. Washington, D.C.: Brookings, 1992.

Thurber, James A., ed. *Divided Democracy: Cooperation and Conflict between the President and Congress.* Washington, D.C.: CQ Press, 1991.

Wayne, Stephen J. *The Legislative Presidency.* New York: Harper and Row, 1978.

Weaver, R. Kent, and Bert A. Rockman, eds. *Do Institutions Matter? Government Capabilities in the United States and Abroad.* Washington, D.C.: Brookings, 1993.

chapter 13

Chief Diplomat

by Meena Bose, Daniel C. Diller, and Stephen H. Wirls

In the nineteenth century, when U.S. foreign interests were limited primarily to trade and western expansion, presidents were able to concentrate largely on domestic policy. Today, the wide array of U.S. economic, political, and military commitments abroad ensures that presidents will spend at least half of their time on foreign affairs. But, in fact, as economic life becomes more globalized, the distinction between domestic and foreign policy is blurring.

The Constitution makes the president the formal head of state. As the "sole representative with foreign nations," the president speaks for the nation as a whole and is often the focus of national hopes and fears, pride and shame.[1] In the role of chief negotiator and national spokesperson, the president has great leverage in any competition with Congress for control of the nation's foreign policies, and important decisions on foreign affairs often have been made by the president after consultations with only a few trusted advisers. The desire of political friends and foes alike to present a united front has frequently produced initial support for and general deference to the president's lead.

Circumstances such as wars or threats of armed conflict enhance this advantage and have allowed presidents to dominate the formulation and implementation of foreign policy. During such times, John F. Kennedy noted, "The big difference [between domestic and foreign policy] is that between a bill being defeated and the country [being] wiped out."[2] Even during periods of relative international calm, foreign affairs issues usually have offered presidents the greatest freedom to exercise their power and the best opportunity to affect policy personally. In contrast, domestic policy decisions commonly involve many officials and interest groups, require less secrecy, and entail the full participation of Congress and its committees. Consequently, presidents may choose to retreat to the refuge of foreign affairs where they can exercise their powers most freely as leader of the nation.

Indeed, foreign affairs often afford the president the opportunity to gain an enduring place in history. Steadfast wartime leadership, the prevention or resolution of dangerous crises, bold policy and diplomatic initiatives, and historic summit meetings with important foreign leaders can create presidential legends: Jefferson's Louisiana Purchase, the Monroe Doctrine, Theodore Roosevelt's Panama Canal, Harry S. Truman's Marshall Plan, Kennedy's peaceful resolution of the Cuban missile crisis, Richard Nixon's trip to China. Following the lead of Theodore Roosevelt, whose successful management of negotiations to end the Russo-Japanese War earned him a Nobel Peace Prize, presidents have used their stature and skills to resolve conflicts less directly related to U.S. interests. Jimmy Carter's Camp David summit led to a peace agreement between Egypt and Israel, and Bill Clinton's participation in the Dayton (Ohio) negotiations helped to move the Bosnia conflict toward a resolution. On the other hand, Clinton's repeated efforts to resolve the conflicts in Northern Ireland and between Israel and the Palestinians were, at best, partial and temporary successes.

The foreign policy records of few administrations are completely triumphant. Although George Washington's administration was honored for a balanced policy of neutrality, the Jay Treaty with Great Britain provoked virulent partisan attacks. Thomas Jefferson's purchase of the Louisiana territory must be paired with the miserable failure of his embargo against Great Britain. Woodrow Wilson, the victorious war leader, was humiliated by the defeat of the Treaty of Versailles and his internationalist foreign policy. Carter's triumph in facilitating an Israeli-Egyptian peace accord at Camp David was followed by his inability to resolve the hostage crisis with Iran. While Ronald Reagan's hard-line anticommunist policies combined with his second-term summit meetings with Soviet leader Mikhail Gorbachev played an important role in ending the cold war, his administration also was mired in the Iran-contra scandal.

Recent presidents who entered office possessing greater expertise and interest in domestic policy have been distracted, seduced, or overwhelmed by foreign affairs. Lyndon B. Johnson's plans for a "Great Society" were undercut by the resource demands of the Vietnam War and the divisions the war created in the American public. Carter, a former governor with little foreign policy experience, became personally absorbed with foreign policy issues such as recognition of the People's Republic of China, arms control, and the Camp David peace process between Egypt and Israel. Events in Somalia, North Korea, Haiti, and Bosnia taught Clinton that even in the post–cold war era no president can avoid the often perilous complications of foreign affairs. Similarly, the terrorist attacks on New York City and Washington, D.C., in September 2001 immediately turned President George W. Bush's agenda from domestic policy to engaging in diplomacy and waging war. The global war on terror will continue to be the focus of presidents for the foreseeable future.

While the Constitution makes presidents the sole head of state, it does not give them sufficient authority to make foreign policy simply on their own. The branches of the federal government share foreign policy powers, and Congress has many means of influence over the substance and execution of general and specific policies. In addition, policy must be coordinated within a complex of often competing advisers, departments, and agencies. Even under the most favorable conditions, presidents frequently struggle to maintain control of policy formulation and implementation. In the current era, which lacks the ideological clarity of the cold war and the unifying fears of nuclear confrontation between two superpowers, achieving presidential leadership and control of foreign policy has become more difficult and complicated.

DISTRIBUTION OF FOREIGN POLICY POWER

On balance, the Constitution gives the president fewer powers related to the making of foreign policy than Congress, and the powers of the presidency are checked in ways that seem designed to prevent the president from making unilateral commitments abroad. The only unshared power in this area is the president's responsibility to "receive Ambassadors and other Public ministers." Presidents may appoint ambassadors only with the "Advice and Consent of the Senate," and the Senate was meant to be involved throughout all treaty negotiations. The executive power is limited by the laws the president is to execute "faithfully." The president's authority as commander in chief is constrained, as a policy-making power, by Congress's constitutional control over both declarations of war and the raising and support of all armed forces.

> He shall have Power, by and with the Advice and Consent of the Senate, to make Treaties, provided two thirds of the Senators present concur; and he shall nominate and, by and with the Advice and Consent of the Senate, shall appoint Ambassadors, other public Ministers and Consuls.... He ... shall receive Ambassadors and other public Ministers.
>
> —from Article II, Sections 2, 3

Besides its influence over the use of force and the powers it shares with the president, Congress has broad foreign policy powers that are checked only by the president's veto. As spelled out in Article I of the Constitution, Congress controls the legal context of international affairs through its powers "to define and punish Piracies and Felonies committed on the high Seas and Offences against the Law of Nations; . . . and make Rules concerning Captures on Land and Water." Most significant is Congress's authority to "regulate Commerce with foreign Nations." These powers are broadened by the so-called elastic power to "make all Laws which shall be necessary and proper for carrying into Execution the foregoing Powers."

Altogether, Congress's formal constitutional authority in foreign affairs is broader and less qualified than the president's. In addition, the legislative branch's general power to make laws, control appropriations, and "provide for the common Defence and general Welfare of the United States" gives it broad authority to become involved in any foreign policy decision or action not specifically reserved for the president by the Constitution.[3] Congress and, especially, the Senate were, it seems, to control general policy and any long-term foreign commitments.

Obviously, this strict reading of the Constitution does not fully or accurately describe the actual distribution of foreign policy responsibilities and influence. A more complete account of the Framers' design must acknowledge that they anticipated and encouraged a presidential ambition that would clash with the other branches. The Framers also expected that this officer, "seated on the summit of his country's honors," would not be content as a mere executive and congressional agent. Rather, the design of the office encourages the president to "undertake extensive and arduous enterprises for the public benefit, requiring considerable time to mature and perfect."[4] This anticipation of a presidential inclination toward grand policy initiation justifies presidential scholar Edward S. Corwin's description of the Constitution as "an invitation to struggle for the privilege of directing American foreign policy."[5]

The affirmative grants of power in the Constitution do not begin to answer all the questions about how foreign policy decisions should be made and implemented, and the actual distribution of shared foreign policy powers between the president and Congress could be established only by events. The particular struggles have produced periods of interbranch stalemate and partnership, presidential subordination and domination.

PRESIDENTIAL DOMINANCE OF FOREIGN POLICY

In 1948, addressing members of the Jewish War Veterans, President Truman stated: "I make foreign policy." [6] Most historians and political scientists would agree that Truman's assessment of presidential power exaggerates only slightly the influence of modern presidents over foreign policy. At least until the end of the cold war with the Soviet Union, Congress retained an important role in foreign affairs; on many occasions it was able to frustrate, delay, modify, or negate presidential foreign policy. The president, however, dominated the formulation and initiation of foreign policy, and Congress's actions were usually responses to presidential policies. Certainly, the American public and foreign governments expect the president to make decisions and to implement them. Particularly in times of crisis, the public looks to the president for leadership, and presidential approval typically records a "rally-around-the-flag" effect, at least for the short term. [7] It is even common for members of Congress from both parties to criticize a president for failing to provide foreign policy leadership. During the cold war, political scientist Aaron Wildavsky concluded that the United States had "two presidencies," one for foreign policy, in which Congress, public opinion, and the courts deferred to executive leadership, and one for domestic policy, in which these constituencies were far more likely to engage in conflict with the president. [8]

Because the constitutional division of power between the executive and legislative branches is relatively ambiguous in the area of foreign affairs, one cannot attribute the establishment of presidential control over foreign relations simply to the affirmative grants of power in the Constitution. The ambiguity of the document ensured that skills, circumstances, public opinion, customs, and precedents would order and reorder the distribution of influence over foreign affairs. The branch most capable of asserting its interests and demonstrating its ability to make effective foreign policy would likely emerge as the more powerful. This branch has proved to be the executive. Yet, at least initially, the principle of "presidential control" seemed to be an inaccurate characterization of foreign policy making in the era that began with the disintegration of the Soviet Union and the Warsaw Pact. Conflicts between President Clinton and Congress over foreign aid, U.S. participation in UN missions, and many other foreign policy issues suggested a return to a sharper struggle for control of foreign policy. On the other hand, President George W. Bush's control of the diplomatic and military policies in response to the September 11, 2001, terrorist attacks indicates that the presidency retains its advantage in these policy arenas. Indeed, the Bush administration has propounded a "unitary executive" theory of presidential power, which holds that the president may ignore legal restrictions on action if national security so requires. [9]

President George W. Bush, right, shakes hands with outgoing British prime minister Tony Blair after their joint press conference, May 17, 2007, in the White House Rose Garden. Early on, ties between Bush and Blair were weaker than those between Bill Clinton and Blair; however, in the wake of the September 11, 2001, attacks, Blair offered Britain's unwaivering support when Bush declared his "war on terrorism."

Presidential Advantages

The history of foreign policy making and the eventual rise of presidential responsibility for leadership and control have been shaped by a mix of more or less mutable influences: presidential skills, public opinion, precedents, constitutional principles, and circumstances. The presidents' enduring advantages are their status as chief of state and the various constitutional powers that establish them as the principal communicator, the "sole organ of the nation in its external relations, and its sole representative with foreign nations." [10] Although presidents do not have the full authority to commit the nation and Congress to a foreign policy, their powers, at the very least, allow them to speak first in defining a policy and course of action for the nation. When coupled with the status as the only nationally elected officer (along with the vice president), these powers give an enterprising and determined president considerable leverage over policy. Insofar as any contradiction to their lead may reflect on the nation, presidents can saddle the congressional opposition with responsibility for embarrassing the nation and harming the general credibility of the presidency in future negotiations.

These advantages are enhanced by the president's other positions. As commander in chief of the armed forces, head of the diplomatic corps, and head of the intelligence agencies, presidents should be in the best position to judge the capacity of the U.S. government to carry out a given foreign policy. Congress has regularly recognized the inherent advantages of the presidency's focused responsibility. Unlike Congress, with its many voices and centers of power, presidents are able to work with speed and secrecy, two capabilities that are indispensable in many diplomatic situations, and especially in crises that threaten the security of the nation. As the most identifiable leaders and visible symbols of the nation, presidents are the most capable of rallying national support in a crisis.

Turning these advantages into enduring presidential dominance depends on other factors. Presidents must establish plausible constitutional principles that support their policy-making ambitions, principles that place within their control the ambiguities and voids in the Constitution, such as the responsibility for policy proclamations, international agreements other than treaties, flexible employment of armed forces, and military actions short of war. A significant constitutional resource is the executive power. Because it is difficult to define precisely where policy making stops and execution begins, even a narrow understanding of the executive power affords presidents some policy influence. Moreover, presidents have claimed that the general executive power authorizes them to fill the constitutional voids and to dominate areas of ambiguity.

Congress retains nonetheless a substantial arsenal of constitutional counterclaims and can at any time reassert itself. The persuasiveness of presidential assertions of authority depends in part on precedent: claims of authority that have received the approbation or acquiescence of Congress, the courts, and public opinion. Successful assertions, and especially those backed by actions with favorable results, tend to strengthen the president's constitutional position and reaffirm the practical advantages of presidential control over policy. Precedents can, however, cut the other way. The war in Vietnam was prosecuted under an expansive interpretation of presidential authority built up through many cold war precedents. However, the immediate effects of the war were a weakened practical argument for presidential control of foreign policy, Congress's reassertion of its constitutional powers, and greater skepticism about the president's claims of broad constitutional authority.

Reaping the full potential of constitutional and practical precedents requires the cooperation of circumstances. Any crisis in foreign affairs that directly or indirectly threat-

ens the security and well-being of U.S. citizens, the nation, or close allies will focus attention on the president as the chief of state and as the officer most able to respond flexibly and decisively in diplomatic and military matters. Congress regularly recognizes its clumsy inability to compete with these presidential qualities. As the French political observer Alexis de Tocqueville noted more than 150 years ago: "If the Union's existence were constantly menaced, and if its great interests were continually interwoven with those of other powerful nations, one would see the prestige of the executive growing, because of what was expected from it and what it did." [11] When Tocqueville wrote this, and for some time after, the United States was following a policy of relative isolation. The enduring elements of foreign policy were westward expansion and commerce. The latter especially was dominated by Congress through its full authority over tariffs and trade. After World War II, the expansive global commitments and permanent national security crises met Tocqueville's conditions and led to a full and enduring realization of the president's constitutional and practical potential in foreign policy leadership and control. In the post–cold war era, the frequent conflicts between Congress and President Clinton over issues such as participation in peacekeeping missions suggest that securing consistent presidential leadership in the future will be much more difficult. On the other hand, Iraq's invasion of Kuwait in 1990 and the September 11, 2001, terrorist attacks on New York City and Washington, D.C., suggest that circumstances can still favor presidential authority and leadership.

Judicial Enhancement of Presidential Power

The president's practical and constitutional advantages in competing with Congress for control of foreign policy are greatly enhanced by the fact that the judicial branch has generally either affirmed presidential assertions or refused to settle conflicts between the president and Congress, especially in this area. *(See box, Supreme Court Cases Related to the President's Foreign Policy Powers, p. 699.)*

The courts have avoided resolving constitutional conflicts in the area of foreign policy through the "political questions" doctrine. Justice Robert Jackson argued that

> the very nature of executive decisions as to foreign policy is political, not judicial. Such decisions are wholly confided by our Constitution to the political departments of the government. . . . They are decisions of a kind for which the Judiciary has neither aptitude, facilities nor responsibility and which has long been held to belong in the domain of political power not subject to judicial intrusion or inquiry. [12]

The Supreme Court has also affirmed broad, inherent national powers in foreign affairs and war, though without settling the exact boundaries between the president and Congress. The most comprehensive of these rulings came in

SUPREME COURT CASES RELATED TO THE PRESIDENT'S FOREIGN POLICY POWERS

Ware v. Hylton, **3 Dall. 199 (1796).** The Court ruled 4–0 that treaties made by the United States overrode any conflicting state laws. The 1783 Treaty of Paris with Britain, which ended the American Revolution, provided that neither Britain nor the United States would block the efforts of the other nation's citizens to secure repayment of debts in the other country. This provision rendered invalid a Virginia law allowing debts owed by Virginians to British creditors to be "paid off" through payments to the state.

Foster v. Neilson, **2 Pet. 253 (1829).** By a 5–0 vote, the Court refused to rule on a boundary dispute involving territory east of the Mississippi River claimed by both the United States and Spain. Chief Justice John Marshall described the matter as a "political question" that was not the business of the judiciary to resolve.

Holmes v. Jennison, **14 Pet. 540 (1840).** A fugitive from Canada, detained in Vermont, sought release through a petition for a writ of habeas corpus. After the state supreme court denied his petition, he asked the Supreme Court to review that action. The Court dismissed the case for lack of jurisdiction, but Chief Justice Roger B. Taney declared in his opinion that states were forbidden by the Constitution to take any independent role in foreign affairs, and thus state governors could not surrender a fugitive within their jurisdiction to a foreign country that sought the fugitive's return.

The Prize Cases, **2 Black 635 (1863).** These cases involved the capture of four ships seized while trying to run the Union blockade of Confederate ports, which Abraham Lincoln instituted in April 1861 and Congress sanctioned in July. By a 5–4 vote, the Court sustained the president's power to proclaim the blockade without a congressional declaration of war. A state of war already existed, the majority said, and the president was obligated "to meet it in the shape it presented itself, without waiting for Congress to baptize it with a name."

Geofroy v. Riggs, **133 U.S. 258 (1890).** The Court ruled 9–0 that it is within the scope of the treaty power of the United States to regulate the inheritance by aliens of land and other property in the United States. The Court declared that the treaty power was unlimited except by the Constitution.

Missouri v. Holland, **252 U.S. 416 (1920).** After lower courts ruled an act of Congress protecting migratory birds to be an unconstitutional invasion of powers reserved to the states, the U.S. government negotiated a treaty with Canada for the protection of the birds. After the Senate approved it, Congress again enacted protective legislation to fulfill the terms of the treaty. The Court sustained this second act by a 7–2 vote. It ruled that to implement a treaty Congress may enact legislation that without a treaty might be an unconstitutional invasion of state sovereignty.

United States v. Curtiss-Wright Export Corp., **299 U.S. 304 (1936).** Although ambiguous, this is the leading case on the general foreign affairs powers. By a 7–1 vote, the Court upheld an act of Congress authorizing the president, at his discretion, to embargo arms shipments to foreign belligerents in a South American war. The Court asserted that the national government has undefined, "inherent" powers in foreign affairs. Justice George Sutherland also argued that the president was "the sole organ of the federal government in … international relations." His powers as the "sole organ" were "plenary and exclusive."

United States v. Belmont, **310 U.S. 324 (1937).** In the executive agreements that established diplomatic relations between the Soviet Union and the United States in 1933, the two nations had agreed that Soviet assets in the United States would be used to pay the claims of U.S. citizens for property seized in the Soviet Union at the time of the Russian Revolution. When U.S. government officials tried to recover funds from the accounts of Russian nationals in New York banks, the state maintained that its laws prohibited the action. The Supreme Court, however, ruled that the executive agreements on which the action was based constituted an international compact that, like a treaty, superseded conflicting state laws.

Goldwater v. Carter, **444 U.S. 996 (1980).** In December 1978 President Jimmy Carter announced that the United States would terminate the 1945 Mutual Defense Treaty with the Republic of China (Taiwan) as part of the process of establishing diplomatic relations with the People's Republic of China. Sen. Barry Goldwater, R-Ariz., brought a suit to stop the action, maintaining that treaty termination, like treaty ratification, required the prior approval of the Senate. The Court tacitly sided with the president by dismissing the case as a political question outside the realm of judicial review.

Hamdi v. Rumsfeld, **542 U.S. 507 (2004).** After the terrorist strikes against New York City and Washington, D.C., on September 11, 2001, Congress passed a resolution authorizing the president to use force against nations, individuals, or organizations connected with the attacks. In 2001 Yaser Esam Hamdi, an American citizen, was arrested in Afghanistan for collaborating with the Taliban regime, which was affiliated with the al Qaeda terrorist network behind the U.S. attacks. Hamdi was classified as an "enemy combatant" and detained in the United States. His father filed a habeas corpus petition, asserting that the U.S. government was violating Hamdi's constitutional rights by holding him indefinitely without criminal charges. The Court ruled that a U.S. citizen must be accorded due process to challenge detention by the government.

Rumsfeld v. Padilla, **542 U.S. 426 (2004).** In 2002 Jose Padilla, a U.S. citizen, was arrested in Chicago for allegedly working with al Qaeda in Pakistan and plotting to set off a radiological, or "dirty," bomb in the United States. He was declared an "enemy combatant" and held without charge in a military prison. Padilla filed a habeas corpus petition, and in 2004 the Court, sidestepping the substantive issue, ruled only that his case needed to be tried in a different jurisdiction. In 2005 the George W. Bush administration moved Padilla to a civilian prison and charged him with conspiring to commit terrorist attacks and supporting al Qaeda. With Padilla's transfer to a civilian prison, the Court in 2006 declined to hear his petition for habeas corpus, declaring it moot.

Hamdan v. Rumsfeld, **126 S.Ct. 2749 (2006).** In 2001 Salim Ahmed Hamdan, a Yemeni national who had worked as a chauffeur for al Qaeda leader Osama bin Laden, was arrested in Afghanistan and detained by the U.S. military in Guantanamo Bay, Cuba. Hamdan challenged his detention in court, but the Bush administration declared that it would employ special military tribunals for "enemy combatants," and that those tribunals would not be subject to requirements that applied to traditional prisoners of war. The Court ruled that military commissions were obligated to comply with U.S. law and the laws of war, including the Geneva Convention adopted after World War II.

United States v. Curtiss-Wright, delivered in 1936. *(See "United States v. Curtiss-Wright Export Corporation," p. 1770, in Reference Materials, Vol. II.)*

In 1934 Congress passed a joint resolution granting the president full discretion in determining the government's policy toward private arms shipments to warring nations in South America. After President Franklin D. Roosevelt used this authority to impose an embargo on Bolivia, the Curtiss-Wright Export Corporation conspired to send arms to Bolivia. In court, lawyers for Curtiss-Wright argued that the law was an unconstitutional delegation to the executive of Congress's legislative power.

The Court's reasoning is rather difficult to follow. It clearly argued for a fundamental distinction between domestic and foreign affairs powers; although the national government's domestic powers are strictly limited by the Constitution, its foreign affairs authority comprises all the powers of a sovereign nation. In other words, the Constitution's specific grants do not define the scope of the government's "inherent" powers, and the government generally has access to an unspecified and undefined range of powers in war and foreign affairs.

The Court argued, moreover, that the president's specific powers establish the office as the "sole organ of the federal government in the field of international relations." However, this seems to be limited to the exclusive authority to "speak or listen as a representative of the nation" and does not imply that the president has full policy-making authority. As Justice George Sutherland indicates in his summary, the president is not independent of Congress in broader questions of policy:

> It is important to bear in mind that we are here dealing not alone with an authority vested in the President by an exertion of legislative power, but with such an authority plus the very delicate, plenary, and exclusive power of the President as the sole organ of the federal government in the field of international relations—a power which does not require as a basis for its exercise an act of Congress, but which, of course, like every other governmental power, must be exercised in subordination to the applicable provisions of the Constitution. It is quite apparent that if, in the maintenance of our international relations, embarrassment—perhaps serious embarrassment—is to be avoided and success for our aims achieved, congressional legislation which is to be made effective through negotiation and inquiry in the international field must often accord to the President a degree of discretion and freedom from statutory restriction which would not be admissible were domestic affairs alone involved.[13]

United States v. Curtiss-Wright was a landmark decision. Although the ruling does not seem to support historian Arthur M. Schlesinger Jr.'s conclusion that the Court "affirmed the existence of an inherent, independent and superior presidential power, not derived from the Constitution and not requiring legislation as the basis for its exercise," the ruling did ground past practices in constitutional doctrine, and it provided the president and Congress with a wealth of possible claims to authority.[14]

Conflicts and Precedents during the Washington Administration

Although George Washington exercised his foreign affairs power with great restraint by today's standards, he and his closest adviser, Secretary of the Treasury Alexander Hamilton, believed the president had the constitutional authority and the practical duty to take the initiative in foreign policy. As a result, Washington set several precedents that enlarged the foreign affairs powers of the young presidency beyond a literal reading of the enumerated powers in the Constitution. He established the president's authority to recognize foreign governments, to demand that foreign ambassadors be recalled, to negotiate treaties without the direction of the Senate, and to withhold from the House documents pertinent to treaty negotiations. Most important, Washington demonstrated that in foreign affairs the president could use the office's inherent executive power to take actions that were authorized neither by Congress nor by a specific presidential foreign policy power in the Constitution. In doing so, his administration initiated a debate that produced history's most complete and enduring constitutional arguments for and against broad presidential authority in foreign affairs.

Neutrality Proclamation of 1793

Washington set the precedent for unilateral presidential policy making by proclaiming the neutrality of the United States in the war between France and Great Britain in 1793. Although the treaty of alliance with France signed in 1778 was still in effect, and many Americans favored the French, Washington was anxious to avoid involving the United States in the conflict, fearing that it would disrupt the strengthening of the American economy and political institutions.

On April 22, 1793, he issued a proclamation that declared that the United States would be "friendly and impartial" toward the belligerents. Although the proclamation was unpopular with many Americans, Congress followed Washington's lead by passing the Neutrality Act of 1794, which endorsed the policy of neutrality already in effect. Washington had shown that the president's executive power could be used to make foreign policy rather than just execute congressional directives.

Hamilton-Madison Debate

Secretary of State Thomas Jefferson was not convinced that the president, without an explicit constitutional grant of power, had the authority to act. Moreover, Jefferson inferred from Congress's exclusive authority to declare war that the president lacked the authority to decide unilaterally that the nation would *not* fight a war. However, his objections to Washington's policy were minor when compared with the horror induced by Hamilton's "Pacificus" essays. Hamilton's defense of the proclamation evolved into a more general argument for broad, inherent presidential powers in war and foreign affairs.

Hamilton's argument took two tacks. First, he argued that Washington was acting within his ordinary authority as chief executive in interpreting the legal obligations of existing treaties and in informing the government and the citizens of their responsibilities under the law. The expansiveness of the other tack was breathtaking. Through a careful, and sometimes clever, analysis of the constitutional text, Hamilton argued that constellations of specific presidential powers implied that the treaty power and the general war power were executive in nature. Therefore, he concluded, Congress's powers in those areas ought to be interpreted narrowly, as strictly construed exceptions to executive power. The crucial argument was that the Constitution grants the president broad and undefined *inherent* powers through the vesting clause of Article II; whereas Congress is given the "legislative Powers *herein granted,*" the executive power is "vested in a President" without a similar limitation. This broad power would not only authorize proclamations but also fill every relevant void in the Constitution. Hamilton acknowledged that the president's use of this power interfered with the free exercise of Congress's power to declare war, but this was an unavoidable consequence, he argued, of the president and Congress having "concurrent powers" in this area.[15]

As a member of Washington's cabinet, Jefferson felt that it would be improper for him to attack Hamilton's argument in public. He urged Madison to respond: "Nobody answers him and his doctrines are taken for confessed. For God's sake, my dear Sir, take up your pen, select the most striking heresies and cut him to pieces in face of the public."[16]

Under the pseudonym Helvidius, Madison's argument rested less on the constitutional text than on a general principle of legislative sovereignty and strict rule of law: "The natural province of the executive magistrate is to execute laws, as that of the legislature is to make laws. All his acts, therefore, properly executive, must presuppose the existence of the laws to be executed."[17] This restrictive interpretation of the executive power then guided his very restrictive reading of all presidential powers in foreign affairs and war. Thus, according to Madison, the president's role in foreign affairs was confined to executing the laws, treaties, and declarations of war made by Congress and performing those duties, strictly construed, that are specifically enumerated in the Constitution. Congress was, according to Madison, the branch of government properly entrusted to formulate foreign policy, including declarations of neutrality.

Although Hamilton's generous reading of the president's constitutional authority has never been fully accepted by the other branches, it has provided presidents with a coherent constitutional foundation for their more adventurous assertions of authority. Indeed, many presidents have spoken and behaved as if they had a general, comprehensive power to conduct foreign affairs, while Congress could only participate if it found an opportunity to use one of its specific powers.

CONGRESSIONAL COOPERATION AND CONFLICT

In spite of their constitutional and practical advantages in the conduct of foreign policy, presidents have regularly struggled, and periodically failed, to control U.S. foreign policy. Congress has significant authority that can be used to thwart and redirect presidential initiatives. At times, Congress has refused to follow the president's leadership and has attempted to legislate its own policy course. Even in eras of presidential domination, Congress has demonstrated that no foreign policy program can be sustained for long without its support. Foreign policy has, therefore, often been shaped through cooperation and accommodation between the two branches.

Early Cooperation and Conflict

Congressional majorities often were willing to cooperate with early presidents on foreign affairs matters. For example, Congress passed the Neutrality Act of 1794 a year after President Washington had declared American neutrality in the war between Britain and France, even though many members of Congress had opposed the original proclamation. In 1803 the Senate followed Jefferson's lead by ratifying the treaty with France that transferred the Louisiana Territory into U.S. control. The full record of these two administrations is, however, more mixed. Although the Senate approved it in 1795, Washington's Jay Treaty with Great Britain ignited a partisan explosion that led to demands from the House for papers related to the negotiations. Against the strong wishes of Jefferson, Congress repealed his embargo policy against Great Britain just before the end of his term.

In 1816 a report by the Senate Foreign Relations Committee reflected Congress's recognition of the practical advantages of presidential leadership in foreign affairs and of the limited practical scope of the Senate's power of advice and consent:

> The President is the Constitutional representative of the United States with regard to foreign nations. He manages our concern with foreign nations and must necessarily be most competent to determine when, how, and upon what subject negotiations may be urged with the greatest

prospect of success. For his conduct he is responsible to the Constitution. The committee considers this responsibility the surest pledge for the faithful discharge of his duties. They think the interference of the Senate in the direction of foreign negotiations [is] calculated to diminish that responsibility and thereby to impair the best security for the national safety. The nature of transactions with foreign nations, moreover, requires caution and unity of design, and their success frequently depends on secrecy and dispatch.[18]

Nineteenth Century

Presidents during much of the last two-thirds of the nineteenth century exerted less foreign policy leadership than had earlier presidents. The resolution of the slavery question, the development of the American West, and the Reconstruction of the South following the Civil War were the most important political issues of the period. The primary foreign relations issues—foreign trade and the acquisition of territory from foreign governments—were two matters in which Congress had a large role. Nonetheless, Presidents Chester A. Arthur, Benjamin Harrison, and William McKinley had significant influence over trade policy.

In the years after the Civil War, congressional power was at its peak. The executive branch suffered some serious setbacks, including the impeachment and near removal of President Andrew Johnson from office and the passage of the Tenure of Office Act in 1867, which allowed the Senate to prevent a president from removing an appointee from office.[19] In general, the Senate controlled the executive branch. Indeed, from 1871 to 1895 no major treaty succeeded in gaining the Senate's consent.[20]

The Spanish-American War in 1898 marked a major turning point in foreign policy, because the nation dropped its traditional policy of nonintervention. Although President McKinley originally sought a peaceful resolution of the conflict with Spain over its rule in Cuba, Congress and public opinion favored intervention. The nation went to war and emerged victorious with overseas territories as

distant as the western Pacific. With the goal of fostering trade, McKinley extended the nation's international interests and engagements. In particular, the annexation of the Philippines involved the nation in a wide range of Far Eastern affairs, especially those affecting trade. This imperial policy helped to merge the president's foreign affairs and war powers, giving the president greater leverage over Congress in making and implementing foreign policy.

Theodore Roosevelt's Administration

After the Spanish-American War, presidents expanded their control over foreign affairs. In 1901 McKinley was assassinated, and his vice president, Theodore Roosevelt, succeeded to the presidency. For the next seven and a half years, Roosevelt frequently ignored or circumvented Congress while boldly asserting a broad executive prerogative to pursue his perception of U.S. interests abroad. In 1903 he used U.S. naval power to back a small Panamanian revolt against Colombian rule; recognized the state of Panama, which emerged from the revolution; and quickly negotiated a treaty

In a bid to end the war between Russia and Japan, President Theodore Roosevelt, middle, meets with delegates from the two countries at the 1905 Portsmouth Conference. Roosevelt won the Nobel Peace Prize for his successful effort, the first U.S. president to receive the award. President Woodrow Wilson won the Nobel Peace Prize in 1919.

with the new Panamanian government giving the United States the right to dig the Panama Canal. In 1905, after the Senate refused to ratify a treaty giving the United States control of the Dominican Republic's customs houses, Roosevelt implemented his policy through an executive agreement. The same year, Roosevelt personally directed mediation efforts between Russia and Japan without consulting Congress. His efforts led to the Portsmouth Conference in New Hampshire, which ended the Russo-Japanese War and won him the Nobel Peace Prize. In 1907 Roosevelt decided to send the U.S. fleet on a world cruise, primarily to impress the Japanese with U.S. naval strength. Congress threatened to deny funding for the mission, but relented when Roosevelt declared he had sufficient funds to send the navy to the Pacific—and Congress would be left to decide whether it wanted the ships back.[21]

President Roosevelt freely admitted that he had avoided involving Congress in major foreign policy actions. In 1909, while still in office, he wrote: "The biggest matters, such as the Portsmouth peace, the acquisition of Panama, and sending the fleet around the world, I managed without consultation with anyone; for when a matter is of capital importance, it is well to have it handled by one man only." [22]

Versailles to World War II

Presidential disregard for Congress's role in foreign policy reached new heights in 1919. Woodrow Wilson traveled to Versailles, France, to participate personally in the negotiation of a peace treaty to end World War I. Under strong pressure from Wilson, the conference agreed to include provisions in the treaty establishing a League of Nations. The president brought the treaty back to the United States and began a vigorous national campaign for Senate approval. During the war, Congress had cooperated with Wilson by granting him unprecedented war powers, but once the threat had passed, the Senate was ready to reassert legislative influence over foreign policy. Wilson, however, ignored the growing opposition within the Senate and refused to involve senators in the Versailles negotiations or even to inform them of U.S. negotiating positions. In 1919 and 1920 the Senate refused to approve the treaty, thus keeping the country out of the League of Nations. (See "The Defeat of the League of Nations," p. 129, in Chapter 2.)

The demise of the Versailles treaty signaled a new period of congressional activism in promoting a foreign policy of isolation. During the next two decades, Congress limited U.S. involvement overseas, with little resistance from the executive branch. When war threatened in Asia and Europe in the late 1930s, Congress, reflecting the isolationism of the public, tried to legislate neutrality through an embargo on arms shipments and strict controls on the president.[23] But when war finally began, Franklin Roosevelt, like presidents before him in times of crisis, acquired enormous powers

through his assertiveness and Congress's grants of authority, which were motivated by the need for national unity.

Postwar Presidential Power

After World War II ended, presidential authority in foreign affairs continued to grow. The period brought many new responsibilities and dangers that required a chief executive capable of quick, decisive action and enhanced presidential stature as an international leader. The United States had emerged from the war as the most powerful nation on earth and the leader of the noncommunist world. The threat of communist expansion brought the whole globe into the sphere of U.S. interest. The United States had swung from isolationism in the late 1930s to unprecedented international involvement in the late 1940s, aligning itself with virtually any willing country and sending billions of dollars in economic and military aid overseas.

More immediate dangers to the security of the United States grew along with its commitments. Advances in missile technology and Soviet development of the atomic bomb in 1949 and the hydrogen bomb in 1953 made a devastating attack on the American homeland a possibility. The fall of China to communist forces in 1949 reinforced the belief of many Americans that the United States had to be ready to use troops if necessary to stop communist expansion.

The continual conjunction of military threats and foreign policy in this complex and hostile international environment contributed to a consensus for strong presidential leadership in foreign policy. Congress recognized that only the executive branch had the means to collect and analyze the huge amount of information on foreign policy issues and to act with the speed and flexibility that seemed necessary to manage U.S. global commitments. In addition, the presidential role of guardian of the nuclear switch magnified the commander in chief's stature as guardian of the free world, thereby enhancing presidential authority in other areas of defense and foreign policy.

Although some major initiatives, such as the Marshall Plan, were developed in close cooperation with congressional leaders, Congress did repeatedly pass resolutions supporting presidential policy discretion and authorizing the president to use force if necessary to deal with particular international problems. In 1955 Congress authorized the president to use force to defend Formosa (Nationalist China) and the neighboring islands if they were attacked by Communist China. An even broader resolution was passed in 1957 that supported the "Eisenhower Doctrine," which announced the intention of the United States to defend Middle Eastern countries "against aggression from any country controlled by international communism." Several years later, in 1962, the House and Senate passed resolutions declaring their support for any presidential action, including the use of force, needed to defend the rights of the United States in the divided city of Berlin. The same year, Congress adopted similar resolutions pertaining to the Cuban missile crisis.

In August 1964 Congress passed the sweeping Tonkin Gulf resolution with only two senators out of the 535 members of Congress in opposition. *(See box, Tonkin Gulf Resolution, p. 753, in Chapter 14)* The resolution had been proposed by the administration of Lyndon Johnson in response to murky evidence that North Vietnamese torpedo boats had attacked U.S. vessels off the coast of Vietnam.[24] The resolution acknowledged and supported the president's full authority to take "all necessary measures to repel any armed attacks against the forces of the United States and to prevent further aggression." At least two months before the incident, Johnson's National Security Council staff had prepared a draft of a similar resolution supporting presidential freedom to act in Vietnam.[25] Because Johnson never asked Congress for a declaration of war, he used the Tonkin Gulf resolution in subsequent years as evidence of congressional support for his expansion of U.S. involvement in the conflict in Vietnam.

Congressional Rebellion and Reassertion

Congress was partly responsible for the expansion of executive power between 1945 and 1969. For the sake of national unity in the fight against communism, the legislature had consented to and even encouraged presidential autonomy in foreign and defense matters. Congress had tended to follow whatever policy direction the president chose and, implicitly or explicitly, accept the enlarged presidential interpretations of executive power.[26] In the late 1960s, however, Congress began to rebel against the growing capacity of presidents to exclude Congress from participation in foreign and defense policy decisions. After passage of the Tonkin Gulf resolution, for example, President Johnson sought the appropriations needed to escalate military involvement in Southeast Asia and never sought congressional approval for any policy or strategy decision about the war. Members of Congress also were unhappy with the increasing number of international commitments made by executive agreement without congressional approval, especially those that expanded the scope of the war.

In June 1969, by a 70–16 vote, the Senate adopted a "national commitments" resolution, which declared the sense of the Senate that a national commitment by the United States results "only from affirmative action taken by the executive and legislative branches of the United States government by means of a treaty, statute, or concurrent resolution of both houses of Congress specifically providing for such a commitment." In 1969 and 1970 some members of Congress repeatedly attempted to terminate funds for U.S. military activities in Indochina. During that period, Congress also used its investigative powers to probe the extent of U.S. commitments abroad.

In the early 1970s, the revelations of a secret Defense Department study of the decision-making process surrounding the Vietnam War (known as the *Pentagon Papers*), the unwillingness of Presidents Johnson and Nixon to include Congress in foreign policy decisions, and the Watergate scandal spurred Congress to seek to recapture the foreign affairs powers it had lost to the executive branch. In 1972 Congress passed the Case Act, which established more rigorous requirements for the reporting of international agreements to Congress by the executive branch. It was followed by passage of the War Powers Resolution of 1973 over President Nixon's veto. The measure set a sixty-day limit on any unauthorized presidential introduction of U.S. troops into hostilities abroad.

In 1974 Congress passed a major trade reform bill, but only after approving the Jackson-Vanik amendment, which linked trade concessions for communist countries to their easing restrictions on the emigration of Jews. The same year Congress imposed a ban on military aid and arms shipments to Turkey. In 1978 the Senate conducted a long and contentious debate on the Panama Canal treaties and approved them only after adding numerous amendments. During this period, Congress also conducted investigations of the intelligence community and began to take a more active interest in the specifics of the Defense Department's budget.

Congressional activism in foreign affairs appears to have become a permanent feature of U.S. foreign policy. Congress was routinely submitting alternative plans for weapons acquisition, arms control, and policies on regional problems. In addition, it was passing nonbinding resolutions stating its concerns on a variety of foreign policy issues. Although Congress often supported President Reagan's actions, many of his foreign policies, such as arms sales to moderate Arab nations, were accompanied by tough and sometimes unsuccessful battles for congressional approval. Military assistance to the Nicaraguan rebels, as part of Reagan's general anticommunist foreign policy, met stiff resistance in Congress, and the administration's attempts to circumvent congressional restrictions led to extensive congressional investigations and general damage to the Reagan administration. President George H.W. Bush began his administration in 1989 by forging a bipartisan accord with Congress to defuse the issue. In 1990, faced with mounting congressional criticism, Bush sought congressional approval for his decision to drive the Iraqi army out of Kuwait. In 1991, in the wake of the 1989 Tiananmen Square massacre of pro-democracy demonstrators by the Chinese government, only the failure to override Bush's veto prevented Congress from imposing a human rights condition on the extension of most-favored-nation status to China.[27]

Congress has significant foreign policy powers. It shares with the president the "plenary power" of the national government in foreign affairs and has "vast powers to define the bounds within which a president may be left to work out a foreign policy." [28] Although Congress has not asserted these powers fully even during periods of presidential weakness such as the second Nixon administration, the potential is there. Congress can dominate any policy involving trade, and contrary to the wishes of presidents, it has imposed trade sanctions, for example, on the former Soviet Union, Uganda, and South Africa. It has used its power over trade to force the president to negotiate, or retaliate, over the trade practices of other countries.

Control over spending is Congress's most powerful and comprehensive power, and it has used this power to control foreign aid and, particularly, arms sales. [29] Congress has blocked and mandated spending contrary to the president's wishes. For example, it forbade Nixon to spend for military operations in Laos and Cambodia (1973) and blocked all military assistance to Angola (1975). In 1986 and 1987 Congress used its control over weapons procurement to prevent the Reagan administration from implementing its controversial interpretations of the ABM and SALT II treaties. President Clinton faced numerous attempts by Congress to dictate policy through its spending power. In 1995, faced with congressional opposition, Clinton had to withdraw his request for emergency funds to support Mexico's collapsing economy. Instead, he used existing executive branch funds to implement the policy. Congress then attempted to require congressional approval for the use of those funds.

In general, Congress can be a potent forum for investigations and public criticism of presidential policy. The effectiveness of this capacity depends on congressional willingness to criticize the president and the willingness of the media and the public to listen. The dramatic changes in international circumstances in the 1990s suggested that Congress would use these resources to greater effect. After the collapse of the Soviet Union, the Warsaw Pact, and European communism in general, both Bush and Clinton lacked the great leverage gained from an ongoing global military and political emergency. The growing independence of the European Union and the ebbing U.S. influence in the North Atlantic Treaty Organization (NATO) lowered the president's stature as a world leader and weakened any argument that deference to presidential preferences was essential to the security of the nation and its allies. As issues such as international trade came to the fore, and as the conjunction of military might and foreign policy became more intermittent, the president became more likely to face a more influential and assertive Congress.

The Clinton presidency confirmed this expectation. President Clinton struggled, like his predecessor, President Bush, to formulate general principles of foreign policy outside of the area of trade. Even in that area, President Clinton's successes with the North American Free Trade Agreement (1993) and the General Agreement on Tariffs and Trade (1994) were notable for the weak support he received from his party. Commitments of U.S. forces in Somalia, Haiti, Bosnia, and Kosovo raised extensive congressional protests as well as proposals and resolutions to limit the president's authority to commit forces. In 1995 Congress passed over Clinton's protests a bill requiring that the U.S. embassy in Israel be relocated to Jerusalem; Clinton claimed such a move would interfere with peace negotiations. He allowed it to become law without his signature and invoked the bill's provisions for delaying the move.

During this period, participation of the United States in multilateral peacekeeping operations was of particular concern to Congress. Initially, the Clinton administration operated under the general principle that international engagements were best undertaken through the United Nations and other multilateral arrangements. But strong congressional reactions led to modifications in specific cases and to a more general retreat from this policy. For example, after the multilateral mission in Somalia was redefined from one of famine relief to a more aggressive policy of subduing the warring factions—a change that resulted in the death of some U.S. soldiers—Congress forced Clinton to negotiate a deadline for withdrawing U.S. forces.

From the start, in 1993, Clinton's policy toward the bloody conflicts among Bosnian Serbs, Croats, and Muslims in the former Yugoslavia generated a stream of congressional criticism and numerous proposals to limit or change the nature of U.S. involvement in the joint UN/NATO relief and mediation efforts. One of the most important of these was the 1994 amendment forcing Clinton to end U.S. enforcement of the arms embargo of Bosnia. This was the first time the United States had withdrawn from a NATO-sponsored operation. Clinton later vetoed a bill that would have lifted the embargo. (*See box, Faces of Foreign Policy: Post–Cold War Era to the Post-9/11 World, p. 706–707.*)

In an effort to ward off more general congressional intrusions, the Clinton administration in 1994 revised its policy on UN missions, restricting U.S. participation to those operations vital to either national or global security. The Serbian assault on ethnic Albanians in Kosovo in 1999 once again brought the president and Congress into conflict. The House and the Senate, however, could not agree on a policy. In the end, Congress did not act to limit Clinton's authority, and he sent ground troops to participate in a peacekeeping mission.

Early in the George W. Bush administration, Congress showed signs of continuing its activist role in foreign policy, especially after the Democratic Party took control of the Senate in June 2001. President Bush's policy toward China, his aggressive promotion of missile defense development, and his withdrawal from a number of UN-sponsored pacts and events, for example, were greeted with legislative resistance and unusually vigorous criticism from Democratic

FACES OF FOREIGN POLICY: POST–COLD WAR ERA TO THE POST-9/11 WORLD

ALLIANCE COMMITMENTS AND PEACEKEEPING IN THE BALKANS

President Bill Clinton's struggle to shape U.S. and alliance policy toward the civil war in the former Yugoslavia illustrates some of the complexities of foreign policy in the post–cold war era. Clinton encountered criticism and resistance for basing foreign policy more on alliance commitments than on clear national interests.

After the end of communist rule, the former Yugoslavia descended into a terrible civil war between Serbs, Croats, and Bosnian Muslims. In 1993 Clinton announced that U.S. involvement in the conflict would be limited strictly to multilateral operations, and the United States began participating in a UN and North Atlantic Treaty Organization (NATO) mission to provide humanitarian relief.[1] In this mission, U.S. air power was used to restrict attacks by Serbs and protect relief operations.

Congressional attitudes toward U.S. involvement were mixed. In 1992 Congress passed a nonbinding resolution calling on the president and the United Nations to act, even with force, to stop the fighting. Yet at the same time, some in Congress were trying to restrict generally the president's authority to commit forces to multilateral operations in Somalia and Haiti as well as the former Yugoslavia. In 1993 Congress passed a nonbinding resolution requiring congressional authorization before ground forces could be sent to the region.

In 1994 President Clinton took a tougher stand, calling for air strikes against the Bosnian Serbs for violating cease-fire agreements, interfering with the relief operation, and besieging various cities that had been designated as protected Muslim "safe areas." After intermittent U.S.-led air strikes failed to halt Serbian aggression, Clinton was unable to lead NATO toward a more consistently forceful response.

President Clinton's policy seemed to be shaped as much by a desire to maintain alliance cohesion as by the situation in Bosnia per se, and in 1994 Congress again attempted to dictate policy. In an extraordinary move, it voted to cut off funds for U.S. enforcement of the UN arms embargo, leading the United States, for the first time, to withdraw from a NATO-approved operation. The Clinton administration tried to repair relations with NATO by shifting its position toward NATO's softer line of seeking a negotiated settlement. On the other side, prominent members of Congress, especially Sen. Robert J. Dole, R-Kan., the majority leader, criticized the "helpless, hopeless," and "maybe irrelevant" NATO for failing to punish and stop Serbian aggression.[2] In summer 1995 Congress passed the Bosnia and Herzegovina Self-Defense Act, which directed the president, under specific conditions, to terminate the U.S. arms embargo against Bosnia and to press for the termination of the UN arms embargo. Clinton vetoed the bill.

The president's general concerns about supporting alliances led to a commitment of additional U.S. forces, including ground troops, to aid in the redeployment or withdrawal of the UN forces being threatened by Serbian forces. Clinton and Congress sparred over any commitment of ground troops for either combat or peacekeeping missions. Then, in a deft move, Clinton deepened his commitments and increased his leverage over Congress by having the United States host the UN-sponsored peace talks, in which Clinton was directly involved. Once the peace accord was signed in Paris in December 1995, Clinton began sending troops on his own authority and without effective congressional resistance. Even former critics such as Senator Dole argued that contradicting the president's commitments would harm the credibility of the United States as an ally and international leader. As for the House, it passed resolutions contradicting the president's

authority to send troops, opposing the mission, and yet supporting the troops deployed. Congress and Clinton continued to argue over a deadline for a conclusion to the mission.

These disputes arose again, in 1999, over the U.S. reaction to the brutal Serbian assaults on ethnic Albanians in Kosovo. General support in Congress for NATO air strikes was coupled with a muddled response to the possibility of U.S. ground forces being deployed for either combat or peacekeeping. Congress refused to authorize the sending of combat troops but failed to mount any strong resistance to Clinton sending ground forces for peacekeeping.

Such operations remain a major issue, in part because they divert forces away from national defense and consume defense dollars that could serve other needs and policies, such as weapons modernization, officer retention, and general military readiness. By one estimate, the cost of U.S. peacekeeping commitments was five times higher in 1996 than in 1989.[3]

COALITION LEADERSHIP IN THE WAR ON TERRORISM

September 11, 2001, abruptly exposed another face of post–cold war foreign policy and a new set of challenges to presidential leadership. More than three thousand people were murdered by terrorists flying hijacked airliners into the two towers of the World Trade Center in New York City, the Pentagon near Washington, D.C., and a field in southeastern Pennsylvania. These were not the first Americans killed by foreign terrorists. In 1983, 241 U.S. Marines were killed by a car bomb in Beirut, Lebanon, and many American lives were lost in the suicide bombings of the Khobar Towers in Saudi Arabia in 1996, of the U.S. embassies in Kenya and Tanzania in 1998, and of the *USS Cole* in Yemen in 2000. The 2001 attack, however, was distinguished from these by a combination of features: it occurred within the U.S. borders; unlike the Oklahoma City bombing, it was planned and executed by foreign terrorists; and the attack's high degree of planning, coordination, boldness, and savagery set it far apart from the 1993 car bombing of the World Trade Center.

The reaction of the U.S. government to this attack also was unprecedented. The government had responded to earlier incidents by retreating, imposing trade sanctions, or retaliating with brief, small-scale military actions. There was an implicit and explicit assumption and policy that international terrorism was, for one reason or another, a problem with which Americans had to live.[4] The potential for a major attack on U.S. soil had been foreseen by many, but the remedies tended to be defensive and remedial: sharpening intelligence capabilities to thwart such plots and enhancing preparedness, from missile defense to emergency logistics to stockpiling medications.[5] Few had argued for a vigorous and international counterterrorism policy.[6] President George W. Bush, however, defined the September 11 attack as an act of war and committed his administration to a war not only against the perpetrators and abettors of these killings but also against international terrorism itself.

On the one hand, the early stages of this campaign bore the earmarks of a bygone era. President Bush could creditably frame the U.S. commitment in terms of both a clear national interest in self-defense and a moral purpose of defending liberty and toleration against their determined enemies. The president's declarations received broad support from the general public and immediate authorization from Congress for the use of force. (See box, *Congressional Authorization for a War on Terrorism, p. 762, in Chapter 14.*) All but absent were the familiar reservations about duration, the use of ground troops in combat, and the loss of American lives. Congress also acted quickly on several otherwise controversial measures: an emergency appropriation of $40 billion for military, intelligence, and security measures, half of which was left to the president's discretion; an airline bailout package; and a broad counterterrorism bill that loosened restrictions on domestic surveillance and detention of suspected terrorists. The U.S.-led military and intelligence campaign received immediate backing from NATO and various levels of support and cooperation from a wide range of nations, including Britain, Germany, Switzerland, and even Russia. The Bush administration also secured the crucial participation of Pakistan and the limited cooperation of some Arab states.

On the other hand, the conflict posed some peculiar domestic and diplomatic problems. To begin with, a war on terrorism seeks not to defeat a state or an alliance of states but rather to disable or destroy a large number of often small and shadowy organizations and networks. How and when would the military objectives of a general antiterrorism operation be met, and what would the obligations of the partners be in the meantime? Concerns over a potentially broad and amorphous conflict led Congress, NATO, and other allies to frame their initial statements of support for military action more narrowly, focusing on the perpetrators of the September 11 attack rather than on international terrorism writ large. Yet even the first battle of the larger war foreshadowed difficulties in managing a broad counterterrorism coalition. Defeating Osama bin Laden and his al Qaeda terrorist network required an assault on the Taliban regime in Afghanistan that was harboring and supporting them.[7] A war on an Islamic state, and particularly one involving civilian casualties, risked the loss of cooperation or acquiescence from other Islamic states.

During the campaign in Afghanistan, the Bush administration was able to maintain the acquiescence of many Islamic countries and the active cooperation of Pakistan. Yet some of those countries, in particular Iran and Saudi Arabia, harbored and financed terrorist groups such as Hezbollah, Hamas, and Islamic Jihad, whose stated aims include the destruction of Israel. Saudi Arabia warned the United States against extending its counterterrorism efforts to these organizations. The Bush administration, at first omitting these groups from its list of terrorist organizations whose assets were to be frozen, later added them as their attacks on Israel grew more violent.[8] In his 2002 State of the Union address, President Bush also named Iran and Iraq as parts of an "axis of evil," which was "arming to threaten the peace of the world." His inclusion of the policies and regimes of these large Islamic states as targets of the war on terrorism was met by criticism and warnings from various allies. Moreover, always hanging over any controversy in the Middle East is the desire to maintain stable and cooperative relations with the regional oil states, which have a large impact on the economic well-being of Europe and the United States.

DEFINING A NATIONAL SECURITY STRATEGY FOR THE WAR ON TERRORISM

In September 2002 the Bush administration presented a comprehensive strategy for how the United States would wage the war on terrorism in the coming years. The thirty-one-page document, first distributed on the White House Web site, neatly summarized the administration's conceptualization of the long-term and multifaceted struggle against terrorism. Historian John Lewis Gaddis described it as "the new grand strategy of transformation."[9]

In many respects, the 2002 National Security Strategy (NSS) consolidated the ideas that President Bush had communicated already in several significant addresses, notably his January 29, 2002, State of the Union message (popularly known as the "axis of evil" speech) and his June 1, 2002, commencement address at the U.S. Military Academy at West Point. In his State of the Union message, Bush had famously identified Iraq, Iran, and North Korea as "an axis of evil, arming to threaten the peace of the world." He went on to declare that "I will not wait on events, while dangers gather. I will not stand by, as peril draws closer and closer."[10] Four months later, Bush announced at West Point that "If we wait for threats to fully materialize, we will have waited too long. . . . [Americans must] be ready for preemptive action when necessary to defend our liberty and to defend our lives."[11] Clearly the cold war strategies of containment and deterrence would not longer be sufficient to protect U.S. interests in the twenty-first century.

The NSS developed these positions further and placed them in the context of broader U.S. goals. The strategy began with a quotation from Bush's West Point speech, declaring that "We will defend the peace. . . . We will preserve the peace. . . . We will extend the peace."[12] After a brief overview, the document went on to discuss aspirations for human dignity, the importance of strengthening alliances to battle global terrorism, and the need to work with other nations to control regional conflicts. The concept of preemption did not emerge explicitly until nearly halfway through the document, which insisted that "the United States has long maintained the option of preemptive actions to counter a sufficient threat to our national security."[13]

Yet preemption marked the most significant change in American national security strategy since the establishment of the containment doctrine after World War II. By declaring that the United States might need to use force to prevent a conflict before it began, and that "traditional concepts of deterrence will not work against a terrorist enemy," the Bush administration was charting a new direction in international affairs. While international law has long held that states may act in self-defense if an aggressor is about to strike, the key question for preemptive warfare is timing: how imminent is the threat? In stating that "we must adapt the concept of imminent threat to the capabilities and objectives of today's adversaries," the NSS seemed to suggest that what traditionally had been defined as preventive war—a strategy that is much more controversial because of the challenge of identifying the likelihood of an attack—would not be viewed as preemptive war.

The implementation of the NSS with the 2003 war in Iraq raised many questions about the need, cost (both domestically and internationally in terms of allied support), ethics, and precedent of preemptive warfare. When the United States did not find the expected stores of weapons of mass destruction (WMD) in Iraq, critics of preemption reinforced their arguments that the strategy would ensnare the United States in conflicts without sustained international support. Nevertheless, the Bush administration continued to endorse the strategy, declaring in 2006 that "the place of preemption in our national security strategy remains the same."[14] The 2006 strategy focused explicitly on the problems that Iran and North Korea presented for nuclear proliferation, but it did not link the possibility of preemptive warfare to a particular case. The strategy also condemned genocide, and it included a new section on globalization, which addressed nontraditional challenges in national security, such as public health and the environment. Thus, although preemption remained part of the administration's strategy, it no longer seemed to be the driving force, as it was in 2002 with the planning for war in Iraq.

President Bush declares a "war on terrorism" after the terrorist attacks on the World Trade Center and the Pentagon on September 11, 2001. The Afghanistan-based al Qaeda terrorist group was suspected of planning the attack. Here U.S. troops prepare to return to their airbase after fighting in villages believed to be strongholds of al Qaeda and the Taliban government that supported them.

ism measures that broaden the government's powers of surveillance and detention. However, Congress killed the president's request for broad authority to waive restrictions on military assistance and weapons exports to certain countries, and it scuttled a plan to turn administration of certain U.S. seaports to a Middle Eastern company. Yet Congress also passed a joint resolution authorizing the president to respond to the 2001 attacks, and the Bush administration used that resolution to justify executive actions in the war on terror. Among Bush's controversial decisions were the authorization of military tribunals for war detainees, the indefinite imprisonment of detainees at the U.S. base in Guantanamo Bay, treatment of detainees, and a National Security Agency program that permitted bypassing traditional legal procedures to wiretap telephone conversations involving U.S. citizens that may be connected to terrorist threats. Congress also authorized the president to use military force in Iraq, although several members subsequently criticized the administration's postwar planning. In the years after 2001, the reassertion of congressional power in foreign policy was continually balanced by executive leadership in international affairs, and congressional reluctance to hinder the war on terror.

leaders. Bush's missile defense requests were slated to be cut, with restrictions placed on how the appropriated funds could be spent.

The September 11, 2001, terrorist attacks on New York City and Washington, D.C., to which Bush responded with a declaration of "war on terrorism," muted some of the criticism and resistance, particularly to missile defense, and fostered a more cooperative relationship that included quick action on an airline bailout bill, a large supplemental defense appropriation, and a controversial package of counterterror-

---

FACES OF FOREIGN POLICY: POST–COLD WAR ERA TO THE POST-9/11 WORLD (continued)

1. Louis Fisher, *Presidential War Power* (Lawrence: University Press of Kansas, 1995), 158.

2. "Republicans Lay Siege to Clinton's Policy," *Congressional Quarterly Weekly Report,* December 3, 1994, 3452–3453.

3. *National Journal,* March 16, 1996, 482.

4. See Jeffrey D. Simon, "Misunderstanding Terrorism," *Foreign Policy* (summer 1987); Charles William Maynes, "Bottom-Up Foreign Policy," *Foreign Policy* (fall 1996).

5. See, for example, Richard K. Betts, "The New Threat of Mass Destruction," *Foreign Affairs* (January/February 1998).

6. See Reuel Marc Gerecht, "A Cowering Superpower," *Weekly Standard,* July 30, 2001.

7. See Ahmed Rashid, "The Taliban: Exporting Extremism," *Foreign Affairs* (November/December 1999).

8. Robert Satloff, "The Other Twin Towers," *Weekly Standard,* October 8, 2001.

9. John Lewis Gaddis, "A Grand Strategy of Transformation," *Foreign Policy* (October/November 2002): 50–57.

10. George W. Bush, "State of the Union Address," January 29, 2002. Available at *(http://whitehouse.gov)*, accessed January 10, 2007.

11. George W. Bush, "Graduation Speech at West Point," June 1, 2002. Available at *(http://whitehouse.gov)*, accessed January 10, 2007.

12. George W. Bush, "The National Security Strategy of the United States of America," September 2002. Available at *(http://whitehouse.gov)*, accessed January 10, 2007.

13. Ibid.

14. George W. Bush, "The National Security Strategy of the United States of America," March 2006. Available at *(http://whitehouse.gov)*, accessed January 10, 2007.

POWER OF COMMUNICATION

The Constitution's separation of powers between independent branches left open the question of which branch had the power to receive communications from foreign countries and to speak for the nation. Under the Articles of Confederation, these responsibilities belonged to Congress. The Constitution assigns to the president the three main communication powers: negotiating treaties, sending ambassadors, and receiving ambassadors. The Framers recognized that communications is a function more suited to an office occupied by a single person than to a large deliberative body. Disputes have arisen over the extent to which communication powers imply policy-making authority.

President Washington was eager to establish the presidency as the only organ of government empowered to communicate officially with foreign governments. He recognized that if both the president and Congress presumed to speak for the nation, diplomacy would be impossible, and foreign governments might try to exploit the confusion. During the first year of his administration, Washington received a letter from King Louis XVI of France notifying "the President and Members of the General Congress of the United States" that Louis's son had died. Washington told Congress that he had received the letter and that he would send a reply to France. The president informed the king that "by the change which has taken place in the national government of the United States, the honor of receiving and answering your Majesty's letter of the 7th of June to 'the President and Members of Congress' has devolved upon me." [30]

In 1793 Washington's secretary of state, Thomas Jefferson, echoed this assertion when he explained to the French ambassador, Edmond Genêt, that the president "being the only channel of communication between this country and foreign nations, it is from him alone that foreign nations or their agents are to learn what is or has been the will of the nation; and whatever he communicates as such, they have the right, and are bound to consider, as the expression of the nation." [31]

Washington's conception of the president's role as national communicator was accepted without serious challenge. In 1799 John Marshall reaffirmed the president's position as the instrument of communication with foreign governments when as a member of the House of Representatives he declared, "The President is the sole organ of the nation in its external relations, and its sole representative with foreign nations." [32] The same year Congress passed the Logan Act, which prohibited any person other than presidents or their agents from communicating with another country with the intention of affecting its policy concerning an issue of contention with the United States. [33] Presumably the Logan Act could be invoked if a senator or representative attempted to usurp the president's power to communicate

officially with foreign nations. Informal discussions with foreign leaders by members of Congress have become accepted practices. Speaker Jim Wright's 1987 attempt, secretly and independent of the Reagan administration, to negotiate a settlement between the Nicaraguan government and the contra rebels was widely criticized across both parties and branches. [34]

More frequently, members of Congress use publicity to affect negotiations. In 1986 the media campaign initiated by Sen. Richard Lugar, R-Ind., helped to persuade President Reagan to withdraw his support for Philippine dictator Ferdinand Marcos in favor of the democratically elected Corazon Aquino. Similarly in 1991, through his use of the press, Sen. Al Gore, D-Tenn., was able to help turn the administration of President George H.W. Bush toward cooperation in negotiating an international treaty on global warming. The initial proposals for a cabinet agency focused on homeland security came from Congress, and the Bush administration adopted the issue after strong public support became evident. In 2005 Sen. John McCain, R-Ariz., successfully pressured the administration to include a prohibition on torture in the Detainee Treatment Act, a position that drew public support in the wake of the Abu Ghraib prison scandals in Iraq.

Foreign Policy Declarations

In practice, the president's exclusive authority to communicate with other nations extends well beyond ceremonial functions as chief of state. Since Washington's day, presidents have found that they can make and influence foreign policy simply by making a statement. Presidents have used their communications power to make commitments, formalize decisions, and establish broad policy goals.

Coming from the chief of state and "the sole representative with foreign nations," presidential declarations are, de facto, national commitments. Consequently, Congress often is left with a choice between supporting a presidential commitment and undermining both the president as the national representative and the confidence of other nations in U.S. policy. Thus how a president expresses U.S. interests and intentions can shape U.S. foreign policy. Kennedy's famous speech at the Berlin Wall in 1963, for example, encouraged the people of Berlin to expect U.S. protection, thereby committing the United States to its defense. Theodore Roosevelt explained the connection between communication and policy:

> The president carries on the correspondence through the State Department with all foreign countries. He is bound in such correspondence to discuss the proper construction of treaties. He must formulate the foreign policies of our government. He must state our attitude upon questions constantly arising. While strictly he may not bind our government as a treaty would bind it, to a definition of its

In 1963 President John F. Kennedy, fourth from right, stands on a platform facing the Berlin Wall and looks toward the Brandenburg Gate. The gate, barely inside East Berlin, was draped with red flags the day before Kennedy's arrival to prevent him from getting a good view of the communist sector of the city.

rights, still in future discussions foreign secretaries of other countries are wont to look for support of their contentions to the declarations and admissions of our secretaries of state in other controversies as in a sense binding upon us. There is thus much practical framing of our foreign policies in the executive conduct of our foreign relations.[35]

Presidential Doctrines

Beyond specific international commitments, presidents have also outlined general tenets of foreign policy, which have come to be labeled "doctrines." The most famous and durable policy statement by a president has been the Monroe Doctrine. In 1823 President James Monroe announced during his annual message to Congress that the United States would resist any attempt by a European power to interfere in the affairs of a Western Hemisphere country that was not already a European colony. Monroe did not consult Congress before his announcement, and some of its members believed the president had overstepped his authority. House Speaker Henry Clay proposed a joint resolution supporting the president's policy, but Congress did not act on it. Not until 1899 did the Monroe Doctrine receive a congressional endorsement.[36]

Theodore Roosevelt built on the Monroe Doctrine in 1904 when he announced in his annual message to Congress what became known as the Roosevelt Corollary. Roosevelt claimed for the United States the right to act as the Western Hemisphere's policeman if "chronic wrongdoing or impotence" in a country required U.S. intervention.

Broad foreign policy "doctrines" are associated with the administrations of many contemporary presidents. The Truman Doctrine stated that "it must be the policy of the United States to support free peoples who are resisting attempted subjugation by armed minorities or outside pressures."[37] The Eisenhower Doctrine, which was supported by a joint resolution, claimed for the United States the right to intervene militarily in the Middle East to protect legitimate governments from attacks by communist forces. The Nixon Doctrine (also known as the Guam Doctrine) proposed to continue giving allies military and economic aid while encouraging them to reduce their reliance on U.S. troops. The Carter Doctrine declared the Persian Gulf area to be a vital U.S. interest and warned that the United States would use force to prevent any attempt by an outside power to gain control of it. The Reagan Doctrine declared the Reagan administration's intention to support anticommunist insurgencies around the world to further a policy of rolling back communism and promoting liberal democratic government in Latin America, South Korea, the Philippines, and Taiwan. Only the president's policy declarations have a chance of being accepted as national policy, yet they are not always accepted by Congress and do not always last beyond the administration that announces them.

In the post–cold war era, the challenge of formulating a presidential strategy comparable to containment after World War II is evident. President George H.W. Bush's vague "New World Order" and President Clinton's similarly ill-defined policy of international engagement through multi-lateral operations illustrate the difficulty of formulating general commitments and principles of action. Actions early in the George W. Bush administration—for example, withdrawals from the Kyoto pact on global warming and from the Antiballistic Missile (ABM) Treaty—signaled a new general policy of unilateral action.[38] Criticism of this policy as "isolationist" was muted by the president's response to the 2001 terrorist attacks, and certainly the president and Congress were united in fighting terrorism. Nevertheless, the problem of translating that long-term goal into a clearly defined doctrine for U.S. action has remained.

THE TREATY POWER

The authors of the Constitution used only one clause to explain how treaties were to be made. Article II, Section 2, Clause 2, declares that the president "shall have the Power, by and with the Advice and Consent of the Senate, to make Treaties, provided two thirds of the Senators present concur." This concise statement blends responsibilities between the legislative and executive branches. Clearly the president is responsible for conducting the actual treaty negotiations; however, the president cannot conclude a treaty without first obtaining the consent of the Senate. The Constitution, therefore, ensures that no formal treaty can be concluded without a strong interbranch consensus, and that presidential negotiations will tend to be influenced by the disposition of the Senate. (See also "Treaty Making and Executive Agreements," p. 1336, in Chapter 29, Vol. II.)

The executive branch has established itself as the more influential branch in treaty making. As the sole organ of communication with foreign countries, commander in chief, and head of the foreign policy bureaucracy, presidents have been equipped with the means necessary to lead in most phases of the treaty-making process. The president dominates decisions concerning whether and when treaty negotiations will be pursued. The president chooses the negotiators, develops the negotiating strategy, and submits completed draft treaties to the Senate for approval.

Moreover, the president's power to "make" treaties is interpreted as including the final power of ratification. Once the Senate has approved a treaty, it does not become law until the president ratifies it. Thus the president has significant leverage over any attempts by the Senate to amend a treaty. If the president decides to ratify a treaty the Senate has approved, an exchange of ratifications occurs between the signatories. Then the treaty is promulgated—that is, officially proclaimed to be law—by the president. At any time

the president may stop the treaty-making process. Thus the president has the power of initiative over a treaty from its conception to its ratification.[39]

Creation of Treaty Power

In the eighteenth century, treaties were considered to be the primary tool of foreign policy, and the authors of the Constitution deliberated extensively on how treaties should be made. Under the Articles of Confederation, the treaty power was completely entrusted to the legislature. It selected negotiators, wrote and revised their orders, and made the final decision on whether a treaty would be accepted or rejected. At the Constitutional Convention, delegates initially assumed that this legislative power would be given to the new Congress and specifically to the Senate, which was designed to be wiser and more stable than the House. Late in the convention's deliberations, and after the executive had been made fully independent of the legislature, the convention divided the treaty-making power between the executive and the Senate.[40]

The Framers recognized that the president, as a single national officer, would be "the most fit agent" for making "preparations and auxiliary measures," for managing delicate and often secret negotiations, and for adapting to often rapidly changing circumstances. John Jay noted other advantages of a single negotiator:

> It seldom happens in the negotiation of treaties, of whatever nature, but that perfect secrecy and immediate dispatch are sometimes requisite. There may be cases where the most useful intelligence may be obtained, if the persons possessing it can be relieved from apprehensions of discovery. . . . and there doubtless are many . . . who would rely on the secrecy of the president, but who would not confide in that of the Senate, and still less in that of a large popular assembly.[41]

Similar considerations favored the exclusion of the House from treaty deliberations. Hamilton and Jay argued in *The Federalist Papers* that the Senate is favored by its smaller size, its wiser membership chosen by the "select assemblies" of the states, and the stability secured by longer and overlapping terms. These features also would encourage the Senate to focus on the long-term interests of the nation as a whole. The extraordinary majority required for treaty approval in the Senate would, it was argued, ensure that no treaty would become law without high levels of scrutiny and approval.[42]

By giving the president the power to "make" treaties "by and with the Advice and Consent of the Senate," the authors of the Constitution bolstered the prestige of the executive. They must have understood that the president's position as chief negotiator would afford him great influence over policy. However, they spoke of the Senate controlling the overall "system" of foreign policy. The Framers seemed to have expected that senatorial "Advice and Consent" would operate throughout the process and that the president would obtain "their sanction in the progressive stages of a treaty." [43]

The Constitution also strengthened the legal status of treaties. One weakness of the national government under the Articles of Confederation was its dependence on the states to implement treaties. Congress could not force the states to recognize treaty provisions as law. As a result, several states had violated certain articles of the Peace Treaty of 1783 with Great Britain. The convention's answer to this problem was Article VI, Clause 2, of the Constitution, which states that "all Treaties made, or which shall be made, under the Authority of the United States, shall be the supreme Law of the Land; and the Judges in every State shall be bound thereby, any Thing in the Constitution or Laws of any State to the Contrary notwithstanding."

Chief Justice John Marshall interpreted this clause in his opinion in *Foster v. Neilson* in 1829. He confirmed that any treaty or portion of a treaty that did not require legislation to fulfill its provisions was binding on the states and had equal force to federal law. Therefore, although Congress may have to enact legislation to carry out acts stipulated by a treaty, any self-executing treaty or part of a treaty automatically attains the status of a law, enforceable by the courts. Provisions of various treaties periodically have been the target of legal challenges, but the Supreme Court has never declared a treaty or provision of a treaty made by the United States to be unconstitutional. [44] *(See "Presidential Powers Directed Abroad," p. 1445, in Chapter 30, Vol. II, and "Treaty Making and Executive Agreements," p. 1336, in Chapter 29, Vol. II.)*

Presidential Primacy in Treaty Negotiations

The Constitution clearly states that both the president and the Senate have a role in treaty making, but the form of the Senate's advice on treaty matters and its influence over negotiations has changed over time.

President Washington's initial interpretation of the treaty-making clause was that "Advice" meant he was to seek Senate opinions in person before his representatives began negotiations. On August 21, 1789, Washington and his secretary of war, Henry Knox, questioned the Senate in its chambers about a treaty to be negotiated with the Creek Indians. After some debate, the Senate decided to postpone its response to Washington's questions until the following week so it could discuss the negotiations further. Washington, who had expected an immediate reply, returned on Monday, August 24, and received answers to his questions, but he was angered by the Senate's indecisiveness and pessimistic that he could rely on that body for timely consultations on treaty matters. He never again attempted to use it as an executive council before treaty negotiations. Nonetheless, during the early years of his presidency Washington conscientiously wrote to the Senate for advice on treaty matters before and during negotiations. He also routinely submitted the negotiators' instructions to the Senate and kept that body informed of the progress of talks. [45]

The Senate's role in treaty negotiations would likely have been enhanced had Washington established a precedent of consulting with that body in person. Subsequent presidents, however, agreed with Washington that the advice and consent of the Senate were best obtained from a distance. Several twentieth-century presidents, including Wilson and Truman, went to the Senate to propose or to lobby for treaties, but no president has ever returned to the Senate chamber to seek direct advice on treaty matters.

Washington's handling of the important Jay Treaty of 1794, which avoided war with Great Britain, demonstrated that he had abandoned his initial interpretation of the Constitution's treaty-making clause. In preparation for the Jay Treaty negotiations, Washington submitted only the appointment of his negotiator, Chief Justice John Jay, to the Senate for approval. He withheld from the Senate Jay's instructions about the sensitive negotiations, and the negotiations were held in London without Senate involvement.

Rather than challenging the president's power to make a treaty independently of the Senate, that body responded by amending the completed Jay Treaty in a manner similar to the method by which it amended legislation. Washington accepted the Senate's authority to do this, and after initial protests, the British ratified the amended treaty. The Jay Treaty established a process of treaty making that subsequent administrations and Senates would emulate. As Corwin observed, "The Senate's function as an executive council was from the very beginning put, and largely by its own election, on the way to absorption into its more usual function as a legislative chamber, and subsequent developments soon placed its decision in this respect beyond all possibility of recall." [46]

The often significant influence the Senate has over treaty negotiations comes more from its power to reject a treaty than from any constitutional provision that the president should consider the Senate's advice when making treaties. The Senate, or a minority thereof, can intrude into negotiations by making the conditions of its final approval quite clear. Presidents have, therefore, often cooperated closely with the Senate in the negotiation of a treaty because they recognize that Senate involvement would increase the chances for approval. Excluding the Senate from the negotiating process has often led to troubles and defeats for presidents. [47]

Moreover, Congress can use its control over other policies to influence a president's treaty negotiations. In 1983 some senators threatened to vote against funding the MX missile, a crucial piece of Ronald Reagan's defense modernization program, unless he modified his negotiating position at the Strategic Arms Reduction Talks (START) in Geneva. [48]

The Treaty-Making Process

The first step in making a treaty is negotiating with a foreign power. This stage is controlled by the president and presidential advisers and representatives. During or before this phase, members of Congress may offer advice to the president or express their views on the negotiations individually or collectively. A resolution communicating Congress's disapproval may cause the president to change negotiating strategies or abandon a treaty altogether. A supportive resolution, however, may contribute to the executive branch's enthusiasm for a particular treaty. In 1948, for example, the Senate's Vandenberg Resolution, which preceded the development of NATO and other alliance systems, advised the president to negotiate regional security agreements.[49] Regardless of congressional protests or encouragement, the president and representatives of the president cannot be prevented from initiating and conducting treaty negotiations with another country.

Although the executive branch has the power to negotiate a treaty without Congress, many presidents have found that involving individual senators in the negotiating process can be a useful political tool. Such involvement can take several forms. During most treaty negotiations, influential senators are at least asked for their opinions on the proceedings, but a president also may ask senators to help select the negotiating team, observe the negotiations, follow the progress of the talks through briefings, or even be negotiators.[50] Until the end of Madison's administration in 1817, the names of treaty negotiators were referred to the Senate for confirmation. The Senate repeatedly protested subsequent presidents' neglect of that practice, but the Senate never was able to establish firmly its right to confirm negotiators.

The practice of sending the instructions of treaty negotiators to the Senate for review, which Washington had followed early in his presidency, proved to be even more temporary. After Washington's administration, no president asked the Senate to consider the terms of a treaty not yet agreed upon, until Polk submitted the skeleton of a treaty ending the war with Mexico in 1846. Preliminary drafts of treaties were sent to the Senate in a few instances by four other presidents—James Buchanan, Lincoln, Andrew Johnson, and Ulysses S. Grant. In 1919 the Senate requested a copy of the proposed Treaty of Versailles as presented to the representatives of Germany. The secretary of state replied: "The president feels it would not be in the public interest to communicate to the Senate a text that is provisional and not definite, and finds no precedent for such a procedure."[51]

President Wilson generally excluded the Senate from the Versailles treaty negotiations, and the Senate rejected this important treaty. Most later presidents grasped the obvious lesson. While World War II was still being fought, Franklin Roosevelt established the Joint Advisory Committee on Postwar Foreign Policy to provide a forum where members of Congress and the executive branch could discuss the composition of an international peace organization. This committee, along with the administration's private consultations with Senate leaders, helped create bipartisan support for the United Nations.[52] When the negotiations on the United Nations Treaty began in 1945, Truman included senators from both parties in the U.S. delegation.

The Carter administration also tried to limit Senate objections to the SALT II (Strategic Arms Limitation Talks) treaty it hoped to negotiate with the Soviet Union by encouraging senatorial participation in the process. Selected senators were allowed to observe the negotiations, and the administration consulted closely with Senate leaders while the negotiations were in progress. During these consultations, senators voiced suggestions and concerns that prompted Carter to instruct his negotiators to modify their position on several issues.[53] The Senate observers in those talks also persuaded the Soviet Union to provide crucial information on their nuclear forces by arguing that the Senate would never approve the treaty without it. In 1991 the Senate Intelligence Committee's concerns over verification procedures in the Intermediate Nuclear Forces (INF) Treaty led President George H.W. Bush to renegotiate the relevant sections.[54]

Once U.S. negotiators have agreed on the terms of a treaty with a foreign government, the president must decide whether to submit the draft to the Senate for consideration. If it appears that Senate opposition to a treaty will make approval unlikely, the president may decide to withdraw the treaty to avoid a political defeat. Also, international events may change the president's mind about the desirability of ratifying a treaty. Carter withdrew the SALT II treaty from Senate consideration to protest the Soviet invasion and occupation of Afghanistan.

If the president decides to submit a treaty to the Senate for consideration, the Constitution requires that two-thirds of the Senate vote in favor of the treaty for it to be approved. The Senate is not compelled by the Constitution either to approve or to reject a treaty as it has been negotiated by the executive branch. It may attach amendments to a treaty that require the president to renegotiate its terms with the other signatories before the Senate grants its approval. In 1978 the Senate added conditions and reservations to the treaty that provided for the transfer of the Panama Canal to Panamanian control after the year 2000. The most notable of these amendments was written by Sen. Dennis DeConcini, D-Ariz. It claimed for the United States the right to take whatever steps were necessary, including military force, to open the canal if its operations ceased.[55] The Panamanian government agreed to accept the Senate amendments without renegotiation.

Although such amendments can often make agreement between the United States and its negotiating partner difficult or impossible, presidents have little choice but to accept the Senate's power to force renegotiation of parts of a treaty. In effect, when the Senate gives its consent on condition that its amendments are accepted by the negotiating partner of the United States, it is rejecting the treaty while outlining a revision of the treaty to which it grants its consent in advance.[56] Presidents in turn may decide not to renegotiate if they believe the senatorial amendments make the treaty undesirable.

The Senate also has the power to add nonbinding written reservations to a treaty before approving it. This option can be used when the Senate accepts the basic terms of a treaty but wishes to impose its interpretation on the document and its implementation. In 1991 the Senate attached a reservation to the Treaty on Conventional Forces in Europe that stated that the United States would consider the Soviet Union's failure to fulfill its pledge to eliminate additional weapons as equivalent to a violation of the treaty.[57] In 1992 the disintegration of the Soviet Union complicated the ratification process for the first Strategic Arms Reduction Treaty (START I). President Bush had to negotiate "protocols" with the newly independent states, committing them to abide by the terms of the treaty, and the Senate then attached a reservation to the treaty stating that these protocols and all other related agreements were fully part of the treaty's formal terms.

Foreign governments may disagree with, or take offense at, such resolutions. Ratification of the 1976 Treaty of Friendship and Cooperation with Spain was delayed several months by Spanish objections to nonbinding Senate resolutions attached to the treaty. The issue was resolved by an agreement between Congress, the Ford administration, and the Spanish government to attach the resolutions to the U.S. instrument of ratification, the document outlining the U.S. understanding of the treaty, but to exclude them from the Spanish instrument of ratification and the treaty ratification document exchanged by the two countries.[58]

After the Senate approves and the president ratifies a treaty, the treaty may require legislation, such as the appropriation of funds or the enactment of criminal laws. Because these tasks can only be accomplished by Congress, such treaties are referred to as "non-self-executing."[59] Consequently, non-self-executing treaties give Congress another chance to pass judgment on them after ratification. Although Congress rarely has chosen to undermine a treaty by refusing to appropriate funds or enact implementing legislation, its right to do so is well established.[60]

Treaty Approval

The Senate has approved without changes about 90 percent of the treaties submitted to it by presidents. This success rate is a less striking testament to presidential leadership than it

may appear. Presidents regularly anticipate senatorial objections in negotiating a treaty, and they must, as in other legislative matters, make deals to gain the votes of particular senators.[61] Moreover, to avoid a political defeat, presidents often have withdrawn treaties from consideration that were in jeopardy of Senate rejection. Other treaties were neither approved nor rejected by the Senate, but instead left in political limbo. For example, the Genocide Treaty, which instructed signers to prevent and punish the crime of genocide, was approved by the Senate in 1986, almost thirty-seven years after Truman submitted it to that body. Many more pacts that could have taken the form of treaties were concluded as less formal executive agreements between the president and a foreign government to avoid the possibility of Senate rejection.

The success rate of treaties probably reflects the inclination of senators, and representatives, to follow the president's lead in foreign affairs in the interest of projecting a united front abroad. As noted, members of Congress do not wish to be seen as saboteurs of presidential policy. Moreover, Congress must balance its reservations about a particular treaty against the damage rejection would inflict on international confidence in the United States and its chief of state. Finally, even senators of the president's party who have reservations about a treaty often will side with the president for the sake of the party. If the president's party happens to be in control of the Senate, obtaining approval for a treaty may require the support of fewer than half of the senators from the opposition party.

Although the Senate's approval record has been overwhelmingly positive, there have been significant exceptions. Between 1871 and 1898, no major treaty was approved. The most famous treaty rejected by the Senate was the Treaty of Versailles, which ended World War I and established the League of Nations. In 1999 the Senate defeated the Comprehensive [Nuclear] Test Ban Treaty, which had been negotiated by President Bill Clinton. *(See Table 13-1.)*

The method by which Congress approves treaties has been the target of periodic criticism. John Hay, the secretary of state under McKinley and Theodore Roosevelt who fought several losing battles with the Senate over treaty approval, called the power of the Senate to veto treaties the "original mistake of the Constitution."[62] After the Senate refused to approve the Versailles treaty, proposals surfaced in both the executive and legislative branches to reduce the fraction of Senate members needed to approve a treaty from two-thirds to three-fifths or to a simple majority. Other proposals would eliminate the requirement of an extraordinary majority in the Senate and replace it with simple majority approval by both houses of Congress. Several resolutions to this effect were introduced in Congress during the 1920s and 1940s, yet none has come close to being implemented.

TABLE 13-1 **Major Treaties Killed by the Senate, 1789–2006**

Date of vote	President	Country	Yea	Vote Nay	Subject
March 9, 1825	J. Q. Adams	Colombia	0	40	Suppression of African slave trade
June 11, 1836	Jackson	Switzerland	14	23	Personal and property rights
June 8, 1844	Polk	Texas	16	35	Annexation
June 15, 1844	Polk	German Zollverein	26	18	Reciprocity
May 31, 1860	Buchanan	Mexico	18	27	Transit and commercial rights
June 27, 1860	Buchanan	Spain	26	17	Cuban Claims Commission
April 13, 1869	Grant	Great Britain	1	54	Arbitration of claims
June 1, 1870	Grant	Hawaii	20	19	Reciprocity
June 30, 1870	Grant	Dominican Republic	28	28	Annexation
January 29, 1885	Cleveland	Nicaragua	32	23	Interoceanic canal
April 20, 1886	Cleveland	Mexico	32	26	Mining claims
August 21, 1888	Cleveland	Great Britain	27	30	Fishing rights
February 1, 1889	B. Harrison	Great Britain	15	38	Extradition
May 5, 1897	McKinley	Great Britain	43	26	Arbitration
March 19, 1920	Wilson	Multilateral	49	35	Treaty of Versailles
January 18, 1927	Coolidge	Turkey	50	34	Commercial rights
March 14, 1934	F. Roosevelt	Canada	46	42	St. Lawrence Seaway
January 29, 1935	F. Roosevelt	Multilateral	52	36	World Court
May 26, 1960	Eisenhower	Multilateral	49	30	Law of the Sea Convention
March 8, 1983	Reagan	Multilateral	50	42	Montreal Aviation Protocol
June 11, 1991	G. H. W. Bush	Multilateral	—	—	Annex II, international convention on load lines[a]
June 11, 1991	G. H. W. Bush	Multilateral	—	—	Amendments to Annex II, international convention on load lines[a]
October 13, 1999	Clinton	Multilateral	48	51	Comprehensive nuclear test ban

SOURCE: Lyn Ragsdale, *Vital Statistics on the Presidency: Washington to Clinton* (Washington, D.C.: Congressional Quarterly, 1998), 321; *CQ Almanac, 1999* (Washington, D.C.: Congressional Quarterly, 1999), C-7.

NOTE: a. Not formally rejected by a roll call vote, but instead returned to the president.

Termination of Treaties

Although Article VI, Clause 2, of the Constitution declares that treaties are the "supreme Law of the Land," the federal government is not legally constrained from terminating a treaty through agreement with the other party in response to the other party's violations of the treaty or for any other reason. However, the Constitution provides no guidelines about which branch determines that a treaty should be revoked and what sort of approval is needed from another branch. Consequently, both the president and Congress at various times have successfully exercised the power to terminate treaties.[63]

In 1979 this issue was brought before the Supreme Court when the Carter administration sought to terminate the 1954 Mutual Defense Treaty with the Republic of China (Taiwan) as part of the process of establishing formal relations with the People's Republic of China. The treaty had a clause permitting withdrawal, but President Carter took the action without consulting the Senate beforehand. Sen. Barry M. Goldwater, R-Ariz., and twenty-three other members of Congress brought suit to prevent Carter's unilateral termination of the treaty.

U.S. district court judge Oliver Gasch ruled in October 1979 that Carter's action violated the principle of separation of powers and that both historical precedents and the text of the Constitution indicate that treaty termination requires the consent of two-thirds of the Senate or a majority of both houses of Congress. A U.S. Court of Appeals overturned Gasch's decision. However, the Supreme Court dismissed the complaint, with five justices arguing that either this case or the issue in general was not fit for judicial resolution.[64]

EXECUTIVE AGREEMENTS

An executive agreement is a pact other than a treaty made by the president or representatives of the president with a foreign leader or government. The executive agreement is a particularly powerful foreign policy tool. Presidents have asserted that their power to execute the laws, command the armed forces, and function as the sole organ of foreign policy gives them the full legal authority to make these pacts without any congressional approval. Unlike treaties, they do not supersede U.S. laws with which they conflict, but in every other respect they are binding.

Although the vast majority of international pacts are executive agreements, most executive agreements either are routine extensions of existing treaties or are based on broad legislative directives.[65] Agreements made by the president to carry out legislation or treaty obligations are often called "congressional-executive international agreements." Other executive agreements have been supported by joint resolutions. Occasionally, presidents seek the approval of a majority of both houses of Congress for executive agreements when they do not have the support of two-thirds of the Senate but they do want, or need, some type of specific congressional consent. This practice has, at times, elicited strong objections from senators, but it is generally supported by partisan majorities and by the House, which is, through this procedure, given a much larger voice in foreign policy.[66] Congressional authorization and joint approval have been used frequently in areas, such as tariffs, where congressional, or House, authority is definitive.

The small percentage of agreements (about 3 percent) that do not fall under these categories are the "pure" executive agreements, which are negotiated and implemented without any congressional approval. The presidents' authority to make such agreements is usually not disputed, especially when presidents are otherwise acting within their sphere of authority and when the practical advantages of a flexible power of agreement are great. For example, the commander in chief must frequently make and alter agreements with allies during the course of a war. However, the proper scope of the president's unilateral authority to commit the nation has often been disputed. As the scope of executive agreements has broadened, these have become the most important and the most controversial pacts.

The use of executive agreements grew dramatically in the twentieth century. From 1789 to 1839, executive agreements made up only 31 percent of all international agreements, whereas more than 95 percent of international pacts made between 1980 and 1990 were executive agreements. As of 1992 the United States had entered into approximately 1,700 treaties and approximately 16,000 executive agreements.[67] Today, executive agreements are used to conduct business once reserved for treaties. Indeed, contemporary presidents can accomplish through an executive agreement almost anything that can be accomplished through a treaty.

Constitutional Dilemma

The Constitution does not prohibit executive agreements, and the Court in *United States v. Curtiss-Wright* explicitly affirmed the power of the national government to make international agreements other than treaties. However, the Founders' careful division of the treaty power in the Constitution must be interpreted as an attempt to ensure that Congress has a direct voice in making international commitments. The use of executive agreements by presidents and their representatives to avoid congressional interference has been widely regarded by constitutional scholars and members of Congress as a serious deterioration of constitutional checks and balances in the area of foreign policy.

The development of the United States into a world power with security commitments and economic interests in every corner of the world has made some degree of executive flexibility in making executive agreements desirable. Like Jefferson, who was confronted with the irresistible opportunity to buy the Louisiana Territory, contemporary presidents are sometimes faced with an international situation that calls for making commitments with speed and secrecy. Also, executive agreements often provide a simpler method of transacting the less important international business that would overload the already tight legislative schedule if treaties were used.

The crux of the problem is that some important international agreements should receive some sort of congressional approval, yet there are no concrete guidelines to indicate which pacts need Senate consent, which need approval by both houses, and which can be handled simply by the president. Presidents may, therefore, use their discretion in deciding how to make a particular agreement. Numerous presidents, faced with the prospect of fighting for two-thirds approval in the Senate, have used executive agreements to skirt the treaty requirements imposed by the Constitution rather than abandon a diplomatic initiative. Treaties, therefore, have become an exception to the rule, which is presidential policy making.

Despite the use of executive agreements to avoid the treaty ratification process, the Supreme Court has repeatedly upheld the president's power to make international agreements without the consent of the Senate. The Court's ruling in *United States v. Belmont* in 1937 was particularly significant. At issue was the president's authority to conclude unilaterally several agreements connected with the 1933 recognition of the Soviet Union. In delivering the Court's opinion, Justice George Sutherland wrote:

> The recognition, establishment of diplomatic relations, the assignment, and agreement with respect thereto, were all parts of one transaction, resulting in an international compact between the two governments. That the negotiations, acceptance of the assignment and agreements and understandings in respect thereof were within the competence of the president may not be doubted. Governmental power over internal affairs is distributed between the national government and the several states. Governmental power over external affairs is not distributed, but is vested exclusively in the national government. And in respect of what was done here, the Executive had the authority to speak as the sole organ of that government.[68]

Justice Sutherland could have based his opinion that the president had the authority to make these agreements on the president's indisputable power to recognize foreign governments. Although he did mention the relevance of this presidential power, he seemed to find authority for the agreements in the president's broader power as the "sole organ" of foreign policy.[69]

Landmark Executive Agreements

The first major executive agreement concluded between a president and a foreign power was the Rush-Bagot agreement with Great Britain.[70] The pact, which imposed limitations on naval forces on the Great Lakes, was concluded under the supervision of President James Monroe in 1817. A year after the agreement was put into operation, Monroe sent the agreement to the House and Senate and asked if they thought it required the consent of the Senate. The Senate endorsed the "arrangement" with a two-thirds vote but did not consider its action to be an approval of a treaty, and instruments of ratification were never exchanged between the United States and Great Britain.[71]

Although Monroe's executive agreement was significant in establishing a precedent, President John Tyler's annexation of Texas by executive agreement in 1845 was even more important, because it was the first time a president had used an executive agreement to accomplish what would have been defeated in the treaty process.[72] Tyler wished to bring Texas into the Union to keep it out of foreign hands and to serve the southern slave interests, but he was not close to having the necessary two-thirds support in the Senate to conclude a treaty of annexation. With sufficient public support for annexation, he called on Congress for a joint resolution to bring Texas into the nation. The resolution passed the House by a 120–98 vote and the Senate by a spare two-vote margin. With this annexation agreement in hand, Tyler invited Texas to become a state. In 1898 McKinley used the same method to annex Hawaii to the United States as a territory.[73]

Predictably, Theodore Roosevelt was not timid about using executive agreements to accomplish foreign policy objectives that would have been delayed or undermined by the treaty process. When Santo Domingo (now the Dominican Republic) fell into heavy debt to European creditors in 1905, Roosevelt oversaw negotiations of a treaty that extended U.S. protection to Santo Domingo and put the United States in control of collecting the country's customs to satisfy the creditors. Roosevelt hoped the Senate would consent to the draft treaty, but when it did not, he continued the arrangement under an executive agreement.[74]

At the outbreak of World War II, Franklin Roosevelt also used an executive agreement to avoid the treaty process when he provided destroyers to the British in 1940. At the time, the United States was still officially neutral, and a predominantly isolationist Senate would not have approved a treaty that provided Britain with ships to defend against

During the eighteenth and nineteenth centuries, no president while in office traveled outside the United States. Theodore Roosevelt broke this precedent when he visited Panama in 1906 to inspect the canal under construction.

German submarines. Roosevelt therefore used an executive agreement to trade old U.S. destroyers for the right to lease several British naval bases in the Western Hemisphere. Because the deal violated two neutrality statutes and altered the neutral status of the United States, it clearly should have been accompanied by some sort of congressional approval.[75]

A dramatic example of the dangers and limits of executive agreements was President Nixon's written assurance to President Nguyen Van Thieu of South Vietnam in 1973 that the United States would "respond with full force" if North Vietnam violated the Paris Peace Agreement, which ended the U.S. military presence in Vietnam. Thieu had consented to the Paris Agreement based on Nixon's personal promise. But Nixon's agreement was little more than the optimistic personal promise of a president who almost certainly would not have had the means to keep it, even if he had remained in office. Thieu, however, regarded Nixon's pledge as a national commitment, and the United States lost credibility when the promise was not kept after the North Vietnamese invaded South Vietnam in 1975.[76]

Yet Congress regularly authorizes the president to avoid the treaty clause, even for major international agreements. In 1993 and 1994 the North American Free Trade Agreement (NAFTA) and a new General Agreement on Tariffs and Trade (GATT), which comprehensively revised the nation's trade policy, were validated only by authorizing legislation passed in the House and Senate. In 2005 Congress narrowly approved the expansion of NAFTA to include the Central America Free Trade Agreement (CAFTA). It has been standard practice for more than a century for Congress to authorize the president to make tariff adjustments through executive agreements, and the House would have had a well-founded complaint if significant changes in tariff laws had been submitted only to the Senate.[77] GATT, however, went beyond the adjustment of tariffs and committed the nation's trade practices to a regime of oversight and sanction by an international body, the World Trade Organization. Even so, the loudest objections were to the agreement itself and not to the mode of approval.

Attempts to Limit Executive Agreements

Since the end of World War II, Congress has made two major attempts to control the president's power to make international agreements and secret commitments. The more intrusive one was a constitutional amendment proposed by Sen. John W. Bricker, R-Ohio, in 1953 that would have placed restraints on the president's power to make executive agreements and decreased the effect of the agreements on domestic law. The second occurred in the early 1970s and culminated in the Case Act of 1972, which was intended to compel the executive branch merely to report all executive agreements to Congress or to selected congressional committees. Except for a clarification of the Case Act passed in 1977, subsequent efforts by Congress to make the executive branch more accountable for its agreements with other nations have been unsuccessful.

Bricker Amendment

Senator Bricker, a conservative Republican, chaired the Senate Interstate and Foreign Commerce Committee for two years beginning in 1953. In the postwar era, when the United States was expanding its defense commitments and its participation in international organizations, the Brickerites argued that the president's broad power to make international agreements that are supreme over the constitutions and laws of states (see *United States v. Belmont*, 1937) threatened the constitutionally guaranteed rights of the states and the American people.[78] Moreover, many senators were alarmed by the growing tendency of presidents to use executive agreements to implement military alliance pacts and UN programs. In January 1953 Bricker and sixty-three

cosponsors introduced an amendment aimed at establishing congressional review of executive agreements and making treaties unenforceable as domestic law without accompanying legislation. Two provisions of the amendment would have radically altered the way the United States enters into agreements with foreign governments. Every treaty and executive agreement would have required implementing legislation to make it enforceable as domestic law, and any executive agreement made by a president would have been subject to regulation by Congress. The ability of presidents to make foreign policy through executive agreements and to negotiate treaties without involving Congress would have been severely curtailed. The amendment did not, however, come to a vote by the time Congress adjourned in August 1953. In 1954 a milder version of the Bricker amendment came within one vote of passing the Senate with a two-thirds majority. Thereafter, support for the amendment ebbed, in part because President Dwight D. Eisenhower strongly opposed it.

Case Act

In the early 1970s, a more modest movement surfaced in Congress to restrain the indiscriminate use of secret agreements. The impetus for this effort was the discovery by a Senate subcommittee in 1969–1970 that the executive branch had made secret commitments and terms of agreements during the 1960s. The Security Agreements and Commitments Abroad Subcommittee of the Senate Foreign Relations Committee, chaired by Sen. Stuart Symington, D-Mo., uncovered secret agreements with Ethiopia, Laos, Thailand, South Korea, Spain, the Philippines, and other countries. The Nixon administration deepened congressional resentment by concluding important executive agreements with Portugal and Bahrain about military bases. The Senate passed a resolution asserting that the agreements should have been made in the form of treaties, which would have required Senate consent.

Congress responded more generally by passing the Case Act in 1972. The act obligates the executive branch to inform Congress of all executive agreements within sixty days of their conclusion. (It also required the executive branch to inform Congress of all executive agreements in existence at the time the law was signed.) The law also provides that the House and Senate committees with jurisdiction over foreign affairs be informed of any executive agreements that the president determines need to be kept secret to ensure national security. The Senate passed the bill by a unanimous 81–0 vote and the House by voice vote.[79] The years following passage of the Case Act saw the emergence of several bills intended to establish a congressional procedure for disapproving executive agreements. Such a bill, introduced by Sen. Sam J. Ervin Jr., D-N.C., passed the Senate in 1974, but the House did not act on it. Hearings on two similar bills were held in 1975 by the Senate Judiciary Subcommittee on the Separation of Powers, but they did not lead to legislation.

After several years, Congress found that many executive agreements were not being reported under the provisions of the Case Act; executive branch officials had labeled them "understandings" rather than executive agreements. Congress reacted by passing legislation in 1977 that required Congress to be informed of any verbal or informal understanding made by any representative of the U.S. government that might constitute a commitment.

Although the Case Act and the legislation that followed it do not limit the president's power to make executive agreements, legislators are better able to check this executive branch power if they know what sort of agreements the president is making. Congress's ability to conduct investigations, issue resolutions, pass legislation, and control appropriations gives it the tools it needs to challenge and refuse to honor executive agreements it believes are unwise or improper. This is especially true of the many executive agreements that depend on supporting legislation.

THE RECOGNITION POWER

Although the Constitution does not explicitly grant presidents the power to recognize foreign governments, Congress has generally accepted that presidents have this power as a consequence of the authority to appoint (Article II, Section 2) and receive (Article II, Section 3) ambassadors. Because the acts of sending an ambassador to a country and receiving its ambassador imply recognition of the legitimacy of the foreign government involved in the exchange, presidents have successfully claimed the general authority to decide which foreign governments will be recognized by the United States. Also, because presidents decide which nations will be recognized, it follows that they have the power to terminate relations with another nation.

This interpretation of presidential power was not universally accepted at the beginning of the Republic. Madison, writing as Helvidius, argued that the duty to receive ambassadors did not give the president the power to rule on the legitimacy of foreign governments.[80] In *The Federalist Papers,* Hamilton did not acknowledge the connection between the ceremonial power to receive ambassadors and the recognition of nations, and he may have considered recognition a power shared with the Senate. Hamilton described the power to receive ambassadors as "more a matter of dignity than of authority. It is a circumstance which will be without consequence in the administration of the government." [81]

The first use of the president's power of recognition occurred in 1793 when Washington agreed to receive Edmond Genêt, the ambassador of the new French Republic.

President George W. Bush sent U.S. secretary of state Colin Powell (right) to meet with Israeli prime minister Ariel Sharon in April 2002 to discuss the possibility of an Israeli-Palestinian cease-fire. Israel had launched extensive military attacks on Palestinian areas following a number of suicide bombings in Israel.

Because most of the members of Congress who were inclined to resist the growth of executive power into areas not specifically granted in the Constitution were also supporters of the new republican regime in France, this expansion of the president's power to receive ambassadors was not questioned.[82] All subsequent presidents have assumed the right to make recognition decisions.

George Washington's decision to accept Genêt's credentials soon began to cause the president problems. Genêt attempted to exploit the American people's sympathy for revolutionary France by privately enlisting their support against his country's enemies, Great Britain and Spain. His activities undercut Washington's Proclamation of Neutrality and threatened to draw the United States into the European hostilities. Washington, therefore, demanded that the French government recall Genêt. The French ordered their ambassador to return home but retaliated by demanding that Washington recall the U.S. minister to France, Gouverneur Morris, on the grounds that he had supported plots to restore the French monarchy.[83] Washington thus established that the president could expel a foreign representative whose conduct was judged unacceptable.

A president also can recognize the rights or interests of national or political groups that do not hold political power. In 1978 Jimmy Carter announced a qualified recognition of the interests of the Palestinians living in Israeli-occupied territories by saying that any Middle East peace settlement must recognize "the legitimate rights of the Palestinian people" and "enable the Palestinians to participate in the determination of their own future." [84] After the agreement of mutual recognition between Israel and the Palestine Liberation Organization (PLO) in 1993, President Clinton and Congress moved to accept the PLO as the legitimate representative of the Palestinians by removing restrictions on, for example, its ability to establish offices in the United States.

Presidents may choose not to exercise the recognition power unilaterally. In 1836 Andrew Jackson realized that the act of recognizing the Republic of Texas could have the effect of a declaration of war against Mexico, which regarded Texas as a Mexican territory. Although Jackson did not repudiate his authority to recognize Texas or any other nation, he announced his willingness to allow Congress to decide if Texas should be recognized: "It will always be considered consistent with the spirit of the Constitution, and most safe, that it [the recognition power] should be exercised when probably leading to war, with a previous understanding with that body by whom war can alone be declared, and by whom all the provisions for sustaining its perils must be furnished." [85]

Congress has powers that it could use to influence recognition decisions. For example, it could implicitly recognize a nation by appropriating funds for the necessary diplomatic positions—and, conversely, eliminate such funding to force the president to withdraw recognition. Only rarely has Congress used its powers to influence presidential decisions. The resolution authorizing President McKinley to expel Spain from Cuba contained an explicit recognition of Cuba's independence as a nation.[86] In 1995 both houses of Congress considered bills that recognized the government in exile as the legitimate government of Tibet, which is occupied by the People's Republic of China, and mandated the appointment of a special envoy with the "personal rank" of ambassador. Otherwise, Congress has no direct role in the recognition process beyond the Senate's approval of the president's nominee for the ambassadorship, which it can refuse to grant. Yet, as with treaties, Congress can pass nonbinding resolutions concerning particular questions of recognition. After France was conquered by the Nazis in World War II, for example, the House and Senate passed resolutions supporting the Roosevelt administration's agreement with other nations in the Western Hemisphere not to allow the transfer of the sovereignty of any European colony in the Americas to another European power.

Recognition as a Policy Statement

A decision to recognize or not to recognize a nation can be a major policy statement that expresses the attitudes and intentions of the United States toward an ideology, toward the character or behavior of a nation's government, and sometimes toward an entire region. Such policy statements can have profound consequences.

For example, in 1913 President Wilson refused to recognize the Mexican regime of Victoriano Huerta on the grounds that it was immoral and did not represent the will of its people.[87] Since Wilson made this decision, the ideology and morality of a foreign regime have become accepted factors in determining whether a government should be recognized. Successive presidents refused to recognize the revolutionary communist regimes in Russia from 1917 to 1933 and in China from 1949 to 1979. President Clinton's 1995 decision to recognize the communist regime in Vietnam was controversial, and the House passed a measure barring the use of funds for an embassy in Hanoi. Closer to home, Clinton continued the policy, begun in 1959, of withholding recognition from Cuba. A president also may deny recognition of a government's legal authority over a part or all of the territory claimed by that government. For example, the United States refused to recognize the legitimacy of the Soviet Union's annexation of Latvia, Lithuania, and Estonia in 1940.

Theodore Roosevelt's recognition of Panama in 1903 after its U.S.-backed revolt from Colombia paved the way to a treaty that gave the United States the right to dig the Panama Canal. It also led to a treaty in 1921 between Colombia and the United States that provided for the United States to pay Colombia $25 million in reparations for the loss of its Panamanian territory.

Harry S. Truman's recognition of Israel on May 15, 1948, was a controversial change of policy. A few minutes after Jews in Palestine proclaimed the state of Israel, Truman rejected the advice of his State Department and made the United States the first nation to recognize the new country. The recognition indicated U.S. support for Israel and effectively blocked a UN plan to keep Palestine under a temporary trusteeship.[88]

The president's power to sever diplomatic relations has been used as an ultimate sanction to protest another country's behavior. Severance of relations is usually reserved for situations in which the differences between the two nations are so great that there is no hope they may be resolved through normal diplomatic procedures. It is customary to break diplomatic ties with a country before declaring war against it, but many events short of war have prompted presidents to terminate relations. In 1979 President Carter ended diplomatic relations with Iran in response to the hostage crisis.

Even when relations have been broken with a particular country, communication usually continues. "Interests sections" may be established in each country's capital in the embassies of a third country. Foreign nations that lack diplomatic relations with the United States also have used their representatives to the United Nations to communicate with U.S. officials. Nevertheless, such measures do not accommodate communication between the two countries with the same efficiency as normal diplomatic exchanges. A less drastic method employed by presidents to communicate their displeasure with another nation is to temporarily recall the U.S. ambassador in that country for "consultations." President Carter used this tactic after the Soviet invasion of Afghanistan.

United Nations and U.S. Foreign Policy

U.S. membership in the United Nations, and particularly in the UN Security Council, often has raised concerns about control of the nation's foreign policy. On the one hand, the UN Participation Act of 1945 assigns control over day-to-day participation in UN affairs to the president; the U.S. permanent representative to the United Nations—more commonly known as the ambassador to the United Nations—is subject to Senate approval but serves "at the pleasure of the president." On the other hand, participation in the United Nations has a potentially large effect on national policy and commitments. Unlike NATO, the United Nations, through its charter, covers peace and security around the globe, without regard to specific U.S. interests. During the cold war, the rivalry between the United States and the Soviet Union effectively halted decision making on matters of international peace and security in the UN Security Council, with such important exceptions as the UN authorization of force in 1950 to repel North Korea's invasion of South Korea (a resolution that passed because the Soviet Union was boycotting the United Nations at the time for its refusal to seat Communist China). In the post–cold war era, however, the potential commitments of the United Nations in its humanitarian and peacekeeping roles multiplied.

The circumstances of the post–cold war era invited an expansion of U.S. participation in multilateral operations. As the United States began losing its cold war status as an essential military and economic ally, its influence even in NATO began to wane. Because fewer conflicts within and between countries had the clear global implications that once supported U.S. intervention and leadership, presidents sought different ways to maintain U.S. influence in international

U.S. LEGAL RELATIONSHIP WITH TAIWAN

The repercussions for U.S. relations with Taiwan from President Jimmy Carter's recognition of the People's Republic of China (PRC) illustrated the effect a recognition decision can have on U.S. laws and relations with other nations. Successive presidents had refused to recognize the PRC since it was established in 1949. Instead, the United States recognized the Republic of China, the nationalist Chinese government that had fled to Taiwan after its defeat by the Communist Chinese armies. Growing cooperation and friendship between the United States and the PRC in the 1970s, however, made the establishment of diplomatic relations with Beijing a matter of practical importance. In December 1978 the Carter administration announced that on January 1, 1979, it intended to recognize the PRC as the "sole legal government of China."

This recognition could be accomplished only by withdrawing U.S. recognition of the Republic of China as China's legal government. Because many laws and agreements involving commercial, cultural, and security relations with other countries depend on a nation's diplomatic status, the legal framework of the U.S. relationship with Taiwan had to be rebuilt. Without new legislation establishing a special relationship with the Republic of China, the United States could not deal with Taiwan as another nation.

Consequently, Congress passed the Taiwan Relations Act in March 1979. The act was intended to ensure that normal relations would continue between Taiwan and the United States, even though the United States no longer recognized the Republic of China regime that governed the island. The legislation established the American Institute in Taiwan through which the United States would conduct relations with Taiwan. The institute was created as a private, nonprofit corporation that was authorized to enter into, execute, and enforce agreements and other transactions with Taiwan and perform consular functions for U.S. citizens. The act also authorized U.S. government employees, especially foreign service officers, to take temporary leaves of absence from their posts to work for the institute. While in Taiwan, they would not be considered U.S. government employees, but they would retain their seniority, pensions, and other benefits when they returned to work for the government. Thus the Taiwan Relations Act created a nonprofit corporation that could do virtually anything done by an embassy.

Besides creating the American Institute in Taiwan, the act recognized the validity of Taiwan domestic law, contracts entered into under Taiwan law, and all U.S. agreements and treaties with Taiwan except the 1954 Mutual Defense Treaty, which was terminated at the end of 1979. It also authorized the president to grant Taiwan's unofficial representatives in the United States diplomatic privileges and treat Taiwan as a nation with an immigration quota equal to that of the PRC. These and dozens of other provisions of the Taiwan Relations Act addressed the legal difficulties created by the withdrawal of U.S. recognition of the Republic of China.

affairs. Yet engagement in global affairs through multilateral efforts was complicated by the inevitable tensions between national interest and alliance policy. On the one hand, a president who limits the nation's participation in UN missions to matters directly affecting U.S. interests would frustrate the global mission of the United Nations. On the other hand, broad participation in that general mission would risk the loss of national control over foreign policy.

From the start, the Clinton administration struggled with this dilemma. President Clinton began his administration with an enthusiastic endorsement of expanded use of UN missions and of broad U.S. participation in them. Given the model of his predecessor, President George H.W. Bush, who had successfully negotiated a UN Security Council resolution (this time with Soviet support) authorizing the use of force to remove Iraqi troops from Kuwait, the prospects for U.S.–UN decision making initially seemed quite promising. Many in Congress, however, criticized the general policy and attempted to limit the president's authority to involve U.S. forces in multilateral missions. Much of the criticism stemmed from the operation in Somalia to relieve the famine, which the United States joined in 1992 with broad congressional and popular support. The operation was transformed in June 1993 after twenty-three UN peacekeepers were killed by one of the warring factions. The United Nations, with President Clinton's approval, then shifted to a more ambitious mission of subduing the armed factions and rebuilding the nation's political order. As a consequence, eighteen U.S. Rangers were killed and eighty were wounded in an assault on one faction's headquarters. The ensuing debates over this operation revolved around the degree to which the United States should involve itself in policing the world in the absence of clear and substantial national security interests.[89] These concerns were reinforced by Clinton's commitments to UN efforts in Haiti and Bosnia.

In late 1993 Congress forced the Clinton administration to set a deadline for the use of funds for the operation and required U.S. forces to remain under U.S. operational command.[90] In response to these and other criticisms and proposals, the Clinton administration announced more restrictive policy guidelines for U.S. participation in UN missions and especially those that may involve combat. Specifically, such missions must involve national interests or "a real threat to international peace and security." Nonetheless, the Clinton administration defended UN missions as effective and as an important part "of our national security policy" and argued that congressional proposals would be an imprudent and unconstitutional intrusion on the president's foreign policy and war powers.[91] Yet after the Somalia debacle, the United States steered clear of enmeshing itself in UN commitments, as was evident with its refusal to support a resolution authorizing force to halt the genocide in Rwanda in 1994. Much of Clinton's second term was devoted to persuading Congress to stop withholding U.S. dues owed to the United Nations. Critics in Congress were angry over the misuse of UN funds, the expanding UN peacekeeping role in violent conflicts, and the removal of the United States from the UN Human Rights Commission.

In 2001 the UN support for a united campaign against international terrorism initially helped to sway opinions in Congress, which acted on bills authorizing payments of dues that had been held up for years. But the George W. Bush administration came into conflict with the United Nations in 2002–2003, when it again sought Security Council endorsement of military force against Iraq, this time because of Iraqi leader Saddam Hussein's failure to comply with arms inspections. Although the Security Council passed a resolution calling for "serious consequences" if Hussein did not comply, it could not reach agreement on a second reso-

lution that explicitly authorized force. Consequently, the United States went to war against Iraq in 2003 without UN backing, though several UN members expressed their support for and participated in the military action. During Bush's second term, the United States pressed strongly for UN reform to make the 192-member organization more efficient and effective, but immediate results were not forthcoming. Thus, while the need for multilateral cooperation to combat terrorism in the twenty-first century was clearly evident, the role of the United Nations as the source of such cooperation was not.

Mutual Security Agreements

Mutual security agreements raise issues similar to those raised by the UN charter. Following World War II, the U.S. policy of containing communist expansion, backed by U.S. military strength, led presidents to offer security commitments and alliance partnerships to countries worried about their ability to defend themselves. Although they have improved relations with many countries, extended U.S. global influence, and strengthened U.S. defenses, these alliances have been politically contentious because such commitments risk drawing the nation into war.

Since World War II, presidents often have entered alliances without formal action by Congress. On August 14, 1941, for example, President Franklin Roosevelt signed the Atlantic Charter, which laid the groundwork for an Anglo-American alliance once the United States had entered World War II. Roosevelt then signed the Declaration by United Nations on January 1, 1942, which pledged the United States and, by the end of the war, forty-five other nations to support the Allied war effort and not make a separate peace with the enemy nations.[92] After the war, Presidents Truman and Eisenhower used executive agreements to expand NATO into a unified defense organization with a standing military structure. Although no formal alliance treaty exists between the United States and Israel, presidents since Truman have maintained the extensive U.S. commitment to Israeli security.

Because alliance disputes may affect the probability and effectiveness of future cooperation, the president is compelled to consider the effect of U.S. foreign and military policy on the cohesion of the nation's alliances and on public opinion within the allied countries. Even when a foreign policy action does not directly involve an alliance, a president must weigh its effect on allied countries. The concerns of Presidents Johnson and Nixon that other U.S. allies would see abandonment of South Vietnam as evidence of U.S. inability to fulfill its commitments contributed to the escalation of U.S. involvement and their refusal to withdraw U.S. troops from Vietnam without attempting to ensure South Vietnamese security.

The United States has been the dominant military power in every alliance it has joined since World War II. As the need for the U.S. deterrent waned with the disintegration of the Soviet Union and the Warsaw Pact, the U.S. influence in alliances weakened. In the absence of an overriding interest in mutual defense, the allies have experienced more conflicts between national interests and alliance cohesion. Although the United States is still the most influential partner, its influence has been further diminished by the development of the European Union.

Insofar as a president can persuade allies to support U.S. foreign policies, alliances can enhance the president's domestic power. However, failure to gain cooperation can be costly, and alliance responsibilities can harm rather than enhance presidential prestige and influence. Congress is less likely to challenge the foreign policy of a president who is perceived as an effective international leader. But a president who has not been able either to deliver allied support for U.S. policies or to ensure that alliance policy serves U.S. interests will face greater congressional criticism and intrusion. President Clinton's policies in Somalia, Haiti, Bosnia, and Kosovo were criticized for serving alliance interests ahead of national interests.

POWER TO APPOINT DIPLOMATIC PERSONNEL

Article II, Section 2, of the Constitution states that the president shall "nominate and, by and with the Advice and Consent of the Senate, shall appoint Ambassadors, other public Ministers and Consuls." The power to appoint, and the power to remove, those individuals who will communicate directly with foreign leaders is crucial in establishing the president as the sole organ of foreign communications. The success of a president's foreign policy program depends greatly on the personalities and abilities of the people who fill important diplomatic and advisory posts.

Although the president appoints officials, Congress has the constitutional power to create offices. Nevertheless, presidents have used executive orders to create the government bodies that required them to make appointments. Kennedy established the Peace Corps in this manner, and Gerald R. Ford unilaterally created the Committee on Foreign Intelligence and the Intelligence Oversight Board.[93] In 2001 President George W. Bush created the Office of Homeland Security in the Executive Office of the President and appointed its first director. One year later Congress and the president approved the creation of a new cabinet agency, the Department of Homeland Security.

Senate confirmation of presidential nominees for diplomatic posts is usually routine, but there have been exceptions. For example, Eisenhower's appointment of Charles E. Bohlen as ambassador to the Soviet Union barely survived the confirmation vote, even though Eisenhower's party controlled the Senate.[94] In 1985 and 1986 Sen. Jesse

Helms, R-N.C., held up the confirmations of some nominees to protest either the nominee or some related matter of policy, and in 1990 Helms's opposition led to the withdrawal or rejection of two of President George H.W. Bush's nominees. In 1989 President Bush faced wider congressional criticism for a slate of nominees that included many who were notable not for diplomatic experience but for having made large contributions to his campaign and the Republican Party.[95] In 1994 a GOP filibuster led by Sen. Robert C. Smith, R-N.H., prevented President Clinton from appointing Sam Brown as U.S. ambassador to the Conference on Security and Cooperation in Europe. In 2005 Senate divisions over the appointment of John R. Bolton as ambassador to the United Nations prompted President George W. Bush to make a recess appointment. In December 2006 Bolton resigned as his appointment was about to expire.

Political Appointees versus the Foreign Service

A question that complicates the diplomatic appointments of contemporary presidents is how to divide ambassadorships and important State Department posts between political appointees and the State Department's career foreign service officers. Senior foreign service officers can offer a president valuable diplomatic experience that can prevent foreign policy mistakes. Also, because they serve successive presidents, they can provide continuity in foreign policy between administrations.[96] Yet presidents often have been reluctant either to waste a source of political rewards or to entrust important ambassadorships and assistant secretary posts to foreign service officers. Because their careers do not depend on the president but on a self-run promotion system, and because many regard foreign policy as an endeavor that should not be subject to partisan politics, foreign service officers have a greater reputation for resisting presidential policies than do political appointees, who are more likely to be politically minded and to appreciate how their jobs fit into the president's domestic and foreign policy goals.

Symbolism and Politics of Appointments

Presidents must take into account more than a candidate's abilities and qualifications when making an appointment. Appointments provide the president with an opportunity to indicate to Congress, the American people, and foreign governments the foreign policy goals the new administration intends to pursue. Ronald Reagan's appointment of conservative Jeane Kirkpatrick as ambassador to the United Nations reaffirmed his intention to make anticommunism a foreign policy theme of his administration, just as Jimmy Carter had underscored his commitment to human rights and developing country issues with his appointment of Andrew Young, an African American civil rights activist, to the same post. In 1986 President Reagan indicated his administration's attitude toward South Africa's racial policies by appointing an African American diplomat, Edward Perkins, as U.S. ambassador to that country.

At times, presidents use appointments to broaden their base of support within their party or to create an atmosphere of bipartisanship. Kennedy tried to disarm potential congressional resistance to his policies by appointing Republicans to senior foreign policy posts. In 1997 President Clinton hoped for a similar result from the appointment of a Republican, former senator William S. Cohen, as secretary of defense.[97] While President George W. Bush made diverse appointments from within the Republican Party, he also placed many longtime personal advisers in top cabinet positions in his second term, notably Condoleezza Rice (foreign policy adviser to Bush during the 2000 presidential campaign and national security adviser in his first presidential term) as secretary of state.

Presidential Envoys

Many presidents have used personal emissaries not subject to Senate confirmation to carry out diplomatic missions. The use of personal envoys allows presidents to inject their own ideas and proposals directly into negotiations without having to go through the State Department or other official channels in which policy could be opposed or compromised. The presence of a personal envoy sent by the president sometimes can stimulate stalemated negotiations by lending greater prestige to the talks and demonstrating the president's interest in them. Presidential representatives also can provide the president with an additional source of information that is relatively free of institutional biases.

The use of presidential envoys is not specifically allowed or disallowed in the Constitution; they fall somewhere between ambassadors and treaty negotiators.[98] Their utility was evident early on. In 1791 Gouverneur Morris, who held no public office at the time, carried out important negotiations with the British at President Washington's direction. By using a personal representative, Washington could explore the possibilities for a treaty without having to involve Congress or deal with the formalities of official treaty negotiations.

The first major controversy over the appointment of diplomats not confirmed by the Senate occurred in 1813, when Madison sent a delegation to the negotiations that produced the Treaty of Ghent, which ended the War of 1812 with Great Britain. The president had dispatched the negotiators without submitting their names for confirmation by the Senate, which was in recess. Madison's critics argued that he could not appoint ministers to offices that had not been authorized by Congress and that the appointments were illegal because the Senate did not have the chance to approve them. The president responded by claiming that it was unnecessary for Congress to create a diplomatic post if the president determined that a need had arisen for one, and

that the president was free to fill any vacancy that happened to occur during a congressional recess.[99] Since Madison's time, however, Congress has enacted legislation that gives it control over the creation of new ambassadorships.

Many presidents have used special envoys or personal representatives instead of ambassadors for specific diplomatic tasks. In 1831 Jackson sent unconfirmed representatives to Turkey to conclude a trade and navigation treaty, and in 1893 Cleveland gave his own emissary, J.H. Blount, "paramount authority" over the Senate-approved resident minister in Honolulu at talks on the annexation of Hawaii.[100] Two twentieth-century presidents, Wilson and Franklin Roosevelt, established the use of personal representatives as a common diplomatic device of the president. Wilson made extensive use of his close friend Col. Edward M. House to perform diplomatic missions in Europe before and during World War I. Harry L. Hopkins, Franklin Roosevelt's personal aide, helped to negotiate and direct the lend-lease agreements under which the United States supplied war materiel to Great Britain and other countries at war with Germany. Early in his first administration, President Reagan used Philip C. Habib as a special envoy to the Middle East to negotiate settlements of the conflict in Lebanon between Israel, Syria, and the Palestine Liberation Organization.

Former president Carter was a curious variation on the special envoy. Carter had presented himself publicly as a willing mediator who could resolve the diplomatic deadlocks with North Korea about its nuclear weapons program and Haiti about the return of its democratically elected government. In accepting Carter as an envoy, President Clinton seemed unwilling to take responsibility for missing a chance to resolve the disputes and avoid armed conflict, even though Carter had clearly demonstrated a willingness to publicize his criticisms of the president's policies and to negotiate settlements that contradicted those policies. More regularly, such unsolicited offers are ignored or rebuffed.

SUMMIT MEETINGS

Although presidents have always been responsible for the conduct of diplomacy, they rarely met personally with foreign leaders until World War II. The difficulties of travel, the isolated location of the United States, and the traditional belief that presidents should stay close to their administrative and legislative responsibilities in the capital inhibited presidents from acting as their own negotiators. Today, if a president were to avoid meetings with leaders of foreign governments, the press and public alike would criticize the chief of state as being uninterested in international affairs, or even isolationist. Presidents have found that a highly publicized summit tends to raise their public approval rating. *(See "Presidential Popularity," p. 557, in Chapter 10.)*

Winston Churchill is credited with coining the term *summit*. In 1953 he used the word when he called for a conference between the leaders of the Soviet Union and the Western powers. The media picked up the term and used it to describe the Geneva conference between Soviet and Western leaders in 1955. After Geneva, meetings between national leaders increasingly were referred to as *summits*.[101] The term is used to distinguish meetings that are actually attended by the recognized leaders of states from meetings between foreign ministers or lower-level officials.

Presidential Diplomacy

Although presidential travel to foreign nations was impractical before the twentieth century, presidents throughout U.S. history have conducted personal diplomacy with foreign leaders through direct exchanges of letters. Personal letters between leaders were able to accomplish some of the goals of the modern summit meeting. They gave a president the chance to send and receive information, ideas, and proposals without using intermediaries and to establish trust through personal rapport with a foreign leader. Presidential letters were especially important to early presidents, who did not have the benefit of an extensive diplomatic network with representatives in many foreign capitals. President Jefferson, whose years as secretary of state under Washington had provided him with extensive diplomatic experience, had an ongoing correspondence with Czar Alexander I of Russia during the Napoleonic wars.[102]

Early presidents also met with foreign emissaries who traveled to the United States. The first high-ranking official of a foreign government to visit the United States was a personal emissary of the ruler of Tunis who came to America in 1805 to discuss the passage of U.S. commercial ships in the Mediterranean. The marquis de Lafayette, who had led colonial troops against the British in the American Revolution, was the first official guest to be invited to the United States by the U.S. government. President Monroe received him in 1824 after he arrived on an American ship that Congress had dispatched to France.[103] During the rest of the nineteenth century, visits to the United States by foreign dignitaries were common. Visits by the heads of state of other nations, however, remained rare. Up to the end of World War I, presidents had received only about thirty heads of state.[104]

Presidential Travel

During the eighteenth and nineteenth centuries, a precedent developed that presidents would not travel outside the country during their term. Theodore Roosevelt became the first

Hoping to stimulate arms control negotiations, President Ronald Reagan and Soviet leader Mikhail Gorbachev meet for the first time at a summit in Geneva in November 1985. Four years later at a summit in Malta, Gorbachev met with President George Bush, acknowledging the end of the cold war.

president to break this precedent when he visited Panama in 1906 to inspect the canal under construction. Presidential travel abroad remained uncommon until Franklin Roosevelt made a series of trips to Canada and overseas to confer with Allied leaders about military strategy and the composition of the postwar world. Truman followed Roosevelt's example by attending the Potsdam Conference in 1945 with Joseph Stalin and Winston Churchill (and, later, Clement R. Attlee).

President Eisenhower, however, broadened the role of the president as international diplomat with his 22,000-mile "Quest for Peace" tour of eleven nations in 1959. He believed that establishing goodwill toward the United States in foreign nations was an important presidential function. Accordingly, many of his stops in foreign countries were devoted to ceremony and speech making. Since Eisenhower, presidential visits abroad have been an accepted part of the president's job and have been highly coveted by the leaders of foreign nations. President Kennedy met with Premier Nikita Khrushchev in Vienna in 1961 and toured Europe in 1963, at which time he delivered his famous "Ich bin ein Berliner" speech. President Johnson initially declined taking trips abroad because he had no vice president, but after the election in 1964 his trips included visits to Australia, the

FDR made a series of trips overseas to confer with Allied leaders about military strategy and postwar issues. In February 1945 an ailing Roosevelt meets with Winston Churchill and Joseph Stalin at Yalta in the Crimea.

Philippines, Vietnam, and Latin America. Nixon embarked on a major European tour in 1969 only a month after he became president. In 1972 he became the first U.S. president to visit the People's Republic of China, which was in itself a momentous change in U.S. policy. All of the more recent presidents have met frequently with foreign leaders overseas, including meetings with Soviet and Russian leaders and the annual economic summits of the Group of Seven (G7) nations: the United States, Canada, France, Germany, Great Britain, Italy, and Japan.

Constitutional Questions

The Constitution clearly establishes the president's right to conduct diplomatic negotiations personally. A more controversial constitutional question about summit meetings was whether a president traveling abroad could properly fulfill the obligations of office.

No one questioned the constitutionality of Theodore Roosevelt's short trip to Panama in 1906 or of William Howard Taft's meeting with the Mexican president just across the border in 1909. When President Wilson announced in late 1918 that he planned to go to Europe to attend the peace conference in Versailles, however, numerous critics objected that Wilson's safety could not be ensured and that he would lose touch with the everyday business of his office during the lengthy Atlantic crossing.[105]

Resolutions were introduced in both houses of Congress that would have declared the presidency vacant and required the vice president to assume the president's powers if Wilson left the country. Former president Taft, however, argued in an article in the *Washington Post* on December 5, 1918, that the president could properly fulfill the duties of his office while overseas. He wrote: "There is no constitutional inhibition, express or implied, to prevent the

president's going abroad to discharge a function clearly given him by the Constitution. That instrument says that he shall make treaties. . . . It is a curious error to assume that the president himself may not attend a conference to which he can send a delegate." [106] Wilson's critics continued to attack the wisdom of his policy, but the congressional resolutions against Wilson's trip never got out of committee.[107]

Today, presidents travel with large staffs and stay in constant touch with administration and congressional officials. They have the means to carry out virtually any presidential function from any place in the world.

In 1972 Richard Nixon became the first U.S. president to visit the People's Republic of China. Here he is greeted by Chinese Communist Party chairman Mao Zedong.

TABLE 13-2 **U.S.-Soviet Summit Meetings, 1945–1991**

Date	Location	Leaders	Topic
July–August 1945	Potsdam, Germany	President Harry S. Truman, Soviet leader Josef Stalin, British prime ministers Winston Churchill and Clement R. Attlee	Partition and control of Germany
July 1955	Geneva	President Dwight D. Eisenhower, Soviet leader Nikolai A. Bulganin, British prime minister Anthony Eden, French premier Edgar Faure	Reunification of Germany, disarmament, European security
September 1959	Camp David, Md.	President Dwight D. Eisenhower, Soviet leader Nikita S. Khrushchev	Berlin problem
May 1960	Paris	President Dwight D. Eisenhower, Soviet leader Nikita S. Khrushchev, French president Charles de Gaulle, British prime minister Harold Macmillan	U-2 incident
June 1961	Vienna	President John F. Kennedy, Soviet leader Nikita S. Khrushchev	Berlin problem
June 1967	Glassboro, N.J.	President Lyndon B. Johnson, Soviet leader Aleksei N. Kosygin	Middle East
May 1972	Moscow	President Richard Nixon, Soviet leader Leonid I. Brezhnev	SALT I, antiballistic missile limitations
June 1973	Washington, D.C.	President Richard Nixon, Soviet leader Leonid I. Brezhnev	Détente
June–July 1974	Moscow and Yalta	President Richard Nixon, Soviet leader Leonid I. Brezhnev	Arms control
November 1974	Vladivostok, Russia	President Gerald R. Ford, Soviet leader Leonid I. Brezhnev	Arms control
June 1979	Vienna	President Jimmy Carter, Soviet leader Leonid I. Brezhnev	SALT II
November 1985	Geneva	President Ronald Reagan, Soviet leader Mikhail Gorbachev	Arms control, U.S.-Soviet relations
October 1986	Reykjavik, Iceland	President Ronald Reagan, Soviet leader Mikhail Gorbachev	Arms control
December 1987	Washington, D.C.	President Ronald Reagan, Soviet leader Mikhail Gorbachev	Intermediate Nuclear Forces (INF) Treaty, Afghanistan
May 1988	Moscow	President Ronald Reagan, Soviet leader Mikhail Gorbachev	Arms control, human rights
December 1988	New York	President Ronald Reagan, Soviet leader Mikhail Gorbachev	U.S.-Soviet relations
December 1989	Malta	President George H. W. Bush, Soviet leader Mikhail Gorbachev	Arms control, eastern Europe
May–June 1990	Washington, D.C.	President George H. W. Bush, Soviet leader Mikhail Gorbachev	Arms control
September 1990	Helsinki	President George H. W. Bush, Soviet leader Mikhail Gorbachev	Middle East crisis
July 1991	Moscow	President George H. W. Bush, Soviet leader Mikhail Gorbachev	Arms control and Soviet economic and political future

Superpower Summitry

The era of nuclear confrontation between the two superpowers, the United States and the Soviet Union, and their allies, made summits an unavoidable, if not always effective, mode of presidential diplomacy. *(See Table 13-2.)* As former president Nixon argued, developing mutual understandings between the superpowers of their respective interests and patterns of behavior was the primary purpose of a superpower summit. These understandings, which he called "rules of engagement," could not resolve differences between the two countries or end their adversarial relationship; rather, they would reduce the possibility that a crisis would lead to war.[108]

Every president from Franklin Roosevelt to George H.W. Bush met with a Soviet leader at least once. Some meetings, such as the summits in Moscow in 1972, Vienna in 1979, Washington in 1987, and Moscow in 1991, were the culmination of the arms control process at which an agreement was signed. At other meetings, such as the 1985 Geneva summit, the 1986 Reykjavik summit, and the 1989 Malta summit, the leaders hoped to stimulate arms control negotiations. The media and public attention that accompanied these meetings was inspired by hopes that they could produce an agreement or understanding that would reduce the chances of nuclear war and lead to a more cooperative coexistence.

The 1989 Malta summit meeting between President Bush and Soviet leader Mikhail Gorbachev marked a dramatic change in the nature of U.S.-Soviet relations and summit meetings. Gorbachev had allowed, and even encouraged, the independence movements in Soviet bloc countries, and at this meeting the two leaders acknowledged the end of the cold war. Later summit meetings focused on advancing arms reduction treaties and normalizing relations. The 1994 meeting between President Bill Clinton and Russian president Boris Yeltsin, and the 2001 meeting between President George W. Bush and Russian president Vladimir Putin, were like ordinary bilateral meetings between the president and the head of an allied country.

Evaluating Summit Diplomacy

Although in the current era summit diplomacy is being used less and for less critical matters than during the cold war, presidents may be tempted to continue to use summits, at the very least to focus attention on their world status and foreign policy leadership. Diplomatic historian Elmer Plischke cites some advantages of summit meetings that can enhance conventional diplomacy. By becoming personally acquainted, a president and a foreign leader may reduce tensions, clarify national interests, and establish mutual respect. Diplomatic impasses may be overcome by shifts in policy that only the top leaders are empowered to make. Summits also allow presidents to focus national attention on specific issues and to improve public understanding of them. And, of course, successful summits can enhance the image of the president and of the United States.[109]

However, after his 1995 meeting with Russian president Yeltsin, President Clinton was criticized by members of Congress for failing to secure changes in Russian policies that opposed the inclusion of eastern European nations in NATO and favored aiding Iran's nuclear development program.

Indeed, there are some disadvantages and risks in using summit meetings rather than conventional diplomacy. For example, the potential for a summit to produce a quick breakthrough in stalemated negotiations also bears the risk that a summit can lead to a hasty, imprudent agreement or commitment. Moreover, an inexperienced or inadequately prepared president can harm relations with other countries or inadvertently undermine U.S. interests. Frequent summits also may harm the morale of professional diplomats if they perceive that their talents are being ignored in favor of direct presidential negotiations.[110] The media attention given summits may distort their substance or lead to popular disillusionment by raising public expectations of improved relations with another country beyond what is warranted. A summit, therefore, is a special diplomatic environment with opportunities and pitfalls. In recent years the term "summit meeting" typically applies to any meeting between the president and another head of state, or group of heads of state, and the president's staff highlights the important communications between leaders, even if they do not result in immediate substantive policy changes. When conflicts with other nations make direct diplomacy difficult, presidents may sometimes ask former presidents to intercede on their behalf. Former president Carter served as an envoy to Haiti and North Korea in 1994 on behalf of President Clinton.

MANAGER OF THE FOREIGN POLICY BUREAUCRACY

The president's management of the foreign policy bureaucracy is less visible than the president's performance as a diplomat, but it is as important to the success of U.S. foreign policy. The "foreign policy bureaucracy" loosely refers to all executive branch personnel whose primary duties pertain to

foreign affairs. Almost every department and agency has employees engaged in activities that affect foreign relations, but the State Department, the Defense Department, the Joint Chiefs of Staff, the intelligence agencies, the National Security Council, and the National Security Council staff dominate the foreign policy-making process. Other agencies, such as the Arms Control and Disarmament Agency (ACDA) and the Agency for International Development (AID), deal with specific aspects of foreign policy.

Although the president is responsible for the conduct of foreign affairs, modern foreign policy cannot be made by one person. Policy results from a process of consultation and compromise among the president and the president's top foreign affairs advisers. Moreover, the lower levels of the administration perform functions that are essential to the success of foreign policy. Presidents Kennedy and Nixon preferred to base their decisions on the advice of a small, close-knit group of advisers, but even presidents such as these need an administrative apparatus to collect information and intelligence, research policy problems, plan for long-range contingencies, represent the United States abroad, and implement presidential directives. A president can attend to only a few of the most pressing matters at one time, and so others must oversee the vast array of daily functions.

It is not only the complexity of this administrative and policy network that makes foreign policy management a massive and continuous presidential headache. Different departments, such as State and Defense, have competing concerns and different modes of operation. As well, more permanent civil servants, such as foreign service officers, tend to resist the president's policy initiatives and to ignore his momentary political needs. Faced with a welter of management problems, each new president reorganizes the policy and administrative structure in the often vain hope of achieving tight control and coherence.

Expansion of the Foreign Policy Bureaucracy

During Washington's administration, the foreign policy bureaucracy consisted of the secretary of state, a small group of clerks, and a few carefully chosen ambassadors to key European states. Although U.S. contacts with other nations expanded during the next hundred years, the foreign policy apparatus of the executive branch remained small. In addition, the low salaries of diplomats and the practice of appointing wealthy campaign contributors and party functionaries to diplomatic posts hindered the development of a professional diplomatic corps.[111] At the end of the nineteenth century, the United States began to upgrade the quality and status of its diplomats to correspond with the nation's growing involvement in international trade and politics. Presidents increasingly relied on the State Department for information, analysis, and staff support.

With the advent of World War II and the emergence of the United States as a superpower with broad international responsibilities, presidents needed greater bureaucratic resources to support their foreign policy decision making. The United States was an international leader and the protector of the free world. In the postwar years, it entered into numerous alliances and mutual defense agreements, distributed massive amounts of military and economic aid, hosted the United Nations, and actively participated in most international organizations. The nation's and the president's foreign policy responsibilities proliferated. An expanded bureaucracy was required to administer the growing number of U.S. programs and activities overseas and to provide the president with the information and analysis needed to construct effective foreign policies.

As a result, the State Department increased in size, and other departments and agencies were created or expanded to provide military, economic, scientific, and intelligence-gathering expertise that the State Department was not equipped to provide. The State Department thus became one player among many in the field of foreign policy. Nevertheless, it has remained the president's primary instrument of negotiation with foreign countries and an important source of information, analysis, and advice on foreign relations.

In 1949 Congress created the Defense Department by unifying the individual armed services. Although the United States demobilized rapidly after World War II, North Korea's invasion of South Korea in 1950 and the growing Soviet threat convinced U.S. leaders that, for the first time in American history, the country needed a large standing military.[112] The size of the unified military budget and the number of people in the armed services ensured that the civilian and military leaders of the new Defense Department would have considerable bureaucratic clout. Moreover, foreign policy had become more thoroughly intertwined with defense and national security. Containing Soviet expansionism, forming and maintaining anticommunist alliances, and remaining ahead in the nuclear arms race were among the

OVERSIGHT OF INTELLIGENCE ACTIVITIES

Because of the need for secrecy, the National Security Act of 1947 gave the president nearly exclusive responsibility for oversight of covert intelligence activities. Before the mid-1970s, Congress rarely investigated covert operations, and the president and the intelligence agencies did not willingly offer information about them. Congress routinely approved billions of dollars in funds for the intelligence community with only a few members of its appropriations committees knowing how the money was being spent.

In the mid-1970s, numerous instances of unethical, unauthorized, and illegal activities by the Central Intelligence Agency (CIA) and other intelligence units were uncovered by congressional investigations. Among other abuses, the CIA was involved in the bloody overthrow of the Socialist government in Chile. In addition, the Federal Bureau of Investigation (FBI) and other intelligence agencies conducted illegal surveillance operations and engaged in other activities that violated the civil liberties of individual Americans.

In response, Congress passed a series of laws that created House and Senate intelligence committees and strengthened congressional oversight of intelligence activities. The Hughes-Ryan Amendment to the 1974 foreign aid bill and the 1980 Intelligence Oversight Act required that the president report all U.S. covert intelligence operations to designated congressional committees in a timely fashion. To complement Congress's actions, President Gerald R. Ford established the Intelligence Oversight Board, a three-member White House panel to oversee intelligence activities and report any questions of illegality to the president through the attorney general.

The 1990s revealed a different defect. In 1994 Aldrich H. Ames, a high-level CIA officer, was arrested on charges of selling classified information to the Soviet Union and, later, Russia. Over the course of nine years, Ames had passed on thousands of documents, compromising more than one hundred intelligence operations and probably leading to the assassinations of a number of double agents working for the United States. The Ames case exposed the inadequacies in the CIA's internal security procedures. Ames's evident drinking problem and his lavish lifestyle, funded by the sales of state secrets, were either not noticed or not investigated. When the CIA director, R. James Woolsey, failed to dismiss any of the negligent officers, Congress intervened.

Citing the CIA's "gross negligence," Congress in 1994 began investigating CIA operations with an eye toward remedies for immediate and long-term problems. The White House argued that intelligence matters ought to be handled within the executive branch, and President Bill Clinton issued a directive that incorporated many of the reform proposals being considered by Congress. Nonetheless, Congress passed, and Clinton signed into law, the Counterintelligence and Security Enhancements Act of 1994 which overhauled the process of internal investigations. The law gave government investigators greater access to the financial and travel records of CIA personnel and turned investigations of all security breaches over to the FBI.

This law also established the blue-ribbon Commission on the Roles and Capability of the United States Intelligence Community, but its 1996 report recommended no major reforms. Troubles continued, nonetheless, as FBI agent Robert P. Hanssen was arrested in 2001 for selling highly classified information to Moscow. His criminal activities had gone undetected by either the FBI or the CIA for fifteen years. His revelations undermined major intelligence and national security operations and led to the assassination of at least one double agent.

In the aftermath of the September 11, 2001, terrorist attacks, a special bipartisan commission (popularly known as the 9/11 Commission) proposed the most significant intelligence reform since the creation of the CIA after World War II. The Intelligence Reform and Terrorism Prevention Act of 2004 created an Office of the Director of National Intelligence (DNI) to coordinate intelligence gathering among the various agencies and report directly to the president. The goal was to centralize the information flow to the president while also ensuring congressional accountability for the DNI.

most important international goals of the United States. Defense officials consequently became important players in foreign policy decision making. *(See "Department of Defense," p. 773, in Chapter 14.)*

Moscow's aggressive use of its intelligence apparatus and the difficulty of extracting information from the closed Soviet society by conventional means seemed to demand a similar intelligence effort by the United States. The National Security Act of 1947 created the Central Intelligence Agency (CIA) to gather and analyze information from every corner of the globe and to provide the president with a covert operations capability. The intelligence community comprises the CIA, the Defense Intelligence Agency, the intelligence offices of the individual armed services, the State Department's Bureau of Intelligence and Research, the Federal Bureau of Investigation, and the massive National Security Agency, which intercepts and analyzes communication signals. The director of central intelligence was given preeminent status in the intelligence community, with primary responsibility for coordinating intelligence activities and advising the president on intelligence matters. *(See box, Oversight of Intelligence Activities, p. 729; and "Control over Intelligence Agencies," p. 1340, in Chapter 29, Vol. II.)* In 2004 Congress enacted the most significant intelligence reform since World War II, responding to the report of the 9/11 Commission that had examined intelligence gathering before the September 11, 2001, attacks. Congress created the Office of the Director of National Intelligence to be responsible for coordinating information from the myriad different intelligence agencies within the federal government and advising the president accordingly.

National Security Council

The 1947 National Security Act also established the National Security Council (NSC) as a means of coordinating the increasingly elaborate array of agencies involved in national security policy. The NSC's responsibility is "to advise the President with respect to the integration of domestic, foreign, and military policies relating to the national security so as to enable the military services and other departments and agencies of the government to cooperate more effectively in matters involving the national security." The statutory members of the NSC are the president, vice president, and secretaries of defense and state. The director of central intelligence and the chairman of the Joint Chiefs of Staff are statutory advisers to the council. Ideally, the NSC is a smaller and more focused forum than the cabinet.

Congress, however, created the NSC not exactly to assist presidents but to force upon them a more collegial decision-making process.[113] In Congress's eyes, decisions in national security matters had become excessively centralized in the White House. Yet presidents cannot be obliged to convene meetings of the NSC or to treat its meetings and delib-

erations as anything more than advisory. Indeed, many presidents have chosen to de-emphasize NSC meetings, preferring to rely on small groups of trusted advisers to make decisions, using the council only to approve them. Others have used the NSC as the formal centerpiece of an extensive web of committees and interagency groups considering foreign policy. Occasionally, the NSC has been used as a decision-making forum during crises, including the North Korean invasion of South Korea in 1950, the Soviet invasion of Czechoslovakia in 1968, and the *Mayaguez* incident in 1975. At various times, the NSC also has been used for less dramatic functions such as policy planning and budget review.[114]

In addition to creating the National Security Council, the National Security Act established an NSC staff to serve the president and the NSC members. *(See "National Security Council," p. 1121, in Chapter 24, Vol. II.)* The most important presidential adaptation of the NSC apparatus has been the use of the NSC staff, contrary to Congress's intention, to centralize decision making and implementation in the White House.

Crucial to the staff's influence has been the evolution of the assistant to the president for national security affairs, a post established by Eisenhower and commonly referred to as the "national security adviser." Originally, the national security adviser was to facilitate foreign policy making by coordinating NSC meetings and overseeing the staff that served the NSC. Under Eisenhower's successors, the national security adviser was often as influential or more so than cabinet members. As a presidential aide, the national security adviser is not confirmed by the Senate and is not burdened by responsibilities for managing an agency or department. The influence of the national security adviser within the administration depends entirely on the president.

Because the national security adviser and most NSC staffers owe their position and status entirely to the president, they have few competing loyalties. Some NSC staffers who were drawn from other departments and agencies may retain institutional loyalty to their parent organization, but during their tenure on the NSC staff they are responsible only to the president. In addition, the NSC staff is beyond the reach of the legislative branch because it has no statutory responsibility to report to Congress. Presidents therefore can use the national security adviser and the NSC staff as a research and advisory arm independent of other agencies and departments. Some national security advisers, such as Henry A. Kissinger and Zbigniew Brzezinski, have served as dominant policy advisers and as negotiators in the most important matters, using the NSC staff to support this work. In the extraordinarily broad and intensive diplomatic efforts of the Nixon administration, Secretary of State William P. Rogers was eclipsed by Kissinger and had no important advisory role.

The accomplishments of Kissinger and Brzezinski built a strong case for the virtues of centralizing foreign policy operations in the White House. On the other hand, investigations of the Iran-contra affair in 1986 and 1987 revealed that the NSC staff could be used to implement not only covert operations but also operations that circumvented the law and were, otherwise, of questionable wisdom. This scandal led to calls for a more collegial decision-making structure, whether oriented around the secretary of state or a reorganized NSC.[115]

President George H.W. Bush made the position of national security adviser stronger than it had been in the Reagan administration. His national security adviser, Brent Scowcroft, played a major role during the Gulf War, and he was generally a voice for more conservative positions on relations with the Soviet Union and Middle East peace prospects. However, foreign policy making during the Bush administration was dominated by Secretary of State James A. Baker III, with whom President Bush had extensive professional and personal ties. Baker shaped policy in the various arms reduction talks with the Soviet Union and was directly involved in all phases of the transition to post–cold war relations with the Soviet Union. His close relationship with Soviet foreign minister Eduard Shevardnadze facilitated agreements on arms control, the fall of the Berlin Wall, and the reunification of East and West Germany. He also assembled and helped to maintain the international coalition opposing Iraq's 1990 invasion of Kuwait.[116]

Similarly, Bill Clinton's national security advisers were less prominent in foreign policy decisions and activities than his secretaries of state, Warren M. Christopher and Madeleine K. Albright. Clinton's first national security adviser, W. Anthony Lake, came from an academic background, and his second-term national security adviser, Samuel R. Berger, had stronger political than national security expertise. In George W. Bush's first term, his national security adviser, Condoleezza Rice, was probably the closest foreign policy adviser to the president. Bush also consulted regularly with Vice President Richard B. Cheney and Secretary of Defense Donald H. Rumsfeld, relegating Secretary of State Colin Powell to a secondary role. In Bush's second term, however, Rice became secretary of state, thus strengthening the power of that position vis-à-vis that of national security adviser Stephen J. Hadley (previously Rice's deputy). In many respects, then, the characteristics of the individual, particularly foreign policy expertise and access to the presi-

In 1989 the dismantling of the Berlin Wall and the reunification of West and East Germany exemplified collapsing Communist control of Eastern Europe and heralded the end of the cold war. Here border guards look through from East Germany after demonstrators pulled down one segment of the wall at Brandenburg gate.

dent, are most significant in determining the importance of the position.

Foreign Policy-making Process

Although the National Security Council and the executive departments and agencies that deal with foreign affairs are established by law, it is up to the president to create and maintain a responsive and effective foreign policy-making process. Because numerous executive branch units are working on foreign policy, their work must be coordinated to minimize the duplication of their efforts and institutional conflict and to ensure that each unit has access to the president. Therefore, as managers of the foreign policy bureaucracy, presidents must establish procedures that determine how policy options and information should be presented to them, who should have access to intelligence, how the efforts of various departments and agencies should be coordinated, how the agendas of foreign policy meetings should be set, who should regularly attend these meetings, who should chair these meetings, and who should be responsible for overseeing policy implementation.

Managing the Foreign Policy-making Process

Since World War II, the central problem within the foreign policy establishment has been deciding who should manage the foreign policy-making process. The president must ultimately referee the inevitable bureaucratic struggle within the administration for influence, resources, and prestige, but the responsibility for determining the substance of policy leaves the president with little time for matters of management. Therefore, some executive branch unit must serve as the facilitator of the foreign policy-making system. The main rivals for this responsibility have been the State Department under the secretary of state and the NSC staff under the national security adviser. From the Kennedy to the Ford administration, presidents tended to look to their national security advisers to manage their foreign policy-making system. Critics of this trend have maintained that the oversight, coordination, and leadership of the foreign policy-making system properly belong to the State Department.[117] They argue that the State Department was intended to be preeminent in foreign affairs and that its foreign policy expertise, accountability to Congress, and network of embassies in foreign capitals make it the best choice to run the president's foreign policy-making system. The presidents from Ford to Clinton have tried various combinations, emphasizing initially the importance of the secretary of state, but often witnessing sharply divisive conflicts between that official and the national security adviser. President George W. Bush initially relied on his national security adviser, Condoleezza Rice, but then made her secretary of state in his second term, thus increasing the importance of that office.

The State Department, however, like the other departments, has institutional interests that inhibit its ability to be an arbiter between competing departments and agencies. Just as the military mission of the Defense Department or the intelligence mission of the CIA disposes those units to approach foreign affairs from a unique perspective, State's diplomatic mission disposes it to prefer its own foreign policy strategies. Even if State Department officials were able to mediate disputes between other bureaucratic units impartially, those units would never regard State as a neutral department.

The perpetual problem in foreign policy management is finding structures and procedures that can accomplish a number of demanding and often incompatible goals: oversight and coordination of the many and varied departments and agencies administering foreign policy; full information and debate in policy formulation; institutional experience and memory; responsiveness to circumstances; and responsiveness to presidential policy decisions and changes of course. Presidents tend to begin their terms with elaborate structures for collegial deliberation and complementary systems of administrative coordination. But over time, they often find these structures to be indecisive, unresponsive, rife with departmental infighting and parochialism, and generally lacking in coherence. Then they tend to turn to a small group or a single adviser, whether the secretary of state, the national security adviser, or the chief of staff.

When decisions are made by a small group, however, wise and successful policy depends on the skills, knowledge, and integrity of the president and his few advisers. Nixon's successes depended on his intense focus on foreign affairs and on the extraordinary qualities and Herculean diplomatic efforts of Henry Kissinger. The same organization but with third-rate national security advisers and a less focused president helped produce the Iran-contra fiasco. President George W. Bush has faced criticism for the insular decision making that led to the 2003 Iraq War.

Even when a more intimate circle of advisers functions well in making policy, a gulf may develop between the policy makers centered in the White House and the administrative arms in the departments and agencies. Then departments and agencies can pursue their distinct and permanent interests by frustrating implementation and by seeking support in the congressional committees with which they are associated.

Foreign Policy Decision-making Systems

Harry Truman's well-founded suspicion that Congress had created the NSC to check his authority and his strained relationships with his first two secretaries of defense, James V. Forrestal and Louis Johnson, initially led him to ignore the NSC. He attended only twelve of the first fifty-seven NSC meetings.[118] During the Korean War, the NSC developed a more important policy-making role. Truman attended most meetings, and he used the group to forge presidential foreign policies. Nevertheless, Truman still emphasized its advisory nature and frequently consulted its individual members or ad hoc groups rather than relying on the entire NSC for policy advice.

Dwight Eisenhower's foreign policy decision-making system reflected his military background. He presided over highly structured weekly meetings of the NSC and created NSC subcommittees to consider specific policy issues. He also established the "Planning Board," a staff body charged with foreign policy planning, and the "Operations Coordinating Board," an interagency committee charged with overseeing implementation of executive decisions.[119] Although Eisenhower's system had the advantages of ensuring that all parties would participate in decision making and that the president would not become bogged down in details better left to subordinates, it often has been criticized as being too rigid and formalistic. Meetings were sometimes held because they were routinely scheduled rather than because they were necessary. Eisenhower also insisted that his top advisers reach a consensus on issues. His demand for unanimity led to policy papers that were too general and vague to provide direction to lower-level personnel charged with implementing policy.

John Kennedy replaced Eisenhower's formal committees with a less structured collegial decision-making system. Kennedy's reliance on the advice of departmental experts who had advocated the disastrous U.S.-supported Bay of Pigs invasion of Cuba by Cuban nationals in April 1961 convinced him that he needed independent sources of national security advice in the White House. As a result, the NSC staff under the direction of the national security adviser, McGeorge Bundy, not only facilitated the decision-making process, it generated and evaluated policy options for the president. Formal NSC meetings were de-emphasized. During the Cuban missile crisis Kennedy relied on an assembly of his closest advisers known as the "Executive Committee." Unlike the NSC, membership in this ad hoc group depended not on statutory requirements, but on the trust and confidence of the president.[120]

Lyndon Johnson made few changes in either Kennedy's national security decision-making system or the personnel who ran it. The number of advisers involved in ad hoc policy-making sessions declined, however, especially when the Vietnam War was the topic. Johnson developed the practice of discussing the war at Tuesday lunch meetings attended by five or six close advisers. The president used NSC meetings primarily to announce and discuss decisions that had already been made. In 1966 Johnson created formal interdepartmental groups to develop and coordinate policy proposals that would flow up to the NSC, but the work of these groups was largely confined to peripheral issues unrelated to the war.[121]

Richard Nixon tried to create a foreign policy-making system that incorporated the best aspects of the Eisenhower and Kennedy-Johnson systems. He created a formal interagency committee structure similar to Eisenhower's to ensure that all departments and agencies would be heard. Unlike Eisenhower's committee system, however, Nixon's was intended to produce several policy options for the president's consideration rather than an interdepartmental consensus. The committees also were designed to make less important decisions, thereby allowing the president and his top advisers to concentrate on the most important issues. Nixon established a strong NSC staff that enabled the president and his national security adviser, Henry Kissinger, to monitor the activities of the committees.

Although most scholars consider Nixon's NSC system to be a well-conceived blueprint for national security decision making, that blueprint was not always followed. His strong interest in national security affairs and the delicate nature of the negotiations to end the Vietnam War and improve relations with the Soviet Union and the People's Republic of China led to a centralization of decision making in the hands of Nixon, Kissinger, and the NSC staff that excluded other top advisers and departments. Late in Nixon's presidency, the Watergate scandal dominated the president's time, causing him to rely even more on Henry Kissinger and a small circle of trusted advisers.[122]

Nixon's successor, Gerald Ford, was able to restore balance to the foreign policy decision-making system. Ford used the NSC staff and national security adviser Brent Scowcroft primarily as coordinators of national security decision making rather than as policy advisers. The president still relied heavily on Kissinger, who had become secretary of state in 1973, but the views of other departments and agencies were integrated more often into national security decisions than they had been during the latter years of Nixon's presidency.

Jimmy Carter simplified the NSC committee system and established a decentralized advisory system of "shops" that would filter proposals up to his office. To ensure that he would not be insulated from a diversity of opinion, he had department and agency leaders report directly to him rather than through the chief of staff or the national security adviser. Initially, his principal adviser was the secretary of state, Cyrus R. Vance, who took the lead in general policy formulation. Over time Carter leaned more heavily on the NSC staff and his national security adviser, Zbigniew Brzezinski. Carter's system suffered from a lack of coherence and from frequent disagreements between Brzezinski and Vance, who resigned his post in May 1980 after opposing the U.S. attempt to rescue American hostages in Iran.

Ronald Reagan initially announced his intention to give dominant roles in national security policy making to his secretaries of defense and state. Nevertheless, Reagan rejected a plan submitted by Secretary of State Alexander M. Haig Jr. to designate the State Department as the manager of foreign policy. The president took a whole year before setting up a formal foreign policy-making system that stressed cabinet predominance.[123] From the beginning of the administration, however, the NSC staff was given a smaller role than under Presidents Nixon, Ford, and Carter. Reagan's first national security adviser, Richard V. Allen, did not even have direct access to the president. Although subsequent national security advisers William Clark, Robert C. McFarlane, John M. Poindexter, Frank C. Carlucci, and Colin Powell did have daily access to the president, none dominated the policy-making process as much as their predecessors Henry Kissinger and Zbigniew Brzezinski.

The most distinguishing feature of the Reagan foreign policy-making system was the president's hands-off administration. Reagan allowed his cabinet secretaries and other subordinates vast discretion in responding to the day-to-day issues affecting their area of foreign policy. He limited his participation primarily to the articulation of broad themes. Some observers during Reagan's presidency praised this style of leadership as an example of how presidents should delegate responsibilities to save their energies for the most important decisions and avoid being overwhelmed by the details of foreign policy. However, the Iran-contra scandal, which was uncovered in 1986, demonstrated the dangers of Reagan's detachment from administration. NSC staff member Lt. Col. Oliver L. North, along with national security adviser Vice Adm. John Poindexter and other administration officials, arranged secret arms sales to Iran, a terrorist state, as barter for U.S. hostages. This contradicted the administration's stated policy and the advice of senior administration officials. In addition, North and Poindexter used the profits from the arms sales to circumvent Congress's prohibition of U.S. government military aid to the contras in Nicaragua. The Tower Commission, appointed by the president to review his NSC system in the wake of the affair, commented on Reagan's management style in its 1987 report:

President George W. Bush's national security adviser, Condoleezza Rice, talks with Secretary of State Colin Powell and White House chief of staff Andrew Card in the White House Oval Office. Both Powell and Rice served in the administration of Bush's father a decade earlier: Powell as chairman of the Joint Chiefs of Staff and Rice as the National Security Council's senior director of Soviet and East European affairs.

Bill Clinton's informal leadership style (in foreign and domestic policy) prompted much criticism in his first year in office, leading Colin Powell, chairman of the Joint Chiefs of Staff, to conclude that "discussions continued to meander like graduate-student bull sessions." [125] After the botched intervention in Somalia, riots in Haiti that deterred the dispatch of U.S. military trainers, and a failure to reach policy consensus on the civil war in Bosnia, Clinton adopted more structure in his decision-making process.

George W. Bush, in sharp contrast to Clinton, insisted on highly structured and punctual meetings, adhering to the leadership approach of a chief executive officer in the corporate world. But that tightly managed system came under attack for ideological rigidity and failure to consider alternatives in the aftermath of the 2003 Iraq war.[126]

> The President's management style is to put the principal responsibility for policy review and implementation on the shoulders of his advisers. Nevertheless, with such a complex, high-risk operation and so much at stake, the President should have ensured that the NSC system did not fail him. He did not force his policy to undergo the most critical review of which the NSC participants and the process were capable. Never did he insist upon accountability and performance review. Had the President chosen to drive the NSC system, the outcome could well have been different.

The scandal forced the resignation and indictment of several White House officials and led the president to project a more visible role in foreign policy making.

George H.W. Bush was directly involved in the foreign policy deliberation and decisions of his administration. He worked closely with his secretary of state, James Baker, on major initiatives. Otherwise, two subgroups within the NSC, the Principals Committee and the Deputies Committee, handled most of the policy decisions and implementation. Bush called few formal NSC meetings and was criticized for the informality of his approach to national security decision making.[124]

The Bureaucracy as a Source of Presidential Power

The foreign policy bureaucracy can be a great asset to presidents in their struggle with Congress for control of foreign policy and their efforts to provide effective foreign policy leadership. The bureaucracy's most obvious benefit is that it enables presidents and their closest advisers to concentrate on the decisions and initiatives they deem most important while the bureaucracy deals with the many small foreign policy matters the executive branch must handle daily. President Nixon and his national security adviser, Henry Kissinger, spent the vast majority of their foreign policy time during Nixon's first term on three problems: ending the Vietnam War, opening up China, and improving relations with the Soviet Union. Most other foreign policy matters were left to the bureaucracy. Although Nixon and Kissinger certainly neglected other important matters as a result, the extraordinary attention they were able to give these principal issues made progress possible.

The bureaucracy's capacity to supply the president with information and advice is another asset. *(See box, Information: A Foreign Policy Commodity, p. 735.)* No institution, including Congress, has information sources on foreign affairs that can compare with the array of channels supplying the president with current intelligence and professional opinions. Most modern presidents have been briefed daily on foreign policy issues by their secretary of state, national security adviser, or other top aides. These officials receive information and proposals that have been distilled and funneled up to them from their respective departments. This information and advice make it possible for a president to address foreign policy issues intelligently without being an expert.

Besides the information available from normal advisory and diplomatic resources, the nation's vast intelligence-gathering capabilities are at the president's service. The director of central intelligence coordinates intelligence activities and relays important intelligence directly to the president. Many foreign policy decisions, particularly those that involve the use of force, cannot be made without access to intelligence information. For example, President Kennedy decided to blockade Cuba during the Cuban missile crisis after he and his advisers had carefully analyzed all intelligence information.[127] The president's access to sensitive intelligence has provided a rationale for presidential autonomy in foreign policy. Congress's recognition of this presidential advantage contributed to its frequent willingness to accept presidential leadership in foreign affairs after World War II. Since the Vietnam War, however, Congress has more

actively sought access to intelligence and has been more reluctant to accept presidential evaluations of international issues.

The professional foreign policy bureaucracy also provides continuity in the policies of successive administrations. When a new president takes office, the general policy directives that provide guidance to the bureaucracy change and the political appointees who head the various departments and agencies are new, but the bureaucrats continue to collect intelligence, write reports, make recommendations, and maintain diplomatic relations with other nations. Useful initiatives begun by the previous president have a chance to find a place in the new administration, and foreign governments that are frustrated by the frequent changes in presidential leadership can take comfort in the continuing presence of career officials with whom they have dealt in the past.

The Bureaucracy as an Impediment to Presidential Power

Although presidents have formal authority over the foreign policy bureaucracy, it is too vast to command and does not always serve their purposes. Indeed, since the end of World War II executive branch departments and agencies often have been a greater obstacle to presidential will in foreign affairs than has Congress. Executive branch obstruction occurs, in large part, because the goals and interests of the

INFORMATION: A FOREIGN POLICY COMMODITY

The administration exerts extensive control over the foreign policy agenda through its control over information held in the federal bureaucracy. The president benefits from the huge operations of the public relations offices of the Pentagon, State Department, and Central Intelligence Agency. Through the power of classification, the president also can control how much information journalists, scholars, and political activists have at their disposal.

Scholars have raised concerns about the effects of the executive's control over information. A constant tension exists between the democratic value of openness and the strategic value of secrecy. Even as the president speaks more and more in public, the president and government also cloak more matters in secrecy. This development may be attributed to the need for different strategies to overcome and control a growing bureaucracy. Political scientist Francis E. Rourke has written:

> To be sure, the bureaucracy did not invent secrecy in American government. The Founding Fathers found it expedient to conduct the deliberations of the Constitutional Convention at Philadelphia in 1787 in private [and] presidents have, through the development of "executive privilege," contributed a great deal to the secrecy surrounding executive activities. . . . But it remains true that the growth of bureaucracy in American government has brought about an enormous expansion in the secretiveness with which policy is made.[1]

The erection of a "national security state," critics have argued, gives the president almost unchallenged power over foreign affairs and even many areas of

domestic policy. Presidents always can assert that "national security" requires withholding information.

Presidents clearly enjoy an important advantage in deciding what information they want released and how they want to do it. President Richard Nixon justified both the "secret" bombing of Cambodia in 1970 and his handling of the Watergate affair on the grounds of national security requirements. The Reagan administration's refusal to allow reporters to witness the invasion of Grenada was based on similar claims. But perhaps more important is the routine information that presidents can keep secret.

After the terrorist attacks of September 11, 2001, the administration of George W. Bush interpreted presidential powers expansively to combat terrorism. One of its most controversial actions was the creation of a secret domestic surveillance program to collect information through overseeing phone calls or e-mails on possible terrorist plans, typically without judicial approval or congressional consultation. When the program was uncovered in 2005, critics maintained that the president lacked the constitutional power to create such a program unilaterally, while supporters declared that the war on terror justified executive action.[2]

1. Francis E. Rourke, *Bureaucracy, Politics, and Public Policy* (Boston: Little, Brown, 1984), 155.
2. James Risen, *State of War: The Secret History of the C.I.A and the Bush Administration* (New York: Free Press, 2006).

bureaucracy conflict with those of the president. Political scientist Richard E. Neustadt has explained why presidents have found it difficult to control the bureaucracy:

> Everything somehow involves the President. But operating agencies owe their existence least of all to one another—and only in some part to him. Each has a separate statutory base; each has its statutes to administer; each deals with a different set of subcommittees at the Capitol. Each has its own peculiar set of clients, friends, and enemies outside the formal government. Each has a different set of specialized careerists inside its own bailiwick. Our Constitution gives the President the "take-care" clause and the appointive power. Our statutes give him central budgeting and a degree of personnel control. All agency administrators are responsible to him. But they also are responsible to Congress, to their clients, to their staffs, and to themselves. In short, they have five masters.[128]

The president cannot, therefore, expect his commands to move bureaucrats, well down the line, exactly as he desires. As Neustadt said, the president must "convince such men that what the White House wants of them is what they ought to do for their sake and on their authority." [129]

The sheer number of people involved in even minor matters makes this task daunting. Moreover, foreign service officers, military personnel, members of the intelligence community, and other career executive branch employees involved in foreign affairs neither depend on the president for their jobs nor necessarily agree with presidential goals and policies. Career bureaucrats are naturally concerned with the long-term welfare of their particular department or agency. They usually will fight against policies that could diminish their responsibilities or resources, and they often will resent decisions that show an obvious disregard for their institutional point of view. In addition, foreign policy bureaucrats may regard presidents and their political appointees as temporary invaders of the foreign policy realm whose political goals harm the permanent interests of the United States.

Members of the foreign policy bureaucracy have several means by which they can resist presidential will in foreign affairs. They can delay or undermine the execution of presidential directives, provide the president only with information and options that do not conflict with their interpretation of an issue, leak details of a controversial or covert policy to Congress or the media, publicly oppose a policy, or resign in protest. The president may have the constitutional power to order an agency to carry out a particular task, but if that agency drags its feet or otherwise undermines implementation of the order, the president's power can be diluted or even neutralized.

The most important means available to presidents of controlling the bureaucracy and communicating to it their foreign policy vision is the power to appoint the officials who will head the departments and agencies. These officials serve as department managers as well as members of the inner circle of presidential advisers. In choosing these appointees the president must reconcile, on the one hand, the need to find qualified persons with administrative talent who will be respected by the departments they head, with, on the other hand, the president's desire to maintain control over the bureaucracy. Even the most loyal presidential appointee, however, usually will develop a competing loyalty to the department or agency, which may at times conflict with the goals of the president.[130]

NOTES

1. *United States v. Curtiss-Wright Export Corp.*, 299 U.S. 304 (1936).

2. Quoted in Theodore C. Sorensen, *Kennedy* (New York: Bantam, 1966), 573.

3. Louis Henkin, *Foreign Affairs and the Constitution* (New York: Norton, 1972), 76–77.

4. James Madison, *Federalist* No. 51, and Alexander Hamilton, *Federalist* No. 72, in Alexander Hamilton, James Madison, and John Jay, *The Federalist Papers* (New York: New American Library, 1961), 321–322, 437.

5. Edward S. Corwin, *The President: Office and Powers, 1787–1984*, 5th ed. (New York: New York University Press, 1984), 201.

6. Quoted in Clinton Rossiter, *The American Presidency*, 2d ed. (New York: Harcourt Brace, 1960), 15.

7. John E. Mueller, *War, Presidents, and Public Opinion* (New York: Wiley, 1973)

8. Aaron Wildavsky, "The Two Presidencies," Reprinted in *Perspectives on the Presidency*, ed. Aaron Wildavsky (Boston: Little, Brown, 1975), 448–461.

9. Jane Mayer, "The Hidden Power," *New Yorker*, July 3, 2006.

10. John Marshall, quoted in *United States v. Curtiss-Wright Export Corp.*, 299 U.S. 304 (1936).

11. Alexis de Tocqueville, *Democracy in America*, ed. J.P. Mayer (Garden City, N.Y.: Anchor, 1969), 126.

12. *Chicago & S. Airlines v. Waterman SS. Corp.*, 333 U.S. 103 (1948), 111.

13. Quoted in Christopher H. Pyle and Richard M. Pious, eds., *The President, Congress, and the Constitution* (New York: Free Press, 1984), 238.

14. Arthur M. Schlesinger Jr., *The Imperial Presidency* (Boston: Houghton Mifflin, 1973), 102–103. See also Henkin, *Foreign Affairs and the Constitution*, 27 n. 19.

15. *The Letters of Pacificus and Helvidius* (Delmar, N.Y.: Scholars' Facsimiles and Reprints, 1976), 5–15.

16. Ibid., ix.

17. Ibid., 57.

18. Quoted in Arthur Bernon Tourtellot, *The Presidents on the Presidency* (Garden City, N.Y.: Doubleday, 1964), 272.

19. Pyle and Pious, *President, Congress, and the Constitution*, 204–205.

20. James M. Lindsay, *Congress and the Politics of U.S. Foreign Policy* (Baltimore: Johns Hopkins University Press, 1994), 15.

21. Richard Harmond, "Theodore Roosevelt and the Making of the Modern Presidency," in *Power and the Presidency*, ed. Philip C. Dolce and George H. Skau (New York: Scribner's, 1976), 72–73.

22. Theodore Roosevelt to H.C. Lodge, January 28, 1909, quoted in Schlesinger, *Imperial Presidency*, 89.

23. Richard M. Pious, *The American Presidency: The Politics of Power from FDR to Carter* (New York: Basic Books, 1979), 53.

24. For a discussion of the Tonkin Gulf incident, see Leslie H. Gelb and Richard K. Betts, *The Irony of Vietnam: The System Worked* (Washington, D.C.: Brookings, 1979), 100–104; and Eugene Windchy, *Tonkin Gulf* (New York: Doubleday, 1971).

25. Gelb and Betts, *Irony of Vietnam*, 103–104.

26. Robert E. DiClerico, *The American President*, 4th ed. (Englewood Cliffs, N.J.: Prentice-Hall, 1995), 58.

27. Lindsay, *Congress and the Politics of U.S. Foreign Policy*, 89–90.

28. Corwin, *President*, 222.

29. Lindsay, *Congress and the Politics of U.S. Foreign Policy*, 86.

30. Quoted in Tourtellot, *Presidents on the Presidency*, 274.

31. Quoted in Pious, *American Presidency*, 334.

32. Quoted in Corwin, *President*, 207–208.

33. Henkin, *Foreign Affairs and the Constitution*, 301.

34. Lindsay, *Congress and the Politics of U.S. Foreign Policy*, 120–121, 126.

35. Quoted in Tourtellot, *Presidents on the Presidency*, 298.

36. Schlesinger, *Imperial Presidency*, 27.

37. Quoted in ibid., 128.

38. Charles Krauthammer, "The Bush Doctrine," *Weekly Standard,* June 4, 2001, 21–25.

39. Cecil V. Crabb Jr. and Pat M. Holt, *Invitation to Struggle: Congress, the President and Foreign Policy*, 4th ed. (Washington, D.C.: CQ Press, 1992), 15.

40. Jack N. Rakove, "Solving a Constitutional Puzzle: The Treaty Making Clause as a Case Study," *Perspectives in American History,* New Series, I:1984, 233–281.

41. John Jay, *Federalist* No. 64, in Alexander Hamilton, James Madison, and John Jay, *The Federalist Papers* (New York: New American Library, 1961), 392–393.

42. George H. Haynes, *The Senate of the United States* (Boston: Houghton Mifflin, 1938), 575.

43. Alexander Hamilton, *Federalist* No. 75, in Alexander Hamilton, James Madison, and John Jay, *The Federalist Papers* (New York: New American Library, 1961), 452–453.

44. Buel W. Patch, "Treaties and Domestic Law," *Editorial Research Reports,* March 28, 1952, 241.

45. Abraham D. Sofaer, *War, Foreign Affairs and Constitutional Power: The Origins* (Cambridge: Ballinger, 1976), 95–96.

46. Corwin, *President*, 240.

47. Louis Fisher, *Constitutional Conflicts between Congress and the President*, 3d rev. ed. (Lawrence: University Press of Kansas, 1991), 219.

48. Lindsay, *Congress and the Politics of U.S. Foreign Policy,* 95.

49. Joseph E. Kallenbach, *The American Chief Executive: The Presidency and the Governorship* (New York: Harper and Row, 1966), 505.

50. Pious, *American Presidency,* 336.

51. F. M. Brewer, "Advice and Consent of the Senate," *Editorial Research Reports,* June 1, 1943, 352.

52. Louis W. Koenig, *The Chief Executive,* 5th ed. (New York: Harcourt Brace and World, 1986), 206.

53. DiClerico, *American President,* 46.

54. Lindsay, *Congress and the Politics of U.S. Foreign Policy,* 65, 123.

55. Theodor Meron, "The Treaty Power: The International Legal Effect of Changes in Obligations Initiated by the Congress," in *The Tethered Presidency: Congressional Restraints on Executive Power,* ed. Thomas M. Franck (New York: New York University Press, 1981), 116–117.

56. Henkin, *Foreign Affairs and the Constitution,* 134.

57. Lindsay, *Congress and the Politics of U.S. Foreign Policy,* 80.

58. Meron, "Treaty Power."

59. Kallenbach, *American Chief Executive,* 507.

60. Corwin, *President,* 205–206.

61. Pious, *American Presidency,* 338–340.

62. Quoted in Henkin, *Foreign Affairs and the Constitution,* 377.

63. Ibid., 168–170.

64. Pyle and Pious, *President, Congress, and the Constitution,* 258–265.

65. Loch K. Johnson, *The Making of International Agreements: Congress Confronts the Executive* (New York: New York University Press, 1984), 12.

66. Lindsay, *Congress and the Politics of U.S. Foreign Policy,* 83.

67. Harold W. Stanley and Richard G. Niemi, *Vital Statistics on American Politics, 2001–2002* (Washington, D.C.: CQ Press, 2001), 334.

68. Quoted in Henkin, *Foreign Affairs and the Constitution,* 177–178. Also see *United States v. Belmont,* 310 U.S. 324 (1937).

69. Henkin, *Foreign Affairs and the Constitution,* 178–179.

70. Schlesinger, *Imperial Presidency,* 86.

71. Ibid., 86–87.

72. Lawrence Margolis, *Executive Agreements and Presidential Power in Foreign Policy* (New York: Praeger, 1986), 7–9.

73. Ibid., 9.

74. Tourtellot, *Presidents on the Presidency,* 277.

75. DiClerico, *American President,* 47–48.

76. Ibid., 48.

77. Corwin, *President,* 245–246.

78. Johnson, *Making of International Agreements,* 86–87.

79. *CQ Almanac, 1972* (Washington, D.C.: Congressional Quarterly, 1972), 619.

80. Corwin, *President,* 212.

81. Alexander Hamilton, *Federalist* No. 69, in Alexander Hamilton, James Madison, and John Jay, *The Federalist Papers* (New York: New American Library, 1961), 420.

82. Schlesinger, *Imperial Presidency,* 14.

83. Kallenbach, *American Chief Executive,* 493.

84. Seth P. Tillman, *The United States in the Middle East* (Bloomington: Indiana University Press, 1982), 221.

85. Quoted in Tourtellot, *Presidents on the Presidency,* 291.

86. Corwin, *President,* 216–219, 486 n. 105.

87. Crabb and Holt, *Invitation to Struggle,* 18.

88. Pious, *American Presidency,* 335.

89. See Richard N. Haass, *The Reluctant Sheriff: The United States after the Cold War* (Washington, D.C.: Council on Foreign Relations Press, 1998).

90. Louis Fisher, *Presidential War Power* (Lawrence: University Press of Kansas, 1995), 153–154.

91. U.S. Department of State Dispatch, vol. 5, no. 20, May 16, 1994; Fisher, *Presidential War Power,* 160–161.

92. R. Gordon Hoxie, *Command Decision and the Presidency* (New York: Reader's Digest Press, 1977), 40.

93. Arthur S. Miller, *Presidential Power in a Nutshell* (St. Paul, Minn.: West, 1977), 37.

94. Koenig, *Chief Executive,* 206–207.

95. *CQ Almanac, 1989* (Washington, D.C.: Congressional Quarterly, 1990), 537–541.

96. Robert E. Hunter, *Presidential Control of Foreign Policy: Management or Mishap* (New York: Praeger, 1982), 79–80.

97. Koenig, *Chief Executive*, 217.

98. Henkin, *Foreign Affairs and the Constitution*, 46.

99. Corwin, *President*, 235.

100. Ibid., 236.

101. Elmer Plischke, *Diplomat in Chief: The President at the Summit* (New York: Praeger, 1986), 13.

102. Kallenbach, *American Chief Executive*, 498–499.

103. Plischke, *Diplomat in Chief*, 121.

104. Kallenbach, *American Chief Executive*, 499.

105. Dorothy Buckton James, *Contemporary Presidency*, 2d ed. (Indianapolis: Pegasus, 1974), 127–128.

106. Quoted in Plischke, *Diplomat in Chief*, 202.

107. Ibid., 200–202.

108. Richard Nixon, "Superpower Summitry," *Foreign Affairs* 64 (fall 1985): 1.

109. Plischke, *Diplomat in Chief*, 456–460.

110. Ibid., 460–473.

111. Marcus Cunliffe, *American Presidents and the Presidency* (New York: American Heritage, 1972), 286.

112. Amos A. Jordan, William J. Taylor, and Lawrence J. Korb, *American National Security: Policy and Process*, 4th ed. (Baltimore: Johns Hopkins University Press, 1984), 167–168.

113. Pious, *American Presidency*, 362.

114. John E. Endicott, "The National Security Council," in *American Defense Policy*, 5th ed., ed. John F. Reichart and Steven R. Sturm (Baltimore: Johns Hopkins University Press, 1982), 521–522.

115. See, for example, Carnes Lord, *The Presidency and the Management of National Security* (New York: Free Press, 1988), chap. 4.

116. Christopher Madison, "Scrambling Vicar," *National Journal*, April 20, 1991, 924–928.

117. For an outline of a state-centered foreign policy-making system, see I.M. Destler, *Presidents, Bureaucrats, and Foreign Policy* (Princeton: Princeton University Press, 1974), 254–294.

118. Endicott, "National Security Council," 522.

119. Zbigniew Brzezinski, "The NSC's Midlife Crisis," *Foreign Policy* 69 (winter 1987–1988): 84–85.

120. Jordan, Taylor, and Korb, *American National Security*, 98.

121. Ibid., 91–92.

122. Charles W. Kegley Jr. and Eugene R. Wittkopf, *American Foreign Policy: Pattern and Process* (New York: St. Martin's Press, 1979), 258–259.

123. Brzezinski, "NSC's Midlife Crisis," 90.

124. Jordan, Taylor, and Korb, *American National Security*, 100, 215–216.

125. Colin Powell, with Joseph E. Persico, *My American Journey* (New York: Random House, 1995), 576

126. George Packer, *The Assassins' Gate: America in Iraq* (New York: Farrar, Straus and Giroux, 2005).

127. Graham T. Allison, *Essence of Decision* (Boston: Little, Brown, 1971), 46–62.

128. Richard E. Neustadt, *Presidential Power and the Modern Presidents* (New York: Free Press, 1990), 34.

129. Ibid., 30.

130. Hunter, *Presidential Control of Foreign Policy*, 18.

SELECTED BIBLIOGRAPHY

Ambrose, Stephen E., and Douglas G. Brinkley. *Rise to Globalism: American Foreign Policy Since 1938*. 8th rev. ed. New York: Penguin, 1997.

Corwin, Edward S. *The President: Office and Powers, 1787–1984*. 5th ed. New York: New York University Press, 1984.

Crabb, Cecil V., Jr., and Pat M. Holt. *Invitation to Struggle: Congress, the President and Foreign Policy*. 4th ed. Washington, D.C.: CQ Press, 1992.

Crabb, Cecil V., Glenn J. Antizzo, and Leila E. Sarieddine. *Congress and the Foreign Policy Process: Modes of Legislative Behavior*. Baton Rouge: Louisiana State University Press, 2000.

Destler, I. M. *Presidents, Bureaucrats, and Foreign Policy*. Princeton: Princeton University Press, 1974.

Fisher, Louis. *Constitutional Conflicts between Congress and the President*. 3d rev. ed. Lawrence: University Press of Kansas, 1991.

Henkin, Louis. *Foreign Affairs and the Constitution*. New York: Norton, 1975.

Hersman, Rebecca K.C. *How Congress and the President Really Make Foreign Policy*. Washington, D.C.: Brookings, 2000.

Howell, William G. *Power Without Persuasion: The Politics of Direct Presidential Action*. Princeton: Princeton University Press, 2003.

Hunter, Robert E. *Presidential Control of Foreign Policy: Management or Mishap*. New York: Praeger, 1982.

Johnson, Loch. *The Making of International Agreements: Congress Confronts the Executive*. New York: New York University Press, 1984.

Kallenbach, Joseph E. *The American Chief Executive: The Presidency and the Governorship*. New York: Harper and Row, 1966.

Koh, Harold Hongju. *The National Security Constitution: Sharing Power After the Iran-Contra Affair*. New Haven: Yale University Press, 1990.

Lindsay, James M. *Congress and the Politics of U.S. Foreign Policy*. Baltimore: Johns Hopkins University Press, 1994.

Margolis, Lawrence. *Executive Agreements and Presidential Power in Foreign Policy*. New York: Praeger, 1986.

Mayer, Kenneth. *With the Stroke of a Pen: Executive Orders and Presidential Power*. Princeton: Princeton University Press, 2002.

Mueller, John E. *War, Presidents, and Public Opinion*. New York: Wiley, 1973.

Neustadt, Richard E. *Presidential Power and the Modern Presidents*. New York: Free Press, 1990.

Pious, Richard M. *The American Presidency: The Politics of Power from FDR to Carter*. New York: Basic Books, 1979.

Plischke, Elmer. *Diplomat in Chief: The President at the Summit*. New York: Praeger, 1986.

Pyle, Christopher H., and Richard M. Pious, eds. *The President, Congress, and the Constitution*. New York: Free Press, 1984.

Rudalevige, Andrew. *The New Imperial Presidency: Renewing Presidential Power After Watergate*. Ann Arbor: University of Michigan Press, 2005.

Schlesinger, Arthur M., Jr. *The Imperial Presidency*. 2d ed. Boston: Houghton Mifflin, 1989.

Wilcox, Francis O. *Congress, the Executive, and Foreign Policy*. New York: Harper and Row, 1971.

Wildavsky, Aaron. "The Two Presidencies." Reprinted in *Perspectives on the Presidency*, 448–461, ed. Aaron Wildavsky. Boston: Little, Brown, 1975.

chapter 14

Commander in Chief

by Meena Bose, Daniel C. Diller, and Stephen H. Wirls

The Framers of the Constitution distrusted both executive and military power and believed the potential for tyranny was great when the two were combined.

Among the colonial grievances cited in the Declaration of Independence were the charges that the British monarch had "kept among us, in times of peace, Standing Armies without the Consent of our legislatures" and "affected to render the Military independent of and superior to the Civil Power." The document also denounced the quartering of troops in American homes, the impressment of American sailors for British warships, and the unjust war being waged against the colonies. The Framers therefore rejected a proposal to grant the president the authority to declare war, divided the war-making power between the executive and Congress, and placed a strict time limit on military appropriations. On the other hand, many of them could recall as well the feeble military and executive powers of the national government both during and after the revolution. The delegates to the Constitutional Convention were determined to find the balance between effective government and safe government. Their main instruments for accomplishing this constitutional goal were adequate powers regulated by checks and balances.

Although many war powers, including the decision to go to war, could be safely placed in the hands of Congress, command of U.S. forces during a conflict required the unified and flexible leadership that only a single person could provide. As Alexander Hamilton noted: "Of all the cares or concerns of government, the direction of war most peculiarly demands those qualities which distinguish the exercise of power by a single hand." [1] The Framers therefore assigned the commander-in-chief power to the presidency. As political scientist Clinton Rossiter summarized the matter: "We have placed a shocking amount of military power in the President's keeping, but where else, we may ask, could it possibly have been placed?" [2]

Few presidents, however, have been as well suited, in skills and integrity, for the role as the first commander in chief, George Washington. Some presidents have mismanaged military affairs, a few have misused their military power, and there have been many confrontations between the executive and legislative branches over the scope and use of the war powers, with charges of usurpation or abuse of power often being leveled at the president. But contrary to the experiences of many other nations, no president has used the forces at his command to interfere with the ordinary course of electoral accountability or the powers and functions of the other branches.

Because conflicts over the executive's use of the war power typically arise during military engagements, efforts to check the president often falter in the face of ongoing events. During the Civil War, World War I, and World War II, presidents boldly and firmly interpreted the commander-in-chief power broadly, and American success in each case largely stymied any subsequent attempts to limit presidential power. The aftermath of the Vietnam War marked the first time that Congress aimed systematically to constrain the president's ability to send troops into combat. After the terrorist attacks of September 11, 2001, the American public and Congress followed the traditional pattern of "rallying 'round the flag" to support the president's foreign and military policies. But as the global war on terror continued, particularly with difficulties occurring in Iraq, attempts to restrict presidential power in military affairs have begun to develop.

DISTRIBUTION OF WAR-MAKING POWER

The Framers of the Constitution made the highest civilian officer also the commander in chief of the nation's military forces. Article II, Section 2, of the Constitution states: "The President shall be Commander in Chief of the Army and Navy of the United States, and of the Militia of the several States, when called into the actual Service of the United States." This statement is all the Constitution says about the president's war-making power.

The Framers did not regard war making as an inherently executive function. Indeed, they originally gave the

The President shall be Commander in Chief of the Army and Navy of the United States, and of the Militia of the several States, when called into the actual Service of the United States.

—from Article II, Section 2

legislature the comprehensive power to "make war." But fearing that a legislature, cumbersome in itself and frequently out of session, might inhibit action in an emergency, the delegates separated the power to declare war from the power to command or direct the military forces. The latter was given to the president. This division of responsibility left the president free to repel invasions and respond to other acts of war.[3] The Framers were careful, though, to prevent the president from initiating a war on his own authority, and Congress was given the bulk of the war-related powers. The clauses outlining Congress's powers (Article I, Section 8) are detailed and specific:

> To declare War, grant Letters of Marque and Reprisal, and make Rules concerning Captures on Land and Water; To raise and support Armies . . .; To provide and maintain a Navy; To make Rules for the Government and Regulation of the land and naval forces; To provide for calling forth the Militia to execute the Laws of the Union, suppress Insurrections and repel Invasions; To provide for organizing, arming, and disciplining, the Militia, and for governing such Part of them as may be employed in the Service of the United States, reserving to the States respectively, the Appointment of the Officers, and the Authority of training the Militia according to the discipline prescribed by Congress.

As Congress's enumerated war powers indicate, the Framers intended Congress to have full control over the size and character of any national armed forces. A president seeking to become a military dictator would be hindered by Congress's exclusive authority to raise, equip, and organize the armed forces. This includes the authority to eliminate all or any part of the standing forces. Presidents might wish to act, but without Congress's support, they would lack the necessary tools to do so.

The exact authority of the commander in chief was left undefined. Nothing is said directly about the president's authority to initiate military actions short of war in the absence of an invasion or attack. Similarly, the Constitution says nothing directly about the power of Congress to control the scope of conflict once war has been declared. The intentions of many of the Framers to "chain the dog of war" and the clear implications of the Constitution suggest that these questions were settled in favor of congressional control. If the Framers gave the commander-in-chief power to a single

federal official to provide for decisive action in emergencies, the balance of constitutional powers still favored Congress.

Textual ambiguities have, nevertheless, allowed presidents to argue that they possess the power or duty traditionally associated with the office of supreme military commander. Consequently, a broad range of actions and powers has been justified under a generous interpretation of the commander-in-chief clause. In addition, foreign policy and chief executive powers give presidents responsibilities in the area of national security that are used in conjunction with the commander-in-chief power to expand the president's war powers.

In practice, controlling the war powers has depended less on precise constitutional provisions and more on the checking capacity of well-balanced institutions.

Power to Declare War

Although Congress's power to raise armies and fund wars and the president's command of the military in times of war are unquestioned, the authority to decide when and where to employ military force has been a source of conflict between the executive and legislative branches. The Framers could have given the president the power to declare war with the "advice and consent of the Senate" as they had with the treaty power. Instead, the Constitution grants Congress the sole authority to take the country from a state of peace into a state of war. By giving Congress the power to declare war, the Framers sought to contain executive ambition and to ensure that these momentous decisions would be made by the deliberative branch and especially by the representatives of the people who would be called on to shoulder the cost in lives and treasure. James Madison wrote:

> Those who are to conduct a war cannot in the nature of things be proper or safe judges whether a war ought to be commenced, continued, or concluded. They are barred from the latter functions by a great principle in free government, analogous to that which separates the sword from the purse, or the power of executing from the power of enacting laws.[4]

The Framers recognized that speed and secrecy, which only a single decision maker could provide, were essential to the safety of the nation. By separating the power to declare war from the power to conduct it, the Framers left the power to repel sudden attacks in the hands of the president. Congress, in short, decides when to go to war unless the hostile actions of another nation thrust the nation in a state of war. In *The Federalist Papers*, Hamilton, one of the foremost advocates of a strong chief executive at the Constitutional Convention, interpreted the commander-in-chief power narrowly:

> The president is to be commander-in-chief of the army and navy of the United States. In this respect his authority

would be nominally the same with that of the King of Great Britain, but in substance much inferior to it. It would amount to nothing more than the supreme command and direction of the military and naval forces, as first general and admiral of the Confederacy; while that of the British king extends to the *declaring* of war and to the raising and *regulating* of fleets and armies—all of which, by the Constitution under consideration, would appertain to the legislature.[5]

This straightforward formula is, however, full of ambiguities. How is war to be defined? Does the power to declare war extend to a power to authorize any or all uses of force short of war? Or are there military missions short of war that the president can order without congressional authorization? Can the president try to prevent an attack by attacking first? Can the president order U.S. forces to invade the territory of a neutral nation in pursuit of enemy forces?

The Framers seemed to have agreed that Congress was to control the initiation of all military actions that might involve the nation in a war. The Constitution gives Congress the power to "grant Letters of Marque and Reprisal." This now antiquated instrument allows Congress to authorize, for example, privateers to operate against enemy boats in U.S. waters. The clause suggests that the Constitution gives Congress power over actions, such as retaliations and reprisals, that are hostile in nature but fall short of war.

In *Bas v. Tingy* (1800), the Supreme Court affirmed the authority of the United States to engage in limited or "imperfect" wars, and it affirmed Congress's full authority in all decisions to take the United States from a state of peace into a state of limited hostility or war. Not only could Congress authorize an "imperfect" war by statute, as opposed to a declaration, but it also had full authority to limit the conflict in relation to places, objects, and time. In other words, congressional authority in limited wars extended beyond initiation and deeply into the strategic and tactical questions that are often understood as the prerogative of a commander in chief.[6]

In sum, the consensus of the founding generation was, as President Washington argued, that the Constitution "vests the power of declaring war with Congress; therefore no offensive expedition of importance can be undertaken until they have deliberated upon the subject, and authorized such a measure." [7] Although some ambiguity remains about what an expedition "of importance" would be, the general thrust is clear. The historical record is, however, far more complicated. Congress has declared war only five times—the War of 1812, the Mexican War, the Spanish-American War, World War I, and World War II—and yet the United States has been involved in more than one hundred violent military conflicts. Only some of these have been explicitly authorized by Congress, and some of the unauthorized actions were quite large in scale and arose from radically expansive interpretations of the commander-in-chief power.

This historical record suggests that presidents, having direct command of military forces and being responsible for defending the nation, have been in a better position than Congress to exploit the constitutional ambiguity. When presidents have believed a war or military action to be necessary, they usually have found ways to maneuver the nation into a conflict. Particularly after a direct attack on the United States, such as Pearl Harbor in 1941 or the terrorist attacks of September 11, 2001, presidents have directed military action with full support from Congress and the public. Even if military action extends beyond the immediate response to the attack, as was the case with the Iraq war in 2003, Congress usually defers to presidential leadership and direction in military affairs.

Power to Declare Neutrality and End Declared Wars

Some students of the Constitution have reasoned that Congress's authority to declare war implies that only Congress has the power to declare that the nation will not become involved in a war. Secretary of State Thomas Jefferson made this argument in 1793 when President Washington proclaimed that the United States would remain "friendly and impartial" in the war between the British and the French.[8] Many Americans favored France, their ally in the American Revolution, but Washington believed the treaty of alliance with France did not require U.S. involvement in the conflict with Britain and that any involvement would disrupt the nation's political and economic development. Jefferson supported Washington despite his reservations about the constitutionality of the president declaring neutrality. As a concession to Jefferson, Washington left the word *neutrality* out of his proclamation.

Washington's proclamation of neutrality set off a famous debate in the *Gazette of the United States* between Hamilton, who justified Washington's action, and Madison, who opposed Hamilton's expansive reading of the executive power. Hamilton and Madison were less concerned with neutrality than with the larger issue of whether a president could declare unilaterally what U.S. foreign policy would be. Hamilton conceded that the legislature had the exclusive right to declare war but asserted that until war is declared, the executive has both the responsibility to maintain peace and broad discretion in the choice of means. Madison saw the proclamation of neutrality as a usurpation of Congress's power to declare war. Over time, Hamilton's expansive account of presidential powers has prevailed. *(See "Hamilton-Madison Debate," p. 700, in Chapter 13.)*

When Washington asked Congress to pass judgment on the proclamation, it eventually ratified the president's action by passing the Neutrality Act of 1794.

Later the custom developed that Congress would not declare war without a presidential request. Yet on two occasions Congress demonstrated that it could move a president to accept a war even if the president had reservations about the wisdom of doing so. In 1812 a majority of members of Congress convinced President Madison that war against the British was necessary. In 1898, with public opinion on its side, Congress pressured a reluctant William McKinley to ask for a declaration of war against Spain.

Congress and the president share the authority to end a war. The commander in chief has the power to order the military to stop fighting or to withdraw from an area of conflict. However, if Congress has declared war, the president cannot unilaterally end the legal state of war that exists. Congress must take some action that supersedes its declaration of war. The Framers considered, but rejected, a clause allowing the Senate to conclude a peace treaty on its own authority. As it stands, wars are usually concluded through Senate ratification of a treaty negotiated by the president ending the war and establishing peaceful relations with the enemy nation. The Mexican War, the Spanish-American War, and hostilities in the Pacific theater of World War II were officially terminated in this manner. Congress also may formally end a state of war by repealing its declaration of war. This method was used in 1921 after Congress had refused to ratify the Versailles treaty at the end of World War I and in 1951 formally to end the war with Nazi Germany.[9]

DEVELOPMENT OF PRESIDENTIAL WAR POWERS

The Constitution's assignment of the office of commander in chief to the president created the basis for presidential war powers, but the practical scope of this and related powers in the context of a major conflict or declared war was not defined. Presidential war powers expanded dramatically to meet the general crises of the Civil War and the two world wars. The flexibility, secrecy, speed, and unity of command associated with the president were understood to be crucial to the preservation and defense of the United States. In the circumstances of these wars, presidential power expanded from purely military issues into ancillary questions of the national budget, the domestic economy, and domestic security. According to political scientist Edward S. Corwin, "The principal canons of constitutional interpretation are in wartime set aside so far as concerns both the scope of national power and the capacity of the President to gather unto himself all constitutionally available powers in order the more effectively to focus them upon the task of the hour."[10] Presidential actions that would have raised a great deal of protest in peacetime have been accepted in the name of necessity when the security of the nation has been at stake.

Extensions of presidential power in wartime have established precedents, which future presidents were able to use to justify broad interpretations of their authority. Woodrow Wilson's expansion of presidential war power paved the way for Franklin D. Roosevelt's extraordinary wartime authority, just as Wilson had referred to Lincoln's exercise of power when justifying his own. Until World War II, however, presidents could not continue to wield exceptional power as if an emergency continued beyond the end of armed conflict. After World War II, circumstances changed. President Harry S. Truman retained his emergency powers, many of which were delegated by congressional action, by refusing to declare that the emergency had passed. Moreover, the rise of the cold war with the Soviet Union fostered the development of more permanent and extensive presidential war and emergency powers.

The cold war and especially the development of nuclear weapons created a more or less permanent state of national security emergency. These circumstances fostered and sustained a high level of discretion in the commander in chief's authority to use force, at least until the late 1960s and early 1970s when Congress reacted to executive branch abuses of power by attempting to reassert its role in national security affairs. Although the executive branch still dominates national security policy and has retained the ability to initiate armed conflicts, Congress has scrutinized national security affairs more closely and has been able to restrict presidential policies on a variety of issues.

Until the latter stages of the Vietnam War, the expansion of the president's war powers usually had been accomplished with Congress's approval and often with its active support. Congress validated many of Lincoln's actions, passed legislation delegating sweeping wartime powers to both Woodrow Wilson and Franklin Roosevelt, and acquiesced to the accumulation of power by presidents after World War II. But Congress also had successfully reasserted its authority following each war. The Supreme Court has occasionally ruled against exercises of presidential war power, but it seldom has done so when a war has been in progress and often has let stand presidential actions on the grounds that they are political matters that should be resolved between the executive and legislative branches. A major exception was *Youngstown Sheet & Tube Co. v. Sawyer* (1952), in which the Court ruled against Truman's extension of his emergency and commander-in-chief powers into domestic economic affairs when he ordered a government takeover of a steel mill that was threatened by a labor strike.[11] However, as the Court's approval of the internment of Americans of Japanese descent during World War II demonstrates, the Court has recognized the authority of the president acting in concert with Congress to take virtually any action in response to a grave national emergency.[12] *(See "Curfew and Exclusion Orders," p. 1442, in Chapter 30, Vol. II.)*

Early Presidents

Early presidents generally adhered to the principle that Congress was responsible for committing the United States to war. John Adams consulted with Congress in 1798 before allowing U.S. naval forces to attack French vessels that were preying on U.S. commercial shipping. Congress refrained from the drastic step of declaring war, but it passed legislation authorizing the president to order U.S. military forces into battle against the French.[13] This action set the precedent, affirmed by the Supreme Court, that the United States could engage in armed conflicts short of war, but only if "authorized" by Congress. Jefferson and Madison also believed presidents should respect Congress's power to authorize war, yet the events of their administrations demonstrated the desirability of a more flexible commander-in-chief power.

Jefferson and the Barbary Pirates

In 1801 American ships in the Mediterranean were being attacked by pirates from Tripoli and the other Barbary Coast states of Algeria, Morocco, and Tunisia. Jefferson, who wanted to take quick action to resolve the problem, immediately dispatched a squadron of ships to the Mediterranean with instructions to offer the rulers of the Barbary Coast states payments to leave U.S. shipping alone. Jefferson anticipated trouble, however, and informed the commodore of the squadron:

> But if you find on your arrival in Gibralter that all the Barbary Powers have declared war against the United States, you will then distribute your forces in such a manner, as your judgment shall direct, so as best to protect our commerce and chastise their insolence—by sinking, burning, or destroying their ships and vessels wherever you shall find them.[14]

Jefferson did not disclose these orders to Congress when he went before that body on December 8, 1801, to request approval to take the offensive in the naval war that was already being fought. Rather, he emphasized the constitutional restraints under which the squadron operated:

> I sent a small squadron of frigates into the Mediterranean, with assurance to that power Tripoli of our desire to remain in peace, but with orders to protect our commerce against the threatened attack. . . . One of the Tripolitan cruisers . . . was captured, after a heavy slaughter of her men, without the loss of a single one on our part. . . . Unauthorized by the Constitution, without the sanction of Congress, to go beyond the line of defense, the vessel, being disabled from committing further hostilities, was liberated with its crew.[15]

Congress passed legislation early in 1802 authorizing the naval war that eventually led to a treaty with the Barbary powers. Jefferson had used deception and a *fait accompli* to secure the Mediterranean for U.S. commercial shipping

while publicly asserting Congress's authority to determine when military force would be used.[16]

Hamilton, however, found Jefferson's consultations with Congress needless. He asserted that the president did not have to ask Congress's permission to turn loose the navy because "when a foreign nation declares or openly and avowedly makes war upon the United States, they are then by the very fact already at war and any declaration on the part of Congress is nugatory; it is at least unnecessary."[17]

Despite Jefferson's willingness to violate his principles in pursuit of objectives he considered important, he generally abided by the principle of congressional authorization. In 1805, when Spanish subjects in Florida made incursions into the newly acquired Louisiana Territory, Jefferson told Congress: "Considering that Congress alone is constitutionally invested with the power of changing our condition from peace to war, I have thought it my duty to await their authority for using force. . . . The course to be pursued will require the command of means which it belongs to Congress exclusively to yield or to deny." When Congress chose not to grant Jefferson the authority to attack the Spanish in Florida, he accepted its decision.[18]

The War of 1812

The War of 1812 was the first declared war in U.S. history. Sentiment for the war had been aroused by British captures of American commercial ships and their crews, allegations that the British were supplying hostile American Indians on the frontier with arms, and a desire to acquire foreign territory in Canada and Florida. The initial advocates of the war were not President Madison and his close advisers, but members of Congress from the South and the West. These "War Hawks" represented areas that were troubled by Indian attacks and falling agricultural prices. In contrast, the Federalist merchants of the Northeast, who were making large profits on export shipments that avoided capture, were against the war. They feared that war would interfere with their commerce much more than sporadic British seizures of their ships.

Especially because Congress, although bent on war, had not provided for an adequate army and navy, Madison tried sincerely to resolve disputes with the British through diplomacy. He was eventually persuaded that the nation must go to war to protect its rights. On June 1, 1812, the president asked Congress for a declaration of war. In his address to lawmakers, Madison called war making a "solemn question which the Constitution wisely confides to the legislative department of the Government."[19] The declaration was passed 79–49 by the House and 19–13 by the Senate. Members of Congress from the South and the West prevailed over their colleagues from the Northeast.

Not only was the nation divided over the war, it was also unprepared to fight. The small U.S. navy was hopelessly overmatched, and despite the war's popularity in the South and West the army had difficulty recruiting volunteers. U.S. forces suffered a string of humiliating defeats, including the capture and burning of Washington, D.C., by the British in August 1814.

After the British forces withdrew from the capital, Congress assembled to consider the war effort. Yet, with the army still at only about half its authorized strength and enlistments falling off, Congress failed to agree on a conscription bill proposed by James Monroe, Madison's secretary of war and state. Fortunately, the British campaign stalled, and peace negotiations revived. The Treaty of Ghent ending the war was signed on December 24, 1814.

U.S. and Mexican forces clash at the Battle of Buena Vista in 1847. In hopes of securing territory occupied by Mexico but claimed by Texas, President James K. Polk maneuvered the country into a "defensive" war after U.S. soldiers were attacked by Mexican forces.

Even in this era, presidents found ways to employ force unilaterally to advance their policies. President Monroe's secret and ambivalent orders allowed Gen. Andrew Jackson to pursue the Seminole Indian raiders into Spanish Florida and to attack Spanish forts suspected of sheltering and aiding the raiders. This action, apparently by design, helped convince the Spanish of the vulnerability of the Florida defenses and move them toward a negotiated sale of the much desired territory.[20]

The Annexation of Texas and the Mexican War

Texas declared its independence from Mexico in 1836 and indicated that it was interested in becoming part of the United States. Although most Americans supported the principle of expansion, the slavery issue made annexation of a new state a tricky political problem for any president. Presidents Andrew Jackson and Martin Van Buren avoided actions on the Texas issue that would anger voters in the North who were opposed to an extension of slavery. However, John Tyler, who succeeded to the presidency after the death of William Henry Harrison in 1841, was a pro-slavery Virginian who wished to strengthen the slave states and limit British influence in Texas.[21] He began secret negotiations on annexation with Texas and initiated a pro-annexation campaign. The Texans, however, were concerned that if they agreed to annexation they would be invaded by Mexico. They informed Tyler that they would be reluctant to agree to annexation without guarantees that he would protect them with U.S. forces. This created a dilemma for Tyler, whose narrow interpretation of the Constitution had led him to reject presidential authority to use military force without congressional approval except in defense of the nation. In early 1844, Tyler showed that he valued the acquisition of Texas more than his strict constructionist principles when he ordered the deployment of U.S. forces in Texas and the Gulf of Mexico while the secret negotiations proceeded. When the needed two-thirds of the Senate refused to approve the annexation treaty produced by the negotiations, Tyler asked Congress to validate the agreement with a majority vote of both Houses. The joint resolution was passed.[22]

Tyler's successor, President James K. Polk, had greater ambitions for expanding the United States, and he used his commander-in-chief power to maneuver the nation into war with Mexico. Polk had decided to ask Congress for a declaration of war, yet he improved the chance of success by provoking an attack. In 1846 he ordered Gen. Zachary Taylor to deploy his army in a strip of territory near the Rio Grande that was claimed by Texas but occupied exclusively by Mexicans. The Mexican forces attacked Taylor's army, killing American soldiers. Polk told Congress: "Now, after reiterated menaces Mexico has invaded our territory and shed American blood on American soil." [23] On May 13, 1846, Congress recognized "a state of war as existing by act of the Republic of Mexico." Polk's successful maneuvering demonstrated the capacity of the commander in chief to weaken congressional control over the initiation of armed conflict.

Lincoln and the Civil War

President Lincoln's extraordinary exercise of power during the Civil War demonstrated how far the authority of the presidency could be expanded in wartime. Lincoln believed he faced a choice between preserving the Union and adhering to a strict interpretation of the Constitution. He feared that if he carefully observed the law he would sacrifice the flexibility needed to prevent the destruction of the nation. *(See box, Lincoln's Interpretation of the Presidential War Powers, right.)*

Lincoln's Expanded Powers

The Civil War began on April 12, 1861, when Confederate forces attacked Fort Sumter in Charleston, South Carolina. Recognizing that the strict constructionists in Congress might object to the emergency measures he thought necessary to deal with the crisis, Lincoln delayed the convocation of Congress until July 4. He used this three-month period to order a series of executive actions to meet the military emergency.[24]

On May 3, 1861, Lincoln called for the mobilization of 75,000 state militia under a 1795 act that authorized the president to issue such a call. Although this action was considered within the powers of the president, most of Lincoln's actions during the early months of the war, from spending government revenues without congressional authorization to suspending *habeas corpus* (the constitutional guarantee against arbitrary detention and imprisonment), had no explicit constitutional or congressional sanction. In the same proclamation used to mobilize the militia, Lincoln unilaterally increased the size of the regular army by 23,000 troops and the navy by 18,000. In addition, he ordered nineteen vessels added to the navy and directed the secretary of the Treasury to advance $2 million to authorized persons to pay for military requisitions. Lincoln also ordered a blockade of southern ports, suspended *habeas corpus* in the vicinity of the routes used by Union forces between Washington, D.C., and Philadelphia, ordered foreign visitors to observe new passport regulations, restricted "treasonable correspondence" from being carried by the Post Office, and directed the military to arrest and detain persons "who were represented to him" as contemplating or participating in "treasonable practices." [25]

When Congress finally convened on July 4, Lincoln asked the members to ratify the actions he had taken in their

---

LINCOLN'S INTERPRETATIONS OF THE PRESIDENTIAL WAR POWERS

To fight a civil war he did not initiate, Abraham Lincoln stretched presidential power until it approached dictatorship. He used the commander-in-chief clause, his oath to protect the Constitution, and his duty "to take Care that the Laws be faithfully executed" to justify these extraordinary powers. As a young member of the House of Representatives, Lincoln had occasion to consider the president's authority to initiate war. He criticized President James K. Polk's use of his peacetime command over troops to provoke a war with Mexico. In a letter to William H. Herndon, his law partner in Illinois, Lincoln explained his view of that power:

Washington, Feb. 15, 1848

Dear William:

. . . Let me first state what I understand to be your position. It is, that if it shall become necessary, to repel invasion, the President may, without violation of the Constitution, cross the line, and invade the territory of another country; and that whether such necessity exists in any given case, the President is to be the sole judge.

. . . Allow the President to invade a neighboring nation, whenever he shall deem it necessary to repel an invasion, and you allow him to do so, whenever he may choose to say he deems it necessary for such purpose—and you allow him to make war at pleasure. Study to see if you can fix any limit to his power in this respect, after you have given him so much as you propose. If, to-day, he should choose to say he thinks it necessary to invade Canada, to prevent the British from invading us, how could you stop him? You may say to him, "I see no probability of the British invading us" but he will say to you "be silent; I see it, if you dont."

The provision of the Constitution giving the war-making power to Congress, was dictated, as I understand it, by the following reasons. Kings had always been involving and impoverishing their people in wars, pretending generally, if not always, that the good of the people was the object. This, our Convention understood to be the most oppressive of all Kingly oppressions; and they resolved to so frame the Constitution that no one man should hold the power of bringing this oppression upon us. But your view destroys the whole matter, and places our President where kings have always stood. Write soon again.

Yours truly,
A. Lincoln[1]

1. The *Collected Works of Abraham Lincoln,* edited by Roy P. Basler (New Brunswick, N.J.: Rutgers University Press, 1953), 451–452.

---

absence. He maintained that some of his emergency measures, "whether strictly legal or not, were ventured upon under what appeared to be a popular demand and a public necessity, trusting then, as now, Congress would readily ratify them." In justifying his suspension of *habeas corpus,* Lincoln made the constitutional argument that in spite of the placement of the provision on *habeas corpus* suspension in Article I, the Framers must have intended the president to share with Congress the suspension authority, because emergencies requiring such action would not always occur when Congress was in session. Yet Lincoln defended his action on practical grounds as well, asking Congress, "Are all the laws but one to go unexecuted, and the Government itself go to pieces lest that one be violated?" In asking this question Lincoln implied that an emergency threatening the existence of the nation may empower the president to ignore parts of the Constitution to defend the whole.[26] In April

In expanding his war-making powers during the Civil War, Lincoln was acutely aware of placing the preservation of the Union above strict adherence to the Constitution. "Was it possible to lose the nation and yet preserve the Constitution?" he wrote. "By general law, life and limb must be protected, yet often a limb must be amputated to save a life."

1864 he explained his reasoning in a letter to Albert Hodges:

> I did understand, however, that my oath to preserve the Constitution to the best of my ability impressed upon me the duty of preserving by every indispensable means, that government—that nation, of which that Constitution was the organic law. Was it possible to lose the nation and yet preserve the Constitution? By general law, life and limb must be protected, yet often a limb must be amputated to save a life; but a life is never wisely given to save a limb. I felt that measures otherwise unconstitutional might become lawful by becoming indispensable to the preservation of the nation. Right or wrong, I assumed this ground and now avow it.[27]

Lincoln did not come to this conclusion lightly. As a member of the House of Representatives, he had questioned the legality and propriety of President Polk's actions that led to the Mexican War. *(See box, Lincoln's Interpretations of the Presidential War Powers, p. 745.)* Lincoln's expansion of his own war-making powers as president, therefore, did not result from a cavalier attitude toward the Constitution but from his recognition of an unprecedented emergency.

During the summer, Congress debated a joint resolution that sanctioned Lincoln's acts. Nagging doubts about the legality of his suspension of *habeas corpus* and blockade of Southern ports prevented a vote on the resolution. Near the end of the session, however, a rider approving Lincoln's actions was attached to a pay bill for army privates that was rushed through Congress. On August 6, 1861, Congress passed the bill and its rider, which declared the president's acts pertaining to the militia, the army, the navy, and the volunteers "in all respects legalized and made valid . . . as if they had been issued and done under the previous express authority and direction of Congress." [28]

Throughout the war, Lincoln continued to extend his commander-in-chief power beyond its constitutional limits. In 1862, when voluntary recruitments were not adequately supplying the army's need for additional troops, Lincoln ordered a draft. The same year he extended his suspension of *habeas corpus* to persons throughout the entire nation who were "guilty of any disloyal practice." He also declared that these persons could be tried by military courts. On January 1, 1863, Lincoln issued the Emancipation Proclamation freeing "all persons held as slaves within any State or designated part of a State, the people whereof shall then be in rebellion against the United States." It was a sweeping confiscation, or destruction, of private property without due process or compensation. Lincoln maintained that his commander-in-chief power gave him the authority to issue the proclamation, which, by liberating the slaves, would reduce the labor force of the South, thereby hindering its ability to carry on the war. It also would provide a new group of army recruits.[29]

The Prize Cases

Although the Supreme Court eventually objected to Lincoln's order that civilians could be tried in military courts, it did sanction his prosecution of a total war against the South. When hostilities began, the president had ordered a blockade of Confederate ports to prevent the South from selling cotton to England and importing supplies. The owners of four vessels seized by the blockade sued for redress on the grounds that the seizures were illegal because Congress had not declared war against the South. Lincoln's duty to suppress the insurrection, they argued, was not equivalent to the power to wage war. Therefore, the president could not legally order an act of war such as a blockade in the absence of a declaration of war.

In 1863 the Supreme Court rejected these arguments in its 5–4 decision on the Prize Cases. Writing for the majority, Justice Robert C. Grier explained:

> It is not necessary to constitute war, that both parties should be acknowledged as independent nations or sovereign states. A war may exist where one of the belligerents claims sovereign rights as against the other. . . . A civil war is never solemnly declared; it becomes such by its accidents—the number, power, and organization of the persons who originate and carry it on. When the party in rebellion occupy and hold in a hostile manner a certain portion of territory; have declared their independence; have cast off their allegiance; have organized armies; have commenced hostilities against their former sovereign, the world acknowledges them as belligerents, and the contest a war.[30]

The decision supported Lincoln's interpretation that the insurrectionist South was without sovereign rights, while the North possessed all rights of a belligerent in wartime. Moreover, the decision gave Lincoln confidence that the Court would not restrict his expansive interpretation of his commander-in-chief powers in the future. Although this case dealt specifically with the president's power to respond to a general insurrection, advocates of a strong presidency have cited it when arguing in favor of a broad interpretation of presidential war power.[31]

The Spanish-American War

The 1895 Cuban rebellion against Spanish rule occurred when the United States was ready to seek a wider role in global affairs. For some Americans, the Cuban crisis offered an opportunity to flex American muscle against a European power and extend U.S. influence. Others, aroused by slanted reports in the press of Spanish atrocities in Cuba, wished to rescue the island's inhabitants from Spanish tyranny. This combination of forces resulted in a popular crusade in the United States to aid Cuban independence.

President Grover Cleveland resisted the temptation to satisfy the nation's appetite for war with Spain during the last two years of his term. In a curious reversal of roles, he even warned members of Congress that, as commander in chief, he would refuse to prosecute any declaration of war.[32] William McKinley entered office in 1897 similarly determined to avoid war. Yet after the mysterious sinking of the

PRESIDENTIAL CLAIMS TO POLICE ACTION

Periodically, presidents have advanced and acted on doctrines that expand the scope of the president's authority to initiate armed conflict. One such doctrine is derived from the executive power and asserts that the president is responsible for protecting the lives and property of U.S. citizens and may deploy armed forces anywhere to fulfill this duty. For example, in 1900 President William McKinley sent troops into China, ostensibly to protect American lives threatened by a domestic insurrection called the Boxer Rebellion. This doctrine affords the president a pretext for intervening in a wide variety of circumstances and places in pursuit of other aims. This doctrine muddled the well-established constitutional principle—designed to control the executive—that Congress has sole authority to take the nation from a state of peace to a state of war.

Similarly, President Theodore Roosevelt's 1904 "corollary" to the Monroe Doctrine expanded the international police power by asserting that the United States would not only resist foreign intervention in the Western Hemisphere, but it would also "police" the hemisphere by intervening in the domestic affairs of other countries if misbehavior or political turmoil—what Roosevelt termed "chronic wrongdoing"—threatened to invite foreign intervention. Many presidents, from Roosevelt to George W. Bush, have assumed that the president alone has the authority to initiate the use of force in other countries, and they have acted on this basis in Colombia, the Dominican Republic, Nicaragua, Honduras, Cuba, Mexico, and Haiti. Moreover, Roosevelt's assertion of authority suggests that a presidential foreign policy proclamation or doctrine can become the basis for extending the president's power to project armed forces and enter into hostile action, the Constitution notwithstanding.[1] President James K. Polk may have embraced the "manifest destiny" of the nation to expand to the Pacific, but he did not act as if his preferences were sufficient authority for going to war with Mexico. Specifically and generally, Roosevelt's bold assertion altered the basis of presidential claims to a broad commander-in-chief power. *(See also "Police Actions and Rescue Missions," p. 000.)*

1. Louis Fisher, *Presidential War Power* (Lawrence: University Press of Kansas, 1995), 35–36, 45–54.

U.S. battleship *Maine* in Havana harbor in February 1898, McKinley could no longer stand up to congressional belligerence and public opinion. He asked Congress on April 11, 1898, to approve U.S. armed intervention in Cuba. Spain had already acceded to many American demands for a settlement of the Cuban crisis, but on April 25 Congress passed a declaration of war authorizing the president to use military force to expel Spain from the island. It was adopted by the Senate 42–35 and by the House 310–6.

The brevity of the war, the ease with which victory was achieved, and the popularity of the conflict made McKinley's job as commander in chief easier. Although he had resisted war, McKinley nevertheless extended the conflict from Cuba to Spanish holdings in the Pacific: the Philippines and Guam. The issue of what to do with the Philippines was quite controversial. McKinley decided to take possession of the islands as part of a broader policy of expanding U.S. trade in the Far East.[33]

On December 10, 1898, Spain signed a treaty relinquishing its control over Cuba and ceding the Philippines along with Puerto Rico and Guam to the United States. The

Senate approved the treaty after a month of debate by a vote of 57–27, only one vote more than the necessary two-thirds majority, and for the first time a president and Congress acquired territory outside the North American continent through war.

The World Wars

The first involvement of the United States in an overseas war of massive scale provided the occasion for the most dramatic expansion of presidential wartime powers since the Civil War. The basis for Woodrow Wilson's power differed from Lincoln's, however, in that Lincoln had taken emergency actions independently of Congress, whereas Wilson was handed most of his expanded war-making authority by statute.[34] Congress gave Wilson not only expanded control of the military and discretion to fight subversion and espionage, but also unprecedented control over industries and the allocation of scarce resources. For example, the Lever Food and Fuel Act of 1917 gave the president "full authority to undertake any steps necessary" for the conservation of food resources. In addition, the 1918 Overman Act gave the president complete authority to reorganize the executive branch. Congress was willing to make these broad delegations of power to Wilson because most members believed that the scope and urgency of the war required unified control and direction of all operations and resources related to the war effort.

In essence, Congress did not just give Wilson broad discretion in implementing its statutes, it abdicated legislative power to him for the duration of the war. Many delegations of authority to the president simply stated their objectives and left Wilson to decide how to achieve them. He commandeered plants and mines, requisitioned supplies, fixed prices, seized and operated the nation's transportation and communications networks, and managed the production and distribution of foodstuffs. The Council of National Defense, an umbrella agency created by Wilson, administered the economy during the war. Wilson created the War Industries Board using his authority as commander in chief. Wall Street broker Bernard Baruch, who had been appointed by Wilson to head the board, became a dictator of sorts over U.S. industry. The president also established by executive order the Committee of Public Information, under whose direction a system of voluntary news censorship was instituted and various government publicity services were organized. On April 28, 1917, Wilson imposed strict censorship of cable messages, which later was extended to other forms of communication with foreign countries under authority of the Trading with the Enemy Act of October 6, 1917.

Presidential war powers reached their apex during World War II. Constitutional scholar Edward S. Corwin wrote: "The relation . . . of the First World War to the Second as regards constitutional interpretation is that of prologue and rehearsal."[35] Like Wilson during World War I, Franklin Roosevelt was delegated wide powers by Congress to manage the economy and direct the war effort, but Roosevelt went beyond Wilson in asserting his power as commander in chief to take any action he deemed necessary to the war effort.

Overcoming Neutrality

The president's war powers were tightly restrained during the 1930s by the prevailing mood of isolationism in Congress and among the American people. Congress enacted and Roosevelt signed a series of laws designed to keep the United States out of the conflicts brewing in Europe and Asia. These laws included the Neutrality Acts of 1935 and 1937, which prohibited shipments of arms, ammunition, or implements of war to any belligerent nation, including those that had been the victims of aggression. After Adolf Hitler's invasion of Poland in September 1939, which brought Great Britain and France into the war against Nazi Germany, Roosevelt began maneuvering the country toward active support of Britain and the other allies, whose survival he believed was crucial to U.S. security.

On September 3, 1940, Roosevelt announced he had concluded an agreement with Great Britain under which that country would receive fifty "overage" destroyers in return for the right to lease certain British territory in the western Atlantic for U.S. naval and air bases. Roosevelt's destroyer deal was accomplished through an executive agreement—a legally binding pact between the president and the British government—rather than a Senate-ratified treaty. The trade violated at least two congressional statutes, but Roosevelt's attorney general, Robert H. Jackson, asserted that the president acted legally under his commander-in-chief authority to "dispose" of the armed forces. It also was argued that the commander in chief was responsible for securing adequate bases for national defense.

On March 11, 1941, Congress passed the Lend-Lease Act, described by Corwin as the most "sweeping delegation of legislative power" ever given to a president.[36] It authorized the president to manufacture any defense article and to "sell, transfer title to, exchange, lease, lend or otherwise dispose of" the defense articles to the "government of any country whose defense the President deems vital to the defense of the United States." The act gave President Roosevelt the power to aid the Allied cause as he saw fit by virtually any means short of using the armed forces.

Yet Roosevelt did use the armed forces to aid the Allied cause despite the absence of any congressional sanction for acts of war. After Germany occupied Denmark in April 1941, Roosevelt ordered U.S. troops to be stationed in Greenland. Three months later, American forces occupied Iceland. Both moves were made without consulting Congress, which had forbidden the deployment of U.S. reserves and draftees outside the Western Hemisphere in the Reserves Act of 1940 and the Selective Service Act of 1941.[37] By the summer of 1941, U.S. naval vessels under presidential orders were escorting Allied convoys across the Atlantic. After the U.S. destroyer *Greer* exchanged shots with a German submarine on September 4, the president declared that henceforth U.S. warships providing protection to supply convoys bound for Britain would be under orders to attack Axis vessels on sight. Three months before Congress declared war, therefore, Roosevelt had already maneuvered the nation into an undeclared naval war in the Atlantic.[38]

Roosevelt's "Dictatorship"

The U.S. entry into World War II was accompanied by the concentration of almost all war powers in the president's hands. Congress delegated vast authority to the president to prosecute the war as it had during World War I, but it also acquiesced to Roosevelt's many unsanctioned appropriations of power and his broad interpretations of congressional statutes. Although Roosevelt saw the wisdom of obtaining Congress's approval for controversial actions, he was far more assertive than Wilson in using his commander-in-chief power to establish complete control over the war effort.

Roosevelt created dozens of executive regulatory agencies that were not based on a specific statute, such as the Office of Emergency Management, Board of Economic Warfare, National War Labor Board, Office of Defense Transportation, and War Production Board. Anything remotely connected to the nation's war effort, including managing national resources and economic activity, was regulated by these war management agencies, which were responsible to the president rather than to existing departments or independent regulatory agencies. Roosevelt justified their creation by citing general delegations of power from Congress, the powers available to him under his emergency proclamations of 1939 and 1941, and his own powers as commander in chief.[39]

On September 7, 1942, the president demonstrated how far he believed his war powers extended. In a speech to Congress, Roosevelt issued an ultimatum to lawmakers to repeal certain provisions contained in the Emergency Price Control Act of 1942:

> I ask the Congress to take this action by the first of October. Inaction on your part by that date will leave me with an inescapable responsibility to the people of this country to see to it that the war effort is no longer imperiled by threat of economic chaos.
>
> In the event that the Congress should fail to act, and act adequately, I shall accept the responsibility and I will act.
>
> At the same time farm prices are stabilized, wages can and will be stabilized also. This I will do.
>
> The President has the power, under the Constitution and under Congressional acts, to take measures necessary to avert a disaster which would interfere with the winning of the war. . . .

> I have given the most thoughtful consideration to meeting this issue without further reference to the Congress. I have determined, however, on this vital matter to consult with Congress. . . .
>
> The American people can be sure that I will use my powers with a full sense of my responsibility to the Constitution and to the country. The American people can also be sure that I shall not hesitate to use every power vested in me to accomplish the defeat of our enemies in any part of the world where our own safety demands such defeat.
>
> When the war is won, the powers under which I act automatically revert to the people—to whom they belong.[40]

With this declaration, Roosevelt claimed, according to Corwin, "the right and power to disregard a statutory provision which he does not deny, and indeed could not possibly deny, that Congress had full constitutional authority to enact, and which, therefore, he was under obligation by the Constitution to 'take care' should be 'faithfully executed.' "[41] Roosevelt was threatening to suspend the Constitution in the interest of national security if Congress did not act. Not even Lincoln during the Civil War had claimed the power to repeal a specific congressional statute.

Many members of Congress were shaken by Roosevelt's ultimatum, and a few denounced it. Republican senator Robert A. Taft of Ohio called the speech "revolutionary and dangerous to the American form of government . . . an assertion that the laws of this country can be made by executive order."[42] The American public, however, supported Roosevelt's position, and with the war raging, there was little desire in Congress to engage the president in a constitutional showdown. Congress therefore amended the Emergency Price Control Act to meet Roosevelt's objections.

Postwar Congressional Acquiescence

After World War II, differences between the United States and the Soviet Union brought on the cold war, a state of continuous international tension that contributed to increased presidential control over national security policy. The specter of an aggressive Soviet Union pushing out wherever the West failed to resist made Congress reluctant to impose restrictions on executive action. A consensus developed that because presidents possessed both the capacity to act immediately and the access to the most detailed and reliable information, they alone were suited to direct foreign and military policy. Their status as leaders of the free world and caretakers of the U.S. nuclear arsenal, the most devastating military force ever created, contributed to their unchallenged authority.

The Korean War

When the North Korean army swept into South Korea on June 24, 1950, President Harry Truman believed he had to act to save South Korea and discourage further communist aggression. The next day the United States called an emergency session of the United Nations Security Council, which passed a resolution condemning the invasion and asking UN members to "render every assistance" to South Korea. By coincidence, the Soviets were boycotting the Security Council to protest the exclusion of the new communist government of China from the UN. Consequently, their representative was not present to veto the resolution. That evening, Truman made up his mind to use air and naval forces to defend South Korea. He authorized Gen. Douglas MacArthur to evacuate Americans from South Korea, transport supplies to the South Koreans, and bomb military targets below the thirty-eighth parallel. After Truman announced his intention to defend South Korea and initiated U.S. involvement, the UN Security Council passed a second resolution explicitly calling on members to give military assistance to South Korea. By June 30, Truman had authorized MacArthur to use U.S. ground forces and to bomb targets in North Korea, thereby completing the U.S. commitment to defend South Korea.[43]

The Korean War involved a massive qualitative change in presidential assertion of war powers. President Truman claimed and exercised an authority to engage the United States in a war without any congressional declaration or authorization. Truman could easily have secured a congressional resolution approving his use of military forces in Korea, but the president wished to avoid an appearance of dependence on Congress. Truman had been advised by Secretary of State Dean G. Acheson and chair of the Senate Foreign Relations Committee Thomas T. Connally, D-Texas, that his commander-in-chief power and the UN Security Council resolution gave him ample authority to use the armed forces. According to Acheson, Truman considered the presidency "a sacred and temporary trust, which he was determined to pass on unimpaired by the slightest loss of power or prestige." [44] Past presidents had ordered U.S. forces to rescue Americans overseas, police the hemisphere, or undertake some other type of limited military mission. The Truman administration cited these precedents in justifying its interpretation of the commander-in-chief power.[45]

The Korean War, however, was quite without precedent in American history. Although by then numerous precedents had established the president's power to use the armed forces for very limited missions, there was no precedent for presidential authority to commit the nation to a large-scale, bloody war of indefinite length involving hundreds of thousands of military personnel. By every definition, the United States was waging war in Korea, regardless of the Truman administration's restrictions on the use of military force against Chinese territory and its assertions throughout the war that U.S. involvement amounted to participation in a UN "police action." [46]

In addition, Truman's use of a UN Security Council resolution as a basis for unilateral presidential action contradicted the language and history of the UN Charter. As constitutional scholar Louis Fisher argues, no treaty can alter the Constitution by delegating the war power to the UN or to the president. Both the Charter and the UN Participation Act specify that any Security Council agreement involving the use of troops is subject to ratification in accordance with each country's "constitutional processes." The congressional debate over the effect of the UN Charter on the war powers revolved around whether the relevant constitutional process was senatorial approval or a two-house resolution. The UN Charter was approved with the understanding that both houses of Congress would have to authorize the use of armed forces in hostilities, and the UN Participation Act clearly affirmed this.[47]

A few Republicans protested Truman's failure to involve Congress in the decision. Influential Republican senator Robert Taft announced on June 28 that although he agreed that U.S. forces should be used in Korea, the president had "no legal authority" to send them without the approval of Congress. In general, though, members of Congress overwhelmingly supported Truman's decision to commit U.S. forces and, initially, did not challenge Truman's sweeping claims of authority. During the fall of 1950, the war remained popular as UN forces were successful in driving the North Koreans up the peninsula. In November General MacArthur's forces had occupied most of North Korea and appeared close to reunifying North and South.[48] In November and December, however, Communist Chinese forces entered the war and drove UN forces back across the thirty-eighth parallel into South Korea.

With Congress already alarmed by reversals in the military campaign, Truman announced on December 19 that he planned to send four more divisions to Europe to bolster Allied defenses under the North Atlantic Treaty Organization (NATO). This time the president's intention to send so many troops abroad without congressional approval triggered a congressional reevaluation of U.S. defense and foreign policy that was known at the time as the "great debate." The debate, which lasted from January to April 1951, was concerned not only with Truman's deployment of troops to Europe, but also with the president's authority to involve the nation in the Korean War. The fear, expressed most fully by Senator Taft, was that the president could use treaties and executive agreements as authority to place U.S. armed forces in situations that would nullify Congress's control over the initiation of war. In the end, the Senate passed two resolutions approving the dispatch of four divisions to Europe. One of the resolutions declared that it was the sense of the Senate that Congress should approve any future deployment of ground troops to Europe.

Truman hailed the resolutions as an endorsement of his policies. They were not. But the Senate and the House failed to pass any binding resolutions that would have put teeth into their assertions of constitutional prerogative in controlling the commitment of the nation's forces. Similar debates leading to similarly weak legislative responses were repeated during the next twenty years.

Truman's actions set the stage for a period of broad presidential control of foreign and national security policy. Truman did suffer a setback in 1952 when the Supreme Court ruled in *Youngstown Sheet and Tube Co. v. Sawyer* that he did not have the authority to take over steel mills to prevent a strike that might damage the Korean War effort.[49] Otherwise, as historian Arthur M. Schlesinger Jr. wrote: "By bringing the nation into war without congressional authorization and by then successfully defending his exercise of independent presidential initiative, Truman enormously expanded assumptions of presidential prerogative."[50] *(See "War-making Powers," p. 1449, in Chapter 30, Vol. II.)*

Joint Resolutions

The period following the Korean War was characterized by the passage of congressional resolutions granting or acknowledging the authority to use such force as presidents deemed necessary to repel armed attacks or threats against designated nations or regions. The purpose behind some of these resolutions was to deter potential aggressors by making it clear that the U.S. government was united in a commitment to respond. Between 1955 and 1962, four joint resolutions of this type were passed. The Formosa Resolution, signed into law on January 29, 1955, authorized presidents to use U.S. forces to protect Formosa and the Pescadores Islands against attack from the People's Republic of China. The Middle East Resolution, signed into law on March 9, 1957, proclaimed U.S. intentions to defend Middle East countries "against any country controlled by international communism." The Cuban Resolution, signed into law on October 3, 1962, authorized presidents to take whatever steps they believed necessary to defend Latin America against Cuban aggression or subversion and to oppose the deployment in Cuba of Soviet weapons capable of threatening U.S. security. The 1962 Berlin Resolution did not have the force of law but expressed the sense of Congress that the United States was determined to defend West Berlin and the access rights of the Western powers to that city.

These resolutions received wide support in Congress, although they did have critics who charged that the resolutions gave too much discretionary power to the president and absolved Congress from any responsibility for national security. Schlesinger describes the extent of congressional abdication during this period:

In the decade after Korea Congress receded not alone from the effort to control the war-making power but almost from the effort to participate in it, except on occasions when national-security zealots on the Hill condemned the executive branch for inadequate bellicosity. Mesmerized by the supposed need for instant response to constant crisis, overawed by what the Senate Foreign Relations Committee later called "the cult of executive expertise," confused in its own mind as to what wise policy should be, delighted to relinquish responsibility, Congress readily capitulated to what Corwin at the start of the fifties had called "high-flying" theses of presidential prerogative.[51]

The Vietnam War

No single president was entirely responsible for U.S. participation in the war in Vietnam; rather, a succession of presidents gradually increased U.S. military involvement in Southeast Asia. In 1954 Vietnamese revolutionary forces defeated the French, who had controlled the region as a colonial power. President Dwight D. Eisenhower had continued the Truman administration's policy of sending aid to the French, but Eisenhower refused to intervene militarily to prevent a French defeat. After the French departed, Vietnam was temporarily partitioned, with the communist government of Ho Chi Minh ruling the North and anticommunists in Saigon controlling the South. Eisenhower undercut reunification efforts, which he feared would result in communist control over the entire country, by ignoring the scheduled reunification elections in 1956 and supporting the noncommunist regime in the South. The North Vietnamese and their supporters in the South launched a guerrilla war in an effort to achieve reunification through force. Although Eisenhower stepped up economic and military aid to the Saigon government, which included a small number of U.S. military advisers, he avoided more extensive U.S. military involvement.

President John F. Kennedy, however, fearing the collapse of the Saigon government, responded to South Vietnamese requests for greater assistance by sending additional military advisers and counterinsurgency units to South Vietnam. By November 1963, the Kennedy administration had deployed 16,500 U.S. military personnel to Vietnam.

President Lyndon B. Johnson continued the gradual escalation of U.S. involvement in the widening war. The Gulf of Tonkin incident in August 1964 resulted in a resolution supporting any presidential effort to combat North Vietnamese aggression. *(See box, Tonkin Gulf Resolution, p. 753, and "Lyndon B. Johnson's Gulf of Tonkin Message," p. 1779, in Reference Materials, Vol. II.)* Armed with this congressional sanction and fearing an imminent communist takeover, Johnson ordered the first regular combat troops to Vietnam in 1965. Their mission was to defend the U.S. airbase at Da Nang, but soon they were conducting patrols and actively engaging the enemy in combat. Although Johnson believed his commander-in-chief powers and the Tonkin

Soldiers of the U.S. 9th Division patrol through an abandoned rice paddy past a flooded shell crater during the Vietnam War. Throughout history presidential ability to wage war had continually expanded until Congress passed the War Powers Resolution in 1973. The resolution reasserted congressional authority to approve military activities begun by the president.

Gulf Resolution gave him the authority to send the troops to Vietnam, he nevertheless wanted Congress on record as approving the move. He therefore requested a specific appropriation of $700 million for U.S. military operations in Vietnam. Within two days, both houses had passed the bill with little dissent.[52] By 1968, Johnson had increased U.S. troop strength in Vietnam to more than 500,000. But the communists' Tet offensive early that year, although a military failure, caused Americans, including Johnson, to begin to lose confidence that the war could be won.

President Richard Nixon began slowly withdrawing U.S. forces from Vietnam in 1969. Nixon's goal was to extricate the United States from the Vietnam quagmire while achieving "peace with honor." In January 1973 the United States and North Vietnam signed a peace accord. The North Vietnamese returned U.S. prisoners of war and allowed the regime of South Vietnamese president Nuygen Van Thieu to remain in power. In return, the United States withdrew its forces from Vietnam and allowed North Vietnamese army units already in South Vietnam to remain there. Without U.S. military support, however, South Vietnam was unable to defend itself against a 1975 North Vietnamese offensive that resulted in the fall of Saigon. Although President Nixon had promised Thieu that the United States would intervene if communist forces threatened to conquer the South, Nixon had already resigned from the presidency in 1974, and Congress refused to fund any further military involvement in Southeast Asia.

Although less so than the Korean War, the Vietnam War was a presidential war. The executive branch dominated decision making about goals and strategy in Vietnam with little congressional influence. Indeed, after 1965 neither Johnson nor Nixon sought congressional approval for their prosecution of the war. Nevertheless, the picture of these presidents carrying on military activities in Indochina without congressional consent often was overdrawn by critics of the war. Congress continually voted in favor of military appropriations and the draft, two resources vital to Johnson's and Nixon's prolongation of the war. Once troops and materiel had been committed to battle, most members of Congress believed that denying U.S. forces the money and reinforcements they needed to wage the war would be perceived as unpatriotic.

Resurgence of Congress

In 1969 the growing number of U.S. casualties in Vietnam, the lack of support for the increased commitment necessary to win the war, and failing public support for the effort encouraged Congress to assert its war powers. In that year, the Senate passed the National Commitments Resolution, which stated that a national commitment "results only from affirmative action taken by the legislative and executive branches . . . by means of a treaty, statute, or concurrent resolution of both houses of Congress specifically providing for such commitment." Although the resolution only expressed the sense of the Senate and had no force of law, it represented Congress's growing dissatisfaction with its exclusion from national security and foreign policy decisions. Later in the year, Congress adopted an amendment supported by President Nixon prohibiting the use of U.S. ground forces in Laos and Thailand. For the first time in three decades, Congress had exercised its authority to limit military activities overseas.[53]

In 1970, even as U.S. forces were being withdrawn from Southeast Asia, President Nixon secretly ordered U.S. forces into Cambodia to attack communist sanctuaries. When Nixon announced the operation on April 30, 1970, many college campuses erupted in protest against the expansion of the war, and four student demonstrators at Kent State University in Ohio were killed by National Guard troops. An estimated 100,000 protesters marched on Washington, D.C. After months of debate, a lame-duck Congress passed an amendment in December 1970 barring the use of U.S.

TONKIN GULF RESOLUTION

Each of the joint resolutions sanctioning presidential use of force passed by Congress between 1955 and 1962 represented a declaration of national policy upon which there was broad agreement. The supporters of these resolutions considered them to be effective means of allowing Congress to create a united front behind presidential action without a formal declaration of war. This was the intention of members of Congress when they voted almost unanimously in favor of the Tonkin Gulf resolution in 1964.

On August 2, 1964, the U.S. destroyer *Maddox,* which the navy contended was on a routine mission in the Tonkin Gulf off the coast of North Vietnam, was attacked by North Vietnamese patrol boats. Two nights later the *Maddox,* which had been joined by another destroyer, the *C. Turner Joy,* reported a second patrol boat attack. Neither ship was damaged. President Lyndon B. Johnson responded to the incidents by ordering U.S. warplanes to bomb North Vietnamese torpedo boat bases.

Johnson informed Congress that U.S. ships had been attacked and asked both houses to pass a resolution empowering him to respond to further North Vietnamese aggression. The administration depicted the incidents as unprovoked acts of belligerence. On August 7, Congress passed the Gulf of Tonkin Resolution by votes of 88–2 and 416–0. The resolution stated that "Congress approves and supports the determination of the President, as Commander-in-Chief, to take all necessary measures to repel any armed attack against the forces of the United States and to prevent further aggression." Within the resolution a broader clause declared that the United States was "prepared, as the President determines, to take all necessary steps, including the use of armed force, to assist any member or protocol state of the Southeast Asia Collective Defense Treaty requesting assistance in defense of its freedom."[1]

By overwhelmingly passing the resolution, Congress was following the practice set during the previous decade of deferring to the president's judgment in national security matters in the name of expediency and unity.

Key members of Congress understood that the Tonkin Gulf Resolution could be interpreted as a "blank check."[2] Members of the Johnson administration and the president himself frequently cited the resolution as evidence of congressional authorization of their policies in Vietnam. Although the resolution in combination with U.S. membership in the Southeast Asia Treaty Organization may not have been the "functional equivalent" of a declaration of war, as Under Secretary of State Nicholas Katzenbach claimed in 1967, it did provide a justification for almost any presidential military decision in Vietnam.

Investigations by the Senate Foreign Relations Committee in 1968 revealed that the *Maddox* was actually gathering sensitive intelligence within the territorial waters claimed by the North Vietnamese and that a South Vietnamese naval attack against North Vietnam was taking place nearby. Furthermore, U.S. intelligence had warned that the North Vietnamese navy was under orders to respond to U.S. vessels in the vicinity of the South Vietnamese operation as if they were part of that operation, and U.S. ships had been moved to reinforce the *Maddox* before it was attacked.[3]

The 1968 revelations about the Tonkin Gulf incidents and growing congressional discontent with the war led to the repeal of the Tonkin Gulf Resolution on December 31, 1970. The repeal provision was added to a foreign military sales bill, which was signed by President Richard Nixon on January 12, 1971. However, the Nixon administration claimed that the president's commander-in-chief power gave him sufficient authority to carry on the war in Vietnam.

1. Quoted in Christopher H. Pyle and Richard M. Pious, *The President, Congress and the Constitution* (New York: Free Press, 1984), 339–340.
2. Quoted in Leslie H. Gelb with Richard K. Betts, *The Irony of Vietnam: The System Worked* (Washington, D.C.: Brookings, 1979), 103.
3. Richard M. Pious, *The American Presidency* (New York: Basic Books, 1979), 387.

ground forces in Cambodia. This amendment had little effect because Nixon had withdrawn U.S. ground troops from Cambodia months before and lawmakers had backed away from prohibiting the use of U.S. aircraft over Cambodia. Later in December, Congress repealed the Tonkin Gulf Resolution.

During the early 1970s, momentum for legislation that would restore Congress's role in the foreign policy process continued to build in Congress. Meanwhile, President Nixon was undertaking a series of controversial military actions without consulting Congress. He provided air support for South Vietnam's 1971 invasion of Laos, ordered North Vietnam's Haiphong harbor mined in May 1972, and launched massive bombing raids against North Vietnam in December 1972. Furthermore, Nixon's "secret" war in Cambodia in 1970, the publication in 1971 of the *Pentagon Papers* (which disclosed the deception of the executive branch during the 1960s), and the revelations about secret

national security commitments uncovered by a Senate Foreign Relations subcommittee chaired by Stuart Symington, D-Mo., contributed to the growing perception of lawmakers that executive branch secrecy was out of control. After three years of work and debate, Congress's attempts to construct a bill that would reestablish its war and national security powers culminated in passage of the War Powers Resolution in 1973.

WAR POWERS RESOLUTION

Implicit in the War Powers Resolution (HJ Res. 542, PL 93-148), which was enacted in November 1973 over President Nixon's veto, was an admission by Congress that it had contributed to the debacle in Vietnam by abdicating its war-making responsibilities to the executive branch. The results of the Vietnam War had cast grave doubts on the assumption that the executive branch, with its superior intelligence resources, its unity of command, and its ability to act quickly, should be largely responsible for determining when and how the nation should go to war. With the passage of the War Powers Resolution Congress attempted to reassert its constitutional prerogative to authorize all significant military engagements. The bill's preamble stated that its purpose was

> to fulfill the intent of the framers of the Constitution of the United States and insure that the collective judgment of both the Congress and the President will apply to the introduction of U.S. armed forces into hostilities, or into situations where imminent involvement in hostilities is clearly indicated by the circumstances, and the continued use of such forces in hostilities or in such situations.

The most important and controversial provisions of the legislation outlined the situations under which presidents could commit troops; permitted Congress at any time by concurrent resolution to order the president to disengage forces involved in an unauthorized military engagement; and required presidents to withdraw armed forces from a conflict within sixty days—ninety if the president certified that more time was necessary to disengage U.S. military personnel safely—unless Congress specifically authorized the continued use of U.S. forces. Other provisions in the act obligated presidents to report to Congress within forty-eight hours on large troop movements abroad and urged them to consult with Congress "in every possible instance" before ordering U.S. forces into hostilities or a situation where hostilities might be imminent.

These provisions are not easily reconciled. On the one hand, the "Purpose and Policy" section seems to confine presidential authority within strict constitutional limits; a president may introduce armed forces into a hostile situation only if Congress has formally authorized the action or if there is a national emergency created by an attack on the United States, its territories, or its armed forces. On the other hand, the procedural sections on reporting, consultation, and time limits seem to suggest otherwise. But they do not actually say that the president has the constitutional authority to engage in hostilities for sixty days. Rather, they acknowledge that the president can and will move troops into hostile or potentially hostile circumstances. The resolution then specifies procedures, including time limits, for congressional scrutiny of such decisions.

To strengthen the resolution's clear purpose that all long-term military engagements must have explicit congressional authorization, Congress included a provision denying that a president could infer congressional authorization for the introduction of troops into hostilities or potentially hostile situations "from any provision of law . . . including any provision contained in any appropriation Act, unless such provision specifically authorizes the introduction of United States Armed Forces into hostilities or into such situations and states that it is intended to constitute specific statutory

authorization within the meaning of this resolution." The provision also denied the president the authority to infer congressional authorization for presidential war making from a ratified treaty. Thus Congress attempted to restrict the means through which it could be said to have approved presidential war making to explicit authorizations of military action.

Passage of the War Powers Resolution was heralded by its supporters as a major step in reasserting Congress's war-making powers. Republican senator Jacob K. Javits of New York, a chief architect of the Senate's version of the legislation, declared:

> With the war powers resolution's passage, after 200 years, at least something will have been done about codifying the implementation of the most awesome power in the possession of any sovereignty and giving the broad representation of the people in Congress a voice in it. This is critically important, for we have just learned the hard lesson that wars cannot be successfully fought except with the consent of the people and with their support.[54]

The resolution was opposed by some conservatives in both houses and a small group of liberals who agreed that the measure was unconstitutional, but for different reasons. The leading liberal opponent of the resolution, Democratic senator Thomas F. Eagleton of Missouri, called the act "the most dangerous piece of legislation" he had seen in his five years in the Senate.[55] Eagleton and other liberal critics of the War Powers Resolution charged that although it may force the president to deal with Congress within ninety days after troops are committed, it sanctions practically any use of the military by the president during those ninety days, thereby enhancing rather than restricting presidential war-making power. He warned: "By failing to define the president's powers in legally binding language, the bill provided a legal basis for the president's broad claims of inherent power to initiate a war. Under the formula, Congress would not participate in the war-making decision until *after* forces had been committed to battle."[56] Although the resolution gave Congress the power to withdraw troops from a conflict, Eagleton believed Congress would rarely have the political will to do so, because such action would be seen by many constituents as unpatriotic or lacking in resolve.

In President Nixon's October 24, 1973, veto message of the war powers bill, he stated that the resolution would impose restrictions on the authority of the president that would be "both unconstitutional and dangerous to the best interests of the nation."[57] On November 7, the House overrode the president's veto by a vote of 284–135—only four votes more than the required two-thirds majority. Later in the day, the Senate followed with a 75–8 override vote. The congressional override was made possible, in part, by the Watergate scandal, which had weakened Nixon's support among legislators of his party.

Legal Questions

Many of the War Powers Resolution's critics and even a few of its supporters have expressed doubts that all of its provisions will stand up to judicial review. President Nixon denounced the war powers bill as unconstitutional when he vetoed it in 1973. The major provisions of the bill, he contended, would "purport to take away, by a mere legislative act, authorities which the president has properly exercised under the Constitution for almost 200 years." These provisions were unconstitutional, he asserted, because "the only way in which the constitutional powers of a branch of the government can be altered is by amending the Constitution—and any attempt to make such alterations by legislation alone is clearly without force." [58]

Neither the executive branch nor a majority of members of Congress has appeared eager to let the Supreme Court decide whether the War Powers Resolution is an unconstitutional legislative intrusion into the powers of the president. It may be that both branches have believed they have more to lose than to win from such a confrontation. On the one hand, because presidents have been able to ignore the most potent provisions of the War Powers Resolution, they have had little incentive to seek a decision on the issue in court that might force them to comply more strictly with its provisions. On the other hand, Congress may have been dissuaded from mounting a legal challenge to presidential war making by the Supreme Court's historic tendency to favor the presidency on matters of foreign policy and national security. A Supreme Court ruling striking down the resolution would deprive lawmakers of any leverage provided by their threats to invoke the resolution and would symbolically weaken Congress's claim to a place in the national security decision-making process.

The Chadha Decision

In 1983 the Supreme Court's decision in an unrelated case called into question at least one crucial provision of the War Powers Resolution. The Court ruled 7–2 in *Immigration and Naturalization Service v. Chadha* that legislative vetoes of presidential actions are unconstitutional. Legislative vetoes are provisions of laws that give Congress the power to review and rescind executive actions otherwise authorized by law. They had been used by Congress for more than fifty years, primarily to maintain some control over executive implementation of congressional policies. The Court in *Chadha* ruled that legislative vetoes circumvent the president's constitutionally granted executive and veto powers. Writing for the majority, Chief Justice Warren Burger emphasized, "The hydraulic pressure inherent within each of the separate branches to exceed the outer limits of its power, even to accomplish desirable objectives, must be resisted." [59]

The *Chadha* ruling raised questions about the sections of the War Powers Resolution empowering Congress to compel the president to withdraw U.S. forces engaged in hostilities by passing a concurrent resolution, which does not require presidential approval. Such a concurrent resolution may constitute a legislative veto over executive action.[60] The War Powers Resolution, however, does not delegate any power to the president, and it denies that introducing armed forces into hostilities is within the president's constitutional authority. The resolution may, therefore, fall outside the reach of the *Chadha* decision. As Louis Fisher argues, the Constitution itself gives Congress a veto insofar as it must authorize military action. Giving the president a veto over any resolution restricting military action would require a two-thirds majority in both houses to control the president's war-making power.[61]

Uses of Force Under the War Powers Resolution

Every president thereafter has denied the constitutionality of the War Powers Resolution, and each of these presidents has used military force, often on a large scale, without complying with its terms. They have seldom consulted Congress before using the military, they have dissembled about the nature of the hostilities, and they have ignored efforts by Congress to force them to start the sixty-day war powers clock. When presidents have reported to Congress, they have generally claimed full constitutional authority for their actions. The many military operations undertaken since the resolution was passed have underscored the inability to control presidential war making in the absence of Congress's firm determination to assert its authority. Some significant and telling examples follow.

Mayaguez *Incident*

The first major test of the War Powers Resolution occurred on May 12, 1975, when Cambodian Communist gunboats seized the U.S. merchant ship *Mayaguez* and its crew of thirty-nine off the disputed island of Poulo Wai in the Gulf of Siam. President Gerald R. Ford unilaterally ordered U.S. forces to free the sailors and their ship and to bomb Cambodian targets in retaliation. The rescue attempt succeeded in freeing the *Mayaguez* and its crew but resulted in the deaths of forty-one marines.

In this case, there was general agreement that the president had the authority to commit U.S. troops without receiving congressional authorization. Ford complied with the war powers provision that required him to report to Congress within forty-eight hours, but he consulted only with selected members of Congress and only after the order to attack had been issued.

Ford, however, defended his approach: "When a crisis breaks out, it is impossible to draw the Congress in with the decision-making process in an effective way." Ford also criticized the resolution itself as "a very serious intrusion on the responsibilities of the President as Commander-in-Chief and the person who formulates and ought to execute foreign policy."[62]

Iranian Hostage Rescue Attempt

In April 1980 President Jimmy Carter sent a small contingent of U.S. forces into Iran in an attempt to rescue forty-nine American embassy personnel held hostage in Tehran. Equipment failure forced the mission to be aborted after eight commandos died in a helicopter crash. Carter justified his decision not to consult with Congress by citing the mission's dependence on secrecy. Many members of Congress agreed with Carter's decision. Sen. John Glenn, D-Ohio, remarked, "If I were on that raid, I wouldn't want it all over Capitol Hill."[63] Carter also maintained that the mission was a "humanitarian" rescue attempt rather than a military action against an enemy nation and therefore fell outside the scope of the War Powers Resolution.[64]

Lebanon

In 1982 President Ronald Reagan sent U.S. troops to Lebanon as part of a multinational peacekeeping force. Marines initially were introduced into that country on August 24, 1982, with the specific mission of observing the evacuation of Palestine Liberation Organization (PLO) forces from Beirut under an agreement mediated by the United States. The marines left Beirut on September 10, after the PLO withdrawal had been completed. Before this operation, the president held constructive consultations with the foreign relations committees of both houses.[65] Reagan had reported to Congress on the deployment of marines the day before it took place. He stated that he was reporting to Congress "consistent" with the resolution rather than "under" it.[66]

After the assassination of President Bashir Gemayel of Lebanon on September 14, 1982, and the massacre of Palestinians at the Sabra and Shatila refugee camps by Lebanese Christian militia on September 16, Reagan ordered twelve hundred U.S. marines to return to Lebanon. The mission of the peacekeeping force, which arrived on September 29, was to join with Italian, French, and British forces in providing a buffer between warring factions, thereby improving stability in Lebanon and the Middle East.

The marines were obviously in a situation in which hostilities were "imminent," but Congress did not demand that the War Powers Resolution's sixty-day clock be started. On August 29, 1983, U.S. forces sustained their first casualties. President Reagan authorized the marines to defend themselves from their positions and ordered warships in the Mediterranean to shell positions in the hills outside Beirut from which the marines had been receiving hostile fire.

Congressional pressure forced the president to negotiate with Congress on terms for keeping the marines there.

On October 12, President Reagan signed a joint resolution that started the War Powers Resolution clock but also authorized him to keep the marines in Lebanon for eighteen months. The compromise resolution stated that the marines had been in a situation of imminent hostilities since August 29, 1983, and that this legislation was "the necessary specific statutory authorization under the War Powers Resolution for continued participation by United States Armed Forces in the Multinational Force in Lebanon." The compromise favored the president and demonstrated Congress's reluctance to apply the War Powers Resolution's strict terms to presidential use of the military.[67] Although the resolution was the basis for the congressional threats that brought the president to the bargaining table, President Reagan denied the constitutionality of the War Powers Resolution and even the legal validity of the joint resolution he was signing:

> I do not and cannot cede any of the authority vested in me under the Constitution as President and as Commander-in-Chief of the United States Armed Forces. Nor should my signing be viewed as any acknowledgment that the President's constitutional authority can be impermissibly infringed by statute, that congressional authorization would be required if and when the period specified in . . . the War Powers Resolution might be deemed to have been triggered and the period had expired, or that the 18-month authorization may be interpreted to revise the President's constitutional authority to deploy United States Armed Forces.[68]

Grenada

On October 25, 1983, two days after the killing of 241 marines in Lebanon, President Reagan ordered nineteen hundred U.S. troops to invade the small Caribbean island of Grenada. The action, which Reagan called a "rescue mission," was undertaken to overthrow Grenada's pro-Cuban, Marxist government, to restore order to the island, and to ensure the safety of approximately one thousand American citizens living there, most of whom were medical students. U.S. forces were joined by troops from six Caribbean nations belonging to the Organization of East Caribbean States, which had officially asked the United States to intervene.

Reagan reported to Congress but claimed that he was acting under his own authority. The House overwhelmingly voted that the sixty-day clock of the War Powers Resolution had begun when U.S. troops invaded Grenada, and the Senate prepared to pass similar legislation. The president declared an end to the fighting on November 2, and he announced plans to withdraw all combat troops by December 23, the end of the sixty-day period.[69]

The invasion, whose objectives were achieved quickly, was viewed favorably by the U.S. public, and Congress generally supported the Grenada action.

In November 1990 President George Bush and General H. Norman Schwarzkopf review U.S. troops stationed in the Persian Gulf region. Two months later the United States led a coalition of twenty-eight nations to a crushing victory over Iraq in liberating Kuwait.

Persian Gulf Naval Escorts

In 1987 during the war between Iran and Iraq, Iranian attacks on Kuwaiti neutral ships threatened to slow the flow of Arab oil through the Persian Gulf. In response to Kuwaiti pleas for assistance, President Reagan offered on March 10, 1987, to place tankers owned by Kuwait under the U.S. flag so they could be escorted through the gulf by U.S. warships. The escort of the Kuwaiti tankers was intended to ensure the flow of oil through the gulf and to prevent the Soviet Union, which Kuwait also had asked for help, from increasing its influence among moderate Arab nations and its naval presence in the gulf.[70]

On July 24, two days after the escort missions began, a reflagged Kuwaiti tanker was damaged by an Iranian mine. Critics of the administration's Persian Gulf strategy pointed to the incident as evidence that the naval escorts could involve the United States in the gulf conflict, and many lawmakers called on the president to invoke the War Powers Resolution. The Reagan administration refused, however, to acknowledge that the escort missions placed U.S. forces into hostilities or an area of imminent hostilities even though military personnel were receiving danger pay.[71]

Panama

In December 1989 President George H. W. Bush sent U.S. forces into Panama. "Operation Just Cause" was a major intervention in a sovereign nation at peace with the United States undertaken without congressional authorization. President Bush justified the invasion as necessary to protect American lives and property, to arrest Panamanian leader Manuel Noriega as a drug trafficker, to ensure the integrity of the Panama Canal Treaty, and to restore democracy to Panama. Factually, and as justifications for an invasion, all of these reasons were highly debatable, especially as bases for presidential authority to invade another nation.[72]

In the period leading up to the invasion, President Bush had kept congressional leaders informed about developments in Panama and the canal zone, and he informed them by phone hours before the invasion was launched. After the operation began, his formal notice to Congress was accompanied by an assertion that the War Powers Resolution was "unconstitutional."[73] Nevertheless, Bush seemed careful to confine the operation to the resolution's sixty- to ninety-day limit.

Persian Gulf War

In August 1990 Iraqi leader Saddam Hussein invaded Kuwait. Citing both the gross violation of national sovereignty and the vital national interest in protecting the flow of critical oil supplies from the Middle East, President Bush responded swiftly with a massive U.S. military buildup in the neighboring nation of Saudi Arabia. These forces were sent without congressional consultation. President Bush notified Congress but denied that the 100,000 troops were in a situation that was likely to evolve into hostilities.[74] Bush also denied any need for congressional authorization even after he sent an additional 150,000 military personnel. Although he claimed that the policy was to establish a defensive "shield," clearly the forces had been increased to offensive capability. Consequently, members of Congress called on Bush to seek authorization for any offensive action.

Instead, President Bush built an international coalition and secured a UN Security Council resolution authorizing UN members to use all necessary means to restore the sovereignty of Kuwait. Bush claimed that this resolution and his constitutional authority as commander in chief gave him sufficient authority to act. Yet, ruling on a suit filed by fifty-four members of Congress seeking an injunction against any offensive action, Judge Harold Greene argued that, although he could not issue an injunction at that time, congressional authorization was required by the Constitution.[75]

In January 1991 Bush asked for congressional support for "Operation Desert Storm," which would drive the Iraqis out of Kuwait. After a lengthy debate in both houses, Congress explicitly "authorized" offensive action under the War Powers Resolution while limiting that action to the terms of the Security Council resolution.[76] Bush, however, denied the validity of the War Powers Resolution and denied that congressional authorization was constitutionally required.

Somalia

Late in his term, and under pressure from Congress, President Bush ordered troops to Somalia, which was suffering from a civil war. The objectives of the mission were limited strictly to assisting in the international effort to relieve the famine-wracked population and to preparing for a more permanent UN force to continue the operation.

The operation was redefined in June 1993 after twenty-three UN peacekeepers were killed by one of the warring factions. U.S. warplanes and ground troops then joined in a retaliatory strike. The United Nations, with President Bill Clinton's approval, shifted to a more ambitious mission of subduing the armed factions and rebuilding the nation's political order. In October eighteen U.S. Rangers were killed and eighty wounded in an assault on one faction's headquarters.

Although U.S. forces were under fire, experiencing casualties, and receiving combat pay for an offensive operation, Clinton did not consult with, or formally report to, Congress on the change in policy. With the death of U.S. soldiers, the operation had become unpopular. Eventually, Congress and the Clinton administration agreed on a deadline for the use of funds for the operation.

Haiti

After the Somalia debacle, congressional criticism of the Clinton policy toward Haiti was less about the War Powers Resolution and more about the president's authority to commit forces in multilateral operations.

In 1991 a military coup overthrew the democratically elected government of Jean-Bertrand Aristide. President Bush declared that the coup "would not stand" and initiated an economic boycott as well as other nonmilitary measures to pressure the military rulers of Haiti. President Clinton continued the Bush policies until the military rulers openly reneged on their July 1993 agreement to cede power and U.S. forces sent to assist the transition were prevented from landing in October 1993. Then Clinton committed his administration to more forceful action to restore the democratically elected government. Congress debated a number of measures to restrict the president's capacity to send armed forces

but passed, in May 1994, only a nonbinding resolution that asserted the need for congressional authorization.[77]

In July 1994 the UN Security Council passed a resolution inviting member nations to use "all necessary means" to restore the democratic government. The Senate passed another nonbinding resolution stating that the Security Council action was not sufficient authority, but Clinton denied that he needed congressional authorization.

Bosnia

In 1993 the United States began participating in a joint UN/NATO effort to relieve the famine caused by the civil war between Serbs, Croats, and Muslims in the former Yugoslavia. U.S. forces were dispatched to help enforce a ban on unauthorized military flights over Bosnia-Herzegovina. President Clinton did not seek congressional authorization either for deployment or for engagement in combat. In 1994 U.S. fighter planes took part in NATO attacks on Bosnian Serb forces. Clinton used his commander-in-chief power as well as the UN and NATO resolutions to claim the full authority to order these missions.

Congress made several attempts to legislate restrictions on the use of additional forces in Bosnia. In 1993 Congress and Clinton agreed on a nonbinding resolution outlining conditions for the placement of U.S. forces under foreign command and stating that funds should not be used to deploy ground forces to oversee a peace agreement.[78] In August 1995 U.S. forces led extensive NATO air strikes against Bosnian Serb positions, and in September President Clinton promised twenty thousand U.S. troops to assist in NATO's oversight of a peace accord. Clinton deepened this commitment by having the United States host the peace talks in Dayton, Ohio. Once the peace accord was signed in Paris on December 14, 1995, Clinton began sending troops on his own authority and with a promise to limit the mission to one year. The House passed resolutions contradicting the president's authority to send troops, opposing the mission, and yet supporting the troops deployed. The Senate passed a resolution supporting the president's commitments while asserting the one-year limit on the mission.

Kosovo

Four years later, the United States again became enmeshed in the Balkans when it led NATO air strikes in Kosovo to halt Serbian leader Slobodan Milosevic's mass attacks in the region. The air strikes followed extensive peace talks that Serbia ultimately rejected.[79] President Clinton conducted the air strikes with divided Senate support, and House opposition, though neither chamber actually tried to stop the military action. The air war concluded successfully in ten weeks, with no ground troops and no U.S. combat casualties. Yet Congress's ability to participate in decision making over the use of military force was questioned once again.

George W. Bush greets troops after arriving at Baghdad International Airport Thursday, Nov. 27, 2003. Bush paid a surprise Thanksgiving day visit to American troops stationed in Iraq during the holiday.

Afghanistan

After the terrorist attacks of September 11, 2001, George W. Bush promised swift retaliation against its perpetrators. As the president said in his address to the nation on September 18, 2001, "Every nation, in every region, now has a decision to make. Either you are with us, or you are with the terrorists." [80] In the speech Bush identified the network of terrorist groups known as Al Qaeda as responsible for the attacks, and he identified their close ties with the repressive and misogynistic Taliban regime in Afghanistan. A few weeks later, on October 7, 2001, the United States attacked al Qaeda camps and Taliban military posts in Afghanistan.

Although Congress had not issued a declaration of war against Afghanistan—and, indeed, had not declared war since World War II—congressional, public, and international support for the U.S. attacks was strong. Just three days after September 11, Congress had passed a joint resolution authorizing the president "to use all necessary and appropriate force against those nations, organizations, or persons he determines planned, authorized, committed, or aided the terrorist attacks of September 11, 2001, or harbored such organizations or persons." [81] Public approval of the president soared to the highest levels ever recorded, surpassing the previous record set by former President George H. W. Bush after the 1991 Gulf War. Countries around the world rallied to support the United States in battling terrorists who posed

a global threat to security. Within a few months, coalition forces had successfully toppled the repressive Taliban regime, albeit without capturing al Qaeda leader Osama bin Laden, and then began the arduous task of building a new regime in Afghanistan. [82]

Iraq

Within a few months of the attacks on Afghanistan, the Bush administration began to hint of forthcoming military action against Iraq as well. In his January 2002 State of the Union address, Bush identified Iraq, Iran, and North Korea as "an axis of evil, arming to threaten the peace of the world." [83] The day after the one-year anniversary of the September 11, 2001, terrorist attacks, Bush addressed the United Nations General Assembly and called for it "to serve the purpose of its founding" [84] by enforcing its many resolutions demanding that Iraq comply with weapons inspections. Although Bush did not explicitly link the September 11, 2001, terrorist attacks with Iraq, he fully iterated the dangers that weapons of mass destruction in this dictatorial regime posed to the world. The next front for the United States in the war on terror was clear.

Following the model that his father had established before the first Gulf War in 1991, Bush sought to secure both congressional and UN approval for the use of military force against Iraq. Congress complied swiftly, passing a joint resolution in October 2002 that authorized the president to use armed force to defend the United States against the threat posed by Iraq and to enforce relevant UN Security Council resolutions. The UN Security Council also seemed initially to support the Bush administration's agenda, unanimously passing a resolution in November 2002 that called for "serious consequences" [85] if Iraq did not comply with arms inspections. Yet the apparent international consensus soon broke down, and ultimately, the United States was unable to secure a second Security Council resolution that explicitly authorized military action against Iraq. The United States waged war against Iraq in 2003 with congressional support but not UN backing, though many member states of the United Nations endorsed U.S. actions.[86]

By early 2007 the American public had grown weary over mounting U.S. causalities and the lack of stability in Iraq. Although Bush had congressional approval for the use of military force, newly empowered Democrats, in control of both houses of Congress for the first time since 1994, began to exert pressure on the president to end the war. Although Congress rarely opposes a president's military strategy during an ongoing conflict, it is easier to do so when that conflict is not going well. In February 2007 the House passed a nonbinding resolution opposing Bush's plan to send 21,500 additional troops to Iraq. In late April Congress moved beyond symbolism and passed a supplemental Iraq spending bill that included a timetable for U.S. troop withdrawal. President Bush vetoed the bill partly because it set an "arbitrary date" for withdrawal. Lacking the votes to override the veto, and not wanting to cut funding to troops already deployed in the field, Congress in late May passed a spending bill that gave Bush what he wanted without a withdrawal deadline. Yet Democratic leaders vowed immediately to keep up pressure for a change of course in the war.

Effects of the War Powers Resolution

The War Powers Resolution has, on the one hand, probably influenced some conflict-related decisions. During President Reagan's deployment of marines to Lebanon in 1982 and 1983, the prospect of the invocation of the resolution helped to produce a formal compromise between the legislative and executive branches on the limits of a military operation. Similarly, President Clinton was forced by an assertive Congress to agree to an even stricter time limit on forces in Somalia. On the other hand, since passage of the resolution in 1973, neither congressional resolutions nor the automatic sixty-day time limit has forced a president to disengage U.S. troops from a conflict. The War Powers Resolution has, then, not been much of a rein on the president's war powers, but mainly because it has never been enforced. Moreover, presidents have appeared undaunted by the resolution's potential to restrict the introduction of American armed forces into hostile situations.

The resolution could be strengthened as law. Currently, it is based on an interpretation of the president's commander-in-chief power, and it has been weakened by the historical precedents that back a president's claims of broad authority to commit armed forces. The resolution could be strengthened by tying the president's authority to commit troops to Congress's clear authority over expenditures.[87] The effectiveness of the resolution depends on the collective will of Congress to challenge presidential actions. If this collective will exists, Congress has ample means to check the president's war-making power and to expand its role in deciding when and how military force should be used. In 1995 Congress considered measures that would repeal the War Powers Resolution, retain the consulting and reporting provisions, and place specific restrictions on U.S. participation in multilateral operations, including UN peacekeeping missions.

MILITARY RESPONSES TO TERRORISM

Periodically, presidents have called on the military to battle not just other nations but also extragovernmental groups that have threatened Americans and their interests. For example, the navy fought pirates in the eighteenth and nineteenth centuries, and in 1916 President Woodrow Wilson sent Gen. John J. "Blackjack" Pershing and six thousand troops into Mexico in pursuit of the Mexican bandit Pancho Villa after he raided Columbus, New Mexico.

Beginning in the 1970s, international terrorist groups have regularly threatened and attacked U.S. citizens, civilian and military alike. The groups committing these acts and the nations that have supported them are generally Arab or Islamic. The motives of these often fanatical groups are largely religious and ideological.

Initially, these attacks were on a relatively small scale. In response, intelligence agencies expanded their efforts to identify terrorists, and the U.S. military stepped up its antiterrorist preparations and formed elite counterterrorist units to provide presidents with a more credible military option should they decide to use force against terrorists. But military operations against terrorists were usually thought to be risky and impractical, and presidents generally refrained from using significant military force against terrorists. The costs of such operations, in lives and diplomatic relations, always appeared to be greater than the possible benefits of what was judged to be unwinnable conflicts.[88] Those directly responsible, moreover, were difficult to identify with precision; they often shielded themselves by locating their operations in densely populated areas. As a result, military operations against terrorists would not only violate sovereign borders, but also risk harming innocent civilians. The more common antiterrorist weapon has been the imposition of economic sanctions on nations such as Syria, Iraq, and Iran that have supported terrorist organizations.

Beginning in the 1980s, terrorists increased the scope and brutality of their attacks. In 1983, 241 marines were killed by a car bomb in Beirut. Many more American lives were lost in other bombings: of a West Berlin discotheque frequented by U.S. military personnel (1986), of the Khobar Towers in Saudi Arabia (1996), of the U.S. embassies in Kenya and Tanzania (1998), and of the *Cole* in Yemen (2000). The Reagan administration began responding with limited military operations. In October 1985 navy fighters intercepted an Egyptian airliner carrying terrorists who had seized a passenger ship and killed a U.S. citizen in the Mediterranean. In April 1986 U.S. warplanes bombed targets in Libya after U.S. intelligence obtained evidence that Libyan leader Col. Muammar Qaddafi sponsored the West Berlin discotheque bombing. President Clinton also used force in ordering cruise missile attacks on terrorist bases in Afghanistan and a possible chemical weapons operation in the Sudan.

The savage September 11, 2001, attacks on New York City and the Pentagon demonstrated the ineffectiveness of sanctions and of short-term, small-scale military actions. President George W. Bush, responding to the attacks, announced that his administration would prosecute a comprehensive "war on terrorism." Unlike in most recent military operations, the commander in chief received immediate support and cooperation from Congress. The controversies that had been occupying Congress and the White House—tax cuts, spending priorities, missile defense, and Medicare and Social Security reform—were pushed aside. With little debate or controversy, Congress passed a $40 billion emergency appropriation and a resolution authorizing the use of force against terrorist organizations and the nations that support them; it said little about avoiding the use of ground troops and minimizing American losses. *(See box, Congressional Authorization for a War on Terrorism, p. 762.)* Congress also passed a controversial counterterrorism bill that expanded the national government's powers of surveillance and detention. Reports of a sweeping intelligence order, authorizing covert actions by the Central Intelligence Agency (CIA) against Osama bin Laden and the Al Qaeda organization, with extraordinary cooperation between CIA and military units, were not greeted with the usual suspicions and con-

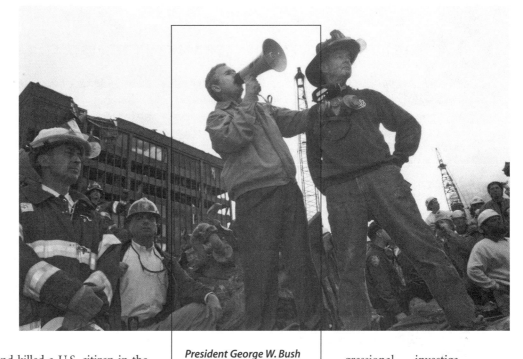

President George W. Bush addresses a crowd of firemen, rescue workers, and volunteers at Ground Zero— the 16-acre plot where the 110-story World Trade Center towers once stood—three days after two hijacked planes struck the buildings on September 11, 2001. The terrorist attack in New York killed almost 2,900 people in the towers and 147 passengers and crew aboard the two airplanes.

gressional investigations.[89] Perhaps most significantly, the president and his advisers propounded a "unitary executive" theory of presidential power, which essentially held that the executive possessed the inherent power to prosecute the war on terrorism without seeking approval from Congress or the courts. The unitary executive concept was used to justify the indefinite detention of terrorist suspects, military tribunals for those detainees, and domestic wiretapping without judicial review for alleged links to terrorist threats.[90]

As a military campaign, a war on terrorism raised questions about war powers. What exactly was the legal and constitutional status of this sort of conflict? With whom, or what, was the nation at war? As with piracy, the immediate enemy was not another country. But was the nation at war if it was not warring on another sovereign state? Also like piracy, however, the immediate enemy needed the cooperation or acquiescence of nation-states to harbor its operations and, especially in the case of terrorism, to fund its activities. This relationship could lead, as it did in Afghanistan, to hostile actions against governments. But because the principal aim of military operations would be to debilitate or destroy a criminal element, they would not necessarily entail

CONGRESSIONAL AUTHORIZATION FOR A WAR ON TERRORISM

In response to the September 11, 2001, terrorist attacks on New York City and Washington, D.C., President George W. Bush committed the nation to what he called a "war on terrorism." Although the president did not acknowledge any need for congressional approval, Congress formally authorized the "use of force" just days after the attacks.[1]

However, the resolution, passed on September 14, 2001, was marked by ambiguity. The authorization seemed to be narrower than the president's commitment. It authorized the use of force against "nations, organizations, or persons" in any way culpable in "recent attacks," with the purpose of preventing "any future acts of international terrorism by such nations, organizations or persons" (section 2a). While permitting a war on the Al Qaeda terrorists responsible for the attacks and their abettors, the resolution was not broad enough to cover the president's general war on international terrorism.

Yet the statement of facts included a more comprehensive statement of purpose: to deter and prevent acts of international terrorism against the United States. This section also seemed to acknowledge that the president had full authority "under the Constitution" to prosecute this broad aim. In other words, the resolution acknowledged that the president's constitutional authority already encompassed the powers that Congress was claiming to authorize.

How expansively the 2001 congressional resolution interpreted presidential power sparked heated debate as the George W. Bush administration vigorously prosecuted the war on terrorism. The president adhered to a "unitary executive" concept of presidential power, which held that the Constitution granted the president broad authority to take action without first seeking congressional authorization.[2] The Bush administration claimed this authority to justify the indefinite detention of prisoners, authorization of military tribunals for "enemy combatants," domestic surveillance of terrorist suspects, and other controversial actions. The 2001 congressional resolution was further cited as evidence of Congress's support for presidential leadership in combating terrorism. The Supreme Court ruled in 2006 that the president did not possess unchecked power to establish military tribunals without attention to international laws governing treatment of prisoners. Nevertheless, the legitimacy of the many executive initiatives following the tragic attacks of September 11, 2001, remained unresolved by early 2007.

1. *CQ Weekly,* September 15, 2001, 2158.
2. Jeffrey Rosen, "Power of One," *New Republic,* July 24, 2006.

military victory over those states, which is the defining objective of a war. Considered in this way, a campaign against terrorist organizations seemed more akin to international policing than to war, and it invited a reconsideration of Theodore Roosevelt's rationale for an international police power. On the other hand, the U.S. operation in Afghanistan turned almost immediately to the defeat of the Afghan government, which brought it much closer to a formal war.

These considerations lead to another set of war powers questions about the scope of the conflict. Congress's authorization of the use of force was ambiguous, but President Bush defined the sides in this conflict sharply: either you are with us or you are with the terrorists. When the Taliban government of Afghanistan refused to arrest the Al Qaeda leadership and dismantle the Al Qaeda terrorist training camps, it became the target of retaliation and antiterrorist operations. If the same reasoning and response were applied to other countries that harbor and finance terrorist organizations, a long-term military campaign against international terrorism could involve the United States in numerous conflicts that would be, in form and fact, wars.

In his January 2002 State of the Union address, President Bush took a step in this direction; he singled out Iraq, Iran, and North Korea for their development of weapons of mass destruction and support for international terrorism. He declared that the United States would vigorously oppose this "axis of evil." Later that year, the Bush administration published its National Security Strategy, in which it explicitly declared that the United States "will, if necessary, act preemptively" to combat terrorist threats.[91] Four years later, the administration stated that "the place of preemption in our national security strategy remains the same." [92] President Bush followed through on this strategy with the 2003 Iraq war, which Congress endorsed. But what role Congress would play in deciding upon a future preemptive attack remained unclear.

INTERNATIONAL AGREEMENTS AND THE WAR POWERS

As events beginning with the Korean War demonstrate, efforts to control presidential use of force have been complicated by U.S. participation in the United Nations and numerous mutual security agreements with other nations. Presidents have used the UN Charter, Security Council resolutions, and other multilateral agreements as authority to commit U.S. forces without additional congressional authorization. They have claimed that Congress granted the authority to act by approving these agreements. They also have used these agreements to invoke their broad foreign policy powers as additional authority for the unilateral use of force.

United Nations Peacekeeping

Presidents often have promoted UN peacekeeping missions and, when appropriate, have offered the services of the U.S. military to those missions. UN peacekeeping missions have

A UN armored personnel carrier rumbles through the streets of Pakrac, Croatia, in May 1995. When the Muslim-led government of Bosnia-Herzegovina declared independence from the central Yugoslavian government in February 1992, the Bosnian war began. Following a relentless "ethnic cleansing" campaign by the Bosnian Serbs to rid the Muslim-held territory of Muslims and Croatian Catholics, the United Nations sent a peacekeeping force. It was largely ineffective because there was no international agreement on how to stop the war. After a brief cease-fire in early 1995, the fighting resumed as Croatian forces captured significant chunks of land from the Serbs.

approval of the council's permanent members. The United States, Russia, Great Britain, France, and the People's Republic of China are permanent members of the Security Council. UN peacekeeping forces have been used to separate combatants, monitor cease-fire agreements, and protect civilians.

During the cold war, UN missions were limited by the veto power of the United States and the Soviet Union. For example, the most dramatic use of the UN security function, the Security Council's resolution to resist the North Korean invasion of South Korea in 1950, was possible only because the Soviets were not present to exercise their veto. When the Soviet Union threatened to exercise its Security Council veto to block the creation of any UN peacekeeping force for the Sinai, as part of the 1979 Camp David peace accords between Egypt and Israel, the United States was compelled to organize a multinational force, which included U.S. troops.

During the late 1980s, the status of UN-sponsored peacekeeping forces grew as UN peacekeepers were awarded the 1988 Nobel Peace Prize and the Soviet Union and United States both advocated the use of UN peacekeeping troops to monitor negotiated settlements of several regional conflicts. The United Nations created new peacekeeping forces to oversee peace accords in Afghanistan, Angola, and Cambodia, and to prevent the war in Bosnia and Serbia from spreading into the former Yugoslav republic of Macedonia. Moreover, in 1992 UN Secretary General Boutros Boutros-Ghali proposed a qualitative change in the type of missions undertaken. He suggested the possibility of a permanent UN force that would not simply oversee peace accords but also intervene forcefully to settle disputes.

This expanded use of UN peacekeepers and the potential for more aggressive use of UN forces led to criticism in Congress and to attempts to restrict U.S. participation in peacekeeping missions. The primary issue was the president's authority, under the UN Charter and Security Council resolutions, to commit armed forces without congressional authorization. Although presidents have argued that their powers in conjunction with UN resolutions provide sufficient authority, such claims are not supported by the text and legislative history of the UN Charter and the United Nations Participation Act.

some advantages over unilateral U.S. action: UN peacekeepers may be less threatening to the nations in which they are deployed, the economic costs to the United States may be lower, and a UN peacekeeping force might promote a spirit of international accountability and cooperation in solving a particular regional problem. Early in his administration, President Clinton was an enthusiastic supporter of an expanded use of UN missions and of broad U.S. participation in them as a way to remain engaged in international affairs in the post–cold war era. Especially after U.S. soldiers were killed in Somalia in 1993, Clinton's policy generated repeated legislative attempts to restrict U.S. participation in UN missions.

The primary responsibility for the peace and security function of the United Nations resides with the Security Council. The council assesses threats to peace and attempts to use peaceful measures to prevent aggression. If nonmilitary actions fail or are inappropriate, the Security Council may vote to use military force.[93] A Security Council decision to use military force or to create a detachment of military observers cannot be adopted without the unanimous

Any UN Security Council actions calling for member nations to supply armed forces are subject to approval through each member nation's "constitutional processes." The most contentious issue in the 1945 Senate debate on U.S. membership in the United Nations was the nature of those "processes": who had the power to commit U.S. forces to Security Council peacekeeping operations? The Senate did not want to hand the executive exclusive authority to provide the United Nations with troops, and the House refused to allow the Senate and the president to usurp its constitutional role.

The clear understanding that emerged from the debate was that majorities in both houses of Congress would be needed to authorize the commitment of armed forces to UN missions.[94] This understanding was affirmed in the United Nations Participation Act of 1945, which stated in part:

> The President is authorized to negotiate a special agreement or agreements with the Security Council which shall be subject to the approval of the Congress by appropriate Act or joint resolution, providing for the numbers and types of armed forces, their degree of readiness and general location, and the nature of facilities and assistance, including rights of passage, to be made available to the Security Council on its call for the purpose of maintaining international peace and security.

Thus presidents are expressly prohibited by the Participation Act from unilaterally concluding an agreement with the Security Council under their powers to negotiate treaties, execute the laws, or defend the United States. The president cannot legally aid or commit U.S. forces to UN military missions without an approving congressional resolution.[95] Nonetheless, Presidents Truman (Korea), George H. W. Bush (Kuwait), and Clinton (Haiti) have used UN resolutions as authorization to commit armed forces without congressional approval.

Early in his administration, President Clinton enthusiastically embraced broad U.S. engagement in world affairs through the United Nations and other multilateral organizations. However, in the absence of the global threat of communist expansion, the U.S. interests served by the expenditure of lives and tax dollars in remote parts of the world are more difficult to define and explain. Unlike the Persian Gulf War, in which the United States had a clear interest in protecting the flow of oil from the Persian Gulf states, the United States had only indirect interests, beyond humanitarian concerns, in Somalia, Haiti, Bosnia, and Kosovo. Therefore, the debates over U.S. participation revolved around the degree to which the United States should involve itself in policing the world in the absence of national or global security interests.

U.S. participation in UN missions can be measured in several ways. On the one hand, the United States supplies only a small number of troops to official UN peacekeeping forces. In 1994 only about 800 of 63,000 UN military personnel were Americans. On the other hand, the United States is extensively involved in UN activities and resolutions. For example, the 1994 Haiti operation was under the aegis of a UN resolution, but the U.S. troops sent were not part of a UN command. In early 1995 more than 60,000 U.S. troops were involved in such "contingency" operations with more than half of those stationed in South Korea. Between 1989 and 1996, U.S. spending on peacekeeping increased 500 percent.[96]

In 1993 Congress passed a nonbinding resolution specifying the conditions under which the president could place U.S. forces under foreign command and under which the United States could participate in UN missions.[97] In 1995 both houses of Congress considered similar measures to restrict U.S. participation in UN missions. One provision would have subtracted the cost of unreimbursed spending on "contingency" operations from U.S. payments to the United Nations for peacekeeping missions. Because the unreimbursed expenses exceed U.S. peacekeeping payments to the United Nations by as much as $500 million a year, the measure would have, as intended by its proponents, hindered UN peacekeeping generally by eliminating all U.S. financial support.

In response to these criticisms and proposals, the Clinton administration announced more restrictive policy guidelines for U.S. participation in UN missions, especially those that may involve combat. Specifically, such missions must involve national interests or "a real threat to international peace and security." These guidelines still asserted that the president had, under the United Nations and other alliances, the full authority to commit armed forces. President Clinton maintained that the congressional proposals would be an imprudent and unconstitutional intrusion on the president's foreign policy and war powers.[98] The fight over UN dues and peacekeeping costs went on for years. Late in the Clinton presidency, Congress, the president, and the United Nations reached an agreement that addressed some of the critics' concerns and committed the United States to paying most of its debt.

Apart from peacekeeping, the president also may seek UN support for military action against aggressor nations. Perhaps the most significant precedent was set in 1990, when President George H. W. Bush, who previously had served as U.S. ambassador to the United Nations, requested a Security Council resolution to authorize the use of force to repel Iraq's invasion of Kuwait. Although the administration maintained that it did not require UN backing, it successfully guided a resolution through the Security Council. In 2002 the administration of President George W. Bush seemed to be following that precedent when it secured a Security Council resolution warning of "serious consequences" if Iraq did not disarm and submit to weapons inspections. But a few months later, the Security Council refused to endorse a second resolution explicitly authorizing force, and the United States ultimately waged war against Iraq without UN support, though many members of the organization supported the United States in what the administration termed a "coalition of the willing." [99]

Alliances and Mutual Security Agreements

Until the post–World War II period, the United States shunned alliances. During most of the nineteenth and early twentieth centuries, the military establishments of the great powers of Europe were concerned primarily with defending against threats from their neighbors. Because the security of the United States did not depend on having allies, Americans generally preferred to remain isolationist. Except for the Franco-American Alliance of 1778, which was effectively voided by George Washington's 1793 neutrality proclamation toward Britain and France, the United States did not participate in a formal peacetime alliance until after World War II.[100] Even when the United States entered World War I against Germany in 1917, U.S. leaders demonstrated the national aversion to alliances by claiming to be only an "associated power" of Britain and France.

World War II shattered the isolationist policies of the United States. The nation emerged from the war not just as a member of the international community, but also as a world leader. Alarmed by the growth of Soviet military power and the establishment of Soviet control over Eastern Europe after World War II, many nations sought the security of an alliance or friendly relationship with the United States. Under Presidents Truman and Eisenhower, the United States responded by enthusiastically erecting a global network of multilateral and bilateral alliances intended to contain Soviet expansionism. The Rio Pact, signed in 1947, reaffirmed the long-standing U.S. commitment to defend the Western Hemisphere. The 1949 North Atlantic Treaty created the North Atlantic Treaty Organization, an alliance between the United States, Canada, and most Western European democracies that developed into the cornerstone of the U.S. containment strategy. Then, in 1951, the ANZUS alliance between Australia, New Zealand, and the United States was created. The United States also joined the Southeast Asia Treaty Organization (SEATO) in 1954 and established ties with, although not membership in, a Middle Eastern alliance known as the Central Treaty Organization (CENTO) in 1956. These multilateral alliances were complemented by bilateral alliances with Japan and the Philippines in 1951, Korea in 1953, Taiwan in 1954, and Iran, Pakistan, and Turkey in 1959.[101]

The purpose of and motivation to maintain these alliances have been in a state of flux in the post–cold war era. Many of them, including SEATO and CENTO, no longer exist. Without an overriding single interest in mutual defense or a dependence on U.S. economic, military, and

especially nuclear power, there are more potential conflicts between national interests and alliance policy. The movement of European NATO nations toward the more Europe-centered defense structure of the Western European Union (WEU) was encouraged by the withdrawal of the United States from the NATO-sponsored naval blockade of the former Yugoslavia.[102] Indeed, the weakening of U.S. influence in NATO was manifest in the many conflicts between the United States and the other NATO nations over alliance policy and actions in that region. President Clinton was committed to working through NATO and the United Nations, and his policy toward Bosnia was shaped by a desire to avoid ruptures between the United States and its NATO allies. In 1995 Clinton vetoed a bill directing him to depart from UN and NATO policy by terminating the U.S. arms embargo against Bosnia, and he committed the United States to providing 20,000 troops to support NATO oversight of a Bosnian peace accord.

In 2001 NATO invoked its charter and declared that the savage terrorist attacks of September 11 would be considered "an attack against all of the parties." Early in the war on terrorism, NATO followed, at least in principle, the U.S. lead.

Alliances and the War Powers

U.S. membership in an alliance creates additional presidential responsibilities and claims to war-making authority. The most important of these is the president's obligation, as commander in chief and the person who executes the laws, to fulfill the terms of a treaty. This obligation depends on the terms of the alliance agreement and the declared policy of the United States. The NATO treaty states that "an attack on one or more [of the parties] shall be considered as an attack against all of the parties." Advocates of presidential power could argue that by ratifying a treaty with such language Congress has given presidents the same authority to repel an invasion of a NATO country as they have to repel an attack on the United States.[103] Those on the other side argue that a treaty, involving only the Senate and the president, cannot alter the Constitution, which gives the House of Representatives a controlling voice in the commitment of armed forces. Indeed, Article II of the North Atlantic Treaty specifies that its provisions shall be "carried out by the Parties in accordance with their respective constitutional processes." [104]

Beyond the language of a treaty, the declared policy of the United States has had significant effects on the president's authority and ability to act in defense of an alliance partner. During the cold war, the president would have been expected to direct U.S. troops to repel an attack on NATO. Similarly, presidents would have assumed they had full authorization to respond to attacks on South Korea and Japan, not only because of treaties with those nations, but because many U.S. troops have been based there and numerous acts of Congress have recognized and supported U.S. defense commitments in East Asia. As the dire general threats recede in the post–cold war era, the effects of such commitments on subsequent policy and presidential latitude in use of force will be weaker.

PRESIDENT AS MILITARY COMMANDER

The commander-in-chief clause gives presidents clear authority to command the military as the nation's first general and admiral. They possess all decision-making powers accorded to any supreme military commander under international law. Presidents not only order troops into battle, but they are also expected to approve major strategic decisions and keep a watchful eye on the progress of any military campaign. Most presidents since World War II have even regarded specific tactical decisions related to certain military operations to be among their commander-in-chief responsibilities.

In making the president the commander in chief, the Framers attempted to ensure that civilian authority would always direct the armed forces. Military leaders who might otherwise use their authority over the army and navy to accumulate political power or enhance their personal reputation would be subordinate to a president who is elected by the entire country and is responsible for the welfare and security of all the people. Designating the president as commander in chief also ensured more effective military leadership; a single leader at the top of the military hierarchy would be recognized by all as the legitimate and indisputable supreme military commander.

Military experience has been fairly common among presidents. Although some presidents with no military experience, such as James Madison and Woodrow Wilson, have led the nation during wartime, as of 2000 twenty-seven of forty-two chief executives had served in the military. A significant number of these were high-ranking officers. Twelve served as generals, and six of these twelve—George Washington, Andrew Jackson, William Harrison, Zachary Taylor, Ulysses S. Grant, and Dwight Eisenhower—attained at least the rank of major

Dwight D. Eisenhower was one of twelve generals who later served as president. On D-Day— June 6, 1944—he personally encouraged American paratroopers of the 101st Airborne Division before their drop into France as the vanguard of the invasion.

general.[105] Three presidents—Grant, Eisenhower, and Carter—graduated from a military academy. Franklin Roosevelt, a wartime president who never entered the military, gained defense-related experience as assistant secretary of the navy.

Presidential Direction of Military Operations

The degree to which presidents have become involved in the direction of military operations has varied according to their military expertise and the circumstances of the military situation. Once troops have been committed to battle, presidents have usually delegated authority for battlefield strategy to their generals and admirals. The Constitution, however, does not prohibit a president from taking direct command of troops in the field. Several delegates to the Constitutional Convention suggested that the president should be prohibited from taking personal command of troops, but the convention rejected these proposals.[106]

George Washington was regarded as the nation's greatest general, and neither Congress nor the American public would have thought it wrong for him to have led U.S. troops into battle while he was president. Indeed, in 1794 Washington came close to doing just that when he personally supervised the organization of the militia charged with putting down the Whiskey Rebellion.[107] In 1799, when an undeclared naval war with France threatened to spread to the North American continent, President John Adams delegated his authority as commander in chief to then-retired Washington. Adams, who recognized his own lack of military experience and the advantages of enabling the country to rally around a national legend if war came, asked Washington to accept the post of "Lieutenant General and Commander-in-Chief of all the armies raised or to be raised in the United States." Washington agreed on the condition that he would not have to take command of the army unless "it became indispensable by the urgency of circumstances." The hostile engagements with France remained confined to the high seas, and Washington never

During the early stages of the Civil War, Abraham Lincoln became deeply involved in battlefield strategy. He occasionally issued direct orders to his generals regarding their troop movements and frequently conferred with them at the front.

had to leave his retirement at Mount Vernon to assume active command of U.S. forces.[108]

The poor performance of Union generals during the early stages of the Civil War and the proximity of the fighting to Washington, D.C., compelled President Abraham Lincoln to become deeply involved in battlefield strategy. He occasionally issued direct orders to his generals regarding their troop movements and frequently conferred with them at the front. Although Lincoln's interference in purely military matters has been criticized by some historians and applauded by others, he did allow his generals broad discretion in their implementation of his orders. After Lincoln gave command of the army to General Grant, in whom he had confidence, the president removed himself from tactical decisions.[109]

President Woodrow Wilson, like John Adams, recognized his lack of military experience and delegated responsibility for strategy and tactics to military leaders. Moreover, the distance between the president and the fighting made personal leadership impractical. He confined his commander-in-chief role during World War I to the domestic war effort and broad military decisions, such as his rejection of a French and British proposal in 1918 that the United States open a major front in Russia to prevent the Germans from transferring troops to the West after the Russians had negotiated a separate peace with Germany.[110]

World War II created conditions that necessitated the involvement of the president in strategic decisions. Because the war effort against Germany and Japan depended on the concerted action of the United States, Great Britain, the Soviet Union, and other nations, Allied strategy had to be determined through negotiations among the leaders of these countries. As a result, Presidents Roosevelt and Truman made decisions, such as when to launch the invasion of Europe and where to concentrate U.S. forces, not just because they were the commander in chief, but also because they were the nation's chief diplomat.

Sophisticated communication technologies also have facilitated presidential involvement in military operations. For example, in April 1988 the pilot of a navy aircraft patrolling the Persian Gulf observed Iranian gunboats attacking a set of oil rigs. Because U.S. forces in the Persian Gulf were authorized to respond only to attacks on American aircraft, ships, and facilities, the pilot radioed his aircraft carrier for permission to attack the Iranian vessels. The pilot's request was transmitted up the chain of command from the aircraft carrier commander to the admiral in charge of the naval task force. Then the request was relayed via satellite through the chief of the U.S. Central Command in Florida to the chairman of the Joint Chiefs of Staff and the secretary of defense at the Pentagon, who called President Reagan. The president authorized U.S. planes to attack the Iranian gunboats, and the order was relayed back through the chain of command to navy pilots who moved to attack only three minutes after permission had been requested.[111]

In the aftermath of the Vietnam War, in which President Lyndon B. Johnson was criticized for micromanaging operational decisions, presidents typically have made a point of not second-guessing the battlefield choices of military commanders.[112] President George W. Bush insisted that he would not direct the operations of his military leaders. But the question of micromanagement arose for Bush's secretary of defense, Donald H. Rumsfeld, in connection with the Iraq war. Several retired military officers, including leaders who had commanded troops in Iraq, called for Rumsfeld's resignation in the spring of 2006, declaring that the secretary of defense had not planned adequately either for the war or postwar reconstruction. Although President Bush strongly affirmed his commitment to keeping Rumsfeld at the Pentagon, the public debate raised questions about the administration's management of military operations in Iraq.[113] Throughout the rest of the year public support of the war and President Bush continued to drop, and after Democrats recaptured both houses of Congress in November 2006, Rumsfeld resigned as defense secretary.

Command of Nuclear Weapons

Despite the absurdity of a modern president ever leading U.S. troops into battle, the realities of nuclear warfare, especially during the cold war, have made the president the nation's "first soldier." The decision to use nuclear weapons is entirely the commander-in-chief's, whose claim on this authority is reinforced by the need for speedy and secret decisions. For example, in the event of a submarine-launched nuclear attack, the president would have no more than ten to twelve minutes to receive positive verification of the attack, decide how to respond, and transmit orders to the military commanders in charge of U.S. nuclear forces. Even if the attack was launched from missile silos in Russia, the president would have little more than twenty to thirty minutes before the weapons detonated.[114] A decision that has to be made this quickly must be assigned to a single individual with indisputable authority.

Although presidents alone have the authority to order the use of nuclear weapons, they do not possess perfect control over them. The U.S. nuclear arsenal consists of thousands of nuclear warheads, delivery vehicles for all types of nuclear missions, and a vast network of personnel, computers, communications equipment, and the information and intelligence gathering and processing systems necessary to manage the weapons.[115] Because of the size and complexity of the U.S. nuclear weapons arsenal and the requirements of deterrence, presidents cannot depend on controlling every weapon by simply pushing a button or making a phone call. Their control could be undermined by the failure or destruction of the U.S. early warning and communications systems, of the personnel who manage the nuclear weapons, or of the weapons themselves.

Presidential control of nuclear weapons has been aided by permissive action links (PALs), which are electronic locks that prevent nuclear weapons from being fired without prior presidential authorization. Intercontinental ballistic missiles (ICBMs) based in missile silos and nuclear warheads carried by U.S. strategic bombers are equipped with PALs. The military commanders of certain other types of nuclear weapons, however, have the physical capability, although not the authority, to launch them without receiving a presidential order. Nuclear missiles deployed in submarines, for example, are not equipped with PALs and therefore could be fired by the officers of a submarine who mistakenly believed that the president had issued a launch order. The navy continually seeks to minimize the danger of an unauthorized nuclear launch through intensive psycho-logical screening of submarine personnel and elaborate launch procedures that require the coordination of several officers aboard any one vessel.

Evolution of Presidential Nuclear Decision Making and Strategies

Since Franklin Roosevelt directed U.S. scientists to build the atomic bomb, presidents have dominated nuclear weapons policy and the formulation of nuclear strategy. Nuclear age presidents during the cold war counted nuclear decision making as among their most important and burdensome responsibilities. Dwight Eisenhower once said in a speech:

> When the push of a button may mean obliteration of countless humans, the President of the United States must be forever on guard against any inclination on his part to impetuosity; to arrogance; to headlong action; to expedience; to facile maneuvers; even to the popularity of an action as opposed to the righteousness of an action. . . . He must worry only about the good—the long-term, abiding, permanent good—of all Americans.[116]

U.S. Nuclear Monopoly

In the summer of 1945, after the war against Nazi Germany had been won, President Truman decided to drop newly manufactured atomic bombs on the Japanese cities of Hiroshima and Nagasaki to bring an end to World War II. Truman maintained that using the atomic bombs was the only way to end the war without an invasion of Japan. In a radio address to the American public on August 9, 1945, Truman explained that he had ordered the attacks "to shorten the agony of war, in order to save the lives of thousands and thousands of young Americans." [117]

Historical evidence suggests that other considerations also were involved. Certainly Truman wanted to end the war quickly to prevent the Soviet Union, which was about to enter the war against the Japanese, from having a role in the occupation of Japan. He also may have regarded the bomb as an impressive demonstration of American power that would cause the Soviets to be more conciliatory toward the West.[118]

From the bombing of Hiroshima to the early 1950s, the United States enjoyed a nuclear monopoly. The Soviet Union tested its first atomic bomb in 1949, but it did not have an operational capability for several more years. The U.S. ability to destroy Soviet population centers with atomic weapons served as an effective deterrent against the threat to Western Europe from superior numbers of Soviet conventional forces.[119] Although the U.S. nuclear advantage prevented war with the Soviet Union through the 1940s and 1950s, the Korean War demonstrated the difficulty of using nuclear weapons in limited wars. Truman rejected their use in Korea because of allied opposition and the need to conserve the U.S. nuclear arsenal to defend against a Soviet attack on Western Europe. A moral prohibition against the use of nuclear weapons also had developed, especially against an underdeveloped nation such as North Korea whose citizens were victims of communist expansion.

U.S. Nuclear Superiority

The Soviet nuclear arsenal early in the 1950s was much inferior in number and quality to the U.S. nuclear force. President Dwight Eisenhower attempted to use U.S. nuclear superiority to deter Soviet aggression. He believed that maintaining a conventional military force capable of countering the Soviets and their clients anywhere in the world would be disastrous for the federal budget and would not be supported by the American public. In addition, a threat to use nuclear weapons against China had helped end the Korean War. The administration therefore declared in 1954 that the United States would use nuclear weapons not only in response to a Soviet attack on Western Europe, but also in response to unspecified lesser provocations.[120]

This strategy, which was known as "massive retaliation," lacked credibility as a response to limited acts of communist aggression such as Soviet-supported guerrilla movements or political subversion. Furthermore, as the Soviet nuclear capability grew during the 1950s, the possibility that the United States could launch a nuclear attack against the Soviet Union without itself and its allies receiving a nuclear counterblow became remote. The successful Soviet launch of the *Sputnik* satellite in 1957 even engendered false speculation that the gap in military technology that Americans assumed to be in their favor actually favored the Soviets.

President Kennedy sought to bring declared nuclear policy in line with current realities. Upon taking office, he announced a new strategy of "flexible response." Kennedy and his advisers saw that improvements in the Soviet nuclear arsenal had diminished the capacity of U.S. nuclear forces to deter anything but a Soviet nuclear attack or massive invasion of Western Europe. Kennedy also recognized that the United States was faced with many forms of communist aggression that called for limited responses. Nuclear deterrence remained the centerpiece of U.S. defense, but conventional and counterinsurgency forces also were built up to be able to wage limited wars.[121]

Soviet placement of medium-range nuclear missiles in Cuba in 1962 precipitated a crisis that pushed the United States to the brink of nuclear war with the Soviet Union. Kennedy refused to accept this alteration of the balance of forces. He ordered a blockade of Cuba to prevent further construction of the Soviet missile sites and demanded that the Soviets withdraw the missiles. After two tense weeks, during which Kennedy estimated the chances of nuclear war at "between one out of three and even," the Soviets agreed to remove their missiles.[122] The Cuban missile crisis highlighted the threat to U.S. security from the growing Soviet

A dark mushroom cloud rises 20,000 feet above Nagasaki, Japan, after the dropping of the atomic bomb on August 9, 1945. President Harry S. Truman ordered the bombing—here and three days earlier on Hiroshima—the only wartime use of nuclear weapons to date.

nuclear arsenal and stimulated a further modernization of nuclear weaponry.

The Era of Parity

Presidents Nixon and Ford subscribed to the basic nuclear strategy established by Kennedy and Johnson. The concept of strategic defense—building defensive weapons systems capable of destroying attacking enemy missiles and bombers—had been widely debated during Johnson's presidency. President Nixon, however, concluded a treaty in 1972 with the Soviet Union that placed strict limitations on antiballistic missile systems. This treaty formalized the doctrine of "mutual assured destruction" (MAD) that had characterized the nuclear relationship between the superpowers since the Soviets achieved strategic nuclear parity in the late 1960s. The MAD doctrine asserted that neither superpower could attack the other with nuclear weapons without its rival launching a devastating counterstrike. Each, therefore, would achieve security by holding the population of the other hostage.

During the Carter administration, U.S. nuclear war strategy was reevaluated. Presidential Directive 59 (PD-59), which was signed by President Carter in July 1980, stressed that the United States had to be prepared to fight a protracted nuclear war lasting up to sixty days. The directive ordered nuclear planners to develop a wider range of limited nuclear war options and assigned a higher priority to destroying the Soviets' leadership, military capabilities, and economic base if nuclear war occurred. It also called for an improvement of U.S. command, control, and communications to ensure that the president and other top leaders could direct a protracted nuclear war effectively.[123] Critics of PD-59 charged that U.S. officials had made nuclear war more likely by promoting the perceptions that a nuclear war could be fought like any other war and that nuclear destruction could be limited to an acceptable degree. On the other hand, the Carter administration argued that preparing to fight a nuclear war was the best way to deter one.

Assuming the presidency in 1981, Reagan vowed to rebuild U.S. defenses, including nuclear forces. He contended that during the 1970s while the United States observed the letter and spirit of nuclear arms control agreements, the Soviets had continued to build nuclear weapons that would give them a first-strike advantage in a nuclear war. Reagan argued that this "window of vulnerability" in the U.S. deterrent could be closed either by building new U.S. weapons or by getting the Soviets to reduce and reconfigure their arsenals. This policy led to a new phase in arms control.

Nuclear Arms Control

Since the development of atomic weapons, presidents have tried to enhance U.S. and world security by controlling the development and deployment of nuclear arms. Arms control agreements have been an important measure of a president's diplomatic success, and, until Clinton, every president from Eisenhower on concluded some agreement with the Soviet Union/Russia or the international community that contributed to the control or reduction of nuclear weapons.

As commander in chief and possessor of the treaty negotiation power, presidents have dominated arms control policy. Congress has tried to goad the president into action by, for example, creating the Arms Control and Disarmament Agency in 1961.[124] However, the president has general control over the initiation and oversight of arms control negotiations. During the cold war, arms control agreements were perceived to be among the most important agreements made by the president, and they generally were concluded as treaties. The Senate usually has approved arms control treaties, but its assent has not been automatic. Three nuclear arms control treaties have remained unapproved: the 1974 Threshold Nuclear Test Ban Treaty, the 1976 Peaceful Nuclear Explosions Treaty, and the 1979 Strategic Arms Limitation Talks Treaty (SALT II).

Presidents may choose to avoid the Senate treaty ratification process, however, by concluding arms control accords in the form of executive agreements, as did President Nixon in 1972 when he signed the SALT I Interim Offensive Arms Agreement, which imposed limitations on the strategic nuclear arsenals of both superpowers. Presidents also may choose to abide by an arms control treaty that the Senate has refused to ratify. President Carter announced in 1980 that the United States would not violate the provisions of the unratified SALT II treaty if the Soviet Union also did not violate it. President Reagan continued Carter's policy of observing SALT II until late 1986 when the administration announced that because of Soviet violations the United States would no longer consider itself bound by the treaty. However, Congress continued to abide by its limits through its appropriations control over weapons development and deployment.

A major shift in arms control policy was initiated by the Reagan administration in 1982. Critics of earlier arms control had argued that agreements limiting the growth of arsenals generally had favored the Soviet Union, which was building massive, multiple warhead rockets. These rockets could deliver a devastating first strike. In conjunction with a weapons modernization program, the Reagan administration announced a new negotiating goal of arms *reductions* to eliminate the Soviet advantage. Because the Soviets would resist any such measure, many observers dismissed this as a ploy by Reagan to avoid all arms negotiations while also shifting the responsibility for stalemate onto the Soviets. Arms talks on this principle did stall during Reagan's first term. However, the end result, driven in part by the political revolutions in the Soviet Union and the Warsaw Pact countries, was four treaties, concluded between 1987 and 1993, that reduced nuclear and conventional arms. Each required the Soviet Union, and later Russia, to make disproportionately large arms cuts. *(See Table 14-1, p. right.)*

The first arms reduction agreement was the Intermediate Nuclear Forces (INF) Treaty, signed in 1987, which mandated the removal and destruction of most medium-range missiles in the European theater. This paved the way for progress on the first Strategic Arms Reduction Treaty (START I), which covered long-range missiles. Before that treaty was completed, President George H. W. Bush signed the Conventional Forces in Europe Treaty in 1990. This treaty addressed the large Soviet/Warsaw Pact advantage in conventional arms, which had to be reduced before any reductions in the U.S./NATO nuclear deterrent could be settled. START I was signed in 1991, but Senate ratification was delayed by the collapse of the Soviet Union. Protocols of agreement to abide by the treaty's terms had to be negotiated between the United States and the newly independent nuclear nations of the former Soviet Union such as Ukraine.[125] Before START I was ratified, President Bush

TABLE 14-1   **Major Arms Control Agreements**

President	Year signed	Agreement	Senate action	Provisions	Parties
Kennedy	1963	Partial Nuclear Test Ban Treaty	Ratified	Prohibits nuclear tests underwater, in the atmosphere, and in outer space	Multilateral
Johnson	1967	Outer Space Treaty	Ratified	Prohibits all military activity, including deployment of nuclear weapons, in outer space	Multilateral
Johnson	1968	Nuclear Nonproliferation Treaty	Ratified	Prohibits acquisition of nuclear weapons by nations not already possessing them and establishes international safeguards to prevent the spread of nuclear weapons capability	Multilateral
Nixon	1971	Sea Bed Treaty	Ratified	Prohibits deployment of nuclear weapons on the ocean floor	Multilateral
Nixon	1972	SALT I ABM Treaty	Ratified	Limits size and number (two) of anti-ballistic missile systems in U.S. and Soviet Union. A 1974 executive agreement reduced number of sites permitted to one	U.S.–Soviet Union
Nixon	1972	SALT I Interim Offensive Arms Agreement	Executive agreement; no action	Established a five-year freeze on number of intercontinental ballistic missiles and submarine-launched ballistic missiles deployed by U.S. and Soviet Union	U.S.–Soviet Union
Nixon	1974	Threshold Nuclear Test Ban Treaty	Unratified	Prohibits underground nuclear test explosions greater than 150 kilotons	U.S.–Soviet Union
Ford	1976	Peaceful Nuclear Explosions Treaty	Unratified	Prohibits nuclear explosions greater than 150 kilotons for excavation and other peaceful purposes	U.S.–Soviet Union
Carter	1979	SALT II Offensive Arms Treaty	Unratified	Limits numbers and types of strategic nuclear weapons	U.S.–Soviet Union
Reagan	1987	Intermediate Nuclear Forces Treaty	Ratified	Mandates the removal and destruction of all land-based nuclear missiles with ranges between 300 and 3,400 miles	U.S.–Soviet Union
Bush, G. H. W.	1991	Conventional Forces in Europe Treaty	Ratified	Reduced conventional weapons and troop strength of NATO and the former Warsaw Pact nations	Multilateral
Bush, G. H. W.	1991	Strategic Arms Reduction Treaty (START I)	Ratified	Mandates a one-third reduction in long-range nuclear warheads and restrictions on delivery systems	U.S.–former Soviet Union nations
Bush, G. H. W.	1993	Strategic Arms Reduction Treaty (START II)	Ratified	Sets a ceiling of 6,500 warheads per nation, requiring a two-thirds reduction in warheads and elimination of multiple warheads (MIRV's)	U.S.–Russia
Clinton	1997	Strategic Arms Reduction Treaty (START III)	Framework proposed, but treaty never negotiated because of failure to implement START II	Proposed destruction of and further reductions in strategic nuclear warheads	U.S.–Russia
Bush, G. W.	2002	Strategic Offensive Reductions Treaty (SORT)	Signed and awaiting ratification by both countries	Commits the United States and Russia to reducing their nuclear arsenals to 1,700 to 2,200 warheads	U.S.–Russia

initiated new force cuts and negotiations toward another reduction treaty (START II), which was signed by Bush and Russian president Boris Yeltsin in January 1993. Both treaties have been ratified.

Arms control efforts continued to concentrate on controlling the development and deployment of nuclear weapons by additional nations and the threat of regional nuclear conflicts. Without great success, Presidents Bush and Clinton worked independently and with the United Nations in trying to enforce the Nuclear Nonproliferation Treaty against Iraq, Iran, North Korea, and Pakistan.

The November 2001 summit meeting between President George W. Bush and Russian president Vladimir Putin signaled an end to the stalemate in U.S.-Russian relations that had marked the Clinton years. The two presidents took steps into a new era of friendly and cooperative relations. Without long and distrustful negotiations over strategic balances, and even without a formal agreement, Bush committed the United States to cutting the number of deployed nuclear warheads by two-thirds during the next decade. Such a step would reduce the U.S. arsenal to less than two thousand warheads (compared with more than ten thousand at the height of the cold war). The Russian president promised to do the same. Putin also reiterated his support for the U.S.-led war on terrorism.

Antiballistic Missile Defense Policy

On March 23, 1983, a proposal by Reagan sparked a significant change in U.S. nuclear strategy. In a nationally televised address he urged the scientific community to develop the technology for a space-based antiballistic missile defense that would some day make nuclear weapons "impotent and obsolete." [126] Implicit in the plan was a rejection of the status quo doctrine of mutual assured destruction. Reagan proposed to achieve security in the future not solely by deterring a Soviet nuclear attack, but also by being able to destroy most incoming Soviet missiles. The Reagan administration was hoping as well that the cost of trying to match U.S. development of strategic defenses would weaken the Soviets and move them toward arms reductions.

Although Reagan's optimistic vision led to an extensive research and development program (called the Strategic Defense Initiative by its supporters and "Star Wars" by its opponents), many scientists admitted that even if insulating the United States from a Soviet missile attack were possible, it would take decades of research and hundreds of billions of dollars to accomplish. (Indeed, by 2000 more than $60 billion had been appropriated.) By 1987, budget constraints and growing scientific skepticism that Reagan's "Peace Shield" could be built led to a reorientation of the plan toward the more attainable goal of using defensive weapons to enhance deterrence. [127] In 1991, with the success of the arms reduction talks (START) and with the collapse of the

Warsaw Pact and the Soviet Union, President George H. W. Bush and Congress again reoriented the development of missile defenses toward defending against a limited nuclear attack or an accidental launching. [128] In 1993 President Clinton pursued this aim with the intention of remaining within the terms of the 1972 Antiballistic Missile (ABM) Treaty, which limits the development and deployment of strategic missile defenses. His "Ballistic Missile Defense" program focused on the development of ground-based systems to be used as "theater" defenses for troops in the field. These systems also would be available to defend the home front. The roles switched after the 1994 midterm elections, with the newly Republican Congress pushing, against Clinton's resistance, for more money and accelerated development of strategic missile defenses.

The advocates of an unrestricted and accelerated program of development and deployment argue that the ABM treaty is outdated. It was designed for a bipolar world of hostile superpowers and a defense strategy of deterring a first strike through an assured and massive retaliation. Moreover, the ABM treaty may be void because one signatory, the Soviet Union, no longer exists. This argument is countered by one that points out that abandoning the treaty will foster another arms race, with Russia and China, and that the treaty ought to be renegotiated, particularly with Russia, before proceeding with the full development and deployment of a missile defense system.

Arguing that the measures would violate the ABM treaty and interfere with progress on arms reductions, Clinton resisted establishing a deadline for deployment. In 1999, however, he signed a bill calling for deployment of a national defense system as soon as possible. Although the bill did not set a specific deadline, it implicitly set aside concerns about the ABM Treaty.

President George W. Bush pushed from the start of his administration for accelerated development, testing, and deployment of a missile defense system. His policy was predicated on the ABM Treaty being outdated and void. While not opposed to pursuing an agreement with Russia on development and deployment of a missile defense system, he declared that he was ready to move ahead in the absence of such an agreement. [129] Democrats, particularly in the Senate, were prepared to cut funding and, in the absence of an agreement with Russia or congressional authorization, prohibit testing that might violate the ABM treaty. After the September 11 terrorist attack, both of these restrictions were dropped from the 2002 appropriations bill. During their summit meeting in November 2001, Bush failed to convince Russian president Putin to accept an interpretation of the ABM Treaty that would permit continued testing and development of missile defense systems, thereby deferring a controversial decision to abandon the treaty until those systems could be deployed. In December

2001 President Bush unilaterally withdrew the United States from the ABM accord.

PRESIDENT AS DEFENSE MANAGER

Before World War II, the isolation and size of the United States rendered it nearly immune to serious invasions by the armies of Europe. This geographic advantage as well as wary attitudes toward standing armies worked to keep the peacetime defense establishments small. When the United States found itself in a war, it mobilized troops and resources until the war was won, and then promptly demobilized its armed forces, returning the country to a state of peace and nonalignment.

After World War II, a national consensus developed that the United States should adopt an internationalist defense policy designed to contain the expansion of communism and limit the coercive potential of Soviet military strength. In pursuit of these regional objectives presidents signed various regional mutual security treaties, the most important of which was the North Atlantic Treaty, which committed the United States to the defense of Western Europe. The expanded defense commitments of the United States and its adversarial relationship with the Soviet Union required the United States to maintain a large peacetime military establishment for the first time in its history.

Although the Constitution gives Congress the authority to raise and equip an army and navy, much of the task of administering the defense bureaucracy and maintaining the nation's defenses in the post–World War II era has been delegated to or assumed by the president and the executive branch. The growth in the size and activities of the military and the perception that nuclear weapons and the cold war had created a condition of constant emergency combined to legitimize the president's role as defense manager. The president functioned not just as the commander in chief in wartime but also as the manager of the routine operations and preparations of the military in peacetime.

The Defense Establishment

The president is positioned at the top of a large and complex defense establishment. The Defense Department is made up of three military services and numerous agencies, offices, and unified multiservice commands, all under the leadership of the secretary of defense. Between the mid-1980s and the mid-1990s, the number of active duty military personnel was cut by about 25 percent, from 2 million to 1.5 million. The Defense Department employs more than 1 million civilians, about one-third of all federal civilian employees. In addition to the Defense Department, other executive departments and agencies have national security roles. The Central Intelligence Agency and the State Department provide intelligence about foreign governments and groups; the Federal Bureau of Investigation is responsible for combating domestic espionage; the Energy Department develops, tests, and produces nuclear warheads; and the Federal Emergency Management Agency (FEMA) oversees civil defense programs. The Defense Department, however, is the president's principal means of executing national security policy.

Department of Defense

Before 1947, the War and Navy Departments functioned independently of each other. Each had its own cabinet-level secretary, military command structure, and procurement operations. The National Security Act of 1947 created the post of secretary of defense, but its occupant was not given a staff or significant power over the individual services. The defense secretary functioned as the coordinator of the loose confederation of the Departments of the Army (the old War Department) and Navy, and the new Department of the Air Force. A 1949 amendment to the National Security Act created the Defense Department and recognized the primacy of the defense secretary, but in practice the individual services retained authority over their budgets and were administered autonomously by the service secretaries. The three services were not unified into one military organization, because reformers believed such an organization could more easily threaten civilian control of the military.

The Department of Defense Reorganization Act of 1958 placed the secretary of defense at the top of the military command structure, second only to the president. The act gave the secretary the means to centralize authority over defense operations and planning within the Office of the Secretary of Defense (OSD). In 1961 Robert S. McNamara became defense secretary with a mandate from President Kennedy to take control of the Defense Department. Under Kennedy and then Lyndon Johnson, McNamara greatly expanded the role of OSD and demanded unequivocal support from the military for the administration's programs.[130] He established the four major roles of the modern defense secretary: principal adviser to the president on defense issues, deputy commander in chief behind the president, director of the Defense Department and its huge military budget, and representative of the Defense Department before Congress and within the executive branch. This enlargement of the role of the secretary of defense gave presidents greater control over the defense establishment and assisted in the integration of defense and foreign policy. *(See "Department of Defense," p. 1184, in Chapter 25, Vol. II.)*

Joint Chiefs of Staff

The Joint Chiefs of Staff (JCS) is the body of military officers responsible for formulating unified military strategy and providing the president with advice on military matters. The JCS comprises a chairman appointed from any of the services, the chiefs of staff of the army and the air force, the

U.S. Secretary of Defense Donald H. Rumsfeld addresses the media at "Camp X-ray," a detention facility for the captured al Qaeda and Taliban terrorists suspected of planning the attacks on the World Trade Center and the Pentagon on September 11, 2001. At the camp, located on the U.S. naval base in Guantanamo Bay, Cuba, Rumsfeld announced that President George W. Bush's administration would not grant prisoner of war status to the detainees because they did not represent a recognized government and their terrorist acts violated internationally accepted laws of warfare.

chief of naval operations, and the commandant of the Marine Corps.

All five of the chiefs are appointed by the president with the advice and consent of the Senate. Since 1967, the chairman has been appointed for a two-year term, which can be renewed once by the president. The four service chiefs serve one nonrenewable four-year term.

A president can appoint several types of officers to the Joint Chiefs of Staff, depending on the president's conception of its advisory role. Most chiefs have been officers nominated by their services and accepted by presidents with little consideration of their political compatibility with the administration. The president may receive the goodwill of the services for endorsing their choices, but the president will have little political control over these nominees. Presidents also have looked beyond the service's candidates and chosen officers whose professional reputation has come to their attention. These appointments may displease the services, but they allow a president to choose an officer with experience and a temperament compatible with the administration. Finally, a few presidents have appointed close associates to the JCS. For example, Kennedy appointed Gen. Maxwell Taylor chairman of the JCS in 1962. Earlier, in 1961,

Taylor had been offered the post of director of the CIA, but he had chosen instead to become a special military representative to the White House. When the general was appointed chairman of the JCS, he quickly became a member of Kennedy's inner circle of advisers. The military usually dislikes such nominees, because their first priority is promoting the policies of the president rather than protecting their service's interests.[131]

In the decades after its creation in 1947, the JCS was criticized by many observers, including influential service chiefs and blue-ribbon panels commissioned to study its organization. These critics identified several problems with the JCS. First, the joint chiefs were given the conflicting tasks of being service chiefs responsible for the welfare of their services and members of the JCS responsible for developing unbiased policy plans and proposals for the president. But the chiefs seldom were able to do both and usually put service interests first. Second, because the entire JCS was considered to be the president's military adviser, the chiefs were compelled to develop consensus positions. As a result, their advice consisted of uncontroversial compromise recommendations of little value to the president. Third, although the JCS was supposed to develop military plans, it was outside the military's chain of command. Consequently, JCS budgetary, procurement, and strategy proposals often were unrelated to the needs of the commanders in chief (CINCs) of the multiservice operational commands in specified geographic areas.[132]

In 1986 President Reagan signed a bill reorganizing the JCS. The legislation was intended to improve interservice coordination and to create an organizational framework that would streamline the chain of command and minimize the influence of service parochialism on the military advice given to the president by the JCS. The reorganization bill sought to accomplish these goals by increasing the authority of the chairman of the JCS. By making the chairman the president's supreme military adviser, the bill's advocates theorized that the chairman would be free to develop advice and options independent of service interests. Among other things, the bill placed the JCS staff under the direct control of the chairman to bolster the chairman's bureaucratic resources and created the post of vice chairman. To ensure that the service chiefs would continue to have an advisory role, the chairman was required to forward their dissenting views to the president and secretary of defense upon the chiefs' request. The bill also enhanced the authority of the CINCs, giving them greater control over the training, supply, organization, and operations of their command.[133]

Homeland Security and the War on Terrorism

Rarely in the history of the United States has its own territory been one of the war fronts. The attack on Pearl Harbor, well off the mainland, put the West Coast on alert and led to extraordinary measures such as the internment of Japanese Americans. *(See* "Korematsu v. United States," *p. 784.)* During World War II, German submarines regularly cruised U.S. coastal waters, and espionage by communists during the cold war was a continuous concern. But outside of the nuclear stalemate of the cold war, imminent military threats against U.S. territory and civilians have been rare. Even attacks on U.S. citizens by international terrorists had been, in the main, overseas. The deaths of more than three thousand civilians in the terrorist attacks of September 11, 2001, clearly demonstrated the will and capacity of foreign terrorist organizations to carry their war on the United States to the U.S. proper. The fact that the terrorists who hijacked and crashed the four airliners—two into New York City's World Trade Center, one into the Pentagon, and one into a Pennsylvania field—trained for their attack while living in the United States, indicated that the war on terrorism would have a broad domestic front.

The relative safety of the U.S. home front had always allowed a fairly strict separation between the two principal and coercive functions of government, domestic police and national defense. The dangers of blending these executive powers were evident in President Nixon's broad claims of extralegal authority in the name of national security. Partly in response to Nixon's abuses, strict limits, more in line with ordinary police procedures, were placed on domestic surveillance and intelligence activities. Yet the 2001 attacks and threats of covert foreign aggression began to break down the distinction between policing and defending, because domestic law enforcement became an important element in national defense. This change was evident in the reorientation of the Federal Bureau of Investigation (FBI). The bureau had devoted its resources mainly to ordinary crime, leaving large-scale foreign threats to the CIA and the Department of Defense. But soon after the 2001 attacks, the FBI began to distribute some of its ordinary crime responsibilities to other agencies, such as the Drug Enforcement Agency (DEA) and the Bureau of Alcohol, Tobacco, and Firearms (ATF) and focus more of its resources instead on counterterrorism activities.[134]

Also in the aftermath of September 11, President George W. Bush and Attorney General John Ashcroft sought and received significant new powers of investigation. Although controversial, the U.S.A. Patriot Act (HR 3162) was passed and signed in late October 2001. It modified many laws, including the restrictive Foreign Intelligence Surveillance Act of 1978, and broadened the national government's powers: of surveillance, including wire tap warrants that cover individuals rather than single phones; of preventative detention of noncitizen suspects; of access to e-mail, voice mail, and other forms of electronic communication; and of search without prior notice. The law also facilitated greater sharing of confidential information from grand juries and financial institutions, and it mandated cooperation between the Justice Department and, for example, the CIA and the Department of Defense.

The complexity of a coordinated domestic counterterrorism effort—involving foreign intelligence, domestic police, disaster relief, disease control, medical facilities, and the myriad state and federal agencies—was recognized by President Bush when he created, by executive order (No. 13228), a new Office of Homeland Security and made the directorship of this office a cabinet-level post. The president appointed the former governor of Pennsylvania Thomas J. Ridge to head the new office. According to the president's order, this office would be responsible for developing "a comprehensive national strategy to secure the United States from terrorist threats or attacks" and for coordinating "the executive branch's efforts to detect, prepare for, prevent, protect against, respond to, and recover from terrorist attacks within the United States."

President Bush's order also created a Homeland Security Council. Similar to the National Security Council, it was intended to advise the president on policy and help coordinate the approximately forty agencies working in the area of domestic security and emergencies. The council members included the president and vice president, the attorney general, the secretaries of defense, health and human services, transportation, and Treasury, and the directors of the FBI, the CIA, and the Federal Emergency Management Agency.

In June 2002, in response to congressional initiatives, President Bush proposed the formation of a Department of Homeland Security (DHS). The creation of the department in late 2002 marked the most significant reorganization of government agencies since the National Security Act of 1947. It placed twenty-two previously independent agencies under the jurisdiction of one cabinet department, including the Citizenship and Immigration Services agency (formerly Immigration and Naturalization Service), Coast Guard, FEMA, and Secret Service. Making homeland security part of the cabinet would ensure both executive and legislative oversight, albeit with sometimes competing visions of the department's responsibilities. *(See box, Department of Homeland Security, p. 1197, in Chapter 25, Vol. II.)*

President Truman pins a medal on Gen. Douglas MacArthur at their October 15, 1950, meeting on Wake Island. Truman called the meeting to discuss MacArthur's strategy in Korea. Six months later, Truman would fire MacArthur for insubordination.

Presidential Control of the Military

Despite the enhanced authority of the civilian leadership of the Defense Department since 1947, presidents have not dominated the military. Like any government organization, the military has its own organizational objectives and is capable of resisting policies it believes are against its interests. Military leaders have been particularly successful in cultivating friends in Congress who pressure the administration to accept the military's perspective on given issues.

In addition to the military's political clout, presidential control of the armed forces is limited by the president's dependence on the military for evaluations of the nation's military capabilities. Civilian advisers can offer opinions on many military problems, but their assessments must depend on the factual information supplied by the military. Moreover, estimates of the force requirements and prospects for success of a given combat operation can only be supplied by the military.[135] The president may be confident that a particular military operation is justified on moral and political grounds, but the president rarely will order the operation if the military is pessimistic about its chances for success. Presidents also depend on the military to implement their military orders. Whereas presidential initiatives in areas such as diplomacy can be accomplished through several channels, only the military can carry out a combat operation.

Because of the political leverage of the armed services and their monopoly on military information and resources, the White House is forced to bargain with the services for cooperation in implementing its programs. Presidents, however, are not always willing and able to compromise with the military. For those presidents who want to reduce their dependence on military sources of defense information and to overcome military opposition to their orders and plans,

several options are available. They can support defense reorganizations, bring a military officer into the White House as an adviser, rely on the secretary of defense and other civilian advisers for military advice, give the Office of Management and Budget (OMB) greater authority over defense spending, and appoint presidential commissions to study defense problems.[136]

Presidents also can exercise control of the military through their appointments of military officers. Congress establishes the ranks to which officers can be promoted, and the Senate confirms presidential appointees, but the power to assign military officers to posts, including the Joint Chiefs of Staff, gives presidents the opportunity to shape the leadership of the military. Moreover, one of the most important instruments of presidential control is the commander in chief's prerogative in wartime to dismiss members of the military who are incompetent or insubordinate. *(See box, Truman and General MacArthur, right.)*

Defense Budget

A frustrating and complicated aspect of presidential defense management is the defense budget. Every year the executive branch must submit to Congress a defense budget, which proposes both the general defense spending level and the specific military programs on which funds will be spent. The general spending level is a highly visible political issue on which many Americans have an opinion—even presidential candidates feel compelled to announce their intentions. The specifics determine force structure and defense strategy, and they are decided through a complicated process of conflict and compromise between the president, Congress, the Defense Department's civilian leadership, and the individual armed services, all under the lobbying pressure of defense contractors and public interest groups.

The amount of money devoted to the defense budget and its distribution among services and weapons systems not only determine the defense policy and capabilities of the United States. They also create a backdrop for U.S. international relations. Adversaries and allies alike scrutinize the defense budget for clues about U.S. global intentions. Increases, decreases, and shifts in defense spending, particularly for items such as naval vessels and aircraft, indicate to foreign governments the nation's specific and general capabilities to project force in the world. Particularly in the late 1980s and 1990s, when large budget deficits were common, all parties in the budget process fought over the redistribution of scarce resources and the redefinition of strategic needs.

TRUMAN AND GENERAL MACARTHUR

The most famous clash between a president and a member of the armed forces was Harry S. Truman's dispute with Gen. Douglas MacArthur during the Korean War. The conflict led to Truman's dramatic firing of MacArthur and tested the principle of presidential control of the military.

Few military leaders in the history of the United States were as respected and revered by the American public as General MacArthur was in the early stages of the Korean War. He had been a decorated hero of World War I, the triumphant commander of U.S. forces in the Pacific in World War II, and the successful military governor of Japan, overseeing that nation's transformation into a modern democratic state. When the Korean War broke out, he was made supreme commander of the UN forces in Korea. His landing at Inchon behind North Korean lines in September 1950 reversed the tide of the war and reinforced his reputation as a tactical genius. Many Americans and members of Congress saw MacArthur as indispensable to the success of the Korean War effort. Republican leaders regarded the eloquent and handsome general as a possible candidate in a future presidential election.

The conflict between Truman and MacArthur arose when they disagreed about the goals to be pursued in the Korean War. When Truman sent forces to Korea in June 1950, he intended to drive the North Korean forces out of South Korea and reestablish a secure border at the thirty-eighth parallel. Once the military campaign succeeded, Truman and his advisers ordered MacArthur to cross into North Korea and attempt to unify the nation.[1] Concerned about provoking Communist China, Truman prohibited MacArthur from attacking North Korean bases in China.

MacArthur, however, envisioned a grand Asian strategy in which the United States would seek to overthrow the government of Communist China. At the least, MacArthur wanted the latitude to bomb North Korean sanctuaries and supply lines inside China. During the fall of 1950, he openly criticized Truman's policies and encouraged his supporters in Congress to press the administration to give him discretion to widen the war.

When in November 1950 Communist China entered the war and pushed U.S. forces back across the thirty-eighth parallel, MacArthur blamed his retreat on Truman's constraints. Truman responded with a presidential directive on December 5 that instructed overseas military commanders and diplomats to clear all public statements with Washington. Unable to accept either Truman's strategy or Gen. Matthew Ridgeway's remarkable progress on the battlefield, MacArthur released a press statement that blamed Truman for the "savage slaughter of Americans."[2]

Later, MacArthur tried to undercut Truman's efforts to arrange cease-fire negotiations with the Chinese by issuing a proclamation that insulted the Communist Chinese government and suggested that the United States might "depart from its tolerant efforts to contain the war to the area of Korea." MacArthur failed to explain or apologize for the communiqué. On April 5, House minority leader Joseph Martin, R-Mass., a MacArthur ally, read a letter from the general on the floor of the House. "If we lose the war to Communism in Asia, the fall of Europe is inevitable. . . . There is no substitute for victory." With that, Truman found he could no longer tolerate MacArthur's insubordination, and it was announced at a news conference at one o'clock in the morning on April 11 that the president was relieving MacArthur of his command.[3]

Truman's public approval ratings, as measured by the Gallup organization, slipped from an abysmal 28 percent in late March to just 24 percent after he fired MacArthur. Sixty-one percent of Americans disapproved of the way the president was doing his job. Impeachment became a frequent topic of conversation as members of Congress accused the president and his top advisers of appeasing communism or even falling under the influence of communist agents.[4] MacArthur's welcome home as a war hero intensified the pressure on the Truman administration. The general delivered an emotional farewell address before Congress on April 19 and received a New York City parade attended by an estimated seven million people.

The Truman administration, however, was able to focus attention on the general's insubordination and the constitutional principle of civilian control of the armed forces. At the joint Senate Foreign Relations and Armed Services Committees' hearings on MacArthur's firing and Korean War strategy, administration officials united behind the president in denouncing MacArthur's actions and endorsing military restraint in Korea. Most important, Truman received the support of the military. Chairman of the Joint Chiefs of Staff Gen. Omar Bradley told the committees that MacArthur's Korean strategy "would involve us in the wrong war, at the wrong place, at the wrong time, and with the wrong enemy."[5] Talk of impeachment subsided, and Congress took no action against the president.

1. John Spanier, *American Foreign Policy Since World War II,* 11th ed. (Washington, D.C.: CQ Press, 1988), 76.
2. David M. McCullough, *Truman* (New York: Simon and Schuster, 1992), 834–835.
3. Ibid., 836–843.
4. James A. Nathan and James K. Oliver, *United States Foreign Policy and World Order,* 2d ed. (Boston: Little, Brown, 1981), 149.
5. McCullough, *Truman,* 853–854.

In recent years, the debate over the defense budget has revolved around two general quandaries. One is the appropriate size of the standing armed forces in the post–cold war world. Some argue that the United States must be prepared to fight two major conflicts simultaneously. Indeed, they point out that given the many areas of potential conflict such as the Korean peninsula, Iraq, Taiwan, and Israel, such a scenario is more than plausible. Moreover, if the country is prepared for only one major conflict, it would resist engaging in any one conflict, because that would leave it unable to respond to another crisis. Those on the other side argue that budget realities, especially in the post–cold war circumstances, require cuts in forces. Both sides have had to contend with how to account for the increasing expenditures on peacekeeping operations. Another debate is over the distribution of available defense dollars. The poor state of current military readiness, including the retention of experienced personnel and the maintenance of equipment, was a regular theme in the criticism of Clinton's diversion of forces and funds for peacekeeping. President George W. Bush's secretary of defense, Donald H. Rumsfeld, argued instead for shifting resources, and even cutting active personnel, for the sake of the modernization of weaponry and the development of a new generation of high-tech weapons. All of these arguments were muted in the immediate aftermath of the September 11, 2001, terrorist bombing attacks. To fund the war on terrorism, Congress increased spending in the fiscal 2002 defense appropriations bill by more than $30 billion, and President Bush's 2003 budget proposal requested a similar increase.

The defense budget has enormous consequences for the U.S. economy. Despite the deep cuts of the 1990s, the current defense budget of more than $300 billion is the largest part of the discretionary budget—the part of the national budget that can be cut or shifted from year to year. (See Chapter 16, Chief Economist.) Defense spending affects the economy in particular ways as well. Although most economists believe the economy is better stimulated by tax cuts than increased military expenditures, boosting defense spending can increase the demand for goods and services, which, in turn, can reduce unemployment and lift the country out of a depression or recession. Defense spending can spur technological development with various commercial applications and is essential to the economies of particular regions.

Defense Budget Process

The annual defense budget, a large and complex document, is prepared with the help of many bureaucratic entities, including the National Security Council, OMB, and various Defense Department agencies. About a year and a half before a fiscal year begins, the defense secretary issues a study assessing military threats and defines departmental goals and spending priorities. Using this outline, the military services develop budget requests. These requests are reviewed and amended by the defense secretary and OMB, who reevaluate them in the context of defense and nondefense spending priorities. The resulting comprehensive defense budget is then submitted to Congress.[137]

Presidential participation in the defense budget process is limited by the size and complexity of the budget. Even if a president has had executive branch experience with the defense budget, the many demands of the presidency would not allow its occupant to become immersed in the details. The president therefore must rely heavily on career military officers and Defense Department bureaucrats familiar with the process.

Nevertheless, presidents, more than any other individual or groups, influence the general outlines of the defense budget, because their assessments of U.S. military capabilities, the threats to U.S. national security, and understandings

of military readiness carry great weight in any debate. Presidents cannot be expected to review every item in the defense budget, but they do determine the approximate level of defense spending, and their general defense policy affects which types of programs will be emphasized. Although a president rarely will participate in discussions of how much to pay privates, a presidential policy of improving the quality of recruits will guide those discussions.

Besides establishing a general national security policy, presidents function as the final arbiter of disputes between executive departments and agencies about specific defense budget decisions. OMB and the Defense Department often disagree on budget issues, because OMB's mission of overseeing spending often clashes with Defense's mission of enhancing national security. Early in his term, President Reagan had to choose between the conflicting defense budget recommendations of defense secretary Caspar Weinberger, who had been charged with building up the nation's defenses, and OMB director David Stockman, who had been given the task of reducing federal spending. Reagan sided with Weinberger, thus subordinating budget reduction to the defense buildup.[138]

After World War II, Congress usually gave presidents most of the funds they requested for defense. Yet especially since the end of the cold war, Congress has scrutinized the defense budget more carefully, though always with an eye toward protecting specific projects that directly benefit states and congressional districts. This sort of parochialism leads to frequent and important disputes over force structure as particular weapons systems are defended against the president's larger policy changes. In particular, Congress had made military bases, large sources of local employment and spending, all but immune to budget cuts. Yet in 1988, under the pressure of chronic budget deficits, Congress and the president initiated a complex base closure process that removed both Congress and the president from specific choices. Under the new procedure, an independent commission studies the utility of the various bases and submits a list of recommended closings. Congress is allowed to vote only on the list as a whole, and its decision is subject to a presidential veto. Since this procedure was initiated, Congress has decisively defeated all attempts to reject the commission's recommendations. In 1996, however, President Clinton violated the spirit of the policy and procedure. He picked two bases off the approved closure list and decided instead to privatize their operations. The two bases were located in key electoral states, Texas and California. Many critics claimed that the president had undermined the integrity of this valuable process by putting his reelection interests ahead of the public good. There were in fact no more rounds of base closings during Clinton's second term, and Congress rejected President George W. Bush's request for another round in 2003. In 2005 the commission recommended closing an additional thirty-three bases, which would provide an estimated annual savings of $5 billion. By early 2007, however, Congress had still not approved funding to begin the closure process.

Overall, the executive branch has retained the initiative in the defense budget process, but Congress has challenged the president on funding for individual weapons systems and defense programs such as the MX missile. In addition, the creation of the Congressional Budget Office in 1974 and the expansion of congressional committee staffs that deal with the defense budget have enhanced Congress's ability to detect waste and fraud in the spending programs that are approved.[139]

Weapons Development and Procurement

Presidents and their scientific and military advisers must choose from a wide variety of options which weapons systems to develop and build. Many different agencies and offices within the Pentagon engage in weapons research, development, and acquisition. In 1986 Congress, in an attempt to centralize oversight and direction of the huge procurement bureaucracy, enacted laws creating the office of under secretary of defense for acquisition and designating the under secretary as the Pentagon's third-ranking official.

Weapons procurement decisions seldom are based solely on rational calculations of how a particular weapons system might contribute to national security. The individual services press presidents and top defense officials to adopt various procurement strategies. The U.S. nuclear triad—the policy of deploying some nuclear weapons on land-based missiles, others on bombers, and the rest on submarines and surface ships—arose in part from the individual services' demands for a nuclear mission. Even groups within the services will maneuver to protect their share of their service's procurement funds.

Technological advances also drive weapons procurement. Since the end of World War II, the defense establishment has operated under the premise that the quality of weapons is more important than their quantity. Presidents must serve as a mediator between competing factions in the procurement process and attempt to develop a mix of weapons that best meets the needs of national security at an affordable cost.

Presidents seldom become personally involved in minor procurement matters, but they must become involved in decisions with significant effects on defense policy. For example, in the early 1980s Reagan's belief that U.S. strategic nuclear forces were threatened by a window of vulnerability led to the deployment of the MX missile and a revival of the B-1 bomber project, which had been scrapped under Carter.

Weapons systems often take more than a decade to move from conception to deployment and may be conceived under one president, tested under another, and mass-produced under a third. Presidents have been reluctant to cancel weapons systems that have reached the production stage because of the time and money already spent on their development. In addition, the longer a weapons program has been around, the more likely it has developed constituencies in the defense bureaucracy and Congress that will resist its cancellation. President Carter's decision not to build the B-1 bomber in 1977 and Secretary of Defense Richard B. Cheney's 1991 decision to cancel the A-12 attack plane are rare examples of executive branch cuts after a weapon was ready for production.

Ultimately, presidents must secure congressional approval for appropriations to pay for the projects they favor. Not only must they contend with members of Congress who do not share their views of procurement priorities, but they also must deal with lawmakers who defend weapons because they happen to be built in their home states and districts.

Budget and Procurement Inefficiency

Distrust of special interests, congressional parochialism, and the huge defense bureaucracy have fed general and long-standing suspicions that the defense budget is filled with fraud and waste. Charges of misuse of defense dollars increased during the Reagan administration defense buildup, giving rise to many anecdotes suggesting that there were serious problems with defense procurement and budgeting procedures. For example, it was reported that military services were purchasing a twelve-cent Allen wrench for $9,606 and toilet seats for $640. Many such horror stories are based on a misunderstanding. To simplify accounting, contractors will distribute their total cost of development and production for an entire system equally across every item within that system. Thus the total cost of, for example, a self-contained toilet for a transport plane would be distributed equally across all parts, including the relatively inexpensive toilet seat. So the "price" of the seat only seems to be high.[140] The problems of procurement lie elsewhere.

Although waste occurs in every government department and agency, several characteristics of the Defense Department have made its problem particularly acute. The enormous size of the defense budget not only creates more opportunities for waste, but also makes central control of its details nearly impossible.[141] Each service, moreover, tends to promote its interests at the expense of the others and often avoids consulting with the other services when developing budget and procurement proposals. Neither the president, the secretary of defense, OMB, nor Congress can assess the worthiness of every one, or even most, of the thousands of line items that make up the defense budget.

In addition, the scope and complexity of weapons development and procurement increase the opportunities for outright fraud. In the late 1980s, several major defense contractors were found guilty of price gouging, bribery, and tax fraud. In June 1988 the Justice Department disclosed evidence of a procurement scandal, involving dozens of defense contracts costing tens of billions of dollars, that threatened to dwarf all previous defense budget scandals.

In response to procurement waste and scandals, a study of procurement reform was commissioned in 1990. The 1993 commission report was incorporated into Vice President Al Gore's general study of government efficiency, the National Performance Review. The major recommendations for streamlining military procurement were part of legislation passed in 1994. Among other changes, the legislation reduced the regulatory requirements for smaller contracts and allowed many contracts with specific providers to be replaced by off-the-shelf purchases from the best available sources.

A crucial problem is how the Defense Department makes and tracks payments. To begin with, the flow of money is staggering. The Defense Department pays out more than $35 million an hour in payroll alone. Added to that are the hundreds of billions of dollars that flow each year through the department and out to private contractors. In 1995 investigations by the General Accounting Office and the Defense Department's comptroller, John J. Hamre, revealed that the department's antiquated accounting sys-

tems could not keep track of who had paid whom and for what. At least $15 billion spent during the preceding decade could not be accounted for. One official estimated that each year the department overpays contractors by at least $500 million. Although an overhaul of the system was begun in 1995, the procurement system cannot be shut down for repairs. The department's comptroller compared any attempt at reform to "changing a tire on a car while driving 60 miles an hour." [142]

Military Personnel Policy

Although the Constitution charges Congress with the responsibility to "make rules for the government and regulation" of the army and navy, the executive branch has substantial authority in military personnel policy. Much of this authority has been delegated to the executive branch by Congress, but authority also has been claimed by presidents under the commander-in-chief power to make regulations that do not conflict with congressional statutes. As a result, the laws passed by Congress governing the armed forces have been supplemented by a body of executive rules and regulations.[143]

Presidents usually take the initiative in proposing changes in the size of the armed forces, the methods by which the ranks are filled, and where U.S. forces will be stationed. Ultimate authority for raising an army resides in Congress, but legislators often accept presidential actions and recommendations on these issues.

Recruitment and the Draft

Conscription was not used in the United States until the Civil War. The 1863 Enrollment Act set up a draft system run by the War Department and administered by military officers. During World War I, Congress again authorized conscription to fulfill troop goals. The 1917 Selective Service Act was challenged in the courts, but the Supreme Court upheld Congress's authority to draft Americans in the *Selective Draft Law Cases.* The Court held that military service was one of a citizen's duties in a "just government."

Not until 1940, however, did Congress pass a draft bill while the nation was at peace. Although the United States had not yet become involved in World War II, President Franklin Roosevelt urged Congress to adopt the measure. In the summer of 1941, with the threat of war looming larger, Roosevelt had a difficult fight before winning enactment of amend-

Homosexuality and Military Service

Attempting to fulfill a campaign pledge, President Bill Clinton stirred up a political storm in 1993 by announcing his determination to end the ban on homosexuals in the armed services. The military's policy was to discharge anyone who engaged in homosexual activities or even disclosed his or her homosexual orientation. Moreover, the military actively sought to ferret out and investigate homosexuals. During the decade leading up to 1993, the armed services had discharged more than fourteen thousand servicemen and women under this policy.[1]

Clinton had the authority to change this policy. The president, as commander in chief, has the constitutional power to "make Rules for the Government and Regulation of the land and naval Forces" as long as these rules do not conflict with congressional decisions. Nevertheless, the president's decision to end the ban was greeted with strong resistance especially from prominent members of the defense establishment, including the Joint Chiefs of Staff and Georgia senator Sam Nunn, a leading congressional authority on defense and a member of the president's party. The criticism may have been amplified by Clinton's lack of credibility in military matters; it was generally known that he had avoided military service during the Vietnam War.

Under a threat from Congress to override the president by writing a ban on homosexual orientation into law, President Clinton settled on a compromise policy known as "don't ask, don't tell." The ban on homosexual conduct was retained, but recruits would no longer be asked about their sexual orientation, and individuals were to keep their orientation to themselves. Investigations would be initiated only by senior officers with reasonable cause to suspect a violation of the ban. Congress then wrote the ban on homosexual conduct into law. These modest changes fell far short of President Clinton's original intentions. In 1995 a federal district court struck down the compromise policy as an unconstitutional infringement of free speech. This ruling was overturned on appeal. The Supreme Court has yet to rule on this issue. As for President Clinton, both his original policy and his handling of the criticism damaged his reputation and political influence.

1. *CQ Almanac, 1992* (Washington, D.C.: Congressional Quarterly, 1993), 454.

ments that widened the draft. The measure was passed in the House by just one vote. Although earlier drafts had been administered by the War Department, the Selective Training and Service Act of 1940 established an independent Selective Service System, headed by a presidential appointee, to oversee the draft.

In 1947 Congress followed President Truman's recommendation to allow the 1940 draft act to expire. A year later when enlistments failed to meet troop needs, Truman proposed a renewal of the draft and universal military training. Truman's plan would have required all physically and mentally able men to receive one year of military training and serve six months in the reserves. Congress rejected universal military training but passed the Selective Service Act of 1948, which renewed the peacetime draft.

After the 1973 signing of the Paris peace accords, ending U.S. involvement in the Vietnam War, Congress followed the recommendation of President Nixon and finally allowed the draft to expire. This was the first step toward an all-volunteer armed forces, an idea that had been under study since 1969. Military pay was raised dramatically to attract volunteers. Since 1973, the armed services have succeeded in meeting their personnel requirements.

In 1980, amid the international tension created in late 1979 by the takeover of the U.S. embassy in Tehran and the invasion of Afghanistan by the Soviet Union, Jimmy Carter asked Congress to reinstitute draft registration, a step intended to reduce the time required to bring draftees into the armed services after a mobilization. The measure that Congress approved provided only for registration and required further authorization from Congress before anyone could be called up for service.[144] Although Reagan opposed draft registration during the 1980 presidential campaign, he ordered its continuation in January 1982. Since then, the few attempts to eliminate funding for registration have failed. By 2007, with military action ongoing in Iraq, the armed services relaxed some requirements to continue to meet recruitment goals.

Peacetime Military Deployments

Presidents have used the commander-in-chief power to justify unilateral decisions on relocating armed forces, but they have generally respected the laws limiting their freedom to redeploy armed forces in peacetime.[145] In 1940 Congress attached a proviso to the Selective Training and Service Act that prohibited troops drafted under the act from being used outside the Western Hemisphere. Franklin Roosevelt accepted this limitation, although he maintained that Iceland was part of the Western Hemisphere and sent troops there in 1941.

A more recent example of a congressional limit on troop deployments occurred in 1982. In that year, Congress attached to a defense appropriations bill an amendment limiting the number of active-duty U.S. military personnel stationed in Europe to 315,000. The Reagan administration opposed the limit, arguing that increases in U.S. troop strength in Europe might be required by changes in the military balance between NATO and the Soviet Union and its allies. Despite the administration's objections, defense secretary Caspar Weinberger assured Congress that the troop ceiling would be observed. The amendment included a provision that allowed the president to waive the troop limit if the president certified that "overriding national security requirements" made such action necessary. By including this provision, Congress was recognizing that the purpose of peacetime military deployments is to deter war and that the president as commander in chief should have wide authority to redeploy troops for that purpose.

If a president does refuse to observe limitations that Congress has placed on peacetime troop deployments, Congress could cut off funds for the base where the troops were stationed or for the supplies needed to sustain the troops. During the Clinton presidency, Congress considered a number of proposals to limit the president's capacity to deploy U.S. forces in, for example, Bosnia, Haiti, and any UN peacekeeping mission without specific congressional authorization.

PRESIDENTIAL WARTIME EMERGENCY POWERS

In 1810, after Thomas Jefferson had left the presidency, he wrote:

> A strict observation of the written laws is doubtless *one* of the high duties of a good citizen, but it is not the *highest*. The law of necessity, of self-preservation, of saving our country when in danger, are of higher obligation. To lose our country by a scrupulous adherence to written law would be to lose the law itself, with life, liberty, property . . . thus absurdly sacrificing the end to the means.[146]

Jefferson maintained that such acts of self-preservation, although justified, were strictly illegal and in no way authorized by the Constitution. Later presidents have derived their emergency powers from a broad reading of constitutional authority and have claimed the authority to violate parts of the Constitution to ensure the security of the nation.

When it is evident that conditions of national peril exist, Congress and the American public turn to the president for leadership. Under such conditions Lincoln and Franklin Roosevelt stretched, reinterpreted, and in some cases brazenly violated the Constitution in the name of national security. Their claims to an inherent executive power to safeguard the nation were accepted because the American people generally agreed with their assessment of

GOVERNING CONQUERED TERRITORY

On many occasions U.S. military forces have occupied enemy territory during hostilities. Presidential authority to administer a recently occupied territory through the armed forces is nearly absolute; neither the Constitution of the United States nor the former laws of a conquered nation constrain the president. Moreover, several hundred Supreme Court cases have upheld the president's authority to function as a dictator over occupied territory subject only to the "laws of war."[1] Presidents and their appointed military representatives may set up new government institutions, make laws by decree, establish a court system, collect taxes, or do anything else they believe necessary to administer the conquered area. Presidential rule over occupied territory lasts until it is annexed to the United States or a treaty is concluded that transfers power back to a local government. The president may not, however, unilaterally annex acquired territory. Article IV of the Constitution grants Congress the power to "dispose of and make all needful Rules and Regulations respecting the Territory or other Property belonging to the United States." Therefore, Congress must approve a treaty of cession or pass legislation annexing the territory before it can become part of the United States.[2]

1. Clinton Rossiter, *The Supreme Court and the Commander in Chief* (Ithaca: Cornell University Press, 1976), 122–123.
2. Joseph E. Kallenbach, *The American Chief Executive: The Presidency and the Governorship* (New York: Harper and Row, 1966), 541.

the gravity of the emergency at hand.[147] Presidential assertions of an inherent executive power based on a doubtful claim of national emergency, however, will likely fail the test of public and judicial scrutiny. President Nixon was not able to convince the American people or the courts that his administration's use of wiretaps and break-ins was justified by dire threats to national security.

Nowhere does the Constitution mention presidential emergency powers, but the courts often have been sympathetic to exercises of emergency power by presidents in wartime, especially when action is taken with the cooperation of Congress. Yet this approval has not been automatic, especially when the rights and property of U.S. citizens are involved. Total war in any age requires sacrifices from civilians and security measures at home, but a wartime emergency does not give the president unrestrained freedom to violate the rights of Americans.

Martial Law and Civil Rights

The most extreme wartime emergency measure a president may take is a declaration of martial law. Under such a declaration, ordinary law and judicial process are temporarily replaced by military rule. Substitution of military for civilian authority may be general or confined to a region. In addition, it may be absolute, or it may apply only to a specific civil function by the military. Even cases of limited martial law, however, entail some curbing of individual rights.

The Constitution does not provide for a power to declare martial law, although it does mention the suspension of *habeas corpus* under Article I, which outlines Congress's powers. The declaration of martial law, however, is usually presumed to be a presidential function flowing from the president's powers to command the armed forces and execute the laws. Because there is no specific constitutional basis for martial law, presidents must justify their decision to proclaim it on the grounds that protecting the welfare and security of the nation requires them to govern through military force rather than ordinary civil institutions and laws.

No president has ever declared a condition of absolute martial law that applied to the entire country. Moreover, not since President Lincoln placed several areas of the nation under martial law during the Civil War has any president directly proclaimed martial law on behalf of the national government. Martial law has been declared, however, by presidential agents or military officers, often with the explicit or implied approval of the president. For example, Gen. Andrew Jackson declared martial law in New Orleans before his battle with the British there in 1814; the commander of federal troops sent to Idaho in 1899 to quell labor unrest declared martial law with President McKinley's approval; and after the Japanese attack on Pearl Harbor on December 7, 1941, the territorial governor of Hawaii declared martial law on the islands with the support of Franklin Roosevelt.[148]

Although the courts may reject the president's assessment of the necessity of martial law, historically they have done so only after the emergency has passed. In 1866 the Supreme Court ruled in *Ex parte Milligan* that Lincoln's suspension of the civil court system in Indiana during the Civil War was illegal.[149] Similarly, in 1946 the Court declared in *Duncan v. Kahanamoku* that the establishment of martial law during World War II in Hawaii by the governor with President Roosevelt's approval had been unlawful.[150] Yet neither decision had any effect on either president's ability to abrogate civil liberties during the wars.

Suspension of Habeas Corpus

The only emergency power mentioned in the Constitution is the crucial provision for the suspension of the writ of *habeas corpus*—the right of prisoners to have the legality of their detention reviewed by the courts and to be released upon the court's orders. The Constitution states: "The Privilege of the Writ of Habeas Corpus shall not be suspended, unless when in Cases of Rebellion or Invasion the public Safety may require it." The Framers did not, however, specify which branch had this authority, although their placement of it in Article I has led many legal scholars, judges, and legislators to argue that it was intended as a congressional power.

The issue of presidential suspension of *habeas corpus* arose most dramatically during the Civil War. In response to sabotage by Confederate sympathizers, President Lincoln ordered in the spring of 1861 that *habeas corpus* be suspended along the route between Washington and Philadelphia. Lincoln believed this and other emergency measures were essential to the survival of the Union. On May 25, John Merryman, a prominent Maryland citizen who had been involved in secessionist activities in that state, was arrested and detained by military authorities. Merryman immediately appealed to Chief Justice Roger Taney for a writ of *habeas corpus*. Taney reviewed the case and ordered the army to release Merryman, but Lincoln defiantly refused to permit his release. Taney denounced Lincoln's action and wrote an opinion asserting that the Constitution had conferred authority to suspend the writ on Congress, not the president. Lincoln maintained that since the suspension of *habeas corpus* was an emergency measure and emergencies could occur when Congress was out of session—as it had been in this case—presidents must have authority to suspend the writ unilaterally.

The conflict between the president and the chief justice showed that a president willing to defy legal procedures during a genuine crisis that was widely recognized as such could suspend *habeas corpus* regardless of whether the president has the constitutional authority to do so. Presidential scholar Clinton Rossiter remarked,

> The one great precedent is what Lincoln did, not what Taney said. Future Presidents will know where to look for historical support. So long as public opinion sustains the President, as a sufficient amount of it sustained Lincoln in his shadowy tilt with Taney and throughout the rest of the war, he has nothing to fear from the displeasure of the courts. . . . The law of the Constitution, as it actually exists, must be considered to read that in a condition of martial necessity the President has the power to suspend the privilege of the writ of habeas corpus.[151]

Trial of Civilians by Military Courts

In addition to suspending *habeas corpus,* President Lincoln also declared that for some crimes civilians could be tried by military courts. On September 24, 1862, he announced that as long as the Civil War continued

> all rebels and insurgents, their aiders and abettors, within the United States, and all persons discouraging volunteer enlistments, resisting militia drafts, or guilty of any disloyal practice affording aid and comfort to rebels against the authority of the United States, shall be subject to martial law and liable to trial and punishment of courts-martial or military commissions.

Lincoln went on to suspend *habeas corpus* for such persons and declared that they could be imprisoned in military facilities. Although Congress had passed legislation approving many of Lincoln's emergency measures, it never approved his subjection of civilians to military courts.[152] *(See "Suspension of the Writ of Habeas Corpus," p. 1443, in Chapter 30, Vol. II.)*

Lambdin P. Milligan, a citizen of Indiana, was arrested in 1864 by military authorities who charged him with aiding a Confederate raid into Indiana from across the Ohio River. On May 9, 1865, Milligan was found guilty and sentenced to death. Milligan's case eventually came before the Supreme Court.

The Court held 9–0 in *Ex parte Milligan* that the president did not have the authority to subject civilians to military tribunals in an area where civilian courts were functioning.[153] The Court also ruled 5–4 that even the president and Congress together lacked power to authorize trials of civilians by military courts outside of a war zone. The majority opinion, written by Justice David Davis, admitted that in regions "where war actually prevails" and makes it "impossible to administer criminal justice according to the law," military government is justified. However, the Court rejected the idea that such conditions existed in Indiana—hundreds of miles from the war front—where civilian courts were functioning normally.

Beyond their verdict, the justices used this case to defend the inviolability of the Constitution. Davis wrote:

> The Constitution of the United States is a law for rulers and people, equally in war and in peace, and covers with the shield of its protection all classes of men, at all times, and under all circumstances. No doctrine involving more pernicious consequences was ever invented by the wit of man than that any of its provisions can be suspended during any of the great exigencies of government.

Milligan is regarded as significant by legal scholars for asserting that constitutional limits to presidential power are not suspended even during the most dire military emergency. *(See "Domestic Trials by Military Authorities," p. 1440, in Chapter 30, Vol. II.)* However, the logic in Lincoln's defense of his policy is also compelling:

> To state the question more directly, are all the laws, *but one,* to go unexecuted, and the government itself go to pieces, lest that one [law] be violated? Even in such a case, would not the official oath to faithfully execute the laws be broken, if the government should be overthrown, when it is believed that disregarding the single law, would tend to preserve it?[154]

When the Supreme Court ruled on *Milligan* in 1866, the war was over and Lincoln was dead. Consequently, the Court was able to strike down a presidential emergency action without confronting an incumbent president during a wartime crisis.

Military Tribunals and Terrorism

In November 2001 President George W. Bush authorized the use of military tribunals for trying foreigners accused of terrorist acts against the United States. The president claimed that emergency powers under the commander-in-chief clause gave him the latitude to institute these extraordinary procedures. The Bush administration cited in particular Franklin Roosevelt's use of a military tribunal to prosecute eight Nazi saboteurs caught in the United States with explosives. All eight were convicted, and six were executed.

Under this order, the president would decide, case by case, which defendants would be tried in a military tribunal. The selection of judges and all the rules of procedure for evidence and witnesses would be left to the secretary of defense. The decision was announced just as the four defendants being tried for the 1986 terrorist bombing of a Berlin discotheque were convicted in an ordinary criminal proceeding, and critics viewed the decision as an unnecessary violation of accepted principles of fairness and the rule of law. The Bush administration defended this decision on several grounds. For one thing, it claimed that the high barriers of evidence and strict standards of fairness in ordinary criminal proceedings, which are designed to prevent an innocent person from being convicted, are not appropriate when the consequences of allowing a guilty party to go free may be so terrible. Ordinary criminal procedures also can result in long trials—the prosecution of the Berlin terrorists took four years—and long trials would make the judges, the jury, and the country in general more inviting targets for intimidation and retaliation. Finally, the secrecy of a military tribunal would help to protect the valuable intelligence sources and methods that are needed in the ongoing struggle against terrorism.

Military tribunals were intended for the several hundred prisoners that the United States had detained at Guantanamo Bay, Cuba, mostly from the 2001 war in Afghanistan. But in 2006, the Supreme Court declared in *Hamdan v. Rumsfeld* that the United States would have to comply with the rule of law in creating such tribunals, including international law such as the post–World War II Geneva Convention, which prescribed rules for treatment of prisoners of war.[155] The Court stated that the president could seek congressional approval for creating special military commissions, but that he could not establish them independently. The Court further held, contrary to the administration's position, that federal courts may adjudicate appeals from detainees held overseas by the United States. The *Hamdan* case raised many questions about whether the president ultimately would, in fact, employ military tribunals to try detainees in the war on terror. *(See box, Supreme Court Cases Related to the President's Foreign Policy Powers, p. 699, in Chapter 13.)*

Nonetheless, a draft of the specific rules that would govern these tribunals seemed to respond to the criticisms. They included a "beyond a reasonable doubt" threshold for conviction, a provision of appeals, and restrictions on secrecy.

Korematsu v. United States

Three-quarters of a century after *Milligan*, a case involving the violation of individual rights by an exercise of wartime emergency power came before the Court while the emergency still existed.

After the Japanese attack on Pearl Harbor on December 7, 1941, President Roosevelt ordered several controversial measures to enhance security on the West Coast. These included the imposition of a curfew on persons of Japanese descent and the relocation of 120,000 Japanese Americans to internment camps in the U.S. interior. Both the curfew and the relocation applied to persons of Japanese ancestry regardless of their citizenship or loyalty. Congress subsequently passed legislation validating the president's directives. *(See "Curfew and Exclusion Orders," p. 1442, in Chapter 30, Vol. II.)*

This wholesale suspension of the rights of American citizens led to several Supreme Court cases. In 1943 the Court ruled unanimously in *Hirabayashi v. United States* that together the president and Congress had the power to impose the curfew and that the extreme emergency created by Japan's threat to the Pacific Coast made the curfew justifiable.[156] The Court did not reach a consensus, however, on the more severe violation of rights involved in the relocation of Japanese Americans. In *Korematsu v. United States*, it ruled 6–3 that the threat to national security justified the joint action of Congress and the president.[157] Writing for the majority, Justice Hugo Black explained: "Compulsory exclusion of large groups of citizens from their homes, except under circumstances of direct emergency and peril, is inconsistent with our basic governmental institutions. But when under conditions of modern warfare our shores are threatened by hostile forces, the power to protect must be commensurable with the threatened danger." In a bitter dissenting opinion, Justice Francis Murphy rejected the premise of the Court's decision that the emergency on the West Coast warranted the exclusion from the West Coast of all persons of Japanese ancestry. "Such exclusion," he wrote, "goes over 'the very brink of Constitutional power' and falls into the abyss of racism."

Justice Robert Jackson's dissenting opinion got closer to the heart of the dilemma. On the one hand, he admitted that there are military emergencies that warrant extraordinary measures. But he also argued that judges are not qualified to assess the circumstances, and the Court ought not to corrupt the law by ruling that momentarily necessary violations of civil rights are also constitutionally permissible.

> But if we cannot confine military expedients by the Constitution, neither would I distort the Constitution to approve all that the military may deem expedient. That is

what the Court appears to be doing. . . . [A] judicial construction of the due process clause that will sustain this order is a far more subtle blow to liberty than the promulgation of the order itself. . . . The principle then lies about like a loaded weapon ready for the hand of any authority that can bring forward a plausible claim of an urgent need. . . . I should hold that a civil court cannot be made to enforce an order which violates constitutional limitations even if it is a reasonable exercise of military authority.[158]

Seizure of Property

During wartime, it is sometimes necessary for a government to seize private property that is vital to the war effort. Congress has traditionally passed legislation governing the seizure of property belonging to U.S. citizens. Before and during World War I, Congress empowered the president to seize transportation and communications systems if such actions became necessary. President Wilson used these statutes to take over railroad, telephone, and telegraph operations, which were returned to civilian control after the war. Similarly, Franklin Roosevelt was authorized by the War Labor Disputes Act of 1943 to seize control of industries important to the war effort that were in danger of being shut down by labor disputes.[159]

But presidents have not always waited for congressional approval before seizing property. Lincoln personally authorized military units to take possession of telegraph lines during the Civil War, and in 1914 Wilson ordered the seizure of a wireless station that refused to comply with naval censorship rules. Several decades later, Franklin Roosevelt took control of several strike-threatened industries before the War Labor Disputes Act of 1943 authorized such action. Yet unilateral seizures of property by presidents have been exceptions to accepted practice, and the courts generally have rejected the proposition that presidents possess inherent emergency powers that authorize them to seize private property.

The most famous court case on this question was *Youngstown Sheet and Tube Co. v. Sawyer,* also known as the *Steel Seizure Case,* in which the Supreme Court ruled on President Truman's authority to seize steel mills during the Korean War. Truman believed that a steelworkers strike, scheduled for April 9, 1952, would damage the Korean War effort, and on April 8, he directed Secretary of Commerce Charles Sawyer to seize and operate the steel mills. He justified his seizure of the mills solely on the basis of his power as commander in chief and his responsibility to execute the laws. Truman conceded in his report to Congress that it had the authority to countermand his directive, but Congress failed to approve or reject the president's action.

The steel companies brought suit against the government, seeking an injunction to stop the president's action. The case quickly reached the Supreme Court, where, by a vote of 6–3, Truman's action was held unconstitutional. The Court claimed that the president had usurped Congress's law-making power. It cited several acts in which Congress had provided procedures for responding to strikes that Truman had ignored. In the debate on one of these laws, the Taft-Hartley Act of 1947, Congress had considered empowering the government to seize an industry to prevent strikes but had refused to include such a provision in the law. Truman, therefore, had not just taken action without congressional authorization; he had taken an action that Congress had rejected.[160]

Although it is unclear whether the Court would have ruled differently had the emergency been more grave or had Congress not rejected the inclusion of property seizure provisions in the Taft-Hartley Act, the decision was generally read as a rejection of inherent emergency powers. In a concurring opinion, Justice William O. Douglas explained:

There can be no doubt that the emergency which caused the president to seize these steel plants was one that bore heavily on the country. But the emergency did not create power; it merely marked an occasion when power should be exercised. And the fact that it was necessary that measures be taken to keep steel in production does not mean that the President, rather than the Congress, had the constitutional authority to act.[161]

In an era of rapidly expanding presidential power, the *Steel Seizure Case,* as Clinton Rossiter observed, "revived, for the moment, the notion that Presidents were subject to congressional limitations in foreign affairs."[162]

ARMED FORCES IN PRESIDENTIAL DIPLOMACY AND FOREIGN POLICY

From the time the Constitution was ratified until the present, presidents have used the military to accomplish limited missions in peacetime—to intimidate potential aggressors, impress trading partners, reassure friends, strengthen alliances, and mediate international disputes. The Constitution does not specifically sanction these peacetime military operations, but presidents have justified them under their power to command the military, defend the United States and its citizens, enforce the laws, and conduct foreign policy. Beyond the use or threat of force in a specific international hot spot, the strength of U.S. armed forces since World War II has allowed presidents to improve relations with other countries by offering them security guarantees and memberships in multinational alliances—although such inducements may prove less potent in the absence of a hostile superpower.

Police Actions and Rescue Missions

Some of the most consequential peacetime military operations have been police actions and rescue missions to protect U.S. citizens and interests abroad. The vast majority of these operations have been minor incidents, and many of them were so brief that Congress had no time even to consider an authorizing resolution. In any case, presidents have argued that these limited missions require no congressional authorization because they have limited goals that otherwise fall under the executive responsibility to protect the lives and property of U.S. citizens. *(See box, Presidential Claims to Police Action, p. 747.)* As long as military operations have not involved the United States in a wider war and casualties have remained low, presidential popularity usually has been bolstered by limited uses of force.

Congress and the courts generally have refrained from challenging the president's authority to protect U.S. citizens and property overseas, even when military actions taken under presidential orders have been unjust. For example, in 1854 a naval commander acting on the vague but belligerent orders of President Franklin Pierce completely destroyed the Nicaraguan city of Greytown when it refused to pay inflated damage claims filed by a U.S. company. Congress investigated the incident but did not condemn the Greytown bombardment or make Pierce account for his actions. A U.S. district court dismissed a suit filed by a Greytown property owner against the naval commander on the grounds that the bombardment was a political matter.[163]

Pierce's successor, James Buchanan, claimed that without the consent of Congress he could not "fire a hostile gun in any case except to repel the attacks of an enemy." [164] Yet most twentieth-century presidents have interpreted the commander-in-chief power to meet the needs and goals of the moment.

No president did more, in principle and in practice, to expand presidential authority to order limited military missions than Theodore Roosevelt. In what became known as the Roosevelt Corollary to the Monroe Doctrine, he asserted the president's right to exercise an "international police power" in Latin America to protect U.S. and hemispheric interests and peace. He argued that if Latin American governments were unable to rule justly, maintain civil order, or meet their international obligations, then they were jeopardizing the security of the hemisphere.

After Roosevelt, presidents exercised the "police power" in the Western Hemisphere with little hesitation or consultation with Congress. William Taft, Woodrow Wilson, Calvin Coolidge, John Kennedy, Lyndon Johnson, Ronald Reagan, George H. W. Bush, and Bill Clinton all used U.S. forces—or foreign troops trained and supplied by the United States—to intervene in the affairs of Latin American nations.[165] Most recently in 1994, President Clinton threatened an invasion of Haiti to restore the democratic government to power. A negotiated settlement with Haiti's military rulers made the invasion unnecessary but still involved U.S. troops in overseeing the transition to democracy.

Even if the president's power to order limited military missions is conceded, there is still the problem of defining which missions fall under the president's police and rescue powers and which should be authorized by a congressional sanction if not a declaration of war. Like the power to repel invasions, the police and rescue powers can be manipulated by presidents to justify military actions that Congress might not sanction. For example, President Reagan ordered nineteen hundred troops to the tiny Caribbean island of Grenada in 1983 on what he called a "rescue mission." The administration maintained that the pro-Cuban military coup had placed U.S. citizens on the island in danger and threatened to turn Grenada into a Cuban-supported communist military base. U.S. troops evacuated about one thousand Americans from the island and proceeded to depose Grenada's new leadership.[166]

The invasion of Grenada was clearly more than a rescue mission. The president used armed force to accomplish geopolitical goals without the consent of Congress. Nevertheless, the historical precedent supporting the authority of presidents to order military missions and the perceived urgency of the situation at hand have influenced presidents and the U.S. public more often than strict interpretations of the Constitution and of international law.

Military Exercises and Shows of Force

Throughout U.S. history presidents have ordered conspicuous deployments of U.S. military power to dissuade potential aggressors, support allies, and reinforce U.S. diplomatic bargaining positions. Demonstrations of force before World War II almost always involved the navy.

In 1853 Millard Fillmore successfully changed Japanese foreign policy by sending a squadron of ships under Commodore Matthew Perry to Japan. The Japanese had excluded Westerners from their ports and had abused U.S. seamen shipwrecked off their shores. This show of U.S. naval power helped to produce the Treaty of Kanagawa, which declared friendship between the United States and Japan, opened several Japanese ports to U.S. commercial vessels, and established provisions for the treatment of U.S. citizens shipwrecked off Japan.

Perhaps the most famous show of force by a president was Theodore Roosevelt's dispatch of the U.S. fleet in 1907 on a cruise around the world. The cruise was primarily intended to impress Japan with U.S. naval power and demonstrate Roosevelt's resolve to oppose any act of aggression by the Japanese. He believed the "Great White Fleet's" cruise also would be a valuable exercise and would promote respect and goodwill for the United States throughout the world. The trip went smoothly, with the navy observing protocol at each port of call. Roosevelt later asserted, "The most important service that I rendered to peace was the voyage of the battle fleet around the world." [167]

In October 1994 President Clinton rushed U.S. forces to Kuwait in response to Iraqi troop movements toward the Kuwaiti border. Clinton's aim was to demonstrate to the Iraqis that the United States was again prepared and willing to resist any aggression in that region.

Shows of force may also be used to reassure a friendly government. On March 17, 1988, President Reagan sent 3,150 additional U.S. troops to Honduras in response to the incursion there of Nicaraguan government troops. The Nicaraguan forces reportedly crossed the Honduran border to destroy a supply depot of the antigovernment Nicaraguan contra rebels, who were supported by the Reagan administration. Secretary of State George P. Shultz said of the troops: "They're not near where the fighting is taking place, but they're designed to say to the Government of Honduras that, 'we are your friend and we stand with you, and if you are invaded you can count on the United States.' " [168] The contingent of troops conducted maneuvers in Honduras and withdrew from the country after ten days without engaging in combat.

Training and Advising Foreign Troops

During the cold war, military advisers became an established part of the superpowers' struggle for influence. Both the United States and the communist bloc sent military personnel into developing countries to instruct the local armed forces in organization, tactics, and the use of weapons. Often these military advisers were sent specifically to teach local troops how to use military equipment that the superpower had given or sold to that nation.

Because U.S. military advisers usually are instructed not to participate in combat, their deployment traditionally has not required congressional approval. Sending military advisers to a foreign country, however, can be controversial. This was certainly true of the U.S. experience in Vietnam, which began with the deployment of fewer than one thousand military advisers in that country by Dwight Eisenhower. During the Kennedy administration, although U.S. forces were still called "advisers," they had active combat roles. By the end of 1963, more than 16,000 advisers were in Vietnam. A year later this number had swelled to 23,210. [169]

When President Reagan introduced military advisers into El Salvador in 1981, critics of Reagan's policy charged that the U.S. military involvement in Central America could escalate as it had in Vietnam. Reagan promised to limit the number of U.S. military advisers in El Salvador to fifty-five, but the House Foreign Affairs Committee was concerned enough to outline in a report what it considered to be unacceptable activities for U.S. military advisers in all countries. These included accompanying local units into combat, arming or fueling combat aircraft, and delivering weapons and supplies to local troops in combat areas. These guidelines did not have the force of law.

★

NOTES

1. Alexander Hamilton, "No. 74," in Alexander Hamilton, James Madison, and John Jay, *The Federalist Papers* (New York: New American Library, 1961), 447.

2. Clinton Rossiter, *The American Presidency,* 2d ed. (New York: Time, 1960), 13.

3. Max Farrand, *The Records of the Federal Convention of 1787* (New Haven: Yale University Press, 1966), 1:318–319.

4. James Madison, *The Gazette of the United States,* August 24, 1793, quoted in *The Power of the Presidency,* ed. Robert S. Hirschenfield (New York: Atherton, 1968), 59.

5. Alexander Hamilton, "No. 69," in Alexander Hamilton, James Madison, and John Jay, *The Federalist Papers* (New York: New American Library, 1961), 417–418.

6. *Bas v. Tingy,* 4 U.S. 37 (1800); Louis Fisher, *Presidential War Power* (Lawrence: University Press of Kansas, 1995), 2–3, 18–19, 23–24.

7. Quoted in Fisher, *Presidential War Power,* 15.

8. Michael P. Riccards, *A Republic, If You Can Keep It: The Foundation of the American Presidency, 1700–1800* (New York: Greenwood Press, 1987), 152–153.

9. Joseph E. Kallenbach, *The American Chief Executive: The Presidency and the Governorship* (New York: Harper and Row, 1966), 535–536.

10. Edward S. Corwin, *The President: Office and Powers, 1787–1984,* 5th rev. ed. (New York: New York University Press, 1984), 297.

11. *Youngstown Sheet and Tube Co. v. Sawyer,* 343 U.S. 579 (1952).

12. Clinton Rossiter, *The Supreme Court and the Commander in Chief* (Ithaca: Cornell University Press, 1976), 48–52.

13. Robert E. DiClerico, *The American President,* 4th ed. (Englewood Cliffs, N.J.: Prentice Hall, 1995), 31.

14. Quoted in Richard M. Pious, *The American Presidency* (New York: Basic Books, 1979), 392.

15. James D. Richardson, *A Compilation of the Messages and Papers of the Presidents, 1789–1910* (New York: Bureau of National Literature, 1917), 1:314–315.

16. Pious, *American Presidency,* 392.

17. Quoted in Corwin, *President,* 229.

18. Quoted in Arthur M. Schlesinger Jr., *The Imperial Presidency* (Boston: Houghton Mifflin, 1989), 23.

19. Quoted in Thomas Eagleton, *War and Presidential Power* (New York: Liveright, 1974), 23.

20. Christopher H. Pyle and Richard M. Pious, eds., *The President, Congress, and the Constitution* (New York: Free Press, 1984), 293–295.

21. Lawrence Margolis, *Executive Agreements and Presidential Power in Foreign Policy* (New York: Praeger, 1986), 9.

22. Schlesinger, *Imperial Presidency,* 39–41.

23. Quoted in Wilfred E. Binkley, *The Man in the White House* (Baltimore: Johns Hopkins University Press, 1964), 192.

24. Schlesinger, *Imperial Presidency,* 58.

25. Corwin, *President,* 264.

26. Ibid., 265.

27. John Nicolay and John Hay, eds., *The Complete Works of Abraham Lincoln* (New York: Francis Tandy, 1891), 10:66.

28. Phillip Shaw Paludan, *The Presidency of Abraham Lincoln* (Lawrence: University Press of Kansas, 1994), 81–82.

29. Binkley, *Man in the White House,* 194.

30. *Prize Cases,* 67 U.S. (2 Black) 635 (1863).

31. Rossiter, *Supreme Court,* 71–75.

32. Fisher, *Presidential War Power,* 42.

33. Louis L. Gould, *The Presidency of William McKinley* (Lawrence: University Press of Kansas, 1980), 96–98.

34. Corwin, *President,* 271–272.

35. Ibid., 272.

36. Ibid.

37. Eagleton, *War and Presidential Power,* 64.

38. Jacob K. Javits, *Who Makes War: The President Versus Congress* (New York: Morrow, 1973), 225–226.

39. Schlesinger, *Imperial Presidency,* 115.

40. Quoted in Corwin, *President,* 285–286.

41. Edward S. Corwin, *Presidential Power and the Constitution* (Ithaca: Cornell University Press, 1976), 114.

42. Quoted in Javits, *Who Makes War,* 230.

43. Cecil V. Crabb Jr. and Pat M. Holt, *Invitation to Struggle: Congress, the President and Foreign Policy,* 4th ed. (Washington, D.C.: CQ Press, 1992), 134–136.

44. Dean Acheson, *Present at the Creation: My Years in the State Department* (New York: Norton, 1969), 415.

45. Schlesinger, *Imperial Presidency,* 133.

46. James L. Sundquist, *Decline and Resurgence of Congress* (Washington, D.C.: Brookings, 1981), 109.

47. Fisher, *Presidential War Power,* 70, 77–81.

48. R. Gordon Hoxie, *Command Decision and the Presidency* (New York: Reader's Digest Press, 1977), 178.

49. *Youngstown Sheet and Tube Co. v. Sawyer,* 343 U.S. 579 (1952).

50. Schlesinger, *Imperial Presidency,* 141.

51. Ibid., 169.

52. Sundquist, *Decline and Resurgence of Congress,* 124–125.

53. Ibid., 249.

54. Quoted in *CQ Almanac, 1973* (Washington, D.C.: Congressional Quarterly, 1974), 906.

55. Ibid., 906–907.

56. Eagleton, *War and Presidential Power,* 203.

57. Quoted in *CQ Almanac, 1973,* 907.

58. Ibid., 907.

59. *Immigration and Naturalization Service v. Chadha,* 462 U.S. 919 (1983).

60. *CQ Almanac, 1983* (Washington, D.C.: Congressional Quarterly, 1984), 568–569.

61. Fisher, *Presidential War Power,* 194–197.

62. Quoted in Larry Berman, *The New American Presidency* (Boston: Little, Brown, 1987), 75.

63. Ibid., 76.

64. DiClerico, *American President,* 41.

65. Jacob Javits, "War Powers Reconsidered," *Foreign Affairs* (fall 1985): 135.

66. Robert J. Spitzer, *President and Congress* (New York: McGraw-Hill, 1993), 176.

67. Javits, "War Powers Reconsidered," 136.

68. Quoted in Crabb and Holt, *Invitation to Struggle,* 148.

69. Fisher, *Presidential War Power,* 141–142.

70. Mary H. Cooper, "Persian Gulf Oil," *Editorial Research Reports,* October 30, 1987, 567.

71. Pat Towell, "New Gulf Incident Rekindles an Old Debate," *Congressional Quarterly Weekly Report,* April 23, 1988, 1051–1058.

72. Fisher, *Presidential War Power,* 145–148.

73. Spitzer, *President and Congress,* 180.

74. Ibid., 182.

75. *Dellums v. Bush,* 752 F. Supp. 1141 (D.D.C. 1990).

76. Fisher, *Presidential War Power,* 150–151.

77. Ibid., 155–156.

78. Ibid., 157–161.

79. David Fromkin, *Kosovo Crossing: The Reality of American Intervention in the Balkans* (New York: Touchstone, 1999).

80. George W. Bush, "Address to a Joint Session of Congress and the American People," 20 September 2001. Available at *(www.whitehouse.gov),* accessed February 8, 2007.

81. Joint Resolution Authorizing Use of United States Armed Forces Against Those Responsible for Recent Attacks on the United States, 14 September 2001. Available through Library of Congress Web site at *(www.thomas.loc.gov),* accessed February 8, 2007.

82. For a discussion of presidential decision making after September 11, 2001, and the war in Afghanistan, see Bob Woodward, *Bush at War* (New York: Simon and Schuster, 2002).

83. George W. Bush, "State of the Union Address," January 29, 2002. Available at *(www.whitehouse.gov),* accessed February 8, 2007.

84. George W. Bush, "Remarks at the United Nations General Assembly," 12 September 2002. Available at *(www.whitehouse.gov),* accessed February 8, 2007.

85. United Nations Security Council Resolution 1441, 8 November 2002. Available at *(www.un.org)* accessed February 8, 2007.

86. The decision-making process leading up to the 2003 Iraq war is discussed in Bob Woodward, *Plan of Attack* (New York: Simon and Schuster, 2004).

87. Fisher, *Presidential War Power,* 192.

88. See Jeffrey D. Simon, "Misunderstanding Terrorism," *Foreign Policy* (summer 1987); Charles William Maynes, "Bottom-Up Foreign Policy," *Foreign Policy* (fall 1996).

89. Bob Woodward, "CIA Told to Do 'Whatever Necessary' to Kill bin Laden," *Washington Post,* October 21, 2001, A1.

90. Jeffrey Rosen, "Power of One," *New Republic,* 24 July 2006.

91. George W. Bush, "The National Security Strategy of the United States of America," September 2002. Available at *(www.whitehouse.gov),* accessed February 8, 2007.

92. George W. Bush, "The National Security Strategy of the United States of America," March 2006. Available at *(www.whitehouse.gov),* accessed February 8, 2007.

93. Corwin, *President,* 249.

94. Sundquist, *Decline and Resurgence of Congress,* 105–106; Fisher, *Presidential War Power,* 77–79.

95. Corwin, *President,* 251; Fisher, *Presidential War Power,* 80–81.

96. Dick Kirschten, "A Contract's Out on U.N. Policing," *National Journal,* January 1, 1995, 231–232; James Kitfield, "Fit to Fight," *National Journal,* March 16, 1996, 5825–5886.

97. 107 Stat. 1478–80, sec. 9001 (1993).

98. U.S. Department of State Dispatch, vol. 5, no. 20 (May 16, 1994); Fisher, *Presidential War Power,* 160–161.

99. Steve Schifferes, "U.S. Names 'Coalition of the Willing,' " BBC News Online in Washington, March 18, 2003. Available at *(http://news.bbc.co.uk/2/hi/americas/2862343.stm),* accessed February 8, 2007.

100. Hoxie, *Command Decision and the Presidency,* 130.

101. Amos A. Jordan and William J. Taylor Jr., *American National Security: Policy and Process* (Baltimore: Johns Hopkins University Press, 1984), 473.

102. "Wooing the WEU," *Economist,* March 4, 1995, 56–57.

103. Pious, *American Presidency,* 395–396.

104. Fisher, *Presidential War Power,* 93–97.

105. Kallenbach, *American Chief Executive,* 531.

106. Charles A. Beard, *The Republic* (New York: Viking, 1944), 101.

107. Riccards, *A Republic, If You Can Keep It,* 164–166.

108. Jacob E. Cook, "George Washington," in *The Presidents: A Reference History,* ed. Henry F. Graff (New York: Scribner's, 1984), 24.

109. Corwin, *President,* 294.

110. Kallenbach, *American Chief Executive,* 530.

111. Molly Moore, "Stricken Frigate's Crew Stitched Ship Together," *Washington Post,* April 22, 1988, A1.

112. For a discussion of Johnson's conflicts with the military over the Vietnam War, see H. R. McMaster, *Dereliction of Duty: Johnson, McNamara, the Joint Chiefs of Staff, and the Lies That Led to Vietnam* (New York: HarperCollins, 1997).

113. The retired generals' public call for Rumsfeld's dismissal is discussed in James Kitfield, "Stakes High in Battle between Rumsfeld Generals," *Government Executive,* May 5, 2006.

114. Jordan and Taylor, *American National Security,* 231.

115. For a detailed description of the U.S. nuclear infrastructure, see William Arkin and Richard W. Fieldhouse, *Nuclear Battlefields* (Cambridge: Ballinger, 1984).

116. *Public Papers of the Presidents of the United States, Dwight D. Eisenhower, 1960–1961* (Washington, D.C.: Government Printing Office, 1963), 851.

117. *Public Papers of the Presidents of the United States, Harry S Truman, 1945* (Washington, D.C.: Government Printing Office, 1961), 212.

118. James A. Nathan and James K. Oliver, *United States Foreign Policy and World Order,* 2d ed. (Boston: Little, Brown, 1981), 41–42.

119. Hoxie, *Command Decision and the Presidency,* 13–14.

120. Miroslav Nincic, *United States Foreign Policy: Choices and Tradeoffs* (Washington, D.C.: CQ Press, 1988), 292.

121. Arthur M. Schlesinger Jr., *A Thousand Days* (Greenwich, Conn.: Fawcett, 1965), 778–783.

122. Theodore Sorensen, *Kennedy* (New York: Harper and Row, 1965), 705.

123. Arkin and Fieldhouse, *Nuclear Battlefields,* 87.

124. James M. Lindsay, *Congress and the Politics of Foreign Policy* (Baltimore: Johns Hopkins University Press, 1994), 102.

125. *CQ Almanac, 1992* (Washington, D.C.: Congressional Quarterly, 1993), 513–514.

126. For text of speech and further commentary, see *Historic Documents of 1983* (Washington, D.C.: Congressional Quarterly, 1984), 305–316.

127. R. Jeffrey Smith, "Pentagon Scales Back SDI Goals," *Washington Post,* March 27, 1988, A1.

128. *CQ Almanac, 1991* (Washington, D.C.: Congressional Quarterly, 1992), 407–408.

129. *CQ Weekly,* July 14, 2001, 1716.

130. Lawrence J. Korb, "The Evolving Relationship between the White House and the Department of Defense in the Post-Imperial Presidency," in *The Post-Imperial Presidency,* ed. Vincent Davis (New Brunswick, N.J.: Transaction, 1980), 103.

131. Richard K. Betts, *Soldiers, Statesmen, and Cold War Crises* (Cambridge: Harvard University Press, 1977), 52–68.

132. For discussions of the problems that led to the reform of the JCS, see James Buck, "The Establishment: An Overview," in *Presidential Leadership and National Security: Style, Institutions, and Politics,* ed. Sam C. Sarkesian (Boulder: Westview Press, 1984), 59–64; and John G. Kestor, "The Role of the Joint Chiefs of Staff," in *American Defense Policy,* ed. John F. Reichart and Steven R. Sturm (Baltimore: Johns Hopkins University Press, 1982), 527–545.

133. Pat Towell, "Major Pentagon Reorganization Bill Is Cleared," *Congressional Quarterly Weekly Report,* September 20, 1986, 2207–2208.

134. Philip Shenon and David Johnston, "Focus of FBI Is Seen Shifting to Terrorism," *New York Times,* October 21, 2001.

135. Morton Halperin, "The President and the Military," in *The Presidency in Contemporary Context,* ed. Norman C. Thomas (New York: Dodd, Mead, 1975), 277.

136. Ibid., 280–284.

137. Alice Maroni, "The Defense Budget," in *Presidential Leadership and National Security: Style, Institutions, and Politics,* ed. Sam C. Sarkesian (Boulder: Westview Press, 1984), 194–196.

138. Ibid., 196.

139. Richard Haass, "The Role of the Congress in American Security Policy," in *American Defense Policy,* ed. John F. Reichart and Steven R. Sturm (Baltimore: Johns Hopkins University Press, 1982), 558–560.

140. James Fairhall, "The Case for the $435 Hammer," *Washington Monthly,* January 1987, 47–52.

141. George F. Brown Jr. and Lawrence Korb, "The Economic and Political Restraints on Force Planning," in *American Defense Policy,* ed. John F. Reichart and Steven R. Sturm (Baltimore: Johns Hopkins University Press, 1982), 583.

142. Quoted in Dana Priest, "Billions Gone AWOL," *Washington Post Weekly Edition,* May 22–28, 1995, 6–7.

143. Kallenbach, *American Chief Executive,* 543.

144. Marc Leepson, "Draft Registration," *Editorial Research Reports,* June 13, 1980, 427–430.

145. Kallenbach, *American Chief Executive,* 537.

146. Quoted in Pyle and Pious, *President, Congress, and the Constitution,* 62 (emphasis in original).

147. Robert S. Hirschfield, "The Scope and Limits of Presidential Power," in *Power and the Presidency,* ed. Philip C. Dolce and George H. Skau (New York: Scribner's, 1976), 301–302.

148. Kallenbach, *American Chief Executive,* 553–554.

149. *Ex parte Milligan,* 4 Wallace 2 (1866).

150. *Duncan v. Kahanamoku,* 327 U.S. 304 (1946).

151. Rossiter, *Supreme Court,* 25.

152. Ibid., 27.

153. *Ex parte Milligan,* 4 Wallace 2 (1866).

154. Quoted in Pyle and Pious, *President, Congress, and the Constitution,* 67 (emphasis in original).

155. *Hamdi v. Rumsfeld,* 542 U.S. 507 (2004).

156. *Hirabayashi v. United States,* 320 U.S. 81 (1943).

157. *Korematsu v. United States,* 323 U.S. 214 (1944).

158. Quoted in Pyle and Pious, *President, Congress, and the Constitution,* 118–119.

159. Kallenbach, *American Chief Executive,* 557.

160. Corwin, *Presidential Power and the Constitution,* 124–125.

161. *Youngstown Sheet and Tube Co. v. Sawyer,* 343 U.S. 579 (1952).

162. Rossiter, *Supreme Court,* xxi.

163. Javits, *Who Makes War,* 104–115.

164. Quoted in Arthur Bernon Tourtellot, *The Presidents on the Presidency* (Garden City, N.Y.: Doubleday, 1964), 326.

165. Donald L. Robinson, *To the Best of My Ability* (New York: Norton, 1987), 224; and Fisher, *Presidential War Power,* 145–148, 154–157.

166. Nincic, *United States Foreign Policy,* 231–233.

167. Theodore Roosevelt, *An Autobiography* (New York: Scribner's, 1920), 548.

168. Quoted in Steven V. Roberts, "3,000 G.I.'s and Questions," *New York Times,* March 18, 1988, A1.

169. Timothy J. Lomperis, *The War Everyone Lost and Won* (Washington, D.C.: CQ Press, 1984), 60.

SELECTED BIBLIOGRAPHY

Corwin, Edward S. *The President: Office and Powers, 1787–1984.* 5th rev. ed. New York: New York University Press, 1984.

Crabb, Cecil V., Jr., and Pat M. Holt. *Invitation to Struggle: Congress, the President and Foreign Policy.* 4th ed. Washington, D.C.: CQ Press, 1992.

Ely, John Hart. *War and Responsibility: Constitutional Lessons of Vietnam and Its Aftermath.* Princeton: Princeton University Press, 1993.

Fisher, Louis. *Presidential War Power.* 2d rev. ed. Lawrence: University Press of Kansas, 2004.

Herspring, Dale R. *The Pentagon and the Presidency: Civil-Military Relations from FDR to George W. Bush.* Lawrence: University Press of Kansas, 2005.

Javits, Jacob K. *Who Makes War: The President Versus Congress.* New York: Morrow, 1973.

Jordan, Amos A., William J. Taylor Jr., and Michael J. Mazarr. *American National Security: Policy and Process.* 5th ed. Baltimore: Johns Hopkins University Press, 1998.

Kallenbach, Joseph E. *The American Chief Executive: The Presidency and the Governorship.* New York: Harper and Row, 1966.

Kelley, Christopher S. *Executing the Constitution: Putting the President Back in the Constitution.* New York: State University of New York Press, 2006.

Koh, Harold Hongju. *The National Security Constitution: Sharing Power after the Iran-Contra Affair.* New Haven: Yale University Press, 1990.

Nincic, Miroslav. *United States Foreign Policy: Choices and Tradeoffs.* Washington, D.C.: CQ Press, 1988.

Pious, Richard M. *The American Presidency.* New York: Basic Books, 1979.

Rossiter, Clinton. *The Supreme Court and the Commander in Chief.* Ithaca: Cornell University Press, 1976.

Sarkesian, Sam C., ed. *Presidential Leadership and National Security: Style, Institutions, and Politics.* Boulder: Westview Press, 1984.

Schlesinger, Arthur M., Jr. *The Imperial Presidency.* Boston: Houghton Mifflin, 1989.

Wilson, George C. *This War Really Matters: Inside the Fight for Defense Dollars.* Washington, D.C.: CQ Press, 2000.

chapter 15

Chief Economist

by Jim Granato, Daniel C. Diller, and Dean J. Peterson

The authors of the Constitution clearly intended Congress to be the branch of government most concerned with the economic affairs of the nation. Article I, Section 8, of the Constitution grants Congress numerous economic powers, including the authority to

> lay and collect taxes, duties, imposts and excises, to pay the debts and provide for the common defense and general welfare of the United States . . . ; borrow money on the credit of the United States . . . ; regulate commerce with foreign nations, and among the several states . . . ; and coin money, regulate the value thereof, and of foreign coin.

In contrast, the Constitution grants the president no specific economic powers. Nevertheless, the Framers expected presidents to have significant influence over the economy. They would, after all, oversee the implementation of Congress's spending and taxing decisions, suggest economic legislation in their State of the Union address and other communications to Congress, negotiate commercial treaties with foreign nations, and have the power to veto legislation on economic matters.

Presidential economic power, however, has developed beyond these constitutional powers. Presidents have effectively used their visibility and their prerogatives in the execution of policy to promote their economic programs. In addition, as management of the economy grew more complex during the twentieth century, Congress gave presidents greater economic power through statutes.

Because the American people associate the presidency—the nation's most powerful and identifiable political office—with the performance of the federal government, they have come to expect presidents to produce economic prosperity for the United States just as presidents are expected to enforce its laws and ensure its security. As political scientist Clinton Rossiter observed near the end of the Eisenhower administration:

> The people of this country are no longer content to let disaster fall upon them unopposed. They now expect their government, under the direct leadership of the President,

to prevent a depression or panic and not simply wait until one has developed before putting it to rout. Thus the President has a new function which is still taking shape, that of Manager of Prosperity.[1]

PRESIDENTIAL POWER OVER THE ECONOMY

Limitations

Despite the expectations of the American people and the president's pivotal role in economic policy making, the president's ability to influence economic conditions does not measure up to presidential responsibility for them. All presidents would like to be able to adjust the economy from a central switch in the White House, but no absolutely reliable controls exist.

When unemployment, inflation, and budget deficits rise, presidents receive most of the blame. Herbert Hoover, Gerald R. Ford, Jimmy Carter, and George H. W. Bush lost their reelection bids in part because of the poor economic conditions that prevailed during their presidencies. The president's party also may suffer in midterm congressional elections if the economy is in a recession.

Presidents themselves are partially responsible for high public expectations of their economic management. As candidates, future presidents usually overestimate their ability to improve the economy.[2] To get elected, presidential candidates must promise to produce economic growth with low inflation and balanced budgets, even if their predecessors have left them with serious economic problems that cannot be corrected quickly or easily.

This relationship between presidential popularity and the economy, however, may also work to a president's advantage. Presidents are quick to take credit for economic growth, price stability, and low unemployment. Presidential candidate Ronald Reagan capitalized on poor economic conditions in 1980 by asking voters, "Are you better off now than you were four years ago?" Voters responded "no" and elected Reagan to succeed Carter. Four years later, when the economy was in the midst of a strong expansion after the recession of 1981–1982, Reagan repeated the question, and the American people reelected him in a landslide.

How the public deals with complex political and economic issues and information also influences presidential actions and may limit policy alternatives. Oftentimes voters mistakenly believe that a specific presidential policy—promoting free trade, for example—that is intended to affect economic activity in the nation as a whole should also affect each individual the same way. Opponents of free trade argue that import restrictions will save jobs, which may be true in the industries that are affected, such as steel manufacturing. Voters may mistakenly believe that this saving of jobs should extend to the entire economy. Economists argue that, in the entire economy, import restrictions are not likely to save jobs outside of the affected industries. This is because more efficient businesses are not allowed to beat out less efficient businesses or more efficient industries are forbidden (by policy) from replacing less efficient ones, which results in a loss in jobs in the economy as a whole as well as fewer innovative products becoming available to the public.

More generally, the advances of technology—the use of the Internet and blogging—have the potential to contribute to rapid transmission of (mis)information on vital political and economic matters.[3] This is particularly true when leaders and politically active citizens in society are more ideologically polarized than the general public.[4]

Even though presidents and their advisers generally understand the benefits of free trade, the politics of governing often trumps economic theory. A good example occurred in early 2002 when President George W. Bush, leader of the Republican Party, which traditionally is associated with free trade, imposed tariffs on steel and lumber imports. Observers noted that certain states, such as Pennsylvania and West Virginia, which were expected to be important to Bush if he sought reelection in 2004, had troubled steel industries, including companies that faced bankruptcy. The lumber industry was also important to influential members of Congress, including Senate minority leader Trent Lott of Mississippi, who were in a position to help the Bush administration win free trade agreements in coming months. Lumber imports from Canada were providing increasingly tough competition to the American suppliers. But these nuances are often lost on the public that often views presidential actions through a narrow lens.

Institutional factors also limit presidential control over the U.S. economy. The chief executive must share power with other individuals and governmental bodies. As the enumeration of congressional economic powers shows, Congress has the constitutional authority to frustrate virtually any presidential economic initiative. Most important, the president cannot levy taxes or appropriate money without the approval of Congress.

Executive branch organizations also cut into presidential economic power. The independent Federal Reserve Board, which sets monetary policy, is not legally obliged to cooperate with the president. Spending and taxing policies adopted by presidents to achieve one economic result may be undercut by monetary policies of the Federal Reserve Board that are designed to achieve a conflicting result. The president's economic advisers also can check presidential power by implementing the chief executive's directives unenthusiastically or by refusing to join a policy consensus. *(See "Monetary Policy," p. 802.)*

Each economic advisory organization has a different mission that disposes it to concentrate on a particular economic problem. The Office of Management and Budget (OMB) looks to trim the budget; the president's Council of Economic Advisers (CEA) focuses on lowering unemployment and inflation and promoting economic expansion; the Treasury Department oversees the national debt and develops international monetary policy; and the heads of other departments and agencies seek to protect funding for projects within their jurisdictions. *(See box, Economic Advisers to the President, p. 793.)* These missions often conflict, making agreement on policy goals difficult and creating rivalries within an administration.

Another factor limiting presidential control of the economy is the highly complex and theoretical nature of the science of economics. Presidents with little formal training in economics may feel overwhelmed, as did Warren G. Harding, who once confided to an associate:

> I don't know what to do or where to turn on this taxation matter. Somewhere there must be a book that tells all about it, where I could go to straighten it out in my mind. But I don't know where the book is, and maybe I couldn't read it if I found it. There must be a man in the country somewhere who could weigh both sides and know the truth. Probably he is in some college or other. But I don't know where to find him, I don't know who he is and I don't know how to get him.[5]

The imprecision of economic information limits presidential power as well. When presidents attempt to adjust the economy, they assume that they have accurate and timely information about the economy's performance. But economic statistics provide, at best, a rough approximation of economic reality. The size and complexity of an evolving economy of 300 million people necessitates that economic statistics be developed from "a slag heap of samples, surveys, estimates, interpolations, seasonal adjustments, and plain guesses." [6]

Toward the end of the twentieth century, economists and public policy makers increasingly questioned the accuracy of economic statistics. In particular, a consensus began to develop that the consumer price index (the primary measure of inflation) was overstating the annual rate of inflation, perhaps by as much as a full percentage point.[7]

ECONOMIC ADVISERS TO THE PRESIDENT

As presidential economic responsibilities increased during the twentieth century, the fulfillment of those responsibilities became increasingly institutionalized. Congress created new organizations, and presidents expanded existing organizations to increase the executive branch's capacity to analyze, coordinate, and manage the American economy and economic relations with other countries. Although White House political advisers and virtually all cabinet secretaries have some influence on economic policy, three executive branch units dominate presidential economic policy making: the Treasury Department, the Council of Economic Advisers (CEA), and the Office of Management and Budget (OMB). The leaders of these three units function as the president's chief economic advisers and meet frequently with one another to coordinate economic policy. Recent presidents also have established working groups beneath the three leaders with representatives from various departments to develop and analyze economic policies.

TREASURY DEPARTMENT

The Treasury Department, one of the original cabinet departments created in 1789 by an act of Congress, was the first executive branch unit to be responsible for advising the president on economic policy and has remained an important participant in economic policy making throughout U.S. history. The department has a variety of economic responsibilities, including collecting taxes and customs, managing the nation's currency and debt, developing tax legislation, and working with foreign governments and the Federal Reserve to adjust the value of the dollar relative to other currencies. Because the Treasury oversees the financing of the debt, the department traditionally has advocated taxes that will bring balanced budgets and monetary policies that yield low interest rates.

The Treasury secretary's position as head of a large cabinet department lends status to the post relative to other top presidential economic advisers. The Treasury secretary's influence on presidential economic decision making, however, may be constrained in some administrations by the amount of time the secretary spends overseeing the many operational responsibilities of the department. As the world's economies have become more interdependent, the Treasury secretary's international economic policy activities have become increasingly important. James A. Baker III, Treasury secretary during Ronald Reagan's second term, spent much of his time formulating exchange rate policies and developing a plan to reschedule Latin American debt payments to the United States. In early 1995, immediately on assuming the post of Treasury secretary, Robert E. Rubin orchestrated the commitment to Mexico of $20 billion in U.S. loans and loan guarantees and an additional $30 billion in international loans to avert severe international repercussions from Mexico's currency crisis. No similar crises arose in the first year and a half of President George W. Bush's term.

COUNCIL OF ECONOMIC ADVISERS

The Council of Economic Advisers is a three-member body appointed by the president and subject to Senate confirmation. It is headed by a chair who oversees the operations of the council's small staff, reports to the president, and represents the CEA before the rest of the executive branch and Congress.

The primary function of the CEA is to provide the president with expert economic advice and analysis. The Employment Act of 1946, which established the CEA as a unit in the Executive Office of the President, states that each member of the council "shall be a person who, as a result of his training, experience and attainments is exceptionally qualified to analyze and interpret economic developments, to appraise programs and activities of the government . . . and to formulate and recommend national eco-

nomic policy." Because the council does not represent a large bureaucratic body and has no responsibilities in operating the government other than preparing the president's annual economic report, Congress hoped that the CEA would have the time and independence to provide presidents with long-term, nonpartisan advice on economic policy and professional analysis of economic conditions. Traditionally, the CEA was primarily concerned with promoting growth and managing the trade-off between inflation and unemployment. In recent years, however, it has addressed a wider range of economic issues, including trade, productivity, pollution, and health care.

The CEA's influence depends almost entirely on the president. If the president values its advice and involves it in decision making, the CEA can have considerable power because its three members and small staff of professional economists usually possess the greatest amount of economic expertise within an administration. Because of this expertise, however, CEA members can be vulnerable to charges from other economic advisers that they approach the realities of economic policy making from a perspective that is too theoretical. CEA members must, therefore, be careful to pay adequate attention to the president's political needs if they wish to retain their influence.

OFFICE OF MANAGEMENT AND BUDGET

In 1921 Congress created the Bureau of the Budget to coordinate and modify the budget estimates of the executive departments. It was originally located within the Treasury Department but was placed under the newly created Executive Office of the President in 1939. In 1970 Richard M. Nixon expanded its staff and duties and renamed it the Office of Management and Budget.

OMB's primary function is to formulate an executive branch budget for the president that considers how much revenue the government is likely to raise through taxes and how much each federal agency and program should receive. OMB, therefore, continually analyzes the merits of budget requests and makes recommendations to the president on what funding should be cut, maintained, or expanded. The office is also responsible for budget forecasts that estimate the size of the budget deficit or surplus. The institutional bias of OMB has been to limit spending. Because department and agency heads tend to request as much funding as is politically possible for their units, OMB has become the central budgetary control within the administration to pare down the budget requests.

The post of budget director has become highly politicized since the Nixon administration. Budget directors frequently testify before Congress and are involved in shaping and promoting the president's social agenda through their budget recommendations. David A. Stockman, budget director under Ronald Reagan from 1981 to 1985, epitomized the budget director's new role. President Reagan gave him a broad mandate to cut items from the budget in pursuit of smaller budget deficits. In the first six months of the Reagan administration, Stockman became not only the dominant presidential adviser on the budget, but also a symbol of Reagan's domestic budget cuts and social agenda, which emphasized a more limited role for the federal government.

The forecasting role of OMB also has pushed it into the political spotlight. Because budgets depend on long-term forecasts of economic growth, tax receipts, and entitlement spending, the assumptions of OMB and its legislative branch counterpart, the Congressional Budget Office (CBO), are critical to plans aimed at reducing the deficit. In 1995 Congress insisted that President Bill Clinton agree to base efforts to balance the budget on forecasts from the traditionally independent CBO. Most observers agree that direct presidential control of OMB has led to the politicization of its budget forecasts under recent presidents. Clinton agreed in November 1995 to use CBO budget estimates that were developed after consultations with OMB.

In addition, economic statistics and indicators do not measure the immediate conditions of the economy but rather the conditions that prevailed between one and four months earlier, depending on the particular economic measure. Consequently, presidents who take action on the basis of the latest economic information may be reacting to a problem that no longer exists or that is much worse than believed. In such cases presidential economic policies may destabilize the economy. A president's attempts to manage the economy, therefore, are only as good as the information on which they are based. When government figures indicate that unemployment is rising and consumer demand is falling, the president may wish to enact spending increases or a tax cut. If, however, the unemployment figures or the estimate of consumer demand is outdated, such anti-recession measures could cause an inflationary spiral.

For example, in 1993, an economic stimulus package proposed by President Bill Clinton had a similar history. After entering office, Clinton proposed a $16 billion spending bill to stimulate the economy, which was not performing well according to the available economic indicators. The proposal was defeated by a Republican filibuster in the Senate. Republicans argued that the stimulus package would have increased the deficit and consisted of federal pork barrel projects designed primarily to reward Democratic mayors, governors, and members of Congress.

A year after the package's defeat, some economists felt that, regardless of the plan's other merits or faults, it could have adversely affected the economy. Clinton and his advisers did not know in early 1993 that the economy was already growing. A fiscal stimulus delivered during the second half of 1993, as the plan envisioned, could have increased inflationary pressures, just as the Federal Reserve Board was working to dampen inflation.

Similarly, an anti-inflation strategy based on inaccurate information can deepen a recession. That occurred at the beginning of 1980 when the inflation rate had sky-rocketed to 18 percent. Economists had predicted that a recession was coming, but President Carter nevertheless imposed credit controls designed to lower inflation. Later in the year, economic statistics showed that the predicted recession was already under way when Carter acted, which contributed significantly to the sharpest decline in gross national product (GNP) in a single three-month period since World War II. Incomplete economic information induced Carter to take measures that exacerbated the economy's troubles.[8]

A final factor limiting presidential control over the economy is forces outside the reach of the federal govern-

British economist Adam Smith promoted a laissez-faire approach to government economic activity. American presidents adhered to his theories until the 1930s, when the Great Depression called for a more activist presidential role in managing the economy.

ment. State and local government policies may undercut those of the federal government; international events such as wars, oil price increases, or recessions in foreign countries may exacerbate U.S. economic problems; bad weather may limit agricultural production; public expectations may make certain economic options such as large cuts in Social Security politically impossible; and corporations may make business decisions that aggravate unemployment, inflation, the trade deficit, and other economic problems. The 2001 collapse of a giant energy company, Enron, and the ensuing controversy about the accuracy and quality of corporate accounting and independent auditing practices contributed to investor wariness about business fundamentals and the stock market, which already had plunged markedly since 2000. While the effects of such developments wear off in time, their immediate impact can offset the best of intentions and policies from government. A president making all the right decisions will not, therefore, necessarily produce a thriving economy, and an economically inexperienced or inept president will not inevitably bring on a national economic disaster or even a recession.

Assets and Opportunities

In spite of these limitations, no person has more influence over the U.S. economy than the president. As chief executive the president oversees the government's economic and regulatory functions and appoints cabinet and Federal Reserve Board members who make many economic decisions; as chief legislator the president proposes federal spending, taxation, and other economy-related legislation and can use the veto—or the threat of the veto—to influence legislation before Congress; as commander in chief the president oversees the multibillion-dollar purchases of the Defense Department; as chief diplomat the president negotiates with foreign governments about trade and currency issues; and as chief of state the president affects the morale, attitudes, and expectations of the American people.

One area of presidential strength is the continued improvement in economic knowledge. For example, in 2006 much agreement existed about the importance of stability in key economic areas. Of first rank is price stability: preventing inflation. This consensus emerged in part from past policy mistakes that contributed to economic hardship such as an unusual combination of inflation and economic stagnation in the 1970s, which became known as "stagflation." It is not an accident that Presidents Clinton, in the 1990s, and Reagan, in the 1980s, despite their large partisan differences, had similar stances on price stability. The George W. Bush administration resembled the Clinton administration in this regard. This should come as no surprise because price stability (stabilizing inflation) is thought to be associated with the longest recorded economic expansions in U.S. economic history.[9]

Another strength may be a president's credibility with the public on particular economic outcomes. Even though a particular policy may create economic troubles for some workers, a president with high public credibility can overcome voter concerns because of a long-noted tendency of Americans to assume the chief executive's actions are in the nation's best interests and to disbelieve that the president will allow hardship to occur. This gives the president leeway to address some social concern with policies that have economic risks attached to them, but that, nevertheless, may be the most effective means to deal with a particular problem.

INTERACTION AND EVOLUTION OF ECONOMIC THEORY, INSTITUTIONS, AND EVENTS

Presidents come to office with a set of policy preferences, which are a function of many factors including personal ideology, personal experience, and political considerations. Yet policy is not made in a vacuum and presidential preferences are not the only factors in decision making. Policy and actions are grounded as well in existing economic understanding and the institutions that exist. A final factor is historical events, some generated by policy mistakes, others unforeseen.

Evolution in Economic Management and Economic Theory

The evolution of presidential economic management has been less on goals than on policies to achieve goals. Every president has been concerned with the U.S. economy, but close presidential supervision of its performance is a relatively recent historical development. Before the Great Depression of the 1930s, Americans generally believed that extensive government intervention in the economy was counterproductive. The human suffering of the Depression, however, convinced the American public and its leaders that the government should intervene to relieve and prevent periods of economic trauma. By the time World War II ended, a national consensus had developed that the government, and especially the president, should use every means available to produce the best economic conditions possible even if the economy was not in trouble. The president had become not just a guardian against economic disaster but an economic manager whose popularity usually depended on a strong and stable economy.

Presidents since the Great Depression have attempted to create the best economic conditions possible through their stabilization policies. The U.S. economy, as with all capitalist economies, experiences cyclical patterns of expansion and contraction in which the levels of inflation, unemployment, and economic growth vary. (See Table 15-1.)

During periods of economic contraction businesses lose sales, investment decreases, unemployment grows, and prices tend to increase at a slow rate or even fall. During expansionary periods consumers spend more, investment increases, unemployment declines, and prices tend to increase at a faster rate. The objective of stabilization policy is to smooth out the natural swings in the economy, so unemployment does not become too severe during contractionary periods and inflation does not get out of control during expansionary periods. Ideally, an administration should achieve these goals while maintaining a steady rate of economic growth and balancing the federal budget, or at least running manageable deficits that can be corrected during periods of prosperity.

The tools presidents use to stabilize the economy are fiscal policy and monetary policy. Fiscal policy refers to the government's taxing and spending decisions. Presidents make fiscal policy in cooperation with Congress, which passes spending and tax bills. The government can choose to combat unemployment and stagnant economic growth by stimulating the economy through tax cuts or increased spending, or both. Congress and the president can choose to fight inflation by contracting the economy through tax increases or reduced spending. Monetary policy refers to decisions about the supply of money. Although presidents do not have legal control over monetary policy, which is determined by the independent Federal Reserve Board, they do exercise much informal influence over it.

Fiscal Policy

Fiscal policy evolved significantly in the last seventy years of the twentieth century. Before the Great Depression most economists believed that the president could best contribute to the health of the economy by working for a balanced federal budget and not overregulating business activity. Deficit spending by the federal government was regarded as an

TABLE 15-1 **Inflation and Unemployment, 1929–2005 (percent)**

Year	Inflation, all items[a]	Unemployment	Year	Inflation, all items[a]	Unemployment	Year	Inflation, all items[a]	Unemployment
1929	0.0%	3.2%	1960	1.7%	5.5%	1983	3.2%	9.6%
1933	−5.1	24.9	1961	1.0	6.7	1984	4.3	7.5
1939	−1.4	17.2	1962	1.0	5.5	1985	3.6	7.2
1940	0.7	14.6	1963	1.3	5.7	1986	1.9	7.0
1941	5.0	9.9	1964	1.3	5.2	1987	3.6	6.2
1942	10.9	4.7	1965	1.6	4.5	1988	4.1	5.5
1943	6.1	1.9	1966	2.9	3.8	1989	4.8	5.3
1944	1.7	1.2	1967	3.1	3.8	1990	5.4	5.6
1945	2.3	1.9	1968	4.2	3.6	1991	4.2	6.8
1946	8.3	3.9	1969	5.5	3.5	1992	3.0	7.5
1947	14.4	3.9	1970	5.7	4.9	1993	3.0	6.9
1948	8.1	3.8	1971	4.4	5.9	1994	2.6	6.1
1949	−1.2	5.9	1972	3.2	5.6	1995	2.8	5.6
1950	1.3	5.3	1973	6.2	4.9	1996	3.0	5.4
1951	7.9	3.3	1974	11	5.6	1997	2.3	4.9
1952	1.9	3.0	1975	9.1	8.5	1998	1.6	4.5
1953	0.8	2.9	1976	5.8	7.7	1999	2.2	4.2
1954	0.7	5.5	1977	6.5	7.1	2000	3.4	4.0
1955	−0.4	4.4	1978	7.6	6.1	2001	2.8	4.7
1956	1.5	4.1	1979	11.3	5.8	2002	1.6	5.8
1957	3.3	4.3	1980	13.5	7.1	2003	2.3	6
1958	2.8	6.8	1981	10.3	7.6	2004	2.7	5.5
1959	0.7	5.5	1982	6.2	9.7	2005	3.4	5.1

SOURCES: The inflation data can be found in the Department of Labor, Bureau of Labor Statistics, *Changes in Consumer Price Indexes for Commodities and Services: Fiscal Years 1929–2005,* Table B-64. The unemployment data can be found in the Department of Labor, Bureau of Labor Statistics, *Civilian Unemployment Rate: Fiscal Years 1959–2005,* Table B-42.

NOTE: a. Average percentage change in consumer price index year to year.

imprudent and irresponsible practice that eroded business confidence in the monetary system and produced inflation.

This economic orthodoxy handcuffed President Herbert Hoover when the stock market crashed and the Depression began in 1929. All of Hoover's efforts to turn the economy around proved ineffectual, and by 1933 unemployment had reached a staggering 25 percent of the workforce—one in every four workers was out of a job. Like presidents before him, Hoover believed in the conventional wisdom that public debt could undermine the economic health of the nation just as private debt could undermine a person's financial well-being. He therefore was suspicious of deficit spending programs that would have reduced the severity of the Depression. Nevertheless, in his search for an answer to the country's economic troubles Hoover did try a variety of measures, including a tax reduction, intended to put more money into the hands of the public. He quickly gave up on this approach, however, when it appeared not to be working and returned to a conservative strategy of cutting expenditures in an effort to balance the budget.[10] This policy, combined with the Federal Reserve Board's failure to expand the money supply, deepened the Depression.[11] In fact, many modern economists believe the Depression would have been limited to a severe recession had the president and the Federal Reserve Board not exacerbated the problem.

While campaigning for the presidency in 1932, Franklin D. Roosevelt did not advocate revolutionary fiscal policies. Like Hoover before him, he promised to cut expenditures and balance the budget. During the campaign Roosevelt attacked Hoover for failing to achieve a balanced budget.

Roosevelt, however, was a pragmatic leader who believed that the government should take emergency measures to fight the Depression. Once in office he initiated "New Deal" policies, government construction and relief programs that threw the federal budget into deficit. The deficit spending, however, was not a fiscal strategy designed to stimulate the economy but a byproduct of the president's decision to spend the money necessary to reduce the suffering of the poor, the elderly, and the unemployed and to begin putting Americans indeed some were terminated within a few years. Other programs, however, including Social Security, federal credit assistance to home buyers, small businesses, and farmers, and unemployment insurance became permanent government commitments.

While the United States and the world struggled through the Depression, the theories of the British economist John Maynard Keynes became widely known. Keynes outlined his theories in *The General Theory of Employment, Interest, and Money,* published in 1936. Keynes's thought focused on unemployment. He argued that recessions occurred when industrial, consumer, or government demand for goods and services fell. This caused unsold inventories to mount, industries to scale back their operations, and unemployment to rise.

Keynes posited that the government could counteract a recession by cutting taxes or increasing its expenditures. Lower taxes would put more money into the hands of consumers, thereby stimulating demand for goods and services. Tax cuts given to industry would create new jobs by boosting businesses' investment in their productive facilities. Greater government expenditures would create jobs and prime the economy through a "multiplier effect." According to Keynes, each dollar spent by the government could stimulate private economic transactions equaling much more than the original dollar.

In May 1937, after the U.S. economy had achieved a partial recovery, a new recession confronted Roosevelt. This recession was caused in part by the Federal Reserve Board, which had again contracted the money supply in its concern to prevent inflation.[12] The president initially ignored the advice of newly converted Keynesians in his administration and attempted to cut spending in an effort to balance the budget. Roosevelt's strategy deepened the recession and solidified a consensus among his advisers in favor of government spending designed to stimulate demand. By April 1938 the president himself was convinced that greater government expenditures were needed to combat the Depression. Roosevelt continued to pay lip service to a balanced budget, but he worked to increase expenditures and accepted growing budget deficits as a necessary evil in a difficult economic period.[13] Unemployment gradually declined from its 1933 high of 25 percent to less than 15 percent in 1940. In the end, the combination of fiscal and regulatory initiatives met with mixed success. The elimination of misery required direct assistance, but the mixture of New Deal policies, some have argued, may have prolonged the Great Depression.[14]

World War II ultimately brought massive government expenditures financed by borrowing that woke the U.S. economy from the nightmare of the 1930s. The war effort required a total mobilization of U.S. productive resources, which ended unemployment.[15] In 1944 unemployment stood at just 1.2 percent. Most economists saw the economic results of New Deal and wartime expenditures as a validation of Keynesian theory.

Since the late 1970s, the budget-making process has been a struggle to limit budget deficits despite erratic eco-

A common sight during the Great Depression was a line of unemployed workers, such as here in 1939, waiting for daily jobs.

nomic growth and dramatic increases in spending for entitlements, social programs, and defense. The American people consistently indicate in surveys that they believe government spending should be reduced. Yet this desire for less government spending is accompanied by a reluctance to sacrifice funding for specific programs that have developed constituencies. The public traditionally has believed the government spends too much in only a few policy areas such as foreign aid, welfare, and space exploration.[16] Thus the budget is one of the most persistent political dilemmas facing presidents. They must try to reduce overall spending while funding the programs that Americans have come to expect.

Budget deficits are not a phenomenon unique to the 1970s, 1980s, and 1990s. The federal government often has been forced to run deficits during wars and other national emergencies, including the Depression. Yet not until the 1970s did budget deficits become a persistent peacetime economic occurrence. Between 1792 and 1946, the federal government produced ninety-three budget surpluses and sixty-one budget deficits. From 1947 to 1969, a period during which two wars were fought, the government produced eight surpluses and fifteen deficits. But from 1970 until the late 1990s, the budget was in deficit every year, often by gigantic amounts.[17] *(See Table 15-2.)*

Unprecedented budget deficits loomed over the otherwise prosperous economy of the mid-1980s. The budget deficit widened sharply from $79.0 billion in 1981 to $221.2 billion in 1986. Annual interest payments to finance the

TABLE 15-2 **U.S. Federal Debt and Budget Deficits, 1940–2005 (billions of dollars)**

Fiscal year	Total federal debt	Federal debt as percentage of GDP	Budget deficit (surplus)	Deficit (surplus) as percentage of GDP
1940	$50.7	0.5	–$2.9	–3.0%
1950	256.9	93.9	–3.1	–1.1
1960	290.5	56.0	0.3	0.1
1970	380.9	37.6	–2.8	–0.3
1975	541.9	34.7	–53.2	–3.4
1976	629	36.2	–73.7	–4.2
1977	706.4	35.8	–53.7	–2.7
1978	776.6	35.0	–59.2	–2.7
1979	829.5	33.1	–40.7	–1.6
1980	909.1	33.3	–73.8	–2.7
1981	994.8	32.5	–79.0	–2.6
1982	1,137.3	35.2	–128.0	–4.0
1983	1,371.7	39.9	–207.8	–6.0
1984	1,564.7	40.8	–185.4	–4.8
1985	1,817.5	43.9	–212.3	–5.1
1986	2,120.6	48.2	–221.2	–5.0
1987	2,346.1	50.5	–149.8	–3.2
1988	2,601.3	51.9	–155.2	–3.1
1989	2,868.0	53.1	–152.5	–2.8
1990	3,206.6	55.9	–221.2	–3.9
1991	3,598.5	60.7	–269.4	–4.5
1992	4,002.1	64.4	–290.4	–4.7
1993	4,351.4	66.3	–255.1	–3.9
1994	4,643.7	66.9	–203.3	–2.9
1995	4,921.0	67.2	–164.0	–2.2
1996	5,181.9	67.3	–107.5	–1.4
1997	5,369.7	65.6	–22.0	–0.3
1998	5,478.7	63.2	69.0	0.8
1999	5,606.1	61.4	125.5	1.4
2000	5,629.0	57.8	236.4	2.4
2001	5,770.3	56.8	128.2	1.3
2002	6,198.40	59.7	-157.8	-1.5
2003	6,760.00	62.6	-377.6	-3.5
2004	7,354.70	63.7	-412.7	-3.6
2005	7,905.30	64.3	-318.3	-2.6

SOURCES: The total federal debt data and budget deficit data can be found in the Department of Commerce (Bureau of Economic Analysis); Treasury Department; and Office of Management and Budget, *Federal Receipts, Outlays, Surplus or Deficit, and Debt: Fiscal Years, 1940–2007,* Table B-78.

The federal debt as percent of GDP data and deficit as percent of GDP data can be found in the Treasury Department and Office of Management and Budget, *Federal Receipts, Outlays, Surplus or Deficit, and Debt as Percent of Gross Domestic Product: Fiscal Years 1934–2007,* Table B-79.

NOTE: GDP = gross domestic product.

national debt had risen from $68.8 billion to $136.0 billion during the same period. By 1985 the enormous budget deficit led legislators to pass the Gramm-Rudman-Hollings Deficit Reduction Act with the support of President Reagan. It was intended to force spending cuts aimed at balancing the budget by 1991. Despite cuts in defense spending and other deficit reduction measures, however, the budget deficit was still $152.5 billion in 1989. During the Reagan administration the national debt had nearly tripled from $994.8 billion in 1981 to $2.868 trillion in 1989.

But a booming economy in the 1990s that generated explosive tax revenues, plus a remarkable agreement to halt deficit spending, forged between Democratic president Clinton and a Republican-controlled Congress, produced a small surplus in fiscal 1998 that grew markedly in the following years. Some cuts in defense spending and to a lesser extent a slowdown in the rate of increase in domestic spending also contributed to this swing.

The surpluses in 1998 through 2000 were the longest consecutive-year surpluses since the period of 1947 through 1949. However, the combination of a mild recession in 2001 and the pressure for additional federal defense and other spending following terrorist attacks on the United States that same year all but ended the hope for continued surpluses for at least a period of years. In addition to these factors the war on terror, expanded starting in 2003 to the war on Iraq, led to budget deficits ranging as high as $400.0 billion and above in the 2002 to 2006 period.

Tax Policy

Traditionally, presidents have exerted less influence over tax policy than over spending matters. Whereas presidents are required to submit an executive budget to Congress outlining their spending proposals each year, tax laws do not require the executive to make major annual revisions. In addition, legislators, especially members of the powerful House Ways and Means and Senate Finance Committees, have historically regarded tax policy as a special province of Congress.

Nevertheless, presidential influence over tax policy is significant and has grown since World War II. This increase in influence has been furthered by the growth in presidential responsibility for economic policy in general.[18] As Congress and the nation have become accustomed to looking to the president for economic initiatives, the chief executive has taken over much of the burden of proposing and campaigning for changes in the tax code.

Within the executive branch, the Treasury Department has primary responsibility for tax policy. Its Office of the Tax Legislative Counsel drafts tax legislation and reviews tax regulations. The Office of Tax Analysis estimates the effect tax changes have on revenues. In addition, the Treasury Department's Internal Revenue Service (IRS) is responsible for collecting taxes and enforcing the tax laws passed by Congress. Other officials in the administration, particularly the OMB director, also are involved in formulating tax strategies.

In addition to proposing tax legislation, presidents influence tax policy by standing ready to veto tax bills passed by Congress that they believe are unfair, excessive, or harmful to the economy. Until a multiyear conflict between President Clinton and a Republican Congress in the late 1990s, presidents after World War II rarely had to veto tax bills because the threat to veto them usually has been enough to stop congressional tax initiatives opposed by the president. President Reagan's success at preventing tax increases during his second term, despite huge budget deficits, demonstrates the president's power over tax policy. Presidents may not be able to get their tax measures passed by Congress, but they will usually be able to stop or at least force the modification of any tax bill they do not like. This was true of the Clinton–Congress standoff, particularly in the 106th Congress in 1999 and 2000. Republicans, in control of both chambers, moved aggressively both to fulfill tax-cutting pledges and to define their party's agenda in contrast to Democrats in preparation for the 2000 presidential elections in which no incumbent was running. The Republicans sent Clinton large tax cut bills

and small tax cut bills, the latter often just pieces of the larger one broken into sizable bites to attract enough Democratic support for passage. But in almost all cases Clinton vetoed the measures and the Republicans did not come close to overriding his vetoes. Congress, however, has similar power to negate the president's tax proposals. Political scientist John F. Witte has written:

> Although the earlier notion that presidents should set only general revenue targets has been replaced by more detailed, almost annual tax proposals, the majority of the tax agenda is still set by Congress. Furthermore, there is no doubt that when presidential requests run counter to legislative momentum or the short run mood of Congress, they can and are summarily dismissed by congressional actions.[19]

The strategy of using tax policy as a tool of fiscal policy is complicated by the government's need for revenue. Although some tax cuts have generated greater revenues, most notably the 1964 tax rate cut that had been proposed the year before by President John F. Kennedy, tax cuts usually result in less revenue and higher deficits than would have ensued had they not been enacted. The supply-side economic theory that cutting tax rates would result in higher revenues became popular in the early 1980s, but the budget deficits that followed Reagan's 1981 tax rate cut diminished public and professional enthusiasm for this concept. Tax cuts meant to stimulate the economy may succeed, but policy makers risk higher budget deficits. Conversely, raising taxes may increase revenues in the short run but also contract the economy, resulting in higher unemployment.

Tax cuts are a popular fiscal policy tool because they directly increase net personal income. Tax cuts have often been used successfully to stimulate the economy. The unpopularity of tax increases, however, has made them difficult to enact with the speed that is necessary if they are to be an effective fiscal policy tool. Godfrey Hodgson has written of President Lyndon B. Johnson's experience with this problem:

> Even a timely shift in the direction of tax policy for macroeconomic reasons is generally beyond the capacity of . . . congressional procedures. Johnson found this to his cost in 1965–1968, when he tried to raise tax revenues to pay for the Vietnam War. His inability to do so may have cost him the presidency. Certainly it spelled the end for his great society programs and gave a sharp new impetus to the inflation combined with economic stagnation that has troubled the economy ever since.[20]

Supply-Side Experiment

During the late 1970s, supply-side economic theory began to gain influential supporters. It was based on the premise that economic growth and low unemployment could best be achieved by promoting investment and increased productivity. Supply-side theorists advocated using tax policy to encourage individuals and businesses to invest more and be more productive. The supply-siders asserted that income tax rates (marginal tax rates) affect people's choice between work and leisure and between saving and consumption. The higher the tax rate, the less incentive they have to work and save. Similarly, the more businesses are taxed, the less money they have to invest in new plant and equipment that can raise their productivity.

By cutting marginal tax rates, the theorists believed, the government could increase personal and corporate productivity and investment, thereby increasing the amount of goods and services produced. Thus, whereas Keynesian economic strategists sought to promote economic growth by stimulating demand for goods and services (typically via targeted increases in government spending), a strategy that often led to inflation, supply-siders focused on increasing the supply of goods and services. Because supply-siders claimed to be able to stimulate the economy without increasing inflation, their theory seemed to provide a promising approach to the economic condition that plagued the 1970s—simultaneous high inflation and high unemployment.

Many supply-side advocates also predicted that the expansion of the economy brought on by a supply-side strategy would generate enough revenue to decrease deficits even though tax rates were lower. This principle was illustrated by the Laffer curve, developed by Arthur B. Laffer of the University of Southern California. Laffer posited that government revenues rise as tax rates rise until they reach a point at which the increases in revenue brought by higher rates are less than the loss of revenue caused by the public's reduced incentive to work. Laffer and his adherents challenged the assumptions of most professional economists by arguing that the tax rates in force under the Carter administration, 1977–1981, were above this optimal level. Therefore, they believed, tax revenues could be increased not by raising rates, which would intensify the disincentives to produce, but by lowering the rates so that they would be closer to the optimal rate of taxation.[21]

Ironically, in 1963 President Kennedy also had argued that his proposed tax rate cut would result in greater revenue. Although Kennedy's reasoning was based on Keynesian theory, not supply-side theory, and his tax rate cut was enacted when economic conditions were very different from those of the late 1970s, some supply-siders pointed to the increase in tax revenue following Kennedy's tax rate cut as evidence of the validity of the Laffer curve.[22]

With the nomination in 1980 of Reagan as the Republican presidential candidate, supply-side theory was thrust into the political limelight. Reagan had become a believer in supply-side theory during the late 1970s as he prepared to run for the Republican presidential nomination. Reagan had been defeated for the nomination in 1976 by incumbent Ford in part because Reagan had advocated an austere policy of budget cuts and the conditioning of tax relief on the success of deficit reduction.[23] Supply-side theory gave Reagan a justification for moving away from painful economic prescriptions without abandoning his conservative philosophies about balancing the budget.

Reagan campaigned on his plan to cut taxes and to balance the budget through increases in revenue that he hoped the tax cut would produce and through domestic budget cuts. Reagan's plan held out the promise of prosperity without increased budget deficits and inflation. During Reagan's campaign for the 1980 nomination, his Republican opponent and eventual vice president, George H. W. Bush, reflected the skepticism of many economists and politicians when he labeled Reagan's supply-side strategy "voodoo economics." The American public, however, elected Reagan in a landslide over incumbent Carter.

The wave of antitax sentiment that hit the United States during the late 1970s and 1980s further diminished the relevancy of anti-inflationary tax measures. Presidential candidates during this period who did advocate a tax increase, such as 1984 Democratic nominee Walter Mondale and 1988 Democratic contender Bruce Babbitt, were praised by many observers for their realism but fared poorly with voters. Mondale won only thirteen electoral votes in his election battle with Reagan, and Babbitt bowed out of the race for the 1988 Democratic nomination after receiving meager support in the early primaries.

During the 1980s and 1990s, reforming the method of taxation became a major issue. In 1986, with Reagan's strong support, Congress passed the bipartisan Tax Reform Act. It was a sweeping attempt to simplify the tax code and eliminate loopholes without increasing or decreasing tax revenues. The initial impetus for the bill came from Reagan, who in January 1984 directed the Treasury Department to develop a plan to simplify the tax code.[24]

The bill that resulted reduced the number of tax brackets from fourteen to just two. It cut the top individual tax rate from 50 to 28 percent and taxed 85 percent of taxpayers at the bottom rate of 15 percent. President Reagan hailed the law as "the best anti-poverty bill, the best pro-family measure, and the best job-creation program ever to come out of the Congress of the United States."

Few Americans, however, believed that the bill had made paying their federal income taxes much easier. By 1993 the number of income tax rates had grown from two back up to five. The income tax's complexity and the intrusiveness of IRS audits stirred a populist movement aimed at finding alternatives to the income tax system. Critics pointed out that the IRS estimated that it failed to collect about $127 billion per year in income taxes. Simultaneously, many economists and policy makers wanted to restructure the tax system so that it would target consumption, thereby raising the low

U.S. savings rate that was weakening productivity gains and causing wages to stagnate.

Virtually all Republican candidates for president in 1996 announced their support for radical tax reform—either a flat tax that would target consumption or a national sales tax. But little changed in the political landscape: Democrat Clinton won reelection to the presidency and the GOP retained a slim but controlling majority in both houses of Congress. Neither party budged at all on basic tax changes for the next four years. The GOP-led Congress sent various tax bills, almost always cutting taxes in one way or another, to the White House, and Clinton invariably vetoed them. Many observers doubted either side wanted to accomplish much, at least nothing that strayed far from core party principles. Instead, the parties used the time to position themselves for the 2000 elections.

In that bitterly contested and controversial election, the voters gave a popular majority to Democrat Al Gore, but the Supreme Court, in a ruling involving disputed votes in Florida, gave that state's electoral votes, and thus the White House, to Republican George W. Bush. In spite of the essentially evenly divided outcome, the Republicans took the victory as a mandate for the tax programs they had been pushing on Clinton for much of his eight years in the White House. Consequently, Bush, with the Republicans still in control of Congress, pushed through to enactment a massive tax cutting bill in 2001 that totaled $1.35 trillion dollars over a ten-year period. A principal feature was a reduction in marginal tax rates. The lowest marginal rate was cut from 15 percent to 10 percent and the top marginal rate was cut from 39.6 percent to 35 percent. Democrats charged that the overall effect was to skew tax reduction to the most wealthy individuals in society.

Economists noted that the legislation would not provide an immediate stimulus because many provisions would take effect only later in the decade. For example, the high-profile tax rate reductions were scheduled to phase in gradually in 2001, 2004, and 2006. The bill did provide an immediate tax rebate to approximately 96 million taxpayers that for married couples generally totaled $600, with lesser amounts to single persons and heads of households.

In the end, arguments on both sides were made regarding the effectiveness of tax rate cuts.[25] Looking at the available evidence from marginal income tax rate cuts from the 1920s, 1960s, and 1980s shows that there appears to be a strong effect in increasing the progressivity of the tax structure. The wealthy appear to report more of their income when rates are lowered. One reason is that tax shelters are

Economic Terms

Classical economic theory: a body of theory developed during the late eighteenth and early nineteenth centuries maintaining that economies naturally tend to achieve full employment and that government intervention in economic matters should be limited.

Contractionary policy: restrictive fiscal or monetary policy designed to decrease demand, thereby reducing inflation.

Deficit: The amount by which government expenditures exceed government receipts during a fiscal year.

Expansionary policy: stimulative fiscal or monetary policy designed to increase demand, thereby decreasing unemployment and promoting economic growth.

Federal Reserve System: the central bank of the United States; oversees the nation's banking system and controls monetary policy.

Fiscal policy: the manipulation of government spending and tax rates for the purpose of altering the levels of unemployment, inflation, and economic growth.

Gross national product: the value of goods and services produced by an economy in a given year; the principal measure of economic growth.

Inflation: a sustained increase in prices.

Keynesian theory: the body of economic theory developed by British economist John Maynard Keynes that advocates government intervention in the economy to stimulate or dampen demand as a way to deal with high unemployment or inflation.

Laissez faire: an approach to economic policy that advocates a limited government role in the economy in favor of a reliance on free-market forces.

Monetarism: an approach to economic policy making that emphasizes the role of the money supply in determining inflation, unemployment, and economic growth.

Monetary policy: the manipulation of the money supply for the purpose of altering the levels of unemployment, inflation, and economic growth.

National debt: The amount of money owed by the federal government to all its foreign and domestic creditors at any given time.

Price stability: the absence of inflation.

Protectionism: an attempt by a government to protect the domestic markets of its industries from foreign competition by erecting trade barriers.

Recession: a prolonged downturn in the economy during which investment, incomes, and employment all decline.

Stabilization policy: monetary and fiscal policies designed to smooth undesirable fluctuations in inflation, unemployment, and the rate of economic growth.

Stagflation: simultaneous high inflation and unemployment.

Supply-side theory: an economic theory that focuses on the role played by incentives in achieving economic growth; supply-siders generally favor lower tax rates and government efforts to stimulate investments.

Tariff: a tax on imports or exports.

Trade barriers: protectionist devices such as tariffs or import quotas that make it more difficult for foreign companies to sell their goods and services in a given country.

Trade deficit: condition when a nation's imports exceed its exports.

more expensive to concoct than paying the lower tax rates. As for tax receipt increases for the government, the results are mixed and the debate on this matter will no doubt continue.

Monetary Policy

Monetary policy, like fiscal policy, is a tool with which the government attempts to stabilize the economy. It is based on the relationship of the supply of money in circulation to the performance of the economy. Because changes in the rate of growth of the money supply profoundly affect unemployment, inflation, and interest rates, the government can regulate economic activity by controlling the supply of money. Increasing the rate of growth of the money supply will stimulate the economy; decreasing it will contract the economy and combat inflation.

In contrast to fiscal policy, which is made through a slow public process of conflict and compromise among the president, Congress, and executive departments, monetary policy is determined within the Federal Reserve System, known as the "Fed." The Fed consists of twelve regional banks, several advisory bodies, and a Board of Governors.

The members of the Board of Governors, who are appointed by the president, are responsible for setting monetary policy and overseeing the operations of the Fed. The chairman of the Federal Reserve Board dominates policy making at the Fed and has often been described as the "second most powerful person" in Washington, after the president.

After 1836, when the charter of the Second Bank of the United States was allowed to expire, the United States did not have a central bank for the rest of the century. In 1907, however, a severe banking crisis prompted policy makers to reexamine the American banking system. In 1912 a commission appointed by Congress recommended that the country establish a central bank to regulate credit conditions and provide stability to the U.S. banking system. With these goals in mind, Congress in 1913 passed with President Woodrow Wilson's support the Federal Reserve Act, which created the Fed.[26]

Congress gave the Fed a permanent charter to avoid the type of political fight that prevented the First and Second Banks of the United States from being rechartered. The Federal Reserve Act does not mention a stabilization policy role for the Fed. This role evolved gradually after the Great Depression, until stabilization of the economy through monetary policy became one of the Fed's primary functions.

Monetary Policy as a Stabilization Tool

The Fed studies the economy and constructs economic forecasts that it uses to determine its monetary policy. As with fiscal policy, the goals of monetary policy include low inflation, low unemployment, and strong economic growth. Fighting inflation, however, has traditionally been the Fed's first priority.

Monetary policy was an attractive policy tool because it is less constrained by politics than is fiscal policy, which is produced through an unwieldy process of negotiation and compromise between the legislative and executive branches.[27] Because the monetary policy-making structure created by Congress was intended to be nonpolitical, politicians usually have tried to avoid the appearance of interfering in the Fed's business. In addition, the complexity of monetary policy discourages many potential critics from looking over the Fed's shoulder.[28]

Over time, monetary policy's primary role in economic stabilization has centered on fighting inflation. This can sometimes lead to restrictive monetary policies. Higher interest rates, higher unemployment, and lower output—for a short period of time—result.

Even though the maintenance of price stability is an important national goal, the political and economic costs can be formidable. Transitions to price stability are not cheap politically or economically. Although economists disagree about the long-term effects of restrictive monetary policies, there is much agreement that, in the short term, monetary actions favor some individuals in society while harming others in direct and palpable ways. Restrictive measures to counter inflation often come at the expense of groups, such as builders, labor, and export-dependent industries that suffer disproportionately from high interest rates, a strong dollar, and high unemployment.

By the same token, expansionary monetary policies may benefit these groups, but those policies' inflationary effects typically hurt others such as investors and persons living on fixed-sum pensions. In general, the very nature of a price-stabilizing monetary policy ensures that, no matter what presidents encourage, their decisions will have important political consequences.

With these types of social and political costs, it would appear that price stability is a foolish goal. But as former Federal Reserve chairman Paul Volcker noted, price stability facilitates activities that lead to greater prosperity:

> In the end there is only one excuse for pursuing such strongly restrictive monetary policies. That is the simple conviction that over time the economy will work better, more efficiently, and more fairly, with better prospects and more saving, in an environment of reasonable price stability.[29]

Price Stability as a Monetary Policy Goal

Changes in presidential thinking on the uses of monetary policy illustrate the linkage between economic thinking, policy mistakes, and real-world events. Widespread agreement has developed that the social cost of a persistent inflation exceeds the social cost of a once-and-for-all return to a stable price level. The experiences of the late 1960s and 1970s show that persistent inflation does not proceed in an orderly way but rather is an erratic process with major uncertainties producing large variations in real growth and high unemployment.

Until the late 1960s the emphasis on fine-tuning was widely accepted. Economists and public policy planners needed only to construct statistical models to accurately determine the effects of monetary and fiscal initiatives on unemployment and output. Walter Heller, who served as chairman of the Council of Economic Advisers under Kennedy, declared in 1967 that "[e]conomics has come of age in the 1960s." [30] Heller and many of his colleagues believed that the combination of Keynesian economic theory, computer technology, and enlightened leaders had made it possible for the government successfully to promote prosperity through stabilization policy. The low unemployment and inflation of the mid-1960s suggested that Heller's optimism was not unfounded.[31]

One major feature of Keynesian fine-tuning was to focus policy on reducing unemployment. The scientific basis for this emphasis centered on the work of A. W. Phillips. In 1958 Phillips showed there was an inverse relationship between wages and unemployment: higher unemployment was associated with lower wages while higher wages were associated with lower unemployment. This relation was extended to incorporate a trade-off between inflation and unemployment. In the late 1950s and up to the late 1960s most economists assumed that there was a stable trade-off between unemployment and inflation. In fact, this stable relationship could be graphically demonstrated, on what is now called the Phillips curve.

This assumption of a stable relationship had powerful appeal to presidents and policy makers. One could simply pick a mix of inflation and unemployment on the Phillips curve and conduct monetary (and fiscal) policy in accordance with those goals in mind.

This optimism was to be short-lived. One problem was that applying Keynesian theory to the management of the economy was that the political process made the Keynesian solution to inflation—cutting spending and raising taxes—difficult to enact. Politicians were predictably unwilling to adopt measures to control inflation because high taxes and cuts in government programs were unpopular with their constituents. Even if an administration were willing to propose a tax increase to combat inflation, it would seldom be able to persuade Congress to risk a recession, especially in election years.[32] Keynesian theory, therefore, offered presidents a politically practicable fiscal response only to reces-

PRESIDENTIAL INFLUENCE OVER MONETARY POLICY

The Federal Reserve System is relatively free of formal congressional or executive control. Although there are other independent agencies, none serves such an important and politically sensitive function as formulating monetary policy.

The Fed ultimately is answerable to Congress, but the only formal powers Congress has over the Fed are Senate confirmation of appointees to the board and the passage of legislation restricting or revising the Fed's powers. Congress can neither pass judgment on nor veto Fed policies. Because the Fed is self-financing (it is funded by the interest it receives from government securities and the fees it charges to banks), Congress also cannot gain leverage by threatening to withhold appropriations. The Fed's independent control of monetary policy is a potent restriction on presidential control of the economy. Except for their power to appoint Federal Reserve Board officials, presidents have no formal means through which they can influence monetary policy. Yet presidents will receive most of the blame or the praise for changes in the economy brought about by monetary policy. Given this situation, presidents naturally try to exert as much informal influence over Fed decisions as possible.

Often this influence is exercised through public statements by presidents or their subordinates suggesting changes in Fed policy. These statements usually are crafted to avoid overt criticisms of the Fed or threats against its independence. For example, on June 1, 1992, with President George H. W. Bush's reelection chances jeopardized by a weak economy, Treasury Secretary Nicholas F. Brady commented: "I think it is clear that if the Fed pulls down the lever of money supply in 1992, as was the case in 1991 when the first appearance of growth started in midsummer, then we are taking a chance with this economic recovery that I don't think is wise for this country." [1] Such statements mark presidential monetary policy positions and distance the president from ensuing Fed policies that conflict with those positions.

Board members recognize a practical need to coordinate fiscal and monetary policy and, despite some prominent exceptions, have usually cooperated with presidential efforts to do so. The Fed also has been mindful that the president is the elected representative of the people who, theoretically, embodies the policy directions preferred by the American electorate.

Although the independence of the Fed is a restraint on presidential control of the economy, it does enable presidents to rely on the Board of Governors to make politically unpopular economic decisions, thus taking some public pressure off the White House. For example, in 1965 President Lyndon B. Johnson's advisers urged him to propose a tax increase to cool down the economy, which was beginning to produce inflation. Johnson, however, refused to propose higher taxes, thus forcing the Fed to bear the responsibility for fighting inflation. When the Fed raised the discount rate, Johnson told reporters, "The Federal Reserve Board is an independent agency. Its decision was an independent action. I regret, as do most Americans, any action that raises the cost of credit, particularly for homes, schools, hospitals, and factories." As political scientist Richard Pious has noted, "Had Johnson fought for the politically unpopular but necessary tax increase, there would have been no need to blame the board for its action." [2]

1. Clyde H. Farnsworth, "Brady Warns That Fed Could Delay Recovery," *New York Times*, June 2, 1992.
2. Richard Pious, *The American Presidency* (New York: Basic Books, 1979), 315.

sion. As a consequence, countercyclical policy emphasized stabilizing unemployment at the expense of ensuring price stability.

The economics profession went through a transformation during the late 1960s as well. In particular, there was a loss of confidence by economists during the 1970s that the economy could be fine-tuned. The inflation dilemma became particularly acute in that decade when rising prices seemed beyond the control of public policy. National leaders found it difficult to muster the political will to fight inflation, and when they did cut government spending and raise taxes, inflation did not fall as expected. The inverse relationship between inflation and unemployment (increases in one had been accompanied by decreases in the other) implicit in Keynesian policies appeared to have disintegrated. Presidents could no longer be confident that a period of higher unemployment would result in lower inflation. Nor could higher inflation be relied on to bring decreased unemployment. The prevailing conditions of high inflation and unemployment, which came to be known as stagflation, defied Keynesian logic and caused presidents to lean heavily on monetary policy. The first sign that the theory and attendant fine-tuning were not working centered on the incorrect economic forecasts. The effects of monetary and fiscal initiatives (fine-tuning) were not having the expected effect on unemployment and output. Robert E. Lucas Jr. notes:

> As recently as 1970, the major U.S. . . . [forecasting] models implied that expansionary monetary and fiscal policies leading to a sustained inflation of about 4 percent [annually] . . . would lead to sustained unemployment rates of less than 4 percent, or about a full percentage point lower than unemployment averaged during any long period of U.S. history.[33]

Another issue was the lack of emphasis on the risks of inflation. An alternative theory to which many national leaders turned was monetarism. The monetarists, led by economist Milton Friedman, argued that inflation occurs when the money supply is allowed to grow faster than the economy, because a greater number of dollars is available to chase the goods and services produced. The best way to control inflation, the monetarists believed, was to reduce the amount of money in circulation.

Coordination of Fiscal and Monetary Policy

Although the organization of the Fed is designed to insulate it from outside influence, monetary policy is most effective when it is coordinated with the administration's fiscal policy. Coordination is accomplished through informal meetings between the Fed chairman and the president's top economic advisers. The Fed chairman, the Treasury secretary, the budget director, and the chairman of the CEA— a group known as the "quadriad"—usually meets at least once a month to discuss coordination of fiscal and monetary policy. Any agreements forged out of these discus-

PRESIDENTIAL APPOINTMENT OF BOARD MEMBERS

The most obvious source of influence presidents have over monetary policy is their power to appoint the members of the Federal Reserve System's Board of Governors. The Fed's Board of Governors consists of a chairman appointed by the president to a four-year term with the approval of the Senate and six members appointed to fourteen-year terms, also subject to Senate confirmation. The members' terms are staggered so that one of their terms expires at the end of January in each even-numbered year. Barring deaths or resignations by board members, a president will appoint two members and a chairman during each four-year term. In practice, however, presidents often make additional appointments to the Board of Governors. Perhaps because salaries paid to board members are generally far below what they can earn in the private sector, board members frequently resign before completing a full fourteen-year term.[1]

The chairman's term, which is renewable, does not coincide with the president's term. Consequently, during the first part of their time in office first-term presidents must work with a chairman appointed by their predecessor.

Given the influence of Fed chairmen and their potential effect on a president's reelection chances, one would expect presidents to choose Fed chairmen from among their closest economic allies. Yet the expectations of the financial and scholarly communities that presidents will appoint board members with high academic credentials and relatively nonpartisan backgrounds serve as a check against overly political appointments. Presidents are mindful that an appointment that appears to conflict with the Fed's traditional goals may cause financial markets to react in a way that hurts the economy (and therefore their own reelection chances). In addition, a president who nominates a close ally to be chairman will be unable to disavow Fed policies that are perceived to be damaging to the economy.

Consequently, presidents often have reappointed Fed chairmen who originally were appointed by their predecessors. In several cases, presidents have even reappointed a chairman who was appointed by a president of a different party. William McChesney Martin was appointed Fed chairman by President Harry S. Truman in 1951. He was reappointed by Dwight D. Eisenhower, John F. Kennedy, and Richard M. Nixon, serving continuously until he retired in 1970. Paul Volcker, a Jimmy Carter appointee, was reappointed by President Ronald Reagan. Alan Greenspan, a Reagan appointee, was reappointed by presidents George H. W. Bush, Bill Clinton, and George W. Bush. Greenspan retired in January 2006 whereupon President George W. Bush nominated Ben Bernanke to succeed him.

The chances that the Fed will cooperate with the president, however, are increased greatly if the Fed chairman is appointed by the incumbent president and shares the president's basic economic philosophy. In 1977 President Carter's expansionary fiscal policy was countered by the anti-inflationary monetary policy of Fed chairman Arthur Burns, the conservative appointee of Nixon. When Burns's term expired in 1978, Carter replaced him with G. William Miller, a Carter associate who worked closely with the president's economic team.[2]

1. Frederic S. Mishkin, *The Economics of Money, Banking, and Financial Markets,* 3d ed. (New York: HarperCollins, 1992), 398.
2. Michael Bradley, *Economics* (Glenview, Ill.: Scott, Foresman, 1980), 576–577.

FISCAL POLICY AND THE ELECTION CYCLE

The performance of the economy during a president's term affects the incumbent's chances for reelection as much as any other issue. In times of peace many Americans will "vote their pocketbooks," basing their votes on whether the American economy has given them the opportunity to meet their economic expectations. Moreover, an economy that improves during the year before an election can erase voters' memories of a longer period of economic stagnation or inflation.

Even second-term or newly elected presidents who are not immediately concerned with their reelection chances understand that economic conditions will affect the outcome of midterm elections, which will determine the strength of their party in Congress. Because the entire House and one-third of the Senate face an election every other year, significant turnover in congressional membership is possible. If an administration loses too many congressional allies, its programs may be threatened and the president's reelection chances in two years may be weakened. Fiscal policy, therefore, is never completely free from the influence of electoral politics and in an election year may be dominated by it.

The connection between economic conditions and the political success of presidents is a powerful incentive for an incumbent administration to try to create short-term improvements in the economy before an election. Economist Edward R. Tufte identified several economic trends that correspond to the U.S. election cycle. His studies of the economy from 1948 to 1976 showed that the unemployment rate on presidential election days tends to be significantly lower than twelve to eighteen months before and after an election.[1]

The elections that occurred during Dwight D. Eisenhower's presidency were notable exceptions to this trend. Eisenhower believed that Americans were more concerned with achieving a balanced budget and low inflation than with low unemployment and economic growth. He therefore opposed short-term stimulations of the economy for political purposes. The Republican losses in Congress in 1954 and 1958 and John F. Kennedy's victory over Richard M. Nixon in 1960, all of which occurred during economic slumps, provide evidence that Eisenhower may have been wrong.[2] After his 1960 defeat, Nixon wrote:

> The bottom of the 1960 dip did come in October and the economy started to move up in November—after it was too late to affect the election returns. In October, usually a month of rising employment, the jobless rolls increased by 452,000. All the speeches, television broadcasts, and precinct work in the world could not counteract that one hard fact.[3]

Tufte also found that increases in Social Security payments—the most direct way to put more money into the hands of voters—usually were enacted with the president's approval in even-numbered years during the ten months preceding an election. Because the increases in payroll taxes required to pay for the higher Social Security payments start at the beginning of a year for administrative reasons, the price of Social Security increases was not felt by taxpayers until after the election.[4] In 1975, however, Social Security benefits were indexed so that recipients automatically receive annual cost-of-living increases to offset inflation, thereby weakening the justification for politically motivated benefit increases.

In addition to stimulative fiscal policies and increased transfer payments, other presidential economic policies have been affected by electoral politics. Lyndon B. Johnson did not press Congress for a tax hike in 1966 partly because he did not wish to focus attention on the growing costs of the Vietnam War before the midterm congressional elections.[5] Despite Nixon's personal distaste for severe government economic intervention, he imposed wage and price controls on the nation in August 1971 because the deteriorating economic situation threatened his upcoming 1972 reelection bid.[6]

Presidential efforts to manipulate the economy for political purposes are seldom in the best interests of the nation's long-term economic health. Although some politicians may argue that election-year economic stimulations are attentive political responses to the desires of voters, the public pays a price for these short-term boosts. Presidents and Congresses do not always have the political will to take away preelection benefits and tax cuts after the election. Consequently, electoral pressures on economic policy contribute to budget deficits and inflation. Even when the president and lawmakers agree on measures to offset their election-year generosity, there is evidence that short-term decreases in unemployment brought about by election-year tax cuts and spending hikes may be more transitory than the increases in inflation that usually accompany them.[7]

Beyond the inflationary and budgetary costs of pandering to voters' short-term economic desires, this practice makes coherent economic policy making difficult. Tufte concluded:

> The electoral-economic cycle breeds a lurching, stop-and-go economy the world over. Governments fool around with transfer payments, making an election-year prank out of the social security system and the payroll tax. There is a bias toward policies with immediate, highly visible benefits and deferred, hidden costs—myopic policies for myopic voters.[8]

1. Edward R. Tufte, *Political Control of the Economy* (Princeton: Princeton University Press, 1978), 19–21.

2. Ibid., 7–9.

3. Richard M. Nixon, *Six Crises* (New York: Doubleday, 1962), 310–311.

4. Tufte, *Political Control of the Economy,* 29–33.

5. Norman C. Thomas and Joseph A. Pika, *The Politics of the Presidency,* 4th ed. (Washington, D.C.: CQ Press, 1996), 371.

6. Dorothy Buckton James, *The Contemporary Presidency,* 2d ed. (Indianapolis: Bobbs-Merrill, 1974), 106.

7. William R. Keech, "Elections and Macroeconomic Policy Optimization," *American Journal of Political Science* 24 (1980): 345–367.

8. Tufte, *Political Control of the Economy,* 143.

sions, however, are nonbinding, and the Fed may pursue a monetary policy at odds with the administration's goals.

The intent of both fiscal and monetary policy is to promote economic stability and prosperity, but the effects of one may cancel, blunt, or distort the intended effects of the other if the president and the Fed do not cooperate. For example, the president may ask Congress to stimulate the economy by spending more than the government receives in revenues. This requires the government to borrow funds, which increases competition for loans, thereby driving up interest rates. The higher interest rates, however, may offset the stimulative effects of the government's spending increases unless the Federal Reserve Board accommodates the president's fiscal policy by increasing the money supply.

The Fed has sometimes "leaned against the wind" to counter administration policies it considered wrong. In 1957 the Fed kept a tight rein on the money supply while the Eisenhower administration was pursuing a moderately expansionary fiscal policy. Similarly, the Fed fought inflation during the late 1960s, while spending on the Vietnam War and Johnson's Great Society social programs stimulated the economy.

The Fed may even use public pressure to attempt to change administration policies. In 1977 Fed chairman Arthur Burns testified against Carter's tax cut proposals, raising the possibility that if the tax cuts were passed, the Fed would use monetary policy to offset their stimulative effect.[34] Fed chairman Alan Greenspan warned the incoming Bush

TRADE POLICY: PROTECTIONISM VERSUS FREE TRADE

The primary question that trade policy must decide is whether to pursue free trade or whether to erect barriers that protect U.S. industries but ultimately risk reducing the overall flow of traade. Few economists or politicians would argue against the proposition that the ideal trade environment for enhancing international prosperity is one in which nations can trade goods and services without trade barriers such as tariffs, import quotas, embargoes, and strict licensing procedures for importing goods. Yet even the most ardent free trade advocates recognize that the threat of protectionism is the most effective negotiating tool the government has to convince other nations to end their unfair trading practices. Appeals for protection from specific industries often have diverted national policy from the ideal of free trade. Nevertheless, since 1934, even when Congress has enacted bills to protect specific industries or to pry open foreign markets, policy makers in the executive branch have maintained the posture that the U.S. economy will benefit from free trade.

Throughout U.S. history, tariffs have been a contentious political issue. The nation's first Treasury secretary, Alexander Hamilton, supported high tariffs, which he hoped would nurture the infant industries of the Northeast. Although the tariffs enacted during the Federalist era were not swept away when Thomas Jefferson took power in 1801, the pro-agrarian Democratic-Republicans favored trade policies that enhanced the ability of farmers to sell their products overseas.

During most of the nineteenth century, the industrial and commercial interests of the North contended with the agricultural interests of the South over national tariff policy. Because the South depended on foreign markets for its agricultural products, it opposed tariffs that could trigger a retaliatory response from its foreign customers. In addition, tariffs raised the price of many goods the South needed to buy from foreign countries. The intersectional tensions over trade policy led to the nullification crisis in South Carolina in 1832. After Congress passed a high-tariff bill in 1832, the South Carolina state legislature passed an ordinance declaring the tariff void in that state. President Andrew Jackson, determined to assert federal authority, threatened to enforce the law in South Carolina with federal troops. Hostilities were averted when Jackson and South Carolina leaders accepted a compromise tariff. Tensions caused by the tariff issue remained, however, and eventually contributed to the secession of Southern states in 1861 that brought on the Civil War.

For the rest of the nineteenth century, tariffs remained high as American industries desirous of protection grew in influence and the protariff Republican Party dominated national politics. Average U.S. tariff rates generally ranged from 35 to 50 percent of the cost of imports subject to tariffs. With the election of President Woodrow Wilson in 1913, tariff policy was reversed. That year, with President Wilson's strong support, Congress enacted the Underwood-Simmons Tariff Act, which cut tariffs sharply. Wilson saw tariff reduction as a way to help American consumers, limit the influence of powerful probusiness lobbyists, and stimulate competition.

America's participation in World War I rekindled the "America first" sentiments in the United States that led to a return of high tariffs. The Tariff Act of 1921 and the Fordney-McCumber Act of 1922, both supported by Republican president Warren G. Harding, returned tariffs roughly to their pre-1913 levels.

When the Depression struck in 1929, the governments of the major industrialized nations reacted by erecting trade barriers to protect their domestic industries. In 1930 Congress passed the Smoot-Hawley Act, which established the highest tariffs the United States had ever erected. The trade war of the early 1930s strangled trade among nations until it was a small fraction of what it had been. Protectionist measures left the world to dig out of the Great Depression without the benefits of international trade.

The counterproductive results of Smoot-Hawley created a consensus among several generations of executive branch policy makers that a U.S. free trade posture was essential to American prosperity and international security. Political scientist I. M. Destler described the role of Smoot-Hawley in solidifying free trade as a goal:

> In this consensus, the Smoot-Hawley Act of 1930 played the same role for economic affairs that Munich played for military. Just as British Prime Minister Neville Chamberlain's sincere search for "peace in our time" had only strengthened those who made war, so too had congressional use of trade barriers to aid Depression-hit American producers backfired, postwar leaders believed. Other nations had retaliated, exports had plummeted even more than imports, and the world economic catastrophe helped to spawn both Adolf Hitler's Nazi regime in Germany and aggressive militarism in Japan. Only by building a more open world could we prevent the sort of mutually destructive, beggar-thy-neighbor competition that had produced national economic disaster and international bloodshed. This meant reducing barriers to trade, and to cross-border economic transactions in general.[1]

Partly because of the president's role as chief negotiator and partly because the presidency's national constituency reduced the pressure that could be brought to bear by labor unions and specific industries seeking protection, presidents, both Democratic and Republican, became the primary force for advancing the free trade agenda. The parochial nature of the legislative branch ensured that Congress would always contain sizable numbers of protectionists. But presidents were generally successful in securing congressional support for initiatives to liberalize trade.

1. I. M. Destler, *American Trade Politics*, 2d ed. (Washington, D.C.: Institute for International Economics, 1992), 6.

administration through testimony before Congress on January 24, 1989, that the Fed would not tolerate an acceleration of inflation. George W. Bush and his economic advisers had placed a high priority on continued strong economic growth, but Greenspan indicated the Fed might slow growth in the near future to combat inflation, saying, "The Federal Reserve policy at this juncture might be well advised to err more on the side of restrictiveness than stimulus." [35]

Presidents, therefore, generally try to coordinate their fiscal policies with the Fed to produce the best economic results and limit political friction between economic policy makers. In 1993 President Clinton went out of his way to establish a good relationship with Greenspan, who had been appointed chairman of the Fed in 1987 by President Reagan and reappointed in 1992 by George H. W. Bush. In a show of their mutual desire for bipartisan coordination of economic policy, Greenspan sat with first lady Hillary Rodham Clinton at the 1993 State of the Union address. Later that year Clinton wrote to House Banking Committee chairman Henry Gonzalez defending Fed policies. Gonzalez had introduced legislation aimed at restricting the Fed's independence. Clinton expressed his opposition to Gonzalez's efforts, saying: "There is a general feeling that the system is functioning well and does not need an overhaul just now."

Yet even as Clinton and Greenspan sought to establish a good working relationship, both demonstrated their independence. Clinton nominated Alan Blinder and Janet Yellen to fill two Federal Reserve Board seats that came open in 1994. The appointment of these economists, who were considered to be more tolerant of inflation than Greenspan, was perceived as signaling Clinton's desire for the Fed to be more growth-oriented. For his part, Greenspan backed up the efforts of congressional Republicans to balance the budget by testifying that if their planned budget cuts deflated the economy, he would lower interest rates. The testimony came in February 1995, as President Clinton led the Democratic opposition to the Republican budget-cutting strategy. Later that year, Greenspan also began lobbying Congress and the president to consider a reduction in the consumer price index (CPI) as a means of limiting the budget's growth. Tax brackets and most entitlements are adjusted upward each year by a percentage that is based on the CPI. This procedure was established so that inflation would not gradually increase taxes or erode the buying power of entitlement benefits. However, many economists believed that the CPI significantly overstated inflation, thereby providing an annual windfall to taxpayers and benefit recipients. In the fall of 1995 congressional Republicans supported the idea of reducing the CPI because it would have reduced the number of politically unpopular budget cuts the Republican leadership had to make in their 1995 proposal to balance the budget in seven years.

Proponents of greater executive control over monetary policy have proposed several reforms. The most radical would be to place the Fed under executive control and allow presidents and their advisers to set monetary policy in addition to performing their other economic functions. This reform would result in the greatest degree of coordination possible between fiscal and monetary policy, because the incumbent administration would be making both. It would, however, allow presidents to use monetary policy for political purposes. Presidents could quietly stimulate the economy through monetary policy in an election year to improve their chances of being reelected.

A more modest reform that has been considered by Congress but never passed is to make the term of the Fed chairman coincide with the president's term of office. This would improve coordination because the president would presumably enter office with a like-minded Fed chairman. The chairman, however, would retain independent control over monetary policy.[36]

THE EVOLUTION OF INSTITUTIONS, LAWS, AND RULES

From the beginning of the Republic presidents understood that promoting the nation's prosperity was as much a part of their job as ensuring its security and enforcing its laws. Presidents did not, however, attempt to affect the performance of the economy through spending and taxing decisions until the Great Depression of the 1930s. Before then, the classical theory of economics, associated with the writings of Adam Smith, the eighteenth-century British economist, generally prevailed. This theory held that a laissez-faire approach to economic activity—one that allowed farmers, merchants, and manufacturers to operate unencumbered by government intervention and regulation—would result in the most prosperous economic conditions. Consequently, if the economy was running smoothly, the president's economic responsibilities were limited primarily to executing the spending and revenue measures passed by Congress, promoting a balanced budget, and working with business leaders and foreign governments to expand industrial development and trade.

The election of Thomas Jefferson as president in 1800 ushered in an economic era in the United States that was dominated by agrarian interests. Jefferson and his successors, most notably Andrew Jackson, rejected the Hamiltonian approach of concentrating the federal government's economic activities on the promotion and protection of industry and business.[37] Most economic regulatory activity and most responsibility for internal improvements that benefited commerce, such as the construction of roads, bridges, and railroads, were left to the states. Even central banking came to be considered outside the government's proper domain.

Although it had refused to recharter the national bank in 1811, Congress chartered the Second Bank of the United States in 1816 after experiencing difficulties with national finance during the War of 1812. In 1832, however, Andrew Jackson vetoed the bill that would have rechartered the Second Bank of the United States. Its charter later expired in 1836. The United States went without a central bank until 1914, when the Federal Reserve System was established.[38]

Nevertheless, the federal government did not entirely abandon business promotion. It maintained tariffs to protect industries from foreign competition, provided systems of money and patents, and in 1817 gave U.S. ships a monopoly on East Coast trade. Yet until the Civil War, the United States remained essentially an agrarian society with the proponents of agriculture dominating national politics.[39]

The Civil War brought both greater industrialization and the political division of northern and southern agrarian interests. The Republican presidents of the second half of the nineteenth century were generally conservatives who favored federal promotion of business affairs, but not federal regulation. These presidents, in cooperation with Congress, aided manufacturing and commercial interests by raising protective tariffs to new highs, giving land to railroads, and continuing to rely on regressive taxes.[40]

As the American business community grew, however, the need for regulation became more apparent. By the 1880s the power of major corporations had begun to alarm many members of the public. State governments no longer were adequate to control companies that operated in many states and functioned as monopolies. The federal government gradually responded to growing demands for regulation. In 1887 Congress passed the landmark Interstate Commerce Act, which created the first independent regulatory agency, the Interstate Commerce Commission, to regulate the nation's railroads.

In the 1890s Congress passed the Sherman Antitrust Act and other laws that gave the president and the executive branch the power to break up monopolies and otherwise regulate business activity. Presidents Theodore Roosevelt and William Howard Taft increased government prosecutions of antitrust cases and expanded other regulatory activities, setting the stage for further economic reforms under President Wilson that would widen presidential authority over the economy.

During his first term, Wilson saw Congress enact legislation establishing the Federal Reserve System, the Federal Trade Commission, and federal aid for agriculture. Wilson also expanded the government's antitrust powers and labor regulations. When the United States entered World War I during his second term, Wilson responded with highly interventionist economic policies, such as the Lever Act of 1917, which included government management of the production, supply, and price of many commodities and govern-

ment takeovers of the railroad, telephone, and telegraph industries. Although these policies ended shortly after the war, they set a precedent for government intrusion in the economy during times of crisis.[41]

Fiscal Policy

The U.S. economy did not always run smoothly, however. As the country became increasingly industrialized in the late nineteenth and early twentieth centuries, fluctuations in employment became more frequent and severe. The growth of industry also created new demands on the nation's financial system and forced the government to protect consumers and workers from the power of monopolies. Americans came to believe that government should work to prevent crises and create a stable and fair business environment. Consequently, presidents in the late nineteenth and early twentieth centuries occasionally abandoned their laissez-faire stance and proposed or supported solutions to pressing economic problems. The public increasingly looked to the president, the symbol of government and the leader of the ruling party, for economic innovation and direction. By the time the Great Depression struck, laissez-faire attitudes toward the executive's economic role had already begun to give way to more activist conceptions of governmental and presidential power.

Financial Foundations of the New Nation

George Washington ensured that economic affairs would have a central place in his administration when he appointed Alexander Hamilton as secretary of the Treasury. Hamilton often worked independently of Washington, who seldom intervened in his Treasury secretary's projects. Hamilton recognized that the international reputation of the United States and its ability to command respect among its citizens—many of whom felt stronger loyalties to their home state than to the new federal government—depended on the government's financial stability and the vibrancy of the American economy. Hamilton, therefore, aggressively promoted the interests of merchants and manufacturers and tried to create an atmosphere of confidence through measures that included the assumption of state debts by the national government and the establishment of a national bank.

Debt Assumption

Both the federal government and the states had gone heavily into debt to finance the Revolutionary War. Congress and the states had borrowed money from virtually anyone who would lend it. The United States owed money to the French government, Dutch bankers, state treasuries, and individual holders of bonds and promissory notes. A comprehensive plan was needed that would allow the government to pay back the debts without imposing burdensome taxes on its citizens, establish good international credit, and reconcile the competing interests of its domestic creditors.

Ten days after Hamilton assumed the office of secretary of the Treasury, the House of Representatives asked him to draft a plan for the "adequate support of the public credit." Hamilton used this simple mandate to construct an ambitious plan to resolve the debt situation and bring fiscal stability to the federal government.[42]

The scope and intricacy of Hamilton's plan surprised Congress when he presented it to that body on January 14, 1790. It called for federal assumption of the $25 million in debts incurred by the states during the Revolutionary War and refunding of the national debt through various bonds and securities. Existing tariffs, which Congress eventually continued at Hamilton's urging, would provide the primary source of revenues to retire the debt gradually.

The most politically divisive aspect of the debt question was how and to what degree the federal government would assume the debts of states. Predictably, the states that had paid their wartime debts, including Georgia, Maryland, North Carolina, and Virginia, were against having the federal government take over the financial burdens of the states with large debts, while the latter, including Connecticut, Massachusetts, and South Carolina, pressed for full assumption.

Division over the assumption question initially led to rejection of Hamilton's plan by a slim margin in both houses of Congress. With Secretary of State Thomas Jefferson's help, however, a compromise was reached whereby the debt assumption bill was linked to a measure moving the capital from New York to Philadelphia for ten years and then to what would become Washington, D.C. This act placated a few southern members of Congress, who changed their votes. The bill was passed, and President Washington signed it on August 4, 1790.[43]

Establishment of Income Tax

During the eighteenth and nineteenth centuries the federal government had financed its activities through excise taxes, sales of the vast national lands that stretched to the Pacific, and, most important, tariffs. Tariffs were simple to administer but were not always an adequate source of income. In wartime, when the government required increased revenue, tariff receipts would fall as trade with other countries was disrupted.[44]

During the Civil War, Congress levied a tax on incomes to help make up the gap between peacetime revenues and wartime expenses. The tax expired in 1872, and no attempt was made to revive it until 1894 when Congress levied a 2 percent tax on personal incomes greater than $3,000. In 1895, however, the Supreme Court declared the income tax unconstitutional in *Pollock v. Farmers' Loan & Trust Co.* The Court held that an income tax was a direct tax that violated Article I, Section 9, Clause 4, of the Constitution, which prohibited direct taxes unless each state paid a share in proportion to its population.

With the support of President Taft, this obstacle was overcome on February 23, 1913, when the Sixteenth Amendment was ratified. It stated: "The Congress shall have power to lay and collect taxes on incomes from whatever source derived, without apportionment among the several states, and without regard to any census or enumeration." Congress passed a 1 percent income tax in 1913 with President Wilson's backing. But the power of the income tax as a source of revenue was not demonstrated until World War I, when an expanded income tax generated the revenues necessary for U.S. participation in the war.

Thereafter income taxes grew in importance. In 1915 customs duties and excise taxes provided 85 percent of federal revenues. By 1930 income taxes were providing more than half of the funds coming into the Treasury, while the share from customs and excises had fallen below 30 percent.[45]

Although the Sixteenth Amendment had given Congress the power to levy income taxes, the amendment greatly expanded presidential power by providing a source of revenue that could finance presidential foreign policy and domestic initiatives. As political scientist Emmet J. Hughes noted, the income tax was "ready for lavish use by future Presidents to meet future needs or crises. And without such a reservoir of funds, there hardly could have followed any grand dreams of Presidential programs in the realms of welfare, education, health, housing, and transport."[46] The tax also enhanced the president's ability to make fiscal policy. Increasing and decreasing income taxes would become one of the methods most commonly used by presidents and Congress to combat inflation and recession.

Budget and Accounting Act of 1921

During the eighteenth and nineteenth centuries presidents had no formal responsibility to submit a budget to Congress or even conduct a comprehensive review of executive branch spending proposals. Executive departments and agencies submitted budget requests directly to Congress in a "Book of Estimates." A number of presidents, such as John Quincy Adams, Martin Van Buren, John Tyler, James K. Polk, James Buchanan, Ulysses S. Grant, and Grover Cleveland, did insist on revising budget estimates, but the budgeting process continued to be dominated by Congress and individual executive departments and agencies.[47]

During the budget process, Congress had no means to balance expenditures with revenues or evaluate alternative spending programs. As a result, the overlapping or extravagant spending proposals submitted by executive departments and agencies could not be weeded out of the budget. Moreover, the lack of central coordination made the use of the budget as an instrument of fiscal policy impossible.[48]

Before and during World War I, the nation had incurred a series of budget deficits that created a debt problem and led Congress to seek to reform the financial machinery of the executive branch. With the 1921 Budget and Accounting Act, Congress set up new procedures and organizations to provide more central coordination of the budget process.[49] The act established two important offices—the Bureau of the Budget (which became the Office of Management and Budget in 1970) and the General Accounting Office. The former was created to centralize fiscal management of the executive branch under the president; the latter was designed to strengthen congressional oversight of spending.

The act also ended the practice of allowing executive departments and agencies to address their annual budget proposals directly to Congress. The Budget Bureau, originally a subdivision of the Treasury Department but later placed under the direct control of the president, became a central clearinghouse for all budget requests. The Budget Bureau evaluated these requests, adjusted them to fit the president's goals, and consolidated them into a single executive branch budget for Congress's consideration. Consequently, the Budget Act of 1921 transformed budget making from a random and fragmented process over which presidents had little control into a tool with which presidents could advance their social, economic, and defense priorities.

The Impoundment Control Act of 1974

The Constitution did not spell out whether presidents were required to promptly spend funds appropriated by Congress or whether they could make independent judgments about the timing and even the necessity of putting appropriated funds to use. Many presidents during the nineteenth century took advantage of this constitutional ambiguity to impound appropriated funds they believed unnecessary or wasteful. In effect, the impoundment power gave presidents a second veto over appropriations because they could withhold funds Congress intended to spend.

After World War II presidents increasingly used impoundments as a fiscal policy tool. Presidents Harry S. Truman, Dwight D. Eisenhower, and Kennedy all clashed with Congress over their withholding of appropriations for defense projects. In 1966 President Johnson impounded $5.3 billion in domestic appropriations to slow inflationary trends brought on by the Vietnam War.

Presidential impoundments reached their zenith after Richard M. Nixon became president in 1969. Nixon impounded billions of dollars of appropriations during the first five years of his presidency. He argued that he was withholding funds only as a financial management technique designed to slow inflation. Democratic leaders in Congress, however, charged that Nixon used impoundments to overturn Congress's spending decisions and further his own

social goals. For example, after Congress overrode a presidential veto to pass the 1972 Clean Water Act, Nixon impounded $9 billion that was intended to implement the act. The conflict between Nixon and Congress over impoundments led to the passage of a law that restricted presidential use of impoundments.[50]

The Impoundment Control Act of 1974 (which was one title of the Congressional Budget and Impoundment Control Act) created new procedures designed to prevent a president from impounding appropriations against the will of Congress. Under the act presidents were required to notify Congress when they decided to impound (rescind) appropriated funds permanently. Congress had forty-five days in which to signal its approval of this permanent impoundment, known as a rescission, by a majority vote of both houses. After forty-five days, if Congress had not approved, presidents were required to spend the money. The law also allowed presidents to defer spending appropriated funds by notifying Congress that they were doing so. The funds could be held until one of the houses of Congress overturned the deferral. In 1983, however, the Supreme Court overturned one-house legislative vetoes in *Immigration and Naturalization Service v. Chadha.* Subsequently, both houses of Congress had to pass legislation directing the president to spend the funds. But in 1987 the Supreme Court ruled that because the deferral authority was contingent on the unconstitutional one-house veto, the president could no longer exercise it.[51]

After presidential impoundment powers were scaled back in 1974, Congress adopted some presidential rescissions but more often it ignored the president's proposed cuts or substituted cuts of its own. As a result many members of Congress argued that the 1974 restrictions on presidential impoundment authority had been a mistake. They wanted a strengthened presidential impoundment power that could help combat wasteful or unnecessary spending by Congress. These sentiments were focused during the 1980s and 1990s on the enactment of a line-item veto.

Line-Item Veto

The *line-item veto* or *item veto* refers generically to a number of proposals intended to strengthen the president's authority to rescind specific spending items within an appropriations bill. The two most prominent forms of the line-item veto are the "enhanced rescission" and the "expedited rescission." *(See "Line-Item Veto," p. 656, in Chapter 12.)*

Enhanced rescission authority would allow presidents to propose rescissions in appropriations bills as they can under the Impoundment Control Act. These rescissions would go into effect automatically, unless both chambers of Congress voted to reject them. The president could then veto the legislation disapproving of the rescissions, forcing both houses to muster a two-thirds vote to override the veto. The enhanced rescission represented a vast expansion of the presidential impoundment power because the president's rescission choices would prevail unless Congress could muster enough votes to clear the high hurdle of a veto override.

This is the approach the Congress took in 1996, with warm support from President Clinton. However, the law—which went into effect in early 1997—was a short-lived experiment. Clinton used it sparingly but on items dear to the heart of congressional members. He vetoed several parts of military construction appropriations bills, which traditionally have been vehicles to bring federal spending to members' districts and states, thereby helping them with voters. Congress promptly rejected the vetoes, Clinton vetoed the rejection, and Congress overrode Clinton's vetoes.

But the death of the idea came at the hands of the Supreme Court in 1998 when it declared the law unconstitutional on a 6–3 vote. The Court ruled that the line-item veto violated provisions of the Constitution that established the procedure for the enactment of laws. Writing for the majority, Justice John Paul Stevens said: "If the Line-Item Veto Act were valid, it would authorize the president to create a different law—one whose text was not voted on by either House of Congress or presented to the president. If there is to be a new procedure in which the president will play a different role in determining the final text of what may 'become a law,' such change must come not by legislation but through . . . [constitutional] amendment."

Although the Court stuck down the enhanced rescission line-item veto, the constitutionality of the expedited rescission version has yet to be tested. Expedited rescission authority is a more modest expansion of presidential power. Under this procedure presidents also would propose a set of rescissions. As under the Impoundment Control Act, these rescissions would not go into effect unless both houses of Congress approved them. But under an expedited rescission, Congress would be required to vote on the rescission proposals within a set time period. Thus, Congress could not overrule the president's rescission proposal merely through inaction.

Monetary Policy

Establishment of the National Bank

In the founding years of the Republic, the assumption of debts by the federal government was one component of Treasury Secretary Alexander Hamilton's plan to bring financial credibility and stability to the new nation. The other component was the establishment of a national bank. Hamilton outlined his bank proposal to Congress in December 1790. He asked Congress to charter a national bank to assist in the financial operations of the United States. It was to be run primarily by private directors and funded by private capital. Of the bank's original $10 million capitalization, only $2 million was to come from the Treasury, while the rest would be provided by individual investors.

Opponents and supporters of the bank saw that it would provide the president with added power over the economy and would serve as a symbol of the preeminence of the federal government. Many of the bank's detractors opposed it because they feared granting more influence to the federal government. Others, including Jefferson, argued that the bank was unconstitutional because the Constitution did not explicitly give the government the power to charter a bank.[52] Legislators in favor of the bill prevailed, however, and the legislation passed both houses by February 1791.

George Washington solicited the opinions of his cabinet on whether to sign the bill. Attorney General Edmund Randolph concurred with Jefferson that no authority existed in the Constitution for the bank's establishment. Washington, who conceived of the president's veto as a tool to prevent the passage of unconstitutional legislation, was concerned about this charge against the bank. Although he favored establishing the bank as a practical step toward a stronger U.S. economy, he was prepared to veto the bill if he became convinced of its unconstitutionality. On February 16, 1791, he asked Hamilton for an assessment of the objections of Jefferson and Randolph. Hamilton responded with his "Defense of the Constitutionality of an Act to Establish a Bank." The paper artfully refuted the Virginians' claim that the bank would be unconstitutional by emphasizing the necessity of a broad interpretation of the government's economic powers. On February 25, Washington signed the bill chartering the bank.[53]

The First Bank of the United States functioned well for twenty years, but Congress refused by one vote to recharter it in 1811. Because the bank was the brainchild of Federalist Hamilton, many members of the Democratic-Republican Party, which dominated U.S. politics in the early nineteenth century, opposed renewing its charter. Some party members agreed with Democratic-Republican Party leaders Thomas Jefferson and James Madison that the bank was unconstitutional. This strong political opposition to the bank, combined with the lobbying efforts of commercial banks that competed for business with the national bank, led to its demise.[54]

Federal Reserve Act of 1913

Congress chartered the Second Bank of the United States in 1816, but the bank existed for only twenty years until forced out of existence by its arch opponent, President Andrew Jackson. *(See "The Evolution of Institutions, Laws, and Rules," p. 807)*

From 1836 to 1913 the United States had no formally constituted monetary authority. During this period monetary policy was governed by the combination of the gold standard and powers vested in the Treasury Department. However, a variety of bank panics and subsequent depressions paved the way for reform. A banking panic and recession in 1907 led to reforms that would create a lender of last resort. In 1908 Congress created the National Monetary Commission that drew up recommendations that culminated in the creation of the Federal Reserve Act of 1913.

While the Fed was created to provide financial stability, sufficient vagueness existed in the law that allowed the Fed to evolve into the policy-making body it is today. In particular, the law gave the Fed flexibility to respond to seasonal fluctuations in the demand for money.

The Accord of 1951

Until 1951 the Treasury Department was the most influential in affecting monetary policy. One consequence of this arrangement was that the Fed had to conduct policy consistent with supporting the prices of government securities and keeping interest rates low. During World War II this was particularly important to keep the cost of financing down.

With the Accord of 1951, the Fed was given the freedom not only to support government securities but also to minimize monetization of the debt. The effect of this agreement between Congress, the Treasury, and the Fed was to provide the Fed with considerable freedom in conducting monetary policy. In effect, countercyclical policy—such as the use of monetary policy to offset inflationary or deflationary pressures—was instituted with this agreement. Modern monetary policy in the United States is in large part a function of the Accord of 1951.

International Monetary Policy

When one nation imports goods from another, it usually must pay for those goods in the seller's currency. The cost of the seller's currency in terms of the buyer's currency is called the exchange rate. Presidents are concerned about exchange rates because they affect a country's ability to export its goods. For example, the higher a country's currency is valued on international markets, the more expensive its goods will be for foreign buyers. Because a dollar that is worth less relative to foreign currencies will make U.S. goods cheaper for foreigners to buy, intervention to lower the value of the dollar is a prominent tool that presidents have used when

PRESIDENTIAL POWER IN INTERNATIONAL ECONOMICS: 1995 MEXICAN FINANCIAL CRISIS

The extent of presidential power in the area of international economics was demonstrated in early 1995 by President Bill Clinton's response to the Mexican financial crisis. On December 20, 1994, Mexico unexpectedly devalued the peso. Concerns in the international currency markets about political instability in Mexico, and about that country's debt level and trade deficit, created strong downward pressure on the peso. The next day, the Mexican government decided to let its currency float freely. The value of the peso plummeted 40 percent within a few days.

The peso's collapse sent the American financial community into a panic. Banks that had made large loans to Mexico feared that they would take huge losses. The value of mutual funds and retirement funds that had invested in Mexico dropped sharply. Businesses in the United States that had expanded to take advantage of the prospect of increased exports to Mexico faced the possibility that Mexicans would no longer be able to afford their products and services. The Clinton administration estimated that 700,000 jobs in the United States depended on reestablishing financial stability in Mexico.

Initially, the president planned to present a financial rescue plan to Congress for its authorization. The plan would have provided $40 billion in American loans and loan guarantees to Mexico in exchange for promises of further Mexican economic reforms. Although congressional leaders of both parties voiced support for such a package, congressional vote-counters doubted that the plan had enough support to pass. Many rank-and-file House members saw a Mexican financial relief plan as an unnecessary taxpayer bailout of a corrupt government and of Wall Street brokers who had made bad investments.

Facing defeat in Congress on the plan, Clinton decided to act without congressional approval. On January 31, 1995, he announced that despite Congress's reluctance to go along with a Mexican rescue plan, the United States would provide $20 billion to Mexico in short-term loans and longer-term loan guarantees. The president also announced that he and Treasury Secretary Robert E. Rubin had secured from the International Monetary Fund and other international lending sources an additional $30 billion in loans to Mexico.

The White House also issued a joint statement by Clinton and congressional leaders saying that the president "has full authority to provide this assistance." Some critics in Congress blasted the president for bypassing Congress, but most members were relieved that they would not have to cast a politically difficult vote on the issue.

The $20 billion in loans came from the Exchange Stabilization Fund (ESF), which has about $25 billion in reserves. The primary role of the fund, which was established in 1934 by the Gold Reserve Act, has been to provide a means by which the Treasury secretary, acting with the approval of the president, could stabilize the dollar on foreign exchange markets. During the Ronald Reagan and George H. W. Bush administrations, the ESF had been used to provide small short-term loans to Latin American nations experiencing financial problems. For example, President Ronald Reagan had authorized an $825 million short-term loan to Mexico from the ESF in response to a 1982 peso crisis. But the Clinton rescue plan far exceeded previous uses of the ESF for bailouts of foreign currencies.

By early 1996 the rescue plan was generally viewed as a qualified success. Mexico had begun to repay the loans, and investment capital was returning to that country. Clinton's use of the ESF undoubtedly established a precedent that future presidents could use to address foreign financial crises of similar magnitude. The action also reaffirmed presidential primacy and flexibility in international economic policy making.

trade balances were a political (as opposed to an economic) problem.

Why are trade balances not necessarily an economic problem? A central fact of economics is that for every buyer there is a seller and for every seller there is a buyer. Accounts must balance, a statement that is never more true than when the discussion is about the balance of payments.

If an American spends a dollar on something from a foreign country, that dollar cannot be spent in the foreign country. It must be exchanged for the country's domestic currency so that in the end the dollar ends up in the United States. How the foreign person spends the dollar dictates where it ends up on the balance of payments. Spending the dollar on goods or services is a credit on the current account. But spending the dollar on some U.S. investment is a credit on the capital account. The dollar is spent in the United States, and it contributes to U.S. economic activity either way, but it is counted differently.

The current and capital account are mirror images of each other. If a deficit is run on the current account, there is a surplus on the capital account. This means more investment in the United States. However, if there is a surplus on the current account, then there will be a deficit between foreign and U.S. investment. In this case, foreign citizens purchase more U.S. goods, but there is more U.S. investment overseas than is coming in.

In the short run, sometimes the two accounts do not cancel each other out. There are many possible reasons for this situation, but when it arises the monetary authority (i.e., central bank) typically steps in to purchase or sell domestic currency (i.e., dollars) to either strengthen or devalue the dollar during this period or to aid another country or country's exchange rate. These actions are usually called Official Settlements.

The focus on how the dollar is counted can cause great political trouble for a president. Protectionist pressures are sown when the current account is the focus. But exclusive attention on the current account ignores the massive amount of economic activity created by what is counted in the capital account. Historically, a current account deficit (capital account surplus) has occurred during decades when the U.S. economy enjoyed sustained economic prosperity. The problem, then, is a political one, not an economic one. In fact, so long as the scope and scale of economic activity is growing, the U.S. economy will continue to prosper.

For substantial parts of its history, the United States has been a debtor nation—and this has generally been a good thing. For example, one factor that helped advance the development of the U.S. economy in the late nineteenth and early twentieth centuries was the inflow of foreign investment, which meant large surpluses on the capital account and large deficits in the current account. Britain, in particular, provided a large amount of investment that led to the construction of canals, factories, and railroads. The result was to enhance U.S. productivity.[55]

Bretton Woods Agreement

After World War II the United States led development of an international monetary system that established stable exchange rates conducive to free trade. Forty-four nations signed an agreement at Bretton Woods, New Hampshire, in 1944 that made gold the standard by which currencies were valued. The Bretton Woods agreement established the International Monetary Fund (IMF) to oversee adjustments in exchange rates and the World Bank to provide loans for postwar reconstruction. The United States sought to build a predictable international currency system that would prevent both destabilizing fluctuations in exchange rates and deliberate currency devaluations that could threaten free trade.

Each member of the IMF was required to declare a par value for its currency in relation to the U.S. dollar, which was pegged to gold at $35 per troy ounce. Official exchange rates of the world's currencies were not allowed to fluctuate more than 1 percent from their par value. Because the United States held most of the world's gold reserves and the U.S. dollar's value was backed by the government's pledge to convert dollars into gold, nations used the dollar as an international trading currency and as a reserve of wealth just like gold. In effect, the United States functioned as banker to the world.[56]

The Bretton Woods arrangement worked well during the 1940s, 1950s, and early 1960s. The stability it produced brought an enormous increase in world trade and the resurgence of economies devastated by World War II. By the mid-1960s, however, the dollar's role as an international reserve currency was causing the United States economic problems. Because other nations wanted to hold dollars to trade and back up their own currencies, dollars flowed overseas but failed to return. The result was a growing U.S. balance-of-payments deficit that weakened international confidence in the dollar and led many foreign investors to exchange their dollars for gold. U.S. gold reserves fell from more than $23 billion in 1949 to just $10 billion in 1971.

In response to this problem, on August 15, 1971, President Nixon stunned the world by announcing that the U.S. Treasury would no longer convert dollars into gold. The dollar's value would be allowed to float to a level determined by international currency markets. Because other currencies depended on the dollar, they, too, would have to float. The dollar, which had been overvalued, declined against other currencies, making U.S. goods cheaper overseas.[57] Nixon's decision ushered in a new era of international monetary relations that required a higher degree of coordination among governments. Although several countries proposed plans to salvage the Bretton Woods system, by

1973 all major currencies adopted some form of a floating exchange rate regime.

Managing the Value of the Dollar

Under the post–Bretton Woods system of floating exchange rates, governments have—for political reasons—often attempted to adjust the value of their currency through intervention in the currency markets. The United States and other governments intervene in currency markets through their central banks. If U.S. policy makers decide that the value of the dollar is too high, they can lower its value by selling dollars on the open market. Conversely, a weak dollar can be strengthened if the central bank shrinks the supply by buying dollars on the open market.

Intervention in currency markets is primarily the responsibility of the secretary of the Treasury, but the Fed also plays a major role. Decisions to intervene are usually made jointly by representatives of the Treasury Department and the Fed. For major interventions, the Treasury secretary and the Fed chairman will usually consult. Treasury and the Fed independently control distinct accounts that can be used for the purpose of currency intervention. The actual transactions from both accounts are conducted by the Federal Reserve Bank of New York. The Fed, therefore, has the means to intervene in currency markets on its own initiative. But in practice, it will not do so if Treasury has an objection.[58]

Currency interventions do not technically require presidential approval. But the central role of the Treasury secretary, who serves at the pleasure of the president, ensures that the chief executive can exercise decisive influence over the process. In addition, even with their sizable reserves, it is difficult for Treasury and the Fed to alter the value of the dollar without cooperation from the central banks of the other industrialized powers. Consequently, coordination of exchange rate policies among the major industrialized countries is usually necessary to affect currency values. The president, as chief economic manager and the official charged with negotiating with foreign countries, must oversee this coordination.

Negotiations with other nations on currency levels are usually led by the Treasury secretary and attended by representatives of the Fed. Currency levels are also frequently discussed by the president and the leaders of the Group of Eight (G-8) nations at their annual economic summits. Negotiations between governments often have resulted in informal agreements to take concerted action to adjust exchange rates. In January 1989, for example, the major industrial nations agreed to slow the rise of the dollar, which was being pushed up near a previously agreed-upon secret limit by rising interest rates in the United States that were attracting foreign capital. At the same time, West Germany wanted its currency to be held up because of fears in that country that a weaker mark would lead to

inflation by increasing the costs of imports. The world's major central banks responded by buying marks with dollars, thereby holding down the dollar's rise and propping up the mark.[59]

The importance of currency intervention was illustrated dramatically in the early 1980s. The strong dollar had encouraged American consumers to buy foreign goods and made American goods too expensive overseas to compete with comparable foreign products, thus contributing to the growing U.S. trade deficit. Early in his first term President Reagan maintained that the exchange markets were inherently stable. His administration largely ignored the dollar's value in the belief that any market fluctuations that occurred were prompted by uncertainty about government intentions. Therefore a policy that consistently avoided intervention would yield the most stable exchange rates.[60] But when the current account deficit jumped from $44.5 billion in 1983 to $99.7 billion in 1984, the Reagan administration for largely political reasons (i.e., pressure from export dependent industries) concluded that it had to act to bring down the value of the dollar. It announced in January 1985, shortly after James A. Baker III had taken over as Treasury secretary, that the United States would intervene in the currency markets to bring down the value of the dollar. U.S. intervention, sometimes with the cooperation of other central banks, probably did temporarily lower the value of the dollar from the peak reached in February 1985.

The president's international economic powers have become increasingly important as nations have become more economically interdependent as a result of high volumes of trade, integrated financial markets, multinational corporations, and other factors that bind the world's economies. Because of this shared economic destiny among industrial nations, presidents must function not just as national economic managers but also as international economic coordinators. They dispatch the U.S. trade representative to international negotiations aimed at reducing trade barriers, oversee the Treasury Department's negotiations with other finance ministries about the value of major currencies, and announce U.S. economic policies to the international community.

Since 1975 presidents also have attended annual economic summits where the leaders of the major industrial nations have met to confer on broad issues of economic policy. These meetings, which are attended by the leaders of the United States, Japan, Germany, France, Great Britain, Italy, and Canada (known collectively as the Group of Seven or G-7), have greatly increased international economic coordination. By 2002 the G-7 and Russia formed the G-8. (Russia was first invited to attend a portion of the G-7 meetings in 1994.) By 2005 the G-7 was to dissolve completely into the G-8, with Russia becoming a full-fledged member of the elite group.

These economic summits have focused attention on the international component of economic policy, forced politicians to develop a better understanding of international economic issues, created a justification for frequent meetings between finance ministers and other economic officials, and provided a forum where economic matters can be discussed in the broader context of allied relations. Because the annual meetings compel the leaders of the world's top industrial powers to face one another, they have had a positive influence on free trade. The leader of a country that has erected protectionist trade barriers or taken other measures contrary to the interests of the group must justify those measures to the other leaders and face their collective pressure to reverse the action.

Trade Policy

Because the Constitution gives Congress the power "to regulate Commerce with foreign Nations," the rules governing foreign trade are set by legislation. Since the Great Depression, however, trade legislation has contained broad grants of power to the president to implement the laws through international negotiations and through tariffs and other trade barriers designed to force other countries to open up their markets to American products.

Congress has granted the executive broad trade powers because only the president has the authority to negotiate with foreign governments. Therefore, when Congress adopted the strategy of pursuing mutual reductions in tariffs through international negotiations in 1934, it had to turn to the president to carry out those negotiations. In addition, Congress wanted to isolate U.S. trade policy from pressures for protectionism from specific industries. Because individual members of Congress have to be concerned with the economic conditions in their states and districts, protectionist sentiments have tended to be stronger in Congress than in the executive branch. If a single industry such as agriculture or steel predominates in a congressional district, then that district's representative often will be disposed to support protectionist measures for that industry. According to political scientist Erwin C. Hargrove, by delegating power to the president Congress is able to respond to the local interests of its constituents without undermining the free trade position of the nation:

> Congress would rather not have responsibility for setting specific tariff levels because the flood of demands for individual industrial areas would be far too intense. Therefore, it has allowed the Executive to set such levels within parameters set by Congress. This permits members of Congress to make their requests in behalf of constituency interests and still permit the President to do what is needed for a national position on international trade.[61]

International Trade Negotiations

After entering office in 1933, President Franklin Roosevelt acted to reverse the onerous Smoot-Hawley tariff that economists later were to conclude contributed significantly to the Great Depression. With the enthusiastic support of his secretary of state, Cordell Hull, Roosevelt asked the Democratic-controlled Congress to delegate to him the authority to reduce U.S. tariffs up to 50 percent in return for equal tariff concessions by other nations. Despite nearly unanimous Republican opposition, Congress passed the Trade Agreements Act of 1934, which delegated this power to the president. Armed with new authority, the Roosevelt

The leaders of the Group of Eight gather in Birmingham, England, for their annual summit, May 1998. Pictured, from left to right, are Jean Chrétien of Canada, Helmut Kohl of Germany, Boris Yeltsin of Russia, Tony Blair of Great Britain, Jacques Chirac of France, Romano Prodi of Italy, Ryutaro Hashimoto of Japan, President Bill Clinton, and Jacques Santer of the European Commission. The group includes seven nations that account for about two-thirds of the world's output plus Russia, which joined the group in 1997.

administration negotiated bilateral agreements with many nations that cut tariffs and increased the flow of trade. The increased access to foreign markets that resulted helped stimulate the U.S. economy. After the initial success of Roosevelt's negotiations, congressional grants of power to the president to negotiate mutual tariff reductions became a regular feature of U.S. trade policy.

After World War II, President Truman sought to establish more sweeping arrangements to reduce international protectionism. At the urging of the United States, twenty-three nations signed the General Agreement on Tariffs and Trade (GATT) in 1947. Since then most nations have signed the agreement. Under GATT, multilateral negotiations aimed at reducing trade barriers were to be held at regular intervals. The signatories also agreed to the most favored nation principle, which committed each nation to apply tariff rates equally to all the other GATT participants. In addition, the agreement prohibited certain restrictive trade practices such as import quotas and set up procedures to mediate trade disputes and implement sanctions against violators of the agreement.

Since 1947, GATT signatories have held eight multinational trade negotiation rounds. The first five rounds produced small but significant tariff reductions. In 1962 Congress passed the Trade Expansion Act with the strong support of the Kennedy administration. The act gave the president broad authority to reduce or eliminate U.S. import duties in return for similar trade concessions from other countries. The sixth round of GATT, known as the Kennedy Round, resulted in tariffs on industrial products being cut by an average of more than 35 percent. In addition, for the first time the GATT participants discussed nontariff barriers to trade. When the round ended in 1967, however, many industries in the United States and in other countries lobbied against further cuts in tariffs because they feared increased foreign competition.

After the Kennedy Round, dozens of bills with protectionist provisions were introduced in Congress. Few were passed, but the drive for trade barrier reduction had temporarily peaked. Congress did not renew the president's authority to participate in multilateral trade negotiations, which had expired in 1967, until it passed the Trade Act of 1974 after the next GATT round was already under way. Although this act extended the president's authority to negotiate reductions of trade barriers, it placed more restrictions on the president's power and reflected the growing pressures from U.S. domestic industries to retaliate against unfair trading practices of foreign countries. The seventh round of GATT (Tokyo Round) was less successful in reducing tariff barriers than the Kennedy Round, although it made some progress on eliminating nontariff barriers.

Throughout much of its history the U.S. economy has experienced trade surpluses as well as deficits. In 1981, how-

ever, the U.S. trade surplus began to decline rapidly as exports failed to keep pace with imports. The following year the U.S. current account, a measure of the net flow of goods and services traded with other countries, dropped into deficit. By 1987 the current account deficit had reached $167 billion. The large current account deficit cost the U.S. economy good jobs because Americans were buying so many products manufactured overseas. In addition, because the United States had to borrow to finance the trade imbalance, the current account deficit was increasing the U.S. dependence on foreign credit and adding to the debts of the nation.

These problems focused public attention on the trade deficit and increased political pressure on Congress to pass legislation to protect American industries from foreign competition. In response to the mounting U.S. trade deficit, Congress enacted the Omnibus Trade Act in 1988, which mandated retaliatory responses to unfair foreign trade practices. President Reagan's firm support of free trade prevented Congress from enacting a more protectionist trade bill.

The continuing trade deficit during the late 1980s and early 1990s, however, sustained protectionist sentiments in Congress and among the American people. With the breakup of the Soviet Union and the end of the cold war, more attention was focused on economic competition with Japan and western Europe. Many Americans viewed the trade deficit as a sign of American economic decline relative to its major industrial allies.[62]

In 1994 the eighth round of GATT (Uruguay Round) was completed. This breakthrough agreement signed by more than one hundred nations provided for tariffs to be reduced on most manufactured items by an average of one-third. The round was the first to reduce barriers on agricultural products, protect intellectual property rights, and establish rules covering trade in services.

The most controversial aspect of the far-reaching agreement, however, was the establishment of the World Trade Organization (WTO), which would replace GATT's existing institutional structure. Some critics charged that it would damage U.S. sovereignty because its dispute resolution procedures could not be vetoed by the United States. If the United States were judged to be at fault in a trade dispute, it would have to accept the WTO's ruling or open itself up to sanctions. But supporters of the agreement argued successfully that such a mechanism was precisely what was needed to protect American commercial interests. Because of the relatively open trading posture of the United States, Americans were far more often the injured party in trade disputes. Therefore, they contended, reforms that put teeth into GATT enforcement procedures would be a great advantage to American exporters.

In 1994 President Clinton, a strong advocate of free trade, lobbied heavily for GATT. On November 29, 1994, a lame-duck House of Representatives passed legislation implementing GATT by a vote of 288–164. The Senate followed on December 1 by passing the act, 76–24. Clinton signed the legislation on December 8, concluding the eight-year effort to negotiate and approve the Uruguay Round.

Since taking office in 2001, George W. Bush has followed tradition to open international markets and remove tariffs. Talks on trade liberalization began in 2001 in Doha, Qatar. In addition to the Doha talks, the Bush administration had by 2004 concluded trade talks with nations around the world including Australia, Bahrain, and Morocco. Since 2004, the Bush administration has been in trade agreement negotiations with many other nations or regional organizations including Colombia, Ecuador, Oman, Peru, the Southern African Customs Union (Botswana, Lesotho, Namibia, South Africa, and Swaziland), Panama, Thailand, and the United Arab Emirates.

North American and Central American Free Trade Agreements

Even as the eighth GATT round was proceeding, the United States embarked on negotiations with Canada and Mexico to establish a single North American free trade area. From start to finish, this was a presidential initiative.

President George H. W. Bush had responded positively to a proposal by President Carlos Salinas de Gortari of Mexico to negotiate a free trade agreement.[63] But then Bush went even further, advocating in June 1990 a long-run goal of creating a free trade area encompassing the entire Western Hemisphere "stretching from the port of Anchorage to the Tierra del Fuego." The first step would be concluding a North American Free Trade Agreement (NAFTA) between Canada, Mexico, and the United States.

The idea of concluding a free trade agreement with Mexico prompted immediate resistance in Congress. Many members, especially those representing districts where older industries and union labor predominated, argued that a free trade agreement with Mexico would cost American jobs. They contended that the elimination of tariffs on goods from Mexico, a relatively poor country where workers were paid low wages, would disadvantage U.S. industry, which had much higher labor costs. They envisioned a scenario in which Mexican exports would undercut American goods in the United States and American businesses would send factories south of the border to take advantage of lower wages and environmental standards.

Presidents Bush and Clinton and their free trade allies in Congress countered that the United States had many economic advantages over Mexico, and these would offset the lower labor costs in Mexico. They reminded critics that the elimination of Mexican trade barriers, which were higher than American trade barriers, would open completely a large and increasingly prosperous market to U.S. businesses, thereby creating jobs in the United States. They also noted that failure to establish open trading relations with Mexico could forfeit this market to competitors in the European Community and Asia.

Unlike GATT, which few American voters understood well, NAFTA had been reduced by supporters and critics to a relatively simple set of propositions. To critics, the free trade agreement meant the loss of American jobs and the erosion of American wages, under pressure from a lower-wage trading partner. To supporters, the agreement would bring all the classic benefits of free trade: more exports, more jobs, more economic growth, and less inflation. As such, the debate on NAFTA became the most emotional and hard-fought debate on trade in the post-Depression era.

President Bush signed the NAFTA accord shortly before he left office in January 1993, leaving the fight for its approval in Congress to President Clinton. Clinton announced his support for the agreement but declared that he would negotiate side agreements with Mexico to address concerns about environmental protection, labor, and import surges. But these side agreements did not satisfy NAFTA's critics, most of whom sought the defeat of the agreement in Congress.

President Clinton demonstrated the centrality of the presidency to the maintenance of the free trade position by mounting a bipartisan campaign for NAFTA's passage in Congress. Despite advice from some advisers in August 1993 that securing approval of NAFTA was a lost cause, Clinton skillfully rallied a bipartisan coalition containing more Republicans than Democrats to pass the agreement.[64] Clinton used every means of presidential power at his disposal to sway undecided members of Congress, including old-fashioned deal making in which he promised to deliver pet projects and other political favors to wavering members in exchange for their votes.

The implementing legislation and side agreements were approved 234–200 by the House on November 17, 1993. The Senate followed three days later with a 61–38 vote of approval. Clinton signed the bill December 8, and the agreement went into effect on January 1, 1994.

The precedent set by NAFTA led to a subsequent regional agreement that would move the United States on a path toward further trade liberalization. The Central American Free Trade Agreement (CAFTA) was an achievement of the George W. Bush administration. CAFTA included the Central American countries of Costa Rica, the Dominican Republic, El Salvador, Guatemala, Honduras, and Nicaragua. Like NAFTA, CAFTA was subject to intense political debate with similar arguments used by both sides of the trade liberalization issue. In the end, while some questions arose as to how much effective reduction in trade barriers existed in CAFTA, both the House and Senate approved the agreement on July 28, 2005. The votes were 217–215 and 55–45, respectively.

Fast-Track Authority

The passage of NAFTA, GATT, and other trade agreements usually depend on a mechanism for congressional consideration of trade agreements known as fast-track authority. This procedure was first established by Congress as part of the Trade Act of 1974, and it was subsequently renewed several times. Using fast-track authority, a president can negotiate a trade agreement, and then submit for Congress's approval a comprehensive, nonamendable piece of legislation implementing the agreement. Congress must consider that legislation within a set time period under expedited rules. Because Congress cannot amend trade agreements negotiated under fast-track authority, the president has broad power over the details of negotiation. When presidents have had this authority, it has greatly expanded their power to conclude trade agreements.

The political consideration behind the establishment of the fast-track authority is that trade agreements have become so complicated and indivisible that they cannot be altered without undermining the entire agreement. For example, presidents and their trade negotiators may make compromises in one area of trade, such as agriculture, to secure concessions from foreign countries in another, such as textiles. But after the agreement is signed, if lawmakers from agricultural states succeed in changing portions of the agreement related to farm products, the compromises on which the agreement is based can be undermined. Therefore, the fast-track procedure gives the president the latitude to negotiate complex trade agreements without having to prevail on multiple votes in Congress designed to chip away pieces of the agreement.

Despite the utility of fast-track procedures, Congress has not been willing to make this authority permanent. From 1974 until 1991, fast-track authority was extended quietly as part of broader trade legislation. In 1991, however, fast-track became a hotly contested issue in Congress. Fast-track was set to expire on June 1, unless it was extended. Under the 1988 Trade Act, which had contained the last fast-track extension, a single, two-year extension of fast-track authority could be obtained by the president as long as neither house disapproved of the president's request. Because fast-track authority has the status of a procedural rule in both houses of Congress, either house acting alone could block the extension.

Opponents of the extension focused on President George H. W. Bush's intention to use it to conclude a free trade agreement with Mexico, which had less support than the ongoing GATT negotiations. They also questioned whether it provided presidents with too much power over trade agreements.[65]

Fast-track authority was extended by votes of 231–192 in the House and 59–36 in the Senate in 1991. Bush signed the NAFTA with Canada and Mexico using this extension, though final approval of the agreement by the U.S. Congress took place under the Clinton administration. But the debate and the relatively close votes on fast-track posed a threat to long-run presidential primacy in trade negotiations, especially because either house acting alone could deny the president fast-track authority. If presidents were unable to secure fast-track authority in the future, they probably would be unable to conclude major trade agreements.

President Clinton was able to renew fast-track authority in 1993 by comfortable votes, but this extension was only for six and a half months and only applied to GATT talks. The limited scope of the extension and the desire of most Democrats to support their new president accounted for its relatively painless enactment. The GATT agreement was concluded under the authority of this extension, but no further extension was forthcoming during the remainder of the Clinton presidency. Between 1994 and 2002, in the absence of fast-track authority for the president, only three agreements were reached (with Canada, Israel, and Mexico).

Following on President Clinton's attempts to restore fast-track authority, President George W. Bush sought a resumption in the first year of his presidency. In early December 2001 the House of Representatives voted 215–214 to restore fast-track authority.[66] The Senate passed a modified version of the measure, 66–30, in May 2002. But the final shape of the bill was uncertain in the face of months of anticipated negotiations between the two chambers. The Senate's version of fast-track authority included two controversial amendments that GOP House leaders had difficulty accepting. One amendment gave increased federal benefits to workers who lost their jobs because of new imports. Another Senate provision gave the Senate the power to amend trade agreements—after passage—to protect U.S. business from unfair foreign trade practices.[67]

Bush signed the bill into law on August 6, 2002. It gave him fast-track authority until July 1, 2005. In contrast to the prior eight years when presidents lacked fast-track authority, from 2002 to 2005 congressional approval of trade agreements with several nations was secured, including Australia, Chile, Jordan, Morocco, and Singapore—as well as CAFTA. In March 2005, President Bush requested a two-year extension to July 2007. In late July and early August of 2005, Congress granted the extension. The House vote was 215–212 and the Senate vote was 64–34, respectively.

HISTORICAL DEVELOPMENT OF STABILIZATION POLICY

Rarely does a presidential administration maintain the same economic policy tack throughout its tenure. Unanticipated, and even predicted, economic developments create political pressures on the president to take action. During the three-quarters of a century since the Great Depression, a variety of administrations, encompassing political views from left to right, have mixed fiscal and monetary policy in the quest for an effective countercyclical policy to achieve economic growth in combination with price stability.

By Franklin Roosevelt's last term in office, which began in early 1945, Keynesianism had become the dominant economic theory in both policy-making and academic circles. Many members of Congress believed that because Keynesian theory had provided the federal government with a tool with which it seemingly could hold down the level of joblessness, the government should be obliged to use that tool to promote full employment. In 1945 proposed legislation in the Senate was titled the Full Employment Act. In mandating that full employment should be a national goal and that the government should run budget deficits when necessary to provide the investment and expenditures required to achieve it, the bill alarmed many business leaders and economic conservatives. They saw the proposal as a gigantic step toward budget deficits, inflation, and excessive regulation of the economy. Despite President Truman's support for the Senate bill, the House favored a more modest version, which eventually was passed by both chambers.[68]

The final version of the legislation was called the Employment Act of 1946. It stated that the government should work for "maximum employment, production and purchasing power" instead of "full" employment, and references to budget deficits as the tool that would be used to achieve high employment were deleted. A statement also was added that measures taken to implement the act must be consistent with the free enterprise system. Economist Herbert Stein wrote of the revision of the bill:

> Given the experience of the 1930s, it was inconceivable that the government would fail to commit itself to maintaining high employment. . . . But the form that commitment took in the United States, as embodied in the Employment Act of 1946, could hardly have been more satisfactory to conservatives. That is, after a major national discussion the Congress rejected an overly ambitious, inflationary definition of the goal, rejected exclusive reliance on deficit financing as the means, and reaffirmed its devotion to the free enterprise system.[69]

Although the proposed Full Employment Act had been watered down, the Employment Act of 1946 nevertheless reflected a new national consensus that government should be involved deeply in the management of the economy. Beyond stating the government's responsibility to work for low unemployment, the act reinforced the president's role as the public official primarily responsible for managing the economy. Although the legislation did not provide presidents with new economic powers, it did require them to report annually to Congress on the state of the economy, and it created the Council of Economic Advisers, which gave presidents an economic advisory body answerable only to

them.[70] These measures encouraged Congress, the business community, and the American public to continue to look to presidents for economic leadership as they had done during the depression.

Truman Administration

When Harry S. Truman succeeded to the presidency following President Roosevelt's death in April 1945, the U.S. economy was booming. Annual federal expenditures had grown from just $8.8 billion in 1939 to $92.7 billion in 1945, and unemployment was virtually nonexistent. Many Americans feared that the economic sluggishness of the 1930s would return when the war ended, but the years following the war saw continued expansion and a relatively smooth transition from a wartime to a peacetime footing. Many women and elderly workers who took jobs during the war because labor was in short supply retired when the war ended, thus making room in the workforce for returning soldiers. The influx of GIs also created greater demand for housing and consumer goods that partially offset the decrease in demand caused by reduced government spending for defense.

Inflation was a more serious problem. Although Truman had enthusiastically supported the original version of the Employment Act, which mandated measures to achieve full employment, as president he followed a pragmatic course that often made fighting inflation the highest economic priority. After the war, inflation was fueled by consumers who demanded goods that had been in short supply during the conflict. Moreover, wartime controls had held the prices of many goods below their true value. As these price controls were lifted in 1946 and 1947, prices rose dramatically to correct the artificial imbalance. Inflation, which had been just 2.3 percent in 1945, rose to 8.3 percent in 1946 and 14.4 percent in 1947. Truman, who had vetoed one price control removal bill but reluctantly signed a second in July 1946, urged labor groups to resist price and wage hikes and sent an anti-inflation program to Congress in October 1947 that included consumer credit controls, rent controls, price ceilings on selected products, and controls over the allocation of some scarce commodities. The Republican Congress put off most of the program until the following year and then enacted only part of it.[71] Inflation, however, peaked in 1947, falling to 8.1 percent in 1948 and then disappearing entirely in 1949 while the economy endured a recession.

In 1947 and 1948 Congress tried to force a tax cut on the president, which, it maintained, would reverse the tax-and-spend policies of Truman and of Roosevelt before him. Truman vetoed three such bills on the grounds that they would lead to budget deficits and greater inflation. Congress, however, overrode the last of Truman's vetoes in April 1948. The tax cut was timely, because the economy fell into a mild recession later in the year. The extra money in the hands of consumers stimulated demand, thereby reducing the recession's severity.

The Korean War, which began on June 24, 1950, when North Korea invaded South Korea, rekindled inflationary pressures that had eased after the post–World War II price acceleration. Growing military expenditures on the war effort stimulated industrial activity. Demand for consumer goods also increased as consumers bought many items in anticipation of wartime shortages. In 1951 inflation shot back up to 7.9 percent. Congress reluctantly granted part of Truman's tax increase request and agreed to wage, price, and credit controls, which succeeded in dropping inflation to 1.9 percent in 1952 and holding it below 1 percent in 1953.

One other significant development during the Truman administration was the Accord of 1951. This agreement between the administration and the Fed allowed for greater independence in monetary policy from administration or congressional preferences. In particular, the accord furthered the Fed's autonomy to conduct restrictive monetary policies. (See "The Accord of 1951," p. 812.)

Eisenhower Administration

In spite of the prominence of Keynesian thought among economists, President Dwight D. Eisenhower entered office skeptical of its utility. He emphasized the traditional conservative economic priorities of balancing the federal budget, limiting government interference in the economy, and, most important, fighting inflation.[72] During Eisenhower's eight years in office, 1953–1961, he produced three budget surpluses.

Throughout his presidency, Eisenhower was willing to accept higher rates of unemployment than his Keynesian critics thought necessary. In response to a recession in 1953 and early 1954, the administration accepted some minor tax decreases and sped up government expenditures. Although the administration took credit for helping the recovery with "speedy and massive actions," the modest antirecession measures of 1954 were an exception to Eisenhower's rule of nonintervention.[73]

During his second term Eisenhower pursued an antiinflationary strategy in defiance not only of his critics but also of several of his advisers, who urged him to support a tax cut. Unemployment averaged a postdepression high of 6.8 percent during the 1958 recession, but Eisenhower remained true to his noninterventionist principles. Moreover, he vetoed a number of spending bills during his last two years in office in pursuit of a balanced budget and low inflation.[74]

When signs of a recession appeared in the spring of 1960, Eisenhower's vice president, Richard Nixon, who was running for president that year, advocated following CEA chairman Arthur Burns's advice to increase defense expenditures and loosen credit. Eisenhower, however, sided with other administration economic advisers who rejected the proposal because they did not believe the recession, if there was one, would be of sufficient magnitude to warrant government intervention.[75] Nixon undoubtedly lost votes because of the economic slump.

Although Eisenhower's stiff resistance to antirecession measures appears old-fashioned, he was successful in holding down consumer prices, which never climbed more than 4 percent in any year of his presidency.

Kennedy Administration

With the election of John F. Kennedy to the presidency in 1960, Democrats believed they could change the economic goals of the nation. Kennedy and his advisers were determined to achieve full employment and sustained economic expansion through fiscal stimulation. They hoped to be able to correct the swings of the business cycle as well as to stimulate the economy to greater growth and productivity. They were motivated by their desire to alleviate poverty and to improve medical care, education, and other social services and by their concern over the apparent rapid growth of the Soviet economy and its military expenditures.

Kennedy believed the economy never would create jobs for everyone without government stimulation. He and his advisers were confident they could direct the economy to greater prosperity. For the first time the Keynesian views of professional economists were fully applied to the political situation.[76]

In the opening months of Kennedy's term, the economy was pulling itself out of the recession that had begun in 1960. Because the budget was in deficit and inflation was a concern, Kennedy hoped that he would not have to use fiscal stimulation to achieve his employment and expansion goals. By early 1962, however, the economy had begun to slow. Kennedy agreed with his advisers that the economy should be stimulated through increased government spending. They believed such a policy would help low-income people and be less controversial than a tax cut at a time when budget deficits persisted. Congress, however, resisted Kennedy's spending plans. Kennedy responded in late 1962 by proposing a tax cut.

The president and his economic advisers attempted to sell the tax cut by promoting the concept of the "full employment budget." The administration argued that, although the government was currently running budget deficits, the greater tax revenues produced by an economy operating at full employment would result in budget surpluses. Therefore, if a tax cut could produce full employment and sustained economic expansion, it would increase government revenues, not decrease, them.[77] Kennedy lobbied Congress to pass the tax cut in 1963 but was assassinated before he could persuade lawmakers to pass the legislation.

The monetary policy of the Kennedy administration was committed to maintaining price stability. Kennedy himself, for all his considerable progrowth beliefs and comments, was wedded to the belief that "a nation was only as strong as the value of its currency." [78] Some of his advisers, in fact, felt Kennedy was too concerned about inflation.[79] Still, his advisers were not prone to support policies that would ignite a new inflation.

Throughout the administration's first year, Walter Heller and other advisers publicly pressured the Fed to lower interest rates. But this abruptly ended in early 1962. Concern about a deteriorating U.S. trade balance prompted the Kennedy administration to emphasize a tighter monetary policy (and an aggressive inflation stance) and a more expansive fiscal policy. The logic behind this was to attract foreign investment from abroad through the higher interest rates and ensure that the higher interest rates did not reduce aggregate demand.

Johnson Administration

Following Kennedy's death in November 1963, President Lyndon B. Johnson delivered an emotional speech to Congress. In that address, on November 27, 1963, he asked lawmakers to honor Kennedy by passing his civil rights bill and asserted: "No act of ours could more fittingly continue the work of President Kennedy than the early passage of the tax bill for which he fought all this long year." Johnson also used his legendary lobbying skills and Congress's feelings for the slain president to push the tax cut through Congress quickly. Johnson signed the Revenue Act of 1964 on February 26. It was the largest tax cut in U.S. history up to that time. The act reduced personal income taxes for 1964 and 1965 by about 20 percent and corporate taxes by 4 percent.[80]

The 1964 tax cut was a milestone in the history of U.S. stabilization policy. It was the first time the president and Congress had intentionally stimulated the economy through a tax cut while the economy was expanding. Unemployment fell from 5.7 percent in 1963 to 4.5 percent in 1965. The impressive results of the tax cut generated enthusiasm and confidence among President Johnson's economic advisers. They believed they could fine-tune the economy through Keynesian stabilization policies.

The Vietnam War, however, forced Johnson to reconsider his economic priorities. By 1966 expenditures on the war and social programs Johnson was pushing under his domestic Great Society initiative had produced a growing budget deficit and rising inflation. Johnson's advisers urged him to correct the overstimulation of the economy caused by the deficit spending through an excise tax or an increase in income taxes. Congress, however, showed no enthusiasm for a tax hike, and Johnson feared that higher taxes would erode public support for the Vietnam War.[81] Consequently, Johnson did not push for an income tax increase, and the task of fighting inflation was left to the Federal Reserve Board's monetary policy.

The anti-inflation monetary policy during Johnson's administration was largely determined by the fiscal policies that followed from the Kennedy-proposed tax cut, spending on Great Society programs, and military expenditures for the Vietnam War. These ambitious undertakings swelled the federal budget deficit from $1.5 billion in 1965 to $25 billion by the end of fiscal year 1968.

As a result the Fed could either provide sufficient credit to make sure that the fiscal stimulus was not choked off by higher interest rates or pursue a restrictive policy that held inflationary pressures in check. Throughout the remainder of his time in office Johnson left no doubt that he favored unrestrictive monetary policy. To achieve this goal, the administration resorted to public pressure on the Fed as well as private negotiations. In both informal and formal meetings, coordination between monetary and fiscal policy was a central topic for the rest of his term. By 1966 a tentative deal was worked out between the administration and the Fed. In exchange for a tax increase to close the deficit, the Fed would agree to keep interest rates down.

By the third quarter of 1966 the Fed again eased credit conditions. Johnson reciprocated by agreeing to reduce federal spending. The central bank continued its policy of monetary ease throughout 1967 and 1968 in the face of a rapidly expanding economy.

By 1967 Johnson recognized that he had to slow inflation and reduce the deficit. He proposed new taxes, but Congress did not react to Johnson's 1967 tax hike plan until the summer of 1968. By that year inflation had risen to 4.2 percent from just 1.6 percent in 1965, and the deficit had expanded to $25.2 billion from only $1.6 billion in 1965. This deficit disappeared in 1969, when Johnson's 10 percent tax increase, combined with the efforts of Johnson's successor, Nixon, to cut government spending, led to the first budget surplus since 1960. This belated fiscal restraint failed, however, to eliminate the long-run inflationary pressures that had been built into the economy or the rising unemployment that was left for Nixon to combat.

Nixon Administration

Richard Nixon entered office intending to fight inflation through small spending cuts coordinated with a tight monetary policy. He hoped his incremental strategy would reduce inflation while holding unemployment near 4 percent.[82] But when he came into the White House in 1969 monetary policy issues were already framed by the onset of combined inflation and low economic growth in the late 1960s. Nixon initially encouraged the Fed to tighten monetary policy to arrest inflation but was not consistent in this course, and he was known to believe that the Fed's tight monetary policy during the 1960 presidential campaign exacerbated already weak economic conditions and contributed to his defeat by Kennedy. This ambivalence diminished prospects for a steady and consistent price stabilization policy. The ensuing upward pressure on interest rates produced dramatic losses in some parts of the economy in 1969 and 1970. In the end Nixon encouraged a shift in monetary policy emphasis that placed more weight on avoiding a major recession than on reducing inflation.

Nixon submitted a budget to Congress for fiscal 1970 that projected a small budget surplus. Congress, controlled by Democrats, trimmed some spending but refused to go along with Nixon's cuts, many of which targeted social programs. The relationship between Nixon and his many intensely partisan Democratic critics in Congress became increasingly confrontational as the president vetoed a number of appropriations bills and resorted to impounding appropriated funds.[83]

By 1970 inflation had reached 5.7 percent. Moreover, the increase in inflation was not accompanied by a corresponding decrease in unemployment, which had risen from 3.6 percent in 1968 to 4.9 percent in 1970. The worsening unemployment situation was exacerbated by the de-escalation of the Vietnam War, which brought thousands of troops back into the civilian workforce.

Congress responded to the bleak economic conditions by passing the Economic Stabilization Act of 1970. Under this act, Congress gave the president the authority to combat inflation through wage and price controls. Nixon signed the act but renounced the use of such controls, saying on June 17, 1970: "I will not take this nation down the road of wage and price controls, however politically expedient they may seem." Nixon objected to wage and price controls because he believed they were an incursion on the rights of Americans and would only postpone a burst of inflation.

In 1971, with his reelection bid less than two years away, Nixon was unwilling to fight inflation by allowing a recession as Eisenhower might have done. Early that year he had abandoned his attempts to achieve a balanced budget and had initiated stimulative fiscal policies to combat rising unemployment, which averaged 5.9 percent for the year. Nixon, like Kennedy, justified deficit spending by arguing that the budget would be balanced if the economy were operating at full employment and output. Nixon admitted to an interviewer in January 1971, "I am now a Keynesian in economics." [84]

Inflation, however, was the more troubling economic problem. The president was being pressured by Congress, the public, and even prominent leaders of his party to take dramatic action against inflation. On August 15, 1971, President Nixon announced that, owing to the economic crisis, he was using the authority granted to him by Congress the previous year to impose a wage and price control policy.

His "New Economic Policy" had several phases. Phase I froze wages, prices, and rents for ninety days. Phase II created a pay board and price commission that acted to limit inflation to 3 percent and wage increases to 5.5 percent per year. In January 1973 Phase III relaxed the controls, and in July of that year Phase IV replaced controls with commitments from businesses to limit price increases for a year. In April 1974 all wage and price control activity ended when Congress refused to extend President Nixon's wage and price control authority.

Initially the controls were successful and popular. Consumer prices rose 4.4 percent in 1971 but just 3.2 percent in 1972. Unemployment fell from 5.9 percent in 1971 to 5.6 percent in 1972 and 4.9 percent in 1973. The brightening economic picture helped Nixon easily win a second term as president in the November 1972 elections.

As Nixon had feared, however, the problems with wage and price controls began to surface during his second term. Shortages of some goods occurred when many manufacturers began exporting a greater share of their products overseas, where prices were higher. In addition, the numerous exemptions from the controls program that had been granted to various industries caused economic distortions. For example, grain prices had been exempted from controls while meat prices remained fixed. Consequently, high feed costs forced many meat producers to slaughter their stock, causing meat shortages and meat price increases later in the decade.

A good deal of blame can be put on Nixon's policy choices. The wage and price controls proved to be only a temporary remedy for inflation—as economic theory predicts. In addition there were numerous problems with policy implementation. For example, in 1972 the growing number of price and wage exemptions weakened the controls, and in the second half of the year the consumer price index began rising again because of the administration's overexpansive monetary policy the preceding year.

By October 1973, the economy received a severe shock when the Arab oil-producing states imposed an embargo on the United States in retaliation for its support of Israel during the Yom Kippur War of 1973. The price of a barrel of oil rose from less than $3 in early 1973 to between $10 and $14 in 1974. Rising oil prices, a poor 1973 harvest, and the phasing out of price controls—begun in 1973 and completed in 1974—led to a dramatic jump in inflation. Prices increased 6.2 percent in 1973 and a painful 11.0 percent in 1974. That year the Nixon administration attempted to fight inflation with more restrictive fiscal and monetary policies, but the Watergate scandal made cooperation with Congress difficult. In August Nixon resigned to avoid impeachment for his part in the Watergate affair.

Ford Administration

Like Nixon, Gerald R. Ford—Nixon's vice president who moved into the presidency on Nixon's resignation—assumed the office intending to fight inflation through moderate fiscal restraint supported by a tight monetary policy. The inflationary effects of the 1973 Arab oil embargo and the removal of the wage and price freeze remained strong after Ford took office. He asked Congress for a 5 percent tax surcharge on corporations and the upper class and for selected spending cuts and deferrals.

A minor part of Ford's economic program, however, received the most attention. He encouraged Americans to fight inflation voluntarily by saving more, conserving energy, increasing charitable contributions, and resisting price and wage increases. The voluntary measures were to be symbolized by "WIN" buttons, which stood for "Whip Inflation Now." The buttons were ridiculed as a symbol of the ineffectuality of the administration's policies.[85]

Ford was forced to abandon his anti-inflationary strategy in early 1975. Data showed that the economy had fallen into a deep recession in 1974 before he took office, partly as a result of the sharp rise in oil prices, which forced businesses to cut back their operations. Unemployment reached 9 percent late in the year.

Ford responded in January 1975 by asking Congress for a $16 billion tax cut and new investment tax credits for business to stimulate the economy. Congress and the president compromised with a $23 billion tax cut bill that favored the lower class. The tax cut, however, was enacted in March 1975 when the recession began to ease. Consequently, by the time the benefits of the cut reached Americans, the economy was already growing.[86]

Despite the persistently high rates of inflation, many Democrats in Congress pressed the president to make low unemployment the nation's first economic priority. During the rest of 1975 and early 1976 Ford battled Congress over economic policy, repeatedly vetoing spending measures he considered inflationary. Nevertheless, Ford compromised on several appropriations bills, which, coupled with large unemployment compensation and welfare payments caused by the recession, increased the federal deficit to new highs of $53 billion in 1975 and $74 billion in 1976.

In early 1976 inflation leveled off, and the economy appeared to be improving just in time for Ford's reelection

In February 1974, cars line up at gas stations, causing traffic jams in New Jersey, right, and across the country. In October 1973, the Arab oil-producing states had imposed an embargo on the United States for its support of Israel during the Yom Kippur War.

bid. Inflation had fallen from 11 percent in 1974 to 9 percent in 1975 and just 5.8 percent in 1976. Meanwhile, unemployment averaged 7.7 percent in 1976, which was an encouraging improvement after 8.5 percent in 1975. The improvements in economic performance by the end of 1976 were of questionable stability and not enough for Ford to win reelection in his own right. The country voted to put Carter in the White House because the incumbent was unable to overcome the recent hard times and, as well, still carried some of the burden of the disgraced Nixon administration.

Carter Administration

Jimmy Carter took over an economy that had improved slightly during the last year of the Ford administration. The Fed's tight monetary policies had brought inflation down to 5.8 percent for 1976, and Carter entered office intending to lower unemployment.

Despite these hopes, the era would be dominated by forces outside Carter's control. During the late 1960s and 1970s, several factors had combined to produce an increasingly difficult economic environment in which astute stabilization policy could not be relied on to produce prosperity. The inflationary pressures built up during the Vietnam War had not yet dissipated. In addition, the Organization of Petroleum Exporting Countries (OPEC) engineered the second major oil price hike of the decade in 1979. Oil prices increased from less than $15 a barrel in 1979 to almost $40 a barrel in 1981. Also, the growth of federal regulation during the 1970s in areas such as environmental protection, job

safety, and consumer protection increased the cost of producing goods and contributed to inflation. Simultaneous
with these inflationary pressures, the economy was declining
in productivity relative to foreign competitors—a trend that
had begun in the 1960s. Finally, the growth of federal benefit programs, especially Social Security and Medicare, had
decreased the controllable portion of the budget that could
be cut from year to year, nearly ensuring budget deficits in
the absence of a tax increase or substantial spending cuts.[87]
Although Carter was not responsible for the underlying economic conditions he faced as president, his policies did little
to help the situation.

At the beginning of his presidency Carter proposed a
stimulative program that included a $50 tax rebate per per-
son. He withdrew the rebate proposal when economic statistics showed that unexpectedly strong economic growth
threatened to spark a renewed surge of inflation, but much
of the rest of his plan, including increased spending for jobs
programs and public works, was enacted. Until late 1979,
Carter gave priority to reducing unemployment.

From 1977 to 1979 Carter encouraged the Fed to pursue a stimulative monetary policy that brought the biggest
expansion of the money supply of any three-year period
since World War II.[88] As a result, the economy continued the
expansion that had begun in late 1975.

During this period, however, the public became
increasingly concerned about inflation. Consumer prices
had risen 7.6 percent in 1978, up from 5.8 percent in 1976.
The OPEC price hike of 1979 triggered a further jump in
inflation, which rose to 11.3 percent for the year. On the eve
of the 1980 election, Carter recognized that inflation had
become the nation's foremost economic problem.

One of Carter's most fateful economic decisions was
the appointment of Paul Volcker as chairman of the Federal
Reserve Board in 1979. On October 6, 1979, Volcker indicated that he would use monetary policy vigorously to fight
inflation. Although in the long run Volcker's contractions of
the money supply were effective in bringing down inflation,
the consumer price index did not respond to the tight monetary policy in 1979 and 1980. Consequently, interest rates
soared without an accompanying drop in inflation. In 1980
inflation rose to 13.5 percent, real per capita income
declined 0.7 percent, and the prime lending rate of banks
stood at a whopping 15.25 percent. Carter complemented
Volcker's tough stand with fiscal restraint designed to combat inflation and lower the budget deficit. Just as the
demands of economic management had induced a conservative Nixon to adopt the liberal tool of wage and price controls, so they led Carter to abandon his liberal goal of
achieving low levels of unemployment and to adopt the traditionally conservative strategy of fighting inflation with
monetary and fiscal policies while pursuing smaller budget
deficits.[89]

However, inflation expectations were not falling as fast
as hoped. For the first time since presidents began submitting an annual economic report thirty years before, Carter's
1980 report forecasted a recession. In the second quarter of
that year the recession came as predicted, while double-digit
inflation remained. In response to lack of downward movement in inflation and inflation expectations, the Carter
administration instituted a far more draconian measure—
credit controls—which had an immediate and severe effect
on borrowing. As one observer, journalist William Greider,
noted this policy caused economic activity not only to slow
down but also come to a crashing halt.

> The recession, long predicted by forecasters, finally began
> in earnest. But it was not the gradual contraction that
> many expected. The loss of economic activity was swift
> and alarmingly steep. Within three months the Gross
> National Product would shrink by 10 percent—the
> sharpest recession in thirty-five years. For a time it looked
> like a free-fall descent.[90]

The anti-inflation policy would be reversed but at great cost
because policy makers had to repudiate their previous anti-
inflation policy stance.

During that year, Republican presidential nominee
Reagan attacked Carter for producing a "misery index" (the
sum of the inflation and unemployment rates) of greater
than twenty. In August 1980 a CBS News/*New York Times*
poll found that only 19 percent of those polled approved of
Carter's "handling of the economy." [91] Although the economy's performance during the first three years of the Carter
administration had not been as dismal as the public perceived, the sharp downturn in 1980 solidified the popular
perception that Carter's policies had undermined the economy.[92] With voters convinced of the president's inability to
manage economic affairs, Reagan defeated Carter in a landslide in the 1980 presidential elections.

Reagan Administration

Ronald Reagan entered office facing the most severe peacetime economic situation since the Great Depression. To deal
with this situation he had some specific policy priorities.
One priority was passing the largest spending and tax cuts in
U.S. history. His landslide victory enabled him to claim a
mandate for his plan to cut personal income taxes by 30 percent, introduce new tax incentives for businesses, and cut
nondefense expenditures sharply.

Some Democrats in Congress attacked the plan as a
disguised attempt to lighten the tax burden of the wealthy
while cutting back on government aid to the poor. Reagan
and his advisers acknowledged that their tax cut would benefit upper-income individuals but argued that these were
precisely the people who would be best able to invest their
tax break in new jobs and productive capacity, thus fueling

the economic expansion for everyone. Reagan's critics called this reasoning a return to a predepression Republican "trickle down" strategy in which benefits for the rich were justified on the grounds that the poor would eventually benefit from a stronger economy.

Although many Americans perceived Reagan's taxing and spending strategy as inequitable, a considerable majority of Americans supported it, and his congressional allies were able to push most of the plan through Congress despite the solid Democratic majority in the House. The president signed the Economic Recovery Tax Act of 1981 in August. It reduced individual tax rates 25 percent—5 percentage points less than Reagan had wanted—over thirty-three months. In addition, the bill indexed the tax system for the first time ever to keep inflation from forcing taxpayers into higher brackets as their incomes kept pace with prices. Reagan also was successful in pushing $35 billion in 1982 nondefense spending cuts through Congress, along with $26.5 billion in defense spending increases.

Reagan had hoped that his tax cut would create an economic boom that would bring increases in tax revenues. These increased revenues along with lower domestic spending would reduce the federal budget deficit until the budget was balanced. In 1980, while running for the presidency, Reagan had attacked Carter and the Democratic-controlled Congress for their deficit spending and promised to balance the budget by 1983. By late 1981, however, economic statistics showed that the country was entering a recession. This recession, the deepest since the Great Depression, lasted through 1982. It widened the budget deficit because tax revenues were depressed by declining industrial output and personal income, while government spending on unemployment insurance and welfare increased.

In addition, after the initial wave of spending cuts, Reagan's budget cutting lost momentum as the administration and Congress refused to make major concessions to each other's priorities. In November 1981, after less than a year in office, Reagan conceded that he probably could not balance the budget in one term. In 1982, despite his position against taxes, Reagan agreed to a tax increase that reduced the 1981 tax cut by about a quarter, with most of the restored revenue coming out of corporate taxes.[93]

A second priority was eliminating inflation. Reagan did not obstruct the Fed's price stabilizing policy, which had a dramatic impact on the economy. Unemployment rose from 7.4 percent in the first quarter of 1981 to nearly 11 percent by the end of the fourth quarter in 1982. But inflation was cut drastically, falling from about 13 percent in 1980 to 3.8 percent by December 1982.

By the middle of 1982, Reagan's popularity had plummeted, and the GOP faced a daunting challenge in that year's congressional elections. Republicans managed to hold their majority in the Senate but lost twenty-six seats in the House,

effectively denying Reagan the working majority of Republicans and conservative Democrats that he enjoyed in his first two years in office.

Beginning in 1983 the economy began a sustained period of economic growth. Inflation stabilized and remained between 3 percent and 4 percent, and interest rates began to fall. The economic expansion would last through the decade. By 1988, the last year of Reagan's term, unemployment had dropped to just 5.5 percent.

Another priority of the Reagan administration was a balanced federal budget. On this score Reagan failed. The combination of Reagan's policies virtually guaranteed a short-run increase in the deficit. His call for monetary restraint in conjunction with an expansive fiscal policy would combine to reduce the rate of increase in government receipts, at least initially.

In 1983 the deficit reached $207.8 billion. Against the recommendation of several advisers, including CEA chairman Martin Feldstein and budget director David A. Stockman, Reagan refused to consider a further tax increase. He maintained that higher taxes would threaten economic growth and would not substantially reduce the budget deficit because Congress would find a way to spend most of the additional revenue.

In addition, the president fought against cuts in defense spending. Reagan had charged that Carter had allowed the nation's defenses to deteriorate while the Soviet Union continued to pursue a massive military buildup. According to Reagan, the growing Soviet advantage in military capability threatened the security of the United States and its allies. During the early 1980s public support for a military buildup and tensions between the United States and the Soviet Union led Congress to accept many of Reagan's defense spending proposals. Military expenditures rose from 5.0 percent of GNP in 1980 to 6.2 percent in 1987.

George H. W. Bush Administration

George H. W. Bush's political dilemma in handling the economy was more acute than that of most new presidents because he could not repudiate the policies of his predecessor. Republican President Reagan, for example, could explain the 1982 recession by blaming conditions that he had inherited from Carter, a Democrat. But Bush had served as Reagan's vice president and had promised to extend the Reagan peacetime economic expansion.

This would not be an easy task. The Reagan expansion had begun in 1983 and had been fueled in part by large tax cuts and defense expenditures. After such a long period of sustained expansion, the business cycle could be expected soon to produce a recession. Moreover, persistently high budget deficits and the collapse of the Soviet Union would create pressure to cut government spending, especially for defense. If recession did come, Bush would have little room to combat it with an expansionary fiscal policy.

Bush complicated his political position by pledging not to raise taxes. At the 1988 Republican convention he threw out a memorable challenge to Congress that was repeatedly quoted back to him during his presidency: "Read my lips: No new taxes." The pledge made Bush appear decisive, and it sharply distinguished his economic platform from that of his Democratic opponent, Michael S. Dukakis. But with Congress firmly in the control of the Democrats and the budget deficit projected to grow, Bush's pledge reduced his capacity to govern. Only by compromising with Congress could President Bush hope to achieve a significant reduction in the deficit. But the Democratic Congress's budget priorities were targeted to benefit its constituencies, which were different from Bush's. Moreover, Democratic leaders were aware that they could wound the president politically either by forcing him to break his "no new taxes" pledge or by allowing the deficit to rise. Congress would never let Bush off the hook by approving a deficit-reduction package without a tax increase, especially when the "no new taxes" pledge had been used as a cudgel against Democrats in the 1988 election.[94]

In 1989 the Bush administration deferred serious budget discussions by releasing highly optimistic estimates of the size of near-term budget deficits. But by May 1990 it was clear to the Bush administration that the deficit would accelerate rapidly in the absence of a significant deficit reduction package. Bush indicated that month that he might accept a tax increase as part of a larger deficit-reduction package. This set in motion highly partisan budget negotiations between the president and Congress.

On June 26 Bush agreed to include tax increases in a deficit-reduction package. Negotiations made little progress, however, until September. By then Congress had the upper hand. The final budget deal passed Congress on October 28 and was signed by Bush on November 5. The five-year package contained discretionary spending cuts of $182.4 billion, most coming from defense. Tax increases, including the elevation of the top marginal income tax rate from 28 percent to 31 percent, totaled $146.3 billion during the period. Minor changes in entitlements, primarily Medicare and farm subsidies, and higher user fees for ports, airports, railroads, Coast Guard inspections, patent processing, and other government services added $99 billion. Lower interest payments resulting from the deficit reduction were projected as saving $68.4 billion.[95]

Bush attempted to put the best face on the budget deal by praising the deficit reduction it contained. He remarked, "I think the spending cuts, when you look at them, are good. The entitlement reform is good. The tough enforcement provisions are tougher than I ever thought we could ever get in any way out of this Congress." The Bush administration attempted to pin responsibility for the higher taxes on congressional Democrats, saying that it had been forced to pay a "ransom" of tax increases to secure congressional approval for spending cuts. But the president was the clear loser in the budget negotiations. Political scientist Stephen Skowronek wrote:

> Bush had made the tax pledge the linchpin of his and his party's credibility, and when he pulled it out, the reaction was swift and predictable. The reversal put Republicans in far more difficult straits than Democrats, and Bush's fellow partisans rose up in revolt, charging their leader with the "big lie."[96]

The public fallout over Bush's broken pledge was less acute than it would have been had not the United States been engaged in the crisis arising from the Iraqi invasion of Kuwait. From August 2, 1990, when Iraq invaded, until February 1991, when the American-led coalition won a speedy victory, public attention was focused on the Middle East. The overwhelming success of the military operation sent President Bush's approval ratings as high as 89 percent. However, Bush could not translate this positive public sentiment into sustained support for his domestic policies.

After the war, Bush's close attention to foreign policy was perceived to come at the expense of economic policy. These perceptions, combined with a shallow but persistent recession that had begun in the summer of 1990, steadily eroded Bush's high level of support. In June 1992, fifteen months after the decisive victory in the Gulf War, a CBS News/*New York Times* poll showed that only 34 percent of the respondents approved of Bush's performance. Only 16 percent approved of his handling of the economy, a rating lower than President Carter's worst rating.[97]

During late 1991 and 1992, the decline of the economy focused voters' minds on Bush's broken pledge on taxes. Real economic growth averaged only about 1 percent per year, and real per capita income fell. Unemployment peaked at 7.5 percent, and the country endured more business failures than during any presidency since the Great Depression.[98]

Bush was criticized in the media for doing nothing to pull the country out of recession. Given the budget problem, however, there was not much that he could do. In the 1990 budget negotiations, he had campaigned for a cut in the capital gains tax as a tool to stimulate economic growth, but Democrats in Congress opposed it as a tax cut for the rich. Having negotiated hard in favor of spending cuts, Bush also could not turn around and offer a stimulus package of government spending.

Bush could not even point to deficit reduction to defend his 1990 budget deal. The 1990 agreement had undoubtedly held the deficit below where it otherwise would have climbed, but its budgetary impact was far below what was needed to solve the budget deficit problem or even reduce the deficit.[99] The cost of the Persian Gulf War, the ongoing government bailout of failed savings and loan institutions, inflation in government health care programs, and increased entitlement costs arising from the recession pushed the deficit from $221.2 billion in 1990 to an all-time high of $290.4 billion in 1992. To the public, Bush's tax increases had yielded nothing.

During the last two years of Bush's presidency, Congress criticized or ignored his economic initiatives. Economic data would later reveal that the nation had pulled out of recession and had begun a strong comeback in the fourth quarter of 1992. But by that time, the voting public had made up its mind. Bush was defeated by Democrat Clinton, who had promised to focus "like a laser beam" on the economy.

Clinton Administration

Bill Clinton was president during almost the entire ten-year run of the longest economic expansion in American history. The president's detractors in the Republican Party instead gave the credit to the American public and business community, as well as to the monetary policies of the Federal Reserve Board, headed by Republican Greenspan. Clinton argued that luck was only part of the equation and that his government's budgetary and economic policies provided a solid basis for the expansion.

The voters apparently sided with Clinton instead of the Republicans in 1996, returning him to office for a second term, making him the first Democrat to serve two full terms in his own right since Franklin Roosevelt more than half a century earlier.

Clinton entered office in January 1993 soon after the federal government reported a budget deficit of $290.4 billion for the 1992 fiscal year that ended just four months earlier and a national debt exceeding $4 trillion. Clinton's economic program, similar to President Bush's immediately before him, would be constrained by the necessity to address the debt problem. But, unlike Reagan's entrance into office in 1981, Clinton was the beneficiary of nearly a decade of price stability and low inflation expectations, and relatively low interest rates.

During the 1992 campaign and immediately after his election, Clinton capitalized on the public perceptions of Bush as detached from economic policy by emphasizing that he would devote himself fully to economic matters. On December 15, 1992, at the conclusion of a two-day economic policy conference in Little Rock, Arkansas, President-elect

Two extended government shutdowns within the period of November 1995 to January 1996 brought Washington to a halt, as President Bill Clinton and Congress battled over how to balance the federal budget. Here a U.S. Park Service employee places a closed sign on the Washington Monument.

Clinton described his commitment to make economic policy his priority:

> I'm not going to stop working and our team is not going to stop working until the economic challenges have been faced and tackled, until we have given it our best shot and our best response. As long as people are out of work and children are left behind, as long as families struggle, as long as the potential of this country is not being fulfilled, we will not rest. We will explore every idea and challenge every prejudice; we won't stop looking or pushing or trying until our job is done.[100]

Clinton's claim to economic leadership was not based on economic theory or ideology; it was based on a promise to put economic management at the core of his agenda and transcend the conflicting economic goals pushed by the left and right. Clinton attempted with considerable success to distance himself from both the traditional image of a Democratic Party rooted in taxing and spending and preference of conservatives to grant business and wealthy individuals lower taxes that they claimed would generate investment and jobs.[101]

Because Clinton was governing in an era of price stability, he did nothing overt to pressure the Fed for a stimulative economic package. In fact, the Fed was already moving in that direction by early 1993. More important, for the whole of his eight-year term, Clinton was to support a monetary policy that reflected in many ways the attitudes of the administrations of Kennedy in the 1960s and Reagan in the 1980s.

During Clinton's tenure in the White House, economic growth averaged 4.0 percent per year, compared with an average growth of 2.8 percent during the expansion of the 1980s. The high point was in 1997 and 1998, when the economy expanded by 4.4 percent (as measured by the real, or inflation-adjusted, gross domestic product), but the growth slowed considerably in 2000, to just 3.4 percent. Most of the slowdown occurred in the second half of 2000, when business investment (especially in high-technology equipment and software) declined sharply.

In terms of fiscal policy initiatives, Clinton's first budget proposal in early 1993 contained three major economic priorities: reducing the deficit, shifting some of the tax burden from poor Americans to wealthy Americans, and expanding public investment—especially in infrastructure, education, environmental protection, and scientific research. He had postponed a campaign promise for a middle-class tax cut out of concern for the deficit. Considering that Republican presidents had been in power for twelve years, this was a relatively modest budgetary agenda.

But even with his party in control of both houses of Congress, Clinton found enactment of his budget priorities difficult. In spite of substantial changes aimed at appeasing conservative Democrats, not a single Republican in either house voted for Clinton's budget. He was able to pass the budget by a 218–216 vote in the House and with Vice President Al Gore breaking a 50–50 tie in the Senate.[102] Clinton signed the Omnibus Budget Reconciliation Act of 1993 into law on August 10, 1993.

The budget contained little new investment, but it did shift some tax burden from the poor to the wealthiest taxpayers. It repudiated policies of the Reagan era, though with its spending cuts and attention to the deficit, it was not a traditionally liberal economic plan. It was instead a pragmatic, deficit-driven compromise for which there was little enthusiasm, even within the Democratic Party. Like the 1990 budget bill that so harmed President Bush, Clinton's budget demonstrated the constraints on presidential authority in budget matters and the central role of accommodation with Congress.[103]

Even as the economy improved, voters continued to feel anxiety. Real wages remained stagnant in spite of declining unemployment. Some of this anxiety was reflected in growing protectionist sentiments. Clinton had achieved some of his most notable legislative successes in free trade, as he led successful bipartisan campaigns to push the North American Free Trade Agreement and the General Agreement on Tariffs and Trade through Congress. Yet large segments of the public, especially labor unions and the followers of billionaire presidential candidate H. Ross Perot, distrusted these agreements. *(See "Trade Policy," p. 815.)*

This undercurrent of economic anxiety contributed to the stunning Republican landslide in the 1994 congressional elections. The Republican victory, in which the GOP won control of both houses in Congress for the first time since 1953 when Eisenhower became president, defied the conventional wisdom that incumbent parties do well when the economy is growing. At the beginning of 1995 the Clinton administration faced what no Democratic administration had faced since Truman: a Republican-controlled Congress. Republicans, led by Speaker Newt Gingrich of Georgia, proposed revolutionary changes, including the achievement of a balanced budget in seven years, the enactment of a significant tax cut, and the passage of a balanced budget amendment and the line-item veto. Most of it came to naught, as Clinton demonstrated once again the power of the presidency to control the public debate and issue agenda even while compromising with adversaries.

Nevertheless, President Clinton had lost the initiative in economic policy. In early 1995 he proposed a budget that was immediately denounced as irrelevant by Republican leaders in Congress. Under Clinton's plan, deficits were projected to remain near $200 billion for the foreseeable future. Many commentators speculated that Clinton's approach was designed to avoid offending constituent groups with spending cuts that would require congressional Republicans to take the initial, politically risky step of making the deep reductions necessary to balance the budget. Clinton appeared ready to wage a fight against the GOP plan, which sharply reduced the growth of Medicare and Medicaid spending.

But during the summer of 1995, Clinton surprised many of his Democratic allies by repudiating his initial budget and embracing a plan to balance the budget in ten years. Although Clinton voiced his opposition to GOP priorities and the pace of the budget cuts, his endorsement of a balanced budget validated the goal of reaching balance within a prescribed time. By the fall, Clinton had indicated he might accept a seven-year balanced budget bill. He rejected, however, the Republicans' choice of spending cuts and the inclusion of tax cuts in the budget.

These differences led to one of the severest budget standoffs in American history. On November 20, 1995, Congress passed the fiscal 1996 budget reconciliation bill that was estimated to balance the budget in seven years. It would have cut $894 billion over that period by slowing the growth of entitlements and mandating cuts in future appropriations for discretionary programs. It also included a $245 billion tax cut. As expected, President Clinton vetoed this bill on December 6, claiming that it cut programs for the needy too deeply; made unsound programmatic reforms in Medicare, Medicaid, welfare, farm subsidies, and environmental programs; and contained an overly generous tax cut. This theme was to be repeated frequently in budget and tax battles between Clinton and the Republican Congress in the president's second term.

In January 1996 House Speaker Gingrich and Senate Majority Leader Bob Dole, R-Kan., began leading their party away from the shutdown strategy. By the end of April—seven months into the fiscal year—President Clinton and Congress finally agreed to a compromise on the final 1996 appropriations bill, essentially ending the crisis.[104]

Thus the stage was set for the fully unexpected accommodations the two parties made early in Clinton's second term that produced the structure for long-range budget savings. Although the outcome—an end to budget deficits—was pushed along by the unprecedented prosperity of the 1990s that saw tax revenues soar, the acceptance by both parties of achieving budget discipline proved to be a primary legacy of the odd combination of a Democrat in the White House and a Republican majority on Capitol Hill. The end of fiscal year 1997 showed a budget deficit at a level (as a percent of the gross domestic product) not seen since 1970. The $22 billion deficit was less than one-tenth of the deficits run at the beginning of the Clinton administration. The last three years of the Clinton administration saw three consecutive surpluses. The achievement demonstrated the malleability of the American political process and the unexpected dexterity of Clinton and his GOP counterparts on the Hill.

But it was a peace of the moment between the parties that faded in Clinton's final years, which were characterized by deadlock with Congress and repeated vetoes that each party seemed to welcome to define its approach to economic policy. The budget surpluses, as welcome as they were, spawned more fundamental controversy between Democrats and Republicans about how to spend the surplus. Clinton's suggested priorities were "saving" the financially troubled Social Security system and paying off the national debt, which stood close to $6 trillion. Congressional Republicans pressed instead for tax cuts for individuals and businesses.

Public opinion polls showed that the voters generally sided with Clinton, and Congress eventually set aside much of the early surpluses to pay off the debt. During fiscal years 1998–2000, the government bought back $363 billion in debt, saving tens of billions of dollars in long-term interest.

But the basic issue of how to use the newfound money was left first to the 2000 elections and then to the totally unexpected exigencies of a new and different kind of war that followed terrorist attacks on the United States on September 11, 2001.

George W. Bush Administration

Texas governor George W. Bush, the son of the president who held office from 1989 to 1993, inherited a vastly improved economic situation. Not since the Kennedy administration in the early 1960s did an incoming president have price stability, relatively low unemployment, and a total federal spending level at about 18 percent of the gross domestic product. However, there was evidence that the U.S. economy was slowing down.

In monetary policy, the Fed was easing back to create lower interest costs. This policy pattern continued throughout all of 2001. On the fiscal side, President Bush had campaigned in 2000 largely on a tax cut. His argument during the campaign, which expressed standard Republican gospel, was that a tax cut was a way to give the predicted generous federal budget surpluses back to the taxpayers. But by early 2001 the Bush administration was also making the traditional supply-side and Keynesian arguments on the utility of the tax cut.

With Congress under narrow but firm Republican control following the 2000 elections, and a Republican in the White House, a major tax-reduction package was all but guaranteed. Over vigorous Democratic opposition,

After terrorists hijacked four commercial airliners, crashing two into the World Trade Center in New York City, one into a field in rural Pennsylvania, and one into the Pentagon outside Washington, D.C., on September 11, 2001, the demand for air travel immediately declined. Congress and the Bush administration provided federal aid to the airline industry and other industries, such as tourism, that were affected by the attacks. One week later, the Continental Airlines ticket counter at the Orlando International Airport in Orlando, Florida, the largest tourist destination in the world, was virtually empty.

Congress passed a huge tax-reduction plan that would cost $1.35 trillion dollars over a ten-year period. The lowest tax rate was cut to 10 percent from 15 percent and the top rate to 35 percent from 39.6 percent. Democrats argued that the size of the reduction in federal revenues would deprive the government of needed funds for programs for years to come. The final package was similar to the bills the previous Congress had sent to President Clinton, who vetoed almost all of them.

The other major economic initiative in 2001, aside from the economic aid in the aftermath of the September terrorist attacks, was restoring fast-track authority, which gives the president substantial flexibility to negotiate trade agreements that lower tariffs among nations. The procedure had been a cornerstone of presidential policy for many administrations but always was controversial with influential interest groups including businesses threatened by overseas competition and by organized labor that feared job losses in those industries. President Clinton, in spite of strong appeals to Congress, was unable to get the authority extended. His successor, George W. Bush, also vigorously sought renewal but by June 2002 Congress had not sent him a bill.

On September 11, 2001, the entire calculus of government policy, including the role of president as chief economist, changed with the terrorist attacks on the United States. In successfully hijacking four commercial airliners, and flying three of them into major U.S. buildings—two into New York City's World Trade Center towers and the third into the Pentagon outside Washington, D.C. (a fourth crashed in rural Pennsylvania)—the terrorists set the Bush administration and the government on a war footing.

The response to the attacks of September 11 displayed a mix of fiscal and monetary policy to ensure economic stability. The Bush administration's reactions were a classic response to both the immediate challenges following the attacks and the longer-term problems resulting from the mild recession that had set in after the long economic boom of the 1990s. In either case, the government's actions were focused on an expansionary fiscal and monetary policy.

In the aftermath of the attack, the airline industry all but collapsed for a time, spreading economic trouble to industries that depended either directly or indirectly on air travel such as tourism. Within a week after the attack an estimated 100,000 jobs in the airline industry alone were eliminated. But many other segments of the economy slowed as uncertainty about the future spread.

Congress and the administration quickly considered a variety of legislation to help industries, particularly airlines, and workers most hurt by the economic effect of the terrorist attacks. The total figure for all assistance, including the airline aid, was nearly $40 billion, which was to be dispensed by no fewer than seventeen federal agencies or departments.

The vigorous U.S. military response that got under way within months promised substantial additional defense spending down the road.

The expansionary fiscal policy reflected in these new government expenditures was bolstered by an expansionary monetary policy. From January to September 2001 the Fed cut interest rates eight times, dropping the level from 6.5 percent to 3.0 percent. Subsequent reductions in interest rates lowered the federal funds rate to 1.0 percent by May 2004. The moves by the Fed, which were under way in response to slowing economic activity even before the attacks, were the most expansionary since the recession of 1991.

Bush's expansionary policies led to large budget deficits for the period 2001–2006, which helped to cushion the economic slowdown. The recession of 2000–2001 was one of the mildest on record. By the election year of 2004, GDP was growing at an average rate of 4.4 percent. The unemployment rate, which had peaked at 6.3 percent in June of 2003, was at 5.4 percent in November of 2004. This downward trend would continue after President Bush's 2004 reelection. The unemployment rate dropped to 4.7 percent by the summer of 2006.

Despite these positive trends, two damaging events occurred in late August and September of 2005. Hurricanes Katrina and Rita, events with immediate economic consequences, devastated the Gulf of Mexico coast. The hardship was palpable. Nearly 800,000 workers were separated from their jobs, unemployment among evacuees was nearly 12 percent by year's end, and the value of the homes destroyed was estimated to be more than $60 billion. In response to this devastation, the Bush administration and Congress authorized $62 billion in disaster relief. Additional support was to follow for flood insurance and tax relief.

Besides the human cost, there was also immediate harm done to energy production in the Gulf. The fourth quarter of 2005 saw total U.S. natural gas production fall by 10 percent because of the devastation in the area. Oil extraction in the United States fell by 1.08 million barrels a day in the third quarter and by 0.7 million barrels in the fourth quarter of 2005. By the middle of 2006, the affected areas were experiencing ongoing recovery and rebuilding efforts, with the harmful effects expected to last for some time.

Another economic challenge—with longer term ramifications—that the Bush administration was forced to wrestle with was the rising cost of energy on world markets. The rapid expansion of China and India meant that the world demand for oil was going to continue its upward trend. The effects of the Hurricanes Katrina and Rita merely reinforced the effect on supply. But the trends were clear. In 2004 consumer energy prices went up 18 percent and in 2005 by an additional 21 percent. Spending on energy goods and services jumped from 4.2 percent in 2002 of personal disposable income to 6.0 percent in 2005. This meant an additional

In August and September 2005 crude oil prices topped $70 per barrel and the price per gallon skyrocketed due in part to the temporary loss of oil production and refining capacity in the aftermath of Hurricane Katrina, which devastated portions of the U.S. Gulf Coast.

$700 of the average household's budget was being diverted to energy expenditures.

The effect of the higher energy prices also put the Federal Reserve in a bind. On the one hand, the higher energy prices could reduce demand in the economy. On the other hand, it could also lead the Fed to pursue overly stimulative policies to help counteract the slowdown. This was the policy error made in the 1970s, and it was unlikely the Fed would make the same mistake twice. While inflation had tripled from 2001 to 2006 to nearly 4 percent (on an annual rate), the Fed had responded since 2004 by raising the federal funds rate from 1.0 percent to 5.25 percent by the fall of 2006. The Fed was erring on the side of price and inflation stability.

FUTURE CHALLENGES: ECONOMIC ISSUES FOR THE TWENTY-FIRST CENTURY

Controlling Government Spending

The 2001 terrorist attacks on the United States increased the likelihood of future surges in government spending as defense spending, and related outlays for homeland security, began to escalate. The budget surpluses that were realized in the late 1990s were eliminated with budget deficits projected to remain for the foreseeable future. However, increased defense and homeland security spending was not the only challenge to public officials who had to make difficult choices between competing claims on government funds or, alternatively, find the additional money needed through taxation and borrowing. Other major reasons included the impending retirement of the baby boom generation, which was predicted to place great demands on retirement systems, and the ability of the national medical system to handle much larger numbers of elderly citizens.

Presidents hoping to limit government spending must face the fiscal difficulties brought by the expenditures that are required from year to year by existing law. These are known as uncontrollable or mandatory budgetary items. Although the term "uncontrollable" is somewhat misleading because these programs can be changed by an act of Congress, it does accurately describe the lack of power presidents have over these items in any given year.

Before the Great Depression, most of the federal budget was devoted to the costs of running the government and, in times of war, the costs of defense. With the establishment of Social Security in the 1930s, however, the government began making large-scale payments directly to people who qualified for them. These entitlements now include Medicare, Medicaid, welfare, job training assistance, student loan guarantees, food stamps, school lunches, farm subsidies, unemployment compensation, and federal retirement benefits. They are intended to alleviate suffering and poverty, promote the health and advancement of individuals, and provide a safety net for those members of society who cannot provide for themselves because of economic recession, poverty, old age, or physical infirmity. Some of these entitlement programs, such as welfare and unemployment insurance, also act as automatic economic stabilizers because they increase the amount of money in the hands of the public when the economy goes into recession.[105]

These payments have consciously been expanded by Congress and several presidents, most notably Franklin Roosevelt and Lyndon Johnson, in an effort to use the wealth generated by the U.S. economy to promote social welfare and care for the less fortunate. Many federal entitlement programs were established or substantially enlarged during the 1960s, when the strong American economy seemed capable of providing funds for virtually any worthy purpose.

Entitlements pose a special problem for presidents because the payments are not based on a yearly congressional appropriation or the government's ability to pay for them. They continue from year to year unless a law is passed that supersedes or alters the measure that created them. Moreover, in 1974 Congress established cost-of-living increases for Social Security payments, thereby ensuring that these benefits would not be reduced by the eroding effects of inflation.[106]

Predictably, presidents and Congress have been hesitant to assume the political risk of significantly reducing entitlement programs as the capacity of the government to pay for them has fallen. The growth of entitlements has been accompanied by an increase in the activities of interest groups that attempt to protect these payments from cutbacks. Lobbyist organizations representing senior citizens, veterans, farmers, and other groups can pressure the president or members of Congress to protect benefits for their constituents by offering or withholding campaign contributions, threatening them with negative publicity, and mobilizing blocs of voters that can make or break their candidacies. The activities of these lobbyists and the negative public reaction to cuts in entitlements received by tens of millions of Americans have made large sections of the budget politically dangerous to touch.[107]

The ability of presidents to propose significant cuts in the budget from year to year has been reduced as federal entitlements have claimed a greater portion of the budget. In 1963 entitlement spending accounted for 22.6 percent of the budget. By fiscal year 1983 it had risen to 45.2 percent of the budget. Ten years later it represented 47.3 percent of the budget. This upward trend continues as entitlement spending is now more than 50 percent of the budget.

Even within the shrinking discretionary spending category, the president's ability to propose budget cuts is limited because the federal government is obligated to pay for items that it has ordered in previous years. For example, large weapon systems such as a new fighter plane or nuclear missile must be paid for over a span of years. Consequently, funds committed to such items cannot be cut from a current budget without breaking contracts and wasting the funds spent on the items in past years. Expenditures for many other items in the budget, such as defense and the costs of operating the government, can be trimmed but not eliminated entirely.

Presidents seeking to reduce government spending in a particular year, therefore, can search for cuts in only a fraction of the budget. According to political scientists Kim Quaile Hill and John Patrick Plumlee, this trend has diminished presidential budgetary power: "Presidential budgetary discretion has been significantly eroded. . . . The President in fact must propose and defend a budget much of which is determined elsewhere and in prior years."[108]

Although presidents acquired control over executive branch budget proposals, Congress often has resisted presidential attempts at budgetary leadership. Legislators are not required to accept the president's recommendations or even to use them as a starting point. The power of presidents to affect budget legislation has depended on their ability to forge congressional coalitions and generate public pressure on Congress to favor their initiatives and priorities.

In 1974 Congress passed the Congressional Budget and Impoundment Control Act, an attempt to revitalize the entire budget process and to link congressional deliberations on spending and revenue legislation. The act created a timetable designed to force action on the budget, moved the start of the fiscal year from July 1 to the following October 1 to give Congress more time to consider budgetary details, and established measures intended to aid Congress in evaluating the budget as a whole instead of as a group of unconnected spending bills. The act created the House and Senate Budget Committees to centralize congressional budget making and the Congressional Budget Office to provide Congress with an expert staff to analyze the budget.[109]

The potential of the 1974 Budget Act as an executive tool was realized in 1981. At that time Reagan used the process to push his dramatic fiscal program of increased military spending, decreased domestic spending, and a large tax cut through Congress. The new centralized budget-making process in Congress allowed him to negotiate with congressional leaders on the substance of his entire budget plan instead of being forced to bargain on a dozen or more appropriations bills, each of which might have been opposed by a different congressional bloc. To get his budget approved, Reagan used his public popularity to build a conservative coalition in the House of Representatives despite the Democratic majority.

Political scientist Louis Fisher explained why the new process improved the position of the president:

> Whereas the politics of incrementalism under the old process had operated as a brake on radical changes, the Budget Act of 1974 strengthened Reagan's hand by requiring Congress to vote on an overall budget policy. . . . Although the administration did not get everything it wanted, the omnibus measure was more of an advantage to the executive branch than to Congress. By packaging all the cuts in a single bill, the White House was able to build a majority for final passage. Members could announce that they objected to specific cuts but supported the bill "on balance." [110]

During a time of divided government, as occurred in all but two years from 1981 to 2002, the president's power to present a budget to Congress remains relevant as a statement of administration priorities. But a far more important budgetary power is the veto. The prospect that the president will veto a budget bill or individual appropriations bills forces Congress to take account of presidential goals. Often this threat of a presidential veto will require direct negotiations between members of Congress and the president on the final form of a budget bill. Yet for its first six years, with Republican control of both houses of Congress for the majority of that time, the Bush administration made little use of the veto threat. More important, the movement to cut government spending had yet to gain significant political traction in either party. What happened instead was that total expenditures (particularly entitlements) continued to increase with partisan differences sometimes developing concerning the mix of expenditures.

In January 2006, however, the new Democratic majority in the House of Representatives passed "Pay-Go" spending control rules, similar to those used in the 1990s, requiring lawmakers to offset tax cuts or entitlement spending increases with cuts elsewhere in the budget.[111]

NOTES

1. Clinton Rossiter, *The American Presidency,* 2d ed. (New York: Harcourt Brace, 1960), 21.

2. Harold M. Barger, *The Impossible Presidency: Illusions and Realities of Executive Power* (Glenview, Ill.: Scott, Foresman, 1984), 320.

3. David M. Anderson and Michael Cornfield, eds., *The Civic Web: Online Politics and Democratic Values* (Lanham, Md.: Rowman and Littlefield, 2003).

4. Morris P. Fiorina, Samuel J. Abrams, and Jeremy C. Pope, *Culture War? The Myth of Polarized America* (New York: Pearson-Longman, 2006).

5. Quoted in Francis Russell, *The Shadow of Blooming Grove* (New York: McGraw-Hill, 1968), 559.

6. Charles Morris, "It's Not the Economy, Stupid," *Atlantic Monthly,* July 1993, 50.

7. See Joseph Spiers, "Washington's Crummy Numbers," *Fortune,* May 15, 1995, 37–38; and James C. Cooper and Aaron Berstein, "Suddenly, the Economy Doesn't Measure Up," *Business Week,* July 31, 1995, 74–76.

8. Rudiger Dornbusch and Stanley Fischer, eds., *Macroeconomics,* 4th ed. (New York: McGraw-Hill, 1987), 450–451.

9. Jim Granato and M. C. Sunny Wong, *The Role of Policymakers in Business Cycle Fluctuations* (New York: Cambridge University Press, 2006).

10. Herbert Stein, *Presidential Economics: The Making of Economic Policy from Roosevelt to Clinton,* 3d rev. ed. (Washington, D.C.: American Enterprise Institute, 1994), 32–33.

11. Anthony S. Campagna, *U.S. National Economic Policy, 1917–1985* (New York: Praeger, 1987), 101.

12. Campagna, *U.S. National Economic Policy,* 131.

13. Ibid., 141.

14. Jim Powell, *FDR's Folly* (New York: Crown Forum, 2003).

15. Norman C. Thomas and Joseph A. Pika, *The Politics of the Presidency,* 4th ed. (Washington, D.C.: CQ Press, 1996), 365.

16. James P. Pfiffner, "The Crisis of Confidence in U.S. Economic Policy," in *The President and Economic Policy,* ed. James P. Pfiffner (Philadelphia: Institute for the Study of Human Issues, 1986), 2.

17. Mary H. Cooper, "Federal Budget Deficit," *Editorial Research Reports,* January 20, 1984, 48–52.

18. John F. Witte, "The President vs. Congress on Tax Policy," in *The President and Economic Policy,* ed. James P. Pfiffner (Philadelphia: Institute for the Study of Human Issues, 1986), 180.

19. Ibid.

20. Godfrey Hodgson, *All Things to All Men* (New York: Simon and Schuster, 1980), 227.

21. Campagna, *U.S. National Economic Policy,* 485–488.

22. Ibid., 486.

23. Stein, *Presidential Economics,* 255–256.

24. Timothy J. Conlan, Margaret T. Wrightson, and David R. Beam, *Taxing Choices: The Politics of Tax Reform* (Washington, D.C.: Congressional Quarterly, 1990), 45–48.

25. See, for example, Paul Krugman, *Peddling Prosperity* (New York: Norton, 1994); and Lawrence Lindsey, *The Growth Experiment* (New York: Basic Books, 1990).

26. Jean R. Schroedel, *Congress, the President and Policymaking: A Historical Analysis* (New York: Sharpe, 1994), 66–80.

27. Dornbusch and Fischer, *Macroeconomics,* 439–446.

28. Paul Peretz, "The Politics of Fiscal and Monetary Policy," in *The Politics of American Economic Policy Making,* ed. Paul Peretz (Armonk, N.Y.: Sharpe, 1987), 149.

29. Paul Volcker and Toyoo Gyohten, *Changing Fortunes* (New York: Times Books, 1992), 176.

30. Quoted in Pious, *The American Presidency,* 297.

31. Charles E. Jacob, "Macroeconomic Policy Choices of Postwar Presidents," in *The President and Economic Policy,* ed. James P. Pfiffner (Philadelphia: Institute for the Study of Human Issues, 1986), 69.

32. Dorothy Buckton James, *The Contemporary Presidency,* 2d ed. (Indianapolis: Bobbs-Merrill, 1974), 96.

33. Robert E. Lucas Jr., "Understanding Business Cycles," *Carnegie Rochester Series on Public Policy* 5 (1977): 14.

34. Pious, *The American Presidency,* 313.

35. John M. Berry and Kathleen Day, "Worker Pay, Benefits Up 4.9% in '88," *Washington Post,* January 25, 1989, F1.

36. Jonas Prager, *Fundamentals of Money, Banking and Financial Institutions* (New York: Harper and Row, 1982), 297.

37. James E. Anderson, *Politics and the Economy* (Boston: Little, Brown, 1966), 9.

38. Jonathan Hughes and Louis P. Cain, *American Economic History,* 4th ed. (New York: HarperCollins, 1994), 194.

39. Anderson, *Politics and the Economy,* 9–10.

40. Ibid., 11–12.

41. John Milton Cooper Jr., "The Great Debate," *Constitution* 6 (spring 1994): 42–43.

42. Michael P. Riccards, *A Republic, If You Can Keep It: The Foundation of the American Presidency, 1700–1800* (New York: Greenwood Press, 1987), 90.

43. Ibid., 91–97.

44. Arthur M. Johnson, *The American Economy* (New York: Free Press, 1974), 52.

45. Witte, "The President vs. Congress on Tax Policy," 166.

46. Emmet J. Hughes, *The Living Presidency* (Baltimore: Penguin, 1974), 216–217.

47. Louis Fisher, *The Politics of Shared Power: Congress and the Executive,* 3d ed. (Washington, D.C.: CQ Press, 1993), 177–178.

48. Anderson, *Politics and the Economy,* 123.

49. George C. Edwards III and Stephen J. Wayne, *Presidential Leadership, Politics, and Policy Making,* 3d ed.(New York: St. Martin's Press, 1994), 391.

50. Viveca Novak, "Defective Remedy," *National Journal,* March 27, 1993, 750.

51. Forrest McDonald, *The American Presidency: An Intellectual History* (Lawrence: University Press of Kansas, 1994), 313.

52. Hughes and Cain, *American Economic History,* 194.

53. Riccards, *A Republic, If You Can Keep It,* 101.

54. Hughes and Cain, *American Economic History,* 200.

55. Mira Watkins, "Foreign Investment in the U.S. Economy before 1914," *Annals of the American Academy of Political and Social Science* 516 (July, 1991): 9–21.

56. Miroslav Nincic, *United States Foreign Policy, Choices. and Trade-offs* (Washington, D.C.: CQ Press, 1988), 337–338.

57. James, *The Contemporary Presidency,* 117–118.

58. Owen F. Humpage, "Institutional Aspects of U.S. Intervention," *Economic Review* 30 (first quarter, 1994): 2–6.

59. Walter S. Mossberg, "Dollar Selling Aimed at Curbing Its Rise," *Wall Street Journal,* January 12, 1989, A2.

60. Humpage, "Institutional Aspects of U.S. Intervention," 6.

61. Erwin C. Hargrove, *The Power of the Modern Presidency* (Philadelphia: Temple University Press, 1974), 159.

62. Stein, *Presidential Economics,* 416.

63. Destler, *American Trade Politics,* 98.

64. R. W. Apple, "A High-Stakes Gamble That Paid Off," *New York Times,* November 18, 1993, A1.

65. Destler, *American Trade Politics,* 98–100.

66. David S. Broder, "A Shaky Victory on Trade," *Washington Post,* December 12, 2001, A35.

67. Warren Vieth, "Fast Track Trade Measure Ok'd by Senate," *Los Angeles Times,* May 24, 2002.

68. Campagna, *U.S. National Economic Policy,* 196.

69. Stein, *Presidential Economics,* 77.

70. James, *The Contemporary Presidency,* 94.

71. Campagna, *U.S. National Economic Policy,* 210–211.

72. Jacob, "Macroeconomic Policy Choices," 65.

73. Campagna, *U.S. National Economic Policy,* 238–243.

74. Jacob, "Macroeconomic Policy Choices," 67.

75. Richard M. Nixon, *Six Crises* (New York: Doubleday, 1962), 309–310.

76. Jacob, "Macroeconomic Policy Choices," 67.

77. Stein, *Presidential Economics,* 106–107.

78. Arthur M. Schlesinger Jr., *A Thousand Days: John F. Kennedy in the White House* (Boston: Houghton Mifflin, 1965), 654.

79. Donald F. Kettl, *Leadership at the Fed* (New Haven: Yale University Press, 1986), 96.

80. Campagna, *U.S. National Economic Policy,* 306–307.

81. Thomas and Pika, *Politics of the Presidency,* 371.

82. Campagna, *U.S. National Economic Policy,* 351.

83. James, *The Contemporary Presidency,* 103.

84. Ibid., 106.

85. Stein, *Presidential Economics,* 214.

86. Campagna, *U.S. National Economic Policy,* 401–402.

87. Jacob, "Macroeconomic Policy Choices," 75.

88. Stein, *Presidential Economics,* 218.

89. Ibid., 228–232.

90. William Greider, *Secrets of the Temple* (New York: Simon and Schuster, 1987), 185.

91. Jacob, "Macroeconomic Policy Choices," 74.

92. Ann Mari May, "Fiscal Policy, Monetary Policy, and the Carter Presidency," *Presidential Studies Quarterly* 23 (fall 1993): 700–701.

93. Pfiffner, "The Crisis of Confidence in U.S. Economic Policy," 10.

94. Stein, *Presidential Economics,* 420–421.

95. George Hager, "One Outcome of Budget Package: Higher Deficits on the Way," *Congressional Quarterly Weekly Report,* November 3, 1990, 3711.

96. Stephen Skowronek, *The Politics Presidents Make: Leadership from John Adams to George Bush* (Cambridge: Harvard University Press, 1993), 438.

97. David E. Rosenbaum, "On the Economy, Bush Followed Reagan's Lead, Not His Success," *New York Times,* June 29, 1992.

98. Sidney M. Milkis and Michael Nelson, *The American Presidency: Origins and Development, 1776–1993,* 2d ed. (Washington, D.C.: CQ Press, 1994), 384.

99. Stein, *Presidential Economics,* 424–425.

100. Robert Solow, James Tobin, and William Jefferson Clinton, *President Clinton's New Beginning, The Complete Text, with Illustrations, of the Historic Economic Conference Conducted by President Bill Clinton & Vice President Al Gore in Little Rock, Arkansas, December 14-15, 1992* (New York: Dutton Adult, 1993).

101. Milkis and Nelson, *American Presidency,* 395–396.

102. George Hager and David S. Cloud, "Democrats Tie Their Fate to Clinton's Budget Bill," *Congressional Quarterly Weekly Report,* August 7, 1993, 2122–2129.

103. Edwards and Wayne, *Presidential Leadership,* 397.

104. George Hager, "Congress, Clinton Yield Enough to Close the Book on Fiscal '96," *Congressional Quarterly Weekly Report,* April 27, 1996, 1155–1157.

105. Anderson, *Politics and the Economy,* 113.

106. Edwards and Wayne, *Presidential Leadership,* 391–392.

107. Ibid., 393.

108. Kim Quaile Hill and John Patrick Plumlee, "Presidential Success in Budgetary Policymaking: A Longitudinal Analysis," *Presidential Studies Quarterly* 12 (spring 1982): 179.

109. Pious, *The American Presidency,* 322–324.

110. Fisher, *The Politics of Shared Power,* 186.

111. Brian Faler and Jonathan D. Salant, "House Approves Democratic 'Pay-Go' Spending-Control Measure," *Bloomberg.com* January 5, 2007.

SELECTED BIBLIOGRAPHY

Anderson, James E. *Politics and the Economy.* Boston: Little, Brown, 1966.

Barger, Harold M. *The Impossible Presidency: Illusions and Realities of Executive Power.* Glenview, Ill.: Scott, Foresman, 1984.

Campagna, Anthony S. *U.S. National Economic Policy, 1917–1985.* New York: Greenwood, 1994.

Destler, I. M. *American Trade Politics.* 3d ed. Washington, D.C.: Institute for International Economics, 1997.

Edwards, George C., III. *Presidential Leadership: Politics and Policy Making.* 5th ed. New York: St. Martin's Press, 1999.

Fisher, Louis. *The Politics of Shared Power: Congress and the Executive.* 3d ed. Washington, D.C.: CQ Press, 1993.

Greider, William. *Secrets of the Temple.* New York: Simon and Schuster, 1987.

Hughes, Jonathan, and Louis P. Cain. *American Economic History.* 5th ed. New York: Addison Wesley Longman, 1997.

Kettl, Donald F. *Leadership at the Fed.* New Haven: Yale University Press, 1986.

Kotlikoff, Laurence J. *Generational Accounting.* New York: Free Press, 1993.

Krugman, Paul. *Peddling Prosperity.* New York: Norton, 1994.

Lindsey, Lawrence. *The Growth Experiment.* New York: Basic Books, 1990.

Mishkin, Frederic S. *The Economics of Money, Banking, and Financial Markets.* 6th ed. New York: Addison Wesley Longman, 2001.

Peretz, Paul, ed. *The Politics of American Economic Policy Making.* Armonk, N.Y.: Sharpe, 1987.

Pfiffner, James P., ed. *The President and Economic Policy.* Philadelphia: Institute for the Study of Human Issues, 1986.

Pious, Richard. *The American Presidency.* New York: Basic Books, 1979.

Schlesinger, Arthur M., Jr. *A Thousand Days: John F. Kennedy in the White House.* Boston: Houghton Mifflin, 1965.

Stein, Herbert. *Presidential Economics: The Making of Economic Policy from Roosevelt to Clinton.* 3d rev. ed. Washington, D.C.: AEI Press, 1997.

Thomas, Norman C., and Joseph A. Pika. *The Politics of the Presidency.* 5th ed. Washington, D.C.: CQ Press, 2001.

Volcker, Paul, and Toyoo Gyohten. *Changing Fortunes.* New York: Times Books, 1992.

chapter 16

Presidential Appearances

by Harold F. Bass Jr. and Charles C. Euchner

Presidents always work at a distance from the American public. Through public opinion polls, interest groups, the media, and relations with Congress and the bureaucracy, presidents gain indirect access to their constituents. Although speaking directly to people helps presidents to create at least the illusion of a direct relationship, it does not help them to develop the relationships they need to assemble coalitions and to govern. To build coalitions, presidents must appeal to many separate groups, or separate publics, as much as to the public at large. Presidents' frequent public appeals have made presidential governance an extension of electoral campaigns.

THE PRESIDENT AS PUBLIC FIGURE

The president occupies the most prominent position in U.S. politics largely because, with the exception of the vice president, the United States has no other nationally elected leader. A related reason for the president's prominence is the availability of what Theodore Roosevelt called the "bully pulpit."

The president's unique ability to promote a national vision and to influence actors in both the public and private spheres has been crucial in disproving the predictions of some observers of early America that the presidency would play a minor role in national government.

In the twentieth century, the president's prominence in American politics increased not only with the growing involvement of the White House in domestic policy and the rise of the United States to international leadership, but also with the expansion of the president's role as the starring preacher in the "bully pulpit" of American politics.[1] Using words and images as well as the actions of the administration, the modern president plays a major role in setting the terms of debate for the entire political system.

Public speaking is one of the most important ties between the president and the public. For many citizens, the clearest memory of the president is of the president delivering a speech.[2] In the half-century since the end of World War II, public speeches by presidents increased by a factor of five.[3] A 1972 report estimated that "a half million words

The setting for a president's speech can be even more important than the words uttered. President Ronald Reagan's speech at the Statue of Liberty celebration on July 3, 1986, is a prime example. Nancy Reagan stands at the president's side.

annually flow out of the White House in a torrent of paper and ink." [4] Not only presidents' words but also their appearances are important in communicating with the public. Academic studies conclude that nonverbal signs, such as physical appearances, have four to ten times the effect of verbal signs on "impression formation." [5]

Political scientist Richard E. Neustadt has argued that the president can exert influence by command only rarely. A more important tool of power is the "power to persuade." [6] Neustadt concentrated on the president's power to persuade other members of the Washington establishment, but the breakdown of many stable institutions has moved presidents to use their persuasive abilities more and more on the public. Even when presidents do not speak out, the threat of "going public" is an important tool.[7]

Communications expert Roderick P. Hart has argued that ubiquitous presidential speech has transformed not only the presidency and the rest of the national government but also the way people perceive politics. The president dominates the public sphere. Working within a "matrix of countervailing forces," the president must maneuver with speech. "Virtually every activity in the modern White House is designed to shape or reshape something that the president has said or will say." [8]

Even when urging change, the president's themes are basically conservative. Political scientist Philip Abbott has written: "President after president, whether advocating reform or retrenchment, attempt[s] to justify policy by calling America back to its origins, restating its basic values, applying them to current problems by seeking to establish an underlying unity amidst current conflict through a call to rededication and sacrifice." [9]

The development of a voluble presidency stems from changes in the U.S. political system as well as from advances in communications and transportation technologies. Modern presidents are inclined to perceive traditional courses of support such as Congress, party organizations, the print media, or the bureaucracy as insufficiently empowered or reliable as foundations to advance their agendas. Less dependent on these mediators of public policy, presidents increasingly must rely on their ability to move people with words.

The connection between presidential speech and the absence of institutional bases was underscored by Richard Nixon's handling of the Watergate scandal in the early 1970s. As Nixon lost support in Congress, in public opinion polls, and among interest groups, he depended increasingly on his rhetorical powers. His last year in office was dominated by behind-the-scenes strategy sessions on how to respond to charges of lawbreaking and by the carefully crafted release of information and public statements.[10]

The disparate parts of the American federal system—from states and localities to the wide variety of economic and social groups—regularly turn to the president for rhetorical as well as administrative and legislative leadership. As political scientist E. E. Schattschneider has noted, battles that originate in a restricted setting often move to higher and higher levels as the combatants seek to attract powerful allies.[11] The president exerts rhetorical force on almost every possible political and economic issue that Americans face, even when the White House plays no direct role in the issue.

Communicating complex policies to the American public is one of the most important—and difficult—tasks of the president. Issues such as interest rates, budget deficits, health care, and trade policy can be numbingly difficult taken alone. When discussed as part of a comprehensive, long-term program, they become even more difficult. Jimmy Carter suffered when he could not explain his complex energy proposals. Carter also addressed so many issues—energy, deregulation, taxes, the Middle East, détente with the Soviet Union, reorganization of the bureaucracy, the environment, urban development—that he could not stay focused in his efforts to sell his policies to the public. Ronald Reagan, in contrast, provided a simple and coherent worldview.

President Bill Clinton initially faced some of the same problems as Carter. Democratic constituencies pressed the new president to address concerns that had been suppressed during the previous twelve years of Republican rule. But Clinton's ambitious agenda often got lost in the minutiae of political battles and policy calculations.

At an early meeting of the Clinton cabinet at Camp David, the Maryland presidential retreat, Clinton's communications advisers and his wife, Hillary Rodham Clinton, tried to get the president's communication with the public back on track. Mrs. Clinton told the group that Clinton's success as governor of Arkansas had hinged on his ability to describe his policy initiatives as a "story" with a beginning, middle, and end, so that the people could follow complex policy initiatives. Clinton had to do the same as president, Mrs. Clinton declared. The story would depict the long journey that the people would travel together—by way of the president's policy initiatives—and it would include tangible signs of progress at regular intervals. Without a coherent storyline, the president would confuse and scare the people who supported him.[12] Clinton used the strategy successfully in his campaigns for the deficit-reduction bill and the North American Free Trade Agreement. During the last six years of his presidency, when the Republicans controlled both houses of Congress, Clinton successfully presented himself as a check on ideological extremism, rhetorically positioning himself in the ideological center, between the congressional Republicans on his right and the congressional Democrats on his left.

Following in Clinton's centrist footsteps, George W. Bush identified himself as a compassionate conservative. He sought to maintain his conservative base by embracing the language of limited government, while reaching across the ideological divide to liberals by signaling his understanding of the need for and his commitment to a social and economic safety net.

However, Bush's agenda, especially in foreign policy, proved to be far more polarizing than Clinton's. Bush demonstrated substantial rhetorical strength in confronting and framing issues in stark fashion. In turn, he sometimes floundered when circumstances called for more circumspect and subtle public remarks. Reputed to have said, "I don't do nuance," [13] his unwillingness and inability to do so diminished his overall effectiveness in using public speeches to promote his policies.

Presidents apply rhetoric to politics in a variety of ways. They meet regularly with reporters and other media representatives, give speeches on television and radio, address large crowds, hold informal meetings with leaders of interest groups, travel abroad to meet foreign leaders, meet and speak by telephone with members of Congress and other elected officials, and attend events that feature celebrities. Every president also commands large research and public relations operations in the White House and federal agencies. Finally, presidential appointees promote the administration's policies.

What presidents say is often less important than how they say it. In other words, the potency of presidential remarks lies not in their content but in the ceremonial way they are delivered. Deference to the president is the norm. As Hart has noted: "Precious few of these ten thousand texts [presidential addresses from Eisenhower to Reagan] were remembered by listeners even a day after their delivery. But what was recalled was the speech event itself—the crowds and the color and the dramaturgy and the physical presence of the chief executive." [14]

Political scientist Murray Edelman argued that the stage on which a president appears can provide a rhetorical advantage because the stage removes the audience from its daily routine. "Massiveness, ornateness, and formality are the most common notes struck in the design of these scenes, and they are presented upon a scale which focuses constant attention on the difference between everyday life and the special occasion," Edelman writes. Such backgrounds make for heightened sensitivity and easier conviction in onlookers, for the framed actions are taken on their own terms. They are not qualified by inconsistent facts in the environment.[15]

Presidents bask in the regal splendor of the presidency whenever they make a public appearance. The podium usually features the presidential seal, and flags often hang somewhere within the audience's frame of vision. Standing alongside the president will likely be a line of dignitaries who look on with respect and even reverence. The distance between the president and the audience increases the sense of the president's "untouchable" status.

When presidents give their annual State of the Union address, they face a rare assemblage of both houses of Congress, the Supreme Court, and the cabinet; the vice president and Speaker of the House are seated behind the president, and a huge flag hangs in the background. The address provides a backdrop for national unity—however brief. Political scientist H. Mark Roelofs notes: "The general impression is of massed cooperation, of forces of every sort coming centripetally together in the president's very person from every corner of the government, the nation, and even the world." [16] When presidents visit military installations, the backdrop likely includes an assemblage of officers and troops in full dress uniforms, an impressive-looking navy ship, or a military band. When they visit a foreign country, presidents are treated to welcomes from dignitaries and bands as well as formal dinners and presentations. When they welcome the winners of the World Series or Super Bowl, they are surrounded by the team's banners and other trappings of the sport.

Even in the most unceremonial situations, the president can use a particular setting to evoke strong national sentiment. After President John F. Kennedy was assassinated in 1963, Lyndon B. Johnson took the oath of office on an airplane to emphasize the suddenness of the tragedy and the swift assumption of power. Soon after the truck bombing of marine barracks in Lebanon in 1983, President Reagan stood in the drizzling rain with his wife and somberly read a statement of tribute to the murdered men and a warning to the forces responsible for the attack. George W. Bush made one of his most effective responses to the September 11, 2001, terrorist attack on New York City during his initial visit to "Ground Zero," where the World Trade Center towers no longer stood. Speaking to relief workers without the benefit of a public address system, he was informed that his words were not being heard. Using a bullhorn, his arm draped around the shoulders of a New York fire chief, he observed that the terrorists would soon be hearing from America.

Although the major television networks occasionally refuse to broadcast an address, presidents almost always have the prestige to gain a wide electronic audience for their speeches and informal discussions. Radio stations generally agree to broadcast short speeches and special events, such as Jimmy Carter's call-in show. The importance of televised speeches has increased since the 1960s as the number of press conferences has declined. The more formal talks give the president greater control over the agenda and tempo of the appearance than does the give-and-take of press conferences. *(See Chapter 18, The President and the News Media.)* However, the advent and proliferation of cable television channels has fragmented a viewing audience that once focused far more on the major television networks. As such, televised presidential speeches in recent decades reach a smaller percentage of the public than was the case decades earlier in the television era.[17]

EARLY ERAS OF PRESIDENTIAL APPEARANCES AND RHETORIC

Even though the president always has been the preeminent single figure in U.S. politics, only since the rise of an activist national government and vast systems of communications and transportation has the president been at the center of constant, partisan, policy-oriented rhetoric. In the early days of the Republic, presidents usually confined their public appeals to written messages and addressed only matters of broad national interest. Presidential messages, at least until Woodrow Wilson's administration (1913–1921), took on the quality of a national civics lesson in constitutional government rather than open appeals for political support.

The nation's history of presidential rhetoric can be divided roughly into three periods: the age of the Founders, the age of economic expansion and reform, and the age of presidential leadership. Abraham Lincoln's speech at Gettysburg in 1863 was a turning point in presidential rhetoric.

The Age of the Founders

The president's role in the nation's rhetoric was set by George Washington (1789–1797) and the rest of the "Virginia Dynasty," which ruled the young nation from 1789 to 1825. Everything Washington did was a conscious precedent for later presidents. Washington's immediate successors—John Adams, Thomas Jefferson, James Madison, and James Monroe—all had direct ties to the nation's founding. They all experienced the same fears about the dangers of democratic or "mob" rule and recognized the importance of the national leadership avoiding rhetorical excess. Thus the same impulse that led the Founders to set limits on democratic rule also led the first presidents to set limits on presidential rhetoric to avoid demagogy.

The sense of rhetorical limits that guided presidential rhetoric for its first century began with Washington's first inaugural address. After hearing recommendations from his advisers, Washington discarded plans to include a seventy-three-page set of policy recommendations in his inaugural speech. Instead, he used the occasion to deliver a more general lecture on virtue and the need for guidance from the Constitution and from God. Washington was the only president to deliver his inaugural address to a select group of members of Congress and other dignitaries rather than to the people at large. As was true throughout his presidency, Washington tried to offer leadership by example, not by argumentation. Fearing that the regal ceremony of his inauguration might give later presidents dangerous dreams of monarchy, Washington issued a simple two-paragraph address at his second inaugural.[18]

With the exception of John Adams (1797–1801), later presidents until Abraham Lincoln (1861–1865) used the inaugural address to explain and extol the principles of republican government, complete with warnings about the potential excesses of democracy. Discussion of specific policy matters was infrequent and always linked directly to the president's conception of American constitutional values. Of the early presidents, James K. Polk (1845–1849) was the most explicit on policy questions; in his inaugural address he pushed for lower tariffs and annexation of Texas and Oregon and opposed creation of a third national bank.

Early presidents also issued a variety of proclamations, mostly written. Those proclamations rarely argued any points; they usually stated government policies, from the institution of Thanksgiving Day to the emancipation of slaves in the South during the Civil War. As political scientist Jeffrey K. Tulis has noted, the proclamations derived their force not from argumentation but from appeals to the Constitution, the nation's sacred document.[19]

The most outstanding example of argumentation in a proclamation was Andrew Jackson's statement denying states the right to "nullify," or declare invalid, laws passed by the national government. Jackson's proclamation was more like a Supreme Court decision, explaining the rationale for an irrevocable decision, than like an attempt to persuade people to join a coalition.

Perhaps the most ceremonious speech presidents deliver regularly is the State of the Union address. Until Woodrow Wilson, however, presidents from Jefferson on had met the constitutional requirement to address the nation's affairs with a written report. Congressional leaders followed up the written report with a response to each of the president's points. The State of the Union address, then, was just the beginning of a formal dialogue about government policies based on constitutional and republican principles.

The nation's early years saw some presidential appeals to the people, but the rhetoric was restrained and the audience limited. Below the level of presidential politics, however, debate could be bitter and divisive. As historian Michael E. McGerr has noted, political debate took place as a public spectacle: "Through participation in torchlight parades, mass rallies, and campaign clubs and marching companies, men gave expression to the partisan outlook of the [fiercely partisan] newspaper press."[20] Political discussions in speeches, pamphlets, and newspapers could be personal and invective. Debates in Congress often took violent turns. City politics was organized by the gangs and political machines that operated in the streets. Mass demonstrations over slavery, labor, and U.S. involvement in wars were a regular part of the American landscape in the nineteenth century. People who worked for presidential campaigns often resorted to caustic language and threats. Through it all, however, the president stood above the fray, speaking little publicly about some of the most important issues of the day.

The Founders resisted unbridled democracy, and their rhetoric sought to dampen whatever political passions might exist at the time. The Constitution includes many mechanisms for blocking democratic processes, such as a federal system, an independent executive, a bicameral legislature, indirect election of presidents and (until 1913) senators, and an independent and tenured judiciary. The ideal political leader was not the man of the people, but rather the statesman who could guide the nation. Alexander Hamilton expressed this ideal in *Federalist* No. 71:

George Washington delivers his inaugural address, April 30, 1789, in New York's old City Hall.

> The republican principle demands that the deliberative sense of the community should guide the conduct of those to whom they entrust the management of their affairs; but it does not require an unqualified complaisance to every sudden breeze of passion, or to every transient impulse which the people may receive from the arts of men, who flatter their prejudices to betray their interests. . . . [W]hen occasions present themselves in which the interests of the people are at variance with their inclinations, it is the duty of the persons whom they have appointed to be the guardians of those interests to withstand the temporary delusion in order to give them time and opportunity for more sedate reflection.[21]

Presidents were expected to account for their actions in public, but not necessarily popular, messages. Written messages explaining vetoes and the "state of the union" would be available to Congress and anyone else educated and interested enough to seek them out, but presidents would not aggressively seek public support.

From the administration of Washington through that of Herbert Hoover (1929–1933), the president spent several hours a week at the White House shaking hands with any citizen interested in glimpsing him. The "open house," usually held on Sundays after church services, did not communicate anything of substance, but it conveyed the message that the president would not be monarchical and removed from the people. After the sounding of trumpets and bands and the announcement that the president was on the way to meet the people, single-file queues would move rapidly through the public room of the Executive Mansion. Presidents often tried to calculate just how many hands they would shake in an afternoon, as well as the handshake-per-minute rate. The conversation consisted of little more than greetings and best wishes, although some citizens occasionally tried to convey an opinion about a pressing policy question.[22]

The change in presidential rhetoric was marked by the way biographers treated presidents before and after 1930. Later biographers expressed puzzlement that the earlier presidents did not turn to rhetoric as a tool of leadership. But earlier biographers underscored the value of the "custom" of limiting public remarks, because such remarks would "sacrifice [the president's] dignity to beg in person for their support." [23]

Tulis found evidence of some one thousand presidential speeches before the twentieth century. Of the twenty-four presidents who served during that period, only four attempted to defend or attack a specific piece of legislation, and only three—Martin Van Buren, Andrew Johnson, and Grover Cleveland—made partisan speeches. The sole president to address the war in which the nation was engaged at the time was Lincoln; Madison and Polk did not. Only nine presidents indicated the general policy directions of the nation in popular speeches. Eighty percent of the speeches were brief.[24]

Throughout the period, presidential rhetoric was circumscribed by the mores that Washington had established. The mores may have changed somewhat—policy issues crept into presidential speeches, even if they were tethered to constitutional principles—but they remained strongly in force. Just how strong the mores remained was underscored by the miserable failure of President Andrew Johnson (1865–1869) in his attempt to rally the public through a national speech-making tour in the early years of Reconstruction.

Washington, the nation's greatest public figure and a symbol of the new nation's unity, made several public tours in which he put himself on display, but the purposes of these excursions were limited. Washington traveled in order to gather information, ease tensions, and simply show himself to the people. He treated the tours "as auxiliary to the president's narrow executive function of carrying out the law and preserving tranquility, rather than his legislative responsibility to initiate new policies."[25] Washington set an important precedent by insisting on making written replies to the remarks of others after his speeches.[26] His farewell address was more scholarly than rhetorical—a document open for careful analysis.

The second president, John Adams, occasionally met with small groups but did not make public tours. Some historians suggest that Adams lost his chance to improve his public standing on issues, particularly foreign affairs, because of his public reticence. Thomas Jefferson (1801–1809), considered the most democratic theorist of early America, limited his public statements to a few meetings with American Indians and his formal, written messages to Congress. Despite a difficult war with Great Britain, James Madison (1809–1817) continued the practice of presidential communication by proclamation rather than speech.

James Monroe (1817–1825) reinstituted Washington's practice of the national tour but otherwise stayed within the limits of unity appeals and limited speech. Despite his background as a teacher of rhetoric at Harvard College, John Quincy Adams (1825–1829) refused to do more than put himself "on display" in public gatherings. His public remarks were simple statements of greetings and congratulations. Adams almost never even referred to the public issues of the day before popular audiences.

After the bitter controversy surrounding the 1824 election of John Quincy Adams over Jackson, the nation experienced major pushes to expand the idea of democratic rule. Suffrage barriers related to property fell during this period as the nation moved westward and politicians from different regions competed for control over the nation's development. Political parties, which put forth radically different views of development and protection, gained legitimacy for the first time and created a regular public clash of ideas. The sectional tensions finally led to the bloody Civil War, which consumed the nation from 1861 to 1865.

Andrew Jackson (1829–1837) rarely gave speeches. He enjoyed popular discourse, but once elected president he limited the number of his appearances and contained his argumentation within the limits set by his predecessors. Jackson's most public campaigns—those against the Bank of the United States and the doctrine of nullification—were quite limited. His public appeals were mediated—that is, he spoke to the public through the formal channels of official documents and proclamations. Jackson's annual messages and the nullification proclamation to Congress were all written appeals.

Jackson's successors also were reluctant to speak. Martin Van Buren (1837–1841) faced a boycott of council members in three New York towns after he delivered a slightly partisan remark, then abandoned any more such rhetoric. John Tyler (1841–1845) delivered no public addresses. James Polk (1845–1849) took one public tour but considered other public appearances a nuisance and therefore avoided them. Zachary Taylor (1849–1850) took one tour but avoided being seen; the journey was more a fact-finding tour than a public relations effort.

Up through the administration of Herbert Hoover, presidents spent several hours a week at the White House shaking hands with citizens. Here the general public is admitted for a New Year's Day reception.

Millard Fillmore (1850–1853) became the first president after Washington to discuss policy in public when he defended the Compromise of 1850 in a series of short speeches. But these speeches took place after policy had been determined; they were not intended to sway action during the policy-making process. Franklin Pierce (1853–1857) expanded presidential rhetoric, discussing the role of tariffs and federalism. As a lame-duck president just before the Civil War, James Buchanan (1857–1861) discussed the nominating process of the Democratic Party and the role of property and popular rule in the states.

Lincoln, Rhetoric, and the New National Ideal

Abraham Lincoln (1861–1865) carefully adhered to the limits of presidential rhetoric. But Lincoln's ruminations about the nation's fragility and destiny during the Civil War challenged Americans to adopt new values to give meaning to the war.

Lincoln appeared before a number of groups but averred that he could not speak about policy except in an appropriate setting. Tulis has outlined five reasons for Lincoln's infrequent public rhetoric: modesty before his inauguration about his own "wisdom," a desire to let problems sort themselves out, the need for flexibility, the dramatic effect that his statements might have, and a desire to lend greater authority to the few public pronouncements he eventually would make.[27]

Still, Lincoln's addresses were an important part of his leadership. As Philip Abbott has noted, Lincoln's speeches focused on specific political problems, such as the lynching of an abolitionist journalist and the economic aspects of slavery. Lincoln carefully articulated principles to guide public opinion on these matters.[28]

Many scholars consider the Gettysburg Address to be the pivotal moment of Lincoln's presidency. The address provided a coherent way for Americans to understand the bitter Civil War that still threatened the Union. More important for the long term, the address helped to change the way Americans understood their government and changed the way in which all politicians talked with the people.

Lincoln appeared at Gettysburg, Pennsylvania, on November 19, 1863, months after the bloody battle that claimed more than forty thousand lives and provoked deep uncertainty on both sides about the strategy and objectives of the war. The occasion was the dedication of the battlefield's cemetery. Realizing the symbolic potency of cemeteries and the uneasy state of the nation one year before his reelection campaign, Lincoln prepared intensely for his appearance. *(See box, The Gettysburg Address, p. 846.)* Edward Everett, an Ivy League scholar, former senator, and diplomat, was actually the major speaker at Gettysburg. He spoke for more than two hours before Lincoln delivered his remarks, and he attracted the most press notice.

Although he was not the main speaker at the dedication of the Union cemetery at Gettysburg, Pennsylvania, on November 19, 1863, Abraham Lincoln's short speech there has become one of the most cherished of the nation.

In his speech, Lincoln worked within the narrow constraints of presidential rhetoric, delivering only general remarks that made no direct reference to such divisive issues as slavery, parties, and elections. But Lincoln's Gettysburg Address was so infused with national symbolism that it eventually became one of the nation's greatest creedal statements. Indeed, Garry Wills and other scholars argue that Lincoln's mere 272 words dramatically changed the basic creed of American politics.[29] In the address, Lincoln raised the Declaration of Independence above the Constitution as the nation's guiding light, stressed the notion of equality of citizens, and began the process of rebuilding the nation so bitterly consumed by the Civil War. Lincoln's brief remarks gave the war a transcendent meaning that was not obvious amid the war's confusion and misery. He declared that the United States was a nation constantly in the process of becoming, not a nation already completed with the establishment of a constitutional system of government. Lincoln called on citizens to undertake "the great task remaining before us," which was to remake the nation.

But the major theme of the speech was the equality of men in the experimental and uncertain American republic. Lincoln had always hedged on the question of the position of blacks in America, expressing opposition to slavery but acceptance of the idea of white superiority over blacks. Lincoln's statement that the Declaration "dedicated [the United States] to the proposition that all men are created equal" established a new foundation for the nation's ongoing struggle to order its affairs.

Lincoln's reference to "government of the people, by the people, for the people" forever fused the notions of liberty, equality, and democracy in American political thought. The importance of that rhetorical move can be appreciated only when the early American aversion to democracy—derisively called "mobocracy" or "Jacobinism" in the years after the Constitution was adopted—is recalled.

The style of Lincoln's speech also changed American discourse. Wills argues that Lincoln's fondness for the new medium of long-distance communications, the telegraph machine, shaped his speech patterns. "The language is itself made strenuous, its musculature easily traced, so even the grammar becomes a form of rhetoric. . . . Lincoln forged a new lean language to humanize and redeem the first modern war." [30]

THE GETTYSBURG ADDRES

On November 19, 1863, President Abraham Lincoln rode a train from Washington to Gettysburg, Pennsylvania, to attend the next day's dedication of a cemetery in which six thousand casualties of the Battle of Gettysburg were buried. The battle, fought in early July, had helped to turn the tide of the Civil War in the Union's favor. Lincoln was not the main speaker at the dedication—that honor fell to former senator and renowned orator Edward Everett, who delivered a lengthy and moving address. Instead, Lincoln spoke briefly after Everett was finished.

The brilliance of the Gettysburg Address is that in the space of about 250 words it solemnly and honestly acknowledges the awful pain of "these honored dead" while placing the war in which they had fought into the context of the struggle to attain "government of the people, by the people, for the people" that had begun "four score and seven years ago" in 1776. That struggle, Lincoln urged, must continue into "a new birth of freedom" so that the soldiers would "not have died in vain."

Four score and seven years ago our fathers brought forth on this continent, a new nation, conceived in Liberty, and dedicated to the proposition that all men are created equal.

Now we are engaged in a great civil war, testing whether that nation or any nation so conceived and so dedicated, can long endure. We are met on a great battle-field of that war. We have come to dedicate a portion of that field, as a final resting place for those who here gave their lives that that nation might live. It is altogether fitting and proper that we should do this.

But, in a larger sense, we can not dedicate—we can not consecrate— we can not hallow—this ground. The brave men, living and dead, who struggled here, have consecrated it, far above our poor power to add or detract. The world will little note, nor long remember what we say here, but it can never forget what they did here. It is for us the living, rather, to be dedicated here to the unfinished work which they who fought here have thus far so nobly advanced. It is rather for us to be here dedicated to the great task remaining before us—that from these honored dead we take increased devotion to that cause for which they gave the last full measure of devotion—that we here highly resolve that these dead shall not have died in vain—that this nation, under God, shall have a new birth of freedom—and that government of the people, by the people, for the people, shall not perish from the earth.

But to call Lincoln's words simple would be wrong. The speech uses Latinate terms to elevate the basic simplicity of the message. Lincoln stated that "four score and seven years ago" the nation was "conceived in Liberty" and "dedicated to the proposition," and that the soldiers "consecrated" the battlefield. If he had wanted to make an ordinary speech, Lincoln would have used more ordinary words. But his goal was to lift the nation to a new public philosophy. Wills comments: "He was a Transcendentalist without the fuzziness." [31]

The Age of Economic Growth and Reform

As the nation recovered from the Civil War, economic growth resumed on a scale never before imagined. Transportation and communications networks stretched across the country, and businesses grew in size and geographic importance. The national government played an important role in the expansion but did not address the negative consequences of rapid industrialization and urbanization. It responded to the economy's swings of boom and bust, but its role was limited by the constrained rhetoric and vision of public action. As politicians recognized the need for more concerted national action, both the rhetoric and the vision expanded.

When Abraham Lincoln was assassinated, Andrew Johnson became president. As a former Southern Democrat, Johnson had no real base of power in Washington. When he found himself under attack from all sides, he fought back with words. But his rhetorical thrusts further undermined his position.[32]

The dilemmas that Johnson faced after succeeding Lincoln resembled the situation of modern presidents. Bereft of a strong party organization, dealing with an independent-minded Congress, facing deep sectional divisions, and lacking control over patronage, Johnson desperately needed a way to build his political strength. Like presidents in the twentieth century, Johnson sought that strength by appealing over the heads of political elites to the power of public opinion. But because the system was not accustomed to such appeals, Johnson's attempt to go public failed. He was one of only two presidents in history to be impeached, and one of the counts against him actually concerned the style of his "intemperate" rhetoric. Johnson committed the most important rhetorical "crimes" while trying to rally public support for his policies toward the defeated states of the Confederacy. Tulis has described Johnson's rhetorical style:

> Like contemporary electoral campaigns, Johnson had one rough outline, carried in his head, on which he rendered variations for particular audiences. In the typical speech, Johnson would begin by disclaiming any intention to speak, proceed to invoke the spirits of Washington and Jackson, claim his own devotion to the principles of Union, deny that he was a traitor as others alleged, attack some part of the audience (depending on the kind of heckles he received), defend his use of the veto, attack Congress as a body and single out particular congressmen (occasionally denouncing them as traitors for not supporting his policies), compare himself to Christ and offer himself as a martyr, and finally conclude by declaring his closeness to the people and appealing for their support.[33]

Johnson's tour of the nation to rally support received bad notices in the Republican-dominated press and was avoided even by Johnson's cabinet and aides. When on February 24, 1868, the House of Representatives resolved to impeach Johnson, the tenth and last article concerned Johnson's bad rhetoric. The Senate acquitted Johnson (by one vote), but no major political figure disagreed with the notion that his public appeals were improper. *(See "Impeachment of Andrew Johnson," p. 482, in Chapter 8, and p. 1763, in Reference Materials, Vol. II.)* The lessons from Johnson's bitter experience were clear: politics is a dirty game, and presidents who become involved in the nasty rhetoric put themselves in danger of getting tarred in the process.

Ulysses S. Grant (1869–1877) and Rutherford B. Hayes (1877–1881), the two presidents immediately after Johnson, limited their public speech making to official greetings and plaudits to veterans and other groups. Both presidents refused to campaign for the White House and issued written statements to indicate policy preferences. Hayes delivered more than one hundred speeches, but they were limited to greetings to groups. This real but unsubstantive expansion of presidential speech might be attributed to the need to shore up national confidence because of the controversy surrounding Hayes's election by the House. *(See "Compromise: 1876," p. 378, in Chapter 6.)* Hayes also took several tours of the country and delivered speeches that addressed policy within the larger philosophical framework of republicanism.

James A. Garfield (1881) campaigned for the White House but did not speak on policy as president. His successor, Chester A. Arthur (1881–1885), also limited his talks to

Seeking to build his political strength, President Andrew Johnson made a speaking tour of the country in 1866.

symbolic statements at public ceremonies. Grover Cleveland (1885–1889, 1893–1897) discussed taxes, civil service, and labor during his presidential campaigns but made few public remarks as president. He also wrote extensively on many issues. Benjamin Harrison (1889–1893) broke with tradition when he discussed policy issues such as the railroads and the postal service during his public tours; still, he was reluctant to go too far. He told a Kingston, New York, crowd, for example: "You ask for a speech. It is not very easy to know what one can talk about on such an occasion as this. Those topics that are most familiar to me, because I am in daily contact with them, namely, public affairs, are in some measure prohibited to me."[34]

William McKinley (1897–1901) vowed to talk on a wide range of issues, but his speeches were formal and philosophical in character like those of the nineteenth-century presidents. McKinley did not make any speeches on the Spanish-American War, the sinking of the battleship *Maine*, the Philippines, or southern race laws.

Theodore Roosevelt (1901–1909), the feisty former New York governor who assumed the presidency upon McKinley's assassination, was the first president since Andrew Johnson to go over the head of Congress to the people, but Roosevelt did not overturn the longtime balance of power between the two branches of government. As political scientist Elmer E. Cornwell Jr. has noted, Roosevelt's tours in behalf of specific policies began and ended before Congress took up the matter.[35]

Roosevelt's handpicked successor, William Howard Taft (1909–1913), pursued even greater presidential leadership of public opinion. Taft regularly issued lists of legislative initiatives he favored. He was more adept as an administra-

FIGURE 16-1 **Public Appearances by Presidents, 1929–2003 (Yearly Averages for First Three Years of First Term)**

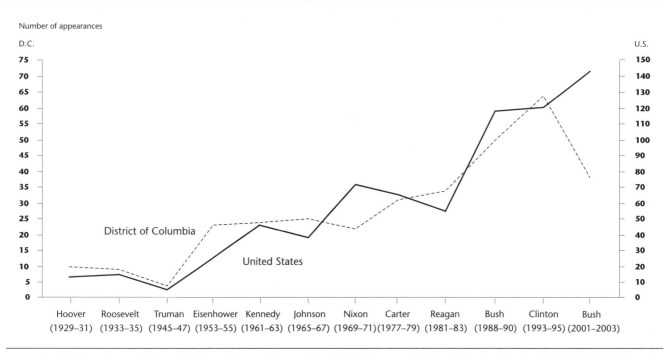

Number of appearances

D.C.		U.S.

Hoover	Roosevelt	Truman	Eisenhower	Kennedy	Johnson	Nixon	Carter	Reagan	Bush	Clinton	Bush
(1929–31)	(1933–35)	(1945–47)	(1953–55)	(1961–63)	(1965–67)	(1969–71)	(1977–79)	(1981–83)	(1988–90)	(1993–95)	(2001–2003)

SOURCES: Data for Hoover, Roosevelt, Truman, Eisenhower, Nixon, and Carter are from William W. Lammers, "Presidential Attention-Focusing Activities," in *The President and the American Public,* ed. Doris A. Graber (Philadelphia: Institute for the Study of Human Issues, 1982), Table 6-2 and 6-3, 154–156. Data for Kennedy, Johnson, Reagan, Bush, and Clinton are from *Public Papers of the Presidents* series. See also Samuel Kernell, "The Presidency and the People: The Modern Paradox," in *The Presidency and the Political System,* ed. Michael Nelson (Washington, D.C.: CQ Press, 1984), 245.

NOTE: To eliminate public activities inspired by concerns of reelection rather than governing, only the first three years have been tabulated. For this reason, Gerald Ford's record of public activities during his two and one-half years of office have been ignored.

tor than as a rhetorician, however. Although his antitrust and environmental policies were in line with Roosevelt's, his hortatory deficiencies were one of the reasons Roosevelt opposed him in the 1912 election.

Woodrow Wilson (1913–1921) was a crucial figure in the transformation of the national government from a congressional to a presidential system. He argued for a more unified system of government with the president as the leader, overcoming the fragmented, plodding committees in Congress. Moving public policy from the darkness of the committee meeting to the bright light of public debate was central to Wilson's system. He argued that the public could judge the president's character; if the public could find a leader to trust, the president could be entrusted with a wide grant of power. Wilson wrote: "Men can scarcely be orators without the force of character, that readiness of resource, that clearness of vision, that earnestness of purpose and that instinct and capacity for leadership which are the eight horses that draw the triumphal chariot of every leader and ruler of free men. We could not object to being ruled by such men." [36]

Wilson's ambitious domestic programs and involvement in World War I and the Versailles peace conference put the presidency in the middle of the nation's rhetorical battles. As historian David Green has argued, Wilson's public comments on the European war left room open for eventual U.S. involvement in the conflict. He promised to keep the United States out of war but contrasted American "liberty" with German "authoritarianism." [37]

Once the United States entered the war and the Allied powers won, Wilson took an active public role. His depiction of the war as the "war to end all wars" helped to overcome many of the deep internal divisions within the United States based on the nationalities of U.S. immigrant citizens. Wilson even traveled to Versailles in 1919 and later joined a parade through the streets of Paris—rare occurrences for an American president. The climax of his public role was his tour of the United States to build support for U.S. membership in the League of Nations. Wilson's moralistic campaign ended, however, when he collapsed from a stroke and the Senate rejected the treaty.

The presidents who succeeded Wilson—Warren G. Harding (1921–1923), Calvin Coolidge (1923–1929), and Herbert Hoover (1929–1933)—were less active rhetorically. Harding, nominated for president because of a backroom bargain at the Republican convention in 1920, limited his public appearances and statements and instituted a written-questions-only policy for the media. He died of a heart attack two years into his term. Coolidge—"Silent Cal"—was best known for his taciturn manner. In his press conferences, Coolidge continued Harding's policy of written press questions. Hoover was the first president to use radio extensively, but the audience was too small and Hoover's speaking style too formal for a strong president-public relationship to develop around his speeches. (*See Chapter 18, The President and the News Media.*)

The Age of Presidential Leadership

During the Great Depression, which began in 1929, the nation turned to Franklin D. Roosevelt (1933–1945) for presidential leadership. Roosevelt was tireless in his efforts to expand the government's involvement in domestic and international politics.

Both Roosevelt's programs and his rhetoric emphasized the need for strong central direction that only a president could provide. For the first time, the government in Washington moved from its traditional role as patronage state to welfare state.[38] As the government became involved in all aspects of everyday life, the need for strong executive direction increased. In the meantime, sophisticated systems of communication tightened the bond between the president and the public. From Franklin Roosevelt to George W. Bush almost sixty years later, the president became more a rhetorical leader on a wide range of issues than an executive who dealt with a limited set of fundamentally national concerns.

By the time FDR took office, millions of American homes were tied together by the airwaves of radio broadcasting. Politics moved from the crowds to the smaller units of a radio-listening audience. Political speeches, once bombastic, became more conversational and intimate. As communications expert Kathleen Hall Jamieson has noted, this shift was reflected in the metaphors used to describe human relations. Warlike words such as *armed, forceful, take, hold, yield, marshal, battle, weapons,* and *onslaught* had often been used to describe political debates. With the dawn of the media age came such warm, electrical words as *wavelength, relayed, channeled, transformed, turned on, fused,* and *defused.*[39]

Roosevelt was the perfect president to begin the new style of debate. Over the radio he delivered a series of "Fireside Chats" to the nation that identified him with everyday concerns. Roosevelt's secretary of labor, Frances Perkins, described the talks:

President Franklin D. Roosevelt gives one of his "fireside chats," national broadcasts from the White House, November 14, 1937.

When he talked on the radio, he saw them gathered in the little parlor, listening with their neighbors. He was conscious of their faces and hands, their clothes and homes. His voice and his facial expression as he spoke were those of an intimate friend. . . . I have seen men and women gathered around the radio, even those who didn't like him or who were opposed to him politically, listening with a pleasant, happy feeling of association and friendship. The exchange between them and him through the medium of the radio was very real. I have seen tears coming to their eyes as he told them of some tragic episode, of the sufferings of the persecuted people in Europe, of the poverty during unemployment, of the sufferings of the homeless, of the sufferings of the people whose sons had died during the war, and they were tears of sincerity and recognition and sympathy.[40]

Since the end of World War II, presidents have spoken in public more than ten thousand times—an average of one speech every working day.[41]

Harry S. Truman (1945–1953) used rhetoric as a tool in his relations with Congress, but it always was directed toward specific policy aims. Truman relied on rhetoric to promote his policies on European redevelopment, relations with the Soviet Union, aid to Greece and Turkey, and civil rights. Truman's 1948 election campaign was a marathon of public speaking—a whistle-stop excoriation of Congress and a call for public support. Perhaps the Truman administration's most important legacy was its rhetoric about the

Soviet Union. Truman acknowledged overstating the Soviet threat to arouse the public during the Greece-Turkey crisis of 1947—after a congressional leader had advised him to "scare the hell out of the country." [42] Harsh anti-Soviet rhetoric starting with the Truman administration may have contributed to the bitterness of U.S.-Soviet relations and the costly nuclear arms race.

Because of improved air transportation, modern presidents have traveled regularly both within the United States and around the world. Presidents through Dwight D. Eisenhower (1953–1961) felt obliged to justify their trips abroad, but international travel has become a regular, expected, and even desired part of the office.

In addition to advanced systems of transportation and communication, the president's expanded role in national politics has stemmed from, among other things, the decline of political party strength, the development of popular nominating systems, the rise of political consultants, the fragmentation of Congress, and the "nationalization" of politics and policy.

MODERN PRESIDENTIAL APPEARANCES AND RHETORIC

Presidential rhetoric in the postwar years shifted fundamentally with the ascension of John Kennedy to the White House. Harry Truman and Dwight Eisenhower used public speech almost solely in pursuit of a specific policy initiative, but later presidents spoke out regularly on a wide range of matters. Indeed, speech became a daily fact of life for modern presidents, who appeared willing and even compelled to talk about every possible aspect of political and social issues—even those about which they were ignorant. Presidents also began to speak before a greater variety of groups.[43]

Today, presidential speech is more personal than ever. Presidents even feel compelled to discuss their own emotions. Whereas earlier presidents spoke formally about issues of great national importance, modern presidents talk in a conversational, intimate way.[44] The shift to the informal style was gradual. Eisenhower spoke formally, but, generally, presidents after Roosevelt at least tried to connect with the public in a casual way.

The number of self-references a president makes increases throughout the term of office. Typical are the following statements by Jimmy Carter: "I've always been proud of the fact that when I came to Virginia to begin my campaign a couple years ago and didn't have very many friends, I went to Henry Howell's home, and he and Betty were nice enough to. . . ." "I would like very much to tell my grandchildren that I slept in the same bed that was used by the governor of Virginia." [45]

Modern political discourse has become deeply personal in other ways as well. Jimmy Carter talked openly about

his experiences as a sinning Christian Baptist; Ronald Reagan described his alcoholic father and "Huck Finn" childhood; and George H. W. Bush discussed the childhood death of his daughter Robin and offered that he had become "born again." Bill Clinton was arguably the most intimate of all, speaking emotionally about his fatherless childhood and proudly about his commitment to carry out his duties of office in the face of scathing personal attacks. Most recently, George W. Bush frequently referred to his deep religious faith and his mediocre academic record.

The Kennedy Style

John Kennedy (1961–1963) may be considered the founder of modern presidential speech making. Indeed, he rose to the presidency in part because of his favorable television appearance during the 1960 election debates with Richard Nixon. Once he occupied the White House, Kennedy used his humor and his ease on camera and in group settings to disarm opponents.

Kennedy was the first president to make regular appearances year-round. Previous presidents and politicians had appeared publicly during elections and campaigns to tout specific policies, but Kennedy stayed in public view even during the slow summer months. Television—which by the early 1960s was in 90 percent of all American households—presented a powerful new opportunity for speaking directly to Americans.

President Kennedy used the presidential news conference to appear on television more frequently than previous presidents. The meetings with the press usually took place during the day, when viewership was lower, because White House aides worried about overexposure and the effect that mistakes would have on the president's public standing. Despite this reluctance, Kennedy was aware that the occupant of the Oval Office intrigued the public, and he moved to exploit that interest. Kennedy's wit played a central part in meetings with the press.

Beyond the development of a personal relationship with the public, speeches were at the center of the most important policy developments of the Kennedy years. The Bay of Pigs invasion, the Cuban missile crisis, the presidential visit to the Berlin Wall, the decision to accelerate the U.S. space program, relations with the Soviet Union, and the civil rights movement—all were marked by important addresses. Unlike the addresses of later presidents, the Kennedy speeches remain important today for their content as much as for the atmosphere in which they were delivered.

Kennedy's inaugural address was one of the most memorable in history, because it was a new expression of national purpose and energy. "And so, my fellow Americans, ask not what your country can do for you—ask what you can do for your country," beseeched the young president. Kennedy had won the presidency in 1960 with the narrowest

President John F. Kennedy developed a personal relationship with the public by pioneering the frequent use of televised press conferences.

margin of victory ever, and he needed a rallying cry to establish his leadership. Congress, though, was skeptical and moved slowly throughout Kennedy's presidency, making the president's stirring calls to action all the more important.

The speech after the failed Bay of Pigs invasion of Cuba in April 1961 is a classic statement of presidential responsibility for failed policy. The invasion by Cuban exiles, who were trained and equipped by the Central Intelligence Agency (CIA) during the Eisenhower administration, was designed to topple Cuban leader Fidel Castro. Kennedy's response to the fiasco was one of his first tests as a world leader. Kennedy quickly reported the incident to the nation and took full responsibility for its failure. The report itself was viewed as an important test of the young president's ability to persevere and learn from mistakes.

In a nationally televised speech, Kennedy told the nation: "There is an old saying that victory has a hundred fathers and defeat is an orphan. . . . I am the responsible officer of government and that is quite obvious." [46] After the speech, Kennedy's poll support increased by ten percentage points. Since then, other presidents—most notably Reagan—have copied the technique of accepting responsibility for a failed undertaking, thereby defusing difficult political situations.

In 1962 President Kennedy used his television address on the Cuban missile crisis as a negotiating tool with the Soviet Union. Kennedy's selective use of information about the stalemate over Soviet placement of nuclear missiles in Cuba gave him flexibility in his private negotiations with Soviet leader Nikita Khrushchev. Later presidents all used dramatic television speeches as levers in their international bargaining. Nixon's speeches on the Vietnam War and Reagan's speeches on arms control are important examples.

Perhaps the most noteworthy recent remarks were made by President George W. Bush, who responded to the September 11, 2001, terrorist attacks on U.S. soil with public declarations that America would bring the "evil-doers," including the nation-states that sponsored and harbored them, to justice.

The Cold War tension over the status of Berlin—a city in the middle of East Germany that was occupied by the four World War II Allied nations—produced two important kinds of public speech. As part of their strategy of public diplomacy, Soviet leaders had threatened the status of the city's "free" sectors. Kennedy countered with a veiled threat of his own, delivered via television. The speech was not an ultimatum, but it evoked the possibility of nuclear war and even discussed the advisability of Americans building bomb shelters. One critic called it "one of the most alarming speeches by an American president in the whole, nerve-wracking course of the cold war." [47] The speech provided an impetus for Congress to mobilize and served as a stark warning to the Soviets.

In June 1963 Kennedy visited Berlin. The famous "Ich bin ein Berliner" [48] speech at the Berlin Wall was a classic statement to foreign publics and a warning to U.S. adversaries. The speech spoke through symbols in a very personal way about major issues of world politics. President Kennedy stood at the wall the Soviets had constructed to halt the free movement of citizens in the city and declared himself and the rest of the Western world citizens of the troubled city.

President Kennedy's speech at American University in Washington, D.C., the same month helped to establish a framework for the later policy of U.S.-Soviet détente. Few presidential speeches have helped to chart major changes in policy as much as that address.

Johnson and Nixon

Lyndon Johnson (1963–1969) was a less graceful speaker than Kennedy, but he spoke even more frequently. Johnson's appearance before a joint session of Congress after Kennedy's assassination was crucial in restoring confidence and stability in the government. After winning election as president on his own in 1964, Johnson used a State of the Union address to outline his ambitious "Great Society" domestic programs.

Johnson also revealed his fondness for public ceremonies, which already had quadrupled from the Eisenhower to the Kennedy administrations. Indeed, he turned his meeting with any group that conceivably could be identified with the nation into a ceremony. It even could be said that, like later presidents, Johnson took refuge in ceremony, especially when polls showed low levels of public support for the president and his policies in Vietnam. Such efforts occasionally backfired. To the president's anger and dismay, a highly publicized 1965 White House Festival of the Arts provided dissident intellectuals with a forum for challenging the escalation of the Vietnam War.

Richard Nixon (1969–1974) ran his public relations campaign on two tracks: national television, where he gave regular addresses and press conferences, and local community and White House meetings, where he appeared before groups likely to support him. On the three issues that occupied Nixon the most—foreign policy (especially the Vietnam War), the economy, and Watergate—Nixon's strategy was closely tied to the way he presented himself to the public. In fact, after his successful 1968 campaign Nixon used public relations to bypass the Washington "establishment." Nixon's presidency was plebiscitary in that he sought public approval after acting on important issues.

Nixon was adept at using foreign travels to build public support. His 1972 trips to the Soviet Union and the People's Republic of China attracted unprecedented television and print coverage and established him as an epoch-making world leader.

Toward the end of his presidency, Nixon's public support fell precipitously—he had the approval of just 23 percent of the public before he resigned—and he tried to revive his fortunes with carefully orchestrated trips to small, friendly communities on the home front. Trips to such places as Nashville's Grand Ole Opry gave the president a chance to escape the insistent questioning of the national press corps. This strategy was lampooned in the newspaper comic strip "Doonesbury," which showed a fictional town called Critters, Alabama, awaiting a presidential motorcade.

Despite his reputation as a cold and even devious politician, Nixon often showed an emotional side to the public and to his staff. The emotional displays were at least partly responsible for many citizens' intense loyalty to the president. In his farewell talk to White House staff after his resignation, Nixon recalled his mother's guidance—he called her a "saint"—and his setbacks as a politician. With tears in his eyes, he spoke of how Theodore Roosevelt fought to rebuild his life after the death of his first wife, implying that he would do the same after losing the presidency. Nixon's staff—and the television audience—was profoundly moved by the speech.

Ford and Carter

When Gerald R. Ford (1974–1977) inherited the presidency after Nixon's resignation, his main job was to restore faith in the badly bruised presidency. In his first address to the nation, Ford declared that "our long national nightmare is over." *(See "Ford's Remarks on Becoming President," p. 1787, in Reference Materials, Vol. II.)* Ford's relaxed style won him broad public support, but his popularity fell dramatically when he pardoned former president Nixon. Ford was unable to recover because of a lack of support in Congress and an inability to stir the nation with his words.

Ford was the nation's most voluble president, even if his many remarks did not win him much public support. Ford made public statements on 1,236 occasions in his less

Jimmy Carter's presidency was filled with symbolic addresses to the nation. Here he wears a cardigan sweater in his televised address asking the nation to make energy sacrifices.

than two and a half years in office.[49] None of his speeches (except his first) was considered memorable, but that was not very important for Ford's immediate purpose of wrapping himself in the prestige of the presidency. The most memorable Ford statements were "gaffes," such as his declaration that Eastern Europeans did not consider themselves to be dominated by the Soviet Union. Ford's aborted public campaign to "Whip Inflation Now" also met with derision.

Jimmy Carter's rise to the presidency (1977–1981) stemmed in part from his intimate statements during the 1976 campaign. Carter's presidency was filled with symbolic events and addresses to the nation; for example, he wore a cardigan sweater in his televised address asking the nation to make energy sacrifices. The crucial moment of the Carter term occurred when, after a ten-day consultation in July 1979 with more than one hundred government officials, economic advisers, business executives, and religious leaders at Camp David, the president spoke on television about a "crisis of confidence" in the nation.

Carter, a tireless public performer, sometimes was very effective. Especially in small groups, Carter's grasp of facts and quiet manner were rhetorically impressive, but his halting speech and southern drawl did not serve him well on television and before larger groups. Moreover, the public did not always receive well his often gloomy assessments of world affairs, such as his descriptions of American moral decay, environmental dangers, human rights abuses, the Vietnam War's legacy, and nuclear war.

Reagan, The "Great Communicator"

Ronald Reagan (1981–1989) presented a rosier picture of the future than Carter. Reagan's training as a movie actor, host of a television show, and speaker on the "mashed potato circuit" for General Electric served him well as a speaker both on television and before crowds. Reagan's optimism gained credibility from his upbeat reactions to such catastrophic events as the attempt on his life. After the 1981 assassination attempt put him in the hospital with a bullet wound, Reagan told his wife, "Honey, I forgot to duck"—a line from an old Hollywood boxing movie.

President Reagan's reputation as the "Great Communicator" underscored the growing separation between the president and the message. All of Reagan's addresses were drafted by professional speechwriters, and even some of his apparently extemporaneous remarks, such as greetings to specific people and jokes, were scripted. Reagan held the fewest press conferences of any modern president, because White House aides doubted his grasp of many policy issues and his ability to make statements that were not written out beforehand.

Several embarrassing extemporaneous remarks seemed to suggest that Reagan was ill-informed about many of the subjects he addressed, such as the role of Americans in

the Spanish Civil War, the effects of budget and tax cuts, weapons systems, the makeup of the nuclear "freeze" movement, Native Americans, monetary policy, and Central American and Soviet politics. Still, Reagan succeeded in promoting his policies because of his apparently deep and consistent convictions and his comfort with public speaking. With the possible exception of Kennedy, Reagan was the first president to have a well-developed affinity for the electronic media. That affinity carried over to live events, because audiences in the media age are comfortable with public performances that resemble television appearances.

Reagan restored the pomp and ceremony stripped from the presidency in the reaction to Nixon's "imperial" administration. A hallmark of his appearances was the grand celebration of American icons, from the Statue of Liberty to ordinary citizens whom Reagan hailed as "heroes" during State of the Union addresses. Reagan basked unabashedly in hearing "Hail to the Chief" before his speeches, and his rhetoric about liberty and opportunity in America and the need to confront the Soviet Union in world politics was inspirational to many Americans weary of the apparent decline the United States had suffered in the 1970s.

Reagan's rhetoric failed conspicuously, however, when he tried to rally public support behind aid to the contra rebels, who were waging guerrilla warfare against the Nicaraguan Sandinista regime, between 1984 and 1986. Reagan delivered a total of thirty-two speeches during this period, all aimed at convincing the public that the Sandinistas posed a threat to their Central American neighbors. But the public did not budge in its opposition to military and financial aid to the rebels. Reagan's evocation of the "threat" posed by "communists," and his equation of the rebels with such groups as the Abraham Lincoln Brigade in the Spanish Civil War, did not resonate with the public. Reagan dropped his appeals after the so-called Iran-contra revelations.[50]

As Kathleen Hall Jamieson has argued, Reagan's speech making fit the intimate manner of public discourse during the age of mass media.[51] His descriptions of firsthand experiences and concrete events were lucid, but his remarks about more abstract policy matters often were disjointed. Earlier presidents had used first-person accounts, but Reagan's personal remarks were particularly effective because they used humor and modesty to portray him as a likable, stable figure. After brief periods in the hospital, Johnson and Nixon used personal anecdotes to attempt to connect with the public. But Johnson's words were cold, Nixon's competitive. Reagan's presidency, by contrast, was a string of self-deflating cracks and yarns about his experiences in Hollywood and politics.[52]

George H. W. Bush

George H. W. Bush (1989–1993) had one of the hardest acts to follow in modern American history when he succeeded

Reagan as president. Bush lacked Reagan's consistent ideology and affable storytelling technique. Partly as the result of a patrician upbringing, when he was taught not to talk about himself, Bush's attempts to relate to ordinary Americans were clumsy.

To make the best of his ordinary speaking ability, Bush's advisers cast him as a modest person who wanted to heal the divisiveness of U.S. politics evident during the Reagan years. In accepting the Republican nomination, Bush promised a "kinder and gentler" nation in which opposing factions would be willing to work out compromises. Bush's inaugural address stressed a desire to work cooperatively with Congress. "The American people await action," he said. "They didn't send us here to bicker." The new president talked about the limits of governmental initiatives and resources: "We have more will than wallet." This modest demeanor continued after the ceremony. Bush and his wife greeted thousands of ordinary citizens in a receiving line at the White House.

Yet Bush was never able to develop a comfortable rapport with the American public. Conservatives in Bush's party viewed the new president suspiciously, as did Democrats who charged that he conducted a dirty campaign in 1988. The problems confronting the nation—unprecedented budget and trade deficits, the breakdown of the savings and loan industry, economic stagnation, and uncertainty abroad from the Soviet Union to Nicaragua—did not lend themselves to sweeping programs. Articulation of the administration's purposes became difficult.

Bush vacillated between the rhetoric of confrontation and the rhetoric of conciliation. Overtures to groups that had been excluded in the Reagan years—African Americans, women, the disabled, urban dwellers—were countered by strident rhetoric on symbolic issues. Bush supported a constitutional amendment banning flag-burning as a mode of expression. His rhetoric on the measure was harsh.

On the foreign policy front, Bush's strongest rhetoric, directed against the dictator of Iraq, Saddam Hussein, ultimately worked to the president's disadvantage. When campaigning in 1990 and 1991 for military action to expel Iraq from neighboring Kuwait, Bush likened Hussein to Hitler and warned that Iraq would obtain a nuclear weapon if Hussein was not defeated. Even though the U.S.-led coalition defeated Iraq decisively, Hussein remained in power. Bush's own rhetoric about Iraq was used against him in the 1992 election.

Similarly, his most memorable rhetorical flourish proved reckless. In accepting the Republican presidential nomination in 1988, Bush proclaimed, "Read my lips: No new taxes." In 1990, he abandoned that commitment, alienating his party's right wing, emboldening his Democratic adversaries, and contributing to his reelection defeat in 1992.

Clinton

Bill Clinton (1993–2001) provided a stark contrast to Bush. He was an exceptionally articulate president, using words precisely and well. He was equally at ease with the subtle language of international diplomacy and the down-home vernacular of his native Arkansas. Clinton combined a commanding presence at the podium, a mastery of delivery and detail, and an uncanny capacity to connect with his audience. He was a tireless and energetic speechmaker who was especially effective in settings where he could demonstrate empathy and provide comfort and solace.

Nevertheless, President Clinton was unable to take full advantage of his formidable rhetorical strengths. Clinton appeared frequently in public to promote his activist agenda, but he jumped from issue to issue; many of his initiatives did not get the follow-up necessary to keep them in the public spotlight; and his rhetoric often strayed off the major themes of the administration. While convincingly demonstrating his familiarity with the arcane details of policy, Clinton often failed to develop and provide a clear, coherent framework for his proposals.

Furthermore, the scandals that plagued his administration constrained his use of the bully pulpit. Unfortunately, most of his memorable phrases uttered during his presidential years emerged in the setting of scandal. These include his assertion that "I did not have sex with that woman, Miss Lewinsky," and the disclaimer, "It depends on what the meaning of 'is' is." His reputation for glibness cost him in observers' assessments of his character and candor. He proved to be so personally polarizing to the American public that his sincere efforts to advance centrist, unifying themes often fell short.

Clinton's best performances came when he could use public appearances to display his vast knowledge of government. In his 1993 health care address to Congress, the TelePrompTer flashed the text of his earlier State of the Union message, but Clinton forged on with a detailed and spirited pitch for his health care reform plan. He also performed well in formal press conferences.

Clinton gave particularly effective speeches on what he called the moral crisis of the nation. In an address at a Memphis church, on November 13, 1993, Clinton challenged African Americans to recover the spirit and aims of the civil rights movement and put an end to inner-city violence and family breakdown. He later gave a well-regarded speech on the breakdown of the American family and community. These addresses were intended to give the administration—and the nation—a focus for Clinton's far-flung agenda. But experts questioned whether rhetoric could make Clinton's agenda coherent in an age fragmented by interest group politics, an explosion of mass media outlets, growing cynicism, and decline in social mores.

George W. Bush

George W. Bush (2001–), like his father, must be ranked among the more rhetorically challenged modern presidents. Before becoming president, he showed neither the inclination nor the capacity to move and inspire audiences with his rhetoric. Exceedingly low expectations worked to his advantage during the presidential campaign and at the outset of his presidency. His speech accepting the party nomination was well received, and his performances in the presidential debates against Vice President Al Gore were surprisingly effective. Similarly, his inaugural address won generally high marks from observers. Still, as his presidency proceeded through its early paces, his speech making was not thought to be one of his major strengths.

However, in responding to the horrific events of September 11, 2001, when terrorist attacks on New York City and Washington, D.C., killed thousands of Americans, Bush found his presidential voice. In the days and weeks that followed, in major and minor speeches as well as impromptu remarks, Bush inspirationally reassured the citizenry and rallied them for the challenging days to come in a protracted war on terrorism. His memorable State of the Union address in January 2002, in which he identified Iran, Iraq, and North Korea as an "axis of evil," received strong support at the time from lawmakers and public alike. Similarly, his second inaugural address, featuring an idealistic clarion call to extend freedom and democracy throughout the world, was generally well received.

Still, Bush continued to appear rather uncomfortable at the podium. He was widely viewed to be much more persuasive and effective speaking informally with small groups than before mass audiences. Moreover, Bush has proven to be an exceptionally polarizing president. The 2001 "rally effect" that unified the nation has given way to bitter partisan division over the Iraq War. In consequence, midway through his second term, his presidential rhetoric more likely reinforced existing dispositions than informs and alters them.

KINDS OF PRESIDENTIAL SPEECHES

The president has different ways and reasons to communicate with the public. One important distinction is whether the communication warrants a "major" or minor label. Political scientist Samuel Kernell has convincingly shown that the number of major speeches has remained relatively stable for decades. However, the incidence of minor speeches has increased both steadily and dramatically. (See Figure 16-2.) Kernell also provides an illustrative list of President George W. Bush's "minor" addresses in a single month. (See Table 16-1.)

How widely the president's remarks will be circulated is the main consideration for the tone and content of a speech. The audience's role in the president's past and future political battles is another consideration. Still another is the president's current political standing with the public and with various interest groups.

Televised presidential addresses cover a wide array of topics. (See Table 16-2.) Foreign policy concerns have predominated throughout, especially in the context of crises. Since the 1970s, domestic issues have been the topic of increased numbers of presidential reports. Herein, the state of the economy has loomed consistently large, along with energy concerns.

The effect of presidential speech making is complex. In one respect, the greater emphasis on rhetoric centers the whole political system on the presidency; the other parts of the system—such as parties, interest groups, and regions—become subordinate to the White House. But as Kernell has argued, presidential speeches are neither a plebiscitary nor a leveling force in U.S. politics. Presidents "go public," in Kernell's words, to assemble temporary coalitions of many different groups on specific policies.[53] Indeed, the explosion in minor addresses supports Kernell's contention that the system remains complex despite the president's primacy.

In addition to the "major" and "minor" distinction, presidential speeches can be broken down by audience, mode of communication, purpose of the address, and political situation at the time of the speech. The six basic categories of presidential addresses are: ceremonial speeches, official state speeches, general persuasive speeches, hortatory or moralistic speeches, crisis speeches, and addresses to specific groups. Some speeches fit more than one category.

Ceremonial Speeches

As the symbolic embodiment of the nation, the president represents the United States in international affairs and in events held abroad and designed to underscore the country's unity and progress. The president also sets the tone for various domestic events, such as award presentations and space shuttle launchings, and issues, such as the fight against drug abuse. (See "Ceremonial Duties and Functions," p. 542, in Chapter 10.)

As Roderick Hart has noted, the increase in presidential speech making since World War II is largely attributable to ceremonial events. The average number of monthly ceremonial speeches increased dramatically from 2.4 under Truman and 3.4 under Eisenhower to 15.2 under Ford and 10.7 under Carter.[54] The monthly average of ceremonial speeches by Reagan—7.85—was not as high as those of his predecessors, but it was still significant. Reagan also made ceremonies out of businesslike events, such as the State of the Union address and policy and interest group speeches. Over the past two decades, this pattern has persisted, in keeping with a larger phenomenon that political scientist Bruce Miroff has labeled the presidential spectacle.[55] Presidents view ceremonial events as potent opportunities

FIGURE 16-2   **Presidential Addresses, 1929–2003 (Yearly Averages for First Three Years of First Term)**

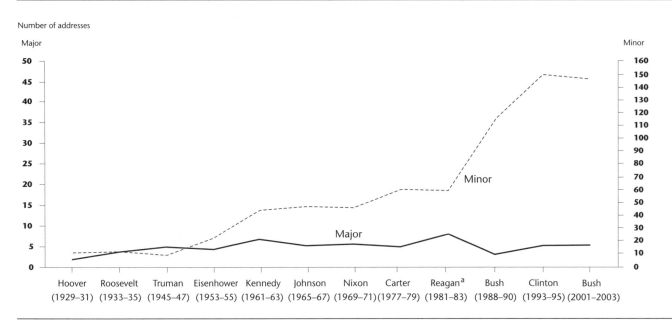

SOURCES: Data for Hoover, Roosevelt, Truman, Eisenhower, Nixon, and Carter are from William W. Lammers, "Presidential Attention-Focusing Activities," in *The President and the American Public,* ed. Doris A. Graber (Philadelphia: Institute for the Study of Human Issues, 1982), Table 6-1, 152. Data for Kennedy, Johnson, Reagan, Bush, and Clinton are from *Public Papers of the Presidents* series. See also Samuel Kernell, "The Presidency and the People: The Modern Paradox," in *The Presidency and the Political System,* ed. Michael Nelson (Washington, D.C.: CQ Press, 1984), 242.

NOTE: To eliminate public activities inspired by concerns of reelection rather than governing, only the first three years have been tabulated. For this reason, Gerald Ford's record of public activities during his two and one-half years of office have been ignored.   a. Major addresses include television addresses only. With radio included, Reagan averaged twenty-four major addresses per year.

and avenues to shape public expectations and understandings in ways that benefit the president's image and agenda.

The chief of state role strengthens the president's efforts to build widespread support for policies and ideas that are part of his political program. Hart has noted: "To stand in this spotlight is to risk comparatively little, for in such situations listeners' defenses are down, the press is prohibited by cultural mandate from being excessively cynical, and the institution of the presidency—its traditions and its emotional trappings—insulate the chief executive from partisan attack." [56]

Hart has identified four kinds of presidential ceremonies. [57] *Initiating ceremonies* mark major transitions—signing legislation or treaties and swearing in government officials. *Honorific ceremonies* bestow some formal recognition of achievement. Testimonial dinners, medals presentations, and university commencements all fit into this category. *Celebrative ceremonies* pay tribute to important national events or values. They include eulogies, dinners for foreign dignitaries, patriotic remembrances, and building dedications. The Statue of Liberty celebration in New York in 1986 was a prime example. *Greeting and departure ceremonies* mark the important travels of presidents and foreign dignitaries.

The inaugural address (an initiating ceremony) is the premier ceremonial speech of the presidency; it sets the tone for an administration. Traditionally delivered at the steps of the Capitol right after the swearing-in, the inaugural address provides the most important hint of the kind of moral leadership the chief executive wants to provide. Furthermore, it helps to unite a nation that has just undergone a partisan election campaign. In the address, the president asks the opposition for help and asserts that the nation's factions have common purposes despite disagreements about how to achieve goals.

The content of most inaugural addresses is usually forgotten soon after the event. Some addresses have been so eloquent or poignant, however, that they have become part of the nation's "civic religion." Thomas Jefferson's first inaugural argued that the nation shared a common purpose despite the bitter battles of the Federalists and the Anti-Federalists. Andrew Jackson asserted the power of the common man in his inaugural. After the horrors of the Civil War, Abraham Lincoln in his second inaugural appealed for national healing ". . . with malice toward none and charity toward all."

Other famous inaugural addresses include Franklin Roosevelt's 1933 admonition that "the only thing we have to fear is fear itself" and John Kennedy's 1961 call for national sacrifice ("Ask not what your country can do for you; ask what you can do for your country"). Kennedy also pledged to "friend and foe alike" that the United States would be an active force in international affairs. George W. Bush used his second inaugural address to commit the United States to the spread of liberty and democracy throughout the world. *(See Documents and Texts, in Reference Materials, Vol. II, for some of these addresses.)*

Eulogies at state funerals (celebrative ceremonies) are considered above partisanship. The speaker attempts to associate with the person being eulogized and to rise above the nation's political divisions. Bill Clinton's eulogy of former president Richard Nixon in 1994 aimed to heal the lingering bitterness of the Vietnam War and the Watergate scandal. "May the day of judging President Nixon on anything less than his entire life and career come to a close," Clinton said. Still, presidents are undoubtedly aware that appearing above politics can be the very best politics. Thus, in the midst of a tight reelection campaign, George W. Bush was eager to associate himself with the Reagan legacy and

bask in its glow as he led the nation in saying goodbye to a beloved former president in 2004.

Presidents' farewell addresses (departure ceremonies) can help to set the tone for the next administration and, more likely, help to shape the nation's memory and assessment of the outgoing executive. The farewell can be an emotional time for the president, the public, and the president's closest political allies. *(See "Speeches of Departing Presidents," p. 870.)*

When moving from active leader to historical figure, presidents are not subject to the same political pressures as an incumbent and cannot muster the same clout. The farewell address can exert great force over time but is not likely to have much of an effect on politics immediately. The purpose is to leave the nation with a lasting statement of principles from an elder statesman to which it can refer. George Washington's farewell set substantive policy and etiquette for future presidents. *(See "Evolution of the Ex-Presidency," p. 1560, in Chapter 34, Vol. II, and Documents and Texts, in Reference Materials, Vol. II.)* Other noteworthy farewell addresses were delivered by Jackson, Cleveland, and Eisenhower.

TABLE 16-1   **President Bush's "Minor" Addresses, February 2006**

Date	Location	Audience	Subject
Feb. 1	Nashville, Tennessee	Speech at Grand Ole Opry House	President discusses 2006 agenda
Feb. 2	Maplewood, Minnesota	3M Corporate Headquarters	President discusses American competitiveness agenda in Minnesota
Feb. 2	Washington, D.C.	Hilton Washington Hotel	Fifty-fourth Annual National Prayer Breakfast
Feb. 3	Rio Rancho, New Mexico	Intel New Mexico	American Competitiveness Panel in New Mexico
Feb. 3	Dallas, Texas	School of Engineering Yvonne A. Ewell Townview Magnet Center	President visits Science and Engineering High School in Texas
Feb. 4	Washington, D.C.	Radio address	American Competitiveness Initiative
Feb. 6	Washington, D.C.	The Federal Reserve	Swearing-in ceremony for Federal Reserve Chair Ben Bernanke
Feb. 7	Atlanta, Georgia	New Birth Missionary Church	President honors Coretta Scott King at Homecoming Celebration
Feb. 8	Manchester, New Hampshire	Radisson Hotel, Manchester	President discusses 2007 budget and deficit reduction
Feb. 9	Washington, D.C.	National Guard Building	Progress in war on terror to National Guard
Feb. 10	Cambridge, Maryland	Hyatt Regency, Chesapeake Bay	President addresses House Republican Conference
Feb. 11	Washington, D.C.	Radio address	Medicare Prescription Drug Coverage
Feb. 15	Dublin, Ohio	Wendy's International Inc.	President discusses health care
Feb. 16	Washington, D.C.	U.S. Department of Health and Human Services	Panel discussion on health care initiatives
Feb. 17	Tampa, Florida	Port of Tampa	Global War on Terror following briefing at CENTCOM
Feb. 17	Lake Buena Vista, Florida	Disney's Contemporary Resort	Remarks at Republican Party of Florida dinner
Feb. 18	Washington, D.C.	Radio address	Advanced Energy Initiative
Feb. 20	Milwaukee, Wisconsin	Johnson Controls Building Efficiency Business	President discusses advanced energy initiative in Milwaukee
Feb. 20	Auburn Hills, Michigan	United Solar Ovonic, LLC	President discusses solar technology and energy initiatives in Michigan
Feb. 21	Golden, Colorado	National Renewable Energy Laboratory	Energy Conservation and Efficiency Panel
Feb. 22	Washington, D.C.	Mandarin Oriental Hotel	President addresses Asia Society, discusses India and Pakistan
Feb. 25	Washington, D.C.	Radio address	Meeting with America's governors and health care providers
Feb. 27	Washington, D.C.	National Building Museum	Republican National Governors Association

SOURCE: *Weekly Compilation of Presidential Documents*, Vol. 42, Numbers 5–8 (http://www.gpoaccess.gov/wcomp/index.html).

TABLE 16-1 **Calendar of Presidential "Reports to the Nation" on National Television, Jan. 1953–Sept. 2006**

	Jan	Feb	Mar.	Apr.	May	June	July	Aug.	Sept.	Oct.	Nov.	Dec.
Eisenhower												
1953						Review						
1954	Review			World affairs				Congress				
1955							Geneva conference					
1956		Reelection announcement		Veto–agriculture						Middle East		
1957		Middle East			Mutual aid				Little Rock		Science security	
1958												
1959			Berlin					Labor reform	Europe			Inter-national peace
Kennedy												
1960		National defense	Latin America		Paris summit	Far East, Europe meetings						
1961							Berlin					
1962			Nuclear tests					Taxes		Cuba	Cuba	
1963						Civil rights		Test ban	Tax cut			
Johnson												
1964				Railroad labor dispute (2)				Tonkin Gulf	Steel strike	International affairs		
1965				Dominican Rep.	Dominican Rep.			Steel strike	Steel strike			
1966	Bombing North Vietnam											
1967							Riots					
1968	Pueblo		Vietnam; noncandidacy	Martin Luther King		Violence				Halt of bombing		
Nixon												
1969					S.E. Asia			Welfare			Vietnam-ization	S.E. Asia
1970	Veto–H.E.W.		Postal strike	Vietnam (2)		Cambodia (2); Economy				Peace initiative		
1971				Vietnam	SALT		China trip	Economy		Economy		
1972	S.E. Asia		Busing	Vietnam	Vietnam							
1973	Vietnam		Economy	Watergate		Economy		Watergate			Energy crisis (2)	
Ford												
1974	Egypt-Israel			Watergate	Middle East crisis		USSR trip (2); economy		Pardon of Nixon			
1975	National issues		Tax cut		Mayaguez (2); energy					Tax cut		
1976												
Carter												
1977		Fireside chat		Energy							Energy	

TABLE 16-1 Calendar of Presidential "Reports to the Nation" on National Television, Jan. 1953–Sept. 2006 (continued)

	Jan	Feb	Mar.	Apr.	May	June	July	Aug.	Sept.	Oct.	Nov.	Dec.
1978		Panama Canal treaty								Inflation		China
1979			Economy									
Reagan												
1981	Farewell (Carter)	Economy					Tax bill		Economy; budget			Poland
1982				Budget					Middle East (2)	Economy	Arms control	Poland
1983			Defense–national security	Central America					Korean airliner	Lebanon, Grenada		
1984					Central America							
1985				Budget	Tax reform						Soviet-U.S. summit	
1986	Space Shuttle explosion	State of the Union; National security	Nicaragua			Independence Day			Drug abuse	Meetings with Gorbachev	Election; Iran and *contra* aid	Iran arms and *contra* aid
1987			Iran arms and *contra* aid			Economic summit		Iran arms and *contra* aid				Soviet-U.S. summit
1988												
1989	Farewell to the nation											Panama
Bush												
1989	Inauguration	Administration goals							Drug control strategy		Thanksgiving	
1990								Kuwait invasion	Persian Gulf; budget deficit	Budget agreement		
1991	Desert Storm	Persian Gulf; Iraqi withdrawal	Persian Gulf						Nuclear weapons reduction		Thanksgiving	Christmas
1992					L.A. riots	Balanced Budget Amendment			Hurricane Andrew			Somalia crisis
Clinton												
1993		Economy (2)				Iraq		Budget	Health care	Somalia crisis	NAFTA	
1994									Haiti (2)	Iraq		Middle-Class Bill of Rights
1995						Budget deficit						Bosnia peace agreement
1996												
1997												
1998											Afghan/Sud. Grand Jury Testimony	Iraq
1999						Yugoslavia			Kosovo			
2000												

(Continued)

TABLE 16-1   Calendar of Presidential "Reports to the Nation" on National Television, Jan. 1953–Sept. 2006 (continued)

	Jan	Feb	Mar.	Apr.	May	June	July	Aug.	Sept.	Oct.	Nov.	Dec.
G. W. Bush												
2001								Stem Cell	9/11 attacks (Sept) War on Terror (Sept)	Afghanistan (Oct.)		Homeland Sec. (Dec.)
2002										Homeland Security		
2003					Iraq							War on Terror
2004												
2005										Katrina		Iraqi Elections
2006					Immigration Reform				9/11 Commemoration			

SOURCE: The entries from 1953 through November 1963 are from "Presidents on TV: Their Live Records," *Broadcasting*, November 8, 1965, 55–58; those from December 1963 through December 1975 are from Denis S. Rutkus, "A Report on Simultaneous Television Network Coverage of Presidential Addresses to the Nation," Congressional Research Service, (Washington, D.C., 1976), mimeograph, appendix; entries since 1976 are from the Public Papers of the Presidents series.

Official State Speeches

The Constitution requires the president to make a statement "from time to time" on the "state of the Union," and since Woodrow Wilson every president has personally addressed a joint session of Congress once a year to propose policies and to assess the nation's problems and achievements. (Thomas Jefferson discontinued the practice of personal, oral delivery of State of the Union reports, which George Washington had begun, choosing instead to present them in writing.)

The State of the Union address has become a major event in presidential leadership and congressional relations. Delivered before a joint session of Congress and before members of the Supreme Court, the cabinet, and honored guests, these addresses survey the range of budgetary and other policies that the administration plans to pursue in the coming year. Even if the administration has not completed the design of its programs, the president announces the major initiatives in the address.

Lyndon Johnson's Great Society and Vietnam initiatives; Richard Nixon's Vietnam, "New Federalism," and economic programs; Jimmy Carter's energy, civil service, welfare and tax reform, and foreign affairs initiatives; Ronald Reagan's tax, budget, regulatory, and military programs; George H. W. Bush's budget and foreign policies; Bill Clinton's health care reform initiative; and George W. Bush's wide-ranging, preemptive war against terrorism—all were outlined in State of the Union addresses.

Because many programs are announced without thorough planning, there is a danger that the State of the Union address will create false expectations and eventual disappointment. Many of Johnson's Great Society programs, for example, were in their nascent stages when announced. The combination of warlike rhetoric and fragmented program designs contributed to the disappointment with many of the programs—among them the Community Action program, which had been designed to "empower" the urban poor. Both supporters and critics of George W. Bush see the possibility of a similar fate for his proclaimed war on terror.

Other state speeches include addresses to foreign bodies such as the British Parliament and the United Nations General Assembly.

General Persuasive Speeches

Most presidential addresses seek to develop a favorable environment for a wide variety of policies, but less than half of presidential speeches try to persuade the public to adopt specific policies and directions.

President Wilson's national campaign after World War I for Senate acceptance of the Versailles Treaty and the League of Nations was perhaps the most dramatic example of persuasive oratory in U.S. history. Unwilling to bargain with the Republican leaders on the treaty, Wilson traveled eight thousand miles in a month, starting on September 3, 1919. He delivered thirty-seven speeches and attended even more public events at which he urged the treaty's passage. Wilson's tour ended when he collapsed of a stroke. The Senate defeated the treaty.

Reagan successfully urged passage of his tax and budget packages in 1981. On February 5, Reagan told a national television audience that the nation faced the "worst economic mess since the Great Depression." Less than two weeks later, Reagan told a television audience about his plans to deal with the problem. After an assassination attempt boosted his popularity, Reagan, in late April 1981, addressed an

Standing in front of the coffin containing the body of Richard Nixon, President Clinton led the eulogizers for the former president in April 1994.

enthusiastic joint session of Congress. In July he returned to national television and asked viewers to pressure Congress to support administration policies. Reagan's appeal generated fifteen million more letters than Congress normally receives in a session.[58]

Other recent examples of major persuasive speeches include Kennedy's addresses on civil rights and economics; Johnson's addresses on Vietnam, social problems, and domestic disorder; Nixon's speeches on Vietnam, the economy, and Watergate; Ford's addresses on the economy and his pardon of Nixon; Carter's energy and economic speeches; the George H. W. Bush's speeches on the Gulf War; Clinton's speeches on health care; and George W. Bush's rhetorical campaign for major tax cuts and social security reform.

Hortatory or Moralistic Speeches

The president sometimes attempts to persuade Americans to set aside personal, selfish aims and to seek goals more in the interest of the general public. Like a high school football coach, the president also attempts to infuse the public with confidence and zeal for tasks that may seem difficult.

Presidential speech making in the nation's first century usually was confined to educational or moralistic messages. On their tours of the expanding nation, presidents discussed constitutional and republican principles, federalism, economic policies, and the place of American values in world politics.

Twentieth-century president Carter spoke frequently on the energy crisis—so frequently that he began to worry that Americans were "inured" to the major problems that the issue presented. In 1979, after a ten-day retreat to Camp David, Carter delivered a speech about what he called the nation's "crisis of confidence" in an attempt to confront the

public's blasé attitude. The speech, with its choppy text, failed to offer a plan of action that matched the spiritual crisis Carter described. Thus, although delivered in an atmosphere of crisis, the address was quickly dismissed. Republican opponents in 1980 revived the speech as evidence of Carter's leadership failures. *(See "Carter's 'Crisis of Confidence' Speech," p. 1789, in Reference Materials, Vol. II.)*

Perhaps Clinton's most acclaimed speech was delivered in November 1993 at the Memphis pulpit where Martin Luther King Jr. gave his last speech before he was assassinated in 1968. Clinton challenged the congregation to live up to King's ideals of nonviolence at the community level and to end the gang and drug violence in the inner city. If Martin Luther King were to reappear, Clinton said, he would decry the violence in America's cities and the breakdown of the African American family.

He would say, "I did not live and die to see the American family destroyed. I did not live and die to see 13-year-old boys get automatic weapons and gun down 9-year-olds just for the kick of it. I did not live and die to see young people destroy their own lives with drugs and then build fortunes destroying the lives of others. This is not what I came here to do. I fought for freedom."

This address exemplified Clinton's inclination to lace his rhetoric with moral and religious themes. Through moralistic speeches he attempted to counter the growing cynicism and defeatism that he felt threatened his activist policy agenda. In his second term, in the wake of the personal scandals surrounding his sexual conduct that imperiled his presidency, Clinton curtailed his use of moralistic rhetoric.

Clinton's successor, George W. Bush, peppered his speeches with frequent references to his evangelical faith and conscience. In one of the defining moments of his presidency before September 11, 2001, he outlined his position on federal funding for stem cell research within the framework of his personal commitment to the sanctity of human life.

Crisis Speeches

The public turns to the president for leadership during crises and other difficult times, partly out of practical considerations—the president is the political figure most familiar to most Americans— and partly out of a psychological need for the reassurance that strong leadership can provide.

A presidential speech in times of crisis can mobilize the nation almost instantly. For example, Franklin Roosevelt's call for war on the Axis powers in World War II after the December 7, 1941, bombing of Pearl Harbor changed the public's mood quite abruptly. Before the dramatic address to a joint session of Congress, the public and Congress were reluctant to enter the foreign war; after the speech, public opinion favored all-out involvement.

John Kennedy's addresses on the failed invasion of the Bay of Pigs, confrontations with the Soviet Union over the status of Berlin, and the Cuban missile crisis were among the most dramatic speeches in modern history. Each suggested the possibility of apocalyptic confrontations. The youthful Kennedy was able to use the speeches to build confidence in his own leadership, even on occasions when his administration had failed, as at the Bay of Pigs.

Lyndon Johnson's first presidential address was another major crisis speech. Five days after President Kennedy's assassination on November 22, 1963, both the traumatized Congress and the public watched the address not only for clues of Johnson's policy intentions but also for signs that the government remained stable. Johnson and his aides worked on the speech almost without interruption throughout those five days and produced an address that reassured the nation of the government's stability and Johnson's own vigor. Johnson was able to outline his own legislative program while paying homage to the martyred Kennedy. "Let us continue," Johnson said, in a reference to Kennedy's "Let us begin." [59]

Through his addresses on the Vietnam War, Richard Nixon slowly but successfully developed a national consensus on the war and blunted opposition to his bombings of Laos and Cambodia.[60]

Carter's "crisis of confidence" speech may fit in this category as well as the hortatory category. Other crisis speeches Carter delivered included those on the Soviet invasion of Afghanistan, on the discovery of Soviet troops in Cuba, and on the American hostages in Iran.

Speeches marking national crises give the president the opportunity to rise above partisan disputes and represent

Just five days after Kennedy's assassination, President Lyndon Johnson delivered a carefully worded speech to Congress. The address reassured the nation during a time of crisis. Speaker of the House John McCormack, D-Mass., and Carl Hayden, D-Ariz., president pro tempore of the Senate, are seated behind Johnson.

the nation as a whole. Gerald Ford's statement that "our long national nightmare is over," after Richard Nixon resigned the presidency in disgrace in 1974, was credited with healing the nation. Ronald Reagan's speech after the explosion of the *Challenger* space shuttle in 1986 promoted a sense of national community and loss.

The wide latitude that the public gives presidents during a crisis invites possible abuse of the crisis speech. President Johnson reported in 1964 that North Vietnam had attacked U.S. ships without provocation in the Gulf of Tonkin and quickly won congressional approval of a resolution that granted him almost unlimited war powers. But the evidence supporting the North Vietnamese attack was questionable at best, as Johnson privately acknowledged. The crisis atmosphere created by Johnson's speech may have been the most important element in the growing U.S. involvement in the war. Critics of George W. Bush accuse him of misusing the acts of terrorism on September 11, 2001, as an ill-advised excuse to begin waging war in Iraq in 2003.

A crisis may give the president an opportunity for rhetorical leadership, but it does not guarantee success. President Carter's address after the Soviet invasion of Afghanistan eventually fueled the arguments of critics on both the left and the right that Carter was too naive and inexperienced to continue as president. Carter stated that the invasion fundamentally changed his perception of the nature of the Soviet Union. The verdict on Bush's global war on terror remains in question as his second term nears its end.

Failure to give an address during a major crisis can undermine the president's support. Herbert Hoover's unpopularity after the Great Crash of 1929 was attributable not so much to his policies as to his inability to convey a sense of national purpose and sympathy for the victims of the economic depression.

Presidents Nixon and Clinton brought a new dimension to this category of crisis speeches, in that circumstances associated with scandals forced both to address the nation amid crisis conditions that pertained more to their personal political survival than to national security. In neither instance did presidential rhetoric prove to be decisive in the resolution of the crisis.

As his second term was getting under way, Nixon was forced to confront growing concerns about White House involvement in the Watergate burglary and cover-up. Over the next eighteen months, as his political support dissipated, Nixon addressed this threat to his presidency in numerous speeches in which he sought, ultimately without success, to deflect the damage. He simply was unable to convince the nation of the credibility of his statements on the Watergate affair. In fact, his many television speeches on the campaign scandal gave rise to more questions and criticisms than they answered. On August 8, 1974, speaking from the Oval Office, he announced his decision to step down from the presidency.

Clinton did not face a major foreign policy crisis during his presidency, and a prosperous economy prevailed throughout his two terms. He did, however, face a crisis related to his personal behavior; allegations emerged early in his second term that he was guilty of sexual improprieties with a young White House intern. These allegations cast their shadow whenever he took to the podium throughout the remainder of his term, adding to the drama of his pronouncements. Critics and supporters alike wondered how he would handle the demands of office while mired in scandal. Generally, Clinton received acclaim for his performance and perseverance under intense pressure.

Nevertheless, after persistent public denials of wrongdoing, Clinton had to provide a deposition under oath to a special prosecutor, in which he attempted to clarify earlier representations. That night, he addressed the nation and acknowledged being less than forthright with the American public. In the months that followed, the House of Representatives impeached him, but his public support remained high, and he prevailed in the ensuing Senate trial.

George W. Bush faced the formidable task of rallying and reassuring the public in the aftermath of terrorist assaults on New York City and Washington, D.C., that left three thousand dead and the World Trade Center towers in ruins. He rose to the challenge with an address to a joint session of Congress. It received enthusiastic bipartisan acclaim from the congressional audience and the general public and established the agenda for a wide-ranging war on international terrorism.

Addresses to Specific Groups

As the government has become more complex and more interest groups have developed permanent ties to the government, presidents have spent more time addressing specific groups. The purpose of such addresses is often nothing more than flattery. Whether delivered to faithful supporters or to skeptical adversaries, these addresses are designed to create a feeling of goodwill toward the presidency. And they often include a specific appeal that is designed for media coverage.

The advantage of appearing before specific constituency groups is that remarks can be tailored to the group, and the president's words will be transmitted to the larger group membership for weeks after the speech. By merely accepting an invitation to address a particular group, a president tells the group that it is important.

Appearances before constituencies also allow the president to see how they might behave during the "bargaining" process over budgetary, tax, and other current legislative matters. The president can then fine-tune the White House approach on those issues. The National Association for the Advancement of Colored People (NAACP) provided presidents from Franklin Roosevelt on with strong signals about the civil rights initiatives it would find meaningful.

Perhaps more important, the president also can use interest group appearances to line up support for policy initiatives. Presidents frequently appear before business and labor groups to seek backing for their economic programs. President Carter tried to build support for his energy program and Panama Canal treaties with appearances before interest groups, but he was opposed by a well-financed cadre of conservatives.[61]

Business organizations are perhaps the most constantly courted in the constellation of interest groups. Presidents of both parties need support from business to pursue their economic and social policies. Some presidents—such as Franklin Roosevelt, Harry Truman, and John Kennedy—publicly attacked business but eventually had to build support among businesspeople.

Other groups to be courted depend on the president's base of support. Almost half of all speeches by postwar presidents were "targeted" appeals to specific constituencies. Most such appeals take place in or around Washington, D.C., where national organizations are housed. Groups ranging from the AFL-CIO to the Christian Coalition attract the sporadic attention of the president. Bill Clinton felt especially at home addressing African American audiences, who proved to be his most dependable and enthusiastic supporters. Social conservatives played a similar role and function for George W. Bush.

Government workers are one of the most important interest groups the president addresses. Especially when morale is low in departments, the president's words can provide a big lift. Speaking before government groups also enables the president to lay out policy positions in the sanctified arena of officialdom. Because the president's words are usually reported widely, the government audience provides an opportunity to talk about a wide range of issues. Carter spoke to government workers on the morality of couples living together outside marriage.

As the leader of the national party, the president also delivers a number of partisan addresses. These appeals usually take place during important election campaigns. President Reagan, for example, was tireless in campaigning for Republican congressional and gubernatorial candidates in the 1980s. An unpopular president is not asked to participate in other campaigns. Democratic candidates studiously avoided Carter in the 1980 campaign and Clinton in the 1994 midterm campaign. George W. Bush was in great demand in 2002 and 2004, but much less so in 2006, when his popular support had plummeted.

Presidents may use appearances before groups to distract them so the administration can pursue other priorities. During his tax and budget initiatives of 1981 and 1982, Reagan relied on rhetoric to allay the concerns of religious organizations, which wanted immediate action on abortion, school prayer, and other social issues. Meanwhile, the president promoted state education reforms in a series of speeches in 1983 and 1984, defusing pressure for national initiatives and spending increases.

Presidents often appear before skeptical groups to co-opt whatever opposition they might present and to portray themselves as leader of all the people. Good examples are Carter's appearances before the Veterans of Foreign Wars and Reagan's speeches to the NAACP. Presidents sometimes deliberately even antagonize certain interest groups to solidify the alliances that have developed in opposition to those groups.[62]

THE IMPERATIVE TO SPEAK

Occupying a role central to U.S. politics, presidents are expected to offer authoritative opinions even on subjects about which they are ignorant or uncertain. As presidents move past the first year or so of their terms, the imperative to speak grows, because they must shore up political standing after an inevitable decline.

Speech is an important strategic tool for the president. Every new administration usually enjoys a honeymoon period of six months to a year in which Congress and the public are inclined to yield to presidential leadership on many important questions. Lyndon Johnson's Great Society legislation of 1965 and Ronald Reagan's budget- and tax-cutting initiatives of 1981 are notable examples. More recently, George W. Bush achieved noteworthy early successes in his commitments to tax cuts and education reform.

After the initial period of goodwill, however, presidents begin to lose their appeal. The president is better known and develops disputes with more groups as the term progresses.

The president also must accept responsibility for many of the nation's problems that were previously blamed on Congress or on a former president. Political scientist John E. Mueller has asserted that the longer the president is in office, the more a "coalition of minorities" develops grievances that cut the president's base of support.[63]

Presidents tend to increase their speech making considerably from the first to the second year in office. For example, Carter delivered 282 speeches in his first year and 323 in his second year; Reagan delivered 211 in his first year and 344 in his second. As the reelection campaign nears, presidents give even more speeches. Ford increased the number of his speeches from 392 to 682 in the year he ran against Carter (1976). During their reelection efforts, Carter increased from 272 speeches in 1979 to 436 in 1980; Reagan from 384 in 1983 to 421 in 1984.[64]

Because presidents have become less reliant on party machinery or congressional leadership for support, they turn to the public. Several presidents have appealed to the public "over the heads of Congress" when Congress has shown reluctance to go along with legislative initiatives. Carter's public statements on western water projects, the Panama Canal treaty, the nation's energy problems, relations with the Soviet Union, and economic problems were all intended to overcome resistance to unpopular programs on Capitol Hill. The psychological demands of the presidency probably contribute to the tendency to speak often, as political scientist Bruce Buchanan has suggested. Stress, deference from underlings, and the search for clear signs of success combine to push the president toward dramatic rhetoric. Frustrated presidents search for scapegoats to pummel in public to improve their relative standing and their leverage over the political process.[65]

The imperative to speak is self-generating. "Presidents have developed a rhetorical reflex, a tendency to resort to public suasion as an initial response to a political situation," Hart has written. Carter displayed the built-in push toward presidential speech. "Always he spoke, and the speaking justified its own continuance: if the coverage were favorable, it stood to reason that more speaking would generate even more flattering responses from the media; if the press disparaged him, more speaking would set matters right." [66]

If presidents need to go public to promote their political agendas, that does not mean they speak all the time about important policy issues. Much of the president's time is occupied with noncontroversial, almost trivial appearances, such as meetings with champion athletes, and proclamations of special days. Even if these talks appear trivial, they strengthen the president's public standing and symbolic hold on the nation and its different "publics." [67]

One of the reasons the president turns to rhetoric is the institutionalization of speech writing and public relations efforts in the White House. An ever-expanding group of presidential aides analyzes the political situation and develops public campaigns for improving it.

The emergence of a public presidency presents dangers as well as opportunities for the chief executive. If the president is blamed by the media or the voters for problems, making regular appearances can aggravate rather than improve the president's position by serving as a constant reminder of the administration's failings.

President Carter suffered politically in 1980 because voters associated him with the Iranian hostage crisis, "stagflation," tense relations with the Soviet Union, and divided leadership in Washington. When Carter appeared on television or before groups, he struck many as tired and ineffectual. But the problem of "overexposure" did not begin with Carter. Both John Kennedy and Lyndon Johnson were criticized for speaking too much. At the outset of his presidency, Clinton's proclivity to discuss any subject was seen as a liability by his advisers, who achieved intermittent success in convincing the president to reduce his daily exposure to the media. Appearing more personally resistant than most of his recent predecessors to this presidential imperative to speak, George W. Bush nevertheless has succumbed to the inevitable demands to mount the bully pulpit at a pace that rivals them.

Presidents are trapped by their public utterances in many ways. Because the media record every public word, presidents must carefully weigh the effect of their statements and take care not to get caught in a tangle of contradictory remarks. The credibility of Presidents Johnson, Nixon, and Clinton came under exceptional assault.

CRITICS OF THE "RHETORICAL PRESIDENCY"

Critics of the new rhetorical style argue that it has led to confusion on the part of both the president and the public about the difference between political action and political speech. The president's dominance in politics also "crowds out" other legitimate actors and issues. [68]

When a presidential address or "photo opportunity" is treated as a meaningful political event, attention is diverted from the complicated process of policymaking and implementation that is the substance of politics. Not only the public but also the president can be deceived about the state of government activity. Media coverage of speeches reinforces the notion that speech is tantamount to substantive action.

As political scientist Bruce Miroff has argued, the president's dominance of U.S. politics starves the political actors and issues not in the president's orbit—that is, the president's "monopolization of public space," as Miroff puts it, simplifies issues and distances politics from the average citizen; politics becomes a spectator sport. The citizen's "vicarious" relationship with important policy issues also reduces important policy decisions to a game. For example, the suspense surrounding George W. Bush's August 2001 decision on federal funding of stem cell research occasionally obscured complex scientific and ethical issues while highlighting the clash of competing political interests and the president's perceived intellectual capacity to confront the question.

Theodore J. Lowi points out that the movement toward a rhetorical presidency has led to an "oversell" of specific policies that breeds disappointment. "Such are the president's channels of mass communication that he must simplify and dramatize his appeals, whether the communication deals with foreign policy, domestic policy, or something else again. Almost every initiative is given a public relations name. Every initiative has to be 'new and improved.' " [69] Steps taken to simplify and dramatize policies remove them from their natural state of uncertainty and complexity—and produce frustration and cynicism when major improvements do not result.

Presidents have taken to more frequent speech making in part to improve the chances of their legislative and other initiatives, but the link between speech making and success has proved tenuous at best. Legislative success is no greater in the modern age of presidential talk than it was in the earlier periods of limited speech. Presidents Eisenhower, Kennedy, Johnson, and Nixon won close to three-quarters of their major tests in Congress while giving an average of 150 policy speeches a year between 1957 and 1972. Presidents Nixon, Ford, and Carter won less than 60 percent of the key issues between 1972 and 1979 while speaking more than 200 times a year. [70]

More frequent presidential communications—not only speech but also written material—do not appear to have increased the understanding between the leaders and the led. Americans continue to exhibit ignorance of most public policy issues despite the ubiquitous media "teaching" of the president. Even more revealing, Americans tell pollsters that they feel increasingly ignored. Voters sense that politicians talk to them but do not listen. [71]

Presidential speech making also reduces the president's control over the job. Because presidents speak so often, they cannot possibly write or even contribute significantly to the drafting of speeches. The White House speech-writing corps drafts all the president's words. If presidents do not have to work on the complex ideas they present to the public, they are less likely to have a thorough and nuanced understanding of issues.

One authority has argued that the "scripted presidency" might have contributed to Reagan's decision to trade arms to Iran in exchange for the release of American hostages in Lebanon. "President Reagan's reliance on speechwriters and before them [movie] scriptwriters played a role in his disposition to accept information about the Iran/Contra dealings uncritically and to trust his aides to act in his best interest." [72]

Proponents of constant presidential talk say it brings the political process into the open. Because presidents are such compelling figures, what they say attracts wide attention and makes politics a more open affair. But presidents must be cautious because their remarks are so thoroughly covered, and that caution can drain public politics of any meaningful content. The effect, ironically, is that open, public politics can drive important policy discussions underground.

The tendency to "go public" was one result of a decline of party strength in Congress. Since World War II, the president and Congress have been from different parties during all or part of the administrations of Eisenhower, Nixon, Ford, Reagan, George H. W. Bush, Clinton, and George W. Bush. Even when the president's party controls Congress, support for specific policies must be developed issue by issue. Public support has therefore become a crucial tool for prodding Congress. Amid resurgent parties over the past quarter-century, going public continues.

THE PRESIDENT AND THE FOREIGN POLICY DEBATE

Every president since Theodore Roosevelt has traveled to foreign countries, but only since the Eisenhower administration have such trips become a regular part of the president's routine.[73] *(See Figure 16-3.)* Many of the trips have been related to diplomatic events, such as treaty negotiations, but most trips have been more for public relations.

The trips usually give the president a temporary lift in the public opinion polls.[74] Longer trips—such as President Nixon's trip to China and President Reagan's trip to the Soviet Union—may have a more permanent effect on the president's standing. More important than the brief surge in popularity, however, is the presentation of the image of the president as a political leader in charge of world affairs.

Presidential travel once was considered a risky proposition with the voters. When President Eisenhower embarked on his first foreign trip, he felt obliged to explain the necessity for the trip in almost apologetic terms:

> Now, manifestly, there are many difficulties in the way of a president going abroad for a period, particularly while Congress is in session. He has many constitutional duties; he must be here to perform them. I am able to go on the trip only because of the generous cooperation of the political leaders in Congress of both political parties who have arranged their work so that my absence for a period will not interfere with the business of the government. On my part, I promised them that by a week from Sunday, on July 24th, I shall be back here ready to carry on my accustomed duties.[75]

The surges in public approval that followed Eisenhower's trip led him—and later presidents—to make travel a regular part of the job.[76] Presidents under political assault at home, Nixon and Clinton in particular, seem to have found opportunities for foreign travel especially enticing. George W. Bush confronted a rather different political dynamic and calculus in his second term. Part of the appeal of foreign travel in the post–World War II era was the opportunity to encounter appreciative foreign audiences, therein hopefully stimulating support on the home front. For Bush, rising international hostility abroad to his foreign policies toward Iraq in particular arguably lessens the prospects of reversing his declining domestic support through foreign travel.

The Importance of Foreign Policy Rhetoric

Control of foreign policy always has been an important political "card" for the president. Especially since the United States became a world economic and military power at the turn of the twentieth century, presidents have been able to increase their prestige with military and diplomatic action. The public often defers to authorities because of its scant knowledge of foreign affairs, so presidents receive a boost in public support even when the action concerns an obscure nation or issue.

Presidents have been able to depend on foreign affairs even more than on economic or social events to enhance their political stock, because they are able to supersede temporarily the divisions engendered by the domestic struggle over "who gets what, when, how." [77] On foreign policy issues, the president acts for the nation as a whole, creating a situation in which Americans are acting, whereas presidential actions on the domestic front almost always create internal divisions. The president can argue that foreign policy involves outside threats to the security of all of the people and therefore requires a unified response. George W. Bush has invoked this argument to sustain support of his commitment to a global war on terror. However, political elites and the general public appear increasingly skeptical.

FIGURE 16-3   **Days of Political Travel by Presidents, 1929–2003 (Yearly Averages for First Three Years of First Term)**

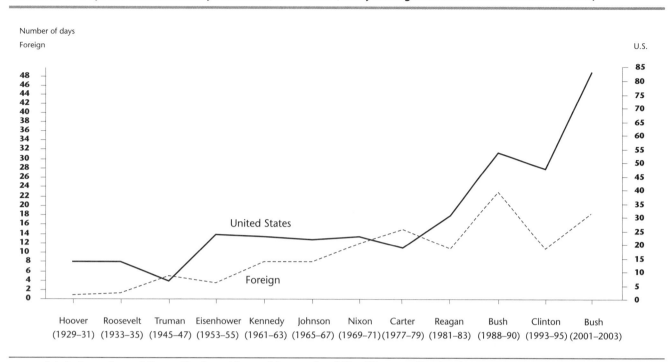

SOURCES: Data for Hoover, Roosevelt, Truman, Eisenhower, Nixon, and Carter are from William W. Lammers, "Presidential Attention-Focusing Activities," in *The President and the American Public,* ed. Doris A. Graber (Philadelphia: Institute for the Study of Human Issues, 1982), Table 6-5, 160. Data for Kennedy, Johnson, Reagan, Bush, and Clinton are from *Public Papers of the Presidents* series. See also Samuel Kernell, "The Presidency and the People: The Modern Paradox," in *The Presidency and the Political System,* ed. Michael Nelson (Washington, D.C.: CQ Press, 1984), 244.

NOTE: To eliminate public activities inspired by concerns of reelection rather than governing, only the first three years have been tabulated. For this reason, Gerald Ford's record of public activities during his two and one-half years of office have been ignored.

Simply appearing at history-making international events can lend the president a bit of glory. In 1993 President Bill Clinton hosted the signing ceremonies in which the Palestine Liberation Organization and Israel ended their formal state of war. Clinton also hosted a ceremony marking the end of hostilities between Israel and Jordan in 1994. The peace talks leading to the White House ceremony occurred long before Clinton became president, but he basked in the rapprochement. For the rest of his presidency, Clinton persistently pursued the cause of peace in the Middle East. In 2000, as his second term was winding down, he brought the leaders of Israel and the Palestinians to Camp David for well-publicized but ultimately unsuccessful deliberations.

The boost that the president gets from foreign policy is usually short-lived. Nevertheless, the president can use a series of foreign events and rhetoric about foreign policy to develop a general disposition among the public to defer to presidential leadership.

But presidents' foreign policy dealings can be a double-edged sword. If presidents do not appear to assert control over crises after the initial period of emergency, the public might develop suspicions about presidential expertise and control. Presidents also may suffer domestically if their actions in the foreign policy arena create or aggravate inter-nal divisions—usually because they asked important domestic constituencies for difficult sacrifices.

George H. W. Bush ascended to unprecedented heights of public support as he assembled an international coalition and then prosecuted the Gulf War in 1990–1991. His foreign policy successes ironically called attention to his comparative weaknesses on the domestic and economic policy fronts, and he failed to win reelection. After September 11, 2001, his son, George W. Bush, followed in the father's footsteps in benefiting from the remarkably strong public support produced by an international crisis. However, in the wake of the 2003 invasion of Iraq, amid ongoing turmoil there, Bush's public support began a precipitous decline that also paralleled his father's, despite the presence of a generally healthy economy. The public became increasingly dissatisfied with his commitment to "stay the course."

Bill Clinton, who struggled to gain credibility in foreign affairs, confronted his credibility gap head-on with speeches before hostile groups. For example, Clinton, who avoided military service in the Vietnam War, became in 1993 the first president to speak at the Vietnam War Memorial in Washington. "Let us continue to disagree, if we must, about the war, but let us not let it divide us as a people any longer," the president told a Memorial Day audience. Some veterans opposed Clinton's appearance, but others expressed respect for his "courage" in speaking to a hostile crowd.[78]

Reaching Foreign Publics

American presidents have "gone public" not only to speak over the heads of their own government, but also to speak directly to foreign publics. Presidents sometimes speak directly to other nations' populations to strengthen their negotiating positions with those nations' leaders. More often, presidents simply try to foster goodwill abroad with their public appeals.

The Cold War and its aftermath provided the backdrop for dramatic moments in rhetoric to foreign audiences. Kennedy's 1963 "Ich bin ein Berliner" speech, Reagan's challenge to Soviet leader Mikhail Gorbachev more than twenty years later to "tear down this wall," and Clinton's 1994 challenge to the Russian leadership to fight resurgent nationalism provided a clear narrative—complete with beginning, middle, and end—of the American struggle with the Soviet empire.

Some of the boldest appeals to foreign audiences took place during President Reagan's 1988 visit to Moscow. Reagan spoke to Soviet citizens on television; later, with Gorbachev at his side, he met crowds at Red Square—an event televised to millions of homes in both the United States and the Soviet Union. Reagan was most outspoken at the University of Moscow. Standing before a huge Soviet flag and a portrait of Vladimir I. Lenin, Reagan challenged the nation to restructure its political and economic institutions and praised the U.S. system.

During his tenure, Reagan also spoke several times about the protests against the placement of U.S. nuclear missiles on European soil. The missiles were strongly opposed by peace activists in Great Britain and West Germany, and Reagan alternately sought to win over opponents of the missiles and to undercut their legitimacy.

A speech at Normandy, France, commemorating the fortieth anniversary of the 1944 U.S. invasion, was a dramatic statement of solidarity among Western nations and values. President Reagan spoke movingly of the soldiers who died in the invasion and their families and of the need for nations to avoid another world war. Clinton's 1994 speech at Normandy was greeted skeptically because of Clinton's avoidance of the military draft as a young man. But Clinton's speech convinced some critics that he was up to the job of commander in chief.

Reagan's foreign appeals sometimes backfired. His trip to Bitburg, West Germany, in 1985 was intended to symbolize the development of ties between the former World War II foes, the United States and Germany. The visit was controversial from the time of its scheduling, however. The discovery that former officers of an elite Nazi brigade were buried in the Bitburg cemetery insulted Jews and others who had fought the Nazis. Reagan defended the trip by saying that German soldiers "were victims, just as surely as the victims in the concentration camps."[79] Despite calls for him to cancel the trip, Reagan went.

George H. W. Bush's 1992 trip to Tokyo was supposed to project an image of strength as Bush demanded trade concessions from Japan. But when an exhausted Bush vomited and passed out at a state dinner, he made a poor impression on his Japanese hosts.

Presidential statements to foreign publics sometimes take the form of threats. Presidents speak frequently about other nations' weapons buildups, terrorist actions, human rights problems, military actions, and trade policies. Although such statements often are intended for domestic consump-

Presidents have often appealed to foreign publics and their leaders to increase their political capital. In December 1918, Woodrow Wilson made a successful European tour to promote his postwar foreign policy agenda.

tion, they also offer flexible ways to communicate with other governments outside the normal channels of diplomacy.

In proclaiming a war on terrorism, President George W. Bush put the international community on notice that the United States would identify and hunt down the perpetrators of the September 11, 2001, attacks on U.S. soil. He went on to say repeatedly that he would bring to justice not only the terrorists themselves but also the governments that sponsored and harbored them. Subsequently, reflecting his dissatisfaction with Palestinian leader Yasser Arafat, Bush made clear his view that U.S. support for a Palestinian state was contingent on the emergence of new leadership for the Palestinian people.

Speeches to foreign bodies such as the United Nations and the Organization of American States—meetings well covered by media across the world—offer additional opportunities to address foreign publics. Because many nations practice censorship, presidents often try to embed their true messages in larger statements that will be reported. Reagan, who sharply criticized the United Nations, also took advantage of the platform of the international body. In his farewell speech in 1988, he attempted to promote internal Soviet political reforms and arms control agreements. Reagan and his UN ambassadors also used the body to criticize the Soviet Union, Nicaragua, and developing countries. Several years later, George H. W. Bush used the United Nations to make a case first for sanctions and then for war against Iraq after Iraq's invasion of Kuwait in 1990.

U.S. presidents lead the world with words in other ways as well. At summit meetings and economic conferences with foreign leaders, presidents speak for the nation on a wide variety of issues. The "news" from most conferences is that the leaders will try to cooperate in pursuit of common goals. But presidents who visibly "takes charge" gain authority in world affairs.

Presidents do not speak to other nations only through their appearances and statements. The U.S. government includes agencies designed to appeal to the "hearts and minds" of foreign peoples. The president's appointments to these agencies can put a distinctive mark on the way the rest of the world sees the United States.

The Voice of America (VOA) is the most noteworthy information provider. An international, multimedia broadcasting service funded by the U.S. government, the VOA broadcasts each week, via radio, satellite television, and the Internet, nine hundred hours of news and other programs to an audience of over ninety million in fifty-three languages. The State Department and Central Intelligence Agency also disseminate information to foreign nations.

The president enjoys a huge advantage in the sheer size of the public relations operations of the government. The public information office of the Pentagon, for example, spends more money each year than any of the major news services. Especially considering that the wire services devote only a small part of their operations to foreign affairs, the Pentagon's public relations work gives the government an awesome advantage in communicating its point of view.

THE TERMS OF PRESIDENTIAL DISCOURSE

Besides dominating the political stage and tilting the balance of opinion on many specific public issues, the president's rhetoric is important in shaping the way political issues are discussed. Many linguistic experts have argued that, for politicians, shaping the political vocabulary is the most important means of gaining public support for a wide range of policies. The president is perhaps the most important political figure in defining and creating a context for such widely used terms as *conservative, progress, liberalism, economic growth, national security,* and *free trade.* The meanings of such terms change over time, sometimes helping and sometimes hurting presidents' abilities to promote their agendas.

Even the most fundamental ideas in American political discourse are constantly changing. The rise and fall of such terms as *people* and *interests* closely parallel the historical development of the nation and the evolution of the presidency. The regular public use of the word *interests,* for example, in the nation's early years was tied to the decline of notions of public virtue and the development of more competitive ideals of politics and society. Theodore Roosevelt and Woodrow Wilson, leaders of the national Progressive movement, used the rhetoric of interests both to decry what Roosevelt called "the ferocious, scrambling rush of an unregulated and purely individualistic industrialism" and to propose government remedies. The upshot was the "pluralistic" idea that a clash of interests managed by popular government would redound to the national interest.[80]

Political scientist Murray Edelman argued that political terms always have multiple meanings that contradict each other. But because people have self-contradictory interests and beliefs, they need catch-all words that cover up the contradictions. These words help to overcome "cognitive dissonance"—the unsettling feeling produced by the realization that one's thoughts are contradictory. These words also provide enough "signposts," or guides for living, enabling people to get along in life without having to reassess their situations and alternatives constantly.

An example of a self-contradictory word is *conservative,* which in U.S. politics is used to denote both stability (family, neighborhoods, local control) and turbulence (economic growth, mobility, exploration, and research). President William McKinley described his "Open Door" policy, which reduced both trade and cultural barriers among nations, as conservative. Although the policy augured unprecedented changes in world trade activities, it also was said to be the surest policy for maintaining traditional American values. President Reagan wove together the contradictory meanings of conservatism. His rhetoric and policies for "unleashing" the dynamic forces of capitalism contradicted his denunciations of the decay of traditional "values."

The complex and changing definitions of political words give presidents wide latitude in shaping the way people talk about political issues at all levels of society. Presidents not only have a "bully pulpit" from which to promote their choices in important policies, as Theodore Roosevelt asserted, but also have the ability to shape the way the population thinks about those choices in the first place.

David Green has chronicled the way twentieth-century presidents have used labels to give themselves a privileged position in policy debates. According to Green, presidents have attempted to use such words as *progressive, liberal, isolationist,* and *conservative* to give their own actions greater legitimacy and to undercut the legitimacy of their opponents.

Franklin Roosevelt's presidency is a thorough case study of adapting, avoiding, and switching labels. Roosevelt avoided using the label *progressive* because it had connotations of confiscation for many members of the older generation. Roosevelt labeled his policies "liberal" and fended off attacks on his policies as "fascist," "socialist," and "communist." The liberal label connoted openness, generosity, and popular support. Roosevelt branded his opponents "conservative" and "reactionary." When it became apparent that the New Deal policies were not ending the Great Depression, Roosevelt stepped up his attacks on opponents, particularly business interests and the wealthy, whom he called "economic royalists."

Roosevelt also went beyond the debate over domestic and economic policy with a move into international affairs. As the United States inched toward involvement in World War II, Roosevelt branded opponents of the war "isolationists," "appeaser fifth columnists," and "propagandists of fear," and linked those terms to his broader argument about reactionaries. Critics who questioned the war or specific tactics found themselves undercut.[81]

What goes around usually comes around in rhetoric. By the 1980s, the word *liberal* was poison. President Reagan's constant labeling of Democrats as "tax and spend liberals" helped to make *liberal* the scarlet letter of politics in the 1980s through the 2000s. Politicians were so scared to identify themselves as liberal, because of the word's negative connotations, that pundits took to calling it the "L-word" as if it were profanity.

Twentieth-century presidents tended to use catch-all phrases to describe their policy programs. Among the phrases were Square Deal (Theodore Roosevelt), New Freedom (Wilson), New Deal (Franklin Roosevelt), Fair Deal (Truman), New Frontier (Kennedy), Great Society (Johnson), New Foundation (Carter), New Federalism (Nixon and Reagan), and New Covenant (Clinton). Such phrases can give the president's program a sense of coherence and completeness, but they also can create false expectations about what the president's policies can accomplish. Johnson's Great Society, for example, was a collection of relatively small and uncoordinated programs, many of which had no viable support system in the state and local governments where they were to be administered. The policies were prepared hurriedly, and funding was restricted before many of the programs were fully implemented. The potent rhetorical force of the Great Society label, David Zarefsky argues, left the domestic programs vulnerable to attack: "The very choices of symbolism and argument which had aided the adoption of the program were instrumental in undermining its implementation and in weakening public support for its basic philosophy."[82]

The use of vague slogans and "sentiments" to promote policies, rather than precisely defined programs, fundamentally undermines the entire U.S. political system, according to Theodore Lowi.[83] When the policies do not work as promised and interest groups gain control over programs, the president is left with the impossible job of gaining control of the federal leviathan. Only clearly defined and circumscribed programs—in the place of sweeping promises—can restore the government's legitimacy and authority.

SPEECHES OF DEPARTING PRESIDENTS

Among the most prominent speeches of any presidency are the addresses delivered at the end of the administration. The farewell addresses of many presidents are remembered long after other speeches have been lost in the bog of presidential rhetoric. Such speeches also gain prominence because they are so infrequent and because they depict politicians jousting to determine their places in history.

George Washington delivered the first and most famous farewell address. *(See "Washington's Farewell Address," p. 1754, in Reference Materials, Vol. II.)* Washington's most lasting advice to the country was to avoid becoming entangled in European alliances, which he predicted would sap the strength and resources of the young nation. Much of the speech was written by Alexander Hamilton, but Washington himself had an active hand in its drafting. Experts agree that it reflects his values and character.

The most influential modern farewell address was Dwight Eisenhower's valedictory of 1961. *(See "Eisenhower's Farewell Address," p. 1775, in Reference Materials, Vol. II.)* He warned the nation against the "military-industrial complex," which, he argued, was beginning to dominate the American system and could endanger democratic processes and liberties. Eisenhower said:

> We must never let the weight of this combination endanger our liberties or democratic processes. We should take

nothing for granted. Only an alert and knowledgeable citizenry can compel the proper meshing of the huge industrial and military machinery of defense with our peaceful methods and goals, so that security and liberty may prosper together.[84]

Farewell addresses give presidents the opportunity to speak more freely than they did as incumbents. Eisenhower's farewell provided a poignant coda to a career in the military and politics. Most presidents, however, simply try to cast their administration in a good light and set challenges for their successors.

★

NOTES

1. Along with the explosion in presidential speech making has come an explosion of research about the development. See Theodore Otto Windt Jr., "Presidential Rhetoric: Definition of a Field of Study," *Presidential Studies Quarterly* 16 (winter 1986): 102–116.

2. Roderick P. Hart, *The Sound of Leadership* (Chicago: University of Chicago Press, 1988), 1.

3. See Lyn Ragsdale, *Vital Statistics on the Presidency,* rev. ed. (Washington, D.C.: Congressional Quarterly, 1998), 183.

4. Quoted in Kathleen Hall Jamieson, *Eloquence in an Electronic Age* (New York: Oxford University Press, 1988), 212–213.

5. Lloyd Grove, "Dukakis: If He Only Had a Heart," *Washington Post,* October 9, 1988, D1.

6. Richard E. Neustadt, *Presidential Power* (New York: Wiley, 1976).

7. Samuel Kernell, *Going Public: New Strategies of Presidential Leadership,* 4th ed. (Washington, D.C.: CQ Press, 2007), 25.

8. Hart, *Sound of Leadership,* 2.

9. Philip Abbott, "Do Presidents Talk Too Much? The Rhetorical Presidency and Its Alternative," *Presidential Studies Quarterly* 18 (spring 1988): 335.

10. Hart, *Sound of Leadership,* 5.

11. E. E. Schattschneider, *The Semisovereign People* (Hinsdale, Ill.: Dryden, 1975).

12. Bob Woodward, *The Agenda: Inside the Clinton White House* (New York: Simon and Schuster, 1994), 109–110.

13. Richard Cohen, "Bush's War on Nuance," *Washington Post,* February 17, 2004, A19.

14. Hart, *Sound of Leadership,* xix.

15. Murray Edelman, *The Symbolic Uses of Politics* (Urbana: University of Illinois Press, 1985), 96.

16. H. Mark Roelofs, *The Poverty of American Politics: A Theoretical Interpretation* (Philadelphia: Temple University Press, 1992), 116.

17. Kernell, *Going Public,* 140.

18. Jeffrey K. Tulis, *The Rhetorical Presidency* (Princeton: Princeton University Press, 1987), 47–49.

19. Ibid., 51–55.

20. Michael E. McGerr, *The Decline of Popular Politics* (New York: Oxford University Press, 1986), 22–23.

21. Alexander Hamilton, *Federalist* No. 71, in *The Federalist Papers,* quoted in Tulis, *Rhetorical Presidency,* 39.

22. Calvin Coolidge once commented on this practice: "At twelve thirty, the doors were opened and a long line passed by who wished merely to shake hands with the president. On one occasion, I shook hands with nineteen hundred in thirty-four minutes." Quoted in Gary King and Lyn Ragsdale, *The Elusive Executive: Discovering Statistical Patterns in the Presidency* (Washington, D.C.: CQ Press, 1988), 249.

23. Tulis, *Rhetorical Presidency,* 63.

24. Ibid., 67, 64–65.

25. Ibid., 69.

26. Ibid., 67–68.

27. Ibid., 79–83.

28. Abbott, "Do Presidents Talk Too Much?" 333–334.

29. See Garry Wills, *Lincoln at Gettysburg: The Words That Remade America* (New York: Simon and Schuster, 1992). Wills's argument that Lincoln's address fundamentally changed the national creed was anticipated by Willmoore Kendall, *The Conservative Affirmation* (New York: Henry Regnery, 1963), 252; and by M. E. Bradford, *Remembering Who We Are: Observations of a Southern Conservative* (Athens: University of Georgia Press, 1985), 145.

30. Wills, *Lincoln at Gettysburg,* 172, 174.

31. Ibid., 174.

32. Tulis, *Rhetorical Presidency,* 87–93.

33. Ibid., 88.

34. Quoted in Tulis, *Rhetorical Presidency,* 86.

35. Elmer E. Cornwell Jr., *Presidential Leadership of Public Opinion* (Bloomington: Indiana University Press, 1965), 24–25.

36. Quoted in Tulis, *Rhetorical Presidency,* 131.

37. David Green, *Shaping Political Consciousness* (Ithaca: Cornell University Press, 1987), 81.

38. Theodore J. Lowi, *The Personal President* (Ithaca: Cornell University Press, 1985), 22–66.

39. Jamieson, *Eloquence in an Electronic Age,* 45–53.

40. Quoted in Daniel J. Boorstin, *The Americans: The Democratic Experience* (New York: Random House, 1973), 475.

41. Hart, *Sound of Leadership,* xix.

42. Kernell, *Going Public,* 22.

43. Hart, *Sound of Leadership,* 11.

44. Ibid., 12–14; see also Jamieson, *Eloquence in an Electronic Age,* 165–201.

45. Quoted in Hart, *Sound of Leadership,* 36.

46. Quoted in Theodore C. Sorensen, *Kennedy* (New York: Harper and Row, 1965), 346.

47. Herbert S. Parmet, *JFK: The Presidency of John F. Kennedy* (New York: Dial Press, 1983), 197.

48. "I am a Berliner."

49. Hart, *Sound of Leadership,* 8. In calculating the total number of Ford's speeches, Hart counted all public occasions at which the president made remarks, including press conferences, dinners, and welcoming ceremonies.

50. Judith D. Horton, "Ronald Reagan's Failure to Secure Contra Aid: A Post-Vietnam Shift in Foreign Policy Rhetoric," *Presidential Studies Quarterly* 24 (summer 1994): 531–541.

51. Jamieson, *Eloquence in an Electronic Age,* 182–200.

52. Kathleen Hall Jamieson contrasts the more awkward style of Johnson and Nixon with the casual, modest style of Reagan (ibid., 186–187). The media critic Mark Crispin Miller makes the same point: "Reagan is unfailingly attractive, not at all like a predator, nor, in fact, like anything other than what he seems—'a nice guy,' pure and simple. . . . We, too, should appreciate the spectacle, after all the bad performances we've suffered through for years: LBJ, abusing his dogs and exposing his belly; Richard Nixon, hunched and glistening like a cornered toad; Jimmy Carter, with his maudlin twang and interminable kin. While each of these men, appallingly, kept lunging at us from behind the

mask of power, Reagan's face and mask are as one." Mark Crispin Miller, *Boxed In* (Evanston, Ill.: Northwestern University Press, 1988), 82.

53. Kernell, *Going Public,* 123.

54. Hart, *Sound of Leadership,* 51.

55. Bruce Miroff, "The Presidential Spectacle," in *The Presidency and the Political System,* 8th ed., ed. Michael Nelson (Washington, D.C.: CQ Press, 2006), 255–282.

56. Hart, *The Sound of Leadership,* 50.

57. Ibid., 219–220.

58. Kernell, *Going Public,* 131.

59. Patricia D. Witherspoon, " 'Let Us Continue': The Rhetorical Initiation of Lyndon Johnson's Presidency," *Presidential Studies Quarterly* 17 (summer 1987): 531–540.

60. Kernell, *Going Public,* 89.

61. Craig Allen Smith, "Leadership, Orientation, and Rhetorical Vision: Jimmy Carter, The 'New Right,' and the Panama Canal," *Presidential Studies Quarterly* 16 (spring 1986): 317–328.

62. King and Ragsdale, *Elusive Executive,* 255.

63. John E. Mueller, *War, Presidents, and Public Opinion* (New York: Wiley, 1973); and Lowi, *Personal President,* 11.

64. Hart, *Sound of Leadership,* 8. Also see Kernell, *Going Public,* 126.

65. Bruce Buchanan, *The Presidential Experience: What the Office Does to the Man* (Englewood Cliffs, N.J.: Prentice Hall, 1978).

66. Hart, *Sound of Leadership,* 33.

67. Ibid., 19.

68. A good overview of the criticism of the trend is James W. Ceaser et al., "The Rise of the Rhetorical Presidency," *Presidential Studies Quarterly* 11 (spring 1981): 158–171. For a response, see Abbott, "Do Presidents Talk Too Much?"

69. Lowi, *Personal President,* 170.

70. Hart, *Sound of Leadership,* 32.

71. Ibid., 30.

72. Jamieson, *Eloquence in an Electronic Age,* 220–222.

73. Ragsdale, *Vital Statistics on the Presidency,* 173.

74. Robert E. Darcy and Alvin Richman, "Presidential Travel and Public Opinion," *Presidential Studies Quarterly* 18 (winter 1988): 85–90.

75. Quoted in Hart, *Sound of Leadership,* 58.

76. Kernell, *Going Public,* 105.

77. Harold D. Lasswell, *Politics: Who Gets What, When, How* (New York: Meridan Books, 1958).

78. Ana Puga, "Amid Boos, Clinton Asks War Healing," *Boston Globe,* June 1, 1993.

79. Quoted in David I. Kertzer, *Ritual, Politics, and Power* (New Haven: Yale University Press, 1988), 94.

80. Daniel T. Rodgers, *Contested Truths* (New York: Basic Books, 1987), 182.

81. Green, *Shaping Political Consciousness,* 119–163.

82. Quoted in Tulis, *Rhetorical Presidency,* 172.

83. Theodore J. Lowi, *The End of Liberalism* (New York: Norton, 1979).

84. Dwight D. Eisenhower, "Farewell Address to the American People," in *Great Issues in American History: From Reconstruction to the Present Day, 1864–1969,* ed. Richard Hofstadter (New York: Vintage, 1969), 451.

SELECTED BIBLIOGRAPHY

Denton, Robert E. Jr., and Dan F. Hahn. *Presidential Communication: Description and Analysis.* New York: Praeger, 1986.

Ellis, Richard, ed. *Speaking to the People: The Rhetorical Presidency in Historical Perspective.* Amherst: University of Massachusetts Press, 1998.

Gelderman, Carol. *All the Presidents' Words: The Bully Pulpit and the Creation of the Virtual Presidency.* New York: Walker and Company, 1997.

Green, David. *Shaping Political Consciousness.* Ithaca: Cornell University Press, 1987.

Hart, Roderick P. *The Sound of Leadership.* Chicago: University of Chicago Press, 1988.

———. *Campaign Talk: Why Elections Are Good for Us.* Princeton: Princeton University Press, 2000.

Jamieson, Kathleen Hall. *Eloquence in an Electronic Age.* New York: Oxford University Press, 1988.

Kernell, Samuel. *Going Public: New Strategies of Presidential Leadership.* 4th ed. Washington, D.C.: CQ Press, 2007.

The Library of Congress Presents: Historic Presidential Speeches (1908–1993). Rhino, compact disc.

Ragsdale, Lyn. *Vital Statistics on the Presidency,* rev. ed. Washington, D.C.: Congressional Quarterly, 1998.

Smith, Craig Allen, and Kathy B. Smith. *The White House Speaks: Presidential Leadership as Persuasion.* Westport, Conn.: Praeger, 1994.

Stuckey, Mary E. *The President as Interpreter-in-Chief.* Chatham, N.J.: Chatham House, 1991.

Tulis, Jeffrey. *The Rhetorical Presidency.* Princeton: Princeton University Press, 1987.

Waldman, Michael. *POTUS Speaks: Finding the Words that Defined the Clinton Presidency.* New York: Simon and Schuster, 2000.

Windt, Theodore Otto Jr. "Presidential Rhetoric: Definition of a Field of Study." *Presidential Studies Quarterly* 16 (winter 1986): 102–116.

Windt, Theodore, with Beth Engold, eds. *Essays in Presidential Rhetoric.* Dubuque, Iowa: Kendall-Hunt, 1983.

chapter 17

The President and Political Parties

by Harold F. Bass Jr.

The president-party relationship gives rise to a significant presidential leadership role, party chief. It also generates noteworthy opportunities and problems for both presidency and party.

National political parties did not exist when the presidency was created in 1787. The emergence of political parties in the decade of the 1790s, however, brought about both an enduring link with the presidency and presidential responsibilities for party leadership. More than two centuries later, in the wake of numerous institutional transformations in both the presidency and the political parties, the linkage and the leadership persist.

Political parties connect citizens with rulers. They also link various public officeholders within the constitutionally designed separated-powers, checks-and-balances federal system that disperses the officers into different branches and levels of government and further positions them as rivals.

In turn, presidential leadership involves role playing. In Harry S. Truman's apt analogy, the president wears many hats: chief executive, chief of state, commander in chief, chief diplomat, chief economic manager, legislative leader, and chief of party. Presidential role playing is simultaneous, however, rather than sequential. A president wears several hats at a time.

This recognition is especially meaningful in considering the presidential role of party chief. Rarely will a president act solely as party leader. It is also rare that other roles will be performed without regard for party leadership.

Paradox pervades the presidential role of party leader. Party chieftainship both stands apart from and connects diverse presidential roles. It is on the periphery, and yet it is also at the center of presidential leadership. It clearly divides, and yet more subtly and significantly it complements and integrates. It is less a power than an opportunity; and yet under certain conditions it becomes an obstacle.

The Constitution does not authorize party leadership. It developed outside the framework formed by the constitutionally enumerated presidential powers. Moreover, the assignment of presidential leadership responsibilities over a specific part of the public conflicts with the general expectation that as head of state the president presides over the entire nation.

Yet because parties play significant linkage roles in politics, party leadership is central to the varied array of presidential responsibilities. Through the party, the president establishes and maintains connections with other elements in the political order, both inside and outside the government. These connections produce cohesion rather than division.

The exercise of presidential party leadership is often shrouded because of perceived presidential role conflicts and public antagonism toward the concept of partisanship. Given the structure and character of the U.S. political order, however, Woodrow Wilson's observation remains pertinent: the president's responsibility as chief of party is virtually inescapable.[1]

Party chieftainship calls for particular leadership skills to be exercised within a problematical structural and cultural setting. Political scientist James MacGregor Burns identifies two basic types of leadership: *transactional* and *transforming*. Transactional leadership operates within the framework of exchange. It features bargaining and negotiation. The more complex and potent transforming leadership has an elevating, even moralistic quality. Burns places party leadership in the transactional category.[2] And yet, certain exercises of party leadership are surely transformational—for example, those that effect a realignment of electoral forces, or those that institute and implement a new policy agenda.

The concept of a major political party in the United States embraces three analytically separate structural elements of membership: the party organization, the party in office (sometimes referred to as "the party in the government"), and the party in the electorate. The party organization consists of the variably linked network of activists who hold membership and leadership positions in party headquarters throughout the country. The party in office comprises the public officials who hold their positions under the banner of the party along with those who aspire to do so.

This group includes both elected officials and those appointed under partisan auspices. According to political scientist Frank J. Sorauf, the president is chief among the officeholders who have "captured the symbols of the party and speak for it in public authority." [3] The party in the electorate refers to those voters who with varying degrees of intensity support the party's candidates and causes.

ORIGINS AND DEVELOPMENT OF PRESIDENTIAL PARTY LEADERSHIP

The presidential role of party leader emerged outside the constitutional framework of expectations and powers established in 1787. As noted earlier, national political parties were not then a part of the political order. Moreover, to the extent that the Founders' generation contemplated the prospect of political parties, it was generally antagonistic toward them. George Washington, the first president, stood second to no one in upholding this position.

Looking from a distance at the Whig and Tory parliamentary factions in Great Britain, the Framers perceived them as divisive and detrimental to national unity. In contrast, the appropriate model of executive leadership appeared in the concept of a patriot king provided a half-century earlier by the British author and statesman Lord Bolingbroke. Such an ideal figure stood above party and faction and ruled benevolently in the public interest.

Nevertheless, almost immediately after the onset of the new government political parties appeared on the national scene. At least in part, their origins could be found in an increasingly acute division within the newly formed cabinet of executive department heads convened by President Washington. This division pitted the secretary of the Treasury, Alexander Hamilton, against the secretary of state, Thomas Jefferson.

Their conflict had roots in ambition, interest, and ideology. Each saw himself as heir to President Washington. Moreover, each realized that the new constitutional order provided a skeletal framework for development that would inevitably need to be fleshed out, and their respective visions of what the new nation should become were at odds.

Hamilton glorified the urban areas and their resident merchants and financiers; Jefferson idealized the rural setting and saw the real America embodied in the hard-working farmer. Hamilton perceived the need for strong, dynamic national government; Jefferson professed not to be the friend of energetic central government. During the early years of the Washington administration, conflict between these two principals rocked the cabinet. Among the issues of controversy were those of assumption of the state debts, establishment of a bank of the United States, and the protective tariff. The foreign policy differences that arose later only intensified the cleavage.

In the federal framework created by the Constitution, with its decentralized separation of powers, these disputes could not be contained within the national executive branch. Inevitably, they extended beyond its bounds into Congress and the states. Consequently, the respective Hamiltonian and Jeffersonian interests organized themselves. The Hamiltonians became the *Federalists,* a name previously

ORIGINS OF PARTY LABELS AND SYMBOLS

Understanding of political party development in the United States is complicated by the considerable confusion surrounding the names of the parties. Contemporary Democrats trace their partisan ancestry back to Thomas Jefferson. In Jefferson's day, however, the party went by two different names, either *Republican* or *Democratic-Republican.* By 1830 the dominant wing of a divided Democratic-Republican Party, led by President Andrew Jackson, abandoned the *Republican* portion of their label, leaving *Democratic* standing alone ever since.

A quarter-century later, in 1854, antislavery sympathizers forming a new party appropriated the name *Republican.* Today's Republicans are their descendants.

The term *democrat* comes from the Greek word *democratia,* a combination of *demos,* meaning "common people," and the suffix *-kratia,* denoting "strength, power." Thus *democratia* means "power of the people," or "the people rule."

The term *republican* derives from the Latin phrase *res publica.* It literally means "public thing," or "public affair," and it connotes a government in which citizens participate. Both party names thus suggest the Democrats' and Republicans' common belief in popular government, conducted by representatives of the people and accountable to them.

Gilded Age political cartoonist Thomas Nast endowed the two major political parties with enduring symbols: the Democratic donkey and the Republican elephant. The association of the Democrats with the donkey actually dates back to the 1830s when Andrew Jackson was characterized by his opponents as a jackass. In the 1870s Nast resurrected this image in a series of compelling political cartoons appearing in *Harper's Weekly.* The donkey aptly symbolized the rowdy, outrageous, tough, durable Democrats. Nast portrayed the Republican Party as an elephant. His initial employment of this symbol lampooned the foolishness of the Republican vote. Nast and other cartoonists later likened the elephant's size and strength advantages over other animals to the GOP's domination of the post–Civil War political landscape. The symbol came to suggest such elephant-like attributes as cleverness, majesty, ponderousness, and unwieldiness.

In an age in which literacy rates were much lower than today, and when information about specific party candidates and their policies was in short supply for the mass public, these party symbols came to serve as valuable cues to prospective voters, providing them with an easy way to distinguish candidates of one party from those of another. For modern electorates, these traditional symbols have diminished significance, but they endure as part of the popular culture.

used by those who favored ratification of the Constitution. Jefferson's followers were variously titled *Republicans* or *Democratic-Republicans*. (*See boxes, Origins of Party Labels and Symbols, p. 874, and When and Why Did Parties Begin? p. 232, in Chapter 5.*) In contrast to Hamilton, Jefferson was not especially visible in the early stages of this process. Rather, his long-standing ally James Madison, a member of the House of Representatives, propelled their common cause and opposed Hamilton's measures in Congress.

Early Presidents' Attitudes toward Parties

President Washington viewed these developments with alarm and despair, in keeping with his virulent antipathy toward party. He implored Hamilton and Jefferson to mute their differences, steadfastly holding himself above the emerging partisan battles dividing the government and indeed the entire political community. The president could not remain oblivious, however, to the disputes over policy. Indeed, his office forced him to take a stand. Regularly, he opted for the Hamiltonian alternative, even as he denied the legitimacy of partisan conflict. Washington's legacy to presidential party leadership was to reject emphatically its propriety while tentatively embracing its inevitability.

Washington's successor as president, John Adams, found himself in an exceedingly awkward position in the ongoing party conflict, which was not of his making. In contrast to Washington, Adams viewed parties as natural and inevitable in a free society. However, his theory of government was built on a similar foundation of disinterested executive leadership. He viewed the executive as the balance wheel in a political order featuring a bicameral legislature that represented distinct class interests.

During the Washington administration, Vice President Adams generally had supported Hamilton's public policies while maintaining his distance from the latter's organizational maneuvers. Personally, he was far closer to Jefferson than to Hamilton. Adams's vice presidency made him the logical successor when Washington chose to retire after two terms, and the Federalists readily embraced his candidacy in 1796, claiming him as their own. Nevertheless, he had not played any significant organizational role within the party— this was indisputably Hamilton's domain. Meanwhile, Jefferson was thrust forward as a candidate by Madison and other Democratic-Republican partisans. Adams won a narrow electoral vote victory in the first presidential election conducted along partisan lines. (*See "The First Succession: 1796," p. 355, in Chapter 6.*)

In the presidency, Adams's exercise of party leadership foundered on his theoretical objections to the president's assumption of the role and on Hamilton's ongoing claims. The tension between Adams and Hamilton and their respective followers grew until, by the end of Adams's term, the Federalist Party clearly had split into two wings. Thus

President Adams can be said to have been the leader of, at most, a party faction.

The third president, Jefferson, is truly the father of presidential party leadership.[4] By the time Jefferson ascended to the presidency, partisan institutions had begun to take shape. Within the executive, appointments to federal positions were being made with party affiliation in mind. Inside the legislature, assemblies or caucuses of like-minded partisans were meeting, not only to plot legislative strategy but also to nominate party candidates for president. Finally, at the state and local level electoral organizations had formed to secure the selection of candidates to public offices.

The Democratic-Republicans looked unequivocally to Jefferson for leadership. While sharing many of his predecessors' prejudices against presidential party leadership, he nevertheless exercised it in a pioneering and exemplary fashion that established high expectations of his successors.

Early on in Washington's presidency, Jefferson acknowledged partisan division as natural but nevertheless deplored its presence. In the ensuing years, he came to defend and justify party activity on grounds of expediency and even honor. Confronted with the realities of Hamilton's initiatives, and disagreeing profoundly with so many of them, he increasingly saw party organization as an exigent and appropriate response. He did not retreat from his antiparty position so much as he superimposed on it a temporary acceptance of party.

For Jefferson, republicanism, or representative government, was preferable to monarchism, which he associated with arbitrary, hereditary government. Republicanism derived governmental authority from popular sovereignty and held public officials accountable to popular control. As such, it had distinctly democratic implications, although Jefferson was not an advocate of direct democracy. The Jeffersonian party promoting this cause was labeled, as noted, "Republican" or "Democratic-Republican."

Significantly, Jefferson did not clearly endorse the notion of institutionalized party competition. He was never really willing to accord legitimacy to those who opposed him and the republican cause he associated with his party. Furthermore, he demonstrated no abiding commitment to the institution of the Democratic-Republican Party. Instead, he viewed the party as dispensable once it had accomplished the restorative tasks for which it had been formed.

Executive-Legislative Relations

Jefferson's party leadership had its chief influence on executive-legislative relations. For Jefferson, presidential party leadership enabled him to overcome an ideological restraint well established in republican thought—namely, an antipathy toward executive power, combined with a corresponding preference for legislative autonomy. Although Jefferson never embraced this position with the enthusiasm and extremism shown by some of his fellow partisans, still he honored it.

For Jefferson, the problem was how to exercise positive presidential leadership in the face of republican ideological objections. Here, the presence of party provided a convenient facade facilitating leadership on his part without compromising a fundamental position of his republican followers. He could justify actions taken under the protection of party that, according to republican ideology, might be considered inappropriate under purely executive auspices. In this sense, from many of his followers' perspectives, President Jefferson the party leader had more legitimacy than President Jefferson the chief executive. In adding party leadership to the president's powers, he substantially increased the president's strength in the political arena.

The tactics and techniques Jefferson developed in using party leadership in legislative relations remain part of the standard presidential repertoire centuries later. He participated in recruiting candidates. He enlisted members of the legislature as his agents and worked through them in pursuit of his objectives. He deployed the executive department secretaries who constituted his cabinet as emissaries to Capitol Hill.

Not content to rely exclusively on surrogates, Jefferson sought to establish personal relations with rank-and-file legislators. He corresponded extensively with members of Congress. He also regularly scheduled dinner parties in which the guest lists were limited to small groups of senators and representatives who shared his partisan affiliation.

Furthermore, the president sought to generate cooperation and goodwill with Democratic-Republican legislators through patronage. Although departmental secretaries and state and local officials also were involved in this process, he consistently solicited recommendations and evaluations from individual legislators for prospective appointees.

On another front, Jefferson discontinued the formal practice followed by his predecessors of delivering in person an annual address to Congress. Instead, he simplified his relations with Congress and preferred to work informally behind the scenes and through his agents. From this vantage point, however, he was quite willing to make suggestions about details of proposed legislation. Indeed, he often provided trusted legislators with drafts of actual bills for them to introduce according to prescribed procedures, accompanying these communications with admonitions of secrecy and disavowals of meddling.

During his presidency, the opposition Federalist press alleged that Jefferson met with and oversaw the deliberations of the Democratic-Republican Party caucus. *Caucus* was the term used to refer to the meetings of the partisan legislators. One well-documented practice was the quadrennial meeting to nominate party candidates for the presidential ticket. In addition, numerous reports mention informal assemblies of sizable numbers of legislators to plot legislative strategy and tactics. However, the historical record cannot clearly establish the nature and extent of the president's relationship with this early partisan institution.

In exercising party leadership through these various processes, President Jefferson based his partisan appeals for support on four main foundations. The first was principle. His correspondence is replete with references to the promotion of common republican principles. The second was the mirror image of this appeal; it invoked the specter of the Federalist opposition. Often nothing produces unity so well as a common adversary, and Jefferson frequently sought to keep his followers together by denouncing the other party. Third, Jefferson traded on the immense personal regard with which he was held by his fellow Democratic-Republicans. Finally, as president he tried to make legislators see that his preferences were in their own self-interests.

Effect of Parties on the Presidency

By the end of Jefferson's presidency, some twenty years into the constitutional era, the unforeseen emergence of political parties had transformed the character of the presidency and the larger U.S. political system. The parties' assertion and assumption of nominating responsibilities for the presidential ticket necessitated a formal change in the balloting arrangements of the Electoral College. Originally, the Constitution required presidential electors to cast a single ballot that listed the names of two presidential candidates. Once the assembled ballots were counted, the candidate with the most votes, provided that number was a majority, was elected president. The candidate with the next largest number of votes became vice president.

Under this procedure, the election of 1800 produced a tie. The Democratic-Republican Party objective before the election was to secure the selection of presidential electors committed to the slate of Jefferson for president and Aaron Burr for vice president. It did so to ensure that as president Jefferson might not be bedeviled by the presence of a Federalist adversary in the secondary slot, as he himself had acted in quiet opposition to President Adams.

The party effort was too successful. Every elector who voted for Jefferson also voted for Burr, and vice versa, and more electors voted for Jefferson and Burr than for any other contenders. The Electoral College tie sent the presidential election to the House of Representatives, where the lame-duck Federalist majority eventually consented to the choice of Jefferson.

Before the next presidential election in 1804, Congress proposed and the state legislatures ratified the Twelfth Amendment. The change separated the ballots for president and vice president, allowing presidential electors effectively to vote for party tickets. This amendment fundamentally altered the status of the electors. They quickly lost the independent agent status envisioned by the Framers. Instead, they became instruments of party will.

Moreover, the parties' monopoly over presidential selection had the result of adding a new, extraconstitutional presidential eligibility requirement above and beyond those enumerated in the Constitution: a party nomination. The expectations and requirements for presidential candidates, which until then had been public service and esteem, came to include not only party affiliation but also party nomination.

In turn, the presence of a party's candidate for president at the head of the party ticket for elective public offices conferred on that individual the status of party leader. Once elected, that figure could presume to be something more than the head of the executive branch. Indeed, there was now a basis for claiming government chieftainship, with the idea and organization of party unifying separated national institutions under the leadership of the president.[5]

The emergence of political parties had a profound and transforming effect on the executive office. The constitutional principle of separation of powers envisioned a clearly divided governmental structure with three distinct branches: executive, legislative, and judicial. Checks and balances, while blurring these divisions, nevertheless were intended to inhibit cooperation by encouraging rivalries among the branches. The appearance of national political parties altered this setting. They provided a foundation and an opportunity for coordination, cooperation, and unity in government.

Evolving President-Party Relationships

Although aspects of presidential party leadership as developed by Jefferson endure to this day, the president-party relationship has not been static since the first decade of the nineteenth century. The changes in the relationship have been mostly gradual and evolutionary, occurring over several presidencies with their essence emerging only in retrospect.

After Jefferson's retirement in 1809, the congressional party caucus that had responded in a generally positive fashion to his leadership proved to be less accommodating to his immediate successors. Indeed, the caucus came to perceive its role in nominating and, absent noteworthy interparty competition, in effect electing presidents as subordinating the president to congressional authority.

By 1828, however, the caucus was in disarray; and the new president, Andrew Jackson, presided over important transformations in the president-party relationship. Two developments in particular were taking form at this time: the growth of national party organization and the emergence of a mass party—ordinary citizens who identified with a political party and provided electoral support for a party's candidates.

Initially, in the 1790s, American political parties were governmental factions. By 1800, however, they were developing organizational means to appeal to the electorate to support the parties' candidates for public offices. Party organization was taking shape, primarily in the form of loosely linked campaign committees, complemented by the partisan press.

In reaching out to the citizenry, positioning themselves as intermediary institutions linking citizens and government, political parties recognized that the constitutional order rested in part on a foundation of popular sovereignty. By the standards of the day, the states' suffrage requirements were liberal and becoming more so, making it easier for the rank and file to vote. Religious tests had been abandoned in the revolutionary era, and property requirements were largely eliminated in the decade of the 1820s. Further, the voters' involvement in presidential selection was enhanced by post-1800 changes in the operation of the Electoral College, most notably the trend toward popular selection of party-nominated presidential electors.

The establishment of the citizen-government link dramatically increased the president's political power. By virtue of the selection process, nationwide in scope and increasingly popular in operation, the president could claim a national, popular constituency above and beyond that of any governmental rival. The "people connection" allowed the president to tap into the wellsprings of popular sovereignty that nourished the exercise of political authority in an increasingly democratic society. As "tribune of the people," the president could claim a prerogative not specifically enumerated in the constitutional allocation of governmental power.

These developments significantly enhanced the president's party leadership role. The presidency became linked with a national party organization that in turn connected state and local party organizations throughout the country. This development came about with the advent of the national party convention as the nominator of the president. Furthermore, the presidency became directly tied to the citizenry of the republic. With Jackson, a general and a popular hero, paving the way, the presidency became the focus of popular attention and representation. Meanwhile, under the astute direction of Jackson's vice president and successor in the White House, Martin Van Buren, presidential patronage assisted the creation and strengthening of the party organizational machinery.

The next important shift in the character of president-party relations occurred in the immediate aftermath of the Civil War. Congressional Republicans reacted against President Abraham Lincoln's assertive wartime leadership by restraining his successors. Also, party leaders at the state and local levels—fortified by patronage resources and strong party identifications and loyalties in the electorate—increased in stature and significance in national politics in the latter part of the nineteenth century. They came to dominate the presidential nomination process, and the presiden-

In the first appearance of the Democratic donkey, this unfavorable 1837 political cartoon shows President Martin Van Buren walking behind his predecessor, Andrew Jackson, who rides the donkey.

tial nominee was usually beholden to the party organization sponsors.

Political scientist Daniel Klinghard credits two late nineteenth-century presidents, Grover Cleveland and William McKinley, with reviving presidential party leadership.[6] After the turn of the twentieth century, the balance of power continued to shift in favor of the president. Strong, assertive occupants of the White House such as Theodore Roosevelt and Woodrow Wilson invigorated the presidency by dint of personality. An increasing world role for the United States enhanced the visibility and power of the presidential office, and advancing communications technology placed the president increasingly in the spotlight. In keeping with these developments, the president's party leadership position became more commanding.

Franklin D. Roosevelt ushered in the modern era in president-party relations with his long presidential tenure, 1933–1945. In responding to the Great Depression and World War II, Roosevelt presided over a dramatic increase in the size and scope of the federal executive. This expansion had important implications for party relations, because Roosevelt came to rely on executive branch personnel to perform many of the political and social service roles that had traditionally been the province of the political party.

Since then, further advancements in communications technology, especially television, have served to connect the

president even more directly with the public, thereby weakening the party's traditional position as intermediary between the two. In addition, and partly in response, party identification in the electorate has declined, and party reforms have reduced the power of the party organization in the nomination of the president.

The Presidency and Two-Party Competition

The emergence of parties transformed American political contention. At first, such conflict mainly divided states. But these rivalries quickly were supplanted by competition between parties. Moreover, contests pitted two major parties against each other. This paradoxically promoted consensus by reducing the potential for fragmentation from among thirteen states to between two parties.

The enduringly dualistic character of party competition in the United States (and in Britain) is in contrast to the multiparty competition prevalent in many European countries and the absence of party competition in the few remaining communist countries and in many of the nation-states of the developing world. In seeking to explain the two-party phenomenon, scholars have pointed to diverse factors such as tradition, culture, and electoral arrangements.

Early on, the political conflicts in America divided the participants into opposing pairs: patriots versus loyalists, Federalists versus Anti-Federalists, Federalists versus Democratic-Republicans. The resulting tradition of two-party competition hindered the emergence of alternatives.

The American political culture contributes to the sustenance of the two-party system because it is supportive of accommodation and compromise. The culture encourages diverse interests to ally under a party banner despite significant differences. Absent this spirit of concession, the various groups would likely form their own, separate political organizations, and a multiparty system would prevail.

Finally, electoral arrangements are critical to understanding the persistence of the two-party system. American elections are for the most part organized on the principle of the single-member district, winner take all. Electoral units designate a single individual—the one who receives the most votes—to occupy a public office. The winner-take-all provision frustrates minor parties that may be capable of assembling sizable numerical minorities but cannot realistically aspire to triumphing in an absolute sense over the two entrenched major parties.

The presidency can be viewed as a special case of, and credited with a critical contribution to, the electoral arrangements explanation. The constitutional standard of an Electoral College majority (not just a plurality) to elect the president discourages competition from parties that cannot hope to attain the high level of support necessary for victory. As such, it supports the maintenance of the two-party system.

In the early years of the Republic, party competition matched the Federalists led by Alexander Hamilton against the Democratic-Republican followers of Thomas Jefferson. In the wake of the Federalists' demise—caused by Jefferson's triumphs in 1800 and 1804 and reinforced by the victories of his lieutenant, James Madison, in 1808 and 1812—a brief period of one-party rule ensued. Jeffersonian heir James Monroe presided over this so-called Era of Good Feelings.

By the mid-1820s, however, intraparty conflict had resulted in the emergence of two rival Democratic-Republican factions. These factions reflected personal ambitions and rivalries in the party leadership, pitting Andrew Jackson and his advocates against an alliance of John Quincy Adams, Henry Clay, and their combined supporters. The Jackson faction represented the emerging claims of the growing southwestern region in party and national politics, as well as those of the lower classes, including immigrants; Adams spoke for the more traditional regional and socioeconomic elements within the party coalition.

The factions quickly evolved into competing political parties. Jackson and his followers styled themselves *Democrats*, the party of the people. Their adversaries borrowed the label *Whigs* from the British. In Britain, Whigs had long supported the cause of legislative supremacy against expansive executive claims, a concern of Jackson's opponents. The partisan battle between the Democrats and the Whigs raged for more than two decades. About the time the Whigs died out in the 1850s, a new party, the *Republicans*, appeared on the scene to challenge the Democrats. Their competition has endured ever since.

Two-party competition has typically taken the form of sustained periods of dominance by one party, measured in terms of control of the presidency. From 1800 to 1860 the

The Republican elephant made its first appearance in a Thomas Nast illustration for Harper's Weekly *on November 7, 1874.*

Democratic Party, in its Jeffersonian and Jacksonian incarnations, ordinarily prevailed in presidential elections.

Amid the upheaval of the Civil War, this pattern gave way to one of Republican ascendancy. The rise of the Republican Party can be attributed initially to the demise of the Whigs and the self-destruction of the Democrats, both precipitated in large part by the slavery controversy. The ultimately successful prosecution of the Civil War under Republican auspices allowed the party to seize the banner of patriotism, while the Democratic opposition was stained in the North and West by its southern roots. Increasingly in the postwar years, the Republican Party developed lasting ties with business interests that provided it with solid financial support. The Republican era endured until 1932, when it was undermined by the Great Depression. That year marked the beginning of a new era of Democratic domination that clearly lasted two decades.

The presidential elections from 1952 until 1988 departed from the previous patterns in that no party was able to sustain its hold on the White House for more than eight years. If two-party competition is measured in terms of alternation in the occupancy of the White House, these years constituted an unprecedented era of competitiveness. In 1988 Republican nominee George H. W. Bush's quest to succeed retiring incumbent Ronald Reagan met with electoral approval, providing the Republicans three consecutive four-year terms in control of the White House.

However, the result of the 1992 election challenged suggestions that a new era of Republican dominance of presidential politics had dawned. President Bush lost to

Democratic nominee Bill Clinton. Two years later, the midterm congressional elections revived Republican electoral prospects. The GOP took control of both chambers of Congress for the first time since Dwight D. Eisenhower's election. Republicans hoped this surprisingly strong showing portended their recapture of the White House in 1996 and a clear, enduring realignment of electoral forces in their favor.

To their disappointment, President Clinton won a convincing reelection, making him the first Democratic president since Franklin Roosevelt to earn a second term. But divided government persisted as the GOP retained majorities on Capitol Hill. In 2001 the Republicans returned to the White House when their presidential nominee, Texas governor George W. Bush, the son of the former president, narrowly prevailed in a disputed election against Vice President Al Gore. With the Republicans remaining in control of Congress, Bush became the first Republican president since Eisenhower to enjoy unified party government. This status was fleeting, for a postinauguration party switch in the Senate placed the Democrats back in the majority. However, the GOP regained its Senate majority in 2002, and Bush's more comfortable reelection in 2004 sustained unified party government through 2006 with a net Republican gain of four Senate seats. However, Democratic victories in the 2006 midterm elections gained them majorities in both chambers and restored divided party government for the remainder of Bush's presidency.

In the first decade of the twenty-first century, the two major parties appear highly competitive in presidential politics, with neither holding a decisive, long-term advantage. Meanwhile, minor parties continue to lurk on the periphery, but the electoral arrangements preclude prospects for winning the White House. Although unlikely to win plurality victories in any states and thus receive electoral votes, minor parties can and do affect outcomes in the states by drawing enough support away from the major parties to determine the winner.

This capacity first manifested itself in 1848, when former president Martin Van Buren bolted the Democratic Party he had once led to run under the label of the Free-Soilers, an antislavery party. He won no states, but his 10 percent of the national popular vote came disproportionately from his native New York. He arguably drew enough votes away from the Democratic ticket to give that state's electoral votes, and thus the presidency, to Zachary Taylor and the Whigs. Most recently, in 2000 Green Party voters nationally cast less than 5 percent of the popular vote. Yet their showing in Florida in behalf of nominee Ralph Nader was sufficient to keep Democrat Al Gore from winning the popular vote there and therefore the presidency. Rhodes Cook has pointed out that 2000 Reform Party candidate Pat Buchanan in a reverse fashion may have siphoned off enough voters

from Bush to keep him from winning a few close states that went to Gore.

On several occasions, minor party nominees have in fact won electoral votes. Indeed, in 1912 former president Theodore Roosevelt, running under the Progressive Party banner, convincingly outpolled his Republican successor, President William Howard Taft, who was seeking reelection. However, the Democratic nominee, Woodrow Wilson, emerged as the landslide victor in the electoral college, although the popular vote for Roosevelt and Taft combined was higher than that for Wilson. Electoral votes for minor party nominees have not clearly altered electoral outcomes in presidential contests.

Parties as Coalitions

Political parties appeal to interest groups, or collections of individuals who share common concerns. Indeed, parties can be seen as broad coalitions of diverse interests: geographic, social, economic, ethnic, and issue. Particularly in presidential elections, parties seek to achieve victory by attracting sufficient electoral support from voters who are members of these varied groups.

Presidential party leadership is part and parcel of the linkages between president and public and between parties and groups. For example, during the decade of the 1930s under the New Deal policies of Franklin Roosevelt, the Democratic Party assembled under its umbrella a formidable electoral coalition that generally included the South, racial minorities, blue-collar laborers, farmers, Catholics, Jews, and middle-class elements brought low by the ravages of the Great Depression. This party coalition successfully supported Roosevelt's presidential candidacies an unprecedented four separate times. It remained sufficiently intact in 1948 to bring victory to his successor, Harry Truman. Vestiges of the declining Roosevelt coalition could still be observed in the electoral support for the victorious Democratic presidential nominees since Truman: John F. Kennedy, Lyndon B. Johnson, Jimmy Carter, and Bill Clinton.

Republican responses to this era of Democratic domination entailed successful presidential campaigns by Dwight Eisenhower, Richard Nixon, Ronald Reagan, and George H. W. Bush that appealed to traditionally Democratic voters. The Eisenhower and Reagan appeals in particular were personalistic. Both presidents enjoyed popularity that transcended partisanship. In addition, all but Bush benefited from public dissatisfaction with the performance of the Democratic incumbents who preceded them. In each instance, the dissatisfaction was fueled by foreign policy problems besetting Democratic administrations: Korea in 1952, Vietnam in 1968, and Iran in 1980.

As presidents, the four Republicans followed up with efforts to reshape electoral alignments into a new winning coalition of interests under the party banner. Over the years, they achieved significant defections to the GOP in the white South, among the middle class, and among blue-collar workers that enabled Reagan's vice president, George H. W. Bush, to win the 1988 presidential election campaigning as a successor. The gains proved ephemeral in 1992 when Bush's reelection effort failed, in large part because Clinton was able to halt, at least temporarily, these inroads.

President Clinton's challenge after 1992 was to expand the electoral coalition that carried him to victory with 43 percent of the vote in a three-person race that had featured a surprisingly strong minor party showing by third party candidate H. Ross Perot (19 percent). Clinton won a more convincing reelection victory in 1996, but he again fell short of a popular vote majority, even though Perot's popular support dropped to 8 percent. In 2000 Clinton sought to pass the torch of presidential party leadership to his designated heir, Vice President Al Gore. By doing so, Clinton believed he could demonstrate his success as party leader in engineering the emergence of an enduring Democratic coalition that could prevail over time not only against Republican onslaughts but also against forces producing fragmentation in the party system and undermining its persistent two-party character.

In the 2000 election Gore achieved a slight popular vote plurality, but he narrowly lost the electoral vote to Republican George W. Bush. The appeal of minor parties continued to fade from the heights of 1992. Meanwhile, the close election indicated that each major party had assembled a competitive coalitional base. One clear point of differentiation was ideological, with the Democrats more liberal and the Republicans more conservative. Another stark division was geographic. The electoral map showed clearly that Democrats controlled the more populous urban America, the Republicans controlled the more spacious rural areas, and the suburbs continued to be a battleground. As such, regionally the Democrats dominated on the East and West Coasts and the Great Lakes region, and the Republicans ruled the South, Central Plains, and Mountain West.

The Democrats' base consisted of minority voters, especially African Americans. The Democrats also attracted women in disproportionate numbers, particularly unmarried women. They were strongest among lower-income, lower-educated voters, but they also demonstrated noteworthy appeal to voters at the upper levels of income and education. The Republican coalition was the mirror image of the Democrats in terms of gender, income, and education. This pattern generally persisted in 2004.

One of the more interesting correlates of electoral behavior in 2000 and 2004 was religious commitment. Voters who attended church services more regularly were more likely to align with the Republican nominee, while the more secular segment of the electorate identified with the Democratic alternative.

These party coalitions essentially divided the electorate into two roughly equal thirds, with the remaining third up for grabs. In this competitive environment, each party aspires to break the deadlock and emerge as the dominant party of the early twenty-first century. A critical question for presidential campaign strategists is whether to pursue electoral victory through conversion or mobilization. George W. Bush prevailed in 2004 with the latter approach.

THE PRESIDENT AND PARTY ORGANIZATION

In the United States the organizational machinery of a major political party parallels the organization of the government. For every level of government in the federal system—national, state, and local—there is a corresponding unit of party organization. Generally, the lower levels of the organization choose members of the higher levels.

Throughout the nineteenth century and well into the twentieth, preponderant party power rested with the state and local organizations. They dominated the national parties, which acted essentially as holding companies. In recent years this balance has shifted, centralizing power at the national level. For the Democrats, centralization was achieved through a codification of national party responsibilities in the party's formal rules and procedures. For the Republicans, a similar result occurred with less resort to rules changes.

The institutions of party organization are the convention, the committee, the chair, and the headquarters staff. The first three typically exist at all levels, but local parties seldom have headquarters or staffs.

Party Organization

National party organization activity traditionally centered on the presidency; relatively little control was exercised over the operations of the state and local entities. More recently, the Democratic and Republican national committees have become increasingly superfluous to presidential politics and removed from them. However, they have assumed more supervision over the lower levels. In the wake of these historic shifts, the national party organization today appears stronger and more vital in many respects than ever before, though less relevant to the presidency.

Within a quarter-century of Jefferson's retirement from the presidency in 1809 a new arena of presidential party leadership opened up with the establishment of national party organizations.[7] These institutions arose after the collapse of the congressional party caucus as a nominating device. Beginning in the 1790s congressional party caucuses had assumed responsibility for nominating the parties' presidential tickets. The gradual demise of the Federalist Party after the electoral success of Jefferson and the

1789 1792 1796 1800 1804 1808 1812 1816 1820 1824 1828 1832 1836 1840 1844 1848 1852 1856 1860 1864 1868 1872 1876 1880 1884 1888 1892 1896 1900 1904 1908 1912 1916 1920 1924 1928 1932 1936 1940 1944 1948 1952 1956 1960 1964 1968 1972 1976 1980 1984 1988 1992 1996 2000

Major Parties

Federalist

Democratic-Republican

National Republican

Democratic

Whig

Republican

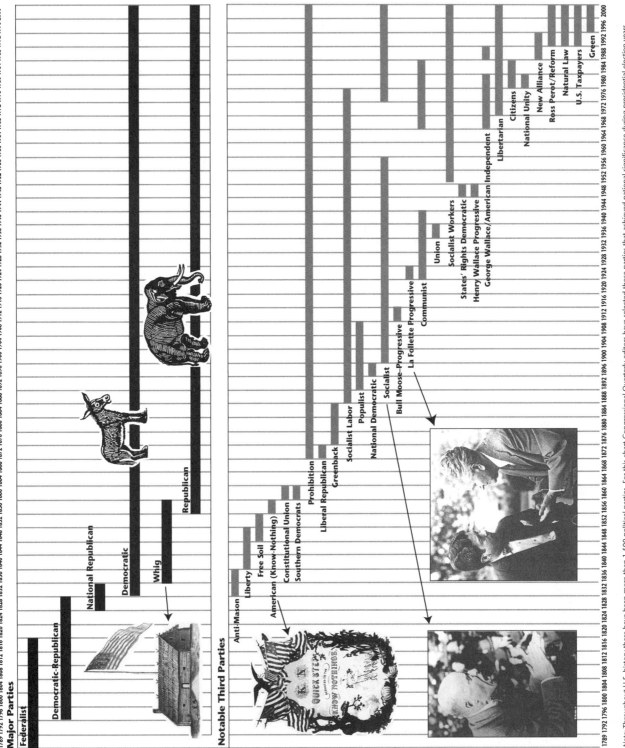

Notable Third Parties

Anti-Mason

Liberty

Free Soil

American (Know-Nothing)

Constitutional Union

Southern Democrats

Liberal Republican

Prohibition

Greenback

Socialist Labor

National Democratic

Populist

Socialist

Bull Moose–Progressive

La Follette Progressive

Communist

Union

Socialist Workers

States' Rights Democratic

Henry Wallace Progressive

George Wallace/American Independent

Libertarian

Citizens

National Unity

New Alliance

Ross Perot/Reform

Natural Law

U.S. Taxpayers

Green

1789 1792 1796 1800 1804 1808 1812 1816 1820 1824 1828 1832 1836 1840 1844 1848 1852 1856 1860 1864 1868 1872 1876 1880 1884 1888 1892 1896 1900 1904 1908 1912 1916 1920 1924 1928 1932 1936 1940 1944 1948 1952 1956 1960 1964 1968 1972 1976 1980 1984 1988 1992 1996 2000

Note: Throughout U.S. history there have been more than 1,500 political parties. For this chart Congressional Quarterly editors have selected those parties that achieved national significance during presidential election years. The spaces between the rules on this chart indicate the election year only. For example, the Constitutional Union Party and the Southern Democrats were in existence for the 1860 election only and were gone by 1864. Similarly, the Green Party first fielded a presidential candidate in 1996.

Democratic-Republicans in 1800 left the latter party's caucus as the designator of the president, with the Electoral College eventually ratifying its choice.

The caucus effected reasonably smooth party leadership transitions from Jefferson to James Madison in 1808–1809 and from Madison to James Monroe in 1816–1817. The culmination of the Virginia dynasty after Monroe's retirement from the White House in 1824 left the party caucus without an obvious consensus choice. Internal division ensued. The decline of interparty competition had served eventually to heighten intraparty competition for the presidential nomination that was tantamount to election.

Furthermore, the very concept of the caucus came under attack from various outside sources. States and congressional districts not in the hands of the dominant Democratic-Republican Party had no voice in the caucus proceedings. These areas found themselves excluded from meaningful participation in presidential selection.

In 1824 the supporters of Andrew Jackson's presidential candidacy assaulted the caucus procedure as elitist. Embracing values of popular participation and reflecting the interests of outsiders in the political order, Jackson's cause drew little support from the members of the Washington-based caucus.

Alternatively, others perceived the caucus to be a de facto denial of the constitutional principle of separation of powers, because it allowed a congressional majority to choose the president. Under the weight of these onslaughts, the caucus as a nominating device virtually disintegrated in the mid-1820s, although for a brief time state legislative party caucuses engaged in nominating activities.

The controversy over the caucus was part of a larger issue, the growing division within the dominant Democratic-Republican Party. Jackson's 1824 candidacy, followed by his successful run for the presidency in 1828, clearly split the party into two irreconcilable wings. Before the 1832 presidential election, with the caucus discredited and inoperative, a new format for presidential nominations came into being.

The Jackson faction, now styling itself the Democrats, along with the anti-Jackson elements, calling themselves National Republicans, and a third group, the Anti-Masons, convened separately to name their presidential tickets. These conventions, the first in U.S. history, brought together delegations from state parties, opening up participation in the nominating process to representatives of the rank-and-file party members. The concept took hold, and since then the quadrennial conventions have been a standard feature of the presidential nominating process.

Convention

The appearance of the nominating convention during the Jacksonian era also marked the beginning of party organization at the national level. Replacing the discredited congressional caucus as a nominating device, the quadrennial convention brought together state delegations to name the party's presidential ticket.[8] (See "The Development of Party Nominating Conventions," p. 239, in Chapter 5.)

At the convention, delegates also agreed on a statement of party principles and issue stances, or platform, on which the party's nominees could run in the upcoming election. The gathering served as a massive party rally where rival factions could be conciliated and unified, and enthusiasm generated, in preparation for the general election campaign. The convention provided a national institutional identity, serving as the party's voice and authority.

In the nineteenth century, state representation at the national convention followed the Electoral College formula,

This 1824 political cartoon criticizes the treatment of Andrew Jackson by the hostile press and the practice of nominating candidates by caucus (especially Republican nominee William Crawford). The snarling dogs are labeled with the names of critical newspapers.

TABLE 17-1   **National Party Nominees and Convention Sites and Dates, 1944–2004**

Year	President	Democrats	Republicans
1944	Roosevelt (D)	Chicago July 19–21 Roosevelt[a]	Chicago June 26–28 Dewey
1948	Truman (D)	Philadelphia July 12–14 Truman[a]	Philadelphia June 21–25 Dewey
1952	Truman (D)	Chicago July 21–26 Stevenson	Chicago July 7–11 Eisenhower[a]
1956	Eisenhower (R)	Chicago August 13–17 Stevenson	San Francisco August 20–23 Eisenhower[a]
1960	Eisenhower (R)	Los Angeles July 11–15 Kennedy[a]	Chicago July 25–28 Nixon
1964	L. Johnson (D)	Atlantic City August 24–27 Johnson[a]	San Francisco July 13–16 Goldwater
1968	L. Johnson (D)	Chicago August 26–29 Humphrey	Miami Beach August 5–8 Nixon[a]
1972	Nixon (R)	Miami Beach July 10–13 McGovern	Miami Beach August 21–23 Nixon[a]
1976	Ford (R)	New York July 12–15 Carter[a]	Kansas City August 16–19 Ford
1980	Carter (D)	New York August 11–14 Carter	Detroit July 14–17 Reagan[a]
1984	Reagan (R)	San Francisco July 16–19 Mondale	Dallas August 20–23 Reagan[a]
1988	Reagan (R)	Atlanta July 18–21 Dukakis	New Orleans August 15–18 G. Bush[a]
1992	G. H. W. Bush (R)	New York July 13–16 Clinton[a]	Houston August 17–20 G. Bush
1996	Clinton (D)	Chicago August 26–29 Clinton[a]	San Diego August 12–15 Dole
2000	Clinton (D)	Los Angeles August 14–17 Gore	Philadelphia July 31–August 3 G. W. Bush[a]
2004	G. W. Bush (R)	Boston July 26–29 Kerry	New York August 30–September 2 G. W. Bush[a]

SOURCE: *National Party Conventions, 1831–2004* (Washington, D.C.: CQ Press, 2005).

NOTE: a. Won election.

at the early nominating conventions were allocated according to the states' representation in Congress: a mixture of population and state equality.

In the twentieth century, both major parties adopted formulas that fixed representation in part according to the states' previous electoral support for the party. In other words, a positive record of support for the party's nominees produced bonus representation at the convention.

The Democrats have moved more decisively in this direction. They also have embraced two alternative representational principles. First, they have systematically sought through affirmative action to offer representation to a variety of population groups—women, racial minorities, and age cohorts, among others. Second, they have seated ex officio "superdelegates," party officeholders chosen apart from the normal delegate selection processes.

Over the years, the conventions have grown dramatically. Early conventions drew fewer than three hundred delegates. In contrast, contemporary Democratic conventions bring together more than four thousand, and today's Republicans assemble about two thousand. Through 2004 twenty-two cities had been designated as convention sites, with Boston, the choice of the Democrats in 2004, joining the ranks most recently. Many have been selected repeatedly. For example, Chicago has hosted twenty-five conventions, most of them for the GOP, but most recently for the Democrats in 1996. *(See Table 17-1.)* The announcement of first-time host cities Minneapolis, Minnesota, and Denver, Colorado, for the 2008 Republican and Democratic conventions respectively indicated the increasing focus of both parties on the evolving political battleground in the Great Lakes and Mountain West regions.

In the nineteenth century, state party organizations tightly controlled the selection of convention delegates. Early in the twentieth century the progressive movement pushed for popular selection of delegates through a party primary. Although a few state parties adopted this mechanism, most kept the party organization in charge.

After 1968, however, some epochal reforms within the Democratic Party lodged far more effective party authority at the national level than had been the case and dramatically increased the number of state parties electing delegates through primaries. These reforms helped to transform the character of convention decision making. Party voters essentially choose the nominee in primaries and caucuses, leaving the convention little to do except ratify the voters' choice. *(See "History of the Primary System," p. 241, in Chapter 5.)*

As a result, every major party convention since 1952 has produced a first-ballot victory. In 2004 the eventual nominees, Democrat John F. Kerry and Republican George W. Bush, solidified their convention majorities through delegate-selection contests in the states well in advance of the

itself an extension of the Constitutional Convention's Great Compromise on congressional apportionment. Under the compromise, the House of Representatives was apportioned according to population, and the Senate according to state equality, two senators for each state. Similarly, delegate seats conventions. For them and their parties, the convention's nominating role was a mere formality.

Elsewhere, the modern convention has become a media event, heightening its traditional function of rallying the party. The target of attention has shifted, however, from the party activists in the hall to the vast television audience viewing the prime-time proceedings. The convention gives the nominee a forum in which to kick off the general election campaign by demonstrating presidential leadership qualities to both party and public. Nominees achieve this by accepting the nomination with a forceful speech and skillfully managing the events of the convention week.[9]

The national convention endures as the formal, legally empowered nominator of the presidential ticket and as the apex of authority within the party. It remains a quadrennial event, though the Democrats experimented with midterm conventions in 1974, 1978, and 1982 to stimulate discussion and development of party positions on issues.

Committee

An institution convening for a few days every four years can hardly exercise effective power and authority within a political party. Early on, in the 1840s, the Democratic national convention established a national committee to oversee the conduct of the presidential campaign and to guide the party's fortunes between conventions. When the Republican Party formed a few years later, it adopted a similar organizational arrangement.[10]

These national committees consisted of representatives of the state and local parties. At the outset, the principle of state equality prevailed: one member from each state party. In the 1920s both parties expanded committee membership to two representatives from each state—one man and one woman. This revision clearly responded to the Nineteenth Amendment that denied states the power to discriminate according to sex in establishing voter qualifications.

In 1952 the Republican Party departed from the historical commitment to state equality as a representational principle. That year, its national convention voted to give ex officio national committee membership to party chairs from states that (1) supported the Republican nominee for president, (2) selected a majority of GOP House members and senators, or (3) selected a Republican governor. This reform gave added weight to those states that consistently voted Republican. Later, the GOP returned to the principle of state equality by designating all state party chairs as committee members. In addition, the District of Columbia, Guam, Puerto Rico, and the Virgin Islands were treated like states for representational purposes. Most recently, the Republicans added the Northern Mariana Islands to this list of nonstates whose parties warrant representation.

In the 1970s the Democrats abandoned state equality by adopting weighted representation. Their national com-

TABLE 17-2 **Composition of the National Party Committees, 2007**

	Number of Members
DEMOCRATIC NATIONAL COMMITTEE	
Chair and highest-ranking officer of opposite sex from each state and from District of Columbia, Puerto Rico, Guam, Virgin Islands, and American Samoa	110
Members apportioned to states on same basis as delegates to national convention (at least two per state)	200
Two additional members, a male and a female, from Guam, Virgin Islands, and American Samoa	6
Chair of Democratic Governors Conference and two additional governors (with gender diversity)	3
Democratic leader and one other member from each chamber of Congress (with gender diversity)	4
Officers of Democratic National Committee	9
Chair of National Conference of Democratic Mayors and two additional mayors (with gender diversity)	3
President of Young Democrats and two additional members (with gender diversity)	3
President of National Federation of Democratic Women and two additional members	3
Chair of Democratic County Officials and two additional members (with gender diversity)	3
Chair of Democratic Legislative Campaign Committee and two additional state legislators (with gender diversity)	3
Chair of National Democratic Municipal Officials Conference and two additional officials (with gender diversity)	3
President and vice president of College Democrats of America	2
Chair and vice chair of National Association of Democratic State Treasurers	2
Chair and vice chair of National Association of Democratic Lieutenant Governors	2
Chair and vice chair of Democratic Association of Secretaries of State	2
Chair of Democratic Attorneys General Association and one additional member, with gender diversity	2
Chair of Democratic Ethnic Coordinating Committee and one additional member, with gender diversity	2
Chair of Democratic Seniors Coordinating Council and one additional member (with gender diversity)	2
Additional members (up to 75)	75
Democrats Abroad has eight members who share the two votes allotted to Democrats Abroad	8
TOTAL	**447**
REPUBLICAN NATIONAL COMMITTEE	
National committeeman, national committeewoman, and the chair from each state and from American Samoa, District of Columbia, Guam, Northern Mariana, Puerto Rico, and Virgin Islands	168

SOURCES: The Charter and Bylaws of the Democratic Party of the United States, and the Rules of the Republican Party.

mittee's greatly expanded membership includes ex officio and gender-specified representatives from the state parties and affiliated party organizations as well. Table 17-2 compares the much larger Democratic National Committee (DNC) with the Republican National Committee (RNC), its GOP counterpart.

Although the convention formally designates the national committee, in practice it ratifies state-level decisions about membership. State parties use a variety of means for choosing their representatives, usually according to their own rules or state laws. In most states, the state convention selects them. Alternatively, the state committee, the national convention delegation, or the party voters through a primary may be authorized to do so. Members serve a four-year term beginning with adjournment of the national convention and ending with adjournment of the next convention.

Party rules currently stipulate the minimal frequency of meetings, annually for the DNC and semi-annually for the RNC. Typically, the party chair issues the call for the meeting. Party rules require the chair to call a special meeting when demanded by the specified portion of the mem-

bership: 25 percent for the DNC and at least sixteen members from at least sixteen states for the RNC.

The committee's major collective function is the election of officers, chief of which is the party chair. Otherwise, the committee has little to do. Most of its assigned functions are undertaken by the chair and headquarters staff, with the committee customarily authorizing and ratifying these decisions.

One noteworthy assignment is to fill vacancies that occur before the election in the nominations for president and vice president. If a convention's nomination is vacated for any reason, it falls to the national committee to meet and fill it. In 1972, when Democratic vice presidential nominee Thomas F. Eagleton withdrew, the Democratic National Committee, on the recommendation of presidential nomi-

TABLE 17-3 **National Party Chairs**

DEMOCRATIC PARTY			REPUBLICAN PARTY		
Name	State	Years of service	Name	State	Years of service
B. F. Hallett	Massachusetts	1848–1852	Edwin D. Morgan	New York	1856–1864
Robert McLane	Maryland	1852–1856	Henry J. Raymond	New York	1864–1866
David A. Smalley	Virginia	1856–1860	Marcus L. Ward	New Jersey	1866–1868
August Belmont	New York	1860–1872	William Claflin	Massachusetts	1868–1872
Augustus Schell	New York	1872–1876	Edwin D. Morgan	New York	1872–1876
Abram S. Hewitt	New York	1876–1877	Zachariah Chandler	Michigan	1876–1879
William H. Barnum	Connecticut	1877–1889	J. Donald Cameron	Pennsylvania	1879–1880
Calvin S. Brice	Ohio	1889–1892	Marshall Jewell	Connecticut	1880–1883
William F. Harrity	Pennsylvania	1892–1896	D. M. Sabin	Minnesota	1883–1884
James K. Jones	Arkansas	1896–1904	B. F. Jones	Pennsylvania	1884–1888
Thomas Taggart	Indiana	1904–1908	Matthew S. Quay	Pennsylvania	1888–1891
Norman E. Mack	New York	1908–1912	James S. Clarkson	Iowa	1891–1892
William F. McCombs	New York	1912–1916	Thomas H. Carter	Montana	1892–1896
Vance C. McCormick	Pennsylvania	1916–1919	Mark A. Hanna	Ohio	1896–1904
Homer S. Cummings	Connecticut	1919–1920	Henry C. Payne	Wisconsin	1904
George White	Ohio	1920–1921	George B. Cortelyou	New York	1904–1907
Cordell Hull	Tennessee	1921–1924	Harry S. New	Indiana	1907–1908
Clem Shaver	West Virginia	1924–1928	Frank H. Hitchcock	Massachusetts	1908–1909
John J. Raskob	Maryland	1928–1932	John F. Hill	Maine	1909–1912
James A. Farley	New York	1932–1940	Victor Rosewater	Nebraska	1912
Edward J. Flynn	New York	1940–1943	Charles D. Hilles	New York	1912–1916
Frank C. Walker	Pennsylvania	1943–1944	William R. Wilcox	New York	1916–1918
Robert E. Hannegan	Missouri	1944–1947	Will Hays	Indiana	1918–1921
J. Howard McGrath	Rhode Island	1947–1949	John T. Adams	Iowa	1921–1924
William M. Boyle Jr.	Missouri	1949–1951	William M. Butler	Massachusetts	1924–1928
Frank E. McKinney	Indiana	1951–1952	Hubert Work	Colorado	1928–1929
Stephen A. Mitchell	Illinois	1952–1954	Claudius H. Huston	Tennessee	1929–1930
Paul M. Butler	Indiana	1955–1960	Simeon D. Fess	Ohio	1930–1932
Henry M. Jackson	Washington	1960–1961	Everett Sanders	Indiana	1932–1934
John M. Bailey	Connecticut	1961–1968	Henry P. Fletcher	Pennsylvania	1934–1936
Lawrence F. O'Brien	Massachusetts	1968–1969	John Hamilton	Kansas	1936–1940
Fred Harris	Oklahoma	1969–1970	Joseph W. Martin Jr.	Massachusetts	1940–1942
Lawrence F. O'Brien	Massachusetts	1970–1972	Harrison E. Spangler	Iowa	1942–1944
Jean Westwood	Utah	1972	Herbert Brownell Jr.	New York	1944–1946
Robert Strauss	Texas	1972–1977	Carroll Reese	Tennessee	1946–1948

nee George McGovern, formally nominated R. Sargent Shriver for the second spot on the ticket. A somewhat similar situation had developed for the Democrats in 1860, when their vice presidential nominee declined the nomination and the national committee replaced him.

Chair and Other Officers

The national chairman or chairwoman presides over the committee and administers the party headquarters. The national chair occupies a highly visible and significant position within the party organization. *(See Table 17-3.)*

To the general public, the occupant of the national chair stands as a symbol and spokesperson for the party. To the president, the chair is a top-level presidential appointee who links White House and party and through whom the president traditionally has exercised considerable party leadership.[11]

The national committee formally elects its top officer. Traditionally, it did so at a meeting immediately after the national convention. This established the presumption that the chair's term of office was four years. In practice, few national party chairs have served that long, especially the chair of the party that lost the last presidential election.

In the 1980s both Republicans and Democrats departed from tradition and opted to elect their chairs after the presidential election instead of after the nominating convention, somewhat separating chair selection from the contest for the party's presidential nomination. The Republicans further established a two-year term for their chair, providing for an election after the midterm elections.

TABLE 17-3 *(Continued)*

DEMOCRATIC PARTY			REPUBLICAN PARTY		
Name	State	Years of service	Name	State	Years of service
Kenneth Curtis	Maine	1977–1978	Hugh D. Scott Jr.	Pennsylvania	1948–1949
John White	Texas	1978–1981	Guy George Gabrielson	New Jersey	1949–1952
Charles Manatt	California	1981–1985	Arthur E. Summerfield	Michigan	1952–1953
Paul Kirk	Massachusetts	1985–1989	C. Wesley Roberts	Kansas	1953
Ronald H. Brown	Washington, D.C.	1989–1993	Leonard W. Hall	New York	1953–1957
David Wilhelm	Illinois	1993–1994	H. Meade Alcorn Jr.	Connecticut	1957–1959
Christopher J. Dodd (general chair)	Connecticut	1995–1997	Thruston B. Morton	Kentucky	1959–1961
Donald Fowler	South Carolina	1995–1997	William E. Miller	New York	1961–1964
Roy Romer (general chair)	Colorado	1997–1999	Dean Burch	Arizona	1964–1965
Steven Grossman	Massachusetts	1997–1999	Ray C. Bliss	Ohio	1965–1969
Edward Rendell (general chair)	Pennsylvania	1999–2001	Rogers C. B. Morton	Maryland	1969–1971
Joe Andrew	Indiana	1999–2001	Robert Dole	Kansas	1971–1973
Terry McAuliffe	Virginia	2001–2005	George Bush	Texas	1973–1974
Howard Dean	Vermont	2005–	Mary Louise Smith	Iowa	1974–1977
			William Brock	Tennessee	1977–1981
			Richard Richards	Utah	1981–1983
			Paul D. Laxalt (general chair)	Nevada	1983–1986
			Frank Fahrenkopf	Nevada	1983–1989
			Lee Atwater (general chair)	South Carolina	1989–1991
			Clayton Yeutter	Nebraska	1991–1992
			Richard Bond	New York	1992–1993
			Haley Barbour	Mississippi	1993–1997
			James Nicholson	Colorado	1997–2001
			James Gilmore	Virginia	2001–2002
			Marc Racicot	Montana	2002–2003
			Edward Gillespie	District of Columbia	2003–2005
			Kenneth Mehlman	Maryland	2005–2007
			Mel Martinez (general chair)	Florida	2007–
			Robert M. "Mike" Duncan	Kentucky	2007–

SOURCE: Hugh A. Bone, *Party Committees and National Politics* (Seattle: University of Washington Press, 1958), 241–243. Updated by the author.

There is an important distinction between the status and activities of the national chair whose party nominee occupies the White House and the one whose party does not. The in-party's chairs serve under the party leadership of the president.

The chair is not the only officer selected by the national committee. The Democrats elect five vice chairs (three of whom are of the opposite sex of the chair), a treasurer, a secretary, a finance chair, and other appropriate officers as the committee deems necessary. The full committee is also empowered to choose an executive committee, determining its size, composition, and term of office.

The Republicans choose a co-chair of the opposite sex, along with eight vice chairs—a man and a woman from each of four different regional state associations: West, Midwest, Northeast, and South. They also select a secretary, treasurer, and such other officers as they desire. Other collective leadership structures include the chair's executive council and the executive committee, with party rules stipulating procedures for selection and responsibilities.

Headquarters

In the nineteenth century, party operations were conducted largely within the context of the convention and the presidential campaign.[12] The chief responsibilities of the committee and its chair were to prepare and conduct the quadrennial nominating convention and direct the ensuing presidential campaign. Once the nominations were completed, headquarters would be established, usually in New York City, and the campaign led by the party chair. After the election, the organization would largely disband. The committee would meet perhaps once a year; at other times the national party would exist in the person of the chair. The pace would pick up again when plans had to be made for the forthcoming convention.

In the 1920s both national parties established year-round headquarters operations with paid staff. The Republicans took the lead here and have continued to emphasize organizational development more than their Democratic counterparts. Initially, both parties rented office space in Washington, D.C. During the Nixon administration, the Republicans moved into their own building adjacent to the House office buildings on Capitol Hill. In the 1980s the Democrats did the same, opening their permanent offices just a few blocks away.

Both parties have expanded their staffs and scope of operations, which swell temporarily before presidential elections. In the intervening years, the staff size remains relatively high. According to political scientists Cornelius P. Cotter and John F. Bibby, since 1950 the Republicans have never had fewer than eighty paid employees and the Democrats never fewer than forty (these figures are for the national party headquarters only). The congressional parties also have campaign organizations, and occasionally the party headquarters will subsidize a White House employee. Overall, off-year staffing for both parties has averaged in excess of seventy.[13]

With this increased staff capacity, the national parties have been shifting away from their traditional presidency-related responsibilities toward party-building activities. But they continue to plan and conduct the national conventions. Each committee issues the convention call, which stipulates procedures for delegate apportionment and selection, along with temporary convention rules. And it designates the membership and leadership of preconvention committees and designates convention presiders and speakers. It establishes the site, date, and order of business, though with in-party committees the White House normally has a significant say in these determinations.

The national headquarters of each party also retains some presidential campaign responsibilities. The Democratic Party charter formally authorizes it to conduct that campaign.[14] The nominee's own campaign organization, however, typically assumes the brunt of the campaign effort, relegating the party organization to the periphery. Nevertheless, the operations of a contemporary presidential campaign are broad enough to occupy the time and energy of an expanded national committee staff throughout the fall campaign.

It is outside the arena of presidential politics, however, that party headquarters are now making increasingly significant contributions, primarily in campaign assistance and other services to the state and local parties. The national parties also are actively engaged in candidate recruitment. They offer training sessions and make available a wide variety of information and expertise for the benefit of the parties' nominees. These include research, polling, data processing, direct mail, consultants, and money in vast amounts.[15] Here again, the Republicans were the pioneers, initially under the leadership of Ray Bliss, party chair from 1965 to 1969. William Brock, chair from 1977 to 1981, emphasized the same approach. The Democrats have followed suit since the late 1970s.

Roles and Interactions with the White House

The traditional patterns of interaction between presidents and national party organizations emerged out of mutual needs. A presidential aspirant needed the party nomination to legitimize the candidacy. Further, a nominee needed the resources of the party organization to conduct the general election campaign. After a successful effort to elect its nominee, the party organization could then justifiably claim the fruits of federal patronage distributed through the executive to its loyal laborers.

During the past half-century, three important developments have altered the traditional nature of that relation-

Jean Westwood, left, was the first woman to head the Democratic National Committee; Ronald Brown, right, was the first African American to hold the post.

ship. The structure of the presidential campaign organization has changed, relegating the party organization to peripheral status; civil service has been extended, reducing the number of political patronage jobs; and the White House Office has been established and expanded, lessening the president's reliance on outside help.

Vast patronage resources once awaited the victorious party assuming control of the executive branch, but the extensive coverage of civil service has reduced drastically the number of political appointments. The remaining appointments are at such high and specialized levels that the party organization is less often able to provide qualified candidates.

Finally, the establishment and expansion of the White House Office have provided the president with an in-house assembly of loyalists willing and able to do the sorts of political chores previously delegated to the national party organization. Their presence, and the president's reliance on them, render the party organization less meaningful in presidential politics. *(See Chapter 22, Executive Office of the President: White House Office, Vol. II.)*

The president and the national party organization interact chiefly in selecting and deploying the party chair. Other avenues to interaction include managing party headquarters, establishing financial and organizational plans, arranging and running the convention, and managing the nominating and election campaigns.

Selection of the Party Chair

At the beginning of the twentieth century, custom and practice clearly dictated that the national committee defer to the party's presidential nominee in electing its postconvention chair. The usual procedure was for a delegation from the committee to call on the nominee to solicit a recommendation. The committee would then convene to ratify that choice. This practice initially developed to tie the nominee's campaign with the national party effort. It had the effect of placing the party organization leadership under the nominee's authority.

After the election, the president-elect could continue to claim that prerogative. Under the revised calendar currently in effect, the party that won the presidency in November defers to its victorious nominee in selecting its chair in January. Therefore, for the party in power the position of chair remains in effect a presidential appointment. The incumbent serves at the pleasure of the president, with the national committee compliantly endorsing the president's choice.

For presidential party leadership, the significance of the recent bipartisan reforms realigning and limiting the term of the party chair is limited. Deferring the formal takeover of the party organization by the presidential nominee until after a victory in the presidential election enables the party organization to prevent an unsuccessful nominee from asserting control over the organization. For the victor's party, however, these reforms have not fundamentally reoriented established patterns and practices.

In the 1970s both major parties elevated their chair into a full-time and salaried position. This action appears to have been in response to an accelerating tendency to place legislators in that office, making it a part-time job. The change both contributed to and resulted from the increasing institutionalization of the national organization, whose members consider themselves ill-served by part-time leaders with primary loyalties to other elements within the party. Moreover, with the increasing amount of responsibility and activity located at the national level, the party headquarters ostensibly requires full-time leadership.

Since the imposition of these rules, there have been several circumventions of them, taking the form of the designation of an elected official as general chair while naming someone else as the titular but subordinate chair. Two Republican presidents (Reagan and George W. Bush) and a Democratic president (Clinton) installed incumbent U.S. senators (Paul D. Laxalt, R-Nev., by Reagan, Christopher J. Dodd, D-Conn., by Clinton, and Mel R. Martinez, R-Fla., by George W. Bush) as general chairs. Clinton subsequently named an incumbent governor, Roy Romer of Colorado, as general chair. When incoming president George W. Bush wanted fellow governor James Gilmore of Virginia to become party chair, with a full year remaining in his gubernatorial term, the Republican National Committee simply waived the rule. Thus developments during the past two decades suggest that these institutionalizing efforts by the national party organization cannot withstand presidential will to the contrary.

Backgrounds. Traditionally, the eligibility requirements for the position of national party chair have been loose, affording the president considerable discretion. Presidents typically have recruited party chairs from three overlapping categories: state party leaders, officeholders, and the preconvention campaign organizations of the presidential nominee. George H. W. Bush, a former House member who headed the Republican Party in the last two years of the Nixon administration, has been the only national chair to date who has gone on to become president. Another former GOP chair, Sen. Robert J. "Bob" Dole, won the presidential nomination in 1996 but lost the fall general election contest. *(See box, The Party Chair as Candidate for National Office, p. 891.)*

Presidential nominees and incumbents have frequently looked to the ranks of the state party organizations in choosing party chairs. Among former state party leaders

chosen while their party controlled the White House after World War II were Republicans H. Meade Alcorn Jr., Mary Louise Smith, Richard Richards, and Frank Fahrenkopf; Democrats Robert E. Hannegan, J. Howard McGrath, Frank E. McKinney, John M. Bailey, and Donald Fowler. Such state party leaders have often already been members of the national committee they are being tapped to head.

Some national chairs have had a congressional connection. Post–World War II chairs of the in-party who had congressional experience before or during their party leadership service included Republicans Leonard W. Hall, Thruston B. Morton, Rogers C. B. Morton, Bob Dole, George H. W. Bush, and general chairs Paul Laxalt and Mel Martinez, and Democrats Howard McGrath and general chair Christopher Dodd.

Apart from Congress, the national-level political office with which the most chairs have been associated has been that of postmaster general, a position abolished when the U.S. Postal Service was created in 1971. The list of chairs who had served previously, subsequently, or simultaneously as head of the former Post Office Department consists of Democrats James A. Farley, Frank C. Walker, Robert Hannegan, and Lawrence F. O'Brien, and Republicans Marshall Jewell, Henry C. Payne, George B. Cortelyou, Harry S. New, Frank H. Hitchcock, Will Hays, and Arthur E. Summerfield.

Gubernatorial linkages have appeared sporadically through the years. Indeed, the two most recent presidents, Bill Clinton and George W. Bush, themselves former governors, have identified gubernatorial colleagues as their choices for national party chairs: Democrat Roy Romer of Colorado (general chair, Clinton) and Republican James Gilmore of Virginia (Bush). In addition, since World War II four former governors have held the national chairmanship of the in-party: Republicans Paul Laxalt (Nevada) and Mark Racicot (Montana), and Democrats Howard McGrath (Rhode Island) and Kenneth Curtis (Maine).

President Clinton's choice of Edward Rendell, mayor of Philadelphia, to succeed Romer as general chair brought a newly elected official to the ranks of incumbent party chairs. It also constituted an unusual selection of a local government leader to head the national party.

Recruits of recent years from preconvention campaign organizations included Republican Lee Atwater (George H. W. Bush), Democrat David Wilhelm (Clinton), and Republican Ken Mehlman (George W. Bush), who came to the national committee after service on the White House staff. Another increasingly prominent background for chairs is that of professional political consultant. These new players in electoral politics have increasingly superseded traditional party managers in the conduct of election campaigns. Their ranks include Atwater, Wilhelm, and Ed Gillespie (George W. Bush).

THE PARTY CHAIR AS CANDIDATE FOR NATIONAL OFFICE

Traditionally, the national party chair performed in the arena of organizational politics and eschewed personal participation in electoral politics at the presidential level. Thus when Democratic national chair James A. Farley ran for the 1940 presidential nomination, it was a major and singular departure from established practice. Since 1960, however, the incumbent national party chair frequently has figured in speculation surrounding the composition of the party's presidential ticket. This connection has taken three forms: (1) a chair was available for the vice presidential nomination; (2) the party chair position was offered as a consolation prize for a loser in the vice presidential sweepstakes; and (3) a former party chair was included in the field of contenders for the party's presidential nomination.

These modern patterns first emerged in 1960 when Sen. Thruston B. Morton of Kentucky, the Republican national chair, was a finalist on nominee Richard Nixon's list of vice presidential prospects. Passed over in favor of former senator Henry Cabot Lodge Jr. (Mass.), Morton retained the chairmanship.

On the Democratic side in 1960, nominee John F. Kennedy placed Sen. Henry M. Jackson of Washington on his short list of potential running mates. After he chose Texas senator Lyndon B. Johnson, Kennedy tapped Jackson to be the Democratic National Committee chair for the duration of the campaign. When Johnson's nomination met with vocal opposition at the convention, the Kennedy camp sent word to Johnson that he could have the party chair job if he declined the offer of the vice presidential nomination.

In 1964 Republican nominee Barry M. Goldwater named as his running mate the incumbent national party chair, Rep. William E. Miller of New York. As of 2007, Miller remained the only incumbent chair ever named to a major party ticket.

The year 1968 marked the return of Richard Nixon to the Republicans' presidential ticket. Nixon seriously considered Rep. Rogers C. B. Morton of Maryland, younger brother of Thruston, as his vice presidential partner, before settling on Maryland governor Spiro T. Agnew. When a vacancy occurred in the party chair after the general election, Nixon recommended Rogers Morton for the post.

In the Democratic contest that year, Sen. Fred Harris of Oklahoma lost out to Sen. Edmund S. Muskie of Maine as Hubert H. Humphrey's choice of running mate. Harris then unsuccessfully sought the party chair post, which on Humphrey's suggestion went to Lawrence F. O'Brien. Harris's persistence paid off when he was named chair in January 1969 amid speculation that he was positioning himself for a future presidential bid.

During the 1972 convention, O'Brien figured prominently in speculation about George McGovern's vice presidential spot before it went to Sen. Thomas F. Eagleton of Missouri. When Eagleton resigned the nomination shortly afterward, O'Brien again was mentioned as a possible choice, but the vice presidential slot went to R. Sargent Shriver.

When President Nixon resigned in 1974, Gerald R. Ford became president, creating a vacancy in the vice presidency. Ford seriously considered nominating George H. W. Bush, then the Republican national chair, but instead Ford chose New York governor Nelson A. Rockefeller. Ford dumped Rockefeller from the 1976 ticket, replacing him with a former national chair, Sen. Robert "Bob" J. Dole of Kansas. One of the people Ford passed over, former Texas governor John B. Connally, was offered the party chair as a consolation prize, but Connally rejected the offer. The Democratic presidential field that year included former party chair Harris.

The 1980 Republican nominating contest featured the candidacies of two former party chairs, Bush and Dole. After both lost out to Ronald Reagan and Bush became Reagan's running mate, the ticket's victory made Bush the first former party chair to be elected vice president.

In 1988, with Reagan's second term due to expire, former party chairs Bush and Dole resumed their presidential rivalry. Early in the campaign season rumors had former senator Paul D. Laxalt of Nevada, who held the position of general chair of the Republican Party from 1983 through 1986, as a possible contender for the GOP nomination, but Laxalt never entered the fray. Bush prevailed, and his November victory made him also the first former party chair to be elected president.

In 1992 the Democratic presidential nomination went to Arkansas governor Bill Clinton, who had been prominently mentioned as a possibility to chair the Democratic National Committee a decade earlier and who did chair the Democratic Leadership Council in 1990–1991. Incumbent party chair Ronald H. Brown figured in speculation about the vice presidential nomination, which went to Sen. Al Gore of Tennessee.

In 1996 Senator Dole became the second former national party chair to win the Republican presidential nomination, following in the footsteps of his successor as chair of the Republican National Committee, George H. W. Bush. In 2005, after losing the Democratic presidential nomination to John F. Kerry, former Vermont governor Howard Dean became the party's chair.

The emergence of the persistent connection between the party chair and the national ticket was rooted in the practice from the late 1950s through the mid-1970s of naming House and Senate incumbents as national party chairs. The visibility of the office made it attractive to electoral figures who sought the role of party spokesperson.

The decision by both parties in the 1970s to make the chair a full-time position seemingly diminished this electoral connection. On several occasions, however, recent presidents have circumvented this practice by naming incumbent senators and governors as party chairs, thus potentially reinstating the linkage. Most have held the title of general chair, serving alongside the national chair. But in the modern media age, even the nonelected officials who serve as party chair have heightened public visibility, which promises to make the connection between the party chair and the national ticket an enduring one. Indeed, in 2007 as the 2008 presidential campaign season got under way, two former national party chairs identified themselves as possible candidates: Democratic senator Christopher Dodd of Connecticut, and former Republican governor James Gilmore of Virginia.

The early chairs were often men of considerable wealth. Although sizable personal fortunes have not been a disqualification in recent years, they are no longer quite so common. Until the 1970s the party chair was exclusively the province of white males. Democrat Jean Westwood broke this pattern in 1972, followed by Republican Mary Louise Smith in 1974. The Democrats also shattered precedent in 1989 and chose an African American, Ronald H.

Brown, as chair. Only Smith chaired the incumbent president's party.

The average tenure for post–World War II national chairs of the party controlling the White House is approximately two and a half years. Thus virtually all presidents have the opportunity to interact with the national party in selecting the national chair. Among modern presidents, only Lyndon B. Johnson never chose a party chair. *(See "Lyndon B. Johnson," p. 927.)*

Customarily, when a vacancy exists, perhaps at the instigation of the president, the national committee sends a delegation of its members to call on the president at the White House to be informed of the president's choice. The White House floats trial balloons before the official visit. The national committee then convenes to elect that person. From that point on, the national committee's interaction with the president typically is limited to occasional presidential addresses and receptions scheduled in conjunction with regular meetings of the committee.

As the leader of the party organization, the party chair unquestionably holds a position highly symbolic in value, especially for those activists who make up the party organization at all levels. Its substantive significance varies considerably according to the expectations of the nominee or president and the orientations of the designated chair.

Patterns in Recruitment. In examining patterns in the recruitment of national party chairs, the paramount considerations are the timing of the selection and whether the party controls the White House. For more than a century, party chairs were routinely chosen in the wake of the nominating conventions, although frequent between-convention vacancies required replacements. The recent realignment of the terms of the national party chairs, beginning in January after the November presidential election and lasting two years for the Republicans and four for the Democrats, introduces a new structure for recruiting party chairs.

Within the party controlling the White House, the president typically dominates the process, unless that incumbent is a lame duck whose successor as party nominee has already been designated. In that case the nominee assumes leadership in selecting the chair, and nominees of both parties have done so. The national committee, nominally authorized to choose its chair, actually does so only when the vacancy occurs between conventions when the party does not control the White House.

Party chairs chosen by nonincumbent presidential nominees soon after the convention tended to be chosen for reasons directly related to the presidential campaign. Typically, they fell into two broad and potentially overlapping categories: personal loyalists from the preconvention campaign organizations or state organization leaders who had delivered crucial delegate support to the nominee. In recruiting a personal loyalist, the nominee rewarded a trusted associate while taking steps to ensure the responsiveness of the party machinery and stamping a personal imprint on it. For state party leaders, the position of national chair often served as a bargaining gambit, offered as a reward for assistance in securing a hotly contested nomination.

Franklin Roosevelt's 1932 selection of James Farley embodies both patterns. Farley was simultaneously Roosevelt's preconvention campaign manager and the leader of the powerful New York state Democratic Party organization.

Nominees traditionally used the prerogative of naming the party chair to cultivate or mollify important party or electoral constituencies. Several demographic variables such as region, ethnicity, religion, and gender came into play here. Nominees sometimes saw in the naming of the party chair an opportunity or a responsibility to recognize and represent a regional center of party power.

For more than three decades in the middle of the twentieth century, every chair of the Democratic Party was an Irish Catholic. This pattern rewarded that powerful constituency within the party organization. Also, it compensated for the absence of a Roman Catholic on the party's presidential ticket between the nominations of Al Smith in 1928 and John Kennedy in 1960.

Democratic nominee George S. McGovern's 1972 selection of Jean Westwood, the first woman to chair a national party committee, reflected two important developments in presidential nominating politics that had relevance for the position of party chair. The first was the growing influence of women in party affairs. The second was the emergence of new bargaining units at the convention transcending the state party delegations—namely, caucuses that represented pressure groups in the larger political order.

Long before the recent rescheduling of the term of the chair, distancing it from the national convention, presidential nominees frequently put aside their prerogative of designating the party chair in favor of retaining the incumbent. In fulfilling their responsibilities, party chairs such as Paul Butler (D, 1956), Thruston Morton (R, 1960), Ray Bliss (R, 1968), Robert Strauss (D, 1976), William Brock (R, 1980), and Charles Manatt (D, 1984) developed strong and vocal personal followings, which provided pressures and incentives for their retention, in recognition of jobs well done and in the interests of party unity.

A final consideration taken into account by the nominee in the selection of the party chair was the primary role anticipated for the chair in the upcoming general election campaign. The traditional role was one of management, concentrating energies and talents on problems of campaign organization and strategy. Subsequently, the role became one of spokesperson, highly visible but largely separated from the centers of campaign decision making.

Presidents-elect and incumbents have tended to make their designations of party chairs for reasons less immediately connected to the presidential campaign. Again, the expectations regarding the role of the party chair greatly affect recruitment. A general distinction can be drawn between chairs recruited primarily as party builders versus those assigned the role of party spokesperson.

Chairs have come from diverse political backgrounds, with state organization leaders and incumbent national legislators predominating. Generally, the state organization leaders have dominated the party-builder category, and the national legislators have acted as party spokespersons. Although these chairs typically have been identified with the political causes and campaigns of their presidents, few qualify as close personal associates.

Changing Role of the Party Chair

The role of the in-party chair has undergone major changes during the past sixty-five years. Once, the national chair was a central actor in presidential politics. By and large, this is no longer the case. Chairs of both the in-party and the out-party today are far more involved in directing ongoing party-building endeavors—national, state, and local—than was previously typical. This shift has come about because of changes in both the presidency and the political parties.

In the past, the national chair customarily directed the party campaign, of which the presidential race was the central feature. The expectation of tying together the overall party effort and specifically the presidential campaign underlay the development of the custom whereby the national committee solicits the presidential nominee's recommendation for its chair. Operating out of party headquarters, the president's choice would direct the campaign.

More recently, the presidential nominees have instead developed and relied on personal campaign organizations. The reasons include strategic considerations related to declining party identification in the electorate, federal election laws effectively mandating the establishment of separate organizations, and, most important, changes in the nature of nominating campaigns.

Years ago, nominating campaigns were low-key efforts designed to elicit the support of a relative handful of party chieftains, who in turn controlled state delegations at the convention. Since the advent of primary contests to select delegates, prospective nominees have had to develop full-scale campaign organizations well in advance of the convention.

The road to the convention nomination now proceeds through delegate-selection primaries in more than thirty states, where campaign organizations are tried and tested. The eventual winner normally is inclined to continue to operate through that organizational vehicle in the general election campaign that follows.

This development relegates the national organization to the periphery of the campaign effort. It similarly places the chair outside the inner circle of campaign decision makers. To be sure, the reelection campaign of an incumbent president may well feature considerable integration of the national party headquarters into the campaign organization, but the national party chair's role clearly remains subordinated to that of campaign officials and White House aides. Thus a major role traditionally performed by the party chair has been rendered negligible.

At the outset, national chairs had important patronage responsibilities. The chair claimed the spoils of electoral victory for the party loyalists. The traditional association between the chair and the postmaster generalship pertained directly to this task, because the Post Office Department provided an abundance of government jobs to be distributed among the party faithful. But with the eventual restructuring of the Post Office Department and the establishment and expansion of the merit system of federal hiring, the role of the party chair as patronage dispenser became passé.

Party chairs in days gone by also served their presidents as key political advisers. They kept chief executives in touch with the perspectives of their counterparts in statehouses and city halls. But modern presidents have perceived much less need for such advice. They now have a sizable personal staff of aides they can rely on as advisers and intermediaries with other political leaders. Polling organizations provide presidents with an abundance of data about the public pulse. Here again, the traditional role of the chair has been supplanted.

Developments within the party organization also have worked to distance the chair from the presidential inner circle. Party chairs have always operated under a norm of neutrality toward competing candidacies for the presidential nomination. Usually, this norm was conveniently ignored by chairs of the party in power, who were serving as presidential appointees and pursuing the interests of their sponsors. As the parties have become more bureaucratic and institutional, the expectations regarding neutrality are growing stronger. In 1999 incoming DNC general chair Edward Rendell had already endorsed the 2000 presidential candidacy of Vice President Al Gore. To conform to modern expectations, Rendell withdrew his formal endorsement of Gore. Federal election laws reinforce the pressure for the chair to remain impartial.[16] As a result, modern party chairs are less likely to occupy the role of key presidential adviser.

Another of the chair's traditional roles—that of fundraiser—endures today, but in an altered form that is generally less focused on presidential politics. At the same time, modern campaign finance practices have strengthened the link between the president and the national party organization. Nineteenth-century chairs tended to be wealthy individuals who made major personal contributions to the presidential campaign, bankrolled a limited party operation that supplemented the campaign, and prevailed upon their similarly disposed friends and associates to do likewise.

National party headquarters operations have expanded beyond the capacity of the chair to underwrite them personally and the growing costs of presidential campaigns are beyond the means of a relative handful of donors, even those of immense personal wealth. Furthermore, federal election laws limit the financial contributions of individuals. They also provide for public funding of presidential campaigns. *(See "The Campaign Finance System," p. 261, in Chapter 5.)*

However, the "soft money" loophole in the federal regulation of campaign finance, which was designed to encourage party building, enhanced the fund-raising role of the national party committee and its chair, and it strengthened the link between the president and the national party organization. The new reality emerged in the mid-1990s as President Clinton geared up for his successful reelection effort. The president and his White House political operatives worked closely and controversially with and through the Democratic National Committee, chaired by Donald Fowler, to raise and spend funds outside the regulatory framework in a manner that clearly benefited the president's reelection.

For example, in 1995 the national Democrats began running generic campaign advertisements designed to put the Republicans on the defensive. This effort continued on into the early months of 1996, while the Republicans contenders for the presidential nomination were focused on fighting each other. It picked up steam in the interim between Sen. Bob Dole's selection as the Republican nominee and the Republican National Convention, a period when the Dole campaign had reached the spending limits imposed on it before the infusion of public funds for the general election. By that time, the Dole campaign was reeling under the partisan assault, and Clinton coasted to an easy victory.

The advent of soft money invigorated and redirected the traditional fund-raising assignment for the national party, but campaign finance reform in 2002 curtailed its use. Nevertheless, today's party chairs are increasingly likely to direct their scarce energies and resources toward fund raising. Alternatively, they may delegate much of it to subordinates. Both national committees have for many years established finance committees—the Republicans since the 1930s and the Democrats some two decades later. The chairs of these committees, while under the authority of the national chair, operate separately, relieving the chair of many traditional fund-raising responsibilities. In addition, the congressional party organizations maintain autonomous fund-raising operations for congressional campaigns.

As these traditional roles have diminished or been refocused in importance, other time-honored functions have attained heightened significance. Three such roles

identified by political scientists Cornelius Cotter and Bernard Hennessy are those of *image-maker, hell-raiser,* and *administrator.*[17]

- Image-Maker. Public relations has always been a major responsibility of the party chair. In the nineteenth century, many national chairs had newspaper backgrounds. Although this has been much less the case since World War I, a sensitivity to and a flair for public relations continue to be expected of the chair.

To promote a positive public image of the party and to position its actions and objectives in the best possible light, the chair personally assumes the role of party spokesperson. Such a chair will regularly make the rounds of the venerable network television interview shows such as NBC's *Meet the Press* and CBS's *Face the Nation,* along with the proliferating cable television presentations such as CNN's *Crossfire* and Fox's *Fox News Sunday.* National chairs are available for interviews and comments to print reporters as well.

- Hell-Raiser. The chair as hell-raiser is the partisan's partisan, seeking to satisfy the expectations of the party faithful by flailing away at the opposition party and righteously defending the party against detractors' assaults. Presidents often rely on their party chairs to emphasize this party leadership role so that they can appear above partisan battles. Senator Dole enthusiastically took on this task for President Nixon in his 1972 campaign against Democratic challenger George McGovern.
- Administrator. As administrators, party chairs supervise the activities of the national headquarters—a role that has grown as the headquarters have expanded. The current expectation that a chair's position be full-time and salaried also serves to emphasize the administrative aspects of the job.

Opportunities for Interaction with the White House

Installed in office by the president, and serving at the president's pleasure, national chairs encounter their party leaders in circumstances that vary considerably in both frequency and substantive significance. The tendency is toward infrequent meetings in rather formal, ceremonial settings. To be sure, President Truman had a standing appointment every Wednesday afternoon with the Democratic national chair to discuss party politics. Somewhat similarly, President Dwight Eisenhower genuinely expected his party chair to be the "political expert" in his delegation of administrative responsibilities.

Still, a facetious anecdote shared by Senator Dole about his tenure as party chair captures well the contemporary character of the relationship. Dole tells of receiving a telephone call from the White House, informing him that his long-standing request to see President Nixon was about to be granted. All he had to do was to turn his television set to the proper channel to receive the president's scheduled campaign address.[18]

Cabinet Meetings. Although no one has served simultaneously as party chair and as a cabinet secretary since 1947, several party chairs have arranged to attend cabinet meetings either regularly or intermittently. At these sessions, party chairs can be kept informed of the administration's public policy proposals, can assess their partisan ramifications, and can seek to present the party's perspective on them. In addition, cabinet meetings can provide the chair with opportunities to request and establish clearance procedures for political appointments. In general, although the party chair's physical presence at cabinet meetings undoubtedly affords an avenue of access to the president, the value is more symbolic than substantive.

President Lyndon Johnson talks with Democratic Party chair John Bailey in the Oval Office in 1968. Serving for seven and one-half years, Bailey had the longest tenure among the post–World War II national party chairs.

White House Staff Meetings. Some recent party chairs have requested and been invited to attend regular meetings between the president and top-level White House staff assistants. This request reflects the chair's recognition that the White House Office has become the epicenter of presidential party leadership. In addition, party chairs often journey to the White House for regular sessions with presidential staff in the absence of the president. On such occasions, the presidential staff's intermediary role between the president and the party chair is heightened.

Congressional Leadership Meetings. The inclination of some modern presidents to name incumbent legislators as party chair introduced a new arena for interaction—the weekly congressional leadership meetings. Although none of these chairs was a ranking member of the party congressional hierarchy, several of them (along with chairs who were not members of Congress) requested permission to attend sessions where legislative strategy was being planned and progress monitored. Here, the presence of the party chair enables coordination of legislative activities with the party's organs of party policy and publicity and provides a forum to bring the chair's point of view directly to the president.

Headquarters Management. Another form of interaction between the White House and the national party is the management of the national party headquarters. Although headquarters management would appear to be the primary responsibility of the chair, few chairs have devoted much

personal attention to this task. Other responsibilities with higher priority and other institutional and professional affiliations typically conflict with that of administrator. The accepted procedure is for the chair to exercise discretion in delegating managerial authority to a chosen subordinate. The chair then remains free in varying degrees to engage in other activities.

On several occasions in recent years, the president or White House aides have deployed at party headquarters a presidential agent with managerial authority. Interventions have been most likely when the chair has simultaneously held an elective office and thus served in a part-time capacity. Such a situation developed during the Truman presidency with the assignment of Truman's old Missouri political assistant William Boyle to a management position at the Democratic National Committee then headed by Sen. Howard McGrath.

A more recent instance of this practice occurred in 2001. With Republican national chair James Gilmore having a year left in his term as Virginia's governor, President George W. Bush placed Jack Oliver, a longtime personal loyalist, at party headquarters as deputy chair.

Financial and Organizational Collaboration

The national party organization engages in a great deal of congenial accommodation in behalf of the White House. Routinely, the White House relies on the financial and organizational structures of the national committee to sponsor what are really White House programs. For example, the White House bills the national committee for travel and living expenses incurred by the president while attending to party leadership responsibilities. Such situations include personal campaigning, campaigning for other party candidates, and appearances at party-sponsored affairs such as fund-raisers, rallies, and the national convention. Occasionally, the national committee can be prevailed upon to carry on its payroll individuals who actually work at the White House. In recent years the national party's contemporary capacity to raise and spend soft money on the president's indirect behalf, and the president's participation in such party fund raising, became the most significant features of this collaboration. However, the Bipartisan Campaign Reform Act of 2002 prohibited the national party committees from accepting this sort of soft money contributions.

During the Clinton presidency, the DNC energetically and visibly solicited public support for presidential policy initiatives. It established a "war room" to provide assistance during the budget battles that dominated Clinton's first year in office, and it similarly, though less successfully, mobilized support for his health care initiative during the second year. George W. Bush established a similar structure and process in his unsuccessful 2005 effort to advance social security reform.

Convention Arrangements and Management

An impending national nominating convention provides the setting for a great deal of interaction between the White House and the national party organization. Although the national committee is responsible for arranging and conducting the convention, it does so under the close supervision of the president, even when the incumbent is not a candidate for reelection.

When the party is out of power, the national committee is supposed to be neutral toward competing candidacies for the nomination. When an incumbent president is seeking the nomination, however, the party headquarters usually strongly supports that candidacy.

Even when the incumbent is not a candidate, White House concern and interest about the party's choice abound. Typically, the retiring president's aides monitor convention arrangements and become deeply involved in maneuvers during the proceedings. In past years, these agents have afforded outgoing presidents considerable influence at the convention. Their presence, and perhaps that of the president, can create tension with their counterparts in the campaign organization of the nominee.

The national committee formally establishes the site of the convention, but the president's preference, if not volunteered, is routinely solicited and accepted. *(See "National Party Conventions," p. 295, in Chapter 5.)* According to Nixon

campaign aide Jeb Stuart Magruder, for personal and political reasons Nixon insisted that the 1972 Republican national convention meet in San Diego, California. The White House sent Magruder, an official of the Committee for the Reelection of the President, to Denver, Colorado, in July 1971 to monitor the meeting of the Republican national committee's site selection committee. The committee was not inclined to choose San Diego, but party chair Bob Dole informed the members that "if the president wanted the convention in San Diego, it would just have to be in San Diego." [19] Although the committee obediently selected San Diego, the convention site subsequently had to be shifted to Miami Beach, Florida. The change took place amid concerns about inadequate hotel facilities in San Diego and fears that security arrangements there would be inadequate to deal with the expected onslaught of anti–Vietnam War demonstrators at the convention site. In 1992 the Republican national convention met in Houston, the home of incumbent President George H. W. Bush.

Similarly, the convention date can be manipulated to the benefit of the incumbent. It is surely no coincidence that modern conventions expected to nominate incumbent presidents have all been scheduled relatively late in the summer, after those of the opposition party. For a unified party led by an incumbent president, a late convention builds momentum for the upcoming general election campaign.

When the president is a candidate, considerable White House effort is usually evident in the preparation of the party platform. Such participation ensures that the president's policies receive party endorsement, equates the party's stance on issues with that of the president, and precludes significant divergence toward an independent position. Even when the president is not a candidate, the presidential presence is likely to hover over platform deliberations. Beyond party policy, recent presidents and White House staffs have concerned themselves with administrative details of convention management, to the point of preparing minute-by-minute scenarios.

Traditionally, the national party has convened only in connection with the nomination of the presidential ticket. In 1974, however, the out-of-power Democrats met in Kansas City for an issues conference midway through the presidential term. Four years later, with Democrat Jimmy Carter in the White House, a similar conference was held in Memphis, which provided an unprecedented opportunity for interaction between the White House and the national party. On this occasion, encountering substantial anti-Carter sentiment in the ranks of the delegates, the White House and presidential agents at the national party headquarters designed and controlled the agenda. They mounted a monitoring operation on the conference floor to ensure that the administration's positions would prevail against intraparty challenges. The effort duplicated the typical pattern of White

House surveillance and supervision repeatedly demonstrated at the nominating conventions. The Democrats have not held a midterm convention since 1982.

Presidential exercises of convention leadership have produced a long string of successes for presidents who wanted to be renominated. Not since Chester A. Arthur in 1884 has an incumbent president who has sought his party's nomination been denied it, and not since Franklin Pierce in 1856 has an elected incumbent been denied.[20] Indeed, most of Arthur's successors have been nominated with ease. Although both Truman and Johnson were constitutionally eligible to seek a second elected presidential term, both chose not to in the face of growing opposition.

In 1976, 1980, and 1992 serious nomination challenges were mounted against the incumbents. Ronald Reagan's contest against President Gerald R. Ford, Sen. Edward M. Kennedy's against President Carter, and Patrick Buchanan's against President Bush suggest that post-1968 reforms in the methods of selecting convention delegates may offset partially the incumbent's traditional advantages. These reforms drastically reduced the state party organizations' control over delegate selection and increased popular participation in that process. Customarily, an incumbent president seeking the nomination could count on the support of the state party leaders. They had been the beneficiaries of presidential favors and attention and would fear presidential reprisal should support be withheld. Thus, even an unpopular president could be quite secure in the face of a nomination challenge. Recent reforms, however, deprive modern presidents of this bulwark of potential support, leaving them potentially more vulnerable to intraparty challengers able to capitalize on popular disenchantment.

Even before the rules changes of the 1980s, which moved the selection of party chair from after the convention to after the general election, incumbent presidents were less inclined than nonincumbent nominees to replace the national chairs. They usually retained the current chair at least through the general election. Put differently, incumbent presidents expecting renomination installed their choices as party chairs well in advance of the nominating convention and retained them in its successful wake.

Presidential Election Campaigns

Journalist Theodore H. White observed that a presidential campaign "starts with a candidate, a handful of men, a theme and a plan. By November of election year it has enlisted hundreds of thousands of volunteers, politicians, state staffs, national staffs, media specialists and has become an enterprise." [21] A key question is: What is the relationship of the national party organization to the presidential campaign?

Traditionally, that role was central. National party committees came into being in the mid–nineteenth century to provide direction to the presidential campaign. Party chairs customarily served as campaign managers. Indeed, the practice of allowing the presidential nominee to name the party chair developed to facilitate integration of the presidential campaign with the party effort.

The campaign manager and a handful of key associates would set up shop at the headquarters of the national party. The party organization provided the nominee with the potent party symbol legitimizing the candidacy. Further, it made available the personnel necessary for the labor-intensive campaign that had to be waged.

More recently, however, presidential nominees have tended instead to establish autonomous campaign organizations, headquartered separately from the national party. Several factors account for this development. Strategic considerations can turn a campaign away from the party organizations. A nominee representing the minority party in the electorate, for example, might prefer to maintain some distance between the candidacy and the party effort in hopes of attracting broader support. Republican Nixon's 1960 and 1968 campaigns took this approach.

On the Democratic side, the relative autonomy of Adlai E. Stevenson's 1952 campaign resulted in part from his ongoing status as governor of Illinois, necessitating the establishment of campaign headquarters in Springfield, the state capital. The Stevenson campaign also wanted to distance itself symbolically from the "mess in Washington," the home base of Democratic president Harry Truman and the national party headquarters.

More recently, in both 1992 and 2000 nominees who were incumbent governors, Democrat Bill Clinton of Arkansas and Republican George W. Bush of Texas, set up official campaign headquarters in their respective state capitals, Little Rock and Austin. Technological developments in communications and transportation facilitate such "outsider" strategies.

Modern presidential nominees seek to appeal to an electorate that is less and less dependent on partisan sources and structures for political information, economic employment, and social services. Moreover, contemporary partisan attachments increasingly appear linked to ideological orientations, amid heightening electoral realignment and polarization. Even when nominees make strongly partisan electoral appeals, they are wary and disinclined to rely primarily on the party organization to carry them to victory.

Modern communications and transportation also have altered the character of election campaigns. Television brings a candidate into living rooms throughout the country. Jet airplanes allow an office seeker to cross the country both rapidly and comfortably. Candidates now can wage far more individualistic efforts than they could previously, and with far less need to rely on the party.

From a different standpoint, changes in the rules governing presidential nominations and elections have contributed to this shift toward more autonomous campaigns. The expansion of presidential primaries has made the coveted presidential nomination increasingly attainable through an appeal directly to the party electorate rather than through the party organization. Indeed, recent nominating conventions have served less as decision-making bodies than as coronations for the party's nominee, already chosen in the fragmented and decentralized delegate selection contests.

This development contributes to autonomy in the campaign organization, because to run in the primaries candidates must assemble an effective campaign staff well before the nominating convention. During the preconvention period, unless an incumbent president is seeking the nomination, the party organization is expected to be neutral toward competing candidacies, which precludes integration of the party and the campaign staffs. Yet after the convention the tested campaign vehicle of the victor remains intact. This both complicates integration and makes it relatively unnecessary.

Finally, federal election laws enacted in the 1970s require a separate campaign organization for a candidate to qualify for public funds. Thus today the likelihood of the traditional sort of integrated campaign, conducted under the auspices of the party apparatus, is virtually nil. In 1996 and 2000 party committees received abundant contributions (soft money) that were spent in the presidential campaign. As a result, the reinvigorated party organization played a significant, but nevertheless peripheral, campaign role. Campaign finance reform designed to restrict soft money as yet does not appear to have undermined the national party organizations' resurgent status in presidential campaign fund-raising. Neither has it fundamentally altered their tangential relationship to autonomous campaign organizations.

All in all, no longer does the presidential campaign provide the context for interaction initiating the president-to-be's leadership relationship with the national party organization. The other traditions on which the relationship was based—political operations and patronage—also have eroded. The national party organization has become increasingly superfluous in presidential politics.

State and Local Party Organizations

The fifty state and countless county and subcounty units of the political parties vary widely. Statewide, the structural components typically replicate those at the national level: convention, committee, chair, and, in recent years, headquarters staff.[22] At the lower levels, the structure persists, though usually with the omission of headquarters staffs.

State Conventions

State conventions ordinarily meet once every two years, preceding the scheduled elections. They bring together representatives of the lower-level party units and vary in size. Most draw fewer than a thousand delegates, but several

exceed this total. In 1994 more than 14,000 delegates assembled for the Virginia Republican convention.

The advent and acceptance of the direct primary in the twentieth century have almost completely taken from these bodies what was originally one of their primary responsibilities—nominating candidates for statewide offices. Contemporary conventions may elect party officers and adopt a party platform. During presidential election years, the state conventions once played an important role in the selection of the state parties' delegates to the nominating convention, but party reforms have substantially reduced this role.

State Committees

State party committees also vary in size, from under fifty to more than five hundred. California, the biggest, assembles more than eight hundred members. Just as at the national level, the state committees are charged with selecting party leaders and guiding the party's fortunes between conventions. By and large, these tasks are delegated to chairs and headquarters staffs. Many state party committees also designate executive committees to act for them.

State Chairs

State party chairs can be categorized into in-party and out-party groups, depending on whether the party's nominee holds the governorship. In-party chairs can be further subdivided into those who act as political agents of their governors and those who act independently. In many state parties, the convention or the committee defers in selecting a chair to the wishes of the governor or the gubernatorial nominee. Party building is a primary concern of state party chairs, who also are involved in fund-raising and campaign-related activities.

State Headquarters

Contemporary state party chairs usually operate out of year-round party headquarters occupied by a small, but full-time, paid staff. This development is relatively recent, dating to the early 1960s. Political scientist Robert Huckshorn attributes this phenomenon to four factors. First, party competition has increased at the state level, especially in the South. Second, new technologies have inspired state parties to take advantage of new methods and approaches in electoral politics. The third factor is pressure from the national parties and government. Reforms in the procedures for the selection of delegates to the national convention have imposed procedural guidelines on the state parties that require considerable attention to detail. Federal campaign finance legislation also has imposed stringent reporting guidelines. Fourth, Huckshorn contends that increased communication among the state chairs in recent years, taking the form of meetings under formal organizational auspices, has encouraged chairs lacking headquarters facilities to emulate those who do by setting up an office and operating in a businesslike manner. The result has been the increased bureaucratization of the state parties.[23]

Local Party Organization

At the local level, the components of convention, committee, and chair exist amid vast variations. The legendary urban party machines are essentially extinct, yet in Chicago, for example, remnants of the once-powerful Daley organization linger. Elsewhere, some local parties are but organizational shells, with positions unoccupied and handfuls of officials quietly tending to procedural regularities. Here as at the other levels, election campaigns provide the primary arena for party activity. A comparative study a couple of decades ago found few signs of organizational decline among local parties.[24]

State and Local Parties and Presidential Politics

The traditional relationship between state and local party organizations and the presidency centered on presidential selection. Changes in the presidential selection process have substantially disengaged connections between the two.

After the national convention became the nominating vehicle in the 1830s, and until recently, state and local party leaders tightly controlled the selection of convention delegates and effectively instructed their delegations in voting on nominees. Astute presidential candidates sought the support of these grassroots political leaders.

The preconvention presidential campaign typically consisted of relatively low-key efforts by candidates and managers to line up commitments from the party bosses. In turn, the bosses had options such as jumping aboard a bandwagon, backing favorite sons, or remaining uncommitted in hopes of ultimately tipping the balance at a divided convention.

Conventions in those days featured "smoke-filled rooms" where the party leaders gathered to wheel and deal for the presidential nomination. The victor would be beholden to the bosses who had authorized the outcome. Around the turn of the twentieth century, Ohio's Mark Hanna epitomized power brokers of this type.

In the years immediately preceding World War II, Frank Hague of New Jersey and "Boss" Crump of Memphis, Tennessee, represented the breed. As late as the 1960s, Mayor Richard J. Daley of Chicago still embodied the traditional pattern.

In campaigns of this era, the presidential nominee relied heavily on personnel resources that the state party leaders could mobilize. Old-time campaigns were much more labor-intensive than they are today. Until about 1960 the state party leaders were able to provide the necessary campaign workers.

After the campaign, the victorious party's bosses would claim the federal patronage as a reward for their workers. Through the spoils system, the presidential selection process clearly linked the state and local parties with the presidency.

Party reforms, beginning in the Progressive Era around 1900 and picking up steam after 1968, have drastically diminished the role of state party leaders in designating and controlling delegations to the national convention. Delegates formerly handpicked by party leaders now are mostly chosen through primaries and, less frequently, participatory caucuses.

In presidential primaries, party voters sometimes vote directly for convention delegates. In many states, they do so in conjunction with a vote for the presidential candidate of their choice. Convention delegate slots usually go to supporters of the various presidential candidates in proportion to their electoral support.

In the caucuses, local party activists gather at specified locations in voting precincts to register their support for particular presidential candidates. Each precinct will send representatives to a county-level assembly in proportion to the initial division of support for the various contenders. At the county level, candidate supporters will be selected, again proportionally, to attend congressional district and finally state conventions. There the national convention delegates will be chosen from among the survivors of the earlier trials. The state parties also provide for at-large representatives to be chosen at the state level. *(See box, How Caucuses Work, p. 244, in Chapter 5.)*

Although modern presidential candidates still court state party leaders' support, they are considerably less dependent on it than were their predecessors. Instead, they pursue appeals to pressure group leaders and party activists in the electorate who, through presidential primaries and participatory caucuses, have the controlling say in delegate selection. The delegations so chosen will be more under the direction of candidate and pressure group organizations, lessening the state party leaders' influence on the convention's choice.

Modern presidential campaigns are capital- and technology-intensive. Where once party workers rang doorbells to solicit support, today through television and the Internet candidates themselves appear in living rooms and on computer screens throughout the land.

The expansion of the civil service, which shrank the resources for patronage, also have helped to disengage state and party leaders from the presidency. This is not to say that the state and local parties have declined organizationally. Indeed, there is considerable evidence to the contrary.[25] President Clinton's 1999 designation of then Philadelphia mayor Edward Rendell as the general chair of the Democratic Party reflects this resurgence. But their organizational activity no longer relates so clearly to the presidency as it once did.

National-State Party Relations

National parties of the past were weak and lacking in resources compared with the state and local political organizations, primarily because the federal system decentralized political power in general and party power in particular.[26] In recent years, a dramatic "nationalization" has taken place as the national parties have expanded authority and influence over their state counterparts. The two parties have taken different paths to similar ends. The Democrats have reformed party rules that primarily address delegate selection procedures for the national convention. The Republican approach has been less legalistic, concentrating instead on making the state parties more reliant on the national party for needed services.

The Democrats' altered course began in the late 1940s in the context of uncertainty about the loyalty of certain southern state parties toward the national ticket and platform. Twice in a twenty-year period sizable elements of the southern Democratic Party bolted to follow a regional favorite son.

In 1948 several southern delegations walked out of the national convention after the passage of a controversial platform plank supporting civil rights. After the convention, several southern state parties held a rump assembly and nominated South Carolina governor J. Strom Thurmond to head a "Dixiecrat" ticket in the presidential election. Thurmond won four states and thirty-nine electoral votes.

In 1968 Alabama governor George C. Wallace mounted a presidential bid under the American Independent Party label. He carried five states and won forty-six electoral votes.

During the two decades of conflict over the loyalty issue, the national party demanded that the state units guarantee support for the convention's decisions. To put teeth in this demand it threatened not to seat noncomplying state delegations at subsequent conventions.

Initially, this controversy was closely associated with the issue of civil rights. The 1964 Democratic national convention resolved to prohibit racial discrimination in delegate selection to the 1968 convention. This promise constituted a historic assertion of national authority over what had previously been the state parties' exclusive prerogative. The national convention also authorized the national chair to appoint a committee to assist the state parties in complying with this new guideline.

This committee and the 1968 convention, along with a new group established by the latter, the Commission on Party Structure and Delegate Selection, broadened the issue beyond that of civil rights to embrace more generally popular participation in delegate selection and other party activities. These various proposals were accepted by the Democratic National Committee and the party's 1972 convention. They culminated at the 1974 midterm convention in the adoption of a charter that clearly subordinates the state parties to their national counterpart. As amended, this charter and the accompanying bylaws remain in force as the party's "constitution."

The nationalization of the Republican Party has placed much less emphasis on formal rules. Where the national Democrats have mandated reform in delegate selection, the Republicans have merely recommended it. In practice, however, many of the Democratic Party guidelines have been incorporated by state legislatures into laws, so that they are similarly binding on the state Republican Parties.

The national Republican Party has amassed a formidable financial foundation that allows it to bestow "favors," such as monetary assistance and campaign and party-building expertise, that bind state and local parties to the national organization. Therefore, although the Republicans have not formally altered their party structure, they too have positioned the national organization in the dominant position.

PRESIDENTIAL PARTY LEADERSHIP WITHIN THE EXECUTIVE BRANCH

Since the 1930s, president-party relations within the executive branch have undergone dramatic structural changes. White House aides have taken over the party management responsibilities once assigned to members of the cabinet, particularly the postmaster general. Appointments once provided the president as party chief with party-building resources, but the decline in the quantity and elevation in the quality of presidential patronage have diminished drastically this party leadership consideration. Although partisanship is still a vital part of presidential appointments, it remains significant primarily as an indicator of policy responsiveness and has become largely divorced from party-building concerns. In other words, as chief executive the president wants and needs appointees with compatible views on public policies, who can be counted on to embrace and implement presidential decisions and perspectives. Partisanship typically provides this expectation of shared vision. However, from the president's perspective as chief executive, party leadership within the executive branch is a means to an end, rather than an end in itself.

The Constitution authorizes the president to act as chief executive—that is, as head of the executive branch. Party leadership augments executive authority in presidential relations with the administration and the bureaucracy.

In the context of party relations in the executive, three conceptual distinctions should be made. First, the word *presidency* refers to the office of the president, those elements within the executive branch most directly under the control of the chief executive. They include the White House Office, support agencies reporting to the president (such as the National Security Council and the Office of Management and Budget), and the people who operate the White House as the president's residence. Second, *administration* is a less precise term that applies to a particular president and the surrounding team of appointed aides, advisers, and managers within the upper echelons of the executive branch. Team members could include the vice president, the president's spouse, cabinet members, the press secretary, and others who derive their authority from their official or de facto association with the current president. Third, the *bureaucracy* is the permanent government, the men and women who are essentially full-time governmental employees more removed from the president's direct supervision.

Party Management in the Executive Branch

The president's exercise of party leadership has long featured the establishment of organizational bases within the executive branch for oversight of party affairs. In the past, the president's cabinet, composed of the executive department heads, included one or more key political advisers who were deeply involved in party management.

The Post Office and Party Politics

For more than a century the post office provided the customary haven for a political adviser or party manager, who was then well positioned to allocate the considerable resources of federal patronage available through the post office. With the strengthening of party organization in the latter half of the nineteenth century, the postmaster generalship regularly went to a prominent party politician. After the turn of the twentieth century it became established practice to place the national party chair in that position.

George Cortelyou (R, appointed in 1905), Frank Hitchcock (R, 1909), Will Hays (R, 1921), James Farley (D, 1933), Robert Hannegan (D, 1945), and Arthur Summerfield (R, 1953) were all incumbent party chairs who became postmasters general. Democrat Frank Walker (D, 1943) reversed the process when, while serving as postmaster general, he became the party chair in 1943. Hitchcock and Summerfield resigned their position as party chair on assuming their responsibilities at the post office; the others held the two positions simultaneously, at least for a time.

The alliance was one of convenience, and the keystone was government patronage, dispensed by the post office to recipients authorized by the party organization. This practice also gave relatively formal representation to the party organization in the inner circles of presidential politics. Thus President Truman could refer to Hannegan as the "political representative of the Democratic Party in the cabinet of the president." [27] No party chair since Hannegan, however, has held the two offices at the same time; and no party chair since Summerfield has been named to head the post office or its successor, the U.S. Postal Service.

Nevertheless, through the 1960s the head of the post office continued to be associated with party politics and political operations. Lyndon Johnson named White House political aide Lawrence O'Brien postmaster general in 1965. O'Brien went on to chair the Democratic National Committee on two occasions, 1968–1969 and 1970–1972. After O'Brien resigned as postmaster general in 1968 to direct Sen. Robert F. Kennedy's presidential campaign, Johnson appointed another White House political assistant, appointments secretary Marvin Watson, a former Texas state Democratic Party chair, as postmaster general. Richard Nixon's choice for that position was Winton Blount, an Alabaman prominent in the growth of the Republican Party in the South and a visible symbol of Nixon's southern strategy, an effort to expand his personal and partisan base in that region.

During the Nixon presidency, administrative reform changed the structure of the post office, removing it from the cabinet and reconstituting it as a government corporation, the U.S. Postal Service. This development ended the historic connection between the post office, party management, and the party chair.

Three important factors brought about this change. First, after World War II the post office had severe financial problems that required effective management at the top. The traditional assumption that the department could run itself, leaving the postmaster general free to tend to partisan politics, had to be discarded. So began a trend toward placing business and public administration executives in this traditional sanctuary of party managers.

Second, presidents began to realize that the major justification for placing a party manager in the post office no longer applied. Even before World War II, the increasing proportion of executive branch positions under civil service protection had greatly depreciated the value of the post office as a strategic operating base for dispensing federal patronage.

Finally, considerations of "good government," rooted in the Progressive Era, contributed to the separation of the post office from party politics. In the years immediately after World War II, influential public administration specialists decried the official coupling of the political and administrative responsibilities. The Hoover Commission officially recommended that the postmaster general "should not be an official of a political party, such as chairman of a national committee." [28]

The Justice Department and Party Politics

In a 1959 study of the president's cabinet, political scientist Richard Fenno observed, "If a party politician lands in the cabinet at some other position [than postmaster general], it is likely to be that of attorney general." [29] Warren G. Harding appointed his 1920 presidential campaign manager, Harry Daugherty, to that position. Homer Cummings, a former chair of the Democratic National Committee, became Franklin Roosevelt's first attorney general in 1933.

Soon after election in his own right in 1948, Truman moved campaign party chair Howard McGrath over to head the Justice Department. Similarly, in 1953 Dwight Eisenhower named former GOP national chair and key campaign strategist Herbert Brownell Jr. to this position.

In 1961 John Kennedy appointed his presidential campaign manager, brother Robert Kennedy, attorney general. Nixon did the same for his 1968 campaign manager, John N. Mitchell. When Mitchell resigned early in 1972 to head up Nixon's reelection effort, his successor was his deputy, Richard G. Kleindienst, an old hand in Republican presidential campaigns.

By the early 1970s the designation of a leading campaign official as attorney general had become a standard feature of the twentieth-century presidency. When the Watergate scandal enveloped both Mitchell and Kleindienst in criminal prosecutions that resulted in convictions, this particular recruitment pattern came under serious attack.

Presidential candidate Jimmy Carter was one of the leading critics of the modern tendency to politicize the Justice Department. Nevertheless, his attorney general, Griffin B. Bell, was an old political ally, adviser, and friend. Indeed, Bell was the only figure with such a background to be named to the cabinet. In the Reagan administration, the attorney generalship went first to the president's California associate William French Smith. After Smith's resignation, Edwin Meese III, an even closer political aide and adviser of Reagan, took over the office.

Criticisms of a politicized Justice Department resurfaced during the Clinton presidency. Attorney General Janet Reno drew Republican fire for her unwillingness to authorize a special prosecutor to investigate allegations of improper 1996 presidential campaign fund-raising by the White House and the Democratic National Committee. Democrats raised similar concerns about a politicized attorney general office when George W. Bush nominated staunch conservative John Ashcroft to head the law enforcement department during Bush's first term. During his tenure Ashcroft received many complaints that his antiterrorism measures not only encroached on civil liberties but advanced the White House's political goals. At the start of his second term, Bush chose Alberto R. Gonzalez to succeed Ashcroft as attorney general. Many felt that Gonzalez, who had served as Bush's general counsel during his governorship in Texas and as White House counsel during Bush's first term, would not have enough political independence from his longtime boss to run the office in a nonpartisan manner. By the spring of 2007 a wave of controversies and scandals concerning operation of his office, especially regarding Gonzalez's unprecedented midterm dismissal of eight U.S. attorneys, resulted in congressional calls for him to step down.

Because the Justice Department always has been politically sensitive and significant, presidents have long recognized that the office of attorney general is one that can occupy profitably the talents of a key political adviser. Several prestigious political appointments are channeled through the Justice Department, including those for U.S. attorneys, assistant U.S. attorneys, and federal marshals. The department also makes important recommendations about presidential nominations of federal judges, including justices of the Supreme Court.

The growing tendency of interest groups to resort to litigation as a means of achieving their objectives has heightened the political sensitivity of the Justice Department. Moreover, expanded government regulation of the economy has placed the Justice Department in the midst of significant government decisions about benefits and penalties. Key political constituencies can be cultivated and managed by lending support and by exercising discretionary aspects of its law enforcement and prosecutorial powers. In the 1990s, during the Clinton presidency, the Anti-Trust Division of the Justice Department vigorously pursued legal action against software giant Microsoft. After the 2000 election the Justice Department, under new leadership appointed by President George W. Bush, a Republican who advanced his party's long-standing ties with big business, agreed to a settlement.

It behooves a president, then, to place a politically astute ally in this crucial post. Moreover, the position itself is a very attractive one, part of the "inner cabinet" made up of the men and women who head the largest and most essential federal departments. Indeed, for some lawyers it has been a steppingstone to a seat on the Supreme Court.

After World War II, the attorney general supplanted the postmaster general as the cabinet position to be occupied by a key political adviser. But, because the attorney general was less affected by explicit party politics than the postmaster general, the party lost institutional representation within the cabinet. Later political pressures to depoliticize the Justice Department left the White House Office without an institutional alternative within the government for the management of political operations.

White House Office

Without a cabinet-based alternative, White House staff assistants today have the major responsibility for conducting political operations and managing party affairs. The White House Office was established in 1939 during Franklin Roosevelt's administration. Previous presidents had received clerical support from a handful of secretaries and personal aides, but the growing size of and demands on the federal government in the New Deal era led a 1937 presidential commission on administrative management to report that "the president needs help."[30] Congress responded by passing a governmental reorganization act creating the White House Office as part of the Executive Office of the President and authorizing the president to hire additional administrative assistants. Since then, White House staff has expanded tremendously. In 2000, the last full year of the Clinton presidency, the *U.S. Government Manual* identified 129 titled assistants under the heading "White House Office." Following Clinton, George W. Bush, substantially reduced the number of titled aides (thirty-four in 2006), but the overall number of White House Office employees was about the same as those of his recent predecessors.

These aides, usually former employees of the campaign organizations of incoming presidents, typically exhibit strong personal loyalty to the president and an organizational responsibility to the presidential office. Their political experience often is limited to their campaign work in behalf of their candidate. Few former elected officials and party warhorses appear on the rosters of the White House staff; the president's political interests dominate the personal and organizational perspectives of White House aides.

With this enlarged staff, Truman and all subsequent presidents have chosen to set up political operations inside the White House. Staff assistants now handle many of the political chores once assigned to the national party organization. Furthermore, such assistants have become the principal instruments through which the president exercises party leadership.

Two ongoing practices have produced this turn of events. The first is the designation of staff assistants as the president's personal contacts with party and political leaders throughout the country, including the national party organization and the congressional party. The second is the employment of personnel and the establishment of an apparatus at the White House for handling political appointments.

As liaison, a presidential staff assistant ostensibly serves merely as a conduit in a two-way flow of advice and information, requests and demands, between the president and representatives of the political party. In speaking and acting for the president in party matters, however, a White House aide inevitably supersedes and supplants the party chair in that central linkage role.

To be sure, the president's primacy as party leader has always made the White House the focus of attention for party representatives. Still, the establishment of a sizable White House staff, sufficient and willing to meet expectations, has enhanced this tendency greatly. In the process of conveying messages, power gravitates to the conveyer, at the expense of those who once dealt with the president directly and now do so through a presidential assistant.

Every White House staff since Truman's has included at least one such figure. This modern pattern of White House staff management of president-party relations first emerged in the deployment of Matthew Connelly, Truman's appointments secretary. During most of the Eisenhower years, Chief of Staff Sherman Adams filled this role. For Kennedy, it was Kenneth O'Donnell. Walter Jenkins and then Marvin Watson served Johnson in this crucial capacity.

The increasing size of the White House staff has resulted in a specialization of function, with a political affairs office usually established under the direction of the chief of staff. Nixon used H. R. "Bob" Haldeman to direct a team of political operators. Ford relied on Donald H. Rumsfeld and later Richard B. Cheney. Hamilton Jordan was Carter's chief political agent. During the Reagan years, the White House chief of staff had overall responsibility for political operations, while subordinates Lyn Nofziger and later Edward Rollins and Mitchell Daniels were primarily in charge of Reagan's interaction with the Republican Party.

During the administration of George H. W. Bush, chiefs of staff John Sununu and later Samuel Skinner supervised the political operations office. Similarly, the Clinton White House designated a midlevel staff member as director of political affairs, under the supervision of the office of the chief of staff. Joan Baggett filled this office for most of the first term. Bruce Lindsey, perhaps the president's closest personal confidant on the staff, did so during the reelection campaign season (1996–1997). Craig Smith and then Minyon Moore finished out the second term. President George W. Bush brought his chief campaign strategist, Karl Rove, into the White House as a senior political adviser. Rove's responsibility was to look after the wide-ranging political interests of the president and his administration. Party politics, including the party organization, were clearly within his domain. Rove's role expanded into the policy domain when he became deputy chief of staff in January 2005, but controversies surrounded his mingling of politics and policy, and he ostensibly withdrew from the latter arena in April 2006.

In recommending the establishment of the White House office, FDR's Commission on Administrative Management envisioned presidential assistants operating with a "passion for anonymity." Instead, these political operators have become very visible and powerful presidential party managers.

In the White House, as in any other office, greater size has been accompanied by a greater division of labor and specialization. A presidential assistant also has been assigned to operate an in-house personnel office managing presidential appointments.

These organizational developments have placed White House aides at the center of what was once a major responsibility of the national party organization. Because partisanship continues to be a major factor in presidential appointments, this element within the White House Office also serves as a major component of presidential party management.[31]

Partisanship and Political Appointments

Political appointments are a chief means by which presidents exercise leadership within the executive branch. The Constitution confers on the president a broad appointment power. Article II, Section 2, provides that the president "shall nominate, and by and with the Advice and Consent of the Senate, shall appoint . . . Officers of the United States, whose Appointments are not herein otherwise provided for, and which shall be established by Law." In addition, it authorizes the houses of Congress to "vest the Appointment of such inferior Officers, as they think proper, in the President alone."

What is the significance of partisanship in presidential appointments and the influence of party in the making of those appointments? Generally, the president's primary concern in making executive appointments is policy responsiveness, so that presidential decisions not only will be accepted and carried out by the administration, but also that policy proposals advanced by the administration will reflect presidential perspectives. Partisanship and party influence are less ends in themselves than instruments for achieving that purpose.

Development of the Spoils System

Ostensibly, partisanship played no role in George Washington's personnel decisions, for at the outset of his administration political parties had yet to appear on the scene. Washington deplored even the idea of partisan division and put forward instead the criterion of fitness of character for consideration as a presidential appointee. Nevertheless, the great majority of the fit characters receiving presidential appointments during the Washington and John Adams administrations turned out to be followers of the policies advocated by Alexander Hamilton.

Thus by the time Thomas Jefferson entered the presidential office in 1801, the executive branch was filled with his partisan adversaries. For the most part, Jefferson did not so much clean house as make new and replacement appointments with partisan considerations in mind. Andrew Jackson, the seventh president, joyfully embraced what came to be called the *spoils system* (from the Roman adage "to the victor belong the spoils"). Under the spoils system, appointive positions were viewed as the rewards of electoral victory, to be doled out to the party of the winning presidential candidate. Thus after a half-century under the Constitution, the principle of partisanship as a criterion for a presidential appointment had become well established.

Presidents needed assistance in making the appointments available. If partisanship was to be a major expectation, who better than the party could provide that help? After the Jacksonian era, the emerging national party organizations quickly asserted claims on the distribution of federal patronage. They had assembled and directed the campaign support essential to electoral victory, and patronage was the means by which they could reward the party faithful. Within the federal government, the post office offered a harvest of available jobs, establishing the long-standing connection between the post office and party politics described earlier. Presidents usually retained personal control over the high-level appointments in the executive branch, but they customarily delegated responsibility for the vast number of lower-level appointments to the party managers.

The operation of the spoils system in the mid–nineteenth century produced extensive partisanship and party control over presidential appointments. Furthermore, it enhanced policy responsiveness within the executive branch. It also was associated, however, with allegations of incompetence and scandal. In response, reformers called for its abolition in favor of a system of civil service based on merit.

Rise of the Merit Principle

The 1881 assassination of President James A. Garfield by Charles Guiteau, who was angry at not being appointed U.S. consul to Paris, led Congress in 1883 to pass the Pendleton Act, also known as the Civil Service Reform Act. This landmark legislation sought to replace partisanship with merit as the essential standard for lower-level positions within the executive branch. It established a nonpartisan Civil Service Commission with authority over certain classes of executive positions.

Initially, only a small minority, about 10 percent, of the total number of executive branch positions came under the coverage of the Civil Service Commission. The majority remained in the hands of the president and continued to be allocated through the party as spoils. Gradually, however, the number and proportion of civil service positions increased. By the beginning of the twentieth century, more than 40 percent were classified. Under President Theodore Roosevelt (1901–1909), a reformer and former civil service commissioner, the merit system covered more than 50 percent of the positions within the executive branch.

In the 1910s civil service classification was extended to 60 and then 70 percent of the positions and the figure hovered around 80 percent by 1930. The percentage declined to 67 percent during the presidency of Franklin Roosevelt, when the numbers of federal positions increased dramatically as the federal government responded to the crises of the Great Depression and World War II. The percentage rose into the mid-1980s shortly after the war and remained relatively constant at that level for more than two decades.[32] Since the 1970s, it has hovered around 90 percent, a rough reversal of the percentage distribution at the outset of the civil service system in the 1880s.

Partisan considerations guided this expansion of civil service coverage. Under the "good government" guise of civil service reform, presidents would extend classification to large groups of their appointees, who had been awarded jobs because of their party affiliations. Their successors in the Oval Office would then find their discretion in making appointments severely limited by the actions of their predecessors.

Establishment of the White House personnel office further changed the procedures for allocating presidential appointments. Partisanship remained important, but the role of the party organization was reduced.

Critical Developments: Roosevelt to Eisenhower

Several critical developments encompassing the presidencies of Franklin Roosevelt and Dwight Eisenhower illustrate these patterns. After Roosevelt's election in 1932, national party chair Jim Farley took on the assignment of patronage distribution. Besieged by job seekers during the depression-ridden early days of the New Deal, Farley allocated government positions by the thousands to "deserving Democrats." According to his testimony, he gave special favor to those members of the FRBC club (For Roosevelt Before Chicago—the site of the 1932 nominating convention). Farley discussed major appointments directly with the president and other high government figures, but he had considerable leeway in making the lower-level appointments. He had intended to deal with applicants at national party headquarters, but he soon found their numbers so great that he moved to the more spacious post office building. Serving as both party chair and postmaster general, Farley could easily make this shift.[33]

In making political appointments, Roosevelt and Farley benefited from New Deal legislation creating several new executive organizations to administer the expansive New Deal social and economic programs. Initially, positions in these new entities were not covered by the civil service. Thus they could be and indeed were awarded to loyal Democrats. Presidents Roosevelt and Truman later extended civil service protection to many of the positions.

Recognizing the partisan character of the executive branch under Roosevelt, Congress passed another landmark law affecting the civil service, the Hatch Act of 1939. It prohibited partisan political activity by federal government workers. A second Hatch Act a year later extended this prohibition to state and local government employees engaged in programs supported by federal funds. According to political scientist Herbert Kaufman, "While the Civil Service Act sought to keep political workers out of the government service, the Hatch Acts operated to keep government workers out of the parties." [34]

Meanwhile, within the Roosevelt administration Farley found his stature diminished considerably after the 1936 reelection campaign. In retirement some years later, Farley attempted to analyze the circumstances surrounding his fall from grace:

National party chair James A. Farley, right, speaks to President Franklin Roosevelt. Using new executive organizations created by New Deal legislation, they collaborated to award jobs to loyal Democrats.

Almost before I knew it, I was no longer called to the White House for morning bedside conferences. My phone no longer brought the familiar voice in mellifluous tones. Months dragged by between White House luncheon conferences. Soon I found I was no longer being consulted on appointments, even in my own state. White House confidence on politics and policy went to a small band of zealots, who mocked at party loyalty and knew no devotion except unswerving obedience to their leader.[35]

During the Truman administration, White House aide Donald Dawson set up a personnel office to serve as a clearinghouse for information on jobs available and potential candidates to fill them. Dawson toiled in relative obscurity at the White House, while the public spotlight continued to focus on the party chair as the administration's patronage dispenser. The party headquarters, which retained a significant patronage role, was by no means ignored or completely supplanted by the White House personnel office, yet an administrative structure, inside the White House and apart from the party, had begun to handle presidential appointments.

During the Eisenhower years, the changing patterns of patronage availability and allocation came sharply into focus. The 1952 presidential election returned the presidency to the Republicans for the first time in twenty years. The party regulars clamoring for jobs discovered to their dismay that patronage of the variety they remembered and expected simply no longer existed. Indeed, the expansion of civil service coverage had the effect of classifying jobs held by Democratic partisans.

Moreover, their standard-bearer was neither attuned nor sympathetic to the idea of using patronage as a tool for party building. Within the White House, Eisenhower assigned responsibilities for managing political appointments to Charles Willis, one of Chief of Staff Sherman Adams's assistants. An energetic young businessman, Willis was an amateur in politics who had cofounded and directed Citizens for Eisenhower, an amalgamation of independents and "discerning" Democrats enthusiastically committed to the Eisenhower presidential candidacy but distinctly uncomfortable with the regular Republican Party organization. The selection of Willis at the outset reflected the new president's organizational and philosophical disposition to keep presidential appointments out of the realm of party politics.

The Republican national organization, under the capable direction of party chair Leonard Hall, sought to assert its traditional prerogatives in the appointment process. Hall was able to institute a procedure whereby the party headquarters was informed of any job openings and was entitled to make recommendations. For a time Willis formally routed employment applications through the Republican National Committee. When press reports publicly exposed this program a few months after its inception, however, the revelation unleashed a volley of criticism from proponents of a depoliticized civil service. The Eisenhower administration quietly abandoned it.

Thus over the years two distinct patterns had developed. The first was the reduction in the number of political appointments available to the president. The second was the shift of influence over the appointment-making process from the national party organization to the White House. These patterns continued in subsequent presidencies.

Diminishing Patronage Categories and Party Role

The decline in patronage coincided with a significant revision of the general categories of available patronage. Over time, then, the classification process virtually eliminated the types of jobs, such as postmaster, that the political party was best able to fill from the ranks of its qualified activists. Since the New Deal era, low-level jobs for deserving partisans have been in exceedingly short supply; and the old-style patronage, associated with party chairs such as Jim Farley, is nearly obsolete.

Today, executive branch presidential patronage applies primarily to a relatively small number of political appointments to upper-level executive positions in the departments and agencies that the president is authorized to fill. Party

affiliation continues to be an important consideration in presidential appointments, but the shift in primary organizational responsibility for handling presidential appointments from the national party to the White House means that patronage has become much less oriented toward party building than was true in the past. The party organization's role has become peripheral. Although it may be called on to make recommendations or to provide political clearances, these requests occur at the discretion of the White House.

Policy responsiveness has always been a primary presidential objective in presidential appointments. In years past, however, it usually went hand in hand with party building. Consider the case of a president doling out jobs to deserving partisans. The very act of placing party loyalists in positions charged with enforcing policies provided, first, the expectation that implementation would occur according to the president's designs, and, second, a significant reward for services rendered to the party. The prospects of such rewards constituted important incentives for partisan involvement. Furthermore, the holders of these positions could be expected to look out for the interests of the party from their strategic vantage points. This party-building practice has become much less the case in the post–World War II era; the two have become separated.

The staffing practices developed by the Reagan White House illustrate well this shift in emphasis in managing presidential appointments. Control over appointments was centralized tightly in the White House, under the supervision of personnel officer E. Pendleton James. Ideological compatibility with the president emerged as the chief standard in making appointments. Indeed, for this reason President Reagan, compared with his predecessors, was able to largely achieve responsiveness from his appointees in the executive branch. Reagan's successor, George H. W. Bush, was less attentive to ideological considerations as was Bill Clinton. The latter emphasized demographic criteria in fulfilling his preelection pledge to form a cabinet that "looked like America." George W. Bush reasserted a Reagan-like concern with ideological responsiveness.

Civil Service Classification and Policy Responsiveness

The extension of civil service classification generated new problems for policy responsiveness. A bureaucracy designed to enhance expertise may well sacrifice accountability in the process. Modern presidents have grown increasingly frustrated with the perceived unresponsiveness of the permanent bureaucracy.

In 1978 President Carter promoted the cause of civil service reform to increase presidential control. In that year Congress enacted the Civil Service Reform Act, which had two important features.

First, the act created the Senior Executive Service (SES), a group comprising mostly high-level career civil servants. From the president's perspective, this innovation was designed to give the White House more flexibility in dealing with the upper echelons of the bureaucracy and to increase the bureaucracy's responsiveness to the White House. According to political scientist Terry Moe, Carter's successor, President Reagan, systematically politicized the SES. He ousted career officials from important positions in the bureaucracy, replacing them with partisans.[36] Reagan's successors have taken less aggressive advantage of this opportunity, and bureaucratic responsiveness remains a problem for modern presidents.

Second, the 1978 Civil Service Reform Act abolished the Civil Service Commission, the bipartisan body created in 1883 to oversee the establishment of the merit principle in the federal bureaucracy. In the commission's stead Congress created the Office of Personnel Management (OPM). Headed by a single presidential appointee, OPM seeks to increase presidential direction of the civil service. Still, even though the president wants a responsive bureaucracy, OPM's concerns are not specifically partisan, thus widening the breach between policy responsiveness and party building.

PRESIDENTIAL PARTY LEADERSHIP IN CONGRESS

Presidential party leadership within the executive branch augments the executive authority the Constitution provides for the president. Such constitutional authority is largely lacking when the chief executive confronts Congress. Rather, the constitutional principle of separation of powers positions the president as an outsider in dealing with the legislature. Moreover, legislative leadership is not an explicit constitutional responsibility. Rather, it emerges out of presidents' ambitions and the expectations of their followers.

Presidents seeking to lead Congress in the enactment of presidential initiatives must do so without formal command authority. Persuasion becomes the key. With the conspicuous exceptions of Thomas Jefferson and, to a lesser extent, Andrew Jackson, nineteenth-century presidents did not seek much in the way of legislative initiatives; nor was Congress disposed to look to the president for legislative direction. In the first half of the twentieth century, however, pivotal presidents such as Theodore Roosevelt, Woodrow Wilson, and Franklin Roosevelt, by dint of their expansive conceptions of the presidential office and in response to new situations and demands, succeeded in altering the political environment, placing the presidency in a much more activist legislative posture. (See "Historical Development," p. 000, in Chapter 12.)

In the separated institutional environment, party emerges as a potentially important unifying force. Presidents can employ their standing as party leaders to secure cooperation from party members in Congress. In

principle, the idea and the organization of party can bridge the constitutionally separated institutions under the leadership of the president. Thus, from the presidential perspective, party leadership provides the foundation for legislative leadership.

Such leadership is, however, extremely problematic. Its success is dependent on numerous structural and stylistic factors. Indeed, relatively few presidents have been able to unlock the party key to legislative leadership.

The Congressional Party

Political parties had no formal standing in 1787 when the Constitution organized and defined the powers of Congress. But today one speaks of the congressional party, or the party in Congress, a concept founded on the fact that for a long time virtually all members of Congress have been elected as nominees of the major political parties. Thus today there are four congressional parties: House Democrats, House Republicans, Senate Democrats, and Senate Republicans.

Furthermore, partisanship provides the basis for the leadership and organization of Congress. A central purpose of congressional party leaders and organizations is to heighten the significance of the party cue in congressional behavior. In each chamber, House and Senate, the members of the congressional parties constitute the party caucuses, or, as the Republicans style themselves, the party conferences. At the outset of each session of Congress, the party caucuses meet to select their party leaders.

Party Leaders

Congressional party leadership includes the constitutional leadership positions within Congress: the Speaker of the House and the president pro tempore of the Senate. These positions are held by members of the majority party. The majority and minority parties elect other leaders as well.

When Congress formally convenes, each party caucus in the House chooses a leader. Both leaders are nominated for Speaker, who is elected by the full House under party lines, with the majority party's victorious candidate becoming Speaker and the loser becoming minority leader. The majority caucus also designates a deputy to fill the position of majority leader under the Speaker. The majority and minority leaders are also called "floor leaders."

In addition, both party caucuses select party whips to assist their leaders in maintaining two-way communication with the party members, especially about party positions and expectations on pending legislation. Both parties have established elaborate yet flexible whip organizations, consisting of deputy whips. The whips extend the congressional party leadership well into the rank and file.

The Senate has no direct counterpart to the House Speaker, who serves both as presiding officer and leader of the majority. The Constitution names the vice president of the United States as the president of the Senate, or presiding officer, who votes only to break a tie. The Constitution also authorizes the designation of a president pro tempore to preside in the absence of the vice president.

The president pro tempore, like the House Speaker, is elected along party lines. The incumbent president pro tempore does not stand for reelection at the outset of each Congress, however, as does the Speaker. Rather, the incumbent remains in office as long as the party retains its majority. A change will occur only with the departure of the incumbent from the Senate or a change in party power.

In the nineteenth century, vice presidents routinely attended to their presiding responsibilities. In their occasional absences, presidents pro tempore were elected ad hoc to serve until the return of the vice president. Beginning in 1890, the position of president pro tempore (usually shortened to president pro tem) became much more stable, with the incumbent now serving until the Senate otherwise orders. Twentieth-century vice presidents virtually abandoned their senatorial presiding duties, so opportunities for the president pro tempore increased. Since 1945, the position of president pro tempore customarily has gone to the member of the majority party who has served the longest. Junior members of the majority typically assume much of the daily burdens of presiding.

At the outset of the George W. Bush presidency in 2001, the Senate was evenly divided. As a result, Vice President Richard Cheney had to preside often, initially to give the GOP the necessary majority to organize the chamber and then to break any tie votes. However, when a Republican senator abandoned the party in June 2001 and caucused with the Democrats as an independent, the Democrats gained majority control and Cheney's presence became less critical.

Despite its constitutional authorization and the status of its incumbent as the senior majority party member, the position of president pro tempore, unlike that of House Speaker, has not emerged as a significant party leadership position. Rather, it is much more an honorific office.

The main party leaders in the Senate are the majority and minority leaders, chosen by the party caucuses. As in the House, each floor leader is assisted by a whip. Because of the smaller size and less formal operating procedures that differentiate the Senate from the House, much less elaborate whip organizations have evolved in the upper chamber.

The power exerted by congressional party leaders ebbs and flows over time, and they find themselves vying with committee chairs for control of the legislative policy process. In the first decade of the twentieth century, House Speaker Joseph G. Cannon, R-Ill., was a virtual czar. Similarly, in the mid-1990s Speaker Newt Gingrich, R-Ga., was unusually influential. At midcentury the balance of power tipped in favor of the committee chairs.

Party Organizations

House and Senate party leadership positions operate within the context of partisan organizations. Traditionally, caucus responsibilities have been limited to presession preparation, but the caucuses have on occasion maintained a presence throughout the session.

In the Jeffersonian era, the Democratic-Republican caucus reportedly met frequently during congressional sessions. More recently, among House Democrats, noteworthy instances of ongoing caucus meetings occurred during the early years of the presidencies of both Woodrow Wilson and Franklin Roosevelt, and again in the mid-1970s when Republicans Richard Nixon and Gerald Ford occupied the White House. For House Republicans, regular meetings of the conference were a standard feature in the 1940s and 1950s. With the return of House Republicans to majority status in the 1994 midterm elections, a revitalized conference provided a regular, lively forum for discussion, if not direction, of party politics and policy.

In recent times, both congressional parties have established "steering" and "policy" committees to work with the leadership on scheduling and strategy. Both also have created ad hoc groups to recommend committee assignments. These various tasks frequently have been combined in single bodies.

The congressional parties play central roles in the committees of Congress. The party caucuses authorize procedures and ratify decisions for the assignments of party members to the committees; the majority party in each chamber controls the chairs of all the committees in that chamber. Positions on all committees are distributed proportionally between the parties—that is, the larger a party's majority within the chamber that term, the larger its majority on each committee.

For example, in the Republican-controlled 109th Congress (2005–2007), thirty-seven Republicans and twenty-nine Democrats sat on the sixty-six-seat House Appropriations Committee. At the outset of the Democratic-controlled 110th Congress (2007–2009), the party composition of the committee was reversed. The majority Democrats now claimed thirty-seven seats, leaving the minority Republicans with twenty-nine.

Within the congressional committees, the "seniority system" has typically governed committee leadership assignments; the position of committee chair goes to the member of the majority party with the most years of continuous service on the committee. However, this custom has been by no means absolute. In the 1970s House Democrats in caucus deposed a handful of senior members from their committee chairs. In the 104th Congress, Republican Speaker Newt Gingrich received conference support for his decisions to abandon seniority in designating committee chairs in several instances. At the outset of the 110th Congress, Democratic

Speaker Nancy Pelosi similarly signaled her commitment to more centralized, party-based leadership by passing over some ranking members in naming committee chairs, an initiative backed by the party caucus.

Additional party organizations in Congress are among the diverse array of special interest caucuses (technically known as legislative service organizations or LSOs) that have proliferated in recent years. These LSOs typically are based on members' ideology, region, or entry "class" (the election or Congress in which members initially took office). Examples of partisan LSOs include the Democratic Study Group, the Republican Study Committee, the California Democratic Congressional Delegation, and the Ninety-ninth New Members Caucus (Democratic). In the 104th Congress (1995–1997), federal funding for such caucuses was slashed drastically. Most lost their federal funding entirely but continued to function in a limited fashion with support from the political parties or private contributors.

Finally, since the Civil War congressional parties have maintained their own campaign committees, devoted to helping party candidates get elected to Congress. Thus the congressional party as a concept embraces a wide variety of specific groups and organizations.

The President and the Congressional Party

How does the president as party leader exert influence in the congressional party? Thomas Jefferson's pioneering exercise of presidential party leadership extended to designating floor leaders and even, according to contemporaneous although inadequately substantiated Federalist reports, meeting with and presiding over the caucus.

Jefferson's successors have fallen far short of these alleged accomplishments. By and large, the congressional party organizes itself and selects its leadership without direct regard to the president's needs and interests. It does so in keeping with the principle of separation of powers and with the institutional need to protect itself against outside, presidential domination.

No direct presidential participation in the congressional party caucuses has even been suggested after the Jeffersonian era. More recent activist presidents such as Woodrow Wilson, Franklin Roosevelt, Bill Clinton, and George W. Bush however, have personally conveyed messages to the caucuses informing the members of presidential concerns.

Congressional Party

Respectful of congressional sentiments, wary of the consequences of unsuccessful initiatives, and aware that hierarchical succession is often the norm, presidents are usually loath to intervene in congressional party leadership contests. A noteworthy exception occurred in 1937 when, after the death of Senate Democratic majority leader Joseph T.

Robinson, President Franklin Roosevelt did not hide his clear preference that the successor be Alben W. Barkley of Kentucky rather than B. Patton "Pat" Harrison of Mississippi. Barkley won a narrow victory.

A more recent instance of presidential involvement occurred in late 2002, in the wake of midterm elections that restored Republican control in the Senate. Erstwhile Minority Leader Trent Lott of Mississippi, poised to resume his role as majority leader, found himself embroiled in controversy surrounding remarks he made praising retiring Sen. Strom Thurmond's 1948 segregationist presidential campaign. White House pressure contributed to Lott's decision to resign his leadership post, and the White House further signaled its desire for William H. Frist of Tennessee to replace him. The Republican Conference unanimously agreed to do so.

Much more typically, presidents view the party leadership contests as internal congressional matters and are content to work with the leaders chosen. Similarly, in the committees the seniority system insulates leadership positions from presidential influence.

This hands-off approach can invest congressional party leadership in individuals antagonistic to the president and presidential objectives. The death of Senate Republican majority leader Robert A. Taft in 1953, early in President Eisenhower's first term, resulted in the elevation of Republican senator William F. Knowland of California. Knowland frequently opposed Eisenhower's legislative objectives. Democratic representative John W. McCormack, who succeeded Sam Rayburn in the Speaker's chair after Rayburn's death in 1961, represented a faction in Massachusetts politics that sometimes was at odds with that of the president, John Kennedy. In neither case, however, did the president exercise effective influence in the determination of the congressional party leadership.

Franklin Roosevelt and the presidents who succeeded him have set up regular meetings with the congressional party leadership. Typically, these sessions have occurred on a weekly basis when Congress is in session. They provide regular opportunities to trace the course of the president's program in Congress, to establish priorities, and to develop and coordinate strategies and tactics.

Depending on the president's style and schedule, these sessions may take place in the early morning with lattes and bagels or in the late afternoon with white wine spritzers (replacing the bourbon and branch water of a bygone era). Should the president's party be in the minority in a congressional chamber, as has been the case more often than not since World War II, then the opposition party leadership may well be invited to participate in some such sessions.

At the outset of his presidency, with nominal partisan control of both chambers, President George W. Bush was not particularly inclined to include the minority Democratic congressional leaders in these meetings. However, once the Republicans lost control of the Senate a more bipartisan approach was in the offing, and Senate majority leader Tom Daschle (D-S.D.) and House minority leader Richard A. Gephardt (D-Mo.) began receiving invitations to join the president, Senate minority leader Trent Lott, and House Speaker J. Dennis Hastert. The frequency of these bipartisan assemblies increased significantly in the immediate aftermath of the September 11, 2001, terrorist attacks on New York City and Washington, D.C. During the next four years, however, amid increasing Democratic criticism of Bush's agenda, sessions including the minority leaders became less routine. The Democratic victories in the 2006 midterm elections portend a shift back toward at least the appearance of more bipartisanship, for the remaining two years of the Bush presidency.

President Ronald Reagan meets with Republican members of Congress in front of the White House in 1984.

In addition to regular meetings with the party leadership, presidents can and do meet with committee chieftains and individual members and groups of the party rank and file in pursuit of their legislative objectives. The frequency with which a president holds such meetings depends very much on considerations of personal style. Lyndon Johnson did so often; Jimmy Carter, less so. In his first two years in office, with Democratic control of Congress, Bill Clinton was much more inclined to do so than either of his predecessors, Ronald Reagan and George H. W. Bush, or his successor, George W. Bush. However, after the GOP took control of Congress in 1994 he rarely did so.

White House Legislative Liaison

The determination of the Brownlow Commission in 1937 that "the president needs help" has had an institutional influence on how presidents conduct legislative leadership. With the expansion of the White House Office, aides received specific presidential responsibilities for congressional relations.

During the Eisenhower administration, the structure of a legislative liaison office took formal shape under Wilton B. "Jerry" Persons, a deputy to Chief of Staff Sherman Adams. When Persons replaced Adams as chief of staff in 1958, Bryce Harlow took charge of the liaison office. These staffers and a handful of associates had the task of establish-ing and maintaining a presidential presence on Capitol Hill. In a word, they became the president's official lobbyists.

Since then, this office has grown in size and stature and has become a vital part of the president's conduct of legislative leadership. It has partisan significance in that it naturally is staffed by members of the president's party, and it normally works more closely and effectively with the leaders and members of the president's party than with the opposition.

Personally, and with the assistance of legislative liaison assistants, presidents put forward a variety of appeals to their fellow partisans in Congress, encouraging them to support the president's legislative initiatives. In many respects, presidents merely overlap with and build on the foundations established at the outset by Thomas Jefferson. In a study of presidential influence in Congress that casts doubt on the ultimate value of these appeals, political scientist George C. Edwards III details a number of diverse approaches.[37]

Appeals may be purely partisan, focusing on the centrality of the measure in question to the party program and calling for support on the basis of party loyalty. Often, this invocation is sufficient. Elected themselves on the party ticket, members of the president's party typically are sympathetic to appeals that call forth their own emotional commitments to the party, its programs, and its leader, particularly if they face a unified partisan opposition.

In his first year in the White House, Clinton faced unanimous Republican opposition to his budget proposals. He narrowly prevailed in both House and Senate by evoking extraordinary party support from his fellow Democrats, making the powerful argument that the votes were a test of the Democratic Party's capacity to govern. Vice President Al Gore's vote was needed in the Senate to break the 50–50 tie on the bill. During the portions of the George W. Bush presidency when the Republicans controlled Congress (early 2001, 2003–2007), the narrowness of their majorities, combined with heightened polarization between the parties, mandated extraordinarily high party support to advance his agenda.

More specific approaches aimed primarily at the partisan audience include patronage and campaign assistance. As noted earlier, the number of political appointments the president can bestow declined markedly in the twentieth century, but party is an important consideration for presidents in making those appointments remaining. These can be used to entice or reward supportive members of Congress—who tend to be vitally interested in presidential appointments in their states and districts—by designating individuals recommended by the members. At the outset of the Kennedy administration, the White House staff functions of patronage distribution and legislative liaison were combined in a single office under the direction of Lawrence O'Brien. This ensured that the congressional party interest in patronage would be addressed. Although later administrations separated these staff functions, the potential linkage endures.

Another service the president as party leader can provide for fellow partisans in the legislature is campaign assistance. The president can agree to campaign for members running a close race, honoring them and their constituencies with the presidential presence and establishing a credit balance for future dealings. The president also may influence the national party organization in deciding whether to offer its financial and organizational resources to a particular legislator's campaign.

Supplementing partisan appeals are those directed at members without regard to partisan affiliation. Some of these bipartisan appeals may be more personal in nature, in which presidents solicit backing as a personal favor. Lyndon Johnson was able to call on congressional and senatorial colleagues of decades-long standing, pleading with them on the basis of friendship to support him on a critical issue. Ronald Reagan may have lacked congressional experience and had few acquaintances in Congress, yet he would resort to his experience as a Hollywood actor, imploring members of Congress to "win one for the Gipper."

Alternatively, the bipartisan appeal may be based on principle. For example, Clinton sought congressional support on both sides of the aisle for two controversial foreign trade initiatives, the North American Free Trade Agreement (NAFTA) and the General Agreement on Tariffs and Trade (GATT). Confronted with significant opposition among his fellow Democrats, he was able to secure enactment of both agreements only by appealing to Republicans on the basis of

mutual commitment to free trade principles. Early on, George W. Bush achieved significant bipartisan legislative success with his "No Child Left Behind" educational initiative that embraced some traditional Democratic policy expectations. Similarly, he found fiscal common ground with a handful of Democrats willing to support his tax cut proposals.

Members of Congress are often quite susceptible to presidential entreaties, for they invoke the prestige of the presidential office and entail direct access to the president, either over the telephone or in person. Furthermore, such appeals are typically linked with an overarching national interest transcending the party one. Among recent presidents, Johnson was particularly prone to invoking nationalistic themes in appealing for congressional support. Although he clearly did so in a calculating fashion, he also was unquestionably sincere and emotional in his personal patriotism.

Similarly, presidents can use the numerous amenities at their disposal to curry favor with members of Congress and thus reinforce these personal appeals. The amenities include visits to the White House or the presidential retreat at Camp David, photo opportunities with the president, flights on *Air Force One,* and the like. The president's desk in the Oval Office is filled with souvenirs bearing the presidential seal, such as cuff links, matches, ash trays, and golf balls. Visitors to Camp David are provided with windbreakers similarly labeled. Members of Congress are not immune to such blandishments.

Conversely, presidents can make themselves available to members of Congress at the members' initiative. Presidents Johnson and Ford took care to return promptly telephone calls from members of Congress, while Nixon and Carter were much less attentive. The accessibility of the president looms large in congressional responses to and evaluations of presidential legislative leadership.

Presidents also can resort to bargaining in pursuit of their legislative objectives. Here, presidents provide favors to members of Congress in return for legislative support. In the congressional vernacular, this is called "logrolling"—you scratch my back and I'll scratch yours.

Edwards has documented several examples of presidential logrolling. In one instance, President Kennedy was attempting with little success to persuade Democratic senator Robert Kerr of Oklahoma, an influential member of the Finance Committee, to support an investment tax credit bill that was languishing in committee. In turn, Kerr expressed his dissatisfaction with the administration's unwillingness to back an Arkansas River project he was pushing. Kerr proposed a trade, to which Kennedy responded, "You know, Bob, I never really understood that Arkansas River bill before today." Thus the deal was done, to the mutual satisfaction of president and senator.[38] Although the president or presidential aides occasionally may initiate bargaining, members of Congress are perhaps more likely to do so, as this anecdote suggests, in response to a presidential request for help. President Clinton's dependency on unified party support in the first two years of his presidency emboldened Democratic members of Congress to extract their pounds of flesh in the form of presidential support for pet ideas and projects in return for crucial votes.

Presidents also have at their disposal a variety of services that can be useful to members of Congress. Making these services available builds goodwill and potential support. Although job-related patronage went into decline a century ago, another brand of patronage—pork barrel patronage, the allocation of federal programs and projects among the states and congressional districts—rose to new heights in the mid–twentieth century with the expansion of the national government. Since the 1980s, however, federal budget deficits have generated pressure for downsizing the federal government, thereby reducing both the availability and attraction of pork barrel patronage.

The president and the president's aides therefore have many incentives or "carrots" to offer for support, but what "sticks" are available to use if Congress chooses not to cooperate? About all the president alone can do is to threaten to withhold the available incentives. Such a step can be effective for members of Congress who are accustomed to the incentives and reliant on them. Independent members who are willing and able to do without presidential support may disregard the president's threats.

During the Johnson presidency, Sen. J. William Fulbright, an Arkansas Democrat, chaired the powerful Senate Foreign Relations Committee. After Fulbright began expressing reservations about the administration's Vietnam War policies, he found that his once warm relationship with

TABLE 17-4 **Presidential Support by Party, House of Representatives, 1953–2006 (percent)**

President	Year	Democrats	Republicans	President	Year	Democrats	Republicans
Eisenhower (R)	1953	49	74		1980	63	40
	1954	45	71		AVERAGE	63	38
	1955	53	60	Reagan (R)	1981	42	68
	1956	52	72		1982	39	64
	1957	50	54		1983	28	70
	1958	55	58		1984	34	60
	1959	40	68		1985	30	67
	1960	44	59		1986	25	65
	AVERAGE	49	65		1987	24	62
Kennedy (D)	1961	73	37		1988	25	57
	1962	72	42		AVERAGE	31	64
	1963	73	32	G. H. W. Bush (R)	1989	36	69
	AVERAGE	73	37		1990	25	63
L. Johnson (D)	1964	74	38		1991	34	72
	1965	74	42		1992	25	71
	1966	64	38		AVERAGE	30	69
	1967	69	46	Clinton (D)	1993	77	39
	1968	64	51		1994	75	47
	AVERAGE	69	43		1995	75	22
Nixon (R)	1969	48	57		1996	74	38
	1970	53	66		1997	71	30
	1971	47	72		1998	74	26
	1972	47	64		1999	73	23
	1973	36	61		2000	73	27
Nixon/Ford (R)	1974	44	57		AVERAGE	74	32
	AVERAGE	46	63	G. W. Bush (R)	2001	31	86
Ford (R)	1975	38	63		2002	32	82
	1976	32	63		2003	26	89
	AVERAGE	35	63		2004	30	80
Carter (D)	1977	63	42		2005	24	81
	1978	60	36		2006	31	85
	1979	64	34		AVERAGE	29	84

SOURCE: *Congressional Quarterly Almanac,* 1953–2005; *CQ Weekly,* January 1, 2007, 49.

NOTE: Congressional Quarterly determines presidential positions on congressional votes by examining the statements made by the president or the president's authorized spokespersons. As defined by Congressional Quarterly, support measures the percentage of the time members voted in accord with the position of the president. Opposition measures the percentage of the time members voted against the president's position.

the president began to cool noticeably. Indeed, where invitations to White House state dinners for visiting foreign dignitaries had once been common, befitting Fulbright's leadership position, they were no longer forthcoming. Fulbright ignored the obvious slights and continued his opposition.

Alternatively, presidents can seek to pressure members of Congress through the use of outside strategies, employing and relying on interest groups and public opinion to encourage or intimidate members to support presidential initiatives. This approach is akin to a bank shot in billiards. The president appeals directly to interest groups and the public, and they in turn exert pressure on the members of Congress. (*See Chapter 21, The Presidency and Interest Groups.*)

For example, a president seeking to influence members of Congress from industrial states to support a presidential program might encourage allies in the labor unions to lobby those members in behalf of the president. Or, in reaching

out to members from farming states the president could deploy supporters from among agricultural interest groups. In the television age, the president has the opportunity to go public with pleas to citizens across the nation to write, call, fax, or e-mail their representatives and senators.

The ultimate "stick" brandished by a president is the threat of a veto. The Constitution authorizes a presidential veto of legislation unacceptable to the chief executive. Its use is thus indicative of unsuccessful legislative leadership. In this fashion, the veto stands as a dramatic negative form of legislative leadership. Interestingly, the president who resorted most often to the veto (more than six hundred times) was Franklin Roosevelt, who is routinely acknowledged as a masterful legislative party leader. President Clinton went through the entire 103d Congress without vetoing a single piece of legislation. He cast his first vetoes in the Republican-controlled 104th Congress. George W. Bush was five and

TABLE 17-5 **Presidential Support by Party, Senate, 1953–2006 (percent)**

President	Year	Democrats	Republicans	President	Year	Democrats	Republicans
Eisenhower (R)	1953	47	67		1980	62	45
	1954	40	71		AVERAGE	67	46
	1955	56	72	Reagan (R)	1981	49	80
	1956	39	72		1982	43	74
	1957	52	69		1983	42	73
	1958	45	67		1984	41	76
	1959	38	72		1985	35	75
	1960	42	65		1986	37	78
	AVERAGE	45	69		1987	36	64
Kennedy (D)	1961	65	37		1988	47	68
	1962	63	40		AVERAGE	41	73
	1963	73	44	G. H. W. Bush (R)	1989	55	82
	AVERAGE	67	40		1990	38	70
L. Johnson (D)	1964	62	45		1991	41	83
	1965	65	48		1992	32	73
	1966	57	43		AVERAGE	42	77
	1967	61	53	Clinton (D)	1993	87	29
	1968	48	47		1994	86	42
	AVERAGE	59	47		1995	81	29
Nixon (R)	1969	47	66		1996	83	37
	1970	45	62		1997	85	60
	1971	41	65		1998	82	41
	1972	44	67		1999	84	34
	1973	37	61		2000	89	46
Nixon/Ford (R)	1974	39	56		AVERAGE	85	40
	AVERAGE	42	63	G. W. Bush (R)	2001	66	94
Ford (R)	1975	47	68		2002	71	89
	1976	39	63		2003	48	94
	AVERAGE	43	66		2004	60	91
Carter (D)	1977	70	52		2005	38	86
	1978	66	41		2006	51	85
	1979	68	47		AVERAGE	56	90

SOURCE: *Congressional Quarterly Almanac,* 1953–2005; *CQ Weekly,* January 1, 2007, 49.

NOTE: Congressional Quarterly determines presidential positions on congressional votes by examining the statements made by the president or the president's authorized spokespersons. As defined by Congressional Quarterly, support measures the percentage of the time members voted in accord with the position of the president. Opposition measures the percentage of the time members voted against the president's position.

one-half years into his presidency before he vetoed a bill. *(See "The Veto," p. 647, in Chapter 12.)*

Congressional Party Voting and Presidential Support

Empirical research on congressional behavior shows that party is the major influence on roll-call voting and that party is the foundation of presidential support in Congress. Yet other factors also affect members' voting decisions, making it difficult to know exactly how much influence the parties have.

It is entirely correct that Democrats tend to vote with other Democrats and Republicans with other Republicans. Similarly, presidents receive stronger support from their fellow partisans in Congress than from the opposition. Moreover, these partisan support indicators are on the rise in recent decades. Yet disquieting questions emerge when one tries to draw conclusions from these findings. Do Democrats vote with other Democrats simply because they belong to the same party? Common policy preferences, constituency pressures, or the personal influence of other members may be the reasons; party affiliation may be merely coincidental. Similar questions surround ostensibly partisan support for presidential initiatives.

These questions notwithstanding, party remains a key to presidential support in Congress. The president's challenge as party leader is to mobilize this base of support by heightening the significance of the party cue. *(See Table 17-4, p. 912, and Table 17-5, p. 913.)*

Limitations on Presidential Party Leadership in Congress

For generations, political scientists have spoken appreciatively of a government model operated by a responsible party. This model contains several components. Initially, parties develop programs to which they commit themselves. Then, they nominate candidates for public office who share those programmatic commitments. Competing parties provide voters with clear policy alternatives. Voters choose between or among the competing parties and authorize one to govern. The elected representatives of the party then demonstrate sufficient discipline and cohesion to enact the party's promises as public policies, responsibly fulfilling its commitments to the voters.

The British party system has long been viewed as an excellent working illustration of responsible parties. American parties, however, have been roundly criticized for falling well short of the mark, particularly with regard to the behavior of the party in the government.

As noted earlier, party does provide the central cue for congressional voting behavior and the primary foundation for presidential support. Moreover, party unity is clearly on the rise in recent Congresses. Still, the members of the congressional party normally exhibit an independence from the party program and leadership in both Congress and the

President Bill Clinton shakes hands with House Democratic leaders at the White House the morning after the House passed the administration's 1993 budget proposal.

White House. That independence is striking when compared with Congress's European counterparts. Why are the party leaders and members in Congress often disinclined to respond positively to presidential leadership? The initial answers can be found in the Constitution.

Separation of Powers

The Constitution does not provide for political parties, nor does it authorize party leadership. However, its separation-of-powers principle places the president largely outside the legislative arena. This is in distinct contrast to a British-style parliamentary model that officially combines executive and legislative authority, establishing the leader of the majority party in the legislature as the chief executive.

The presence of party competition within the context of separation of powers makes possible divided party government, again impossible under the classic parliamentary system. Should the president encounter an entire Congress or a chamber controlled by the opposition party, the limitations of party leadership are obvious. Moreover, a president can hardly be expected to pursue legislative objectives primarily in a partisan fashion when the president's party constitutes a legislative minority. *(See table, "Party Affiliations in Congress and the Presidency: 1789–2006," p. 1869, in Reference Materials, Vol. II.)* In such circumstances, legislative leadership demands a bipartisan approach.

Significantly, divided government has been the norm in the post–World War II era. All the Republican presidents have confronted it. Eisenhower had to deal with Democratic majorities in both houses for six of his eight years in office.

Nixon and Ford faced opposition party control throughout their presidencies. During the Reagan years, the Democrats prevailed throughout in the House and for the last two years in the Senate. George H. W. Bush encountered a Democratic Congress throughout his term. His son, George W. Bush, began his presidency with narrow partisan majorities in both Houses, but the his party lost control of the Senate only four months into his term when a Republican senator switched his affiliation to independent and voted with Democrats to reorganize the chamber. After restoring Republican control in the 2002 midterm elections, the voters elected Democratic congressional majorities four years later.

Only two modern Democrats have had to deal with Republican control of Congress. Harry Truman experienced it in the wake of the midterm 1946 elections until his successful election effort in 1948. Almost fifty years later, Bill Clinton presided over the 1994 midterm elections that saw the Republicans retake the Senate and House for the first time since 1986 and 1954, respectively. The GOP retained control of both chambers for the remainder of his presidency.

Only two modern presidents, Democrats Johnson and Carter, have had the benefit of unified party control of the executive and legislative branches of government for a full four-year term. Democrat John Kennedy also had Democratic Party majorities throughout his abbreviated presidency. In contrast, four Republicans—Nixon, Ford, Reagan, and George H. W. Bush—experienced nothing but divided government. Four presidents—Truman (D), Eisenhower (R), Clinton (D), and George W. Bush (R)—had periods of both unified and divided party government.

Scholars and journalists disagree on the implications and repercussions of divided party government for the process and substance of policymaking. There is no doubt, however, that divided government undermines presidential party leadership in the legislative arena.

As an offshoot of separation of powers, the constitutional principle of checks and balances consciously breeds antagonism between the two separated branches. In James Madison's view, protection against concentration of power, leading toward tyranny, necessitated not merely separating the executive and the legislature, but also pitting the two against each other, providing "constitutional means and personal motives to resist encroachments. . . . Ambition must be made to counteract ambition." [39]

Bicameralism further divides the congressional party into House and Senate bodies. Institutionally, the members of each chamber are conditioned to preserve and protect their particular prerogatives, against each other as well as the president.

Federalism

Federalism, the division of governmental power between the central government and the states, inhibits the president's party leadership in Congress in several ways. First, it works to decentralize party organization in the United States. Party organization parallels government organization at each level—national, state, and local—separating national parties from their state and local counterparts.

The power to nominate candidates for congressional offices clearly rests with the local party organizations. Furthermore, the advent of the direct primary method of party nomination places control of nominations in the hands of party voters in the states and districts, far removed from the president's party leadership. Indeed, those nominations could go even to men and women openly antagonistic to the president and the party program.

Second, the federal principle provides for different electoral constituencies—national for the president, state and local for senators and representatives. Diverse constituencies undermine the unifying potential of party. In the heterogeneous American society, regional variations persist. Massachusetts Democrats and Arkansas Democrats may be two different breeds, as can Pennsylvania and California Republicans.

Staggered Elections

In addition, the Constitution staggers electoral terms and schedules. Presidents serve four-year terms, representatives two, and senators six. In the context of a presidential election, all the representatives and one-third of the senators are elected simultaneously. Two years later, all the representatives and another third of the senators are up for election—midway through the president's term. These disjointed elections undermine the unity that party can bring to the political order. Moreover, the midterm congressional elections typically reduce the numbers of the president's party in Congress. This development weakens the president's influence on the legislature by undermining the base of party support and encouraging the partisan opposition.

In the November 1994 congressional elections, the Democratic Party suffered massive losses that reduced it to minority status in both the House and the Senate, shifting control of the legislative agenda to the Republicans and immensely complicating President Clinton's exercise of legislative leadership. Four years later, the Democrats unexpectedly gained seats at midterm. Not since Franklin Roosevelt in 1934 had the president's party done so. However, the GOP retained its majorities in both Houses, so Clinton's constraints continued.

In 2002 the president's party, now the Republicans, again gained seats in the House, augmenting their narrow majority, while regaining majority control of the Senate. These outcomes enhanced George W. Bush's legislative leadership position. However, four years later the 2006 midterm elections proved devastating, as the Republicans lost control of both chambers, reinstituting divided government.

In large measure because of these constitutional features of separation of powers, federalism, and staggered elections, political parties in the United States have not developed the discipline and responsibility demonstrated by their counterparts in parliamentary systems. Many of the limitations on party leadership by the president also hold true for the congressional party leadership. Take, for example, the regional differences enhanced by the federal system. Democratic president Jimmy Carter, a Georgia native, lacked rapport with many northern liberals in the congressional party, and some southern conservative Democrats viewed House Speaker Thomas P. "Tip" O'Neill Jr. with suspicion because of his Massachusetts background. Neither Carter nor O'Neill, both representing central, national party leadership, had much say over whom the voters in the 435 congressional districts and the fifty states sent to Congress. Of course, should congressional party leaders be antagonistic toward the president, presidential problems intensify.

Political Culture

The political culture in the United States—that is, the widely held attitudes and beliefs about politics and the political order—is another limitation on presidential party leadership in Congress. In the United States, the general public has long viewed political parties with considerable disfavor. In part this negative view can be traced to the antiparty position of the Framers in the late eighteenth century. It was reinforced about a century later by the progressive reformers' intellectual assault on parties.

Furthermore, the U.S. political culture is individualistic. Americans expect their political representatives to look out for them and not to subordinate their needs and interests to the party's. The public effectively discourages members of Congress from acting out of a fundamental commitment to party loyalty.

Presidential Influence on Congressional Elections

All these specific and general limitations notwithstanding, the fact remains that members of the president's party in Congress are more inclined to support presidential legislative initiatives than are the partisan opposition. Therefore, among the most potentially effective exercises of presidential party leadership are those that influence the election of fellow partisans to Congress. Presidential coattails, midterm campaigning, and party purges are three ways presidents have tried to affect the partisan composition of Congress.

Presidential Coattails

"Presidential coattails" is the voting phenomenon by which voters attracted to a presidential candidacy tend to cast their ballots in congressional elections for the nominees of the president's party. In turn, the coattails effect presumably translates into increased presidential support in Congress.

Because shared party affiliation produces a predisposition to support the president, a swelling of the ranks of the congressional partisans should increase presidential support. Furthermore, the members who have ridden into office on the president's coattails should be particularly grateful to their benefactor and thus inclined to be particularly supportive. *(See Table 29-9, p. 1365, Vol. II.)*

This theory of presidential coattails as an influence on Congress is, however, both riddled with holes and difficult to test. In the first place, not all presidents have "coattails." In the post–World War II presidential elections, several presidents appear to have been associated with minimal changes in the size of the congressional parties. There is also the possibility of reverse coattails. On five occasions—1956, 1960, 1988, 1992, and 2000—the elected president's party actually lost seats in the House, and in five contests—1972, 1984, 1988, 1996, and 2000—it lost seats in the Senate.

It is not uncommon for the presidential nominee to run behind the congressional party nominees in their states and districts. For example, in 1960 Democratic presidential nominee John Kennedy, a Massachusetts Catholic, ran behind the party's congressional and senatorial nominees throughout the South. Likewise, in 1976 the party's presidential nominee, Carter of Georgia, trailed the party ticket in many northern states and districts. Truman, Kennedy, Nixon (1968), Clinton (twice), and George W. Bush (2000) were all elected president without popular vote majorities. Their victorious congressional party counterparts, typically facing only one opponent, routinely outpolled them.

The Democratic Party's domination of Congress in the post–World War II era also complicates the theory of a coattails effect. The Democrats seized control of both houses of Congress in the election of 1948, when Truman, a Democrat, won by a narrow margin. They relinquished it in 1952 when Eisenhower, a Republican, won the presidency. Only two years later, however, the Democrats reestablished majority control of the House that they maintained for forty years. But they lost it again in the 1994 midterm elections. After a twenty-six year drought, the Republicans gained control of the Senate in 1980 when Reagan won the presidency. Six years later, the Democrats returned to power in the Senate, once again giving them majorities in both chambers. But the Democrats then lost control of the Senate in 1994, regaining it in 2001, although not via an election outcome. Rather, with the Senate evenly divided, a disgruntled Republican senator declared himself an independent and voted with the Democrats to reorganize the chamber. Losing the Senate in 2002, the Democrats came back to win control of both chambers in 2006, for the first time since 1994.

Only the elections of Presidents Truman and Eisenhower coincided with shifting party control of both chambers; Reagan's coincided with shifting party control of only one. The gains and losses of the president's party in the remaining presidential elections affected the size of existing party majorities, to be sure, but not the majorities themselves. From an empirical examination of the coattails effect in the House, political scientist George Edwards identified specific coattail victories in elections from 1952 through 1980. He credited Johnson in 1964 with the most, seventeen, and Carter in 1980 with the fewest, four.[40] Edwards concluded that "the coattail effect on congressional elections has been minimal for some time" and attributed this result primarily to the decreasing competitiveness within congressional districts.[41] In other words, safe seats have become pervasive in Congress, and they severely reduce presidential opportunities to influence electoral outcomes. He finds the explanation for this phenomenon in the heightened congressional responsiveness to the voters.

Overall, the decline of the coattails effect hinders the president's ability to exercise party leadership in Congress. If presidents are unable to carry partisan supporters into office, they have lost a key incentive in winning congressional support.

Midterm Campaigning

The Constitution mandates that midway through the president's term elections be held for the entire House and one-third of the Senate. By campaigning for party nominees, the president may influence the partisan composition of Congress.

Midterm campaigning is one of the most visible manifestations of presidential party leadership. Here the president departs from an above-partisanship stance to assume openly the mantle of party chief. Among the forms this activity can take are public speeches, statements and gestures of support for the party ticket, appearances throughout the country in behalf of selected party congressional nominees, mobilization and deployment of administrative personnel such as cabinet members, access to the national party's organizational resources, and fund-raising.

Of those activities, presidential fund-raising has taken on special significance in recent years. Political scientist James Davis reports that in 1990 President George H. W. Bush raised an unprecedented $80 million for the party ticket.[42] President Clinton was unusually attentive to fund-raising responsibilities in his two midterm campaigns. His success in seeking soft money contributions enriched the party coffers in an unprecedented fashion. In the aftermath of campaign finance legislation restricting soft money, George W. Bush similarly set records, generating more than $200 million in each of his midterm cycles.[43]

Midterm campaigning has emerged only relatively recently as a dimension of presidential party leadership. Political scientist Roger Brown points to President Woodrow Wilson as the inaugurator of the practice in 1918.[44] In that year Wilson put forward an unprecedented plea to the elec-

torate to vote Democratic to demonstrate support for and to protect the integrity of his foreign policy objectives.

More recently, the allegedly nonpolitical Eisenhower has been credited with extending presidential involvement in midterm campaigns. Indeed, his participation in the 1954 campaign went well beyond the precedents already established. According to Eisenhower biographer Stephen E. Ambrose, the president initially expressed an unwillingness to participate in the midterm campaign. He viewed such participation as improper, unlikely to succeed, and threatening to his health. In mid-October, with clear indications that party fortunes were in peril, Eisenhower responded belatedly to the pleas of party leaders. He embarked on a tour of the states east of the Mississippi River that covered more than ten thousand miles and required nearly forty speeches.[45] In 1962 President Kennedy exceeded his predecessor's pace, and since then, presidential midterm campaigning has become an important component of the expectations and responsibilities of presidential party leadership.

These exercises of presidential party leadership cannot be associated with conspicuous success. Indeed, one of the abiding truisms of electoral politics in the United States is that the president's party loses seats in the House at the midterm elections. However, in both 1998 and 2002, this pattern was broken, as the president's party gained seats for the first time since 1934.[46] The record in the Senate is less clear, but significant gains have not been the norm. (See Table 29-4, p. 1367, Vol. II.)

The 1994 election campaign was an extreme example of this phenomenon of midterm in-party losses in Congress. President Clinton, despite his low popularity ratings, was extraordinarily energetic in his campaign for Democratic nominees. He contributed to a heightened nationalization of the congressional elections, presenting them as a referendum pitting his leadership and policies against those of his Republican predecessors. The elections resulted in an overwhelming rejection of Democratic nominees, transferring majority control of both houses of Congress to the Republicans. Similarly, in 2006 voters repudiated George W. Bush's Republican Party, resulting in the loss of majorities in both chambers.

Efforts to explain the consistent pattern of midterm losses for the president's party point in a variety of directions. Although some analysts view the president as a central actor in accounting for election outcomes, others focus attention elsewhere, alternatively contending that different electorates are present in presidential and midterm elections, that economic conditions have a significant influence, or that incumbency is the critical variable.

Whatever the explanation, midterm campaigning appears more an effort to minimize losses than to maximize gains. One of the most visible exercises of presidential party leadership therefore appears, at least on the surface, to be one of the least productive. Perhaps the most conspicuous exception to this generalization occurred in 2002, when George W. Bush's energetic campaigning loomed large in explanations for the Republican advances in both chambers.

When one party controls the presidency and another controls at least one chamber of Congress, midterm campaigning carries potentially severe disadvantages for presidential legislative leadership. It can inflame partisan opposition, making the president's subsequent bipartisan appeals less effective. Further, some presidents have found members of the opposition party to be more consistently supportive than their own partisans. They have therefore been reluctant to campaign against those members. Party polarization in recent years has diminished the likelihood of this eventuality.

For this and other reasons, presidents occasionally delegate certain of their midterm campaign chores to their vice presidents. Most notably, President Eisenhower asked Nixon to campaign in 1954 and 1958, and President Nixon assigned campaign tasks to Vice President Spiro Agnew in 1970. In the 1958 and 1970 elections, a Republican president confronted a Congress controlled by Democratic majorities.

When presidents place their vice presidents at the forefront of the party effort in midterm congressional campaigns, it can be interpreted as an attempt to fulfill party leadership responsibilities while avoiding direct personal involvement that might antagonize the leaders and members of the opposition party and impair presidential stakes in the upcoming Congress.

Party Purges

In the decentralized parties, presidents usually are far removed from the selection of party senatorial and congressional nominees. This is the task of the voters in party primaries in the states and districts. Furthermore, one of the fundamental norms of U.S. party politics is that the party organization should be neutral toward competing candidacies for a nomination, and then it should willingly support whoever secures that nomination. Departures from this norm, when they do occur, are to shore up incumbents against intraparty challengers.

Nevertheless, on rare occasions presidents have assumed a high profile in primary elections to bring about the defeat of party members in Congress who have consistently opposed them and their policy initiatives. The most well known and widespread of these efforts occurred in 1938 when President Franklin Roosevelt openly sought the defeat of several congressional party incumbents who had voted against New Deal legislation. According to political scientist Sidney M. Milkis, "In the dozen states within which the president acted against entrenched incumbents, he was successful in only two of them."[47] The blatant purge effort must be judged a failure.

In the 1970 general election the Nixon administration undertook to purge a single Republican senator in New York by supporting the candidacy of Conservative Party nominee James L. Buckley over the incumbent Republican Charles E. Goodell. Although President Nixon stopped short of an endorsement of Buckley, confining himself to a statement of appreciation, Vice President Agnew was openly critical of Goodell as a betrayer of party interests. Aided by administration support, Buckley succeeded in his campaign to unseat Goodell.

This incident notwithstanding, presidents are unlikely to exercise party leadership by seeking the removal from Congress of antagonistic partisans. Party purges are rarely successful and therefore are not a very realistic option available to the president.

PRESIDENT, PARTY, AND JUDICIARY

The federal judiciary consists of the Supreme Court of the United States, explicitly provided for in the Constitution, and inferior courts, established by Congress under constitutional authorization. The system of inferior federal courts consists of district courts and courts of appeals, or circuit courts.

The constitutional principles of separation of powers and checks and balances frame the relationship between the executive and judicial branches. The chief executive check is the president's responsibility for nominating federal judges. The judiciary's check on the presidency is its capacity to exercise judicial review, which holds the president's actions accountable to the Supreme Court's interpretation of presidential power under the Constitution.

Partisan considerations rarely surface directly in analyses of the federal judiciary. Unlike the chief executive and members of Congress, federal judges are not elected in the wake of party nominations. Rather, they are appointed. Moreover, unlike the legislature, the judiciary is not organized along partisan lines, with majority and minority institutions. Judges do not take action as overt partisans. Indeed, the judicial role ostensibly requires a nonpartisan stance.

One should not assume, however, that partisan considerations and presidential party leadership have no relevance in the federal judiciary. They do, but in an indirect and often shrouded fashion. In the judicial arena, partisanship manifests itself perhaps most clearly in the appointment of judges.

Appointment in turn is a two-stage process consisting of nomination and confirmation. Article III of the Constitution specifically empowers the president to nominate justices of the Supreme Court. It empowers the Senate to confirm the president's nomination. The appointment process for lower-court federal judges also consists of presidential nomination and senatorial confirmation.

Partisanship and Supreme Court Appointments

According to the Constitution, Congress determines the size of the Supreme Court. Before 1869, the number of justices fluctuated between five and ten; ever since the number remained at nine.

In making nominations to the Supreme Court when vacancies occur, the president normally considers several factors. Partisanship looms large among them. Certainly, the record of appointments to date indicates that presidents are strongly inclined to name persons who share their party affiliation. Political scientist Henry J. Abraham found that presidents do so about 85 percent of the time. From his examination of the 112 presidential appointees who have actually served on the Court since 1789, Abraham was able to identify only fourteen instances in which a president crossed partisan lines in the appointment process.[48] (See Table 17-6.) The latest instance of a nonpartisan nomination occurred in 1971, when Republican Nixon named Lewis F. Powell, a conservative southern Democrat. The heightened polarization that has characterized the party system since then makes it much more difficult for presidents to identify and recommend judges from the opposing party who could be expected to share their policy orientations.

Thus the question is not whether partisanship is associated with presidential nominations to the Supreme Court, but why partisanship is important. Do Supreme Court nominations constitute a presidential party leadership opportunity? The answer is a qualified yes. In the words of President Theodore Roosevelt,

> In the ordinary and low sense which we attach to the words "partisan" and "politician," a judge of the Supreme Court should be neither. But in the highest sense, in the proper sense, he is not in my judgment fitted for the position unless he is a party man, a constructive statesman constantly keeping in mind his adherence to the principles and policies under which this nation has been built up and in accordance with which it must go on.[49]

Supreme Court nominations are probably the highest form of presidential patronage. They can be used to reward persons for previous services rendered to the president and the party. Several presidents, for example, have elevated members of their cabinets to the Court, with the attorney generalship in particular being a steppingstone. In the twentieth century, five attorneys general were named to the high court: James C. McReynolds (1914), Harlan Fiske Stone (1925), Frank Murphy (1940), Robert H. Jackson (1941), and Tom C. Clark (1949).

From a slightly different and more symbolic perspective, Supreme Court nominations provide presidents as party leaders with opportunities to reward supportive groups or to broaden the party coalition by reaching out to new groups within the electorate. Here persons appointed

TABLE 17-6 **Nonpartisan Presidential Supreme Court Nominations**

Year	President	President's party	Nominee	Nominee's party
1845	Tyler	Whig	Samuel Nelson	Dem.
1863	Lincoln	Rep.	Stephen J. Field	Dem.
1893	B. Harrison	Rep.	Howell E. Jackson	Dem.
1909	Taft	Rep.	Horace H. Lurton	Dem.
1910			Edward D. White[a]	Dem.
1910			Joseph R. Lamar	Dem.
1916	Wilson	Dem.	Louis D. Brandeis	Rep.
1922	Harding	Rep.	Pierce Butler	Dem.
1932	Hoover	Rep.	Benjamin Cardozo	Dem.
1939	F. Roosevelt	Dem.	Felix Frankfurter	Ind.
1941			Harlan F. Stone[a]	Rep.
1945	Truman	Dem.	Harold D. Burton	Rep.
1956	Eisenhower	Rep.	William Brennan	Dem.
1971	Nixon	Rep.	Lewis F. Powell	Dem.

SOURCE: Henry J. Abraham, *The Judicial Process,* 7th ed. (New York: Oxford University Press, 1998).

NOTE: a. Elevated from associate justice to chief justice.

can be identified with larger groups of which they are a part. Consider the long-standing customs of maintaining geographical, Catholic, and Jewish seats on the Court, along with the more recent appointments of African Americans and women.

In 1967, in an era featuring dramatic advances in federal civil rights policies, President Johnson nominated noted African American civil rights advocate Thurgood Marshall to a Court seat. In 1981, with women's groups becoming increasingly visible and assertive in the political process, President Reagan named Sandra Day O'Connor to the Court, fulfilling a campaign promise to choose a woman if the opportunity arose. In each instance, the president recognized an important political constituency and achieved a historic first by choosing a member of a previously unrepresented group.

Both these precedents subsequently received reinforcement, providing them with staying power. In 1991, after Marshall's resignation, President George H. W. Bush nominated Clarence Thomas, an African American conservative whom Bush had previously named to a seat on a federal circuit court. Bush thus maintained the Johnson precedent and also sought to make Republican inroads in the Democratic hold on black voters established in the New Deal era and solidified in the 1960s. President Clinton awarded his first Supreme Court nomination to a female federal judge, Ruth Ginsburg. This action, which doubled the number of women on the Court, fulfilled Clinton's expressed commitment to greater gender diversity in the federal government and recognized the importance of women voters to his recent election and his prospective reelection.

Notwithstanding presidential initiatives, organized interests can and do put pressure on the president for representation on the Court. Similarly, party managers encourage the president to be attentive to party interests in making Supreme Court nominations. In 1969, with two vacancies to be filled by President Nixon, national party chair Rogers Morton encouraged the president to "think Republican." [50]

Party leadership considerations, however, are not the primary motivations underlying Supreme Court nominations. Rather, as in executive branch appointments, presidents first seek policy responsiveness—that is, presidents want justices on the Court who share their general orientations toward public policy. The stakes are much higher in naming Supreme Court nominees because of their tenure. Executive appointees serve at the pleasure of the president, but justices, according to the Constitution, hold office during good behavior, which is tantamount to a lifetime term. Thus presidential nominees on the Court can influence the course of public policy long after the departure of the president.

From this vantage point, partisanship takes on significance mostly as an indicator of policy orientation. Ideological compatibility emerges as the overriding presidential expectation, with party-building considerations of secondary importance. In the Clarence Thomas nomination, certainly the first President Bush was more certain of Thomas's ideological conservatism than of the prospect of attracting black voters to the Republican banner. Thus the Thomas nomination can be properly interpreted as an effort by Bush to solidify his own vulnerable standing among Republican conservative activists.

In 2005 a new generation of Republican conservative activists confounded the efforts of President George W. Bush to nominate a personal loyalist, White House Counsel Harriet Miers, to fill a Supreme Court vacancy created by the retirement of Justice Sandra Day O'Connor. The Miers nomination would have kept the number of women on the court at two. However, conservatives objected vociferously to the nomination, on the grounds that Miers' ideological qualifications were insufficient. With Democrats piling on by objecting to Miers's lack of constitutional law experience, she withdrew, enabling Bush to nominate Samuel Alito, who was confirmed with enthusiastic conservative approval.

Republican president Theodore Roosevelt illustrated his endorsement of this partisan-ideological distinction in an observation to Henry Cabot Lodge about the prospect of nominating Democrat Horace H. Lurton: "The nominal politics of the man has nothing to do with his actions on the bench. His real politics are all important." [51]

Partisan considerations can reinforce ideological ones in the senatorial confirmation process. Presidential strength influences outcomes, and divided party government contributes possible complications.[52] In 1969–1970 the Democratic-controlled Senate rejected two of Republican president Nixon's nominations. More recently, the return of the Democrats to majority status in the Senate in the 1986 elections set the stage for the Senate's 1987 rejection of Republican president Reagan's nominee Robert H. Bork.

Partisanship and Lower Federal Court Appointments

In 2007 the lower federal court system comprised ninety-one U.S. district courts, with 645 judges, and thirteen U.S. courts of appeals, with 177 judges.[53] The formal appointments process for judges on lower federal courts is the same as for justices of the Supreme Court: presidential nomination and senatorial approval. The president tends to be much less involved in these nominations, however, because of the larger number of appointments. Typically, the attorney general and Justice Department associates play a critical role in the recruitment process, as well as White House staff.

The long-standing practice known as senatorial courtesy also comes into play in lower-court nominations. Under this tradition, senators of the president's party from the state in which the nominee is to serve have effective veto power over that nomination. Thus presidents or their agents usually consult the relevant senators before making the nomination.

Presidents may well encourage recommendations from these senators, or the senators may volunteer candidates. In practice, senators' recommendations for district court judges carry more weight than those for the appeals courts.

Should a judicial vacancy occur in a state in which the president's party is not represented in the Senate, the senatorial role remains important. The opposition senators normally are at least consulted. In this case, a bipartisan consensus or perhaps an allocation of nominations between the senators and the president may occur.

State and local party leaders may play significant roles in such nominations. In addition, members of the state delegation in the House of Representatives who share the president's party affiliation may assume and assert influence over presidential nominations. Their participation is not institutionalized like that of senatorial courtesy; indeed, there is no guarantee they will be consulted. Rather, their influence depends on considerations such as power relationships, friendships, and favors owed and claimed. State party leaders sometimes mediate disagreements within the state's senatorial delegation over judicial appointments. Alternatively, if the state delegation in Congress does not include a member of the president's party, the state party leader may play a more assertive role.

Other persons and groups who may influence judicial nominations include the American Bar Association, sitting judges, and interest groups. In these cases, partisan and party leadership considerations recede in importance.

Lower federal court judges share the president's party affiliation in even higher percentages than do Supreme

Court justices—about 90 percent according to Abraham's study.[54] As with Supreme Court nominations, policy responsiveness has become the overriding consideration. Ideological compatibility may even transcend partisanship. Party leadership considerations probably receive greater weight in staffing the lower federal courts than in filling Supreme Court vacancies because of the vast number of positions, the key role of the senatorial party, and the pressure from state party leaders.

Because members of the Senate are more directly involved in the recruitment of lower-court judges, the confirmation process itself is rarely controversial or overtly partisan. The Judiciary Committee receives the nomination, typically holds brief hearings, and then recommends the nomination to the entire Senate. On the Senate floor, lower federal court nominations ordinarily pass by voice votes.

Still, as in the case of Supreme Court nominations, the presence of divided party government can complicate the presidential nomination of lower-court judges, making senatorial confirmation potentially more problematic. In such cases the president is likely to designate noncontroversial nominees rather than risk senatorial rejection. Presidents Bill Clinton and George W. Bush had difficulties in getting the Senate Judiciary Committee, controlled by the opposition party, to report judicial nominations to the floor for a confirmation vote. Even with a party majority in the Senate, George W. Bush discovered that the opposition Democrats could effectively threaten a filibuster and thereby keep his nominees bottled up in committee.

PRESIDENT, PARTY, AND THE ELECTORATE

For parties there is strength in numbers. Like its rivals, the president's party is constantly competing to attract more adherents and maintain good relations with them as well as with the party faithful. Thus the party in the electorate forms a crucial part of the president's core constituency. The concept of the party in the electorate refers to people who are qualified to vote and who identify with the party, its causes, and its candidates.

Party Identification in the U.S. Electorate

Party identification is an attachment a person feels toward a political party. It is ascertained by self-classification and manifests itself most significantly in voting behavior.

Survey research during the past half-century indicates that most Americans develop partisan attachments that are relatively persistent for individual voters and, in the aggregate, are stable over time. Since the New Deal, the percentage of self-proclaimed Democratic identifiers has ranged from the midthirties to the low fifties. Democrats reached their high-water marks early on, in the 1930s, and again in the mid-1960s. Their nadir came in the mid-1990s. Meanwhile,

the Republicans reached the 40 percent level only once, in 1946; and even sunk into the low twenties during the 1970s. Beginning with Ronald Reagan in the 1980s, the Republicans have narrowed their long-standing deficit and approached parity by the mid-1990s. Since then, their support has declined. Measurements of partisan identification vary with regard to categorizing self-styled independents who regularly support one particular party. Thus, on the one hand, Americans appear decreasingly inclined to make these enduring partisan attachments, and the percentage of independent identifiers has risen to a level above either of the major parties. On the other, strong partisans are on the rise in the electorate, amid relative stability in overall party identification over time.[55]

Party identification develops through political socialization—the acquisition of political information and attitudes. Students of political socialization have learned that party loyalties often emerge relatively early in a person's life and are usually in place by the elementary school years. This finding points to the family as a primary agent for determining a person's party identity. Surveys of elementary school children indicate that although they may know little else about politics, they are fully aware of the identity of the president and generally associate the president with a political party.[56]

The president's extremely high public visibility combines with the public's awareness of the president's political party to make the chief executive's status as party leader perhaps clearest from the perspective of the party in the electorate. Here, there is no real appreciation for the conflicts, rivalries, and tensions that can beset exercises of presidential party leadership of the party organization or the congressional party. Rather, the president's party leadership is readily and uncritically acknowledged.

Partisanship and Presidential Support

Partisanship in the electorate influences evaluations of the president by providing filters or screens through which people see the chief executive. As Gallup poll surveys show, voters who identify with the president's party are inclined to be supportive, while opposition party identifiers invariably are less so inclined. *(See Table 17-7, p. 922.)* In addition, evidence indicates that members of the president's party think of themselves and the president as having similar policy positions. On the one hand, they tend to believe the president shares their stances. On the other, they may alter theirs to conform to the president's.[57]

This link between the president and the party in the electorate emerged during the presidency of Andrew Jackson; it was not part of Thomas Jefferson's pioneering presidential party leadership. In Jefferson's day, voter eligibility was restricted by state law to Christian, white, male property holders.

TABLE 17-7 **Partisanship and Public Approval of the President, 1953–2006 (percent)**

President	Year	Democrats	Republicans	Independents
Eisenhower (R)	1953	56	87	67
	1954	49	87	69
	1955	56	91	74
	1956	56	93	75
	1957	47	86	66
	1958	36	82	56
	1959	48	88	66
	1960	44	87	64
Kennedy (D)	1961	87	58	72
	1962	86	49	69
	1963	79	44	62
L. Johnson (D)	1964	84	62	69
	1965	79	49	69
	1966	65	31	64
	1967	59	26	38
	1968	58	27	36
Nixon (R)	1969	50	83	61
	1970	42	83	57
	1971	36	79	49
	1972	41	86	67
	1973	26	71	43
Nixon/Ford (R)	1974	25	60	35
Ford (R)	1975	33	66	45
	1976	36	71	51
Carter (D)	1977	73	46	60
	1978	56	28	42
	1979	47	25	35
	1980	54	26	36
Reagan (R)	1981	38	83	57
	1982	24	79	46
	1983	28	80	49
	1984	32	88	59
	1985	35	89	62
	1986	40	86	60
	1987	26	79	50
	1988	30	85	53
G. H. W. Bush (R)	1989	46	82	53
	1990	53	86	63
	1991	58	89	70
	1992	18	65	36
Clinton (D)	1993	70	22	42
	1994	75	21	46
	1995	76	20	47
	1996	85	23	54
	1997	85	30	54
	1998	89	36	64
	1999	88	31	61
	2000	90	29	59
G. W. Bush (R)	2001	46	92	63
	2002	53	95	69
	2003	33	92	56
	2004	15	91	45
	2005	14	87	38
	2006	9	80	29

SOURCES: Gallup poll; George C. Edwards III, *The Public Presidency* (New York: St. Martin's Press, 1983), 214; and updated by author from *Gallup Poll Monthly*, various issues, 1981–1998, and data provided by the Gallup Poll, 1999–2007.

Moreover, the Constitution had placed presidential selection in the hands of electors, themselves chosen by methods determined by the state legislatures. At the outset, the state legislatures divided between those making the choice of electors themselves and those authorizing the popular vote to do so. More opted for the former than the latter.

Gradually, however, more democratic norms and practices began to prevail. During the next three decades, revised state constitutions eliminated religious tests and property requirements for voting, and the constitutions of the new states entering the Union omitted them. Also, the state legislatures that initially had retained control over selection of presidential electors passed that power to the voters. By the time of the Jackson presidency in 1828, the country was more democratic than it had been at its birth. A connection between the president and the party in the electorate had been established.

In turn, Jackson was a popular hero who seized this opportunity unavailable to his predecessors to fashion the public link. In doing so, he dramatically increased the political power of the president. Henceforth, the president could claim to have been chosen by the people and derive power from their sovereignty.

Twentieth-century innovations in the realm of communications technology enhanced this popular connection. First radio and then television brought the president into the living rooms of partisan supporters throughout the nation, heightening the sense of identification. In this fashion, the president emerged as the embodiment of the party in the eyes of the voters.

An intriguing question arises about a president's capacity to influence and even induce party identification within the electorate. Most studies of the distribution of party loyalties point toward social class, region, religion, race, and sex as controlling factors. But individual politicians' personalities, and issues, have short-term importance in explaining departures from party loyalty.

For example, in the 1950s millions of Americans could like Ike (Dwight Eisenhower) without abandoning their traditional Democratic loyalties. Similarly in the 1980s, even though the Democrats continued to surpass Republicans in holding the allegiance of voters, Ronald Reagan was able to attract droves of Democratic voters in his sweeping electoral victories.

This being said, fundamental realignments of party loyalties can occur, elevating new parties into positions of dominance. Contextual factors, especially economic ones producing depressions, remain an important explanation of these phenomena. But the potential contribution of presidential party leadership cannot be ignored. One of the president's major challenges is to establish or maintain the party in the dominant position. By this standard, Franklin Roosevelt was eminently successful, while Eisenhower fell short.

Partisanship in the electorate experiences ebbs and flows, amid controversies associated with measurement issues. Studies in the 1950s and 1960s generally found party identification to be strong and stable. In the 1970s the "decline of party" thesis emerged, addressing a weakening in the commitments of the professed party identifiers and a corresponding rise in split ticket voting. In the 1980s and 1990s partisanship appeared to heighten, amid significant ideological realignment that produced a more coherently liberal Democratic Party and conservative Republican Party. In the first decade of the twenty-first century, this pattern persists, alongside signs of resurgent independence in the electorate.[58] Such shifts have great significance for presidential relationships with the electorate that rely on partisanship and party leadership.

Group Bases of Party Electoral Coalitions

To speak of the party in the electorate is to recognize that the electorate is divided into many different groups. Parties seek to enlist the support of these groups in behalf of their nominees. In turn, appealing nominees can point voters in these groups toward their parties. In the electorate, a president's personal and party leadership interests converge in an effort to maintain and expand the party's electoral coalition.

In the context of presidential campaigns, candidates make specific overtures to various groups in seeking their support. The most common approach takes the form of an issue or policy stance proposed to gain favor with the group. A candidate seeking to appeal to Jewish voters, for example, might emphasize a commitment to aid for Israel. In 1980 Ronald Reagan solidified traditional business support for the Republican Party by strongly advocating deregulation.

Political parties assemble platforms, or wide-ranging statements of issue positions, and present them to voters as promises in return for support. The party's presidential nominee usually has a significant role in the development of the platform. The positions that presidential nominees and incumbent presidents take inevitably are attributed to the nominating party.

Presidential Patronage

Patronage provides presidents with opportunities to develop and maintain support from interest groups. Appointments to positions in the executive and judicial branches, particularly those with high visibility, enable the president to recognize and to reward representatives of key interest groups in the electoral coalition. Presidents also can reach out to new constituencies through an astute use of the appointing power.

As mentioned earlier, President Lyndon Johnson's 1967 nomination of Thurgood Marshall, an African American, to a seat on the Supreme Court had immense symbolic and substantive value. It recognized the contribution of black voters to the electoral successes of the president

and the Democratic Party. It also demonstrated the abiding commitment of the Johnson administration to the cause of civil rights.

Political scientist Nelson W. Polsby identifies "clientele representation" as one of three strategies presidents use in forming cabinets. Presidents acknowledge that many federal departments serve as advocates for major interests, and they appoint as departmental secretaries leaders who reflect these interests.[59] Recent examples of cabinet appointments that fit this pattern include George H. W. Bush's designation of Clayton Yeutter as secretary of agriculture and Clinton's decision to name Bruce Babbitt secretary of the interior. Yeutter had a lifelong background in agriculture concerns, while Babbitt maintained close ties with environmental groups.

In seeking a cabinet that "looked like America," President Clinton reached out to women and minorities in identifying leaders for the executive departments. In addition to including women and African Americans in significant policymaking positions, President George W. Bush demonstrated his awareness of the rising electoral presence of Hispanics, and his hopes of enlisting them in the Republican ranks, through cabinet nominations of Mel Martinez (Housing and Urban Development), Alberto Gonzales (Justice), and Carlos Gutierrez (Commerce).

Public Liaison

In addition to electoral and symbolic appeals to distinct groups, presidents since Franklin Roosevelt have made the White House a point of direct access for representatives of supportive interest groups. Earlier presidents, of course, had to be attentive to the groups that composed the party coalitions. The modern presidency, however, has developed an organizational unit, the White House Office of Public Liaison, to work with a variety of interests.

As with any organization, the expansion of the White House Office has been accompanied by a division of labor and specialization. Early on, in the Truman White House, one task of presidential assistant David Niles was to maintain relations with representatives of minority groups. Subsequent presidents built on this foundation and broadened it by designating specific aides as liaisons with specific interest groups. For example, in the Eisenhower administration Frederick Morrow, the first African American ever appointed to the White House staff, served as a contact point for the black community on issues related to civil rights. Through designated staff assistants, Lyndon Johnson reached out to Catholics and Jews.

During the Nixon years, plans to organize and give more official standing to this activity took shape. Ford established the Office of Public Liaison, with a director and a staff, in the White House. The institution has continued under Ford's successors, and it is now established firmly as part of the White House Office.

Confronting divisive policy issues, presidents may well provide differential access and encouragement to organized interests and their electoral constituencies. For example, since the elevation of the abortion issue, prochoice forces found the Clinton White House to be more attentive and receptive to their concerns than his predecessors or successor. The George W. Bush administration was conspicuously conscientious in reaching out to social conservatives on the religious right.

Public liaison aides play an intermediary role. On the one hand, they communicate to the president the needs and interests of the various groups. On the other, they seek to build support for the president and presidential policies within and among the groups.

In institutionalizing this liaison function in the White House Office, presidents have in one sense advanced the cause of presidential party leadership. Because the public so clearly identifies the president with a party, the party can benefit from the president's successful efforts to call forth support from interest groups.

Sometimes, though, this establishment of direct presidential communications with interest groups can work to the detriment of the political party. Historically, parties served as intermediary associations connecting the electorate, including groups, with the government. The development and maintenance of direct ties between interest groups and the presidency largely bypass the party as an intermediary. To the extent that the president can assemble interest groups into a coalition of supporters, they constitute themselves as a presidential party, in a manner of speaking.

This aggregation must then be linked in an enduring fashion with the existing party organization. The capacity to do so constitutes a measure of considerable success in presidential party leadership. Failure, in turn, intensifies separation between president and party and can contribute to antagonism in president-party relations.

FDR TO GEORGE W. BUSH: PARTY LEADERSHIP PORTRAITS

Presidential style is an elusive concept. As used in this section, it refers to the distinctive behavior of the president as party leader. The presidency is an extremely personal office that takes on the character of its immediate occupant. In a study of presidential character, political scientist James David Barber pointed out the significance of the personal dimensions of the presidency.[60]

Presidents exercise leadership within a structural framework that provides opportunities in some situations and constraints in others. A critical assessment of individual presidents as party leaders therefore must consider both personal and structural factors.

The background and experiences of the president, particularly as they pertain to party politics, are highly relevant. Structurally balancing these characteristics are, first, the distribution and significance of partisanship in both the electorate and Congress during the president's tenure, and, second, the vitality of the party organization. Linking the two are the assistance the party is able to provide toward achievement of the president's political objectives and the personal contributions of the president to the structure of party competition. What follows are brief biographical characterizations of recent presidents as party leaders.

Franklin D. Roosevelt

Franklin Roosevelt, a transformative figure in American government history, presided over the emergence of the modern presidency. As party leader, he set in motion developments and patterns that have become standard features for his successors. Roosevelt was an enthusiastic partisan who was instrumental in remaking the Democratic Party.

Roosevelt came from a distinguished New York family. His branch of Roosevelts settled in Hyde Park, where they were known as the Democratic Roosevelts. This label distinguished them from their Oyster Bay cousins, led by Theodore, who were Republican to the core.

While still in his twenties, Franklin Roosevelt entered party politics and ran successfully for a seat in the New York senate. He supported Woodrow Wilson's presidential candidacy in 1912. After Wilson was elected, he named Roosevelt assistant secretary of the navy. Roosevelt held this position until the end of the Wilson administration. Then in 1920 the Democratic Party nominated FDR for the vice presidency and James M. Cox for the presidency.

Unsuccessful in that quest, Roosevelt retired to private life and underwent a debilitating bout with polio. That did not prevent him, however, from laboring in behalf of fellow Democrat Al Smith's quest for the Democratic presidential nomination in 1924 and 1928. After Smith's nomination in 1928, Roosevelt received the state party nomination to succeed Smith as governor. Elected in 1928 and reelected in 1930, he sought his party's presidential nomination in 1932 with a clear and long-standing identity as a Democrat.

Roosevelt's successful nomination campaign was spearheaded by party chieftain James A. Farley, who traveled the country lining up support among key party activists. For the general election campaign, he named Farley as party chair and emphasized his party affiliation. His electoral victory accompanied Democratic successes in the congressional elections.

Thus Roosevelt entered the White House as an unabashed partisan with comfortable party majorities in Congress. Not surprisingly, he openly grasped the mantle of party leadership. The Democrats in Congress responded by enacting a broad social and economic program called the "New Deal."

Roosevelt's relations with congressional Democrats also featured considerable conflict, however. Not only did the president fail dramatically in his effort to gain legislative approval to add justices to the Supreme Court (the "Court-packing" plan), but he also vetoed a record number of congressional bills.

Both inside and outside Congress, Roosevelt sought to remake the Democratic Party in a modified image that would alter its structure and its ideological orientation. This effort entailed bringing new groups and forces into the Democratic electoral coalition. It also meant moving the party in a more liberal direction ideologically. This required extraordinary efforts to influence the composition of the party in office by openly campaigning against recalcitrant incumbents in congressional party primaries.

Finally, Roosevelt sought to relocate control within the party away from the traditional bosses in the states and localities, replacing them as leaders with his agents in positions of responsibility within the federal government. It was partly this development that led to a widely publicized falling-out between Roosevelt and party chair Farley.

Although he fell short of fully achieving these ambitious objectives, Roosevelt otherwise enjoyed conspicuous success in his exercise of presidential party leadership. Furthermore, his extraordinarily long tenure, spanning both the Great Depression and World War II, established him as the exemplar of the modern presidency. Roosevelt provides the benchmark for evaluating subsequent presidents as party leaders.

Harry S. Truman

On Roosevelt's death in 1945, Harry Truman succeeded to the presidency. In his rise to the vice presidency, Truman had developed an intimate association with Democratic Party politics. Indeed, he began his political career in the Kansas City area of his native Missouri toiling for the Pendergast machine, renowned for its strength and its corruption. He served as county judge and received the party nomination for the U.S. Senate in return for his loyalty to and services in behalf of the party organization. Party loyalty marked his senatorial career, placing him in position to receive the vice presidential nomination in 1944. He had held that office for less than three months when Roosevelt died.

A vice president elevated to the presidency through a vacancy inherits certain constitutionally based roles and responsibilities. The presidential role of party leader, however, operates outside the specific constitutional framework. Truman's exercise of party leadership as an accidental president illustrates a variation on the normal pattern in which the party's presidential nomination initially confers leadership status that is confirmed by the victory in the general election.

Truman became party leader without the legitimacy of nomination and election. Nevertheless, he benefited from Robert Hannegan's presence in the national party chair. Hannegan was an old Missouri political ally who held that position in part because of Senator Truman's earlier recommendation. In turn, Hannegan had been instrumental in pushing for Truman's selection as Roosevelt's vice presidential running mate in 1944.

Thus the relationship between President Truman and the party organization began on a positive note. After Hannegan's departure, Truman did not hesitate to exercise his presidential prerogative in recommending a successor to the national committee. His choice, Sen. J. Howard McGrath of Rhode Island, quickly received committee approval.

Truman began his presidential tenure with Democratic Party majorities in both houses of Congress. The foreign and defense policy tasks of concluding World War II and preparing for peace in the postwar world precluded, however, any major domestic policy initiatives at the outset. In the 1946 midterm congressional elections, the Republicans won majorities in both houses. The president pursued a combative strategy in dealing with the Republican congressional leadership in domestic affairs for the next two years.

In 1948 Truman won an upset victory over his Republican challenger, Gov. Thomas E. Dewey of New York. The Democrats also regained control of Congress and maintained it for the duration of Truman's presidency. During these years, Truman sought without noteworthy success to secure the enactment of his domestic policy agenda, the Fair Deal.

Developing strains in the Democratic Party coalition posed a serious problem for Truman. A major controversy over the party's commitment to civil rights split the 1948 national convention, resulting in a walkout by several southern delegations and the formation of the States' Rights or Dixiecrat Party for the general election. The Democrats also experienced ideological conflict that led the same year to the departure of a portion of the party's left wing under the banner of former vice president Henry Wallace and the Progressive Party.

In sum, Truman followed Roosevelt in openly and enthusiastically embracing partisanship. He was a Democrat to the core, fully comfortable with the mantle of party leadership in spite of the extraordinary conditions surrounding his accession. Yet his presidential party leadership did not demonstrate the transformational character of his predecessor's.

Dwight D. Eisenhower

Dwight Eisenhower entered national politics at the presidential level after a distinguished military career; he lacked any background or experience in party politics. Courted by representatives of both major parties, he cast his lot with the

Republicans at a time when they had not won a presidential election in more than two decades and they held the allegiance of a distinct minority of the electorate.

Eisenhower's presidential candidacy attracted legions of enthusiastic amateurs under the organizational umbrella of Citizens for Eisenhower. In the years to come, the president labored without noteworthy success to integrate this element into the regular party organization. In that effort, he encountered resistance from amateurs and party regulars alike.

As president, Eisenhower exhibited a leadership style that political scientist Fred I. Greenstein has characterized as "hidden hand." [61] He self-consciously and systematically sought to obscure his political activities. Although all presidents are aware of the political benefits to be derived from a nonpolitical posture, Eisenhower appreciated this reality more than most.

He was acutely aware of his lack of formal authority over the Republican Party. This is clearly evident in his comments at two press conferences about midway through his tenure. In the first, weeks away from his 1956 reelection victory, he observed:

> Now, let's remember, there are no national parties in the United States. There are forty-eight state parties, and they are the ones that determine the people that belong to those parties.
>
> There is nothing I can do to say that one is not a Republican. The most I can say is that in many things they do not agree with me. Therefore, in looking for help to get over a program, which is the sole purpose of political leadership, as I see it, for the good of the country, I can't look to them for help. But we have got to remember that these are state organizations, and there is nothing I can do to say so-and-so is a Republican and so-and-so is not a Republican.[62]

In the second statement, less than six months into his second term, Eisenhower noted: "He, the president, is the leader not of the, you might say, hierarchy of control in any political party. What he is is the leader who translates the platform into a legislative program in collaboration with his own executive departments and with the legislative leaders." [63]

Eisenhower regularly bemoaned his inability to move the party in the direction of the "modern Republicanism" he espoused. In turn, party activists often viewed him as inattentive to their interests. Certainly, he demonstrated little concern with or enthusiasm for the exercise of patronage power as a party-building device.

His administrative style featured extensive delegation of authority, and he tended to view "politics" as the special province of the party chair. The party chairs who served during his presidency found themselves more within the presidential circle than has been typical since World War II. His 1956 reelection campaign, under the general direction of party chair Leonard Hall, featured extensive integration with the national party effort.

In Congress the Republican Party gained a majority of seats in both houses in the 1952 elections that brought Eisenhower to the White House. The party lost control of Congress in the midterm 1954 elections, however, and remained in the minority for the remainder of his presidency. This development forced Eisenhower to look beyond the party ranks in seeking support for his policy initiatives and further muted his partisanship.

For Eisenhower, personal and structural factors combined to diminish the emphasis on presidential partisanship compared with that evident during the Roosevelt and Truman years. He was not personally comfortable with its exercise. Nor did the political climate encourage presidential partisanship. Indeed, Eisenhower perceived political benefits in denying it. Moreover, the efforts he made to reshape the Republican Party and make it over as a majority party failed. Still, he remained a revered and unifying figure in the eyes of most of his fellow Republicans.

John F. Kennedy

In contrast with his predecessor, John Kennedy ardently embraced partisanship. His family was closely identified with the Democratic Party, and successful congressional and senatorial contests under the party banner had preceded his race for the presidency. In the early days of that candidacy, he proclaimed his leadership responsibilities in the party arena.

> No president, it seems to me, can escape politics. He has not only been chosen by the nation—he has been chosen by his party. And if he insists that he is "president of all the people" and should, therefore, offend none of them—if he blurs the issues and differences between the parties—if he neglects the party machinery and avoids his party's leadership—then he has not only weakened the political party . . . he has dealt a blow to the democratic process itself.[64]

Kennedy installed a longtime political ally, Connecticut party chair John Bailey, as the national party chair, but Bailey lacked direct access to the president. White House appointments secretary Kenneth P. O'Donnell provided primary liaison between the party organization and the president.

In Congress, Democratic majorities controlled both chambers during the Kennedy administration, but a large portion of the party and committee leadership consisted of southern conservatives who were not keen on some of his policy initiatives and were adamantly opposed to others. As a result, at the time of the president's assassination the Kennedy administration had failed to achieve noteworthy legislative successes.

As party leader, President Kennedy reverted to the Roosevelt-Truman pattern of unabashed partisanship in his rhetoric. His substantive accomplishments in this realm were not particularly noteworthy. Any evaluation of his presidency must take into account, however, his short tenure in office.

Presidential candidate John F. Kennedy and running mate Lyndon B. Johnson talk with Eleanor Roosevelt at a Democratic Party rally in New York City on November 5, 1960.

Lyndon B. Johnson

Although clearly identified as a Democrat, Lyndon Johnson sought consensus throughout his political career. He came to Washington with a background in the one-party politics of his native Texas, where party organization was notoriously weak. In his rise to the presidency he served consecutively as congressional assistant, New Deal bureaucrat, representative, senator, and vice president.

On assuming the presidency after Kennedy was assassinated, Johnson inherited the party management team assembled by his predecessor. He retained the team members not only in the interest of party unity but also because he needed their expertise in his upcoming quest for a presidential term of his own. Still, he felt he could not fully trust the Kennedy loyalists to act in his behalf.

Johnson interspersed his own trusted associates amid the Kennedy holdovers. In the realm of party relations, the main responsibilities initially were assigned to Walter Jenkins at the White House and Clifton Carter, who went to the national committee as the president's untitled representative. Later, Marvin Watson took over the White House end, and John Criswell succeeded Carter at the national headquarters. Having established this structure, Johnson generally was inattentive and occasionally even antagonistic to the needs and interests of the party organization.

In Johnson's 1964 campaign for president, his agents supervised the convention proceedings closely. The national party headquarters, however, was much less visible within the campaign organization than its counterpart had been during President Eisenhower's 1956 reelection campaign. After the Republicans nominated Barry M. Goldwater, a strong ideological conservative, Johnson was able to draw support from disaffected Republicans. In doing so, he blurred his own partisanship and undertook a nonpartisan effort. The result was a landslide victory of historic proportions.

The 1964 elections also brought impressive Democratic majorities to both houses of Congress, giving Johnson a strengthened partisan base on which to seek the enactment of his party's legislative program. At this task, he was much more successful than Kennedy, not only because of the improved arithmetic but also because of his considerable skill as a legislative leader. He clearly appealed to party loyalty and unity, but he also worked closely and cooperatively with the opposition leadership, particularly on civil rights legislation, to offset southern Democratic opposition and to promote national unity.

As his term wore on, Johnson faced increasing opposition within his party to both his domestic initiatives and his foreign policies. The Vietnam War was especially divisive. At the beginning of the 1968 presidential campaign season, Sen. Eugene McCarthy of Minnesota announced his challenge to Johnson's expected renomination. McCarthy's impressive early showing in the New Hampshire primary encouraged Sen. Robert F. Kennedy of New York to join the race. In a dramatic nationally televised address on March 31, 1968, President Johnson announced that he would neither seek nor accept the party's presidential nomination. For the remainder of his term, Johnson affected a nonpartisan stance, although his agents were very visible at that summer's Democratic national convention.

President Johnson never appeared fully comfortable in his role as party leader. His consensus style did not allow the exclusion of significant elements of Congress or the electorate from his domain.

During his retirement years, the vehement opposition Johnson had engendered within the party lingered, precluding his assumption of a role as party elder statesman. Indeed, at the 1972 national convention, he received none of the accolades customarily accorded a former nominee and president. He died in 1973.

Richard Nixon

Richard Nixon began his campaign for the White House in 1968 with a well-deserved reputation as a slashing Republican partisan. He had earned this designation during his years as a member of the House and Senate from 1947 to 1953. He reinforced it as Eisenhower's vice president from 1953 to 1961. As vice president he assumed many of the responsibilities of party leadership with which Eisenhower was uncomfortable. He gained the enduring gratitude of Republican activists for his extensive party-building efforts. His scathing attacks on Democratic personalities and programs simultaneously generated emotional public support and antagonism. In his successful 1968 presidential campaign, however, Nixon labored to appear above partisanship and called for a lowering of voices and an end to divisiveness.

In the Oval Office, President Nixon frequently disappointed party regulars with his general disregard and occasional animosity toward the party organization. Indeed, his team of personal loyalists demonstrated a low regard for the needs and interests of that organization, and they largely excluded the four national party chairs—Ray Bliss, Rep. Rogers Morton, Sen. Robert J. "Bob" Dole, and George H. W. Bush—from any White House efforts to conduct party leadership.

In Congress, Nixon encountered Democratic Party majorities in both houses. This reality forced on him a nominal posture of bipartisanship, although the opposition Democrats were not inclined to support his policy initiatives.

In organizing his 1972 reelection effort, Nixon chose to ignore the Republican National Committee in favor of the Committee to Re-elect the President, a personal electoral vehicle. The presidential effort went forward with little attention paid to the needs of other Republicans on the party ticket. In seeking reelection, Nixon gave only rhetorical support to the concept of a "new American majority" that would realign the party coalitions with greater ideological consistency.

In June 1972 agents of the president's campaign organization were arrested on charges of breaking into the Democratic National Committee's headquarters at the Watergate office building in Washington. The scandal that ensued, known as "Watergate," had little effect on the election. President Nixon won an overwhelming victory that portended a new era of Republican domination in presidential elections.

Eventually, however, Watergate and related scandals drove the president from office. By the time Nixon resigned on August 9, 1974, he had lost the support of the many party activists and officeholders he had treated so cavalierly throughout his presidency. Nixon also left the Republican Party tainted by the scandal.

Like his predecessor Lyndon Johnson, Nixon was viewed as a pariah in party circles in the years immediately after his departure, although he regained considerable respect and status in the latter years of his lengthy retirement. His death in 1994 was accompanied by accolades of appreciation for his insights and abilities as a political strategist and party coalition builder.

Gerald R. Ford

Gerald Ford became president after Nixon resigned on August 9, 1974. Ford received his political training in Congress, where he had toiled from 1949 until 1973 in behalf of the Republican Party. He served as minority leader from 1965 until his elevation to the vice presidency in 1973 upon the resignation of Nixon's vice president, Spiro Agnew.

The unique circumstances that produced Ford's accession, and his struggle to maintain his incumbency in the face of vigorous nomination and general election challenges, elevated the significance of party leadership considerations. Ford was not only the first president to come to office via the resignation of his predecessor; he was also the first person to become vice president via the procedures spelled out in the Twenty-fifth Amendment—nomination by the president and confirmation by majority vote of both houses of Congress. In no way had the national party legitimized his incumbency.

In certain respects, the pattern of Ford's dealings with the national party organization did not differ significantly from Nixon's. A vacancy in the party chair occurred when Ford sent George H. W. Bush to head the U.S. Liaison Office in China. The incumbent vice chair, Mary Louise Smith, received the president's blessing as Bush's successor and thus became the first woman to chair the Republican National Committee. Meanwhile, White House political advisers provided liaison with the party headquarters.

The initial expectation that Ford might be a caretaker president and not seek the 1976 presidential nomination for himself, and the later realization that former California governor Ronald Reagan might mount a serious nomination challenge, produced an unusual relationship between the party chair and the president. Although Smith publicly supported Ford, she did not overtly forestall or hinder the Reagan challenge in a manner comparable with that of previous party chairs favoring incumbent presidents.

Ford's postnomination choice of Kansas senator Bob Dole as his vice presidential running mate signaled his intention to assume an above-the-battle, presidential stance in the upcoming general election campaign. A former party chair, Dole spiritedly took on the tasks of partisan attacks on the Democratic opposition.

Ford's dealings with the Democratic-controlled Congress were more congenial (if no less partisan) than Nixon's had been during the latter years of his presidency. During Ford's long years of service in the House of Representatives, he had established comfortable social and working relationships with the Democratic Party leaders in Congress. Executive-legislative relations during his presidency, however, suffered not only from conflicts over policy and ideology but also from the legislators' institutional desires to assert themselves against a presidency weakened by the ravages of Vietnam and Watergate.

As party leader, President Ford openly and willingly embraced his party. He asserted his presidential prerogatives in party affairs despite his unique status as an accidental president. He strove with some success to restore the party's credibility in the aftermath of Watergate. His 1976 electoral defeat paved the way for Reagan to lead the Republican Party in a decisive shift toward stronger and more consistent ideological conservatism. As is true of John Kennedy, Ford's brief tenure as president makes evaluation inconclusive.

Jimmy Carter

In 1976 former Georgia governor Jimmy Carter came out of obscurity to win the Democratic presidential nomination and then to defeat President Ford in the general election. He assumed the reins of party leadership as an outsider unfamiliar with national party politics.

In his dealings with the national party organization, Carter closely followed the pattern of his recent predecessors. After receiving the party nomination, he retained the incumbent party chair, Robert Strauss, while keeping intact and relying on his personal campaign organization to conduct the general election campaign. After the election, he brought Strauss into the administration and designated former Maine governor Ken Curtis as the party chair.

But the White House controlled political operations, which did not set well with the party regulars. Carter set up an apparatus and process for conducting political operations and supervising those of the national party organization. Similarly, the White House personnel office established a recruitment and management program for presidential nominations that largely ignored the patronage claims of state party leaders. When the Democratic National Committee convened in April 1977, it showed its displeasure by directing a formal rebuke to the White House.[65]

One year into his presidency, Carter attempted to make amends. He replaced Curtis as party chair with Texas politico John C. White and pledged increased accommodation and sensitivity in the future. For the remainder of his presidency, the national committee supported the president without incident. This support was an important factor in the president's success in thwarting the major challenge to his renomination mounted by Massachusetts senator Edward M. Kennedy.

In dealing with Congress, Carter had the benefit of comfortable party majorities in both houses. Still, he achieved little success for his legislative initiatives. His difficulties stemmed from several sources. First, his electoral victory had been narrow, and he had run behind Democratic senatorial and congressional victors in most districts and states. He therefore could not claim that his coattails had secured the positions of many legislators. Second, his ideological leanings were moderate, placing him at odds with many of his fellow partisans of a more liberal bent. As an outsider, he was unfamiliar with the norms and procedures of Congress. Finally, he appeared uncomfortable with expectations of many legislators that presidents seeking their support shower them with personal attention and engage in lengthy bargaining sessions.

President Carter was never comfortable with the cloak of party leadership. His approach to presidential leadership was more administrative and technical than political and partisan. His antiestablishment campaign placed him at odds with both the party organization and the congressional party.

Ronald Reagan

Ronald Reagan came to Republican Party politics relatively late in life. After a lengthy career as a Hollywood actor, mostly spent as a Democrat, he gradually shifted allegiance during the 1950s to the Republican Party. In 1960 he openly supported Nixon's presidential candidacy; and in 1964 he was highly visible working in behalf of Barry Goldwater. By this time, Reagan clearly identified with the ideological conservatives of the Republican Party's right wing and served as one of that faction's chief public voices.

Reagan successfully sought the Republican nomination for the governorship of California in 1966, and he went on to win in the general election. In 1968 he conducted a late and tentative campaign for the GOP presidential nomination that failed to ignite. He won reelection as governor in 1970, retiring at the end of his second term in 1974. In 1976 he challenged incumbent president Gerald Ford for the party's presidential nomination and came close to success. In 1980 he won a comfortable nomination victory, followed by his election in November over the incumbent Jimmy Carter.

Although late blooming, Reagan's Republican Party loyalty had become extremely strong by the time he reached the White House. He willingly accepted the responsibilities of party leadership. Structurally, the relationship between Reagan and the Republican National Committee developed along the lines of those of his presidential predecessors, with White House aides assuming responsibility for political operations, including party liaison. Rumors of White House dissatisfaction with Richard Richards's performance accompanied his resignation as national party chair after two years in office.

Nevertheless, the spirit of the relationship between the party chair and the White House was much more positive than it had been during the Johnson, Nixon, and Carter presidencies. Cooperation and goodwill prevailed as President

Reagan provided strong support and encouragement for the party-building efforts undertaken by the national headquarters. In staffing his administration, Reagan demanded unprecedented ideological loyalty that identified the Republican Party more clearly with conservatism.

In dealing with Congress, Reagan benefited from the 1980 senatorial elections that placed the Republican Party in a majority position for the first time in a quarter-century. He worked closely and cooperatively with the congressional party leadership in pursuit of economic policy objectives.

Reagan's relations with the House of Representatives, still controlled by the Democrats, were more antagonistic. He tried to expand the boundaries of his secure party base by enlisting the support of conservative House Democrats. In that respect, he emphasized ideology over partisanship.

In 1984 Reagan won a massive reelection victory over Democratic challenger Walter F. Mondale. The party majorities in the House and Senate remained stable. In 1986, however, the Democrats recaptured control of the Senate, preventing the president from relying primarily on the party symbol in pursuing his policy objectives there. Increasingly, he resorted to threats of presidential vetoes in congressional relations.

Reagan's record of party leadership may be regarded as among the most successful in the modern era. He was a committed partisan who established and maintained congenial relations with the congressional party and the party organization.

Moreover, Reagan's electoral successes attracted new groups of voters to the Republican ranks. Ever since the New Deal, the Democrats had been the majority party. Reagan's efforts essentially leveled the playing field for the GOP.

Significantly, the 1988 electoral victory of Reagan's anointed successor, Vice President George H. W. Bush, was the first by a nonincumbent nominee of the party controlling the presidency since Herbert C. Hoover succeeded Calvin Coolidge in 1928, and the first by an incumbent vice president since Martin Van Buren succeeded Andrew Jackson in 1836. Clearly, Ronald Reagan restored a positive aura to the presidential role of party leader following a sequence of negative experiences.

George H. W. Bush

In background and experience George H. W. Bush had unmatched preparation for assuming the mantle of presidential party leadership. As the son of a Republican U.S. senator, he brought to the role a noteworthy familial heritage of party identity and accomplishment, complemented by his impressive record of party organization leadership at the county and national levels, high-level executive branch appointments, and party nominations and elections to positions in both Congress and the executive.

In the 1988 presidential campaign, the national party organization, under the leadership of holdover chair Frank Fahrenkopf, played its now customary peripheral role, with central direction coming from the personal campaign organization headed by Lee Atwater. Atwater, an astute and creative electoral strategist, had played a key role in building the modern South Carolina Republican Party before coming on the national scene. The relationship between the personal campaign organization and the national party was quite amicable. The party's main contributions to Bush's victory came in the areas of fund raising and generic advertising.

After the election, when Fahrenkopf's term expired, Bush named Atwater to head the national committee. The selection of a highly visible presidential insider, along with the belief that Bush as a former national chair would be especially attentive to the party's needs and interests, promised to elevate the prestige of the office of national chair and restore it to its traditional role as the political arm of the administration.

Although optimism initially prevailed, some fourteen months later, in the wake of controversies that had already forced him to assume a lower public profile, Atwater became incapacitated by a brain tumor. While continuing to occupy the chair for the remainder of his two-year term, Atwater's attention shifted from partisan responsibilities to his fight for life.

The national party's hopes for a central role in presidential politics became a casualty of Atwater's illness, as White House aides, led by chief of staff John Sununu, came to dominate the conduct of presidential politics in a manner now typical of the modern presidency. To succeed Atwater as national chair, Bush called on agriculture secretary Clayton Yeutter, who lacked Atwater's forceful presence and was disinclined to challenge the preeminence of the White House staff in the conduct of partisan political operations.

Although he claimed to be the heir to the Reagan legacy, President Bush was more pragmatic than ideological in style. Less insistent than Reagan on ideological conformity, Bush tolerated among some principal appointees moderate views that generated sustained criticism from party conservatives. More generally, this group expressed increasing disenchantment with Bush for his perceived lack of vision and direction, particularly in domestic policy.

In his relations with the Republican Party in Congress, Bush was well served by his previous membership in those ranks. He worked comfortably with old congressional colleagues, and he clearly understood, appreciated, and embraced the traditional congressional norms of compromise and accommodation.

However, the minority status of the Republican Party in Congress throughout Bush's presidency created noteworthy tensions for his party leadership, particularly among Republican right-wingers on Capitol Hill who bemoaned the apparent lack of ideological vision and commitment manifested in his willingness to seek necessary bipartisan support for legislative initiatives.

Public approval of the Bush presidency skyrocketed in early 1991, in the context of the Persian Gulf War, reaching an unprecedented high of almost 90 percent. After the war, however, with the economy in recession, Bush's popularity with the electorate plummeted. Once headed for certain reelection, by fall 1991 the president appeared suddenly vulnerable.

Patrick Buchanan, a conservative political commentator, mounted a challenge to Bush's party renomination. Bush rather easily defeated Buchanan in the spring primaries, successfully relying on his base of support in the party organization, now headed by his old deputy, Richard Bond. Disaffection with Bush from party conservatives was increasingly apparent, however, as was his declining level of support among middle-class voters, many of whom deserted him in favor of either Democratic nominee Bill Clinton or independent candidate H. Ross Perot.

In the November balloting, Bush suffered an electoral repudiation, winning only 38 percent of the popular vote and eighteen states with 168 electoral votes. His convincing electoral defeat left his initially promising presidential party leadership in tatters. In retirement, his elder statesman status took on atypical and heightened significance following the 2000 nomination and election of his son and namesake as president.

Bill Clinton

Prior to his successful 1992 bid for the presidency, Bill Clinton had spent virtually his entire adult life in electoral politics in his native state of Arkansas. The traditional dominance of the state's Democratic Party had persisted for the most part, although the Republican Party was making strong inroads elsewhere in the South. In this hospitable arena, Clinton usually prospered under the Democratic banner, winning election to a single term as attorney general and five terms as governor.

Clinton unequivocally embraced the Democratic Party label. However, he shared with Presidents Johnson and Carter an identification with the "no-party politics" of the traditionally Democratic South. In his dealings with the Arkansas legislature as governor, he never had to worry about a Republican opposition spearheading and energizing a coalition capable of defeating his policy initiatives. Yet Clinton's adherence to no-party politics also meant that party loyalty was unavailable to him as an effective cue to generate legislative support.

As governor, Clinton made his presence felt on the national party scene. He was a leader in the formation and development of the centrist Democratic Leadership Council (DLC), chairing the body in 1990–1991. Campaigning for the Democratic presidential nomination, Clinton effectively used his DLC affiliation to promote himself as a "New Democrat," one who could lead his party away from its perceived liberal leanings back toward the center.

At the outset of his presidency, Clinton confronted a complex and contradictory political environment for party leadership. On the one hand, he started out with comfortable party majorities in both houses of Congress, the first president since Carter to so benefit. However, his political base was weak, because he had been elected with only a 43 percent plurality in a three-candidate race that featured the best popular vote showing by an independent candidate, Perot, since Theodore Roosevelt's in 1912. As president, Clinton put forward an ambitious policy agenda, seeking legislative enactment of several high-profile, controversial measures. In his first year in office, he achieved narrow but noteworthy successes relying on two distinct leadership strategies.

In the first instance, Clinton's budget proposal passed without the vote of a single Republican member of Congress. His impressive effort to mobilize party support was costly, as emboldened Capitol Hill Democrats advanced their special interests in negotiations with the White House in return for their necessary support. In contrast, the Clinton-supported NAFTA passed Congress despite substantial Democratic defections, because Clinton was able to enlist strong support from the Republicans.

Congressional relations took a distinct turn for the worse in Clinton's second year. He failed to marshal either partisan or bipartisan backing for the centerpiece of his legislative agenda, his heralded health care initiative. Clinton's Capitol Hill problems were attributable in considerable measure to his inability to generate sustained public support for himself, his policy proposals, or his party. The midterm 1994 congressional elections produced a historic landslide victory for the opposition Republicans that placed them in control of both chambers. Clinton became the first Democratic president since Truman to face a Congress dominated by Republicans. A casualty of this deteriorating political environment was Clinton's national party chair, David Wilhelm, who had served with distinction as his 1992 campaign manager.

Midway through his term, Clinton's party leadership was imperiled. The electoral fortunes of the party he led were in decline, largely because of public disenchantment with him and his policies. In 1995 and 1996, however, Clinton's political fortunes revived. He skillfully and successfully pursued a policy of "triangulation" that centrally positioned him between the polarized congressional parties, thereby generating popular support and thwarting objectionable policy initiatives advanced by the GOP. He also benefited from a booming economy.

Unable to accomplish much in advancing a Democratic agenda, Clinton nonetheless maintained strong partisan support by presenting himself as the indispensable obstacle to Republican domination of national government and politics. He succeeded in sustaining his "New Democrat" image by embracing the cause of welfare reform, shaping successful legislation in a fashion that frustrated both his party's left wing and the Republican right.

Clinton faced no opposition to his renomination to a second term in 1996, and he breezed to a comfortable reelection victory. Clinton joined the illustrious ranks of Woodrow Wilson and Franklin Roosevelt as the only twentieth-century Democratic presidents to win reelection. However, the Republicans held on to their congressional majorities, and divided government persisted.

In anticipation of and throughout the 1996 presidential campaign, Clinton aggressively pursued fund raising, nominally on behalf of the Democratic Party but mostly to enhance his prospects for reelection. He proved extraordinarily effective in his role of fund-raiser-in-chief, especially in taking advantage of the recently identified soft money loophole in the federal regulation of campaign finance. However, his high visibility and the presence of some questionable contributors raised questions of ethical propriety, triggering media criticism and congressional investigations. Moreover, the fund-raising controversies soiled the reputation of the Democratic National Committee.

In 1997 Clinton continued his successful practice of triangulation that confounded the Republican congressional majorities and edged the Democrats toward the center of the ideological spectrum. In early 1998, however, allegations of a sexual affair with a White House intern threatened Clinton's presidency. He weathered the initial firestorm, fortified by high public approval ratings for his job performance and economic prosperity. However, Whitewater special prosecutor Kenneth Starr turn over the results of his investigation to the House of Representatives, which then undertook an impeachment inquiry.

As the House conducted its investigation, the midterm elections loomed. In November the Democrats unexpectedly picked up five House seats, but the Republicans retained control of both chambers. Clinton thus became the first president since Franklin Roosevelt in 1934 whose party did not lose House seats midway through his term. In December the House voted along largely partisan lines to impeach Clinton on charges of perjury and obstruction of justice. As the drama moved across the Capitol to the Senate, Clinton retained the steadfast support of the Democratic minority, which provided him with the assurance that the two-thirds majority required for conviction and removal was unattainable.

Acquitted, Clinton continued to enjoy high job approval ratings for the rest of his term, buoyed by the booming economy. Core Democratic constituencies adored him. He continued his prolific party fund-raising with great success. Vice President Al Gore received Clinton's unequivo-

cal support in his campaign to win the Democratic presidential nomination. Gore then coasted to an easy nomination victory, but he found himself locked in a close general election contest with Republican George W. Bush.

Clinton's presence proved a mixed blessing for the Gore campaign. The president was beloved by the party faithful; but he evoked a much less favorable image among undecided swing voters, and he was anathema to the Republican opposition. This reality contributed to rising tensions between the president and his designated heir as the campaign progressed. Ultimately, the close, disputed election went to the Republicans, who also maintained their narrow control of Congress.

Clinton left office without the affirmation that the election of his vice president would have provided. Nevertheless, he remained a potent force in party politics. His close friend Terry McAuliffe became chair of the Democratic National Committee, and his wife, Hillary, won election to the Senate from her newly adopted state of New York.

Overall, Clinton earned decidedly mixed marks for his presidential party leadership. He developed, implemented, and embodied a centrist electoral strategy whereby Democrats could win and hold the presidency. After a faltering start, the general public, and especially fellow Democratic partisans, consistently applauded his job performance. He was effective and inspiring in rallying partisans and raising funds on their behalf.

Still, the Clinton presidency proved disappointing in many respects for Democrats. In spite of his ideological centrism, he was personally polarizing. The Republicans governed both houses of Congress throughout the last six years of his presidency, their longest tenure in control since the advent of the New Deal, and incessant scandals plagued him and his administration. Inevitably, they tainted the Democratic Party and contributed to its narrow loss of the presidency in 2000. Nevertheless, in retirement he has come closer to any president since Theodore Roosevelt in embracing the role of postpresidential party leader.

George W. Bush

The son of a former president, George W. Bush was twice elected governor of Texas. There, he benefited from a clear shift in the electorate toward the Republican Party. In addition, he demonstrated a capacity to forge bipartisan support for his policy agenda in the state legislature where the Democrats remained a potent force.

Bush campaigned for the presidency in 2000 as a "compassionate conservative." He sought to reassure the potent right wing of the Republican Party that he was committed to its ideological agenda while convincing centrist voters that he accepted a legitimate role for the federal government in promoting social and economic welfare. His bifurcated campaign appeal proved barely sufficient. Despite narrowly losing the popular vote, he prevailed in his quest for an Electoral College majority by a scant five votes, and that occurred only after an unprecedented intervention by the Supreme Court that halted the recounting of popular votes in the pivotal state of Florida.

Bush entered office with narrow partisan majorities in both houses of Congress, giving the GOP unified control of Congress and the presidency for the first time in almost fifty years, since the beginning of the Eisenhower presidency. However, the exceedingly close outcomes of the elections cast doubt on his capacity to accomplish much in his presidency.

In his first months in office, Bush won congressional approval for his chief campaign promise, a significant tax cut, as well as noteworthy education reform, but his other initiatives got bogged down in the legislative process amid heightened partisanship. In May 2001 his difficulties mounted when Sen. James Jeffords of Vermont announced he was abandoning the Republican Party to become an independent and to caucus with the Democrats, providing them with majority control of the chamber. Nevertheless, by the time of the August congressional recess Bush had demonstrated that he could function with some dexterity and success in the context of divided party government, using his party majority in the House, presidential persuasion, and veto threats to shape pending legislation to his satisfaction.

On the party organization front, Bush named Virginia governor James Gilmore as his choice to head the Republican National Committee. Bush's personal loyalist, Jack Oliver, became deputy chair, handling day-to-day administration and representing presidential interests. From the White House, senior adviser Karl Rove oversaw political operations, including party politics, working closely and generally compatibly with Gilmore and his several successors.

Early on, Bush received generally favorable, but far from overwhelming, public support. As expected, Republicans constituted his base, with Democrats less enthusiastic. Indeed, a sizable minority continued to question the legitimacy of his disputed election, and the partisan acrimony surrounding the contested election pervaded the political landscape.

The political climate changed dramatically on September 11, 2001, when terrorist attacks on American soil left thousands dead. Congress and the public rallied behind the president. His public approval reached unprecedented heights in support of and in response to his efforts to deal with the crisis. In turn, Bush initially assumed a more bipartisan style, presenting himself as president of all the people and promoting national unity in a war on terrorism. Among the more significant legislative accomplishments of this period were the Patriot Act and the creation of the Department of Homeland Security.

However, as the 2002 midterm elections approached, Bush adopted a more partisan tone, leading the Republicans

to gain seats in both chambers and reclaim their Senate majority and thus restoring unified party government. The price he paid for this significant achievement was heightened antagonism from opposition Democrats in both Congress and the electorate. His Republican Party support in Congress, the party organization, and the electorate, remained phenomenally high, contributing to increased party polarization.

Bush's 2003 decision to wage war in Iraq initially received considerable bipartisan support, but it deteriorated over time. Nevertheless, Bush won reelection in 2004, defeating Sen. John F. Kerry of Massachusetts, while the Republicans remained in control of Congress. Despite a substantially more impressive electoral performance than in 2000, Bush had the smallest margin of victory by an incumbent president seeking reelection since Woodrow Wilson in 1916.

Bush began his second term with an ambitious domestic policy agenda, the centerpiece of which was social security reform. However, he was unable to generate sufficient partisan support, in the face of unyielding Democratic opposition, to advance it. His efforts to pursue immigration reform ran aground amidst opposition in his party's ranks. He was able the secure the appointment of two conservative justices to the Supreme Court, with the potential to shape the Court's policy direction for decades to come. However, one of his initial nominees, White House counsel Harriett Miers, had to be withdrawn in the face of vigorous opposition from conservatives within Bush's party and electoral coalition.

His administration's mishandling of the Katrina disaster in the Gulf Coast in 2005 and declining public support for the ongoing Iraq War dragged his poll ratings by 2006 down to historic low levels associated with the presidencies of Truman, Nixon, and Carter. Bush's deteriorating fortunes coincided with a Democratic takeover of Congress in the 2006 midterm elections, restoring divided party government and portending a rocky conclusion to his White House years. Events and developments following his 2004 reelection seriously undermined his impressive performance as a presidential party leader to that date.

Comparing the Presidents as Party Leaders

The experiences of the modern presidents as party leaders have differed in numerous and significant ways, yet they were similar in some respects. The variations appear to be threefold. They pertain first to the presidents' personal orientations toward partisanship, generally positive or negative; second to the tone of president-party relations, relatively congenial or hostile; and third to the political circumstances confronted by the incumbents, either favorable or unfavorable for the exercise of party leadership. These factors can either reinforce one another or diverge for particular presidents.

Among modern presidents, Roosevelt, Truman, Kennedy, Ford, Reagan, both Bushes, and Clinton viewed partisanship in a generally positive fashion. Eisenhower, Johnson, Nixon, and Carter were less affirmatively disposed. Party relations were relatively congenial for presidents Roosevelt, Truman, Eisenhower, Kennedy, Reagan, and George W. Bush through 2006, but they were more hostile for presidents Johnson, Nixon, and Carter. Ford, George H. W. Bush, and Clinton occupy intermediate positions on this continuum.

Political circumstances relate primarily to party competition in the electorate and in the government. For five decades following the Great Depression, the Democratic Party consistently claimed more professed loyalists than its Republican opposition, measured by public opinion surveys and voter registration totals. In the quarter-century since 1980, the gap between the two parties narrowed to the point of relative parity. Democrats currently enjoy a growing lead.

Furthermore, the Democratic Party controlled Congress the great majority of the time from the 1930s into the 1990s. The only exceptions were 1947–1949, 1953–1955, and 1981–1987. On the first two occasions, the GOP held both houses; on the third, the Senate. The Republicans assumed control of both chambers in 1995. They held the House of Representatives until 2007. In the Senate, they lost their majority for most of the 107th Congress (2001–2003), before regaining it from 2003–2007. The 110th Congress, 2007–2009, was back under Democratic domination.

Thus, for most the time period considered Democratic presidents were better positioned to exercise party leadership in the political arena than their Republican counterparts. Roosevelt, Kennedy, Johnson, and Carter all experienced unified party government throughout their presidencies, while Truman had it for all but two years of his tenure. Clinton only had it for his first two years, making him the one modern Democratic president who faced divided party government most of his time in office. In contrast, Nixon, Ford, and George H. W. Bush served with Democrats always in control of both chambers. Eisenhower, like Clinton, enjoyed two years of unified party government, followed by six years of division. Republicans held the Senate for the first six years of Reagan's presidency, but they failed to claim the House. For George W. Bush, unified party government prevailed for five months in 2001, and from 2003–2007. In mid-2001 the GOP lost the Senate when a Republican senator left the party, and in 2007 they surrendered control of both chambers to the Democrats.

Roosevelt, Eisenhower, Johnson, Nixon (1972), Reagan, George H. W. Bush, and Clinton (1996) all won comfortable, if not landslide, electoral victories. Truman, Kennedy, Nixon (1968), Carter, Clinton (1992), and George W. Bush (twice) had much narrower winning margins. Ford was an unelected president throughout his brief tenure. The general expectation is that a generous margin of electoral victory should enhance the prospects for presidential party leadership.

Taking these factors together, Roosevelt most clearly combined personal partisan commitment, positive party relations, and a favorable political context for the exercise of presidential party leadership. Before his political fortunes began to decline in 2005, George W. Bush appeared poised to join Roosevelt at the peak. However, it now appears that he belongs in the ranks of with Truman, Kennedy, Ford, Reagan, George H. W, Bush, and Clinton, all of whom generally shared FDR's positive orientations and relatively congenial relations amid less favorable political circumstances.

Alternatively, although Eisenhower's party relations were relatively congenial, he lacked partisan commitment and confronted a political setting that inhibited party leadership. Johnson, Nixon, and Carter faced very different political circumstances—positive in Johnson's case and less so for the others. They not only appeared personally uncomfortable with party leadership, but also experienced and contributed to generally antagonistic relations with the parties they nominally led.

PARTY LEADERSHIP AND PRESIDENTIAL POWER

In a constitutional sense, party leadership conveys no power. The president derives no legal power from the role, and within the party the president lacks command authority. Rather, party leadership operates within the transactional domains of bargaining and negotiation.

Party leadership ordinarily is intertwined with other leadership roles and responsibilities. The reason other elements in the party—elected and appointed public officials, party organization officials and activists, and party supporters in the electorate—look to the president for leadership has less to do with party power per se than with power coming from other sources, such as the Constitution and the laws, or public support.

The exercise of party leadership often enables the president to perform successfully in other roles. Policy responsiveness is an important presidential expectation in making executive appointments. Although partisanship is not an absolute requirement for policy responsiveness, it serves as a convenient indicator. Presidents' effectiveness as chief executive turns in part on their success as party leader.

Similarly, by acting as party leader the president can be an effective legislative leader, another presidential role that has no constitutional authority. The party connection can unite the separated executive and legislative branches under presidential leadership. In a situation of divided party government, however, where opposing parties control the White

House and Congress, presidential party leadership can become less an opportunity than an obstacle.

Party leadership is relevant to the president's powers and responsibilities as chief economic manager because the general public identifies the president with the party. The president's success in controlling the economy can influence the electoral fortunes of the party's nominees, including the president.

Furthermore, presidential approaches to economic management can reflect ideological positions associated with the party. For example, the more ideologically conservative Republican presidents have tended to view monetary policy (dealing with the supply and circulation of money) as a more appropriate response than fiscal policy (on taxing and spending). The more liberal Democratic presidents have tended to prefer fiscal to monetary policy.

Presidential party leadership has less obvious relevance for the president's responsibilities in the diplomatic and military aspects of foreign affairs. The United States has a long heritage of foreign policy bipartisanship. Nevertheless, the electoral and ideological considerations just described can come into play here as well, along with those elements of partisanship associated with political appointments. For example, the Democratic Senate rejected President George H. W. Bush's 1989 nomination of former senator John Tower to serve as secretary of defense. The substantial bipartisan support undergirding George W. Bush's decision to go to war in Iraq in 2003 quickly dissipated into partisan strife.

The presidential role of chief of state surely has the least relevance for party leadership. In symbolizing the nation undivided, the president ostensibly puts partisanship aside. In the wake of the terrorist attacks in 2001, George W. Bush transcended the prevailing partisan divisions and, for a short time successfully projected a nonpartisan image. The problem here is that presidential roles cannot simply be discarded like hats. The basic contradiction between these two roles produces tension for the president and confusion throughout the political system.

President Nixon's attempts to deal with allegations concerning his involvement in the Watergate scandal while pursuing his ongoing presidential responsibilities illustrate this situation. In his January 1974 State of the Union address, Nixon bemoaned that "one year of Watergate is enough," and he asserted that in responding to congressional demands, he would never do "anything that weakens the office of the president of the United States or impairs the ability of the presidents of the future to make the great decisions that are so essential to this nation and to the world." [66]

A few weeks later, during a March 19 question-and-answer session before the National Association of Broadcasters, the president urged the House Judiciary Committee considering the issue of presidential impeachment to resolve the question quickly, asserting that "dragging out Watergate drags down America." [67]

The paradoxes of the president's role as party chief will remain unresolved. The president of all the people is the champion of a specific part of the electorate and the antagonist of another. Yet, in acknowledging the divisiveness inherent in presidential party leadership, Americans also must credit it with providing the means for presidential leadership in other roles. Without embodying specific powers, party leadership nevertheless typically enhances the president's power position in the political order. Contemporary trends that undermine presidential party leadership and widen the separation between president and party could diminish both the presidency and the party system.

★

NOTES

1. Woodrow Wilson, *Constitutional Government in the United States* (New York: Columbia University Press, 1980/1908), 67.

2. James MacGregor Burns, *Leadership* (New York: Harper and Row, 1978), 4.

3. Frank J. Sorauf, *Party Politics in America* (Boston: Little, Brown, 1968), 11–12.

4. This section draws on Harold F. Bass Jr., "Thomas Jefferson's Presidential Party Leadership" (Paper presented at the annual meeting of the American Political Science Association, Chicago, September 3–6, 1987). See also three works by Noble Cunningham Jr., *The Jeffersonian Republicans: The Formation of Party Organization, 1798–1801* (Chapel Hill: University of North Carolina Press, 1957); *The Jeffersonian Republicans in Power: Party Operations, 1801–1809* (Chapel Hill: University of North Carolina Press, 1963); and *The Process of Government under Jefferson* (Princeton: Princeton University Press, 1978).

5. Robert V. Remini, "The Emergence of Political Parties and Their Effect on the Presidency," in *Power and the Presidency*, ed.

Philip C. Dolce and George H. Skau (New York: Scribner's, 1976), 30–32.

6. Daniel P. Klinghard, "Grover Cleveland, William McKinley, and the Emergence of the President as Party Leader," *Presidential Studies Quarterly* 35 (December 2005): 736–760.

7. This section draws on Harold F. Bass Jr., "The President and the National Party Organization," in *Presidents and Their Parties: Leadership or Neglect?* ed. Robert Harmel (New York: Praeger, 1984), 59–89.

8. The traditional role and status of the national party convention is developed at length in Paul T. David, Ralph M. Goldman, and Richard C. Bain, *The Politics of National Party Conventions* (Washington, D.C.: Brookings, 1960).

9. See Byron E. Shafer, *Bifurcated Politics: Evolution and Reform in the National Party Convention* (Cambridge: Harvard University Press, 1988).

10. Three instructive studies of the national party committees are Hugh A. Bone, *Party Committees and National Politics* (Seattle: University of Washington Press, 1958); Cornelius P. Cotter and

Bernard C. Hennessy, *Politics without Power: The National Party Committees* (New York: Atherton, 1964); and Philip A. Klinkner, *The Losing Parties: Out-Party National Committees, 1956–1993* (New Haven: Yale University Press, 1994).

11. Generally, see Cotter and Hennessy, *Politics without Power,* chaps. 4–5, for a consideration of the traditional role and status of the national party chair.

12. See Bone, *Party Committees and National Politics,* chap. 2; Cotter and Hennessy, *Politics without Power,* chaps. 6–9; and Cornelius P. Cotter and John F. Bibby, "Institutional Development of Parties and the Thesis of Party Decline," *Political Science Quarterly* 95 (spring 1980): 6–7.

13. Cotter and Bibby, "Institutional Development of Parties," 5.

14. *Charter and the Bylaws of the Democratic Party of the United States* (Washington, D.C.: Democratic National Committee, 1999), 3.

15. Paul Allen Beck and Frank J. Sorauf, *Party Politics in America,* 7th ed. (New York: HarperCollins, 1992), 104–105.

16. Cotter and Bibby, "Institutional Development of Parties," 6–7.

17. Cotter and Hennessy, *Politics without Power,* 67–71, 78–80.

18. Theodore H. White, *The Making of the President, 1972* (New York: Atheneum, 1973), 61.

19. Jeb S. Magruder, *An American Life: One Man's Road to Watergate* (New York: Atheneum, 1975), 178.

20. None of the nineteenth-century "accidental" presidents received a subsequent major party nomination. By contrast, all of their twentieth-century counterparts were nominated to succeed themselves as president.

21. Theodore H. White, *Breach of Faith: The Fall of Richard Nixon* (New York: Atheneum, 1975), 97.

22. Sources for this discussion include Malcolm E. Jewell and David Olson, *Political Parties and Elections in the American States,* 3d ed. (Belmont, Calif.: Wadsworth, 1988), chap. 3; Robert J. Huckshorn, *Party Leadership in the States* (Amherst: University of Massachusetts Press, 1976); and Cornelius P. Cotter, James L. Gibson, John F. Bibby, and Robert J. Huckshorn, *Party Organizations in American Politics* (New York: Praeger, 1984).

23. Huckshorn, *Party Leadership in the States,* 254–257.

24. Cotter et al., *Party Organizations in American Politics,* chap. 2.

25. Ibid., passim.

26. See E. E. Schattschneider, *Party Government* (New York: Rinehart, 1942), 129–133; and Morton Grodzins, "American Political Parties and the American System," *Western Political Quarterly* (December 1960): 974–998.

27. Harry S. Truman, "The President's News Conference of October 31, 1945," *Public Papers of the Presidents of the United States, Harry S. Truman, 1945* (Washington, D.C.: Government Printing Office, 1953), 456.

28. Hoover Commission, *Report on Organization of the Executive Branch of Government* (New York: McGraw-Hill, 1949), 224–225.

29. Richard Fenno, *The President's Cabinet: An Analysis in the Period from Wilson to Eisenhower* (Cambridge: Harvard University Press, 1959), 70.

30. President's Committee on Administrative Management, *Administrative Management of the Government of the United States* (Washington, D.C.: Government Printing Office, 1937), 5.

31. See Thomas J. Weko, *The Politicizing Presidency: The White House Personnel Office, 1948–1994* (Lawrence: University Press of Kansas, 1995).

32. Herbert Kaufman, "The Growth of the Federal Personnel System," in *The Federal Government Service,* 2d ed., ed. Wallace S. Sayre (Englewood Cliffs, N.J.: Prentice-Hall, 1965), 40–53.

33. James A. Farley, *Behind the Ballots: The Personal History of a Politician* (New York: Harcourt, Brace, 1938), 223–238.

34. Kaufman, "Growth of the Federal Personnel System," 55.

35. James A. Farley, *Jim Farley's Story: The Roosevelt Years* (New York: Whittlesey House, 1948), 68.

36. Terry M. Moe, "The Politicized Presidency," in *The New Direction in American Politics,* ed. John E. Chubb and Paul E. Peterson (Washington, D.C.: Brookings, 1985), 260–261.

37. George C. Edwards III, *Presidential Influence in Congress* (San Francisco: Freeman, 1980), 125–188 passim. See also George C. Edwards III, *At the Margins: Presidential Leadership of Congress* (New Haven: Yale University Press, 1989).

38. Edwards, *Presidential Influence in Congress,* 129, citing Harry McPherson, *A Political Education* (Boston: Little, Brown, 1972), 197; and Russell D. Renka, "Legislative Leadership and Marginal Vote-Gaining Strategies in the Kennedy and Johnson Presidencies" (Paper presented at the annual meeting of the Southwestern Political Science Association, Houston, Texas, April 1978), 26–27.

39. James Madison, *Federalist* No. 51, in Alexander Hamilton, James Madison, and John Jay, *The Federalist Papers* (New York: Bantam, 1982), 262.

40. George C. Edwards III, *The Public Presidency: The Pursuit of Public Support* (New York: St. Martin's Press, 1983), 83–88.

41. Edwards, *Presidential Influence in Congress,* 77.

42. James W. Davis, *The President as Party Leader* (New York: Praeger, 1992).

43. John King, "White House: We've Made History," CNN, November 6, 2002 *(www.cnn.com/inside politics),*; Alexander Bolton, "Rove Raises $1.2 million in 2006 Cycle," *The Hill,* October 11, 2006 *(www.hillnews.com).*

44. Roger G. Brown, "Presidents and Midterm Campaigners," in *Presidents and Their Parties: Leadership or Neglect?* ed. Robert Harmel (New York: Praeger, 1984), 127.

45. Stephen E. Ambrose, *Eisenhower,* vol. 2, *The President* (New York: Simon and Shuster, 1984), 218–219.

46. Previous exceptions were in 1902, 1838, and 1830. However, in both 1902 and 1838, the House expanded in size, limiting the significance of the added seats.

47. Sidney M. Milkis, "Presidents and Party Purges: With Special Emphasis on the Lessons of 1938," in *Presidents and Their Parties: Leadership or Neglect?* ed. Robert Harmel (New York: Praeger, 1984), 167.

48. Henry J. Abraham, *The Judicial Process: An Introductory Analysis of the Courts of the United States, England, and France,* 7th ed. (New York: Oxford University Press, 1998), 70–71. One of these, Felix Frankfurter, a nominal independent designated by Franklin Roosevelt, while a nonpartisan appointment, did not belong to an opposing party.

49. Walter F. Murphy and C. Herman Pritchett, *Courts, Judges, and Politics: An Introduction to the Judicial Process,* 4th ed. (New York: Random House, 1986), 150; citing Henry Cabot Lodge, *Selections from the Correspondence of Theodore Roosevelt and Henry Cabot Lodge, 1894–1918* (New York: Scribner's, 1925), 1: 517–519.

50. Abraham, *Judicial Process,* 76; citing *New York Times,* May 17, 1969, 1.

51. Ibid., 78; citing Lodge, *Correspondence of Theodore Roosevelt and Henry Cabot Lodge,* 2: 228.

52. See Jeffrey A. Segal and Harold J. Spaeth, *The Supreme Court and the Attitudinal Model* (New York: Cambridge University Press, 1993).

53. *The United States Government Manual, 2006–2007* (Washington, D.C.: Government Printing Office, 2000), 66–72.

54. Abraham, *Judicial Process,* 77.

55. "Gallup Trend on Party Identification, 1937–1995," *Gallup Poll Monthly,* August 1995, 45; Lydia Saad, "Independents Rank as

the Largest U.S. Political Group," April 9, 1999 (www.gallup.com); Jeffrey M. Jones, "Democrats Have Advantage on Party Ratings, Affiliation, and Issues," *Gallup Poll Briefing*, September 2006, 33–35; Marjorie Random Hershey, *Party Politics in America*, 11th ed. (New York: Longman, 2005), 104–106.

56. See Fred I. Greenstein, *Children and Politics* (New Haven: Yale University Press, 1965); and Robert D. Hess and Judith V. Torney, *The Development of Political Attitudes in Children* (Chicago: Aldine, 1967).

57. Edwards, *Public Presidency*, 213.

58. The classic study on party identification and electoral behavior was Angus Campbell, Philip E. Converse, Warren E. Miller, and Donald E. Stokes, *The American Voter* (New York: Wiley, 1960). The party decline thesis finds expression in Walter Dean Burnham, *Critical Elections and the Mainsprings of American Politics* (New York: Norton, 1970); Gerald M. Pomper, "The Decline of the Party in American Elections," *Political Science Quarterly* 92 (spring 1977): 21–41; William J. Crotty and Gary C. Jacobson, *American Parties in Decline*, 2d ed. (New York: Harper and Row, 1987); and Martin P. Wattenberg, *The Decline of American Political Parties, 1952–1992* (Cambridge: Harvard University Press, 1994). For a more recent consideration that considers indications of party resurgence, see Jeffrey E. Cohen, Richard Fleisher, and Paul Kantor, eds., *American Political Parties: Decline or Resurgence* (Washington, D.C.: CQ Press, 2001). For a "textbook" summary of these issues, see Hershey, *Party Politics in America*, chap. 6.

59. Nelson W. Polsby, "Presidential Cabinet Making: Lessons for the Political System," *Political Science Quarterly* 93 (spring 1978): 19.

60. James David Barber, *The Presidential Character: Predicting Performance in the White House*, 4th ed. (New York: Prentice Hall, 1992).

61. Fred I. Greenstein, *The Hidden Hand Presidency: Eisenhower as Leader* (New York: Basic Books, 1982).

62. Dwight D. Eisenhower, "The President's Press Conference of October 11, 1956," *Public Papers of the Presidents, Dwight D. Eisenhower, 1956* (Washington, D.C.: Government Printing Office, 1956), 891.

63. Dwight D. Eisenhower, "The President's News Conference of June 5, 1957," *Public Papers of the Presidents, Dwight D. Eisenhower, 1957* (Washington, D.C.: Government Printing Office, 1957), 435.

64. *New York Times*, January 15, 1960, 14.

65. See Warren Weaver Jr., "National Committee Scolds Carter for Bypassing State Party Chiefs," *New York Times*, April 2, 1977, 12.

66. Quoted in *Watergate: Chronology of a Crisis*, vol. 2 (Washington, D.C.: Congressional Quarterly, 1974), 228.

67. Ibid., 286.

SELECTED BIBLIOGRAPHY

Bond, Jon R., and Richard Fleisher, eds. *Polarized Politics: Congress and the President in a Partisan Era*. Washington, D.C.: CQ Press, 2000.

Bone, Hugh A. *Party Committees and National Politics*. Seattle: University of Washington Press, 1958.

Brown, Roger G. "Party and Bureaucracy: From Kennedy to Reagan." *Political Science Quarterly* 97 (summer 1982): 279–294.

———. "The Presidency and the Political Parties." In *The Presidency and the Political System*, edited by Michael Nelson. Washington, D.C.: CQ Press, 1985.

Brown, Roger G., and David M. Welborn. "Presidents and Their Parties: Performance and Prospects." *Presidential Studies Quarterly* 12 (summer 1982): 302–316.

Cotter, Cornelius P. "Eisenhower as Party Leader." *Political Science Quarterly* 98 (summer 1983): 255–284.

Cotter, Cornelius P., and John F. Bibby. "Institutional Development of Parties and the Thesis of Party Decline." *Political Science Quarterly* 95 (spring 1980): 1–27.

Cotter, Cornelius P., and Bernard D. Hennessy. *Politics without Power: The National Party Committees*. New York: Atherton, 1964.

Cotter, Cornelius P., James L. Gibson, John F. Bibby, and Robert J. Huckshorn. *Party Organizations in American Politics*. New York: Praeger, 1984.

Crockett, David A. *The Opposition Presidency: Leadership and the Constraints of History*. College Station: Texas A&M University Press, 2002.

Cronin, Thomas E. "The Presidency and the Parties." In *Party Renewal in America*, edited by Gerald M. Pomper. New York: Praeger, 1980.

Davis, James W. *The President as Party Leader*. New York: Praeger, 1992.

Goldman, Ralph M. "Titular Leadership of Presidential Parties." In *The Presidency*, edited by Aaron Wildavsky. Boston: Little, Brown, 1969.

Harmel, Robert, ed. *Presidents and Their Parties: Leadership or Neglect?* New York: Praeger, 1984.

Kessel, John H. *Presidential Parties*. Homewood, Ill.: Dorsey, 1984.

Ketcham, Ralph. *Presidents above Party: The First American Presidency, 1789–1829*. Chapel Hill: University of North Carolina Press, 1984.

Milkis, Sidney M. "The Presidency and the Political Parties." In *The Presidency and the Political System*, edited by Michael Nelson. 6th ed. Washington, D.C.: CQ Press, 2000.

———. *The President and the Parties: The Transformation of the American Party System since the New Deal*. New York: Oxford University Press, 1993.

Odegard, Peter H. "Presidential Leadership and Party Responsibility." *Annals of the American Academy of Political and Social Science* 307 (September 1956): 66–81.

Seligman, Lester. "The Presidential Office and the President as Party Leader (with a Postscript on the Kennedy-Nixon Era)." In *Parties and Elections in an Antiparty Age*, edited by Jeff Fishel. Bloomington: Indiana University Press, 1978.

Skowronek, Stephen. *The Politics Presidents Make: Leadership from John Adams to Bill Clinton*. Cambridge, Mass.: Belknap Press, 1997.

chapter 18

The President and the News Media

by Matthew R. Kerbel, Dom Bonafede, Martha Joynt Kumar, and John L. Moore

The relationship between the president and the news media changed profoundly with the terrorist attacks on America of September 11, 2001. It took several years before this relationship began to revert to its testy characteristic of a time when terrorism was not a major American concern.

The attacks, which took nearly three thousand lives, and the war on terrorism that they engendered presented new challenges to President George W. Bush and his successors and emphasized their need to communicate through the media with the nation and the world. Unlike other wartime presidents, Bush faced a more complex, geographically diffuse enemy. More even than in Vietnam, the war on terrorism was a battle for the hearts and minds of people not in a single country but in many lands where American ideals of religious freedom were little understood and even less appreciated.

President Bush approached the war on terrorism more like a third world war than a regional overseas conflict, and he repeatedly warned Americans that they were in for a long siege. At a news conference on March 13, 2002, he told reporters: "I believe this war is more akin to World War II than it is to Vietnam. This is a war in which we fight for the liberties and freedom of our country."

Barely seven months before the September 11 attacks, Bush had seemed unprepared for such a monumental challenge. Besides his tendency to mangle the English language and lack of foreign policy experience, he had lost the 2000 popular vote to Democrat Al Gore by more than a half-million votes. He owed his Electoral College victory to a 5–4 Supreme Court decision halting the disputed Florida recount, prompting humorist Mark Russell to quip, "The people have spoken—all five of them."

As commander in chief of the armed forces and as leader of the sole remaining world power, President Bush needed the media's help in overcoming the public's low expectations of his ability to cope with the terrorist threat. And during his first term of office he succeeded. He assembled a 174-nation coalition to support the U.S. war on terrorism, and within weeks of the attacks, American troops were in Afghanistan, helping to dismantle the extremist Muslim Taliban government and pursue Osama bin Laden, mastermind of the September attacks, and his terrorist al Qaeda network. At home, Bush's public approval ratings soared. For a time, it seemed almost unpatriotic to criticize the president, even on matters unrelated to the war, and administration supporters tried not very subtly to squelch dissent on that basis.

Just as President Bush relied on the media to help rally the nation and its allies behind his war on terrorism, reporters needed his administration's cooperation to cover the war thoroughly without divulging secrets to the enemy or endangering themselves needlessly. Despite the precautions, several journalists were killed covering the war and one, Daniel Pearl of the *Wall Street Journal*, was kidnapped and murdered. On the whole, relations between the U.S.-led military and the press were cooperative. Defense secretary Donald H. Rumsfeld won praise for his accessibility and his frequent on-the-record news briefings.

But by Bush's second term, the Iraq War had become a political liability. Americans and Iraqis continued to die in steady numbers long after the president had declared an end to hostilities. Although Iraqis went to the polls to choose a democratic government, insurgent violence grew to the point where by 2006 the military situation began to resemble civil war. Retired senior military leaders began to publicly call for Rumsfeld's ouster. Questions arose about whether the administration had been completely open with the public about the threat posed by Saddam Hussein before the war started. These events, coupled with doubts about the administration's handling of the devastation delivered in August 2005 by Hurricane Katrina to the Gulf Coast, and the president's failure to advance his second-term domestic agenda steadily drove down the president's public support. As large majorities of Americans registered the opinion that the nation was heading in the wrong direction, the war president had become unpopular. Reporters consequently began asking difficult questions of the president and his surrogates, and the relationship between President Bush and the press soured in a manner reminiscent of his predecessors.

The layer of hostility at the surface of the modern-day relationship between the White House and news organizations is perhaps its most conspicuous feature. "I have long since given up the thought that I could disabuse some of you of turning any substantive decision into anything but a political process," retorted President Bill Clinton in 1993 to a question directed to him by Brit Hume, then the White House correspondent for ABC News.[1] The president was seething with frustration over what he considered to be frivolous and inaccurate coverage of him and his administration. But his comments were typical of remarks delivered at some point by almost every one of his predecessors, and by his immediate successor, George W. Bush. For their part, reporters have grievances against just about every president they encounter. When reporters believe the White House is withholding information, complaints abound. The resulting tension between the two sides receives great play in the pages of newspapers and on television news programs.

The harsh veneer that overlays the interaction between the president and news organizations belies the continuing working relationship existing below its surface. Two fundamental features characterize this enduring relationship: the mutual benefit of the president–news media association and the cooperation that suffuses the dealings of the White House and news organizations. Without these features, the relationship would not have the importance it currently holds for each partner. Presidents need news organizations to reach their constituents, and reporters depend on the president for their copy. The president is central to the concept of news that is shared by a news organization's viewers and readers: people want to hear what the president is doing, thinking, and planning.

All presidents have valued the press. They have not necessarily liked the people who report or who publish or air the news, but they have understood that the media are an important vehicle for reaching the public. When the first president, George Washington (1789–1797), needed to explain to the public his rationale for leaving his presidency, he did so through the press. His farewell address was not spoken directly to Congress nor was it even presented as a speech. *(See "Washington's Farewell Address," p. 1754, in Reference Materials, Vol. II.)* Instead, at President Washington's request it was published as a communication to the people in Pennsylvania's *Daily American Advertiser* on September 19, 1796. Philadelphia was the nation's capital at that time, so Washington chose a local newspaper as his venue. His choice for such an important statement confirmed his high regard for the press as a presidential resource. His successors also have recognized the value of news organizations. When President Ronald Reagan

addressed the American public at the end of his eight years in office, he delivered a televised farewell speech from the Oval Office. He too chose the media as the vehicle to deliver his message to the people collectively.

Through the decades, new forms of media have changed the ways in which people receive information. Beginning in the late seventeenth century, newspapers played an active part in the political debate that surrounded the founding of the United States. The first colonial newspaper, *Publick Occurrences Both Forreign and Domestick,* was published in Boston on September 25, 1690, and its first issue happened to be its last. The *Boston News-Letter,* which followed in 1704, was the first continually published newspaper in colonial America. While the Constitution was being drafted in the late eighteenth century, the citizens of major cities were able to read in more than one newspaper timely, solid political discussions of the emerging document. In New York, for example, newspapers were available four days a week,[2] and political information, either by subscription or through quick perusal in taverns or coffee houses, was plentiful. Indeed, essays by Alexander Hamilton, John Jay, and James Madison in support of the Constitution initially appeared as letters published in New York's *Independent Journal;* they then were reprinted in newspapers around the country. The documents collectively became *The Federalist Papers.*

Unfortunately, once the Constitution was adopted, what had become a partisan and often vituperative press frequently failed to raise and seriously discuss important political questions in anything but the most partisan manner. Presidents and the members of their administrations spoke through newspapers designated as the vehicles for their official statements and viewpoints. The opposition regularly used the partisan press to launch attacks against specific presidents and their administrations.

In 1800, as Washington began to function as the nation's capital, the establishment of a newspaper, the *National Intelligencer,* marked the city's development. Similarly, as communities around the young nation matured, newspapers became an important aspect of their civic lives. At the start of the nineteenth century, 202 newspapers were being published nationwide.[3]

From 1861 to 1900 a second period emerged as the press changed its focus from serving presidential interests to getting a story quickly and attracting the largest number of readers possible. During these years, the White House began to take shape as an institution as the staff assumed new responsibilities, including daily dealings with reporters.

A third period, 1901–1932, covering the administration of Theodore Roosevelt through that of Herbert Hoover, saw the White House become a distinct beat for the press. Presidents began to hold regular meetings with reporters to receive their questions, and the position of presidential press secretary was established and the operating procedures of the office were developed. When Franklin D. Roosevelt became president, the modern period in president-press relations began.

ORIGINS OF PRESS COVERAGE: 1789–1860

In 1789, the federal government's first year, press access to the government was extremely limited. Earlier, neither the press nor the public had been admitted to the Constitutional Convention. After American independence, state legislatures generally were not open to the public nor was the Continental Congress. Moreover, no one in the government or in the press thought it their duty to provide a literal transcript of either debate or the statements of elected officials. Verbatim reports of congressional debates were not available until the *Congressional Globe* provided them for both houses beginning in 1851.[4] The *Congressional Record* became the publisher of debate in 1873. Both publications, however, made generous allowance for transcript "corrections" by the members.

At least four significant patterns established during this period continue to define relations between the president and the news media today. First, it was clearly recognized that the press—newspapers in those days—was a valuable resource for a governing president. Second, the reciprocity or mutual benefit that underlies the present-day relationship between the president and the news media was established. Third, presidential opponents came to see the news media as a major venue. Partisans acquired a means to oppose the president and his programs. Congress was their stage, but their line to the public was through the media. Fourth, few rules governed political reporting as it developed in Washington. "Reporters" during this time included editors operating as journalists, letter writers who sent polemic messages back home, government employees who wrote newspaper copy on the side, and journalists who also lobbied for legislation. Some reporters were viewed as outsiders in the political system; others were among those consulted by the president. Some newspaper figures, such as early– and mid–nineteenth-century newspaper publishers Joseph Gales, William Seaton, Francis Blair, and Amos Kendall, were among the glitterati of their time, socially and professionally recognized.

The Press as an Executive Resource

When George Washington took office, there were no national political parties. Nevertheless, a newspaper associated with the incoming president and his governing principles began to take shape just as the new president was to take the oath of office. The *Gazette of the United States* published its first issue in New York on April 15, 1789, fifteen days before Washington's inauguration. It moved to Philadelphia the next year when the government seat was relocated to that city.

In 1754 Benjamin Franklin drew what is considered the first American editorial cartoon. In his **Pennsylvania Gazette,** *Franklin published the drawing of a reptile divided into separate parts, each representing one of the colonial states.*

Political parties grew out of the programs that government leaders endorsed and sought to enact, and officials found party organizations useful for articulating their ideas and broadening their coalitions of support. According to political scientist Richard Rubin, "newspapers formed around leadership blocs . . . linking political leaders to their mass constituencies."[5] Alexander Hamilton, a political figure with his own agenda, saw to the creation of the *Gazette of the United States;* John Fenno served as its editor. Hamilton, Vice President John Adams, and other Federalists contributed editorially and financially to the paper, which rapidly became the voice of the developing Federalist Party.[6] In fact, when Vice President Adams wrote a series of articles on American political history, he published them in the *Gazette* in 1790 and 1791. Later, as president, Adams (1797–1801) took no active role in establishing a newspaper as an organ for the government.

Washington Newspapers and the Patronage Factor

Washington newspapers got their start with assistance from Thomas Jefferson, who foresaw the need for an outlet to carry his voice beyond the center of government. When the capital moved to the new federal town on the banks of the Potomac, Jefferson recommended to Samuel Harrison Smith, the owner of the Philadelphia newspaper the *Independent Gazetteer,* that he move to Washington and establish a newspaper there that would become the new administration's official voice. He did so, and on October 31, 1800, he published the first issue of the *National Intelligencer,* which began as a four-page paper appearing three times a week.

Once Jefferson became president (1801–1809), the fledgling newspaper became the official channel for information coming from the executive branch of government. "Over a faithful and comprehensive detail of facts will preside a spirit of investigation, a desire to enlighten, not only by fact, but by reason," editor Smith stated in the *National Intelligencer*'s second issue November 3, 1800. "The tendency of public measures, and the conduct of public men, will be examined with candour and truth." [7] Although generally a source of anti-Federalist and later Whig views, the paper was never seen as partisan in the way many party organs were in the decades that followed.

The imprimatur of the new administration guaranteed the *Intelligencer*'s success. With no rivals in the new town, the *Intelligencer* could establish its roots and dominate an industry that would inevitably grow. James Madison (1809–1817) continued the governmental role of the *Intelligencer*, as did James Monroe (1817–1825) and John Quincy Adams (1825–1829). The *Intelligencer* thereby served as the president's agent until President Andrew Jackson (1829–1837) moved first to the *United States Telegraph* and then in 1830 to the *Washington Globe*.[8] President Martin Van Buren (1837–1841) continued the presidential association with the *Globe*. The *Intelligencer* came back into favor with William Henry Harrison (1841), John Tyler (1841–1845), although not for all of his term, and Millard Fillmore (1850–1853). The Washington *Union*, a new paper, was favored by President James K. Polk (1845–1849), Franklin Pierce (1853–1857), and James Buchanan (1857–1861). Yet another paper, the Washington *Republic*, was created when President Zachary Taylor (1849–1850) took office. Other papers, then, sprouted up in Washington during the terms of the thirteen presidents from 1801 to 1860, but none lived so long or was so closely associated with the institutions of government as the *Intelligencer*, which firmly established its reputation as the most reliable reporter of congressional debates.

Although both the administration and the nascent newspapers benefited from the popular press's role as a voice of the administration, the newspapers received another reward for their endeavor–patronage. According to historian William Ames, the federal government paid the newspapers to print proclamations, advertisements for bids, and other notices, as well as official documents such as treaties. Some of the documents were copied by other papers, thereby enhancing the *Intelligencer*'s importance as a news source.[9] Local and state newspapers regularly used information from the *Intelligencer* in their pages. At its high point, approximately six hundred papers were reprinting information gleaned from its pages.[10] Along with official administration pronouncements, speeches in both houses of Congress were reported, as well as news reports from the federal city.

In time the *Intelligencer* paid more attention to Congress than to the administration through whose efforts

it had been established. Interestingly, the patronage potential at the congressional level was about equal to that at the executive branch level. Congressional patronage took the form of offers to the newspapers to publish debates, and the executive branch was profitable through the publication of newly enacted laws.

In 1829, when Jackson became president, reciprocity between the president and the press took a new form. Long comfortable with journalists, the new president surrounded himself with several ad hoc advisers (known as his kitchen cabinet), who included three journalists: Francis Blair, Amos Kendall, and Duff Green. Jackson also appointed his supporters to government positions, and, in a change from the way government positions had been filled previously, his appointees included journalists as well as party functionaries. Ben Perley Poore, a journalist in Washington in its early days, observed that the editors who supported President Jackson "claimed their rewards." But what they sought was different from the rewards given earlier to newspaper editors supporting a president. "They were not to be appeased by sops of Government advertising, or by the appointment of publisher of the laws of the United States in the respective States, but they demanded some of the most lucrative offices as their share of the spoils," Poore said.[11] In 1832 the *National Intelligencer* published the names of fifty-seven journalists who received appointments to positions in the federal government during Jackson's first term.[12]

Newspapers as Venues for Presidential Opponents

As Hamilton pressed for government policies based on a broad reading of the Constitution, his opponents were quick to match his *Gazette of the United States* with a news outlet of their own. Madison and Jefferson encouraged Philip Freneau to publish a newspaper in Philadelphia, which was at that time America's capital. The *National Gazette* was established October 31, 1791.

Then as now, no political figure was immune from the attack of newspapers. On the day he left office, Washington found himself characterized most unfavorably in the *Aurora*, rival newspaper to Washington's *Gazette of the United States*. Editor Benny Bache described Washington as a "man who is the source of all the misfortunes of our country . . . no longer possessed of power to multiply evils upon the United States." [13] This was not the first stinging criticism of President Washington by the *Aurora* or other critics. Editor Bache, the grandson of Benjamin Franklin, was the most vitriolic of the critics of the Federalists. The severest attacks began with the discussion of the Jay Treaty between the United States and Great Britain, the first sharply partisan issue of the young nation.

At the end of his administration, President John Adams also had to contend with the attacks leveled at him by the Republican-slanted *National Intelligencer*. On its very first front page an anonymous writer—"A Republican"—queried the legality of President Adams's actions as an executive. The Framers of the Constitution "understood that he should exercise *no participation in making the laws,* further than that of assenting to, or rejecting them, when submitted to him, after their formation." [14]

The Federalists responded to the vilification directed their way by enacting laws to stop the attacks on them. In 1798 Congress passed the Alien and Sedition Acts, making it a crime to write or to publish "any false, scandalous and malicious" criticism of the federal government. The effect was to slow down, if not silence, the opposition. In total, twenty-five people were arrested and twelve trials were held, with eleven people convicted, including editors of newspapers as well as members of Congress. When Jefferson became president, he pardoned all convicted under the act.[15]

At this time, neither the stalwarts of the president nor the opposition newspapers believed it their duty to present both sides of a national political issue. Newspapers supporting a president did so wholeheartedly. Among papers, however, there was a difference in the vehemence of support. The *Intelligencer* was perhaps the most objective of the lot.

Birth of the Washington Press Corps

With a twofold increase in the national population between 1790 and 1820 and a burgeoning electorate (property ownership as a prerequisite for voting was abandoned), newspapers found themselves catering to an expanding audience. Concurrently, the Republican coalition began to break apart, and regional differences and splits over trade and tariffs began to surface. The result was that editors outside Washington were no longer willing to rely solely on the *Intelligencer* for news and views of the national government; only the *Intelligencer's* debate summaries remained acceptable. By the 1820s correspondents from around the country were being sent to report on the government—the first Washington correspondents had arrived.

The nature of these reporters' work bore little semblance to the activities of the modern professional press corps. The beat then included purchasing news and, sometimes, even running for office. The job did not require focusing on a particular institution or territory; in fact, until the Civil War reporters roamed all around Washington, placing little emphasis on any special agency or activity. Actually, Congress, not the president, was the dominant source of national government news. It was not until the late nineteenth century that the White House had news people assigned to it permanently. The White House itself lacked the staff to exploit the publicity opportunities available to it.

Congressional press galleries came into being in the 1840s. James Gordon Bennett, publisher of the *New York Herald,* sought congressional floor space for his stenographers and was granted some desks in what was called a "Reporters' Gallery." Created in July 1841, the gallery was located above the vice president's chair in the Senate. Here began the formal press's coverage of government institutions in Washington.

The first Washington correspondents were letter writers who sent back their impressions of the government at work. Beginning with the opening of the second session of the Seventeenth Congress in December 1822, Nathaniel Carter wrote articles for the *Albany Statesman and Evening Advertiser* under the title "Washington Correspondence." By 1827 the group of out-of-town staffers included Samuel Knapp, who wrote for the *Boston Gazette, Charleston Courier,* and *New York Advertiser;* Joseph Buckingham, who reported for the *Boston Gazette;* and James Gordon Bennett, who began his long career with a stint as the correspondent for the *New York Enquirer.* F. B. Marbut, in his *News from the Capital: The Story of Washington Reporting,* marked the year 1827 as the founding of the Washington press corps as a permanent institution. But there still was no organization and no rules to govern behavior.[16]

By their nature, the letter writers were able to engender stronger feelings in their work than the feelings aroused by the fairly bland summaries of debates and pamphlets typical of the *Intelligencer:* "Miserable slanderers-hirelings, hanging on to the skirts of literature, earning a miserable subsistence from their vile and dirty misrepresentations of the proceedings here, and many of them writing for both sides," complained Sen. John M. Niles of Connecticut, who felt the sting of their attacks.[17]

Without rules, there were no restrictions to participation in the press corps. Women, who were admitted to the House of Representatives in 1827 as floor observers, were able to work alongside their male colleagues so long as they reported to a newspaper.[18] Originally sent to Washington in 1850 to write a column for Horace Greeley's *New York Tribune,* Jane Swisshelm was the first woman gallery reporter and the first woman political correspondent. She recorded a session from the Senate press gallery on April 17, 1850, "greatly to the surprise of the Senators, the reporters, and others on the floor and in the galleries." [19] Other women failed to occupy the gallery as she had anticipated. While never a large group in the nineteenth century, women eventually made up 12 percent of the 167 correspondents accredited to the press galleries of the two houses of Congress until their temporary disappearance from the scene in 1880.[20]

From the beginning, women's interests tended to differ from those of their male colleagues. In addition to reporting on Washington social activities, they were especially interested in the issues surrounding slavery. In 1831 Anne Royall, the woman whom journalism historian Frank Luther Mott has identified as writing the "forerunner of the modern Washington gossip column," published a weekly paper that focused on gossip and religion.[21] But she, like her successor

Horace Greeley used his newspaper for crusades and causes. His New York Tribune *was the first major paper to endorse the abolition of slavery and the first to introduce a separate editorial page.*

Jane Swisshelm, was regarded as an outsider with little influence on those who governed.

Diversity also created differences in influence. Some news people were widely accepted in the halls of government and had close connections with those in power. President Andrew Jackson and *Globe* editor Amos Kendall had such a relationship, reports journalism historian Thomas C. Leonard. "The president himself called in Amos Kendall when he wished to make an address. This experienced newspaper editor took down what Jackson said and usually recast it before reading it back. Only after a lengthy exchange did Jackson know what he wished to say." [22]

Emerging Independence of the Press

From 1789 to 1860 the media played a unique role in linking together national political institutions and the electorate and in enhancing the evolving two-party system. As Rubin observed,

> Unlike the situation of present-day politics, both of the chief instruments of mass mobilization and communications, the party and the press, served to increase partisan organizational activity and reinforce lines of electoral cleavage. More effectively than substantive issues alone, the extensiveness of the press's political coverage, the penetrating partisanship of its new journalistic style, and the press's tight organizational links to the parties, all helped make possible a new and tumultuous era of American politics—the politics of mass mobilization in a firmly entrenched two-party system. [23]

Throughout the seventy years, the press, while becoming increasingly independent, remained an important presidential resource as each president's party sought to build a stable group of supporters with whom it could communicate. Also during this time the number of newspapers grew in enormous increments, from approximately two hundred at the beginning of the nineteenth century to twelve hundred by the middle of Andrew Jackson's presidency. Newspapers had doubled again by 1860, but the vast growth came primarily through the proliferation of rural weeklies that accompanied the western expansion taking place during the first half of the nineteenth century. [24] At the same time, in the cities inexpensive dailies proliferated. The affordable price of these dailies earned them the name "penny press." Their sensational style of coverage was aimed at a wide popular audience. The papers did not espouse or depend on party principles or political subsidies. Financially independent through mass circulation and high advertising revenues, they proved harder for politicians to control. [25]

Technology also played an important part in the emerging independence of the press. Publishing costs plummeted with advances in printing and the use of advertising. The telegraph allowed news organizations to gather information more quickly but at a greater cost. In 1844 Samuel F. B. Morse tested his experimental telegraph cable, which ran from the Capitol to the Democratic convention assembled in Baltimore. The exchange between the two political centers demonstrated the validity of the telegraph and "demolished forever the Washington papers' monopoly on Washington reporting," noted Donald A. Ritchie, an authority on nineteenth-century reporting from Washington. [26]

The outbreak of the Mexican War in 1846 put news organizations on notice that the news must be provided as quickly as possible. Distance proved to be an obstacle to timely reporting. According to historian Frank Luther Mott, most news about the event took from two to four weeks to reach print. [27] Some newspapers, however, were willing to spend large sums of money to scoop the competition. In New Orleans, which was serving as a source of military supplies and thus a national combat center, there was great competition for news of the war. With nine newspapers jockeying for the latest information, the tab ran high. According to one account, "The *Picayune* sometimes sent fast boats equipped with composing rooms out to sea to meet the slower steamers from Vera Cruz; and by the time the boat had returned to harbor the type for the latest story was set and ready to be rushed to the *Picayune* presses." [28]

Papers in the East incurred even greater expenses because of gaps in the railroad system, requiring fill-in horseback transmittal to get information out of the South. Not until Richmond, Virginia, the southernmost point of the telegraph, could the news be put on the wire. The cost was so high that several news organizations joined forces to share both the news and the expenses incurred in gathering it. In May 1848, six papers assembled at the offices of the *New York Sun* to form an informal association to share foreign news. In 1856 a more formal association with the same membership became incorporated; it was known as the New York Associated Press.

The establishment of the Government Printing Office (GPO) in 1860 contributed to the growing independence of the press from parties. With its creation, the newspapers lost their patronage plum. Coincidentally, Joseph Gales, senior editor of the *Intelligencer*, died in 1860, bringing to an end an era and the influence of a paper that at one time had so dominated the newspaper industry in Washington.

ESTABLISHMENT OF ROUTINES: 1861–1900

Between 1861 and 1900 several key developments transformed the news business and its relations with the White House. First, technological improvements allowed the diffusion of more news to a greater number of people throughout a larger geographical area. The telegraph, distribution of the news through wire services, and the invention of the linotype machine in 1886 made it possible to quickly mass-produce and circulate papers featuring the latest information. Second, the rising professionalism of reporters added a new dimension to relations between the press and government institutions. For the first time, journalists established rules governing eligibility of persons to cover Congress. The aim was to limit access to congressional institutions to those who worked for valid news-gathering organizations. Third, in this period, too, the importance of the president as a center of news became clear and the White House itself became a distinct news beat. Fourth, the increased attention to the White House led to the establishment of White House routines for the distribution of news.

As the White House staff grew during the latter part of the nineteenth century, the distribution of information to journalists was among its important functions. And, increasingly, the president dealt directly with reporters but not on a routine basis. Not until shortly after the turn of the century could reporters expect to see and to question the president regularly.

Technology and Consolidation

In this significant period, newspapers began to worry about the costs of news gathering—especially about how to transmit information quickly and at a lower cost. Efficiency in gathering news took precedence over a newspaper's relationship with the president; getting a story as soon as possible and making it dramatic was of primary importance. But with the country expanding, speed and accuracy were becoming more difficult. The creation in 1856 of the New York Associated Press led to the rapid distribution of news through press associations. By 1914 participation in the Associated Press had risen from the original six newspapers to one hundred newspapers.[29]

Newspaper advances and consolidation made ties to political parties even less important. News became market-driven. The invention of the linotype machine allowed newspapers to run pictures and advertisements with graphics, making papers livelier. This development translated into more revenue to cover the burgeoning costs of printing the news. The telephone sped news to the home office. As rag replaced wood pulp, paper costs fell dramatically. Presidential scholar Elmer E. Cornwell Jr. found that the entire financial structure of journalism changed as the price of newsprint dropped from about 12 cents a pound in 1872 to 3 cents a pound in 1892.[30] Lower costs meant increased circulation, so between 1870 and 1890 daily circulation went up 222 percent with only a 63 percent increase in population. Cornwell suggested that increased literacy and the wider availability of cheap newspapers in attractive formats accounted for the rise.[31]

PUBLISHERS AND POLITICS

In the late nineteenth century, elected officials found publishers such as Horace Greeley a force to be reckoned with. In 1872 Greeley ran for president on the Democratic ticket, receiving 44 percent of the vote. Other influential publishers of the time included Charles Dana of the *New York Sun*, James Gordon Bennett of the *New York Herald*, Henry J. Raymond of the *New York Times*, Joseph Pulitzer of the *New York World*, and William Randolph Hearst of the *New York Journal*.

None was wary about speaking on the issues of the day or about telling the president what course he should follow. They guided the growth of their newspapers, expressed their opinions in print and in person, and believed in the correctness of their high level of activity in the political world. Even policy positions were within their ken. In the spring of 1869, for example, Dana served as temporary chair of a public meeting advocating Cuban independence from Spain; the mayor of New York was the permanent chair.[1]

When Oscar King Davis, the *New York Times'* Washington, D.C., correspondent during Theodore Roosevelt's last years in office, spoke with the president about taking a position as a newspaper editor after leaving the White House, they discussed the influence of Dana. According to Davis, Dana was a great editor because of his "keen and constant interest in everything that was going on all around the world and his determination to have something about it to print in the 'Sun.'"[2] The group proposing the position to Roosevelt wanted him for his "inspiration" because "that is what makes a great newspaper."[3]

Inspiration is what Dana and the other publishers provided for their newspapers. They employed people to gather, edit, and write news, but the notion of what constituted news came from the direction of the publishers.

1. James Pollard, *The Presidents and the Press* (New York: Macmillan, 1947), 444.
2. Oscar King Davis, *Released for Publication* (New York: Houghton Mifflin, 1925), 138.
3. Ibid.

Adoption of Rules and Standards

With so many of the Civil War battlefields located near the nation's capital, the new correspondents coming into Washington more than doubled the size of the press corps. By the end of the war, there were forty-nine correspondents listed in the congressional galleries.[32]

Out of the reporting of the war came demands from news organizations for objective news reports. "The heads of the Associated Press were troubled by the warped opinions and twisted reports in news columns, which had helped stir sectional antipathies before the war," noted Douglass Cater, a chronicler of the Washington press corps.[33] As the Associated Press developed, it required objectivity from its correspondents so that they would be able to appeal equally to all of its member newspapers.

In another development, reporters developed name recognition in a way they had not previously. The War Department, which designed and enforced censorship regulations, ruled that stories detailing the actions of war had to carry the name of the correspondent writing it. That began the practice of bylines for reporters, a custom retained after the war.

Despite all these rules, only after the Civil War were standards and rules for congressional coverage formalized. News organizations, in particular, wanted to make sure that journalists with congressional privileges were actually working for news organizations devoted to objective coverage of the government. There was no room in the press galleries for agents of persons or organizations seeking government actions in their behalf.

The line between lobbying and journalism became particularly murky during the years of industrial expansion. When the Crédit Mobilier scandal arose in the 1870s, the investigations disclosed that Washington correspondents were lobbying for the passage of specific bills. In 1875 the House decided to expel all journalists who had acted in behalf of legislation.[34]

The resulting questions that arose about the objectivity of the congressional community of correspondents led to the adoption of rules governing admittance to the press galleries and the use of its facilities. In 1879 a set of rules was adopted specifying who could serve as an accredited congressional correspondent. "These rules defined an accreditable correspondent as one whose primary salary came from sending telegraphic dispatches to daily newspapers. The rules also barred lobbying by any member of the press gallery; and prohibited all clerks from executive agencies (although not from congressional committees)," reported Donald Ritchie.[35]

As benign as the gallery rules sounded, their effect was to exclude women from representation because they either worked for weeklies or mailed in their columns on Washington society news to their newspapers.[36] Generally, editors did not believe women to be as astute as men or their

pieces to be worth the transmittal costs. Women, however, continued to report from Washington because social reporting was such a central element of both Washington and the White House. Emily Briggs of the *Philadelphia Press* was an exception to the gallery rule as she became one of the first women correspondents to use the telegraph for "spot news" (important late-breaking information). Her dispatches contained "detailed accounts of the people and events she observed from the reporters' galleries or at an evening's social gathering."[37]

The President as a News Story

Down the road from the Capitol, the press was beginning to take an increased interest in the president. On the eve of the Civil War, the Associated Press assigned a correspondent, Henry Villard, to shadow the newly elected Abraham Lincoln (1861–1865) from December until he left Springfield, Illinois, for Washington in early February. Villard was to supply the Associated Press with regular dispatches about events in Springfield, which "was to become for a time the center of political gravitation."[38] The correspondent sat in on Lincoln's morning meetings with political visitors and was privy to all matters under review, including cabinet appointments. Villard went on to become an exceptionally inventive war correspondent who provided first-hand reports of important battles. His dispatches were closely followed by government officials, including the president. After the Union loss in the battle of Fredericksburg in December 1862, Villard was summoned by Lincoln to relate his account of the fighting and to discuss with the president his assessments of the war.[39]

A White House press corps eventually evolved from the reporters who came to the White House for specific purposes. In the case of President Andrew Johnson (1865–1869), many reporters talked with him before his impeachment trial. Both the president and the press recognized the benefits their relationship could have: the president could explain his beliefs about the errors of the impeachment proceedings, and members of the press could report the results of the individual interviews each had had with the president.

In the years after Johnson left office, the presidency faced considerable congressional opposition, and presidents were forced to turn to the public for support of legislation favored by the White House. Interviews and presidential visits to other cities were particularly useful tools for eliciting public support. In fact, between 1860 and 1901, the availability of information about the president changed from episodic to routine. Once individual presidential interviews and the distribution of information about the president were in place, reporters did not want to give up the regular presidential and staff contact.

With the cutting of political ties between newspaper editors and presidents, press relationships had become inherently less cozy. Gone were the days when a president could expect the counsel of an editor on the release of information. Instead, there was an emphasis on recording presidential statements and views. The interview replaced the edited speech. This innovation became a distinctive characteristic of American reporting built, in most respects, on the earlier tradition of printing the statements, debates, and speeches of elected officials. Now, however, reporters also were recording the intentions and desires of officials, including the president.[40]

The modern presidential interview has its roots in Andrew Johnson's presidency. In October 1865, Col. A. K. McClure of the *Franklin Repository* of Chambersburg, Pennsylvania, interviewed President Johnson.[41] McClure, in fact, simply asked the president about his policy intentions and published the president's answers in his newspaper. Over the next two and a half years, President Johnson, as noted earlier, held a dozen more interviews with reporters, seven of them in the year of his 1868 impeachment proceedings. Finally, his lawyers put an end to the sessions.

Henry Villard, from the Associated Press, was the first reporter ever assigned to cover a president-elect full-time. He followed Abraham Lincoln from 1860 to 1861, thus becoming a forerunner of modern White House correspondents.

President Johnson's interviews were complemented by his tours through cities in the Midwest, including Chicago and St. Louis. On such tours, known as "swings around the circle," the president took his message to people outside of Washington. Although his appearances were heavily covered by the local media, in Johnson's case the local newspaper coverage worked to his detriment because his speeches led to the desertion of many of his supporters. As journalism historian Mark Wahlgren Summers described it,

> When the president used an address to accuse members of Congress of plotting his assassination or to brand two of the most prominent Republicans on Capitol Hill traitors, when he compared himself to Christ or, in the presence of disabled veterans, posed the rhetorical question of who had suffered for the Union more than himself, he did himself more damage than the most hostile editorial that radical partisans could have penned.[42]

Although Johnson's successor, Ulysses S. Grant (1869–1877), regularly gave interviews when he was in the field as a general, he gave few as president. Rutherford B.

Hayes (1877–1881) also had few formal meetings or interviews with the press. President James A. Garfield (1881) had friends among the media, including Whitelaw Reid, the editor and publisher of the *New York Tribune,* but he gave only one interview, appearing April 24, 1881, just days before his assassination.[43] Chester A. Arthur (1881–1885), who followed him, kept his distance from the press. "From the standpoint of publicity," historian James Pollard noted, "he was perhaps less conspicuous than he had been . . . as customs collector." [44] By the time of Grover Cleveland's administration (1885–1889; 1893–1897) the press had expectations about what information the White House would provide journalists. Overcoming his natural antipathy for the press, Cleveland realized he needed to respond to press inquiries and issue statements through the newspapers when necessary, but he rarely confided in the press or had direct contacts.[45]

Like other presidents, Cleveland received press attention as he traveled. Local reporters chronicled his every move as he took a "swing around the circle" through the western and southern United States. To the South, he brought a message of healing: "There is . . . fairness enough abroad in the land to insure a proper and substantial recognition of the good faith which you have exhibited. . . . [T]he educational advantages and the care which may be accorded to every class of your citizens have a relation to the general character of the entire country." [46]

Development of White House Press Operations

The president's staff was quite minimal during the late nineteenth century. In 1871 President Grant was allowed only a private secretary, stenographer, a few executive clerks, a steward, and a messenger. They were paid out of a total payroll of $13,800, according to Leonard D. White, who has chronicled the development of administrations.[47]

Unfortunately, White House staff positions, including the position of private secretary, held little allure for would-be appointees. Yet President Garfield was wise enough to know that "the man who holds that place can do very much to make or mar the success of an administration" and "ought to be held in higher estimation than Secretary of State." [48]

Candidates for the position shared neither his enthusiasm nor his confidence.

Dan Lamont, Grover Cleveland's secretary, counted among his responsibilities that of dispensing routine scheduling and other discretionary information to the press. David Barry, a Washington correspondent during those days, described Cleveland's press habits:

> When he had something to communicate to the public he wrote it out and gave it to his private secretary to hand to representatives of the press associations. Mr. Cleveland early developed a fondness for making announcements in this formal way and it is a fact perhaps worth noting that he invariably selected Sunday evening for having his messages promulgated, evidently believing that on Monday morning the newspapers had ample space to devote to his utterances.[49]

President Cleveland released information primarily through a press syndicate headed by George F. Parker, one of the few members of the newspaper business Cleveland counted among his friends. This daily contact with the president allowed Parker to make specific recommendations to Cleveland such as suggesting that he provide advance texts of speeches to both friendly and oppositional news organizations. Cleveland's eagerness to reach the public overcame his reticence, and he saw that competent staff people provided reporters with solid presidential information. A Washington correspondent of that time, commenting on Lamont's importance to both reporters and to the president, observed that Lamont "had tact, judgment, knew what to say and how to say it, and what to do and how to do it. He let the 'boys' do most of the talking and guessing, but never allowed them to leave the White House with a wrong impression, or without thinking that they had got about all there was in the story." [50] For the first time, the White House staff was at the heart of the news operation.

Meanwhile, the interest in presidential activities was building. In 1896 William W. Price of the *Washington Evening Star* became the first correspondent to be based at the White House, and he brought to his beat a different approach than those of his predecessors. Price found that his old *modus operandus* from his days with a weekly newspaper in South Carolina—his main assignment had been to interview people leaving the trains as they arrived in town each day[51]—also was suited to the White House in 1896. According to historian George Juergens:

> The idea of rounding up news simply by standing outside the White House and interviewing visitors as they arrived and departed was at once obvious and inspired. Price immediately struck a rich lode. It may be that the people he accosted opened up to him because of the sheer surprise at being asked questions under such circumstances. Within a few hours he had accumulated enough material to scrawl hurriedly a story that appeared in the *Star* that evening

under the headline "AT THE WHITE HOUSE," the first installment of what would be a regular Price feature in the paper for the next two decades.[52]

The importance of news organizations to William McKinley's administration was presaged in his 1896 campaign. President McKinley (1897–1901) used the press to carry his advertisements and to report on his prepared speeches, which carefully enunciated his campaign themes. In addition, McKinley was the first presidential candidate to be filmed.[53]

Also during the McKinley administration, Congress appropriated the funds for a "secretary and two assistant secretaries, two executive clerks and four clerks, two of whom were telegraphers, as well as numerous doorkeepers and messengers," raising the total White House staff to approximately thirty.[54] Only this additional staff assistance made it possible to provide for the daily needs of the press.

Creation of a White House Press Facility

By 1898, one year into the McKinley administration, White House routines for dealing with the press were in place, White House facilities were being made available on a regular basis for the exclusive use of reporters, and unwritten conventions were being observed by reporters in their dealings with the president. During the Spanish-American War noted journalist Ida Mae Tarbell described the White House press arrangements:

> The President, as a matter of fact, has the newspaper man always with him. He is as much a part of the White House personnel as ... the big police inspector at the door. Accommodations are furnished him there, and his privileges are well-defined and generally recognized. Thus in the outer reception-room of the business part of the White House, a corner containing a well furnished table and plenty of chairs is set aside for reporters. Here representatives of half a dozen or more papers are always to be found, and during Cabinet meetings and at moments of grave importance the number increases many fold. Here they write, note the visitors who are admitted to the President, catch the secretaries as they come and go, and here every evening about ten o'clock they gather around Secretary [John Addison] Porter for a kind of family talk, he discussing with them whatever the events of the day he thinks it wise to discuss.
>
> It is in "Newspaper Row," as the east side of the great north portico is called, that the White House press correspondents flourish most vigorously. Here they gather by the score on exciting days, and, in the shadow of the great white pillars, watch for opportunities to waylay important officials as they come and go. Nobody can get in or out of the Executive Mansion without their seeing him, and it is here that most of the interviews, particularly with the cabinet officers, are held. Close to "Newspaper Row" is a long line of wheels belonging to messengers and telegraph boys, alert, swift little chaps, a half dozen of whom are always in

waiting at the foot of the big columns, discussing the war, or on warm days catching the forty winks of sleep they are always sadly in need of.

It is part of the unwritten law of the White House that the newspaper men shall never approach the President as he passes to and fro near their alcove or crosses the portico to his carriage, unless he himself stops and talks to them. This he occasionally does, for he knows all of the reporters by name and treats them with uniform kindness. If a man disappears, Mr. McKinley is sure to inquire soon what has become of him, and if one falls ill, he asks regularly after him.[55]

Therefore under McKinley, for the first time, a place was set aside in the White House for the exclusive use of reporters and the staff assigned to deal with reporters on a regular basis. According to historian Lewis L. Gould, the "president's secretary, John Addison Porter, circulated constantly, and at noon and 4:00 p.m. he spoke formally with the newsmen."[56] By the end of the McKinley administration, the staff was clipping information and editorial opinion from newspapers for the president's daily perusal. Moreover, the release of major presidential messages and speeches had been coordinated so that all newspapers and press services would receive equal treatment.[57] By the time of McKinley's assassination in 1901, the following procedures were in place: presidential speeches and texts were distributed regularly to news organizations on an equal basis; permanent space was available for reporters in the White House; senior staff were responsible for the president's press relations; the White House was involved in making arrangements for the press traveling with the president; a press briefing was held daily; a rudimentary news summary was prepared for the president to read; and a press corps was assigned to cover the White House. These procedures remain at the heart of the arrangements provided today for those covering the president.

The current contours of the relationship between the president and the press were in place as well. Presidential statements and speeches were made available to reporters, and the president's staff answered questions about his actions and the nuances of policy. The White House had begun its routines of providing the reporters with information in forms they could best use, with an adequate amount of lead time to prepare their stories, and in a permanent place set aside for their use. Reporters, for their part, had established the White House as a beat. In addition, they had settled on the ways in which they gathered information and the importance of the interview to their concept of a story. Those interviews could be with staff members, department secretaries, or members of Congress. Their most important interview was the presidential one, but those interviews were not a hallmark of this period. That would come in the next stages.

THE PRESIDENT MEETS THE PRESS: 1901–1932

Many of the formal structures and tacit understandings that underlie today's relationship between the president and the news media were shaped significantly in the period from 1901 to 1932. Four important developments marked this period.

First, the president became a central actor in a federal government expanding its scope of activity. At the turn of the century, and under the aegis of Theodore Roosevelt, the United States had become a world power and its president a world leader. On the domestic front, the president's policy agenda included railroad regulation, passage of a Pure Food and Drug Act, and initiation of government-sponsored conservation activities, including a conservation corps. The increase in activity generated a commensurate increase in public attention to the chief executive's activities.

A second development of this period was the establishment of the presidential press conference as an instrument through which the president could inform and respond to the Washington press corps. From a rather informal exchange in Roosevelt's administration, it assumed a more formal, public, and egalitarian form in the Woodrow Wilson administration and continuing into those of Warren Harding, Calvin Coolidge, and Herbert Hoover. Since its inception in March 1913, the press conference has proved enduring as a central meeting place for presidents and those who cover them and their administrations, even though recent presidents have held them less frequently than their mid–twentieth-century counterparts. In a related development, rules were established to govern both small private and large public meetings between the president and reporters. Many of these rules remain the basis of today's interactions between the president and the press. Their mutual dependency evolved naturally as reporters struggled to define the nature of their relationship with the president in the larger context of news gathering. Over the course of this struggle, several prominent correspondents became confidants and advisers to presidents. This aspect of the relationship waned, however, in later periods as procedures established at the beginning of the century gradually shifted toward a more egalitarian model.

Third, in this era the White House press staff, headed by a presidential press secretary, became fully responsible for handling the president's daily relations with news organizations and for servicing the news needs of a White House press corps.

And, fourth, the presidency became an important institution for prominent news organizations to cover regularly.

Photographers covering the White House pose on the South Lawn in 1918.

The President on Center Stage

When President Theodore Roosevelt (1901–1909) came into office, he was an important official but hardly a national news center; Congress, and particularly the Senate, held center stage. But all that soon changed. Washington correspondent Louis Ludlow described how:

> It would not be stating the whole truth to say that [Roosevelt] made news. He was news. His very personality reflected news. He exuded news at every pore. Even the way in which he said and did things made news.
>
> The ordinary person's conventional "I'm pleased to meet you" suggests nothing to write about, but when President Roosevelt exclaimed, "Dee-lighted!" and showed two glistening rows of ivories, he made copy for the press.[58]

Earlier presidents had chosen to distance themselves from reporters. Roosevelt preferred instead to capitalize on a personal relationship with the correspondents. He sought their friendship and encouraged their reporting. A magnetic force resulted, which drew correspondents to the White House when he was there and around the country when he was on the road on one of his many swings around the circle.

Because President Roosevelt viewed the White House as a "bully pulpit" for reaching the voters, he turned to reporters to publicize himself and his policies. For him, the correspondents—not the publishers or editors—were important. Leo Rosten, chronicler of the creation of the Washington press corps, noted that Roosevelt, in what was fairly typical of his publicity style, called in about fifty correspondents to announce the creation of the First Conservation Congress.[59] Roosevelt "knew the value and potent influence of a news paragraph written as he wanted it written and disseminated through the proper influential channels better than any man

who ever occupied the White House, before him, or since," commented David Barry, a journalist who covered his administration. He also knew that "editorial articles do not mold public opinion" and that "editors are nowadays more apt to follow public opinion than to lead it."[60]

For Roosevelt, caring about news articles meant getting involved in their direction and preparation. He did not hesitate to suggest possible news articles and news paragraphs to reporters, and once he even drafted himself what he wanted sent over the wires. When a bill to control railroad rates was being considered by the Senate, an attorney working for the Standard Oil Company sent a letter to selected senators suggesting how they should vote on individual elements of the bill. According to Barry, "The newspaper account of that incident created a worldwide sensation, and blocked the attempt of those who sought to amend the bill in behalf of certain interests, and the man who gave the story to the newspapers and who wrote the preliminary news item that was sent to the afternoon papers was the President of the United States himself."[61] When an issue was important to the president, he put his redoubtable energy into the publicity element in its passage.

In the spring of 1905, when congressional action on railroad rate regulation was stymied, President Roosevelt launched a publicity campaign that took him through the Southwest and the Midwest. He continued in October with a trip to the South. "Invoking the name of his mother as a native of Georgia, and of his two uncles as Confederate veterans, he made such legislation almost a matter of sectional loyalty. It was as if he 'himself fired the last two shots for the *Alabama* instead of his uncles.' "[62] Back at the White House, Roosevelt kept up his campaign for railroad regulation by providing reporters with information on malfeasance by the railroad companies. His multipronged publicity attack featured local as well as national reporters and news writers from both magazines and newspapers.

President William Howard Taft (1909–1913), in contrast, paid little attention to publicity preparations, including major speeches such as one on the Payne-Aldrich Bill, which he lauded as the "best tariff bill the Republican party ever passed." [63] The bill was in fact extremely unpopular, particularly in the congressional district of James A. Tawney of Minnesota whom Taft was trying to aid with a campaign appearance. Later, Taft confessed that he had not prepared the speech until he was on the train to Winona.[64] Moreover, he had not sought information about the nature of the district and the issues alive in it. Unfortunately for Taft, Tawney went down to a resounding defeat.

President Woodrow Wilson (1913–1921), who shared with Roosevelt a sense of the importance of a public address, revived the custom of delivering his State of the Union address in person, a practice moribund since Jefferson's presidency. The more he had a hand in public addresses or in press conferences, he believed, the more likely that his words would be recorded faithfully and prominently displayed. His was a public presidency, and his choice of forums continually reinforced that theme. Wilson also used personal addresses before joint sessions of Congress to concentrate public attention on particular issues. Political scientist Elmer Cornwell calculated that in his first term Wilson made twelve appearances before the Congress, in addition to his State of the Union addresses.[65]

If vehicles other than newspapers had then existed, Wilson would have had an even larger choice of strategies for getting to the public. One of Wilson's few close associates in the press, Ray Stannard Baker, suggested that "the radio, if it had been in use at that time, might have proved a godsend to Wilson: for he would have been able to secure direct contact with his public, broadening his influence as the fragmentary reporting of his addresses could not do." [66]

America's entry into World War I stimulated President Wilson to establish a special vehicle to coordinate publicity information. The Committee on Public Information became the first sustained effort to coordinate White House information with that from the executive branch departments and agencies. George Creel, a Wilson appointee heading the group, carefully constructed an image of the president as chief executive and commander in chief. According to Cornwell, the Creel Committee saw the war in Wilsonian terms. "Mobilization, diplomacy, and peacemaking" were all orchestrated to "impress on the public a heightened sense of the importance of the presidency" and Wilson.[67] Among the publicity strategies devised by Creel was the *Official Bulletin,* which was distributed to post offices throughout the country as well as to military installations.

Succeeding presidents Harding, Coolidge, and Hoover relied primarily on press conferences to communicate their messages to the public but added professional speechwriters and use of the radio to the presidential communications arsenal. President Warren Harding (1921–1923) hired speechwriter Judson Welliver, who proved so successful that President Calvin Coolidge kept him on. Coolidge (1923–1929) was the first president to give his State of the Union message not only in person but also on radio. Recognizing that the new medium allowed him to speak directly with the citizens of the country and communicate both his persona and his brand of leadership, Coolidge began to broadcast a monthly radio program in 1924. President Herbert Hoover (1929–1933), too, used radio but preferred it only for traditional occasions such as the State of the Union address. "Radio as a presidential tool would not and could not come into its own until it was realized that only speeches prepared exclusively with an unseen radio audience in mind would make possible full exploitation of the medium," Cornwell suggested.[68] Presidential radio would have to wait for Franklin Roosevelt to shape fully its contours into a powerful force to promote programs and policy.

Presidential Press Conference

Theodore Roosevelt was the first president to make himself regularly available to reporters. He met with them at all hours of the day, individually and in groups, while he was at his desk, over a meal, and at unusual locations. Often his group meetings meant receiving a half-dozen reporters while he was being shaved. Oscar King Davis, a correspondent for the *New York Times,* described the scene as he met the president at shaving time:

> Every day, at one o'clock, Delaney, a colored messenger employed at the Treasury Department, came over to the White House and shaved the President. There was, of course, no regular barber's chair, but Delaney did the best he could with a big armchair. The shaving hour was always a good one to see the President, for it gave the interviewer a better chance to say what he wanted to say in full, as the President, with his face covered with lather and Delaney's razor sweeping over it, was rather at a disadvantage as to talking.[69]

Unlike his predecessors, Roosevelt was no stranger to regular give and take with reporters. As governor of New York, he had held daily press meetings and recognized the value of direct dealings with reporters and the efficient use of staff. Both this practice and his skillful staff followed him into the White House after McKinley's assassination in 1901. William Loeb, his assistant from Albany, who had both an ability to deal with reporters and a knowledge of news gathering, was able to enhance the likelihood of good play in what reporters produced.

Taft had a very different view of press relations. On the day of his inauguration reporters received their "first, emphatic demonstration that it was not only a new President in the White House, but, in fact, a new man, and not at all the pleasant, genial, helpful, good-natured man we had known as Secretary of War." [70] Taft was no longer as cooperative with reporters as when he was a cabinet officer. The president's secretary, Fred Carpenter, informed reporters that the president would send for them when he wanted to talk to them. Wednesdays were a possibility, but such meetings were totally at Taft's direction. Reporters, then, had to resort to other means of acquiring presidential information—ones less favorable to the president. "Correspondents took advantage of the four mornings a week from 10:30 a.m. to noon that Taft set aside to see senators and representatives," historian George Juergens recounted. "They would feed questions to the president through their congressional contacts, on the understanding that nothing would be said about who was actually doing the asking." [71] Leaks also proved to be a fruitful source of information on the executive branch.

Woodrow Wilson, too, was most comfortable dealing with reporters at arm's length. But Wilson brought reporters together as a group, which was the first step in the evolution of the formal modern press conference. These regularly scheduled gatherings were open to all reporters on an equal basis. Members of the press chose the questions; and the president chose how and when to answer. The first formal press conference was held March 15, 1913, at 12:45 on a Saturday afternoon, eleven days after Wilson's inauguration. "Although no transcript exists of the dialogue in the Oval Office between the president and approximately 125 reporters, it is clear the session went badly," wrote Juergens.[72] A week later, the second conference attracted almost two hundred reporters, who this time headed for the East Room, the only White House room large enough to handle a group of that size. Clearly, then, the press conference was a successful idea even if Wilson did not enjoy the meetings.

Like Roosevelt, Wilson felt the press conference was a valuable publicity tool and one particularly suited to current issues; these gatherings led to positive articles on the front pages of major newspapers. In June 1913, for example, the president called on Congress to create a Federal Reserve system, and the next day the *New York Times* featured the story, commenting that "in the course of the day the President made a splendid defense of the currency bill." Generally, the *Times,* Cornwell found, gave great play to a presidential initiative, including a page-one story on the message and the press conference text.[73] In another conference, the president became his own assertive publicist when he suggested, " 'There is one question, which, if I am properly informed, I would ask me, if I were you.' " He then emphasized that he had no intention of compromising on a wool provision in

tariff legislation: " 'When you get a chance, just say that I am not the kind that considers compromises when I once take my position. Just note that down, so that there will be nothing more of the sort transmitted in the press.' " [74]

Reporters, having grown used to individual meetings with presidents, did not like Wilson's group sessions. The president reverted to his schoolmaster role toward undergraduates, noted Barry: "The newspaper men would, when they screwed up courage enough to do so, ask questions bearing upon various phases of the news of the day, and the president would answer or sidestep them as he chose, sometimes elucidating the subject with a little inside information but as a rule not throwing any new light on the subject." [75]

The reporters sensed the president disliked those meetings and always looked forward to their conclusion. In the early days of his term, conferences were held regularly on Mondays and Thursdays, but they dwindled early in 1915 to each Tuesday before being abandoned altogether. The sinking of the ocean liner *Lusitania* in May 1915 seemed to provide the excuse Wilson needed to cut back. His annoyance was directed generally at what he considered the time wasted in preparation and the poor quality of the questions posed to him.

Other presidents used press conferences to attract attention to matters of particular interest. Harding structured his conferences to stimulate the exchange between the president and correspondents and thoroughly enjoyed the encounters. As former publisher of an Ohio newspaper, the Marion *Star*, Harding was used to the news-gathering business. He discussed cabinet meetings and problems in the conduct of his office at twice-weekly sessions. Not reluctant to talk, Harding spoke on a background basis (his words could be used but without attributing them to the president), but he often went "off the record" (neither the words nor their source could be cited). (*See box, Classifications of White House Information, p. 988.*) Reporters were expected to keep these off-the-record discussions private, but there was inevitable seepage into the public domain. Harding's concern with this eventuality stemmed more from possible inadvertent errors than unwanted publicity. Ground rules, therefore, were initiated to require reporters to submit in writing the questions to be put to the president. The rules were relaxed over the course of Harding's term, but they did not prevent a presidential gaffe when Harding responded to a written question about the provisions in the Four Power Treaty being negotiated by the Conference for the Limitation of Armaments related to the protection of the Japanese islands.[76] While those negotiating the treaty intended such protection, the president responded that the treaty itself did not. Secretary of State Charles Evans Hughes intervened, and that evening the White House issued a statement correcting the president's misstatement.

President Coolidge continued to require that questions be submitted in advance when he succeeded Harding, and, like Harding, Coolidge spoke with reporters from his office in the West Wing of the White House. But without the bond of a shared profession he lacked ease in dealing with the press. "As the reporters, between fifty and one hundred in number, stood silently in the executive office taking notes, the president leafed through the pile of written queries and answered those which he wished to answer, ignoring the others," wrote F. B. Marbut.[77] Another Washington correspondent, J. Fred Essary, who covered the administration, told of one conference when reporters collectively responded to this habit by all writing the same question. Leafing through the pile, Coolidge picked out the final one in the stack. "I have here a question about the condition of the children in Porto Rico," said Coolidge to the group of journalists, none of whom had asked that question.[78] Neither the reporters nor the president divulged the true content of the question they had actually submitted.

What frustrated reporters most was the paucity of material for their stories. "What he says is mostly noncommittal, neutral, evasive," complained Frank Kent of the Baltimore *Sun*. "To many questions he replies that he has no exact information on the subject but expects to have it shortly, or that he is informed some department has the matter in hand and is handling it in a satisfactory manner. Even when his replies are definite, which is rare, they are flat and meatless." [79] Other Coolidge practices rankled reporters as well. For example, they chafed under the new rule that the president could not be quoted either directly or indirectly. To use information, reporters created a contrivance: the White House spokesperson.[80]

President Hoover also required presubmitted questions, but he tightened the time frame to twenty-four hours in advance and, like Coolidge, made his choice of responses. Reporters, however, became restive, and they regarded Hoover as a roadblock to the release of information. As the economy worsened in 1931, so did Hoover's press relations. From the beginning of June until the end of November 1932, Hoover held only eight press conferences.[81] By the end of the administration, not many reporters attended the few conferences that were held.

New Rules Governing the Relationship

As open as President Theodore Roosevelt was to certain reporters, he had a set of rules—and punishments—governing his relationships with correspondents and news organizations. Roosevelt's rules were not negotiated, they were announced. On his first day in office he invited David Barry and three colleagues to the White House to discuss his relationship with them. His confidence in them would be demonstrated by keeping them apprised, he declared, but "if any of the reporters should at any time violate a confidence or publish news that the President thought ought not to be published, he should be punished by having legitimate news

withheld from him." [82] During his years as governor, such a punishment had been leveled against a reporter in Albany, Roosevelt told them, and that man still would not be privy to any White House news.[83] Members of the press corps consigned to the Roosevelt-invented Ananais Club faced a news blackout.

President Taft, like Roosevelt, set the rules. Taft kept personal contacts with reporters at a minimum, allowing press relations to be handled through his staff and only occasionally meeting with individual correspondents, such as Oscar King Davis. He selected the publications he would favor with a response, usually those with which he had had a long-standing acquaintance or friendship. President Wilson's rules, in contrast, focused on group settings and equal presidential access. Press conference information was "just between us" when the president said so. Otherwise, material could be used without attribution to the president himself.

Herbert Hoover established a formal set of rules to govern the terms of the release of information provided in press conferences. His rules included three tiers of information. First, information on the record could be quoted directly as the president's words. For the second tier, material could be used but without the president's name. At the third tier was information given on a confidential basis with the understanding that it would not be used in any way. The device of the "White House spokesman" was put to rest in the Hoover years,[84] but these three distinctions continue to form the basis of White House information policies. (*See box, Classifications of White House Information, p. 988.*)

President Hoover had trouble with reporters—not over the rules but over the manner in which he sought to apply them. The Hoover White House attempted to prevent the distribution of official information, something it could not accomplish. At a press conference on October 6, 1931, Hoover tried to prevent the publication of reports that a conference on the Depression and unemployment would be held at the White House. "He said there would be no announcement, not even a statement of the persons attending or of the general program discussed," wrote Leo Rosten. "He told the newspapermen not to 'waylay' participants as they left the conference." But waylay them they did. Richard Oulahan of the *New York Times* and Hay Hayden of the *Detroit News* warned "the President that it would be out of the question to expect the newspapermen not to supply the public with information about one of the most important events of the year." [85] Rebellion was not the reporters' only recourse. Armed with a petition of more than one hundred signatories, they appealed to the Board of Governors of the National Press Club to create a committee to consider the problem of the administration's refusal to provide information on government activities.[86]

Press Corps Confidants and Advisers

As the twentieth century began, there was a well-laid history of journalistic advice to presidents. During Andrew Jackson's administration, Amos Kendall had helped the president to craft speeches. Journalist George F. Parker had advised President Cleveland on the release of information to the press, and, to facilitate the process, Parker had formed a press syndicate to handle the distribution of White House information. By his own account, Parker met frequently with the president, and in Cleveland's second term the two discussed cabinet selections. Cleveland had not yet decided on any appointees, Parker said. "At this interview, I had occasion to bring forward and to discuss the names of five men fitted to become Mr. Cleveland's advisers," Parker related. "Of these, two declined appointment, and the remainder were sworn into his Cabinet after his second inauguration." [87] The definition of *conflict of interest* was fuzzy in those days. There was no widely held understanding among reporters that newspaper work precluded participation in White House decision making.

When reporters eagerly sought a close relationship with Theodore Roosevelt, he, in turn, gave credence to their opinions and, most especially, to their knowledge. Correspondents often served as his foils and advisers, as illustrated by the role they played in preparing presidential speeches. His preparation for a major address on transportation suggested the routine he often employed. "The President had laboriously prepared his great speech on the transportation problem . . . and Secretary [William] Loeb called in the correspondents in order that the President might 'try it on the dog' before he went out to Indianapolis to deliver it," observed journalist Louis Ludlow. When the president read his speech, "warm words of approbation came from different correspondents." Only one correspondent remained silent—Judson Welliver, who only recently had come to Washington from Iowa. When Roosevelt asked Welliver what he thought, the correspondent responded that he did not "think much of it." After prodding by the president, Welliver continued, "I have studied this subject a long time and I tell you that you are going about this business in the wrong way." Welliver's fellow correspondents were astonished. "No other correspondent had ever dared to start a rough house with the impetuous President. But Roosevelt craved fuller information. He pressed Welliver for his detailed views," recounted Ludlow. At a second encounter the next evening, President Roosevelt and Welliver redrafted the Indianapolis speech and the president "from that night became a staunch advocate of the railroad valuation plan," wrote Ludlow. Welliver emerged as a valuable informal aide. He remained at the White House for several administrations and, among other things, handled press relations and speech writing for President Harding. In the Roosevelt administration, however, he was

there as a journalist, yet that did not preclude his involvement in White House decisions and actions. [88]

As much as William Howard Taft disdained reporters' advice, there were times when he paid attention. During the 1908 general election campaign, Oscar Davis was concerned that Taft had not defined a theme in his speeches. Davis and fellow Washington correspondent Dick Lindsay, representing the *Kansas City Star and Times,* urged Taft to become more involved in developing speeches with specific themes. "So Lindsay and I kept at Mr. Taft to prepare some speeches," Davis said. "We pointed out several issues that he might well discuss, and he replied that he had handled them all in his speech of acceptance." That night, Davis and Lindsay spent hours tearing apart the nomination acceptance speech. The next day they gave Taft a series of speeches dealing with discrete topics. Ultimately he did not give them, but, significantly, the correspondents had felt free to make their suggestions. [89]

Office of Press Secretary

The foundation for the office of press secretary was laid in the late–nineteenth-century administrations of Cleveland and McKinley with the work of staff members Dan Lamont, George Cortelyou, and John Addison Porter. They stood in for the reluctant presidents and for the first time provided official White House information and guidance in behalf of the chief executives they served. (Earlier, the presidential private secretary, the equivalent of the contemporary chief of staff, had served as the president's surrogate, preparing information and providing news-gathering arrangements.) George Cortelyou, secretary to McKinley, handled all press relations as well as the president's congressional contacts. This role required him to organize whatever information the president might need and also to preside over the White House staff. Employed by three presidents, Cortelyou saw his work for Theodore Roosevelt bring him particular attention, in part because as a master publicist the president added luster to his secretaries' reputations. Both Cortelyou and William Loeb had more press exposure than their predecessors precisely because Roosevelt was so publicity-prone.

Notable also before the formal creation in 1930 of the press secretary's position were Joseph P. Tumulty (Wilson), who shaped and broadened the task of presidential press relations still further, and secretaries Charles Norton (Taft), Judson Welliver (Harding), and George B. Christian (Harding), who maintained the traditions set by their predecessors, paving the way for many of the practices in use today. They provided the speech texts reporters needed, arranged press conferences, held daily briefings, answered questions, and sought to represent the interests of reporters to press-shy presidents.

William Loeb's familiarity with press routines and with Roosevelt's penchant for publicity went back to his service during Roosevelt's New York governorship. This relationship was of inestimable value to both the president and the press, according to Henry L. Stoddard, a Washington correspondent at the time:

> No one ever knew every thought, purpose and mood of a President as Loeb knew Roosevelt's. He was in truth the President's other self—he was the one man who could act for Roosevelt in full confidence that he was doing as the President would have him to do. There is not much in the Roosevelt Administration that does not, in some way, bear the impress of Loeb's judgment.[90]

Loeb also knew the rules reporters lived by, and he worked on stories with individual reporters.

The styles of those handling presidential press relations usually reflected the interests of their presidents. A press-shy president, Taft, first chose Fred Carpenter, a man with curiously little interest in either directing press inquiries to the president or pleading the cases of journalists. After Carpenter was succeeded by Charles Norton, relations with reporters took an upswing. As described by Oscar Davis, "We began to get back into something of our old status with Mr. Taft, and it was no longer such a rare thing to get an appointment with him, even on very short notice."[91]

Joseph Tumulty, secretary to President Wilson, struggled to pick up the slack when Wilson's news conferences ceased in 1915. Tumulty became the intermediary between "these two entities whose contacts otherwise remained at best formal and reserved."[92] In addition, Tumulty was able to interpret successfully Wilson's thoughts and actions. David Lawrence, who served as a Washington correspondent during that period, reported that "time and again, Secretary Tumulty revealed the President's views and articulated the administration viewpoint with more skill than the President showed in his conferences with the newspapermen."[93] He put the best face on the president's actions and made a good case with his boss for release of information to reporters. Tumulty also was familiar with reporters' routines and persuaded the president that advance preparation of speeches encouraged wide public circulation. Press associations required a full week to distribute speeches to member papers. Once World War I had begun and President Wilson's clearinghouse for the release of all government information, the Committee on Public Information, was established, Tumulty discontinued his daily briefings and his publicity work.

In the Coolidge White House, for the first time, the responsibility for arrangements for the press traveling with the president was added to other staff duties. In the Hoover administration the first presidential press secretary, George Akerson, was appointed. With Congress providing funding for three secretarial positions instead of the traditional one, the president was able to have one senior aide devote his full attention to press matters. Akerson instituted twice-daily briefings and also provided space for photographers in the renovated White House West Wing. But he was not regarded as an especially able staff person and his successor, Theodore G. Joslin, was held in even lower esteem.[94] It remained for Stephen T. Early to shape the position during his years as the press secretary to President Franklin Roosevelt.

Organization of the Press Corps

After the congressional Standing Committee on the Press Galleries was formed, needs beyond the creation of rules of appropriate professional conduct for the press emerged. In 1908 news organizations banded together to form the National Press Club. Located in a building across from the Treasury Department, the Press Club provided a place where Washington institutions could quickly distribute press releases to a large number of news organizations. "The news from the Government departments and various publicity agencies are delivered at the club every day and are spread out on a long table. Every member of the club is at liberty to help himself to this literary free lunch," Louis Ludlow reported.[95] The National Press Club, however, did not coordinate or distribute the news. With many bureaus for out-of-town newspapers located in the building, the assembled journalists fell into a social as well as professional camaraderie.

Common interests brought together another group. On February 25, 1914, the White House Correspondents Association was established. Its first task was to address the difficulty of getting reporters to accept certain tacit understandings that arose from presidential press conferences. On July 17, 1913, when President Wilson went off the record, several reporters violated the unspoken agreement that governed the reporting of such remarks. Before this incident, the president had indicated when something was off the record and reporters had respected his wish. "The violation threatened for a time to end the conferences altogether," reported George Juergens. Instead, reporters allowed Joseph Tumulty, the president's secretary, to decide who would be allowed to attend conferences. "When eleven charter members came together several months later to found an organization through which reporters would handle the responsibility themselves, the press demonstrated a new level of professionalism," noted Juergens.[96] The organization was most important for legitimating the notion that there was an amorphous group that could be characterized as the White House press corps. (In reality, the organization has not served as much more than a social one, organizing an annual dinner attended by the president and those who cover the White House.)

THE MODERN WHITE HOUSE PUBLICITY APPARATUS

When Franklin D. Roosevelt (1933–1945) assumed the office of president, approximately thirty-five people were on the White House payroll.[97] By 1995 that figure had increased to 430—four hundred full-time employees plus thirty detailees from government agencies.[98] The enormous increase in staff is related directly to the development of the presidency and the White House as the policy center of the American political system. In the twentieth century, the public and the various elites in and around government came to expect the president to initiate policy action. With this responsibility came the need to communicate an administration's programs to the president's many constituencies.

Publicizing Administration Policy

The turbulent times of the early 1930s saw the president become the dominant force in the U.S. political system. Congress depended on the chief executive to introduce legislation to serve as its agenda, its members waited on the president's budget before formulating its appropriations and revenue measures, and the people depended on the president to give notice of the condition of the nation. When Franklin Roosevelt took office in 1933, financial disaster was looming. The public prayed for the president to find a way to create a stable economy and to communicate a sense of hope for the future to each citizen.

Those in government also expected two things from the president: action and communication. They wanted something done to restore the nation and expected the president to communicate with them about his plans. Roosevelt delivered on both points. In his administration, executive action and communication reached new levels. Indeed, the high level of public expectation of a president's policy performance that crystallized in the Roosevelt years served as a base on which to build for those who followed him. Through his policy initiatives and his explanations of his actions, President Roosevelt established the standards by which his successors would be judged.

On March 5, 1933, the nation tuned in to Roosevelt's inauguration speech to hear him articulate the path to stability. His specific solutions were laid out in only the most general of terms, but here was leadership. "In declaring there was nothing to fear but fear, Roosevelt had minted no new platitude; Hoover had said the same thing repeatedly for three years," wrote historian William E. Leuchtenburg. "Yet Roosevelt had nonetheless made his greatest single contribution to the politics of the 1930's: the instillation of hope and courage in the people."[99] Later that day, Roosevelt ordered a national bank holiday and called for Congress to come into session March 9. The strong inaugural speech, together with the promise to pay attention to the instability of the banks, lent confidence to a shaken populace. The president's banking message was read to Congress on March 9, and the accompanying bill was considered and passed by both houses within six and a half hours. It was signed by the chief executive an hour later. One week after his inauguration, the president reported to the nation through a new medium, radio. In what became the first of twenty-seven "fireside chats," the president called on Americans to return their money to the banks. What followed, then, was not the drain on the banks that many observers had expected. Instead, people heeded the president's request and deposited funds in the reopened banks. In seven days, noted Leuchtenburg, Roosevelt was able to "make an impression

The forceful FDR transformed presidential press relations. He held 998 Oval Office news conferences during his twelve years in office.

which Hoover had never been able to create—of a man who knew how to lead and had faith in the future." [100]

Through radio, Roosevelt was able to go directly to the public. The president had a voice that could and did soothe a nation, and he appreciated the lack of distortion radio could provide. "Radio for the first time put the president and his public in face-to-face contact," observed Elmer Cornwell in *Presidential Leadership of Public Opinion.* "Cutting, paraphrasing, quoting out of context, adverse editorial comment, and other alleged newspaper practices which annoyed Chief Executives were ruled out." [101]

Fireside chats built support for the president and his programs, and only occasionally for his legislative initiatives (in only four out of the twenty-seven chats did the president very clearly discuss legislation under consideration).[102] The first half dozen chats, wrote Cornwell, "found the President carefully reviewing . . . the steps that the New Deal had taken to deal with the Depression, the new legislation that had been passed, and the programs that had been set up." [103] Later presidents adopted his strategy of using the latest electronic technology to make direct contact with the people.

From 1933 to 1968 the federal government assumed an even more central role in addressing domestic problems. The period saw new government programs for consumer protection, medical care for the poor and elderly, rent subsidies for the poor, housing, food stamps, automobile safety, airport and hospital construction, environmental protection, aid to higher education, and equal employment. The initiative for most of these pieces of legislation came from the president, and only under his aegis was the legislation passed.

The nature of the times also led to a concentration of presidential power. Crisis was the prevailing condition. Sometimes, as during the Depression, it was an economic crisis; at other times a war gripped the nation. World War II, the Korean War, and the Vietnam War all took place during this thirty-five-year period. The cold war that existed between the United States and the Soviet Union precipitated the undercurrents that ran through most foreign and defense policies. Crises involve a president as do few other situations. It was only natural that the president became the focal point of the nation and that the news media became his path to its citizens. Presidents and news organizations alike become more prominent in crisis situations.

The demands for new policies were matched by expectations that presidents would effectively communicate their actions to their various publics. This required the existence of a communications operation that would provide in a timely way the information on those actions and the people to elaborate on their importance. To meet these expectations, presidents and their staffs created a publicity operation that could respond to the increased communications demands on the president. From 1933 to 1968 the duties of the presidential press secretary were further defined and

The Washington Post's *Bob Woodward, left, and Carl Bernstein, right, broke many of the Watergate stories that led to President Nixon's eventual resignation.*

developed and a Press Office was created to handle the distribution of information. Today, the White House press corps has come to rely on the press secretary's daily briefing and on the regular distribution of information through Press Office officials to reporters as they put together their stories on presidential activities.

Growing Presidential Vulnerability

Beginning in 1968 the presidency developed a vulnerability it did not have earlier. The president and his staff were required to perform as the public expected in an environment of declining political resources. With the decentralization of Congress in the 1970s and the greater authority it invested in subcommittee chairs, presidential policy action became a much more difficult process because so many more people had the power to shape legislation. Political parties began to have less meaning to the average voter than in Roosevelt's time, making it more difficult for presidents to appeal successfully for public support. Presidents themselves became particularly vulnerable. When Richard Nixon entered office in 1969, he replaced a president, Lyndon B. Johnson, who had lost public support through a discredited Vietnam policy. In 1974 Nixon became the first president to resign. He was threatened with impeachment because of the illegal activities undertaken by those who worked in his name and because of evidence that he had obstructed justice in his attempts to thwart a federal investigation. Two young *Washington Post* reporters, Carl Bernstein and Bob Woodward, were instrumental in exposing the Watergate abuses that led to Nixon's resignation.

In the years 1933–1968 the president represented the public trust. When a problem surfaced in the society, it was directed his way for solution. Since 1969, however, some presidents and many White House staff members have been charged—in print, on the air, and in the halls of Congress—with misusing that trust. Presidents or their staffs have been accused of, among other things, violating the law, using the office for private gain, having financial irregularities in previous business transactions and political campaigns, promoting failed policies, manipulating intelligence to justify war, and being "out of touch" with public sentiment and need. Perhaps reflecting this trend, only two presidents, Ronald Reagan and Bill Clinton, served two full terms in the period 1969–2001—and Clinton had to survive impeachment to do it. George W. Bush, reelected in 2004, will presumably become the third.

In the face of an increasingly restless and skeptical press, the White House has sought new avenues of publicity and additional communications structures to direct the selling of the president and the president's program. President Nixon overhauled the White House communications structure to take account of the new vulnerability. He created additional structures and redesigned the traditional ones. Because the Press Office operation was focused on only one segment of the nation's press—the Washington press corps—the Nixon administration, concluding correctly that there were other press elements on which to draw, created the Office of Communications as a complement to the existing Press Office. The Office of Communications handled three aspects of presidential publicity: the out-of-town press (newspapers with regional and local focus—not national papers such as the *New York Times, Washington Post,* or *Wall Street Journal*) and the specialty press (newspapers and magazines that target a specific audience, such as Hispanic readers), long-range planning, and coordination of executive branch public information officers. The parallel staff organizations of daily operations and future planning continued to define the White House communications operations into the twenty-first century.

Today, one of the central activities of the White House staff is publicizing the president and the president's program. The approximately one hundred staff members (out of the four hundred full-time White House employees)[104] of the frontline publicity units—including the Press Office and the Office of Communications—answer the questions of reporters, make arrangements for their travel, and prepare documents, such as transcripts of the press secretary's daily briefing. The Press Office also ensures that reporters are able to see and question the president regularly. In recent years, the Office of Communications has expanded the White House press functions to include the preparation of materials for the out-of-town and specialty press. In addition, its functions include managing the television appearances of

administration spokespersons, coordinating administration information, and supplying speeches for the president.

Others in the White House who are concerned with the communications element of the president's program and publicity matters are the chief of staff, who manages the president's time and the information going into the Oval Office; the people who schedule the president's appointments and make advance preparations for presidential appearances; and those responsible for managing the president's relations with Congress, interest groups, and political constituencies. Almost all of the White House senior staff are concerned in one way or another with presidential publicity.

A brief salary survey of the president's top staff indicates the importance of publicity in their work. In early 2002 nineteen White House staff members were at the top annual salary level of $140,000, including chief of staff Andrew H. Card Jr. Of those nineteen people, four (Counselor to the President Karen P. Hughes, Press Secretary L. Ari Fleischer, Senior Presidential Adviser Karl C. Rove, and Counselor to the Vice President and Assistant to the President Mary Matalin) had jobs directly related to communications.

Of the remaining fifteen, several had a significant communications element in their job descriptions. For example, National Security Adviser Condoleezza Rice and Director of Homeland Security Thomas J. Ridge briefed the press at times on important administration initiatives and crises. Other staff members, such as those who handled legislative relations, public liaison, and political affairs, used publicity as a major strategy in building support for the president's program.

Those at the next-highest salary level, $120,000, included Michael J. Gerson, director of speech writing. When Hughes returned to Texas in July 2002, communications director Dan Bartlett took over many of her duties and received a pay raise. As a deputy to Hughes, Bartlett, along with several other communications staffers, had been in the $110,000 bracket.[105] These figures suggest that presidential publicity is important in the operations of practically every warren within the White House. After all, the decisions that rise to the presidential level are those that cannot be solved elsewhere. Once a presidential judgment is made, acceptance most often has to be sold to the reluctant.

The Presidential Press Secretary

In the years from Franklin Roosevelt's administration through that of Lyndon Johnson, the White House press operation consisted of the press secretary and the Press Office. In the Nixon administration, however, the press operation was bifurcated. As noted, a long-range planning operation, the Office of Communications, was created to emphasize coordination among units of the White House and the executive departments. The Press Office continued to handle the daily publicity routines under the guidance of the press secretary. *(See Table 18-1.)*

Standard-Setters: Stephen T. Early and James C. Hagerty

"Steve and I thought that it would be best that straight news for use from this office should always be without direct quotations," declared Franklin Roosevelt at his first presidential press conference. "In other words, I do not want to be directly quoted, unless direct quotations are given out by Steve in writing." [106] With these words, Roosevelt defined an important role for his press secretary. Steve Early listened to the president, who relied on him to serve daily as his spokesperson throughout his administration. He would provide a presidential or administration viewpoint with skillful accuracy.

Early had known the future president since 1913 when the young Roosevelt came to Washington as assistant secretary of the navy. Early was then a reporter for the Associated Press covering the military beat. The two kept in touch over the next twenty years and earned each other's trust. Roosevelt viewed Early as a person who knew his craft. He had faith in Early's recommendation to establish a different press relationship outside of the prevailing rules. "This new deal in press relations was largely the handiwork of Roosevelt's hard-driving, hot-tempered press secretary, Steve Early," wrote Patrick Anderson in *The President's Men*.[107] "Before accepting the job, Early demanded Roosevelt's assurance that he would cooperate in a liberalized press policy." Mutual trust and respect served both men well.

President Eisenhower had similar confidence in his press secretary, James C. Hagerty. At a crucial juncture in his presidency, Eisenhower confirmed this stance. While on vacation in Denver in September 1955, President Eisenhower suffered a heart attack. Afterward, Eisenhower reportedly told his doctor: "Tell Jim to take over." Once Hagerty arrived in Denver, he did in fact take over. "Jim represented the sole link between the presidential sick room and the anxious public," noted Cornwell. "As such he held the center of news interest to the unheard of extent of having *his* press conferences reproduced verbatim in the *New York Times*." [108] Because President Eisenhower had three illnesses—the heart attack, ileitis (1956), and a minor stroke (1957)—Hagerty was the president's only link with the public for several months at a time. Eisenhower did not have a press conference for five months after his heart attack and two months after his ileitis operation. "In a sense, then," observed Cornwell, "the mythical 'White House spokesman' of the Coolidge era had at last been clothed with flesh and respectability." [109] Even in good health, Eisenhower kept his

TABLE 18-1   Presidential Press Secretaries, 1929–

Press secretary	President	Years	Background[a]
George Akerson	Hoover	1929–1931	Reporter
Theodore G. Joslin	Hoover	1931–1933	AP reporter
Stephen T. Early	F. Roosevelt	1933–1945	AP, UPI reporter
Charles Ross	Truman	1945–1950	Reporter
Joseph H. Short	Truman	1950–1952	Reporter
Roger Tubby	Truman	1952–1953	Journalist
James C. Hagerty	Eisenhower	1953–1961	Reporter
Pierre E. Salinger	Kennedy	1961–1963	Investigative writer
	L. Johnson	1963–1964	
George Reedy	L. Johnson	1964–1965	UPI reporter
Bill Moyers	L. Johnson	1965–1967	Associate director, Peace Corps
George Christian	L. Johnson	1967–1969	Reporter
Ronald L. Ziegler	Nixon	1969–1974	Advertising
Jerald F. terHorst	Ford	1974	Bureau chief, newspaper
Ron H. Nessen	Ford	1974–1977	Journalist
Jody L. Powell	Carter	1977–1981	Advertising
James S. Brady[b]	Reagan	1981–1989	Congressional press aide
Larry Speakes	Reagan	1981–1987	Reporter
Marlin Fitzwater	Reagan	1987–1989	Government information aide
	G. H. W. Bush	1989–1993	
Dee Dee Myers	Clinton	1993–1994	Campaign aide
Michael McCurry	Clinton	1995–1998	Congressional press aide
Joe Lockhart	Clinton	1998–2000	Television reporter
L. Ari Fleischer	G. W. Bush	2001–2003	Congressional press aide
Scott McClellan	G. W. Bush	2003–2006	Campaign press aide
Tony Snow	G. W. Bush	2006–	Speechwriter, Fox News anchor

NOTES: a. Early training.   b. Although Brady was severely wounded in the 1981 assassination attempt, his title remained press secretary until 1989. Speakes's title was assistant to the president and principal deputy press secretary; Fitzwater's title was assistant to the president for press relations. Fitzwater's title became White House press secretary in the George H. W. Bush administration.

press secretary well informed. According to Hagerty, "For eight years I knew everything he did, and if I wasn't in his office when he made a decision, even including the secretary of state, he'd tell John Foster Dulles, 'stop in at Jim's office as you go out and tell him what we decided.' " [110] Eisenhower depended on the press secretary in a way that the presidents before and after him have not.

Previous contact with the press appears to be a significant determinant of presidential inclinations. "[Theodore] Roosevelt, Truman, Kennedy, and Johnson had all dealt with the press for decades before entering the White House," Patrick Anderson wrote, and

> all rightly felt that they could more skillfully persuade, inform, or deceive the press, as the case demanded, than their Press Secretaries. Eisenhower was different. He disliked the cajolery, the deception, the self-promotion of press relations, and he was happy to delegate it all to Hagerty, as he delegated political affairs to [Chief of Staff Sherman] Adams.[111]

The president's inclinations have served as a particularly important element in the nature of the duties of the press secretary. In the case of Pierre Salinger (1961–1963, John

Kennedy; 1963–1964, Lyndon Johnson), the inclinations of his presidents were to conduct their own dealings with reporters and not report contacts to Salinger.

Early and Hagerty were model press secretaries because each was able to serve his president's interests effectively. Yet each could at the same time convey to reporters that they too were being taken care of and that the press secretary was their best source of information. One White House reporter who worked under both men compared the strengths of each:

> Early could give you a long think-piece on the Administration's attitude toward the gold standard. Hagerty knows just what makes a good still picture, the exact amount of lighting needed for television, and exactly when to break up a press conference in order to make deadlines for home editions on the East Coast.[112]

Such a scene could not be repeated today.

Press Secretary Marlin Fitzwater described a different relationship with the White House press corps during his ten years on the job in the administrations of Ronald Reagan and George H. W. Bush. "The White House press corps gathers every morning like a pride of lions. It snarls and growls, sleeps and creeps, and occasionally loves, but it is always hungry," Fitzwater observed.[113] The relationship between the White House and the press plays itself out in the daily briefing. In that spotlight,

> each reporter has a hold on you, an invisible string tied to your belt buckle that pulls and tugs with each question, as if you were tied to the ground near anthills, and they torture you with repetitive questions. When they see that your mouth is dry, and you have squandered every ounce of knowledge, and you have probably made at least one embarrassing slip that will elicit ridicule from White House colleagues and a frown from the president, then Helen [Thomas] twists until she can see over her shoulder, and decides if the lions have any fight left.[114]

The senior White House correspondent (a position United Press International reporter Helen Thomas held in the 1980s through the early 2000s, when she left UPI and joined Hearst News Service) calls an end to the briefing, not the press secretary. The tenor of the briefing provides an indicator of the mutual mistrust evident in public White House settings.

The atmosphere of acrimony is fueled by the formal setting that now dominates the dissemination of official White House information. When Hagerty was Eisenhower's press secretary, reporters were stationed right across the hall from his room on the first floor of the West Wing. Checking in with the press secretary was quite easy given the short distance between their quarters. Douglass Cater described the scene:

> A special room has been set aside for the press, its typewriters, its telephones, its poker table. There are twenty to thirty White House . . . 'regulars'—reporters whose sole assignment is to cover this tiny beat. . . . Just across the entrance hall, the Press Secretary has offices, connected by private corridor to the President's own office. He is the hourly spokesman of the President, the constant stand-in for the public image of the Presidency. Two and three times daily he meets with the regulars and any other reporters who may wander in.[115]

Today the informality is gone, the poker table an artifact. The press secretary steps behind a podium in the briefing room at an announced time—a time not always observed— to respond to the queries of those who are seated in the forty-eight assigned seats. A formal setting, it emphasizes the differences between those on either side of the dais. In these sessions, routine information coexists with requests for a response to a president's policy critics. If a secretary is weak in providing information, the secretary's influence both inside and outside the White House is strongly reduced.

Functions of the Press Secretary

From administration to administration, there is continuity in the tasks performed by the press secretary. No matter who is serving in the post, the demands made by the president, the White House staff, and the press corps all call for the individual to serve as an accurate and sensitive conduit of information, to bring together and then organize a press staff, to advise the president on communications policy and then be responsible for its implementation, and, finally, to serve as an agent responsible for meeting the interests of the press corps, the White House staff, and the president.[116] From a staff point of view, the press secretary manages Press Office personnel and whatever units are subsumed in this domain. The secretary also is responsible for implementing and disseminating communications policy for the administration. As agent, the press secretary must carefully interweave representation of the interests of the president, the press, and the White House staff. Although the secretary is chosen by and is solely responsible to the president, the appointee must be able to articulate skillfully the interests of all three and help each to understand the others' points of view.

Conduit of Presidential Information. The conduit function includes the transmittal of information from the White House to the president's various publics. In this, the daily briefing is key. At the daily briefing reporters can expect to uncover a president's thinking on specific issues of interest to them. Often an hour or longer when there is a hot issue, briefings are held once a day and cover a broad range of topics. Good press secretaries must be able to field questions on diverse topics because the fast-moving queries cover a broad spectrum of concerns. Often the secretary must deal with an issue for which there are no instructions or guidelines. In fact, the value of a press secretary to an administration lies in his or her ability "to go before reporters and articulate the administration's position without being instructed on what to say, as well as . . . to provide the right emphasis on information the White House wishes reporters to present to their audiences." [117]

In something of a juggling act, a press secretary must be articulate in accurately representing the president's positions and at the same time provide informed answers to correspondents' queries. Without this dual skill, the secretary's influence will be minimal and reporters will look elsewhere for answers. Such was the case with the Clinton administration's first press secretary, Dee Dee Myers. Never in the information loop, Myers was not even given the office occupied by her predecessors. Reporters liked her but saw her as amiable rather than well informed. "She is often left out of what is going on," said one reporter. "She came out and said she didn't know anything about a staff shakeup and five minutes later the President in the Oval Office said they had been discussing it for five weeks." [118] Myers was not the first press secretary to be perceived as uninformed. Others who acknowledged they felt left out of the information loop or about whom reporters expressed lack of confidence were Ronald L. Ziegler (1969–1974, Richard Nixon), Jerald F. terHorst (1974, Gerald R. Ford), Ron H. Nessen (1974–1977, Ford), and Larry Speakes (1981–1987, Ronald Reagan).

At the end of 1994 Myers left the Clinton administration and was replaced by Michael McCurry, who moved to the White House from his perch behind the podium at the State Department. McCurry, trained through answering tough questions but in a less-charged atmosphere, made a smooth and effective transition to the White House podium. Because many reporters already were well acquainted with McCurry from his years as a press secretary on Capitol Hill, he came to the White House with the benefit of recognition and respect. And in a symbolic victory, he was given the press secretary's office, a trophy denied to Myers.

Becoming the full-fledged press secretary proved to be small compensation for what befell McCurry three years later. In January 1998, Internet reporter Matt Drudge broke the sensational news of President Clinton's affair with a White House intern, Monica Lewinsky, which began in 1995 when she was twenty-one years old and lasted until 1997. Newspapers and other media flashed the news around the world. From then on McCurry faced a daily barrage of questions about the allegations, most of which he turned aside. McCurry deliberately took himself "out of the loop" so that he could truthfully plead ignorance of the affair, which Clinton at first denied. McCurry was never subpoenaed. He resigned in July 1998, before Clinton was impeached. McCurry's deputy, Joe Lockhart, became the new press secretary and as such confronted excruciating questions through the remainder of Clinton's tenure.[119] *(See box, A Press Secretary's Nightmare, p. 962, and "Clinton Impeachment," p. 492, Chapter 8.)*

Press relations were hardly better for Scott McClellan, who served as press secretary to President George W. Bush in the early portion of his second term, when questions about the efficacy of the president's Iraq war policy were becoming increasingly difficult to address. McClellan's approach to questions he could not easily answer was to avoid answering them entirely, while giving the appearance of saying something meaningful. In the process, he drew heat from frustrated reporters while distancing the president from their inquiries. In this 2005 exchange with Terry Moran of ABC News regarding a comment by Vice President Richard B. Cheney that the Iraqi insurgency was in its "last throes," McClellan insisted that he had answered the reporter's ques-

George W. Bush shakes hands with outgoing White House press secretary Scott McClellan, right, after announcing the appointment of Tony Snow, left, as his new press secretary on April 26, 2006.

A PRESS SECRETARY'S NIGHTMARE

In January 1998 Bill Clinton's press secretary Michael McCurry and deputy press secretary Joe Lockhart found themselves in the most difficult situation White House officials could imagine: trying to speak for a popular president who allegedly had sexual encounters with a young woman within steps of the sacrosanct Oval Office. On the morning of January 21, 1998, when the story of the young intern, Monica Lewinsky, and President Clinton exploded on the front page of the *Washington Post,* shock waves rippled around the world. Even most members of the Washington press corps were caught unawares.

Tales of illicit White House liaisons were nothing new: Warren G. Harding, Franklin D. Roosevelt, John F. Kennedy, to name a few, had similar rumors floating around the press corps. But these whispers never appeared in print until after the participants were dead. Such stories were not considered newsworthy. In his book on the Clinton-Lewinsky scandal, former CBS-TV journalist Marvin Kalb recalled an incident one night at New York's Carlyle Hotel, where President Kennedy was staying. Despite the efforts of Secret Service men to block his view, Kalb caught a glimpse of a "woman with stunningly attractive legs" entering a private elevator. Kalb never got the woman's name and "never for one moment did I consider pursuing and reporting what I had seen and experienced that evening. . . . In those days, the possibility of a presidential affair, while titillating, was not considered 'news'; by the mainstream press." [1]

That Kennedy did have affairs was obliquely confirmed by his press secretary, Pierre Salinger, in his 1995 memoir.[2] He wrote, "While in the White House, on several occasions, President Kennedy encouraged me to take a lover, an obvious sign he also had some himself." Now happily married, Salinger confessed that he formerly did have "scores" of mistresses. But Salinger never had to endure daily interrogation about Kennedy's sex life, or his own. "Back in 1960, when Kennedy ran for office," he said, "the media were not interested in his private life. But now a candidate's life is of paramount interest to the media." [3]

As McCurry and Lockhart could attest, this interest has grown tenfold for a president's private life. Both were on duty that fateful morning when the Lewinsky story broke. Lockhart recalled later that usually "people used to fight to get into" meetings to brief the president for interviews. But that morning "there was a very small group of people who showed up. There was no big fuss at the door." People were wary of attending. Clinton himself, he said, was "a little more serious. He was not quite as sure-footed as he normally was when there was some sensational story." [4]

For the next nine months McCurry bore the brunt of the daily inquisition. His strategy, honed from months of avoiding a subpoena in the Paula Jones litigation, was to stay away from fact-gathering. "His job was to repeat whatever facts or assertions the lawyers had approved for public consumption," said *Washington Post* media columnist Howard Kurtz.[5] At his final briefing on October 1, 1998, McCurry said he had always tried not to lie to or mislead reporters. But he admit-

ted that "the president misled me, too, so I came here and misled you on occasion. And that was grievously wrong of him, but he has acknowledged that." As he left, the reporters applauded, but one of them wrote that at times McCurry had been "lying by omission rather than commission." [6]

After taking over for McCurry in October 1998, Lockhart was featured in a PBS documentary "The Press Secretary." It showed for three days in September 2000 when the Press Office was preparing for Clinton's final news conference, a joint conference with India's prime minister. During the filmed interview, Lockhart recalled that his first day facing the press as secretary was like "an out-of-body experience." It happened to be the first day that the House began to debate impeaching Clinton for perjury and obstruction of justice. "During that entire terrible period," Lockhart said, "it was nonstop coverage, Monica and the president twenty-four hours a day." Lockhart described it in another way in an October 2000 interview. Although most people in the White House were doing their jobs despite the scandal, he said, "nobody was paying attention. I mean, [chief economic adviser] Gene Sperling could have stood on the White House roof taking his clothes off—people still wouldn't have trained a camera up there unless he yelled something about Monica." [7]

In the end, Lockhart's preparations for Clinton's final news conference as president were for naught because of the Indian prime minister's minor illness; the joint session was downgraded to a brief Oval Office session for pool reporters. The few questions allowed dealt with neither Monica nor India's problems.

Meanwhile, Clinton's approval ratings remained high, and in the 1998 midterm elections the president's party gained five House seats—not enough to return control to the Democrats but impressive still. No president since Franklin Roosevelt in 1934 had gained even one House seat at midterm. When the Senate in February 1999 fell short of the two-thirds vote needed to remove Clinton from office, the impeachment ordeal was over.

In a bit of irony, the PBS documentary closed with footage showing President Kennedy with the visiting Indian prime minister at that time, Jawaharlal Nehru. The narrator noted it was shot in black-and-white film with wind-up cameras— a graphic illustration of how television's voracious appetite, which now consumes much of the West Wing's time and energies, had changed in four decades.

1. Marvin Kalb, *One Scandalous Story: Clinton, Lewinsky and Thirteen Days that Tarnished American Journalism* (New York: Free Press), 2001, 5–6.
2. Pierre Salinger, *P.S.: A Memoir* (New York: St. Martin's Press, 1995), x.
3. Ibid., ix.
4. Joe Lockhart, interview by Chris Bury, "The Clinton Years," *Nightline,* ABC News, October 2000.
5. Howard Kurtz, *Spin Cycle: Inside the Clinton Propaganda Machine* (New York: Free Press), 1998, xiv.
6. Howard Kurtz, "The First Flack's Last Stand," *Washington Post,* October 2, 1998, D1.
7. Lockhart, interview by Chris Bury, "The Clinton Years."

tion while Moran, through repetition of his question, suggested McClellan was being nonresponsive:

Q: Scott, is the insurgency in Iraq in its "last throes"?

McCLELLAN: Terry, you have a desperate group of terrorists in Iraq that are doing everything they can to try to

derail the transition to democracy. The Iraqi people have made it clear that they want a free and democratic and peaceful future. And that's why we're doing everything we can, along with other countries, to support the Iraqi people as they move forward. . . .

Q: But the insurgency is in its last throes?

McCLELLAN: The Vice President talked about that the other day—you have a desperate group of terrorists who recognize how high the stakes are in Iraq. A free Iraq will be a significant blow to their ambitions.

Q: But they're killing more Americans, they're killing more Iraqis. That's the last throes?

McCLELLAN: Innocent—I say innocent civilians. And it doesn't take a lot of people to cause mass damage when you're willing to strap a bomb onto yourself, get in a car and go and attack innocent civilians. That's the kind of people that we're dealing with. That's what I say when we're talking about a determined enemy.

Q: Right. What is the evidence that the insurgency is in its last throes?

McCLELLAN: I think I just explained to you the desperation of terrorists and their tactics.

Q: What's the evidence on the ground that it's being extinguished?

McCLELLAN: Terry, we're making great progress to defeat the terrorist and regime elements. You're seeing Iraqis now playing more of a role in addressing the security threats that they face. They're working side by side with our coalition forces. They're working on their own. There are a lot of special forces in Iraq that are taking the battle to the enemy in Iraq. And so this is a period when they are in a desperate mode.

Q: Well, I'm just wondering what the metric is for measuring the defeat of the insurgency.

McCLELLAN: Well, you can go back and look at the Vice President's remarks. I think he talked about it.

Q: Yes. Is there any idea how long a 'last throe' lasts for?

McCLELLAN: Go ahead, Steve.[120]

Press relations did not improve for Tony Snow, who moved from FOX News to the press secretary's podium in 2006, just before a stinging defeat for President Bush's Republican Party in that year's congressional elections. Democrats assumed control of the House and Senate, promising close oversight of the White House in what quickly became a confrontational political environment. With the administration already on the defensive because of public dissatisfaction with the course of the Iraq War, Snow had to navigate the press during the president's low public approval ratings. His approach reflected the combative nature of the rough-and-tumble FOX network, which was short on sympathy for administration opponents. As press secretary, Snow could exhibit impatience with reporters whose coverage might have been considered less than friendly to the White House.

Earlier in the post–Early and Hagerty period, Jimmy Carter's press secretary, Jody L. Powell, was the closest to Early and Hagerty in terms of his ability to speak for his president. "There was only one source [of information] when

Jimmy Carter's press secretary, Jody Powell, left, was highly regarded by the press for his ability to speak for the president. A fellow Georgian, Powell had been a confidant, aide, and adviser to Carter for about ten years before his White House appointment.

Carter was here," said Sam Donaldson, who served as the ABC White House correspondent in those years. "As long as you talked with Jody, you knew you weren't going to get beaten and if he didn't know, he would find out."[121] Powell had worked and traveled with Carter not only during his gubernatorial years but also through the long presidential campaign. He knew the president well and had honed the ability to speak for him even on individual issues they had not discussed. In relating the importance of Powell's access to Carter, Larry Speakes, principal deputy press secretary to Ronald Reagan, indicated that he was hurt by Reagan's reluctance to keep him fully informed. "In fairness to [Reagan], ninety percent of the politicians deal with press secretaries in the same fashion," Speakes related. "Two exceptions were Jimmy Carter, who gave extraordinary access to Jody Powell, and Dwight Eisenhower, who did the same with Jim Hagerty. It's no accident that Hagerty and Powell were two of the best press secretaries of all time."[122] Solid information, given in a timely manner, glosses over many imperfections. In Powell's case, that meant overlooking the administrative clutter that resulted from the press secretary's penchant for trying to control too many organizational units in the White House. Although no press secretaries in the post–Hagerty period have been able to speak for their presidents so effectively as Powell, two press secretaries whom reporters found valuable for the reliability of their information and their understanding of what reporters needed were George Christian (1967–1969, Lyndon Johnson) and Marlin Fitzwater (1987–1989, Ronald Reagan; 1989–1993, George H. W. Bush).[123]

The press secretary's conduit role also includes informal contacts with correspondents and news organizations. The press secretary must steer individual reporters toward an accurate story or away from an incorrect one. A press secretary who is wrong suffers publicly for it. Larry Speakes had such an experience as the principal spokesperson for President Reagan. In late October 1983, Bill Plante, CBS White House correspondent, went to Speakes for verification of a story. Plante said he had information that the United States was amassing forces for an invasion of the island nation of Grenada. Speakes went to Adm. John Poindexter, deputy director of the National Security Council, to check out Plante's story and was told in no uncertain terms that there was nothing to the allegation. Speakes repeated Poindexter's words and deflected what would have been a scoop for Plante.[124] The subsequent invasion of Grenada by U.S. marines on October 25, 1983, raised serious questions about Speakes's capacity to speak knowledgeably about White House activities.

Authenticity of information is sacrosanct. Use of one's own thoughts or words instead of those of the president is risky for any press secretary. In his book *Speaking Out: The Reagan Presidency from Inside the White House,* Speakes confessed to manufacturing presidential quotations:

> I polished the quotes and told the press that while the two leaders stood together . . . the President said to [Soviet leader Mikhail] Gorbachev, "There is much that divides us, but I believe the world breathes easier because we are talking here together." CBS had me on the news Wednesday evening . . . and Chris Wallace said, "The talks were frank. The President's best statement came off-camera, aides quoting him as saying, 'The world breathes easier because we are talking together.' "[125]

Speakes was not the only one to venture into such muddy waters. Among correspondents covering the administration of Lyndon Johnson, press secretary Bill Moyers had a similar reputation: "I never fully trusted Bill Moyers," said one doubter; "he was interested in promoting himself and his programs. He ingratiated himself with the press corps. He was serving two masters and I distrust anyone who tries that."[126] Moyers, a divinity school graduate who became a respected television journalist after Johnson left office, appreciated policy and enjoyed talking about the merits of particular courses of action. Press secretaries, however, are judged according to their fidelity in representing the president, not their own abilities to explain the value of alternative courses of action.

Overstepping that boundary can be dangerous, as George W. Bush press secretary Ari Fleischer discovered in

March 2002. The usually cautious Fleischer was forced to issue a retraction after he, in effect, blamed the 2000 peacemaking efforts of former president Clinton for renewed violence in the Middle East. Without naming Clinton, Fleischer had told reporters, "You could make the case that in an attempt to shoot the moon and get nothing, more violence resulted; that as a result of an attempt to push the parties beyond where they were willing to go, that it led to expectations that were raised to such a high level that it turned to violence." Shortly thereafter, Fleischer read a statement that declared that what he had said "is not the position of the administration. . . . No United States president, including President Clinton, is to blame for violence in the Middle East. The only people to blame for violence are the terrorists who engage in it. I regret any implication to the contrary." [127]

Even in embarrassing situations, a press secretary ensures that press reports reach the president and the president's staff. Transcripts of the briefings are an extremely valuable source of press intelligence, which Cheney learned before he became vice president. As chief of staff in the Ford administration, Cheney regularly read the transcripts to get "a feel for what is on the minds of the press." [128] The repetition of a question in one briefing can serve as an alert to staff members that the matter merits attention.

Secretary as Staff Chief. When Steve Early was press secretary, his staff consisted of one assistant, William Hassett, and secretarial help. James Hagerty's office operation was not much larger. He had two aides, Murray Snyder and Anne Wheaton, and secretarial help. The White House staff then was small by today's standards. In both cases, the secretary could talk regularly in an informal way with the president and with other staff members, eliminating the need for elaborate coordination mechanisms. In fact, both men, but especially Early, also often dealt with cabinet officers and members of Congress. Early's diary noted, "Throughout the day was kept busy on the telephones, as I am the only secretary here to talk with governors, Senators, and Cabinet officers, etc." [129] Hagerty had a more difficult time keeping up with the larger White House staff. He also was very particular that both White House staff and reporters coordinate any statements through him so that one clear voice would emerge. Moreover, the juggling act included bringing together the departmental information officers and keeping in touch with both White House staff members and even cabinet officers. *Time* noted the effectiveness of Hagerty's efforts to keep "the news systems of all the departments of Federal Government under his sure thumb." He met regularly with the press officers for the departments, scanned departmental news bulletins before they were released, and advised cabinet members who may have gotten themselves out on a limb and needed help.[130]

Other press secretaries have tried to maintain such control but failed. The daily routines exact too many demands to manage effectively departmental press officers who are bent on avoiding any curbs. Since the Nixon administration, the responsibility for coordinating public information officers has shifted to the purview of the communications adviser. In the Carter administration, Jody Powell tried to establish control, but both he and his deputy, Walter Wurfel, were snowed under just trying to attend to the daily routines.

To manage the Press Office staff today, a press secretary must fit in a daily series of meetings, unlike the single gathering Early faced. In the morning staffers go over issues raised in the day's newspapers and television and radio programs, which are the first clues to questions likely to come up at reporters' briefings. At the senior staff meeting later in the morning, the press secretary looks for guidance on the

ONE PICTURE IS WORTH A . . .

The White House Photo Office is entrusted with the mission of making a historical record of the presidency. And it is no small task. In his 1988 book *The Ring of Power: The White House Staff and Its Expanding Role in Government,* Bradley Patterson recounted the enormity of the photo enterprise: "Every year, the photographer and his five assistants put 7,000 rolls of film into their cameras; some 150,000 frames are snapped, 70 percent of them producing pictures of archival quality." [1] During the Reagan years, six photographers worked in the White House photo shop, aided by four assistants; the technical processing staff of military personnel numbered forty.

Recording a president's time in office involves photographs of many types of occasions, official and personal. "Personal meetings, classified meetings, just personal things that happen," observed George H. W. Bush photographer David Valdez about the subjects of his photographs, which included the president's grandchildren and dogs. [2] All presidential occasions—official and personal—are appropriate subjects for official photographs. The presence of the president is what makes a scene worth recording.

Presidential photographs are distributed to news organizations and also displayed on White House walls and in the homes of the president's supporters around the country. At the end of the Reagan administration, Reaganites queued up from the Roosevelt Room in the West Wing to the far corners of the White House lobby to have their pictures taken with the president who appointed them. At the annual White House reception for correspondents, journalists and their spouses lined up to have their pictures taken with the president they covered. To their satisfaction, within days they received from the White House the photographs of them signed by the president.

The photographs distributed to news organizations usually are ones that will complement a theme the White House is then emphasizing in presidential speeches and appearances, in the press secretary's briefing, in the public remarks of senior White House staff members appearing on television news programs, and in officially released White House statements. In late 1995, for example, President Bill Clinton was spending much of his time debating the shape of the federal budget with Republican congressional leaders. In one such session, the president, harking back to his days as a professor at the University of Arkansas Law School, stood pointer in hand next to a board brought into the Oval Office to allow the president to lecture his "students"—Senate Majority Leader Robert J. "Bob" Dole, Speaker of the House Newt Gingrich, and House Majority Leader Richard B. Armey, among others—who were seated comfortably around him. [3] When the picture later appeared in *Time,* the three congressional leaders objected to being used as presidential props.

What the Clinton communications team was trying to do in this instance differed little from the practices of most earlier administrations, which used presi-

dential photographs to advance the personal and policy interests of the president. With the capacity to determine what pictures should be released and when, the White House can use its photographs to create positive impressions of the president.

Beginning with the administration of Franklin D. Roosevelt, the job of recording the president's activities was assigned to photographers employed by the National Park Service. The appointment of an official presidential photographer began with the administration of Lyndon B. Johnson, who appointed Yoichi R. Okamoto to the position. Although Okamoto was assigned to the Press Office, his salary was paid by the Defense Department and his film was processed by the White House Communications Agency, a division of the Army Signal Corps. Once Okamoto came onto the White House staff and the Photo Office was finally formed, the unit was maintained in succeeding administrations even though some, such as the Jimmy Carter administration, did not designate an official photographer.

Clinton was the second president to name a member of a minority group as official photographer. (Johnson, who appointed Okamoto, an Asian, was the first.) In 1999 Clinton promoted an African American woman, Sharon Farmer, to be director of White House photography, succeeding Robert McNeely. As a member of McNeely's staff in 1993, Farmer photographed the historic handshake between Israeli prime minister Yitzhak Rabin and Palestine Liberation Organization chairman Yasser Arafat on the White House lawn. "Every day I pinch myself to see if I'm dreaming that I have this job here, in this time, in this world," Farmer told an interviewer. [4]

President George W. Bush appointed Associated Press photographer Eric Draper as his official photographer. Another photographer, Paul Morse, quit the *Los Angeles Times* and joined Draper's staff after his top editors cited "conflict of interest" because he helped Draper to take an official portrait of Bush. Lower-echelon editors had given Morse permission to do the job, but higher-ups balked when he sought further permission to portray Vice President Richard B. Cheney. [5]

Some official presidential photographers have had a high profile, such as David Hume Kennerly, the Pulitzer Prize–winning photographer from *Time* who held that post in the Ford administration. Michael Evans in the first Reagan term also was well known.

1. Bradley Patterson, *The Ring of Power: The White House Staff and Its Expanding Role in Government* (New York: Basic Books, 1988).
2. David Valdez, interview by Martha Joynt Kumar, Washington, D.C., January 12, 1993.
3. Nancy Gibbs, "The Inner Game," *Time,* January 15, 1996, 12–14.
4. "Inside the White House," fall 1999, *(clinton 3.nara.gov/WH/kids/inside/html/ fall 99/html/farmer.html).*
5. Dorothy Ho, "People on the Move," *Photo District News,* February 28, 2001, 2.

issues that have emerged and have been presented to the assembled group. The deputies will have spent the morning checking with the public information officers in the departments, particularly State and Defense, and, when relevant, domestic departments and agencies will be asked to comment on pertinent material arising at the senior staff meeting. When not in meetings, the press secretary and deputy secretaries may pick up more signals from White House reporters who visit their offices or who are in the press room. Clinton press secretary Michael McCurry got early warning of press corps interests at the 9:15 morning meeting with reporters in his office—known as the "gaggle." There, reporters asked questions arising from overnight stories and reviewed information on the day's schedule.

The Press Office has jurisdiction over the White House photographers and the staffers who manage the advance operation, news summary, and radio operation. *(See box, One Picture Is Worth a . . . , p. 965.)* Begun in the Nixon administration, the news summary operation brings together in one place articles from regional and local papers. President Nixon analyzed the summary to provide an agenda for media action, and, according to Nixon senior aide John Ehrlichman, Nixon's marginal notes contained the responses he wanted his staff to make to news items found in the document. Other administrations have used summaries to emphasize coverage of the administration at state and local levels. As a similar resource, the Carter administration added a "radio actuality" line to its database, and it, too, has been maintained by successors. Audio clips of presidential speeches and statements are available daily for taping by local radio stations.

The Office of Communications

The Office of Communications was created shortly after President Nixon took office in 1969, primarily to handle relations with the out-of-town and specialty press. The office serves multiple functions, which vary from administration to administration. As a White House organization, its parts are more distinct than the whole. Each administration determines its publicity functions, and many place them differently on organizational charts. During the Carter administration, for example, there was a distinct Office of Communications for only one year. More specifically, Carter press secretary Jody Powell kept speech writing under his wing for most of the administration, while in the Ford, Reagan, Clinton, and George W. Bush administrations it was largely located in the Office of Communications.

Such administrative flexibility does not seem to affect continuity. Although each unit appears in many different locations on the organizational chart, physically the units continue to occupy the same offices as their predecessors. The news summary staff, for example, remains housed in a warren on the top floor of the Eisenhower Executive Office Building, formerly the Old Executive Office Building, where President Eisenhower held the first televised news conference, in 1955. Speechwriters are well established on the first floor across from the media affairs people.

Although the Office of Communications has been controlled by the press secretary at times, the communications adviser, a senior-level official, is usually in charge. *(See Table 18-2, right.)*

Media Affairs Unit

The media affairs unit lies at the heart of the Office of Communications. It maintains a television studio in the Eisenhower Executive Office Building. The unit arranges radio and television interviews with administration figures—both on and off the premises. Most especially, the office deals with the news organizations that exist outside of Washington and have no local bureau—a group that includes television stations and the print press at the regional and local levels, as well as newspapers that target identified ethnic, racial, or gender groups. When there is a presidential statement or appearance of interest to a specific group, the White House sends information to the relevant news organizations. In addition, the office deals with a satellite technology base of organizations. Conus Communications, for example, is a satellite cooperative that provides news spots to independent television stations around the country. If a station asks for an interview with a home state official who is visiting the president that day, the White House correspondent for Conus provides the footage. To set up such an event, the correspondent would have to go through the designated television specialist in the media affairs office.

Recent presidents have been particularly receptive to appearances on radio and television news programs and talk shows. In his first year, President Clinton had interviews with 161 correspondents from local television stations. Media affairs arranged these sessions because most occurred while the president was visiting the cities where the stations were located. Although the staff had visions of regularly connecting the president with local television anchors around the country, the budget for such activities proved meager. "The technique is an inefficient way of communicating because there are six hundred TV stations in the country, and the White House has no budget for satellite work and has to beg and borrow the money from various contingency funds or from federal agencies," explained Tom Rosenstiel, media critic for the *Los Angeles Times*.[131]

Satellites may be outside of budget range, but computers can be used to connect the White House to interested individuals and to news organizations. For the White House, contacting the local media once meant sending statements and speeches by surface mail. Today, such contacts are made by electronic mail via the Internet. Anyone with a computer and a modem can go to the White House Web site (www.whitehouse.gov) and download the press secretary's briefing, selected presidential speeches, and interviews.

Public Affairs Unit

Under several recent administrations, the public affairs office coordinated administration spokespersons, including department publicity officers and administration officials appearing in behalf of the president and his programs. It also assembled information for administration spokespersons making public appearances, particularly the latest facts and figures proving administration successes. In the Reagan administration, it was a significant support unit, which included among its functions arranging television appearances. The Clinton administration closed the office and the Bush administration left it that way.

Advance Unit

The advance unit, in carrying out its task of making arrangements for correspondents traveling with the president on trips outside of Washington, arranges hotels and locations where reporters can write and file their stories, and it facilitates communications links. This unit works closely with scheduling operations, which makes travel arrangements for the president and the White House staff. Reporters and camera crews do not travel at government expense, however. Their employers pay their airplane, hotel, and other expenses.

How the president is covered is a major concern in setting up the locations and choosing the times for presidential appearances. Michael Deaver, Reagan's trusted aide who designed and scripted the president's first-term appearances, was especially good at matching location and message. "The trip of the Demilitarized Zone on the border between North and South Korea was a symbolic high point of the Reagan years," said Deaver. "Standing there, staring across that buffer zone, drawing the contrast between freedom and oppression, this was what Ronald Reagan did best." [132] When President George W. Bush spoke about homeland security at Mt. Rushmore on August 15, 2002, his aides choreographed his presentation to make Bush the visual equal of his four granite predecessors, positioning him so that his profile was in line with the presidents on the mountain.

TABLE 18-2 **Directors of the White House Office of Communications, 1969–**

President	Director	Term
Richard Nixon	Herbert G. Klein	January 1969–June 1973
	Ken W. Clawson	January 1974–August 1974
Gerald R. Ford	Paul Miltich and James Holland[a]	August 1974–November 1974
	Gerald L. Warren[a]	November 1974–June 1975
	Margita White[a]	June 1975–June 1976
	David R. Gergen	July 1976–January 1977
Jimmy Carter	None[b]	January 1977–June 1978
	Gerald Rafshoon	July 1978–August 1979
	None[b]	September 1979–January 1981
Ronald Reagan	Frank A. Ursomarso	February 1981–June 1981
	David R. Gergen	June 1981–January 1984
	Michael A. McManus Jr. (acting director)	January 1984–January 1985
	Patrick Buchanan	February 1985–February 1987
	John O. Koehler	February 1987–March 1987
	Thomas C. Griscom	April 1987–June 1988
	Mari Maseng	July 1988–January 1989
George H. W. Bush	David F. Demarest Jr.	January 1989–August 1992
	Margaret Tutwiler	August 1992–January 1993
Bill Clinton	George R. Stephanopoulos	January 1993–May 1993
	Mark D. Gearan	May 1993–August 1995
	Donald Baer	August 1995–January 2001
George W. Bush	Karen P. Hughes[c]	January 2001–July 2002
	Dan Bartlett	July 2002–January 2005
	Nicolle Devenish Wallace	January 2005–July 2006
	Kevin Sullivan	July 2006–

SOURCE: Through Clinton's first term, John Anthony Maltese, *Spin Control* (Chapel Hill: University of North Carolina Press, 1994), 243. Updated by the authors.

NOTES: a. Communications Office under the jurisdiction of the Press Office. b. The functions of the Office of Communications performed by the deputy press secretaries and the Office of Media Liaison. c. In the George W. Bush administration, communications director Dan Bartlett reported to Hughes, who was counselor to the president until she left the White House in mid-2002.

Speech-Writing Unit

Since the Reagan administration, speech writing usually has been housed in the Office of Communications. The staff is responsible for preparing the president's major addresses as well as routine remarks, such as those delivered in brief Rose Garden ceremonies. Message coordination is critical. An administration needs a strong presidential message to focus the attention of its personnel on one subject or issue.

Communications directors especially concerned with message—David R. Gergen (Ford, Reagan); Gerald Rafshoon (Carter); and Patrick Buchanan, Thomas C. Griscom, Mari Maseng (Reagan); and, until mid-2002, Karen Hughes (George W. Bush), among others—have kept speech writing within their organizational base. Interestingly, four communications directors—Gergen, Buchanan, Maseng, and Clinton director Donald Baer—had served earlier as presidential speechwriters. This exposure provided a sense of the importance of speech writing within the communications framework.

Presidential speech writers usually receive little or no credit for their work. Their words become the president's words and the president receives the praise (or blame) for the phraseology. Playwright Robert Sherwood was an exception to the rule. He reportedly penned Roosevelt's famed "date which will live in infamy" line after the Japanese attack on Pearl Harbor in 1941.

In January 2002, President Bush's description of Iran, Iraq, and North Korea as an "axis of evil" drew attention, not all of it favorable, to an otherwise unspectacular State of the Union message. The author, assistant speechwriter David Frum, made headlines after his wife sent e-mails identifying her husband as the originator of the controversial phrase. Frum's resignation was announced shortly thereafter, but he insisted he had submitted it well before the January 29 speech. He said he was returning to journalism.

Relationship with Press Secretaries

Since the creation of the Office of Communications in the Nixon administration, Jody Powell, who served under President Carter, has been the only press secretary with the extraordinary responsibility of stage managing long-range planning, speech writing, photographers, the news summary, radio actuality, and the out-of-town and specialty press operations. In the Ford, Reagan, George H. W. Bush, and Clinton administrations, communications advisers were responsible individually for functions such as planning, speech writing, and the out-of-town and specialty press, but not for the daily operation as well. Until she resigned after eighteen months on the job, Karen Hughes came closest to Powell in wielding overall control of a presidential communications apparatus. Indeed, she may even have exceeded Powell's breadth of responsibility. As counselor to President George W. Bush, Hughes managed virtually every facet of his communications with the people, including oversight of Ari Fleischer's office. At a meeting with top advisers the day before he took office, Bush pointed to Hughes and said, "I don't want any important decision made without her in the room." By one account, his order was strictly enforced, making Hughes "perhaps the most influential woman ever to have served a president." [133]

The Office of Communications was subjected to exceptional scrutiny after the Watergate scandal that drove President Nixon from office in 1974. It was recognized that at times under Nixon

> the office stepped over the line that separates legitimate appeals for public support from illegitimate tactics to induce or fabricate that support through the use of administration-sponsored letters and telegrams, the creation of supposedly independent citizens' committees to praise administration policy, and even threat of Internal Revenue Service investigations and antitrust suits against media organizations that painted the White House in an unfavorable light. [134]

In recent years, instead of controlling the office the press secretary has had to fight for independence from the office. In the Reagan years, communications advisers Tom Griscom and David Gergen had the Press Office within their domain. In the Clinton administration, the Press Office again was placed under the direction of the communications adviser until Michael McCurry joined as the press secretary. Under George W. Bush, the Press Office reverted to the control of the communications adviser.

The Communications Adviser

The Office of Communications is headed by a senior-level official, whose duties are primarily administrative but also include participation in communications strategies. With a staff that ranges between fifty and one hundred people, the adviser spends a significant amount of time keeping management running smoothly. The "adviser" aspect of the role refers to developing and coordinating the president's public messages. Depending on the individual strengths of the office's occupant, the adviser also helps to build political support for the president and the administration's program.

An effective communications adviser provides news organizations with a persuasive interpretation of presidential actions and policies and designs strategies to coordinate and integrate administration ideas. Equally important are the creation of a presidential message and the coalescence of administration support around it.

The communications adviser also provides reporters with information on a background basis. In some administrations, for example, the communications adviser has regularly conducted a weekly briefing for the news magazines and another for the networks. The communications adviser sometimes has a public role as well. During the Clinton administration, two communications advisers appeared frequently on television to provide a presidential version of events. Clinton advisers George R. Stephanopoulos and Mark D. Gearan were seen regularly on the weekday and Sunday morning television news show circuit.

The right surrogate needs to speak for the president in the right place at the right time. Communications advisers are responsible for finding that right person and coordinating the statements provided by public information officers from the departments with messages coming from the White House. Personnel from all sections of an administration must speak with one voice if they are to consolidate the sources of presidential support. During the Reagan administration, Friday or Saturday meetings were regularly devoted to long-range planning for coordinating legislative and communications strategy.[135] Without these meetings, the effective establishment of a presidential message relevant to the progress of the administration's legislative program would have been difficult if not impossible.

But communications advisers have not served without controversy in the White House. In the first thirty-six years that the Office of Communications existed (1969–2005), there were twenty-two presidential communications advisers, twelve press secretaries, and seven presidents. Only six communications advisers served two years or more: Herbert G. Klein (1969–1973, Nixon), David Gergen (1976, Ford; 1981–1984, Reagan), Patrick Buchanan (1985–1987, Reagan), David F. Demarest Jr. (1989–1992, George H. W. Bush), Mark Gearan (1993–1995, Clinton), and Dan Bartlett (2002–2005, George W. Bush). The relatively high turnover of advisers points up the difficult nature of their tasks and the complexity of relationships. The adviser is charged with the smooth operation of the various units contained within the Office of Communications, yet the adviser's status derives from the ability to create and execute a successful presidential communications plan. The adviser's success depends on the president's success. If things go sour for the president, the communications adviser is often the first casualty.

Three general models have to date characterized the communications adviser: staff director, campaign adviser, and coalitions coordinator.

The staff chief type of director concentrates on administrative tasks. During his four and a half years in office, Klein, the longest-serving communications adviser, set up the operation and established the routines for disseminating information to the out-of-town press. He also focused on taking Nixon's message to groups of news organizations, such as the American Society of Newspaper Editors. In the George H. W. Bush administration, David Demarest directed his attention to the administrative aspects of the job rather than to developing a tightly coordinated message to sell to news organizations. With three and a half years of service, he stayed at his post almost as long as Klein. As a model, the communications adviser as an administrator seems to offend few.

In the campaign model, the director has the added responsibility of coordinating the president's reelection communications efforts. Gergen assumed the adviser role during Ford's presidential campaign and was followed by Gerald Rafshoon (1978–1979), who arrived to prepare for President Carter's reelection effort. Gergen and Rafshoon had the added burden of having to create a general strategy and set the tone for a presidential campaign in addition to the staff coordination required. Something had to give, and their strategies were devised to enhance the president's political strengths rather than the day-to-day unit operations.

Gergen remained until the end of the Ford administration, but Rafshoon left his desk after a year to run Carter's reelection campaign. Because Ford lost the election, the strength of Gergen's early success in the Ford administration was little noticed beyond Washington. During his tenure, however, Ford's support climbed dramatically. Part of the credit belonged to the controlled publicity operation that featured President Ford amid the trappings of the office as he carried out his duties.

During Reagan's reelection campaign, senior adviser Michael Deaver was able to closely control the communications operation by having his deputy, Michael A. McManus Jr., serve as its acting director during 1984. Reagan's last communications adviser, Mari Maseng, directed a campaign of another sort at the end of his second term. Focused on the notion of the legacy of the Reagan years, the campaign was designed to establish a strong finish for a president who was under fire in his last years in office.

During George H. W. Bush's reelection campaign, the communications adviser was Margaret Tutwiler, longtime assistant to James A. Baker III, who was responsible for directing the campaign. The resources of the office were used to emphasize the general communications assets of the president. In George W. Bush's administration, Tutwiler became U.S. ambassador to Morocco.

An example from the Reagan administration illustrates the third model, coalitions coordinator. In his second tour of duty as communications adviser, Gergen directed his energies toward shaping political coalitions for governing. During the first three years of the Reagan administration, under Gergen's guidance, the office held 150 briefings for media and elite groups from outside Washington.[136] These meetings were specifically geared toward generating political support for the president's program. Along with senior advisers Deaver, who understood the communications strengths of Ronald Reagan as well as the dynamics of television, and Baker, who was familiar with the workings of power in Washington, Gergen developed clear messages together with strong communications plans to implement them. He also maintained a tightly controlled "line-of-the-day" operation throughout the administration. "Not only was the line spread to the departments through morning conference calls, but it was also accessible throughout the executive branch by computer," political scientist John Anthony Maltese reported.[137] When the reelection effort got under way, the system was broadened to include campaign officials.

At the beginning of Reagan's second term, Patrick Buchanan introduced an agenda different from Gergen's. Buchanan spent less time with reporters and gave more time to a conservative agenda. Instead of speaking on background to reporters about the president's program, he expressed his policy preferences publicly. For example, he wrote an article published in the *Washington Post* calling for congressional support of the Nicaraguan rebels. In participating in the upcoming vote, Buchanan wrote that "the Democratic Party will reveal whether it stands with Ronald Reagan and the resistance—or Daniel Ortega and the communists." [138] When the details of the Iran-contra affair became public, the White House sought a less combative communications director and one centered on the restoration of the presidential image. Thomas C. Griscom accompanied former senator Howard Baker to the White House when the latter became chief of staff. Having served as press secretary to Baker when he was majority leader, Griscom had the knowledge and skills to work smoothly with the representatives of news organizations. He was followed as communications director by Mari Maseng, who took over to conduct "the legacy" campaign.

In 1993 the broad scope and the burdensome nature of the communications adviser's duties came under closer scrutiny when George Stephanopoulos left the position after four months. He had tried to develop overall communications planning while at the same time splitting the briefing duties with Press Secretary Dee Dee Myers. "As chief White House spokesman he was giving daily press briefings and returning some 150 telephone calls a day," wrote Maltese. "As a policy advisor, he met regularly with [Chief of Staff] McLarty and the president to discuss substantive issues." [139] But as Jody Powell had discovered, involvement in daily operations leaves no time to handle long-range planning. Thus Stephanopoulos gave up the communications and the briefing roles and took instead a less-visible senior position. The communications post then was taken by Mark D. Gearan, who held it for two years before leaving the White House to head the Peace Corps. Although Gearan made many public appearances to explain the president's positions and actions, others, including Stephanopoulos, also helped to create the administration's messages.

But Clinton often carried the message himself. His chief speechwriter, Michael Waldman, explained:

> Most fundamentally, he [Clinton] changed the way a president uses the bully pulpit to lead. Consider this fact: In a typical year, Clinton spoke in public 550 times. In a similar year, Reagan spoke 320 times; Harry Truman, 88 times. It wasn't just that Clinton liked to talk (which he most assuredly did). Rather, he was forced to find new ways to break through, to connect with the public amid the clamor of four competing twenty-four-hour cable networks, the bitterly partisan Congress, and seemingly permanent investigations. [140]

Political scientist Doris Graber attributes Clinton's skill in using the media to his ability to talk " 'kitchen-table style,' friend to friend—about middle-class concerns, involving issues such as college costs and health care and teen pregnancy.... Thanks to television, much of the world knew Clinton's expressive face, his thrust of jaw while he bit his lower lip, and his engaging speaking style. Millions loved it."

But Graber noted, "those who live by the tube are also at risk of dying from it." Consequently, the constant media scrutiny of Clinton exposed his personal misbehavior, resulting in his impeachment. [141]

In the succeeding Bush administration, counselor Karen Hughes oversaw all aspects of White House communications. She reportedly reviewed and sometimes rewrote every statement the president made. A former television reporter, Hughes had been Texas communications director when Bush was governor. She also handled communications for his 2000 presidential campaign.

Hughes's team included press secretary Ari Fleischer, a former press aide to Sen. Pete Domenici, a New Mexico Republican; communications director Dan Bartlett, formerly of Karl Rove's political consulting firm; and director of media affairs Tucker A. Eskew. After she left the White House in July 2002 to return to Texas, Hughes remained a top adviser to Bush, under a contract with the Republican Party. In 2005 she became Under Secretary of State for Public Diplomacy and Public Affairs to lead the State Department's effort to improve the image of the United States abroad.

THE MODERN PRESIDENTIAL NEWS CONFERENCE

The most important of the direct exchanges of information between the president and the press is the presidential news (or press) conference. (See "Presidential Press Conference," p. 951.) Although each side has groused about the conduct and performance of the other in these exchanges, the news conference has proved to be a durable institution. Every president since Woodrow Wilson convened the first news conference on March 15, 1913, has held conferences designed around a question-and-answer format. Reporters have asked the questions and presidents have responded. The exchange itself has evolved from the "just-between-us" basis in the Wilson administration to the public nature of today's conference, and the evolution from an off-the-record session to an official event has brought with it a variation in the way presidents have used press conferences.

Many presidents have not been enthusiastic about the use of press conferences and have tried to use them to suit their own purposes. Presidents from Dwight Eisenhower through Lyndon Johnson held approximately two news conferences a month. Since President Johnson, there has been little stability either in the numbers or in the location of press conferences; the only presidents to hold at least two conferences a month have been George H. W. Bush and Bill Clinton. In the administrations of Richard Nixon, Ronald Reagan, and George W. Bush, news conferences were reduced to the lowest numbers the presidents and their staffs could manage. Although the younger Bush often answered reporters' questions, especially in joint appearances with foreign leaders, through his first term he held fewer formal news conferences than his immediate predecessors. *(See Table 18-3.)*

Presidential press conferences have endured because presidents and reporters alike have found them to be useful. For the president, the primary distinction of the press conference is its usefulness in advancing policy and electoral goals; it is an opportunity to explain policies and seek support for them. Moreover, conferences can be timed to coincide with legislative initiatives or foreign policy events.

The press conference is the closest the president gets to having a conversation with the nation. In response to a reporter's question at one of the gatherings, President Eisenhower spoke of the importance of the press conference as a communication device:

President George H. W. Bush preferred casual press conferences, such as this one at his vacation home in Kennebunkport, Maine, in September 1989.

> The presidency is not merely an institution. In the minds of the American public, the President is also a personality. They are interested in his thinking.... At the same time, they believe the President, who is the one official with the Vice President that is elected by the whole country, should be able to speak to the whole country in some way.... I believe [what] they want to see is the President, probably, capable of going through the whole range of subjects that can be fired at him and giving to the average citizen some concept of what he is thinking about the whole works.... [T]he press conference is a very fine latter-day American institution.[142]

Other than the press conference, there is no established forum where a president regularly submits to questions. Advisers and cabinet officers cannot be expected to engage in the rigorous questioning of the president that reporters favor in press conferences. The president is, however, in a vulnerable position when appearing before correspondents. Reporters and the public may find this an attractive feature of the press conference, but it represents an element of concern for the president and the White House staff. For that reason, as the event has become increasingly public, presidents and their staffs have had to invest a considerable amount of time in preparations for the conference. The presidential briefing books that appeared in the Truman administration have been maintained ever since. Staff members also pose questions to the president in preparatory rounds. Both of these practices reduce the risks the president faces when appearing before reporters. It is fairly easy to predict almost all the questions that will be raised.

Besides presenting the president with an opportunity to communicate with the public, the conference has the added advantage of ensuring that the president is brought up to speed on existing problems and what is going on in the bureaucracy on particular policies. *Washington Post* reporter David S. Broder has explained the importance of a press conference to a president: "The reporters' questions often short-circuit the official channels, layers of bureaucracy, and tiers of staff advisers that insulate a President from the real world." [143] In this way, President Nixon found out about problems in the Veterans Administration through a question posed by Sarah McClendon, owner of a news service providing Washington political information to small newspapers and radio stations.

Presidents who do not invest attention and time in preparation for press conferences put themselves at some risk. Because President Reagan, for example, did not like to prepare for press conferences, his staff sometimes had to correct his statements after he made them. *Washington Post* media critic Howard Kurtz explained the dramatic appeal of Reagan's press conferences: "The old actor was John Wayne, swaggering into the saloon to do battle with the villains of the press corps. Would he say something outrageous? Would he mangle the facts and force the White House to put out a correction?" [144] Even when Reagan made mistakes, the public did not seem to mind. But the president did, and he preferred to make speeches when he had a message to deliver. The Oval Office, joint sessions of Congress, and settings around the country and abroad with dramatic backdrops were the venues he preferred for delivering messages. He wanted a script to follow and a stage where he could deliver his lines.

Until the George H. W. Bush administration (1989–1993) a president could reasonably expect his press conferences to be televised, but conferences held in the early

TABLE 18-3　**Solo Presidential News Conferences with White House Correspondents, 1929–2005**

President	Average number of press conferences per month	Total number of press conferences
Hoover (1929–1933)	5.6	267
F. Roosevelt (1933–1945)	7.0	984
Truman (1945–1953)	3.4	311
Eisenhower (1953–1961)	2.0	192
Kennedy (1961–1963)	1.9	65
L. Johnson (1963–1969)	2.2	118
Nixon (1969–1974)	0.6	39
Ford (1974–1977)	1.3	39
Carter (1977–1981)	1.2	59
Reagan (1981–1989)	0.5	46
G. H. W. Bush (1989–1993)	3.0	84
Clinton (1993–2001)	2.0	62
G. W. Bush (2001–2005)	2.0	22

SOURCE: Harold W. Stanley and Richard G. Niemi, *Vital Statistics on American Politics, 2005–2006* (Washington, D.C.: CQ Press, 2006), Table 4-3.

NOTE: On March 28, 2001, White House spokesperson Ari Fleischer said President George W. Bush planned to conduct no formal news conferences but intended to be accessible to reporters during public appearances. Any count of news conferences is only an approximation, given the variety of contacts presidents have with the press. Congressional Quarterly's lists and the editors' update attempt to count only formal news conferences, almost always at the White House. The largest category of news conferences excluded are joint appearances with foreign leaders that take place in conjunction with meetings at the White House and abroad.

afternoon attracted much smaller audiences than those held in the evening. Neither Bush nor Clinton favored the evening East Room event, preferring less formal settings. Bush held only two press conferences at eight o'clock in the evening, and the second one was not televised by the regular networks because it was too close to the election and network executives believed that "equal time" questions could be raised. With cable television in so many homes today, the networks are no longer willing to commit evening time to a presidential press conference. If people want to watch a press conference, the networks contend, they can tune in to CNN or C-SPAN (Cable-Satellite Public Affairs Television).

Reporters also find press conferences useful. The gatherings give them an opportunity to take the president's measure—that is, they learn a great deal about a president as a person when the president must respond publicly and extemporaneously to their questions. The absence of other forums in which the president must respond to questions posed by people outside the administration increases the significance of the presidential news conference. In addition, reporters become part of a presidential event in a news conference. In televised conferences, their colleagues in the press corps, back at the office, and at corporate headquarters can watch them at work.

Franklin Roosevelt and the Press Conference

President Franklin Roosevelt converted the presidential press conference "from the comatose institution he inherited from Herbert Hoover to a distinctly American device for informing the nation of what the President is contemplating and the President of what the nation is thinking."[145] He set a standard that, for frequency (an average of 6.9 conferences a month) has yet to be repeated.[146] At his twice-weekly Oval Office meetings, reporters no longer had to submit written questions, which allowed better access to the facts. Information could be attributed to the president, but direct quotations still were not used, except when Press Secretary Steve Early wrote out the quotations cleared for publication. Confident in his relationship with the press, Roosevelt was generous in sharing with reporters information that he would classify as "background" or "off the record." In more than half of his first 250 news conferences, the president raised the issues.[147] In the others, he left it to reporters to choose the questions and direct the flow of conversation. A true master of the press conference, Roosevelt had no imitators. For frequency, consistency, and close control, he was unmatched and a tough act to follow.

Truman and the Press: Formalizing the Relationship

President Harry Truman's feisty, often irascible nature provided colorful copy and made him popular with White House reporters. But the feeling was not always reciprocal. When they complained because he gave an exclusive interview to Arthur Krock of the *New York Times,* Truman bristled, "I'll give interviews to anybody I damn please." And when *Washington Post* music critic Paul Hume criticized daughter Margaret Truman's operatic singing, Truman fired off a famed letter saying Hume would need "a new nose and plenty of beefsteak" if they ever met.

Truman's speaking voice and delivery were no match for those that made his predecessor, Roosevelt, a master of radio speeches. The advent of television posed an even more daunting medium for the man from Missouri. For these and other reasons, Truman sought a more formal relationship with the White House reporters, who often followed him, breathlessly shouting questions as he took his brisk morning walk. Truman cut back his news conferences to once a week and he moved them from the Oval Office to the Indian Treaty Room in the Executive Office Building. Here "the whole tone was shifted in the direction of a rather stiff interpellation, far removed from 'family' gatherings, as F.D.R. liked to call them."[148] Reporters now had seats instead of standing in haphazard fashion around the president's desk. When correspondents asked a question, they had to identify themselves and their publication. The formal setting robbed the conference of the spontaneity that had characterized sessions in the Roosevelt years. Transcripts were taken and audio recordings were made. Snippets of both were released under the president's name and with his voice. For the first time, electronic media competed for attention alongside the pencil press.

As the relationship between the president and the press became more formal during the Truman years, so did the preparation for the press conferences. And as the conferences became more public, measures had to be introduced to reduce the risks inherent in open, public exchanges. Opening presidential statements at the conference provided such a buffer because they gave the president an opportunity to state his positions on issues of his choosing, as did the process of briefing the president before the conference. Elmer Cornwell found that President Truman began with formal statements in 63 percent of the conferences held his first two years in office and 52 percent of the conferences held the last two years as president.[149] Not only did this practice reduce the inherent risks of openness by directing attention to the issues of the president's choosing, but also, as with Roosevelt's issue statements, the president could selectively respond to the news media when the attention was focused on him.

Presidential preparations for the press conferences were the responsibility of Truman's press secretary and consisted mainly of preparing the president to answer questions the secretary anticipated would be asked. Staff members joined the press secretary for collective sessions to brief the president. By the end of the Truman administration, the briefing book—introduced by Roger Tubby, who became acting press secretary after the death of Joseph H. Short— was being used. It included about forty possible questions for the president's perusal the night before the conference.[150] The staff might then go over the material with the president one last time before the conference began.

Eisenhower and Kennedy: Televised Conferences

By the time Dwight Eisenhower was elected, the serendipitous encounter between president and press of Theodore Roosevelt's day had metamorphosed to the scripted event of the Truman administration. President Eisenhower proceeded to build on the formal and public nature of the press conference, with reporters kept even farther at arm's length. Radio had allowed Truman extra space; Eisenhower used television in the same way. Although the technology for trans-

Eisenhower was the first president to hold a televised news conference. But before the film was released to the public, it was edited by his press secretary, James Hagerty.

mission was still cumbersome, James Hagerty, Eisenhower's press secretary, capitalized on this direct link to the public and encouraged the improvement of lighting.

Hagerty's real innovation was to provide virtually full television coverage of news conferences, beginning in 1955. The conferences were filmed for release to television later in the day. Aides edited the films to remove the worst examples of Eisenhower's sometimes garbled syntax, but otherwise the complete content was provided. Before videotape came into widespread use beginning in 1956, television images were preserved in black and white kinescope, often of poor quality. President Kennedy was the first president to have his press conferences broadcast live.

Hagerty's interest lay in having the public serve as the main audience rather than reporters who might be critical. After one conference in 1954 Hagerty wrote in his diary: "[President Eisenhower] upset at press reaction. . . . I'm glad we released the tape of the statement to radio, TV, and newsreels. . . . [W]e'll go directly to the people."[151] He also noted in his diary that reporters would drop by and tell him what questions they were going to ask. "[Chalmers] Roberts of the *Washington Post* told me that he was going to ask the President the same question he had asked Churchill. Namely, what are the possibilities for peaceful co-existence between Soviet Russia and Communist China on the one hand and non-communist nations on the other?"[152] Press conferences, then, were not always as spontaneous as they appeared. Eisenhower, too, used prepared statements but not nearly so frequently as some of his predecessors. Retreating even further from President Roosevelt's twice-weekly and

Truman's once-a-week conferences, President Eisenhower held press conferences only once every two weeks, or an average of 2.0 a month for a total of 193 during his administration.

By President Kennedy's election in 1960, new electronic equipment offered new opportunities for presidential publicity. The president's news conferences could be televised live without concern about lighting difficulties. By then, more than four-fifths of the households in the United States had television sets. President Kennedy, long comfortable with the print and electronic media, had no hesitation about live conferences and held them about as often as Eisenhower. While in office, Kennedy held sixty-five conferences, or an average of 1.9 per month. As the press conference became a higher-profile event, preparations became more extensive. Briefing books, practice sessions, and increasing amounts of staff time were devoted to conferences. The conferences, broadcast live throughout the country, were held in the afternoons in the State Department auditorium, which could accommodate a large press contingent.

President Gerald R. Ford holds an impromptu press conference in the Oval Office, in another attempt to restore openness to the presidency after the closed administration and secrets of Richard Nixon.

Johnson, Nixon, and Reagan: Avoiding the Traditional Conference

Beginning with President Johnson, the notion of what constituted a press conference changed. Instead of counting as press conferences only those meetings held in a set forum, such as the Indian Treaty Room or the State Department auditorium, and announced in advance, Johnson often included impromptu sessions where few questions were asked. He might appear in the press room at five o'clock or take a walk around the residence and have reporters ask him questions while he moved at a fair speed. Of the forty-one press conferences he held in 1966, for example, twenty were impromptu sessions and most did not have television coverage. His average was 2.2 a month, for a total of 135.

President Nixon did not like the formal setting either, but he saw no need to include other types of sessions with reporters. Instead, he avoided them altogether. His average was 0.6 a month, for a total of thirty-nine. And when he did meet the press, it was an extremely contentious event.

Ronald Reagan also avoided press conferences. Like Nixon, he averaged 0.6 a month, for a total of fifty-three. His conferences were not contentious in the same way that Nixon's were, but in some, such as the ones he held to answer questions on the Iran-contra affair, he came off poorly. Because Reagan was able to present himself and his policies in so many other venues, he avoided press conferences. When he did have them, he used the East Room as a venue. In addition, Reagan held them at night to minimize the impact of the analysis of news organizations. If the sessions were held in the afternoon before the evening news programs, the networks assessed his performances and pointed out where his answers were weak. Evening conferences avoided those assessments. Because President Reagan was so successful in communicating his message from a set stage, he could afford to opt for few press conferences.

Ford, Carter, and George H. W. Bush: Regular Conferences

President Ford sought to eliminate the bitterness that pervaded the relationship between the president and the press after Watergate. He was open with reporters, offering to hold press conferences and to schedule interviews regularly. He held thirty-nine conferences, with an average of 1.3 a month during his time in office. He also conducted interviews with television anchors, such as Walter Cronkite, Tom Brokaw, and Barbara Walters, and with leading columnists and journalists. In addition to holding comparatively regular conferences, Ford met with local correspondents when he traveled around the country. Meetings with the press were an aspect of restoring trust in the presidency.

Jimmy Carter had no liking for the White House press corps. To expand his contacts with the press, he scheduled meetings with out-of-town editors. Carter generally met with the White House press corps every two weeks and with the out-of-town press on alternate weeks. He had far more press appearances than his predecessors. But counting only his regular press conferences with the White House press corps, he held an average of 1.2 a month. These fifty-nine press conferences were almost evenly matched by the number of question-and-answer sessions he held with the out-of-town press in the Cabinet Room. His conferences fell off during his last two years, however, with only six held in his last year and twelve the year before. Carter reduced the number of conferences his final year because he felt the coverage he received did not justify the work that went into preparing for them.

Almost all of Carter's press conferences were held in Room 450 of the Old Executive Office Building, an auditorium lacking the trappings of office. Five of his last seven conferences, however, were held in the opulent setting of the East Room, with four of those held at nine o'clock in the evening when the viewing audience would be the greatest. In preparing for his reelection campaign, Carter found the formal White House setting an appropriate one to dramatize his incumbency.

Unlike Reagan, who dealt with reporters chiefly through the intermediary of the White House staff, his successor, George H. W. Bush, preferred to deal directly with the press. Bush also followed earlier precedents by bringing back the press conference as a tool for communicating regularly with the public. He did not, however, hold the high-profile evening events favored by President Reagan. President Bush made frequent use of the conference during his first three years in office. His total of sixty-four averaged out to 1.3 a month. Bush's conferences were almost always held in the Press Office briefing room, and he added a new aspect to the press conference by frequently holding joint sessions with visiting heads of state (35.2 percent of his press conferences were joint sessions). In his final year, especially once he began his reelection campaign, he no longer held conferences with the same regularity.

Like his predecessors, he found them of diminishing use, and so he found other ways to deal with news organizations.

Clinton and George W. Bush: Joint Press Conferences

Presidents Clinton and George W. Bush followed the practice first established by Bush's father of regularly holding joint press conferences with visiting foreign leaders. Between his solo conferences on October 11, 2001, and March 13, 2002, George W. Bush held no others. But during that same six-month period he met the press numerous times with a foreign leader at his side, usually an ally in the war on terrorism.

Journalists generally dislike this type of forum because they get fewer chances to ask questions, and sometimes it is just a photo opportunity with no questions permitted. The president also may be at a disadvantage. For example, Bush was clearly annoyed at a November 2001 joint conference with Indian prime minister Atal Bilhari Vajpayee because several Indian reporters kept interrupting Bush's replies. The president finally terminated the exchange by saying, "Our food is getting cold." [153]

A veteran Washington reporter, Carl Leubsdorf of the *Dallas Morning News,* recalled the time during the 1992 campaign when a woman from CNN asked the senior Bush, standing outside his Maine vacation home with Israeli prime minister Yitzhak Rabin, about a newspaper story alleging an affair between the president and an aide. Bush angrily dismissed the rumor and chastised the woman for asking the question at a serious foreign policy occasion. Leubsdorf said he disagreed with his paper's decision to report the exchange, "but we did, on page one. Why? Because it was out there." [154]

Despite their dissatisfaction with joint conferences as a rule, reporters covering Clinton and George W. Bush had many other opportunities to see and hear the president. Both men were often available for questions from the pool reporters at photo opportunities. In addition, they spoke in Washington, at the White House, and around the country on a regular basis, and they were often available for radio and television interviews with hosts from stations around the country. Clinton appeared on MTV and CNN's *Larry King Live,* venues that had proven

Addressing the terrorist attacks on the World Trade Center and the Pentagon, President George W. Bush holds the first prime-time presidential press conference since 1995.

so successful for him during the campaign. Clinton's final news conference in September 2000 also was to have been with Prime Minister Vajpayee. But because the prime minister was not feeling well the conference was first called off and then changed to a brief "pool spray" with reporters in the Oval Office. Clinton never held a formal farewell news conference. *(See box, A Press Secretary's Nightmare, p. 962.)*

Bush continued Clinton's practice of answering reporters' questions often in settings less formal than a news conference. In January 2002 Bush and First Lady Laura Bush gave an interview to NBC *Nightly News* anchor Tom Brokaw in conjunction with *The Real West Wing*, which depicted a day in the president's life with some of his top White House staffers. The idea for the show grew out of the popular fictional television series *The West Wing*.

THE MODERN WHITE HOUSE PRESS CORPS

"The White House is the gilded cage of American journalism," declared media critic Howard Kurtz.[155] It is an assignment that fills the new recruit with anticipation of journalistic bravura. After all, few people can say that they spend their days in the West Wing of the White House less than fifty feet from where the president is meeting with officials, digesting information and preparing to take actions, and making decisions. But correspondents soon realize that the only information accessible is that scrupulously selected, either officially or unofficially, for dissemination. A White House press pass provides merely the privilege to wait—wait for a briefing; wait to see the president; wait until a press conference is called; wait to see the press secretary; wait to see senior officials; wait to have phone calls returned. There may be propinquity to power, but there is little control over when and how the news is gathered.

Who Covers the White House

A White House press pass is issued to relatively few correspondents—currently they number 1,700, almost unchanged from the Reagan years.[156] Even fewer correspondents, about seventy, cover the White House regularly.[157] The first step toward qualification is accreditation to the congressional press galleries. Accredited correspondents in the four congressional press galleries fall into the following categories: newspapers, 1,830; periodicals, 1,800; radio and television, 2,452, plus 519 technicians; and photographers, 400.[158] To qualify for a pass for any of the congressional press galleries, a person must work for an independent news organization with a Washington bureau and live in or around Washington. The second step toward qualification for the White House press corps is a formal request to the White House from the bureau chief of the correspondent's news organization seeking clearance for the correspondent to represent the bureau at the White House on a regular

basis. A Secret Service review follows. For a valid reason, the Secret Service can deny entrance to a correspondent, but a negative decision can be appealed through the court system.

Beyond those with press credentials, others can apply for a day's admittance to the White House. If, for example, several out-of-town reporters wish to attend a presidential press conference, they can apply through their news organization's Washington bureau. Accordingly, an almost limitless number can come in for specified reasons on a short-term basis. Nevertheless, rarely are all forty-eight seats in the briefing room filled. Exceptions occur when it is believed the president will come in to personally name an appointee to a major administration post, or the president is ready to present legislation to Capitol Hill, or the scent of trouble prevails. Then the seats fill up and people stand along the walls.

The White House is among the prestige beats in Washington. Some, like correspondent Stewart Alsop in 1968, found it to be the assignment with the greatest status. But in his 1981 study of the Washington press corps, Stephen Hess found that the White House beat had slipped in prestige—from first place to fifth.[159] Diplomacy, law, and politics are equally lustrous and are distinguished by the flexibility of the subjects the reporters might cover and of the approaches that reporters can take toward structuring their stories. Coverage of the White House has less latitude.

Demographically, in 1981 the White House reporter was male (86.2 percent), white (89.7 percent), and thirty to thirty-nine years old (58.6 percent); more than half of reporters (55.2 percent) had had some graduate school work.[160] Today, one clear difference is the growing number of women assigned to the White House beat and the importance of the copy they produce. Since the Hess study was completed, the *New York Times* and *Washington Post* have regularly posted women to presidential coverage, as have the regular and cable television networks.

On a day-to-day basis it is the White House press corps to whom the president and the president's staff pitch their best stuff. Nevertheless, in the larger scheme of things news outlet owners, columnists, and television anchors may receive special attention. Columnists may get special interviews with senior officials, and, on occasion, with the president. Television anchors also may get one-on-one time, and, occasionally, publishers are invited to dine with the president, especially when the poll numbers fall or successes seem in doubt. But it is the nature of the news itself that makes the regulars important. "A large part of the success of public affairs depends on the newspapermen—not so much the editorial writers, because we can live down what they say, as upon the news writers, because the news is the atmosphere of public affairs," Woodrow Wilson suggested in his first presidential press conference.[161] News is the context in which an administration operates. Maintaining some control over its content is essential to laying a foundation for policy initiatives and for the president's personal popularity. Time spent advancing either one is regarded as time efficiently spent.

The Official Story

Through the Press Office, the press secretary, senior staff officials, and the president, the official story is available to all reporters who cover the White House. On a typical day, reporters may have access to written announcements, briefings, individual meetings with White House staffers, and presidential appearances from which they prepare their coverage. The official story is the basic story. For Carl Cannon, White House correspondent for the Baltimore *Sun* and later for the *National Journal*, President Clinton himself provided a good measure of what was needed for a story. "If you want to cover something, you have to listen to Clinton," Cannon said. "He will give you a road map of where he is going. You can write off of what he is saying and then call the Press Office and then call sources." [162] With Clinton, who talked to a large number of people, building a presidential story was not so difficult as it was in some earlier administrations.

Unlike Clinton, who did not hide his annoyance with press criticism, George W. Bush tried to appear unbothered by what reporters said about him. This proved more difficult in his second term, when his popularity plummeted amid criticism of his handling of the Iraq war. "The reality is that he pores over the newspapers each morning," wrote media critic Howard Kurtz. As an example, Kurtz cited Bush's irritation with a *New York Times* story two days after the president called Iran, Iraq, and North Korea an "axis of evil." Citing anonymous White House sources, the story implied Bush was already backing down from the statement he made in his January 2002 State of the Union address. "I don't like unnamed sources, frankly," Bush told Kurtz. "I know it's part of the process. I happen to view it as quite cowardly for people to read into my intentions when they don't know me." [163]

Some White House reporters themselves were angry "unnamed sources" in June 2002 when they were excluded from an Alberta, Canada, summit of Bush and other world leaders making up the Group of Eight. Except for one pool reporter, the correspondents were kept sixty miles away in Calgary, trying to cover the summit by watching television. "This has been, without a doubt, the worst-run event in my experience," said one of the unidentified reporters. "The credibility of this administration has gone right down the tubes with this fiasco." Not hiding his identity or fury was Bob Deans of Cox News Service, who gained access to the meeting site as a pool reporter. Even he did not see Bush. Deans wrote, "It was only a matter of time, perhaps, but what passes for White House coverage these days has finally devolved into a Lewis Carroll absurdity in which correspondents can travel on a three-day foreign trip and not once lay eyes on the president." [164]

As a rule, reporters do not get "the official story" from the president personally. Instead, they rely on information from the press secretary's staff. In the morning as they enter the White House, correspondents go to the Press Room. (Occupying a one-story building that links the West Wing to the main White House, it was the site of Franklin Roosevelt's swimming pool. In 1969 President Nixon filled in the pool and had press facilities built on top. Run-down and cramped, it was renovated in 2006.) A reporter's typical day is fairly routine. The first item of business is to check the bins on a wall near the entrance to the Press Room for printed announcements, statements, and schedules. These items provide early indications of the shape of the day's activities. At about a quarter past nine reporters begin to assemble outside the office of the press secretary, awaiting entry to the "gaggle." For about fifteen minutes, the secretary goes through the president's schedule for the day and answers questions for the perhaps twelve to twenty assembled reporters. In addition, the secretary provides a White House response to overnight developments. The correspondents gathered there heavily represent the wire services, radio, and television—that is, those who need a continual flow of news. They cannot wait until the afternoon briefing to get information for their news audiences.

While press officers prepare for the afternoon briefing, reporters call in to their news organization's Washington bureau to set up their schedules and then perhaps check around with people in the White House to see if and when there will be an opportunity to see the president. If the president is making an appearance, such as brief remarks in the Rose Garden to the Future Farmers of America, will there be an opportunity to ask questions? The Rose Garden is large enough to accommodate all reporters for presidential appearances. By contrast, only a few reporters are allowed in the Oval Office.

Each day press pools are established to allocate coverage when the president appears in a limited space such as the Oval Office or the Cabinet Room. The pool is composed of representatives of all of the television networks (including the independent ones), the wire services, and radio; photographers representing newspapers, magazines, and the wire services; technicians to operate the lights and the sound recording system; and a representative of the print press. Once the group is ushered into a presidential meeting, it may be allowed, or even encouraged, to ask the president a question or two. It is the responsibility of the representative of the print press to write up a "pool report" for distribution to the entire White House press corps. The Press Office then distributes the official transcripts of the presidential question-and-answer sessions along with copies of the pool reports. In instances where official transcripts are made available, the pool reports focus almost exclusively on providing color. If, however, as happens on the road, the president speaks informally to people he meets publicly or exchanges remarks with citizens, the print pool reporter must report exchanges of words as well as describe the event itself.

All the facts must be included in the pool report to guarantee that those who were not present will have everything, not just a summary. The pool report for a typical White House ceremony provides an example. In May 1993 President Clinton met at the White House with a group of Cuban Americans to commemorate the ninety-first anniversary of Cuban independence. The group gathered under a tent on the South Lawn. "HRC [Hillary Rodham Clinton] wore a blue skirt, red blazer and a red, white, and blue star-spangled scarf. The President, with not a hair out of place, wore his customary ventless blue suit," the report stated. "He then launched into a defense of his budget plan and a plea for the group's help in getting it passed. Nothing particularly new here; he criticized the Boren plan as 'this so-called alternative proposal' and said, in effect, it would rob from the poor and give to the rich." The report ended with identifications of those on the dais.[165]

The press secretary's briefing is the central event in the daily distribution of official White House information. Whatever the president and the president's staff decide must be highlighted is presented in an opening statement. The press secretary then takes questions from the media. After the briefing, which may last from a half hour to an hour, depending on the day's issues, reporters call their home offices to discuss their stories. When the Press Office puts on a "lid," there is an interruption in distribution, and the media can feel free to go to lunch as no news will be distributed in their absence. If something newsworthy occurred, the Press Office staff would page reporters on their beepers and summon them back to the White House.

Other briefings also take place in a normal day. A senior official, such as the national security adviser, the head of the Office of Management and Budget, or the head of the Council of Economic Advisers, might give a briefing on a policy or action under discussion.

In the late afternoon when reporters have their stories together, some may want to check the accuracy of their information with the Press Office. The press secretary or staff members are available to check the validity of a story. Those from the "prestige press" (*New York Times, Washington Post,* and *Wall Street Journal*) and the networks are more likely to get first priority, but others also can rely on verification. Inaccurate stories, even in obscure publications, are a hazard as far as the Press Office is concerned, because that information can leach into the prestige press.

The Unofficial Record

Official presidential news is distributed to all correspondents at approximately the same time and in the same format, but not all presidential information is distributed in an official

manner. Certain kinds of news are released on the basis of whom the reporter represents, the identity of the reporter, or the kind of information in which he or she specializes. Special consideration is generally given to television, prestige newspapers, news magazines, and the wire services. In some cases, a particular reporter is sought out, and in others it is the news organization the person represents, such as the *New York Times, Washington Post, Newsweek, Time,* or one of the big three networks.

Images for Television

Since the Eisenhower administration, most Press Offices have paid particular attention to television. Television offers the direct access to the public that the other news formats do not. Television coverage has increased immeasurably since Eisenhower's day. In 2000, 98 percent of U.S. households had television sets and 68 percent had cable compared with 9 percent with televisions in 1950 and 87 percent in 1960.[166] Only negligible numbers of Americans had cable until 1980.

As long ago as 1962, media critic Ben Bagdikian wrote that "television has become the president's medium. . . . What necessarily comes across on live television and radio is what the public figures would like to see of themselves in print if they could manage it—their own words verbatim and without the filtration by reporters and editors."[167]

Larry Speakes, press secretary to Ronald Reagan—the president who made perhaps the most effective use of the medium—told how television was woven into strategies for presenting the administration's policies. "Underlying our whole theory of disseminating information in the White House was our knowledge that the American people get their news and form their judgments based largely on what they see on television," Speakes wrote. The Reagan White House, then, learned to think "like a television producer" to dramatize its story. The formula was

> a minute and thirty seconds of pictures to tell the story, and a good solid soundbite with some news. So when Reagan was pushing education, the visual was of him sitting at a little desk and talking to a group of students, or with the football team and some cheerleaders, or in a science lab. Then we would have an educators' forum where the President would make a newsworthy statement. We knew very quickly that the rule was no pictures, no television piece, no matter how important our news was.[168]

Although the White House was using television, its correspondents also profited. The public tuned in to watch the president when he spoke, whether it was from the Oval Office or the shores of Normandy. And they liked what they saw. Television reporters basked in the reflected glory of the president they covered. Sam Donaldson got his own evening television magazine program, which he shared with former Nixon White House Press Office aide Diane Sawyer. Lesley Stahl, the CBS White House correspondent, was selected to cohost the television news magazine program *60 Minutes.* Earlier, she had had the host position on *Face the Nation.* When she left to go to *60 Minutes, Face the Nation* was taken over by Bob Schieffer, another former CBS White House correspondent. Judy Woodruff, an NBC White House correspondent, moved on to a co-anchor position on the Public Broadcasting System's news program the *MacNeil-Lehrer News Hour.* From there she moved to the anchor slot on CNN's *Inside Politics.* White House television correspondents during the Reagan years did very well. Reagan's good pictures included them.

In the years since Ronald Reagan, television news has not fared so well at the White House. George H. W. Bush avoided comparisons with the master performer by choosing other venues in which to release information. With his decidedly less aggressive policy agenda, Bush did not need prime-time exposure to the public. After all, he was a Washington hand of long standing, and so was comfortable talking with reporters in less formal settings. While Reagan's venues included prime-time television appearances, which guaranteed maximum exposure, Bush chose nonpeak hours for his press conferences—held in the Press Office briefing room—which ensured minimum attention.

Although Bill Clinton lacked Reagan's acting experience, he proved adept at using visuals to get television exposure. As a candidate in 1992 he played the saxophone on the *Arsenio Hall Show* and he and running mate Al Gore, with their wives, boarded buses instead of airplanes for an offbeat start to their general election campaign. As president, Clinton took consultants' advice and tailored remarks, gestures, and even his bearing to suit the public taste. Instead of strolling off *Air Force One,* he began striding off in a military manner.

For a time in the Clinton years network correspondents found their air time shrinking. After the Republicans took control of the House of Representatives and the Senate in the 1994 midterm elections, political momentum moved from the White House to Capitol Hill. Soon, however, the president was again at the top of the news, even though he was often sharing top billing with the Republicans heading the House and the Senate. In 1996 Clinton became the first Democrat elected to a second full term since Franklin Roosevelt in 1938. Although the Republicans retained control of Congress, Clinton regained his ability to dominate the nightly television news—but not always in the most favorable circumstances.

After the news broke in January 1998 of his affair with Monica Lewinsky, Clinton tried to use television to deflect the tidal wave of negative publicity headed his way. Wagging his finger for emphasis, Clinton told the viewers: "I did not have sexual relations with that woman, Ms. Lewinsky. I never told anybody to lie, not a single time. Never. These allegations are false." Clinton later apologized to the American people and conceded he had had a relationship with Lewinsky "that was not appropriate." He was impeached by the House for lying to a grand jury but escaped conviction (and removal from office) by the Senate in February 1999. *(See "The Clinton Impeachment," p. 492, Chapter 8.)*

George W. Bush's ability to laugh at himself on television helped him to overcome an almost legendary reputation for gaffes and malapropisms. As of mid-2002 the online magazine *Slate* had compiled some two hundred "Bushisms: The President's Accidental Wit and Wisdom," which it had put together as a book of the same name. Bush himself introduced the book at the 2001 White House Correspondents Association dinner, saying, "I'm kind of proud my words are in book form." The Bushisms included "malfeance" (for malfeasance); "gracious" (for grateful); "Do you have blacks, too?" (to the president of Brazil); and, fifty-one years after the Japanese attack on Pearl Harbor, "For a century and a half now, America and Japan have formed one of the great and enduring alliances of modern times."

Although such awkwardness might be considered a liability, many Americans initially found it endearing and a reminder of themselves. Along with Bush's self-deprecating humor, his affability became an asset, especially on television. In the opinion of New York University media studies professor Marc Crispin Miller, among others, television enabled Bush to persuade voters that he was qualified to be president and, later, a wartime leader. Miller, author of *The Bush Dyslexion: Observations on a National Disorder,* told an interviewer that Bush's TV persona after the terrorist attacks on America "came across like Churchill, or like FDR, despite his lack of stature which, prior to the shock, had been quite clear to most observers." [169]

As in the Reagan and Clinton administrations, staged television events were an important element in crafting this image. Most famously, when President Bush appeared on the aircraft carrier *USS Abraham Lincoln* in May 2003 to (as it turned out, prematurely) declare the end to hostilities in Iraq, every detail was choreographed by the White House staff to communicate the persona of a strong, dynamic commander-in-chief. The carrier was positioned so that television viewers could not see the coast of California in the background, as Bush arrived on board a military jet and appeared under a broad banner declaring "Mission Accomplished." Assisted by an expert team of aides that understood and appreciated how to communicate on television, Bush honed an image of strength and decisiveness that remained until his second term, when events in Iraq eroded public support for his policies and leadership.

Prestige Newspapers

All newspapers are not equal at the White House, nor anywhere else in Washington. The *Washington Post, Wall Street*

Journal, New York Times, and, sometimes, *Los Angeles Times* are more likely to get the big stories and explanations of policy decisions and presidential actions than the regional papers because of their broad and deep reach into the Washington political community. "In dealing with the daily newspapers, [the Reagan administration's] starting point was always the *Washington Post,*" explained Press Secretary Larry Speakes. "It had a slight edge in importance over *The New York Times,* simply because it hit the doorstep first, and all of Washington spun off the *Post*—including Congress, the Supreme Court, and everybody in the administration." [170]

The solid financial bases of both the *Post* and the *New York Times* and the keen interests their readers have in White House activities combine for strong institutional and personal coverage of the president and the president's staff. Each paper has two correspondents covering the White House, which allows a certain flexibility in coverage: only one person needs to do the "body watch"—that is, close coverage of the president. That person picks up official announcements, hears the press secretary's pronouncements, and views the president. Being there when and if the unexpected or the unthinkable occurs is essential. The other correspondent is free to work the phones and seek information from the unofficial sources. *(See box, How a Reporter Gets the Story, below.)*

Without identifying the *Post* by name, President Bush provided an example in 2002 of how a newspaper can surprise the president with embarrassing news of his own administration. At a March 13 meeting with the press Bush said, "I could barely get my coffee down [this morning] when I opened my local newspaper. Well, a newspaper." The front-page *Post* story he read said a flight school had just received student visa approvals for two of the hijackers in the September 11 terrorist attacks. Bush said he had already given the Immigration and Naturalization Service "a wake-up call" that it needed to be reformed, and that now he would give it another one. "I was plenty hot," the president said.

News Magazines

Each administration treats news magazines with care. *Time, Newsweek,* and *U.S. News and World Report* all receive special consideration from the White House, traditionally at the end of the week. These background briefings allow the White House to give them what they need for their weekend deadlines. During the first Reagan term, the White House paid obeisance to the three news magazines in a way Reagan's predecessors did not. "Every news magazine would see every senior official for thirty minutes every week," said Larry Speakes, who managed the policy. "No newspaper or network enjoyed that privilege. The senior staff liked the idea that they could remain totally anonymous, that they would never identify you." [171] In the George H. W. Bush administration the White House continued a policy of special attention. On Thursday afternoons, Press Secretary Marlin Fitzwater arranged special briefings attended only by the magazines.

But news magazine reporters, like all good journalists, are not averse to biting the hand that feeds them if they find wrongdoing in government. For example, it was a *Newsweek* reporter, Michael Isikoff, who tracked down the story of the Clinton-Lewinsky affair. Isikoff lost the scoop out of an abundance of journalistic caution—an ethic that was less of a deterrent to the Internet gossip columnist who broke the story.[172]

HOW A REPORTER GETS THE STORY

How do reporters sniff out a good story? Ann Devroy of the *Washington Post,* known to be particularly enterprising in her White House coverage, wrote a sweeping series of articles in the early 1990s on the finances of President George H. W. Bush's Chief of Staff John H. Sununu, and Sununu's propensity to travel at the expense of others, including businesses and taxpayers.[1] A look at how the series was developed demonstrates the way a good story comes about.

The elements here were an enterprising reporter, a newspaper that supported the development of the story, and the willingness of people with collaborative information to come forward. According to *Washington Post* media critic Howard Kurtz, Devroy noticed that Sununu was traveling most weekends, yet his financial standing did not suggest that his salary could support that level of travel. Devroy and Charles Babcock of the *Post* used the Freedom of Information Act to pry loose Sununu's travel records. The result was a string of stories on his misuse of privilege during his tenure as chief of staff. Sununu, however, refused to cooperate with reporters or, for that matter, with staff members seeking information on his con-

duct. "I'm not going to give them a damn thing," Sununu told Press Secretary Marlin Fitzwater. "It's none of their business. Every trip I made was authorized on behalf of the president." [2]

But once Sununu was wounded, the many people he had offended during his two years in office sensed his vulnerability. "Those who provide reporters with their daily scraps of information—congressmen, Cabinet aides, Republican activists, midlevel staffers—had also been trampled by Sununu, and were only too happy to use the press to even the score." [3] In the end the disgruntled staff and critics got what they wanted: the resignation of Sununu from his post as chief of staff.

1. Howard Kurtz, *Media Circus: The Trouble with America's Newspapers* (New York: Times Books, 1993), 255–260.
2. Marlin Fitzwater, *Call the Briefing: Bush and Reagan, Sam and Helen: A Decade with Presidents and the Press* (New York: Times Books, 1995), 177.
3. Kurtz, *Media Circus,* 256.

Niche magazines such as *CQ Weekly* and the *National Journal* specialize in in-depth coverage of Congress and the executive branch, respectively. Despite their relatively small circulations, they are closely read on Capitol Hill and the White House.

Finally, in the computer age online magazines (or e-zines) such as *Salon* or *Slate* have become staples of the news magazine industry.

Wire Services

The wire services (Associated Press, Hearst, Reuters, and United Press International) continually transmit information to their member news outlets—such as newspapers, radio, television, and online services—so their correspondents must generate a steady flow of material. But carrying on this service in competition with the Internet has been financially difficult for the wire services. UPI, which had been in and out of bankruptcy since 1984, was taken over in May 2000 by News World Communications, an offshoot of Sun Myung Moon's controversial Unification Church. Helen Thomas, dean of the White House press corps, promptly left UPI for the Hearst News Service. The Associated Press survived by reinventing itself for the twenty-first century, making use of the Internet and other advances in technology. In 1998, according to writer Brent Cunningham, "It took just six seconds for the AP to transmit the entire [Kenneth] Starr report, 130,000 words long. . . . To move that many words when the Watergate story broke in 1972 would have taken more than thirty hours." [173]

Reporters with Niches

Some reporters covering the White House have carved out information niches, which may be particularly useful in describing the operations of the White House or the personality of a president. *New York Times* correspondent Maureen Dowd, for example, explained an important aspect of George W. Bush and his administration by focusing on the personalities and behavior of those in power. Because Bush came into office without a long, articulated agenda, who he was became unusually important. "What I'm interested in is character and how character can be traced in terms of its effect on policy and people—what compromises they're willing to make, how they see women, how they see blacks because of their background," Dowd explained. She found character especially pertinent to understanding the Bush administration: "His whole attitude is, we know best. We are the elite ruling class. We've been bred to run the country." [174]

In an earlier time, John Osborne was known for the details he collected on the operation of the Nixon White House. His *New Republic* column, "The Nixon Watch," was later retitled "White House Watch" during the years he chronicled the Ford and Carter administrations. His column was particularly useful for those who were following palace intrigues and the elements of an administration's decision-making process. For those providing the information to Osborne, there was a reward. James Fallows, chief speechwriter for President Carter, noted that Osborne was "kind to his sources, which makes him worthwhile to talk to." [175] After all, the higher one is on the White House staff chain, the greater the need to bank credit with a news source. In the Reagan years, *Washington Post* White House correspondent Lou Cannon commandeered much of the same kind of information that Osborne had once featured; he collected and published "Reaganisms" of the week. Regular readers of his column looked forward to their publication, and insiders no doubt knew that there was mileage in providing them.

The Internet

As the reach of the Internet increases with each passing year, it poses a new challenge to the mainstream press as the disseminator of news. By one account, there were fifty Web sites when Bill Clinton took office in 1993. By 2000 there were 25 million and growing. Most of these sites have little direct influence on the shape of the news, but a few are widely read weblogs or "blogs" operated by individuals or organizations giving their own "take" on the content and meaning of the news. [176]

It was a one-man, Hollywood-based news service, the *Drudge Report,* that scooped the media heavyweights on the Clinton-Lewinsky scandal. Operating in a free-wheeling atmosphere presented both opportunities and risks. "The Internet has diminished the traditional news media's tight control over access to large mass audiences," wrote Doris Graber. "Politicians, for example, who have felt victimized by journalists who paraphrased their comments and boiled them down to meaningless nuggets, can now reach audiences directly via e-mail and Web technology, and they often do." By 2002 "Internet users thought it was the most up-to-date medium, the easiest to use, and the most enjoyable," Graber continued. "Nonetheless, when asked to express a preference among media, television was still the first choice at the turn of the century. It was deemed as accurate as the Internet." [177]

Unlike traditional media, blogs can be openly partisan, drawing readers who agree with the philosophy espoused on the site. The more widely read blogs on the right and left, like the conservative Instapundit *(www.instapundit.com)* and the progressive Daily Kos *(www.dailykos.com),* can receive more daily traffic than a major metropolitan newspaper. And, they can get results. Conservative bloggers took credit for the resignation of CBS News anchor Dan Rather after they called attention to a CBS report on President Bush's National Guard service that used apparently bogus documents. Liberal bloggers took credit for keeping alive a story that led to the resignation of Senator Trent Lott from the position of majority leader following remarks he made about the late Senator Strom Thurmond, which some took to have racist overtones.

The potential for Internet communication to influence political outcomes became a bit more evident during the 2006 congressional elections. With the promotion and active backing of progressive blogs and progressive Web-based organizations like ActBlue (*www.actblue.com*), Democracy for America (*www.democracyforamerica.com*), and Moveon.org, a number of underdog Democratic candidates were able to achieve a level of success that might have eluded them in the pre-Internet era.

In March 2007, during the gearing up of the 2008 presidential campaign, the power of yet another Internet means of communication, the self-publishing video site YouTube (*www.youtube.com*), became evident. An anonymous video entitled "Vote Different" posted at the site offered a critique of two of the leading Democratic presidential candidates, New York senator Hillary Clinton and Illinois senator Barack Obama. The one-minute clip, a near copy of the famous Orwellian ad for Apple computer in 1984, portrayed Clinton in the role of Big Brother and Obama as the anti-establishment candidate. Within a few days, more than one million YouTube visitors had viewed the political ad. Revealed as the ad's creator, Phillip de Vellis, a marketer and Obama supporter, admitted he "made the ad on a Sunday afternoon in my apartment using my personal equipment . . . because I wanted to express my feelings about the Democratic primary, and because I wanted to show that an individual citizen can affect the process." Pundits were quick to declare that a new era in political advertising had begun. "This is an historic shift from a world in which a few important media outlets kind of control the dialogue to a game where anyone can play," said media critic Howard Kurtz. It remained to be seen whether the "Vote Different" ad or similar ones would have any lasting political effect. However, presidential candidates or, for that matter, presidents in office trying to advance a particular policy or program, may have to learn to deal with this type of unexpected grass-roots viewpoint disseminated quickly to millions of Americans via the Internet.[178]

DYNAMICS OF THE CURRENT RELATIONSHIP

The relationship between an administration and the White House press corps is shaped by the continuing need each has for the other. The administration, for its part, seeks to provide reporters with a continual flow of news. Reporters try to get from the press secretary and from others in the White House, including the president, answers to the questions they believe to be important. Along the way, skirmishes erupt. In part, the contention that exists between them flows from the mistrust that has in recent decades colored how each views the other.

A Legacy of Mutual Mistrust

Perhaps nowhere is the veneer of hostility in the relationship between the White House and the press more apparent than in the public statements traded between the press corps and recent former press secretaries, each of whom feels victimized by the other. Reporters believe they are used by the White House. "You are a stenographer for functionaries determined to put their spin on events," observed Howard Kurtz.[179] Press Secretary Larry Speakes saw his role as one of the few against the many. "For my six years as White House spokesman, it was Us Against Them," he wrote. "Us was a handful of relatively underpaid but dedicated public servants in the White House press office. Them was the entire White House press corps, dozens strong, many of them Rich and Famous and Powerful." [180] It was a no-win game. Each viewed the other as having the advantage, yet each needed the other's cooperation to do an effective job.

Watergate was the primary source of the mistrust that exists today between the two sides. The press has yet to recover from the stream of lies from the Press Office and from other White House locations, including President Nixon himself. But the mistrust also had earlier roots in the way in which reporters were misinformed by President Eisenhower and his administration during the U-2 affair in May 1960. An American intelligence plane had been shot down over the Soviet Union and its pilot captured. Believing that all evidence of the plane and pilot would disintegrate, the government first stated that the aircraft was a weather plane that had strayed slightly off course. When the Soviets produced the pilot and evidence that it was an intelligence plane, President Eisenhower admitted the truth and defended the need for such surveillance now and in the future.

Mistrust escalated on an almost daily basis during Lyndon Johnson's years as president. In the early days of the administration, the press found the president unwilling to answer questions about his relationship as Senate majority leader with his protégé Bobby Baker, who held the position of secretary of the Senate. Eventually, Baker pleaded guilty to corruption charges and went to jail. Even then, Johnson remained silent about their relationship. As the administration progressed, reporters deplored other silences. By far the greatest source of friction was over the lack of accurate information on the progress of the Vietnam War. The misinformation provided by President Johnson on the circumstances surrounding the attacks by the North Vietnamese on two U.S. destroyers, the *Maddox* and the *C. Turner Joy*, resulted in congressional passage in 1964 of the Tonkin Gulf Resolution, which commended the president for his handling of the crisis. After the first reports of torpedo attacks were sent to the Pentagon, the task force commander on the *Maddox* sent a telegram asking for a complete evaluation of the incident. "Review of action makes many recorded contacts and torpedoes fired appear doubtful. Freak weather effects and overeager sonarman may have accounted for many reports. No actual sightings by *Maddox*," the telegram read.[181] But President Johnson chose not to review the facts, and only much later did the telegram become public. When it did become public, along with other facts about the alleged attack on the destroyers, members of the press corps questioned the versions of events provided by the president and the White House staff. Other incidents during the Johnson years also raised the issue of the value of information coming from the White House.

This, then, was the legacy carried into the Nixon administration. By the time President Nixon resigned his office, mistrust had been a major element in the relationship between the president and the news media for a full fifteen years. And it has not disappeared in the years since. Reporters are quick to question a president's motives or to go with a story calling a president's action into question. The details can come later. President Clinton acknowledged the mistrust existing between himself and the press: "I think the most important thing is that we attempt, you and I, to create an atmosphere of trust and respect and that you at least know that I'm going to do my best to be honest with you and I think you're going to be honest with me." [182]

Five years after Clinton uttered those words, his deceptions about his relationship with Monica Lewinsky shattered any illusion that he would always be honest with the press and the people. After that, the level of mistrust between the president and the press was at least as high as it had been during the Watergate scandal. Clinton could barely disguise his dislike for the news media.

But *Washington Post* reporter John F. Harris, a long-time Clinton observer, believed that Clinton's disdain for his press coverage predated independent prosecutor Kenneth Starr's investigation of the matter. Writing just before Clinton left office, Harris contended that

> reporting as it is conducted in modern Washington, with a heightened emphasis on the personal and political motives behind the actions and statements of public officials, clashed with Clinton's perception of himself, and with his conviction that his own noble motives should not be questioned. . . . In the 1990s, both Clintons believed that Washington should take them as they presented themselves, and they felt violated when the press corps wouldn't go along.

About Clinton's successor, Harris wrote, "When Bush is challenged on his motives, he seems every bit as quick to take umbrage as Clinton. 'Do not judge my heart,' Bush rasped more than once on the campaign trail. And he seems to share the illusion of the early Clintonites that it is possible, by taking a hard line, to get reporters to report only on what he wants them to know."

Initially, Bush appeared to have a friendly relationship with the press. "On his campaign plane, he had nicknames for the regular reporters," wrote Harris, with a warning that the "once-chummy spirit" would evaporate as soon as Bush faced a wave of bad news. "No modern president has press corps friends." [183] Not all of Bush's pet names for reporters were complimentary, however. At a Chicago campaign stop, Bush, not realizing the microphone was open, told his running mate, Richard Cheney, "There's Adam Clymer—major league asshole—from the *New York Times*." Cheney replied, "Yeah, big time." [184]

With the nation at war following the attacks of September 11, 2001, President Bush was the recipient of deferential press coverage by a press corps that treated him primarily as commander-in-chief. In this regard, press relations in Bush's first term were notably devoid of the hostility that characterized previous administrations. In his second term, Bush began to feel the heat of probing questions. Reporters, who had a first-hand view of the widely criticized government response to the devastation caused by Hurricane Katrina in 2005, pointedly raised doubts about the administration's competence. As it became apparent that Iraq did not have weapons of mass destruction before the U.S. invasion, as the Bush administration had asserted, reporters started to pepper Press Secretary Scott McClellan with questions about whether the administration had been forthcoming about what it knew of Iraq's offensive capability—questions that had a faint echo of Watergate and Vietnam. Although the nation was still at war, presidential press relations began to resume a familiar atmosphere of mistrust.

The Twenty-Four-Hour News Day

In the past, the news cycle was built around information coming out of the morning public events, the daily briefing, and whatever afternoon activity there was. Television spots and newspaper stories came together in the late afternoon when all of the day's pieces were fitted together. Today, the dynamics of coverage are different because day and night the events that unfold around the world are featured on the television news programs and the Internet. Questions asked at the press secretary's daily briefing are frequently drawn from stories developed during the day and reported on radio and television news programs, especially CNN. Press secretaries do not have the same control over the briefings they once had. At times, the pace of events is so fast that the briefing becomes less of a White House publicity resource than it was traditionally. "In 1980 the White House dealt with three networks who controlled 90 percent of the viewing audience. The news cycle ended at 6:30 with the network news broadcasts," said Tom Rosenstiel of *Newsweek*. "Today the news cycle never ends." [185] *(See box, How the Twenty-Four-Hour News Day Works, p. 984.)*

In a sense, today's news cycle is much shorter than twenty-four hours. "Now the news cycle has shrunk to minutes," said former Clinton speechwriter Michael Waldman.

How THE TWENTY-FOUR-HOUR NEWS DAY WORKS

During the early months of the Clinton administration, seven members of the White House Travel Office were fired. Press Secretary Dee Dee Myers stated in her briefing that the people were relieved of their jobs because of "serious misman-agement. We believe that all of the seven individuals were part of a poor manage-ment operation." [1] Questions immediately were directed her way calling for solid information backing up the charges. As the week wore on, supporting information was hard to find. Although five of the seven were later rehired by the federal gov-ernment, only one person, Billy Dale, the head of the office, was brought to trial on criminal charges. He later was found innocent. [2]

The incident crested on a Friday when the Press Office altered its normal brief-ing routine. Myers canceled her usual briefing and Communications Adviser George R. Stephanopoulos continually put off his afternoon one. During the day the White House staff consistently remained behind events. Around noon, Wolf Blitzer, CNN's senior White House correspondent, filed a news story from the White House. At the same time, Stephanopoulos and his staff could be seen in his office clustered around the television set watching Blitzer's report. Blitzer gave details of a memo raising questions of whether the Travel Office malfeasance issue was first brought up by someone who earlier had proposed to take over the travel opera-

tion. The memo raised the issue of personal gain as an element in the firings of the Travel Office staff.

At about 1:30 p.m., Robert J. "Bob" Dole, minority leader of the Senate, rose to the floor demanding that the White House get out information on the misman-agement charges. His information came from a Reuters wire story based on Blitzer's CNN news spot. "There are media reports that now suggest the firings were planned as long as three months ago, as part of [a] political coup at the non-partisan White House travel office," Dole stated. "It had never been done before," he added. [3] All these activities took place in less than two hours. By the time Stephanopoulos held his news briefing three hours later, he found himself having to respond to news reports and official statements that he had had no hand in shaping. The story clearly had washed over the White House with little staff con-trol. That is what happens in a twenty-four-hour news cycle.

1. Press briefing by Dee Dee Myers, May 19, 1993, 5.
2. Toni Locy, "Fired Travel Office Director Acquitted of Embezzlement," *Washington Post*, November 17, 1995, A1.
3. U.S. Congress, Senate, *Congressional Record*, daily ed., 103d Cong., May 21, 1993, S6314.

"Presidents have to work harder to be heard at all. They can no longer order up an Oval Office address without wran-gling with the television networks for time." As an example, Waldman cited a Clinton request for time in May 2000 to address U.S.-China relations. The president was rebuffed by two of the three major networks. "Are you crazy? It's sweeps month!" was the networks' reaction. "Eventually, he canceled the speech." [186]

Even with a war going on, Clinton's successor also ran into problems with the network viewership ratings system. During the November 2001 sweeps, ABC was the only major network to carry a prime-time speech by President Bush. Even public television did not air the speech live. [187]

A Question of Standards

The expansion and diversification of news brought about by developments such as the Internet, cable television, and satellite technology have had a profound effect on the news business. Today, newspapers work on the assumption that their readers already know about, through television, the major news developments occurring overnight. When offi-cials in Washington go to their doorsteps in the morning, they are ahead of the newspaper lying there and that fact changes the aims of news organizations. More emphasis is now placed on explaining why something has happened than on describing the outlines of the actions. Even the net-works have been affected by the rapid transmittal of infor-mation. David Gergen told of a conversation he had with

veteran network executive Larry Grossman: "When Larry Grossman became president of NBC News he told me that his greatest challenge was figuring out how to make the news fresh when so many people had already seen the national and international news stories that the network provided to local stations." [188] When cable arose in the 1980s, it put increasing pressure on news organizations to come up with a new angle for their traditional morning and evening news programs and their Sunday morning interviews. In 1981, 25.2 percent of American households received cable pro-gramming, and in 2000 that number was 68.0 percent. [189]

The need to find an attractive way to package informa-tion has grown more critical with the demise of many news-papers. In 1909 there were 2,600 daily newspapers. That number fell to 1,482 in 1999. In the time between the admin-istrations of Harry Truman and Bill Clinton, the percentage of the population receiving newspapers dropped from 37.0 percent to 20.2 percent. [190] Often a fresh angle on events takes the form of news analysis. "A lot of what we do is what I call soufflé journalism," said John Broder, White House corre-spondent for the *Los Angeles Times*. [191] The mix of story-as-soufflé includes "a recipe that calls for one part information mixed with two parts attitude and two parts conjecture. And after twenty-four hours or so, the analysis it contains has fallen flat." Each newspaper has to provide something differ-ent and that often can turn out to be the perspective of the reporter. For the *Los Angeles Times* that has meant allowing reporters more latitude in describing presidential initiatives.

James Risen, economics correspondent for the paper, told Tom Rosenstiel that "we definitely are willing to write what we think about [the Clinton] budget in a way we were not, say, in the budget package of 1990."[192] Such latitude leads to statements predicting the road ahead. Rosenstiel cited one budget article written by Risen that began by saying: "A few simple statistics go a long way toward explaining why the [Clinton budget deficit plan] may not work, despite the best intentions of its authors." Predictions of doom precede a discussion of the facts of the plan itself.

The impact of news analysis is made more dramatic by the trend among news organizations toward cutting back the space they provide for a president's version of events. In the 1960s newspapers regularly provided the transcripts of news conferences. Today, press conference information is contained in news articles, not verbatim transcripts, and the same is true for speeches. Transcript space is provided only for the most important statements, addresses, and speeches. Newspaper editors feel less obligated to provide transcripts because many are easily available from Web sites operated by the White House, government agencies, and various organizations.

With the expansion of cable television, the networks are less compelled to give the president prime time for a news conference. In fact, when President Clinton gave his first prime-time conference in June 1993, NBC was the only one of the three networks to carry it live, and it cut away after thirty minutes. The networks give presidents less attention than they once received, but cable television provides contemporaneous coverage of their actions. Major presidential addresses are regularly carried live on CNN. C-SPAN provides interviews with White House reporters and officials as well as full-length coverage of presidential speeches and the press secretary's daily briefing. Major news organizations continue to commit resources to important stories and reporters provide extensive coverage of presidential remarks on prominent issues. "The president ought to be allowed to say what he wants to say to the American people before it is dissected and taken apart," observed *Washington Post* correspondent Ann Devroy.[193]

When the U.S. government recognized the government of Vietnam in 1995, the *Washington Post* provided a transcript of perhaps 75 percent of President Clinton's speech; a piece by Devroy focusing on the speech, the ceremony, and those who opposed the action; a color piece featuring an area draft resister then living in Stockholm; and an article on the mixed emotions stirred by the presidential action. The Devroy piece reviewed the president's statement, quoted the detractors of the policy, including Senate Majority Leader Robert Dole, and provided a description of the scene in the White House East Room, including who was there supporting the presidential action. The *New York Times* provided the full text, a White House story, a news analysis, and four separate articles viewing the action from the perspectives of investors, families, those in Vietnam, and refugees in California. All in all, both publications provided the reader with what President Clinton had earlier asked reporters that he be granted: "The only thing I ever ask is, if I have a response and I have a side, let that get out, and we'll let this conflict unfold."[194]

Notwithstanding the November 2001 sweeps shutout, after the commencement of the war on terrorism President George W. Bush generally had little trouble gaining print space or television time in his roles as commander in chief of the armed forces and booster of morale on the home front. He appeared almost daily in all media, often against a backdrop of American flags and other trappings of the patriotic fervor that swept the nation after the attacks.

From the very beginning, a communications strategy was part of Bush's war strategy. He was in Florida when the attackers struck on September 11. Even as *Air Force One* circuitously returned him to Washington, Bush was working with aides on a statement to be given the press by communications adviser Karen Hughes. As originally drafted by speechwriter Michael Gerson, the president's statement said in part, "This is not just an act of terrorism, this is an act of war." Bush told Hughes to take that sentence out, not because he disagreed, he later told *Washington Post* writers Dan Balz and Bob Woodward, but because he "wanted to calm nerves. . . . I felt like I had a job as the commander in chief to first, not be warlike, but to be more—as good as I could to be firm, but to be as comforting as possible, in a very difficult moment for the country."[195]

President Bush spoke to the nation on television later on September 11, but again as comforter, not warrior. By September 20 the gloves were off. Eighty million Americans watched as the president delivered a carefully crafted speech in which he vowed to use "every necessary weapon of war, to the disruption and to the defeat of the global terror network." In the speech he targeted Osama bin Laden by name as leader of the al Qaeda terror network. Within days, U.S. troops were on the ground in Afghanistan, waging the shooting war against terrorism.

On the one-month anniversary of the attacks on America, Bush took over the press secretary's lectern to brief the nation on the state of the war. "Appearing far more comfortable and polished than he had at earlier news conferences, Bush leaned on the lectern at times and sought to relate the war to common Americans with families and children," wrote the *Washington Post*'s Dana Milbank. "In soothing tones, he presented a more nuanced, complex view of the month-old conflict. Without a text, Bush did not exercise the Churchillian phrases that he has invoked in recent speeches, and he stumbled at times. But while losing something in eloquence, Bush presented a homier, common sense discussion of the war."[196]

One result of Bush's war on terrorism was that it enhanced the president's standing with the voters and put a damper on dissent. His public approval ratings soared to record highs, creating a "halo" that made it difficult for the press to be very critical of Bush or for congressional Democrats to oppose his conservative agenda.[197] Bush's handling of the terrorism war was not without missteps, however. The president drew criticism for linking Iran, Iraq, and North Korea together in his January 29, 2002, State of the Union speech as an "axis of evil" that supports terrorism. Some world leaders complained that the label harmed efforts to improve relations with Iran and North Korea and had no effect on the worst of the three, Iraq, which some believed was developing weapons of mass destruction, possibly nuclear weapons.

The Bush administration briefly considered creation of a Pentagon "office of strategic information" to coordinate the use of propaganda as a military weapon. After reports circulated that the agency would put out false information if necessary to deceive an enemy, protests from the press and other quarters prompted defense secretary Rumsfeld to kill the idea.[198]

Whether it was an accidental or deliberate part of the propaganda war was not clear, but on March 9, 2001, the *Los Angeles Times* published a leaked story that the administration "has directed the military to prepare contingency plans to use nuclear weapons against seven countries and to build smaller nuclear weapons for use in certain situations, according to a classified Pentagon report." The report revived fears of nuclear war and speculation that Bush was considering an attack or invasion of Iraq, where dictator Saddam Hussein still ruled despite his defeat by forces the senior Bush had led ten years earlier. If nothing else, the true or false "strategic information" again showed the power of words and images in modern warfare.

President Bill Clinton takes questions during a Rose Garden press conference.

PHASES IN THE RELATIONSHIP WITH THE NEWS MEDIA

No matter who is president and who is reporting, the chief executive and news organizations need one another. When governing requires building support on an issue-by-issue basis to create coalitions, news organizations provide the strongest support-building link to an attentive public. For that reason and others, the president invests large personal and staff resources to ensure that certain media serve the administration's interests. Weekly radio addresses, occasional press conferences and speeches, and White House appearances are effective channels for conveying the president's words and image. Both for the president personally and for the White House staff, news organizations provide not only the hardware to connect technically with the citizenry but also the interpretive link to relay the significance and meaning of the president's words and actions.

The White House press and communications advisers choose settings where the images and words transmitted by the media showcase the president in the way they prefer. In response, the media transmit their judgments on the importance of what the president said and did not say. To news organizations, the president is a top story—the most important continuing subject in national politics. On a day-in and day-out basis, the president receives more air time and print space than any other individual in the national government.

With mutual need creating the context of the relationship between the president and the news media, continuities tend to define the relationship more clearly than differences. Indeed, the relation between the two institutions becomes one of oscillating rhythms as within the span of each administration patterns repeat themselves with predictable regularity. As described in *Portraying the President: The White House and the Media* by Michael B. Grossman and Martha Joynt

Kumar, the phases of alliance, competition, and detachment appear sequentially in most administrations.[199] The number of months and years making up each phase will vary, but every incoming president can expect to experience similar cycles. In short, the president and the press contend with one another in different degrees of cooperation and contention but with enduring regularity.

Alliance

At the outset of most administrations, the interests and needs of both partners are fairly similar—and, indeed, they soon converge. The central stories of this period tend to introduce the new president and the presidential team, as well as their goals. For their part, presidents generally promise an open administration. Richard Nixon, for example, declared that he and his aides would be "open to new ideas . . . open to the critics as well as those who support us." [200] Others made similar declamations, and, in fact, an open administration works well in the early months. For their part, reporters want to write the kinds of stories that will generate goodwill for the president. For that reason, most chief executives and their staff come into office with the intention of making information available to reporters. Only when reporters begin asking for information that White House staff members do not want to release does the information flow reduce to a trickle.

Almost every modern president has realized his advantage and acted on the early opportunities to use news organizations as they announce staff decisions and describe goals. President Clinton, however, was an exception to this rule. He came into office believing erroneously that the news media would grant him a "honeymoon." But grace periods never have been a formal practice. Instead, it has been the merging of interests that has resulted in early favorable stories. Less than six months after coming into office, Clinton complained aloud that he had not been given the honeymoon he anticipated. From the start, then, a contentious relationship was established between the president and the press.

The Clinton administration got off to a bad start by banning reporters from the upper Press Office, an area traditionally open to them. As a result, the stories about denied access sat side by side—and dominated—the routine stories on the new administration and its personnel. Even the traditional stories on new appointees did not work favorably for the Clinton team. Beginning with Zöe Baird, a corporate lawyer nominated to head the Justice Department, several high-profile nominees ran headfirst into a wall of negative publicity. The health care task force proceedings that were not released to the public suffered the same fate. Through diffidence or arrogance, then, the new administration created and shaped its own elective crises. To further exacerbate its problems, a group of critics presented themselves earlier than normal when a new president takes office. In most administrations, critics are reluctant to surface in the early postelection months. Instead, they prefer to show support for the new team and to become critics only when they sense some weakening in the coalition behind the new leader. But as early as election night, Senate Minority Leader Robert Dole indicated that he would not provide the new president with any automatic support. Because he had received only 43 percent of the popular vote, Bill Clinton's critics gave him no allowances for mistakes.

The unusually early and negative stories about the Clinton team were the product of two factors: elective crises unwittingly fueled by the administration and the immediate surfacing of critics. Reporters sometimes will write negative postelection stories, but rarely to the extent that they were evident in the opening days of the Clinton administration.

In retrospect, it is clear that some of the negative press stemmed from a concerted effort by wealthy conservatives to discredit Clinton through stories about his business and sexual behavior as governor of Arkansas. In his 2002 book *Blinded by the Right: The Conscience of an Ex-Conservative*, David Brock, who wrote some of those sensational stories, documents the existence of the so-called Arkansas Project aimed at removing Clinton from office. Brock was then a reporter for the conservative *American Spectator* magazine, which first published the Paula Jones, "troopergate," and other allegations against Clinton.

Even those early stories, however, could not match in intensity or frequency stories that almost brought down the Clinton administration after disclosure of the Monica Lewinsky affair. In this case it was not the president and the press needing each other, it was another arm of government needing the news media, and vice versa, to expose the president's wrongful behavior. In his book *One Scandalous Story: Clinton, Lewinsky, and Thirteen Days that Tarnished American Journalism*, former television journalist Marvin Kalb cites the deal that *Newsweek* reporter Michael Isikoff made with the Office of Independent Counsel (OIC) that ultimately put in his hands copies of the Linda R. Tripp tapes that confirmed the rumored affair. Because the OIC wanted more time for its investigation before *Newsweek* ran the story of the president's rumored affair with the White House intern, Isikoff agreed to hold off until the last minute, 4:00 p.m., Friday, January 16, 1998, before calling Lewinsky to confirm the facts he planned to reveal in his story. According to Kalb,

> Isikoff's bargain with the OIC's [Jackie] Bennett was highly unusual. Ever since the Vietnam War and the Watergate scandal, relations between reporters and government officials have been prickly. Reporters are skeptical, even cynical, about the government; officials are distrustful and disdainful of the press. In this case, both sides cooperated, in part because both sides, for different reasons, were intent on "getting" the president. They needed each other.[201]

CLASSIFICATIONS OF WHITE HOUSE INFORMATION . . . ON OR OFF THE RECORD, BACKGROUND, LEAKS

A president can elect to speak in an official posture or to make unofficial statements. The standard distinctions presidents and their surrogates use to release information fall into three categories: on the record, on background, and off the record.

ON-THE-RECORD INFORMATION

"On the record" means that a government official is speaking for attribution. The statement is officially given and made publicly available. An example of an official statement was President Bill Clinton's declaration of recognition of the government of Vietnam: "Saying the time was at hand to 'bind up our own wounds,' President Clinton today extended full diplomatic recognition to Vietnam." [1] Reporters can use official statements in whatever form they wish.

BACKGROUND INFORMATION

"On background" means that the information may be used but not attached to the name of the official who gave it, even if that official was the president. An example of information coming out of a background session appeared in a *Washington Post* article: "Clinton, sources said, also probably will recommend new efforts to prevent companies from benefiting from affirmative action if they are not really owned by minorities." [2] No name is attached to the information provided; instead, epithets such as "an administration official" or "sources" are used.

Background information has become the coin of the realm for members of the White House staff whose many different voices often find their way into reporters' copy. Dissenting words frequently appear in the prestige newspapers and in the news magazines. And sometimes staff members intentionally provide reporters with a statement that is at cross-purposes with a presidential proposal. During the Gerald R. Ford administration, White House memoranda appeared in print so persistently that Donald H. Rumsfeld, President Ford's chief of staff, warned White House staff members with one of his Rumsfeld's Rules: "Assume that most everything you say or do will be on the front page of the *Washington Post* the next morning. It may well be. For many reasons, including that, conduct yourself accordingly." [3]

Background briefings are used on a regular basis to prepare reporters for legislative and administrative initiatives, such as the budget; trips, particularly foreign travel; and important speeches, such as the State of the Union address. Background information also is used to set up a policy proposal so that when the president gives a speech, reporters understand what actually is being said. In addition, the buildup brings the president a stream of articles beforehand that actually set up the speech. Such articles most likely will appear in the *Washington Post,* especially if the speech is to be delivered locally.

When President Clinton spoke at the National Archives on July 19, 1995, outlining his affirmative action proposals, advance publicity provided a prepared audience. During the week before the event, the *Post* published two articles by John F. Harris announcing the speech and detailing its elements. The first article appeared on July 12. The piece, "Clinton Reassures Black Caucus on Affirmative Action Policies," indicated that Clinton would present his conclusions on what affirmative action policies the government should adopt. Three days later, Harris's second article, "Clinton to Push Set-Aside Programs for Poor," this one on the front page, detailed the direction of the speech with some degree of specificity about "set-aside" programs and the president's intention to reaffirm "what the government is already doing." The article cited "administration officials" (five times), "sources"

(once), and "senior officials" (once). The one official named in the body of the piece was Clinton's press secretary, Michael McCurry. From that one citation, one can extrapolate where, either directly or indirectly, much of the remaining information originated. News of the speech was later broadcast on television and radio and carried in other newspapers. Through careful use of background strategies, the White House was able to get a week's worth of page-one and -two publicity.

From time to time the background information on policy proposals is provided by the major administration figures who are knowledgeable about a policy or issue up for discussion. If it is a budget briefing, the director of the Office of Management and Budget may conduct the briefing for reporters. Any reporter covering the issue, not just White House correspondents, may attend these briefings. Typically, they are held in Room 450 of the Eisenhower Executive Office Building.

Another use of background information is to float "trial balloons." If a policy turns out to be unpopular, the president and the staff can back away without having made a solid commitment to it. Theodore Roosevelt regularly used "trial balloons." Succeeding administrations have found them an equally important device because of the flexibility they provide. For example, staff members in the Ford and Jimmy Carter administrations mentioned the idea of placing heavy energy taxes on gasoline. But the administrations backed off when it was clear that strong coalitions, and perhaps insurmountable ones, would oppose the idea. In 2005 President George W. Bush floated the possibility of raising payroll taxes on high-income workers as a way of advancing his stalled efforts to overhaul Social Security, then dropped the idea when the trial balloon met with resistance from some of the president's closest supporters.

Prestige publications, in particular, benefit from being in the White House information loop. When the *Washington Post* was able to scoop its competition with the news that President George H. W. Bush was planning to lift the next day the economic sanctions that the U.S. government had imposed on goods from South Africa, the news of the impending action was put on the front page. President Bush's statement about the lifting of sanctions and related actions, when it finally appeared, was placed near the end of section A. [4] From a White House staff member's point of view, providing such information banks credits with a reporter.

OFF-THE-RECORD INFORMATION

Off-the-record information is supposed to stay under one's hat. The terms under which it is given call for the reporter not to use the material in any way. At the beginning of the 1900s, presidents spoke only on an off-the-record basis. Reporters understood that they were to keep the president's counsel when they spoke with Theodore Roosevelt while he was being shaved. They also understood the consequences of breaking the rule. At the beginning of the 2000s, however, a president's statements are made for attribution with almost no off-the-record statements. Even a president's brief responses to a reporter's queries during daily activities—climbing into a helicopter, walking with a head of state, responding to a tourist's question while jogging—are recorded by television, radio, and reporters' tape recorders. All become public and officially uttered statements.

In social situations, however, where reporters or members of news organizations are present, a president's remarks are off the record. Some recent presidents—Kennedy, Lyndon B. Johnson, Ford, Carter, and George H. W. Bush—occasionally or regularly hosted social events, especially dinners, designed to have

reporters get to know them. Presidents Kennedy, Johnson, and George H. W. Bush also met informally with reporters as social friends. President Kennedy dined with reporters such as Stewart Alsop, columnist Charles Bartlett of the *Chattanooga Times,* Rowland Evans of the *Herald Tribune,* and Ben Bradlee, who at the time was with *Newsweek.* A longtime member of the Washington scene, President Johnson had friends among the press from his years in Congress. At the behest of his communications adviser Gerald Rafshoon, President Carter held a group of off-the-record dinners for members of news organizations, including publishers, network executives, anchors for television news programs, editors, and bureau chiefs. The idea was to let them meet the president in an informal setting since few in Washington had a sense of who Carter, the former governor of Georgia, was. President George H. W. Bush enjoyed reporters' company when fishing, boating, playing horseshoes, golf, and tennis. All of the contacts that presidents have with news organization personnel are helpful in that each side gets to know the other. But that does not necessarily translate into positive copy. That depends on what the president does.

PROVIDING AND PLUGGING LEAKS

Although a large portion of the information provided to reporters on a background basis from White House officials carries the imprimatur of the president and the president's senior staff, there are unauthorized disclosures as well. Those are the ones that make presidents angry; every president, in fact, gets upset about leaked information. Lyndon Johnson had a White House staff member, Marvin Watson, check the visitor logs to see which reporters staff members were talking to. He also directly asked staff members to tell him of their contacts with reporters. Often the information provided is given on background in an effort to distance the information from its source. The senior staff themselves sometimes leak information. For example, Carter press secretary Jody Powell floated what proved to be a false rumor that Republican senator and political foe Charles Percy of Illinoishad used business aircraft and offices while serving in his capacity as a senator.[5] When the *Chicago Sun-Times* revealed Powell as the source he came in for heavy criticism.

President Ronald Reagan's chief of staff James A. Baker III regularly provided reporters with background information, but some Reagan administration staffers, such as senior adviser Edwin Meese, regarded this practice as leaking. What Meese viewed as a leak, Reagan consultant David Gergen explained, was an instance in which "the goal was to talk it through, to give us a historical context and some background to *why* things were going the way they were and what the President was trying to accomplish." [7]

Despite pervasive leaking in the Reagan years, President George H. W. Bush made clear his antipathy toward leaks. Presidential speechwriter John Podhoretz described the policy:

> He signaled the seriousness of his intent during the 1988 transition when he informed a longtime friend and aide that she would not be given a job in the administration because she had had unauthorized conversations with reporters. The example terrified White House staffers, and with the exception of the focused and controlled leaking campaigns against [unpopular chiefs of staff] John Sununu and subsequently Sam Skinner, Bush mostly got his wish.[7]

One of the reasons for the low level of unauthorized disclosures was Sununu's interest in tracking leaks. "This was due in part to Ed Rogers, John Sununu's assistant, who was official Leak Inquisitor—if a staffer was told by his secretary that Ed Rogers was on the line, it would fill him with fear and trembling." But the person who cared most about leaks was Bush himself. When the *New York Times* obtained a cable sent by William Reilly, administrator of the Environmental Protection Agency, from the 1992 summit on the environment held in Rio de

Janeiro, President Bush sought to find out who had given it to *Times* reporter Keith Schneider:

> He ordered an investigation of all outgoing White House phone calls and selected his favorite suspect, David Mcintosh, a member of Dan Quayle's staff. On a Saturday morning from Camp David, the president called Quayle and began reading from the logs: At 4:09 Tuesday afternoon the staffer had called Keith Schneider's office, and he'd better have a damn good explanation.[8]

Like most presidents who chase leaks, Bush did not find conclusive results. But the search process let off some presidential steam.

President George W. Bush was publicly just as adamant about unauthorized leaks as his father, when he faced a leak with national security ramifications. After former ambassador Joseph Wilson challenged the administration's claim that Iraq was developing nuclear weapons—a claim that was central to the case against Saddam Hussein used to justify the invasion of Iraq—classified information was leaked to the press about the covert status of Wilson's wife, Valerie Plame, who worked for the Central Intelligence Agency (CIA). Administration critics alleged the leak was retribution against Wilson for undermining the administration's justification for invading Iraq. On a trip to Niger Wilson found that the country had not provided uranium to Iraq for use in nuclear weapons as the administration had asserted. President Bush promised, "if there's a leak out of my administration, I want to know who it is."

The leak became the subject of an investigation headed by federal attorney Patrick Fitzgerald, which led to an indictment of I. Lewis Libby, Vice President Richard B. Cheney's chief of staff, for lying about his role in the incident. In the course of preparations for his trial, Libby acknowledged that both the president and vice president had knowledge of the leak, although the possibility that the president had authorized it was never proven. Libby was convicted of four counts in February 2007—two counts of perjury, and one count each of obstruction of justice and lying to the FBI. His lawyers immediately said they would seek a new trial or appeal the conviction. Except for expressing sadness for Libby and his family, President Bush said he would have no comment on the case until the appeals process was exhausted. Although no other members of Bush's White House staff were charged with breaking the law, the trial revealed a coordinated effort by high-level administration officials to use classified information to silence Wilson. In Bush's defense, administration sources contended that because the president can declassify any material, the leak in question could not be considered breaking the law. House Speaker Nancy Pelosi saw it otherwise: "The testimony unmistakably revealed—at the highest levels of the Bush administration—a callous disregard in handling sensitive national security information and a disposition to smear critics of the war in Iraq." [9]

1. Alison Mitchell, "U.S. Grants Full Ties to Hanoi; Time for Healing, Clinton Says," *New York Times,* July 12, 1995, A1.

2. John F. Harris, "Clinton to Push Set-Aside Programs for Poor," *Washington Post,* July 15, 1995, A5.

3. Donald Rumsfeld, "Rumsfeld's Rules," in *The Presidency in Transition,* vol. 6, ed. James P. Pfiffner and Gordon Hoxie (New York: Center for the Study of the Presidency, 1989), 40.

4. Howard Kurtz, *Media Circus: The Trouble with America's Newspapers* (New York: Times Books, 1993), 242.

5. Michael B. Grossman and Martha Joynt Kumar, *Portraying the President: The White House and the News Media* (Baltimore: Johns Hopkins University Press, 1981), 175.

6. Mark Hertsgaard, *On Bended Knee: The Press and the Reagan Presidency* (New York: Farrar, Straus, Giroux, 1988), 41.

7. John Podhoretz, *Hell of a Ride: Backstage at the White House Follies, 1989–1993* (New York: Simon and Schuster, 1993), 56.

8. Ibid., 60.

9. NBC News and news services, "Jurors Convict Libby on Four of Five Charges," March 6, 2007, (*http://www.msnbc.msn.com/id/17479718/*).

As a result of the bargain, Tripp's lawyer, Jim Moody, delivered one of the crucial tapes to *Newsweek*'s Washington bureau after midnight on January 17, still in time for Isikoff to break the story. Isikoff and others listened to the tape, but his editors decided the story needed more checking. The magazine went to press without it. The matter did not end there, however. That weekend Drudge tipped off his readers that *Newsweek* had killed a "blockbuster report" of a former White House intern's "sex relationship with the president."

How did Drudge learn about *Newsweek*'s decision? According to Kalb, "Once again, it was the anti-Clinton legal cabal," one of whom e-mailed what he knew to Drudge. If they "couldn't get their story out by way of the mainstream press, through Isikoff, they didn't mind getting it out by way of Drudge." [202]

President-Press Competition

When negative stories begin, an administration must decide whether to tamper with the information flow. Generally, two types of information control are available to the new president: shutting off the information spigot altogether or generating more positive stories. Some presidents find that their staff members are leaking damaging information to the press about the administration and its programs. Lyndon Johnson monitored reporters' communications with senior assistants and tracked the journalists' copy to determine what presidential aides might have said. Some presidents may even manipulate the access enjoyed by reporters as they cover the White House.

To generate more positive coverage of the president, the president's press and communications aides must prepare presidential appearances with great care. The settings and frequency of public presentations are manipulated to emphasize the president's strong points. For Ronald Reagan, who sometimes performed poorly at press conferences, that meant holding down the number of press conferences in favor of Oval Office speeches; Jimmy Carter preferred the opposite mix. George H. W. Bush curried favor with reporters rather than deny them access or manipulate the settings of his presentations. Bill Clinton, who moved almost directly into the competition phase because of the prominent place taken by his critics, sought to establish an advantage in his relationship with the press by avoiding the White House press corps. He turned instead to less-established settings, such as radio call-in programs, CNN's *Larry King Live*, and MTV.

As for George W. Bush, by July 2002 his war-induced "halo" had evaporated and his relations with the press had moved to the competitive phase, according to political scientist Martha Joynt Kumar. With Enron, WorldCom, and other corporate scandals undermining confidence in the stock market, reporters pressed Bush to disclose records of his sale of Harken Energy Corporation stock before he became president. Bush, who had been a Harken director at the time, insisted, "I can't release something I don't have." [203]

Detachment

After expending a great deal of effort manipulating settings and people, presidents and their staffs ultimately realize that all the effort produces less than what they sought. As a result, the staff cuts back on its effort to shape reporters' stories through direct presidential-press contact. Jimmy Carter drastically reduced the number of his press conferences in his final year and a half in office, and George H. W. Bush did the same. Even Reagan, who held few press conferences, staged fewer his last year in the White House. Detachment also means that the president spends little time entertaining the members of news organizations, until perhaps, as the clock winds down, the president begins to think about a spot in the history books.

Although Bill Clinton often kept his distance from reporters, he sorely lacked detachment, in the opinion of *Post* writer John Harris:

> What Bill Clinton lacks, for all his high intelligence, is a quality that modern reporters covet in politicians and their aides: detachment. This is the ability to step outside their public roles and comment, preferably with humor and irony, on their own performance. Clinton's boyhood hero, John F. Kennedy, had this ability in abundance, and it endeared him to a generation of political reporters. (It was Clinton's 1996 opponent, Bob Dole, who showed that detachment had its limits as a political strategy.) [204]

In his first years in office, George W. Bush showed flashes of the self-deprecating wit that Kennedy used so effectively, and it served him well, as his relationship with the press was generally positive. As things soured for Bush in his second term, he began to show flashes of irritation when challenged. The genial president who had pet names for reporters could be defensive and ill-at-ease when his competence was questioned.

From administration to administration, alliance, competition, and detachment are predictable phases in the relationship between the president and the press. The phases begin and end depending on the kinds of activity the president undertakes at key junctures in the term. The president may be upset at the information appearing in news stories, but articles generally reflect real political problems. Perception of problems with the press is endemic to the office, but, in fact, reporters are not the president's problem; the problem lies with the critics who talk with reporters. Yet most presidents persist in seeing reporters as the problem.

NOTES

1. "The One-Question News Conference," *Washington Post,* June 15, 1993, A13.

2. Richard B. Morris, *The Forging of the Union, 1781–1789* (New York: Harper and Row, 1987), 23.

3. Frank Luther Mott, *American Journalism, A History: 1690–1960* (New York: Macmillan, 1962), 113 n. 1.

4. Donald A. Ritchie, *Press Gallery: Congress and the Washington Correspondents* (Cambridge: Harvard University Press, 1991), 30.

5. Richard Rubin, *Press, Party, and Presidency* (New York: Norton, 1981), 10.

6. Ibid., 12.

7. *National Intelligencer and Washington Advertiser,* November 5, 1800.

8. Mott, *American Journalism,* 179.

9. William Ames, *A History of the National Intelligencer* (Chapel Hill: University of North Carolina, 1972), 114.

10. Ritchie, *Press Gallery,* 17.

11. Ben Perley Poore, *Perley's Reminiscences of Sixty Years in the National Metropolis,* vol. 1 (Philadelphia: Hubbard Brothers, 1886), 96.

12. Mott, *American Journalism,* 180.

13. James Pollard, *The Presidents and the Press* (New York: Macmillan, 1947), 26.

14. *National Intelligencer and Washington Advertiser,* October 31, 1800, 1.

15. This discussion comes from James Morton Smith, "Alien and Sedition Acts," *Encyclopedia of the American Presidency,* vol. 1, ed. Leonard W. Levy and Louis Fisher (New York: Simon and Schuster, 1994), 47.

16. F. B. Marbut, *News from the Capital: The Story of Washington Reporting* (Carbondale: Southern Illinois University Press, 1971), 30–31.

17. See the discussion in Ritchie, *Press Gallery,* 22.

18. Poore, *Perley's Reminiscences,* 77–78.

19. As quoted in Marbut, *News from the Capital,* 96.

20. Poore, *Perley's Reminiscences,* 77–78.

21. Mott, *American Journalism,* 312.

22. Thomas C. Leonard, *The Power of the Press: The Birth of American Political Reporting* (New York: Oxford University Press, 1986), 78–79.

23. Rubin, *Press, Party, and Presidency,* 52.

24. Ritchie, *Press Gallery,* 23.

25. Ibid., 23.

26. Ibid., 30.

27. Mott, *American Journalism,* 250.

28. Ibid., 249.

29. By 1940 the AP had increased to fourteen hundred newspapers. From this success other wire services, including the United Press International, which was established in 1907, came into being and expanded from approximately five hundred clients in 1914 to fourteen hundred clients in 1940. Ibid., 710.

30. Elmer E. Cornwell Jr., *Presidential Leadership of Public Opinion* (Bloomington: Indiana University Press, 1965), 11.

31. Ibid.

32. Douglass Cater, *The Fourth Branch of Government* (New York: Vintage, 1959), 85.

33. Ibid., 85–86.

34. Ritchie, *Press Gallery,* 108.

35. Ibid., 109.

36. Ibid., 145.

37. Ibid., 154.

38. Henry Villard, *Memoirs of Henry Villard: Journalist and Financier, 1835–1900,* vol. 1 (Boston: Houghton Mifflin, 1904), 140.

39. Pollard, *Presidents and the Press,* 351.

40. The first published discussion with a president came as a result of an interview that James Gordon Bennett conducted with Martin Van Buren. James Pollard, who chronicled the relationship of each president with the press, characterized the interview as more of a recitation of the publisher's impressions after talking with Van Buren than an interview. It appeared on January 12, 1839, and "although it caused no sensation at the time," Pollard noted, "it set a precedent." Ibid., 189–190.

41. Ibid., 413. There is some dispute as to which was the first interview granted by President Johnson. Frank Luther Mott indicated that J. B. McCullagh of the St. Louis *Globe-Democrat* was the first to interview a president. See Mott, *American Journalism,* 370.

42. Mark Whalgren Summers, *The Press Gang: Newspapers and Politics 1865–1878* (Chapel Hill: University of North Carolina Press, 1994), 32.

43. Pollard, *Presidents and the Press,* 485.

44. Ibid., 491.

45. Ibid., 501.

46. W. U. Hensel, *Life and Public Services of Grover Cleveland* (Philadelphia: Hubbard Brothers, 1888), 233–234.

47. Leonard D. White, *The Republican Era: A Study in Administrative History, 1869–1901* (New York: Free Press, 1965), 101.

48. Ibid., 103.

49. As quoted in Pollard, *Presidents and the Press,* 517.

50. O. O. Stealey, *Twenty Years in the Press Gallery* (New York: Publishers Printing, 1906), 34.

51. George Juergens, *News from the White House: The Presidential-Press Relationship in the Progressive Era* (Chicago: University of Chicago Press, 1981), 14–15.

52. Ibid., 15.

53. Lewis L. Gould, *The Presidency of William McKinley* (Lawrence: Regents Press of Kansas, 1980), 3, 11–12.

54. Ibid., 241; White, *Republican Era,* 102.

55. Ida Mae Tarbell, "President McKinley in War Times," *McClure's Magazine,* May 1898–October 1898, 98, 214.

56. Gould, *Presidency of William McKinley,* 38.

57. Ibid., 241.

58. Louis Ludlow, *From Cornfield to Press Gallery* (Washington, D.C.: W. F. Roberts, 1924), 321.

59. Leo Rosten, *The Washington Correspondents* (New York: Harcourt, Brace, 1937), 22.

60. David Barry, *Forty Years in Washington* (Boston: Little, Brown, 1924), 270.

61. Ibid., 271.

62. A *Washington Star* correspondent, as quoted in Juergens, *News from the White House,* 55–56.

63. Ibid., 114.

64. Oscar King Davis, *Released for Publication* (New York: Houghton Mifflin, 1925), 176.

65. Cornwell, *Presidential Leadership of Public Opinion,* 46.

66. Ibid., 45.

67. Ibid., 49.

68. Ibid., 113.

69. Davis, *Released for Publication,* 136.

70. Ibid., 157.

71. Juergens, *News from the White House,* 97.

72. Ibid., 140.

73. Cornwell, *Presidential Leadership of Public Opinion,* 39.

74. Ibid., 41.

75. Barry, *Forty Years in Washington,* 309.

76. Marbut, *News from the Capital,* 174.

77. Ibid., 175.

78. Pollard, *Presidents and the Press,* 717–718.

79. Ibid., 719.

80. Marbut, *News from the Capital,* 175.

81. Rosten, *Washington Correspondents,* 46.

82. Barry, *Forty Years in Washington,* 268.

83. Ibid., 269.

84. Rosten, *Washington Correspondents,* 40.

85. Ibid., 44.

86. Ibid., 46.

87. George F. Parker, *Recollections of Grover Cleveland* (New York: Century, 1909), 174–176.

88. Ludlow, *From Cornfield to Press Gallery,* 328–329.

89. Davis, *Released for Publication,* 102.

90. Henry L. Stoddard, *As I Knew Them: Presidents and Politics from Grant to Coolidge* (New York: Harper and Brothers, 1927), 299–300.

91. Davis, *Released for Publication,* 184.

92. Cornwell, *Presidential Leadership of Public Opinion,* 43.

93. As quoted in ibid., 44.

94. Ibid., 109.

95. Ludlow, *From Cornfield to Press Gallery,* 269.

96. Juergens, *News from the White House,* 151.

97. John Hart, "White House Staff," in *Encyclopedia of the American Presidency,* vol. 4, ed. Leonard W. Levy and Louis Fisher (New York: Simon and Schuster, 1994), 1641.

98. Ann Devroy, "Keeping a Campaign Pledge to Rein in Costs," *Washington Post,* July 3, 1995, A21.

99. William E. Leuchtenburg, *Franklin D. Roosevelt and the New Deal, 1932–1940* (New York: Harper Torchbooks, 1963), 42.

100. Ibid.

101. Cornwell, *Presidential Leadership of Public Opinion,* 255.

102. Ibid., 263.

103. Ibid.

104. Lyn Ragsdale, *Vital Statistics on the Presidency: Washington to Clinton* (Washington, D.C.: CQ Press, 1998), 268.

105. *Washington Post,* "OnPolitics" *(www.washingtonpost.com).*

106. Marbut, *News from the Capital,* 178.

107. Patrick Anderson, *The President's Men* (Garden City, N.Y.: Doubleday, 1968), 59.

108. Cornwell, *Presidential Leadership of Public Opinion,* 218.

109. Ibid., 220.

110. Transcript, James Hagerty oral history interview, March 2, 1967, Columbia Oral History Project, 56, as quoted in Michael B. Grossman and Martha J. Kumar, *Portraying the President: The White House and the News Media* (Baltimore: Johns Hopkins University Press, 1981), 153.

111. Anderson, *President's Men,* 193.

112. Ibid., 182.

113. Marlin Fitzwater, *Call the Briefing: Bush and Reagan, Sam and Helen, A Decade with Presidents and the Press* (New York: Times Books, 1995), 3.

114. Ibid., 105–106.

115. Douglass Cater, *The Fourth Branch of Government* (New York: Vintage, 1959), 23.

116. See the discussion of roles performed by the press secretary in Grossman and Kumar, *Portraying the President,* 136–149.

117. Ibid., 137–138.

118. A reporter on background, as quoted in Martha Joynt Kumar, "Freelancers and Fogmeisters: Party Control and White House Communications Activities" (Paper presented at the annual meeting of the American Political Science Association, Washington, D.C., September 2–5, 1993), 37.

119. Helen Thomas, *Front Row at the White House: My Life and Times* (New York: Scribner's, 1999), 160.

120. White House, Press Briefing by Scott McClellan, June 16, 2005 *(http://www.whitehouse.gov/news/releases/2005/06/20050616-5.html#3).*

121. Kumar, "Freelancers and Fogmeisters."

122. Larry Speakes with Robert Pack, *Speaking Out: The Reagan Presidency from Inside the White House* (New York: Scribner's, 1988), 155.

123. James S. Brady retained the title of press secretary throughout Reagan's presidency, even though he could not return to work after being critically wounded in the March 30, 1981, attempt on the president's life. On February 11, 2000, President Clinton named the White House briefing room in Brady's honor. The plaque said Brady "served his nation with honor and distinction, strengthening the bond between government and press." Clinton praised Brady and his wife, Sarah, for their help in passing the 1993 "Brady Bill," requiring a waiting period for background checks of gun purchasers.

124. Speakes, *Speaking Out,* chap. 10.

125. Ibid., 136.

126. As quoted in Grossman and Kumar, *Portraying the President,* 152.

127. Mike Allen, "Fleischer Rebuffed for Remarks on Mideast: White House Regrets Statement Linking Violence to Failed Clinton Peace Moves," *Washington Post,* March 1, 2002, A16.

128. Grossman and Kumar, *Portraying the President,* 58.

129. As quoted in ibid., 153.

130. From Cornwell, *Presidential Leadership of Public Opinion,* 228.

131. Tom Rosenstiel, *The Beat Goes On: President Clinton's First Year with the Media* (New York: Twentieth Century Fund, 1994), 14.

132. Michael K. Deaver, with Micky Herskowitz, *Behind the Scenes* (New York: Morrow, 1987), 175.

133. Associated Press, "Mrs. Hughes Leaves Washington," July 8, 2002 *(www.ap.org).*

134. John Anthony Maltese, "White House Office of Communications," in *Encyclopedia of the American Presidency,* vol. 4, ed. Leonard W. Levy and Louis Fisher (New York: Simon and Schuster, 1994), 1633–1634.

135. John Anthony Maltese, *Spin Control: The White House Office of Communications and the Management of Presidential News* (Chapel Hill: University of North Carolina, 1994), 186–187.

136. Ibid., 194.

137. Ibid., 198.

138. Ibid., 208.

139. Ibid., 235.

140. Michael Waldman, *POTUS Speaks: Finding the Words that Defined the Clinton Presidency* (New York: Simon and Schuster, 2000).

141. Doris A. Graber, *Mass Media and American Politics,* 6th ed. (Washington, D.C.: CQ Press, 2002), 271–272.

142. As quoted in David S. Broder, *Behind the Front Page* (New York: Simon and Schuster, 1987), 198–199.

143. Ibid., 200.

144. Howard Kurtz, *Media Circus: The Trouble with America's Newspapers* (New York: Times Books, 1993), 251.

145. As quoted in Pollard, *Presidents and the Press,* 781.

146. Harold W. Stanley and Richard G. Niemi, *Vital Statistics on American Politics, 2001–2002* (Washington, D.C.: CQ Press, 2001), 174.

147. Cornwell, *Presidential Leadership of Public Opinion,* 157.

148. Ibid., 173.

149. Ibid., 170.

150. Ibid., 172.

151. Grossman and Kumar, *Portraying the President,* 243.

152. Ibid., 140.

153. Mike Allen, *Washington Post,* November 10, 2001, A18.

154. Marvin Kalb, *One Scandalous Story: Clinton, Lewinsky, and Thirteen Days that Tarnished American Journalism* (New York: Free Press, 2001), 252.

155. Kurtz, *Media Circus,* 238.

156. Speakes, *Speaking Out,* 258.

157. Graber, *Mass Media and American Politics,* 289.

158. The figures, as of July 24, 2002, were provided by the four separate congressional galleries. They are subject to fluctuations within a year.

159. Stephen Hess, *The Washington Reporters* (Washington, D.C.: Brookings, 1981), 49.

160. Ibid., 156–157.

161. As quoted in Cater, *Fourth Branch of Government,* 32.

162. Carl Cannon, telephone interview by Martha Joynt Kumar, July 8, 1995.

163. Howard Kurtz, "Straight Man," *Washington Post Magazine,* May 19, 2002, 19.

164. Joseph Curl, "Press Angered over Isolation at Summit," June 28, 2001 (*www.washtimes.com*).

165. Pool report #1, May 20, 1993.

166. Stanley and Niemi, *Vital Statistics,* Table 4-1.

167. Ben H. Bagdikian, quoted in *Columbia Journalism Review,* November–December 2001, 52.

168. Speakes, *Speaking Out,* 220.

169. As quoted by Norman Solomon in "The Televised Greatness of George W. Bush," FAIR (Fairness and Accuracy in Reporting) Media Beat, October 19, 2001 (*www.fair.org*).

170. Speakes, *Speaking Out,* 227.

171. Ibid., 231.

172. Kalb, *One Scandalous Story,* 80.

173. Graber, *Mass Media and American Politics,* 392.

174. Kurtz, *Media Circus,* 255.

175. As quoted in Grossman and Kumar, *Portraying the President,* 171.

176. Ted Boghosian, *The Press Secretary,* documentary, Public Broadcasting System, WGBH Boston, 2001.

177. Graber, *Mass Media and American Politics,* 395.

178. cnn.com, "Source behind Internet Attack on Clinton Revealed," March 22, 2007 (*http://www.cnn.com/2007/POLITICS/03/21/clinton.you.tube/index.html*).

179. Kurtz, *Media Circus,* 238.

180. Speakes, *Speaking Out,* 217.

181. David Wise, *The Politics of Lying: Government Deception, Secrecy, and Power* (New York: Vintage, 1973), 62–63. In this, one of the most complete accounts of the incidents, Wise calls the Tonkin Gulf incident "the most crucial and disgraceful episode in the modern history of government lying."

182. Gwen Ifill, "President, in Prime Time, Is Spurned by Two Networks," *New York Times,* June 18, 1993, A19.

183. John F. Harris, "Clinton Never Liked the Media, But Don't Ask Him Why," *Washington Post,* December 31, 2000, B1.

184. Jake Tapper, September 4, 2000 (*www.Salon.com*).

185. Tom Rosenstiel, telephone interview with Martha Joynt Kumar, July 13, 1995.

186. Waldman, *POTUS Speaks,* 267. "Sweeps" are periodic measurements of radio or television audiences.

187. Lisa de Moraes, "The TV Column: Networks Decide Bush's Speech Doesn't Rate," *Washington Post,* November 9, 2001, C1.

188. David Gergen, "Commentary," in *The Future of News: Television, Newspapers, Wire Services, Newsmagazines,* ed. Philip S. Cook, Douglas Gomery, and Lawrence W. Lichty (Baltimore: Johns Hopkins University Press, 1992), 207.

189. Stanley and Niemi, *Vital Statistics,* Table 4-1.

190. Ibid., Table 4-2.

191. Quoted in Rosenstiel, *Beat Goes On,* 31.

192. Ibid.

193. Ann Devroy, telephone interview, July 5, 1995.

194. Ifill, "President, in Prime Time," A19.

195. Dan Balz and Bob Woodward, "Ten Days in September: Inside the War Cabinet" (Part I), January 27, 2002, A13.

196. Dana Milbank, "Analysis: For President, Reassuring a Jittery Nation: Bush Takes on the Role of Comforter," *Washington Post,* October 12, 2001, A19.

197. John Lancaster, " 'Halo' Cows Democrats: Popular Support for Bush, Republicans Makes Mounting Challenges Difficult," *Washington Post,* February 11, 2002, A1.

198. Thomas E. Ricks, "Rumsfeld Kills Pentagon Propaganda Unit: News Reports Decried As Damaging, Inaccurate," *Washington Post,* February 27, 2002, A21.

199. Grossman and Kumar, *Portraying the President,* 273–298.

200. As quoted in Rowland Evans Jr. and Robert D. Novak, *Nixon in the White House* (New York: Random House, 1971), 33–34.

201. Kalb, *One Scandalous Story,* 47.

202. Ibid., 64, 80.

203. Dana Milbank, "The Minute Waltz and a Skeptical Press Corps," *Washington Post,* July 16, 2002, A15.

204. Harris, "Clinton Never Liked the Media."

SELECTED BIBLIOGRAPHY

Brock, David. *Blinded by the Right: The Conscience of an Ex-Conservative.* New York: Crown, 2002.

Broder, David S. *Behind the Front Page.* New York: Simon and Schuster, 1987.

Bruni, Frank. *Ambling into History: The Unlikely Odyssey of George W. Bush.* New York: HarperCollins, 2002.

Cater, S. Douglass. *The Fourth Branch of Government.* New York: Vintage, 1959.

Cronkite, Walter. *A Reporter's Life.* New York: Knopf, 1996.

Davis, Oscar King. *Released for Publication.* New York: Houghton Mifflin, 1925.

Downie, Leonard, Jr., and Robert G. Kaiser. *The News About the News: American Journalism in Peril.* New York: Knopf, 2002.

Fitzwater, Marlin. *Call the Briefing! Bush and Reagan, Sam and Helen: A Decade with Presidents and the Press.* New York: Times Books, 1995.

Graber, Doris A. *Mass Media and American Politics,* 6th ed. Washington, D.C.: CQ Press, 2002.

Graber, Doris A., Denis McQuail, and Pippa Norris, eds. *The Politics of News: The News of Politics.* Washington, D.C.: CQ Press, 1998.

Grossman, Michael B., and Martha Joynt Kumar. *Portraying the President: The White House and the News Media.* Baltimore: Johns Hopkins University Press, 1981.

Hayden, Joseph M. *Covering Clinton: The President and the Press in the 1990s.* New York: Praeger, 2001.

Hertsgaard, Mark. *On Bended Knee: The Press and the Reagan Presidency.* New York: Farrar, Straus, Giroux, 1988.

Hess, Stephen. *The Washington Reporters.* Washington, D.C.: Brookings, 1981.

Isikoff, Michael. *Uncovering Clinton: A Reporter's Story.* New York: Crown, 1999.

Juergens, George. *News from the White House: The Presidential-Press Relationship in the Progressive Era.* Chicago: University of Chicago Press, 1981.

Kalb, Marvin. *One Scandalous Story: Clinton, Lewinsky, and Thirteen Days that Tarnished American Journalism.* New York: Free Press, 2001.

Kurtz, Howard. *Media Circus: The Trouble with America's Newspapers.* New York: Times Books, 1993.

———. *Spin Cycle: Inside the Clinton Propaganda Machine.* New York: Free Press, 1998.

Leonard, Thomas C. *The Power of the Press: The Birth of American Political Reporting.* New York: Oxford University Press, 1986.

Liebovich, Louis W. *The Press and the Modern Presidency: Myths and Mindsets from Kennedy to Clinton.* New York: Praeger, 1998.

Ludlow, Louis. *From Cornfield to Press Gallery.* Washington, D.C.: W. F. Roberts, 1924.

Maltese, John Anthony. *Spin Control: The White House Office of Communications and the Management of Presidential News.* Chapel Hill: University of North Carolina Press, 1994.

Marbut, F. B. *News from the Capital: The Story of Washington Reporting.* Carbondale: Southern Illinois University Press, 1971.

Pollard, James. *The Presidents and the Press.* New York: Macmillan, 1947.

Poore, Ben Perley. *Perley's Reminiscences of Sixty Years in the National Metropolis.* Vol. I. Philadelphia: Hubbard Brothers, 1886.

Powell, Jody. *The Other Side of the Story.* New York: Morrow, 1984.

Ritchie, Donald A. *Press Gallery: Congress and the Washington Correspondents.* Cambridge: Harvard University Press, 1991.

Rosenstiel, Tom. *The Beat Goes on: President Clinton's First Year with the Media.* New York: Twentieth Century Fund, 1994.

Rosten, Leo. *The Washington Correspondents.* New York: Harcourt, Brace, 1937.

Rubin, Richard. *Press, Party, and Presidency.* New York: Norton, 1981.

Salinger, Pierre. *P.S.: A Memoir.* New York: St. Martin's Press, 1995.

Shogun, Robert. *Bad News: Where the Press Goes Wrong in the Making of the President.* Chicago: Ivan R. Dee, 2002.

Speakes, Larry, with Robert Pack. *Speaking Out: The Reagan Presidency from Inside the White House.* New York: Scribner's, 1988.

Summers, Mark Whalgren. *The Press Gang: Newspapers and Politics, 1865–1878.* Chapel Hill: University of North Carolina Press, 1994.

Thomas, Helen. *Front Row at the White House: My Life and Times.* New York: Scribner's, 1999.

Thompson, Kenneth W. *Three Press Secretaries on the Presidency and the Press: Jody Powell, George Reedy, and Jerry terHorst.* Lanham, Md.: University Press of America, 1983.

chapter 19

The Presidency and Popular Culture

by Mary Stuckey and Greg M. Smith

There are few cultural icons as central as the president, few symbols that speak as loudly of "The United States" as do the symbols of that office.[1] When nightly newscasts seek to show an image of the American government, the one most likely to be chosen is that of the White House. Presidents are the individuals most able to interrupt regularly scheduled programming on any of the national media outlets. They are most likely to be the topic on the nation's talk radio shows on any given day, and about ten plays—three of them musicals, one a Pulitzer Prize winner[2]—and about 450 movies and television shows have been made concerning presidents.[3] There is no doubt that the occupant of the Oval Office is the single most recognizable and central person in American political life.

In addition, American presidents have significant power regarding popular culture. The executive branch, through the Federal Communications Commission and other executive branch departments and agencies, can influence national policy on copyright laws, broadcasting policies, trade policies, censorship, education policy, and other regulations governing communications in the United States and with other nations. In all of these areas, presidents exercise at least some power vis-á-vis popular culture.[4]

Presidents also have unmatched cultural power. Their hobbies can become national hobbies; their likes and dislikes can influence the behavior of the nation's citizens; their endorsement of causes can increase the attention paid to those causes and the donations they receive. Through their role of chief of state, presidents seek to amplify and exploit that cultural power, which they understand as contributing to their institutional power. Presidents do this by working hard to portray themselves as "common men," participants in the common popular culture. Examples of this include their penchant for watching televised team sports and inviting winning teams to the White House;[5] by appearing on popular television shows (Richard Nixon asked the actors to "sock it to" him on *Laugh-In*, Bill Clinton donned sunglasses and played his saxophone on the *Arsenio Hall Show*, and George W. Bush met with all of the winners from *American Idol*). In all of these cases, the president in question was positioning himself as a "regular guy," just another citizen.[6] As political scientist Bruce Miroff notes, "Much of what the modern presidency does, in fact, involves the projection of images whose purpose is to shape public understanding and gain popular support."[7]

Such positioning may help the president overcome the American cultural fear of power and of those who wield it.[8] While citizens are fascinated by power and the powerful, they are also leery of that power. The president is thus the locus of both approbation and a certain amount of dismay. Both of these are played out through the vehicle of popular culture.[9]

President Bush greets 2005 NASCAR Nextel Cup champion Tony Stewart on the South Lawn of the White House on January 24, 2006. Presidents regularly invite championship winning athletes to the White House to enhance their "common man" appeal.

Gov. Bill Clinton, sitting with the band, turns out an impressive version of "Heatrbreak Hotel" as Arsenio Hall gestures approvingly in the musical opening of "The Arsenio Hall Show" taping at Paramount Studios in Hollywood, June 3, 1992.

As John Street says, "Popular culture can . . . become a form of resistance. It can provide a form of defiance, a weapon with which to deny power."[10] Popular culture magnifies both presidents' virtues and their failures; it can thus serve as a sort of "fifth estate," working as an informal, unregulated, uneven, and often chaotic check on the power of the nation's chief executive.

DEFINING POPULAR CULTURE

"Popular culture" is not necessarily the same as "mass media," although mass media are the primary means of disseminating pop culture. Mass media[11] circulate images, words, sounds, ideas, and stories on television, movies, the Internet, computer games, radio, newspapers, books, magazines, and so on. The term "mass media" is defined by the channel that carries the content, not by the content itself. Although people talk about "television" or "film" as if they were coherent entities, the medium itself is a delivery system that can relay vastly different forms of culture.

Popular culture, on the other hand, is less defined by the medium that carries it and more by the way it circulates (or is intended to circulate). Popular culture is integrated into people's everyday lives. People receive it from mass media, and they use it for their own purposes. They talk about it at home and at the workplace, stick it on their bumpers, sing along with it on their iPods, circulate it to friends via e-mail, and wear it on their T-shirts. Popular culture is widely shared across a culture or subculture, but it is also intimately experienced: in American living rooms and cars, in a darkened theater, at the beauty salon. Popular culture is expressive of an individual's thoughts, preferences, and identity, but it tends to be seen as having minimal direct impact on the official culture. A bumper sticker can tell people how they should feel, but it does not count in the same way that a vote on election day does. Popular culture is generally seen as a fairly playful arena where the rules are less strict, where people can experiment with real world concepts without bearing the real life consequences of their actions.

Top-Down Popular Culture

An item (be it a television show or an action figure) can become popular culture through one of two processes. One is the process of actually producing an object that is intended to be integrated into people's everyday lives. Making a Halloween mask of a president or doing a satiric television comedy sketch are both examples of popular culture. The intent in production is for the object to circulate within the realm of popular culture. This differs from other forms of mass media, which may be intended for many people's eyes and ears without participating in everyday popular recirculation. The overt intent of a presidential press conference is to disseminate information (or at least to appear to do so) to the press and the populace. The policies announced in that conference may have great bearing on citizens' lives, and the conference may be seen by more people than a particular T-shirt, and yet the T-shirt is popular culture, while the press conference in all likelihood is not. A presidential press conference is intended to be an official pronouncement, one that is carried on mass media without becoming part of the fabric of people's continuing lived experience.

The "popular" in popular culture, therefore, is not a simple matter of counting people; instead, it has to do partly with the overt intent of production. Popular culture artifacts can be unsuccessful, failing to find a sizable market as a consumer item or as a cultural phenomenon. An object that fails to become popular in one era may find a second life in another. Although a particular comedy sketch may fail to provide the U.S. culture with memorable character or catchphrase or a particular presidential mask may end up on the bargain shelf after Halloween, these somewhat unpopular items nonetheless qualify as "popular culture" because they were intended to become popular.

Objects can be considered popular culture regardless of who produces them. A bumper sticker is intended to be integrated into people's lives, whether it is mass manufactured by the millions by a president's official campaign or cheaply produced by the hundreds by an underground organization. When people place "W" bumper stickers on their vehicles to demonstrate their support for George W. Bush's election, they are participating in popular culture, even though they are using an item created by a political party campaign. The same is true for people who place commercially produced "Voldemort (the evil wizard in the fictional *Harry Potter* book series) Votes Republican" stickers on their bumpers. A presidential library can sell presidential paper dolls and collections of presidential speeches; although both are packaged by an official arm of the federal government, the first is popular culture and the second is not. It does not matter who makes the object or how they create it; one way to distinguish popular culture is that it is made to be used by people for their own purposes.[12]

Bottom-Up Popular Culture

The other process for creating popular culture has less to do with its manufacture and more to do with its circulation. People can repurpose items that were not intended for popular circulation, thus making them popular culture in spite of the original intended use. The intended use may shape the way many people handle an object, but this intended purpose does not govern everyone's interaction with a piece of culture. The forces of popular culture are too playful to be so restricted. An official portrait of a president's face can be placed on another person's body for satiric purposes using photo doctoring software, or a clip from a presidential news conference can be repeated within a rapper's music video. In these instances, the impact of popular culture involves doing symbolic violence to the official original intent of the text. Using presidents' own words and images against them gives a satiric power to these pop culture texts.[13]

Popular culture, therefore, can be both "top down" and "bottom up." It can be created specifically for the purposes of popular recirculation, although not all such items succeed in finding widespread acceptance. It also can be formed by the efforts of "the people": individuals or grass-roots organizations who appropriate official symbols and pronouncements,

Actress Geena Davis takes questions during a presentation of ABC's new series Commander In Chief *at the Television Critic's Association 2005 Summer press tour in Beverly Hills, Calif., Wednesday, July 27, 2005. Davis depicted female president Mackenzie Allen in the series.*

turning them on their heads, placing them outside official contexts, relocating them into everyday situations.

VERSIONS OF THE PRESIDENT IN POPULAR CULTURE

When popular culture presents narratives about the presidency, it tends to present utopian or dystopian visions of the executive office. The utopian depiction is a gentler critique of the status quo, asking why can the real president not look more like this? Why can the American people not elect someone as intelligent as a Nobel Prize–winning economist, like Martin Sheen's Jed Bartlett of the television show *The West Wing* (1999–2006) who could solve the Middle East crisis? Why can the United States not have a noble, benevolent father figure like those presidents of the past, whose rise to greatness is depicted in hagiographic films such as director Henry King's *Wilson* (1944) or director John Ford's *Young Mister Lincoln* (1939) triumphing over or ignoring the criticisms that these real-life historical figures once faced? Why can the nation not elect a female president, such as Mackenzie Allen (Geena Davis) on the television show *Commander in Chief* (2005–2006), or a member of a minority race, such as David Palmer (Dennis Haysbert) of *24* (2001–) or Matt Santos (Jimmy Smits) of *The West Wing*? Or why can the U.S. president not be a man of forceful action like James Marshall (Harrison Ford) of the film *Air Force One* (1997), capable of fending off terrorists single-handedly?

The central figure in these utopian depictions is the heroic president. The distance between these visionary figures and the all-too-human actual occupant of the White House encourages the American people to envision a better alternative, although at the same time these larger-than-life figures exist in an impossibly utopian universe. It is much easier for a fictional president to defeat an enemy or create successful new policy initiatives than it is for a real-life executive to gain support for an unpopular war or forge a congressional coalition to pass a bill. The heroic president gives a particular shape to the desire for better government, one that operates within the expectations of popular narrative form, and owes more to Hollywood conventions than to the structure of the executive office.

Hollywood has conventions for presenting dystopian alternate futures as well, and so when presidents appear in such narratives, they allow U.S. citizens to see their worst fears about the possible excesses of the president's power. If the heroic president allows citizens to envision their dreams for the office, the villainous president shows their nightmares about the chief executive. Popular narrative has developed a formal language for making characters look menacing or devious or conniving. When those conventions are applied to the president, they depict a cautionary tale, a warning against trusting too much in the president. Such depictions illustrate that the power wielded for the people by the heroic president can also be used against the people by the villainous president. If the villainous president is defeated, then the ideological work of the narrative closure reassures the American public that the U.S. political system can withstand an evil individual in the seat of power. This comforting closure cannot entirely contain the frightening possibility that the narrative has raised: that an individual president can be far from the heroic figure people hope for at election time.

There are also other visions that have both dystopian and utopian elements, and in these, the president will often appear as a ridiculous character, relying on the president as fool. Kevin Kline's president in the movie *Dave* (1993) played something of a heroic incompetent (who was still more talented than the career politicians with whom he contended). *Dave* has utopian elements—as president the title character works determinedly for the national good—and dystopian ones—he is president only as sham and is surrounded by venal characters in Washington. In such portrayals, popular culture provides a leveling device—if people can laugh at a president, they do not need to be too much in awe of him. This is the president of late night comedy and, often, editorial page cartoons. Laughter is an important, if informal, check on political power.

In all of these cases, popular culture interacts with official political institutions in ways that support and promote the democratic system—whether the specific artifact presents the president as hero, villain, or fool, the effect is usually to offer an image of democracy that is worth preserving, and one that allows the system to be challenged from the inside without really being seriously threatened.

The Heroic President

For much of U.S. history, presidents were portrayed as heroes. From the time that Parson Weems penned the largely fictional hagiographic biography of George Washington giving the nation a president who never told a lie and who could throw a silver dollar across the Potomac River, Americans have been treated to laudatory depictions of their presidents. These depictions have led to what political scientist Thomas E. Cronin has called the "textbook presidency,"

or a reliance on an overly optimistic view of the president.[14] Some scholars argue that reliance on this model contributes to unrealistic expectations of the capacities of the presidency and the capabilities of individual presidents.[15]

Political scientists Richard Waterman, Robert Wright, and Gilbert St. Clair, for instance, have noted that three types of images dominate portrayals of presidents: the president as common man, as master politician, and as Washington outsider.[16] Each of these is associated with specific historical time periods, and each represents one way in which the American public as a culture has understood the heroic possibilities of the office—presidents have represented the American public in Washington (common man), have worked for the public within its confines (master politician), and have crusaded for the masses against its worst tendencies (Washington outsider). In all of these images, presidents are understood as worthy of support, either as part of government or as its antagonist.

There are numerous examples of this type of presidential portrayal, which comes in many forms. The iconic painting of Washington crossing the Delaware is one early example, as is the enormous statue in the Smithsonian, which portrays him as a Roman senator, complete with toga. Examples from film include the almost invisible but nonetheless magisterial president who listens to George M. Cohan unfold his life story in *Yankee Doodle Dandy* (1942). Such a president offers a picture of a removed, yet benign power. This set of images follows the depiction of Washington as "father of the country" and depends on a sort of paternalistic benevolence. Any time a president is presented as the most recent in a long line of presidents, this heroic model is implied.

Then there is the quietly moral president, the one who returns power to the people where it rightfully belongs, as in *Dave*, and the compassionate and caring, yet politically astute and policy savvy presidents of the Michael Douglas film *The American President* (1995) and the television series *The West Wing*. These presidents are less distant, more contemporary, and more likely to be welcomed into U.S. living rooms, but their benevolence—and often their paternalism—remains the same. These are presidents who look out for the American people, who protect them, sometimes from themselves. They are the presidents who speak to the "better angels of our nature."

Another version of the heroic president includes the aggressively protective president from *Air Force One* who commands the movie's villains to "get off my plane" before kicking one of them into oblivion, or the equally pugnacious chief executive, portrayed by Bill Pullman, who was instrumental in the defeat of aliens in the film *Independence Day* (1996). These presidents are heroic in the way that Hollywood often understands heroism and owe the least to any real understanding of how the office actually functions.

The cast of **The West Wing** *poses backstage after the show won best drama series at the 54th Annual Primetime Emmy Awards, on Sept. 22, 2002, in Los Angeles. From left: Martin Sheen, Rob Lowe, John Spencer, Stockard Channing, Richard Schiff, Bradley Whitford, Allison Janney, and Dule Hill.*

They are the most macho of heroic presidents, who exercise power through physical force rather than strategic acumen or moral suasion.

These heroic presidents are not just artifacts of motion pictures. The heroic presidency is memorialized in presidential museums, birthplaces, libraries, and commemorative coins and in locations such as Mount Rushmore and the Hall of Presidents at Disney World, where animatronic chief executives speak in turn on the achievements of their various administrations.[17] They are the presidents as the American people wish them to be: larger than life, able to see the public good clearly and to act decisively to protect it.

From time to time, the president is portrayed as an ancillary character, whose need to be protected and supported provides the foil for the narrative's hero—see, for instance, *In the Line of Fire* (1993) starring Clint Eastwood. On the one hand, this vulnerable president would seem to be problematic—witness the furor over the fictional death of the real President George W. Bush in the 2006 film *Death of a President*—but generally these presidents display bravery in the face of threat, and when the action centers around protecting them, the films encourage positive feelings toward the office and its occupant.

Communication professors Trevor Parry-Giles and Shawn Parry-Giles have proposed the term "presidentiality" to describe the "ideological rhetoric that helps shape and order the cultural meaning of the institution of the presidency." [18] They emphasize that multiple voices contribute to the public's understanding of what the presidency is, including the input of popular culture as well as more official voices. Although presidentiality is broadly defined as a concept that incorporates all forms of ideological rhetoric, their examples focus on the heroic president within the historical structure of the "romance narrative." The romance narrative emphasizes the struggle between larger-than-life heroes and villains, extending from Medieval dramas to today's action films, encompassing most of television drama. *The West Wing* presents a complicated portrait of the office, intermingling "postmodern" complexity of character with the simpler force of the romance narrative.

This is the presidency as presidents and their supporters want the public to see it. These presidents are seen as somehow more than human. They are smarter, and braver, and more moral than normal people. These are the presidents who represent the idealized nation and an idealized version of its most prominent national official. It is the presidency that actual presidents seek to portray in their role as chief of state, and it is the one most likely to lead people to admire the office and its occupant.

Indeed, this version of the presidency has clear civic functions, the most obvious of which is to encourage citizens to trust the presidency, and by implication, the government as well. American children are socialized in school to believe in a benign presidency, and to regard the institution with reverence and respect.[19] Through the depiction of the heroic presidency, this early learning is reinforced, and citizens are encouraged to maintain positive feelings toward the president.

This in turn contributes to the president's ability to aggrandize the powers of the office. For if citizens trust the president, and if they also trust the government, they are more likely to award both entities more power than would otherwise be the case. There is a tension here, because while faith in the president and in the political system is necessary to the survival of both, such faith can lead to unbalanced power among the branches of the federal government and to unrealistically high expectations. These problems can be partially mitigated by the corrective offered by the villainous and foolish presidencies.

The Villainous President

One corrective to an unrestrained view of the president as wise, noble, protective, and benign are depictions of its polar opposite, presenting the president as evil, manipulative, corrupt, and self-aggrandizing. During the early republic, for instance, villainy was portrayed as identical to monarchy, and villainous presidents were shown with crowns and other trappings of Old World rule. Such depictions present a picture of power as always and inevitably destructive of the public good. In popular culture narratives, these presidents are almost always found out and removed from office, thus vindicating the system as a whole, but casting doubt on the integrity of the individual president. More rarely, the president is shown as "getting away with it," and, potentially, this can have damaging consequences for the public understanding of the presidency and of the system in which it is embedded.

First, there is the villainous president who is caught in his (or her) villainy, and is removed from office. Examples of this include most narratives of Richard Nixon's presidency, some depictions of Lyndon B. Johnson, film portrayals such as *Absolute Power* (1997), and *Murder at 1600* (1997), and the evil president Charles Logan, who met his political downfall at the hands of hero Jack Bauer in the television show *24* (2001–). The fate of the television show *Prison Break's* (2005–) corrupt female president, Caroline Reynolds, who attained her office by conspiring in the murder of her predecessor, remained uncertain, but given the narrative arc of the story, it was not likely to end happily for her.

Actor Gregory Itzin speaks at a program called "24 and America's Image in Fighting Terrorism: Fact, Fiction or Does it Matter?" sponsored by the Heritage Foundation, June 23, 2006, in Washington, D.C.. Itzin plays President Charles Logan on the TV series **24**.

These narratives and depictions center on the president as an individual who abuses the considerable power of the office. Sometimes, the remedy is an extra-institutional force—the journalists Bob Woodward and Carl Bernstein (Robert Redford and Dustin Hoffman) of *All the President's Men* (1976), the cat burglar (Clint Eastwood) in *Absolute Power*—but more often the corrective is supplied from within the system, such as the police officer (Wesley Snipes) in *Murder at 1600*. Real presidents are threatened with impeachment (Nixon, for the Watergate scandal) or choose not to run for reelection because they assume they cannot be reelected (Johnson, who became consumed by Vietnam). In this way, the system is vindicated, either because the corrupt element was removed, and/or because it was removed through the natural operation of the system itself. The lesson is: if there is a problem with a president, it will be temporary, and any problem is with the individual not with the inherent nature of the office.

Second, there are villainous presidents who are not caught or killed, and who continue to wreak havoc on an innocent (or even a complicit) nation. Thus are the powerful portrayed in many spy novels and other, darker genres of literature and film. These depictions are rare because they are both angry and implausible. They may exist in small arenas and in pockets of the popular culture (such as bumper stickers that declared after George W. Bush's 2000 election that "Frodo Failed: Bush has the Ring"), but they are not likely to have wider influence.

Narratively speaking, presidents make particularly good villains, because their power is so all-encompassing, their resources so vast, and the scope of their concerns is so great. There are few political or economic pies in which presidents do not have the power to put their fingers. Fictional presidents have conspired with oil companies (*Prison Break*), with foreign interests (*JFK*), and with terrorists (*24*). Villainous presidents have been involved with sex and murder scandals (*Murder at 1600* and *Absolute Power*).

When illustrated in cartoons and the like, these presidents tend to be portrayed as large, if not overwhelming, with grossly exaggerated features. They may be seen as animals, or as looming presences. They are something more—

and something less—than human; they are thus not quite real. The dark fantasy of villainous presidents requires that presidents be somehow less upstanding than the rest of the citizenry; presidents are usually something of one-dimensional figures, representing the underbelly of the American dream.

It is quite rare to have depictions of president—especially real presidents—as wholly villainous, although some of the images of Nixon and Johnson come close. In part, this may reflect the widespread acceptance of presidential power, and of the pervasive belief in the office, if not in the individual who may hold it at any given time.

Depictions of the villainous president can serve as a useful corrective to the idea of the heroic presidency, because they promulgate the idea that the president is not immune to the temptations of power. Such depictions, therefore, can moderate expectations of the office to more realistic levels. On the other hand, however, these portrayals can also increase citizen mistrust of the government in general and of the president in particular. Because of their potential to foster ill feeling toward the president and the political system, these depictions tend to be confined to smaller pockets of the popular culture. Their potential to break through and become more widely accepted is important, however, for there is an implicit understanding that if presidents go too far in the exercise of power, that these images await and can be summoned and used against them if the images start to resonate widely.

Comedian Rich Little impersonates former president Richard Nixon as he receives the 1,765th star on the Hollywood Walk of Fame July 27, 1983.

The Foolish President

There is a long and important tradition of misrule, dating back to the monarchies of Europe. At specified times, the peasants were both allowed and encouraged to make fun of those who governed them, choosing for themselves a "King of Misrule" and temporarily overturning the hierarchies of power. These spectacles provided both amusement for the masses and functioned to release some of the resentment caused by those hierarchies. By sanctioning brief, hypothetical reversals of the political order, those in power hoped to prevent actual, permanent reversals in the form of revolutions.[20]

Both the traditions of carnival and misrule have long been part of the American political culture, and both have important political consequences. Carnival, now most frequently associated with Mardi Gras and New Orleans, once held an important place in American—and Old World—political culture. Associated with market days and the celebration of holidays, carnival provided the powerless with an

opportunity to engage in disruptive and often corrective behavior without fear of sanctions. Officials and magistrates could be mocked and the power of the state could be both questioned and, in the questioning, affirmed.[21]

Misrule functioned in much the same way, allowing colonists and their descendents to protect the social order through informal practices of the popular culture. Misrule dates back to peasant England and the tradition of allowing the locals to elect their own "lords" who would (briefly) "govern" in the actual lords' stead. Misrule occurs whenever a collection of the mass populace takes it upon itself to enforce an informal understanding of "proper" behavior against the rules of the state. The Boston Tea Party is probably the most famous example of misrule in the American colonies, as are other examples of social protest that allowed groups of citizens to enforce their will on the institutionalized authorities.

Aspects of both carnival and misrule appear in depictions of the president as fool. Whereas the villainous president is often depicted as larger than life, the president as fool is often small. In fact, one can almost measure the status of a contemporary president by his relative size as depicted in political cartoons. As Ronald Reagan gained in the polls on incumbent president Jimmy Carter, for instance, it was possible to chart the weakening stature of Carter as his cartoon likenesses visibly shrank until by the end of the campaign one cartoon showed him sitting in an Oval Office chair much too large for him—a visible statement that the job was too big for its occupant. Conversely, Reagan grew, while his shock of hair was tamed as his image transformed from candidate to a more presidential demeanor. Such exaggerations—of size, or of particularly distinctive characteristics (Carter's teeth, Reagan's hair, George H. W. Bush's glasses, Clinton's nose, George W. Bush's ears) are hallmarks of depictions of the president as fool. By exaggerating specific features, these depictions seek to cut the president down to size, to make him a figure of fun rather than of awe. It is one way of managing presidential power.

There is a long and distinguished history of political cartooning, which carries misrule in small ways into everyday life. Comic depictions of the president are a fact of life for inhabitants of the Oval Office. They may have seemed daring when Rich Little developed his impersonation of Richard Nixon, or when Chevy Chase famously portrayed Gerald Ford as both stumbling and bumbling, but such caricature is now almost routine.

Many presidents would be pleased if this lampooning ended with impersonations, but such is not the case. Jon Stewart, of Comedy's Central's *The Daily Show* (1996–), is especially famous as a professional gadfly, attracting both approbation (in the form of Emmy and Peabody Awards) and criticism (both from the White House and from news outlets such as Fox News).[22] At the 2006 annual meeting of the National Communication Association, for instance, a panel of academics "tried" Stewart in absentia during a panel called "The Wages of Cynicism: A Heresy Trial for Jon Stewart." The prosecution's case rested on the claim that he

Comedian Stephen Colbert arrives at a party following The White House Correspondents' Dinner on April 29, 2006. Though his biting comedic performance initially failed to attract mainstream media attention, it was widely discussed in the blogosphere.

was fostering cynicism and apathy among America's youth. The defense, on the other hand, argued that he advocated an engaged and an active polity. The jury is apparently still out.

The Internet is a particularly vibrant source of depictions for the president as fool, for of all forms of present-day mass media, it is the one most open to unregulated and uncontrolled input from ordinary citizens. Most blogs do not function within the standardized norms of professional journalism, and thus there is little to deter people from depicting the president as buffoon. Political jokes no longer circulate solely by word of mouth, but through e-mail. Satiric content produced by professionals can gain new life via the Web: political cartoons from online newspapers or uploaded video clips at sites such as YouTube and Google Video can be easily attached to emails. When mainstream news outlets paid little attention to Stephen Colbert's comic diatribe against George W. Bush at the White House Correspondents' Dinner in 2006, video of his performance reappeared online where it was heralded for its biting commentary.[23] Although the Internet tends not to "broadcast" in the quantities that mainstream television can, its relative ease of production and its relative lack of censoring bureaucracy can give it both qualities of immediacy and illicitness.

Portrayals of the foolish president, because they depend so heavily on contemporary humor, can be quite transient (Bush as Voldemort), or incredibly durable (the president as monarch). Also because of their dependence on humor, these depictions are considerably less stark than the ones of the villainous president, though there is some concern that foolish portrayals legitimate cynicism, thereby rendering politics a spectator sport and discouraging citizen participation.[24] Nonetheless, depictions of the foolish president provide some of the same corrective value as do the villainous presidents, fostering healthy skepticism about those in power and allowing for criticism of the government by the governed, but in ways that are less overtly jarring, and less obviously detrimental to the citizenry's overall faith in the system than images of the president as villain.

POPULAR CULTURE AS THE FIFTH ESTATE

Popular culture both reflects and refracts presidential power. Some scholars, like Thomas Langston, worry that the president's relationship with the American people is best understood as dysfunctional, that the images of the president and the presidency that are transmitted through popular culture encourage the American people "to be passive but insistent, hopeful yet despairing. As for the president, he is too often either a tragic or a sinister figure." [25] This ignores the possibility that popular culture is both the locus of the problem and a potential site for its corrective. As Lee Sigelman notes, popular fiction (and culture) should not be treated as a simple reflection of the real world but should be examined as ways of refracting that world through new perspectives:

> [F]or political and social theorists, the analytic appeal of popular fiction should not lie in objective accuracy (a quality for which writers of fiction are constitutionally ill suited), but rather in its ability to provide new contexts—beyond the theorists' own experience—for analyzing existing models of political and social phenomena or, in some instances, to provide new models in the form of imagined characters, situations, and words. [26]

Viewed in this way, popular culture is neither frivolous fluff that has little bearing on ways of thinking, nor is it a deceptive denigration of some objective political reality. Popular culture can serve a valuable function alongside more established political institutions.

The executive branch of the federal government exists within a constitutionally established system of checks and balances, with the legislative and judicial branches setting limits on presidential power. Although not explicitly part of the government, the press has historically also served as a check on executive power within civil society, having the ability to call attention to violations of the public trust and even to cause the downfall of a president (in Nixon's case). Most see the operation of the free press to be so vital to democracy that the institution of journalism is called the "fourth estate," whose established purpose is to monitor, investigate, and criticize the actions of more official estates of power. But popular culture also helps

in this critical function in a messier, less officially recognized manner that gives it particular advantages as a check on power, helping it to serve as a "fifth estate." *(See Chapter 18, The President and the News Media.)*

The practice of journalism is not bound so much by law (except for slander, libel, and so on) as much as it is by long-standing institutional norms. [27] There is no law requiring a reporter to check for a corroborating source before using information in a story, but journalistic training and editorial practice makes journalism a more careful and deliberate institution. It is rule-bound and dedicated (at least overtly) to goals of fairness and objectivity, and those goals and rules give the institution its credibility and limit its ability to make claims that are less than fully substantiated. [28] The fourth estate's institutional status depends on these restraints, working to ensure that the press's claims are taken seriously. [29]

The statements made by late night talk show hosts in comedy monologues are clearly not intended as "serious." They can insult the president or make unsubstantiated allegations without fear of legal consequences. This freedom means that the comedians' criticism of the president may range more broadly and make more outlandish assertions, but those assertions lack the gravity of the official charges of the press. What popular culture loses in official status, it makes up for in vigor and assertiveness. Although much popular culture does have an institutional, industrial basis, the norms of that institution are not as strongly binding as those in journalism.

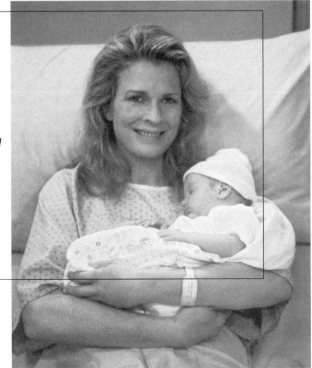

Actress Candice Bergen, in character as "Murphy Brown," cradles her newborn baby which the character delivered in May 1992. Vice President Dan Quayle attacked the character for having a child out of wedlock, but White House spokesman Marlin Fitzwater said the character displayed pro-life values for having the child after becoming pregnant by her ex-husband.

In fact, the lack of seriousness in popular culture is what allows it to consider criticisms that the fourth estate cannot. By refusing to be "serious," pop culture bypasses normal political radar, launching a rhetorical attack that may be more powerful because it is unclear how official channels can respond. In 1992, when Vice President Dan Quayle attacked the depiction of a single woman (played by actress Candice Bergen) intentionally giving birth to and raising a child out of wedlock on the television show *Murphy Brown* (1988–1998), he ventured into territory where he did not have the advantage of his institutional power. When a president or vice president takes a fictional character seriously or when they respond testily to a pop culture barb, they risk being seen as humorless or lowering themselves to the same level as a comedian (as opposed to interacting with other heads of state). Presidents can use popular culture for their own purposes to make them seem more like a "man of the people," but the messy charges levied by pop culture criticisms are difficult to answer without legitimating them.

The function of popular culture as a fifth estate acknowledges the limitations of the other institutions' criticisms. The American republic depends on governmental checks and balances and on journalistic monitoring, but these alone are inadequate to the task of limiting political excesses. The functioning of the republic requires a less rigid, more unruly critique that can humble the lofty. Because popular culture circulates within people's everyday lives, it reaches places that other mediated criticisms do not penetrate. As John Street noted, "Popular culture can function as an instrument of political change, not merely reflecting reform, but actually prompting it." [30] By voicing observations that are constrained by the ethical or professional standards of journalism, business, and government, pop culture's criticism ranges more widely and attacks more vigorously. In airing both the American people's utopian dreams and dystopian fears, popular culture frames the true limits of expectations for the real-life president.

★

NOTES

1. Thomas S. Langston, *With Reverence and Contempt: How Americans Think About Their President* (Baltimore: Johns Hopkins University Press, 1995), xii.

2. The musicals include *Of Thee I Sing*, by George Gershwin, the first musical to win the Pulitzer; *Let 'Em Eat Cake*, its sequel; and *I'd Rather Be Right*, by Rodgers and Hart. Other plays include Gore Vidal's *The Best Man*; *Sunrise at Campobello*, which was also made into a movie; *Abe Lincoln in Illinois*; and several more about Richard Nixon.

3. For a list of television episodes and movies, see the Internet Movie Data Base Web site at *www.imdb.com*.

4. John Street, *Politics and Popular Culture* (Philadelphia: Temple University Press, 1997), 6.

5. Michael David Hester, "America's #1 Fan: A Rhetorical Analysis of Presidential Sports Encomia and the Symbolic Power of Sports in the Articulation of Civil Religion in the United States" (Ph.D., diss. Georgia State University, Department of Communication, 2005).

6. Presidents have become so embedded in popular culture, in fact, that Shawn J. Parry-Giles and Trevor Parry-Giles have termed Clinton's presidency "hyperreal" in that his presidency was dominated and defined mediation by representation. See Shawn J. Parry-Giles and Trevor Parry-Giles, *Constructing Clinton: Hyperreality and Presidential Image-Making in Postmodern Politics* (New York: Peter Lang, 2002), 1.

7. Bruce Miroff, "The Presidency and the Public: Leadership as Spectacle," in *The Presidency and the Political System*, 6th ed., ed. Michael Nelson (Washington, D.C.: CQ Press, 2000), 301–324.

8. Langston, *With Reverence and Contempt*, 52.

9. See Bruce Miroff, "From 'Midcentury' to 'Fin-de-Siecle': The Exhaustion of the Presidential Image," *Rhetoric and Public Affairs* 1 (summer 1998): 185–199; Street, *Politics and Popular Culture*, 3. For discussion of the aesthetics of politics and how it may work through popular culture, see Murray Edelman, *From Art to Politics: How Artistic Creations Shape Political Conceptions* (Chicago: University of

Chicago Press, 1995), 91; Murray Edelman, *Constructing the Political Spectacle* (Chicago: University of Chicago Press, 1998).

10. Street, *Politics and Popular Culture*, 12.

11. "Mass media" here is akin to Dwight MacDonald's concept of "mass culture," except that (unlike MacDonald) we do not assume that the term is pejorative. See Dwight MacDonald, "A Theory of Mass Culture," in *Mass Culture: The Popular Arts in America*, ed. Bernard Rosenberg and David Manning White (New York: Free Press, 1957), 59–73.

12. This first component process of popular culture is grounded in Noël Carroll's discussion of "mass art." Carroll's definition concentrates on how mass art is intentionally designed to be accessible to the largest number of untutored audiences. Carroll's account deals with arts such as film and television, though he is not averse to expanding this definition to include a wider range of culture, as we do here. See Noël Carroll, *A Philosophy of Mass Art* (Oxford, England: Clarendon Press, 1998).

13. The second component process of popular culture owes much to John Fiske's definition, which emphasizes that popular culture is something that people do instead of something that the media make. See John Fiske, *Understanding Popular Culture* (Boston: Unwin Hyman, 1989). Our definition of popular culture blends Carroll's emphasis on production with Fiske's focus on recirculation.

14. Thomas Cronin, "Superman: Our Textbook President," *Washington Monthly*, October 1970, 47–54.

15. Ernest Giglio, *Here's Looking at You: Hollywood, Fun, and Politics*, 2d ed. (New York: Peter Lang, 2005), 133; Donnalyn Pompper, "*The West Wing*: White House Narratives That Journalists Cannot Tell," in *The West Wing: The American Presidency as Television Drama*, ed. Peter C. Rollins and John E. O'Connor (Syracuse, N.Y.: Syracuse University Press, 2003), 17–31.

16. Richard Waterman, Robert Wright, and Gilbert St. Clair, *The Image-Is-Everything Presidency* (Boulder: Westview Press, 1999).

17. Such portrayals are common among presidential scholars as well; see the discussion by Brice Miroff in "From 'Midcentury' to

'Fin-de-Siecle,' " 186; and by Michael Nelson who astutely analyzes the conceptions of presidents among scholars as "Savior," "Satan," and "Samson" in "Evaluating the Presidency," in *The Presidency and the Political System,* 6th ed., ed. Michael Nelson (Washington, D.C.: CQ Press, 2000), 3–28.

18. Trevor Parry-Giles and Shawn J. Parry-Giles, "*The West Wing*'s Prime-Time Presidentiality: Mimesis and Catharsis in a Postmodern Romance," *Quarterly Journal of Speech* 88 (May 2002): 209.

19. Fred I. Greenstein, "The Benevolent Leader: Children's Images of Political Authority," *American Political Science Review* 54 (1960): 934–943.

20. For a good discussion of this phenomenon, see Philip Deloria, *Playing Indian* (New Haven: Yale University Press, 1999).

21. Mikhail Bakhtin, *Rabelais and His World* (Bloomington: Indiana University Press, 1984).

22. For details, see the *Daily Show with Jon Stewart* official Web site at *www.comedycentral.com/shows/the_daily_show/index.jhtml.*

23. See *http://mediamatters.org/items/200605010005.*

24. Roderick P. Hart, *Seducing America: How Television Charms the Modern Voter* (Thousand Oaks, Calif.: Sage Publications, 1998).

25. Langston, *With Reverence and Contempt,* 9.

26. Lee Sigelman, "Taking Popular Fiction Seriously," in *Reading Political Stories: Representations of Politics in Novels and Pictures,* ed. Maureen Whitebrook (Lanham, Md.: Rowman and Littlefield, 1992), 160.

27. See Timothy E. Cook, *Governing with the News Media as a Political Institution* (Chicago: University of Chicago Press, 1998); Doris A. Graber, *Mass Media and American Politics,* 7th ed., (Washington, D.C.: CQ Press, 2005).

28. Shanto Iyengar, *Is Anyone Responsible? How Television Frames Political Issues* (Chicago: University of Chicago Press, 1991).

29. Danil C. Hallin, *We Keep America on Top of the World: Television Journalism and the Public Sphere* (New York: Routledge, 1994).

30. Street, *Politics and Popular Culture,* 28.

SELECTED BIBLIOGRAPHY

Buchanan, Bruce. *The Citizen's Presidency: Standards of Choice and Judgment.* Washington, D.C.: CQ Press, 1987.

Caretta, Vincent. *The Snarling Muse: Verbal and Visual Political Satire from Pope to Churchill.* Philadelphia: University of Philadelphia Press, 1983.

Carroll, Noël. *A Philosophy of Mass Art.* Oxford, England: Clarendon Press, 1998.

———. "The Power of Movies," *Daedalus* 114 (fall 1985): 79–103.

Castriota, David, ed. *Artistic Strategy and the Rhetoric of Power: Political Uses of Art from Antiquity to the Present.* Carbondale: Southern Illinois Press, 1986.

Christensen, Terry. *Reel Politics: American Political Movies from Birth of a Nation to Platoon.* New York: Basil Blackwell, 1987.

Combs, James. *Polpop: Politics and Popular Culture in America.* Bowling Green, Ohio: Bowling Green University Press, 1984.

Diamond, Edwin, and Robert A. Silverman *White House to Your House: Media and Politics in Virtual America.* Cambridge: MIT Press, 1995.

Edelman, Murray. *From Art to Politics: How Artistic Creations Shape Political Conceptions.* Chicago: University of Chicago Press, 1995.

———. *Constructing the Political Spectacle.* Chicago: University of Chicago Press, 1998.

Fiske, John. *Understanding Popular Culture.* Boston: Unwin Hyman, 1989.

Gianos, Phillip. *Politics and Politicians in American Film.* Westport, Conn.: Praeger, 1998.

Giglio, Ernest. *Here's Looking at You: Hollywood, Film, and Politics.* 2d ed. New York: Peter Lang, 2005.

Langston, Thomas S. *With Reverence and Contempt: How Americans Think About Their President.* Baltimore: Johns Hopkins University Press, 1995.

MacDonald, Dwight. "A Theory of Mass Culture," in *Mass Culture: The Popular Arts in America,* edited by Bernard Rosenberg and David Manning White, 59–73. New York: Free Press, 1957.

Miroff, Bruce. "From 'Midcentury' to 'Fin-de-Siecle': The Exhaustion of the Presidential Image," *Rhetoric and Public Affairs* 1 (summer) 1998: 185–199.

———. *Icons of Democracy: American Leaders as Heroes, Aristocrats, Dissenters, and Democrats.* Lawrence: University Press of Kansas, 2000.

———. "The Presidency and the Public: Leadership as Spectacle," in *The Presidency and the Political System,* 6th ed., edited by Michael Nelson, 301–324. Washington, D.C.: CQ Press, 2000.

Parry-Giles, Shawn J., and Trevor Parry-Giles. *Constructing Clinton: Hyperreality and Presidential Image-Making in Postmodern Politics.* New York: Peter Lang, 2002.

Parry-Giles, Trevor, and Shawn J. Parry-Giles. "*The West Wing*'s Prime-Time Presidentiality: Mimesis and Catharsis in a Postmodern Romance," *Quarterly Journal of Speech* 88 (May 2002): 209–227.

Rollins, Peter C., and John E. O'Connor, eds. *The West Wing: The American Presidency as Television Drama.* Syracuse, N.Y.: Syracuse University Press, 2003.

Sigelman, Lee. "Taking Popular Fiction Seriously," in *Reading Political Stories: Representations of Politics in Novels and Pictures,* edited by Maureen Whitebrook, 149–163. Lanham, Md.: Rowman and Littlefield, 1992.

Street, John. *Politics and Popular Culture.* Philadelphia: Temple University Press, 1997.

Waterman, Richard, Robert Wright, and Gilbert St. Clair. *The Image-Is-Everything Presidency.* Boulder: Westview Press, 1999.

Whitebrook, Maureen, ed. *Reading Political Stories: Representations of Politics in Novels and Pictures.* Lanham, Md.: Rowman and Littlefield, 1992.

chapter 20

Public Support and Opinion

by David A. Crockett, Charles C. Euchner, and Harold F. Bass Jr.

A republic is founded on the consent of the governed. Its legitimacy depends in part on the sense among citizens that government policies are responsive to the popular will. The Framers of the U.S. Constitution recognized that fact and were committed to constructing a government based on democratic principles. At the same time, however, the Framers recognized that several other objectives were essential for republican government to be successful. For example, it would do little good for government to be responsive to public opinion if the majority sought policies that violated the rights and liberties of others. Similarly, the Framers understood the importance of ensuring the security and stability of the new nation. The Framers also recognized that a government based on public support would be susceptible to the weaknesses of popular opinion, and so they hoped to construct a system in which the popular will was modified and refined through a deliberative process.[1] Thus, while the Framers adhered to the preference for republican government, they also understood the weaknesses that plagued republics.

The Framers constructed the separation of powers system in part to regulate these at times competing objectives, a regulation accomplished in part through such mechanisms as institutional structure, selection process, and term length. Congress is a plural institution designed to be responsive to the popular will in a way that employs the deliberative process to make policies conducive to the common good. Two-year terms in the House of Representatives make that legislative chamber the most responsive institution in the federal government, while six-year terms in the Senate provide what James Madison called "an anchor against popular fluctuations."[2] The Senate is, by design, less responsive to public opinion than the House. The federal court system is made up of panels of learned experts who enjoy job security, enabling them to make decisions presumably free from considerations of popularity. Thus, the federal judiciary is designed to be the least responsive of our institutions. The presidency is a unitary entity designed in part to respond energetically to threats to national security, to help set the national agenda, and to ensure the steady administration of the law. The four-year term of the office places it in an institutional context midway between the House and the Senate. Like the Senate, the presidency was designed to be a product of popular support, although that support is filtered through the mechanism of the electoral college.

Alexander Hamilton made it clear, however, that the term length gives the president the incentive, when facing popular opinion that runs contrary to the common good, to resist public pressure to give the people "time and opportunity for more cool and sedate reflection." According to this argument, the president at times should be willing to resist popular opinion rather than follow it. Hamilton was realistic, however, and understood that when a president faced reelection in the term's fourth year, "his confidence, and with it his firmness, would decline."[3] Thus, the Framers designed the presidency to be an office capable of resisting public opinion for the sake of the common good, while also recognizing that public opinion would still influence the chief executive, especially during election years. Since the time of the Framers, greater democratization, changing mores in campaigning and governance, and technological developments have made the role of public opinion more central to American politics, but the tension in the presidency between leading or resisting public opinion and following it remains.

Elections are the most obvious way that people register their support and voice their opinion. But elections are blunt instruments: they occur periodically, the issues in campaigns change, the positions of candidates and parties often are unclear, and the electorate's decision rarely sends an unambiguously clear message. The people also communicate with the government in other ways as well. They call, write, fax, or send electronic mail and telegrams to elected officials. They march in Washington to show their intensity and numbers. They express their views in letters to newspapers or calls to radio or television programs. They work through interest groups and political parties to make their views known. Most recently, they organize and mobilize through the use of Internet-based web-logs (or blogs).

Elected officials closely monitor the public's reaction to government policies. Officials even try to influence or manufacture public opinion in their favor. Public support is seen as a political resource, and presidents believe they can bolster their bargaining positions with Congress by referring to their high approval ratings in public opinion surveys. Likewise, presidents believe they can bolster institutional support for their policy initiatives by referring to public support for those initiatives. Even when it comes to such things as political bargaining, negotiations with foreign countries, interpretations of statutes, and administrative management, public opinion is rarely far from the president's consideration. Over time, therefore, an institution designed in part to resist public opinion, and to be sheltered from the vagaries of public support, has become more attuned to it.

Understanding the role of public opinion in the presidency requires first understanding the fundamental levels and sources of support for the presidency as an office and then determining how specific presidents work with that support. All presidents enjoy a basic reserve of support because of the public's near reverence for the office. But individual presidents experience complex, constantly changing levels of support for their programs and styles of leadership.

THE PRESIDENT'S RELATIONSHIP WITH THE PUBLIC

The American public has deep psychological bonds with all of its presidents. Those bonds may be strained by specific events and the conflicting interests of the population, but they are a foundation for the president's oscillating relationship with the public.[4]

Most schools teach Americans to respect the presidency, even when they find fault with a specific president on important issues. The media, economic enterprises, voluntary associations, cultural events, and even some religious institutions also promote a general respect for the office. This fundamental support for the presidency creates a basic reserve of popular support that occupants of the Oval Office can use in developing backing for their specific programs and actions.

The presidency is revered largely because the chief executive is the most visible single figure in American life. All but a tiny segment of the population knows who the president is at a given moment. In comparison, a 1995 national survey found that only 48 percent of the respondents knew the name of one of their two senators, 33 percent could name their House member, and 24 percent could name both of their senators. In fact, the U.S. president is well known throughout the world.[5]

The single most visible figure in American life, the president is covered by the media as both a personality and government official.

As the only government officials who represent the entire population, the president and the vice president are unique in American politics. Other elected officials have parochial outlooks. The Supreme Court has a national constituency, but its members are appointed, and its role in American politics is obscure and often limited to narrow legal argumentation. The president is the only person who can profess to speak for the "national interest" and the "general will" of the people. As commander in chief, the president projects this appearance to the rest of the world.

The prestige of the presidency is enhanced by the president's role as head of state as well as the top government official. Other nations, such as Great Britain and Japan, give symbolic functions to a queen or emperor and leave the job of governing to someone else. But the president is the embodiment of the state in the United States. Much of the emotional attachment that Americans have for the nation as a whole, therefore, also is transferred to the president.

On a more basic level, the first political figure that children learn about is the president. Children often perceive this figure to be a uniquely benevolent, intelligent, powerful, and even-handed person. Although people grow up to be more skeptical of specific presidents, they retain the early lesson that the presidency is a special, important, stabilizing office usually deserving of awe.[6] One of the first tests of presidential candidates is that of "looking presidential," and political actors use this generalized support for the office to generate specific support for the incumbent in times of scandal and during reelection campaigns. It is common for the president's backers in difficult times to ask for public support by referring to "the president" rather than the specific name of the president. For example, Richard Nixon's 1972 campaign slogan was "Reelect the President" rather than "Reelect Richard Nixon."

The childhood lesson that the president is benign and patriotic comes to the surface any time the nation faces a crisis. A military attack such as that on Pearl Harbor in 1941, a terrorist attack such as the September 11, 2001, assaults on U.S. soil, a technological challenge such as the *Sputnik* launch, or a sudden tragedy such as the assassination of John F. Kennedy caused the public to offer the president unquestioned, almost paternal loyalty for at least a short period.

Because the average citizen knows little about politics, he or she tends to identify with the president's personality as a shortcut to dealing with the complexities of the government. If citizens can develop "trust" in the president's personality, they can feel safe leaving the complexities of governing to the chief executive. Because the president is covered in the media as a personality as well as a government official, citizens are able to develop a vicarious relationship with the president.

On this subject, Murray Edelman, a leading student of the political uses of symbols and language, has written:

> Because it is apparently intolerable for men to admit the key role of accident, or ignorance, and of unplanned processes in their affairs, the leader serves a vital function by personifying or reifying the processes. As an individual, he can be blamed and given "responsibility" in a way that processes cannot. Incumbents of high public office therefore become objects of acclaim for the satisfied, scapegoats for the unsatisfied, and symbols of aspiration or of whatever is opposed.[7]

The public's emotional attachment to the president does not always work in the president's favor. Presidents who have complex or contradictory personas can confuse and even anger the public. According to scholar Garry Wills, President Bill Clinton's early drop in popularity stemmed from his frequent movement between the world of "dogpatch" Arkansas politics and culture and the sophisticated and calculating world of national politics. "He was as much at home with his mother, the Elvis groupie, as he was with his wife, the legal scholar. Not bad training for a politician— or so one would think. But onlookers can be puzzled by the blur of transitions as he takes them through time warps from one world to the other." [8] A president needs a consistent persona to exploit the national psychological yearning for a strong father figure.

As for their overall views of government and politics, Americans tend to be less ideological and more pragmatic than citizens of other countries. Surveys show that most Americans place themselves in the "moderate," or middle, part of the political spectrum.[9] They share common fears about big government, suspicion of elites, support for basic political rights, and the desire to assert American interests in foreign policy surely but quickly. America's cultural consensus, however, has frayed in the past generation. Since the late 1960s, sociologist James Davison Hunter writes, Americans have been engaged in bitter "culture wars" over the very meaning of the ideas and symbols, such as family, once central to a common national ethos.[10] These tensions have made presidential leadership more difficult. Presidents dare not stray too far from the national symbols, yet the meanings of the symbols are being increasingly contested.

FORMS OF PUBLIC EXPRESSION

In the years before public opinion polling became a regular part of politics and government, the measures of public support were rough and sporadic. This unscientific measurement of public support fit the desires of the Framers, who were wary of the pressures that public sentiments could have on government. The Constitution therefore contains limits to the influence of public opinion, such as indirect election of and lengthy terms for the president and Senate (before the Seventeenth Amendment), "checks and balances" among the branches of government, a divided legislature, an independent national judiciary appointed for life, and a federal system of national and state governments.

Institutions usually mediated public opinion in the nation's first century. As former corporate executive Chester Barnard has noted, to gauge public opinion nineteenth-century legislators "read the local newspapers, toured their districts, and talked with voters, received letters from the home state, and entertained delegations which claimed to speak for large and important blocks of voters." [11]

Polling dominates modern presidents' efforts to gauge public opinion, but the White House still pays attention to the more traditional means of assessing public opinion. These vehicles provide the much-needed "texture" for understanding the mood of the country that is not captured by polling data. Other vehicles for measuring opinion—such as blogs and the Internet—are fast becoming more important.[12]

Party and Other Organizations

Until World War II, state and local party organizations provided the most regular and reliable information on political attitudes. Party leaders were in touch with voters about issues ranging from trade to internal improvements.

Attitudes toward political matters were revealed by local party meetings, as well as by the outside efforts of reform organizations and petition drives. If an issue persisted, officials at higher levels often began to pay attention to it. Much of the reform impulse in national politics around the turn of the century came from the activities of parties and reform organizations in states and cities.

As states and localities passed reform legislation for the organization of city government and the regulation of business, national leaders began to shift their ways of doing business. Woodrow Wilson's legislative program was, for some, a response to the demands of reform organizations in the states. Franklin D. Roosevelt kept a regular watch on party organizations in cities such as New York, Chicago, Philadelphia, and Detroit.

Party organizations did not just offer a rough measurement of public opinion; parties also stabilized and developed the support of particular groups. Because party membership demanded some commitment, political figures could be more certain of their popular standing with active citizens. The rise of third parties in the prepolling years provided a dramatic demonstration of changes in public opinion. When the two major parties did not address developing political issues, new parties developed to give voice to those concerns. Public opinion found expression in third parties on issues such as slavery, immigration, agriculture policy, monetary policy, women's rights, and labor relations.

Interest groups and elected officials also have long been vehicles for transmitting opinion information to the president. The Kennedy administration kept a finger on the pulse of the civil rights movement through contacts with leaders of the NAACP (formerly the National Association for the Advancement of Colored People) and other organizations. Presidents regularly visit economic leaders in groups such as the U.S. Chamber of Commerce and the Business Roundtable, as well as social groups and the organizations of causes such as environmentalism and women's rights.

Public Demonstrations

Public events—demonstrations, parades, strikes, and riots—have provided the president and other government leaders with dramatic expressions of public opinion throughout U.S. history. Protests and demonstrations have taken on, among other issues, slavery, tariffs, women's rights, gay rights, ethnic and religious divisions, Prohibition, wars, abuses of monopolies, capital-labor disputes, agricultural problems, the death penalty, civil rights, welfare rights, school busing, abortion, education, and drug abuse. But with the development of more regular and "scientific" means of measuring public opinion, public events have declined in importance.

Despite the dominance in recent years of polls as expressions of public opinion, citizens have used demonstrations since the 1950s to express their opinions on civil rights, abortion, gay and women's rights, and involvement in war. People who either do not have the ballot or find the ballot to be an empty gesture tend to favor protest as a way of expressing their opinions. Political scientist Benjamin Ginsberg has found that nations with well-established voting procedures are not the scene of demonstrations when economic conditions change for the worse. But the citizens of nations with less reliable voting procedures, such as Latin American countries, must take to the streets to express their opinions.[13] These findings suggest that formal procedures for expressing opinion preclude the spontaneous development and expression of opinion.

A policeman stands guard along the inaugural parade route in Washington, D.C., on January 20, 2001, as a group of demonstrators protest George W. Bush's election. After a prolonged and bitterly contested presidential election that was ultimately decided by the Supreme Court, Bush was sworn in as the forty-third president of the United States.

Demonstrations continue to offer a gauge of the sentiments of selected groups. In 1982 one million people gathered in New York City's Central Park to protest against President Ronald Reagan's nuclear arms buildup and refusal to rule out U.S. initiation of nuclear conflict with the Soviet Union. The administration publicly dismissed the demonstration, the largest in American history, but understood its intensity. Reagan's political strategists attempted to put Reagan in situations where he could assuage the fears of people concerned about the danger of nuclear war.[14]

In the closing decade of the twentieth century, activists staged protests to express themselves, pro and con, on such things as abortion, the Persian Gulf War, and the admission of gays to the military. In October 1995 Nation of Islam leader Louis Farrakhan organized a "Million Man March" in Washington. African American men from all across the country came to the march and pledged to commit themselves to their families and their communities. Scandals associated with the Clinton presidency encouraged small groups of protesters to assemble wherever the president made a public appearance in the last three years of his second term.

In 2001 President George W. Bush's proclamation and prosecution of a war on terrorism met with broad public support. Nevertheless, a few protests and demonstrations were staged over perceived abuses of civil liberties and in support of pacifist principles. Before the invasion of Iraq in March 2003, however, the number and size of demonstrations protesting President Bush's policies rose considerably. More than 125,000 people opposing war gathered in New York City before the invasion, and similar demonstrations drawing out thousands of individuals have taken place in many cities, both in the United States and worldwide against the war in Iraq, especially during the anniversary month of the U.S. invasion. War protestor Cindy Sheehan made a name for herself in the summer of 2005 by launching a lengthy peace demonstration outside President Bush's ranch in Crawford, Texas. These latest examples of public demonstrations, however, highlight their uncertain effect on government policies. Antiwar protests did not prevent the invasion of Iraq, nor did they prompt the administration to change its policies. Public demonstrations are one expression of public opinion, but they do not necessarily affect presidential decision making.

Newspapers, Television, and Radio

Until the Civil War, newspapers were partisan sheets designed not so much to deliver news as to persuade or agitate a fiercely partisan audience. The fortunes of a newspaper provided a rough barometer of the public mood. Newspapers also indicated party strength because they depended on the parties for advertising and readership, and party strength provided clues about the popularity of presidents. Presidents also made use of partisan newspapers to communicate with the public.[15]

With the newspaper boom of the late nineteenth century, newspapers dropped their blatant partisan ties. Readership of the New York *World*, the nation's first mass-circulation newspaper, rose from 15,000 to 1.5 million between 1883 and 1898.[16] Because newspapers were cheap and geared toward the general public, they reached every class of people. Many cities had a dozen or more newspapers with distinct readerships. The news pages, letter columns, and advertising space all gave indications about the tenor and trend of popular opinion. Today, with daily newspaper readership in decline, news and opinion columns have become less reliable indicators of the public mood. Other media provide vehicles for gauging elite and mass opinion.

Since the 1980s, radio and television talk shows have become major forces in the creation and expression of political opinions. Programs featuring personalities such as Larry King, Rush Limbaugh, and humorist Al Franken offer running commentary with call-ins from listeners across the country. Callers to such programs tend to express intense viewpoints on issues. The radio hosts, in particular, feed into public passions with their strong rhetoric and exhortations to flood government offices in Washington with telephone calls, faxes, and electronic mail. Even when the shows do not take calls from listeners, their ratings-conscious hosts are savvy pulse-takers of their listeners.

The White House has attempted to tap into the passions of talk radio. President Clinton invited talk-show hosts to set up their broadcasting operations on the White House lawn during an early push for health care reform in 1994, and he appeared several times on the nationally syndicated *Imus in the Morning* radio program. In October 2006 George W. Bush hosted a similar gathering of radio talk-show hosts on the White House lawn to get out the administration's message for the upcoming congressional elections. Operatives and surrogates from both the Clinton and Bush administrations regularly appeared on the radio programs as guests to promote or defend White House policies and rally support.

Letter Writing

One of the most common forms of public expression is letter writing to the president and other public officials.[17] In the nation's early years, letter writing was a practice used mostly by economic and educational elites. As the nation expanded its notion of democracy, and as the government extended its reach during times of crisis, the letter-writing population grew to include not only elites but the whole literate public. Then, with the growth of mass communications, the letter became a regular tool of instantaneous public opinion pressure. The first major letter-writing campaign persuaded George Washington to seek a second term as president in 1792.

Like other forms of political activity, letter-writing booms during periods of national crisis. During periods of calm before the New Deal, the number of letters written per 10,000 literate adults ranged from 4.7 in 1900 during William McKinley's administration to 11.8 during Herbert C. Hoover's administration before the 1929 economic crash. The letter-writing rate increased during the crises of the Civil War (44 letters per 10,000 literate adults) and World War I (47). A major—and permanent—change came with the presidency of Franklin Roosevelt. Roosevelt's mail rate reached 160 during the Great Depression and fell to 111 during the relative calm of the late 1930s.

Headline events are most likely to spur letter writing. State of the Union addresses, presidential speeches on television, press conferences, congressional hearings, wars and other military events, major appointments, Supreme Court decisions, international summits or meetings, and political scandals spark mass letter writing. The top letter-writing events in recent decades included the Vietnam War, the Watergate scandal, the energy crisis, the proposed nomination of Robert H. Bork to the Supreme Court, crisis events in the Middle East and in the cold war with the Soviet Union, the Iran-contra affair, and various scandals associated with the Clinton presidency.

Many letter-writing campaigns are instigated by prominent officials during controversial political events. Sen. Joseph R. McCarthy of Wisconsin, for example, initiated a deluge of letters to President Dwight D. Eisenhower urging that the United States cut ties with countries doing business with the People's Republic of China. Members of Congress who regularly correspond with voters urge constituents to write letters to the president on key issues.

The president, too, sometimes calls for letters to the White House and to Congress to indicate support for presidential policies. Full-time White House staffers read and keep track of letters the president receives to determine the general flow of opinion. The flow of letters into the Clinton White House was so overwhelming that the administration recruited volunteers from the Washington area to process them. In the wake of the terrorist attacks and anthrax scares of 2001, however, most White House mail is now opened and screened at offsite facilities.

Interest groups have begun to play a more prominent role in spurring letter writing. National organizations and grass-roots organizations often circulate postcards and letters on specific issues for supporters to sign and send to the White House and Congress. Interest groups also print advertisements in newspapers urging a barrage of letters to elected officials. Interest groups with vast memberships are capable of managing letter-writing blitzkriegs to the president, to members of Congress, and to state officials. But those letters often rate only cursory consideration because the recipients can see that they are not spontaneous. They

do, however, reinforce the sense of vulnerability of some elected officials.

Although letter writing still influences public policy, this once intimate form of communication has become part of the larger process of technologically sophisticated politics, driven by advances in computers and telecommunications technologies.

E-mail and the Internet

In recent years, many citizens have begun to use electronic mail or e-mail to provide the president with their reactions to major policy initiatives. The incidence of this form of communication has increased dramatically as more and more Americans have access to computers and the Internet. Most computer network services also provide forums for members to speak out on major issues.[18] The Clinton administration, which received unprecedented numbers of letters, telephone calls, and other communications during its first year in office, assigned a full-time staffer to gather and analyze the e-mail messages to the president and vice president. Political offices now make regular use of e-mail, and citizens can contact public officials via the Internet. The White House Office of Public Liaison now regularly uses e-mail to keep in contact with administration supporters, and the national parties use e-mail extensively for fundraising and organizational purposes.

In addition to e-mail, political leaders and interest groups make use of Web sites to garner public attention. Just as partisan newspapers were once used to disseminate information to the party faithful and rally public support, now Web sites are becoming increasingly more important. All serious candidates make use of Web sites, and the White House itself employs the technology for a variety of purposes.[19] As more and more people have access to the Internet, both at home and at work, more and more people can be reached through this technology. In fact, there are times during the day, mostly during working hours, when the Internet audience greatly exceeds that of television. An important and influential Web site in recent years has been MoveOn.org, a site begun during 1998 to attack lawmakers who supported the impeachment of President Clinton. More than 100,000 people signed the Web-based petition the first week it was posted, a number that rose to 450,000 by the time the House of Representatives voted for impeachment.[20] Since impeachment, MoveOn has morphed into a genuine force in Democratic party politics, supporting candidates for public office and mobilizing people for political action.

Finally, the Internet is witnessing an explosion in the use of "blogs"—Web-based diaries and journals in which "bloggers" recount their views about contemporary issues. Many pundits and political leaders manage blogs, but they are also easily established by grass-roots activists. In fact, those who operate in these circles call this arena of public opinion "netroots." Bloggers now run their own conventions, which attract the attention of political leaders, who feel compelled to court these activists as they contemplate reelection bids or jumps into presidential politics.

It remains unclear what effect these virtual communities will have on politics. Certainly they helped Howard Dean become a viable presidential candidate due to his ability to raise money via the Internet in the run-up to the 2004 Democratic nomination battle, but Dean was unable to transform his Internet popularity into votes. Currently it appears that many Web sites and blogs tend toward the ideological extremes, making it unclear how reliable they are as mirrors of public opinion in general, rather than of those who are politically active. On the other hand, sixty-three million people made use of the Internet to access political information during the 2004 presidential campaign, a number that is sure to increase in future elections. Research shows that in 2004 forty-three million people discussed politics over e-mail, and thirteen million people used the technology to contribute money and organize volunteer efforts. As time passes, the ability of groups to raise money and garner attention and pressure political leaders seems to grow stronger, making it impossible for political leaders to ignore them.

Telephone Calls and Telegrams

For immediate reactions to political events, other than Internet-based venues, telephone calls and telegrams have augmented the increasing use of overnight polls.

Telegrams provide a tangible if biased indication of support. White House officials referred to the volume of positive telegrams they received to bolster their credibility during crises such as the Watergate scandal, Vietnam War, explosion of the space shuttle *Challenger,* and congressional hearings over the Reagan administration's secret dealings in the Iran-contra affair.

Vice-presidential candidate Richard Nixon survived a major crisis in 1952 when he appealed on television for telegrams expressing support for his continued candidacy. Nixon's "Checkers speech" produced, according to Nixon's own reckoning, between one million and two million telegrams and permitted him to stay on the Republican ticket despite the controversy over the propriety of a fund for his personal expenses.

During the Iran-contra investigation in 1987, White House officials and backers pointed to the thousands of telegrams sent to fired National Security Council aide Oliver North as a sign of public support. North brought bags of the telegrams to the congressional hearings, giving both himself and the White House a boost during the administration's greatest crisis.

Also during the Iran-contra affair, Reagan referred to the deluge of supportive telephone calls he had received. "After my speech, some 84 percent of those people who

called in supported me," Reagan said. "It was the biggest outpouring of calls they've ever had. The letters coming in are in my favor." [21]

The advent of more modern and virtually instantaneous forms of long-distance communication has rendered telegrams increasingly anachronistic. They persist, nevertheless, and they continue to have an effect on the recipients who, in turn, refer to them in subsequent efforts to shape public opinion.

FORMAL SURVEYS AND POLLING

Presidents and other political figures have used surveys since the early nineteenth century, but only since the development of sophisticated systems of communications and analysis have surveys and polls become a major part of White House efforts to measure and shape public opinion.

Polling data are often sketchy and contradictory, but they at least reduce the uncertainty under which the president operates. As President Reagan's pollster, Richard Wirthlin, suggested, polling is "the science of ABC—almost being certain." [22]

Early Polls

The first poll in the United States was a straw poll measuring support for presidential candidates John Quincy Adams and Andrew Jackson; it appeared in the *Harrisburg Pennsylvanian* in 1824. With the rise of mass-circulation newspapers in the 1880s, polls became regular features. Newspapers such as the *New York Herald Tribune, Los Angeles Times,* and *St. Louis Republic* all regularly published poll results. A 1936 survey of *Literary Digest* readers, which predicted that Alfred Landon would defeat Franklin Roosevelt for the presidency, both damaged polling's credibility and helped to pave the way for more sophisticated surveys. The *Digest's* huge mistake—Roosevelt won by a landslide—was attributed to the built-in bias of the polling sample, which consisted of the magazine's predominantly Republican, well-to-do readers.

The founder of modern polling was George Gallup, whose surveys helped his mother-in-law to win election as secretary of state in Iowa in 1932. Gallup wrote a doctoral thesis on sampling techniques and in 1935, with Elmo Roper and Archibald Crossley, founded the independent Gallup poll, which was the leader in scientific polling for decades. Gallup was a key figure in giving polling its scientific credentials by using large, representative sample sizes and carefully worded questions.

Franklin Roosevelt was the first president to use polling data regularly to interpret the public's reactions to the political and policy actions of the administration. As U.S. involvement in World War II became more likely in the late 1930s, Roosevelt received advice from Gallup on how to frame his rhetoric on possible U.S. involvement. Harry S. Truman in 1948 and Dwight Eisenhower in 1952 used polls to develop campaign appeals. With the availability of regular information about voter attitudes, elections and governing became more and more intertwined.

John F. Kennedy hired pollster Louis Harris two years before his successful 1960 presidential campaign to gauge support and develop strategy. After that, polls gradually developed into a daily part of government action and the flow of news and academic analysis. By 1962 virtually all gubernatorial candidates, two-thirds of all Senate candidates, and half the winning candidates for the House of Representatives were commissioning polls sometime during their campaigns.

Lyndon B. Johnson was the first president to hire a pollster for the White House staff. Throughout his term, Johnson kept a steady stream of polling data flowing into the White House from every state. Academics working at Johnson's presidential library in Austin, Texas, have found dozens of memorandums and poll results among Johnson's papers.

When faced with growing opposition to the Vietnam War, Johnson frequently referred to polls that suggested that a majority of Americans favored the administration's war policies. Johnson rejected arguments that most of the nation was uninformed and that those who were knowledgeable about the war opposed it. When polls showed a majority of Americans opposing the war effort, Johnson moved toward a decision against seeking a second full term in office.

Nixon's public relations campaigns were based on the notion of the "silent majority." These Americans, the president claimed, backed his administration's policies on Vietnam, civil rights, crime, regulation, social programs and budget priorities, and the Watergate affair. The lack of widespread opposition to his policies, Nixon argued, could be interpreted to be approval. Nixon's argument, in effect, gave as much weight to people with no strong feelings or knowledge as to those with well-informed, strong views.

Nixon regularly used polls to help formulate policy statements and to plan strategies for dealing with Congress and interest groups. When polls showed that he was personally popular with blue-collar workers, Nixon decided to ignore the opposition of labor union leadership on issues such as wage and price controls.

Current Public Opinion Efforts

Polls became pervasive in U.S. politics in the 1970s. In 1972 no newspapers conducted their own polls; they relied on private polling organizations. But by the end of the decade, most major news organizations were conducting regular surveys, which became an important part of determining which stories were "news." Today, dozens of newspapers and magazines, television and radio stations, government agencies, business firms, universities, and private organizations commission surveys of political and social attitudes and habits. Surveys are so pervasive that pollsters now ask survey questions about polling itself.[23] Polling also has become a daily part of White House operations. This practice began with the presidency of Jimmy Carter.

Carter's Use of Polls

Jimmy Carter became president with no Washington experience and an uncertain ideology; he therefore did not have a strong sense of his role in the government. His campaign was successful partly because of the work of Patrick Caddell, a pollster who was one of the top architects of the campaign agenda. Once in the White House, Carter regularly sought advice from Caddell, and polling data assumed a prominent role in presidential decision making.[24]

Perhaps the most significant moment of Carter's presidency was the nationally televised speech he delivered about the country's moral lassitude. During a gas shortage in the summer of 1979, Carter planned to deliver a speech to pro-

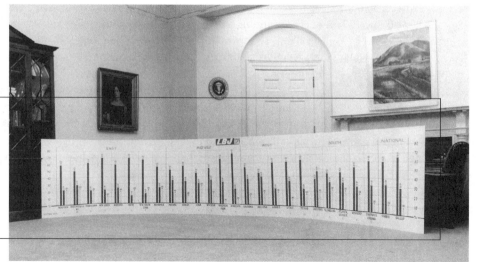

In a room across from the Oval Office, President Lyndon B. Johnson set up charts displaying his private polls before the 1964 election.

mote a variety of energy conservation and development initiatives. While working on the address, however, he decided that it would fail to move a public that already had heard four such presidential speeches. Caddell gave Carter polling data and a memorandum recommending a shift in emphasis. Carter's decision to act on the data was one of his presidency's fateful moments.

Caddell's data suggested that the public would react cynically to another call for energy conservation. The memorandum said that the public had become "completely inured" to warnings about the energy crisis and would not make sacrifices because of cynicism about both the government and the oil industry.[25] Caddell argued that the breakdown of faith in U.S. institutions could be overcome only with a dramatic call for common cause and sacrifice. Caddell had been making that argument to Carter at least since the 1976 campaign.[26]

Carter's speech—which analyzed the American public's "crisis of confidence" in its government—originally was well received. But then a series of cabinet firings, which Carter acknowledged handling "very poorly," created an atmosphere of crisis—not so much in the nation as in the administration.[27] The "malaise" speech, as it came to be known, became a source of ridicule rather than national unity.

Reagan's Use of Polls

Despite widespread criticism of Carter's reliance on polls, Reagan brought campaign pollster Richard B. Wirthlin with him to the White House in 1981. While consistently articulating the basic themes of small government and international power, Reagan developed his rhetoric and policy proposals based on data supplied by polls and focus groups. Annual funding from the Republican National Committee (RNC) of about $900,000 allowed Wirthlin's firm, Decision Making Information, to conduct the most extensive and expensive polls ever undertaken on behalf of a president.

Wirthlin's surveys and regular "tracking" polls—in which changes in a sample of opinion were followed daily—affected administration policy in several areas. Reagan's "honeymoon" poll results encouraged the president to seek dramatic tax and budget legislation in early 1981. Later data, as well as an outcry from legislative leaders and interest groups, persuaded Reagan to drop plans for wholesale changes in Social Security. Early in 1982 administration officials feared that the economic slump would lead to big midterm losses for congressional Republicans. Polling data showed widespread support for giving the administration's tax policies a chance, but they also revealed disturbing declines in support from blue-collar voters. When polls began to show a decline in the percentage of the public urging the administration to "continue as is," Reagan agreed to budget and tax compromises with Congress.[28] Polling data also guided administration actions on the nomination of

Sandra Day O'Connor to the Supreme Court, U.S. involvement in the Lebanese civil war, Reagan's visit to the Bitburg cemetery in West Germany, and tax reform.

Wirthlin's most extensive polling took place in early 1987, when the administration struggled to control the effects of disclosures that the White House had secretly sold arms to Iran in exchange for help in releasing American hostages in Lebanon and that profits from the sales went to help rebels fight the government of Nicaragua. During the first six or seven weeks of the year, Wirthlin conducted rounds of interviews with 25,000 people—more people than most pollsters interview in an entire year.[29]

Wirthlin's polling measured not only the public's attitudes toward issues, but also the public's emotional response to the president and his program. Wirthlin asked voters about how they felt toward President Reagan and his political rivals. When voters expressed doubts about the president's empathy and stability in international affairs, Wirthlin scripted public events and television advertisements that depicted Reagan as a person concerned about ordinary people's lives. The spots helped to strengthen the public's trust and emotional attachment to Reagan.

Polling in the George H. W. Bush Presidency

George H. W. Bush lacked Reagan's strong ideology, and he could not claim that his election was a mandate for particular policies. He therefore had to rely increasingly on survey data over the course of his term—he rarely used pollsters during his first year in office, however—to help him formulate his policy pronouncements and to demonstrate to Congress that these policies had public support. Because of his tenuous mandate, Bush needed concrete evidence of public support as an extra political resource. With high approval ratings, the president could tell Congress and other parts of the political establishment that "the people" supported White House initiatives.

After the first Persian Gulf War, President Bush may have paid too much attention to the polls, which showed his public approval ratings hovering near 90 percent. Bush and his advisers concluded that the American public was solidly behind the president, when in fact the polls represented a temporary surge of support. Because the president is the symbol of the nation as a whole, Bush benefited from the inclination of Americans to "rally 'round the flag" in a national emergency. But soon the nation turned its attention to other concerns, such as a slack economic recovery and a crisis in the health care system.

Bush's inability to develop a coherent domestic policy agenda has been attributed to his overreliance on polls. Bush reacted to public opinion on such things as the budget deficit, economic recession, civil rights, and the Los Angeles riots of 1992. His overreaction to some opinion surveys prompted him to expend valuable time and resources advocating constitutional amendments mandating a balanced budget and banning flag burning as a form of protest. The president, however, did not have an overall policy framework. Thus the public viewed his disconnected initiatives skeptically. Bush's reliance on survey data in his unsuccessful reelection campaign of 1992 reveals one of the main pitfalls of polling. Surveys underscored the importance of shoring up the conservative movement within the Republican Party, and Bush attempted to do just that during the party convention and fall campaign. Yet in the process he alienated his broader pool of potential voters, many of whom cast their ballots for Democrat Bill Clinton or independent H. Ross Perot.

Clinton: The Perils and Profits of a Poll-Driven Presidency

Bill Clinton devoted unprecedented presidential attention to the enterprise of polling. Far more than his predecessors, he understood and appreciated how to develop and interpret public opinion surveys. Clinton was singularly adept in framing and phrasing survey questions and astute in analyzing public responses.

Clinton won the presidency in 1992 with only 43 percent of the popular vote. Sensitive to the need to attract a broader base, Clinton used polls to figure out how to appeal to the independents who had voted for Texas billionaire Perot. But Clinton's desire to appeal to the broad electorate undermined his focus and resulted in the image of a waffling politician.

All recent presidents have arranged for their national party organizations to pay for polling that assists the White House. Thus the Democratic National Committee paid pollster Stanley Greenberg $1,986,410 for polling in Clinton's first year in the White House. Greenberg conducted several polls and focus groups each week for Clinton.

Clinton's aides denied that the president used polling data to guide basic decisions, but they admitted that polling was used to help package and sell the president's proposals. One adviser to the president said: "With Bill Clinton, you are working with someone who knows what he believes and wants to know better ways of describing those positions. We shouldn't change [policy positions], but we should help him communicate them. Stan does an excellent job testing and analyzing the different options for the messages." [30] In 1993 Clinton used polling data to package his budget deficit reduction proposal. Clinton described his plan as "5-3-1" at a press conference—$5 in budget cuts for every $3 in additional taxes on the wealthy and $1 in additional taxes on the middle

class—after surveys showed the formulation resonated with voters. [31]

Reliance on polling data, however, can provide a false sense of support. When they first announced their intention to overhaul the nation's health care system in 1993, President Clinton and First Lady Hillary Rodham Clinton appeared to enjoy the broad support of the public. But support for reform was "soft." When the blueprint for reform was delayed for months, Republican opponents and interest groups mounted a long-term campaign to cast the plan as dangerous "social engineering." By the time congressional allies had scheduled a vote, public support had dropped precipitously.

After the disastrous 1994 midterm elections, in which the Democrats lost control of both houses of Congress, Clinton increased his reliance on polling. He instituted a White House–based polling operation directed by his longtime political adviser Dick Morris. Poll data and analysis played a prominent role in successful Clinton White House efforts to counter Republican congressional initiatives and to position the president in the middle for his reelection effort. [32] This polling infrastructure remained intact, and Clinton's poll ratings remained strong for the rest of his presidency.

In Clinton's second term, polling data were crucial in framing the president's response to the allegations that he

Two months before he was sworn in as president, President-elect Bill Clinton solicited opinions from residents and business owners of a Washington, D.C., neighborhood.

had engaged in improper behavior with a White House intern, Monica Lewinsky. Although this scandal humiliated the president and ultimately resulted in his impeachment, he was fortified throughout by his strong, stable public support, and he survived this assault on his presidency. During his presidency, Clinton and his aides consistently claimed that polls were never used to set presidential policies; rather, they helped him to prioritize and present his policies in a fashion that facilitated public approval and support. They pointed to Clinton's persistent and largely successful promotion of initiatives such as the North American Free Trade Agreement (NAFTA) and intervention in Haiti and Kosovo, despite the lack of public support as evidenced in polls. The critics, however, decried his apparent reluctance to confront controversial domestic issues, such as reform of Social Security and Medicare, that might threaten his popularity.

President George W. Bush declares the end of major combat in Iraq as he speaks aboard the aircraft carrier U.S.S. *Abraham Lincoln, May 1, 2003.*

Thus the Clinton presidency illustrates both the appeals and perils of reliance on public opinion polls for presidential leadership. Through his masterful use of the polls, he was able to stay in touch daily with the public's attitudes and moods, which enabled him to elevate his level of public support and to sustain it in the face of political attack. Yet his perceived dependence on polls undermined the image of a strong, decisive leader that he sought to project.

George W. Bush: The Anti-Clinton?

In his campaign for the presidency, and in office, George W. Bush presented himself as the antithesis of Clinton in the use of polling. He professed disdain for "leaders" who appeared to test the winds of public opinion before taking positions and making decisions. Still, his aides and advisers enjoyed constant access to public opinion polls commissioned by the campaign, the Republican Party, and later the White House. Certainly, Bush was much more disengaged than Clinton from the polling operation, but polling has become an institution in the contemporary presidency.

One might have expected Bush to take close account of polls because of the exceptional narrowness of his election. Having lost the popular vote but won the office in a disputed recount ended by a controversial Supreme Court decision, it would be hard to imagine a scenario in which public expectations of the president could be lower. Indeed, a significant percentage of the population felt cheated by the election result. Despite these constraints, Bush chose to govern as though he had won a landslide victory. Although he had run a "compassionate conservative" campaign focused on being "a uniter, not a divider," once in office he pursued a

governing strategy concentrated on winning conservative policy victories through the narrow Republican majorities in Congress. After some initial success, Bush's poll numbers softened until the terrorist attacks of September 11, 2001. His decisive rhetoric and leadership after the attacks propelled his poll numbers to record highs. Bush took advantage of this opportunity to win passage of several antiterror and security measures, prosecute the war in Afghanistan, and campaign vigorously for Republicans in the 2002 midterm elections, defying history by leading his party to rare advances in Congress.

The critical public relations effort by the Bush administration during this time was its outreach to partisan supporters. While the 2001 terrorist attacks rallied broad support for the president, Bush's greatest support always came from his partisan base. Even before the attacks, 87 percent of Republicans approved of his job performance, with 71 percent strongly approving. At a similar time in Clinton's presidency, only 39 percent of Democrats strongly approved of his job performance. Republican support held steady long after Democratic approval waned as war in Iraq approached, with the gap between approval by Republicans of Bush and approval by Democrats of Bush reaching historic levels.[33] That partisan gap remained, making it imperative that Bush reach out to his ideological base in his 2004 reelection bid. In a closely divided electorate that held such divergent opinions of the president, the administration's campaign strategy focused on mobilizing its true believers. Closely divided opinion polls were less relevant than motivating Bush supporters to vote.

The Bush administration worked as hard as any previous presidency to make use of attractive images to garner public support. For example, Bush's May 2003 carrier landing at the end of the major combat phase of the war in Iraq presented the image of a strong and confidant military leader. Such tactics, however, reveal the danger of visuals, which have to appear to the public to cohere with reality. As the insurgency in Iraq developed, the "Mission Accomplished" banner prominently displayed on the aircraft carrier appeared to be a premature claim of victory. Similarly, news footage of Bush flying over hurricane-ravaged New Orleans in 2005 gave the impression of an aloof president not personally engaged in a crisis. Bush was successful in winning reelection partly because of the skillful mobilization of Republican voters, but as his second term progressed declining support from within his party led to lower approval numbers that seemed to threaten his political objectives.

FACTORS IN PRESIDENTIAL POPULARITY

Presidential popularity tends to decline throughout the four-year term in office, with short-term increases after important international events and at the beginning of a reelection campaign or at the end of the term. Since 1945, the Gallup poll has surveyed Americans about once a month to determine popular support for the president. The identical question—"Do you approve or disapprove of the way [the incumbent] is handling his job as president?"—has produced data that track presidents' relations with the public.

Between 1953 and 1969 presidents attracted the support of 75 percent of the public, with a standard deviation of 3.1 percentage points; the approval ratings of presidents serving between 1969 and 1984 was 59.7 percent, with a standard deviation of 8.6 percentage points. The overall mean was 62 percent in the early period and 48.1 percent in the later period.[34]

Most presidents enjoy a honeymoon period in which the nation gives the new chief executive broad, general support.[35] Indeed, for several presidents, public support has peaked at the outset of their tenures. After his third month in office, Truman received a rating of 87 percent; for the same period Kennedy received a rating of 83 percent. Lyndon Johnson had a rating of 80 percent after his second month, and Gerald R. Ford and Carter had early 71 percent ratings.[36] An administration's early days are considered by many the best time for a president to pass difficult legislation, such as Carter's energy program or Reagan's tax- and budget-cutting packages. However, the fact that an administration's early days are ideal for passing difficult legislation does not mean such legislation cannot be passed later on. Several studies demonstrate that significant legislation can be passed even in times of great conflict between Congress and the presidency, or when public support for the president is collapsing. The connection between public approval and achievement is not as clear as some think.[37]

Political scientist Samuel Kernell has argued that a president's popularity throughout the four-year term is partly determined by the results of previous polls.[38] Poll results do not vary much from month to month—mostly because only a small segment of the population is likely to veer very far from its orientations, but also because of the public's inertia and use of previous polls to judge the president. Presidents therefore have a strong base of support at the beginning of their term. The key question for the president is how quickly the support will decline.

Since the beginning of the Gallup survey, public approval of the president has ranged from a low of 14 percent for Carter to a high of 90 percent for George W. Bush.[39] The approval rating for Nixon during the final days of perhaps the greatest crisis of the modern presidency—the Watergate affair, which led to Nixon's resignation on August 8, 1974—was 24 percent.

The oscillation of support within an administration was greatest during the Truman presidency. Truman's support varied by as much as 64 percentage points, from a low of 23 percent to a high of 87 percent. Eisenhower had the most consistent support. In his first term, approval scores were almost always between 60 and 80 percent, and in his second term the scores largely ranged between 50 and 70 percent. With a much shorter tenure, and somewhat greater fluctuation, Kennedy had the smallest overall variation, from a high of 83 percent to a low of 56 percent.

Of the more recent presidents, George H. W. Bush experienced the greatest highs and lows. Bush's popularity fell 60 points in Gallup surveys from a high of 89 percent in March 1991 after the Persian Gulf War, to a low of 29 percent in late July 1992. Major events, such as the invasion of Panama and the Persian Gulf War, gave Bush increased support. Other developments, such as the stalemate with Congress over the budget and the controversy over White House chief of staff John Sununu, hurt the president.[40] Bush's approval ratings after the 1991 war in the Persian Gulf probably caused complacency in the White House. Advisers justified Bush's inattention to major domestic issues by pointing to his poll ratings. When his ratings fell, Bush struggled to define his goals and achievements. Bill Clinton's job approval ranged from a high of 73 percent to a low of 37 percent. Immediately following the terrorist attacks of September 11, George W. Bush's Gallup numbers soared to a record high of 90 percent. Controversy over the war in Iraq and the administration's response to Hurricane Katrina, however, dropped that number to a low of 31 percent by

April 2006, a drop of 59 points, almost as large as that experienced by Bush's father.

The average levels of support for presidents have varied widely. Kennedy received the highest average rate of support, 70 percent, during his shortened presidency. Other average levels of support were: Eisenhower, 65 percent; Johnson, 55 percent; Nixon, 49 percent; Ford, 47 percent; Carter, 45 percent; Reagan, 53 percent; George H. W. Bush, 61 percent; and Clinton, 55 percent. In his first term, George W. Bush averaged 62 percent, but his fifth year average dropped to 46 percent due to lingering problems in Iraq and the effect of Hurricane Katrina.[41] *(See Table 20-1.)*

Public orientations change between, as well as during, administrations. Political scientist Stephen Skowronek has argued that presidents live in "political time"—that is, they are forced to respond to the legacies and ideals of their predecessors. Reagan responded to the problems Carter faced by redefining the terms of political debate, inaugurating a new conservative era in American politics. George H. W. Bush promised to manage more effectively the system he inherited from Reagan rather than move in a new direction. After early missteps, Clinton shifted his policy agenda toward the center to adjust to a newly energized conservative Congress. Then, George W. Bush governed with an eye toward his conservative coalition, working to complete the "Reagan revolution" that started two decades earlier. Thus, to the extent that presidents are constrained by the larger political context that they inherit, they may have a limited ability to relate to and lead public opinion on their own terms.[42]

Patterns of Support

Studies by political scientists John E. Mueller and James A. Stimson suggest that public support of the president follows regular patterns, no matter who is president and what policies the president pursues. Mueller argues that the president's popularity declines steadily, virtually in a straight line, after the first several months in office.[43] Stimson points out that popularity ratings follow the form of a parabola, a curve that slowly declines before flattening out and then rising slightly late in the term.[44] Stimson writes: "The president, in this theory, is largely a passive observer of his downsliding popularity."[45]

Both Mueller and Stimson agree that the trend is interrupted—but only temporarily—by "rally points" such as U.S. military involvement overseas, the release of favorable economic news, assassination attempts, and campaign activities. Such events can give a president a spurt of approval. But even if a president benefits from public attention to highly visible news, the basic trend of decline is immutable.[46] According to Mueller, after an average approval rating of 69 percent early in the term, the president's rating will fall about six percentage points each year. Because of a "coalition of minorities" effect—in which groups aggrieved by administration policies

TABLE 20-1   **Overall Presidential Approval Ratings, 1953–2005 (percent)**

	Average	High	Low
Kennedy (1961–1963)	70	83	56
Eisenhower (1953–1961)	65	79	48
G. W. Bush (2001–2005)	62	90	31
G. H. W. Bush (1989–1993)	61	89	29
Clinton (1993–2001)	55	73	37
L. Johnson (1963–1969)	55	79	35
Reagan (1981–1989)	53	65	35
Nixon (1969–1974)	49	67	24
Ford (1974–1977)	47	71	37
Carter (1977–1981)	45	74	28

SOURCE: Gallup Organization, "Poll Topics and Trends, Presidential Ratings—Job Approval" (www.gallup.com).

slowly but steadily build an antiadministration coalition—presidential popularity ratings steadily decline.

Stimson and Mueller disagree, however, about the dynamic aspects of public opinion. A president's popularity at a given point cannot be considered an isolated judgment of the president, Stimson argues. Instead, one month's approval rating feeds into and influences the next. Rather than simply reflecting the accumulation of grievances, as Mueller argues, the decline in popularity results from the public's changing psychological relationship with the president. Early in the term, the president benefits from a sense of excitement and promise. As the term progresses, the president not only disappoints different parts of the public, but also develops an overall persona that many people come to dislike. The popularity decline, in other words, is greater than the sum of the disappointments.

Although the public usually pays little attention to politics and does not know much about presidents, from the media excitement and soaring rhetoric accompanying a new administration the public develops high expectations of the new president. The two factors—inattentiveness and high expectations—are a dangerous combination for presidents. As political scientist Thomas E. Cronin has observed,

> The significance of the textbook presidency is that the whole is greater than the sum of the parts. It presents a cumulative presidential image, a legacy of past glories and impressive performances ... which endows the White House with a singular mystique and almost magical qualities. According to this image ... only men of the caliber of Lincoln, the Roosevelts, or Wilson can seize the chalice of opportunity, create the vision, and rally the American public around that vision.[47]

The public, in effect, wants the president to lead them to the Promised Land, but it does not appreciate the rockiness of the terrain.

The public's response, Stimson points out, is not just a steady decline of support but a deep disappointment, reflected in the fast decline of support. The decline then bottoms out and rises slightly at the end of the term, both because of the public's desire to correct its overreaction and because of the president's return to more simplistic rhetoric as the reelection campaign approaches. A study by political scientists Paul Brace and Barbara Hinckley found the same pattern of decline followed by resurgence.[48]

President Reagan's first-term surge in popularity was unusual. After first- and second-year approval ratings similar to Carter's and Nixon's, Reagan's support surged in his third and fourth years. A January 1983 poll put Reagan's popularity at 35 percent; by his second inauguration it was almost 62 percent. Scholars attributed the surge to favorable economic trends, such as lower inflation and interest rates, and to adept use of public events to rally the nation around the president's leadership. Another cause might have been the nation's desire for a leader in whom it could place faith. After the assassination of President Kennedy and the failed presidencies of Johnson, Nixon, Ford, and Carter, the public may have decided to believe in Reagan's leadership just to give the nation the stability it had lacked since the 1950s. Reagan's ability to redefine the public debate in response to these earlier perceived failed presidencies demonstrated an astute understanding of historical context.

Job approval ratings during Clinton's first term reflected this anticipated pattern of decline and resurgence. Missteps in the opening months of his administration resulted in a dramatic decline, from 58 percent at the outset to 37 percent in early June 1993. By the end of his first year, he had regained his footing, elevating his support well above 50 percent. In 1994 he experienced a gradual descent that again dropped him below 40 percent for a brief time and culminated in a disastrous showing for his party in the midterm congressional elections. From that low point, his support steadily increased during the last two years of his term, reflecting an improving economy, his centrist policy orientations, and public disenchantment with his Republican rivals now in control of Congress. By the fall of 1996 he had reached a high of 60 percent support, leaving him about where he had been at his inauguration and signaling a comfortable reelection victory.

In his first year in office, George W. Bush experienced a noteworthy variation on this pattern. He saw his approval ratings gradually decline from 57 percent in January to 51 percent in early September. At that point, the terrorist attacks on the United States and his forceful, immediate response sent his popularity rising to unprecedented heights.[49] Although Bush's popularity remained at an exceptionally high level for an unusually long period of time, the normal pattern of decline began. Because his popularity reached such a high point, and the decline was slow and gradual, Bush helped his party to defy the historical pattern in the 2002 midterm elections. By the time of his reelection

bid in 2004, however, Bush's popularity had declined to the point that the presidential race was uncommonly tight, and the decline continued as his second term began.

Brace and Hinckley contend that presidents tend to lose support in greater and greater increments through the first thirty months of their presidencies, at which point approval ratings begin to climb. Presidents and their supporters then take steps to boost popularity in anticipation of the reelection campaign. If a president is reelected, the inauguration period is marked by even greater popularity, but it diminishes quickly in the new term.[50]

According to Brace and Hinckley, four main types of events affect presidential popularity. *Positive acts* are events that a president can control and that produce gains in popularity, such as foreign policy initiatives and announcements of aid to groups and regions. *Hard choices* are events that the president can control but that can produce declines in popularity, such as budget cutbacks or controversial domestic policy initiatives. *Good luck* and *bad luck* refer to events beyond the president's control, such as changes in the world economy, that produce positive and negative effects on public support. In recent history, nondiscretionary events—ones the president cannot control—have outnumbered discretionary events by a ratio of almost two to one. Among these, negative events outnumber positive events.

Presidents often respond to "bad luck" events by taking actions on other issues where they can exert greater control. Reagan's reactions to negative events was a case study in using the office's control over some policies to neutralize the negative effects of others. Brace and Hinckley discovered that

> Reagan showed a more reactive pattern [than Eisenhower and Nixon] in his second term. Action in the Persian Gulf occurred within the same month as the beginning of the Iran-contra hearings in May 1987. In June, as the hearings on the scandal continued, the reflagging of Kuwaiti tankers began. In April 1988, as the Edwin Meese scandal led to an investigation of the Justice Department, the Marines entered Panama. Reagan's polls fell somewhat during this period, but they remained remarkably stable given the barrage of negative events.[51]

Second-term presidents are generally less popular than first-term presidents. Eisenhower, Johnson, Nixon, Reagan, and G. W. Bush all had lower support scores after their second inaugurations. Johnson and Nixon were driven from the White House at least partly by depressed opinion scores.[52] Reagan's second term was marred by the Iran-contra scandal, an uncertain domestic agenda, and splits within the ranks of the Republican Party.

The second-term decline has several explanations. First, the president is a "lame duck," without the prospect of a bold reelection campaign to inspire supporters. The public, Congress, and key bureaucrats expect to be involved in national politics after the president's departure, which makes the president's position on long-term issues less and less relevant. Second, problems are more difficult to explain away with reference to the mistakes of the previous president. Reagan constantly referred to the "mess" left him by Carter, but the public was less willing to blame Carter the longer Reagan was in office. Third, the best members of the administration often leave office soon after the president's reelection, creating the aura of a provisional and "second-string" team less deserving of respect. The president also loses top political operatives as they go to work for other politicians who will be involved in public life after the president leaves office. Finally, other politicians, who want to develop an independent base and perhaps succeed the president, try to develop their own political messages distinct from that of the president, reducing the reinforcement that the president's message receives.

Bill Clinton was a conspicuous exception to the general expectation that presidential support declines in the second term. To the contrary, his support clearly increased. He averaged 50 percent job approval during his first term, which rose to an average of 61 percent over his second term. His job approval rating throughout his second term showed remarkable stability, never dipping below 55 percent while rising no higher than 73 percent. This consistently high public support was all the more remarkable in that it accompanied revelations of scandalous personal behavior on his part that led to his impeachment and a Senate trial that ended in his acquittal. Throughout the course of these tumultuous developments, the public differentiated between its evaluation of Clinton as a person and Clinton as a president, rating him much higher in the latter role. His public support can be attributed to a booming economy, foreign policy successes, his capacity to demonstrate empathy for the needs and interests of the American people, his success in casting his political adversaries in a negative light, and his nimbleness in adjusting his policy agenda in a more centrist direction.

Patterns of support also have their partisan aspects. Public approval seems to work differently for Republican and Democratic presidents. Because of their more diverse constituencies, and a lower level of loyalty from their own party followers, Democratic presidents suffer greater declines in popularity than do Republican presidents. The key groups in Democratic coalitions—nonwhites, Jews, easterners, manual laborers, and union families—sometimes disagree with each other on major issues. The Republican coalitions—whites, Protestants, midwesterners, westerners, and southerners—usually share basic values and so are less likely to be critical of their own presidents than the more diverse Democrats of their top officeholders. For example, Johnson lost 34 percentage points in approval ratings among Democrats between June 1965 and August 1968, and Carter lost 38 points between March 1977 and April 1980. By contrast, Republicans Nixon and Reagan did not lose significant support within their own party until scandals developed in their second terms. Even then, Reagan rallied at the end of his term.[53]

George H. W. Bush and Bill Clinton were exceptions to this general rule. Bush lost support among all segments of the population—Republicans, Democrats, and independents—between the elections of 1988 and 1992, when his support among Republican voters fell from 91 to 73 percent; his share among Democrats fell from 17 to 10 percent, and his support from independents fell from 55 to 32 percent.[54] Independent Perot's visibility in the last year of Bush's presidency played a major part in the declines. Bush's uncertain political agenda, especially after the Persian Gulf War, also contributed. Still, Bush's Republican drop-off in support was smaller than the typical Democratic drop-off.

Clinton, by contrast, became increasingly popular among Democratic partisans as his presidency progressed, with his job approval rating rising from 70 percent approval in 1993 to 90 percent approval in 2000.[55] Clinton won the 1992 Democratic nomination and the ensuing general election campaigning as a "New Democrat" who was seeking to move the party to the center. As such, he was viewed with suspicion by some traditional party constituencies on the ideological left. In office, he continued to promote centrist policies, but he successfully cultivated the more liberal elements of the party. In particular, African Americans rallied to his cause. Meanwhile, Clinton was able to turn the rising tide of Republicanism in Congress to his advantage within his own party. He presented himself as the indispensable obstacle standing in the way of Republican control of the entire government. In addition, Clinton benefited among Democrats from the perception that ideological extremists on the right were bent on his personal destruction, and fellow partisans rallied to his defense. *(See Table 17-7, p. 922.)*

George W. Bush enjoyed consistently strong support from Republican partisans throughout his first term in office. The 2001 terrorist attacks caused his support among Republicans to jump from 83 percent to 96 percent. The reason for his exceptionally high popularity among the population as a whole following the attacks is that support among Democrats jumped from 28 percent to 81 percent. Over time, however, while Republican support remained strong, Democratic support declined, returning to 35 percent within a year, and dropping lower after that.[56] Controversies over the war in Iraq and the administration's handling of Hurricane Katrina, as well as partisan divisions over immigration, caused Bush's support among Republicans to decline in his second term, leading to lower overall public support.

Steadiness during the Cycles

Throughout the cycles of presidential approval, some groups within the public consistently support or oppose the president, while "swing" groups fluctuate greatly and cause the ups and downs of presidential approval. Segments of the population react to public events according to their education, income, gender, and political involvement.

The president usually can depend on support from "partisans," citizens who are members of the same party, and opposition from members of the opposing party. The groups expressing support for the Vietnam War switched with Republican Nixon's move into the White House and Johnson's move out—that is, Republicans generally opposed the war under Johnson but supported it under Nixon. Unless presidents deeply offend the basic tenets of their party, they usually can count on party identifiers for support. Many of those people actually will be registered with the party, and others will just "lean" toward the party—and rely on the party for cues—on most issues.

Besides these "partisans," the president also must deal with a set of "believers," a small minority of the population with fully developed ideological stances on a wide range of economic, social, and political issues. Believers are committed to a cause, such as the security of Israel or free-market values. They also have "psychological predispositions" on issues ranging from military activity to community values. Presidents can count on consistent behavior by believers, just as they can count on consistent behavior by partisans. But the consistency depends on the issue rather than the party affiliation.

Another group—the "followers"—is willing to follow the president's lead on a wide range of issues, especially foreign affairs, simply because the president is the president. This group often associates its support for the president with patriotism—a "my president, right or wrong" attitude.[57]

The battle for public opinion, then, centers on the opinions of the less aligned, more independent citizens. Among the best-educated and involved elements of the citizenry, those who identify with a party rely on partisan cues in assessing the president. Independents, by contrast, react to shifting news events without the anchoring effects of partisanship. If they know that a president is struggling with Congress, they may lower their opinions of that person because of the conflict. If they see the president take a strong stand on an issue, they may raise their opinions of the office-holder.[58] In addition, changes in presidential evaluations tend to occur most rapidly among the best-educated citizens and those who are most attentive to news events. Those with less education and involvement do not closely follow political news and so are less able to react to changing political fortunes.

Why Support Declines

No matter which model best depicts the trends of approval, it is clear that presidential approval usually declines throughout a term of office. There are several explanations for the decline:

- Inevitable disappointment after high expectations. Presidential campaigns are exercises in popular education and excitement. As the nation prepares to select its next leader, the candidates attempt to depict the positive changes that would occur in their administrations as dramatically as possible.[59]

The public—usually inattentive to politics—gradually gets to know prospective presidents and develops personal attachments to the personalities of the leading contenders. As the media explore the candidates' personal backgrounds, voters get an intimate view of the persons who might lead the next government.

When the president takes office, the public has unrealistic expectations of what might be accomplished. Thus when people begin to see the president's weaknesses, they view the president less and less favorably. Even when the public supports the president's stances and policies on specific issues, it might be critical of the administration's inability to achieve all that was promised. And even when the president is able to deliver on a specific program, support among certain groups may decline because the program yields less impressive results than were expected.

Political scientist Jeffrey K. Tulis describes this phenomenon as an expectations gap between presidential power and performance, one that actually is exacerbated by the tendency of modern presidents to court public opinion and be responsive to it. Presidents try to please their popular audiences by promising more, under the assumption that high public approval will lead to policy success. Unfortunately for presidents, their efforts run straight into all of the institutional constraints of the constitutional checks and balances system. The strategy of "going public" by appealing to the people is often unsuccessful, presidential performance rarely matches the public's raised expectations, and the result is declining approval.[60]

- Accumulation of grievances. When taking the oath of office for the first time, the president has not yet damaged the material fortunes of any segment of society. Even the most skeptical observers—such as business leaders under a Democratic administration or labor leaders under a Republican administration—are willing to suspend judgment of the new president.

As the president submits federal budgets, adopts legislative programs, and uses the "bully pulpit" to promote various social causes, different groups develop specific grievances with the administration. Any public policy decision helps some groups at the expense of others. Even defense and economic policies—which, the president argues, benefit all members of society—have clear winners and losers. High levels of military spending helps out defense contractors and towns where bases are located but undermines other programs facing severe funding restrictions in the budget.

As the president builds a record, some groups develop into consistent winners and others into consistent losers. The greater the number of policy areas affected by White House involvement, the greater is the number of groups affected negatively by policy decisions. Even if a group receives some benefits as well as losses because of the administration's policies, the group's support for the president likely will decline because of unhappiness with the losses. The result of the accumulation of grievances—or the "coalition of minorities effect"—is that groups dissatisfied with government policy are more likely to organize than groups satisfied with the government.[61]

Political scientist Richard A. Brody has linked presidential popularity to the amount of "good" and "bad" news the public receives in the media. Brody's model posits that the public keeps a running score of the news about politics and the economy and rewards presidents who have presided over periods full of good news—regardless of their role in creating that news.[62]

- Manipulation of the political calendar for electoral advantage. When first taking office, the president has one overriding goal: to create the best possible circumstances for a reelection campaign four years later. Secondary goals include passage of important policies and improvement of the president's party strength in Congress and state governments.

These goals demand different kinds of presidential popularity at different points in the nation's electoral cycles. The president will try to time the administration's policies and pronouncements to produce the support necessary for the crucial electoral and policy-making decisions. Most presidents, for example, are willing to see their popularity decline after the first year in office. The first year is usually the best time for achieving budgetary and other legislative goals, which require high levels of popularity. After a couple of years of lower levels of support—during which the White House might pursue policy goals through executive action and more modest or bipartisan legislative action—the president seeks to boost public support in time for the reelection campaign.

- Persistent problems. Major national problems—many of which, when first exposed publicly, gain the president broad support—can develop into liabilities for the president if they are not resolved quickly.

When they first came to the public's attention, the Korean War, Vietnam War, Watergate scandal, Iran hostage crisis, and the second Gulf War all gained the president in office at the time broad public support. But after those problems remained unsolved for one or more years, the public became disenchanted and public support declined.

President Carter's experience with Iran was a dramatic example. When Iranian students stormed the U.S. embassy in Tehran and took fifty-two Americans hostage on November 4, 1979, Carter's popularity jumped dramatically. His approval rating, which was 14 percent on October 30, rose to 38 percent on November 13 and to almost 58 percent the next January 22. But as the crisis dragged into the summer months, Carter's popularity ratings dipped into the low 30s. Similarly, when President George W. Bush launched the invasion of Iraq in March 2003, his approval rating jumped from 58 percent to 71 percent. Four years later, with American forces still fighting in Iraq, Bush's popularity dropped into the low 30s.

- Evidence of a breach of faith. Because they feel they have a highly personal relationship with the president, Americans are more likely to lose confidence in the chief executive over a personal moral failing, such as lying, than over ineffective, dangerous, or even immoral policies.

President Nixon's slide in public opinion did not come with revelations that his administration had undertaken questionable activities, such as illegally bombing Cambodia during the Vietnam War, destabilizing the Marxist regime of Chilean leader Salvador Allende, and presiding over unethical campaign practices. The slide came instead with revelations that he had consistently covered up such activities.

Controversial Reagan administration policies in Central America, the Middle East, Iran, and South Africa did not cause Reagan as much trouble as the public's concern that he may have lied about his activities. When former White House aide Oliver North acknowledged and even bragged about breaking the law (shredding government documents, lying to Congress, diverting government funds to Nicaraguan rebels), the White House lost public support.

Bill Clinton battled the "character" question throughout his presidency. Before he even entered the White House his marital fidelity, draft record, and business dealings came under critical scrutiny from the media, and the business dealings, especially the Whitewater land deal, were the subject of official investigations by Congress and a special prosecutor during his presidential terms. In addition, Clinton faced a civil suit alleging sexual harassment while he was governor of Arkansas. In the course of the latter inquiries, new charges of illicit sexual activity, perjury, and obstruction of justice arose. Remarkably, Clinton's job approval rating increased as the scandals accelerated. Clearly, in the president's case the public made a crucial distinction between its evaluation of him as a person and as the president.

George W. Bush's decline in public approval following the invasion of Iraq was predictable, but its continuing slide was due in part to the absence of any weapons of mass destruction in Iraq—the principal justification for the war—leading many to believe that the administration either exaggerated the case for war or deliberately misled the public as to its motives.

Issues Affecting Presidential Popularity

The relative importance of foreign affairs and domestic politics to presidential popularity is difficult to determine. In foreign affairs, the public is quick to unite behind the president because the source of concern is external. Domestic policy, however, usually involves internal divisions, so public support is less monolithic.

Domestic Affairs

The condition of the national economy can help or hurt a president's level of popularity, but not always in simple ways. People who hold the government responsible for the economy's overall performance are likely to judge the president according to data about inflation, unemployment, interest rates, and so on. But about half of the population is likely to take responsibility for their economic fortunes. Generally, the more a person follows media accounts of the economy, the more that person holds the president responsible for the state of the economy. Partisanship also biases a person's assessment of the economy. People are more willing to excuse poor economic trends when a president of their party is occupying the White House.[63]

Some students of public opinion maintain that a president is only as popular as the economic conditions allow. During periods of high unemployment or high inflation, the president's popularity is bound to suffer. As the nation's most visible public figure, the president bears the brunt of voter anxiety about the economic health of the country. Likewise, presidents benefit when economic conditions are good.

The experience of twentieth-century presidents lends some support to the pocketbook interpretation of presidential popularity. The most dramatic example of a president suffering from poor economic conditions was Herbert Hoover, president when the Great Crash

of October 1929 plunged the nation into its severest depression. The popularity of Hoover's successor, Franklin Roosevelt, appeared to decline at the end of his second term when the nation experienced another economic downturn. Historian David Green has argued that the failure of the New Deal to produce prosperity forced Roosevelt to shift political tactics by 1938. To distract the nation from the economic slump, Roosevelt launched public campaigns against "reactionaries" at home and fascists abroad.[64]

Eisenhower's popularity ratings declined when the nation entered a deep recession in 1958. The first poll of the year gave Eisenhower a 60 percent approval rate; by the time of the midterm congressional elections, it was down to 52 percent. Eisenhower also had the highest disapproval scores of his two terms during 1958—as high as 36 percent. More important, Eisenhower's Republicans were thrashed in the congressional campaign, losing forty-seven House seats and fifteen Senate seats.

Presidents occupying the Oval Office during periods of economic stagnation have struggled to maintain a moderate level of popularity. Johnson, Nixon, Ford, Carter, Reagan, and George H. W. Bush all suffered in the polls during perilous economic times. As political scientist Kristen R. Monroe has pointed out, economic factors such as unemployment and inflation may have both an immediate and a cumulative effect. The public has a "lagged response" to inflation—that is, one single monthly increase in inflation will have a political effect for as many as eleven months. Monroe has written: "The lagged impact suggests that the public has a long memory. The public is not easily distracted by sudden declines in inflation which directly precede an election."[65]

President Clinton presided over a strong economy throughout his presidency. Initially, prosperity did not cor-

With high rates of unemployment and food lines like this across the nation, in 1932 Americans voted their "pocketbooks" and gave Franklin D. Roosevelt a landslide victory over the incumbent Herbert Hoover.

RALLYING 'ROUND THE FLAG: RONALD REAGAN AND GEORGE W. BUSH

International crises typically coincide with dramatic upturns in presidential popularity as the public rallies behind its chief of state. Two noteworthy illustrations of this phenomenon are the invasion of Grenada in 1983 and the terrorist assaults on the World Trade Center and the Pentagon in 2001. Both incumbents, Ronald Reagan and George W. Bush, experienced significant surges in their job approval ratings from the American public. However, each such spike in presidential approval has its own distinctive contextual features. In Reagan's case, a presidential address appears to have been the critical factor in stimulating support. For Bush, the upturn cannot be so easily tied to a specific presidential statement or action. Rather, the event itself was sufficient.

The U.S. invasion of the Caribbean island of Grenada came on the heels of the deaths of 241 Marines stationed in Beirut, Lebanon, on October 23, 1983—a traumatic event that called into question the validity of the administration's actions in the Middle East. Two days later, President Reagan ordered the invasion of Grenada. On October 27, Reagan delivered a nationally televised address effectively explaining and justifying the invasion. Polls conducted by the *Washington Post*/ABC News the day before and the day after the speech indicate that Reagan's job approval moved upward from 54 percent to 63 percent. Approval of the invasion itself advanced from 51 percent on the eve of the speech to 65 percent in its wake. Moreover, approval of the president's handling of the Lebanon situation shot upward from 41 percent to 52 percent. Before the speech, 58 percent responded positively to the question "Would you say the United States is trying to do too much with its armed forces overseas, or not?" Afterward, that number declined to 48 percent. These data point to the speech itself as the critical factor in shaping the public response, and they indicate why Reagan was known as the "Great Communicator."

On the eve of the September 11, 2001, terrorist attacks on New York City and Washington, D.C., George W. Bush's job approval rating stood at 51 percent, the low mark of his first year in office, according to a Gallup poll taken September 7–10. The next Gallup poll, taken September 14–15, revealed that the president's job approval rating had soared to 86 percent. A week later, after a presidential address from Capitol Hill, Bush's approval rating stood at an unprecedented 90 percent. In contrast with the Grenada situation, the 2001 crisis was of far greater immediacy and magnitude, sufficient in itself to account for the dramatic shift in public support. Presidential rhetoric, though assuredly effective in this case as well, provides a more incremental and less compelling explanation for the rally.

SOURCES: Barry Sussman, *What Americans Really Think* (New York: Pantheon Books, 1988), 70; "Presidential Ratings—Job Approval," Gallup Organization (www.gallup.com); David W. Moore, "Bush Job Approval Highest in Gallup History: Widespread Public Support for War on Terrorism," Gallup Organization, September 24, 2001 (www.gallup.com).

---

relate with impressive approval ratings, but eventually it did so. In particular, Clinton claimed and received public credit for economic policies that produced rising government revenues, wiping out deficits and generating surpluses for the first time in a generation. Early in the presidency of George W. Bush, the economy went into recession, but his national security successes in the war on terrorism kept his public support at unprecedented heights. Later, despite low inflation and positive job growth, high gas prices helped lower that support significantly. The connection of gas prices to lingering conflict in the Middle East demonstrates that domestic issues are not always easily separable from foreign policy issues.

Pocketbook issues affecting presidential popularity include tax rates, the strength of social welfare programs, and perceptions of government efficiency. All these factors affect the public's sense of economic well-being and its view of the president's performance. Studies show that economic problems are more likely to damage a president's popularity than economic well-being is likely to boost the president's standing.[66]

Domestic events outside the economic sphere affect presidential popularity as well. Domestic disturbances such as the urban riots of the 1960s, controversial issues such as abortion and gay and lesbian rights, presidential appointments, and domestic scandals all tend to damage the president's popularity.

The Foreign Policy Explanation

Because pocketbook and other domestic issues do not provide the popularity boosts that most presidents seek, they often turn instead to a series of foreign policy events to help them achieve higher approval ratings.[67] Most analysts attributed President Reagan's strong rebound from low poll ratings during his first term to improvements in the economy. Theodore Lowi maintains, however, that the economic improvements took place too gradually and affected people too little to produce Reagan's dramatic turnaround.[68] According to Lowi, Reagan's approval rating improved significantly after *foreign policy events* with which he associated publicly, such as the bombing of the U.S. embassy in Lebanon, the Soviet attack on the Korean Air Lines plane, the redeployment of Marines in Lebanon, changes of leadership in the Soviet Union, and the invasion of Grenada. (*See box, Rallying 'Round the Flag: Ronald Reagan and George W. Bush, above.*)

Thus as Lowi has suggested, foreign policy events of short duration help a president's public standing, even if the event itself is not considered a "success" for the president. Domestic politics has a less certain effect on ratings. Positive economic news is considered the most useful domestic event for a president, but many experts question how much it can help a president's overall standing. Other domestic events—such as the passage of major spending programs or regulatory policies—are more divisive because they almost

Presidents often visit American troops abroad to build public support back home for military operations. President George H. W. Bush spent Thanksgiving Day 1990 with U.S. troops stationed in the Persian Gulf region before the outbreak of the Gulf War.

always produce clear losers as well as winners.

The president's tendency to become more involved in foreign policy as the term progresses may be an indicator of the public's inclination to "rally 'round the flag." The steady decline in approval ratings may give the president a reason to look to foreign affairs as a way of boosting, at least temporarily, public support. For example, the March 1947 announcement of the Truman Doctrine increased President Truman's public support by twelve percentage points (from 48 percent to 60 percent); the surge endured over nine months. Likewise, trips to Europe in 1970 and Russia in 1972 upped Nixon's popularity by seven and nine percentage points, respectively, but the surges in support were short-lived—only two months.

The public's willingness to back a president in times of international crisis is almost complete. Franklin Roosevelt, for example, saw his public support rise from 72 percent to 84 percent after Japan bombed Pearl Harbor in 1941. President Kennedy marveled at his public support after an event that he acknowledged to be a complete failure: the aborted invasion of Cuba and attempted overthrow of Fidel Castro at the Bay of Pigs. Kennedy's public approval rating jumped from 73 to 83 percent after the disaster, with only 5 percent of the public giving negative views.

Kennedy also experienced surges of support after the Cuban missile crisis, the construction of the Berlin Wall to separate the eastern and western parts of Berlin, and the assassination of South Vietnamese president Ngo Dinh

Diem. Incidents producing gains in other presidents' approval ratings have included: the Gulf of Tonkin crisis (Johnson); the early bombing of North Vietnam and Cambodia (Nixon); the *Mayaguez* incident and the fall of Saigon (Ford); the taking of American hostages at the U.S. embassy in Iran and the Soviet invasion of Afghanistan (Carter); terrorist attacks in Europe, the attack on a Korean Air Lines plane that strayed into Soviet territory, the Grenada invasion, the U.S. bombing of Libya, and the U.S. response to crises in the Philippines and Haiti (Reagan); the invasion of Panama, events leading up to the Gulf War, and the period during and after the war (George H. W. Bush); and the American bombing of Iraq in retaliation for an alleged assassination plot against President Bush (Clinton). The most recent, and most dramatic, example of this phenomenon occurred in September 2001. Immediately before terrorist attacks on U.S. soil, President George W. Bush could claim the support of a bare majority of the public. Afterward, his support level reached an unprecedented 90 percent.[69] *(See box, Rallying 'Round the Flag: Ronald Reagan and George W. Bush, p. 1025.)* Bush also experienced a surge of support immediately following the invasion of Iraq, but that support gradually dissipated as the war continued.

The rally effect is counteracted when major "opinion leaders" such as public figures and the mass media express doubts about the president's policy. When the opinion leaders are divided or opposed to a president's policy, the public decides whether to support the president based on its judgment of the policy's success or failure.[70] President George H. W. Bush's ups and downs in public approval during and after the Persian Gulf crisis reflected the shift from elite unanimity to ambivalence. Bush rallied the public when he spoke frequently and clearly on the subject, but his ratings fell when he let others define or obscure the issues.[71] Similarly, as the war in Iraq moved from a swift invasion to a lengthy insurgency, elite opinion became more and more divided, contributing to President George W. Bush's declining support.

Without decisive responses, foreign policy crises can produce "slump points" as well. Initially, Clinton's foreign policy was dogged by doubts from opinion leaders, and the policy actions in Somalia and Bosnia tended to produce ambiguous results. Yet Clinton's successes in other areas throughout his presidency—assistance to Russia's reform government, engagement in the peace process in the Middle East and Northern Ireland, negotiation of world trade treaties, and intervention in Kosovo—did not produce significant jumps in public support. Early on, because the foreign policy victories were not accompanied by dramatic and continual good news in the media, they were easily overshadowed by his troubles on other issues. Later, his popularity stabilized at a high level that did not fluctuate much in correlation with foreign policy successes.

In the post–cold war era, a time of uncertainty about the U.S. role in the world, foreign policy presented mixed opportunities for presidents. For example, some 74 percent of the public approved of President Clinton's 1994 deployment of the U.S. military to the Persian Gulf in response to Iraq's massing of troops along the Kuwaiti border. But while 84 percent said they would support military action if Iraq invaded Kuwait, only 30 percent said they would support U.S. intervention without direct Iraqi belligerence. That put Clinton in a position of talking loudly but only occasionally being permitted to use the "stick" of American power.[72] The events of September 11, 2001, changed this situation dramatically for President George W. Bush, granting him broad public support for the invasion of Afghanistan, and fairly strong support for his move against Iraq. Again, however, as war in the Middle East lengthened, casualties rose, and doubts grew about the war's justification and cost, public opinion returned to its more ambivalent mode.

Often, presidents are able to use the political structure of their support and opposition to initiate major changes in policy. In this context, they count on their supporters to back them despite their new policy and on their opponents to back them because of it. President Nixon, for example, was able to establish a political relationship with the People's Republic of China because of his career as an anticommunist. Nixon's allies could not resist their own president. Reagan also used his record of anticommunism to justify a risky initiative with the communists—ambitious arms-limitation negotiations with the Soviet Union. Polls showed that Reagan's record as an anticommunist helped him to neutralize right-wing opposition to agreements with the Soviets. As political scientist Lee Sigelman noted, "Americans may well reconsider their opposition on those dramatic occasions when the president rises above his own deeply held principles."[73]

It may be incorrect to ascribe paramount importance to either domestic or foreign policy issues for presidential popularity; both policy areas can increase or decrease the president's range of options. But perhaps domestic concerns provide a more durable base of popularity. Foreign policy events, by contrast, provide a dramatic but fleeting opportunity for the president to build popularity.

LINKS BETWEEN OPINION AND PUBLIC DEBATE

Especially since the dawn of the media age, presidential popularity has been an important tool for attaining public policy goals. Presidents use information about their levels of public support to persuade Congress to go along with their proposals for foreign and domestic policies.

Particularly on issues on which the public has not formed strong opinions, presidents can shape public opinion simply by speaking out. The public's deep-seated desire to support its president gives the president opportunities to bring people's thinking more in line with that of the administration. Some surveys have determined that the public is more willing to support an initiative if it knows the president proposed or backed the measure. For example, one researcher, Corey Rosen, found different samples showing different levels of support for proposals when respondents were either told or not told that the president backed the proposals.[74] Identification of the proposal with the president served to "personify" the policy and therefore to increase public support.

An unpopular president may produce a "reverse Midas" effect, damaging potentially popular policies. President Clinton's low popularity during congressional debate over health care reform in 1994 may have undermined public support for a compromise on the measure. When the Republican Party took control of Congress in 1995 for the first time in forty years, Clinton faced competition as the nation's leading agenda-setter. The new Speaker of the House, Newt Gingrich of Georgia, temporarily dominated headlines with his leadership of the Republican campaign platform dubbed the "Contract with America." By the end of 1995, however, the Republican Congress had squandered its initiative on trying to force through cuts in Medicaid and Medicare, and President Clinton had regained his political footing.

Political scientist Lee Sigelman used one sample to determine that public support for a policy rises when respondents are told of the president's position. But Sigelman found that the public is less willing to go along with the president's policies as the president's position becomes more "radical."[75] The latter finding suggests that the president's prestige depends to a great extent on a strong base of public respect for the president's office. That respect is one of the nation's fundamental values. As presidents move away from the nation's other fundamental values with "radical" proposals, they might lose the public's automatic support.

History offers additional evidence for the academic findings of Rosen and Sigelman. Public support for President Truman's proposed aid to Greece and Turkey—which was not a prominent issue at the time—rose dramatically after Truman's 1947 speech on the matter.[76] Support for bombing Hanoi and Haiphong increased from 50 to 80 percent after the bombing there began in 1966.[77] Before Lyndon Johnson announced a halt to the bombing of North Vietnam on March 31, 1968, only 40 percent of the public opposed bombing the enemy. In early April polls showed that 64 percent approved the bombing halt.

Influencing Capitol Hill

The link between presidential approval ratings and support on Capitol Hill for the White House is not clear. Political scientist Richard E. Neustadt has argued that high approval ratings and poll support for specific policies help the president to persuade Congress to support key policy proposals.[78] But the record of postwar presidents suggests that the link is indirect and that other factors enter into the calculations of Congress and other actors.

One reason Congress pays attention to presidential popularity is that many members of Congress have no other regular barometer of the public mood. The president is the dominant figure in national politics, and when the public reacts to administration stands, members of Congress gain a sense of public opinion. Another reason is that the public generally expects Congress to cooperate with the president.[79]

Kent Hance, a Democratic representative from Texas, explained his support for Republican president Reagan's tax and budget initiatives in 1981: "Reagan won 72 percent of the vote in my district and he's a lot more popular now than he was on Election Day. It's mighty tough to go against a popular president in a district like mine." [80] Speaker Thomas P. "Tip" O'Neill Jr. pleaded with conservative Democrats to oppose the president's plan, but he concluded that the marginal representatives "go along with the will of the people, and the will of the people is to go along with the president." [81] When in November Reagan's public approval fell below 50 percent—a drop of nineteen points since May—the White House encountered difficulties pushing the rest of its program. Budget cuts never made it to the floor of either chamber.[82]

In his statistical analysis of congressional roll call votes and presidential popularity polls, political scientist George C. Edwards III confirmed that constituents expect their representatives to cooperate with the president, and that members of Congress respond to the general desires of their major supporters back home. According to Edwards, the relationship between presidential public support and success on Capitol Hill is modest. As a rule of thumb, the president gains 1.5 percentage points in congressional support for every 10 percentage point increase in public approval.[83] An increase in presidential support of 10 percentage points among Democrats produces a 3 to 4 percent increase in Democratic support in the House of Representatives.[84] These strong results do not hold for Democrats in the Senate and Republicans in both chambers.

Yet Edwards notes that measures of aggregate support for the president may not tell the whole story. More revealing, he says, is congressional attention to the constituents in the district or state who support members. Edwards writes:

> Presidential approval is likely to have its greatest positive impact on Congress when members of the legislature sense that the public supports the chief executive for his positions on issues as well as his general leadership or other characteristics. The strongest negative influence is likely to occur when there is dramatic, rapid decline in the president's approval level, undermining other sources of support. Neither of these situations is typical.[85]

Jon R. Bond and Richard Fleisher find Edwards's correlations "spurious" because of his failure to account for the natural biases of congressional party members regardless of the president's popularity.[86] Oddly, the correlation between presidential popularity and the success of the White House program on Capitol Hill is weaker on votes on important issues, to which the public pays more attention.[87] The president's popularity produces a greater effect on foreign policy votes in the House and domestic issues in the Senate. Of the presidents serving since the 1950s, Johnson demonstrated the closest correlation between popularity and success in Congress.[88]

Among members of Congress from the party not occupying the Oval Office, the relationship between presidential popularity and congressional support is mixed. Members of the party's "base" tend to respond somewhat favorably to a popular president of the other party. But members of Congress of the same party who face "cross pressures" about the White House program actually oppose the president more when the president is popular. "Most members of Congress know that very few voters are likely to have information about their votes on specific roll calls or about their support for the president," Bond and Fleisher write. "Voters are, however, more likely to be aware of a representative's general voting patterns reflected by party and ideology. Incumbents seldom lose because they support a popular president too little or support an unpopular president too much; they are more likely to lose because they are too liberal or too conservative for their constituents." [89]

Shaping Public Opinion

The regularity of polling on every conceivable issue gives the president and other political figures the opportunity to try to shape public opinion and react to it. Pollsters gather information daily about the ways all kinds of citizens think on a variety of issues, including many hypothetical situations. Polling data include combinations of conditions to which the polling subject can respond. Thus the president can anticipate the way the population—and specific groups of the population—will react to large and small initiatives on any issue imaginable. By analyzing polling data, the president can know, for example, what the Jewish population thinks about the administration's policies in the Middle East and what that group thinks about different approaches to the broad problems as well as the minor elements of the situation. Presidents then can attempt to move public opinion in their direction through vigorous use of the "bully pulpit."

Some political scientists argue that the attempt to move public opinion through rhetorical efforts is now the core presidential strategy for governing. According to George C. Edwards III, the assumptions behind this governing strategy are that public support is an important political resource for the president; that the president "must actively take his case to the people;" and that the president is, in fact, able to "successfully persuade or even mobilize the public." [90] The problem with this strategy, according to Edwards, is that it rarely works. Whether examining "great communicators" such as Reagan or presidents with lesser rhetorical gifts, Edwards finds that presidents cannot lead the public where it does not want to go. Personal charisma does not help, and neither do frequent addresses to the public. The constitutional separation of powers prevents presidents from imposing their will on Congress, and presidents face too much competition for attention in the modern media-saturated world. Edwards concludes that "presidents typically do not succeed in their efforts to change public opinion," and the "bully pulpit has proved ineffective not only for achieving majority support but also for increasing support from a smaller base." [91]

Nevertheless, because presidents are faced with the inevitable decline in popularity, they are inclined to take dramatic, public actions to improve poll ratings. Presidential leadership, then, "tilts" toward dramatic actions designed to bolster approval ratings rather than concerted efforts and cooperation with other government officials to deal with complex problems.

George Gallup relates the public's desire for strong leadership to the president's sometimes feverish activity to boost ratings:

> I would say that any sharp drop in popularity is likely to come from the president's inaction in the face of an important crisis. Inaction hurts a president more than anything else. A president can take some action, even a wrong one, and not lose his popularity. . . . People tend to judge a man by his goals, what he's trying to do, and not necessarily by what he accomplishes or how well he succeeds. People used to tell us over and over again about all the things that Roosevelt did wrong and then they would say, "I'm all for him, though, because his heart is in the right place; he's trying." [92]

Recent events appear to support Gallup's statement. Nixon's trips to the Soviet Union in 1974 during the height of the Watergate controversy, Ford's military action against Cambodia after the attack on the *Mayaguez,* Carter's dramat-ic disavowal of his previous approach to the Soviet Union after its invasion of Afghanistan, Carter's high-profile response to the Iranian seizure of hostages, and Reagan's attacks on Grenada and Libya—all led to a boost in the president's ratings. President Clinton's eventual decision in 1995 to send troops to Bosnia was in this context preferable to his continued stance of noncommitment of U.S. forces. The same could be said for his deployment of the U.S. military on behalf of the North Atlantic Treaty Organization (NATO) in the Kosovo conflict, although as noted previously neither of these episodes produced a dramatic surge in presidential popularity. In the wake of terrorist attacks, George W. Bush became far more visible as well as formidable on the political stage. It was his perceived inaction in the wake of Hurricane Katrina, in addition to the perception of lack of progress in Iraq, that began to undermine Bush's public support.

THE JUDGMENT ON PUBLIC OPINION POLLING

Changes in the measurement of public opinion fundamentally altered the way groups press political demands and political leaders respond to those demands. Scholars have disagreed about whether a system with constant polling promotes or damages democracy.

Some argue that regular polling, more than infrequent elections, makes political leaders responsive to the wishes of the electorate. George Gallup, one of the pioneers of modern polling, has maintained that elected officials do a better job when they have "an accurate measure of the wishes, aspirations, and needs of different groups within the general public." [93] Behavior in office that is influenced by polls is a kind of rolling election campaign, with officials constantly on the lookout for ways to please and avoid displeasing the public.

Proponents of polling also stress the "scientific" nature of findings and the increasingly sophisticated views of the political landscape that well-done polls offer. If conducted comprehensively, proponents say, polls can offer a more complete picture of the political landscape than any other single tool.

On the other hand, other scholars argue that the persistent reliance on public opinion polling serves to drain the presidency of its constitutional authority. Political scientist James W. Ceaser argues that the Framers believed the presidency needed some degree of independence from public opinion, but that modern practices reverse this dynamic. Presidents want to lead through polls, which they believe are the primary source of presidential authority in the modern era. But the multiplication of polls now serves as an ongoing referendum on presidential performance, updated almost daily, placing limits on the president's constitutional discretion. Whereas at one time the presidential election granted the chief executive legitimacy to pursue his objectives through constitutional means, now constant polling actually robs the chief executive of independence. What is often seen as a source of power has become a severe constraint.[94]

The reliability of public opinion surveys varies widely. Polls with carefully worded questions and random samples of at least a thousand respondents are considered the most reliable. Polls with smaller sample sizes can be useful if designed well and analyzed rigorously. Even large opinion samples can misjudge the mood of the population, because they gauge the intensity of public preferences only roughly. "Focus groups"—small groups of selected voters, gathered for intensive interviews with professional surveyors—help to tap the more visceral feelings of key segments of the public. Early in his administration, President Clinton decided to postpone his promise for a middle-class tax cut after focus groups revealed that Clinton and Perot voters would not blame him for breaking the pledge.[95]

Surveys also can be misleading because of the way the data are presented. In 1976 reporters seeking to understand Carter's appeal speculated that Carter's religiosity tapped a wellspring of conservatism in the electorate. But when polls showed that Carter was as popular among nonreligious as religious people, reporters dropped the idea. One polling expert, however, took the analysis a step further by examining young voters. "Sure enough, those young, non-churchgoing Carter fans were masking the religion effect. When age was held constant, religion effect appeared. Revealing it took nothing more complicated than a three-way table."[96] A look at a single factor, then, can obscure the complex truths hidden in polling data.

Reliance on polling data in making policy and strategic decisions can be risky; especially on volatile issues, survey results can be erratic and inaccurate. Differences in the wording of survey questions—as well as different arrangements of the questions—can produce dramatically different responses. Dramatic events also can produce reactions that do not last long. For example, American public opinion in the months before the Persian Gulf War of 1991 was extremely unsteady. In some polls, the public appeared to favor the use of military force; in others, the public appeared reluctant. On the surface, public opinion seemed to change dramatically. But, according to Mueller, "the most remarkable aspect of public opinion on such matters was that it changed very little." Events such as failed peace talks increased the public's hawkishness, but such hawkishness "was essentially ephemeral."[97] Presidents, then, who do not carefully interpret polling data can find themselves embarking on policies that have only fleeting support.

Some students of American politics take the critique of polling a step further, arguing that polls can be a tool of manipulation. Political scientist Benjamin Ginsberg argues that polls have the effect of stifling public expression rather than measuring it in a neutral manner for voter-conscious political leaders. According to Ginsberg, a regular assessment of a wide variety of public attitudes, in which a diverse range of issues is assessed according to the many demographic characteristics of survey respondents, enables the government to "manage" demands rather than deal with the complex problems that produce political demands. By determining which groups in society would object to certain governmental actions, the government is able to adapt its policies and presentation of those policies to avoid conflict. Many issues, then, never receive the full public discussion that they might receive if the public pulse were not so regularly tested.

Presidents Carter, Reagan, and Clinton employed full-time White House pollsters who monitored the vagaries of public opinion among all imaginable demographic groups, and all recent presidents have had access to extensive public opinion data generated on their behalf. Today, other parts of the federal government—from executive departments and agencies to Congress—also use polls regularly to monitor and shape public opinion. To the extent that such polling allows public officials to head off a full discussion of major issues, critics argue, democracy is thwarted.

Also concerned about the way polling shapes the expression of public opinion, Ginsberg has pointed out that polling data channel political expression into formulations provided by the pollster that discourage group political action. Besides allowing government officials to manage public opinion, polls have four possible negative effects on democratic expression.

First, polling eliminates the cost of expressing an opinion, which reduces the influence of the people most concerned and knowledgeable about various issues. Polls tally the preferences of cross sections of the population, which include people who do not know or care about issues. The respondent's knowledge and the issue's salience are usually ignored. "Polls, in effect, submerge individuals with strongly held views in a more apathetic mass public."[98]

Second, polls shift the concern of public debate from behavior to attitudes. The demonstrations that once informed elites of mass opinion required people to engage directly in politics. Simply responding to survey questions, in contrast, requires just a few moments of time of a small sample of the public. Polls give the government the opportunity to shape opinion before it can enjoy full debate, thereby reducing public engagement.

Third, polls shift politics from the group to the individual. Before polls, citizens needed to band together to express their desires and demands. Such a requirement served to build political institutions such as parties, unions, neighborhood groups, and farmer cooperatives. Active involvement in many such groups—especially parties and unions—has declined as public officials have turned to polls for information about public opinion.

Fourth, polls shift political expression from assertions to responses. Survey subjects can react only to the agenda of the pollster; they rarely make an independent assertion. The subjects that respondents—and therefore, the public—can discuss are thereby limited to the interests of pollsters.

Daniel Yankelovich, a leading analyst of public opinion, has called for the simplicity of opinion polls to be replaced by a more complex process of "public judgment." Most polls ask questions that people do not know much about, so their answers are shaky at best. For example, 63 percent of respondents in one poll said they favored a constitutional amendment to balance the federal budget. But when respondents were told that such a measure might require higher taxes, only 39 percent said they favored the amendment.[99]

Political scientist Philip E. Converse puts the proper use of polls and surveys into perspective:

> Acquiring relevant public opinion data is not unlike the riverboat captain buying the latest mapping of sandbar configurations before embarking on a voyage. Few politicians consult poll data to find out what they should be thinking on the issues, or to carry out errands. But they have very little interest in flouting the will of their constituency in any tendentious, head-on way. Such data give them a sense of what postures to emphasize and avoid.[100]

★

NOTES

1. Jeffrey K. Tulis, *The Rhetorical Presidency* (Princeton: Princeton University Press, 1987).

2. Alexander Hamilton, James Madison, and John Jay, *The Federalist Papers,* ed. Clinton Rossiter (New York: Mentor, 1961) 353.

3. Ibid., 400–402.

4. This discussion relies mostly on the following studies by Fred I. Greenstein: "Popular Images of the President," *American Journal of Psychiatry* 122, no. 5 (November 1965): 523–529; "The Benevolent Leader: Children's Images of Presidential Authority," *American Political Science Review* 54 (December 1960): 934–943; "College Student Reactions to the Assassination of President Kennedy," in *The Kennedy Assassination and the American Public: Social Communication in Crisis,* ed. Bradley S. Greenberg and Edwin B. Parker (Stanford: Stanford University Press, 1965); and "What the President Means to Americans," in *Choosing the President,* ed. James David Barber (Englewood Cliffs, N.J.: Prentice Hall, 1974), 121–147. Also see Roberta S. Sigel, "Image of the American Presidency, Part II of an Exploration into Popular Views of Presidential Power," *Midwest Journal of Political Science* 10 (February 1966): 123–137.

5. Greenstein, "What the President Means to Americans," 125, 128–129. Percentages are from *Washington Post,* January 29, 1996, 6.

6. The respect for the presidency is not uniformly strong. Groups that are left out of the mainstream of economic and political life, such as African Americans and Appalachian whites, respond less favorably to mention of the presidency and specific presidents.

7. Murray Edelman, *The Symbolic Uses of Politics* (Urbana: University of Illinois Press, 1985), 78.

8. Garry Wills, "Clinton's Troubles," *New York Review of Books,* September 22, 1994, 6. However, throughout his second term Clinton consistently maintained job approval ratings in excess of his personal favorability figures, suggesting that the public can and does make a crucial distinction between the two.

9. For examinations of consensus in U.S. politics, see Louis Hartz, *The Liberal Tradition in America* (New York: Harcourt, Brace, Jovanovich, 1955); Daniel Boorstin, *The Genius of American Democracy* (Chicago: University of Chicago Press, 1958); Daniel Bell, *The End of Ideology* (Glencoe, Ill.: Free Press, 1960); and Samuel H. Beer, "In Search of a New Political Philosophy," in *The New American Political System,* ed. Anthony King (Washington, D.C.: American Enterprise Institute, 1978), 5–44.

10. James Davison Hunter, *Culture Wars: The Struggle to Define America* (New York: Basic Books, 1991).

11. Quoted in Benjamin Ginsberg, *The Captive Public* (New York: Basic Books, 1986), 61.

12. For a suggestive survey of new opinion media, see William G. Mayer, "The Rise of the New Media," *Public Opinion Quarterly* 58 (spring 1994): 124–146.

13. Ginsberg, *Captive Public,* 56–57.

14. See Pam Solo, *From Protest to Policy: Beyond the Freeze to Common Security* (Cambridge: Ballinger, 1988).

15. See Mel Laracey, *Presidents and the People: The Partisan Story of Going Public* (College Station: Texas A&M University Press, 2002).

16. Daniel Boorstin, *The Americans: The Democratic Experience* (New York: Random House, 1973), 403.

17. Leila Sussman, "Dear Mr. President," in *Readings in American Public Opinion,* ed. Edward E. Walker et al. (New York: American Book, 1968).

18. Graeme Browning, "Hot-Wiring Washington," *National Journal,* June 26, 1993, 1624–1629.

19. See the White House Web site at *www.whitehouse.gov.*

20. Michael Cornfield and Jonah Seiger, "The Net and the Nomination," in *The Making of the Presidential Candidates 2004,* ed. William G. Mayer (Lanham, Md.: Rowman and Littlefield, 2004), 199–228.

21. Sussman, *What Americans Really Think,* 226.

22. Quoted in James R. Beniger and Robert J. Guiffra Jr., "Public Opinion Polling: Command and Control in Presidential Campaigns," in *Presidential Selection,* ed. Alexander Heard and Michael Nelson (Durham, N.C.: Duke University Press, 1987), 189.

23. Herbert Asher, *Polling and the Public,* 3d ed.(Washington, D.C.: CQ Press, 1995), 15.

24. For a critique of Caddell's conception of politics and polling, see Sidney Blumenthal, "Mr. Smith Goes to Washington," *New Republic,* February 6, 1984, 17–20.

25. Jimmy Carter, *Keeping Faith* (New York: Bantam Books, 1982), 114.

26. Larry J. Sabato, *The Rise of Political Consultants,* (New York: Basic Books, 1981), 74–75.

27. Carter, *Keeping Faith,* 123.

28. Laurence I. Barrett, *Gambling with History* (New York: Doubleday, 1983), 351–352.

29. Sussman, *What Americans Really Think,* 35–36.

30. Quoted in James A. Barnes, "Polls Apart," *National Journal,* July 7, 1993, 1751.

31. Ibid., 1753.

32. Dick Morris, *Behind the Oval Office: Winning the Presidency in the Nineties* (New York: Random House, 1997).

33. Michael A. Dimock, "Bush and Public Opinion," in *Considering the Bush Presidency,* eds. Gary L. Gregg II and Mark J. Rozell (New York: Oxford University Press, 2004), 76–81.

34. Jon R. Bond and Richard Fleisher, *The President in the Legislative Arena* (Chicago: University of Chicago Press, 1990), 179.

35. Some scholars argue that the honeymoon is no longer something a new president can rely on. See Karen S. Johnson, "The Honeymoon Period: Fact or Fiction," *Journalism Quarterly* 62 (winter 1985): 869–876. Theodore J. Lowi has argued that the honeymoon period offers the president's only real opportunity to achieve major policy initiatives—and that that period is getting shorter and shorter. See Lowi, *The Personal President: Power Invested, Promise Unfulfilled* (Ithaca: Cornell University Press, 1985), 7–11.

36. Lyn Ragsdale, *Vital Statistics on the Presidency: Washington to Clinton* (Washington, D.C.: Congressional Quarterly, 1996), 194–209.

37. See David R. Mayhew, *Divided We Govern* (New Haven: Yale University Press, 1991) and Charles O. Jones, *The Presidency in a Separated System,* 2d ed. (Washington, D.C.: Brookings Institution Press, 2005).

38. Samuel Kernell, "Explaining Presidential Popularity," *American Political Science Review* 72 (1978): 506–522.

39. John Mueller, "The Polls—A Review: American Public Opinion and the Gulf War," *Public Opinion Quarterly* 57 (1993): 84, 85; Gary King and Lyn Ragsdale, *The Elusive Executive: Discovering Statistical Patterns in the Presidency* (Washington, D.C.: Congressional Quarterly, 1988), 292–293; Gallup Organization, "Poll Topics and Trends: Presidential Ratings—Job Approval" *(www.gallup.com)*; David W. Moore, "Bush Job Approval Highest in Gallup History," Gallup News Service, September 24, 2001 *(www.gallup.com)*.

40. "Bush Job Performance—Trend," *Gallup Poll Monthly,* November 1992, 24–27.

41. Ragsdale, *Vital Statistics on the Presidency,* 189; Gallup Organization, "Poll Topics and Trends, Presidential Ratings—Job Approval" *(www.gallup.com)*.

42. Stephen Skowronek, *The Politics that Presidents Make: Leadership from John Adams to George Bush* (Cambridge: Belknap Press, 1993).

43. See John E. Mueller, *War, Presidents, and Public Opinion* (Lanham, Md.: University Press of America, 1985). Mueller's shorter works include "Presidential Popularity from Truman to Johnson," *American Political Science Review* 64 (March 1970): 18–34; and "Trends in Popular Support for the Wars in Korea and Vietnam," *American Political Science Review* 65 (June 1971): 358–375.

44. James A. Stimson, "Public Support for American Presidents: A Cyclical Model," *Public Opinion Quarterly* 40 (spring 1976): 1–21.

45. Ibid., 10.

46. See the work by Mueller and Jong R. Lee, "Rallying Around the Flag: Foreign-Policy Events and Presidential Popularity," *Presidential Studies Quarterly* 7 (fall 1977): 252–256.

47. Thomas E. Cronin, *The State of the Presidency* (Boston: Little, Brown, 1980), 84.

48. Paul Brace and Barbara Hinckley, "The Structure of Presidential Approval: Constraints within and across Presidencies," *Journal of Politics* 53 (November 1991): 1003, 1012.

49. Richard A. Brody, "Is the Honeymoon Over? The American People and President Bush," *PRG Report* (fall 2001; addendum published October 8, 2001): 1, 23–28.

50. Paul Brace and Barbara Hinckley, *Follow the Leader: Opinion Polls and the Modern Presidents* (New York: Basic Books, 1992), 101.

51. Ibid.

52. King and Ragsdale, *Elusive Executive,* 296–307.

53. David J. Lanoue, "The 'Teflon Factor': Ronald Reagan and Comparative Presidential Popularity," *Polity* 21 (spring 1989): 291.

54. Paul J. Quirk, "The Election," in *The Elections of* 1988, ed. Michael Nelson (Washington, D.C.: CQ Press, 1989), 82; Paul J. Quirk and Jon K. Dalager, "The Election: A 'New Democrat' and a New Kind of Presidential Campaign," in *The Elections of 1992,* ed. Michael Nelson (Washington, D.C.: CQ Press, 1993), 78.

55. *Gallup Poll Monthly,* various issues, 1993–2000; data provided by the Gallup poll.

56. Dimock, "Bush and Public Opinion," 76–81.

57. This discussion relies on John E. Mueller, "Public Opinion and the President," in *The Presidency Reappraised,* ed. Rexford G. Tugwell and Thomas E. Cronin (New York: Praeger, 1974), 133–147. The categories just described overlap; for example, a citizen can have elements of both the partisan and the follower.

58. See ibid. and Richard A. Brody and Benjamin I. Page, "The Impact of Events on Presidential Popularity: The Johnson and Nixon Administrations," in *Perspectives on the Presidency,* ed. Aaron Wildavsky (Boston: Little, Brown, 1975), especially p. 145: "Foreign events reach people through news reports, [while] some domestic events, like real personal income, may be perceived without mediation."

59. Eric B. Herzik and Mary L. Dodson have suggested that the "climate of expectations" has more to do with the president's personal appeal than with programmatic plans. "The President and Public Expectations: A Research Note," *Presidential Studies Quarterly* 12 (spring 1982): 168–173.

60. Tulis, *Rhetorical Presidency.*

61. Mueller, "Presidential Popularity," 20–21.

62. Richard A. Brody, "Public Evaluations and Expectations and the Future of the Presidency," in *Problems and Prospects of Presidential Leadership in the 1980's,* ed. James Sterling Young (New York: University Press of America, 1982), 45–49. Also see Stanley Kelley, *Interpreting Elections* (Princeton: Princeton University Press, 1983), for a similar view of how voters make judgments.

63. Alan I. Abramowitz, David J. Lanoue, and Subha Ramesh, "Economic Conditions, Causal Attributions, and Political Evaluations in the 1984 Presidential Election," *Journal of Politics* 50 (November 1988): 848–863.

64. David Green, *Shaping Political Consciousness* (New York: Oxford University Press, 1988), 126–134.

65. Kristen R. Monroe, "Inflation and Presidential Popularity," *Presidential Studies Quarterly* 9 (summer 1979): 339. Also see Kristen R. Monroe, "Economic Influences on Presidential Popularity," *Public Opinion Quarterly* (1978): 360–370. Kim Ezra Sheinbaum and Ervin Sheinbaum, in "Public Perceptions of Presidential Economic Performance: From Johnson to Carter," *Presidential Studies Quarterly* 12 (summer 1982): 421–427, find a strong link between prosperity and popularity. Henry C. Kenski, in "The Impact of Economic Conditions on Presidential Popularity," *Journal of Politics* 39 (1977): 764–773, argues that high unemployment and inflation rates affect Republican and Democratic presidents differently.

66. Henry C. Kenski, "The Impact of Unemployment on Presidential Popularity from Eisenhower to Nixon," *Presidential Studies Quarterly* 7 (spring–summer 1977): 114–126.

67. Lowi's analysis of the spurts in presidential popularity is part of his overall critique of the public presidency. See Lowi, *Personal President.*

68. Lowi points to other evidence against the pocketbook explanation for presidential popularity. Economic conditions improved in both 1968 and 1976 but did not help Presidents Johnson and Ford,

whose high negative ratings and intense public opposition prevented one from campaigning for, and the other from winning, reelection.

69. For an analysis of this phenomenon, see Mueller, *War, Presidents, and Public Opinion.*

70. Richard A. Brody and Catherine R. Shapiro, "A Reconsideration of the Rally Phenomenon in Public Opinion," in *Political Behavior Annual,* ed. Samuel Long (Boulder: Westview Press, 1989), 77–102.

71. Brigitte Lebens Nacos, "Presidential Leadership during the Persian Gulf Conflict," *Presidential Studies Quarterly* 24 (summer 1994): 543–561.

72. David W. Moore and Lydia Saad, "Public Supports Actions against Iraq," *Gallup Poll Monthly,* October 1994, 14.

73. Lee Sigelman, "Disarming the Opposition: The President, the Public, and the I.N.F. Treaty," *Public Opinion Quarterly* 54 (spring 1990): 46.

74. Corey Rosen, "A Test of Presidential Leadership of Public Opinion: The Split Ballot Technique," *Polity* 6 (1972): 282–290.

75. Lee Sigelman, "Gauging the Public Response to Presidential Leadership," *Presidential Studies Quarterly* 10 (summer 1980): 427–433.

76. Samuel Kernell, "The Truman Doctrine Speech: A Case Study of the Dynamics of Presidential Opinion Leadership," *Social Science History* 1 (fall 1976): 20–45.

77. See Mueller, *War, Presidents, and Public Opinion.*

78. Richard E. Neustadt, *Presidential Power* (New York: Wiley, 1980), 64–73.

79. See George C. Edwards III, "Presidential Influence in the House: Presidential Prestige as a Source of Presidential Power," *American Political Science Review* 70 (March 1976): 101–113.

80. Quoted in George C. Edwards III, *At the Margins: Presidential Leadership of Congress* (New Haven: Yale University Press, 1989), 116.

81. Ibid., 116.

82. Ibid., 117.

83. Ibid., 118.

84. Ibid., 120.

85. Ibid., 124–125.

86. Jon R. Bond and Richard Fleisher, *The President in the Legislative Arena* (Chicago: University of Chicago Press, 1990), 187.

87. Ibid., 182.

88. Ibid., 182–183.

89. Ibid., 194.

90. George C. Edwards III, *On Deaf Ears: The Limits of the Bully Pulpit* (New Haven: Yale University Press, 2003), 4–5.

91. Ibid., 241.

92. Quoted in Edelman, *Symbolic Uses of Politics,* 78.

93. Quoted in Ginsberg, *Captive Public,* 237.

94. James W. Ceaser, "Presidential Selection," in *The Presidency in the Constitutional Order,* eds. Joseph M. Bessette and Jeffrey Tulis (Baton Rouge: Louisiana State University Press, 1981).

95. Bob Woodward, *The Agenda: Inside the Clinton White House* (New York: Simon and Schuster, 1993), 72, 97.

96. Philip Meyer, "Polling as Political Science and Polling as Journalism," *Public Opinion Quarterly* 54 (1990): 451.

97. Mueller, "The Polls," 84, 85.

98. Ginsberg, *Captive Public,* 65.

99. Daniel Yankelovich, *Coming to Public Judgment: Making Democracy Work in a Complex World* (Syracuse, N.Y.: University of Syracuse Press, 1991), 25.

100. Philip E. Converse, "Changing Conceptions of Public Opinion in the Political Process," *Public Opinion Quarterly* 51 (1987): 22.

SELECTED BIBLIOGRAPHY

Asher, Herbert. *Polling and the Public.* 3d ed. Washington, D.C.: CQ Press, 1995.

Bond, Jon R., and Richard Fleisher. *The President in the Legislative Arena.* Chicago: University of Chicago Press, 1990.

Brody, Richard A. *Assessing the President: The Media, Elite Opinion, and Public Support.* Stanford: Stanford University Press, 1991.

Edelman, Murray. *The Symbolic Uses of Politics.* Urbana: University of Illinois Press, 1985.

Edwards, George C., III. *At the Margins: Presidential Leadership of Congress.* New Haven: Yale University Press, 1989.

———. *Presidential Approval: A Sourcebook.* Baltimore: Johns Hopkins University Press, 1990.

———. *On Deaf Ears: The Limits of the Bully Pulpit.* New Haven: Yale University Press, 2003.

Ginsberg, Benjamin. *The Captive Public.* New York: Basic Books, 1986.

Greenberg, Stanley. *Middle Class Dreams.* New York: Times Books, 1995.

Kernell, Samuel. *Going Public: New Strategies of Presidential Leadership.* 3d ed. Washington, D.C.: CQ Press, 1997.

Langston, Thomas. *With Reverence and Contempt: How Americans Think about Their President.* Baltimore: Johns Hopkins University Press, 1995.

Lanoue, David J. *From Camelot to the Teflon Presidency.* New York: Greenwood Press, 1988.

Laracey, Mel. *Presidents and the People: The Partisan Story of Going Public.* College Station: Texas A&M University Press, 2002.

Lowi, Theodore J. *The Personal President.* Ithaca: Cornell University Press, 1985.

Morris, Dick. *Behind the Oval Office: Winning the Presidency in the Nineties.* New York: Random House, 1997.

Mueller, John E. *War, Presidents, and Public Opinion.* Lanham, Md.: University Press of America, 1985.

Ragsdale, Lyn. *Vital Statistics on the Presidency: Washington to Clinton.* Washington, D.C.: Congressional Quarterly, 1996

Tulis, Jeffrey K. *The Rhetorical Presidency.* Princeton: Princeton University Press, 1987.

chapter 21

The President and Interest Groups

by Daniel J. Tichenor, Charles C. Euchner, and Harold F. Bass

Modern presidents have long maintained an ambivalent relationship with the extensive interest group system that has been a fixture in Washington, D.C., for more than a century. Americans tend to form private associations to pursue their political ends. Balancing the demands of these organized interests has been a major—and difficult—part of the president's job, particularly since the days of the New Deal and World War II.

An interest group is a set of people who form an association to promote ideals or pursue material benefits. Groups may know what ends they desire, but their tactics evolve according to their relationship with other forces in society. Because interest groups usually are seeking the kind of assistance available only from the public, they often go to the government with their claims.[1]

Modern presidents have considerable incentive to be wary of interest groups given the political hazards of appearing to be captured by "special interests." The ability of organized interests to derail presidential policy initiatives and to logjam both judicial and executive branch nominations has frustrated most contemporary presidents, leading more than a few to describe the Washington lobbying community as a chief obstacle to addressing national problems and serving the common good. Despite these sources of tension, presidential candidates lean on interest groups for various forms of electoral support, and modern presidents rely on them to help build governing coalitions and to advance their programmatic agenda in Congress and other venues. The relationship between the presidency and the national interest group system is inevitable, necessary, and often uneasy.

CONSTITUTIONAL DEBATE ABOUT FACTIONS

Debate over the U.S. Constitution framed the major issues of interest group politics that occupy students of U.S. government today. After completion of the Constitution in Philadelphia in 1787, Federalists and Anti-Federalists debated how best to achieve adequate "energy" in the federal government and the presidency without stifling free debate and competition among social groups—notions central to a democratic society. The debate's basic tension has persisted to the modern day.

James Madison presented what has come to be the main justification for interest group politics.[2] In *Federalist* No. 10, Madison argued that separate, competing interests were inevitable in a free society and that efforts to snuff out this competition would require the drastic step of curbing free thought and action. The goal of government should not be to ban interest groups, Madison asserted, but to control them by competition. In *Federalist* No. 10, Madison wrote:

> As long as the reason of man continues fallible, and he is at liberty to exercise it, different opinions will be formed. . . . From the protection of different and unequal faculties of acquiring property, the possession of different degrees and kinds of property immediately results; and from the influence of these on the sentiments and views of the respective proprietors ensues a division of the society into different interests and parties.[3]

Alexis de Tocqueville, a nineteenth-century French aristocrat, argued in his classic study *Democracy in America* that the "equality of conditions" and the lack of a feudal tradition in the United States gave Americans the freedom to pursue their interests by using large and small associations. Tocqueville wrote:

> Americans of all ages, all conditions, and all dispositions, constantly form associations. They have not only commercial and manufacturing companies, but associations of a thousand other kinds—religious, moral, serious, futile, general or restricted, enormous or diminutive. . . . Wherever, at the head of some new undertaking, you see the government in France, or a man of rank in England, in the United States you will be sure to find an association.[4]

This being said, Tocqueville pointed out that the American condition was a double-edged sword. He feared that the United States would develop into a "tyranny of the majority" because equality would undermine citizens' willingness to be tolerant of people who expressed unpopular ideas or had different characteristics. But, he observed, equality and freedom of expression also enabled a variety of institutions—newspapers, the legal profession, and interest groups—to break the tendency of majorities to impose their wills on the entire population.

When Tocqueville published his work in 1835 and 1840, interest groups existed mainly at the local level. State and local governments had control over most matters of public life, including property laws, banking and commerce, morals, education, use of land and resources, and criminal procedures. The states and localities also played an important part in developing "internal improvements," such as roads, canals, railroads, schools, hospitals, and agricultural enterprises.[5]

John C. Calhoun, one of the South's great champions in the nineteenth century, developed another doctrine of interest groups that had a profound effect on U.S. history. Calhoun's theory of "concurrent majorities" asserted that the legitimacy of national government action depended on the acquiescence of the interests affected by the action. The distinct interests of the states, Calhoun said, deserved protection from the larger interests of the nation. Calhoun argued that a state could "nullify," or veto, federal actions that usurped state independence.

Calhoun's home state of South Carolina invoked the doctrine of nullification after enactment of a tariff bill in 1828 that state officials considered discriminatory against the South. President Andrew Jackson responded by sending warships to the harbor of Charleston, and the state legislature soon revoked the act of nullification.

Even though Jackson defeated the most extreme form of concurrent majorities, the theory remained a part of U.S. politics. The notion that states' rights had priority over the national interest helped to bring about the Civil War. After the war, the states' rights view held considerable sway in the national political debate. In the compromise over the 1876 presidential election, the national government ceded considerable autonomy to the states over the issues of basic civil rights and commerce. (See "Compromise: 1876," p. 378, in Chapter 6.)

The states' rights view crumbled as the national government gained strength in the twentieth century, but a doctrine similar in many ways to Calhoun's theory arose. Especially since the Great Society of the 1960s, a practice that might be called "representational democracy" has guided policy making in national politics. This practice encourages or requires the government to gain the consent of groups affected by legislation or regulations before it implements such policies.

Recent critics charge that the American system too easily accommodates groups of all kinds. Whereas Madison counted on interest groups to guard jealously against rivals, in fact groups reinforce each others' actions. Jonathan Rauch writes in *Demosclerosis* that interest groups seek to avoid conflict that would threaten a stable working environment. According to Rauch:

> So why don't all these lobbies cancel each other out? . . . Lobbies work hard to avoid head-on confrontations with other lobbies, for exactly the same reason that politicians work to avoid confrontations with lobbies: challenge someone's sinecure, and you get his fist in your face. If the farmers tell the government, "We want you to kill the ranchers' subsidy and give us the money," they can count on a bruising fight with the cattlemen's association. On the other hand, if they say, "The ranchers are getting land-use subsidies, so please raise our price supports," they avoid antagonizing any powerful group directly.[6]

This kind of accommodation is likely to continue. Interest groups do not have incentives to give up benefits, and the federal government lacks the political support to develop comprehensive policies that are accepted across the nation.

THE RISE OF MODERN INTEREST GROUP POLITICS

During the first decades of the twentieth century, the Washington lobbying community grew markedly in size, variety, and sophistication. Unprecedented numbers of organized interests became actively engaged in the national policy-making process during the Progressive Era, including an explosion of trade associations, private corporations, labor organizations, professional associations, and citizens groups activated by diverse social, economic, and international issues. During the First World War, the federal government directly spurred further development of the national interest group system by encouraging better organization of business and labor sectors to better coordinate wartime industrial production. As the political scientist E. Pendleton Herring noted soon after the war, "In mobilizing the full strength of the country these special interest units gave the government cohesive and responsible organizations with which to deal."[7] Presidents such as Theodore Roosevelt and Woodrow Wilson viewed the rise of an increasingly centralized and professional interest group politics with foreboding. "I am genuinely independent of the big monied men all matters where I think the interests of the public are concerned," Roosevelt noted. "But . . . it is out of the question for me to expect them to grant favors to me in return. The sum of this is that I can make no private or special appeals to them, and I am at my wits' end how to proceed."[8] Nearly every modern president since has decried what Ronald Reagan called a "Washington colony" of "special interest groups" that undermines the public good.[9]

The growth of the national interest group system continued during the New Deal of Franklin D. Roosevelt (FDR),

President Calvin Coolidge meets with members of the Sioux Indian Republican Club in March 1925.

as subsidies to farmers, but they had strings attached. Enterprises, then, recognized the need to establish a permanent presence in Washington to influence the federal agencies and committees that controlled the strings. As the government's regulation of many aspects of economic and social life increased, interest groups sprang up to influence the way the government controlled their affairs.

and today organized interests are an important fixture in national political life. According to political scientist Theodore J. Lowi, the United States has seen two distinct styles of government, which he calls the first and second "republics." In its early years, the national government was a "patronage state" (its first republic) based on the demands for internal improvements by governments and businesses at the state and local levels.[10] The national party system, with the president at its apex, played an important role in the process of internal development. But that process remained fundamentally parochial—congressional and party leaders from the states merely vied for a fair share of patronage—until Franklin Roosevelt's New Deal programs of the 1930s.

Beginning with the administrations of Theodore Roosevelt and Woodrow Wilson, and gaining full strength during Franklin Roosevelt's New Deal, the federal government expanded its reach over general regulation of the economy (the second republic). Instead of simply doling out resources to discrete states and constituencies, the government began to play an important role in almost all aspects of political and economic life.

In time, the federal government regulated the everyday activities of a wide range of enterprises, such as banking, labor relations, transportation systems, the media, mining and development of natural resources, manufacturing, product safety, farming, the environment, and civil rights. Thus instead of simply seeking direct material rewards from the government—and then using those rewards as they wished—a wide variety of enterprises saw even the most mundane business practices regulated by the government. The government continued to offer material rewards, such

The national interest group system grew over time from a few thousand in the early twentieth century to the nearly ten thousand groups listed in the *Encyclopedia of Associations* in 1970.[11] By 1990, that figure had doubled to twenty thousand interest groups, and it continues to grow at a dramatic rate during the twenty-first century.

Significantly, even these robust numbers underestimate the amount of interest group activity because of the even more extensive activity of national organizations at the state and local levels. For example, the Chamber of Commerce and the American Federation of Labor-Congress of Industrial Organizations (AFL-CIO) each count as one interest group in the Washington surveys, but they have many subdivisions across the nation. In 2002 the chamber claimed to represent 3,000,000 businesses, 3,000 state and local chapters, and 830 business associations, as well as 92 U.S. Chambers of Commerce Abroad. The AFL-CIO included more than thirteen million dues-paying members in sixty-six affiliated unions.[12]

Political action committees (PACs) boomed in the 1970s and 1980s after election finance laws were changed in 1974.[13] PACs are essentially checkbook organizations run by interest groups that depend on, PACs have become a major contributor to federal and statewide campaigns. PACs do not, however, have the active membership programs and tangible benefits of other groups such as the AFL-CIO. Originally, PACs were mostly connected to labor groups, but in the last two decades, PACs have proliferated and expanded to a wide range of interest groups. In 1974, 608 PACS registered with the newly established Federal Election Commission; by century's end, there were nearly 4,000.[14]

In subsequent years, interest group involvement in campaigns and elections incorporated two new dimensions to circumvent campaign finance regulation. Interest groups began making substantial contributions of "soft (unregulated) money" to the national political parties. This exercise enabled them to funnel funds far in excess of federal limits indirectly to favored candidates. In addition, interest groups began focusing much of their campaign activity on "issue advocacy," efforts that implicitly, but not explicitly, endorsed or attacked candidates. As such, it also fell outside the jurisdiction of campaign finance regulation. Campaign finance reform enacted in 2002 sought to limit these activities. *(See "The Campaign Finance System," p. 261, in Chapter 5.)*

Interest groups have increased their role in national politics partly because of the decline of political parties, the increased fragmentation of Congress, the rise of regulatory politics, the greater complexity of many government issues, and changes in the style of campaigning. Interest groups represent the politics of specialization, whereas the political style in the United States previously was majority rule. Interest groups continued to heighten in significance amid noteworthy party resurgence in the 1990s.

Modern Theories of Interest Groups

Since the rise of the modern bureaucratic state, scholars have developed theories to justify or explain the place of interest groups in politics. One of the predominant theories of U.S. politics used a market model to justify the role of interest groups in policy making. Sociologist Arthur F. Bentley argued in 1908 that pursuit of the public interest was misguided. The sum total of government, he asserted, was the result of groups competing for position and favor. Interest groups had a "representative quality" that ensured a degree of democratic activity as groups competed for influence.[15]

Political scientist David Truman argued in 1951 that the result of interest group competition and bargaining was a consensus on the public interest.[16] Truman's model resembled the economic model of British economist Adam Smith, which held that an "invisible hand" guided self-interested competition among firms toward the public interest. According to Truman, the interaction of groups enabled a variety of viewpoints and material interests to get a public hearing. The result was a democratic contest over policy at all levels. Political scientist Robert A. Dahl reached similar conclusions in a 1961 study of community power.[17]

Later students of interest groups disputed the cheery views of such pluralists as Bentley, Truman, and Dahl. Political scientist E. E. Schattschneider and sociologists C. Wright Mills and Floyd Hunter argued that the interests of economically disadvantaged groups did not receive adequate representation simply because they did not have the resources to press their causes.[18] These scholars maintained that the makeup of the interest group universe had an elite bias.[19]

In perhaps the most influential work to question the assumption that citizens easily form groups to represent their interests, economist Mancur Olson pointed out that many groups with a definite stake in government actions have difficulty organizing because of limited resources and limited incentives for individuals to join the cause.[20] Group formation is most likely to occur when groups offer material incentives or even coerce prospective members. Labor unions, which automatically deduct dues from workers' paychecks, exercise a form of membership coercion. Because the less-advantaged groups in society have a smaller surplus to spend on political action, they lose out in the competition for influence over the government.

Another critique of interest group politics stresses the overload of modern bureaucratic politics. Sociologist Daniel Bell argues that economic conflicts have increasingly fallen to the federal government to resolve, needing entitlements to paper over fundamental contradictions between forces, such as the management–labor and business–environmentalist schisms. "One large question that the American system now confronts is whether it can find a way to resolve these conflicts. Lacking rules to mediate claims, the system will be under severe strains."[21]

A growing danger of the increased influence of interest groups is the erosion of government authority and legitimacy. Instead of integrating citizens into a process of mutual accommodation with a goal of the public interest, interest groups often isolate citizens from one another. The common purpose that is the hallmark of republican theory is lost to self-interested competition that does not recognize common social destiny.[22]

The autonomy given to many interest groups removes many policies from democratic deliberation and reduces the maneuvering room on issues that are on the public agenda. For example, the control given farmers over prices and land cultivation removes agriculture policy from the general debate about how society should allocate resources. And because they often are nonnegotiable, policies on agriculture, Social Security, Medicare, job training, and military spending reduce the options for the president and Congress on a wide variety of budget and social issues. In Theodore Lowi's view, by giving groups autonomy over parts of public policy, the public loses control over the wide range of interrelated issues. The system becomes inflexible and policy options close.[23]

How Interest Groups View and Interact with the White House

Most students of U.S. national politics conclude that interest group activity is concentrated on the specific bureaucratic agencies and congressional committees that address the particular concerns of organized interests—not on the White House. For example, farmers deal with the Department of

Agriculture and the congressional committees that allocate money to farm programs.

Interest groups do not concentrate on the White House for a number of reasons. First, the schedules of the president and top presidential aides are tight, so it is difficult even to get the president's time and attention. It is much easier to get the attention of a member of Congress or of a civil servant. One aide to President Lyndon B. Johnson explained: "There are 535 opportunities in Congress and only one in the White House. You get an hour to present your case before each representative, and only fifteen minutes once a year with the president. Where would you put your effort?" [24]

Second, the president's tenure in office is short compared with the terms of key bureaucrats and members of Congress. Postwar presidents have served on average about five and a half years. Much of the president's time is spent learning the ropes or struggling with lame duck status.

Third, presidents usually devote their time to a few top priorities—and those priorities are shaped by previous alliances. Only occasionally can an interest group alter a president's set agenda.

Finally, the president is the nation's most public political figure, and interest groups usually operate best out of the glare of public attention where they can promote their interests through small legislative and regulatory means. Seeking a shift in import duties, for example, is a matter best addressed by Commerce Department bureaucrats, not by the president.

Even though interest groups favor the predictability of agencies and committees, many still maintain a relationship with the presidency. Since World War II, the White House has developed regular channels for interest groups to make and receive appeals. The size of the White House staff has increased greatly, with many officials assigned in some way to keeping track of interest groups. The most formal mechanism in the White House for dealing with interest groups is the Office of Public Liaison, created in the administrations of Richard M. Nixon and Gerald R. Ford.

Political scientist Robert H. Salisbury has noted that interest groups often "tend to gravitate toward the effective centers of power in a given political system." As the White House has become the initiator of the national political agenda, it has become the focus for at least some policy areas such as economic and security policy, and even matters such as prayer in schools—even if the bulk of policies are better addressed in the bureaucracy and congressional committees. The White House may not be the focus of all interest group activity, but neither is it a place of last resort for groups.[25]

Interest groups do not become active only when a policy directly affects them. Effective lobbies make regular contact with political figures, often offering financial or logistical assistance and useful information even when no policy proposals are under discussion. Such assistance helps them to secure access when the issues about which they would like to have a say do arise.

Corporate interests have consistently demonstrated their willingness to fund presidential inaugural festivities. They picked up most of the $33 million tab for Bill Clinton's first inauguration in 1993 and provided $23.7 million to underwrite his second inauguration four years later. In 2001 corporate interests donated more than $35 million for the inaugural festivities honoring George W. Bush.[26] Such gifts could put subtle pressure on the White House to at least consider appeals of donors on controversial issues.

When the president attempts a major initiative—such as Ronald Reagan's tax- and budget-cutting initiatives of 1981 and his tax reform of 1986, or Clinton's deficit-reduction program of 1993 and health care legislation of 1994—interest groups respond in two ways. First, they recruit their members to contact congressional representatives. Second, they attempt to shape public opinion with advertising campaigns in the mass media. Both strategies effectively eliminated most of the important aspects of Clinton's health care reform plan.

Some authorities maintain that the president has an advantage in dealing with interest groups. For example, the White House "is less likely to be besieged at its most vulnerable points because lobbyists are less likely to know where those points are," observe political scientists Martha Joynt Kumar and Michael Baruch Grossman.[27] But the growth of the White House staff also has produced a separate arena in which interest groups can concentrate their appeals. White House officials who have served as unofficial spokespersons for interest groups include George H. W. Bush's first chief of staff, John H. Sununu (nuclear power interests), and Clinton's first chief of staff, Thomas F. "Mack" McLarty (natural gas producers). In the George W. Bush's administration, the vice president, Richard B. Cheney, not to mention the president himself, had extensive ties to the energy sector of the economy.

Although interest groups may sometimes have difficulty finding a point of entry into the White House, they do know their way around the executive bureaucracy. The White House must then struggle to exercise control over the huge and complex bureaucracy.

How the White House Views and Interacts with Interest Groups

Interest group politics have continued to grow and change with the inclusion of new groups in the political process. Since the 1970s, a proliferation of groups on both the right and left has presented new challenges to presidents from both parties. Especially pronounced has been the challenge from the right, since its forces were better financed.

Former governors Jimmy Carter, Ronald Reagan, Bill Clinton, and George W. Bush had no national political experience before becoming president. All but Carter also faced the daunting problems of divided party government, and he received little benefit from Democratic Party majorities in both chambers of Congress, owing to division within the ranks of congressional Democrats. The only nongovernor to serve as president in the past quarter-century, George H. W. Bush, also suffered under divided party government.

The fortunes of their legislative agendas turned in part on the bewildering welter of interest groups. These presidents attempted to assemble viable coalitions on an issue-by-issue basis. But as they ventured into interest group politics, opposing groups allied to thwart their agendas—and party coalitions became even more vulnerable. Political scientist Joseph A. Pika has written, "In this way, presidents may have weakened political parties just at the time they were most needed as mechanisms to organize effective coalitions to pass legislative initiatives." [28]

Intraparty cohesion, as well as interparty division, increased during the 1990s. Still, presidents lacking disciplined party majorities in both houses of Congress must cobble together legislative majorities for their proposals by appealing to interest group allies.

An important part of Republican presidential candidate Reagan's electoral strategy in 1980 was harnessing the so-called New Right, a wide range of groups that promoted an agenda that included tax cuts, reduced federal regulation, an end to legal abortions, a return to prayer in the schools, federal tax breaks for parochial schools, restricted gay rights, and a more rigid interpretation of civil rights. Reagan provided hortatory leadership, submitted legislation on some of these issues, and involved Christian organizations in drafting tuition tax credit legislation. But overall, the New Right agenda was a low priority in Reagan's first term. Reagan held on to the groups' support, however, because they had nowhere else to go.

President Clinton's noteworthy legislative successes—the 1993 tax and budget bill, passage of the North American Free Trade Agreement (NAFTA), anticrime legislation, and welfare and lobbying reforms—carried the visible imprint of interest group politics. Clinton's strategy involved attacking as well as negotiating with important interest groups. In his more successful efforts, Clinton assigned a staff member to assemble a workable coalition of interest groups that could be used to prod reluctant legislators. One such effort, the NAFTA campaign, was managed by Chicago political operative William Daley, the son and brother of two powerful Chicago mayors.

As with his father and Clinton before him, George W. Bush's most successful domestic initiatives—most notably education reform in 2001 and Medicare reform in 2003—were centrist measures that relied on compromise and bipartisan coalitions. The administration's more controversial legislative proposals, such as its initiative to involve faith-based organizations in the delivery of government-funded social services, efforts to authorize oil drilling in Alaska's Arctic National Wildlife Refuge, and blueprints for restructuring Social Security to permit a measure of privatization were all frustrated by resistant interest groups.

Calculating Interest Group Politics

The ongoing calculations of interest group politics at the White House take into account a number of factors. Perhaps the most important is which interests have supported the president's political campaigns and government initiatives. Just as when dealing with public opinion, the president must maintain the steady backing of a basic core of supporters and bring independents and opposition figures into alliances that will support different issues. At the same time, chief executives must avoid the appearance of being beholden to powerful special interests. The political fallout produced by the Jack Abramoff lobbying scandal is only the most recent illustration of the risks of too close an association with well-heeled interests. Abramoff was one of the most influential lobbyists and Republican activists in Washington working since the mid-1990s. In January 2006, Abramoff pled guilty to felony counts of conspiracy, fraud, and tax evasion stemming from a scheme to bilk Native American casino interests he represented out of $85 million. He also admitted to bribing elected officials, such as powerful Ohio Republican representative Bob Ney.

Interest group alliances shift from issue to issue. Most groups do not get involved in legislative or regulatory activity outside their direct interests; they only become active when they see a possible gain or threat in government initiatives. Large-scale policy making entails a wider array of competing groups than incremental policy making. As a result, presidents must consider the extent to which their initiatives will activate interest groups. Business and organized labor often switch sides depending on the issue. The two groups may work together on such issues as construction projects, banking regulation, and other legislation affecting economic growth. But they will oppose each other on issues affecting the organization of the workplace, such as "common site" picketing (picketing of a workplace by workers not directly involved in the dispute), "right to work" rules (restrictions on union organizing), and workplace safety legislation.

Other factors in the calculations of shifting interest group politics are the salience of issues and the timing of events. As economist Anthony Downs has noted, issues are subject to a cycle of attention. [29] After a period of high publicity, most issues tend to fade from public consciousness. The president may try to focus attention on particular issues, but the public and interest groups will still react

according to their priorities at the time.

The president must
respond to issues put on
the public agenda by
concerted interest group
efforts. Likewise, the
president must take into
account—and influence,
if possible—just how
much attention the pub-
lic is giving an issue and
how groups are respond-
ing to that attention.

A final factor in the
calculations is the relative
strength of different
interest groups. The
membership, wealth, and
status of advocacy organ-
izations vary greatly. Most interest groups have just a few
hundred members and budgets in the hundreds of thousands of dollars. Others, such as the American Association of
Retired Persons (AARP), have multimillion dollar budgets,
large memberships that can be deployed swiftly on various
campaigns, and professional staffs and consultants to advise
them. Many are connected with corporations that they can
use for overhead expenses, expert advice, technology, and
membership lists.

The White House examines the balance of power
among interest groups on specific issues as it plans its strategy on how to deal with a particular issue. This is not to say
that the president decides which side of the issue to take
based on this balance of power, only whether to attempt to
influence the issue and, if so, what tactics to use. For example, President Reagan decided to pursue omnibus budget
reconciliation legislation in 1981 when a wide range of interest groups appeared ready to defeat the administration, issue
by issue, in congressional committees. The package cut
$130.6 billion from the federal budget over four years.[30]

The president's relationship with interest groups develops according to issue. The president can rely on certain
groups always to be supportive and others always to offer
opposition. The president usually must seek the support of
many fence-straddling groups. Groups traditionally aligning
with Republican presidents include business, oil companies,
conservative social and religious groups, and some farm
groups. Traditional Democratic allies include many multinational firms, labor, environmental groups, feminists, and
minorities.

Working behind the scenes, interest groups attempt to
shape the details of major White House policy initiatives.
Mark Bloomfield and Charls Walker developed the Bush

During his presidency, Ronald Reagan frequently criticized federal coercion of states. In 1984, however, after a lengthy campaign by Mothers Against Drunk Driving, he signed legislation to penalize states that did not increase the mandatory drinking age to twenty-one.

administration's 1990
capital gains tax-cut
proposal. The propos-
al expanded the types
of investments receiv-
ing tax preference
from stocks and bonds
to include other pas-
sive assets such as real
estate and corporate
structures. "Inclusion
of timber and other assets," a confidential memorandum
outlining the initiative advised, would bring the "timber
industry, agricultural interests, heretofore reluctant small
business organizations, and others into the private-sector
capital-gains coalition." The memo also urged Bush to work
more closely with the Capital Gains Coalition, a group of
businesses actively lobbying on Capitol Hill.[31] Although the
legislation did not pass, it helped to shape Bush's legislative
relations.

Interest groups also pursue public strategies to promote their causes. As one example, interest groups have
played an increasing role in the confirmation process for
U.S. Supreme Court nominations. After bruising battles over
Reagan's nomination of Robert H. Bork and George H. W.
Bush's nomination of Clarence Thomas, President Clinton
was careful to select candidates with little in their records to
spark controversy from interest groups. Thus it was only
after lengthy searches that Clinton nominated Ruth Bader
Ginsburg and Stephen G. Breyer to the high court. During
the searches, Clinton floated many possibilities that were
later withdrawn after objections from organized groups. In a
trickle-down effect, interest groups occasionally have

extended their focus on judicial confirmations to lower-court nominations as well. Charles W. Pickering, nominated by Republican George W. Bush for a position on the Fifth Circuit Court of Appeals, attracted significant opposition from liberal interest groups. The Senate Judiciary Committee with a slight Democratic majority, on a party-line vote, declined to send the Pickering nomination to the floor, effectively killing it. Clearly, the presence of divided party government heightens the significance of interest groups in judicial nominations.

Cabinet positions also are subject to intense public lobbying. Casualties of interest group opposition included former Texas senator John G. Tower, President George H. W. Bush's first nominee for secretary of defense. Morton Halperin, director of the Washington office of the American Civil Liberties Union (ACLU), saw his nomination for a high-level State Department position in the Clinton administration withdrawn after conservative groups complained about his past writings criticizing government policies on defense and intelligence gathering. George W. Bush's nominee for attorney general, John Ashcroft, survived a withering confirmation process that featured intense interest group mobilization both in opposition and in support of his candidacy.

Using technologies that allow almost instant contact with organization members and key political figures, interest groups have undertaken a number of public campaigns in recent years to rouse the public on specific issues. Liberal organizations mobilized against the policies and nominees of the Reagan and both Bush administrations. When Clinton won the presidency in 1992, conservatives mobilized. Floyd Brown, an independent political operative, sent a newsletter to 175,000 subscribers and regularly publicized charges against Clinton. Brown even sold an audiotape of Clinton talking with a woman who claimed to have had an affair with him. The Center for Security Policy, a conservative group that successfully opposed Clinton nominations, sent out triweekly "attack faxes" to one thousand public officials and opinion leaders.[32]

Inevitably, interest groups that support the president during election campaigns become disenchanted with the administration's performance. Organized labor, civil rights groups, mayors, social workers, and advocates of a national health system were disappointed with President Carter's policies, particularly after his budget and defense priorities shifted in a conservative direction during the second half of his term. This disappointment led many to urge Sen. Edward M. Kennedy of Massachusetts to challenge Carter for the 1980 Democratic nomination. The far right groups that supported George H. W. Bush's candidacy in 1988 later were upset that Bush was not more vigorous in promoting their agenda, including prayer in the schools, tuition tax credits for private schools, and an antiabortion constitu-tional amendment. Many in the right wing found a new voice in Patrick J. Buchanan, whose challenge of Bush in the 1992 primaries weakened the unity of the party and contributed to Bush's defeat. President Clinton in 1993 clashed bitterly with organized labor, a major Democratic constituency, over the North American Free Trade Agreement. Labor claimed that NAFTA would cost Americans jobs and damage the environment. The tensions over NAFTA lasted long after the successful, but very close, vote in Congress. The George W. Bush administration advanced the policy goals of its closest interest group allies through unilateral actions such as executive orders and control over the implementation and regulatory processes. For example, the Bush White House used its regulatory influence to advance the positions of allies in policy areas such as consumer protection, environmental control, labor standards, drug safety, and stem cell research, to name a few.

The President's Staff and Interest Groups

Since the earliest days of the American republic, presidents have assigned staff members to monitor important interest groups. Andrew Jackson's aides, for example, carefully gauged the activities and strength of bankers and businesses opposed to the administration (1829–1837). A little over a century later, Franklin Roosevelt's New Deal initiated governmental growth that gave hundreds of new groups reason to have a regular relationship with Washington politicians, including the president. Today, interest groups are so important to the presidency that the White House has an office—the Office of Public Liaison—devoted exclusively to monitoring and cajoling interest groups.

The president's relations with interest groups have not always been so direct as they are today. Before the expansion of the White House staff in the postwar era, the cabinet served as the main link between interest groups and the administration.[33] Cabinet officials tended to have strong ties to the groups whose affairs their departments oversaw, and over the years they developed an appreciation of the concerns of interest groups. Administrations also developed relations with interest groups through political parties and campaign organizations.

Many of the cabinet-level departments were designed to serve the interests of specific groups. The Departments of Agriculture, Commerce, and Labor were created after years of lobbying by farmers, business leaders, and unions. At first designed to be research centers, the departments later gave their clients influence over a wide range of programs. Other federal agencies created at the urging of interest groups include the Federal Reserve Board, Federal Trade Commission, and Environmental Protection Agency (EPA). Agencies even helped to create organizations for interest groups, as when the Department of Commerce helped to organize the U.S. Chamber of Commerce.

Departments develop strong ties to interest groups even if they were not created specifically to serve those groups. Political scientists have used images of enduring "iron triangles" and more fluid "issue networks" to express the common outlooks and interests that develop among agencies and congressional committees and the groups they regulate.[34] Even some administration appointees develop protective views toward their agencies and the interest groups with whom they work.

To the extent that presidents need advice on issues, they rely on the information provided by the departments as well as the advice of a small staff in the White House and informal advisers. The interest-dominated departments are the incubators of presidential legislative initiatives. Bureaucrats interested in improving the status of their agencies develop programs that enlarge their involvement with interest groups.

Presidents frequently appoint interest group representatives to administration posts to gain their support. Less than 1 percent of the federal bureaucracy today is filled with presidential appointees, but strategic use of those posts can improve presidential relations with interest groups. The president appoints interest group representatives for a number of reasons: to gain insight into constituent groups or leverage in bargaining, to co-opt groups by giving them formal involvement in policy discussions, and simply to establish a common ground for dealing with those groups. Political scientist Nelson Polsby refers to this pattern of presidential cabinet making as "clientele-oriented."[35]

For some agencies, interest groups have almost absolute authority over presidential nominations and appointments. For example, from Dwight D. Eisenhower through Clinton, the Justice Department formally solicited ratings of judicial nominations by the American Bar Association. Appointments for the Federal Reserve Board, Treasury Department, Central Intelligence Agency (CIA), and Defense Department will likely require the approval of their interest group establishments—bankers, businesses, academic experts, and defense contractors. President Carter dropped his nomination of Theodore C. Sorensen as CIA director after the intelligence community and conservative activists criticized it strongly.

Democratic presidents must solicit the blessings of African Americans, women's groups, environmental activists, consumer groups, real estate developers, multinationals, social workers, and organized labor for their major appointments because these groups are an important part of the Democratic coalition. Republican presidents must satisfy developers of natural resources, multinational and small business concerns, financial and insurance interests, conservative social and religious groups, and defense contractors. President Carter withdrew his proposed nomination of John Dunlop for secretary of labor in 1976 because of opposition

from African American and women's groups. Later, President Reagan consulted Moral Majority leader Jerry Falwell before appointing Sandra Day O'Connor to the Supreme Court, because he was concerned that Falwell might oppose O'Connor over her vote as an Arizona state legislator for funding abortions.[36]

Who does not get an important cabinet position is often as revealing as who gets the post. Some Republican presidents have reached out to groups outside their coalition by appointing moderates to the Environmental Protection Agency and the Labor, Interior, and Energy Departments. Reagan, however, rebuffed those agencies' key clients by making appointments antagonistic to their concerns. Reagan's first secretary of interior, James G. Watt, had been a lawyer for a firm strongly opposed to restrictions on the development of natural resources. (Watt himself was associated with the Mountain States Legal Foundation, an interest group for developers and oil concerns.) Reagan's first energy chief, James B. Edwards, had no experience in the field and was told to do all he could to close down the department.

Tasks of the White House Staff

Kumar and Grossman have argued that the presidency's relationship with interest groups involves four basic roles, representing four distinct tasks for the administration. To enact its policies, the administration usually must deal with all four tasks at the same time. Assigned within the White House to carry out these tasks, the "marker" keeps track of the president's debts to particular groups and attempts to help those groups; the "communicant" gathers information about current interest group concerns; the "constructor" builds coalitions for specific policy initiatives; and the "broker" helps the administration and groups with different interests to negotiate their differences to give the president sufficiently broad backing for policy initiatives.[37]

The Reagan administration's action on its tax cuts in 1981 illustrates all four tasks. Partly to repay the business community for its support in the 1980 election, the administration proposed and shepherded through Congress legislation that would reduce the marginal tax rates on individuals by 30 percent over three years and would provide massive corporate tax relief. The original decision to push the legislation illustrates the "marker" task.

Before and after taking up the legislation, the White House acted as a communicant, sounding out diverse groups on tax and other issues. Staffers gathered information about which groups were likely to support and oppose the legislation and how strong and reliable they were.

White House constructors helped to build a coalition to back the legislation in Congress. A wide variety of groups joined the coalition, including the U.S. Chamber of Commerce, Business Roundtable, National Small Business

First Lady Eleanor Roosevelt was one of Franklin Roosevelt's most important emissaries to interest groups such as African Americans and labor. Here she speaks to members of the CIO, AFL, and unaffiliated unions in West Park, New York.

House staff can settle the differences.

In the Reagan administration, the Office of Management and Budget (OMB) played an important role not only in arbitrating budget claims but also in developing new federal regulations. Under a presidential order, OMB studied the impact of new regulations before they went into effect. White House and OMB purview over the budget and regulations meant a reduced role for interest groups. Before, public action on regulations extended simply to publication of the public's comments in the *Federal Register*. Under Reagan, regulations came under the control of OMB. The close relationship that interest groups enjoyed with specific agencies was not enough for their wishes to prevail.

Critics of these developments focused on lack of expertise among the White House staff and OMB officials on the many complex matters under agency jurisdiction. The Reagan White House staff, as in previous administrations, was made up of political operatives, and OMB was staffed by political professionals and accountants—few of whom knew much if anything about the chemical issues involved in environmental regulations, for example, or the complex interrelationships between different components of tax and welfare policy.

Stung by criticism that his White House was not aggressively restricting the growth of regulations, President George H. W. Bush created the Council on Competitiveness, chaired by Vice President Dan Quayle. The council, deliberating in strict secrecy, attempted to deal with contentious regulatory issues—issues dear to many special interests. Once again much criticism arose of this arrangement, which gave the impression of allowing private interests a chance at "backdoor rulemaking." One of the first executive orders President Clinton issued in 1993 disbanded the Council on Competitiveness and limited the role of OMB in reviewing new regulations. Clinton's executive order also required that OMB disclose all communications with federal agencies or outside parties during the course of its review. In turn, President George W. Bush took immediate action on the Saturday of his inauguration to block implementation of several executive orders expanding the scope of federal reg-

Association, Moral Majority, and National Conservative Political Action Committee. Wayne Valis, a special assistant to the president, oversaw the coordination of interest group efforts.

Finally, the administration served as a broker to settle differences among the administration, congressional leaders, and interest groups. One result of the bargaining was a reduction of the tax cut from 30 to 25 percent and a delay of the legislation's implementation.

Interest group relations with the White House are most routine—and important—on budgetary matters. Interest groups develop relationships with bureaucrats in federal agencies throughout the year, and those agencies develop budget proposals in the last three months of the calendar year. The proposals work their way up the system to the cabinet secretaries and the president.

As it has grown in size, the White House staff has played a greater role in overseeing budget recommendations. The White House, often distrusting departmental recommendations, wants to create coherent domestic and foreign programs that often are impossible without top-down control. When departments and agencies do not agree on budget and program authorities, only the president and the White

ulatory authority issued by Clinton in the waning days of his presidency.

THE INTEREST GROUP SYSTEM TODAY

Most of today's active interest groups are the offspring of past political and economic movements, and their survival and involvement in politics are one of the constraints on the activities of the president, the executive bureaucracy, and Congress. Yet the interest groups serve not just as constraints; they also offer politicians a means of mobilizing political activity.

Interest groups represent every conceivable group in the United States: big and small business, domestic and multinational manufacturers and services, banks and insurance companies, real estate developers, teachers, miners, lawyers, blue-collar workers, opponents of unions, senior citizens, peaceniks, military contractors, consumers, evangelicals, Jews, Arabs, Hispanics, gays, feminists, guardians of different notions of the public interest, states and cities, government workers, secretaries, custodians, athletes, actors, environmentalists, developers of natural resources—and the list goes on and on. The interest group universe is so large that it contains innumerable internal contradictions. Within the set of interest groups concerned about military affairs, for example, keen competition often exists. Recent presidents sold weapons to influence the balance of power in the Middle East, provoking opposition from the nations or interests that felt put at a disadvantage.

To understand interest groups, it is important to understand their different goals and functions, resources, everyday activities, and long-term strategies.

Goals and Functions

Interest groups form to promote a group's material interests in budget, tax, and regulatory proceedings in Washington; to express a group's ideology and desires; or to provide a group with a forum, services, and standards.

The U.S. Chamber of Commerce is an umbrella organization for more than three million businesses, three thousand state and local chapters, and more than eight hundred business associations. The chamber's annual $100 million budget provides about $10 million for direct lobbying of both the federal and state governments. The chamber is dedicated to one overriding goal: improving the conditions for business expansion. Active in issues such as tax legislation, labor laws, and regulatory relief, the group has a definite ideology, but it is interested primarily in material concerns.

The chamber is the largest business organization in the United States. Other active business groups designed strictly to produce better conditions for economic activity include the Business Roundtable, oil lobbies, and the National Small Business Association.

Hoping to persuade the Clinton administration to impose quotas and broad tariffs on foreign steel imports, steelworkers protest in Washington, D.C., January 1999. A few thousand steelworkers and supporters marched from the Capitol to the White House.

The AFL-CIO also is designed to advance the material benefits of its members. The organization has more than thirteen million dues-paying members in sixty-six affiliated unions, including the Teamsters, the United Auto Workers, the United Mine Workers, and American Federation of Teachers. The AFL-CIO's job is simple: bargain for the best wages, benefits, and working conditions possible, and make the task of organizing workers as easy and efficient as possible.

The Chamber of Commerce and the AFL-CIO are interested mainly in material benefits for their members. Other interest groups have more expressive agendas. Rather than simply seeking a share of federal largesse, they exist to promote their ideological or cultural values. Many of the evangelical and conservative groups that fall under the New Right umbrella were founded to promote values rather than material interests. Frustrated with what they perceive to be a decline in the moral values of the family, groups such as the Christian Coalition, National Right to Life Committee, and National Conservative Political Action Committee contribute generously to political campaigns and lobby hard in the White House and on Capitol Hill. They have promoted an antiabortion amendment to the Constitution, prayer in the schools, and tuition tax credits for private schools. They also have spoken out on foreign policy issues such as arms control. Other important ideologically oriented organizations include the Americans for Democratic Action, American Civil Liberties Union, Cato Institute, the Heritage Foundation, and People for the American Way.

Professional organizations take on both material and expressive functions. The American Bar Association, American Medical Association (AMA), and American Association of State Colleges and Universities serve as protectors of professional standards and ideals, but they also want to defend the privileges of their members. The AMA, for example, is among the biggest contributors to political campaigns and actively defends the profession's material interests whenever Congress considers issues such as Medicare or hospital cost-containment legislation.

Since the 1970s there has been a boom in public interest lobbies. These groups do not promote the interests of any single sector but instead promote their nonpartisan vision of the general interest of all society. The members of these groups do not stand to receive special material benefits if their ideals are realized, but the policies they promote would help some groups at the expense of others. Prominent public interest groups include Common Cause, the League of Women Voters, the U.S. Public Interest Research Group and other organizations set up by consumer activist Ralph Nader and the Consumer Federation of America.

Resources and Everyday Activities

The influence of interest groups differs according to their resources. Money, size of membership, technological sophistication (such as computer networks, direct-mail operations, fax machines, telephone banks, polling operations), expertise on issues, familiarity with the political process, political reputation and contacts, motivation, and leadership are the important factors defining an organization's strength.[38]

The everyday activities of most lobbies consist of unglamorous work such as monitoring legislation on Capitol Hill and regulatory action in agencies, researching issues, fund raising, surveying and responding to the concerns of membership, and staying in touch with congressional staff members.

Most interest groups have a legislative agenda that they would like to pursue, but they rarely have the opportunity to press specific proposals at the White House or on Capitol Hill. Usually they must form alliances with other groups on specific issues that the president, Congress, or federal departments are considering. An interest group's agenda, then, is pursued bit by bit rather than as a whole. This helps to explain why interest groups often become disenchanted

with an administration that considers itself an ally: the interest group may consider its program to be the president's program, but presidents also must serve other, often conflicting groups and goals.

Long-term Strategies

Because of the slow pace of legislative action in Washington, lobbies must be content to pursue incremental change most of the time. But groups must do what they can to develop a wide range of large and small initiatives so they are able to act when opportunities for exerting influence arise.

Interest groups must decide whether they are going to use insider or outsider strategies to influence the president and the rest of the Washington establishment.[39] Insiders establish ties with a number of White House, agency, and congressional staffers and, depending on the administration, can play a role in writing legislation and regulations that affect their interests. Outsiders attempt to pressure the administration by putting the public spotlight on the issues they consider important.

Interest groups often move from outsider to insider roles with a change in administration. Many consumer protection and environmental protection groups moved from the outside to the inside with the election of Carter in 1976. Carter appointed a number of "Naderites"—disciples of activist Ralph Nader—to top agency positions. Likewise, before Reagan was elected president, the Moral Majority and other conservative groups relied on public relations campaigns and insurgent candidates. After Reagan became president, however, the White House consulted these groups on many social initiatives. They helped to write tuition tax credit legislation.

Public Efforts by Interest Groups

Textbooks of U.S. politics stress the cozy, behind-the-scenes relationships between interest groups and government agencies and congressional committees. But many groups are not part of the federal establishment and must orchestrate large public demonstrations to influence the president and other parts of the government.

In recent years, protest has become a regular part of American politics. Protest traditionally was a political strategy of groups excluded from the mainstream of American life, such as minorities and poor people. But middle-class movements are increasingly resorting to advocacy and protest to promote their interests.

A number of groups representing the public interest have arisen in recent years to pressure the president and Congress on a wide range of issues. United We Stand America, a rump group formed by 1992 independent presidential candidate H. Ross Perot, rallied followers to conduct door-to-door campaigns against the Clinton administration's trade, budget, health care, and Haiti initiatives. The

Protesters and supporters of the United States' involvement in the Vietnam War walk on opposite sides of Pennsylvania Avenue in front of the White House, January 1967.

Concord Coalition, founded in 1992 by former senators Warren B. Rudman, a New Hampshire Republican, and Paul Tsongas, a Massachusetts Democrat, lobbied for efforts to reduce the federal budget deficit and national debt. In the late 1990s Common Cause's abiding advocacy of campaign finance reform helped bring that issue to the attention of policy makers.

Other outstanding examples of interest group efforts to influence the president and the rest of the government by "going public" include: the civil rights marches, starting in the 1950s; gay rights marches, beginning in the early 1970s; the protests against the Vietnam War and the movements for and against ratification of the Equal Rights Amendment in the 1970s; expressions of support and opposition to the Reagan administration's policies in Central America, particularly the activities of Lt. Col. Oliver North, in the late 1980s, as well as protests against Reagan's nuclear weapons policies; and the pro- and antiabortion movements of the 1980s and 1990s.

In the latter half of the twentieth century, the most sustained public protests in the United States were those over the issues of civil rights and the Vietnam War. When African American organizations confronted the limits of the legal strategies of the National Association for the Advancement of Colored People (NAACP) and the state-by-state actions to protect rights, a series of protests helped to put the issue on the national agenda. Demonstrations and other outsider efforts by civil rights organizations forced Presidents Eisenhower, John F. Kennedy, and Johnson to deal with the issue. The most dramatic demonstration was the 1963 march on Washington, capped by the Rev. Dr. Martin Luther King's "I Have a Dream" speech and a visit by civil rights leaders to the White House.

President Johnson first dismissed Vietnam War protests as unrepresentative of public opinion, but the protests succeeded in drawing attention to moral and tactical questions about the war in elite circles such as the media and universities. Extensive war coverage after protests helped to shift public opinion against the war and persuade Johnson to halt bombing in 1968.

Many protests fail to move the president, at least in any direct way. President Reagan stood by his nuclear arms policies—including the decision to base Pershing missiles in Europe—despite massive demonstrations in West Germany, Great Britain, and the United States. Reagan dismissed the protests, including a gathering of several hundred thousand people in New York's Central Park, and claimed that they were inspired and organized in part by Soviet agents. Reagan's aggressive moves toward arms control in his second term, however, suggest that the peace movement may have had an effect on him after all. More recently, anti-Iraq war protests that were coordinated worldwide on February 15–16, 2003, failed to dissuade the George W. Bush administration from launching the Iraq war.

Sociologists Frances Fox Piven and Richard Cloward have argued that public protest and disruption historically have been necessary for poor people to obtain benefits from the federal government and the states. Protests develop when economic conditions decline, compelling the government to provide social welfare programs to serve as a safety net. When the economy improves and public pressure declines, the government adopts restrictions on benefits.[40]

Public protest opens or narrows the space for political discussion and negotiation. On the one hand, demonstrations have brought new issues to the table of public debate—among them, civil rights, the Vietnam War, gay rights, military spending, abortion, and environmental protection. Debates about Social Security, however, have been restricted by the climate created by public lobbying against cuts in benefits. On the other hand, protest sometimes blunts the

Frequently interest groups organize large public demonstrations in the nation's capital in attempts to influence the government. In August 1963 the leaders of the March on Washington led the way along Constitution Avenue to the Lincoln Memorial, where a racially integrated crowd of almost a quarter-million people gathered to hear the Reverend Martin Luther King Jr. deliver his "I Have a Dream" speech. The march gave immense impetus to the civil rights movement and sped passage of legislation aimed at aiding African Americans.

Franklin Roosevelt provides a textbook example of presidential influence over interest group alignment. Roosevelt gave a number of groups—such as senior citizens, African Americans, labor, and the "third of a nation" that was poor—a positive new identity that led to their involvement in Democratic politics. The New Deal offered a wide range of incentives to certain businesses to support the president, thereby chipping them away from a strong business alliance that had been hostile to previous liberal initiatives. Finally, by stressing the common desire for economic security, Roosevelt forged an alliance of ethnic groups in similarly vulnerable economic positions.[42]

Postwar presidencies steadily expanded the number of interest groups involved in national politics. The expansion of federal regulation of civil rights, workplace safety, consumer products, the environment, trade, energy production and prices, air travel, and home building continued through the Carter administration, regardless of the president's party. That regulatory expansion, added to the hundreds of federal programs and studies, increased the stake of interest groups in the federal government.

President Johnson's Great Society also led to the creation of many new interest groups. Domestic initiatives in housing, community development, job training, education, and health care included specific instructions to involve the communities and interests affected by the programs. The most famous example was the Economic Opportunity Act of 1964, which required some urban programs to be "developed, conducted, and administered with the maximum feasible participation of residents of the areas and members of the groups served." The "maximum feasible participation" provision was among the most controversial found in the 1960s programs. Proponents maintained that the provision allowed poor people to develop self-esteem and political skills so they could become self-sufficient members of society. Opponents argued that it simply gave antagonistic groups resources to undermine the government's efforts.[43]

A president's program does not need an explicit demand for participation to promote interest groups. In

edge of a movement. Groups that mobilize followers for rallies may have difficulty translating their activism to sustained research and lobbying on Capitol Hill. Followers may mistake their expressions of opinion to be adequate political action.

INFLUENCING THE BALANCE OF POWER

Even if presidents are limited in their dealings with interest groups on particular issues, they influence the balance of power among competing interest groups. Presidential use of public opinion, budget priorities, and White House staff can enhance some groups and undercut others. In this way, the president can "set the table" for later political conflicts.

Political scientists Benjamin Ginsberg and Martin Shefter have identified three strategies that a president can use to shape the makeup of the interest group universe.[41] First, the president can try to transform the identities of established and nascent groups. Second, the president can "divide and conquer" existing alliances of groups and attempt to bring fragments of the old alliance under White House influence. Third, the president can attempt to bring estranged groups together on an issue in a movement where they find common interest.

fact, such provisions have a minor effect compared with the way a president's budget priorities provide the resources and incentives for interest groups. Robert Reischauer, an official of the Urban League, has explained:

> In each area of federal involvement a powerful network of interest groups developed. First there were the representatives of the recipient governments. These included not only interest groups representing governors, mayors, city managers, county executives, state legislators, and the like, but also recipient agency organizations such as chief state school officers, public welfare directors, and highway commissioners. All told, some seventy-two groups of this sort existed. A second element of the network consisted of the general providers of the services provided by the grants—organized teachers, builders of public housing, and so forth. The recipients of the services also formed an element in this network—ranging from welfare recipients to P.T.A. [Parent-Teacher Association] organizations to automobile clubs. Private-sector suppliers of the inputs needed to provide the services also joined the effort. These organizations might represent the producers of library shelves, manufacturers of school buses, book publishers, or asphalt suppliers. The academics and private-sector consulting firms that made a living evaluating existing programs and planning and designing new programs also formed an element in the support group for the grants strategy.[44]

The Reagan administration skillfully transformed the interest group balance of power.[45] First, the president gave greater visibility to many groups. Reagan attracted the support of southern white conservative groups by appealing not to past racial issues but also to the moral concerns of their evangelical churches and organizations. The network of churches throughout the South served as a base for organizing on issues ranging from school prayer to nuclear arms policy. Reagan also helped to shift the focus of many blue-collar workers to patriotism and devotion to family issues such as opposition to abortion. The president appealed to middle-class voters not on the basis of federal programs—most of which they favored and he wanted to cut—but as overburdened taxpayers.

Reagan helped to ally groups long at odds. Protestants and Catholics came together with common concerns about abortion and other moral issues pertaining to personal values. Corporations and small domestic businesses—longtime antagonists on tariff, trade, and tax issues—united on environmental, consumer, and other regulatory concerns. Middle-class professionals, who often had sided with Democrats and liberals on social issues, were drawn to the Reagan camp with tax cuts.

Many groups and alliances split over Reagan initiatives—business and labor on issues of regulation, college-educated professionals over taxes, and beneficiaries of federal programs over tax and budget cuts. Business and labor, which previously had joined forces on many regulatory issues, for example, split in the late 1970s and early 1980s as deregulation led to the rise of nonunion firms that undersold unionized firms. Consumer groups also opposed former allies in business and labor.

Reagan managed as well to shift the focus of much interest group activity downward. His emphasis on nonfederal programs for addressing social problems increased the work of interest groups at the state level. The increased reliance on public-private partnerships and voluntarism limited the notion of public responsibility for social problems. Even though Reagan's tax policies reduced incentives for corporate giving, his celebration of voluntary action took some of the political pressure off the administration for its budget cuts.[46]

Finally, Reagan came to Washington determined to defund what he considered to be irresponsible liberal interest groups. Many groups, such as antipoverty, environmental, and legal advocacy groups, depended on the federal government for some support, but Reagan cut that support in 1981. However, the Reagan White House had largely ignored the possibility that resourceful opposition groups might transform open hostility from a powerful conservative president into a catalyst for liberal organizational growth. National environmental groups, for example, prospered during the 1980s. Denied access to once friendly federal agencies, environmental organizations launched an effective drive that included aggressive fund raising, publicity, and coordinated action with congressional allies.[47] As private donations to these groups increased, environmental leaders quipped that James Watt, Reagan's unpopular, anticonservation secretary of the interior, was the "Fort Knox of the environmental movement."[48]

President Clinton entered office having an ambivalent approach toward interest groups. On the one hand, he considered himself a reformer sent to attack special interest domination of the capital. On the other hand, he was a pragmatic politician eager to get along with powerful figures and enact a wide range of initiatives. "How can a new president turn his back on dozens of his advisers from inside the Beltway who make their living trading on influence and access?" asked Charles Lewis, president of the Center for Public Integrity. "He wants to be known as the candidate of change, but he's using all those old insider types because he wants to be effective."[49] The Washington establishment awaited Clinton's presidency nervously. The public policy magazine National Journal said the interest group "winners" from the change in administrations included the AIDS Action Council, American Gas Association, American Israel Public Affairs Committee, Association of Trial Lawyers of America, Progressive Policy Institute, and Cuban-American National Fund. Losers included the American Nuclear Energy Council, Association of Bank Holding Companies, Pharmaceutical Manufacturers Association, and Heritage Foundation.[50]

Interest groups with ties to the Democratic and liberal causes were initially uncertain whether to help Clinton or maintain their independence. Pamela Gilbert of Congress Watch said that liberal causes felt "emotionally odd" as Clinton took office. "We need a little group therapy, because we have these competing pressures on us," she said. "One is to work with a new Democratic administration and the other is to play our traditional outsider role, publicly criticizing what we don't like." [51] In the constantly shifting coalitions of modern American politics, most interest groups support the president on a case-by-case basis.

Congressional consideration of President Clinton's health care reform proposals in 1993 and 1994 dramatically displayed the modern role of interest groups. Groups representing business, labor, and the health care industry attacked Clinton's proposals one by one. The administration's options were limited from the beginning. Two solid Democratic allies—labor unions and senior citizens—opposed any changes in the tax status of worker health care benefits and reforms of Social Security and Medicare.

The most influential interests in the medical industry were the insurance companies and medical associations. Insurance companies such as Aetna and Prudential supported the president's plan for "managed competition" because it put them at the center of delivery systems. Doctors' groups, led by the American Medical Association, resisted the president's plan for regulation of fees and the alliances that would oversee doctor-patient relationships. Smaller insurance companies, fearing that the giants would drive them out of business, opposed the Clinton plan. Pharmaceutical companies also criticized the plan because of the proposed regulation of drug prices. Teaching and research hospitals resisted the reform because of its emphasis on basic delivery and the fear that they would lose federal grants. Meanwhile, some citizens groups attempted to steer policy making toward a more public plan such as that used in Canada. Citizens groups in California succeeded in placing an initiative on the ballot that would mandate such a single payer plan in that state.

The decisive blow to comprehensive reform came from the National Federation of Independent Businesses (NFIB). The lobby of 600,000 owners of small businesses attacked the proposal for "employer mandates" to pay for health care. The NFIB claimed that Clinton's plan, which would have required businesses to pay up to 80 percent of health insurance costs, would eliminate as many as 1.5 million jobs. NFIB lobbyists wrote letters, attended rallies, and met personally with members of Congress and their staffers. NFIB members also appeared on television and other media outlets. The lobby focused its attention on undecided members of Congress from districts with high proportions of small businesses.

President Clinton and his wife, Hillary Rodham Clinton, the chief architect of the proposal, by turns took a hard line and a conciliatory line toward the interest groups. The first lady delivered blistering speeches against the pharmaceutical industry and doctors who benefited from the health care inflation of the 1980s. But she and the president also sought common ground with interest groups. When the usual politicking seemed to fail, the White House turned to parody, lampooning television commercials critical of the Clinton plan.

Clinton both encountered and generated unprecedented ideological polarization among interest groups during his presidency. Gaining momentum after the Republican takeover of Congress in 1994, and persisting throughout the remainder of his presidency, this polarization often appeared to be based more on personality than on policy. Conservative groups consistently attacked him, even though his policy orientations on many issues were decidedly centrist. In turn, liberal groups sprang to his defense, despite their reservations regarding his willingness to compromise with and accommodate their adversaries. [52]

Any president's policies are bound to rouse interest groups that oppose the administration. Many groups develop or improve their organization in response to threats they perceive from the White House. President Nixon's grain export policies led to the creation of the American Agriculture Movement. [53] Independent oil companies organized on a large scale for the first time when President Carter pushed a windfall profits tax. [54] Labor, environmental, women's rights, Social Security, civil rights, and public interest groups improved their membership and fund-raising efforts in response to Reagan administration policies. Those groups used the negative images of administration officials such as Interior Secretary James G. Watt, Attorney General Edwin Meese III, and Judge Robert Bork as part of their direct-mail fund-raising appeals and rallies. The Sierra Club's membership almost doubled from 180,000 to 300,000 during Watt's tenure at the Department of Interior. [55] A number of grassroots organizations developed sophisticated operations and national bases in their campaigns against Reagan's policies on Central America, nuclear arms, South Africa, and the environment. Some fifty thousand canvassers knocked on doors every night in the early 1980s with petitions and requests for donations for one cause or another. [56] Still, the intensity of interest group opposition to Clinton appears remarkable for its relative disengagement from presidential policies.

White House Efforts to Rouse Interest Group Support

Presidents' interest group strategies fit somewhere between their attempts to control the huge bureaucracy and their efforts to appeal to the public at large. Interest groups have many of the open characteristics involved in public appeals, but groups also become intricately involved in the everyday machinery of the hundreds of agencies that develop and execute federal policy. Whatever the situation, the president needs interest group support for difficult policy battles. To gain support, the White House must mobilize both the public and the elites who are important players in the complex negotiations of congressional and bureaucratic politics.

Whether a president can persuade Congress to adopt the administration's policy proposals depends on how much pressure interest groups can bring to an issue. Interest groups offer the president a number of tools that can be used to prod Congress.

- Expertise and legitimacy. An organization that includes respected analysts of a political problem not only serves as a school for the president and the White House staff but also puts the reputations of the experts behind the White House.
- Membership and organization. Most interest groups do not have large, active memberships, but many have access to mailing lists and expertise in mobilizing the important participants in a political battle.
- Money for media campaigns. Even the most skeletal organizations often have financial resources for a media campaign. Battles over telecommunications and health care reform and passage of NAFTA involved extensive broadcast and newspaper advertising to sway public opinion.
- A system of balancing political concerns. The participation of many interest groups in the policy-making process enables the president and members of Congress to engage in extensive bartering that goes far beyond the specific controversy. Votes for highly visible initiatives are won by promising members of Congress support on other, unrelated matters.
- Leadership. Interest groups include many nationally recognized names—such as John Sweeney of the AFL-CIO, Phyllis Schlafly of the Eagle Forum, and Charlton Heston for the National Rifle Association—as well as sophisticated organizational operators. These groups can offer the kind of leadership that mobilizes whole segments of the population on issues important to the president.

Political battles occasionally develop into battles between two sets of interest groups and their White House and congressional allies. NAFTA-implementing legislation, passed under Clinton, and the 1981 budget cuts, enacted under Reagan, were two cases in which the battle lines between supporters and opponents were fairly clear, and uncommitted members of Congress were courted vigorously by both sides. Often, however, on a highly complex issue such as telecommunications reform, the lines are more fluid, and more negotiation occurs between interest groups and executive and legislative branch officials. In these cases, as legislation evolves, interest groups constantly reevaluate it,

based on an assessment of how the legislation affects their core values and goals. Interest group activity determines the extent of the propaganda battle and the intricacy and duration of the maneuvering between the president and key members of Congress.

Campaign Promises and Debts: How the White House Deals with Its Allies

Despite the cynical view that candidates forget campaign promises as soon as they enter public office, studies have found that presidents attempt to honor most of their pledges. Presidential candidates usually target those pledges to specific interest groups, so in a sense interest group influence on the White House begins before a president even takes office.[57]

An analysis of Carter's 1976 campaign promises and later policies shows that he pursued the policies he promised in seven of ten policy areas. But because Carter's ambitious legislative agenda did not lead to success on many major issues, he often was attacked by interest groups even though he pursued many of his promises.

The areas in which Carter tried to honor campaign pledges included creation of a cabinet-level Department of Education (a promise to the National Education Association), creation of a consumer protection agency (Ralph Nader organizations), common-site picketing legislation (AFL-CIO), amnesty for Vietnam-era draft dodgers (peace groups), deregulation of businesses such as the airline industry (business and labor groups), expansion of environmental regulations (the Wilderness Society and other environmental groups), and a new public works program (AFL-CIO and big-city mayors).

Other presidents have had similar records of seeking to honor campaign pledges. The Congress Kennedy faced was just as reluctant to enact his programs as the Congress faced years later by Carter. Kennedy, however, not only tried to honor campaign promises but also succeeded in a number of areas: the Peace Corps, minimum wage legislation, job training, trade expansion, regional development, arms control, the Alliance for Progress, and civil rights protections. Presidents Nixon and Reagan followed up on a number of campaign themes, such as a devolution of power to states and localities, a stronger U.S. military posture, free-trade policies, cuts in domestic programs, and reduced federal regulation of business and the environment. Nixon departed from his promises to some interest groups, however, by supporting improved relations with the Union of Soviet Socialist Republics and the People's Republic of China and strict regulation of the economy.

President Clinton was criticized by interests that had supported his candidacy for abandoning campaign pledges. Early in his administration, Clinton postponed fulfillment of his pledge for a middle-class tax cut. Later, he had to compromise on issues such as homosexuals in the military and the treatment of Haitian refugees.

But Clinton risked his presidency to meet other campaign commitments. He pushed health care reform, free-trade treaties, and a package of tax increases and budget cuts to reduce the federal budget deficit. He also followed up on pledges to create a national service program for youths, make voter registration simpler, and require employers to give leaves of absence to workers with family medical emergencies.

Despite their dedication to their candidate's campaign agenda, interest groups that see their candidate elected will later complain that the president should do better. In some cases, such as Clinton's support for the Defense of Marriage Act, presidents have moved to the political center and away from former allies. More commonly, modern presidents have demonstrated a propensity to frustrate their interest group allies by failing to advance controversial policy goals. The Reagan administration's interactions with the Religious Right is illustrative.

Reagan and the Christian Right: Courting and Frustrating Interest Group Allies

During the late 1970s the Christian right emerged as a new force in conservative politics. For decades after the Scopes trial of 1925 and the repeal of Prohibition in 1933, religious conservatives had retreated from the political sphere into a separate subculture of churches and sectarian educational and social institutions.[58] In the 1960s and 1970s many social and political changes deeply offended Christian fundamentalists, evangelicals, Pentecostals, and charismatics, who strongly believed that they must resist culturally liberal government policies that favored secular humanism over faith-based morality. Organizations formed to advocate what leaders of the new Christian right described as a pro-family agenda, including tax credits for private school tuition, promotion of school prayer, and restrictions on abortion and pornography. The most prominent new group was the Moral Majority, led by televangelist Jerry Falwell. Other new organizations included the Religious Roundtable, which brought together reform-minded fundamentalist and evangelical clergy, the National Christian Action Council, Christian Voice, and Pat Robertson's Freedom Council.[59]

During the presidential campaign of 1980, Ronald Reagan openly courted conservative Christian leaders. Sharing their enthusiasm for restoring traditional values, Reagan pledged his support for their social agenda. He won an early endorsement from Christian Voice, which organized an effective political action committee—Christians for Reagan—on his behalf. The Religious Roundtable invited Reagan to address more than fifteen thousand ministers at one of its public affairs briefings in summer 1980, another event that helped to coalesce conservative Christians behind his candidacy. The Moral Majority and other groups mobilized voters at the fundamentalist and evangelical grass roots, urging followers to express their religious convictions at the polls.[60] Reagan openly appealed to conservative religious leaders and constituents by supporting the removal of a pro–Equal Rights Amendment plank from the Republican platform and the insertion of an antiabortion plank.[61] His 1980 presidential bid served as an important catalyst for unifying and mobilizing the Christian right, making it a formidable electoral force in American politics.

As president, Reagan appointed a number of Christian right activists to visible administration positions. Morton Blackwell, who served as a liaison between evangelicals and the Reagan campaign organization, was named a special assistant on the White House staff. Robert Billings, the former executive director of the Moral Majority, received a prominent post in the Department of Education. Gary Bauer, a future director of the Family Research Council, became domestic policy adviser in Reagan's second term White House. Reagan also used his bully pulpit to advocate Christian right causes, including frequent endorsements of constitutional amendments to prohibit abortion and restore school prayer.[62] Reagan exercised his executive powers to bar the disbursement of public funds to any family planning organization that discussed abortion as an option with patients. The White House also threw its support behind fundamentalist Bob Jones University in its lawsuit against the Internal Revenue Service, which had revoked the institution's tax-exempt status because of alleged racially discriminatory practices.[63]

If Christian right activists expected the Reagan administration to expend significant political capital on behalf of their social reform agenda, however, they soon discovered that the White House had other priorities. Reagan strategists focused instead on economic issues and a defense buildup. James Baker, the politically moderate White House chief of staff, and Robert H. Michel, the House Republican leader, set the tone early by serving notice that social issues would not be the administration's top priority. Reagan even reneged on a campaign promise to appear at the 1981 March for Life in Washington, offering instead to meet privately with antiabortion leaders in the Oval Office. Several of them boycotted the meeting in protest. Paul Weyrich, a central figure in the Christian right movement, organized a conference call among conservative religious leaders in hopes of rallying them to press their social policy goals with the president. Yet few of these leaders were prepared to battle the Reagan White House. Falwell, for instance, argued that to antagonize the administration would be self-defeating.[64] Significantly, at the same time that the White House was placing Christian right issues on the back burner, the Moral Majority and other conservative religious organizations dutifully joined a broad coalition of conservative interest groups in rallying behind the president's 1981 Omnibus Budget Reconciliation Act and his Economic Recovery Tax Act.[65] In 1984, although they had few tangible policy gains to show for their alliance with Reagan, prominent Christian right groups threw their full support behind the president's reelection campaign.

The Reagan presidency gave the Christian right and its conservative social agenda enormous symbolic recognition. It also forged an enduring alliance between conservative religious groups and the Republican Party. In every presidential election since 1980, the Christian right has focused its energies on electing the Republican candidate. Ralph Reed, a prominent movement figure, credits Reagan with leading religious conservatives "out of the wilderness" and "giving their concerns a viability in the political system that they had never had before." [66] To be sure, he and many other Christian right activists also lament that they received little more from the Reagan administration than "consolation prizes like speeches by the Gipper to their annual conventions or schmooze sessions in the Roosevelt Room." [67] Yet the Christian right had few alternatives but to remain loyal. Presidents who dominate the political system for a time, such as FDR and Reagan, largely control the terms of their relationship with interest group allies.

Co-optation is often the price interest groups pay for their engagement in collaborative breakthrough politics. Sometimes the price is high. Unlike organized labor in the 1930s, which benefited from the reform program that Roosevelt framed, however, the Christian right accepted a form of co-optation from Reagan that ensured that its policy goals would be frustrated.

By contrast, presidents increasingly have sought to help friendly interest groups through regulatory means that often evade public scrutiny and afford enormous discretion to the White House. George W. Bush's regulatory policies illuminate this capacity for presidents to pay back campaign debts and aid organized interests in their camp.

George W. Bush's Regulatory Regime: Assisting Friends

Regulatory action allows an administration to advance its agenda and assist allied organized interests unilaterally, incrementally, and with little public or media attention. In contrast to high-profile lawmaking efforts such as Clinton's ill-fated campaign for sweeping health care reform, an administration can write or revise regulations largely on the president's own authority. Although the George W. Bush White House was certainly not the first to pursue its policy goals through regulation, it proved exceptionally aggressive and successful in its use of this strategy during the first term.

The administration's air quality policies are illustrative. During the 2000 presidential race, Bush pledged to impose controls on power plant emissions of carbon dioxide. In her first days as Bush's director of the Environmental Protection Agency, Christie Todd Whitman, a former Republican governor of New Jersey, announced plans to carry out this promise. Interest groups representing electric power companies expressed alarm. One of their main lobbyists, Haley Barbour, a former Republican Party chairman, threw down the gauntlet in a memorandum to Vice President Richard B. Cheney: "The question is whether environmental policy still prevails over energy policy with Bush–Cheney, as it did with Clinton–Gore." Barbour urged Cheney, who was heading a task force established by the president to conduct a broad review of energy policy, to show that environmental issues did not "trump good energy policy." [68] In March 2001, Bush announced that he would not impose carbon dioxide controls, explaining that "the reality is that our nation has a real problem when it comes to energy." [69]

Industrywide lobbying groups such as the Edison Electric Institute and the Electric Reliability Coordinating Council soon pressed the White House for new regulatory changes. One of their targets was a set of rules known as the New Source Review program, which required companies to add new pollution controls when they upgraded or expanded their plants. In a memorandum to Cheney, Whitman warned that any administration effort to undercut New Source Review rules would make it "hard to refute the charge that we are deciding not to enforce the Clean Air Act." In November 2002, however, the administration quietly released a statement from EPA's assistant administrator outlining revisions of the New Source Review program. The rules stipulated that companies would not have to add new pollution control devices if their plant upgrades and construction projects did not cost more than 20 percent of the plant's total value. The rules changes also raised the amount of pollution permitted an entire facility, instead of targeting emissions from individual pieces of equipment, and exempted plants that had installed modern pollution controls from having to make further improvements for ten years regardless of their emission levels. Twelve states, twenty cities, and numerous environmental groups sued the EPA in response. "Our powerful, bipartisan court challenge says to this administration: 'No, you cannot repeal the federal Clean Air Act by dictatorial edict,' " declared Connecticut attorney general Richard Blumenthal.

Even as opponents of Bush's air quality policies fought these rules changes in the courts, environmental groups noted that lax regulatory enforcement had already paid huge dividends for affected power companies.[70] In addition to loosening air quality controls, Bush's EPA has proved far less vigorous than previous administrations in cracking down on companies that violate federal environmental laws. The number of lawsuits initiated against companies for environmental violations during Bush's first term declined 75 percent from the number initiated during that last four Clinton years. The $56.8 million in civil penalties that the EPA collected in fiscal 2004 was the lowest amount since 1990.[71]

The Bush White House's approach to environmental policy does not represent an isolated example. New regulations adopted during Bush's first term revised health rules, work safety standards, product safety disclosure requirements, energy regulations, and other measures in a manner that usually favored business and industry allies and drew fire from interest groups representing consumers, labor, the elderly, medical patients, racial minorities, and other constituencies. At the behest of automakers, the National Highway Traffic Safety Administration published a regulation forbidding the public release of some data related to unsafe motor vehicles because the information might cause "substantial competitive harm" to manufacturers. The Mine Safety and Health Administration proposed a new regulation that would dilute rules intended to protect coal miners from black lung disease. Responding to industry complaints, the Department of Labor dropped a rule requiring employers to keep a record of employees' ergonomic injuries. A rule that required hospitals to install facilities to protect workers against tuberculosis was also jettisoned by the administration. In response to lobbying by groups representing lumber and paper companies, Forest Service managers were authorized to approve logging in federal forests without the usual environmental reviews.

These regulatory initiatives inspired little or no public attention. It is the unilateral, low-profile character of regulatory change that makes it so attractive to presidents whose efforts to get what they want from Congress are frustrated. During his first term, George W. Bush pursued favorable policy outcomes for his administration and its interest group allies through incremental, regulatory means.

Navigating Rival Interests

As much as modern presidents have confronted strong demands from interest group allies, they also have had to negotiate a diverse array of organized interests when advancing major reforms. The budget battles of 1981 and telecommunications reform of 1996 capture the necessity of navigating rival interests well.

Budget Cuts of 1981: Set Battle Lines

President Reagan's budget-cutting victory in the summer of 1981 was a classic contest between two sets of interest groups. Here, too, the outcome of the struggle was determined by bartering, public appeals, strong presidential leadership, and the organizational strength of interest groups.

The prospect of more than $160 billion in budget cuts over Reagan's first term in office activated a wide range of interest groups involved with domestic policy. The usual strategy of such groups was to work with the staff members of congressional committees and the federal agencies to restore proposed cuts, piece by piece, to the budget. This "micro" activity was to be supplemented by a publicity cam-

paign that would show low public support for the budget cutting and put both the president and Congress on the defensive. The groups opposing the budget cut proposals included the AFL-CIO, NAACP, Urban League, U.S. Conference of Mayors, Children's Defense Fund, U.S. Public Interest Research Group, National Organization for Women, Operation PUSH, and American Association of Retired Persons.

President Reagan and his lieutenants thwarted the two-pronged interest group attack, however. First, the White House reduced the chances for "micro" response to the cuts by asking Republican Senate leaders to consider the cuts as a single budget package—that is, Congress would have one up-or-down vote on all the cuts. The all-or-nothing legislation reduced the possibilities for interest groups to appeal to friendly members of congressional committees. One observer noted: "Many hundreds of lobbying groups that had built strong relationships over the years with authorizing and appropriations committee members and aides have found themselves not so much without a sympathetic ear as without a way to leverage that sympathy to get more money." [72]

Second, by including in the package authorizing legislation as well as spending legislation—that is, legislation that allowed funding as well as legislation that funded the programs—Reagan forced Congress to deal with otherwise protected entitlement programs. If the authorization for a program were cut, it could not be funded later in that budget year.

And, third, the Reagan administration led supportive interest groups in its own public offensive in favor of the cuts. The groups Reagan brought into the administration's alliance included the Chamber of Commerce, National Association of Manufacturers, National Conservative Political Action Committee, Moral Majority, National Jaycees, National Federation of Independent Business, and American Medical Association. The White House managed the interest groups' campaign. It selected key congressional districts where the administration might find support and instructed the interest groups to pressure House members from those districts. Lee Atwater, the president's assistant political director, explained:

> The way we operate, within forty-eight hours any Congressman will know that he has had a major strike in his district. All of a sudden, Vice President Bush is in your district, Congressman Jack Kemp is in your district. Ten of your top contributors are calling you, the head of the local AMA, the head of the local realtors' group, local officials. Twenty letters come in. Within forty-eight hours, you're hit by paid media, free media, mail, phone, all asking you to support the president. [73]

The interest group politics of the budget cuts had an elaborate system of rewards and punishments. As Reagan sought congressional approval, he co-opted the United Auto

Workers union by going along with import relief on Japanese automobiles. The president also punished two of his biggest Democratic foes, House Speaker Thomas P. "Tip" O'Neill Jr. and Sen. Edward Kennedy, by lifting duties on Taiwan and Korea—a move that hurt the shoe-making industry in their home state of Massachusetts.[74]

Under such a system of lobbying, the president depends on interest groups when bartering with reluctant budget-cutters in Congress. The cozy system of backroom bargaining between the White House staff and key congressional figures is not replaced, but it is supplemented by the mobilization of interest groups for the district pressure campaigns.

Reagan was not always so skillful in shaping interest group politics. During consideration of his tax-cut bill in 1981, Reagan watched as congressional leaders engaged interest groups in negotiations over tax benefits. David A. Stockman, Reagan's budget director, remembered: "Everyone was accusing everyone else of greed, and in the same breath shouting 'What's in it for me?' " If the budget no longer offered ornaments to constituents, the tax code did. The competition between White House and congressional versions of the tax bill gave interest groups the opportunity to expand their tax breaks. "Try as I have," Stockman mused, "it is virtually impossible to discern rationality in the behavior of any of the principal players."[75]

Interest group politics engages all modern presidents. President Carter won Senate approval of the Panama Canal treaties because of his ability to assemble a broad coalition of interest groups and his willingness to barter for the final crucial votes. Treaty opponents included Reagan, who had found the issue to be potent in the 1976 presidential campaign. Groups fighting the treaty included the American Conservative Union, Liberty Lobby, National States' Rights Party, and John Birch Society. Some fifteen hundred State Department officials led the fight for the treaty, backed by Common Cause, the National Education Association, AFL-CIO, National Jaycees, and business leaders. The interest groups were troops in a battle for public opinion to sway skeptical senators. At the beginning, only 8 percent of the public supported "giving up" the canal; by the time of the Senate vote, a majority favored the treaties. The emotional debate eventually worked to Carter's detriment, however. Leaders of the New Right later said the canal issue was the catalyst for their activism in the 1980 election campaign for Reagan and against Carter. The issue strengthened the memberships, treasuries, organization, and technological sophistication of groups within the New Right.

On issues affecting a wide number of groups, even presidents with less popular support can fashion a coalition strong enough to win on a particular vote. Clinton won approval of the 1993 budget and tax legislation and NAFTA by playing the insider game. On NAFTA, for example, Clinton used patronage agreements to gain the support of more than fifty members of the House of Representatives. Some of these deals provided special benefits for constituents—such as sugar growers, citrus farmers, and defense contractors—in the congressional districts of the representatives whose NAFTA votes Clinton obtained. Even if presidents do not enjoy a high personal standing with the public, they are able to use the executive branch's prodigious resources to pull together disparate groups.

Conversely, broad-based popular support for the president can discourage interest groups in opposition to his policies. Clinton's capacity to sustain high job-approval ratings amid personal scandals proved maddening to his interest group adversaries. The remarkably and persistently high public approval ratings George W. Bush enjoyed in the aftermath of the terrorist attacks of September 2001 stifled at least some of the opposition he faced in the first few months of his presidency.

In a highly polarized political environment, interest group opposition to a president can rally support from the other side of the ideological divide. Early in the Clinton presidency, labor and civil rights groups expressed concerns about the administration's priorities, which they perceived as insufficiently attentive to their interests. However, as Clinton came increasingly under fire from conservative interests, these groups flocked to his defense. They came to view Clinton as their indispensable bulwark against control of the national policy agenda by right-wingers who would surely proceed in directions disadvantageous to their positions. By the time his presidency ended, Clinton had no stronger, more reliable and enthusiastic supporters than the labor and civil rights groups.

Telecommunications Overhaul: Freewheeling Negotiation

On February 8, 1996, President Clinton signed a long-awaited overhaul of the telecommunications industry into law. Appropriately for the measure that was designed to take American telecommunications into the twenty-first century, Clinton logged onto the Internet and signed an electronic version of the bill in real time—the first president to do so. The passage of the Telecommunications Act of 1996 was a classic high-stakes contest among many affected interest groups. The outcome of the struggle was determined by bartering, public appeals, presidential leadership (much of it behind the scenes, in contrast to the highly public fight to round up votes for NAFTA), and the organizational strength of the various interest groups.

Billions of dollars were at stake when on November 22, 1993, bills were introduced in the House of Representatives to overhaul the U.S. telecommunications industry for the first time in sixty years. Technological innovations in data processing and communications had rendered existing legislation anachronistic. New digital technologies promised a convergence of telephone, television, and computer services, but existing legislation carefully separated and regulated the spheres in which local phone companies, long-distance phone companies, and cable television companies could operate. This regulation of the industry was stifling innovation. By unleashing full-blown competition in telecommunications, some argued, Congress would give companies more incentive to invest in these technologies and to realize more fully the potential of the "information superhighway."

Deregulation, however, would create winners and losers among many players. To gain support for passage of the legislation, Congress and the president would have to weigh the interests and organizational strength of the regional Bell companies, the cable industry, the long-distance phone companies, consumer advocates, supporters of service to rural (and therefore, high-cost) communities, family-values interest groups concerned with violence on television and pornography on the internet, First Amendment groups such as the ACLU, broadcast television interests and advertisers, equipment manufacturers, alarm-service providers, public television proponents and opponents, public utilities, electronic publishers, satellite companies, cellular phone service providers, and the members of Congress with ties to each of these players.

On a number of occasions between introduction of the legislation in November 1993 and enactment in February 1996 it appeared as though the whole effort would come to nothing. Every change, no matter how small, that was made to appease one interest group led other groups to reevaluate their support for the legislation.

In the end, no one was completely satisfied with the outcome. Bradley Stillman, telecommunications policy director of the Consumer Federation of America, for example, complained that the law deregulated cable TV rates without any assurance that a major competitor would come along.[76] Many Republican congressional leaders, including Dick Armey of Texas, objected that it did not deregulate the industry quickly enough or thoroughly enough.[77]

All players, including President Clinton, found something objectionable in the bill. But the final consensus was that any additional tinkering would invite the whole, fragile house of cards to come crashing down.

REGULATION OF LOBBYING

Lobbying is protected by First Amendment guarantees of the freedom of speech, but Congress has acted several times to monitor and regulate the kinds of contacts that interest groups can make with the president and members of Congress.

In the late 1970s Congress, concerned about conflicts of interest in the White House and the bureaucracy, passed restrictions on the lobbying activities of former administration officials. Under the Ethics in Government Act of 1978, administration officials are not permitted to lobby for a year after they leave the government.

LOBBYING REFORM AND ETHICS LEGISLATION

A bill signed by President Bill Clinton in December 1995 opened the world of lobbying, which long operated behind closed doors, to public scrutiny. The legislation stipulated that lobbyists who spent at least 20 percent of their time meeting with top executive branch officials, members of Congress, or their staff had to disclose the names of their clients, the issues they lobbied for, and the amount of money they spent. Lobbyists who were paid $5,000 or less, or organizations that used their own employees to lobby and spent $20,000 or less on those efforts, did not have to register.

The legislation closed loopholes in the 1946 Federal Regulation of Lobbying Act that allowed most lobbyists to avoid registering and required those who did to disclose only limited information about their activities. In July 1991 the General Accounting Office reported that almost 10,000 of the 13,500 individuals and organizations listed in the *Washington Representatives* directory were not registered as lobbyists.

In the Republican-dominated Congress, reluctant House Republican leaders brought the bill to the floor in 1995 after proponents showed they had the votes either to attach the measure to another bill or to discharge the measure from committee. Veteran Republicans who had supported such a change for years, members of the feisty Republican class of 1994, and minority Democrats joined to force the bill to the floor. Once there, passage was all but assured because few lawmakers were willing to oppose the bill in an era of low public opinion of Congress.

In 2006, two aides of former House majority leader Rep. Tom DeLay (R-Texas) and Rep. Bob Ney (R-Ohio) were among those implicated in the growing scandal surrounding lobbyist Jack Abramoff, who pleaded guilty to bribing public officials. DeLay subsequently resigned his seat in Congress and chose not to run for reelection in the 2006 general election. Ney resigned from Congress in November 2006 and was found guilty on federal corruption charges. He was sentenced to prison in early 2007.

Democrats took control of both houses of Congress as a result of the 2006 midterm elections and at the outset of the 110th Congress in January 2007 began forwarding ethics legislation designed to address what many had decried during the campaign season as a "culture of corruption."

SOURCES: Jonathan D. Salant, "Bill Would Open Windows on Lobbying Efforts," *Congressional Quarterly Weekly Report,* December 2, 1995, 3631–3633; Kate Barrett, "Indian Lobbying Abuses Detailed," *CQ Weekly Online* (June 23, 2006): 1796–1796; Jonathan Allen, "Former Rep. Ney Gets 30 Months for Corruption," *CQ Weekly Online* (January 19, 2007): 261–261; and Martin Kady II and Jonathan Allen, "Senate Passes Ethics Overhaul," *CQ Weekly Online* (January 19, 2007): 250–252.

Two top Reagan advisers—Lyn Nofziger and Michael K. Deaver—were indicted for illegally contacting their former Reagan administration colleagues on behalf of clients after the two men had become lobbyists. Nofziger was convicted of illegal lobbying for a military contractor, and Deaver was convicted on three counts of perjury in connection with his lobbying work for the Canadian government.

The history of regulating lobbies has been spotty. Congress and the president have faced intense interest group resistance to any regulation of their activities. The legislation that has passed has been either so vaguely defined or restricted that lobbies' activities have been barely controlled.

The Revenue Act of 1934 denied tax-exempt status to groups that devoted a substantial part of their activities to influencing legislation. The provision enumerated vague definitions and no sanctions, and courts applied the law inconsistently. The Foreign Agents Registration Act of 1938 required representatives of foreign governments and organizations to register with the U.S. government. The act was the source of controversy when President Carter's brother, Billy, was hired by the Libyan government as a U.S. representative.

The Revenue Acts of 1938 and 1939 denied tax exemptions to corporations devoting a substantial part of their activities to propaganda and lobbying. The acts also stated that citizens' donations to such corporations were not tax deductible. The Federal Regulation of Lobbying Act of 1946, the most comprehensive legislation up to that time, required registration of anyone who was hired by someone else to lobby Congress. The act also required quarterly reports from registered lobbyists.

One of the issues Clinton campaigned on in 1992 was lobby reform. Three years later, in December 1995, Congress broke more than forty years of gridlock and passed legislation that required most lobbyists to disclose twice a year the issues that they lobbied on, the specific federal agencies or houses of Congress they contacted, and the amount of money spent on the effort.[78] *(See box, Lobbying Reform of 1995, p. 1056.)*

When Clinton took office in 1993, he instituted new ethics standards for more than one thousand top appointees. Among other ethics guidelines, Clinton's executive order increased from one year to five years the period during which former executive branch officials are prohibited from lobbying their former agencies.

The regulation of interest groups is always several years behind the modern methods of lobbying. While former White House aides are forbidden from lobbying the executive branch, for example, they can still influence the political process directly as members of law firms or indirectly by giving advice to colleagues in lobbying firms. Activities of think

tanks also are immune from the rules of lobbying. As his presidency neared its end, Clinton reduced the time frame on the "revolving door."

Momentum for further lobbying reform advanced on the watch of Clinton's successor, George W. Bush. The Bush administration came under fire early in 2001 for the perceived access it granted to lobbyists from the energy industry in the development of energy policy. When one giant energy trading company, Enron—which had made numerous contacts with administration officials—suffered a spectacular bankruptcy in the fall of 2001, the outcry intensified.

At most, the government can create incentives that encourage or discourage the different kinds of petitioning of the government undertaken by parties, interest groups, and the mass media. As the Framers of the Constitution recognized, attempts to stifle factions would endanger democracy. The government cannot eliminate the pressures of interest groups, but it can direct them in ways more conducive to deliberation and the public interest.

Political interactions between presidents and national interest groups are an intrinsic feature of contemporary American politics. Despite these significant disincentives to close relations between presidents and interest groups, rarely can either disregard the other. They do so at their political peril. Organized interests are crucial elements of presidents' electoral coalitions. In an era of candidate-centered campaigns, interest groups provide money, organizational support, and votes for presidential hopefuls during their primary and general election bids.[79] Once in office, modern presidents largely stake their claims as successful leaders on whether they can build supportive coalitions for their policies with any regularity. Along with political parties, organized interests can offer the White House a potent and efficient means of expanding support for the president's agenda in Congress and other venues. Presidents must also consider, however, that interest groups can just as surely serve as continuous sources of mobilized opposition.

In turn, interest groups cannot ignore the enormous power that modern executives wield in public agenda setting, policy formation, budget making, and crucial details of implementation. Presidents also can alter the prevailing interest group system they encounter. They can encourage the creation of new organized interests, actively work to demobilize others, and even influence how interest groups frame their preferences in the first place.[80] In short, the modern presidency presents interest groups with significant opportunities and constraints. Whether as allies or as rivals, policy-minded presidents and interest groups cannot discount each other in a political system constitutionally designed to "counteract ambition with ambition." [81]

NOTES

1. For a comparative perspective on interest groups, see Frances Millard, *Pressure Politics in Industrial Societies* (London: Macmillan, 1986).

2. *Federalist* No. 10 was largely ignored by historians and theorists of American democracy until the early twentieth century. See David Rodgers, *Contested Truths* (New York: Basic Books, 1987), 185.

3. Alexander Hamilton, James Madison, and John Jay, *The Federalist Papers,* ed. Clinton Rossiter (New York: New American Library, 1961).

4. Alexis de Tocqueville, *Democracy in America* (New York: New American Library, 1956), 198.

5. Theodore J. Lowi, *The Personal President* (Ithaca: Cornell University Press, 1985), 22–41.

6. Jonathan Rauch, *Demosclerosis: The Silent Killer of American Government* (New York: Times Books, 1994), 135.

7. E. Pendleton Herring, *Group Representation Before Congress* (Baltimore: Johns Hopkins University Press, 1929), 51.

8. Roosevelt is quoted in Lewis Eigen and Jonathan Siegel, *The Macmillan Dictionary of Political Quotations* (New York: Macmillan, 1993), 382.

9. Ronald Reagan, "Remarks to Administration Officials on Domestic Policy, December 13, 1988," *Weekly Compilation of Presidential Documents,* vol. 24 (Washington, D.C.: Government Printing Office, 1988), 1615–1619.

10. Theodore J. Lowi, *The End of Liberalism* (New York: Norton, 1979), 3–63.

11. Rauch, *Demosclerosis,* 39; current totals from the *Encyclopedia of Associations* are available at its Web site, www.library.dialog.com

12. Information provided on the Web sites of the U.S. Chamber of Commerce, www.uschamber.com; and AFL-CIO, www.aflcio.org.

13. The Federal Election Campaign Act amendments of 1974 limited donations to individual candidates to $1,000 and donations to groups to $5,000. This provision encouraged donors to give to PACs instead of to candidates. The campaign reform legislation signed in 2002 increased the individual candidate limit to $2,000. *(See "The Campaign Finance System," p. 261, in Chapter 5.)*

14. Federal Election Commission reports cited in Paul Allen Beck and Marjorie Randon Hershey, *Party Politics in America,* 9th ed., (New York: Longman, 2001). See also Harold W. Stanley and Richard G. Niemi, *Vital Statistics on American Politics,* 5th ed. (Washington, D.C.: CQ Press, 1995), 161. Congressional PAC spending increased from $23 million in 1976 to $190 million in 1994. See also Martha Joynt Kumar and Michael Baruch Grossman, "The President and Interest Groups," in *The Presidency and the Political System,* ed. Michael Nelson (Washington, D.C.: CQ Press, 1984), 288.

15. Arthur F. Bentley, *The Process of Government,* rev. ed. (San Antonio, Texas: Principia Press, 1949).

16. David Truman, *The Governmental Process* (New York: Knopf, 1951).

17. Robert A. Dahl, *Who Governs?* (New Haven: Yale University Press, 1961).

18. E. E. Schattschneider, *The Semisovereign People* (New York: Holt, Rinehart, and Winston, 1960); C. Wright Mills, *The Power Elite* (New York: Oxford University Press, 1959); and Floyd Hunter, *Community Power Structure* (Chapel Hill: University of North Carolina Press, 1953).

19. For a concise examination of the bias of interest group representation, see Kay Lehman Schlozman, "What Accent the Heavenly Chorus? Political Equality and the American Pressure System," *Journal of Politics* 46 (1984): 1006–1031.

20. Mancur Olson, *The Logic of Collective Action* (Cambridge: Harvard University Press, 1965).

21. Daniel Bell, "The Revolution of Rising Entitlements," *Fortune,* April 1975, 99.

22. For a critique of the breakdown of a civic ethic because of individualist and interest group liberalism, see Benjamin Barber, *Strong Democracy* (Berkeley: University of California Press, 1984), especially pages 3–114. For a conservative statement of similar concerns, see Robert Nisbet, *The Twilight of Authority* (New York: Oxford University Press, 1975).

23. Lowi, *The End of Liberalism,* 62.

24. Quoted in Paul Light, *The President's Agenda* (Baltimore, Md.: Johns Hopkins University Press, 1982), 94.

25. Joseph A. Pika, "Interest Groups and the Executive: Presidential Intervention," in *Interest Group Politics,* ed. Allen J. Cigler and Burdett A. Loomis (Washington, D.C.: CQ Press, 1983), 312.

26. Leslie Wayne, "Big Companies Picking Up Tab in Inauguration," *New York Times,* January 18, 2001, A1. See also Michael Kranish, "Corporate Cash Paves Way for Inaugural," *Boston Globe,* January 17, 1993.

27. Kumar and Grossman, "The President and Interest Groups," 289.

28. Pika, "Interest Groups and the Executive," 301.

29. Anthony Downs, "Up and Down with Ecology—The Issue Attention Cycle," *Public Interest* 28 (summer 1972): 38–50.

30. Reagan's budget-cutting strategy is discussed in Allen Schick, *Reconciliation and the Congressional Budget Process* (Washington, D.C.: AEI Press, 1981).

31. Jeffrey H. Birnbaum, *The Lobbyists: How Influence Peddlers Work Their Way in Washington* (New York: Times Books, 1993), 205–206.

32. Mary Curtius and John Aloysius Farrel, "Conservatives Hitting Hard at Clinton Policies," *Boston Globe,* March 21, 1994.

33. The size of the White House staff increased from a few dozen under Franklin Roosevelt to 660 under Richard Nixon in 1971. After falling to 362 under President Reagan, the staff increased again under Bush and Clinton, to 400 by 1998. The Executive Office of the President was at its largest—5,751—in 1974. See Lyn Ragsdale, *Vital Statistics on the Presidency,* rev. ed. (Washington, D.C.: CQ Press, 1998), 264–268.

34. Thomas E. Cronin, *The State of the Presidency* (Boston: Little, Brown, 1980), 84.

35. Nelson W. Polsby, "Presidential Cabinet Making: Lessons for the Political System," *Political Science Quarterly* 93 (spring 1978): 15–25.

36. Nelson W. Polsby, "Interest Groups and the Presidency: Trends in Political Intermediation in America," in *American Politics and Public Policy,* ed. Walter Dean Burnham and Martha Wagner Weinberg (Cambridge: MIT Press, 1978), 46.

37. See Kumar and Grossman, "The President and Interest Groups," 290–307.

38. Ornstein and Elder, *Interest Groups, Lobbying, and Policymaking,* 69–79.

39. Ibid., 82–93.

40. Frances Fox Piven and Richard Cloward, *Regulating the Poor: The Functions of Public Relief* (New York: Random House, 1972).

41. The following discussion relies on Benjamin Ginsberg and Martin Shefter, "The Presidency and the Organization of Interests,"

in *The Presidency and the Political System,* ed. Michael Nelson (Washington, D.C.: CQ Press, 1988), 311–330.

42. Ibid., 311–333.

43. Maximum feasible participation never played as important a role as its promoters and detractors argued. Most organizations created by the provision eventually came under the control of local governments and other more conservative groups such as local businesses. But the principles behind the program—that interest groups can be created to promote policies and that interested parties should be consulted before policies affecting them are implemented—have remained part of American politics. Perhaps most important, the provision led to the development of a wide range of interest groups and trained a generation of government and interest group leaders. See Dennis R. Judd, *The Politics of American Cities: Power and Public Policy,* 2d ed. (Boston: Little, Brown, 1984), 311; and Daniel Patrick Moynihan, *Maximum Feasible Misunderstanding* (New York: Free Press, 1970).

44. Robert D. Reischauer, "Fiscal Federalism in the 1980's: Dismantling or Rationalizing the Great Society," in *The Great Society and Its Legacy,* ed. Marshall Kaplan and Peggy Cuciti (Durham, N.C.: Duke University Press, 1986), 187–188.

45. Ginsberg and Shefter, "The Presidency and the Organization of Interests," 313–327.

46. Marc Bendick Jr. and Phyllis M. Levinson, "Private-Sector Initiatives or Public-Private Partnerships," in *The Reagan Presidency and the Governing of America,* ed. Lester M. Salamon and Michael S. Lund (Washington, D.C.: Urban Institute, 1984), 455–479.

47. Mark Peterson and Jack Walker have shown that Reagan ushered in "a virtual revolution" in the access of interest groups to bureaucratic agencies of the federal government. See Mark Peterson and Jack Walker, "Interest Group Responses to Partisan Change," in *Interest Group Politics,* 2nd ed., ed. Allan J. Cigler and Burdett A. Loomis (Washington, D.C.: CQ Press, 1986), 172.

48. Michael S. Greve, "Why 'Defending the Left' Failed," *Public Interest* 89 (fall 1987): 99.

49. Quoted in Peter H. Stone, "Lying in Wait," *National Journal,* November 21, 1992, 2661.

50. Ibid., 2656–2661.

51. Quoted in Kirk Victor, "Asleep at the Switch?" *National Journal,* January 16, 1993, 131.

52. For a perceptive account of this aspect of the Clinton presidency, see Mark A. Peterson, "Clinton and Organized Interests: Splitting Friends, Unifying Enemies," in Colin Campbell and Bert Rockman, eds., *The Clinton Legacy* (New York: Seven Bridges Press, 2000), 140–168.

53. Allan J. Cigler, "From Protest Group to Interest Group: The Making of the American Agriculture Movement, Inc.," in *Interest Group Politics,* ed. Allan J. Cigler and Burdett A. Loomis (Washington, D.C.: CQ Press, 1988), 46–69.

54. Thomas Byrne Edsall, *The New Politics of Inequality* (New York: Norton, 1984), 99–103.

55. Jeff Fishel, *Presidents and Promises* (Washington, D.C.: CQ Press, 1985), 168.

56. John Herbers, "Grass-Roots Groups Go National," *New York Times Magazine,* September 4, 1983, 22–23, 42, 46, 48.

57. See Fishel, *Presidents and Promises.*

58. Eric Larson, *Summer for the Gods* (Cambridge: Harvard University Press, 1997), 232–235.

59. John C. Green, "The Spirit Willing: Collective Identity and the Development of the Christian Right," in *Waves of Protest,* ed. Jo Freeman and Victoria Johnson (New York: Rowman and Littlefield, 1999), 156–159.

60. Kenneth Wald, *Religion and Politics in the United States* (Washington, D.C.: CQ Press, 1992), 234–235.

61. See Ralph Reed, *Active Faith: How Christians Are Changing the Soul of American Politics* (New York: Free Press, 1996), 113–114.

62. A. James Reichley, *Religion in American Public Life* (Washington, D.C.: Brookings Institution, 1985), 324–325.

63. Duane Oldfield, *The Right and the Righteous: The Christian Right Confronts the Republican Party* (New York: Rowman and Littlefield, 1996), 118–121.

64. See Reed, *Active Faith,* 114–115.

65. Reichley, *Religion in American Public Life,* 325.

66. Reed, *Active Faith,* 116.

67. Ibid., 115.

68. Christopher Drew and Richard Oppel Jr., "Air War: Remaking Energy Policy," *New York Times,* March 6, 2004, A1.

69. Ibid.

70. Matthew Wald, "E.P.A. Says It Will Change Rules Governing Industrial Pollution," *New York Times,* November 23, 2002, A1; Drew and Oppel, "Air War," 1; and Don Hopey, "Groups Score Bush on Environment," *Pittsburgh Post-Gazette,* November 10, 2004, 1.

71. Hopey, "Groups Score Bush on Environment," 1.

72. Wolman and Teitelbaum, "Interest Groups and the Reagan Presidency," 308.

73. Quoted in Hedrick Smith, "The President as Coalition Builder: Reagan's First Year," in *Rethinking the Presidency,* ed. Thomas E. Cronin (Boston: Little, Brown, 1982), 280.

74. Ibid., 281.

75. David Alan Stockman, *The Triumph of Politics: The Inside Story of the Reagan Revolution* (New York: Avon Books, 1987), 257.

76. Dan Carney, "Congress Fires Its First Shot in Information Revolution," *Congressional Quarterly Weekly Report,* February 3, 1996, 290.

77. Dan Carney, "Telecommunications: Key Agreements, Remaining Problems for Telecommunications Conferees," *Congressional Quarterly Weekly Report,* December 23, 1995, 3883.

78. Jonathan D. Salant, "Bill Would Open Windows on Lobbying Efforts," *Congressional Quarterly Weekly Report,* December 2, 1995, 3631–3633.

79. Stephen Wayne, "Interest Groups on the Road to the White House: Traveling Hard and Soft Routes," in *The Interest Group Connection,* ed. Paul Herrnson, Ronald Shaiko, and Clyde Wilcox (Chatham, N.J.: Chatham House Publishers, 1998), 65–79.

80. See Benjamin Ginsburg and Martin Shefter, "The Presidency and the Organization of Interests," in *The Presidency and the Political System,* 5th ed., ed. Michael Nelson (Washington, D.C.: CQ Press, 1988).

81. See Alexander Hamilton, James Madison, and John Jay, *The Federalist Papers,* ed. Clinton Rossiter (New York: New American Library, 1961).

SELECTED BIBLIOGRAPHY

Baumgartner, Frank, and Beth Leech. *Basic Interests: The Importance of Groups in Politics and in Political Science.* Princeton: Princeton University Press, 1998.

Beck, Paul Allen, and Marjorie Randon Hershey. *Party Politics in America,* 9th ed. New York: Longman, 2001.

Berry, Jeffrey. *The Interest Group Society.* Boston: Little, Brown, 1984.

Berry, Jeffrey. *The New Liberalism: The Rising Power of Citizen Groups.* Washington, D.C.: Brookings Institution, 2000.

Cigler, Allan J., and Burdett A. Loomis. *Interest Group Politics.* 6th ed. Washington, D.C.: CQ Press, 2002.

Clemens, Elisabeth. *The People's Lobby.* Chicago: University of Chicago Press, 1997.

Heclo, Hugh. "Issue Networks and the Executive Establishment." In *The New American Political System,* ed. Anthony King. Washington, D.C.: AEI Press, 1978.

Lowi, Theodore J. *The End of Liberalism.* New York: Norton, 1979.

Ornstein, Norman J., and Shirley Elder. *Interest Groups, Lobbying, and Policymaking.* Washington, D.C.: CQ Press, 1978.

Peterson, Mark A. "The Presidency and Organized Interest Groups: White House Patterns of Interest Group Liaison." *American Political Science Review* 86 (1992): 612–625.

Schlozman, Kay Lehman. "What Accent the Heavenly Chorus: Political Equality and the American Pressure System." *Journal of Politics* 46 (1984): 1006–1031.

Skocpol, Theda. *Diminished Democracy: From Membership to Management in American Public Life.* University of Oklahoma Press, 2004.

Wilcox, Clyde, and Ronald G. Shaiko, eds. *The Interest Group Connection: Electioneering, Lobbying, and Policy Making in Washington.* New York: Seven Bridges Press, 1997.

★ INDEX

Italic page numbers indicate illustrations. Boxes, notes, and tables are indicated by "b," "n," and "t" following the page number. Alphabetization is letter by letter (e.g., "Campbell" precedes "Camp David").

A

AARP. *See* American Association of Retired
Persons
Abbott, Philip, 840, 845
Abdullah, Saudi crown prince, 1527
Abell, Bess, 1545
Aberbach, Joel D., 594
Abolitionists, 367, 368
See also Liberty Party
Abortion
demonstrations on, 1047
election of 1984 and rights to, 419
family planning funding and counseling
on, 1052, 1408
federal funding restricted, 1498
gag rule enforcement, 521
judicial jurisdiction regulation and cases
on, 1415
legal precedents and judicial restraint on,
1410–1411
Abraham, Henry J., 919, 919t, 921, 1405
Abraham, Spencer, 1178, 1193
Abramoff, Jack, 1040, 1056b, 1368
Abramowitz, Alan I., 283
Absentee voting, 248
Absolute veto, 648
Abu Ghraib prison, 533, 709
Academic figures, 678
Acceptance speeches, 305–306
Access to president, 689, 1083, 1161
See also White House
Accountability for Intelligence Activities Act
(1980), 1341
Achenbach, Joe, 1288b
Acheson, Dean G., 750, 1161, 1162, 1163,
1169, 1170, 1216, 1327
Acheson's Rule of the Bureaucracy, 1467b
Achievement, presidents of, 1507
Ackley, Gardner, 1134
Acronym list, agencies and departments,
1470b
Acting President, 445, 447, 450–451b, 457,
459, 1094–1095
Act to Prevent Pernicious Political Activities,
1308, 1309b
See also Hatch Act (1939)
Adams, Abigail, 1252, 1282, 1536
adviser to John, 1537
biography of, 1702–1703
ranking of, 1557t
Adams, Bruce, 1106, 1107, 1108, 1168, 1176,
1296
Adams, Charles Francis, 326, 377
Adams, John
amnesty by, 1430
on appointment and removal power, 70
appointments, 904
biography of, 1579–1581, 1660
burden of presidency and, 564
cabinet meetings and, 203, 1096, 1155
as commander in chief, 766
Congress and, 1355
congressional appearances by, 670t
*Defense of the Constitutions of Government
of the United States of America,* 4

election of 1789, 231, *231,* 354
election of 1792, 355
election of 1796, 72–73, 233, 262, 356
election of 1800, 187n34, 233–234,
334–335, 356
election of 1820, 360–361
executive branch employees under, 1300
executive orders by, 522t
French diplomacy and, 73–75
Gazette of the United States and, 741, 941
Hamilton and, 73–74, 231, 875
Jefferson and, 1561
leadership style of, 1281
memorialization of, 568
as minority president, 331t
newspaper criticism of, 942–943
oath of office of, 340
on political parties, 875
prayer for White House, 1261
presidency, 73–75, 77, 278b, 1398
presidential ceremonial duties and, 552b
presidential election of, 207b
on presidential title, 68
as president of Senate, 1093
previous government service of, 277b
public reticence of, 844
rating as president, 219, 220t, 221t, 222t,
223t
retirement, 1560t, 1561
as Senate vote tie-breaker, 203
State of the Union messages, 544, 669
veto use by, 649t, 651t
on vice presidency, 201, 202–203
as vice president, 1155
war power and, 743
on Washington's farewell address, 552b
as White House resident, 1252, 1282
wife of. *See* Adams, Abigail
Adams, John Quincy, *334*
American plan of, 84, 235–236
biography of, 1587–1589
Calhoun and, 205, 498
Congress and, 1355
election of 1820, 361
election of 1824, 81–82, 235, 335, 361–362,
430
election of 1828, 262
executive branch employees under, 1301
executive orders by, 522t
National Republican Party and, 80, 82
party affiliation and leadership, 879
Pinckney Plan and, 16b
polling by, 1013
presidency, 78, 82
on presidency, 1562
previous government service of, 277b
public appearances by, 844
rating as president, 220t, 221t, 222t, 223t
retirement, 1560t, 1562, 1563
as secretary of state, 81–82
Supreme Court nominations, 1426t
threats to, 478
on Tyler Precedent, 462
veto use by, 649t, 651t
Washington, D.C., newspapers and, 941

White House elm tree and, 1265
wife of. *See* Adams, Louisa
Adams, John T., 886t
Adams, Louisa, 1536, 1557t
biography of, 1704–1705
Adams, Samuel, 10, *10*
Adams, Sherman
domestic policy and, 1077, 1126
Eisenhower and, 405, 1067
as Eisenhower's chief of staff, 148, 585,
603, 903, 1075t, 1076, 1085, *1085,*
1164
Eisenhower's illnesses and, 502
Adams, William, 283
Addresses, presidential. *See* Speeches,
presidential
Adenauer, Konrad, 549
Adet, Pierre, 356
Ad Hoc Commissions, 1234–1235
Adjournment *sine die,* 655, 656
Adkins v. Children's Hospital (1923), 1428b
Administration, EOP Office of, 1073t, 1103,
1104t, 1116, 1145
Administration, meaning of, 901
Administration Building, Agriculture
Department, 1271
Administration press, 86, 188n87
See also Partisan newspapers
Administrative activities. *See* Bureaucracy;
Executive branch; Executive Office of
the President (EOP)
Administrative Careers with American
(ACWA), 1311
Administrative Management, Commission
on, 903
Administrative presidency, 1362
See also Executive Office of the President
(EOP); White House Office
Clinton's, 177
development of, 139–140
Nixon's, 156–157
origins of term, 193n367
Reagan's, 163–164
Administrative Procedures Act (1946), 522,
1476
Administrative style
Bush (G. H. W.) administration, 588
Bush (G. W.) administration, 590–591
Carter administration, 586–587
circular, 585
Clinton administration, 589–590
Eisenhower administration, 563
hierarchical, 585
Johnson (Lyndon) administration, 563
overview of, 584–585
patterns of organizational change, 586
Reagan administration, 563, 587–588
Roosevelt (Franklin) administration,
563
Wilson administration, 563
Admiral's House, Naval Observatory, *1269,*
1269–1270, 1296
Admiralty and maritime jurisdiction, f
ederal courts and, 1394
Advance Office, White House, 1073t, 1081

conservative backlash to, 157
Department of Housing and Urban
    Development, *1200*
domestic policy council and, 1126
election of 1968, 411
electoral process and, 260
federal bureaucracy growth and, 1462
implementation of, 1492
interest groups and, 1048, 1059*n*43
legislative leadership and, 152–153, 668
legislative scope of, 476
Medicare, 1195
organized labor and, 1212
origin of, 120, 410, 668
place in history and, 668, 695–696
State of the Union announcement of, 852,
    860, 864, 870
success of, 1381–1382
Vietnam War and, 1356
"Great White Fleet" cruise, 703, 786
Greeley, Horace, 108, 369, 377–378, 685, *944,
    945b*
    Daily National Intelligencer, 461
Green, David, 848, 870, 1024
Green, Duff, 942
Green, James A., 461
Green, Joyce, 1412
Green, Theodore Francis, *1382*
Greenback Party, 327, 383–384, 882*t*
Greenberg, Sanford E., 1237
Greenberg, Stanley, 294, 313, 1016, 1110
Greene, Harold, 758, 1450–1451
Green Party, 326, 330, 433, 444*n*210, 880,
    882*t*
Green Room, White House, 1260
Greenspan, Alan, 337, 804*b*, 806–807, 827,
    1134–1135
Greenstein, Fred I.
    on Clinton and populist personae, 548
    on Eisenhower, 146, 221*b*, 926
    on Nixon and Congress, 157
    on Nixon and Reagan's use of executive
        power, 164
    on Roosevelt (Franklin), 192*n*349
Greer (ship), 749
Greeting ceremonies, 856–857
Greider, William, 824
Grenada invasion, 735*b*, 756, 786, 1025*b*,
    1026, 1330–1331
Grier, James, 93
Grier, Robert C., 747, 1449–1450
Griffin, Patrick, 1358
Griles, J. Stephen, 1346
Grimes, James, 377
Griscom, Thomas C., 967, 967*t*, 968, 970
Gross, Bertram, 663
Grossman, Jonathan, 1211
Grossman, Larry, 984
Grossman, Michael Baruch, 986–987, 1039,
    1043
Grossman, Steven, 887*t*
Grossman, Ex parte (1925), 1430
Gross national product, 801*b*
Ground Floor Corridor, White House, 1258
Ground Zero. *See* World Trade Center
Group of Eight (G8) economic summits,
    814–815, *815*
Group of Seven (G7) economic summits,
    726, 814
Grunwald, Mandy, 314, 1110
GSA. *See* General Services Administration
Guam, 748
Guam Doctrine, 710

Guantanamo Bay, Cuba, detention facility,
    532–533, 699*b, 774,* 784, *1441,* 1442
Guarantee clause, 1411
Guinier, Lani, 1208, 1346
Guinn and Beall v. United States (1965), 60
Guiteau, Charles J., 111, 379, 469*t,* 471, 904,
    1303, 1461
Gulf of Tonkin Resolution. *See* Tonkin Gulf
    resolution (1964)
Gulf War. *See* Persian Gulf War
Gulick, Luther, 140, 595, 1064
Gulley, Bill, 1282, 1298
Gustafson, Merlin, 566
Gutierrez, Carlos, 447*b,* 923, 1183

H

Habeas corpus
    border states and, 1443
    Constitution on, 782–783
    executive authority and, 513
    Lincoln's suspension of, 98–99, 745–746,
        1419, 1449
    Milligan and, 1442
    petition for writ of, 699*b,* 1441
    Vallandigham and, 1440
Habeas Corpus Act (1863), 513–514
Habib, Phillip C., 724
Hadley, Stephen J., 731, 1077, 1125
Hagerty, James C.
    as Eisenhower's press secretary, 147,
        959–960, 959*t,* 961, 973, 1067, 1080
    staff support and management by, 964–965
    television use by, 150
Hagin, Joseph W., 1076
Hagner, Belle, 1545
Hague, Frank, 899
Haig, Alexander M., Jr., 421, 447*b,* 499, 733,
    1075*t,* 1164, 1217
Haig v. Agee (1981), 1445
"Hail to the Chief," 158, 159, 557*b,* 566, 1282
Haiti
    U.S. foreign policy and, 174, 526, 696, 705,
        706*b,* 722, 724, 1506
    U.S. war power and, 758, 764, 786, 1332,
        1451
Halberstam, David, 411, 1124, 1172–1173
Haldeman, H. R., *586*
    Nixon protection by, 1493
    as Nixon's chief of staff, 585–586, 587, 903,
        1069, 1075*t,* 1076, 1083, 1086, 1358,
        1490
    Secret Service and, 1532
    staff perquisites and, 1298
    Watergate and, 488, 489, 1070, 1423
Hale, Eugene, 118
Hale, John P., 370
Half-breed Republicans, 190*n*208, 471
Hall, David B., 382
Hall, Gus, 326
Hall, Leonard W., 887*t,* 890, 906, 926
Hallett, B. F., 886*t*
Halliburton, 438
Halperin, Morton, 1042, 1570
Hamas and war on terrorism, 707*b*
Hamby, Alonzo, 147
Hamdan, Salam Ahmed, 181
Hamdan v. Rumsfeld (2006), 181, 533–534,
    539*n*128, 699*b,* 784, 1401*b*
Hamdi, Yaser, 533
Hamdi v. Rumsfeld (2004), 533,
    539*nn*123–124, 699*b,* 1442
Hamilton, Alexander, *9, 69, 1154*
    Adams and, 73–74, 231, 875, 1155

Annapolis Convention and, 9
Bank of the United States and, 363
budgetary policy and, 90
burden of presidency and, 564
Burr's duel with, 203
Coast Guard and, 635
Committee of Style and, 21
at Constitutional Convention (1787), 6*b,*
    9*b,* 13*b*
constitutional plan of, 17, 63*n*28
on council of state, 1153
death of, 203, 498
domestic policy, 874
draft legislation for Washington by, 673
election of 1796, 233, 356
election of 1800, 187*n*34, 233, 334–335,
    357
on electoral college flaws, 354
on elector selection, 48, 231
on executive power, 511–512, 513, 1417
Federalist Papers and, 43–44, 648, 663, 940
Federalists and, 74, 232, 232*b,* 874–875
foreign policy and, 700–701, 711
Gazette of the United States and, 248, 941
on ideal political leader, 843
on impeachment power, 480, 641
Jefferson and, 71–72, 77, 355, 673, 700–701,
    874, 875, 1155
on judiciary, 1395–1396, 1396*b,* 1415
on leadership style, 1281
legislative process and, 673
national bank and, 811, 1419
"Pacificus" essays, 71–72, 118, 701, 1440
on pardon power, 34, 1431*b*
party leadership role of, 874, 879, 904
on political parties, 228–229
on presidency, 1281
on president's leadership, 663
on Proclamation of Neutrality, 1326
qualifications for president and, 38
on reception of ambassadors, 545
as Secretary of Treasury, 69, 673, 808–809,
    1154, 1222
Secretary of Treasury salary, 1296
succession plan of, 40
tariffs and, 806*b*
on term of office, 27, 1007
on treaty power, 34, 701, 1336
on veto power, 32, 70, 648
veto power and, 1348
on war power, 701, 739, 740–741, 743,
    1388*n*28
war power debate with Madison, 700–701,
    741
as Washington's legislative lobbyist, 664
as Washington's speechwriter, 870
Hamilton, John, 886*t*
Hamilton, Lee, 186, 538*n*76, 678, 1244
Hamilton v. Kentucky Distilleries Co. (1919),
    1445
Hamlin, Hannibal, 205, 371
    biography of, 1671–1672
Hamre, John J., 780
Hance, Kent, 1028
Hancock, John, 45, 354, 552*b*
Hancock, Winfield Scott, 110, 303, 376, 379
Handgun assaults on presidents, 573*n*68
Handgun Control Inc., 271, 1486
Hanna, Mark A., *263*
    brokered conventions and, 304, 346*n*92
    election of 1892, 382
    election of 1896, 384
    election of 1900, 474

Military aid to foreign countries. *See* Foreign military aid; Peacekeeping missions; Police actions
Military Appeals Court, U.S., 1400, 1440
Military arrests and detentions, 746
Military bases, 778–779, 1284
Military budget. *See* Defense budget
Military bureaucracy. *See* Defense bureaucracy
Military command by president. *See* Commander-in-chief power; War powers
Military Commissions Act (2006), 182, 534
Military courts. *See* Military tribunals
Military draft system, 746, 752, 780–781, 1456*n*291
Military exercises and shows of force, 703, 786–787
Military heroes as candidates, 274
Military-industrial complex, 1502
Military interventions, 1328–1329*b*
Military personnel policy
  commander-in-chief power and, 780
  defense budget and, 776, 780–781
  desegregation and, 1436
  draft system and, 780–781
  homosexuality and, 171, 196*n*516, 323, 523, 780*b*
  Internet-based voting systems, 248
  submarine personnel and, 768
  war power and, 745, 746
Military power, 627–628, 1327–1336
Military Reconstruction Act (1867), 104
Military responses to terrorism, 760–762, 762*b*
  See also War on terrorism
Military service as duty. *See* Draft system, military
Military tribunals
  Civil War trials of civilians, 98–99, 746, 782, 783
  Nazi saboteur trial, 784
  terrorism and, 142, 180–181, 699*b*, 708, 762*b*, 784
  WW II, 142
Militia
  Constitution on calling up, 20
  primacy of federal government and, 80, 552*b*
  war power and, 739, 740*b*, 745, 746
Milkis, Sidney M., 918
Miller, G. William, 804*b*
Miller, James C., III, 1118
Miller, Mark Crispin, 871*n*52, 979
Miller, Samuel, 623
Miller, William E., 409, 886*t*, 891*b*
Miller, Zell, 241, 300, 438
Milligan, Ex parte (1866), 99, 142, 514, 536*n*23, 782, 783, 784, 1440
Milligan, Lambdin P., 783, 1440
"Million Man March" (October 1995), 1011
Mills, C. Wright, 1038
Mills, Ogden, 138
Mills, Robert, 1276
Milošević, Slobodan, 174, 177, 758
Miltich, Paul, 967*t*
Minerals Management Service, 1205
Mine Safety and Health Administration, 1054
Mineta, Norman Y., 1174*b*, 1221
Ministerial powers, 1429–1430
Minnesota
  presidential primary in, 242–243
Minor v. Happersett (1920), 1415

Minority Business Development Agency, 1184
Minority presidents, 331, 331*t*, 916
Minority representation on commissions, 1237
Mint, U.S., 1224
Miranda v. Arizona (1966), 1410, 1415
Miroff, Bruce, 150, 661, 865, 995
Misrule, tradition of, 1001
Missile defense
  commander-in-chief power and, 768, 769, 771, 772
  defense budget and, 712, 779
Missile technology advances
  foreign policy and, 703
Missing, Exploited, and Runaway Children, White House Conference on, 1235
Mississippi v. Johnson (1867), 1411
Mississippi, secession by, 96
Mississippi Freedom Democratic Party (MFDP), 298–299
Missouri v. Holland (1920), 699*b*, 1441, 1447
Missouri Compromise (1820), 80, 92, 95, 187*n*61, 360, 370
  Dred Scott and, 1419–1420
Mistretta v. United States (1989), 1429
Mitchell, George, 173
Mitchell, Greg, 396
Mitchell, John, 120
Mitchell, John N.
  as attorney general, 630*b*, 678, 902, 1162, 1407
  Democratic National Headquarters robbery and, 490
  Nixon and, 1168, 1173
  Watergate and, 414, 488, 489, 1206, 1423
Mitchell, Stephen A., 886*t*
Mixner, David, 270
Mob rule, Framers' fears of, 228, 365, 684, 842, 843
Model Cities program, 411
Modus vivendi, 1448
Moe, Terry, 907
Moley, Raymond, 138, 585, 1064, 1554
Mona Lisa (da Vinci), 1530
Monarchy
  See also Foreign monarchs; Imperial presidency
  Anti-Federalists on, 41–42
  Aristotle on, 3
  British monarchs, U.S. presidents' meetings with, 555
  continuity in politics and, 554
  U.S. war power and, 745*b*
  villainy and, 1000
Mondale, Joan, 1541*b*
Mondale, Walter F.
  African American votes for, 60
  biography of, 1693–1694
  campaign strategy of, 285
  as Carter advisor, 1098, 1101
  Carter's ticket balancing and, 319
  delegated travel by Carter, 570
  delegate lead in 1984, 284
  early knockout campaign strategy of, 285
  election of 1976, 415
  election of 1984, 244–245, 260, 287, 288, 290, 295, 418–420, 930
  exploratory strategies, 280
  Ferraro selection as running mate, 209, 310, 319
  general election campaign 1984, 323
  government experience of, 209

preconvention vice-presidential search by, 209
presidential campaign of, 207*b*
presidential nomination of, 202, 213, 884*t*
as president of Senate, 1094
primaries and caucuses in 1984 and, 283, 284
on regional primaries, 309
role of, 1323
as special envoy for Carter, 1099
superdelegates and, 292
tax policy and, 800
travel by, 570
on vice presidency as training, 214
as vice president, 211–212, *212*, 1100–1101, 1296
as vice president and candidate for president, 1099–1100
on vice president role, 39*b*, 1098
vice president's residence and, 1270
Monetarism, 801*b*, 804
Monetary policy
  See also Gold standard
  economic theory, institutions, events, and, 795, 801*b*, 802–804
  institutions, laws, and rules, 811–812
  international, 812–815
Monroe, Elizabeth, 1536, 1544, 1557*t*
  biography of, 1704
Monroe, James
  biography of, 1586–1587
  Congress and, 1355
  election of 1808, 358–359
  election of 1816, 235, 359–360
  election of 1820, 235, 360–361
  executive branch employees under, 1301
  executive orders by, 522*t*
  foreign policy and, 695, 710, 717, 725
  as governor of Virginia, 277*b*
  inaugural address of, 342
  inauguration of, 340
  one-party rule during presidencies of, 879
  opposition to presidency by, 42
  presidency, 78, 80–83
  previous government service of, 277*b*
  rating as president, 220*t*, 221, 221*t*, 222*t*, 223*t*
  retirement, 1282, 1560*t*, 1561
  State of the Union address, 81
  travel by, 844
  veto use by, 80, 649*t*, 651*t*, 1321
  war power and, 514, 744
  Washington, D.C., newspapers and, 941
  as White House resident, 1253, 1282
  wife of. *See* Monroe, Elizabeth
  workday of, 564
Monroe, Kristen R., 1024
Monroe Doctrine, 81, 360, 695, 710
  Roosevelt (Teddy) Corollary to, 122, 474, 710, 747*b*, 786
Montana, presidential primary in, 242–243
Montesquieu, Baron de, 4, 29, 42, 1417
Moody, Jim, 990
Moore, Frank, 338, 1105, 1358, 1383
Moore, Minyon, 903
Moore, Sara Jane, 469*t*, 479, 1533
Moot cases, Supreme Court on, 1409
Moral and religious references in speeches, 561, 861–862
Morality
  civil service appointments and, 1306
  voting rights, tests for, 246